THE
WRITERS
DIRECTORY
THIRTIETH EDITION

THE WRITERS DIRECTORY

THIRTIETH EDITION
VOLUME 2: D-G

Editor
Lisa Kumar

ST. JAMES PRESS
A part of Gale, Cengage Learning

GALE
CENGAGE Learning·

Detroit • New York • San Francisco • New Haven, Conn • Waterville, Maine • London

Writers Directory, 30th Edition

Project Editor: Lisa Kumar

Editorial Support Services: Natasha Mikheyeva

Manufacturing: Rita Wimberley

For product information and technology assistance, contact us at
Gale Customer Support, 1-800-877-4253.
For permission to use material from this text or product,
submit all requests online at **www.cengage.com/permissions.**
Further permissions questions can be emailed to
permissionrequest@cengage.com

Gale
27500 Drake Rd.
Farmington Hills, MI, 48331-3535

ISBN-13: 978-1-4144-8712-0 (set)   ISBN-10: 1-4144-8712-6 (set)
ISBN-13: 978-1-4144-8713-7 (vol. 1)   ISBN-10: 1-4144-8713-4 (vol. 1)
ISBN-13: 978-1-4144-8714-4 (vol. 2)   ISBN-10: 1-4144-8714-2 (vol. 2)
ISBN-13: 978-1-4144-9901-7 (vol. 3)   ISBN-10: 1-4144-9901-9 (vol. 3)
ISBN-13: 978-1-4144-9902-4 (vol. 4)   ISBN-10: 1-4144-9902-7 (vol. 4)
ISBN-13: 978-1-4144-9903-1 (vol. 5)   ISBN-10: 1-4144-9903-5 (vol. 5)
ISBN-13: 978-1-4144-9904-8 (vol. 6)   ISBN-10: 1-4144-9904-3 (vol. 6)

ISSN 0084-2699

Printed in the United States of America
1 2 3 4 5   16 15 14 13 12

FD157

Contents

Preface

The Writers Directory is the newly revised and expanded thirtieth edition of this acclaimed reference work. It lists 26,615 writers—writing under 29,776 names—from all countries of the world who have had at least one work published in English.

The Directory is published in 6 individual volumes, with content divided as follows:

Volume 1: Lists entries from A-C
Volume 2: Lists entries from D-G
Volume 3: Lists entries from H-L
Volume 4: Lists entries from M-Q
Volume 5: Lists entries from R-U
Volume 6: Lists entries from V-Z, Obituaries, Index to Writing Categories, and Country of Citizenship Index

The Directory lists approximately 26,526 living writers of fiction and non-fiction who have published at least one full-length work in English. Listees run the gamut from the best-known, best selling authors of fiction and the most prominent non-fiction writers to those writers just embarking on their literary careers. The thirtieth edition includes nearly 1,000 writers whose listings have not appeared in a previous edition of The Writers Directory.

The **Obituaries** Section contains the entries for approximately 89 writers whose listings have appeared in previous editions of The Writers Directory and whose passing was made known to us in preparing this edition.

Compilation Methods

Selection of writers to appear in The Writers Directory is based primarily on reference value. Biographical and career information is researched for each writer, then a copy of the entry is sent to the writer for his or her approval and updates. By this process, the editors can assure comprehensive, current information. At the same time, entries in the previous edition were rigorously reviewed with an eye toward their current research value. As a result, some writers' entries have been retired to make way for those of new writers.

How to Read a Citation

Entries in The Writers Directory contain some or all of the following elements (please note that this is a sample entry-for demonstration purposes only):

▌1▐ WILLIAMS, Mae. ▌2▐ (Allison May Williams) ▌3▐ Also writes as William Allison. ▌4▐ American (born Malta), ▌5▐ b. 1945. ▌6▐ **Genres:** Novels, Biography. ▌7▐ **Career:** Freelance writer. ▌8▐ **Publications:** Paris, L'amour, 1972; (ed.) Running through the Weeds, 1982; (as William Allison) Louis, My Love (biography), 1987; The Waves at My Back, 1997. ▌9▐ **Address:** 27500 Drake Rd., Farmington Hills, MI 48331 U.S.A. ▌10▐ **Online address:** maewil@aol.com ▌11▐ Died 1997.

▌1▐ Name of writer with fuller name information in parentheses

▌2▐ Full name of writer if different from writing name or pseudonyms but not used for writing

▌3▐ Pseudonym information

▌4▐ Nationality—if birthplace is different from nationality, it will follow the nationality in parentheses

▌5▐ Birth year

▌6▐ Genres—corresponds to **Index to Writing Categories**

▌7▐ Brief career information

▌8▐ Publications: title, year of publication, pseudonym if used, special awards

▌9▐ Address

▌10▐ Online address and/or web site

▌11▐ Death notation and year (in **Obituaries** Section only)

Cross references appear in the following form:

To main entry in main section: **ALLISON, William.** See **WILLIAMS, Mae.**

From main section to main entry in **Obituaries** section: **WILLIAMS, Mae.** See Obituaries.

From pseudonym in main section to main entry in **Obituaries** section: **ALLISON, William.** See **WILLIAMS, Mae** in the Obituaries.

Writers (and cross references) are listed alphabetically by surname which are sorted letter-by-letter. In cases where surnames are identical, writers are listed first by surname, then by given and middle names, and finally by suffixes such as Jr., Sr., II, or III. Surnames beginning with a prefix (such as Du, Mac, or Van), however spaced, are listed alphabetically under the first letter of the prefix and treated as if there were no space. Other compound surnames, hyphenated names, and names with apostrophes are alphabetized as if there were no space or punctuation. Surnames beginning with Saint or St. appear after names beginning with Sains and before names beginning with Sainu.

Entries in the **Obituaries** Section follow the same style as those in the main entries with the addition of the notation *Died* and the death year (if known) at the end of the entry.

Features

The Writers Directory contains many features to enhance its usefulness:

Boldface Rubrics allow quick and easy scanning for specifics on genre, career, publication, and mailing and online addresses.

The Obituaries Section lists the entries for those writers whose listing appeared in previous editions of The Writers Directory and whose passing was made known to us in preparing this edition. Cross references have been provided in the main body of the Directory to those deceased writers.

Indexing

The Writers Directory includes two indexes. In the **Index to Writing Categories**, one can locate writers by the type of works they write. New categories are added to The Writers Directory as needed to reflect new topics of interest and to define a writer's body of work more accurately. The **Country of Citizenship Index** lists writers by their country of citizenship as provided by the writer. Users are advised that one writer with multiple citizenship may appear under one country grouping (e.g., Canada-England) while another with the same citizenships may appear under a different grouping (e.g., England-Canada) depending on how the writer submitted the information.

The **Index to Writing Categories and Country of Citizenship Index** can be found in Volume 6 of the Directory following the **Obituaries** Section.

Also Available in Electronic Formats

Licensing. The Writers Directory is available for licensing. The complete database is provided in a fielded format and is deliverable on such media as disk or CD-ROM. For more information, contact Gale's Business Development Group at 1-800-877-GALE, or visit us on our web site at gale. cengage. com.

Online. The Writers Directory is accessible as part of Gale's Biography in Context database, as well as through the Gale Biographies database (File GALBIO) through Lexis-Nexis. For more information on Biography in Context, visit us on our web site at gale.cengage.com. For more information on Gale Biographies, contact LexisNexis, P.O. Box 933, Dayton, OH 45401-0933; phone (937) 865-6800; toll- free: 800-227-4908.

Suggestions Welcome

Comments and suggestions from users of *The Writers Directory* on any aspect of the product as well as suggestions for writers to be included in a future edition are cordially invited. Please write:

The Editor

The Writers Directory

St. James Press

Gale, a part of Cengage Learning

27500 Drake Rd.

Farmington Hills, Michigan 48331-3535.

Entry in *The Writers Directory* is at the discretion of the editor.

Abbreviations Used In The Writers Directory

A

AB	Alberta
ABC	American Broadcasting Company
ACT	Australian Capital Territory
AK	Alaska
AL	Alabama
Apt.	Apartment
AR	Arkansas
Assn.	Association
Assoc.	Associate
Asst.	Assistant
Ave.	Avenue
AZ	Arizona

B

b.	born
BBC	British Broadcasting Corporation
BC	British Columbia
Beds.	Bedfordshire
Berks.	Berkshire
Bldg.	Building
Blvd.	Boulevard
Brig.	Brigadier
Bros.	Brothers
Bucks.	Buckinghamshire

C

CA	California
Cambs.	Cambridgeshire
Can.	Canada
Capt.	Captain
CBC	Canadian Broadcasting Company
CBS	Columbia Broadcasting System (US)
CIA	Central Intelligence Agency (US)
CO; co.	Colorado; Company; County
Co-ed.	Co-editor
Co-trans.	Co-translator
Col.	Colonel
Contrib.	Contributor; Contributing
Corp.	Corporation
CPA	Certified Public Accountant
Cres.	Crescent
CT; Ct.	Connecticut; Court

D

DC	District of Columbia
DE	Delaware
Dept.	Department
Derbys.	Derbyshire
Dir.	Director
Div.	Division
Dr.	Doctor; Drive

E

E.	East
Ed.	Editor; Edition
Exec.	Executive

F

FBI	Federal Bureau of Investigation (US)
FL	Florida
Ft.	Fort

G

GA	Georgia
Gen.	General
Glam.	Glamorgan
Glos.	Glouchestershire
Gov.	Governor
Govt.	Government

H

Hants.	Hampshire
HE	His Eminence; His/Her Excellency
Herts.	Hertfordshire
HI	Hawaii
HM	His/Her Majesty
HMS	His/Her Majesty's Ship; His/Her Majesty's Service
Hon.	Honorable; Honorary

I

IA	Iowa
ID	Idaho
IL	Illinois
IN	Indiana
Inc.	Incorporated
Inst.	Institute
Intl.	International

J

Jr.	Junior

K

KS	Kansas
KY	Kentucky

L

LA	Louisiana
Lab.	Laboratory
Lancs.	Lancashire
Leics.	Leicestershire
LI	Long Island
Lincs.	Lincolnshire
Lt.	Lieutenant
Ltd.	Limited

M

MA	Massachusetts
Mag.	Magazine
Maj.	Major
MB	Manitoba
MD	Maryland
ME	Maine
Mgr.	Manager
MI	Michigan
Middx.	Middlesex
MN	Minnesota
MO	Missouri
MP	Member of Parliament
MT; Mt.	Montana; Mount, Mountain

N

N.	North
NASA	National Aeronautics and Space Administration
NATO	North Atlantic Treaty Organization
NB	New Brunswick
NBC	National Broadcasting System (US)
NC	North Carolina
NE	North East
NF	Newfoundland
NH	New Hampshire
NJ	New Jersey
NL	Newfoundland and Labrador
NM	New Mexico
No.	Number

Northants.	Northamptonshire
Notts.	Nottinghamshire
nr.	Near
NS	Nova Scotia
NSW	New South Wales
NT	Northern Territory (Australia); Northwest Territories (Canada)
NU	Nunavut
NV	Nevada
NW	North West
NWT	Northwest Territories
NY	New York
NYC	New York City

O

OH	Ohio
OK	Oklahoma
ON	Ontario
OR	Oregon
Orch.	Orchestra
Org.	Organization
Oxon.	Oxfordshire

P

PA	Pennsylvania
PE, PEI	Prince Edward Island
PEN	Poets, Playwrights, Essayists, Editors, Novelists
Pl.	Place
PO	Post Office
Pres.	President
Prof.	Professor
Prog.	Program
Publrs.	Publishers
Publs.	Publications

Q

QC	Quebec
QLD	Queensland

R

Rd.	Road
Rep.	Representative
Rev. ed.	Revised edition
RI	Rhode Island
RR	Rural Route
Rte.	Route

S

S.	South
SA	South Australia
Salop.	Shropshire
SC	South Carolina
Sch.	School
SD	South Dakota
SE	South East
Sec	Secretary
SK	Saskatchewan
Soc.	Society
Sq.	Square
Sr.	Senior
St.	Saint; Street
Staffs.	Staffordshire
Ste.	Suite
Supt.	Superintendent
SW	South West

T

Tas.	Tasmania
Terr.	Terrace
TN	Tennessee
Trans.	Translator; Translation
Treas.	Treasurer
TX	Texas

U

UK	United Kingdom
UN	United Nations
Unesco	United Nations Educational, Scientific and Cultural Organization

Unicef	United Nations Children's Emergency Fund
Univ.	University
US;	USA United States, United States of America
USS	United States Ship; United States Service
USSR	Union of Soviet Socialist Republics
UT	Utah

V

VA	Virginia
VIC	Victoria
Vol(s).	Volume(s)
VT	Vermont

W

W.	West
WA	Washington; Western Australia
Warks.	Warwicks; Warwickshire
WHO	World Health Organization
WI	Wisconsin
Wilts.	Wiltshire
Worcs.	Worcestershire
WV	West Virginia
WY	Wyoming

Y

YM-YWHA	Young Men's-Young Women's Hebrew Association
YMCA	Young Men's Christian Association
Yorks.	Yorkshire
YWCA	Young Women's Christian Association
YT	Yukon Territory

D

D, John. (John D'Emilio). American (born United States), b. 1948. **Genres:** Civil Liberties/Human Rights, Gay And Lesbian Issues, History, Sex, Social Sciences, Biography. **Career:** University of North Carolina, Department of History, assistant professor, 1983-88, associate professor, 1988-92, director of graduate studies, 1988-93, professor, 1992-98; Center for Advanced Studies in the Behavioral Sciences, fellow, 1990-91; Australian National University, Humanities Research Centre, fellow, 1993; National Gay and Lesbian Task Force Policy Institute, founding director, 1995-97; University of Illinois, Department of History, professor, 1999-, Gender and Women's Studies Program, director, 2002-04; director of graduate studies, 2005-06. Writer. **Publications:** The Civil Rights Struggle: Leaders in Profile, 1979; Sexual Politics, Sexual Communities: The Making of a Homosexual Minority in the United States, 1940-1970, 1983; (with E.B. Freedman) Intimate Matters: A History of Sexuality in America, 1988, 2nd ed., 1997; Making Trouble: Essays on Gay History, Politics, and the University, 1992; Sexual Politics, Sexual Communities: the Making of a Homosexual Minority in the United States, 1940-1970, 1998; (ed. with W.B. Turner and U. Vaid) Creating Change: Sexuality, Public Policy, and Civil Rights, 2000; The World Turned: Essays on Gay History, Politics, and Culture, 2002; Lost Prophet: The Life and Times of Bayard Rustin, 2003; (ed. and intro.) My Desire for History: Essays in Gay, Community, and Labor History, 2011. Contributor to books and periodicals. **Address:** Department of Gender & Women, University of Illinois, 1812 University Hall, 601 S Morgan St., PO Box 360, Chicago, IL 60607-7109, U.S.A. **Online address:** demilioj@aol.com

DAALDER, Ivo H. American/Dutch (born Netherlands), b. 1960. **Genres:** International Relations/Current Affairs, Social Sciences, Law. **Career:** Harvard University, Center for Science and International Affairs, Harvard-MacArthur pre-doctoral fellow, 1985-87; International Institute for Strategic Studies, research associate, 1987-88, senior research fellow, 1988-89; Center for International and Security Studies, research fellow, 1989-91, director of research, 1991-88; University of Maryland, research fellow, 1989-91, director of research, 1991-98, School of Public Affairs, adjunct professor, 1991, visiting assistant professor, 1991-93, assistant professor, 1993-95, associate professor and director of international security and economic policy, 1995-98; National Security Council, director for global affairs, 1995-96, director for European affairs, 1996-97; Brookings Institution, senior fellow in foreign policy studies; North Atlantic Treaty Organization, United States permanent representative ambassador, 2009-. Writer. **Publications:** The SDI Challenge to Europe, 1987; Strategic Defences in the 1990s: Criteria for Deployment, 1991; The Nature and Practice of Flexible Response: NATO Strategy and Theater Nuclear Forces since 1967, 1991; Cooperative Arms Control: A New Agenda for the Post-Cold War Era, 1992; Getting to Dayton: The Making of America's Bosnia Policy, 2000; (with M.E. O'Hanlon) Winning Ugly: NATO's War to Save Kosovo, 2000; (co-author) Protecting the American Homeland, 2002, rev. ed., 2003; (with J.M. Lindsay) America Unbound: The Bush Revolution in Foreign Policy, 2003; (with I.M. Destler) In the Shadow of the Oval Office: Profiles of the National Security Advisers and the Presidents They Served-From JFK to George W. Bush, 2009. EDITOR: (with T. Terriff) Rethinking the Unthinkable: New Directions in Nuclear Arms Control, 1993; (with F.G. Burwell) The United States and Europe in the Global Arena, 1998; (with P. Gordon and N. Gnesotto) Crescent of Crisis: US-European Strategy for the Greater Middle East, 2006; Beyond Preemption: Force and Legitimacy

in a Changing World, 2007. Contributor to periodicals and newspapers. **Address:** The Brookings Institution, 1775 Massachusetts Ave. NW, Washington, DC 20036, U.S.A. **Online address:** idaalder@brookings.edu

DABASHI, Hamid. American/Iranian (born Iran), b. 1951. **Genres:** Philosophy, Social Sciences. **Career:** Columbia University, Institute for Comparative Literature and Society, director of graduate studies, 2001-05, Hagop Kevorkian professor of Iranian studies and comparative literature; University of Texas, teacher; University of Utah, teacher; Harvard University, teacher; New York University, teacher; Dreams of a Nation (a Palestinian film project), founder. Writer. **Publications:** (Ed.) Shiism: Doctrines, Thought, and Spirituality, 1988; (ed.) Expectation of the Millennium: Shiism in History, 1989; Authority in Islam: From the Rise of Muhammad to the Establishment of the Umayyads, 1989; (ed.) Parviz Sayyad's Theater of Diaspora: Two Plays, The Ass and The Rex Cinema Trial, 1993; Theology of Discontent: The Ideological Foundations of the Islamic Revolution in Iran, 1993, 2nd ed., 2006; (with P. Chelkowski) Staging a Revolution: The Art of Persuasion in the Islamic Republic of Iran, 1999; Truth and Narrative: The Untimely Thoughts of Ayn al-Qudāt al-Hamadhānī, 1999; Onomadopean: Visite à Amir Parsa, 2000; Close Up: Iranian Cinema, Past, Present, and Future, 2001; Shirin Neshat: La última palabra, 2005; (ed. and intro.) Dreams of a Nation: On Palestinian Cinema, 2006; Iran: A People Interrupted, 2007; Masters & Masterpieces of Iranian Cinema, 2007; Islamic Liberation Theology: Resisting the Empire, 2008; Post-Orientalism: Knowledge and Power in Time of Terror, 2009; Iran, The Green Movement and the USA: The Fox and the Paradox, 2010; Conversations with Mohsen Makhmalbaf, 2010; Shi'ism: A Religion of Protest, 2010; (ed. with A. Dacison) The World is My Home: A Hamid Dabashi Reader, 2010. **Address:** Department of Middle Eastern, South Asian, and African Studies, Columbia University, 606 W 122nd St., New York, NY 10027, U.S.A. **Online address:** hd14@columbia.edu

DABNEY, Joseph Earl. American (born United States), b. 1929. **Genres:** Food And Wine, History, Air/Space Topics, Military/Defense/Arms Control, Mythology/Folklore, Sciences, Business/Trade/Industry. **Career:** Gainesville Daily Times, managing editor, 1954-56; Florence Morning News, managing editor, 1956-60, associate editor, 1961-62; South Carolina Associated Press Association, president, 1960; Atlanta Journal, state news editor, 1963-64; Lockheed-Georgia Co., public relations representative, 1965-; Lockheed Aeronautical Systems Co., public relations officer, 1965-90; Georgia Association of Business Communicators, president, 1969; Southern Association of Business Communicators, vice-president, 1974, president, 1975. **Publications:** Mountain Spirits: A Chronicle of Corn Whiskey from King James' Ulster Plantation to America's Appalachians, 1974; HERK, Hero of the Skies, 1979, 3rd ed., 2003; More Mountain Spirits: The Continuing Chronicle of Moonshine Life and Corn Whiskey, Wines, Ciders & Beers in America's Appalachians, 1985; Smokehouse Ham, Spoon Bread and Scuppernong Wine: The Folklore and Art of Southern Appalachian Cooking, 1998; The Food, Folklore, and Art of Lowcountry Cooking: A Celebration of the Foods, History, and Romance Handed down from England, Africa, the Caribbean, France, Germany, and Scotland, 2010. **Address:** Lockheed-Georgia Co., Marietta, GA 30063, U.S.A. **Online address:** joedabney@aol.com

DABYDEEN, Cyril. Canadian/Guyanese (born Guyana), b. 1945. **Genres:**

Novels, Novellas/Short Stories, Poetry. **Career:** Teacher, 1961-70; Algonquin College, communications lecturer, 1975-81; Ottawa Journal, reviewer, 1975-78; University of Ottawa, professor of creative writing and English, 1982-, part-time professor, teacher of creative writing, 1986-97; World Literature Today, reviewer. Writer and consultant. **Publications:** NOVELS: The Wizard Swami, 1985; Dark Swirl, 1989; Sometimes Hard, 1994; Drums of My Flesh, 2005. POETRY: Poems in Recession, 1972; Goatsong, 1977; Distances, 1977; Heart's Frame, 1979; This Planet Earth, 1980; Elephants Make Good Stepladders, 1982; Islands Lovelier Than a Vision, 1987; Coastland: New and Selected Poems, 1989; (co-author) Six Ottawa Poets, 1990; Stoning the Wind, 1994; Born in Amazonia, 1995; Discussing Columbus, 1997; Hemisphere of Live, 2003; Play a Song Somebody: New and Selected Stories, 2004. STORIES: Still Close to the Island, 1980; Monkey Jungle, 1988; Jogging in Havanna, 1992; Berbice Crossing, 1996; Black Jesus and Other Stories, 1996; My Brahmin Days and Other Stories, 2000; North of the Equator, 2001; Uncharted Heart, 2008; Unanimous Night, 2009. EDITOR: A Shapely Fire: Changing the Literary Landscape, 1987; Another Way to Dance, 1990, 2nd ed., 1996. OHTERS: Islands Lovelier than a Vision, 1990; Uncharted Heart, 2008. Works appears in anthologies. **Address:** Department of English, University of Ottawa, Rm. 338, Arts Hall, 70 Laurier Ave. E, Ottawa, ON K1N 6N5, Canada. **Online address:** cdabydeen@ncf.ca

DABYDEEN, David. British (born England), b. 1956. **Genres:** Novels, Poetry, Art/Art History, Literary Criticism And History, Social Sciences, inspirational/Motivational Literature. **Career:** Community Education Officer, 1982-84; Warwick University, professor of literature, 1984-, Centre for Caribbean Studies, director. **Publications:** Slave Song (poetry), 1984; (ed.) The Black Presence in English Literature, 1985; Hogarth's Blacks: Images of Blacks in Eighteenth-Century English Art, 1987; (ed. with B. Samaroo) India in the Caribbean, 1987; (with N. Wilson-Tagoe) Reader's Guide to West Indian and Black British Literature, 1987; Hogarth, Walpole and Commercial Britain, 1987; (ed.) A Handbook for Teaching Caribbean Literature, 1988; (ed.) Rented Rooms, 1988; Coolie Odyssey, 1988; (ed. and intro. with P. Edwards) Black Writers in Britain, 1760-1890, 1991; (ed. with B. Samaroo.) Across the Dark Waters: Ethnicity and Indian Identity in the Caribbean, 1996; (ed.) Cheddi Jagan: Tributes in Verse and Prose, 1998; (ed.) The USA in South America and Other Essays, 1998; (ed.) Poesiias escogidas/Selected poems, 1999; (ed. with J. Gilmore) No Island is an Island: Selected Speeches of Sir Shridath Ramphal, 2000; (ed.) Cheddi Jagan: Selected Correspondences 1953-1965, 2004; (ed. with J. Gilmore and C. Jones) The Oxford Companion to Black British History, 2007; (ed.) Selected Poems of Egbert Martin, 2007; (co-ed.) First Crossing, 2007. NOVELS: The Intended (novel), 1990; Disappearance (novel), 1993; Turner (poetry), 1994; The Counting House (novel), 1996; A Harlot's Progress (novel), 1999; Our Lady of Demerara, 2004; Molly and the Muslim Stick, 2008. **Address:** Centre for Caribbean Studies, University of Warwick, Kirby Corner Rd., Coventry, WM CV4 8JY, England. **Online address:** d.dabydeen@warwick.ac.uk

DACE, Letitia. See DACE, Tish.

DACE, Tish. (Letitia Dace). American (born United States), b. 1941. **Genres:** Literary Criticism And History, Theatre, Writing/Journalism. **Career:** Kansas State University, instructor in speech and associate director of theatre, 1967-71; City University of New York, John Jay College of Criminal Justice, assistant professor, 1971-74, associate professor of speech, drama and English, 1975-80, Department of Speech and Theatre, chairman, 1979-80; Greenwich Village News, theatre editor, 1976-77; University of Massachusetts, College of Arts and Sciences, dean, 1980-86, professor of English and drama, 1986-97, chancellor professor, 1997-2002, chancellor professor emeritus, 2002-. **Publications:** LeRoi Jones (Imamu Amiri Baraka): A Checklist of Works by and about Him, 1971; (with W. Dace) The Theatre Student: Modern Theatre Drama, 1973; (co-author) Black American Writers, 1978; (ed.) Langston Hughes: The Contemporary Reviews, 1997; Martin Sherman: Skipping over Quicksand, 2012. Contributor to books and periodicals. **Address:** Kaya Mars 12, Bonaire, AN BES, Netherlands Antilles. **Online address:** tdace@umassd.edu

DACEY, Austin. American (born United States), b. 1972. **Genres:** Humanities, Young Adult Non-fiction, Politics/Government. **Career:** United Nations representative for the Center for Inquiry, director of research and education; FREEMUSE, advisor; Polytechnic Institute of New York University, faculty; Philo, executive editor. **Publications:** (With L. Vaughn) The Case for Humanism: An Introduction, 2003; The Secular Conscience: Why Belief Belongs in

Public Life, 2008; Future of Blasphemy: Speaking of the Sacred in an Age of Human Rights, 2011. Contributor to periodicals. **Address:** The Continuum International Publishing Group, 80 Maiden Ln., 704 Ste., New York, NY 10038, U.S.A. **Online address:** info@austindacey.com

DACEY, Philip. American (born United States), b. 1939. **Genres:** Poetry. **Career:** Miles College, instructor, 1966; University of Missouri, instructor in English, 1967-68; Southwest State University, assistant professor, professor of English and coordinator of creative writing, 1970-90, director of international film series, 1981-82; Crazy House, editor, 1971-76; Minnesota Writers' Festival, founder and director, 1978; Wichita State University, poet-in-residence, 1985, Fulbright lecturer in creative writing, 1988; Marshall Festivals, founder and director, 1986, 1989; Lyon College, White River Writers Workshop, faculty, 1996; University of Idaho, visiting writer, 1999; Mankato State University, Eddice Barber Visiting Writer, 2003; Southwest Minnesota State University, Department of English, now professor emeritus. **Publications:** How I Escaped from the Labyrinth and Other Poems, 1977; The Condom Poems, 1979; The Boy Under the Bed, 1979, 2nd ed., 1981; Gerard Manley Hopkins Meets Walt Whitman in Heaven and Other Poems, 1982; Fives, 1984; (ed. with D. Jauss) Strong Measures: Contemporary American Poetry in Traditional Forms, 1986; The Man with Red Suspenders: Poems, 1986; The Condom Poems II, 1989; Night Shift at the Crucifix Factory: Poems, 1991; The Deathbed Playboy: Poems, 1999; The Paramour of the Moving Air, 1999; The Adventures of Alixa Doom and Other Love Poems, 2003; The Mystery of Max Schmitt: Poems on the Life and Work of Thomas Eakins, 2004; Mister Five-by-Five, 2005; Three Shades of Green: Poems of Fatherhood, 2006; The New York Postcard Sonnets: A Midwesterner Moves to Manhattan, 2007; Vertebrae Rosaries: 50 Sonnets, 2009; Mosquito Operas: New and Selected Short Poems, 2010. **Address:** 102 W 76th St., Ste. 2R, New York, NY 10023, U.S.A. **Online address:** philipdacey@gmail.com

D'ADAMO, Francesco. Italian (born Italy), b. 1949?. **Genres:** Young Adult Fiction, History, Plays/Screenplays. **Career:** Writer. **Publications:** Lupo Omega, 1999; Mille Pezzi Al Giorno, 2000; Storia di Iqbal, 2001; Bazar, 2002; Johnny il Seminatore, 2005; Storia di Ouiah Che Era un Leopardo, 2006; My Brother Johnny, 2008. **Address:** Atheneum Books, 1230 Ave. of the Americas, New York, NY 10020, U.S.A.

D'ADAMO, Peter J. American (born United States), b. 1956. **Genres:** Medicine/Health, Sports/Fitness. **Career:** Southwest College of Naturopathic Medicine, adjunct clinical professor; National College of Naturopathic Medicine, adjunct clinical professor; University of Bridgeport, College of Naturopathic Medicine, instructor, Health Sciences Center, supervising physician; American Association of Naturopathic Physicians, board director; Institute for Human Individuality (IfHI), founder, chairman and academic dean; The Journal of Naturopathic Medicine, founder and editor emeritus. Writer. **Publications:** WITH C. WHITNEY: Eat Right 4 (for) Your Type: The Individualized Diet Solution to Staying Healthy, Living Longer and Achieving Your Ideal Weight, 1996; Live Right 4 Your Type: The Individualized Prescription for Maximizing Health, Metabolism, and Vitality in Every Stage of Life, 2001; Complete Blood Type Encyclopedia: The A-Z Reference guide for the Blood Type Connection to Symptoms, Disease, Conditions, Vitamins, Supplements, Herbs, and Food, 2002; Eat Right for Your Baby: The Individualized Guide to Fertility and Maximum Health During Pregnancy, Nursing, and Your Baby's First Year, 2003; Diabetes: Fight it with the Blood Type Diet, 2004; Cardiovascular Disease: Fight it with the Blood Type Diet, 2004; Cancer: Fight It with the Blood Type Diet, 2004; Arthritis: Fight it with the Blood Type Diet, 2004; Aging: Fight It with the Blood Type Diet, 2005; Fatigue: Fight it with the Blood Type Diet, 2005; Menopause: Manage Its Symptoms with the Blood Type Diet, 2005; Allergies: Fight Them with the Blood Type Diet, 2005; The Genotype Diet, 2007. OTHER: Cook Right 4 Your Type: The Practical Kitchen Companion to Eat Right 4 Your Type, Including more than 200 Original Recipes, as well as Individualized 30-day Meal Plans for Staying Healthy, Living Longer, and Achieving Your Ideal Weight, 1998. **Address:** Putnam Berkeley Group Inc., 375 Hudson St., New York, NY 10014-3658, U.S.A.

DADLEZ, E(va) M(aria). American (born United States), b. 1956. **Genres:** Philosophy, Ethics. **Career:** Syracuse University, teaching assistant, 1984-86, 1987-88, teaching fellow, 1986, part-time instructor in philosophy, 1988-89, 1991, professional writing instructor, 1989-92, philosophy writing consultant, 1990-91; Cornell University, teaching associate, 1989; Ithaca College, assistant professor of philosophy and religion, 1992-93; University of Central

Oklahoma, Department of Humanities and Philosophy, assistant professor, 1993-98, associate professor, 1998-2002, professor, 2002-. Writer. **Publications:** What's Hecuba to Him? Fictional Events and Actual Emotions, 1997; Mirrors to One Another: Emotion and Value in Jane Austen and David Hume, 2009. Contributor of articles to journals. **Address:** Department of Humanities and Philosophy, University of Central Oklahoma, Rm. 205A, 100 N University Dr., Edmond, OK 73034, U.S.A. **Online address:** edadlez@uco.edu

DA FONSECA, Eduardo Giannetti. Brazilian (born Brazil), b. 1957. **Genres:** Economics, Philosophy, Business/Trade/Industry. **Career:** Cambridge University, St. John's College, research fellow and professor, 1984-87, Joan Robinson memorial lecturer, 1992-93; University of São Paulo, professor in economics, 1988-99; Instituto Fernand Brandel de Economia Mundial, Octavio Gouvea de Bulhoes Professor, 1992-; Ibmec Educacional SA, School of Economics and Business Administration, professor, 2000-. Writer. **Publications:** Adol(eddência), 1976; Liberalismo x pobreza: a liberdade vencendo amiséria, 1989; Livre para Crescer, 1990; Beliefs in Action: Economic Philosophy and Social Change, 1991; (with D.C. Cyrillo and J. Gonçalves) Arrecadação e Distribuiçãodo Salário-Educação em São Paulo, 1993; Vícios Privados, Benefícios Públicos?: a ética na Riqueza das Nações, 1993; As Partes & o Todo, 1995; (ed. with M.J.F. Willumsen) Brazilian Economy: Structure and Performance in Recent Decades, 1997; Nada é Tudo: ética, Economia e Brasilidade, 2000; Valor do amanhã: ensaio sobre a natureza dos juros, 2005; livro das Citações, 2008. **Address:** Ibmec Educacional SA, 1170 Rua Maestro Cardim, Aclimação, Sao Paulo, SP 01323-001, Brazil. **Online address:** eduardogf@isp.edu.br

DAFTARY, Farhad. British/Belgian (born Belgium), b. 1938. **Genres:** Cultural/Ethnic Topics, History, Theology/Religion. **Career:** Plan Organization of Iran, senior adviser, 1972; Central Bank of Iran, Research Department, director, 1973; Yekom Consultants, founder, 1974, director, 1974-80; Institute of Ismaili Studies, professor of history, 1988-, Department of Academic Research and Publications, associate director and head, 1991-, co-director; Encyclopaedia Islamica, co-editor; Encyclopaedia Iranica, consulting editor. **Publications:** The Ismā'īliWMCNs: Their History and Doctrines, 1990, 2nd ed., 2007; The Assassin Legends: Myths of the Isma'ilis, 1992, 2nd ed., 1995; (ed.) Mediaeval Isma'ili History and Thought, 1996; A Short History of the Ismailis, 1998; (ed.) Intellectual Traditions in Islam, 2000; (contrib.) Sunnat'hā-yi 'aqlānī dar Islām, 2001; (ed. with J.W. Meri) Culture and Memory in Medieval Islam, 2003; Mukhtasare dar tarikhi ismoiliia, 2003; Ismaili Literature: A Bibliography of Sources and Studies, 2004; Ismailis in Medieval Muslim Societies, 2005; (with Z. Hirji) Ismailis: An Illustrated History, 2008; (with W. Madelung) Encyclopaedia Islamica, 2008; (foreword) The Epistles of the Brethren of Purity: The Ikhwan al-Safa' and their Rasa'il An Introduction, 2009; (ed. with E. Fernea and A. Nanji) Living in Historic Cairo: Past and Present in an Islamic City, 2010; (ed.) A Modern History of the Ismailis: Continuity and Change in a Muslim Community, 2011; Historical Dictionary of the Ismailis, 2012. Contributor to journals. **Address:** Institute of Ismaili Studies, 210 Euston Rd., London, GL NW1 2DA, England. **Online address:** fdaftary@iis.ac.uk

DAGBOVIE, Pero Gaglo. American (born United States), b. 1971. **Genres:** History. **Career:** Michigan State University, Department of History, assistant professor, 1999-2007, associate professor of African American history, 2008-, became graduate director; Wayne State University, Department of Interdisciplinary Studies, visiting assistant professor, 2000-03. Writer. **Publications:** Black History: Old School Black Historians and the Hip-hop Generation, 2005; The Early Black History Movement, Carter G. Woodson, and Lorenzo Johnston Greene, 2007; African American History Reconsidered, 2010; Willing to Sacrifice: Carter G. Woodson (1875-1950) and the Carter G. Woodson Home, NHS, 2010. Contributor to books and periodicals. **Address:** Department of History, Michigan State University, 301 Morrill Hall, East Lansing, MI 48824, U.S.A. **Online address:** dagbovie@msu.edu

DAHL, Arlene. American (born United States), b. 1928. **Genres:** Adult Nonfiction, Film, Theology/Religion. **Career:** Arlene Dahl Enterprises, president, 1951-75; A.N. Saab & Co., sleepwear designer, 1952-57; Kenyon & Eckhart Advertising Co., vice president, president of woman's world division, 1967-72; Sears, Roebuck & Co., national beauty director, 1970-75; O.M.A., fashion consultant, 1975-78; Dahlia Perfumes Inc., president, 1975-80; Vogue Patterns, designer, 1978-85; Dahlia Productions, president and chief executive officer, 1978-81; Dahlmark Productions, president and chief executive officer, 1981-; Lasting Beauty Ltd., president and chair, 1986-; Broadway Walk of Stars Foundation, founder and president, 1998-. Writer and actress. **Publications:** Scene of the Crime, 1949; Always Ask a Man, 1963; Your Beauty Scope, 12 vols., 1969, rev. ed., 1978; Arlene Dahl's Secrets of Skin Care, 1971; Arlene Dahl's Secrets of Hair Care, 1978; The Reminiscences of Arlene Dahl, 1978; Your Beauty Scope: Gemini, May 21-June 21, 1978; Beyond Beauty: A Three-Part Journey to Help You Reach Your Full Potential as a Woman, 1980; Arlene Dahl's Lovescopes: The Astrological Key to a More Exciting, Fulfilling Love Life, 1983. **Address:** Dahlmark Productions, PO Box 116, Sparkill, NY 10976, U.S.A.

DAHL, Robert (Alan). American (born United States), b. 1915. **Genres:** Economics, Politics/Government, Social Sciences. **Career:** U.S. Department of Agriculture, management analyst, 1940; War Production Board, economist, 1940-42; Office of Production Management, economist, 1941; Yale University, faculty, 1946, instructor, 1946-47, assistant professor, 1948-52, associate professor, 1953-57, Ford research professor, 1957, chair, 1957-62, Eugene Meyer professor of political science, 1957-63, Sterling professor of political science, 1963-, Sterling professor emeritus of political science and senior research scientist of sociology; University of Chicago, Walgreen lecturer, 1954; Center for the Advanced Study of the Behavioral Science, fellow, 1955-56, 1967; lecturer in Chile, 1967. Writer. **Publications:** Congress and Foreign Policy, 1949; (with R. Brown) Domestic Control of Atomic Energy, 1951; (ed.) The Impact of Atomic Energy, 1953; (with C.E. Lindblom) Politics, Economics and Welfare: Planning and Politico-economic Systems Resolved into Basic Social Processes, 1953; A Preface to Democratic Theory, 1956; (with M. Haire and P.F. Lazarsfeld) Social Science Research on Business: Product and Potential, 1960; (co-author) Power and Democracy in America, 1961; Who Governs? Democracy and Power in an American City, 1961; Modern Political Analysis, 1963, 6th ed. 2002; L'avenir de l'opposition dans les démocraties, trans. as Political Oppositions in Western Democracies, 1966; Pluralist Democracy in the United States: Conflict and Consent, 1967; (ed. with D.E. Neubauer) Readings in Modern Political Analysis, 1968; After the Revolution? Authority in a Good Society, 1970, rev. ed. 1990; The New Haven Community Study: Yale University, Summer 1959, 1971; Polyarchy: Participation and Opposition, 1971; Democracy in the United States: Promise and Performance, 1972, 4th ed., 1981; (ed.) Regimes and Oppositions, 1973; (with E.R. Tufte) Size and Democracy, 1973; Vorstufen zur Demokratie-Theorie, trans. as Preface to Democratic Theory, 1976; Dilemmas of Pluralistic Democracy: Autonomy vs. Control, 1982; A Preface to Economic Democracy, 1985; Controlling Nuclear Weapons: Democracy Versus Guardianship, 1985; Democracy, Liberty and Equality, 1986; I Sistemi dipartito, 1986; Democracy and Its Critics, 1989; The New American Political (Dis)order, 1994; Toward Democracy: A Journey, Reflections, 1940-1997, 1997; On Democracy, 1998; On Democracy, Arabic, 2000; How Democratic is the American Constitution, 2001; (ed. with I. Shapiro and J.A. Cheibub) Democracy Sourcebook, 2003; After the Gold Rush: Growing Up in Skagway, 2005; On Political Equality, 2006. Contributor to periodicals. **Address:** Department of Political Science, Yale University, Rm. 209, 124 Prospect St., PO Box 208301, New Haven, CT 06520-8301, U.S.A. **Online address:** robert.dahl@yale.edu

DAHL, Victoria. American (born United States), b. 1973?. **Genres:** Novels. **Career:** Writer. **Publications:** ROMANCE NOVELS: To Tempt a Scotsman, 2007; A Rake's Guide to Pleasure, 2008; One Week as Lovers, 2009; A Little Bit Wild, 2010. TUMBLE CREEK SERIES ROMANCE NOVELS: Talk Me Down, 2009; Start Me Up, 2009; Lead Me On, 2010. Contributor to books. Works appear in anthologies. **Online address:** victoria@victoriadahl.com

DAHLBERG, Maurine F. American (born United States), b. 1951?. **Genres:** Novels, Children's Fiction, Romance/Historical, Literary Criticism And History. **Career:** Navy Research Institute, editor. **Publications:** Play to the Angel, 2000; The Spirit and Gilly Bucket, 2002; Escape to West Berlin, 2004; The Story of Jonas, 2007. **Address:** c/o Author Mail, Farrar, Straus & Giroux, 19 Union Sq. W, New York, NY 10003, U.S.A.

DAHLEN, Beverly. (Beverly Jean Dahlen). American (born United States), b. 1934. **Genres:** Poetry, Education, Language/Linguistics. **Career:** Poetry Center, assistant & secretary, 1967-73; California Poetry-in-the-Schools Project, creative writing teacher, 1970-74; East Bay Community Arts Project, creative writing teacher, 1974-80; City College of San Francisco, Adult Learning Center, staff, 1980-; San Francisco State University, College of Marin, creative writing teacher; Foothill College, teacher of summer writing. **Publications:** Out of the Third, 1974; A Letter at Easter: To George Stanley, 1976; The Egyptian Poems, 1983; A Reading (1-7), 1985; A Reading (11-17), 1989;

A Reading (8-10), 1992; A Reading (18-20), 2006. Contributor to periodicals. **Address:** 15 1/2 Mirabel Ave., San Francisco, CA 94110, U.S.A.

DAHLEN, Beverly Jean. *See* DAHLEN, Beverly.

DAHLIE, Hallvard. Canadian/Norwegian (born Norway), b. 1925. **Genres:** Literary Criticism And History, Young Adult Fiction. **Career:** Teacher, 1951-64; University of Calgary, assistant professor, 1967-71, associate professor, 1971-76, head of department, 1974-79, professor of English, 1976-90, professor emeritus of English, 1990-. Writer. **Publications:** Brian Moore, 1969; (contrib.) Common Wealth, 1971; (ed. with R. Chadbourne) The New Land: Studies in a Literary Theme, 1978; Alice Munro and Her Works, 1984; Varieties of Exile: The Canadian Experience, 1986; Isolation and Commitment: Frederick Philip Grove's Settlers of the Marsh, 1993. **Address:** Deparment of English, University of Calgary, 2500 University Dr. NW, Calgary, AB T2N 1N4, Canada.

DAHLSTROM, Carol Field. American (born United States) **Genres:** Food And Wine, Crafts. **Career:** Carol Field Dahlstrom Inc., Brave Ink Press (publishing house), president. Writer. **Publications:** Simply Christmas, 2000; Christmas, Make It Sparkle: 225 Simple Crafts, Food & Decorating Ideas for Your Holiday Home, 2003; Beautiful Christmas: 250 Best Ideas for a Memorable Holiday, 2004; An Ornament a Day: 25 Sparkling Holiday Trims to Make, 2004; Cool Crafts to Make: Even If You Don't Have a Creative Bone in Your Body! Or Even If You Do!, 2005; College Kids Cook, 2005; Easy Decorating Projects: Even if You Don't have a Creative Bone in your Body! Or Even if You Do, 2005; Christmas Together, 2005; Christmas Happy & Bright: Trees, Wreaths, Trims, Stockings, Gifts, Cookies, Memories, 2006; Christmas in the Nick of Time, 2008; (with E.D. Burnley and M.S. Dahlstrom) Gluten-Free made Simple, 2011. EDITOR: Mary Engelbreit Cross-Stitch for All Seasons, 1997; Great Patchwork Collection: A Step-by-Step Guide to Quilting, 1997; 101 Full-size Quilt Blocks and Borders, 1998; Simply Handmade: 365 Easy Gifts & Decorations You Can Make, 1998; Hey, Kids! Come Craft with Me, 1999; Crafts to Decorate Your Home, 1999; Simply Handmade: 365 Easy Projects for Every Occasion, 2000; Crafts to Make & Sell, 2000; Halloween: 101 Frightfully Fun Ideas, 2000; New Junior Craft Book, 2000; Decorating Ideas: Projects to Make for Indoors and Out, 2001; 501 Fun-to-Make Family Crafts, 2001; Stitching Pretty: 101 Lovely Cross Stitch Projects to Make, 2002; Grandma's Best Full-Size Quilt Blocks: Pieces of the Past for Today's Quilter, 2002; Collections: Projects & Ideas to Display Your Treasures, 2002; Christmas Ornaments to Make: 101 Sparkling Holiday Trims, 2002; Paint It!: 101 Ideas, Designs, & Patterns for Decorating Any Surface, 2002; Scrapbooking: Everything You Need to Know to Preserve Your Memories, 2003; Crafts for Girls Only, 2004; Scrapbooking for Girls Only, 2004; Spider-Man Party Book, 2004; Two-Color Quilts, 2004; Hip Knits: 65 Easy Projects from Hot Designers, 2004; Crafting with 4 Supplies, 2004; Beautiful Cross-Stitch: Designs and Projects Inspired by the World around You, 2004; Pretty Printed Paper Squares, 2005; Merry Christmas Ideas: 225 Projects for Crafting, Cookie-Baking, Gift-Giving, Decorating, and Memory-Making, 2007. **Address:** Carol Field Dahlstrom Inc., PO Box 663, Ankeny, IA 50021, U.S.A. **Online address:** braveink@aol.com

DAIGLE, Evelyne. Canadian (born Canada), b. 1965. **Genres:** Environmental Sciences/Ecology, Zoology, Illustrations, Education. **Career:** Biodome of Montreal, environmental educator, 1992-. Writer and biologist. **Publications:** As Long as There Are Whales, 2004; The World of Penguins, 2007. **Address:** Biodome of Montreal, 4777 Pierre De Coubertin, Montreal, QC H1V 1B3, Canada. **Online address:** edaigle@ville.montreal.qc.ca

DAILEY, Janet. American (born United States), b. 1944. **Genres:** Romance/ Historical, Westerns/Adventure, Novels, Children's Fiction, Young Adult Fiction, Young Adult Non-fiction, inspirational/Motivational Literature. **Career:** Writer. **Publications:** Something Extra, 1975; No Quarter Asked, 1976; Boss Man from Ogallala, 1976; Savage Land, 1976; Fire and Ice, 1976; The Homeplace, 1976; After the Storm, 1976; Land of Enchantment, 1976; Dangerous Masquerade, 1976; The Night of the Cotillion, 1976; Valley of the Vapours, 1976; Fiesta San Antonio, 1977; Show Me, 1977; Bluegrass King, 1977; A Lyon's Share, 1977; The Widow and the Wastrel, 1977; The Ivory Cane, 1978; The Indy Man, 1978; Darling Jenny, 1978; Reilly's Woman, 1978; To Tell the Truth, 1978; Sonora Sundown, 1978; Big Sky Country, 1978; Something Extra, 1978; The Master Fiddler, 1978; Beware of the Stranger, 1978; Giant of Mesabi, 1978; The Matchmakers, 1978; Touch the Wind, 1979; For Bitter or Worse, 1979; Green Mountain Man, 1979; Six White Horses, 1979;

Summer Mahogany, 1979; The Bride of the Delta Queen, 1979; Tidewater Lover, 1979; Strange Bedfellow, 1979; Low Country Liar, 1979; Sweet Promise, 1979; For Mike's Sake, 1979; Sentimental Journey, 1979; A Land Called Deseret, 1979; The Rogue, 1980; Ride the Thunder, 1980; Kona Winds, 1980; That Boston Man, 1980; Bed of Grass, 1980; That Boston Man, 1980; The Thawing of Mara, 1980; The Mating Season, 1980; Lord of the High Lonesome, 1980; Southern Nights, 1980; Enemy in Camp, 1980; Difficult Decision, 1980; Heart of Stone, 1980; One of the Boys, 1980; Night Way, 1981; This Calder Sky, 1981; The Hostage Bride, 1981; The Lancaster Men, 1981; For the Love of God, 1981; Wild and Wonderful, 1981; A Tradition of Pride, 1981; The Traveling Kind, 1981; Dakota Dreamin', 1981; This Calder Range, 1982; Terms of Surrender, 1982; Foxfire Light, 1982; Northern Magic, 1982; With a Little Luck, 1982; That Carolina Summer, 1982; Wildcatter's Woman, 1982; The Second Time, 1982; Mistle Toe and Holly, 1982; Separate Cabins, 1983; Western Man, 1983; The Best Way to Lose, 1983; Stands A Calder Man, 1983; Calder Born, Calder Bred, 1983; Leftover Love, 1984; Silver Wings, Santiago Blue, 1984; The Pride of Hannah Wade, 1985; The Glory Game, 1985; The Great Alone, 1986; Heiress, 1987; Rivals, 1989; Masquerade, 1990; Aspen Gold, 1991; Tangled Vines: A Novel, 1992; The Proud and the Free, 1994; The Healing Touch, 1994; Legacies, 1995; Notorious, 1996; (co-author) A Spring Bouquet, 1996; Flower Girls, 1996; (with J. Blake and E. Gage) Unmasked, 1997; Homecoming, 1997; Illusions, 1997; Calder Pride, 1999; A Capital Holiday, 2001; (with S. Steffen and K. Adams) The Only Thing Better Than Chocolate, 2002; Scrooge Wore Spurs, 2002; Green Calder Grass, 2002; Shifting Calder Wind, 2003; Calder Promise, 2004; Lone Calder Star, 2005; Calder Storm, 2006; Eve's Christmas, 2006; Man of Mine, 2007; Something More, 2007; Wearing White, 2007; With This Kiss, 2007; Mistletoe and Molly, 2007; Searching For Santa, 2008; American Dreams, 2009; Santa in a Stetson, 2009; Close To You, 2010; That Loving Feeling, 2010; Santa in Montana, 2010; To Santa With Love, 2011; Trust, 2011; Drawing Fire, 2011; Honor, 2012; A Cowboy Under My Christmas Tree, 2012. **Address:** PO Box 1190, Branson, MO 65615-1190, U.S.A. **Online address:** janetdailey@janetdailey.com

DAILY, David W. American (born United States), b. 1965?. **Genres:** Politics/Government. **Career:** University of the Ozarks, assistant professor of religion, 2000-. Writer. **Publications:** Battle for the BIA: G.E.E. Lindquist and the Missionary Crusade against John Collier, 2004. **Address:** University of the Ozarks, 415 N College Ave., Clarksville, AZ 72830, U.S.A. **Online address:** ddaily@ozarks.edu

DAITCH, Susan. American (born United States), b. 1954?. **Genres:** Novels, Novellas/Short Stories, Young Adult Fiction. **Career:** Barnard College, faculty; Hunter College, adjunct faculty. Writer. **Publications:** L.C., 1987; The Colorist, 1990; Storytown, 1996; The Dreyfus Book, 2011, The Paper Conspiracies, 2011. Contributor to periodicals. **Address:** Hunter College, Rm. 1235 HW, 695 Park Ave., New York, NY 10065, U.S.A. **Online address:** sed372@aol.com

DALAI LAMA. Indian/Tibetan (born Tibet), b. 1935. **Genres:** Theology/ Religion, Autobiography/Memoirs, Self Help, inspirational/Motivational Literature. **Career:** Emory University, presidential distinguished professor, 2007-. Writer. **Publications:** The International Position of Tibet, 1959; My Land and My People (autobiography), 1962; An Introduction to Buddhism, 1965; The Opening of the Wisdom-Eye and the History of the Advancement of the Buddhadharma in Tibet, 1968; Happiness, Karma, and Mind, 1969; The Key to Madhyamika, 1974; The Buddhism of Tibet and the Key to the Middle Way, 1975; The Sadhana of the Inseparability of the Spiritual Master and Avalokiteshvara, A Mahayana Method for Accomplishment, 1975; Universal Responsibility and the Good Heart: The Message of His Holiness the XIV Dalai Lama of Tibet on His First Visit to the West in 1973, 1976; Teachings of His Holiness the Dalai Lama, 1981; Four Essential Buddhist Commentaries, 1982; The Collected Statements, Articles, and Interviews of His Holiness the Dalai Lama, 1982; Advice from Buddha Shakyamuni: An Abridged Exposition of the Bikkshu's Precepts, 1982; A Human Approach to World Peace, 1984; (co-author) Emerging Consciousness for a New Humankind: Asian Interreligious Concern, 1985; Opening the Eye of New Awareness, 1985, rev. ed., 1999; The Kalachakra Tantra: Rite of Initiation for the Stage of Generation: A Commentary on the Text of Kay-drup-ge-lek-bel-sang-bo, 1985; The Bodhgaya Interviews: His Holiness the Dalai Lama, 1988; The Dalai Lama at Harvard: Lectures on the Buddhist Path to Peace, 1988; Tibet, China, and the World, 1989; Oceans of Wisdom: Guidelines for Living, 1989; Freedom in Exile: The Autobiography of the Dalai Lama, 1990; The Meaning of Life, 1990; My Tibet, 1990; (co-author) Mind Science: An East-West Dialogue, 1991; Cultivating a Daily Meditation, 1991; Path to Bliss, 1991; (with T. Jinpa) The World of Tibetan Buddhism: An Overview of Its Philosophy and Practice, 1995; Violence and Compassion, 1995; The Power of Compassion, 1995; Essential Teachings: His Holiness the Dalai Lama, 1995; The Path to Enlightenment, 1995; Beyond Dogma: Dialogues & Discourses, 1996; The Good Heart: A Buddhist Perspective on theTeachings of Jesus, 1996; The Joy of Living and Dying in Peace: Core Teachings of Tibetan Buddhism, 1997; (with A. Berzin) The Gelug/Kagyu Tradition of Mahamudra, 1997; Awakening the Mind, Lightening the Heart, 1997; The Way to Freedom, 1997; The Heart of Compassion: A Dalai Lama Reader, 1997; The Buddha Nature, 1997; The Four Noble Truths, 1998; (with H.C. Cutler) The Art of Happiness: A Handbook for Living, 1998; Spiritual Advice for Buddhists and Christians, 1998; The Dalai Lama's Book of Wisdom, 1999; The Heart of the Buddha's Path, 1999; (with A. Benson and F. Ouaki) Imagine All the People: A Conversation with the Dalai Lama on Money, Politics, and Life As It Could Be, 1999; The Transformed Mind: Reflections on Truth, Love, and Happiness, 1999; The Path to Tranquility: Daily Wisdom, 1999; Stages of Meditation, 2000; A Simple Path: Basic Buddhist Teachings by His Holiness the Dalai Lama, 2000; (with J.K. Rinpoche) Buddha Heart, Buddha Mind: Living the Four Noble Truths, 2000; Transforming the Mind: Teachings on Generating Compassion, rev. ed. as The Dalai Lama's Book of Transformation, 2000; Ethics for the New Millennium, 2000; (with R. Matthieu) The Spirit of Tibet: The Life and World of Khyentse Rinpoche, Spiritual Teacher, 2001; Live in a Better Way: Reflections on Truth, Love, and Happiness, 2001; Words of Wisdom: Selected Quotes from His Holiness the Dalai Lama, 2001; Dzogchen: The Heart Essence of the Great Perfection, 2001; An Open Heart: Practicing Compassion in Everyday Life, 2001; Advice on Dying, 2002; Illuminating the Path to Enlightenment, 2002; The Heart of Compassion: A Practical Approach to a Meaningful Life, 2002; The Compassionate Life, 2003; Warm Heart Open Mind, 2003; 365 Dalai Lama Daily Advice from the Heart, 2003; Many Ways to Nirvana?, 2004; The Wisdom of Forgiveness, 2004; The Universe in a Single Atom-The Convergence of Science and Spirituality, 2005; Yoga Tantra: Paths to Magical Seats, 2005; (foreword) Way of the Bodhisattva, 2006; (intro.) Beyond Seven Years in Tibet, 2007; (foreword) Business and the Buddha, 2007; Mind in Comfort and Ease, 2007; (foreword) Truthful Heart, 2008; Phyi yul du raṅ dbaṅ, 2008; In My Own Words, 2008; Worlds in Harmony: Compassionate Action for a Better World, 2008; (with L. van den Muyzenberg) Leader's Way, 2009; Lam gtsói sgron me, 2009; (foreword) Boy on the Lion Throne, 2009; Grub mtha'i rnam bśad, 2009; (with H. Cutler) Art of Happiness in a Troubled World, 2009; Bod gaṅs-can gyi khyad nor: The unique Tibetan heritage, 2009; Toward a True Kinship of Faiths, 2010; (with H.C. Cutler) Essence of Happiness: A Guidebook to Living, 2010; (with L.J. Jiao and D.Y. Yi) Wo de tu di, wo de ren min, 2010; My Spiritual Journey, 2010; (contrib.) Spyi nor gon sa skyab mgon chen po mchog nas stsal ba'i Dol-rgyal skor gyi lam ston bka slob, 2010; (contrib.) Spyi nor goṅ sa skyab mgon chen po mchog nas stsal ba'i Kun-bzoṅ bla ma'i zal luṅ sñon 'gro'i gsuṅ chos thar lam gsal ba'i sgron me zes bya ba bzugs so, 2010; (contrib.) 365 méditations quotidiennes pour éclairer votre vie, 2010; (contrib.) Kun khyab sems 'khur daṅ 'dzam gliṅ zi bde, 2010; Beyond Religion, 2011; (contrib.) Goṅ sa skyabs mgon chen po mchog nas Bod-kyi Dgu-bcu-gsum Las-gul Tshogs-par bstsal ba'i bka' slob phyogs bsgrigs rmoṅs mun sel ba'i ñin byed, 2011; Bod kyi naṅ chos ṅo sprod sñiṅ bcud, 2011; From here to Enlightenment, 2011; How to be Compassionate, 2011; A Profound Mind, 2011. Contributor to books. **Address:** The Office of His Holiness the Dalai Lama, Thekchen Choeling, PO Mcleod Ganj, Dharamsala, HP 176219, India. **Online address:** ohhdl@dalailama.com

DALBY, Liza Crihfield. American (born United States), b. 1950?. **Genres:** Anthropology/Ethnology, Novels, inspirational/Motivational Literature, Cultural/Ethnic Topics. **Career:** University of Chicago, faculty. Writer, consultant and anthropologist. **Publications:** (Ed.) Ko-uta: Little Songs of the Geisha World, 1979; Geisha, 1983; (co-author) All-Japan: The Catalogue of Everything Japanese, 1984; Kimono: Fashioning Culture, 1993; (contrib.) The Women of the Pleasure Quarter: Japanese Paintings and Prints of the Floating World, 1995; The Tale of Murasaki (novel), 2000; (ed.) Little Songs of the Geisha: Traditional Japanese Ko-uta, 2000; (foreword) Ariake: Poems of Love and Longing by the Women Courtiers of Ancient Japan, 2000; (intro.) Kimono, 2001; East Wind Melts the Ice: A Memoir through the Seasons, 2007;

Hidden Buddhas: A Novel of Karma and Chaos, 2009. Contributor to books and journals. **Address:** c/o Author Mail, Nan A. Talese Books, 1745 Broadway, New York, NY 10019, U.S.A. **Online address:** lizadalby@gmail.com

DALCOURT, Gerard Joseph. American (born United States), b. 1927. **Genres:** Philosophy. **Career:** University of Kansas, librarian, 1954-56; Villanova University, instructor in philosophy, 1957-62; Seton Hall University, assistant professor, 1962-66, associate professor, 1966-75, professor of philosophy, 1975-97, professor emeritus, 1997-, department chairman, 1988-91. Writer. **Publications:** The Philosophy of St. Thomas Aquinas, 1965; (ed.) The Great Dialogue of Nature and Space, 1970; The Methods of Ethics, 1983. Contributor to journals. **Address:** Department of Philosophy, Seton Hall University, 246 Fahy Hall, 400 S Orange Ave., South Orange, NJ 07079-2646, U.S.A.

DALE, Anna. British (born England), b. 1971?. **Genres:** Novels. **Career:** Novelist. **Publications:** Whispering to Witches, 2004; Dawn Undercover, 2005; Spellbound, 2008; Magical Mischief, 2010. **Address:** c/o Author Mail, Bloomsbury Publishing Plc., 50 Bedford Sq., London, GL WC1B 3DP, England.

DALE, Peter. British (born England), b. 1938. **Genres:** Plays/Screenplays, Poetry, Education, Literary Criticism And History, Translations, Psychology, Biography. **Career:** Knaphill County Secondary School, assistant teacher of English, 1963; Howden C.S. School, assistant teacher of English, 1964-65; Glastonbury C.S. School, assistant teacher of English, 1965-72; Hinchley Wood C.S. School, English Department, head, 1972-93; Agenda, co-editor, 1982-96; full-time writer, 1993-; Oxford Today, poetry editor; Between the Lines, editorial director. **Publications:** Walk from the House, 1962; The Storms, 1968; Mortal Fire, 1970; Mortal Fire: New and Selected Poems and Translations, 1976; Cross Channel, 1977; One Another: A Sonnet Sequence, 1978; Too Much of Water: Poems 1976-82, 1983; (with W.S. Milne and R. Richardson) A Set of Darts: Epigrams, 1990; Earth Light: New Poems, 1991; Edge to Edge, New and Selected Poems, 1996; Da Capo: A Sequence, 1997; Under the Breath: New Poems, 2002; Peter Dale in Conversation with Cynthia Haven, 2005; Eight by Five, 2007; Local Habitation: A Sequence of Poems, 2009. TRANSLATOR: The Legacy and Other Poems, 1971, rev. ed. as Poems of Francois Villon, 2001; (with K. Subbiah) The Seasons of Cankam, 1975; Francois Villon, 1978; Narrow Straits, 1985; The Poems of Jules Laforgue, 1986, rev. ed., 2001; The Divine Comedy: Hell, Purgatory, Heaven, 1996; T. Corbiere, Way-Blue Loves and Other Poems, 2005. PROSE: Michael Hamburger in Conversation with Peter Dale, 1998; An Introduction to Rhyme, 1998; Anthony Thwaite in Conversation with Peter Dale and Ian Hamilton, 1999; Richard Wilbur in Conversation with Peter Dale, 2000. **Address:** 10 Selwood Rd., Sutton, SR SM3 9JU, England.

DALE, Richard. American (born United States), b. 1932. **Genres:** International Relations/Current Affairs, Politics/Government, History, Essays. **Career:** University of New Hampshire, instructor in government, 1962-63; Northern Illinois University, assistant professor of political science, 1963-66; Southern Illinois University, Department of Political Science, adjunct professor, 1966-67, assistant professor, 1967-71, associate professor, 1971-97, 1997-, associate professor emeritus. Writer. **Publications:** Botswana and Its Southern Neighbor: The Patterns of Linkage and the Options in Statecraft, 1970; The Racial Component of Botswana's Foreign Policy, 1971; (ed. with C.P. Potholm) Southern Africa in Perspective: Essays in Regional Politics, 1972; Botswana's Search for Autonomy in Southern Africa, 1995. Contributor of articles to journals. **Address:** PO Box 18635, Fountain Hills, AZ 85269-8635, U.S.A.

DALE, Rodney A. M. British (born England), b. 1933?. **Genres:** Medicine/Health, Music, Mythology/Folklore, Technology, Biography, Reference, Autobiography/Memoirs, History, History. **Career:** Fern House Publishing, owner. Writer. **Publications:** BIOGRAPHY: Louis Wain: The Man Who Drew Cats, 1968, rev. ed., 1991; (intro.) Catland, 1977; The Sinclair Story, 1985; (ed.) Walter Wilson: Portrait of an Inventor, 1986; Cats in Books: A Celebration of Cat Illustration Through the Ages, 1997. TECHNOLOGY: Bridges, 1973; Inland Waterways, 1974; Iron Roads, 1974; From Ram Yard to Milton Hilton: A History of Cambridge Consultants Ltd. 1960-1979, 1979; Die Manna Maschine, 1979; (with J. Gray) Edwardian Inventions 1901-1905, 1979; (with I. Williamson) BASIC Programming, 1979; (co-author) Understanding Microprocessors with the Science of Cambridge MK-14, 1980; The Myth of the Micro, 1980; Monde du jazz, 1980; (with R. Weaver) Machines in the Home, 1992; Early Flying Machines, 1992; (with H. Dale) The Industrial Revolution, 1992; Timekeeping, 1992; Home Entertainment, 1994; Machines in the Office, 1994; Early Railways, 1994; Early Cars, 1994; (with C. Fiddy) The Fern House Design & Technology Pack, 1995. CAREERS: (ed.) Hobsons Engineering Casebook, 1979; (ed.) Hobsons Computing Casebook, 1980; Becoming an Architect, 1983; (ed.) Hobsons Sixth Form Science, Technology and Engineering Casebook, 1985. FOLKLORE: The Tumour in the Whale: A Collection of Modern Myths, 1978; Its True, It Happened to a Friend: A Collection of Urban Legends, 1984. MUSIC: The World of Jazz, 1980; A History of Jazz, 1983; Teach Yourself Jazz, 1997, rev. ed., 2004; Jazz, 1998. COSMOLOGY: (with G. Sassoon): The Manna Machine, 1978; (co-ed.) The Kabbalah Decoded: A New Translation of the Ancient of Days Texts of the Zohar, 1978. OTHER: (ed.) O-level English (textbook), 1982; (with J. Starkie) Understanding AIDS (medicine), 1988; Puss in Boots (pantomime), 1990, rev. ed., 2001; The Tinder Box (pantomime), 1993; About Time (novel), 1995; (with S. Puttick) The Wordsworth Dictionary of Abbreviations & Acronyms (reference), 1997; Hello, Mrs. Fish (humor), 1997; Halcyon Days (autobiography), 1999; The Wordsworth Dictionary of Culinary & Menu Terms (reference), 2000; Haddenham & Aldreth Past and Present, 2000; The Wordsworth Dictionary of Culinary and Menu Terms, 2000; A Treasury of Love Poems, 2003; A Treasury of Proverbs, 2003; A Treasury Of Essential Proverbs, 2003; (comp. and ed.) The Book of WHAT?, 2004; (comp. and ed.) The Book of WHEN?, 2004; (comp. and ed.) The Book of WHERE?, 2004; (comp. and ed.) The Book of WHO?, 2004; Book of Urban Legend, 2005; Dickens Dictionary, 2005; Mrs. Fish Swims Again, 2005; Mrs. Fish On Tour, 2005; Sayings Usual and Unusual, 2007. **Address:** Fern House Publishing, 19 High St., Haddenham, Ely, CB CB6 3XA, England. **Online address:** info@fernhouse.com

DALEY, Michael J. American (born United States), b. 1968?. **Genres:** Science Fiction/Fantasy, Technology, Children's Fiction. **Career:** Dartmouth College, Energy Educator; St. Xavier High School, teacher. Citizen Lobbyist and writer. **Publications:** At Home with the Sun: Solar Energy for Young Scientists, 1995; Nuclear Power: Promise or Peril?, 1997; Amazing Sun Fun Activities, 1998; Getting Around without Gasoline, 2002; Space Station Rat, 2005; Shanghaied to the Moon, 2007; Rat Trap, 2008; Pinch and Dash and the Terrible Couch, 2012. **Address:** c/o Author Mail, Holiday House, 425 Madison Ave., New York, NY 10017, U.S.A. **Online address:** mjdaley@sover.net

DALEY, Robert (Blake). French/American (born United States), b. 1930. **Genres:** Novels, History. **Career:** New York Giants, publicity director, 1953-58; New York Times, foreign correspondent, war correspondent 1959-64; New York Police Department, deputy commissioner, 1971-72. Writer. **Publications:** The World beneath the City, 1959; Cars at Speed, 1961; The Bizarre World of European Sports, 1963; The Cruel Sport, 1963; The Swords of Spain, 1966; The Whole Truth, 1967; Only a Game, 1967; A Priest and a Girl, 1969; A Star in the Family, 1971; Target Blue, 1973; Strong Wine Red as Blood, 1974; To Kill a Cop, 1976; Death of a Cop, 1976; Treasure, 1977; The Fast One, 1978; Prince of the City: The True Story of a Cop Who Knew Too Much, 1979; An American Saga: Juan Trippe and His Pan Am Empire, 1980; Year of the Dragon, 1981; The Dangerous Edge, 1983; Hands of a Stranger, 1985; Man with a Gun, 1988; A Faint Cold Fear, 1990; Portraits of France, 1991; Tainted Evidence, 1993; Wall of Brass, 1994; Nowhere to Run, 1996; The Innocents Within, 1999; The Enemy of God, 2005; Pictures, 2006; Cars at Speed: Classic Stories from Grand Prix's Golden Age, 2007. **Address:** c/o Esther Newburg, International Creative Management, 730 5th Ave., New York, NY 10019, U.S.A. **Online address:** rivierapro@aol.com

DAL LAGO, Enrico. Italian (born Italy), b. 1966. **Genres:** History. **Career:** University of Rome, faculty, 1988; University College London, teaching fellow in history, 1995-99; National University of Ireland, lecturer in American history, 1999-. Writer and historian. **Publications:** (Ed. with R. Halpern and contrib.) The American South and the Italian Mezzogiorno: Essays in Comparative History, 2002; (ed. with R. Halpern and contrib.) Slavery and Emancipation, 2002; Agrarian Elites: American Slaveholders and Southern Italian Landowners, 1815-1861, 2005; (ed. and contrib. with C. Katsari) Slave Systems: Ancient and Modern, 2008; (ed. with C. Katsari) From Captivity to Freedom: Themes in Ancient and Modern Slavery, 2008; American Slavery, Atlantic Slavery, and Beyond: The U.S. Peculiar Institution on International Perspective, 2011. **Address:** Department of History, National University of

Ireland, Rm. 403, Twr. I, University Rd., Galway, City, Ireland. **Online address:** enrico.dallago@nuigalway.ie

DALLAIRE, Romeo A. Canadian/Dutch (born Netherlands), b. 1946. **Genres:** History, Social Sciences. **Career:** Canadian Government, special adviser on war-affected children, 2000; Canadian Armed Forces, Department of Defence, advisor, 2002; Canadian Senate, staff, 2005-. Writer. **Publications:** (With B. Beardsley) Shake Hands with the Devil: The Failure of Humanity in Rwanda (memoir), 2003. **Address:** Senate of Canada, Ottawa, ON K1A 0A4, Canada. **Online address:** dallar@sen.parl.gc.ca

DALLAS, Gregor. French/British (born England), b. 1948. **Genres:** History, Travel/Exploration. **Career:** Rutgers University, teacher; Smith College, teacher; British Conservatives in Paris, Constitution Study Group, chair. Writer. **Publications:** The Imperfect Peasant Economy: The Loire Country, 1800-1914, 1982; At the Heart of a Tiger-Clemenceau and His World, 1841-1929, 1993; 1815: The Roads to Waterloo, 1996; The Final Act: The Roads to Waterloo, 1997; 1918: War and Peace, 2000; 1945: The War that Never Ended, 2005; Poisoned Peace: 1945 - The War that Never Ended, 2006; Metro Stop Paris: Underground Tales from the City of Light, 2008. Contributor of periodicals to journals. **Address:** c/o Author Mail, Overlook Press, 141 Wooster St., Ste. 4B, New York, NY 10012, U.S.A. **Online address:** gregor.dallas@free.fr

DALLAS, Roland. American (born United States) **Genres:** Biography, Local History/Rural Topics, Business/Trade/Industry, Travel/Exploration. **Career:** Reuters, correspondent. **Publications:** The Economist Pocket Africa, 1994; Pocket Latin America: Profiles, Facts, and Figures about Latin America, 1994; Pocket Middle East and North Africa, 1995; King Hussein: A Life on the Edge, 1999; Fromm International, 1999. **Address:** Foreign Report, Jane's Information Group, Sentinel House, 163 Brighton Rd., Coulsdon, SR CR5 2YH, England.

DALLEK, Robert. American (born United States), b. 1934. **Genres:** History, International Relations/Current Affairs, Biography. **Career:** Columbia University, instructor in history, 1960-64; University of California, Department of History, assistant professor, 1964, associate professor, 1969-73, professor, 1973-94, vice chair, 1972-74, professor emeritus; Southern California Psychoanalytic Institute, research associate, 1981-85; University of Oxford, Harmsforth visiting professor, 1994-95; University of Texas, LBJ School of Public Affairs, visiting professor, 1996; Boston University, professor of history, 1996-2003; Dartmouth College, Montgomery fellow and visiting professor of history, 2004; Stanford University, professor. Writer. **Publications:** Democrat and Diplomat: The Life of William E. Dodd, 1968; Franklin D. Roosevelt and American Foreign Policy, 1932-1945, 1979; The American Style of Foreign Policy: Cultural Politics and Foreign Affairs, 1983; Ronald Reagan: The Politics of Symbolism, 1984; (co-author) The Great Republic: A History of the American People, 4th ed., 1991; Lone Star Rising: Lyndon Johnson and His Times, 1908-1960, 1991; Hail to the Chief: The Making and Unmaking of American Presidents, 1996; Flawed Giant: Lyndon Johnson and His Times, 1961-1973, 1998; Ronald Reagan: The Politics of Symbolism: With a New Preface, 1999; An Unfinished Life: John F. Kennedy, 1917-1963, 2003; Lyndon B. Johnson: Portrait of a President, 2004; Let every Nation know: John F. Kennedy in his Own Words, 2006; Nixon and Kissinger: Partners in Power, 2007; Lost Peace: Leadership in a Time of Horror and Hope, 1945-1953, 2010; John F. Kennedy, 2011. EDITOR: The Roosevelt Diplomacy and World War II, 1978; Western Europe, vol. I: Dynamics of World Power: A Documentary History of American Foreign Policy 1945-1973, 1973; (with T. Golway) Let Every Nation Know: John F. Kennedy in his Own Words, 2004; Harry S. Truman, 2008. **Address:** Stanford in Washington, 2661 Connecticutt Ave. NW, Washington, DC 20008, U.S.A. **Online address:** rdallek@aol.com

DALLISON, Robert L. Canadian (born Canada), b. 1935?. **Genres:** Social Sciences, History, Military/Defense/Arms Control. **Career:** Kings Landing Historical Settlement, Prince William, director, 1992-2002; York Sunbury Museum, Hope Restored and Fredericton Loyalists Exhibits, curator. Writer and soldier. **Publications:** Hope Restored: The American Revolution and the Founding of New Brunswick, 2003; Turning Back the Fenians: New Brunswick's Last Colonial Campaign, 2006. **Address:** York Sunbury Museum, 571 Queen St., PO Box 1312, Sta. A, Fredericton, NB E3B 5C8, Canada.

DALOZ, Laurent A. See **DALOZ, Laurent A. Parks.**

DALOZ, Laurent A. Parks. (Laurent A. Daloz). American (born United States), b. 1940. **Genres:** Education, Business/Trade/Industry. **Career:** Konawaena High School, social studies teacher, 1966-67; Port Moresby, educational planner, 1969-71; Community College of Vermont, founding academic dean, 1972-76; Johnson State College, faculty mentor for external degree program, 1977-84, 1979-80; Vermont College, faculty adviser for adult degree program, 1980-85; Harvard University, Harvard Institute for the Management of Lifelong Education, faculty, 1987-88, Harvard Graduate School of Education, consultant on faculty development, 1989-90; Lesley College, instructor, 1988-96, professor, 1996-; Columbia University, Teachers College, adjunct professor, 1996, 2001; The Whidbey Institute, core faculty and associate director, 1997-, senior fellow. Writer. **Publications:** Effective Teaching and Mentoring: Realizing the Transformational Power of Adult Learning Experiences, 1986; (co-author) Common Fire: Lives of Commitment in a Complex World, 1996; Mentor: Guiding the Journey of Adult Learners, 1999. Contributor to books and periodicals. **Address:** The Whidbey Institute, 6449 Old Pietila Rd., PO Box 57, Clinton, WA 98236-0057, U.S.A.

DALRYMPLE, Theodore. *See* **DANIELS, Anthony.**

DALSIMER, Katherine. American (born United States), b. 1944?. **Genres:** Young Adult Fiction, Psychiatry, History. **Career:** Columbia University, Center for Psychoanalytic Training and Research, lecturer in psychiatry, Mental Health Service, consultant; Cornell University, Weill Medical College, clinical associate professor of psychology in psychiatry. Writer. **Publications:** Female Adolescence: Psychoanalytic Reflections on F Literature, 1986; Virginia Woolf: Becoming a Writer, 2001. **Address:** Center for Psychoanalytic Training and Research, Columbia University, 275 Central Park W, Ste. 1D, New York, NY 10024, U.S.A. **Online address:** kd81@columbia.edu

DALTON, Annie. British (born England), b. 1948. **Genres:** Science Fiction/Fantasy, Children's Fiction, Novels. **Career:** Writer. **Publications:** FANTASY NOVELS: Out of the Ordinary, 1988; Night Maze, 1989; The Witch Rose, 1990; The Alpha Box, 1991; Demon-Spawn, 1991; Naming the Dark, 1992; Swan Sister, 1992; (reteller) The Starlight Princess and Other Princess Stories, 1999; Aliens at Paradise High, 2000; Friday Forever, 2001; Isabel: Taking Wing: Girls of Many Lands, 2002; Ferris Fleet the Wheelchair Wizard, 2005; Invisible Threads, 2006; Zack Black and The Magic Dads, 2007; Ways to Trap a Yeti, 2010. ANGELS UNLIMITED SERIES: Winging It, 2001; Losing the Plot, 2001; Flying High, 2001; Calling the Shots, 2002; Fogging Over, 2002; Fighting Fit, 2003; Making Waves, 2003; Budding Star, 2004; The Cos Keeping It Real, 2005; Going For Gold, 2007; Feeling the Vibes, 2008; Burning Up, 2008; Living the Dream, 2008; How to Save a Dragon, 2011; Moonbeans and the Dream Cafe, 2012; Moonbeans and the Shining Star, 2012. LILAC PEABODY SERIES: Lilac Peabody and Sam Sparks, 2004; Lilac Peabody and Bella Bright, 2004; Lilac Peabody and Charlie Chase, 2005; Lilac Peabody and Honeysuckle Hope, 2005. AFTERDARK SERIES: The Afterdark Princess, 1990; Dream Snatcher, 2001; The Midnight Museum, 2001; Rules of Magic, 2004. TILLY BEANY SERIES: The Real Tilly Beany, 1991; Tilly Beany and the Best Friend Machine, 1993; Tilly Beany Saves the World, 1997. PICTURE BOOKS: Ugly Mug, 1994; Space Baby, 1998; Tyler and the Talkstalk, 1998; Paradise High, 1999; Dozy Rosy, 1999; The Jam Jar Genie, 1999; The Frog Files, 2000; The Hut That Grew, 2010; Noah's Ark, 2012. **Address:** c/o Laura Cecil, 17 Alwyne Villas, London, GL N1 2HG, England.

DALTON, Russell J. American (born United States) **Genres:** Politics/Government. **Career:** University of Cologne, German Electoral Data Project, co-project director, 1973-74; University of Michigan, Inter-University Consortium for Political and Social Research Summer Program, instructor, 1973-75, Institute for Social Research, Political Action Project, assistant study director, 1975-76; United States Information Agency, Office of Research, foreign affairs specialist, 1976-77; Florida State University, Department of Government, assistant professor of government, 1977-82, Department of Political Science, associate professor of political science, 1982-86, professor of political science, 1986-90, Survey Research Center, Policy Studies Program, founding director, 1979-80; University of California, School of Social Sciences, Department of Political Science, professor of political science, 1990-, chair, 1992-97; Center for the Study of Democracy, founding director, 1995-2004. Writer. **Publications:** NON-FICTION: Values in Change: A Panel Study of German Youth, 1980; (with K.L. Baker and K. Hildebrandt) Germany Transformed: Political Culture and the New Politics, 1981; (ed.

with S. Flanagan and P.A. Beck) Electoral Change in Advanced Industrial Democracies: Realignment or Dealignment?, 1984; Citizen Politics in Western Democracies: Public Opinion and Political Parties in the United States, Great Britain, West Germany, and France, 1988, 2nd ed. as Citizen Politics: Public Opinion and Political Parties in Advanced Industrial Democracies, 1996, 5th ed., 2008; Politics and Culture in West Germany, 1988; Politics in West Germany, 1989; (ed. with M. Kuechler) Challenging the Political Order: New Social and Political Movements in Western Democracies, 1990; Politics in Germany, 2nd ed., 1993; (ed.) The New Germany Votes: Unification and the Creation of a German Party System, 1993; The Green Rainbow: Environmental Groups in Western Europe, 1994; (ed.) Germans Divided: The 1994 Bundestag Elections and the Evolution of the German Party System, 1996; (ed. with G.A. Almond and G.B. Powell, Jr.) European Politics Today, 1999, 2nd ed., 2002; (co-author) Critical Masses: Citizens, Nuclear Weapons Production, and Environmental Destruction in the United States and Russia, 1999; (ed. with M.P. Wattenberg) Parties without Partisans: Political Change in Advanced Industrial Democracies, 2000; (ed. with B. Cain and S. Scarrow) Democracy Transformed? Expanding Political Opportunities in Advanced Industrial Democracies, 2003; Democratic Challenges, Democratic Choices: The Erosion of Political Support in Advanced Industrial Democracies, 2004; (with G.A. Almond, G.B. Powell, Jr. and K. Strom) Comparative Politics: A Theoretical Framework, 4th ed., 2004, (with G.B. Powell, Jr. and K. Strom) 6th ed. as Comparative Politics Today: A Theoretical Framework, 2012; (ed. with G.A. Almond and G.B. Powell, Jr.) Comparative Politics Today, 8th ed., 2005, (ed. with G.B. Powell, Jr. and K. Strom) 10th ed. as Comparative Politics Today: A World View, 2012; (ed. with D.C. Shin) Citizens, Democracy, and Markets around the Pacific Rim: Congruence Theory and Political Culture, 2006; (ed. with H. Klingemann) Oxford Handbook of Political Behavior, 2007; Good Citizen: How a Younger Generation is Reshaping American Politics, 2008, rev. ed., 2009; (ed. with D.C. Shin and Y. Chu) Party Politics in East Asia: Citizens, Elections, and Democratic Development, 2008; (ed.) Engaging Youth in Politics: Debating Democracy's Future, 2011; (ed. with C.J. Anderson) Citizens, Context, and Choice, 2011. Contributor of articles to books and journals. **Address:** Department of Political Science, University of California, 5279 Social Science Plz., PO Box 5100, Irvine, CA 92697-5100, U.S.A. **Online address:** rdalton@uci.edu

DALTON, Sheila. Canadian/British (born England), b. 1949?. **Genres:** Children's Fiction, Young Adult Fiction, Novels, Poetry. **Career:** Richmond Hill public library, head of reference department, 1972-79; Owl Magazine, contributing editor, 1980-82; freelance writer and poet, 1982-; Toronto Public Library, North York Central Library, staff. **Publications:** Bubblemania (picture book), 1992; Blowing Holes Through the Everyday (poetry), 1993; Tales of the Ex-Fire Eater: A Novel, 1994; Doggerel (picture book), 1996; Catalogue (picture book), 1998; Trial by Fire (young adult), 1998. **Address:** The Writers' Union of Canada, 90 Richmond St. E, Ste. 200, Toronto, ON M5C 1P1, Canada. **Online address:** b0396@freenet.toronto.on.ca

D'ALUISIO, Faith. American (born United States), b. 1957?. **Genres:** Women's Studies And Issues, Animals/Pets, Sciences. **Career:** Material World Books, editor and lead writer. **Publications:** (With P. Menzel) Women in the Material World, 1996; (with P. Menzel) Man Eating Bugs: The Art and Science of Eating Insects, 1998; (with P. Menzel) Robo Sapiens: Evolution of a New Species, 2000; (with P. Menzel) Hungry Planet: What the World Eats, 2005, rev. ed., 2008; What I Eat: Around the World in 80 Diets, 2010. **Address:** Material World Books, 199 Kreuzer Ln., Napa, CA 94559, U.S.A. **Online address:** fda@menzelphoto.com

DALY, Brenda O. American (born United States), b. 1941. **Genres:** Literary Criticism And History, Women's Studies And Issues, Autobiography/Memoirs, Literary Criticism And History, Young Adult Fiction. **Career:** High school English teacher, 1964-71; University of Minnesota-Twin Cities, visiting assistant professor of English and women's studies, 1985, instructor in English, 1985-86; Macalester College, lecturer, 1985-86; St. Olaf College, visiting assistant professor, 1986-87; Iowa State University, associate professor of English, 1987-, professor of English and women's studies, 2004-, Center for Excellence in the Arts and Humanities, director, 2005-08, emeritus professor of English; NWSA Journal, editor, 2003-07. **Publications:** (Ed. with M.T. Reddy) Narrating Mothers: Theorizing Maternal Subjectivities, 1991; Lavish Self-Divisions: The Novels of Joyce Carol Oates, 1996; Authoring a Life: A Woman's Survival in and Through Literary Studies, 1998; Rich Soil for Stories: A Geological Memoir of the Midwest, forthcoming. Contributor to literature journals and books. **Address:** Department of English, Iowa State University, 203 Ross Hall, Ames, IA 50011-1201, U.S.A. **Online address:** bdaly@iastate.edu

DALY, Leo (Arthur). *See* Obituaries.

DALY, M(artin) W. American (born United States), b. 1950. **Genres:** Area Studies, Humanities, History. **Career:** New England College, lecturer in history, 1978-79; University of Durham, research fellow in arts, 1980-83; University of Khartoum, Institute of African and Asian Studies, Fulbright visiting professor, 1984-85; Arkansas State University, assistant professor of history, 1985-87; Memphis State University, assistant professor, 1987-89, associate professor, 1989-91, Humanities Center, fellow, 1989, professor of history, 1991-92; University of Tennessee at Chattanooga, professor of history, 1992-97, head of department, 1992-95; Kettering University, professor of humanities and social science and head of department, 1997-; Richmond College, lecturer, 1978-79; Woodrow Wilson International Center for Scholars, fellow, 1986; Oxford University, St. Antony's College, senior associate member, 1987; University of Durham, Leonard Slater lecturer, 1989; Tel Aviv University, Fulbright visiting professor, 1994-95; University of East Anglia, archival researcher. **Publications:** (With P.M. Holt) The History of the Sudan: From the Coming of Islam to the Present Day, 3rd ed., 1979, 6th ed., 2011; British Administration and the Northern Sudan, 1917-1924, 1980; Sudan, 1983, 2nd ed., 1992; Empire on the Nile: The Anglo-Egyptian Sudan, 1898-1934, 1986; (with Deng) Bonds of Silk: The Human Factor in the British Administration of the Sudan, 1989; Imperial Sudan: The Anglo-Egyptian Condominium, 1934-1956, 1991; On Trek in Kordofan: Diaries of a British District Officer in the Sudan, 1931-33, 1994; (with L.E. Forbes) The Sudan, 1994; The Sirdar: Sir Reginald Wingate and the British Empire in the Middle East, 1997; (with J.R. Hogan) Images of Empire: Photographic Sources for the British in the Sudan, 2005; Darfur's Sorrow: A History of Destruction and Genocide, 2007, 2nd ed., 2010. EDITOR: The Road to Shaykan: Letters of Major General William Hicks Pasha Written during the Sennar and Kordofan Campaigns, 1883, 1983; Modernization in the Sudan: Studies in Honor of Richard Hill, 1985; Al-Majdhubiyya and Al-Mikashfiyya: Two Sufi Tariqas in the Sudan, 1985; (with G. Benavides and contrib.) Religion and Political Power, 1989; (with A.A. Sikainga and contrib.) Civil War in the Sudan, 1993; The Cambridge History of Egypt, vol. II: Modern Egypt, 1998; (ed.) The Cambridge History of Egypt (series), 1998. Contributor of articles to books and journals. **Address:** Department of Humanities & Social Science, Kettering University, Rm. 4502-AB, 1700 W 3rd Ave., Flint, MI 48504, U.S.A. **Online address:** mdaly@kettering.edu

DALY, Michael. American (born United States), b. 1952. **Genres:** Novels, Young Adult Non-fiction. **Career:** Daily News, columnist. Writer. **Publications:** Under Ground: A Novel, 1995; The Book of Mychal: The Surprising Life and Heroic Death of Father Mychal Judge (nonfiction), 2008. **Address:** New York News Inc., 220 E 42nd St., New York, NY 10017-5806, U.S.A.

DALY, Niki. South African (born South Africa), b. 1946. **Genres:** Children's Fiction, Illustrations. **Career:** CBS Record Co., singer and songwriter, 1971-73; Advertising Agencies, junior art director, 1973-75; East Ham Technical College, graphics teacher, 1976-79; Stellenbosch University, head of design department, 1983-89; Songololo Books, director, 1989-93; The Inkman Co., facilitator of childrens picture books, 1993-. Writer. **Publications:** SELF-ILLUSTRATED: Joseph's Other Red Sock, 1982; Not So Fast, Songololo, 1985; Papa Lucky's Shadow, 1992; Mary Malloy and the Baby Who Wouldn't Sleep, 1993; The Boy on the Beach, 1999; Jamela's Dress, 1999; What's Cooking, Jamela?, 2001; Yebo Jamela!, 2001; Old Bob's Brown Bear, 2002; Once upon a Time, 2003; Where's Jamela?, 2004; Ruby Sings the Blues, 2005; Happy Birthday, Jamela!, 2006; Pretty Salma, 2006; Welcome to Zanzibar Road, 2006; A Song for Jamela, 2009; Next Stop-Zanzibar Road!, 2012. OTHERS: The Little Girl Who Lived Down the Road, 1978; Vim the Rag Mouse: Story and Pictures, 1979; Leo's Christmas Surprise, 1983; Ben's Gingerbread Man, 1985; Teddy's Ear, 1985; Monsters Are Like That, 1985; Just Like Archie, 1986; Look at Me!, 1986; Thank You Henrietta, 1986; (with I. Mennen) Ashraf of Africa, 1990; Mama, Papa and Baby Joe, 1991; Papa's Lucky Shadow, 1991; (with I. Mennen) Somewhere in Africa, 1992; My Dad: Stories and Pictures, 1995; Why the Sun & Moon Live in the Sky, 1995; (with N. Turkington) The Dancer, 1996; (with W. Hartmann) The Dinosaurs Are Back and It's All Your Fault, Edward!, 1997; Bravo, Zan Angelo!: A Commedia dell'Arte tale with Story & Pictures, 1998; Pa's Perfect Pizza, 2000; The Wanderer in Og: An Amphigory Devised for Your Amusement, 2005; Pretty Salma: A Little Red Riding Hood Story from Africa, 2007; Bettina Valentino and the Picasso Club, 2009. Contributor to periodicals. **Address:** c/o Laura Cecil, 17 Alwyne Villas, London, GL N1 2HG, England. **Online address:** inkman@iafrica.com

DALYELL, Tam. Scottish (born Scotland), b. 1932. **Genres:** History, International Relations/Current Affairs, Politics/Government, Sciences. **Career:** Bo'ness High School, teacher, 1956-62; Dunera Ship School, deputy director of studies, 1961-62; British Parliament, labour member for West Lothian, 1962-, opposition spokesman on science, 1980-82; House of Commons, member of Parliament, 1962-2005, retired, 2005; New Scientist Magazine, columnist, 1967-; Parliamentary Labour Party's Defense and Foreign Affairs Groups, vice chair, 1972-74; Scottish Labour Group's Members of Parliament, vice chair, 1973-75; European Parliament, member of parliament, 1975-79; University of Edinburgh, rector, 2003-06. **Publications:** The Case of Ship-Schools, 1960; Ship-School Dunera, 1963; Devolution: The End of Britain?, 1977; A Science Policy for Britain, 1983; Thatcher's Torpedo, 1983; One Man's Falklands, 1982; Thatcher: Patterns of Deceit, 1986; Misrule: How Mrs. Thatcher Has Misled Parliament from the Sinking of the Belgrano to the Wright Affair, 1987; Dick Crossman: A Portrait, 1989. **Address:** Weidenfeld & Nicholson, 91 Clapham High St., London, GL SW4 7TA, England.

DALZELL, Alexander. Canadian/Irish (born Ireland), b. 1925. **Genres:** Literary Criticism And History, Translations, History. **Career:** University of London, King's College, assistant lecturer in classics, 1951-53; University of Sheffield, assistant lecturer in classics, 1953-54; Trinity College, honorary fellow, lecturer, professor of classics, 1954-88, now emeritus; Classical Association of Canada, president, 1980-82. Writer. **Publications:** (Ed. with C. Fantazzi and R.J. Schoeck) Acta Conventus Neo-Latini Torontonensis, 1991; (trans.) The Correspondence of Erasmus, vol. X (with R. Mynors and J. Estes), 1992, vol. XI (with C. Nauert), 1994, vol. XII (with C. Nauert), 2003; The Criticism of Didactic Poetry, 1996. **Address:** Trinity College, 6 Hoskin Ave., Toronto, ON M5S 1H8, Canada. **Online address:** adalzell@nbnet.nb.ca

DALZELL, Frederick. American (born United States) **Genres:** Novels, Business/Trade/Industry. **Career:** The Winthrop Group Inc., senior consultant, partner; Harvard University, faculty of history; Williams College, faculty of history, Harvard Business School, researcher, research associate. Writer. **Publications:** (With G.D. Smith) Wisdom from the Robber Barons: Enduring Business Lessons from Rockefeller, Morgan, and the First Industrialists, 2000; (co-author) Changing Fortunes: Remaking the Industrial Corporation, 2002; (co-author) Rising Tide: Lessons from 165 Years of Brand Building at Procter & Gamble, 2004; Financing the Dream: The Federal Home Loan Bank of Indianapolis, 2007; (with M. Brewster) Driving Change: The UPS Approach to Business, 2007; Engineering Invention: Frank J. Sprague and the U.S. Electrical Industry, 2010; A Joyous Adventure. **Address:** The Winthrop Group Inc., 2 Canal Pk., Cambridge, MA 02141, U.S.A.

DAMASCENE, Hieromonk. *See* CHRISTENSEN, Damascene.

DAMASIO, Antonio R. American (born United States), b. 1944. **Genres:** Medicine/Health, Psychology. **Career:** University of Lisbon Medical School, professor auxiliar in neurology, 1974-75; University of Iowa, visiting assistant professor, 1975-76, associate professor, 1976-80, Division of Behavioral Neurology and Cognitive Neuroscience, chief, 1977-2005, professor of neurology, 1980-2005, Alzheimer's Disease Research Center, director, 1985-2000, head of department, 1986-2005, Van Allen distinguished professor, 1989-2005, distinguished adjunct professor, 2005-; Salk Institute, adjunct professor, 1989-; University of Southern California, Language Research Laboratory, Center de Estudos Egas Moniz, chief, 1971-75; Brain and Creativity Institute, director, 2005-; professor of psychology, neuroscience and neurology, 2005-; David Dornsife professor of neuroscience, 2006-, David Dornsife chair in neuroscience, university professor, 2011-. Writer. **Publications:** (With H. Damasio) Lesion Analysis in Neuropsychology, 1989; Descartes's Error: Emotion, Reason and the Human Brain, 1994; (ed. with H. Damasio and Y. Christen) Neurobiology of Decision-making, 1996; (co-author) Cervelli che parlano, 1997; The Feeling of What Happens: Body and Emotion in the Making of Consciousness, 1999; (intro.) The Scientific American Book of the Brain, 1999; (co-ed.) Unity of Knowledge: The Convergence of Natural and Human Science, 2001; Looking for Spinoza: Joy, Sorrow, and the Feeling Brain, 2003; Ao encontro de Espinosa: As emoções sociais e a neurologia do sentir, 2003; Self Comes to Mind: Constructing the Conscious Brain, 2010. Contributor to periodicals. **Address:** College of Letters, Arts and Sciences, University of Southern California, 126 HNB, 3551 Trousdale Pkwy., ADM 304, Los Angeles, CA 90089-4012, U.S.A. **Online address:** damasio@usc.edu

D'AMATO, Anthony. American (born United States), b. 1937. **Genres:** Plays/Screenplays, Law, Philosophy, Politics/Government, Social Sciences. **Career:** Hudson Institute, consultant, 1962-63; Wellesley College, instructor in political science, 1963-66; Ethiopia and Liberia in 'The South West Africa Cases', International Court of Justice, 1965-66, assistant counsel; Misco Management Co., Social Science Research Council, fellow in statistics, 1967-68; Northwestern University, assistant professor, 1968-71, associate professor, 1971-74, professor of law, 1974-90, School of Medicine, lecturer of professional ethics, 1976-91, Perkins-Bauer teaching professor of law, 1984-85, Stanford Clinton Sr. research professor, 1989-90, Judd and Mary Morris Leighton professor of law; Oregon Law School, visiting professor of law, 1973-74; International League for the Rights of Man, consultant; Cardozo Law School, Yeshiva University, visiting professor of Law, 1986. Writer. **Publications:** Law of the Use of Force Short of War, 1963; (ed. with W.C. Beal) Realities of Vietnam; A Ripon Society Appraisal, 1968; The Concept of Custom in International Law, 1971; (with R.M. O'Neil) The Judiciary and Vietnam, 1972; (co-author) The Politics of Ecosuicide, 1972; (co-author) The Political Calculus (philosophy), 1972; (co-author) International Law and Vietnam, vol. III, 1973; The Magic Man (play), 1974; (ed. with J.L. Hargrove) Environment and the Law of the Sea, a Report, 1974; (with S.L. Wasby and R. Metrailer) Desegregation from Brown to Alexander: An Exploration of Supreme Court Strategies, 1977; (with B. Weston and R. Falk) International Law and World Order: A Problem-Oriented Course book, 1980, 2nd ed., 1990; (comp. and ed. with B.H. Weston and R.A. Falk) Basic Documents in International Law and World Order, 1980, 2nd. ed., 1990; R.S.V.P. Broadway (musical play), 1981; Assyrian Case for Autonomy, 1982; Jurisprudence: A Descriptive and Normative Analysis of Law, 1984; International Law: Process and Prospect, 1987, rev. ed., 1995; How to Understand the Law, 1989; (with A.J. Jacobson) Justice and the Legal System: A Course book, 1992; International Law Course Book, 1994; (ed.) International Law Anthology, 1994; International to Law and Political Reality, 1995; (ed. with K. Engel) International Environmental Law Anthology, 1996; (ed.) Analytic Jurisprudence Anthology, 1996; Introduction to Law and Legal Thinking, 1996; (ed. with D.E. Long) International Intellectual Property Anthology, 1996; (co-ed.) International Environmental Property Law, 1997; International Law Studies, 1997; (ed. with Long) International Intellectual Property Law, 1997; (ed. with R.G. Steinhardt) The Alien Tort Claims Act: An Analytical Anthology, 1999; (with D.E. Long) Course Book in International Intellectual Property, 2000; International Law Sources, 2004; (with J. Abbassi) International Law Today: A Handbook, 2006. **Address:** School of Law, Northwestern University, 357 E Chicago Ave., Chicago, IL 60611, U.S.A. **Online address:** a-damato@northwestern.edu

D'AMBROSIO, Charles. American (born United States), b. 1960?. **Genres:** Novellas/Short Stories, Young Adult Fiction, Literary Criticism And History. **Career:** University of Iowa, visiting professor, 2006; Tin House Summer Writers Workshop, instructor; University of Montana, William Kittredge professor of English literature; Warren Wilson College, faculty, 2008-; University of Chicago, faculty. Freelance writer. **Publications:** The Point (short stories), 1995; Orphans, 2004; (intro.) Cooking and Stealing: The Tin House Nonfiction Reader, 2004; Dead Fish Museum, 2006. Contributor to periodicals. **Address:** Little Brown, 3 Center Plz., Ste. 100, Fl. 3, Boston, MA 02108, U.S.A.

D'AMBROSIO, Jay S. American (born United States), b. 1971. **Genres:** Education, Philosophy. **Career:** Seneca Valley School District, middle-school teacher of ancient and world history, 1995-; Atlantis Web Solutions, owner and web site developer, 2001-; Northway Counseling Services, conflict mediator and mentor, 2004-; Hampton Middle School, history teacher. Writer. **Publications:** E-Teaching: Creative Web Sites and Student Web Portfolios Using Microsoft PowerPoint, 2003; Teaching the Spirit: Connecting to the Next Generation through Story, 2005; Rethinking Adolescence: Using Story to Navigate Life's Uncharted Years, 2006. Contributor to periodicals. **Address:** Seneca Valley School District, 122 Seneca School Rd., Harmony, PA 16037, U.S.A.

DAMMAN, Gregory C. American (born United States) **Genres:** Law. **Career:** Hecht, Sweet, Alesio, Morrow, Poppe & Otte (law firm), associate attorney, attorney, 1989-91; Damman Law Office, Lincoln, attorney, 1991-96; Damman Legal Research, owner and operator, 1991-96, sole practitioner, 1996-99; Damman Law Office, Seward, attorney, 1996-99; Blevens & Damman, attorney and partner, 1999-. Writer. **Publications:** How to Form and Operate a Limited Liability Company, 1995, 3rd ed., 2005; Collecting Child Support: Twelve Effective Strategies, 1997. Contributor to periodicals and journals. **Address:** Blevens & Damman, 129 N 5th St., PO Box 98, Seward, NE 68434-2100, U.S.A. **Online address:** gregdamman@alltel.net

DAMON, William. American (born United States), b. 1944. **Genres:** Psychology, Human Relations/Parenting, Self Help. **Career:** Clark University, Department of Psychology, assistant professor, 1973-78, associate professor, 1978-82, dean of the graduate school, 1983-87, professor, 1982-89, chair of education, 1988-89; University of Puerto Rico, distinguished visiting professor, 1988; Brown University, professor of education, 1989-98, chair of education, 1989-92, Center for the Study of Human Development, The Mittlemann Family director, 1992-98, university professor, 1996-98, adjunct professor of human development, 1998-; Center for Advanced Study in Behavioral Sciences, fellow, 1994-95; Stanford University, professor of education and director of center on adolescence, 1997-, Hoover Institution on War, Revolution, and Peace, senior fellow, 1999-. Writer. **Publications:** The Social World of the Child, 1977; (ed.) Moral Development, 1978; (ed.) Social Cognition, 1978; Social and Personality Development: Infancy through Adolescence, 1983; (ed.) Social and Personality Development: Essays on the Growth of the Child, 1983; Self-Understanding in Childhood and Adolescence, 1988; Moral Child: Nurturing Children's Natural Moral Growth, 1988; (ed.) Child Development Today and Tomorrow, 1989; The Moral Child, 1990; (with A. Colby) Some Do Care: Contemporary Lives of Moral Commitment, 1992; Greater Expectations: Overcoming the Culture of Indulgence in America's Homes and Schools, 1995; Greater Expectations: Overcoming the Culture of Indulgence in Our Homes and Schools, 1996; Youth Charter: How Communities Can Work Together to Raise Standards for All Our Children, 1997; (ed.) Handbook of Child Psychology, 1998, 6th ed., (ed. with R.M. Lerner), 2006; (co-ed.) Variability in the Social Construction of the Child, 2000; (co-author) Good Work: When Excellence and Ethics Meet, 2001; (ed.) Bringing in a New Era in Character Education, 2002; Noble Purpose: The Joy of Living a Meaningful Life, 2003; Moral Advantage: How to Succeed in Business by Doing the Right Thing, 2004; (ed. with S. Verducci) Taking Philanthropy Seriously: Beyond Noble Intentions to Responsible Giving, 2006; (ed. with R.M. Lerner) Handbook of Child Psychology, 2006; (ed. with R.M. Lerner) Child and Adolescent Development: An Advanced Course, 2008; Path to Purpose: Helping Our Children Find Their Calling in Life, 2008; Failing Liberty 101, 2011. **Address:** Center on Adolescence, Stanford University, BC 202, 505 Lasuen Mall, Stanford, CA 94305-3083, U.S.A. **Online address:** wdamon@stanford.edu

DAMROSCH, Phoebe. American (born United States), b. 1978. **Genres:** Autobiography/Memoirs, Biography, Humor/Satire. **Career:** Freelance writer. **Publications:** Service Included: Four-Star Secrets of an Eavesdropping Waiter (memoir), 2007. Contributor to periodicals. **Address:** c/o Paul Cirone, The Friedrich Agency, 136 E 57th St., New York, NY 10022-2707, U.S.A. **Online address:** phoebedamrosch@yahoo.com

DAMS, Jeanne M(artin). American (born United States), b. 1941. **Genres:** Mystery/Crime/Suspense, Novels. **Career:** Writer. **Publications:** MYSTERY NOVELS: The Body in the Transept, 1995; Trouble in the Town Hall, 1996; Holy Terror in the Hebrides, 1997; Malice in Miniature, 1998; Death in Lacquer Red, 1999; Victim in Victoria Station, 1999; Red, White, and Blue Murder, 2000; Killing Cassidy, 2000; Green Grow the Victims, 2001; To Perish in Penzance, 2001; Silence Is Golden, 2002; Sins Out of School, 2003; Winter of Discontent, 2004; Crimson Snow, 2005; Indigo Christmas, 2008; (with B. D'Amato and M.R. Zubro) Foolproof, 2009; A Dark and Stormy Night, 2011; The Evil That Men Do, 2011; Murder in Burnt Orange, 2011; Murder in the Tower, 2012; The Orkneys Murder, 2013. **Address:** c/o Kimberley Cameron, Kimberley Cameron & Associates, 98 Main St., Ste. 704, Tiburon, CA 94920, U.S.A. **Online address:** jeannedams@sbcglobal.net

DANAKAS, John. Canadian (born Canada), b. 1963. **Genres:** Young Adult Fiction. **Career:** Winnipeg Sun, journalist, 1986-91; University of Manitoba, media relations officer, 1996-, director of public affairs, 1999-. Writer. **Publications:** Curve Ball, 1993; Lizzie's Soccer Showdown, 1994; Hockey Night in Transcona, 1995; Hockey Heroes, 1998; Brothers on Ice, 2001; Choice of Colours, 2007. **Address:** Public Affairs Office, University of Manitoba,

137 Education Bldg., 423 University Cres., Winnipeg, MB R3T 2N2, Canada. **Online address:** john_danakas@umanitoba.ca

DANBOM, David B. (David Byers Danbom). American (born United States), b. 1947. **Genres:** History. **Career:** North Dakota State University, professor of history, 1974-, North Dakota Institute for Regional Studies, co-editor, 1982-92; New Deal, book review editor, 2000-; Agricultural History, associate editor, 2003-. **Publications:** The Resisted Revolution: Urban America and the Industrialization of Agriculture, 1900-1930, 1979; The World of Hope: Progressives and the Struggle for an Ethical Public Life, 1987; Our Purpose Is to Serve: The First Century of the North Dakota Agricultural Experiment Station, 1990; Born in the Country: A History of Rural America, 1995, 2nd ed., 2006; Going It Alone: Fargo Grapples with the Great Depression, 2005. **Address:** Department of History, North Dakota State University, 402 Minard Hall, PO Box 5075, Fargo, ND 58105-5075, U.S.A. **Online address:** david.danbom@ndsu.edu

DANBOM, David Byers. See **DANBOM, David B.**

DANCE, Daryl Cumber. American (born United States), b. 1938. **Genres:** Cultural/Ethnic Topics, Mythology/Folklore, Bibliography, Essays, Biography, History, Autobiography/Memoirs. **Career:** Virginia State University, instructor in English, 1963-72; Virginia Commonwealth University, associate professor, 1972-85, professor of English, 1985-92; University of California, visiting professor of black studies, 1986-87; University of Richmond, professor of English, 1993-. Writer. **Publications:** Shuckin' and Jivin': Folklore from Contemporary Black Americans, 1978; Folklore from Contemporary Jamaicans, 1985; (ed.) Fifty Caribbean Writers: A Bio-Bibliographical-Critical Casebook, 1986; Long Gone: The Mecklenburg Six and the Theme of Escape in Black Folklore, 1987; New World Adams: Conversations with West Indian Writers, 1992; (ed.) Honey, Hush! An Anthology of African American Women's Humor, 1998; The Lineage of Abraham: The Biography of a Free Black Family in Charles City, 1999; (ed.) From My People: 400 Years of African American Folklore, 2002. Contributor to periodicals and journals. **Address:** Department of English, University of Richmond, Rm. 323, Ryland Hall, 28 Westhampton Way, Richmond, VA 23173, U.S.A. **Online address:** ddance@richmond.edu

DANCHEV, Alex. British (born England) **Genres:** Politics/Government. **Career:** University of Nottingham, School of Politics and International Relations, professor of international relations, 2004-, director of admissions. Writer. **Publications:** NONFICTION: Very Special Relationship: Field-Marshall Sir John Dill and the Anglo-American Alliance, 1941-1944, 1986. EDITOR: Establishing the Anglo American Alliance: The Second World War Diaries of Brigadier Vivian Dykes, 1990; The Franks Report: The Falkland Islands Review, 1992; International Perspectives on the Falklands Conflict: A Matter of Life and Death, 1992; (with D. Keohane) International Perspectives on the Gulf Conflict, 1990-1991, 1994; Fin de Siècle: The Meaning of the Twentieth Century, 1995; (with T. Halverson) International Perspectives on the Yugoslav Conflict, 1996; Alchemist of War: The Life of Basil Liddell Hart, 2000; (with D. Todman) War Diaries, 1939-1945: Field Marshal Lord Alanbrooke, 2001; (with J. MacMillan) The Iraq War and Democratic Politics, 2005. OTHERS: Oliver Franks: Founding Father, 1993; On Specialness: Essays in Anglo-American Relations, 1998; Georges Braque: A Life, 2005; On Art and War and Terror, 2009. **Address:** The School of Politics & International Relations, University of Nottingham, Rm. C103, University Pk., Nottingham, NG7 2RD, England. **Online address:** alex.danchev@nottingham.ac.uk

D'ANCONA, Matthew. (Matthew Robert Ralph d'Ancona). British (born England), b. 1968. **Genres:** Theology/Religion, History. **Career:** Times, trainee, assistant editor, 1990-95; Sunday Telegraph, deputy comment editor and political columnist, deputy editor, 1996-2009; Index on Censorship, education correspondent, assistant editor, fellow, 1989-96; Oxford University, All Souls College, fellow, 1989-96; The Spectator, editor, 2006-09. **Publications:** (With C.P. Thiede) Eyewitness to Jesus: Amazing New Manuscript Evidence About the Origin of the Gospels in UK as The Jesus Papyrus, 1996; The Ties That Bind Us, 1996; The Quest for the True Cross, 2000; Going East, 2004; (intro.) The Emmaus Mystery: Discovering Evidence for the Risen Christ, 2005; Confessions of a Hawkish Hack: The Media and the War On Terrorism, 2006; Tabatha's Code, 2006; Nothing to Fear, 2008; (ed.) Being British: The Search for the Values That Bind the Nation, 2009. **Address:** Hodder & Stoughton, 338 Euston Rd., London, GL NW1 3BH, England.

D'ANCONA, Matthew Robert Ralph. See **D'ANCONA, Matthew.**

DANDRIDGE, Rita B(ernice). (Rita Dandridge Simons). American (born United States), b. 1940. **Genres:** Literary Criticism And History, Cultural/Ethnic Topics, Bibliography, Language/Linguistics, Writing/Journalism, Poetry. **Career:** Morgan State University, instructor, assistant professor of English, 1964-71; University of Toledo, assistant professor of English, 1971-74; Norfolk State University, associate professor, professor of English and and foreign languages, 1974-; University of Virginia, Center for the Humanities, fellow-in-residence, 1987-. Writer. **Publications:** (As Rita Dandridge Simons with D.M. Flemons) Relevant Expository Techniques and Programmed Grammar, 1971; (comp.) Ann Allen Shockley: An Annotated Primary and Secondary Bibliography, 1987; Black Women's Blues: A Literary Anthology, 1934-1988, 1992; The Oxford Companion to African American Literature, 1992; (co-ed.) Empowering the Hip Hop Nation: The Arts and Social Justice, 2000; Black Women's Activism: Reading African American Women's Historical Romances, 2004. Contributor of articles to periodicals. **Address:** Department of English, Norfolk State University, 106 James Bowser Bldg., 700 Park Ave., Norfolk, VA 23504, U.S.A. **Online address:** rbdandridge@nsu.edu

DANE, Eva. See **DAWES, Edna.**

DANEFF, Stephen Constantine. See **CONSTANT, Stephen.**

DANER, Paul. See **STOKOE, E(dward) G(eorge).**

DANESH, Abol Hassan. American/Iranian (born Iran), b. 1952. **Genres:** Economics, Business/Trade/Industry, Social Sciences, Local History/Rural Topics. **Career:** University of California, associate in sociology, 1981-84; Colby College, visiting assistant professor of sociology, 1985-89; University of Rhode Island, assistant professor of sociology and anthropology, 1989-92, associate professor of sociology, 1992-. Writer and consultant. **Publications:** An Introduction to a Theory of Irregular Rural-Urban Migration, 1983; Causes of Unproductive Jobs in the Third World, 1984; Rural Exodus and Squatter Settlements in the Third World: Case of Iran, 1987; The Informal Economy: Underground Economy, Moonlighting, Subcontracting, Household Economy, Unorganized Sector, Barter, Ghetto Economy, Second Economy: A Research Guide, 1991; The Informal Economy: A Research Guide, 1991; The Informal Economy and Informalization in Photography, 1994; Corridor of Hope: A Visual View of Informal Economy, 1999. Contributor to periodicals. **Address:** University of Rhode Island, Kingston, RI 02881, U.S.A. **Online address:** hassan@uri.edu

DANFORTH, John C(laggett). American (born United States), b. 1936. **Genres:** History, Politics/Government. **Career:** Ordained Episcopal deacon, 1963; assistant rector, 1963-66; priest, 1964; Davis, Polk, Wardwell, Sunderland and Kiendl (law firm), tax lawyer, 1964-66; associate rector, 1966-68; Bryan, Cave, McPheeters and McRoberts (law firm), private law practice, 1966-68; attorney general, 1969-76; Grace Church, associate rector, 1969; Missouri Law Enforcement Assistance Council, chair, 1973-74; United States senator, 1976-94, retired, 1994; St. Alban's, associate rector, 1977-94; Church of the Holy Communion, associate priest, 1995-; Bryan Cave L.L.P.(law firm), lawyer, 1995-, partner; USUN, ambassador, 2004-05; Memorial Sloan-Kettering Cancer Center, assistant chaplain; Church of Epiphany, assistant rector; Church of St. Michael, assistant rector. Writer. **Publications:** (Contrib.) Government Regulation: Where Do We Go From Here?: A Round Table Held on December 19, 1977 And Sponsored By The American Enterprise Institute for Public Policy Research, 1977; Resurrection: The Confirmation of Clarence Thomas, 1994; Budgeting: Ourselves or Our Children, 1996; Faith and Politics: How the Moral Values Debate Divides America and How to Move forward Together, 2006; (foreword) Leadership, Vision, Change: The Blunt Years, 2005-2009, 2009. **Address:** Bryan Cave L.L.P., 1 Metropolitan Sq., 211 N Broadway, Ste. 3600, St. Louis, MO 63102, U.S.A. **Online address:** jcdanforth@bryancave.com

DANFORTH, Paul M. See **ALLEN, John E(lliston).**

DANGAREMBGA, Tsitsi. Zimbabwean (born Zimbabwe), b. 1959. **Genres:** Novels, Plays/Screenplays, Novellas/Short Stories, Westerns/Adventure, Mystery/Crime/Suspense, Young Adult Fiction. **Career:** Nyeria Films, founder, 1992. Author and filmmaker. **Publications:** The Letter, 1987; She No Longer Weeps (play), 1987; Nervous Conditions (novel), 1988; The Book of Not, 2006. Contributor to books and periodicals. **Address:** The Women's Press, 27 Goodge St., London, GL W1T 2LD, England.

DANGL, Benjamin. American (born United States), b. 1980?. Genres: Young Adult Non-fiction, History. Career: Andean Information Network, staff; UpsideDownWorld.org, founder and editor; TowardFreedom.com, editor; Burlington College, teacher. Writer and journalist. Publications: The Price of Fire: Resource Wars and Social Movements in Bolivia, 2007. Contributor to periodicals. Address: U.S.A. Online address: ben@upsidedownworld.org

DANGLER, Jean. American (born United States), b. 1961. Genres: History, Literary Criticism And History, Women's Studies And Issues, Politics/Government. Career: Mount Holyoke College, visiting instructor, 1996-97; Florida State University, assistant professor, 1997-2002; Tulane University, Department of Spanish and Portuguese, assistant professor, 2002-04, associate professor, 2004-. Writer. Publications: Mediating Fictions: Literature, Women Healers, and the Go-Between in Medieval and Early Modern Iberia, 2001; Making Difference in Medieval and Early Modern Iberia, 2005. Address: Department of Spanish and Portuguese, Tulane University, 304 Newcomb Hall, New Orleans, LA 70118, U.S.A. Online address: jdangler@tulane.edu

DANIEL, G. Reginald. American (born United States), b. 1949?. Genres: Race Relations, Social Sciences. Career: University of California, lecturer, 1988-96, Department of Sociology, lecturer of Latin American studies/African American studies, 1992-98, assistant professor, 1998-2003, associate professor, 2003-, professor, American Sociological Association, coordinator and mentor, 1996-98, Latin American and Iberian Studies Center, faculty, 1998-, MOST, mentor, 1998-, Department of Asian American studies, faculty, 1998-, Department of Black Studies, faculty, 2006-. Writer. Publications: More Than Black? Multiracial Identity and the New Racial Order, 2001; (ed. with P. Spickard) Racial Thinking in the United States: Uncompleted Independence, 2004; Race and Multiraciality in Brazil and the United States: Converging Paths?, 2006. Contributor to periodicals. Address: Department of Sociology, University of California, 2834 Ellison Hall, Santa Barbara, CA 93106-9430, U.S.A. Online address: rdaniel@soc.ucsb.edu

DANIEL, Pete. American (born United States), b. 1938. Genres: Art/Art History, Essays, Photography. Career: University of North Carolina, instructor in history, 1963-66; University of Maryland, Booker T. Washington papers, assistant editor, 1969-70; University of Tennessee, assistant professor, 1971-73, associate professor, 1973-77, professor of history, 1978; U.S. Senate, legislative aide to Senator Robert B. Morgan, 1979-81; University of Massachusetts, visiting professor, 1974-75; Smithsonian National Museum of American History, Division of Agriculture and Natural Resources, curator, supervisor, 1982-94, Kenneth E. Behring Center, Division of Work and Industry, curator, 1994-; Southern Historical Association, president, 2005-06. Writer. Publications: Shadow of Slavery: Peonage in the South, 1901-1969, 1972; Talent for Detail: The Photographs of Miss Frances Benjamin Johnston, 1889-1910, 1974; Deep'n As It Come: The 1927 Mississippi River Flood, 1977; Breaking the Land: The Transformation of Cotton, Tobacco and Rice Cultures Since 1880, 1985; Standing at the Crossroads: Southern Life Since 1900, 1986; (co-author) Official Images: New Deal Photography, 1987; (with A.W. Tucker) Carry Me Home: Louisiana Sugar Country Photographs (essays), 1990; Standing at the Crossroads: Southern Life in the Twentieth Century, 1996; Lost Revolutions: The South in the 1950s, 2000; Toxic Drift: Pesticides and Health in the Post-World War II South, 2005. Address: Division of Work and Industry, Kenneth E Behring Ctr., National Museum of American History, PO Box 37012, Washington, DC 20002, U.S.A. Online address: pedaniel@aol.com

DANIEL, Tony. American (born United States), b. 1963. Genres: Novels, Science Fiction/Fantasy, inspirational/Motivational Literature. Career: Seattle Pacific University, teacher, 1991; Vashon High School, assistant debate coach, 1992-93; Automatic Vaudeville, writer and director, 1998-99; Seeing Ear Theater, producer and story editor, 2000. Publications: NOVELS: Ascension, 1991; Warpath, 1993; Earthling, 1997; Adrenalynn: Weapon of War, 2001; Silke, 2002; Vampires, 2002. TENTH SERIES: Abuse of Humanity, 1997; The Tenth, 1998; Blackout, 2001; No Sweets After Dark, 2002. METAPLANETARY SERIES: Metaplanetary: A Novel of Interplanetary Civil War, 2001; Superluminal, 2004; (contrib.) Batman: The Black Glove, 2008; (contrib.) Batman R.I.P., 2009. COLLECTIONS: The Robot's Twilight Companion, 1999. OTHER: Guardian of Night, 2012. Contributor of articles to periodicals. Address: Baen Publishing Enterprises, PO Box 1403, Riverdale, NY 10471, U.S.A.

DANIEL, Wayne W. American (born United States), b. 1929. Genres: Mathematics/Statistics, Medicine/Health, Music, Biology, Sciences. Career: Teacher, 1949-50, 1954-57; Georgia Department of Public Health, statistical research assistant, 1957-58, research statistician, 1959-60, Biostatistics Service, Mental Health Statistics Section, chief, 1965-67, Biostatistics Service, director, 1967-68; Milledgeville State Hospital, biostatistical analyst, 1960-63; Georgia State University, assistant professor, professor of decision sciences, 1968, now professor emeritus. Writer. Publications: Biostatistics: A Foundation for Analysis in the Health Sciences, 1974, 9th ed., 2009; (with J.C. Terrell) Business Statistics: Basic Concepts and Methodology, 1975, 7th ed., 1995; Introductory Statistics with Applications, 1977; Applied Nonparametric Statistics, 1978; Lost Letter Technique: An Annotated Bibliography, 1978; Collecting Sensitive Data by Randomized Response: An Annotated Bibliography, 1979, 2nd ed., 1993; Decision Trees for Management Decision Making: An Annotated Bibliography, 1979; On Nonparametric and Robust tests for Dispersion: A Selected Bibliography, 1979; Questionnaire Design: A Selected Bibliography for the Survey Researcher, 1979; Use of Monetary and Other Gift Incentives in Mail Surveys: An Annotated Bibliography, 1979; Statistical Adjustment for Nonresponse in Sample Surveys: A Selected Bibliography with Annotations, 1979; Use of Dummy Variables in Regression Analysis: A Selected Bibliography with Annotations, 1979; Use of Random Digit Dialing in Telephone Surveys: An Annotated Bibliography, 1979; Goodness-of-Fit: A Selected Bibliography for the Statistician and the Researcher, 1980; Outliers in Research Data: A Selected Bibliography, 1980; Nonparametric, Distribution-free and Robust Procedures in Regression Analysis: A Selected Bibliography, 1980; Multiple Comparison Procedures: A Selected Bibliography, 1980; Ridge Regression: A Selected Bibliography, 1980; Essentials of Business Statistics, 1984, 2nd ed., 1988; Picking on Peachtree: A History of Country Music in Atlanta, Georgia, 1990; Business Statistics: For Management and Economics, 7th ed., 1995. Contributor of articles. Address: Georgia State University, PO Box 3965, Atlanta, GA 30302-3965, U.S.A. Online address: wwdaniel@gsu.edu

DANIELL, Ellen. American (born United States), b. 1947. Genres: Sciences. Career: University of California, assistant professor of microbiology, 1976-84; Cetus Corp., senior scientific recruiter, 1984-85, personnel director, 1985-88; PCR Division, director of business development, 1988-91; Roche Molecular Systems Inc., director of licensing and business development, 1991-; consultant, 1991-. Writer. Publications: Every Other Thursday: Stories and Strategies from Successful Women Scientists, 2006. Address: Yale University Press, 302 Temple St., PO Box 209040, New Haven, CT 06511-8909, U.S.A. Online address: ellen_daniell@earthlink.net

DANIELS, Angie. American (born United States) Genres: Novels, Romance/Historical, Mystery/Crime/Suspense. Career: Writer. Publications: Intimate Intentions, 2000; Hart & Soul, 2003; Endless Enchantment, 2003; Time is of the Essence, 2004; When It Rains..., 2005; Love Uncovered, 2005; Destiny in Disguise, 2005; A Will to Love, 2005; When I First Saw You, 2006; In the Company of My Sistahs, 2006; A Delight before Christmas, 2006; (with K.K. Terry and L.G. Riley) Big Spankable Asses, 2007; The Second Time Around, 2007; Trouble Loves Company, 2007; The Playboy's Proposition, 2008; Careful of the Company You Keep, 2008; The Player's Proposal, 2008; For You I Do, 2009; Before I Let You Go, 2010. Works appear in anthologies. Address: PO Box 1954, Columbia, MO 65201, U.S.A. Online address: angie@angiedaniels.com

DANIELS, Anthony. (Theodore Dalrymple). British (born England), b. 1949. Genres: Travel/Exploration, Psychology, Medicine/Health, Autobiography/Memoirs, Social Sciences. Career: Manhattan Institute for Policy Research, Weismann fellow. Psychiatrist and writer. Publications: Coups and Cocaine: Two Journeys in South America, 1986; Fool or Physician: The Memoirs of a Sceptical Doctor, 1987; Zanzibar to Timbuktu, 1988; Sweet Waist of America: Journeys around Guatemala, 1990; Utopias Elsewhere: Journeys in a Vanishing World in UK as The Wilder Shores of Marx: Journeys in a Vanishing World, 1991; Monrovia Mon Amour: A Visit to Liberia, 1992. AS THEODORE DALRYMPLE: If Symptoms Persist: Anecdotes from a Doctor, 1995; So Little Done: The Testament of a Serial Killer, 1996; Mass Listeria: The Meaning of Health Scares, 1998; An Intelligent Person's Guide to Medicine, 2001; Life at the Bottom: The Worldview That Makes the Underclass, 2002; Our Culture, What's Left of It: The Mandarins and the Masses, 2005; Romancing Opiates: Pharmacological Lies and the Addiction Bureaucracy, 2006; Junk Medicine: Doctors, Lies and the Addiction Bureaucracy, 2007; In Praise of Prejudice: The Necessity of Preconceived Ideas, 2007; (foreword) Pit of Shame: The Real Ballad of Reading Gaol, 2007; Not with a Bang but a Whimper: The Politics and Culture of Decline, 2008; Second Opinion: A Doctor's Dispatches from the Inner City, 2009; Spoilt Rotten: The Toxic Cult of Sentimentality, 2010; The new Vichy Syndrome: Why European Intellectuals Surrender to Barbarism, 2010; Litter, 2011. Contributor to periodicals. **Address:** Hodder Education, 338 Euston Rd., London, GL NW1 3BH, England.

DANIELS, Connie. *See* **LAUX, Constance.**

DANIELS, Elizabeth Adams. American (born United States), b. 1920. **Genres:** Biography, Education. **Career:** Vassar College, instructor, 1948-54, assistant professor, 1954-60, dean of freshmen, 1955-58, associate professor, 1960-63, professor of English, 1964-85, dean of studies, 1966-73, chairman of the English department, 1974-76, dean of faculty, 1976-78, professor emeritus of English and Vassar historian, 1986-. Writer. **Publications:** Jessie White Mario: Risorgimento Revolutionary, 1972; Possedutadall'angelo, 1977; (ed.) Vassar: The Remarkable Growth of a Man and His College, 1984; Main to Mudd, 1987; Matthew Vassar, More than a Brewer, 1992; Bridges to the World: Henry Noble MacCracken and Vassar College, 1994; Main to Mudd, and More, 1996; (with M. Bruno) Vassar College, 2001; (with C. Griffen) Full Steam Ahead in Poughkeepsie, The Story of Coeducation at Vassar, 2001. **Address:** Vassar College, Rm. 100, Maria Mitchell Observatory, 124 Raymond Ave., PO Box 74, Poughkeepsie, NY 12604, U.S.A.

DANIELS, Jeff. American (born United States), b. 1955. **Genres:** Film, Novels, Young Adult Fiction. **Career:** Writer and Actor. **Publications:** Shoeman, 1991; The Tropical Pickle, 1992; The Kingdoms Coming, 1994; Boomtown, 1998; Apartment 3A, 2000; The Vast Difference, 2000; Escanaba in da Moonlight, 2000; Super Sucker, 2002; Across the Way, 2002. **Address:** 8942 Wilshire Blvd., Beverly Hills, CA 90211, U.S.A.

DANIELS, Karen. American (born United States), b. 1957. **Genres:** Science Fiction/Fantasy, Children's Fiction, Adult Non-fiction, Literary Criticism And History, Human Relations/Parenting. **Career:** Writer. **Publications:** THE ZADDACK TALES: Dancing Suns, 2000; Mentor's Lair, 2000; (with E.M. Vukich) City and County Jails in the State of Washington, 2000; Mind Spark, 2001. OTHERS: Meditation Strategies: A Booklet For Getting Through the Day/Finding Yourself Creative; The Baby About to Be Born: A Story of Spirit for Adoptive and A.R.T. Families, 2005. **Address:** c/o Author Mail, 2 Neptune Rd., Poughkeepsie, NY 12601, U.S.A. **Online address:** kdauthor@aol.com

DANIELS, Mark R. American (born United States), b. 1952. **Genres:** Politics/Government, Social Sciences. **Career:** Slippery Rock University, Department of Government and Public Affairs, associate professor, 1997-2002, Master of Public Administration Program, director, 1997-2000, professor, 2002-, chairperson, 2004-10. Writer. **Publications:** Terminating Public Programs: An American Political Paradox, 1997; Medicaid Reform and the American States: Case Studies on the Politics of Managed Care, 1998; (ed.) Creating Sustainable Community Programs: Examples of Collaborative Public Administration, 2001. Contributor to journals. **Address:** Department of Political Science, Slippery Rock University of Pennsylvania, 1 Morrow Way, Slippery Rock, PA 16057-1326, U.S.A. **Online address:** mark.daniels@sru.edu

DANIELS, Max. *See* **GELLIS, Roberta (Leah Jacobs).**

DANIELS, Olga. *See* **SINCLAIR, Olga (Ellen).**

DANIELS, Rebecca. American (born United States), b. 1949. **Genres:** Plays/Screenplays, Theatre. **Career:** National Onion Singing Telegram Service, public relations manager, branch manager and performer, 1977-79; Murphy, Symonds and Stowell, executive recruiter, 1979-82; Artists Repertory Theatre, founder, 1982, producing director and artistic director, 1982-88; Pacific Lutheran University, visiting assistant professor of theatre, 1988-89; University of Portland, adjunct instructor in theatre, 1989-90; Seattle Pacific University, visiting lecturer in theatre, 1989-90; St. Lawrence University, assistant professor, 1992-98, department chair, 1997-2002, Birdsong associate professor in the arts, 1998-, department co-chair, 2004-06, 2008-; Portland Area Theatre Alliance, board director. Writer. **Publications:** Women Stage Directors Speak: Exploring the Influence of Gender on Their Work, 1996. Contributor to periodicals. **Address:** Department of Performance and Communication Arts, St. Lawrence University, 105 Noble Ctr., 23 Romoda Dr., Canton, NY 13617, U.S.A. **Online address:** rdaniels@stlawu.edu

DANIELS, Sarah. British (born England), b. 1957. **Genres:** Plays/Screenplays, Novels, Music, Art/Art History, Poetry. **Career:** Royal Court Theatre, associate resident writer, 1984; Albany Empire, resident writer, 1989-90. **Publications:** Neaptide, 1986; Ripen Our Darkness and The Devil's Gateway, 1986; Byrthrite, 1987; The Gut Girls: A Play, 1989; Masterpieces, 1991; Beside Herself, 1991; (and intro.) Plays, Two, 1994; Morning Glory, 2001; Come As You Are, 2001. **Address:** Judy Daish Associates Ltd., 2 St. Charles Pl., London, GL W10 6EG, England.

D'ANIERI, Paul J. D. American (born United States), b. 1965?. **Genres:** Politics/Government, History, Adult Non-fiction, Economics, Business/Trade/Industry, Education. **Career:** University of Kansas, College of Liberal Arts and Sciences, Department of Political Science, assistant professor, 1991-98, associate professor, 1998-2007, professor, 2007-, Center for Russian and European Studies, associate dean of international programs, 1999-2003, director, 2003-04, associate dean for humanities, 2004-08, dean, 2008-. Writer. **Publications:** Economic Interdependence in Ukrainian-Russian Relations, 1999; (with R. Kravchuk and T. Kuzio) Politics and Society in Ukraine, 1999; (ed. with T. Kuzio and R.S. Kravchuk) State and Institution Building in Ukraine, 1999; (ed. with T. Kuzio) Dilemmas of State-Led Nation Building in Ukraine, 2002; Understanding Ukrainian Politics: Power, Politics, and Institutional Design, 2007; (ed. with T. Kuzio) Aspects of the Orange Revolution I, 2008; International Politics: Power and Purpose in Global Affairs, 2010; (ed.) Orange Revolution and Aftermath: Mobilization, Apathy, and the State in Ukraine, 2010. Contributor to periodicals. **Address:** Department of Political Science, College of Liberal Arts and Sciences, University of Kansas, Rm. 200, Strong Hall, 1541 Lilac Ln., Lawrence, KS 66045-7594, U.S.A. **Online address:** danieri@ku.edu

DANILOWITZ, Brenda. American/South African (born South Africa) **Genres:** Design, Fash Ion/Costume. **Career:** University of the Witwatersrand, faculty, 1980-86; Josef and Anni Albers Foundation, curator, 1990-, chief curator. Art historian and writer. **Publications:** (Ed. and intro.) Anni Albers: Selected Writings on Design, 2000; The Prints of Josef Albers: A Catalogue Raisonné 1915-1976, 2001, rev. ed., 2009; (with N.F. Weber) The Prints of Anni Albers: Catalogue Raisonné, 1963-1984, 2009. Contributor to books and periodicals. **Address:** Josef and Anni Albers Foundation, 88 Beacon Rd., Bethany, CT 06524, U.S.A. **Online address:** danilowitz@albersfoundation.org

DANKO, William D(avid). American (born United States), b. 1952. **Genres:** Biography, Social Sciences. **Career:** State University of New York, School of Business, professor of marketing, 1976-2007, professor emeritus, 2007-, chair. Writer. **Publications:** (With T.J. Stanley) The Millionaire Next Door: The Surprising Secrets of America's Wealthy, 1996. Contributor to periodicals. **Address:** School of Business, State University of New York, 1400 Washington Ave., Albany, NY 12222-0001, U.S.A. **Online address:** danko@albany.edu

DANLEY, John R(obert). American (born United States), b. 1948. **Genres:** Economics, Philosophy, Business/Trade/Industry, Sociology. **Career:** Southern Illinois University, College of Arts and Sciences, Department of Philosophy, faculty, 1976-, interim dean, professor, now professor emeritus. Writer. **Publications:** The Role of the Modern Corporation in a Free Society, 1994. **Address:** Department of Philosophy, College of Arts and Sciences, Southern Illinois University, Rm. 3212, Peck Hall, PO Box 1433, Edwardsville, IL 62026-1433, U.S.A. **Online address:** jdanley@siue.edu

DANN, Colin (Michael). British (born England), b. 1943. **Genres:** Children's Fiction, Natural History, Novels, Picture/Board Books. **Career:** William Collins Sons & Company Ltd. (publishing company), sales administration manager, 1966-78; writer, 1979-. **Publications:** The Beach Dogs, 1970; A Great Escape, 1970; Fox's Feud, 1970; A Legacy of Ghosts, 1970; (with C. Guthrie) Looking at Insects, 1978; The Animals of Farthing Wood, 1979; In the Grip of Winter, 1981; Fox Cub Bold, 1983; The Siege of White Deer Park, 1985; Ram of Sweetriver, 1986; King of The Vagabonds, 1987; Just Nuffin, 1989; In the Path of the Storm, 1989; The City Cats, 1991; Battle for the Park, 1992; Farthing Wood: The Adventure Begins, 1994; (with S. Mongredien) Weasel's Adventure, 1995; Copycat, 1997; Nobody's Dog, 1999; (with R. Perry) Spooky Stories, 1999; Journey to Freedom, 1999; Lion Country, 2000; Pride of the Plains, 2002. Contributor to periodicals. **Address:** Castle Oast, Ewhurst Green, Robertsbridge, ES TN32 5TD, England.

DANN, Jack. Australian/American (born United States), b. 1945. **Genres:** Novels, Novellas/Short Stories, Romance/Historical, Science Fiction/Fantasy, Poetry, Young Adult Fiction, Horror. **Career:** Science Fiction and Fantasy Writers of America Bulletin, assistant editor, 1970-72, managing editor, 1973-75; Science Fiction Writers Speakers Bureau, lecturer, 1971-; Broome Community College, instructor of writing and science fiction, 1972, 1990-91; Cornell University, assistant professor, 1973; Tor Books, consulting editor, 1994-. **Publications:** Starhiker (novel), 1977; Christs and Other Poems, 1978; Junction (novel), 1981; The Man Who Melted (novel), 1984; (with J.C. Haldeman II) Echoes of Thunder (novel), 1991; (with J.C. Haldeman II) High Steel, 1993; The Memory Cathedral, 1995; The Silent, 1998; Counting Coup, 2001; (with R. Campbell and D. Etchison) Gathering the Bones, 2003; The Rebel, 2004; (co-author) Fiction Factory, 2005; Man Who Melted, 2007; Nebula Awards 39, forthcoming. SHORT STORIES: Timetipping, 1980; (co-author) Slow Dancing through Time, 1990; Jubilee, 2001; Visitations, 2003. EDITOR: Wandering Stars (anthology), 1974; (with G. Zebrowski) Faster Than Light (anthology), 1976; Immortal, 1977; More Wandering Stars, 1981; (with J.V.B. Dann) In the Field of Fire, 1987; (with P. Sargent and G. Zebrowski) Three in Time: White Wolf Rediscovery Trio, vol. I, 1997; (with P. Sargent and G. Zebrowski) Three in Space: White Wolf Rediscovery Trio No. 2, vol. I, 1998; (with J. Webb) Dreaming Down-Under, 1998; (with G. Davidson) Everybody Has Somebody in Heaven, 2000; Dreaming Again: Thirty-five New Stories Celebrating the Wild Side of Australian Fiction, 2008; (with J. Strahan) Legends of Australian Fantasy, 2010; (with N. Gevers) Ghosts by Gaslight, 2011. EDITED WITH G. DOZOIS: Future Power, 1976; Aliens!, 1980; Unicorns! 1984; Magicats! 1984; Bestiary!, 1985; Mermaids!, 1986; Sorcerers!, 1986; Demons!, 1987; Dogtails!, 1988; Seaserpents!, 1989; Dinosaurs!, 1990; Little People!, 1991; Magicats II, 1991; Unicorns II, 1992; Dragons!, 1993; Invaders!, 1993; Horses!, 1994; Angels!, 1995; Dinosaurs II, 1995; Hackers!, 1996; Timegates, 1997; Immortals!, 1998; Nanotech!, 1998; Armegeddons, 1999; Aliens among Us, 2000; Genometry, 2001; Space Soldiers, 2001; Future Sport, 2002; Beyond Flesh, 2002; Future Crime, 2003; A.I.S, 2004; Robots, 2005; Beyond Singularity, 2005; Future Past, 2006; Escape from Earth: New Adventures in Space, 2006; Wizards, 2007; Dangerous Games, 2007; Dragon Book, 2009. **Address:** PO Box 101, Foster, VI 3960, Australia. **Online address:** jackdann@jackdann.com

DANNER, Mark (David). American (born United States), b. 1958. **Genres:** Documentaries/Reportage, Adult Non-fiction. **Career:** New York Review of Books, editorial assistant, 1981-84, contributor, 1993-; Harper's Magazine, senior editor, 1984-86; New York Times Magazine, foreign affairs and politics story editor, 1986-90; New Yorker, staff writer, 1990-2001, contributor, 2001-; New York University, New York Institute for the Humanities, fellow, 1993-; ABC News, writer and producer, 1994-95, Peter Jennings Reporting, staff; University of California, Berkeley Graduate School of Journalism, visiting professor, 1998, professor of journalism, 1999-2010, Chancellors professor of English, journalism and politics, 2010-, Center for Human Rights, senior research fellow, 1998, Goldman Forum on the Press and Foreign Affairs, founding director, 2002-05; Bard College, Henry R. Luce professor of human rights and journalism, 2003-07, James Clarke Chace professor of foreign affairs, politics, and humanities, 2007-. **Publications:** The Massacre at El Mozote: A Parable of the Cold War, 1994; The Road to Illegitimacy: One Reporter's Travels Through the 2000 Florida Vote Recount, 2004; Torture and Truth: America, Abu Ghraib, and the War on Terror, 2004; The Secret Way to War: The Downing Street Memo and the Iraq War's Buried History, 2006; Stripping Bare the Body: Politics, Violence, War, 2009. Contributor to periodicals. **Address:** New York Review of Books, 435 Hudson St., New York, NY 10014, U.S.A. **Online address:** mark@markdanner.com

DANO, Linda. American (born United States), b. 1943. **Genres:** Romance/Historical, Fash Ion/Costume, Homes/Gardens, Architecture, Novels, Sports/Fitness. **Career:** Writer, actress and consultant. **Publications:** (As Felicia Gallant with R. Flanders) Dreamweaver (romance novel), 1984; (with A. Kyle) Looking Great: Daytime Television Star Linda Dano Shares Her Fashion, Beauty and Style Secrets to Help You Look Your Best, 1997; (with A. Kyle) Living Great: Style Expert and Television Star Linda Dano Shows You How to Bring Style Home with Her Easy, Affordable Decorating Ideas and Techniques, 1998. **Address:** c/o VSMP, The Marketing Group, 1010 Nautilus, Mamaroneck, NY 10543, U.S.A. **Online address:** linda@lindadano.com

DANOPOULOS, Constantine P. American/Greek (born Greece), b. 1948. **Genres:** Military/Defense/Arms Control, Adult Non-fiction, Social Commentary, Politics/Government. **Career:** Southwest Missouri State University, faculty, 1978-81; Ball State University, faculty, 1981-82; San Jose State University, faculty, 1983, professor of political science, department vice chair;

Journal of Political and Military Sociology, associate editor, 1985-; Journal of Political and Military Sociology, editor, 1993-96; Armed Forces and Society, associate editor, 1993-2004; Mediterranean Quarterly, associate editor, 2003-; Library of Congress, Federal Research Division for Project on European Civil-Military Relations, consultant, 2004; The Carson: Journal of Environmental Studies, consulting editor, 2004-. **Publications:** Warriors and Politicians in Modern Greece, 1984. EDITOR: The Decline of Military Regimes: The Civilian Influence, 1988; Military Disengagement from Politics, 1988; From Military to Civilian Rule, 1992; Civilian Rule in the Developing World: Democracy on the March?, 1992; (with K.P. Magyar) Prolonged Wars: A Post-Nuclear Challenge, 1994; (with C. Watson) The Political Role of the Military: An International Handbook, 1996; (with D. Zirker) Civil-Military Relations in the Soviet and Yugoslav Successor States, 1996; (with K.G. Messas) Crises in the Balkans: Views from the Participants, 1997; (with D. Zirker) The Military and Society in the Former Eastern Bloc, 1999; (with D. Vajpeyi and A. Bar-or) Civil-military Relations, Nation Building and National Identity: Comparative Perspectives, 2004. Contributor to books and journals. **Address:** 6188 Northland Terr., Fremont, CA 94555, U.S.A. **Online address:** cdanopou@email.sjsu.edu

DANOW, David K. American (born United States), b. 1944. **Genres:** Literary Criticism And History, Essays, Reference. **Career:** University of California, professor of Russian and comparative literature, director, College of Humanities, Arts and Social Sciences, Comparative Literature and Foreign Languages, professor emeritus. Writer. **Publications:** The Thought of Mikhail Bakhtin: From Word to Culture, 1991; The Dialogic Sign: Essays on the Major Novels of Dostoevsky, 1991; The Spirit of Carnival: Magical Realism and the Grotesque, 1995; Models of Narrative: Theory and Practice, 1997; Transformation as the Principle of Literary Creation from the Homeric Epic to the Joycean Novel, 2004. **Address:** Department of Comparative Literature and Foreign, Languages, University of California, HMNSS 2304, Riverside, CA 92521, U.S.A. **Online address:** david.danow@ucr.edu

DANQUAH, Meri Nana-Ama. American/Ghanaian (born Ghana), b. 1967. **Genres:** Autobiography/Memoirs, Social Sciences. **Career:** Writer. **Publications:** Willow Weep for Me (memoir), 1998; (ed. and intro.) Becoming American: Personal Essays by First Generation Immigrant Women, 2000; (ed.) Shaking the Tree: A Collection of New Fiction and Memoir by Black Women, 2003; (ed.) Black Body, 2009. Contributor to periodicals. **Address:** 7095 Hollywood Blvd., Ste. 447, Los Angeles, CA 90028-8912, U.S.A. **Online address:** outloud@danquah.com

DANSON, Edwin. British (born England), b. 1948. **Genres:** Social Commentary, Earth Sciences, History, Geography, Institutions/Organizations. **Career:** Wimpol Ltd., development manager, 1983-94; Kongsberg AS, communal director, 1994-95; Fugro NV, business manager, 1996-2000; Swan Consultants Ltd., managing director, 2000-; Island Fibre, Netherlands Antilles, consultant, 2002; University of Plymouth, external examiner, 2003-07; Institution of Civil Engineering Surveyors, vice president, 2004, president, 2006-07; India Card Technologies Ltd., technical director; Admiralty Coastal Surveys, business manager; Hydrographic Survey Panel, chair; Geospatial Engineering Board, chairman. Writer and surveyor. **Publications:** Drawing the Line: How Mason and Dixon Surveyed the Most Famous Border in America, 2001; Weighing the World: The Quest to Measure the Earth, 2006. Contributor to journals. **Address:** Swan Consultants Ltd., Deers Leap, Bubwith Farm, Wookey Hole, SM BA5 1BA, England. **Online address:** edanson@aol.com

DANTICAT, Edwidge. American (born United States), b. 1969. **Genres:** Novels, Novellas/Short Stories, Plays/Screenplays, Young Adult Fiction. **Career:** Clinica Estetico, production and research assistant, 1993-94; novelist, 1994-; New York University, professor, 1996-97; University of Miami, visiting professor of creative writing, 2000. **Publications:** Breath, Eyes, Memory (novel), 1994; Krik? Krak! (short stories), 1995; The Farming of Bones (novel), 1998; (ed.) The Butterfly's Way, 2001; Behind the Mountains, 2002; After the Dance: A Walk through Carnival in Jacmel, Haiti, 2002; (trans. and afterword) Espace d'un cillement, 2002; The Dew Breaker, 2004; Anacaona, Golden Flower: Haiti, 1490, 2005; Brother, I'm Dying, 2007; Create Dangerously: The Immigrant Artist at Work, 2010; Eight Days: a Story of Haiti, 2010. **Address:** Soho Press, 853 Broadway, Ste. 1903, New York, NY 10003, U.S.A.

DANTO, Arthur C(oleman). American (born United States), b. 1924. **Genres:** Philosophy, Essays. **Career:** University of Colorado, instructor,

1950-51; Columbia University, instructor, 1951-54, assistant professor, 1954-59, associate professor 1959-66, professor of philosophy, 1966-75, Johnsonian professor of philosophy, 1975-92, head, 1979-87, Johnsonian professor emeritus of philosophy, 1992-, Center for Study of Human Rights, co-director, 1978-; Princeton University, visiting professor, 1965, visiting lecturer; University of California-San Diego, visiting lecturer, 1965, visiting professor, 1973; University of California-Santa Barbara, visiting professor, 1965; Amnesty Intl., director, 1970-75; The Nation Magazine, art critic; Amnesty Intl., board director, 1970-75; Catholic University of America, visiting professor, 1972; American Philosophical Association, vice-president and president; Journal of Philosophy, editor, consulting editor. **Publications:** (Ed. and intro. With S. Morgenbesser) Philosophy of Science, 1960; Analytical Philosophy of History, 1965; Nietzsche as Philosopher, 1965; Analytical Philosophy of Knowledge, 1968; What Philosophy Is, 1968; Mysticism and Morality, 1972; Analytical Philosophy of Action, 1973; Jean-Paul Sartre, 1975; Sartre, 1975; (co-author) Handlungstheorie, 1976; The Transfiguration of the Commonplace, 1981; Narration and Knowledge, 1985; The Philosophical Disenfranchisement of Art, 1986; The State of the Art, 1987; Politics of Imagination, 1988; Connections to the World, 1989; Encounters and Reflections: Art in the Historical Present, 1990; Beyond the Brillo Box: The Visual Arts in Post-Historical Perspective, 1992; Embodied Meanings: Critical Essays and Aesthetic Meditations, 1994; Playing with the Edge, 1996; Sean Scully, 1996; After the End of Art: Contemporary Art and the Pale of History, 1997; Cy Twombly, 1997; IdaApplebroog, 1998; Wake of Art, 1998; The Body/Body Problem, 1999; (with M.J. Jacob and P. Sims) Howard Ben Tré, 1999; Philosophizing Art, 1999; Madonna of the Future: Essays in a Pluralistic Art World, 2000; (contrib.) Made in Oakland, 2001; (with R. Enright and S. Martin) Eric Fischl, 1970-2000, 2001; (contrib.) Ursula von Rydingsvard: Cedar Lace and Tossing Loops, 2002; (contrib.) Kimura, 2003; (contrib.) Michele Oka Doner: Natural Seduction, 2003; The Abuse of Beauty: Aesthetics and the Concept of Art, 2003; Joel Shapiro, 2003; Robert Mangold, 2003; (with M. Livingstone and T. Hyman) Redgrooms, 2004; Unnatural Wonders: Essays from the Gap between Art and Life, 2005; Wave Music, 2005; (with R. Fleck and B. Söntgen) Peter Fischli, David Weiss, 2005; Cuatro Cuartetos, 2005; (contrib.) Betty Woodman, 2006; (ed. with J. Simon and N. Stritzler-Levine) Sheila Hicks Weaving as Metaphor, 2006; (contrib.) The Sculpture of Louise Nevelson, 2007; (contrib.) June Wayne, the Art of Everything, 2007; (with R. Enright and S. Martin) Eric Fischl, 1970-2007, 2008; Andy Warhol, 2009; (intro.) Night Shift, 2009. **Address:** Department of Philosophy, Columbia University, 708 Philosophy Hall, 1150 Amsterdam Ave., PO Box 4971, New York, NY 10027-7051, U.S.A. **Online address:** acd1@columbia.edu

DANTO, Elizabeth Ann. American (born United States), b. 1952. **Genres:** Humanities, Social Work, Intellectual History, Social Sciences, Psychology. **Career:** United Store Workers Union, coordinator of social services, 1983-86; Office of Mayor, employee assistance program director, 1986-91; City University of New York, Hunter College School of Social Work, associate professor, 1997-, professor, Human Behavior and Social Environment, chair. Writer. **Publications:** Freud's Free Clinics: Psychoanalysis & Social Justice, 1918-1938, 2005; Historical Research, 2008. Contributor to books and periodicals. **Address:** School of Social Work, Hunter College, City University of New York, Rm. 435, 129 E 79th St., New York, NY 10021, U.S.A. **Online address:** edanto@hunter.cuny.edu

D'ANTONIO, Michael. American (born United States), b. 1955. **Genres:** Adult Non-fiction, History, Ghost Writer, Biography, Money/Finance, Theology/Religion, Natural History, Sports/Fitness, Sports/Fitness. **Career:** Dover Democrat, reporter, 1976-77; Portland Press Herald, reporter, 1977-78; Guy Gannet Newspapers, Washington correspondent, 1979-83, Newsday, writer, 1983-90; Center for Policy Research, research associate; Dana-Farber Cancer Institute, consultant; Pfizer Corp., consultant. **Publications:** Fall from Grace: The Failed Crusade of the Christian Right, 1989; Heaven on Earth: Dispatches From America Spiritual Frontier, 1992; Atomic Harvest: Hanford and the Lethal Toll of America's Nuclear Arsenal, 1993; (with M. Magee) The Best Medicine: Doctors, Patients, and the Covenant of Caring, 1999; (with R. Acampora) The Fourth Mega-Market, Now through 2011: How Three Earlier Bull Markets Explain the Present and Predict the Future, 2000; Tin Cup Dreams: A Long Shot Makes It on the PGA Tour, 2000; (with A. Spielman) Mosquito: A Natural History of Our Most Persistent and Deadly Foe, 2001; Tour '72, 2002; (with B. McNall) Fun While it Lasted: My Rise and Fall in the Land of Fame and Fortune, 2003; The State Boys Rebellion, 2004; Hershey: Milton S. Hershey's Extraordinary Life of Wealth, Empire, and Utopian Dreams, 2006; A Ball, A Dog, and A Monkey: 1957-The Space Race Begins,

2007; Forever Blue: The True Story of Walter O'Malley, Baseball's Most Controversial Owner, and the Dodgers of Brooklyn and Los Angeles, 2009; A Full Cup: Sir Thomas Lipton's Extraordinary Life and His Quest for the America's Cup, 2010; (with J. Gerzema) Spend Shift: How the Post-Crisis Values Revolution Is Changing the Way We Buy, Sell, and Live, 2011. Contributor to periodicals. **Address:** Jossey-Bass, 1 Montgomery St., Ste. 1200, San Francisco, CA 94104, U.S.A. **Online address:** michael@michaeldantonio.net

DANTZER, Robert. American/French (born France), b. 1944. **Genres:** Medicine/Health, Psychology. **Career:** National Institute of Agronomic Research, staff, 1968-, Laboratory of Behavioural Neurobiology, director, 1981-93; National Institute of Health and Medical Research, Laboratory of Integrative Neurobiology, director, 1994-; University Paul Sabatier, Department of Animal Sciences, Neuroscience Program, professor, Integrative Immunology and Behavior Program, director, Department of Pathology, professor of psychoneuroimmunology; University of Illinois, Department of Pathology, professor of psychoneuroimmunology, Integrative Immunology and Behavior Program, director, Neuroscience Program, professor, Department of Animal Sciences, professor. Consultant and writer. **Publications:** Le stress en elevage intensif, 1979; Les emotions, 1988, 2nd ed., 1994; Illusion psychosomatique, 1989; (ed. with N. Rothwell) Interleukin-1 in the Brain, 1992; The Psychosomatic Delusion: Why the Mind is Not the Source of all Our Ills, 1993; (co-ed.) Cytokines, Stress, Depression, 1999. Contributor to books and scientific journals. **Address:** Departmental of Animal Sciences, 227 Edward R. Madigan Laboratory, 1207 W Gregory Dr., Urbana, IL 61801, U.S.A. **Online address:** dantzer@illinois.edu

DANZ, Harold P. American (born United States), b. 1929. **Genres:** Animals/Pets, History, Zoology. **Career:** U.S. Department of the Interior, National Park Service, staff, 1955-74, associate regional director, 1974-91; Danz and Associates, owner, 1991-92; writer, 1993-. **Publications:** Historical Listing of National Park Service Officials, 1986, rev. ed., 1991; Of Bison and Man: From the Annals of a Bison Yesterday to a Refreshing Outcome from Human Involvement with America's Most Valiant of Beasts, 1997; Cougar!, 1999. Contributor to periodicals. **Address:** 6751 S Callaway Dr., Chandler, AZ 85249-4451, U.S.A.

DANZIGER, Charles. American (born United States), b. 1962. **Genres:** Adult Non-fiction, Local History/Rural Topics. **Career:** Museum of Modern Art, assistant general counsel, 1990-94; Milbank, Tweed, Hadley & McCloy, staff; Danziger & Danziger, partner and specialist in art law, 1994-; Crunchyworld, co-founder, animator; The Journal of International Law and Politics, editor. **Publications:** The American Who Couldn't Say Noh: Almost Everything You Need to Know about Japan, 1994; Japan for Starters, 2002; (with M. Sakamoto) Harvey And Etsuko's Manga Guide To Japan, 2007. Contributor to magazines and newspapers. **Address:** Danziger, Danziger & Muro L.L.P., 405 Park Ave., Ste. 502, New York, NY 10022, U.S.A. **Online address:** charles@danziger.com

DANZIGER, Daniel (Guggenheim). (Danny Danziger). American (born United States), b. 1953. **Genres:** Novels, Art/Art History, Architecture. **Career:** Independent, columnist, 1990-95; Daily Mail, columnist, 1996-97; Cover Magazine, co-founder and co-editor, 1997-; Sunday Times, columnist, 1999-. **Publications:** AS DANNY DANZIGER: (comp.) The Happiness Book, 1980; All in a Day's Work, 1987; Eton Voices, 1988; The Cathedral: A Portrait of Lincoln Cathedral, 1989; The Year Zero, 1989; The Noble Tradition: Intimate Interviews withthe Medical Profession, 1990; Lost Hearts: Talking about Divorce, 1992; The Orchestra: The Lives behind the Music, 1995; (with R. Lacey) The Year 1000: What Life Was Like at the Turn of the First Millennium, 1999; (with J. Gillingham) 1215: The Year of Magna Carta, 2003; (with N. Purcell) Hadrian's Empire: When Rome Ruled the World, 2005; Museum: Behind the Scenes at the Metropolitan Museum of Art, 2007; The Thingummy, 2008; (with M. McCrum) Whatchamacallit: Those Everyday Objects You just Can't Name: (And Things You Think You Know about but Don't), 2009. **Address:** The Sunday Times, 1 Virginia St., London, GL E98 1SS, England.

DANZIGER, Danny. See **DANZIGER, Daniel (Guggenheim).**

DAOUST, Jean-Paul. Canadian (born Canada), b. 1946. **Genres:** Poetry, Social Sciences. **Career:** Cegep Edouard-Montpetit, professor. Writer. **Publications:** POETRY: Oui, cher: Recit, 1976; Chaise longues, 1977; Portrait d'interieur, 1981; Poemes de Babylone, 1982; Taxi, 1984; Dimanche apres-midi, 1985; La peau du coeur et son opera, 1985; Les garcons magiques, 1986; Suite contemporaine, 1987; Rituels d'Ameriques, 1990; Les cendres bleues, 1990, rev. ed., 2001; Du Dandysme, 1991; Les chambres de la mer, 1991; Les poses de la lumiere, 1991; L'Amerique, 1993; Levres ouvertes, 1993, rev. ed., 2001; Fusions, 1994; (with L. Desjardins and M. Latif-Ghattas) Poemes faxes, 1994; 111 Wooster Street, 1996; Taxi pour Babylone, 1996; Les saisons de l'Ange, 1997, vol. II, 1999; Amérique: poème, 1999; Le poeme deshabille, 2000; Désert rose, 2000; Versets Amoureux, 2001; Roses labyrinthes, 2002; Cinéma gris: poésie, 2006; Cobra et colibri, 2006; Fleurs lascives, 2007. OTHER: Soleils d'acajou, 1983; Le Desert rose, 2000; élégie nocturne, 2008; Le vitrail brisé, 2009; Carnets de Moncton: scénes de la vie ordinaire, 2010; Libellules, couleuvres et autres merveilles, 2011. Contributor to periodicals. **Address:** 151 rue Champoux, Ste-Melanie, QC J0K 3A0, Canada. **Online address:** mesanges@pandore.qc.ca

DARBY, Andrew. Australian (born Australia), b. 1953?. **Genres:** History, Natural History. **Career:** Australian Associated Press, staff. Journalist. **Publications:** Harpoon: Into the Heart of Whaling, 2007. Contributor to newspapers. **Address:** The Age, PO Box 257C, Melbourne, VI 3001, Australia.

DARBY, Ann. American (born United States) **Genres:** Novels, Adult Nonfiction, Animals/Pets. **Career:** Scientific American Medicine, associate editor, editor and science writer. **Publications:** Finny the Lovesick Frog, 1996; The Orphan Game, 1999; (with T.P. Mauriello) The Dollhouse Murders: A Forensic Expert Investigates 6 Little Crimes, 2004; The Sweet, Sad Songs of W.F. Pine, forthcoming. **Address:** c/o Emma Sweeney, Emma Sweeney Agency L.L.C., 245 E 80th St., Ste. 7E, New York, NY 10075-0506, U.S.A. **Online address:** ann@anndarby.com

DARBY, J. See DARBY, John.

DARBY, John. Also writes as J. Darby, John P. Darby. American (born United States), b. 1940. **Genres:** History, Social Sciences. **Career:** Saint Malachy's College, teacher, 1963-71, Department of History, head, 1967-71; Northern Ireland Community Relations Commission, research and publications officer, 1971-74; University of Ulster, lecturer in social administration, 1974-85, professor of ethnic studies, 1985-98, Centre for the Study of Conflict, director, 1999-2000; Harvard Graduate School of Education, associate in education, 1980; Duke University, Center for International Studies, visiting professor, 1988; Ethnic Studies Network, founder and director, 1990-99, president, 2000-03; United Nations University, Feasibility Study, chairman, 1991, The Initiative on Conflict Resolution and Ethnicity (INCORE), founding director, 1991-97, research director and senior research fellow, 1997-2001; United States Institute of Peace, Jennings Randolph fellow, 1998; University of Notre Dame, Joan B. Kroc Institute for International Peace Studies, professor of comparative ethnic studies, 1999-, visiting fellow, 1999-2000, Research Initiative for the Resolution of Ethnic Conflict, director, 2002-06, Peace Accords Matrix, director, 2004-, Kroc-Uppsala Initiative on Post-agreement Issues in Peace Processes, co-director, 2008-; University of Sunderland, adjunct professor, 2000-02; Nepal Transition to Peace, external advisor, 2009-10. Writer. **Publications:** Conflict in Northern Ireland, 1976; (ed. with A. Williamson) Violence and the Social Services in Northern Ireland, 1978; (with D. Murray) Vocational Aspirations and Expectations of School Leavers in Londonderry and Strabane, 1980; Cartoons and Conflict, 1982; A Regulated Conflict, 1983; (ed.) Northern Ireland: Background to the Conflict, 1983; Dressed to Kill: Cartoonists and the Northern Irish Conflict, 1983; (ed.) Register of Economic and Social Research on Northern Ireland, 1980-83, 1983; Intimidation and the Control of Conflict in Northern Ireland, 1986; (ed. with N. Dodge and A.C. Hepburn) Political Violence: Northern Ireland in a Comparative Perspective, 1990; Northern Ireland: Managing Difference, 1995; Scorpions in a Bottle, 1997; The Management of Peace Processes, 2000; Effects of Violence on Peace Processes, 2001; (with R.M. Ginty) Guns and Government: The Management of the Northern Ireland Peace Process, 2002; (ed. with R.M. Guinty) Contemporary Peacemaking: Conflict, Violence and Peace Processes, 2003, 2nd ed., 2008; (ed.) Violence and Reconstruction, 2006. **Address:** Joan B. Kroc Institute for International Peace Stu, University of Notre Dame, 330 Hesburgh Ctr., Notre Dame, IN 46556, U.S.A. **Online address:** darby.3@nd.edu

DARBY, John P. See DARBY, John.

DARBY, Mary Ann. American (born United States), b. 1954. **Genres:** Bibliography, Education, Social Sciences. **Career:** English Teacher, 1976-88, 1993-; Jefferson State Community College, English teacher. Writer. **Publications:** (With M. Pryne) Hearing All the Voices: Multicultural Books for Adolescents, 2002. Contributor of articles to periodicals. **Address:** Egan Junior High School, 100 W Portola, Los Altos, CA 94022, U.S.A. **Online address:** ma.darby@gmail.com

DARBY, William D(uane). American (born United States), b. 1942. **Genres:** Film, Sports/Fitness, Art/Art History, Reference. **Career:** Davenport University, instructor, professor in English, 1991-. Writer. **Publications:** Necessary American Fictions, 1987; (with J. DuBois) American Film Music: Major Composers, Techniques, Trends, 1915-1990, 1990; Masters of Lens and Light: A Checklist of Major Cinematographers and Their Feature Films, 1991; (with D.F. Darby) Major League Baseball, 1979-1992: A Year-by-Year History Using Fan-oriented Statistics, 1993; John Ford's Westerns: A Thematic Analysis, with a Filmography, 1996; Deconstructing Major League Baseball, 1991-2004: How Statistics Illuminate Individual and Team Performances, 2006; Anthony Mann: The Film Career, 2009. **Address:** 13168 E Outer Dr., Detroit, MI 48224-2735, U.S.A.

DARCY, Emma. See BRENNAN, Wendy.

DARDEN, Robert. American (born United States), b. 1954. **Genres:** Documentaries/Reportage, Ghost Writer, Music. **Career:** Waco Tribune-Herald, arts and entertainment editor, 1978-86; Billboard Magazine, Gospel music editor, 1984-94; The Door, senior editor, 1987-; Texas State Technical College, teacher, 1988; Baylor University, adjunct professor, 1988-99, assistant professor of English, 1999, associate professor of journalism and media arts, 2006-, professor in department of journalism. **Publications:** Drawing Power: Knott, Ficklen, and McClanahan, Editorial Cartoonists of the Dallas Morning News, 1983; (comp.) Into the End Zone, 1989; (with P.J. Richardson) The Way of an Eagle, 1996; Come to the Temple, 1996; Wheels Like a Whirlwind, 1996; I, Jesus: Stories from the Savior, 1997; (with P.J. Richardson) Wheels of Thunder, 1997; (with C.B. Simmons) Little Mo's Legacy: A Mother's Lessons, A Daughter's Story, 2001; (with P.J. Richardson) Corporate Giants: Personal Stories of Faith and Finance, 2002; Secret Recipe: Why KFC is Still Cookin' After 50 Years, 2002; People Get Ready: A New History of Black Gospel Music, 2004; People Get Ready: A New History of Black Gospel Music, 2005; Reluctant Prophets and Clueless Disciples: Introducing the Bible by Telling its Stories, 2006; Jesus Laughed: The Redemptive Power of Humor, 2008. EDITOR: What a World! The Collected Essays of Dr. Ralph Lynn, 1998; On the 8th Day God Laughed, 2000. AS OTHERS: The Option Play, 1990; FastForward, 1991; (with W.R. Spence) December Champions, 1993; (with B. Bailey) Mad Man in Waco, 1993; (with K. Saunders) There's Always a Way, 1993; The Young Messiah, 1994. Contributor to books and periodicals. **Address:** Department of Journalism, Public Relations and, New Media, Baylor University, 1 Bear Pl., PO Box 97353, Waco, TX 76798, U.S.A. **Online address:** robert_darden@baylor.edu

DARION, R. F. See STACEY, Cherylyn.

DARKE, Marjorie (Sheila). British (born England), b. 1929. **Genres:** Children's Fiction, Young Adult Fiction. **Career:** John Lewis Partnership, textile designer, 1951-54; writer, 1962-. **Publications:** Ride the Iron Horse, 1973; The Star Trap, 1974; Mike's Bike, 1974; A Question of Courage, 1975; What Can I Do?, 1975; The Big Brass Band, 1976; Kipper's Turn, 1976; My Uncle Charlie, 1977; The First of Midnight, 1978; A Long Way to Go, 1978; Kipper Skips, 1979; Carnival Day, 1979; Comeback, 1981; Tom Post's Private Eye, 1983; Messages: A Collection of Shivery Tales, 1984; Imp, 1985; The Rainbow Sandwich, 1989; A Rose from Blighty, 1990; Night Windows, 1990; Emma's Monster, 1992; Just Bear and Friends, 1996. Work appears in anthologies. **Address:** c/o Rogers, Coleridge & White Ltd., 20 Powis Mews, London, GL W11 1JN, England.

DARLING, David J. British (born England), b. 1953. **Genres:** Adult Nonfiction, Astronomy, Children's Non-fiction, Philosophy, Physics, Sciences, Theology/Religion, Young Adult Non-fiction, Biography. **Career:** Cray Research, manager of applications software, 1978-82; writer, 1982-; The Worlds of David Darling, owner, 1999-. **Publications:** JUVENILE NON-FICTION. DISCOVERING OUR UNIVERSE SERIES: Comets, Meteors and Asteroids, 1984; The Moon: A Spaceflight Away, 1984; The Planets: The Next Frontier, 1984; The Sun: Our Neighborhood Star, 1984; Where are We Going in Space?, 1984; Other Worlds: Is There Life Out There?, 1985; The Galaxies: Cities of Stars, 1985; The New Astronomy, 1985; The Stars, 1985; The Universe, 1985. WORLD OF COMPUTERS SERIES: Computers at Home, 1986; Fast, Faster, Fastest: The Story of Supercomputers, 1986; Inside Computers, 1986; The Microchip Revolution, 1986; Robots and the Intelligent Computer, 1986. COULD YOU EVER... SERIES: Build a Time Machine?, 1990; Dig a Hole to China?, 1990; Fly to the Stars?, 1990; Meet an Alien?, 1990; Speak Chimpanzee?, 1990; Could You Ever?, 1991; Live Forever?, 1991. EXPERIMENT SERIES: Making Light Work: The Science of Optics, 1991; Up, Up and Away: The Science of Flight, 1991; Spiderwebs to Skyscrapers: The Science of Structures, 1991; Sounds Interesting: The Science of Acoustics, 1991; Between Fire and Ice: The Science of Heat, 1992; From Glasses to Gases: The Science of Matter, 1992. ADULT NONFICTION: Deep Time, 1989; Equations of Eternity, 1993; Soul Search: A Scientist Explores the Afterlife, 1995; Zen Physics, 1996; The Extraterrestrial Encyclopedia, 2000: Life Everywhere: The Maverick Science of Astrobiology, 2001; The Complete Book of Spaceflight, 2003; Universal Book of Astronomy from the Andromeda Galaxy to the Zone of Avoidance, 2004; Universal Book of Mathematics: From Abracadabra to Zeno's Paradoxes, 2004; Teleportation: The Impossible Leap, 2005; Gravity's Arc: The Story of Gravity, from Aristotle to Einstein and Beyond, 2006. BEYOND 2000 SERIES: Genetic Engineering, 1995; Micromachines and Nanotechnology, 1995; After Life: in Search of Cosmic Consciousness, 1995; Computers of the Future, 1996; The Health Revolution: Surgery and Medicine in the 21st Century, 1996. OTHER: Diana, the People's Princess (biography), 1984. Contributor of articles to periodicals. **Address:** 8776 Dorothy Ave., Brainerd, MN 56401-7084, U.S.A.

DARLING, Diana. Indonesian/American (born United States), b. 1947. **Genres:** Novels, Young Adult Fiction. **Career:** Writer and sculptor. **Publications:** Committee, a Novel, 1936; The Painted Alphabet: A Novel, 1992; Marc Jurt, Anatomies of the Invisible, 1997. **Address:** Laura Gross Literary Agency, 39 Chester St., Ste. 301, Newton Highlands, MA 02461, U.S.A.

DARLING, Mary Albert. American (born United States), b. 1956. **Genres:** Theology/Religion. **Career:** Spring Arbor College (now Spring Arbor University), secretary to vice president for student affairs, 1978-79, administrative assistant, 1979-86, assistant and instructor, 1986-90, director of chapel program, 1990-92, assistant professor of communication, associate professor, 1990-; Greater Jackson Habitat for Humanity, board director, 1989-92. Writer. **Publications:** (With T. Campolo) The God of Intimacy and Action: Reconnecting Ancient Spiritual Practices, Evangelism, and Justice, 2007; (with T. Campolo) Connecting like Jesus: Practices for Healing, Teaching, and Preaching, 2010. **Address:** Spring Arbor University, 106 E Main St., Spring Arbor, MI 49283-9701, U.S.A. **Online address:** mdarling@arbor.edu

DARLING, T. H. See HARRIS, Thomas Walter.

DARLINGTON, Ralph. British (born England), b. 1954?. **Genres:** History, Industrial Relations, Organized Labor, Business/Trade/Industry. **Career:** University of Salford, lecturer, 1991-, Industrial Relations, senior lecturer, faculty of business, law and the built environment, 2001-, professor of employment relations, director of business management. Writer. **Publications:** The Dynamics of Workplace Unionism: Shop Stewards' Organization in Three Merseyside Plants, 1994; The Political Trajectory of J.T. Murphy, 1998; (ed. and intro.) Suffragette and Socialist, 1998; (with D. Lyddon) Glorious Summer: Class Struggle in Britain, 1972, 2001; Syndicalism and the Transition to Communism: An International Comparative Analysis, 2008; (ed.) What's the Point of Industrial Relations?: In Defence of Critical Social Science, 2009. **Address:** School of Management, University of Salford, 313 B Maxwell Bldg., 43 The Cres., Salford, GM M5 4WT, England. **Online address:** r.r.darlington@salford.ac.uk

DARLISON, Bill. Irish (born Ireland) **Genres:** Novels. **Career:** Writer. **Publications:** The Shortest Distance: 101 Stories from the World's Spiritual Traditions, 2006; The Gospel and the Zodiac: The Secret Truth about Jesus, 2007; The Penultimate Truth and Other Incitements (sermons), 2007; Enlightenment and Ice Cream, 2007. **Address:** Unitarian Church, 112 St. Stephen's Green W, Dublin, 2, Ireland.

DARLOW, Stephen. See DARLOW, Steve.

DARLOW, Steve. (Stephen Darlow). British (born England), b. 1966. **Genres:** Military/Defense/Arms Control, History. **Career:** England Basketball, staff, 1988-, development officer, national club development manager and national academies officer; Fighting High Ltd., founder and publisher. Writer. **Publications:** Lancaster Down! The Extraordinary Tale of Seven Young Bomber Aircrew at War, 2000; Sledgehammers for Tintacks: Bomber Command Combats the V-1 Menace, 1943-1944, 2002; (as Stephen Darlow) D-Day Bombers: The Veterans' Story: RAF Bomber Command and the US Eighth Air Force Support to the Normandy Invasion 1944, 2004 in US as D-Day Bombers: The Stories of Allied Heavy Bombers during the Invasion of Normandy, 2010; (as Stephen Darlow) Victory Fighters: The Veterans' Story: Winning the Battle for Supremacy in the Skies over Western Europe, 1941-1945, 2005; Five of the Few: Survivors of the Battle of Britain and the Blitz Tell Their Story, 2006; Five of the Many: Survivors of the Bomber Command Offensive from the Battle of Britain to Victory Tell Their Story, 2007; Special Op: Bomber; Daring Missions That Changed the Shape of WWII, 2008; (comp. and ed.) Fighting High: World War Two-Air Battle Europe, vol. I, 2009, vol. II, 2010; Flightpath to Murder: Death of a Pilot Officer, 2010; (with R. Pinkham) On Wings of Fortune: A Bomber Pilot's War from the Battle of Britain, to Germany, North Africa, and Accident Investigation in the Far East, 2010. **Address:** Fighting High Ltd., 23 Hitchin Rd., Stotfold, Hitchin, HF SG5 4HP, England. **Online address:** stephen.darlow@btinternet.com

DARNAY, Arsen J. American/Hungarian (born Hungary), b. 1936. **Genres:** Science Fiction/Fantasy, Environmental Sciences/Ecology, Information Science/Computers, Mathematics/Statistics. **Career:** J.F. Pritchard & Co. (consulting engineers), technical writer, 1961-65; Midwest Research Institute, program manager, 1965-73, director of north star project, 1977-81; U.S. Environmental Protection Agency, deputy assistant administrator, 1973-75; Carborundum Co., Solid Waste Conversion Division, general manager, 1975-77; Arsen Darnay & Associates, principal, 1981-; Government and Industry Executive, publisher; Editorial Code and Data Inc., president, 1990-. **Publications:** (With W.E. Franklin) The Role of Packaging in Solid Waste Management 1966 to 1976, 1969; (with W.E. Franklin) Salvage Markets for Materials in Solid Wastes, 1972; A Hostage for Hinterland, 1976; Karma, 1978; The Siege of Faltara, 1978; The Karma Affair: A Novel of Retribution and Transcendence, 1979; The Purgatory Zone, 1981; The Splendid Freedom, 1980; Manufacturing USA, 1989; Market Share Reporter, 1990; American Salaries and Wages Survey, 1990; Services Industry USA, 1991; Economic Indicators Handbook, 1992; (comp. and ed.) Statistical Record of the Environment, 1992; Finance, Insurance, Real Estate USA, 1992; American Cost of Living Survey, 1993; (ed.) Statistical Record of Older Americans, 1994; Transportation and Public Utilities USA, 1997; Agriculture, Mining and Construction U.S.A., 1998; Manufacturing & Distribution U.S.A.: Industry Analyses, Statistics, and Leading Companies, 2000; (co-ed.) Social Trends & Indicators USA, 2003; (ed. with M.D. Magee) Encyclopedia of Small Business, 2007; (ed. with P.J. Bungert) Encyclopedia of Products & Industries-Manufacturing, 2008. **Address:** Editorial Code & Data Inc., 814 Wolverine Dr., Ste. 2, Walled Lake, MI 48390-2377, U.S.A.

DARNELL, Regna (Diebold). Canadian/American (born United States), b. 1943. **Genres:** Anthropology/Ethnology, Biography, Language/Linguistics, Politics/Government. **Career:** University of Pennsylvania, Department of Anthropology, research assistant, 1966-69; University of Alberta, assistant professor of anthropology, 1969-73, Cree Language Teaching Program, coordinator and instructor, 1970-84, associate professor of anthropology, 1973-79, professor of anthropology, 1979-90; Yale University, visiting professor of anthropology, 1985, Canadian Studies of anthropology, bicentennial visiting professor, 2000; University of Western Ontario, Department of Anthropology, chair, 1990-93, professor of anthropology, 1990-, First Nations Studies Program, founding director, 2003-06, distinguished professor, 2005-, Killam research fellow, 2006-08; Centre for Research and Teaching of Canadian Native Languages, director, 1992-; McMaster University, adjunct professor of anthropology, 1994-. Writer. **Publications:** (Ed.) Linguistic Diversity in Canadian Society, 1971; (ed. and intro.) American Anthropology, 1971-1995; (ed.) Canadian Languages in Their Social Context, 1973; Readings in the History of Anthropology, 1974; Daniel Garrison Brinton: The Fearless Critic of Philadelphia, 1988; (ed. with M.K. Foster) Native North American Interaction Patterns, 1988; Edward Sapir: Linguist, Anthropologist, Humanist, 1990; (ed. with J. Irvine) Collected Works of Edward Sapir 4: Ethnology, 1994; And Along Came Boas: Continuity and Revolution in Americanist Anthropology, 1998; (ed. with J. Irvine and R. Handler) Collected Works of Edward Sapir 3: Ethnology, 1999; (ed.) Culture, 1999; (ed. with L. Valentine) Theorizing the

Americanist Tradition, 1999; Invisible Genealogies: A History of Americanist Anthropology, 2001; (ed. with F.W. Gleach) Celebrating a Century of the American Anthropological Association: Presidential Portraits, 2002; (ed. with F.W. Gleach) Papers From the American Anthropologist, 2002; (ed. with F.W. Gleach) Histories of Anthropology Annual I, 2005; (ed.) Historicizing Canadian Anthropology, 2006; (ed. with F.W. Gleach) Histories of Anthropology Annual II, 2007; (with L.Valentine and A. McDougall) Contemporary First Nations: Discourse, Identity and Power, forthcoming. **Address:** Department of Anthropology, University of Western Ontario, Social Science Ctr., London, ON N6A 5C2, Canada. **Online address:** rdarnell@uwo.ca

DARNTON, Robert. American (born United States), b. 1939. **Genres:** History, Literary Criticism And History, Theology/Religion. **Career:** The New York Times, reporter, 1964-65; Harvard University, Society of Fellows, junior fellow, 1965-68, Carl H. Pforzheimer University professor, 2007-, University Library, director, 2007-; Princeton University, assistant professor, 1968-71, associate professor, 1971-72, professor of history, 1972-2008, Shelby Cullom Davis professor of European history, 1985-2007, Program in European Cultural Studies, director, 1987-95, Center for the Study of Books and Media, director, 2002-07, professor emeritus, 2007-; Stanford University, Center for Advanced Study in the Behavioral Sciences, fellow, 1973-74; Netherlands Institute for Advanced Study, fellow, 1976-77; Oxford University, George Eastman visiting professor, 1986-87; Institute for Advanced Study, fellow, 1989-90, 1993-94; University of Warwick, honorary professor, 1996-2000; St. John's College, honorary fellow, 2000-; Siemens Foundation, fellow, 2005. Writer. **Publications:** Mesmerism and the End of the Enlightenment in France, 1968; (with B. Fabian and R.M. Wiles) The Widening Circle: Essays on the Circulation of Literature in Eighteenth-Century Europe, 1976; The Business of Enlightenment: A Publishing History of the Encyclopédie, 1979; The Literary Underground of the Old Regime, 1982; Bohème littéraire et révolution: le monde des livres au XVIIIe siècle, 1983; The Great Cat Massacre and Other Episodes in French Cultural History, 1984; The Kiss Lamourette: Reflections in Cultural History, 1989; Kiss of Lamourette: Reflections in Cultural History, 1990; What was Revolutionary about the French Revolution?, 1990; Edition et sédition: L'universe de la littérature clandestine au XVIIe siecle, 1991; Berlin Journal, 1989-1990, 1991; Gens de lettres, gens du livre, 1992; The Forbidden Best-sellers of Pre-revolutionary France, 1995; The Corpus of Clandestine Literature in France, 1769-1789, 1995; J.P. Brissot, His Career and Correspondence (1779-1878), 2001; Pour les Lumieres: Defense, illustration, methode, 2002; Wissenschaft des Raubdrucks: ein zentrales Element im Verlagswesen des 18. Jahrhunderts, 2003; George Washington's False Teeth: An Unconventional Guide to the Eighteenth Century, 2003; (contrib.) Media and Political Culture in the Eighteenth Century, 2005; Case for Books, 2009; Devil in the Holy Water or the Art of Slander from Louis XIV to Napoleon, 2010; Poetry and the Police, 2010. EDITOR: (with D. Roche) Revolution in Print: The Press in France, 1775-1800, 1989; (with O. Duhamel) Démocratie, 1998; Bohémiens, 2010. **Address:** Department of History, Harvard University, Rm. 212, Robinson Hall, 35 Quincy St., Cambridge, MA 02138-3880, U.S.A. **Online address:** robert_darnton@harvard.edu

DARRELL, Elizabeth. See DAWES, Edna.

DARRIEUSSECQ, Marie. French (born France), b. 1969. **Genres:** Novels, Ghost Writer. **Career:** University of Lille, part-time lecturer, 1994-97. Writer. **Publications:** Naissance des Fantômes: Roman, 1998; Le Mal de Mer: Roman, 1999; Brefséjour chez les vivants: Roman, 2001; Le Bébé, 2002; Brief Stay with the Living, 2003; White: Roman, 2003; Dolorès Marat: Illusion, 2003; (with P. Rahm and J. Vilmouth) Ghostscape, 2004; Bernard Faucon, 2005; Le Pays: Roman, 2005; (co-author) Naissances: récits, 2005; Marie Darrieussecq parle des éditions P.O.L, 2006; Tom est mort: Roman, 2007; Le musé de la mer: pièce en deux parties pour cinq, six, sept ou huit acteurs, 2009; Rapport de Police, 2010; (contrib.) Portrait of the Artist as a Young Mother, 2011; Clèves, 2011. Contributor to periodicals. **Address:** The Fund for Independent Publishing, 38 Greene St., Fl. 4, New York, NY 10013-2505, U.S.A.

DARROCH, James L. Canadian (born Canada), b. 1951. **Genres:** Economics. **Career:** University of Toronto, Erindale College, teaching assistant, 1978-79; McMaster University, lecturer in European history, 1979; Queen's University, assistant professor of European history, 1980-82; Wilfrid Laurier University, assistant professor of business policy, 1985-86; York University, Faculty of Administrative Studies, course director, 1985, sessional assistant professor, 1986-88, assistant professor, 1988-93, Schulich School of Business, associate professor of policy studies and director of entrepreneurial studies, 1993-, Financial Services Program, associate director, 1998-2004, co-director, 2004-07, director, 2007; York Consulting Group, director, 1997-98, co-director, 1998-2005. Writer. **Publications:** Canadian Banks and Global Competitiveness, 1994. Contributor of articles to books and journals. **Address:** Schulich School of Business, York University, Rm. N305K, 4700 Keele St., North York, ON M3J 1P3, Canada. **Online address:** jdarroch@schulich.yorku.ca

DARROW, Sharon. American (born United States), b. 1948?. **Genres:** Novels, Children's Fiction. **Career:** Waubonsee Community College, faculty; College of DuPage, faculty; Vermont College, MFA in Writing for Children; Columbia College, Department of English, faculty. Writer. **Publications:** Old Thunder and Miss Raney, 2000; Through the Tempests Dark and Wild: A Story of Mary Shelley, 2003; The Painters of Lexieville, 2003; Trash, 2006; BOTTLEKATZ: A Complete Care Guide for Orphan Kittens, 2006. Contributor to books and periodicals. **Address:** Candlewick Press, 99 Dover St., Somerville, MA 02144, U.S.A. **Online address:** sharondarrow@hotmail.com

DART, Iris Rainer. American (born United States), b. 1944?. **Genres:** Novels, Young Adult Fiction, Psychology, Romance/Historical, Children's Fiction. **Career:** Writer. **Publications:** NOVELS: The Boys in the Mail Room, 1980; Beaches, 1985; 'Til the Real Thing Comes Along, 1987; I'll Be There, 1991; The Stork Club, 1992; Show Business Kills, 1995; When I Fall in Love, 1999; Some Kind of Miracle, 2003; (with J. Brotman) Larry, The King of Rock and Roll, 2007; All the Rage, forthcoming. **Address:** Markson Thoma Literary Agency, 44 Greenwich Ave., New York, NY 10011, U.S.A.

DARTON, Eric. American (born United States), b. 1950. **Genres:** Novels, History, Urban Studies. **Career:** Hunter College, faculty; New York University, faculty; Goddard College, MFA in Creative Writing Program, faculty. Writer. **Publications:** Radio Tiranë (fiction collection in Conjunctions 10), 1991; Free City (novel), 1996; Divided We Stand: A Biography of New York's World Trade Center (history), 1999, rev. ed., 2011; Beaky Chronicles (fiction collection), 2008; Orogene (novel), 2009; Notes of a New York Son, 1995-2007 (cultural memoir in five volumes), vol. I, 2010, vol. II, 2011. Contributor to periodicals. Works appear in anthologies. **Address:** Watkins Loomis Agency Inc., 133 E 35th St., Ste. 1, New York, NY 10016-3886, U.S.A. **Online address:** ericdartonbooks@earthlink.net

DART-THORNTON, Cecilia. Australian/British/Irish (born Ireland) **Genres:** Novels, Science Fiction/Fantasy, Young Adult Fiction, Mythology/Folklore, Paranormal, Novellas/Short Stories, Poetry, Romance/Historical, Romance/Historical. **Career:** Writer, educator, book designer and musician. **Publications:** The Ill-Made Mute, 2001; The Lady of the Sorrows, 2002; The Battle of Evernight, 2003; The Iron Tree, 2005; The Well of Tears, 2006; Weatherwitch, 2006; Fallowblade, 2007. Works appear in anthologies. **Address:** PO Box 9113, Brighton, VI 3186, Australia. **Online address:** dartthornton@yahoo.co.uk

DARTY, Peggy. American (born United States) **Genres:** Novels, Romance/Historical, Young Adult Fiction, Literary Criticism And History. **Career:** Columbia Broadcasting System Inc. (CBS), researcher. Writer. **Publications:** FICTION: Mountain to Stand Strong, 1984; Kincaid of Cripple Creek, 1985; Cimarron Sunset, 1986; The Wailing Winds of Juneau Abbey, 1990; The Crimson Roses of Fountain Court, 1991; The Captured Bride of Aspenwood, 1992; The Widowed Bride of Raven Oaks, 1992; The Precious Pearls of Cabot Hall, 1992; Angel Valley, 1995; Morning Mountain, 1995; Sundance, 1996; Seascape, 1996; Song of the Dove, 1997; Moonglow, 1997; Promises, 1997; Memories, 1998; Spirits, 1998; Summer Place, 1998; Look Homeward, Angel, 2000; My Beloved Waits, 2001; Lilly's Dream, 2004. COZY MYSTERY SERIES: When the Sandpiper Calls, 2005; When Bobbie Sang the Blues, 2007; When Zeffie Got a Clue, 2008. **Address:** Random House Inc., 1745 Broadway, 7th Fl., New York, NY 10019, U.S.A. **Online address:** peggydarty@aol.com

DARVILLE, Helen (Fiona). (Helen Demidenko). Australian (born Australia), b. 1972. **Genres:** Novels. **Career:** The Courier-Mail, columnist. Educator and writer. **Publications:** NOVELS: (as Helen Demidenko) The Hand That Signed the Paper, 1994. Contributor to books and periodicals. **Address:** Allen & Unwin, PO Box 8500, St. Leonards, NW 1590, Australia.

DARWISH, Adel. British/Egyptian (born Egypt), b. 1945. **Genres:** Politics/Government, Cultural/Ethnic Topics, International Relations/Current Affairs, History, Military/Defense/Arms Control, Third World, Area Studies, Translations, Translations, Autobiography/Memoirs, Ghost Writer. **Career:** Freelance writer and foreign correspondent, 1966-84; Arab News Group (Asharq al-Awsat), foreign news reporter and editor, 1984; Ashara Al-Ansal, editor, 1984-86; The Independent, reporter on the Middle East and foreign affairs, 1986-98; consultant and commentator, 1986-; Middle East Monthly Magazine, political editor (Parliamentary Press Lobby), 1999-. **Publications:** Secret Diplomacy and Islamic Fundamentalism in Egypt, 1983; The Muslim Brotherhood and Britain in the 1950s, 1984; Iraqi Defence Strategy in the Gulf War, 1987; Shape of Wars to Come the Spread of Missile Technology in the Middle East, 1988; Between the Quill and the Sword: The Political Background to the Satanic Verses Affair, 1989; (with G. Alexander) Unholy Babylon: The Secret History of Saddam's War, 1991; (with J. Bulloch) Water Wars: Coming Conflicts in the Middle East, 1993; Anti-Americanism in Arabic Language Media, 2003. Contributor to periodicals. **Address:** The Middle East Magazine, IC Publications, 7 Coldbath Sq., London, GL EC1R 4LQ, England. **Online address:** a_d@mideastnews.com

DARY, David Archie. American (born United States), b. 1934. **Genres:** Communications/Media, History, Social Commentary, Bibliography, Biography, Autobiography/Memoirs, Social Sciences, Animals/Pets, Animals/ Pets. **Career:** WIBW-Radio and Television, morning news editor, 1956-57; KWFT-Radio, news editor, 1957-60; KTSA-Radio, managing news editor, 1960; Columbia Broadcasting System Inc., reporter and editor, 1960-63; National Broadcasting Company Inc., manager of local news, 1963-67; Studio Broadcasting System, director of news, 1967; University of Kansas, assistant professor, 1969-75, associate professor, 1975-81, professor of journalism, 1981-89; University of Oklahoma, School of Journalism and Mass Communication, professor of journalism, director, 1989-2000, now professor emeritus; Western Writers of America, president, 1989-90. **Publications:** Radio News Handbook, 1967; TV News Handbook, 1971; How to Write News for Broadcast and Print Media, 1973; The Buffalo Book: The Full Saga of the American Animal, 1974; Tales of the Old-Time Plains, 1979; Cowboy Culture: A Saga of Five Centuries, 1981; Lawrence, Douglas County, Kansas, an Informal History, 1982; True Tales of Old-Time Kansas, 1984; Entrepreneurs of the Old West, 1986; More True Tales of Old Time Kansas, 1987; Kanzana, 1854-1900: A Selected Bibliography of Books, Pamphlets and Ephemera of Kansas, 1986; Lawrence, Douglas County Kansas: An Informal History, 1982; Pictorial History of Lawrence, Douglas County Kansas, 1992; Seeking Pleasure in the Old West, 1995; Red Blood and Black Ink: Journalism in the Old West, 1998; The Santa Fe Trail: Its History, Legends and Lore, 2000; Oklahoma Publishing Company's First Century: The Gaylord Family Story, 2003; The Oregon Trail: An American Saga, 2004; Texas Cowboy's Journal: Up the Trail to Kansas in 1868, 2006; True Tales of the Prairies and Plains, 2007; Frontier Medicine: From the Atlantic to the Pacific, 1492-1941, 2008; Stories of Old-Time Oklahoma, 2011. **Address:** c/o Eleanor Wood, Spectrum Literary Agency, 320 Central Pk. W, Ste. 1-D, New York, NY 10025, U.S.A.

DAS, Lama Surya. American (born United States), b. 1950. **Genres:** inspirational/Motivational Literature, Theology/Religion. **Career:** English teacher, Kyoto, 1973-74; Karma Triyana Dharma Chakra Monastery, Woodstock, founder, 1977, director, 1977-80; Lama in the Non-Sectarian Practice Lineage of Tibetan Buddhism; meditation workshop and retreat teacher in Dzogchen, Vajrayana and Mahayana Buddhism; Dzogchen Foundation, founder. Writer. **Publications:** The Snow Lion's Turquoise Mane: Wisdom Tales from Tibet, 1992; (with N.K. Rinpoche) Natural Great Perfection: Dzogchen Teachings and Vajra Songs, 1995; Dancing with Life: Dzogchen View, Meditation and Action, 1996; Awakening the Buddha Within: Tibetan Wisdom for the Western World, 1997; The Facts of Life from a Buddhist Perspective; Awakening to the Sacred: Creating a Spiritual Life from Scratch, 1999; Awakening the Buddhist Heart: Intergrating Love, Meaning and Connection into Every Part of Your Life, 2000; Letting Go of the Person You Used to Be: Lessons on Change, Loss and Spiritual Transformation, 2003; Natural Radiance, 2005; Buddha is as Buddha Does: A Practical Guide to Enlightened Living, 2007; Big Questions: How to Find Your Own Answers to Life's Essential Mysteries, 2007; Words of Wisdom, 2008; Mind is Mightier than the Sword: Enlightening the Mind, Opening the Heart: New Dharma Talks, 2009; Buddha Standard Time, 2011; New Dharma Talks: Buddhism for Today and Tomorrow, forthcoming. Contributor of articles to periodicals. **Address:** 1770 Mass Ave., Ste. 127, Cambridge, MA 02140, U.S.A. **Online address:** surya@surya.org

DAS, Suranjan. Indian (born India), b. 1954. **Genres:** Civil Liberties/Human Rights, Cultural/Ethnic Topics, Local History/Rural Topics, Politics/Govern-

ment. **Career:** Visva-Bharati University, lecturer in history, 1978-81; Vidyasagar College, Department of History, lecturer; University of Calcutta, Department of History, UGC junior research fellow, lecturer, 1981-89, reader in history, 1989-95, professor, 1995-, pro-vice-chancellor for academic affairs, 2002-08, vice-chancellor; Netaji Institute For Asian Studies, honorary director; University of Hull, honorary professor. Writer. **Publications:** Communal Riots in Bengal, 1905-1947, 1991; Fort William: A Historical Perspective, 1995; (with J.K. Ray) The Goondas: Towards a Reconstruction of the Calcutta Underworld, 1996; Kashmir and Sindh: Nation-Building, Ethnicity, and Regional Politics in South Asia, 2001. EDITOR: (with S. Bandopadhyay) Caste and Communal Politics in South Asia, 1993; Electoral Politics in South Asia, 2000; (with P.K. Bandhyopadhay) Food Movement of 1959: Documenting a Turning Point in the History of West Bengal, 2004; (with S.D. Muni) India and China: The Next Decade: Papers and Proceedings of a Seminar Organised by the Observer Research Foundation and the University of Calcutta, 2009; (ed. with S. Chakrabarti) Challenges of Nation-building in Developing Societies: Vignettes from West and South Asia, 2009. Work appears in anthologies. Contributor of articles. **Address:** Department of History, University of Calcutta, 1 Reformatory St., Alipore Campus, 4th Fl., Calcutta, WB 700027, India. **Online address:** suranjandas2000@yahoo.co.in

DASA, Drutakarma. See **CREMO, Michael (A.).**

DASCAL, Marcelo. Israeli/Brazilian (born Brazil), b. 1940. **Genres:** Language/Linguistics, Philosophy, Speech/Rhetoric, History, Translations. **Career:** University of Sao Paulo, instructor, 1964; Hebrew University of Jerusalem, researcher and lecturer, 1967-72; Ben Gurion University of the Negev, lecturer, senior lecturer, 1967-76, chair of department of philosophy, 1969-73; Tel Aviv University, instructor, professor of philosophy, 1967-, now professor emeritus, Faculty of Humanities, dean, 1995-2000; University of Massachusetts, visiting lecturer, 1973-74; Universidade Estadual de Campinas, professor, 1974-85; Young Persons Institute for Arts and Sciences, teacher, 1975-92; Manuscrito, editor, 1975-92; University of California, visiting associate professor of philosophy, 1980; Pragmatics and Cognition, editor, 1991-. **Publications:** Filosofia das Ciencias, 1964; La Sémiologie de Leibniz, 1978; Pragmatics and the Philosophy of Mind, 1983; Leibniz: Language, Signs, and Thought, 1987; Interpretation and Understanding, 2003; Mashav Ha-ruach, 2004. EDITOR: (with A. Parush) Harationali Vehairatzionali, 1975; Fundamentos Metodologicos da Linguistica, 4 vols., 1978-82; (with M. Brinker and D. Nesher) Baruch de Spinoza: Kovetz ma'amarim al mishnato, 1979; Tekstim Filosofi'im, 1979; (with J. Gracia, E. Rabossi and E. Villanueva) Philosophical Analysis in Latin America, 1984; Dialogue: An Interdisciplinary Approach, 1985; (with O. Gruengard) Knowledge and Politics, 1989; (with A. Cohen) The Institution of Philosophy, 1989; Conhecimento, Linguagm, Ideologia, 1989; Cultural Relativism and Philosophy, 1991; (with D. Gerhardus, K. Lorenz and G. Meggle) Philosophy of Language, 2 vols., 1993-95; (with E. Yakira) Leibniz and Adam, 1993; (with R. Gibbs and J. Nuyts) Human Cognitive Processes, 1996; (co-ed.) Eucuentros and Desencuentros: Spanish-Jewish Cultural Interactions, 2000; (with E. Weigand) Negotiation and Power in Dialogic Interaction, 2001; (with P. Barrotta) Controversies and Subjectivity, 2005; (and trans. and intro.) G.W. Leibniz, The Art of Controversies, 2006; (with H. Chang) Traditions of Controversy, 2007; The Practice of Reason: Leibniz and his Controversies, 2010. Contributor to journals. **Address:** Department of Philosophy, Tel Aviv University, PO Box 39040, Ramat Aviv, Tel Aviv, 69978, Israel. **Online address:** dascal@post.tau.ac.il

DASGUPTA, Amit. Australian/Indian (born India), b. 1953?. **Genres:** Young Adult Fiction. **Career:** Government of India, Central Civil Services, Indian Foreign Service, staff, 1979-, Ministry of Labour, staff, Ministry of External Affairs, staff, Indian Council for Cultural Relations, director of budget and finance and deputy director-general, Public Diplomacy Division, head, Consulate General of India-Sydney, consul general, 2009-. Writer. **Publications:** FICTION: In the Land of the Blue Jasmine (novel), 2006; (contrib.) Indian by Choice, 2009. NONFICTION: (ed. with S.H. Whang) High Temperature Superconducting Compounds: Processing & Related Properties: Proceedings of the 1989 Symposium on High Temperature Superconducting Oxides-Processing & Related Properties, Which Was Sponsored by the Superconducting Materials Committee and Held in Las Vegas, NV, February 27 and 28, 1989, at the 118th Annual Meeting of the Minerals, Metals & Materials Society, 1989; (ed. with S.H. Whang and R. Laibowitz) High Temperature Superconducting Compounds II, 1990; (ed. with S.H. Whang and E. Collings) High Temperature Superconducting Compounds III: Processing and Microstructure Property Relationships: Proceedings of a Symposium by the

Superconducting Materials Committee, the Structural Materials Division and the Electronic Materials Division of the Minerals, Metals, and Materials Society, New Orleans, Louisiana, February, 1991, 1991; (ed. with K.S. Murty) The Divine Peacock: Understanding Contemporary India, 1995; (ed. with S. Ramakrishna) Le Mahatma Gandhi 125 Années, 1995; Telling Tales: Children's Literature in India, 1995; (ed. with K.S. Murty) The Perennial Tree: Select Papers for the International Symposium on Indian Studies, 1996; (ed. with B. Debroy) Salvaging the WTO's Future: Doha and Beyond, 2002; (ed.) The Strategic Shape of the World: Proceedings of MEA-IISS Foreign Policy Dialogue, 2008; (ed.) India for a Billion Reasons, 2010. **Address:** Consulate General of India, Level 27, 25 Bligh St., Sydney, NW 2000, Australia. **Online address:** cg@indianconsulatesydney.org

DASGUPTA, Rana. Indian/British (born England), b. 1971. **Genres:** Novels. **Career:** Writer. **Publications:** Tokyo Cancelled, 2005; Solo, 2009. **Address:** c/o Sarah Chalfant, The Wylie Agency, 17 Bedford Sq., London, GL WC1B 3JA, England. **Online address:** rana@ranadasgupta.com

DASGUPTA, Shamita Das. American/Indian (born India), b. 1949. **Genres:** Psychology. **Career:** Franklin University, adjunct faculty of behavioral sciences, 1982-83; Rutgers University, teacher of psychology and women's studies, 1985-90, director of honors program, 1989-90; Yale University, lecturer; Manavi, co-founder, 1985, coordinator, 1985-; Kean College, adjunct faculty, 1987-90; New School for Social Research, faculty in Adult Division, 1989-90; Women's Resources of Monroe County, executive director, 1990-92; Rutgers University, lecturer, 1992-95, assistant professor of psychology, 1996-, adjunct assistant professor of clinical law; Cornell University, lecturer; Asian American Legal Defense and Education Fund, director, 1992-94; Women's Law Project, director, 1996-98; University of Illinois, lecturer; Columbia University, lecturer; Williams College, lecturer; Health Research and Educational Trust, consultant; U.S. Marine Corps, consultant; Bell Laboratories, consultant. Writer. **Publications:** All that Glitters: An Assessment of Feminist Consciouness in Hindi films, 1986; (with S. Warrier) In Visible Terms: Domestic Violence in the Asian Indian Context, 1995, rev. ed., 1997; (with I. Sinha) Mothers for Sale: Women in Kolkata's Sex Trade, 2009. EDITOR: (with S. Das Gupta) The Demon Slayers and Other Stories: Bengali Folk Tales, 1995; A Patchwork Shawl: Chronicles of South Asian Women in America, 1998; Body Evidence: Intimate Violence Against South Asian Women in America, 2007. Contributor to books and periodicals. **Address:** Sage Publications, 2455 Teller Rd., Thousand Oaks, CA 91320, U.S.A.

DASGUPTA, Subrata. American/Canadian (born Canada), b. 1944. **Genres:** Novels, Information Science/Computers, Intellectual History, Psychology, Autobiography/Memoirs. **Career:** International Business Machines World Trade Corp., programmer and systems analyst, 1967-71; University of Alberta, teaching assistant in computer science, 1972-74, associate professor of computer science, 1980-82; Simon Fraser University, assistant professor of computer science, 1975-79; Ohio State University, assistant professor of computer science and information science, 1979-80; University of Louisiana, associate professor, 1982-84, professor, 1984-86, Edmiston professor of computer science, 1986-93, endowed chair in computer science, 1993-, professor of history, 2000-, Institute of Cognitive Science, director, 2000-; Indian Institute of Science, Centre for Development in Advanced Computing, visiting scientist, 1991; Victoria University of Manchester, Institute of Science and Technology, Dowty professor of computer systems engineering, 1992-93. Writer. **Publications:** The Design and Description of Computer Architectures, 1984; Computer Architecture: A Modern Synthesis, vol. I: Foundations, vol. II: Advanced Topics, 1989; Design Theory and Computer Science: Processes and Methodology of Computer Systems Design, 1991; Creativity in Invention and Design: Computational and Cognitive Explorations of Technological Originality, 1994; Technology and Creativity, 1996; Jagadis Chandra Bose and the Indian Response to Western Science, 1999; Three Times a Minority (novel), 2003; Twilight of the Bengal Renaissance: R.K. Dasgupta & His Quest for a World Mind, 2005; Salaam, Stanley Matthews (a memoir), 2006; The Bengal Renaissance: Identity and Creativity from Rammohun Roy to Rabindranath Tagore, 2007; The Awakening: The Story of the Bengal Renaissance, 2010; Macaulay's Ghost: The Indo-Western Mind After the Awakening, forthcoming; The Golden Jubilee (a novel), forthcoming; Born Again India (a memoir), forthcoming. Contributor to books. **Address:** Institute of Cognitive Science, University of Louisiana, PO Box 43772, Lafayette, LA 70504-3772, U.S.A. **Online address:** subrata@louisiana.edu

DASH, Julie. American (born United States), b. 1952. **Genres:** Plays/Screen-plays, Novels. **Career:** Geechee Girls Multimedia Productions Inc., founder. Writer. **Publications:** Daughters Of The Dust: The Making Of An African American Woman's Film, 1992; Daughters of the Dust, 1997; Vetiver, Jasmine and Zen, 2007. **Address:** c/o Dutton, 375 Hudson St., New York, NY 10014, U.S.A. **Online address:** jdash@mac.com

DASO, Dik A. (Dik Alan Daso). American (born United States), b. 1959. **Genres:** History. **Career:** U.S. Air Force Academy, history instructor, 1992, lieutenant colonel, now retired; Air Force Historical Research Center, research associate, 1993-94; U.S. Air Force Science Advisory Board, historian, 1994-95; U.S. Government, The Pentagon, U.S. Air Force Doctrine, chief, 1995-97; Smithsonian Institution, National Air and Space Museum, A. Verville Fellow, 1997-98, Modern Military Aircraft, curator, 1998-. Writer, military historian and museum curator. **Publications:** (ed. with G.E. Brooks, M. Hitchens and H. Roupp) The Aspen World History Handbook: An Organizational Framework, Lessons, and Book Reviews for NonCentric World History, 1994; Architects of American Air Supremacy: Gen. Hap Arnold and Dr. Theodore von Kármán, 1997; Hap Arnold and the Evolution of American Air Power, 2000; (as Dik Alan Daso) Doolittle: Aerospace Visionary, 2003; U.S. Air Force: A Complete History, 2006; (ed.) America's Hangar: The Steven F. Udvar-Hazy Center, 3rd ed., 2007. **Address:** National Air and Space Museum, Smithsonian Institution, NASM MRC 312, PO Box 3702, Washington, DC 20013-7012, U.S.A. **Online address:** dasod@si.edu

DASO, Dik Alan. See **DASO, Dik A.**

DASSANOWSKY, Robert. (Robert von Dassanowsky). American/Austrian (born Austria), b. 1960. **Genres:** Plays/Screenplays, Poetry, Literary Criticism And History, Documentaries/Reportage, Translations, Language/Linguistics, Humanities, Popular Culture, Popular Culture, Reference, Communications/Media, Film, Institutions/Organizations, International Relations/Current Affairs. **Career:** Professional actor, 1976-83; University of Colorado, assistant professor of German, 1993-99, associate professor of German and film studies, 1999-2006, professor of German and film studies, 2006-, German studies, head, 1993-, Film Studies Program, director, 1993-, Department of Visual and Performing Arts, interim chair, 2000-01, Department of Languages and Cultures, chair, 2001-06; Stone-Stanley Television Productions and Disney Channel, writer and researcher, 1990-92; J. Paul Getty Conservation Institute, consultant and translator, 1991-93; University of California, visiting assistant professor of German, 1992-93, visiting professor of German, 2007-08; Colorado P.E.N., founding president, 1994-99; Austrian American Film Association, founding vice president, 1997-2009; International Alexander Lernet-Holenia Society, founding vice president, 1998-; independent film producer 1999-; Belvedere Film L.L.C., co-head, 1999-2007, head, 2007-, chief executive officer and producer; Celluloid Magazine, columnist, 2002-; Royal Historical Society, fellow, 2007; Elfi von Dassanowsky Foundation, director, 2009-; European Academy of Sciences and Arts (EASA), delegate, 2009-; Royal Society for the Arts, fellow, 2010; Austrian Studies Association (formerly Modern Austrian Literature and Culture Association), vice president, 2011-. **Publications:** Phantom Empires: The Novels of Alexander Lernet-Holenia and the Question of Postimperial Austrian Identity, 1996; (trans.) H. Raimund, Verses of a Marriage, 1996; Telegrams from the Metropole: Selected Poetry, 1999; (ed. with J. Lehman as Robert von Dassanowsky) Gale Encyclopedia of Multicultural America, 2nd ed., 2000; (trans. and afterword as Robert von Dassanowsky) A. Lernet-Holenia, Mars in Aries, 2003; (as Robert von Dassanowsky) Austrian Cinema: A History, 2005; Soft Mayhem: Poems, 2010; (ed. with O.C. Speck as Robert von Dassanowsky) New Austrian Film, 2011; (ed. with M. Liebscher and C. Fricker) The Nameable and the Unnameable: Hugo von Hofmannsthal's Der Schwierige Revisited, 2011; (ed.) Tarantino's Inglorious Basterds: Negotiations with Metacinema, 2011; (ed.) World Film Locations: Vienna, 2011. Contributor to books and periodicals. **Address:** Department of Languages & Cultures, University of Colorado, 1420 Austin Bluffs Pkwy., Colorado Springs, CO 80919, U.S.A. **Online address:** rvondass@uccs.edu

DATE, C. J. American/British (born England), b. 1941. **Genres:** Sciences, Education. **Career:** Leo Computers (and successor companies), mathematical programmer and instructor, 1962-67; International Business Machines, Development Laboratory, database technologist, language designer and instructor, 1967-74; Programming Center, database technologist, language designer and instructor, 1974-77; Santa Teresa Laboratory, database technologist, language designer and instructor, 1977-83; author, lecturer and researcher, 1983-; Codd Date Intl., founding partner, 1985-89. Writer. **Publications:** An

Introduction to Database Systems, 1975, 8th ed., 2004; Database: A Primer, 1983; A Guide to DB2, 1984, 4th ed., 1993; Relational Database: Selected Writings, 1986; A Guide to Ingres, 1987; A Guide to the SQL Standard, 1987, 4th ed., 1997; (with C.J. White) A Guide to SQL/DS, 1988; Relational Database Writings, 1985-1989, 1990; (with H. Darwen) Relational Database: Writings 1989-1991, 1992; (with D. McGoveran) A Guide to SYBASE and SQL Server, 1992; Relational Database Writings, 1991-1994, 1995; (with H. Darwen and D. McGoveran) Relational Database Writings, 1994-1997, 1998; (with H. Darwen) Databases, Types and the Relational Model: The Third Manifesto, 1998, 3rd ed., 2006; (with H. Darwen) Foundation for Object/Relational Databases, 1998, 2nd ed. as Foundation for Future Database Systems, 2000; What Not How: The Business Rules Approach to Application Development, 2000; The Database Relational Model: A Retrospective Review and Analysis, 2001; (with H. Darwen and N.A. Lorentzos) Temporal Data and the Relational Model, 2003; Database in Depth: Relational Theory for Practitioners, 2005; Relational Database: Selected Writings 1997-2000, 2006; Date on Database: Writings 2000-2006, 2006; The Relational Database Dictionary, 2006; Logic and Databases: The Roots of Relational Theory, 2006; SQL and Relational Theory: How to Write Accurate SQL Code, 2009. **Address:** PO Box 1000, Healdsburg, CA 95448, U.S.A.

D'ATH, Justin. Australian/New Zealander (born New Zealand), b. 1953. **Genres:** Novels, Science Fiction/Fantasy, Children's Fiction, Young Adult Fiction. **Career:** Bendigo Regional Institute, TAFE teacher of professional writing. Writer. **Publications:** The Initiate (novel), 1989; Das Mädchen mit den magnetischen Fingern, 2005; Extreme Adventures: Man Eater, 2007; Extreme Adventures: Spider Bite, 2007; Pool, 2007; Killer Whale, 2008; Tiger Trouble, 2010. FOR CHILDREN: Infamous, 1996; Humungous, 1997; Fantabulous, 1998; Why Did the Chykkan Cross the Galaxy?, 1998; SNIWT, 1999; The Upside Down Girl, 2000; Koala Fever, 2000; Terrors of Nature, 2000; Aussie Nibbles: Topsy and Turvy, 2001; Aussie Bites: Goldfever, 2001; Hunters and Warriors, 2001; Phoebe Nash Detective, 2001; Echidna Mania, 2001; Aussie Nibbles: Snowman Magic, 2002; Astrid Spark, Fixologist, 2003; Shaedow Master, 2004; Extreme Adventures: Crocodile Attack, 2005; Extreme Adventures: Bushfire Rescue, 2005; Extreme Adventures: Shark Bait, 2006; Extreme Adventures: Scorpion Sting, 2006; The Quentaris Chronicles: Skyflower, 2006; Robbie and the Dolphins, 2006; Shark Bait, 2008; Grizzly Trap, 2009; Anaconda Ambush, 2009; Devil Danger, 2009; Monkey Mountain, 2010; Phoebe Nash, Girl Warrior, 2010; Sous La Piscine, 2010; Mission Fox: Snake Escape, 2011; Mission Fox: Panda Chase, 2011; Mission Fox: Dolphin Rescue, 2011; Mission Fox: Horse Hijack, 2011. **Address:** c/o Fiona Inglis, Curtis Brown Ltd., PO Box 19, Paddington, NW 2021, Australia. **Online address:** jd@justindath.com

DAUBER, Philip M. American (born United States), b. 1942. **Genres:** Plays/Screenplays, Documentaries/Reportage, Sciences, Astronomy. **Career:** Alameda High School, teacher of physics and astronomy, 1994-. Writer. **Publications:** (Ed.) Isotopic Composition of the Primary Cosmic Radiation: Proceedings of a Symposium, 1971; The Search for Antiworlds, 1976; (with R.A. Muller) The Three Big Bangs: Comet Crashes, Exploding Stars, and the Creation of the Universe, 1996. Contributor to journals. **Address:** Alameda High School, 2201 Encinal Ave., Alameda, CA 94501-4412, U.S.A.

DAUER, Lesley. American (born United States), b. 1965. **Genres:** Poetry, Literary Criticism And History. **Career:** Project Read Literacy Program, volunteer teacher, 1987-88; University of Massachusetts, instructor in English and creative writing, 1989-91; Johns Hopkins University, Center for Talented Youth, instructor in English, 1993-97; Foothill College, Language Arts Division, instructor in English and creative writing, 1996-; Cabrillo College, instructor, 1996-97. Writer. **Publications:** The Fragile City: Poems, 1996. Contributor to journals. Works appear in anthologies. **Address:** Language Arts Division, Foothill College, Rm. 6035, 12345 El Monte Rd., Los Altos Hills, CA 94022-4504, U.S.A. **Online address:** dauerlesley@foothill.edu

DAUGHARTY, Janice. American (born United States), b. 1944. **Genres:** Novels, Novellas/Short Stories. **Career:** Valdosta State University, writer-in-residence; Abraham Baldwin Agriculture College, writer-in-residence. Librarian and writer. **Publications:** NOVELS: Dark of the Moon, 1994; Necessary Lies, 1995; Pawpaw Patch, 1996; Earl in the Yellow Shirt, 1997; Whistle, 1998; Like a Sister, 1999; Just Doll, 2004; The Little Known, 2010. OTHER: Going through the Change (short stories), 1994. **Address:** Abraham Baldwin Agriculture College, 2802 Moore Hwy., Tifton, GA 31793, U.S.A. **Online address:** janic826@bellsouth.net

DAUGHERTY, Greg(ory Ash). American (born United States), b. 1953. **Genres:** Money/Finance, Art/Art History, Reference. **Career:** Success, articles editor, 1981-84, managing editor, 1984-85; Sylvia Porter's Personal Finance, managing editor, 1985-86; Consumer Reports, economics editor, 1989-; World: The Magazine for Decision Makers, contributing editor, 1987-; Writer's Digest, correspondent, 1987-. **Publications:** The Consumer Reports Mutual Funds Book, 1994; You Can Write for Magazines, 1999. Contributor to newspapers and magazines. **Address:** Consumer Reports, 101 Truman Ave., Yonkers, NY 10703-1044, U.S.A.

DAUGHTRY, Herbert D(aniel). American (born United States), b. 1931. **Genres:** Theology/Religion. **Career:** House of the Lord Churches, national presiding pentecostal minister, 1960-; Bedford Stuyvesant Youth in Action, director and vice-chair, 1968; Operation Breadbasket, vice chair, 1969; Coalition of Concerned Leaders and Citizens to Save Our Children, founding member and president, 1977; Commission on African Solidarity, founder, 1977; Randolph Evans Memorial Scholarship Fund, director, 1978-; National Black United Front, founder, chair, 1979-86, chairman emeritus, 1986-; National Black United Fund of New York, director, 1980-; African People's Christian Organization, president; Downtown Brooklyn Neighborhood Alliance, president and founder; Darfur Inc., National Religious Leaders of African Ancestry, founding chair. Writer. **Publications:** From Magnificence to Wretchedness: The Sad Saga of Black Humanity: A Special Message to Men of African Ancestry, 1981; A Special Message to Men of African Ancestry, 1981; Seize the Future: Two Speeches, 1981; Jesus Christ: African in Origin, Revolutionary and Redeeming Action, 1986; No Monopoly on Suffering: Blacks and Jews in Crown Heights, 1997; My Beloved Community: Sermons, Lectures, and Speeches of Rev. Daughtry, 2001; The House of the Lord Pentecostal Church: Official Orientation Material; Inside the Storm; In My Life Time: Towards the Presidency of Barack Obama, 2010. Contributor to periodicals. **Address:** Downtown Brooklyn Neighborhood Alliance, 415 Atlantic Ave., Brooklyn, NY 11217, U.S.A.

DAUVERGNE, Peter. Canadian (born Canada) **Genres:** Politics/Government, International Relations/Current Affairs, Local History/Rural Topics, Environmental Sciences/Ecology. **Career:** Australian National University, Department Of International Relations, faculty; University of British Columbia, professor of political science and Canada research chair in global environmental politics, 2002-, Liu Institute for Global Issues, director, Environment Program, director, 2003-05, Faculty of Arts, associate dean for strategic initiatives and development, 2006-08, senior advisor to the president, 2008-09, University of British Columbia Press, founding editor, 2001-08; Massachusetts Institute of Technology, Global Environmental Politics, founding editor, 2001-08. **Publications:** Shadows in the Forest: Japan and the Politics of Timber in Southeast Asia, 1997; (contrib.) Southeast Asia and Globalization: New Domains of Analysis/L'Asie du Sud-Est face A la mondialisation: les nouveaux champs d'analyse, 1997; (ed.) Weak and Strong States in Asia-Pacific Societies, 1998; Loggers and Degradation in the Asia-Pacific: Corporations and Environmental Management, 2001; (contrib.) Japan and East Asian Regionalism, 2001; (contrib.) Development and Security in Southeast Asia, 2002; (ed.) Handbook of Global Environmental Politics, 2005; (with J. Clapp) Paths to a Green World: The Political Economy of the Global Environment, 2005, 2nd ed., 2011; (contrib.) The Business of Global Environmental Governance, 2005; (contrib.) Global Political Economy, 2nd ed., 2008; Shadows of Consumption: Consequences for the Global Environment, 2008; Historical Dictionary of Environmentalism, 2009; (with J. Lister) Timber, 2011. Contributor to books and periodicals. **Address:** Department of Political Science, University of British Columbia, Rm. C425, 1866 Main Mall, Vancouver, BC V6T 1Z1, Canada. **Online address:** peter.dauvergne@ubc.ca

D'AVENI, Richard. (Richard A. D'Aveni). American (born United States) **Genres:** Adult Non-fiction, Administration/Management, Business/Trade/Industry, Economics. **Career:** Massachusetts Legislature, legislative staff, 1975-76, Energy Office, project manager, 1977-78; Coopers & Lybrand, senior associate, 1979-82; University of North Carolina, Graduate School of Business, assistant professor of business, 1986-88; Dartmouth College, Tuck School of Business, assistant professor of business administration, 1988-92, associate professor of business administration, 1992-96, professor of strategic management, 1996-, Bakala professor of strategy, coordinator; International University of Japan, visiting professor, 1993; DUXX Graduate School of Business, visiting faculty, 1995-2002; University of Pennsylvania, Wharton

School, faculty, 1996-99, 2001, 2004; Hanoi School of Business, visiting faculty, 1997-2002; Hebrew University of Jerusalem, Executive MBA Program, visiting faculty, 1998; SDA Bocconi School of Management, visiting research professor, 2008, 2010; Rad Strat.com, chief executive officer and founder. Writer. **Publications:** AS RICHARD A. D'AVENI: (with R.E. Gunther) Hypercompetition: Managing the Dynamics of Strategic Maneuvering, 1994; (with R.E. Gunther) Hypercompetitive Rivalries: Competing in Highly Dynamic Environments, 1995; (with R.E. Gunther and J. Cole) Strategic Supremacy: How Industry Leaders Create Growth, Wealth, and Power through Spheres of Influence, 2001; Beating the Commodity Trap: How to Maximize Your Competitive Position and Increase Your Pricing Power, 2010; Escaping Commoditization: Winning the Battle Against Price Erosion, forthcoming. OTHER: (ed. with A.Y. Ilinitch and A.Y. Lewin) Managing in Times of Disorder: Hypercompetitive Organizational Responses, 1998. Contributor to journals. **Address:** Tuck School of Business, Dartmouth College, 100 Tuck Hall, Hanover, NH 03755-9000, U.S.A. **Online address:** richard.a.d'aveni@tuck.dartmouth.edu

D'AVENI, Richard A. See **D'AVENI, Richard.**

DAVENPORT, John. American (born United States), b. 1960. **Genres:** Adult Non-fiction, Poetry, History. **Career:** Saint Raymond Elementary School, social-studies and language-arts teacher, 1997-2002; Corte Madera Middle School, teacher of social studies, 2002. Writer. **Publications:** Saladin, 2003; The Mason-Dixon Line, 2004; C.S. Lewis, 2004, 2nd ed., 2010; The U.S.-Mexico Border: The Treaty of Guadalupe Hildalgo, 2004; The Louisiana Territory, 2005; Nat Turner: Slave Revolt Leader, 2005; W.E.B. Du Bois: Scholar and Activist, 2005; Marcus Garvey: Black Nationalist Lleader, 2005; Dante: Poet, Author and Proud Florentine, 2006; The Nuremberg Trials, 2006; The American Revolution, 2007; (ed.) Democracy in the Middle East, 2007; (ed.) The American Empire, 2007; A Brief Political and Geographic History of the Middle East: Where are Persia, Babylon, and the Ottoman Empire, 2007; (ed.) Global Extremism and Terrorism, 2007; The Age of Feudalism, 2007; A Brief Political and Geographic History of Africa: Where are Belgian Congo, Rhodesia and Kush?, 2008; Attack on Pearl Harbor: The United States enters World War II, 2009; Internment of Japanese Americans during World War II: Detention of American Citizens, 2010; Bolshevik Revolution, 2010; D-Day and the Liberation of France, 2010; The French Revolution and the Rise of Napoleon, 2011; The Thirty Years' War, 2012. **Address:** Corte Madera Middle School, 4575 Alpine Rd., Portola Vally, CA 94028-8040, U.S.A. **Online address:** johncdaven@aol.com

DAVENPORT, John (Chester). British (born England), b. 1938. **Genres:** Medicine/Health, Sciences. **Career:** Bristol Dental School, senior house officer, 1964, registrar, 1965-66; University of Birmingham, lecturer, 1966-79, senior lecturer in dental prosthetics, 1979-95, professor of primary dental care, 1995-2000, emeritus professor, 2000-; Birmingham Area Health Authority, senior registrar, 1966-79. Writer. **Publications:** (With R.M. Basker and H.R. Tomlin) Prosthetic Treatment of the Edentulous Patient, 1976, (with J. M. Thomason and R.M. Basker) 5th ed., 2011; A Colour Atlas of Removable Partial Dentures, 1988; (co-author) Clinical Guide to Removable Partial Denture Design, 2000. **Address:** John Wiley & Sons Inc., 111 River St., Hoboken, NJ 07030-5774, U.S.A. **Online address:** john.davenport@btclick.com

DAVENPORT, Paul. American (born United States), b. 1946. **Genres:** Economics. **Career:** McGill University, professor of economics, 1973-89; Planning and Computer Services, vice principal, 1986-89; University of Alberta, president and vice-chancellor, 1989-94; University of Western Ontario, president and vice-chancellor, 1994-2009, president emeritus, 2009-. Writer. **Publications:** University Education in Quebec: An Economic Perspective, 1979; (co-author) Industrial Policy in Ontario and Quebec, 1982; (ed. with R.H. Leach) Reshaping Confederation: The 1982 Reform of the Canadian Constitution, 1984. Contributor to periodicals. **Address:** University of Western Ontario, Stevenson-Lawson Bldg., Rm. 113, 1151 Richmond St., Ste. 2, London, ON N6A 5B8, Canada. **Online address:** pdavenpo@uwo.ca

DAVENPORT, Randi. American (born United States), b. 1957. **Genres:** Autobiography/Memoirs. **Career:** University of North Carolina, faculty, James M. Johnston Center for Undergraduate Excellence, executive director; Hobart and William Smith Colleges, faculty; Duke University, faculty. Writer. **Publications:** The Boy Who Loved Tornadoes (memoir), 2010. Contributor to books. **Address:** c/o Julie Barer, Barer Literary L.L.C., 270 Lafayette St., Ste. 1504, New York, NY 10012, U.S.A. **Online address:** rdavenpo2@gmail.com

DAVENPORT, Roger (Hamilton). British (born England), b. 1946. **Genres:** Children's Fiction, Young Adult Fiction, Novels, Children's Non-fiction, Children's Fiction. **Career:** Actor, 1967-80; advertising executive, 1980-82; theater manager, 1983-84; writer, 1985-. **Publications:** JUVENILE NOVELS: Onlooker, 1989; Pieces of the Game, 1993; Out of His Mind, 1996; Lowlake, 2000; Ortho's Brood, 2000. **Address:** Cecily Ware Literary Agents, 19C John Spencer Sq., Canonbury, GL N1 2LZ, England. **Online address:** roger.davenport@gmail.com

DAVENPORT-HINES, Richard (Peter Treadwell). British (born England), b. 1953. **Genres:** Art/Art History, Literary Criticism And History, Sex, Biography. **Career:** University of London, London School of Economics and Political Science, research officer and research fellow, 1982-86; London Library, trustee, 1996-2005. Writer, journalist, historian and radio broadcaster. **Publications:** Dudley Docker: The Life and Times of a Trade Warrior, 1984; Sex, Death and Punishment: Attitudes to Sex and Sexuality in Britain since the Renaissance, 1990; Glaxo: A History to 1962, 1992; The Macmillans, 1992; Vice, 1993; Auden, 1995; Gothic: 400 Years of Excess, Horror, Evil and Ruin, 1998; The Pursuit of Oblivion: A Global History of Narcotics, 2001; A Night at the Majestic, 2005; Proust at the Majestic: the Last Days of the Author Whose Book Changed Paris, 2006; Ettie: The Intimate Life and Dauntless Spirit of Lady Desborough, 2008; Titanic Lives: Atlantic Voyagers and The Worlds They Came From, 2012. EDITOR: Speculators and Patriots: Essays in Business Biography, 1986; Markets and Bagmen: Studies in the History of Marketing and British Industrial Performance, 1830-1939, 1986; (with J. Liebenau) Business in the Age of Reason, 1987; (with G. Jones) Enterprise, Management and Innovation in British business, 1914-80, 1988; (with G. Jones) The End of Insularity: Essays in Comperative Business History, 1988; (with G. Jones) British Business in Asia since 1860, 1989; Business in the Age of Depression and War, 1990; Capital, Entrepreneurs and Profits, 1990; Letters from Oxford: Hugh Trevor-Roper to Bernard Berenson, 2006. Contributor to periodicals. **Address:** 51 Elsham Rd., London, GL W14 8HD, England. **Online address:** jdavenp225@aol.com

DAVEY, H. E. American (born United States) **Genres:** Art/Art History, How-to Books, inspirational/Motivational Literature, Medicine/Health, Philosophy, Self Help, Sports/Fitness. **Career:** Sennin Foundation, primary instructor, president, Center for Japanese Cultural Arts, director and founder; Kokusai Budoin, councilor, director of U.S. branch; Nihon Jujutsu and kobudo, teacher; Elite Shudokan Martial Arts Association, director. Writer. **Publications:** The Way of the Universe, 1985; Unlocking the Secrets of Aiki-jujutsu, 1997; Brush Meditation: A Japanese Way to Mind and Body Harmony, 1999; (with A.H. Kameoka) The Japanese Way of the Flower: Ikebana as Moving Meditation, 2000; Japanese Yoga: The Way of Dynamic Meditation, 2001; Living the Japanese Arts & Ways: 45 Paths to Meditation & Beauty, 2003; The Japanese Way of the Artist, 2007. Contributor of articles to periodicals. **Address:** Center For Japanese Culutral Arts, Sennin Foundation, 1053 San Pablo Ave., Albany, CA 94706, U.S.A. **Online address:** hedavey@aol.com

DAVID, Anna. American (born United States) **Genres:** Novels. **Career:** Parenting and Premiere, staff; The Fix, executive editor. Columnist. **Publications:** Party Girl, 2007; Bought, 2009; Reality Matters, 2010. **Address:** 5850 W 3rd St., Ste. 116, Los Angeles, CA 90036, U.S.A. **Online address:** anna@annadavid.com

DAVID, Catherine. French (born France), b. 1954?. **Genres:** Art/Art History, Architecture, Photography. **Career:** Musee National d'Art Moderne, Centre Georges Pompidou, curator, 1981-90; Ecole du Louvre, professor of contemporary art, 1989-91; University of Paris, professor of anthropology and aesthetics, 1990-93; Galerie Nationale de Jeu de Paume, curator, 1990-. Writer. **Publications:** Gilberto Zorio, 1986; (ed. with B. Blistene and A. Pacquement) L'Epoque, La mode, la Morale, la Passion: Aspects de l'art d'aujourd'hui, 1977-1987, 1987; (with J. Chevrier) Suzanne Lafont, 1992; (with C. Merewether and L.S. Sims) Wifredo Lam: A Retrospective of Works on Paper, 1992; (with M. Mendès-France) L'esprit de Liberté, 1992; Art & Language, 1993; (with A. Barzel) Raymundo Sesma: Dies Solis, Estudio Para Una Ultima Cena: Video installazione, 1993; Day After Day, 1994; La Beaute du Geste, 1994 in US as The Beauty of Gesture: The Invisible Keyboard of Piano and T'ai Chi, 1996; (contrib.) Bordering on Fiction: Chantal Akerman's D'Est, 1995; (with J.F. Chevrier) Politics, Poetics: Documenta X, the Book, 1997; Christos Papoulias, Hypertopos: Zwei Architekturprojekte: Two Architectural Projects, 1998; (with U. Küster and B.V.K. Blomberg) Jörg Herold:

(Kunstpreis der Leipziger Volkszeitung 1999), 1999; Outro Começa Onde Nossos Sentidos Se Encontram Com o Mundo, 2002. Contributor to books. **Address:** Galerie Nationale de Jeu de Paume, 1 Pl. de la Concorde, Paris, 75008, France.

DAVID, Catherine. American (born United States), b. 1949?. **Genres:** Biography, Novels, Photography. **Career:** Writer. **Publications:** NOVELS: L'océan Miniature, 1983; Beauté Du Geste, 1994; The Beauty of Gesture: The Invisible Keyboard of Piano and T'ai Chi, 1996; Passage De L'ange, 1995; Little Bang: Le Roman Des Commencements, 1999; L'homme Qui Savait Tout, 2001; Clandestine: Récit, 2003; Sous Le Regard Des Dieux, 2003; Crescendo: Avis Aux Amateurs, 2006; Les Violons Sur le Moi: Pourquoi la Celebrite nous Fascine, 2010. BIOGRAPHIES: Simone Signoret, 1993. OTHERS: (comp.) L'Occident Enquête De Sens, 1996; (comp.) Egyptes: Anthologie De L'ancien Empire a Nos Jours, 1997; (ed.) Entretiens Sur La Fin Des Temps, 1998; (with Jean-Philippe de Tonnac) Little Bang: Le Roman Des Commencements, 1999; (ed.) Conversations About the End of Time, 2000; (contrib.) Christiane Deroches-Noblecourt, Souls Le Regard Des Dieux, 2003. **Address:** North Atlantic Books, 1456 4th St., Berkeley, CA 94710-1336, U.S.A.

DAVID, Esther. Indian (born India), b. 1945. **Genres:** Literary Criticism And History. **Career:** Femina, columnist, 1995-; Times of India, columnist, 1995-, art critic; writer, 1997-; Center for Environmental Planning and Technology University, sculptor, art critic and professor of history of art and art appreciation; National Institute of Fashion Technology, teacher; Eve Times, advisory editor. **Publications:** The Walled City, 1997; By the Sabarmati, 1999; Book of Esther, 2002; Book of Rachel, 2006; Shalom India Housing Society, 2007; My Father's Zoo (for teenagers), 2007. **Address:** Ahmedabad, GJ , India. **Online address:** esther@estherdavid.com

DAVID, James F. American (born United States), b. 1952. **Genres:** Science Fiction/Fantasy, Young Adult Fiction, Novels, Mystery/Crime/Suspense, Psychology, Novellas/Short Stories. **Career:** George Fox University, professor of psychology, School of Behavioral and Health Sciences, dean, undergraduate psychology department, chairperson. Writer. **Publications:** Footprints of Thunder, 1995; Fragments, 1997; Ship of the Damned, 2000; Before the Cradle Falls, 2002; Judgment Day: A Novel, 2005; Thunder of Time: A Novel, 2006; The Book of Summer, 2008. **Address:** c/o Tor Books, 175 5th Ave., New York, NY 10010, U.S.A. **Online address:** jfoster@georgefox.edu

DAVID, Laurie. American (born United States), b. 1958. **Genres:** Sciences. **Career:** David Letterman Show, talent coordinator; Fox Broadcasting, vice president of comedy development, 1993-95; StopGlobalWarming.org, founder; Stop Global Warming College Tour, founder, 2007. Writer. **Publications:** The Solution Is You! An Activist's Guide, 2006, 2nd ed. as Stop Global Warming: The Solution Is You! An Activist's Guide, 2008; (with C. Gordon) The Down-to-Earth Guide to Global Warming, 2007; (with K. Uhrenholdt) The Family Dinner: Great Ways to Connect with Your Kids, One Meal at a Time, 2010. Contributor to periodicals. **Address:** Stop Global Warming, 15332 Antioch St., Ste. 168, Pacific Palisades, CA 90272, U.S.A.

DAVID, Thomas. Austrian/Hungarian (born Hungary), b. 1940. **Genres:** Travel/Exploration. **Career:** Oesterreichisches Zellkultur-Forschungslabor, president and chief scientist. Writer. **Publications:** Griechenland (art and photography), 1981; (with S. Worm) Kreta, 1982; Istria (art and photography), 1983; Crete (art and photography), 1984; Salzburg (art and photography), 1985; (ed. with B. Etemad and J. Batou) Pour une histoire économique et sociale internationale, 1995; Miracle Medicines of the Rainforest: A Doctor's Revolutionary Work With Cancer and AIDS Patients, 1997; (with B. Etemad and J.M. Schaufelbuehl) La Suisse et l'esclavage des noirs, 2005; (intro. with O. Pavillon and J.M. Schaufelbuehl) Seul au milieu de 128 nègres, 2008; (with V. Groebner, J.M. Schaufelbuehl and B. Studer) Die Produktion von Ungleichheiten, 2010. **Address:** Juergen Braunschweiger, Grendelstrasse 15, Lucerne, 1, Switzerland. **Online address:** codtea-nutritional@mail.xpoint.at

DAVIDAR, David. Indian (born India), b. 1959?. **Genres:** Novels, Young Adult Fiction, Literary Criticism And History. **Career:** Gentleman magazine, executive editor, 1985; Penguin Books India, chief executive officer and publisher, 1985-; Dorling Kindersley India, managing director, 2000-04; Penguin Books Canada Ltd., publisher, 2004-. **Publications:** The House of Blue Mangoes, 2002; The Solitude of Emperors, 2007. Contributor to periodicals. **Address:** c/o Author Mail, HarperCollins, 10 E 53rd St., 7th Fl., New York, NY 10022, U.S.A.

DAVIDOFF, Leonore. British/American (born United States), b. 1932. **Genres:** History, Sociology, Women's Studies And Issues, Adult Non-fiction, Humanities. **Career:** University of Birmingham, research officer, 1956-57; University of London, tutor, 1956-60; University of Essex, research officer, 1969-74, lecturer, 1975-88, senior lecturer, 1988-90, research professor, 1990-, professor, Centre for Cultural and Social History, founding director; University of Wisconsin, visiting professor, 1987; Rutgers University, visiting professor, 1988; Gender and History, founder and editor, 1989-95; University of Melbourne, visiting fellow, 1993; Swedish Collegium for Advanced Study in Social Science, visiting fellow, 1996; Lucy Cavendish College, researcher. Writer. **Publications:** The Best Circles: Society, Etiquette and The Season, 1973; (with R. Hawthorn) A Day in the Life of a Victorian Domestic Servant, 1976; Life is Duty, Praise, and Prayer, 1981; (ed. with B. Westover) Our Work, Our Lives, Our Words: Women's History and Women's Work, 1986; (with C. Hall) Family Fortunes: Men and Women of the English Middle Class 1780-1850, 1987, rev. ed., 2002; Worlds Between: Historical Perspectives on Gender and Class, 1995; (with M. Doolittle, J. Fink and K. Holden) The Family Story: Blood, Contract and Intimacy 1830-1960, 1998. **Address:** Department of Sociology, University of Essex, Rm. 5A, Wivenhoe Pk., Colchester, EX C04 3SQ, England. **Online address:** davidoff@essex.ac.uk

DAVIDSEN, Susanna L. American (born United States) **Genres:** How-to Books, Librarianship, Information Science/Computers. **Career:** University of Michigan, Research Press, indexer, cataloger and editor, reference librarian, School of Information Science, adjunct lecturer on government information and policy, associate director for academic outreach and practical experience programs; Concordia University, head of public services; Library of Michigan, government information librarian; Internet Public Library, managing director; MLink, technology librarian, operations manager and creator of GoM-Link; Michigan Electronic Library, director; ProQuest, product manager; Michlib-L, creator and moderator. **Publications:** (With E. Yankee) Web Site Design with the Patron in Mind: A Step-by-Step Guide for Libraries, 2004. **Address:** University of Michigan, 500 S State St., Ann Arbor, MI 48109-1382, U.S.A. **Online address:** davidsens@michigan.gov

DAVIDSON, Craig. (Patrick Lestewka). Canadian (born Canada), b. 1976?. **Genres:** Young Adult Fiction. **Career:** Writer. **Publications:** Rust and Bone: Stories, 2005; A Mean Utility, 2006; The Fighter, 2007; Sarah Court, 2010; In the Pit, forthcoming. AS PATRICK LESTEWKA: Mother Bitchfight, 2003; Confessions of the Archivist, 2003; The Preserve (novel), 2004; Imprint (novel), 2006. Contributor to periodicals. **Address:** The Helen Heller Agency Inc., 4-216 Heath St. W, Toronto, ON M5P 1N7, Canada. **Online address:** craigdavidson11@gmail.com

DAVIDSON, Dana. American (born United States), b. 1967?. **Genres:** Novels, Young Adult Fiction, Romance/Historical. **Career:** Lewis Cass Technical High School, English teacher. Writer. **Publications:** NOVELS: Jason & Kyra, 2004; Played, 2005. **Address:** Hyperion Books, 77 W 66th St., 11th Fl., New York, NY 10023-6201, U.S.A.

DAVIDSON, Denise Z. American (born United States), b. 1967. **Genres:** History. **Career:** Georgia State University, professor. Writer. **Publications:** France after Revolution: Urban Life, Gender, and the New Social Order, 2007. **Address:** U.S.A. **Online address:** ddavidson2@gsu.edu

DAVIDSON, Diane Mott. American (born United States), b. 1949. **Genres:** Mystery/Crime/Suspense, Literary Criticism And History. **Career:** Episcopal Church, lay preacher. Writer and educator. **Publications:** MYSTERIES: Catering to Nobody, 1990; Dying for Chocolate, 1992; The Cereal Murders, 1993; The Last Suppers, 1994; Killer Pancake, 1995; The Main Corpse, 1996; The Grilling Season, 1997; Prime Cut, 1998; Tough Cookie, 2000; Sticks & Scones, 2001; Chopping Spree, 2002; Double Shot, 2004; Dark Tort, 2006; Sweet Revenge, 2007; Fatally Flaky, 2009; Crunch Time, 2011. Contributor to periodicals. **Address:** c/o Taryn Fagerness, Sandra Dijkstra Literary Agency, 1155 Camino Del Mar, PO Box 515, Del Mar, CA 92014-3115, U.S.A.

DAVIDSON, Gordon. American (born United States), b. 1944?. **Genres:** Theology/Religion, Human Relations/Parenting, Self Help. **Career:** Sirius Educational Resources, co-founder; Sirius School of Spiritual Science, co-founder; The Center for Visionary Leadership, co-founder, president; The American University, Department of Government, adjunct faculty; University of Massachusetts, adjunct faculty; Social Investment Forum, founding director, executive director. Writer and consultant. **Publications:** WITH C.

MCLAUGHLIN: Builders of the Dawn: Community Lifestyles in a Changing World, 1985; Spiritual Politics: Changing the World from the Inside Out, 1994; Practical Visionary: A New World Guide for Spiritual Growth and Social Change, 2010. **Address:** Sirius Educational Resources, PO Box 1101, Greenbelt, MD 20768, U.S.A.

DAVIDSON, Jamie S. Singaporean/American (born United States), b. 1971?. **Genres:** Politics/Government. **Career:** National University of Singapore, associate professor of political science. Writer and political scientist. **Publications:** (Ed. with D. Henley) The Revival of Tradition in Indonesian Politics: The Deployment of Adat from Colonialism to Indigenism, 2007; From Rebellion to Riots: Collective Violence on Indonesian Borneo, 2008. Contributor to books, periodicals and journals. **Address:** Singapore. **Online address:** poldjs@nus.edu.sg

DAVIDSON, Jeff. American (born United States), b. 1961. **Genres:** Business/Trade/Industry, How-to Books, Human Relations/Parenting, Self Help, Ghost Writer, inspirational/Motivational Literature, Autobiography/Memoirs, Marketing, Marketing. **Career:** Profiles Inc., project manager, 1975-77; Emay Corp., senior project manager, 1977-80; IMR Systems, vice-president marketing, 1980-84; Breathing Space Institute, founder, 1984-. Author, columnist, and professional speaker. **Publications:** Checklist Management, 1987; (with D. Beveridge) How to Be a 10 in Business, 1987; The Marketing Sourcebook for Small Business, 1989; Marketing for the Home-Based Business, 1990, 2nd ed., 1999; Marketing Your Consulting and Professional Services, 1990, 3rd ed., 1997; (with D. Yoho) How to Have a Good Year Every Year, 1991; Selling to the Giants, 1991; Avoiding the Pitfalls of Starting Your Own Business, 1991; Power and Protocol for Getting to the Top, 1991; You Can Start Your Own Business, 1991; Marketing to Home-Based Business, 1991; (with D. Vlcek) The Domino Effect, 1992; Your Bank, 1992; Cash Traps, 1992; Getting New Clients, 1993; Breathing Space, 1993, 2nd ed., 1999; Marketing on a Shoestring, 2nd ed., 1994; The Complete Idiot's Guide to Managing Stress, 1997, 2nd ed., 1999; The Complete Idiot's Guide Series: Assertiveness, 1997; Reaching Your Goals, 1998; Managing Your Time, 2nd ed., 1999; Marketing Your Career and Yourself, 1999; The Joy of Simple Living, 1999; The Ten Minute Guide to Project Management, 2000; Change Management, 2001; 101 Internet Marketing Tips, 2002; The Complete Guide to Public Speaking, 2003; The Christian Family Guide to Organizing, 2003; The 60-Second Procrastinator, 2004; The 60-Second Organizer, 2005, 2nd ed., 2008; Getting Things Done, 2005; The 60-Second Self-Starter, 2008; The 60-Second Innovator, 2009; Simpler Living, 2010. **Address:** Breathing Space Institute, 3202 Ruffin St., Raleigh, NC 27607-4024, U.S.A. **Online address:** jeff@breathingspace.com

DAVIDSON, Larry. American (born United States), b. 1960. **Genres:** Medicine/Health, Psychology, Psychiatry. **Career:** Yale University, postdoctoral fellow in clinical and community psychology, 1990-92, instructor, 1992-93, assistant professor, 1993-99, associate professor of psychology, 1999-, professor of psychology, Calhoun College, fellow and director of mental health education program, 1996-, senior clinical officer, director of program for recovery and community health, 2000-; Connecticut Mental Health Center, assistant director for outpatient program development and research, 1994-96, coordinator of outpatient psychology training, 1995-96, associate director of outpatient division, 1996-97, director of psychosis program, 1996-2001, deputy director of clinical services, 1997-98, president of medical and professional staff, 1998-2000, director of clinical services, 1998-2000, director of behavioral health policy and research, 2000-. Writer. **Publications:** Living outside Mental Illness: Qualitative Studies of Recovery in Schizophrenia, 2003; (ed. with C. Harding and LeRoy Spaniol) Recovery from Severe Mental Illnesses: Research Evidence and Implications for Practice, 2005; (coauthor) Practical Guide to Recovery-oriented Practice: Tools for Transforming Mental Health Care, 2009; (with J. Rakfeldt and J. Strauss) Roots of the Recovery Movement in Psychiatry: Lessons Learned, 2010. **Address:** Yale University School of Medicine, 319 Peck St. Bldg. 1, New Haven, CT 06513, U.S.A. **Online address:** larry.davidson@yale.edu

DAVIDSON, Michael. American (born United States), b. 1944. **Genres:** Poetry, Literary Criticism And History. **Career:** Time Magazine, reporter, 1967-70; San Diego State University, lecturer, 1973-76; University of California, Department of Literature, assistant professor, 1976-81, associate professor, 1981-, professor of American literature, vice chair, distinguished professor, Archive for New Poetry, curator, 1976-85, director; Future Presentations Inc., lecturer, 1978-79; Proteus Inc., president and founder, 1983-. **Publications:**

Exchanges, 1972; Two Views of Pears, 1973; The Mutabilities and the Foul Papers, 1976; Summer Letters, 1976; Grillwork, 1980; Discovering Motion, 1980; The Prose of Fact, 1981; The Landing of Rochambeau, 1985; Analogy of the Ion, 1988; The San Francisco Renaissance, 1989; Post Hoc, 1990; (with L. Hejinian, R. Silliman and B. Watten) Leningrad, 1991; Ghostlier Demarcations: Modern Poetry and the Material Word, 1997; The Arcades, 1999; (ed. and intro.) The New Collected Poems, 2002; Guys Like Us: Citing Masculinity in Cold War Poetics, 2004; Concerto for the Left Hand: Disability and the Defamiliar Body, 2008; On the Outskirts of Form: Practicing Cultural Poetics, 2011. Contributor to periodicals. **Address:** Department of Literature, University of California, Rm. LIT 442, 9500 Gilman Dr., La Jolla, CA 92093-0410, U.S.A. **Online address:** mdavidson@ucsd.edu

DAVIDSON, Nicole. See JENSEN, Kathryn.

DAVIDSON, Osha Gray. American (born United States), b. 1954. **Genres:** Urban Studies, Politics/Government, Photography. **Career:** The County magazine, assistant editor, 1972; The Grapevine, publisher, 1982-85; freelance writer, 1984-; Iowa Divestment Coalition, state coordinator, 1984-85; University of Iowa Alumni, chief writer and associate editor, 1985-87. **Publications:** Broken Heartland: The Rise of America's Rural Ghetto, 1990, rev. ed., 1996; Under Fire: The NRA and the Battle for Gun Control, 1993, rev. ed., 1998; The Best of Enemies: Race and Redemption in the New South, 1996; Enchanted Braid: Coming to Terms with Nature on the Coral Reef, 1998; Fire in the Turtle House: The Green Sea Turtle and the Fate of the Ocean, 2001, rev. ed., 2003; Enchanted by Prairie, 2009. Contributor to periodicals. **Address:** c/o Alison Picard, PO Box 2000, Cotuit, MA 02635, U.S.A. **Online address:** contact@oshadavidson.com

DAVIDSON, Pamela. British/Dutch (born Netherlands), b. 1954. **Genres:** Literary Criticism And History, Biography, How-to Books, History, Young Adult Fiction, Reference. **Career:** University of Birmingham, lecturer in Russian, 1981-84; University of Surrey, lecturer and tutor in Russian, 1984-93; University College London, School of Slavonic and East European Studies, 1993-, senior lecturer, 1996-, reader in Russian literature, 2001-, head of Russian department, 2003-06, professor of Russian literature, 2007-. Freelance translator, consultant on Russian culture and writer. **Publications:** (With J. Norman) Russian Phrase Book, 2nd ed., 1980, 3rd ed., 1989; The Poetic Imagination of Vyacheslav Ivanov: A Russian Symbolist's Perception of Dante, 1989; Viacheslav Ivanov: A Reference Guide, 1996; (ed. and contrib.) Russian Literature and Its Demons, 2000; Vyacheslav Ivanov and C.M. Bowra: A Correspondence from Two Corners on Humanism, 2006. Contributor to books. **Address:** School of Slavonic & East European Studies, University College London, 16 Taviton St., London, GL WC1H 0BW, England. **Online address:** p.davidson@ssees.ucl.ac.uk

DAVIDSON, Robyn. Australian (born Australia), b. 1950. **Genres:** Novels, Travel/Exploration. **Career:** Writer. **Publications:** TRAVEL BOOKS: Tracks, 1980; (with P. Adam-Smith and T. Keneally) Australia: Beyond the Dreamtime, 1987; Travelling Light, 1989; From Alice to Ocean: Alone across the Outback, 1992; Desert Places, 1996; (ed.) The Picador Book of Journeys, 2001; (contrib.) Desert, Mountain, Sea, 2008. OTHER: Ancestors (novel), 1989. Contributor to periodicals. **Address:** Addison Wesley Publishing, Finchampstead Rd., Wokingham, BR RG11 2NZ, England. **Online address:** robyn@dircon.co.uk

DAVIDSON, Roger H(arry). American (born United States), b. 1936. **Genres:** Politics/Government, Public/Social Administration, Economics. **Career:** Fort Collins Coloradoan, municipal reporter, 1957-59; Brookings Institution, research assistant, 1960; Dartmouth College, assistant professor of government, 1962-68; W.E. Upjohn Institute for Employment Research, staff associate, 1965-66; University of California, associate professor, 1968-71, professor of political science, 1971-82, chairman, 1976-78, associate dean, 1978-80; U.S. Library of Congress, Congressional Research Service, senior specialist on American government, 1980-87; University of Maryland, professor of government and politics, 1987, now professor emeritus of government and politics; University of Debrecen, John Marshall chair in political science, 2001-02; Governance Institute, Dirksen Congressional Center, board director. **Publications:** (With D.M. Kovenock and M.K. O'Leary) Congress in Crisis: Politics and Congressional Reform, 1966; (with J.F. Bibby) On Capitol Hill: Studies in the Legislative Process, 1967, 2nd ed., 1972; (with S.A. Levitan) Antipoverty Housekeeping: The Administration of the Economic Opportunity Act, 1968; The Role of the Congressman, 1969; The Politics of

Comprehensive Manpower Legislation, 1972; (with W.J. Oleszek) Congress Against Itself, 1977; (with S.C. Patterson and R.B. Ripley) A More Perfect Union: Introduction to American Government, 1979, 4th ed., 1989; (with W.J. Oleszek) Congress and Its Members, 1981, rev. ed., 2008; (with S.W. Hammond and R.W. Smock) Masters of the House: Congressional Leadership Over Two Centuries, 1998. EDITOR: (with W.J. Oleszek) Governing: Readings and Cases in American Politics, 1987, 2nd ed., 1992; Understanding Congress: A Bicentennial Research Conference, 1989; (with U. Thaysen and R.G. Livingston) U.S. Congress and the German Bundestag: Comparisons of Democratic Processes, 1990; The Postreform Congress, 1992; (with R.A. Baker) First Among Equals: Outstanding Senate Leaders of The Twentieth Century, 1992; (with J.A.Thurber) Remaking Congress: Change and Stability in the 1990s, 1995; (with W.J. Oleszek) 104th Congress: A Congressional Quarterly Reader: A Supplement to Congress and Its Members, 1995; (with D.C. Bacon and M. Keller) Encyclopedia of the United States Congress, 1995; (with J.P. Pfiffner) Understanding the Presidency, 1997, 5th ed., 2009; (with L.D. Longley) New Roles of Parliamentary Committees, 1998; Understanding the Presidency, 2000, rev. ed., 2007; WorkWays of Governance: Monitoring Our Government's Health, 2003. **Address:** Department of Government and Politics, University of Maryland, 3140 Tydings Hall, College Park, MD 20742, U.S.A.

DAVIDSON, Sol M. American (born United States), b. 1924. **Genres:** Children's Fiction, Young Adult Fiction, Administration/Management, Education, History, Human Relations/Parenting, Mythology/Folklore, Social Commentary, Cartoons, Humor/Satire. **Career:** Baton Rouge Morning Advocate, assistant sports editor, 1945; Beneficial Finance Co., educational director, 1948-59; Maplewood-South Orange, Department of Adult Education, instructor, 1957; Dial Finance Co., director of personnel, 1959-66, director of operations, 1967-73; Des Moines Public Schools, Adult Education Advisory Council, chairman, 1962; Northwestern Bell Telephone Co., assistant to the president, 1974-76; Davidson, Wyatt and Associates, president, 1976-; The Sandpiper, editor-in-chief, 1999-2002; Des Moines Board of International Education, president; Des Moines Human Rights Commission, chairman; Ships Editorial Association, managing editor. **Publications:** Culture and the Comic Strips, 1959; The Cultivation of Imperfection, 1965; The Value of Friction, 1968; Power of Friction in Business, 1968; Philbert the Flea, 1989; Wild Jake Hiccup: America's First Frontiersman, 1992. Contributor of articles to magazines. **Address:** PO Box 2974, Palm Beach, FL 33480, U.S.A.

DAVIES, Brian. American/British (born England), b. 1951. **Genres:** Philosophy, Theology/Religion, Essays. **Career:** Oxford University, lecturer, 1982-95, Blackfriars Hall, regent, 1994-95; Fordham University, professor, 1995-. Writer, catholic priest and theologian. **Publications:** An Introduction to the Philosophy of Religion, 1982, 3rd ed., 2004; (ed.) Language, Meaning, and God: Essays in Honour of Herbert McCabe, 1987; The Thought of Thomas Aquinas, 1992; (ed.) Philosophy of Religion: A Guide to the Subject, 1998; (ed. and intro. with G.R. Evans) Anselm of Canterbury: The Major Works, 1998; (ed.) Philosophy of Religion: A Guide and Anthology, 2000; (ed. and intro.) The De Malo of Thomas Aquinas, 2001; (ed.) Thomas Aquinas: Contemporary Philosophical Perspectives, 2002; Aquinas, 2002, rev. ed. as Aquinas: An Introduction, 2003; (ed. and intro.) On Evil, 2003; (ed. and intro.) God, Christ and Us, 2003; (ed. with B. Leftow) The Cambridge Companion to Anselm, 2004; (ed.) God Still Matters, 2005; (ed. and intro.) The Good Life: Ethics and the Pursuit of Happiness, 2005; (ed.) Aquinas's Summa Theologiae: Critical Essays, 2006; The Reality of God and the Problem of Evil, 2006; (ed. with B. Leftow) Summa Theologiae: Questions on God, 2006; (ed. and intro.) Faith within Reason, 2007; (ed. and intro.) On Aquinas, 2008. Contributor of articles to books and journals. **Address:** Department of Philosophy, Fordham University, Collins Hall, 441 E Fordham Rd., Bronx, NY 10458-5149, U.S.A.

DAVIES, Charles E. American (born United States) **Genres:** International Relations/Current Affairs, Intellectual History. **Career:** University of Exeter, Centre for Arab Gulf Studies, honorary research fellow; historian; barrister. Writer. **Publications:** After the War: Iran, Iraq, and the Arab Gulf, 1990; Global Interests in the Arab Gulf, 1992; The Blood-Red Arab Flag: An Investigation into Qasimi Piracy, 1797-1820, 1997. **Address:** Institute of Arab & Islamic Studies, University of Exeter, Stocker Rd., Exeter, DN EX4 RND, England.

DAVIES, Charlotte Aull. Welsh (born Wales), b. 1942. **Genres:** Human Relations/Parenting, History, Politics/Government, Philosophy, Local History/Rural Topics. **Career:** University of Wales, lecturer, 1989-; University of South Carolina, visiting professor. Writer. **Publications:** Welsh Nationalism in the Twentieth Century: The Ethnic Option and the Modern State, 1989; Reflexive Ethnography: A Guide to Researching Selves and Others, 1999, 2nd ed., 2008; (ed. with S. Jones) Welsh Communities: New Ethnographic Perspectives, 2003; (with N. Charles and C. Harris) Families in Transition: Social Change, Family Formation, and Kin Relationships, 2008. Contributor of articles to books and journals. **Address:** Deppartment of Sociology and Anthropology, School of the Environment and Society, University of Wales, Margam Bldg., Singleton Pk., Swansea, WG SA2 8PP, Wales. **Online address:** c.a.davies@swansea.ac.uk

DAVIES, Christie. British (born England), b. 1941. **Genres:** Children's Fiction, Criminology/True Crime, Ethics, Sociology, Humor/Satire. **Career:** University of Adelaide, tutor, 1964; BBC Third Program, radio producer, 1967-69; University of Leeds, lecturer in sociology, 1969-72; University of Reading, lecturer, 1972-81, senior lecturer, 1975-81, acting department head, 1976-77, reader, 1981-84, department head, 1982-94, professor of sociology, 1984-2002, department chair, 1990, established professor, 1990-2002, professor emeritus, 2002-; International Society for Humor Studies, president. Writer. **Publications:** (With R. Brandon) Wrongful Imprisonment, Mistaken Convictions and Their Consequences, 1973; (with R. Lewis) The Reactionary Joke Book, 1973; Permissive Britain: Social Change in the Sixties and Seventies, 1975; Welsh Jokes, 1978; (ed. with R. Dhavan) Censorship and Obscenity, 1978; Ethnic Humor around the World: A Comparative Analysis, 1990; Jokes and Their Relation to Society, 1998; (with M. Neal) The Corporation Under Siege, 1998; The Mirth of Nations, 2002; The Strange Death of Moral Britain, 2004; The Right to Joke, 2004; Dewi the Dragon Finds a Wife, 2005; Jokes and Targets, 2011. Contributor to journals. **Address:** Department of Sociology, University of Reading, FOLS 292A, Reading, BR RG6 6AA, England. **Online address:** j.c.h.davies@reading.ac.uk

DAVIES, Gareth. British (born England), b. 1965. **Genres:** Education, History. **Career:** Oxford University, St. Anne's College, university lecturer in American history; Old Boys' High School, faculty. Writer. **Publications:** From Opportunity to Entitlement: The Transformation and Decline of Great Society Liberalism, 1996; See Government Grow: Education Politics from Johnson to Reagan, 2007; (ed. with C. Hudson) Ronald Reagan and the 1980s: Perceptions, Policies, Legacies, 2008. Contributor to books and periodicals. **Address:** Faculty of History, Old Boys' High School, George St., Oxford, OX OX1 2RL, England. **Online address:** gareth.davies@history.ox.ac.uk

DAVIES, Hunter. British (born England), b. 1936. **Genres:** Novels, Children's Fiction, Travel/Exploration, Biography, Autobiography/Memoirs. **Career:** Evening Chronicle, reporter, 1958-60; Sunday Times, reporter, 1960, chief feature writer, 1960-84; Colour magazine, editor, 1975-77; Punch, columnist, 1979-89; BBC, presenter, 1983-86; The Independent, journalist, 1989-; Cumbria Wildlife Trust, president. **Publications:** Here We Go Round the Mulberry Bush, 1966; The Other Half, 1966; (ed.) The New London Spy, 1966; The Beatles, 1968; The Rise and Fall of Jake Sullivan, 1969; (ed.) I Knew Daisy Smuten, 1970; A Very Loving Couple, 1971; The Glory Game, 1972; Body Charge, 1972; A Walk Along the Wall, 1974; George Stephenson, 1975; The Creighton Report, 1976; The Sunday Times Book of Jubilee Year, 1977; A Walk Around the Lakes, 1979; The Book of British Lists, 1980; William Wordsworth, 1980; The Grades, 1981; Father's Day, 1981; A Walk Along the Tracks, 1982; Great Britain: A Celebration, 1982; Flossie Teacake's Fur Coat, 1982; A Walk Round London's Parks, 1983; The Joy of Stamps, 1983; The Good Guide to the Lakes, 1984; Flossie Teacake Strikes Back, 1984; Come On Ossie, 1985; The Grand Tour, 1986; Ossie Goes Supersonic, 1986; The Good Quiz Book to the Lakes, 1987; Back in the USSR, 1987; Beatrix Potter's Lakeland, 1988; Saturday Night, 1989; S. T. A. R. S., 1989; My Life in Football, 1990; In Search of Columbus, 1991; Striker, 1992; Teller of Tales, 1992; Wainwright, 1995; Living on the Lottery, 1996; Quarrymen, 2001; Best of Lakeland, 2002; Glory Game, 2002; (with J. Prescott) Prezza: My Story: Pulling No Punches, 2008; Confessions of a Collector, 2009; Postcards from the Edge of Football, 2010. Contributor to periodicals. **Address:** The Independent, 2 Derry St., London, GL W8 5HF, England.

DAVIES, Jennifer (Eileen). British (born England), b. 1950. **Genres:** Homes/Gardens, Education, Local History/Rural Topics, Horticulture. **Career:** Writer. **Publications:** The Victorian Kitchen Garden, 1987; The Victorian Kitchen Garden Companion, 1988; The Victorian Kitchen, 1992; The Victorian Flower Garden, 1992; Harry Dodson's Practical Kitchen Garden,

1992; The Wartime Kitchen and Garden, 1993; Safe in Print, 1994; Tales of the Old Country Horseman, 1997; Tales of the Old Gypsies, 1999; Saying It with Flowers: The Story of the Flower Shop, 2000; Tales of the Old Horsemen, 2006. Contributor to journals and magazines. **Address:** Park Barn, Ledbury, Herefordshire, HW HR8 2JB, England.

DAVIES, J(ohn) D(avid). British/Welsh (born Wales), b. 1957. **Genres:** Military/Defense/Arms Control, History, Literary Criticism And History. **Career:** History teacher, 1979-82; Bedford Modern School, history teacher and head of general studies, 1987-; Combined Cadet Force, sub-lieutenant, 1988-94. Writer and historian. **Publications:** Gentlemen and Tarpaulins: The Officers and Men of the Restoration Navy, 1991; Pepys's Navy: Ships, Men and Warfare, 1649-1689, 2008; Gentleman Captain, 2009. Works appear in anthologies. Contributor to history and journals. **Address:** Ampersand Agency Ltd., Ryman's Cottages, Little Tew, Chipping Norton, OX7 4JJ, England. **Online address:** j.d.davies@net.ntl.com

DAVIES, Katharine. British (born England), b. 1968?. **Genres:** Novels, Literary Criticism And History. **Career:** Writer. **Publications:** NOVELS: A Good Voyage, 2004; The Madness of Love, 2005; Hush, Little Baby, 2006. Contributor to periodicals. **Address:** c/o Caroline Dawnay, PFD, Drury House, 34-43 Russell St., London, GL WC2B 5HA, England.

DAVIES, Kristian. American/Hong Kong (born Hong Kong) **Genres:** Art/ Art History, History, Photography. **Career:** Writer and art historian. **Publications:** Artists of Cape Ann: A 150 Year Tradition, 2001; The Orientalists: Western Artists in Arabia, the Sahara, Persia, and India, 2006. **Address:** Twin Lights Publishers Inc., 8 Hale St., Ste. 2, Rockport, MN 01966, U.S.A. **Online address:** kristiandavies@hotmail.com

DAVIES, Linda. Scottish (born Scotland), b. 1963?. **Genres:** Novels, Young Adult Fiction, Mystery/Crime/Suspense, Science Fiction/Fantasy. **Career:** Writer. **Publications:** NOVELS: A Nest of Vipers, 1994; Wilderness of Mirrors, 1995; Into the Fire, 1999; Something Wild, 2001; Final Settlement, 2007. DJINN SERIES: Sea Djinn, 2009; Fire Djinn, 2010; Storm Djinn, 2010. **Address:** Jerboa Books, PO Box 333838, Dubai, 1, United Arab Emirates.

DAVIES, Martin (Brett). British (born England), b. 1936. **Genres:** Psychology, Social Work, Sociology, Adult Non-fiction, Politics/Government. **Career:** Home Office, research officer, 1964-71; University of Manchester, senior lecturer, 1971-75; University of East Anglia, director of social work program, 1975-79, professor of social work, 1979-, emeritus professor, 2002- ; Social Work Monographs, editor, 1982-2000. **Publications:** Use of the Jesness Inventory on a Sample of British Probationers, 1967; Probationers in Their Social Environment: A Study of Male Probationers Aged 17-20, Together with an Analysis of Those Re Convicted Within Twelve Months, 1969; Financial Penalties and Probation, 1970; (with A. Knopf) Social Enquiry Reports and the Probation Service, 1973; An Index of Social Environment, 1973; (with M. Rayfield, A. Calder and T. Fowles) Social Work in the Environment: A Study of One Aspect of Probation Practice, 1974; Prisoners of Society: Attitudes and After-Care, 1974; Support Systems in Social Work, 1977; The Role of Social Workers in the Rehabilitation of Ex-Prisoners, 1979; The Essential Social Worker: A Guide to Positive Practice, 1981, rev. ed., 1985; Towards a Classification of Unemployment, 1986; Skills, Knowledge and Qualities in Probation Practice, 1988; The Nature of Probation Practice Today: An Empirical Analysis of the Skills, Knowledge, and Qualities Used by Probation Officers, 1989; (ed.) The Sociology of Social Work, 1991; Contemporary Probation Practice, 1993; (ed.) The Blackwell Companion to Social Work, 1997, 3rd ed., 2008; (ed.) Blackwell Encyclopaedia of Social Work, 2000; (as Martin Brett Davies) Doing a Successful Research Project: Using Qualitative or Quantitative Methods, 2007. **Address:** School of Social Work & Psychosocial Studies, University of East Anglia, Norwich, NF NR4 7TJ, England. **Online address:** m.davies@uea.ac.uk

DAVIES, Martin L. British (born England), b. 1948. **Genres:** Literary Criticism And History, History, Humanities, Education. **Career:** University of Leicester, The School of Historical Studies, reader in the history of the European enlightenment, Stanley Burton Centre for Holocaust Studies, director. Writer. **Publications:** Identity or History?: Marcus Herz and the End of the Enlightenment, 1995; (ed. with M. Meskimmon) Breaking the Disciplines: Reconceptions in Knowledge, Art and Culture, 2003; Historics: Why History Dominates Contemporary Society, 2006; (ed. with C.W. Szejnmann) How the Holocaust Looks Now: International Perspectives, 2006; Imprisoned by History: Aspects of Historicized Life, 2010. Contributor to books and periodicals. **Address:** School of Historical Studies, University of Leicester, 509 Attenborough, University Rd., Leicester, LE LEI 7RH, England. **Online address:** mld@le.ac.uk

DAVIES, Nicola. (Stevie Morgan). British (born England), b. 1958. **Genres:** Novels, Children's Non-fiction, Animals/Pets, Young Adult Non-fiction, Sciences. **Career:** Writer. **Publications:** Big Blue Whale, 1997; Dolphin: Habitats, Life Cycles, Food Chains, Threats, 2000; Bat Loves the Night, 2001; One Tiny Turtle, 2001; Wild about Dolphins, 2001; Currants Pats and Poops, 2003; Unexpected Sharks, 2003; Birds, 2003; Surprising Sharks, 2003; Oceans and Seas, 2004; Poop: A Natural History of the Unmentionable, 2004; Deserts, 2005; Ice Bear: In the Steps of the Polar Bear, 2005; Extreme Animals: The Toughest Creatures on Earth, 2006; Home, 2006; What's Eating You?: Parasites--The inside Story, 2007; White Owl, Barn Owl, 2007; Up On The Hill, 2008; (with J. Lovelock) Gaia Warriors, 2009; Just the Right Size, 2009; Talk Talk Squawk: A Human's Guide to Animal Communication, 2011; Grow Your Own Monsters, 2011; A Girl Called Dog, 2011; Monsters of the Deep, 2011; Aboard at Silver Street Farm, 2011; Dolphin Baby!, 2012; Welcome to Silver Street Farm, 2012. AS STEVIE MORGAN: Delphinium Blues, 1999; Fly Away Peter, 2000; Checking Out, 2002. **Address:** Ed Victor Ltd., 6 Bayley St., Bedford Sq., London, GL WC1B 3HE, England. **Online address:** nicola.davies@btinternet.com

DAVIES, Oliver. American (born United States), b. 1956?. **Genres:** Theology/Religion. **Career:** Saint Leonhard Gymnasium, fremdsprachen assistent, 1977-78; Merton and Balliol College, part-time tutor in German language and literature, 1979-82; University of Cologne, lecturer in English language and literature, 1982-84; University of Wales, Department of Theology and Religious Studies, honorary lecturer and part-time lecturer, 1989-93, lecturer, 1993-2004, senior lecturer, 1995, reader in systematic theology, 1997; King's College London, professor of Christian doctrine, 2004-. Writer. **Publications:** God Within: The Mystical Tradition of Northern Europe, 1988; Meister Eckhart: Mystical Theologian, 1991; (ed. and trans.) Selected Writings, 1994; Celtic Christianity in Early Medieval Wales: The Origins of the Welsh Spiritual Tradition, 1996; A Theology of Compassion: Metaphysics of Difference and the Renewal of Tradition, 2003; The Creativity of God: World, Eucharist, Reason, 2004; (with P.D. Janz and C. Sedmak) Transformation Theology: Church in the World, 2007. OTHER: (trans.) Beguine Spirituality: Mystical Writings of Mechthild of Magdeburg, Beatrice of Nazareth and Hadewijch of Brabant, 1989; (ed., trans. and intro.) The Rhineland Mystics: Writings of Meister Eckhart, Johannes Tauler and Jan van Ruusbroec and Selections from the Theologia Germanica and the Book of Spiritual Poverty, 1990; (ed. and intro. with F. Bowie) Mystical Writings, with New Translations by Robert Carver, 1990; (ed.) Gateway to Paradise: Basil the Great, 1991; (ed.) Born to New Life, 1992; (ed. and trans. with A.I. Jones) Promise of Good Things: The Apostolic Fathers, 1993; (trans. with J. Hirshfield) Ecstatic Meditations: For SSAATTBB Choir a Capella, 1998; (ed. with F. Bowie) Celtic Christian Spirituality: An Anthology of Medieval and Modern Sources, 1999; (trans. and intro.) Celtic Spirituality, with the Collaboration of Thomas O'Loughlin, 1999; (ed. with D. Turner) Silence and the Word: Negative Theology and Incarnation, 2002. Contributor of translations. **Address:** Department of Theology and Religious Studies, King's College London, Rm. 1E, Chesham Bldg., Strand Campus, Strand, GL WC2R 2LS, England. **Online address:** oliver.davies@kcl.ac.uk

DAVIES, Owen. British (born England), b. 1969. **Genres:** History. **Career:** University of Hertfordshire, instructor. Writer and educator. **Publications:** A People Bewitched: Witchcraft and Magic in Nineteenth-Century Somerset, 1999; Witchcraft, Magic and Culture, 1736-1951, 1999; Cunning-Folk: Popular Magic in English History, 2003 in UK as Popular Magic: Cunning Folk in English History, 2007; (ed. with W. de Blecourt) Witchcraft Continued: Popular Magic in Modern Europe, 2004; (ed. with W. de Blecourt) Beyond the Witch Trials: Witchcraft and Magic in Enlightenment Europe, 2004; Murder, Magic, Madness: The Victorian Trials of Dove and the Wizard, 2005; The Haunted: A Social History of Ghosts, 2007; (ed. with J. Barry) Palgrave Advances in Witchcraft Historiography, 2007. **Address:** University of Hertfordshire, Hatfield, HF AL10 9AB, England. **Online address:** o.davies@herts.ac.uk

DAVIES, Peter Ho. American/British (born England), b. 1966. **Genres:** Novellas/Short Stories, Young Adult Fiction, Novels. **Career:** Emory University, lecturer, 1996-97; Fine Arts Work Center, fellow, 1996-; University of Oregon, assistant professor, 1997-99; National Endowment for the Arts, fellow, 1998; University of Michigan, assistant professor, 1999-, associate professor and director of the MFA Program in Creative Writing, 2002-, Department of English Language and Literature, professor; Northwestern University, faculty. Writer. **Publications:** The Ugliest House in the World, 1997; Equal Love, 2000; The Welsh Girl, 2007. Contributor to periodicals. Works appear in anthologies. **Address:** Abner Stein Agency, 10 Roland Gardens, London, GL SW7 3PH, England. **Online address:** phdavies@umich.edu

DAVIES, Peter J. Australian (born Australia), b. 1937. **Genres:** Medicine/Health, Music, Psychiatry, Psychology, Biography. **Career:** St. Vincent's Hospital, physician in internal medicine and gastroenterology, 1971-86; private practice of medicine, 1971-98. Writer. **Publications:** (With A.W. Galston) Control Mechanisms in Plant Development, 1971; The Sign of the Smiling Lion, 1979; (with A.W. Galston) Life of The Green Plant, 1980; British Silver Coins Since 1816: With Engravers' Patterns and Proofs and Unofficial Pieces, 1982; Mozart in Person: His Character and Health, 1989; Mozart's Health Illnesses and Death, in The Pleasures and Perils of Genius: Mostly Mozart, 1993; Beethoven in Person: His Deafness, Illnesses and Death, 2001; Beethoven in Profile: The Character of a Genius, 2001; The Character of a Genius: Beethoven in Perspective, 2002; World Encyclopedia of Trucks, 2005; The Debate on the French Revolution (Issues in Historiography), 2006. Contributor to periodicals. Illustrated A-Z of World Trucks, 2001; The Character of a Genius: Beethoven in Perspective, 2002; World Encyclopedia of Trucks, 2005; The Debate on the French Revolution (Issues in Historiography), 2006. **Address:** 14 Hamilton St., East Kew, VI 3102, Australia.

DAVIES, Philip John. British (born England), b. 1948. **Genres:** Area Studies, Politics/Government, Social Sciences, History. **Career:** University of Maryland, faculty, 1972-74; Lanchester (Coventry) Polytechnic, lecturer, 1975-76; Manchester University, lecturer, 1976-91, American Studies Exchange and Junior Year Program, director, 1985-91; University of Massachusetts, John W. McCormack Institute of Public Affairs, visiting professor, 1984-85; De Montfort University, principal lecturer and director of international office, 1991-93, American Studies Program, reader and head, 1993-, professor of American studies, 1993-, now professor emeritus of American studies; Creighton University, visiting professor, 1996; Wartburg College, visiting professor, 1996; British Association for American Studies, chair; British Library, Eccles Centre for American Studies, director, 2001-, American Politics Group, chair, 2010; Academy of the Social Sciences, College of Academicians, chairman; American Politics Group, chair; QAA subject benchmarking group, chair; U.K. Council of Area Studies Associations, chair. Writer. **Publications:** Metropolitan Mosaic, 1980; The History and Evolution of the Constitution, 1989; Elections USA, 1992, new ed. as U.S. Elections Today, 1999; (co-author) History Atlas of North America, 1998. EDITOR: (with B. Neve) Cinema, Politics, and Society in America, 1981; (with F. Waldstein) Political Issues in America Today, 1987; Science Fiction, Social Conflict and War, 1990; (with Waldstein) Political Issues in America: The 1990s, 1991; An American Quarter Century, 1995; Political Issues in America Today: The 1990s Revisited, 1996; Representing and Imagining America, 1996; (with J.K. White) Political Parties and the Collapse of the Old Orders, 1998; (with P. Wells) American Film and Politics from Reagan to Bush Jr., 2002; (with G.C. Edwards) New Challenges for the American Presidency, 2004; (with B.I. Newman) Winning Elections with Political Marketing, 2006; (with I.W. Morgan) The Federal Nation, 2008; (with I.W. Morgan) Assessing George W. Bush's Legacy: The Right Man?, 2010. Contributor to books and journals. **Address:** Eccles Centre for American Studies, British Library, St Pancras, 96 Euston Rd., London, GL NW1 2DB, England. **Online address:** pjd@dmu.ac.uk

DAVIES, Piers Anthony David. New Zealander/Australian (born Australia), b. 1941. **Genres:** Plays/Screenplays, Poetry, Law. **Career:** Grey Lynn Neighbourhood Law Office, chairman, 1979-80; Wackrow, Williams and Davies, barrister and solicitor, partner, 1970-, consultant, 2001-; New Zealand Film Commission, Short Film Fund, chairman, 1987-91. Writer. **Publications:** East and Other Gong Songs, 1967; Day Trip from Mount Meru, 1969; Deus Vult, 1971; Diaspora, 1974; Bourgeois Homage to Dada, 1974; (ed.) Central Almanac, 1974; Jetsam, 1984. Contributor to books. **Address:** Wackrow Williams and Davies Ltd., Level 14, 48 Emily Pl., PO Box 461, Auckland, 01010, New Zealand. **Online address:** piers@wwandd.co.nz

DAVIES, Robert William. British (born England), b. 1925. **Genres:** Area Studies, Economics, History, Politics/Government, Business/Trade/Industry.

Career: University of Glasgow, assistant in department of Soviet institutions, 1954-56; University of Birmingham, Centre for Russian and East European Studies, research fellow, 1956-59, lecturer, 1959-62, senior lecturer, 1962-63, Center for Russian and East European Studies, director, 1963-79, professor of Soviet economic studies, 1965-89, professor emeritus, 1989-. Writer. **Publications:** The Development of the Soviet Budgetary System, 1958; (with E.H. Carr) Foundations of a Planned Economy 1926-1929, vol. I, 1969; (with E. Zaleski and others) Science Policy in the U.S.S.R., 1969; The Socialist Offensive: The Collectivization of Soviet Agriculture, 1929-1930, 1980; The Soviet Collective Farm 1929-1930, 1980; Soviet Defence Industries During the First Five-Year Plan, 1987; The Soviet Economy in Turmoil 1929-1930, 1989; Soviet History in the Gorbachev Revolution, 1989; Soviet History, 1917-53, 1995; Crisis and Progress in the Soviet Economy, 1931-1933, 1996; Soviet History in the Yeltsin Era, 1997; Soviet Economic Development from Lenin to Khrushchev, 1998. EDITOR: The Technological Level of Soviet Industry, 1977; The Soviet Union, 1978, 2nd ed., 1989; Soviet Investment for Planned Industrialisation 1929-37: Policy and Practice: Selected Papers from the Second World Congress for Soviet and East European Studies, 1984; (with S.G. Wheatcroft) Materials for a Balance of the Soviet National Economy 1928-30, 1985; E.H. Carr's What Is History?, 2nd ed., 1986; From Tsarism to the New Economic Policy: Continuity and Change in the Economy of the USSR, 1990; (with M. Harrison and S.G. Wheatcroft) The Economic Transformation of the Soviet Economy, 1913-1945, 1994; (with S.G. Wheatcroft) The Years of Hunger: Soviet Agriculture, 1931-1933, 2003; (with O. Khlevniuk and E.A. Rees) The Stalin-Kaganovich Correspondence 1931-1936, 2003; Introduction to E.H. Carr's The Russian Revolution from Lenin to Stalin, 2004. **Address:** Center for Russian & East European Studies, University of Birmingham, Birmingham, B15 2TT, England. **Online address:** r.w.davies@bham.ac.uk

DAVIES, Sharon L. American (born United States), b. 1960?. **Genres:** Medicine/Health, Race Relations. **Career:** Steptoe and Johnson, litigation associate, 1987-88; Lord Day & Lord, Barrett Smith, litigation associate, 1988-90; United States Attorney's Office, Southern District of New York, Criminal Division, assistant United States attorney, 1990-95; Ohio State University, assistant professor, 1995-99, associate professor, 1999-2002, professor, 2002, John C. Elam/Vorys Sater designated professor of law, 2001-, associate dean for faculty, 2004-06; University of Michigan, School of Law, visiting professor of law, 2003. Writer and public speaker. **Publications:** (With T.S. Jost) The Law of Medicare and Medicaid Fraud and Abuse, 1997 as Medicare and Medicaid Fraud and Abuse, 2003; Rising Road: A True Tale of Love, Race, and Religion in America, 2010. Contributor to periodicals and journals. **Address:** Moritz College of Law, Ohio State University, Rm. 321, Drinko Hall, 55 W 12th Ave., Columbus, OH 43210, U.S.A. **Online address:** davies.49@osu.edu

DAVIES, Stephanie. (Stevie Davies). Welsh (born Wales), b. 1946. **Genres:** Novels, Literary Criticism And History, Young Adult Non-fiction, Young Adult Fiction. **Career:** Victoria University of Manchester, English Language and Literature, faculty, 1971-84; full-time author, 1984-94; Salford University, part-time lecturer in English literature, 1989-90; Roehampton Institute, senior research fellow, 1994-; Swansea University, professor, fellow, 2001-03, Creative and Media Writing Research Group, director; Royal Society of Literature, fellow; Manchester University, Centre for Continuing Education, senior tutor in English; University of Wales, senior tutor in creative writing. **Publications:** EDITOR: The Bronte Sisters: Selected Poems, 1976; Renaissance Views of Man, 1978; Anne Bronte, The Tenant of Wildfell Hall, 1996. NONFICTION AS STEVIE DAVIES: Images of Kingship in Paradise Lost: Milton's Politics and Christian Liberty, 1983; Emily Brontë: The Artist as a Free Woman, 1983; The Feminine Reclaimed: The Idea of Woman in Renaissance Literature, 1986; William Shakespeare: Twelfth Night, 1993; John Donne, 1994; Emily Brontë: Heretic, 1994; Henry Vaughan, 1995; Shakespeare, The Taming of the Shrew, 1995; Emily Bronte, 1998; Unbridled Spirit: Women of the English Revolution, 1640-1660, 1998. FICTION AS STEVIE DAVIES: Boy Blue, 1987; Primavera, 1990; Arms and the Girl, 1992; Closing the Book, 1994; Four Dreamers and Emily, 1996; The Web of Belonging, 1997. OTHER: Milton, 1991; Unbridled Spirits: Women of the English Revolution, 1640-1660, 1998; Impassioned Clay, 1999; Element of Water, 2001; (ed.) Dreams and Other Aggravations, 2003; Kith & Kin, 2004; Eyrie, 2008; Into Suez, 2010. Contributor to periodicals. **Address:** Department of English, University of Wales, Rm. 215, Singleton Pk., Swansea, SA2 8PP, Wales. **Online address:** stephanie.davies@swansea.ac.uk

DAVIES, Stevie. See **DAVIES, Stephanie.**

DAVIES-MITCHELL, Margaret (Constance). (Mitchell). British (born England), b. 1923. **Genres:** Novels, Literary Criticism And History, Young Adult Fiction. **Career:** Harrow County School for Girls, French mistress, 1951-53; University of Reading, French tutor, 1961-63, lecturer, 1964-70, reader in French studies, 1969-74, professor of French, 1974-88, professor emeritus, 1988-; University of London, Westfield College, lecturer, 1963; St. Paul's Girls Preparatory School, governor; University of Nottingham, visiting professor, 1988-92. Writer. **Publications:** Two Gold Rings (novel), 1958; Colette, 1961; Apollinaire, 1964; Une saison en enfer d'Arthur Rimbaud: analyse du texte, 1975. **Address:** Department of French Studies, University of Reading, Whiteknights, PO Box 217, Reading, BR RG6 6AH, England.

DÁVILA, Arlene M. American/Puerto Rican (born Puerto Rico), b. 1965. **Genres:** Anthropology/Ethnology. **Career:** Harvard University, Peabody Museum of Archaeology and Ethnology, curatorial intern, 1985-86; Brooklyn Museum, Department of African, Oceanic, and New World Art, curatorial intern, 1988; Museum of Contemporary Hispanic Art, director of education, 1989; El Museo del Barrio, curatorial assistant, 1990-93; Herbert H. Lehman College of the City University of New York, adjunct lecturer in Puerto Rican studies, 1992-93; Hunter College of the City University of New York, adjunct lecturer in anthropology, 1994-95; Syracuse University, assistant professor of anthropology, 1995-; New York University, visiting research associate at Center for Media, Culture, and History, 1998-, associate professor of anthropology and American studies, 1998-, professor. Writer. **Publications:** Sponsored Identities: Cultural Politics in Puerto Rico, 1997; Latinos, Inc.: The Marketing and Making of a People, 2001; (ed. with A. Laó-Montes) Mambo Montage: The Latinization of New York, 2001; Barrio Dreams: Puerto Ricans, Latinos, and the Neoliberal City, 2004; Latino Spin: Public Image and the Whitewashing of Race, 2008; Culture Works, 2012. Contributor to books and journals. **Address:** Department of Social/Cultural Analysis-Africana, Studies, New York Unversity, 20 Cooper Sq., 4th Fl., New York, NY 10003-7112, U.S.A. **Online address:** arlene.davila@nyu.edu

DAVIS, Alan (R.). American (born United States), b. 1950. **Genres:** Novellas/Short Stories, Politics/Government, Young Adult Fiction. **Career:** Parish Library, assistant reference librarian, 1974-75; Louisiana Department of Corrections, counselor and technical writer, 1975-77; Loyola University, lecturer, 1980-81; University of North Carolina, lecturer, 1981-85; Charlotte Business Quarterly and Charlotte Business and Finance, editorial assistant, 1984; Minnesota State University, Department of English, assistant professor, professor of English, 1985-, chair, 1991-98, MFA Program, coordinator, 1991-95, director, 1999-, co-director of creative writing, 1991-98; New Rivers Press, senior editor, 2002-. **Publications:** (With N. McIntosh and J. Williams) Management of Deprivation, 1978; Rumors from the Lost World: Stories, 1993; (with J. George) States of Health: Health and Illness in Australia, 1998; Fun Also Rises Travel Guide International: The World's Most Fun Places to Be at the Right Time, 1999; Alone with the Owl, 2000; So Bravely Vegetative: Stories, 2011. EDITOR: (with M.C. White) American Fiction '87: The Best Unpublished Short Stories by Emerging Writers, 1987; (with M.C. White) American Fiction '88: The Best Unpublished Short Stories by Emerging Writers, 1988; (with M.C. White) American Fiction, vol. IX: The Best Unpublished Short Stories by Emerging Writers, 1997; (with M.C. White) American Fiction: The Best Unpublished Short by Emerging Writers, 10 vols., 1999; Beginning Years: Illinois Manufactured Housing Association, 1949-1999, 2000. Contributor of articles to books and periodicals. **Address:** Department of English, Minnesota State University, 202 Weld Hall, 1104 7th Ave. S, Moorhead, MN 56563, U.S.A. **Online address:** davisa@mnstate.edu

DAVIS, Albert Belisle. American (born United States), b. 1947. **Genres:** Novels, Poetry, Young Adult Fiction, Literary Criticism And History. **Career:** Nicholls State University, University College, dean, Alcee Fortier distinguished professor, distinguished service professor of English and literature, novelist-in-residence. **Publications:** What They Wrote on the Bathhouse Walls: Yen's Marina, Chinese Bayou, Louisiana (poems), 1988; Leechtime (novel), 1989; Marquis at Bay (novel), 1992; Virginia Patout's Parish (poetry), 1999. Works appear in anthologies. Contributor to journals. **Address:** Department of English, Nicholls State University, 233 Elkins Hall, PO Box 2008, Thibodaux, LA 70310, U.S.A. **Online address:** albert.davis@nicholls.edu

DAVIS, Allen F. American (born United States), b. 1931. **Genres:** History, Biography. **Career:** Temple University, professor of history, 1968-99, emeritus professor of history, 1999-, Center for Public History, director; Wayne State University, instructor, 1959-60; University of Missouri, assistant professor, 1960-63, associate professor of history, 1963-68; University of Texas, visiting professor, 1983; University of Amsterdam, John Adams Chair, 1986-87; American civilization, visiting professor. Writer. **Publications:** (With J. Cooke and R. Daly) March of American Democracy, vol. V, 1965; (with H.D. Woodman) Conflict and Consensus in Early American History, 1967, 8th ed., 1992; Spearheads for Reform, 1967; American Heroine: The Life and Legend of Jane Addams, 1973, 2nd ed., 2000; (with J. Watts) Generations, 1974, 3rd ed., 1983; (co-author) Still Philadelphia, 1983; (co-author) The American People, 1986, 6th d., 2003; (co-author) Philadelphia Stories, 1988; Postcards from Vermont, 2002. EDITOR: (with H. Woodman) Conflict and Consensus in American History, 1966, 9th ed., 1997; (with H.D. Woodman) Conflict and Consensus in Modern American History, 1968, 8th ed., 1992; (with M. McCree) Eighty Years at Hull House, 1969; (with M. Haller) The Peoples of Philadelphia, 1973; Jane Addams on Peace, War and International Understanding, 1976; For Better or Worse, 1981; (with M.L.M. Bryant) One-Hundred Years at Hull House, 1990. **Address:** Department of History, Temple University, 908 Gladfelter Hall, 1115 W Berks St., Philadelphia, PA 19122-6089, U.S.A. **Online address:** davisafd@aol.com

DAVIS, Amelia. American (born United States), b. 1968?. **Genres:** Photography, Biography, Adult Non-fiction, Essays, Autobiography/Memoirs. **Career:** VisionWorks Foundation Inc., president; Jim Marshall Photography L.L.C., owner and manager. Photographer and author. **Publications:** (Co-ed.) Glimpses Into Our Lives: Memories of Harrisburg's Black Senior Citizens, 1978; The First Look, 2000; My Story: A Photographic Essay on Life with Multiple Sclerosis, 2004; Faces of Osteoporosis, 2006. **Address:** c/o Author Mail, Demos Medical Publishing, 11 W 42nd St., 15th Fl., New York, NY 10036, U.S.A. **Online address:** order@ameliadavisphotography.com

DAVIS, Andrew. American (born United States), b. 1946. **Genres:** Film, Communications/Media, Mathematics/Statistics, Crafts, Education. **Career:** Director, producer, cinematographer and screenwriter. **Publications:** (Ed. with D. Pettitt) Developing Understanding in Primary Mathematics, 1994; (with J. Suggate and M. Goulding) Mathematical Knowledge for Primary Teachers, 1998, 4th ed., 2010; Craft, 2000. Contributor to periodicals. **Address:** Creative Artists Agency, 9830 Wilshire Blvd., Beverly Hills, CA 90212-1825, U.S.A.

DAVIS, Anita (Grey) P(rice). American (born United States), b. 1943. **Genres:** Adult Non-fiction, Education, Military/Defense/Arms Control, History, Biography. **Career:** Teacher, 1963-68; Converse College, instructor, 1969-72, assistant professor, 1972-76, associate professor, 1976-83, professor, 1983-88, Charles A. Dana professor of education, 1988-, department chair, 1978-83, 1986-2000. Writer. **Publications:** HISTORY AND BIOGRAPHY MATERIALS: The South in the American Revolutionary War, 1993; (with E. Hall) Harriet Quimby: An Activity Book for Children, 1993; (with M. Selvidge) Focus on Women, 1995; (with K. Preston) Discoveries, 1996; (with E. Hall) Harriet Quimby: America's First Lady of the Air-A Biography for Intermediate Readers, 1998; Walnut Grove Plantation: A Fun and Learn Book, 2000; Real Heroes: Rutherford County (NC) Men Who Made the Supreme Sacrifice during World War II, 2002; (with B. Hambright) Chimney Rock and Rutherford County, 2002; North Carolina during the Great Depression: A Documentary Portrait of a Decade, 2003; Rutherford County, North Carolina, in World War II, 2003; A Tribute: Rutherford County Vets, 2003; (with J. Walker) Rutherford County in World War II, vol. II, 2004; (with J. Walker) Spartanburg County in World War II, 2004; (with K. Slemenda) Discoveries, 2004; (with J. Walker) Cleveland County in World War II, 2005; (with J. Walker) Forest City, 2006: (with J. Walker) Rutherford County in the Korean War, 2006; Margaret Mitchell: A Link to Atlanta and the World (A Teacher's Guide to the Author of Gone With the Wind), 2006; (with M. Selvidge) Women Nobel Peace Prize Winners, 2006; (with L. Hunt) Women on U.S. Postage Stamps, 2008; Georgia During the Great Depression, 2008; New Deal Art in North Carolina: The Murals, Sculptures, Reliefs, Paintings, Oils and Frescoes and Their Creators, 2008; New Deal Art in Virginia: The Murals, Sculptures, Reliefs, Paintings, Oils and Frescoes and Their Creators, 2009. EDUCATION AND TEST PREPARATION MATERIALS: (co-author) The Graduate Management Admission Test: The Best and Most Comprehensive in Test Preparation, 1990; (co-author) The Best Test Preparation for the Graduate Record Examination, 1990; (co-author) The Best Test Preparation for the Scholastic Aptitude Test, 1990; (co-author) The Best Test Preparation for the NTE Core Battery (and Tests of Professional Knowledge), 1991; (co-author) The Best Test Preparation for the Medical College Admission Test, 1991; (co-author) The Best Test Preparation for the Law School Admissions

Test, 1992; (co-author) Verbal Skill Builder, 1992; (co-author) The Best Test Preparation for the New PSAT/NMSQT: The Preliminary SAT/National Merit Scholarship Qualifying Test, 1994; Max Notes: To Kill a Mockingbird, 1994; Max Notes: I Know Why the Caged Bird Sings, 1994; Max Notes: The Inferno, 1995; (co-author) The Best Test Preparation for the ACT Test, 1995; (co-author) The Best Test Preparation for the CLEP Exam, 1996; Reading Instruction Essentials, 1996, rev. ed., 2004; (co-author) SAT I, 1997; (co-author) Regents Test for Reading in the Elementary School, 1997; Max Notes: Sula, 1998; The Best Test Preparation for the High School Proficiency Test, 1999; NTE Study Guide, 1999; (ed.) Max Notes: Tar Baby, 1999; Florida Teacher Certification Exam Study Guide, 1999, rev. ed., 2006; Children's Literature Essentials, 1999, rev. ed., 2004; The Best Test Preparation for the PRAXIS II, 2000; (co-author) The Best Test Preparation for the Cooperative Admissions Examination and the High School Placement Test, 2001; (co-ed.) ACT Assessment: The Very Best Coaching and Study Course for the ACT, 2002; (co-ed.) GMAT CAT: The Best Test Preparation for the Graduate Management Admission Test, Computer-Adaptive Testing, 2002; The Best Teachers' Test Preparation for the PRAXIS PLT Test: K-6, 2002, rev. ed., 2004; The Best Teachers' Test Preparation for the PRAXIS PLT Test: 5-9, 2002, rev. ed., 2004; The Best Teachers' Test Preparation for the PRAXIS PLT Test: 7-12, 2002, rev. ed., 2004; (co-ed.) MCAT: The Very Best Test Preparation for the Medical College Admission Test, 2002; The Best Test Preparation for the COOP and HSPT, 2002; (co-ed.) PSAT/NMSQT Assessment: The Best Coaching and Study Course for the Preliminary Scholastic Test/National Merit Scholarship Qualifying Test, 2002; Davis, Anita P. (co-author) The Best Test Preparation for the Pre-GED, 2003; The Best Test Preparation for the PRAXIS II: 20012 and 20014, 2006; The Best Test Preparation for the Arizona Teacher Certification Exam, 2007; The Best Test Preparation for the PRAXIS English Examinations, 2009; (with S. Grey) The Best Test Preparation for the PRAXIS II: Elementary Education (Content Knowledge 0014), 2008; (with S. Grey) The Best Test Preparation for the PRAXIS II: Elementary Education: Curriculum, Instruction, and Assessment 0011, 2008. OTHERS: The Best Teacher's Test Preparation for the Praxis Elementary Education with Testware, 2006; The Best Test Preparation for the GMAT, 2006; The Best Teachers; Test Preparation for Praxis Plt Test Grades 7-12, 2nd ed., 2006; The Best Teachers' Test Preparation for the Aepa in Elementary Education K-6, 2007; (with L. Hunt) Women on United States Postage Stamps, 2008; The Best Teachers' Test Preparation for the Praxis II English Subject Assessments W/testware, 2009; The Best Teachers' Test Preparation for the Praxis II English Subject Assessments, 2009; Praxis II Plt Grades 7-12, 3rd ed., 2011; Praxis II English Subject Assessments, 2nd ed., 2011; GMAT, Graduate Management Admission Test, 5th ed., 2011; (with M. Rhyne and S. Withrow) Colfax Township, 2011. **Address:** Converse College, 580 E Main St., Spartanburg, SC 29302, U.S.A. **Online address:** anita13@charter.net

DAVIS, Ann. Canadian (born Canada), b. 1946. **Genres:** Art/Art History, Antiques/Furnishings. **Career:** Winnipeg Art Gallery, staff, 1973-76, administrative curator, 1976-79; University of Winnipeg, associate professor, 1976-79; Carleton University, faculty, 1980; University of Western Ontario, faculty, 1982-91; National Museum of Singapore, museum adviser, 1983; London Regional Art and Historical Museums, director of education, 1990-91; University of Calgary, Nickle Arts Museum, curator and director, 1992-, Museum and Heritage Studies, director, 1996-. Writer. **Publications:** Old English Sheepdog, 1973, 4th ed., 1978; Frontiers of Our Dreams: Quebec Painting in the 1940's and 1950's, 1979; Griffiths brothers=Les frères Griffiths, 1989; Somewhere Waiting: The Life and Art of Christiane Pflug, 1991; The Logic of Ecstasy: Canadian Mystical Painting, 1920-1940, 1992; (ed. with B.A. Sandalack) Sense of Place: A Catalogue of Essays, 2005; (ed. with B.A. Sandalack) Excursions into the Cultural Landscapes of Alberta, 2005; Down by the Back River Light, 2006; (with V.E. Cree) Social Work: Voices from the Inside, 2006; No More Indians: Or, No Book on Earth has Lied More Sincerely than My Ol' Virginia Text, 2007. Contributor to journals. **Address:** The Nickle Arts Museum, University of Calgary, 2500 University Dr. NW, NM 213, Calgary, AB T2N 1N4, Canada. **Online address:** adavis@ucalgary.ca

DAVIS, Anna. British (born England), b. 1971?. **Genres:** Literary Criticism And History, Romance/Historical. **Career:** Curtis Brown Literary Agency, staff. Writer. **Publications:** The Dinner, 1999; Melting, 2001; Cheet, 2003; The Shoe Queen, 2007; The Jewel Box, 2009. Works appear in anthologies. Contributor to periodicals. **Address:** London, GL, England. **Online address:** annaceedavis@gmail.com

DAVIS, Barbara Steincrohn. See **DAVIS, Maggie S.**

DAVIS, Bridgett M. American (born United States) **Genres:** Novels, Adult Non-fiction. **Career:** City University of New York, associate professor of English, professor. Writer. **Publications:** Shifting Through Neutral, 2004; Lagos, forthcoming. Contributor to periodicals. **Address:** Department of English, Weissman School of Arts & Sciences, Baruch College, CUNY, 7-265 Vertical Campus, 1 Bernard Baruch Way, New York, NY 10010, U.S.A. **Online address:** bridgett.davis@baruch.cuny.edu

DAVIS, Bryan. American (born United States), b. 1958. **Genres:** Theology/Religion. **Career:** Writer. **Publications:** The Story of Jesus' Baptism and Temptation: Matthew 3: 13-4: 11; Mark 1: 9-13; Luke 3: 21-4: 13; and John 1: 31-34 for Children, 1997; The Story of the Empty Tomb: John 20 for Children, 1998; Jacob's Dream: The Story of Jacob's Ladder: Genesis 28: 1-22 for Children, 2001; Spit and Polish for Husbands: Becoming Your Wife's Knight in Shining Armor, 2004; The Image of a Father: Reflections of God for Today's Father, 2004. DRAGONS IN OUR MIDST SERIES: Raising Dragons, 2004; The Candlestone, 2004; Circles of Seven, 2005; Tears of a Dragon, 2005. ORACLE OF FIRE SERIES: Eye of the Oracle, 2006; Enoch's Ghost, 2008; Last of the Nephilim, 2008; The Bones of Makaidos, 2009. ECHOES FROM THE EDGE TRILOGY: Beyond the Reflection's Edge, 2008; Eternity's Edge, 2008; Nightmare's Edge, 2009. **Address:** PO Box 512, Middleton, TN 38052, U.S.A. **Online address:** bryan@daviscrossing.com

DAVIS, Caitlyn. See **CLARK, Catherine.**

DAVIS, Christopher. American (born United States), b. 1928. **Genres:** Novels, Adult Non-fiction, Children's Fiction, Plays/Screenplays. **Career:** University of Pennsylvania, lecturer in creative writing, 1958-69; Bowling Green State University, lecturer, 1970; Drexel University, part-time lecturer, 1970-76; Indiana University of Pennsylvania, part-time lecturer, 1970-76; Franklin & Marshall College, part-time lecturer, 1970-76; Bryn Mawr College, senior lecturer in creative writing, 1977-95. Freelance writer and sculptor. **Publications:** Lost Summer, 1958; Scotty, 1959; First Family, 1961; A Kind of Darkness, 1962; Belmarch a Legend of the First Crusade, 1964; Sad Adam-Glad Adam (children's fiction), 1966; The Shamir of Dachau, 1966; Ishmael, 1967; A Peep into the 20th Century, 1970; The Producer (nonfiction), 1972; The Sun in Mid-Career, 1975; Suicide Note, 1977; Waiting for It (nonfiction), 1980; Dog, Horse, Rat, 1990; Working Words (nonfiction), 2007; Blue Sky: A Novel, 2008; The Conduct of Saints, 2013. Contributor to periodicals. **Address:** 2284 Norwic Pl., Altadena, CA 91001-2565, U.S.A. **Online address:** kitdavis@earthlink.net

DAVIS, David Brion. American (born United States), b. 1927. **Genres:** History, Literary Criticism And History, Race Relations, Medicine/Health. **Career:** Cornell University, assistant professor, 1955-58, associate professor, 1958-63, Ernest I. White professor of history, 1963-69; Yale University, professor of history, 1969-72, Farnham professor of history, 1972-78, Sterling professor of history, 1978-2001, Gilder Lehrman Center for the Study of Slavery, Resistance and Abolition, director emeritus; Oxford University, Harold Vyvyan Harmsworth professor, 1969-70; Ecole de Hautes Etudes en Sciences Sociales, chair in American Civilization, 1980-81; Gilder Lehrman Center for the Study of Slavery, Resistance and Abolition, director, 1998-2003. Writer. **Publications:** Homicide in American Fiction, 1957; The Problem of Slavery in Western Culture, 1967; The Slave Power Conspiracy and the Paranoid Style, 1969; The Problem of Slavery in the Age of Revolution, 1975; (co-author) The Great Republic, 1977; Slavery and Human Progress, 1984; From Homicide to Slavery: Studies in American Culture, 1986; Slavery in the Colonial Chesapeake, 1986; Revolutions: Reflections on American Equality and Foreign Liberations, 1990; (co-author) The Antislavery Debate, 1992; (co-author) The Boisterous Sea of Liberty: A Documentary History of American from Discovery through the Civil War, 1998; In the Image of God: Religion, Moral Values, and Our Heritage of Slavery, 2001; Challenging the Boundaries of Slavery, 2003; Inhuman Bondage: The Rise and Fall of Slavery in the New World, 2006. EDITOR: Antebellum Reform, 1967; The Fear of Conspiracy, 1971; Antebellum American Culture, 1979. **Address:** HI, U.S.A. **Online address:** david.b.davis@yale.edu

DAVIS, David (Howard). American (born United States), b. 1941. **Genres:** Politics/Government, Natural History, Sciences. **Career:** Rutgers University, assistant professor of political science, 1971-77; Environmental Protection Agency, staff, 1973-74; Cornell University, associate professor of government, 1977-78; Library of Congress, Congressional Research Service, staff, 1979-80; Energy and Minerals, special assistant, deputy assistant secretary of Interior, 1980-81; International Energy Associates Ltd., senior associate consultant, 1981-84; University of Wyoming, associate professor of political science, 1984-89; Social Science Journal, editor, 1986-89; University of Toledo, Department of Political Science and Public Administration, associate professor, 1989-92, professor of political science, 1992-; PA Times, commentary page editor, 1993-95. Writer. **Publications:** How the Bureaucracy Makes Foreign Policy an Exchange Analysis, 1972; Energy Politics, 1974, 4th ed., 1992; American Environmental Politics, 1998; Ignoring the Apocalypse: Why Planning to Prevent Environmental Catastrophe Goes Astray, 2007. **Address:** Department of Political Science and and Public, Administration, University of Toledo, SH 2047, 2801 Bancroft St., Toledo, OH 43606-3390, U.S.A. **Online address:** david.davis@utoledo.edu

DAVIS, David R. American (born United States), b. 1948. **Genres:** Humor/Satire, Cartoons, Young Adult Non-fiction. **Career:** Writer, cartoonist and speaker. **Publications:** A Redneck Night before Christmas, 1997; Trucker's Night Before Christmas, 1999; Jazz Cats, 2001; Nurse's Night Before Christmas, 2003; Ten Redneck Babies: A Southern Counting Book, 2004; Librarian's Night Before Christmas, 2006; Texas Zeke and The Longhorn, 2006; Rock 'n' Roll Dogs, 2006; Texas Mother Goose, 2006; Texas Aesop's Fables, 2008; Southern Child's Garden of Verses, 2010; (with J. Peck) Green Mother Goose: Saving the World One Rhyme at a Time, 2010; Fandango Stew, 2011; The Twelve Days of Christmas- in Texas, That is, 2011. Contributor of articles to journals. **Address:** 704 Parker Dr., Clinton, MS 39056, U.S.A. **Online address:** ddavis7@bellsouth.net

DAVIS, Dee. American (born United States), b. 1959?. **Genres:** Romance/Historical, Novels, Novellas/Short Stories, Human Relations/Parenting. **Career:** Writer. **Publications:** A Match Made on Madison (novel), 2007; Chain Reaction, 2007; Set up in SoHo, 2009; Dangerous Desires, 2010; Desperate Deeds, 2010; Deep Disclosure, 2011; Deadly Dance, 2012. ROMANCE FICTION: Everything in Its Time, 2000; After Twilight, 2001; Just Breathe, 2001; Dark of the Night, 2002; Midnight Rain, 2002; The Promise, 2002; Dancing in the Dark, 2003; Wild Highland Rose, 2003; (with C. Dain and E. Rogers) Silent Night, 2004; Endgame, 2005; Enigma, 2005; Exposure, 2005; (with J. Kenner and K. O'Reilly) Hell with the Ladies (novellas), 2006; Eye of the Storm, 2006; (with J. Kenner and K. O'Reilly) Hell on Heels (novellas), 2007; Dark Deceptions, 2010; (contrib.) Fall in Love Like a Romance Writer, 2011. **Address:** PO Box 7231, New York, NY 10150, U.S.A. **Online address:** dee@deedavis.com

DAVIS, Dick. American/British (born England), b. 1945. **Genres:** Poetry, Translations, Social Sciences. **Career:** Teacher, 1967-69, 1970-87; University of Tehran, teacher, 1970-78, instructor, 1970-71, College of Literature and Foreign Languages, instructor, 1971-78; Margaret McMillan College, instructor, 1969-70; freelance writer, 1978-80, 1981-85; University of Durham, northern arts literary fellow, 1985-87; Newcastle University, northern arts literary fellow, 1985-87; University of California, poet-in-residence, 1985-87, visiting associate professor, 1987-88; Ohio State University, assistant professor of Persian, 1988-93, associate professor, 1993-94, professor of Persian, 1998, Department of Near Eastern Languages and Cultures, chair. **Publications:** (With C. Wilmer and R. Wells) Shade Mariners, 1970; In the Distance, 1975; Seeing the World, 1980; (ed.) The Selected Writings of Thomas Traherne, 1980; Wisdom and Wilderness: The Achievement of Yvor Winters, 1983; What the Mind Wants, 1984; The Covenant, 1984; (trans. and intro. with A. Darbandi) F.U.D. Attar, The Conference of the Birds; (trans.) N. Ginzburg, The Little Virtues, 1985; (trans.) N. Ginzburg, The City and the House, 1987; (ed. with D. Williams) New Writing from the North, 1988; (ed.) The Ruba'iyaat of Omar Khayyaam, 1989; Devices and Desires: New and Selected Poems 1967-1987, 1989; A Kind of Love: New and Selected Poems, 1991; Epic and Sedition: The Case of Ferdowsi's Shahnameh, 1992; (trans. and intro.) A. Ferdowsi, The Legend of Seyavash, 1992, rev. ed., 2004; (trans.) I. Pezeshkzad, My Uncle Napoleon, 1996; Touchwood, 1996; Borrowed Ware, 1996; (trans.) E. Yarshater, The Lion and the Throne, 1997; (trans.) Fathers and Sons, 2000; Belonging, 2002; Panthea's Children, 2002; Sunset of Empire, 2004; (trans.) A. Ferdowsi, The Shahnameh, 2006; A Trick of Sunlight, 2006; N. Batmanglij, From Persia to Napa: Wine at the Persian Table, 2006; (with R. Hadas and T. Steele) Three Poets in Conversation, 2006; (trans. and intro.) A. Ferdowsi, Rostam: Tales of Love & War From Persias Book of Kings, 2007; (trans., ed. and intro.) F. Gorgani, Vis & Ramin, 2008; (contrib.) Obeyd-e Zakani, 2nd ed., 2008; At Home, and Far from Home: Poems on Iran and Persian Culture, 2009. Contributor of articles to periodicals. **Address:** Department of Near Eastern Languages and Cultures, Ohio State University, 300-G Hagerty Hall, 1775 College Rd., Columbus, OH 43210, U.S.A. **Online address:** davis77@osu.edu

DAVIS, Donald. American (born United States), b. 1944. **Genres:** Novellas/Short Stories, Young Adult Fiction, Children's Fiction, Social Sciences, Art/Art History, Humor/Satire, Autobiography/Memoirs. **Career:** United Methodist minister, 1967-88; nationwide storyteller, 1967-; National Association for the Preservation and Perpetuation of Storytelling, chairperson, 1983-88. Writer. **Publications:** My Lucky Day, 1983; Listening for the Crack of Dawn, 1990; Barking at a Fox-Fur Coat, 1991; Jack Always Seeks His Fortune: Authentic Appalachian Jack Tales, 1992; Telling Your Own Stories: A Guide to Family, Classroom and Personal Storytelling, 1993; Thirteen Miles from Suncrest, 1994; Jack and the Animals, 1995; See Rock City, 1996; The Big-Screen Drive-in Theater, 1996; Writing as a Second Language, 2000; Ride the Butterflies, 2000; Telling Your Arkansas Stories: For Family and Classroom Storytelling, Public Speaking and Personal Journaling, 2002; Mama Learns to Drive, 2005; Don't Kill Santa!: Christmas Stories, 2006; Tales from a Free-Range Childhood, 2011. Contributor of articles and fiction to periodicals. **Address:** Storyteller Inc., PO Box 397, Ocracoke Island, NC 27960, U.S.A. **Online address:** donald@ddavisstoryteller.com

DAVIS, Donald A. (Donald Alan Davis). American (born United States), b. 1939. **Genres:** Novels. **Career:** Athens Banner- Herald, reporter, 1961-62; Savannah Morning News, reporter, 1962; United Press International (UPI), journalist, 1963-65, 1967- 83, Vietnam correspondent, 1971-73, New England editor, 1977-80, White House correspondent, 1981-83; St. Petersburg Times, reporter and editor, 1965-66; San Diego Union, political reporter & columnist, 1983-91; Boston University, instructor in journalism, 1979; University of Colorado, instructor in writing, 1998-99; U.S. Naval War College, lecturer, 1983; Queen Elizabeth 2, lecturer, 1991. **Publications:** UNDER NAME DON DAVIS: The Nanny Murder Trial, 1993; Fallen Hero: The Shocking True Story behind the O.J. Simpson Tragedy, 1994; Bad Blood: The Shocking True Story behind the Menendez Killings, 1994; Appointment with the Squire (novel), 1995; Hush Little Babies, 1997; (with S. Thomas) JonBenet: Inside the Ramsey Murder Investigation, 2000; (with L. Vyborny) Dark Waters: An Insider's Account of the NR-1, the Cold War's Undercover Nuclear Sub, 2003; UNDER NAME DONALD A. DAVIS: Lightning Strike: The Secret Mission to Kill Admiral Yamamoto and Avenge Pearl Harbor, 2005; (with J. Coughlin and C. Kuhlman) Shooter: The Autobiography of the Top-Ranked Marine Sniper, 2005; (with J. Coughlin) Kill Zone (novel), 2007; Stonewall Jackson (biography), 2007. **Address:** Boulder, CO , U.S.A. **Online address:** tedsalad@mesanetworks.net

DAVIS, Donald Alan. See **DAVIS, Donald A.**

DAVIS, Donald Edward. American (born United States), b. 1959?. **Genres:** History. **Career:** Dalton State College, assistant professor of sociology, 1993-, professor; University System of Georgia, European Council, Study Abroad Program, assistant professor, 1998, 1999. Writer. **Publications:** Ecophilosophy: A Field Guide to the Literature, 1989; (with J. Rifkin) Biosphere Politics: A New Consciousness for the 21st Century, 1991; Where There Are Mountains: An Environmental History of the Southern Appalachians, 2000; The Land of Ridge and Valley: A Photographic History of the Northwest Georgia Mountains, 2001; Homeplace Geography: Essays for Appalachia, 2006; (ed.) Voices from the Nueva Frontera: Latino Immigration in Dalton, Georgia, 2009. Contributor to periodicals. **Address:** Dalton State College, Rm. 242, Liberal Arts Bldg., 650 College Dr., Dalton, GA 30720, U.S.A. **Online address:** ddavis@daltonstate.edu

DAVIS, (Edmund) Wade. American/Canadian (born Canada), b. 1953. **Genres:** Anthropology/Ethnology, Biology, Adult Non-fiction. **Career:** Jardin Botanico Antonio Uribe, plant collector, 1974-75; U.S. Department of Agriculture, plant explorer, 1974-75; MacMillan Bloedel, axman and topographer, 1977-78; ethnobotanical researcher and writer, 1982-; Center for Field Research, lecturer, 1982; Tufts university, lecturer, 1984; National Geographic Society, explorer-in-residence, lecturer, 1985-; Institute of Economic Botany, honorary research associate in ethnobiology, 1986-; Smithsonian Institution, lecturer, 1986; American Museum of Natural History, lecturer, 1987; Instituto Caribe de Antropologia y Sociologia, honorary research associate in ethnobiology, 1990-; Endangered Peoples Project, executive director, 1990-. Writer. **Publications:** The Serpent and the Rainbow (nonfiction), 1985; Passage of Darkness: The Ethnobiology of the Haitian Zombie (nonfiction), 1988; (with T. Henley) Penan: Voice for the Borneo Rain Forest, 1990; (with I. Mackenzie and S. Kennedy) Nomads of the Dawn, 1995; One River: Explorations and Discoveries in the Amazon Rain Forest, 1996, 2nd ed., 2004; The Clouded Leopard, 1998; Shadows in the Sun: Travels to Landscapes of Spirit and Desire, 1998; (contrib.) Rainforest: Ancient Realm of the Pacific Northwest, 1998; Light at the Edge of the World: A Journey Through the Realm of Vanishing Cultures, 2001; Río, 2004; The Lost Amazon, 2004; (ed. with K.D. Harrison) Book of Peoples of the World: A Guide to Cultures, 2007; Wayfinders, 2009; (contrib.) La amazonia perdida: el viaje fotográico del legendario Richard Schultes, 2009; Into the Silence: The Great War, Mallory, and the Conquest of Everest, 2011. **Address:** Institute of Economic Botany, New York Botanical Garden, 2900 Southern Blvd., Bronx, NY 10458-5126, U.S.A.

DAVIS, Eleanor. American (born United States), b. 1983?. **Genres:** Graphic Novels, Illustrations, Humor/Satire. **Career:** Little House Comics, co-founder and publisher. Writer and illustrator. **Publications:** SELF-ILLUSTRAT-ED: Stinky, 2008; The Secret Science Alliance and the Copycat Crook (graphic novel), 2009. **Address:** Little House Comics, PO Box 1926, Athens, GA 30603, U.S.A. **Online address:** eleanor@doing-fine.com

DAVIS, Ellen F. American (born United States), b. 1950. **Genres:** Philosophy. **Career:** Union Theological Seminary, assistant professor, 1987-89; Yale Divinity School, assistant professor, 1989-91, associate professor of Old Testament, 1991-96; Virginia Theological Seminary, associate professor, 1996-99, professor of Old Testament and language, 1999-2001; Duke Divinity School, associate professor, 2001-04, professor of Bible and practical theology, 2004-09, Renk Sudan Visiting Teachers Program, founder and co-director, 2004-, associate dean for faculty development, 2008-, Amos Ragan Kearns distinguished professor of Bible and practical theology, 2009-; Cambridge University, Hulsean lecturer, 2005-06. Writer and theologian. **Publications:** Swallowing the Scroll: Textuality and the Dynamics of Discourse in Ezekiel's Prophecy, 1989; Imagination Shaped: Old Testament Preaching in the Anglican Tradition, 1995; Proverbs, Ecclesiastes and the Song of Songs, 2000; Getting Involved with God: Rediscovering the Old Testament, 2001; (ed. with R.B. Hays) The Art of Reading Scripture, 2003; (trans.) Who Are You, My Daughter? Reading Ruth through Image and Text, 2003; Wondrous Depth: Preaching the Old Testament, 2005; Scripture, Culture, and Agriculture: An Agrarian Reading of the Bible, 2009; Prophecy and Contemporary Ministry, Interpretation Resources Series, 2014. Contributor to books and periodicals. **Address:** Duke Divinity School, Duke University, 211 Gray, 407 Chapel Dr., PO Box 90967, Durham, NC 27708-0967, U.S.A. **Online address:** edavis@div.duke.edu

DAVIS, (Elvis) Clark. American (born United States), b. 1964. **Genres:** Literary Criticism And History, Young Adult Fiction, Humanities. **Career:** Northeast Louisiana University, assistant professor of English, 1992-96, associate professor, 1996-2000; University of Denver, Department of English, associate professor, 2000-07, professor 2007-, department chair. Writer. **Publications:** After the Whale: Melville in the Wake of Moby-Dick, 1995; Hawthorne's Shyness: Ethics, Politics and the Question of Engagement, 2005. **Address:** Department of English, University of Denver, 487B Sturm, 2000 E Asbury, Denver, CO 80208, U.S.A. **Online address:** cldavis@du.edu

DAVIS, Emma. See **DAVIS, Maggie S.**

DAVIS, Francis. American (born United States), b. 1946. **Genres:** Cultural/Ethnic Topics, Music, Young Adult Non-fiction, Art/Art History, Literary Criticism And History. **Career:** WHYY-FM Radio, producer and host, 1978-83; Philadelphia Inquirer, jazz critic, 1982-; Musician, jazz editor, 1982-85; Atlantic Monthly, music critic, 1984-, contributing editor, 1992-; National Public Radio, jazz critic, 1987; 7 Days, staff writer, 1988-90; University of Pennsylvania, instructor in folk and blues, 1995-. **Publications:** In the Moment: Jazz in the 1980s, 1986, 2nd ed., 1990; Outcats: Jazz Composers, Instrumentalists, and Singers, 1990; The History of the Blues, 1995; Bebop and Nothingness: Jazz and Pop at the End of the Century, 1996; Like Young: Jazz and Pop, Youth and Middle Age, 2001; Afterglow: A Last Conversation with Pauline Kael, 2002; Jazz and Its Discontents: A Francis Davis Reader, 2004. **Address:** The Atlantic Monthly, 77 N Washington St., Ste. 5, Boston, MA 02114-1908, U.S.A.

DAVIS, Frank Joseph. American (born United States), b. 1942. **Genres:** Food And Wine. **Career:** WWL Radio, host; WWL TV, In the Kitchen with Frank Davis, host. Writer, chef, public speaker and consultant. **Publications:**

The Frank Davis Seafood Notebook, 1983; The Frank Davis Fishing Guide to Lake Pontchartrain and Lake Borgne, 1988; Frank Davis Cooks Naturally N'Awlins, 1990; Frank Davis Cooks Cajun, Creole, and Crescent City, 1994; The Fisherman's Tackle Box Bible, 2003; Frank Davis Makes Good Groceries! A New Orleans Cookbook, 2008. **Address:** New Orleans, LA , U.S.A. **Online address:** frankd@frankdavis.com

DAVIS, Hank. American (born United States), b. 1941. **Genres:** Psychology, Sports/Fitness. **Career:** WKCR 89.9 FM, host, 1961-63; Naval Medical Research Institute, psychologist, 1965-67; California State University, assistant professor of psychology, 1968-70; University of Guelph, associate professor of psychology, 1971-, professor of psychology, Centre for the Study of Animal Welfare, co-founder, now professor emeritus. Writer and journalist. **Publications:** Small-Town Heroes: Images of Minor League Baseball, 1997; Classic Cliffhangers: vol. II 1941-1955, 2008; Caveman Logic: The Persistence of Primitive Thinking in a Modern World, 2009. EDITOR: (with H.M.B. Hurwitz) Operant-Pavlovian Interactions, 1977; (with D. Balfour) The Inevitable Bond: Examining Scientist-Animal Interactions, 1992. Contributor of articles to journals. **Address:** Department of Psychology, University of Guelph, MacKinnon Bldg., Rm. 3002, Guelph, ON N1G 2W1, Canada. **Online address:** hdavis@uoguelph.ca

DAVIS, Harold. American (born United States), b. 1953. **Genres:** Photography. **Career:** Writer and photographer. **Publications:** Publishing Your Art as Cards & Posters: The Complete Guide to Creating, Designing & Marketing, 1990, rev. ed., 1993; Photographer's Publishing Handbook, 1991; Successful Fine Art Photography: How to Market Your Art Photography, 1992; (with P. Norton and P. Davis) Peter Norton's Guide to Visual Basic 4 for Windows 95, 4th ed., 1995; Delphi Power Toolkit for Windows: Cutting-Edge Tools & Techniques for Programmers, 1995; Visual Basic 4 Secrets, 1996; Web Developer's Secrets, 1997; Visual Basic 5 Secrets, 1997; Visual Basic 6 Secrets, 1998; Red Hat Linux 6, 1999; Visual Basic 6, 2000; Visual Basic 2002; (with R. Mansfield) The Wi-Fi Experience: Everyone's Guide to 802.11b Wireless Networking, 2002; Visual Basic.NET for Windows, 2003; Absolute Beginner's Guide to Wi-Fi Wireless Networking, 2004; Learn How to Program: Using Any Web Browser, 2004; (with J. Merlino and K. Wrightson) Red Hat Linux 9, 2004; Digital Photography: Digital Field Guide, 2005; Building Research Tools with Google for Dummies, 2005; Google Advertising Tools, 2006; Anywhere Computing with Laptops: Making Mobile Easier, 2006; Practical Artistry: Light and Exposure for Digital Photographers, 2007; The Photographer's Guide to Yosemite and the High Sierra: Where to Find Perfect Shots and How to Take Them, 2008; 100 Views of the Golden Gate, 2008; Creative Close-Ups: Digital Photography Tips and Techniques, 2009; Creative Night: Digital Photography Tips & Techniques, 2009; Creative Composition: Digital Photography Tips & Techniques, 2009; The Photoshop Darkroom: Creative Digital Post-Processing, 2009; Photographing Flowers, 2012. **Address:** c/o Matt Wagner, Fresh Books Literary Agency, 231 Diana St., Placerville, CA 95667-3315, U.S.A. **Online address:** info@photoblog2.com

DAVIS, Heather. American (born United States), b. 1970?. **Genres:** Young Adult Fiction, Novels. **Career:** Writer and educator. **Publications:** YOUNG-ADULT NOVELS: Never Cry Werewolf, 2009; The Clearing, 2010; Wherever You Go, 2011. Contributor of stories to periodicals. **Address:** c/o Stephen Barbara, Foundry Literary & Media, 33 W 17th St., New York, NY 10011, U.S.A. **Online address:** heather@heatherdavisbooks.com

DAVIS, James Calvin. American (born United States), b. 1970. **Genres:** Theology/Religion. **Career:** Middlebury College, associate professor of religion. Writer, biographer, educator and historian. **Publications:** The Moral Theology of Roger Williams: Christian Conviction and Public Ethics, 2004; (ed. and intro.) On Religious Liberty: Selections from the Works of Roger Williams, 2008. **Address:** Middlebury College, Munroe Hall 103, Middlebury, VT 05753, U.S.A. **Online address:** jcdavis@middlebury.edu

DAVIS, Jennifer S. American (born United States), b. 1973. **Genres:** Novellas/Short Stories. **Career:** Mack-Fil School, English instructor, 1997-98; University of Alabama, graduate teaching assistant, 1998-2001; University of Miami, English instructor, 2001-02; New College of Florida, instructor; Eastern Washington University, assistant professor, 2002-04, Willow Springs Journal, editor, 2002-04; University of California, online English instructor, 2003-; University of Colorado, assistant professor of English, 2006-; Copper Nickel Magazine, faculty editor. **Publications:** Her Kind of Want (collection of short stories), 2002; Our Former Lives in Art, 2007; Confederados, forthcoming. Contributor to periodicals and short stories. Works appear in anthologies. **Address:** Department of English, University of Colorado Denver, Rm. 1061, 1015 9th Street Pk. 201, PO Box 173364, Denver, CO 80204, U.S.A. **Online address:** jennifer.davis@ucdenver.edu

DAVIS, John W. American (born United States), b. 1943. **Genres:** History. **Career:** Worland, attorney. Writer. **Publications:** Worland before Worland, 1987; Sadie & Charlie, 1989; A Vast Amount of Trouble: A History of the Spring Creek Raid, 1993; Goodbye, Judge Lynch: The End of a Lawless Era in Wyoming's Big Horn Basin, 2005; Wyoming Range War: The Infamous Invasion of Johnson County, 2010. Contributor to periodicals. **Address:** John W. Davis, Attorney at Law P.C., PO Box 953, 718 Big Horn Ave., Worland, WY 82401, U.S.A. **Online address:** jwdavis@rtconnect.net

DAVIS, Jon. American (born United States), b. 1952. **Genres:** Poetry. **Career:** Fine Arts Work Center, Shankpainter, managing editor, 1986-87, co-ordinator of writing program, 1987-88; Salisbury State University, visiting assistant professor of creative writing, 1988-89, visiting assistant professor of American literature, 1989-90; Institute of American Indian Arts, professor of creative writing and literature, 1990-, department head, 1990-91, 1993-94, chair of creative writing; University of Montana, faculty; College of Santa Fe, Countermeasures, co-editor, 1995-. **Publications:** Preliminary Report, 2010. POETRY: West of New England, 1983; Dangerous Amusements, 1987; The Hawk; The Road; The Sunlight after Clouds, 1995; Local Color, 1995; Scrimmage of Appetite, 1995; How is This Fun: The Poems of Chuck Calabreze, forthcoming; Heteronymy: An Anthology, forthcoming. Works appear in anthologies. Contributor of articles to periodicals. **Address:** Creative Writing Program, Institute of American Indian Arts, 83 Avan Nu Po Rd., Santa Fe, NM 87508-1300, U.S.A. **Online address:** jdavis@iaia.edu

DAVIS, Julie Nelson. American (born United States), b. 1963?. **Genres:** History. **Career:** University of Pennsylvania, assistant professor of art history, 2002-, associate professor and undergraduate chair; University of East Anglia, Sainsbury Institute for the Study of Japanese Arts and Cultures, Robert and Lisa Sainsbury fellow; University of London, School of Oriental and African Studies (SOAS), Robert and Lisa Sainsbury fellow, 2003. Writer. **Publications:** (With F.L. Chance) Dramatic Impressions: Japanese Theatre Prints from the Gilbert Luber Collection, 2006; Utamaro and the Spectacle of Beauty, 2007. Contributor to books and journals. **Address:** School of Arts & Sciences, University of Pennsylvania, 307 Jaffe Bldg., Philadelphia, PA 19104, U.S.A.

DAVIS, Kathy E. American (born United States), b. 1949. **Genres:** Medicine/Health. **Career:** Utrecht University, associate professor of women's studies, 1990-, Institute of History and Culture, senior researcher; European Journal of Women's Studies, editor. Researcher and clinical psychologist. **Publications:** Reshaping the Female Body: The Dilemma of Cosmetic Surgery, 1995; Dubious Equalities and Embodied Differences: Cultural Studies on Cosmetic Surgery, 2003; The Making of Our Bodies, Ourselves: How Feminism Travels across Borders, 2007; (with M. Evans) Transatlantic Conversations: Feminism as Travelling Theory, 2011. EDITOR: (with M. Leijenaar and J. Oldersma) The Gender of Power, 1991; (with S. Fisher) Negotiating at the Margins: The Gendered Discourses of Power and Resistance, 1993; Embodied Practices: Feminist Perspectives on the Body, 1997; (with M. Evans and J. Lorber) Handbook of Gender and Women's Studies, 2006. **Address:** Institute of History and Culture, Utrecht University, Janskerkhof 13, Utrecht, 3512, Netherlands. **Online address:** k.e.davis@uu.nl

DAVIS, Kenneth C. American (born United States) **Genres:** Cultural/Ethnic Topics, History, Social Commentary, Travel/Exploration. **Career:** Writer. **Publications:** Strictly Legal, A Novelette, 1934; Two-Bit Culture: The Paperbacking of America, 1984; Foul Plays And Other Dubious Achievements in Sports, 1988; Don't Know Much About History: Everything You Need to Know About American History but Never Learned, 1990; Oklahoma History in Light of the Cross, 1991; Don't Know Much About Geography: Everything You Need to Know About the World but Never Learned, 1992; Don't Know Much About the Civil War: Everything You Need to Know About America's Greatest Conflict but Never Learned, 1996; Don't Know Much About the Bible: Everything You Need to Know About the Good Book but Never Learned, 1998; Don't Know Much About the Solar System, 2001; Don't Know Much About the Universe: Everything You Need to Know About the Cosmos but Never Learned, 2001; Don't Know Much About Space, 2001;

Don't Know Much About the Fifty States, 2001; Don't Know Much About the Pilgrims, 2001; Don't Know Much About the Planet Earth (for Kids!), 2001; Don't Know Much About the Presidents, 2002; Don't Know Much About the Kings and Queens of England, 2002; Don't Know Much About the Pioneers, 2003; Don't Know Much About Sitting Bull, 2003; Don't Know Much About George Washington, 2003; Don't Know Much About American History, 2003; Don't Know Much About Abraham Lincoln, 2004; Don't Know Much About the Dinosaurs, 2004; Don't Know Much About World Myths, 2005; Don't Know Much About Mummies, 2005; Don't Know Much About Mythology: Everything You Need to Know About the Greatest Stories in Human History but Never Learned, 2005; Don't Know Much About Rosa Parks, 2005; Don't Know Much About Thomas Jefferson, 2005; Don't Know Much About Martin Luther King, Jr, 2006; Don't Know Much About Anything, 2007; Don't Know Much About Anything Else: Even More Things You Need to Know but Never Learned About People, Places, Events and More!, 2008; America's Hidden History: Untold Tales of the First Pilgrims, Fighting Women and Forgotten Founders who Shaped a Nation, 2008; (with J. Davis) Don't Know Much About Literature, 2009; Nation Rising: Untold Tales of Flawed Founders, Fallen Heroes and Forgotten Fighters from America's Hidden History, 2010. Contributor to periodicals. **Address:** c/o Nat Sobel, Sobel Weber Associates Inc., 146 E 19th St., New York, NY 10003-2404, U.S.A.

DAVIS, Lexi. American (born United States) **Genres:** Novels. **Career:** Novelist. **Publications:** Pretty Evil, 2005; The After Wife, 2009. **Address:** c/o Author Mail, Pocket Books, 1230 Ave. of the Americas, 11th Fl., New York, NY 10020-1513, U.S.A. **Online address:** lexi@lexidavis.com

DAVIS, Linda W. American (born United States), b. 1945. **Genres:** Biology, Horticulture, Agriculture/Forestry. **Career:** Kansas State University, Division of Biology, instructor, 1988-. Writer. **Publications:** Weed Seeds of the Great Plains: A Handbook for Identification, 1993. **Address:** Division of Biology, Kansas State University, 116 Ackert Hall, Manhattan, KS 66506-4900, U.S.A. **Online address:** lwdavis@ksu.edu

DAVIS, Lindsey. British (born England), b. 1949. **Genres:** Romance/Historical, Mystery/Crime/Suspense, Novels, Young Adult Fiction, Reference. **Career:** Civil servant and full-time writer. **Publications:** HISTORICAL MYSTERIES: The Silver Pigs, 1989; Shadows in Bronze: A Marcus Didius Falco Novel, 1990; Venus in Copper: A Marcus Didius Falco Novel, 1991; The Iron Hand of Mars, 1992; Poseidon's Gold: A Marcus Didius Falco Mystery, 1994; Last Act in Palmyra, 1994; Time to Depart, 1997; A Dying Light in Corduba, 1998; The Course of Honor, 1997; The Descent to Avernus, with Ticket Office, 1998; Two for the Lions, 1999; Three Hands in the Fountain, 1999; One Virgin Too Many, 2000; Ode to a Banker, 2001; A Body in the Bathhouse, 2002; The Jupiter Myth, 2002; The Accusers, 2003; Scandal Takes a Holiday, 2004; See Delphi and Die: A Marcus Didius Falco Novel, 2005; The Silver Pigs: A Marcus Didius Falco Mystery, 2006; Saturnalia, 2007; Alexandria, 2009; Rebels and Traitors, 2009; Nemesis, 2010; Falco: The Official Companion, 2010. OTHERS: (foreword) Life in Ancient Rome, 2005; Master & God, 2012. **Address:** Century Publishing Ltd., Random House, 20 Vauxhall Bridge Rd., London, GL SW1V 2SA, England. **Online address:** readers@lindseydavis.co.uk

DAVIS, Maggie S. Also writes as Barbara Steincrohn Davis, Emma Davis, Maggie Steincrohn Davis, M. E. Cooper. American (born United States), b. 1942. **Genres:** Children's Fiction, Children's Non-fiction, Young Adult Non-fiction, Young Adult Fiction. **Career:** Reese Air Force base, director of nursery, 1967; University of Miami Reading Clinic, teacher for learning-disabled children, 1967-68; McGlannan Language Arts Center, teacher for learning-disabled children, 1967-73; Poets-in-the-Schools Program, staff, 1973; Citizens Dispute Settlement Center, counselor, public relations representative, 1977-79; freelance editor and rewrite specialist, 1981-86; Left Bank Bakery and Cafe, co-owner; Heartsong Books, co-founder and publisher; Neighborcare, co-founder, publisher. **Publications:** FOR YOUNG READERS: (as Barbara Steincrohn Davis) Scrubadubba Dragon, 1971; (as Barbara Steincrohn Davis) Forest Hotel: A Counting Story, 1972; The Best Way to Ripton, 1982; Grandma's Secret Letter, 1982; Rickety Witch, 1984; Forbidden Objects, 1986; (as M.E. Cooper) Something New, 1987; (as Emma Davis) A Dog for Jessie, 1988; Eagles, 1988; The Rinky-Dink Café, 1988; Something Magic, 1991; (as Maggie Steincrohn Davis) A Garden of Whales, 1992. NONFICTION: Blooming!: Choices of a Growing Woman, 1981 as Choices of a Growing Woman, 1994; Roots of Peace, Seeds of Hope: A Journey for Peacemakers, 1994; Glory! to the Flowers, a Celebration, 1995; Caring in

Remembered Ways: The Fruit of Seeing Deeply, 1999. AS M.E. COOPER: Sworn Enemies, 1985; Made for Each Other, 1985; Moving too Fast, 1985; Crazy Love, 1985; Bad Love, 1986; Secrets, 1986; Changing Partners, 1986; Summer Heat!, 1986; Picture Perfect, 1986; Coming on Strong, 1986; Dance with Me, 1986; Broken Hearts, 1986; Kiss and Run, 1986; Sweet and Sour, 1987; Slow Dancing, 1987; Teacher's Pet, 1987; Be Mine!, 1987; Beach Party!, 1987; Making Promises, 1986; Mean to Me, 1988; Bye Bye Love, 1987; Lovestruck, 1987; Love Exchange, 1987; Don't get Close, 1988; Take Me Back, 1988; Prom Date, 1988; Hold Me Tight, 1988; Falling for You, 1988; Head over Heels, 1987. **Address:** Heartsong Books, PO Box 370, Blue Hill, ME 04614, U.S.A. **Online address:** maggie@downeast.net

DAVIS, Maggie Steincrohn. *See* **DAVIS, Maggie S.**

DAVIS, Margaret Leslie. American (born United States), b. 1958. **Genres:** Biography, Adult Non-fiction, Autobiography/Memoirs, History, Art/Art History, Law. **Career:** Lawyer and writer. **Publications:** Lovers, Doctors and the Law: Your Legal Rights and Responsibilities in Today's Sex-Health Crisis, 1988; Rivers in the Desert: William Mulholland and the Inventing of Los Angeles, 1993, new ed., 2001; Bullocks Wilshire, 1996; Dark Side of Fortune: Triumph and Scandal in the Life of Oil Tycoon Edward L. Doheny, 1998; (with A. Vertikoff) The Los Angeles Biltmore: The Host of the Coast, 1998; Children's Hospital and the Leaders of Los Angeles: The First 100 Years, 2002; (with W.M. Karmer) A Lone Traveler: Einstein in California, 2004; The Culture Broker: Franklin D. Murphy and the Transformation of Los Angeles, 2007; Mona Lisa in Camelot: How Jacqueline Kennedy and Da Vinci's Masterpiece Charmed and Captivated a Nation, 2008; Purse Strings of Phoebe Hearst: Her Philanthropy, Social Vision and Dreams for Her Son William Randolph Hearst, 2010. **Address:** Da Capo Press, 11 Cambridge Ctr., Cambridge, MA 02142, U.S.A. **Online address:** margaretlesliedavis@gmail.com

DAVIS, Margaret (Thomson). Scottish (born Scotland), b. 1926. **Genres:** Novels, History. **Career:** Writer, 1967-. Educator. **Publications:** The Breadmakers, 1972; A Baby Might Be Crying, 1973; A Sort of Peace, 1973; The Prisoner, 1974; The Prince and the Tobacco Lords, 1976; Roots of Bondage, 1977; Scorpion in the Fire, 1977; The Dark Side of Pleasure, 1981; The Making of a Novelist, 1982; A Very Civilized Man, 1982; Light and Dark, 1984; Rag Woman, Rich Woman, 1987; Mothers and Daughters, 1988; Wounds of War, 1989; A Woman of Property, 1991; A Sense of Belonging, 1993; Hold Me Forever, 1994; Kiss Me No More, 1995; The Tobacco Lords Trilogy, 1999; The Glasgow Belle, 1999; A Tangled Web, 1999; Clydesiders, 1999; The Gourlay Girls, 2000; The Breadmakers Saga, 2001; Clydesides at War, 2002; The Clydesiders Trilogy, 2003; Write from the Heart, 2006; A Darkening of the Heart, 2007. **Address:** 11 Hanover Gardens, Keir Hardie Ct., Bishopbriggs, G64 1AQ, Scotland.

DAVIS, Mark H. American (born United States), b. 1953?. **Genres:** Psychology, Psychiatry, Medicine/Health. **Career:** University of Texas at Austin, research associate, 1979-80; Indiana University, postdoctoral program in measurement, 1980-83; Eastern Illinois University, assistant professor, 1983-86; Eckerd College, Department of Psychology, assistant professor, 1986-91, associate professor, 1991-99, professor, 1999-; Journal of Personality and Social Psychology, consulting editor, 1996-2002; Personality and Social Psychology Bulletin, consulting editor, 2006-. **Publications:** Empathy: A Social Psychological Approach, 1996, rev. ed., 2003; (with S. Capobianco and L.A. Kraus) Managing Conflict Dynamics: A Practical Approach, 2004; (with S. Capobianco and L.A. Kraus) Conflict Dynamics Profile, Individual Version: Development Guide, 2005; Test your EQ: Find Out How Emotionally Intelligent You Really Are, 2005. **Address:** Department of Psychology, Eckerd College, Continuing Education Ctr., 4200 54th Ave. S, St. Petersburg, FL 33733, U.S.A. **Online address:** davismh@eckerd.edu

DAVIS, Martyn P(aul). British (born England), b. 1929. **Genres:** Communications/Media, Advertising/Public Relations, Business/Trade/Industry. **Career:** Inter-Varsity Club, trustee; Buland Publishing Co., publicity controller, 1953-56; Robert Brandon & Partners, associate director, 1956-58; T. Booth Waddicor and Partners, senior executive, 1958-60; College for the Distributive Trades, head of marketing services, 1960-88; marketing communications consultant, 1989-. Writer. **Publications:** (Ed.) Impact Yellow Book, 1957; A Career in Advertising, 1963; Handbook for Media Representatives, 1967; The Effective Use of Advertising Media, 1981, 5th ed., 1996; Business to Business Marketing and Promotion, 1990; (with K. Davis) Families: A Handbook Of Concepts And Techniques For The Helping Professional, 1995; Successful

Advertising: Key Alternative Approaches, 1997. **Address:** 1 Pk. Steps, St. George's Fields, Albion St., London, GL W2 2YQ, England.

DAVIS, Matthew J. American (born United States), b. 1977?. **Genres:** Autobiography/Memoirs, Children's Fiction. **Career:** Gotham Writer's Workshop, writing instructor. Memoirist and journalist. **Publications:** The Magic Horse Fiddle (for children), 2002; When Things Get Dark: A Mongolian Winter's Tale (memoir), 2010. Contributor to periodicals. **Address:** Washington, DC , U.S.A. **Online address:** matthew.davis.j@gmail.com

DAVIS, Mildred (B.). American (born United States), b. 1930?. **Genres:** Mystery/Crime/Suspense, Novels. **Career:** Writer. **Publications:** The Room Upstairs, 1948; They Buried a Man, 1953; Suicide Hour (novella), 1954; The Dark Place, 1955; The Voice on the Telephone, 1964; The Sound of Insects, 1966; Strange Corner, 1967; Walk into Yesterday, 1967 as Nightmare of Murder, 1969; The Third Half, 1969; Three Minutes to Midnight, 1972; The Invisible Boarder, 1974; Tell Them What's-Her-Name Called, 1975; Scorpion, 1977; (with K. Davis) Lucifer Land (historical novel), 1977. MURDER IN MAINE SERIES WITH K. ROOME: The Avenging of Nevah Wright, 2006; The Fly Man Murders, 2007; The Butterfly Effect, 2008. **Address:** McIntosh & Otis Inc., 353 Lexington Ave., New York, NY 10016, U.S.A. **Online address:** md1@mildreddavis.com

DAVIS, Nageeba. American (born United States) **Genres:** Mystery/Crime/Suspense, Young Adult Fiction, Horror. **Career:** Antelope Trails Elementary School, International Baccalaureate Program, coordinator. Writer. **Publications:** MAGGIE KEAN MYSTERY SERIES: A Dying Art (mystery fiction), 2001; An Opening for Murder (mystery fiction), 2002. **Address:** c/o Author Mail, Berkeley Prime Crime, Penguin Publishing Group, 375 Hudson St., New York, NY 10014-3658, U.S.A. **Online address:** ndavis@d20.co.edu

DAVIS, Nancy Yaw. American (born United States), b. 1936. **Genres:** Anthropology/Ethnology, Literary Criticism And History, Business/Trade/Industry, History, Politics/Government, Social Sciences. **Career:** Alaska Methodist University, instructor, 1960-62; Anchorage Community College, lecturer, 1963-67, 1970, assistant professor, 1971-72; University of Alaska, assistant professor, 1972-75; Cultural Dynamics, president, 1976-89, sole proprietor, 1989-. Writer. **Publications:** Steps toward Understanding Rapid Culture Change in Native Rural Alaska, 1976; Historical Indicators of Alaska Native Culture Change, 1978; Kodiak Native Sociocultural Impacts, 1979; A Sociocultural Description of Small Communities in the Kodiak-Shumag in Region, 1986; (with R.P. McConochie and D.R. Stevenson) Research and Consulting as a Business, 1987; (comp. and ed. with W.E. Davis) Adventures through Time: Readings in the Anthropology of Cook Inlet, Alaska, 1996; The Zuni Enigma: A Native American People's Possible Japanese Connection, 2000; And the City Came All Around, All Around, 2003; Do Something Respectable, 2004; Priests across the Pacific, 2005. Contributor to journals and periodicals. **Address:** Cultural Dynamics, 719 N St., Ste. 3, Anchorage, AK 99501, U.S.A. **Online address:** nydavis@gci.net

DAVIS, Patrick. British (born England), b. 1925. **Genres:** Travel/Exploration, Autobiography/Memoirs, History, Animals/Pets. **Career:** CMS Bookshops, bookseller, 1952-55; Oxford University Press, publicity and sales, 1955-59; J.M. Dent & Sons Ltd., publicity manager and editor, 1959-64; University of London, London School of Economics and Political Science, publications officer, 1964-91. **Publications:** (As Patrick David Channer Davis with A.A. Dent) Animals That Changed The World, 1966; A Child at Arms, 1970, rev. ed., 1986; An Experience of Norway (travel), 1974: It's a Mind Thing, 1993; (with S. Gilmore) A Connecticut Yankee in the 8th Gurkha Rifles: A Burma Memoir, 1995. **Address:** Bolt & Watson Ltd., 8 Storey's Gate, London, GL SW1P 3AT, England. **Online address:** mary.patrick.davis@talk21.com

DAVIS, Peter G(raffam). American (born United States), b. 1936. **Genres:** Music, Biography, Art/Art History. **Career:** New York Times, staff writer, 1969-81; New York (magazine), music critic, 1981-. **Publications:** The American Opera Singer: The Lives and Adventures of America's Great Singers in Opera and Concert, From 1825 to the Present, 1997. Contributor to periodicals. **Address:** New York Magazine, 444 Madison Ave., 4th Fl., New York, NY 10022, U.S.A. **Online address:** pgdavis@aol.com

DAVIS, Philip Maurice. British (born England) **Genres:** Novels. **Career:** University of Liverpool, professor. Writer. **Publications:** Memory and Writing: From Wordsworth to Lawrence, 1983; In Mind of Johnson: A Study of

Johnson the Rambler, 1989; The Experience of Reading, 1992; Experimental Essays on the Novels of Bernard Malamud: Malamud's People, 1995; Sudden Shakespeare: The Shaping of Shakespeare's Creative Thought, 1996; Real Voices on Reading, 1997; The Oxford English Literary History: Volume 8, 1830-1880: The Victorians, 2002; The Human Sentence: The Life and Work of Bernard Malamud, 1914-1986, 2007; Bernard Malamud: A Writer's Life, 2007; Shakespeare Thinking, 2007. **Address:** School of English, University of Liverpool, Cypress Bldg., Chatham St., Liverpool, L69 7ZR, England. **Online address:** p.m.davis@liverpool.ac.uk

DAVIS, Pierre. See OUELLETTE, Pierre.

DAVIS, Rachel. See JAMES, Deana.

DAVIS, Richard. American (born United States), b. 1955. **Genres:** Politics/Government, Communications/Media, Law. **Career:** Brigham Young University, Department of Political Science, professor of political science. Writer. **Publications:** (Ed.) Politics and the Media, 1994; Decisions and Images: The Supreme Court and the Press, 1994; The Press and American Politics: The New Mediator, 2nd ed., 1996, 3rd ed., 2001; (with D. Owen) New Media and American Politics, 1998; The Web of Politics: The Internet's Impact on the American Political System, 1999; (with B. Bimber) Campaigning Online: The Internet in U.S. Elections, 2003; Politics Online: Blogs, Chatrooms, and Discussion Groups in American Democracy, 2005; Electing Justice: Fixing the Supreme Court Nomination Process, 2005; Typing Politics: The Role of Blogs in American Politics, 2009; Justices and Journalists: The U.S. Supreme Court and the Media, 2011. **Address:** Department of Political Science, Brigham Young University, 754 SWKT, Provo, UT 84602, U.S.A. **Online address:** richard_davis@byu.edu

DAVIS, Richard A. (Richard Albert Davis). American (born United States), b. 1937. **Genres:** Earth Sciences. **Career:** Western Michigan University, Department of Geology, faculty, 1965-73; University of South Florida, Department of Geology, faculty, 1973-, distinguished research professor, now emeritus distinguished research professor. Writer. **Publications:** (Co-author) Field Trip Guide Book for Cambrian-Ordovician Geology of Western Wisconsin, 1970; Principles of Oceanography, 1972, 2nd ed., 1977; (ed.) Beach and Nearshore Sedimentation, 1976; (with B.C. Delporte and M.A.R. Marsden) Morphology, Surface Facies and Sediment Distribution, 1977; (ed.) Coastal Sedimentary Environments, 1978, 2nd rev. ed., 1985; Depositional Systems: A Genetic Approach to Sedimentary Geology, 1983, 2nd ed., 1992; (ed. with B. Greenwood) Hydrodynamics and Sedimentation in Wave-Dominated Coastal Environments, 1984; Oceanography: An Introduction to the Marine Environment, 1987, 2nd ed., 1991; (with J.C. Gibeaut) Historical Morphodynamics of Inlets in Florida: Models for Coastal Zone Planning, 1990; (ed.) Geology of Holocene Barrier Island Systems, 1994; The Evolving Coast, 1994; Geology of Holocene Barrier Island Systems, 1994; Coasts, 1996; (with D.M. FitzGerald) Beaches and Coasts, 2004; Sea-level Changes in the Gulf of Mexico, 2011. **Address:** Department of Geology, University of South Florida, SCA 106, 4202 E Fowler Ave., Tampa, FL 33620, U.S.A. **Online address:** rdavis@cas.usf.edu

DAVIS, Richard Albert. See DAVIS, Richard A.

DAVIS, Richard Whitlock. American (born United States), b. 1935. **Genres:** History, Biography, Politics/Government. **Career:** The Making of Modern Freedom, general editor; Cambridge University, Christ's College, supervisor in history, 1960-62, distinguished visiting professor, 1981-82; University of Rhode Island, instructor, 1962-64; University of California, assistant professor, 1964-69; Washington University, Department of History, associate professor, 1969-73, chairman, 1974-77, professor of history, 1973-2003, emeritus professor, 2003-, Center for the History of Freedom, director, 1973-2003. **Publications:** Dissent in Politics, 1780-1830, 1971; Political Change and Continuity, 1760-1885: A Buckinghamshire Study, 1972; (with F.C. Davis) Somers: The History of a Connecticut Town, 1973; Disraeli, 1976; The English Rothschilds, 1983; (co-author) 1984, Orwell's and Ours, 1984; A Political History of the House of Lords, 1811-1846: From the Regency to Corn Law Repeal, 2008; The Grenvilles, A Great Political Family, forthcoming. EDITOR: (with R.J. Helmstadter) Religion and Irreligion in Victorian Society, 1992; Lords of Parliament: Studies, 1714-1914, 1995; The Origins of Modern Freedom in the West, 1995; Leaders in the Lords: Government Management and Party Organization in the Upper Chamber, 1765-1902, 2003; (with C. Jones and P. Salmon) Partisan Politics, Principle and Reform

in Parliament and the Constituencies, 1689-1880: Essays in Memory of John A. Phillips, 2005. Contributor of articles to journals. **Address:** Department of History, Washington University, Rm. 113, Busch Hall, Academy Bldg., 1 Brookings Dr., PO Box 1062, St. Louis, MO 63130-4899, U.S.A. **Online address:** rwdavis@wustl.edu

DAVIS, Robert C. American (born United States), b. 1948?. **Genres:** History, Social Sciences, Autobiography/Memoirs, History. **Career:** Ohio State University, associate professor, professor of Italian Renaissance and early modern Mediterranean history. Writer. **Publications:** Shipbuilders of the Venetian Arsenal: Workers and Workplace in the Preindustrial City, 1991; The War of the Fists: Popular Culture and Public Violence in Late Renaissance Venice, 1994; (ed. with J.C. Brown) Gender and Society in Renaissance Italy, 1998; (ed. with B. Ravid) The Jews of Early Modern Venice, 2001; Christian Slaves, Muslim Masters: White Slavery in the Mediterranean, the Barbary Coast and Italy, 1500-1800, 2003; (with G.R. Marvin) Venice, The Tourist Maze: A Cultural Critique of the World's Most Touristed City, 2004; Holy War and Human Bondage, 2009; (with B. Lindsmith) Renaissance People: Lives That Shaped the Modern Age, 2011. **Address:** Department of History, Ohio State University, 248 Dulles Hall, 230 W 17th Ave., Columbus, OH 43210, U.S.A. **Online address:** davis.711@osu.edu

DAVIS, Robin W(orks). American (born United States), b. 1962. **Genres:** Education, Language/Linguistics, Art/Art History, Children's Fiction, Information Science/Computers, Social Sciences. **Career:** Richardson Public Library, youth services librarian, 1987-91; Hurst Public Library, youth services librarian, 1991-. Consultant and workshop presenter. Writer. **Publications:** Creature Features, 1989; Camp Wanna Read, 1991; Promoting Reading with Reading Programs: A How-to-do-it Manual, 1992; An Alphabet of Books: Literature-Based Activities for Schools and Libraries, 1995; An Alphabet of Authors, 1996; Art Information through Children's Literature, 1995; Art and Children: Using Literature to Expand Creativity, 1996; Toddle on Over: Developing Infant and Toddler Literature Programs, 1998; Big Books for Little Readers, 1999; Multimedia Storytimes, 2000. **Address:** 901 Precinct Line Rd., Hurst, TX 76053, U.S.A.

DAVIS, Rocio G. Spanish (born Spain), b. 1964?. **Genres:** Autobiography/Memoirs, History, Human Relations/Parenting. **Career:** University of Navarra, assistant professor of English and American Literature, 1992-2004, associate professor of English and American literature, 2004-, Department of Modern Languages, assistant director, 1993-98, director, 1998-2001, Department of Humanities, assistant director, 1998-2000, Diploma of English and American Studies, director, 1998-, Institute of Liberal Arts, director, 2005-, School of Philosophy, Linguistics Department of Spanish and Modern Languages, assistant professor, associate professor, department head; University of Illinois, visiting professor of Asian American literature, 2000-01; City University of Hong Kong, Department of English, professor. Writer. **Publications:** Transcultural Reinventions: Asian American and Asian Canadian Short-Story Cycles, 2001; Begin Here: Reading Asian North American Autobiographies of Childhood, 2007; Relative Histories: Mediating History in Asian American Family Memoirs, 2011. EDITOR: (with R. Baena) Tricks with a Glass: Writing Ethnicity in Canada, 2000; (with R. Baena) Small Worlds: Transcultural Visions of Childhood, 2001; (with W. Boelhower and C. Birkle) Sites of Ethnicity: Europe and the Americas, 2004; (with S. Ludwig) Asian American Literature in the International Context: Readings on Fiction, Poetry, and Performance, 2004; (with S. Lee) Literary Gestures: The Aesthetic in Asian American Writing, 2005; (with J. Aurell and A.B. Delgado) Ethnic Life Writing and Histories: Genres, Performance, and Culture, 2007; (ed. with D. Fischer-Hornung and J.C. Kardux) Aesthetic Practices and Politics in Media, Music, and Art: Performing Migration, 2010. **Address:** Department of Modern Languages, University of Navarra, Edificio Library Bldg., Navarra, 31080, Spain. **Online address:** rgdavis@unav.es

DAVIS, R(oland) P(arker) Stephen. American (born United States), b. 1951. **Genres:** Archaeology/Antiquities, History, Local History/Rural Topics. **Career:** University of North Carolina, archaeological laboratory assistant, 1971-74, Research Laboratories of Archaeology, archaeologist I-II, 1983-88, research archaeologist, 1988-2000, acting director, 1999-2000, associate director, 2000-, adjunct professor of anthropology, 2001-, North Carolina Archaeology, editor, 1997-; University of Calgary, teaching assistant in archaeology, 1974-75, research assistant in archaeology, 1975-76; Wright State University, Archaeological Field School, instructor, 1975; University of Tennessee, archaeological field supervisor, 1976, archaeological laboratory assistant, 1979-80, research associate in archaeology, 1980-82; West Virginia Antiquities Commission, staff archaeologist, 1976-77; West Virginia Geological Survey, staff archaeologist, 1977-78; U.S. Forest Service, cultural resource paraprofessional training instructor, 1979; Southern Indian Studies, secretary and editor, 1988-91, editor, 1994-96; Southeastern Archaeology, editor, 1990-93. **Publications:** Bibliography of West Virginia Archeology, 1978; 1975 Excavations at the Wiser-Stephens I Site, 1978; (contrib.) Structure and Process in Southeastern Archaeology, 1985; (ed. wiith R.S. Dickens, Jr. And H.T. Ward) The Siouan Project: Seasons I and II, 1987; (contrib.) The Evolution of Ranked Agricultural Societies in the Eastern Woodlands, 1990; Aboriginal Settlement Patterns in the Little Tennessee River Valley, 1990; (with H.T. Ward) Indian Communities on the North Carolina Peidmont, AD 1000 to 1700, 1993; (contrib.) Handbook of North Carolina History, 1998; (with H.T. Ward) Time Before History: The Archaeology of North Carolina, 1999; (contrib.) Societies in Eclipse: Eastern North America at the Dawn of Civilization, 2001. Contributor to journals. **Address:** Research Laboratories of Archaeology, University of North Carolina, Alumni 101, PO Box 3120, Chapel Hill, NC 27599-3120, U.S.A. **Online address:** rpsdavis@unc.edu

DAVIS, Rose Parkman. (Rose Parkman Marshall). American (born United States), b. 1947. **Genres:** Poetry, Education, Librarianship, Bibliography, Genealogy/Heraldry, Local History/Rural Topics, Essays. **Career:** Jackson State University, instructor of English, 1970-72; high school English teacher, 1972-78; Tougaloo College, instructor in English and director of writing center, 1979-84; freelance writer, 1984-88; City of Jackson, Community Arts Program, coordinator, 1985-87; Mary Holmes College, reference and technical services librarian, 1989-91; Mississippi State University, branch librarian and assistant professor, 1991-95; Winthrop University, coordinator of library instruction and assistant professor, 1996-2000; University of South Carolina, coordinator of library instruction, 2000-05, library instruction coordinator, 2005-. Writer. **Publications:** Black History Every Month: Puzzles for Learning, 1982; A Guide to Training Peer Tutors, 1983; Women's Studies: Bibliographic Essay and List of Electronic Resources, 1994-95, 1995; (comp.) Zora Neale Hurston: An Annotated Bibliography and Reference Guide, 1997; (as Rose Parkman Marshall) Unbuckle My Soul, 2004; The Family History of Richard (Ex-Slave) and Mary Bridges Parkman, 2005; The Genealogy of James Houston and Mattie Moore Oatis, 2006; Possession! (poems), forthcoming; First Class: Audre Lorde, Warrior Poet, forthcoming. Contributor to periodicals. **Address:** PO Box 4528, Columbia, SC 29240-4528, U.S.A. **Online address:** rosem@gwm.sc.edu

DAVIS, Sampson. American (born United States), b. 1973. **Genres:** Biography, Autobiography/Memoirs, Children's Non-fiction, Science Fiction/Fantasy. **Career:** Beth Israel Medical Center, resident; St. Michael's Medical Center, emergency physician; Eaton Hospital, emergency physician; Raritan Bay Medical Center, assistant medical director of emergency department; Three Doctors Foundation, co-founder; Physician Recruitment for Physician Practice Enhancement, vice-president. Writer. **Publications:** (With G. Jenkins, R. Hunt and L.F. Page) The Pact: Three Young Men Make a Promise and Fulfill a Dream, 2002; (with G. Jenkins, R. Hunt and S.M. Draper) We Beat the Street: How a Friendship Pact Helped Us Succeed, 2005; (with G. Jenkins, R. Hunt and M. Bernstein) The Bond: Three Young Men Learn to Forgive and Reconnect with Their Fathers, 2007. **Address:** Three Doctors L.L.C., 65 Hazelwood Ave., Newark, NJ 07106, U.S.A. **Online address:** drdavis@threedoctors.com

DAVIS, Shelley L(orraine). American (born United States), b. 1956. **Genres:** History. **Career:** Office of Air Force History, historian, 1979; Air Force Communications Command, historian, 1980-82; Air Force Logistics Command, historian, 1982-83; Air Force Space Communications Division, historian, 1983-84; Tactical Air Command, historian, 1984-87; Defense Mapping Agency, historian, 1987-88; Internal Revenue Service, historian, 1988-95; freelance writer, 1996-; Stars and Stripes, historian, 2000-. **Publications:** History of the Memphis Service Center: Yesterday, Today and Tomorrow, 1972-1992, 1992; Unbridled Power: Inside the Secret Culture of the IRS, 1997. Contributor to periodicals. **Address:** 6203 Sierra Ct., Manassas, VA 20111, U.S.A. **Online address:** shelley@stripes.com

DAVIS, Steven J(oseph). American (born United States), b. 1957. **Genres:** Business/Trade/Industry, Economics, Mathematics/Statistics, Literary Criticism And History, Science Fiction/Fantasy. **Career:** Brown University, teaching fellow, 1983-85; University of Chicago, assistant professor, 1985-89, associate professor, 1989-94, professor of economics, 1994-, William H. Abbott professor of international business and economics, 1994-; Stanford Univer-

sity, national fellow, 1988-89; University of Maryland at College Park, visiting associate professor, 1990; Federal Reserve Bank of Chicago, consultant and research associate of corporate studies group, 1991-93; Massachusetts Institute of Technology, visiting associate professor, 1993-94; Chicago Partners (consulting firm), principal, 1995-2006; Chicago Economics and Finance Experts, president; American Economic Journal: Macroeconomics, editor, 2006-07; CRA Intl., senior consultant, vice president, 2007; John McCain Presidential Campaign 2008, economic adviser, 2007-08; National University of Singapore, distinguished visitor, 2009; Brookings Papers on Economic Activity, senior adviser, 2010-; U.S. Congressional Budget Office, panel on economic adviser, 2010-. **Publications:** (With J.C. Haltiwanger and S. Schuh) Job Creation and Destruction, 1996; (contrib.) Labor Economics, Employment Policy, and Job Creation, 1996; (with M. Henrekson) Foeretagandets Villkor: Spelregler foer sysselsaettning och tillvaext, 1996; (contrib.) The Welfare State in Transition, 1997; (contrib.) Labor Statistics Measurement Issues, 1998; (with M. Henrekson) Tax Effects on Work Activity, Industry Mix and Shadow Economy Size: Evidence from Rich-Country Comparisons, 2004; (with R.J. Faberman and J.C. Haltiwanger) The Flow Approach to Labor Markets: New Data Sources, Micro-Macro Links and the Recent Downturn, 2005; (with L. Rivera-Batiz) The Climate for Business Development and Employment Growth in Puerto Rico, 2005; Measuring The Dynamics of Young and Small Businesses, 2007; Sivad and Chorn: The Adventures Begin, 2009; (co-author) Private Equity and Employment, 2009; e Sweden and the United States, forthcoming. Contributor to journals. **Address:** Graduate School of Business, University of Chicago, 5807 S Woodlawn Ave., Chicago, IL 60637, U.S.A. **Online address:** steve.davis@chicagobooth.edu

DAVIS, Steven L. American (born United States), b. 1963. **Genres:** History. **Career:** Texas State University-San Marcos, assistant curator, 1997-; University of Texas Press, series editor, 2006-. **Publications:** Texas Literary Outlaws: Six Writers in the Sixties and Beyond, 2004; (ed. with B. Cunningham and R.K. Newsom) Lone Star Sleuths: An Anthology of Texas Crime Fiction, 2007; (ed.) Land of the Permanent Wave: An Edwin Bud Shrake Reader (anthology), 2008; J. Frank Dobie: A Liberated Mind, 2009. **Address:** Wittliff Collections, Alkek Library, Texas State University-San Marcos, 601 University Dr., San Marcos, TX 78666-4604, U.S.A. **Online address:** sdtx@sbcglobal.net

DAVIS, Val. See IRVINE, Angela.

DAVIS, Wendi. See HOLDER, Nancy L.

DAVISON, Carol Margaret. Canadian/Scottish (born Scotland), b. 1963. **Genres:** Literary Criticism And History, Bibliography. **Career:** Concordia University, lecturer in English, 1991-98; McGill University, lecturer in English, 1998-99; University of Toronto, assistant professor of English, 1999-2000; University of Windsor, assistant professor of English, 2000-, Women's Studies Program, acting director. Writer. **Publications:** (ed.) Bram Stoker's Dracula: Sucking through the Century, 1897-1997, 1997; (contrib.) Gothic Writers: A Critical and Bibliographical Guide, 2001; Anti-Semitism and British Gothic Literature, 2004; British Gothic Literature, 1764-1824, 2009. Contributor to periodicals. **Address:** Dt of English Language, Lit, and Creative Writing, University of Windsor, 2-104 Chrysler Hall N, Windsor, ON N9B 3P4, Canada. **Online address:** cdavison@uwindsor.ca

DAVISON, Eddy W. American (born United States), b. 1955?. **Genres:** Military/Defense/Arms Control, History. **Career:** Federal Bureau of Prisons, Department of Justice, officer, 1985-91, Special Operations and Response Team, staff, through, 1987, senior officer specialist, through 1991; Ottawa University, criminal justice instructor, 1993-, adjunct professor of history; International Institute of the Americas, criminal justice teacher. Writer. **Publications:** (With D. Foxx) Nathan Bedford Forrest: In Search of the Enigma, 2007. Contributor to periodicals. **Address:** Ottawa University, 10020 N 25th Ave., Phoenix, AZ 85021, U.S.A.

DAVISON, Liam. (Liam Patrick Davison). Australian (born Australia), b. 1957. **Genres:** Novels, Novellas/Short Stories, Young Adult Non-fiction, History, Travel/Exploration, Reference. **Career:** Freelance writer, 1988-; Peninsula College of Technical and Further Education, instructor in creative writing; Chisholm Institute of Technology, instructor in creative writing. **Publications:** NOVELS: The Velodrome, 1988; Soundings, 1993; The White Woman, 1994; The Betrayal, 1999; Florilegium, 2001. OTHERS: The Shipwreck Party (short stories), 1989; The Spirit of Rural Australia, 1999; Collected Stories, 2001. **Address:** Penguin Group, 250 Camberwell Rd., PO Box 701, Camberwell, VI 3124, Australia.

DAVISON, Liam Patrick. *See* **DAVISON, Liam.**

DAVISON, Peter (Hobley). British (born England), b. 1926. **Genres:** Literary Criticism And History, Bibliography, Autobiography/Memoirs. **Career:** University of Birmingham's Shakespeare Institute, fellow, 1964-65, 1971-72; University of Birmingham, lecturer, 1965-70, senior lecturer, 1970-73; St. David's University College, professor of English, 1973-79; University of Kent, professor of English and American literature, 1979-85; University of Leeds, Cecil Oldman lecturer, 1984; Westfield College, visiting professor in performing arts, 1986-89; De Montfort University, research professor, 1992-2001, senior research professor, acting head of department, 1994-95; OBE, 1999; North East Wales Institute of Higher Education, research professor, 2001-. Writer. **Publications:** Futures Valuing of Greasy Wool Clips, 1961; The Contexts of English: An Inaugural Lecture Delivered at Saint David's University College, Lampeter on 22 May 1975, 1975; The Seven Deceits (dance drama), 1978; Henry V in the Context of the Popular Dramatic Tradition (monograph), 1981; Contemporary Drama and the Popular Dramatic Tradition in England, 1982; Popular Appeal in English Drama to 1850, 1982; Hamlet: Text and Performance, 1983; Sheridan: A Case Book, 1986; Henry V: Masterguide, 1986; (comp. and contrib.) Pelican Guide to American Literature, 1987; Othello: The Critical Debate, 1988; George Orwell: A Literary Life, 1996; (comp.) The Lost Orwell: Being a Supplement to The Complete Works of George Orwell, 2006. EDITOR: Merchant of Venice, 1967; Dutch Courtesan, 1968; Songs of the British Music Hall, 1971; (and contrib.) New Cambridge Bibliography of English Literature, 1900-1950, 1972; (and contrib.) Theatrum Redivivum, 17 vols., 1972; Second Part of King Henry the Fourth, 1977; (and contrib.) Year's Work in English Studies, 1984-85; Nineteen Eighty-Four: The Facsimile of the Extant Manuscript, 1984; Book Encompassed: Studies in Twentieth-Century Bibliography, 1992; First Quarto of King Richard III, 1996; The Complete Works of George Orwell, vol. XX, 1998; Our Job is to make Life Worth Living: 1949-50, 2002; It is What I Think: 1947-48, 2002; Diaries, 2009. EDITOR WITH R. MEYERSOHN AND E. SHILS: Literary Taste, Culture and Mass Communication, vol. XIV, 1978-80; Literature and Society, 1978; Mass Media and Mass Communication, 1978; Sociology of Literature, 1978; Theatre and Song, 1978; Uses of Literacy: Media, 1978; Art and Changing Civilization, 1978; Art and Social Life, 1978; Bookselling, Reviewing, and Reading, 1978; Content and Taste: Religion and Myth, 1978; Cultural Debate, 1978; Writer and Politics, 1978; Orwell in Spain, 2001; Orwell and Politics, 2001; Orwell and the Dispossessed, 2001; Orwell's England, 2001; Service for Worship, 2001. Contributor to periodicals. **Address:** c/o Bill Hamilton, A M Heath & Company Ltd., 6 Warwick Ct., Holborn, GL WC1R 5DJ, England.

DAWE, (Donald) Bruce. Australian (born Australia), b. 1930. **Genres:** Poetry, Novellas/Short Stories. **Career:** Downlands College, faculty, 1968-71; University of Southern Queensland, Darling Downs Institute of Advanced Education, lecturer in literature, 1971-78, senior lecturer and teaching fellow, 1979-89, associate professor, 1990-93, now emeritus professor. Freelance writer. **Publications:** No Fixed Address, 1962; A Need of Similar Name, 1965; An Eye for a Tooth: Poems, 1968; Beyond the Subdivision: Poems, 1969; Heat-wave, 1970; Condolences of the Season, 1971; Bruce Dawe Reads from His Own Work, 1971; Just a Dugong at Twilight, 1975; Sometimes Gladness: Collected Poems 1954-1978, 1978, 5th ed. as Sometimes Gladness: Collected Poems 1954 to 1997, 1997; Over Here, Harv! and Other Stories, 1983; Towards Sunrise: Poems 1979-1986, 1986; This Side of Silence: Poems, 1987-1990, 1990; Bruce Dawe: Essays and Opinions, 1990; Tributary Streams, 1992; Mortal Instruments: Poems, 1990-1995, 1995; A Poet's People, 1999; Hier und anderswo: ausgewählte Gedichte, 2003. EDITOR: Dimensions, 1975; Speaking in Parables: A Reader, 1987. Contributor to periodicals. **Address:** Darling Downs Institute of Advanced Education, University of Southern Queensland, Toowoomba, QL 1, Australia.

DAWE, Margaret. American (born United States), b. 1957. **Genres:** Criminology/True Crime, Young Adult Fiction. **Career:** East Hampton Star, reporter, 1981-86; Brooklyn College, adjunct lecturer, 1986-93; Wichita State University, assistant professor, 1993-99, associate professor, 1999-, chair, 2001-, professor, director of creative writing. Writer. **Publications:** Nissequott, 1992; The Geography of Hope, forthcoming. **Address:** Departmentt of English, Wichita State University, 1845 Fairmount St., Wichita, KS 67260-

0014, U.S.A. **Online address:** margaret.dawe@wichita.edu

DAWE, R(oger) D(avid). British (born England), b. 1934?. **Genres:** Classics, Literary Criticism And History, Poetry. **Career:** Cambridge University, Caius College, research fellow, 1957-63; Trinity College, teaching fellow, 1963-, senior research fellow, 1998-2001. Writer and editor. **Publications:** Collation and Investigation of Manuscripts of Aeschylus, 1964; Repertory of Conjectures on Aeschylus, 1965; Studies on the Text of Sophocles, 1973; EDITOR: Sophoclis Tragoediae, 1975; (ed. with J. Diggle and P.E. Easterling) Dionysiaca: Nine Studies in Greek Poetry, 1978; Oedipus Rex/Sophocles, 1982, 2nd ed., 2006; Sophocles: The Classical Heritage, 1996; Aiax/Sophoclis, 1996; Electra/Sophoclis: Tertium Edidit, 1996; Philogelos, 2000. **Address:** Trinity College, Cambridge University, Trinity St., Cambridge, CB CB2 1TQ, England.

DAWES, Casey. American (born United States), b. 1951. **Genres:** Romance/Historical, Novellas/Short Stories, Business/Trade/Industry. **Career:** American Telephone and Telegraph, manager, 1986-90; United Parcel Service (UPS), manager, 1990-94; RYC Inc., consultant, 1994-98; International DB2 Users Group, president, 1996-98; International Business Machines Co. (IBM), manager, 1998-2005; Wise Woman Shining, small business coach and consultant. 2003-. Writer. **Publications:** Exploring IBM E-Business Software: Become an Instant Insider on IBM's Internet Business Tools, 2001, 2nd ed., 2003; Mountain Vines, Mountain Wines: Exploring the Wineries of the Santa Cruz Mountains, 2003; From the Highlands to the Sea: Exploring the Wineries of Monterey County, 2005; Ariel Wines, 2006. Contributor to periodicals. **Address:** c/o Author Mail, Wise Woman Shining, 715 Walker Dr., Missoula, MT 59804, U.S.A. **Online address:** casey@wisewomanshining.com

DAWES, Edna. Also writes as Emma Drummond, Eva Dane, Elizabeth Darrell. British (born England), b. 1931. **Genres:** Novels. **Career:** Writer. **Publications:** Dearest Tiger, 1975; Pink Snow, 1975; A Hidden Heart of Fire, 1976; Burn All Your Bridges, 1976; Fly with My Love, 1978; The Burning Land, 1979; The Rice Dragon, 1980; Beyond All Frontiers, 1983; Scarlet Shadows, 1984; Forget the Glory, 1985; The Bridge of a Hundred Dragons, 1986; A Captive Freedom, 1987; Some Far Elusive Dawn, 1991; That Sweet and Savage Land, 1991; A Question of Honour, 1992; Concerto, 1993; We Will Remember, 1996; A Distant Hero, 1997; Act of Valour, 1998; Flight to Anywhere, 2001; Unsung Heroes, 2001; Shadows over the Sun, 2005; Russian Roulette, 2005. AS ELIZABETH DARRELL: The Jade Alliance, 1979; The Gathering Wolves, 1980; At the Going Down of the Sun, 1985; And in the Morning, 1986; The Flight of the Flamingo, 1989. AS EMMA DRUMMOND: Scarlet Shadows, 1978; Burning Land, 1979; The Rice Dragon, 1980; Beyond All Frontiers, 1983; Forget the Glory, 1985; The Bridge of a Hundred Dragons, 1986; T A Captive Freedom, 1987; Some Far Elusive Dawn, 1991; That Sweet and Savage Land, 1991; A Question of Honour, 1992; A Distant Hero, 1997; Act of valour, 1998. AS EVA DANE: A Lion by the Mane, 1975; Shadows in the Fire, 1975; The Vaaldorp Diamond, 1978. Contributor to periodicals. **Address:** St. Martins Press, 175 5th Ave., New York, NY 10010, U.S.A.

DAWES, Gregory W. New Zealander (born New Zealand), b. 1957. **Genres:** History, Theology/Religion. **Career:** University of Otago, teaching fellow, 1994-96, lecturer, 1997-2000, senior lecturer, 2001-, part-time associate professor in religious studies. Writer. **Publications:** The Body in Question: Metaphor and Meaning in the Interpretation of Ephesians 5: 21-33, 1998; (ed.) The Historical Jesus Quest: Landmarks in the Search for the Jesus of History, 1999; The Historical Jesus Question: The Challenge of History to Religious Authority, 2001; Introduction to the Bible, 2007; Theism and Explanation, 2009. Contributor of articles to books and periodicals. **Address:** Department of Theology and Religion, University of Otago, Rm. 4S10, Burns Arts Bldg., 4th Fl., PO Box 56, Dunedin, 9001, New Zealand. **Online address:** gregory.dawes@otago.ac.nz

DAWICK, John. British/New Zealander (born New Zealand), b. 1934. **Genres:** Biography, Literary Criticism And History. **Career:** Massey University, lecturer, senior lecturer in English, 1964-95. Writer. **Publications:** Pinero: A Theatrical Life, 1993; Late Victorian Theatre: Gilbert, Pinero, Wilde, and Shaw, forthcoming. Contributor to periodicals. **Address:** 130 Acaster Ln., Bishopthorpe, York, NY YO2 1TD, England. **Online address:** dawickjohn@hotmail.com

DAWID, Annie. American (born United States), b. 1960. **Genres:** Novels, Novellas/Short Stories, Photography, Writing/Journalism, Film, Ethics. **Ca-**

reer: San Francisco Phoenix, copy editor, 1982; Denver Quarterly, managing editor, 1988-89; University of North Dakota, assistant professor of English, 1989-90; Lewis and Clark College, professor of English, director of creative writing, 1990-2006; Custer County High School, AP English instructor, 2005-; BloomsburyWest, founder, 2006-; Poetica magazine, Canon Beat Literary, page editor, 2009-, short story editor, 2010. **Publications:** York Ferry (novel), 1993; Lily in the Desert (short stories), 2002; And Darkness was Under His Feet: Stories of a Family, 2009; Paradise Undone: A Novel of Jonestown, forthcoming. Contributor to periodicals. **Address:** PO Box 1637, Westcliffe, CO 81252, U.S.A. **Online address:** annie@anniedawid.com

DAWIDOFF, Nicholas. American (born United States), b. 1962. **Genres:** Travel/Exploration, Sports/Fitness, Biography. **Career:** Sports Illustrated, staff writer. general assignment reporter, 1985-91; freelance writer, 1989-; Princeton University, Anschutz distinguished fellow, 2008, Department of English, visiting professor. **Publications:** The Catcher Was a Spy: The Mysterious Life of Moe Berg, 1994; In the Country of Country: People and Places in American Music, 1997; The Fly Swatter: How My Grandfather Made His Way in the World, 2002; (ed.) Baseball: A Literary Anthology, 2002; The Crowd Sounds Happy: A Story of Love, Madness and Baseball, 2008. Contributor to periodicals. **Address:** Department of English, Princeton University, 22 McCosh Hall, Princeton, NJ 08544, U.S.A. **Online address:** dawidoff@princeton.edu

DAWN, Marva J. American (born United States), b. 1948. **Genres:** Theology/Religion. **Career:** University of Idaho, instructor in English, 1970-72, campus minister, 1972-75; Washington State University, campus minister, 1972-75; Concordia Lutheran Church, director of youth and education, 1972-75; Lutheran church, director of special ministries, 1976-79; Christians Equipped for Ministry, co-founder, 1979, director of teaching and writing ministry, 1979-; Regent College, adjunct professor of spiritual theology, teaching fellow in spiritual theology; Western Evangelical Seminary, visiting professor, 1981; Pittsburgh Theological Seminary, Schaff lecturer, 2000. Writer. **Publications:** To Walk and Not Faint, 1980, rev. ed., 1997; To Walk in the Kingdom, 1982; I'm Lonely, Lord-How Long?, 1983, rev. ed., 1998; Keeping the Sabbath Wholly, 1989; The Hilarity of Community, 1992, as Truly the Community, 1997; Sexual Character, 1993; Joy in Our Weakness, 1994, rev. ed., 2002; Reaching Out without Dumbing Down, 1995; Is It a Lost Cause?, 1997; A Royal Waste of Time, 1999; (with E.H. Peterson) The Unnecessary Pastor, 2000; Powers, Weakness, and the Tabernacle of God, 2001; Morning by Morning, 2001; How Shall We Worship?, 2003; Unfettered Hope, 2003; Talking the Walk: Letting Christian Language Live Again, 2005; Corrupted Words Reclaimed, 2005; Joy in Divine Wisdom: Practices of Discernment from Other Cultures and Christian Traditions, 2006; Sense of the Call: A Sabbath Way of Life for Those Who Serve God, the Church, and the World, 2006; My Soul Waits: Solace for the Lonely from the Psalms, 2007; Being Well When We're Ill: Wholeness and Hope in Spite of Infirmity, 2008; In the Beginning, GOD: Creation, Culture, and the Spiritual Life, 2009. EDITOR and TRANSLATOR: G. von Rad, Holy War in Ancient Israel, 1991; Sources and Trajectories: Eight Early Articles by Jacques Ellul that Set the Stage, 1997. Works appear in anthologies. Contributor to periodicals. **Address:** Christians Equipped for Ministry, 304 N Fredericksburg Way, Vancouver, WA 98664, U.S.A.

DAWSON, Carol. American (born United States), b. 1951. **Genres:** Novels, Poetry, Business/Trade/Industry. **Career:** Jeweler, 1965-79. Writer and painter. **Publications:** Job (poems), 1975. NOVELS: The Waking Spell, 1992; Body of Knowledge, 1994; Meeting the Minotaur, 1997; The Mother-in-Law Diaries, 1999; (with C. Dawson) House of Plenty: The Rise, Fall and Revival of Luby's Cafeterias, 2006. Contributor to magazines. **Address:** Witherspoon Associates, 235 E 31st St., New York, NY 10016, U.S.A.

DAWSON, David. See **DAWSON, John David.**

DAWSON, Elizabeth. See **GEACH, Christine.**

DAWSON, George Glenn. American (born United States), b. 1925. **Genres:** Economics, Adult Non-fiction, Education, Business/Trade/Industry, Politics/Government, Reference. **Career:** RCA Communications, radio operator, 1947-55; New York University, part-time instructor, 1957-59, assistant professor, 1959-64, associate professor, 1964-65, professor of social studies, Division of Social Studies, head, Center for Economic Education, director, 1965-70; Peace Corps Somalia Project, director, 1962-64; Joint Council on

Economic Education, director of research and publications and managing editor of journal of economic education, 1970-75; Empire State College of the State University of New York, dean and professor of economics, 1975, now professor emeritus. Writer. **Publications:** Communism and Freedom, 1962; (with R. McClain) Collier Quick and Easy Guide to Economics, 1963; Economics: Book One, 1965, Book Two, 1965; (with McClain) Economics for Businessmen and Investors, 1966; (ed.) Economic Education Experiences of Enterprising Teachers, vol. IV-XV, 1966-78; College Level Economics, 1968; Our Nation's Wealth, 1968; Foundations of the American Economy, 1969; (with S. Gordon and J. Witchel) The American Economy, 1969; (with S.D. Gordon) Introductory Economics, 1972, 7th ed., 1991; (with E. Prehn) Teaching Economics in American History, 1973, 2nd ed., 1984; (with L. Leamer) Suggestions for a Basic Economics Library, 1973; (ed.) Economics and Our Community, 1973; (ed.) Government and the Economy, 1974; (with A.T. Nappi and W. Luksetich) Learning Economics Through Children's Stories, 1978. CONTRIBUTOR: Theory, Structure and Application, 1975; Foundations of Education for Business, 1975; Teaching Economics, 1975; Handbook on Contemporary Education, 1976; Perspective on Economic Education, 1977. OTHER: Foundations of the American Economy, 1969. **Address:** Department of Economics, Empire State College, State University of New York, PO Box 130, Old Westbury, NY 11568, U.S.A. **Online address:** gdawsonnabad@aol.com

DAWSON, Geralyn. American (born United States) **Genres:** Novels, Young Adult Fiction, Literary Criticism And History, Romance/Historical. **Career:** Author. **Publications:** NOVELS: The Texan's Bride, 1993; Capture the Night, 1993; Tempting Morality, 1995; The Wedding Raffle, 1996; The Bad Luck Wedding Dress, 1996; The Wedding Ransom, 1998; The Bad Luck Wedding Cake, 1998; The Kissing Stars, 1999; Simmer All Night, 1999; The Kissing Stars, 1999; Sizzle All Day, 2000; The Bad Luck Wedding Night, 2001; The Pink Magnolia Club, 2002; My Big Old Texas Heartache, 2003; My Long Tall Texas Heartthrob, 2004; Give Him the Slip, 2006; Never Say Never, 2007; Always Look Twice, 2008; The Loner, 2008. OTHERS: Her Bodyguard, 2005; Her Scoundrel, 2005; Her Outlaw, 2007. **Address:** Pocket Books, 1230 Ave. of the Americas, New York, NY 10020, U.S.A. **Online address:** geralyn@geralyndawson.com

DAWSON, Greg. American (born United States), b. 1949?. **Genres:** Young Adult Fiction. **Career:** Orlando Sentinel, television critic, 1986-94, state and local columnist, 1994-2000, consumer rights columnist, 2003-; Indianapolis Star, staff, 2000-03. Writer. **Publications:** Hiding in the Spotlight: A Musical Prodigy's Story of Survival, 1941-1946, 2009. Contributor to periodicals. **Address:** Orlando, FL , U.S.A. **Online address:** candycdawson@gmail.com

DAWSON, Janet. American (born United States), b. 1949. **Genres:** Mystery/Crime/Suspense. **Career:** U.S. Navy, journalist; University of California, faculty, Office of the President, staff; MWA NorCal, president. **Publications:** Kindred Crimes, 1990; Till the Old Men Die, 1993; Take a Number, 1993; Don't Turn Your Back on the Ocean, 1994; Nobody's Child, 1995; Credible Threat: A Jeri Howard Mystery, 1996; Witness to Evil, 1997; Where the Bodies are Buried, 1998; A Killing at the Track: A Jeri Howard Mystery, 2000; Scam and Eggs: Stories, 2002; Bit Player: A Jeri Howard Mystery, 2010. **Address:** Office of the President, University of California, 1111 Franklin St., 9th Fl., Oakland, CA 94607-5201, U.S.A. **Online address:** janet.dawson@ucop.edu

DAWSON, John David. (David Dawson). American (born United States), b. 1957?. **Genres:** Cultural/Ethnic Topics. **Career:** Haverford College, professor of religion, 1987-2011, provost, 2002-07, Constance and Robert MacCrate professor in social responsibility, through 2011, Humanities Center, director; Earlham College, president and professor of religion, 2011-. Writer. **Publications:** (As David Dawson) Allegorical Readers and Cultural Revision in Ancient Alexandria, 1992; (as David Dawson) Literary Theory, 1995; Christian Figural Reading and the Fashioning of Identity, 2002. **Address:** President's Office, Earlham College, 801 National Rd. W, Richmond, IN 47374-4095, U.S.A. **Online address:** davidd@earlham.edu

DAWSON, Melanie. American (born United States), b. 1967. **Genres:** Adult Non-fiction, Communications/Media, History. **Career:** College of William & Mary, Department of English, visiting assistant professor, assistant professor. Writer. **Publications:** (Ed. with S.H. Smith) The American 1890s: A Cultural Reader, 2000; Laboring to Play: Home Entertainment and the Spectacle of Middle-Class Cultural Life, 1850-1920, 2005. **Address:** Department of English, College of William & Mary, 316 Tyler Hall, 300 James Blair Dr., PO Box 8795, Williamsburg, VA 23185, U.S.A. **Online address:** mvdaws@wm.edu

DAWSON, Roger. American/British (born England), b. 1940. **Genres:** Business/Trade/Industry, How-to Books. **Career:** Real estate broker, 1976-82. Speaker, writer, 1982-. **Publications:** You Can Get Anything You Want, But You Have to Do More Than Ask, 1985; You Can Get Anything You Want: Secrets of Power Negotiating, 1987; Secrets of Power Persuasion, 1992; Secrets of Power Persuasion: Everthing You'll Ever Need to Get Anything You'll Ever Want, 1992; The Confident Decision Maker: How to Make the Right Business and Personal Decisions Every Time, 1993; The 13 Secrets of Power Performance, 1994; Roger Dawson's Secrets of Power Negotiating, 1995; Secrets of Power Negotiating for Salespeople: Inside Secrets from a Master Negotiator, 1999, 2nd ed., 2009; Secrets of Power Negotiating: Inside Secrets from a Master Negotiating from a Master Negotiator, 1999; Secrets of Power Persuasion for for Salespeople, 2003; (with M. Summey) Weekend Millionaire's Secrets to Investing in Real Estate, 2004; (with M. Summey) Weekend Millionaire Mindset, 2005; (with M. Summey) Weekend Millionaire Real Estate FAQ, 2006; Secrets of Power Salary Negotiating: Inside Secrets from a Master Negotiator, 2006; (with M. Summey) Weekend Millionaire Secrets to Negotiating Real Estate: How to Get the Best Deals to Build Your Fortune in Real Estate, 2008; Secrets of Power Problem Solving, 2011. **Address:** Power Negotiating Institute, 1045 East Rd., La Habra Heights, CA 90631, U.S.A. **Online address:** rogdawson@aol.com

DAY, Aidan. British (born England), b. 1952. **Genres:** Literary Criticism And History. **Career:** University of Hull, research fellow, 1978-79, lecturer in English, 1979-82; University of Edinburgh, lecturer in English literature, 1984-92, reader in English literature, 1992-99, professor of nineteenth century and contemporary literature, 1999-2001; University of Aarhus, professor of British literature and culture, 2001-07; University of Dundee, professor of English, 2007-. Writer. **Publications:** Bob Dylan: Escaping on the Run, 1984; Jokerman: Reading the Lyrics of Bob Dylan, 1988; Romanticism, 1996, 2nd ed., 2012; Angela Carter: The Rational Glass, 1998; Tennyson's Skepticism, 2005. EDITOR: (with C. Ricks) The Tennyson Archive, 31 vols., 1987-93; Robert Browning: Selected Poetry and Prose, 1991; Alfred Lord Tennyson: Selected Poems, 1991. Contributor of articles to periodicals. **Address:** School of Humanities, University of Dundee, Rm. 3.2 Tower Extension, George Sq, Dundee, DD1 4HN, Scotland. **Online address:** a.z.day@dundee.ac.uk

DAY, Alan. (Alan Edwin Day). British (born England), b. 1932. **Genres:** History, Archaeology/Antiquities, Bibliography, Education. **Career:** Oxford City Libraries, central lending librarian, 1962-65; Leeds Polytechnic, senior lecturer and principal lecturer, 1965-79; Manchester Polytechnic, head of department of library and information studies, 1979-90, now retired. Writer. **Publications:** The British Library: A Guide to Its Structure, Publications, Collections and Services, 1988; (ed. with P. Lea) Printed Reference Material and Related Sources of Information, 1990; (ed. with J.M. Harvey) Walfords Guide to Reference Material, vol. II: Social and Historical Sciences, 1990, 6th ed., 1994; (comp.) England, 1993; The New British Library, 1994; (comp.) The Falkland Islands, South Georgia and the South Sandwich Islands, 1996; (comp.) St. Helena, Ascension and Tristan da Cunha, 1997; Inside the British Library, 1998; (ed.) By Tram from Bruddersford: Papers Read to a Meeting of the J.B. Priestley Society at Bradford Central Library, 27th February 1999, 1999; A Supplement, 2001; Historical Dictionary of the Discovery and Exploration of Australia, 2003; Historical Dictionary of the Discovery and Exploration of the Northwest Passage, 2006. AS ALAN EDWIN DAY: History: A Reference Hand Book, 1977; Archaeology: A Reference Book, 1978; Discovery and Exploration: A Reference Handbook, 1980; J.B. Priestley: An Annotated Bibliography, 1980; Search for the Northwest Passage: An Annotated Bibliography, 1986. Contributor to journals. **Address:** ABC-Clio Press, 130 Cremona Dr., PO Box 1911, Santa Barbara, CA 93117, U.S.A.

DAY, Alan Edwin. *See* **DAY, Alan.**

DAY, Alexandra. American (born United States), b. 1941. **Genres:** Children's Fiction, Illustrations, Picture/Board Books. **Career:** The Art Studentsi League, teacher; Green Tiger Press (children's book publishing company), founder and owner, 1975-86; Blue Lantern Studio, owner, 1993-. Writer and illustrator. **Publications:** The Blue Faience Hippopotamus, 1984; Good Dog, Carl, 1985; (with C. Edens) Helping the Flowers & Trees, 1987; (with C. Edens) Helping the Night, 1987; (with C. Edens) Helping the Animals, 1987; (with C. Edens) Helping the Sun, 1987; (with C. Edens and W. Poltarnees)

Children from the Golden Age, 1880-1930, 1987; Frank and Ernest, 1988; Paddy's Pay-Day, 1989; Carl Goes Shopping, 1989; (ed. with W. Poltarnees) A.B.C. of Fashionable Animals, 1989; Frank and Ernest Play Ball, 1990; Carl's Christmas, 1990; River Parade, 1990; Carl's Afternoon in the Park, 1991; Carl's Masquerade, 1992; Carl Pops Up, 1992; Carlito en el parque una tarde, 1992; Carl Goes to Daycare, 1993; Frank and Ernest on the Road, 1994; Carl Makes a Scrapbook, 1994; My Puppy's Record Book, 1994; Carl's Birthday, 1995; Carl's Baby Journal, 1996; Bouquet, 1996; (with C. Darling) The Mirror, 1997; (with C. Edens) The Christmas We Moved to the Barn, 1997; Follow Carl!, 1998, Boswell Wide Awake, 1999; (with C. Edens) Darby, the Special Order Pup, 2000; (with C. Edens) Special Deliveries, 2001; Puppy Trouble, 2002; Flight of a Dove, 2004; Not Forgotten: A Consolation for the Loss of an Animal Friend, 2004; Carl's Sleepy Afternoon, 2005; You're a Good Dog, Carl, 2007; Carl Goes on Vacation, 2008; Carl's Summer Vacation, 2008; Carl's Snowy Afternoon, 2009; Carl and the Kitten, 2011; Carl at the Dog Show, 2012. Illustrator of books by others. **Address:** Farrar Straus Giroux Books, 19 Union Sq. W, New York, NY 10003, U.S.A.

DAY, Alyssa. *See* **HOLLIDAY, Alesia.**

DAY, A(rthur) Colin. British (born England), b. 1935. **Genres:** Information Science/Computers, Theology/Religion, Reference. **Career:** Wycliffe Bible Translators, translator, 1959-67; University College London, Computer Centre, head of applications, 1967-92; Writer, 1992-. **Publications:** Fortran Techniques with Special Reference to Non-numerical Applications, 1972; A London Fortran Course, 1972; Getting the Edge on Card Files, 1976; Compatible Fortran, 1978; Illustrating Computers, 1982; Text Processing, 1984; Using Ventura Publisher, 1988; Roget's Thesaurus of the Bible, 1992; Collins Thematic Thesaurus of the Bible, 2005. **Address:** Hillcroft, Thornton Rust, Leyburn, NY DL8 3AW, England. **Online address:** acolinday@aol.com

DAY, Cathy. American (born United States), b. 1968. **Genres:** Young Adult Fiction. **Career:** University of Alabama, instructor, 1995-97; Minnesota State University, assistant professor, 1997-2000; College of New Jersey, assistant professor of creative writing, 2000-05, Governor's School for the Arts, writer-in-residence, 2001-02; University of Pittsburgh, assistant professor, 2005-10; Mercyhurst College, Pennsylvania Governor's School for the Arts, visiting writer, 2006; Ball State University, assistant professor, 2010-, Creative Writing Area, secretary, 2010-11. Writer. **Publications:** The Circus in Winter, 2004; Comeback Season: How I Learned to Play the Game of Love, 2008. **Address:** c/o Jill Siegel, Simon & Schuster Inc., 1230 Ave. of the Americas, New York, NY 10020-1513, U.S.A. **Online address:** cday@bsu.edu

DAY, Charles R. Canadian (born Canada), b. 1936. **Genres:** Education, History, Business/Trade/Industry. **Career:** Foothill College, instructor, 1964-66; Simon Fraser University, assistant professor, 1966-80, professor, 1980-2001, professor emeritus, 2001-. Writer. **Publications:** Education for the Industrial World: The écoles d'Arts et Métiersand the Rise of French Industrial Engineering, 1987; Les écoles d'Artset Métiers. L'enseignement technique en France, XIX-XX siècle, 1991; Schools and Work: Technical and Vocational Education in France Since the Third Republic, 2001. Contributor to periodicals. **Address:** Simon Fraser University, 8888 University Dr., Burnaby, BC V5A 1S6, Canada. **Online address:** cday@sfu.ca

DAY, Edward C. American (born United States), b. 1932. **Genres:** Children's Fiction, Travel/Exploration, Young Adult Fiction, Westerns/Adventure. **Career:** Harvard University Press, assistant sales manager, advertising manager, 1957-69; Itek Corp., public relations representative, 1969-70; Bates College, part-time staff writer, 1970-72; Bath Art Shop and Gallery, owner and operator, 1973-74; Whitcoulls Publishers, assistant publishing manager, 1974-77, 1979-80; Alaska Northwest Publishing Co., associate editor, 1977-78; Summer Street Studios, landscape photographer, 1980-83; Wooden-Boat (magazine), merchandise manager, 1983-85; Colby College, development writer, director of corporate and foundation relations, 1985-90; freelance writer, 1990-92; Vermont Foodbank, director of development, 1993-94, executive director, 1995-97. **Publications:** John Tabor's Ride, 1989. Contributor to magazines and newspapers. **Address:** 1670 Center Rd., Montpelier, VT 05602-8534, U.S.A. **Online address:** edjoday@sover.net

DAY, Holliday T. American (born United States), b. 1936. **Genres:** Art/Art History, Bibliography, Photography. **Career:** Freelance art critic, 1975-80; Joslyn Art Museum, curator of American art, 1980-85; Indianapolis Museum of Art, senior curator of contemporary art, 1985-2000. Writer and educator.

Publications: Seven Sculptors, 1978; Europe in the Seventies (bibliography), 1979; Stacked, Packed and Hung, 1980; Dennis Kowalski, 1980; I-80 Series, 1980-82; The Shape of Space: The Sculpture of George Sugarman, 1981; (co-author) Ed Paschke: Selected Works, 1982; New Art of Italy: Chia, Clemente, Cucchi, Paladino, 1985; Elyn Zimmerman, 1985; Painting and Sculpture Today, 1986; (with H. Sturges) Art of the Fantastic: Latin America, 1920-1987, 1987; (ed. with H. Sturges, E. Simak and J.L. Farber) Joslyn Art Museum: Paintings and Sculpture from the European and American Collections, 1987; (ed.) Indianapolis Museum of Art: Collections Handbook, 1988; Joseph Cantor: Connoisseur, 1988; Rick Paul, 1989; Power: Its Myths and Mores in American Art, 1961-1991, 1991; Forefront Series, 1991-2000; (with Harris and Waller) The Poetry of Form: Richard Tuttle Drawings from the Vogel Collection, 1993; (with F. Coleman) Felrath Hines, 1995; Crossroads of American Sculpture, 2000. Contributor to periodicals. **Address:** Indianapolis Museum of Art, 4000 N Michigan Rd., Indianapolis, IN 46208-3326, U.S.A.

DAY, Laura (Globus). American (born United States), b. 1959. **Genres:** How-to Books, Psychology, inspirational/Motivational Literature, Business/Trade/Industry, Homes/Gardens. **Career:** Teacher, 1982-. Writer and consultant. **Publications:** Practical Intuition: How to Harness the Power of Your Instinct and Make It Work for You, 1996; Practical Intuition for Success: A Step-by-Step Program to Increase Your Wealth Today, 1997; Practical Intuition in Love: Start a Journey through Pleasure to the Love of Your Life, 1998; The Circle: How the Power of a Single Wish Can Change Your Life, 2001; Welcome to Your Crisis: How to Use the Power of Crisis to Create the Life You Want, 2006; How to Rule the World from Your Couch, 2009; (with R. Martine) Strangled by Wild Geese, 2010; Cómo Controlar el Mundo Desde su Sofá: Utilice su Intuición Para Realizar Todos sus Sueños, 2010. **Address:** c/o Melanie Jackson, Melanie Jackson Agency, 250 W 57th St., Ste. 1119, New York, NY 10107, U.S.A. **Online address:** info@practicalintuition.com

DAY, Marele. Australian (born Australia), b. 1947. **Genres:** Mystery/Crime/Suspense, Writing/Journalism, Adult Non-fiction, Mystery/Crime/Suspense. **Career:** Teacher, 1984-87; writer and freelance editor, 1988-; Sydney Writers' Centre, Crime Writing Workshop, faculty. **Publications:** FICTION: Shirley's Song, 1984; The Life and Crimes of Harry Lavender, 1988; The Case of the Chinese Boxes, 1990; The Last Tango of Dolores Delgado, 1993; The Disappearances of Madalena Grimaldi, 1994 in US as The Disappearances of Madalena Grimaldi: A Claudia Valentine Mystery, 1996; Lambs of God, 1998; Mrs. Cook: The Real and Imagined Life of the Captain's Wife, 2002; The Sea Bed, 2002. NONFICTION: The Art of Self-Promotion for Writers, 1993; (ed.) How to Write Crime, 1996; (ed. with S.B. Smith and F. Knight) Making Waves: 10 Years of the Byron Bay Writers Festival, 2006; The Sea Bed, 2009. Works appear in anthologies. **Address:** Allen & Unwin, 9 Atchison St., PO Box 8500, Saint Leonards, NW 2065, Australia.

DAY, M. H. *See* **DAY, Michael Herbert.**

DAY, Michael Herbert. (M. H. Day). British (born England), b. 1927. **Genres:** Anthropology/Ethnology, Archaeology/Antiquities. **Career:** British Broadcasting Corp., writer; University of London, Royal Free Hospital School of Medicine, assistant lecturer, 1958-63; Middlesex Hospital Medical School, lecturer, 1964-66, senior lecturer in anatomy, 1966-69, reader in physical anthropology, 1969-72; United Medical and Dental Schools, professor of anatomy, 1972-89; St. Thomas's Hospital Medical School, professor of anatomy, 1972-; The Natural History Museum, senior research fellow; British Museum, Department of Paleontology, professor, 1989-; Anatomical Society of Great Britain and Ireland, president. **Publications:** Guide to Fossil Man, 1965, 4th ed., 1986; Fossil Man, 1969; (ed.) Human Evolution, 1973; The Fossil History of Man, 2nd ed., 1977; (ed.) Vertebrate Locomotion: (The Proceedings of a Symposium Held at the Zoological Society of London on 27 and 28 March 1980), 1981. **Address:** 26 Thurlow Rd., Hampstead, London, GL NW3 5PR, England. **Online address:** m.day@mailbox.ulcc.ac.uk

DAY, Nancy. American (born United States), b. 1953. **Genres:** Young Adult Non-fiction, Advertising/Public Relations, Marketing, Social Sciences. **Career:** BBL Microbiology Systems, advertising manager, 1976-79; M.A. Bioproducts, director of marketing communications, 1979-81; West Co., business development manager, 1982-83; Cooper Biomedical, director of marketing communications, 1983-85; freelance marketing consultant, 1985-2000; Sakaduski Marketing Solutions Inc., co-founder and president, 2000-. Writer and marketing consultant. **Publications:** The Horseshoe Crab, 1992; Animal Experimentation: Cruelty or Science?, 1994, rev. ed., 2000; Abortion: Debat-

ing the Issue, 1995; Sensational TV: Trash or Journalism?, 1996; Violence in Schools: Learning in Fear, 1996; Advertising: Information or Manipulation?, 1999; The Death Penalty for Teens: A Pro/Con Issue, 2000; Killer Superbugs: The Story of Drug-Resistant Diseases, 2001; Malaria, West Nile, and Other Mosquito-borne Diseases, 2001; Censorship, or Freedom of Expression? 2001; Strategies for Motivation: Learning Ways to Get Unstuck, 2004; (with R.A. Day) Scientific English: A Guide for Scientists and Other Professionals, 2011. PASSPORT TO HISTORY SERIES: Your Travel Guide to Renaissance Europe, 2001; Your Travel Guide to Colonial America, 2001; Your Travel Guide to Ancient Greece, 2001; Your Travel Guide to Civil War America, 2001; Your Travel Guide to Ancient Mayan Civilization, 2001; Your Travel Guide to Ancient Egypt, 2001. Contributor to periodicals. **Address:** Sakaduski Marketing Solutions Inc., 100 Wedgewood Dr., Chadds Ford, PA 19317, U.S.A. **Online address:** nancy@sakaduskimarketing.com

DAY, Richard J. F. Canadian (born Canada), b. 1964?. **Genres:** Sociology, Social Sciences, Politics/Government, History. **Career:** Simon Fraser University, teacher of sociology, 1996-97, 1999-2000; Charles Square Housing Cooperative, president, 1997-98; Kwantlen University College, teacher of social sciences, 1998; Douglas College, teacher of sociological theory, 2000-01; Critical U. (community education project), co-organizer, 2000-01; Queen's University, Department of Sociology, assistant professor, 2001-07, associate professor, 2007-; Kingston Social Action Centre, director, 2003-. Writer. **Publications:** Multiculturalism and the History of Canadian Diversity, 2000; Gramsci Is Dead: Anarchist Currents in the Newest Social Movements, 2005; (ed. with M. Coté and G.D. Peuter) Utopian pedagogy: Radical Experiments Against Neoliberal Globalization, 2007. **Address:** Department of Sociology, Queens University, D413 Mackintosh-Corry Hall, 99 University Ave., Kingston, BC K7L 3N6, Canada. **Online address:** richard.day@queensu.ca

DAY, Stacey B. American/British (born England), b. 1927. **Genres:** Novels, Plays/Screenplays, Poetry, Medicine/Health, Philosophy, Sociology, Autobiography/Memoirs, Communications/Media, Sciences. **Career:** Royal College of Surgeons, Dublin, Ireland, graduate in medicine and surgery, 1955; University of Minnesota, faculty, 1955-60; McGill University, faculty, 1964; University of Cincinnati, associate director, Basic Medical Research, Shriner's Burn Institute, faculty, 1969-71; University of Minnesota, assistant professor, associate professor, Bell Museum of Pathology, head, 1971-73; Sloan-Kettering Institute for Cancer Research, professor and head of lab communications and medical education, 1973-80; Cornell University Medical College, professor of biology, 1974-80; New York Medical College, clinical professor of behavioral medicine, 1980-92; University of Calabar, Nigeria, chairman and professor of community and biopsychosocial medicine, 1982-85; World Health Collaborating Center, Meharry Medical College, founding director and professor of international health, 1985-90, director of NAAFEO/US-AID; University of Arizona, adjunct professor of family and community medicine, 1985-89; Charles University, Czech Republic, Fulbright professor, 1990, visiting professor of international health, 1989-93; Oita Medical University, Japan, visiting professor of medical education, 1992-99. Writer. **Publications:** Collected Lines, 1966; By the Waters of Babylon (play), 1966; American Lines, 1967; The Music Box (play), 1967; Rosalita (novella), 1968; Poems and Etudes, 1968; The Idle Thoughts of a Surgical Fellow, 1968; Edward Stevens (Translation of De Alimentorum Concoctine with Notes on Life), 1969; Bellechasse, 1970; (with B.G. MacMillan and W.A. Altmeier) Curling's Ulcer, 1971; Ten Poems and a Letter from America for Mr. Sinha, 1971; Tuluak and Amaulik: Death and Dying in Eskimos of Alaska, 1973; East of the Navel and Afterbirth: Song Poetry from Easter Island (Isla de Pascua), 1976; Image of Science and Society, 1977; Health Communications, 1979; (with F. Lolas and M. Kusinitz) Biopsychosocial Health, 1981; Man in Search of Health, 1983; Primary Health Care Guide Lines: Akampka, Calabar, 1984; Cancer, Stress, and Death 2E, 1986; (with T.A. Lambo) Contemporary Issues in International Health, 1989; (with H. Koga) Hagakure: Spirit of Bushido, 1993; (with K. Inokuchi) The Wisdom of Hagakure, 1995; Developing Health in the West African Bush, 2 Parts, 1995; (with M. Kobayashi and K. Inokuchi) 21-Seiki ni okeru igakusei oyobi igaku no shimei, 1996; Letters of Owen Wangensteen to a Surgical Fellow, with a Memoir, 1996; Man and Mu, 1997; Selected Poems and Embers of a Medical Life, 1997; The Surgical Treatment of Ischemic Heart Disease, 1999; W. Von Humboldt, Ueber die unterdem namen Bhagavadghita, with Commentary (Ethics), 2001; A Vitaesophia of Integral Humanism and Japanese Lectures, 1990-2000, 2001; Letters to Ivana from Calabar, 2001; The Klacelka in a Slavic Woodland, 2002; Pliskova's Butterflies: Az Buhrekne Dost: When God Says Enough, 2002; (with I.P. Day) A Season of Flowers in Death Valley and the California Deserts, 2005; (with I.P. Day) In

Search of the Desert Five Spot, 2006; Nensokan: Moon in a Dewdrop, 2007; (trans. and intro.) T.G. Masaryk, Problém Malého Národa (title means: 'Problem of a Small Nation'), 2010; (with K. Inokuchi) Hangakure: Tricentennial Anniversary, 2011. EDITOR: Death and Attitudes towards Death, 1972; (with R.A. Good) Membranes and Viruses in Immunopathology, 1972; Proceedings: Ethics in Medicine in a Changing Society, 1973; Communication of Scientific Information, 1975; Health Communications and Informatics, 1975; Trauma, 1975; (with R.A. Good and J. Yunis) Molecular Pathology, 1975; (with R.A. Good) Comprehensive Immunology, 9 vols., 1975-2003; Cancer Invasion and Metastasis, 1977; The American Biomedical Network, 1978; A Companion to the Life Sciences, vol. I, 1978, vol. II: Integrated Medicine, 1980, vol. III: Life Stress, 1982; (with F. Lolas and M. Kusinitz) Biopsychosocial Health, 1980; Readings in Oncology, 1980; (co-ed.) Computers for Medical Office and Patient Management, 1982; (co-ed.) Health and Quality of Life in Central Europe in the Year 2000, 1992. **Address:** The American Institute of Stress, 124 Park Ave., Yonkers, NY 10703, U.S.A. **Online address:** sbday@stgregorys.edu

DAYAN, Colin. (Joan Dayan). American (born United States), b. 1949?. **Genres:** Biography, Literary Criticism And History. **Career:** Princeton University, Shelby Cullom Davis Center for Historical Study, fellow, 1990-91; Yale University, Department of English, assistant professor, 1981-86; City University of New York Graduate Center, associate professor of comparative literature and French, 1986-90; University of Arizona, African-American Studies Program, visiting associate professor, 1991-92, professor, 1992-2001; regents professor, 1998-2001; Princeton Program in Law and Public Affairs, fellow, 2000-01; University of Pennsylvania, professor of English, 2001-04, Africana Studies, core faculty, 2002-04, professor of comparative literature and literary theory, 2003-04; University of Michigan, visiting professor, 2001; Vanderbilt University, Robert Penn Warren professor of the humanities, 2004-. Writer. **Publications:** (Trans. and intro. as Joan Dayan) Rene Depestre, A Rainbow for the Christian West, 1977. AS JOAN DAYAN: Fables of Mind: An Inquiry into Poe's Fiction, 1987; Haiti, History, and the Gods, 1995; The Story of Cruel and Unusual, 2007; The Law is a White Dog: How Legal Rituals Make and Unmake Persons, 2011. CONTRIBUTOR: Critical Essays on Edgar Allan Poe, 1987; Poe and His Times, 1990; Displacements: Women, Tradition, Literatures in French, 1991; Reading World Literature: Theory, History, Academic Practice, 1994; After Colonialism: Imperialism and the Colonial Aftermath, 1995; Repenser la Creolite, 1995; Subjects, Nations, and Citizens, 1995; The American Face of Edgar Allan Poe, 1995; Postcolonial Subjects: Francophone Women Writers, 1996; Sacred Possessions, 1997; Making Worlds: Gender, Metaphor, Materiality, 1998; The Woman, the Writer, and Caribbean Society: Essays on Literature and Culture, 1998; Caribbean Francophone Writing: An Introduction, 1999; History, Memory, and the Law, 1999; Slavery in the Francophone World: Forgotten Acts, Forged Identities, 2000; For the Geography of a Soul: In Honor of Kamau Brathwaite, 2001; Women at Sea: Travel Writing and the Margins of Caribbean Discourse, 2001; Romancing the Shadow: Poe and Race, 2001; Sisyphus and Eldorado: Magical and Other Realisms in Caribbean Literatures, 2002; Materializing Democracy, 2002; Colonial Saints, 2002; Cities without Citizens: Statelessness and Settlements in Early America, 2003; Histoires et identite dans la Caribe, 2004. OTHERS: The Law Is a White Dog, 2011. Contributor to journals and periodicals. **Address:** Department of English, Vanderbilt University, 319 Benson Hall, 2301 Vanderbilt Pl., Nashville, TN 37235, U.S.A. **Online address:** colin.dayan@vanderbilt.edu

DAYAN, Joan. *See* **DAYAN, Colin.**

DAY-LEWIS, Sean (Francis). British (born England), b. 1931. **Genres:** Biography, Autobiography/Memoirs, Art/Art History, Technology, History, Photography, Reference. **Career:** Daily Telegraph, television and radio editor, 1970-86; London Daily News, television editor, 1986-87. **Publications:** Bulleid: Last Giant of Steam, 1964, 2nd ed., 1968; C. Day Lewis: An English Literary Life, 1980; (ed.) One Day in the Life of Television, 1989; TV Heaven, 1992; Talk of Drama: Views of the Television Dramatist Now and Then, 1998. **Address:** Restorick Row, 1 Rosemary Ln., Colyton, DN EX24 6LW, England. **Online address:** seandaylewis@tesco.net

DAYTON, Charles (W.). American (born United States), b. 1943. **Genres:** Education, Medicine/Health, Self Help. **Career:** Cayuga Community College, English teacher, 1968-71; American Institutes for Research, research scientist, 1972-84; Stanford Urban Coalition, director of peninsula academies, 1982-84; University of California, Graduate School of Education, Ca-

reer Academy Support Network, co-founder, 1998-, coordinator, 1998-2011, education consultant and national liaison. Writer. **Publications:** (Co-author) Safeguarding Your Education: A Student's Consumer Guide to College and Occupational Education, 1977; (contrib.) New Horizons in Counseling Psychology, 1977; The Job Search and Youth Employment, 1980; (contrib.) Environmental Variables and the Prevention of Mental Illness, 1980; (with R.J. Rossi and K.J. Gilmartin) Agencies Working Together: A Guide to Co-ordination and Planning, 1982; (with D. Stern and M. Raby) Career Academies: Partnerships for Reconstructing American High Schools, 1992; Net Impact Evaluation of School-to-Work: Exploring Alternatives, 1996; (with M. Raby) Career Academies and High School Reform, 1998; (with M. Raby) Youth Development in Career Academies, 1999. Contributor to periodicals. **Address:** Career Academy Support Network, Graduate School of Education, University of California, Berkeley, CA 94720-1670, U.S.A. **Online address:** charleswdayton@gmail.com

DEÀK, Erzsi. French/American (born United States), b. 1959. **Genres:** Children's Fiction. **Career:** Society of Children's Book Writers and Illustrators, international coordinator. Journalist, editor and writer. **Publications:** (With K.E. Litchman) Period Pieces: Stories for Girls, 2003; (ed. with S. Becker and K.B. Narisetti) Urban Crayon Paris: The City Guide for Parents with Children, 2008. Contributor to periodicals. **Address:** c/o Author Mail, HarperCollins, 10 E 53rd St., 7th Fl., New York, NY 10012, U.S.A. **Online address:** erzsi.deak@gmail.com

DEAK, Istvan. American/Hungarian (born Hungary), b. 1926. **Genres:** History. **Career:** German Academic Exchange fellow, 1960-61; University of Maryland Overseas Program, lecturer, 1961; Smith College, instructor, 1962-63; Columbia University, instructor, 1963-64, assistant professor, 1964-67, associate professor, 1967-71, professor of history, 1971-93, Institute on East Central Europe, director, 1967-78, acting director, 1979-80, 1983, Seth Low professor of history, 1971-2000, Seth Low professor emeritus of history, 2000-; Yale University, visiting lecturer, 1966; University of California, visiting professor, 1975; Conference Group for Slavic and East European History, vice president, 1975-77, president, 1985; Universitaet Siegen, visiting professor; 1981. Writer. **Publications:** Villamos Gépek, 1959; Weimar Germany's Left-Wing Intellectuals: A Political History of the Weltbühne and Its Circle, 1968; The Lawful Revolution: Louis Kossuth and the Hungarians 1848-49, 1979; Assimilation and Nationalism in East Central Europe during the Last Century of Habsburg Rule, 1983; Beyond Nationalism: A Social and Political History of the Habsburg Officer Corps, 1848-1914, 1990; Jewish Soldiers in Austro-Hungarian Society, 1990; K. (u.) k. Offizier, 1848-1918, 1991; Volt egyszer egy tisztikar: a Habsburg-monarchia katonatisztjeinek társadalmi és politikai története, 1848-1918, 1993; Essays on Hitler's Europe, 2001. EDITOR: (with S. Sinanian and P.C. Ludz) Eastern Europe in the 1970's, 1972; (and comp. with A.C. Mitchell) Everyman in Europe: Essays in Social History, 1974, 3rd ed., 1990; (with J.T. Gross and T. Judt) The Politics of Retribution in Europe: World War II and Its Aftermath, 2000; Essays on Hitler's Europe, 2001. Contributor to books. **Address:** East Central European Center, Harriman Institute, Columbia University, MC 3336, 420 W 118th St., New York, NY 10027, U.S.A. **Online address:** id1@columbia.edu

DEAN, Cornelia. American (born United States) **Genres:** Environmental Sciences/Ecology, Business/Trade/Industry. **Career:** Providence Journal, reporter and editor, 1969-84; New York Times, staff, 1984-2003, assistant science editor, 1985, deputy science editor, 1987, Washington Bureau, deputy Washington editor, 1994, science editor, 1997-2003; Harvard University, Joan Shorenstein Center on the Press, Politics and Public Policy, fellow, Center for the Environment, associate; University of Rhode Island, professor; Columbia University, Graduate School of Journalism, professor; Vassar College, professor. Journalist. **Publications:** (Co-ed.) The Environment from Your Backyard to the Ocean Floor, 1994; (ed. with N. Wade and W.A. Dicke) New York Times Book of Science Literacy, 1994; Against the Tide: The Battle for America's Beaches, 1999; Am I Making Myself Clear?: A Scientist's Guide to Talking to the Public, 2009. **Address:** Center for the Environment, Harvard University, 24 Oxford St., 3rd Fl., Cambridge, MA 02138, U.S.A. **Online address:** cdean@fas.harvard.edu

DEAN, Debra. American (born United States), b. 1957. **Genres:** Novels, Literary Criticism And History. **Career:** Teacher and writer. **Publications:** The Madonnas of Leningrad, 2006; Confessions of a Falling Woman: And

Other Stories, 2008. **Address:** Marly Rusoff & Associates Inc., PO Box 524, Bronxville, NY 10708, U.S.A. **Online address:** debra@literarydelights.com

DEAN, Eric T. American (born United States), b. 1950. **Genres:** History, Medicine/Health. **Career:** Legal Services Program of Northern Indiana, attorney, 1978-81; Purdue University, instructor in history, 1989; Yale University, Mellon fellow, 1992-93, instructor in history, 1993, 1995, John F. Enders fellow, 1994, Whiting fellow in humanities, 1995-96; Marcus Law Firm, real estate attorney, 1996-; Law Offices of Eric T. Dean Jr., owner. Writer. **Publications:** Shook Over Hell: Post-Traumatic Stress, Vietnam and the Civil War, 1997. Contributor to journals. **Address:** Law Offices of Eric T. Dean Jr., 40 Twin Brook Rd., Hamden, CT 06514, U.S.A. **Online address:** eric@deank1k3visas.com

DEAN, Margaret Lazarus. American (born United States), b. 1972?. **Genres:** Novels, Essays. **Career:** University of Michigan, lecturer; University of Tennessee, assistant professor. Writer. **Publications:** The Time It Takes to Fall, 2007. **Address:** c/o Julie Barer, Barer Literary L.L.C., 156 5th Ave., Ste. 1134, New York, NY 10010-7745, U.S.A. **Online address:** margaret.lazarus.dean@gmail.com

DEAN, Martin. American (born United States), b. 1962?. **Genres:** History, Military/Defense/Arms Control. **Career:** Center for Advanced Holocaust Studies, U.S. Holocaust Memorial Museum, Pearl Resnick post-doctoral fellow, 1997-98. Historian and writer. **Publications:** Collaboration in the Holocaust: Crimes of the Local Police in Belorussia and Ukraine, 1941-44, 2000; (ed. with C. Goschler and P. Ther) Robbery & Restitution: The Conflict Over Jewish Property in Europe, 2007; Robbing the Jews: The Confiscation of Jewish Property in the Holocaust, 1933-1945, 2008. **Address:** St. Martin's Press, 175 5th Ave., New York, NY 10010, U.S.A.

DEAN, Pamela. See DEAN (Dyer-Bennett), Pamela (Collins).

DEAN, Rebecca. See PEMBERTON, Margaret.

DEAN, Trevor. British (born England), b. 1956. **Genres:** Essays, History. **Career:** Roehampton University, professor. Writer. **Publications:** Land and Power in Late Medieval Ferrara: The Rule of the Este, 1350-1450, 1988; City and Countryside in Late Medieval and Renaissance Italy: Essays Presented to Philip Jones, 1990; (ed. with K.J.P. Lowe) Crime, Society, and the Law in Renaissance Italy, 1994; (with D.S. Chambers) Clean Hands and Rough Justice: An Investigating Magistrate in Renaissance Italy, 1997; (ed. with K.J.P. Lowe) Marriage in Italy, 1300-1650, 1998; The Towns of Italy in the Later Middle Ages, 2000; Crime and Justice in Late Medieval Italy, 2007. **Address:** England. **Online address:** t.dean@roehampton.ac.uk

DEAN, William Denard. American (born United States), b. 1937. **Genres:** Theology/Religion, Philosophy, Literary Criticism And History, Intellectual History. **Career:** Northland College, assistant professor of philosophy and religion, 1966-68; Gustavus Adolphus College, assistant professor, 1968-73, associate professor, 1973-80, professor of religion, 1980-96, Florence and Raymond Sponberg chair in ethics, 1996; Iliff School of Theology, professor of constructive theology, 1996-2004, professor emeritus, 2004-. Writer. **Publications:** Coming To: A Theology of Beauty, 1972; Love before the Fall, 1976; American Religious Empiricism, 1986; (co-ed.) The Size of God: The Theology of Bernard Loomer in Context, 1987; History Making History: The New Historicism in American Religious Thought, 1988; The Religious Critic in American Culture, 1994; The American Spiritual Culture: And the Invention of Jazz, Football, and the Movies, 2002; (co-ed.) Republic of Faith: The Search for Agreement Amid Diversity in American Religion, 2003. **Address:** 4565 E Mexico, Ste. 9, Denver, CO 80222, U.S.A. **Online address:** wdean@Iliff.edu

DEAN (DYER-BENNETT), Pamela (Collins). (Pamela Dean). American (born United States), b. 1953?. **Genres:** Science Fiction/Fantasy, Novels, Young Adult Fiction, Poetry. **Career:** Writer. **Publications:** FANTASY NOVELS: The Dubious Hills, 1994; Juniper, Gentian & Rosemary, 1998; Hidden Land, 2003; The Secret Country, 2003; The Hidden Land, 2003; The Whim of the Dragon, 2003; Secret Country, 2003; Tam Lin, 2006. Works appear in anthologies. **Address:** Tom Doherty Associates Inc., 175 5th Ave., New York, NY 10010, U.S.A. **Online address:** pddb@demesne.com

DEANE-DRUMMOND, Anthony (John). British (born England), b. 1917.

Genres: International Relations/Current Affairs, Autobiography/Memoirs, Travel/Exploration. **Career:** Paper and Paper Products Ltd., director, 1971-79; Cotswold Conversions, director, 1983-88; British Army, major, now retired. Writer. **Publications:** Return Ticket, 1953; Riots, 1974; Arrows of Fortune, 1991. **Address:** Royal Bank of Scotland, 67 Lombard St., London, GL EC3, England.

DEANGELIS, Camille. American (born United States), b. 1980. **Genres:** Travel/Exploration, Novels. **Career:** HarperCollins, editorial assistant, 2002-04. Travel writer and novelist. **Publications:** (With T. Haslow) Hanging Out in Ireland (travel book), 2001; Mary Modern (novel), 2007; Moon Ireland (travel book), 2007; Second Life of Mary Morrigan: A Novel, 2007; Petty Magic: A Novel, 2010. **Address:** c/o Kate Garrick, DeFiore and Company L.L.C., 47 E 19th St., 3rd Fl., New York, NY 10003, U.S.A. **Online address:** mealey@gmail.com

DE ANGELIS, Lissa G. American (born United States), b. 1954. **Genres:** Food And Wine, Medicine/Health. **Career:** Teacher, 1975-82; Natural Gourmet Cookery School, associate director and professor, 1981-91; freelance nutritionist, chef and writer, 1991-. **Publications:** (With M. Siple) Recipes for Change: Gourmet Wholefood Cooking for Health and Vitality at Menopause, 1996; (with B. Adderly) The Arthritis Cure Cookbook, 1998; (with M. Siple) SOS for PMS: Whole-Food Solutions for Premenstrual Syndrome, 1999. Contributor to periodicals. **Address:** 67 Revere Blvd., Edison, NJ 08820-1908, U.S.A. **Online address:** lissad@optonline.net

DEANS, Bob. American (born United States) **Genres:** Novels, History. **Career:** Fairchild Publications, reporter, 1980, editor, 1981-83; Post and Courier, reporter, 1983; Atlanta Journal-Constitution, business reporter, 1984; Cox Newspapers, chief Asia correspondent, 1987-91, national correspondent, White House, correspondent, 1992, White House Correspondents Association, president, 2002-03. **Publications:** Behind the Headlines, 1996; The River Where America Began: A Journey along the James, 2007; (with F. Beinecke) Clean Energy Common Sense: An American Call to Action on Global Climate Change, 2010. Contributor to periodicals. **Address:** Cox Newspapers, Washington Bureau, 400 N Capitol St. NW, Ste. 750, Washington, DC 20001-1536, U.S.A.

DEANS, Sis Boulos. American (born United States), b. 1955. **Genres:** Novellas/Short Stories, Children's Fiction, Young Adult Fiction, Biography, Sports/Fitness, Psychology, Self Help, Mythology/Folklore, Mythology/Folklore. **Career:** Mercy Hospital, surgical technician, 1985-. Writer. **Publications:** CHILDREN'S FICTION: Chick-a-dee-dee-dee: A Very Special Bird, 1987; Emily Bee and the Kingdom of Flowers, 1988; The Legend of Blazing Bear, 1992. YOUNG ADULT NOVELS: Brick Walls, 1996; Racing the Past, 2001; Every Day and All the Time, 2003. OTHERS: Decisions and Other Stories (adult short stories), 1995; His Proper Post: A Biography of Gen. Joshua Lawrence Chamberlain, 1996; Brick Walls, 1996; Rainy, 2005. Contributor to periodicals. **Address:** 260 Gray Rd., Gorham, ME 04038, U.S.A.

DEAR, Peter. American (born United States), b. 1958. **Genres:** Adult Nonfiction, Sciences. **Career:** Cornell University, professor, President Andrew D. White professor of the history of science. Writer. **Publications:** Mersenne and the Learning of the Schools, 1988; (ed.) The Literary Structure of Scientific Argument: Historical Studies, 1991; Discipline & Experience: The Mathematical Way in the Scientific Revolution, 1995; (ed.) The Scientific Enterprise in Early Modern Europe: Readings from Isis, 1997; Revolutionizing the Sciences: European Knowledge and Its Ambitions, 1500-1700, 2001, 2nd ed., 2009; The Intelligibility of Nature: How Science Makes Sense of the World, 2006; (ed. with L. Roberts and S. Schaffer) Mindful Hand: Inquiry and Invention from the Late Renaissance to Early Industrialisation, 2007. **Address:** Department of Science and Technology Studies, Cornell University, 306 Rockefeller Hall, Ithaca, NY 14853, U.S.A. **Online address:** prd3@cornell.edu

DEARDEN, James Shackley. British (born England), b. 1931. **Genres:** Literary Criticism And History, Biography, Autobiography/Memoirs. **Career:** Tantivy Press (publishers), advertising manager, 1952-57; Bembridge School, Ruskin Galleries, curator, 1957-96; Brantwood, curator, 1959-96, now retired. Writer. **Publications:** A Short History of Brantwood, 1967; Books Are for People, 1969; Facets of Ruskin: Some Sesquicentennial Studies, 1970; Ruskin & Coniston, 1971; John Ruskin: An Illustrated Life of John Ruskin, 1819-1900, 1973; Turner's Isle of Wight Sketchbook, 1979; (contrib.) Studies in Ruskin, 1982; John Ruskin's Camberwell, 1990; John Ruskin and Victorian Art, 1993; Ruskin, Bembridge, and Brantwood: The Growth of the Whitehouse Collection, 1994; Hare Hunting on the Isle of Wight, 1996; John Ruskin, a Life in Pictures, 1999; King of the Golden River, 1999; John Ruskin's Dogs, 2003. EDITOR: The Professor: Arthur Severn's Memoir of John Ruskin, 1967; Iteriad or Three Weeks Among the Lakes, 1969; Tour to the Lakes in Cumberland: John Ruskin's Diary for 1830, 1990. Contributor to journals. **Address:** 4 Woodlands, Foreland Rd., Bembridge, IW PO35 5PN, England.

DEARIE, John. American (born United States) **Genres:** Young Adult Fiction, Novels. **Career:** Federal Reserve Bank of New York, foreign exchange staff, policy and analysis staff, officer, 1996; Financial Services Volunteer Corps (FSVC), managing director, through 2001; Financial Services Forum, senior vice president for policy and research, 2001-, executive vice president for policy. Writer. **Publications:** Love and Other Recreational Sports, 2003. **Address:** The Financial Services Forum, 601 13th St. NW, Ste. 750 S, Washington, DC 20005, U.S.A. **Online address:** john.dearie@financialservicesforum.org

DEARING, Sarah. Canadian (born Canada) **Genres:** Novels, Young Adult Non-fiction, Young Adult Fiction, Mystery/Crime/Suspense. **Career:** Writers Guild of Canada, agreement administrator. Writer and communications specialist. **Publications:** The Bull is Not Killed, 1998; Courage My Love: A Novel, 2001. **Address:** Writers Guild of Canada, 366 Adelaide St. W, Ste. 401, Toronto, ON M5V 1R9, Canada. **Online address:** s.dearing@wgc.ca

DEATHRIDGE, John (William). British (born England), b. 1944. **Genres:** Music. **Career:** Cambridge University, reader-in-music, 1983-96; King's College, King Edward professor of music, 1996-, department head, fellow, director of studies in music; Royal Musical Association, president, 2005-08; University of Princeton, faculty; University of Chicago, faculty. Writer. **Publications:** Wagner's Rienzi: A Reappraisal Based on a Study of the Sketches and Drafts, 1977; (with C. Dahlhaus) The New Grove Wagner, 1984; (with M. Geck and E. Voss) Verzeichnis der musikalisohn Werke, 1986; Wagner Beyond Good and Evil, 2008. EDITOR: The Family Letters of Richard Wagner, 1991; (with U. Muler and P. Wapnewski) The Wagner Handbook, 1992; Lohengrin WWV75, 1996; Wagner Beyond Good and Evil, 2008. Contributor to books and journals. **Address:** Department of Music, King's College, The Strand, London, GL WC2R 2LS, England. **Online address:** john.deathridge@kcl.ac.uk

DEATS, Richard L. American (born United States), b. 1932. **Genres:** Human Relations/Parenting, International Relations/Current Affairs, Theology/Religion, Third World. **Career:** Union Theological Seminary, associate professor, professor, 1959-72; Southeast Asia Graduate School of Theology, professor, 1968-72; Fellowship of Reconciliation, faculty, 1972, retired, 2005; Fellowship Magazine, editor, director of inter-faith activities, 1972-79, 1984-93, executive secretary, 1979-84; Methodist Social Center, chairman, board director; Wesleyan University-Philippines, trustee; United Nations-Washington Christian Citizenship Seminar, chairman. **Publications:** The Story of Methodism in the Philippines, 1964; Nationalism and Christianity in the Philippines, 1968; (ed. with V.R. Gorospe) The Filipino in the Seventies: An Ecumenical Perspective, 1973; (ed.) Ambassador of Reconciliation: A Muriel Lester Reader, 1991; How to Keep Laughing Even Though You've Considered All the Facts, 1994; Martin Luther King, Jr.: Spirit-Led Prophet, 2000; Mahatma Gandhi: Non-Violent Liberator: A Biography, 2005; Marked for Life: The Story of Hildegard Goss-Mayr, 2008. Contributor of articles to periodicals. **Address:** 117 N Broadway, Nyack, NY 10960, U.S.A. **Online address:** deatspeace@optonline.net

DEAVER, Jeff. See **DEAVER, Jeffery Wilds.**

DEAVER, Jeffery Wilds. Also writes as Jeff Deaver, William Jefferies. American (born United States), b. 1950. **Genres:** Mystery/Crime/Suspense, E-books, Novels, Children's Non-fiction, Young Adult Non-fiction, Young Adult Fiction, Novellas/Short Stories. **Career:** Writer. **Publications:** RUNE SERIES: Manhattan Is My Beat, 1989; Death of a Blue Movie Star, 1990; Hard News, 1991. MYSTERY AND SUSPENSE NOVELS: Voodoo, 1988; Always a Thief, 1988; Mistress of Justice, 1992; The Lesson of Her Death, 1993; Praying for Sleep, 1994; A Maiden's Grave, 1995; The Devil's Teardrop, 1999; Speaking in Tongues, 2000; The Blue Nowhere, 2001; Garden Of Beasts, 2004; The Sleeping Doll, 2007; The Bodies Left Behind, 2008; Roadside Crosses, 2009; Watchlist: A Serial Thriller, 2009. LINCOLN RHYME: The Bone Collector, 1997; The Coffin Dancer, 1998; The Empty Chair, 2000;

The Stone Monkey, 2002; The Vanished Man, 2003; The Twelfth Card, 2005; The Cold Moon, 2006; The Broken Window, 2008; The Burning Wire, 2010. LOCATION SCOUT MYSTERIES AS WILLIAM JEFFERIES: Shallow Graves, 1992; Bloody River Blues, 1993; Hell's Kitchen, 2001. OTHERS: (as Jeff Deaver) The Complete Law School Companion (nonfiction), 1984, rev. ed. as The Complete Law School Companion: How to Excel at America's Most Demanding Post-Graduate Curriculum, 1992; (ed.) A Hot and Sultry Night for Crime, 2003; Twisted: The Collected Stories of Jeffery Deaver, 2003; More Twisted: Collected Stories, 2 vols., 2006; (contrib.) Mystery Writers of America Presents In the Shadow of the Master: Classic Tales, 2009; Edge, 2010; Carte Blanche: The New James Bond Novel, 2011; XO, 2012. Contributor to periodicals. **Address:** c/o Deborah Schneider, Gelfman Schneider Literary Agents Inc., 250 W 57th St., Ste. 2515, New York, NY 10107, U.S.A. **Online address:** info@jefferydeaver.com

DEAVER, Julie Reece. American (born United States), b. 1953. **Genres:** Young Adult Fiction, Social Commentary, Mystery/Crime/Suspense. **Career:** Writer, illustrator and freelance artist. **Publications:** Say Goodnight, Gracie, 1988; First Wedding, Once Removed, 1990; You Bet Your Life, 1993; Chicago Blues, 1995; The Night I Disappeared, 2002. **Address:** c/o Author Mail, HarperCollins Publishers Inc., 10 E 53rd St., New York, NY 10022, U.S.A. **Online address:** juliedeaver@aol.com

DE BECKER, Gavin. American (born United States), b. 1954. **Genres:** How-to Books, Politics/Government, Social Sciences. **Career:** Gavin de Becker and Associates Inc. (consulting firm), founder and chief executive; UCLA School of Public Policy and Social Research, senior fellow; MOSAIC Threat Assessment Tool, designer; Federal Research Project, principal advisor; Rand Corp., senior advisor. Writer and consultant. **Publications:** (Intro.) To Have Or To Harm, 1994; The Gift of Fear: Survival Signals That Protect Us from Violence, 1997; Protecting the Gift: Keeping Children and Teenagers Safe (and Parents Sane), 1999; Thinking Caps: Mind Puzzles for Sharper Intuition, 2001; (intro.) Beauty Bites Beast: Awakening the Warrior Within Women and Girls, 2001; Fear Less: Real Truth about Risk, Safety and Security in a Time of Terrorism, 2002; (with T. Taylor and J. Marquart) Just 2 Seconds, 2008; (foreword) On Combat, 2008; (foreword) Mortal Shield, 2008. Contributor to books. **Address:** Gavin de Becker and Associates, 11684 Ventura Blvd., Ste. 440, Studio City, CA 91604, U.S.A. **Online address:** infoline@gavindebecker.com

DEBELJAK, Erica Johnson. Slovenian/American (born United States), b. 1961?. **Genres:** Autobiography/Memoirs, Translations. **Career:** Writer and translator. **Publications:** Srecko Kosovel: Pesnik in Jaz, 2004; Tako si moj, 2008; Forbidden Bread: A Memoir, 2009; Prepovedani kruh, 2010. AS TRANSLATOR: M. Jesih, The Name on the Tip of the Tongue, 1997; Z. Petan, Aphorisms, 1998; V. Kreslin and Z. Drava, Songs, 1998; I. Luksic, The Political System of the Republic of Slovenia: A Primer, 2001; K. Kovic, The Story of Radenska, 2001; A. Hodalic, Voyage into the Illusory Mirror: Photography 1998-2000, 2001; (with J. Cedilnik) A. Hrausky and J. Kozelj, Architectural Guide to Ljubljana: 100 Selected Buildings, 2002; Proverbs and Sayings: The Months of the Year in Slovenian Folk Wisdom, 2003; Traditional Slovene Folk Songs, 2004; D. Zajc, Barren Harvest: Selected Poems, 2004; M. Dekleva, Blind Spot of Time: Selected Poems, 2007; F. Lainscek, Murisa, 2009; B. Pahor, A Difficult Spring, 2009; B. Mozetic, Lost Story, 2011. Works appear in anthologies. Contributor to periodicals. **Address:** Ljubljana, Slovenia. **Online address:** info@ericajohnsondebeljak.com

DE BELLAIGUE, Christopher. Iranian/British (born England), b. 1971?. **Genres:** Local History/Rural Topics. **Career:** St. Antony's College, visiting fellow, 2007-08; India Today, journalist; The Economist, correspondent. **Publications:** In the Rose Garden of the Martyrs: A Memoir of Iran, 2005; Struggle for Iran, 2007; Rebel Land: Among Turkey's Forgotten Peoples, 2009. Contributor to periodicals. **Address:** HarperCollins Publishers, 10 E 53rd St., 7th Fl., New York, NY 10022, U.S.A.

DEBERG, Betty A. American (born United States), b. 1953. **Genres:** Theology/Religion, Bibliography. **Career:** Vanderbilt University, Divinity School, director of admissions and financial aid, 1980-88; Valparaiso University, assistant professor, 1988-94, associate professor of theology, 1994-96; Center for the Study of Religion and American Culture, fellow, 1992-93; University of Northern Iowa, Department of Philosophy and Religions, professor of religion and head, 1997-, National Study of Campus Ministries, director. Writer. **Publications:** Ungodly Women: Gender and the First Wave of American Fundamentalism, 1990; Women and Women's Issues in North American Lutheranism: A Bibliography, 1992; (with C. Cherry and A. Porterfield) Religion on Campus, 2001. Contributor of articles to journals. **Address:** Department of Philosophy and Religions, University of Northern Iowa, 1227 W 27th St., Cedar Falls, IA 50614-0501, U.S.A. **Online address:** betty.deberg@uni.edu

DE BERNIERES, Louis. British (born England), b. 1954. **Genres:** Novels, History, inspirational/Motivational Literature. **Career:** Writer and educator. **Publications:** The War of Don Emmanuel's Nether Parts (novel), 1990; Senor Vivo and the Coca Lord, 1991; The Troublesome Offspring of Cardinal Guzman, 1994; Captain Corelli's Mandolin, 1994; Labels, 1997; (intro.) The Book of Job, 1998; A Day Out for Mehmet Erbil, 1999; Red Dog, 2001; Gunter Weber's Confession, 2001; Sunday Morning at the Centre of the World: A Play For Voices, 2001; Birds Without Wings, 2004; A Partisan's Daughter, 2008; Notwithstanding: Stories from an English Village, 2009. **Address:** c/o Lavinia Trevor, 6 The Glass House, 49A Goldhawk Rd., London, GL W12 8QP, England.

DEBIN, David. Also writes as Smith and Doe. American (born United States), b. 1942. **Genres:** Mystery/Crime/Suspense, Adult Non-fiction, Plays/Screenplays, Human Relations/Parenting. **Career:** Antioch University, instructor in creative writing; Santa Barbara City College, faculty; The Third Age Foundation, co-founder. Writer. **Publications:** MYSTERY NOVELS: Nice Guys Finish Dead, 1992; The Big O, 1994; Murder Live at Five, 1995. ADULT NON-FICTION: (with M. Smith as Smith and Doe) What Men Don't Want Women to Know, 1998; The Book of Horrible Questions, 1999; The Ultimate Sex Test, 2000; Worst Case Scenarios: A Survivalist Guide to Love, Sex, and Romance, 2001. Living Your Creative Spirit, forthcoming; Resolving Your Unfinished Business: The Key to a Longer, Happier, Healthier Life, forthcoming. **Address:** c/o Peter Matson, Sterling Lord Literistic, 65 Bleeker St., New York, NY 10012, U.S.A. **Online address:** Al.b.marx@verizon.net

DE BLASI, Marlena. Italian/American (born United States), b. 1952. **Genres:** Food And Wine, Novels, Autobiography/Memoirs, Young Adult Fiction, Travel/Exploration, Biography. **Career:** Writer. **Publications:** COOKBOOKS: Regional Foods of Northern Italy: Recipes and Remembrances, 1997; Regional Foods of Southern Italy, 1999; A Taste of Southern Italy: Delicious Recipes and a Dash of Culture, 2006. MEMOIRS: A Thousand Days in Venice: An Unexpected Romance, 2002; A Thousand Days in Tuscany: A Bittersweet Adventure, 2004; The Lady in the Palazzo: At Home in Umbria, 2006; A Sequel to A Thousand Days in Venice, forthcoming. OTHERS: Dolce e Salata: A Bittersweet Adventure in Tuscany, 2005; That Summer in Sicily: A Love Story, 2008; Amandine: A Novel, 2010. Contributor to periodicals. **Address:** Algonquin Books, PO Box 2225, Chapel Hill, NC 27515-2225, U.S.A.

DE BLIJ, Harm J(an). American/Dutch (born Netherlands), b. 1935. **Genres:** Environmental Sciences/Ecology, Geography, Travel/Exploration. **Career:** University of Natal, lecturer in geology and geography, 1959-60; Northwestern University, visiting lecturer, 1959, visiting assistant professor, 1960-61, visiting associate professor, 1963-64; Michigan State University, assistant professor, 1961-63, associate professor, 1964-67, professor of geography, 1967-69, associate director of African studies center, 1964-69, distinguished professor of geography, 1999-, professor and associate director, John A. Hannah professor; University of Miami, Geography Department, chairman, 1969-76, College of Arts and Sciences, associate dean, 1976-78, professor of geography, 1978-94; The Journal of Geography, editor, 1970-74; Institute for Shipboard Education, University of Colorado, visiting professor of geography, 1978; University of Hawaii, visiting professor of geography, 1979; Colorado School of Mines, presidential professor, 1981-82; National Geographic Research, editor, 1984-90; Georgetown University, George Landegger distinguished professor, 1989-94; Marshall University, John Deaver Drinko professor of geography; Georgetown University, George Landegger distinguished professor; Miami Geographical Society, founder. **Publications:** Africa South, 1962; (contrib.) Economic Framework of South Africa, 1962; Dar es Salaam: A Study in Urban Geography, 1963; Geography of Subsaharan Africa, 1964; Systematic Political Geography, 1967, 4th ed., 1989; Mombasa: An African City, 1968; A Guide to Subsaharan Africa, 1968; (contrib.) Islam in Africa, 1969; Geography: Regions and Concepts, 1971, 3rd ed., 1981, rev. ed., 2000; Essentials of Geography: Regions and Concepts, 1974; Man Shapes the Earth: A Topical Geography, 1974; (contrib.) Contemporary Africa, 1976; African Survey, 1977; (contrib.) Almanac, 1977; Human Geography: Culture, Society, and Space, 1977, (with A.B. Murphy) 7th ed., 2003, (with A.B. Murphy and E.H. Fouberg) 8th ed. as Human Geography: People, Place, and Cul-

ture, 2007; (with D. Greenland) Earth in Profile: A Physical Geography, 1977; (contrib.) The Association of American Geographers: The First Seventy-five Years, 1979; Earth: A Topical Geography, 1980; (comp.) African Perspectives: An Exchange of Essays on the Economic Geography of Nine African States, 1981; Geography of Viticulture, 1981; (co-ed. and contrib.) African Perspectives: An Exchange of Essays on the Economic Geography of Nine African States, 1981; Wine-A Geographic Appreciation, 1983; Wine Regions of the Southern Hemisphere, 1985; Earth: A Physical and Human Geography, 1987; (ed.) Earths 88: Changing Geographic Perspectives: Proceedings of the Centennial Symposium, 1988; (with P.O. Muller) Physical Geography of the Global Environment, 1993, rev. ed., 2004; Nature on the Rampage, 1994; Geography: Realms, Regions and Concepts, 1994, 14th ed., 2010; Earth: An Introduction to Physical and Human Geography, 1995; Harm de Blijs Geography Book: A Leading Geographers Fresh Look at Our Changing World, 1995; Wartime Encounter with Geography, 2000; (with P.O. Muller) Concepts and Regions in Geography, 2003, 2nd ed., 2005; (with R. Cole) Survey of Subsaharan Africa: A Regional Geography, 2005; Why Geography Matters: Three Challenges Facing America: Climate Change, The Rise of China, and Global Terrorism, 2005; (ed.) Atlas of the United States, 2006; (ed.) Atlas of North America, 2005; (with P.O. Muller) The World Today: Concepts and Regions in Geography, 2007, (with P.O. Muller and A.M.G.A. WinklerPrins) 4th ed., 2009; College Atlas of the World/National Geographic Society, 2007; Power of Place: Geography, Destiny, and Globalizations Rough Landscape, 2009; The Endarkenment, 2010. Contributor to periodicals. **Address:** PO Box 608, Boca Grande, FL 33921, U.S.A. **Online address:** deblij@c4.net

DEBNAM, Aaron. American (born United States), b. 1979?. **Genres:** Novellas/Short Stories. **Career:** British Transport Police, constable. Writer. **Publications:** One Morning in July: The Man Who Was First on the Scene Tells His Story, 2007. Contributor to Periodicals. **Address:** John Blake Publishing Ltd., 3 Bramber Ct., 2 Bramber Rd., London, GL W14 9PB, England.

DE BONDT, Gabe J. German/Dutch (born Netherlands), b. 1969. **Genres:** Economics, Money/Finance, Business/Trade/Industry. **Career:** Nederlandsche Bank, staff, 1994-2000; European Central Bank, staff, 2001-, Capital Markets and Financial Structure Division, principal economist. Writer. **Publications:** Financial Structure and Monetary Transmission in Europe: A Cross-Country Study, 2000. **Address:** European Central Bank, Kaiserstrasse 29, PO Box 16 03 19, Frankfurt am Main, 60311, Germany. **Online address:** gabe.de_bondt@ecb.int

DEBONIS, Steven. American (born United States), b. 1949. **Genres:** History, Adult Non-fiction. **Career:** Phanat Nikhom, U.S. Refugee Program, instructor, 1980-81; U.S. Refugee Program, educational supervisor, 1982-92; St. Ursula High School, English teacher, 1993-; Allen College, English teacher, 1995. Writer. **Publications:** Children of the Enemy: Oral Histories of Vietnamese Amerasians, 1995. **Address:** 133 Egret Cir., West Palm Beach, FL 33413, U.S.A. **Online address:** harp88@yahoo.com

DE BONO, Douglas. American (born United States), b. 1957. **Genres:** Young Adult Fiction, Military/Defense/Arms Control, Technology. **Career:** Systems Consulting Inc., owner. Database administrator, consultant and technical writer. **Publications:** THE TERROR WAR SERIES: Point of Honor, 2002; Blood Covenant, 2002; Reap the Whirlwind, 2002; Rogue State, 2002; Firewall, 2003; No Safe Harbor, 2006. **Address:** c/o Author Mail, Metropolis Ink, 22870 S Metate Forest Trl., PO Box 682, Yarnell, AZ 85362-0682, U.S.A. **Online address:** readermail@douglasdebono.com

DE BONO, Edward (Francis Charles). Maltese/British (born England), b. 1933. **Genres:** Administration/Management, Education, Philosophy, Psychology, Technology, Theology/Religion, Information Science/Computers, inspirational/Motivational Literature, inspirational/Motivational Literature. **Career:** Oxford University, research assistant, 1957-60, lecturer, 1960-61; University of London, lecturer, 1961-63, St. Thomas Hospital Medical School, research associate; Cambridge University, assistant director of research, 1963-76, lecturer in medicine, 1976-83; Boston City Hospital, consultant, 1965-66; Harvard Medical School, research associate. Writer and consultant. **Publications:** The 5-Day Course in Thinking, 1967; The Use of Lateral Thinking in US as New Think: The Use of Lateral Thinking in the Generation of New Ideas, 1967; The Mechanism of Mind, 1969; Lateral Thinking: Creation Step by Step in UK as Lateral Thinking: A Textbook of Creativity, 1970; The Thinking Class, 1970; The New Word Po, 1970;

The Dog Exercising Machine, 1970; Lateral Thinking for Management: A Handbook: Creativity, 1971; Practical Thinking: Four Ways To Be Right, Five Ways To Be Wrong, Five Ways To Understand, 1971; Children Solve Problems, 1972; About Think, 1972; PO: A Device for Successful Thinking, 1972 in UK as PO: Beyond Yes and No, 1973; Think Tank, 1973; Teaching Thinking, 1976; The Case of the Disappearing Elephant: A 3G Mystery, 1977; The Happiness Purpose, 1977; Word Power: An Illustrated Dictionary: Vital Words, 1977; Opportunities: A Handbook of Business Opportunity Search, 1978; Future Positive, 1979; Atlas of Management Thinking, 1981; De Bono's Thinking Course, 1982, rev. ed., 1994; (with M. de Saint-Arnaud) Learn-to-think: Coursebook and Instructor's Manual, 2nd ed., 1982; Tactics: The Art and Science of Success, 1984; Conflicts: A Better Way to Resolve Them, 1985; Six Thinking Hats, 1985, rev. ed., 1999; Masterthinker's Handbook, 1985; Letters to Thinkers: Further Thoughts on Lateral Thinking, 1987; CoRT Thinking Program, 1987; Thinking Skills for Success, 1990; Handbook for the Positive Revolution, 1991; I Am Right, You Are Wrong: From This To The New Renaissance: From Rock Logic To Water Logic, 1990; Six Action Shoes, 1991; Serious Creativity: Using the Power of Lateral Thinking to Create New Ideas, 1992; Sur/petition: Creating Value Monopolies When Everyone Else Is Merely Competing, 1992; Teach Your Child How to Think, 1993; Water Logic, 1993; Parallel Thinking, 1994; Teach Yourself to Think, 1995; Mind Power, 1995; The Creative Fource: Operations Handbook, 1995; Edward De Bono's Textbook of Wisdom, 1996; How to Be More Interesting, 1997, 2nd ed., 2000; Edward de Bono's Direct Attention Thinking Tools, 1997; Alti şapkali düşünme tekniği, 1997; Simplicity, 1998; Edward de Bono's Thinking for Action, 1998; Why I Want to Be King of Australia, 1999; How You Can Be More Interesting, 2000; New Thinking for the New Millennium, 2000; How to Have a Beautiful Mind, 2004; Six Value Medals, 2005; H + (Plus) A New Religion?, 2006; (contrib.) Malta Diaries, 2006; H+ Plus: A New Religion: How to Live Your Life Positively through Happiness, Humour, Help, Hope and Health, 2006; How to Have Creative Ideas: 62 Games to Develop the Mind, 2007; Free or Unfree?: Are Americans Really Free?, 2007; Six Frames: For Thinking About Information, 2008; Creativity Workout: 62 Exercises to Unlock Your Most Creative Ideas, 2008; Think!: Before It's Too Late, 2009. EDITOR: Technology Today, 1971; Eureka!: An Illustrated History of Inventions From The Wheel To The Computer, 1974; The Greatest Thinkers: The Thirty Minds That Shaped Our Civilization, 1976. Contributor of articles to journals. **Address:** PO Box 17, Sliema, SLM 01, Malta. **Online address:** edwdebono@msn.com

DE BOTTON, Alain. British (born England), b. 1969. **Genres:** Sex, Adult Non-fiction. **Career:** Novelist and journalist; London University, director of graduate philosophy program; Seneca Productions, owner; The School of Life, founder and chairman. **Publications:** Essays in Love, 1993 in US as On Love, 1993; The Romantic Movement: Sex, Shopping and the Novel, 1995; Kiss & Tell, 1996; How Proust Can Change Your Life: Not a Novel, 1997; The Consolations of Philosophy, 2000; The Art of Travel, 2002; Status Anxiety, 2004; The Architecture of Happiness, 2006; Week at the Airport: A Heathrow Diary, 2009; Pleasures and Sorrows of Work, 2009; Religion for Atheists, 2012; How To Think More About Sex, 2012. Contributor to periodicals. **Address:** 73 Sterndale Rd., London, GL W14 0MU, England. **Online address:** adb@netcomuk.co.uk

DE BREADUN, Deaglan. Irish (born Ireland) **Genres:** Novellas/Short Stories, History, Politics/Government, Local History/Rural Topics, Social Commentary, Young Adult Non-fiction, Philosophy. **Career:** Irish Times, Belfast bureau chief, political reporter, foreign affairs correspondent. **Publications:** Scealloga, 1990; The Far Side of Revenge: Making Peace in Northern Ireland, 2000. Contributor to periodicals. **Address:** The Irish Times, 10-16 D'Olier St., Dublin, DU 2, Ireland. **Online address:** ddebreadun@irish-times.ie

DEBRIX, François. American/French (born France), b. 1968. **Genres:** Politics/Government, History, Social Sciences. **Career:** The University of Memphis, Department of Political Science, visiting adjunct professor, 1997-98; Florida International University, Department of International Relations, adjunct professor, 1997-98, assistant professor, 1998-2003, associate professor, 2003-, Department of Politics and International Relations, associate chair. Writer. **Publications:** Re-Envisioning Peacekeeping, 1999; Tabloid Terror: War, Culture and Geopolitics, 2007. EDITOR: (with C. Weber) Rituals of Mediation: International Politics and Social Meaning, 2003; Language, Agency and Politics in a Constructed World, 2003; (with M.J. Lacy) Geopolitics

of American Insecurity: Terror, Power and Foreign Policy, 2009; (with A.D. Barder) Beyond Biopolitics: Theory, Violence, and Horror in World Politics, 2011. **Address:** Department of International Relations, Florida International University, DM 432, University Pk., 11200 SW 8th St., Modesto A. Maidique Campus, Miami, FL 33199, U.S.A. **Online address:** debrixf@fiu.edu

DEBRY, Roger K. American (born United States), b. 1942. **Genres:** Information Science/Computers, Children's Fiction. **Career:** IBM Corp., senior technical staff, 1964-98; Denver University, Management Program, instructor in technology; Utah Valley University, Department of computer sciences and networking services, assistant professor, associate professor, professor. Writer. **Publications:** Communicating with Display Terminals, 1985; Bartholomew's Christmas Adventure: A Bear's Tale (children's fiction), 1995. Contributor to journals. **Address:** Department of Computing & Networking Sciences, Utah Valley University, CS 520, 800 W University Pkwy., Orem, UT 84058-6703, U.S.A. **Online address:** debryro@uvu.edu

DEBS, Victor. American (born United States), b. 1949. **Genres:** Sports/Fitness, Biography. **Career:** Board of Education, teacher, 1970-92; Rutgers University, instructor in baseball history. Writer. **Publications:** They Kept me Loyal to the Yankees, 1993; Still Standing after All These Years, 1996; Baseball Tidbits, 1997; Missed It by That Much: Baseball Players Who Challenged the Record Books, 1998; That Was Part of Baseball Then: Interviews With 24 Former Major League Baseball Players, Coaches and Managers, 2002. **Address:** 175 Lewiston St., PO Box 131800, Staten Island, NY 10314-6203, U.S.A. **Online address:** tkmlty7@aol.com

DEBURON, Nicole. French/Tunisian (born Tunisia), b. 1929?. **Genres:** Novels, Autobiography/Memoirs, Women's Studies And Issues, Psychology, History. **Career:** Writer. **Publications:** Drole de Sahara, 1956; Et vogue la gondole!, 1957; To the Gondolas, 1958; Les pieds sur le bureau, 1959; Pies sobre el escritorio, 1959; Bride and the Bugatti, 1959; Meisjes van Parijs (in Dutch), 1961; Girls of Paris, 1962; Sainte Chérie, 1964, new ed. as Les saintes chéries, 1995; Sainte Chérie en vacances, 1967; Vas-y, maman!, 1978; Dix-jours-de-rêve (novel): Roman, 1982; Qui c'est ce garçon? (novel): Roman, 1985; Où sont mes lunettes?, 1991; Arrêtez de piquer mes sous!, 1992; Arrête ton cinéma!, 1995; Mais t'as-tout pour-être heureuse!, 1996; Chéri, tu m'écoutes' Alors, répète ce que je viens de dire, 1998; Mon coeur, tu penses à quoi: A rien, 2000; C'est fou ce qu'on voit de choses dans la vie!: souvenirs vrais et faux, 2006. **Address:** 7 rue Daru, Paris, 8, France.

DECANDIDO, Keith R.A. American (born United States), b. 1969. **Genres:** Science Fiction/Fantasy, Novels. **Career:** Library Journal, assistant editor, 1990-93; Chronic Rift (talk show), co-host and producer, 1990-94; Byron Preiss Visual Publications and Multimedia Co., associate editor, editor of science fiction, fantasy and horror, 1993-98; Albe-Shiloh Inc., president, 1998-. Writer. **Publications:** (With J.R. Nieto) Spider-Man: Venom's Wrath, 1998; (with C. Golden and N. Holder) Buffy the Vampire Slayer: The Watchers Guide, 1998; Buffy: The Vampire Slayer: The Xander Years, 1999; Young Hercules: Cheiron's Warriors, 1999; Young Hercules: The Ares Alliance, 1999; Star Trek: Fatal Error, 2000; Star Trek: Invincible, 2000; Star Trek: Cold Fusion, 2001; Star Trek: The Next Generation 61: Diplomatic Implausibility, 2001; Deep Space Nine: Gateways Book 4: Demons of Air and Darkness, 2001; Farscape: House of Cards, 2001; Darkness Falls, 2002; S.C.E. Book 1: Have Tech, Will Travel, 2002; S.C.E. Book 2: Miracle Workers, 2002; The Brave & the Bold Books 1 & 2, 2002; Brave and the Bold, 2002; S.C.E. Book 3: Some Assembly Required, 2002; The Lost Era: The Art of the Impossible, 2003; I.K.S. Gorkon Book 1: A Good Day to Die, 2003; I.K.S. Gorkon Book 2: Honor Bound, 2003; Gene Roddenberrys Andromeda: Destruction of Illusions, 2003; Resident Evil: Genesis, 2004; Dragon Precinct, 2004; Resident Evil: Apocalypse, 2004; A Time for War, a Time for Peace, 2004; Tales of the Dominion War, 2004; S.C.E. Book 6: Wildfire, 2004; I.K.S. Gorkon Book 3: Enemy Territory, 2005; Satisfaction is not guaranteed, 2005; Articles of the Federation, 2005; Spider-Man: Down These Mean Streets, 2005; Serenity, 2005; Mirror Image, 2006; The Madness of King George, in Star Wars on Trial, 2006; Buffy the Vampire Slayer: Blackout, 2006; Star Craft: Ghost: Nova, 2006; World of Warcraft: Cycle of Hatred, 2006; Extinction, 2007; (co-author) Twist of Faith, 2007; Tiberium Wars, 2007; Supernatural: Nevermore, 2007; (with P. David and S. Shaw) Star Trek: Mirror Universe: Obsidian Alliances Four Walls: A Novel, 2008; A Burning House, 2008; Bone Key, 2008; (with G. Trowbridge and C. Roberson) Echoes and Refractions, 2008; Star Trek Destiny: A Singular Destiny, 2009; Heart of the Dragon, 2010; Unicorn Precinct, 2011; (with Nieto) Spider-Man: Venoms Rage, forthcoming. EDI-

TOR: (with B. Preiss and J.G. Betancourt) The Ultimate Alien, 1995; (with Preiss and Betancourt) The Ultimate Dragon, 1995; (with B. Preiss and R. Silverberg) Virtual Unrealities: The Short Fiction of Alfred Bester, 1997; (with J. Sherman) Urban Nightmares (short stories), 1997; Tales from the Captains Table, 2005. (with L. Wein) Pryde of the X-Men, In The Unauthorized X-Men, 2006; (with M. Millar) Actor and Superactor, In The Boy from Krypton, 2006; (with L.L. Coleman) Meiyo, In Age of War: A Classic Battle Tech Anthology, 2006; Deathless, 2007; Spectres, 2010. Contributor of articles to periodicals. **Address:** PO Box 4976, New York, NY 10185-4976, U.S.A. **Online address:** keith@decandido.net

DECARO, Louis A. American (born United States), b. 1957. **Genres:** Theology/Religion, Social Sciences, History. **Career:** Nyack College, assistant professor of church history. Writer. **Publications:** On the Side of My People: A Religious Life of Malcolm X, 1996; (ed. with R.D. Carle) Signs of Hope in the City: Ministries of Community Renewal, 1997, rev. ed., 1999; Malcolm and the Cross: The Nation of Islam, Christianity and Malcolm X, 1998; Fire from the Midst of You: A Religious Life of John Brown, 2002; John Brown: The Cost of Freedom, 2007. **Address:** Nyack College & Alliance Theological Seminary, 350 N Highland Ave., Nyack, NY 10960, U.S.A. **Online address:** louis.decaro@nyack.edu

DE CARVALHO, Mário. German/Portuguese (born Portugal), b. 1944. **Genres:** Novels, Romance/Historical, Translations. **Career:** Lawyer, 1975-. Writer. **Publications:** Contos Da'setima Esfera, 1981; Casos do Beco Das Sardinheiras, 1982; OLivro Grande de Tebas Navio e Mariana, 1982; A Inaudita Guerra da AvenidaGago Coutinho, 1983; Fabulário, 1984; Era Uma Vez Um Alferes, 1984; Contos Soltos, 1986; (with C.P. Correia) E Se Tivesse A Bondade De MeDizer Porque, 1986; A Paixao Do Conde de Fróis, 1986; Os Alferes, 1989; Quatrocentos Mil Sestetrcios, 1991; Agua Em Pena de Pato, Teatro Do Quotidiano, 1991; Um Deus Passeando Pela Brisa da Tarde: Romance, 1994, trans. as A God Strolling in the Cool of the Evening, 1997; Era Bom Que Trocassemos Umas Ideias Sobre O Assunto, 1995; Haja Harmonia, 1997; Se Perguntarem por mim, não Estou; Seguido de, Haja Harmonia: Teatro, 1999; Contos Vagabundo, 2000; Fantasia Para Dois Coronéis E UmaPiscina, 2003; O Homem que Engoliu a Lua, 2003; Sala magenta: romance, 2008; Arte de morrer longe, 2010; Homem do turbante verde e outras histórias, 2011; Quando o diabo reza: vadiário breve, 2011. **Address:** c/o Ray-Guede Mertin, Friedrichstrasse 1, Bad Homburg, D-6138, Germany. **Online address:** mariodecarvalho@mail.telefac.ht

DECK, Allan Figueroa. American (born United States), b. 1945. **Genres:** Literary Criticism And History, Theology/Religion, Biography, Social Sciences, Sociology. **Career:** Pontifical University of Comillas, lecturer in Latin American literature, 1972; St. Louis University, lecturer in Brazilian literature, 1972-73; University of Santa Clara, lecturer in Mexican American history, 1973-75; Immaculate Heart College, lecturer, 1976-77; Centro Pastoral Guadalupe, director, 1976-78; Diocese of Orange, director of Hispanic ministry, 1979-85; Jesuit School of Theology at Berkeley, adjunct professor, 1987-88, assistant professor of Hispanic ministry and missiology, 1988-92; National Catholic Council for Hispanic Ministry, founder, executive director, 1991-; Catholic University of Portugal, visiting professor, 1990; Loyola Marymount University, lecturer in Chicano studies and theology, 1992-93, coordinator of Hispanic pastoral studies, 1992-, associate professor of theological studies, 1993-, Cultural Orientation Program for International Ministers, director; University of St. Mary of the Lake, visiting professor, 1992; Lutheran School of Theology, visiting professor, 1992; Loyola Institute for Spirituality, executive director; United States Conference of Catholic Bishops (USCCB), executive director, 2008-. Writer. **Publications:** Francisco Javier Alegre: A Study in Mexican Literary Criticism, 1976; The Second Wave: Hispanic Ministry and the Evangelization of Culture, 1989; (ed. and intro.) Frontiers of Hispanic Theology in the United States, 1992; (ed. with J.P. Dolan) The Notre Dame History of Hispanic Catholics in the U.S., vol. III: Hispanic Catholic Culture in the U.S.: Issues and Concerns, 1994; (ed. with Y. Tarango and T. Matovina) Perspectivas: Hispanic Ministry, 1995; (ed. with V. Elizondo and T. Matovina) Treasure of Guadalupe, 2006. Contributor to books. **Address:** Loyola Institute for Spirituality, 480 S Batavia St., Orange, CA 92868-3907, U.S.A. **Online address:** diversity@usccb.org

DE COSTA, Elena M. American (born United States), b. 1949. **Genres:** Cultural/Ethnic Topics, Literary Criticism And History, Language/Linguistics, Theatre, Third World, Art/Art History, Education. **Career:** University of Wisconsin, instructor in Spanish, 1975-76; College of Wooster, assistant professor of Spanish, 1977-82; Indiana University of Pennsylvania, assistant professor of Spanish language and Hispanic and comparative literature, 1982-85; Santa Clara University, assistant professor of Spanish, 1987-; Santa Clara County Unified School District, instructional aide for migrant education program, 1988; Carroll University, associate professor of Spanish, 1995-; Waukesha County, coordinator of interpreters for health and human services. Writer. **Publications:** Collaborative Latin American Popular Theatre: From Theory to Form, From Text to Stage, 1992. Works appear in anthologies. Contributor of articles to periodicals. **Address:** Department of Modern Languages & Literatures, Carroll University, MacAllister B003A, 100 N East Ave., Waukesha, WI 53186-3103, U.S.A. **Online address:** edecosta@carrollu.edu

DECOSTA-WILLIS, Miriam. American (born United States), b. 1934. **Genres:** Cultural/Ethnic Topics, Race Relations, Women's Studies And Issues, Language/Linguistics, Literary Criticism And History, Local History/Rural Topics. **Career:** LeMoyne College, associate, 1957-58; Owen College, instructor, 1960-65; Memphis State University, associate professor of Spanish, 1966-70; Howard University, Department of Romance Languages, associate professor, 1970-74, professor of Spanish and chair, 1974-76; LeMoyne-Owen College, professor of Spanish, DuBois Scholars Program, director, 1979-89; George Mason University, commonwealth professor of Spanish, 1989-91; University of Maryland, professor in Africana studies, 1991-99, now retired; SAGE: A Scholarly Journal on Black Women, associate editor; Memphis Black Writers Workshop, co-founder and chair. Writer. **Publications:** Notable Black Memphians, 2008. EDITOR: (intro.) Blacks in Hispanic Literature: Critical Essays, 1977; (with F.P. Delk and P. Dotson) Homespun Images: An Anthology of Black Memphis Writers and Artists, 1989; (co-ed.) Double Stitch: Black Women Write about Mothers and Daughters, 1991; (with R.P. Bell and R. Martin) Erotique Noire/Black Erotica, 1992; The Memphis Diary of Ida B. Wells, 1995; Singular Like a Bird: The Art of Nancy Morejon, 1999; Daughters of the Diaspora: Afra-Hispanic Writers, 2003. Contributor to books and periodicals. **Address:** 700 7th St., SW, Ste. 205, Washington, DC 20024, U.S.A. **Online address:** decosta2@umbc.edu

DECREDICO, Mary A. American (born United States), b. 1959. **Genres:** History, Local History/Rural Topics, Business/Trade/Industry. **Career:** U.S. Naval Academy, assistant professor of history, 1986-, professor, chair, vice academic dean; The National Civil War Museum, director. Writer. **Publications:** Patriotism for Profit: Georgia's Urban Entrepreneurs and the Confederate War Effort, 1990; Mary Boykin Chesnut: A Confederate Woman's Life, 1996. **Address:** Department of History, U.S. Naval Academy, 107 Maryland Ave., 121 Blake Rd., Annapolis, MD 21402, U.S.A. **Online address:** decredic@usna.edu

DE CRESPIGNY, (Richard) Rafe (Champion). Australian (born Australia), b. 1936. **Genres:** History. **Career:** Australian National University, lecturer, 1965-70, senior lecturer, 1970-74, reader in Chinese, 1974-98, University House, master, 1991-2001, adjunct professor of Asian studies, 1998-, now professor emeritus; University of Melbourne, visiting lecturer, 1966-70; 28 Intl. Congress of Orientalists, secretary general, 1971; University of Washington, Han Project, senior research fellow, 1971; Cambridge University, Clare Hall, visiting fellow, 1971-72; University of Hawaii, Asian Studies Program, visiting professor, 1978; University of Leiden, Sinologisch Instituut, visiting fellow, 1986. Writer. **Publications:** The Biography of Sun Chien, 1966; (comp.) Official Titles of the Former Han Dynasty, 1967; (trans.) The Last of the Han: Being the Chronicle of the Years 181-220 A.D. as Recorded in Chapters 54 to 59 of the Tzu-chih t'ung-chien of Ssu-ma Kuang, 1969; The Records of the Three Kingdoms: A Study in the Historiography of San-kuo Chih, 1970; China: The Land and Its People, 1971; China This Century, 1975; Portents of Protest in the Later Han Dynasty: The Memorials of Hsiang Kai to Emperor Huan, 1976; Northern Frontier: The Policies and Strategy of the Later Han Empire, 1984; Emperor Huan and Emperor Ling: Being the Chronicle of Later Han for the Years 157-189 AD as Recorded in Chapters 54 to 59 of the Zizhi tongjian of Sima Guang, 1989; Generals of the South: The Foundation and Early History of the Three Kingdoms State of Wu, 1990; Man from the Margin: Cao Cao and the Three Kingdoms, 1990; To Establish Peace: Being the Chronicle of Later Han for the Years 189 to 220 AD as Recorded in Chapters 59 to 69 of the Zizhi tongjian of Sima Guang, 1996; A Biographical Dictionary of Later Han to the Three Kingdoms (23-220 AD), 2007; Imperial Warlord: A Biography of Cao Cao 155-220, 2010. Contributor to journals. **Address:** Faculty of Asian Studies, Australian National University, Canberra, AC 0200, Australia. **Online address:** rafe.decrespigny@anu.edu.au

DECROW, Karen. American (born United States), b. 1937. **Genres:** Education, Law, Women's Studies And Issues, Civil Liberties/Human Rights, Social Commentary, Psychology. **Career:** Golf Digest, fashion and resorts editor, 1959-60; Zoning Digest, editor, 1960-61; Center for the Study of Liberal Education of Adults, writer and editor, 1961-64; Holt, Rinehart & Winston Inc., social studies and adult education editor, 1965; L.W. Singer Company Inc., social science editor, 1965-66; Eastern Regional Institute for Education, writer, 1967-69; National Organization for Women, Eastern regional director and political chairwoman, 1968-77, president, 1974-77; World Woman Watch, co-founder, 1988; Syracuse Post-Standard, columnist. Attorney. **Publications:** (With R. DeCrow) University Adult Education: A Selected Bibliography, 1967; (ed.) The Pregnant Teenager, 1968; The Young Woman's Guide to Liberation; Alternatives to A Half-Life While The Choice is Still Yours, 1971; (ed. with R. Seidenberg) Corporate Wives, Corporate Casualties, 1973; Sexist Justice, 1974; (with R. Seidenberg) Women Who Marry Houses: Panic and Protest in Agoraphobia, 1983; (with J. Kammer) Good Will Toward Men, 1994. **Address:** 7599 Brown Gulf Rd., Jamesville, NY 13078-9636, U.S.A.

DEDMAN, Stephen. Australian (born Australia), b. 1959?. **Genres:** Science Fiction/Fantasy, Novellas/Short Stories. **Career:** Freelance writer, 1977-; Department of Education, Employment and Training, administrative service officer, 1993-2002; Australian Physicist, editorial assistant; Eidolon, associate editor, 1995-2003; A Touch of Strange Science Fiction and Fantasy Bookshop, purchasing manager, 1997-2000; Nova Express, book reviewer, 1998-2003; Central Metro College of TAFE, lecturer, 1999; The West Australian, book reviewer, 2000-; Driftwood Manuscripts, manuscript assessor, 2001-; Clarion South, reader, 2003-; Borderlands Magazine, fiction editor, 2003-; University of Western Australia, tutor and lecturer, 2003-; Fantastic Planet Bookshop, purchasing manager, 2005-. **Publications:** (Co-author) GURPS Martial Arts Adventures, 1993; The Art of Arrow Cutting, 1997; Foreign Bodies, 1999; Shadows Bite, 2001; Never Seen by Waking Eyes: Stories, 2005; Shadowrun, 2006; Fistful of Data, 2006. Contributor of fiction to periodicals. **Address:** Tor Books, 175 5th Ave., 14th Fl., New York, NY 10010, U.S.A. **Online address:** dedmans@ii.net

DEE, Barbara. American (born United States), b. 1958. **Genres:** Young Adult Fiction. **Career:** Freelance writer and educator. **Publications:** Just Another Day in My Insanely Real Life, 2006; Solving Zoe, 2009; This Is Me from Now On, 2010; Trauma Queen, 2011. **Address:** c/o Jill Grinberg, Jill Grinberg Literary Management, 224 5th Ave., New York, NY 10001, U.S.A. **Online address:** barbara@barbaradeebooks.com

DEE, Ed(ward J.). American (born United States), b. 1940. **Genres:** Novels, Novellas/Short Stories, Mystery/Crime/Suspense, Criminology/True Crime. **Career:** New York Police Department, police officer, 1962-82, Crime Control Bureau, lieutenant and supervisor of detectives. Writer. **Publications:** 14 Peck Slip, 1994; Bronx Angel, 1995; Little Boy Blue, 1997; Nightbird, 1999; The Con Man's Daughter, 2003. Contributor to periodicals. **Address:** c/o Gail Hochman, Brandt & Hochman, 1501 Broadway, New York, NY 10036, U.S.A. **Online address:** edee58@cs.com

DEE, Jonathan. American (born United States), b. 1962?. **Genres:** Adult Non-fiction. **Career:** Paris Review, senior editor, 1987-90; The New York Times Magazine, staff writer; New School University, teacher of creative writing; Young Men's Hebrew Association, Unterberg Poetry Center, teacher of creative writing; Columbia University, teacher of creative writing; Queens University, faculty. **Publications:** The Lover of History, 1990; The Liberty Campaign, 1993; St. Famous, 1996; Chronicles of Ancient Egypt, 1998; Palladio, 2002; Isis: Queen of Egyptian Magic: Her Book of Divination and Spells, 2003; (with L. Taylor) Beginner's Guide to Color Therapy, 2004; Privileges: A Novel, 2010. Contributor to publications. **Address:** New School University, 66 W 12th St., Rm. 507, New York, NY 10011, U.S.A.

DEE, Tim. British (born England), b. 1961?. **Genres:** Animals/Pets, Natural History. **Career:** British Broadcasting Corp. (BBC), producer and art host. Writer. **Publications:** The Running Sky: A Bird-Watching Life in US as A Year on the Wing: Four Seasons in a Life with Birds, 2009; (ed. with S. Armitage) The Poetry of Birds, 2009. **Address:** c/o Sarah Ballard, United Agents, 12-26 Lexington St., London, GL W1F OLE, England.

DEEB, Lara. American (born United States), b. 1974?. **Genres:** Gay And Lesbian Issues, History, Theology/Religion, Women's Studies And Issues. **Career:** University of California, associate professor of women's studies,

through 2009; Scripps College, Department of Anthropology, assistant professor, 2004-09, associate professor, 2009-, chair of department; Middle East Research and Information Project, editor. **Publications:** An Enchanted Modern: Gender and Public Piety in Shi'i Lebanon, 2006. Contributor to books and periodicals. **Address:** Scripps College, Vita Nova 113, 1030 Columbia Ave., Claremont, CA 91711-3905, U.S.A. **Online address:** ldeeb@uci.edu

DEEM, James M(organ). American (born United States), b. 1950. **Genres:** Children's Fiction, Young Adult Fiction, Archaeology/Antiquities, Children's Non-fiction, Education, History, Paranormal, Writing/Journalism, Writing/Journalism. **Career:** Detroit Institute of Technology, Learning Center, director, 1976-78; Mohawk Valley Community College, assistant professor, department chair of developmental studies, 1979-84; John Jay College of Criminal Justice, associate professor of communication skills, 1984-2003. Writer. **Publications:** YOUNG ADULT NOVELS: Frog Eyes Loves Pig, 1988; Frogburger at Large, 1990; 3 NBs of Julian Drew, 1994. MIDDLE GRADE NOVELS: The Very Real Ghost Book of Christina Rose, 1996. MIDDLE-GRADE NONFICTION: How to Find a Ghost, 1988; How to Catch a Flying Saucer, 1991; How to Hunt Buried Treasure, 1992; Ghost Hunters, 1992; How to Travel through Time, 1993; How to Read Your Mother's Mind, 1994; How to Make a Mummy Talk, 1995; Bodies from the Bog, 1998; Zachary Taylor, 2002; Millard Fillmore, 2003; The Vikings, 2004; El Salvador, 2004; Bodies From the Ash, 2005; Primary Source Accounts of the Mexican-American War, 2006; Primary Source Accounts of the Revolutionary War, 2006; Bodies from the Ice: Melting Glaciers and the Recovery of the Past, 2008; Auschwitz: Voices from the Death Camp, 2011; Kristallnacht: The Nazi Terror that Began the Holocaust, 2011. OTHER: Study Skills in Practice, 1993. Contributor to books and periodicals. **Address:** c/o Author Mail, Houghton Mifflin Children's Books, 222 Berkeley St., 8th Fl., Boston, MA 02116, U.S.A. **Online address:** jamesmdeem@yahoo.com

DEEN, Hanifa. Australian (born Australia), b. 1941. **Genres:** Literary Criticism And History. **Career:** Multicultural and Ethnic Affairs Commission of Western Australia, deputy commissioner, Human Rights and Equal Opportunity Commission of Western Australia, hearing commissioner; Monash University, Centre for Muslim Minorities and Islamic Policy, senior research fellow. Writer. **Publications:** Caravanserai: Journey among Australian Muslims, 1995, rev. ed., 2003; Broken Bangles, 1998, 2nd ed., 2000; The Crescent and The Pen: The Strange Journey of Taslima Nasreen, 2006; The Jihad Seminar, 2008; Ali Abdul v The King, 2011. **Address:** Jenny Darling & Associates Pty Ltd., PO Box 413, Toorak, VI 3142, Australia. **Online address:** hanifa.deen@arts.monash.edu.au

DEENA, Seodial F(rank) H(ubert). Guyanese (born Guyana), b. 1956. **Genres:** Adult Non-fiction, Theology/Religion. **Career:** East Carolina University, Department of English, associate professor of English, 1994-, professor of multicultural and postcolonial, transnational literature and criticism, Graduate Multicultural and Transnational Literatures Program, coordinator; Journal of Caribbean Studies, editor; Region and Nation Literature Association Journal, founder and editor. **Publications:** Canonization, Colonization, Decolonization: A Comparative Study of Political and Critical Works by Minority Writers, 2001; Situating Caribbean Literature and Criticism in Multicultural and Postcolonial Studies, 2003; From Around the Globe: Secular Authors and Biblical Perspectives, 2004. Contributor to periodicals. **Address:** Department of English, East Carolina University, Bate 2105, Greenville, NC 27858-4353, U.S.A. **Online address:** deenas@ecu.edu

DEFAZIO, Albert J. American (born United States) **Genres:** Literary Criticism And History. **Career:** George Mason University, Department of English, adjunct professor, assistant professor; Northern Virginia Writing Project, teacher consultant, Student Summer Institute, teacher. Writer. **Publications:** Literary Masterpieces: The Sun Also Rises, 2000; (ed.) Dear Papa, Dear Hotch: The Correspondence of Ernest Hemingway and A.E. Hotchner, 2005. Contributor to periodicals. **Address:** Department of English, George Mason University, Rm. A 119B, Robinson Hall, 4400 University Dr., 3E4, Fairfax, VA 22030, U.S.A. **Online address:** adefazio@gmu.edu

DE FERRARI, Gabriella. American (born United States), b. 1941. **Genres:** Adult Non-fiction, Biography, Literary Criticism And History. **Career:** Institute of Contemporary Art, director, 1975-77; Harvard University, Busch Reisinger Museum, acting curator, 1978-79, Fogg Art Museum, assistant director of curatorial affairs, 1979-82; New School for Social Research, Vera List Center for Art and Politics, founding chair, 1988-. Freelance writer and historian. **Publications:** A Cloud on Sand, 1989; Gringa Latina: A Woman of Two Worlds, 1995; (with D. Merriam) Lika Mutal, 1996; Machu Picchu, forthcoming. Contributor to periodicals. **Address:** c/o Lynn Nesbit, Janklow & Nesbit Associates, 445 Park Ave., New York, NY 10022-2606, U.S.A. **Online address:** gdferrari@aol.com

DEFFAA, Chip. American (born United States), b. 1951. **Genres:** Music, Plays/Screenplays, Autobiography/Memoirs. **Career:** New York Post, jazz critic, 1986-; Chip Deffaa Productions L.L.C., owner. Writer. **Publications:** Swing Legacy, 1989; Voices of the Jazz Age: Profiles of Eight Vintage Jazz Men, 1990; In the Mainstream: Eighteen Portraits in Jazz, 1992; Traditionalists and Revivalists in Jazz, 1993; (with D. Cassidy) C'Mon Get Happy ... Fear and Loathing on the Partridge Family Bus, 1994; Blue Rhythms: Six Lives in Rhythm and Blues, 1996; Jazz Veterans: A Portrait Gallery, 1996; (ed. and intro.) F. Scott Fitzgerald: The Princeton Years, 1996; George M. Cohan, in His Own Words, 2004. Contributor to periodicals. **Address:** Chip Deffaa Productions L.L.C., 50 Quartz Ln., Paterson, NJ 07501-3345, U.S.A.

DEFORD, Frank. American (born United States), b. 1938. **Genres:** Novels, Social Commentary, Sports/Fitness, Literary Criticism And History. **Career:** Sports Illustrated, senior writer, 1962-89, senior contributing writer, 1998-; National Public Radio (NPR), commentator, 1980-; Cable News Network (CNN), commentator, 1980-86; National Broadcasting Co. (NBC), sports commentator, 1986-89; National Sports Daily, editor, 1989-91; The National, daily sports newspaper, editor-in-chief, 1990-91; ESPN, commentator, 1991-94; Newsweek, columnist, 1992, 1996-98; Home Box Office, correspondent and writer, 1995-; Cystic Fibrosis Foundation, chairman, through 1999, chairman emeritus. **Publications:** (With D. Budge) A Tennis Memoir, 1968; Five Strides on the Banked Track: The Life and Times of the Roller Derby, 1971; There She Is: The Life and Times of Miss America, 1971, rev. ed., 1978; Cut 'n' run, 1973; (with A. Ashe) Arthur Ashe, Portrait in Motion, 1975; Owner, 1976; Big Bill Tilden: The Triumphs and the Tragedy, 1976; (with J. Kramer) The Game: My 40 Years in Tennis, 1979; Everybody's All-American, 1981; Autobiography of Billie Jean King, 1982; Alex, The Life of a Child, 1983; Lite Reading, 1984; Spy in the Deuce Court, 1986; World's Tallest Midget: The Best of Frank Deford, 1987; (with P. Shriver and S.B. Adams) Passing Shots: Pam Shriver on Tour, 1987; Sports People, 1988; (contrib.) Fireside Book of Pro Football, 1989; Casey on the Loose, 1989; Love and Infamy, 1993; Alex: The Life of a Child, 1997; Best of Frank Deford: I'm just Getting Started, 2000; Other Adonis: A Novel of Reincarnation, 2001; An American Summer: A Novel, 2002; Heart of a Champion: Celebrating the Spirit and Character of Great American Sports Heroes, 2002; Old Ball Game: How John Mcgraw, Christy Mathewson and the New York Giants Created Modern Baseball, 2005; Entitled: A Tale of Modern Baseball, 2007; Bliss, Remembered, 2010. **Address:** c/o Sterling Lord, Sterling Lord Literistic, 65 Bleecker St., New York, NY 10012, U.S.A.

DEFRANK, Thomas M. American (born United States), b. 1945. **Genres:** Politics/Government, Documentaries/Reportage, Autobiography/Memoirs, Biography. **Career:** Fort Worth Star-Telegram, reporter; Bryan Daily Eagle, reporter; Minneapolis Star, reporter; United States Department of Defense, Pentagon, public affairs officer, 1968-70; Newsweek, Washington, intern to deputy bureau chief and senior White House correspondent, 1968-95; freelance writer, 1995-96; New York Daily News, Washington Bureau chief, 1996-. **Publications:** (Co-author) Quest for the Presidency 1984, 1985; (co-author) Quest for the Presidency 1988, 1989; (co-author) Quest for the Presidency 1992, 1994; The Politics of Diplomacy: Revolution, War, and Peace, 1989-1992, 1995; (with E. Rollins) Bare Knuckles and Back Rooms (autobiography), 1996; Write It When I'm Gone: Remarkable Off-The-Record Conversations With Gerald R. Ford, 2007. **Address:** 608 S Carolina Ave. SE, Washington, DC 20003, U.S.A.

DEFREES, Madeline. Also writes as Mary Madeline DeFrees, Mary Gilbert, Mary Gilbert. American (born United States), b. 1919. **Genres:** Novellas/Short Stories, Poetry, Writing/Journalism, Autobiography/Memoirs, Social Sciences. **Career:** Elementary school teacher, 1938-39; St. Monica's School, teacher, 1939-40; St. Francis School, teacher, 1940-42; St. Mary's Academy, teacher, 1942-44, 1946-49; St. Mary's, teacher, 1944-46; Holy Names College (now Fort Wright College), instructor, 1950-55, assistant professor, 1955-63, associate professor of English and journalism, 1963-67; Seattle University, visiting professor, 1965-66, 1972; University of Montana, visiting associate professor, 1967-69, associate professor, 1969-72, professor of English, 1972-79; Marylhurst College, visiting professor, 1969; University of Washington,

visiting professor, 1970; University of Victoria, visiting professor, 1974; University of Massachusetts, professor of English, 1979-85, MFA Writing Program, director, 1980-83, professor emeritus, 1985-; Full-time writer, 1985-; Bucknell University, poet-in-residence, 1988; Eastern Washington University, distinguished visiting writer, 1988; Wichita State University, distinguished visiting poet-in-residence, 1993; Richard Hugo House, creative writing teacher, 1998-99; Pacific University, faculty; Northwest Institute of Literary Arts, lecturer of low-residency MFA program, 2009-. **Publications:** AS SISTER MARY GILBERT: Springs of Silence (autobiography), 1953; Later Thoughts from the Springs of Silence, 1962; From the Darkroom (poetry), 1964. AS MADELINE DEFREES: When Sky Lets Go, 1978; Imaginary Ancestors, 1978; Magpie on the Gallows, 1982; The Light Station on Tillamook Rock (poetry), 1989; Imaginary Ancestors (poetry), 1990; Possible Sibyls, 1991; Blue Dusk: New and Selected Poems, 1951-2001, 2001; Spectral Waves: New and Uncollected Poems, 2006. **Address:** Northwest Institute of Literary Arts, PO Box 639, Freeland, WA 98249, U.S.A.

DEFREES, Mary Madeline. See **DEFREES, Madeline.**

DEGEORGE, Richard T(homas). American (born United States), b. 1933?. **Genres:** Philosophy, Ethics, Information Science/Computers. **Career:** University of Kansas, assistant professor, 1959-62, associate professor, 1962-64, professor, 1964-72, university distinguished professor of philosophy, 1972-. Writer. **Publications:** Patterns of Soviet Thought, 1966; (co-author) Science and Ideology in Soviet Society, 1967; The New Marxism, 1968; Soviet Ethics and Morality, 1969; Guide to Philosophical Bibliography and Research, 1971; The Philosopher's Guide, 1980; Business Ethics, 1982, 7th ed., 2010; The Nature and Limits of Authority, 1985; Competing with Integrity in International Business, 1993; Freedom and Tenure: Ethical Issues, 1997; The Ethics of Information Technology and Business, 2003. EDITOR: Classical and Contemporary Metaphysics, 1962; (co-ed.) Reflections on Man, vol. II: Dialectical Thought, 1966; Ethics and Society, 1966; (with F.M. DeGeorge) The Structuralists from Marx to Levi-Strauss, 1972; (with J.P. Scanlan) Marxism and Religion in Eastern Europe, 1976; (with J. Pichler) Ethics, Free Enterprise and Public Policy, 1978; Semiotic Themes, 1981. **Address:** Department of Philosophy, University of Kansas, 1445 Jayhawk Blvd., Rm. 3090, Lawrence, KS 66045-7590, U.S.A. **Online address:** degeorge@ku.edu

DEGRAAFF, Robert M(ark). American (born United States), b. 1942. **Genres:** Animals/Pets, Poetry, Natural History. **Career:** St. Lawrence University, instructor, 1966-69, assistant professor, 1972-76, associate professor, 1976-85, London Program, coordinator, 1981-83, professor of English, 1985-2008, professor emeritus, 2008-, Chorus, tenor, Catch Club (singing group), leader. Writer. **Publications:** The Book of the Toad: A Natural and Magical History of Toad-human Relations, 1991. Contributor of articles to journals. **Address:** Department of English, St. Lawrence University, 23 Romoda Dr., Canton, NY 13617, U.S.A. **Online address:** rdegraaff@stlawu.edu

DE GRAVE, Kathleen. (Kathy). American (born United States), b. 1950. **Genres:** Novels, Novellas/Short Stories, Literary Criticism And History, Women's Studies And Issues. **Career:** Social Security Administration, claims representative, 1978-82; University of Wisconsin, lecturer in English, 1983-84; Saint Norbert College, affiliate, 1983-84; Pittsburg State University, lecturer, 1987-89, professor of English, 1989-, associate professor of English, 1989-, director of writing across the curriculum program, 1989-, director of Western Athletic Conference program, 1989-. Writer. **Publications:** Company Woman: A Novel, 1995; Swindler, Spy, Rebel: The Confidence Woman in Nineteenth Century America (literary study), 1995; (author of intro.) The Jungle, 2003. Works appear in anthology. Contributor of to periodicals. **Address:** English Department, Pittsburg State University, 449 Grubbs Hall, 1701 South Broadway, Pittsburg, KS 66762, U.S.A. **Online address:** kdegrave@pittstate.edu

DEGRAZIA, Emilio. American (born United States), b. 1941. **Genres:** Novels, Novellas/Short Stories, Humanities. **Career:** Winona State University, assistant professor, 1969-79, associate professor, 1979-86, professor of English, 1986-, now professor emeritus. Writer. **Publications:** Enemy Country (short stories), 1984; (co-author) Today's Gift, 1985; Billy Brazil (novel), 1991; Seventeen Grams of Soul (short stories), 1994; 26 Minnesota Writers (anthology), 1996; A Canticle for Bread and Stones (novel), 1997; (ed. with M. DeGrazia) 33 Minnesota Poets (anthology) 2000; Winona: A Romantic Tragedy (play) 2002; Burying the Tree (essays) 2006; Walking on Air in a Field of Greens (memoir) 2009. **Address:** Winona State University, 175

West Mark St., PO Box 5838, Winona, MN 55987, U.S.A. **Online address:** edegrazia@winona.edu

DE GROEN, Alma. Also writes as Alma Margaret De Groen. New Zealander (born New Zealand), b. 1941. **Genres:** Plays/Screenplays, Novels, Women's Studies And Issues. **Career:** National Library Service, library assistant, 1958-64; playwrighter, 1968-; West Australia Institute of Technology, writer-in-residence, 1986; Griffin Theatre Co., dramaturg, 1987. **Publications:** The Joss Adams Show, 1970; Going Home and Other Plays, 1977; Vocations, 1984; The Rivers of China, 1988; Chidley, 1991; The Girl Who Saw Everything, 1992; The Woman in the Window, 1999; Wicked Sisters, 2003. Contributor to periodicals. **Address:** RGM Associates, 64-76 Kippax St., Level 2, Ste. 202, PO Box 128, Surry Hills, NW 2010, Australia.

DE GROEN, Alma Margaret. *See* **DE GROEN, Alma.**

DE GROOT, Gerard J. Scottish/American (born United States), b. 1955. **Genres:** Military/Defense/Arms Control, History. **Career:** University of St. Andrews, Department of Modern History, chair and professor, 1985-. Writer. **Publications:** Liberal Crusader: The Life of Sir Archibald Sinclair, 1993; Blighty: British Society in the Era of the Great War, 1996; (ed. with C.M. Peniston-Bird) A Soldier and a Woman: Sexual Integration in the Military, 2000; The First World War, 2001; The Bomb: A Life, 2005; Dark Side of the Moon: The Magnificent Madness of the American Lunar Quest, 2006; The Sixties Unplugged: A Kaleidoscopic History of a Disorderly Decade, 2008; Seventies Unplugged: A kaleidoscopic Look at a Violent Decade, 2010. **Address:** School of History, University of St Andrews, St Katharine's Lodge, The Scores, St Andrews, FF KY16 9BA, Scotland. **Online address:** gjdg@st-and.ac.uk

DE GRUCHY, John W(esley). South African (born South Africa), b. 1939. **Genres:** Area Studies, Theology/Religion, Humanities, Biography. **Career:** United Congregational Church, ordained minister, 1961, pastor, 1961-73, president, 1980-81; University of Cape Town, lecturer, 1973-75, senior lecturer, 1975-80, associate professor, 1980-86, Robert Selby Taylor professor of Christian studies, 1986-, Robert Selby Taylor chair of Christian studies, Graduate School in Humanities, director, 2000-; South African Council of Churches, director, 1968-73; United Congregational Church, president, 1980-81. Writer. **Publications:** The Church in Our Cities, 1970; The Church Struggle in South Africa, 1979, 2nd ed., 1986; Bonhoeffer and South Africa, 1985; Cry Justice!: Prayers, Meditations and Readings from South Africa, 1986; Theology and Ministry in Context and Crisis, 1987; Dietrich Bonhoeffer: Witness to Jesus Christ, 1987; In Word and in Deed: Towards a Practical Theology of Social Transformation, 1991; Liberating Reformed Theology, 1991; Christianity and Democracy: A Theology for a Just World Order, 1995; (with J. Wiersma) A Distant View, 1997; Christianity, Art and Transformation: Theological Aesthetics in the Struggle for Justice, 2001; Reconciliation: Restoring Justice, 2002; Daring, Trusting Spirit: Bonhoeffer's Friend Eberhard Bethge, 2005; Confessions of a Christian Humanist, 2006; (with L. Holness) The Emerging Researcher: Nurturing Passion, Developing Skills, Producing Output, 2007; John Calvin: Christian Humanist & Evangelical Reformer, 2009; (with P. Grassow) Christianity and the Colonisation of South Africa ...: A Documentary History, 2009. EDITOR: E. Bethge, Bonhoeffer: Exile and Martyr, 1975; (with C. Villa-Vicencio) Apartheid Is a Heresy, 1983; (with C. Villa-Vicencio) Resistance and Hope: South African Essays in Honour of Beyers Naudé, 1985; (with L. Rasmussen) Reinhold Niebuhr, 1988; (with C. Green) Karl Barth: Theologian of Freedom, 1989; (with G. Kelly) Karl Rahner: Theologian of the Graced Search for Meaning, 1989; (with H.M. Rumscheidt) Adolf Von Harnack: Liberal Theology at Its Height, 1989; (with M. Prozesky) A South African Guide to World Religions, 1991; (with C. Villa-Vicencio) Doing Theology in Context, 1994; (with C. Villa-Vicencio) Doing Ethics in Context: South African Perspectives, 1994; Religion and the Reconstruction of Civil Society: Papers from the Founding Congress of the South African Academy of Religion, January 1994, 1995; (with M. Prozesky) Living Faiths in South Africa, 1995; Bonhoeffer for a New Day: Theology in a Time of Transition, 1997; D. Bonhoeffer, Creation and Fall: A Theological Exposition of Genesis 1-3, 1997; (with J. Cochrane and S. Martin) Facing the Truth: South African Faith Communities and the Truth & Reconciliation Commission, 1999; The Cambridge Companion to Dietrich Bonhoeffer, 1999; The London Missionary Society in Southern Africa, 1799-1999: Historical Essays in Celebration of the Bicentenary of the LMS in Southern Africa, 2000; Letters and Papers from Prison, 2010. Contributor to journals. **Address:** Graduate School in Humanities, University of

Cape Town, PO Box X01, Rondebosch, 7701, South Africa. **Online address:** jdeg@humanities.uct.ac.za

DE HAAS, Margaret. (Margaret R. De Haas). British (born England), b. 1954. **Genres:** Law, Medicine/Health, Business/Trade/Industry. **Career:** Queen Elizabeth II Law Courts, circuit judge. Writer. **Publications:** WITH I.S. GOLDREIN: (as Margaret R. de Haas) Property Distribution on Divorce, 1983, rev. ed., 1989; Butterworths Personal Injury Litigation Service, 1985; (as Margaret R. de Haas) Structured Settlements: A Practice Guide, 1993, 2nd ed., 1997; Medical Negligence, 1997; (and with J. Frenkel) Personal Injury Major Claims Handling: Cost Effective Case Management, 2000. OTHER: (as Margaret R. de Haas) Domestic Injunctions, 1987, 2nd ed., 1997. **Address:** Queen Elizabeth II Law Courts, Derby Sq., Liverpool, L2, England. **Online address:** goldhaas@netcomuk.co.uk

DE HAAS, Margaret R. *See* **DE HAAS, Margaret.**

DEHAENE, Stanislas. French (born France), b. 1965. **Genres:** Sciences, Mathematics/Statistics. **Career:** Institut National de la Sante et de la Recherche Medicale (INSERM), research scientist, 1989-99, research director, 1997-2005, INSERM-CEA Cognitive Neuroimaging Unit, director, 2002-; University of Oregon, Institute of Cognitive and Decision Sciences, postdoctoral fellow, 1992-94; Collège de France, professor and chair of experimental psychology, 2005-; Cognition, associate editor. Cognitive neuroscientist. **Publications:** La bosse des maths, 1997, trans. as The Number Sense: How the Mind Creates Mathematics, 1997; Vers une science de la vie mentale, 2006; Les neurones de la lecture, 2007, trans. as Reading in the Brain: The Science and Evolution of a Human Invention, 2009. EDITOR: Numerical Cognition, 1993; Le cerveau en action: imagerie cerebrale fonctionnelle en psychologie cognitive, 1997; The Cognitive Neuroscience of Consciousness, 2001; (co-ed.) From Monkey Brain to Human Brain: A Fyssen Foundation Symposium, 2005; (with C. Petit) Parole et musique: aux origines du dialogue humain: colloque annuel 2008, 2009. Contributor of articles to journals. **Address:** CEA Cognitive Neuroimaging Unit, Institut National de la Sante et de la, Recherche Medicale, Point Courrier 156, Bat 145, Gif-sur-Yvette, 3 F-91191, France. **Online address:** stanislas.dehaene@cea.fr

DE HAMEL, Joan (Littledale). *See* Obituaries.

DE HAVEN, Tom. American (born United States), b. 1949. **Genres:** Novels, Novellas/Short Stories, Graphic Novels. **Career:** Magazine Associates, managing editor, 1973-76; freelance magazine editor, 1977-80; Hofstra University, adjunct professor of creative writing, 1981-87; Rutgers University, assistant professor of American studies, 1987-90; Virginia Commonwealth University, associate professor of American studies and creative writing, 1990-, professor. **Publications:** Freak's Amour (novel), 1978; Jersey Luck (novel), 1980; Funny Papers (novel), 1985; Sunburn Lake: A Trilogy, 1988; Joe Gosh (young adult novel), 1988; Pixie Meat (fiction), 1990; Derby Dugan's Depression Funnies, 1996; The Orphan's Tent, 1996; Green Candles (graphic novel), 1997; Dugan Under Ground, 2001; Funny Papers, 2002; It's Superman, 2005; Our Hero: Superman on Earth, 2010; (ed. with A. Blossom and B. Castleberry) Richmond Noir, 2010. CHRONICLE OF THE KING'S TRAMP SERIES: Walker of Worlds, 1990; The End-of-Everything Man, 1991; The Last Human, 1992. Contributor to periodicals. **Address:** English Department, Virginia Commonwealth University, 404A Hibbs Hall, Richmond, VA 23284, U.S.A. **Online address:** tdehaven@vcu.edu

DE HERRERA, Nancy Cooke. American (born United States) **Genres:** Autobiography/Memoirs, Theology/Religion. **Career:** U.S. Information Service, U.S. ambassador of fashion. Writer. **Publications:** Beyond Gurus: A Woman of Many Worlds (memoir), 1993, rev. ed. as The Socialite and the Holy Man, 1999; All You Need Is Love: An Eyewitness Account of When Spirituality Spread from the East to the West, 2003. **Address:** 9300 Beverlycrest Dr., Beverly Hills, CA 90210-2504, U.S.A. **Online address:** ndeherrera@sbcglobal.net

DEICHMANN, Ute. German (born Germany), b. 1951. **Genres:** Biology, Chemistry, History, Philosophy. **Career:** Teacher, 1975-87; University of Cologne, research fellow and lecturer, 1987-96, 1997-98, Institute of Genetics, research group leader, 2000-; Leo Baeck Institute, research professor, 2003-07, Ben-Gurion University of the Negev, adjunct associate professor, Jacques Loeb Centre for the History and Philosophy of the Life Sciences, director, 2007-. Writer. **Publications:** Biologen unter Hitler: Vertreibung, Karrieren,

Forschung, 1992, 2nd ed. as Biologen unter Hitler: Porträt einer Wissenschaft im NS-Staat, 1995; Flüchten, Mitmachen, Vergessen: Chemiker und Biochemiker in der NS-Zeit, 2001; (ed. with S. Wenkel) Max Delbrück and Cologne: An Early Chapter of German Molecular Biology, 2007; (ed. with U. Charpa) Jews and Sciences in German Contexts: Case Studies from the 19th and 20th Centuries, 2007. **Address:** Jacques Loeb Centre for the History and Philosophy, of the Life Sciences, Ben-Gurion University of the Negev, Rm. 347, 3rd Fl., 74 Diller Bldg., PO Box 653, Beer Sheva, 84105, Israel. **Online address:** uted@bgu.ac.il

DEIGHTON, Len. British (born England), b. 1929. **Genres:** Novels, Mystery/Crime/Suspense, Food And Wine, History, Novellas/Short Stories, Military/Defense/Arms Control, Children's Non-fiction. **Career:** British Overseas Airways Corp. (BOAC), steward, 1956-57. Writer, photographer, producer and artist. **Publications:** The Ipcress File, 1962; Horse Under Water, 1963; Funeral in Berlin, 1964; (ed.) Drinksmanship: Town's Album of Fine Wines and High Spirits, 1964; Action Cook Book, 1965; Ou est le Garlic?, 1965; The Billion Dollar Brain, 1966; Len Deighton's Cookstip Cook Book, 1966; An Expensive Place to Die, 1967; (ed.) Len Deighton's London Dossier, 1967; (comp. with M. Rand and H. Loxton) The Assassination of President Kennedy, 1967; Len Deighton's Continental Dossier: A Collection of Cultural Culinary, 1968; Only When I Larf, 1968; Bomber: Events Relating to the Last Flight of an R.A.F. over Germany on the Night of June 31, 1943, 1970; Declarations of War (stories), 1971; Close-Up, 1972; Spy Story, 1974; Yesterday's Spy, 1975; Eleven Declarations of War, 1975; Twinkle, Twinkle, Little Spy in US as Catch a Falling Spy, 1976; Fighter: The True Story of the Battle of Britain, 1977; (with P. Mayle) How to Be a Pregnant Father: An Illustrated Survival Guide for the First-time Father, 1977; SS-GB: Nazi-occupied Britain, 1941, 1978; (with A. Schwartzman) Airshipwreck, 1978; Basic French Cooking, 1979; Basic French Cooking: Including Chapters on L'art Culinaire, Les Viandes, Les Fromages, Les Corps Gras, La Carte Des Vins, La Cuisine Française Et Le Froid, Le Lexique, La Batterie De Cuisine and 50 Cookstrips, 1979; (ed. and intro.) Tactical Genius in Battle, 1979; Blitzkrieg, From the Rise of Hitler to the Fall of Dunkirk, 1980; (with M. Hastings) Battle of Britain, 1980; XPD, 1981; Goodbye, Mickey Mouse, 1982; Berlin Game, 1983; Mexico Set, 1984; London Match, 1985; Game, Set and Match, 1986; Only When I Laugh, 1987; Winter: A Berlin Family, 1899-1945, 1987; Spy Hook, 1988; Spy Line, 1989; ABC of French Food, 1990; Spy Sinker, 1990; Basic French Cookery Course, 1990; MAMista, 1991; City of Gold, 1992; Violent Ward, 1993; Three Complete Novels, 1993; Blood, Tears and Folly: An Objective Look at World War II, 1993; Pests: A Play in Three Acts, 1994; Faith, 1994; Hope, 1995; Charity, 1996; Len Deighton's French Cooking for Men, 2010; Billion-Dollar Brain, 2011; Bomber, 2011. **Address:** Jonathan Clowes Ltd., 10 Iron Bridge House, Bridge Approach, London, GL NW1 8BD, England.

DEJOHN, Jacqueline. American (born United States) **Genres:** Novels, Young Adult Fiction. **Career:** Writer. **Publications:** Antonio's Wife: A Novel, 2004. **Address:** c/o Author Mail, HarperCollins Publishers, 10 E 53rd St., New York, NY 10022-5244, U.S.A.

DEJOHNSON, Shervene. American (born United States) **Genres:** Women's Studies And Issues. **Career:** Beanie Publishing, publisher and writer. **Publications:** Forever Outcast, 2003; Choices!, 2004; Frienemy, forthcoming. **Address:** Beanie Publishing Co., PO Box 8506, Chicago, IL 60680, U.S.A. **Online address:** beaniepublishing@shervene.com

DE JONGE, Alex. American/British (born England), b. 1938. **Genres:** Literary Criticism And History, Sports/Fitness, Biography, Translations, History. **Career:** Oxford University, New College, tutorial fellow in French and Russian, 1964-86; University of Arizona, professor of Russian and comparative literature, 1986-; James Madison University, professor of French and Russian. Writer. **Publications:** Nightmare Culture, Lautreamont and les Chants de Maldoror, 1973; (co-author) Nineteenth Century Russian Literature, 1973; Nightmare Culture, Lautreamont and Les Chants de Maldoror, 1973, 2nd ed., 2005; Dostoevsky and the Age of Intensity, 1975; Baudelaire Prince of Clouds: A Biography, 1976; (ed.) Weimar Chronicle: Germany between the Wars, 1977; (trans. and intro.) Napoleon's Last Will and Testament, 1977; The Weimar Chronicle: Prelude to History, 1978; Fire and Water: A Life of Peter the Great, 1979; The Life and Times of Grigorii Rasputin, 1982; Stalin and the Shaping of the Soviet Union, 1986; (trans.) E. Sue, The Godolphin Arabian, 2003. **Address:** Department of Foreign Languages, Literatures, and Cultures, James Madison University, 800 S Main St., Harrisonburg, VA 22807-0002, U.S.A. **Online address:** dejongah@jmu.edu

DE JOUVENEL, Hugues Alain. French/Swedish (born Sweden), b. 1946. **Genres:** Institutions/Organizations, International Relations/Current Affairs, Sciences, Technology, Translations. **Career:** Study and Documentation Economiques, Industrial and Social, secretary general, 1968-72; International Center of Research and Training on the Future, affiliate, 1969-71, general delegate and secretary general, 1974-; United Nations Institute for Training and Research, research associate, 1972-73; Ministry of Defence, press secretary, 1972, news editor; Futuribles Group, chief executive officer, 1974-, director of media; National School of Public Administration, professor; Association for the Development of Science Applied Social, secretary general, 1974; Center for Economic, Industrial and Social Studies and Documentation, secretary and acting director, 1974. Writer. **Publications:** (Co-author) The United Nations and the Future, 1972; Sciences, Technology and the Future, 1979; Le Point Critique, 1980; (with C. Charpy) Protection Sociale: Trois Scénarios Contrastés à L'horizon 2000, 1986; (with M. Roque) Cataluna a Horizonte 2010, 1993; La France a l'Horizon 2010, 1995; The Knowledge Base of Future Studies, 1996; Changing Europe, 1996; Vers une Prospective des Retraites en France a L'horizon 2030, 1998; (with V. Gollain and A. Sallez) Emploi et Territoires en Ile-de-France: Prospective, 1999; La Tour d'Aigues, 1999; Decision, Prospective, auto Organisation, 2000; Dáwah ilá Al-istishrāq, 2008. TRANSLATOR: C.A. Doxiades, Between Dystopia and Utopia; J.S. Coleman, Changes in Educational Structures. **Address:** Futuribles Group, 55 rue de Varenne, Paris, 75007, France. **Online address:** hjouvenel@futuribles.com

DEKA, Connie. See **LAUX, Constance.**

DE KERCKHOVE, Derrick. Canadian/Belgian (born Belgium), b. 1944?. **Genres:** Information Science/Computers, Architecture. **Career:** University of Toronto, Department of French, professor, 1967-, Information Studies and the Knowledge Media Design Institute, faculty, McLuhan Program in Culture and Technology, co-director, director, 1983-, St. Michael's College, fellow, 2008-; Centre for Culture and Technology, associate, 1972-80; Marshall McLuhan, translator, assistant and co-author; ICT trade, co-chair, 2003; University Federico II, faculty. Writer. **Publications:** McLuhan e la metamorfosi dell'uomo, 1984; Brainframes: Technology, Mind and Business, 1991; Connected Intelligence: The Arrival of the Web Society, 1997; Les nerfs de la culture, 1998; Architecture of Intelligence, 2001; (with M. Federman) McLuhan for Managers: New Tools for New Thinking, 2003; Dopo la democrazia, 2006; (with M. Leeker and K. Schmidt) McLuhan neu lesen, 2008; (with V. Susca) Transpolitica, 2008. EDITOR: (with C.H. Lumsden) The Alphabet and the Brain: The Lateralization of Writing, 1988; (with C. Dewdney) The Skin of Culture: Investigating the New Electronic Reality, 1995. Contributor to books. **Address:** St. Michael College, 81 St.Mary St., Toronto, ON M5S 1J4, Canada.

DEKEYSER, Stacy. American (born United States), b. 1959?. **Genres:** Novels. **Career:** Writer. **Publications:** Sacagawea, 2004; The Wampanoag, 2005; Jump the Cracks (young-adult novel), 2008. **Address:** Adams Literary, C4 215, 7845 Colony Rd., Charlotte, NC 28226, U.S.A. **Online address:** stacy@stacydekeyser.com

DE LA BARQUE, Robert Louis Marie. See **SCHUITEN, François Louis Marie.**

DE LA BÉDOYÈRE, Guy. British (born England), b. 1957?. **Genres:** History, Archaeology/Antiquities, Military/Defense/Arms Control. **Career:** BBC Radio News, sound engineer, 1981-98; full-time freelance writer and broadcaster, 1998-; Kesteven and Sleaford High School, teacher of history and classical civilization. Historian. **Publications:** NONFICTION: The Roman Site at Billingsgate Lorry Park, London: A Catalogue of the Samian and Other Finds, 1986; Samian Ware, 1988; The Finds of Roman Britain, 1989; The Buildings of Roman Britain, 1991; Book of Roman Towns in Britain, 1992; English Heritage Book of Roman Villas and the Countryside, 1993; (ed.) The Diary of John Evelyn, 1994; (ed.) The Writings of John Evelyn, 1995; (ed.) Particular Friends: The Correspondence of Samuel Pepys and John Evelyn, 1997; Hadrian's Wall: History and Guide, 1998; The Golden Age of Roman Britain in UK as Companion to Roman Britain, 1999; Battles over Britain: The Archaeology of the Air War, 2000; Voices of Imperial Rome, 2000; Pottery in Roman Britain, 2000; (co-author) An Illustrated Dictionary of Irish History, 2001; Eagles over Britannia, 2001; Aviation Archaeology in Britain, 2001; Architecture in Roman Britain, 2002; The Home

Front, 2002; Gods with Thunderbolts: Religion in Roman Britain, 2002; Defying Rome: The Rebels of Roman Britain, 2003; (co-author) World History: A Source Book, 2003; The Discovery of Penicillin, 2006; Roman Britain: A New History, 2006; The First Polio Vaccine, 2006; The Romans for Dummies, 2006; The First Computers, 2006; (ed.) The Letters of Samuel Pepys, 1656-1703, 2006. Contributor to journals. **Address:** Kesteven and Sleaford High School, Jermyn St., Sleaford, LI NG34 7RS, England. **Online address:** guydelabed@yahoo.co.uk

DE LA BILLIERE, Peter (Edgar de la Cour). American/British (born England), b. 1934. **Genres:** Autobiography/Memoirs. **Career:** Writer. **Publications:** Storm Command: A Personal Account of the Gulf War, 1992; Looking for Trouble: SAS to Gulf command (autobiography), 1994; Supreme Courage: Heroic Stories from 150 Years of the VC, 2005. Contributor to periodicals. **Address:** Curtis Brown Ltd., 28/29 Haymarket, London, GL SW1Y 4SP, England.

DELACROIX, Claire. Also writes as Claire Cross, Deborah Cooke. Canadian/American (born United States), b. 1951. **Genres:** Romance/Historical, Novels. **Career:** Writer. **Publications:** Romance of the Rose, 1993; Honeyed Lies, 1994; Roarkes Folly, 1994; Unicorn Bride, 1994; The Sorceress, 1994; Unicorn Vengeance, 1995; The Magician's Quest, 1995; Pearl beyond Price, 1995; My Lady's Champion, 1996; Enchanted, 1997; The Princess, 1998; My Lady's Desire, 1998; The Damsel, 1999; The Heiress, 1999; The Countess, 2000; The Beauty, 2001; The Temptress, 2001; The Rogue, 2002; The Scoundrel, 2003; (co-author) To Weave a Web of Magic, 2004; The Warrior, 2004; The Snow White Bride, 2005; The Rose Red Bride, 2005; The Beauty Bride, 2005; (co-author) The Queen in Winter, 2006; Fallen, 2008; Guardian, 2009; Rebel, 2010. AS CLAIRE CROSS: The Last Highlander, 1998; Silent Night, 1998; Once upon a Kiss, 1998; The Moonstone, 1999; Love Potion #9, 1999; Third Time Lucky, 2000; Double Trouble, 2001; One More Time, 2006; All or Nothing, 2007. AS DEBORAH COOKE: DRAGONFIRE SERIES: Kiss of Fire, 2008; Kiss of Fury, 2008; (contrib.) The Mammoth Book of Vampire Romance 2, 2009; Kiss of Fate, 2009; Winter Kiss, 2009; Whisper Kiss, 2010; Harmonia's Kiss, 2010; Darkfire Kiss, 2011; Winging It, 2011; Flying Blind, 2011; Blazing the Trail, 2012; Flashfire, 2012. **Address:** c/o Dominick Abel, Dominick Abel Literary Agency Inc., 146 W 82nd. St., Ste. 1A, New York, NY 10024-5530, U.S.A. **Online address:** chestwick@delacroix.net

DE LA CRUZ, Melissa. American/Filipino (born Philippines), b. 1971?. **Genres:** Novels, Young Adult Fiction, Fash Ion/Costume, Adult Non-fiction, How-to Books. **Career:** Computer programmer, 1993-2001. Freelance magazine writer. **Publications:** NOVELS: Cat's Meow, 2001; The Au Pairs, 2004; Fresh Off the Boat, 2005; Sun-Kissed, 2006; Skinny-Dipping, 2006; Masquerade: A Blue Bloods Novel, 2007; Crazy Hot: A Novel, 2007; The Ashleys!, 2008; The Ashleys: Jealous?, 2008; The Ashleys, 2008; Birthday Vicious, 2008. NON-FICTION: (with K. Robinovitz) How to Become Famous in Two Weeks or Less, 2003; (with K. Robinovitz) Fashionista Files: Adventures in Four-inch Heels and Faux Pas, 2004; Fresh Off the Boat, 2005; Blue Bloods, 2006; Mistletoe, 2006; (ed. with T. Dolby) Girls who Like Boys: True Tales of Love, Lust and Friendship between Straight Women and Gay Men, 2007; Angels on Sunset Boulevard, 2007; Revelations: A Blue Bloods Novel, 2008; Jealous?, 2008; Girl Stays in the Picture: A Girl Novel, 2009; Van Alen Legacy: A Blue Bloods Novel, 2009; Misguided Angel, 2010; Wolf Pact, 2011. OTHERS: (ed. with T. Dolby) Girls who like boys who like boys, 2007; There's a New Name in Schoo, 2007; Lip Gloss Jungle, 2008; Angels Lie, 2009; The Strip, 2009; (contrib.) Reality Matters, 2010; Keys to the Repository, 2010; Bloody Valentine: A Blue Bloods Novella, 2010; Witches of East End, 2011; Lost In Time, 2011; Witches 101: A Witches of East End Prime, 2011; Blue Bloods: The Graphic Novel, 2012; Serpent's Kiss, 2012; The Gates of Paradise, 2013. Works appear in anthologies. Contributor to periodicals. **Address:** 12400 Ventura Blvd., Ste. 1268, Studio City, CA 91604, U.S.A. **Online address:** melissa@melissa-delacruz.com

DELAGE, Denys. Canadian (born Canada), b. 1942. **Genres:** Sociology. **Career:** Laval Universite, professor of sociology, 1981-, chair of department, 1991-95, professor emeritus, retired associate. Writer. **Publications:** Pays Renversé: Amérindiens et Européens en Amérique du Nord-Est, 1600-1664, 1985; Familles de Saint-Sauveur, 1986; La religion dans l'alliance franco-amerindienne, 1991; L'influence des Amerindiens sur les Canadiens et les Francais au temps de la Nouvelle-France, 1992; The Bitter Feast: Amerindians and Europeans in Northeastern North America, 1600-64, 1993; Les Traites des Sept Feux avec les Britanniques, 2001; (with Y. Chrtien and S. Vincent)

Au croisement de Nos Destins, 2009. **Address:** Department of Sociology, Laval Universite, House Charles-With Koninck, Office 6463, Quebec City, QC G1V 0A6, Canada. **Online address:** denys.delage@soc.ulaval.ca

DELAHAYE, Michael (John). British (born England), b. 1946?. **Genres:** Mystery/Crime/Suspense, Novels, Young Adult Fiction, Politics/Government. **Career:** British Institute, teacher of English, 1968-69; BBC, News and Current Affairs Department, television reporter and correspondent, 1969-79; BBC TV, reporter and producer, 1988-98. Writer. **Publications:** The Sale of Lot 236, 1981; On the Third Day in UK as The Third Day, 1984; Stalkinghorse: A Novel of Political Intrigue, 1987. **Address:** David Higham Associates, 5-8 Lower John St., Golden Sq., London, GL W1F 9HA, England.

DELAHUNT, Meaghan. British/Scottish/Australian (born Australia), b. 1961. **Genres:** Novels, Psychology. **Career:** St Andrews University, writer-in-residence, 2004, lecturer in creative writing. Writer. **Publications:** In the Blue House, 2001; In the Casa Azul: A Novel of Revolution and Betrayal, 2002; The Red Book, 2008; The Prayer Wheel, forthcoming. Works appear in anthologies. Contributor to periodicals. **Address:** School of English, University of St. Andrews, Rm. CH12, Castle House, London, GL KY16 9AL, England. **Online address:** md50@st-andrews.ac.uk

DE LA ISLA, José. American (born United States), b. 1944?. **Genres:** Adult Non-fiction. **Career:** National Public Radio/KPFT-FM Radio, World Radio Morning News, commentator; Cable News Network, commentator; University of Oregon, faculty; University of California, faculty. Writer. **Publications:** The Rise of Hispanic Political Power, 2003. Contributor to newspapers. **Address:** c/o Author Mail, Archer Books, PO Box 1254, Santa Maria, CA 93456-1254, U.S.A. **Online address:** joseisla3@yahoo.com

DELANEY, Denis. See GREEN, Peter (Morris).

DELANEY, Diane Meier. See MEIER, Diane.

DELANEY, Edward J. American (born United States), b. 1957. **Genres:** Novels. **Career:** Denver Post, staff writer; Colorado Springs Gazette, columnist; Colorado State University, Gannett Foundation professional-in-residence; University of Colorado, professional-in-residence; Chicago Tribune Magazine, contributing writer; Providence Journal Magazine, contributing writer; Atlantic Monthly, contributing writer; Roger Williams University, professor of communications and creative writing, 1990-; Harvard University, The Nieman Foundation, The Nieman Journalism Lab, assistant editor, 2008-09. Educator and journalist. **Publications:** The Drowning and Other Stories, 1999; Warp and Weft, 2004; (co-author) Born to Play, 2009. Contributor to periodicals. **Address:** Roger Williams University, 1 Old Ferry Rd., Bristol, RI 02809, U.S.A. **Online address:** edelaney@rwu.edu

DELANEY, Gayle (M. V.). American (born United States), b. 1952. **Genres:** Psychology, Self Help, Sex, Medicine/Health. **Career:** Association for the Study of Dreams, founding president; California Institute of Integral Studies, assistant professor, 1980-85; Delaney and Flowers Dream and Consultation Center, co-founder and co-director, 1981-; Institute of Transpersonal Psychology, visiting associate professor, 1987-. Writer and radio host. **Publications:** Living Your Dreams: Using Sleep to Solve Problems and Enrich Your Life, 1979, rev. ed., 1996; Breakthrough Dreaming: How to Tap the Power of Your 24-Hour Mind, 1991; (ed.) New Directions in Dream Interpretation, 1993; Sexual Dreams: Why We Have Them, What They Mean, 1994 as Sensual Dreaming, 1995; The Dream Kit: An All-in-One Toolkit for Understanding Your Dreams, 1995; In Your Dreams: Falling, Flying and Other Dream Themes: A New Kind of Dream Dictionary, 1997; All about Dreams: Everything You Need to Know about Why We Have Them, What They Mean, and How to Put Them to Work for You, 1998. Contributor of articles to periodicals. **Address:** Delaney & Flowers Dream & Consultation Center, 16 Manzanita Pl., Mill Valley, CA 94941, U.S.A. **Online address:** dreams@gdelaney.com

DELANEY, Kathleen. American (born United States) **Genres:** Novels, Mystery/Crime/Suspense. **Career:** Writer. **Publications:** ELLEN MCKENZIE SERIES: Dying for a Change, 2002; Give First Place to Murder, 2004; And Murder for Dessert, 2007; Murder Half Baked, 2011. **Address:** Poisoned Pen Press, 6962 E 1st Ave., Ste. 103, Scottsdale, AZ 85251, U.S.A. **Online address:** kathleen@kathleendelaney.net

DELANEY, Michael. American (born United States), b. 1955. **Genres:** Children's Fiction, Illustrations, Sciences. **Career:** Gourmet magazine, freelance illustrator, 1981-96; J. Walter Thompson, advertising copywriter, 1985-90. Writer and illustrator. **Publications:** AS M.C. DELANEY: The Marigold Monster, 1983; Henry's Special Delivery, 1984; Not Your Average Joe, 1990; Birdbrain Amos, 2002; The Great Sockathon, 2004; Obi, Gerbil on the Loose!, 2008; Obi, Gerbil on a Mission!, 2012. SELF-ILLUSTRATED: Deep Doo Doo, 1996; Deep Doo-Doo and the Mysterious E-Mail, 2001; Birdbrain Amos, Mr. Fun, 2006. Contributor to periodicals. **Address:** c/o Author Mail, Dutton Publicity, 345 Hudson St., New York, NY 10014, U.S.A. **Online address:** chauck@discovernet.net

DELANEY, Norman. American (born United States), b. 1932. **Genres:** History, Biography, Autobiography/Memoirs, Young Adult Fiction. **Career:** Bridgewater State Teachers College (now Bridgewater State College), instructor in history, 1959-62; University of Houston, instructor in history, 1966-67; Del Mar College, assistant professor, 1967-71, associate professor, 1971-74, professor of history, 1974-2006, Piper professor, 1996, now retired; Naval War College, dean. Writer. **Publications:** John McIntosh Kell of the Raider Alabama, 1973; (co-ed.) Historical Times Illustrated Encyclopedia of the Civil War, 1986; Ghost Ship: The Confederate Raider Alabama, 1989; An Oral History of Naval Air Station Corpus Christi during World War II, 1997; (with W.N. Still, Jr. and J.M. Taylor) Raiders & Blockaders: The American Civil War Afloat, 1998. Contributor of articles to books, journals and magazines. **Address:** 3747 Aransas St., Corpus Christi, TX 78411-1305, U.S.A. **Online address:** kelltheluff@yahoo.com

DELANEY, Shelagh. British (born England), b. 1939. **Genres:** Plays/Screenplays, Novellas/Short Stories, Literary Criticism And History, Poetry. **Career:** Metro-Vickers, photography assistant. Playwright and television screenwriter. **Publications:** Sweetly Sings the Donkey (short stories), 1963; Writing Woman, 1984. PLAYS: A Taste of Honey, 1959; The Lion in Love, 1961. Contributor of articles to periodicals. **Address:** The Sayle Literary Agency, 1 Petersfield, Cambridge, CB CB1 1BB, England.

DELANO, Anthony. American/British/Australian (born Australia), b. 1930?. **Genres:** Novels, Education, Writing/Journalism, Documentaries/Reportage, Criminology/True Crime, Young Adult Fiction, Reference. **Career:** Daily Mirror, Rome correspondent, 1956-60, Paris correspondent, 1960-63, American correspondent, 1963-70, London Diary, editor and roving correspondent, 1970-74, chief American correspondent, 1975-79, chief European correspondent, managing editor, 1980-, editor; Mirror Group, director, 1984-87; University of Queensland, senior lecturer, 1989-92; London College of Communication, visiting professor, 2003-. **Publications:** Breathless Diversions (novel), 1973; Slip-up: Fleet Street, Scotland Yard and the Great Train Robbery, 1975; Slip-Up: How Fleet Street Found Ronnie Biggs and Scotland Yard Lost Him: The Story Behind the Scoop (documentary), 1977; Joyce McKinney and the Manacled Mormon, 1978; Maxwell, 1988; The News Breed, 1995; Joyce McKinney and the Case of the Manacled Mormon, 2009. **Address:** Daily Mirror, 220 East 42nd St., Ste. 3103, New York, NY 10017, U.S.A. **Online address:** t.delano@lcp.liust.ac.uk

DELANY, Samuel R(ay). American (born United States), b. 1942. **Genres:** Science Fiction/Fantasy, Autobiography/Memoirs, Novels, Novellas/Short Stories, inspirational/Motivational Literature, Biography, Essays, Adult Nonfiction, Adult Non-fiction. **Career:** University of Buffalo, Butler professor of English, 1975, professor of English, 1999-2001; University of Wisconsin, Center for Twentieth-Century Studies, senior fellow, 1977; Cornell University, Society for the Humanities, senior fellow, 1987; University of Massachusetts, professor of comparative literature, 1988-99; Temple University, professor of English and creative writing, 2001-. Writer. **Publications:** The Jewels of Aptor, 1962; Captives of the Flame, 1963, rev. ed. as Out of the Dead City, 1968; The Towers of Toron, 1964; City of a Thousand Suns, 1965; The Ballad of Beta-2, 1965; Empire Star, 1966; Babel-17, 1966; The Einstein Intersection, 1967; Nova, 1968; The Fall of the Towers, 1970; Drift Glass: Ten Tales of Speculative Fiction, 1971; The Tides of Lust, 1973 as Equinox, 1994; Dhalgren, 1975; Triton, 1976 as Trouble on Triton: An Ambiguous Heterotopia, 1996; The Jewel-hinged Jaw: Notes on the Language of Science Fiction, 1977, rev. ed., 2009; Empire: A Visual Novel, 1978; The American Shore, 1978; Tales of Nevèrÿon, 1979; Heavenly Breakfast: An Essay on the Winter of Love, 1979; Distant Stars, 1981; Neveryóna, or, The Tale of Signs and Cities, 1983, rev. ed. as Neveryóna, or, The Tale of Signs and Cities, Some

Informal Remarks towards the Modular Calculus, Part Four, 1993; Stars in My Pocket like Grains of Sand, 1984; Starboard Wine: More Notes on the Language of Science Fiction, 1984; Flight from Nevèrÿon, 1985; The Complete Nebula Award-winning Fiction, 1986; The Bridge of Lost Desire, 1987, rev. ed. as Return to Nevèrÿon, 1994; The Motion of Light in Water: Sex and Science-Fiction Writing in the East Village, 1957-65, 1988; The Star Pits, 1989; Straits of Messina, 1989; They Fly at Çiron, 1993; Silent Interviews: On Language, Race, Sex, Science Fiction, and Some Comics: A Collection of Written Interviews, 1994; The Mad Man, 1994; Atlantis: Three Tales, 1995; Hogg, 1995, 2nd ed., 2004; Longer Views: Extended Essays, 1996; Bread and Wine: An Erotic Tale of New York City; An Autobiographical Account, 1998; Shorter Views: Queer Thoughts and the Politics of the Paraliterary, 1999; Times Square Red, Times Square Blue, 1999; 1984: Selected Letters, 2000; (intro.) Black Gay Man, 2001; Aye, and Gomorrah: And Other Stories, 2003; Phallos, 2004; About Writing: Seven Essays, Four Letters, and Five Interviews, 2005; Dark Reflections, 2007; Through the Valley of the Nest of Spiders, 2008; (ed.) Conversations with Samuel R. Delany, 2009. Contributor to periodicals. **Address:** Department of English, Temple University, 955 Anderson Hall, 1114 W Berks St., Philadelphia, PA 19122-6090, U.S.A. **Online address:** sdelany@temple.edu

DELANY, Vicki. Canadian (born Canada), b. 1951?. **Genres:** Mystery/Crime/Suspense, Novels. **Career:** Royal Bank of Canada, computer programmer and systems analyst, through 2007, retired, 2007. Writer. **Publications:** Whiteout, 2002; Murder at Lost Dog Lake, 2003; Scare the Light Away, 2005; Burden of Memory, 2006; In the Shadow of the Glacier, 2007; Gold Digger, 2009; Valley of the Lost, 2009; Winter of Secrets, 2009; Negative Image, 2010; Gold Fever, 2010; Among the Departed, 2011; Gold Mountain, 2012. Works appear in anthologies. **Address:** Poisoned Pen Press, 6962 E 1st Ave., Ste. 103, Scottsdale, AZ 85251, U.S.A. **Online address:** vdelany@sympatico.ca

DE LA PEDRAJA, René. American/Cuban (born Cuba), b. 1951. **Genres:** History, Military/Defense/Arms Control. **Career:** Universidad de los Andes, research professor of economics, 1976-85; business consultant, 1984-86; Kansas State University, assistant professor of history, 1986-89; Canisius College, assistant professor, 1989-92, associate professor of history, 1992-97, professor of history, 1997-, president of faculty senate, 2000-. Writer. **Publications:** Historia de la Energia en Colombia, 1985; FEDEMETAL y la industrializacion de Colombia, 1986; Energy Politics in Colombia, 1989; The Rise and Decline of U.S. Merchant Shipping in the Twentieth Century, 1992; Historical Dictionary of the U.S. Merchant Marine, 1994; Oil and Coffee: The Merchant Shipping of Latin America, 1998; Latin American Merchant Shipping in the Age of Global Competition, 1999; Wars of Latin America, 1899-1941, 2006. Contributor to periodicals. **Address:** Department of History, Canisius College, CT 609, 2001 Main St., Buffalo, NY 14208-1098, U.S.A. **Online address:** delapedr@canisius.edu

DELARA, Ellen. American (born United States), b. 1949. **Genres:** Human Relations/Parenting, Education. **Career:** Cornell University, Department of Human Service Studies, Policy Analysis and Management, lecturer and faculty liaison, 1985-87, 1993-97, Department of Field and International Studies, lecturer, 1992, Family Life Development Center, faculty fellow, 2001-; Syracuse University, College of Human Services and Health Professions, School of Social Work, assistant professor, 2003-09, associate professor, 2009-; Suicide Prevention and Crisis Center, consultant. Writer. **Publications:** (With J. Garbarino) And Words Can Hurt Forever: How to Protect Adolescents from Bullying, Harassment, and Emotional Violence, 2002; (with J. Garbarino) Educator's Guide to School-Based Interventions, 2003. Contributor to books and periodicals. **Address:** School of Social Work, Syracuse University, 305 Sims Hall, Syracuse, NY 13244, U.S.A. **Online address:** edelara@syr.edu

DE LAS CASAS, Walter. American/Cuban (born Cuba), b. 1947. **Genres:** Poetry, Education, History. **Career:** Teacher, 1970-79; Sarah J. Hale High School, Spanish teacher, 1979-93; Science Skill Center High School, teacher of Spanish language and literature, 1994-96. Writer. **Publications:** POEMS: La Niñez Que Dilata, 1986; Libido (in Spanish), 1989; Tributes, 1993; Discourse, 1999; Human, 2004. Contributor to periodicals. **Address:** 323 Dahill Rd., Apt. 1A, Brooklyn, NY 11218-3848, U.S.A. **Online address:** delascasis2@netzero.net

DE LA TORRE, Miguel A. American/Cuban (born Cuba), b. 1958. **Genres:** Theology/Religion, History. **Career:** Goshen Baptist Church, pastor, 1993-94; Temple University, instructor, 1995-99; Rutgers University, visiting professor, 1997; Immaculata College, visiting professor, 1999; West Chester University, visiting professor, 1999; Hope College, assistant professor, 1999-2005; Iliff School of Theology, Justice and Peace Institute, director, associate professor of social ethics, 2005-10, professor, 2010-; Ethics Daily, columnist; American Academy of Religion Ethics Sectio, co-chair, 2006-09; American Academy of Religion, board director, 2009-11. **Publications:** (With E.D. Aponte) Introducing Latino/a Theologies, 2001; Reading the Bible from the Margins, 2002; The Quest for the Cuban Christ: A Historical Search, 2002; La Lucha for Cuba: Religion and Politics on the Streets of Miami, 2003; Doing Christian Ethics from the Margins, 2004; Santeria: The Beliefs and Rituals of a Growing Religion in America, 2004; (ed.) Handbook on U.S. Theologies of Liberation, 2004; Leer la Biblia desde los Marginados, 2005; (ed. with E.D. Aponte) Handbook on Latina/o Theologies, 2006; (ed. with G. Espinosa) Rethinking Latino(a) Religion and Identity, 2006; Liberating Jonah: Forming an Ethics of Reconciliation, 2007; A Lily among the Thorns: Imagining a New Christian Sexuality, 2007; (ed.) AAR Career Guide for Racial and Ethnic Minorities in the Profession, 2007; (ed.) The Hope of Liberation in World Religions, 2008; Trails of Hope and Terror: Testimonies on Immigration, 2009; (ed.) Hispanic American Religious Culture, 2009; (ed.) Out of the Shadows, Into the Light: Christianity and Homosexuality, 2009; Latina/o Social Ethics: Moving Beyond Eurocentric Moral Thinking, 2010; (with A. Hernandez) The Quest for the Historical Satan, 2011; (ed. with S. Floyd-Thomas) Beyond the Pale: Reading Christian Ethics from the Margins, 2011; Genesis: A Theological Commentary on the Bible, 2011; (ed. with S. Floyd-Thomas) Beyond the Pale: Reading Christian Theology from the Margins, 2011. **Address:** Iliff School of Theology, Iliff Hall 404, 2201 S University Blvd., Denver, CO 80210, U.S.A. **Online address:** mdelatorre@iliff.edu

DELBANCO, Francesca. American (born United States) **Genres:** Novels, Young Adult Fiction, Literary Criticism And History. **Career:** Seventeen (magazine), staff; University of Michigan, instructor. Writer. **Publications:** Ask Me Anything, 2004 in UK as Midnight in Manhattan, 2005. Contributor to periodicals. **Address:** c/o Author Mail, W. W. Norton, 500 5th Ave., New York, NY 10110, U.S.A.

DELBANCO, Nicholas F(ranklin). American/British (born England), b. 1942. **Genres:** Novels, Novellas/Short Stories, Plays/Screenplays, Autobiography/Memoirs. **Career:** Bennington College, Department of Language and Literature, faculty, 1966-84, writing workshop director, 1977-84; Skidmore College, professor of English, 1984-85; University of Michigan, Robert Frost collegiate professor of English, 1985-, Robert Frost distinguished university professor of English language and literature, chair, MFA Program, director, through 2002, Hopwood Awards Program, director, through 2002, retired, 2002. Writer. **Publications:** The Martlet's Tale, 1966; Grasse, 3/23/66, 1968; Consider Sappho Burning, 1969; News, 1970; In the Middle Distance: A Novel, 1971; Fathering, 1973; Small Rain, 1975; Possession, 1977; Sherbrookes, 1978; Stillness, 1980; Group Portrait: Joseph Conrad, Stephen Crane, Ford Madox Ford, Henry James, and H.G. Wells, 1982; About My Table and Oher Stories, 1983; The Beaux Arts Trio: A Portrait, 1985; (ed. and intro.) Stillness, and, Shadows, 1986; Running in Place: Scenes from the South of France (memoir), 1989; The Writers' Trade and Other Stories, 1990; (ed. with L. Goldstein) Writers and Their Craft: Short Stories & Essays on the Narrative, 1991; In the Name of Mercy, 1995; (ed. with A. Cheuse) Talking Horse: Bernard Malamud on Life and Work, 1996; Old Scores, 1997; The Lost Suitcase: Reflections on the Literary Life, 2000; What Remains, 2000; The Countess of Stanlein Restored, 2001; The Vagabonds: A Novel, 2004; (ed.) Ann Arbor Writes, 2004; Sincerest Form: Writing Fiction by Imitation, 2004; Anywhere Out of the World: Essays on Travel, Writing, Death, 2005; (ed. with A. Beauchamp and M. Barrett) Hopwood Awards: 75 Years of Prized Writing, 2006; Spring and Fall, 2006; Count of Concord, 2008; (ed. and intro.) Hopwood Lectures: Sixth Series, 2009; (with A. Cheuse) Literature: Craft and Voice, 2010; Lastingness: The Art of Old Age, 2011. **Address:** Department of English Language and Literature, University of Michigan, 1168 Angell Hall, 435 S State St., Ann Arbor, MI 48109, U.S.A. **Online address:** delbanco@umich.edu

DEL CARO, Adrian. American (born United States), b. 1952. **Genres:** Humanities, Intellectual History, Literary Criticism And History, Philosophy. **Career:** University of California, lecturer in German and comparative literature, 1979-80; Louisiana State University, assistant professor, 1980-83, associate professor, 1983-89, professor of German, 1989-92; University of Colorado, Department of Germanic and Slavic Languages and Literature, professor and chair, 1992-, associate vice-chancellor for graduate educa-

tion, Graduate School, interim associate dean. Writer. **Publications:** Dionysian Aesthetics: The Role of Destruction in Creation as Reflected in the Life and Works of Friedrich Nietzsche, 1981; Nietzsche Contra Nietzsche, 1989; (trans.) Puntigam, or, The Art of Forgetting, 1990; Hölderlin: The Poetics of Being, 1991; Hugo von Hofmannsthal: Poets and the Language of Life, 1993; The Early Poetry of Paul Celan: In the Beginning Was the Word, 1997; (ed. with J. Ward) German Studies in the Post-Holocaust Age, 2000; (trans.) The Gay Science, 2001; Grounding the Nietzsche Rhetoric of Earth, 2004; (trans.) Thus Spoke Zarathustra, 2006. Contributor to journals. **Address:** Department of Germanic and Slavic Languages, University of Colorado, McKenna 207, PO Box276, Boulder, CO 80309-0276, U.S.A. **Online address:** adrian.delcaro@colorado.edu

DELEON, Peter. American (born United States), b. 1943. **Genres:** Criminology/True Crime, Politics/Government. **Career:** University of Colorado, professor of public affairs, 1985-, director of Office of International Education, 1994-, PHD Program, director; Rand Corp., senior researcher; European Center for Social Welfare, consultant; Swedish Colloquium for Advanced Study in the Social Sciences and Science Center, consultant. Writer. **Publications:** Scenario Designs: An Overview, 1973; (with J. Enns) The Impact of Highways Upon Metropolitan Dispersion, St. Louis, 1973; The Laser-Guided Bomb: Case History of a Development: A Report Prepared for United States Air Force Project Rand, 1974; (co-author) The Prosecution of Adult Felony Defendants in Los Angeles County, 1976; A Comparative Analysis of High Technology Programs: The Development and Diffusion of the Nuclear Power Reactor in Six Nations, 1978; The Development and Diffusion of the Nuclear Power Reactor: A Comparative Analysis, 1979; (with G.D. Brewer) The Foundations of Policy Analysis, 1983; (with H. Nowotny and B. Wittrock) Choosing Futures: Evaluating the Secretariat for Futures Studies, 1985; (co-author) A Reassessment of Potential Adversaries to U.S. Nuclear Programs, 1986; The Altered Strategic Environment: Towards the Year 2000, 1987; Advice and Consent: The Development of the Policy Sciences, 1988; (with B. Hoffman, K. Konrad and B. Jenkins) The Threat of Nuclear Terrorism: A Reexamination, 1988; Thinking about Political Corruption, 1993; Democracy and the Policy Sciences, 1997; (ed. with J.E. Rivera) Voluntary Environmental Programs: A Policy Perspective, 2010. Contributor to journals. **Address:** Graduate School of Public Affairs, University of Colorado, CB 142, 1380 Lawrence St., Ste. 500, PO Box 173364, Denver, CO 80204, U.S.A. **Online address:** peter.deLeon@ucdenver.edu

DELERM, Philippe. French (born France), b. 1950. **Genres:** Novels, Children's Fiction. **Career:** Writer and school teacher. **Publications:** La cinquième saison, 1983; Un été pour mémoire, 1985; Lebonheur: Tableux et Bavardages, 1986; Rouen, 1987; Le Buveur de Temps, 1987; Le Miroir de ma Mère, 1988; Autumn, 1990; C'est bien, 1991; Les Amoureux de l'hôtel de Ville (novel), 1993; Mister Mouse, Ou, la Métaphysique du terrier, 1994; En Pleine Lucarne, 1995; L'envol, 1996; Sundborn, ou, les Jours de Lumière (novel), 1996; Sortilège au muséum, 1996; La Première gorgée de Bièreet Autres Plaisirs Minisucles, 1997; Les Chemins Nous Inventent, 1997; La Malédiction des Ruines, 1997; Il Avait plu tout le dimanche, 1998; Panier de Fruits, éditionsdu Rocher, 1998; Elle S'appelait Marine (children's stories), 1998; Quiproquo, 1999; La Portique (novel), 1999; We Could Almost Eat Outside: An Appreciation of Life's Small Pleasures, 1999; Small Pleasures of Life, 1999; Eitei Pourmeimoire, 2001; Intérieur: Vilhelm Hammershøi, 2001; Sieste assassinée, 2001; Buveur de Temps: Roman, 2002; Paris l'instant, 2002; Enregistrements pirates, 2003; Dickens, barbe à papa: Et Autres Nourritures Dèlectables: Rècits, 2005; Bulle de Tiepolo: Roman, 2005; Ce voyage, 2005; Tranchèe d'Arenberg et Autres Voluptèssportives, 2006; Maintenant, foutez-moi la paix!: Essai, 2006; Tranchee D Arenberg, 2008; Ma Grand-mere Avait Les Memes. Les Dessous Affriolants Des Petites Phrases, 2008; Traces, 2008; Quelque chose en lui de Bartleby: roman, 2009; Trottoir au soleil, 2011. **Address:** Editions Gallimard, 5 rue Sebastien-Bottin, Paris, 75328, France.

DELESSERT, Jacquine. See **REITER, Victoria (Kelrich).**

DELETANT, Dennis. British (born England), b. 1946. **Genres:** History, Language/Linguistics. **Career:** University College London, School of Slavonic and East European Studies, professor of Romanian studies. Writer and linguist. **Publications:** Colloquial Romanian: A Complete Language Course, 1983, (with R. Gönczöl-Davis) 3rd ed. as Colloquial Romanian: The Complete Course for Beginners, 2002, 4th ed., 2011; Studies in Romanian History, 1991; (with Y. Alexandrescu) Romanian: A Complete Course for Beginners, 1992, new ed. in US as Romanian, 2004; Ceausescu and the Securitate: Coercion and Dissent in Romania, 1965-1989, 1995; (with M. Pearton) Romania Observed: Studies in Contemporary Romanian History, 1998; Communist Terror in Romania: Gheorghiu-Dej and the Police State, 1948-1965, 1999; Romania under Communist Rule, 1999; (with K. Williams) Security Intelligence Services in New Democracies: The Czech Republic, Slovakia and Romania, 2001; (intro.) Banalitatea Raului: O Istorie a Securitatii în Documente 1949-1989, 2002; Hitler's Forgotten Ally: Ion Antonescu and His Regime, Romania 1940-44, 2006 . EDITOR: (with A. Deletant) Romania, 1985; (with H. Hanak) Historians as Nation-Builders: Central and Southeast Europe, 1988; Occasional Papers in Romanian Studies, No. 1, 1995; (with Y. Alexandrescu) Romanian Phrase Book, 2000; (with M.E. Ionescu) Romania and the Warsaw Pact, 1955-1989: Selected Documents, 2004; (with O. Trasca) The Third Reich and the Rumanian Holocaust, 1940-1944: Documents from the German Archives, 2007. **Address:** England. **Online address:** d.deletant@ssees.ucl.ac.uk

DELFATTORE, Joan. American (born United States), b. 1946. **Genres:** Education, Civil Liberties/Human Rights, Law, Theology/Religion. **Career:** Secondary school teacher, 1967-76; University of Delaware, assistant professor, 1979-84, associate professor, 1984-92, professor of English, 1992-2001, professor of English and legal studies, 2001-, College of Arts and Science, director of teacher education. Writer. **Publications:** What Johnny Shouldn't Read: Textbook Censorship in America, 1992; The Fourth R: Conflicts Over Religion in America's Public Schools, 2004; The Myth of Academic Freedom in America's Schools and Universities, 2007; Knowledge in the Making: Academic Freedom and Free Speech in America's Schools and Universities, 2010; The Myth of Academic Freedom in America's Schools and Universities, forthcoming. **Address:** Department of English, University of Delaware, 062 Memorial Hall, 401 Academy St., Newark, DE 19716-2537, U.S.A. **Online address:** jdel@udel.edu

DELGADO, Aidan. American (born United States), b. 1981. **Genres:** Autobiography/Memoirs, Military/Defense/Arms Control. **Career:** Writer and activist. **Publications:** The Sutras of Abu Ghraib: Notes from a Conscientious Objector in Iraq, 2007. **Address:** Beacon Press, 25 Beacon St., Boston, MA 02108-2824, U.S.A. **Online address:** mail@aidandelgado.com

DELGADO, Hector L. American (born United States), b. 1949. **Genres:** Sociology. **Career:** Rutgers University, assistant director of admissions services and coordinator of Latino student recruitment, 1971-73, vice-chairperson of academic foundations department and coordinator of Hispanic affairs, 1978-80; Princeton University, assistant dean of student affairs, 1980-83; University of Michigan, instructor in sociology and Latino studies, 1984-86; Occidental College, assistant professor of sociology and anthropology, 1988-92; University of Arizona, assistant professor of sociology and assistant research social scientist at Mexican-American studies and research center, 1993; University of La Verne, associate professor of sociology, professor. Writer. **Publications:** New Immigrants, Old Unions: Organizing Undocumented Workers in Los Angeles, 1993; EDITOR WITH F.N. MAGILL: Survey of Social Science, 1994; International Encyclopedia of Sociology, 1995. Contributor to books and journals. **Address:** University of La Verne, Hoover Bldg. 111, Central Campus, 1950 3rd St., La Verne, CA 91750, U.S.A. **Online address:** delgadoh@ulv.edu

DELGADO, Ricardo. American (born United States) **Genres:** Humor/Satire, Sciences, Graphic Novels, Science Fiction/Fantasy. **Career:** Comic book artist, illustrator, storyboard artist/conceptual designer for films and writer. **Publications:** Age of Reptiles: Tribal Warfare (collection), 1996; Age of Reptiles: Carnivores (collection), 1997-1998; Age of Reptiles: The Hunt (collection), 1997; Hieroglyph, 1999. **Address:** c/o Author Mail, Dark Horse Comics, 10956 SE Main St., Milwaukie, OR 97222, U.S.A.

D'ELIA, Anthony F. Canadian/American (born United States), b. 1967. **Genres:** History, Translations. **Career:** Queen's University, associate professor of history, professor. Editor, translator, historian and educator. **Publications:** The Renaissance of Marriage in Fifteenth-Century Italy, 2004; (ed. and trans.) Bartolomeo Platina, Lives of the Popes: Antiquity, 2008; A Sudden Terror: The Plot To Murder The Pope In Renaissance Rome, 2009. Contributor to periodicals and journals. **Address:** Department of History, Queen's University, Rm. 238, Watson Hall, 49 Bader Ln., Kingston, ON K7L 3N6, Canada. **Online address:** deliaa@queensu.ca

DELIGIORGI, Katerina. British (born England), b. 1965. **Genres:** Philoso-

phy, History, Politics/Government. **Career:** Anglia Ruskin University, faculty; University of Sussex, senior lecturer in literature and philosophy, 2006-. Writer. **Publications:** Kant and the Culture of Enlightenment, 2005; (ed.) Hegel: New Directions, 2006. Contributor to books and journals. **Address:** Department of Philosophy, University of Sussex, Arts B Bldg., Falmer, Brighton, ES BN1 9QN, England. **Online address:** K.deligiorgi@sussex.ac.uk

DELILLO, Don. (Cleo Birdwell). American (born United States), b. 1936. **Genres:** Novels, Plays/Screenplays, Novellas/Short Stories, History, Literary Criticism And History. **Career:** Writer. **Publications:** Americana, 1971; End Zone, 1972; Great Jones Street, 1973; Ratner's Star, 1976; Players, 1977; Running Dog, 1978; (as Cleo Birdwell) Amazons: An Intimate Memoir by the First Woman Ever to Play in the National Hockey League, 1980; The Names, 1982; White Noise, 1985; Day Room: A Play, 1987; Libra, 1988; Mao II, 1991; Underworld, 1997; Valparaiso: A Play, 1999; The Body Artist: A Novel, 2001; Pafko at the Wall: A Novella, 2001; Cosmopolis: A Novel, 2003; Love-Lies-Bleeding: A Play, 2005; Conversations with Don DeLillo, 2005; Falling Man: A Novel, 2007; Point Omega: A Novel, 2010. The Angel Esmeralda, 2011. Works appear in anthologies. Contributor to periodicals and magazines. **Address:** c/o Lois Wallace, Wallace Literary Agency Inc., 177 E 70th St., New York, NY 10021-5162, U.S.A.

DELINSKY, Barbara (Ruth Greenberg). Also writes as Bonnie Drake, Billie Douglass. American (born United States), b. 1945. **Genres:** Novels. **Career:** Children's Protective Services, sociological researcher, 1968-69; Dover-Sherborn School System, instructor in photography, 1978-82; Belmont Herald, reporter. **Publications:** Bronze Mystique, 1984; A Special Something, 1984; Fingerprints, 1984; First Things First, 1985; Secret of the Stone, 1986; Threats and Promises, 1986; Straight from the Heart, 1986; Cardinal Rules, 1987; A Single Rose, 1987; Heat Wave, 1987; First, Best and Only, 1987; Twelve Across, 1987; Twilight Whispers, 1987; T.L.C., 1988; Commitments, 1988; Fulfillment, 1988; Through My Eyes, 1989; Heart of the Night, 1989; Montana Man, 1989; Having Faith, 1990; Crosslyn Rise: The Dream, 1990; Crosslyn Rise: The Dream Unfolds, 1990; Crosslyn Rise: The Dream Comes True, 1990; Facets, 1990; A Woman Betrayed, 1991; With this Ring: Father of the Bride, 1991; The Stud, 1991; The Outsider, 1992; The Passions of Chelsea Kane, 1992; Three Complete Novels, 1993; More Than Friends, 1993; Suddenly, 1994; For My Daughters, 1994; Together Alone, 1995; Shades of Grace, 1995; A Woman's Place: A Novel, 1997; Three Wishes: A Novel, 1997; Within Reach, 1997; Fast Courting, 1997; Coast Road: A Novel, 1998; Lake News, 1999; Rekindled, 1999; The Vineyard, 2000; The Woman Next Door, 2001; Uplift: Secrets From the Sisterhood of Breast Cancer Survivors, 2001; An Accidental Woman: A Novel, 2002; Flirting with Pete: A Novel, 2003; The Summer I Dared: A Novel, 2004; Does a Lobsterman Wear Pants?, 2005; Looking for Peyton Place: A Novel, 2005; Family Tree, 2007; Secret between Us, 2008; While My Sister Sleeps, 2009; Not my Daughter, 2010; Escape, 2011. AS BILLIE DOUGLASS: A Time to Love, 1982; Knightly Love, 1982; Search for a New Dawn, 1982; An Irresistible Impulse, 1983; Beyond Fantasy, 1983; Fasting Courting, 1983; Flip Side of Yesterday, 1983; Sweet Serenity, 1983; The Carpenter's Lady, 1983; Variation on a Theme, 1984. AS BONNIE DRAKE: Sensuous Burgundy, 1981; Surrender by Moonlight, 1981; Sweet Ember, 1981; The Passionate Touch, 1981; Amber Enchantment, 1982; Lilac Awakening, 1982; The Ardent Protector, 1982; Whispered Promise, 1983; Gemstone, 1983; Lover from the Sea, 1983; Passion and Illusion, 1983; The Silver Fox, 1983; Moment to Moment, 1984. **Address:** Writers House Inc., 21 W 26th St., New York, NY 10010, U.S.A.

DE LISLE, Harold F. American (born United States), b. 1933. **Genres:** Botany, Biology, Natural History. **Career:** University of Pasadena, assistant professor of biology, 1979-89; Moorpark College, professor of biology, 1989-. Writer. **Publications:** Common Plants of the Southern California Mountains, 1961; Wildlife of the Southern California Mountains, 1963; (ed.) Proceedings of the Conference on California Herpetology, 1989; The Natural History of Monitor Lizards, 1996. **Address:** Krieger Publishing Co., 1725 Krieger Dr., Malabar, FL 32950, U.S.A.

DELLAMONICA, A. M. Canadian (born Canada), b. 1968?. **Genres:** Science Fiction/Fantasy. **Career:** University of California, Extension Writer's Program, creative writing instructor. Writer. **Publications:** Indigo Springs, 2009. Contributor to periodicals. **Address:** Linn Prentis Literary Agency, 155 E 116th St., New York, NY 10029, U.S.A. **Online address:** alyx@sff.net

DELLASEGA, Cheryl. American (born United States), b. 1953. **Genres:**

Young Adult Non-fiction, Adult Non-fiction, Novels. **Career:** University of Pennsylvania Hospital, staff nurse, 1974-75; Medox Nursing Pool, staff nurse, 1975-76; Lancaster General Hospital, CCU staff nurse, 1976, recovery room staff nurse, 1980-81, School of Nursing, clinical instructor, 1982; Muhlenburg Hospital, CCU staff nurse, 1977; Centre Community Home Health Agency, visiting nurse and team coordinator, 1977-78; St. Joseph's Hospital and Health Care Center, infirmary charge nurse, 1978-80; Millersville University, instructor, 1982-84; Messiah College, instructor, 1984-85; Susquehanna Nursing Services, nurse practitioner, 1985; Pennsylvania State University, School of Nursing, instructor, 1986-88, assistant professor, 1988-95, associate professor of humanities, 1995-99, professor of humanities, 1999-, professor of women's studies, 2005-; Rehab Hospital for Special Services, nurse practitioner, 1987; South Huntingdon County Family Health Center, nurse practitioner in rural primary care, 1988; Halshogskolan University, visiting professor, 1992, 1997; Geisinger Medical Group, State College, geriatric nurse practitioner, 1994-96. Consultant and writer. **Publications:** Surviving Ophelia: Mothers Share Their Wisdom in Navigating the Tumultuous Teenage Years, 2001; (with C. Nixon) Girl Wars: 12 Strategies That Will End Female Bullying, 2003; Artolescence: Ten Art Based Activities for Adolescent Girls to Overcome Relational Aggression, 2005; The Starving Family: Caregiving Mothers and Fathers Share Their Eating Disorder Wisdom, 2005; Mean Girls Grown Up: Adult Women Who Are Still Queen Bees, Middle Bees, and Afraid-to Bees, 2005; The Girl's Friendship Journal, 2006; Forced to be Family: A Guide for Living with Sinister Sisters, Drama Mamas and Infuriating In-Laws, 2007; NuGrl90 (Sadie), 2007; (with S.O. Morris) Girl Grudges: Learning How to Forgive and Live, 2008; Sistrsic92 (Meg), 2009; The Testings of Devotion, 2009; When Nurses Hurt Nurses, 2011. Contributor of articles to periodicals. **Address:** Department of Humanities, Pennsylvania State University, H134, 500 University Dr., Hershey, PA 17033, U.S.A. **Online address:** opheliasmother@aol.com

DELLER, John J. American (born United States), b. 1931. **Genres:** Gerontology/Senior Issues, Medicine/Health. **Career:** Letterman General Hospital, chief of medicine, 1966, 1977; Letterman Army Medical Center, Department of Medicine, chief, 1969-76; University of California, associate clinical professor, 1976-77; Eisenhower Medical Center, physician, 1978-91, Center for Healthy Living, director and director of diabetes program, 1989-, chief of staff, 1992-93, director of education and research, now retired. Writer. **Publications:** Achieving Agelessness: Retirement is a New, Exciting Career: Here's How to Make It All It Can Be, 1991; The Palm Springs Formula for Staying Healthier and Living Longer, 1995. Contributor to periodicals and journals. **Address:** 346 Crest Lake Dr., Palm Desert, CA 92211-1704, U.S.A.

DELMAN, Carmit. American/Israeli (born Israel), b. 1975. **Genres:** Autobiography/Memoirs, Young Adult Non-fiction. **Career:** Writer. **Publications:** Burnt Bread and Chutney: Growing Up Between Cultures: A Memoir of an Indian Jewish Girl, 2002. **Address:** Ballantine/Del Rey/Fawcett/Ivy Books, 1540 Broadway, New York, NY 10036, U.S.A.

DEL MORAL, Roger. American (born United States), b. 1943. **Genres:** Environmental Sciences/Ecology, Sciences, Social Sciences. **Career:** University of Washington, professor of botany, 1968-, professor of biology, 2003-; University of Melbourne, CSIRO research fellow, 1976-77. Writer and botanist. **Publications:** (With L.R. Walker) Primary Succession and Ecosystem Rehabilitation, 2003; (with L.R. Walker) Environmental Disasters, Natural Recovery and Human Responses, 2007. Contributor to journals. **Address:** Department of Biology, University of Washington, Rm. HCK 226, 24 Kincaid Hall, PO Box 355325, Seattle, WA 98195-5325, U.S.A. **Online address:** moral@uw.edu

DEL NEGRO, Giovanna P. American (born United States) **Genres:** Cultural/Ethnic Topics, History, Mythology/Folklore. **Career:** Texas A&M University, assistant professor of English, associate professor of English. Writer. **Publications:** Looking through My Mother's Eyes: Life Stories of Nine Italian Immigrant Women in Canada, 1997, 2nd ed., 2003; (with H.M. Berger) Identity and Everyday Life: Essays in the Study of Folklore, Music and Popular Culture, 2004; The Passeggiata and Popular Culture in an Italian Town: Folklore and the Performance of Modernity, 2004. Contributor to journals. **Address:** Department of English, Texas A&M University, 219E Blocker Bldg., PO Box 4227, College Station, TX 77843, U.S.A. **Online address:** delnegro@tamu.edu

DE LOMELLINI, C. A. See **KELLEY, (Kathleen) Alita.**

DE LONG, David G. (David Gilson De Long). American (born United States), b. 1939. **Genres:** Architecture, Art/Art History. **Career:** John Carl Warnecke and Associates, associate, 1971-75; University of Pennsylvania, School of Design, professor of architecture, 1984-2003, professor emeritus of architecture, 2003-, Graduate School of Fine Arts, associate dean, 1992-94; Columbia University, Program in Historic Preservation, chair, 1984-96; Frank Lloyd Wright Conservancy, director; National Council for Preservation Education, director; Philadelphia Historic Preservation Corp., director; Middle East Technical University, visiting critic in architectural design; University of Sydney, visiting professor. Writer. **Publications:** (As David Gilson De Long) The Architecture of Bruce Goff: Buildings and Projects, 1916-1974, 2 vols., 1977; (ed.) Historic American Buildings, 14 vols., 1977-80; (intro.) Historic American Buildings, California, 1980; (ed. with H. Searing and R.A.M. Stern) American Architecture: Innovation and Tradition, 1986; Bruce Goff: Toward Absolute Architecture, 1988; (with D.B. Brownlee) Louis I. Kahn: In the Realm of Architecture, 1991; (ed.) James Gamble Rogers and the Architecture of Pragmatism, 1994; (contrib.) The Architecture of Bruce Goff, 1904-1982: Design for the Continuous Present, 1995; (ed.) Frank Lloyd Wright: Designs for an American Landscape, 1922-1932, 1996; (ed.) Frank Lloyd Wright and the Living City, 1998; (co-author) Out of the Ordinary: Robert Venturi and Denise Scott Brown, 2001; Auldbrass: Frank Lloyd Wright's Southern Plantation, 2003, 2nd ed., 2011; (ed. with C.F. Peatross) Eero Saarinen: Buildings from the Balthazar Korab Archive, 2008; (ed.) Sunnylands: Art and Architecture of the Annenberg Estate in Rancho Mirage, California, 2010. **Address:** School of Design, University of Pennsylvania, 102 Meyerson Hall, 210 S 34th St., Philadelphia, PA 19104-6311, U.S.A. **Online address:** ddelong@design.upenn.edu

DE LONG, David Gilson. See **DE LONG, David G.**

DELONG-BAS, Natana J. American (born United States) **Genres:** Theology/Religion, Adult Non-fiction. **Career:** Brandeis University, visiting lecturer in Islamic studies, 2005-, professor; Boston College, adjunct professor of theology; Georgetown University, Center for Muslim-Christian Understanding, senior research assistant. Consultant and writer. **Publications:** NONFICTION: (with J.L. Esposito) Women in Muslim Family Law, 2001; Wahhabi Islam: From Revival and Reform to Global Jihad, 2004; Notable Muslims: Muslim Builders of World Civilization and Culture, 2006. Contributor of books. **Address:** Near Eastern and Judaic Studies, Brandeis University, 415 South St., Waltham, MA 02454-9110, U.S.A. **Online address:** delongba@brandeis.edu

DELORIA, Philip J. Also writes as Philip Joseph Deloria. American (born United States) **Genres:** History, Social Sciences. **Career:** University of Michigan, Department of History, assistant professor, 1994-2000, associate professor, 2001-04, American Culture Program, director and professor of history, 2004-, associate dean for undergraduate education; American Studies Association, president, 2008-09. Historian and writer. **Publications:** Playing Indian, 1998; (ed. with N. Salisbury) A Companion to American Indian History, 2002; Indians in Unexpected Places, 2004. **Address:** Department of History, University of Michigan, 3700 Haven Hall, 500 S State St., Ann Arbor, MI 48109-1003, U.S.A. **Online address:** pdeloria@umich.edu

DELORIA, Philip Joseph. See **DELORIA, Philip J.**

DELORS, Catherine. American (born United States) **Genres:** Novels. **Career:** Lawyer and writer. **Publications:** Mistress of the Revolution, 2008. **Address:** Los Angeles, CA , U.S.A. **Online address:** catherine@catherinedelors.com

DE LOS SANTOS, Marisa. American (born United States), b. 1966?. **Genres:** Poetry, Novels. **Career:** University of Delaware, English instructor. Writer. **Publications:** From the Bones Out: Poems, 2000; Love Walked In: A Novel, 2006; Belong to Me, 2008; Falling Together: A Novel, 2011. **Address:** William Morrow Publishers, 10 E 53rd St., New York, NY 10022-5299, U.S.A. **Online address:** marisa@marisadelossantos.com

DEL PASO, Fernando. Mexican (born Mexico), b. 1935. **Genres:** Poetry, Novels, Literary Criticism And History, Social Sciences, Biography, Novellas/Short Stories. **Career:** British Broadcast Corp., publicist and newscaster, 1970-; Radio France Intl., staff, 1985-; Mexican Embassy, cultural attaché, general consultant, through 1986; Bibliotheca Iberoamericana Octavio Paz, director. Novelist, diplomat, painter and journalist. **Publications:** Sonetos del amor y de lo diario (poetry), 1958; José Trigo, 1966; Palinuro de México, 1977; Noticias del imperio, 1987; La loca de Miramar (monolog), 1988; De la A a la Z por un poeta (for children), 1990; Paleta de diez colores (for children), 1992; (prologue) Flores en México, 1992; Palinuro en las escalera (play), 1992; Memoria y olvido de Juan José Arreola, 1920-1947 (biography), 1994, 2nd ed., 1996; Linda 67: historia ed un crimen, 1996; (with M.L. Portilla) Yo soy un hombre de letras: discurso (speech), 1996; La muerte se va a Granada: poema dramático en dos actos, 1998; Cuentos dispersos (stories), 1999; Obras (collected works), 2 vols., 2000; Ensayo y obra periodística, 2002; PoeMar, 2004; Viaje alrededor de El Quijote, 2004; News from the Empire, 2009. Contributor to periodicals. **Address:** c/o Author Mail, Random House Mondadori, Homero 544, Col. Chapultepec Morales, DF 11570, Mexico.

DEL RE, Giuseppe. Italian (born Italy), b. 1932. **Genres:** Chemistry, Education, Philosophy. **Career:** University of Naples, assistant professor of chemistry, 1956-58, associate professor of spectroscopy, 1963-68, professor of theoretical chemistry, 1969-; RIAS, research group leader, 1959-62; University of Montreal, visiting professor, 1971; University of Waterloo, visiting professor, 1973, 1976, 2001; University of Erlangen, visiting professor, 1981-; International Centre for Transdisciplinary Research and Studies, founding member. Writer. **Publications:** (With G. Berthier and J. Serre) Electronic States of Molecules and Atom Clusters, 1980; The Cosmic Dance: Science Discovers the Mysterious Harmony of the Universe, 2000. EDITOR: Brain Research and the Mind-Body Problem: Epistemological and Metaphysical Issues, 1992; Scienza moderna e sense del divino, 1992. Contributor to books and journals. **Address:** Via della Giuliana 58, Rome, I-00195, Italy. **Online address:** g.delre@agora.stm.it

DELRIO, Martin. *See* MACDONALD, James D.

DELRIO, Martin. *See* DOYLE, Debra.

DELSEN, Lei. Dutch (born Netherlands), b. 1952. **Genres:** Business/Trade/Industry, Economics. **Career:** European Centre for Work and Society, research fellow, 1978-84; Radboud University Nijmegen, Nijmegen School of Management, Department of Economics and Business Economics, assistant professor, 1987-2001, associate professor of economics, 2002-, Institute for Management Research, faculty. Writer. **Publications:** Atypical Employment: An International Perspective: Causes, Consequences and Policy, 1995; (ed. with G. Reday-Mulvey) Gradual Retirement in the OECD Countries: Macro and Micro Issues and Policies, 1996; (ed. with G. Reday-Mulvey and A. Scarioni) La pensione flessibile: Politiche statali e strategie imprenditoriali, 1997; (ed. with E. de Jong) The German and Dutch Economies: Who Follows Whom?, 1998; Exit poldermodel?: Sociaal-economische ontwikkelingen in Nederland, 2000, trans. as Exit Polder Model?: Socioeconomic Changes in the Netherlands, 2002; (co-ed.) Social Security and Solidarity in the European Union, 2000; (co-ed.) Solidariteit in polder?: Armoede en sociale uitsluiting in Nederland bezien Vanuit de Economie en de Theologie, 2006; (co-ed.) Operating Hours and Working Times: A Survey of Capacity Utilisation and Employment in the European Union, 2007; (co-ed.) Comparative Analyses of Operating Hours and Working Times in the European Union, 2009. **Address:** Department of Economics and Business, Radboud University Nijmegen, Thomas van Aquinostraat 5.1.54, PO Box 9108, Nijmegen, 6525 GD, Netherlands. **Online address:** l.delsen@fm.ru.nl

DELSOHN, Gary. American (born United States), b. 1952. **Genres:** Adult Non-fiction, Writing/Journalism, Social Sciences, Biography. **Career:** Denver Rocky Mountain News, reporter, 1978-83; Denver Post, reporter, 1983-89; Sacramento Bee, senior writer, 1989-2006; State of California, Office of Governor, chief speech writer and deputy communications director, 2006-. **Publications:** (With A. English) The English Language, 1986; The Prosecutors: A Year in the Life of a District Attorney's Office, 2003. Contributor to periodicals. **Address:** c/o Author Mail, PENGUIN GROUP Inc., 375 Hudson St., New York, NY 10014, U.S.A. **Online address:** gdelsohn@sacbee.com

DELSON, Rudolph. American (born United States), b. 1975. **Genres:** Novels, Literary Criticism And History. **Career:** U.S. Department of Justice, Antitrust Division, paralegal; U.S. Court of Appeals for the Ninth Circuit, law clerk; Simpson, Thacher & Bartlett LLP, litigation associate; New York University, Law Review, notes editor. **Publications:** Maynard & Jennica (novel), 2007. Contributor to periodicals. **Address:** Brooklyn, NY , U.S.A. **Online address:** benjamin@rudolphdelson.com

DEL TORO, Guillermo. Mexican (born Mexico), b. 1964. **Genres:** Novels. **Career:** Cha Cha Cha Films, co-founder, 2009. Writer, director and producer. **Publications:** NOVELS: Hellboy: A Novelization, 2004; (with C. Hogan) The Strain, 2009; (With C. Hogan) The Fall, 2010. NONFICTION: (with A. Cruz) Bertha Navarro: Cineasta Sin Fronteras, 2008; Hitchcock, 2009. Contributor to periodicals. **Address:** William Morris Agency, 151 El Camino Dr., Beverly Hills, CA 90212, U.S.A.

DELVES, Peter J(ohn). British (born England), b. 1951. **Genres:** Medicine/Health, Biology, Education. **Career:** Imperial Cancer Research Fund, research officer, 1974-79; University of London, Department of Immunology, senior lecturer, professor, faculty, 1979-. Writer. **Publications:** (Ed. with I.M. Roitt) Encyclopedia of Immunology, 1992, 2nd ed., 1998; (with I.M. Roitt) Slide Atlas of Essential Immunology, 1992; (ed.) Cellular Immunology Labfax, 1994; (with I.M. Roitt) Essential Immunology Review, 1995; Essential Techniques: Antibody Applications, 1995; Antibody Production: Essential Techniques, 1997; (with I.M. Roitt) Roitt's Essential Immunology, 12th ed., 2011; (with I.M. Roitt and A.I. Rabson) Really Essential Medical Immunology, 2005. Contributor to periodicals. **Address:** Department of Immunology, University College London, Rm. 1.3.03, Cruciform Bldg., Gower St., London, GL WC1E 6BT, England. **Online address:** p.delves@ucl.ac.uk

DELYSER, Dydia. American (born United States), b. 1965?. **Genres:** Travel/Exploration. **Career:** Louisiana State University, Department of Geography and Anthropology, instructor, 1998-99, assistant professor, 1999-2005, associate professor, 2005-; Association of American Geographers, Qualitative Research Specialty Group, co-chair, 2005-. Writer. **Publications:** (Co-ed.) Historical Geography, 1999-; Ramona Memories: Tourism and the Shaping of Southern California, 2005; The SAGE Handbook of Qualitative Geography, 2010. Contributor to journals. **Address:** Department of Geography & Anthropology, Louisiana State University, 227 Howe-Russell Geoscience Complex, Baton Rouge, LA 70803-0001, U.S.A. **Online address:** dydia@lsu.edu

DEMACOPOULOS, George E. American (born United States), b. 1970?. **Genres:** Theology/Religion, History. **Career:** Fordham University, associate professor of theology. Writer. **Publications:** Five Models of Spiritual Direction in the Early Church, 2007; (ed. with A. Papanikolaou) Orthodox Readings of Augustine, 2008. **Address:** Department of Theology, Fordham University, 441 E Fordham Rd., Bronx, NY 10458-9993, U.S.A. **Online address:** demacopoulos@fordham.edu

DEMARAIS, Ann. American (born United States), b. 1959. **Genres:** Novels, Psychology, Self Help. **Career:** First Impressions Consulting, founder and president; Columbia University Business School, Social Intelligence Program, consultant. Psychologist and writer. **Publications:** (With V. White) First Impressions: What You Don't Know about How Others See You, 2004. **Address:** First Impressions Inc., 22 Prince St., Ste. 318, New York, NY 10012, U.S.A. **Online address:** ann@firstimpressionsconsulting.com

DEMARAY, Donald E(ugene). American (born United States), b. 1926. **Genres:** Theology/Religion, Biography. **Career:** Seattle First Free Methodist Church, minister of youth, 1952-53; Seattle Pacific College, School of Religion, dean, 1959-66; Asbury Theological Seminary, associate professor, 1966-67, professor of preaching and speech, 1966-92, dean of students, 1967-75, Senior Beeson professor of preaching, 1992-, now professor emeritus of biblical preaching. Writer. **Publications:** Basic Beliefs, 1958, rev. ed., 1996; Loyalty to Christ, 1958; Amazing Grace, 1958; The Book of Acts, 1959; Pulpit Manual, 1959; Questions Youth Ask, 1961; Acts (in Aldersgate series), 2 vols., 1961; Layman's Guide to the Bible, 1964 as Sourcebook of the Bible, 1971; Cowman Handbook of the Bible, 1964; Alive to God through Prayer, 1965; Preacher Aflame!, 1972; Pulpit Giants, 1973; An Introduction to Homiletics, 1974, 3rd ed., 2006; A Guide to Happiness, 1974; The Minister's Ministries, 1974; The Practice of the Presence of God (paraphrase), 1975, 2nd ed., 1997; Near Hurting People: The Pastoral Ministry of Robert Moffat Fine, 1978; Proclaiming the Truth, 1980, rev. ed., 2001; Watch Out for Burnout, 1983; How Are You Praying?, 1985; People Called Free Methodist: Snapshots, 1985; Snapshots, 1985; Laughter, Joy, and Healing, 1986, rev. ed., 1995; The Innovation of John Newton 1725-1807, 1988; Listen to Luther, 1989; The Little Flowers of St. Francis (paraphrase), 1992; The Daily Wesley, 1993, rev. ed., 1996; The Daily Roberts, 1996; Prayers and Devotions of John Wesley, 1998; Wesley's Daily Prayers, 1998; Experiencing Healing and Wholeness, 1999; With His Joy: The Life and Ministry of David McKenna, 2000; Daily Asbury: Excerpts for Every Day in the Year, 2001; Proclaiming the Truth: Guides to

Scriptural Preaching, 2001; (with K. Pickerill) A Robust Ministry, 2004; Mile Markers: 40 Intimate Journeys with Jesus, 2007; (with R. Johnson) Spiritual Formation for Christian Leaders, 2007; Healing, Wholeness, and Holiness, 2008. EDITOR: Prayers and Devotions of John Wesley, 1957; Prayers and Devotions of C. H. Spurgeon, 1960; Blow, Wind of God (anthology), 1975; Imitation of Christ, 1982; The Wesleys' Hymns and Poetry, 2003. **Address:** Asbury Theological Seminary, 204 N Lexington Ave., Wilmore, KY 40390, U.S.A. **Online address:** donald.demaray@asburyseminary.edu

DEMARCE, James L. Also writes as Virginia Easley DeMarce. American (born United States), b. 1940. **Genres:** History. **Career:** U.S. Department of the Interior, Office of Federal Acknowledgement, Bureau of Indian Affairs, historian, through 2004; Northwest Missouri State University, faculty; George Mason University, faculty; California Department of Agriculture, staff. Writer. **Publications:** AS VIRGINA EASLEY DEMARCE: A Tentative Outline of U.S. Easley Lines Primarily to the Year 1800, rev. ed., 1970; Data on Demers/Dumais Families in Quebec, 1648-1835: Background for Emigration to the United States, 1974; (Comp.) The Family and Ancestry of Hermann Joseph Jongebloed and His Wife Marie Emma Zuhlke in Germany and America, 1974; Supplement to a Tentative Outline of U.S. Easley Lines Primarily to the Year 1800, 1978; Canadian Participants in the American Revolution: An Index, 1980; An Annotated List of 317 Former German Soldiers Who Chose to Remain in Canada after the American Revolution, 1981; The Settlement of Former German Auxiliary Troops in Canada after the American Revolution, 1982; Carter of Deerfield, Mass., and Norwalk, Conn., Chartier of Quebec Province, Canada, and New York: A Study in Multilingualism and Multiculturalism in Eighteenth-Century America, 1983, rev. ed., 1985; Mercenary Troops from Anhalt-Zerbst, Germany, Who Served with the British Forces during the American Revolution, 1984; (Comp. with A.L. Stratton and V. Gassette) Notebook, French-Canadian Settlement in the Champlain Islands, Grand Isle County, Vermont before the Year 1880, 1985; The French-Canadian Settlement in Waterville Township, Pepin Co., Wisconsin, 1987; (Comp.) Clues to the Ancestry of Solomon Mace of Boone Co., Mo., the Mase/Mace Family of Ralls and Pike Cos., Mo., the Mase/Mace Family of Bourbon and Bath Cos. Ky., the Mace Family of Hampshire/Hardy Cos., VA/WV Preliminary Draft, 1989; (Comp.) Baptisms and Burials: St. Edmund's, Ellenburg, New York, St. Philomene's, Churubusco, New York, St. James, Cadyville, New York, Clinton County, 18641881, 1990; Now Living in Boone County, Missouri: Our Family Genealogies, 1990. ASSITI SHARDS SERIES SCIENCE FICTION NOVELS WITH ERIC FLINT: 1634: The Ram Rebellion, 2006; 1634: The Bavarian Crisis, 2007; 1635: The Dreeson Incident, 2008; 1635: The Tangled Web, 2009. Works appear in anthologies. Contributor to periodicals. **Address:** PO Box 1188, Wake Forest, NC 27588, U.S.A. **Online address:** virginiademarce@yahoo.com

DEMARCE, Virginia Easley. See DEMARCE, James L.

DEMARCO, Kathleen. See DEMARCO, Kathy.

DEMARCO, Kathy. Also writes as Kathleen van Cleve, Kathleen DeMarco. American (born United States), b. 1966. **Genres:** Novels. **Career:** University of Pennsylvania, School of Arts and Sciences, Department of English, faculty, senior lecturer in cinema studies; Lower East Side Films, producer; New York University, Tisch School of the Arts, consultant. Writer. **Publications:** AS KATHLEEN DEMARCO: Cranberry Queen, 2001; The Difference between You and Me: A Novel, 2003. OTHER: (as Kathleen Van Cleve) Drizzle, 2010. **Address:** Laura Dail Literary Agency Inc., 350 7th Ave., Ste. 2003, New York, NY 10001, U.S.A. **Online address:** kathydemarco@writing.upenn.edu

DEMARCO-BARRETT, Barbara. American (born United States) **Genres:** Reference, Writing/Journalism. **Career:** KUCI-FM, radio-show host and producer, public affairs director, 2000-02; University of California, writing instructor, 2000-, distinguished instructor; Gotham Writers Workshop, instructor; Pen on Fire Writers Salon, founder. Writer. **Publications:** (Contrib.) Conversations with Clarence Major, 2002; (contrib.) The ASJA Guide to Freelance Writing, 2003; Pen on Fire: A Busy Woman's Guide to Igniting the Writer Within, 2004. Contributor to periodicals and journals. **Address:** Van Haitsma Literary Agency, 204 N El Camino Real, Ste. E-431, Encinitas, CA 92024-2867, U.S.A. **Online address:** penonfire@earthlink.net

DE MARINIS, Marco. Italian (born Italy), b. 1949. **Genres:** Theatre, Art/Art History. **Career:** University of Bologna, researcher, 1981-87, associate professor, 1992-2000, professor of theater, 2000-; University of Macerata,

associate professor of theater, 1988-91; International School of Theater Anthropology, staff scientific collaborator. Writer. **Publications:** (With G. Bettetini) Teatro e Comunicazione, 1977; (ed.) Teatro e Semiotica, 1978; (ed.) Mimo e mimi, 1980; Semiotica del teatro, 1982, 2nd ed., 1992; Al limite del teatro, 1983; Il nuovo teatro, 1947-1970, 1987, 4th ed., 2000; Capire il teatro, 1988, 4th ed., 2000; Mimo e teatro nel Novecento, 1993; Visioni di teatro: Aristotle, Rousseau, Barthes, 1994; (ed.) Drammaturgia dell'attore, 1997; La Danza alla Rovescia di Artaud: Il Secondo Teatro Della Crudeltà (1945-1948), 1999; In Cerca Dell'attore: Un Bilancio del Novecento Teatrale, 2000; Visioni della Scena: Teatro e Scrittura, 2004; En busca del Actor y del Espectador, 2005. **Address:** Department of Music and Entertainment, University of Bologna, Via Barberia 4, Bologna, 40123, Italy. **Online address:** marco.demarinis@unibo.it

DE MARINIS, Rick. American (born United States), b. 1934. **Genres:** Novels, Novellas/Short Stories, Young Adult Fiction. **Career:** University of Montana, instructor in English, 1967-69; San Diego State University, associate professor of English, 1969-76; Arizona State University, visiting writer, 1980-81; Wichita State University, distinguished writer-in-residence, 1986; University of Texas, professor of English, 1988-89, now professor emeritus of English. Writer. **Publications:** A Lovely Monster: The Adventures of Claude Rains and Dr. Tellenbeck: A Novel, 1975; Scimitar: A Novel, 1977; Cinder, 1978; Jack & Jill: Two Novellas and a Story, 1979; The Burning Women of Far Cry: A Novel, 1986; Under the Wheat (stories), 1986; The Coming Triumph of the Free World: Stories, 1988; The Year of the Zinc Penny, 1989; The Voice of America (stories), 1991; The Mortician's Apprentice (novel), 1994; Borrowed Hearts: New and Selected Stories, 1999; The Art & Craft of the Short Story, 2000; A Clod of Wayward Marl, 2001; Sky Full of Sand, 2003; Apocalypse Then: Stories, 2004; Mama's Boy: A Novel, 2010. Contributor of to periodicals. **Address:** Department of English, University of Texas, 500 W University Ave., Ste. 210, El Paso, TX 79902-5816, U.S.A.

DE MARNEFFE, Daphne. American (born United States), b. 1959?. **Genres:** Psychology, Women's Studies And Issues. **Career:** Therapist, 1994-. Psychologist and writer. **Publications:** Maternal Desire: On Children Love and the Inner Life, 2004. Contributor to periodicals. **Address:** Little Brown Co., Time Warner Book Group, 1271 Ave. of the Americas, New York, NY 10020, U.S.A.

DEMARR, Mary Jean. American (born United States), b. 1932. **Genres:** Literary Criticism And History, Bibliography. **Career:** Junior high school English and German teacher, 1955-56; Willamette University, visiting assistant professor of English, 1964-65; Indiana State University, assistant professor, 1965-70, associate professor, 1970-75, professor of English and women's studies, 1975-95, now professor emeritus, 1995-. Writer. **Publications:** (With J.S. Bakerman) Adolescent Female Portraits in the American Novel, 1961-1981: An Annotated Bibliography, 1983; (with J.S. Bakerman) The Adolescent in the American Novel since 1960, 1986; (ed. and contrib.) In the Beginning: First Novels in Mystery Series, 1995; Colleen McCullough: A Critical Companion, 1996; Barbara Kingsolver: A Critical Companion, 1999; Kaye Gibbons: A Critical Companion, 2003. Contributor of articles to periodicals and books. **Address:** Indiana State University, 200 N 7th St., Terre Haute, IN 47809-1902, U.S.A. **Online address:** mjd594@msn.com

DEMASTES, William. (William W. Demastes). American (born United States), b. 1956. **Genres:** History, Adult Non-fiction, Art/Art History. **Career:** University of Georgia, teaching assistant, 1978-79; University of Wisconsin, teaching assistant, 1979-81, 1982-86; Alabama State University, instructor in English, 1981-82; Mount Senario College, instructor in English, 1984-86; University of Tennessee, instructor in English, 1986-89; Louisiana State University, Department of English, assistant professor, 1989-91, associate professor, 1991-95, director of graduate studies, 1992-94, 2005-06, professor of English, 1995-, alumni professor of English, associate chair, 1998-99, director of undergraduate studies, 1999-2001, 2010-11, Master of Arts in Liberal Arts Program, director, 1996-2004, faculty athletics representative, 2012-, College of Arts and Sciences, associate dean, 2000-04. Writer. **Publications:** AS WILLIAM W. DEMASTES: Beyond Naturalism: A New Realism in American Theatre, 1988; Clifford Odets: A Research and Production Sourcebook, 1991; Theatre of Chaos: Beyond Absurdism, Into Orderly Disorder, 1998; Staging Consciousness: Theater and the Materialization of Mind, 2002; Comedy Matters: From Shakespeare to Stoppard, 2008; Spalding Gray's America, 2008; The Cambridge Introduction to Tom Stoppard, 2012; Understanding John Guare, forthcoming. EDITOR: American Playwrights, 1880-1945: A

Research and Production Sourcebook, 1995; (with K.E. Kelly) British Playwrights, 1880-1956: A Research and Production Sourcebook, 1996; British Playwrights, 1956-1995: A Research and Production Sourcebook, 1996; Realism and the American Dramatic Tradition, 1996; (with B. Schrank) Irish Playwrights, 1880-1995: A Research and Production Sourcebook, 1997; (with I.S. Fischer) Interrogating America through Theatre and Performance, 2007. **Address:** Department of English, Louisiana State University, 219-C Allen Hall, Baton Rouge, LA 70803, U.S.A. **Online address:** wdemast@lsu.edu

DEMASTES, William W. See **DEMASTES, William.**

DEMBSKA, Anna. American (born United States) **Genres:** Music, Art/Art History. **Career:** Flying Leap Music, co-founder, 1999-; Singin' Local (vocal ensemble group), performer and director; The Schoodic Summer Chorus, director. Writer, educator and composer. **Publications:** (With J. Harkness) You've Got Rhythm: Read Music Better by Feeling the Beat, 2000; (with J. Harkness) Piano Body and Soul: Learn to Play and Bethe Musician You Always Wanted to Be, 2003; Edly's Music Theory for Practical People, 2005; Double Bounce: Ten Piano Duets for Older Beginners, forthcoming. **Address:** Flying Leap Music, 53599 Hwy. 245, Pinehurst, CO 93641, U.S.A. **Online address:** anna@fleap.com

DE MEDICI, Lorenza. Italian (born Italy), b. 1926. **Genres:** Food And Wine, Children's Non-fiction, Children's Fiction. **Career:** Novita, editor of living section, 1949-54; writer, 1954-; Vogue Italia, food editor, 1962-66; Public Broadcasting Service, host, 1982-. **Publications:** CHILDREN'S BOOKS: Giochiamo alla cucina, 1966; Giochiamo con i fiori, 1966; Giochiamo con i filo, 1966; Giochiamo con gli animali, 1966. OTHERS: I mille menu, 3 vols., 1967-68; La cucina dello zodiaco, 1968; I jolly della cucina, 12 vols., 1970-72; Menu dell'estate, 1973; Ricette del picnic, 1973; Antipasti, 1973; Menu economici, 1973; Menu dell'ultima ora, 1973; Menù delle occasioni, 1973; Cucina quasi pronta, 1973; Insalate, 1973; Libro dei mille menù, 1974; La cucina dello zodiaco: con un'appendice sulla cucina magica, 1974; Cucina internazionale, 1977; Tutto in tavola, 6 vols., 1980-82; La cucina Mediterranea, 1986; La cucina della badia, 1986; Il grande libro dei dolci, 1988 in US as Great Desserts, 1989; The Renaissance of Italian Cooking, 1989; Italy the Beautiful Cookbook, 1989; The Heritage of Italian Cooking, 1990; The Renaissance of Italian Gardens, 1990; The de' Medici Kitchen, 1992; Tuscany the Beautiful Cookbook, 1992; Pasta, 1992; Pizza, 1993; Florentines: A Tuscan Feast, 1993; The Villa Table: 300 Classic Italian Recipes, 1993; Lorenza's Pasta: 200 Recipes for Family and Friends, 1996; Italy Today the Beautiful Cookbook: Contemporary Recipes Reflecting Simple, Fresh Italian Cooking, 1997; Lorenza's Antipasti, 1998; Passion for Fruit, 1999. Contributor to periodicals. **Address:** Badia a Coltibuono, Gaiole in Chianti, Siena, 53013, Italy.

DEMELLO, Margo. American (born United States), b. 1964. **Genres:** Adult Non-fiction, Animals/Pets, Social Sciences, Popular Culture. **Career:** House Rabbit Society, president and executive director; Central New Mexico Community College, faculty; Animals and Society Institute, Human-Animal Studies, director. Writer. **Publications:** Bodies of Inscription: A Cultural History of the Modern Tattoo Community, 2000; (with S.E. Davis) Stories Rabbits Tell: A Natural and Cultural History of a Misunderstood Creature, 2003; Low-Carb Vegetarian, 2004; (with E.E. Williams) Why Animals Matter: The Case for Animal Protection, 2007; Encyclopedia of Body Adornment, 2007; Feet and Footwear: A Cultural Encyclopedia, 2009; (ed.) Teaching the Animal: Human-Animal Studies across the Disciplines, 2010; Teaching the Animal. The Social Sciences, 2010; Teaching the Animal. The Humanities, 2010; Faces Around the World: A Cultural Encyclopedia of the Human Face, 2012; Animals and Society: An Introduction to Human-Animal Studies, forthcoming; Speaking for Animals: Animal Autobiographical Writing, forthcoming. **Address:** New Mexico House Rabbit Society, PO Box 95226, Albuquerque, NM 87199, U.S.A. **Online address:** margo@rabbit.org

DEMERS, David (Pearce). American (born United States), b. 1953. **Genres:** Writing/Journalism, Communications/Media, Essays, History. **Career:** University of Wisconsin, assistant professor of communication, 1991-95; University of Minnesota, assistant professor of communications, 1995-96; Washington State University, Edward R. Murrow School of Communication, associate professor of communications, 1996-; Marquette Books L.L.C., publisher, 2001-; Mass Communication and Society, founding editor; University of Laval, Centre D'études sur les Médias, research consultant; Center for Global Media Studies, founder. **Publications:** (With R. Best) Investigation Report on the MGM Grand Hotel Fire, Las Vegas, Nevada, November 21, 1980: Report

Revised January 15, 1982, 1982; (with S. Nichols) Precision Journalism: A Practical Guide, 1987; Breaking Your Child's TV Addiction, 1989; The Menace of the Corporate Newspaper: Fact or Fiction?, 1996; Global Media: Menace or Messiah?, 1999, rev. ed., 2002; (ed. with K. Viswanath) Mass Media, Social Control and Social Change: A Macrosocial Perspective, 1999; (ed.) Global Media News Reader, 2002, rev. ed., 2003; (ed.) Terrorism, Globalization & Mass Communication: Papers Presented at the 2002 Center for Global Media Studies Conference, 2003; The Media Essays: From Local to Global, 2003; China Girl: One Man's Adoption Story, 2004; An Interpretive Introduction to Mass Communication, 2004; Dictionary of Mass Communication & Media Research: A Guide for Students, Scholars and Professionals, 2005; My Grandpa Loves Trains: A Picture Storybook for Preschoolers, 2006; History and Future of Mass Media: An Integrated Perspective, 2007; The Ivory Tower of Babel: Why the Social Sciences have Failed to Live up to Their Promises, 2011; The Last Professor of the Enlightenment: An American Odyssey, forthcoming; (with T. Kim) How the Mass Media Really Work: An Introduction to the Role and Function of Mass Media in Society, forthcoming; Why the Decline in Traditional Mass Media isn't Necessarily Bad for Democracy, forthcoming. **Address:** Edward R. Murrow School of Communication, Washington State University, MURE 219B, 101 Communication Addition, PO Box 642520, Pullman, WA 99164, U.S.A. **Online address:** ddemers@wsu.edu

DEMERS, Joanna Teresa. American (born United States), b. 1975. **Genres:** Music. **Career:** University of Southern California, Thornton School of Music, assistant professor. Writer. **Publications:** Steal This Music: How Intellectual Property Law Affects Musical Creativity, 2006. Contributor to journals. **Address:** Department of Musicology, University of Southern California, School of Music, Los Angeles, CA 90089-0851, U.S.A. **Online address:** jtdemers@usc.edu

DEMERS, Patricia. Canadian (born Canada), b. 1946?. **Genres:** Literary Criticism And History, Language/Linguistics, Art/Art History. **Career:** University of Alberta, Department of English and Film Studies, chair, 1995-98, professor of English and film studies; Social Sciences and Humanities Research Council of Canada, vice president, 1998-2002. Writer and researcher. **Publications:** NONFICTION: P.L. Travers (biography), 1991; Women As Interpreters of the Bible, 1992; Heaven upon Earth: The Form of Moral and Religious Children's Literature to 1850, 1993; The World of Hannah More (biography), 1996; (contrib.) Science and Ethics: Proceedings of a Symposium Held in November 2000 under the Auspices of the Royal Society of Canada, 2001; Women's Writing in English: Early Modern England, 2005; (trans. with N.L. McIlwraith and D. Thunder and intro.) The Beginning of Print Culture in Athabasca Country: A Facsimile Edition and Translation of a Prayer Book in Cree Syllabics By Émile Grouard: Prepared and Printed at Lac La Biche in 1883, 2010. EDITOR: (with G. Moyles) From Instruction to Delight: An Anthology of Children's Literature to 1850, 1982; A Garland from the Golden Age: An Anthology of Children's Literature from 1850 to 1900, 1983; (and intro.) The Creating Word: Papers from an International Conference on the Learning and Teaching of English in the 1980s, 1986; Scholarly Publishing in Canada: Evolving Present, Uncertain Future, 1988; Cœlebs in Search of a Wife: Comprehending Observations on Domestic Habits and Manners, Religion and Morals, 2007. **Address:** Department of English and Film Studies, University of Alberta, 4-43 Humanities Ctr., Edmonton, AB T6G 2E5, Canada. **Online address:** patricia.demers@ualberta.ca

DEMIDENKO, Helen. See **DARVILLE, Helen (Fiona).**

D'EMILIO, John. See **D, John.**

DEMILLE, Nelson (Richard). Also writes as Brad Matthews, Kurt Ladner. American (born United States), b. 1943. **Genres:** Novels, Mystery/Crime/Suspense, Literary Criticism And History, Young Adult Fiction. **Career:** Novelist, 1973-. **Publications:** Hammer of God, 1974; Sniper, 1974; Smack Man, 1975; Quest, 1975; Cannibal, 1975; (as Kurt Ladner) Hitler's Children, 1976; (as Brad Mathews) Killer Sharks, 1977; By the Rivers of Babylon, 1978; (with T.H. Block) Mayday, 1979; Cathedral, 1981; The Talbot Odyssey, 1984; Word of Honor, 1985; The Charm School, 1988; The Gold Coast, 1990; The General's Daughter, 1992; Three Complete Novels, 1992; Spencerville, 1994; Plum Island, 1997; Mary Higgins Clark Presents the Plot Thickens, 1997; The Lion's Game, 2000; Getting Your Book Published for Dummies, 2000; Take-off!, 2000; Up Country, 2002; Night Fall, 2004; The Best American Mystery Stories, 2004; Dangerous Women, 2005; Wild Fire: A Novel, 2006; The Book that Changed My Life, 2007; Gate House, 2008; In the Shadow of the Master,

2009; Lion, 2010; (ed.) Mystery Writers of America Presents the Rich and the Dead, 2011. Works appear in anthologies. **Address:** c/o Author Mail, Grand Central Publishing, 237 Park Ave., New York, NY 10017, U.S.A. **Online address:** nelson@nelsondemille.net

DEMING, Alison Hawthorne. American (born United States), b. 1946. **Genres:** Poetry, Essays. **Career:** University of Southern Maine, instructor, 1983-87; Vermont College, visiting lecturer in writing, 1983-85; Fine Arts Work Center, coordinator of writing fellowship program, 1988-90; University of Arizona Poetry Center, director, 1990-2000, Department of English, professor of creative writing, 1998-2003, professor, 2003-present. Writer. **Publications:** Science and Other Poems, 1994; Temporary Homelands (essays), 1994; (ed.) Poetry of the American West: A Columbia Anthology, 1996; The Monarchs: A Poem Sequence, 1997; The Edges of the Civilized World: A Journey in Nature and Culture, 1998; Writing the Sacred into the Real, 2001; (ed. with L.E. Savoy) Colors of Nature: Culture, Identity and the Natural World, 2002; Genius Loci, 2005; The Poet's Guide to the Birds, 2009; Rope, 2009. Contributor to periodicals. Works appear in anthologies. **Address:** Department of English, University of Arizona, ML438, PO Box 210067, Tucson, AZ 85721, U.S.A. **Online address:** ademing@email.arizona.edu

DEMING, Sarah. American (born United States) **Genres:** Novels, Essays, Ghost Writer, Mystery/Crime/Suspense. **Career:** Writer and educator. **Publications:** Iris, Messenger, 2007. **Address:** c/o George Nicholson, Sterling Lord Literistic Inc., 65 Bleecker St., New York, NY 10012, U.S.A. **Online address:** sarahlynndeming@gmail.com

DEMIRGUC-KUNT, Asli. American/Turkish (born Turkey), b. 1961. **Genres:** Money/Finance. **Career:** Ohio State University, Departments of Economics and Mathematics, instructor, 1983-88; Federal Reserve Bank of Cleveland, visiting economist, 1988-89; World Bank, lead economist in development economics, 1989-2003, finance research manager for development economics and advisor on financial sector operations and policy, 2003-05, Finance and Private Sector, Financial Sector Operations and Policy, senior research manager, 2005-06, Development Research Group, Finance and Private Sector Development, senior research manager, 2006-09, Financial and Private Sector Network, senior research manager, chief economist, 2010-; Journal of Financial Services Research, associate editor, 1999-. **Publications:** (With I. Diwan) Menu Approach to Developing Country External Debt: An Analysis of Commercial Banks' Choice Behavior, 1990; (co-author) Capital Positions of Japanese Banks, 1991; (R. Erzan) Role of Officially Supported Export Credits in Sub-Saharan Africa's External Financing, 1991; (with H. Huizinga) Official Credits to Developing Countries: Implicit Transfers to the Banks, 1991; Brady Plan, 1989 Mexican Debt-Reduction Agreement, and Bank Stock Returns in the United States and Japan, 1992; (with E. Detragiache) Interest Rates, Official Lending, and the Debt Crisis: A Reassessment, 1992; Developing Country Capital Structures and Emerging Stock Markets, 1992; (with E. Fernández-Arias) Burden-Sharing among Official and Private Creditors, 1992; (H. Huizinga) Barriers to Portfolio Investments in Emerging Stock Markets, 1992; Creditor Country Regulations and Commercial Bank Lending to Developing Countries, 1992; (co-author) North American Free Trade Agreement: Issues on Trade in Financial Services from Mexico, 1993; (with R. Levine) Stock Market Development and Financial Intermediary Growth: A Research Agenda, 1993; (with R. Levine) Financial System and Public Enterprise Reform: Concepts and Cases, 1994; (with V. Maksimovic) Capital Structures in Developing Countries: Evidence from Ten Country Cases, 1994; (with V. Maksimovic) Stock Market Development and Firm Financing Choices, 1995; (with R. Levine) Stock Market Development and Financial Intermediaries: Stylized Facts, 1995; (with A. Schwarz) Costa Rican Pension System: Options for Reform, 1995; Institutions, Financial Markets, and Firms' Choice of Debt Maturity, 1996; (with V. Maksimovic) Financial Constraints, Uses of Funds, and Firm Growth: An International Comparison, 1996; (with E. Detragiache) Determinants of Banking Crises: Evidence from Industrial and Developing Countries, 1997; (with G. Caprio, Jr.) Role of Long Term Finance: Theory and Evidence, 1997; (with E. Detragiache) Financial Liberalization and Financial Fragility, 1998; (co-author) How does Foreign Entry Affect the Domestic Banking Market?, 1998; Determinants of Commercial Bank Interest Margins and Profitability: Some International Evidence, 1998; (with R. Levine) Bank-Based and Market-based Financial Systems: Cross-Country Comparisons, 1999; (H. Huizinga) Market Discipline and Financial Safety Net Design, 1999; (with E. Detragiache) Monitoring Banking Sector Fragility: Multivariate Logit Approach with an Application to the 1996-97 Banking Crises, 1999; (with R. Levine) Financial Structure and Economic Growth: A Cross-Country Comparison of Banks Markets and Development, 2001; (co-ed.) Deposit Insurance Around the World: Issues of Design and Implementation, 2008; (co-author) Finance for All?: Policies and Pitfalls in Expanding Access, 2008; (ed. with D.D Evanoff and G.G Kaufman) The International Financial Crisis: Have the Rules of Finance Changed?, 2011. **Address:** World Bank, Rm. MC 3-445, 1818 H St., Washington, DC 20433, U.S.A. **Online address:** ademirguckunt@worldbank.org

DEMOS, John Putnam. American (born United States), b. 1937. **Genres:** History, Social Sciences. **Career:** Brandeis University, Department of History, assistant professor, 1968-72, professor, 1972-86, chairman, 1984-86; Center for Psychosocial Studies, director, 1974-75; Yale University, Department of History, professor of history, Samuel Knight professor of history, 1986-2008, Samuel Knight professor emeritus of history, 2008-. Writer and consultant. **Publications:** A Little Commonwealth: Family Life in Plymouth Colony, 1970, 2nd ed., 1999; (ed. and intro.) Remarkable Providences, 1600-1760, 1972, (comp.) rev. ed. as Remarkable Providences: Readings on Early American History, 1991; (ed. with S.S. Boocock) Turning Points: Historical and Sociological Essays on the Family, 1978; Entertaining Satan: Witchcraft and the Culture of Early New England, 1982; Past, Present, and Personal: The Family and the Life Course in American History, 1986; The Unredeemed Captive: A Family Story from Early America, 1994; The Tried and the True: Native American Women Confronting Colonization, 1995; Circles and Lines: The Shape of Life in Early America, 2004; Enemy Within: 2, 000 Years of Witch-Hunting in the Western World, 2008; Albanie, 2008. Contributor to journals and periodicals. **Address:** Department of History, Yale University, PO Box 208324, New Haven, CT 06520-8324, U.S.A. **Online address:** john.demos@yale.edu

DEMOTT, Robert (James). American (born United States), b. 1943. **Genres:** Poetry, Essays, Literary Criticism And History, Recreation. **Career:** Ohio University, assistant professor, 1969-74, associate professor, 1973-79, professor of American literature, 1979-, Edwin and Ruth Kennedy distinguished professor, 1998-; Back Door Magazine, co-editor, 1971; San Jose State University, Steinbeck Research Center, director, 1984-85, visiting professor of English, 1984-85. **Publications:** A Concordance to the Poems of Hart Crane, 1973; (ed. with S.E. Marovitz) Artful Thunder: Versions of the Romantic Tradition in American Literature in Honor of Howard P. Vincent, 1975; Steinbeck's Reading: A Catalogue of Books Owned and Borrowed, 1984; (ed.) Working Days: The Journals of the Grapes of Wrath, 1938-1941, 1989; (intro.) The Grapes of Wrath, 1992; Poetry: News of Loss, 1995; (ed. with D.V. Coers and P.D. Ruffin) After the Grapes of Wrath: Essays on John Steinbeck in Honor of Testsumaro Hyashi, 1995; Steinbeck's Typewriter: Essays on His Art, 1996; Dave Smith: A Literary Archive, 2000; The Weather in Athens: Poems, 2001; (ed.) Conversations with Jim Harrison, 2002; (ed. with B. Railsback) Travels with Charley and Later Novels, 1947-1962, 2007; Brief and Glorious Transit: Prose Poems, 2007; (with D. Smith) Afield: American Writers on Bird Dogs, 2010. Contributor to periodicals. **Address:** Department of English, Ohio University, 331 Ellis Hall, Athens, OH 45701, U.S.A. **Online address:** demott@ohio.edu

DEMOTT, Wes. American (born United States), b. 1952. **Genres:** Mystery/Crime/Suspense, Novels, Literary Criticism And History. **Career:** Federal Bureau of Investigation, special agent, 1982-85; independent businessperson, 1985-95; writer, 1995-; Aetna, property claims representative. **Publications:** SUSPENSE NOVELS: Walking K, 1998; Vapors, 1999; The Fund, 2004; Heat Sync, 2005; Jasperville, forthcoming; Never Pet a Burning Dog, forthcoming. **Address:** c/o Judith Buckner, Judith Buckner Literary Agency, 12721 Hart St., North Hollywood, CA 91605, U.S.A. **Online address:** wdemott@aol.com

DEMPSEY, Charles (Gates). American (born United States), b. 1937. **Genres:** Art/Art History, Cultural/Ethnic Topics, History. **Career:** American Academy, fellow in the history of art; Bryn Mawr College, faculty, 1965-80, assistant professor, professor of history of art, chair, 1975-80; Johns Hopkins University, visiting professor of history of art, 1971-73, professor of Italian renaissance and baroque art, 1980-, Johns Hopkins Center for Italian Studies, director of studies, 1980-85; Melbourne University, Department of Fine Arts, senior associate, 1977; Folger Institute of Renaissance and Eighteenth-century Studies, senior consultant, 1977, 1995; Princeton University, Council of the Humanities Class of 1932, Department of Art and Archaeology, visiting senior fellow and lecturer, 1985; École des Hautes Études en Sciences Sociales, associate director of studies, 1995; Collège de France, associate director of studies, 1996. Educator, art historian and writer. **Publications:** Annibale Carracci and the Beginnings of Baroque Style, 1977, 2nd. ed., 2000; La galerie des Carrache, 1984; (contrib.) Pietro Testa, 1612-1650: Prints and Drawings, 1988; (intro.) Scritti dei Carracci: Ludovico, Annibale, Agostino, Antonio, Giovanni Antonio, 1990; The Portrayal of Love: Botticelli's Primavera and Humanist Culture at the Time of Lorenzo the Magnificent, 1992; Annibale Carracci, the Farnese Gallery, Rome, 1995; (with E. Cropper) Nicolas Poussin: Friendship and the Love of Painting, 1996; (ed. and intro.) Quattrocento Adriatico: Fifteenth-Century Art of the Adriatic Rim: Papers from a Colloquium Held at the Villa Spelman, Florence, 1994, 1996; Inventing the Renaissance Putto, 2001; (contrib.) Captured Emotions: Baroque Painting in Bologna, 1575-1725, 2008; Early Renaissance and Vernacular Culture, 2012. Contributor of articles to books, periodicals and journals. **Address:** Department of the History of Art, Johns Hopkins University, 269 Mergenthaler Hall, 3400 N Charles St., Baltimore, MD 21218, U.S.A. **Online address:** charles.dempsey@jhu.edu

DEMSKI, Joel S. American (born United States), b. 1940. **Genres:** Business/Trade/Industry, Essays, Education. **Career:** Columbia University, research associate in business, 1966-67, assistant professor of business, 1967-68; Stanford University, assistant professor, 1968-70, associate professor, 1970-73, professor of information and accounting systems, 1973-79; University of Chicago, visiting faculty, 1974-75; University of Michigan, visiting faculty, 1981-82; Yale University, Milton Steinbach professor of information and accounting systems, 1985-94; Odense University, visiting faculty, 1990; American Accounting Association, president; University of Florida, faculty. Writer. **Publications:** Information Analysis, 1972, 2nd ed., 1980; (with N. Dopuch and J.G. Birnberg) Cost Accounting: Accounting Data for Management's Decisions, 2nd ed., 1974, 3rd ed., 1982; (with G. Feltham) Cost Determination: A Conceptual Approach, 1976; (ed. with Dopuch and S. Zeff) Essays in Honor of William A. Paton, 1979; Information Economics and Accounting Research: A Workshop, 1980; Managerial Uses of Accounting Information, 1994, 2nd ed., 2008; (with J.A. Christensen) Accounting Theory: An Information Content Perspective 2003. Contributor to books and journals. **Address:** Fisher School of Accounting, College of Business Administration, University of Florida, 333 GER, PO Box 117166, Gainesville, FL 32611-7166, U.S.A. **Online address:** joel.demski@cba.ufl.edu

DEMSKY, Issur Danielovitch. See **DOUGLAS, Kirk.**

DE MUNCK, Victor C. American/Dutch (born Netherlands), b. 1948. **Genres:** Anthropology/Ethnology. **Career:** University of South Carolina, Department of Anthropology, visiting assistant professor, 1990-91; University of California, Department of Anthropology, visiting assistant professor, 1992-93; University of New Hampshire, visiting assistant professor, 1993-95, assistant professor, 1995-96; State University of New York College, Department of Anthropology, assistant professor of anthropology, 1996-2003, associate professor, 2003-. Writer. **Publications:** Seasonal Cycles, 1993; (ed. and contrib.) Romantic Love and Sexual Behavior: Perspectives from the Social Sciences, 1998; (co-ed.) Using Methods in the Field: A Practical Introduction and Casebook, 1998; Culture, Self and Meaning, 2000; Experiencing Vilnius: Voices on the Process of Othering, 2008; Research Design and Field Methods, 2009; A Primer for Anthropological Field Research, forthcoming; Research Design and Methods for Studying Culture in the Field, forthcoming. **Address:** Department of Anthropology, State University of New York, Wooster Science Bldg. 228, 1 Hawk Dr., New Paltz, NY 12561-2499, U.S.A. **Online address:** victor@bestweb.net

DENDINGER, Roger E. American (born United States), b. 1952. **Genres:** Novels, Travel/Exploration, Education. **Career:** South Dakota School of Mines & Technology, Department of Social Sciences, associate professor of geography and chair, 1998-. Writer. **Publications:** Scotland, 2002; Costa Rica, 2003; Guatemala, 2004; Honduras, 2008. **Address:** Department of Social Sciences, South Dakota School of Mines & Technology, CB 311 / SS, 501 E Saint Joseph St., Rapid City, SD 57701-3995, U.S.A. **Online address:** roger.dendinger@sdsmt.edu

DE NEUFVILLE, Richard. American (born United States), b. 1939. **Genres:** Engineering, Technology, Transportation. **Career:** Massachusetts Institute of Technology, assistant professor, 1966-70, associate professor of engineering,

1970-75, Civil Engineering Systems Laboratory, director, 1970-73, Technology and Policy Program, professor and chairman, 1975-99; Systems Analysis, owner, 1969-; Imperial College of Science and Technology, visiting professor, 1973-74; London Graduate School of Business, visiting professor, 1973-74; University of California, visiting professor, 1974-75; Ecole Centrale de Paris, visiting professor, 1981-82; Ecole des Ponts et Chaussees, adjunct professor, 1984-94; Oxford University, visiting fellow, 2000; Harvard University, Kennedy School, affiliate staff, 2000-10; Judge School of Business, visiting professor, 2002-; Instituto Superior Tecnico Lisbon, visiting professor, 2007-. Writer. **Publications:** (With J. Stafford) Systems Analysis for Engineers and Managers, 1971; (ed. with D. Marks) Systems Planning and Design: Case Studies in Modeling, Optimization, and Evaluation, 1974; Airport Systems Planning: A Critical Look at the Methods and Experience, 1976; Applied Systems Analysis: Engineering Planning and Technology Management, 1990; (with A.R. Odoni) Airport Systems: Planning, Design and Management, 2003; (with S. Scholtes) Flexibility in Engineering Design, 2011. **Address:** Engineering Systems Division, Massachusetts Institute of Technology, 77 Massachusetts Ave., Ste. E40-261, Cambridge, MA 02139-4307, U.S.A. **Online address:** ardent@mit.edu

DENEUVE, Catherine. French (born France), b. 1943. **Genres:** Children's Fiction, Autobiography/Memoirs, Art/Art History, Biography. **Career:** Films de la Citrouille (film production Co.), founder, 1971; A Strange Place to Meet, producer, 1988; UNESCO, co-chair, 1994. Writer, actor, producer, composer, designer and memoirist. **Publications:** (With P. Modiano) Elle s'appelait Franoise, 1996; A L'ombre De Moi-même: Carnets de Tournage & Entretien Avec Pascal Bonitzer (memoir), 2004 in UK as Close Up and Personal, 2005; (with A. Desplechin) Une certaine lenteur, 2010. **Address:** Artmedia, 20 Ave. Rapp, Paris, 75007, France.

DENG, Francis Mading. American (born United States), b. 1938. **Genres:** Area Studies, History, Novels. **Career:** Sudanese ambassador to Scandinavia, 1972-74; Sudanese ambassador to the United States, 1974-76; Minister of State for Foreign Affairs, 1976-80; Sudanese ambassador to Canada, 1980-83; Brookings Institution, senior fellow, 1989-, non-resident senior fellow; Yale Law School, visiting lecturer; Johns Hopkins University, School of Advanced International Studies, research professor, director; City University of New York, distinguished professor of political science and senior fellow and co-director, 2001-02; Khartoum University, faculty; United Nations Secretariat, human rights officer; Wilson Center, senior research associate. Writer. **Publications:** Tradition and Modernization: A Challenge for Law among the Dinka of the Sudan, 1971; The Dinka of the Sudan, 1972; The Dinka and Their Songs, 1973; Dynamics of Identification: A Basis for National Integration in the Sudan, 1973; Dinka Folktales: African Stories from the Sudan, 1974; Africans of Two Worlds: The Dinka in Afro-Arab Sudan, 1978; Dinka Cosmology, 1980; (as Francis M. Deng) Security Problems: An African Predicament, 1981; Recollections of Babo Nimir, 1982; (as Francis Deng) Seed of Redemption: A Political Novel, 1986; The Man Called Deng Majok: A Biography of Power, Polygyny and Change, 1986; Cry of the Owl (novel), 1989; (as Francis M. Deng with M.W. Daly) Bonds of Silk: The Human Factor in the British Administration of the Sudan, 1990; (as Francis M. Deng with L. Minear) The Challenges of Famine Relief: Emergency Operations in the Sudan, 1992; (as Francis M. Deng) Protecting the Dispossessed: A Challenge for the International Community, 1993; (as Francis M. Deng) War of Visions: Conflict of Identities in the Sudan, 1995; (as Francis M. Deng) Sovereignty as Responsibility: Conflict Management in Africa, 1996; (as Francis M. Deng) Preventive Diplomacy, the Case of Sudan, 1997; Partners for Peace, 1998; (as Francis M. Deng) Masses in Flight: The Global Crisis of Internal Displacement, 1998; (as Francis M. Deng) Internally Displaced Persons: Compilation and Analysis of Legal Norms, 1998; (co-author as Francis M. Deng) Critical Choices: The United Nations, Networks and the Future of Global Governance, 2000; (co-author as Francis M. Deng) A Strategic Vision for Africa: The Kampala Movement, 2002; (foreword) Darfur Diaries: Stories of Survival, 2006; Identity, Diversity and Constitutionalism in Africa, 2008; (co-ed.) Self-Determination and National Unity, 2009; Frontiers of Unity: An Experiment in Afro-Arab Co-operation, 2010; Sudan at the Brink: Self-Determination and National Unity, 2010; Customary Law in the Modern World: the Crossfire of Sudan's War of Identities, 2010. EDITOR: (as Francis M. Deng with R.O. Collins) The British in the Sudan, 1898-1956: The Sweetness and the Sorrow, 1984; (with P. Gifford) The Search for Peace and Unity in the Sudan, 1987; (as Francis M. Deng with A. An-Naim) Human Rights in Africa: Cross-Cultural Perspectives, 1990; (as Francis M. Deng with I.W. Zartman) Conflict Resolution in Africa, 1991; (as Francis M. Deng with T.

Lyons) African Reckoning: A Quest for Good Governance, 1998; (as Francis M. Deng with R. Cohen) The Forsaken People: Case Studies of the Internally Displaced, 1998; New Sudan in the Making?: Essays on a Nation in Painful Search of Itself, 2010. **Address:** The Brookings Institution, 1775 Massachusetts Ave. NW, Washington, DC 20036, U.S.A.

DENG, Yong. American/Chinese (born China), b. 1966?. **Genres:** International Relations/Current Affairs, Economics, Young Adult Non-fiction. **Career:** Benedictine University, assistant professor of political science, 1995-99; United States Naval Academy, faculty, 1999-, professor of political science. Writer. **Publications:** NONFICTION: Promoting Asia-Pacific Economic Cooperation: Perspectives from East Asia, 1997; (ed. with F. Wang) In the Eyes of the Dragon: China Views the World, 1999; (ed. with F. Wang) China Rising: Power and Motivation in Chinese Foreign Policy, 2005; China's Struggle for Status: The Realignment of International Relations, 2008. Contributor to journals. **Address:** United States Naval Academy, 121 Blake Rd., Annapolis, MD 21402-5000, U.S.A.

DENG XIAO HUA. (Can Xue). Chinese (born China), b. 1953. **Genres:** Novels. **Career:** Writer. **Publications:** A Performance of Breakthrough (novel), 1988; Dialogues in Paradise, 1989; Old Floating Cloud: Two Novellas, 1991; Yellow Mud Street, 1991; Ren lei wen hua yu yan xue, 1993; (with L. Meizhen) Kejia fang yan, 1995; The Embroidered Shoes, 1997; Mei fang zhi li nan xia ri, 2000; Qi yi de mu ban fang, 2000; Cang lao de fu yun, 2001; Mo shi ai qing, 2006; Blue Light in the Sky and Other Stories, 2006; Qu guang yun dong: hui su tong nian de jing shen tu jing, 2008; Five Spice Street, 2009; Vertical Motion: Short Stories, 2011; The Last Lover, forthcoming. **Address:** Rm. 1512, Mu Dan Bei Li 5, Hai Dian Qu, Beijing, 100083, China. **Online address:** dengxiaohua2001@sina.com.cn

DENHAM, Andrew. British (born England) **Genres:** Politics/Government, Biography, Social Sciences. **Career:** University of Nottingham, School of Politics and International Relations, faculty of law and social sciences, reader in government, PhD Admissions, director, Learning Community Forum, chair, Centre for British Politics, deputy director. Writer. **Publications:** Think-Tanks of the New Right, 1996; (with M. Garnett) British Think-Tanks and the Climate of Opinion, 1998; (with M. Garnett) Keith Joseph (biography), 2001; (with K. O'Hara) Democratising Conservative Leadership Selection: From Grey Suits to Grass Roots, 2008; (with P. Dorey and M. Garnett) From Crisis to Coalition: The Conservative Party, 2011. EDITOR: (with D. Stone and M. Garnett) Think Tanks across Nations: A Comparative Approach, 1998; (with D. Stone) Think Tank Traditions, 2004. Contributor to periodicals. **Address:** School of Politics and International Relations, University of Nottingham, Rm. C7, University Pk., Nottingham, NT NG7 2RD, England. **Online address:** andrew.denham@nottingham.ac.uk

DENHAM, James M. American (born United States), b. 1957. **Genres:** History, Criminology/True Crime. **Career:** Georgia Southern University, instructor, 1987; Limestone College, assistant professor of history, 1987-91; Florida Southern College, assistant professor, 1991-96, associate professor of history, 1996-2000, professor, 2000-, Lawton M. Chiles Center for Florida History, director, 2001-. Writer. **Publications:** A Rogue's Paradise: Crime and Punishment in Antebellum Florida, 1821-1861, 1997; (ed. with C. Brown, Jr.) Cracker Times and Pioneer Lives: The Florida Reminiscences of George Gillette Keen and Sarah Pamela Williams, 2000; (with W.W. Rogers) Florida Sheriffs: A History, 1821-1945, 2001; (ed. with K. Huneycutt) Echoes from a Distant Frontier: The Brown Sisters' Correspondence in Antebellum Florida, 2004. Contributor to books. **Address:** Lawton M. Chiles Center for Florida History, Florida Southern College, 111 Lake Hollingsworth Dr., Lakeland, FL 33801-5698, U.S.A. **Online address:** jdenham@flsouthern.edu

DEN HARTOG, Kristen. Canadian (born Canada), b. 1965. **Genres:** Adult Non-fiction. **Career:** Author and florist. **Publications:** Water Wings (novel), 2001; The Perpetual Ending (novel), 2002; Origin of Haloes: A Novel, 2005; (with T. Kasaboski) The Occupied Garden: A Family Memoir of War-Torn Holland, 2009. Works appear in anthologies. Contributor to periodicals. **Address:** c/o Author Mail, MacAdam/Cage, 280 Columbine St., Ste. 303, Denver, CO 80206-4719, U.S.A. **Online address:** authors@theoccupiedgarden.com

DENIZET-LEWIS, Benoit. American (born United States), b. 1975?. **Genres:** Social Sciences. **Career:** Boston Magazine, staff writer; San Francisco Chronicle, staff writer; New York Times Magazine, contributing writer; Tufts University, instructor in magazine and nonfiction writing; Emerson College, instructor in magazine and nonfiction writing; Northeastern University, instructor in magazine and nonfiction writing. Journalist and public speaker. **Publications:** America Anonymous: Eight Addicts in Search of a Life, 2009; American Voyeur: Dispatches from the Far Reaches of Modern Life, 2010. Contributor to periodicals and newspapers. **Address:** Jamaica Plain, MA , U.S.A. **Online address:** benoitsf@gmail.com

DENKER, Henry. American (born United States), b. 1912. **Genres:** Novels, Plays/Screenplays. **Career:** Lawyer, 1935-58; Research Institute of America, executive, 1938-40; Standard Statistics, tax consultant, 1940-42; CBS, Radio Readers Digest, writer, 1945; novelist and writer for radio, television, stage and screen, 1947-97; American Theatre Wing, drama instructor, 1961-63; College of the Desert, drama instructor, 1970. **Publications:** I'll Be Right Home, Ma, 1947; My Son, the Lawyer, 1949; Salome: Princess of Galilee, 1951; The First Easter, 1951; God's Selfless Men, 1952; Valour will Weep, 1955; Time Limit! (play), 1957; Far Country (play), 1961; Give us Barabbas, 1961; A Case of Libel (play), 1963; What did We Do Wrong? (play), 1967; The Director, 1970; The Kingmaker, 1972; A Place for the Mighty, 1973; The Soft Touch, 1974; The Physicians, 1975; The Experiment, 1976; The Headhunters (play), 1974; The Starmaker, 1977; The Scofield Diagnosis, 1977; The Second Time Around (play), 1977; The Actress, 1978; Error of Judgment, 1979; Horowitz and Mrs. Washington, 1979; The Warfield Syndrome, 1981; Outrage, 1982; The Healers, 1983; Kincaid, 1984; Robert, My Son, 1985; Judge Spencer Dissents, 1986; The Choice, 1987; The Retreat, 1988; Gift of Life, 1989; Payment in Full, 1991; Doctor on Trial, 1992; Mrs. Washington and Horowitz, Too, 1993; Labyrinth, 1994; This Child is Mine, 1995; To Marcy with Love, 1996; A Place for Kathy Cameron, 1997; Clarence, 1998; Class Action, 2000; Benjie (novel), 2001; Class Action: The Novel, 2002. **Address:** c/o Mitch Douglas, International Creative Management, 730 5th Ave., New York, NY 10019, U.S.A.

DENMAN, K. L. Canadian (born Canada), b. 1957?. **Genres:** Novels. **Career:** Writer. **Publications:** NOVELS: Battle of the Bands, 2006; Mirror Image, 2007; Rebel's Tag, 2007; The Shade, 2008; Spiral, 2008; Perfect Revenge, 2009; Me, Myself and Ike, 2009. **Address:** Powell River, BC , Canada. **Online address:** write@shaw.ca

DENNETT, Nolan A. American (born United States), b. 1950. **Genres:** Novels. **Career:** St. Louis Conservatory and School for the Arts, director of dance, 1974-78; Metro Theater Circus, principal performer and choreographer, 1975-78; Dance Kaleidium of St. Louis, artistic director, 1976-78; Chicago Moving Co., artist-in-residence, 1978-81; DePaul University, Goodman School of Drama, faculty member, 1980-81; University of California, teacher of drama and dance, 1981-88; Repertory-West Dance Co., principal dancer, 1981-88, artistic director, 1987-88; San Jose State University, associate professor of dance, 1988-89; San Francisco Moving Co., principal dancer, 1988-89; Western Washington University, Theater Department, movement specialist and member of theater arts faculty, 1989-, professor, Western's Dance Program, director; American College Dance Festival Association, national board director. Producer, director and writer. **Publications:** Place of Shelter (novel), 1994. Work appear in anthologies. Contributor of articles and stories to periodicals. **Address:** Dance Program, Western Washington University, 516 High St., Carver Gym, Rm. 28, Bellingham, WA 98225, U.S.A. **Online address:** nolan.dennett@wwu.edu

DENNIS, Felix. British (born England), b. 1947. **Genres:** Poetry, Biography. **Career:** Blues musician, 1967-68; Oz Magazine, editor, 1969-73; Dennis Publishing Group, owner and managing director, 1973-83, chair, 1983-; Microwarehouse Inc., director and founder, 1986; Macuser Magazine, director and founder, 1985-87. **Publications:** (With P. Simmons) The Beginner's Guide to Kung-Fu, 1974; (with D. Atyeo) Bruce Lee, King of Kung-Fu, 1974; (with D. Atyeo) The Holy Warrior, Muhammad Ali: An Illustrated Biography, 1975; (ed.) Man Eating Sharks: Deadly Jaws of the Deep, 1975; (with D. Atyeo) Muhammad Ali: The Glory Years, 2003; How to Get Rich, 2006 in US as How to Get Rich: One of the World's Greatest Entrepreneurs Shares His Secrets, 2008; Tales From the Woods, 2010; The Narrow Road, 2011. POETRY: A Glass Half Full, 2002; Lone Wolf, 2004; When Jack Sued Jill, 2006. **Address:** Dennis Publishing Group, 9-11 Kingly St., London, GL W1B 5PN, England.

DENNIS, Michael. Canadian (born Canada), b. 1967. **Genres:** Civil Liberties/Human Rights, Economics. **Career:** Acadia University, Department of History and Classics, assistant professor, 1999, associate professor. Writer.

Publications: Lessons in Progress: State Universities and Progressivism in the New South 1880-1920, 2001; Luther P. Jackson and a Life for Civil Rights, 2004; The New Economy and the Modern South, 2009; The Memorial Day Massacre and the Movement for Industrial Democracy, 2010. **Address:** Department of History and Classics, Acadia University, Rm. 407, Beveridge Arts Ctr., 15 University Ave., Wolfville, NS B4P 2R6, Canada. **Online address:** michael.dennis@acadiau.ca

DENSON, Andrew. American (born United States) **Genres:** History, Cultural/Ethnic Topics, Young Adult Non-fiction. **Career:** Butler University, affiliated, through 2004; Western Carolina University, Department of History, assistant professor, 2004-, associate professor. Writer. **Publications:** Demanding the Cherokee Nation: Indian Autonomy and American Culture, 1830-1900, 2004. Contributor to periodicals. **Address:** Department of History, Western Carolina University, 203B McKee Bldg., Cullowhee, NC 28723, U.S.A. **Online address:** denson@email.wcu.edu

DENT, David J. American (born United States) **Genres:** Cultural/Ethnic Topics, Social Sciences. **Career:** American Broadcasting Companies Inc. (ABC), television reporter; Black Entertainment Television News, contributing correspondent; New York University, associate professor of journalism and mass communication; Open Society Institute of the Soros Foundation, media fellow, 2004; Court TV, commentator. Journalist, educator and author. **Publications:** In Search of Black America: Discovering the African American Dream, 2000; American Extremes, forthcoming. Contributor to magazines and newspapers. **Address:** Department of Journalism, New York University, Arthur Carter Hall, 10 Washington Pl., New York, NY 10003-6604, U.S.A. **Online address:** david.dent@nyu.edu

DENT, Grace. British (born England), b. 1973?. **Genres:** Novels. **Career:** Marie Claire (magazine), editorial assistant; Guardian, television critic, journalist. **Publications:** YOUNG-ADULT NOVELS: Curse of the Mega-Boobed Bimbos, 2006; Trainers v. Tiaras, 2007. LBD SERIES: LBD: It's a Girl Thing, 2003; LBD: The Great Escape, 2004; LBD: Live and Fabulous!, 2006; LBD: Friends Forever!, 2006; Too Cool for School, 2008; The Ibiza Diaries, 2008; The Fame Diaries, 2008; Diary of a Chav, 2008; Posh and Prejudice, 2009; Keeping It Real, 2009; Poor Little Rich Girl, 2009; Money Can't Buy Me Love, 2010. **Address:** Little, Brown Book Group, 100 Victoria Embankment, London, GL EC4Y 0DY, England. **Online address:** worldoflather@hotmail.com

DENT, Harry S. American (born United States), b. 1950?. **Genres:** Business/Trade/Industry, History. **Career:** HS Dent Investment Management, founder; H.S. Dent Foundation, president; H.S. Dent Publishing, president. Writer, economic analyst, investment analyst and consultant. **Publications:** Our Power to Predict: Revolutionary New Tools for Predicting Our Economy and the Future of Business, 1989; The Great Boom Ahead: Your Comprehensive Guide to Personal and Business Profit in the New Era of Prosperity, 1993; The Great Jobs Ahead: Your Comprehensive Guide to Surviving and Prospering in the Coming Work Revolution, 1995; Job Shock: Four New Principles Transforming Our Work and Business, 1995; The Roaring 2000s: Building the Wealth and Lifestyle You Desire in the Greatest Boom in History, 1998; The Roaring 2000s Investor: Strategies for the Life You Want, 1999; The Next Great Bubble Boom: How to Profit from the Greatest Boom in History 2005-2009, 2004; The Next Great Bubble Boom: How to Profit from the Greatest Boom in History, 2006-2010, 2006; The Great Depression Ahead: How to Prosper in the Crash following the Greatest Boom in History, 2009. **Address:** 15310 Amberly Dr., Ste. 390, Tampa, FL 33647, U.S.A.

DENT, Richard J. American (born United States), b. 1951. **Genres:** Anthropology/Ethnology. **Career:** American University, Department of Anthropology, associate professor and head, 1988-, American Studies Program, director, Department of History, affiliate associate professor. Writer. **Publications:** Chesapeake Prehistory: Old Traditions, New Directions, 1995. **Address:** Department of Anthropology, American University, Battelle Tompkins-T-43, 4400 Massachusetts Ave., NW, Washington, DC 20016-8001, U.S.A. **Online address:** potomac@american.edu

DENTON, Terry. Australian (born Australia), b. 1950?. **Genres:** Children's Fiction, Illustrations, Cartoons. **Career:** Australian Childrens Television Foundation, Lift-off, co-creator and puppet designer, 1991-92. Writer and artist. **Publications:** SELF-ILLUSTRATED: Felix and Alexander, 1985; Flying Man, 1985; At the Café Splendid, 1987; Home is the Sailor, 1988; The School

for Laughter, 1989; Gasp!: The Breathtaking Adventures of a Fish Left Home Alone, 1995; Zapt!: The Electrifying Adventures of a Fish Left Home Alone (also see below), 1997; (co-author) Bedtime Stories (includes Felix and Alexander), 1997; Splat!: The Explosive Adventures of a Fish Left Home Alone (also see below), 1998; (with M. Dumbarton) Passing On, 2001; Crash!, 2003; Gasp! Zapt! Splat!: The Explosive, Breathtaking and Electrifying Adventures of a Mad Fish on the Loose!, 2003; It's True! Pigs Do Fly, 2004; Squish!, 2004; Chomp!, 2006; Wombat and Fox: Tales of the City, 2006; Wombat and Fox: Summer in the City, 2007; Wombat and Fox: Thrillseekers, 2009. SELF-ILLUSTRATED STORY MAZE GRAPHIC-NOVEL SERIES: The Ultimate Wave, 1999; The Eye of Ulam, 2001; The Wooden Cow, 2002; The Golden Udder, 2002; The Minotaur's Maze, 2003; The Obelisk of Eeeno, 2003. **Address:** Booked Out Speakers Agency, PO Box 580, South Yarra, VI 3141, Australia. **Online address:** terry@terrydenton.com

DENVER, Rod. See EDSON, J(ohn) T(homas).

DENZEY, Nicola. American/Canadian (born Canada), b. 1966. **Genres:** Adult Non-fiction, History, Theology/Religion. **Career:** Bowdoin College, visiting assistant professor of religion, 1997-98, visiting assistant professor, 2002-06; Skidmore College, assistant professor of religion, 1998-2002; Dartmouth College, visiting assistant professor, 2006-07; Harvard University, lecturer in the study of religion, 2006-09; Brown University, visiting assistant professor of religious studies, 2007-. Writer. **Publications:** The Bone Gatherers: The Lost Worlds of Early Christian Women, 2007. **Address:** Department of Religious Studies, Brown University, 59 George St., PO Box 1927, Providence, RI 02912-9025, U.S.A. **Online address:** ndenzey@brown.edu

DE PALCHI, Alfredo. American/Italian (born Italy), b. 1926. **Genres:** Poetry. **Career:** Chelsea Literary Journal, editor, publisher. Poet and translator. **Publications:** POETRY: Sessioni con l'analista, 1967; Mutazioni, 1988; La buia Danza di Scorpione, 1993; Costellazione Anonima, 1997; Le Viziose Avversioni, 1999; Paradigma, 2001. EDITOR: (with M. Palma) The Metaphysical Streetcar Conductor: Sixty Poems by Luciano Erba, 1998. Contributor of poems to magazines. **Address:** Chelsea Literary Journal, PO Box 773, Cooper Sta., New York, NY 10276-0773, U.S.A. **Online address:** katpoet13@aol.com

DEPAOLA, Tomie. American (born United States), b. 1934. **Genres:** Novellas/Short Stories, Children's Fiction, Children's Non-fiction, Illustrations, Picture/Board Books, Social Sciences. **Career:** Professional artist, designer and teacher of art, 1956-; Newton College of the Sacred Heart, instructor, 1962-63, assistant professor of art, 1963-66; San Francisco College for Women (now Lone Mountain College), assistant professor of art, 1967-70; Chamberlayne Junior College, instructor in art, 1972-73; Colby-Sawyer College, associate professor, designer and technical director in speech and theater department, Childrens Theater Project, costume designer, 1973-76; New England College, associate professor of art, 1976-78, artist-in-residence, 1978-79. Writer. **Publications:** SELF-ILLUSTRATED: Here We All Are, 2000; On My Way, 2001; Meet the Barkers: Morgan and Moffat Go to School, 2001; What a Year, 2002; A New Barker in the House, 2002; Four Friends at Christmas, 2002; Adelita: A Mexican Cinderella Story, 2002; Trouble in the Barkers' Class, 2003; Things Will Never Be the Same, 2003; Marcos Counts: One, Two, Three, 2003; Marcos Colors: Red, Yellow, Blue, 2003; Four Friends in Summer, 2003; Pascual and the Kitchen Angels, 2004; Guess Who's Coming to Santa's for Dinner?, 2004; Four Friends in Autumn, 2004; Stagestruck, 2005; I'm Still Scared, 2006; Why?, 2007; For the Duration: The War Years, 2009; Strega Nona: An Original Tale, 2010. OTHERS: The Wonderful Dragon of Timlin, 1966; Fight the Night, 1968; Joe and the Snow, 1968; Parker Pig, Esquire, 1969; The Journey of the Kiss, 1970; The Monsters' Ball, 1970; The Wind and the Sun, 1972; Andy, That's My Name, 1973; Charlie Needs a Cloak, 1973; Nana Upstairs and Nana Downstairs, 1973; The Unicorn and the Moon, 1973; Watch Out for the Chicken Feet in Your Soup, 1974; The Cloud Book: Word and Pictures, 1975, trans. as El Libro de las Arenas Movedizas, 1993; Michael Bird-Boy, 1975; Strega Nona: An Old Tale, 1975 in UK as The Magic Pasta Pot, 1979; Things to Make and Do for Valentine's Day, 1976; When Everyone Was Fast Asleep, 1976; Four Stories for Four Seasons, 1977; Helga's Dowry: A Troll Love Story, 1977; The Quicksand Book, 1977, trans. as El Libro De Las Nubes, 1993; Bill and Pete, 1978; The Christmas Pageant, 1978, rev. ed. as The Christmas Pageant Cut-out Book, 1980; (adapter) The Clown of God: An Old Story, 1978; Criss-Cross, Applesauce, 1978; Pancakes for Breakfast, 1978; The Popcorn Book, 1978; Big Anthony and the Magic Ring, 1979; Flicks, 1979; The Kids' Cat Book, 1979; Oliver Button is a Sissy,

1979; Songs of the Fog Maiden, 1979; The Family Christmas Tree Book, 1980; The Knight and the Dragon, 1980; The Lady of Guadalupe, 1980; The Legend of Old Befana: An Italian Christmas Story, 1980; The Prince of the Dolomites: An Old Italian Tale, 1980; (reteller) Fin M'Coul: The Giant of Knockmany Hill, 1981; The Friendly Beasts: An Old English Christmas Carol, 1981; The Hunter and the Animals: A Wordless Picture Book, 1981; Now One Foot, Now the Other, 1981, rev. ed., 2005; Francis, the Poor Man of Assisi, 1982; Giorgio's Village, 1982; Strega Nona's Magic Lessons, 1982; (adapter) The Legend of the Bluebonnet: An Old Tale of Texas, 1983; Marianna May and Nursey, 1983; Noah and the Ark, 1983; Sing, Pierrot, Sing: A Picture Book in Mime, 1983; (adapter) The Story of the Three Wise Kings, 1983; Tomie dePaola's Country Farm, 1984; Tomie dePaola's Mother Goose Story Streamers, 1984; (adapter) The Mysterious Giant of Barletta: An Italian Folktale, 1984; (adapter) David and Goliath, 1984; The First Christmas: A Festive Pop-up Book, 1984; Tomie dePaola's Mother Goose, 1985; Tomie dePaola's Favorite Nursery Tales, 1986; Merry Christmas, Strega Nona, 1986; (adapter) Queen Esther, 1986; Katie and Kit at the Beach, 1986; Katie's Good Idea, 1986; Katie, Kit and Cousin Tom, 1986; Pajamas for Kit, 1986; (co-author) Once upon a Time: Celebrating the Magic of Children's Books in Honor of the Twentieth Anniversary of Reading Is Fundamental, 1986; Bill and Pete Go Down the Nile, 1987; (ed.) Tomie dePaola's Book of Christmas Carols, 1987; An Early American Christmas, 1987; The Parables of Jesus, 1987; The Miracles of Jesus, 1987; Tomie dePaola's Diddle, Diddle, Dumpling and other Poems and Stories from Mother Goose, 1987; Tomie dePaola's Three Little Kittens and other Poems and Songs from Mother Goose, 1987; The Legend of the Indian Paintbrush, 1988; Tomie dePaola's Book of Poems, 1988; Baby's First Christmas, 1988; Hey Diddle Diddle: And other Mother Goose Rhymes, 1988; Charlie needs A Cloak, 1988; Tomie de Paola's Kitten Kids and the Big Camp-out, 1988; Tomie de Paola's Kitten Kids and the Haunted House, 1988; Tomie de Paola's Kitten Kids and the Missing Dinosaur, 1988; Tomie de Paola's Kitten Kids and the Treasure Hunt, 1988; Haircuts for the Woolseys, 1989; Too Many Hopkins, 1989; The Art Lesson, 1989; Tony's Bread: An Italian Folktale, 1989; My First Chanukah, 1989; Little Grunt and the Big Egg, 1990; Tomie dePaola's Book of Bible Stories, 1990; My First Easter, 1991; My First Passover, 1991; Bonjour, Mr. Satie, 1991; My First Halloween, 1991; My First Thanksgiving, 1992; Jamie O'Rourke and The Big Potato: An Irish Folktale, 1992; Jingle the Christmas Clown, 1992; Patrick, Patron Saint of Ireland, 1992; Stega Nona, 1993; Tom The Legend of the Persian Carpet, 1993; The Legend of the Poinsettia, 1994; Kit and Kat, 1994; Unicorn and the Moon, 1994; Christopher, the Holy Giant, 1994; Country Angel Christmas, 1995; Wind and the Sun, 1995; Strega Nona Meets Her Match, 1996; Get Dressed, Santa, 1996; The Baby Sister, 1996; The Bubble Factory, 1996; Mary: The Mother of Jesus, 1997; Days of the Blackbird: A Tale of Northern Italy, 1997; Tomie's Little Mother Goose, 1997; Antonio the Bread Boy, 1997; Bill and Pete to the Rescue, 1998; Big Anthony: His Story, 1998; 26 Fairmount Avenue, 1999; The Night of Las Posadas, 1999; Jamie O'Rourke and the Pooka, 2000; Tomie dePaola's Mother Goose Favorites, 2000; Strega Nona Takes a Vacation, 2000; Boss for a Day, 2001; Tomie's Little Christmas Pageant, 2002; T-Rex Is Missing!, 2002; Hide-and-Seek All Week, 2002; Tomie's Little Book of Poems, 2004; Tomie's Baa Baa Black Sheep and Other Rhymes, 2004; Tomie's Three Bears and Other Tales, 2004; Mary Had a Little Lamb, 2004; Tomie's Mother Goose Flies Again, 2005; Angels, Angels Everywhere, 2005; Christmas Remembered, 2006; Little Grunt and the Big Egg: A Prehistoric Fairy Tale, 2006; Tomie Depaola's Big Book of Favorite Legends, 2007; Tomie DePaola's Front Porch Tales & North Country Whoppers, 2007; Tomie's Little Book of Love, 2007; Tomie dePaola's More Mother Goose Favorites, 2007; (with R. Sabuda and M. Reinhart) Brava, Strega Nona!: A Heartwarming Pop-up Book, 2008; Song of Francis, 2009; Strega Nona's Harvest, 2009; My Mother is so Smart!, 2010; Joy to the World: Christmas Stories and Songs, 2010; Let the Whole Earth Sing Praise, 2011; Strega Nona's Gift, 2011; Birds of Bethlehem, 2012. Contributor of periodicals. Illustrator of books by others. **Address:** c/o Author Mail, Penguin Group Inc., 375 Hudson St., New York, NY 10014-3657, U.S.A.

DE PAOR, Louis. Irish (born Ireland), b. 1961?. **Genres:** Poetry, Literary Criticism And History. **Career:** Three Words for Green (group of musicians and dancers), founder, 1987-96; National University of Ireland, director of Irish studies; University of Sydney, faculty. Poet and educator. **Publications:** Próca solais is luatha: dánta 1980-87, 1988; Innti 13 (poems), 1990; (with S.O. Tuama) Coiscéim na haoise seo (poems), 1991; Faoin mblaoisc bheag sin (criticism), 1991; 30 dán, 1992; Aimsir bhreicneach/Freckled Weather (poems), 1993; Seo., siúd., agus uile. (poems), 1996; Goban cré is cloch/Sentences of Earth and Stone (poems), 1996; (with S.O. Tuama) Leabhar Sheáin Uí

Thuama (poems), 1997; Corcach agus Danta Eile, 1999; (ed.) An Illuminated Celtic Book of Days, 1999; (ed.) Freacnairc mhearcair: rogha dánta 1970-1998/The Oomph of Quicksilver: Selected Poems 1970-1998, 2000; Agus rud eile de, 2002; Ag greadadh bas sa reilig = Clapping in the Cemetery, 2005; Uimhir A Seacht, 2010. Contributor to books and periodicals. **Address:** Center for Irish Studies, National University of Ireland, Martha Fox House, Distillery Rd., Galway, 4, Ireland. **Online address:** louis.depaor@nuigalway.ie

DEPARLE, Jason. American (born United States) **Genres:** Novels, Adult Non-fiction. **Career:** New York Times, observer, senior writer. **Publications:** American Dream: Three Women, Ten Kids and a Nation's Drive to End Welfare, 2004. Contributor to periodicals. **Address:** c/o Yen Cheong, Viking Penguin, 375 Hudson St., 4th Fl., New York, NY 10014, U.S.A. **Online address:** jdeparle@nytimes.com

DEPASTINO, Todd Allan. American (born United States), b. 1966?. **Genres:** Novels. **Career:** Penn State Beaver, instructor in history; Waynesburg College, instructor in history. Writer. **Publications:** Citizen Hobo: How a Century of Homelessness Shaped America, 2003; (ed. with Jack London) The Road, 2006; Bill Mauldin: A Life Up Front, 2008; (ed. with B. Mauldin) Willie & Joe: The WWII Years, 2008, Commissioned in Battle: A Combat Infantryman in the Pacific, 2012. **Address:** c/o Jacques de Spoelberch, J de S Associates Inc., 9 Shagbark Rd., Norwalk, CT 06854, U.S.A. **Online address:** todd@billmauldinbiography.com

DE PILLIS, John E. American (born United States) **Genres:** Mathematics/Statistics. **Career:** Writer, research mathematician and illustrator; University of California, Department of Mathematics, professor, now professor emeritus. **Publications:** Linear Algebra, 1969; 777 Mathematical Conversation Starters, 2002; Special Relativity Illustrated: A Fusion of Linear Algebra, Graphics, and Reality, forthcoming. **Address:** Department of Mathematics, University of California, 0208 Surge Bldg., 900 University Ave., Riverside, CA 92521, U.S.A. **Online address:** jdp@math.ucr.edu

DEPOY, Phillip. American (born United States), b. 1950?. **Genres:** Young Adult Fiction, Mystery/Crime/Suspense, Literary Criticism And History. **Career:** Georgia State University, television writer, 1971-77, visiting instructor, 2001-04; Georgia Council for the Arts, artist-in-residence, 1980-90; Academy Theatre, composer-in-residence, 1982-88; Theatrical Outfit, artistic director, 1991-95; Townsend Center for the Performing Arts, director, 1995-98; University of West Georgia, head of theater department, 1997-; St. Martin Press, author, 1997-; Clayton State University, theater director; Metropolitan Theatre Alliance, playwright-in-residence; Atlanta Theatre Coalition, director; Georgia Tech, faculty of English department; Mercer University, faculty; Callanwolde Fine Arts Center, head of creative writing program; Abraham Baldwin Agricultural College, faculty. Writer. **Publications:** FLAP TUCKER MYSTERY SERIES: Angels, 1995; Beggar's Opera, 1995; The Beggar's Opera: A New Performing Version, 1996; Easy, 1997; Too Easy, 1998; Easy as One, Two, three, 1999; Dancing Made Easy, 1999; Dead Easy, 2000; FEVER DEVILIN MYSTERY SERIES: The Devil's Hearth, 2003; The Witch's Grave, 2004; A Minister's Ghost, 2006; A Widow's Curse, 2007; Drifter's Wheel, 2008; King James Conspiracy, 2009; A Corpse's Nightmare: A Fever Devilin Novel, 2011. **Address:** Clayton State University, 2000 Clayton State Blvd., Morrow, GA 30260, U.S.A. **Online address:** phillipdepoy@clayton.edu

DE PREE, Christopher G. (Christopher Gordon De Pree). American/Hong Kong (born Hong Kong), b. 1966. **Genres:** Astronomy, Sciences, Physics. **Career:** King and Low-Heywood Thomas Schools, physics and chemistry instructor, 1988-89; Cardinal Gibbons High School, physical science and computer science instructor, 1989-90; UNC Chapel Hill, Department of Physics and Astronomy, teaching assistant, 1990-93, research assistant, 1993-94; National Radio Astronomy Observatory, junior research associate, 1994-96; Oglethorpe University, Department of Physics, lecturer in physical science, 1996-97; Agnes Scott College, Department of Physics and Astronomy, visiting assistant professor, 1996-98, research associate, 1996-97, director of bradley observatory, 1997-, assistant professor, 1998-2003, associate professor, 2003-09, professor, 2009-, chair, 2003-07; Emory University, Physics Department, visiting associate professor, 2004-05, adjunct associate professor, 2004-. Writer. **Publications:** (With A. Axelrod) The Complete Idiot's Guide to Astronomy, 1998, 4th ed., 2008; (with K. Marvel and A. Axelrod) Recent Advances and Issues in Astronomy, 2003; (co-ed.) Van Nostrand Concise Encyclopedia of Science, 2003; Physics Made Simple, 2004; Seven Astronomical Events That Will Change Your Life, 2005. **Address:** Department of

Physics & Astronomy, Agnes Scott College, 141 E College Ave., Decatur, GA 30030, U.S.A. **Online address:** cdepree@agnesscott.edu

DE PREE, Christopher Gordon. *See* **DE PREE, Christopher G.**

DERBY, Pat. American/British (born England), b. 1942?. **Genres:** Novels, Human Relations/Parenting, Animals/Pets. **Career:** Writer. **Publications:** (With P. Beagle) The Lady and Her Tiger, 1976; Visiting Miss Pierce, 1986; Goodbye Emily, Hello, 1989; Grams, Her Boyfriend, My Family, and Me, 1994; (with P. Beagle) In the Presence of Elephants, 1995; Away to the Goldfields!, 2004. **Address:** c/o Author Mail, Farrar, Straus and Giroux, 19 Union Sq. W, New York, NY 10003-3304, U.S.A.

DERBY, Sally. American (born United States), b. 1934. **Genres:** Children's Fiction, Picture/Board Books. **Career:** Educator and writer. **Publications:** The Mouse Who Owned the Sun, 1993; Jacob and the Stranger, 1994; King Kenrick's Splinter, 1994; My Steps, 1996; Taiko on a Windy Night, 2001; Hannah's Bookmobile Christmas, 2001; Two Fools and a Horse, 2003; The Wacky Substitute, 2005; Whoosh Went the Wind, 2006; No Mush Today, 2008; Kyle's Island, 2010. **Address:** 770 Southmeadow Cir., Cincinnati, OH 45231, U.S.A. **Online address:** derbymiller@fuse.net

DERESKE, Jo. American (born United States), b. 1947. **Genres:** Mystery/Crime/Suspense, Children's Fiction, Young Adult Fiction, inspirational/Motivational Literature. **Career:** Western Washington University, inter-library loan librarian, 1978-88; Corridor Information Services, owner-operator, 1983-87; Whatcom Community College, librarian. Freelance writer. **Publications:** CHILDREN'S BOOKS: Glom Gloom, 1985; The Lone Sentinel, 1989; My Cousin, the Poodle, 1991. MYSTERY NOVELS: Miss Zukas and the Library Murders, 1994; Miss Zukas and the Island Murders, 1995; Miss Zukas and the Stroke of Death, 1996; Miss Zukas and the Raven's Dance, 1996; Savage Cut, 1996; Cut and Dry, 1997; Out of Circulation, 1997; Final Notice, 1998; Short Cut, 1998; Miss Zukas in Death's Shadow, 1999; Miss Zukas Shelves the Evidence, 2001; Bookmarked to Die, 2006; Catalogue of Death: A Miss Zukas Mystery, 2007; Index to Murder, 2008; Farewell, Miss Zukas, 2011. Contributor of articles to books and periodicals. **Address:** PO Box 305, Everson, WA 98247, U.S.A. **Online address:** email@jodereske.com

DERFLER, (Arnold) Leslie. American (born United States), b. 1933. **Genres:** History, Literary Criticism And History, Politics/Government, Social Sciences. **Career:** City University of New York, City College, lecturer, 1960-62; Carnegie-Mellon University, assistant professor, associate professor, 1962-68; University of Massachusetts, associate professor, 1968-69; Florida Atlantic University, Dorothy F. Schmidt College of Arts and Letters, Department of History, professor of history, 1969-2002, professor emeritus, 2002-, chairman, 1978-. Writer. **Publications:** The Dreyfus Affair: Tragedy of Errors, 1963; The Third French Republic, 1870-1940, 1966; Socialism Since Marx: A Century of the European Left, 1973; (ed.) Alexandre Millerand: The Socialist Years, 1977; (ed.) Hindi, 1977; President and Parliament: A Short History of the French Presidency, 1983; (ed.) An Age of Conflict: Readings in Twentieth-Century European History, 1990, (comp. with P. Kollander) 3rd ed., 2002; Paul Lafargue and the Founding of French Marxism, 1842-1882, 1991; Paul Lafargue and the Flowering of French Socialism, 1882-1911, 1998; Fall and Rise of Political Leaders: Olof Palme, Olusegun Obasanjo, and Indira Gandhi, 2010. Contributor to journals. **Address:** Department of History, Dorothy F. Schmidt College of Arts and Letters, Florida Atlantic University, 777 Glades Rd., Boca Raton, FL 33431-6424, U.S.A. **Online address:** deflerl@fau.edu

DERIAN, James (Arthur) Der. American (born United States), b. 1955. **Genres:** Politics/Government, History. **Career:** Oxford University, lecturer, 1982-83; Columbia University, adjunct assistant professor of political science, 1984; University of Massachusetts, professor of political science, 1984-2003; Gardner and Lancaster State Prisons, visiting professor, 1986-91; University of Southern California, Center for International Studies, senior research fellow, 1988; Oxford University, St. Antony's College, senior associate, 1995; Brown University, Watson Institute for International Studies, visiting professor, 1998, Global Security Program, director, 2003-08, Information Technology, professor of international studies; Institute for Advanced Study, School of Social Science, faculty, 2000-01; War and Peace Project, founder and principal investigator; Global Media Project, founder and principal investigator. Writer. **Publications:** On Diplomacy: A Genealogy of Western Estrangement, 1987; (ed. with M. Shapiro) International/Intertextual Relations:

Postmodern Readings of World Politics, 1989; Antidiplomacy: Spies, Terror, Speed, and War, 1992; (contrib.) Global Voices: Dialogues in International Relations, 1993; (ed.) International Theory: Critical Investigations, 1995; Virtual Security, 1996; (ed.) The Virilio Reader, 1998; Virtuous War: Mapping the Military-Industrial-Media-Entertainment Network, 2001, 2nd ed., 2009; Critical Practices in International Theory: Selected Essays, 2009; (ed. with C.M. Constantinou) Sustainable Diplomacies, 2010. Contributor of articles to books and periodicals. **Address:** Watson Institute, Brown University, 111 Thayer St., PO Box 1970, Providence, RI 02912-1970, U.S.A. **Online address:** james_der_derian@brown.edu

DERICKSON, Alan. American (born United States), b. 1948. **Genres:** Social Sciences. **Career:** University of California, Health Arts and Sciences Program, teaching associate, 1982-83, Institute for Health Policy Studies, Pew health policy research fellow, 1983-85; chancellor's research fellow, 1985; Pennsylvania State University, Department of Labor Studies and Employment Relations, assistant professor, 1987-90, associate professor, 1990-99, professor, 1999-2004, Center for Health Care and Policy Research, senior scientist, 1991-, Department of History, faculty, 1996-2004, affiliate professor, 2004-, professor of American history. Writer and historian. **Publications:** Workers' Health, Workers' Democracy: The Western Miners' Struggle, 1891-1925, 1988; Black Lung: Anatomy of a Public Health Disaster, 1998; Health Security for All: Dreams of Universal Health Care in America, 2005. Contributor to periodicals and journals. **Address:** Department of History & Religious Studies Program, Pennsylvania State University, 311 Weaver Bldg., University Park, PA 16802, U.S.A. **Online address:** avd3@psu.edu

DERISO, Christine Hurley. American (born United States), b. 1961?. **Genres:** Children's Fiction. **Career:** Medical College of Georgia, publications editor, 1988-; Augusta Chronicle, restaurant critic, 1998-2005, reporter. Writer. **Publications:** JUVENILE FICTION: Dreams to Grow On, 2002; Do-Over, 2006; The Right-Under Club, 2007; Talia Talk, 2009. OTHERS: (with S. Hsu) Green Tea and Beyond, 2010; Then I Met My Sister, 2011. **Address:** c/o Courtney Colton, Midnight Ink, 2143 Wooddale Dr., Woodbury, MN 55125-2989, U.S.A. **Online address:** christine@christinehurleyderiso.com

DE RIVAS, Bárbara Ganson. *See* **GANSON, Barbara.**

DERKSEN, Jeff. Canadian (born Canada), b. 1958?. **Genres:** Poetry, Young Adult Fiction. **Career:** Kootenay School of Writing, founding member, 1984-; Artspeak Gallery, founding member, 1986-95; Writing Magazine, editor, 1989-93; City University of New York, Center for Place, Culture and Politics, research fellow; Simon Fraser University, lecturer in English, associate professor. **Publications:** POETRY: Memory is the Only Thing Holding Me Back, 1984; Until (chapbook), 1987; Down Time, 1990; Selfish (chapbook), 1993; Dwell, 1993; Transnational Muscle Cars, 2003; (with B. Clausen and M. Herrmann) Andrea Geyer: Secession, 2003. OTHER: (contrib. with K. Scott) Ken Lum Works with Photography, 2002. **Address:** Kootenay School of Writing, 309-207 W Hastings St., Dominion Bldg., Vancouver, BC V6B 1H6, Canada. **Online address:** jderksen@sfu.ca

DERMOND, Susan Usha. American (born United States) **Genres:** Human Relations/Parenting. **Career:** Education for Life School, teacher; Living Wisdom School, director. Librarian and writer. **Publications:** Calm and Compassionate Children: A Handbook, 2007. **Address:** Living Wisdom School, 4855 SW Watson, Beaverton, OR 97005, U.S.A. **Online address:** susanusha@yahoo.com

DEROGATIS, Jim. American (born United States), b. 1964. **Genres:** History, Music, Military/Defense/Arms Control, Adult Non-fiction. **Career:** Rolling Stone, deputy music editor, 1995-96; Chicago Sun-Times, pop music critic; Chicago Public Radio, co-host of Sound Opinions weekly talk show; Request magazine, assistant editor; Columbia College Chicago, Department of English, faculty, 2010-. **Publications:** NONFICTION: Kaleidoscope Eyes: Psychedelic Rock from the '60s to the '90s, 1996, rev. ed. as Turn On Your Mind: Four Decades of Great Psychedelic Rock, 2003; Let It Blurt: The Life and Times of Lester Bangs, America's Greatest Rock Critic, 2000; Milk It! Collected Musings on the Alternative Music Explosion of the '90s, 2003; (ed. with C.C. DeRogatis) Kill Your Idols: A New Generation of Rock Writers Reconsiders the Classics, 2004; Staring at Sound: The True Story of Oklahoma's Fabulous Flaming Lips, 2006; Sheperd Paine: The Life and Work of a Master Modeler and Military Historian, 2008; (with B. Bentley) The Velvet Underground: An Illustrated History of a Walk on the Wild Side, 2009; (with

G. Kot) Beatles vs. the Rolling Stones: Sound Opinions on the Great Rock 'n' Roll Rivalry, 2010; The Best Thirty Minutes of My Life, forthcoming. **Address:** Department of English, Columbia College Chicago, 600 S Michigan Ave., Chicago, IL 60605, U.S.A. **Online address:** jimdero@jimdero.com

DE ROSNAY, Tatiana. French (born France), b. 1961. **Genres:** Novels. **Career:** Christie's (auction house), president attaché; Vanity Fair (magazine), editor, through 1993; Elle magazine, journalist for French edition; Psychologies Magazine, literary critic; author. **Publications:** NOVELS: L'appartement temoin, 1992; Mariés, pères de famille: romans d'adulteres, 1995; Le dîner des ex, 1996; Le coeur d'une autre, 1998; Le voisin, 2000; La mémoire des murs, 2002; Spirales, 2004; Moka, 2006; Sarah's Key, 2007; Secret Kept, 2010. **Address:** St. Martin's Press, 175 5th Ave., New York, NY 10010, U.S.A. **Online address:** tatianacom@hotmail.com

DERR, Mark (Burgess). American (born United States), b. 1950. **Genres:** History, Natural History, Geography, Environmental Sciences/Ecology, Biography, Zoology, Essays, Sciences, Sciences. **Career:** Writer. **Publications:** NONFICTION: Some Kind of Paradise: A Chronicle of Man and the Land in Florida, 1989; Over Florida, 1992; The Frontiersman: The Real Life and Many Legends of Davy Crockett (biography), 1993; Dog's Best Friend: Annals of the Dog-Human Relationship, 1997; A Dog's History of America: How Our Best Friend Explored, Conquered, and Settled a Continent, 2004. Contributor to periodicals. **Address:** 4245 Sheridan Ave., Miami Beach, FL 33140, U.S.A. **Online address:** mark.derr@gmail.com

DERRETT, (John) Duncan (Martin). British (born England), b. 1922. **Genres:** Law, Theology/Religion, History, Essays, Cultural/Ethnic Topics. **Career:** University of London, School of Oriental and African Studies, lecturer in Hindu law, 1949-56, reader in Oriental laws, 1956-65, professor of Oriental laws, 1965-82, professor emeritus, 1982-; Inns of Court School of Law, lecturer in Hindu law, 1965-79; University of Oxford, Wilde lecturer in natural and comparative religion, 1978-81. Writer. **Publications:** The Hoysalas, 1957; Hindu Law, Past and Present, 1957; Introduction to Modern Hindu Law, 1963; (ed. and co-author) Studies in the Law of Succession in Nigeria, 1965; Religion, Law and the State in India, 1968; (ed.) Introduction to Legal Systems, 1968; Law in the New Testament, 1970; Critique of Modern Hindu Law, 1970; Jesus's Audience, 1973; (trans. and ed.) R. Lingat, Classical Law of India, 1973; Henry Swinburne 1551-1624, 1973; Dharmasastra and Juridical Literature, 1973; Bharuci's Commentary on the Manusmrti, 1975; Essays in Classical and Modern Hindu Law, 4 vols., 1976-78; Studies in the New Testament, 6 vols., 1977-95; Death of a Marriage Law, 1978; (ed. with W.D. O'Flaherty) The Concept of Duty in South Asia, 1977; Beitrage zu Indischem Rechtsdenken, 1979; The Anastasis: The Resurrection of Jesus as an Historical Event, 1982; A Textbook for (Buddhist) Novices, 1983; The Making of Mark, 1985; New Resolutions of Old Conundrums (on Luke), 1986; The Ascetic Discourse, 1989; The Victim, the Johannine Passion Narrative, 1993; The Sermon on the Mount, 1994; Prophecy in the Cotswolds, 1803-1947, 1994; Two Masters: The Buddha and Jesus, 1995; Some Telltale Words in New Testament, 1996; Law and Morality, 1998; The Bible and the Buddhists, 2000. **Address:** Half Way House, High St., Blockley, Moreton-in-Marsh, GC GL56 9EX, England.

DERRY, John (Wesley). British (born England), b. 1933. **Genres:** History, Biography. **Career:** Emmanuel College, research fellow, 1959-61; London School of Economics, assistant lecturer, 1961-63, lecturer, 1963-65; Downing College, director of studies in history and fellow, 1965-70; University of Newcastle, lecturer, 1970-73, senior lecturer, 1973-77, reader 1977-92, professor, 1992-98, emeritus professor of modern British history, 1998-. Writer. **Publications:** William Pitt, 1962; Reaction and Reform, 1963, 3rd ed., 1970; The Regency Crisis and the Whigs, 1963; Parliamentary Reform, 1966; The Radical Tradition: Tom Paine to Lloyd George, 1967; Political Parties, 1968; (ed.) Cobbett's England: A Selection from the Writings of William Cobbett, with Engravings by James Gillray 1968; The Story of Sheffield, 1971; Charles James Fox, 1972; Castlereagh, 1976; English Politics and the American Revolution, 1976; Politics in the Age of Fox, Pitt and Liverpool, 1990; Charles, Earl Grey: Aristocratic Reformer, 1992; Politics in the Age of Fox, Pitt, and Liverpool, 2001. **Address:** Department of History, University of Newcastle, Newcastle upon Tyne, Tyne and Wear, NE1 7RU, England.

DERSHOWITZ, Alan M. American (born United States), b. 1938. **Genres:** Civil Liberties/Human Rights, Criminology/True Crime, Law, Psychiatry.

Career: Civil liberties lawyer, 1963-; Harvard University, associate professor, 1964-67, professor of law, 1967-93, Felix Frankfurter professor of law, 1993-; National Institute of Mental Health, consultant; United Features Syndicate, syndicated columnist; Penthouse Magazine, columnist; Hebrew University, visiting professor of law, 1988. Writer. **Publications:** (Co-author) Psychoanalysis, Psychiatry and the Law, 1967; (with J. Goldstein and R. Schwartz) Criminal Law: Theory and Process, 1974; (with J. Goldstein and R.D. Schwartz) Fair and Certain Punishment: Report of the Twentieth-Century Fund Task Force on Criminal Sentencing, 1976; (with T. Taylor) Courts of Terror, 1976; The Best Defense, 1982; Reversal of Fortune: Inside the Von Bulow Case, 1986; Taking Liberties: A Compendium of Hard Cases, Legal Dilemmas and Bum Raps, 1988; Chutzpah, 1991; Contrary to Popular Opinion, 1992; The Abuse Excuse and Other Cop-Outs, Sob Stories and Evasions of Responsibility, 1994; The Advocate's Devil, 1994; Reasonable Doubts, 1996; The Vanishing American Jew, 1997; Sexual McCarthyism, 1998; Just Revenge, 1999; The Genesis of Justice, 2000; Supreme Injustice, 2001; Letters to a Young Lawyer, 2001; Why Terrorism Works, 2002; Shouting Fire: Civil Liberties in a Turbulent Age, 2002; Tsedek miBe reshit: aśarah ma aśe I tsedek ba-derekh le áśeret ha dibrot vela mishpat ha moderni, 2003; The Case for Israel, 2003; America Declares Independence, 2003; America on Trial: Inside the Legal Battles That Transformed Our Nation, 2004; Rights from Wrongs, 2005; The Case for Peace: How the Arab-Israeli Conflict Can Be Resolved, 2005; (ed.) What Israel Means to Me, 2006; Preemption: A Knife That Cuts Both Ways, 2006; (ed.) What Israel Means to Me, 2006; Blasphemy: How the Religious Right is Hijacking Our Declaration of Independence, 2007; Case against Israel's Enemies: Exposing Jimmy Carter and Others who Stand in the Way of Peace, 2008; Is There a Right to Remain Silent?: Coercive Interrogation and the Fifth Amendment after 9/11, 2008; Finding Jefferson: A Lost Letter, A Remarkable Discovery and the First Amendment in an Age of Terrorism, 2008; Trials of Zion, 2010; (forward) Postcards from the Holy Land: A Pictorial History of the Ottoman Era, 1880-1918, 2010; Israel on Trial, 2011. Contributor to periodicals. **Address:** Harvard Law School, Hauser Hall 520, 1575 Massachusetts Ave., Cambridge, MA 02138, U.S.A. **Online address:** dersh@law.harvard.edu

DERVAES, Claudine. American (born United States), b. 1954?. **Genres:** Travel/Exploration, Language/Linguistics, Geography, Reference, Translations, Transportation, How-to Books. **Career:** Ocala Star Banner, travel writer; Gainesville Sun, travel writer. **Publications:** Travel Agent's Dictionary, 1985; The Travel Dictionary, 1985, rev. ed., 1986; The Travel Dictionary, rev. ed., 2000; The U.K. to U.S.A. Dictionary, 1994, new ed., 2005; International Travel, 1998; Sales and Marketing Techniques, 1998; Teaching Travel: A Handbook for the Educator, 2000; Travel and Tourism Student Handbook, 2000; Video on Careers in Travel, 2000; Travel Geography, 2000; Domestic Travel and Ticketing, 2000; Selling Independent Travel (Hotels, Car Rentals, Tours) The Travel Dictionary, 2000; Selling Cruises, 2003. **Address:** Solitaire Publishing, 1090 S Chateau Pt., Inverness, FL 34450-3565, U.S.A. **Online address:** psolitaire@aol.com

DERY, Dominika. Czech (born Czech Republic), b. 1975. **Genres:** Poetry, Biography, Autobiography/Memoirs. **Career:** National Ballet Co., dancer; National Theater, dancer; SBS, journalist. **Publications:** Přebolení: První Sbírka Básń z Obdobi Mezi Lety 1991-1997, 1999; Č eský orloj, 2000; Křížová cesta, 2001; The Twelve Little Cakes, 2004. Contributor to periodicals. **Address:** c/o Author Mail, Riverhead Books Publicity, 375 Hudson St., New York, NY 10014-3658, U.S.A. **Online address:** dominika.dery@gmail.com

DERY, Mark. American (born United States), b. 1959. **Genres:** Information Science/Computers, Adult Non-fiction, Essays, Social Sciences. **Career:** New York University, Occidental College, Department of Journalism, professor; University of California, Chancellors distinguished fellow, 2000. Full-time cultural critic and freelance journalist. **Publications:** (Ed.) Flame Wars: The Discourse of Cyberculture (nonfiction anthology), 1994; Escape Velocity: Cyberculture at the End of the Century (nonfiction), 1996; El Paseante, 1998; The Pyrotechnic Insanitarium: American Culture on the Brink (essays), 1999; The Pyrotechnic Insanitarium, 1999; I Must Not Think Bad Thoughts, 2011. Contributor to books and periodicals. **Address:** C/o Andrew Stuart, The Andrew Stuart Agency, 260 W 52 St., Suite 24C, New York, NY 10019, U.S.A. **Online address:** markdery@markdery.com

DESAI, Anita. American/Indian (born India), b. 1937. **Genres:** Novels, Children's Fiction, Young Adult Fiction, History, Young Adult Non-fiction. **Ca-**

reer: Smith College, Elizabeth Drew professor of English, 1987-88; Mount Holyoke College, Purington professor of English, 1988-93; Massachusetts Institute of Technology, John E. Burchard professor of writing, 1993-, now John E. Burchard professor emeritus of humanities; Girton College, Helen Cam visiting fellow, 1986-87, honorary fellow, 1988, Clare Hall, Ashby fellow, 1989, honorary fellow, 1991. Writer. **Publications:** Cry, The Peacock, 1963; Voices in the City: A Novel, 1965; Bye-Bye, Blackbird, 1971; The Peacock Garden, 1974; Where Shall We Go This Summer?, 1975; Cat on a Houseboat, 1976; Fire on the Mountain, 1977; Games at Twilight: And Other Stories, 1978; Clear Light of Day, 1980; A Village by the Sea: An Indian Family Story, 1982; In Custody, 1984; Baumgartner's Bombay, 1988; Journey to Ithaca, 1995; Fasting, Feasting, 1999; Diamond Dust: Stories, 2000; (foreword) Arctic Summer, 2003; The Zig Zag Way, 2004; (foreword) Daughters of the Vicar, 2004; Hill of Silver, Hill of Lead, 2005; Artist of Disappearance, 2011. Works appear in anthologies. Contributor of articles to journals. **Address:** Program in Writing & Humanistic Studies, Massachusetts Institute of Technology, Rm. 14E-303, Cambridge, MA 02139-4307, U.S.A. **Online address:** andesai@mit.edu

DESAI, Boman. American/Indian (born India), b. 1950. **Genres:** Novels, Essays, Adult Non-fiction, Young Adult Fiction. **Career:** Sears, Roebuck and Co., secretary, 1976. Writer and educator. **Publications:** The Memory of Elephants, 1988; Asylum, USA, 2000; A Woman Madly in Love, 2004; Trio, 2004; Servant, Master, Mistress, 2005; Trio 2, 2006. Contributor of articles to periodicals. **Address:** 567 W Stratford, Ste. 305, Chicago, IL 60657-2642, U.S.A. **Online address:** boman@megsinet.net

DESAI, Kiran. American/Indian (born India), b. 1971. **Genres:** Novels, Literary Criticism And History. **Career:** Writer. **Publications:** Hullabaloo in the Guava Orchard, 1998; Inheritance of Loss, 2006. Works appear in anthologies. Contributor to periodicals. **Address:** Aragi Agency, 143 W 27th St., Ste. 4F, New York, NY 10001-6230, U.S.A.

DESAIX, Deborah Durland. American (born United States) **Genres:** Novellas/Short Stories, Illustrations. **Career:** University of Hartford, professor of illustration; School of Visual Arts, instructor in illustration. Writer and illustrator. **Publications:** SELF-ILLUSTRATED: In the Back Seat, 1993; Returning Nicholas, 1995; (with K.G. Ruelle) Hidden on the Mountain: Stories of Children Sheltered from the Nazis in Le Chambon, 2007. OTHER: (with K.G. Ruelle) The Grand Mosque of Paris: A Story of How Muslims Saved Jews During the Holocaust, 2008. Illustrator of books by others. **Address:** Holiday House, 425 Madison Ave., New York, NY 10017, U.S.A. **Online address:** karenanddeb@gmail.com

DESALLE, Rob. American (born United States) **Genres:** Environmental Sciences/Ecology, Sciences. **Career:** Field Museum of Natural History, research technician, 1975-77; University of Chicago, research technician, 1977-79; University of California, NIH postdoctoral fellow, 1984-85; Washington University, NIH postdoctoral fellow, 1985-86; Yale University, Department of Biology, assistant professor, 1986-91; American Museum of Natural History, assistant curator of entomology, 1991-93, associate curator of entomology, 1993-99, curator of entomology, 1999-; Columbia University, adjunct professor; City University of New York, adjunct professor; New York University, adjunct professor. **Publications:** (With D. Lindley) The Science of Jurassic Park and the Lost World; or, How to Build a Dinosaur, 1997; (with M. Yudell) Welcome to the Genome: A User's Guide to the Genetic Past, Present, and Future, 2005; (with I. Tattersall) Bones, Brains and DNA: The Human Genome and Human Evolution, 2007; (with M.A. DiSpezio) Your 21st Century Brain: Amazing Science Games to Play with Your Mind, 2010; (with P.J. Wynne) Brain: A 21st Century Look at a 400 Million Year Old Organ, 2010; (with I. Tattersall) Race?, 2011. EDITOR: (with B. Schierwater) Molecular Approaches to Ecology and Evolution, 1998; Epidemic!: The World of Infectious Diseases, 1999; (with M. Yudell) The Genomic Revolution: Unveiling the Unity of Life, 2002; (with G. Giribet and W. Wheeler) Molecular Systematics and Evolution: Theory and Practice, 2002; (with G. Giribet and W. Wheeler) Techniques in Molecular Systematics and Evolution, 2002; (with B. Schierwater) Key Transitions in Animal Evolution, 2010; (with B. Schierwater) Key Transitions in Animal Evolution, 2011. Contributor to journals. **Address:** Division of Invertebrate Zoology, American Museum of Natural History, Central Pk. W, 79th St., New York, NY 10024-5192, U.S.A. **Online address:** desalle@amnh.org

DESAN, Suzanne. American (born United States), b. 1957. **Genres:** Theology/Religion, Law, History. **Career:** University of California, teaching assistant, 1980-82, acting instructor, 1984-85; University of Wisconsin, assistant professor, 1985-90, associate professor, 1990-98, professor, 1998-; Northwestern University, advisory professor, 2004-05. Historian and writer. **Publications:** Reclaiming the Sacred: Lay Religion and Popular Politics in Revolutionary France, 1990; The Family on Trial in Revolutionary France, 2004; (with J. Merrick) Family, Gender, and Law in Early Modern France, 2009. Contributor of articles to books and periodicals. **Address:** Department of History, University of Wisconsin, 3211 Humanities, 455 N Park St., Madison, WI 53706-1405, U.S.A. **Online address:** smdesan@wisc.edu

DESARTHE, Agnès. French (born France), b. 1966. **Genres:** Children's Fiction, Novels, Illustrations. **Career:** Author, translator and educator. **Publications:** (Co-author) Compte les étoiles, 1990; (co-author) Anastasia, demandeà ton psy!, 1990; Je ne t'aime pas, Paulus, 1990; Juanita, Le Pingouin, 1990; Le Roi Ferdinand, 1991; Dur de Dur, 1991; La centièmechose que j'aime chez toi, Caroline, 1991; Le Mariage de Simon, 1992; Les peurs de Conception, 1992; Abo, le minable homme des neiges, 1992; LeFête des Pères, 1993; Tout ce qu'on ne dit pas, 1993; Quelquesminutes de bonheur absolu, 1993; L'expèdition, 1994; BenjaminHéros solitaire, 1994; La femme du bouc èmissaire, 1995; Poètemaudit, 1995; Un secret sans importance, 1996; Je manque d'assurance, 1997; Cinq photos de ma femme, 1998; Les grandes questions, 1999; Les Bonnes Intentions, 2000; Petit Prince Pouf, 2002; Leronde d'e cooté, 2002; Principe de Frédelle, 2003; (with G. Brisac) V.W.: le mélange des genres, 2004; Eat Me, 2006; Chez moi, 2008; Le remplaçant, 2009; Dans la nuit brune, 2010. Illustrator of books by others. **Address:** c/o Author Mail, HarperCollins Publishers Ltd., 77-85 Fulham Palace Rd., Hammersmith, London, GL W6 8JB, England.

DESAUTELS, Denise. Canadian (born Canada), b. 1945. **Genres:** Poetry, Literary Criticism And History. **Career:** Poet. **Publications:** Comme miroirs en feuilles (poems), 1975; Marie, tout s'éteignait en moi, 1977; La promeneuse et l'oiseau suivi de Journal de la promeneuse, 1980; écran, précédé de, Aires du temps, 1983; (with A. Alonzo and R. April) Nous en reparlerons sans doute, 1986; Un livre de Kafka à la main, 1987; Lecons de Venise, 1990; Mais la menace estune belle extravagance suivi de Le Signe Discret, avec huit photographiesd Ariane Theze, 1991; Le Saut de l'ange: autour de quelques objets de Martha Townsend, 1992; (with A. Alonzo) Lettres à Cassandre, 1994; Ma joie, crie-t-elle, 1996; Ce fauve, le bonheur: Récit, 1998; Tombeau de Lou, 2000; Pendant la mort, 2002; Mémoires parallèles: choix de poèmes, 2004; Ce désir toujours: un abécédaire, 2005; Œil au ralenti, 2007; Angle noir de la joie, 2011. **Address:** éditions du Noroît, 4609, rue d'Iberville, espace 202, Montreal, QC H2H 2L9, Canada.

DESCH, Michael C. American (born United States), b. 1960?. **Genres:** Military/Defense/Arms Control, Politics/Government, History. **Career:** University of California, assistant professor, 1991-96; Harvard University, John M. Olin Institute for Strategic Studies, assistant director and senior research associate, 1993-98; University of Kentucky, assistant professor, 1998-2002, professor, 2002-04, Patterson School of Diplomacy and International Commerce, associate director, 1998-2003, director, 2003-04; Texas A&M University, professor, 2004-08, George Bush School of Government and Public Service, Robert M. Gates chair in intelligence and national security Decision-Making, 2004-08, Scowcroft Institute of International Affairs, director, 2007-08; University of Notre Dame, Department of Political Science, professor of political science, 2008-, chair, 2009-, Joan B. Kroc Institute for International Peace Studies, fellow, 2008-; Department of State, Bureau of Intelligence and Research, staff; Congressional Research Service, Foreign Affairs and National Defense Division, staff. Writer. **Publications:** When the Third World Matters: Latin America and United States Grand Strategy, 1993; (ed. with J.I. Domínguez and A. Serbín) From Pirates to Drug Lords: The Post-Cold War Caribbean Security Environment, 1998; Civilian Control of the Military: The Changing Security Environment, 1999; (ed.) Soldiers in Cities: Military Operations on Urban Terrain, 2001; Power and Military Effectiveness: The Fallacy of Democratic Triumphalism, 2008. Contributor to books and periodicals. **Address:** U.S.A. **Online address:** mdesch@nd.edu

DESCOLA, Philippe. French (born France), b. 1949. **Genres:** Anthropology/Ethnology, Young Adult Non-fiction, History. **Career:** Ecole des Hautes Etudes en Sciences Sociales, temporary lecturer, 1981-84, assistant professor, 1984-89, professor of anthropology, director of studies, 1989-2000; College dé France, professor and chair of the nature of anthropology, 2000-. Writer. **Publications:** La nature domestique: Symbolisme et praxis dans l'écologie des

Achuar, 1986; Les lances du crépuscule: Relations jivaros, Haute-Amazonie 1993; (ed. with G. Palsson and contrib.) Nature and Society: Anthropological Perspectives, 1996. IN FRENCH: (with G. Lenclud, C. Severi and A.C. Taylor) Les idees de l'anthropologie, 1988; (co-ed.) Dictionnaire de l'ethnologie et de l'anthropologie, 1991; Production dusocial: autour de Maurice Godelier, 1999; Par-delà nature et culture, 2005; Diversité Des Natures, Diversité Des Cultures, 2010; Fabrique des Images: Visions du Monde Et Formes de La Représentation, 2010. Contributor to books, journals and periodicals. **Address:** Department of Anthropology, Collège de France, 11 place Marcelin Berthelot, Paris, 75231, France. **Online address:** descola@msh-paris.fr

DESENA, Carmine. American (born United States), b. 1957. **Genres:** Humor/Satire, Writing/Journalism, Women's Studies And Issues, How-to Books, Literary Criticism And History, Young Adult Fiction. **Career:** Vocational Rehab Services, Intensive Psychological Rehabilitation Treatment Program, manager, 1979-; OK So We Lied, co-founder. Writer. **Publications:** Lies: The Whole Truth (humor), 1993; (with G.C. Alicea) The Air Down Here: True Tales from a South Bronx Boyhood, 1995; The Comedy Source (writer's handbook), 1996; The Comedy Market: A Writer's Guide to Making Money Being Funny, 1996; Satan's Little Instruction Book (humor), 1996; (with J. DeSena) Girl Power: Women on Winning, 2001. Contributor to magazines and newspapers. **Address:** c/o Barbara Zitwer, Barbara Zitwer Agency, 525 W End Ave., Apt. 29E, New York, NY 10024, U.S.A.

DESFOR, Gene. Canadian/American (born United States), b. 1942. **Genres:** Politics/Government, Administration/Management, Social Commentary. **Career:** York University, Changing Urban Waterfronts Project, principal investigator, Faculty of Environmental Studies, associate professor, professor of environmental studies, now professor emeritus. Writer. **Publications:** (Coauthor) Impact of Suburban Rapid Transit Station Location, Fare, and Parking Availability on Users' Station Choice Behavior: Analysis of the Philadelphia-Lindenwold High-Speed Line: Final Report to Office of the Secretary, U.S. Department of Transportation, 1974; (with L. Haas) Energy Requirements for Urban Goods Movement, 1979; Urban Waterfront Industry: Planning and Developing Green Enterprise for the 21st Century: Symposium Report, 1990; (ed. with D. Barndt and B. Rahder) Just Doing It: Popular Collective Action in the Americas, 2002; (with R. Keil) Nature and the City: Making Environmental Policy in Toronto and Los Angeles, 2004; (co-ed.) Transforming Urban Waterfronts: Fixity and Flow, 2011; (ed. with J. Laidley) Reshaping Toronto's Waterfront, 2011. Contributor to periodicals and journals. **Address:** Faculty of Environmental Studies, York University, 109 Health, Nursing & Environmental Studies Bldg., 4700 Keele St., Toronto, ON M3J 1P3, Canada. **Online address:** desfor@yorku.ca

DE-SHALIT, Avner. Israeli (born Israel), b. 1957. **Genres:** Politics/Government, Philosophy. **Career:** Hebrew University, lecturer, 1991-94, senior lecturer, 1994-99, associate professor, 1999-2007, professor of science and chair of department, 2007-, Max Kampelman professor of democracy and human rights, Social Sciences Faculty, dean, 2010-; Oxford Centre for Environment, Ethics, and Society, associate fellow; Politika: The Israeli Journal of Political Science, founding editor. **Publications:** NONFICTION: (ed. with S. Avineri) Communitarianism and Individualism, 1992; Sotsyalizm, 1994; Why Posterity Matters: Environmental Policies and Future Generations, 1995; Liberalism and Its Practice, 1999; The Environment: Between Theory and Practice, 2000; (ed. with A. Light) Moral and Political Reasoning in Environmental Practice, 2003; (ed. with D.A. Bell) Forms of Justice: Critical Perspectives on David Miller's Political Philosophy, 2003; Adom-yarok: Demokratyah, tsedek ve-ekhut ha-sevivah, 2004; Power to the People: Teaching Political Philosophy in Skeptical Times, 2006; (with J. Wolf) Disadvantage, 2007. **Address:** Department of Political Science, Hebrew University of Jerusalem, Jerusalem, 91905, Israel. **Online address:** msads@mscc.huji.ac.il

DESHPANDE, Chris. (Christine Lydia Deshpande). British (born England), b. 1950. **Genres:** Children's Non-fiction, Young Adult Fiction, Food And Wine, Crafts, Social Sciences. **Career:** Teacher, 1972-; Author, 1985-. **Publications:** Diwali, 1985; Finger Foods, 1988; Five Stones and Knuckle Bones, 1988; Scrape, Rattle and Blow, 1988; Tea, 1989; Bangles, Badges and Beads, 1990; Silk, 1991; (with J. Eccleshare) Spring Tinderbox, 1992; Celebrations, Food, 1993; Festival Crafts, 1994; Food Crafts, 1994. **Address:** A & C Black Ltd., 35 Bedford Row, London, GL WC1R 4JH, England.

DESHPANDE, Christine Lydia. See **DESHPANDE, Chris.**

DES JARDINS, Julie. American (born United States), b. 1972?. **Genres:** Women's Studies And Issues. **Career:** Brown University, faculty; Tufts University, faculty; Simmons College, faculty; Augsburg College, faculty; Hamline College, faculty; Harvard University, lecturer in history and literature; City University of New York, Baruch College, assistant professor of modern American history. Writer. **Publications:** Women and the Historical Enterprise in America: Gender, Race, and the Politics of Memory, 1880-1945, 2003; The Madame Curie Complex: The Hidden History of Women in Science, 2010. **Address:** City University of New York, Baruch College, 55 Lexington Ave., New York, NY 10010, U.S.A. **Online address:** julie.desjardins@baruch.cuny.edu

DESJARLAIS, John. (John Joseph Desjarlais). American/German (born Germany), b. 1953. **Genres:** Novels, Writing/Journalism, Essays, Poetry. **Career:** 2100 Productions, associate producer, 1984-92; University of Wisconsin, instructor in writing, 1990-93; Illinois Central College, adjunct faculty in English, 1992-93; Illinois State University, instructor in writing, 1993-95; Wisconsin Public Radio, producer, 1992-93; Kishwaukee College, journalism and English instructor, 1995-; John Desjarlais, founder and novelist, 1995-. **Publications:** The Throne of Tara, 1990. AS JOHN J. DESJARLAIS: Relics, 1993; Bleeder: A Mystery, 2009; Viper: A Mystery, 2011. Contributor to periodicals. **Address:** Kishwaukee College, U-201, 21193 Malta Rd., Malta, IL 60150-9600, U.S.A. **Online address:** jjdesjarlais@johndesjarlais.com

DESJARLAIS, John Joseph. See **DESJARLAIS, John.**

DESLANDES, Paul R. American (born United States), b. 1965. **Genres:** History. **Career:** University of Toronto, Department of History, tutor, 1989-91, 1993-95, lecturer, 1993-95; Trinity College, visiting assistant professor of history, 1997-98; Sweet Briar College, visiting assistant professor of history, 1998-99; Texas Tech University, assistant professor of history, 1999-2004; University of Vermont, associate professor of history, 2004-. Writer. **Publications:** Oxbridge Men: British Masculinity and the Undergraduate Experience, 1850-1920, 2005. Contributor of articles to periodicals. **Address:** Department of History, University of Vermont, Wheeler House, 133 S Prospect St., Burlington, VT 05405, U.S.A. **Online address:** paul.deslandes@uvm.edu

DESMANGLES, Leslie G. American/Haitian (born Haiti), b. 1941. **Genres:** Theology/Religion, Novels. **Career:** First Baptist Church, assistant minister, 1965-66; Ardmore United Methodist Church, assistant minister, 1966-67; Arch Street Methodist Church, campus minister, 1967-68; Eastern University, lecturer in religion, 1968-69; Temple University, teaching assistant in religion, 1968-70; Ohio Wesleyan University, assistant professor of religion, 1969-76; Miami University, curriculum consultant, 1972-73; Ohio University, Correctional Institution for Men and the Ohio Correctional Institution for Women, visiting lecturer in the social sciences, 1975-76; DePaul University, assistant professor of religion, 1976-78; Trinity College, assistant professor, 1978-82, associate professor, 1982-93, professor of religion and international studies, 1993-2009, Charles A. Dana research professor of religion and international studies, 2009-, Area Studies Program, director, 1982-88, acting affirmative action officer, 1992-2004, Hartford Consortium professor in Caribbean studies, 1994-95, Department of religion, chair, 1994-97; University of Connecticut Medical School, visiting lecturer, 1989; Hartford College for Women, visiting associate professor of religion, 1989-91; Trinity College-Rome, Barbieri Center, professor of religion, 2001-02. Writer. **Publications:** The Faces of the Gods: Vodou and Roman Catholicism in Haiti, 1992. Contributor of articles to journals. **Address:** Department of Religion and International Studies, Trinity College, McCook 211, 300 Summit St., Hartford, CT 06106-3100, U.S.A. **Online address:** leslie.desmangles@trincoll.edu

DESMOINAUX, Christel. French (born France), b. 1967. **Genres:** Children's Fiction, Illustrations, Humor/Satire. **Career:** Illustrator, 1988-. Writer. **Publications:** SELF-ILLUSTRATED FOR CHILDREN: Comme Il Rougit, M. Souris!, 1989; Julia N'En Rate Pas Une!, 1991; Panique dans L'Ascenseur, 1992; Henri, Tete-en-L'Air, 1992; L'Oeuf de Madame Poule, 1998; Dis-moi, Qu'est-ce Que c'est Halloween?, 1998; Rosa Veut Maigrie, 1999; Marius le minus, 1999; Emile et Lucette, 1999; Prends-moi Dans te bras, 2000; Le Meilleur ami de Suzette, 2000; Mrs. Hen's Big Surprise, 2000; Courage Gaston, 2001; Aldo au Marriege, 2001; Aldo Prend son bain, 2001; Aldo est Grognon, 2001; Aldo est Malade, 2001; Aldo et son Doudou, 2002; Aldo au Square, 2002; L'anniversaire d'Aldo, 2002; Aldo au Supermarche, 2002; Lucie la Raleux, 2002; Plouk, 2002; Hallo-What?, 2003; Arsene le Glouton, 2003; Lolotte la Marmotte, 2003; L'elephant qui Voulait etre Papa,

2004. Illustrator of books by others. **Address:** Children's Division, Simon & Schuster Inc., 1230 Ave. of the Americas, New York, NY 10020, U.S.A. **Online address:** desmoino@free.fr

DE SOIGNÉE, Jacqueline. *See* DRUCKER, Lisa.

DE SOMOGYI, Nick. British (born England) **Genres:** Humor/Satire, Novels. **Career:** College of Arms, genealogist; New Theatre Quarterly, contributing editor; Globe Quartos series, founding editor; Shakespeare's Globe, visiting curator, 2003-06, Department of Education, teacher. Freelance writer and researcher. **Publications:** Jokermen and Thieves: Bob Dylan and the Ballad Tradition, 1986; Shakespeare's Theatre of War, 1998; (ed.) Twelfth Night: Twelfe Night, or, What You Will, 2001; (ed.) Henry V: The Life of Henry the Fifth, 2001; (ed.) Hamlet: The Tragedie of Hamlet, Prince of Denmarke, 2001; (ed.) Measure for Measure: The First Folio of 1623 and a Parallel Modern Edition, 2002; (ed.) Othello: The Tragedie of Othello, the Moore of Venice, 2002; (ed.) Richard III: The Tragedy of Richard the Third, 2002; (ed.) Macbeth: The Tragedie of Macbeth, 2003; (ed.) Richard II: The Life and Death of King Richard the Second, 2003; (ed.) As You Like It, 2003; (ed.) The Merry Wives of Windsor, 2008. **Address:** Nick Hern Books, The Glasshouse, 49A Goldhawk Rd., Shepherds Bush, London, GL W12 8QP, England.

DE SOUZA, Eunice. Indian (born India), b. 1940. **Genres:** Poetry, Children's Non-fiction, Novels, Literary Criticism And History. **Career:** St. Xavier's College, Department of English, lecturer in English, 1969, head, 1990-2007, retired, 2007; Economic Times, arts columnist, 1973-84; Indian Post, literary editor, 1987. **Publications:** All about Birbal, 1969; Himalayan Tales, 1973; (ed. with A. Jussawalla) Statements: An Anthology of Indian Prose in English, 1976; Dangerlok, 2001; (intro.) Women's Voices: Selections from Nineteenth and Early-Twentieth Century Indian Writing in English, 2002; Dev & Simran: A Novel, 2003; (ed.) Purdah: An Anthology, 2004; 101 Folktales From India, 2004; (ed. and intro.) The Satthianadhan Family Album, 2005. POETRY: Fix, 1979; Akbar Padamsee, 1980; Women in Dutch Painting, 1988; Ways of Belonging: Selected Poems, 1990; Selected and New Poems, 1994; (ed.) Nine Indian Women Poets: An Anthology, 1997; Talking Poems: Conversations with Poets, 1999; (ed. and intro.) Early Indian Poetry in English: An Anthology: 1829-1947, 2005; (ed.) Both Sides of the Sky: Post-Independence Indian Poetry in English, 2008; Necklace of Skulls: Collected Poems, 2009. Contributor to books. **Address:** Penguin Books India Private Ltd., 11 Community Ctr., Panchsheel Pk., New Delhi, DH 110017, India.

DESPAIN, Pleasant. American (born United States), b. 1943. **Genres:** Mythology/Folklore, Young Adult Fiction, Picture/Board Books. **Career:** University of Massachusetts, instructor in literature and speech, 1966-68; University of Washington, instructor in literature and speech, 1970-72; professional storyteller and author, 1973-; KING-TV, producer, writer and host of children's storytelling show, 1975-80; Rose Studios, consultant and author, 1994-. **Publications:** Pleasant Journeys, 1979, 2nd ed. as Twenty-two Splendid Tales to Tell from around the World, 2nd ed., 1990, 3rd ed., 1994; Thirty-three Multicultural Tales to Tell, 1993; Eleven Turtle Tales: Adventure Tales from around the World, 1994; Tales to Tell from Around the World, 1995; Strongheart Jack and the Beanstalk, 1995; The Mystery Artist, 1996; Eleven Nature Tales, 1996; The Dancing Turtle: A Folktale from Brazil, 1998; (comp.) Sweet Land of Story: Thirty-Six American Tales to Tell, 2000; Books of Nine Lives, vol. I, 2001, vol. IX, 2003; Tales of Wisdom & Justice, 2001; Tales of Nonsense & Tomfoolery, 2001; Tales of Tricksters, 2001; Tales of Holidays, 2002; Tales of Insects, 2002; Tales of Heroes, 2002; Tales of Cats, 2003; Tales of Enchantment, 2003; Tales to Frighten and Delight, 2003; The Magic Pot, 2007. Contributor to periodicals. **Address:** 405 3rd St., Troy, NY 12180, U.S.A. **Online address:** pleasant@storypro.com

DESPLECHIN, Marie. French (born France), b. 1959. **Genres:** Children's Fiction, Young Adult Fiction, Animals/Pets, Novels. **Career:** Freelance journalist. Writer, 1994-. **Publications:** Et Dieu dans tout ça? (novel), 1994; (contrib.) Trésors des galions, 1994; Tu seras un homme, monneveu, 1995; Trop Sensibles, 1995; Verte, 1996; J'envie ceux qui sont dans ton coeur, 1997; Un vague d'amoursur un lac d'amitié, 1997; Sans Moi, 1998; La prédication de Nadia, 1999; Copiedouble, 2000; Le monde Joseph, 2000; Le coup dukiwi, 2000; Dragons, 2003; Un pas de plus: Nouvelles, 2005; (contrib.) Chroniques d'ici et d'ailleurs: Florence Miailhe, 2006; (with D. Darzacq) Bobigny Centre Ville, 2006; La galerie de Psyché, 2009. Contributor to periodicals. **Address:** c/o Author Mail, St. Martin's Press, 175 5th Ave., New York, NY 10010-7703, U.S.A.

DESPRES, Loraine. American (born United States) **Genres:** Novels, Plays/Screenplays. **Career:** University of California, instructor. International screenwriting consultant and writer. **Publications:** NOVELS: The Scandalous Summer of Sissy LeBlanc, 2001; The Southern Belle's Handbook: Sissy LeBlanc's Rules to Live By, 2003; The Bad Behavior of Belle Cantrell, 2005. Contributor of articles to magazines. **Address:** c/o Katherine Herring, HarperCollins Publishers, 10 E 53rd St., New York, NY 10022-5299, U.S.A. **Online address:** loraine@lorainedespres.com

DESPUTEAUX, Hélène. Canadian (born Canada), b. 1959. **Genres:** Children's Fiction, Illustrations, Picture/Board Books, Young Adult Fiction. **Career:** Illustrator, educator and art specialist. **Publications:** SELF-ILLUSTRATED LOLLYPOP SERIES (in English): Lollypop: My Clothes, 1991; Lollypop: My Food, 1991; Lollypop: My House, 1991; Lollypop's Animals, 1992; Lollypop's Colors, 1992; Lollypop's Numbers, 1992; Lollypop's Playtime, 1992; Lollypop's Baby Book, 1993; Lollypop's Travels, 1995; Lollypop's Farm, 1996; Lollypop's Music, 1996; Lollypop's Zoo, 1996; Mella: Have a Good Day Mella, 2007; Mella: In a Bad Mood, 2008; Mella: Polka Dot Underpants, 2008; Caillou: My House and Me, 2008; Caillou: Nighty Night!, 2009; Caillou: My Daddy and Me, 2010; Caillou: My Mommy and Me, 2010; Mella: Where is Pouit?, 2010; Mella: One, Two, Three...Pouit!, 2010; Caillou: My Grandpa and Me, 2010; Caillou: My Grandma and Me, 2010. **Address:** 235 Case postale, Succursale Beloeil, Beloeil, QC J3G 4T1, Canada.

DES RIVIÈRES, Jim. Canadian (born Canada), b. 1953. **Genres:** Information Science/Computers, Engineering. **Career:** Carleton University, Computer Centre, programmer, 1972-83, assistant professor of computer science, 1981-82; Xerox Palo Alto Research Center, System Sciences Laboratory, computer scientist, 1982-84, 1989-93; Object Technology International Inc., computer scientist, 1993-. Writer. **Publications:** (With G. Kiczales and D.G. Bobrow) The Art of the Metaobject Protocol, 1991. **Address:** Object Technology International Inc., 2670 Queensview Dr., Ottawa, ON K2B 8K1, Canada. **Online address:** jeem@acm.org

DESROCHERS, Diane. American (born United States), b. 1937. **Genres:** Novels, Science Fiction/Fantasy, Civil Liberties/Human Rights, Paranormal, Theology/Religion, Writing/Journalism, Self Help. **Career:** Apple Star Seminars, founder and director; Temple of Apple Moon Coven & Teaching Grove Inc., founder and high priestess; Witches Anti-Discrimination Lobby, New England regional director; Sacred Paths Alliance Network, founding member; AppleMoon and Friends, coordinator. Writer. **Publications:** Walker between the Worlds: A Novel, 1995; Shadow Walker, forthcoming. **Address:** 38 Fitch Bridge Rd., Groton, MA 01450-1253, U.S.A. **Online address:** firstamendmt@aol.com

DESSAIX, Robert. Australian (born Australia), b. 1944. **Genres:** Literary Criticism And History, Novels, Autobiography/Memoirs, Biography. **Career:** Australian National University, teacher, through 1985; University of New South Wales, lecturer in Russian language and literature; ABC Radio National, Books and Writing Program, producer and presenter, 1985-95. Translator and writer. **Publications:** Turgenev: The Quest for Faith (criticism), 1980; (trans. with Ulman) B. Vakhtin, The Sheepskin Coat and An Absolutely Happy Village (novellas), 1990; A Mother's Disgrace (autobiography), 1994; Night Letters (fiction), 1996; And So Forth, 1998; Corfu, 2001; Twilight of Love: Travels with Turgenev, 2004; Arabesques: A Tale of Double Lives, 2008; On Humbug, 2009. EDITOR: (and trans. With M. Ulman) A History of Post-War Soviet Writing: The Literature of Moral Opposition (criticism), 1981; Australian Gay and Lesbian Writing: An Anthology, 1993; (with H. Daniel) Picador New Writing (anthology), 1993; Speaking Their Minds: Intellectuals and the Public Culture in Australia, 1998. **Address:** c/o Lyn Tranter, Australian Literary Management, 2 Buckland St., Sydney, NW 2008, Australia.

DESSART, George Baldwin. American/German (born Germany), b. 1925. **Genres:** Communications/Media. **Career:** Station WCAU-TV, writer, producer, director, 1953-65, director of public affairs, 1952-54; University of Pennsylvania, Annenberg School of Communications, lecturer in charge of TV labs, 1961-69; WCBS TV, Documentary Unit, executive producer, 1965-67, director of community services, 1967-71, executive assistant, 1971-; City University of New York, Lehman College, adjunct associate professor of education, 1969-72, adjunct professor, 1972-; CBS Broadcast Group, senior executive, through 1988, vice president of of program practices; Brooklyn

College, Center for the Study of World Television, director, Graduate Studies in Television and Radio, deputy chairman, Department of TV/RADIO, professor, now professor emeritus; American Cancer Society, national chairman, 1996-98; CBS School of Management, instructor of broadcasting; New York University, adjunct faculty; Hunter College, adjunct faculty. Consultant. **Publications:** (Contrib.) Puss in Boots: A Musical Television Play, 1959; (ed. and contrib.) Television in the Real World: A Case Study Course in Broadcast Management, 1978; More Than You Want to Know About Public Service Announcements: A Guide to Production & Placement of Effective Public Service Announcements on Radio and Television, 1982; (with W.F. Baker) Down the Tube: An Inside Account of the Failure of American Television, 1998. **Address:** Department of Television and Radio, Brooklyn College, 304 Whitehead Hall, 2900 Bedford Ave., Brooklyn, NY 11210-2889, U.S.A.

DESSER, David. American (born United States), b. 1953. **Genres:** Film, History, Art/Art History. **Career:** University of Illinois-Urbana-Champaign, professor emeritus of cinema studies, 1981-, Unit for Cinema Studies, director, now EALC research professor emeritus, program in Jewish Culture and Society, professor, institute of communication research, research professor, now professor emeritus of criticism and interpretive theory; Cinema Journal, editor; Journal of Japanese and Korean Cinema, co-editor. **Publications:** The Samurai Films of Akira Kurosawa, 1983; Eros Plus Massacre: An Introduction to the Japanese New Wave Cinema, 1988; (ed. with A. Nolletti, Jr.) Reframing Japanese Cinema: Authorship, Genre, History, 1992; (with L. Friedman) American-Jewish Filmmakers: Traditions and Trends, 1993, 2nd ed., 2004; (ed. with G. Studlar) Reflections in a Male Eye: John Huston and the American Experience, 1993; (ed. with L. Ehrlich) Cinematic Landscapes: Observations on The Visual Arts and Cinema of China and Japan, 1994; (with L.D. Friedman) American Jewish Directors: Three Visions of the American Jewish Experience, 1995; (ed.) Ozu's Tokyo Story, 1997; (ed. with P. Fu) The Cinema of Hong Kong: History, Arts, Identity, 2000; (ed. with G.S. Jowett) Hollywood Goes Shopping, 2000. **Address:** Department of Speech Communication, University of Illinois at Urbana-Champaign, 2090A Foreign Languages Bldg., 707 S Mathews Ave., Urbana, IL 61801, U.S.A. **Online address:** desser@illinois.edu

D'ESTE, Carlo. American (born United States), b. 1936?. **Genres:** Military/Defense/Arms Control, Bibliography, History. **Career:** Military historian and biographer, 1978-; William E. Colby Military Writers' Symposium, co-founder; United States Army Command and General Staff College, School of Advanced Military Studies, lecturer; Norwich Public Library, Friends of the Norwich Library, president. Writer. **Publications:** Decision in Normandy: The Unwritten Story of Montgomery and the Allied Campaign, 1983; Bitter Victory: The Battle for Sicily, 1943, 1988; World War II in the Mediterranean, 1942-1945, 1990; Bitter Victory: The Battle for Sicily, July-August 1943, 1991; Fatal Decision: Anzio and the Battle for Rome, 1991; Patton: A Genius for War, 1995; Eisenhower: A Soldier's Life, 2002; Warlord: A Life of Winston Churchill at War, 1874-1945, 2008. **Address:** HarperCollins Publishers, 1000 Keystone Industrial Pk., Scranton, PA 18512, U.S.A.

DE STEFANO, George. American (born United States), b. 1955?. **Genres:** Cultural/Ethnic Topics, Gay And Lesbian Issues, Popular Culture, Film, Adult Non-fiction. **Career:** Author and critic. **Publications:** An Offer We Can't Refuse: The Mafia in the Mind of America, 2006. Contributor to books. **Address:** c/o Author Mail, Faber and Faber Inc., 19 Union Sq. W, New York, NY 10003-3304, U.S.A. **Online address:** gdsnyc@nyc.rr.com

DESTEFANO, Stephen. American (born United States), b. 1956. **Genres:** Natural History, Environmental Sciences/Ecology. **Career:** University of Massachusetts, professor; U.S. Geological Survey, Massachusetts Cooperative Fish and Wildlife Research Unit, leader. Writer and biologist. **Publications:** (With G.R. McPherson) Applied Ecology and Natural Resource Management, 2003; Coyote at the Kitchen Door: Living with Wildlife in Suburbia, 2010. **Address:** Department of Natural Resources Conservation, University of Massachusetts, 160 Holdsworth Way, Amherst, MA 01003, U.S.A. **Online address:** sdestef@nrc.umass.edu

DES VALLIRES, Nathalie. French (born France), b. 1952?. **Genres:** Art/Art History, Literary Criticism And History, Poetry. **Career:** Writer. **Publications:** (With R. de Ayala) Le plus beaux manuscrits de Saint Exupéry, 2003; (with R. de Ayala) Les plus beaux manuscrits de Arthur Rimbaud, 2004. **Address:** Rizzoli Universe International Publications Inc., 300 Park Ave. S, 3rd Fl., New York, NY 10010, U.S.A.

DE SYON, Guillaume. American/French (born France), b. 1966. **Genres:** History, Adult Non-fiction. **Career:** Aviation Data Centre, freelance press correspondent, 1983-89; Albright College, Department of History, assistant professor of history, 1995-2001, associate professor of history, 2001-09, professor of history, 2009-; Franklin & Marshall College, Department of History, research associate, 1998-. Writer. **Publications:** Zeppelin!: Germany and the Airship, 1900-1939, 2001; (ed.) 1905-2005: 100 Years of Motoring Progress: Geneva International Motor Show, 2004; (ed.) A Century of Motoring Progress, 2005; Science and Technology in Modern European Life, 2008. **Address:** Department of History, Albright College, 128 Masters Hall, 13th and Bern Streets, PO Box 15234, Reading, PA 19612, U.S.A. **Online address:** gdesyon@alb.edu

DE TAGYOS, Paul Rátz. American (born United States), b. 1958. **Genres:** Children's Fiction, Illustrations. **Career:** Writer. **Publications:** Showdown at Lonesome Pellet, 1994; (contrib.) Rooster Can't Cock-A-Doodle-Doo, 2004; Ready, Set, School!, 2007; Maybelle Goes to Tea, 2008. **Address:** Clarion Books, 215 Park Ave. S, New York, NY 10003, U.S.A. **Online address:** paulratz@paulratz.com

DETERRE, Veronica. *See* **HOLLAND, JoJean.**

DETTMAR, Kevin J(ohn) H(offmann). American (born United States), b. 1958. **Genres:** Literary Criticism And History, Humanities, Music. **Career:** Loyola Marymount University, visiting assistant professor of English, 1990-91; Clemson University, assistant professor, associate professor of English, 1991-, professor of English, through 1999; Southern Illinois University, professor of English, 1999-2008; Princeton University, trustee; Pomona College, W.M. Keck professor of English, 2008-, Department of English, chair; Columbia University, faculty. Writer. **Publications:** The Illicit Joyce of Postmodernism: Reading Against the Grain, 1996; Is Rock Dead, 2005; Irony in the Public Sphere: History and Theory, forthcoming. EDITOR: Rereading the New: A Backward Glance at Modernism, 1992; (with S. Watt) Marketing Modernisms: Self-Promotion, Canonization, Rereading, 1996; Reading Rock and Roll: Authenticity, Appropriation, Aesthetics, 1999; (with D. Damrosch) The Longman Anthology of British Literature, 2006; (with D. Bradshaw) A Companion to Modernist Literature and Culture, 2006; (with D. Damrosch) Masters of British Literature, 2008; Cambridge Companion to Bob Dylan, 2009; Think Rock, 2011. Works appear in anthologies. Contributor to journals. **Address:** Department of English, Pomona College, Crookshank 103, 140 W 6th St., Claremont, CA 91711, U.S.A. **Online address:** kevin.dettmar@pomona.edu

DETZ, Joan (Marie). American (born United States), b. 1951. **Genres:** Speech/Rhetoric, Writing/Journalism, Business/Trade/Industry, Economics. **Career:** James Blair School, teacher, 1974-76; Wells, Rich and Greene Advertising, writer and researcher, 1976-80; Brooklyn Union Gas, speechwriter, scriptwriter and editor, 1980-84; communications consultant, 1984-; Joan Detz Speechwriting, Coaching, director, 1985-. **Publications:** How to Write and Give a Speech: A Practical Guide for Executives, PR People, Managers, Fundraisers, Politicians, Educators and Anyone Who has to Make Every Word Count, 1984, 2nd rev. ed., 2002; You Mean I Have to Stand Up and Say Something?, 1986; Can You Say a Few Words?, 1991; It's Not What You Say, It's How You Say It, 2000; Can You Say a Few Words?: How to Prepare and Deliver a Speech for any Special Occasion, 2006. Contributor to periodicals. **Address:** Joan Detz Speechwriting/Coaching, 73 Harvey Ave., Doylestown, PA 18901, U.S.A. **Online address:** jdetz@joandetz.com

DEUKER, Carl. American (born United States), b. 1950. **Genres:** Children's Fiction, Young Adult Fiction, Sports/Fitness, Novels. **Career:** Saint Luke School, teacher, 1977-90; Seattle Sun, film and book critic, 1980-85; Northshore School District, Shelton View Elementary School, teacher, 1991-. **Publications:** On the Devil's Court, 1988; Heart of a Champion, 1993; Painting the Black, 1997; Night Hoops, 2000; High Heat, 2003; Runner, 2005; Gym Candy, 2007; Payback Time, 2010. Contributor to short stories. **Address:** 2827 NW 62nd St., Seattle, WA 98107-2513, U.S.A. **Online address:** carl1989@hotmail.com

DEUTSCH, Sarah (Jane). American (born United States), b. 1955. **Genres:** History, Women's Studies And Issues, Cultural/Ethnic Topics, Social Sciences. **Career:** Massachusetts Institute of Technology, assistant professor, associate professor of history, 1985-89; Clark University, associate professor of history; University of Arizona, associate professor, professor of history; Duke

University, Department of History, professor, 2004-, chair, 2004-06, dean of social sciences, 2006-; Organization of American Historians, distinguished lecturer, 2004-08. Writer. **Publications:** No Separate Refuge: Culture, Class, and Gender On an Anglo-Hispanic Frontier in the American Southwest, 1880-1940, 1987; From Ballots to Breadlines: American Women, 1920-1940, 1994; Women and the City: Gender, Space, and Power in Boston, 1870-1940, 2000. Contributor to books and periodicals. **Address:** Department of History, Duke University, 326 Carr Bldg., PO Box 90719, Durham, NC 27708-0719, U.S.A. **Online address:** sarah.deutsch@duke.edu

DEUTSCHER, Irwin. American (born United States), b. 1923. **Genres:** Sociology, History, Social Sciences. **Career:** University of Missouri, instructor in sociology and anthropology, 1950-53; Community Studies Inc., project director of metropolitan nurse studies, 1953-58, director of research in health and welfare, 1958-59; Syracuse University, associate professor, 1959-64, professor of sociology, 1964-68, Youth Development Center, director, 1959-68; Case Western Reserve University, professor of sociology, 1968-75; University of Amsterdam, visiting professor, 1971-72; University of Akron, professor, 1975-83, professor emeritus of sociology, 1983-; U.S. Office of Education, consultant; National Institute of Mental Health, chairman. Writer. **Publications:** (With E.C. and H.M. Hughes) Twenty Thousand Nurses Tell Their Story, 1958; (ed. with E.J. Thompson) Among the People: Encounters with the Poor, 1968; What We Say/What We Do: Sentiments and Acts, 1973; (with F.P. Pestello and H.F. Pestello) Sentiments and Acts, 1993; Making a Difference: The Practice of Sociology, 1999; Accommodating Diversity: National Policies That Prevent Ethnic Conflict, 2002; (with L. Lindsey) Preventing Ethnic Conflict: Successful Cross-National Strategies, 2005. **Address:** Olin Hall 247, Akron, OH 44325-1905, U.S.A. **Online address:** ideutscher@juno.com

DEVALLE, Susana B. C. Mexican/Argentine (born Argentina), b. 1945. **Genres:** Cultural/Ethnic Topics, Politics/Government. **Career:** Buenos Aires National University, Institute of Anthropology, researcher, 1966-67; El Colegio de Mexico, Center for Asian and African Studies, researcher, 1970-72, research professor of Asian and African studies, 1973-, director of research group on ethnicity and nationalisms in Asia, Africa, and Latin America, 1994-, coordinator of research group on the culture of violence, coexistence, and human rights, 1994-; Mexican Ministry of Education, national researcher in the social sciences, Sistema Nacional de Investigadores, staff, 1987-; University of Hawaii, visiting fellow in ethnic studies, 1990; Universidad Iberoamericana, lecturer. Writer. **Publications:** (Co-author) Movimientos Agrarios y Cambio Social en Asia y Africa, 1974; La Palabra de la Tierra: Protesta Campesina en India, siglo XIX, 1977; Multi-Ethnicity in India: The Adivasi Peasants of Chota Nagpur and Santal Parganas, 1980; (co-ed. and contrib.) Peasantry and National Integration, 1981; (ed. and contrib.) La Diversidad Prohibida: Resistencia Étnica yPoder de Estado, 1989; Discourses of Ethnicity: Culture and Protest in Jharkhand, 1992; Saadatj Hasan Manto: Antología de cuentos, 1996; (comp.) Poder y cultura de la violencia, 2000; Etnicidad e Identidad: Continuidad y Cambio: continuidad y cambi, 2002; Identidad y etnicidad: continuidad y cambio, 2002; Augustus Cleveland y el colonialismo en la India, 2008; Augustus Cleveland and Colonialismin India, 2008. Contributor to journals. Works appear in anthologies. **Address:** Center for Asian and African Studies, El Colegio de Mexico, Camino al Ajusco No. 20, Pedregal de Santa Teresa, Mexico City, DF 10740, Mexico. **Online address:** sdevalle@colmex.mx

DEVANE, Terry. See **HEALY, Jeremiah.**

DE VARONA, Frank J. Cuban (born Cuba), b. 1943. **Genres:** Area Studies, History, Social Sciences. **Career:** Junior high school, social studies teacher, 1967-70; high school social studies teacher, 1970-72; Miami Senior High Adult Education Center, assistant principal, 1973-75; Miami Coral Park Senior High Adult Education Center, principal, 1975-77; West Miami Junior High School, principal, 1977-79; Miami Edison Senior High School, principal, 1979-82; Dade County Public Schools, South Central area director, 1982-85, area superintendent, 1985-87, associate superintendent of bureau of education, 1987-91, region I superintendent, 1991; Florida International University, Department of Curriculum and Instruction, visiting associate professor, 1997-. Writer, consultant and historian. **Publications:** (Co-author) Hispanics in United States History: Through 1865, 1989, vol. II as Hispanics in United States History: 1865 to the Present, 1989; Bernardo de Gálvez, 1990; (ed.) Hispanic Presence in the United States: Historical Beginnings, 1993; Florida Government Activities, 1993; Simón Bolívar: Latin American

Liberator, 1993; Benito Juárez, President of Mexico, 1993; Miguel Hidalgo y Costilla: Father of Mexican Independence, 1993; (co-author) The Cuban Educational System: Past, Present and Future, 1993; Latino Literacy: The Complete Guide to Our Hispanic History and Culture, 1996. Contributor to newspapers, magazines and books. **Address:** Department of Education Leadership & Policy, Studies, Florida International University, 355B ZEB Bldg., 11200 SW 8th St., Miami, FL 33199, U.S.A. **Online address:** devaronf@fiu.edu

DE VASCONCELOS, Erika. Canadian (born Canada), b. 1965. **Genres:** Novels, Young Adult Fiction. **Career:** Novelist. **Publications:** My Darling Dead Ones, 1997; Between the Stillness and the Grove: A Novel, 2000. **Address:** c/o Author Mail, Random House Canada Ltd., 1 Toronto St., Unit 300, Toronto, ON M5C 2V6, Canada.

DEVASHISH, Donald Acosta. American (born United States), b. 1956. **Genres:** Novels, Translations, Literary Criticism And History. **Career:** Writer. **Publications:** (Trans.) Shabda Cayanika, vol. I, 1995, vol. II, 1996, vol. III, forthcoming; Felicitavia: A Spiritual Journal (novel), 1997; Conversations, 1998; When the Time Comes Conversations with Acharya Chandranath Kumar, 1998; Cuando Lllega El Momento, 2005. **Address:** PNS 265, PO Box 5075, San German, PR 00683, U.S.A. **Online address:** devashisa@igc.org

DEVAUX, Claudia. American (born United States), b. 1946. **Genres:** inspirational/Motivational Literature, Biography, Education, Cultural/Ethnic Topics, Economics. **Career:** Hewlett-Packard Co., marketing executive; Sichuan International Studies University, Postgraduate Department, teacher; California Polytechnic State University, lecturer; Guli Institute, owner, 2002-; Holy Land Institute, leader. Writer and consultant. **Publications:** (With G.B. Wong) Bamboo Swaying in the Wind: A Survivor's Story of Faith and Imprisonment in Communist China, 2000. **Address:** Guli Institute, 1044 Vista Collados, San Luis Obispo, CA 93405-4822, U.S.A. **Online address:** claudiadevaux@guligroup.com

DE VECCHI, Nicolo. Italian (born Italy), b. 1943. **Genres:** Economics, Translations. **Career:** University of Trento, associate professor, 1971-73, professor of economics, 1972-74; University of Pavia, associate professor, 1973-81, professor of political economy, 1981-. Writer. **Publications:** Interdipendenze strutturali e contabilità nazionale: le tavole delle transazioni riferite all'economia italiana, 1975; Valore e distribuzione nell'economia politica classica, 1976; Jevons: il calcolo logico in economia politica, 1976; Schumpeter viennese: imprenditori, istituzioni e riproduzione del capitale, 1993; (ed. with M.C. Marcuzzo) A cinquant'anni da Keynes: teorie dell'occupazione, interesse e crescita, 1998. Contributor to books and periodicals. **Address:** Department of Economics, University of Pavia, Strada Nuova, Pavia, 27100, Italy. **Online address:** ndevecchi@eco.unipv.it

DEVEREAUX, Robert. American (born United States), b. 1947. **Genres:** Novels. **Career:** Pulphouse Magazine, staff; Hewlett Packard, software engineer. Writer. **Publications:** The Principles of Turkism, 1968; Deadweight, 1994; Walking Wounded, 1996; Santa Steps Out: A Fairy Tale for Grown-ups, 1998; Caliban and Other Tales, 2002; A Flight of Storks and Angels, 2003; Santa Claus Conquers the Homophobes, 2008; Slaughterhouse High: A Tale of Love and Sacrifice, 2010; Baby's First Book of Seriously Fucked-Up Shit, 2011. Contributor to journals. **Address:** c/o Jane Dystel, Dystel Goderich Literary Management, 1 Union Sq. W, Ste. 904, New York, NY 10003, U.S.A. **Online address:** contact@robertdevereaux.com

DEVEREUX, David. British (born England), b. 1971?. **Genres:** Autobiography/Memoirs. **Career:** Athanor Consulting, senior field officer, through 2008. Writer and professional exorcist. **Publications:** Memoirs of an Exorcist, 2007; Hunter's Moon, 2008; Eagle Rising, 2009. **Address:** London, GL , England. **Online address:** mail@david-devereux.com

DE VILLIERS, Marq. Canadian/South African (born South Africa), b. 1940?. **Genres:** History, Writing/Journalism, Race Relations, Adult Nonfiction, Natural History, Economics. **Career:** South African Newspapers, reporter and writer, 1959-60; Toronto Telegram, reporter and editorial writer, 1962-65, feature writer, 1967, Moscow Bureau, staff, 1969-71; Toronto Life, executive editor, 1978-82, editor, 1982, publisher, 1992-93; WHERE Magazines Intl., editorial director, 1993-; Reuters Wire Service, reporter; Lost Magazine, contributor. **Publications:** White Tribe Dreaming: Apartheid's Bitter Roots: Notes of an Eighth-generation Afrikaner, 1987 in US as White Tribe

Dreaming: Apartheid's Bitter Roots as Witnessed by Eight Generations of an Afrikaner Family, 1988; White Tribe Dreaming: Apartheid's Bitter Roots: Notes of an Eighth-Generation Afrikaner, 1987; Down the Volga in a Time of Troubles: A Journey Revealing the People and Heartland of Post-Perestroika Russia, 1991 in US as Down the Volga: A Journey through Mother Russia in a Time of Troubles, 1992; The Heartbreak Grape: A California Winemaker's Search for the Perfect Pinot Noir, 1994, rev. ed. as The Heartbreak Grape: A Journey in Search of the Perfect Pinot Noir, 2006; (with G. Drabinsky) Closer to the Sun: An Autobiography, 1995; (with S. Hirtle) Blood Traitors, 1997; (with S. Hirtle) Into Africa: A Journey through the Ancient Empires, 1997; The Water Wars: The Looming Crisis in Global Fresh Water, 1999; Water, 1999 in US as Water: The Fate of Our Most Precious Resource, 2001, rev. ed., 2003; Guide to America's Outdoors: Eastern Canada, 2001; (with S. Hirtle) Sahara: A Natural History, 2002; (with S. Hirtle) Sable Island: The Strange Origins and Curious History of a Dune Adrift in The Atlantic, 2004; Windswept: The Story of Wind and Weather, 2006; Witch in the Wind: The True Story of the Legendary Bluenose, 2007; (with S. Hirtle) Timbuktu: The Sahara's Fabled City of Gold, 2007; A Short History of Natural Calamities, 2008; Dangerous World, 2008; End: Natural Disasters, Manmade Catastrophes, and the Future of Human Survival, 2008; Our Way Out, 2012. Contributor to books and periodicals. **Address:** Westwood Creative Artists Ltd., 94 Harbord St., Toronto, ON M5S 1G6, Canada. **Online address:** jacobus@fox.nstn.ca

DEVINCENT-HAYES, Nan. American (born United States) **Genres:** Novels, Novellas/Short Stories, Horror, Romance/Historical, Science Fiction/Fantasy, Young Adult Fiction, Adult Non-fiction, Cultural/Ethnic Topics, Education, Humanities, Politics/Government, Women's Studies And Issues, Writing/Journalism. **Career:** Salisbury State University, adjunct professor, 1985-90, assistant professor of English, 1989-92, adjunct professor of communications, 1995-; Wor-Wic College, adjunct professor of English, 1985-89; Mount Aloysius College, associate professor of English and chair, 1989-91; University of Maryland Eastern Shore, visiting lecturer and adjunct professor of English, 1992-94. Writer. **Publications:** Move It, 1988; The Last of the Wallendas, 1993; Ocean City: vol. I, 1999; (with B. Bennett) Chincoteague and Assateague Islands, 2000; (with B. Bennett) Wallops Island, 2001; Rehobeth and the Quiet Resorts, 2002; (with B. Bennett) Rehoboth Beach, Delaware, 2002; Zambelli: The First Family of Fireworks, 2003. NOVELS: 22 Friar Street, 2001; Thy Brothers' Reaper, 2001; Jacob's Trouble, 2001; Heartbroken Love, 2002. TEXTBOOKS: Troublesome Grammar; Grammar and Sentence Diagramming, 1998. Contributor to periodicals and magazines. **Address:** 5736 Royal Mile Blvd., Salisbury, MD 21801, U.S.A. **Online address:** ndhayes@att.net

DE VINCK, José M. G. A. American/Belgian (born Belgium), b. 1912. **Genres:** Poetry, Human Relations/Parenting, Philosophy, Sex, Theology/Religion, Translations, Social Sciences. **Career:** Seton Hall University, professor of philosophy, 1950-54; Saint Anthony Guild Press, editor and translator, 1955-70; Tombrock College, professor of philosophy and theology, 1967-74; Sunday Publications, associate editor, 1974; Alleluia Press, owner. **Publications:** Images, 1940; (co-author) Le Cantique de la Vie, 1943, as écris-moi du désert, auz horizons de l'unité, 1955; The Virtue of Sex, 1966; (with J.T. Catoir) The Challenge of Love: Practical Advice for Married Couples and Those Planning Marriage, 1969; The Yes Book: An Answer to Life, 1972; The Words of Jesus, 1977; (ed.) Byzantine Altar Gospel, 1979; (ed.) Byzantine Altar Epistles, 1980; Revelations of Women Mystics: From the Middle Ages to Modern Times, 1985; Faith in The New Age, A Critical Survey, 1997; Allegories of Exchange: Anthropology, Semiotics, Narrative, Culture, 1999. TRANSLATOR: (ed. with J. Raya) Byzantine Missal for Sundays and Feast Days, 1958; The Works of Bonaventure: Cardinal, Sepharic Doctor, and Saint, vol. I: Mystical Opuscula, 1960, vol. II: The Breviloquim, 1963, vol. III: Opuscula, Second Series, 1966, vol. IV: Defense of the Mendicants, 1966, vol. V: Collations on the Six Days, 1970; G. Bougerol, Introduction to the Works of St. Bonaventure, 1964; (ed. with J. Raya) Byzantine Daily Worship, 1969; (with L.C. Contos) The Psalms, 1993; The Quest for the Golden Dove: Thoughts on Love Human and Divine, 1994. **Address:** Alleluia Press, PO Box 103, Allendale, NJ 07401-0103, U.S.A.

DEVITA, James. American (born United States) **Genres:** Novels, Science Fiction/Fantasy. **Career:** First Stage Children's Theater, resident playwright; American Players Theater, actor, 1995-. Writer. **Publications:** NOVELS: Blue, 2001; The Silenced, 2007. PLAYS: The Christmas Angel, 1998; Excavating Mom, 1999; The Swiss Family Robinson, 2002; The Three Musketeers, 2002; The Rose of Treason: A Fictional Dramatization Based on the True Story of Sophie Scholl and the White Rose, 2003; Dickens in America, 2006. **Address:** American Players Theatre, 5950 Golf Course Rd., PO Box 819, Spring Green, WI 53588, U.S.A. **Online address:** jibvii@charter.net

DEVITO, Joseph A. American/Italian (born Italy), b. 1938. **Genres:** Communications/Media, Speech/Rhetoric. **Career:** Lehman College, faculty, 1964-71; City University of New York, Queens College, professor, 1972-85, Hunter College, professor, 1985-94, now professor emeritus. Writer. **Publications:** The Psychology of Speech and Language, 1970; General Semantics, 1971, new ed., 1974; Psycholinguistics, 1971; The Interpersonal Communication Book, 1976, 12th ed., 2009; Human Communication: The Basic Course, 1978, 12th ed., 2012; Elements of Public Speaking, 1981, 7th ed., 2000; Communication Handbook: A Dictionary, 1986; The Nonverbal Communication Workbook, 1989; Messages: Building Interpersonal Communication Skills, 1990, 6th ed., 2005; The Interpersonal Challenge, 1992, 3rd ed., 1997; Essentials of Human Communication, 1993, 7th ed., 2011; Studying Communication, 1995; The Essential Elements of Public Speaking, 2003, 4th ed. 2012; Interpersonal Messages, 2008, 2nd ed., 2011; The Interviewing Guidebook, 2nd ed., 2010. EDITOR: Communication: Concepts and Processes, 1971, 3rd ed., 1981; Language, 1973; (with M.L. Hecht) The Nonverbal Communication Reader, 1990, (with L.K. Guerrero and M.L. Hecht) 2nd ed., 1999. **Address:** 12 St. Josen Rd., Accord, NY 12404, U.S.A. **Online address:** jadevito@earthlink.net

DEVJI, Faisal Fatehali. Tanzanian (born Tanzania, United Republic of), b. 1964?. **Genres:** History. **Career:** Harvard University, Cambridge, Society of Fellows, Junior Fellow, 1993-96; Institute of Ismaili Studies, lecturer and research associate, 1997-99, head of graduate studies, 1999-2003; New School, assistant professor of history, 2005-06, associate professor of history, 2006-09. University of Chicago, Department of History, visiting lecturer, 1996-97; Yale University, Department of History, Singh visiting lecturer, 2003-05. Writer. **Publications:** Landscapes of the Jihad: Militancy, Morality, Modernity, 2005; The Terrorist in Search of Humanity: Militant Islam and Global Politics, 2008. Contributor of articles to books. **Online address:** devji@post.harvard.edu

DEVLIN, Albert J. American (born United States) **Genres:** Administration/Management, Young Adult Fiction, Literary Criticism And History, inspirational/Motivational Literature. **Career:** PBS television documentary, academic advisor; University of Missouri, Catherine Payne Middlebush Professor, now professor emeritus. Writer. **Publications:** Eudora Welty's Chronicle: A Story of Mississippi Life, 1983. EDITOR: Conversations with Tennessee Williams, 1986; Welty: A Life in Literature, 1987; (with N.M. Tischler) The Selected Letters of Tennessee Williams, vol. I: 1920-1945, 2000, vol. II, 1945-1957, 2004. Contributor to periodicals. **Address:** Department of English, University of Missouri, 366 McReynolds, 218 Tate Hall, Columbia, MO 65211-1500, U.S.A. **Online address:** devlina@missouri.edu

DEVLIN, Anne. British/Irish (born Ireland), b. 1951?. **Genres:** Novellas/Short Stories, Plays/Screenplays, Photography. **Career:** Teacher, 1974-78; Royal Court Theatre, writer associate, 1985-; University of Birmingham, visiting lecturer in playwriting, 1987; University of Lund, writer-in-residence, 1990; Trinity College, fellow, 2003-04. **Publications:** PLAYS: Ourselves Alone: With, The Long March and A Woman Calling, 1986; (with S. Bill and D. Edgar) Heartlanders: A Community Play to Celebrate Birmingham's Centenary, 1989; After Easter, 1994; Ourselves Alone, 1999. OTHER: The Way Paver (short stories), 1986. **Address:** Dramatists Play Service Inc., 440 Park Ave. S, New York, NY 10016, U.S.A. **Online address:** anne.devlin@virgin.net

DEVLIN, Dean. American (born United States), b. 1962. **Genres:** Plays/Screenplays. **Career:** Electric Entertainment, founder, producer. Screenwriter. **Publications:** (Co-author) Universal Soldier, 1992; Stargate, 1994; (with R. Emmerich) Independence Day, 1996; (contrib.) Godzilla, 1998; (contrib.) The Official Godzilla Movie Fact Book, 1998; (with R. Emmerich) Resistance, 1999. **Address:** Creative Artists Agency, Astaire Bldg., 9830 Wilshire Blvd., Ste. 2610, Beverly Hills, CA 90212-1825, U.S.A.

DEVLIN, Keith. British/American (born United States), b. 1947. **Genres:** Mathematics/Statistics, Sciences. **Career:** University of Oslo, scientific visitor, 1971, scientific assistant in mathematics, 1972-73; Victoria University of Manchester, temporary lecturer in mathematics, 1973; University of Heidelberg, scientific assistant in mathematics, 1974; University of Bonn, scientific assistant in mathematics, 1974-76; University of Toronto, assistant professor of mathematics, 1976; University of Lancaster, lecturer, 1977-79, reader in mathematics, 1979-87; Stanford University, visiting associate professor of mathematics, 1987-88, Center for the Study of Language and Information, senior researcher, 1987-, associate professor of mathematics and philosophy, 1988-89; Colby College, Carter professor, Department of Mathematics and Computer Science, chair, 1989-93; St. Mary's College of California, professor of mathematics, School of Science, dean, 1993-2001; Stanford University, senior research scientist, H-STAR Institute, executive director, 2001-. Writer. **Publications:** Aspects of Constructibility, 1973; (with H. Johnsbraaten) The Souslin Problem, 1974; The Axiom of Constructibility: A Guide for the Mathematician, 1977; Fundamentals of Contemporary Set Theory, 1979, 2nd ed., 1993; Sets, Functions, and Logic, 1981, 2nd ed., 1992; Constructibility, 1984; Microchip Mathematics, 1984; Micro Maths, 1984; Mathematics: The New Golden Age, 1988, 2nd ed., 1999; Logic and Information, 1991; The Joy of Sets, 1993; All the Math That's Fit to Print, 1994; Mathematics: The Science of Patterns, 1994; Plato's Mirror: Mathematical Reflections of Mind and Universe, 1994; (with D. Rosenberg) Language at Work-Analyzing Communication Breakdown in the Workplace to Inform Systems Design, 1996; Goodby Descartes-The End of Logic and the Search for a New Cosmology of the Mind, 1997; Life by the Numbers, 1998; The Language of Mathematics: Making the Invisible Visible, 1998; Infosense: Turning Information into Knowledge, 1999; The Math Gene: How Mathematical Thinking Evolved and Why Numbers Are like Gossip, 2000; The Millennium Problems: The Seven Greatest Unsolved Mathematical Puzzles of Our Time, 2002; The Math Instinct: Why You're a Mathematical Genius, 2005; (with G. Lorden) The Numbers behind NUMB3RS: Solving Crime with Mathematics, 2007; (with J. Borwein) The Computer as Crucible, 2008; The Unfinished Game: Pascal, Fermat, and the Seventeenth Century Letter that Made the World Modern, 2008; Mathematics Education for a New Era: Video Games as a Medium for Learning, 2011; The Man of Numbers: Fibonacci's Arithmetic Revolution, 2011. **Address:** H-STAR Institute, Stanford University, Cordura Hall, 210 Panama St., Stanford, CA 94305-4115, U.S.A. **Online address:** devlin@stanford.edu

DEVLIN, Linda. *See* **JONES, Linda Winstead.**

DEVNEY, Darcy C(ampion). American (born United States), b. 1960. **Genres:** Administration/Management, How-to Books, Public/Social Administration, Young Adult Non-fiction. **Career:** Harvard University, faculty, Harvard Magazine, staff, Cabot House, staff, Office for Sponsored Research, staff, 1979-91. Writer. **Publications:** Organizing Special Events and Conferences: A Practical Guide for Busy Volunteers and Staff, 1990, rev. ed., 2001; The Volunteer's Survival Manual: The Only Practical Guide to Giving Your Time and Money, 1992. **Address:** Practical Press, PO Box 2296, Cambridge, MA 02238, U.S.A.

DEVON, Paddie. Irish (born Ireland), b. 1953. **Genres:** Children's Fiction, Plays/Screenplays, Theology/Religion, Illustrations, Novellas/Short Stories. **Career:** Tudor Publications, graphic artist and art director, 1974-82; Sweet Inspirations, interior design consultant, 1984-. Writer. **Publications:** SELF-ILLUSTRATED: The Grumpy Shepherd, 1995. OTHER: (A. Tomos) Bugail Blin, Y, 1996. **Address:** Ballywooley Cottage, 175 Crawfordsburn Rd., Bangor, County Down, BT19 1BT, Northern Ireland.

DEVOR, Aaron H. (Holly Devor). Canadian (born Canada), b. 1951. **Genres:** Sociology, Gay And Lesbian Issues, History, Medicine/Health, Psychology, Sex, Civil Liberties/Human Rights, Social Sciences, Women's Studies And Issues, Biography. **Career:** Simon Fraser University, Women's Studies for Prison Education Program, instructor, 1986-88, instructor in women's studies, 1988-89; University of Victoria, visiting lecturer of sociology, 1989-90, assistant professor of sociology, 1990-94, associate professor 1994-97, professor 1997-, associate dean of social sciences, 2000-02, dean of graduate studies, 2002-12. Writer. **Publications:** AS HOLLY DEVOR: Gender Blending: Confronting the Limits of Duality, 1989; FTM: Female-to-Male Transsexuals in Society, 1997. **Address:** Department of Sociology, University of Victoria, PO Box 3050, Victoria, BC V8W 3P5, Canada. **Online address:** ahdevor@uvic.ca

DEVOR, Holly. *See* **DEVOR, Aaron H.**

DE VORSEY, Louis. American (born United States), b. 1929. **Genres:** Geography, History. **Career:** East Carolina College (now University), assistant professor of geography, 1962-65; University of North Carolina, assistant professor of geography, 1965-67; University of Georgia, associate professor, 1967-73, professor, 1973-88, professor emeritus of geography, 1988-. Writer. **Publications:** The Indian Boundary in the Southern Colonies, 1763-1775, 1966; West Europe-East Europe, 1968; Europe and Asia, 1968; Neighbors in Eurasia, 1968; American Revolution, 1972; (comp.) American Revolution, 1775-1783: An Atlas of 18th Century Maps and Charts, Theatres of Operations, 1972; The Peoples of Western Europe, 1972; Collection of Eighteenth Century Maps: With Introductory Notes, 1974; The Atlantic Pilot, 1974; Georgia, the Home Place, 1979; A Land in Time, 1979; (co-author) Coast, Rivers and Inlets of the Province of Georgia, 1981; The Georgia-South Carolina Boundary: A Problem in Historical Geography, 1982; (contrib.) New Map Map of Georgia, with Part of Carolina, Florida and Louisiana, 1986; The Canada-United States Boundary in the Gulf of Maine and Over Georges Bank, 1990; Keys to the Encounter: A Library of Congress Resource Guide for the Study of the Age of Discovery, 1992; (with M.J. Rice) The Plantation South: Atlanta to Savannah and Charleston, 1992; (co-author) Columbus and the Land of Ayllón: The Exploration and Settlement of the Southeast, 1992; (with W.P. Cumming) The Southeast in Early Maps, 1998. EDITOR: (and intro.) De Brahm's Report of the General Survey in the Southern District of North America, 1971; (with J. Parker) In the Wake of Columbus: Islands and Controversy, 1985; (with D.G. Dallmeyer) Rights to Oceanic Resources: Deciding and Drawing Maritime Boundaries, 1989. **Address:** Department of Geography, University of Georgia, Rm. 204, GG Bldg., 210 Field St., Athens, GA 30602, U.S.A. **Online address:** loudev@aol.com

DE VOS, Susan. (Susan M. De Vos). American/Japanese (born Japan), b. 1953. **Genres:** Demography, Social Sciences, Medicine/Health. **Career:** University of Wisconsin, Institute on Aging, postdoctoral fellow, 1982-84, Center for Demography and Ecology, research associate, 1984-, postdoctoral fellow, 1986-87, Department of Sociology, research scientist, senior scientist, Center for Demography and Ecology, researcher, Center for Demography of Health and Aging, staff; University of Zimbabwe, Department of Sociology, visiting lecturer, 1989. Writer. **Publications:** The Old-age Economic Security Value of Children in the Philippines and Taiwan, 1984; (as Susan M. De Vos) Household Composition in Latin America, 1995. Contributor to journals. **Address:** Department of Sociology, University of Wisconsin, 2409 William H. Sewell Social Sciences Bldg., 1180 Observatory Dr., Madison, WI 53706-1393, U.S.A. **Online address:** devos@ssc.wisc.edu

DE VOS, Susan M. *See* **DE VOS, Susan.**

DE VRIES, Hent. American/Dutch (born Netherlands), b. 1958. **Genres:** Theology/Religion, Politics/Government, Young Adult Non-fiction. **Career:** Johns Hopkins University, professor of modern European thought; University of Amsterdam, professor of philosophy, chair of metaphysics and its history; Amsterdam School for Cultural Analysis, director. Writer. **Publications:** NONFICTION: Die Aktualität der Dialektik der Aufklärung: Zwischen Moderne und Postmoderne, 1989; Theologie im pianissimo & zwischen Rationalität und Dekonstruktion: Die Aktualität der denkfiguren Adornos und Levinas, 1989; (ed. with H. Kunneman) Enlightenments: Encounters between Critical Theory and Contemporary French Thought, 1993; (ed. with S. Weber) Violence, Identity, and Self-Determination, 1997; Philosophy and the Turn to Religion, 1999; (ed. with H.A. Krop and A.L. Molendijk) Post-Theism: Reframing the Judeo-Christian Tradition, 2000; (ed. with S. Weber) Religion and Media, 2001; Religion and Violence: Philosophical Perspectives from Kant to Derrida, 2002; (ed. with L.E. Sullivan) Political Theologies: Public Religions in a Post-Secular World, 2006; (ed.) Religion: Beyond a Concept, 2008. **Address:** Johns Hopkins University, Dell House 302A, 3400 N Charles St., Baltimore, MD 21218-2608, U.S.A. **Online address:** hentdevries@jhu.edu

DEVRIES, Kelly. American (born United States), b. 1956. **Genres:** History, Military/Defense/Arms Control, Biography, Literary Criticism And History, Technology. **Career:** University of Toronto, Department of History, The Institute of History, Philosophy of Science and Technology, teaching assistant, 1983-87; Ryerson Poly Technical Institute, Department of History, instructor, 1987-88; University of British Columbia, Department of History, sessional lecturer, 1988-89; Wilfrid Laurier University, Department of History, assistant professor, 1989-91; Loyola College, Department of History, assistant professor, 1991-95, associate professor of history, 1995-2002, full professor, 2002-. Writer. **Publications:** Medieval Military Technology, 1992, 2nd ed., 2008; Infantry Warfare in the Early Fourteenth Century, 1996; The Norwegian Invasion of England in 1066, 1999; Joan of Arc: A Military Leader, 1999; Guns and Men in Medieval Europe, 1200-1500: Studies in Military History and Technology, 2002; A Cumulative Bibliography of Medieval Military History and Technology, 2002; (ed.) The Battle of the Golden Spurs, 2002; (with R.D. Smith) Artillery of the Dukes of Burgundy, 1363-1477, 2005; (co-author) Battles of the Medieval World, 1000-1500: From Hastings to Constantinople, 2006; (with R.D. Smith) Medieval Weapons: An Illustrated History of Their Impact, 2007; Battles of the Crusades, 2007; (ed. with J. France) Warfare in the Dark Ages, 2008; Strategic Battles, 2008; (co-author) Battles of the Ancient World: From Kadesh to Catalaunian Fields, 2008; (with R.D. Smith) Rhodes Besieged, 2011. **Address:** Department of History, Loyola College, Humanities 312, 4501 N Charles St., Baltimore, MD 21210-2699, U.S.A. **Online address:** kdevries@loyola.edu

DE VRIES, Rachel (Guido). American (born United States), b. 1947. **Genres:** Novels, Poetry, Essays, Gay And Lesbian Issues, History, Autobiography/Memoirs, Biography, Young Adult Fiction, Young Adult Fiction. **Career:** Nurse, 1968-78; Syracuse University, Humanistic Studies Center, part-time instructor of creative writing, 1978-, teacher; Women's Writers Center, resident faculty and co-director, 1978-82; Community Writers' Project Inc., co-founder, 1984-, co-director, 1984-95; Central New York Psychiatric Center, poet-in-residence, 1984-; State University of New York, Morrisville College, instructor, 1985. **Publications:** An Arc of Light, 1978; (contrib.) Learning Our Way: Essays in Feminist Education, 1983; Tender Warriors, 1986; Anthology: The Voices We Carry: Recent Italian American Women's Fiction, 1994; How to Sing to a DAGO and Other Canzonetti (poetry), 1996; Gambler's Daughter, 2001; Teeny Tiny Tino's Fishing Story, 2007; The Brother Inside Me, 2008. Works appear in anthologies. **Address:** Community Writers' Project Inc., PO Box 6884, Syracuse, NY 13217, U.S.A.

DEW, Andrea J. American (born United States) **Genres:** Politics/Government. **Career:** JET Program, teacher, 1993-96; Kyoto YWCA, volunteer coordinator of a Conflict Resolution Training Program and English language coordinator, 1998- 2001; Tufts University, Fletcher Writing Program coordinator, 2003-06, research associate for International Security Studies Program, 2003- 06; Harvard University, Kennedy School of Government, Belfer Center for Science and International Affairs, International Security Studies Fellow, 2006; U.S. Naval War College, assistant professor, 2007-; Tufts University, Jebsen Center for Counter-Terrorism senior fellow, 2007-08. Academic, historian and writer. **Publications:** (with R.H. Shultz) Insurgents, Terrorists and Militias: The Warriors of Contemporary Combat, 2006; (with M.M. Mohamedou) Empowered Groups, Tested Laws and Policy Options, Program on Humanitarian Policy and Conflict Research, 2007. Contributor to books. **Address:** U.S. Naval War College, 686 Cushing Rd., Newport, RI 02841, U.S.A. **Online address:** andrea.dew@gmail.com

DE WAAL, Ronald Burt. American (born United States), b. 1932. **Genres:** Literary Criticism And History, Autobiography/Memoirs, Bibliography. **Career:** University of New Mexico, special collections librarian, 1958-59; New Mexico Military Institute, head librarian, 1959-60; Sperry Utah Co., head librarian, 1961-64; Westminster College, staff, 1964-66; Colorado State University, humanities librarian, 1966-88. Writer. **Publications:** The World Bibliography of Sherlock Holmes and Dr. Watson: A Classified and Annotated List of Materials Relating to Their Lives and Adventures, 1887-1972, 1974; The International Sherlock Holmes, 1980; The Universal Sherlock Holmes, 1985, vol. IV, 1994, (with L.S. Klinger) vol. V: The Indexes to The Universal Sherlock Holmes, 1995; Pages from the Journal of Ron De Waal, 1993-2002, 2003. Contributor to periodicals. **Address:** 638 12th Ave., Salt Lake City, UT 84103, U.S.A.

DEWALD, Paul A. See Obituaries.

DEWALT, Gary W(eston). American (born United States) **Genres:** Natural History, Environmental Sciences/Ecology. **Career:** Freelance journalist, investigative filmmaker and author. **Publications:** NONFICTION: (with A. Boukreev) The Climb: Tragic Ambitions on Everest, 1997. **Address:** St. Martin's Press, 175 5th Ave., New York, NY 10010-7703, U.S.A.

DEWART, Gilbert. American (born United States), b. 1932. **Genres:** Travel/Exploration, History, Sports/Fitness. **Career:** Arctic Institute of North America, geophysicist and glaciologist, 1956-58; Seismological Laboratory, research engineer and field geophysicist, 1958-63; Byrd Polar Research Cen-

ter, research associate and fellow, 1963-71; ESD Geophysics (consultants), proprietor, 1972-85; Moorpark College, part-time lecturer, 1986-. Writer. **Publications:** Antarctic Comrades: An American with the Russians in Antarctica, 1989; Journey to the Ice Age, 2003. Contributor to journals. **Address:** Department of Environmental Studies, Moorpark College, Rm. LMC-103, 7075 Campus Rd., Moorpark, CA 93021-1695, U.S.A. **Online address:** dewartg@hotmail.com

DEWBERRY, Elizabeth. (Elizabeth Dewberry Vaughn). American (born United States), b. 1962. **Genres:** Plays/Screenplays, Novels. **Career:** Emory University, instructor of English, 1987-88, visiting assistant professor of English, 1989-90; Samford University, adjunct lecturer of English, 1991-92; Ohio State University, assistant professor of English, 1992-94; Wesleyan Writers Conference, teaching fellow, 1993; University of Southern California, visiting lecturer of creative writing, 1993; Sewanee Writers' Conference, faculty member, 1994; Bread Loaf Writers Conference, faculty member, 1994; University of the South, Tennessee Williams Fellow, 1995; Florida State University, playwright-in-residence. Writer. **Publications:** NOVELS: (as E.D. Vaughn) Many Things Have Happened Since He Died and Here Are the Highlights, 1990; (as E.D. Vaughn) Break the Heart of Me, 1994; Sacrament of Lies, 2002; His Lovely Wife, 2006. Contributor to books and periodicals. **Address:** c/o Elaine Markson, Elaine Markson Literary Agency, 44 Greenwich Ave., New York, NY 10011, U.S.A.

DEWDNEY, A(lexander) K(eewatin). Canadian (born Canada), b. 1941. **Genres:** Information Science/Computers, Biology, Mathematics/Statistics. **Career:** University of Western Ontario, lecturer, 1968-74, Department of Computer Science, research report editor, 1973-75, assistant professor, associate professor, 1974-96, professor emeritus, 1996-, graduate chairman, 1978-80, 1981-82, Department of Biology, adjunct professor; Algorithm, editor and founder, 1989-93; University of Waterloo, professor, 2000-04, professor emeritus, 2004-; Turing Omnibus Inc., president; Newport Forest Conservation Area, owner and operator. **Publications:** The Planiverse: Computer Contact with a Two-dimensional World, 1984; The Armchair Universe: An Exploration of Computer Worlds, 1988; The Turing Omnibus: 61 Excursions in Computer Science, 1989; The Magic Machine: A Handbook of Computer Sorcery, 1990; Two Hundred Percent of Nothing: An Eye-opening Tour Through the Twists and Turns of Math Abuse and Innumeracy, 1993; The New Turing Omnibus: 66 Excursions in Computer Science, 1993; The Tinkertoy Computer and Other Machinations, 1993; Introductory Computer Science: Bits of Theory, Bytes of Practice, 1996; Yes, We Have No Neutrons: An Eye-Opening Tour through the Twists and Turns of Bad Science, 1997; (ed.) Daylight in the Swamp: Memoirs of Selwyn Dewdney, 1997; Hungry Hollow: The Story of a Natural Place, 1998; A Mathematical Mystery Tour: Discovering the Truth and Beauty of the Cosmos, 1999; Beyond Reason: Eight Great Problems that Reveal the Limits of Science, 2004. Contributor to periodicals. **Address:** Department of Computer Science, Middlesex College, University of Western Ontario, Rm. 355, Toronto, ON N6A 5B7, Canada. **Online address:** akd@julian.uwo.ca

DEWEESE, Gene. Also writes as Thomas Stratton, Victoria Thomas, Jean DeWeese. American (born United States), b. 1934. **Genres:** Novellas/Short Stories, Mystery/Crime/Suspense, Horror, Romance/Historical, Science Fiction/Fantasy, Children's Fiction, Young Adult Fiction, Crafts, Crafts. **Career:** General Motors, Delco Electronics, electronics technician, 1954-59, technical writer, 1959-74; freelance writer, 1974-. **Publications:** WITH ROBERT COULSON AS THOMAS STRATTON: The Invisibility Affair, 1967; The Mind-Twisters Affair, 1967. OTHER: (with G. Rogowski) Making American Folk Art Dolls (non-fiction), 1975; Computers in Entertainment and the Arts (non-fiction), 1984; (with C. Kugi as Victoria Thomas) Ginger's Wish, 1987. WITH ROBERT COULSON: Gates of the Universe, 1975; Now You See It/Him/Them..., 1975; Charles Fort Never Mentioned Wombats, 1977; Nightmare Universe, 1985. NOVELS: Jeremy Case, 1976; The Wanting Factor, 1980; Something Answered, 1983; King of the Dead, 1996; Lord of the Necropolis, 1997; The Vault, 1999; Murder in the Blood (mystery), 2002; Three Deaths Of Jeremy Case, 2002. GOTHIC NOVELS AS JEAN DeWEESE: The Reimann Curse, 1975, rev. ed. as A Different Darkness, 1982; The Moonstone Spirit, 1975; The Carnelian Cat, 1975; Cave of the Moaning Wind, 1976; Web of Guilt, 1976; The Doll with Opal Eyes, 1976; Nightmare in Pewter, 1978; Hour of the Cat, 1980; The Backhoe Gothic, 1981. JUVENILE SCIENCE FICTION: Major Corby and the Unidentified Flapping Object, 1979; Nightmares from Space, 1981; Adventures of a Two-Minute Werewolf, 1983; Black Suits from Outer Space, 1985; The Dandelion Caper, 1986; The Calvin

Nullifier, 1987; Whatever Became of Aunt Margaret?, 1990; Firestorm, 1997. STAR TREK NOVELS: Chain of Attack, 1987; The Peacekeepers, 1988; The Final Nexus, 1988; Renegade, 1991; Into the Nebula, 1995; Engines of Destiny, 2005. Contributor to periodicals. Works appear in anthologies. **Address:** 2718 N Prospect, Milwaukee, WI 53211, U.S.A. **Online address:** gdeweese@wi.rr.com

DEWEESE, Jean. *See* **DEWEESE, Gene.**

DEWEESE, Pamela J. American (born United States), b. 1951. **Genres:** Literary Criticism And History, Translations. **Career:** College of Charleston, assistant professor, 1987-90; Sweet Briar College, assistant professor, 1990-93, associate professor, 1993-, professor of Spanish, 1999-. Writer and translator. **Publications:** Approximations to Luis Goytisolo's Antagonia, 2000; (trans.) L. Goytisolo, 360 Diary, 2008; (trans.) L. Freixas, Love . or Whatever, forthcoming; (trans.) L. Goytisolo, Statute with Doves, forthcoming. Contributor to books and periodicals. **Address:** Department of Modern Languages & Literatures, Sweet Briar College, 134 Chapel Rd., Sweet Briar, VA 24595, U.S.A. **Online address:** deweese@sbc.edu

DEWEY, Donald O(dell). American (born United States), b. 1930. **Genres:** History, Politics/Government, Biography. **Career:** City editor of newspapers, managing editor, 1952-54; University of Chicago, instructor in history, 1960-62, The Papers of James Madison, assistant editor, associate editor, 1960-62; California State University, assistant professor, 1962-65, associate professor, 1965-69, professor of history, 1969, School of Letters and Science, dean, 1970, now professor emeritus of history, dean emeritus; California State University Emeritus and Retired Faculty Association, president. **Publications:** Marshall versus Jefferson: The Political Background of Marbury Vs Madison, 1970; That's a Good One: Cal State LA at Fifty, 1997; (with B.B. Peterson) James Madison: Defender of the American Republic, 2009. CO-AUTHOR: Becoming Informed Citizens: Lessons on the Constitution for Junior High School Students, 1988; Invitation to the Dance: An Introduction to Social Dance, 1991; Becoming Informed Citizens: Lessons on the Bill of Rights and Limited Government, 1994; Controversial Presidential Elections, 2001; The Federalists & Anti-Federalists, 2001. EDITOR: (co-ed.) The Papers of James Madison, 3 vols., 1962-64; (co-ed.) The Continuing Dialogue, 2 vols., 1964-65; Union and Liberty: A Documentary History of American Constitutionalism, 1969; The Federalist and Anti-Federalist Papers, 1998. **Address:** Department of History, California State University, Los Angeles, CA 90032, U.S.A. **Online address:** ddewey@calstatela.edu

DEWEY, Joseph (Owen). American (born United States), b. 1957. **Genres:** Literary Criticism And History, Adult Non-fiction, Novels. **Career:** University of Pittsburgh, Humanities Division, assistant professor, 1987-91, associate professor of American literature, 1991-. Writer. **Publications:** In a Dark Time: The Apocalyptic Temper in the American Novel of the Nuclear Age, 1990; Novels from Reagan's America: A New Realism, 1999; Understanding Richard Powers, 2002; Beyond Grief and Nothing: A Reading of Don DeLillo, 2006. EDITOR: (with B. Horvath) The Finer Thread, The Tighter Weave: Essays on the Short Fiction of Henry James, 2001; (with S.G. Kellman and I. Malin) Underwords: Perspectives on Don DeLillo's Underworld, 2002; The Catcher in the Rye, by J.D. Salinger, 2012. Contributor of articles to books and periodicals. **Address:** Department of English, University of Pittsburgh, 234 Biddle Hall, 450 Schoolhouse Rd., Johnstown, PA 15904-2912, U.S.A. **Online address:** dewey@pitt.edu

DEWEY, Scott Hamilton. American (born United States), b. 1968. **Genres:** Novels, Politics/Government, Technology, Science Fiction/Fantasy, Social Commentary. **Career:** Rice University, lecturer, 1989-96; California State University, adjunct professor, 1994-2000; Chambers of Judge Manella, judicial extern, 2002. Writer. **Publications:** Don't Breathe the Air: Air Pollution and U.S. Environmental Politics, 1945-1970, 2000; Irreconcilable Differences, forthcoming. Contributor to periodicals. **Address:** Texas A&M University Press, 4354 TAMU, John H. Lindsey Bldg., Lewis St., College Station, TX 91011-3961, U.S.A. **Online address:** dewey@2003.law.ucla.edu

DEWHIRST, Ian. British (born England), b. 1936. **Genres:** Poetry, History, Novellas/Short Stories. **Career:** Keighley Public Library, library assistant, 1960-65, lending librarian, 1965-67, reference librarian, 1967-91; Library Association, associate; Keighley Civic Society, vice chairman, 1977-. Writer. **Publications:** The Handloom Weaver and Other Poems, 1965; The Haworth Water-Wolf, and Other Yorkshire Stories, 1967; Scar Top, and Other Po-

ems, 1968; Gleanings from Victorian Yorkshire, 1972; More Old Keighley as It Was, 1973; A History of Keighley, 1974; Yorkshire Through the Years, 1975; Gleanings from Edwardian Yorkshire, 1975; The Story of a Nobody: A Working-Class Life, 1890-1939, 1980; You Don't Remember Bananas, 1985; Keighley in Old Picture Postcards, 1987; Keighley in the 1930s and 1940s, 1989; Victorian Keighley Characters, 1990; In the Reign of the Peacemaker, 1993; Down Memory Lane, 1993; Images of Keighley, 1996. EDITOR: A Poet Passed...Poems by Alfred Holdsworth, 1968; A Century of Yorkshire Dialect, 1997. COMPILER: Old Keighley in Photographs, 1972; More Old Keighley in Photographs, 1973. **Address:** Keighley Public Library, North St., Keighley, WY BD21 3SX, England.

DEWHURST, Eileen (Mary). British (born England), b. 1929. **Genres:** Mystery/Crime/Suspense, Novels, Literary Criticism And History. **Career:** London University, administrator, 1953-64; Liverpool University, administrator, 1953-64; freelance journalist, 1964-80. **Publications:** Death Came Smiling, 1975; After the Ball, 1976, 2nd ed., 1989; Curtain Fall, 1977, 3rd ed., 1983; Drink This, 1981; Trio in Three Flats, 1981; Whoever I Am, 1982; The House that Jack Built, 1983; There Was a Little Girl, 1984; Playing Safe, 1985; A Private Prosecution, 1986; Nice Little Business, 1987; The Sleeper, 1988; Dear Mr. Right, 1990; The Innocence of Guilt, 1991; Death in Candie Gardens, 1992; Now You See Her, 1995; The Verdict on Winter, 1996; Alias the Enemy, 1997; Roundabout, 1998; Death of a Stranger, 1999; Double Act, 2000; Closing Stages, 2001; No Love Lost, 2001; Easeful Death, 2003; Naked Witness, 2003. Contributor to periodicals. **Address:** Gregory & Co., 3 Barb Mews, Hammersmith, GL W6 7PA, England.

DEWILDE, Dennis M. American (born United States), b. 1950. **Genres:** Business/Trade/Industry. **Career:** American Electric Power, vice president for planning and engineering, 1972-84; Old Ben Coal Co., vice-president for engineering, 1984-85; Standard Oil of Ohio, corporate controller, 1985-88; British Petroleum, vice president and general manager, 1988-95; American School of Aberdeen, board director, 1992-94; ISP Associates Inc., principal, 1995-. **Publications:** (With G. Anderson) The Performance Connection, 2006. Contributor to periodicals. **Address:** ISP Associates Inc., 916 Elywood Dr., Elyria, OH 44035-3601, U.S.A. **Online address:** dennis@theperformanceconnection.org

DEWITT, Calvin B. American (born United States), b. 1935?. **Genres:** Environmental Sciences/Ecology, Ethics, Theology/Religion, Natural History, Zoology, Environmental Sciences/Ecology. **Career:** University of Michigan, assistant professor, 1963-66, associate professor, 1966-69, professor of biology, 1969-71; University of Wisconsin, honorary fellow in zoology, 1970, professor of environmental studies, 1972-; Au Sable Institute, director, 1980-2004, president, 2004-05; University of Wisconsin, Nelson Institute for Environmental Studies, professor; International Evangelical Environmental Network, co-founder; Academy of Evangelical Scientists and Ethicists, president; American Society of the Green Cross, chair. Writer. **Publications:** (Ed. with E. Soloway) Wetlands, Ecology, Values, and Impacts, 1977; (with R.M. Friedman and T.K. Kratz) Simulating Postglacial Wetland Formation, 1979; (with R.M. Friedman and T.K. Kratz) A Spatial Simulation Model of Lake-Edge Wetland Formation, 1979; The Environment and the Christian, 1991; (co-author) Earthkeeping in the Nineties, 1991; (with G.T. Prance) Missionary Earthkeeping, 1992; Caring for Creation: Responsible Stewardship of God's Handiwork, 1998; Earth-Wise: A Biblical Response to Environmental Issues, 1994, 3rd ed., 2011. **Address:** Nelson Institute for Environmental Studies, University of Wisconsin, 550 N Park St., Madison, WI 53706-1404, U.S.A. **Online address:** cbdewitt@wisc.edu

DEWITT, Helen. German/American (born United States), b. 1957?. **Genres:** Novels. **Career:** Writer. **Publications:** The Last Samurai, 2000; (with I. Gridneff) Your Name Here, 2007; Lightning Rods, 2011. **Address:** c/o Author Mail, Hyperion, 114 5th Ave., New York, NY 10011, U.S.A. **Online address:** helen.dewitt@gmx.net

DEWITT, Patrick. American/Canadian (born Canada), b. 1975. **Genres:** Novels, Literary Criticism And History, Humor/Satire. **Career:** Writer. **Publications:** Help Yourself Help Yourself (nonfiction), 2007; Ablutions: Notes for a Novel (novel), 2009; Sisters Brothers, 2011. **Address:** Foundry Literary & Media, 33 W 17th St., New York, NY 10011, U.S.A. **Online address:** info@patrickdewitt.net

DEXTER, N. C. *See* **DEXTER, (Norman) Colin.**

DEXTER, (Norman) Colin. (N. C. Dexter). British (born England), b. 1930. **Genres:** Mystery/Crime/Suspense, Sports/Fitness. **Career:** Wyggeston School, assistant classics master, 1954-57; Loughborough Grammar School, sixth form classics master, 1957-59; Corby Grammar School, senior classics master, 1959-66; Oxford Local Examination Board, assistant secretary, 1966-76, senior assistant secretary, 1976-87; University of Oxford, Delegacy of Local Examinations, senior assistant secretary, 1966-88, retired, 1988; writer, 1973-. **Publications:** (As N.C. Dexter with E.G. Rayner) Liberal Studies: An Outline Course, 1964; (as N.C. Dexter with E.G. Rayner) Guide to Contemporary Politics, 1966; Last Bus to Woodstock, 1975; Last Seen Wearing, 1976; The Silent World of Nicholas Quinn, 1977; Service of All the Dead, 1979; The Dead of Jericho, 1981; The Riddle of the Third Mile, 1983; The Secret of Annexe 3, 1986; The Wench is Dead, 1989; The Jewel That was Ours, 1991; The Way through the Woods, 1992; Morse's Greatest Mystery, 1993; The Daughters of Cain, 1994; Death is Now My Neighbour, 1996; The Remorseful Day, 1999; Silent World of Nicholas Quinn, 2005; Cracking Cryptic Crosswords, 2009. **Address:** 456 Banbury Rd., Oxford, OX OX2 7RG, England.

DEXTER, Pete. American (born United States), b. 1943. **Genres:** Novels, Plays/Screenplays, Young Adult Non-fiction, Essays, Reference, Literary Criticism And History. **Career:** West Palm Beach Post, reporter, 1971-72; Philadelphia Daily News, columnist, 1972-84; Sacramento Bee, columnist, 1985-; Seattle Post-Intelligencer, columnist. Screenwriter and journalist. **Publications:** NOVELS: God's Pocket, 1983; Deadwood, 1986; Paris Trout, 1988; Brotherly Love, 1991; The Paperboy, 1995; Train, 2003; Paper Trails: True Stories of Confusion, Mindless Violence and Forbidden Desires, A Surprising Number of Which Are Not About Marriage, 2007; Spooner, 2009. Contributor to periodicals. **Address:** c/o Esther Newberg, International Creative Management, 40 W 57th St., New York, NY 10019-4001, U.S.A.

DEXTER, Ross. *See* STOKOE, E(dward) G(eorge).

DE ZEGHER, M. Catherine. Dutch (born Netherlands), b. 1955. **Genres:** History, Art/Art History. **Career:** Kanaal Art Foundation, curator, co-founder, 1985, director, 1987-; Institute of Contemporary Art, visiting curator, 1995-97; October Books, executive editor, 1997; The Drawing Center, director, 2000-08, chief curator; University of Leeds, lecturer; Royal College of Art, lecturer; University of London, lecturer; Art Gallery of Ontario, director, 2008-. Writer. **Publications:** Inside the Visible: An Elliptical Traverse of Twentieth Century Art, in, of and from the Feminine, 1996; The Precarious: Art and Poery of Cecilia Vicuna and Quipoem, 1997; (with M. Archer and G. Brett) Mona Hatoum, 1997; Martha Rosler: Rights of Passage, 1997; (ed.) Martha Rosler: Positions in the Life World, 1998; (ed.) Between Street and Mirror: The Drawings of James Ensor, 2001; (with M. Wigley) The Activist Drawing: Retracing Situationist Architectures from Constant's New Babylon to Beyond, 2001; (ed. with C. Armstrong) Ocean Flowers: Impressions from Nature, 2004; (co-ed.) 3 X Abstraction: New Methods Of Drawing, 2005; (ed. with C. Armstrong) Women Artists at the Millennium, 2006; (ed.) Eva Hesse Drawing, 2006; Julie Mehretu: Drawings, 2007; Angelika Hoerle, 2009; (with C. Butler) On Line: Drawing Through The Twentieth Century, 2010. Contributor to books. **Address:** Kanaal Art Foundation, Pottelberg 73A, Kortrijk, 8500, Belgium.

DHAMI, Narinder. British (born England), b. 1958. **Genres:** Children's Fiction. **Career:** Teacher, 1980-90; full-time writer, 1990-. **Publications:** (With K. Rogers) A Medal for Malina, 1990; (with J. Park) Cat's Eyes, 1993; Angel Face, 1995; My Secret Love, 1995; The Hero, 1996; The Sun of the Sea, 1996; Starring Alice Mackenzie, 1996; Me and My Big Mouth, 1996; Oh Brother!, 1998; Spotlight on Sunita, 1998; The Cool Rule, 1998; (adapter) The Case of the Disappearing Dragon (screenplay novelization), 1998; Who's Who?, 1998; Annie's Game, 1998; It's Not Fair, 2000; Animal Crackers, 2000; Genius Games, 2001; (adapter) Charles Dickens, Christmas Carol: The Movie, 2001; (adapter) Gurinder Chadha, Guljit Bindra and Paul Mayeda Berges, Bend It Like Beckham (screenplay novelization), 2002; Changing Places, 2002; (adapter) Cinderella, 2003; (adapter) Disney's The Lion King, 2003; (adapter) Disney's The Jungle Book, 2003; (adapter) Disney's The Aristocats, 2003; (adapter) Disney's Lady and the Tramp, 2003; (adapter) Sleeping Beauty, 2003; Bindi Babes, 2004; The Barber's Clever Wife, 2004; Bollywood Babes, 2005; Bhangra Babes, 2005; Sunita's Secret, 2006; Grow Up, Dad!, 2007; Outcast, 2007; Dani's Diary, 2007; Superstar Babes, 2008; Lauren's Best Friend, 2009; Bang Bang You're Dead, 2009; Hannah's Secret, 2009; Team Jasmin; 2010; Golden Girl Grace, 2010; Georgie's War, 2010;

A Tiger for Breakfast, 2011; Flora to the Rescue, 2011; Olly the Octopus, 2011; Katy's Real Life, 2011. SLEEPOVER CLUB SERIES: Starring the Sleepover Club, 1997; The Sleepover Club Sleeps Out, 1997; Sleepover in Spain, 1998; Sleepover Girls and Friends, 1999; Sleepover Girls Go Designer, 1999; Vive le Sleepover Club!, 2000; Sari Sleepover, 2000; Sleepover Club Down Under, 2000; Sleepover Girls Go Karting, 2001; Sleepoverclub.com, 2001; Sleepover Girls on the Ball, 2001. Contributor to journals. **Address:** Rosemary Canter, PFD, Drury House, 34-43 Russell St., London, GL WC2B 5HA, England.

DHAVAMONY, Mariasusai. Italian/Indian (born India), b. 1925. **Genres:** Philosophy, Theology/Religion. **Career:** Sacred Heart College, assistant professor of philosophy, 1962-64; Gregorian University, associate professor, professor of history of religions and Hinduism, 1966-, dean of faculty of missiology, 1975-, now emeritus; Studia Missionalia periodical, chief editor; Vatican Secretariate for Non-Christian Religions, consultant. **Publications:** Subjectivity and Knowledge according to St. Thomas Aquinas, 1965; Love of God according to Saiva Sidhanta, 1971; (with C. Papali and P. Fallon) For Dialogue with Hinduism, 1972; Phenomenology of Religion, 1973; Classical Hinduism, 1982; La luce di Dio nell'Induismo, 1987; L'Induismo, 1991; (co-author) Le grandi figure dell'Induismo, 1992; L'Hindouisme et Foi Chretienne, 1995; Christian Theology of World Religions, 1997, 3rd ed., 2002; Teologia delle religioni, 1997; Christian Theology of Inculturation, 1997; La Spiritualité Hindoue, 1997, trans. as Hindu Spirituality, 1999; La teologia de las religiones, 1998; Pluralismo Religioso e Missione della Chiesa, 2001; Madre Teresa, 2002; Ecumenical Theology of World Religions, 2003; The Kingdom of God and World Religions, 2004; World Religions in the History of Salvation, 2004; Jesus Christ in the Understanding of World Religions, 2004; Il Dialogo indu-cristiano e Missione della Chiesa, 2004; Hindu-Christian Dialogue: Theological Soundings and Perspectives, 2009. EDITOR: Evangelization, Dialogue and Development, 1972; Evangelisation, 1975; (co-ed.) Buddhism and Christianity, 1979; Prospettive di Missiologia oggi, 1982; La meditazione nelle grandi religioni, 1989; Teologia Cristiana delle religioni e della Missione Ad Gentes, 2002. Contributor to books and periodicals. **Address:** Gregorian University, Piazza della Pilotta 4, Rome, 00187, Italy. **Online address:** dhavamony@unigre.it

DI, Zhu Xiao. American/Chinese (born China), b. 1958. **Genres:** Autobiography/Memoirs, Education, Reference. **Career:** Jiangsu Education College, assistant professor of English, supervisor of field education, liaison officer and interpreter, 1982-87; Harvard University, Fairbank Center for East Asian Research, research assistant, 1987-89, Joint Center for Housing Studies, research associate, 1997-, senior research analyst; Cognetics Inc., research assistant, 1989-90; Management Strategies Inc., assistant, 1991-92; University of Massachusetts, Center for Survey Research, assistant study director, 1992-93, senior assistant director, 1993-97; Arthur Andersen & Co., management consultant, 1995-96. Writer. **Publications:** (With J.M. Chen) English-Speaking Nations (textbook), 1984; Thirty Years in a Red House: A Memoir of Childhood and Youth in Communist China, 1998; (contrib.) Father: Famous Writers Celebrate the Bond Between Father and Child, 2000; Tales of Judge Dee, 2006; Leisure Thoughts on Idle Books, 2009. Contributor to journals and periodicals. **Address:** Joint Center for Housing Studies, Harvard University, 1033 Massachusetts Ave., 5th Fl., Cambridge, MA 02138-5366, U.S.A. **Online address:** zhu_xiao_di@harvard.edu

DIAL-DRIVER, Emily. American (born United States), b. 1946. **Genres:** Education, Writing/Journalism, Plays/Screenplays, Art/Art History. **Career:** Ohio State University, Children's Hospital Research Foundation, dietary interviewer, 1968-69; Rogers State University, School of Liberal Arts, Department of English and Humanities, instructor, 1971-74, professor, 1980-, ACHIEVE Program, coordinator, 1996-99; Oklahoma State University, OSU Writing Project, teacher consultant. Writer. **Publications:** EDITOR: (and intro.) Maggie Fry, The Cherokee Female Seminary Years: A Cherokee National Anthology, 1990; (with S. Emmons and J. Ford) Fantasy Media in the Classroom: Essays on Teaching with Film, Television, Literature, Graphic Novels, and Video Games, 2012. OTHERS: Composition II: Multiple Learning Opportunities, 1989; Write Right, 1993; College Writing: Discovering the Writing Spiral, 1994; A Guide to College Writing, 1996, 11th ed., 2009; September-June, May-December: What It Means I Can't Remember, forthcoming. EDITOR AND CONTRIBUTOR: The Competitive Edge II, 1992; The Truth of Buffy: Essays on Fiction Illuminating Reality; Voices from the Heartland, 2007. Contributor of articles to periodicals. **Address:** Department of English and Humanities, School of Liberal Arts, Rogers State University,

Rm. 215, Baird Hall, 1701 W Will Rogers Blvd., Claremore, OK 74017, U.S.A. **Online address:** edial-driver@rsu.edu

DIALLO, Kadiatou. American/Guyanese (born Guyana), b. 1959. **Genres:** Autobiography/Memoirs, Biography, Social Sciences. **Career:** Amadou Diallo Foundation, founder. Writer. **Publications:** (With C. Wolff) My Heart Will Cross This Ocean: My Story, My Son, Amadou, 2003. Contributor to periodicals. **Address:** c/o Author Mail, Random House Inc., 1745 Broadway, New York, NY 10019-4368, U.S.A.

DIAMANT, Anita. American (born United States), b. 1951. **Genres:** Novels, How-to Books, Essays, Theology/Religion, Human Relations/Parenting, Reference, Literary Criticism And History, Young Adult Fiction, Young Adult Fiction. **Career:** Writer, 1975-; Equal Times, editor, 1977-78; Boston Phoenix, columnist and staff writer, 1980-83; New England Monthly, contributing editor, 1984-86; Boston, senior staff writer, 1986-88; Boston Globe magazine, columnist, 1988-94, Parenting, columnist, 1993-95. **Publications:** The New Jewish Wedding, 1985, rev. ed., 2001; The Jewish Baby Book, 1988; What to Name Your Jewish Baby, 1989; (with H. Cooper) Living a Jewish Life: A Guide for Starting, Learning, Celebrating and Parenting, 1991; New Jewish Baby Book: Names, Ceremonies, Customs-A Guide for Today's Families, 1994, 2nd. ed., 2005; Bible Baby Names: Spiritual Choices from Judeo-Christian Tradition, 1996; (with H. Cooper) Living a Jewish Life: Jewish Traditions, Customs, and Values for Today's Families, 1996, rev. ed., 2007; Choosing a Jewish Life: A Handbook for People Converting to Judaism and for Their Family and Friends, 1997; Saying Kaddish: How to Comfort the Dying, Bury the Dead and Mourn as a Jew 1998; (with K. Kushner) How to Be a Jewish Parent, 2000; Pitching My Tent: On Marriage, Motherhood, Friendship and Other Leaps of Faith (essays), 2003; (with K. Kushner) How to Raise a Jewish Child: A Practical Handbook for Family Life, 2008. NOVELS: The Red Tent, 1997; Good Harbor, 2001; The Last Days of Dogtown, 2005; Day After Night, 2009. Contributor to periodicals. **Address:** c/o Amanda Urban, ICM Agency, 825 8th Ave., New York, NY 10019, U.S.A. **Online address:** anitaweb@aol.com

DIAMOND, Arthur. American (born United States), b. 1957. **Genres:** Children's Non-fiction, Biography, History, Autobiography/Memoirs, Sports/Fitness, Cultural/Ethnic Topics, Social Sciences. **Career:** St. John's University, adjunct professor of English, 1990-91. Writer. **Publications:** The Romanian Americans, 1988; Paul Cuffe, 1989; The Bhopal Chemical Leak, 1990; Smallpox and the American Indian, 1991; Alcoholism, 1992; Jackie Robinson, 1992; Egypt: Gift of the Nile, 1992; Prince Hall: Social Reformer, 1992; Malcolm X: A Voice for Black America, 1994; Anwar Sadat, 1994; Charlie Chaplin, 1995; Muhammad Ali, 1995. **Address:** 80-17 209th St., Queens Village, NY 11427, U.S.A. **Online address:** aidiamondfamily@aol.com

DIAMOND, Hanna Elizabeth. British (born England), b. 1962. **Genres:** Women's Studies And Issues, History, Politics/Government. **Career:** University of Bath, faculty, 1993-, senior lecturer in French history, reader in French history and European studies and deputy head, Center for Women's Studies, director. Writer. **Publications:** Women and the Second World War in France, 1939-1948: Choices and Constraints, 1999; (ed. with A. Bull and R. Marsh) Feminisms and Women's Movements in Contemporary Europe, 2000; (ed. with S. Kitson) Vichy, Resistance, Liberation: New Perspectives on Wartime France, 2005; Fleeing Hitler: France 1940, 2007. **Address:** Department of Politics, Languages & International, Studies, University of Bath, 1 NW 4.2, Bath, SM BA2 7AY, England. **Online address:** h.e.diamond@bath.ac.uk

DIAMOND, Jared (Mason). American (born United States), b. 1937. **Genres:** Environmental Sciences/Ecology, Geography, Sciences, Adult Non-fiction. **Career:** Trinity College, Cambridge, fellow in physiology, 1961-65; Harvard University, Society of Fellows, junior fellow, 1962-65, Harvard Medical School, associate in biophysics, 1965-66; University of California, David Geffen School of Medicine, associate professor of physiology, 1966-68, professor of physiology, 1968-, professor of geography; American Museum of Natural History, Department of Ornithology, research associate, 1973-; Los Angeles County Museum of Natural History, research associate, 1985-. Writer, physiologist, ecologist and geographer. **Publications:** NONFICTION: Avifauna of the Eastern Highlands of New Guinea, 1972; (with M. Lecroy) Birds of Karkar and Bagabag Islands, New Guinea, 1979; The Third Chimpanzee: The Evolution and Future of the Human Animal in UK as The Rise and Fall of the Third Chimpanzee, 1992; Why Is Sex Fun? The Evolution of Human Sexuality, 1997; Guns, Germs and Steel: The Fates of

Human Societies, 1997; (with E. Mayr) The Birds of Northern Melanesia: Speciation, Ecology & Biogeography, 2001; Why Did Human History Unfold Differently on Different Continents for the Last 13, 000 Years?, 2001; Collapse: How Societies Choose to Fail or Succeed, 2005. EDITOR: (with M.L. Cody) Ecology and Evolution of Communities, 1975; (with T.J. Case) Community Ecology, 1986; (with J. Brockman) What are You Optimistic About?: Today's Leading Thinkers on Why Things are Good and Getting Better, 2007; (with J.A. Robinson) Natural Experiments of History, 2010. Contributor to magazines. **Address:** Department of Geography, University of California, 1255 Bunche Hall, Los Angeles, CA 90095-1524, U.S.A. **Online address:** jdiamond@geog.ucla.edu

DIAMOND, Jed. American (born United States), b. 1943?. **Genres:** Psychology, Sciences, Human Relations/Parenting. **Career:** University of California, faculty; John F. Kennedy University, faculty; Esalen Institute, faculty; The Omega Institute, faculty; MenAlive, Health Program, director; Men's Health Network, advisor. Writer. **Publications:** Looking for Love in All the Wrong Places: Romantic and Sexual Addictions, 1988; The Warrior's Journey Home: Healing Men, Healing Planet, 1994; Male Menopause, 1997; Surviving Male Menopause: A Guide for Women and Men, 2000; The Whole Man Program: Reinvigorating Your Body and Spirit after Forty, 2002; The Irritable Male Syndrome: Managing the 4 Key Causes of Depression & Aggression, 2004; Mr. Mean: Saving Your Relationship from the Irritable Male Syndrome, 2010; Male Depression: The Hidden World-Wide Epidemic, forthcoming; The Future of Men: Decline and Fall or Growth and Transformation, forthcoming. **Address:** 34133 Shimmins Ridge Rd., Willits, CA 95490, U.S.A. **Online address:** jed@menalive.com

DIAMOND, Petra. See SACHS, Judith.

DIAMOND, Raymond T. American (born United States), b. 1952?. **Genres:** Law. **Career:** Office of Robert Livingston, legislative counsel, 1977-78; Federal Trade Commission, Bureau of Competition, staff attorney, 1978-81; Jefferson, Bryan & Gray P.C., associate, 1981-84; Louisiana State University, Paul M. Hebert Law Center, assistant professor, 1984-89, associate professor, 1989-90, Jules F. and Frances L. Landry distinguished professor of law, 2008-; Tulane University, Law School, associate professor, 1990-92, professor, 1992-2009, C.J. Morrow Research professor, 2003-04, John Koerner professor of law, 2005-09, adjunct professor of African diaspora studies, 1993-2009. Writer. **Publications:** (With R.J. Cottrol and L.B. Ware) Brown v. Board of Education: Caste, Culture, and the Constitution, 2003. **Address:** Paul M. Hebert Law Center, Louisiana State University, Rm. 440, 1 E Campus Dr., Baton Rouge, LA 70803-1000, U.S.A. **Online address:** ray.diamond@law.lsu.edu

DIAMOND, Rickey Gard. American (born United States), b. 1946. **Genres:** Novels, Novellas/Short Stories, Environmental Sciences/Ecology, Women's Studies And Issues, Essays. **Career:** Central Vermont Community Action Council, director of communications, 1981-85; Community College of Vermont, instructor, 1984, 1985; Vermont Children's Forum, board director, 1984; Vermont Woman Publishing, founding editor, 1985-88, contributing editor; Washington County Parent-Child Center, board director, 1986-87; Johnson State College, tutorial instructor, 1987, instructor, 1993; Central Vermont Community Action Council, director of development, 1988-93; Norwich University, Vermont College Campus, part-time adjunct faculty, 1990-95, visiting professor, 1990-95; assistant professor of liberal studies, 1995-2001, Central Vermont Community Action, director of development, 1998-95; Union Institute and University, professor, 2001-, Vermont Academic Center, faculty chair, 2008-; Multicultural Media (music distributors and producers), co-owner. **Publications:** Vermont Odysseys: Essays on the New Vermont, 1991; Second Sight (novel), 1997. Contributor to periodicals. **Address:** Vermont Woman Publishing, 307 Rte. 2, PO Box 490, South Hero, VT 05486, U.S.A. **Online address:** rickey.diamond@myunion.edu

DIAMOND, Sara. American (born United States), b. 1958?. **Genres:** Politics/Government. **Career:** Banff New Media Institute, curator, Media and Visual Arts, artistic director; University of California, adjunct professor; Z Magazine, columnist; JFK University School of Law, faculty of sociology and journalism. Writer. **Publications:** Spiritual Warfare: The Politics of the Christian Right, 1989; Roads to Dominion: Right-Wing Movements and Political Power in the United States, 1995; Facing the Wrath: Confronting the Right in Dangerous Times, 1996; Not by Politics Alone: The Enduring Influence of the Christian Right, 1998. **Address:** 1936 University Ave., Ste. 380, Berkeley, CA 94704, U.S.A. **Online address:** sara@saradiamondattorney.com

DIANE, Nana. *See* **KAIMANN, Diane S.**

DIAZ, Tony. American (born United States), b. 1968?. **Genres:** Novels. **Career:** Central American Resource Center, assistant director; Houston Immigration and Refugee Coalition, coordinator, 2000; University of Houston, faculty; Inprint Houston, staff; St. Charles Church, staff; High School for the Performing and Visual Arts, staff; Chicano Family Center, staff; Houston Community College-Central, English professor; Kansas State University, faculty; Rice University, faculty. Writer. **Publications:** The Aztec Love God (novel), 1998; (ed.) Latino Heretics, 1999. Contributor to anthologies and periodicals. **Address:** Red Lat Writings, PO Box 540181, Houston, TX 77245, U.S.A. **Online address:** tony.diaz@hccs.edu

DÍAZ-STEVENS, Ana María. American/Puerto Rican (born Puerto Rico), b. 1942. **Genres:** Cultural/Ethnic Topics, Theology/Religion, Social Sciences, Anthropology/Ethnology. **Career:** New York Catholic Archdiocese, administrative coordinator of Spanish speaking apostolate, 1969-72; Centro de Evangelizacion, Ministerioe Investigacion, co-founder, editor and investigator, 1974-78; City University of New York, Queens College, adjunct assistant professor of modern languages, sociology and Puerto Rican studies, 1978-86; Aspira of America Inc., editor and public relations specialist, 1981-83; Fordham University, assistant professor of social science, 1986-87; Rutgers University, assistant professor of Puerto Rican and Hispanic studies, 1989-93; Union Theological Seminary, associate professor of church and society, 1993-; Program for the Analysis of Religion Among Latinos, co-founder; Macmillan Encyclopedia of Contemporary Religion, associate editor. **Publications:** Oxcart Catholicism on Fifth Avenue: The Impact of the Puerto Rican Migration Upon the Archdiocese of New York, 1993; The Religious Experience of Latinos in the United States: An Interdisciplinary Perspective, 1994; (with A.M. Stevens-Arroyo) An Enduring Flame: Popular Religiosity of Latinos, 1994; (with A.M. Stevens-Arroyo) Recognizing the Latino Resurgence in U.S. Religion: The Emmaus Paradigm, 1998; Devocionario de Nuestra Señora de la Altagracia, forthcoming; Descripción de la Isla de San Juan Bautista, forthcoming. Contributor to books and journals. **Address:** Union Theological Seminary, AD 418, 3041 Broadway, 121st St., New York, NY 10027, U.S.A. **Online address:** dstevens@uts.columbia.edu

DIBARTOLOMEO, Albert. American (born United States), b. 1952. **Genres:** Novels. **Career:** Philadelphia School Board, library assistant, 1975-80; self-employed cabinetmaker, 1980-89; Temple University, instructor, 1986-88; Delaware County Community College, instructor, 1990; Community College of Philadelphia, instructor in creative writing and expository writing, 1990; Drexel University, adjunct assistant professor of English, 1990-95, auxiliary faculty, instructor of English, 1996-, professor of English, ASK Journal, editor-in-chief; Philadelphia College of Pharmacy and Science, adjunct faculty, instructor of English, 1994-96; University of Pennsylvania, visiting lecturer creative writing, 1995-; Drexel Publishing Group, co-director; Drexel Online journal, editor. **Publications:** The Vespers Tapes: A Novel, 1991; Blood Confessions, 1992; Fool's Gold, 1993. Contributor of stories. **Address:** Department of English and Philosophy, Drexel University, Rm. 5026, MacAlister Hall, 3141 Chestnut St., Philadelphia, PA 19104, U.S.A. **Online address:** dibartoa@drexel.edu

DIBBELL, Julian. American (born United States), b. 1963. **Genres:** Communications/Media, Information Science/Computers, Money/Finance, Technology, Autobiography/Memoirs, Anthropology/Ethnology, Writing/Journalism, Economics, Economics. **Career:** Nadine, co-founder and co-editor, 1985-86; Freelance journalist, 1986-; Newsweek, freelance editor and copyeditor, 1988-; Village Voice, assistant editor, 1988-96, columnist, 1992-96; Time, contributing writer on technology, 1995-97; Harper, proofreader, 1997; Stanford Law School, Center for Internet and Society, fellow, 2003; Wired, contributing editor, 2004-; University of Oklahoma, Leadership Enrichment Program, teacher, 2009. **Publications:** My Tiny Life: Crime and Passion in a Virtual World, 1998; Play Money: Or How I Quit My Day Job and Made Millions Trading Virtual Loot, 2006; The Best Technology Writing 2010, 2010. Contributor to periodicals. **Address:** 1309 E 50th St., Chicago, IL 60615, U.S.A. **Online address:** julian@juliandibbell.com

DIBBERN, Mary. American (born United States), b. 1951. **Genres:** Music, Translations. **Career:** University of Miami, faculty; Lotte Lehmann Foun-

dation, advisor; University of Nevada, artist-in-residence; Nadia and Lili Boulanger Foundation, fellow, 1985. Vocal coach, accompanist, pianist and author. **Publications:** Carmen: A Performance Guide, 2000; The Tales of Hoffmann: A Performance Guide, 2001; (with C. Kimball and P. Choukroun) Interpreting the Songs of Jacques Leguerney: A Guide for Study and Performance, 2001; Roméo et Juliette/Faust: A Performance Guide, 2006; Manon: A Performance Guide, 2011. **Address:** c/o Author Mail, Pendragon Press, 52 Whitehill Ln., PO Box 190, Hillsdale, NY 12529-0190, U.S.A. **Online address:** marydibbern@mac.com

DIBBLE, J(ames) Birney. American/Indian (born India), b. 1925. **Genres:** Novels, Travel/Exploration, Mystery/Crime/Suspense, Biography, Novellas/Short Stories, Poetry, Young Adult Fiction. **Career:** Cook County Hospital, resident in surgery, 1953-57; Luther Memorial Hospital, chief of surgery, 1970-72; Sacred Heart Hospital, chief of surgery, 1975-; Chippewa Valley Ethological Society, co-founder; WYNOT Alcoholic Rehabilitation Center, co-founder; Kiomboi Lutheran Mission Hospital, staff. Writer. **Publications:** In This Land of Eve, 1965; The Plains Brood Alone, 1973; Pan (fiction), 1980; Brain Child (fiction), 1987; Outlaw for God, 1992; The Taking of Hill 1052 (novel), 1995; The Same God? Comparing the Bible with the Koran, 2006. **Address:** W 4290 Jene Rd., Eau Claire, WI 54701, U.S.A. **Online address:** dibble@discover-net.net

DI BLASI, Debra. American (born United States), b. 1957. **Genres:** Novellas/Short Stories, Plays/Screenplays, Poetry, Novels, Illustrations, Young Adult Fiction. **Career:** Oppenheimer Industries, executive assistant, 1980-85; Robert Half of Northern California, advertising manager, 1986-89; MacWeek Magazine, advertising production manager, 1988-89; Accessible Arts Inc., assistant, 1990-92; Sprint Communications, Department of International Network Design and Engineering, senior secretary, 1992-95; Kansas City Art Institute, writing tutor, 1994, writing instructor, 1995-2003, learning specialist, 1995-2000, adjunct instructor, 1998-99; Jaded Ibis Productions, founder, owner, publisher, president, 2002-, publisher-in-chief, 2009-, Jaded Ibis Press, prose editor. **Publications:** Drought: Say What You Like (novellas), 1997; Prayers of an Accidental Nature (short stories), 1998; The Jirí Chronicles & Other Fictions, 2007; What the Body Requires, 2009; Skin of the Sun: New Writing, 2011. Contributor of articles to periodicals. **Address:** Jaded Ibis Productions, PO Box 61122, Seattle, WA 98141-6122, U.S.A. **Online address:** debra@debradiblasi.com

DIBUA, Jeremiah I. American/Nigerian (born Nigeria), b. 1956. **Genres:** Economics, Business/Trade/Industry, History, Politics/Government, International Relations/Current Affairs. **Career:** Morgan State University, Department of History and Geography, professor and graduate faculty. Writer and historian. **Publications:** Modernization and the Crisis of Development in Africa: The Nigerian Experience, 2006. Contributor to books, journals and periodicals. **Address:** Department of History and Geography, Morgan State University, 326-B Holmes Hall, 1700 E Cold Spring Ln., Baltimore, MD 21251-0001, U.S.A. **Online address:** jdibua@morgan.edu

DI CERTO, J(oseph) J(ohn). American (born United States), b. 1933. **Genres:** Novels, Children's Fiction, Communications/Media, Air/Space Topics, Social Commentary, History, Natural History. **Career:** Curtiss Wright Corp., senior technical writer, 1956-59; American Machine and Foundry, technical writer and editor, 1959-62; Sperry Gyroscope, publication engineer, 1962-66; Sylvania Electric Products, advertising supervisor, 1966-72; Al Paul Lefton Company Inc. (advertising agency), staff, 1972-73; Marstella Advertising Agency, staff, 1973-74; Sperry Rand Corp., manager of special projects, 1974-78; CBS-TV Stations, director of sales promotions, 1978-80; CBS Cable, director of communications, 1980-81; CBS Broadcast Intl., director of communications, 1981-. **Publications:** SELF-ILLUSTRATED: The Electric Wishing Well: The Solution to the Energy Crisis, 1976; From Earth to Infinity: A Guide to Space Travel, 1980; Star Voyage, 1981. OTHERS: Planning and Preparing Data Flow Diagrams, 1963; Missile Base beneath the Sea, 1967; Looking into TV, 1983; The Wall People: In Search of a Home, 1985, rev. ed., 2004; The Pony Express: Hoofbeats in the Wilderness, 1989; The Saga of the Pony Express, 2002. Contributor to magazines. **Address:** 1646 1st Ave., New York, NY 10028-4629, U.S.A.

DICHTL, John R. American (born United States), b. 1965?. **Genres:** History. **Career:** Indiana University-Purdue University Indianapolis, adjunct professor of history; National Council on Public History, executive director; Organization of American Historians, deputy executive director. Writer and historian. **Publications:** Frontiers of Faith: Bringing Catholicism to the West in the Early Republic, 2008. **Address:** Indiana University-Purdue University Indianapolis, 327 Cavanaugh Hall, Indianapolis, IN 46202, U.S.A. **Online address:** jdichtl@iupui.edu

DICK, Bernard F. American (born United States), b. 1935. **Genres:** Film, Literary Criticism And History, Biography. **Career:** Iona College, Classics Department, instructor, 1960-63, assistant professor of classics, 1963-67, associate professor of classics and chairman of department, 1967-70; Fairleigh Dickinson University, associate professor, 1970-73, professor of English and comparative literature, 1973-95, professor of communication and English, 1995-, School of Communication Arts, director, 1996-97; M.A. Program in Media and Professional Communication, coordinator, 2005-, Media Studies Program, co-director. Writer. **Publications:** William Golding, 1967, rev. ed., 1987; The Hellenism of Mary Renault, 1972; The Apostate Angel: A Critical Study of Gore Vidal, 1974; Anatomy of Film, 1978, 6th ed., 2010; Billy Wilder, 1980, rev. ed., 1996; (ed. with intro.) Dark Victory, 1981; Hellman in Hollywood, 1982; Joseph L. Mankiewicz, 1983; The Star-Spangled Screen, 1985, rev. ed., 1996; William Golding, 1987; Radical Innocence: A Critical Study of the Hollywood Ten, 1989; Columbia Pictures: Portrait of a Studio, 1992; The Merchant Prince of Poverty Row: Harry Cohn of Columbia Pictures, 1993; City of Dreams: The Making and Remaking of Universal Pictures, 1997; Engulfed: The Death of Paramount Pictures and the Birth of Corporate Hollywood, 2001; Hal Wallis: Producer to the Stars, 2004; Forever Mame: The Life of Rosalind Russell, 2006; Claudette Colbert: She Walked in Beauty, 2008; Hollywood Madonna: Loretta Young, 2011. Contributor of articles to periodicals. **Address:** School of Art & Media Studies, Fairleigh Dickinson University, Rm. R-22, Robison Hall, 285 Madison Ave., Madison, NJ 07940, U.S.A. **Online address:** bfdick@fdu.edu

DICKASON, Christie. British/American (born United States), b. 1942?. **Genres:** Novels, Poetry, Young Adult Non-fiction. **Career:** Royal Shakespeare Co., choreographer. Writer, director, composer and educator. **Publications:** Experience and Experiment: New Theatre Workshops, 1979-1982 (nonfiction), 1987; The Balancing Dance (poems), 2006. HISTORICAL NOVELS: The Dragon Riders, 1986; Indochine, 1987 in UK as The Tears of the Tiger, 1990; The Firemaster's Mistress, 2005; The Principessa, 2007; The King's Daughter, 2010. LADY TREE TRILOGY: HISTORICAL FICTION: The Lady Tree, 1993; Quicksilver, 1999; The Memory Palace, 2003. Contributor to newspapers and periodicals. **Address:** c/o Richard Kirby, United Agents, 12-26 Lexington St., London, GL W1F 0LE, England.

DICKE, Thomas S(cott). American (born United States), b. 1955. **Genres:** History, Economics, Business/Trade/Industry, Reference. **Career:** High school teacher of history, geography and American government, 1979-81; Ohio State University, instructor, 1987-88, lecturer, 1988-89; University of Georgia, temporary assistant professor, 1989-90; Southwest Missouri State University, Department of History, assistant professor, 1990-93, associate professor of history, 1993, professor, acting department head. Writer. **Publications:** Franchising in America: The Development of a Business Method, 1840-1980, 1992. Contributor of articles to journals. **Address:** Department of History, Southwest Missouri State University, 423 Strong Hall, 901 S National Ave., Springfield, MO 65897, U.S.A. **Online address:** tomdicke@missouristate.edu

DICKERSON, Dennis C. American (born United States), b. 1949. **Genres:** History. **Career:** Williams College, Stanfield professor of history and head of department, 1976-99, Department of History, chairman, Afro-American Studies Program, chairman; African Methodist Episcopal Church, historiographer, 1988-; Vanderbilt University, Department of History, professor, 1999-, James M. Lawson Jr. professor of history; A.M.E. Church Review, editor, 2000-; American Society of Church History, president, 2004; Rhodes College, faculty; Yale Divinity School, faculty; Payne Theological Seminary, faculty; Williamstown Savings Bank, corporator. Writer. **Publications:** Out of the Crucible: Black Steelworkers in Western Pennsylvania, 1875-1980, 1986; Religion, Race and Region: Research Notes on A.M.E. Church History, 1995; Militant Mediator: Whitney M. Young, Jr., 1998; A Liberated Past: Explorations in A.M.E. Church History, 2003; African Methodism and Its Wesleyan Heritage, 2009; African American Preachers and Politics: The Careys of Chicago, 2010; Protestant Preachers in the Public Square: The Careys of Chicago, forthcoming; Brother in the Spirit of Gandhi, forthcoming; A Short History of the African Methodist Episcopal Church, forthcoming. Work appears in anthologies. Contributor to journals and books. **Address:** Department of History, Vander-

bilt University, Benson 209, 2301 Vanderbilt Pl., PO Box 351802, Nashville, TN 37235-1802, U.S.A. **Online address:** dennis.c.dickerson@vanderbilt.edu

DICKERSON, Matthew. See **DICKERSON, Matthew T.**

DICKERSON, Matthew T. (Matthew Dickerson). American (born United States), b. 1963. **Genres:** Young Adult Non-fiction, Music, Science Fiction/Fantasy. **Career:** Middlebury College, professor. Writer. **Publications:** NONFICTION: The Finnsburg Encounter, 1991; (as Matthew Dickerson) Hammers & Nails: The Life and Music of Mark Heard, 2003; Following Gandalf: Epic Battles and Moral Victory in the Lord of the Rings, 2003; (as Matthew Dickerson with J. Evans) Ents, Elves, and Eriador: The Environmental Vision of J.R.R. Tolkien, 2006; (with D. O'Hara) From Homer to Harry Potter: A Handbook on Myth and Fantasy, 2006; (with D. O'Hara) Narnia and the Fields of Arbol: The Environmental Vision of C.S. Lewis, 2008. **Address:** Middlebury College, Middlebury, VT 05753, U.S.A. **Online address:** dickerso@middlebury.edu

DICKERSON, Vanessa D. American (born United States), b. 1955. **Genres:** Literary Criticism And History. **Career:** University of Virginia, faculty; Rhodes College, faculty; DePauw University, director of Black studies and professor of English. Writer. **Publications:** (Ed.) Keeping the Victorian House: A Collection of Essays, 1995; Victorian Ghosts in the Noontide: Women Writers and the Supernatural, 1996; (ed. with M. Bennett) Recovering the Black Female Body: Self-Representations by African American Women, 2001; Dark Victorians, 2008. **Address:** U.S.A. **Online address:** vdickerson@depauw.edu

DICKEY, Eric Jerome. American (born United States), b. 1961. **Genres:** Novels, Plays/Screenplays. **Career:** Rockwell (now Boeing), software developer and technical writer, 1983-92; Rowland Unified School District, educator, 1994-97. Writer. **Publications:** NOVELS: Sister, Sister, 1996; Friends and Lovers, 1997; Milk in My Coffee, 1998; Cheaters, 1999; Liars' Game, 2000; Cafe Noisette, 2000; Between Lovers 2001; La Grosse Triche, 2001; Petit mensonge deviendra grand, 2002; Thieves' Paradise, 2002; The Other Woman, 2003; Naughty or Nice, 2003; Drive Me Crazy, 2004; Genevieve, 2005; Chasing Destiny, 2006; Sleeping With Strangers, 2007; Waking With Enemies, 2007; Pleasure, 2008; Dying for Revenge, 2008; Resurrecting Midnight, 2009; Tempted By Trouble, 2010; An Accidental Affair, 2012. ANTHOLOGIES: River Crossings: Voices of the Diaspora, 1994; Mothers and Sons, 2000; (with C. Channer and E.L. Harris and M. Major) Got To Be Real, 2001; Griots Beneath the Baobab, 2002; Black Silk, 2002; Gumbo: A Celebration of African American Writing, 2002; Voices from the Other Side: Dark Dreams II, 2006. COMIC BOOKS: Storm (Six-issue mini-series), 2006; Storm Premiere Hardcover, 2007. CALENDAR: Black Expressions, Celebrating our Male Authors, 2007. **Address:** c/o Dutton, 375 Hudson St., New York, NY 10014, U.S.A. **Online address:** ejdickeyfanmail@aol.com

DICKEY, Page. American (born United States), b. 1940. **Genres:** Homes/Gardens, Animals/Pets, Horticulture. **Career:** Garden designer, author, columnist and lecturer. **Publications:** Duck Hill Journal: A Year in a Country Garden, 1991; Breaking Ground: Portraits of Ten Garden Designers, 1997; Inside Out: Relating Garden to House, 2000; Dogs in Their Gardens, 2001; Cats in Their Gardens, 2002; Gardens in the Spirit of Place, 2005; Embroidered Ground: Revisiting the Garden, 2011. **Address:** c/o Helen Pratt, Helen F. Pratt Inc., 1165 5th Ave., New York, NY 10029, U.S.A. **Online address:** pdickey@optonline.net

DICKIE, John. British/Scottish (born Scotland), b. 1963. **Genres:** Young Adult Non-fiction. **Career:** University College London, School of European Languages, Culture and Society, Department of Italian, reader, professor. Writer. **Publications:** NONFICTION: Darkest Italy: The Nation and Stereotypes of the Mezzogiorno, 1860-1900, 1999; (ed. with J. Foot and F.M. Snowden) Disastro! Disasters in Italy since 1860: Culture, Politics, Society, 2002; Cosa Nostra: A History of the Sicilian Mafia, 2004; Delizia! The Epic History of the Italians and Their Food, 2008; Una Catastrofe Patriottica: 1908, Il Terremoto di Messina, 2008; Blood Brotherhoods: The Rise of the Italian Mafias, 2011. **Address:** Department of Italian, School of European Languages, Culture and Society, University College London, Gower St., London, GL WC1E 6BT, England. **Online address:** j.dickie@ucl.ac.uk

DICKIE, Matthew W(allace). American/Scottish (born Scotland), b. 1941. **Genres:** Classics, History. **Career:** Swarthmore College, instructor, 1967-68, associate professor of classics, 1972-78; University of Illinois, professor of classics, 1978-, now professor emeritus. Writer. **Publications:** (Ed. with O. Andersen) Homer's World: Fiction, Tradition, Reality, 1995; Magic and Magicians in the Greco-Roman World, 2001; Philostratus' Life of Apollonius of Tyana, forthcoming; Evil Eye in Greece and Rome, forthcoming. Contributor to periodicals. **Address:** Department of Classics and Mediterranean Studies, University of Illinois, 1722 University Hall, 601 S Morgan St., PO Box 4348, Chicago, IL 60607-7112, U.S.A. **Online address:** theurgy@uic.edu

DICKINSON, Amy. American (born United States), b. 1959. **Genres:** Autobiography/Memoirs, Biography. **Career:** National Broadcasting Co., producer; Chicago Tribune, syndicated advice columnist, 2003-. Educator. **Publications:** The Mighty Queens of Freeville: A Mother, a Daughter, and the People Who Raised Them (memoir), 2009. Contributor to periodicals. **Address:** Chicago Tribune, 435 N Michigan Ave., Chicago, IL 60611, U.S.A. **Online address:** allison.mcgeehon@abc.com

DICKINSON, Don(ald Percy). Canadian (born Canada), b. 1947. **Genres:** Novels, Novellas/Short Stories, Literary Criticism And History. **Career:** British Columbia, English teacher, 1993-2003, retired, 2003; University of British Columbia, writing instructor, 2004-05; Thompson River University, writing instructor, 2004-06. Writer. **Publications:** (With B. Dempster and D. Margoshes) Third Impressions, 1982; Fighting the Upstream (stories), 1987; Blue Husbands (stories), 1991; The Crew (novel), 1993; Robbiestime (novel), 2000. Works appear in anthologies. **Address:** 554 Victoria St., PO Box 341, Lillooet, BC V0K 1V0, Canada. **Online address:** ongole@cablelan.net

DICKINSON, Harry Thomas. British (born England), b. 1939. **Genres:** History, Biography. **Career:** Washington Grammar School, history master, 1961-64; University of Newcastle, Earl Grey research fellow and researcher in history, 1964-66; University of Edinburgh, lecturer and reader, 1966-80, professor of history, 1980-2006, emeritus professor, 2006-; Nanjing University, professor of history, 1987-. Writer. **Publications:** Bolingbroke, 1970; Walpole and the Whig Supremacy, 1973; Liberty and Property: Political Ideology in 18th Century Britain, 1977; Radical Politics in the North-East of England in the Later 18th Century, 1979; British Radicalism and the French Revolution, 1789-1815, 1985; Caricatures and the Constitution, 1760-1832, 1986; The Politics of the People in 18th Century Britain, 1995. EDITOR: Correspondence of Sir James Clavering, 1708-1740, 1967; Politics and Literature in the 18th Century, 1974; The Political Works of Thomas Spence, 1982; Britain and the French Revolution, 1789-1815, 1989; Britain and the American Revolution, 1998; A Proper Reply to a Late Scurrilous Libel In Titled Sedition and Defamation Displayed (1731), 1998; (with M. Lynch) The Challenge to Westminster: Sovereignty, Devolution and Independence, 2000; A Companion to Eighteenth-Century Britain, 2002; (co-ed.) Reactions to Revolutions: The 1790s and Their Aftermath, 2007; British Pamphlets on the American Revolution, 8 vols., 2007-08. Contributor of articles to periodicals. **Address:** School of History, Classics and Archaeology, University of Edinburgh, West Wing, Teviot Pl., Edinburgh, EH8 9AG, Scotland. **Online address:** harry.dickinson@ed.ac.uks

DICKINSON, Janice. American (born United States), b. 1955. **Genres:** Autobiography/Memoirs, Biography, Art/Art History. **Career:** Model, photographer and writer. **Publications:** No Lifeguard on Duty: The Accidental Life of the World's First Supermodel (memoir), 2002; Everything about Me Is Fake - And I'm Perfect, 2004; Check Please! Dating Mating & Extricating, 2006. Contributor to books and periodicals. **Address:** 9972 W Wanda Dr., Beverly Hills, CA 90210, U.S.A.

DICKINSON, John. British (born England), b. 1962?. **Genres:** Novels, Science Fiction/Fantasy, History. **Career:** Ministry of Defense, affiliate. Writer. **Publications:** YOUNG ADULT FANTASY NOVELS: The Cup of the World, 2004; The Widow and the King, 2005; The Fatal Child, 2008. HISTORICAL NOVEL: The Lightstep, 2008. SCIENCE FICTION: We, 2010. **Address:** c/o Author Mail, David Fickling Books, 20 Vauxhall Bridge Rd., London, GL SW1V 2SA, England. **Online address:** john@john-dickinson.net

DICKINSON, Margaret. See MUGGESON, Margaret Elizabeth.

DICKINSON, Mary-Anne. See RODDA, Emily.

DICKINSON, Matt. British (born England) **Genres:** Documentaries/Reportage, Westerns/Adventure, Travel/Exploration, Adult Non-fiction, Essays. **Career:** British Broadcasting Corp., researcher and production manager, 1984-88; freelance producer and director, 1988-. Writer. **Publications:** The Death Zone: Climbing Everest Through the Killer Storm, 1997 in US as The Other Side of Everest: Climbing the North Face through the Killer Zone, 1999; High Risk, 2000; Everest: Triumph and Tragedy on the World's Highest Peak, 2002; Black Ice, 2003; Mortal Chaos, 2012; Deep Oblivion, 2012. Contributor to periodicals. **Address:** c/o Author Mail, Random House, 20 Vauxhall Bridge Rd., London, GL SW1V 2SA, England. **Online address:** dickinson_matt@hotmail.com

DICKINSON, Mike. See HUTSON, Shaun P.

DICKINSON, Peter. British/Zambian (born Zambia), b. 1927. **Genres:** Novels, Mystery/Crime/Suspense, Science Fiction/Fantasy, Children's Fiction, Young Adult Fiction, Poetry, Literary Criticism And History, Young Adult Non-fiction, Young Adult Non-fiction. **Career:** Punch Magazine, assistant editor, 1952-69. **Publications:** FOR CHILDREN: The Weathermonger, 1968; Heartsease, 1969; The Devil's Children, 1970; Emma Tupper's Diary, 1971; The Iron Lion, 1972; The Dancing Bear, 1972; The Gift, 1973; Chance, Luck and Destiny, 1975; Presto!: Humorous Bits and Pieces, 1975; The Blue Hawk, 1976; Annerton Pit, 1977; Hepzibah, 1978; Tulku, 1979; City of Gold and Other Stories from the Old Testament, 1980; The Seventh Raven, 1981; Healer, 1983; Giant Cold, 1984; (ed.) Hundreds and Hundreds, 1984; Mole Hole, 1987; Merlin Dreams, 1988; A Box of Nothing, 1988; Eva, 1989; AK, 1992; A Bone from a Dry Sea, 1993; Time and the Clock Mice, etcetera, 1994; Shadow of a Hero, 1994; Chuck and Danielle, 1996; The Lion Tamer's Daughter and Other Stories, 1997; The Ropemaker, 2001; (with R. McKinley) Water: Tales of Elemental Spirits, 2002; The Tears of the Salamander, 2003; Inside Grandad, 2004; Angel Isle, 2007; (with R. McKinley) Fire: Tales of Elemental Spirits, 2009. KIN SERIES YOUNG ADULT NOVELS: Noli's Story, 1998; Po's Story, 1998; Suth's Story, 1998; Mana's Story, 1999; The Kin, 2003; The Gift Boat, 2005. MYSTERY NOVELS FOR ADULTS: The Glass-Sided Ants' Nest, 1968 in UK as Skin Deep, 1968; A Pride of Heroes in US as The Old English Peep-Show, 1969; The Seals in US as The Sinful Stones, 1970; Sleep and His Brother, 1971; The Lizard in the Cup, 1972; The Green Gene, 1973; The Poison Oracle, 1974; The Lively Dead, 1975; King and Joker, 1976; Walking Dead, 1977; One Foot in the Grave, 1979; The Last Houseparty, 1982; Hindsight, 1983; Death of a Unicorn, 1984; Skeleton-in-Waiting, 1989; Play Dead, 1991; The Yellow Room Conspiracy, 1994; Some Deaths before Dying, 1999. OTHER: The Great Detectives, 1978; The Flight of the Dragons, 1979; (contrib.) Verdict of Thirteen, 1979; A Summer in the Twenties, 1981; Tefuga: A Novel of Suspense, 1986; Perfect Gallows: A Novel of Suspense, 1988; The Weir: Poems, 2007. Works appear in anthologies. Contributor to periodicals. **Address:** AP Watt Ltd., 20 John St., London, GL WC1N 2DL, England. **Online address:** hahoro@peterdickinson.com

DICKINSON, Terence. Canadian (born Canada), b. 1943. **Genres:** Children's Non-fiction, Young Adult Non-fiction, Astronomy, Natural History, Photography, Physics, Sciences. **Career:** Ontario Ministry of Transportation and Communications, technician, 1964-67; McLaughlin Planetarium, Royal Ontario Museum, scientific assistant, 1967-70; Stasenburgh Planetarium, assistant director, 1970-73; Astronomy, editor, 1973-75; Ontario Science Centre, editor of publications, 1975-76; science writer, 1976-; Whig-Standard, astronomy columnist, 1976-82; St. Lawrence College, teaching master, 1977-; CBC Radio, Quirks and Quarks, astronomy commentator, 1978-94; Discovery Channel, commentator, 1994-; Sky News Magazine, editor, 1995-. **Publications:** CHILDREN'S AND YOUNG ADULT NONFICTION: Exploring the Night Sky: The Equinox Astronomy Guide for Beginners, 1987; Exploring the Sky by Day: The Equinox Guide to Weather and the Atmosphere, 1988; From the Big Bang to Planet X: The Fifty Most-asked Questions about the Universe and Their Answers, 1993; (with A. Schaller) Extraterrestrials: A Field Guide for Earthlings, 1994; Other Worlds: A Beginner's Guide to Planets and Moons, 1995. ADULT NONFICTION: Exploring the Moon and the Solar System, 1971; (with S. Brown) Edmund Sky Guide, 1977; (with G. Chaple and V. Costanzo) The Edmund Mag 6 Star Atlas, 1982; NightWatch: An Practical Guide to Viewing the Universe, 1983, 4th ed., 2006; Halley's Comet: Mysterious Visitor from Outer Space, 1985; The Universe and Beyond, 1986, 4th ed., 2004; (with A. Dyer) Backyard Astronomer's Guide, 1991, 3rd ed., 2008; Summer Stargazing: A Practical Guide for Recreational Astronomers for Use Anywhere in North America through 2010, 1996; (with J. Newton) Splendors of the Universe: A Practical Guide to Photographing the Night Sky, 1997. Contributor to magazines and newspapers. **Address:** SkyNews Magazine, PO Box 10, Yarker, ON K0K 3N0, Canada. **Online address:** skynewseditor@reztel.net

DICKINSON, W(illiam) Calvin. American (born United States), b. 1938. **Genres:** Local History/Rural Topics, Bibliography, Military/Defense/Arms Control. **Career:** Chowan College, instructor, 1961-63, department head, 1965-71; Tennessee Technological University, associate professor, 1971-76, professor of history, 1976-2000, professor emeritus, 2000-; Macalester College, visiting lecturer, 1971; Upper Cumberland Humanities and Social Sciences Institute, associate director, 1982-2000; Tennessee Historical Commission, Architectural Survey Program, associate director, 1983-2000; College of Charleston, visiting lecturer, 1986. Writer. **Publications:** James Harrington's Republic, 1983; (co-ed.) Lend an Ear: Heritage of the Tennessee Upper Cumberland, 1983; Morgan County, 1987; (with L.H. Whiteaker) Letters of Cornelius Tenure, Civil War Soldier, 1989; (ed. with L.H. Whiteaker) Civil War Letters of the Tenure Family: Rockland County, N.Y., 1862-1865, 1990; Sidney Godolphin, Lord Treasurer, 1702-1710, 1990; (ed. with L.H. Whiteaker) Tennessee in American History, 1991; (with H.G. Neufeldt) Search for Identity: A History of Tennessee Technological University, 1915-1985, 1991; Cumberland County, Tennessee, 1800-1985, 1992; (with L.H. Whiteaker) Tennessee: State of the Nation, 1994, 2nd ed., 1995; (comp. with E.R. Hitchcock) The War of the Spanish Succession, 1702-1713: A Selected Bibliography, 1996; (ed. with E.R. Hitchcock) Bibliography of Tennessee History, 1973-1996, 1999; (with Ivey and Rand) Tennessee Tales That Textbooks Don't Tell, 2002; (with M. Johnson) Tennessee Technological University, 2002; (with M.E. Birdwell and H.D. Kemp) Upper Cumberland Historic Architecture, 2002; (ed. with M.E. Birdwell) Rural Life and Culture in the Upper Cumberland, 2004; (with J. Ivey and L.W. Rand) E is for Elvis: The Elvis Presley Alphabet: A Parody, 2006; (ed. with K.T. Dollar and L.H. Whiteaker) Sister States, Enemy States: The Civil War in Kentucky and Tennessee, 2009. Contributor of articles to books, journals and periodicals. **Address:** Department of History, Tennessee Technological University, 1 William L. Jones Dr., PO Box 5064, Cookeville, TN 38505, U.S.A. **Online address:** cdickinson@tntech.edu

DICKMAN, Thomas. American (born United States), b. 1955. **Genres:** Translations, Adult Non-fiction, Economics, Social Sciences, Politics/Government, Theology/Religion. **Career:** Clinical social worker and writer. **Publications:** (Trans. with A. Lefebvre) M. Beaud, A History of Capitalism, 1500-1980, 1983; Of Sex and Sin, 1986; (trans.) M. Beaud, Socialism in the Crucible of History, 1993; Inside the Millennium (novel). **Address:** 1784 South 800 East, Salt Lake City, UT 84105, U.S.A.

DICKS, Shirley. American (born United States), b. 1940. **Genres:** Criminology/True Crime, Military/Defense/Arms Control, Social Commentary, Biography, Children's Non-fiction. **Career:** Murfreesboro Writers Club, president and founder, 1987-; The Jeff Dicks Medical Coalition, president and founder; Authors For Charity, president and founder. Writer. **Publications:** Death Row: Interviews with Inmates, Their Families, and Opponents of Capital Punishment, 1990; From Vietnam to Hell: Interviews with Victims of Post-Traumatic Stress Disorder, 1990; Victims of Crime and Punishment: Interviews with Victims, Convicts, Their Families, and Support Groups, 1991; They're Going to Kill My Son, 1992; Easy Guide for Beginner Writers, 2000; Poison Passion, 2000; Road Angels: Women Who Ride Motorcycles, 2002; A Long Journey Home, 2003; The Choice Is Yours, 2003; The Devil's Playground: Behind Prison Walls, 2003; A Mother's Torment, 2008; There is Life After Fifty, 2009. EDITOR: Congregation of the Condemned: Voices against the Death Penalty, 1992; Young Blood: Juvenile Justice and the Death Penalty, 1995. Contributor to magazines. **Address:** The Jeff Herman Agency, PO Box 1522, Stockbridge, MA 01262, U.S.A. **Online address:** sdicks@bloomand.net

DICKSON, Athol. American (born United States), b. 1955?. **Genres:** inspirational/Motivational Literature, Novels. **Career:** Writer and teacher. **Publications:** Whom Shall I Fear? 1996; Every Hidden Thing, 1998; Kate and Ruth: A Novel, 1999; They Shall See God, 2002; The Gospel according to Moses: What My Jewish Friends Taught Me about Jesus, 2003; River Rising, 2005; The Cure, 2007; Winter Haven, 2008; Lost Mission, 2009; The Opposite of Art, 2011. **Address:** Zondervan Publishing House, 5300 Patterson Ave. SE, Grand Rapids, MI 49530, U.S.A.

DICKSON, Paul (Andrew). American (born United States), b. 1939.

Genres: History, Recreation, Social Commentary, Speech/Rhetoric, Sports/Fitness, Humor/Satire, Young Adult Non-fiction. **Career:** McGraw-Hill Book Co., editor, 1966-69; Washingtonian Magazine, consulting editor; writer, 1968-; Dover Publications Inc., consulting editor, 2008-. **Publications:** Think Tanks, 1971; The Great American Ice Cream Book, 1972; The Future of the Workplace, 1975 in UK as Work Revolution, 1977; The Electronic Battlefield, 1976; The Mature Person's Guide to Kites, Yo-Yo's, Frisbees and Other Childlike Diversions, 1977; The Future File, 1977; Out of This World: American Space Photography, 1977; Chow: A Cook's Tour of Military Food, 1978; The Official Rules, 1978; The Official Explanations, 1980; Toasts, 1981, 2nd ed., 2009; Words, 1982; (with J.C. Goulden) There Are Alligators in Our Sewers, 1983; Jokes, 1984 as Too Much Saxon Violence, 1986; On Our Own, 1985; Names, 1986; The Library in America, 1986; Family Words, 1988; The New Official Rules, 1989; The Dickson Baseball Dictionary, 1989, 3rd ed., 2009; Timelines, 1990; What Do You Call a Person from..., 1990; Slang!, 1990, rev. ed., 2008; (ed.) Baseball's Greatest Quotations, 1991; (with D. Evelyn) On This Spot, 1992, 3rd ed., 2008; Dickson Word Treasury, 1992; Dickson's Joke Treasury, 1992; (with J.C. Goulden) Myth Informed, 1993; (with P. Clancy) The Congress Dictionary, 1993; (with W.B. Mead) Baseball: The President's Game, 1993; The Worth Book of Softball, 1994; War Slang, 1994, 2nd ed., 2003; The Book of Thanksgiving, 1995; (with R. Skole) The Volvo Guide to Halls of Fame, 1996; The Joy of Keeping Score, 1996; The Official Rules at Home, 1996; What's in a Name?, 1996; The Official Rules for Lawyers, 1996; The Official Rules at Work, 1997; The Official Rules of Golfers, 1997; Labels for Locals, 1997; The New Dickson Baseball Dictionary, 1999; From Elvis to E-Mail: Trends, Events, and Trivia from the Postwar Era to the End of the Century, 1999; (with W.D. Hickman) Firestone: A Legend, A Century, A Celebration, 2000; The Official Rules for Life, 2000; Sputnik: The Shock of the Century, 2001; The Hidden Language of Baseball, 2003; (with T.B. Allen) The Bonus Army: An American Epic, 2004; Unwritten Rules of Baseball, 2009; Dictionary of the Space Age, 2009; Drunk: The Definitive Drinkers Dictionary, 2009; The Dickson Baseball Dictionary, Third Edition, 2009; Baseball Is, 2011. Contributor to magazines. **Address:** PO Box 280, Garrett Park, MD 20896, U.S.A. **Online address:** newdefiner@aol.com

DICKSON, (W.) Michael. American (born United States), b. 1968. **Genres:** Mathematics/Statistics. **Career:** Indiana University, assistant professor, 1996-98, associate professor of history, 1998-2000, Ruth N. Halls professor of history and philosophy of science, 2002-04; University of South Carolina, professor of philosophy of science, 2004-, department chair; University of Chicago, adjunct professor, 2000. Writer. **Publications:** Quantum Chance and Non-locality: Probability and Non-locality in the Interpretations of Quantum Mechanics, 1998; (with R. Clifton) Structuring Reality: Mathematica and Philosophical Foundations of Quantum Theory, forthcoming. Contributor books and journals. **Address:** Department of Philosophy, College of Arts & Sciences, University of South Carolina, Rm. Byrnes 401-C, James F. Byrnes Bldg., Columbia, SC 29208, U.S.A. **Online address:** dickson@sc.edu

DIDION, Joan. American (born United States), b. 1934. **Genres:** Novels, Social Commentary, Novellas/Short Stories, Plays/Screenplays, Adult Nonfiction, Essays, Young Adult Fiction, Autobiography/Memoirs, Autobiography/Memoirs. **Career:** Vogue, promotional copywriter, associate feature editor, 1956-63; University of California, visiting regents lecturer in English, 1976. **Publications:** Run River, 1963; Slouching Towards Bethlehem (essays), 1968; Play It as It Lays: A Novel, 1970; (with A. Edwards and J.G. Dunne) A Star Is Born, 1976; A Book of Common Prayer (novel), 1977; Telling Stories, 1978; The White Album, 1979; Salvador, 1982; Joan Didion: Essays & Conversations, 1984; Democracy: A Novel, 1984; Miami, 1987; Robert Graham: The Duke Ellington Memorial in Progress, 1988; (intro.) Some Women, 1989; After Henry, 1992 in UK as Sentimental Journeys, 1992; The Last Thing He Wanted, 1996; Political Fictions (essays), 2001; Where I was From, 2003; Fixed Ideas: America since 9.11, 2003; Vintage Didion, 2004; The Year of Magical Thinking, 2005; We Tell Ourselves Stories In Order To Live: Collected Nonfiction, 2006; (contrib.) Companionship in Grief, 2010; Blue Nights, 2011. Contributor of articles to periodicals. **Address:** c/o Lynn Nesbit, Janklow & Nesbit Associates, 445 Park Ave., New York, NY 10022-2606, U.S.A.

DIECKHOFF, Alain. French (born France), b. 1958. **Genres:** Young Adult Non-fiction. **Career:** National Center for Scientific Research, Center for International Studies and Research (CNRS/CERI), research director. Writer. **Publications:** NONFICTION: Les espaces d'IsraEl: Essai sur la strategie territoriale israelienne (title means: 'Spaces of Israel: Essay on the Israeli

Territorial Strategy'), 1987; L'invention d'une nation: IsraEl et la modernite politique, 1993, trans. as The Invention of a Nation: Zionist Thought and the Making of Modern Israel, 2003; Rescapes du genocide: L'action Musy'une operation de sauvetage de juifs europeens en 1944-1945 (title means: 'Escape from Genocide: The Musy Action A Rescue Operation of European Jews in 1944-1945'), 1995; Israeliens et palestiniens: L'epreuve de la paix (title means: 'Israelis and Palestinians: The Test of Peace'), 1996; La nation dans tous ses etats: Les identites nationales en mouvement (title means: 'The Nation in All Its States: National Identities in Motion'), 2000. EDITOR: L'Italie, une nation en suspens (title means: 'Italy, a Nation in Uncertainty'), 1995; Belgique: La force de la desunion (title means: 'Belgium: The Force of Disunion'), 1996; (with N. Gutierrez) Modern Roots: Studies of National Identity, 2001; (with R. Kastoryano) Nationalismes en mutation en Mediterranee Orientale (title means: 'Changing Nationalisms in the Eastern Mediterranean'), 2002; (with R. Leveau) Israeliens et palestiniens: La guerre en partage (title means: 'Israelis and Palestinians: Sharing War'), 2003; La constellation des appartenances: Nationalisme, liberalisme et pluralisme, 2004, trans. as The Politics of Belonging: Nationalism, Liberalism and Pluralism, 2004; (with C. Jaffrelot) Repenser le nationalisme: Theories et pratiques, 2006, trans. as Revisiting Nationalism: Theories and Processes, 2006; L'etat D'IsraEl (title means: 'The State of Israel'), 2008. Contributor to books and journals. **Address:** CERI-Sciences Po-CNRS (UMR 7050), 56 rue Jacob, Paris, 75006, France. **Online address:** dieckhoff@ceri-sciences-po.org

DIEHN, Gwen. American (born United States), b. 1943. **Genres:** Art/Art History, Communications/Media, Crafts, Children's Non-fiction, Photography. **Career:** Indiana Vocational Technical Community College, instructor of oral and written communications, 1979-84; Asheville City Schools, teacher, 1985-89; Warren Wilson College, professor of fine arts, 1989-2009, now retired. Writer. **Publications:** (With J. Comeau) Communication on the Job (textbook), 1986; (with S. Griesmaier) Streamwalking with Kids, 1988; Mt. Mitchell, 1991; (with T. Krautwurst) Nature Crafts for Kids: Fifty Fantastic Things to Make with Mother Nature's Help, 1992; (with T. Krautwurst) Science Crafts for Kids: 50 Fantastic Things to Invent and Create, 1994; (with T. Krautwurst) Kid Style Nature Crafts, 1995; (with A. Anderson and T. Krautwurst) Geology Crafts for Kids, 1996; Making Books that Fly, Fold, Wrap, Hide, Pop Up, Twist, and Turn: Books for Kids to Make, 1998; Simple Printmaking, 2000; The Decorated Page, 2002; (co-author) Science Smart: Cool Projects for Exploring the Marvels of the Planet Earth, 2003; (wit T. Krautwurst and B. Needham) Nature Smart, 2003; The Decorated Journal: Creating Beautifully Expressive Journal Pages, 2005; Real Life Journals, 2010; Complete Decorated Journal, 2011. **Address:** Department of Art, Warren Wilson College, PO Box 9000, Asheville, NC 28815-9000, U.S.A. **Online address:** gdiehn@mindspring.com

DIEM, Max. German (born Germany), b. 1947. **Genres:** Sciences, Medicine/Health. **Career:** Syracuse University, postdoctoral fellow, 1976-78; City University of New York, Hunter College, instructor, professor in chemistry, 1996-97, now professor emeritus; Northeastern University, Department of Chemistry and Chemical Biology, research faculty, 2005-. Writer. **Publications:** Introduction to Modern Vibrational Spectroscopy, 1993; (ed. with P.R. Griffiths and J.M. Chalmers) Vibrational Spectroscopy for Medical Diagnosis, 2008. Contributor to scientific journals. **Address:** Department of Chemistry, Hunter College, City University of New York, 695 Park Ave., New York, NY 10021, U.S.A. **Online address:** mdiem@hunter.cuny.edu

DIERKER, Larry. American (born United States), b. 1946. **Genres:** Humor/Satire, Sports/Fitness, Medicine/Health, Biography. **Career:** Houston Astros (originally Houston Colts), baseball pitcher, 1964-76, director of group and season sales office, 1977-79, radio and television color analyst, 1979-97, manager, 1997-2001; St. Louis Cardinals, pitcher, 1977. Writer and sports commentator. **Publications:** This Ain't Brain Surgery: How to Win the Pennant without Losing Your Mind, 2003; My Team: Choosing My Dream Team from My Forty Years in Baseball, 2006. Contributor to periodicals. **Address:** MLB Advanced Media L.P., 75 9th Ave., 5th Fl., New York, NY 10011-7076, U.S.A.

DIETERICH, Michele M. American (born United States), b. 1962. **Genres:** Recreation, Sports/Fitness, Young Adult Fiction, Children's Fiction. **Career:** Mountain Biker Intl., itinerant correspondent; Happenings Magazine, staff writer and art critic. Artist. **Publications:** All Action: Skiing, 1991; Skiing, 1992. Contributor to books and periodicals. **Address:** PO Box 7273, Bozeman, MT 58715, U.S.A.

DIETRICH, William A. American (born United States), b. 1951. **Genres:** Novels, Environmental Sciences/Ecology, Romance/Historical, Adult Non-fiction, History, Local History/Rural Topics, Natural History. **Career:** Bellingham Herald, political reporter, 1973-76; Gannett News Service, reporter, 1976-78; Vancouver Columbian, reporter and columnist, 1978-82; Seattle Times, reporter, 1982-2008; writer, 1992-; Western Washington University, Huxley College of the Environment, Department of Environmental Studies, assistant professor of environmental journalism, 2006-11. **Publications:** The Final Forest: The Battle for the Last Great Trees of the Pacific Northwest, 1992; Northwest Passage: The Great Columbia River, 1995; Natural Grace: The Charm, Wonder and Lessons of Pacific Northwest Animals and Plants, 2003; On Puget Sound, 2007, Green Fire, 2011. NOVELS: Ice Reich, 1998; Getting Back, 2000; Dark Winter, 2001; Hadrian's Wall, 2004; The Scourge of God, 2005; Napoleon's Pyramids, 2007; The Rosetta Key, 2008; The Dakota Cipher, 2009; The Barbary Pirates, 2010, Blood of the Reich, 2011. **Address:** 11660 Marine Dr., Anacortes, WA 98221-8427, U.S.A. **Online address:** williamdietrich@comcast.net

DIETZ, Laura. American (born United States), b. 1976?. **Genres:** Novels, Mystery/Crime/Suspense, Literary Criticism And History. **Career:** Anglia Ruskin University, Department of English, Communication, Film and Media, lecturer. Writer. **Publications:** In the Tenth House, 2007; The Spells for Going Forth By Day, forthcoming. **Address:** c/o Esmond Harmsworth, Zachary Shuster Harmsworth, 1776 Broadway, Ste. 1405, New York, NY 10019, U.S.A. **Online address:** info@lauradietz.com

DIETZ, Maribel. American (born United States), b. 1966. **Genres:** Travel/Exploration, Theology/Religion, History. **Career:** Louisiana State University, Department of History, associate professor. Writer. **Publications:** Wandering Monks, Virgins, and Pilgrims: Ascetic Travel in the Mediterranean World, A.D. 300/800, 2005. **Address:** Department of History, Louisiana State University, 224 Himes Hall, Baton Rouge, LA 70803, U.S.A. **Online address:** maribel@lsu.edu

DIETZ, Peter (John). British (born England), b. 1924. **Genres:** Autobiography/Memoirs, Military/Defense/Arms Control, History, Young Adult Fiction, Politics/Government. **Career:** Royal Military College of Science, department head, 1968-71; Open University, lecturer, 1982-89. Writer. **Publications:** (Ed.) Garrison: Ten British Military Towns, 1986; The Last of the Regiments: Their Rise and Fall, 1990; The British in the Mediterranean, 1994. Contributor to periodicals. **Address:** c/o Kernow, Pannier Ln., Carbis Bay, St. Ives, CW TR26 2RF, England.

DIETZ, Steven. American (born United States), b. 1958. **Genres:** Novels, Plays/Screenplays. **Career:** Playwrights' Center, staff, 1980-91; Quicksilver Stage, co-founder, 1983-86; Midwest Playlabs, artistic director, 1987-89; Sundance Institute, resident director, 1990; Contemporary Theatre, associate artist, 1990-91; University of Texas, College of Fine Arts, Department of Theatre and Dance, faculty. Writer. **Publications:** Foolin' around with Infinity, 1990; God's Country, 1990; More Fun than Bowling, 1990; Lonely Planet, 1994; Trust, 1995; Halcyon Days, 1995; Dracula, 1996; Private Eyes, 1998; Still Life with Iris, 1998; Force of Nature, 2003; Rocket Man, 2003; Nina Variations, 2003; Inventing Van Gogh, 2004; Fiction, 2005; Sherlock Holmes: The Final Adventure, 2007; Last of the Boys, 2008. Contributor to periodicals. **Address:** Department of Theatre and Dance, College of Fine Arts, University of Texas, 300 E 23rd St., PO Box D3900, 1 University Sta., Austin, TX 78712-0362, U.S.A. **Online address:** sjdietz@mail.utexas.edu

DIFFILY, Deborah. American (born United States), b. 1955. **Genres:** Education, Children's Non-fiction, Social Sciences, Philosophy. **Career:** Southern Methodist University, assistant professor of early childhood education, 2000, associate professor, 2006-. Writer and educator. **Publications:** (Ed. with K. Morrison) Family Friendly Communication for Early Childhood Programs, 1996, 2nd ed., forthcoming; (with M.P. Puckett) Teaching Young Children: An Introduction to the Early Childhood Profession, 1999, 2nd ed., 2004; (with E. Donaldson and C. Sassm) The Scholastic Book of Early Childhood Learning Centers: Complete How-to's, Management Tips, Photos and Activities for Delightful Learning Centers That Teach Early Reading, Writing, Math & More!, 2001; (with C. Sassm) Project-based Learning with Young Children, 2002; Creating a Video About Hurricanes: Experiences in Project-Based Learning, 2003; Teachers and Families Working Together, 2004; Teaching Effective Classroom Strategies: Establish Structure in the Classroom to Foster Children's Learning-From the First Day of School and

All through the Year, 2004; (with C. Sassman) Positive Teacher Talk for Better Classroom Management, 2006. FOR CHILDREN: Jurassic Shark, 2004; (with C. Sassman) Teacher Talk: Supporting Young Children's Learning and Development, forthcoming; (with C. Sassman) Service Learning Project for Elementary Students, forthcoming; (with C. Sassman) Project-Based Learning Prepares Young Children for Successful Adult Lives, forthcoming; Math Games: Real World Learning through Projects, forthcoming. **Address:** School of Education and Human Development, Southern Methodist University, 6116 N Central Expy., Ste. 1080, Dallas, TX 75205, U.S.A. **Online address:** ddiffily@smu.edu

DI FILIPPO, Paul. (Philip Lawson). American (born United States), b. 1954. **Genres:** Novels, Novellas/Short Stories, Science Fiction/Fantasy. **Career:** Rhode Island Blue Cross, programmer, 1980-82; Brown University Bookstore, staff, 1987-94; full-time writer, 1994-. **Publications:** SHORT STORIES: The Steampunk Trilogy, 1995; Ribofunk, 1996; Destroy All Brains!, 1996; Fractal Paisleys, 1997; Lost Pages, 1998; Strange Trades, 2001; Little Doors, 2002; Babylon Sisters, 2002; Neutrino Drag, 2004; Emperor of Gondwanaland, and Other Stories, 2005; Shuteye for the Timebroker, 2006; Plumage from Pegasus, 2006; Harsh Oases, 2009; Roadside Bodhisattva, 2010. NOVELS: Ciphers, 1997; Would It Kill You to Smile?, 1998; Joe's Liver, 2000; (with M. Bishop as Philip Lawson) Muskrat Courage, 2000; A Year in the Linear City, 2002; A Mouthful of Tongues, 2002; Spondulix, 2003; Fuzzy Dice, 2003; Harp, Pipe, and Symphony, 2004; Creature from the Black Lagoon: Time's Black Lagoon, 2006; Cosmocopia, 2008. Works appear in anthologies. Contributor of articles to magazines. **Address:** 2 Poplar St., Providence, RI 02906, U.S.A. **Online address:** author@pauldifilippo.com

DIFONZO, Nicholas. American (born United States), b. 1959. **Genres:** Psychology, Sports/Fitness. **Career:** Rochester Institute of Technology, Department of Psychology, assistant professor, 1994-99, associate professor, 2000-06, professor, 2006-, Rumor and Gossip Research Group, founder and administrator, 2003-; Journal of Social Psychology, consulting editor, 2000-08; Social Influence, consulting editor, 2008-; Computers in Human Behavior, consulting editor, 2009-. Psychologist. **Publications:** (With P. Bordia) Rumor Psychology: Social and Organizational Approaches, 2007; The Watercooler Effect: A Psychologist Explores the Extraordinary Power of Rumors, 2008. Contributor to journals and periodicals. **Address:** Rochester Institute of Technology, 3176 George Eastman Bldg., 18 Lomb Memorial Dr., Rochester, NY 14623, U.S.A. **Online address:** Nicholas.DiFonzo@rit.edu

DIGBY-JUNGER, Richard. American (born United States), b. 1954. **Genres:** Literary Criticism And History, Writing/Journalism. **Career:** Northern Illinois University, assistant professor, 1989-96; Western Michigan University, School of Communication, associate professor of English, 1996-, director of journalism program. Writer. **Publications:** The Journalist as Reformer: Henry Demarest Lloyd and Wealth against Commonwealth, 1996. **Address:** School of Communication, Western Michigan University, 317 Sprau Twr., 1903 West Michigan Ave., Kalamazoo, MI 49008-5318, U.S.A. **Online address:** richard.digby-junger@wmich.edu

DI GREGORIO, Mario A(urelio Umberto). Italian/British (born England), b. 1950. **Genres:** Natural History, Humanities. **Career:** Milan Conservatoire, teacher of Italian, Latin, history, 1974; Cambridge University, Darwin College, research fellow, 1978-81, lecturer in history, 1979-92; Hiram College, visiting professor, 1989; University of L'Aquila, associate professor of the history of science, 1992-, Department of Comparative Cultural Studies, professor, coordinator. Writer. **Publications:** T.H. Huxley's Place in Natural Science, 1984; (ed.) Charles Darwin's Marginalia, vol. I: Books, 1990; From Here to Eternity: Ernst Haeckel and Scientific Faith, 2005. Contributor to books and periodicals. **Address:** Dipartimento di Culture Comparate, University of L'Aquila, Piazza S Margherita Z, La'quila, 67100, Italy. **Online address:** didomenico@cc.univaq.it

DIGREGORIO, Mario J. American (born United States) **Genres:** Horticulture, Biology. **Career:** U.S. Government, National Park Service, park ranger, U.S. Army Corps of Engineers, park resource manager, 1976-86; Sabatia Inc. (environmental consultants), owner, professional wetland scientist and botanist, 1983-; Town of Brewster, municipal conservation administrator, 1986-88; Commonwealth of Massachusetts, Natural Heritage and Endangered Species Program, consulting ecologist and rare plant specialist; expert witness in superior, district and land courts on issues related to wetlands and wildlife; Cape Cod and Islands Botany Club, co-founder, president. Writer. **Publica-**

tions: (With J. Wallner) Wildflowers of the Cape Cod Canal: An Annotated Checklist, 1985; (with Wallner) A Vanishing Heritage: Cape Cod's Wildflowers, 1989; (co-author) A Guide to the Natural History of Cape Codand the Islands, 1990; (with J. Wallner) New England's Mountain Flowers: A High Country Heritage, 1997; (with J. Wallner) Cape Cod Wildflowers: A Vanishing Heritage, 2003. Contributor to periodicals. **Address:** 913 W Falmouth Hwy., Falmouth, MA 02540, U.S.A. **Online address:** sabatia@aol.com

DIJON, Jon. See **GRANT, Pete.**

DIKÖTTER, Frank. Dutch (born Netherlands), b. 1961. **Genres:** Adult Non-fiction, International Relations/Current Affairs, Medicine/Health, Social Commentary. **Career:** University of London, School of Oriental and African Studies, Wellcome Research Fellow, 1993-2000, professor of the modern history of China, 2002-; University of Hong Kong, visiting professor, 2004-05, chair of humanities in the faculty of arts, 2006-; Contemporary China Institute, board director. Historian and writer. **Publications:** The Discourse of Race in Modern China, 1992; Sex, Culture and Modernity in China: Medical Science and the Construction of Sexual Identities in the Early Republican Period, 1995; (ed.) The Construction of Racial Identities in China and Japan: Historical and Contemporary Perspectives, 1997; Imperfect Conceptions: Medical Knowledge, Birth Defects and Eugenics in China, 1998; Crime, Punishment and the Prison in Modern China, 1895-1949, 2002; (with L. Laamann and Z. Xun) Narcotic Culture: A History of Drugs in China, 2004; Exotic Commodities: Modern Objects and Everyday Life in China, 2006 in UK as Things Modern: Material Culture and Everyday Life in China, 2006; (ed. with I. Brown) Cultures of Confinement: A History of the Prison in Africa, Asia and Latin America, 2007; The Age of Openness: China before Mao, 2008; Mao's Great Famine: The History of China's most Devastating Catastrophe, 1958-1962, 2010. CONTRIBUTOR: Racial Identities in East Asia, 1995; Ethnicity, 1996; Sex, Disease and Society: A Comparative History of Sexually Transmitted Diseases and HIV/AIDS in Aisa and the Pacific, 1997; The Construction of Racial Identities in China and Japan: Historical and Contemporary Perspectives, 1997; Le corps violente: Du geste A la parole, 1998; Hair: Its Power and Meaning in Asian Cultures, 1998; Encyclopedia of Historians and Historical Writing, 1999; Racism, 1999; Neue Geschichten der Sexualität: Beispiele aus Ostasien und Zentraleuropa, 1700-2000, 1999; Nationalism: A Reader, 1999; Societes asiatiques face au Sida, 2000; Si you gong: Jindai Zhongguo geti yu zhengti zhi chongjian, 2001; International Encyclopedia of the Social and Behaviour Sciences, 2002; A Companion to Racial and Ethnic Studies, 2002; An Introduction to Women's Studies: Gender in a Transnational World, 2002; The Cambridge History of Science, 2003; Das grosse China-Lexikon, 2003; Race and Ethnicity, 2003; State, Market and Ethnic Groups Contextualized, 2003; China since 1919: Revolution and Reform: A Sourcebook, 2003; Tobacco in History and Culture: An Encyclopedia, 2004; China Inside Out: Contemporary Chinese Nationalism and Transnationalism, 2005; Crime, Policing and Criminology in China, 2005; Zhongguo de chengshi shenghuo, 2005; New Makers of Modern Culture, 2006; Encyclopedia of Legal History, 2007; Drugs and Empires, 2007. Contributor to journals. **Address:** School of Oriental and African Studies, University of London, Russell Sq., Thornhaugh St., London, GL WC1 H0XG, England. **Online address:** dikotter@mac.com

DI LELLA, Alexander Anthony. American (born United States), b. 1929. **Genres:** Language/Linguistics, Theology/Religion. **Career:** Holy Name College, lecturer in Old Testament, 1964-67; Catholic University of America, assistant professor, 1966-68, associate professor of Semitic languages, 1968-76, Andrews-Kelly-Ryan distinguished professor of biblical studies, 1976-, professor emeritus, 2005-; Washington Theological Coalition, adjunct professor, 1969-72. Writer. **Publications:** The Hebrew Text of Sirach: A Text-Critical and Historical Study, 1966; (intro.) The Book of Daniel, 1978; Proverbs, in The Old Testament in Syriac, 1979; (intro.) The Wisdom of Ben Sira, 1987; (ed.) New Revised Standard Version of the Bible: Catholic Edition, 1993; Il libro di Daniele, 14 vols., 1995-1996; Daniel: A Book for Troubling Times, 1997; (contrib.) Intertextual Studies in Ben Sira and Tobit, 2005. **Address:** School of Theology & Religious Studies, Catholic University of America, 620 Michigan Ave. NE, Washington, DC 20064, U.S.A. **Online address:** dilella@cua.edu

DILLARD, Annie. American (born United States), b. 1945. **Genres:** Novels, Poetry, Literary Criticism And History, Autobiography/Memoirs, Essays, Adult Non-fiction, Philosophy. **Career:** Harper's Magazine, editor, 1974-81, 1983-85; Wesleyan University, distinguished visiting professor, 1979-81, full adjunct professor, 1983-98, writer-in-residence, 1987-98, professor emeritus,

1999-. **Publications:** Tickets for a Prayer Wheel, 1974; Pilgrim at Tinker Creek, 1974; Holy the Firm, 1977; Living by Fiction, 1978; Weasel, 1981; Living by Fiction, 1982; Teaching a Stone to Talk, 1982; Encounters with Chinese Writers, 1984; An American Childhood, 1987; The Writing Life, 1989, (contrib.) Hollins, 1991; (with W.R. Robinson) Seeing Beyond, 2001; The Living, 1992; (ed. with C. Conley) Modern American Memoirs, 1995; Mornings Like This, 1995; For the Time Being, 1999; Maytrees, 2007; Give it All, Give it Now, 2009. **Address:** c/o Timothy Seldes, Russell & Volkening Inc., 50 W 29th St., New York, NY 10001, U.S.A.

DILLARD, R(ichard) H(enry) W(ilde). American (born United States), b. 1937. **Genres:** Literary Criticism And History, Novels, Plays/Screenplays, Poetry, Autobiography/Memoirs. **Career:** University of Virginia, instructor in English, 1961-64; Hollins University, Graduate Center, assistant professor, 1964-68, associate professor, 1968-74, professor of English, 1974-, The Hollins Critic, contributing editor, 1966-77, editor, 1996-; The Film Journal, vice president, 1973-. **Publications:** (Intro.) The Vicar of Wakefield, 1965; (intro.) She Stoops to Conquer, 1965; The Day I Stopped Dreaming About Barbara Steele, and Other Poems, 1966; (contrib.) Man and the Movies, 1967; (ed. with L.D. Rubin, Jr.) The Experience of America: A Book of Readings, 1969; News of the Nile: A Book of Poems, 1971; (ed. with G. Garrett and J.R. Moore) The Sounder Few: Essays from The Hollins Critic, 1971; After Borges: A Sequence of New Poems, 1972; The Book of Changes: A Novel, 1974; Horror Films, 1976; The Greeting: New & Selected Poems, 1981; The First Man on the Sun: A Novel, 1983; Understanding George Garrett, 1988; Just Here, Just Now: Poems, 1994; Omniphobia: Stories, 1995; Sallies: Poems, 2001; (with A. Dillard) Seeing Beyond: Movies, Visions, and Values: 26 Essays, 2001; (ed. with A. Cockrell) Twayne Companion to Contemporary Literature in English from the Editors of the Hollins Critic, 2003; What Is Owed the Dead, 2006. Contributor to journals. **Address:** Graduate Center, Hollins University, 8009 Hill House Rd., PO Box 9603, Roanoke, VA 24012, U.S.A.

DILLER, Harriett. American (born United States), b. 1953. **Genres:** Adult Non-fiction, Young Adult Fiction, Crafts, Homes/Gardens, Social Sciences. **Career:** Freelance writer, 1979-. **Publications:** Celebrations That Matter: A Year-Round Guide to Making Holidays Meaningful, 1990; Grandaddy's Highway, 1993; The Waiting Day, 1994; The Faraway Drawer, 1996; Big Band Sound, 1996. Contributor to periodicals. **Address:** 590 E King St., Chambersburg, PA 17201, U.S.A.

DILLINGHAM, William B. American (born United States), b. 1930. **Genres:** Literary Criticism And History, Education, Humanities, Humor/Satire. **Career:** Emory University, instructor, 1956-62, assistant professor, 1962-66, associate professor, 1966-68, professor of English, 1968-, Charles Howard Candler professor of American literature, 1986-96, now Charles Howard Candler professor emeritus; University of Oslo, American Institute, Fulbright visiting professor, 1964-65. Writer. **Publications:** (Ed. with H. Cohen) Humor of the Old Southwest, 1964, 3rd ed., 1994; (with F.C. Watkins and E.T. Martin) Practical English Handbook, 1965, (with F.C. Watkins and J. Hiers) 11th ed., 2001; Frank Norris: Instinct and Art, 1969; An Artist in the Rigging: The Early Work of Herman Melville, 1972; Melville's Short Fiction, 1853-1856, 1977; (with F.C. Watkins) English Handbook, 1979; Melville's Later Novels, 1986; Melville and His Circle: The Last Years, 1996; Rudyard Kipling: Hell and Heroism, 2005; Being Kipling, 2008. Contributor of articles to periodicals. **Address:** Emory University, 201 Dowman Dr., Atlanta, GA 30322-1007, U.S.A. **Online address:** wdillin@emory.edu

DILLON, Anna. *See* **SCOTT, Michael.**

DILLON, Anne. British (born England) **Genres:** Theology/Religion. **Career:** Cambridge University, Lucy Cavendish College, instructor. Writer. **Publications:** The Construction of Martyrdom in the English Catholic Community, 1535-1603, 2002. **Address:** Lucy Cavendish College, Cambridge, CB3 0BU, England. **Online address:** akd31@cam.ac.uk

DILLON, Kathleen M. (Hynek). American (born United States), b. 1947. **Genres:** Psychology, Biography, Autobiography/Memoirs. **Career:** Western New England College, College of Arts and Sciences, professor of psychology, 1968-, now professor emeritus, provost; Massachusetts Department of Mental Health, psychiatric social worker, 1969; Springfield College, adjunct faculty, 1970-74; University of Massachusetts, adjunct faculty, 1982, professor of psychology; University of California, UC Language Consortium, associate director. Writer. **Publications:** Living with Autism: The Parents' Stories,

1995: Living with Pain, 2002. Contributor to journals. **Address:** College of Letters and Science, University of California, 200 Social Science & Humanities Bldg., 1 Shields Ave., Davis, CA 95616-8572, U.S.A. **Online address:** kedillon@ucdavis.edu

DILLON, Patrick. American (born United States), b. 1945. **Genres:** Adult Non-fiction. **Career:** Forbes ASAP magazine, editor; California Monthly Magazine, executive editor; San Jose Mercury News, assistant managing editor, columnist, editor; Quokka Sports, director; Stamen Design, executive producer, 2010-11. **Publications:** The Last Best Thing: A Classic Tale of Greed, Deception, and Mayhem in Silicon Valley, 1996; Dangerous Waters, 1997; Lost at Sea: An American Tragedy, 1998; (with C.M. Cannon) Circle of Greed: The Spectacular Rise and Fall of the Lawyer Who Brought Corporate America to Its Knees, 2010. Contributor to periodicals. **Address:** c/o Author Mail, Bantam Dell Publishing Group, Random House, 1745 Broadway, New York, NY 10019-4368, U.S.A.

DILLON, Sam(uel). American (born United States), b. 1951?. **Genres:** Politics/Government. **Career:** Associated Press, chief of El Salvador bureau, 1981-82; Miami Herald, San Salvador bureau chief, 1982-95, Nicaraguan bureau chief, 1987-89, South America bureau chief, 1990-92, Latin American correspondent, 1995-97; New York Times, metropolitan reporter, 1992-95, Mexico bureau chief, 1995-2000, foreign and national correspondent, 2001. **Publications:** Comandos: The CIA and Nicaragua's Contra Rebels, 1991; (with J. Preston) Opening Mexico: The Making of a Democracy, 2004. **Address:** c/o Author Mail, Farrar, Straus & Giroux, 19 Union Sq. W, New York, NY 10003, U.S.A.

DILLON, Wilton Sterling. American (born United States), b. 1923. **Genres:** Anthropology/Ethnology, Area Studies, History, Economics. **Career:** U.S. Government, information specialist, 1946-49; journalist, 1946-49; Hobart and William Smith Colleges, instructor in sociology and anthropology, 1953-54; Society for Applied Anthropology, Human Organization, director of clearinghouse for research, 1954-56, vice-president, 1956-57; Phelps-Stokes Fund of New York, director of research and executive secretary, 1957-63, Hazen Foundation Research Program, director, 1961-62; Smithsonian Institution, Office of Symposia and Seminars, director, 1969-; University of Alabama, adjunct professor of anthropology, 1971-; Columbia University, Teachers College, lecturer, 1955-56, 1957-58, New School for Social Research, lecturer, 1959-60; Cancer Hospital, lay reader, 1957-59; Institute of Intercultural Studies, president; Institute for Psychiatry and Foreign Affairs, secretary-treasurer; Bryn Mawr College, consultant on international programs. Writer. **Publications:** Gifts and Nations: The Obligation to Give, Receive and Repay, 1969; (ed. with J.F. Eisenberg) Man and Beast: Comparative Social Behavior, 1971; (with G. Kennan and L. Gordenker) South Africa: Three Visitors Report, 1971; (ed.) The Cultural Drama: Modern Identities and Social Ferment, 1974; (contrib.) The Nature of Scientic Discovery, 1975; (contrib.) Arab and American Cultures, 1977; (ed. with N.G. Kotler) The Statue of Liberty Revisited: Making a Universal Symbol, 1994. Contributor of articles to periodicals. **Address:** Smithsonian Institution, Rm. 153, SI Bldg., MRC 010, PO Box 37012, Washington, DC 20013-7012, U.S.A. **Online address:** mcelroym@op.si.edu

DILLOW, Gordon. American (born United States) **Genres:** Money/Finance, Law, Social Sciences. **Career:** Orange County Register, regional reporter, metro columnist, war correspondent; Los Angeles Herald Examiner, reporter, war correspondent; Los Angeles Times, reporter; Brownsville Herald, reporter; Missoulian, reporter. **Publications:** (With W.J. Rehder) Where the Money Is: True Tales from the Bank Robbery Capital of the World, 2003; (with B. White) Uppity: My Untold Story about the Games People Play, 2011. **Address:** Orange County Register, 625 N Grand Ave., Santa Ana, CA 92701-4347, U.S.A. **Online address:** gldillow@aol.com

DILMORE, Kevin. American (born United States) **Genres:** Novels. **Career:** Republic Newspaper, news editor, reporter and photographer, 1988-2003; Star Trek Communicator Magazine, contributing writer, 1997-, reporter. **Publications:** (With D. Ward) Interphase, vol. I-II, 2001; (with D. Ward) Foundations, vol. I-III, 2002; (co-author) Have Tech Will Travel, 2002; Miracle Workers, 2002; (with D. Ward) Home Fires, 2003; (with D. Ward) A Time to Harvest, 2004; Grand Designs, 2004; Where Time Stands Still, 2004; (with D. Ward) A Time to Sow, 2004; (with D. Ward) Summon the Thunder, 2006; (with D. Ward) 4400: Wet Work, 2008. Contributor of articles to magazines. **Address:** c/o Author Mail, Pocket Books, 1230 Ave. of the Americas, 11th Fl., New York, NY 10020-1513, U.S.A. **Online address:** dilmore@kc.rr.com

DILS, Tracey E. (Tracey Herrold). American (born United States), b. 1958. **Genres:** Children's Fiction, Writing/Journalism. **Career:** Frontier Press, associate editor, 1980-81; Merrill Publishing Co., production editor, 1982-84, developmental editor, 1984-86; Willowisp Press, managing editor and editorial project manager, 1986-89, editor-in-chief, 1989-90; Thurber House, instructor, 1989; Ohio State University, Department of Psychiatry, consultant, Press, marketing manager, 1990-93; A Writer's Place, owner, manager, director, author, 1993-; Romance Writers of America National Convention, instructor; Institute of Children's Literature, faculty, 1993-; Guideposts for Kids Magazine, consultant; Black Oak Books, consultant. **Publications:** Words, Words, Words, 1988; (as Tracey Herrold) The Puppy Who Needed a Friend, 1989; The Scariest Stories You've Ever Heard, vol. III, 1990; Grandpa's Magic, 1990; Whatever I Do, the Monster Does Too, 1991; George Washington: Country Boy, Country Gentleman, 1992; Boytalk: How to Talk to Your Favorite Guy, 1992; A Look around Coral Reefs, 1995; Annabelle's Awful Waffle, 1995; Real-Life Scary Places, 1996; Real-Life Strange Encounters, 1998; You Can Write Children's Books, 1998, 2nd ed., 2009; Samuel L. Jackson, 2000; Exxon Valdez, 2001; Mother Teresa, 2001; Oil Spill Cleaner, 2010. **Address:** 1759 Bedford Rd., Columbus, OH 43212, U.S.A.

DILSAVER, Lary M. American (born United States), b. 1949?. **Genres:** Environmental Sciences/Ecology, Travel/Exploration, Geography, Adult Nonfiction. **Career:** University of South Alabama, assistant professor, 1982-88, associate professor, 1988-92, professor of geography, 1992-; National Park Service, environmental history researcher. Writer. **Publications:** NONFICTION: The Effects of International Tourism: A Bibliography, 1977; (with W.C. Tweed) Challenge of the Big Trees: A Resource History of Sequoia and Kings Canyon National Parks, 1990; (ed. with C.E. Colten) The American Environment: Interpretations of Past Geographies, 1992; (ed.) America's National Park System: The Critical Documents, 1994; (ed. with W. Wyckoff) The Mountainous West: Explorations in Historical Geography, 1995; (contrib.) Western Spaces, American Places, 2003; Cumberland Island National Seashore: A History of Conservation Conflict, 2004. Contributor to periodicals. **Address:** Department of Earth Sciences, University of South Alabama, 1504 Spring Hill Ave., Ste. 3531, Mobile, AL 36604-3207, U.S.A. **Online address:** ldilsaver@usouthal.edu

DIMARCO, Cris K. A. (Cris Newport). American (born United States), b. 1960?. **Genres:** Novels, Mythology/Folklore, Social Sciences, Romance/Historical, Young Adult Fiction. **Career:** Freelance book reviewer and editor, 1988-; New Hampshire Technical Institute, associate professor of English, 1991-97; Windstorm Creative Ltd., senior editor, 1996-, co-owner; Colby Sawyer College, adjunct faculty; Women of Power magazine, managing editor. **Publications:** NOVELS: (as Cris Newport) Sparks Might Fly, 1994; The White Bones of Truth, 1996; Queen's Champion: The Legend of Lancelot Retold (fantasy), 1997; Virtual Rock, 2002; Kresh, 2006. OTHER: 1001 Nights: Exotica 1, 2000; 1002 Nights: Exotica 2, 2001. Contributor of book to periodicals. **Address:** Windstorm Creative, 7419 Ebbert Dr. SE, Port Orchard, WA 98367, U.S.A. **Online address:** crisnewport@aol.com

DIMARCO, Damon. American (born United States), b. 1971. **Genres:** History. **Career:** New River Dramatists Play Development Center, playwright, collaborator, 1999-. **Publications:** (Ed.) Tower Stories: The Autobiography of September 11th, 2004, 2nd ed. as Tower Stories: An Oral History of 9/ 11, 2007; (co-author) Out of Bounds: Coming Out of Sexual Abuse, Addiction and My Life of Lies in the NFL Closet, 2006; (Comp.) Heart of War: Soldiers' Voices from the Front Lines in Iraq, 2007; (with W. Esper) The Actor's Art and Craft: William Esper Teaches the Meisner Technique, 2008; (Comp.) The Quotable Actor: 1001 Pearls of Wisdom from Actors Talking about Acting, 2009. **Address:** The Martha Kaplan Agency, 115 W 29th St., New York, NY 10001, U.S.A. **Online address:** mail@damondimarco.com

DIMBLEBY, Jonathan. British (born England), b. 1944. **Genres:** International Relations/Current Affairs, Biography. **Career:** The World at One, reporter, 1970; ITV, staff, 1972; National Commission for UNESCO, staff, 1978-79; Yorkshire Television, 1979; TV-am News Ltd., staff, 1985, director; Council for the Protection of Rural England, president, vice-president; Soil Association, vice president, Voluntary Service Overseas, president; Index on Censorship, chairman; University of California, honorary fellow; freelance broadcaster, television presenter and journalist. **Publications:** Unknown Famine: A Report on Famine in Ethiopia, 1974; Richard Dimbleby: A Biography, 1975; The Palestinians, 1979; The Prince of Wales: A Biography, 1994; (foreword) Derbyshire: Detail and Character: A Celebration of Its Towns

and Villages, 1996; The Last Governor, 1997; Xianggang Mo Dai Zong Du Peng Dingkang, 1997; The Organic Directory: Your Guide to Buying Natural Foods, 1999; (with P. Conford) The Origins of the Organic Movement, 2001; Russia: A Journey to the Heart of a Land and Its People, 2008. **Address:** David Higham Associates Ltd., 5-8 Lower John St., Golden Sq., London, GL W1R 4HA, England.

DIMBLEBY, Josceline (Rose). British (born England), b. 1943?. **Genres:** Food And Wine, Autobiography/Memoirs, Travel/Exploration. **Career:** Sainsbury's, food writer, 1978-97; Sunday Telegraph, food editor, 1982-97. Public speaker. **Publications:** A Taste of Dreams: Josceline Dimbleby's Cookery Book, 1976 as Taste of Dreams: Cookery Book, 1979; Party Pieces: Special Recipes to Celebrate the Queen's Silver Jubilee, 1952-1977, 1977; Cooking for Christmas, 1978; Cooking with Herbs and Spices, 1979; Family Meat and Fish Cookery, 1979; Josceline Dimbleby's Book of Puddings, Desserts, and Savouries, 1979; Curries and Oriental Cookery, 1980; Salads for All Seasons, 1981; Festive Food and Party Pieces, 1982; Favourite Food, 1983; Sweet Dreams: Puddings and Pies, Gateaux and Ices, and Lots More, 1983; Marvellous Meals with Mince, 1983; First Impressions, 1984; Main Attractions, 1985; A Traveller's Tastes: Recipes from around the World, 1986; The Josceline Dimbleby Christmas Book, 1987; The Essential Josceline Dimbleby, 1989; Soups and Starters, 1991; Puddings and Desserts, 1991; Josceline Dimbleby's Christmas, 1994; The Practically Vegetarian Cookbook, 1994; Sainsbury's the Almost Vegetarian Cookbook, 1994; The Josceline Dimbleby Complete Cookbook, 1997; Josceline Dimbleby's Almost Vegetarian Cookbook, 1999; Josceline Dimbleby's Cooking Course, 1999; The Cooking Enthusiast: An Illustrated Culinary Encyclopedia, 2000; A Profound Secret: May Gaskell, Her Daughter Amy, and Edward Burne-Jones, 2004 as May and Amy: A True Story of Family, Forbidden Love, and The Secret Lives of May Gaskell, Her Daughter Amy, and Sir Edward Burne-Jones, 2004; Josceline Dimbleby's Christmas, 2006; Orchards in the Oasis: Recipes, Travels and Memories, 2010. Contributor to periodicals. **Address:** 18 Ashchurch Park Villas, London, GL W12 9SP, England. **Online address:** jossy@dircon.co.uk

DIMMICK, Barbara. American (born United States), b. 1954?. **Genres:** Novels. **Career:** Freelance writer and educator. **Publications:** In the Presence of Horses, 1998; Heart-Side Up, 2002. **Address:** PO Box 8, Scottsville, NY 14546, U.S.A. **Online address:** email@barbaradimmick.com

DIMOCK, Wai Chee. American/Macanese (born Macao), b. 1953. **Genres:** Literary Criticism And History, Law, Philosophy. **Career:** Rutgers University, assistant professor, 1982-88, associate professor of English, 1988-90; University of California, associate professor of literature, 1990-92; Brandeis University, associate professor 1992-94, professor of English, 1994-97; Harvard University, visiting associate professor of English, 1994; Yale University, professor, 1997-2002, William Lampson professor of English and American studies, 2003-; Peking University, visiting lecturer; Tel Aviv University, visiting lecturer; Central European University, visiting lecturer; University of Turku, visiting lecturer. Writer. **Publications:** Empire for Liberty: Melville and the Poetics of Individualism, 1989; Rethinking Class: Literary Studies and Social Formations, 1994; Residues of Justice: Literature, Law, Philosophy, 1996; Through Other Continents: American Literature across Deep Time, 2006; (ed. with L. Buell) Shades of the Planet: American Literature as World Literature, 2007. Contributor to books and periodicals. **Address:** Department of English, Yale University, 63 High St., Ste. 109, PO Box 208302, New Haven, CT 06520-8302, U.S.A. **Online address:** wai.chee.dimock@yale.edu

DIMOND, Peter. British (born England) **Genres:** Music, Art/Art History. **Career:** School teacher, 1961-65; Somerset Education Authority, music adviser, 1965-82; Open University, lecturer, 1971-2004; Trinity College, examiner in music, 1982-92. Writer. **Publications:** Music Made Simple, 1982; The Art of Beethoven, 1993; Mozart Diary: A Chronological Reconstruction of the Composer's Life, 1761-1791, 1997. **Address:** Golden Pheasant, Stocklinch, Ilminster, Somerset, SM TA19 9JF, England. **Online address:** ptrdmnd@aol.com

DIMSON, Wendy. *See* BARON, Wendy.

DINAN, Desmond. American/Irish (born Ireland), b. 1957?. **Genres:** History, Politics/Government. **Career:** George Mason University, faculty, 1986-, assistant professor, 1987-94, associate professor, 1994-2004, professor of public policy, Ad Personam Jean Monnet professor, Jean Monnet professor of public policy, Jean Monnet chair in European public policy, Ad Personam

Jean Monnet chair, 2002-, Center for European Community Studies, director, 1989-97, Undergraduate Minor in The New Europe, director, 2000-09, International Commerce and Policy Program, director, 2002-06; College of Europe, Directorate General for Education, Communication and Culture, adviser, 1993-94, visiting professor, 1997-2000, 2005-08, research fellow; Netherlands Institute for International Relations, fellow, 1997-2000; College of Europe-Natolin Campus, visiting professor, 2005-08. Writer. **Publications:** The Politics of Persuasion: The British Policy and French African Neutrality, 1940-1942, 1988; Historical Dictionary of the European Community, 1993; Ever Closer Union: An Introduction to the European Community, 1994, 4th ed., 2010; Encyclopedia of the European Union, 1998, rev. ed., 2000; (ed. with L. Cram and N. Nugent) Developments in the European Union, 1999; Europe Recast: A History of European Union, 2004; Developments in the European Union 2, 2004; (ed.) Origins and Evolution of the European Union, 2006; Ever Closer Union: An Introduction to European Integration, 2010. **Address:** George Mason School of Public Policy, George Mason University, MS 3B1, 3351 Fairfax Dr., Arlington, VA 22201, U.S.A. **Online address:** ddinan@gmu.edu

DINAN, Susan E. (Susan Eileen Dinan). American (born United States), b. 1965. **Genres:** Women's Studies And Issues, Theology/Religion, History. **Career:** University of Wisconsin, lecturer, 1994-96; Long Island University, assistant professor, 1997-2003, associate professor of history, 2003-05, assistant dean, 2002-03, history department chair, 2003-05; Folger Shakespeare Library, institute fellow, 1998; National Endowment for the Humanities, Sumner Institute, fellow, 1998; William Paterson University, Honors College, director, 2005-. Writer, academic and historian. **Publications:** (ed. with D. Meyers) Women and Religion in Old and New Worlds, 2001; Women and Poor Relief in Seventeenth-Century France: The Early History of the Daughters of Charity, 2006. **Address:** William Paterson University, 126-129 Raubinger Hall, 300 Pompton Rd., Wayne, NJ 07470-2103, U.S.A. **Online address:** dinans@wpunj.edu

DINAN, Susan Eileen. See DINAN, Susan E.

DINE, Janet. British (born England), b. 1951. **Genres:** Law, Politics/Government, Social Sciences. **Career:** Barrister in London, 1974-80; King's College, lecturer, 1978-86, Center of European Law, director, 1990-; Institute of Advanced Legal Studies, senior research fellow, 1987-89, senior visiting fellow, 2000-; LUISS University, faculty, 1990; University of South Africa, faculty, 1990; WITS University, faculty, 1990; WITS University, faculty, 1990; Russian People's Friendship University, faculty, 1990; University of the West Indies, faculty; RAU University, faculty, 1990; University of Essex, reader, 1992-94, Law Department, professor and head, 1994-97, senior fellow, 2004-; United Kingdom HM Treasury, commissioner for friendly society, 1992-93; TACIS Project, staff, 1999-2000; Queen's University, visiting professor, 2000-03, honorary professor, 2003-; University of London, Queen Mary College, Centre for Commercial Law Studies, professor, 2004-, director, 2005-08, AKC professor of international economic development law. Writer. **Publications:** (With S. Douglas-Scott and I. Persaud) Procedure and the European Court, 1991; (with M. Andeans) Eastern and Central European Company Laws, 1994; Criminal Law in the Company Context, 1995; (with J. Gobert) Cases and Materials on Criminal Law, 2nd ed., 1998, (with J. Gobert and W. Wilson) 6th ed., 2011; (contrib.) Developments in European Company Law, vol. III, 2001; New Perspectives on Property Law: Obligations and Restitution, 2003; The Governance of Corporate Groups, 2000; Criminal Law and the Privilege against Self- Incrimination, 2004; Companies, International Trade and Human Rights, 2005; (ed. with A. Fagan) Human Rights and Capitalism: A Multidisciplinary Perspective on Globalisation, 2006; (with M. Koutsias and M. Blecher) Company Law in the New Europe: The EU Acquis, Comparative Methodology and Model Law, 2007. Contributor to professional journals. **Address:** School of Law, Queen Mary College, University of London, Mile End Rd., London, GL E1 4NS, England. **Online address:** j.m.dine@qmul.ac.uk

DINELLO, Paul. American (born United States), b. 1962. **Genres:** Science Fiction/Fantasy, Young Adult Fiction. **Career:** Allstate Insurance Co., staff; Chicago Mercantile Exchange, staff. Writer, comedian and actor. **Publications:** (With A. Sedaris and S. Colbert) Wigfield: The Can-Do Town That Just May Not, 2003; (contrib.) I Like You: Hospitality Under the Influence, 2006; (contrib.) I Am America (And So Can You!), 2007; Simple Times, 2010. **Address:** c/o John Huddle, United Talent Agency, 9560 Wilshire Blvd., Beverly Hills, CA 90212, U.S.A. **Online address:** caitlin@pauldinello.net

DINER, Dan. German (born Germany), b. 1946?. **Genres:** History, Essays. **Career:** University of Marburg, Department of Political Science, acting professor, 1982-84; University of Osnabrück, Department of Political Science, acting professor, 1984, 1985; University of Southern Denmark, assistant professor, 1984-85; University of Essen, Department of History, professor, 1985-99; Tel Aviv University, Department of History, professor, 1987-99, Institute for German History, director, 1994-99, Benyamin and Chaya Schapelski chair of holocaust studies, 1997-99; University of the Negev, Department of History, professor, 1999-2001; University of Leipzig, Department of History, professor, 1999-, Simon Dubnow Institute for Jewish History and Culture, director, 1999-; Hebrew University of Jerusalem, professor of modern European history, 2001-; University of Odense, professor; Babylon, co-editor. **Publications:** Der Einfluss von Kriegsbegriff und Waffenstillstandsvertrag auf das Kriegsende im modernen Volkerrecht, 1973; Israel in Palastina: über Tausch Und Gewalt Im Vorderen Orient, 1980; Keine Zukunft auf den Gräbern der Palastinenser: Eine Historisch-politische Bilanz der Palästinafrage, 1982; (co-author) Zerbrochene Geschichte: Leben und Selbstverständnis der Juden in Deutschland, 1991; Der Krieg der Erinnerungen und die Ordnung der Welt, 1991; Verkehrte Welten: Antiamerikanismus in Deutschland: Ein Historischer Essay, 1993; Kreislaufe: Nationalsozialismus und Gedächtnis, 1995; Das Jahrhundert Verstehen: Eine Universalhistorische Deutung, 1999; Beyond the Conceivable: Studies on Germany, Nazism, and the Holocaust, 2000; Versiegelte Zeit: über den Stillstand in der Islamischen Welt, 2005; (contrib.) Jüîdische Geschichte als allgemeine Geschichte: Festschrift fùir Dan Diner zum 60. Geburtstag, 2006; Gegenläufige Gedächtnisse: über Geltung und Wirkung des Holocaust, 2007; (with G. Wunberg) Restitution and Memory: Material Restoration in Europe, 2007; Cataclysms: A History of the Twentieth Century from Europe's Edge, 2008; (contrib.) Kanon und Diskurs: über Literarisierung jüdischer Erfahrungswelten, usanne Zepp, 2009; Lost in the Sacred: Why the Muslim World Stood Still, 2009. EDITOR: Ist der Nationalsozialismus Geschichte? Zu Historisierung und Historikerstreit, 1987; Zivilisationsbruch: Denken Nach Auschwitz, 1988; (with J. Frankel) Dark Times, Dire Decisions: Jews and Communism, 2004; Synchrone Welten: Zeitenräume Jüdischer Geschichte, 2005; (with G. Wunberg) Restitution and Memory: Material Restoration in Europe, 2007. **Address:** University of Leipzig, Goldschmidtstrase 28, Leipzig, 04103, Germany.

DINERMAN, Beatrice. American (born United States), b. 1933. **Genres:** Medicine/Health, Politics/Government, Urban Studies, Social Sciences, History. **Career:** University of California, Bureau of Governmental Research, public administration analyst, 1956-62; Welfare Planning Council, director, 1962-65; Economic and Youth Opportunities Agency, social science research analyst, 1965-66; University of California, School of Public Health, research associate, 1966-67; University of Southern California, School of Public Administration, consultant, 1967-68, Regional Research Institute in Social Welfare, research consultant, 1970-72; Comprehensive Health Planning Council of Los Angeles, chief of research and information, 1972-. Writer. **Publications:** Chambers of Commerce in the Modern Metropolis, 1958; Hospital Development and Communities, 1961; Administrative Decentralization in City and County Government, 1961; Structure and Organization of Local Government in the United States, 1961; (with R. Clayton and R.D. Yerby) Metropolitan Services: Studies of Allocation in a Federated Organization, 1961; (with W.W. Crouch) Southern California Metropolis, A Study in Development of Government for a Metropolitan Area, 1963; Citizen Participation in the Model Cities Program, 1971. Contributor to journals. **Address:** 15434 Vista Haven Pl., Sherman Oaks, CA 91403, U.S.A.

DINES, Gail. American/British (born England), b. 1958. **Genres:** Education. **Career:** Wheelock College, professor of sociology and women's studies, 1986-; American Studies Department, chair; Haifa, Israel, founder; Stop Porn Culture (educational and activist group), founding member, 2007; National Feminist Anti-Pornography Movement, co-founder. Writer. **Publications:** (Ed. with J.M. Humez) Gender, Race, and Class in Media: A Text-Reader, 1995, 2nd ed., 2003, 3rd ed. as Gender, Race, and Class in Media: A Critical Reader, 2011; (with R. Jensen and A. Russo) Pornography: The Production and Consumption of Inequality, 1998; (contrib.) The Strength to Resist: Beyond Killing Us Softly, Produced and Directed by Margaret Lazarus and Renner Wunderlich, 2000; Pornland: How Porn Has Hijacked Our Sexuality, 2010. Contributor of articles to periodicals. **Address:** School of Arts and Sciences, American Studies, Wheelock College, 200 The Riverway, Boston, MA 02215, U.S.A. **Online address:** gdines@wheelock.edu

DINH, Linh. American/Vietnamese (born Vietnam), b. 1963. **Genres:** Novellas/Short Stories, Poetry, Adult Non-fiction, Novels. **Career:** The Drunken Boat, co-founder and editor, 1991-93; Art in General, critic-in-residence, 1994; The Fabric Workshop, artist-in-residence, 1994; University of Pennsylvania, visiting faculty. **Publications:** FICTION: (ed.) Night, Again: Contemporary Fiction from Vietnam (short story anthology), 1996, 2nd ed., 2006; Fake House: Stories, 2000; Blood and Soap: Stories, 2004; Love Like Hate: A Novel, 2010. POETRY: Drunkard Boxing, 1998; A Small Triumph Over Lassitude (chapbook), 2001; A Glass of Water, 2001; All Around What Empties Out, 2003. OTHER: (ed. and trans.) Three Vietnamese Poets, 2001; Vietnam Postcards, 2002; (ed.) Night, Again: Contemporary Fiction from Vietnam, 2006; (trans.) Night, Fish and Charlie Parker, 2006. Contributor to journals. **Address:** c/o Author Mail, Seven Stories Press, 140 Watts St., New York, NY 10013, U.S.A. **Online address:** linhdinh99@yahoo.com

DINNERSTEIN, Leonard. American (born United States), b. 1934. **Genres:** History. **Career:** New York Institute of Technology, instructor, 1960-65; City University of New York, Brooklyn College, lecturer, 1965, City College, instructor in American history, 1966-67; Fairleigh Dickinson University, assistant professor, 1967-70; University of Arizona, associate professor, 1970-72, professor of American history, 1972-2004, Judaic Studies, director, 1993-2000, professor emeritus, 2003-. Writer. **Publications:** The Leo Frank Case, 1968, rev. ed., 2008; (with D.M. Reimers) Ethnic Americans: A History of Immigration and Assimilation, 1975, (with D.M. Reimers) 5th ed. as Ethnic Americans: A History of Immigration, 2009; (with R.L. Nichols and D.M. Reimers) Natives and Strangers, 1979, 5th ed., 2009; America and the Survivors of the Holocaust, 1982; Uneasy at Home: Anti-Semitism and the American Jewish Experience, 1987; Antisemitism in America, 1994. EDITOR: (with F.C. Jaher) The Aliens, 1970 as Uncertain Americans, 1977; (with K.T. Jackson) American Vistas, 1971, 7th ed., 1995; Anti-Semitism in the United States, 1971; (with M.D. Palsson) Jews in the South, 1973; (with J. Christie) Decisions and Revisions: Interpretations of Twentieth-Century American History, 1975; (with J. Christie) America Since World War II: Historical Interpretations, 1976. **Address:** Department of History, University of Arizona, 1981 E Miraval Cuarto, Rm. 215, Social Sciences, 1145 SE Campus Dr., Tucson, AZ 85718-3032, U.S.A. **Online address:** dinnerst@u.arizona.edu

DINSDALE, Ann. British (born England), b. 1960. **Genres:** History, Social Sciences. **Career:** Bronte Parsonage Museum, librarian, collections manager, 1996-. Writer. **Publications:** Old Haworth, 1999; The Brontes at Haworth, 2006; The Bronte Collection, 2007; (with M. Ward and R. Swindells) A Guide to Historic Haworth and the Brontes, 2007. **Address:** The Bronte Parsonage Museum, Haworth, Keighley, WY BD22 8DR, England. **Online address:** ann.dinsdale@bronte.org.uk

DINTENFASS, Mark L. American (born United States), b. 1941. **Genres:** Novels, Literary Criticism And History. **Career:** Haile Selassie I University, teacher, 1964-66; Lawrence University, professor of English, 1968, professor emeritus, 2006-. Writer. **Publications:** (Ed.) How to Adapt and Use Reading Materials: A Teacher's Guide, 1967; Make Yourself an Earthquake, 1969; The Case Against Org, 1970; Figure 8, 1974; Montgomery Street, 1978; Old World, New World, 1982; The Loving Place, 1986. Contributor to periodicals. **Address:** Department of English, Lawrence University, 711 E Boldt Way, PO Box 599, Appleton, WI 54911, U.S.A. **Online address:** mark.l.dintenfass@lawrence.edu

DINTIMAN, George B. (George Blough Dintiman). American (born United States), b. 1936. **Genres:** Sports/Fitness, Education, Young Adult Non-fiction. **Career:** South Williamsport High School, physical education teacher and coach, 1958-59; Inter-American University, instructor, 1959-61, associate professor of physical education, 1961-65; Southern Connecticut State College, associate professor and head basketball coach, 1965-68; Virginia Commonwealth University, division chair and professor, 1968-98, professor emeritus, 1998-; National Association of Speed and Explosion (NASE), founder and president. Writer. **Publications:** NONFICTION: (with L.M. Barrow) A Comprehensive Manual of Physical Education Activities for Men, 1970; Evaluation Manual in Health and Physical Education, 1970; Sprinting Speed: Its Improvement for Major Sports Competition, 1971; The Art and Science of Coaching, 1972; What Research Tells the Coach about Sprinting, 1974; How to Run Faster as How to Run Faster: Step-by-Step Instructions on How to Improve Foot Speed, 1979; A Comprehensive Manual of Foundations and Activities for Men and Women, 1979; (with J. Unitas) Improving Health

and Performance in the Athlete, 1979; Doctor Tennis: A Complete Guide of Conditioning and Injury Prevention for Tennis, 1980; Health through Discovery, 1980, 4th ed. (with J.S. Greenberg), 1989; Teacher's Manual for Health through Discovery, 1980; (with J. Unitas) The Athlete's Handbook, 1982; Discovering Lifetime Fitness, 1984; (with B. Ward) Train America!: Achieving Peak Performance and Fitness for Sports Competition, 1988; (with R.D. Ward) Sports Speed, 1988, 3rd ed., 2003; College Student Self-Care Diary, 1991; (with J.S. Greenberg) Exploring Health: Expanding the Boundaries of Wellness, 1992; Exploring Fitness, 1994; (co-author) Physical Fitness and Wellness, 3rd ed., 2004; (with J.S. Greenberg and B.M. Oakes) Wellness: Creating a Life of Health and Fitness, 1997; (with J.S. Greenberg) The Manatech Exercise Program, 1999; High Performance Sports Training, 2001; Speed Improvement for Young Athletes: How to Sprint Faster in Your Sport in 30 Workouts, 2002; (with J.S. Greenberg and B.M. Oakes) Physical Fitness and Wellness: Changing the Way You Look, Feel, and Perform, 2004; Managing Athletic Performance Stress, 2009; Encyclopedia of Sports Speed, 2009. **Address:** National Association of Speed & Explosion (NASE), 1400 W 1st St., PO Box 1784, Kill Devil Hills, NC 27948-8009, U.S.A. **Online address:** naseinc@earthlink.net

DINTIMAN, George Blough. See **DINTIMAN, George B.**

DINTRONE, Charles V. American (born United States), b. 1942. **Genres:** Communications/Media, Film, History, Bibliography. **Career:** Fresno State University, assistant government publications librarian, 1968-72; San Diego State University, head of government publications at university library, 1972-89, coordinator of library instruction, 1989-92, reference librarian, 1992-, general reference division, 1999-2002, head, 2002-05, now librarian emeritus. Writer. **Publications:** Television Program Master Index: Access to Critical and Historical Information on 1002 Shows in 341 Books, 1996, 2nd ed. as Television Program Master Index: Access to Critical and Historical Information on 1, 927 Shows in 925 Books, Dissertations, and Journal Articles, 2003. **Address:** Library, San Diego State University, 5500 Campanile Dr., San Diego, CA 92182, U.S.A. **Online address:** charles.dintrone@sdsu.edu

DIOGUARDI, Joseph J. American (born United States), b. 1940. **Genres:** Politics/Government, Literary Criticism And History. **Career:** Arthur Andersen & Co., certified public accountant, 1962-84, partner, 1972-84; U.S. House of Representatives, congressman, 1985-89; Truth in Government, chairman, 1989-; Albanian American Civic League, president, 1989-, chairman; Congressional Long Island Sound and Hudson River Caucuses, founder and co-chairman. Writer. **Publications:** (Co-author) House of Ill Repute, 1987; Unaccountable Congress: It Doesn't Add Up, 1992. **Address:** Albanian American Civic League, PO Box 70, Ossining, NY 10562-0070, U.S.A. **Online address:** jjd@aacl.com

DIONNE, E(ugene) J. American (born United States), b. 1952. **Genres:** Adult Non-fiction, Politics/Government. **Career:** New York Times, reporter, 1976-90; Washington Post, reporter, 1990-93, columnist, 1993-; Brookings Institution, senior fellow, 1996-; Georgetown University, Public Policy Institute, Foundations of Democracy and Culture, university professor, 2003-; Saint Anselm College, senior research fellow; NPR, commentator. **Publications:** Why Americans Hate Politics: The Death of the Democratic Process, 1991, rev. ed., 1992; They Only Look Dead: Why Progressives Will Dominate the Next Political Era, 1996, rev. ed., 1997; (ed.) Community Works: The Revival of Civil Society in America, 1998; (ed. with J.J. Dilulio, Jr.) What's God Got to Do with the American Experiment?, 2000; (ed. with W. Kristol) Bush v. Gore: The Court Cases and the Commentary, 2001; (ed. with M.H. Chen) Sacred Places, Civic Purposes: Should Government Help Faith-Based Charity?, 2001; (ed. with R.E. Litan and K.M. Drogosz) United We Serve: National Service and the Future of Citizenship, 2003; (ed. with K.M. Drogosz and J.B. Elshtain) One Electorate under God?: A Dialogue of Religion and American Politics, 2004; Stand Up, Fight Back: Republican Toughs, Democratic Wimps, and the Politics of Revenge, 2004; Souled Out: Reclaiming Faith and Politics after the Religious Right, 2008. Contributor to periodicals. **Address:** Department of Government, Georgetown University, 210 Old N, PO Box 571034, Washington, DC 20057, U.S.A. **Online address:** ejd25@georgetown.edu

DIOTALEVI, Dave A. American (born United States), b. 1951. **Genres:** Novels, Theology/Religion. **Career:** Writer. **Publications:** God's Questions: Prayerful Answers for Daily Life, 1998; Miracle Myx (novel), 2008. Contributor to periodicals. **Address:** MA , U.S.A. **Online address:** wheresmyx@yahoo.com

DIOUF, Sylviane A. American/French (born France), b. 1952. **Genres:** Race Relations, Cultural/Ethnic Topics. **Career:** Libreville University, assistant professor, 1976-79; Jeune Afrique (weekly magazine), journalist, 1979-82; Senegalese Diplomatic Service, counselor, 1982-84, 1985-89, 1989-99; New York University, adjunct professor, 1999-2001; New York Public Library, Schomburg Center for Research in Black Culture, researcher and content manager, 2001-. Writer. **Publications:** (With K. Gravelle) Growing up in Crawfish Country, 1998; (with K. Gravelle) A Cajun Childhood, 1998; Servants of Allah: African Muslims Enslaved in the Americas, 1998; Kings and Queens of East Africa, 2000; Growing Up in Slavery, 2001; Bintou's Braids, 2001; (ed.) Fighting the Slave Trade: West African Strategies, 2003; Tranas de Bintou, As, 2004; (ed. and comp. with H. Dodson) In Motion: The African-American Migration Experience, 2004; Dreams of Africa in Alabama: The Slave Ship Clotilda and the Story of the Last Africans Brought to America, 2007. **Address:** Zachary Shuster Harmsworth, 1776 Broadway, Ste. 1405, New York, NY 10019, U.S.A.

DI PIERO, W(illiam) S(imone). American (born United States), b. 1945. **Genres:** Poetry, Art/Art History, Essays, Translations. **Career:** Louisiana State University, instructor, 1976-79, assistant professor of English, 1979-80; Northwestern University, visiting lecturer in English, 1980-82; Stanford University, assistant professor, 1982-85, associate professor, 1985-90, professor of English, 1990-99; Northwestern University, Center for the Writing Arts, poet-in-residence, 2000, 2004. Writer. **Publications:** Memory and Enthusiasm: Essays, 1975-1985, 1989; Out of Eden: Essays on Modern Art, 1991; Shooting the Works: On Poetry and Pictures (essays), 1996; City Dog (essays), 2009; When Can I See You Again: New Art Writings, 2010. POETRY: Country of Survivors, 1974; Solstice, 1981; The First Hour, 1982; The Only Dangerous Thing, 1984; Early Light, 1985; The Dog Star, 1990; The Restorers, 1992; Shadows Burning, 1995; Skirts and Slacks, 2001; Brother Fire, 2004; Chinese Apples: New and Selected Poems, 2007; Nitro Nights, 2011. TRANSLATOR: Giacomo Leopardi, Pensieri, 1981; This Strange Joy: The Collected Poems of Sandro Penna, 1982; The Ellipse: Selected Poems of Leonardo Sinisgalli, 1982; Photography: A History; Ion, 1996; Night of Shooting Stars: Poems by Leonardo Sinisgalli, 2011. Contributor of poems and essays to periodicals. **Address:** 225 Downey St., Ste. 5, San Francisco, CA 94117, U.S.A. **Online address:** dipiero@stanford.edu

DIPIETRO, Cary. Canadian (born Canada), b. 1971. **Genres:** Poetry, History. **Career:** Japan Exchange and Teaching Programme, assistant language teacher, 1996-98; Brave New Shakespeare, founder and educational workshop coordinator, 1999-2002; Kyoto University, visiting lecturer in English, 2002-05; University of Toronto, lecturer, 2005-, undergraduate instructor. Writer. **Publications:** Shakespeare and Modernism, 2006; (ed.) Bradley, Greg, Folger, 2010; (contrib.) The Shakespeare Encyclopedia, forthcoming. **Address:** Department of English and Drama, University of Toronto, 294A North Bldg., 3359 Mississauga Rd. N, Mississauga, ON L5L 1C6, Canada. **Online address:** cary.dipietro@utoronto.ca

DIPPEL, John V(an) H(outen). American (born United States), b. 1946. **Genres:** History. **Career:** Stevens Institute of Technology, adjunct professor of humanities, 1978-80; Jan Krukowski and Associates, senior associate and promotional writer, 1981-; Community Playgroup of Piermont, board director, 1984-89, president, 1988-89; Rockland Council for Young Children, board director, 1988-96. **Publications:** Two Against Hitler: Stealing the Nazis' Best-Kept Secrets, 1992; Bound upon a Wheel of Fire: Why So Many German Jews Made the Tragic Decision to Remain in Nazi Germany, 1996; Race to the Frontier: White Flight and Westward Expansion, 2005; War and Sex: A Brief History of Men's Urge for Battle, 2010. Contributor to magazines. **Address:** 333 Hudson Terr., Piermont, NY 10968-1062, U.S.A. **Online address:** jvdippel@yahoo.com

DIPPLE, Geoffrey. (Geoffrey Luke Dipple). American (born United States), b. 1960?. **Genres:** History, Essays. **Career:** Queen's University, teaching assistant, 1984-86, head teaching assistant, 1986-87, Department of History, instructor, 1991-93, 1994-96; University of Ottawa, assistant professor, 1993-94; University of Toronto, Department of History, instructor, 1995-97, assistant professor, 1997-98; Augustana College, Department of History, assistant professor, 1998-2003, associate professor, 2003-09, chair, 2003-, Stanley L.

Olsen chair of moral values, 2005-07, professor, 2009-. Writer and historian. **Publications:** Antifraternalism and Anticlericalism in the German Reformation: Johann Eberlin Von Günzburg and the Campaign against the Friars, 1996; (ed. with W.O. Packull as Geoffrey L. Dipple) Radical Reformation Studies: Essays Presented to James M. Stayer, 1999; Just as in the Time of the Apostles: Uses of History in the Radical Reformation, 2005. Contributor to books and periodicals. **Address:** Department of History, Augustana College, 236 Madsen Ctr., 2001 S Summit Ave., PO Box 763, Sioux Falls, SD 57197, U.S.A. **Online address:** geoffrey.dipple@augie.edu

DIPPLE, Geoffrey Luke. *See* **DIPPLE, Geoffrey.**

DI PRIMA, Diane. American (born United States), b. 1934. **Genres:** Novels, Plays/Screenplays, Poetry, Autobiography/Memoirs, Translations, Novellas/Short Stories, Women's Studies And Issues, Literary Criticism And History, Literary Criticism And History. **Career:** Floating Bear (magazine), co-editor, 1961-63, editor, 1963-69; New York Poets Theater, director and co-founder, 1961-65; Kulchur, contributing editor, 1961-62; Signal Magazine, associate editor, 1963-65; Poets Press, publisher and editor, 1963-69; Eidolon Editions, editor and publisher, 1972-76; Naropa Institute School of Poetics, instructor, 1974-; New College of California, poetry instructor, 1980-87; San Francisco Institute of Magical and Healing Arts, co-founder and instructor, 1983-92; California College of Arts and Crafts, instructor, 1990-93; San Francisco Art Institute, instructor, 1992; California Institute of Integral Studies, instructor, 1993-95; Atlantic Center for the Arts, master artist-in-residence, 1994; Columbia College, master poet-in-residence, 2000-; Napa State Hospital, instructor; American Theater for Poets, co-founder; Poets Institute, founder. **Publications:** POETRY: The Monster, 1961; This Kind of Bird Flies Backward, 1963; The New Handbook of Heaven, 1963; Unless You Clock In, 1963; Combination Theater Poem and Birthday Poem for Ten People, 1965; Poems for Freddie, 1966, as Freddie Poems, 1974; Haiku, 1966; New Mexico Poem, 1967; Earthsong: Poems, 1957-1959, 1968; Hotel Albert: Poems, 1968; The Star, the Child, the Light, 1968; L.A. Odyssey, 1969; New As, 1969; Notes on the Summer Solstice, 1969; The Book of Hours, 1970; Kerhonkson Journal, 1966, 1971; Prayer to the Mothers, 1971; So Fine, 1971; XV Dedications: Poems, 1971; The Revolutionary Letters, 1971; as The Revolutionary Letters, Etc., 1973; Loba, Part I, 1973; North Country Medicine, 1974; Brass Furnace Going Out: Song, After an Abortion, 1975; Selected Poems, 1956-1975, 1975; Loba As Eve, 1975; Loba, Part II, 1976; Loba, Parts I-VIII, 1978; Wyoming Series, 1988; The Mysteries of Vision, 1988; Pieces of a Song: Selected Poems, 1990; Seminary Poems 1991; The Mask Is the Path of the Star, 1993; 22 Death Poems, 1996. OTHER: Various Fables from Various Places, 1960; Dinners and Nightmares, 1961, rev. ed., 1998; (trans.) Seven Love Poems from the Middle Latin, 1965; (trans.) J. Genet, The Man Condemned to Death: Le condamné à mort, 1965; Spring and Autumn Annals, 1966; (intro.) The Hermetic and Alchemical Writings of Paracelsus, 1967; (ed.) War Poems, 1968; (intro.) The First Cities, 1968; Memoirs of a Beatnik (novel), 1969, rev. ed., 1998; The Calculus of Variation (novel), 1972; (co-author) City for Sale: Ed Koch and the Betrayal of New York, 1988; Only in America: The Life and Crimes of Don King, 1995; Recollections of My Life as a Woman, the New York Years: A Memoir, 2001; Fun with Forms, 2001; Towers Down, 2002; The Ones I Used to Laugh With, 2003; Time Bomb, 2006. Contributor to magazines and newspapers. Works appear in anthologies. **Address:** Wingbow Press, 2940 W 7th St., Berkeley, CA 94710, U.S.A. **Online address:** ddiprima@earthlink.net

DIRCK, Brian R. American (born United States), b. 1965?. **Genres:** Politics/Government, Law. **Career:** Anderson University, assistant professor, associate professor, professor. Writer and historian. **Publications:** Lincoln & Davis: Imagining America, 1809-1865, 2001; Waging War on Trial: A Handbook with Cases, Laws and Documents, 2003; The Executive Branch of Federal Government: People, Process, and Politics, 2007; (ed. and contrib.) Lincoln Emancipated: The President and the Politics of Race, 2007; Lincoln the Lawyer, 2007; Executive Branch of Federal Government: People, Process and Politics, 2007. **Address:** Department of History, Anderson University, 367 Decker, 100 E 5th St., Anderson, IN 46012, U.S.A. **Online address:** brdirck@anderson.edu

DIRENZO, Anthony. American/Italian (born Italy), b. 1960. **Genres:** Novels, Novellas/Short Stories, Administration/Management, Advertising/Public Relations, Business/Trade/Industry, Cultural/Ethnic Topics, Literary Criticism And History, Cartoons, Essays, Humor/Satire, Biography. **Career:** WNNJ/WIXL Radio, copy chief, news writer, production director, 1982-83; WMGQ-

FM Radio, copywriter, 1983-84; Timely Advertising, copy chief, 1984-85; S&L Productions, copywriter and technical writer, 1985-86; Syracuse University, technical assistant, 1986-90, adjunct professor of English, 1990-93; Torvex Studios Inc., technical writer, 1987-90; freelance consultant, 1990-; Ithaca College, associate professor in writing program, 1990-. **Publications:** American Gargoyles: Flannery O'Connor and the Medieval Grotesque, 1993; If I Were Boss: The Early Business Stories of Sinclair Lewis, 1997; Design Discourse: Composing and Revising Programs in Professional and Technical Writing, 2010; Bitter Greens: Essays on Food, Politics, and Ethnicity from the Imperial Kitchen, 2010; Trinacria: A Tale of Bourbon Sicily, forthcoming; After the Fair Is Over, forthcoming. Works appear in anthologies. Contributor of articles to journals. **Address:** Department of Writing, Ithaca College, 430 Smiddy Hall, 953 Danby Rd., Ithaca, NY 14850, U.S.A. **Online address:** direnzo@ithaca.edu

DISALVO, Jackie. (Jacqueline DiSalvo). American (born United States), b. 1943. **Genres:** History, Literary Criticism And History, Organized Labor, Social Commentary, Women's Studies And Issues, Psychology, Writing/Journalism, Novels, Poetry, Adult Non-fiction. **Career:** Antioch College (now University), instructor in English, 1969; Rutgers University, Livingston College, assistant professor of English, 1972-83; City University of New York, Bernard M. Baruch College, associate professor of English, 1984-; City University of New York, Graduate Center, associate professor, 1990-, Ph.D. Program in English, faculty. Writer. **Publications:** War of Titans: Blake's Critique of Milton and the Politics of Religion, 1984; (ed. with G.A. Rosso and C. Hobson) Blake, Politics and History, 1998. Work appear in anthologies. Contributor of articles and poems to magazines. **Address:** Department of English, Bernard M. Baruch College, City University New York, Rm. VC 7-256, 365 5th Ave., 1 Bernard Baruch Way, New York, NY 10016, U.S.A. **Online address:** jacqueline.disalvo@baruch.cuny.edu

DISALVO, Jacqueline. See **DISALVO, Jackie.**

DISILVESTRO, Roger L. American (born United States) **Genres:** Animals/Pets, Travel/Exploration, History, Military/Defense/Arms Control. **Career:** Audubon magazine, senior editor; National Wildlife magazine, senior editor; Audubon Television, chief staff writer; BioScience magazine, features editor. **Publications:** NOVELS: Ursula's Gift, 1988; Living with the Reptiles (science fiction), 1990. NONFICTION: The Endangered Kingdom: The Struggle to Save America's Wildlife, 1989; Audubon Perspectives: Fight for Survival: A Companion to the Audubon Television Specials, 1990; The African Elephant: Twilight in Eden, 1991; Audubon Perspectives: Rebirth of Nature: A Companion to the Audubon Television Specials, 1992; Reclaiming the Last Wild Places: A New Agenda for Biodiversity, 1993; Audubon: Natural Priorities, 1994; In the Shadow of Wounded Knee: The Untold Story of the Indian Wars, 2005; Fair Funding for Wildlife: Investing in Our Commitment to Save America's Endangered Wildlife, 2007; Theodore Roosevelt in the Badlands: A Young Politician's Quest for Recovery in the American West, 2010. **Address:** c/o Author Mail, Walker & Co., 104 5th Ave., New York, NY 10011, U.S.A.

DISKI, Jenny. British (born England), b. 1947. **Genres:** Novels, Young Adult Fiction, Adult Non-fiction, inspirational/Motivational Literature. **Career:** Teacher, 1973-82. Writer. **Publications:** NOVELS: Nothing Natural, 1986; Rainforest, 1987; Like Mother, 1988; Then Again, 1990; Happily Ever After, 1992; Monkeys Uncle, 1994; Vanishing Princess, 1995; The Dream Mistress, 1996; Skating to Antarctica, 1997; Don't, 1998; Only Human: A Comedy, 2000 in US as Only Human: A Divine Comedy, 2001; Skating to Antarctica: Skating to the End of the World, 2001; Stranger on a Train: Daydreaming and Smoking around America with Interruptions, 2002; The View from the Bed and Other Observations, 2003; After These Things, 2004; On Trying to Keep Still, 2006; Apology For the Woman Writing, 2008; What I Don't Know About Animals, 2010; The Sixties, 2010. **Address:** c/o Derek Johns, AP Watt Ltd., 20 John St., London, GL WC1N 2DR, England. **Online address:** info@jennydiski.co.uk

DISPIRITO, Rocco. American (born United States), b. 1966. **Genres:** Food And Wine. **Career:** Aujourd'hui, assistant chef; Adrienne, assistant chef; Lespinasse, chef de partie; Dava Restaurant, founder and executive chef, 1995; Union Pacific, owner and executive chef, 1997-2004; Tuscan, consulting chef, 2003; Rocco's on 22nd, founder and executive chef, 2003-04. Writer. **Publications:** (With K. Sherer) Flavor, 2003; (with N. DiSpirito and N. Lalli) Rocco's Italian-American, 2004; (with K. Kurek) Rocco's 5 Minute Flavor,

2005; Rocco's Real-Life Recipes, 2007; Rocco Gets Real: Cook at Home Every Day, 2008; Now Eat This!: 150 of America's Favorite Comfort Foods, all Under 350 Calories, 2010; Now Eat This! Diet, 2011; Now Eat This! Quick Calorie Solutions at Home, 2011; Now Eat This! Italian: Favorite Dishes from the Real Mamas of Italy, All Under 350 Calories, 2012. Contributor to journals. **Address:** c/o Author Mail, Scribner Publicity, Simon & Schuster, Inc., 1230 Ave. of the Americas, New York, NY 10020, U.S.A.

DITCHFIELD, Christin. American (born United States), b. 1973?. **Genres:** Children's Fiction, Theology/Religion, Children's Non-fiction. **Career:** Take It to Heart (two-minute daily devotional radio program), host. Writer, speaker and educator. **Publications:** FOR CHILDREN: Cowlick!, 2007. SERIES NONFICTION; FOR CHILDREN: Sports Great Michael Chang, 1999; Kayaking, Canoeing, Rowing and Yachting, 2000; Swimming and Diving, 2000; Top 10 American Women's Olympic Gold Medalists, 2000; Wrestling, 2000; Gymnastics, 2000; Cycling, 2000; Martina Hingis, 2001; Wood, 2002; Water, 2002; Soil, 2002; Coal, 2002; Joseph E. Johnston: Confederate General, 2002; Oil, 2002; Condoleezza Rice: National Security Advisor, 2003, rev. ed. as Condoleezza Rice: America's Leading Stateswoman, 2007; Johnny Appleseed, 2003; Golf, 2003; Ice Hockey, 2003; Memorial Day, 2003; Presidents' Day, 2003; The Shoshone, 2003; Tennis, 2003; Volleyball, 2003; Bible Heroes of the Old Testament, 2004; Knowing Your Civil Rights, 2004; Serving Your Community, 2004; Freedom of Speech, 2004; Clara Barton: Founder of the American Red Cross, 2004; The Comanche, 2005; Louisa May Alcott: Author of Little Women, 2005; The Choctaw, 2005; The Blackfoot, 2005; The Shoshone, 2005; The Chippewa, 2005; The Arapaho, 2005; The Crow, 2005; The Lewis and Clark Expedition, 2006; Spanish Missions, 2006; Bono, 2008; OTHERS: A Family Guide to Narnia: Biblical Truths in C.S. Lewis's the Chronicles of Narnia, 2003; Take It to Heart: Sixty Meditations on God and His Word, 2005; The 3 Wise Women: A Christmas Reflection, 2005; A Family Guide to the Lion, the Witch and the Wardrobe, 2005; A Family Guide to Prince Caspian, 2007; A Family Guide to the Bible, 2009; Shwatsit!: No One Knows just what it Means, 2009; A Way with Words: What Women should Know about the Power they Possess, 2010; Bible Stories of Boys and Girls, 2010; (with P. Broughton) Little Golden Book Bible Favorites, 2011; Northeast Indians, 2012; Plateau Indians, 2012; The Story behind Plastic, 2012; The Story behind Soap, 2012; The Story behind Wool, 2012; The Story behind Water, 2012. Contributor to periodicals. **Address:** Take It to Heart Ministries, PO Box 1000, Osprey, FL 34229, U.S.A. **Online address:** christin@takeittoheartradio.coms

DITCHOFF, Pamela J. Canadian/American (born United States), b. 1950. **Genres:** Novels, Poetry, History, Novellas/Short Stories. **Career:** WFSL-TV, head copywriter and creative consultant, 1982-84; Quality Dairy, advertising agent, 1984-85; ASAP Copywriting, owner and sole operator, 1985-87; Haslett Middle School and elementary schools, instructor in Quest Program for Gifted Children, 1985-89; Lansing Community College, instructor in communication and business, 1986-87; Michigan State University, graduate teaching assistant, 1986-89; instructor in creative writers in schools program, 1989-93. Writer. **Publications:** Poetry: One, Two, Three (textbook), 1989; Lexigram Learns America's Capitals (textbook), 1994; The Mirror of Monsters and Prodigies (novel), 1995; Mrs. Beast: A Novel, 1998; Seven Days & Seven Sins: A Novel in Short Stories, 2003; Princess Beast, 2010. Works appear in anthologies. Contributor to periodicals. **Address:** Jane Dystel Literary Management, 1 Union Square W, Ste. 904, New York, NY 10003, U.S.A. **Online address:** pamela@voyager.net

DITTMAR, Trudy. See **DITTMAR, Trudy Addis.**

DITTMAR, Trudy Addis. (Trudy Dittmar). American (born United States), b. 1944. **Genres:** Natural History. **Career:** Chicago City College, Malcolm X Campus, instructor in English, 1967-68; English and social studies teacher, 1970-74; Brookdale Community College, instructor in writing, 1974-81; Estee Lauder Inc., transactional writer, 1989-91; freelance writer, 1993-. **Publications:** (As Trudy Dittmar) Fauna and Flora, Earth and Sky: Brushes with Nature's Wisdom, 2003. **Address:** c/o Jin Auh, The Wylie Agency, 250 W 57th St., Ste. 2114, New York, NY 10107-2199, U.S.A. **Online address:** tdittmar@wyoming.com

DIVAKARUNI, Chitra Banerjee. American/Indian (born India), b. 1956. **Genres:** Poetry, Novels, Novellas/Short Stories, Language/Linguistics, Art/Art History, Literary Criticism And History. **Career:** Diablo Valley College, professor of creative writing, 1987-89; Foothill College, professor of creative writing, 1989-; Mid Peninsula Support Network for Battered Women, staff, 1990-; MAITRI (help-line for South Asianwomen), president, 1991-; University of Houston, professor of creative writing, Betty and Gene McDavid professor of writing. Writer. **Publications:** Dark Like the River (Poem), 1987; The Reason for Nasturtiums (Poems), 1990; Black Candle: Poems about Women from India, Pakistan and Bangaladesh, 1991, rev. ed., 2000; Multitude: Cross-Cultural Readings for Writers, 1993, 2nd ed., 1997; Arranged Marriage, 1995; Leaving Yuba City: New and Selected Poems, 1997; The Mistress of Spices (novel), 1997; Sister of My Heart, 1999; The Unknown Errors of Our Lives: Stories, 2001; Neela, Victory Song, 2002; The Vine of Desire, 2002; The Conch Bearer: A Novel, 2003; Queen of Dreams: A Novel, 2004; The Mirror of Fire and Dreaming: The Brotherhood of the Conch: Book II, 2005; The Palace of Illusions: A Novel, 2008; Shadowland: A Novel, 2009; One Amazing Thing, 2010. EDITOR: We, Too, Sing America, 1998; (with W.E. Justice and J. Quay) California Uncovered: Stories for the 21st Century, 2004. Contributor to periodicals. **Address:** c/o Sandra Dijkstra, Sandra Dijkstra Literary Agency, 1155 Camino Del Mar, PO Box 515, San Diego, CA 92104-2605, U.S.A. **Online address:** chitra.divakaruni.list@gmail.com

DIVALE, William T(ulio). American (born United States), b. 1942. **Genres:** Anthropology/Ethnology, Autobiography/Memoirs, Bibliography. **Career:** City University of New York, York College, professor of anthropology, 1973-, coordinator of anthropology, 1974-, chair of social sciences, 2001-03, deputy chairman of social sciences, School for Professional Studies, professor, 2006-; Society for Cross-Cultural Research, president, 2004-05, 2009-. Writer. **Publications:** (With J. Joseph) I Lived Inside the Campus Revolution, 1970; Warfare in Primitive Societies, 1971, rev. ed., 1973; Matrilocal Residence in Pre-Literate Society, 1984. Contributor to journals. Works appear in anthology. **Address:** Department of Anthropology, York College, City University of New York, AC-3A01, 94-20 Guy R. Brewer Blvd., Jamaica, NY 11451-0001, U.S.A. **Online address:** divale@york.cuny.edu

DIVER, Lucienne. American (born United States), b. 1971?. **Genres:** Young Adult Fiction, Horror. **Career:** Spectrum Literary Agency, literary agent, 1993-2008; Knight Agency, literary agent, 2008-. Writer. **Publications:** (As Kit Daniels) Playing Nice, 2006; Vamped, 2009; ReVamped, 2010. Contributor to periodicals. **Address:** FL , U.S.A. **Online address:** lucienne@luciennediver.com

DIVINE, Robert A(lexander). American (born United States), b. 1929. **Genres:** History, Politics/Government. **Career:** University of Texas at Austin, instructor, 1954-57, assistant professor, 1957-61, associate professor, 1961-63, professor of history, 1963-81, chair of department, 1963-68, George W. Littlefield professor, 1981-96, George W. Littlefield professor emeritus in American history, 1996-; Institute for Advanced Study in the Behavioral Sciences, fellow, 1962-63. Writer. **Publications:** American Immigration Policy 1924-52, 1957; The Illusion of Neutrality, 1962; The Reluctant Belligerent: American Entry into World War II, 1965; Second Chance: The Triumph of Internationalism in America During World War II, 1967; Roosevelt and World War II, 1969; Foreign Policy and U.S. Presidential Elections 1940-1960, 2 vols., 1974; Since 1945: Politics and Diplomacy in Recent American History, 1975; Blowing on the Wind, 1978; Eisenhower and the Cold War, 1981; (co-author) America: Past and Present, 1984, 9th ed., 2010; The Sputnik Challenge, 1993; Perpetual War for Perpetual Peace, 2000. EDITOR: American Foreign Policy, 1960; The Age of Insecurity: America, 1920-1945; Interpretive Articles and Documentary Sources, 1968; (with J.A. Garraty) Twentieth Century America: Contemporary Documents and Opinions, 1968; Causes and Consequences of World War II, 1969; American Foreign Policy since 1945, 1969; The Cuban Missile Crisis, 1971; Exploring the Johnson Years, 1981; The Johnson Years, vol. II, 1987, vol. III, 1994; America, The People and the Dream, 1991; (co-author) The American Story, 2005, 4th ed., 2011. **Address:** Department of History, University of Texas, PO Box Z, Austin, TX 78713, U.S.A. **Online address:** rdivine@austin.rr.com

DIVINSKY, Nathan (Joseph). (N. J. Divinsky). Canadian (born Canada), b. 1925. **Genres:** Mathematics/Statistics, Recreation, Sports/Fitness, Biography. **Career:** University of Manitoba, assistant professor in mathematics, 1951-59; Canadian Chess Chat, editor, 1959-74; University of British Columbia, professor of mathematics, 1959-, assistant dean of science, now professor emeritus; Vancouver School Board, staff, 1974-80; Vancouver City Council, alderman, 1980-81; International Chess Federation, Canadian delegate, 1987. Chess writer. **Publications:** Rings and Radicals, 1965; Around the World in 80 Years, 1965; Linear Algebra, 1975; (with R. Keene) Warriors of the Mind:

A Quest for the Supreme Genius of the Chess Board, 1989; Batsford Chess Encyclopedia, 1990; The Chess Encyclopedia, 1991; Life Maps of the Great Chess Master, 1993; (contrib.) Jewish Chess Masters on Stamps, 2000. **Address:** Department of Mathematics, University of British Columbia, 2329 West Mall, Vancouver, BC V6T 1Z4, Canada.

DIVINSKY, N. J. See **DIVINSKY, Nathan (Joseph).**

DIX, Robin C. See Obituaries.

DIX, Shane. Australian/American (born United States), b. 1960?. **Genres:** Science Fiction/Fantasy, Novels, Young Adult Fiction, Westerns/Adventure. **Career:** Writer. **Publications:** (WITH S. WILLIAMS): COGAL SERIES: The Unknown Soldier, 1995. EVERGENCE SERIES: The Prodigal Sun, 1999; The Dying Light, 2000; The Dark Imbalance, 2001. ORPHANS: Echoes of Earth, 2002; Orphans of Eart, 2002; Heirs of Earth, 2003. GEODESICA SERIES: Asscent, 2005; Descent, 2006. STAR WARS SERIES: Remnant: Force Heretic I, 2003; Refugee: Force Heretic II, 2003; Reunion: Force Heretic III, 2003. **Address:** c/o Author Mail, Ace Books, 375 Hudson St., New York, NY 10014, U.S.A.

DIXON, Ann R. American (born United States), b. 1954. **Genres:** Children's Fiction, Poetry, Young Adult Non-fiction, Adult Non-fiction. **Career:** Hoedads Inc., reforestation contractor, 1977-81; freelance writer, 1981-; Matanuska-Susitna Borough, librarian, 1987-97; Willow Elementary School, librarian and consultant, 2007-. **Publications:** (Reteller) How Raven Brought Light to People, 1992; (reteller) The Sleeping Lady, 1994; Merry Birthday, Nora Noël, 1996 as Waiting for Noël: An Advent Story, 2000; Trick-or-Treat!, 1998; Blueberry Shoe, 1999; (with P. Flowers) Alone across the Arctic: One Woman's Epic Journey by Dog Team, 2001; Winter Is, 2002; (with P. Flowers) Big-Enough Anna: The Little Sled Dog Who Braved the Arctic, 2003; When Posey Peeked at Christmas, 2008. Contributor to periodicals and magazines. **Address:** Willow Elementary School, PO Box 69, Willow, AK 99688, U.S.A. **Online address:** ann@anndixon.com

DIXON, Bernard. British (born England), b. 1938. **Genres:** Medicine/Health, Sciences. **Career:** University of Newcastle, research microbiologist, 1961-65, research fellow, 1965; World Medicine, assistant editor and deputy editor, 1965-68; New Scientist Magazine, science writer, deputy editor, 1968-69, editor, 1969-79; Association of British Science Writers, chairman, 1971-72; Omni Magazine, European editor, 1979-82; Science 80 Magazine, editor, 1980-86; Biotechnology, European editor, 1980-96; Scientist Newspaper, European editor, 1986-90; Medical Science Research, editor, 1989-2003; American Society for Microbiology News, European editor, 1996-. **Publications:** What is Science for?, 1973; Magnificent Microbes, 1976; Invisible Allies: Microbes and Man's Future, 1976; Beyond the Magic Bullet, 1978; Ideas of Science, 1984; Health and the Human Body, 1986; Engineered Organisms in the Environment, 1988; (contrib.) The Encyclopedic Dictionary of Science, 1988; The Society and Science, 1989; Science of Science, 1989; How Science Works, 1989; Science and Society: Changing the Way We Live, 1989; Power Unseen: How Microbes Rule the World, 1994; Animalcules: The Activities, Impacts and Investigators of Microbes, 2009. EDITOR: Journeys in Belief, 1968; Health and the Human Body: An Illustrated Guide to Modern Medical Knowledge, 1986; From Creation to Chaos: Classic Writings in Science, 1989. **Address:** American Society for Microbiology, 1752 North St. NW, Washington, DC 20036-2904, U.S.A.

DIXON, Dougal. British/Scottish (born Scotland), b. 1947. **Genres:** Science Fiction/Fantasy, Earth Sciences, Natural History, Animals/Pets. **Career:** Mitchell-Beazley Ltd., researcher and editor, 1973-78; Blandford Press, researcher and editor, 1978-80; Open University, part-time tutor in earth sciences, 1976-78; Bournemouth Science Fiction and Fantasy Group, vice chairman, 1980-81, chairman, 1981-82, secretary, 1990-2007; freelance writer, 1980-. **Publications:** (Ed. with E. Abranson) Physical Earth, 1977; Doomsday Planet (comic strip), 1980; After Man, 1981; Discovering Earth Sciences, 1982; Science World: Geology, 1982, Geography, 1983; Picture Atlas: Mountains, 1984, Forests, 1984, Deserts, 1984; Find Out about Prehistoric Reptiles, 1984; Find Out about Jungles, 1984; (with J. Burton) The Age of Dinosaurs in US as Time Exposure, 1984; Nature Detective Series: Minerals, Rocks, and Fossils, 1984; Time Machine 7: Ice Age Explorer, 1985; Secrets of the Earth, 1986; Find Out about Dinosaurs, 1986; The First Dinosaurs, 1987; Hunting the Dinosaurs, 1987; The Jurassic Dinosaurs, 1987; The Last Dinosaurs, 1987; Be a Dinosaur Detective, 1987; The New Dinosaurs, 1988;

Dino Dots, 1988; (ed.) The Macmillan Illustrated Encyclopedia of Dinosaurs and Prehistoric Animals, 1988; My First Dinosaur Library, 1989; When Dinosaurs Ruled the Earth, 1989; Air and Oceans, 1990; The Changing Landscape, 1990; Man after Man, 1990; The Giant Book of Dinosaurs, 1990; The Big Book of Prehistoric Life, 1990; Equinox Junior Animals Series, Animal Evolution, 1992; The Big Book of the Earth, 1991; The Practical Geologist, 1992; Explore the World of Prehistoric Life on Earth, 1992; Dinosaurs: Giants of the Earth, 1992; Dinosaurs: The Real Monsters, 1992; Dinosaurs: All Shapes and Sizes, 1992; Dinosaurs: The Fossil Hunters, 1992; Geography Facts, 1992; Earth Facts, 1992; Young Geographer: The Changing Earth, 1992; Dougal Dixon's Dinosaurs, 1993, 3rd ed., 2007; Tell Me about Dinosaurs, 1993; Spotlights: Prehistoric Life, 1993; Questions and Answers about Dinosaurs, 1995; Digging up the Past, 1995; Ladybird Discovery, 1995; Collins Gem, Dinosaurs, 1996; The Earth, Its Wonders, Its Secrets: Natural Disasters, 1996; Dinosaurs, 1996; Amazing Dinosaurs, 2000, 2nd ed. as Amazing Dinosaurs: More Feathers, More Claws, Big Horns, Wide Jaws!, 2007; (co-author) Cassell's Atlas of Evolution, 2001; Dinosaurs: The Good, the Bad, and the Ugly, 2001; My First Book of Dinosaurs, 2001; Megabytes, Dinosaurs, 2001; (ed.) Atlas of the Earth, 2002; The Magic Facet Machine: Dinosaurs, 2002; History Hunters: The Dinosaur Skull, 2003; History Hunters: The Mammoth's Tomb, 2003; (with J. Adams) The Future Is Wild, 2003; Volcano Evacuation, 2004; Hurricane Destruction, 2004; Frozen Mammoth, 2004; Forest Fire, 2004; Earthquake Emergency, 2004; (with J. Malam) Dinosaur, 2004, rev. ed., 2006; Dinosaur Dig, 2004; Triceratops and Other Forest Dinosaurs, 2005; Stegosaurus and Other Plains Dinosaurs, 2005; Plateosaurus and Other Desert Dinosaurs, 2005; Dinosaurs, 2005; Dinosaur Explorer, 2005; Deltadromeus and Other Shoreline Dinosaurs, 2005; Centrosaurus and Other Dinosaurs of Cold Places, 2005; Ankylosaurus and Other Mountain Dinosaurs, 2005; Scutellosaurus and Other Small Dinosaurs, 2006; Saltopus and Other First Dinosaurs, 2006; Prehistoric World: Triassic Life, 2006; Prehistoric World: The Age of Mammals, 2006; Prehistoric World: Jurassic Life, 2006; Prehistoric World: Early Life, 2006; Prehistoric World: Cretaceous Life, 2006; Ornithomimus and Other Fast Dinosaurs, 2006; Istoric world: The Ice Age, 2006; Giganotosaurus and Other Big Dinosaurs, 2006; Ceratosaurus and Other Fierce Dinosaurs, 2006; Styracosaurus and Other Last Dinosaurs, 2006; Nodosaurus and Other Dinosaurs of the East Coast, 2007; Neovenator and Other Dinosaurs Of Europe, 2007; Minmi and Other Dinosaurs of Australia, 2007; Maiasaura and Other Dinosaurs of the Midwest, 2007; If Dinosaurs were Alive Today, 2007; Dromaeosaurus and Other Dinosaurs of the North, 2007; Coelophysis and Other Dinosaurs of the South, 2007; Allosaurus and Other Dinosaurs of the Rockies, 2007; Aletopelta and Other Dinosaurs of the West Coast, 2007; Agustinia and Other Dinosaurs of Central and South America, 2007; Tyrannosaurus and Other Dinosaurs of North America, 2007; Therizinosaurus and Other Dinosaurs of Asia, 2007; Spinosaurus and Other Dinosaurs of Africa, 2007; World of Dinosaurs and Other Prehistoric Life, 2008; Tsintaosaurus and Other Duck-billed Dinosaurs, 2008; Pawpawsaurus and Other Armored Dinosaurs, 2008; Diceratops and Other Horned Dinosaurs, 2008; Deinocheirus and Other Big, Fierce Dinosaurs, 2008; Chungkingosaurus and Other Plated Dinosaurs, 2008; Bambiraptor and Other Feathered Dinosaurs, 2008; Xiaosaurus and Other Dinosaurs of the Dashanpu Digs in China, 2009; Torosaurus and Other Dinosaurs of the Badlands Digs in Montana, 2009; Saurophaganax and Other Meat-eating Dinosaurs, 2009; Masiakasaurus and Other Fish-eating Dinosaurs, 2009; Mahakala and Other Insect-eating Dinosaurs, 2009; Iguanodon and Other Leaf-eating Dinosaurs, 2009; Camarasaurus and Other Dinosaurs of the Garden Park Digs in Colorado, 2009; Baryonyx and Other Dinosaurs of the Isle of Wight Digs in England, 2009; Ultimate Guide to Dinosaurs, 2010; Meat-eating Dinosaurs, 2011; Plant-eating Dinosaurs, 2011; Prehistoric Oceans, 2011; Prehistoric Skies, 2011. Contributor of articles to books and periodicals. **Address:** 55 Mill Ln., Wareham, DS BH20 4QY, England. **Online address:** afterman@tiscali.co.uk

DIXON, John E. British/Australian (born Australia), b. 1946. **Genres:** Social Work, Social Sciences. **Career:** Dun & Bradstreet, business analyst, 1968-70; Australian National University, research assistant in administrative studies in economics, 1974-75; Canberra College of Advanced Education (now University of Canberra), lecturer, 1975-82, associate professor, 1983-90, Management and Policy Studies Centre, director, 1983-90; Monash University, associate professor of management, 1991-92, David Syme Management Education Centre, executive director, 1991-92; Lingnan College (now University), associate professor of sociology and politics and head of social sciences department, 1993-97; University of Plymouth, senior lecturer, professor of international social policy, 1997-2003, professor of public policy and management, 2003-, now professor emeritus, Business School, research

coordinator, 2003-, Governance Network, director; The Kazakhstan Institute of Management, Economics and Strategic Research, College of Social Sciences, dean, Department of Public Administration, distinguished professor. Writer. **Publications:** EDITOR: (with D.L. Jayasuriya) Social Policy in the 1980s, 1983; (with J. Ratnatunga) Australian Small Business, 1984; (with H.S. Kim) Social Welfare in Asia, 1985; Social Welfare in the Middle East, 1987; Social Welfare in Africa, 1987; (with R.P. Scheurell) Social Welfare in Developed Market Countries, 1989; (with R.P. Scheurell) Social Welfare in Latin America, 1990; (with D. Macarov) Social Welfare in Socialist Countries, 1992; (with J. Ratnatunga and D. Tweed) Australia and New Zealand Small Business Manual, 1992; (with R.P. Scheurell) Social Welfare with Indigenous Populations, 1994; (with R.P. Scheurell) Social Security Programs: A Cross-Cultural Comparative Perspective, 1995; (with R.P. Scheurell) Social Welfare with Indigenous Peoples, 1995; (with D. Macarov) Poverty: A Persistent Global Reality, 1997; (with M. Hyde) The Marketization of Social Security: International Perspectives, 2001; (with R.P. Scheurell) The State of Social Welfare: The Twentieth Century in Cross-National Review, 2002; (with M. Hyde) Comparing How Various Nations Administer Retirement Income: Essays on Social Security, Privatisation, and Inter-generational Covenants, 2010. OTHERS: (with J. Cutt and B. Nagorcka) Income Support Policy in Australia, 1977; Australia's Policy towards the Aged, 1890-1972, 1977; The Chinese Welfare System, 1949-1979, 1981; (with D. Newman) Entering the Chinese Market: Risks and Discounted Rewards, 1998; Social Security in Global Perspective, 1999; (with D. Goodwin and J. Wing) Responses to Governance: Governing Corporations, Societies, and the World, 2003; (with M. Hyde and G. Drover) Privatization of Mandatory Retirement Income Protection: International Perspectives, 2006; (with R. Dogan and A. Sanderson) Situational Logic of Social Actions, 2009; (with R. Dogan and A. Sanderson) Reading a Relational Situation: The Contending Lenses, 2009. **Address:** Department of Public Administration, The Kazakhstan Institute of Management, Economics and Strategic Research, 311 a/ac Hall, 4 Abay Ave., Almaty, 050100, Kazakhstan. **Online address:** dixon@kimep.kz

DIXON, Keith. American (born United States), b. 1971?. **Genres:** Young Adult Fiction, Mystery/Crime/Suspense. **Career:** New York Times, Department of News Technology, editor, 1993-. **Publications:** Ghostfires, 2004; The Art of Losing, 2007; Cooking for Gracie, 2011. **Address:** Department of News Technology, The New York Times, 620 8th Ave., New York, NY 10018, U.S.A. **Online address:** kdwriter@gmail.com

DIXON, Larry. American (born United States), b. 1966. **Genres:** Science Fiction/Fantasy, Novels, Young Adult Non-fiction, Theology/Religion. **Career:** Novelist and artist. **Publications:** FANTASY NOVELS WITH M. LACKEY: The Free Bards, 1997. SERRATED EDGE SERIES WITH M. LACKEY: Born to Run, 1992; Chrome Circle, 1994; The Chrome Borne, 1999. MAGE WARS SERIES WITH M. LACKEY: The Black Gryphon, 1994; The White Gryphon, 1995; The Silver Gryphon, 1996. DARIENS TALE WITH M. LACKEY: Owlflight, 1997; Owlsight, 1998; Owlknight, 1999. **Address:** c/o Author Mail, Baen Publishing Enterprises, PO Box 1403, Riverdale, NY 10471-0605, U.S.A.

DIXON, Simon M. British (born England) **Genres:** History, Biography, Autobiography/Memoirs. **Career:** University of Leeds, professor of modern history, School of History, chair; Sidney Sussex College, junior research fellow; University of Glasgow, lecturer in modern history; University College London, School of Slavonic and East European Studies, Arts and Humanities Research, faculty, 2008, Sir Bernard Pares professor of Russian history; Kritika, associate editor. **Publications:** (Co-trans. and co-ed.) Britain and Russia in the Age of Peter the Great: Historical Documents, 1998; The Modernisation of Russia, 1676-1825, 1999; (ed. with J. Klein and M. Fraanje) Reflections on Russia in the Eighteenth Century, 2001; Catherine the Great, 2009. **Address:** School of Slavonic and East European Studies, University College London, 16 Taviton St., London, GL WC1H 0BW, England. **Online address:** s.dixon@ssees.ucl.ac.uk

DIXON, Stephen. American (born United States), b. 1936. **Genres:** Novels, Novellas/Short Stories, Bibliography, Young Adult Fiction. **Career:** News Associates, reporter, 1959-60; Radio Press, reporter, 1959-60; Stanford University, Stegner fellow, 1964-65; New York University, School of Continuing Education, lecturer, 1979-80; Johns Hopkins University, assistant professor, 1980-83, associate professor, 1984-89, professor of fiction, 1990-, now retired. **Publications:** SHORT STORIES: No Relief, 1976; Quite Contrary: The Mary and Newt Story, 1979; 14 Stories, 1980; Movies, 1983; Time to

Go, 1984; The Play and Other Stories, 1988; Love and Will, 1989; All Gone, 1990; Friends: More Will and Magna Stories, 1990; Long Made Short, 1993; The Stories of Stephen Dixon, 1994; Sleep, 1999. NOVELS: Work, 1977; Too Late, 1978; Fall & Rise, 1985; Garbage, 1988; Frog (novel, novellas and stories), 1991; Interstate, 1995; Gould, 1997; 30, 1999; Tisch, 2000; I, 2002; Old Friends, 2004; Phone Rings, 2005; End of I, 2006; Meyer, 2007. OTHERS: Man on Stage (play stories), 1996. **Address:** Melville House Publishing, 145 Plymouth St., Brooklyn, NY 11201, U.S.A.

DIXON, Steve. British (born England), b. 1956?. **Genres:** Art/Art History, Social Sciences, Politics/Government. **Career:** Salford University, head of performance and director of performance research; The Chameleons Group, director, 1994; Brunel University, head of school of arts, professor of performance and technology, Bit Lab Research Centre, deputy director, 2005, pro-vice-chancellor of development. Writer. **Publications:** The Hawaiian Voyages of the Ono Jimmy, 1998; Digital Performance: A History of New Media in Theater, Dance, Performance Art and Installation, 2007. **Address:** Brunel University, Uxbridge Campus, Middlesex, GL UB8 3PH, England. **Online address:** steve.dixon@brunel.ac.uk

DIZIKES, John. American (born United States), b. 1932?. **Genres:** History, Music. **Career:** University of California, staff, 1965-, professor of history and American studies, through 2005, professor emeritus, 2005-; Cowell College, provost. Writer. **Publications:** Britain, Roosevelt, and the New Deal: British Opinion, 1932-1938, 1979; Sportsmen and Gamesmen: American Sporting Life in the Age of Jackson, 1981; Opera in America: A Cultural History, 1993; Yankee Doodle Dandy: The Life and Times of Tod Sloan, 2000; Sportsmen and Gamesmen, 2002. **Address:** Department of American Studies, University of California, 209 Humanities 1, 1156 High St., Santa Cruz, CA 95064, U.S.A.

DJERASSI, Carl. American/Austrian (born Austria), b. 1923. **Genres:** Novels, Novellas/Short Stories, Plays/Screenplays, Poetry, Chemistry, Sex, Autobiography/Memoirs, Adult Non-fiction, Adult Non-fiction, Essays. **Career:** Ciba Pharmaceutical Products, research chemist, 1942-43, 1945-49; Syntex S.A., associate director of research, 1949-52, research vice president, 1957-60, Syntex Research, vice president, 1962-68, president, 1968-72, Syntex Laboratory, vice president, 1960-62; Wayne State University, associate professor, 1952-53, professor of chemistry, 1953-59; Stanford University, professor of chemistry, 1959-2002, professor emeritus, 2002-; Zoecon Corp., chief executive officer, 1968-83, chairman, 1968-88. Writer. **Publications:** Optical Rotatory Dispersion: Applications to Organic Chemistry, 1960; (ed.) Steroid Reactions: An Outline for Organic Chemists, 1963; (with H. Budzikiewicz and D.H. Williams) Structure Elucidation of Natural Products by Mass Spectrometry, 1964; (co-author) Interpretation of Mass Spectra of Organic Compounds, 1964; (with H. Budzikiewicz and D.H. Williams) Mass Spectrometry of Organic Compounds, 1967; The Politics of Contraception, 1979; The Futurist and Other Stories, 1988; Cantor's Dilemma, 1989; Steroids Made It Possible, 1990; The Clock Runs Backward, 1991; The Pill, Pygmy Chimps, and Degas' Horse, 1992; From the Lab into the World, 1994; The Bourbaki Gambit, 1994; Marx, Deceased, 1996; Menachem's Seed, 1996; NO, 1998; An Immaculate Misconception, 1999; (with R. Hoffmann) Oxygen, 2001; This Man's Pill, 2001; (ed. with C. Aigner and contrib.) Paul Klee: Masterpieces of the Djerassi Collection, 2002; Calculus, 2002; (with D. Pinner) Newton's Darkness: Two Dramatic Views, 2003; Dalla pillola alla penna, 2004; Ego: Three on a Couch, 2004; Phallacy, 2005; Taboos, 2006; Four Jews on Parnassus, 2008; Sex in an Age of Technological Reproduction, 2008; Foreplay, 2011. Contributor to periodicals. **Address:** Department of Chemistry, Stanford University, Rm. 121, Mudd Bldg., 333 Campus Dr., Stanford, CA 94305-5080, U.S.A. **Online address:** djerassi@stanford.edu

DJOLETO, (Solomon Alexander) Amu. Ghanaian (born Ghana), b. 1929. **Genres:** Adult Non-fiction, Children's Fiction, Poetry, Novels, Young Adult Non-fiction. **Career:** Ghana Ministry of Education, Government Secondary Technical School, education officer, 1958, senior education officer and head of English department, 1963, assistant headmaster, 1964; Ghana Ministry of Education, editor of Ghana Teachers Journal, 1966, principal education officer in charge of information, public relations and publications, 1967, deputy chief education officer and head of planning division, 1973, Ghana Book Development Council, executive director, 1975-89; Authorship Development Fund, vice-chairperson of board; United Nations Educational, Scientific and Cultural Organization, consultant on book development councils to several African countries, 1981-88; United Nations University, consultant, 1988-89;

Ghana Ministry of Education, textbooks consultant, 1989-. **Publications:** NONFICTION: English Practice for the African Student (textbook), 1967, rev. ed. as English Practice, 1990. EDITOR: (ed. with T. Kwami) West African Prose Anthology, 1972; Ten Stories from Chaucer, 1979; Books and Reading in Ghana, 1985; Chaucer's Prologue and Five Stories, 1987. FICTION: The Strange Man, 1967; Money Galore, 1975; Hurricane of Dust, 1987. POETRY: Amid the Swelling Act, 1992. CHILDREN'S BOOKS: Obodai Sai (novel), 1990; Twins in Trouble, 1991; The Frightened Thief, 1992; Kofi Loses His Way, 1996; The Girl Who Knows about Cars, 1996; Akos and the Fire Ghost, 1997. Contributor to books. **Address:** Dzorwulu Bookshop, Cantonments Communications Centre, PO Box C2217, Accra, 4, Ghana.

DJUPE, Paul A. American (born United States), b. 1971. **Genres:** Young Adult Non-fiction, Institutions/Organizations, Theology/Religion, Politics/Government. **Career:** Denison University, associate professor of political science, 1999-. Writer. **Publications:** (ed. with L.R. Olson) Encyclopedia of American Religion and Politics (nonfiction), 2003; (ed. with L.R. Olson) Religious Interests in Community Conflict: Beyond the Culture Wars (nonfiction), 2007. NONFICTION WITH CHRISTOPHER P. GILBERT: (with D.A.M. Peterson and T.R. Johnson) Religious Institutions and Minor Parties in the United States, 1999; The Prophetic Pulpit: Clergy, Churches and Communities in American Politics, 2003; The Political Influence of Churches, 2009. **Address:** Department of Political Science, Denison University, Granville, OH 43023, U.S.A. **Online address:** djupe@denison.edu

DJWA, Sandra (Ann). Canadian (born Canada), b. 1939. **Genres:** Poetry, Essays, Biography, Essays, Language/Linguistics, Law, Autobiography/Memoirs. **Career:** Simon Fraser University, Department of English, assistant professor, 1968-73, associate professor, 1973-80, professor, 1980-, chair, 1986-94. Writer. **Publications:** E.J. Pratt: The Evolutionary Vision, 1974; (with M.G. Flitton) An Inventory of Research-in-Progress and Suggested Research Projects in English-Canadian Literature, 1978-1979, 1979; The Politics of the Imagination: A Life of F.R. Scott, 1987; F.R. Scott and His Works, 1989; F.R. Scott: Une Vie, 2001; Professing English: A Life of Roy Daniells, 2002. EDITOR: (and intro.) Saul and Selected Poetry of Charles Heavysege, 1976; (with R. St. J. Macdonald) On F.R. Scott: Essays on His Contributions to Law, Literature and Politics, 1983; (with R.G. Moyles) E.J. Pratt: Complete Poems, 2 vols., 1989; Giving Canada a Literary History: A Memoir by Carl F. Klinck, 1991; (with W.J. Keith and Z. Pollock) Selected Poems, 2000. **Address:** Department of English, Simon Fraser University, 6117 AQ, 8888 University Dr., Burnaby, BC V5A 1S6, Canada. **Online address:** djwa@sfu.ca

D'LACEY, Chris. British/Maltese (born Malta), b. 1954. **Genres:** Novels, Children's Fiction, Novellas/Short Stories, Sports/Fitness. **Career:** Leicester University, histologist, 1978, confocal microscopist. Writer. **Publications:** A Hole at the Pole, 1994; Juggling with Jeremy, 1996; Henry Spaloosh!, 1997; The Snail Patrol, 1998; The Table Football League, 1998; A Break in the Chain, 1998; Fly Cherokee Fly, 1998; Lofty, 1999; Bubble and Float, 1999; Riverside United, 1999; Scupper Hargreaves Football Genie!, 2000; From E to You, 2000; Dexters Journey, 2000; The Salt Pirates of Skegness, 2001; Pawnee Warrior, 2002; The Prompter, 2003; Franklin's Bear, 2003; Falling 4 Mandy, 2003; Horace: A Teddy Bear Story, 2004; Shrinking Ralph Perfect, 2005; The Fire Within, 2005; Icefire, 2005; Fire Star, 2005; Franklin's Bear, 2006; Fire Star, 2007; The Fire Eternal, 2007; Gruffen: Dragons of Wayward Crescent, 2008; Gauge, 2008; Glade, 2009; Dark Fire, 2009; Grabber, 2010; Fire World, 2011; The Fire Ascending, 2012. Works appear in anthologies. **Address:** Scholastic Inc., 557 Broadway, New York, NY 10012, U.S.A. **Online address:** ldc@le.ac.uk

DOAK, Wade (Thomas). New Zealander (born New Zealand), b. 1940. **Genres:** Anthropology/Ethnology, Children's Non-fiction, Environmental Sciences/Ecology, History, Marine Sciences/Oceanography, Natural History, Young Adult Non-fiction, Zoology, Zoology. **Career:** Teacher, 1963-81; Dive South Pacific Magazine, publisher. Writer. **Publications:** Elingamite and Its Treasure, 1969; Beneath New Zealand Seas, 1971; Fishes of the New Zealand Region, 1972; Sharks and Other Ancestors: Patterns of Survival in the South Seas, 1975; Islands of Survival, 1976; The Cliffdwellers, 1979; Dolphin, Dolphin, 1982; The Burning of the Boyd: A Saga of Culture Clash, 1984; Ocean Planet, 1984; Encounters with Whales and Dolphins, 1989; Wade Doak's World of New Zealand Fishes, 1991; Swimming with Dolphins in New Zealand, 1994; Friends in the Sea: Solo Dolphins in New Zealand & Australia, 1995; Deep Blue: A South Pacific Odyssey, 1996; I Am a Fish, 1999; Photographic Guide to Sea Fishes of New Zealand, 2003, Gaia Calls: South

Sea Voices, Dolphins, Sharks and Rainforests, 2012. **Address:** PO Box 20, Whangarei, 01500, New Zealand. **Online address:** wade@wadedoak.com

DOANE, Janice (L.). American (born United States), b. 1950. **Genres:** Literary Criticism And History, Women's Studies And Issues, Novels, Gay And Lesbian Issues. **Career:** Canisius College, instructor, 1980-82; State University of New York College, instructor in English, 1980-83; Medaille College, instructor, 1981; St. Mary's College of California, assistant professor, 1984-89, associate professor of English, 1989-, professor of English, department head, 1993-, Department of Women's Studies, faculty. Writer. **Publications:** Silence and Narrative: The Early Novels of Gertrude Stein, 1986; (with D. Hodges) Nostalgia and Sexual Difference: The Resistance to Contemporary Feminism, 1987; (with D. Hodges) From Klein to Kristeva: Psychoanalytic Feminism and the Search for the Good Enough Mother, 1992; (with D. Hodges) Telling Incest: Narratives of Dangerous Remembering from Stein to Sapphire, 2002. Contributor to books and journals. **Address:** Department of English, St. Mary's College of California, 306 Dante Hall, 1928 Saint Mary's Rd., PO Box 4730, Moraga, CA 94556, U.S.A. **Online address:** jdoane@stmarys-ca.edu

DOBBIN, Murray. Canadian (born Canada), b. 1945. **Genres:** Economics, Politics/Government, Biography. **Career:** Freelance writer, 1971-; educator, 1978-86; Financial Post, columnist; Winnipeg Free Press, columnist. **Publications:** The One-and-a-Half Men, 1981; Preston Manning and the Reform Party, 1991; The Politics of Kim Campbell, 1993; The Remaking of New Zealand, (radio documentary), 1994; The Myth of the Good Corporate Citizen: Democracy Under the Rule of Big Business, 1998; Paul Mortin: CEO for Canada?, 2003; Myth of the Good Corporate Citizen: Canada and Democracy in the Age of Globalization, 2003; Paul Martin: un PDG à la barre, 2004. **Address:** 903 9th Ave. N, Saskatoon, SK S7K 2Z3, Canada. **Online address:** mdobbin@telus.net

DOBBS, Michael. British (born England), b. 1948. **Genres:** Politics/Government, Novels. **Career:** Adviser to Margaret Thatcher, 1975-90; U.K. government adviser, 1983-87; Saatchi & Saatchi Advertising, deputy chairman, 1983-86, 1988-91; Conservative Party, chief of staff, 1986-87; Conservative Party, deputy chairman, 1994-95; adviser to John Major, 1994-97; playwright and broadcaster, 1995-. Writer. **Publications:** HARRY JONES NOVELS: The Lord's Day, 2007; Edge of Madness, 2008; The Reluctant Hero, 2010; Old Enemies 2011; The Sentimental Traitor, 2012. FRANCIS URQUHART NOVELS: House of Cards, 1989; To Play the King, 1992; The Final Cut, 1995. THOMAS GOODFELLOWE NOVELS: Goodfellowe MP, 1997; The Buddha of Brewer Street, 1998; Whispers of Betrayal, 2001. WINSTON CHURCHILL NOVELS: Winston's War, 2002; Never Surrender, 2003; Churchill's Hour, 2004; Churchill's Triumph, 2005. OTHERS: Wall Games, 1990; Last Man to Die, 1992. **Address:** Bell Lomax Moreton Agency, 1 James House, Babmaes St., London, GL SW1Y 6HF, England. **Online address:** michldobbs@aol.com

DOBBS, Ricky F. American (born United States) **Genres:** Politics/Government, History, Biography. **Career:** Texas A&M University, assistant professor, associate professor of history, University College, dean. Writer. **Publications:** Yellow Dogs and Republicans: Allan Shivers and Texas Two-Party Politics, 2005. **Address:** Department of History, Texas A&M University, Commerce, TX 75429-3011, U.S.A. **Online address:** ricky_dobbs@tamu-commerce.edu

DOBIE, Kathy. American (born United States) **Genres:** Autobiography/Memoirs, Young Adult Non-fiction, Social Sciences. **Career:** Writer. **Publications:** The Only Girl in the Car: A Memoir, 2003. Contributor to periodicals and web sites. **Address:** c/o Author Mail, Dial Press, Bantam Dell Publishing Group, Random House, 1745 Broadway, New York, NY 10019, U.S.A.

DOBREZ, Patricia. Australian (born Australia), b. 1943. **Genres:** Biography, Art/Art History. **Career:** Australian National University, faculty, visiting fellow; Australian Catholic University, teacher. Writer. **Publications:** (With P. Herbst) The Art of the Boyds: Generations of Artistic Achievement, 1990; Michael Dransfield's Lives: A Sixties Biography, 1998. Contributor to periodicals. **Address:** Australian National University, Manning Clark Ctr., Canberra, AC 0200, Australia.

DOBRIN, Lyn. American (born United States), b. 1942. **Genres:** Children's Fiction, Civil Liberties/Human Rights, Food And Wine, Homes/Gardens,

Medicine/Health, Travel/Exploration. **Career:** World Hunger Year, editor, 1976-80; Adelphi University, School of Social Work, Community Relations, director, 1981-95. Public relations consultant and freelance writer, 1995-. **Publications:** (With J. Ibongia) The Magic Stone, 1967; (with T. Liotti and A. Dobrin) Convictions: Political Prisoners, Their Stories, 1981; Look to This Day: Voices Affirming the Human Spirit, 1988. **Address:** 613 Dartmouth St., Westbury, NY 11590, U.S.A. **Online address:** lyndobrin@optonline.net

DOBSON, Alan P. Scottish/British (born England), b. 1951. **Genres:** Politics/Government, History, International Relations/Current Affairs, Air/Space Topics. **Career:** University of Wales, University College of Swansea, lecturer, 1978-91, senior lecturer in politics, 1991-96, reader, 1996; Norwegian Nobel Institute, senior research fellow, 1997; University of Dundee, School of Humanities, Department of Politics, professor, 1999-, Institute for Transatlantic, European and American Studies, director, 2003-; Baylor University, McBride Centre for International Business Studies, distinguished visiting research professor, 2008. Writer. **Publications:** US Wartime Aid to Britain, 1940-1946, 1986; Politics of the Anglo-American Economic Special Relationship, 1940-1987, 1988; Peaceful Air Warfare: The United States, Britain, and the Politics of International Aviation, 1991; Flying in the Face of Competition: The Policies and Diplomacy of Airline Regulatory Reform in Britain, the USA, and the European Community, 1968-94, 1995; Anglo-American Relations in the Twentieth Century: Of Friendship, Conflict, and the Rise and Decline of Superpowers, 1995; (ed. with S.P. Malik and G. Evans) Deconstructing and Reconstructing the Cold War, 1999; (with S. Marsh) US Foreign Policy since 1945, 2000, 2nd ed., 2006; US Economic Statecraft for Survival, 1933-1991: Of Sanctions, Embargoes, and Economic Warfare, 2002; Globalization and Regional Integration: The Origins, Development and Impact of the Single European Aviation Market, 2007; FDR and Civil Aviation: Flying Strong, Flying Free, 2011. **Address:** Department of Politics, School of Humanities, University of Dundee, Nethergate, Dundee, DD1 4HN, Scotland. **Online address:** a.p.dobson@dundee.ac.uk

DOBSON, Andrew (Nicholas Howard). British (born England), b. 1957. **Genres:** Philosophy, Politics/Government, Social Sciences. **Career:** St. John's College, E.S.R.C. research fellow, 1984-87; University of Keele, lecturer in politics, 1987-93, professor of politics, 1993-2002, 2006-; Lulea University of Technology, visiting professor, 1996-2003; Open University, professor of politics, 2002-06. Writer. **Publications:** An Introduction to the Politics and Philosophy of Jose Ortega y Gasset, 1989; Green Political Thought: An Introduction, 1990, 4th ed., 2007; Jean-Paul Sartre and the Politics of Reason, 1993; Justice and the Environment: Conceptions of Environmental Sustainability and Theories of Distributive Justice, 1998; Fairness and Futurity: Essays on Environmental Sustainability and Social Justice, 1999; Citizenship and the Environment, 2003. EDITOR/CO-EDITOR: The Green Reader, 1991; (with P. Lucardie) The Politics of Nature: Explorations in Green Political Theory, 1993; (with D. Bell) Environmental Citizenship, 2005; (with J. Huysmans and R. Prokhovnik) The Politics of Protection: Sites of Insecurity and Political Agency, 2006; (with R. Eckersley) Political Theory and the Ecological Challenge, 2006; Contemporary Environmental Politics: From Margins to Mainstream, 2006; (with A.V. Saiz) Citizenship, Environment, Economy, 2006. **Address:** Keele University, CBB 2.024, Keele, ST ST5 5BG, England. **Online address:** a.n.h.dobson@pol.keele.ac.uk

DOBSON, Barrie. See **DOBSON, R(ichard) Barrie.**

DOBSON, James C. American (born United States), b. 1936. **Genres:** Medicine/Health, Psychology, Women's Studies And Issues, Human Relations/Parenting. **Career:** Hudson School District, teacher, 1960-63; psychometrist, 1962-63; Charter Oak Unified School District, psychometrist and coordinator, 1963-64, school psychologist and coordinator of pupil personnel services, 1964-66; University of Southern California, School of Medicine, Department of Medical Genetics and Child Development, Children's Hospital of Los Angeles, assistant professor, 1969-77, associate clinical professor of pediatrics, 1978-83, Division of Medical Genetics, co-director of research; Focus on the Family, founder, 1977-, president and chief executive officer, 1977-2003, board director, board chairman, through 2009, now chairman emeritus. Writer. **Publications:** Dare to Discipline, 1970; (ed. with R. Koch) The Mentally Retarded Child and His Family: A Multidisciplinary Handbook, 1971, rev. ed., 1976; Discipline with Love, 1972; Hide or Seek, 1974, 3rd ed., 1979; What Wives Wish Their Husbands Knew about Women, 1975; The Strong-Willed Child, 1978; Prescription for a Tired Homemaker, 1978; Preparing for Adolescence, 1978; (with D. Dobson) Woof!: A Bedtime Story about a Dog,

1979; Straight Talk to Men and Their Wives, 1980, rev. ed., 1991; Emotions: Can You Trust Them?, 1980; Dr. Dobson Answers Your Questions, 1982; Love Must Be Tough, 1983; Dr. Dobson Answers Your Questions about Confident, Healthy Families, 1986; Dr. Dobson Answers Your Questions about Marriage and Sexuality, 1986; Dr. Dobson Answers Your Questions about Raising Children, 1986; Temper Your Child's Tantrums, 1986; Love for a Lifetime, 1987; Parenting Isn't for Cowards, 1987; Christ in Christmas: A Family Advent Celebration, 1989; Counsels You on Romantic Love: Using Your Head in Matters of the Heart, 1989; Romantic Love, 1989; Children at Risk, 1990; Help for Home and Family, 1990; The New Dare to Discipline, 1992; When God Doesn't Make Sense, 1993; Life on the Edge, 1996; Love for a Lifetime: Building a Marriage That Will Go the Distance, 1996; Home with a Heart: Encouragement for Families, 1996; In the Arms of God, 1997; Solid Answers, 1997; Coming Home: Timeless Wisdom for Families, 1998; Night Light, 2000; Stories of the Heart and Home, 2000; Keys to a Lifelong Love, 2000; Straight Talk to Men: Recovering the Biblical Meaning of Manhood, 2000; Finding God's Will for Your Life, 2000; Bringing up Boys, 2001; Emotions: Friend or Foe, 2001; New Hide Or Seek: Building Confidence In Your Child, 2001; Getting Along with Your Parents, 2001; Key to Lifelong Love, 2001; 38 Values To Live By, 2001; Money and Success, 2001; Trusting God When Life Goes Wrong, 2001; (with S. Dobson) Night Light for Parents, 2002; Family Christmas, 2002; Wonderful World of Boys, 2003; Seven Solutions for Burned-Out Parents, 2004; Dr. James Dobson on Parenting, 2004; Marriage Under Fire: Why We Must Win This War, 2004; Romantic Love: How to Be Head Over Heels and Still Land on Your Feet, 2004; The New Strong-Willed Child, 2004; Preparing for Adolescence Group Guide, 2005; Father, A Hero: Inspiration and Insights for Every Dad, 2005; 5 essentials for Lifelong Intimacy, 2005; Love Must Be Tough: New Hope for Families in Crisis, 2007; Bringing Up Girls, 2010; Dads and Daughters, 2011. **Address:** Focus on the Family, 8605 Explorer Dr., Colorado Springs, CO 80920-0500, U.S.A. **Online address:** backpacker18@juno.com

DOBSON, Jill. British (born England), b. 1969?. **Genres:** Young Adult Fiction. **Career:** The Moscow Times, copy editor; Australian Department of Defence, employee; International Institute for Strategic Studies, assistant editor. Educator. **Publications:** YOUNG ADULT FICTION: The Inheritors, 1988; Time to Go, 1991; A Journey to Distant Mountains, 2001. **Address:** c/o Author Mail, University of Queensland Press, Staff House Rd., PO Box 6042, St. Lucia, QL 4067, Australia.

DOBSON, Joanne. American (born United States), b. 1942. **Genres:** Novels, Literary Criticism And History. **Career:** Amherst College, visiting professor of English and American studies, 1985-86; Tufts University, visiting assistant professor of English, 1986-87; Fordham University, assistant professor, 1987-92, associate professor of English, 1992-; Journal of American Women Writers, founding editor, 1983-93. **Publications:** (Ed. and intro.) The Hidden Hand, 1988; Dickinson and the Strategies of Reticence: The Woman Writer in Nineteenth-Century America, 1989. NOVELS: Quieter than Sleep, 1997; The Northbury Papers, 1998; The Raven and the Nightingale, 1999; Cold and Pure and Very Dead, 2000; The Maltese Manuscript, 2003; Death Without Tenure, 2010. Contributor of books to periodicals. **Address:** Department of English, Fordham University, 441 E Fordham Rd., Bronx, NY 10458, U.S.A. **Online address:** jadobson@aol.com

DOBSON, Julia. See TUGENDHAT, Julia.

DOBSON, R(ichard) Barrie. (Barrie Dobson). British (born England), b. 1931. **Genres:** History, Theology/Religion, Politics/Government, Essays, Social Sciences. **Career:** University of St. Andrews, lecturer in medieval history, 1958-64; University of York, lecturer, 1964-68, senior lecturer, 1968-76, professor of history, 1976-88, honorary professor of history, 1999-; honorary visiting professor; York Film Theatre, founder and chairman, 1968-74; Cambridge University, professor of medieval history, 1988-99. Writer. **Publications:** Selby Abbey and Town, 1969; (with M.J. Angold) The World of the Middle Ages, 1971; Durham Priory, 1400-1450, 1973; The Jews of Medieval York and the Massacre of March 1190, 1974; (with J. Taylor) Rymes of Robyn Hood: An Introduction to the English Outlaw, 1976, (ed. with J. Taylor) rev. ed., 1997; (with S. Donaghey) The Nunnery of Clementhorpe, 1984; Preserving the Perishable: Contrasting Communities in Medieval England: An Inaugural Lecture Delivered in the University of Cambridge on 22 February 1990, 1991; Church and Society in the Medieval North of England, 1996; Plantagenet England (History of Medieval Britain), 2003. EDITOR: The Peasants' Revolt of 1381, 1970; York City Chamberlains' Account Rolls,

1396-1500, 1980; (as Barrie Dobson) The Church, Politics, and Patronage in the Fifteenth Century, 1984; (as Barrie Dobson with P. Biller) Medieval Church: Universities, Heresy, and the Religious Life: Essays in Honour of Gordon Leff, 1999; (co-ed.) Foundations of Medieval English Ecclesiastical History: Studies Presented to David Smith, 2005. Contributor to journals. **Address:** Department of History, University of York, Heslington, York, NY YO10 5DD, England.

DOBYNS, Jay Anthony. See DOBYNS, Jay Jaybird.

DOBYNS, Jay Jaybird. (Jay Anthony Dobyns). American (born United States), b. 1961. **Genres:** Autobiography/Memoirs. **Career:** U.S. Bureau of Alcohol, Tobacco, and Firearms (ATF), agent, 1987-, ATF National Academy, undercover instructor, 1989-; Jay Dobyns Group L.L.C. (a motivational speaking and consulting business), owner and operator. Writer, public speaker, consultant and law enforcement officer. **Publications:** (With N. Johnson-Shelton) No Angel: My Harrowing Undercover Journey to the Inner Circle of the Hell's Angels (memoir), 2009. **Address:** U.S.A. **Online address:** jay@jaydobyns.com

DOCHERTY, James. See DOCHERTY, Jimmy.

DOCHERTY, James C(airns). Australian (born Australia), b. 1949. **Genres:** History, Demography, Reference. **Career:** Australian National University, research assistant, 1974, research assistant in political science, 1974, 1977; Australian Bureau of Statistics, Australian Federal Government, research officer, 1978-79; Australian Department of Industrial Relations, clerk, executive officer, head of Trends Section, 1983-87, administrative service officer, 1984-, branch publications editor, 1992-93, Department of Immigration and Multicultural Affairs, staff, 1996-2004; Monash University, National Centre for Australian Studies, honorary research associate, 1990-96. Writer. **Publications:** Selected Social Statistics of New South Wales, 1861-1976 (monograph), 1982; Newcastle: The Making of an Australian City, 1983; (with M. Mellman and S.B. Lilien) Discovery Techniques, 1987; Historical Dictionary of Australia, 1992, rev. ed., 1999; (ed. with D. Peetz and A. Preston and contrib.) Workplace Bargaining in the International Context: First Report of the Workplace Bargaining Research Project, 1993; A Historical Dictionary of Organized Labor, 1996, rev. ed., 2004; Historical Dictionary of Socialism, 1997. **Address:** 59 Devonport St., Lyons, AC 2606, Australia.

DOCHERTY, Jimmy. (James Docherty). Scottish/British (born England), b. 1976. **Genres:** Children's Fiction, Social Sciences, Art/Art History. **Career:** Radio Clyde, producer, 1987-. Writer. **Publications:** SELF-ILLUSTRATED: The Global Art Grab, 2004; The Ice Cream Con, 2008. **Address:** Coatbridge, Scotland. **Online address:** jimmy.docherty@gmgradio.com

DOCHERTY, Paddy. British/Scottish (born Scotland) **Genres:** History, Travel/Exploration, Essays. **Career:** Global Union, director of oil and gas investment; PricewaterhouseCoopers, staff; Oxford University, Brasenose College, junior dean; Phoenix Africa Development Co., chief executive officer. Writer and adventurer. **Publications:** The Khyber Pass: A History of Empire and Invasion, 2007. **Address:** c/o Robert Caskie, MacFarlane Chard Associates Ltd., 33 Percy St., London, GL W1T 2DF, England. **Online address:** contact@paddydocherty.com

DOCKER, John. Australian (born Australia) **Genres:** Young Adult Non-fiction, History. **Career:** Australian National University, Humanities Research Centre, visiting fellow; University of Sydney, School of Philosophical and Historical Inquiry, honorary professor, adjunct professor. Writer. **Publications:** NONFICTION: Australian Cultural Elites: Intellectual Traditions in Sydney and Melbourne, 1974; (ed. with S. Dermody and D. Modjeska) Nellie Melba, Ginger Meggs, and Friends: Essays in Australian Cultural History, 1982; The Nervous Nineties: Australian Cultural Life in the 1890s, 1991; Postmodernism and Popular Culture: A Cultural History, 1994; (with G. Fischer) Race, Colour and Identity in Australia and New Zealand, 2000; 1492: The Poetics of Diaspora, 2001; (ed. with G. Fischer) Adventures of Identity: European Multicultural Experiences and Perspectives, 2001; Sheer Perversity: Anti- Zionism in the 1940s, 2001; (with A. Curthoys) Is History Fiction?, 2005, 2nd ed., 2010; (ed. with D. Ganguly) Rethinking Gandhi and Nonviolent Relationality Origins of Violence, 2007; Religion, History and Genocide, 2008; (ed. with F. Peters-Little and A. Curthoys) Passionate Histories, 2010; Sheer Folly and Derangement: Disorienting Europe and the West, forthcoming. **Address:** School of Philosophical and Historical Inquiry, University of Sydney, Rm. 715, MacCallum Bldg., Quadrangle A14, Sydney, NW 2006, Australia. **Online address:** john.docker@usyd.edu.au

DOCKERY, Kevin. American (born United States), b. 1954. **Genres:** History, Intellectual History, Military/Defense/Arms Control. **Career:** Richard Nixon, president's guard; Gerald Ford, president's guard; The Morrow Project, co-creator, 1980; grade-school teacher, radio broadcaster and writer. **Publications:** The Armory: A Compendium of Weaponry for Gamers and Students of Ordnance, 1983; SEALs in Action, 1991; (with J. Watson) Point Man: Inside the Toughest and Most Deadly Unit in Vietnam by a Founding Member of the Elite Navy SEALs, 1993; Special Warfare: Special Weapons: The Arms and Equipment of the UDT and SEALs from 1943 to the Present, 1996; (with J. Watson) Walking Point: The Experiences of a Founding Member of the Elite Navy SEALs, 1997; (ed. with B. Fawcett) The Teams: An Oral History of the U.S. Navy SEALs, 1998; (with D.C. Chalker) The United States Navy SEALs Workout Guide: The Exercise and Fitness Programs Based on the U.S. Navy SEALs and BUD/S Training, 1998; Free Fire Zones: SEALs Missions, 2000; Navy SEALs: A History of the Early Years, 2001; (with D. Chalker) Hell Week: SEALs in Training, 2002; One Perfect Op: An Insider's Account of the Navy SEALs' Special Warfare Teams, 2002; Navy SEALs: A History Part II: From Vietnam to Desert Storm, 2002; Navy SEALs: A History Part II: The Vietnam Years, 2002; Navy Seals: A History Part III: Post-Vietnam to the Present, 2003; Special Forces in Action: Missions, Ops, Weapons, and Combat, Day by Day, 2004; The Home Team: Undeclared War, 2004; Weapons of the Navy SEALs, 2004; (with D. Chalker) Home Team: Hostile Borders, 2005; (with D. Chalker) Home Team: Weapons Grade, 2006; Stalkers and Shooters: A History of Snipers, 2006; Future Weapons, 2007; (with D. Niles) Starstrike: Task Force Mars, 2007; Operation Thunderhead: The True Story of Vietnam's Final POW Rescue Mission- and the Last Navy SEAL Killed in Country, 2008. Contributor to periodicals. **Address:** c/o Author Mail, Berkley Books, Penguin Group Publicity, 375 Hudson St., 11th Fl., New York, NY 10014, U.S.A.

DOCKREY, Karen. American (born United States), b. 1955. **Genres:** Theology/Religion, inspirational/Motivational Literature, Human Relations/Parenting. **Career:** Youth minister, 1980-; writer, 1984-. **Publications:** Getting to Know God, 1984; Friends: Finding and Keeping Them, 1985; Getting to Know God Study Guide, 1986; Dating: Making Your Own Choices, 1987; What's Your Problem?, 1987; Family Survival Guide (leader's and student's versions), 1988; Living until Jesus Comes, 1989; When Everyone's Looking at You, 1989; Jr. High Retreats and Lock-Ins, 1990; (with J. Hall) Holiday Specials and Boredom Busters, 1990; Youth Workers and Parents: Sharing Resources for Equipping Youth, 1990; Why Does Everybody Hate Me?, 1991; The Youth Worker's Guide to Creative Bible Study, 1991, rev. ed., 1999; Does Anybody Understand?: Devotions for Teens on Family Survival, 1992; What's a Kid like Me Doing in a Family like This?: Leader's Book, 1992; From Frustration to Freedom, 1992; It's Not Fair!: Through Grief to Healing, 1992; (with J. Godwin and P. Godwin) Holman Student Bible Dictionary, 1993; Will I Ever Feel Good Again?: When You're Overwhelmed by Grief and Loss, 1993; Are You There, God?, 1993; When a Hug Won't Fix the Hurt, 1993; I Thought You Were My Friend!, with Leader's Guide, 1994; (with B. Matthews and A. Adams) I Only See My Dad on Weekends: Kids Tell Their Stories about Divorce and Blended Families, 1994; (co-author) Ready for Life, 1994; Tuned-Up Parenting: Eight Studies to Invite Harmony in Your Home, 1994; (with E. Dockrey) You'll Never Believe What They Told Me: Trusting God through Cancer and Other Serious Illness, 1994; Alone but Not Lonely, 1994; Curing the Self Hate Virus, 1994; Growing a Family Where People Really Like Each Other, 1996; Fun Friend-Making Activities for Adult Groups, 1997; Am I in Love? Twelve Youth Studies on Guy/Girl Relationships, 1997; YouthCare: Giving Real Help That Makes a Real Difference, 1997; (co-author) Facing Down the Tough Stuff, 1998; The Youth Worker's Guide to Creative Bible Study, 1999; (contrib.) Innovative Worship, 1999; When a Hug Won't Fix the Hurt: Walking with Your Child through Crisis, 2000; Reaching Your Kids: A Team Strategy for Parents and Youth Workers, 2002; Bold Parents, Positive Teens: Loving and Guiding Your Child Through the Challenges of Adolescence, 2002. Contributor to books and periodicals. **Address:** 8CPH, 3558 S Jefferson Ave., St. Louis, MO 63118, U.S.A. **Online address:** kdockrey@mindspring.com

DOCTOROW, E(dgar) L(awrence). American (born United States), b. 1931. **Genres:** Novels, Novellas/Short Stories, Plays/Screenplays, Essays, Young Adult Fiction. **Career:** Columbia Pictures Industries Inc., script reader, 1956-58; New American Library, senior editor, 1959-64; Dial Press, editor-in-chief, 1964-69, vice president and publisher, 1968-69; University of California, writer-in-residence, 1969-70, visiting writer; Sarah Lawrence College, faculty, 1971-78; Yale School of Drama, creative writing fellow, 1974-75; University of Utah, visiting professor, 1975; Princeton University, visiting senior fellow, 1980-81; New York University, professor of English, Lewis and Loretta Glucksman professor in American letters, 1982-, Glucksman chair in American letters, 1982-. **Publications:** Welcome to Hard Times: A Novel, 1960 in UK as Bad Man from Bodie, 1961; Big as Life, 1966; The Book of Daniel: A Novel, 1971; Ragtime, 1975; Drinks before Dinner: A Play, 1979; Loon Lake: A Novel, 1980; American Anthem, 1982; E.L. Doctorow, Essays And Conversations, 1983; Lives of the Poets: Six Stories and a Novella, 1984; World's Fair: A Novel, 1985; E.L. Doctorow: An Annotated Bibliography, 1988; Billy Bathgate: A Novel, 1989; Scenes and Sequences: Fifty-eight Monotypes, 1989; The People's Text: A Citizen Reads the Constitution, 1992; Jack London, Hemingway, and the Constitution: Selected Essays 1977-1992, 1993; Three Complete Novels, 1994; The Waterworks, 1994; City of God: A Novel, 2000; (ed. with K. Kenison) The Best American Short Stories, 2000; Lamentation 9/11, 2002; Reporting the Universe, 2003; Three Screenplays, 2003; Sweet Land Stories, 2004; The March: A Novel, 2005; Creationists: Selected Essays, 1993-2006, 2006; Homer and Langley: A Novel, 2009; All the Time in the World: New and Selected Stories, 2011; (with A, Ginsberg and D. Mamet) Poems for Life: A Special Collection of Poetry, 2011. Contributor to periodicals. **Address:** Department of English, New York University, 19 University Pl., 5th Fl., New York, NY 10003-4556, U.S.A. **Online address:** eld1@nyu.edu

DOCX, Edward. British (born England), b. 1972?. **Genres:** Novels, Young Adult Fiction. **Career:** London Express, literary editor and Sunday columnist; British Broadcasting Corp., cultural critic, consultant and commentator. Journalist and columnist. **Publications:** The Calligrapher (novel), 2003; Self Help (novel), 2007 in US as Pravda, 2008; The Devil's Garden, 2011. Contributor to periodicals. **Address:** London, GL , England. **Online address:** mail@edwarddocx.com

DODD, Christina. American (born United States) **Genres:** Romance/Historical, Novels. **Career:** Writer. **Publications:** Candle in the Window, 1991; Treasure of the Sun, 1991; Priceless, 1992; Lady in Black, 1993; Castles in the Air, 1993; The Greatest Lover in All England, 1994; Outrageous, 1994; Move Heaven and Earth, 1995; Once a Knight, 1996; A Knight to Remember, 1997; A Well Pleasured Lady, 1997; A Well Favored Gentleman, 1998; That Scandalous Evening, 1998; Someday My Prince, 1999; The Runaway Princess, 1999; (with C. Brockway) Once upon a Pillow, 2002; One Kiss from You, 2003; Scandalous Again, 2003. LOST TEXAS HEARTS SERIES: Just the Way You Are, 2003; Almost like Being in Love, 2004; Close to You, 2005. GOVERNESS BRIDES SERIES: Rules of Surrender, 2000; Rules of Engagement, 2000; Rules of Attraction, 2001; In My Wildest Dreams, 2001; Lost in Your Arms, 2002; My Favorite Bride, 2002; My Fair Temptress, 2005; In Bed with the Duke, 2010; Taken by the Prince, 2011. LOST PRINCESS SERIES: Some Enchanted Evening, 2004; The Prince Kidnaps a Bride, 2006; The Barefoot Princess, 2006. CHOSEN ONES SERIES: Storm of Shadows, 2009; Storm of Visions, 2009; Chains of Ice, 2010; Chains of Fire, 2010. FORTUNE HUNTERS SERIES: Trouble in High Heels, 2006; Tongue in Chic, 2007; Thigh High, 2008; Danger in a Red Dress, 2009. DARKNESS CHOSEN SERIES: Scent of Darkness, 2007; Touch of Darkness, 2007; Into the Shadow, 2008; Into the Flame, 2008. SCARLET DECEPTION SERIES: Secrets of Bella Terra, 2011; Revenge at Bella Terra, 2011; Betrayal in Bella Terra, 2012. **Address:** c/o Author Mail, William Morrow, 10 E 53rd St., 7th Fl., New York, NY 10022, U.S.A. **Online address:** christina@christinadodd.coms

DODD, Christopher J. American (born United States), b. 1944. **Genres:** History, Law, Biography. **Career:** Connecticut United States senator, 1959-71, 1981-2011; Bar of Connecticut, staff, 1973; Suisman, Shapiro, Wool & Brennan, attorney, 1973-74; U.S. Congressman representing Second District of Connecticut, 1975-80; Picture Association of America, chairman and chief executive officer, 2011-. Writer. **Publications:** Letters from Nuremberg: My Father's Narrative of a Quest for Justice, 2007. **Address:** United State Senate, 448 Russell Senate Bldg., Washington, DC 20510-0001, U.S.A. **Online address:** sen_dodd@dodd.senate.gov

DODD, Elizabeth Caroline. American (born United States), b. 1962. **Genres:** Poetry, Essays. **Career:** Kansas State University, professor of English, 1989-; DePauw University, faculty. Writer. **Publications:** Like Memory, Caverns: Poems, 1992; The Veiled Mirror and the Woman Poet: H.D., Louise Bogan, Elizabeth Bishop and Louise Glück, 1992; Archetypal Light: Poems, 2001; Prospect: Journeys and Landscapes, 2003; In the Mind's Eye: Essays Across the Animate World, 2008. **Address:** Department of English, Kansas State University, 113-A, 108 E/CS Bldg., Manhattan, KS 66506-6501, U.S.A. **Online address:** edodd@ksu.edu

DODD, Lynley Stuart (Weeks). New Zealander (born New Zealand), b. 1941. **Genres:** Children's Fiction, Illustrations. **Career:** Queen Margaret College, art mistress, 1963-68, faculty; freelance author and illustrator, 1968-. **Publications:** (With E. Sutton) My Cat Likes to Hide in Boxes, 1974. SELF-ILLUSTRATED: The Nickle Nackle Tree, 1976; Titimus Trim, 1979; The Smallest Turtle, 1982; The Apple Tree, 1982; Hairy Maclary from Donaldson's Dairy, 1983; Hairy Maclary's Bone, 1984; Hairy Maclary, Scattercat, 1985; Wake Up, Bear, 1986; Hairy Maclary's Caterwaul Caper, 1987; A Dragon in a Wagon, 1988; Hairy Maclary's Rumpus at the Vet, 1989; Slinky Malinki, 1990; Find Me a Tiger, 1991; Hairy Maclary's Show business, 1991; The Minister's Cat ABC, 1992; Slinky Malinki, Open the Door, 1993; Schnitzel Von Krumm's Basketwork, 1994; Sniff-Snuff-Snap!, 1995; Schnitzel Von Krumm, Forget-Me-Not, 1996; Hairy Maclary, Sit, 1997; Slinky Malinki Catflaps, 1998; Hairy Maclary and Zachary Quack, 1999; Hedgehog Howdedo, 2000; Hairy Maclary Scattercat, 2000; Scarface Claw, 2001; Schnitzel Von Krumm, Dogs Never Climb Trees, 2002; The Other Ark, 2004; Zachary Quack, Minimonster, 2005; Hairy Maclary's Hat Tricks, 2007; Dudgeon is Coming, 2008; Hairy Maclary, Shoo, 2009. **Address:** Edward Ave., RD 3, Tauranga, 3144, New Zealand.

DODD, Wayne. (Donald Wayne). American (born United States), b. 1930. **Genres:** Novels, Children's Fiction, Poetry, Literary Criticism And History. **Career:** University of Colorado, instructor, 1960-64, assistant professor of English, 1964-68; Wesleyan University, Center for Advanced Studies, fellow, 1964; Ohio University, associate professor, 1968-73, professor of English, 1973-94, Edwin and Ruth Kennedy distinguished professor of English, 1994-2001, distinguished professor emeritus, 2001-; The Ohio Review, editor, 1971-2001; Ohio Review Books, editor. **Publications:** (As Donald Wayne) The Adventures of Little White Possum, 1970; We Will Wear White Roses: Poems, 1974; Made in America, 1975; A Time of Hunting, 1975; The Names You Gave It: Poems, 1980; The General Mule Poems, 1980; Sometimes Music Rises: Poems, 1986; Echoes of the Unspoken: Poems, 1990; Toward the End of the Century: Essays into Poetry, 1992; Of Desire and Disorder, 1993; The Blue Salvages, 1997; Is: Poems, 2003. Works appear in anthologies. Contributor to periodicals and journals. **Address:** 11292 Peach Ridge Rd., Athens, OH 45701, U.S.A. **Online address:** doddw@ohiou.edu

DODDS, Bill. American (born United States), b. 1952. **Genres:** Young Adult Fiction, Human Relations/Parenting, Humor/Satire, How-to Books, Theology/Religion. **Career:** Catholic Youth Organization, retreat leader, 1974-76; King County Advocates for Retarded Citizens, recreation center assistant director, 1976-78; The Progress, reporter and editor, 1978-88; My Daily Visitor, editor; freelance writer, 1988-. **Publications:** JUVENILE: The Hidden Fortune, 1991; My Sister Annie, 1993; Bedtime Parables, 1993. HUMORS: The Parents' Guide to Dirty Tricks: How to Con, Hoodwink and Outsmart Your Children, 1989 as How to Outsmart Your Kids: The Parents' Guide to Dirty Tricks, 1993; How to Be a Catholic Mother, 1990; Dads, Catholic Style, 1990; How to Survive Your 40th Birthday, 1990. OTHERS: (co-author) Speaking Out, Fighting Back: Personal Experiences of Women Who Survived Childhood Sexual Abuse in the Home, 1985; O Father: A Murder Mystery, 1991; How I Flunked Penmanship and Other Tales of Growing up Catholic, 1991; (with M. Dodds) Joy of Marriage: Inspiration and Encouragement for Couples, 1994; Are You over the Hill?: Find Out Before It's Too Late!, 1994; (with M.J. Dodds) Happily Ever After Begins Here and Now: Living the Beatitudes Today, 1997; (with M. Dodds) Caring for your Aging Parents: A Guide for Catholic Families, 1997; (with M. Dodds) Seeker's Guide to 7 Life-Changing Virtues, 1999; 1, 440 Reasons to Quit Smoking, 2000; Your One-Stop Guide to How Saints are Made, 2000; What you Don't Know about Retirement: A Funny Retirement Quiz, 2000; (with D. Fushek) Your One-Stop Guide to the Mass, 2000; Your Grieving Child: Answers to Questions on Death and Dying, 2001; Your One-Stop Guide to Heaven, Hell and Purgatory, 2001; Ride of Your Life: A Catholic Road Trip for Teens, 2002; Seekers Guide to the Holy Spirit: Filling Your Life with Seven Gifts of Grace, 2003;

Managing Customer Value: Essentials of Product Quality, Customer Service, and Price Decisions, 2003; (with D. Fushek) Your One-Stop Guide to the Sacraments, 2003; What You Don't Know about Turning 40: A Funny Birthday Quiz, 2006; (with M. Dodds) Encyclopedia of Mary, 2007. Contributor to books and periodicals. **Address:** Boyds Mills Press, 815 Church St., Honesdale, PA 18431, U.S.A. **Online address:** billdodds@billdodds.com

DODER, Joshua. *See* LACEY, Josh.

DODGE, Peter. American (born United States), b. 1926. **Genres:** History, Sociology, Biography. **Career:** State University of New York, Harpur College, instructor in sociology, 1958-61, assistant professor of sociology, history and anthropology, 1961-64, Division of Social Sciences, assistant chairman, 1962-64; University of New Hampshire, associate professor of sociology, 1963-95, department chair, Graduate Program in Sociology, director, 1967-71, now professor emeritus; University of Wales, visiting professor, 1973. Writer. **Publications:** Beyond Marxism: The Faith and Works of Hendrik de Man, 1966; (ed. and trans.) Documentary Study of Hendrik de Man, Socialist Critic of Marxism, 1979. Contributor to journals. **Address:** University of New Hampshire, Thompson Hall, 105 Main St., Durham, NH 03824-2512, U.S.A. **Online address:** peterdodge@comcast.net

DODGE, Tom. American (born United States), b. 1939. **Genres:** Poetry, Adult Non-fiction, Sports/Fitness, Bibliography, Medicine/Health. **Career:** High school English teacher, 1965-68; Blinn College, instructor in English, 1968-70; Mountain View College, professor of English, 1970-94; KERA-Radio, commentator, 1988-. Writer. **Publications:** (Trans.) A Generation of Leaves (poems), 1977; (comp.) A Literature of Sports (anthology), 1980; Oedipus Road: Searching For A Father In A Mother's Fading Memory (non-fiction), 1996; Tom Dodge Talks about Texas: Radio Vignettes and Other Observations, 1989-1999 (non-fiction), 2000; Fair Warrior. **Address:** 302 Stiles Dr., Midlothian, TX 76065, U.S.A. **Online address:** tomdodgebooks@yahoo.com

DODGSHON, Robert A(ndrew). British/Welsh (born Wales), b. 1941. **Genres:** Geography, History, Social Commentary, Local History/Rural Topics, Adult Non-fiction. **Career:** University of Reading, Museum of English Rural Life, assistant keeper, 1966-70; The University of Wales, Institute of Geography and Earth Sciences, senior lecturer, 1970-84, reader in geography, 1984-, professor, 1988, chair, 1988-, Gregynog chair of human geography, 2002-07, director, 1998-2003; Society for Landscape Studies, president, 1998; Aberystwyth University, Gregynog professor of human geography, 2002-07, professor emeritus, 2007-. Writer. **Publications:** (Ed. with R.A. Butlin) An Historical Geography of England and Wales, 1978, 2nd ed., 1990; The Origins of British Field Systems: An Interpretation, 1980; Land and Society in Early Scotland, 1981; The European Past: Social Evolution and Spatial Order, 1987; (ed. with R.A. Butlin) Historical Geography of Europe, 1998; From Chiefs to Landlords: Social and Economic Change in the Western Highlands and Islands, c. 1493-1820, 1998; Society in Time and Space: A Geographical Perspective on Change, 1998; Age of the Clans: The Highlands from Somerled to the Clearances, 2002; (ed. with R.A. Butlin) Európa Türténeti Füldrajza, 2007; Writing the Environmental History of Mountains Areas, 2007; Traditional Livestock Farming in the Highlands and Islands Before and After the Clearances, 2008; Highland Townships Before the Clearances, 2008; Bones, Bows and Byres: The Nature of Early Dairying in the Scottish Highlands and Islands, 2008; The Longhouse and the Housing of Stock in the Scottish Highlands and Islands Prior to 1900, 2008; Everyday Structures, Rhythms and Spaces of the Scottish Countryside, 1600-1800, 2008; Geography's Place in Time, 2008; In What Way is the World Really Flat: Debates Over Geographies of the Moment, 2008. FORTHCOMING: Everyday Structures, Rhythms and Spaces of the Scottish Countryside, 1600-1800; Traditional Livestock Farming in the Highlands and Islands Before and After the Clearances; Highland Townships Before the Clearances. **Address:** Institute of Geography & Earth Sciences, Aberystwyth University, L2, Llandinam Bldg., Penglais Campus, Aberystwyth, SY23 3DB, England. **Online address:** rad@aber.ac.uk

DODMAN, Nicholas H. American/British (born England), b. 1946. **Genres:** Animals/Pets, Medicine/Health. **Career:** Tufts University, Cummings School of Veterinary Medicine, Department of Clinical Sciences, professor, section head and program director of animal behavior, 1982-; PetPlace.com, senior editor. Veterinarian. **Publications:** The Dog Who Loved Too Much: Tales, Treatments, and the Psychology of Dogs, 1996; The Cat Who Cried for Help: Attitudes, Emotions, and the Psychology of Cats, 1997; (ed. with L. Shuster) Psychopharmacology of Animal Behavior Disorders, 1998; Dogs Behaving Badly: An A to Z Guide to Understanding and Curing Behavioral Problems in Dogs, 1999; If Only They Could Speak: Stories About Pets and their People, 2002; (ed.) Best Behavior: Unleashing Your Dog's Instinct to Obey, 2004; (ed. with L. Lindner) Puppy's First Steps: The Whole-Dog Approach to Raising a Happy, Healthy, Well-Behaved Puppy, 2007; The Well-Adjusted Dog: Dr. Dodman's Seven Steps to Lifelong Health and Happiness for Your Best Friend, 2008; (ed. with L. Lindner) Good old Dog: Expert Advice for Keeping Your Aging Dog Happy, Healthy, and Comfortable, 2010; (foreword) Your Dog: The Owner's Manual, 2011. **Address:** Department of Clinical Sciences, Cummings School of Veterinary Medicine, Tufts University, 200 Westboro Rd., North Grafton, MA 01536, U.S.A. **Online address:** nicholas.dodman@tufts.edu

DOEBLER, Bettie Anne. American (born United States), b. 1931?. **Genres:** Poetry, Literary Criticism And History, Biography. **Career:** Mundelein College, lecturer, 1960-61; Dickinson College, instructor, 1961-62, assistant professor, 1962-67, associate professor of English, 1968-70; Arizona State University, associate professor, 1971-77, professor of English, 1976-96, professor emeritus, 1996-, Center for Humanities, acting chair, 1976-77, chair, 1978, 1980, director humaities, philosophy, and humanities, 1983-85, director humanities graduate and undergraduate programs, 1985-92, director graduate studies, interdisciplinary humanities program, 1994, Bachelor of Interdisciplinary Studies, professor emeritus, 2006-09; writer, 1995-; Grand Canyon University, visiting professor of English, 2003-05. **Publications:** The Quickening Seed: Death in the Sermons of John Donne, 1970; Rooted Sorrow: Dying in Early Modern England, 1994; (with R. Slotten and J. Thiem) The Book of the Mermaid, 2001; (with R. Slotten and J. Thiem) Nine Waves (poems), 2003. EDITOR/CO-EDITOR AND INTRODUCTION: Willet, Sacrorum Emblematum Centura Una, 1984; Deaths Advantage Little Regarded, 1993; (with R.M. Warnicke) The Pilgrim's Profession, 1995; (with R.M. Warnicke) Deaths Sermon unto the Living, 1999; (with R.M. Warnicke) The Praise of a Godly Woman, 2001; (with R.M. Warnicke and J. Barlow) A True Guide to Glory, 2004; (with R.M. Warnicke) A Sermon Preached at Constantinople at the Funeral of Lady Anne Glover, 2005; (with R.M. Warnicke) A Sermon of Commemoration of the Lady Danvers, Late Wife of Sr. John Danvers, 2006. Contributor of poems to periodicals. **Address:** Department of English, Arizona State University, UCENT 324AB, PO Box 870302, Tempe, AZ 85287-0302, U.S.A. **Online address:** bettie.doebler@asu.edu

DOERR, Anthony. American (born United States), b. 1973. **Genres:** Novellas/Short Stories, Novels, Natural History, Sciences, Travel/Exploration, Young Adult Fiction, Biography, Autobiography/Memoirs, Autobiography/Memoirs. **Career:** Bowling Green State University, affiliate; Boise State University, distinguished writer-in-residence, 2002-03; Princeton University, Hodder fellow, 2004; Boston Globe, columnist; Warren Wilson College, faculty. **Publications:** The Shell Collector: Stories, 2002; About Grace (novel), 2004; Four Seasons in Rome: On Twins, Insomnia, and the Biggest Funeral in the History of the World, 2007; Memory Wall: Stories, 2010. Contributor to books and periodicals. **Address:** The Wendy Weil Agency Inc., 232 Madison Ave., Ste. 1300, New York, NY 10016, U.S.A. **Online address:** adoerr@cableone.net

DOGNIEZ, Cecile. French (born France), b. 1953. **Genres:** Theology/Religion. **Career:** Centre National de la Recherche Scientifique, Centre Lenain de Tillemont, researcher. Writer. **Publications:** (With M. Harl) La Bible d'Alexandrie LXX, tome 5: Le Deuteronome, 1992; Bibliography of the Septuagint (1970-1993), 1995; Les Douze Prophetes, 1999; Le Pentataique d'Alexandre, 2001. **Address:** Center National de la Recherche Scientifique, Sorbonne, 1 rue Victor Cousin, Paris, 75005, France. **Online address:** cecile.dogniez@wanadoo.fr

DOHERTY, Berlie. British (born England), b. 1943. **Genres:** Novels, Children's Fiction, Plays/Screenplays, Poetry, Picture/Board Books, Young Adult Fiction, Adult Non-fiction. **Career:** Leicestershire Child Care Services, child care officer, 1966-67; teacher, 1978-80; British Broadcasting Corp. Radio, schools broadcaster, 1980-82; full-time writer, 1983-; Calderdale Libraries, writer-in-residence, 1985. **Publications:** How Green You Are!, 1982; The Making of Fingers Finnigan, 1983; Tilly Mint Tales, 1984; White Peak Farm, 1984; Children of Winter, 1985; Granny Was a Buffer Girl, 1986; Tough Luck, 1988; Tilly Mint and the Dodo, 1989; Paddiwak and Cosy, 1989; Spellhorn, 1989; Requiem, 1991; Dear Nobody, 1991; Snowy, 1993; Walk-

ing on Air, 1993; Old Father Christmas, 1993; Willa and Old Miss Annie, 1994; The Vinegar Jar, 1994; Street Child, 1994; The Golden Bird, 1995; The Magic Bicycle, 1995; Our Field, 1996; The Snake-Stone, 1996; Walking on Air, 1996; Running on Ice, 1997; Bella's Den, 1997; Daughter of the Sea, 1997; Tales of Wonder and Magic, 1997; (ed.) The Forsaken Merman and Other Story Poems, 1998; The Midnight Man, 1998; The Sailing Ship Tree, 1998; Yel Ban-Golden Bird, 1998; The Snow Queen, 1998; Paddiwak and Cozy, 1999; Garreg Neidr, 2000; Fairy Tales, 2000; The Famous Adventures of Jack, 2001; Zzaap and the Word Master, 2001; Holly Starcross, 2002; The Nutcracker, 2002; Coconut Comes to School, 2002; Blue John, 2003; Beauty and the Beast, 2003; Cinderella, 2003; Hansel and Gretel, 2003; Rapunzel, 2003; Rumpelstiltskin, 2003; The Sleeping Beauty in the Forest, 2003; Jeannie of White Peak Farm, 2003; Snow White, 2003; Aladdin and the Enchanted Lamp, 2003; The Wild Swans, 2003; Deep Secret, 2003; The Starburster, 2004; Tricky Nelly's Birthday Treat R/I, 2004; Jinnie Ghost, 2005; Abela-The Girl Who Saw Lions, 2007; A Beautiful Place for a Murder, 2008; The Goblin Baby, 2009; (with K. Lewis) Valentine's Day, 2009; Nightmare: Two Ghostly Tales, 2009; Classic Fairy Tales, 2009; The Frog Prince, 2010; Sleeping Beauty, 2010; Aladdin, 2010; The Three Princes, 2011; Treason, 2011; Haunted, 2011; Collins Big Cat - Wild Cat, 2012. Contributor to magazines and newspapers. **Address:** c/o Veronique Baxter, David Higham Associates, 5-8 Lower John St., Golden Sq., London, GL W1R 4HA, England.

DOHERTY, Brian. American (born United States), b. 1968?. **Genres:** Politics/Government, Young Adult Non-fiction. **Career:** Cherry Smash Records, founder, 1993; Regulation Magazine, managing editor, 1993-94; Reason, associate editor and reporter, 1994-2003, senior editor, 2004-; Cato Institute, staff. Journalist and writer. **Publications:** This is Burning Man: The Rise of a New American Underground, 2004; Radicals for Capitalism: A Freewheeling History of the Modern American Libertarian Movement, 2007; Gun Control on Trial: Inside the Supreme Court Battle Over the Second Amendment, 2008. Contributor to periodicals. **Address:** Reason, 3415 S Sepulveda Blvd., Ste. 400, Los Angeles, CA 90034, U.S.A. **Online address:** bdoherty@reason.com

DOHERTY, Craig A. American (born United States), b. 1951. **Genres:** Children's Non-fiction, Architecture, History, Travel/Exploration. **Career:** Berlin High School, English teacher, 1987-. Writer. **Publications:** WITH K.M. DOHERTY: The Apaches and Navajos, 1989; The Iroquois, 1989; Benazir Bhutto, 1990; Arnold Schwarzenegger: Larger than Life, 1993; The Zunis, 1993; King Richard the Lionhearted and the Crusades in World History, 2002; Southeast Indians, 2007; Northwest Coast Indians, 2007; Great Basin Indians, 2007; Southwest Indians, 2007; California Indians, 2007; Subartic Peoples, 2008; Arctic Peoples, 2008; Plateau Indians, 2008; Plains Indians, 2008; Northeast Indians, 2008. NATIVE AMERICAN PEOPLE SERIES: WITH K.M. DOHERTY: The Cahuilla, 1994; The Chickasaw, 1994; The Crow, 1994; The Huron, 1994; The Narragansett, 1994; The Ute, 1994. BUILDING AMERICA SERIES: WITH K.M. DOHERTY: The Wampanoag, 1995; The Penobscot, 1995; The Gateway Arch, 1995; The Golden Gate Bridge, 1995; The Hoover Dam, 1995; Mount Rushmore, 1995; The Sears Tower, 1995; The Washington Monument, 1995; The Erie Canal, 1997; The Statue of Liberty, 1996; The Houston Astrodome, 1997; The Seattle Space Needle, 1997; The Empire State Building, 1998; The Alaska Pipeline, 1998. THIRTEEN COLONIES SERIES: WITH K.M. DOHERTY: North Carolina, 2005; Delaware, 2005; Maryland, 2005; New Hampshire, 2005; Virginia, 2005; South Carolina, 2005; New Jersey, 2005; New York, 2005; Rhode Island, 2005; Pennsylvania, 2005; Connecticut, 2006; Georgia, 2005; Massachusetts, 2006. Contributor to periodicals. **Address:** Infobase Publishing, 132 W 31st St., 17th Fl., New York, NY 10001, U.S.A.

DOHERTY, Gillian M. Irish (born Ireland) **Genres:** History, Autobiography/Memoirs. **Career:** University College Cork, Department of History, lecturer. Historian, educator and writer. **Publications:** The Irish Ordnance Survey: History, Culture and Memory, 2004. Contributor to books and periodicals. **Address:** Department of History, University College, 5 Perrott Ave., Cork, 47545, Ireland. **Online address:** gm.doherty@ucc.ie

DOHERTY, Justin (Francis). British (born England), b. 1960. **Genres:** Literary Criticism And History, Cultural/Ethnic Topics, Sports/Fitness. **Career:** Queen's University of Belfast, lecturer in Russian, 1989-95; Trinity College, lecturer in Russian, 1995-, Centre for European Studies, director. Writer. **Publications:** Culture and the Word: Aspects of Acmeist Poetic Theory and Practice, 1989; The Acmeist Movement in Russian Poetry: Culture and the Word, 1995; (trans.) G. Gazdanov, Night Roads: A Novel, 2009; What it Means to be a Badger: Barry Alvarez and Wisconsin's Greatest Players, 2011. **Address:** Department of Russian, Trinity College, Rm. 5047, Arts Bldg., Dublin, 2, Ireland. **Online address:** jdoherty@tcd.ie

DOHERTY, Katherine M(ann). American (born United States), b. 1951. **Genres:** Children's Non-fiction, Architecture. **Career:** New Hampshire Community Technical College, director of learning resources, 1986-, Basic Health Sciences Library, coordinator. Writer. **Publications:** CO-AUTHOR WITH C.A. DOHERTY: The Apaches and Navajos, 1989; The Iroquois, 1989; Benazir Bhutto, 1990; Arnold Schwarzenegger: Larger than Life, 1993; The Zunis, 1993; The Wampanoag, 1995; Penobscot, 1995; The Houston Astrodome, 1997; The Seattle Space Needle, 1997; The Alaska Pipeline, 1998; The Empire State Building, 1998; King Richard the Lionhearted and the Crusades in World History, 2002; North Carolina, 2005; Delaware, 2005; Maryland, 2005; Massachusetts, 2005; New Hampshire, 2005; Virginia, 2005; South Carolina, 2005; New Jersey, 2005; New York, 2005; Rhode Island, 2005; Pennsylvania, 2005; Connecticut, 2006; Georgia, 2006; Northeast Indians, 2006; Great Basin Indians, 2007; California Indians, 2007; Southwest Indians, 2007; Southeast Indians, 2007; Northwest Coast Indians, 2007; Plains Indians, 2008; Subartic Peoples, 2008; Plateau Indians, 2008; Arctic Peoples, 2008. NATIVE AMERICAN PEOPLE SERIES WITH C.A. DOHERTY: The Cahuilla, 1994; The Chickasaw, 1994; The Crow, 1994; The Huron, 1994; The Narragansett, 1994; The Ute, 1994. BUILDING AMERICA SERIES WITH C.A. DOHERTY: The Gateway Arch, 1995; The Golden Gate Bridge, 1995; Hoover Dam, 1995; Mount Rushmore, 1995; Sears Tower, 1995; The Washington Monument, 1995; The Astrodome, 1996; The Erie Canal, 1996; The Statue of Liberty, 1996. **Address:** New Hampshire Community Technical College, 2020 Riverside Dr., Berlin, NH 03570, U.S.A. **Online address:** kdoherty@nhctc.edu

DOHERTY, Kieran. American (born United States), b. 1945. **Genres:** History, Novels, Biography, Autobiography/Memoirs, Politics/Government. **Career:** American Writers and Artists Institute, copywriter and mentor, 1998-. Journalist. **Publications:** William Penn: Quaker Colonist, 1998; Congressional Medal of Honor Recipients, 1998; Soldiers, Cavaliers, and Planters: Settlers of the Southeastern Colonies, 1999; Puritans, Pilgrims, and Merchants: Founders of the Northeastern Colonies, 1999; William Bradford: Rock of Plymouth, 1999; Explorers, Missionaries, and Trappers: Trailblazers of the West, 2000; To Conquer Is to Live: The Life of Captain John Smith of Jamestown, 2001; Ranchers, Homesteaders, and Traders: Frontiersmen of the South-Central States, 2001; Marjory Stoneman Douglas: Guardian of the 'Glades, 2002; Andrew Jackson: America's 7th President, 2003; Voyageurs, Lumberjacks, and Farmers: Pioneers of the Midwest, 2003; William Howard Taft: America's 27th President, 2004; John F. Kennedy: America's 35th President, 2005; Ronald Reagan: America's 40th President, 2005; Sea Venture: Shipwreck, Survival, and the Salvation of the First English Colony in the New World, 2007; Sea Venture: Shipwreck, Survival, and the Salvation of Jamestown, 2008. Contributor to periodicals. **Address:** 1 N Golfview Rd., Lake Worth, FL 33460, U.S.A.

DOHERTY, P(aul) C. Also writes as Ann Dukthas, Anna Apostolou, C. L. Grace, Vanessa Alexander, Paul Harding. British (born England), b. 1946. **Genres:** Mystery/Crime/Suspense, Novels, Young Adult Non-fiction, History. **Career:** Trinity Catholic High School, headmaster, 1981-; writer, 1985-. **Publications:** HUGH CORBETT NOVELS: Satan in St. Mary's, 1986; The Crown in Darkness, 1987; Spy in Chancery, 1988; The Angel of Death, 1990; The Prince of Darkness, 1992; Murder Wears a Cowl, 1992; The Assassin in the Greenwood, 1993; The Song of a Dark Angel, 1994; Satan's Fire, 1995; The Devil's Hunt, 1996; The Demon Archer, 1999; The Treason of the Ghosts, 2000; Corpse Candle, 2001; The Magician's Death, 2004; The Waxman Murders, 2006; Nightshade, 2008; The Mysterium, 2010. CANTERBURY TALES/NICHOLAS CHIRKE NOVELS: An Ancient Evil, Being the Knight's Tale, 1994; A Tapestry of Murders, Being the Man of Law's Tale, 1994; A Tournament of Murders, Being the Franklin's Tale, 1996; Ghostly Murders, Being the Priest's Tale, 1997; The Hangman's Hymn, Being the Carpenter's Tale, 2002; A Haunt of Murder, Being the Clerk's Tale, 2003. BROTHER ATHELSTAN NOVELS: (as Paul Harding) The Nightingale Gallery, 1991; The House of the Red Slayer, 1992 in US as Red Slayer, 1992; (as Paul Harding) Murder Most Holy, 1992; Anger of God, 1993; (as Paul Harding) By Murder's Bright Light, 1994; The House of Crows, 1995; (as Paul Harding) The Assassin's Riddle, 1996; The Devil's Domain, 1998; The Field of Blood, 1999; The House of Shadows, 2003. EGYPTIAN NOVELS: The Mask of Ra, 1998; The Horus Killing, 1999; The Anubis Slayings, 2000;

The Slayers of Seth, 2001; An Evil Spirit Out of the West, 2003; The Assassins of Isis, 2004; The Season of the Hyaena, 2004; The Year of the Cobra, 2006; The Poisoner of Ptah, 2007; The Spies of Sobeck, 2008. ALEXANDER THE GREAT MYSTERY NOVELS: The House of Death, 2001; The Godless Man, 2002; The Gates of Hell, 2003. NON-FICTION: Isabella and Edward, 2002; The Mysterious Death of Tutankhamun, 2002; Isabella and the Strange Death of Edward II, 2003; Alexander the Great: The Death of a God, 2004; The Great Crown Jewels Robbery of 1303, 2005; The Secret Life of Elizabeth I, 2006. SIR ROGER SHALLOT NOVELS AS MICHAEL CLYNES: The White Rose Murders, 1991; Poisoned Chalice, 1992; The Grail Murders, 1993; A Brood of Vipers, 1994; The Gallows Murders, 1995; The Relic Murders, 1997. NICHOLAS SEGALLA NOVELS AS ANN DUKTHAS: A Time for the Death of a King, 1994; The Prince Lost to Time, 1995; The Time of Murder at Mayerling, 1996; In the Time of the Poisoned Queen, 1998. KATHERINE SWINBROOK NOVELS AS C.L. GRACE: Shrine of Murders, 1993; The Eye of God, 1994; The Merchant of Death, 1995; The Book of Shadows, 1996; Saintly Murders, 2001; A Maze of Murders, 2003; A Feast of Poisons, 2004. AS VANESSA ALEXANDER: The Love Knot, 1999; Of Love and War, 2000; The Loving Cup, 2001. MATHILDE OF WESTMINSTER SERIES: The Cup of Ghosts, 2005; The Poison Maiden, 2007; The Darkening Glass, 2009. TEMPLARS SERIES: The Templar, 2007; The Templar Magician, 2009. OTHERS: The Death of a King, 1982, rev. ed., 2003; The Prince Drakulya, 1986; The Lord Count Drakulya, 1986; King Arthur (juvenile biography), 1987; The Whyte Harte, 1988; The Fate of Princes, 1991; The Masked Man, 1991; Dove Amongst the Hawks, 1990; The Serpent among the Lilies, 1990; Tapestry of Murders: The Man of Law's Tale of Mystery and Murder as he goes on Pilgrimage from London to Canterbury, 1996; The Rose Demon, 1997; The Haunting, 1997; (as Anna Apostolou) Murder in Macedon, 1997; The Soul Slayer, 1997; (as Anna Apostolou) Murder in Thebes, 1998; Domina, 2002; The Plague Lord, 2002; Murder Imperial, 2003; The Song of the Gladiator, 2004; The Queen of the Night, 2006; The Death of the Red King, 2006; Murder's Immortal Mask, 2008. **Address:** Trinity Catholic High School, Mornington Rd., Woodford Green, EX IG8 0TP, England. **Online address:** paulcdoherty@gmail.com

DOHERTY, Paul (Michael). American (born United States), b. 1948. **Genres:** Sciences, Children's Fiction, Art/Art History. **Career:** Oakland University, professor of physics, 1974-86; Exploratorium Teacher Institute, staff physicist, 1986-, co-director, 1990-, senior staff scientist, 1997-; Center for Teaching and Learning, founding director, 1992; Tom Tits Experiment, visiting scientist; San Francisco State University, adjunct professor of physics. Writer. **Publications:** Atlas of the Planets, 1980; Building and Using an Astronomical Observatory, 1986; The Arrival of Halley's Comet, 1986; (with J. Cassidy) The Klutz Book of Magnetic Magic, 1994; (with D. Rathjen) The Cheshire Cat and Other Eye-popping Experiments on How We See the World, 1995; (with D. Rathjen) The Magic Wand and Other Bright Experiments on Light and Color, 1995; (with D. Rathjen) The Cool Hot Rod and Other Electrifying Experiments on Energy and Matter, 1996; (with D. Rathjen) The Spinning Blackboard and Other Dynamic Experiments on Force and Motion, 1996; (with P. Murphy) Color of Nature, 1996; The Photographic Atlas of the Stars, 1997; (with J. Cassidy and P. Murphy) Zap Science, 1998; (with K. Pottner) The Best Paper Airplanes You'll Ever Fly, 1998; (with P. Murphy) Traces of Time, 2000; (with D. Rathjen) Square Wheels: And Other Easy-to-Build, 2002; (with J. Cassidy) Awesome! Magnet Magic, 2007. Contributor to periodicals. **Address:** Exploratorium Teacher Institute, 3601 Lyon St., San Francisco, CA 94123, U.S.A. **Online address:** pauld@exploratorium.edu

DOHERTY, Robert. See MAYER, Bob.

DOIDGE, Norman. American/Canadian (born Canada) **Genres:** Psychology. **Career:** Books in Canada-The Canadian Review of Books, editor-in-chief, 1995-98; ToroNational Post, columnist, 1998-2001; University of Toronto, Clarke Institute of Psychiatry, head of the psychotherapy centre and the assessment clinic, instructor in philosophy, political science, law and psychiatry, research faculty; Columbia University, Center for Psychoanalytic Training and Research, research faculty. **Publications:** The Brain That Changes Itself: Stories of Personal Triumph from the Frontiers of Brain Science, 2007. Contributor to periodicals. **Address:** Psychoanalytic Ctr., Columbia University, 1051 Riverside Dr., Ste. 63, New York, NY 10032-1007, U.S.A. **Online address:** normandoidge.com@me.com

DOIG, Ivan. American (born United States), b. 1939. **Genres:** Novels, Communications/Media, Social Commentary, Autobiography/Memoirs. **Career:**

Lindsay-Schaub Newspapers, editorial writer, 1963-64; The Rotarian, assistant editor, 1964-66; freelance journalist and novelist, 1969-. **Publications:** (With C.M. Doig) News: A Consumer's Guide, 1972; The Streets We have Come Down: Literature of the City, 1975; Early Forestry Research: A History of the Pacific Northwest Forest & Range Experiment Station, 1925-1975, 1976; (ed.) Utopian America: Dreams and Realities (non-fiction), 1976; This House of Sky: Landscapes of a Western Mind (non-fiction), 1978, 15th ed., 1992; Winter Brothers: A Season at the Edge of America (non-fiction), 1980; The Sea Runners, 1982; (with D. Kelso) Inside This House of Sky (non-fiction), 1983; English Creek, 1984; Dancing at the Rascal Fair, 1987; Ride with Me, Mariah Montana, 1990; Heart Earth (non-fiction), 1993; Bucking the Sun, 1996; Mountain Time, 1999; Prairie Nocturne, 2003; (contrib.) Building Tradition: Gifts in Honor of the Northwest Art Collection, 2003; Ride with Me, Mariah Montana, 2005; English Creek, 2005; Whistling Season, 2006; The Eleventh Man, 2008; Work Song, 2010. Contributor to periodicals. **Address:** 17277 15th Ave. NW, Seattle, WA 98177, U.S.A.

DOKEY, Cameron. American (born United States), b. 1956. **Genres:** Children's Fiction, Young Adult Fiction, Novels. **Career:** Oregon Shakespeare Festival, actor, 1977-81; Pacific Science Center, exhibit copywriter, 1989-93; novelist, 1993-. **Publications:** YOUNG ADULT NOVELS: Eternally Yours, 1994; The Talisman, 1994; Love Me, Love Me Not, 1995; Blue Moon, 1995; Heart's Desire, 1995; Katherine: Heart of Freedom, 1997; Charlotte: Heart of Fire, 1997; Stephanie: Heart of Gold, 1998; Carrie: Heart of Courage, 1998; Together Forever, 1997; Lost and Found, 1999; Hindenburg, 1937, 1999; Washington Avalanche, 1910, 2000; Here Be Monsters, 2000; Haunted by Desire: An Original Novel, 2000; Charmed Haunted by Desire, 2000; The Summoned, 2001; Picture Perfect, 2005; (co-author) The Warren Witches, 2005. SHORT STORIES: (with M.G. Lee and D.C. Regan) New Year, New Love, 1996; (with K. Jensen, J. Thesman and S.D. Wyeth) Be Mine, 1997; How I Survived My Summer Vacation, vol. I, 2000. OTHER: Midnight Mysteries (children's): A Fright Light Book, 1997; Graveside Tales (children's): A Fright Light Book, 1997; Dance of Death, 1997; Winning is Everything, 1998; The Crimson Spell, 2000; Storyteller's Daughter, 2002; J.T: Opposites Attract, 2002; Beauty Sleep, 2002; (with C.M. Burge) Truth and Consequences: An Original Novel, 2003; Everything I Want, 2004; How Not to Spend Your Senior Year, 2004; Sunlight and Shadow, 2004; Picture Perfect, 2005; Golden, 2006; Retelling of Cinderella, 2007; Before Midnight, 2007; Belle: A Retelling of Beauty and the Beast, 2008; The Wild Orchid: A Retelling of the Ballad of Mulan, 2009; Winter's Child, 2009; The World Above, 2010; Ghost Hunt, 2011; Once, 2012. Contributor to periodicals. **Address:** c/o Fran Lebowitz, Writers House Inc., 21 W 26th St., New York, NY 10010-1003, U.S.A.

DOLAN, David. American (born United States), b. 1955. **Genres:** Area Studies, Novels, Theology/Religion. **Career:** Voice of Hope radio station, news director, 1982-84; IMS News, correspondent, 1984-87; Israel News Digest, editor, 1986; Middle East Television, reporter, 1987; CBS Radio News, correspondent, 1988-2000; Moody Radio Network, reporter; METV, free lance reporter, international speaker. **Publications:** Holy War for the Promised Land: Israel's Struggle to Survive, 1991, 3rd ed. as Israel at the Crossroads: Fifty Years and Counting, 1998; Israel: The Struggle to Survive, 1992; End of the Age, 1995; The End of Days (novel), 1997; Israel in Crisis: What Lies Ahead?, 2001. Contributor to magazines and newspapers. **Address:** Jerusalem Capital Studios Ltd., 206 Jaffa St., Jerusalem, 91131, Israel. **Online address:** dolan@grmi.org

DOLAN, Frederick Michael. American (born United States), b. 1955. **Genres:** Adult Non-fiction, Essays, Humanities, Philosophy, Literary Criticism And History, Politics/Government. **Career:** University of California, assistant professor, 1988-94, associate professor of rhetoric, 1994-, professor through 2006, professor emeritus of rhetoric, 2006-, Doreen B. Townsend Center for the Humanities, fellow, 1989-90, Rhetoric 1A/1B Program, coordinator, 1993-94, 1997-99; California College of the Arts, professor of humanities, 2006-, associate dean of graduate studies, 2006-08; MySpace.com, consultant. Writer. **Publications:** (Ed. with T.L. Dumm) Rhetorical Republic: Governing Representations in American Politics, 1993; Allegories of America: Narratives, Metaphysics, Politics, 1994; (ed. with S. Goi) Between Terror and Freedom: Politics, Philosophy, and Fiction Speak of Modernity, 2006; Political Theory and the Problem, forthcoming; Political Philosophy and Truth, forthcoming; Wonder and Worldliness, forthcoming; Heidegger for Artists, forthcoming. Contributor of articles to journals. **Address:** California College of the Arts, University of California, 1111 8th St., San Francisco, CA 94107, U.S.A. **Online address:** fdolan@cca.edu

DOLAN, Harry. American (born United States), b. 1966?. **Genres:** Young Adult Fiction. **Career:** Social Philosophy and Policy, editor. **Publications:** Bad Things Happen, 2009. **Address:** Ann Arbor, MI , U.S.A. **Online address:** harry.c.dolan@gmail.com

DOLAN, Sean J. American (born United States), b. 1958. **Genres:** Biography, Children's Non-fiction, Young Adult Fiction, Children's Fiction. **Career:** Chelsea House, senior editor, 1986-. **Publications:** Chiang Kai-shek, 1988; Robert F. Kennedy, 1989; Christopher Columbus: The Intrepid Mariner, Columbine, 1989; Lewis and Clark, 1990; Daniel Boone, 1990; Junipero Serra, 1991; West Germany: On the Road to Reunification, 1991; James Beckwourth, 1992; Matthew Henson, 1992; The Polish Americans, 1992; Roald Amundsen, 1992; The Irish-American Experience, 1993; Ray Charles, 1993; Thurgood Marshall, 1993; W.E.B. DuBois, 1993; Earvin Magic Johnson, 1993; Gabriel Garcia Marquez, 1994; Michael Jordan, 1994; Lady Bird, 1994; Johnny Cash, 1995; Juan Ponce de Léon, 1995; Charles Barkley, 1996; Bob Marley, 1997; Pursuing the Dream, 1965-1971, 1998; Germany, 1999; Everything You Need to Know about Cults, 2000; Mexico, 2002; Canada, 2002; Helen Keller, 2005; Minnesota, 2005. **Address:** Chelsea House Publishers, 2080 Cabot Blvd., Ste. 201, Langhorne, PA 19047-1813, U.S.A.

DOLIN, Eric Jay. American (born United States), b. 1961. **Genres:** Biology, History, Social Sciences. **Career:** National Marine Fisheries Service, fishery-policy analyst, 2002-07; U.S. Environmental Protection Agency, environmental consultant and program manager; Business Week, writing fellow; Harvard University, Museum of Comparative Zoology, Mollusk Department, curatorial assistant; National Wildlife Federation, intern; Harvard Law School, Pew research fellow; U.S. National Oceanic and Atmospheric Administration, Knauss Sea Grant fellow. **Publications:** The U.S. Fish and Wildlife Service, 1989; Dirty Water Clean Water, 1990; (ed. with L.E. Susskind and J.W. Breslin) International Environmental Treaty Making, 1992; (with B. Dumaine) The Duck Stamp Story: Art, Conservation, History, 2000; Smithsonian Book of National Wildlife Refuges, 2003; Snakehead: A Fish Out of Water, 2003; Political Waters: The Long, Dirty, Contentious, Incredibly Expensive but Eventually Triumphant History of Boston Harbor; A Unique Environmental Success Story, 2004; The Ph.D. Survival Guide, 2005; Leviathan: The History of Whaling in America, 2007; Fur, Fortune and Empire: The Epic History of the Fur Trade in America, 2010. Contributor to periodicals. **Address:** c/o Russell Galen, Scovil, Chichak, Galen, Literary Agency Inc., 276 5th Ave., Ste. 708, New York, NY 10001, U.S.A. **Online address:** eric.dolin@noaa.gov

DOLIN, Sharon. American (born United States), b. 1956. **Genres:** Poetry, Literary Criticism And History, Humanities, Education, Essays. **Career:** Rebus Inc., executive editor, 1988-90; Cooper Union, instructor in humanities, 1988-98; 92nd Street Y, teacher, 1995-, Unterberg Poetry Center, teacher; New School for Social Research, instructor in poetry, 1997-98; New York University, teacher; The Center for Book Arts, director, 1996-; Eugene Lang College, writer-in-residence, 2006-. **Publications:** POETRY: Mind Lag, 1982; Heart Work, 1995; Climbing Mount Sinai, 1996; Mistakes, 1999; The Seagull, 2001; Serious Pink: Ekphrastic Poems, 2003; Realm of the Possible, 2004; Entreaty to Indecision, 2006; Burn and Dodge, 2008; Whirlwind, 2012. **Address:** The Center for Book Arts, 28 W 27th St., 3rd Fl., New York, NY 10001, U.S.A. **Online address:** sdolin@earthlink.net

DOLIS, John. American (born United States), b. 1945. **Genres:** Literary Criticism And History, Poetry, Humanities, Philosophy, Psychology. **Career:** High school English teacher, 1969-70; Columbia College, instructor in television department, 1970-71; Neil Stewart and Associates Inc., copywriter and music writer, 1973-74; Loyola University-Chicago, lecturer in English, 1974-76; Playboy Clubs Intl., translator of foreign correspondence, 1975-78; Northeastern Illinois University, instructor, 1978-80; Loyola University, lecturer in English, 1978-80; University of Turin, Fulbright lecturer in English and American literature, 1980-81; University of Kansas, instructor in English, 1981-85; University of Bucharest, Fulbright senior lecturer in philology, 1989-90; Pennsylvania State University, assistant professor, 1985-92, associate professor, 1992-2005, professor of English and American studies, 2005-; Bilkent University, visiting professor, 1995-96. Writer. **Publications:** Bl( )nk Space, 1993; The Style of Hawthorne's Gaze: Regarding Subjectivity, 1993; Time Flies: Butterflies, 1999; Tracking Thoreau: Double-Crossing Nature and Technology, 2005; Enlightenment, 2008; Picture Perfect, 2009; (P)ear, 2009. Contributor of articles to books and journals. **Address:** Department of English, Pennsylvania State University, Worthington Scranton Campus, Dawson 213C, Dunmore, PA 18512, U.S.A. **Online address:** jjd3@psu.edu

DOLL, Mary A(swell). American (born United States), b. 1940. **Genres:** Literary Criticism And History, Mythology/Folklore, Women's Studies And Issues, Language/Linguistics. **Career:** Garrison Forest School, teacher, 1962-65; Sidwell Friends School, teacher, 1965-66; Park School, teacher and chair of senior program, 1966-70; Community College, teacher, 1970-71; State University of New York College, instructor, 1978-82, assistant professor of English, 1982-84; University of Redlands, instructor in English, 1985-88; California State University, instructor in writing and supervisor of student teachers, 1986-88; Loyola University, instructor in English, 1988; Tulane University, visiting assistant professor of literature, 1988-89; Holy Cross College, associate professor, Department of English, chair, 1989-94, professor, 1995-2000; Savannah College of Art and Design, professor, 2000-. Writer. **Publications:** Beckett and Myth: An Archetypal Approach, 1988; (ed. with C. Stites) In the Shadow of the Giant: Thomas Wolfe, 1988; Joseph Campbell and the Ecological Imperative, Joseph Campbell, Uses of Comparative Mythology, 1992; Tom Stoppard and the Theatre of Unknowing, British Literature since 1960, 1993; Ghosts of Themselves: The Demeter Myth in Beckett, Images of Persephone in Literature, 1993; To the Lighthouse and Back: Writings on Teaching and Living, 1996; Like Letters in Running Water: A Mythopoetics of Curriculum, 1999; (ed. with M. Morris and W.F. Pinar) How We Work, 1999; (with D. Wear and M.L. Whitaker) Triple Takes on Curricular Worlds, 2006; The More of Myth: A Pedagogy of Diversion, forthcoming. **Address:** Savannah College of Art & Design, Savannah, GA 31405, U.S.A. **Online address:** mdoll4444@aol.com

DOLLE, Raymond F. American (born United States), b. 1952. **Genres:** Literary Criticism And History, Writing/Journalism, Travel/Exploration. **Career:** Pennsylvania State University, Department of English, teaching assistant, 1978-85, lecturer, 1985-86; Indiana State University, assistant professor of English, 1986-90, associate professor of English, 1990-, undergraduate advisor, 1991-. Writer. **Publications:** Anne Bradstreet: A Reference Guide, 1990. Contributor to books and periodicals. **Address:** Department of English, Indiana State University, A-286 Root Hall, 400 N 7th St., Terre Haute, IN 47809-0001, U.S.A. **Online address:** raymond.dolle@indstate.edu

DOLLIMORE, Jonathan. British (born England), b. 1948. **Genres:** Literary Criticism And History, Cultural/Ethnic Topics, Plays/Screenplays, Classics. **Career:** Freelance journalist and correspondent, 1964-69; University of Sussex, School of English and American Studies, lecturer, 1976-89, senior lecturer, 1989-90, reader, 1990-93, professor of English, 1993-95, Graduate Research Centre for the Humanities, professor, 1995-99, honorary professor, 2003-; National Humanities Center, Mellon fellow, 1988-89; University of British Columbia, visiting professor, 1997; University of York, professor of English and related literature, 1999-2004; University of London, Royal Holloway College, honorary research fellow; University of Tel Aviv, Cohen-Porter visiting professor, 2002; LeHigh University, Selfridge lecturer in philosophy, 2002; Johns Hopkins University, Department of English, Hinkley visiting professor of English. **Publications:** (Ed. with A. Sinfield) The Selected Plays of John Webster, 1983; Radical Tragedy: Religion, Ideology, and Power in the Drama of Shakespeare and His Contemporaries, 1984, 3rd ed., 2004; (ed. with A. Sinfield) The Tragedy of State, 1987; (ed. with A. Sinfield) Political Shakespeare: New Essays in Cultural Materialism, 1985, 2nd ed. as Political Shakespeare: Essays in Cultural Materialism, 1994; Sexual Dissidence: Augustine to Wilde, Freud to Foucault, 1991; Death, Desire, and Loss in Western Culture, 1998; (co-author) Nuevo Historicismo, 1998; Sex, Literature, and Censorship, 2001. Contributor of articles to periodicals. **Address:** Department of English, Johns Hopkins University, 1101C Dell House, 3400 N Charles St., Baltimore, MD 21218, U.S.A. **Online address:** skodajag@aol.com

DOLLING-MANN, Patricia May. British (born England), b. 1939. **Genres:** Romance/Historical, Young Adult Fiction, Novels. **Career:** Writer. **Publications:** WESSEX CHRONICLES (historical fiction): Weatherbury Farm, 1999 as Weatherbury Farm: A Sequel to Thomas Hardy's Far From the Madding Crowd, 2008; A Claim to Kin, 2001; The d'Urberville Inheritance, 2001. **Address:** 27 Cottingham Grove, Bletchley, BK MK3 5AA, England. **Online address:** patmann@ouvip.com

DOLNICK, Barrie. American (born United States), b. 1960. **Genres:** Self Help, Romance/Historical, Business/Trade/Industry, Psychology, Sports/Fitness, Antiques/Furnishings. **Career:** Madison Avenue Advertising, executive; Executive Mystic Services, founder, 1993. Writer, consultant and astrologer. **Publications:** Simple Spells for Love: Ancient Practices for Emotional Fulfillment, 1994; Simple Spells for Success: Ancient Practices for Creating Abundance and Prosperity, 1996; (with J. Condon and D. Limoges) Sexual Bewitchery: And Other Ancient Feminine Wiles, 1998; The Executive Mystic: Psychic Power Tools for Success, 1998; (with D. Baack) How to Write a Love Letter: Putting What's in Your Heart on Paper, 2000; Simple Spells for Hearth and Home: Ancient Practices for Creating Harmony, Peace and Abundance, 2000; Instructions for Your Discontent: How Bad Times Can Make Life Better, 2003; Minerva Rules Your Future: Goddess-Given Advice for Smart Moves at Work, 2003; DreamBabe: Understanding Dreams and Using Them to Make Your Dreams Come True, 2004; AstroBabe: A Girl's Guide to the Planetary Powers of Romance, 2004; Enlighten Up: The Keys to Kabbalah, 2005; Karma Babe: Deciphering Your Karmic Code for Your Best Possible Life, 2005; Luck: Understanding Luck and Improving the Odds, 2007; Zodiaction: Fat-Burning Fitness Tailored to Your Personal Star Quality, 2007. Contributor to periodicals. **Address:** c/o Author Mail, Harmony Books, 1745 Broadway, Ste. B1, New York, NY 10019, U.S.A. **Online address:** barriedolnick@gmail.com

DOLNICK, Ben. American (born United States), b. 1982?. **Genres:** Children's Fiction, Novels. **Career:** Educator and writer. **Publications:** Zoology: A Novel, 2007; You Know Who You Are: A Novel, 2011. **Address:** Vintage Contemporaries, 3612 Vintage Pl., Dallas, TX 75214, U.S.A. **Online address:** zoologynovel@gmail.com

DOMAN, Glenn. American (born United States), b. 1919. **Genres:** Education, Medicine/Health, How-to Books. **Career:** Temple University Hospital, staff member, 1941; Pennsylvania Hospital, staff member, 1945-48; Norwood Rehabilitation Center, director, 1948-55; Institutes for the Achievement of Human Potential, founder and director, 1955, chairman of the board, 1980-89; International Rehabilitation Forum, president, 1959; Centro de Reabilitacao Nossa Senhora da Gloria, associate director, 1959-; Avery Postgraduate Institute, professor, 1963-; University of Plano, professor of human development, 1965-72; Instituto Para La Organisation, associate director, 1967; World Organization for Human Potential, president, 1968-72. Writer. **Publications:** How to Teach Your Baby to Read: The Gentle Revolution, 1964; Reading and Writing before School, 1971; What to Do About Your Brain-Injured Child, 1974; Teach Your Baby Math, 1979; (with J.M. Armentrout) The Universal Multiplication of Intelligence, 1980; (intro.) The Path to Math, 1980; How to Multiply Your Baby's Visual Intelligence between Birth and Six, 1980; Babies Manual and Intelligence, 1980; (with G. Kerr and M. Britt) Babies, Mobility, and Intelligence, 1980; (with M. Kett and C. Coombs) Babies, Vision, and Intelligence, 1980; (with G. Kerr and L. van Dyk) Babies Manual and Intelligence, 1980; How to Measure Your Baby's Mobility Intelligence: Between Birth and Six, 1980, rev. ed., 2005; How to Multiply Your Baby's Mobility Intelligence, 1981; How to Measure Your Baby's Manual Intelligence: Between Birth and Six, 1981; How to Measure Your Baby's Auditory Intelligence between Birth and Six, 1982; Nose is Not Toes, 1983; (with J. Doman and S. Aisen) How to Give Your Baby Encyclopedic Knowledge, 1984, rev. ed., 2005; (with J. Doman) How to Multiply Your Baby's Intelligence, 1984, rev. ed., 2005; (co-author) How to Measure Your Baby's Tactile Intelligence between Birth and Six, 1987; (with D. Doman and B. Hagy) How to Teach Your Baby to be Physically Superb: Birth to Age Six, 1988; How to Teach your Baby Math, 1991; What to Do about Your Brain-Injured Child: Or Your Brain-Damaged, Mentally Retarded, Mentally Deficient, Cerebral-Palsied, Spastic, Flaccid, Rigid, Epileptic, Autistic, Athetoid, Hyperactive, Down's Child, 1994; Nose is Not Toes (children's book), 3rd ed., 1995; (with J. Doman) How Smart is Your Baby?: Develop and Murture Your Newborn's Full Potential, 2006. **Address:** Institutes for the Achievement of Human Potential, The Gentle Revolution Press, 8801 Stenton Ave., Wyndmoor, PA 19038, U.S.A.

DOMBROWSKI, Daniel A. American (born United States), b. 1953. **Genres:** Philosophy, Sports/Fitness, Recreation, Theology/Religion, Animals/Pets, Sciences, Humanities. **Career:** Saint Joseph's University, assistant professor of philosophy, 1978-82; Creighton University, associate professor of philosophy, 1982-88; Seattle University, professor of philosophy, 1988-. Writer. **Publications:** Plato's Philosophy of History, 1981; The Philosophy of Vegetarianism, 1984; Thoreau the Platonist, 1986; Hartshorne and the Metaphysics of Animal Rights, 1988; Christian Pacifism, 1991; St. John of the Cross, 1992; Analytic Theism, Hartshorne and the Concept of God, 1996; Babies and Beasts: The Argument from Marginal Cases, 1997; Kazantzakis and God, 1997; (with R. Deltete) A Brief, Liberal, Catholic Defense of Abortion, 2000; Not Even a Sparrow Falls: The Philosophy of Stephen R.L. Clark,

2000; Rawls and Religion: The Case for Political Liberalism, 2001; Divine Beauty: The Aesthetics of Charles Hartshorne, 2004; A Platonic Philosophy of Religion: A Process Perspective, 2005; Rethinking the Ontological Argument: A Neoclassical Theistic Response, 2006; Contemporary Athletics & Ancient Greek Ideals, 2009; Rawlsian Explorations in Religion and Applied Philosophy, 2011. **Address:** Department of Philosophy, Seattle University, Casey 420, 901 12th Ave., PO Box 222000, Seattle, WA 98122, U.S.A. **Online address:** ddombrow@seattleu.edu

DOMINGUEZ, Carlos Maria. Uraguayian/Argentine (born Argentina), b. 1955?. **Genres:** Translations. **Career:** Writer. **Publications:** Pozo de Vargas, 1985; Bicicletas negras (novel), 1990; ConstrucciOn de la noche: La vida de Juan Carlos Onetti, 1993; Contando Historia, 1995; La mujer hablada: Historia de tres ciudades, 1995; El bastardo: La vida de Roberto de las Carreras y su madre Clara, 1997; (ed.) Dario GirO, Una joya por cada rata: Memorias de un asaltante de bancos, 2001; Delitos de amores crueles: Las mujeres uruguayas frente a la justicia (1865-1911), 2001; Tola Invernizzi: La rebeliOn de la ternura, 2001; Escritos en el agua: Aventuras, personajes y misterios de Colonia y el Rio de la Plata, 2002; Historias del polvo y el camino, 2002; La casa de papel (novel), 2002; Tres muescas en mi carabina, 2003; El norte profundo: Viaje por Tacuarembo, Artigas, Rivera y Cerro Largo, 2004; Mares baldios, 2005; Las puertas de la tierra: La escena de acero de los puertos y los marinos uruguayos, 2007. **Address:** Av. Independencia 1668, Buenos Aires, C1100ABQ, Argentina. **Online address:** adastra@adinet.com

DOMINIAN, Jack. British/Greek (born Greece), b. 1929. **Genres:** Human Relations/Parenting, Psychology, Theology/Religion, Sex. **Career:** Central Middlesex Hospital, consultant physician, 1965-88; One Plus One, founder, chairman. Writer. **Publications:** Psychiatry and the Christian, 1962; Christian Marriage, 1967; Marital Breakdown, 1968; The Future of Christian Marriage, 1969; The Church and the Sexual Revolution, 1971; The Marriage Relationship Today, 1974; Cycle of Affirmation, 1975; Cycles of Affirmation, 1975; Affirming the Human Personality: Psychological Essays in Christian Living, 1975; Depression: What is It? How Do We Cope?, 1976; Authority: A Christian Interpretation of the Psychological Evolution of Authority, 1976; (with A.H. Peacocke) From Cosmos to Love: The Meaning of Human Life, 1976; Proposals for a New Sexual Ethic, 1977; Marital Pathology, 1980; Marriage, Faith and Love, 1981; The Growth of Love and Sex, 1982; Make or Break: An Introduction to Marriage Counselling, 1984; The Capacity to Love, 1985; Sexual Integrity: The Answer to AIDS, 1988; (with H. Montefiore) God, Sex & Love: An Exercise in Ecumenical Ethics, 1989; Passionate and Compassionate Love, 1991; Dynamics of Marriage: Love, Sex and Growth from a Christian Perspective, 1993; Marriage, 1995; One Like Us: A Psychological Interpretation of Jesus, 1998; Let's Make Love: The Meaning of Sexual Intercourse, 2001; Living Love, 2004. **Address:** One Plus One Marriage & Partnership Research, 1 Benjamin St., London, EC1M 5QG, England. **Online address:** info@oneplusone.org.uk

DONAHUE, Tina. American (born United States) **Genres:** Novels, Novellas/Short Stories, Romance/Historical, E-books. **Career:** Writer. **Publications:** ROMANTIC FICTION: Lady Love, 1999; Take a Chance, 1999; Once in a Blue Moon, 1999; Just One Kiss, 1999; O'Toole's Promise, 2000; Force of Nature, 2000; My Man, 2000; Finally and Forever (Irish Eyes), 2002; Let the Games Begin, 2005; Close to Perfect, 2005; Take My Breath Away, 2005; Tempt Me, Tease Me, Thrill Me, 2007; Close to Perfect, 2008; Adored, 2009; Deep, Dark, Delicious, 2010; Lush Velvet Nights, 2010; In His Arms, 2010; Sensual Stranger, 2010; The Yearning, 2011; Take Me Away, 2011; Unending Desire, 2011. **Address:** c/o Author Mail, Kensington Brava, 119 W 40th St., 21st Fl., New York, NY 10018, U.S.A. **Online address:** tina@tinadonahue.com

DONALD, Diana. British (born England), b. 1938. **Genres:** Art/Art History, Natural History, Translations, Humanities. **Career:** Manchester Metropolitan University, Department of History of Art and Design, head, 1986-97, professor of art history and design, 1990-97, retired, 1997; Yale University, Center for British Art, visiting fellow, 1987. Writer. **Publications:** (Comp.) Reynolds, 1986; The Age of Caricature: Satirical Prints in the Reign of George III, 1996; (trans. and ed. with C. Banerji) Gillray Observed: The Earliest Account of His Caricatures in London und Paris, 1999; What Is Popular Print, 2000; (ed. with F. O'Gorman) Ordering the World in the Eighteenth Century, 2006; Picturing Animals in Britain: 1750-1850, 2007; (ed. with J. Munro) Endless Forms: Charles Darwin, Natural Science and the Visual Arts, 2009. Contributor to journals. **Address:** Yale University Press, 47 Bedford Sq., London, GL WC1B 3DP, England. **Online address:** dianadonald@ukonline.co.uk

DONALD, Merlin (Wilfred). Canadian (born Canada), b. 1939. **Genres:** Psychology. **Career:** Yale University, School of Medicine, Department of Neurology, assistant professor, 1970-72; West Haven Veterans Administration Medical Center, research neuropsychologist; Queen's University, Department of Psychology, assistant professor, 1972-73, associate professor, 1974-82, Department of Psychiatry, assistant professor, 1980-90, professor of psychology, 1982-2005, faculty of education, professor, 1995-2005, Department of Psychology, chair, 2002-04, emeritus professor; Case Western Reserve University, Department of Cognitive Science, professor and founding chair, 2005-, now adjunct professor; Cleveland Museum of Natural History, research associate, 2005-; University College, visiting professor, Harvard University, visiting professor; Stanford University, visiting professor; University of California, visiting professor. Writer. **Publications:** Origins of the modern mind, 1991; A Mind So Rare: The Evolution of Human Consciousness, 2001. Contributor journals and magazines. **Address:** Department of Psychology, Queens University, Rm. 232, Humphrey Hall, 62 Arch St., Kingston, ON K7L 3N6, Canada. **Online address:** donaldm@queensu.ca

DONALD, Peter (Harry). Scottish (born Scotland), b. 1962. **Genres:** History, Theology/Religion. **Career:** University of London, Institute of Historical Research, research fellow, 1986-87; Church of Scotland, assistant minister, 1990-91, parish minister, 1991-, vice-convener; Edinburgh University, Cunningham fellow, 1990; Centre of Theology and Public Issues, affiliate. Writer. **Publications:** An Uncounselled King: Charles I and the Scottish Troubles, 1637-1641, 1990; (ed. with W. Storrar) God in Society: Doing Social Theology in Scotland Today, 2003. Contributor of essays to periodicals. **Address:** Crown Church, Kingsmills Rd., Inverness, HI 1V2 3JT, Scotland. **Online address:** pdonald7@aol.com

DONALD, Robyn Elaine. New Zealander (born New Zealand), b. 1940. **Genres:** Novels. **Career:** Teacher, 1960-64, 1971-72, 1973-, 1974-77. Writer. **Publications:** NOVELS: Bride at Whangatapu, 1977; Dilemma in Paradise, 1978; Summer at Awakopu, 1978; Shadow of the Past, 1979; Wife in Exchange, 1979; Bay of Stars, 1980; Iceberg, 1980; The Dark Abyss, 1981; The Interloper, 1981; An Old Passion, 1982; Mansion for My Love, 1982; The Gates of Rangitatau, 1983; The Guarded Heart, 1983; Return to Yesterday, 1983; A Durable Fire, 1984; Durable Line, 1984; An Unbreakable Bond, 1986; Long Journey Back, 1986; A Willing Surrender, 1986; Captives of the Past, 1986; Country of the Heart, 1987; A Late Loving, 1987; Smoke in the Wind, 1987; The Sweetest Trap, 1988; A Matter of Will, 1989; Love's Reward, 1989; A Bitter Homecoming, 1989; No Guarantees, 1990; The Darker Side of Paradise, 1990; A Summer Storm, 1990; No Place Too Far, 1990; Storm Over Paradise, 1991; Some Kind of Madness, 1991; The Stone Princess, 1991; The Golden Mask, 1992; Once Bitten, Twice Shy, 1992; Such Dark Magic, 1993; Island Enchantment, 1993; Pagan Surrender, 1993; Paradise Lost, 1993; Dark Fire, 1994; The Colour of Midnight, 1994; Tiger Eyes, 1994; Element of Risk, 1994; Prince of Lies, 1995; Indiscretions, 1995; Meant to Marry, 1996; The Final Proposal, 1996; The Mirror Bride, 1996; Tiger, Tiger, 1997; A Forbidden Desire, 1997; Surrender to Seduction, 1998; Forbidden Pleasure, 1998; (with D. Clair) Writing Romantic Fiction, 1999; The Paternity Affair, 1999; A Reluctant Mistress, 1999; Sanchia's Secret, 2000; A Ruthless Passion, 2001; Forgotten Sins, 2001; The Devil's Bargain, 2001; Wolfe's Temptress, 2002; One Night at Parenga, 2002; The Prince's Pleasure, 2002; The Temptress of Tarika Bay, 2003; The Millionaire's Virgin Mistress, 2003; A Spanish Vengeance, 2003; By Royal Command, 2004; His Pregnant Princess, 2004; The Billionaire's Passion, 2004; The Royal Baby Bargain, 2005; The Blackmail Bargain, 2005; By Royal Demand, 2005; By Royal Demand, 2006; The Rich Man's Royal Mistress, 2006; The Prince's Convenient Bride, 2007; The Prince's Forbidden Virgin, 2007; Virgin Bought and Paid for, 2007; His Majestys Mistress, 2008; The Mediterranean Prince's Captive Virgin, 2008; Innocent Mistress, Royal Wife, 2008; Ruthless Billionaire, Inexperienced Mistress, 2009; The Rich Man's Blackmailed Mistress, 2009; Rich, Ruthless and Secretly Royal, 2009; The Virgin and His Majesty, 2009; Brooding Billionaire, Impoverished Princess, 2010; Powerful Greek, Housekeeper Wife, 2010; The Disgraced Princess, 2011; Innocent Mistresses, 2011; Bought for His Bed, 2011; One Night in the Orient, 2011; Revenge, Secrets & Seduction, 2011. **Address:** c/o Author Mail, Harlequin Mills & Boon Ltd., Eton House, 18-24 Paradise Rd., Richmond, SR TW9 1SR, England. **Online address:** robyn@robyndonald.com

DONALDSON, Gary A. American (born United States) **Genres:** History, Humanities. **Career:** Xavier University of Louisiana, faculty, 1987-, associate professor of history, Keller Family Foundation chair in American history, Center for Undergraduate Research, director. Writer. **Publications:** The History of African Americans in the Military: Double V, 1991; America at War since 1945: Politics and Diplomacy in Korea, Vietnam and the Gulf War, 1996; Abundance and Anxiety: America, 1945-1960, 1997; Truman Defeats Dewey, 1999; Second Reconstruction: A History of the Modern Civil Rights Movement, 2000; Liberalism's Last Hurrah: The Presidential Campaign of 1964, 2003; First Modern Campaign: Kennedy, Nixon and the Election of 1960, 2007; (ed.) Modern America: A Documentary History of the Nation Since 1945, 2007; The Making of Modern America: The Nation from 1945 to the Present, 2009. Contributor to periodicals. **Address:** Department Of History, Xavier University of Louisiana, 1 Drexel Dr., PO Box 147, New Orleans, LA 70125, U.S.A. **Online address:** gdonalds@xula.edu

DONALDSON, Islay (Eila) Murray. Scottish (born Scotland), b. 1921. **Genres:** Biography, Local History/Rural Topics, Autobiography/Memoirs, Literary Criticism And History. **Career:** Kirkby Stephen Grammar School, teacher of English, 1947-48; Queen's University, assistant lecturer in English, 1948-49; Workers' Educational Association, teacher, 1949-; University of Edinburgh, part-time lecturer and courier, 1971-79; Scottish Arts Council, lecturer on graveyards and Staffordshire portrait figures. Writer. **Publications:** The Life and Work of Samuel Rutherford Crockett, 1989; East Lothian Gravestones, 1991; (contrib.) Transactions of East Lothian Antiquarian and Natural History Society, 1991; Midlothian Gravestones, 1994. Contributor to periodicals. **Address:** 7 Custom House Sq., Dunbar, LT EH42 1HY, Scotland.

DONALDSON, Joan. American (born United States), b. 1953. **Genres:** Adult Non-fiction, Young Adult Fiction, Children's Fiction. **Career:** Organic fruit farmer, 1977-; Hope College, teaching associate of dance, 1981-84. Writer. **Publications:** The Real Pretend, 1992; A Pebble and a Pen, 2000; The Secret of the Red Shoes, 2006; On Viney's Mountain, 2009. Contributor of articles to magazines. **Address:** Pleasant Hill Farm, 585 124th Ave., Fennville, MI 49408, U.S.A. **Online address:** mail@joandonaldson.com

DONALDSON, John Scott. *See* **DONALDSON, Scott.**

DONALDSON, Julia. British (born England), b. 1948. **Genres:** Children's Fiction, Plays/Screenplays, Food And Wine, Picture/Board Books, Songs/Lyrics And Libretti, Poetry. **Career:** Writer. **Publications:** A Squash and a Squeeze, 1993; Turtle Tug, 1995; The Magic Twig 1995; The Boy Who Cried Wolf, 1995; The Three Billy Goats Gruff, 1995; Mr. Snow, 1996; Strange Sue, 1996; The Town Mouse and the Country Mouse, 1996; Counting Chickens, 1996; The King's Porridge, 1996; Top of the Mops, 1997; The Wonderful Smells, 1997; All Gone, 1998; Books and Crooks, 1998; Waiter! Waiter!, 1998; The Brownie in the Teapot, 1998; The Gruffalo, 1999; Clever Katya, 1999; The Noises Next Door, 1999; The King's Ears, 2000; The Strange Dream, 2000; The Boy Who Talked to the Birds, 2000; Monkey Puzzle, 2000; Steve's Sandwiches, 2000; One Piece Missing, 2000; Jumping Jack, 2000; Cat Whispers, 2000; The Giant Jumperee, 2000; Problem Page, 2000; Fox's Socks, 2000; Hide and Seek Pig, 2000; Rabbit's Nap, 2000; Postman Bear, 2000; The Gruffalo Song and Other Songs, 2000; Stop Thief!, 2001; The Monster in the Cave, 2001; Room on the Broom and Other Songs, 2001; The Smartest Giant in Town, 2002; Night Monkey Day Monkey, 2002; Follow the Swallow, 2002; The Dinosaur's Diary, 2002; Hamlet, 2002; Midsummer Dream, 2002; The Trial of Wilf Wolf, 2002; Conjuror Cow, 2003; The Head in the Sand, 2003; Bombs and Blackberries, 2003; Brick-a-Breck, 2003; I Don't Want To, 2003; The Magic Paintbrush, 2003; Princess Mirror-Belle, 2003; Spiffiest Giant in Town, 2003; The Snail and the Whale, 2003; The False Tooth Fairy, 2004; Giants and the Joneses, 2005; Gruffalo's Child, 2005; Worm Looks for Lunch, 2005; Rosie's Hat, 2005; Wrong Kind of Bark, 2005; Crazy Mayonnaisy Mum, 2005; Wriggle and Roar!: Rhymes to Join in with, 2005; Spinderella, 2006; (with J. Henderson) Fly, Pigeon, Fly, 2006; One Ted Falls Out of Bed, 2006; Quick Brown Fox Cub, 2006; Charlie Cook's Favorite Book, 2006; Bricks for Breakfast, 2006; Songbirds, 2006; The Mermaid and the Octopus, 2006; The Pot of Gold, 2006; Julia Donaldson: A Biography, 2006; Sharing a Shell, 2007; The Princess and the Wizard, 2007; Tales from Acorn Wood, 2008; Tyrannosaurus Drip, 2008; Where's My Mom?, 2008; Gruffalo Colouring Book, 2008; Gruffalo Pop-up Theatre Book, 2008; Stick Man, 2008; The Troll, 2008; The Fish Who Cried Wolf, 2008; Chocolate Mouse for Greedy Goose, 2009; One Mole Digging a Hole, 2009; The Tyrannosaurus Drip Song, 2009; Gruffalo Magnet Book, 2009; Gruffalo's Child

Activity Book, 2009; Running on the Cracks, 2009; Hippo Has a Hat, 2009; What the Ladybug Heard, 2010; Gruffalo Sound Book, 2010; Freddie and the Fairy, 2010; Cave Baby, 2010; Chocolate Mousse for Greedy Goose, 2010; Tabby McTat, 2010; Toddle Waddle, 2010; Charlie Cook's Favourite Book, 2010; Tiddler, 2010; Zog, 2010; What the Ladybird Heard, 2010; Gruffalo Red Nose Day Book, 2011; Gruffalo's Child Song: And Other Songs, 2011; My First Gruffalo: Touch-and-Feel, 2011; Animal Actions, 2011; Colours, 2011; Gruffalo, What Can You See?, 2011; Hello Gruffalo! Buggy Book, 2011; Numbers, 2011; Opposites, 2011; Rhyming Rabbit, 2011; Jack and the Flumflum Tree, 2011; Highway Rat, 2011; Goat Goes To Playgroup, 2012; Gold Star for Zog, 2012. **Address:** 2 Chapelton Ave., Glasgow, CN G61 2RE, Scotland.

DONALDSON, Loraine. American (born United States) **Genres:** Demography, Economics, Third World, Social Sciences. **Career:** Georgia State University, Andrew Young School of Policy Studies, assistant professor, 1964-66, associate professor, 1966-70, professor of economics, 1970-, now professor emeritus. Writer. **Publications:** Development Planning in Ireland, 1966; Economic Development: Analysis and Policy, 1984; Fertility Transition: The Social Dynamics of Population Change, 1991. Contributor to journals. **Address:** Andrew Young School of Policy Studies, Georgia State University, 14 Marietta St. NW, Atlanta, GA 30303-2813, U.S.A.

DONALDSON, Molla S(loane). American (born United States), b. 1944. **Genres:** Medicine/Health. **Career:** George Washington University, research assistant, 1972-76, research instructor, 1976-78, assistant research professor of health care sciences, 1978-83, associate professor, 1983-94, Medical Decision Center, senior health services researcher, 1985-88, adjunct professor, 1994-, Health Plan, Research and Quality Assurance Program, director, 1983-88; CIMA, Risk Control Services, risk control consultant, 1984-86; National Academy of Sciences, Institute of Medicine, senior staff officer, 1988-2001, project co-director; University of Michigan, Pew fellow, 1994-; National Institutes of Health, National Cancer Institute, senior scientist, 2001-06; American Society of Clinical Oncology, Quality Division, director, 2006; MSD Health Care Consulting Group, founder and president, 2006-. Writer. **Publications:** (Co-author) Autobiographical Memory for Health-Related Events: Enhanced Memory for Recurring Incidents, 1988. EDITOR: (with J. Harris-Wehling and K.N. Lohr) Medicare-New Directions in Quality Assurance, 1991; (ed. with A.M. Capron) Patient Outcomes Research Teams: Managing Conflict of Interest, 1991; (with C. Sox, Jr.) Setting Priorities for Health Technology Assessment: A Model Process, 1992; (co-ed.) Clinical Applications of Mifepristone and other Antiprogestins, 1993; (with K.L. Lohr) Health Data in the Information Age: Use, Disclosure and Privacy, 1994; (with K.N. Lohr, K.D. Yordy and N.A. Vanselow) Primary Care: America's Health in a New Era, 1996; Measuring the Quality of Health Care, 1999; Collaboration among Competing Managed Care Organizations for Quality Improvement, 1999; (L.T. Kohn and J.M. Corrigan) To Err Is Human: Building a Safer Health System, 2000. Contributor to books and periodicals. **Address:** George Washington University, 2121 I St. NW, Washington, DC 20052, U.S.A. **Online address:** molla@msdhealth.com

DONALDSON, Ross I. American (born United States), b. 1975?. **Genres:** Medicine/Health. **Career:** University of California, professor of medicine; Los Angeles Trauma Center, emergency physician. Writer. **Publications:** The Lassa Ward: One Man's Fight against One of the World's Deadliest Diseases, 2009. **Address:** Venice Beach, CA , U.S.A. **Online address:** info@rossdonaldson.com

DONALDSON, Scott. (John Scott Donaldson). American (born United States), b. 1928. **Genres:** Literary Criticism And History, Social Commentary, Biography, Poetry. **Career:** Minneapolis Star, reporter, 1956-58; Bloomington Sun-Suburbanite, editor and publisher, 1959-63; University of Minnesota, instructor in humanities and American literature, 1963-66; College of William and Mary, assistant professor, 1966-69, associate professor, 1969-74, professor, 1974-84, Louise G.T. Cooley professor of English, 1984-, now emeritus; University of Leeds, visiting professor, 1972-73, Bruern fellow; Princeton University, visiting fellow, 1978; Fulbright Alumni Association, founding director; Hemingway Foundation, president, 2000-02. **Publications:** The Suburban Myth, 1969; Poet in America: Winfield Townley Scott, 1972; By Force of Will: The Life and Art of Ernest Hemingway, 1977; (with A. Massa) American Literature: Nineteenth and Early Twentieth Centuries, 1978; Fool for Love, F. Scott Fitzgerald, 1983; John Cheever: A Biography, 1988; Archibald MacLeish: An American Life, 1992; Hemingway vs. Fitzgerald: The Rise and

Fall of a Literary Friendship, 1999; Edwin Arlington Rohinson: A Poet's Life, 2007; Fitzgerald and Hemingway: Works and Days, 2009. EDITOR: On the Road, 1979; Critical Essays on F. Scott Fitzgerald's The Great Gatsby, 1984; Conversations with John Cheever, 1987; New Essays on A Farewell to Arms, 1990; The Cambridge Companion to Hemingway, 1996; Robinson: Poems, 2007. **Address:** 10040 E Happy Valley Rd., Desert Highlands 303, Scottsdale, AZ 85255, U.S.A. **Online address:** scottd10@mac.com

DONALDSON, Terence L. Canadian (born Canada), b. 1948. **Genres:** Theology/Religion. **Career:** College of Emmanuel and St. Chad, professor of New Testament and biblical languages, 1984-99; University of Toronto, Wycliffe College, School of Theology, Lord and Lady Coggan professor of New Testament studies, 1999-, director of advanced degree programs. Theologian and writer. **Publications:** Jesus on the Mountain: A Study in Matthean Theology, 1985; Paul and the Gentiles: Remapping the Apostle's Convictional World, 1997; Judaism and the Gentiles: Jewish Patterns of Universalism (to 135 CE), 2007; Jews and Anti-Judaism in the New Testament: Decision Points and Divergent Interpretations, 2010. Contributor of articles to journals. **Address:** School of Theology, Wycliffe College, University of Toronto, 5 Hoskin Ave., Toronto, ON M5S 1H7, Canada. **Online address:** terry.donaldson@utoronto.ca

DONALDSON, Thomas. American (born United States), b. 1945. **Genres:** Ethics, Business/Trade/Industry, Essays, Philosophy. **Career:** Loyola University of Chicago, assistant professor, 1976-81, associate professor, 1981-84, Henry J. Wirtenberger Professor of Ethics, 1984-88, Graduate Program in philosophy, director, 1982-84; University of Virginia, C. Stewart Sheppard visiting professor of business Administration, 1988-89; Georgetown University, John F. Connelly Professor of Business Ethics, 1990-96; University of Pennsylvania, Wharton School, professor of legal studies and business ethics, Mark O. Winkelman Professor, 1996-, Wharton PhD Program in Ethics and Legal Studies, director, 2002-08, Academy of Management Review, associate editor, 2003-07, Social Issues in Management Division of the Academy of Management, chairman, 2007-08, Zicklin Center for Research in Business Ethics, director. Writer. **Publications:** (Ed. with P.H. Werhane) Ethical Issues in Business: A Philosophical Approach, 1979, 8th ed., 2008; Corporations and Morality, 1982; (ed.) Case Studies in Business Ethics, 1984, (with A.R. Gini) 4th ed., 1996; (comp.) Issues in Moral Philosophy, 1986; Ethics of International Business, 1989; (ed. with R.E. Freeman) Business as a Humanity, 1994; (co-ed.) Uncompromising Integrity: Motorola's Global Challenge: 24 Global Case Studies with Commentaries, 1998; (with T.W. Dunfee) Ethics in Business and Economics, 2 vols., 1998; Business Ethics: Corporate Competitiveness and Ethics Compliance Management Systems, 1999; (with T.W. Dunfee) The Ties that Bind: A Social Contracts Approach to Business Ethics, 1999. Contributor of articles to journals. **Address:** Wharton School, University of Pennsylvania, 644 Jon M. Huntsman Hall, 3730 Walnut St., Philadelphia, PA 19104-6369, U.S.A. **Online address:** donaldst@wharton.upenn.edu

DONATI, Sara. See **LIPPI(-GREEN), Rosina.**

DONEGAN, Greg. See **MAYER, Bob.**

DONGALA, Emmanuel Boundzeki. American/Congolese (born Congo), b. 1941. **Genres:** Poetry. **Career:** Institut de Chimie, instructor, 1973-75; école Nationale Supérieure de Chimie de Paris, research assistant, 1976-78; Université de Brazzaville, professor of chemistry, 1979-98; Théatre de l'éclair, founder, 1981; Conseil Africain et Malgache de l'Enseignement Suoerieure, Math and Physical Sciences Section, vice-president, 1995-97; Simon's Rock College, professor of chemistry and French, 1998-, Richard B. Fisher Chair in Natural Sciences, Bard College, professor of French, 1998-. Writer. **Publications:** Un Fusil Dans la main, un Poeme Dans la Poche, 1973; Jazz et vin de Palme, 1982; Le Feu des origines, 1987; Les Petits garçons Naissent Aussi Des étoiles, 1998; Little Boys Come From the Stars, 2001; Johnny Chien Méchant, 2002; Johnny Mad Dog, 2005; Photo de groupe au bord du fleuve: Roman, 2010. Contributor to journals. **Address:** Fisher Science and Academic Ctr., Bard College at Simons' Rock, Rm. 207, 84 Alford Rd., Great Barrington, MA 01230, U.S.A. **Online address:** edongala@simons-rock.edu

DONG YU-DE See **Donnithorne, Audrey Gladys.**

DONIA, Robert J(ay). American (born United States), b. 1945. **Genres:** History, Theology/Religion. **Career:** University of Michigan, lecturer in Russian and eastern European studies, 1977, research associate; University

of Windsor, assistant professor of history, 1977-78; Ohio State University, assistant professor of history, 1978-; University of Sarajevo, associate professor of history. Writer. **Publications:** Islam under the Double Eagle: The Muslims of Bosnia and Hercegovina, 1878-1914, 1981; Into all the World: Hope College and International Affairs: Essays in Honor of Paul G. Fried, 1985; (with J.V.A. Fine, Jr.) Bosnia and Hercegovina: A Tradition Betrayed, 1994; Sarajevo: A Biography, 2006. Contributor to periodicals. **Address:** Department of History, Ohio State University, 4300 Campus Dr., Lima, OH 45804, U.S.A.

DONKER, Marjorie. (Marjorie J. Donker). American (born United States), b. 1926. **Genres:** Language/Linguistics, Literary Criticism And History, Reference. **Career:** Western Washington University, instructor, 1967-70, assistant professor, 1970-73, associate professor, 1973-82, professor of English, 1982-, now professor emeritus of English. Writer. **Publications:** (With G. Muldrow) A Dictionary of Literary-Rhetorical Conventions of the English Renaissance, 1982; Shakespeare's Proverbial Themes: A Rhetorical Context for the Sententia as Res, 1992. **Address:** Department of English, Western Washington University, 329 Humanities, 516 High St., Bellingham, WA 98225, U.S.A.

DONKER, Marjorie J. See **DONKER, Marjorie.**

DONLEAVY, J(ames) P(atrick). Irish/American (born United States), b. 1926. **Genres:** Novels, Novellas/Short Stories, Plays/Screenplays, Social Commentary, Language/Linguistics, Children's Fiction, Young Adult Fiction, Humanities, Literary Criticism And History. **Career:** Writer. **Publications:** The Ginger Man: A Novel, 1955; A Singular Man, 1963; Meet My Maker the Mad Molecule (short stories), 1964; The Saddest Summer of Samuel S., 1966; The Beastly Beatitudes of Balthazar B., 1968; The Onion Eaters: A Novel, 1971; The Collected Plays of J.P. Donleavy, 1972; A Fairy Tale of New York, 1973; The Unexpurgated Code: A Complete Manual of Survival and Manners, 1975; The Destinies of Darcy Dancer, Gentleman, 1977; Schultz, 1979; Leila: Further in the Destinies of Darcy Dancer, Gentleman in UK as Leila: Further in the Life and Destinies of Darcy Dancer, Gentleman, 1983; De Alfonce Tennis: The Superlative Game of Eccentric Champions, Its History Accountrements, Rules, Conduct, and Regimen, 1984; J.P. Donleavy's Ireland: In All Her Sins and in Some of Her Graces, 1986; Are You Listening, Rabbi Löw?, 1987; A Singular Country, 1989; That Darcy, That Dancer, That Gentleman, 1990; The History of the Ginger Man (memoirs), 1994; The Lady Who Liked Clean Rest Rooms: The Chronicle of One of the Strangest Stories Ever to Be Rumored About Around New York, (novella), 1995; An Author and His Image: The Collected Shorter Pieces, (short stories), 1997; Wrong Information is Being Given Out at Princeton (novel), 1998; Letter Marked Personal, 2000. Contributor of periodicals. **Address:** Levington Pk., Mullingar, WE 2, Ireland. **Online address:** dlhartz@earthlink.net

DONN, Linda. American (born United States) **Genres:** Novels, Young Adult Non-fiction, Young Adult Fiction, Romance/Historical, Biography, Autobiography/Memoirs. **Career:** Historian and writer. **Publications:** Freud and Jung: Years of Friendship, Years of Loss, 1988; The Roosevelt Cousins: Growing Up Together, 1882-1924, 2001; The Little Balloonist, 2006; Himalaya/ Dreams, forthcoming. **Address:** c/o Author Mail, Dutton Publicity, 375 Hudson St., New York, NY 10014-3658, U.S.A.

DONNACHIE, Ian. (Ian Lowe Donnachie). Scottish (born Scotland), b. 1944. **Genres:** History, Economics, Business/Trade/Industry. **Career:** University of Strathclyde, Department of History, research assistant, 1967-68; Napier University, lecturer in history, 1968-70; Industrial Archaeology, assistant editor, 1968-77; Open University in Scotland, Faculty of Arts, staff tutor in history, 1970-85, senior lecturer, 1985-, reader in history, professor, now professor emeritus; Industrial Archaeology Review, assistant editor, 1975-78; Deakin University, visiting lecturer in social sciences, 1982; University of Dundee, honorary lecturer in history, 1998-; University of Sydney, faculty. **Publications:** (With J. Butt and J.R. Hume) Industrial History: Scotland, 1968; (with J. Butt) The Industries of Scotland, 1969; Industrial Archaeology of Galloway, 1971; War and Economic Growth in Britain 1793-1815, 1973; (with I. Macleod) Old Galloway, 1974; Roads and Canals, 1976; (with A. Hogg) The War of Independence and the Scottish Nation, 1976; (with J. Hume and M. Moss) Historic Industrial Scenes: Scotland, 1977; A History of the Brewing Industry in Scotland, 1979; (with J. Butt) Industrial Archaeology in the British Isles, 1979; (intro. with I. Macleod) Victorian and Edwardian Scottish Lowlands in Old Photographs, 1979; (with G. Hewitt) Scottish History 1560-1980, 1982; (with G. Hewitt) Companion to Scottish History,

1989; (with G. Hewitt) Historic New Lanark, 1993, 2nd ed., 1999; Robert Owen: Owen of New Lanark and New Harmony, 2000; Scottish History, 2003; Robert Owen: Social Visionary, 2005, new ed., 2011; (with G. Hewitt) Birlinn Companion to Scottish History, 2007. EDITOR: (with C. Harvie and I.S. Wood) Forward! Labour Politics in Scotland 1888-1988, 1989; (with C. Whatley) The Manufacture of Scottish History, 1992; Studying, Literature and Culture, 1996; Modern Scottish History 1707 to the Present, 5 vols., 1998; (with C. Larvin) From Enlightenment to Romanticism: Anthologies I and II, 2004. **Address:** Department of History, Faculty of Arts, Open University, Walton Hall, Milton Keynes, MK7 6AA, England. **Online address:** i.donnachie@open.ac.uk

DONNACHIE, Ian Lowe. *See* **DONNACHIE, Ian.**

DONNELLY, Deborah. American (born United States) **Genres:** Science Fiction/Fantasy, Human Relations/Parenting. **Career:** Writer and librarian. **Publications:** Veiled Threats, 2002; Died to Match, 2002; May the Best Man Die, 2003; Death Takes a Honeymoon, 2005; You May Now Kill The Bride, 2006; Bride and Doom, 2006. Contributor to magazines. **Address:** c/o Author Mail, Bantam Doubleday Dell Publishing Group Inc., 1745 Broadway, New York, NY 10019, U.S.A.

DONNELLY, Jane. British (born England) **Genres:** Romance/Historical, Young Adult Fiction, Novels. **Career:** Novelist. **Publications:** Don't Look Back, 1965; A Man Apart, 1968; Don't Walk Alone, 1969; This Hell Called Love, 1969; Whispering Ones, 1969; Stranger in the Dark, 1969; Shadows from the Sea, 1969; Take the Far Dream, 1970; Never Turn Back, 1970; The Man in the Next Room, 1970; Halfway to the Stars, 1971; The Mill in the Meadow, 1972; A Stranger Came, 1972; The Long Shadow, 1973; Rocks under Shining Water, 1973; A Man Called Mallory, 1974; Collision Course, 1975; The Man Outside, 1975; Ride Out the Storm, 1975; Dark Pursuer, 1976; The Silver Cage, 1976; Dear Caliban, 1977; Four Weeks in Winter, 1977; The Intruder, 1977; Forest of the Night, 1979; Love for a Stranger, 1978; Spell of the Seven Stones, 1978; The Black Hunter, 1978; Touched by Fire, 1978; A Man to Watch, 1979; A Savage Sanctuary, 1979; Behind a Closed Door, 1979; No Way Out, 1980; When Lightning Strikes, 1980; Flash Point, 1981; So Long a Winter, 1981; The Frozen Jungle, 1981; Diamond Cut Diamond, 1982; A Fierce Encounter, 1983; Call Up the Storm, 1983; Face the Tiger, 1983; Moon Lady, 1984; Ring of Crystal, 1985; To Cage a Whirlwind, 1985; Force Field, 1987; The Frozen Heart, 1987; Ride a Wild Horse, 1987; No Place to Run, 1987; Fetters of Gold, 1988; When We're Alone, 1989; The Devil's Flower, 1990; The Jewels of Helen, 1991; Once a Cheat, 1991; Hold Back the Dark, 1993; The Trespasser, 1994; Shadow of a Tiger, 1994; Cover Story, 1994; Sleeping Beauty, 1995; Living with Marc, 1996; (ed. with D. Nicole) Mighty Giants of the Wild, 1996; (and ed. with D. Nicoll) Fearsome Hunters of the Wild, 1996; Max's Proposal, 1998; A Very Private Man, 1999; Fiance for Real, 2000. **Address:** Harlequin Mills and Boon Ltd., Eton House, 18-24 Paradise Rd., Richmond, SR TW9 1SR, England.

DONNELLY, Joe. Scottish (born Scotland), b. 1950. **Genres:** Horror, Children's Fiction, Novels, Young Adult Fiction. **Career:** Evening Times, staff writer, 1976-80; Sunday Mail, journalist, 1980-. **Publications:** Bane, 1989; Stone, 1990; The Shee, 1992; Still Life, 1993; Shrike, 1994; Havock Junction, 1995; Incubus, 1996; Twitchy Eyes, 1997; Dark Valley, 1998; Jack Flint and the Redthorn Sword, 2008; Jack Flint and the Spellbinder's Curse, 2008; Jack Flint and the Dark Ways, 2009. **Address:** Michael Joseph Ltd., Penguin Books, 27 Wrights Ln., London, GL W8 5TZ, England.

DONNER, Rebecca. American/Canadian (born Canada) **Genres:** Novels, Graphic Novels. **Career:** KGB Sunday Fiction Series, literary director, 1998-2002; KGB Bar Fiction Series, director. Writer. **Publications:** (Ed.) On the Rocks: The KGB Bar Fiction Anthology, 2002; Sunset Terrace (novel), 2003; Burnout (graphic novel), 2008. **Address:** c/o Jennifer Carlson, Dunow, Carlson & Lerner, 27 W 20th St., Ste. 1107, New York, NY 10011, U.S.A. **Online address:** rebecca@rebeccadonner.com

DONNISON, David Vernon. Scottish/Myanmar (born Myanmar), b. 1926. **Genres:** Regional/Urban Planning, Social Sciences. **Career:** University of Manchester, assistant lecturer in social administration, 1950-53; University of Toronto, lecturer in social work, 1953-55; University of London, London School of Economics and Political Science, reader, 1956-61; professor of social administration, 1961-69; Public Schools Commission, chair, 1968-70; Centre for Environmental Studies, director, 1969-75; Supplementary Benefits

Commission, chairman, 1975-80; University of Glasgow, Town and Regional Planning, professor, 1980-90, chair, honorary research fellow, 1990-, Department of Urban Studies, honorary senior research fellow, now professor emeritus. Writer. **Publications:** The Neglected Child and the Social Services, 1954; Welfare Services in a Canadian Community, 1958; (with P. Jay and M. Stewart) The Ingleby Report: Three Critical Essays, 1962; Social Policy and Administration: Studies in the Development of Social Services at the Local Level, 1965, rev. ed., 1975; The Government of Housing, 1967; (intro.) Housing Problems and Policies, 1968; A Pattern of Disadvantage: A Commentary on From Birth to Seven, 1972; (with P. Soto) The Good City: A Study of Urban Development and Policy in Britain, 1980; The Politics of Poverty, 1982; (with C. Ungerson) Housing Policy, 1982; A Radical Agenda: After the New Right and the Old Left, 1991; Social Policies and Moral Principles, 1993; Act Local, 1994; Policies for a Just Society, 1998; Speaking to Power: Advocacy for Health and Social Care, 2009. EDITOR: (with D. Eversley) London: Urban Patterns, Problems and Policies, 1973; (with A. Middleton) Regenerating the Inner City: Glasgow's Experience, 1987; (with D. Maclennan) The Housing Service of the Future, 1991. **Address:** Department of Urban Studies, University of Glasgow, 25 Bute Gardens, Glasgow, G12 8RS, Scotland.

DONNITHORNE, Audrey Gladys. (Dong Yu-de). British (born England), b. 1922. **Genres:** Economics. **Career:** Yenching University-in-Chengdu, English faculty, 1942; War Office London, junior civil assistant, 1943-44; University of London, University College, research assistant, 1948-51, lecturer in political economy, 1951-66, reader in Chinese economic studies, 1966-68; Australian National University, professorial fellow, 1969-85; Contemporary China Centre, foundation head, 1970-77; AITECE Ltd., director, 1988-2000. Writer. **Publications:** Economic Developments since 1937 in Eastern and Southeastern Asia and their Effects on the United Kingdom, 1950; (with G.C. Allen) Western Enterprise in Far Eastern Economic Development: China and Japan, 1954; (with G.C. Allen) Western Enterprise in Indonesia and Malaya, 1957; British Rubber Manufacturing, 1958; China's Economic System, 1967; China's Grain: Output, Procurement, Transfers and Trade, 1970; The Budget and the Plan in China: Central-Local Economic Relations, 1972; Centre-Provincial Economic Relations in China, 1981. Contributor to periodicals. **Address:** 73 Bonham Rd., Flat A3, 18th Fl., Kingsfield Twr., Hong Kong, 852, Hong Kong. **Online address:** agd@netvigator.com

DONNITHORNE, Larry R. American (born United States), b. 1944. **Genres:** Military/Defense/Arms Control, Administration/Management. **Career:** U.S. Military Academy, teacher of leadership and moral philosophy; College of the Albemarle, president. Writer. **Publications:** The West Point Way of Leadership: From Learning Principled Leadership to Practicing It, 1994. **Address:** College of the Albemarle, PO Box 2327, Elizabeth City, NC 27906-2327, U.S.A.

DONOFRIO, Beverly. American (born United States), b. 1950?. **Genres:** Autobiography/Memoirs. **Career:** San Miguel Workshops, San Miguel de Allende, founder; Riding in Cars with Boys, co-producer, 2001. Writer and memoirist. **Publications:** Riding in Cars with Boys: Confessions of a Bad Girl Who Makes Good, 1990; (with R. Bonanno) Mafia Marriage: My Story, 1990; Looking for Mary or The Blessed Mother and Me (memoir), 2000; Mary and the Mouse, the Mouse and Mary, 2007; Thank You, Lucky Stars, 2008. Contributor to periodicals. **Address:** Crestone, CO , U.S.A. **Online address:** bevdono@yahoo.com

DONOGHUE, Daniel. American (born United States), b. 1956. **Genres:** Literary Criticism And History. **Career:** Harvard University, Department of English, assistant professor, 1986-91, professor of English, 1991-, John P. Marquand professor of English, director of undergraduate studies. Writer. **Publications:** Style in Old English Poetry: The Test of the Auxiliary, 1987; (ed.) Beowulf: A Verse Translation: Authoritative Text, Contexts, Criticism, 2002; Lady Godiva: A Literary History of a Legend, 2003; Old English Literature: A Short Introduction, 2004; (ed. with J. Simpson and N. Watson) Morton W. Bloomfield Lectures, 1989-2005, 2010. **Address:** Department of English, Harvard University, 208 Barker Ctr., 12 Quincy St., Cambridge, MA 02138, U.S.A. **Online address:** dgd@wjh.harvard.edu

DONOGHUE, Emma. Irish/Canadian (born Canada), b. 1969. **Genres:** Literary Criticism And History, Gay And Lesbian Issues, Women's Studies And Issues, Theatre, History, Novels, Novellas/Short Stories, Plays/Screenplays, Plays/Screenplays, Adult Non-fiction. **Career:** Irish Times Prize for Irish

Literature, judge, 1997; University of Western Ontario, writer-in-residence, 1999-2000; University of York, writer-in-residence, 1999-2000. Writer. **Publications:** NOVELS: Stir-Fry, 1994; Hood, 1995; (co-author) Ladies Night at Finbar's Hotel (novel), 1999; Slammerkin, 2000; Life Mask, 2004; Landing, 2007; The Sealed Letter, 2008; Room, 2010. OTHER: Passions between Women: British Lesbian Culture, 1668-1801 (nonfiction), 1993; I Know My Own Heart: A Lesbian Regency Romance (play), 1994; Kissing the Witch: Old Tales in New Skins (stories), 1997; (ed.) Poems between Women, 1997 as What Sappho Would Have Said: Four Centuries of Love Poems between Women, 1997; Ladies and Gentleman, 1998; We Are Michael Field (biography), 1998; (ed.) The Mammoth Book of Modern Lesbian Short Stories, 1999; The Woman Who Gave Birth to Rabbits: Stories, 2002; Touchy Subjects: Stories, 2005; Inseparable: Desire Between Women in Literature, 2010; Astray, 2012. Contributor to periodicals. **Address:** c/o Caroline Davidson, Caroline Davidson Literary Agency, 5 Queen Anne's Gardens, London, GL W4 1TU, England. **Online address:** emma@emmadonoghue.com

DONOGHUE, Francis Joseph. *See* **DONOGHUE, Frank J.**

DONOGHUE, Frank J. (Francis Joseph Donoghue). American (born United States), b. 1958?. **Genres:** History, Literary Criticism And History, Business/Trade/Industry. **Career:** Stanford University, assistant professor, 1986-89; Ohio State University, Department of English, assistant professor, 1989-95, associate professor, 1995-, professor. Writer. **Publications:** The Fame Machine: Book Reviewing and Eighteenth-Century Literary Careers, 1996; The Last Professors: The Corporate University and the Fate of the Humanities, 2008. Contributor to books, periodicals and journals. **Address:** Department of English, Ohio State University, 556 Denney Hall, 164 W 17th Ave., Columbus, OH 43210, U.S.A. **Online address:** donoghue.1@osu.edu

DONOGHUE, Mildred R(ansdorf). American (born United States), b. 1929?. **Genres:** Education, Language/Linguistics, Art/Art History. **Career:** Immaculate Heart College, instructor in elementary education, 1961-62; California State University, Department of Elementary and Bilingual Education, assistant professor, 1962-66, associate professor, 1966-71, professor of education and reading, 1971-. Writer. **Publications:** Foreign Languages and the Schools, 1967; Foreign Languages and the Elementary School Child, 1968; The Child and the English Language Arts, 1971, 5th ed., 1990; (with J.F. Kunkle) Second Languages in Primary Education, 1979; Using Literature Activities to Teach Content Areas to Emergent Readers, 2001; Language Arts: Integrating Skills in the Classroom, 2009. **Address:** Department of Elementary and Bilingual Education, California State University, 2600 Nutwood, Ste. 500, PO Box 6868, Fullerton, CA 92831, U.S.A. **Online address:** mdonoghue@fullerton.edu

DONOHUE, A. A. (Alice A. Donohue). American (born United States), b. 1952?. **Genres:** Archaeology/Antiquities. **Career:** Bryn Mawr College, professor of classical and Near Eastern archaeology & acting graduate advisor. Writer. **Publications:** Xoana and the Origins of Greek Sculpture, 1988; (ed. with M.D. Fullerton) Ancient Art and Its Historiography, 2003; Greek Sculpture and the Problem of Description, 2005; (ed, with C.C. Mattusch and A. Brauer) Proceedings of the XVIth International Congress of Classical Archaeology, Boston, August 23-26, 2003: Common Ground: Archaeology, Art, Science and Humanities, 2006. **Address:** Dept. of Classical & Near Eastern Arch., Bryn Mawr College, 101 North Merion Ave., Bryn Mawr, PA 19010-2899, U.S.A. **Online address:** adonohue@brynmawr.edu

DONOHUE, Alice A. *See* **DONOHUE, A. A.**

DONOHUE, Keith. American (born United States), b. 1960?. **Genres:** Novels. **Career:** National Endowment for the Arts, speechwriter, 1981-94, director of publications, 1994-97; U.S. General Services Administration, senior advisor on work-life and child care issues; Center for Arts and Culture, creative director; National Historical Publications and Records Commission, communications director and editor; Open Studio: The Arts Online, creator and producer. **Publications:** (Ed.) Imagine! Introducing Your Child to the Arts, 1997; The Irish Anatomist: A Study of Flann O'Brien, 2002; The Stolen Child, 2006; Angels of Destruction: A Novel, 2009; Centuries of June, 2011. **Address:** c/o Peter Steinberg, The Steinberg Agency, 47 E 19th St., 3rd Fl., New York, NY 10003, U.S.A. **Online address:** donohuebooks@gmail.com

DONOHUE, Laura K. American (born United States), b. 1969. **Genres:** Social Sciences. **Career:** Judge John T. Noonan, Ninth Circuit Court of Appeals, clerk, 2008-09; Stanford University, Center for International Security and Cooperation (CISAC), fellow; Stanford Law School, Center for Constitutional Law, fellow; Harvard University, John F. Kennedy School of Government, fellow; University of Cambridge, Churchill College, by-fellow; Georgetown Law School, associate professor of law, Center on National Security and the Law, faculty. Writer and attorney. **Publications:** Counter-terrorist Law and Emergency Powers in the United Kingdom, 1922-2000, 2001; The Cost of Counterterrorism: Power, Politics and Liberty, 2008. Contributor to periodicals and journals. **Address:** Center for International Security and Cooperation, Stanford University, 600 New Jersey Ave., Washington, DC 20001, U.S.A. **Online address:** lkd27@law.georgetown.edu

DONOHUE, William A. (William Anthony Donohue). American (born United States), b. 1947. **Genres:** Civil Liberties/Human Rights, Politics/Government, Adult Non-fiction, Social Sciences. **Career:** St. Lucy's School, teacher, 1973-77; La Roche College, professor of sociology, 1977-93; Catholic League for Religious and Civil Rights, president, 1993-. Writer. **Publications:** The Politics of the American Civil Liberties Union, 1985; The New Freedom: Individualism and Collectivism in the Social Lives of Americans, 1990; Twilight of Liberty: The Legacy of the ACLU, 1994; On the Front Line of the Culture War: Recent Attacks on the Boy Scouts of America, 1996; Secular Sabotage: How Liberals are Destroying Religion and Culture in America, 2009. **Address:** Catholic League for Religious and Civil Rights, 450 7th Ave., 34th Fl., New York, NY 10023, U.S.A.

DONOHUE, William Anthony. *See* **DONOHUE, William A.**

DONOUGHUE, Bernard. British (born England), b. 1934. **Genres:** Politics/Government, Biography, Autobiography/Memoirs. **Career:** The Economist, editorial staff, 1959-60; Political and Economic Planning (PEP), senior research officer, 1960-63; London School of Economics, senior lecturer in politics, 1963-74; senior policy adviser to the Prime Minister, 1974-79; London Symphony Orchestra, chairman, 1979-91; Economist Intelligence Unit, director, 1979-81; The Times, assistant editor, 1981-82; Kleinwort Grieveson & Co., head of research, 1982-86; Kleinwort Grieveson Securities Ltd, head of international research and director, 1986-88; LBI, executive vice-chair, 1988-91; Towcester Racecourse Ltd, director, 1992-97; Minister of Agriculture, 1997-99; Government of LSE, visiting professor, 2000-. **Publications:** (Ed.) Oxford Poetry 1956, 1956; Trade Unions in a Changing Society, 1963; British Politics and the American Revolution: The Path to War, 1965; (with W.T. Rodgers) People into Parliament: A Concise History of the Labour Movement in Britain, 1966; (with W.T. Rodgers) People into Parliament: An Illustrated History of the Labour Party, 1966; (with G.W. Jones) Herbert Morrison: Portrait of a Politician, 1973; Prime Minister: The Conduct of Policy Under Harold Wilson and James Callaghan, 1987; Heat of the Kitchen: An Autobiography, 2003; Downing Street Diary: With Harold Wilson in No. 10, 2005; Downing Street Diary Volume Two: With James Callaghan in No. 10, 2008. **Address:** 71 Ebury Mews E, London, GL SW1W 9QA, England.

DONOVAN. Also writes as Donovan Leitch, Donovan P. Leitch. Irish/Scottish (born Scotland), b. 1946. **Genres:** Autobiography/Memoirs, Songs/Lyrics And Libretti, Music, Photography. **Career:** Writer. **Publications:** Dry Songs and Scribbles, 1971; (as Donovan Leitch) The Autobiography of Donovan: The Hurdy Gurdy Man, 2005. **Address:** c/o Author Mail, St. Martin's Press, 175 5th Ave., New York, NY 10010-7703, U.S.A.

DONOVAN, Anne. Scottish (born Scotland), b. 1956?. **Genres:** Novellas/Short Stories, Novels. **Career:** Writer and educator. **Publications:** Environmental Regulations and Technology: Managing Used Motor Oil, 1994; Hieroglyphics & Other Stories, 2001; Women's Basketball: The Post Player's Handbook, 2001; Buddha Da (novel), 2003; Hieroglyphics, 2004; Being Emily, 2008. Contributor to periodicals. **Address:** c/o Author Mail, Carroll and Graf, 245 W 17th St., 11th Fl., New York, NY 10011, U.S.A.

DONOVAN, Brian. American (born United States), b. 1941. **Genres:** Social Sciences. **Career:** Alicia Patterson Foundation, fellow. Investigative journalist. **Publications:** Hard Driving: The Wendell Scott Story: The American Odyssey of NASCAR'S First Black Driver, 2008. Contributor to periodicals. **Address:** c/o Robert Guinsler, Sterling Lord Literistic Inc., 65 Bleecker St., New York, NY 10012, U.S.A. **Online address:** briandonovan@harddriving.us

DONOVAN, Brian. American (born United States), b. 1971. **Genres:** History. **Career:** University of Kansas, assistant professor, associate professor, 2001-. Sociologist and writer. **Publications:** White Slave Crusades: Race, Gender, and Anti-Vice Activism, 1887-1917, 2006. Contributor of articles to periodicals. **Address:** Department of Sociology, University of Kansas, Rm. 716, Fraser Hall, 1415 Jayhawk Blvd., Lawrence, KS 66045-7556, U.S.A. **Online address:** bdonovan@ku.edu

DONOVAN, Felicia. American (born United States), b. 1960. **Genres:** Mystery/Crime/Suspense, Novellas/Short Stories. **Career:** Teacher, through 1998. Writer. **Publications:** The Black Widow Agency, 2007; Spun Tales, 2008; (with K. Bernier) Cyber Crime Fighters: Tales from the Trenches, 2009. **Address:** c/o Jill Grosjean, The Jill Grosjean Literary Agency, 1390 Millstone Rd., Sag Harbor, NY 11963, U.S.A. **Online address:** felicia@feliciadonovan.com

DONOVAN, Gerard. American/Irish (born Ireland), b. 1959?. **Genres:** Poetry, Novels, Novellas/Short Stories. **Career:** Long Island University, Southampton College, professor of graduate and undergraduate writing; Suffolk County Community College, professor; Bread Loaf Writers' Conference, teacher, 2000; New England Young Writers' Conference, teacher, 2000; Eastern Illinois University, instructor in writing, 2007-. Writer. **Publications:** POETRY: Columbus Rides Again, 1992; Kings and Bicycles, 1995; The Light-House, 2000. NOVELS: Schopenhauer's Telescope, 2003; Doctor Salt, 2005; Julius Winsome, 2006; Sunless, 2007. SHORT STORIES: Young Irelanders, 2008; Country of the Grand, 2008. **Address:** Department of English, Eastern Illinois University, 600 Lincoln Ave., 3762 Coleman, Charleston, IL 61920-3099, U.S.A. **Online address:** gadonovan@eiu.edu

DONOVAN, Katie. Irish (born Ireland), b. 1962. **Genres:** Poetry, Literary Criticism And History, Essays, Young Adult Fiction. **Career:** Teacher of English to foreign students, 1987-88; Irish Times, features writer, editor and literary critic, 1988-2002. **Publications:** Irish Women Writers (essay), 1988. POEMS: Watermelon Man, 1993; Entering the Mare, 1997; Day of the Dead, 2002; Rootling: New & Selected Poems, 2010. EDITOR: (with B. Kennelly and A.N. Jeffares) Ireland's Women: Writings Past and Present, 1994; (with B. Kennelly) Dublines, 1996. **Address:** An Tigh Thuas, Torca Rd., Dalkey, DU 1, Ireland.

DOOLEN, Andy. American (born United States), b. 1968. **Genres:** History, Politics/Government. **Career:** Clemson University, assistant professor of English, 2001-03; University of Kentucky, Department of English, assistant professor, associate professor of American literature and American studies, 2003-. Writer. **Publications:** Fugitive Empire: Locating Early American Imperialism, 2005. Contributor to journals. **Address:** Department of English, University of Kentucky, 1337 Patterson Office Twr., Lexington, KY 40506-0027, U.S.A. **Online address:** andy.doolen@uky.edu

DOOLEY, Allan C(harles). American (born United States), b. 1943. **Genres:** Humanities, Literary Criticism And History, Bibliography. **Career:** Kent State University, assistant professor, 1969-77, associate professor, 1978-92, professor of English, 1993-, now professor emeritus; Institute for Bibliography and Editing, fellow, 1988-. Writer. **Publications:** Author and printer in Victorian England, 1992; (ed.) The Complete Works of Robert Browning, vol. XV, 2007, vol. XVII, 2012. Works appear in anthologies. Contributor of articles and reviews to periodicals. **Address:** Department of English, Kent State University, Main Campus, PO Box 5190, Kent, OH 44242-0001, U.S.A. **Online address:** adooley@kent.edu

DOOLEY, Brendan Maurice. American/German (born Germany), b. 1953. **Genres:** Social Sciences. **Career:** University of Notre Dame, assistant professor, 1985-87; Cleveland State University, assistant professor, 1990-91; Harvard University, associate professor, 1991-99; Jacobs University, professor of history, 1999-; Medici Archive Project, chief of research, 1999-2002. Writer, historian, editor, translator and educator. **Publications:** (with H. Seifert and R. Strohm) Giovanna Gronda, La Carriera Di Un Librettista: Pietro Pariati Da Reggio Di Lombardia, 1990; Science, Politics and Society in Eighteenth-Century Italy: The Giornale De' Letterati D'Italia and Its World, 1991; (ed. and trans.) Italy in the Baroque: Selected Readings, 1995; The Social History of Skepticism: Experience and Doubt in Early Modern Culture, 1999; (ed. with S.A. Baron) The Politics of Information in Early Modern Europe, 2001; Giovanni Baldinucci, Quaderno: Peste, Guerra E Carestia Nell'Italia Del Seicento, 2001; Science and the Marketplace in Early Modern Italy, 2001; Morandi's Last Prophecy and the End of Renaissance Politics, 2002; Energy

and Culture: Perspectives on the Power to Work, 2006. Contributor to books, periodicals and journals. **Address:** Jacobs University, PO Box 750 561, Bremen, D-28725, Germany. **Online address:** b.dooley@jacobs-university.de

DOOLEY, Brian J. American (born United States), b. 1954. **Genres:** Information Science/Computers, Technology, Air/Space Topics, Communications/Media, Business/Trade/Industry, Essays, Marketing. **Career:** Datapro Corp., senior analyst and senior associate editor, 1983-88; Okidata Corp., senior technical writer, 1988-89; Unisys Corp., senior product information analyst, 1989-92; Aoraki Corp., senior technical writer, 1993-94; B.J. Dooley Technical Information Services, director, 1994-; New Zealand Chapter of the Society for Technical Communication, founder. **Publications:** Desktop Publishing for WordPerfect for Windows, 1992; Learn Windows in a Day: For Versions 3.0 and 3.1, 1992; Learn OS/2 2.1 in a Day, 1993; The Complete Guide to Single-Engine Cessnas, 4th ed., 1993; Learn Microsoft Powerpoint 4.0 for Windows in a Day, 1995. Contributor to periodicals. **Address:** 28A Mcbratneys Rd., Dallington, Christchurch, 8061, New Zealand. **Online address:** bjd@bjdooley.com

DOOLEY, David (Allen). American (born United States), b. 1947. **Genres:** Poetry, Literary Criticism And History, Young Adult Fiction. **Career:** Matthews and Branscomb, paralegal, 1982-; Sheppard, Mullen, Richter & Hampton, paralegal. Writer. **Publications:** Isolated in the Absurd: Drawings, 1969; The Volcano Inside, 1988; The Revenge by Love, 1995; The Zen Garden, 2004. **Address:** c/o Author Mail, WorldTech Editions, PO Box 541106, Cincinnati, OH 45254-1106, U.S.A.

DOOLEY, Maura. British (born England), b. 1957. **Genres:** Novellas/Short Stories, Poetry, Adult Non-fiction. **Career:** Newport School, teacher of English, 1981-82; Arvon Foundation, director of writing center, 1982-87; South Bank Board, director of literature program, 1987-93; freelance literature consultant, 1993-97; consultant to performing arts labs, 1994-2002; Jim Henson Films, script adviser, 1997-2000; Poetry Book Society, chair, 1999-2003; University of London, Goldsmiths College, convener of MA in creative writing, 2000-, senior lecturer in creative writing. Writer. **Publications:** POETRY: Ivy Leaves and Arrows, 1986; Turbulence, 1988; Explaining Magnetism, 1991; Kissing a Bone, 1996; Sound Barrier: Selected Poems, 2002; Life Under Water, 2008. EDITOR: (with D. Hunter) Singing Brink, 1987; (with D. Morley and P. Callow) Northern Stories II, 1990; (with J. Shapcott) New Poetry International, 1993; Making for Planet Alice: New Women Poets, 1997; How Novelists Work, 2000; The Honey Gatherers: Love Poetry, 2003. Contributor to periodicals. **Address:** Bloodaxe Books Ltd., Highgreen, PO Box 1SN, Tarset, NH NE48 1RP, England. **Online address:** m.dooley@gold.ac.uk

DOOLING, Richard (Patrick). (Eleanor Druse). American (born United States), b. 1954. **Genres:** Novels, Novellas/Short Stories, Young Adult Fiction. **Career:** Bryan, Cave, McPheeters and McRoberts, law associate, 1987-91; University of Nebraska, College of Law, faculty of law, literature and entertainment law, 2008-, visiting professor, 2010-. Writer. **Publications:** Critical Care (novel), 1992; White Man's Grave, 1994; Bush Pigs (short story), 1994; Blue Streak: Swearing, Free Speech, and Sexual Harassment, 1996; Brainstorm, 1998; Watsons Brainstorm: Roman, 1998; Bet Your Life, 2002; (as Eleanor Druse) The Journals of Eleanor Druse, 2004; Rapture for the Geeks: When AI Outsmarts IQ, 2008. Contributor of short fiction to periodicals. **Address:** 816 S 95th St., Omaha, NE 68114-5072, U.S.A. **Online address:** rpdooling@yahoo.com

DOOLITTLE, Amity A. American/Australian (born Australia), b. 1964. **Genres:** Social Sciences, Politics/Government. **Career:** Yale School of Forestry and Environmental Studies, lecturer, 2001-05, associate research scientist and lecturer, 2005-08, lecturer and research scientist, 2009-, Tropical Resources Institute, program director, 2001-08. Writer. **Publications:** Property & Politics in Sabah, Malaysia: Native Struggles over Land Rights, 2005; (ed. with M.R. Dove and P.E. Sajise) Beyond the Sacred Forest: Complicating Conservation in Southeast Asia, 2011. **Address:** Yale School of Forestry & Environmental Studies, Rm. 121, Kroon Hall, 195 Prospect St., New Haven, CT 06511-8499, U.S.A. **Online address:** amity.doolittle@yale.edu

DORAN, Colleen. American (born United States), b. 1963. **Genres:** Illustrations. **Career:** Colleen Doran Studios, owner; Smithsonian Institute, artist-in-residence, 2006. Illustrator, conceptual artist, cartoonist and writer. **Publications:** SELF-ILLUSTRATED: A Distant Soil: Immigrant Song, 1987; A Distant Soil: Knights of the Angel, 1989 as The Ascendant, 2001; A Distant

Soil: The Aria, 2001; A Distant Soil: Coda, 2006; Girl to Grrrl Manga: How to Draw the Hottest Shoujo Manga, 2007; Manga Pro Superstar Workshop: How to Create and Sell Comics and Graphic Novels, 2008. Contributor to books and periodicals. **Address:** Colleen Doran Studios, 435-2 Oriana Rd., PO Box 610, Newport News, VA 23608, U.S.A.

DORAN, David K. British (born England), b. 1929. **Genres:** Engineering. **Career:** G. Wimpey, chief structural engineer, 1965-85; consulting civil and structural engineer, 1985-; Journal of the International Association for Bridge and Structural Engineering, Structural Engineering International Journal, correspondent. Writer. **Publications:** Newnes Construction Materials Pocket Book, 1994. EDITOR: Construction Materials Reference Book, 1991; Construction Materials Pocket Book, 1994; Eminent Civil Engineers: Their 20th Century Life and Times, 1999; Site Engineers Manual, 2004, 2nd ed., 2009; (with J. Douglas and R. Pratley) Refurbishment and Repair in Construction, 2009. **Address:** 17 Blake Hall Cres., London, GL E11 3RH, England. **Online address:** david.doran@btinternet.com

DORAN, Phil. American (born United States), b. 1944?. **Genres:** Plays/Screenplays. **Career:** Television writer and producer, 1971-95. **Publications:** The Reluctant Tuscan: How I Discovered My Inner Italian, 2005. **Address:** Gotham Books Publicity, 375 Hudson St., New York, NY 10014, U.S.A. **Online address:** phil@reluctanttuscan.com

DORAN, Robert. American/Australian (born Australia), b. 1940. **Genres:** Theology/Religion, History. **Career:** Amherst College, professor of religion, 1978-, Samuel Williston professor of Greek and Hebrew religion. Writer. **Publications:** Temple Propaganda: The Purpose and Characters of 2 Maccabees, 1981; (trans.) Lives of Simeon Stylites, 1992; Birth of a Worldview: Early Christianity in Its Jewish and Pagan Context, 1995; (trans. and intro.) Stewards of the Poor: The Man of God, Rabbula and Hiba in Fifth-Century Edessa, 2006. **Address:** Department of Religion, Amherst College, 206 Chapin Hall, PO Box AC 2252, Amherst, MA 01002, U.S.A. **Online address:** rdoran@amherst.edu

DORE, Elizabeth W. British (born England), b. 1946. **Genres:** Politics/Government, Business/Trade/Industry. **Career:** University of Southampton, Faculty of Humanities, professor of Latin American studies, now professor emeritus; University of Portsmouth, senior lecturer in Latin American studies. Writer. **Publications:** (With J. Weeks) Basic Needs in Development Strategies: The Journey of a Concept, 1979; Acumulación y crisis en la minería peruana, 1900-1977, 1986; The Peruvian Mining Industry: Growth, Stagnation, and Crisis, 1988; (ed.) Gender Politics in Latin America: Debates in Theory and Practice, 1997; (ed. with M. Molyneux) Hidden Histories of Gender and the State in Latin America, 2000; Myths of Modernity: Peonage and Patriarchy in Nicaragua, 2006. **Address:** Faculty of Humanities, University of Southampton, Rm. 65/3023, 65 Bldg., Avenue Campus, Highfield, Southampton, HM SO17 1BF, England. **Online address:** e.dore@soton.ac.uk

DOREMUS, Paul N. American (born United States), b. 1960?. **Genres:** Business/Trade/Industry. **Career:** Congressional Office of Technology Assessment, project director, 1992-95; Office of Technology Assessment, analyst; Commerce Department's Office of Technology Policy, senior analyst, 1995-97; National Institute of Standards and Technology, strategic planning analyst, director of strategic planning and performance, 2005, Program Office, director, through 2005, acting deputy assistant administrator; National Oceanic and Atmospheric Administration, Office of Program Planning and Integration, acting assistant administrator, acting deputy assistant administrator and director of strategic planning, 2005-. Writer. **Publications:** (Co-author) The Myth of the Global Corporation, 1998. Contributor to books and periodicals. **Address:** National Oceanic and Atmospheric Administration, Office of Program Planning and Integration, 1315 E West Hwy., Silver Spring, MD 20910, U.S.A. **Online address:** paul.n.doremus@noaa.gov

DORF, Fran. American (born United States), b. 1953. **Genres:** Novels, Mystery/Crime/Suspense, Young Adult Fiction, Psychology. **Career:** Esquire, merchandising manager, 1976-77; International Playtex, promotion manager, 1978-81. Writer. **Publications:** A Reasonable Madness, 1990; Flight, 1992; Saving Elijah, 2000. **Address:** William Morris Agency, 1325 Ave. of the Americas, New York, NY 10019, U.S.A.

DORFLINGER, Carolyn. American (born United States), b. 1953. **Genres:** Children's Fiction, Young Adult Fiction. **Career:** Branchburg Central School,

Spanish and French teacher, 1975-80; Shenendehowa Schools, staff, 1988-89; Harding Township School, staff, 1995-. Writer. **Publications:** Tomorrow is Mom's Birthday, 1994. Contributor to Guideposts for Kids. **Address:** 131 Chatham St., Chatham, NJ 07928-2023, U.S.A.

DORIANI, Beth Maclay. American (born United States), b. 1961. **Genres:** Literary Criticism And History, Business/Trade/Industry, Biography. **Career:** Religion and Literature, staff, 1986-88; Northwestern College, assistant professor, associate professor of English, department chair, department head and coordinator of faculty development, 1990-98; Malone College, academic dean, 1998-2000; Montreat College, vice president, dean of academics and associate professor of English, 2000-. Writer. **Publications:** Emily Dickinson: Daughter of Prophecy, 1996; For All You're Worth: Getting That Academic Job in Today's Market, 1998. Contributor of articles to books and journals. **Address:** Montreat College, PO Box 1267, Montreat, NC 28757, U.S.A. **Online address:** bdoriani@montreat.edu

DORKIN, Evan. American (born United States), b. 1965. **Genres:** Graphic Novels, Young Adult Fiction, Illustrations, Humor/Satire, Picture/Board Books. **Career:** Writer and artist. **Publications:** Superman and Batman: World's Funnest, 2000. SELF-ILLUSTRATED: Fun with Milk and Cheese (collection of Milk & Cheese issues), 1997; Hectic Planet, vol. I: Dim Future 1998, vol. II: Checkered Past, 1998, vol. III: The Young and the Reckless, 2001; Dork!: Who's Laughing Now?, 2001; Circling the Drain, 2003. **Address:** c/o Author Mail, SLG Publishing, 577 S Market St., San Jose, CA 95113, U.S.A. **Online address:** evandorkin@aol.com

DORMAN, Daniel. American (born United States), b. 1936?. **Genres:** Psychiatry, Biography, Autobiography/Memoirs, Psychology. **Career:** University of California School of Medicine, assistant clinical professor of psychiatry. Writer. **Publications:** Dante's Cure: A Journey out of Madness, 2003. **Address:** c/o Author Mail, Other Press L.L.C., 2 Park Ave., 24th Fl., New York, NY 10001, U.S.A. **Online address:** drdorman@dantescure.com

DORMAN, Michael L. American (born United States), b. 1932. **Genres:** Politics/Government, Adult Non-fiction, Civil Liberties/Human Rights, Criminology/True Crime, History, Law, Race Relations, Writing/Journalism, Writing/Journalism. **Career:** Wall Street Journal, editorial assistant, 1949-; New York Times, staff; Associated Press, reporter, 1953; Houston Press, reporter, 1953-58; Newsweek, 1959; Newsday, reporter, 1959-64, 1999-; freelance writer, 1965-99. **Publications:** We Shall Overcome, 1964; The Secret Service Story, 1967; The Second Man, 1968; King of the Courtroom, 1969; Under 21, 1970; Payoff: The Role of Organized Crime in American Politics, 1972; The Making of a Slum, 1972; Confrontation, 1974; Vesco: The Infernal Money-Making Machine, 1975; Witch Hunt: The Underside of American Democracy, 1976; The George Wallace Myth, 1976; Detectives of the Sky: Investigating Aviation Tragedies, 1976; Dirty Politics: From 1776 to Watergate, 1979; Blood and Revenge: A True Story of Small-Town Murder and Justice, 1991. **Address:** McIntosh & Otis Inc., 353 Lexington Ave., New York, NY 10016, U.S.A.

DORMANDY, Thomas. British (born England) **Genres:** Sciences, Medicine/Health. **Career:** Whittington Hospital, consultant and chemical pathologist, professor of chemical pathology, retired; University of London, consultant and chemical pathologist; University of Brunel, consultant and chemical pathologist; Royal College of Pathologists, fellow; Royal College of Surgeons, fellow. Writer. **Publications:** The White Death: A History of Tuberculosis, 1999; Moments of Truth: Four Creators of Modern Medicine, 2003; The Worst of Evils: The Fight against Pain, 2006; Opium: Reality's Dark Dream, 2012. Contributor to journals and periodicals. **Address:** c/o Author Mail, Yale University Press, PO Box 209040, New Haven, CT 06520-9040, U.S.A.

DORMENT, Richard. British/American (born United States), b. 1946. **Genres:** Art/Art History, Photography. **Career:** Philadelphia Museum of Art, assistant curator of European painting, 1973-76; Daily Telegraph, art critic, 1987-, chief art critic. Writer. **Publications:** Alfred Gilbert, 1985; Alfred Gilbert, Sculptor and Goldsmith, 1986; British Painting in the Philadelphia Museum of Art, 1986; (with M.F. MacDonald) James McNeill Whistler, 1995; (co-author) Whistler: 1834-1903, 1995. Contributor to books and periodicals. **Address:** The Daily Telegraph, 111 Buckingham Palace Rd., London, GL SW1W 0DT, England.

DORNENBURG, Andrew. American (born United States), b. 1958. **Genres:**

Food And Wine, Young Adult Non-fiction. **Career:** Rosemarie's (restaurant), sous-chef; America Online, host, 1995-. Writer. **Publications:** Nonfiction (with K. Page): Becoming a Chef: With Recipes and Reflections from America's Leading Chefs, 1995, rev. ed., 2003; Culinary Artistry, 1996; Dining Out: Secrets from America's Leading Critics, Chefs, and Restaurateurs, 1998; Chef's Night Out, 2001; New American Chef: Cooking with the Best Flavors and Techniques from Around the World, 2003; What to Drink with What You Eat: The Definitive Guide to Pairing Food with Wine, Beer, Spirits, Coffee, Tea-Even Water-Based On Expert Advice from Americas Best Sommeliers, 2006; Flavor Bible: The Essential Guide to Culinary Creativity, Based On the Wisdom of America's Most Imaginative Chefs, 2008; Food Lover's Guide to Wine, 2011. **Address:** 527 3rd Ave., Ste. 130, New York, NY 10016, U.S.A. **Online address:** dornenburg@aol.com

DORNER, Marjorie. American (born United States), b. 1942. **Genres:** Novels, Plays/Screenplays, Novellas/Short Stories, Mystery/Crime/Suspense, Young Adult Fiction. **Career:** Wisconsin State University, instructor in English, 1965-66; Saint Norbert College, instructor in English, 1966-68; Winona State University, professor of English, 1971-, now professor emeritus. Writer. **Publications:** NOVELS: Nightmare, 1987; Family Closets, 1989; Freeze Frame, 1990; Blood Kin, 1992; Seasons of Sun and Rain, 1999. OTHER: Winter Roads, Summer Fields (short story collection), 1992. Contributor to magazines. **Address:** Winona State University, PO Box 5838, Winona, MN 55987, U.S.A. **Online address:** mdorner@vax2.winona.msus.edu

DORRÉ, Gina M. American (born United States), b. 1963. **Genres:** Literary Criticism And History. **Career:** University of Nevada, lecturer in English. Writer. **Publications:** Victorian Fiction and the Cult of the Horse, 2006. **Address:** Department of English, University of Nevada, Rm. 0098, 1664 N. Virginia St., Reno, NV 89557-0042, U.S.A. **Online address:** dgina@unr.edu

DORRESTEIN, Renate. Dutch (born Netherlands), b. 1954. **Genres:** Novels, Young Adult Fiction, Architecture. **Career:** Journalist, 1972-; Panorama Magazine, staff, reporter, through 1977; Side Magazine, staff; Viva Magazine, staff; Time Magazine, staff; Anna Bijns Foundation, founder, 1986; University of Michigan, writer-in-residence, 1986-87; Leiden University, writer-in-residence, 2007; Free University, writer-in-residence. **Publications:** Buitenstaanders, 1983; Vreemde Streken, 1984; Noorderzon, 1986; Een Nacht om Te Vliegeren, 1987; Het Perpetuum Mobile Van De Liefde, 1988; Korte Metten, 1988; Vóór Alles Een Dame: Een Vrolijke Geschiedenis Indagelijkse Afleveringen, 1989; (co-author) Nieuwe Man, 1990; Het Hemelse Gerecht, 1991; Heden Ik, 1992; Ontaarde Moeders, 1992; Een Sterke Man, 1994; Verborgen Gebreken, 1996; Want Dit is Mijn Lichaam, 1997; Een Hart Van Steen, 1998; Het Geheim Van de Schrijver, 1999; Zonder Genade, 2001; Het Duister Dat Ons Scheidt, 2003; Zolang er Leven is, 2004; (with K. Kleijn and H. Strak) Behind the Facades: Gardens of Canal Houses in Amsterdam, 2005; Echt Sexy, 2007; Laat Me Niet Alleen, 2008; Is er Hoop, 2009; Heiligenlevens En Bananenpitten, 2009; Leesclub, 2010. **Address:** c/o Author Mail, Veen Uitgevers Groep, 125 St Jacobsstraat, PO Box 14095, Utrecht, 3511 BP, Netherlands.

DORRIEN, Gary J. American (born United States), b. 1952. **Genres:** Philosophy, Politics/Government, Theology/Religion, Social Sciences. **Career:** Parsons Center (school for emotionally disturbed children), teacher, 1979-82; St. Andrew's Episcopal Church, assistant pastor, 1982-87; Doane Stuart School, chaplain, 1982-87; Kalamazoo College, professor of religion, 1987-, Stetson Chapel, dean, 1987-, chair of religious studies and chair of humanities, 1987-2000, Ann V. and Donald R. Parfet distinguished professor, 2000; Union Theological Seminary, Reinhold Niebuhr professor of social ethics; Columbia University, professor of religion. Writer. **Publications:** Logic and Consciousness: The Dialectics of Mind, 1985; The Democratic Socialist Vision, 1986; Reconstructing the Common Good: Theology and the Social Order, 1990; The Neoconservative Mind: Politics, Culture and the War of Ideology, 1993; Soul in Society: The Making and Renewal of Social Christianity, 1995; The Word as True Myth: Interpreting Modern Theology, 1997; The Remaking of Evangelical Theology, 1998; The Barthian Revolt in Modern Theology: Theology without Weapons, 2000; The Making of American Liberal Theology: Imagining Progressive Religion, 1805-1900, 2001; The Making of American Liberal Theology: Idealism, Realism and Modernity, 1900-1950, 2003; Imperial Designs: The New Pax Americana, 2004; The Making of American Liberal Theology: Crisis, Irony and Postmodernity, 1950-2005, 2006; Social Ethics in the Making: Interpreting an American Tradition, 2009; Economy, Difference and Empire: Social Ethics for Social Justice, 2010; The Obama Ques-

tion: A Progressive Perspective, 2012; Kantian Reason and Hegelian Spirit: The Idealistic Logic of Modern Theology, 2012. **Address:** Union Theological Seminary, 3041 Broadway, AD 413, New York, NY 10027, U.S.A. **Online address:** gdorrien@uts.columbia.edu

DORRIL, Stephen. American (born United States) **Genres:** Writing/Journalism, History, Biography, Adult Non-fiction. **Career:** University of Huddersfield, senior lecturer in print journalism; Lobster, founder, editor and writer, 1983-; researcher and investigative journalist, 1986-. **Publications:** Honeytrap: The Secret Worlds of Stephen Ward, 1987; Smear!: Wilson and the Secret State, 1991; The Silent Conspiracy: Inside the Intelligence Services in the 1990s, 1994; MI6: Inside the Covert World of Her Majesty's Secret Intelligence Service, 2000; Gladio: MI6 and the European Stay-behind Networks, 1945-1990, 2000; Sir Oswald Mosley and British Fascism, 2006; Blackshirt: Sir Oswald Mosley and the Rise of Fascism, 2007. **Address:** Department of Media and Journalism, University of Huddersfield, JM2/09, Oldham Cromwell St., Queensgate, WY HD1 3DH, England. **Online address:** s.dorril@hud.ac.uk

DORROS, Arthur (M.). American (born United States), b. 1950?. **Genres:** Children's Fiction, Young Adult Fiction, Children's Non-fiction, Young Adult Non-fiction, Illustrations, Novels, Writing/Journalism, Picture/Board Books, Picture/Board Books. **Career:** Writer and illustrator, 1979-. **Publications:** Pretzels, 1981; Alligator Shoes, 1982; Yum Yum, 1987; Splash Splash, 1987; (contrib.) Magic Secrets, 1990; Me and My Shadow, 1990; Abuela, 1991; Tonight Is Carnaval, 1991; Radio Man/Don Radio: A Story in English and Spanish, 1993; Elephant Families, 1994; Isla, 1995; A Tree is Growing, 1997; The Fungus That Ate My School, 2000; Ten Go Tango, 2000; When the Pigs Took Over, 2002; City Chicken, 2003; Under the Sun, 2004; Julio's Magic, 2005; Winner, 2006; (with A. Dorros) Número Uno, 2007; Papa and Me, 2008; Mama and Me, 2011. SELF-ILLUSTRATOR: Ant Cities, 1987; Feel the Wind, 1989; Rain Forest Secrets, 1990; Follow the Water from Brook to Ocean, 1991; This Is My House, 1992; Animal Tracks, 1991; Ciudades De Hormigas, 1995. Illustrator of books by others. **Address:** c/o Author Mail, HarperCollins Publishers, 1350 Ave. of the Americas, New York, NY 10019-4703, U.S.A. **Online address:** arthur@arthurdorros.com

DORSCHT, Susan Rudy. See RUDY, Susan Arlene.

DORSEN, Norman. American (born United States), b. 1930. **Genres:** Civil Liberties/Human Rights, Law. **Career:** Dewey, Ballantine, Bushby, Palmer and Wood, law associate, 1958-60; New York University School of Law, Arthur Garfield Hays Civil Liberties Program, co-director, 1961, assistant professor of law, 1961-, associate professor, professor of law, 1965-, Frederick I. and Grace A. Stokes professor of law, 1981-, Hauser Global Law School Program, founding director, 1994-96, faculty chair, 1996-2002, counselor to president of university, 2002; American Civil Liberties Union, general counsel, 1969-76, president, 1976-91; Society of American Law Teachers, president, 1972-73; U.S. Association of Constitutional Law, president, 2000-05. Writer. **Publications:** (With T. Emerson and D. Haber) Political and Civil Rights in the United States, 3rd ed., 1967, 4th ed., 1979, supplement, 1982; Frontiers of Civil Liberties, 1968; Discrimination and Civil Rights, 1969; (with L. Friedman) Disorder in the Court, 1973; (with P. Bender and B. Neuborne) Emerson, Haber, And Dorsen's Political And Civil Rights In the United States, 1973, 4th ed., 1977; (contrib.) Areru hōtei, 1978; (with S. Gillers) Regulation of Lawyers: Problems of Law and Ethics, 1985; (with D. Rudovsky and L. Whitman) Human Rights in Northern Ireland, 1991; (intro.) Rights of Racial Minorities, 1998; (intro.) Rights of Women and Girls, 1998; (co-author) Comparative Constitutionalism: Cases and Materials, 2003, 2nd ed., 2010; (co-author) History of the Hays Program: 1958-2008, 2008. EDITOR: The Rights of Americans, 1971; (with S. Gillers) None of Your Business-Government Secrecy in America, 1974; Our Endangered Rights: The ACLU Report on Civil Liberties Today, 1984; (and foreword) The Evolving Constitution: Essays on the Bill of Rights and the U.S. Supreme Court, 1987; (with P. Gifford) Democracy and the Rule of Law, 2001; The Unpredictable Constitution, 2002. **Address:** School of Law, New York University, 40 Washington Sq. S, 308C, New York, NY 10012, U.S.A. **Online address:** norman.dorsen@nyu.edu

DORSET, Phyllis (Flanders). American (born United States), b. 1924. **Genres:** Novels, Novellas/Short Stories, History, Military/Defense/Arms Control, Autobiography/Memoirs, Sciences. **Career:** Sandia Corp., editorial assistant in publications section, 1952-54, technical writer and editor in weapons effects department, 1954-56; Stanford Research Institute, Physics Division, technical writer and editor, 1956-63; freelance technical writer and editor, 1963-. **Publications:** Technical Writing Handbook, 1955; (co-author) Measuring Military Effects of Nuclear Weapons, A Manual for the Conduct of Full-Scale Field Tests, 1958; (contrib.) Nuclear Geoplosics: A Sourcebook of Underground Phenomena and Effects of Nuclear Explosions, 1962; Historic Ships Afloat, 1967; The New Eldorado: The Story of Colorado's Gold and Silver Rushes, 1970; (ed.) My Life at Fort Ross, 1987; (with S.W. Miller) A Finite Difference: 1950-1969, 2003. **Address:** 460 Sherwood Way, Menlo Park, CA 94025, U.S.A.

DORSEY, Candas Jane. Canadian (born Canada), b. 1952. **Genres:** Poetry, Novels, Novellas/Short Stories. **Career:** Edmonton Bullet, editor and manager, 1983-88; Grant MacEwan College, Professional Writing Program, instructor, 1983-; Alberta Social Services and Community Health Public Communications, public affairs officer III, 1984-85; River Books, publisher and editor-in-chief, 1992-2006; The Books Collective, founding member and publisher, 1992-2006; Tesseract Books, publisher and editor-in-chief, 1994-2003; Wooden Door and Associates (communications consulting), founder partner, 1992-; Writers' Guild of Alberta, executive; SF Canada, executive. **Publications:** POETRY: This Is for You, 1973; Orion Rising, 1974; Results of the Ring Toss, 1976; Leaving Marks, 1992. NOVELS: (with N. Abercrombie) Hardwired Angel, 1985; (with R. Deegan) Dark Earth Dreams, 1994; Black Wine, 1997; A Paradigm of Earth, 2001. SHORT STORIES: Machine Sex and Other Stories, 1988; (ed. with G. Truscott) Tesseracts Three: Canadian Science Fiction, 1990; Vanilla and Other Stories, 2000. OTHERS: (ed. with J.B. McCrosky) Land/Space: An Anthology of Prairie Speculative Fiction, 2002. Contributor to books. **Address:** Porcepic Books, 4252 Commerce Cir., Victoria, BC V8Z 4M2, Canada. **Online address:** cdorsey@istream.com

D'ORSO, Michael. American (born United States), b. 1953. **Genres:** Essays, Humor/Satire, Sports/Fitness, Biography. **Career:** The Virginia Gazette, writer; Commonwealth Magazine, staff writer, 1981-84; Virginian-Pilot, features writer, 1984-93. **Publications:** (With D.S. Redford) Somerset Homecoming: Recovering a Lost Heritage, 1988; (as Mike D'Orso) Fast Takes: Slices of Life through a Journalist's Eye, 1990; (with C. Elliott, Sr.) The Cost of Courage: The Journey of an American Congressman, 1992; (with M. Cartwright) For the Children: Lessons from a Visionary Principal-How We Can Save Our Public Schools, 1993; (with D. Byrd) Rise and Walk: The Trial and Triumph of Dennis Byrd, 1993; (as Mike D'Orso) Pumping Granite and Other Portraits of People at Play, 1994; (with D. Byrd) Dennis Byrd, 1995; Like Judgment Day: The Ruin and Redemption of a Town Called Rosewood, 1996; (with D. Hakala) Thin is Just a Four-Letter Word, 1997; (with L. Steinberg) Winning With Integrity: Getting What You're Worth Without Selling Your Soul, 1998; (with J. Lewis) Walking With the Wind: A Memoir of the Movement, 1998; (with B. Phillips) Body-For-Life: 12 Weeks to Mental and Physical Strength, 1999; (with J.I. Lieberman) In Praise of Public Life, 2000; Plundering Paradise: The Hand of Man on the Galapagos Islands, 2002; (with T. Daschle) Like No Other Time: The 107th Congress and the Two Years That Changed America Forever, 2003; Eagle Blue: A Team, a Tribe and a High School Basketball Season in Arctic Alaska, 2006; (with T. Danson) Oceana: Our Endangered Oceans and What We can do to Save Them, 2011. Contributor to periodicals. **Address:** David Black Literary Agency, 156 5th Ave., Ste. 608, New York, NY 10010, U.S.A. **Online address:** dorsonic@gmail.com

DOSS, Erika. (Erika Lee Doss). American (born United States) **Genres:** Art/Art History, Language/Linguistics, Area Studies. **Career:** University of Minnesota, Honors Department, instructor, 1981-82; Minneapolis College of Art and Design, instructor in art history, 1981-83, Art Museum, consultant, 1982-83; Carleton College, visiting assistant professor of art history, 1983-84; Cleveland State University, Department of Art, assistant professor, 1984-86, co-curator, 1984-86; SPACES Gallery, consultant, 1985; University of Colorado, Department of Fine Arts, assistant professor, 1986-91, associate professor, 1991-96, professor, 1996-, associate chair, 1994-95, interim chair, 1997-98, London Study Abroad Program, director, 1988, American Studies Program, director, 1991-2002, Film Studies Program, interim director, 1998-99, American Studies Program, director, 1991-2002; Autry National Center, Autry Museum of Western Heritage, consultant, 1993-95; Canadian Centre for Architecture, consultant, 1955-97; University of Sydney, senior Fulbright lecturer, 1996; Culture America Series, editor, 1997-; University Press of Kansas, editor, 1997-; The Encyclopedia of the Midwest, senior consulting editor, 2000-04; University of Notre Dame, Department of American Studies, professor and chair; American Studies Association, Indiana University

Press, senior consulting editor, 2000-04; American Quarterly, advisory editors, 2001-04; Brigham Young University Museum of Art, consultant, 2002-. **Publications:** Benton, Pollock, and the Politics of Modernism: From Regionalism to Abstract Expressionism, 1991; Spirit Poles and Flying Pigs: Public Art and Cultural Democracy in American Communities, 1995; Elvis Culture: Fans, Faith and Image, 1999; (ed. and contrib.) Looking at LIFE: Cultural Essays on America's Favorite Magazine, 2001; Twentieth-Century American Art, 2002; (with V.T. Clayton and E. Stillinger) Drawing on America's Past: Folk Art, Modernism, and the Index of American Design, 2002; John Wilde: Recent Work, April 10-May 3, 2003; (contrib.) Coming Home!: Self-Taught Artists, the Bible, and the American South, 2004; Duane Hanson: Portraits from the Heartland, 2004; (contrib.) Sublime Spaces and Visionary Worlds: Built Environments of Vernacular Artists, 2007; Memorial Mania: Self, Nation, and the Culture of Commemoration in Contemporary America, 2010; Memorial Mania: Public Feeling in America, 2010; Saint Elvis: Audiences and Cultural Production in Contemporary America, forthcoming; Picturing Faith: Twentieth-Century American Artists and Issues of Religion, forthcoming. Contributor of articles journals. **Address:** Department of American Studies, University of Notre Dame, 1044 Flanner Hall, Notre Dame, IN 46556, U.S.A. **Online address:** erika.doss@colorado.edu

DOSS, Erika Lee. See **DOSS, Erika.**

DOS SANTOS, Joyce Audy. (Joyce Audy Zarins). American (born United States), b. 1949. **Genres:** Children's Fiction, Young Adult Fiction, Art/Art History, Children's Non-fiction, Illustrations, Young Adult Non-fiction, Natural History. **Career:** ATSA Associates, designer, 1980-81; Merrimack Publishers Circle, designer, 1982-84; Ayer Publishing Co., designer, 1985-86; writer and illustrator, 1986-. **Publications:** SELF-ILLUSTRATED FOR CHILDREN: Sand Dollar, Sand Dollar, 1980; (and reteller) The Diviner, 1980; Henri and the Loup-Garou, 1982; Giants of Smaller Worlds: Drawn in Their Natural Sizes, 1983; (as Joyce Audy Zarins) Toasted Bagels: A Break-of-the-Day Book, 1988. Contributor of articles to periodicals. **Address:** 19 Woodland St., Merrimac, MA 01860, U.S.A. **Online address:** joyce.zarins@verizon.net

DOSSEY, Larry. American (born United States), b. 1940?. **Genres:** Medicine/Health, Psychology, Novels, Sports/Fitness, Medicine/Health. **Career:** Dallas Diagnostic Association, physician of internal medicine, 1974-88, Biofeedback Department, director, 1976-88; Medical City Dallas Hospital, chief of staff, 1982; Isthmus Institute of Dallas, president, 1987-89; National Institutes of Health, Office of Alternative Medicine, Panel on Mind/Body Interventions, co-chair, 1992-94; Alternative Therapies, executive editor, 1995-2003; EXPLORE: The Journal of Science and Healing, executive editor, 2005-. **Publications:** Space, Time & Medicine, 1982; Consciousness and Health, 1982; Beyond Illness: Discovering the Experience of Health, 1984; Non-Violence in Medical Science: Lectures Delivered at the Gujarat Vidvapith, Ahmedabad, India on 18th and 19th January 1988, 1988; Recovering the Soul: A Scientific and Spiritual Search, 1989; Meaning & Medicine: Lessons from a Doctor's Tales of Breakthrough and Healing, 1991; Healing Words: The Power of Prayer and the Practice of Medicine, 1993; Prayer Is Good Medicine: How to Reap the Healing Benefits of Prayer, 1996; Be Careful What You Pray for You Just Might Get It: What We Can Do about the Unintentional Effects of Our Thoughts, Prayers, and Wishes, 1997; (co-author) The Power of Meditation and Prayer, 1997; Scientific and Pastoral Perspectives on Intercessory Prayer: An Exchange between Larry Dossey, M.D. and Health Care Chaplains, 1998; (with W.B. Jonas and J. Jacobs) Healing with Homeopathy: The Doctor's Guide, 1998; (with G. Feuerstein) The Mystery of Light: The Life and Teaching of Oraam Mikhael Aivanhov, 1998; Reinventing Medicine: Beyond Mind-Body to a New Era of Healing, 1999; Prayer for Healing: 365 Blessings, Poems, and Meditations from Around the World, 2000; Healing beyond the Body: Medicine and the Infinite Reach of the Mind, 2001; (with J. Kane) The Healing Companion: Simple and Effective Ways Your Presence Can Help People Heal, 2001; Extraordinary Healing Power of Ordinary Things: Fourteen Natural Steps to Health and Happiness, 2006; Power of Premonitions: How Knowing the Future can Shape Our Lives, 2009. Contributor to periodicals. **Address:** c/o Author Mail, HarperCollins Publishers, 10 E 53rd St., 7th Fl., New York, NY 10022, U.S.A. **Online address:** nospamhere@dosseydossey.com

DOTI, Lynne Pierson. American (born United States), b. 1948. **Genres:** Economics, Money/Finance, Business/Trade/Industry. **Career:** Chapman

University, The George L. Argyros School of Business and Economics, professor of economics, 1971-, associate professor and tenure, 1980, David and Sandra Stone professor of economics, 2005-; California State University, visiting professor, 1979-80; Plaza Bank, director; Eldorado Bank, director; California Bankers Association, consultant. Writer. **Publications:** (With L. Schweikart) Banking in the American West: From the Gold Rush to Deregulation, 1991; (with L. Schweikart) California Bankers 1848-1993, 1994; Banking in an Unregulated Environment: California 1879-1905, 1995; (with L. Schweikart) American Entrepreneur: The Fascinating Stories of the People Who Defined Business in the United States, 2010. Contributor of articles to periodicals. **Address:** George L. Argyros School of Bus. and Economics, Chapman University, BK 307C, Orange, CA 92866-1099, U.S.A. **Online address:** ldoti@chapman.edu

DOTSON, Bob. (Robert Charles Dotson). American (born United States), b. 1946. **Genres:** Documentaries/Reportage, Communications/Media, Autobiography/Memoirs, Social Sciences, History. **Career:** KMBC-TV, reporter, photographer and documentary producer, 1967-68; University of Oklahoma, visiting professor, 1969-73; WKY-TV, director of special projects, 1969-75; WKYC-TV, correspondent, 1975-77; NBC-TV News Bureau, correspondent, 1977-79; Today Show, correspondent, 1978-85; Prime Time Saturday, correspondent, 1979-80; NBC-TV's Nightly News, correspondent, 1985-; Dateline NBC, correspondent, 1994. **Publications:** ...In Pursuit of the American Dream (nonfiction vignettes), 1985; Make it Memorable: Writing and Packaging TV News with Style, 2000. **Address:** c/o Paul Millman, 111 N Central Park Ave., 9th Fl., Ste. 470, Hartsdale, NY 10530, U.S.A.

DOTSON, Rand. American (born United States), b. 1967?. **Genres:** History. **Career:** Louisiana State University, instructor, Louisiana State University Press, senior acquisitions editor. Writer. **Publications:** Roanoke, Virginia, 1882-1912: Magic City of the New South, 2007. **Address:** U.S.A. **Online address:** pdotso1@lsu.edu

DOTSON, Robert Charles. See **DOTSON, Bob.**

DOTT, Brian R. (Brian Russell Dott). American (born United States), b. 1964. **Genres:** Young Adult Non-fiction. **Career:** University of Pittsburgh, Department of History, teaching fellow, 1991-92, 1995-96, lecturer, 1996, 1997; Kalamazoo College, Department of History, visiting assistant professor, 1998-99; Kenyon College, Department of History, visiting assistant professor, 1999-2000; Fort Lewis College, Department of History, assistant professor, 2001-02; Whitman College, Department of History, assistant professor, 2002-. Writer. **Publications:** Identity Reflections: Pilgrimages to Mount Tai in Late Imperial China (nonfiction), 2004. Contributor to journals. **Address:** Department of History, Whitman College, Walla Walla, WA 99362, U.S.A. **Online address:** dottbr@whitman.edu

DOTT, Brian Russell. See **DOTT, Brian R.**

DOTY, Mark. American (born United States), b. 1953. **Genres:** Poetry, Autobiography/Memoirs. **Career:** University of Houston, teacher of creative writing, Graduate Program, John and Rebecca Moores professor; Rutgers, The State University of New Jersey, distinguished writer, 2009-, professor of English, Writers House, acting director. Poet and memoirist. **Publications:** POETRY: Turtle, Swan, 1987; Bethlehem in Broad Daylight, 1991; My Alexandria, 1993; Atlantis, 1995; Sweet Machine, 1998; Murano, 2000; Source, 2001; Still Life with Bysters and Lemon, 2001; School of the Arts, 2005; (ed.) Collected Poems, 2006; Fire to Fire: New and Selected Poems, 2008. NONFICTION: Heaven's Coast: A Memoir, 1996; Firebird: A Memoir, 1999; Still Life with Oysters and Lemon, 2001; (contrib.) Seeing Venice: Bellotto's Grand Canal, 2002; (ed.) Open House: Writers Redefine Home, 2003; Dog Years: A Memoir, 2007. OTHERS: Theories and Apparitions, 2008; The Art of Description, 2010; Lost Dallas, 2011. Contributor to books and magazines. **Address:** Department of English, Rutgers, The State University of New Jersey, Rm. 040A, Murray Hall, 77 Hamilton St., New Brunswick, NJ 08901, U.S.A. **Online address:** markdoty@rci.rutgers.edu

DOUCET, Julie. Canadian (born Canada), b. 1965. **Genres:** Graphic Novels. **Career:** Weirdo, staff. Independent cartoonist, writer and artist. **Publications:** GRAPHIC NOVELS: Lift Your Leg, My Fish Is Dead!, 1993; My Most Secret Desire: A Collection of Dream Stories, 1995; Ciboire de Criss, 1996; My New York Diary, 1999; The Madame Paul Affair, 2000; Long Time Relationship, 2001; Journal, 2004; J comme Je, 2006; Elle Humour, 2006; 365 Days:

A Diary by Julie Doucet, 2007. Works appear in anthologies. Contributor to periodicals. **Address:** c/o Author Mail, Drawn & Quarterly, PO Box 48056, Montreal, QC H2V 4S8, Canada. **Online address:** info@juliedoucet.net

DOUDERA, Vicki. American (born United States), b. 1961. **Genres:** Novels, Travel/Exploration. **Career:** Camden Real Estate, agent; Midcoast Habitat for Humanity, president; Children's Hospital, development officer. Writer. **Publications:** Moving to Maine: The Essential Guide to Get You There, 2000, rev. ed., 2007; Where to Retire in Maine, 2003; A House to Die For (novel), 2010. Contributor of articles to periodicals. **Address:** U.S.A. **Online address:** vicki@vickidoudera.com

DOUGAN, Terrell. See **DOUGAN, Terrell Harris.**

DOUGAN, Terrell Harris. Also writes as Terrell Harris, Terrell Dougan. American (born United States), b. 1939. **Genres:** Autobiography/Memoirs. **Career:** U.S. Information Agency, journalist and magazine writer. Activist and memoirist. **Publications:** (As Terrell Dougan comp. with L. Isbell and P. Vyas) We Have Been There: A Guidebook for Families of People with Mental Retardation, 1983; That Went Well: Adventures in Caring for My Sister (memoir), 2008. Contributor to periodicals and magazines. **Address:** Salt Lake City, UT , U.S.A. **Online address:** tdougan@that-went-well.com

DOUGHERTY, James E(dward). American (born United States), b. 1923. **Genres:** International Relations/Current Affairs, Military/Defense/Arms Control, Area Studies, Politics/Government, Theology/Religion. **Career:** Saint Joseph's University, Department of Political Science, instructor, 1951-60, professor of political science, 1960-97, emeritus professor of political science, 1997-, executive vice-president, 1968-73, 1976-77; Foreign Policy Research Institute, research associate, 1955-68; National War College, professor, 1964-65; Institute for Foreign Policy Analysis, senior staff, 1976-89. Writer. **Publications:** (Co-author) Protracted Conflict, 1959; (co-author) Building the Atlantic World, 1963; (with A.J. Cottrell) The Politics of the Atlantic Alliance in UK as The Atlantic Alliance: A Short Political Guide, 1964; (ed. with J.F. Lehman, Jr.) The Prospects for Arms Control, 1965; Arms Control and Disarmament: The Critical Issues, 1966; (ed. with J.F. Lehman, Jr.) Arms Control for the Late Sixties, 1967; How to Think about Arms Control and Disarmament, 1973; (co-author) SALT: Arms Control in the 1970s, 1973; Security through World Law and World Government: Myth or Reality?, 1974; British Perspectives on a Changing Global Balance, 1975; (with D.K. Pfaltzgraff) Eurocommunism and the Atlantic Alliance, 1977; (with A.J. Cottrell) Iran's Quest for Security: U.S. Arms Transfers and the Nuclear Option, 1977; (with P.H. Nitze and F.X. Kane) The Fateful Ends and Shades of SALT: Past... Present... and Yet to Come?, 1979; The Horn of Africa: A Map of Political-Strategic Conflict, 1982; The Bishops and Nuclear Weapons: The Catholic Pastoral Letter on War and Peace, 1984; (co-author) Ethics, Deterrence, and National Security, 1985; JCS Reorganization and U.S. Arms Control Policy, 1986. WITH R.L. PFALTZGRAFF, JR.: Contending Theories of International Relations: A Comprehensive Survey, 1971, 5th ed., 2001; (ed.) Shattering Europe's Defense Consensus: The Antinuclear Protest Movement and the Future of NATO, 1985; American Foreign Policy: FDR to Reagan, 1986. Contributor to periodicals. **Address:** Department of Political Science, Saint Joseph's University, 5600 City Ave., Philadelphia, PA 19131, U.S.A.

DOUGHTY, Robert A. (Robert Allan Doughty). American (born United States), b. 1943. **Genres:** History, Military/Defense/Arms Control, Technology. **Career:** U.S. Military Academy, Department of History, instructor, 1972-75, associate professor, 1981-84, professor and head, 1985-2005; U.S. Army Command and General Staff College, Department of Strategy, instructor, 1976-79; Pierson College, associate fellow, 1983-93; U.S. Army War College, Military History Institute, visiting professor, 1995-96. Writer. **Publications:** MILITARY HISTORY: The Evolution of U.S. Army Tactical Doctrine, 1946-76, 1979; (as Robert Allan Doughty) The Seeds of Disaster: The Development of French Army Doctrine, 1919-1939, 1985; (as Robert Allan Doughty) The Breaking Point: Sedan and the Fall of France, 1940, 1990; (contrib.) The Making of Strategy: Rulers, States and War, 1994; (co-author) Warfare in the Western World, vol. I: Military Operations from 1600 to 1871, vol. II: Military Operations since 1871, 1995; (co-author) American Military History and the Evolution of Warfare in the Western World, 1996; (co-author) American Civil War, 1996; (contrib.) Challenging the United States Symmetrically and Asymmetrically, 1998; (contrib.) Mai-juin 1940: Defaite franaise, victoire allemande, sous l'oeil des historiens Etrangers, 2000; (contrib.) Les Batailles de la Marne de l'Ourcq A Verdun (1914 et 1918), 2004; Pyrrhic Victory: French Strategy and Operations in the Great War, 2005; (contrib.) 1917: Tactics, Training and Technology, 2007. Contributor to periodicals. **Address:** Belknap Press, 79 Garden St., Cambridge, MA 02138, U.S.A. **Online address:** robert.doughty@yahoo.com

DOUGHTY, Robert Allan. *See* DOUGHTY, Robert A.

DOUGLAS, Ann. American (born United States), b. 1942?. **Genres:** Literary Criticism And History, Women's Studies And Issues. **Career:** Princeton University, Department of English, professor, 1970-74; Columbia University, professor of English and comparative literature, 1974-, Parr professor of English and comparative literature; American Academy of Arts and Sciences, fellow, 2002. Writer. **Publications:** The Feminization of American Culture, 1977; Terrible Honesty: Mongrel Manhattan in the 1920s, 1994; Noir Nation: Cold War U.S. Culture 1945-1960, forthcoming; If You Live You Burn: Cold War Culture in the United States: 1939-1965, forthcoming. EDITED WITH INTRODUCTION: Uncle Tom's Cabin: Or, Life Among the Lowly, 1981; Charlotte Temple and Lucy Temple, 1991. Studs Lonigan, 2004; The Subterraneans, 2001; The Dharma Bums, 2006. Contributor of articles to periodicals. **Address:** Institute for Resarch on Women & Gender, Columbia University, 405 Philosophy, 1200 Amsterdam Ave., PO Box 4927, New York, NY 10027, U.S.A. **Online address:** ad34@columbia.edu

DOUGLAS, Arthur. *See* HAMMOND, Gerald (Arthur Douglas).

DOUGLAS, Deborah G. American (born United States), b. 1962. **Genres:** History, Air/Space Topics, Women's Studies And Issues. **Career:** Old Dominion University, adjunct assistant professor, 1994-99; NASA Langley Research Center, visiting historian, 1994-99; Smithsonian Institution, National Air and Space Museum, pre-doctoral fellow; Massachusetts Institute of Technology, MIT Museum, staff member, 1999-, curator of science and technology. Researcher and author of nonfiction. **Publications:** Out of Thin Air: A History of Air Products and Chemicals, Inc., 1940-1990, 1990; United States Women in Aviation, 1940-1985, 1990; American Women and Flight since 1940, 2004. **Address:** MIT Museum, Massachusetts Institute of Technology, Bldg. N51, 265 Massachusetts Ave., Cambridge, MA 02139, U.S.A.

DOUGLAS, Edward. *See* AMBURN, Ellis.

DOUGLAS, Ian. *See* KEITH, William H(enry).

DOUGLAS, John (Frederick James). (Sean McGrath). British (born England), b. 1929. **Genres:** Geography, Photography, Travel/Exploration, Technology, History. **Career:** Geoslides Photo Agency, library director, 1969-; Geo Group and Associates, coordinating director, 1989-; Geo Aerial Photography, managing director, 1993-; Nyala Publishing, director, 1996-. Writer. **Publications:** South Downs, 1969; The Arctic Highway: A Road and its Setting, 1972; Town and Village in Northern Ghana, 1973; Water Problems in the Third World, 1973; Kampong Tengah, a Malay Village, 1974; Kuala Lumpur: A Third World City, 1974; A Dyak Longhouse in Borneo, 1975; Environmental Viewpoint: Water, 1976; Shelter and Subsistence, 1976; Ice and Snow, 1976; Off the Beaten Track, 1977; Expedition Photography, 1979; The Independent Travellers Handbook, 1980; The Travellers Handbook, 1982; Creative Techniques in Travel Photography, 1982; (with K. White) Spectrum Guide to Malawi, 2003; Norway's Arctic Highway, 2003. Contributor of articles to magazines and newspapers. **Address:** Geo Group & Associates, 4 Christian Fields, London, GL SW16 3JZ, England. **Online address:** jd@geo-group.co.uk

DOUGLAS, Kirk. Also writes as Issur Danielovitch Demsky, George Spelvin. American (born United States), b. 1916. **Genres:** Novels, Autobiography/Memoirs, Theology/Religion. **Career:** Greenwich House Settlement, drama coach, 1939-41; Bryna Production Co., founder and president, 1955-; Joel Productions, founder and president, 1962-. Writer, actor, producer and director. **Publications:** MEMOIRS: The Ragman's Son, 1988; Climbing the Mountain: My Search For Meaning, 1997; My Stroke of Luck, 2002; Let's Face It: 90 Years of Living, Loving and Learning, 2007. NOVELS: Dance with the Devil, 1990; The Gift, 1992; Last Tango in Brooklyn, 1994. OTHERS: Star in the Window, 1945; The Broken Mirror (children), 1997; Young Heroes of the Bible: A Book For Family Sharing, 1999. **Address:** The Bryna Co., 141 S El Camino Dr., Ste. 209, Beverly Hills, CA 90212-2731, U.S.A.

DOUGLAS, L. Warren. American (born United States), b. 1943. **Genres:**

Novels, Science Fiction/Fantasy, Young Adult Fiction, Children's Fiction, Earth Sciences. **Career:** Muskegon River Archaeological Sites, staff, 1966; Toledo University, archaeology field crew supervisor, 1967; University of Alberta, Anthropology and Prehistory, instructor, 1972-; regional planning commission artist, 1973-; woodcarver, 1973-. **Publications:** NOVELS: A Plague of Change, 1992; Bright Islands in a Dark Sea, 1993; Cannon's Orb, 1994; Simply Human, 2000. ARBITER SERIES: Stepwater, 1995; Glaice, 1996; The Wells of Phyre, 1996. THE SORCERESS'S TALE SERIES: The Sacred Pool, 2001; The Veil of Years, 2001; The Isle beyond Time, 2003. Contributor to periodicals. **Address:** c/o Author Mail, Roc Publicity, 375 Hudson St., New York, NY 10014, U.S.A. **Online address:** ldouglas@lugthart.org

DOUGLAS, Mark. American (born United States), b. 1966. **Genres:** Theology/Religion, Philosophy, Psychology. **Career:** University of Virginia, teaching assistant, 1994-96; University Hospital, clinical intern, 1995; Virginia Commonwealth University, adjunct professor, 1997; Tabor Presbyterian Church, associate pastor, 1997-99; Columbia Theological Seminary, assistant professor, 1999-2005, associate professor of Christian ethics, 2005-. Writer and theologian. **Publications:** Confessing Christ in the Twenty-first Century, 2005. Contributor to books, periodicals and journals. **Address:** Columbia Theological Seminary, PO Box 520, Decatur, GA 30031, U.S.A. **Online address:** douglasm@ctsnet.edu

DOUGLAS, Matthew M. American/American (born United States), b. 1949. **Genres:** Biography, Sciences, Science Fiction/Fantasy, Biology. **Career:** California State University, assistant professor of entomology, 1978-79; Boston University, assistant professor of biophysical ecology, 1979-81; Harvard University, assistant professor of zoology, 1980; University of Kansas, Snow Entomological Museum, senior research scientist, 1981; Monarch Communications, president, 1981; University of Michigan Press, series editor, 1995-; Michigan State University, adjunct professor of entomology, 2005-; Grand Rapids Community College, Department of biology, head. Writer. **Publications:** The Lives of Butterflies, 1986; The Ark of Polaris, 2001; (with J.M. Douglas) Butterflies of the Great Lakes Region, 2005; Mary's Voyage, 2008; The One Arm Bandit, 2008; (with K.T. Patton and G.A. Thibodeau) Essentials of Anatomy and Physiology, 2011. Contributor of articles to periodicals and scientific journals. **Address:** 7131 Oran SE, 7131 Oran SE, 7131 Oran SE, Grand Rapids, MI 49546, U.S.A. **Online address:** matt.thewriter@yahoo.com

DOUGLAS, Shirley Stewart. *See* TEPPER, Sheri S.

DOUGLAS, Susan J(eanne). American (born United States), b. 1950?. **Genres:** Communications/Media, Human Relations/Parenting, Social Sciences, Photography. **Career:** Hampshire College, assistant professor, 1981-87, associate professor, 1987-92, professor of media and American studies, 1992-96; Skidmore College, visiting professor in American studies, 1986-87; University of Michigan, Department of Communication Studies, professor of communication studies, 1996-, Program in American Culture, faculty associate, 1996-, Catherine Neafie Kellogg professor, 1998-, Arthur F. Thurnau professor, 1999-2002, chair, 2004-. Writer. **Publications:** Inventing American Broadcasting, 1899-1922, 1987; Where the Girls Are: Growing up Female with the Mass Media, 1994; Listening In: Radio and the American Imagination: From Amos N Andy and Edward R. Murrow to Wolfman Jack and Howard Stern, 1999, 2004; (with M.W. Michaels) The Mommy Myth: The Idealization of Motherhood and How It has Undermined Women, 2004; Enlightened Sexism: The Seductive Message that Feminism's Work is Done, 2010. Contributor to periodicals. **Address:** Department of Communication Studies, University of Michigan, 1225 S University Ave., Ann Arbor, MI 48104-2523, U.S.A. **Online address:** sdoug@umich.edu

DOUGLAS-HAMILTON, James. *See* DOUGLAS-HAMILTON, James Alexander.

DOUGLAS-HAMILTON, James Alexander. (James Douglas-Hamilton). Scottish/British (born England), b. 1942. **Genres:** History, Biography, Military/Defense/Arms Control. **Career:** Practising Scots advocate, 1968-77; Edinburgh District Council, councillor, 1972-74; MP for Edinburgh West, 1974-97; opposition, government whip, 1977-81; Malcolm Rifkind MP, parliamentary private secretary, 1983-87; State for Scotland, parliamentary under secretary, 1987-95; State at the Scottish Office, minister, 1995-97; privy counsellor and queen's counsel, 1996; Douglas-Hamilton 'D' Company Ltd., director, 1997-; Scottish Conservative Group of MSPs, chief whip and business manager, 1999-2001; Home Affairs, lead spokesman, 2001-03. Writer. **Publications:** AS JAMES DOUGLAS-HAMILTON: Motive for a Mission: The Story behind Hess's Flight to Britain, 1971; Air Battle for Malta: The Diaries of a Fighter Pilot, 1981; Roof of the world: Man's First Flight Over Everest, 1983; The Truth about Rudolf Hess, 1993. Contributor to books. **Address:** Hamilton QC MSP, Scottish Parliament, Holyrood, Edinburgh, EH99 1SP, Scotland. **Online address:** james.douglas-hamilton.msp@scottish.parliament.uk

DOUGLASS, Billie. *See* **DELINSKY, Barbara (Ruth Greenberg).**

DOUGLASS, Sara. *See* **WARNEKE, Sara.**

DOVAL, Alexis J. (Alexis James Doval). American (born United States), b. 1953. **Genres:** Theology/Religion. **Career:** La Salle High School, instructor, 1976-81; St. Mary's College High School, instructor, 1984-88; University of Oxford, Centre for Medieval and Renaissance Studies, instructor, 1989-93; St. Mary's College of California, associate professor, 1993-2002, professor, 2002-. Writer. **Publications:** Cyril of Jerusalem, Mystagogue: The Authorship of the Mystagogic Catecheses, 2001; (ed.) Duties of a Christian to God, 2002. **Address:** St. Mary's College, 109 Garaventa, 1928 Saint Mary's Rd., PO Box 4730, Moraga, CA 94556, U.S.A. **Online address:** adoval@stmarys-ca.edu

DOVAL, Alexis James. *See* **DOVAL, Alexis J.**

DOVAL, Teresa de la Caridad. *See* **DOVALPAGE, Teresa.**

DOVALPAGE, Teresa. (Teresa de la Caridad Doval). American/Cuban (born Cuba), b. 1966. **Genres:** Writing/Journalism, Gay And Lesbian Issues, Novels, Women's Studies And Issues. **Career:** University of Havana, faculty; Havana Dentist School, faculty; University of California, faculty. Writer. **Publications:** (As Teresa de la Caridad Doval) A Girl like Che Guevara, 2004; Posesas de la Habana, 2004; Muerte de un murciano en La Habana, 2006; Por culpa de Candela y otros cuentos escandalosos, forthcoming. **Address:** c/o Author Mail, Soho Press Inc., 853 Broadway, New York, NY 10003, U.S.A. **Online address:** dovalpage@aol.com

DOVE, Rita (Frances). American (born United States), b. 1952. **Genres:** Novels, Novellas/Short Stories, Plays/Screenplays, Poetry. **Career:** University of Iowa, research assistant, 1975, teaching assistant, 1976-77; Arizona State University, assistant professor of creative writing, 1981-84, associate professor, 1984-87, professor of English, 1987-89; University of Virginia, professor of English, 1989-93, commonwealth professor of English, 1989- ; Library of Congress, consultant, 1993-95, 1999-2000; United States, poet laureate, 1993-95; Commonwealth of Virginia, poet laureate, 2004-06; Yale University, Chubb fellow, 2007. **Publications:** POETRY: Ten Poems, 1977; The Only Dark Spot in the Sky, 1980; The Yellow House on the Corner, 1980; Mandolin, 1982; Museum, 1983; Thomas and Beulah, 1986; The Other Side of the House, 1988; Grace Notes, 1989; Selected Poems, 1993; To Make a Prairie, 1993; Lady Freedom among Us, 1994; Mother Love, 1995; Three Days of Forest, a River, Free, 1996; On the Bus with Rosa Parks, 1999; American Smooth, 2004; One Volume Missing, 2006; Sonata Mulattica, 2009. OTHER: Fifth Sunday (stories), 1985; The Siberian Village (play), 1991; Through the Ivory Gate (novel), 1992; The Darker Face of the Earth (play), 1994, The Poet's World (essays), 1995; (foreword) Multicultural Voices: Literature from the United States, 1995; Evening Primrose, 1998; Seven for Luck (song cycle) 1998; (ed.) The Best American Poetry 2000, 2000. Works appear in anthologies. **Address:** Department of English, University of Virginia, 219 Bryan Hall, PO Box 400121, Charlottesville, VA 22904-4121, U.S.A.

DOVER, Michael A. American (born United States) **Genres:** Literary Criticism And History, Business/Trade/Industry. **Career:** Fordham University, School of Social Work, part-time instructor, 1989-91; Adelphi University, School of Social Work, Urban Center, part-time faculty advisor, 1990-91; Eastern Michigan University, School of Social Work, instructor, 1997-98; Central Michigan University, Department of Sociology, Anthropology and Social Work, assistant professor, 2003-07, Social Work Program, director, 2003-07; Cleveland State University, School of Social Work, visiting assistant professor, 2007-09, assistant professor, 2009-. Writer. **Publications:** (With D.H. Smith and R.A. Stebbins) A Dictionary of Nonprofit Terms and Concepts, 2006. **Address:** School of Social Work, Cleveland State University, 326 Chester Hall, 2121 Euclid Ave., Cleveland, OH 44115-2214, U.S.A. **Online address:** m.a.dover@csuohio.edu

DOW, David R. American (born United States), b. 1959. **Genres:** Autobiography/Memoirs, Law. **Career:** University of Houston, Law Center, faculty, 1988-, university distinguished professor of law; Texas Defender Service (a nonprofit law firm representing death row inmates), litigation director; Texas Innocence Network (an advocacy and legal assistance group), founder; Smyser Kaplan & Veselka, of counsel, 1995-. Writer. **Publications:** (Ed. with M. Dow) Machinery of Death: The Reality of America's Death Penalty Regime, 2002; (with C. Smyser) Contract Law, 2005; Executed on a Technicality: Lethal Injustice on America's Death Row, 2005; America's Prophets: How Judicial Activism Makes America Great, 2009; The Autobiography of an Execution (memoir), 2010; Killing Time: One Man's Race to Stop an Execution, 2010. Contributor to journals and periodicals. **Address:** U.S.A. **Online address:** ddow@uh.edu

DOW, James. (James Raymond Dow). American (born United States), b. 1936. **Genres:** Literary Criticism And History, Language/Linguistics, Cultural/Ethnic Topics. **Career:** University of Iowa, teaching assistant and instructor in German, 1959-66; University of Wyoming, Department of Modern and Classical Languages, assistant professor, 1966-70; Iowa State University, Department of Foreign Languages, assistant professor, 1971-74, associate professor, 1974-80, professor of German, 1980-, Department of Foreign Languages and Literatures, chair, 1991-97, chair of linguistics program, 1998-2004, now professor emeritus; Universität Essen, visiting professor, 1990; Universität Bremen, visiting professor, 2003. Writer. **Publications:** AS JAMES R. DOW: Eine Sibirische Märchenerzählerin, 1974; Internationale Volkskundliche Bibliographie, 1979-80, 1985; Internationale Volkskundliche Bibliographie, 1981-82, 1986; (ed. and trans. with H. Lixfield) German Volkskunde: A Decade of Theoretical Confrontation, Debate, and Reorientation (1967-1977), 1986; Internationale Volkskundliche Bibliographie, 1983-84, 1988; Focus on Language and Ethnicity, 1991; (ed.) Language and Ethnicity, 1991; (co-ed.) Sprachminoritäten/Minoritätensprachen, 1991; Gesunkenes Kulturgut-primitive Gemeinschaft: Der Germanist Hans Naumann (1886-1951) in seiner Bedeutung für die Volkskunde, 1993; (ed. and trans. with H. Lixfeld.) The Nazification of an Academic Discipline: Folklore in the Third Reich, 1993; (ed. with W. Enninger and J. Raith) Old and New World Anabaptists: Studies on the Language, Culture, Society, and Health of the Amish and Mennonites, 1994; (ed. and trans.) Folklore and Fascism: The Reich Institute for German Volkskunde, 1994; (co-ed.) Völkische Wissenschaft? Gestalten und Tendenzen in der deutschen und österreichischen Volkskunde in der ersten Hälfte des 20, Jahrhunderts, 1994; (ed. with M. Wolff) Languages and Lives: Essays in Honor of Werner Enninger, 1997; (with A.S. Mercatante) The Facts on File Encyclopedia of World Mythology and Legend, 2004, 3rd ed., 2009; (with O. Bockhorn) The Study of European Ethnology in Austria, 2004; (with T. Stolz) Das Zimbrische zwischen Germanisch und Romanisch, 2005; German Folklore: A Handbook, 2006; Zimbrische Gesamtgrammatik: Vergleichende Darstellung Der Zimbrischen Dialekte, 2008; (ed. and intro. with R.L. Welsch) Wyoming Folklore: Reminiscences, Folktales, Beliefs, Customs and Folk Speech, 2010. **Address:** Department of Foreign Languages and Literatures, Iowa State University, 300 E Pearson, 3102 Pearson Hall, Ames, IA 50011-2205, U.S.A. **Online address:** jrdow@iastate.edu

DOW, James Raymond. *See* **DOW, James.**

DOW, Vicki. *See* **MCVEY, Vicki.**

DOWDY, Cecelia D. American (born United States), b. 1966. **Genres:** Novels. **Career:** Writer. **Publications:** (With A. Ford and L. Meredith) Promises to Keep, 2002; First Mates, 2005; John's Quest, 2008; Milk Money, 2008; Bittersweet Memories, 2009; Chesapeake Weddings, 2010. **Address:** PO Box 951, Greenbelt, MD 20768-0951, U.S.A. **Online address:** ceceliadowdy@ceceliadowdy.com

DOWELL, Frances O'Roark. American/German (born Germany), b. 1964. **Genres:** Children's Fiction, Children's Non-fiction, Young Adult Fiction. **Career:** Dream Girl, editor and co-publisher. Writer. **Publications:** Dovey Coe, 2000; Where I'd Like to Be, 2003; The Secret Language of Girls, 2004; Chicken Boy, 2005; Phineas L. MacGuire Erupts!: The First Experiment, 2006; Phineas L. MacGuire-Gets Slimed!, 2007; Phineas L. MacGuire-Blasts Off!, 2008; Shooting the Moon, 2008; Kinds of Friends We Used To Be, 2009; Falling In, 2010; Ten Miles Past Normal, 2011. **Address:** Simon & Schuster Children's Publishing, 1230 Ave. of the Americas, New York, NY 10020, U.S.A. **Online address:** fdowell@mindspring.com

DOWER, John W(illiam). American (born United States), b. 1938. **Genres:** Area Studies, Cultural/Ethnic Topics, Design, History, Photography, Race Relations, Bibliography. **Career:** Kanazawa Joshi Tanki Daigaku, instructor of English, 1962-63; John Weatherhill Inc. (publishers), assistant editor, 1963-65; Harvard University, Department of History, teaching assistant, 1968-69; University of Nebraska, instructor of history, 1970-71; University of Wisconsin, assistant professor of history, 1971-75, associate professor of history, 1975-79, professor of history, 1979-85; University of California, Joseph Naiman professor of history and Japanese studies, 1986-91; Massachusetts Institute of Technology, professor of history and Henry R. Luce professor of international cooperation and global stability, 1991-96, Elting E. Morison professor of history, 1996-2003, Ford International professor of history, 2003-10, professor emeritus, 2010-; American Academy of Arts & Sciences, fellow, 1991-. **Publications:** The Elements of Japanese Design: A Handbook of Family Crests, Heraldry, and Symbolism, 1971; (contrib.) Peace with China? U.S. Decisions for Asia, 1971; Empire and Aftermath: Yoshida Shigeru and the Japanese Experience, 1878-1945, 1979; A Century of Japanese Photography, 1980; Japanese History and Culture from Ancient to Modern Times: Seven Basic Bibliographies, 1985, (with T.S. George) 2nd ed., 1995; War without Mercy: Race and Power in the Pacific War, 1986; Japan in War and Peace, 1993; Embracing Defeat: Japan in the Wake of World War II, 1999; (with L. Rubinfien and S.S. Phillips) Shomei Tomatsu: Skin of the Nation, 2004; (co-author) Wearing Propaganda: Textiles on the Home Front in Japan, Britain, and the United States, 1931-1945, 2005; (contrib.) A Letter from Japan: The Photographs of John Swope, 2006; Cultures of War: Pearl Harbor: Hiroshima: 9-11: Iraq, 2010. EDITOR: (and intro.) Origins of the Modern Japanese State: Selected Writings of E.H. Norman, 1975; (with J. Junkerman) The Hiroshima Murals: The Art of Iri Maruki and Toshi Maruki, 1985. Contributor to books. **Address:** Department of History, Massachusetts Institute of Technology, 77 Massachusetts Ave., Bldg. E51-287, Cambridge, MA 02139-4301, U.S.A.

DOWER, Laura. American (born United States), b. 1967. **Genres:** Novels, Children's Fiction, Cartoons, Young Adult Non-fiction, Children's Nonfiction. **Career:** Writer. **Publications:** Bubble Trouble, 2000; Paste Makes Waste, 2000; Monkey See, Doggy Do, 2000; Mojo Jojo's Rising, 2000; Bought and Scold, 2001; The Powerpuff Girls: Beat Your Greens, 2001; Fishy Business, 2001; The Powerpuff Girls Save Valentine's Day!, 2001; I Will Remember You: What to Do When Someone You Love Dies: A Guidebook through Grief for Teens (nonfiction), 2001; The Valentine's Day Mix-Up, 2002; Three Girls and a Monster, 2002; Let the Fur Fly, 2002; Bubbles Bedazzled!, 2003; 'Twas the Fight before Christmas, 2003; Not-So-Awesome Blossom, 2004; Bf4e: Best Friends Forever, 2006; Rewind, 2006; All Shook Up, 2006; The Boy Next Door, 2006; Friends till the End, 2007; For Girls Only: Everything Great about Being a Girl, 2008; The Slime That Would Not Die, 2009; Return of Mega Mantis, 2009; The Beast with 1000 Eyes, 2009; They Came from Planet Q, 2010; Curse Of The Lake Monster, 2010. FROM THE FILES OF MADISON FINN SERIES: Only the Lonely, 2001; Boy, Oh Boy!, 2001; Play It Again, 2001; Caught in the Web, 2001; Thanks for Nothing, 2001; Lost and Found, 2002; Save the Date, 2002; Picture Perfect, 2002; Just Visiting, 2002; Give and Take, 2002; Heart to Heart, 2003; Lights Out!, 2003; Sink or Swim, 2003; Double Dare, 2003; Off the Wall, 2004; Three's a Crowd, 2004; On the Case, 2004; Give Me a Break, 2004; To Have and to Hold, 2004; Keep It Real, 2005; All That Glitters, 2005; Forget Me Not, 2005; Only the Lonely, 2006; Hit the Beach, 2006. **Address:** Stimola Literary Studio, 306 Chase Ct., Edgewater, NJ 07020, U.S.A.

DOWLAH, Abu Faij. See DOWLAH, Caf.

DOWLAH, A. F. See DOWLAH, Caf.

DOWLAH, Alex F. See DOWLAH, Caf.

DOWLAH, C. A. F. See DOWLAH, Caf.

DOWLAH, Caf. Also writes as Alex F. Dowlah, Abu Faij Dowlah, A. F. Dowlah, C. A. F. Dowlah. American/Bangladeshi (born Bangladesh), b. 1958. **Genres:** Politics/Government. **Career:** State University of New York, Agricultural and Technical Institute, assistant professor of economics and government, 1991-96; Financial Express, columnist, 1993-95; DCCI Monthly Review, editor, 1993-94; Industrial Policy Quarterly, editor, 1994-95; World Bank, Dhaka Office, Private Sector Development and Rural Development Units, policy economist, 1997-; City University of New York, Queensborough Community College, Department of Social Sciences, associate profes-

sor of economics, Center of Economics Education, director, International Center for Environmental Resources and Development, Division of Economic Analysis and Global Cooperation, head; U.S. Agency for International Development, consultant; United Nations Development Program, consultant; Bangladesh Ministry of Industries, consultant. **Publications:** (As Abu Faij Dowlah) Perestroika: Historical and Intellectual Roots, 1990; (as A.F. Dowlah) Soviet Political Economy in Transition: From Lenin to Gorbachev, 1992; (as Alex F. Dowlah with J.E. Elliott) The Life and Times of Soviet Socialism, 1997; (as C.A.F. Dowlah) The Consequences of the GATT Uruguay Round for the Textile and Garments Sector in Bangladesh, 1998; Backwaters of Global Prosperity: How Forces of Globalization and GATT/WTO Trade Regimes Contribute to the Marginalization of the World's Poorest Nations, 2004. Contributor of articles to books and periodicals. **Address:** Department of Social Sciences, Queensborough Community College, City University of New York, Rm. M-104, Medical Arts Bldg., 222-05 56th Ave., Bayside, NY 11364, U.S.A. **Online address:** cdowlah@qcc.cuny.edu

DOWLING, Terry. Australian (born Australia), b. 1947. **Genres:** Science Fiction/Fantasy, Novellas/Short Stories, Graphic Novels, Novels. **Career:** June Dally-Watkins Business Finishing College, Business Communication and English, tutor. Writer. **Publications:** TOM RYNOSSEROS SERIES: Rynosseros, 1990; Blue Tyson, 1992; Twilight Beach, 1993; Rynemonn, 2007. COLLECTIONS: Wormwood, 1991; The Man Who Lost Red (novellas), 1994; An Intimate Knowledge of the Night, 1995; Antique Futures: The Best of Terry Dowling, 1999; Blackwater Days, 1999; Basic Black: Tales of Appropriate Fear, 2006; (ed.) The Jack Vance Reader, 2008; Amberjack: Tales of Fear and Wonder, 2009; Make Believe, 2009. NOVELS: Beckoning Nightframe, 1995; His Own, The Star Alphecca, 1995; The Ichneumon and the Dormeuse, 1995; Clowns at Midnight, 2009. OTHERS: (ed. and intro. with R. Delap and G. Lamont) The Essential Ellison: A 35-Year Retrospective, 1987, rev. ed. as Essential Ellison: A 50-Year Retrospective, 2001; (ed. with V. Ikin) Mortal Fire: Best Australian Science Fiction, 1993; The Mars You Have in Me (short stories), 2000; (co-author) Flinch, 2009. Works appear in anthologies. Contributor to periodicals. **Address:** 11 Everard St., Hunters Hill, NW 2110, Australia.

DOWNER, Lesley. British (born England), b. 1949. **Genres:** Travel/Exploration, Food And Wine, Autobiography/Memoirs, Biography, History. **Career:** Gifu Women's University, lecturer in English, 1978-81; Tokyo Broadcasting System, personal assistant, 1984-86; Japanese Embassy, lecturer, 1984-; freelance writer, journalist and broadcaster, 1986-. Writer. **Publications:** (With M. Yoneda) Step-by-Step Japanese Cooking, 1986; Japanese Vegetarian Cookery, 1986; (contrib. and ed.) The Economist Business Traveller's Guide to Japan, 1987, rev. Ed., 1990; Japanese Food and Drink, 1988; Japan, 1989; On the Narrow Road: Journey into a Lost Japan in UK as On the Narrow Road to the Deep North: Journey into a Lost Japan, 1989; A Taste of Japan, 1991; At the Japanese Table: New and Traditional Recipes, 1993; The Brothers: The Saga of the Richest Family in Japan, 1994 in US as The Brothers: The Hidden World of Japan's Richest Family, 1995; Hard Currency in Amazonian: Penguin Book of Women's New Travel Writing, 1998; Geisha: The Secret History of a Vanishing World, 2000 in US as Women of the Pleasure Quarters: The Secret History of the Geisha, 2001; Madame Sadayakko: The Geisha Who Bewitched the West in UK as Madame Sadayakko: The Geisha Who Seduced the West, 2003; Last Concubine, 2008; The Courtesan and the Samurai, 2010; Across A Bridge of Dreams, 2012. Contributor to periodicals. **Address:** c/o Bill Hamilton, A M Heath & Company Ltd., 6th Warwick Ct., Holborn, London, GL WC1R 5DJ, England. **Online address:** lesleydowner@email.msn.com

DOWNES, Alexander B. American (born United States), b. 1969. **Genres:** History. **Career:** Harvard University, Olin Institute for Strategic Studies, fellow, 2002-03; Duke University, assistant professor of political science, 2004-; George Washington University, Department of Political Science, associate professor, 2011-, Elliott School of International Affairs, associate professor, 2011-. Writer and political scientist. **Publications:** Targeting Civilians in War, 2008. Contributor to periodicals. **Address:** Elliott School of International Affairs, George Washington University, Rm. 605B, 1957 E St. NW, Washington, DC 20052, U.S.A. **Online address:** downes@gwu.edu

DOWNES, Bryan T(revor). Canadian/American (born United States), b. 1939. **Genres:** Local History/Rural Topics, Politics/Government, Public/Social Administration, Urban Studies. **Career:** San Francisco State College, assistant professor, 1966-67; Michigan State University, assistant professor,

1967-70, associate professor 1970-71; University of Missouri, associate professor of political science, 1971-76; University of Oregon, Wallace School of Community Service and Public Affairs, associate professor, 1976-78, associate dean and professor, 1978-82, Public Affairs and International Development Division, chair, 1976-78, Community Service Division, 1977-78, professor of public affairs, 1981-2001, Department of Planning, professor, 1982-88, director of public affairs graduate program, 1982-88, 1994-96, department head, 1996-99, professor emeritus, 2001-. Writer. **Publications:** (Ed.) Cities and Suburbs: Selected Readings in Local Politics and Public Policy, 1971; Politics, Change, and Urban Crisis, 1976. **Address:** Department of Planning, Public Policy and Management, University of Oregon, 1209, 119 Hendricks Hall, Eugene, OR 97403-1209, U.S.A. **Online address:** downesb@uoregon.edu

DOWNES, David A(nthony). American (born United States), b. 1927. **Genres:** Novels, Literary Criticism And History, Autobiography/Memoirs, History, Young Adult Fiction. **Career:** Gonzaga University, instructor in English, 1950-53; Seattle University, assistant professor, professor of English, chairman of department, 1964-68; California State University, dean of humanities, 1968-72, professor, 1972-91, director of graduate studies, 1977-78, chairman of English department, 1978-84, now professor emeritus; University Journal, editor, 1974-78. **Publications:** Gerard Manley Hopkins: A Study of His Ignatian Spirit, 1959; Victorian Portraits: Hopkins and Pater, 1965; The Temper of Victorian Belief: Studies in the Victorian Religious Fiction, 1972; Ruskin's Landscape of Beatitude, 1980; The Great Sacrifice: Studies in Hopkins, 1983; Hopkins' Sanctifying Imagination, 1985; The Ignatian Personality of G.M. Hopkins, 1990; (ed. with M.E. Allsopp) Saving Beauty: Further Studies in Hopkins, 1994; Hopkins' Achieved Self, 1996, rev. ed., 2002. **Address:** Department of English, California State University, 209 Taylor Hall, 400 W 1st St., Chico, CA 95929, U.S.A. **Online address:** ddownes@mail.csuchico.edu

DOWNES, Jeremy M. American (born United States), b. 1961?. **Genres:** Poetry, Humanities, Women's Studies And Issues, Literary Criticism And History. **Career:** Auburn University, professor of English. Writer. **Publications:** Recursive Desire: Rereading Epic Tradition, 1997; The Lost Atlas of Desire, 2006; Dark Village Haiku, 2008; The Female Homer: An Exploration of Women's Epic Poetry, 2010; Poems Too Small to Read, 2011. **Address:** Department of English, Auburn University, 9030 Haley Ctr., Auburn, AL 36849, U.S.A. **Online address:** downejm@auburn.edu

DOWNEY, Tom. American (born United States), b. 1965?. **Genres:** Economics, History, Business/Trade/Industry. **Career:** University of South Carolina, Papers of Henry Laurens, assistant editor, 1998-2000, South Carolina Encyclopedia Project, managing editor, 2000-04; Princeton University, Papers of Thomas Jefferson, assistant editor, 2004-. Historian. **Publications:** (ed.) The South Carolina Encyclopedia, 2006; Planting a Capitalist South: Masters, Merchants, and Manufacturers in the Southern Interior, 1790-1860, 2006. **Address:** Papers of Thomas Jefferson, Princeton University, Firestone C-9-J, Princeton, NJ 08544, U.S.A. **Online address:** downey@princeton.edu

DOWNIE, Leonard. American (born United States), b. 1942. **Genres:** Law, Urban Studies, Writing/Journalism. **Career:** The Ohio State University Alumni Association, managing editor, 1963-64; The Washington Post, reporter, 1964-70, assistant city editor, 1970-71, deputy metro editor, 1972-74, assistant managing editor, 1974-79, London correspondent, 1979-82, national editor, 1982-84, managing editor, 1984-91, executive editor, 1991-2008, vice president-at-large, 2008-; American University, instructor in communications, 1972-73; Arizona State University, Walter Cronkite School of Journalism and Mass Communication, Weil Family professor of journalism, 2009-; Los Angeles Times, Washington Post News Service, board director; International Herald Tribune, board director; Missouri School of Journalism, Investigative Reporters and Editors Inc., board director, 2009-; Center for Investigative Reporting, board director, 2009-. **Publications:** Justice Denied: The Case for Reform of the Courts, 1971; Mortgage on America, 1974; The New Muckrakers, 1976; (with R.G. Kaiser) The News about the News: American Journalism in Peril, 2002; The Rules of the Game, 2009. Contributor to books and periodicals. **Address:** Walter Cronkite School of Journalism and, Mass Communication, Arizona State University, Rm 389, 555 N Central Ave., Ste. 302, Phoenix, AZ 85004, U.S.A. **Online address:** leonard.downie@asu.edu

DOWNIE, Mary Alice. Canadian (born Canada), b. 1934. **Genres:** Essays, Children's Fiction, Young Adult Fiction, Poetry, Songs/Lyrics And Libretti, Botany, Children's Non-fiction, Homes/Gardens, Local History/

Rural Topics, Mythology/Folklore, Picture/Board Books, Translations. **Career:** Maclean-Hunter, stenographer, 1955; Marketing Magazine, reporter, 1955-56; Canadian Medical Association Journal, editorial assistant, 1956-57; Oxford University Press, librarian and publicity manager, 1958-59; Kingston Whig-Standard, book review editor, 1973-78; Newnham College, staff, 1988-. Writer and critic. **Publications:** (With J. Downie) Honor Bound, 1971; The King's Loon, 1980; Snow Paws, 1996; Bright Paddles, 1999; (with J. Downie) Danger in Disguise, 2000; Pioneer ABC, 2005. FICTION: (with J. Downie) Honor Bound, 1971, rev. ed., 1981; Scared Sarah, 1974; Dragon on Parade, 1974; ; The Last Ship, 1980; (with G. Rawlyk) A Proper Acadian, 1981; Jenny Greenteeth, 1984; (with J. Downie) Alison's Ghosts, 1984; The Cat Park, 1993. OTHERS: (ed. with B. Robertson) The New Wind Has Wings: Poems from Canada, 1968; (trans.) The Magical Adventures of Pierre, 1974; The Witch of the North: Folktales from French Canada, 1975; (with M. Hamilton) And Some Brought Flowers: Plants in a New World, 1980; (with J.H. Gilliland) Seeds and Weeds: A Book of Country Crafts, 1981; The Wicked Fairy Wife, 1983; (with J.H. Gilliland) Stones and Cones: Country Crafts for Kids, 1984; (with B. Robertson) The New Wind Has Wings, 1984; (with E. Greene and M.A. Thompson) The Window of Dreams, 1986; (with B. Robertson) The Well-Filled Cupboard: Everyday Pleasures of Home and Garden, 1987; How the Devil Got His Cat, 1988; (with M.H. Huang-Hsu) The Buffalo Boy and the Weaver Girl, 1989; (ed. with B. Robertson) Doctor Dwarf and Other Poems for Children by A.M. Klein, 1990; Cathal the Giant Killer and the Dun Shaggy Filly, 1991; (with M.A. Thompson) Written in Stone: A Kingston Reader, 1993; (with B. Robertson) Early Voices, 2010. **Address:** 190 Union St., Kingston, ON K7L 2P6, Canada. **Online address:** downiej@queensu.ca

DOWNIE, R(obert) S(ilcock). Scottish (born Scotland), b. 1933. **Genres:** Education, Ethics, Humanities, Medicine/Health, Philosophy, Biography, Music. **Career:** University of Glasgow, lecturer, 1959-67, senior lecturer, 1968-69, professor of moral philosophy, 1969-, Stevenson lecturer in medical ethics, 1985-88, honorary professor research fellow; University of Syracuse, visiting professor of philosophy, 1963-64, University of Sydney, visiting professor 1997. Writer. **Publications:** Government Action and Morality, 1964; (with E. Telfer) Respect for Persons, 1969; Roles and Values: An Introduction to Social Ethics, 1971; (with E. Telfer and E.M. Loudfoot) Education and Personal Relationships, 1974; (co-author) Values in Social Work, 1976; (with E. Telfer) Caring and Curing, 1980; Healthy Respect: Ethics in Health Care, 1987, 2nd ed., 1994; (with C. Fyfe and A. Tannahill) Health Promotion: Models and Values, 1990; (with B. Charlton) The Making of a Doctor: Medical Education in Theory and Practice, 1992; Francis Hutcheson, 1994; The Healing Arts: An Illustrated Oxford Anthology, 1994; (with F. Randall) Palliative Care Ethics, 1996, 2nd ed., 1999; (ed.) Medical Ethics, 1996; (with J. Macnaughton and F. Randall) Clinical Judgement: Evidence in Practice, 2000; (with F. Randall) The Philosophy of Palliative Care: Critique and Reconstruction, 2006; (with J. Macnaughton) Bioethics and the Humanities, 2007; (with F. Randall) End of Life Choices, 2009. **Address:** Department of Moral Philosophy, University of Glasgow, Glasgow, G12 8QQ, Scotland. **Online address:** r.downie@philosophy.arts.gla.ac.uk

DOWNING, David A(lmon). (Russell Almon). American (born United States), b. 1958. **Genres:** Novels, Children's Fiction, Sports/Fitness, Young Adult Fiction. **Career:** University of Washington Extension, instructor in fiction writing, 1990-; CNA Companies (an architectural and engineering firm), marketing writer, 1992-. Writer. **Publications:** (As Russell Almon with W.R. Clevenger) The Kid Can't Miss!, 1992. **Address:** 143 NW 79th St., Seattle, WA 98117-3022, U.S.A.

DOWNING, David C(laude). American (born United States), b. 1951. **Genres:** Literary Criticism And History, Biography, Novels. **Career:** University of California, teaching fellow, 1974-77; Westmont College, Department of English, assistant professor, 1977-83, associate professor, 1983-89, professor, 1989-94; Elizabethtown College, visiting assistant professor of English, 1994-97, associate professor of English, 1997-2001, R.W. Schlosser associate professor of English, 2001-03, R.W. Schlosser professor of English, 2003-. Writer. **Publications:** What You Know Might Not Be So: 220 Misinterpretations of Bible Texts Explained, 1987; 303 Dumb Spelling Mistakes (sic): And What You Can Do about Them, 1990; Imagine Yourself a Perfect Speller, 1990; NTC's Dictionary of American Spelling, 1991; NTC's Pocket Guide for Doubtful Spellers, 1992; NTC's Spell it Right Dictionary, 1992; Planets in Peril: A Critical Study of C.S. Lewis's Ransom Trilogy, 1992; The Most Reluctant Convert: C.S. Lewis's Journey to Faith, 2002; Into the Region of

Awe: Mysticism in C.S. Lewis, 2005; Into the Wardrobe: C.S. Lewis and the Narnia Chronicles, 2005; (with D.K. Williams) McGraw-Hill Dictionary of Misspelled and Easily Confused Words: Choose the Right Word and Spell it Correctly!, 2006; A South Divided: Portraits of Dissent in the Confederacy, 2007; Looking for the King: An Inklings Novel, 2010. **Address:** Department of English, Elizabethtown College, Rm. 100, Wenger Ctr., 1 Alpha Dr., Elizabethtown, PA 17022-2290, U.S.A. **Online address:** downindc@etown.edu

DOWNING, Michael (Bernard). American (born United States), b. 1958. **Genres:** Novels, History, Plays/Screenplays, Essays, Adult Non-fiction. **Career:** Harvard College, Harvard-Shrewsbury fellow, 1980-81; Oceanus Periodical, senior editor, 1983-84; FMR Periodical, senior editor, 1984-86; Bentley College, instructor in English, 1987-88; Wheelock College, instructor, 1988-91, assistant professor of humanities and director of writing program, 1992-97; Tufts University, lecturer in creative writing, 1998-. **Publications:** A Narrow Time, 1987; Mother of God, 1990; Perfect Agreement, 1997; Breakfast With Scot: A Novel, 1999; Shoes Outside the Door: Desire, Devotion and Excess at San Francisco Zen Center, 2001; Spring Forward: The Annual Madness of Daylight Saving Time, 2005; Life with Sudden Death: A Tale of Moral Hazard and Medical Misadventure, 2009. Contributor to periodicals. **Address:** Harold Matson Company Inc., 276 5th Ave., New York, NY 10001, U.S.A. **Online address:** michael.downing@tufts.edu

DOWNS, Dorothy. American (born United States), b. 1937. **Genres:** Art/Art History, Humanities. **Career:** University of Miami, Lowe Art Museum, registrar, 1977-78, New Gallery, director, 1986-87; instructor in art history, 1996, Native American Art Collection, curatorial consultant, 2000; Tribal Art Society, founder and president; Four Corners Gallery, director, 1978-79; art dealer, consultant and appraiser, 1979-80; Center for the Fine Arts, Center Art Store, manager, 1982-84; Florida Keys Community College, instructor in art history, 1995. Writer. **Publications:** (Contrib.) Miccosukee Arts & Crafts, 1982; Art of the Florida Seminole and Miccosukee Indians, 1995; Patchwork: Seminole and Miccosukee Art and Activities, 2005. Contributor to magazines and newspapers. **Address:** 5650 SW 87th St., Miami, FL 33143, U.S.A. **Online address:** dordow@earthlink.net

DOWNS, Robert C. S. American (born United States), b. 1937. **Genres:** Novels, Novellas/Short Stories, Plays/Screenplays. **Career:** Phillips Exeter Academy, instructor in English, 1962-63; City University of New York, Hunter College, lecturer in English, 1965-66; Life, sales promotion writer, 1966-68; Colby Junior College, assistant professor of English, 1968-73; University of Arizona, associate professor of English and director of creative writing program, 1973-80; Pennsylvania State University, professor of English and director of writing program, 1980-98, professor emeritus, 1998-. Writer. **Publications:** Going Gently, 1973; Peoples, 1974; Country Dying (novel), 1976; White Mama, 1980; Living Together, 1983; White Mama, 1980; The Fifth Season, 2000; The Cape May Stories, 2008. Contributor of articles to periodicals. **Address:** Department of English, Pennsylvania State University, 111 Sparks Bldg., University Park, PA 16802, U.S.A. **Online address:** rcd4@psu.edu

DOWTY, Alan K. American (born United States), b. 1940. **Genres:** International Relations/Current Affairs, Politics/Government, History. **Career:** City College of Chicago, instructor in political science, 1962-63; Hebrew University of Jerusalem, instructor, 1964-65, lecturer, 1965-72, senior lecturer, 1972-75, International Relations Department, chairman, 1974-75; Tel Aviv University, lecturer, 1968-69; Northeastern Illinois University, visiting assistant professor, 1970-71; University of Chicago, visiting research fellow, 1970-71; University of Illinois, visiting assistant professor, 1971; Institute for International Relations, executive director, 1972-74; Planning Branch of Israeli, staff, 1974-75; University of Notre Dame, associate professor, 1975-78, professor of political science, 1978-2004, professor emeritus, 2004-, Institute for International Peace Studies, senior associate; Twentieth Century Fund project, director, 1983-85; Haifa University, visiting professor, 1985-87; University of Calgary, Kahanoff chair professor of Israel studies, 2004-06; Association for Israel Studies, president, 2005-07. Consultant and writer. **Publications:** The Limits of American Isolation: the United States and the Crimean War, 1971; The Role of Great Power Guarantees in International Peace Agreements, 1974; Middle-East Crisis: U.S. Decision-Making in 1958, 1970 and 1973, 1984; Closed Borders: The Contemporary Assault on Free Movement, 1987; The Arab-Israeli Conflict: Perspectives, 1984, 2nd ed., 1991; The Jewish State: A Century Later, 1998; (ed.) Critical Issues in Israeli Society, 2004;

Israel/Palestine, 2005. Contributor to periodicals. **Address:** College of Arts & Letters, University of Notre Dame, 100 O'Shaughnessy Hall, Notre Dame, IN 46556, U.S.A. **Online address:** dowty.1@nd.edu

DOYLE, Brian. Canadian (born Canada), b. 1935. **Genres:** Children's Fiction, Young Adult Fiction, Natural History, Social Sciences, Literary Criticism And History. **Career:** Glebe Collegiate, Department of English, teacher, head; Ottawa Technical School, English teacher, 1969-91, now emeritus; Ottawa Board of Education, Queen's University, faculty; Toronto Telegram, journalist. **Publications:** (Ed. and comp.) Who's Who of Boy's Writers and Illustrators, 1964; (ed. and comp.) The Who's Who of Children's Literature, 1968; Hey Dad!, 1978; You Can Pick Me up at Peggy's Cove, 1979; Up to Low, 1982; Angel Square, 1984; Easy Avenue, 1988; Covered Bridge, 1990; Spud Sweetgrass, 1992; Spud in Winter, 1995; Uncle Ronald, 1996; Dam Lies, 1998; The Low Life: Five Great Tales From Up and Down the River, 1999; Mary Ann Alice, 2001; Boy O'Boy, 2003; à la Guerre Comme à la Guerre!, 2006; Pure Spring, 2007. Contributor to newspapers and magazines. **Address:** c/o Author Mail, Groundwood/Douglas & McIntyre Children's Books, 585 Bloor St. W, 2nd Fl., Toronto, ON M6G 1K5, Canada.

DOYLE, Charles (Desmond). (Mike Doyle). Canadian/British (born England), b. 1928. **Genres:** Poetry, Literary Criticism And History, Politics/Government, Biography. **Career:** University of Auckland, lecturer, 1961-66, senior lecturer in English and American literature, 1966-68; Yale University, visiting fellow in American studies, 1967-68; University of Victoria, associate professor, 1968-76, professor of English, 1976-93, professor emeritus, 1993-; Tuatara Magazine, editor, 1969-74. **Publications:** A Splinter of Glass: Poems 1951-55, 1956; Distances: Poems 1956-61, 1963; Messages for Herod, 1965; A Sense of Place: Poems, 1965; (as Mike Doyle) Noah, 1970; R.A.K. Mason, 1970; Earth Meditations, 1971; Abandoned Sofa, 1971; Earth shot, 1972; Preparing for the Ark, 1973; Planes, 1975; Stone dancer, 1976; James K. Baxter, 1976; William Carlos Williams and the American Poem, 1982; A Steady Hand, 1983; Richard Aldington: A Biography, 1989; The Urge to Raise Hats, 1989; Separate Fidelities, 1991; Intimate Absences: Selected Poems, 1993; Trout Spawning at Lardeau River, 1997; Living Ginger, 2004; Paper Trombones, 2007; The Watchman's Dance, 2009. EDITOR/CO-EDITOR: Recent Poetry in New Zealand, 1965; William Carlos Williams: The Critical Heritage, 1980; The New Reality: The Politics of Restraint in British Columbia, 1984; Wallace Stevens: The Critical Heritage, 1985; After Bennett: A New Politics for British Columbia, 1986; Richard Aldington: Reappraisals, 1990. **Address:** 641 Oliver St., Victoria, BC V8S 4W2, Canada. **Online address:** doylec@uvic.ca

DOYLE, Debra. Also writes as Robyn Tallis, Victor Appleton, Martin Delrio, Nicholas Adams. American (born United States), b. 1952?. **Genres:** Science Fiction/Fantasy, Novellas/Short Stories, Novels, Biography, Literary Criticism And History. **Career:** Computer Assisted Learning Center, teacher of fiction writing. Novelist. **Publications:** ALL WITH J.D. MACDONALD: CIRCLE OF MAGIC SERIES: The Prisoners of Bell Castle, 1989; School of Wizardry, 1990; Tournament and Tower, 1990; City by the Sea, 1990; The Prince's Players, 1990; The High King's Daughter, 1990. AS ROBYN TALLIS: Night of Ghosts and Lightning, 1989; Zero-Sum Games, 1989. AS NICHOLAS ADAMS: Pep Rally, 1991. AS VICTOR APPLETON: Monster Machine, 1991; Aquatech Warriors, 1991. OTHER NOVELS: Timecrime Inc., 1991; Night of the Living Rat, 1992; Knight's Wyrd, 1992; Groogleman, 1996; Requiem for Boone, 2000; Land of Mist and Snow, 2006; Lincoln's Sword, 2010. MAGEWORLDS SERIES: The Price of the Stars, 1992; Starpilot's Grave, 1993; By Honor Betray'd, 1994; The Gathering Flame, 1995; The Long Hunt, 1996; The Stars Asunder, 1999; A Working of Stars, 2002. BAD BLOOD SERIES: Bad Blood, 1993; Hunters' Moon, 1994; Judgment Night, 1995. AS MARTIN DELRIO: Mortal Kombat, 1995; Spider-Man Super-Thriller: Midnight Justice, 1996; Spider-Man Super-Thriller: Global War, 1996; Prince Valiant, 1997. Wroks appear in anthologies. **Address:** c/o Russ Galen, Scovil Chichak Galen Literary Agency, 276 5th Ave., Ste. 708, New York, NY 10001, U.S.A. **Online address:** doylemacdonald@sff.net

DOYLE, Dennis M(ichael). American (born United States), b. 1952. **Genres:** Theology/Religion, Humanities. **Career:** Xavier University, part-time instructor, 1981-82; Ohio University, prison program, part-time instructor, 1981-84; University of Dayton, Department of Religious Studies, assistant professor, 1984-89, associate professor, 1989-2000, professor, 2000-.

Educator and writer. **Publications:** The Church Emerging from Vatican II: A Popular Approach to Contemporary Catholicism, 1992, rev. ed., 2002; Communion Ecclesiology, 2000; (with P. Doyle) Rumors at School, 2000. Contributor to periodicals. **Address:** Department of Religious Studies, University of Dayton, 333 Humanities, 300 College Pk., Dayton, OH 45469-1530, U.S.A. **Online address:** dennis.doyle@notes.udayton.edu

DOYLE, Jeff. Australian (born Australia), b. 1952. **Genres:** Local History/Rural Topics, Mystery/Crime/Suspense. **Career:** University of New South Wales, Australian Defence Force Academy Campus, lecturer, senior lecturer, 1983-, visiting fellow; University of New South Wales, Duntroon Campus, professor. Writer. **Publications:** (Ed. with B. Moore) England and the Spanish Armada: Papers Arising from the 1988 Conference University College University of New South Wales Australian Defence Force Academy Canberra Australia, 1990; (ed. with J. Grey and P. Pierce) Vietnam Days: Australia and the Impact of Vietnam, 1991; (ed. with J. Grey) Vietnam: War Myth and Memory; Comparative Perspectives on Australia's War in Vietnam, 1992; (comp. with S. Ballyn) Douglas Stewart: A Bibliography, 1996; (with J. Grey and P. Pierce) Australia's Vietnam War, 2002; Silver Lining, 2004; Irresistible Leverage, 2006. **Address:** School of Humanities and Social Sciences, Australian Defence Force Academy Campus, University of New South Wales, Northcott Dr., PO Box 7916, Canberra, AC 2600, Australia. **Online address:** j.doyle2@adfa.edu.au

DOYLE, Larry. American (born United States), b. 1958. **Genres:** Humor/Satire, Novels, Science Fiction/Fantasy. **Career:** United Press Intl., medical and science reporter, 1983-89; First Comics, editor-in-chief, 1989; National Lampoon, editor, 1991; Spy Magazine, deputy editor, 1992-93; New York Magazine, deputy editor, 1994-97; The Simpsons, supervising producer, 1997-2001. Writer. **Publications:** NOVELS: I Love You, Beth Cooper, 2007; Go, Mutants!, 2010. COLLECTION: Deliriously Happy and Other Bad Thoughts, 2011. OTHERS: This Sucks, Change It!: Giant Inactivity Book with Handy Remote Control, 1995; Huh Huh for Hollywood, 1996. **Address:** Ecco Press, 10 E 53rd St., New York, NY 10022-5244, U.S.A.

DOYLE, Mike. See **DOYLE, Charles (Desmond).**

DOYLE, Paul E. American (born United States), b. 1946?. **Genres:** Autobiography/Memoirs. **Career:** Bureau of Narcotics, agent; Dangerous Drugs, agent; Drug Enforcement Administration, agent; New England Chapter of the Association, chairman; Mir Pace Intl., director. Writer. **Publications:** Hot Shots and Heavy Hits: Tales of an Undercover Drug Agent, 2004. Contributor to periodicals. **Address:** Mir Pace Intl., 1173 Nantasket Ave., Ste. C-6, Hull, MA 02045, U.S.A. **Online address:** hotshotsheavyhits@hotmail.com

DOYLE, Paul I(gnatius). American (born United States), b. 1959. **Genres:** Business/Trade/Industry, Economics, Money/Finance. **Career:** Delta Management Group, vice president, 1987-92; Donnelly Corp., operations development manager, 1992-, global director organizational development, 1993-99; GHSP Inc., vice president of human resources, 1999-2004, vice president of sales and marketing, 2004-07, president and chief executive officer, 2007-. Writer. **Publications:** (With R.J. Doyle) Gain-Management: A Process for Building Teamwork, Productivity, and Profitability Throughout Your Organization, 1991. Contributor to periodicals. **Address:** AMACOM Books, 1601 Broadway, New York, NY 10019, U.S.A. **Online address:** paul.doyle@donnelly.com

DOYLE, Robert Charles. American (born United States), b. 1946. **Genres:** History, Military/Defense/Arms Control, Documentaries/Reportage, Humanities. **Career:** Checkered Flag Motor Car Co., automobile salesperson, 1972; Public Schools in Philadelphia, substitute teacher, 1972; Joint Personnel Recovery Agency, historical consultant; professional musician and band leader, 1972-86; Pennsylvania State University, University Park, lecturer in American studies, 1974-77; Bob Doyle Talent Agency, owner, 1978-86; Pennsylvania State University, University Park, American studies program, Department of English, lecturer, 1987-94; Wilhelms University, Department of English, Fulbright lecturer, 1994-95; Marc Bloch University, American studies, visiting professor, 1995-98; Franciscan University, Department of History, instructor, 2000-01, associate professor, 2001-07, professor, 2007-. Writer. **Publications:** (Intro.) Learning the Fiddler's Ways, 1980; Voices from Captivity: Interpreting the American POW Narrative, 1994; A Prisoner's Duty: Great Escapes in U.S. Military History, 1997; (contrib.) Shaw and Other Matters, 1998; (contrib.) War and Literature, 1999; Enemy in Our Hands:

America's Treatment of Enemy Prisoners of War From the Revolution to the War on Terror, 2010. Contributor of articles to periodicals. **Address:** Department of History, Franciscan University, 1235 University Blvd., Steubenville, OH 43952, U.S.A. **Online address:** rdoyle@franciscan.edu

DOYLE, Robert J. American (born United States), b. 1931. **Genres:** Administration/Management, Business/Trade/Industry, Money/Finance. **Career:** Ford Motor Co., personnel administrator, 1957-64; Wolverine World Wide, training director, 1964-67; Donnelly Mirrors Inc., director of human resources, 1967-74; Precision Castparts Corp., director of personnel, 1974-75; Hay Associates, principal, 1975-77; Delta Management Group, president, 1977-; Scanlon Plan Associates, co-founder, president; Widener University, Graduate School of Management, adjunct professor of taxation; American College, associate professor of finance and insurance; Wharton School of the University of Pennsylvania, Huebner fellow; Mandeville Financial Services Inc., senior vice president. Writer. **Publications:** Tuffy, 1942; Gainsharing and Productivity, 1983; (with P.I. Doyle) Gain-Management: A Process for Building Teamwork, Productivity and Profitability throughout Your Organization, 1992; (with S.R. Leimberg) The Tools and Techniques of Life Insurance Planning, 1993, 3rd ed., 2004; (co-author) Tools and Techniques of Investment Planning, 2006; (co-author) Tools and Techniques of Financial Planning, 8th ed., 2007. **Address:** 3617 224th Pl SE, Issaquah, OR 98029, U.S.A.

DOYLE, Roddy. Irish (born Ireland), b. 1958. **Genres:** Novels, Plays/Screenplays, Novellas/Short Stories, Young Adult Non-fiction. **Career:** Greendale Community School, English and geography teacher, 1980-93; full-time writer, 1993-. **Publications:** NOVELS: War, 1989; Paddy Clarke Ha Ha Ha, 1993; Brownbread: And War, 1994; The Woman Who Walked into Doors, 1996; Not Just for Christmas, 1999; (co-author) Yeats is Dead!: A Mystery by Fifteen Irish Writers, 2001; Paula Spencer, 2006; Mad Weekend, 2006; Wilderness, 2007; Deireadh seachtaine craiceáilte, 2007; Her Mother's Face, 2008; A Greyhound of a Girl, 2011. THE BARRYTOWN TRILOGY: The Commitments, 1987; The Snapper, 1990; The Van, 1992. THE LAST ROUNDUP SERIES: A Star Called Henry, 1999; Oh, Play that Thing: Volume Two of The Last Roundup, 2004. FOR CHILDREN: The Giggler Treatment, 2000; Rover Saves Christmas, 2001; Rory & Ita, 2002; Meanwhile Adventures, 2004. SHORT STORIES: Teaching, 2007; Black Hoodie, 2007; The Dog, 2007; The Deportees and Other Stories, 2007. The Extra Big Rover Adventures, 2009; The Dead Republic, 2010; Bullfighting, 2011. Contributor to books and periodicals. **Address:** Secker & Warburg Ltd., 20 Vauxhall Bridge Rd., London, GL SW1V 2SA, England.

DOYLE, William. British (born England), b. 1942. **Genres:** History. **Career:** University of York, lecturer, 1967-78, senior lecturer in history, 1978-81; University of South Carolina, visiting professor, 1969-70; Universite de Bordeaux III, visiting professor, 1976; University of Nottingham, professor of history, 1981-85, head of department, 1982-85; University of Bristol, head of department, 1986-90, professor of history, 1990-2008, emeritus professor and senior research fellow, 2008-; Ecole des Hautes Etudes en Sciences Sociales, visiting professor, 1988; Oxford University, All Souls College, visiting fellow, 1991-2000; University of Richmond, Douglas Southall Freeman Visiting Professor, 2010. Writer. **Publications:** The Parlement of Bordeaux and the End of the Old Regime, 1771-90, 1974; The Old European Order, 1660-1800, 1978, 2nd ed., 1992; Origins of the French Revolution, 1980, 3rd ed., 1998; (trans.) G. Chaussinand-Nogaret, The French Nobility in the Eighteenth Century: From Feudalism to Enlightenment, 1985; The Ancien Regime, 1986, 2nd ed., 2001; The Oxford History of the French Revolution, 1989, 2nd ed., 2002; Officers, Nobles and Revolutionaries: Essays on Eighteenth-Century France, 1995; Venality: The Sale of Offices in Eighteenth Century France, 1996; Jansenism: Catholic Resistance to Authority: From the Reformation to the French Revolution, 1999; (ed.) Old Regime France, 1648-1788, 2001; The French Revolution: A Very Short Introduction, 2001; Aristocracy and Its Enemies in the Age of Revolution, 2009; Aristocracy: A Very Short Introduction, 2010. EDITOR: (with C. Haydon) Robespierre, 1999; (with M. Crook and A. Forrest) Enlightenment and Revolution: Essays in Honour of Norman Hampson, 2004; The Oxford Handbook of the Ancien Regime, 2011. CO-EDITOR: The Blackwell Dictionary of Historians, 1988; The Impact of the French Revolution on European Consciousness, 1989. **Address:** Department of Historical Studies, University of Bristol, G.51 13 Woodland Rd., Bristol, SM BS8 1TB, England. **Online address:** william.doyle@bristol.ac.uk

DOZIER, Cheryl. American (born United States), b. 1960. **Genres:** Education, Literary Criticism And History. **Career:** Vassar College, visiting professor; State University of New York, assistant professor. Writer. **Publications:** (With P. Johnston and R. Rogers) Critical Literacy/Critical Teaching: Tools for Preparing Responsive Teachers, 2006; Responsive Literacy Coaching: Tools for Creating and Sustaining Purposeful Change, 2006. **Address:** University at Albany, State University of New York, School of Education-349, Albany, NY 12222, U.S.A. **Online address:** cldnsc@aol.com

DOZIER, Zoe. *See* **BROWNING, Dixie Burrus.**

DRABBLE, Margaret. British (born England), b. 1939. **Genres:** Novels, Young Adult Fiction, Plays/Screenplays, Literary Criticism And History, Biography, Poetry, Young Adult Non-fiction. **Career:** Writer. **Publications:** NOVELS: A Summer Bird Cage, 1963; The Garrick Year, 1964; The Millstone, 1965 in US as Thank You All Very Much, 1973; Jerusalem the Golden, 1967; The Waterfall, 1969; (ed. with B.S. Johnson) London Consequences, 1972; The Needle's Eye, 1972; The Realms of Gold, 1975; The Ice Age, 1977; The Middle Ground, 1980; The Radiant Way, 1987; A Natural Curiosity, 1989; The Gates of Ivory, 1991; The Witch of Exmoor, 1996; The Peppered Moth, 2001; The Seven Sisters, 2002; The Red Queen: A Transcultural Tragicomedy, 2004; The Sea Lady: A Late Romance, 2006. OTHERS: Wordsworth, 1966; Virginia Woolf: A Personal Debt, 1973; Arnold Bennett: A Biography, 1974; (ed. and intro.) Lady Susan: The Watsons: Sanditon, 1974; (ed.) Genius of Thomas Hardy, 1976; (ed. with C. Osborne) New Stories 1, 1976; For Queen and Country: Britain in the Victorian Age, 1978 in US as For Queen and Country: Victorian England, 1979; A Writer's Britain: Landscape in Literature, 1979; The Oxford Companion to English Literature, 1985, 6th ed., 2006; (ed. with J. Stringer) The Concise Oxford Companion to English Literature, 1987, 3rd ed., 2007; Stratford Revisited, 1989; Safe As Houses, 1990; (ed.) Wuthering Heights and Poems, 1993; Angus Wilson: A Biography, 1996; (intro.) The Woodlanders, 1997; (intro.) Far from the Madding Crowd, 2001; (intro.) Mansfield Park, 2008; (intro.) Pride and Prejudice, 2008; The Pattern in the Carpet: A Personal History with Jigsaws, 2009; (intro.) The Time Machine: The Invisible Man, 2010; A Day in the Life of a Smiling Woman: Complete Short Stories, 2011. Works appear in anthologies. **Address:** Peters Fraser & Dunlop, The Rights House, 34-43 Russell St., London, GL WC2B 5HA, England.

DRACUP, Angela. Also writes as Angela Drake, Caroline Sibson. British (born England), b. 1943. **Genres:** Novels, Romance/Historical, Young Adult Fiction, Biography, Autobiography/Memoirs, Children's Fiction. **Career:** Educational psychologist, 1964-72, 1975-78, 1981-; College of Ripon and York St. John, senior lecturer, 1975-78. Writer. **Publications:** AS CAROLINE SIBSON: The Chosen One, 1988; Birds of a Feather, 1990. AS ANGELA DRACUP: The Placing, 1991; The Split, 1993; The Ultimate Gift, 2000; Voices from the Past, 2000; Where Darkness Begins, 2004; A Kind of Justice, 2005; Retribution, 2006; The Burden of Doubt, 2007; The Killing Club, 2010. RAINBOW ROMANCE SERIES: An Independent Spirit, 1984; Bavarian Overture, 1986; A Tender Ambition, 1986; A Man to Trust, 1987; Dark Impulse, 1987; Star Attraction, 1988; Dearest Pretender, 1989; Venetian Captive, 1989; Mozart's Darling, 1996. AS ANGELA DRAKE: The Mistress Woman of Dreams, 1996; Master of Destiny, 2000; Stay Very Close, 2001. **Address:** Jane Conway-Gordon Ltd., 1 Old Compton St., London, GL W1D 5JA, England. **Online address:** frank@fdracup.freeserve.co.uk

DRAGOMÁN, György. Hungarian/Romanian (born Romania), b. 1973?. **Genres:** Novels. **Career:** Writer and translator. **Publications:** Pusztítás Könyve, 2002; Fehér Király: Regény, 2005. **Address:** Budapest, Hungary. **Online address:** dragoman.gy@gmail.com

DRAKE, Albert (Dee). American (born United States), b. 1935. **Genres:** Novels, Novellas/Short Stories, Poetry, Young Adult Non-fiction, Young Adult Fiction, Transportation. **Career:** Oregon Research Institute, research assistant, 1963-64; University of Oregon, research assistant, 1965, teaching assistant, 1965-66; Michigan State University, assistant professor, 1966-70, associate professor, 1970-79, professor of English, 1979-91, professor emeritus, 1991-. Writer. **Publications:** POETRY: Crap Game, 1968; (ed. and contrib.) Michigan Signatures: An Anthology of Current Michigan Poetry, 1969; (with L. Inada and D. Lawder) 3 Northwest Poets, 1970; Poems, 1972; Riding Bike in the 'Fifties, 1973; By Breathing In and Out, 1974; Cheap Thrills: Poems, 1975; Returning to Oregon: Poems, 1975; Roadsalt, 1976; Reaching for the Sun, 1979; Garage: Poems, 1980; Homesick, 1988. FICTION: The Postcard Mysteries & Other Stories, 1976; Tillamook Burn, 1977; In the

Time of Surveys & Other Stories of Americans Abroad, 1978; One Summer, 1979; Beyond the Pavement, 1981; I Remember the Day James Dean Died and Other Stories, 1983. NONFICTION: Assuming the Position, 1973; The Big Little GTO Book, 1982; Street Was Fun in '51, 1982; A 1950's Rod & Custom Builder's Wishbook, 1985; Herding Goats, 1989; Hot Rodder!, 1992; Flat Out, 1994; Fifties Flashback, 1998; Overtures to Motion, 2003; Age of Hot Rods: Essays on Rods, Custom Cars and Their Drivers from the 1950s to Today, 2008. Contributor of articles to magazines. Works appear in anthologies. **Address:** Department of English, Michigan State University, 400 Albert Ave., East Lansing, MI 48823-4407, U.S.A.

DRAKE, Alicia. French/American (born United States), b. 1968. **Genres:** Art/Art History, Biography, Autobiography/Memoirs, Fash Ion/Costume, Photography, Social Sciences. **Career:** Writer. **Publications:** A Shopper's Guide to Paris Fashion, 1997; The Beautiful Fall: Lagerfeld, Saint Laurent, and Glorious Excess in 1970s Paris, 2006. **Address:** c/o Lizzy Kramer, David Higham Associates, 5-8 Lower John St., Golden Sq., London, GL W1F 9HA, England.

DRAKE, Angela. *See* **DRACUP, Angela.**

DRAKE, Bonnie. *See* **DELINSKY, Barbara (Ruth Greenberg).**

DRAKE, Charles D. (Charles Lum Drake). British (born England), b. 1924. **Genres:** Law. **Career:** Drake and Noone, partner, 1954-57; Newcastle upon Tyne Polytechni, lecturer in law 1957-64; University of Durham, lecturer, 1964-68, senior lecturer in law, 1968-72; University of Leeds, professor of English law, 1972-, faculty of law, dean, 1974-78, head of department, 1978-82; University of South Carolina, visiting professor, 1978-79; Vanderbilt University, visiting professor, 1981, 1985-86. Writer. **Publications:** Law of Partnership, 1972, 2nd ed., 1977; Labour Law, 1969, 3rd ed., 1981; (with B. Bercusson) The Employment Acts 1974-1980, 1981; (with F. Wright) Law of Health and Safety at Work, 1983; Trade Union Acts, 1985. Contributor to books. **Address:** Sweet & Maxwell, Cheriton House, PO Box 2000, Andover, SP10 9AH, England.

DRAKE, Charles Lum. *See* **DRAKE, Charles D.**

DRAKE, David A. American (born United States), b. 1945. **Genres:** Novels, Novellas/Short Stories, Science Fiction/Fantasy. **Career:** Town of Chapel Hill, assistant town attorney, 1972-80. Freelance writer, 1981-. **Publications:** HAMMER'S SLAMMERS SERIES: Hammer's Slammers, 1979; Cross the Stars, 1984; At Any Price, 1985; Counting the Cost, 1987; Rolling Hot, 1989; The Warrior, 1991; The Sharp End, 1993; The Voyage, 1993; Paying the Piper, 2002. STAR HUNTERS SERIES: (comp.) Men Hunting Things, 1988; Things Hunting Men, 1988; Bluebloods, 1990. NORTHWORLD SERIES: Northworld, 1990; Vengeance, 1991; Justice, 1992. GENERAL SERIES WITH S.M. STIRLING: The Forge, 1991; The Hammer, 1992; The Anvil, 1993; The Steel, 1993; The Sword, 1995; The Chosen, 1996; The Reformer, 1999. REACHES SERIES: Igniting the Reaches, 1994; Through the Breach, 1995; Fireships, 1996. ARC RIDERS SERIES WITH J. MORRIS: Arc Riders, 1995; The Fourth Rome, 1996. LORD OF THE ISLES SERIES: Lord of the Isles, 1997; Queen of Demons, 1998; Servant of the Dragon, 1999; Mistress of the Catacombs, 2001; Goddess of the Ice Realm, 2003; Master of the Cauldron, 2004. BELISARIUS SERIES WITH E. FLINT: An Oblique Approach, 1998; In the Heart of Darkness, 1998; Destiny's Shield, 1999; Fortune's Stroke, 2000; The Tide of Victory, 2001; The Dance of Time, 2006. LT. LEARY SERIES: With the Lightnings, 1998; Lt. Leary, Commanding, 2000; The Far Side of The Stars, 2003; The Way to Glory, 2005; Some Golden Harbor, 2006; When the Tide Rises, 2008; In the Stormy Red Sky, 2009; What Distant Deeps, 2010. CROWN OF THE ISLES SERIES: The Fortress of Glass, 2006; The Mirror of Worlds, 2007; The Gods Return, 2008. BELISARIUS OMNIBUS SERIES WITH E. FLINT: Thunder at Dawn, 2008; Storm at Noontide, 2009; The Flames of Sunset, 2009. BOOKS OF THE ELEMENTS SERIES: The Legions of Fire, 2010; Out of the Waters, 2011. NOVELS: The Dragon Lord, 1979; Skyripper, 1983; Birds of Prey, 1984; The Forlorn Hope, 1984; (with K.E. Wagner) Killer, 1985; (with J. Morris) Active Measures, 1985; Strangers and Lovers, 1985; Fortress, 1986; Ranks of Bronze, 1986; Lacey and His Friends, 1986; Bridgehead, 1986; (with J. Morris) Kill Ratio, 1987; Vettius and His Friends, 1989; (with J. Morris) Target, 1989; (with L.S. de Camp) The Undesired Princess and the Enchanted Bunny, 1990; Surface Action, 1990; (with J. Kjelgaard) The Hunter Returns, 1991; The Jungle, 1991; Old Nathan, 1991; Starliner, 1992; Tyrannosaur, 1994; (with B. Ohlander) Enemy of My Enemy, 1995; Patriots, 1996; Redliners, 1996; All the Way to the Gallows, 1996; Seas of Venus, 2002; Other Times Than Peace, 2006; (with J. Lambshead) Into the Hinterlands, 2011. COLLECTIONS: Time Safari, 1982; From the Heart of Darkness, 1983; The Military Dimension, 1991; The Military Dimension Mark II, 1995; (with E. Flint and D. Weber) The Warmasters, 2002; Grimmer than Hell, 2003; (with E. Flint, H. Kuttner and R.E. Spoor) Mountain Magic, 2004; Balefires, 2007. CRISIS OF EMPIRE SERIES: (with T.T. Thomas) An Honorable Defense, 1988; (with W.C. Dietz) Cluster Command, 1989; (with R.M. Allen) The War Machine, 1989; (with C.Q. Yarbro) Crown of Empire, 1994. OTHERS: (with N. Gingrich and M. Gingrich) Window of Opportunity: A Blueprint for the Future, 1984; Dagger, 1988; (with J. Morris) Explorers in Hell, 1989; The Square Deal, 1992; (with G.R. Dickson, C. Stasheff and Q. Yarbro) Blood and War, 1993; (with E. Flint) Changer of Worlds, 2001; (with E. Flint) The Tyrant, 2002; Loose Cannon, 2011; Voyage Across the Stars, 2012; Road of Danger, 2012. SHORT STORIES: (with K.E. Wagner) Killer, 1974; The Shortest Way, 1974; Under the Hammer, 1974; Awakening, 1975; The Barrow Trol, 1975; But Loyal to His Own, 1975; Dragon's Teeth, 1975; Something Had to Be Done, 1975; Blood Debt, 1976; Children of the Forest, 1976; Firefight, 1976; The Hunting Ground, 1976; Smokie Joe, 1977; Best of Luck, 1978; Nemesis Place, 1978; The Red Leer, 1979; Hangman, 1979; Standing Down, 1979; Cultural Conflict, 1979; The Automatic Rifleman, 1980; Men Like Us, 1980; Than Curse the Darkness, 1980; The Dancer in the Flames, 1982; Out of Africa, 1983; The Fool, 1987; Rescue Mission, 1988; The End of the Hunt, 1989; Cannibal Plants From Heck, 1994; A Very Offensive Weapon, 1995; Caught in the Crossfire, 1998; The Butcher's Bill, 1998; Dragon, the Book, 1999; The Tradesmen, 2000. EDITOR: (with B. Fawcett) The Fleet, 1988; (with B. Fawcett) Counterattack, 1988; (with B. Fawcett) Breakthrough, 1989; (with S. Miesel) A Separate Star, 1989; (with M.H. Greenberg and C.G. Waugh) Space Gladiators, 1989; (with S. Miesel) Heads to the Storm, 1989; (with M.H. Greenberg and C. Waugh) Space Infantry, 1989; (with M.H. Greenberg and C. Waugh) Space Dreadnaughts, 1990; (with B. Fawcett) Sworn Allies, 1990; (with B. Fawcett) Total War, 1990; (with M.H. Greenberg and C. Waugh) The Eternal City, 1990; (with B. Fawcett) Crisis, 1991; (with B. Fawcett) Battlestation, 1992; (with B. Fawcett) Vanguard, 1993; Dogs of War, 2002; (with E. Flint and J. Baen) World Turned Upside Down, 2005; (with E. Flint) Transgalactic, 2006. Contributor of articles to magazines. **Address:** PO Box 904, Chapel Hill, NC 27514-0904, U.S.A. **Online address:** dad@david_drake.com

DRAKE, Jane. Canadian (born Canada), b. 1954. **Genres:** Children's Non-fiction, Recreation, Environmental Sciences/Ecology, Sciences. **Career:** Author. **Publications:** My Grandfather and Me, 1999; My Grandmother and Me, 1999; My Mother and Me, 2000; My Father and Me, 2000; My Baby Brother and Me, 2000; My Baby Sister and Me, 2000; My Best Friend and Me, 2001; My Family and Me, 2002. WITH A. LOVE: Take Action: An Environmental Book for Kids, 1993; The Kids' Cottage Book, 1993 in UK as The Kids' Summer Handbook, 1994; The Kids Campfire Book, 1995; Farming, 1996; Forestry, 1996; Mining, 1997; Fishing, 1997; The Kids Guide to the Millennium, 1998; The Kids Cottage Games Book, 1998; The Kids Book of the Far North, 2000; Kids Winter Cottage Book, 2001; Cool Woods: A Trip Around the World's Boreal Forest, 2003; Kids Book of the Night Sky, 2004; Snow Amazing: Cool Facts and Warm Tales, 2004; Trash Action: A Fresh Look at Garbage, 2006; Sweet!: The Delicious Story of Candy, 2007; Alien Invaders: Species that Threaten Our World, 2008; Yes You Can! Your Guide To Becoming An Activist, 2010; Talking Tails: The Incredible Connection Between People and Their Pets, 2010. **Address:** 95 Ridge Dr., Toronto, ON M4T 1B6, Canada. **Online address:** jane.drake@rogers.com

DRAKE, Timothy A. American (born United States), b. 1967. **Genres:** Theology/Religion, Children's Non-fiction, Autobiography/Memoirs, Theology/Religion. **Career:** Educator, 1989-94; Science Museum, promotions specialist, 1995-97; Public Group, staff writer, 1997-98; Morris Sun Tribune, editor, 1998; Catholic Charities, communications assistant, 1998-99; Fidelitas Web Design, co-founder, 1999-; Drake Wordsmithing, owner, 1999-; National Catholic Register, features correspondent, 1999-2000, senior editor; Circle Media, journalist and features correspondent, 1999-, managing editor, 2001-; The Write Stuff E-zine, publisher, 1999-; Envoy Magazine, contributing editor, 2000-; Catholic.net, editor, 2001-. **Publications:** (With R.J. Neuhaus) There We Stood, Here We Stand: 11 Lutherans Rediscover Their Catholic Roots, 2001; (co-author) Saints of the Jubilee, 2002; Young and Catholic: The Face of Tomorrow's Church, 2004; Behind Bella: The Amazing Stories of Bella and the Lives It's Changed, 2008. EDITOR: (with H. Graham) Where We Got the Bible, 1997; (with C. Hartman) Physicians Healed, 1998; (with

P. Madrid) Where Is That in the Bible?, 2001. FOR CHILDREN: Viva Cristo Rey! The Courageous Saints of the Knights of Columbus, 2003; From an Angel in a Dream: The Story of St. Joseph, 2005. CONTRIBUTOR: (with P. Madrid) Surprised by Truth 2, 2000; (with L. Nordhagen) When Only One Converts, 2001; No Wonder They Call it the Real: Lives Changed by Christ In Eucharistic Adoration, 2002; 201 Inspirational Stories of the Eucharist, 2004. Contributor to magazines. **Address:** 35474 Co. Rd. 2, Saint Joseph, MN 56374, U.S.A. **Online address:** tdrake@tdrake.clearwire.net

DRAKULIĆ, Slavenka. (Slavenka Drakulic-Ilic). Swedish/Croatian (born Croatia), b. 1949. **Genres:** Novels, History, Adult Non-fiction, Young Adult Fiction, Women's Studies And Issues, Essays. **Career:** Start (bi-weekly newspaper), staff writer, 1982-92; Danas, staff writer, 1982-92; The Nation, writer, contributing editor; La Stampa, writer; Dagens Nyheter, writer; Frankfurter Allgemeine Zeitung, writer; Politiken, writer. **Publications:** Smrtni Grijesi Feminizma: Ogled o Mudologiji, 1984; Hologrami Straha: Roman 1988, trans. as Holograms of Fear, 1992; Mramorna koza (novel), 1989; How We Survived Communism and Even Laughed, 1992; Balkan Express: Fragments from the Other Side of War, 1993; Bozanska Glad, 1995; Café Europa: Life After Communism, 1997; The Taste of a Man, 1997; Kao da me Nema: Roman, 1999; S: A Novel, 1999 as As If I Am Not There, 2001; Sabrani Romani, 2003; Oni ne bi ni Mrava Zgazili, 2003; They Would Never Hurt a Fly: War Criminals on Trial in The Hague, 2004; Sabrani Eseji, 2005; Tijelo njenog tijela: price o dobroti, 2007; Frida, ili, O boli, 2008; Frida's Bed: A Novel, 2008; Two Underdogs and a Cat: Three Reflections on Communism, 2009; Basne o komunizmu: iz pera domaćih, divljih i egzoticnih zivotinja, 2009; A Guided Tour Through the Museum of Communism: Fables from a Mouse, A Parrot, A Bear, A Cat, A Mole, A Pig, A Dog, and A Raven, 2011. Contributor to periodicals. **Address:** c/o Anneli Hoier, Leonhardt & Hoier Literary Agency A/S, Studiestraede 35, Copenhagen, DK-1455, Denmark. **Online address:** info@slavenkadrakulic.com

DRAKULIC-ILIC, Slavenka. See **DRAKULIĆ, Slavenka.**

DRAPER, Alfred Ernest. British (born England), b. 1924. **Genres:** Novels, Biography, History, Autobiography/Memoirs, Young Adult Non-fiction. **Career:** Daily Herald, staff; Daily Express, journalist, 1950-72; Daily Mail, journalist, 1950-72; writer, 1972-; British Broadcasting Corp., staff. **Publications:** NOVELS: Swansong for a Rare Bird, 1970; The Death Penalty, 1972; Smoke Without Fire (biography), 1974; The Prince of Wales, 1975; Amritsar, the Massacre that Ended the Raj, 1981 as The Amritsar Massacre: Twilight of the Raj, 1985; The Con Man, 1988; (with H. Challenor) Tanky Challenor: SAS & the Met, 1990; A Crimson Splendour, 1991; Operation Midas, 1993. NON-FICTION: (with J. Austin and H. Edgington) The Story of the Goons, 1977; Operation Fish: The Race to Save Europe's Wealth, 1939-1945, 1979; Dawns Like Thunder: Retreat from Burma, 1942, 1987; Scoops and Swindles: Memoirs of a Fleet Street Journalist, 1988. SERIES: Grey Seal, 1981; Restless Waves, 1983; Raging of the Deep, 1985; Storm over Singapore, 1987; The Great Avenging Day, 1990. Contributor to magazines. **Address:** 31 Oakridge Ave., Radlett, HF WD7 8EW, England.

DRAPER, Hastings. See **JEFFRIES, Roderic.**

DRAPER, Maureen McCarthy. American (born United States), b. 1941. **Genres:** Music, Medicine/Health, Self Help, Psychology. **Career:** Teacher, 1971-98; Fine Arts Museum, art docent, 1987-92; Stanford Hospital, Music for Health Program, coordinator, 2001-. Writer and consultant. **Publications:** The Nature of Music: Beauty, Sound, and Healing, 2001; (ed. with H.H. Houghton) Music Lover's Poetry Anthology, 2007. **Address:** 18800 Montebellow Rd., Cupertino, CA 95014, U.S.A. **Online address:** modraper1@yahoo.com

DRAPER, Polly. American (born United States), b. 1955. **Genres:** Plays/Screenplays, Young Adult Fiction. **Career:** Actress, producer and writer. **Publications:** The Making of the Naked Brothers Band, 2007. **Address:** The Gersh Agency Inc., 9465 Wilshire Blvd., 6th Fl., PO Box 5617, Beverly Hills, CA 90212, U.S.A.

DRAPER, Robert. American (born United States), b. 1959?. **Genres:** Biography, Novels, Philosophy, Music. **Career:** Texas Monthly, writer and editor, senior editor; GQ Magazine, staff writer and national correspondent; The New York Times Magazine, contributor. **Publications:** ZZ Top, 1985; Huey Lewis and the News, 1986; Rolling Stone Magazine: The Uncensored History, 1990; Hadrian's Walls (novel), 1999; Dead Certain: The Presidency of George W. Bush, 2007. Contributor to periodicals. **Address:** c/o Author Mail, Knopf Publishing, 1745 Broadway, New York, NY 10019-4368, U.S.A.

DRAPER, Sharon Mills. American (born United States), b. 1950?. **Genres:** Children's Fiction, Young Adult Fiction, Social Sciences, Biography, Education, Crafts. **Career:** Walnut Hills High School, Department of English, English teacher and head, 1970-; Cincinnati Public Schools, teacher, 1970-97; Mayerson Academy for Professional Development of Teachers, associate; Writer, 1991-. **Publications:** Tears of a Tiger, 1994; Ziggy and the Black Dinosaurs, 1994; Ziggy and the Black Dinosaurs: Lost in the Tunnel of Time, 1996; Forged by Fire, 1997, rev. ed. as Forged by Fire: Hazelwood High Trilogy, 2005; Shadows of Caesar's Creek, 1997; Romiette and Julio, 1999; Jazz Imagination: A Journal to Read and Write, 1999; Teaching from the Heart: Reflections, Encouragement and Inspiration, 2000; Not Quite Burned Out but Crispy around the Edges: Inspiration, Laughter and Encouragement for Teachers, 2001; Darkness Before Dawn, 2001; Double Dutch, 2002; The Battle of Jericho 2003; We Beat the Street 2005; Ziggy and the Black Dinosaurs: The Space Mission Mystery, 2006; Copper Sun, 2006; The Backyard Animal Show, 2006; The Space Mission Adventure, 2006; November Blues, 2007; Fire From The Rock, 2007; Just Another Hero, 2009; Sassy: Little Sister is not my Name, 2009; Sassy: The Birthday Storm, 2009; Sassy: The Silver Secret, 2010; Out of My Mind, 2010; Sassy: The Dazzle Disaster Dinner Party, 2010. **Address:** c/o Janell Agyeman, Marie Brown Associates Inc., 6640 Akers Mill Rd., Ste. 580, Atlanta, GA 30339, U.S.A. **Online address:** sharondraper@mindspring.com

DRAUT, Tamara. American (born United States), b. 1971?. **Genres:** Young Adult Fiction. **Career:** Demos (public policy center), director of economic opportunity program, vice president of policy and programs. Writer. **Publications:** Strapped: Why America's 20- and 30-Somethings Can't Get Ahead, 2006. Contributor to periodicals. **Address:** Demos, 220 5th Ave., 5th Fl., New York, NY 10001, U.S.A. **Online address:** tdraut@demos.org

DRAWE, D. Lynn. American (born United States), b. 1942. **Genres:** Botany, Environmental Sciences/Ecology, Sciences. **Career:** Texas A&M University, assistant professor of agriculture, 1970-74; Welder Wildlife Foundation, assistant director, 1974-98, director, 1999-. Writer and consultant. **Publications:** (With J.H. Everitt) Trees, Shrubs, and Cacti of South Texas, 1993, rev. ed., 2002; (with S.L. Hatch and J.L. Schuster) Grasses of the Texas Gulf Coastal Prairies and Marshes, 1999; (with J.H. Everitt and R. Lonard) Field Guide to the Broad-Leaved Herbaceous Plants of South Texas: Used by Livestock and Wildlife, 1999. Contributor to journals. **Address:** Welder Wildlife Foundation, PO Box 1400, Sinton, TX 78387, U.S.A. **Online address:** welderwf@aol.com

DRAY, Philip. American (born United States) **Genres:** Documentaries/Reportage, Social Sciences. **Career:** New School University, professor of African-American history. Writer. **Publications:** (With S. Cagin) Hollywood Films of the Seventies: Sex, Drugs, Violence, Rock n Roll and Politics, 1984, 2nd ed. as Born to Be Wild: Hollywood and the Sixties Generation, 1994; (with S. Cagin) We Are Not Afraid: The Story of Goodman, Schwerner and Chaney and the Civil Rights Campaign for Mississippi, 1988; (with S. Cagin) Between Earth and Sky: How CFCs Changed Our World and Endangered the Ozone Layer, 1993; At the Hands of Persons Unknown: The Lynching of Black America, 2002; Stealing God's Thunder: Benjamin Franklin's Lightning Rod and the Invention of America, 2005; Yours for Justice, Ida B. Wells the Darling Life of Crusading Journalist, 2008; Capitol Men: The Epic Story of Reconstruction through the Lives of the First Black Congressmen, 2008; There is Power in a Union, 2010. Contributor to periodicals. **Address:** c/o Author Mail, Random House, 1745 Broadway, New York, NY 10019, U.S.A.

DRAZIN, Israel. American (born United States), b. 1935. **Genres:** Theology/Religion, Philosophy. **Career:** Drazin and Drazin (law firm), senior partner, 1974-98; private practice, 1974-93. Writer. **Publications:** Targum Onkelos to Deuteronomy: An English Translation of the Text with Analysis and Commentary, 1982; Targum Onkelos to Exodus: An English Translation of the Text with Analysis and Commentary, 1990; Targum Onkelos to Leviticus: An English Translation of the Text with Analysis and Commentary, 1994; (with C.B. Currey) For God and Country: The History of a Constitutional Challenge to the Army Chaplaincy, 1995; Targum Onkelos to Numbers: An English Translation of the Text with Analysis and Commentary, 1998; (with S.M. Wagner) Onkelos on the Torah: Understanding the Bible Text, 2006; A Rational Approach to Judaism and Torah Commentary, 2006; Miamonides: The Exceptional Mind, 2008; Maimonides: And the Biblical Prophets, 2009; (with S.M. Wagner) Deuteronomy, 2010. Contributor to magazines. **Address:** Drazin & Drazin, 10420 Little Patuxent Pkwy., Amdahl Bldg., Ste. 100, Columbia, MD 21044, U.S.A. **Online address:** iddrazin@aol.com

DREHER, Henry. American (born United States), b. 1955. **Genres:** Medicine/Health, Administration/Management, Psychology, Social Commentary, Sports/Fitness, Autobiography/Memoirs, Children's Fiction. **Career:** Cancer Research Institute Inc., staff, 1979, staff writer, 1980-85; Kallir Phillips Ross Inc., freelance writer, 1990-97; Mediphacs Inc., freelance writer, 1995-98; Forhealers.com, expert consultant, 2000-; Sage Publications, Integrative Cancer Therapies, assistant editor, 2002-; Cancer Guide Consultations, director; The Centre for Mind Body Medicine, course faculty. **Publications:** Your Defense against Cancer, 1988; (with L. Temoshok) The Type C Connection: The Mind-Body Links to Cancer and Your Health, 1991; The Immune Power Personality: Seven Traits You Can Develop to Stay Healthy, 1995; (with A.D. Domar) Healing Mind, Healthy Woman: Using the Mind-Body Connection to Manage Stress and Take Control of Your Life, 1996; (with J. Torre) Joe Torre's Ground Rules for Winners: 12 Keys to Managing Team Players, Tough Bosses, Setbacks and Success, 1999; (with A.D. Domar) Self-Nurture: Learning to Care for Yourself as Effectively as You Care for Everyone Else, 2000; (with S. Chiel) For Thou Art with Me: The Healing Power of Psalms, 2000; (with J. Davidson) The Anxiety Book: Developing Strength in the Face of Fear, 2003; Mind-Body Unity: A New Vision for Mind-Body Science and Medicine, 2003; (with S. Chiel) The Healing Power of Psalms: Renewal, Hope and Acceptance from the World's Most Beloved Ancient Verses, 2007. CHILDREN'S BOOKS: Great Sports Thrills, 1981; Beware: This House Is Haunted!, 1982. Contributor to periodicals. **Address:** Cancer Guide Consultations, 84 E 3rd St., Ste. 2C, New York, NY 10003, U.S.A. **Online address:** hendreh2@aol.com

DREHER, Rod. American (born United States), b. 1967. **Genres:** Politics/Government, Social Sciences, Sociology, Economics. **Career:** Dallas Morning News, editor and columnist, 2003-09; John Templeton Foundation, publications director, 2010-; National Review, senior editor; Big Questions Online, editor; South Florida Sun-Sentinel, film reviewer; The New York Post, chief film critic. Advocate and arts critic. **Publications:** Crunchy Cons: How Birkenstocked Burkeans, Gun-Loving Organic Gardeners, Evangelical Free-Range Farmers, Hip Homeschooling Mamas, Right-Wing Nature Lovers and Their Diverse Tribe of Countercultural Conservatives Plan to Save America (or at Least the Republican Party); Crunchy Cons: The New Conservative Counterculture and Its Return to Roots, 2006. Contributor to periodicals. **Address:** John Templeton Foundation, 300 Conshohocken State Rd., Ste. 500, West Conshohocken, PA 19428, U.S.A. **Online address:** rdreher@dallasnews.com

DREHLE, Dave Von. *See* **DREHLE, David Von.**

DREHLE, David Von. (Dave Von Drehle). American (born United States), b. 1961. **Genres:** Adult Non-fiction. **Career:** The Denver Post, sports writer, 1978-83; Miami Herald, staff writer, 1983-91; Washington Post, staff writer, 1991-95, assistant managing editor, 1995-99, senior writer, 1999-, national political writer, magazine staff writer, New York bureau chief, 1991, assistant managing editor; Time Magazine, editor-at-large, 2006. Journalist. **Publications:** Among the Lowest of the Dead: Inside Death Row (nonfiction), 1995; Triangle: The Fire that Changed America, 2003; Among the Lowest of the Dead: The Culture of Capital Punishment, 2004. Contributor to books. **Address:** Time Inc., 1271 Ave. of the Americas, New York, NY 10020-1393, U.S.A. **Online address:** vondrehled@washpost.com

DRESSER, Norine. Also writes as Margaret N. Stone, Jessie Lattimore. American (born United States), b. 1931. **Genres:** Novellas/Short Stories, Cultural/Ethnic Topics, Mythology/Folklore, How-to Books, Gay And Lesbian Issues. **Career:** California State University, teacher of American folklore, American pop culture, basic writing, freshman composition and American food ways, 1972-, now retired; University of California, Center for the Study of Comparative Folklore and Mythology, research associate, 1985-91. Freelance writer. **Publications:** (As M.N. Stone with G.I. Sugarman) Your Hyperactive Child, 1974; (as Jessie Lattimore with M. Fontes) High Contrast, 1988; American Vampires, 1989; Our Own Stories: Cross-Cultural Communication Practice, 1993; I Felt Like I was from Another Planet, 1993; Multicultural Manners: New Rules of Etiquette for a Changing Society, 1996, rev.

ed., 2005; Multicultural Celebrations: Today's Rules of Etiquette for Life's Special Occasion, 1999; Our Own Journeys: Readings for Cross-Cultural Communication, 2003; Come As You Aren't!: Feeling at Home with Multicultural Celebrations, 2005; (with F. Wasserman) Saying Goodbye to Someone You Love: Your Emotional Journey Through End of Life and Grief, 2010. **Address:** c/o Michael R. Shapiro, 612 Sepulveda, Ste. 11, Los Angeles, CA 90049, U.S.A. **Online address:** norinedresser@yahoo.com

DRESSLER, Alan (Michael). American (born United States), b. 1948. **Genres:** Air/Space Topics, Sciences, Mathematics/Statistics. **Career:** Hale Observatory, Carnegie Institution of Washington fellow, 1976-78; Las Campanas fellow, 1978-81; Carnegie Institution of Washington, Mt. Wilson and Las Campanas observatories, scientific staff, 1981-, acting associate director, 1988-89. Writer. **Publications:** Voyage to the Great Attractor: A Journey through Intergalactic Space, 1994; (co-author) Future Research Direction and Visions for Astronomy, 2002; (co-ed.) Clusters of Galaxies: Probes of Cosmological Structure and Galaxy Evolution, 2004. **Address:** Carnegie Observatory, 813 Santa Barbara St., Pasadena, CA 91101, U.S.A.

DRESSLER, Joshua. American (born United States), b. 1947. **Genres:** Law, Criminology/True Crime, Politics/Government, Education. **Career:** San Fernando Valley College of Law, assistant professor of law, 1975-77; Hamline University, School of Law, associate professor of law, 1977-79, professor of law, 1979-82; Wayne State University, Law School, professor of law, 1982-93, career development chair, 1986; University of the Pacific, McGeorge School of Law, professor of law, 1993-2000, distinguished professor, 2000-01; Ohio State University, Michael E. Moritz College of Law, Frank R. Strong chair in law, 2001-, university distinguished lecturer, 2005, Ohio State Journal of Criminal Law, founder and co-editor, 2002-. **Publications:** Understanding Criminal Law, 1987, 5th ed., 2009; Casenote Law Outlines Criminal Law, 1990; Casenote Law Outlines Criminal Procedure, 1991, 2nd ed., 1993; Understanding Criminal Procedure, 1991, (with A.C. Michaels) 5th ed., 2010; Cases and Materials on Criminal Law, 1994, 4th ed., 2007; (with G.C. Thomas, III) Criminal Procedure: Principles, Policies, and Perspectives, 1999, 4th ed., 2010; (ed.) Encyclopedia of Crime & Justice, 2002; Criminal Law, 2005, 2nd ed., 2010. Contributor to journals. **Address:** Michael E. Moritz College of Law, Ohio State University, Drinko 305, 55 W 12th Ave., Columbus, OH 43210-1391, U.S.A. **Online address:** dressler.11@osu.edu

DRESSLER, Mylène. American/Dutch (born Netherlands), b. 1963?. **Genres:** Novels, Young Adult Fiction. **Career:** University of St. Thomas, professor of literature; University of Texas, visiting writer. **Publications:** NOVELS: The Medusa Tree, 1997; The Deadwood Beetle, 2001; My Little Blue Dress, 2003; The Floodmakers, 2004; The Wedding of Anna F., forthcoming. **Address:** Alison M. Bond Literary Agency, 171 W 79th St., New York, NY 10025, U.S.A. **Online address:** author@mylenedressler.com

DREW, Alan. American (born United States), b. 1970. **Genres:** Novels. **Career:** Villanova University, faculty of fiction writing. Writer. **Publications:** Gardens of Water (novel), 2008. **Address:** c/o Karen Fink, Random House Inc., 1745 Broadway, MD 17-1, New York, NY 10019, U.S.A. **Online address:** alandrewauthor@yahoo.com

DREW, Bettina. American (born United States), b. 1956. **Genres:** Literary Criticism And History, Social Sciences. **Career:** City College of the City University of New York, lecturer in English, 1981-90; New York University, lecturer in humanities, 1990-93; West Side Young Men's Christian Association (YMCA), workshop instructor at Writer's Voice, 1994-95; Yale University, instructor, 1995-99; Mercy College, lecturer; Bronx Community College, lecturer; New York Technical College, lecturer; University of Missouri, assistant professor of English and creative writing, 2001-10. Writer. **Publications:** Nelson Algren: A Life on the Wild Side, 1989; (ed. and intro.) The Texas Stories of Nelson Algren, 1995; Crossing the Expendable Landscape, 1998; Travels in Expendable Landscapes (essays), 1998. Contributor of articles to magazines. **Address:** c/o Theresa Park, Sanford J. Greenburger Associates Inc., 55 5th Ave., New York, NY 10003, U.S.A. **Online address:** drewb@missouri.edu

DREW, Horace R. Australian/American (born United States), b. 1955. **Genres:** Medicine/Health, Technology, Engineering, Physics. **Career:** Medical Research Council Laboratory, staff, 1981-86; CSIRA Molecular Science, principal research scientist, 1987-. Writer. **Publications:** (With C.R. Calladine) Understanding DNA: The Molecule & How It Works, 1992, 2nd ed.,

1997; (ed. with S. Pellegrino) New Approaches to Structural Mechanics, Shells, and Biological Structures, 2002. Contributor of articles to magazines. **Address:** 125 Charles St., Putney, NW 2112, Australia. **Online address:** horace.drew@csiro.au

DREW, Philip. Australian (born Australia), b. 1943. **Genres:** Architecture, Cultural/Ethnic Topics, Design, Regional/Urban Planning, Art/Art History. **Career:** The Architectural Press, technical editor, 1970-71; University of Idaho, visiting assistant professor of architecture, 1972-73; University of Newcastle, senior lecturer in architecture, 1977-; Australian Correspondent, 1978-; Business Review Weekly, design critic; Washington University, visiting associate professor, 1982-83. Writer. **Publications:** Third Generation: The Changing Meaning of Architecture, 1972; Frei Otto: Form and Structure, 1976; Tensile Architecture, 1979; Two Towers: Harry Seidler, 1980; The Architecture of Arata Isozaki, 1982; Leaves of Iron: Glenn Murcutt, Pioneer of an Australian Architectural Form, 1985; (with K. Frampton) Harry Seidler: Four Decades of Architecture, 1992; Veranda: Embracing Place, 1992; Real Space: The Architecture of Martorell, Bohigas, Mackay, Puigdomenech, 1993; The Coast Dwellers: Australians Living on the Edge, 1994; Sydney Opera House: Jørn Utzon, 1995; Edward Suzuki: Buildings & Projects, 1996; Church on the Water, Church of the Light: Tadao Ando, 1996; The Museum of Modern Art, Gunma, Arata Isozaki, 1996; Touch this Earth Lightly: Glenn Murcutt in His Own Words, 1999; The Masterpiece: Jørn Utzon, a Secret Life, 1999; New Tent Architecture, 2008. **Address:** Department of Architecture, University of Newcastle, Cnr King and Auckland St., Newcastle, NW 2308, Australia. **Online address:** pdrew@idx.com.au

DREW, Simon. British (born England), b. 1952. **Genres:** Art/Art History, Humor/Satire, Graphic Novels, Animals/Pets. **Career:** Art gallery director and writer. **Publications:** Book of Bestial Nonsense, 1986; Nonsense in Flight: Drawings And Verses, 1987; Puffin's Advice: Drawings And Verse, 1989; Cat With Piano Tuna And Other Feline Nonsense: Drawings And Verse, 1990; Still Warthogs Run Deep And Other Free Range Nonsense, 1990; Camp David, 1994; Handel's Warthog Music, 1995; Simon Drew's Beastly Birthday Book, 1995; Great Mistakes of Civilisation, 1996; Dogsbodies, 1998; The Very Worst of Simon Drew, 1999; Spot the Author, 1999; Spot the Book Title, 2000; Pie Aaaaaggh (Squared), 2001; The Quotations of Oscar Wilde, 2004; And so I Face the Vinyl Curtain, 2005; Address Book, 2006; Pointless Verses, 2007; Shepherd Spy: A Tale of Violence and Intrigue and Terrorist Sheep, 2007. **Address:** 13 Foss St., Dartmouth, DN TQ6 9DR, England. **Online address:** info@simondrew.co.uk

DREWE, Robert. (Robert Duncan Drewe). Australian (born Australia), b. 1943. **Genres:** Novels, Plays/Screenplays, Novellas/Short Stories. **Career:** Perth West Australian, cadet journalist, 1961-64; Sydney Bureau, reporter, 1964-65, head, 1965-70; The Australian, daily columnist, 1970-73, features editor, 1971-72, literary editor, 1972-74; The Bulletin, special writer, 1975-76, contributing editor, 1980-83; University of Western Australia, writer-in-residence, 1979; Mode, Sydney and Sydney City Monthly, columnist, 1981-83; La Trobe University, writer-in-residence, 1986; The West Australian, junior reporter. **Publications:** NOVELS: The Savage Crows, 1976; A Cry in the Jungle Bar, 1979; Fortune, 1986; Bondi, 1986; Our Sunshine, 1991; The Drowner, 1997; The Penguin Book of the City, 1998; Walking Ella, 1998; The Shark Net: Memories and Murder, 2000; (ed.) Penguin Book of the Beach, 2001; Kelly Gang, 2003; Ned Kelly, 2004; Grace, 2005; (foreword) Perth, 2005; Mangrove Point, 2007; (with J. Kinsella) Sand, 2010. SHORT STORIES: The Bodysurfers, 1983; The Bay of Contented Men, 1989; (ed.) The Picador Book of The Beach, 1993; The Rip, 2008. Contributor to periodicals. **Address:** Hickson Associates Private Ltd., PO Box 271, Woollahra, NW 2025, Australia.

DREWE, Robert Duncan. See **DREWE, Robert.**

DREWES, Athena A. American (born United States), b. 1948. **Genres:** Psychology, Bibliography, Human Relations/Parenting, Social Sciences. **Career:** Maimonides Hospital, Division of Parapsychology and Psychophysics, research assistant, 1969-75; Jewish Board of Family and Children's Services, Child Development Center, play therapist and and psychometrician, 1974-82; Child Study Center, play therapist and psychometrician, 1982-85; Warwick Special Education Preschool, play therapist and psychometrician, 1985-91; Astor Home for Children, senior psychologist and clinical coordinator, 1992-. Writer. **Publications:** (With S.A. Drucker) Parapsychological Research with

Children: An Annotated Bibliography, 1991; (ed. with L.J. Carey and C.E. Schaefer) School-Based Play Therapy, 2001, (with C.E. Schaefer) 2nd ed., 2010; (ed. with E. Gil) Cultural Issues in Play Therapy, 2005; (ed. with J.A. Mullen) Supervision Can be Playful: Techniques for Child and Play Therapist Supervisors, 2007; (ed.) Blending Play Therapy with Cognitive Behavioral Therapy: Evidence-based and Other Effective Treatments and Techniques, 2009; (ed. with S.C. Bratton and C.E. Schaefer) Integrative Play Therapy, 2011. Contributor to periodicals. **Address:** Astor Home for Children, 6339 Mill St., PO Box 5005, Rhinebeck, NY 12572-5005, U.S.A. **Online address:** adrewes@astorservices.org

DREXLER, Rosalyn. (Julia Sorel). American (born United States), b. 1926. **Genres:** Novels, Plays/Screenplays, Writing/Journalism, Film, Art/Art History, Literary Criticism And History, Young Adult Fiction. **Career:** University of Iowa, writer's workshop, 1976-77; University of Colorado, art teacher. Playwright and novelist. **Publications:** I am the Beautiful Stranger, 1965; The Bold New Women, 1966; Line of Least Existence and Other Plays, 1967; (co-author) Collision Course, 1968; The Investigation and Hot Buttered Roll, 1969; One or Another, 1970; Was I Good?, 1972; To Smithereens, 1972 in UK as Submissions of a Lady Wrestler; 1976; The Ice Queen, 1973; She Who Was He, 1974; Travesty Parade, 1974; The Cosmopolitan Girl, 1975; (as Julia Sorel) Unwed Widow, 1975; (as Julia Sorel) Dawn: Portrait of a Teenage Runaway, 1976; (as Julia Sorel) Rocky, 1977; (as Julia Sorel) Alex: Portrait of a Teenage Prostitute, 1977; (as Julia Sorel) See How She Runs, 1978; Starburn: The Story of Jenni Love, 1979; Vulgar Lives, 1979; The Writer's Opera, 1979; Tomorrow is Sometimes Temporary When Tomorrow Rolls Around, 1979; Graven Image, 1980; Wonder, 1980; Bad Guy, 1982; Room 17-C, 1983; Delicate Feelings, 1984; Rosalyn Drexler: Intimate Emotions, 1986; Transients Welcome, 1986; What Do You Call It?, 1986; The Heart That Eats Itself, 1987; Black Ice, 1992; The Flood, 1992; Art Does (Not) Exist, 1996; Dear: A New Play, 1997; I am the Beautiful Stranger: Paintings of the '60s, 2007. Works appear in anthologies. Contributor of articles to periodicals. **Address:** Georges Borchardt Inc., 136 E 57th St., New York, NY 10022, U.S.A. **Online address:** wrestlerarm@msn.com

DREYER, Eileen. (Kathleen Korbel). American (born United States), b. 1952?. **Genres:** Novels, Romance/Historical, Mystery/Crime/Suspense. **Career:** Writer. **Publications:** CRIME NOVELS: A Man to Die For, 1991; If Looks Could Kill, 1992; Nothing Personal, 1993; Bad Medicine, 1995; Brain Dead, 1997; With a Vengeance, 2003; (co-author) The Sunken Sailor, 2004; Head Games, 2004; Sinners and Saints, 2005; (with J. Crusie and A. Stuart) The Unfortunate Miss Fortunes, 2007; Barely a Lady, 2010; Never a Gentleman, 2011; Always the Temptress, 2011. ROMANCE NOVELS; UNDER PSEUDONYM KATHLEEN KORBEL: Playing the Game, 1986; A Stranger's Smile, 1986; Worth Any Risk, 1987; A Prince of a Guy, 1987; Edge of the World, 1987; The Princess and the Pea, 1988; The Road to Mandalay, 1989; Perchance to Dream, 1989; The Ice Cream Man, 1989; Hotshot, 1990; Lightening Strikes, 1990; A Rose for Maggie, 1991; A Fine Madness, 1991; Jake's Way, 1991; Isn't It Romantic?, 1992; Walk on the Wild Side, 1992; Timeless, 1993; Simple Gifts, 1994; A Soldier's Heart, 1995; Don't Fence Me In, 1996; Sail Away, 1998; Some Men's Dreams, 2003; Dangerous Temptation, 2006; Dark Seduction, 2008; Deadly Redemption, 2008. Works appears in anthologies. **Address:** Jane Rotrosen Agency, 318 E 51st St., New York, NY 10022, U.S.A. **Online address:** eileendreyer@eileendreyer.com

DREYER, Elizabeth A. American (born United States), b. 1945. **Genres:** Theology/Religion, Women's Studies And Issues, Humanities. **Career:** Washington Theological Union, faculty; Fairfield University, professor of religious studies. Writer. **Publications:** Passionate Women: Two Medieval Mystics, 1989; Manifestations of Grace, 1990; Earth Crammed with Heaven: A Spirituality of Everyday Life, 1994; A Retreat with Catherine of Siena: Living the Truth in Love, 1999; (ed.) The Cross in Christian Tradition: From Paul to Bonaventure, 2000; (ed. with M.S. Burrows) Minding the Spirit: The Study of Christian Spirituality, 2005; Passionate Spirituality: Hildegard of Bingen and Hadewijch of Brabant, 2005; Holy Power, Holy Presence: Rediscovering Medieval Metaphors for the Holy Spirit, 2007; Making Sense of God: A Woman's Perspective, 2008. Contributor to periodicals. **Address:** Fairfield University, 1073 N Benson Rd., Fairfield, CT 06824-5171, U.S.A.

DREYFUSS, Robert. American (born United States) **Genres:** Politics/Government, Sciences, Social Sciences. **Career:** Freelance journalist. **Publications:** (With T. LeMarc) Hostage to Khomeini, 1980; Devil's Game: How the United States Helped Unleash Fundamentalist Islam, 2005. Contributor to journals. **Address:** c/o Author Mail, Henry Holt and Company Inc., 175 5th Ave., New York, NY 10010, U.S.A. **Online address:** robert@robertdreyfuss.com

DREZ, Ronald J(oseph). American (born United States), b. 1940. **Genres:** History. **Career:** Bonded Carbon and Ribbon Company Inc., salesperson, 1969-72; Dockside Elevators, operations manager, 1973-82; Delta Transload, general manager, 1982-86; self-employed, 1987-; University of New Orleans Metro College Eisenhower Center, assistant director, 1987-; Stephen Ambrose Tours, president, 1999-. Writer. **Publications:** (Ed.) Voices of D-Day: The Story of the Allied Invasion, Told by Those Who Were There, 1994; Twenty Five Yards of War: The Extraordinary Courage of Ordinary Men in World War II, 2001; Remember D-day: The Plan, The Invasion, Survivor Stories, 2004; Voices of Valor: D-Day, June 6, 1944, 2004; (with D. Brinkley) Voices of Courage: The Battle for Khe Sanh, Vietnam, 2005; Heroes Fight Like Greeks, The Greek Resistance Against the Axis Powers in WWII, 2009. Contributor to periodicals. **Address:** Stephen Ambrose Historical Tours, 1515 S Salcedo St., Ste. 230, PO Box 19354, New Orleans, LA 70125, U.S.A. **Online address:** rdrez@aol.com

DRÈZE, Jean. Indian/Belgian (born Belgium), b. 1959. **Genres:** Economics, Politics/Government, Third World. **Career:** University of London, London School of Economics and Political Science, lecturer in economics, 1987-88; freelance development economist, 1988-; University of Delhi, Delhi School of Economics, Centre for Development Economics, visiting professor, 1993-, honorary professor; G.B. Pant Social Science Institute, visiting professor. Writer. **Publications:** Famine Prevention in India, 1988; (with A. Sen) Hunger and Public Action, 1989; (with S.E. Ahmad, J. Hills) Social Security in Developing Countries, 1991; (with A. Sen) India: Economic Development and Social Opportunity, 1995; (with N. Sharma) Palanpur 1957-93, 1997; (co-author) Public Report on Basic Education in India, 1999; (with A. Sen) India: Development and Participation, 2002; The Future of Mid-Day Meals, 2003. EDITOR: (with A. Sen) The Political Economy of Hunger, 3 vols., 1990; (co-author) Social Security in Developing Countries, 1991; (with A. Sen) Indian Development: Selected Regional Perspectives, 1997; (with M. Samson and S. Singh) The Dam and the Nation: Displacement and Resettlement in the Narmada Valley, 1997; Economics of Famine, 1999; (ed. with B. Bhatia and K. Kelly) War and Peace in the Gulf: Testimonies of the Gulf Peace Team, 2001. **Address:** Department of Economics, Delhi School of Economics, University of Delhi, New Delhi, DH 110007, India. **Online address:** jean@econdse.org

DREZNER, Daniel W. (Daniel William Drezner). American (born United States), b. 1968. **Genres:** Politics/Government. **Career:** RAND Corp., research consultant, 1994; University of Colorado, assistant professor of political science, 1996-99; University of Chicago, assistant professor of political science, 1999-2006; U.S. Department of the Treasury, Office of International Banking and Securities Markets, international economist, 2000-01; Tufts University, Fletcher School of Law and Diplomacy, professor of international politics, 2006-; Donetsk Technical University, Civic Education Project, visiting lecturer in economics, 1993-94; Cable-Satellite Public Affairs Network (C-SPAN), commentator; Cable News Network Financial (CNNfn), commentator; CNN International, commentator; American Broadcasting Co., commentator. Writer. **Publications:** The Sanctions Paradox: Economic Statecraft and International Relations, 1999; (ed.) Locating the Proper Authorities: The Interaction of Domestic and International Institutions, 2003; All Politics Is Global: Explaining International Regulatory Regimes, 2007. Contributor to periodicals. **Address:** Fletcher School, Tufts University, 160 Packard Ave., Medford, MA 02155, U.S.A. **Online address:** ddrezner@gmail.com

DREZNER, Daniel William. *See* **DREZNER, Daniel W.**

DRIEDGER, Leo. Canadian (born Canada), b. 1928?. **Genres:** Area Studies, Cultural/Ethnic Topics, Sociology, Social Sciences. **Career:** University of Manitoba, professor of ethnic relations, urban sociology and sociology of religion, 1966-99, professor emeritus, 1999-; Elizabethtown College, Young Center for the Study of Anabaptist and Pietist Groups, fellow. Writer. **Publications:** (Ed.) The Canadian Ethnic Mosaic: A Quest for Identity, 1978; (with N.L. Chappell) Aging and Ethnicity: Toward an Interface, 1987; (ed.) Ethnic Canada: Identities and Inequalities, 1987; Mennonite Identity in Conflict, 1988; The Ethnic Factor, 1989; Mennonites in Winnipeg, 1990; (ed. with L. Harder) Anabaptist-Mennonite Identities in Ferment, 1990; (ed. with S.S. Halli and F. Trovato) Ethnic Demography: Canadian Immigrant, Racial and Cultural Variations, 1990; The Urban Factor, 1991; (with J.H. Kauffman) The

Mennonite Mosaic: Identity and Modernization, 1991; (with D.B. Kraybill) Mennonite Peacemaking: From Quietism to Activism, 1994; Multi-Ethnic Canada: Identities and Inequalities, 1996; (with S. Halli) Immigrant Canada, 1999; Mennonites in the Global Village, 2000; (with S.S. Halli) Race and Racism: Canada's Challenge, 2000; Race and Ethnicity: Finding Identities and Equalities, 2003; At the Forks: Mennonites in Winnipeg, 2010. Contributor to journals. **Address:** Department of Sociology, University of Manitoba, 307 Isbister Bldg., Winnipeg, MB R3T 2N2, Canada. **Online address:** driedge1@cc.umanitoba.ca

DRIESEN, David M. American (born United States), b. 1958. **Genres:** Law, Sciences, Economics. **Career:** Freelance trumpet performer and teacher, 1980-86; Washington State Supreme Court, law clerk to Justice Robert Utter, 1989-90; Office of the Washington State Attorney General, Special Litigation Division, assistant attorney general, 1990-91; Natural Resources Defense Council, Air and Energy Program, project attorney, 1992-94, senior project attorney, 1994-95; Syracuse University, assistant professor, 1995-99, associate professor of law, 1999-2004, professor, 2004-06, Angela S. Cooney professor, 2006-08, university professor, 2008-; University of Michigan, Law School, visiting professor, 2006; State University of New York, College of Environmental Science and Forestry, adjunct associate professor. Writer. **Publications:** The Economic Dynamics of Environmental Law, 2003; (with R. Adler) Environmental Law: A Conceptual and Pragmatic Approach, 2007; (with R. Adler and K. Engel) Environmental Law: A Conceptual and Pragmatic Approach, 2007, 2nd ed., 2011; Economic Thought and U.S. Climate Change Policy, 2010; (ed. with A.C. Flournoy) Beyond Environmental Law, 2010. Contributor of articles to journals. **Address:** College of Law, Syracuse University, E. I. White Hall, Syracuse, NY 13244-1030, U.S.A. **Online address:** ddriesen@law.syr.edu

DRISCOLL, Jeremy. American (born United States), b. 1951. **Genres:** Theology/Religion, Novels. **Career:** Benedictine monk, 1973-; Roman Catholic priest, 1981-; Mount Angel Seminary, faculty, 1983-, professor, 2000-; Pontificio Ateneo Sant Anselmo, faculty, 1994-, associate professor in theology, professor of theology, 2002-; Congregation for Divine Worship, Vox Clara Commission, advisor, 2002; St. Paul Center for Biblical Theology, senior fellow, distinguished fellow; Gregorian University, visiting professor; AIM, consultant. Writer. **Publications:** The Ad Monachos of Evagrius Ponticus: Its Structure and a Select Commentary, 1991; Some Other Morning, 1992; (trans. and intro.) The Mind's Long Journey to the Holy Trinity: The Ad Monachos of Evagrius Ponticus, 1993; (ed. with M. Sheridan) Spiritual Progress, 1994; Theology at the Eucharistic Table: Master Themes in the Theological Tradition (essays), 2003; (trans.) Evagrius Ponticus: Ad Monachos, 2003; Steps to Spiritual Perfection: Studies on Spiritual Progress in Evagrius Ponticus, 2005; What Happens at Mass, 2005, rev., ed. 2011; A Monk's Alphabet: Moments of Stillness in a Turning World (essays), 2006. Contributor to journals. **Address:** St. Paul Center for Biblical Theology, 2228 Sunset Blvd., Ste. 2A, Steubenville, OH 43952-3707, U.S.A.

DRISDELLE, Rosemary. Canadian (born Canada), b. 1959?. **Genres:** Animals/Pets, Sciences. **Career:** Suite101.com, birds feature writer, 2006-09, Science and Nature, section editor, 2009-. **Publications:** Parasites: Tales of Humanity's Most Unwelcome Guests, 2010. Contributor to journals and magazines. **Address:** NS , Canada. **Online address:** info@rosemarydrisdelle.com

DRISKILL, J. Lawrence. American (born United States), b. 1920. **Genres:** Children's Non-fiction, Cultural/Ethnic Topics, Gerontology/Senior Issues, Theology/Religion, Self Help, Social Sciences. **Career:** University of Dubuque seminary, visiting professor, 1961-62; Trinity University, visiting professor, 1972-73; Highland Presbyterian Church, pastor, 1973-82; Madison Square Presbyterian Church, interim pastor, 1973; Maryville College, part-time professor, 1974-75; Grace Presbyterian Church, interim pastor, 1984-85; Christ Presbyterian Church, interim pastor, 1987-89; First Presbyterian Church, pastor, 1990-99; San Gabriel Presbytery, mission advocate. Writer. **Publications:** Mission Adventures in Many Lands, 1992; (with L.C. Driskill) Japan Diary of Cross-Cultural Mission, 1993; Mission Stories from Around the World, 1994; Cross-Cultural Marriages and the Church: Living the Global Neighborhood, 1995; Worldwide Mission Stories for Young People, 1996; (ed.) Christmas Stories from Around the World: Honoring Jesus in Many Lands, 1997; Adventures in Senior Living: Learning How to Make Retirement Meaningful and Enjoyable, 1997; (co-author) Kingship in the Bible and Japan's Emperor System, 1998. **Address:** 1420 Santo Domingo Ave., Duarte, CA 91010, U.S.A.

DRIVER, C(harles) J(onathan). British/South African (born South Africa), b. 1939. **Genres:** Novels, Poetry. **Career:** National Union of South African Students, president, 1963, 1964; Sevenoaks School, staff; Matthew Humberstone Comprehensive School, staff; University of York, research fellow, 1976; Island School, principal, 1978-83; Berkhamsted School, headmaster, 1983-89; Wellington College, master, 1989-2000; University of East Anglia, School of Literature, Drama and Creative Writing, honorary senior lecturer, 2007-. Writer. **Publications:** Elegy for a Revolutionary, 1969; Send War in Our Time, O Lord, 1970; Death of Fathers, 1972; A Messiah of the Last Days, 1974; Patrick Duncan (biography), 1980; Shades of Darkness, 2004. POETRY: (with J. Cope) Occasional Light, 1979; I Live Here Now, 1979; Hong Kong Portraits, 1986; In the Water-Margins, 1994; Holiday Haiku, 1997; Requiem, 1998; So Far: Selected Poems, 1960-2004, 2005. Works appear in anthologies. Contributor to periodicals. **Address:** c/o Andrew Hewson, Johnson & Alcock Ltd., Clerkenwell House, 45-47 Clerkenwell Green, London, GL EC1R 0HT, England. **Online address:** jontydriver@hotmail.com

DRLICA, Karl. American (born United States), b. 1943. **Genres:** Medicine/Health, Ethics. **Career:** University of Rochester, assistant professor to associate professor, 1977-85; New York University, associate research professor, research professor, 1985-, Department of Microbiology, adjunct professor, 2005-; Public Health Research Institute, principal investigator, 2005-. Writer. **Publications:** Understanding DNA and Gene Cloning: A Guide for the Curious, 1984, 4th ed., 2004; (ed. with M. Riley) Bacterial Chromosome, 1990; Double-Edged Sword: Risks and Opportunities of the Genetic Revolution, 1994; (ed. with I.W. Fong) Reemergence of Established Pathogens in the 21st Century, 2003; (ed. with I.W. Fong) Antimicrobial Resistance and Implications for the 21st Century, 2008; (with D.S. Perlin) Antibiotic Resistance: Understanding and Responding to an Emerging Crisis, 2011. Contributor to books and journals. **Address:** Department of Microbiology, New York University, Rm. 217, Medical Science Bldg., 550 1st Ave., 2nd Fl., New York, NY 10016, U.S.A. **Online address:** drlicaka@umdnj.edu

DROGIN, Bob. American (born United States) **Genres:** History. **Career:** United Nations Children's Fund, program associate, 1973-75; Charlotte Observer, police/investigative reporter, 1977-79; Philadelphia Enquirer, environment reporter, 1981-83; Los Angeles Times, national correspondent, 1983-89, bureau chief in southeast asia, 1989-93, bureau chief in south africa, 1993-97, intelligence/national security correspondent, 1998-2006, investigative reporter, 2007-; kampuchean emergency relief co-ordinator, 1980. Writer. **Publications:** Curveball: Spies, Lies and the Con Man Who Caused a War, 2007. **Address:** Silver Spring, MD , U.S.A. **Online address:** curveball@bobdrogin.com

DROMGOOLE, Dominic. British (born England), b. 1964. **Genres:** Autobiography/Memoirs, How-to Books, Literary Criticism And History, History, Art/Art History, Biography. **Career:** Bush Theatre, assistant director, artistic director, 1990-96; Oxford Stage Co., director, (now known as Headlong), staff, 1999-2005; Old Vic, staff; Shakespeare's Globe Theatre, artistic director, 2006-. Writer. **Publications:** The Full Room: An A-Z of Contemporary Playwriting, 2000; Will and Me: How Shakespeare Took Over My Life, 2006. Contributor to periodicals. **Address:** Department of Theatre, Shakespeare's Globe, 21 New Globe Walk, Bankside, London, GL SE1 9DT, England.

DROSNIN, Michael. American (born United States), b. 1946. **Genres:** Documentaries/Reportage, Young Adult Non-fiction, Biography, Theology/Religion. **Career:** Washington Post, staff reporter, 1966-68; Wall Street Journal, staff reporter, 1969-70; freelance journalist, 1970-. **Publications:** NONFICTION: Citizen Hughes, 1985; The Bible Code, 1997; Bible Code II: The Countdown, 2003. **Address:** c/o John Brockman, Brockman Inc., 5 E 59th St., New York, NY 10022, U.S.A.

DRUCKER, Joel. American/Canadian (born Canada), b. 1960?. **Genres:** Biography. **Career:** Writer and television commentator. **Publications:** Jimmy Connors Saved My Life, 2004. **Address:** 3239 Kempton Ave., Ste. 14, Oakland, CA 94611, U.S.A. **Online address:** jdruck@aol.com

DRUCKER, Johanna. American (born United States), b. 1952. **Genres:** Art/Art History. **Career:** East Bay Regional Parks Exhibit Lab, assistant preparator, 1980; University of California-Berkeley, Summer Film Program, teaching assistant, 1981, Environmental Design, teaching assistant, 1982, teaching associate, 1991; University of Texas, assistant professor, 1986-88; Harvard University, Mellon faculty fellow in fine arts, 1988-89; Columbia University, assistant professor of modern art, 1989-94; San Francisco State University, Center for Experimental and Interdisciplinary Arts, lecturer/visiting artist, 1992, Purchase College, professor, 1998-99; Yale University, associate professor of history of art, 1994-98; Feminist Art and Art History Conference, coordinator, 1995-96; University of Virginia, Department of English, professor, director of media studies, Robertson chair in media studies, 1999-2008; University of California-Los Angels, Department of Information Studies, Martin and Bernard Breslauer professor, 2008-. Writer. **Publications:** Dark, the Bat Elf, 1972; As No Storm, 1975; Twenty-Six '76 Let Hers, 1976; From A to Z: The Our An Bibliography, 1977; Fragile, 1977; The Surprize Party, 1977; Netherland: (How) So Far, 1978; Experience of the Medium, 1978; Kidz, 1980; Jane Goes Out W' the Scouts, 1980; 'S Crap 'S Ample, 1980; Italy, The Figures, 1980; Dolls of the Spirit, 1981; It Happens Pretty Fast, 1982; Tongues, 1982; Just As, 1983; Against Fiction, 1983; Spectacle, 1984; Through Light and the Alphabet, 1986; (with E. McVarish) Sample Dialogue, 1989; The Word Made Flesh, 1989; Simulant Portrait, 1990; The History of the/My Wor(l)d, 1990; Books: 1970 to 1994, 1994; (with K.D. Jackson and E. Vos) Experimental, Visual, Concrete: Avant-garde Poetry Since the 1960s, 1996; Figuring the Word: Essays on Books, Writing and Visual Poetics, 1998; Night Crawlers on the Web, 2000; John Eric Broaddus: Arts of the Book Collection, 2001; (with B. Freeman) Emerging Sentience, 2001; (with S. Bee) Girl's Life, 2002; (contrib.) Typographically Speaking, 2002; Damaged Spring, 2003; Sweet Dreams: Contemporary Art and Complicity, 2005; Damaged Nature, Salvage Culture: Specific Fragments, 2005; Events: Particle Zoo, 2005; Cuba, 2006; (contrib.) Seeing Double, 2006; Testament of Women: A New Translation to & from the Texts, 2006; (contrib.) The Book as Art, 2007, 2nd ed., 2011; SpecLab: Digital Aesthetics and Projects in Speculative Computing, 2009; (with E. McVarish) Graphic Design History: A Critical Guide, 2009; (ed. and afterword) Petit Journal des Refusées, 2009. OTHERSPACE: (with B. Freeman): Martian Ty/opography, 1993; Theorizing Modernism: Visual Art and the Critical Tradition, 1994; The Visible Word: Experimental Typography and Modern Art, 1909-1923, 1994; Dark Decade (fiction), 1994; Narratology: Historical Romance, Sweet Romance, Science Fiction, Romantic Suspense, Supernatural, Horror, Sensual Romance, Adventure, Thriller, Glitz, 1994; Three Early Fictions, Potes and Poets Press, 1994; The Alphabetic Labyrinth: The Letters in History and Imagination, 1995; The Century of Artists Books, 1995; The Current Line, 1996. Works appear in anthologies. Contributor to periodicals. **Address:** Department of Information Studies, University of California, GSE&IS 203, 300 N Charles E Young Dr., PO Box 951521, Los Angeles, CA 90095, U.S.A. **Online address:** drucker@gseis.ucla.edu

DRUCKER, Lisa. (Jacqueline de Soignée). American (born United States), b. 1967. **Genres:** Young Adult Fiction, Humor/Satire, Romance/Historical. **Career:** HCI Books, senior editor, 1997-2004. Freelance writer and editor, 2004-. **Publications:** (As Jacqueline de Soignée) The Princess-in-Training Manual, 2003. **Address:** c/o Author Mail, Red Dress Ink, PO Box 5190, Buffalo, NY 14240-5190, U.S.A. **Online address:** hrhjacquie36@aol.com

DRUCKER, Mort. American (born United States), b. 1929. **Genres:** Humor/Satire, Illustrations, Picture/Board Books, Young Adult Fiction, Science Fiction/Fantasy. **Career:** National Periodicals, staff artist, 1948-50, retoucher; freelance commercial artist, 1951-; Mad Magazine, contributing artist, 1956-. Writer. **Publications:** (With P. Laikin) The JFK Coloring Book, 1961; Mort Drucker's Show-Stoppers, 1985; (with P. Laikin) The Ollie North Coloring Book, 1987; (with D.D. Duncan) Familiar Faces: The Art of Mort Drucker, 1988; (with P. Laikin) The Ronald Reagan Coloring Book, 1988; (with L.J. Ames) Draw Fifty Famous Caricatures, 1990; (with A. Yorinks) Whitefish Will Rides Again, 1994. Contributor to periodicals. **Address:** 42 Juneau Blvd., Woodbury, NY 11797, U.S.A.

DRUCKER, Olga Levy. American/German (born Germany), b. 1927. **Genres:** Autobiography/Memoirs. **Career:** Audio Video Engineering Co., president, 1989-2004; Temple Beth Am, board director, 1990-92. Writer and educator. **Publications:** Kindertransport (young adult autobiography), 1992; House of Levy and Children of Levy, forthcoming; The First Passover, forthcoming; Eight Nights of Hanukkah, forthcoming. Contributor of articles to periodicals. **Address:** 1 Pineapple Ln., Stuart, FL 34996-6341, U.S.A. **Online address:** odrucker@gate.net

DRUCKER, Peter. American (born United States), b. 1958. **Genres:** Biography, History, Translations, Autobiography/Memoirs. **Career:** Against the Current (bi-monthly socialist magazine), editor, 1984-; National Mobi-

lization for Survival, program coordinator, 1989-91; National Campaign for Peace, co-founder and leader, 1990-91; International Institute for Research and Education, co-director, 1993-2006, director; Polytechnic Institute, lecturer in history and political science; New College of California, lecturer in history and political science. Writer. **Publications:** Max Shachtman and His Left: A Socialist's Odyssey through the American Century, 1994; (trans.) C. Samary, Yugoslavia Dismembered, 1995. Contributor to periodicals. **Address:** International Institute for Research and Education, Willemsparkweg 202, PO Box 53290, Amsterdam, 1007 RG, Netherlands. **Online address:** peter.iire@antenna.nl

DRUM, Alice. American (born United States), b. 1935. **Genres:** Education, Money/Finance. **Career:** American University, instructor in English, 1976; Antioch University, adjunct professor of general studies, 1976-78; Gettysburg College, adjunct assistant professor of English, 1977-80; Georgetown University, lecturer in general studies, 1980-81; University of Maryland, lecturer, 1980-83; Hood College, assistant professor of English, 1981-85, coordinator of writing program, 1981-83, Learning Center, assistant director, 1982-83, associate dean of academic affairs, 1983-85; Franklin and Marshall College, adjunct associate professor of English, 1985-2001, dean of freshmen, 1985-88, vice president of the college, 1988-2001, dean of educational services, 1988-94; Franklin and Marshall College, visiting professor of English and women's studies, vice president, 1988-2001, vice president emeritus, 2001-, chairman, 2001, president, through 2008, professor of English literature and womens' studies, director of the women's and gender studies program; Lancaster County District Attorney Commission, chairperson, 1990. Writer. **Publications:** (With R. Kneedler) Funding a College Education: Finding the Right School for Your Child and the Right Fit for Your Budget, 1996. Contributor to books, articles and poems to periodicals. **Address:** Office of the Vice President, Franklin and Marshall College, PO Box 3003, Lancaster, PA 17604-3003, U.S.A. **Online address:** adrum@fandm.edu

DRUMM, D. B. See NAHA, Ed.

DRUMMOND, Edward H. American (born United States), b. 1953. **Genres:** Medicine/Health, Psychiatry, Self Help. **Career:** Seacoast Mental Health Center, associate medical director, 1986-. Writer. **Publications:** Overcoming Anxiety without Tranquilizers: A Groundbreaking Program for Treating Chronic Anxiety, 1997; The Complete Guide to Psychiatric Drugs: Straight Talk for Best Results, 2000, rev. ed., 2006. Contributor to periodicals. **Address:** Seacoast Mental Health Ctr. Inc., 1145 Sagamore Ave., Portsmouth, NH 03801, U.S.A. **Online address:** tedd@seacoastmentalhealth.org

DRUMMOND, Emma. See DAWES, Edna.

DRUMMOND, Jack. See O'BRIEN, Martin.

DRUMMOND, June. See Obituaries.

DRUMMOND, Michael. American (born United States), b. 1964?. **Genres:** Biography, Autobiography/Memoirs, History. **Career:** San Diego Union-Tribune, business writer. **Publications:** Renegades of the Empire: How Three Software Warriors Started a Revolution Behind the Walls of Fortress Microsoft, 1999. Contributor to periodicals. **Address:** San Diego Union-Tribune, 350 Camino de la Reina, PO Box 120191, San Diego, CA 92108, U.S.A.

DRURY, John. (John Henry Drury). American/British (born England), b. 1936. **Genres:** Theology/Religion, Photography. **Career:** St. John's Wood Church, curate, 1963-66; Downing College, chaplain, 1966-69; Exeter College, chaplain and fellow, 1969-73; Norwich Cathedral and Examining chaplain to Bishop of Norwich, resident canon, 1973-79, vice-dean of Norwich, 1978; Sussex University, lecturer in religious studies, 1979-81; Cambridge University, dean, 1981-91; University of Oxford, dean of Christ church, 1991-2003, faculty of theology; All Soul's College, chaplain and fellow, 2003-. Writer. **Publications:** Angels and Dirt: An Enquiry into Theology and Prayer, 1972; Luke, 1973; Tradition and Design in Luke's Gospel: A Study in Early Christian Historiography, 1976; Parables in the Gospels: History and Allegory, 1985; (ed. and trans.) An Evolutionary Approach to Jesus of Nazareth, 1988; (ed.) Critics of the Bible, 1724-1873, 1989; (intro.) The New Testament: The Authorized or King James Version of 1611, 1998; Painting the Word: Christian Pictures and Their Meanings, 1999. **Address:** All Souls College, Oxford University, Christ Church, Oxford, OX OX1 4AL, England.

DRURY, John Henry. See **DRURY, John.**

DRURY, Sally. British (born England), b. 1960. **Genres:** Homes/Gardens, Horticulture, History. **Career:** Haymarket Publishing, technical editor, 1982-88; freelance writer, 1988-; Horticulture Week, technical editor, 2000-; Institute of Horticulture, The Horticulturist, consultant editor, 2000-. **Publications:** (Co-author) Gardens of England, 1991. Contributor to periodicals. **Address:** Horticulture Week, 174 Hammersmith Rd., London, GL W6 7JP, England. **Online address:** sally.drury@haymarket.com

DRURY, Thomas Jay. See **DRURY, Tom.**

DRURY, Tom. (Thomas Jay Drury). American (born United States), b. 1956?. **Genres:** Novels, Novellas/Short Stories. **Career:** St. Petersburg Times, editor; Wesleyan University, visiting lecturer and writing instructor, 2001-, distinguished writer, 2000-03; Yale University, visiting writer; Florida State University, visiting writer; LaSalle University, visiting writer; University of Southern Mississippi, visiting writer; Los Angeles County Museum of Art, senior editor. Journalist. **Publications:** The End of Vandalism, 1994; The Black Brook, 1998; Hunts in Dreams, 2000; Driftless Area, 2006. Works appear in anthologies. Contributor to periodicals. **Address:** c/o Author Mail, Houghton Mifflin, 222 Berkeley St., Boston, MA 02116-3764, U.S.A. **Online address:** tdrury@wesleyan.edu

DRUSE, Eleanor. See **DOOLING, Richard (Patrick).**

DRYDEN, Konrad. American (born United States), b. 1963. **Genres:** Biography, Autobiography/Memoirs. **Career:** University of Maryland, professor of music and humanities. Writer. **Publications:** Riccardo Zandonai: A Biography, 1999; Leoncavallo: Life and Works, 2007; Franco Alfano: Transcending Turandot, 2010. **Address:** Markusplatz 16, Bamberg, 96047, Germany. **Online address:** konrad_dryden@yahoo.com

DRYFOOS, Joy G. American (born United States), b. 1925. **Genres:** Psychology, Sex, Business/Trade/Industry, Economics, Social Sciences. **Career:** Research, Writing and Editing Associates, research associate, 1960-66; Planned Parenthood Federation of America, research associate, 1967-68; Alan Guttmacher Institute, director of research and planning, fellow and consultant, 1969-81; Sarah Lawrence College, National Commission on Community Health Services, research associate, 1981-. Writer. **Publications:** Putting Boys in the Picture: A Review of Programs to Promote Sexual Responsibility among Male Adolescents, 1988; Adolescents-at-Risk: Prevalence and Prevention, 1990; Full Service Schools: A Revolution in Health and Social Services for Children, Youth, and Families, 1994; Safe Passage: Making It through Adolescence in a High Risk Society, 1998; Inside Full Service Community Schools, 2002; (ed. with J. Quinn and C. Barkin) Community Schools in Action: Lessons from a Decade of Practice, 2005; Adolescence: Growing Up in America Today, 2006. Contributor of articles to books and periodicals. **Address:** 32 Russell St., Brookline, MA 02446-2414, U.S.A. **Online address:** joy@joydryfoos.com

DRYZEK, John S. Australian/British (born England), b. 1953. **Genres:** Politics/Government. **Career:** Glasgow College of Technology, lecturer, 1977; Ohio State University, Department of Political Science, assistant professor, 1980-86; University of Oregon, assistant professor, 1986-88, associate professor, 1988-91, professor 1991-95, Department of Political Science, head; University of Melbourne, Department of Political Science, professor, 1995-2000; Australian Journal of Political Science, editor, 1995-99; ACritical Review of International Social and Political Philosophy, corresponding editor, 1998-; Journal of Political Philosophy, associate editor, 2000-01; Australian National University, Social and Political Theory Program, Research School of Social Sciences, professor, 2001-, Australian Research Council, federation fellow. **Publications:** Conflict and Choice in Resource Management: The Case of Alaska, 1983; Rational Ecology: Environment and Political Economy, 1987; (with D.B. Bobrow) Policy Analysis by Design, 1987; Discursive Democracy: Politics, Policy, and Political Science, 1990; (ed. with J. Farr and S.T. Leonard) Political Science in History: Research Programs and Political Traditions, 1995; Democracy in Capitalist Times: Ideals, Limits, and Struggles, 1996; The Politics of the Earth: Environmental Discourses, 1997, 2nd ed., 2005; (ed. with D. Schlosberg) Debating the Earth: The Environmental Politics Reader, 1998, 2nd ed., 2005; Deliberative Democracy and Beyond: Liberals, Critics, Contestations, 2000; (with L. Holmes) PostCommunist Democratization Political Discourses across Thirteen Countries, 2002;

(co-author) Green States and Social Movements: Environmentalism in the United States, United Kingdom, Germany, and Norway, 2003; Deliberative Global Politics: Discourse and Democracy in a Divided World, 2006; (ed. with B. Honig and A. Phillips) The Oxford Handbook of Political Theory, 2006; (with P. Dunleavy) Theories of the Democratic State, 2009; (with S. Niemeyer) Foundations and Frontiers of Deliberative Governance, 2010. **Address:** Political Science Program, Research School of Social Sciences, Australian National University, Rm. 4035, Coombs Bldg., Canberra, AC 0200, Australia. **Online address:** john.dryzek@anu.edu.au

D'SOUZA, Tony. American (born United States), b. 1974. **Genres:** Novels, Romance/Historical. **Career:** Writer. **Publications:** Whiteman, 2006; Discovering Awareness: A Guide to Inner Peace, Strength and Freedom, 2006; Konkans, 2008; Mule: A Novel of Moving Weight, 2011. Contributor to periodicals. **Address:** c/o Liz Darhansoff, Feldman Literary Agents, 236 W 26th St., Ste. 802, New York, NY 10001, U.S.A.

DUBBER, Markus Dirk. American (born United States) **Genres:** Essays, Law. **Career:** Chambers of Gerald B. Tjoflat, U.S. Court of Appeals for the Eleventh Judicial Circuit, judicial clerk, 1991-92; University of Chicago Law School, Harry A. Bigelow teaching fellow and lecturer in law, 1992-93; State University of New York-Buffalo, School of Law, associate professor, 1993-99, professor of law, 1999-; Buffalo Criminal Law Review, editor, 1996-; Buffalo Criminal Law Center, founding director, 1996-; Universität München, Institut für Rechtsphilosophie, Humboldt research fellow, 2000-01; University of Michigan Law School, visiting professor, 2001; Stanford University Press, Critical Perspectives on Crime and Law, series editor, 2005-; New Criminal Law Review, founding editor-in-chief, 2006-08; University of Toronto, Centre for Ethics, visiting faculty fellow, 2007-08. **Publications:** (Ed. with B. Schunemann) Die Stellung des Opfers im Strafrechtssystem: Neue Entwicklungen im deutschen und amerikanischen Recht, 2000; Criminal Law: Model Penal Code, 2002; Victims in the War on Crime: The Use and Abuse of Victims' Rights, 2002; Einfuhrung in das US-amerikanische Strafrecht, 2004; (with M. Kelman) American Criminal Law: Cases, Statutes and Comments, 2005; The Police Power: Patriarchy and the Foundations of American Government, 2005; The Sense of Justice: Empathy in Law and Punishment, 2006; (ed. with M. Valverde) The New Police Science: The Police Power in Domestic and International Governance, 2006; (ed. with L. Farmer) Modern Histories of Crime and Punishment, 2007; New York Penal Law and Related Provisions, 2008; New York Criminal Law: Cases and Materials, 2008; (ed. with M. Valverde) Police and the Liberal State, 2008; Handbook of Comparative Criminal Law, 2011; American Criminal Law: A Treatise, forthcoming; Comparative Perspectives on Criminal Law, forthcoming; German Criminal Law: A Critical Introduction, forthcoming; A Theory of Penal Law: Autonomy and the Legitimacy of State Punishment, forthcoming. Contributor of articles to books and periodicals. **Address:** School of Law, State University of New York at Buffalo, North Campus, 712 O'Brian Hall, North Campus, Buffalo, NY 14260, U.S.A. **Online address:** dubber@buffalo.edu

DUBENS, Eugene (M.). British (born England), b. 1957. **Genres:** Novels, Mystery/Crime/Suspense, Young Adult Fiction. **Career:** Writer. **Publications:** The Hypnotist, 2000; The Hypnotist II, forthcoming. **Address:** 73 Wagner Close, Basingstoke, HM RG22 4JD, England. **Online address:** eugeneathome@hotmail.com

DUBERMAN, Martin. (Martin Bauml Duberman). American (born United States), b. 1930. **Genres:** Plays/Screenplays, Gay And Lesbian Issues, History, Literary Criticism And History. **Career:** Harvard University, tutor, 1955-57; Yale University, instructor and assistant professor, 1957-62; Yale University, Morse fellow, 1961-62; Princeton University, assistant professor, 1962-65, associate professor, 1965-67, professor of history, 1967-71; City University of New York, Graduate Center and Lehman College, distinguished professor, 1971-, distinguished professor of history emeritus; Center for Lesbian and Gay Studies (CLAGS), founder and director. Writer. **Publications:** Charles Francis Adams, 1807-1886, 1961; In White America, 1964; James Russell Lowell, 1966; Metaphors, 1968; The Colonial Dudes, 1969; The Uncompleted Past (essays), 1969; The Memory Bank, 1970; Guttman Ordinary Scale, 1972; Black Mountain: An Exploration in Community (nonfiction), 1972; Male Armor: Selected Plays 1968-1974, 1975; Visions of Kerouac, 1977; Uncompleted Past, 1984; About Time: Exploring the Gay Past, 1986, 1991; Paul Robeson, 1989; Hidden from History: Reclaiming Gay and Lesbian Past, 1989; Cures, 1991, rev. ed., 2002; Mother Earth, 1991; Stonewall, 1993; Midlife Queer, 1996; Left Out: The Politics of Exclusion/Essays

1964-99, rev. ed., 2002; Haymarket, 2003; Worlds of Lincoln Kirstein, 2007; Radical Acts, 2008; Waiting to land: A (Mostly) Political Memoir, 1985-2008, 2009; A Saving Remnant: The Radical Lives of Barbara Deming and David McReynolds, 2011. EDITOR: The Antislavery Vanguard: New Essays on the Abolitionists, 1965; Psychiatry, Psychology, and Homosexuality, 1995; Liberace, 1995; Lesbians and Gays and Sports, 1995; Oscar Wilde, 1995; Gay Men, Lesbians, and the Law, 1997; Beyond Gay or Straight, 1997; A Queer World, 1997; Queer Representations, 1997. Contributor to periodicals. **Address:** Department of History, Lehman College, 202 C Carman Hall, 250 Bedford Park Blvd., Bronx, NY 10468-1589, U.S.A.

DUBERMAN, Martin Bauml. *See* **DUBERMAN, Martin.**

DUBERSTEIN, Helen (Laura). American (born United States), b. 1926. **Genres:** Plays/Screenplays, Poetry, Novellas/Short Stories, Novels, Women's Studies And Issues, Illustrations, Autobiography/Memoirs, Songs/Lyrics And Libretti, Songs/Lyrics And Libretti, Young Adult Fiction. **Career:** Theatre for the New City, artistic director, 1974-75; Playwrights Group Inc., president, 1974-76; Hartford University, playwright-in-residence, 1977-78; New York University, faculty, 1987. Writer. **Publications:** POEMS: Succubus, Incubus, 1970; The Human Dimension, 1970; The Voyage Out, 1978; Arrived Safely, 1979; The Shameless Old Lady, 1993. FICTION: Dream of Rewards, 1987; Hotel Europe and Other Tales, 1991. OTHER: Changes, 1978; Shadow Self, 1979; Hotel Europe, 1979; In Pursuit of the Goddess, 1991; A Thousand Wives Dancing, 2001; Roma, 2002; Skip to My Lou, forthcoming. **Address:** Helmut Meyer Literary Agency, 330 E 79th St., New York, NY 10021, U.S.A. **Online address:** ghohel@aol.com

DUBERSTEIN, Larry. American (born United States), b. 1944. **Genres:** Novels, Novellas/Short Stories, Essays, Biography, Autobiography/Memoirs, Literary Criticism And History. **Career:** Writer, 1971-; Darkhorse Builders, staff; Squarehorse Builders, staff; Brimstone Corner Builders, staff; Clark & Duberstein, staff. **Publications:** NOVELS: The Marriage Hearse, 1987; Carnovsky's Retreat, 1988; Postcards from Pinsk, 1991; The Alibi Breakfast, 1995; The Handsome Sailor, 1998; The Mt. Monadnock Blues, 2003; The Day the Bozarts Died, 2006; The Twoweeks, 2011. STORIES: Nobody's Jaw, 1979; Eccentric Circles, 1992. Contributor to periodicals. **Address:** 117 Hamilton St., Cambridge, MA 02139-4526, U.S.A.

DUBIN, Michael J. American (born United States), b. 1938. **Genres:** Politics/Government, History, Social Sciences. **Career:** John F. Kennedy High School, social studies teacher, 1966-96. Writer. **Publications:** (With S.B. Parsons and W.W. Beach) United States Congressional Districts and Data, 1843-1883, 1986; (with S.B. Parsons and K.T. Parsons) United States Congressional Districts, 1883-1913, 1990; United States Congressional Elections, 1788-1997: The Official Results of the Elections of the 1st through 105th Congresses, 1998; United States Presidential Elections 1788-1860: The Official Results by County and State, 2002; United States Gubernatorial Elections 1776-1860: The Official Results by State and County, 2003; Party Affiliations in the State Legislatures: A Year by Year Summary, 1796-2006, 2007; United States Gubernatorial Elections, 1861-1911, 2010. **Address:** McFarland, 960 NC Hwy 88 W, PO Box 611, Jefferson, NC 28640, U.S.A. **Online address:** mik323@aol.com

DUBOIS, Ellen Carol. American (born United States), b. 1947. **Genres:** Women's Studies And Issues, History, Social Sciences. **Career:** State University of New York, assistant professor, 1971-78, associate professor of history, 1978-, professor of history and American studies; University of California, visiting professor, professor of history, 1988-; Stanford University, visiting professor; New York University, visiting professor; University of Massachusetts, Stanton-Anthony Archival Project, editor. **Publications:** Feminism and Suffrage: The Emergence of an Independent Women's Movement in America, 1848-1869, 1978; (ed.) Elizabeth Cady Stanton, Susan B. Anthony: Correspondence, Writings, Speeches, 1981, rev. ed., 1992; (co-author) Feminist Scholarship: Kindling in the Groves of Academe, 1985; (ed. with V.L. Ruiz) Unequal Sisters: A Multicultural Reader in U.S. Women's History, 1990, 4th ed., 2008; (with K. Kearns) Votes for Women: A 75th Anniversary Album, 1995; Harriet Stanton Blatch and the Winning of Woman Suffrage, 1997; Woman Suffrage and Womens Rights, 1998; (with L. Dumenil) Through Women's Eyes: An American History with Documents, 2005, 2nd ed., 2009. Contributor to periodicals. **Address:** Department of History, University of California, 6244 Bunche Hall, 405 Hilgard Ave., Los Angeles, CA 90024-1473, U.S.A. **Online address:** edubois@ucla.edu

DUBOIS, Muriel L. American (born United States), b. 1950. **Genres:** Children's Non-fiction, Novels. **Career:** Publisher and writer. **Publications:** FOR CHILDREN: Abenaki Captive (historical fiction), 1994; Alaska Facts and Symbols, 2000; Maryland Facts and Symbols, 2000; New Hampshire Facts and Symbols, 2000; Wyoming Facts and Symbols, 2000; I Like Music, What Can I Be?, 2001; Ethiopia, 2001; Dominican Republic, 2001; I Like Sports, What Can I Be?, 2001; I Like Computers, What Can I Be?, 2001; I Like Animals, What Can I Be?, 2001; Argentina, 2001; Out and About at the Firehouse, 2002; Pro Stock Cars, 2002; Snowmobiles, 2002; The Vietnam Veterans Memorial, 2002; The Washington Monument, 2002; Rosa Parks, 2003; Helen Keller, 2003; John Adams, 2003; (with K.W. Deady) Ancient China, 2004; The U.S. Senate, 2004; The U.S. House of Representatives, 2004; The U.S. Supreme Court, 2004; The U.S. Presidency, 2004; Ancient Rome, 2004; Michigan, 2005; Virginia, 2005; New Jersey, 2005; Delaware, 2005; Connecticut, 2005; Peru, 2005; Cuba, 2005; Liberia, 2005; For My Countrywomen: The Life of Sarah Josepha Hale, 2006; Women of Granite: 25 New Hampshire Women You Should Know, 2008; (co-author) Women of the Bay State: 25 Massachusetts Women You Should Know, 2009. **Address:** Apprentice Shop Books L.L.C., PO Box 375, Amherst, NH 03031, U.S.A. **Online address:** apprenticeshpbks@aol.com

DU BOIS-REYMOND, Manuela. Dutch/German (born Germany), b. 1940. **Genres:** Children's Fiction, Social Sciences, Sociology. **Career:** Fachhochschule für Sozialpädagogih und Sozialarbeit Wiesbaden, assistant professor, 1976-77; University of Leiden, professor of sociology of education, 1977-85, professor of youth sociology, 1985-2005, now professor emeritus of education; University of Dresden, visiting professor, 1992; University of Siegen, visiting professor, time. Writer and social scientist. **Publications:** (With B. Söll) Neuköllner Schulbuch, 1974; (ed. with H. Sunker and Heinz-Hermann Kruger) Childhood in Europe: Approaches-Trends-Findings, 2001; (co-ed.) Misleading Trajectories-Integration Policies for Young Adults in Europe?, 2002; Lernfeld Europa. Eine kritische Analyse der Lebenslund Lernbedingungen von Kindern und Jungendlichen in Europa (title means: 'Learnfield Europe. An Analysis of the Conditions of Life and Learning of Children and Young People in Europe'), 2004; (ed. with L. Chisholm) The Times are a Changing: Modernising Youth Transitions in Europe, 2006; (ed. with A. Walther and A. Biggart) Participation in Transition: Motivation of Young Adults in Europe for Learning and Working, 2006; Family, School, Youth Culture. International Perspectives of Pupil Research, 2008; In Sociological Problems Special Issue Work-Life Dilemmas: Changes in Work and Family Life in the Enlarged Europe, 2009; Handbook on Youth and Young Adulthood, 2009; Integrated Transition Policies for European Young Adults: Contradictions and Solutions, 2009; Up2Youth: Youth-actor of Social Change, forthcoming. Contributor to books and periodicals. **Address:** Faculty of Social Sciences, University of Leiden, Wassenaarseweg 52, Leiden, NL-3434, Netherlands. **Online address:** dubois@fsw.leidenuniv.nl

DUBOSARSKY, Ursula. Australian (born Australia), b. 1961. **Genres:** Children's Fiction, Young Adult Fiction, Children's Non-fiction, Adult Non-fiction, Picture/Board Books. **Career:** Government Public Service, research officer; Australian Public Service, Australian Capital Territory, researcher, 1983-84; Reader's Digest Magazine, freelance researcher, 1986-; The New South Wales School Magazine, editorial assistant. Writer. **Publications:** YOUNG ADULT FICTION: High Hopes, 1990; Zizzy Zing, 1991; The Last Week in December, 1993; The White Guinea-Pig, 1994; The First Book of Samuel, 1995; Bruno and the Crumhorn, 1996; Black Sails, White Sails, 1997; My Father is not a Comedian!, 1999; The Game of the Goose, 2000; Abyssinia, 2003; How to Be a Great Detective, 2004; Theodora's Gift, 2005; The Red Shoe, 2006; The Golden Day, 2011. CHILDREN'S FICTION: Maisie and the Pinny Gig, 1989; The Strange Adventures of Isador Brown, 1998; Honey and Bear, 1998; The Two Gorillas, 1999; The Even Stranger Adventures of Isador Brown, 2001; Fairy Bread, 2001; The Magic Wand, 2002; Special Days for Honey and Bear, 2002; Isador Brown's Strangest Adventures of All, 2003; Rex, 2005; The Puppet Show, 2006; Jerry, 2008; Tibby's Leaf, 2009; The Terrible Plop, 2009; The Cubby House, 2009; The Honey and Bear Stories, 2010; The Deep End, 2010. OTHER: The Word Spy: Come and Discover the Secrets of the English Language, 2008 in US as The Word Snoop, 2009; The Return of the Word Spy, 2010. **Address:** Penguin Books Australia Ltd., 250 Camberwell Rd., Camberwell, VI 3124, Australia. **Online address:** dubosar@dodo.com.au

DUBOSE, Lou(is H.). American (born United States), b. 1948. **Genres:** Politics/Government, Biography. **Career:** Texas Observer, editor, 1987-;

Washington Spectator, editor; Austin Chronicle, politics editor. **Publications:** (With M. Ivins) Shrub: The Short but Happy Life of George W. Bush, 2000; (with M. Ivins) Bushwhacked: Life in George W. Bush's America, 2003; (with J. Reid and C. Cannon) Boy Genius: Karl Rove, the Brains Behind the Remarkable Political Triumph of George W. Bush, 2003; (with J. Reid) The Hammer, Public Affairs, 2004; (with J. Bernstein) Vice: Dick Cheney and the Hijacking of the American Presidency, 2006; (with M. Ivins) Bill of Wrongs: The Executive Branch's Assault on America's Fundamental Rights, 2007; (foreword) Stirring it up with Molly Ivins: A Memoir with Recipes, 2011. Contributor to periodicals. **Address:** Washington Spectator, 611 Pennsylvania Ave. SE, Ste. 1950, Washington, DC 20003, U.S.A.

DUBOST, Thierry. French (born France), b. 1958. **Genres:** Literary Criticism And History, Translations. **Career:** Schoolteacher, 1985-93; University of Caen, assistant professor, 1993-94, associate professor, 1994-2001, professor of English, 2001-; Open University of Caen, dean of distance learning center and head of English studies. **Publications:** (Trans.) W. Soyinka, Death and the King's Horseman, 1986; Struggle, Defeat, or Rebirth: Eugene O'Neill's Vision of Humanity, 1997; Le Theatre de Thomas Kilroy, 2001; The Plays of Thomas Kilroy: A Critical Study, 2007. EDITOR: (with A. Mills) La femme Noire américaine: Aspects d'une crise d'identité, 1997; (with P. Brennan) Regards croises sur G.B. Shaw, 1998; Le Théâtre de Thomas Kilroy, 2001; Drama Reinvented: Theatre Adaptation in Ireland, 1970-2007, 2011. **Address:** Department of English, University of Caen, Esplanade de la Paix, PO Box 5186, Caen, 14032, France. **Online address:** dubost@cte.unicaen.fr

DUBROW, Gail Lee. American (born United States) **Genres:** History, Women's Studies And Issues, Architecture. **Career:** University of Washington, associate professor, professor of architecture, urban design and planning, associate dean for research and computing, adjunct professor of history and women's studies, director of preservation planning and design certificate program; University of Minnesota, Graduate School, dean and vice provost, 2005-09, Department of History, professor. Writer. **Publications:** The Library Book: A Good Book for a Rainy Day, 1991; (with D. Graves) Sento at Sixth and Main: Preserving Landmarks of Japanese American Heritage, 2002; (ed. with J.B. Goodman) Restoring Womens History Through Historic Preservation, 2003. Contributor to periodicals. **Address:** Department of History, University of Minnesota, 1016 Heller Hall, 271 19th Ave. S, PO Box 7062, Minneapolis, MN 55455, U.S.A. **Online address:** dubrow@umn.edu

DUBROW, Heather. American (born United States), b. 1945?. **Genres:** Poetry. **Career:** University of Wisconsin, Tighe-Evans professor, John Bascom professor; Fordham University, professor, Rev. John Boyd, S.J. chair. Writer. **Publications:** Genre, 1982; Captive Victors: Shakespeare's Narrative Poems and Sonnets, 1987; (ed. with R. Strier) The Historical Renaissance: New Essays on Tudor and Stuart Literature and Culture, 1988; A Happier Eden: The Politics of Marriage in the Stuart Epithalamium, 1990; Echoes of Desire: English Petrarchism and Its Counterdiscourses, 1995; Shakespeare and Domestic Loss: Forms of Deprivation, Mourning, and Recuperation, 1999; The Challenges of Orpheus: Lyric Poetry and Early Modern England, 2008. Works appear in anthologies. Contributor to periodicals. **Address:** Fordham University, Lincoln Center Campus, New York, NY 10023, U.S.A. **Online address:** hdubrow@fordham.edu

DU BRUL, Jack B. American (born United States), b. 1968. **Genres:** Novels, Mystery/Crime/Suspense. **Career:** Writer. **Publications:** PHILIP MERCER SERIES: Vulcan's Forge, 1998; Charon's Landing, 1999; The Medusa Stone, 2000; Pandora's Curse, 2001; River of Ruin, 2002; Deep Fire Rising, 2003; Havoc, 2005. OREGON FILES WITH C. CUSSLER: Dark Watch, 2005; Skeleton Coast, 2006; Plague Ship, 2008; Corsair, 2009; The Silent Sea, 2009; The Jungle, 2011; Mirage, 2012. **Address:** c/o Author Mail, Onyx Books, 375 Hudson St., New York, NY 10014-3658, U.S.A. **Online address:** jack@jackdubrul.com

DUBUS, Andre. American (born United States), b. 1959. **Genres:** Novels, Novellas/Short Stories, Autobiography/Memoirs, Mystery/Crime/Suspense, Young Adult Fiction. **Career:** Boulder Community Treatment Center, counselor, 1982-83; Emerson College, writing instructor; Harvard University, faculty; Tufts University, faculty; University of Massachusetts, Department of English, Jack Kerouac writer-in-residence, 2001, assistant professor. Writer. **Publications:** The Cage Keeper and Other Stories, 1989; Bluesman, 1993; House of Sand and Fog, 1999; (afterword) The Stories of Breece D'J Pancake, 2002; The Garden of Last Days: A Novel, 2008; Townie: A Memoir, 2011.

Contributor to periodicals. **Address:** Philip G. Spitzer Literary Agency Inc., 50 Talmage Farm Ln., East Hampton, NY 11937-4300, U.S.A. **Online address:** andre_dubus@uml.edu

DUCEY, Michael T. (Michael Thomas Ducey). American (born United States), b. 1960. **Genres:** History. **Career:** University of Colorado Denver, associate professor of history & director of international studies major. Writer, historian and educator. **Publications:** A Nation of Villages: Riot and Rebellion in the Mexican Huasteca, 1750-1850, 2004. Contributor to periodicals. **Address:** Department of History, College of Liberal Arts & Sciences, University of Colorado Denver, PO Box 173364, Denver, CO 80217-3364, U.S.A. **Online address:** michael.ducey@cudenver.edu

DUCEY, Michael Thomas. See DUCEY, Michael T.

DUCHAC, Joseph. American (born United States), b. 1932. **Genres:** Literary Criticism And History, Poetry, Education. **Career:** Long Island University, library staff, periodicals librarian and head of public services, head reference librarian, 1964-95; Brooklyn Philharmonic, vocal soloist. Writer. **Publications:** The Poems of Emily Dickinson: An Annotated Guide to Commentary Published in English, 1890-1977, 1979; The Poems of Emily Dickinson: An Annotated Guide to Commentary Published in English, 1978-1989, 1993. Contributor to periodicals. **Address:** 25 Parade Pl., Ste. 6D, Brooklyn, NY 11226-1003, U.S.A.

DUCHARME, Diann. American (born United States), b. 1971?. **Genres:** Novels. **Career:** Writer. **Publications:** The Outer Banks House: A Novel, 2010. Contributor to periodicals. **Address:** Manakin-Sabot, VA, U.S.A. **Online address:** contact@diannducharme.com

DUCKWORTH, Eleanor. Canadian (born Canada), b. 1935. **Genres:** Education, Translations, Essays, How-to Books. **Career:** Harvard University, associate professor, 1981-89, professor of education, 1989-; United for Justice with Peace, coordinator and contributing editor. Educator and writer. **Publications:** (Trans.) J. Piaget, Genetic Epistemology, 1971; African Primary Science Program: An Evaluation and Extended Thoughts, 1978; Learning with Breadth and Depth, 1979; Inventing Density, 1986; The Having of Wonderful Ideas and Other Essays on Teaching and Learning, 1987, 3rd ed., 2006; (co-author) Science Education: A Minds-On Approach for the Elementary Years, 1990; (co-author) Teacher to Teacher: Learning from Each Other, 1997; (ed.) Tell Me More: Listening to Learners Explain, 2001. **Address:** Harvard University, Longfellow 301, 13 Appian Way, Cambridge, MA 02138, U.S.A. **Online address:** eleanor_duckworth@gse.harvard.edu

DUCKWORTH, Marilyn. New Zealander (born New Zealand), b. 1935. **Genres:** Novels, Novellas/Short Stories, Poetry, Autobiography/Memoirs, Biography. **Career:** Writer. **Publications:** NOVELS: A Gap in the Spectrum, 1959; The Matchbox House, 1960; A Barbarous Tongue, 1963; Over the Fence is Out, 1969; Disorderly Conduct, 1984; Married Alive, 1985; Rest for the Wicked, 1986; Pulling Faces, 1987; A Message from Harpo, 1989; Unlawful Entry, 1992; Seeing Red, 1993; Leather Wings, 1995; (ed.) Cherries on a Plate: New Zealand Writers Talk about Their Sisters, 1996; Studmuffin, 1997; Swallowing Diamonds, 2003; Playing Friends, 2007. OTHERS: Other Lover's Children: Poems 1958-74, 1975; Explosions On the Sun (stories), 1989; Fooling (novella), 1994; Camping on the Faultline: Memoir, 2000. Contributor to books and periodicals. Works appear in anthologies. **Address:** 41 Queen St., Mt. Victoria, Wellington, 6011, New Zealand. **Online address:** marilynduckworth@paradise.net.nz

DUCKWORTH, William (Ervin). American (born United States), b. 1943. **Genres:** Music, Biography, Art/Art History, Reference. **Career:** Atlantic Christian College, instructor, associate professor of music, 1966-73; Media Press, president, 1969-72; Bucknell University, professor of music, 1973-2011, Ringling Museum of Art, artistic director, 1986-88, Ellen Williams professor of music; South Bank Precinct, inaugural cultural arts fellow; Griffith University, Queensland Conservatorium, senior Fulbright specialist. Writer. **Publications:** (With E. Brown) Theoretical Foundations of Music, 1978; A Creative Approach to Music Fundamentals, 1981, 10th ed., 2007; (ed. with R. Fleming) John Cage at Seventy-Five, 1989; Talking Music: Conversations with John Cage, Philip Glass, Laurie Anderson, and Five Generations of American Experimental Composers, 1995; (ed. with R. Fleming) Sound and Light: La Monte Young & Marian Zazeela, 1996; 20/20: Twenty New Sounds of the Twentieth Century, 1999; Virtual Music: How the Web

Got Wired for Sound, 2005; (intro.) Jazz: American Popular Music, 2006. **Address:** Department of Music, Bucknell University, 208 Sigfried Weis Music Bldg., Moore Ave., Lewisburg, PA 17837, U.S.A. **Online address:** duckwrth@bucknell.edu

DUDDEN, Alexis. American (born United States), b. 1969. **Genres:** History. **Career:** University of Connecticut, associate professor, 1998-, professor of history, director of program in humanitarian research. Writer. **Publications:** (Contrib.) Tokens of Exchange: The Problem of Translation in Global Circulations, 1999; (contrib.) Truth Claims: Representation and Human Rights, 2002; Japan's Colonization of Korea: Discourse and Power, 2005; Troubled Apologies among Japan, Korea and the United States, 2008. Contributor of books to periodicals. **Address:** Department of History, University of Connecticut, Rm. 326, Wood Hall, 241 Glenbrook Rd., Storrs, CT 06269-2103, U.S.A. **Online address:** alexis.dudden@uconn.edu

DUDER, Tessa. New Zealander (born New Zealand), b. 1940. **Genres:** Children's Fiction, Young Adult Fiction, Plays/Screenplays, Adult Non-fiction, Novellas/Short Stories, Writing/Journalism, Novellas/Short Stories, Novels, Novels. **Career:** Daily Express, reporter, 1964-66; freelance journalist and editor, 1976; writer, 1982-; Spirit of Adventure Trust, staff, 1986-; Storylines Children's Literature Foundation of New Zealand, staff, 1991-; Waikato University, writer-in-residence, 1991. **Publications:** Kawau, 1980; Night Race to Kawau, 1982; The Book of Auckland, 1985; Spirit of Adventure, 1985; Jellybean, 1985, new ed., 1986; Play It Again, Sam, 1987; Dragons, 1987; In Lane Three, Alex Archer, 1987; Simply Messing about in Boats, 1988; Waitemata: Harbour of Sail, 1989; Alex in Winter, 1991; Songs for Alex, 1992; Alessandra: Alex in Rome, 1992; The Making of Alex: The Movie, 1993; Mercury Beach, 1997; The Tiggie Tompson Show, 1999; (with W. Taylor) Hot Mail, 2000; Tiggie Tompson All at Sea, 2001; In Search of Elisa Marchetti: A Writer's Search For Her Italian Family, 2002; Tiggie Tompson's Longest Journey, 2003; Margaret Mahy: A Writer's Life, 2005; Carpet of Dreams, 2006; Too Close to the Wind and other stories, 2006; Is She Still Alive?, 2008. EDITOR: Nearly Seventeen, 1993; (with A. Nieuwenhuizen) Crossings: Australian and New Zealand Short Stories, 1995; Falling in Love: Romantic Stories for Young Adults, 1995; Mercury Beach, 1997; A Book of Pacific Lullabies, 1998; Salt Beneath the Skin: Seafaring Kiwis Tell Their Stories, 1999; Seduced by the Sea, 2002; Storylines: The Anthology, 2003; (with K Thompson) Spirit of Youth: Thirty years of the Spirit of Adventure Trust, 2003; Down to the Sea Again: True Sea Stories for Young New Zealanders, 2005; (with L. Orman) Out of the Deep, Stories from New Zealand and the Pacific, 2007; The Word Witch, the Magical Verse of Margaret Mahy, 2009; DIY Graffiti, 2009. **Address:** 2/126 Selwyn Ave., Mission Bay, Auckland, 1071, New Zealand. **Online address:** tessa.duder@ihug.co.nz

DUDLEY, Ellen. American (born United States), b. 1938?. **Genres:** Travel/Exploration, Recreation, Social Sciences, Young Adult Non-fiction. **Career:** Union for Concerned Scientists, media relations director. Writer. **Publications:** (With E. Seaborg) Hiking and Backpacking, 1994; (with E. Seaborg) American Discoveries: Scouting the First Coast-to-Coast Recreational Trail, 1996; Savvy Adventure Traveler: What to Know Before You Go, 1999. **Address:** c/o Mountaineers Books, 1001 SW Klickitat Way, Ste. 201, Seattle, WA 98134, U.S.A.

DUDLEY-SMITH, Timothy. British (born England), b. 1926. **Genres:** Songs/Lyrics And Libretti, Theology/Religion, Bibliography, Biography, Music, Reference, Autobiography/Memoirs. **Career:** Ordained deacon, 1950; priest, 1951; Crusade magazine, 1954-59; Church Pastoral-Aid Society, assistant secretary, 1959-65, secretary, 1965-73; Evangelical Alliance, editorial secretary, 1955-59, president; Archdeacon of Norwich, 1973-81; Bishop of Thetford, 1981-91, retired, 1991. Writer. **Publications:** Christian Literature and the Church Bookstall, 1963; What Makes a Man a Christian?, 1965; A Man Named Jesus, 1971; (ed.) Someone Who Beckons: Readings and Prayers for 60 Days, 1978; Lift Every Heart: Collected Hymns 1961-1983 and Some Early Poems, 1984; The Lion Book of Stories of Jesus, 1986; A Flame of Love, 1987; Songs of Deliverance: Thirty-Six New Hymns, 1988; (comp.) The Lion Book of Classic Bible Passages: One Hundred Selected Quotations, from Genesis to Revelation, 1989; Praying with the English Hymn Writers, 1989; A Voice of Singing: Thirty-Six New Hymns, 1988-1992, 1993; (intro.) Authentic Christianity, 1995; John Stott: A Comprehensive Bibliography, 1995; Great Is the Glory: Thirty-Six New Hymns, 1993-1996, 1997; John Stott: The Making of a Leader, 1999; John Stott: A Global Ministry, 2001; Beneath a Travelling Star, 2001; A House of Praise: Collected Hymns 1961-

2001, 2003; A Door for the Word: Thirty-Six New Hymns 2002-2005, 2006; A Calendar of Praise, 2006; High Days and Holy Days, 2007; Our God and Father, Whose Eternal Mind, 2007; Snakes and Ladders: A Hymn Writer's Reflections, 2008; Praise to the Name, 2009; Beyond Our Dreaming, 2011. **Address:** 9 Ashlands Ford, Salisbury, WT SP4 6DY, England. **Online address:** web@timothydudley-smith.com

DUDZIAK, Mary L. American (born United States), b. 1956. **Genres:** History, Politics/Government, Military/Defense/Arms Control, Civil Liberties/Human Rights. **Career:** Center for Independent Living, administrative assistant, 1978-80; Fourth Circuit Court of Appeals, law clerk, 1984-85; University of Iowa, associate professor, 1986-90, professor, 1990-98; University of Southern California, visiting professor, 1997-98, professor, 1998-, Judge Edward J. and Ruey L. Guirado professor of law, history and political science, 2001-; Princeton University, Program in Law and Public Affairs, fellow, 2002; Harvard Law School, William Nelson Cromwell visiting professor of law, 2005-06. Writer and lawyer. **Publications:** Cold War Civil Rights: Race and the Image of American Democracy, 2000; (ed. and contrib.) September 11 in History: A Watershed Moment?, 2003; (ed. with L. Volpp) Legal Borderlands: Law and the Construction of American Borders, 2006; Exporting American Dreams: Thurgood Marshall's African Journey, 2008; War time: An Idea, Its History, Its Consequences, 2012. Contributor of articles to books, journals and periodicals. **Address:** Gould School of Law, University of Southern California, Rm. 404, 699 Exposition Blvd., Los Angeles, CA 90089-0071, U.S.A. **Online address:** mdudziak@law.usc.edu

DUDZINSKI, Kathleen. American (born United States), b. 1967. **Genres:** Animals/Pets, Natural History. **Career:** University of Connecticut, teaching assistant, 1986-87, laboratory assistant, 1986-89; Mystic Clipper Cruises, shipboard naturalist, 1989; Yale University, School of Medicine, research technician, 1989-90; Texas A&M University, National Science Foundation, fellow, 1990-95, teaching assistant, 1992, 1996; Oceanic Society Expeditions-Bahamas, shipboard naturalist, 1991-95; Oceanic Society Expeditions-Belize, naturalist, 1992; MacGillivray Freeman Films, documentary film consultant, 1997-2000; Mie University, postdoctoral fellow, 1997-2000; Dolphin Communication Project, director and founder, 2000-; University of Southern Mississippi, adjunct faculty, 2002-; University of Rhode Island, adjunct faculty, 2004-; Mystic Aquarium and Institute for Exploration, scientist-in-residence, 2003-07, director of development, 2004-07; Alaska Pacific University, adjunct faculty, 2005-; Geo-Marine Inc., senior marine scientist, 2008-; Aquatic Mammals, co-editor. **Publications:** Meeting Dolphins: My Adventures in the Sea, 2000; (with T. Frohoff) Dolphin Mysteries: Unlocking the Secrets of Communication, 2008. Contributor of articles to periodicals. **Address:** Stonington, CT , U.S.A. **Online address:** kdudzinski@dolphincommunicationproject.org

DUE, Tananarive. American (born United States), b. 1966. **Genres:** Novels, Young Adult Fiction, History, Autobiography/Memoirs, Young Adult Non-fiction. **Career:** Miami Herald, reporter, feature writer and columnist, 1988-98; Dark Dream Productions, screenwriter, 1998-; New York Times, intern; Wall Street Journal, intern; Antioch University, M.F.A. in Creative Writing Program, associate faculty, 2007-; DiamondHour.com, writing coach, 2009-. Journalist. **Publications:** NOVELS: The Between, 1995; (co-author) Naked Came the Manatee, 1996; My Soul to Keep, 1997; The Black Rose, 2000; The Living Blood, 2001; The Good House, 2003; Joplin's Ghost, 2005; My Soul to Take, 2011; (with S. Barnes) Devil's Wake, 2012. MEMOIRS: (with P.S. Due) Freedom in the Family: A Mother-daughter Memoir of the Fight for Civil Rights, 2003; (with S. Barnes and B. Underwood) Casanegra: A Tennyson Hardwick Story, 2007; Blood Colony, 2008; (with L.A. Banks and B. Massey) The Ancestors, 2008; (with S. Barnes and B. Underwood) In the Night of the Heat: A Tennyson Hardwick Novel, 2008; (with S. Barnes and B. Underwood) From Cape Town with Love, 2010; (with S. Barnes and B. Underwood) South by Southeast, 2012. Contributor to books and periodicals. **Address:** John Hawkins and Associates Inc., 71 W 23rd St., Ste. 1600, New York, NY 10010-4185, U.S.A. **Online address:** thelivingblood@gmail.com

DUECK, Adele. Canadian (born Canada), b. 1955. **Genres:** Young Adult Fiction, Children's Fiction. **Career:** Wheatland Regional Library, director, 1993-; Lucky Lake Community Band, treasurer, 1995-97; Western People Magazine, columnist. Writer. **Publications:** Anywhere But Here (young adult novel), 1996; Nettie's Journey, 2006; The New Calf, 2007; Racing Home, 2011. Contributor to periodicals. **Address:** PO Box 152, Lucky Lake, SK S0L 1Z0, Canada. **Online address:** adeledueck@books4kids.ca

DUELFER, Charles A. American (born United States), b. 1952?. **Genres:** History, Social Commentary, Politics/Government. **Career:** White House Office of Management and Budget, Department of Defense Strategic Nuclear Forces and Space Programs, director, 1977-83; U.S. State Department, Office of International Security Policy, deputy director, 1984-85, director, 1985-90, Task Force in Support of Desert Storm, director, 1991; Center for Defense Trade, director and deputy to the assistant secretary of state for politico-military matters, 1990-92; UN Special Commission on Iraq (UNSCOM), deputy executive chair, chair, 1993-2000; Central Intelligence Agency (CIA), special advisor to the director of central intelligence for Iraq WMD and leader of Iraq survey group, 2000-04; Omnis Inc., advisor to the chief executive officer; Transformational Space Corp. (a small space launch company), chief executive officer. Writer. **Publications:** Comprehensive Report of the Special Advisor to the DCI on Iraq's WMD, with Addendums, 2005; Hide and Seek: The Search for Truth in Iraq, 2009. Contributor to books and periodicals. **Address:** c/o Tessa Shanks, Public Affairs Books, 250 W 57th St., Ste. 1321, New York, NY 11017, U.S.A. **Online address:** info@charlesduelfer.com

DUEY, Kathleen. American (born United States), b. 1950. **Genres:** Children's Fiction, Young Adult Fiction, Children's Non-fiction, Young Adult Non-fiction, Picture/Board Books. **Career:** Writer. **Publications:** AMERICAN DIARIES SERIES: Emma Eileen Grove: Mississippi, 1865, 1996; Mary Alice Peale: Philadelphia, 1777, 1996; Sarah Anne Hartford: Massachusetts, 1651, 1996; Anisett Lundberg: California, 1851, 1996; Willow Chase: Kansas Territory, 1847, 1997; Ellen Elizabeth Hawkins: Mobeetie, Texas, 1886, 1997; Evie Peach: St. Louis, 1857, 1997; Alexia Ellery Finsdale: San Francisco, 1905, 1997; Celou Sudden Shout: Idaho, 1826, 1998; Summer MacCleary: Virginia, 1749, 1998; Agnes May Gleason: Walsenberg, Colorado, 1933, 1998; Amelina Carrett: Bayou Grand Coeur, Louisiana, 1863, 1999; Josie Poe: Palouse, Washington, 1943, 1999; Rosa Moreno: Hollywood, California, 1928, 1999; Nell Dunne: Ellis Island, 1904, 2000; Maddie Retta Lauren: Sandersville, Georgia, C.S.A, 1864, 2000; Francesca Vigilucci: Washington, DC, 1913, 2000; Janey G. Blue: Pearl Harbor, 1941, 2001; Zellie Blake: Massachusetts, 1836, 2002. SURVIVAL! SERIES WITH K.A. BALE: Earthquake, 1906, 1998; Cave-In: St. Claire, Pennsylvania, 1859, 1998; Stranded: Death Valley, 1850, 1998; Flood: Mississippi, 1927, 1998; Blizzard: Estes Park, Colorado, 1886, 1998; Fire: Chicago, 1871, 1998; Titanic: April 14, 1912, 1998; Hurricane: Open Seas, 1844, 1999; Train Wreck: Kansas, 1892, 1999; Swamp: Bayou Teche, Louisiana, 1851, 1999; Forest Fire: Hinckley, Minnesota, 1894, 1999; Hurricane: New Bedford, Massachusetts, 1784, 1999; San Francisco Earthquake, 1906, 1999; Louisiana Hurricane, 1860, 2000; Terremoto, 2002; The Story of Peter Rabbit, 2004. SPIRIT OF THE CIMARRON SERIES: Esperanza, 2002; Bonita, 2002; Sierra, 2002; Spirit: Stallion of the Cimarron (adaptation), 2002. UNICORN'S SECRET SERIES: Moonsilver, 2001; The Silver Thread, 2001; The Silver Bracelet, 2002; Mountains of the Moon, 2002; The Sunset Gates, 2002; Beyond the Sunset, 2002; True Heart, 2003; Castle Avamir, 2003; The Journey Home, 2003. OTHERS: Double-Yuck Magic, 1991; Mr. Stumpguss Is a Third-Grader, 1992; The Third Grade's Skinny Pig, 1993; (with K.A. Bale) Three of Hearts, 1998; Nowhere to Run, Nowhere to Hide!, 2000; Stay Out of the Graveyard!, 2000; Bogeyman in the Basement!, 2000; Beware the Alien Invasion!, 2000; (with M. Barnes) Freaky Facts about Natural Disasters, 2000; (with M. Barnes) More Freaky Facts about Natural Disasters, 2001; Time Soldiers book 2 -Rex 2, 2003; Spider-Man, Ultimate Picture Book, 2003; Rex, 2003; Arthur, 2004; Mummy, 2005; Lara at Athenry Castle, 2005; Lara and the Silent Place, 2005; Lara and the Moon-colored Filly, 2005; Lara and the Gray Mare, 2005; Samurai, 2006; Patch, 2006; (with R. Gould and E. Epstein) Escapade Johnson in Mayhem at Mount Moosilauke, 2006; 100 Easy Ways to get Your Kids Reading: A Busy Mom's Guide, 2006; Rex 2, 2006; Skin Hunger, 2007; Silence and Lily: 1773, 2007; Margret and Flynn, 1875, 2008; Nanuq, 2008; Leo, 2008; Tahi, 2009; Sacred Scars, 2009. FAERIES' PROMISE: Silence and Stone, 2010; Following Magic, 2010; Wishes and Wings, 2011; Full Moon, 2011. PICTURE BOOKS: The Easter Morning Surprise, 1996; The Big Blue Easter Egg, 1996; Hogger the Hoarding Beastie, 1999; Moogie the Messy Beastie, 1999; Glumby the Grumbling Beastie, 2001; Crassy the Crude Beastie, 2001; X-Men, 2003; Ella the Baby Elephant, 2008. Contributor to periodicals. **Address:** 345 Hudson St., PO Box 1665, Fallbrook, CA 92028, U.S.A. **Online address:** kathleen@kathleenduey.com

DUFAULT, Peter Kane. American (born United States), b. 1923. **Genres:** Poetry, Literary Criticism And History, Young Adult Non-fiction. **Career:** Journalist, 1950-64; musician and teacher, 1964-2000; Williams College, critic-in-residence, 1968-69; Cheltenham Festival of Literature, poet-in-resi-

dence, 1978, 1993. Writer. **Publications:** Angel of Accidence, 1954; For Some Stringed Instrument, 1957; A Westchester Farewell and Other Poems, 1968; On Balance, 1978; Memorandum to the Age of Reason, 1988; New Things Come into the World, 1993; Looking in All Directions: Selected Poems, 1954-2000, 2000; To Be in the Same World, 2007; The Ponderable World, forthcoming. Contributor to magazines. **Address:** 56 Hickory Hill Rd., Hillsdale, NY 12529-6116, U.S.A. **Online address:** peterkanedufault@hotmail.com

DUFAULT, Roseanna Lewis. American (born United States), b. 1954?. **Genres:** Literary Criticism And History, Women's Studies And Issues. **Career:** University of Colorado, instructor in French, 1979-85; Colorado State University, assistant professor of French, 1986-89; Ohio Northern University, assistant professor, 1989-92, associate professor of French, 1992-, professor of French, chair; Alliance Francaise, instructor, 1980-83; Universite de Bordeaux III, lecturer, 1985-86; Ohio Council on World Affairs, representative, 1989. Writer. **Publications:** Metaphors of Identity: The Treatment of Childhood in Selected Québécois Novels, 1991. EDITOR: Women by Women: The Treatment of Female Characters by Women Writers of Fiction in Quebec Since 1980, 1997 (with P.R. Gilbert) Doing Gender: Franco-Canadian Women Writers of the 1990s, 2001; (with J. Ricouart) Les secrets de la Sphinxe: Lectures de l'œuvre d'Anne-Marie Alonzo, 2004; (with M. Suzuki) Diversifying the Discourse: The Florence Howe Award for Outstanding Feminist Scholarship, 1990-2004, 2006; (with J. Ricouart) Visions poétiques de Marie-Claire Blais, 2008. Contributor to journals. Works appear in anthologies. **Address:** Department of Modern languages, Ohio Northern University, 220 Dukes Memorial Bldg., 525 S Main St., Ada, OH 45810-1599, U.S.A. **Online address:** r-dufault@onu.edu

DUFF, Alan. New Zealander (born New Zealand), b. 1950. **Genres:** Novels, Social Sciences, Young Adult Fiction, Autobiography/Memoirs. **Career:** Freelance writer, 1985-. **Publications:** Once Were Warriors, 1991; One Night Out Stealing, 1992; Maori: The Crisis and the Challenge, 1993; State Ward, 1994; What Becomes of the Broken Hearted?, 1996; Both Sides of the Moon, 1998; Out of the Mist and Steam: A Memoir, 1999; Alan Duff's Maori Heroes, 2000; Szabad, 2001; Jake's Long Shadow, 2002; Dreamboat Dad, 2008; Who Sings for Lu?, 2009. **Address:** 51 Busby Hill, Havelock North, 4130, New Zealand.

DUFFEY, Betsy (Byars). American (born United States), b. 1953. **Genres:** Children's Fiction, Humor/Satire. **Career:** Writer. **Publications:** The Math Wiz, 1990; A Boy in the Doghouse, 1991; The Gadget War, 1991; Lucky in Left Field, 1992; Puppy Love, 1992; How to Be Cool in the Third Grade, 1993 in UK as How to Be Cool in Junior School, 1996; Lucky on the Loose, 1993; Wild Things, 1993; Throw-Away Pets, 1993; Lucky Christmas, 1994; Coaster, 1994; Utterly Yours, Booker Jones, 1995 in UK as Buster and the Black Hole, 1996; Hey, New Kid!, 1996; Camp Knock Knock, 1996; The Camp Knock Knock Mystery, 1997; Virtual Cody, 1997; Cody's Secret Admirer, 1998; Spotlight on Cody, 1998; Alien for Rent, 1999; Cody Unplugged, 1999; (with B. Byars and L. Myers) My Dog, My Hero, 2000; Fur-Ever Yours, Booker Jones, 2001; (with B. Byars and L. Myers) SOS File, 2004; (with B. Byars and L. Myers) Dog Diaries: Secret Writings of the WOOF Society, 2007; (with B. Duffey and L. Myers) Cat Diaries: Secret Writings of the MEOW Society, 2010. **Address:** 4825 Franklin Pond Rd., Atlanta, GA 30342, U.S.A.

DUFFIELD, Gervase E. British (born England), b. 1935. **Genres:** Ethics, History, Intellectual History, Theology/Religion, Essays. **Career:** News Extra, editor, 1964-79, 1985-; General Synod of Church of England for Oxford Diocese, staff, 1960-80; The Churchman, editor, 1967-72; News Today, editor, 1980-; Sutton Courtenay & Appleford, staff; Vale of White Horse District Council, Councillor. **Publications:** (Ed.) Paul Report Considered: An Appraisal of Mr. Leslie Paul's Report, The Deployment and Payment of the Clergy: Thirteen Essays, 1964; Admission to Holy Communion, 1964; The Work of William Tyndale, 1965; (ed.) The Work of Thomas Cranmer, 1965; (ed.) John Calvin, 1966; Revision and the Layman, 1966; (ed.) Anglicans/Methodists: A Popular Appraisal by Leading Anglicans and Methodists Who Believe that the Proposals in the Report Anglican-Methodist Unity Remain Defective, 1968; (ed. with M. Bruce) Why Not? Priesthood and the Ministry of Women: A Theological Study, 1972, rev. ed., 1976; (with J.I. Packer and G.O. Buchanan) Fellowship in the Gospel: Evangelical Comment on Anglican-Methodist Unity and Intercommunion Today, 1968; Martin Bucer's Psalter of David 1530, 1973; Bunyan of Bedford, 1978; Tyndale's 1525 New Testament Fragment, 1994; Across the Divide, 1978; The Prayer Book Noted 1550, 1982;

William Barlowe's Dialogue of Lutheran Factions 1531, 1983; The Work of Peter Martyr, 1990. **Address:** Appleford House, Abingdon, Oxford, AV OX14 4PB, England. **Online address:** gervase.duffield@whitehorsedc.gov.uk

DUFFIELD, John S. American (born United States), b. 1958?. **Genres:** Politics/Government, Military/Defense/Arms Control, History. **Career:** International University of Mexico, instructor, 1986; University of Southern California, Center for International Studies, visiting fellow, 1988; Harvard University, Center for Science and International Affairs, research fellow, 1989-90; University of Virginia, assistant professor, 1990-97, research associate, 1997-98; University of Georgia, assistant professor, 1998-2000, associate professor of political science, 2000-01; Georgia State University, associate professor, 2002-06, professor of political science, 2006-. Writer. **Publications:** Power Rules: The Evolution of NATO's Conventional Force Posture, 1995; World Power Forsaken: Political Culture, International Institutions, and German Security Policy after Unification, 1998; Over a Barrel: The Costs of U.S. Foreign Oil Dependence, 2008; (ed. with P.J. Dombrowski) Balance Sheet: The Iraq War and U.S. National Security, 2009. Contributor to books and periodicals. **Address:** Georgia State University, PO Box 3965, Atlanta, GA 30302-3965, U.S.A. **Online address:** duffield@gsu.edu

DUFFIELD, Wendell. American (born United States), b. 1941. **Genres:** Geography. **Career:** U.S. Geological Survey, research geologist, 1965-97, retired, 1997; Northern Arizona University, adjunct geology professor, 1997-; writer, 1997-. **Publications:** Structure and Origin of the Koae Fault System, Kilauea Volcano, Hawaii, 1975; (with R.V. Sharp) Geology of the Sierra Foothills Melange and Adjacent Areas, Amador County, California, 1975; (with R.D. Weldin) Mineral Resources of the South Warner Wilderness, Modoc County, California, 1976; (with D.A. Swanson and R.S. Fiske) Displacement of the South Flank of Kilauea Volcano, 1976; (with M. Guffanti) Geothermal Research Program of the U.S. Geological Survey, 1982; (with J.H. Sass and M.L. Sorey) Tapping the Earth's Natural Heat, 1994; Volcanoes of Northern Arizona: Sleeping Giants of the Grand Canyon Region, 1997; Chasing Lava: A Geologist's Adventures at the Hawaiian Volcano Observatory, 2003; (with J.H. Sass) Geothermal Energy: Clean Power from the Earth's Heat, 2003; When Pele Stirs: A Volcanic Tale of Hawaii, Hemp, and High-Jinks, 2003; Poems, Song Lyrics, Essays and Short Stories by Nina Hatchitt Duffield, 2005; From Piglets to Prep School: Crossing a Chasm, 2005; Yucca Mountain Dirty Bomb, 2007; What's So Hot About Volcanoes, 2011. **Address:** Department of Geology, Northern Arizona University, PO Box 4099, Flagstaff, AZ 86011, U.S.A. **Online address:** wendell.duffield@nau.edu

DUFFIN, Jacalyn. Canadian (born Canada), b. 1950. **Genres:** Medicine/Health, Intellectual History, History. **Career:** Ontario Cancer Treatment and Research Foundation, hematologist and oncologist, 1980-82; University of Ottawa, Hannah postdoctoral fellow in the history of medicine, 1985-88; Queen's University, Department of Philosophy, Hannah chair in the history of medicine and Hannah professor, 1988-, Department of Medicine, faculty, Department of History, faculty, Faculty of Education, faculty; Kingston General Hospital, consulting hematologist, 1988-. Writer. **Publications:** (Trans. with R.C. Maulitz) M.D. Grmek, History of AIDS: Emergence and Origin of a Modern Pandemic, 1990; Langstaff: A Nineteenth-Century Medical Life, 1993; (contrib.) French Medical Culture in Nineteenth-Century Atlanta, 1994; (contrib.) Muse and Reason: The Relation of Arts and Sciences, 1650-1850, 1994; To See with a Better Eye: A Life of R.T.H. Laennec, 1998; History of Medicine: A Scandalously Short Introduction, 1999; (contrib.) Oxford Companion to Canadian History, 2004; Lovers and Livers: Disease Concepts in History, 2005; (ed.) Clio in the Clinic: History in Medical Practice, 2005; (ed. with A. Sweetman) SARS in Context: Memory, History, Policy, 2006; (contrib.) Poetics of Biography, 2007; Medical Miracles: Doctors, Saints, and Healing in the Modern World, 2009. Contributor to periodicals. **Address:** Department of Philosophy, Queen's University, John Watson Hall, 78 Barrie St., Kingston, ON K7L 3N6, Canada. **Online address:** duffinj@queensu.ca

DUFFY, Bruce. American (born United States), b. 1953?. **Genres:** Novels, Literary Criticism And History. **Career:** Writer. **Publications:** The World As I Found It, 1987; Last Comes the Egg: A Novel, 1997; World as I Found It, 2010; Disaster was My God, 2011. Contributor to periodicals. **Address:** Simon & Schuster, 1230 Ave. of the Americas, New York, NY 10020, U.S.A.

DUFFY, Eamon. American/Irish (born Ireland), b. 1947. **Genres:** Theology/Religion, History. **Career:** St Mary's College, honorary fellow; University of Cambridge, Magdalene College, university reader in church history, univer-

sity lecturer in ecclesiastical history, professor of the history of Christianity, Faculty Board of Divinity, chair, 1997-2000, director of studies, fellow and president, 2001-. Writer. **Publications:** Peter and Jack: Roman Catholics and Dissent in Eighteenth Century England, 1982; The Stripping of the Altars: Traditional Religion in England, 1400-1580, 1992; The Creed in the Catechism, 1996; Saints and Sinners: A History of the Popes, 1997; (contrib.) Medieval Theology and the Natural Body, 1997; The Voices of Morebath: Reformation and Rebellion in an English Village, 2001; Faith of Our Fathers: Reflections on Catholic Tradition, 2004; Creed in the Catechism: The Life of God for Us, 2005; Walking to Emmaus, 2006; Marking the Hours: English People and their Prayers 1240-1570, 2006; Fires of Faith: The Reconstruction of Catholicism in Mary Tudor's England, 2009; (contrib.) Object of Devotion, 2010; Ten Popes Who Shook the World, 2011. EDITOR: Challoner and His Church: A Catholic Bishop in Georgian England, 1981; (with B. Bradshaw) Humanism, Reform, and Reformation: The Career of John Fisher, Bishop of Rochester, 1989; (with D. Loades)The Church of Mary Tudor, 2006; (and intro.) Reign of Mary Tudor, 2009. Contributor to books. **Address:** Faculty of Divinity, University of Cambridge, West Rd., Cambridge, CB3 9BS, England. **Online address:** ed10000@cam.ac.uk

DUFFY, James H(enry). (Haughton Murphy). American (born United States), b. 1934. **Genres:** Novels, Mystery/Crime/Suspense, Politics/Government, Young Adult Fiction, Children's Fiction, Criminology/True Crime. **Career:** American Bank of Albania, director; Cravath, Swaine & Moore L.L.P. (law firm), associate lawyer, 1959-67, partner, 1968-88, retired, 1988. Writer. **Publications:** Domestic Affairs: American Programs and Priorities, 1978; Dog Bites Man: City Shocked! (novel), 2001. REUBEN FROST MYSTERY NOVEL SERIES AS HAUGHTON MURPHY: Murder for Lunch, 1986; Murder Takes a Partner, 1987; Murders and Acquisitions, 1988; Murder Keeps a Secret, 1989; Murder Times Two, 1990; Murder Saves Face, 1991; A Very Venetian Murder, 1992. **Address:** c/o Lois Wallace, Wallace Literary Agency Inc., 301 E 79th St., Ste. 14-J, New York, NY 10075, U.S.A. **Online address:** jduffy@global.net

DUFFY, Margaret. British (born England), b. 1942. **Genres:** Mystery/Crime/Suspense, Novels, Horror. **Career:** Inland Revenue, clerical officer, 1958-66; Ministry of Defense, clerical officer, 1969-74. Writer and garden designer. **Publications:** A Murder of Crows, 1987; Death of a Raven, 1988; Brass Eagle, 1988; Who Killed Cock Robin?, 1990; Rook-Shoot, 1990; Man of Blood, 1992; Gallows Bird, 1993; Dressed to Kill, 1994; Mindspinner, 1994; Corpse Candle, 1995; Prospect of Death, 1995; Music in the Blood, 1997; A Fine Target, 1998; A Hanging Matter, 2001; Dead Trouble, 2004; So Horrible a Place, 2004; Tainted Ground, 2006; Cobweb, 2007; Blood Substitute, 2008; Souvenirs of Murder, 2009; Corpse in Waiting, 2010; Rat Poison, 2012. **Address:** The Crossing, Iron Mine Ln., Dousland, DN PL20 6NA, England.

DUFFY, Maureen (Patricia). (D. M. Cayer). British (born England), b. 1933. **Genres:** Novels, Plays/Screenplays, Poetry, History, Biography, Translations, Adult Non-fiction, Young Adult Non-fiction, Autobiography/Memoirs. **Career:** Novelist and teacher. **Publications:** (As D.M. Cayer) Scarborough Fear, 1982; Critical Quarterly, 1987; England: The Making of the Myth: From Stonehenge to Albert Square (history), 2001; Alchemy, 2004. NOVELS: That's How It Was, 1962, rev. ed., 1984; The Single Eye, 1964; The Microcosm, 1966, rev. ed., 1990; The Paradox Players, 1968; Wounds, 1969; Love Child, 1971; The Erotic World of Faery, 1972, rev. ed., 1989; All Heaven in a Rage in US as I Want to Go to Moscow, 1973; Capital, 1975; Housespy, 1978; Gor Saga, 1981; Londoners: An Elegy, 1983; Change, 1987; Illuminations, 1991; Occam's Razor, 1993; Restitution, 1998; The Orpheus Trial, 2009. POETRY: (trans.) D. Rea, A Blush of Shame, 1963; Lyrics for the Dog Hour: Poems, 1968; The Venus Touch (poetry), 1971; Actaeon, 1973; Evesong (poetry), 1975; Memorials of the Quick and the Dead, 1979; Collected Poems, 1949-84, 1985; Family values, 2008. OTHER: (trans.) A Blush of Shame, 1963; The Passionate Shepherdess: Aphra Behn (biography), 1977, rev. ed., 2000; (ed. with A. Brownjohn) New Poetry (anthology), 1977; Inherit the Earth: A Social History, 1979; Men and Beasts: An Animal Rights Handbook, 1984; (ed. and intro.) Oroonoko and Other Stories, 1986; A Thousand Capricious Chances: A History of the Methuen List 1889-1989, 1990; (ed.) Five Plays, 1990; Henry Purcell, 1994; The Orpheus Trail, 2009. **Address:** c/o Jonathan Clowes, 22 Prince Albert Rd., London, GL NW1 7ST, England. **Online address:** 113714.1610@compuserve.com

DUFFY, Michael. American (born United States), b. 1958. **Genres:** History,

Biography. **Career:** Defense Week, military affairs reporter, 1980-85; Time (magazine), political correspondent, 1985-97, bureau chief, 1997-2005, assistant managing editor, 2005-. Freelance reporter and writer, 2005-. **Publications:** (With D. Goodgame) Marching in Place: The Status Quo Presidency of George Bush, 1992; (with N. Gibbs) The Preacher and the Presidents: Billy Graham in the White House, 2007. Contributor to periodicals. **Address:** Time Inc., 1271 Ave. of the Americas, New York, NY 10020, U.S.A. **Online address:** michaelrwduffy@gmail.com

DUFFY, Susan. American (born United States), b. 1951?. **Genres:** Bibliography, Politics/Government, Theatre, Adult Non-fiction, History, Intellectual History. **Career:** California Polytechnic State University, College of Liberal Arts, professor and chair of liberal studies, Department of Liberal Studies, chair and director. Writer. **Publications:** (Comp.) Shirley Chisholm: A Bibliography of Writings by and about Her, 1988; (ed. with M. Slann) Morality and Conviction in American Politics: A Reader, 1990; (comp.) The Political Left in the American Theater of the 1930s: A Bibliographic Source book, 1992; American Labor on Stage: Dramatic Interpretations of the Steel and Textile Industries in the 1930s, 1996; (comp. with P.T. Adalian, Jr.) A Comprehensive Index to Artist and Influence: The Journal of Black American Cultural History, 1981-1999, 2000; (intro.) The Political Plays of Langston Hughes, 2000; (with S. Duffy) Mortal Wounds, 2001 (co-author) Keystones of Entrepreneurship Knowledge, 2005. Contributor to periodicals. **Address:** College of Liberal Arts, California Polytechnic State University, 1 Grand Ave., San Luis Obispo, CA 93407, U.S.A. **Online address:** sduffy@calpoly.edu

DUFRESNE, Jim. American (born United States), b. 1955. **Genres:** Travel/Exploration, Reference, Art/Art History. **Career:** Booth Newspapers, outdoor writer, 1987-. **Publications:** Isle Royale National Park: Foot Trails and Water Routes, 1984, 3rd ed., 2002; Voyageurs National Park: Water Routes, Foot Paths and Ski Trails, 1986; (with K. Leghorn) Glacier Bay National Park: A Backcountry Guide to the Glaciers and Beyond, 1987; Michigan: Off the Beaten Path, 1988, 4th ed., 1996; Michigan State Parks: A Complete Guide for Campers, Boaters, Anglers, Hikers and Skiers, 1989, 2nd ed. as Michigan State Parks: A Complete Recreation Guide, 1998; Michigan's Best Outdoor Adventures with Children, 1990; Fifty Hikes in Lower Michigan: The Best Walks, Hikes and Backpacks from Sleeping Bear Dunes to the Hills of Oakland County, 1991, 2nd ed. as 50 Hikes in Michigan: The Best Walks, Hikes, and Backpacks in the Lower Peninsula, 1999; Wild Michigan, 1992; Porcupine Mountains Wilderness State Park: A Backcountry Guide for Hikers, Campers, Backpackers and Skiers, 1993; Alaska: A Travel Survival Kit, 4th ed., 1994; Backpacking in Alaska: A Lonely Planet Walking Guide, 1995; Trekking in Alaska: A Walking Guide, 1995; (with J. Williams) Tramping in New Zealand: A Walking Guide, 1995, 4th ed., 1998; Best Hikes with Children in Michigan, 2001; Michigan, 2001; The Complete Guide to Michigan Sand Dunes, 2005; Backpacking in Michigan, 2007; Twelve Classic Trout Streams in Michigan A Handbook for Fly Anglers, rev. ed., 2009; Michigan's Best Campgrounds: A Guide to the Best 150 Public Campgrounds in the Great Lakes State, 2011. **Address:** PO Box 852, Clarkston, MI 48347, U.S.A. **Online address:** kidven@aol.com

DUFRESNE, John. American (born United States), b. 1948. **Genres:** Novels, Novellas/Short Stories, Plays/Screenplays, Young Adult Fiction, Children's Fiction, Self Help, Writing/Journalism, Literary Criticism And History, Literary Criticism And History. **Career:** Northeast Louisiana University, instructor in composition and creative writing, 1984-87; Augusta College, instructor in composition, creative writing and humanities, 1988-89; Florida International University, associate professor in creative writing, 1989-98, professor, 1999-; University of Texas, Michener Center for Writers, visiting professor, 2005. Writer. **Publications:** STORIES: The Way That Water Enters Stone, 1991; Johnny Too Bad, 2005. NOVELS: Louisiana Power & Light, 1994; Love Warps the Mind a Little, 1997; Deep in the Shade of Paradise, 2002; Requiem, Mass.: A Novel, 2008; Is Life Like This?: A Guide to Writing your First Novel in Six Months, 2010. OTHER: The Lie That Tells a Truth: A Guide to Writing Fiction, 2003. **Address:** Department of English, Florida International University, AC1, 3000 NE 151 St., North Miami, FL 33181, U.S.A. **Online address:** johndufresne@mindspring.com

DUGAN, Ellen. American (born United States), b. 1963. **Genres:** Psychology, Theology/Religion. **Career:** Writer and educator. **Publications:** Garden Witchery: Magick from the Ground Up, 2003; Elements of Witchcraft: Natural Magick for Teens, 2003; 7 Days of Magic: Spells, Charms & Correspondences for the Bewitching Week, 2004; Cottage Witchery: Natural Magick for

Hearth and Home, 2005; Autumn Equinox: The Enchantment of Mabon, 2005; Herb Magic for Beginners: Down-to-Earth Enchantments, 2006; The Enchanted Cat: Feline Fascinations, Spells & Magick, 2006; Natural Witchery: Intuitive, Personal & Practical Magick, 2007; How to Enchant a Man: Spells to Bewitch, Bedazzle & Beguile, 2008; Book of Witchery: Spells, Charms & Correspondences for Every Day of the Week, 2009; Garden Witch's Herbal: Green Magick, Herbalism & Spirituality, 2009; Practical Protection Magick: Guarding & Reclaiming Your Power, 2011; Seasons of Witchery: Celebrating the Sabbats with the Garden Witch, 2012; Witches Tarot, 2012. **Address:** Llewellyn Worldwide Ltd., 2143 Wooddale Dr., Woodbury, MN 55125-2989, U.S.A. **Online address:** edugan_gardenwitch@yahoo.com

DUGATKIN, Lee Alan. American (born United States), b. 1962. **Genres:** Animals/Pets, Sciences, History. **Career:** University of Louisville, professor of biological sciences. Writer. **Publications:** Cooperation among Animals: An Evolutionary Perspective, 1997; (ed. with H.K. Reeve) Game Theory & Animal Behavior, 1998; Cheating Monkeys and Citizen Bees: The Nature of Cooperation in Animals and Humans, 1999; The Imitation Factor: Evolution beyond the Gene, 2000; (ed.) Model Systems in Behavioral Ecology: Integrating Conceptual, Theoretical, and Empirical Approaches, 2001; Principles of Animal Behavior, 2004, 2nd ed., 2009; The Altruism Equation: Seven Scientists Search for the Origins of Goodness, 2006; Mr. Jefferson and the Giant Moose, 2009. Contributor to periodicals. **Address:** Department of Biological Sciences, University of Louisville, Louisville, KY 40292, U.S.A. **Online address:** lee.dugatkin@louisville.edu

DUGAW, Dianne. American (born United States), b. 1948. **Genres:** History, Women's Studies And Issues. **Career:** University of California, visiting lecturer in composition, 1982-85; University of Colorado, assistant professor of English, 1985-89; Harvard University, Mellon teaching fellow, 1989-90; University of Oregon, associate professor, 1991-99, professor of English, 1999-. Writer. **Publications:** (Ed.) The Female Soldier, 1989; Warrior Women and Popular Balladry 1650-1850, 1989; (ed.) The Anglo-American Ballad: A Folklore Casebook, 1995; Deep Play: John Gay and the Invention of Modernity, 2001; The Hidden Baroque in Britain, 1600-1750, forthcoming. Contributor to books. **Address:** Department of English, University of Oregon, PLC 458, 1585 E 13th Ave., Eugene, OR 97403-1286, U.S.A. **Online address:** dugaw@uoregon.edu

DUGGAN, Christopher. British (born England), b. 1957. **Genres:** Area Studies, History, Social Commentary, Young Adult Non-fiction. **Career:** Oxford Polytechnic, part-time lecturer, 1983-85; Wolfson College, junior research fellow, 1983-85; All Soul's College, thesis fellow, 1985-97; University of Reading, lecturer in Italian history and director of the center for the advanced study of Italian society (CASIS), 1987-94, reader in Italian history, 1994-2002, professor of modern Italian history, 2002-, Centre for Modern Italian History, director, School of Literature & Languages, head. Writer. **Publications:** (With M.I. Finley and D.M. Smith) A History of Sicily, 1986; Fascism and the Mafia, 1989; A Concise History of Italy, 1994; (ed. with C. Wagstaff) Italy in the Cold War: Politics, Culture and Society, 1948-58, 1995; Francesco Crispi, 1818-1901: From Nation to Nationalism, 2002; The Force of Destiny: A History of Italy Since 1796, 2007. Contributor of articles to journals and newspapers. **Address:** Department of Italian Studies, University of Reading, Whiteknights, Reading, BR RG6 6AA, England. **Online address:** c.j.h.duggan@reading.ac.uk

DUGGLEBY, John. American (born United States), b. 1952. **Genres:** Art/Art History, Biography, Children's Non-fiction, Ghost Writer, Education, History, Marketing, Popular Culture, Travel/Exploration, Zoology, Biography, Ghost Writer. **Career:** Allstate Insurance, magazine editor, 1976-78; American Telephone and Telegraph-Chicago, communications staff, 1978-81; Burson-Marsteller Public Relations, creative staff, 1981-84; Duggleby Communications, owner, 1984-. Writer, biographer, public speaker and musician. **Publications:** The Sabertooth Cat, 1989; Pesticides, 1990; Doomed Expeditions, 1990; Impossible Quests, 1990; Artist in Overalls: The Life of Grant Wood, 1996; Story Painter: The Life of Jacob Lawrence, 1998; Uh Huh!: The Story of Ray Charles, 2005; Revolution: The Story of John Lennon, 2007. Contributor to periodicals. **Address:** Duggleby Communications, 5322 Norma Rd., McFarland, WI 53558-9396, U.S.A. **Online address:** duggleby@charter.net

DUGONI, Robert. American (born United States), b. 1961. **Genres:** Novels, Young Adult Non-fiction. **Career:** Los Angeles Times, reporter; Gordon and Rees, partner; Schlemlein Goetz Fick & Scruggs P.L.L.C., of counsel. Journalist. **Publications:** (With J. Hilldorfer) The Cyanide Canary, 2004; The Jury Master, 2006; Damage Control, 2007; Wrongful Death, 2009; False Justice, 2010; Bodily Harm: A Novel, 2010; Murder One, 2011; The Conviction, 2012. **Address:** Simon & Schuster Inc., 1230 Ave. of the Americas, New York, NY 10020, U.S.A. **Online address:** rvd@soslaw.com

DUGUID, Paul. American/British (born England), b. 1954?. **Genres:** Technology, Adult Non-fiction. **Career:** Granville Publishing, senior editor, 1981-87; Institute for Research on Learning, research scientist, 1987-90; Xerox Corp., consultant, 1989-2001; University of California, research associate in social and cultural studies in education, 1992-2004, School of Information, adjunct professor, 2005-; Duke University, Center for the Public Domain, fellow, 2001-02; Copenhagen Business School, Department of Organisational and Industrial Sociology, part-time visiting professor, 2002-05; Santa Clara University, Center for Science, Technology and Society, visiting fellow, 2005-06, senior researcher; Queen Mary University, professorial research fellow, 2005-; Lancaster University, Institute for Entrepreneurship and Enterprise Development, honorary research fellow, 2005-; York University, School of Management, visiting research fellow in business history, 2008-. **Publications:** (Contrib. with J.S. Brown) Automation for Usability, 1992; (contrib.) The Future of the Book, 1996; (contrib. with J.S. Brown) Web-Weaving: Intranets, Extranets and Strategic Alliances, 1998; (with J.S. Brown) The Social Life of Information, 2000; (contrib.) Contradictions et Dynamique des Organisations, 2005; (contrib.) Organizing for the Creative Economy: Community, Practice and Capitalism, 2008; French Connections: The Propagation of Trade Marks in the Nineteenth Century, 2009; (ed. with T.S. Lopes) Trademarks, Brands and Competitiveness, 2010. Contributor to books and periodicals. **Address:** School of Information, University of California, 203A South Hall, Berkeley, CA 94720-4600, U.S.A. **Online address:** duguid@ischool.berkeley.edu

DUHL, Leonard J. American (born United States), b. 1926. **Genres:** Medicine/Health, Psychiatry, Urban Studies, Regional/Urban Planning. **Career:** Jewish Hospital, intern, 1948-49; Winter Veterans Administration Hospital, resident in psychiatry, 1949-54; Menninger Foundation School of Psychiatry, fellow, 1949-54; California Public Health Service, senior assistant surgeon, 1951-53; U.S. Public Health Service, medical director, 1954-72; National Institute of Mental Health, Professional Services Branch, psychiatrist, 1954-66, Office of Planning, chief, 1964-66; George Washington University, clinical instructor, 1958-61, assistant clinical professor, 1963-68; U.S. Department Housing and Urban Development, special assistant to secretary, 1966-68; University of California, professor of urban social policy and public health, 1968-, now professor emeritus; University of California's San Francisco Medical Center, clinical professor, 1969-; Antioch College, adjunct professor, 1970-; Berkeley Unified School District, co-director of documentation and evaluation of experimental schools programs, 1971-. Writer. **Publications:** Approaches to Research in Mental Retardation, 1959; The Urban Condition: People and Policy in the Metropolis, 1963; Urban America and the Planning of Mental Health Services, Symposium No. 10, 1964; Mental Health and Urban Social Policy, 1968; (ed.) A Symposium on the Urban Crisis, 1969; (with M. Myerson, C. Rapkin and J. Collins) The City and the University, 1969; (with D.A. Schon) Deliberate Social Change in the City, 1972; Making Whole: Health for a New Epoch, 1980; (with C. Cousins) Technology and Learning Disabilities, 1983; The Mental Health Complex: It's a New Ball Game, 1985; Healthy Social Change, 1985; Health Planning and Social Change, 1986; (ed. with N.A. Cummings) The Future of Mental Health Care, 1987; The Social Entrepreneurship of Change, 1990; The Urban Condition-20 Years Later, 1993. Contributor to periodicals. **Address:** School of Public Health, University of California, 410 Warren Hall, Berkeley, CA 94720-1329, U.S.A. **Online address:** lduhl@berkeley.edu

DUIGAN, John. American/British (born England), b. 1949. **Genres:** Plays/Screenplays, Novels, Literary Criticism And History. **Career:** University of Melbourne, teacher; La Trobe University, teacher. Writer and director. **Publications:** NOVELS: Badge, 1975; Room to Move, 1985; Players, 1988. Contributor to periodicals. **Address:** Creative Artists Agency, 9830 Wilshire Blvd., Beverly Hills, CA 90212-1825, U.S.A.

DUINA, Francesco G. American (born United States), b. 1969?. **Genres:** Politics/Government, Sociology. **Career:** Monitor Co., editor and consultant, 1996-2008; Harvard University, lecturer, 1998-2000; Bates College, Department of Sociology, assistant professor, 2000-06, associate professor, 2006-, chair, 2008-; Copenhagen Business School, International Center for Business and Politics, visiting professor, 2004-; The JLJ Group, director, 2009-. **Publications:** Harmonizing Europe: Nation-States within the Common Market, 1999; The Social Construction of Free Trade: The European Union, NAFTA and MERCOSUR, 2006; Institutions and the Economy, 2011; Winning: Reflections on an American Obsession, 2011. **Address:** Department of Sociology, Bates College, Rm. 263, Pettengill Hall, Lewiston, ME 04240, U.S.A. **Online address:** fduina@bates.edu

DUKE, Anna Marie. Also writes as Anna Astin, Patty Duke. American (born United States), b. 1946. **Genres:** Women's Studies And Issues, Autobiography/Memoirs, Biography. **Career:** Screen Actors Guild, president, 1985-88. Writer and actor. **Publications:** AS PATTY DUKE: Miracle Worker, 1959; Surviving Sexual Assault, 1983; (with K. Turan) Call Me Anna: The Autobiography of Patty Duke, 1987; (with G. Hochman) A Brilliant Madness: Living with Manic-Depressive Illness, 1992. **Address:** Creative Artists Agency, 1888 Century Pk. E, Ste. 1400, Los Angeles, CA 90067, U.S.A.

DUKE, Martin. American/British (born England), b. 1930. **Genres:** Medicine/Health, Essays, Novellas/Short Stories, History. **Career:** Manchester Memorial Hospital, director of medical education, 1963-84; self-employed internist and cardiologist, 1963-93. Writer. **Publications:** The Development of Medical Techniques and Treatments: From Leeches to Heart Surgery, 1991; Tales My Stethoscope Told Me, 1998. Contributor to journals. Works appear in anthologies. **Address:** 1 Heritage Pl., 945 Main St., Manchester, CT 06040-6064, U.S.A.

DUKE, Michael S. Canadian/American (born United States), b. 1940. **Genres:** Novellas/Short Stories, Literary Criticism And History, Translations, History. **Career:** George Washington University, assistant professor of Chinese, 1974-76; University of Vermont, assistant professor of Chinese, 1976-77; Oberlin-in-Taiwan Program, resident director, 1978-80; National Taiwan University, assistant professor of European literature, 1979-80; University of Wisconsin, visiting assistant professor of Chinese, 1980-81; University of British Columbia, assistant professor, 1982-85, associate professor, 1985-90, professor of Asian studies, 1990-, head of department, 1991-96, now professor emeritus; Peking University, resident director of Council on International Educational Exchange, 1986-87; New York Times, cultural informant for Beijing Bureau, 1986-87. Writer. **Publications:** Lu You, 1977; Blooming and Contending: Chinese Literature in the Post-Mao Era, 1985; The Iron House: A Memoir of the Chinese Democracy Movement and the Tiananmen Massacre, 1990; (trans.) Raise the Red Lantern: 3 Novellas by Su Tong, 1993; (trans.) C. Koonchung, Fat Years, 2011. EDITOR, AUTHOR OF INTRODUCTION AND CONTRIBUTOR: Contemporary Chinese Literature: An Anthology of Post-Mao Fiction and Poetry, 1985; Modern Chinese Women Writers: Critical Appraisals, 1989; Worlds of Modern Chinese Fiction: Short Stories & Novellas from the People's Republic, Taiwan & Hong Kong, 1991. **Address:** Department of Asian Studies, University of British Columbia, 1871 W Mall, Vancouver, BC V6T 1Z2, Canada. **Online address:** michael.duke@ubc.ca

DUKE, Patty. See DUKE, Anna Marie.

DUKE, Steven B. American (born United States), b. 1934. **Genres:** Law, Politics/Government. **Career:** Supreme Court of the United States, law clerk, 1959-60; Yale Law School, assistant professor, 1961-64, associate professor, 1965-66, professor of law, 1966-82, 2003-, law of science and technology professor, 1981-2003; University of California-Berkeley, visiting professor, 1965-66; University of California-Hastings, visiting professor, 1981-82. Writer. **Publications:** (With A.C. Gross) America's Longest War: Rethinking Our Tragic Crusade Against Drugs, 1993. Contributor to journals. **Address:** Yale Law School, Rm. 215, 127 Wall St., PO Box 208215, New Haven, CT 06520-8215, U.S.A. **Online address:** steven.duke@yale.edu

DUKERT, Joseph M(ichael). American (born United States), b. 1929. **Genres:** Technology, Environmental Sciences/Ecology, Physics, International Relations/Current Affairs. **Career:** Baltimore News Post, copy reader, late news editor, reporter and feature writer, 1953-55; Martin Co., information services staff, 1956-59, Nuclear Division, director of public relations, 1960-62, Research Institute for Advanced Studies, staff, 1962-65; Baltimore City Jail Board, officer, 1963-68; energy consultant, 1965-; Center for Strategic and International Studies, senior associate; North American Commission for Environmental Cooperation, energy agency consultant and senior adviser.

Publications: Atompower, 1962; This is Antarctica, 1965, rev. ed., 1972; Thorium and the Third Fuel, 1970; Nuclear Ships of the World, 1973; Atoms on the Move: Transporting Nuclear Material, 1975; High-Level Radioactive Waste: Safe Storage and Ultimate Disposal, 1975; Nuclear Power and the Environment, 1976; Energy History of the United States, 1776-1976, 1976; (ed.) Energy in America's Future: The Choices before Us, 1979; A Short Energy History of the United States: And Some Thoughts about the Future, 1980; (with H.H. Landsberg) High Energy Costs: Uneven, Unfair, Unavoidable?, 1981; The Evolution of the North American Energy Market, 1999; North American Energy: At Long Last, One Continent, 2005; Energy, 2009. Contributor of articles to books. **Address:** Center for Strategic and International Studies, 1800 K St. NW, Washington, DC 20006, U.S.A. **Online address:** dukert@verizon.net

DUKES, Paul. British (born England), b. 1934. **Genres:** Area Studies, History, Philosophy. **Career:** University of Maryland, lecturer, 1959-64; University of Aberdeen, professor of history, now professor emeritus, King's College, lecturer, 1964-71, senior lecturer in history, 1972-, reader, 1975-. Writer. **Publications:** Catherine the Great and the Russian Nobility, 1967; The Emergence of the Super-Powers, 1970; A History of Russia, 1974, 3rd ed., 1998; (ed.) Russia Under Catherine the Great, 2 vols., 1977-78; October and the World: Perspectives on the Russian Revolution, 1979; The Making of Russian Absolutism, 1613-1801, 1982, 2nd ed., 1990; A History of Europe, 1985; The Last Great Game: USA versus USSR, 1989; (ed. with J. Dunkley) Culture and Revolution, 1990; (ed.) Russia and Europe, 1991; (ed. with T. Brotherstone) Trotsky Reappraisal, 1992; (ed.) Muscovy and Sweden in the Thirty Years' War, 1630-1635, 1996; World Order in History: Russia and the West, 1996; (ed.) Frontiers of European Culture, 1996; The Superpowers, 2000; Russia and the Wider World in Historical Perspective, 2000; USA in the Making of the USSR: The Washington Conference, 1921-1922, and Uninvited Russia, 2004; (with Graeme P. Herd, Jarmo Kotilaine) Stuarts and Romanovs, 2009; Minutes to Midnight, 2011. **Address:** School of Divinity, History and Philosophy, King's College, University of Aberdeen, Rm. G13, Crombie Annexe, Aberdeen, AB24 3FX, England. **Online address:** p.dukes@abdn.ac.uk

DUKORE, Bernard F. American (born United States), b. 1931. **Genres:** Literary Criticism And History, Theatre, Literary Criticism And History, Plays/Screenplays, Film. **Career:** City University of New York, Hunter College, instructor of speech and drama, 1957-60, associate professor, professor of drama, 1966-72; University of Southern California, assistant professor of drama, 1960-62; California State University, assistant professor, associate professor of drama, 1962-66; Stanford University, visiting associate professor of drama, 1965-66; University of Hawaii, professor of drama, 1972-86; Virginia Tech, university distinguished professor of theatre and humanities, 1986-97, university distinguished professor emeritus, 1997-. Writer. **Publications:** (With M. Rohrberger and S.H. Woods) Introduction to Literature, 1969; (comp.) Drama and Revolution, 1970; (comp.) Documents for Drama and Revolution, 1971; Bernard Shaw, Director, 1971; Drama and Revolution, 1971; Bernard Shaw, Playwright: Aspects of Shavian Drama, 1973; (comp.) Dramatic Theory and Criticism: Greeks to Grotowski, 1974; 17 Plays: Sophocles to Baraka, 1976; Where Laughter Stops, 1976; Money and Politics in Ibsen, Shaw and Brecht, 1980; The Theatre of Peter Barnes, 1981; (comp.) Bernard Shaw's Arms and the Man, 1982; Harold Pinter, 1982, 2nd ed., 1985; American Dramatists 1918-1945, 1984; Death of a Salesman and The Crucible, 1989; Barnestorm: The Plays of Peter Barnes, 1995; Sam Peckinpah's Feature Films, 1999; Shaw's Theatre, 2000. EDITOR: (and intro.) The Man of Mode (play), 1962; A Bibliography of Theatre Arts Publications in English, 1963; (with R. Cohn) Twentieth Century Drama: England, Ireland, the United States (anthology), 1966; (with R. O'Brien) Tragedy: Ten Major Plays (anthology), 1969; (with D.C. Gerould) Avant-Garde Drama (anthology), 1969; (with J. Gassner) A Treasury of the Theatre, 1970; (and intro.) The Collected Screenplays of Bernard Shaw, 1980; Alan Ayckbourn: A Casebook, 1991; Shaw and the Last Hundred Years, 1992; Bernard Shaw: The Drama Observed, vol. IV, 1994; Bernard Shaw and Gabriel Pascal, 1996; Not Bloody Likely!: And Other Quotations from Bernard Shaw, 1996; (and intro.) Bernard Shaw on Cinema, 1997; Sam Peckinpah's Feature Films. 1999; Shaw's Theater, 2000. **Address:** 2510 Plymouth St., Blacksburg, VA 24060-8256, U.S.A. **Online address:** bdukore@vt.edu

DUKTHAS, Ann. See **DOHERTY, P(aul) C.**

DULANEY, W. Marvin. American (born United States), b. 1950. **Genres:** History, Race Relations, Education, Politics/Government. **Career:** Wittenberg University, upward bound instructor, 1978, academic and career counselor, 1978-81; Texas Christian University, intercultural affairs adviser, 1981-83; University of Texas, Upward Bound Program, assistant director, 1983-85, assistant professor, 1986-93, associate professor of history, 1993-94, African American Museum, curator of history, 1987-94, Walter Prescott Webb lecturer, 1991; St. Olaf College, assistant professor of history, 1985-86; Juanita Jewel Craft House Civil Rights Museum, curator, 1993; College of Charleston, director of African-American studies, 1994-, Avery Research Center for African American History and Culture, director, 1994-, Department of History, chair, 1998-2004, associate professor; Texas African-American History Journal, co-editor. **Publications:** (Ed. with K. Underwood) Essays on the American Civil Rights Movement, 1993; Black Police in America, 1996; (with E.L. Drago) Charleston's Avery Center: From Education And Civil Rights To Preserving The African American Experience, 2006. Contributor of articles to books and periodicals. **Address:** Department of History, College of Charleston, 66 George St., Charleston, SC 29424-0001, U.S.A. **Online address:** dulaneyw@cofc.edu

DULLY, Howard. American (born United States), b. 1948. **Genres:** Novels, Biography, Autobiography/Memoirs. **Career:** Newsweek, staff writer. **Publications:** (With C. Fleming) My Lobotomy: A Memoir, 2007; (with C. Fleming) Messing with My Head, 2009. **Address:** Vermilion, 20 Vauxhall Bridge Rd., London, GL SW1V 2SA, England. **Online address:** howarddully@comcast.net

DUMAS, Firoozeh. American/Iranian (born Iran), b. 1966?. **Genres:** Biography, Autobiography/Memoirs, Travel/Exploration. **Career:** Writer. **Publications:** Funny in Farsi: A Memoir of Growing Up Iranian in America, 2003; Laughing Without an Accent: Adventures of an Iranian American, at Home and Abroad, 2008. Contributor to periodicals. **Address:** c/o Mel Berger, William Morris Agency L.L.C., 1325 Ave. of the Americas, New York, NY 10019-6026, U.S.A. **Online address:** author@firoozehdumas.com

DUMBLETON, Mike. Australian/British (born England), b. 1948. **Genres:** Young Adult Non-fiction, Novels. **Career:** South Australian Education Department, English teacher, 1973-74, faculty coordinator, 1975-87, deputy principal, 1988, literacy project coordinator, 1989-; Adelaide High School, English and literacy coordinator. Author and consultant. **Publications:** Dial-a-Croc, 1991; Granny O'Brien and the Diamonds of Selmore, 1993; Mrs. Watson's Goat, 1993; Mr Knuckles, 1993; Ms MacDonald's Farm, 1994; I Hate Brussels Sprouts, 1994; Pumped Up! (short stories), 1995; Let's Escape, 1997; Downsized, 1999; Muddled-up Farm, 2001; Passing On, 2001; Watch Out for Jamie Joel (young-adult novel), 2003; Giraffe in a Scarf, 2007; Hippopotamouse, 2007; You Must Be Joking!, 2007; Cat, 2007; Jet-ball, 2008; One Cool Kangaroo, 2008; What Will Baby Do?, 2009. NONFICTION: Can Cards, 1989; (with J. Guess) Hands on Poetry: A Practical Anthology, 1993; Real Writing across the Curriculum: A Practical Guide to Improving and Publishing Student Work, 1993; (with K. Loutain) Addressing Literacy in Society and Environment, 1999; (with K. Loutain) Addressing Literacy in Science, 1999; (with K. Loutain) Addressing Literacy in the Arts, 1999. **Address:** Jenny Darling & Associates, PO Box 413, Toorak, VI 3142, Australia.

DUMBRELL, John. British (born England), b. 1950. **Genres:** Politics/Government, History, Social Sciences. **Career:** Manchester Metropolitan University, lecturer in American studies, 1978-94; Keele University, senior lecturer in American studies, 1994-; Durham University, School of Government and International Affairs, professor of government, acting head; Open University, tutor. Writer. **Publications:** (Ed.) Vietnam and the Antiwar Movement, 1989; The Making of U.S. Foreign Policy, 1990; Vietnam, 1992; The Carter Presidency: A Re-Evaluation, 1993, 2nd ed., 1995; American Foreign Policy: Carter to Clinton, 1997; A Special Relationship: Anglo-American Relations in the Cold War and After, 2001, 2nd ed., 2006; President Lyndon Johnson and Soviet Communism, 2004; (ed. with D. Ryan) Vietnam in Iraq: Tactics, Lessons, Legacies and Ghosts, 2007; (ed. with J.E. Jones) America's War on Terrorism: New Dimensions in U.S. Government and National Security, 2008; Clinton's Foreign Policy: Between the Bushes, 1992-2000, 2009; (ed. with A.R. Schäfer) America's Special Relationships: Foreign and Domestic Aspects of the Politics of Alliance, 2009. Contributor to periodicals. **Address:** School of Government and International Affairs, Durham University, The Al-Qasimi Bldg., Elvet Hill Rd., Durham, DU DH1 3TU, England. **Online address:** j.w.dumbrell@durham.ac.uk

DUMMETT, (Agnes Margaret) Ann. British (born England), b. 1930.

Genres: Civil Liberties/Human Rights, Plays/Screenplays, Novels, Criminology/True Crime. **Career:** Local Voluntary Organisation for Race Equality, community relations officer, 1966-69; College of Further Education, English teacher, 1969-71; Institute of Race Relations, researcher on the teaching of history, 1971-73; Joint Council for Welfare of Immigrants, researcher, 1978-84; Runnymede Trust, director, 1984-87; Commission for Racial Equality, consultant, 1990-99. Writer. **Publications:** A Portrait of English Racism, 1973; (with M. Hollings) Restoring the Streets: Catholics in Multiracial Britain, 1974; Citizenship and Nationality, 1976; Who Is My Neighbour?: The Race Question in the United Kingdom, 1977; A New Immigration Policy, 1978; Moral Philosophy, 1979; (with I. Martin) British Nationality: A Guide to the New Law, 1982; (ed.) Towards a Just Immigration Policy, 1986; (with A. Nicol) Subjects, Citizens, Aliens, and Others, 1990; Racially Motivated Crime, 1997. Contributor to periodicals. **Address:** Commission for Racial Equality, Elliot House, 10-12 Allington St., London, GL SW1E 5EH, England.

DUMMETT, Michael (Anthony Eardley). *See* Obituaries.

DUMONT, Ninda. *See* FRANKLIN, Linda Campbell.

DUNANT, Peter. *See* DUNANT, Sarah.

DUNANT, Sarah. (Peter Dunant). British (born England), b. 1950. **Genres:** Mystery/Crime/Suspense, Essays, Plays/Screenplays, Novels. **Career:** BBC-Radio, producer, 1974-76; freelance writer and broadcaster, 1977-; BBC, presenter and anchor woman; Guardian, critic and writer; The Times, critic and writer. Observer. **Publications:** AS PETER DUNANT: Exterminating Angels, 1983; Intensive Care, 1986. NOVELS: Snow Storms in a Hot Climate, 1988; Transgressions, 1997; Mapping the Edge, 1999; The Birth of Venus, 2003; In the Company of the Courtesan, 2006; Sacred Hearts, 2009. HANNAH WOLFE MYSTERY SERIES: Birth Marks, 1991; Fatlands, 1993; Under My Skin, 1996. EDITOR: The War of the Words (essays), 1994; (with R. Porter) The Age of Anxiety (essays), 1997. **Address:** 17 Tytherton Rd., London, GL N19 4QB, England.

DUNAWAY, Finis. American/Canadian (born Canada) **Genres:** Environmental Sciences/Ecology, Politics/Government, International Relations/Current Affairs, History. **Career:** Trent University, assistant professor, associate professor. Writer. **Publications:** Natural Visions: The Power of Images in American Environmental Reform, 2005. Contributor to periodicals. **Address:** Trent University, 1600 W Bank Dr., Peterborough, ON K9J 7B8, Canada. **Online address:** finisdunaway@trentu.ca

DUNAWAY, Wilma A. American (born United States), b. 1944. **Genres:** Economics. **Career:** Virginia Polytechnic Institute and State University, professor of sociology. Writer. **Publications:** The First American Frontier: Transition to Capitalism in Southern Appalachia, 1700- 1860, 1996; New Theoretical Directions for the 21st Century World-System, 2003; Crises and Resistance in the 21st Century World-System, 2003; The African-American Family in Slavery and Emancipation, 2003; (ed.) Emerging Issues in the 21st Century World-System, 2003; Slavery in the American Mountain South, 2003; Women, Work, and Family in the Antebellum Mountain South, 2008. **Address:** School of Public & International Affairs, Virginia Polytechnic Institute, and State University, 105 Architecture Annex, Blacksburg, VA 24061-0113, U.S.A. **Online address:** wdunaway@vt.edu

DUNBAR, Gary S(eamans). American (born United States), b. 1931. **Genres:** Geography, History, Essays, Translations. **Career:** Longwood College, instructor in geography and history, 1956-57; University of Virginia, visiting assistant professor, 1957-58, assistant professor, 1958-62, associate professor of geography, 1962-67, department chair, 1963-67; Ahmadu Bello University, visiting professor, 1965-67; University of California, Los Angeles, visiting associate professor, 1967, associate professor, 1968-70, professor of geography, 1970-88, professor emeritus, 1988-; State University of New York, College at Oneonta, adjunct lecturer, 1997. Writer. **Publications:** African Ranches Ltd., 1914-1931: An Ill-Fated Stockraising Enterprise in Northern Nigeria, 1971; élisée Reclus, Historian of Nature, 1978; (comp.) A Biographical Dictionary of American Geography in the Twentieth Century, 1992, 2nd ed., 1996; The History of Geography: Collected Essays, 1996. EDITOR: Historical Geography of the North Carolina Outer Banks, 1958; The History of Geography: Translations of Some French and German Essays, 1983; The History of Modern Geography: An Annotated Bibliography of Selected Works, 1985; Modern Geography: An Encyclopedic Survey, 1991; Geogra-

phy: Discipline, Profession and Subject since 1870, 2001. **Address:** Department of Geography, University of California-Los Angeles, 856 CHS, 1255 Bunche Hall, PO Box 951524, Los Angeles, CA 90095-1524, U.S.A. **Online address:** gdunbar1@stny.rr.com

DUNBAR, Joyce. British (born England), b. 1944. **Genres:** Children's Fiction, Adult Non-fiction, Novels, Education, Picture/Board Books. **Career:** English teacher, 1968-89. Writer. **Publications:** CHILDREN'S BOOKS: Jugg, 1980; (with J. Dunbar) The Magic Rose Bough, 1984; Mundo and the Weather-Child, 1985; Cake for Barney, 1987; A Bun for Barney, 1987; Software Superslug, 1987; Tomatoes and Potatoes, 1988; Billy and the Brolly Boy, 1988; The Raggy Taggy Toys, 1988; Mouse Mad Madeline, 1988; One Frosty Friday Morning, 1989; Joanna and the Bean-Bag Beastie, 1989; Software Superslug and the Great Computer Stupor, 1989; Ollie Oddbin's Skylark, 1989; I Wish I Liked Rice Pudding, 1989; Software Superslug and the Nutty Novelty Knitting, 1990; Ten Little Mice, 1990; Five Mice and the Moon, 1990; The Scarecrow, 1991; Giant Jim and Tiny Tim, 1991; I Want a Blue Banana, 1991; Why Is the Sky Up?, 1991; Lollopy, 1991; Four Fierce Kittens, 1991; Can Do, 1992; Mouse and Mole, 1993; Mouse and Mole Have a Party, 1993; My First Read Aloud Story Book: For Young Children, 1993; The Spring Rabbit, 1993; The Wishing Fish Tree, 1994; Brown Bear, Snow Bear, 1994; Seven Sillies, 1994; (reteller) Little Eight John, 1994; Oops-A-Daisy: And Other Tales for Toddlers, 1995; Indigo and the Whale, 1996; This Is the Star, 1996; Freddie the Frog, 1996; Happy Days for Mouse and Mole, 1996; A Very Special Mouse and Mole, 1996; The Selfish Snail, 1997; Doodledragon, 1997; Doodling Daniel (x4), 1997; Doodlecloud, 1997; Doodlemaze, 1997; If you Want to Be a Cat..., 1997; Hansel and Gretel, 1997; Tell Me Something Happy before I Go to Sleep, 1998; Baby Bird, 1998; The Sand Children, 1999; Panda and Gander, 1999; The Pig Who Wished, 1999; Gander's Pond, 1999; Secret Friend, 1999; Bowl of Fruit, 1999; The Glass Garden, 1999; Panda's New Toy, 1999; Eggday, 1999; The Very Small, 2000; (ed.) Kingfisher Read-Aloud Storybook, 2000; Hip-Dip-Dip with Mouse and Mole, 2000; The Ups and Downs of Mouse and Mole, 2001; Tell Me What It's Like to be Big, 2001; Magic Lemonade, 2002; Chick Called Saturday, 2003; Love-Me Bird, 2004; Shoe Baby, 2005; Voices and Visions A Celebration of Norwich Market, 2005; Where's My Sock?, 2006; (with J. Ray) Moonbird, 2007; (with J. Liao) Monster Who Ate Darkness, 2008; Oddly, 2009. Works appear in anthologies. **Address:** c/o Hilary Delamere, The Agency Ltd., 24 Pottery Ln., Holland Pk., London, GL W11 4LZ, England.

DUNBAR, Leslie W(allace). American (born United States), b. 1921. **Genres:** Philosophy, Politics/Government, Race Relations, History. **Career:** Emory University, assistant professor of political science, 1948-51; Atomic Energy Commission, Savannah River Plant, chief of community affairs, 1951-54; Mount Holyoke College, assistant professor of political science, 1955-58; Southern Regional Council, director of research, 1958-61, executive director, 1961-65; Field Foundation, executive director and secretary, 1965-80; University of Arizona, visiting professor, 1981; Ford Foundation, senior associate, 1985-87; United Negro College Fund, Book Review, Southern Changes, editor, 1989-93; Nation Institute, president. **Publications:** Republic of Equals, 1966; (with K. Wagenheim) Puerto Ricans in the U.S., 1983; (ed.) Minority Report: What Has Happened to Blacks, Hispanics, American Indians and Other American Minorities in the Eighties, 1984; Common Interest: How Our Social Welfare Policies Don't Work and What We Can Do about Them, 1988; Just Entitlements: What it Means to be Poor in America, 1988; Reclaiming Liberalism, 1991; Shame of Southern Politics: Essays and Speeches, 2002; Collected Essays, 2002. **Address:** 3050 Military Rd. NW, Washington, DC 20015, U.S.A.

DUNBAR-ORTIZ, Roxanne. American (born United States), b. 1939. **Genres:** Adult Non-fiction, Trivia/Facts, History, Autobiography/Memoirs. **Career:** Activist, 1967-72; California State University, Native American Studies Program, teacher, Department of Ethnic Studies, professor of ethnic studies, now professor emeritus; Indigenous World Association, co-founder. Writer. **Publications:** NONFICTION: The Great Sioux Nation: Sitting in Judgement on America: Based on and Containing Testimony Heard at the Sioux Treaty Hearing held December, 1974, in Federal District Court, Lincoln, Nebraska, 1977; Roots of Resistance: Land Tenure in New Mexico, 1680-1980, 1980; Indians of the Americas: Human Rights and Self-Determination, 1984; La Cuestión Miskita En La Revolución Nicaragüense, 1986; The Miskito Indians of Nicaragua, 1988; Red Dirt: Growing Up Okie (autobiography), 1997; Outlaw Woman: A Memoir of the War Years, 1960-1975 (autobiography), 2001; Blood on the Border: A Memoir of the Contra War (autobiography), 2005; Roots of Resistance: A History of Land Tenure in New Mexico, 2007. **Address:** Department of Ethnic Studies, California State University, 4099 Meiklejohn Hall, 25800 Carlos Bee Blvd., Hayward, CA 94542, U.S.A. **Online address:** rdunbaro@pacbell.net

DUNCAN, A. A. M. Scottish (born Scotland), b. 1926. **Genres:** History, Biography, Social Sciences. **Career:** Oxford University, Balliol College, lecturer in history, 1950-51; Queen's University of Belfast, lecturer in medieval history, 1951-53; University of Edinburgh, lecturer in medieval history, 1953-62; University of Glasgow, School of Historical Studies, professor of Scottish history and literature, 1962-93, dean of faculty of arts, 1974-76, clerk of Senate, 1978-83, honorary research fellow, professor emeritus, 1993-Writer. **Publications:** (With J.M. Webster) Regality of Dunfermline Court Book 1531-1538, 1953; Introduction to Scottish History for Teachers, 1967; The Nation of Scots and the Declaration of Arbroath (1320), 1970; Scotland: The Making of the Kingdom, 1975, rev. ed., 1978; James I, 1424-1437, 1976; The Kingship of the Scots, 842-1292: Succession and Independence, 2002. EDITOR: Scottish Independence 1100-1328, 1971; Formulary E: Scottish Letters and Brieves, 1286-1424, 1976; Scotland from the Earliest Times to 1603, 3rd. ed., 1977; The Acts of Robert I, King of Scots, 1306-1329, 1988; The Bruce, 1997. **Address:** School of Humanities, University of Glasgow, 1 University Gardens, Glasgow, G12 8QQ, Scotland. **Online address:** archibald.duncan@glasgow.ac.uk

DUNCAN, Alice Faye. American (born United States), b. 1967. **Genres:** Children's Non-fiction, Civil Liberties/Human Rights. **Career:** Memphis City School System, school librarian, 1993-. Writer. **Publications:** The National Civil Rights Museum Celebrates Everyday People, 1995; Willie Jerome, 1995; Miss Viola and Uncle Ed Lee, 1999; Honey Baby Sugar Child, 2003; (with P. Dooley) Christmas Soup, 2005. **Address:** c/o Kendra Marcus, 67 Meadow View Rd., Orinda, CA 94563-3246, U.S.A. **Online address:** afduncan@aol.com

DUNCAN, Andy. American (born United States), b. 1964. **Genres:** Science Fiction/Fantasy. **Career:** News andamp; Record, features writer and copy editor, 1986-93; University of Alabama, assistant director of student media, 2002-; Overdrive, senior editor; Frostburg State University, assistant professor of English. **Publications:** Beluthahatchie and Other Stories, 2000; (ed. with F.B. Cox) Crossroads: Tales of the Southern Literary Fantastic, 2004; Alabama Curiosities, 2005; The Man Who Rode the Mule around the World, forthcoming. Contributor to periodicals. **Address:** Overdrive, PO Box 264, Frostburg, MD 21532, U.S.A. **Online address:** aduncan@rrpub.com

DUNCAN, Carol Greene. American (born United States), b. 1936. **Genres:** Art/Art History, Romance/Historical, Literary Criticism And History. **Career:** Ramapo College of New Jersey, professor of art history, through 1972, professor emeritus, 1972-. Writer. **Publications:** The Pursuit of Pleasure: The Rococo Revival in French Romantic Art, 1976; Strangers on the Shore, 1989; The Aesthetics of Power: Essays in Critical Art History, 1993; Civilizing Rituals: Inside Public Art Museums, 1995; How to Have a Museum with Brains: John Cotton Dana and the Making of a Democratic Culture for America, 2009. **Address:** Department of Art History, Ramapo College of New Jersey, Rm. BC232, 505 Ramapo Valley Rd., Mahwah, NJ 07430, U.S.A. **Online address:** cduncan@ramapo.edu

DUNCAN, Christine H. American (born United States) **Genres:** Mystery/Crime/Suspense, Novels, Literary Criticism And History, Young Adult Fiction. **Career:** Writer. **Publications:** Safe Beginnings (mystery novel), 2002; Safe House, 2009; Safe Reunion, forthcoming. **Address:** c/o Author Mail, Treble Heart Books, 1284 Overlook Dr., Sierra Vista, AZ 85635-5512, U.S.A. **Online address:** chduncan@christineduncan.com

DUNCAN, Colin A.M. Canadian (born Canada), b. 1954. **Genres:** Agriculture/Forestry, Environmental Sciences/Ecology, History, Adult Non-fiction. **Career:** University of Edinburgh, research technician in microbiology, 1979-81; Queen's University, historian of England and of the environment, postdoctoral research fellow, instructor and assistant professor, 1987-98, adjunct associate professor, 2010-11; McGill University, assistant professor of history of the environment, 1997-, adjunct associate professor. Writer. **Publications:** (Ed. with D.W. Tandy) From Political Economy to Anthropology: Situating Economic Life in Past Societies, 1994; The Centrality of Agriculture: Between Humankind and the Rest of Nature, 1996. Contributor to periodicals. **Address:** Department of History, Queen's University, 129 Wat-

son Hall, 49 Bader Ln., Kingston, ON K7L 3N6, Canada. **Online address:** colin.duncan@mcgill.ca

DUNCAN, Cynthia M. American (born United States) **Genres:** Sociology, Business/Trade/Industry, Economics, Social Sciences, Young Adult Non-fiction. **Career:** Mountain Association for Community Economic Development, research director; Aspen Institute, Rural Economic Policy Program, director, through 1989; University of New Hampshire, associate professor, professor of sociology and department chair, 1989-2000, Carsey Institute, founding director, 2004-; Ford Foundation's Community and Resource Development Unit, director, 2000-04. Writer. **Publications:** (Ed.) Rural Poverty in America, 1992; (with N. Lamborghini and E. Pank) Young Families and Youth in the North Country: A Report to the Northern New Hampshire Foundation, 1993; Worlds Apart: Why Poverty Persists in Rural America, 1999. Contributor to journals. **Address:** The Carsey Institute, University of New Hampshire, 73 Main St., Huddleston Hall, Durham, NC 03824, U.S.A.

DUNCAN, Dave. Also writes as Ken Hood. Canadian/Scottish (born Scotland), b. 1933. **Genres:** Science Fiction/Fantasy, Novels. **Career:** Geologist, 1955-76; geological consultant, 1976-86. Writer. **Publications:** THE SEVENTH SWORD FANTASY SERIES: The Reluctant Swordsman, 1988; The Coming of Wisdom, 1988; The Destiny of the Sword, 1988. A MAN OF HIS WORD FANTASY SERIES: Magic Casement, 1990; Faery Lands Forlorn, 1991; Perilous Seas, 1991; Emperor and Clown, 1992. A HANDFUL OF MEN FANTASY SERIES: The Cutting Edge, 1992; Upland Outlaws, 1993; The Stricken Field, 1993; The Living God, 1994. THE GREAT GAME FANTASY SERIES: Past Imperative, 1995; Present Tense, 1996; Future Indefinite, 1997. YEARS OF LONGDIRK HISTORICAL FANTASY SERIES AS KEN HOOD: Demon Sword, 1995; Demon Rider, 1997; Demon Knight, 1998. TALES OF THE KING'S BLADES FANTASY SERIES: The Gilded Chain, 1998; Lord of the Fire Lands, 1999; Sky of Swords, 2000. CHRONICLES OF THE KING'S BLADES FANTASY SERIES: Paragon Lost, 2002; Impossible Odds, 2003; The Jaguar Knights, 2004; Children of Chaos (Unnamed Series), 2006; Mother of Lies, 2007. THE ALCHEMIST, HISTORICAL MYSTERY FANTASY SERIES: The Alchemist's Apprentice, 2007; The Alchemist's Code, 2008; The Alchemist's Pursuit, 2009. OTHER FANTASY: A Rose-Red City, 1987; The Reaver Road, 1992; The Hunters' Haunt, 1995; The Cursed, 1995; Ill Met in the Arena, 2008; Speak to the Devil, 2010; Pock's World, 2010; When the Saints, 2011; Against the Light, forthcoming. SCIENCE-FICTION NOVELS: Shadow, 1987; West of January, 1989; Strings, 1990; Hero!, 1991. YOUNG ADULT FANTASY SERIES, THE KING'S DAGGERS: Sir Stalwart, 1999; The Crooked House, 2000; Silvercloak, 2001. HISTORICAL NOVEL: (as Sarah B. Franklin) Daughter of Troy, 1998. **Address:** c/o Richard Curtis, Richard Curtis Associates Inc., 171 E 74th St., New York, NY 10021, U.S.A. **Online address:** himself@daveduncan.com

DUNCAN, David Douglas. French/American (born United States), b. 1916. **Genres:** Photography, Homes/Gardens, Art/Art History. **Career:** Freelance photo journalist, 1938-39, 1956; American Museum, photographer, 1940-41; co-ordinator for inter-american affairs, 1941-42; Life Magazine, photographer, 1946-56; American Broadcasting Corporation (ABC) television, photo-correspondent, 1967-68. Writer. **Publications:** This Is War!: A Photo-Narrative in Three Parts, 1951; The Private World of Pablo Picasso, 1958; The Kremlin, 1960; Picasso's Picassos, 1961; Yankee Nomad: A Photographic Odyssey (autobiography), 1966; I Protest: Khe Sanh, Vietnam, 1968; Great Treasures of the Kremlin, 1968; Self-Portrait: U.S.A., 1969; War without Heroes, 1970; Prismatics: Exploring a New World, 1973; Goodbye Picasso, 1974; Atelier Silencieux, 1976; The Silent Studio, 1976; Magic Worlds of Fantasy: Dorle Lindner, Oscar Forel, Hsueh Shao-Tang, Ariane, 1978; The Fragile Miracle of Martin Gray, 1979; Great Treasures of the Kremlin, 1979; Viva Picasso: A Centennial Celebration, 1881-1981, 1980; The World of Allah, 1982; New York, New York: Masterworks of a Street Peddler, 1984; Sunflowers for Van Gogh, 1986; (with M. Drucker) Familiar Faces: The Art of Mort Drucker, 1988; This is War!: A Photo-Narrative of the Korean War, 1990; Picasso and Jacqueline, 1988; A Secret Garden, 1992; Thor, 1993; Picasso Paints a Portrait, 1996; Yo-Yo: Kidnapped in Providence, 2000; Faceless: The Most Famous Photographer in the World, 2000; Photo Nomad, 2003; Picasso & Lump: A Dachsund's Odyssey, 2006. **Address:** Castellaras 53, Mouans-Sartoux, 06370, France.

DUNCAN, David James. American (born United States), b. 1952. **Genres:** Novellas/Short Stories, Young Adult Non-fiction. **Career:** Writer. **Publica-**

tions: The River Why, 1983; The Brothers K, 1992 (fiction); River Teeth: Stories and Writings, 1995; My Story as Told by Water: Confessions, Druidic Rants, Reflections, Bird-watchings, Fish-stalkings, Visions, Songs and Prayers Refracting Light, from Living Rivers, in the Age of the Industrial Dark, 2001; God Laughs & Plays: Churchless Sermons in Response to the Preachments of the Fundamentalist Right, 2006; River Teeth: Stories and Writings, 2006; (with K. Stafford) Frank Boyden: The Empathies, 2006; (with R. Bass) The Heart of the Monster, 2011. Contributor to periodicals. **Address:** Doubleday Adult Trade, 1540 Broadway, New York, NY 10036, U.S.A.

DUNCAN, Glen. British (born England), b. 1965. **Genres:** Novels, Young Adult Fiction, Psychology, Mystery/Crime/Suspense. **Career:** Dillons, bookseller, 1990-94. Writer, 1994-. **Publications:** Hope, 1998; Love Remains, 2000; I Lucifer, 2002; Weathercock, 2003; Death of an Ordinary Man, 2004; The Bloodstone Papers, 2006; A Day and a Night and a Day, 2009; The Last Werewolf, 2011. **Address:** Simon Schuster Inc., Africa House, 64-78 Kingsway, London, GL WC2B 6AH, England.

DUNCAN, Hal. Scottish (born Scotland), b. 1971?. **Genres:** Adult Nonfiction, Novels, Horror. **Career:** Writer and computer programmer. **Publications:** BOOK OF ALL HOURS SERIES: Vellum (fantasy fiction), 2005; Ink: The Book of All Hours, 2007. NOVELS: Escape from Hell!, 2007. **Address:** c/o Author Mail, Ballantine Books Inc., 1745 Broadway, New York, NY 10019-4368, U.S.A. **Online address:** hal_duncan@hotmail.co.uk

DUNCAN, Karen A. American (born United States), b. 1955. **Genres:** Social Sciences, Psychology. **Career:** Wellness Center for Women Inc., founder; The Right to Be Safe Inc., founder; Marian College, adjunct faculty; Indiana University-Purdue University (IUPUI), Departments of Psychology and Women's Studies, adjunct faculty. Therapist, counselor, social worker, speaker and writer. **Publications:** Healing from the Trauma of Childhood Sexual Abuse: The Journey for Women, 2004; (contrib.) VISTA: Compelling Perspectives on Counseling, 2005; Female Sexual Predators: Understanding Them to Protect Our Children and Youths, 2010. Contributor to periodicals. **Address:** Greenwood, IN , U.S.A. **Online address:** karenduncan@healing4women.com

DUNCAN, Kirsty E. (Kirsty Ellen Duncan). Canadian (born Canada), b. 1969. **Genres:** Medicine/Health, Environmental Sciences/Ecology. **Career:** University of Windsor, faculty, 1993-2000; University of Toronto, Michael Lee-chin Family Institute for Corporate Citizenship, Joseph L. Rotman School of Management, adjunct professor of medical geography; Parliament of Canada, member of parliament, Writer. **Publications:** Hunting the 1918 Flu: One Scientist's Search for a Killer Virus, 2003; Environment and Health: Protecting Our Common Future, 2008; (ed. with C.A. Brebbia) Disaster Management and Human Health Risk: Reducing Risk, Improving Outcomes, 2009. Contributor to periodicals. **Address:** Department of Geography, Joseph L. Rotman School of Management, University of Toronto, 105 St. George St., Toronto, ON M5S 3E6, Canada. **Online address:** kirsty.duncan@utoronto.ca

DUNCAN, Kirsty Ellen. See **DUNCAN, Kirsty E.**

DUNCAN, Lois. (Lois Kerry). American (born United States), b. 1934. **Genres:** Novels, Mystery/Crime/Suspense, Children's Fiction, Young Adult Fiction, Poetry, Songs/Lyrics And Libretti, Paranormal, Young Adult Nonfiction, Essays, Children's Non-fiction, Adult Non-fiction, Criminology/True Crime, Autobiography/Memoirs, Picture/Board Books. **Career:** University of New Mexico, Department of Journalism, instructor, 1971-82. Writer and photographer. **Publications:** YOUNG ADULT NOVELS: Debutante Hill, 1958; (as Lois Kerry) Love Song for Joyce, 1958; (as Lois Kerry) A Promise for Joyce, 1959; The Middle Sister, 1960; Game of Danger, 1962; Season of the Two-Heart, 1964; Ransom, 1966 as Five Were Missing, 1972; They Never Came Home, 1969; Peggy, 1970; I Know What You Did Last Summer, 1973; Down a Dark Hall, 1974; Summer of Fear, 1976; Killing Mr. Griffin, 1978; Daughters of Eve, 1979; Stranger with My Face, 1981; The Third Eye, 1984 in UK as The Eyes of Karen Connors, 1985; Locked in Time, 1985; The Twisted Window, 1987; Don't Look Behind You, 1989; Gallows Hill, 1997. FOR CHILDREN: The Littlest One in the Family, 1960; Silly Mother, 1962; Giving Away Suzanne, 1963; Hotel for Dogs, 1971; A Gift of Magic, 1971; From Spring to Spring: Poems and Photographs, 1982; The Terrible Tales of Happy Days School (poetry), 1983; Horses of Dreamland, 1985; Wonder Kid Meets the Evil Lunch Snatcher, 1988; The Birthday Moon, 1989; Songs from Dreamland: Original Lullabies, 1989; The Circus Comes Home: When the Greatest Show on Earth Rode the Rails, 1993; The Magic of Spi-

der Woman, 1996; The Longest Hair in the World, 1999; I Walk at Night, 2000; Song of the Circus, 2002; News for Dogs, 2009; Movie For Dogs, 2010. OTHERS: Point of Violence, 1966; Major Andre: Brave Enemy, 1969; When the Bough Breaks, 1974; How to Write and Sell Your Personal Experiences, 1979; Chapters: My Growth as a Writer (autobiography), 1982; Who Killed My Daughter?: The True Story of Duncan's Search for Her Own Daughter's Murderer, 1992; (with W. Roll) Psychic Connections: A Journey into the Mysterious World of Psi, 1995; (ed.) Night Terrors: Stories of Shadow and Substance, 1996; (ed.) Trapped! Cages of Mind and Body, 1998; (ed.) On the Edge: Stories at the Brink, 2000; (ed.) Seasons of the Heart (poetry), 2007. Contributor of articles to periodicals. **Address:** Sterling Lord Literistic Inc., 65 Bleecker St., New York, NY 10012-2420, U.S.A. **Online address:** loisduncan123@arquettes.com

DUNCAN, Patrick Sheane. American (born United States), b. 1947. **Genres:** Novels, Plays/Screenplays, Young Adult Fiction. **Career:** Writer and director, 1989-. **Publications:** Eighty-four Charlie Mopic, 1992; Live! From Death Row (teleplay), 1992; A Home of Our Own, 1993; The Pornographer, 1994; Nick of Time, 1995; Mr. Holland's Opus, 1996; Courage under Fire, 1996. NOVELS: Courage under Fire, 1996; A Private War, 2002. **Address:** Putnam Berkley Group Inc., 375 Hudson St., 200 Madison Ave., New York, NY 10014, U.S.A.

DUNCAN, Sarah. British (born England) **Genres:** Young Adult Fiction, Romance/Historical, Novels. **Career:** Writer, 1990-; University of Bristol, teacher of creative writing and fellow; University of Bath, teacher of creative writing. **Publications:** How to Become a Working Actor, 1990; Adultery for Beginners, 2004; Nice Girls Do, 2006; A Single to Rome, 2009; Kissing Mr. Wrong, 2010. **Address:** c/o Lavinia Trevor, Lavinia Trevor Literary Agency, 29 Addison Pl., London, GL W11 4RJ, England. **Online address:** sarah@sarahduncan.co.uk

DUNCAN, Stephen M. American (born United States), b. 1941. **Genres:** Military/Defense/Arms Control, Politics/Government, Young Adult Non-fiction. **Career:** Federal District of Colorado, assistant U.S. attorney; Systems Engineering and Information Technology Co., president and chief executive officer; National Defense University, Institute of Homeland Security Studies, director, Institute for National Strategic Studies, distinguished visiting fellow; Dartmouth College, assistant professor of naval science; Center for Strategic and International Studies, adjunct fellow; Duncan Worldwide, staff. Writer. **Publications:** NONFICTION: Citizen Warriors: America's National Guard and Reserve Forces & the Politics of National Security, 1997; A War of a Different Kind: Military Force and America's Search for Homeland Security, 2004. **Address:** Naval Institute Press, 291 Wood Rd., Annapolis, MD 21402, U.S.A. **Online address:** duncans@ndu.edu

DUNCAN, Terence. See **NOLAN, William F(rancis).**

DUNCAN, William (Robert). British (born England), b. 1944. **Genres:** Business/Trade/Industry, Marketing, Travel/Exploration, Law, Social Sciences. **Career:** Egon Ronay Organisation, editor, 1971-75; Kluwer Publishing, editorial manager, 1975-79; Oyez Publishing, managing editor, 1979-80; Duncan Publishing, managing partner, 1980-93; University College Northampton, senior lecturer in marketing, 1990-. Writer. **Publications:** A Guide to Japan, 1970; Japanese Markets Review, 1974; Doing Business with Japan: A Guide to Setting-Up Operations, Trading, Travel and Leisure, 1976; Thailand: A Complete Guide, 1976; The Case for Divorce in the Irish Republic: A Report Commissioned by the Irish Council for Civil Liberties, 1982; (with P.E. Scully) Marriage Breakdown in Ireland: Law and Practice, 1990; (with R. Byrne) Developments in Discrimination Law in Ireland and Europe, 1997; (co-author) The Operating Environment (textbook), 1999. Contributor to magazines. **Address:** Northampton Business School, University College Northampton, Boughton Green Rd., Northampton, NH NN2 7AL, England. **Online address:** william.duncan@northampton.ac.uk

DUNCKER, Patricia. British/Jamaican (born Jamaica), b. 1951. **Genres:** Literary Criticism And History, Novels, Young Adult Non-fiction, Mystery/Crime/Suspense. **Career:** University of Wales (University of Aberystwyth), teacher of writing, literature and feminist theory, developer of writing courses, 1993-2002; University of East Anglia, professor of prose fiction, teaching writing at undergraduate and postgraduate levels, 2002-06; University of Manchester, professor of modern literature, 2007-. Writer. **Publications:** Sisters and Strangers: An Introduction to Contemporary Feminist Fiction,

1992; Hallucinating Foucault, 1996; (with S. Dodd and R.M. Kempher) Insides Out: Stories by Susan Dodd, Patricia Duncker and Ruth Moon Kempher, 1997; Monsieur Shoushana's Lemon Trees, 1997; Monsieur Shoushana's Lemon Trees: Stories, 1998; The Doctor: A Novel, 1999; James Miranda Barry, 1999; Writing on the Wall: Essays on Writing, Feminism and Contemporary Women's Literature, 2002; The Deadly Space Between, 2002; Seven Tales of Sex and Death, 2003; Contains Small Parts: UEA Creative Writing Anthology 2003, 2003; Miss Webster and Chérif, 2006; The Strange Case of the Composer and His Judge, 2010. EDITOR: In and Out of Time: Lesbian Feminist Fiction, 1990; (with V. Wilson and contrib.) Cancer through the Eyes of Ten Women, 1996; (with J. Thomas) The Woman Who Loved Cucumbers: Contemporary Short Stories by Women from Wales, 2002; (with J. Thomas) Mirror, Mirror, 2004; (with J. Thomas) Safe World Gone, 2007. **Address:** School of Arts, Histories and Cultures, University of Manchester, Oxford Rd., Manchester, LC M13 9PL, England. **Online address:** patricia.duncker@manchester.ac.uk

DUNCOMBE, Stephen. American (born United States) **Genres:** Novels, Adult Non-fiction. **Career:** U.S. Department of Education, Jacob K. Javits fellow, 1989-93; New School, instructor in master of arts in media studies, instructor, 1992-94; State University of New York, assistant professor in American Studies and media and mass communications, 1994-99; New York University, Gallatin School, assistant professor, 1999-2002, associate professor of sociology, 2002-, associated faculty in department of culture and communications, 2005-; Gallatin, faculty co-chair, 2004-06; Eyebeam Center for Art and Technology, research associate, 2009; Communications and Journalism, Fulbright senior specialist, 2009-14; Moscow State University, Fulbright Summer School in the Humanities, lead instructor, 2009; Eyebeam Center for Art and Technology, College of Tactical Culture, co-organizer and instructor, 2009; USC/MIT, Futures of Entertainment fellow, 2011-12; Open Society Foundations, School for Creative Activism, co-organizer and instructor, 2011. Writer. **Publications:** Notes from Underground: Zines and the Politics of Alternative Culture, 1997; Cultural Resistance Reader, 2002; (with A. Mattson) The Bobbed Haired Bandit: A True Story of Crime and Celebrity in 1920s New York, 2006; Dream: Re-imagining Progressive Politics in an Age of Fantasy, 2007; (ed. with M. Tremblay) White Riot: Punk Rock and the Politics of Race, 2011; Democratic Persuasion: The Art of Propaganda during the New Deal, forthcoming; (with S. Lambert) How to Win: Understanding the Efficacy of Political Art, forthcoming. Contributor to periodicals. **Address:** Gallatin School, New York University, 1 Washington Pl., New York, NY 10012, U.S.A. **Online address:** stephen.duncombe@nyu.edu

DUNHAM, Tracy. American (born United States) **Genres:** Novels, Mystery/Crime/Suspense. **Career:** Writer. **Publications:** WESTERNS: Morgan's Land, 1983; On the Terror Trail, 1989; The Trail to Medicine Lodge, 1994; The Trail of Mythmaker, 1995; The Long Trail Home, 1996; The Ghost Trail, 1997; The Changing Trail, 1998; The Eureka Trail, 1999; The Last Campaign, 2002. MYSTERY NOVELS: Wishful Sinful, 2004; Yes, the River Knows, 2005. **Address:** c/o Author Mail, Berkeley Prime Crime Publicity, 375 Hudson St., New York, NY 10014, U.S.A. **Online address:** tracy@tracydunham.com

DUNHAM, William. American (born United States), b. 1947. **Genres:** Mathematics/Statistics, Adult Non-fiction, Biography, Sciences. **Career:** Ohio State University, lecturer in mathematics, 1974-75, visiting associate professor, 1987-89; Hanover College, assistant professor, 1975-81, associate professor, 1981-90, professor of mathematics, 1990-92; Muhlenberg College, Truman Koehler professor of mathematics, 1992-; Harvard University, visiting professor, 2008. Writer. **Publications:** Journey Through Genius: The Great Theorems of Mathematics, 1990; The Mathematical Universe: An Alphabetical Journey Trough the Great Proofs, 1994; Euler: The Master of Us All, 1999; The Calculus Gallery: Masterpieces from Newton to Lebesgue, 2005; (ed.) Genius of Euler: Reflections on His Life and Work, 2007. **Address:** Department of Mathematics & Computer Science, Muhlenberg College, 110 Trumbower, 2400 W Chew St., Allentown, PA 18104, U.S.A. **Online address:** wdunham@muhlenberg.edu

DUNK, Thomas W. (Thomas William Dunk). Canadian (born Canada), b. 1955. **Genres:** Anthropology/Ethnology, Sociology, Social Sciences. **Career:** McGill University, teaching assistant, 1987; Concordia University, part-time lecturer, 1987-88; McMaster University, assistant professor and research fellow, 1988-89; Lakehead University, assistant professor, 1989-93, Centre for Northern Studies, associate professor, 1993-96, Department of Sociology, as-

sociate professor, 1996-2002, chair, 1998-2006, professor, 2002-; University of Toronto, Department of Anthropology, visiting lecturer, 1989; University of Warwick, Department of Sociology, visiting fellow, 1994. Writer. **Publications:** It's a Working Man's Town, 1991, 2nd. ed., 2003; Social Relations in Resource Hinterlands, 1991; (ed. with S. McBride and R.W. Nelsen) The Training Trap: Ideology, Training, and the Labour Market, 1996. **Address:** Department of Sociology, Lakehead University, 955 Oliver Rd., Thunder Bay, ON P7B 5E1, Canada.

DUNK, Thomas William. See **DUNK, Thomas W.**

DUNKERLEY, James. British (born England), b. 1953. **Genres:** Politics/Government, Cultural/Ethnic Topics, Essays. **Career:** Latin America Bureau, researcher, 1979-80, 1983-84; University of London, Institute for Latin American Studies, research fellow, 1981-82, Queen Mary and Westfield College, reader in politics, 1986, professor of politics, Institute of Latin American Studies, professor in politics, director, 1998, honorary research fellow; University of Liverpool, Centre for Latin American Studies, research fellow, 1982-83; University of Notre Dame, Kellogg Institute, faculty fellow, 1985; Universidad Boliviana Mayor de San Andres, visiting professor; Institute for the Study of the Americas, director. Writer. **Publications:** (With C. Whitehouse) Unity Is Strength: Trade Unions in Latin America: A Case for Solidarity, 1980; Bolivia: Coup D'état, 1980; The Long War: Dictatorship and Revolution in El Salvador, 1982; Bolivia, 1980-1981: The Political System in Crisis, 1982; Rebellion in the Veins: Political Struggle in Bolivia, 1952-1982, 1984; (with F. Amburseley) Granada: Whose Freedom?, 1984; Origenes Del Poder Militar on Bolivia, 1879-1935, 1987; Power in the Isthmus: A Political History of Central America, 1988; Political Suicide in Latin America and Other Essays, 1992; The Pacification of Central America: Political Change in the Isthmus, 1987-1993, 1994; (ed. with V. Bulmer-Thomas) The United States and Latin America: The New Agenda, 1999; Americana: The Americas in the World Around 1850, 2000; Warriors and Scribes: Essays on the History and Politics of Latin America, 2000; (ed. with P. Preston and M. Partridge) British Documents on Foreign Affairs: Reports and Papers from the Foreign Office Confidential Print. Part IV, From 1946 through 1950. Series D, Latin America, 1946, 2000; Tercer Hombre: Francisco Burdett O'Connor y Laemancipación de las Américas, 2000; (ed. with P. Preston and M. Partridge) British Documents on Foreign Affairs--Reports and Papers from the Foreign Office Confidential Print. Part V, from 1951 through 1956. Series D, Latin America, 1951, 2005. Contributor of articles to magazines. **Address:** Institute of Latin American Studies, 31 Tavistock Sq., London, GL WCH1 9HA, England. **Online address:** j.dunkerley@sas.ac.uk

DUNKLEY, Graham (Royce). Australian (born Australia), b. 1946. **Genres:** Economics. **Career:** Victoria University, research associate in economics and senior lecturer in economics, 1975-, Centre for Alternative Economic Policy Research, co-founder and president; John Shaw Neilson Society, president. Writer. **Publications:** (Ed.) Technology, Economics and Change, 1981; The Japanese Social Contract 1974-1980, 1988; The Greening of the Red: Sustainability, Socialism, and the Environmental Crisis, 1992; The Free Trade Adventure: The Uruguay Round and Globalism-A Critique, 1997, 2nd. ed., 2000; The Free Trade Adventure: The WTO, The Uruguay Round and Globalism: A Critique, 2000; Free Trade: Myth, Reality, and Alternatives, 2003; Consuming Our First Planet, 2004; The Americanization of Australia, 2005. **Address:** Victoria University, Victoria University, PO Box 14428, Melbourne, VI 8001, Australia. **Online address:** graham.dunkley@vu.edu.au

DUNLAP, Julie. American (born United States), b. 1958. **Genres:** Children's Fiction, Children's Non-fiction, Marine Sciences/Oceanography, Natural History, Biography, Picture/Board Books, Animals/Pets, Environmental Sciences/Ecology, Recreation, Social Sciences, Young Adult Non-fiction, Zoology, Essays. **Career:** Yale University, post-doctoral researcher, 1987-88; The Humane Society of the United States, associate director of higher education, 1989-90; writer and consultant, 1990-. **Publications:** BIOGRAPHIES: Aldo Leopold: Living with the Land, 1993; Parks for the People: A Story about Frederick Law Olmsted, 1994; Eye on the Wild: A Story about Ansel Adams, 1995; Birds in the Bushes: A Story about Margaret Morse Nice, 1996. OTHERS: Extraordinary Horseshoe Crabs (natural history), 1999; (with M. Lorbiecki) Louisa May and Mr. Thoreau's Flute (historical fiction picture book), 2002; (with M. Lorbiecki) John Muir and Stickeen: An Icy Adventure with a No-Good Dog (historical fiction picture book), 2004; Parks for the People: The Life of Frederick Law Olmsted, Fulcrum, 2011; (ed. with S.R. Kellert) Companions in Wonder: Children and Adults Exploring Nature

Together, 2012. Contributor of articles to periodicals. **Address:** 6371 Tinted Hill, Columbia, MD 21045, U.S.A. **Online address:** juliedunlap@excite.com

DUNLAP, Susan D. (Sullivan). American (born United States), b. 1943. **Genres:** Mystery/Crime/Suspense, Young Adult Fiction, Novels. **Career:** Department of Social Services, social worker, 1966-67, 1967, 1968-84; full-time writer, 1984-; Sisters in Crime, president, 1990-91. Social services professional. **Publications:** (Ed. with R.J. Randisi) Deadly Allies II: Private Eye Writers of America and Sisters in Crime Collaborative Anthology, 1994; The Celestial Buffet and Other Morsels of Murder, 2001; Karma and Other Stories, 2002; Fast Friends, 2004. DARCY LOTT MYSTERY: A Single Eye, 2006; Hungry Ghosts, 2008; Civil Twilight, 2009; Power Slide, 2010; No Footprints, 2012. VEJAY HASKELL MYSTERY SERIES: An Equal Opportunity Death: A Mystery, 1984; The Bohemian Connection, 1985; The Last Annual Slugfest, 1986. JILL SMITH MYSTERY SERIES: Karma, 1981; As a Favor: A Mystery, 1984; Not Exactly a Brahmin, 1985; Too Close to the Edge, 1987; A Dinner to Die For, 1987; Diamond in the Buff, 1990; Death and Taxes, 1992; Time Expired, 1993; Sudden Exposure, 1996; Cop Out, 1997. KIERNAN O'SHAUGHNESSY MYSTERY SERIES: Pious Deception, 1989; Rogue Wave, 1991; High Fall: A Kiernan O'Shaughnessy Mystery, 1994; No Immunity, 1998. Contributor to periodicals. **Address:** c/o Dominick Abel, Dominick Abel Literary Agency Inc., 146 W 82nd St., Ste. 1A, New York, NY 10024, U.S.A. **Online address:** sddunlap@gmail.com

DUNLAP, Susanne Emily. American (born United States), b. 1955?. **Genres:** Novels, History. **Career:** The Hutton Co., copywriter, 1980-82; Draft Worldwide, senior copywriter, 1998-99; Connecticut Opera, director of development, 2000-05; Commonwealth Opera, consultant, 2003-04; Quinn Fable Advertising, associate creative director, 2005-10; AppeProPo L.L.C., president, 2011-. **Publications:** Emilie's Voice (novel), 2005; Liszt's Kiss (novel), 2007; The Musician's Daughter, 2009; Anastasia's Secret, 2010; In The Shadow of The Lamp, 2011; The Academie, 2012. **Address:** Bloomsbury Publishing, 175 5th Ave., Newyork, NY 10010, U.S.A. **Online address:** sdunlap@optonline.net

DUNLEAVY, Deborah. Canadian (born Canada), b. 1951. **Genres:** Music, Songs/Lyrics And Libretti, Young Adult Non-fiction, Children's Non-fiction. **Career:** Writer and musician. **Publications:** The Language Beat, 1992; The Jumbo Book of Music (juvenile), 2001; The Jumbo Book of Drama, 2004. Contributor to periodicals. **Address:** PO Box 205, Brockville, ON K6V 5V2, Canada. **Online address:** kgp@ripnet.com

DUNLOP, Eileen (Rhona). Scottish (born Scotland), b. 1938. **Genres:** Children's Fiction, History, Mythology/Folklore, Travel/Exploration, Biography, Novels, Education, Adult Non-fiction, Social Sciences, Picture/Board Books. **Career:** Eastfield Primary School, assistant mistress, 1959-62; Abercromby Primary School, assistant mistress, 1962-64; Sunnyside School, assistant mistress, 1964-70, headmistress, 1970-79; Dollar Academy, headmistress of preparatory school, 1980-90. Writer. **Publications:** CHILDREN'S FICTION: Robinsheugh, 1975 in US as Elizabeth, Elizabeth, 1977; A Flute in Mayferry Street in US as The House on Mayferry Street, 1976; Fox Farm, 1978; The Maze Stone, 1982; Clementina, 1985; The House on the Hill, 1987; The Valley of Deer, 1989; The Chip Shop Ghost, 1991; Finn's Island, 1991; Red Herring, 1992; Tales of St. Columba, 1992; Green Willow, 1993; Green Willow's Secret, 1993; Finn's Roman Fort, 1994; Finn's Search, 1994; Stones of Destiny, 1994; Castle Gryffe in US as Websters' Leap, 1995; Waters of Life, 1996; The Ghost by the Sea, 1996; Tales of St. Patrick, 1996; Warrior's Bride, 1998; St. Andrew for Beginners, 1998; A Royal Ring of Gold: Stories from the Life of Mungo, 1999; Ghoul's Den, 2000; The Haunting of Alice Fairlie, 2001; Nicolas Moonlight, 2002; Weerdwood, 2003; Queen Margaret of Scotland, 2005; Heroes and Heroines, 2007; Robert Louis Stevenson: The Travelling Mind, 2008; Scottish Myths and Legends: Scotties, 2009; Supernatural Scotland, 2011. WITH A. KAMM: Edinburgh, 1982; The Story of Glasgow, 1983; (comp.) A Book of Old Edinburgh, 1983; Kings and Queens of Scotland, 1984; Scottish Heroes and Heroines of Long Ago, 1984; Scottish Homes through the Ages, 1985; (comp.) The Scottish Collection of Verse to 1800, 1985; (comp.) Scottish Traditional Rhymes, 1985; Wallace, Bruce and the War of Independence, 1994; Saints of Scotland, 1996. **Address:** 46 Tarmangie Dr., Dollar, FK14 7BP, Scotland.

DUNLOP, Ian (Geoffrey David). Scottish/Indian (born India), b. 1925. **Genres:** Architecture, Biography. **Career:** Teacher, 1952-54; Church of England, curate, 1956-59; Westminster School, chaplain, 1959-62; Vicar of

Bures, 1962-72; Salisbury Cathedral, canon and chancellor, 1972-92; Society of Antiquaries, fellow. Writer. **Publications:** Versailles, 1956; Palaces and Progresses of Elizabeth I, 1962; Modern Britain, 1968; Chateaux of the Loire, 1969; Practical Techniques in the Teaching of Oral English, 1970; The Teaching of English in Swedish Schools: Studies in Methods of Instruction and Outcomes, 1975; Collins Companion Guide to the Ile de France, 1979, 2nd ed. as The Country Round Paris; The Cathedrals' Crusade, 1982; (with H. Schrand) Matters of Moment, 1980; (with H. Schrand) In and about English, 1980; (with H. Schrand) Communication for Business: Materials for Reading Comprehension and Discussion, 1982; Royal Palaces of France, 1985; The Companion Guide around Paris, 1985; Thinking It Out: Christianity in Thin Slices, 1986; Donald Sultan, 1987; Burgundy, 1990; Marie-Antoinette: A Portrait, 1993; Louis XIV, 2000; Edward VII and the Entente Cordiale, 2004. Contributor to periodicals. **Address:** Gowanbrae, The Glebe, Selkirk, TD7 5AB, Scotland.

DUNLOP, Nic. Irish (born Ireland), b. 1969?. **Genres:** Photography, Local History/Rural Topics, Area Studies. **Career:** Writer and photojournalist. **Publications:** The Lost Executioner: A Story of the Khmer Rouge, 2005; The Lost Executioner: A Journey to the Heart of the Killing Fields, 2006; (with H. Hānkehn) Bejjhagāt pât khluan ryan muay knun rapap Khmaer Kraham, 2006; Burma Betrayal, forthcoming. Contributor of photographs to periodicals. **Address:** c/o Pat Kavanagh, Peters Fraser & Dunlop Group Ltd. (PFD), Drury House, 34-43 Russell St., London, GL WC2B 5HA, England. **Online address:** info@nicdunlop.com

DUNMORE, John. (Jason Calder). New Zealander/French (born France), b. 1923. **Genres:** Education, History, Autobiography/Memoirs, Biography. **Career:** Massey University, senior lecturer, 1961-66, professor of French, 1966-84, Department of Modern Languages, head, dean of humanities; Dunmore Press, editor, 1969-84; Heritage Press, managing editor, 1985-2004. **Publications:** French Explorers in the Pacific, vol. I, 1965, vol. II, 1969; Le Mystere d'Omboula, 1966; Aventures dans le Pacifique, 1967; Success at University, 1968; Success at School, 1969; The Fateful Voyage of the St. Jean Baptiste, 1969; Meurtre a Tahiti, 1971; Norman Kirk: A Portrait, 1972; (trans.) In Search of the Maori, 1974; (trans.) Kunie, or, The Isle of Pines, 1978; How to Succeed as an Extra-Mural Student, 1983; (trans.) R. Herve, Chance Discovery of Australia and New Zealand, 1983; Pacific Explorer: The Life of Jean-Francois de la Perouse, 1985; New Zealand: The North Island, 1988; New Zealand: The South Island; Who's Who in Pacific Navigation, 1992; A Playwright's Workbook, 1993; The Journal of La Perouse, 1995; Visions and Realities, 1997; I Remember Tomorrow, 1998; (foreword) Laplace in New Zealand, 1831, 1998; Chronology of Pacific History, 2000; Playwrights in New Zealand, 2001; Monsieur Baret: First Woman Around the World, 2002; Louis de Bougainville's Pacific Journal 1767-68, 2002; Storms and Dreams: The Life of L.A. de Bougainville, 2005; Where Fate Beckons: The Life of Jean-François de la Pérouse, 2006; From Venus to Antarctica: The Life of Dumont D'Urville, 2007. EDITOR: The Map Drawn, 1964; Towards Nationhood, 1969; An Anthology of French Scientific Prose; (and trans.) The Expedition of the St. Jean-Baptiste to the Pacifique, 1769-70, 1981; Le Journal de Laperouse, 1985; The Book of Friends, 1989; New Zealand and The French, 1990; The French and the Maori, 1992. AS JASON CALDER: The Man Who Shot Rob Muldoon, 1976; A Wreath for the Springboks, 1978; The O'Rourke Affair, 1979; Target Margaret Thatcher, 1981. **Address:** New Zealand. **Online address:** john_dunmore@hotmail.com

DUNN, Douglas (Eaglesham). Scottish (born Scotland), b. 1942. **Genres:** Novellas/Short Stories, Poetry, History. **Career:** Renfrew County Library, junior library assistant, 1959-62; University of Strathclyde, Andersonian Library, library assistant, 1962-64; Akron Public Library, assistant librarian, 1964-66; University of Glasgow, Chemistry Department Library, librarian, 1966; University of Hull, Brynmor Jones Library, assistant librarian, 1969-71, writer-in-residence, 1974-75; University of Dundee, writer-in-residence, 1981-82, honorary visiting professor, 1987-89; University of New England, writer-in-residence, 1984; Duncan of Jordanstone College of Art, Dundee District Library, librarian, 1986-88; University of St. Andrews, faculty, 1989-91, professor of English language and literature, 1991-, St. Andrews Scottish Studies Centre, founding director, 1993-, The MLitt School in Creative Writing, founder, 1993-. **Publications:** Terry Street, 1969; Backwaters, 1971; Night, 1971; The Happier Life, 1972; Love or Nothing, 1974; Barbarians, 1979; St. Kilda's Parliament, 1981; Europa's Lover, 1982; Elegies, 1985; Secret Villages: Stories, 1985; Selected Poems, 1964-1983, 1986; Under The Influence: Douglas Dunn on Philip Larkin, 1987; Northlight, 1988; New and

Selected Poems 1966-1988, 1989; Poll Tax: The Fiscal Fake, 1990; (trans.) J. Racine, Andromache, 1990; Dante's Drum-Kit, 1993; Boyfriends and Girlfriends (short stories), 1995; The Donkey's Ears, 2000; The Year's Afternoon, 2000; New Selected Poems, 1964-2000, 2003; (with N. Ackroyd) Line in the Water, 2009. EDITOR: New Poems 1972-73, 1973; (and intro.) A Choice of Byron's Verse, 1974; Two Decades of Irish Writing: A Critical Survey, 1975; What Is to Be Given: Selected Poems of Delmore Schwartz, 1976; The Poetry of Scotland, 1979; Poetry Book Society Supplement, 1979; A Rumoured City: New Poets from Hull, 1982; To Build a Bridge, 1982; (and intro.) The Essential Browning, 1990; Scotland: An Anthology, 1992; Faber Book of Twentieth-century Scottish Poetry, 1992; Oxford Book of Scottish Short Stories, 1995; (and intro.) Selected Poems, 1997; Robert Browning: Poems, 2003; Twentieth-century Scottish Poetry, 2006. Contributor to periodicals. **Address:** School of English, University of St. Andrews, Rm. 20, Castle House, St. Andrews, FF KY16 9AL, Scotland. **Online address:** ded@st-andrews.ac.uk

DUNN, Durwood. American (born United States), b. 1943. **Genres:** Local History/Rural Topics, Social Commentary, Adult Non-fiction, Biography, History. **Career:** Hiwassee College, instructor in history and political science, 1970-74; University of Tennessee, instructor in history, 1975; Tennessee Wesleyan College, Department of History and Political Science, instructor, 1975-77, chair, 1976-, assistant professor, 1977-79, associate professor, 1979-81, professor, 1981-; University of Tennessee Press, Appalachian Echoes Series, editor, 1997-. Writer. **Publications:** Cades Cove: The Life and Death of a Southern Appalachian Community, 1818-1937, 1988; (ed.) These Are Our Lives: McMinn Countians in the Twentieth Century, 1992; (afterword) Florence Cope Bush, Dorie: Woman of the Mountains, 1992; An Abolitionist in the Appalachian South: Ezekiel Birdseye on Slavery, Capitalism and Separate Statehood in East Tennessee, 1841-1486, 1997. Contributor to periodicals. **Address:** Department of History and Political Science, Tennessee Wesleyan College, Durham Hall, 204 E College St., Athens, TN 37371, U.S.A. **Online address:** durwooddunn@twcnet.edu

DUNN, Herb. *See* **GUTMAN, Dan.**

DUNN, Joe P. American (born United States), b. 1945. **Genres:** Intellectual History, History. **Career:** University of Maryland, lecturer, 1973-76; Converse College, assistant professor, 1976-81, associate professor, 1981-88, professor, 1988-, department chair, 1990-, Charles A. Dana professor of history and politics, 1991, Summer Programs, director; University of Iceland, visiting professor of history, 2005. Writer. **Publications:** Teaching the Vietnam War: Resources and Assessments, 1990; (ed. with H.W. Preston) The Future South: A Historical Perspective for the Twenty-first Century, 1991; Desk Warrior: Memoirs of a Combat REMF, 1999, 2nd ed., 2005; (ed. with M. Walker and J.R. Dunn) Southern Women at the Millennium: A Historical Perspective, 2003; A Good and Ordinary Life, forthcoming. Contributor of articles to periodicals and journals. **Address:** Department of History and Politics, Converse College, Rm. 308D, Carmichael Hall, 580 E Main St., Spartanburg, SC 29302, U.S.A. **Online address:** joe.dunn@converse.edu

DUNN, John M. American (born United States), b. 1949. **Genres:** History, Social Sciences, Education. **Career:** Paulding County Junior High School, English teacher, 1972-76; U.S. Department of Defense American Junior High School, English teacher, 1976-80; Asheville-Buncombe County Technical College, instructor in adult education and writing, 1980-81; Osceola Middle School, English teacher, 1981-82; Forest High School, teacher of history, sociology, law and ethics, 1982-; Central Florida Community College, part-time instructor, 1990-96. Writer. **Publications:** The Russian Revolution, 1994; The Relocation of the North American Indian, 1995; The Spread of Islam, 1996; Issues in Advertising, 1997. FOR YOUNG ADULTS: The Civil Rights Movement, 1998; The Enlightenment, 1999; Life during the Black Death, 2000; The Vietnam War: A History of U.S. Involvement, 2001; Computer Revolution, 2002; French Revolution: The Fall of the Monarchy, 2003; (ed.) Northerners, 2003; (ed.) Confederate Soldiers, 2003; (ed.) Union Soldiers, 2003; (ed.) Southerners, 2003; Relocation of the Native American Indian, 2006; Constitution and Founding of America, 2007; Prohibition, 2010; Modern-Day Pirates, 2012. Contributor to newspapers and periodicals. **Address:** 222 SE 29th Terr., Ocala, FL 34471, U.S.A.

DUNN, John (Montfort). British (born England), b. 1940. **Genres:** Politics/Government, Philosophy, Social Sciences, History, Essays. **Career:** Jesus College, fellow, 1965-66; University of Cambridge, Kings College, director

of studies in history and fellow, 1966-72, lecturer in political science, 1972-77, reader in politics, 1977-87, professor of political theory, 1987-, now professor emeritus; University of Ghana, visiting lecturer, 1968-69; University of British Columbia, Cecil H. and Ida Green visiting professor, 1977; University of Bombay, visiting professor, 1979; Tokyo Metropolitan University, visiting professor, 1983; Chiba University, Graduate School of Social Sciences and Humanities, visiting professor. Writer. **Publications:** The Political Thought of John Locke: An Historical Account of the Argument of the 'Two treatises of Government', 1969; (contrib.) John Locke: Problems and Perspectives, 1969; (contrib.) Anarchy and Culture: The Problem of the Contemporary University, 1969; (contrib.) The Cambridge Mind, 1970; (contrib.) Philosophy, Politics and Society, 1972; Modern Revolutions: An Introduction to the Analysis of a Political Phenomenon, 1972; (with A.F. Robertson) Dependence and Opportunity: Political Change in Ahafo, 1973; (contrib.) Politicians and Soldiers in Ghana 1966-1972, 1975; (contrib.) The Making of Politicians: Studies from Africa and Asia, 1976; (contrib.) Action and Interpretation: Studies in the Philosophy of Social Science, 1978; (ed.) West African States: Failure and Promise: A Study in Comparative Politics, 1978; Western Political Theory in the Face of the Future, 1979, 2nd ed., 1993; Political Obligation in its Historical Context: Essays in Political Theory, 1980; (contrib.) John Locke: Symposium Wolfenbuettel 1979, 1981; (contrib.) Social Theory and Political Practice, 1983; Politics of Socialism: An Essay in Political Theory, 1984; Locke, 1984, rev. ed. as Locke: A Very Short Introduction, 2003; Rethinking Modern Political Theory: Essays, 1979-83, 1985; (ed. with D.B.C. O'Brien and R. Rathbone) Contemporary West African States, 1989; Modern Revolutions: An Introduction to the Analysis of a Political Phenomenon, 2nd ed., 1989; (ed.) The Economic Limits to Modern Politics, 1990; Interpreting Political Responsibility: Essays 1981-1989, 1990; (ed.) Democracy: The Unfinished Journey, 508 BC to AD 1993, 1992; (contrib.) Politica, 1993; (ed.) Contemporary Crisis of the Nation State?, 1996; The History of Political Theory and Other Essays, 1996; (ed. with I. Harris) Aquinas, 1997; (ed.) Great Political Thinkers, 1997; (ed. with I. Harris) Aristotle, 1997; (ed. with I. Harris) Augustine, 1997; (ed. with I. Harris) Grotius, 1997; (ed. with I. Harris) Hobbes, 1997; (ed. with I. Harris) Hume, 1997; (ed. with I. Harris) Machiavelli, 1997; (ed. with I. Harris) Plato, 1997; (contrib.) What is Left?: il futuro della sinistrademocratica in Europa, 1997; (ed. with I. Harris) More, 1998; The Cunning of Unreason: Making Sense of Politics, 2000; (ed.) Pensare la politica, 2002; Setting the People Free: The Story of Democracy, 2005; Democracy: A History, 2005; (with J. Foran, D. Lane and A. Zivkovic) Understanding Revolution: Social Identities, Globalisation and Modernity, 2007; Capitalist Democracy: Elective Affinity or Beguiling Illusion, 2007. Contributor to journals and periodicals. **Address:** Department of Social and Political Sciences, University of Cambridge, Rm. E6 left, POLIS, 17 Mill Ln., Cambridge, GL CB2 1RX, England. **Online address:** jmd24@cam.ac.uk

DUNN, Mark (Rodney). American (born United States), b. 1956. **Genres:** Novels, Plays/Screenplays, Geography, Language/Linguistics, Young Adult Non-fiction. **Career:** Thirteenth Street Repertory Co., playwright-in-residence, 1988-97; New Jersey Repertory Co., playwright-in-residence, 1998-; Community Theatre League, playwright-in-residence, 1999-; People United for Libraries in Africa, co-founder, 2002-. **Publications:** NOVELS: Ella Minnow Pea: A Progressively Lipogrammatic Epistolary Fable, 2001; Welcome to Higby, 2002; Ibid: A Life, 2004; Under the Harrow, 2009; PIGmalion, 2010. PLAYS: Belles: A Play in Two Acts and Thirty-Nine Phone Calls, 1989; Minus Some Buttons: A Play in Two Acts, 1991; Sand Pies and Scissorlegs: A Play in Two Acts 1992; Frank's Life, 1992; Five Tellers Dancing in the Rain (two-act), 1994; Judge and Jury (two-act), 1994; Oh Revoir, 1996; Gendermat (one-act), 1999; Cabin Fever: A Texas Tragicomedy, 2000; The Deer and the Antelope Play, 2001; Helen's Most Favorite Day: A Romantic Fantasy in Two Acts, 2005; Dix Tableaux: A Play in Ten Scenes, 2007. NONFICTION: (with M. Dunn) United States Counties, 2003; Zounds! A Browser's Dictionary of Interjections, 2005; Reluctant Chrononauts, 2009. **Address:** PO Box 40, Old Chelsea Sta., New York, NY 10011, U.S.A. **Online address:** montydunn@aol.com

DUNN, Peter Norman. American/British (born England), b. 1926. **Genres:** Literary Criticism And History, Adult Non-fiction, Young Adult Fiction, History. **Career:** University of Aberdeen, assistant lecturer, 1949-50, lecturer in Spanish, 1950-66; Case Western Reserve University, visiting professor, 1964-65; University of Rochester, professor of Spanish literature, 1966-77; Wesleyan University, professor of romance languages, 1977, Hollis professor of romance languages and literatures, now Hollis professor emeritus of romance languages and literatures. Writer. **Publications:** Castillo Solórzano and the

Decline of the Spanish Novel, 1952; (ed. and intro.) El alcalde de Zalamea, 1966, 2nd ed., 1968; Fernando de Rojas, and La Celestina, 1975; The Spanish Picaresque Novel, 1979; Spanish Picaresque Fiction: A New Literary History, 1993; (with Y. Jehenson) Utopian Nexus in Don Quixote, 2006; Cervantes: Narrative Strategies, forthcoming. Contributor to journals. **Address:** Department of Romance Languages, Wesleyan University, 300 High St., Middletown, CT 06459, U.S.A. **Online address:** pdunn@wesleyan.edu

DUNN, Robert J. American (born United States), b. 1981?. **Genres:** Astronomy, Sciences. **Career:** Southampton University, postdoctoral researcher, 2006, faculty. Astrophysicist and writer. **Publications:** (With J. Wilkins) 300 Astronomical Objects: A Visual Reference to the Universe, 2006. **Address:** School of Physics & Astronomy, University of Southampton, University Rd., Southampton, HM SO17 1BJ, England. **Online address:** r.j.dunn@phys.soton.ac.uk

DUNN, Stephen. American (born United States), b. 1939. **Genres:** Poetry, Essays, Autobiography/Memoirs, Novellas/Short Stories. **Career:** National Biscuit Co., copywriter, 1963-66; Ziff-Davis Publishing Co., assistant editor, 1967-68; Southwest Minnesota State College, assistant professor, 1970-73; Syracuse University, lecturer in poetry, 1973-74; Richard Stockton State College, distinguished professor of creative writing, 1974-; University of Washington, visiting professor, 1980; Columbia University, visiting professor of poetry, 1983-87; University of Michigan, visiting professor, 2000; New York University, visiting professor. **Publications:** 5 Impersonations, 1971; Looking for Holes in the Ceiling, 1974; Full of Lust and Good Usage, 1976; (ed.) A Cat of Wind, an Alibi of Gifts (poetry), 1977; (ed.) Silence Has a Rough, Crazy Weather (poetry), 1978; A Circus of Needs, 1978; Work and Love, 1981; Not Dancing, 1984; Local Time, 1986; Between Angels: Poems, 1989; Landscape at the End of the Century: Poems, 1991; Walking Light: Essays & Memoirs, 1993; New & Selected Poems, 1974-1994, 1994; (intro.) Ransom Street Quartet: Poems and Stories, 1995; Loosestrife: Poems, 1996; Riffs & Reciprocities: Prose Pairs, 1998; Different Hours: Poems, 2000; Unrequited: Poems, 2003; Local Visitations: Poems, 2003; Insistence of Beauty: Poems, 2004; Everything Else in the World: Poems, 2006; What Goes On: Selected & New Poems, 1995-2009, 2009; Here and Now: Poems, 2011. **Address:** 790 Piney Run Rd., Frostburg, MD 21532-4241, U.S.A. **Online address:** sdunn55643@aol.com

DUNN, Suzannah. British (born England), b. 1963. **Genres:** Novels, Young Adult Fiction, Novellas/Short Stories. **Career:** University of Manchester, faculty of creative writing, programming director in novel-writing. Writer. **Publications:** Darker Days than Usual (short fiction), 1990; Quite Contrary, 1991; Blood Sugar, 1994; Past Caring, 1995; Venus Flaring, 1996; Tenterhooks, 1998; Commencing Our Descent, 1999; The Queen of Subtitles, 2004; The Sixth Wife, 2007; Queen's Sorrow, 2009; The Confession of Katherine Howard, 2010. **Address:** c/o Antony Topping, Greene & Heaton, 37 Goldhawk Rd., London, GL W12 8QQ, England.

DUNNAGE, Jonathan (Michael). British (born England), b. 1963. **Genres:** History, Politics/Government, Social Sciences. **Career:** University of Wales, University College of Swansea, lecturer in Italian, 1993-, senior lecturer, History Postgraduate Taught Masters Schemes, coordinator . Writer. **Publications:** The Italian Police and the Rise of Fascism: A Case Study of the Province of Bologna, 1897-1925, 1997; (contrib.) Pouvoirs et Polices au XXe Siecle, 1997; Policing Politics in the Twentieth Century: Comparative Perspectives, 1997; (ed.) After the War Was Over: Violence, Justice, Reparation and the State in Italy, 1943-1948, 1999; Twentieth Century Italy: A Social History, 2003; Mussolini's Policemen: Behaviour, Ideology and Institutional Culture in Representation and Practice, forthcoming. Contributor to books and periodicals. **Address:** Department of Italian, University of Wales Swansea, Singleton Pk., Swansea, SA2 8PP, United Kingdom. **Online address:** j.dunnage@swansea.ac.uk

DUNNE, Gillian A(nne). British/Irish (born Ireland), b. 1956. **Genres:** Gay And Lesbian Issues, Social Sciences, Politics/Government. **Career:** Anglia Polytechnic University, lecturer in human geography, 1992-95; Cambridge University, senior research associate in social and political sciences, 1994-98; University of London, London School of Economics and Political Science, Gender Institute, research fellow, 1998-, senior research fellow; University of Plymouth, Sociology Department, lecturer, 2001; University of Leeds, institutions of higher learning, lecturer; University of Glamorgan, institutions of higher learning, lecturer; University of York, institutions of higher learning,

lecturer; University of Essex, institutions of higher learning, lecturer; York University, institutions of higher learning, lecturer. Writer. **Publications:** (Contrib.) Working Out: New Directions for Women's Studies, 1991; Lesbian Lifestyles: Women's Work and the Politics of Sexuality, 1997; (ed.) Living Difference: Lesbian Perspectives on Work and Family Life, 1998; (contrib.) The New Family?, 1998; Who Essentially Cares? Towards a Reformulation of the Gender Dynamics of Care Giving: In International Perspectives on Mothers and Daughters, 2000; (contrib.) Relating Intimacies: Power and Resistance, forthcoming. Contributor to books and periodicals. **Address:** Gender Institute, London School of Economics and Political Science, University of London, Houghton St., London, GL WC2A 2AE, England. **Online address:** gdunne@jasmine.u-net.com

DUNNE, John S(cribner). American (born United States), b. 1929. **Genres:** Theology/Religion. **Career:** University of Notre Dame, instructor, 1957-60, assistant professor, 1960-65, associate professor, 1965-69, professor of theology, 1969-, John A. O'Brien chair, 1988-, John A. O'Brien professor of theology; Yale University, visiting lecturer and Riggs chair, 1972-73; Oxford University, Sarum lecturer, 1976-77. Writer. **Publications:** The City of the Gods: A Study in Myth & Mortality, 1965; A Search for Godin Time and Memory, 1969; The Way of All the Earth, 1972; Time and Myth, 1973; The Reasons of the Heart: A Journey into Solitude and Back Again into the Human Circle, 1978; Way of all the Earth: Experiments in Truth and Religion, 1978; The Church of the Poor Devil, 1982; The House of Wisdom, 1985; The Homing Spirit: A Pilgrimage of the Mind, of the Heart, of the Soul, 1987; The Peace of the Present: An Unviolent Way of Life, 1991; Love's Mind: An Essay on Contemplative Life, 1993; The Music of Time: Words and Music and Spiritual Friendship, 1996; The Mystic Road of Love, 1999; Reading the Gospel, 2000; The Road of the Heart's Desire, 2002; A Journey with God in Time, 2003; Vision Quest, 2006; Deep Rhythm and the Riddle of Eternal Life, 2008; The Circle Dance of Time, 2010. Contributor to periodicals. **Address:** Department of Theology, University of Notre Dame, 238 Malloy Hall, Notre Dame, IN 46556, U.S.A. **Online address:** john.s.dunne.1@nd.edu

DUNNE, Pete. American (born United States), b. 1951. **Genres:** Natural History, Sciences. **Career:** Cape May Bird Observatory, sanctuary director, 1976-99, director; World Series of Birding, founder, 1984, Operation Flight Path (protects habitats of migratory birds), founder, 1987; New Jersey Audubon Magazine, editor, publisher. **Publications:** Tales of a Low-Rent Birder, 1986; (with D. Keller and R. Kochenberger) Hawk Watch: A Guide For Beginners, 1986; (with D. Sibley and C. Sutton) Hawks in Flight: The Flight Identification of North American Migrant Raptors, 1988; (ed. with R. Kane and P. Kerlinger) New Jersey at the Crossroads of Migration, 1989; The Feather Quest: A North American Birder's Year, 1992; More Tales of a Low-Rent Birder, 1994; Before the Echo: Essays on Nature, 1995; The Wind Masters: The Lives of North American Birds of Prey (fiction), 1995; Small-Headed Flycatcher: Seen Yesterday, He Didn't Leave His Name and Other Stories, 1998; Golden Wings and Other Stories about Birders and Birding, 2003; (foreword) Photographic Guide to North American Raptors, 2003; Peter Dunne on Bird Watching: The How-To, Where-To and When-To of Birding, 2003; Pete Dunne's Essential Field Guide Companion, 2006; The Art of Pishing: How to Attract Birds by Mimicking Their Calls, 2006; Prairie Spring, 2009; Bayshore Summer, 2010; Art of Bird Finding, 2011; Arctic Autumn: A Journey to Season's Edge, 2011; Art of Bird Identification, 2012. Contributor to periodicals. **Address:** Cape May Bird Observatory, 701 E Lake Dr., PO Box 3, Cape May Point, NJ 08212, U.S.A. **Online address:** pete.dunne@njaudubon.org

DUNS, Jeremy. Swedish/British (born England), b. 1973. **Genres:** Novels. **Career:** Journalist and novelist. **Publications:** Free Agent, 2009. Contributor to magazines. **Address:** Stockholm, Sweden. **Online address:** jeremyduns@yahoo.com

DUNSTER, Julian A. Canadian/British (born England), b. 1954. **Genres:** Agriculture/Forestry, Natural History, Sciences. **Career:** Clogwyn Climbing Gear and Troll Products, technical consultant, 1973-77; Pugh-Lewis Ltd., forestry manager, 1979-80; British Columbia Ministry of Forests, district planning forester, 1981-84; Association of British Columbia Professional Foresters, professional forester, 1984-; Dunster and Associates Ltd. (environmental consulting firm), owner and principal, 1984-; Canadian Institute of Forestry, secretary, 1986-87, vice chair, 1987-88, director and chair, 1988-89; University College of North Wales, visiting scientist in department of forestry and wood science, 1986; University of Toronto, sessional lecturer in department of geography, 1988; Simon Fraser University, assistant professor in natural resources management program, 1989-90; Bowen Island Forest and Water Management Society, founding director and chair, 1993-96; Bowen Island Conservancy, founding director, 1997. Writer. **Publications:** (With R.B. Gibson) Forestry and Assessment: Development of the Class Environmental Assessment for Timber Management in Ontario, 1989; A Proposed Forest Practices Code for British Columbia: Backgrounds Papers, 1993; (with K. Dunster) Dictionary of Natural Resource Management, 1996; (with S.M. Murray) Arboriculture and the Law in Canada, 1997. Contributor to periodicals. **Address:** Dunster & Assoc Environmental Consultants Ltd., 4621 Cliffwood Pl., Victoria, BC V8Y 1B6, Canada. **Online address:** jd@dunster.ca

DUNTEMANN, Jeff. American (born United States), b. 1952. **Genres:** Information Science/Computers, Science Fiction/Fantasy, How-to Books, Theology/Religion, Technology, Autobiography/Memoirs. **Career:** Xerox Corp., programmer and analyst, 1978-85; PC Tech Journal (Ziff-Davis), senior technical editor, 1985-87; Borland, Turbo Technix Magazine, creator and editor, 1987-89; The Coriolis Group, Book Publishing Division, co-founder and editorial director, 1989-2002; Paraglyph Press, co-founder, 2002-07; Copperwood Media, founder, 2007-. **Publications:** Complete Turbo Pascal, 1985, rev. ed., 1989; Turbo Pascal Solutions, 1987; Assembly Language from Square One: For the PC AT and Compatibles, 1990; Assembly Language: Step-by-Step, 1992, rev. ed. as Assembly Language Step-by-Step: Programming with DOS and Linux, 2000, rev. ed. as Assembly Language Step-By-Step: Programming with Linux, 2009; (with K. Weiskamp) PC Techniques C/C++ Power Tools: HAX, Techniques and Hidden Knowledge, 1992; (ed.) Borland Pascal 7 Insider, 1993; (ed.) Macro Magic with Turbo Assembler, 1993; Borland Pascal from Square One, 1993; (with R. Pronk) Inside the Power PC Revolution, 1994; (with P. Cilwa) Windows Programming Power with Custom Controls, 1994; (ed.) Visual Basic Multimedia Adventure Set, 1994; (ed.) The Developer's Guide to Win Help. Exe: Harnessing the Windows Help Engine, 1994; (with U.A. Le Jeune) Mosaic and Web Explorer, 1995; (with U.A. LeJeune) Netscape and HTML Explorer, 1995, rev. ed. as The New Netscape and HTML Explorer, 1996; (with R. Pronk and P. Vincent) Web Explorer Pocket Companion, 1995; (with R. Pronk and P. Vincent) Mosaic Explorer Pocket Companion, 1995; All-in-One Web Surfing and Publishing Kit, 1995; (with J. Mischel and D. Taylor) Delphi Programming Explorer, 1995, rev. ed. as The New Delphi 2 Programming Explorer, 1996; (with J. Mischel) Borland C++ Builder Programming Explorer, 1997; Jeff Duntemann's Drive-by Wi-Fi Guide, 2003, rev. ed. as Jeff Duntemann's Wi-Fi Guide, 2004; (with J. Ballew) Degunking Windows, 2004, rev. ed., 2005; Degunking Your Email, Spam and Viruses, 2004; (with J. Ballew) Degunking Your PC, 2005; The Cunning Blood, 2005; Souls in Silicon, 2008; Cold Hands and Other Stories, 2009; Drumlin Circus, 2011. Contributor of articles to periodicals. **Address:** Copperwood Media L.L.C., 145 Stanwell St., Colorado Springs, CO 80906, U.S.A. **Online address:** jeff@duntemann.com

DUNTEMANN, Jeff. American (born United States), b. 1952. **Genres:** Information Science/Computers. **Career:** Xerox Corp., technical representative, 1974-76, data specialist, 1976-79, programmer and analyst, 1979-85; PC Tech Journal, technical editor, 1985-86; Turbo Technix, editor-in-chief, 1987-88; PC Techniques (now Visual Developer Magazine), editor-in-chief, 1989-2000; Coriolis Group Books, co-founder, executive vice president and editorial director, 1993-2002; Paraglyph Press, partner and editor at large, 2002-07; freelance writer and editor, 2007-. **Publications:** Complete Turbo Pascal, 1985, 3rd ed., 1989; Turbo Pascal Solutions, 1987; Assembly Language from Square One: For the PC AT and Compatibles ("Assembly Language Programming" series), 1989; Assembly Language: Step-by-Step, 1992, rev. ed. as Assembly Language Step-by-Step: Programming with DOS and Linux, 2000, 3rd ed., 2010; Borland Pascal 7 from Square One, 1993; All-in-One Web Surfing and Publishing Kit (includes CD-ROM), 1995; Jeff Duntemann's Drive-By Wi-Fi Guide, 2003, 2nd ed., 2004; Degunking Your Email, Spam, and Viruses, 2004. CO-AUTHOR: (with K. Weiskamp) PC Techniques C/C+ + Power Tools: HAX, Techniques, and Hidden Knowledge (includes disk), 1992. (With P.S. Cilwa) Windows Programming Power with Custom Controls (includes listings disk), 1993. (With R. Pronk) Inside the PowerPC Revolution, 1994. (With U.A. LeJeune) Mosaic and Web Explorer (includes laser optical disk), 1995; (With U.A. LeJeune) Netscape and HTML Explorer, 1995, rev. ed. as The New Netscape and HTML Explorer (includes laser optical disk), 1996; (with R. Pronk and P. Vincent) Web Explorer Pocket Companion, 1995; (with R. Pronk and P. Vincent) Mosaic Explorer Pocket Companion, 1995; (with J. Mischel and D. Taylor) Delphi Programming Explorer (includes one disk), 1995, rev. ed. as The New Delphi 2 Programming

Explorer, 1996; (with J. Mischel) Borland C+ + Builder Programming Explorer (includes laser optical disk), 1997; (with J. Ballew) Degunking Windows, 2004, 2nd ed., 2005. (with J. Ballew) Degunking Your PC, 2005. EDITOR: (with P.S. Cilwa) Borland Pascal 7 Insider ("Wiley Insider" series), 1993; (with J. Mischel) Macro Magic with Turbo Assembler (includes disk), 1993; (with S. Jarol) Visual Basic Multimedia Adventure Set, 1994; (with J. Mischel) The Developer's Guide to WinHelp.Exe: Harnessing the Windows Help Engine (includes disk), 1994. SCIENCE FICTION: The Cunning Blood, 2005; Souls in Silicon, 2008; Cold Hands and Other Stories, 2010. Contributor of articles to periodicals. **Address:** Colorado Springs, CO , U.S.A. **Online address:** jeff@duntemann.com

DUPLESSIS, Rachel Blau. American (born United States), b. 1941. **Genres:** Poetry, Literary Criticism And History, Essays, Social Sciences. **Career:** Columbia University, School of General Studies, preceptor, 1966, Columbia College, preceptor, 1967-70; Rijksuniversiteit te Gent, suppleant, 1970-71; Universite de Lille III, maitre de conference associe, 1970-72; Trenton State College, assistant professor, 1972-73; Rutgers University, Douglass College, lecturer, 1973-74; Temple University, assistant professor, 1974-83, associate professor, 1983-87, professor, 1987-; Katholieke Universiteit, Fulbright professor, 1985. Writer. **Publications:** POETRY: American Women, 1972; Wells, 1980; Gypsy/Moth, 1984; Tabula Rosa, 1987; Draft X: Letters, 1991; Drafts (3-14), 1991; Essais: quatres poemes, 1996; Drafts 15-XXX, The Fold, 1997; Renga: Draft 32, 1998; Drafts 1-38, Toll, 2001; Draft, Unnumbered: Precis, 2004; Blue Studios: Poetry and Its Cultural Work, 2006. DRAFTS. Drafts 39-57, Pledge, with Draft, unnumbered: Precis, 2004, Torques: Drafts 58-76, 2007; Pitch: Drafts 77-95, 2010. EDITOR: (with S.S. Friedman) Signets: Reading H.D., 1990; The Selected Letters of George Oppen, 1990; (with A. Snitow) The Feminist Memoir Project: Voices from Women's Liberation, 1998; (with P. Quartermain) The Objectivist Nexus: Essays in Cultural Poetics, 1999. OTHERS: Writing beyond the Ending: Narrative Strategies of Twentieth-Century Women Writers (literary criticism), 1985; H.D: The Career of That Struggle (criticism), 1986; The Pink Guitar: Writing as Feminist Practice, 1990; Genders, Races and Religious Cultures in Modern American Poetries, 1908-1934, 2001; Torques, 2007; Purple Passages: Pound, Eliot, Zukofsky, Olson, Creeley and the Ends of Patriarchal Poetry, 2012. Works appear in anthologies. Contributor to periodicals and books. **Address:** Department of English, Temple University, 954 Anderson Hall, 1114 W Berks St., Philadelphia, PA 19122-6090, U.S.A. **Online address:** rdupless@temple.edu

DUPRAU, Jeanne. American (born United States), b. 1944. **Genres:** Adult Non-fiction, Children's Fiction, Children's Non-fiction. **Career:** Writer. **Publications:** NONFICTION: Adoption: The Facts, Feelings, and Issues of a Double Heritage, 1981; (with M. Tyson) The Apple IIgs Book, 1986; The Earth House, 1992; Cloning, 2000; Cells, 2002; The American Colonies, 2002. FICTION: The City of Ember, 2003; The People of Sparks, 2004; Car Trouble, 2005; The Prophet of Yonwood, 2006; The Diamond of Darkhold, 2008. OTHERS: Golden God, 1981; Books of Ember, 2008; Princess and the Goblin, 2010. Contributor to periodicals. **Address:** PO Box 754, Menlo Park, CA 94025, U.S.A. **Online address:** jduprau@mac.com

DUPRÉ, Louis. American/Belgian (born Belgium), b. 1926?. **Genres:** Philosophy, Theology/Religion, Cultural/Ethnic Topics. **Career:** Georgetown University, instructor, 1958-59, assistant professor, 1959-64, associate professor, 1964-67, professor in philosophy, 1967-; Yale University, Department of Religious Studies, professor, 1973-, T. Lawrason Riggs professor, through 1998, now T.L. Riggs professor emeritus; American Catholic Philosophical Association, president; Hegel Society of America, president. Writer. **Publications:** Het Vertrekpunt der Marxistische Wijsbegeerte: de kritiek op Hegels staatsrecht, 1954; Kierkegaard as Theologian, 1963; Contraception and Catholics, 1964; The Philosophical Foundations of Marxism, 1966; The Other Dimension: A Search for the Meaning of Religious Attitudes, 1972; Transcendent Selfhood: The Loss and Rediscovery of the Inner Life, 1976; A Dubious Heritage: Studies in the Philosophy of Religion after Kant, 1977; The Deeper Life: An Introduction to Christian Mysticism, 1981; Terugkeer naar Innerlijkheid, 1981; Marx's Social Critique of Culture, 1983; The Common Life: The Origins of Trinitarian Mysticism and its Development by Jan Ruusbroec, 1984; Passage to Modernity: An Essay in the Hermeneutics of Nature and Culture, 1993; Metaphysics and Culture, 1994; Religious Mystery and Rational Refection: Excursions in the Phenomemology and Philosophy of Religion, 1998; Symbols of the Sacred, 2000; Enlightenment and the Intellectual Foundations of Modern Culture, 2004; Religion and the Rise of Modern Culture, 2008. EDITOR: Faith and Reflection, 1968; (with J.A. Wiseman)

Light from Light: An Anthology of Christian Mysticism, 1988; (with D.E. Saliers and J. Meyendorff) Christian Spirituality: Post-Reformation and Modern, 1989. Contributor of articals. **Address:** Department of Religious Studies, Yale University, 451 College St., New Haven, CT 06511, U.S.A. **Online address:** louis.dupre@yale.edu

DUPREE, Nathalie. American (born United States), b. 1939. **Genres:** Food And Wine. **Career:** Restaurant chef, country restaurant owner, cook show host and food consultant; Rich's Cooking School, founder, chef and teacher, 1975-84. Professional chef and writer. **Publications:** Cooking of the South, 1982; New Southern Cooking, 1988; Nathalie Dupree's Matters of Taste, 1990; Nathalie Dupree Cooks for Family and Friends, 1991; Nathalie Dupree's Southern Memories: Recipes and Reminiscences, 1993; Nathalie Dupree Cooks Great Meals for Busy Days: Delicious Food And Easy Entertaining For A Less Than Perfect World, 1994; Nathalie Dupree Cooks Everyday Meals from a Well-Stocked Pantry: Strategies For Shopping Less and Eating Better, 1995; Nathalie Dupree Cooks Quick Meals for Busy Days, 1996; Nathalie Dupree's Comfortable Entertaining: At Home with Ease & Grace, 1998; (foreword) Savoring Savannah: Feasts From the Low Country, 2001; Nathalie Dupree's Southern Memories: Recipes and Reminiscences, 2004; New Southern Cooking, 2004; (with M. Sullivan) Nathalie Dupree's Shrimp & Grits Cookbook, 2006; (with C.S. Graubart) Southern Biscuits, 2011. Contributor to periodicals. **Address:** Gibbs Smith, PO Box 667, Layton, UT 84041, U.S.A. **Online address:** nathalie@nathalie.com

DUPREE, Sherry Sherrod. American (born United States), b. 1946. **Genres:** Education, History, Librarianship, Bibliography, Biography, Reference, Social Sciences. **Career:** Ann Arbor Public Schools, Tappan Junior High School Media Center, instructional media specialist and department chair, 1970-76; University of Michigan Hospital, summer dietetic supervisor, 1970-73; Eastern Michigan University, visiting professor, 1975; University of Florida Libraries, associate Afro-American and religion specialist, 1977-83; University of Florida, Institute of Black Culture, project director, 1982-93; Santa Fe Community College, reference librarian, 1983-; PNEUMA, associate editor, 1985-; Bethune Cookman College, Daytona Beach, extension professor of teacher education, 1986-89; DuPree African-American Pentecostal and Holiness Collection New York Public Library's Schomburg Center for Research in Black Culture, founder and organizer; Tappan Middle School, instructional media specialist. Writer. **Publications:** NONFICTION: (ed. and comp.) Biographical Dictionary of African-American, Holiness-Pentecostals: 1880-1990, 1990; (with H.C. DuPree) African-American Good News (Gospel) Music, 1993; 1993 Yearbook of American and Canadian Churches, 1993; (comp.) Exposed!!!: Federal Bureau of Investigation (FBI) Unclassified Reports on Churches and Church Leaders, 1993; African-American Holiness Pentecostals Movement: An Annotated Bibliography, 1996. Contributor to books and periodicals. **Address:** Santa Fe Community College Library, S-212 Bldg., 3000 NW 83rd St., Gainesville, FL 32606, U.S.A. **Online address:** sherry.dupree@santafe.cc.fl.us

DUPREE, Stephen A. American (born United States), b. 1942. **Genres:** Sciences. **Career:** Sandia National Laboratories, distinguished technical staff; Journal of Nuclear Materials Management, assistant technical editor. Nuclear scientist, consultant and historian. **Publications:** (With S.K. Fraley) A Monte Carlo Primer: A Practical Approach to Radiation Transport, 2 vols., 2002; Planting the Union Flag in Texas: The Campaigns of Major General Nathaniel P. Banks in the West, 2008. **Address:** U.S.A. **Online address:** mcp@fraleys.com

DUPUIS, Robert. American (born United States), b. 1926. **Genres:** Music, Biography, Dance/Ballet, Literary Criticism And History. **Career:** Detroit Public Schools, teacher, 1950-57, counselor, 1957-63, assistant principal, 1963-66, principal, 1966-84; Wayne County Intermediate School District, teacher and training consultant, 1984-87. Writer. **Publications:** Bunny Berigan: Elusive Legend of Jazz, 1993. Contributor to books and periodicals. **Address:** 725 Lincoln Rd., Grosse Pointe, MI 48230-1221, U.S.A. **Online address:** bunnyrob@aol.com

DUQUETTE, David A. American (born United States), b. 1949. **Genres:** Philosophy. **Career:** St. Norbert College, professor of philosophy, 1985-, assistant divisional chair for humanities and fine arts, 1990-93, coordinator for philosophy discipline, 1994-96, faculty chair, 2004-06, associate dean of humanities and fine arts, 2008-. Writer. **Publications:** G.W.F. Hegel: Social and Political Thought, Internet Encyclopedia of Philosophy, 2001; (ed.)

Hegel's History of Philosophy: New Interpretations, 2003. Contributor of articles to books and periodicals. **Address:** St. Norbert College, Rm. 402, Boyle Hall, 100 Grant St., De Pere, WI 54115-2099, U.S.A. **Online address:** david.duquette@snc.edu

DURAN, Jane. American (born United States), b. 1944?. **Genres:** Education, Philosophy. **Career:** Rutgers University, co-adjutant, 1981; Trenton State College, visiting assistant professor, 1982-83; Hamilton College, visiting assistant professor, 1983-84; University of California, fellow in education, 1984-85, research associate and lecturer in philosophy, 1988-98, Department of Black Studies. lecturer; California Polytechnic State University, lecturer, 1985-86; Mount St. Mary's College, assistant professor, 1987-88; Johns Hopkins University, Center for Research on Students Placed at Risk, associate, 1995-98. Writer. **Publications:** Epistemics: Epistemic Justification Theory Naturalized and the Computational Model of Mind, 1989; Toward a Feminist Epistemology, 1991; Knowledge in Context: Naturalized Epistemology and Sociolinguistics, 1994; Philosophies of Science/Feminist Theories, 1998; Worlds of Knowing: Global Feminist Epistemologies, 2001; Eight Women Philosophers: Theory, Politics, and Feminism, 2006; Women, Philosophy and Literature, 2007. Contributor of articles to books and journals. **Address:** Department of Black Studies, University of California, Rm. 3718, South Hall, Santa Barbara, CA 93106-3150, U.S.A. **Online address:** jduran@education.ucsb.edu

DURAND, Alain-Philippe. American (born United States), b. 1968. **Genres:** Novels. **Career:** North Carolina Central University, visiting instructor of romance languages, 1998-99; University of Rhode Island, assistant professor of French, film studies and comparative literature, 1999-2004, associate professor, 2004-08, honors professor of French, English and film media, 2008-10, interim director of film media, 2008-09, interim chair of English, 2007-08, French and Francophone Studies, head, 2005-10, Honors Program, faculty, 2006-10; University of Arizona, School of International Languages, Literatures, and Cultures (SILLC), director, professor of French, 2010-. Writer. **Publications:** Black Blanc Beur: Rap Music and Hip Hop Culture in the Francophone World, 2002; Un monde techno: nouveaux espaces electroniques dans le roman francais des annees 1980-1990, 2004; (ed. with N. Mandel) Novels of the Contemporary Extreme, 2006; Frederic Beigbeder et ses doubles, 2008. **Address:** School of International Languages, Literatures, an, University of Arizona, 1512 E First St., PO Box 210105, Tucson, RI 85721, U.S.A. **Online address:** adurand@email.arizona.edu

DURANG, Christopher. American (born United States), b. 1949. **Genres:** Plays/Screenplays, Humor/Satire. **Career:** Yale Repertory Theatre, actor, 1974; Southern Connecticut College, teacher of drama, 1975; Yale University, teacher of playwriting, 1975-76; playwright, 1976-. **Publications:** A History of the American Film, 1978; The Vietnamization of New Jersey: A American Tragedy, 1978; The Nature and Purpose of the Universe/Death Comes to Us All, Mary Agnes/Dentity Crisis, 1979; Beyond Therapy, 1981; (with A. Innaurato) Idiots Karamazov, 1981; Sister Mary Ignatius Explains It All for You and The Actor's Nightmare, 1982; Titanic, 1983; Christopher Durang Explains It All for You, 1983; Baby with the Bathwater, 1984; The Marriage of Bette and Boo, 1985; Laughing Wild, 1988; 27 Short Plays, 1995; Durang/Durang, 1996; Laughing Wild, 1996; Complete Full Length Plays, 1975-1995, 1997; Naomi in the Living Room & Other Short Plays: A Collection of One-Acts, 1998; Betty's Summer Vacation, 1999; Monologues, 2002; Mrs. Bob Cratchit's Wild Christmas Binge, 2005; Miss Witherspoon and Mrs. Bob Cratchit's Wild Christmas Binge, 2006. Contributor to periodicals. **Address:** c/o Kenneth Ferrone, International Creative Management, 40 W 57th St., 16th Fl., New York, NY 10019, U.S.A.

DURANT, Michael J. American (born United States), b. 1961. **Genres:** Military/Defense/Arms Control, Young Adult Fiction. **Career:** Rockwell Collins Simulation & Training Solutions, program manager. Writer and American pilot. **Publications:** (With S. Hartov) In the Company of Heroes, 2003; (with S. Hartov and R.L. Johnson) The Night Stalkers: Top Secret Missions of the U.S. Army's Special Operations Aviation Regiment, 2006. **Address:** Rockwell Collins Simulation & Training Solutions, 22626 Sally Ride Dr., Sterling, VA 20164-7104, U.S.A. **Online address:** mike@mikedurant.com

DURBACH, Nadja. American/Canadian/British (born England), b. 1971?. **Genres:** History, Adult Non-fiction. **Career:** University of Utah, assistant professor of history, 2000-05, associate professor of history, 2005-, associate professor of comparative gender and sexuality, associate professor of colonialism and imperialism, associate professor of European history, associate chair of History. Writer. **Publications:** Bodily Matters: The Anti-Vaccination Movement in England, 1853-1907, 2005; Spectacle of Deformity: Freak Shows and Modern British Culture, 2009. Contributor to periodicals. **Address:** Department of History, University of Utah, Rm. 211, 223 CTIHB, 215 S Central Campus Dr., Salt Lake City, UT 84112, U.S.A. **Online address:** n.durbach@utah.edu

DURBAN, Pam. American (born United States), b. 1947. **Genres:** Novels, Novellas/Short Stories, Human Relations/Parenting, Young Adult Fiction, Sociology. **Career:** Atlanta Gazette, editor and writer, 1974-75; State University of New York, visiting assistant professor of creative writing, 1979-80; Murray State University, assistant professor of creative writing, 1980-81; Ohio University, associate professor of creative writing, 1981-86; Georgia State University, professor of English and creative writing, 1986-2001; Five Points Literary Magazine, founding editor, 1986-; University of North Carolina, professor of English, 2000-, Doris Betts distinguished professor of creative writing. **Publications:** (Ed.) Cabbagetown Families, Cabbagetown Food, 1976; All Set About with Fever Trees and Other Stories, 1985. CONTRIBUTOR: The Editor's Choice: New American Stories, vol. II, 1986; Necessary Fictions, 1986; New Writers of the South, 1987; New Stories from the South: The Year's Best 1988, 1988; The Laughing Place (novel), 1993; Best American Short Stories 1997, 1997; Best American Short Stories of the Century, 1999; So Far Back, 2000. Contributor to books and periodicals. **Address:** Department of English and Comparative Literature, University of North Carolina, Greenlaw Hall, PO Box 3520, Chapel Hill, NC 27599-3520, U.S.A. **Online address:** durban@email.unc.edu

DURCAN, Liam. Canadian (born Canada), b. 1967?. **Genres:** Young Adult Fiction, Novels, Novellas/Short Stories. **Career:** Montreal Neurological Institute and Hospital, neurologist; McGill University, Department of Neurology and Neurosurgery, assistant professor, neurologist-in-chief. Writer. **Publications:** A Short Journey by Car, 2004; García's Heart, 2007. Contributor to periodicals. **Address:** Montreal Neurological Hospital and Institute, 3801 University St., Montreal, QC H3A 2B4, Canada. **Online address:** ldurcan@hotmail.com

DURDEN, Robert F(ranklin). American (born United States), b. 1925. **Genres:** History, Biography, Autobiography/Memoirs, Politics/Government. **Career:** Duke University, instructor, 1952-56, assistant professor, 1956-60, associate professor, 1961-64, professor, 1965-, chairman of the department, 1974-80, professor emeritus; Johns Hopkins School for Advanced International Studies, Fulbright professor of history, 1965-66; College of William and Mary, James Pinckney Harrison professor of history, 1970-71. Writer. **Publications:** James Shepherd Pike: Republicanism and the American Negro, 1850-1882, 1957; Reconstruction Bonds and Twentieth-Century Politics: South Dakota v. North Carolina, 1904, 1962; The Climax of Populism: The Election of 1896, 1965; (contrib.) The Abolitionist Vanguard, 1965; (ed. and intro.) The Prostrate State: South Carolina under Negro Government, 1968; The Populists in Historical Perspective, 1968; The Gray and the Black: The Confederate Debate on Emancipation, 1972; The Dukes of Durham, 1865-1929, 1975; (with J.J. Crow and D.L. Russell) Maverick Republican in the Old North State: Political Biography of Daniel L. Russell, 1977; The Self-Inflicted Wound: Southern Politics in the Nineteenth Century, 1985; The Launching of Duke University, 1924-49, 1993; Lasting Legacy to the Carolinas: The Duke Endowment, 1924-1994, 1998; Carter G. Woodson: Father of African-American History, 1998; Electrifying the Piedmont Carolinas: The Duke Power Company, 1904-1997, 2001; Bold Entrepreneur: A Life of James B. Duke, 2003. Contributor of articles to journals. **Address:** Department of History, Duke University, 319 Carr Bldg., PO Box 90719, Durham, NC 27708, U.S.A. **Online address:** durdenrf@duke.edu

DURFEE, Mary. (Mary H. Durfee). American (born United States), b. 1951. **Genres:** Philosophy, Adult Non-fiction. **Career:** NCR Corp., staff, 1980-81; Colgate University, lecturer, 1983-84; Canisius College, assistant professor, 1985-86; Antioch University, Center for Adult Learning, adjunct assistant professor, 1987-89; University of Dayton, adjunct assistant professor, 1987-90, 1992; Wittenberg University, visiting assistant professor, 1990-91; Michigan Technological University, assistant professor of social sciences, 1992-98, associate professor of social sciences, 1998-, Michigan Tech Graduate Faculty Council, president, 2001-02, Department of Social Sciences, MS Environmental Policy, graduate director, 2001-03, national scholarships advisor, 2002-, special assistant to the provost, 2002-05, assistant provost for Academ-

ic Improvement, 2005-07, assistant provost, 2006-07, faculty, 2008-. Writer. **Publications:** (With J.N. Rosenau) Thinking Theory Thoroughly: Coherent Approaches to an Incoherent World, 1995, 2nd ed., 2000. Contributor to periodicals. **Address:** Department of Social Sciences, Michigan Technological University, 216 Academic Office Bldg., 1400 Townsend Dr., Houghton, MI 49931-1295, U.S.A. **Online address:** mhdurfee@mtu.edu

DURFEE, Mary H. *See* **DURFEE, Mary.**

DURGIN, Doranna. American (born United States), b. 1960. **Genres:** Science Fiction/Fantasy. **Career:** Columbus Metroparks, park naturalist, 1982-; freelance technical writer, 1996-. **Publications:** FANTASY NOVELS: Dun Lady's Jess, 1994; Changespell, 1996; Touched by Magic, 1996; Barrenlands, 1998; Wolf Justice, 1998; Wolverine's Daughter, 1999; Seer's Blood, 2000; Tooth and Claw, 2001; A Feral Darkness, 2001; Gene Roddenberry's Earth: Final Conflict-Heritage, 2001; Heritage, 2001; Changespell Legacy, 2002; Dark Debts, 2003; Fearless, 2003; Impressions, 2003; Exception to the Rule, 2004; Khamsin's Heir, 2004; Nose for Trouble, 2005; Checkmate, 2005; (with M. Fletcher and V. Hinze) Smokescreen, 2005; Beyond the Rules, 2005; Survival Instinct, 2006; Comeback, 2006; Scent of Danger, 2008; Revenge, 2008; Hidden Steel, 2008; Ghost Whisperer, 2008; Sentinels: Jaguar Night, 2009; Sentinels: Lion Heart, 2009; Ghost Trap, 2009; Wolf Hunt, 2010; Deep River Reckoning, 2010; The Reckoners, 2010; Sentinels: Wolf Hunt, 2010; Storm of Reckoning, 2011. **Address:** PO Box 31123, Flagstaff, AZ 86003-1123, U.S.A. **Online address:** doranna@sff.net

DURHAM, Walter T. American (born United States), b. 1924. **Genres:** History, Local History/Rural Topics, Biography. **Career:** Durham Manufacturing Company Inc., partner, 1948-73, chairperson, 1973-98; Gallatin Aluminum Products Company Inc., co-founder and treasurer, 1958-63, president, 1963-73; Tennessee Historical Society, president, 1974-78; Tennessee Historical Commission, chair, 1975-85; Tennessee Library Advisory Council, chairperson, 1991-93; White House Conference on Library and Information Services, member of task force, 1991-98; Tennessee State, historian, 2002-. Writer. **Publications:** The Great Leap Westward: A History of Sumner County, Tennessee, from Its Beginnings to 1805, 1969; Old Sumner: A History of Sumner County, Tennessee, from 1805 to 1861, 1972; A College for This Community, 1974; Daniel Smith, Frontier Statesman, 1976; The Building Supply Dealer in Tennessee: A History of the Tennessee Building Material Association, 1925-1976, 1976; James Winchester, Tennessee Pioneer, 1979; Rebellion Revisited: A History of Sumner County, Tennessee, from 1861 to 1870, 1982; Nashville, the Occupied City: The First 17 Months, 1985; (with J.W. Thomas) A Pictorial History of Sumner County, Tennessee, 1796-1986, 1986; Reluctant Partners: Nashville and the Union, July 1, 1863 to June 30, 1865, 1987; Before Tennessee: The Southwest Territory, 1790-1796, 1990; Wynnewood, Bledsoe's Lick, Castalian Springs, Tennessee, 1994; (with J.F. Creasy) A Celebration of Houses Built before 1900 in Sumner County, Tennessee, 1995; Volunteer 49ers: Tennessee and the California Gold Rush, 1997; The Life of William Trousdale, Soldier, Statesman, Diplomat, 2001; (with G. Milliken) Gallatin 200: A Time Line History Celebrating the Bicentennial of Gallatin, Tennessee, 2002; Josephus Conn Guild and Rosemont: Politics and Plantation in 19th Century Tennessee, 2002; Balie Peyton of Tennessee: 19th Century Politics and Thoroughbreds, 2004; Reluctant Partners: Nashville and the Union, 1863-1865, 2008; Nashville, the Occupied City: 1862-1863, 2008; Grasslands, A History of the Southern Grasslands Hunt and Racing Foundation 1929-1932, 2010. Contributor to books and journals. **Address:** 1010 Durham Dr., Gallatin, TN 37066, U.S.A. **Online address:** wtdurham@bellsouth.net

DURKEE, Sarah. American (born United States), b. 1955?. **Genres:** Novels, Humor/Satire. **Career:** Songwriter, television lyricist, screenwriter, and author. **Publications:** (Co-author) The Book of Sequels: The Greatest Stories Ever Retold!, 1990; Strk C African Animals Alph Is, 1997; The African Animals Alphabet, 1998; The Lucky Duck, 2000; Over the Hedge Movie Storybook, 2006; The Fruit Bowl Project (young-adult novel), 2006. **Address:** c/o Author Mail, Random House Trade, 1745 Broadway, New York, NY 10019, U.S.A.

DURRANT, Lynda. American (born United States), b. 1954. **Genres:** Novels, Social Sciences, History, Children's Fiction. **Career:** Writer and teacher. **Publications:** Echohawk, 1996; The Beaded Moccasins: The Story of Mary Campbell, 1998; Turtle Clan Journey, 1999; Betsy Zane, the Rose of Fort Henry, 2000; The Sun, the Rain, and the Apple Seed: A Novel of Johnny Appleseed's Life, 2003; My Last Skirt: The Story of Jennie Hodgers, Union

Soldier, 2006; Imperfections, 2008. Contributor to periodicals. **Address:** PO Box 123, Bath, OH 44210, U.S.A.

DURRELL, Julie. American (born United States), b. 1955. **Genres:** Children's Fiction, Illustrations, Young Adult Fiction. **Career:** Writer and illustrator. **Publications:** SELF-ILLUSTRATED FOR CHILDREN: Mouse Tails, 1985; Tickety-Tock, What Time is It?, 1990; It's My Birthday!, 1990; The Colorful Mouse, 1991; Little Mouse's Book of Colors, 1991. **Address:** c/o Paige Gillies, Publisher Graphics, 251 Greenwood Ave., Bethel, CT 06801-2422, U.S.A.

DURRENBERGER, E. Paul. American (born United States), b. 1943. **Genres:** Anthropology/Ethnology, Archaeology/Antiquities. **Career:** Smithsonian Institution, Texas Memorial Museum, Texas Archaeological Research Laboratory, archaeological researcher and field worker, 1962-65; Washington State University, teaching assistant, 1965-66; Eastern New Mexico University, instructor in anthropology, 1966; University of Illinois, research associate, 1968-70; Antioch College, assistant professor of anthropology, 1971-72; University of Iowa, assistant professor, 1972-76, associate professor, 1976-82, professor of anthropology, 1982-87, acting department executive officer, 1995, department executive officer, 1996-97; Council on Thai Studies, president, 1978-80; University of Iceland, Fulbright professor, 1984; University of South Alabama, visiting professor, 1987-89; National Public Radio, commentator, 1995-96; Pennsylvania State University, professor, 1997-; Central States Anthropological Society, second vice president, 2000-01, president 2001-04. Writer. **Publications:** A Socio-Medical Study of the Lisu of Northern Thailand, 1969; A SocioEconomic Study of a Shan Village in Maehongson Province, 1977; Agricultural Production and Household Budgets in a Shan Peasant Village in Northwestern Thailand: A Quantitative Description, 1978; Lisu Religion (monograph), 1989; (with N. Tannenbaum) Analytical Perspectives on Shan Agriculture and Village Economics, 1990; (with D. Durrenberger) The Saga of Gunnlaugur Snake's Tongue, with an Essay on the Structure and Translation of the Saga, 1992; It's All Politics: South Alabama's Seafood Industry, 1992; The Dynamics of Medieval Iceland: Political Economy and Literature, 1992; Icelandic Essays: Explorations in the Anthropology of a Modern Nation, 1995; Gulf Coast Soundings: People and Policy in the Mississippi Shrimp Industry, 1996; (with D. Durrenberger) The Saga of Havardur of Isafjordur, with an Essay on the Political, Economic, and Cultural Background of the Saga, 1996; (with Kendall M. Thu) Pigs, Profits, and Rural Communities, 1998; State and Community in Fisheries Management: Power, Policy, and Practice, 2000; (with S. Erem) Class Acts: An Anthropology of Service Workers and Union, 2005; (ed. with J.E. Marti) Labor in Cross-Cultural Perspective, 2006; (with S. Erem) On the Global Waterfront: The Fight to Free the Charleston 5, 2007; (with S. Erem) Anthropology Unbound: A Field Guide to the 21st Century, 2007, 2nd ed., 2010; Paradigms for Anthropology: An Ethnographic Reader, 2010; The Anthropology of Labor Unions, 2010. EDITOR: (and contrib.) Chayanov, Peasants, and Economic Anthropology, 1984; (with G. Palsson and contrib.) The Anthropology of Iceland, 1989; (with L. Maril and J.S. Thomas) Marine Resource Utilization, 1989; (with Palsson and contrib.) Images of Contemporary Iceland: Everyday Lives and Global Contexts, 1996; State Power and Culture in Thailand: An Historical View, 1996; Class and Consciousness, forthcoming. Contributor of articles. **Address:** Department of Anthropology, Pennsylvania State University, 409 Carpenter Bldg., University Park, PA 16802-3404, U.S.A. **Online address:** epd2@psu.edu

DURROW, Heidi W. American (born United States), b. 1969. **Genres:** Novels. **Career:** Oregonian, reporter, 1990; Newsday, reporter, 1991; Newsweek, reporter, 1992; Milbank, Tweed, Hadley & McCloy, legal associate, 1993; Blanc, Williams, Johnston & Kronstadt, legal associate, 1994; Cravath, Swaine & Moore, attorney, 1995-97; Improvisational Ensemble, founder and performer, 1997-2003; Greif Co., associate producer, 2001-03; Essence Magazine, freelance writer, 2004-05; Zinc Sports Consulting, life skills trainer, 2000-07; Mixed Chicks Chat, podcaster and blogger, 2007-. **Publications:** The Girl Who Fell from the Sky: A Novel, 2010. Contributor to books and periodicals. **Address:** c/o Wendy Weil, Wendy Weil Agency, 232 Madison Ave., Ste. 1300, New York, NY 10016, U.S.A. **Online address:** heididurrowats@hotmail.com

DURSCHMIED, Erik. French/Austrian (born Austria), b. 1930. **Genres:** Plays/Screenplays, History, Autobiography/Memoirs, Documentaries/Reportage, Philosophy. **Career:** Canadian Broadcasting Corp., camera operator, 1956-60, war correspondent; British Broadcasting Corp., staff, 1959-, camera operator for Panorama, 1960-72, war correspondent; independent film producer, 1973-80; Columbia Broadcasting System, film director and camera operator, 1981-86; Austrian Military Staff College, lecturer of military history. Writer. **Publications:** Shooting Wars: My Life as a War Cameraman, from Cuba to Iraq, 1990; Don't Shoot the Yanqui: The Life of a War Cameraman (autobiography), 1990; Armee Rouge: Le dernier Combat, 1991; The Hinge Factor: How Chance and Stupidity Have Changed History, 2000; Der Untergang Grosser Dynastien, 2000; The Weather Factor: How Nature Has Changed History, 2001; Whisper of the Blade, 2001; Blood of Revolution: From The Reign of Terror to the Rise of Khomeini, 2002; From Armageddon to the Fall of Rome: How the Myth Makers Changed the World, 2002; The Hinges of Battle: How Change and Incompetence Have Changed the Face of History, 2002; Unsung Heroes: The Twentieth Century's Forgotten History-makers, 2003; Whores of the Devil: Witch-Hunts and Witch-Trials, 2005; How Chance and Stupidity Have Changed History, 2005; Beware the Dragon: China-A Thousand Years of Bloodshed, 2008. **Address:** Sheil Land Associates Ltd., 52 Doughty St., London, GL WC1N 2LS, England.

DURST, Sarah Beth. American (born United States), b. 1974. **Genres:** Children's Fiction, Young Adult Fiction, Novels. **Career:** Writer. **Publications:** JUVENILE FICTION: Into the Wild, 2007; Out of the Wild, 2008; Ice, 2008; Enchanted Ivy, 2010; Drink, Slay, Love, 2011; Vessel, 2012. **Address:** c/o Andrea Somberg, Harvey Klinger Inc., 300 W 55th St., Ste. 11V, New York, NY 10019, U.S.A. **Online address:** sarah@sarahbethdurst.com

DU SAUTOY, Marcus Peter Francis. British (born England), b. 1965. **Genres:** Mathematics/Statistics. **Career:** University of Oxford, Wadham College, professor of mathematics, 2002-, fellow, 2005-08, New College, Simonyi professor for the Public Understanding of Science and fellow, 2008-; The Music of the Primes, BBC 4, presenter, 2005; Mind Games, BBC 4, presenter; Royal Institution Christmas Lecturer, 2006; ecole Normale Superieure, visiting professor; Max Planck Institute, visiting professor; Hebrew University of Jerusalem, visiting professor; Australian National University, visiting professor; EPSRC committee on Public Engagement, member, 2007; Royal Society panel to assess URF applications, member, 2007-; Oxford University, Steering Group on Public Engagement for MPLS division, member, 2008; LMS Mathematics Promotion Unit steering committee member, 2008; All Souls College, General Purposes Committee, member, 1996-2001; Aventis Science Book Prize, judge, 2003. Writer. **Publications:** (with D. Segal) Analytic Prop Groups, 1999; (ed. with D. Segal and A. Shalev) New Horizons in Pro-p Groups, 2000; The Music of the Primes: Searching to Solve the Greatest Mystery in Mathematics, 2003; Finding Moonshine: A Mathematician's Journey through Symmetry, 2007 in US as Symmetry: A Journey into the Patterns of Nature, 2008; (with L. Woodward) Zeta Functions of Groups and Rings, 2008; The Story of Maths, 2008. Contributor to periodicals. **Address:** Mathematical Institute, University of Oxford, 24-29 Saint Giles, Oxford, OX OX1 3LB, England. **Online address:** dusautoy@maths.ox.ac.uk

DUSSEL PETERS, Enrique. Mexican/German/French (born France), b. 1965. **Genres:** Economics, Area Studies. **Career:** Universidad Nacionál Autónoma de México, professor of economics, 1993-, China/Mexico Studies Center, coordinator. Writer and consultant. **Publications:** (Ed. with M. Piore and C.R. Durán) Pensar globalmente y actuar regionalmente: Hacia un nuevo paradigma industrial para el siglo XXI, 1997; (with C.R. Durán and T. Taniura) Changes in Industrial Organization of the Mexican Automobile Industry by Economic Liberalization, 1997; La economía de la polarización: Teoría y evolución del cambio estructural de las manufacturas mexicanas, 1982-1996, 1997; (with C.R. Durán) El reto de la educación superior en la sociedad del conocimiento, 1997; (with C.R. Durán) Dinámica Regional y Competitividad Industrial, 1999; Las industrias farmacéutica y farmoquímica en México y el distrito federal, 1999; El tratado de libre comercio de Norteamérica y el desempeño de la economía en México, 2000; Polarizing Mexico: The Impact of Liberalization Strategy, 2000; Claroscuros, 2001; Estrategias y políticas de competitividad en Centroamérica: De la integración externa a la integración interna, 2001; Territorio y competitividad en la agroindustria en México: condiciones y propuestas de política para los clusters del limón mexicano en Colima y la piña en Veracruz, 2002; (contrib.) La industria electrónica en México, 2003; (contrib.) Perspectivas y retos de la competitividad en México, 2003; (contrib.) Condiciones y efectos de la inversión extranjera directa y del proceso de integración regional en México durante los años noventa, 2003; (with L.X. Dong) Economic Opportunities and Challenges Posed by China for Mexico and Central America, 2005; (co-author) Inversión extranjera directa en México, 2007; (ed. with R. Jenkins) China and Latin America, 2009.

Contributor to periodicals. **Address:** Faculty of Economics, City University, Universidad Nacional Autonoma de Mexico, Av Revolución 2040, Mexico City, 04510, Mexico. **Online address:** dussel@servidor.unam.mx

DUSSLING, Jennifer. American (born United States), b. 1970. **Genres:** Children's Fiction, Humor/Satire. **Career:** Writer and children's book editor. **Publications:** Balto, Beware, 1995; Finger Painting, 1995; In a Dark, Dark House, 1995; Under the Sea, 1995; Bossy Kiki, 1996; Stars, 1996; Kermit's Teeny Tiny Farm, 1996; Creep Show, 1996; A Very Strange Dollhouse, 1996; Don't Call Me Names!, 1996; Muppet Treasure Island, 1996; Top Knots!: The Ultimate Bracelet and Hair-Wrapping Kit, 1996; The Princess Lost Her Locket, 1996; The Bunny Slipper Mystery, 1997; A Simple Wish, 1997; Bug Off!, 1997; The Dinosaurs of the Lost World, Jurassic Park, 1997; A Dozen Easter Eggs, 1997; Jewel the Unicorn, 1997; Construction Trucks, 1998; Tall Tale Trouble, 1998; Small Soldiers: The Movie Storybook, 1998; A Heart for the Queen of Hearts, 1998; Slinky, Scaly Snakes, 1998; The Magic Carpet Ride, 1998; Bugs! Bugs! Bugs!, 1998; Pink Snow and Other Weird Weather, 1998; Gargoyles: Monsters in Stones, 1999; Giant Squid: Mystery of the Deep, 1999; The 100-Pound Problem, 2000; Planets, 2000; Dinosaur Eggs, 2000; (adapt.) L.M. Montgomery, Anne of Green Gables, 2001; Looking at Rocks, 2001; The Rainbow Mystery, 2002; Lightning: It's Electrifying, 2002; Gotcha!, 2003; Fair Is Fair!, 2003; Earthquakes, 2004; Whatcha Got?, 2004; Picky Peggy, 2004; Longest Yawn, 2005; Lo justo es justo!, 2007; Deadly Poison Dart Frogs, 2009; One Little Flower Girl, 2009; El misterio del arco iris, 2009. Contributor to periodicals. **Address:** c/o Author Mail, Kane Press, 240 W 35th St., Ste. 300, New York, NY 10001, U.S.A.

DUTHU, N. Bruce. American (born United States), b. 1958?. **Genres:** Law, History. **Career:** Dartmouth College, Native American Program, director, 1986-89, associate dean of freshmen and director ofIntensive academic support program, 1989-91, professor of ative American studies, 2008; Vermont Law School, director, professor of law, 1991-, associate dean for academic affairs, 2002-05; University of Wollongong, Faculty of Law, visiting fellow, 1999; Harvard Law School, visiting professor, 2000; University of Trento, faculty of law, 2003; Sun Yat-sen University, director. Writer. **Publications:** American Indians and the Law, 2008. Contributor to journals. **Address:** Vermont Law School, Chelsea St., PO Box 96, South Royalton, VT 05068, U.S.A. **Online address:** bduthu@vermontlaw.edu

DUTKINA, Galina (Borisovna). Russian (born Russia), b. 1952. **Genres:** Essays, History, Adult Non-fiction, Social Sciences. **Career:** Moscow Radio, Japanese Section, editor and announcer, 1974-79; Progress Publishing House, Oriental Department, senior editor, 1980-83; Raduga Publishing House, Foreign Literature Department, expert editor, 1983-93; Center for Postgraduate Training of High School Professors, professor, 1993-95; freelance journalist and translator, 1995-; Moscow Publishing House, editor and translator. **Publications:** Misuteri Mosukuwa, 1993. Contributor to periodicals. **Address:** 116 Leningradskoe shosse, Flat 90, Moscow, 125445, Russia.

DUTOIT, Ulysse. American (born United States), b. 1944?. **Genres:** Art/Art History, Humor/Satire. **Career:** Ecole Normale, instructor of film studies; University of Lausanne, instructor of film studies; Rutgers University, instructor of film studies; Hunter College, instructor of film studies; University of California, lecturer in French cinema, 1975-, lecturer emeritus. Writer. **Publications:** WITH L. BERSANI: The Forms of Violence: Narrative in Assyrian Art and Modern Culture, 1985; Arts of Impoverishment: Beckett, Rothko, Resnais, 1993; Caravaggio's Secrets, 1998, trans. as Les secrets du Caravage, 2002; Caravaggio, 1999; Forming Couples: Godard's Contempt, 2003. Contributor to periodicals. **Address:** Department of French, University of California, 4307 Dwinelle, Berkeley, CA 94720-2580, U.S.A.

DUTTON, Donald G. Canadian (born Canada), b. 1943. **Genres:** Psychology, Criminology/True Crime, Law, Women's Studies And Issues. **Career:** West Coast Social and Behavioral Research Enterprises, president, 1974-; University of British Columbia, professor, 1974-; British Columbia Police College, domestic dispute intervention trainer, 1975-79; Assaultive Husbands Project, therapist, 1979-95; America on Violence, executive director, 1999-2002; Simon Fraser University, adjunct professor; Royal Canadian Mounted Police, psychologist, 2003-. **Publications:** (with B.R. Levens) The Social Service Role of Police: Domestic Crisis Intervention, 1980; The Domestic Assault of Women: Psychological and Criminal Justice Perspectives, 1988, rev. ed., 1995; (with S.K. Golant) The Batterer: A Psychological Profile, 1995; The Abusive Personality: Violence and Control in Intimate Relationships,

1998, 2nd ed., 2007; (ed. with D.J. Sonkin) Intimate Violence: Contemporary Treatment Innovations, 2002; Rethinking Domestic Violence, 2006; The Psychology of Genocide, Massacres, and Extreme Violence: Why Normal People Come to Commit Atrocities, 2007. Contributor to periodicals. **Address:** Department of Psychology, University of British Columbia, 2136 West Mall, Vancouver, BC V6T 1Z4, Canada. **Online address:** dondutton@shaw.ca

DUTTON, J. T. American (born United States), b. 1964. **Genres:** Novels, Young Adult Fiction. **Career:** Writer. **Publications:** Freaked (novel), 2009; Stranded (novel), 2010. **Address:** Harper Teen, 10 E 53rd St., New York, NY 10022, U.S.A. **Online address:** jt@jtdutton.com

DUTTON, Michael. See **DUTTON, Michael R.**

DUTTON, Michael R. Also writes as Michael Dutton, Michael Robert Dutton. Australian/British (born England), b. 1957. **Genres:** Politics/Government, Area Studies, Humanities. **Career:** University of Adelaide, Asian Studies Centre, lecturer in Chinese politics and language, 1988-90; University of Melbourne, Department of Political Science, lecturer, 1990-93, senior lecturer in Chinese politics and social theory, 1994-95, reader and associate professor, 2000-05; University of London, Goldsmiths College, Department of Politics, professor, 2005-, chair; Griffith University, Griffith Asia Institute, research professor of political cultures, 2007-; Institute of Postcolonial Studies, founding fellow; Academy of the Social Sciences in Australia, fellow. Writer. **Publications:** (As Michael Robert Dutton) The Crisis of Marxism in China, 1983; Policing and Punishment in China: From Patriarchy to The People, 1992; (ed.) Streetlife China, 1998; Policing Chinese Politics: A History, 2005; (with H.S. Lo and D.D. Wu) Beijing Time, 2008. **Address:** Department of Political Science, Goldsmiths College, University of London, Rm. 605, Warmington Twr., New Cross, London, GL SE14 6NW, England. **Online address:** m.dutton@gold.ac.uk

DUTTON, Michael Robert. See **DUTTON, Michael R.**

DUTTON, Paul Edward. Canadian (born Canada), b. 1952. **Genres:** History, Biography, Autobiography/Memoirs, Humanities. **Career:** Simon Fraser University, professor of medieval history, 1983-, Jack and Nancy Farley endowed university professor, 2005-; Medieval Academy of America, fellow. Writer. **Publications:** (Ed. and intro.) The Glosae super Platonem of Bernard of Chartres, 1991; Carolingian Civilization: A Reader, 1993, 2nd ed., 2004; The Politics of Dreaming in the Carolingian Empire, 1994; (with E. Jeauneau) The Autograph of Eriugena, 1996; (with H.L. Kessler) The Poetry and Paintings of the First Bible of Charles the Bald, 1997; (ed. and trans.) Charlemagne's Courtier: The Complete Einhard, 1998; Charlemagne's Mustache and Other Cultural Clusters of a Dark Age, 2004; The Mystery of the Missing Heresy Trial of William of Conches, 2006. **Address:** Department of Humanities, Simon Fraser University, AQ 6231, 8888 University Dr., Burnaby, BC V5A 1S6, Canada. **Online address:** dutton@sfu.ca

DUVALL, Aimee. See **THURLO, Aimee.**

DUVOISIN, Roger C(lair). American (born United States), b. 1927. **Genres:** Medicine/Health, How-to Books. **Career:** Lenox Hill Hospital, rotating intern, 1954-55, assistant resident in neurology, 1955-56; Columbia Presbyterian Medical Center, Neurological Institute, assistant resident, 1956-58; Presbyterian Hospital, assistant attending neurologist, 1962-69, associate attending neurologist, 1969-72, attending neurologist, 1972-73; Columbia University, College of Physicians and Surgeons, research associate, 1962-64, assistant professor, 1964-69, associate professor, 1969-72, professor of neurology, 1972-73; Helen Hayes Hospital, consulting neurologist, 1965-73; City University of New York, Mount Sinai School of Medicine, professor of neurology, 1973-79; King's College Hospital, visiting scientist, 1973; Institute of Psychiatry, visiting scientist, 1973; University of London, visiting scientist, 1973; University of Medicine and Dentistry of New Jersey, Rutgers Medical School, professor of neurology, 1979-, Department of Neurology, chairman, 1979-, now retired, Robert Wood Johnson Medical School, William Dow Lovett professor of neurology, 1990-96, professor emeritus, 1996-, now Lovett professor emeritus; Robert Wood Johnson University Hospital, Neurology Service, chief, 1979-95, Prognosis Committee, chair, 1980-87, chair of ad hoc committee on brain death certification, 1983-84; Veterans Administration Medical Center, consultant, 1980. Writer. **Publications:** (Ed. with W. Birkmayer) Extrapyramidal Disorders, 1983; (ed. with A. Plaitakis and contrib.) The Olivopontocerebellar Atrophies, 1985; (ed. with E. Tolosa and F.F.

Cruz-Sánchez) Progressive Supranuclear Palsy: Diagnosis, Pathology and Therapy, 1994; Parkinson's Disease: A Guide for Patient and Family, 1978, (with J. Sage) 5th ed., 2001. Contributor of articles to journals. **Address:** Department of Neurology, Robert Wood Johnson Medical School, University of Medicine & Dentistry of New Jersey, CN-19, 1 Robert Wood Johnson Pl., New Brunswick, NJ 08901-1928, U.S.A.

DUYFHUIZEN, Bernard. American (born United States), b. 1953. **Genres:** Literary Criticism And History. **Career:** University of Tulsa, teaching fellow, 1977-80, assistant instructor in English, 1980-83, visiting lecturer in English, 1983-84; University of Wisconsin, Department of English, assistant professor of English, 1984-89, associate professor of English, 1989-92, professor of English, 1992-, head, 1992-98, director of graduate studies, 1987-93, College of Arts and Sciences, assistant dean, 1999, associate dean, 1999-, interim dean, 2003-04; Pynchon Notes (journal), editor, 1989-; King Alfred's College, faculty exchange teacher, 1992. **Publications:** Narratives of Transmission, 1992. Contributor of articles to periodicals. **Address:** Department of English, College of Arts and Sciences, University of Wisconsin, 138 Schofield Hall, 105 Garfield Ave., Eau Claire, WI 54702-4004, U.S.A. **Online address:** pnotesbd@uwec.edu

DWIGHT, Jeffry. American (born United States), b. 1958. **Genres:** Science Fiction/Fantasy, Young Adult Fiction, Young Adult Non-fiction, Novellas/Short Stories. **Career:** Greyware Automation Products Inc., chief executive officer; SFF.net (Website), owner and operator. Writer. **Publications:** FICTION: (contrib.) Platinum Edition Using HTML 3.2, Java 1.1 and CGI, 1996; (contrib.) Web Publishing Electronic Resource Kit, 1996; (with R. Niles) CGI by Example, 1996; (co-author) Using CGI, 1996, 2nd ed., 1997; Windows NT4 Systems Programming: The Best Way to Learn How NT Works under the Hood, 1997; (ed.) Between the Darkness and the Fire: Twenty-three Tales of Imaginative Fiction from the Internet, 1998; (ed. with K. Roth) The Age of Reason, 1999; (ed.) The Age of Wonders, 2000. **Address:** c/o Author Mail, Wildside Press, PO Box 301, Holicong, PA 18928-0301, U.S.A. **Online address:** jay@jeffrydwight.net

DWORKIN, Shari L. American (born United States), b. 1968. **Genres:** Sports/Fitness, Adult Non-fiction. **Career:** University of Southern California, teaching assistant, 1994-98, research assistant, 1998-2000; Pitzer College, visiting assistant professor, 2000-02; Columbia University, HIV Center for Clinical and Behavioral Studies, postdoctoral research fellow, 2002-05, Department of Psychiatry, assistant professor of clinical behavioral medicine, 2005-, Post-Doctoral Fellowship Program in HIV Infection, associate training director, 2007-, MAC AIDS Fund Leadership Initiative, program director, 2007-; New York State Psychiatric Institute, HIV Center for Clinical and Behavioral Studies, post-doctoral research fellow, 2002-05, research scientist, 2005-; University of California-San Francisco, School of Nursing, Department of Social and Behavioral Sciences, associate professor; University of California-Los Angeles, MAC AIDS Fund Leadership Initiative, program director, 2007-. Writer. **Publications:** (With L. Heywood) Built to Win: The Female Athlete As Cultural Icon, 2003; (with F.L. Wachs) Body Panic: Gender, Health and the Selling of Fitness, 2009; Men and HIV/AIDS Prevention, forthcoming. Contributor to periodicals. **Address:** HIV Center for Clinical and Behavioral Studies, Columbia University, 1051 Riverside Dr., Ste. 5, New York, NY 10032, U.S.A. **Online address:** sld2011@columbia.edu

DWYER, Augusta (Maria). Canadian (born Canada), b. 1956. **Genres:** Environmental Sciences/Ecology, Reference, Travel/Exploration. **Career:** Marquee (music and life-styles weekly), staff writer, 1977; free-lance writer, 1982-85, 1987-; translator and broadcaster, 1982-85; Maclean's Magazine, correspondent, 1984, 1985, researcher and reporter, 1985-87. **Publications:** Into the Amazon: Chico Mendes and the Struggle for the Rain Forest, 1990; On the Line: Life on the US-Mexican Border, 1994; Broke but Unbroken: Grassroots Social Movements and their Radical Solutions to Poverty, 2011. Contributor to periodicals. **Address:** c/o David Johnson, 89 Collier St., Top Fl., Toronto, ON M4M 1X1, Canada.

DWYER, Deanna. See KOONTZ, Dean R(ay).

DWYER, Jim. American (born United States), b. 1949. **Genres:** Poetry, Environmental Sciences/Ecology, Literary Criticism And History, Bibliography, Natural History. **Career:** State University of New York, librarian, 1973-76; University of Oregon, librarian, 1976-82; Northern Arizona University, librarian, 1982-86; California State University, Meriam Library, head of bib-

liographic services, 1986-2011, Department of Collection Management and Technical Services, librarian; Sacramento River Preservation Trust, board director and secretary, 1989-; Chico Natural Foods, vice president, 1992-93, president, 1993-94. Writer. **Publications:** Earth Works: Recommended Fiction and Nonfiction about Nature and the Environment for Adults and Young Adults, 1996; The Sun, the Stars, the Moondog (poetry), 1999; Where the Wild Books Are: A Field Guide to Ecofiction, 2010. **Address:** Sacramento River Preservation Trust, PO Box 5366, Chico, CA 95927, U.S.A.

DWYER, K. R. See KOONTZ, Dean R(ay).

DWYER, Richard A. American (born United States), b. 1934. **Genres:** History, Biography, inspirational/Motivational Literature, Classics. **Career:** Purdue University, instructor, 1964-66; University of Florida, assistant professor, associate professor, 1966-71; Florida International University, professor of English, 1971-90; R&R Travel Inc., treasurer, 1985-. Writer. **Publications:** Boethian Fictions: Narratives in the Medieval French Versions of the Consolatio Philosophiae, 1976; Always on the Stretch: An Imus Family History, 2003. WITH RICHARD E. LINGENFELTER: The Nonpareil Press of T.S. Harris, 1957; The Songs of the Gold Rush, 1964; (comp. and ed. with D. Cohen) Songs of the American West, 1968; Lying on the Eastern Slope: James Townsend's Comic Journalism on the Mining Frontier, 1984; Death Valley Lore: Classic Tales of Fantasy, Adventure and Mystery, 1988; Dan De Quille, the Washoe Giant: A Biography and Anthology, 1990; Sagebrush Trilogy: Idah Meacham Strobridge and Her Works, 1990. **Address:** University of Nevada Press, PO Box 166, Reno, NV 89557, U.S.A. **Online address:** rdwyer@networld.com

DYAL, Donald H(enriques). American (born United States), b. 1947. **Genres:** Bibliography, Reference, History, Biography, Architecture. **Career:** Texas A&M University, serials acquisitions librarian, 1973-76, serials and separates acquisitions librarian, 1976-77, head of special collections division, 1977-91, adjunct professor of history, 1985, head of special collections, manuscripts and archives, 1992-94, Cushing Memorial Library, associate university librarian director, 1994-2001; Texas Tech University, dean of libraries, 2001-. Consultant and writer. **Publications:** (With S. Smith) Texas Library Journal Index, 1924-1975, 1977; I am My Work; My Work is Me (monograph), 1980; The Twentieth Century Stadium, 1982; An International Bibliography of Doors and Doorways, 1982; Sun, Sod and Wind: A Bibliography of Ranch House Architecture, 1982; The Staircase: An International Bibliography, 1982; A Selected Bibliography of Memorial and Triumphal Arches, 1983; Norman Bel Geddes: Designer of the Future, 1983; The Architecture of Power Plants: Symbols and Reality: A Bibliography of Periodical Articles, 1983; The English Country House: A Periodical Bibliography, 1970-1982, 1984; A Periodical Bibliography of Continental European Country House, 1984; Ceilings: A Bibliography, 1984; The Irish, Scottish and Welsh Country Houses: A Periodical Bibliography, 1984; Addison Mizner: The Palm Beach Architect, 1985; (ed.) A Vanished Landscape, 1986; (with H. Dethloff) A Special Kind of Doctor: A History of Veterinary Medicine in Texas, 1991; (with M.P. Kelsey) The Courthouses of Texas, 1993, 2nd ed., 2008; Historical Dictionary of the Spanish American War, 1996; (ed. with E. Smith and C.A. Hastedt) American Book and Magazine Illustrators to 1920, 1998; Biography of Harry Igo, 2004. Contributor to books and periodicals. **Address:** University Library, Texas Tech University, Rm. MS 0002, 18th and Boston, Lubbock, TX 79409, U.S.A. **Online address:** donald.dyal@ttu.edu

DYCHTWALD, Maddy Kent. American (born United States), b. 1952. **Genres:** Advertising/Public Relations, Natural History. **Career:** Actress, 1974-83; Dychtwald & Associates (marketing consultants), director of special projects, 1983-86; Age Wave Inc. (generational marketing consultants), co-founder, 1986-, director of communications, 1986, vice president of communications, 1987-90, senior vice president of communications, 1990-95, senior vice president of business development, 1995-. Writer. **Publications:** Cycles: How We Will Live, Work, and Buy, 2003; (co-author) Gideon's Dream: A Tale of New Beginnings, 2008; (with C. Larson) Influence: How Women's Soaring Economic Power Will Transform Our World for the Better, 2010; Shift Happens, forthcoming. Contributor to journals. **Address:** Age Wave Inc., 2000 Powell St., Ste. 1090, Emeryville, CA 94608-1861, U.S.A. **Online address:** mdychtwald@maddydychtwald.com

DYER, Charles (Raymond). Also writes as C. Raymond Dyer, Charles Stretton. British (born England), b. 1928. **Genres:** Plays/Screenplays, Novels, Mystery/Crime/Suspense, Humor/Satire, Gay And Lesbian Issues. **Career:**

Royal Shakespeare Co., playwright. Freelance actor and director. **Publications:** Time, Murderer, Please A Comedy Thriller, 1956; Wanted, One Body, 1956; Rattle of a Simple Man: A Novel, 1963; Staircase (play), 1966; Staircase: or, Charlie Always Told Harry Almost Everything, 1969; Mother Adam, 1972; Lovers Dancing, 1984. **Address:** Old Wob, Austenwood, Gerrards Cross, BK SL9 8SF, England.

DYER, C. Raymond. *See* **DYER, Charles (Raymond).**

DYER, Davis. American (born United States) **Genres:** Institutions/Organizations, Administration/Management, Business/Trade/Industry. **Career:** The Winthrop Group Inc., co-founder, director and head of editorial services; Monitor University, faculty; Harvard Business Review, associate editor. Consultant. **Publications:** (With P.R. Lawrence) Renewing American Industry, 1983; (ed. with R.H.K. Vietor) Telecommunications in Transition, 1986; (with M.S. Salter and A.M. Webber) Changing Alliances, 1987; (with D.B. Sicilia) Labors of a Modern Hercules: The Evolution of a Chemical Company, 1990; Architects of Information Advantage: The Mitre Corporation since 1958, 1998; TRW: Pioneering Technology and Innovation since 1900, 1998; (ed. with A. Brinkley) The Reader's Companion to the American Presidency, 2000; Corning: A Story of Discovery and Reinvention, 2001; (with D. Gross) The Generations of Corning: The Life and Times of a Global Corporation, 2001; (with N. Nohria and F. Dalzell) Changing Fortunes: Remaking the Industrial Corporation, 2002; (with F. Dalzell and R. Olegario) Rising Tide: Lessons from 165 Years of Brand Building at Procter and Gamble, 2004; (ed. with A. Brinkley) The American Presidency, 2004; (with C.F. Knight) Performance Without Compromise: How Emerson Consistently Achieves Winning Results, 2005; (with J. Heskel) After the Harkness Gift: A History of Phillips Exeter Academy Since 1930, 2008. **Address:** The Winthrop Group Inc., 2 Canal Pk., Cambridge, MA 02141, U.S.A. **Online address:** ddyer@winthropgroup.com

DYER, Gwynne. Canadian (born Canada), b. 1943. **Genres:** Adult Non-fiction, Military/Defense/Arms Control. **Career:** Royal Military Academy Sandhurst, lecturer in military studies, 1973-77; Canadian Broadcasting Corporation (CBC), producer and host of radio and television series, 1978; American Broadcasting Companies (ABC), producer and host of radio and television series, 1978; The Gorbachev Revolution and The Human Race, host, 1994; military commentator in Canada during Gulf War; Oxford University, instructor; journalist; military analyst; Order of Canada, officer, 2010. Writer. **Publications:** NONFICTION: War, 1985; (with T. Viljoen) The Defence of Canada: In the Arms of the Empire, 1990; Ignorant Armies: Sliding into War in Iraq, 2003; Future: Tense: The Coming World Order, 2004; With Every Mistake, 2005; Fighting Decline, 2007; After Iraq: Anarchy and Renewal in the Middle East, 2008; The Mess They Made: The Middle East After Iraq, 2007; Climate Wars, 2008; After Iraq: Anarchy and Renewal in The Middle East, 2008; Crawling from the Wreckage, 2010. **Online address:** gwynnedyer@gmail.com

DYER, James (Frederick). British (born England), b. 1934. **Genres:** Children's Fiction, Archaeology/Antiquities, Children's Non-fiction, History, Local History/Rural Topics, Social Sciences. **Career:** School teacher, 1958-66; The Bedfordshire Magazine, editor, 1965-74; Putteridge Bury College of Education, principal lecturer in archaeology, 1966-76; Shire Publications, archaeological editor, 1968-; Harlington Upper School, teacher of archaeology and head of department, 1976-; freelance archaeologist and broadcaster. **Publications:** (With J. Dony) The Story of Luton, 1964, 3rd ed., 1975; Discovering Regional Archaeology: Eastern England, 1969; Discovering Archaeology in England and Wales, 1969, 6th ed., 1997; Discovering Regional Archaeology: The Cotswolds and the Upper Thames, 1970; Discovering Regional Archaeology: Wessex, 1971; Discovering Archaeology in Denmark, 1972; Southern England: An Archaeological Guide, the Prehistoric and Roman Remains, 1973; Your Book of Prehistoric Britain, 1974; (ed.) From Antiquary to Archaeologist: William Cunnington 1754-1810, 1975; Worthington Smith 1835-1917, 1978; The Penguin Guide to Prehistoric England and Wales, 1981; Hillforts of England and Wales, 1981, 2nd ed., 1992; Teaching Archaeology in Schools, 1983; Shire Guide to Bedfordshire, 1987, 2nd ed., 1995; Ancient Britain, 1990, 2nd ed., 1995; The Ravens, 1990; Discovering Prehistoric England, 1993, 2nd ed., 2001; The Stopsley Book, 1998; The Stopsley Picture Book, 1999; Rhubarb and Custard: The Luton Modern School History, 2004. **Address:** 6 Rogate Rd., Luton, BD LU2 8HR, England.

DYER, Joel. American (born United States), b. 1958?. **Genres:** Documenta-ries/Reportage, Social Sciences, Economics, Politics/Government. **Career:** Boulder Weekly, editor-in-chief, 1992-; tv series commentator. **Publications:** Harvest of Rage: Why Oklahoma City Is Only the Beginning, 1997; Crime or Punishment, 1998; The Perpetual Prisoner Machine: How America Profits from Crime, 2000. Contributor to magazines and newspapers. **Address:** Boulder Weekly, 690 S Lashley Ln., Boulder, CO 80305, U.S.A. **Online address:** joeldyer@aol.com

DYER, Joyce. American (born United States), b. 1947. **Genres:** Essays, Autobiography/Memoirs, Literary Criticism And History, Local History/Rural Topics, Writing/Journalism. **Career:** Hiram College, faculty, 1991-, John S. Kenyon professor of English. Writer. **Publications:** The Awakening: A Novel of Beginnings (criticism), 1993; In a Tangled Wood: An Alzheimer's Journey (memoir), 1996; (ed.) Bloodroot: Reflections on Place by Appalachian Women Writers (essays), 1998; Gum-Dipped: A Daughter Remembers Rubber Town (memoir), 2003; My Mother's Singer (chapbook), 2009; Goosetown: Reconstructing an Akron Neighborhood (memoir), 2010. **Address:** Hiram College, 6811 Hinsdale St., Writing House, Hiram, OH 44234, U.S.A. **Online address:** dyerja@hiram.edu

DYER, K. C. Canadian (born Canada), b. 1961. **Genres:** Novels, Young Adult Non-fiction, Children's Fiction. **Career:** New Westminster Secondary School, writer-in-residence. **Publications:** Seeds of Time, 2002; Secret of Light, 2003; Shades of Red, 2005; Ms. Zephyr's Notebook, 2007; A Walk Through A Window, 2009; Facing Fire, 2010. **Address:** PO Box 516, Lions Bay, BC V0N 2E0, Canada. **Online address:** kcdyer@telus.net

DYER, Sarah L. British (born England), b. 1978. **Genres:** Young Adult Fiction, Children's Fiction. **Career:** Kingston University, part-time lecturer, lecturer. Writer and illustrator. **Publications:** SELF-ILLUSTRATED: Five Little Fiends, 2002; Clementine and Mungo, 2004; Princess for a Day: A Clementine and Mungo Story, 2007; Mrs Muffly's Monster, 2008; The Girl with the Bird's Nest Hair, 2009. OTHERS: Monster Day at Work, 2010; Batty, 2011. **Address:** Kingston University, River House, 53-57 High St., Kingston, SR KT1 1LQ, England. **Online address:** sarah@sarahdyer.com

DYER, Wayne W(alter). American (born United States), b. 1940. **Genres:** Novels, Psychology, Children's Fiction, Biography. **Career:** Pershing High School, resource teacher and counselor, 1965-67; Mercy High School, director of guidance and counseling, 1967-71; Wayne State University, instructor in counselor education and practicum supervisor, 1969-71; St. John's University, education counselor and assistant professor, 1971-74, associate professor, 1974-77; Board of Cooperative Educational Services, Drug Information and Service Center, staff consultant, 1972-75; Mental Health Association of Nassau Co., staff consultant, 1973-75; Half Hollow School District, trainer and staff consultant, 1973-75; Herman Kiefer Hospital, Detroit Hospital Drug Treatment Program, staff consultant, 1974-75; North Shore University Hospital, Drug Treatment and Education Center, teaching staff and adjunct consultant, 1974-75. Writer. **Publications:** (With J. Vriend) Counseling Effectively in Groups, 1973; (with J. Vriend) Counseling Techniques That Work: Application to Individual and Group Counseling, 1974; Your Erroneous Zones: Bold But Simple Techniques for Eliminating Unhealthy Behavior Patterns, 1976; Pulling Your Own Strings, 1977; The Sky's the Limit, 1980; Gifts from Eykis (novel), 1982; Group Counseling for Personal Mastery, 1980; What Do You Really Want for Your Children, 1985; Happy Holidays, 1986; You'll See It When You Believe It, 1989; No More Holiday Blues, 1990; Real Magic: Creating Miracles in Everyday Life, 1992; Your Sacred Self, 1994; Everyday Wisdom, 1994; Staying on the Path, 1995, rev. ed., 2004; A Promise Is a Promise, 1995; Manifest Your Destiny, 1997; Wisdom of the Ages: A Modern Master Brings Eternal Truths into Everyday Life, 1998; Dr. Wayne Dyer's 10 Secrets for Success and Inner Peace, 2001; There's a Spiritual Solution to Every Problem, 2001; Getting in the Gap: Making Conscious Contact with God Through Meditation, 2003; Power of Intention: Learning to Co-Create Your World Your Way, 2004; Incredible You!: 10 Ways to Let Your Greatness Shine Through, 2005; Being in Balance: 9 Principles for Creating Habits to Match Your Desires, 2006; Everyday wisdom for success, 2006; (with K. Tracy) Unstoppable Me!: 10 Ways to Soar Through Life, 2006; Inspiration: Your Ultimate Calling, 2006; Change Your Thoughts, Change Your Life: Living the Wisdom of the Tao, 2006; Invisible Force: 365 Ways to Apply the Power of Intention to Your Life, 2007; (with K. Tracy) It's Not What You've Got: Lessons for Kids on Money and Abundance, 2007; Living the wisdom of the Tao: The Complete Tao Te Ching and Affirmations, 2008; New Way of Thinking, A New Way of Being: Experiencing the Tao Te Ching, 2009; (with K. Tracy)

No Excuses!: How What You Say Can Get in Your Way, 2009; Excuses Begone!, 2009; The Shift: Taking Your Life from Ambition to Meaning, 2010. **Address:** Hay House Inc., PO Box 5100, Carlsbad, CA 92018-5100, U.S.A.

DYRNESS, William A. American (born United States), b. 1943. **Genres:** Art/Art History, Cultural/Ethnic Topics, Theology/Religion. **Career:** Hinson Memorial Baptist Church, minister to students, 1971-73; Asian Theological Seminary, professor of theology, 1972-82; New College, president, 1982-86, professor of theology, 1986-89; Fuller Theological Seminary, School of Theology, dean, 1990-, professor of theology and culture, 1990-. Writer. **Publications:** Rouault: A Vision of Suffering and Salvation, 1971; Christian Critique of American Culture, 1974; Themes of Old Testament Theology, 1979; Christian Art in Asia, 1979; Let the Earth Rejoice! 1983; A Christian Apologetics in a World Community, 1983; How Does America Hear the Gospel?, 1989; Learning About Theology from the Third World, 1990; Invitation to Cross-Cultural Theology, 1992; The Earth is God's: A Theology of American Culture, 1997; Visual Faith: Art Theology and Worship in Dialogue, 2001; Reformed Theology and Visual Culture, 2004; Senses of the Soul: Art and the Visual in Christian Worship, 2008; Primer on Worship, 2009; Poetic Theology: God and the Poetics of Everyday Life, 2011. **Address:** School of Theology, Fuller Theological Seminary, 135 N Oakland Ave., Pasadena, CA 91101, U.S.A. **Online address:** wdyrness@fuller.edu

DYSART, Joshua. American (born United States), b. 1971. **Genres:** Graphic Novels, Military/Defense/Arms Control. **Career:** Graphic novelist. **Publications:** Violent Messiahs: Genesis, vol. I-II, 2000; (adapter) The Demon Ororon, vol. I, 2004; Captain Gravity and the Power of the Vril, 2006; Swamp Thing: Love in Vain, 2006; Swamp Thing: Healing the Breach, 2006; (with C. d'Errico) Avril Lavigne's Make 5 Wishes, vol. I-II, 2007; Unknown Soldier, vol. I: Haunted House, 2009, vol. II: Easy Kill, 2010; Neil Young's Greendale, 2010. **Address:** U.S.A. **Online address:** dysart@gmail.com

DYSON, Esther. American/Swiss (born Switzerland), b. 1951. **Genres:** Information Science/Computers, Technology, Medicine/Health. **Career:** Forbes magazine, reporter, 1974-77, columnist, 1987-; New Court Securities, securities analyst, 1977-79; Oppenheimer & Co., president, 1980-82; Release 1.0, editor and publisher, 1982-; Eddventure Holdings, owner and president, 1982-; Computer Industry Daily, editor and publisher, 1985; Mayfield Software Partners Ltd., partner; Guardian Magazine, columnist; Content Magazine, columnist; National Public Radio, commentator; Electronic Frontier Foundation, vice chair; Cygnus Support, director; Poland Online, founding investor. **Publications:** Release 2.0: A Design for Living in the Digital Age, 1997; Release 2.1: A Design for Living in the Digital Age, 1998. Contributor of articles to journals and periodicals. **Address:** EDventure Holdings, 632 Broadway, 10th Fl., New York, NY 10012, U.S.A. **Online address:** edyson@boxbe.com

DYSON, Freeman (John). American/British (born England), b. 1923. **Genres:** Physics, Autobiography/Memoirs, Science Fiction/Fantasy. **Career:** RAF Bomber Command, High Wycombe, civilian scientist, 1943-45; Cornell University, commonwealth fellow, 1947-49, professor of physics, 1951-53, Institute for Advanced Study, professor of physics, 1953-94, professor emeritus, 1994-; Trinity College, research fellow, 1946-49; University of Birmingham, Warren research fellow, 1949-51; Orion Project, chief theoretician for propulsion system, 1958-59; Arms Control and Disarmament Agency, consultant, 1962; Yeshiva University, visiting professor, 1967-68; Princeton University, Institute for Advanced Study, professor, professor emeritus, 1994; Gustavus Adolphus College, Rydell professor, 1999. Writer. **Publications:** (Ed.) Symmetry Groups in Nuclear and Particle Physics, 1966; Neutron Stars and Pulsars, 1971; Disturbing the Universe (autobiography), 1979; (with R. Aron and J. Robinson) Values at War: Selected Tanner Lectures on the Nuclear Crisis, 1983; Weapons and Hope, 1984; Origins of Life, 1986, rev. ed., 1999; Infinite in All Directions, 1988; From Eros to Gaia, 1992; Selected papers of Freeman Dyson with Commentary, 1996; Imagined Worlds, 1997; The Sun, the Genome and the Internet, 1999; The Scientist as Rebel, 2006; Heretical Thoughts about Science and Society, 2006; A Many-Colored Glass: Reflections on the Place of Life in the Universe, 2007; Advanced Quantum Mechanics, 2007. **Address:** 105 Battle Road Cir., Princeton, NJ 08540, U.S.A. **Online address:** dyson@ias.edu

DYSON, John. New Zealander (born New Zealand), b. 1943. **Genres:** Travel/Exploration, History, Children's Fiction, Children's Non-fiction, Sports/Fitness, Recreation, Reference, Biography, Biography. **Career:** Journalist, 1959-72; author, 1972-; Reader's Digest Magazine, roving editor, 1988-. **Publications:** NONFICTION: (co-author) The Magnificent Continent, 1976; Business in Great Waters, 1977; The Hot Arctic, 1979; The South Seas Dream: An Adventure in Paradise, 1982; (with J. Fitchett) Sink the Rainbow!: An Enquiry Into the Greenpeace Affair, 1986; Spirit of Sail: On Board the World's Great Sailing Ships, 1987; Columbus: For Gold, God and Glory, 1991; The Montana Badmen, 1996. FICTION: The Prime Minister's Boat Is Missing, 1974; Blue Hurricane, 1983; China Race, 1984. JUVENILE: Yachting the New Zealand Way, 1965; Behind the Wheel, 1974; In a Garage, 1974; (with K. Dyson) Fun with Kites, 1976; The Pond Book, 1976; The Motorcycling Book, 1977; The Young Yachtsman, 1978; Westward with Columbus, 1991. **Address:** 27 The Terr., Barnes, London, GL SW13 0NR, England.

DYSON, Michael Eric. American (born United States), b. 1958. **Genres:** Essays, Cultural/Ethnic Topics, History. **Career:** Thankful Baptist Church, preacher and minister; Princeton University, Mathy College, assistant master; Hartford Seminary, assistant director of poverty project, 1988-89; Chicago Theological Seminary, instructor, assistant professor, 1989-92; Brown University, assistant professor, 1993-95; University of North Carolina, professor, 1995-97, Institute of African-American Research, director, 1995-97; Columbia University, visiting distinguished professor of African-American studies, 1997-99; DePaul University, Ida B. Wells-Barnett university professor and professor of religious studies, 1999-2002; University of Pennsylvania, Avalon Foundation professor; Georgetown University, Department of Sociology, university professor of sociology, 2007-. Writer. **Publications:** Reflecting Black: African-American Cultural Criticism (essays), 1993; Making Malcolm: The Myth and Meaning of Malcolm X, 1995; Between God and Gangsta Rap: Bearing Witness to Black Culture (essays), 1996; Race Rules: Navigating the Color Line, 1996; I May Not Get There With You: The True Martin Luther King, Jr., 2000; Holler if You Hear Me: Searching for Tupac Shakur, 2001; Open Mike: Reflections on Philosophy, Race, Sex, Culture, and Religion, 2003; Why I Love Black Women, 2003; Mercy, Mercy Me: The Art, Loves, and Demons of Marvin Gaye, 2004; Michael Eric Dyson Reader, 2004; Is Bill Cosby Right?: Or Has the Black Middle Class Lost its Mind?, 2005; Pride: The Seven Deadly Sins, 2006; Come Hell or High Water: Hurricane Katrina and the Color of Disaster, 2006; Debating Race, 2007; Know What I Mean?: Reflections on Hip-Hop, 2007; April 4, 1968: Martin Luther King, Jr.'s Death and How It Changed America, 2008; Can You Hear Me Now?, 2009; (co-ed.) Born to Use Mics: Reading Nas's Illmatic, 2010. Contributor to books and periodicals. **Address:** Department of Sociology, Georgetown University, 307 Healy Hall, Car Barn, 3520 Prospect St. NW, Ste. 209, PO Box 571037, Washington, DC 20057, U.S.A. **Online address:** med52@georgetown.edu

DZIELSKA, Maria. Polish (born Poland), b. 1942. **Genres:** Classics, Education. **Career:** Jagiellonian University, History Institute, Department of Byzantine History, assistant, 1967-73, assistant professor, 1973-87, dozent, 1987-92, professor of Roman history, 1992-. Writer. **Publications:** Apolloniusz z Tiany: legenda i rzeczywistość, 1983; Hypatia z Aleksandrii, 1993. **Address:** Department of Byzantine History, Institute of History, Jagiellonian University, Studencka 3, Krakow, 31-116, Poland.

DZUBACK, Mary Ann. American (born United States), b. 1950. **Genres:** History, Women's Studies And Issues, Social Sciences. **Career:** Washington University, assistant professor of education, 1987-94, associate professor of education and associate professor of history, 1994-, associate professor of women, gender, and sexuality studies and director of women, gender, and sexuality studies, 2006-, adjunct associate professor of history, advisor for educational studies; History of Education Quarterly, associate editor, 1993-99; AERA, Division F, vice-president, 1995-97. Writer. **Publications:** Robert M. Hutchins: Portrait of an Educator, 1991. **Address:** Department of Education, Washington University, 138 Seigle Hall, 1 Brooking Dr., PO Box 1183, St. Louis, MO 63130-4899, U.S.A. **Online address:** madzubac@wustl.edu

E

EADY, Cornelius. American (born United States), b. 1954?. **Genres:** Poetry, Literary Criticism And History. **Career:** Sarah Lawrence College, teacher; New York University, faculty; The Writer's Voice, teacher; The College of William and Mary, teacher; Sweet Briar College, teacher; City College of New York, distinguished writer-in-residence; University of Notre Dame, faculty of the Creative Writing MFA program; State University of New York at Stony Brook, associate professor of English, director of Poetry Center; Cave Canem, co-founder, 1996-; University of Missouri, Miller chair. Poet and playwright. **Publications:** POETRY: Kartunes, 1980; Victims of the Latest Dance Craze, 1986; BOOM BOOM BOOM, 1988; The Gathering of My Name, 1991; You Don't Miss Your Water, 1995; The Autobiography of a Jukebox: Poems, 1997; Brutal Imagination, 2001; (with T. Derricotte) Gathering Ground: A Reader Celebrating Cave Canem's First Decade, 2006; Hardheaded Weather: New and Selected Poems, 2008. Works appear in anthologies. **Address:** University of Notre Dame, 261 Decio Faculty Hall, Notre Dame, IN 46556, U.S.A. **Online address:** cornelius.r.eady.1@nd.edu

EAGLE, Kin. *See* **ADLERMAN, Danny.**

EAGLE, Kin. *See* **ADLERMAN, Kimberly M.**

EAGLES, Charles W. American (born United States), b. 1946. **Genres:** History, Race Relations, Race Relations. **Career:** Research Triangle Institute, district supervisor, 1969-71; North Carolina State University, assistant professor of history, 1977-80; Southeast Missouri State University, assistant professor of history, 1980-82; Vanderbilt University, assistant professor of history, 1982-83; University of Mississippi, professor of history, 1983-, William F. Winter professor of history, 2008-. Writer. **Publications:** Jonathan Daniels and Race Relations: The Evolution of a Southern Liberal, 1982; Democracy Delayed: Congressional Reapportionment and Urban-Rural Conflict in the 1920s, 1990; Outside Agitator: Jon Daniels and the Civil Rights Movement in Alabama, 1993; Price of Defiance: James Meredith and the Integration of Ole Miss, 2009. EDITOR: The Civil Rights Movement in America, 1986; The Mind of the South: Fifty Years Later, 1992; Is There a Southern Political Tradition?, 1996. **Address:** Department of History, University of Mississippi, PO Box 1848, University, MS 38677-1848, U.S.A. **Online address:** eagles@olemiss.edu

EAGLETON, Terry. British (born England), b. 1943. **Genres:** Novels, Plays/Screenplays, Literary Criticism And History, Politics/Government. **Career:** Cambridge University, Jesus College, fellow, 1964-69; University of Oxford, Wadham College, fellow and tutor in poetry, 1969-89, Linacre College, lecturer in critical theory, 1989-92, St. Catherine's College, Thomas Warton professor of English literature, 1992-2001; University of Manchester, John Edward Taylor professor of English literature, 2001-08; Lancaster University, Department of English and Creative Writing, chair, distinguished professor of English literature, 2008-; National University of Ireland, visiting professor. Writer. **Publications:** The New Left Church, 1966; Shakespeare and Society: Critical Studies in Shakespearean Drama, 1967; (ed. with B. Wicker) From Culture to Revolution: The Slant Symposium, 1967; (ed.) Directions: Pointers for the Post-Conciliar Church, 1968; The Body as Language: Outline of a New Left Theology, 1970; Exiles and émigrés: Studies in Modern Literature, 1970; Myths of Power: A Marxist Study of the Brontës, 1975, 2nd ed., 1988;

Marxism and Literary Criticism, 1976; Criticism and Ideology: A Study in Marxist Literary Theory, 1976, new ed., 2006; Walter Benjamin, or, Towards a Revolutionary Criticism, 1981; The Rape of Clarissa: Writing, Sexuality and Class Struggle in Samuel Richardson, 1982; Literary Theory: An Introduction, 1983, 2nd ed., 2008; The Function of Criticism: From the Spectator to Post-Structuralism, 1984; (ed.) Alexander Pope, 1985; (ed.) Emily Bronte, 1985; (ed.) W.H. Auden, 1985; William Shakespeare, 1986; Against the Grain: Selected Essays, 1975-1985, 1986; Saints and Scholars, 1987; (ed.) Hard Times, 1987; (ed.) Raymond Williams: A Critical Reader, 1989; Saint Oscar, 1989; The Ideology of the Aesthetics, 1990; (with F. Jameson and E.W. Said) Nationalism, Colonialism and Literature, 1990; The Significance of Theory, 1990; Ideology: An Introduction, 1991; Wittgenstein: The Terry Eagleton Script, 1993; Heathcliff and the Great Hunger: Studies in Irsih Culture, 1995; (ed. with D. Milne) Marxist Literary Theory: A Reader, 1996; The Illusions of Postmodernism, 1997; Saint Oscar and Other Plays, 1997; Marx and Freedom, 1997; Crazy John and the Bishop and Other Essays on Irish Culture, 1998; Marx, 1999; Scholars and Rebels in Nineteenth-Century Ireland, 1999; The Idea of Culture, 2000; (co-author) Modernity, Modernism, Postmodernism, 2000; The Truth about the Irish, 2000; The Gatekeeper: A Memoir, 2001; After Theory, 2003; Figures of Dissent: Critical Essays on Fish, Spivak, žižek and Others, 2003; Sweet Violence: The Idea of the Tragic, 2003; English Novel: An Introduction, 2005; Function of Criticism: From the Spectator to Post-structuralism, 2005; Holy Terror, 2005; (co-author) 18: Beckett: Blackwood Gallery, University of Toronto at Mississauga, 2006; How to Read a Poem, 2007; (intro.) Gospels, 2007; The Meaning of Life: A Very Short Introduction, 2007; Trouble with Strangers: A Study of Ethics, 2009; Reason, Faith, and Revolution: Reflections on the God Debate, 2009; (with M. Beaumont) Task of the Critic, 2009; (co-author) Now is The Time: Art & Theory in the 21st Century, 2009; (contrib.) God and Evil in the Theology of St Thomas Aquinas, 2010; On Evil, 2010; Why Marx was Right, 2011; Event of Literature, 2012. Contributor to periodicals. **Address:** Department of English and Creative Writing, Lancaster University, B193 County College, Lancaster, LC LA1 4YD, England.

EAKINS, Patricia. American (born United States), b. 1942. **Genres:** Adult Non-fiction. **Career:** Writer and book coach, 1974-; New York Institute of Technology, instructor, 1979-86, adjunct assistant professor, 1986-; Trinity College, visiting assistant professor, 1990-94; New School, instructor, 1992-97; Woodstock Guild, writer-in-residence; Frigate, editor-in-chief. **Publications:** Oono (chapbook), 1982; The Hungry Girls and Other Stories, 1988; The Marvelous Adventures of Pierre Baptiste: Father and Mother, First and Last (novel), 1999; Writing for Interior Design, 2004; Affamées et Autres Nouvelles, 2010; Hoodoo Dreams: A Meditation on Culture and Landscape, forthcoming. Contributor to periodicals. **Address:** c/o Martha Millard, Martha Millard Literary Agency, 420 Central Pk. W, Ste. 5H, New York, NY 10025, U.S.A. **Online address:** eakins@fabulara.com

EAMES, Anne. American (born United States), b. 1945. **Genres:** Romance/Historical, Novels, Human Relations/Parenting, Young Adult Fiction. **Career:** Peanut Gallery (children's store), owner, 1960; Old Town Playhouse, business manager; Associated Builders and Contractors, executive director, 1980; full-time writer, 1990-. **Publications:** MONTANA MALONES SERIES: The Best Little Joeville Christmas, 1997; A Marriage Made in Joeville,

1997; The Last of the Joeville Lovers, 1998; The Unknown Malone, 1999. NOVELS: Two Weddings and a Bride, 1996; You're What?!, 1996; Christmas Elopement, 1996; The Pregnant Virgin, 2001. **Address:** c/o Author Mail, Silhouette Books, Harlequin Enterprises, PO Box 5190, Buffalo, NY 14240-5190, U.S.A.

EARL, Maureen. American/Egyptian (born Egypt), b. 1944. **Genres:** Novels, Plays/Screenplays, Young Adult Fiction. **Career:** Writer and film maker. **Publications:** NOVELS: Gulliver Quick, 1992; Boat of Stone, 1993. Contributor to magazines. **Address:** 1423 Sanchez St., San Miguel Allende, San Francisco, CA 94131, U.S.A.

EARL, Riggins R. American (born United States), b. 1942. **Genres:** History, Theology/Religion, Young Adult Non-fiction, Social Sciences. **Career:** University of Tennessee, assistant professor of religious studies, 1974-82; Interdenominational Theological Center, professor of ethics and theology, 1990-; Berea College, Martin L. King, Jr. lecturer; Baptist church in Atlanta, weekly Bible lecturer, 1995-. Writer. **Publications:** (Ed.) To You Who Teach in the Black Church, 1972; Dark Symbols, Obscure Signs: God, Self and Community in the Slave Mind, 1993; Dark Salutations: Rituals, God and Greetings in the Black Community, 2001. FORTHCOMING: Dark Status: Black America's Quest to Be; Dark Testimony: Black America's Witness; Religion, Politics and Morality in the Rhetoric of Booker T. Washington; The Mosaic of Black Religious Leadership; The Jesus as Lord and Savoir Problem: Blacks' Double Consciousness Self-Worth Dilemma. Contributor to books and periodicals. **Address:** Interdenominational Theological Ctr., Classroom Bldg. 308, 700 Martin Luther King Jr. Dr. SW, Atlanta, GA 30314, U.S.A. **Online address:** rearl@itc.edu

EARLE, Jonathan. (Jonathan Halperin Earle). American (born United States), b. 1968. **Genres:** Politics/Government, History, Humanities. **Career:** University of Kansas, Department of History, professor, 1997-; Robert J. Dole Institute of Politics, associate director, 2003-, director; Occidental College, Ray Allen Billington chair in U.S. history, 2006-07. Writer. **Publications:** The Routledge Atlas of African American History, 2000; Jacksonian Antislavery and the Politics of Free Soil, 1824-1854, 2004; (with S. Wilentz and T. Paterson) Major Problems in the Early Republic, 1787-1848: Documents and Essays, 2007; John Brown's Raid on Harpers Ferry: A Brief History with Documents, 2008. **Address:** Department of History, University of Kansas, 3642 Wescoe Hall, 1445 Jayhawk Blvd., Lawrence, KS 66045-7594, U.S.A. **Online address:** jonearle@ku.edu

EARLE, Jonathan Halperin. See **EARLE, Jonathan.**

EARLE, Rebecca. British (born England), b. 1964. **Genres:** History. **Career:** University of Warwick, instructor. Writer. **Publications:** (Ed.) Epistolary Selves: Letters and Letter-Writers, 1600-1945, 1999; Entre Tintas y Plumas: Historias de la Prensa Chilena del Siglo XIX, 2004; The Return of the Native: Indians and Myth-Making in Spanish America, 1810-1930, 2007. **Address:** England. **Online address:** r.earle@warwick.ac.uk

EARLE, Sylvia A. (Sylvia Alice Earle). American (born United States), b. 1935. **Genres:** Marine Sciences/Oceanography. **Career:** Cape Haze Marine Laboratories, resident director, 1966; Harvard University, Farlow Herbarium, research fellow, 1967-81; California Academy of Sciences, research biologist and curator, 1976; University of California, research associate, 1969-81; Natural History Museum, fellow, 1976; Deep Ocean Technology & Deep Ocean Engineering, founder, president and chief executive officer, 1981-90; National Oceanic and Atmospheric Administration, chief scientist, 1990-92; Deep Ocean Exploration and Research, founder and chairman, 1992-; Global Marine Conservation for Conservation Intl., executive director; Harte Research Institute, program coordinator and advisory council chair; Monterey Bay Aquarium Research Institute, adjunct scientist; Kerr-McGee Inc., director; Common Heritage Corp., director. Writer. **Publications:** Humbrella, a New Red Alga of Uncertain Taxonomic Position From the Juan Fernandez, 1969; (with J.R. Young) Siphonoclathrus, A New Genus of Chlorophyta (Siphonales: Codiaceae) from Panama, 1972; (with A. Giddings) Exploring the Deep Frontier: The Adventure of Man in the Sea, 1980; Sea Change: A Message of the Oceans, 1996; Dive!: My Adventures in the Deep Frontier, 1999; Hello Fish, 1999; (with W. Henry) Wild Ocean: America's Park under the Sea, 1999; Sea Critters, 2000; (with E.J. Prager) The Oceans, 2001; National Geographic Atlas of the Ocean: The Deep Frontier, 2001; Coral Reefs, 2003; Jump into Science, 2003; Fathoming the Ocean, 2005; (intro.) Coral Reefs

of the Southern Gulf of Mexico, 2007; (with L. Glover) Ocean, 2008; (with J. Cancelmo) Texas Coral Reefs, 2008; The World is Blue, 2010. EDITOR: (with B.C. Collette) Results of the Tektite Program: Ecology of Coral Reef Fishes, 1972; (with R.J. Lavenberg) Results of the Tektite Program, Coral Reef Invertebrates and Plants, 1975; (with L.K. Glover) Defying Ocean's End: An Agenda for Action, 2004; (co-ed.) Gulf of Mexico Origin, Waters, and Biota, 2009. **Address:** DOER Marine, 1827 Clement Ave., Bldg. 19, Alameda, CA 94501, U.S.A. **Online address:** searle@literati.net

EARLE, Sylvia Alice. See **EARLE, Sylvia A.**

EARLEY, Pete. American (born United States), b. 1951. **Genres:** Documentaries/Reportage, Adult Non-fiction, Young Adult Fiction, Young Adult Non-fiction, Novels. **Career:** Enid News & Eagle, reporter, 1972-73; Emporia Gazette, staff writer, 1973-75; Tulsa Tribune, investigative reporter, 1975-78, correspondent, 1978-80; Washington Post, reporter, 1980-86; freelance writer, 1986-; Goucher College, visiting faculty, 2006. **Publications:** Family of Spies: Inside the John Walker Spy Ring, 1988; Prophet of Death: The Mormon Blood-Atonement Killings, 1991; The Hot House: Life Inside Leavenworth Prison, 1992; Circumstantial Evidence: Death, Life, and Justice in a Southern Town, 1995; Confessions of a Spy: The Real Story of Aldrich Ames, 1997; Super Casino: Inside the New Las Vegas, 2000; (with G. Shur) WITSEC: Inside the Federal Witness Protection Program, 2002; Deep Cover, 2004; The Big Secret, 2004; Lethal Secrets, 2005; Crazy: A Father's Search through America's Mental Health Madness, 2006; The Apocalypse Stone, 2006; Comrade J: The Untold Secrets of Russia's Master Spy in America After the End of the Cold War, 2007; The Serial Killer Whisperer, 2012. Contributor to periodicals. **Address:** Putnam Publishing Group, 375 Hudson St., New York, NY 10014, U.S.A. **Online address:** peteearley.speeches@gmail.com

EARLEY, Tony. American (born United States), b. 1961?. **Genres:** Novels, Novellas/Short Stories, Young Adult Fiction. **Career:** University of the South, Williams visiting writer; Carnegie-Mellon University, instructor; Daily Courier, columnist and sports editor; Vanderbilt University, assistant professor of English, 1997-, professor of English, 1997-, Samuel Milton Fleming associate professor of English, Samuel Milton Fleming chair in English; University of Alabama, faculty, 1997-. **Publications:** Here We Are in Paradise (stories), 1994; Jim the Boy (novel), 1999; Somehow Form a Family: Stories that are Mostly True, 2001; The Blue Star, 2008. Contributor to periodicals. **Address:** Department of English, Vanderbilt University, 413 Benson Hall, 2201 W End Ave., Nashville, TN 37235-0001, U.S.A. **Online address:** tony.l.earley@vanderbilt.edu

EARLS, Nick. Australian/Irish (born Ireland), b. 1963. **Genres:** Novellas/Short Stories, Novels, Young Adult Fiction. **Career:** Freelance writer, 1988-; Medical Observer, continuing medical education editor, 1994-; War Child, founding chair, ambassador; Mater Foundation, honorary ambassador; Abused Child Trust, honorary ambassador. **Publications:** Passion (short stories), 1992; After January (young adult novel), 1996; Zigzag Street (novel), 1996; Bachelor Kisses, 1998; Headgames, 1999; 48 Shades of Brown, 1999; Perfect Skin, 2000; World of Chickens, 2001; Making Laws for Clouds, 2002; (co-author) Big Night Out, 2002; (ed. with J. Adams and J. Partridge) Kid's Night In, 2003; Two to Go, 2003; The Thompson Gunner, 2004; After Summer, 2004; Monica Bloom, 2006; (with R. Sparrow) Joel and Cat Set the Story Straight, 2007; The True Story of Butterfish, 2009; The Fix. 2011. Works appear in anthologies. **Address:** Curtis Brown, PO Box 19, Paddington, NW 2021, Australia. **Online address:** nickearls@optusnet.com.au

EARLY, Jack. See **SCOPPETTONE, Sandra.**

EARLY, Joseph E. American (born United States), b. 1970. **Genres:** Biography, Theology/Religion, History. **Career:** Baylor University, faculty; University of the Cumberlands, assistant professor of religion. Author of nonfiction. **Publications:** A Handbook of Texas Baptist Biography, 2004; A Texas Baptist History Sourcebook: A Companion to McBeth's Texas Baptists, 2004; A Texas Baptist Power Struggle: The Hayden Controversy, 2005; A Student's Guide to the New Testament, 2005; A Student's Guide to the Old Testament, 2005; Readings in Baptist History: Four Centuries of Selected Documents, 2008. Contributor of articles to journals. **Address:** University of the Cumberlands, 6191 College Station Dr., Williamsburg, KY 40769-1372, U.S.A. **Online address:** joeearly@cumblerlandcollege.edu

EARNSHAW, Micky. (Spencer Wright Earnshaw). American (born United

States), b. 1939. **Genres:** Music. **Career:** University of Vermont, instructor of mathematics, 1969-73; drum-set instructor, 1974-84; freelance musician, 1974; Courtenay Youth Music Center, drum instructor, 1976-90; University of Hawaii, instructor of mathematics. Musician and writer. **Publications:** The Essence of Rhythm, 1994; Eighth-Note Rhythms in Common Time; Developing Rhythmic Independence. **Address:** Department of Mathematics, University of Hawaii, WH-B1, 200 W Kawili St., Hilo, HI 96720-4091, U.S.A. **Online address:** earnshaw@hawaii.edu

EARNSHAW, Spencer Wright. *See* **EARNSHAW, Micky.**

EARNSHAW, Steven. British (born England), b. 1962. **Genres:** Literary Criticism And History, Humanities. **Career:** Walsall College, lecturer in English, 1988-89; University of Leicester, part-time lecturer, 1990-94; Nene College, part-time lecturer, 1990-94, lecturer, 1994-95; Sheffield Hallam University, professor of English literature, 1995-. Writer. **Publications:** (Ed. with J. Dowson) Postmodern Subjects/Postmodern Texts, 1995; The Direction of Literary Theory: Generations of Meaning, 1996; (ed.) Just Postmodernism, 1997; The Pub in Literature: England's Altered State, 2000; (co-ed.) Ten Hallam Poets, 2005; Existentialism: A Guide for the Perplexed, 2006; (ed.) The Handbook of Creative Writing, 2007; Beginning Realism, 2010. Contributor to books and journals. **Address:** Department of English, Sheffield Hallam University, City Campus, Howard St., Sheffield, SY S1 1WB, England. **Online address:** s.l.earnshaw@shu.ac.uk

EASON, Alethea. Chilean/American (born United States), b. 1957?. **Genres:** Social Sciences, Travel/Exploration, Children's Fiction, Science Fiction/Fantasy. **Career:** Middletown Unified School District, teacher. Writer. **Publications:** Hungry, 2007. Works appear in anthologies. **Address:** Concon, Chile. **Online address:** aletheaeason1@yahoo.com

EAST, Churchill. *See* **HARNER, Stephen M.**

EASTBURN, Kathryn. American (born United States) **Genres:** Food And Wine, Autobiography/Memoirs. **Career:** Colorado Springs Independent, founding editor, co-founder; Lighthouse Writers Workshop, faculty; Colorado College, faculty. Journalist and freelance writer. **Publications:** Simon Says: A True Story of Boys, Guns and Murder in the Rocky Mountain West, 2007; A Sacred Feast: Reflections on Sacred Harp Singing and Dinner on the Ground, 2008. Contributor to periodicals. **Address:** University of Nebraska Press, 1111 Lincoln Mall, Lincoln, NE 68588-0630, U.S.A. **Online address:** kathryneastburn@mac.com

EASTER, Gerald. *See* **EASTER, Gerald M.**

EASTER, Gerald M. (Gerald Easter). American (born United States) **Genres:** Politics/Government, Social Commentary, History, Adult Non-fiction. **Career:** Columbia University, Department of Political Science, teaching assistant, 1984-86, instructor, 1986-89, Center for Social Science Research, research associate for project on labor movement in late imperial Russia, 1985-87; Georgetown University, visiting assistant professor, 1992-95; Miami University, visiting assistant professor, 1995-97; Boston College, assistant professor, 1999-2003, associate professor of history, 2003-, director of masters program, 2010-; Harvard University, Davis Center for Russian and Eurasian Studies Center, associate, 2000-. Writer and historian. **Publications:** Reconstructing the State: Personal Networks and Elite Identity in Soviet Russia, 2000; (ed. with S. Harter) Shaping the Economic Space in Russia: Decision Making Processes, Institutions, and Adjustment to Change in the El'tsin Era, 2000. FORTHCOMING: Capital, Coercion, and Post-Communist States; Out of the Red: Building Fiscal Capacity in Post-Communist States; Regional Governors and the Making of the Russian Federation; (co-ed.) Shaping the Economic Space in Russia: Policy-making, Institutions, Actors. **Address:** Boston College, Political Science Department, 229 McGuinn Hall, 140 Commonwealth Ave., Chestnut Hill, MA 02467, U.S.A. **Online address:** easterg@bc.edu

EASTERBROOK, Gregg. American (born United States), b. 1953. **Genres:** Novels, Politics/Government, Young Adult Non-fiction. **Career:** New Republic Magazine, contributing editor, senior editor; Beliefnet.com, co-founder and senior editor; Brookings Institution, visiting fellow; writer, 1977-; U.S. News & World Report, contributing editor; Newsweek Magazine, contributing editor; Atlantic Monthly Magazine, staff writer, national correspondent, contributing editor; Entertainment and Sports Programming Network.

com, columnist; National Football League.com, columnist; The Washington Monthly, contributing editor, editor. **Publications:** This Magic Moment (novel), 1986; Surgeon Koop, 1991; A Moment on the Earth (non-fiction), 1995; Beside Still Waters: Searching for Meaning in an Age of Doubt (non-fiction), 1998; Tuesday Morning Quarterback: Haiku and other Whimsical Observations to Help you Understand the Modern Game (humor), 2001; The Here and Now (novel), 2002; The Progress Paradox (non-fiction), 2004; Sonic Boom (non-fiction), 2009. Contributor to periodicals. **Address:** c/o Michael Carlisle, Inkwell Management, 521 5th Ave., 26th Fl., New York, NY 10175, U.S.A. **Online address:** gregg@greggeasterbrook.com

EASTERLY, William. (William R. Easterly). American (born United States), b. 1957?. **Genres:** Economics, Adult Non-fiction. **Career:** Economist; professor; Data Resources Inc., economist for Latin American service, 1980-81; El Colegio de Mexico, research fellow, 1983-84; Massachusetts Institute of Technology, consultant to government of Jamaica, 1983, teaching assistant, 1984-85; World Bank, economist in operations, 1985-87, economist, 1988, senior advisor, 1989-2001; Georgetown University, adjunct professor, 1992-95, 1997-98; Johns Hopkins University, adjunct professor, 1992-95; University of Maryland, faculty visitor, 1996; Institute for International Economics and Center for Global Development, 2001-03; New York University, professor of economics, 2003-; Development Research Institute, co-director, 2003-; Center for Global Development, non-resident senior fellow, 2003-, senior fellow; Brookings Institution, non-resident senior fellow, 2008-; National Bureau of Economic Research, research associate; Journal of Development Economics, co-editor. **Publications:** NONFICTION: (ed. with C.A. Rodríguez and K. Schmidt-Hebbel) Public Sector Deficits and Macroeconomic Performance, 1994; The Elusive Quest for Growth: Economists' Adventures and Misadventures in the Tropics, 2001; (ed. with L. Servén) The Limits of Stabilization: Infrastructure, Public Deficits and Growth in Latin America, 2003; The White Man's Burden: Why the West's Efforts to Aid the Rest Have Done So Much Ill and So Little Good, 2006; (ed.) Reinventing Foreign Aid, 2008. OTHERS: Consistency Framework for Macroeconomic Analysis, 1989; (as William R. Easterly) Policy Distortions, Size of Government and Growth, 1989; (as William R. Easterly) Fiscal Adjustment and Deficit Financing during the Debt Crisis, 1989; (as William R. Easterly with D.L. Wetzel) Policy Determinants of Growth: Survey of Theory and Evidence, 1989; (with P Honohan) Financial Sector Policy in Thailand: A Macroeconomic Perspective, 1990; (co-author) Modeling the Macroeconomic Requirement of Policy Reforms, 1990; (co-author) How do National Policies Affect: Long-Run Growth?, 1991; (with K. Schmidt-Hebbel) Macroeconomics of Public Sector Deficits: A Synthesis, 1991; Macroeconomics of the Public Sector Deficit: The Case of Colombia, 1991; Economic Stagnation, Fixed Factors and Policy Thresholds, 1991; (co-author) How do National Policies affect Long-Run Growth?: A Research Agenda, 1992; (with S. Rebelo) Marginal Income Tax Rates and Economic Growth in Developing Countries, 1992; (with P. Mauro and K. Schmidt-Hebbel) Money Demand and Seignorage-Maximizing Inflation, 1992; How much do Distortions affect Growth?, 1993; When is Fiscal Adjustment an Illusion?, 1999; (with A. Kraay) Small States, Small Problems?, 1999; (with D. Dollar) The Search for the Key: Aid, Investment and Policies in Africa, 2009; (ed. with J. Cohen) What Works in Development?: Thinking Big and Thinking Small, 2009; (co-ed.) Tesoros o bombas de tiempo?, 2009. **Address:** Department of Economics, New York University, Rm. 705, 19 W 4th St., New York, NY 10012, U.S.A. **Online address:** william.easterly@nyu.edu

EASTERLY, William R. *See* **EASTERLY, William.**

EASTERMAN, Daniel. *See* **MACEOIN, Denis.**

EASTMAN, Susan Tyler. American (born United States), b. 1939. **Genres:** Theatre, Technology, Sciences, Communications/Media. **Career:** Bowling Green State University, instructor and fellow, 1974-77; Temple University, assistant professor, 1977-81; Indiana University, associate professor, 1981-97, Department of Telecommunications, professor, 1997-2003, professor emeritus, 2003-. Writer. **Publications:** (With S.W. Head and L. Klein) Broadcast Programming: Strategies for Winning Television and Radio Audiences, 1981; (ed. with R.A. Klein) Strategies in Broadcast and Cable Promotion: Commercial Television, Radio, Cable, Pay-Television, Public Television, 1982; (with S.W. Head and L. Klein) Broadcast/Cable Programming: Strategies and Practices, 2nd ed., 1985, (with D.A. Ferguson) 8th ed. as Media Programming: Strategies and Practices, 2009; (ed. with R.A. Klein) Promotion and Marketing for Broadcast and Cable, 2nd ed., 1991, (ed. with D.A. Ferguson and R.A. Klein) 5th ed. as Media Promotion and Marketing for Broadcasting, Cable and the Internet, 2006; (ed.) Research in Media Promotion, 2000. **Address:** Department of Telecommunications, Indiana University, Radio-TV 240, Bloomington, IN 47405, U.S.A. **Online address:** eastman@indiana.edu

EASTON, David. American/Canadian (born Canada), b. 1917. **Genres:** Politics/Government, Social Sciences. **Career:** Harvard University, teaching fellow, 1944-47; University of Chicago, Department of Political Science, assistant professor, 1947-53, associate professor, 1953-55, professor, 1955-84, Andrew MacLeish distinguished service professor emeritus, 1984-; Brookings Institution, consultant, 1953; University of Michigan, Mental Health Research Institute, consultant, 1955-56; Ford Foundation, Ford Professor, 1960-61; Royal Commission on Bilingualism and Biculturalism, consultant, 1965-67; Educational Testing Service, consultant, 1966-68; American Political Science Association, president, 1968-69; International Committee on Social Science Documentation, president, 1969-71; Queen's University, Sir Edward Peacock professor of political science, 1971-80; University of California, School of Social Sciences, Department of Political Science, distinguished research professor of political science, 1982-, now distinguished research professor emeritus of political science; American Academy of Arts and Sciences, vice president. Writer. **Publications:** The Political System: An Inquiry into the State of Political Science, 1953, 2nd ed., 1971; A Framework for Political Analysis, 1965; A Systems Analysis of Political Life, 1965; Varieties of Political Theory, 1966; (with J. Dennis and S. Easton) Children in the Political System: Origins of Political Legitimacy, 1969; The Analysis of Political Structure, 1990. EDITOR: (with J.G. Gunnell and L. Graziano) The Development of Political Science: A Comparative Survey, 1991; (with C.S. Schelling) Divided Knowledge: Across Disciplines, Across Cultures, 1991; (with J.G. Gunnell and M.B. Stein) Regime and Discipline: Democracy and the Development of Political Science, 1995. Contributor to journals. **Address:** Department of Political Science, University of California, 4251 Social Science Plz. B, PO Box 5100, Irvine, CA 92697-5100, U.S.A. **Online address:** deaston@uci.edu

EASTON, Elizabeth Wynne. American (born United States), b. 1956. **Genres:** Art/Art History. **Career:** Brooklyn Museum, assistant curator of European paintings, 1988-91, associate curator, 1992-98, curator, 1998-, Department of European Painting and Sculpture, chair, 1999-; Association of Art Museum Curators, president, 2003-06; Center for Curatorial Leadership, co-founder and director, 2007-; New York University, Department of Art History, adjunct professor. Writer. **Publications:** The Intimate Interiors of Edouard Vuillard, 1989; (ed.) Snapshot: Painters and Photography, Bonnard to Vuillard, 2011. Contributor to journals. **Address:** Center for Curatorial Leadership, 174 E 80th St., New York, NY 10075, U.S.A. **Online address:** eweaston@hotmail.com

EASTON, Laird M. (Laird McLeod Easton). American (born United States), b. 1956. **Genres:** History, Travel/Exploration. **Career:** Stanford University, instructor, 1990-91; California State University, Department of History, professor, 1991-, chair, Humanities Center, director. Writer. **Publications:** (As Laird McLeod Easton) The Red Count: The Life and Times of Harry Kessler, 2002; (ed., trans. and intro) Journey to the Abyss: The Diaries of Count Harry Kessler, 1880-1918, 2011. Contributor to periodicals. **Address:** Department of History, California State University, Rm. 223, Trinity Hall, Chico, CA 95929-0735, U.S.A. **Online address:** leaston@csuchico.edu

EASTON, Laird McLeod. See **EASTON, Laird M.**

EASTON, Malcolm Coleman. (Clare Coleman). American (born United States), b. 1942?. **Genres:** Mystery/Crime/Suspense, Novels, Young Adult Fiction, Science Fiction/Fantasy. **Career:** Writer. **Publications:** AS CLARE COLEMAN: Daughter of the Reef, 1992; Sister of the Sun, 1993; Child of the Dawn, 1994. KYALA SERIES: Masters of Glass, 1985; Iskiir, 1986; The Fishermans Curse, 1987; Spirits of Cavern and Hearth, 1988. NOVEL: Swimmers Beneath the Bright, 1987. **Address:** Jove Books, Penguin Group, 375 Hudson St., New York, NY 10014, U.S.A.

EASTON, Nina J(ane). American (born United States), b. 1958. **Genres:** Novels, Biography, Autobiography/Memoirs. **Career:** The American Banker, journalist; BusinessWeek, journalist; Legal Times, journalist; Center for Study of Responsive Law, staff writer, 1981-82; Legal Times, staff writer, 1983; American Banker, staff writer, 1985-87; Los Angeles Times, Sunday Magazine, staff writer, 1988-98; Boston Globe, lead editor, senior assistant

national editor of Washington bureau, 1998-2006, deputy Washington bureau chief, lead political writer; Fortune Magazine, Washington bureau chief, 2006-, senior editor-at-large; Fox News Channel, commentator. **Publications:** Reagan's Squeeze on Small Business: How the Administration Plan Will Increase Economic Concentration, 1981; (with R. Brownstein) Reagan's Ruling Class: Portraits of the President's Top 100 Officials, 1982; Gang of Five: Leaders at the Center of the Conservative Crusade, 2000; (with M. Kranish and B.C. Mooney) John F. Kerry: The Complete Biography by the Boston Globe Reporters Who Know Him Best, 2004. **Address:** Time Inc., 1271 Ave. of the Americas, New York, NY 10020, U.S.A. **Online address:** nina_easton@fortune.com

EASUM, Bill. See **EASUM, William M.**

EASUM, William M. (Bill Easum). American (born United States), b. 1939. **Genres:** Theology/Religion, inspirational/Motivational Literature, Human Relations/Parenting, Adult Non-fiction. **Career:** United Methodist church, senior pastor, 1969-93; 21st Century Strategies Inc., founder, president and senior consultant, 1993-99; Easum, Bandy and Associates, president, senior consultant, senior managing partner, 1999-; Resource Shelf, editor; Today's Leader, contributing editor. **Publications:** The Church Growth Handbook: Includes Complete Ministry Audit, 1990; How to Reach Baby Boomer, 1991; Dancing with Dinosaurs: Ministry in a Hostile and Hurting World, 1993; Sacred Cows Make Gourmet Burgers: Ministry Anytime, Anywhere, by Anybody, 1995; The Complete Ministry Audit: How to Measure 20 Principles for Growth, 1996, 2nd ed., 2006; (with T.G. Bandy) Growing Spiritual Redwoods, 1997; (as Bill Easum) Leadership on the Otherside: No Rules, Just Clues, 2000; (as Bill Easum) Unfreezing Moves: Following Jesus into the Mission Field, 2001; (as Bill Easum with D.Travis) Beyond the Box: Innovative Churches That Work, 2003; (as Bill Easum with L.N. Capshaw) Put on Your Own Oxygen Mask First: Rediscovering Ministry, 2004; (as Bill Easum with P. Theodore) The Nomadic Church: Growing Your Congregation without Owning the Buildings, 2005; (as Bill Easum with B. Tenny-Brittian) Under the Radar: Learning from Risk-Taking Churches, 2005; (with W. Cornelius) Go Big: Lead Your Church to Explosive Growth, 2006; (as Bill Easum) A Second Resurrection: Leading Your Congregation to New Life, 2007; (as Bill Easum with J. Atkinson) Go Big with Small Groups: Eleven Steps to an Explosive Small Group Ministry, 2007; (as Bill Easum with J. Griffith) Ten Most Common Mistakes Made by Church Starts, 2008; (as Bill Easum) Ministry in Hard Times, 2010; (as Bill Easum) Preaching for Church Transformation, 2010. **Address:** Easum, Bandy & Associates, 1126 Whispering Sands, Port Aransas, TX 78373, U.S.A. **Online address:** easum@aol.com

EATON, Jack. British (born England), b. 1947. **Genres:** Administration/Management, Organized Labor, Young Adult Non-fiction, Social Sciences. **Career:** Vanden Berghs, personnel management trainee; Oxford University, research associate and senior research fellow, 1971-72; University of Wales, lecturer in industrial relations, 1972-; University of Cranfield, lecturer, 2002; North East London Polytechnic, lecturer; University of Nottingham, lecturer; Open University, lecturer. Writer. **Publications:** (With C.G. Gill and R. Morris) Industrial Relations in the Chemical Industry, 1978; (with C.G. Gill) Trade Union Directory: A Guide to All TUC Unions, 1981; Judge John Bryn Roberts: A Biography, 1989; (contrib.) British Trade Union Directory, 1990; (with M.F. Bott, A. Coleman and D. Rowland) Professional Issues in Software Engineering, 2nd ed., 1994, 3rd ed., 2000; Globalization and Human Resource Management in the Airline Industry, 1996, 2nd ed., 2001; Comparative Employment Relations, 2000. Contributor of articles to books and periodicals. **Address:** School of Management & Business, University of Wales, Cledwyn Bldg., Penglais Campus, Aberystwyth, Ceredigion, SY23 3DD, Wales. **Online address:** jke@aber.ac.uk

EATON, J. H. See **EATON, John Herbert.**

EATON, John Herbert. (J. H. Eaton). British (born England), b. 1927. **Genres:** Theology/Religion, Biography, Reference. **Career:** St. George's Upper School, teacher, 1953-56, acting headmaster, 1954-55; University of Birmingham, assistant lecturer, 1956-59, lecturer, 1959-69, senior lecturer, 1969-77, Department of Theology, reader, 1977-92, now retired. Writer. **Publications:** Obadiah, Nahum, Habakkuk and Zephaniah: Introduction and Commentary, 1961; Psalms: Introduction and Commentary, 1967; Kingship and the Psalms, 1976; Festal Drama in Deutero-Isaiah, 1979; First Studies in Biblical Hebrew, 1980; Vision in Worship, 1981; Readings in Biblical Hebrew, 1982; The Psalms Come Alive, 1984; Job, 1985; The Contemplative

Face of Old Testament Wisdom, 1989; Interpreted by Love: Expositions of Great Old Testament Passages, 1994; Psalms of the Way and the Kingdom, 1995; The Circle of Creation: Animals in the Light of the Bible, 1995; Mysterious Messengers: A Course on Hebrew Prophecy from Amos Onwards, 1998; The Psalms: A Historical and Spiritual Commentary on the Psalms, with a New Translation, 2003; Meditating on the Psalms, 2004; Job, 2004; Psalms for Life: Hearing and Praying the Book of Psalms, 2006. **Address:** 19 Sandhills Ln., Barnt Green, Birmingham, WM B45 8NU, England.

EATON, Richard M. (Richard Maxwell Eaton). American (born United States), b. 1940. **Genres:** History, Area Studies, Essays. **Career:** Teacher, 1964-65; University of Arizona, assistant professor, 1972-78, associate professor, 1978-94, professor of history, 1994-; Brown University, visiting professor, 1998-99. Writer. **Publications:** (As Richard Maxwell Eaton) Sufis of Bijapur, 1300-1700: Social Roles of Sufis in Medieval India, 1978; Islamic History as Global History (pamphlet), 1990; (with G. Michell) Fīrūzābād: Palace City of the Deccan, 1990; The Rise of Islam and the Bengal Frontier, 1204-1760, 1993; Essays on Islam and Indian History, 2000; (ed.) India's Islamic Traditions, 711-1750, 2003; (ed.) Temple Desecration and Muslim States in Medieval India, 2004; Social History of the Deccan, 1300-1761: Eight Indian Lives, 2005; (with M.C. Smith) Eugene O'Neill Production Personnel: A Biographical Dictionary of Actors, Directors, Producers and Scenic and Costume Designers in Stage and Screen Presentations of the Plays, 2005; (ed. with I. Chatterjee) Slavery & South Asian History, 2006. **Address:** Department of History, University of Arizona, SS 111B, 1145 E South Campus Dr., PO Box 210027, Tucson, AZ 85721, U.S.A. **Online address:** reaton@u.arizona.edu

EATON, Richard Maxwell. See **EATON, Richard M.**

EATON, Trevor (Michael William). British (born England), b. 1934. **Genres:** Language/Linguistics, Literary Criticism And History, Psychology. **Career:** University of Erlangen, lecturer in English, 1958-60; University of New South Wales, lecturer in English language, 1961-65; Norton Knatchbull School, teacher, 1965-87, Philosophy Department, head, 1974-87; Linguistics Association of Great Britain, Linguistics and Literature Section, section convener, 1972-76; Journal of Literary Semantics, founder and editor, 1972-2002; International Association of Literary Semantics, founder. **Publications:** The Semantics of Literature, 1966; The Foundations of Literary Semantics, 1970; Theoretical Semics, 1972; (ed.) Poetries: Their Media and Ends, 1974; (ed.) Essays in Literary Semantics, 1978. **Address:** Honeywood Cottage, 35 Seaton Ave., Hythe, KT CT21 5HH, England.

EATWELL, Roger. British (born England), b. 1949. **Genres:** Politics/Government, Local History/Rural Topics, Adult Non-fiction. **Career:** University of Bath, reader in politics, 1974-, professor of politics, 1974-97, professor of comparative European politics, 1997-, Faculty, Humanities and Social Sciences, dean, 2008-; University of Kent, MA in Politics and Democracy Studies, external examiner, 2002-05; University of Cardiff, BA/BSc Politics, external examiner, 2004-06, MA European Studies, external examiner, 2005-07. Writer. **Publications:** POLITICAL SCIENCE: The 1945-1951 Labour Governments, 1979; Fascism: A History, 1995; Fascismo: verson un modello nuovo, 1999. EDITOR: (with N. O'Sullivan) The Nature of the Right: European and American Politics and Political Thought since 1789, 1989; (with A. Wright) Contemporary Political Ideologies, 1993, 2nd ed., 1999; European Political Cultures, 1997; (with C. Mudde) Western Democracies and the New Extreme Right Challenge, 2004; Fascism And The Extreme Right, 2004; Explaining Fascism and Ethnic Cleansing, 2006; Community Cohesion and Cumulative Extremism in Contemporary Britain, 2006; (with M.J. Goodwin) New Extremism in 21st century Britain, 2010. **Address:** European Studies and Modern Languages, University of Bath, 1 West North, Bath, SM BA2 7AY, England. **Online address:** r.eatwell@bath.ac.uk

EAVES, Will. British (born England), b. 1967?. **Genres:** Novels. **Career:** Times Literary Supplement, arts editor, 1995-2001; University of Warwick, associate professor, faculty. **Publications:** The Oversight, 2001; Nothing to Be Afraid Of, 2005; Small Hours, 2006; Sound Houses, 2011; This Is Paradise, 2012; The Ancestors, forthcoming; The Point of Distraction, forthcoming. **Address:** c/o David Miller, Rogers, Coleridge & White Ltd., 20 Powis Mews, London, GL W11 1JN, England. **Online address:** arts@the-tls.co.uk

EBADI, Shirin. Iranian (born Iran), b. 1947. **Genres:** Humanities, Local History/Rural Topics, Autobiography/Memoirs. **Career:** Justice Department, judge, 1969-79, city court of Tehran, president, 1975-79; lawyer in private practice, 1992-; Tehran University, lecturer; Defenders of Human Rights Center, founder. Writer. **Publications:** (With A. Moaveni) Iran Awakening: A Memoir of Revolution and Hope, 2006. Contributor to periodicals. **Address:** Random House Inc., 1745 Broadway, New York, NY 10019-4368, U.S.A.

EBAUGH, Helen Rose (Fuchs). American (born United States), b. 1942. **Genres:** Theology/Religion, Social Sciences, Sociology, Politics/Government. **Career:** University of Houston, Department of Sociology, assistant professor, 1973-79, associate professor, 1979-89, chairman of department, 1985-87, professor of sociology, 1993-. Writer. **Publications:** Out of the Cloister: A Study of Organizational Dilemmas, 1977; Becoming an Ex: The Process of Role Exit, 1988; Women in the Vanishing Cloister: Organizational Decline in Catholic Religious Orders in the United States, 1993; (ed. with J.S. Chafetz) Religion and the New Immigrants: Continuities and Adaptations in Immigrant Congregations, 2000; (ed. with J.S. Chafetz) Religion Across Borders: Transnational Immigrant Networks, 2002; (ed.) Handbook of Religion and Social Institutions, 2005; The Gülen Movement: A Sociological Analysis of a Civic Movement Rooted in Moderate Islam, 2009. Contributor of articles to journals. **Address:** Department of Sociology, University of Houston, 450 Philip G. Hoffman Hall, 4800 Calhoun Rd., Houston, TX 77204-3012, U.S.A. **Online address:** ebaugh@uh.edu

EBBESMEYER, Curtis Charles. American (born United States), b. 1943. **Genres:** Natural History, Environmental Sciences/Ecology, Autobiography/Memoirs. **Career:** Mobil Oil Corp., consulting oceanographer, 1965-74; Evans-Hamilton Inc., freelancer; retired, 2003; Beachcombers Alert, president and editor. Radio host. **Publications:** (With W.J. Ingraham, Jr.) Atlas of Pilot Charts, North Pacific Ocean, 1994; (with E. Scigliano) Flotsametrics and the Floating World: How One Man's Obsession with Runaway Sneakers and Rubber Ducks Revolutionized Ocean Science, 2009. Contributor to journals. **Address:** Smithsonian Books, 10 E 53rd St., New York, NY 10022, U.S.A. **Online address:** curtisebbesmeyer@comcast.net

EBBETT, Eve. (Eva Burfield). New Zealander/British (born England), b. 1925. **Genres:** Novels, History, Novellas/Short Stories, Young Adult Nonfiction, Military/Defense/Arms Control, Young Adult Fiction, Social Sciences. **Career:** Freelance writer, 1946-. **Publications:** AS EVA BURFIELD: Yellow Kowhai, 1957; A Chair to Sit On, 1958; The Long Winter, 1964; Out of Yesterday, 1965; After Midnight, 1965; The White Prison, 1966; The New Mrs. Rainier, 1967; The Last Day of Summer, 1968. OTHERS: Give Them Swing Bands, 1969, 2nd ed., 1996; To the Garden Alone, 1970; In True Colonial Fashion: A Lively Look at What New Zealanders Wore 1977; Victoria's Daughters: New Zealand Women of the Thirties, 1981; When the Boys Were Away, 1984. Contributor to periodicals. **Address:** 908 Sylvan Rd., Hastings, 4122, New Zealand.

EBEL, Roland H. American (born United States), b. 1928. **Genres:** Politics/Government, Social Sciences, History. **Career:** Western Michigan University, assistant professor, 1960-64; Tulane University, associate professor of political science, 1964-94, professor emeritus, 1994-. Writer. **Publications:** (Ed.) Proceedings of the VI Inter-American University Seminar on Municipal Affairs, 1968; Political Modernization in Three Guatemalan Indian Communities, 1969; (ed. and contrib.) Cambio politico en tres comunidad es indigenas de Guatemala, 1969; (ed. with H.F. Hrubecky and contrib.) Perspectives on the Energy Crisis, 1976; (with J.D. Cochrane and R. Taras) Political Culture and Foreign Policy in Latin America: Case Studies from the Circum-Caribbean, 1991; Misunderstood Caudillo: Miguel Ydigoras Fuentes and the Failure of Democracy in Guatemala, 1998. **Address:** Department of Political Science, Tulane University, 316 Norman Mayer Bldg., New Orleans, LA 70118, U.S.A. **Online address:** tanglewild@juno.com

EBERHART, Mark E. American (born United States) **Genres:** Sciences, Technology, Engineering. **Career:** Nova, Public Broadcasting, consultant; Massachusetts Institute of Technology, Department of Materials Science, postdoctoral research associate, 1983-85, Materials Processing Center, research associate, 1985-90, Laboratory for Materials Synthesis, direcotr, 1990-92; Los Alamos National Laboratory, staff scientist, 1985-90; Imperial College, Blackett Laboratory, visiting scientist, 1987, 1991-92; Harvard University, Department of Chemistry, visiting scientist, 1990-91; Colorado School of Mines, Department of Metallurgical and Materials Engineering, research associate professor, 1992-98, Molecular Theory Group, head, 1993-, Department of Chemistry and Geochemistry, associate professor, professor,

Faculty Senate, president, 2009-10. Writer. **Publications:** Why Things Break: Understanding the World by the Way It Comes Apart, 2003; Feeding the Fire: The Lost History and Uncertain Future of Mankind's Energy Addiction, 2007. **Address:** Department of Chemistry & Geochemistry, Colorado School of Mines, Coolbaugh Hall 106B, 1500 Illinois St., Golden, CO 80401, U.S.A. **Online address:** meberhar@mines.edu

EBERHART, Sheri S. See **TEPPER, Sheri S.**

EBERLE, Gary. American (born United States), b. 1951. **Genres:** Novels, Novellas/Short Stories, Social Commentary, Theology/Religion, History. **Career:** Aquinas College, Department of English, associate professor, 1981-2007, professor of English, 2007-, chairman, 2007-09. Writer. **Publications:** Haunted Houses of Grand Rapids, 1982; The Geography of Nowhere: Finding One's Self in the Postmodern World, 1994; Angel Strings (novel), 1995; A City Full of Rain: Collected Stories, 2001; Sacred Time and the Search for Meaning, 2003; Dangerous Words: Talking About God in an Age of Fundamentalism, 2007; Aquinas College: The First 125 Years, 2011. Works appear in anthologies. Contributor to periodicals. **Address:** Department of English, Aquinas College, 1607 Robinson Rd. SE, Grand Rapids, MI 49506-1979, U.S.A. **Online address:** eberlgar@aquinas.edu

EBERSTADT, Nicholas (Nash). American (born United States), b. 1955. **Genres:** Politics/Government, Social Sciences. **Career:** Harvard University, visiting fellow, 1980-2002; American Enterprise Institute for Public Policy Research, Henry Wendt chair in political economy, 1999-; National Board of Asian Research, senior adviser. Writer. **Publications:** Poverty in China, 1979; (ed.) Fertility Decline in the Less Developed Countries, 1981; Foreign Aid and American Purpose, 1988; The Poverty of Communism, 1988; (with J. Banister) The Population of North Korea, 1992; Korea Approaches Reunification, 1995; The Tyranny of Numbers: Mismeasurement and Misrule, 1995; The End of North Korea, 1999; Prosperous Paupers and Other Population Problems, 2000; (ed. with J. Tombes) Comparing the US and Soviet Economies, 2000; (ed. with R.J. Ellings) Korea's Future and the Great Powers, 2001; (ed. with A. Choong-yong and L. Young-Sun) New International Engagement Framework for North Korea?: Contending Perspectives, 2004; Health and the Income Inequality Hypothesis: A Doctrine in Search of Data, 2004; Global Population Trends, 2006; North Korean Economy: Between Crisis and Catastrophe, 2007; (with H. Groth) Europe's Coming Demographic Challenge: Unlocking the Value of Health, 2007; Poverty of The Poverty Rate: Measure and Mismeasure of Want in Modern America, 2008; Policy and Economic Performance in Divided Korea during the Cold War Era: 1945-91, 2008. **Address:** American Enterprise Institute, 1150 Seventeenth St. NW, Washington, DC 20036, U.S.A. **Online address:** eberstadt@aei.org

EBERT, James I(an). American (born United States), b. 1948. **Genres:** Archaeology/Antiquities, Anthropology/Ethnology. **Career:** National Park Service, archaeologist, 1973-84; NASA/University of New Mexico, Technology Application Center, research associate, 1980-84; Ebert & Associates Inc., co-founder and vice president, 1983-, chief scientist, secretary and treasurer, 1984-; New York State Police, Medicolegal Investigations Unit, Photogrammetrist, 1985-. Writer. **Publications:** (Contrib.) Aerial Remote Sensing Techniques in Archeology, 1977; (ed. with T.R. Lyons) Remote Sensing and Non-Destructive Archeology, 1978; Distributional Archaeology, 1992. Contributor to books. **Address:** Ebert & Associates Inc., 3700 Rio Grande Blvd. NW, Ste. 3, Albuquerque, NM 87107, U.S.A. **Online address:** jebert@ebert.com

EBERT, Roger (Joseph). American (born United States), b. 1942. **Genres:** Plays/Screenplays, Film, History. **Career:** News-Gazette, staff writer, 1958-66; Daily Illinois, editor, 1963-64; U.S. Student Press Association, president, 1963-64; Chicago City College, instructor in English, 1967-68; Chicago Sun Times, film critic, 1967-; University of Chicago, Fine Arts Program, lecturer on film, 1969-; University of Illinois Alumni Association, director, 1975-77; Sneak Previews, PBS-TV, co-host, 1977-82; At the Movies, co-host, 1982-86; Ebert and Roeper, Syndicated TV Program, co-host, 1986-. Consultant and writer. **Publications:** An Illini Century, One Hundred Years of Campus Life, 1967; A Kiss Is Still a Kiss: Roger Ebert at the Movies, 1984; Roger Ebert's Movie Home Companion, 1985; (with D. Curley) The Perfect London Walk, 1986; Two Weeks in the Midday Sun: A Cannes Notebook, 1987; Roger Ebert's Movie Yearbook, 1991; (with G. Siskel) Future of the Movies: Interviews with Martin Scorsese, Steven Spielberg and George Lucas, 1991; Behind the Phantom's Mask: A Serial, 1993; (ed.) Ebert's Little Movie Glossary: A Compendium of Movie clichés, Stereotypes, Obligatory Scenes,

Hackneyed Formulas, Shopworn Conventions and Outdated Archetypes, 1994; (with J. Kratz) Computer Insectiary: A Field Guide to Viruses, Bugs, Worms, Trojan Horses and Other Stuff That Will Eat Your Programs and Rot Your Brain, 1994; Roger Ebert's Book of Film, 1996; Questions for the Movie Answer Man, 1997; Roger Ebert's Movie Yearbook, 1999; Roger Ebert's Bigger Little Movie Glossary, 1999; I Hated, Hated, Hated This Movie, 2000; The Great Movies, 2002; Awake in the Dark: The Great Movies II, 2005; The Best of Roger Ebert: Forty Years of Reviews, Essays and Interviews, 2006; Roger Ebert's Four-Star Reviews, 1967-2007, 2007; Your Movie Sucks, 2007; Scorsese by Ebert, 2008; The Great Movies III, 2010; The Pot and How to Use it: The Mystery and Romance of the Rice Cooker, 2010; Roger Eber's Movie Yearbook 2011, 2010; Life Itself, 2011; Roger Ebert's Movie Yearbook 2012, 2011; Horrible Experience of Unbearable Length, 2012. **Address:** Chicago Sun-Times, Rm. 110, 401 N Wabash, Chicago, IL 60611, U.S.A.

EBISCH, Glen Albert. American (born United States), b. 1946?. **Genres:** Young Adult Fiction, Literary Criticism And History. **Career:** Western New England College, professor of philosophy. Writer. **Publications:** FICTION: Behind the Mask, 1986; Shock Effect, 1987; Angel in the Snow, 1988; The Secret of Bluefish Point, 2000; A Special Power, 2000; Woven Hearts, 2001; Unwanted Inheritance, 2001; To Breathe Again, 2001; A Rocky Road, 2004; The Crying Girl, 2007; Grave Justice, 2008; To Grandmother's House, 2009; Ghosts from the Past, 2009. LOU DUNLOP SERIES FOR YOUNG ADULTS: Lou Dunlop: Private Eye, 1987; Lou Dunlop: Cliffhanger, 1987. **Address:** Western New England College, 1215 Wilbraham Rd., Springfield, MA 01119, U.S.A.

EBLE, Connie. American (born United States), b. 1942. **Genres:** Language/ Linguistics. **Career:** University of Kentucky, instructor, 1968-71; University of North Carolina, assistant professor, professor of English, 1971-, Graduate Studies in English, director, 1981-84, 1985-87, Humanities Division, faculty chair, 1998-2001, 2001-04; Linguistic Association of Canada and the United States, secretary-treasurer, 1993-98, vice president, 2003, president, 2004; South Atlantic Modern Language Association, acting chair, 1996, vice-president, 2001, 2002, president, 2003; American Dialect Society, vice president and program chair, 2007-08; Modern Language Association, president. Writer. **Publications:** College Slang 101, 1989; Slang & Sociability: In-Group Language among College Students, 1996. **Address:** Department of English & Comparative Literature, University of North Carolina, Greenlaw Hall, PO Box 3520, Chapel Hill, NC 27599-3520, U.S.A. **Online address:** cceble@email.unc.edu

ECHENIQUE, Alfredo Bryce. Puerto Rican (born Puerto Rico), b. 1939. **Genres:** Novels, Young Adult Fiction, Romance/Historical. **Career:** University of Nanterre, reader of Spanish, 1968-73; Sorbonne, faculty, 1971-74; University of Vincennes, assistant of literature and Latino American civilization, 1973-80; Paul Valery (Montpellier) University, assistant of Latino American literature and civilization, 1980-82; University of Austin, visiting professor, 1987; University of Puerto Rico, visiting professor, 1991, 1997; Yale University, visiting professor, 1995. Writer. **Publications:** Huerto cerrado cuentos, 1968; Un Mundo para Julius, 1970; Muerte de Sevilla en Madrid; Antes de la cita conlos Linares, 1972; La Felicidad, ja, ja, 1974; La Pasión según San Pedro Balbuena que fue tantas veces Pedro y que nunca pudo negar a nadie, 1977; A vuelo de buen cubero y otras cronicas, 1977; Todos los cuentos, 1979; Je suis le roi, 1980; Cuentos completos, 1981; La vida exagerada de Martín Romana, 1981; Cuentistas hispanoamericanos en la Sorbona, 1984; Magdalena peruana y otros cuentos, 1986; Lectura de un cuento: teoríay práctica del análisis del relato Al agua patos! de Alfredo Bryce Echenique, 1986; Goig, 1987; Tantas veces pedro, 1987; La ultima mudanzade Felipe Carrillo, 1988; Crónicas personales; 1988; El hombre quehablaba de Octavia de Cadiz: cuaderno de navegación en un silloin Voltaire, 1988; Silvio en el rosedal, 1989; Dos señoras conversan; Un sapo el desierto; Los grandes hombres son asi, y tambien asa, 1990; Permiso para vivir: antimemorias, 1993; Antología personal, 1995; No me esperen en abril, 1995; Cuentos completes, 1995; Para que duela menos, 1995; A trancas y barrancas, 1996; 15 cuentos de amor y humor, 1996; La Amigdalitis de Tarzan, 1998; Charla magistral, 1998; Guía triste de Paris, 1999; Reo de nocturnidad, 1997; Sirenas, Monstruos y Leyendas: Bestiario Maritimo, 1998; La historia personal de mis libros, 2000; Crónicas Perdidas, 2001; (co-author) Hemingway desde Espana, 2001; Tarzan's Tonsillitis, 2001; El Huerto de Mi Amada, 2002; Doce cartas a dosamigos, 2003; Entrevistas escogidas, 2004; Entre la soledad y el amor, 2005; Permiso para sentir, 2005; Las obras infames de Pancho Marambio, 2007; Martín Chambi, 2007; Esposa del Rey de las Curvas: cuentos, 2008; Penúltimos escritos: retazos de vida y literatura, 2009; Alfredo Bryce Echenique, una vida de novela, 2010; La suprema ironía cervantina, 2010. **Address:** Editorial Planeta SA, Edifici Planeta, Diagonal, 662-664, Barcelona, 08034, Spain.

ECHENOZ, Jean. French (born France), b. 1947. **Genres:** Novels, Plays/ Screenplays. **Career:** Writer. **Publications:** Le Méridien de Greenwich (novel), 1979; Cherokee (novel), 1983; L'équipée malaise (novel), 1986; L'occupation des Sols (novel), 1988; Lac (novel) 1989; Ayez des Amis, 1991; J'arrive, 1992; Nous Trois (novel), 1992; Les Grandes blondes (novel), 1995; Un An (novel), 1997; Je m'en Vais (novel), 1999; Jérôme Lindon, 2001; (contrib.) Luxembourg, 2002; Au Piano (novel), 2003; Ravel, 2006; Courir, 2008; Des éclairs, 2010. Contributor to newspapers and periodicals. **Address:** Les éditions de Minuit, 7 rue Bernard-Palissy, Paris, 75006, France.

ECHERUO, Michael. (Michael J.C. Echeruo). American/Nigerian (born Nigeria), b. 1937. **Genres:** Poetry, Literary Criticism And History, Language/ Linguistics, History, Cultural/Ethnic Topics. **Career:** Nigerian College of Arts and Technology, lecturer, 1960-61; University of Ibadan, lecturer, 1961-70, senior lecturer, 1970-73, professor, 1973-74, professor of English, 1974-90, head, 1974-78, dean of postgraduate school, 1978-80; University of Nigeria, Department of English, head, 1972-74; Imo State University, President, 1981-88, vice-chancellor, 1981-; University of Houston, distinguished visiting professor of the humanities, 1980-81; University of California, Department of English, visiting professor, 1988-89; Indiana University, Department of English, visiting professor, 1989-90; Syracuse University, William Safire professor in modern English, 1990-. Writer. **Publications:** AS MICHAEL J.C. ECHERUO: Mortality: Poems, 1968; (ed. and intro. with E.N. Obiechina) Igbo Traditional Life, Culture and Literature, 1971; Joyce Cary and the Novel of Africa, 1973; Distanced: New Poems, 1975; Victorian Lagos: Aspects of Nineteenth Century Lagos Life, 1977; The Conditioned Imagination from Shakespeare to Conrad: Studies in the Exo-Cultural Stereotype, 1978; Joyce Cary and the Dimensions of Order, 1979; (ed.) Shakespeare's The Tempest, 1980; Igbo-English Dictionary: Comprehensive Dictionary of the Igbo Language, With an English-Igbo Index, 1998; (ed. and intro.) A Concordance to the Poems of Christopher Okigbo, 2008. Contributor of articles to books and periodicals. Works appear in anthologies. **Address:** Department of English, Syracuse University, 425 Hall of Languages, Syracuse, NY 13244, U.S.A. **Online address:** mecheruo@syr.edu

ECHERUO, Michael J.C. See ECHERUO, Michael.

ECHEVARRIA, Jana. American (born United States), b. 1956. **Genres:** Cultural/Ethnic Topics, Education. **Career:** Whittier Union High School, resource specialist, 1980-82; Feng Chia University, visiting instructor, 1982-83; Maikel Language Services, Spanish instructor, 1984-85; Loyola Marymount University, research associate, visiting instructor, bilingual special education grant coordinator, 1985-93; California State University, professor of educational psychology, administration and counseling, 1993-2006, chair, 2002-, professor emeritus, 2006-; SIOP Institute, writer and consultant. Writer. **Publications:** (With A. Graves) Sheltered Content Instruction: Teaching Students with Diverse Abilities, 1998, 4th ed., 2011; (with D.J. Short and M. Vogt) Making Content Comprehensible for English Language Learners: The SIOP Model, 2000, 3rd ed., 2008; (with D.J. Short and K. Powers) School Reform and Standards-based Education: An Instructional Model for English Language Learners, 2006; (with M. Vogt) Teaching Ideas for Implementing: The SIOP Model, 2006; (with M.E. Vogt and D.J. Short) Implementing the SIOP Model through Effective Professional Development and Coaching, 2008; (with M.E. Vogt) 99 Ideas and Activities for Teaching English Learners with the SIOP Model, 2008; (with M. Vogt and D.J. Short) The SIOP Model for Administrators, 2008; (with M. Vogt and D.J. Short) Making Content Comprehensible for Elementary English Learners: The SIOP Model, 2010; (with M. Vogt and D.J. Short) The SIOP Model for Teaching Mathematics to English Learners, 2010; (with M. Vogt and D.J. Short) The SIOP Model for Teaching English-language Arts to English Learners, 2010; (with M. Vogt) RTI and English Learners: Making It Happen, 2011; (with D.J. Short and M. Vogt) The SIOP Model for Teaching Science to English Learners, 2011; (with D.J. Short and M. Vogt) The SIOP Model for Teaching History-Social Studies to English Learners, 2011; (with M. Vogt) Response to Intervention (RTI) and English Learners: Making it Happen, 2011; (with D.J. Short and C. Peterson) Using the SIOP Model with Pre-k and Kindergarten English Learners, 2012. Contributor to books. **Address:** Department of Advanced Studies, in Education and Counseling, California State University, 1250 Bellflower Blvd., Long Beach, CA 90840-0004, U.S.A. **Online address:** jechev@csulb.edu

ECK, Joe. American (born United States), b. 1946?. **Genres:** Homes/Gardens, Young Adult Non-fiction. **Career:** North Hill Garden Design Inc., co-founder and partner, 1977-. Writer and educator. **Publications:** NONFICTION: Elements of Garden Design, 1995. WITH W. WINTERROWD: A Year at North Hill: Four Seasons in a Vermont Garden, 1995; Living Seasonally: The Kitchen Garden and the Table at North Hill, 1999; Our Life in Gardens, 2009. **Address:** North Hill Garden Design Inc., PO Box 327, Old Westbury, NY 11568, U.S.A. **Online address:** northhillgarden@gmail.com

ECK, Matthew. American (born United States), b. 1974. **Genres:** Philosophy, Military/Defense/Arms Control. **Career:** University of Central Missouri, assistant professor of English; U.S. Army, 1992-. Writer. **Publications:** The Farther Shore, 2007. **Address:** Department of English & Philosophy, University of Central Missouri, 336Q Martin Bldg., Warrensburg, MO 64093, U.S.A. **Online address:** meckwriter@yahoo.com

ECKARD, Paula G. (Paula Gallant Eckard). American (born United States), b. 1950. **Genres:** Medicine/Health, Adult Non-fiction. **Career:** Carolinas Medical Center, registered nurse, 1972-73; Lamaze Association of Charlotte, childbirth educator, 1973-80; University of North Carolina at Charlotte, lecturer, 1990-2002, American Studies Program, director, 2002-, professor; Juvenile Diabetes Research Foundation, government relations representative and grassroots lobbyist, board director. Writer. **Publications:** (As Paula Gallant Eckard) Maternal Body and Voice in Toni Morrison, Bobbie Ann Mason and Lee Smith, 2002; Lost Children in Southern Literature and Culture, forthcoming. Contributor of articles to periodicals. **Address:** Department of English, University of North Carolina, 245 G Fretwell, 9201 University City Blvd., Charlotte, NC 28223, U.S.A. **Online address:** pgeckard@uncc.edu

ECKARD, Paula Gallant. See ECKARD, Paula G.

ECKART, Gabriele. American/German (born Germany), b. 1954. **Genres:** Novellas/Short Stories, Poetry. **Career:** Havelobst (agricultural cooperative), cultural worker, 1979-82; University of Texas, writer-in-residence, 1988; University of Minnesota, teaching assistant, 1988-93; Spring Hill College, assistant professor, 1994-97; Southeast Missouri State University, Department of Global Cultures and Languages, professor of foreign languages, 1999-. **Publications:** Gabriele Eckart, 1974; Tagebuch, 1979; Per Anhalter, 1982; So sehe ick die Sache, 1984; Sturzacker, 1985; Der Seidelstein, 1986; Wie mag ich alles was beginnt, 1987; Seidelstein, 1988; Frankreich heisst Jeanne, 1989; Der gute fremde Blick, 1992; Sprachtraumata in den Texten Wolfgang Hilbigs, 1996. **Address:** Department of Global Cultures and Languages, Southeast Missouri State University, 309 Art Bldg., 1 University Plz., PO Box 4150, Cape Girardeau, MO 63701, U.S.A. **Online address:** geckart@semo.edu

ECKERT, Kathryn Bishop. (Kathryn Bishop Omoto). American (born United States), b. 1935. **Genres:** Architecture, History. **Career:** Michigan Department of State, Michigan Historical Center, architectural historian, deputy state historic preservation officer, acting state historic preservation officer, 1974-92, state historic preservation officer, 1992-97, state historic preservation officer emeritus, 1997-. Writer. **Publications:** Buildings of Michigan, 1993, rev. ed., 2012; Sandstone Architecture of the Lake Superior Region, 2000; Cranbrook, 2001. Contributor to periodicals. **Address:** Michigan Historical Center, 717 W Allegan St., Lansing, MI 48915-6362, U.S.A. **Online address:** katheckert@charter.net

ECKLAR, Julia (Marie). American (born United States), b. 1964. **Genres:** Science Fiction/Fantasy. **Career:** Secretary; data processor; freelance writer, 1987-. **Publications:** Star Trek: The Kobayashi Maru, 1989; (with L A Graf) Ice Trap, 1992; Regenesis, 1995. Contributor of novellas to magazines. **Address:** c/o Karen Cercone, 521 7th St., Trafford, PA 15085-1052, U.S.A. **Online address:** j.ecklar1@genie.com

ECKLER, Rebecca. Canadian (born Canada), b. 1973. **Genres:** Novels, Biography, Humor/Satire, Young Adult Fiction. **Career:** Calgary Herald, entertainment reporter; Modern Manners (television show), host; Canadian Broadcasting Corp., Pamela Wallin Live, producer; Global television, reporter; National Post, columnist and feature writer, 2000-05; Post City Magazines, columnist. **Publications:** Knocked Up: Confessions of a Hip Mother-to-Be, 2004; Wiped!: Life with a Pint-size Dictator, 2007; Rotten Apple, 2008; (with S. Benvie) Toddlers Gone Wild, 2008; (with E. Ehm) The Mischievous Mom at the Art Gallery, 2010; Apple's Angst, 2010; How to Raise a Boyfriend,

2011; The Lucky Sperm Club, 2011. Contributor to periodicals. **Address:** The Bukowski Agency, 14 Prince Arthur Ave., Ste. 202, Toronto, ON M5R 1A9, Canada. **Online address:** rebeccaeckler@yahoo.com

ECKLUND, Elaine Howard. American (born United States), b. 1973. **Genres:** Theology/Religion. **Career:** Rice University, postdoctoral fellow, 2004-06, Department of Sociology, assistant professor, 2008-, Center on Race, Religion, and Urban Life, associate director, 2008-; State University of New York, University at Buffalo, assistant professor, 2006-08. Writer and researcher. **Publications:** Korean American Evangelicals: New Models for Civic Life, 2006; Science vs. Religion: What Scientists Really Think, 2010. Contributor of articles to periodicals and magazines. **Address:** Department of Sociology, Rice University, 6100 S Main St., Houston, TX 77005-1892, U.S.A. **Online address:** ehe@rice.edu

ECKSTEIN, A. M. See **ECKSTEIN, Arthur M.**

ECKSTEIN, Arthur M. (A. M. Eckstein). American (born United States), b. 1946. **Genres:** History. **Career:** University of North Carolina, assistant professor, 1978-80; University of Maryland, assistant professor, associate professor, professor, 1980-, director of Undergraduate Honors Program in History. Writer. **Publications:** Senate and General: Individual Decision-Making and Roman Foreign Relations, 264-194 B.C., 1987; Moral Vision in the Histories of Polybius, 1994; (ed. with P. Lehman) The Searchers: Essays and Reflections on John Ford's Classic Western, 2004; Mediterranean Anarchy, Interstate War and the Rise of Rome, 2006; Rome Enters the Greek East: From Anarchy to Hierarchy in the Hellenistic Mediterranean, 230-170 B.C., 2008. **Address:** University of Maryland, 2115 Francis Scott Key, College Park, MD 20742, U.S.A. **Online address:** ameckst1@umd.edu

ECKSTEIN, Rick. American (born United States), b. 1960. **Genres:** Sociology, Sports/Fitness, Recreation. **Career:** State University of New York, graduate instructor, 1985-89, director of teaching assistant development, 1989-90; Villanova University, Department of Sociology, assistant professor, 1990-96, associate professor, 1997-2004, professor, 2005-, Center for Peace and Justice Education, staff, 1992-2010, director, 2008-, acting director, 2010-11. Writer. **Publications:** Nuclear Power and Social Power, 1997; (with K.J. Delaney) Public Dollars, Private Stadiums: The Battle Over Building Sports Stadiums, 2003. **Address:** Deparment of Sociology and Criminal Justice, Villanova University, Rm. 285, St Augustine Ctr Liberal Arts, 800 Lancaster Ave., Villanova, PA 19085-1603, U.S.A. **Online address:** rick.eckstein@villanova.edu

ECONOMOU, George. American (born United States), b. 1934. **Genres:** Poetry, Literary Criticism And History, Translations. **Career:** Wagner College, lecturer, 1958-60; Chelsea Review, editor, 1958-60; Trobar, editor, 1960-64; Long Island University, assistant professor, 1961-69, associate professor, 1969-73, professor of English, 1973-83, chairman of department, 1982-83; University of Oklahoma, professor of English, 1983, 1990-2000, chairman of department, 1983-90, director of creative writing, 1990-2000, emeritus professor, 2000-. **Publications:** The Georgics, 1968; Landed Natures, 1969; Poems for Self-Therapy, 1972; The Goddess Natura in Medieval Literature, 1972; (ed.) Geoffrey Chaucer: A Collection of Criticism, 1975; (co-editor) In Pursuit of Perfection: Courtly Love in Medieval Literature, 1975; Ameriki: Book One and Selected Earlier Poems, 1977; (ed. and intro.) Proensa: An Anthology of Troubadour Poetry, 1978; Voluntaries, 1984; Harmonies and Fits, 1987; (and trans.) William Langland's Piers Plowman, The C Version, a Verse Translation, 1996; Century Dead Center and Other Poems, 1998; (ed. and foreword) Poem of the Cid: A Modern Translation with Notes, 1998; (trans.) Acts of Love: Ancient Greek Poetry from Aphrodite's Garden, 2006; (trans.) Ananios of Kleitor, 2009. **Address:** Department of English, University of Oklahoma, 760 Van Vleet Oval, Gittinger Hall, Norman, OK 73019-2055, U.S.A. **Online address:** gero@mymailstation.com

EDDIE, David. Canadian/American (born United States), b. 1961. **Genres:** Documentaries/Reportage, Biography, Young Adult Fiction. **Career:** Newsweek magazine, Letters Department, staff, letters correspondent; East Hampton Star, reporter; Canadian Broadcasting Corporation (CBC), television news writer, producer. **Publications:** Chump Change, 1999; Housebroken: Confessions of a Stay-at-Home Dad (biography), 1999; (with P. Lynch) Damage control: How To Tiptoe Away from the Smoking Wreckage of Your Latest Screw-up with a Minimum of Harm to Your Reputation, 2010. Contributor to periodicals. **Address:** Riverhead Books Publicity, 375 Hudson St., New York, NY 10014, U.S.A. **Online address:** david@davideddie.com

EDDINS, Dwight L. American (born United States), b. 1939. **Genres:** Poetry, Literary Criticism And History, History. **Career:** University of Alabama, Department of English, instructor, 1966-67, assistant professor, 1967-70, associate professor, 1972-76, professor, 1976-2006, chair, professor emeritus. Writer. **Publications:** Yeats: The Nineteenth Century Matrix, 1971; Of Desire, and the Circles of Hell, 1980; The Gnostic Pynchon, 1990; (ed. and intro.) The Emperor Redressed: Critiquing Critical Theory, 1995. **Address:** Department of English, University of Alabama, 323-A Russell, PO Box 870244, Tuscaloosa, AL 35487-0244, U.S.A. **Online address:** deddins@english.as.ua.edu

EDE, Piers Moore. British (born England), b. 1975?. **Genres:** Travel/Exploration, Philosophy, Young Adult Fiction, Essays. **Career:** Writer and educator. **Publications:** Honey and Dust: Travels in Search of Sweetness, 2005; All Kinds of Magic, 2009. Contributor to periodicals. **Address:** c/o Peter Straus, Rogers, Coleridge & White Ltd., 20 Powis Mews, London, GL W11 1JN, England.

EDELHEIT, Abraham J. American (born United States), b. 1958. **Genres:** Cultural/Ethnic Topics, History, International Relations/Current Affairs, Politics/Government, Social Commentary, Bibliography, Literary Criticism And History. **Career:** City University of New York, Kingsborough Community College, adjunct professor of holocaust studies, 1985-86, assistant professor of history, Csengeri Institute Holocaust Lecture Series, moderator, 1988-90, Department of History, Philosophy and Political Science, professor; Edelheit Research Institute for Contemporary History, co-founder and assistant director, 1985-; Touro College, Flatbush Evening Program, adjunct professor of history, 1987-90, visiting professor of history, 1991-93; Macmillan Publishing Company Inc., Reference Book Division, editorial consultant, 1988-89; U.S. Holocaust Memorial Museum, researcher and writer, 1990-91; Holocaust Educational Resource Center, Project Witness, consultant. **Publications:** (With H. Edelheit) Bibliography on Holocaust Literature, 1986; (with H. Edelheit) The Jewish World in Modern Times: A Selected, Annotated Bibliography, 1988; (with H. Edelheit) A World in Turmoil: An Integrated Chronology of the Holocaust and World War II, 1991; (ed. with H. Edelheit) The Rise and Fall of the Soviet Union: A Selected Bibliography of Sources in English, 1992; (with H. Edelheit) The History of the Holocaust: A Handbook and Dictionary, 1994; (with H. Edelheit) Israel and the Jewish World, 1948-1993: A Chronology, 1995; The Yishuv in the Shadow of the Holocaust: Zionist Politics and Rescue Aliya, 1933-1939, 1996; (with H. Edelheit) East European Jewry, 1919-1939, 1996; (with H. Edelheit) History of Zionism: A Handbook and Dictionary, 2000; (ed. with R. Lichtenstein and M. Berenbaum) Witness to History, 2009. Contributor to periodicals. **Address:** Department of History, Philosophy and, Political Science, Kingsborough Community College, Rm. D219, 2001 Oriental Blvd., Brooklyn, NY 11235-2333, U.S.A. **Online address:** abraham.edelheit@kbcc.cuny.edu

EDELMAN, Amy Holman. American (born United States), b. 1958. **Genres:** Novels. **Career:** Self-employed publicist, 1994-97; Tiffany & Co., staff; Barnes & Noble, staff. Writer & publicist, 1997-. **Publications:** The Little Black Dress, 1997; Manless in Montclair: A Novel: How a Happily Married Woman Became a Widow Looking for Love in the Wilds of Suburbia, 2007. **Address:** Montclair, NJ , U.S.A. **Online address:** amy@amyedelman.com

EDELMAN, Marian Wright. American (born United States), b. 1939. **Genres:** Civil Liberties/Human Rights. **Career:** National Association for the Advancement of Colored People (NAACP), Legal Defense and Education Fund Inc., staff attorney, 1963-64, director of office in Jackson, 1964-68; Washington Research Project of Southern Center for Public Policy, founder, partner, 1968-73; Children's Defense Fund, founder and president, 1973-, leader, principal spokesperson; Harvard University, W.E.B. Du Bois Lecturer, 1986, Center for Law and Education, director, 1971-73; Marian Wright Edelman Institute, founder. Writer. **Publications:** School Suspensions: Are They Helping Children?, 1975; Portrait of Inequality: Black and White Children in America, 1980; Families in Peril: An Agenda for Social Change, 1987; The Measure of Our Success: A Letter to My Children and Yours, 1992; Guide My Feet: Prayers and Meditations on Loving and Working for Children, 1995; (intro.) The Best of The Brownies' Book, 1996; Stand for Children, 1998; Lanterns: A Memoir of Mentors, 1999; I'm Your Child, God: Prayers for Children and Teenagers, 2002; (foreword) Susan Shreve, 2004; (afterword) Juan Williams, My Soul Looks Back in Wonder: Voices of the Civil Rights Experience, 2004; (ed.) I Can make a Difference, 2005; The Sea Is so Wide and My Boat Is so Small: Charting a Course for the Next Generation, 2008; (foreword) If it Takes a Village, Build One: How I Found Meaning Through a Life of Service and 100+ Ways you can Too, 2010; You and me Together, 2010. Contributor to books. **Address:** Children's Defense Fund, 25 E St. NW, Washington, DC 20001, U.S.A.

EDELMAN, Ric. American (born United States), b. 1958. **Genres:** Economics, Adult Non-fiction, Business/Trade/Industry. **Career:** Edelman Financial Services L.L.C., founder, 1987, chairman and chief executive officer; Edelman Financial Group, chief executive officer, president and director; WMAL Radio, show host, 1991-2007; Georgetown University, faculty, 1992-2001; Sanders Morris Harris Group, president and director; United Way of the National Capital Area, chairman, 2005-07; American Broadcasting Companies Inc. (ABC) Radio Networks, host, 2007. Writer. **Publications:** The Truth about Money, 1996, 3rd ed., 2004; The New Rules of Money: 88 Strategies for Financial Success Today, 1998; Ordinary People, Extraordinary Wealth: The 8 Secrets of How 5, 000 Ordinary Americans Became Successful Investors, and How You Can Too, 2000; Financial Security in Troubled Times: What You Need to Do Now, 2001; Discover the Wealth within You: A Financial Plan for Creating a Rich and Fulfilling Life, 2002; What You Need to Do Now: An 8-Point Action Plan to Secure Your Financial Independence, 2003; The Lies about Money: Achieving Financial Security and True Wealth by Avoiding the Lies Others Tell Us-and the Lies We Tell Ourselves, 2007; Rescue Your Money, 2009. Contributor to periodiacls. **Address:** Edelman Financial, 4000 Legato Rd., 9th Fl., Fairfax, VA 22033, U.S.A. **Online address:** money@ricedelman.com

EDELSTEIN, Robert. American (born United States), b. 1960. **Genres:** Sports/Fitness, Biography. **Career:** TV Guide, executive motor sports writer. **Publications:** NASCAR Generations: The Legacy of Family in NASCAR Racing, 2000; Full Throttle: The Life and Fast Times of NASCAR Legend Curtis Turner, 2005; NASCAR Legends: Memorable Men, Moments and Machines in Racing History, 2011. Contributor of articles to periodicals. **Address:** c/o Author Mail, Overlook Press, 141 Wooster St., New York, NY 10012-3163, U.S.A.

EDGAR, David. British (born England), b. 1948. **Genres:** Plays/Screenplays, Novels, Music, Poetry. **Career:** Telegraph and Argus, lecturer and reporter, 1969-72; Leeds Polytechnic, fellow in creative writing, 1972-74; Birmingham Repertory Theatre, resident playwright, 1974-75; University of Birmingham, playwriting tutor, 1975-78, honorary professor, 1992-95, professor, 1995-99. Writer. **Publications:** Dick Deterred: A Play in Two Acts, 1974; Destiny, 1976; Wreckers, 1977; Ball Boys, 1978; Jail Diary of Albie Sachs, 1978; (with S. Todd) Teendreams, 1979; (co-author) Ah! Mischief: The Writer and Television, 1982; Maydays, 1983; Entertaining Strangers: A Play for Dorchester, 1986; That Summer, 1987; Plays One: The Jail Diary of Albie Sachs, Saigon Rose, Mary Barnes, O Fair Jerusalem, Destiny, 1987; The Second Time as Farce: Reflections on the Drama of Modern Times, 1988; Shorts: Short Plays, 1989; (with S. Bill and A. Devlin) Heartlanders: A Community Play to Celebrate Birmingham's Centenary, 1989; The Shape of the Table, 1990; Plays Two: Ecclesiastes, The Life and Adventures of Nicholas Nickleby, Entertaining Strangers, 1990; Plays Three: Teendreams, Our Own People, That Summer, Maydays, 1991; The Strange Case of Dr. Jekyll and Mr. Hyde, 1991; Pentecost, 1996; Dr. Jekyll and Mr. Hyde: A New Version of the Novel by Robert Louis Stevenson, 1996; (contrib.) The State of Play: Playwrights on Playwriting, 1999; Edgar-Shorts: Short Plays, 2000; How Plays Work, 2000; Albert Speer, 2000; Prisoner's Dilemma, 2002; Continental Divide: Daughters of the Revolution, 2005; Playing with Fire, 2005; Continental Divide: Mothers Against, 2005; (with S. Dale) Time to Keep, 2007; Testing the Echo, 2008; The Master Builder, 2010; Arthur & George, 2010. Contributor to periodicals. **Address:** Alan Brodie Representation Ltd., Fairgate House, 211 Piccadilly, London, GL W1J 9HF, England. **Online address:** davidedgar@compuserve.com

EDGAR, Stacey L. American (born United States), b. 1940. **Genres:** Information Science/Computers, Philosophy, Technology, Young Adult Non-fiction, Ethics. **Career:** General Electric Co., computer programmer and analyst, 1960-67; State University of New York College, instructor in computer science and philosophy, 1969-75, lecturer, 1976-91, assistant professor of philosophy, 1991-97, associate professor of philosophy, 1997-. Writer. **Publications:** Advanced Problem Solving with FORTRAN 77, 1989; (with W.J. Edgar and E. Daly) Introduction to Logic, 1992; Fortran for the '90s, 1992; Morality and Machines: Perspectives on Computer Ethics, 1997, 2nd ed., 2002. **Address:** Department of Philosophy, State Universiity of New York,

103 Welles, 1 College Cir., Geneseo, NY 14454, U.S.A. **Online address:** edgar@geneseo.edu

EDGE, Marc. Canadian (born Canada), b. 1954?. **Genres:** Communications/Media, Writing/Journalism. **Career:** Vancouver Province, newspaper journalist, 1974-93; Calgary Herald, newspaper journalist, 1974-93; Ohio University, educator; Nanyang Technological University, School of Communication and Information, assistant professor, 2001-04; Sam Houston State University, associate professor; Simon Fraser University, faculty; University of Texas, faculty; Thompson Rivers University, faculty. Media critic. **Publications:** Pacific Press: The Unauthorized Story of Vancouver's Newspaper Monopoly, 2001; Red Line, Blue Line, Bottom Line: How Push Came to Shove between the National Hockey League and Its Players, 2004; Asper Nation: Canada's Most Dangerous Media Company, 2007. **Address:** Canada. **Online address:** mail@marcedge.com

EDGECOMBE, David. American (born United States), b. 1952. **Genres:** Plays/Screenplays, Novels. **Career:** Radio announcer and journalist, 1970-71; Antilles Radio Corp., radio announcer, 1971, director of education, 1977-80; Lagos Festival, administrator, 1976-77; WE Garments, manager, 1983-85; Montserrat Reporter, editor, 1985-90; University of the Virgin Islands, instructor in speech and theater, 1990-92, playwright, Reichhold Center for the Arts, director, 1992-, associate professor of communication. Actor and theater administrator. **Publications:** For Better, For Worse, 1973; Sonuvabitch, 1975; Strong Currents, 1977; Coming Home to Roost: A Play in Two Acts, 1978; A View from the Bridge, 1979; Kirnon's Kingdom, 1981; Heaven, 1991; Heaven and Other Plays, 1993; Marilyn, 1997; Smile, Natives, Smile, 2000; Theatrical Training during the Age of Shakespeare, 1995; (ed. with E.J. Waters) Contemporary Drama of the Caribbean, 2000. **Address:** Reichhold Center for the Arts, University of the Virgin Islands, John Brewers Bay, Ste. 2, St. Thomas, 00802-9990, Virgin Islands (US). **Online address:** dedgeco@uvi.edu

EDGERTON, Clyde. American (born United States), b. 1944. **Genres:** Novels. **Career:** Southern High School, English teacher, 1972-73; English Teaching Institute, co-director, 1976; North Carolina Central University, visiting lecturer, 1977; Campbell University, assistant professor, 1977-82, associate professor of education and psychology, 1982-85; writer, 1978-, 1989-98; St. Andrews Presbyterian College, associate professor of English and education, 1985-89; Agnes Scott College, visiting writer-in-residence, 1991; Duke University, visiting professor, 1992; Millsaps College, Eudora Welty visiting professor and Eudora Welty co-chair of southern studies, 1996; University of North Carolina-Wilmington, Department of Creative Writing, professor, 1998-; University of North Carolina, distinguished visiting professor, 1998-2002, professor of creative writing, 2002-. Writer. **Publications:** Raney (novel), 1985; Walking across Egypt, 1987; The Floatplane Notebooks, 1988; Killer Diller, 1991; In Memory of Junior, 1992; Redeye: A Western, 1995; Where Trouble Sleeps, 1997; Lunch at the Piccadilly, 2003; (contrib.) North Carolina, 2003; Solo: My Adventures in the Air, 2005; Bible Salesman: A Novel, 2008; The Night Train: A Novel, 2011. Contributor to books and periodicals. **Address:** Department of Creative Writing, University of North Carolina, 601 S College Rd., Wilmington, NC 28403, U.S.A. **Online address:** clyde_edgerton@yahoo.com

EDGERTON, David. British/Uraguayian (born Uruguay), b. 1959. **Genres:** History, Business/Trade/Industry, Essays. **Career:** Victoria University of Manchester, lecturer in economics of science and technology, 1984-85, Institute for Science and Technology, lecturer, 1985-88, lecturer in history of science and technology, 1988-92; University of London, Imperial College of London, Center for the History of Science, Technology and Medicine, faculty, 1993-, Hans Rausing professor, Hans Rausing chair, Leverhulme major research fellow. Writer. **Publications:** England and the Aeroplane: An Essay on a Militant and Technological Nation, 1992; Science, Technology and the British Industrial Decline, 1870-1970, 1996; (ed.) Industrial Research and Innovation in Business, 1996; Warfare State: Britain, 1920-1970, 2006; The Shock of the Old: Technology and Global History Since 1900, 2007; Britain's War Machine: Weapons, Resources, and Experts in the Second World War, 2011; How Britain Won, forthcoming. Contributor to books and journals. **Address:** Center for the History of Science,, Technology and Medicine, Imperial College London, S Kensington Campus, London, GL SW7 2AZ, England. **Online address:** d.edgerton@imperial.ac.uk

EDGERTON, Teresa (Ann). (Madeline Howard). American (born United States), b. 1949?. **Genres:** Science Fiction/Fantasy, Children's Fiction,

Young Adult Fiction, Novellas/Short Stories. **Career:** Writer. **Publications:** THE GREEN LION TRIOLOGY: Child of Saturn, 1989; The Moon in Hiding, 1989; The Work of the Sun, 1990. THE GOBLIN DUOLOGY: Goblin Moon, 1991; The Gnome's Engine, 1991. CHRONICLES OF CELYDONN SERIES: The Castle of the Silver Wheel, 1993; The Grail and the Ring, 1994; The Moon and the Thorn, 1995. SHORT STORIES: Weird Tales from Shakespeare, 1994; Enchanted Forests, 1995; The Shimmering Door, 1996; Tarot Fantastic, 1997; Highwaymen: Robbers and Rogues, 1997; Assassin Fantastic, 2001. FOREIGN LANGUAGE BOOKS: Das Kind des Saturn, 1998; Der verborgene Mond, 1998; Das Werk der Sonne, 1998; Under dem Trollmond, 1999; Die Gnomen-Maschine, 1999; Die grünen Löwen, 2002. OTHERS: The Queen's Necklace, 2001; (as Madeline Howard) The Hidden Stars: Book One of the Rune of Unmaking, 2004; (as Madeline Howard) A Dark Sacrifice: Book Two of the Rune of Unmaking, 2007. Works appear in anthologies. **Address:** Ace Publishing, Berkeley Publishing Group, Penguin Group USA, 375 Hudson St., New York, NY 10014-3657, U.S.A. **Online address:** goblin49@pacbell.net

EDGETTE, Janet. (Janet Sasson Edgette). American (born United States), b. 1956. **Genres:** Psychology. **Career:** Milton H. Erickson Institute of Philadelphia, co-director, 1987-; Devereux Foundation, staff psychologist, 1987-90; HCA Rockford Center, psychology consultant, 1990-91; Immaculata College, coordinator of clinical training, 1990-91; Practical Horseman Magazine, columnist and consulting sport psychologist, 1994-; Brief Therapy Center of Philadelphia, founder and co-director, 1996-; Jewish Family and Children's Services, consultant, 1998-; Comprehensive Behavioral Health Care Inc., consultant, 1998-99. **Publications:** (With J.H. Edgette)The Handbook of Hypnotic Phenomena in Psychotherapy, 1995; Heads Up! Practical Sport Psychology for Riders, Their Families and Their Trainers, 1996; Candor, Connection and Enterprise in Adolescent Therapy, 2002; Stop Negotiating with Your Teen: Strategies for Parenting Your Angry, Manipulative, Moody or Depressed Adolescent, 2002; Rider's Edge: Overcoming the Psychological Challenges of Riding, 2004; Adolescent Therapy that Really Works: Helping Kids who Never Asked for Help in the First Place, 2006; Clinical Pearls of Wisdom 21 Leading Therapists Offer Their Key Insights, 2009. Contributor to books and journals. **Address:** Rosemont Plz., 1062 Lancaster Ave., Ste. 25, Bryn Mawr, PA 19010, U.S.A. **Online address:** janetedgette@cs.com

EDGETTE, Janet Sasson. See **EDGETTE, Janet.**

EDGHILL, Rosemary. See **BES-SHAHAR, Eluki.**

EDIN, Kathryn. American (born United States), b. 1962?. **Genres:** Women's Studies And Issues, Social Commentary, Adult Non-fiction, Human Relations/Parenting, Social Sciences. **Career:** Rutgers University, assistant professor of sociology, 1993-97; University of Pennsylvania, Department of Sociology and Population Studies Center, assistant professor, 1997-2000 associate professor, 2004-06, professor, 2006-07; Northwestern University, associate professor of sociology, 2000-04, Institute for Policy Research, faculty fellow, 2000-04; Harvard University, Harvard Kennedy School, John F. Kennedy School of Government, professor of public policy and management; Multidisciplinary Program on Inequality and Social Policy, acting chair. Writer. **Publications:** Theres a Lot of Month Left at the End of the Money: How Welfare Recipients Make Ends Meet in Chicago, 1993; (with L. Lein) Making Ends Meet: How Single Mothers Survive Welfare and Low-Wage Work, 1997; (with K.M. Harris and G. Sandefur) Welfare to Work: Opportunities and Pitfalls: Congressional Seminar March 10 1997, 1998; Making a Way Out of No Way: How Low Income Single Mothers Meet Basic Family Needs while Moving from Welfare to Work, 2004; Juggling Low-Wage Work and Family Life: What Mothers Say about Their Children's Well-being in the Context of Welfare Reform, 2004; (with M. Kefalas) Promises I Can Keep: Why Poor Women Put Motherhood before Marriage, 2005; (ed. with P. England) Unmarried Couples with Children, 2007. Contributor to periodicals. **Address:** Harvard Kennedy School, Harvard University, 466 Taubman, 79 JFK St., PO Box 103, Cambridge, MA 02138, U.S.A. **Online address:** kathy_edin@hks.harvard.edu

EDINGER, Ray. American (born United States) **Genres:** Novellas/Short Stories, History. **Career:** Bibliophile Society of Rochester, president emeritus. Journalist and Writer. **Publications:** Fury Beach: The Four-Year Odyssey of Captain John Ross and the Victory, 2003; Love and Ice: The Tragic

Obsessions of Dr. Elisha Kent Kane, Arctic Explorer, 2011. **Address:** Penguin Group, Berkley Books Publicity, 375 Hudson St., New York, NY 10014, U.S.A. **Online address:** readermail@rayedinger.com

EDISON, Mike. American (born United States), b. 1964. **Genres:** Autobiography/Memoirs. **Career:** Backbeat Books, editor; Wrestling Magazine, Main Event, editor, 1985-; High Times Magazine, publisher, 1998-2001, editor, 2003-06; Screw Magazine, editor, 2003-06; Heeb (Jewish culture magazine), editorial director. Musician. **Publications:** I Have Fun Everywhere I Go: Savage Tales of Pot, Porn, Punk Rock, Pro Wrestling, Talking Apes, Evil Bosses, Dirty Blues, American Heroes, and the Most Notorious Magazines in the World (memoir), 2008. **Address:** New York, NY , U.S.A. **Online address:** rockettrain@hotmail.com

EDLOW, Jonathan A. American (born United States), b. 1952. **Genres:** History, Medicine/Health. **Career:** Harvard Medical School, Beth Israel Deaconess Medical Center, Department of Emergency Medicine, assistant professor of medicine, associate professor of medicine, professor, vice-chair, David Rockefeller Center for Latin American Studies, fellow. Writer and physician. **Publications:** Bull's-Eye: Unraveling the Medical Mystery of Lyme Disease, 2003, 2nd ed., 2004; Stroke, 2008; Deadly Dinner Party: And Other Medical Detective Stories, 2009; (ed. with M.H. Selim) Neurology Emergencies, 2011. Contributor of articles to periodicals. **Address:** c/o Author Mail, Yale University Press, 302 Temple St., PO Box 209040, New Haven, CT 06511-8909, U.S.A. **Online address:** jedlow@bidmc.harvard.edu

EDMISTEN, Patricia Taylor. American (born United States), b. 1939. **Genres:** International Relations/Current Affairs, Autobiography/Memoirs, History. **Career:** University of West Florida, associate professor, professor of sociology of education, educational psychology and special education, 1977-, director of international education and programs; United Nations consultant; West Florida Literary Federation, president; Peru, staff. Poet and novelist. **Publications:** Nicaragua Divided: La Prensa and the Chamorro Legacy, 1990; (trans., intro. and afterword) Autobiography of Maria Elena Moyano the Life and Death of a Peruvian Activist, 2000; The Mourning of Angels (novel), 2001; Treasures of Pensacola Beach (poetry), 2003; Wild Women with Tender Hearts (poetry), 2006; A Longing for Wisdom: One Woman's Conscience and Her Church, 2010. Contributor to periodicals. **Address:** College of Education, University of West Florida, 11000 University Pkwy., Pensacola, FL 32514, U.S.A. **Online address:** pedmiste@uwf.edu

EDMUNDS, John C. American (born United States), b. 1947. **Genres:** Young Adult Non-fiction, Business/Trade/Industry. **Career:** Instituto Superior de Agricultura, professor and management advisor, 1972-74; INCAE, Export Management, associate professor, 1976-80, 1982-85; Northeastern University, Finance Group, professor, 1979-82, 1985-88; Hult International Business School, professor of quanitiative methods and finance, 1980-82, 1985-90; Instituto de Empresa, Asesores Bursatiles professor of capital markets, 1991-92; Greenpoint Mortgage Securities, director, 1997-; Babson College, professor of finance and research director, Institute for Latin American Business Studies, research director; Boston University, Fletcher School of Law and Diplomacy, faculty. Writer. **Publications:** The Wealthy World: The Growth and Implications of Global Prosperity, 2001; Brave New Wealthy World, 2003; (with J.E. Marthinsen) Wealth by Association: Global Prosperity through Market Unification, 2003. **Address:** Babson College, Forest St., Wellesley, MA 02457, U.S.A. **Online address:** edmunds@babson.edu

EDMUNDS, R(ussell) David. American (born United States), b. 1939. **Genres:** Anthropology/Ethnology, History, Bibliography, Education, Humanities. **Career:** University of Wyoming, instructor, 1971-72, assistant professor of history, 1972-75; The University of Texas, assistant professor, 1975-78, associate professor, 1978-81, professor of American history, 1982-, Anne and Chester Watson chair in history professor; University of California, visiting professor, 1978; Macalester College, Michael Burris lecturer, 1979; San Diego State University, visiting professor, 1984; Smithsonian Institution, consultant; Center for the History of the American Indian, consultant; Newberry Library, consultant. Writer. **Publications:** The Otoe-Missouria People, 1976; The Potawatomis: Keepers of the Fire, 1978; Shawnee Prophet, 1983; Tecumseh and the Quest for Indian Leadership, 1984, 2nd ed., 2007; Kinsmen through Time: An Annotated Bibliography of Potawatomi History, 1987; (with J.L. Peyser) The Fox Wars: The Mesquakie Challenge to New France, 1993; (contrib.) Indians and a changing Frontier: The Art of George Winter, 1993; (with F.E. Hoxie and N. Salisbury) The People: A History of Native America, 2007.

EDITOR: American Indian Leaders: Studies in Diversity, 1980; New Warriors: Native American Leaders Since 1900, 2001; Enduring Nations: Native Americans in the Midwest, 2008. Works appear in anthologies. Contributor to periodicals and books. **Address:** School of Arts & Humanities, The University of Texas at Dallas, 5.414 JO, 800 W Campbell Rd., Richardson, TX 75080-3021, U.S.A. **Online address:** edmunds@utdallas.edu

EDSEL, Robert M. American (born United States), b. 1956?. **Genres:** History. **Career:** Gemini Exploration, owner; Monuments Men Foundation, founder and president. Writer and photographer. **Publications:** Rescuing Da Vinci: Hitler and the Nazis Stole Europe's Great Art: America and Her Allies Recovered It, 2006; (with B. Witter) The Monuments Men: Allied Heroes, Nazi Thieves, and the Greatest Treasure Hunt in History, 2009. **Address:** Dallas, TX , U.S.A. **Online address:** redsel@monumentsmen.com

EDSON, J(ohn) T(homas). Also writes as Chuck Nolan, Rod Denver. British (born England), b. 1928. **Genres:** Westerns/Adventure, Young Adult Fiction. **Career:** Writer. **Publications:** FLOATING OUTFIT SERIES: Trail Boss, 1961; The Ysabel Kid, 1962; Quiet Town, 1962; Rio Guns, 1962; The Texan, 1962; Waco's Debt, 1962; The Hard Riders, 1962; The Half Breed, 1963; Gun Wizard, 1963; The Rio Hondo Kid, 1963; Wagons to Backsight, 1964; Trigger Fast, 1964; The Rushers, 1964; The Rio Hondo War, 1964; Troubled Range, 1965; The Wildcats, 1965; The Fortune Hunters, 1965; The Man from Texas, 1965; A Town Called Yellowdog, 1966; The Law of the Gun, 1966; Return to Backsight, 1966; Guns in the Night, 1966; Sidewinder, 1967; The Fast Gun, 1967; The Floating Outfit, 1967; Terror Valley, 1967; The Hooded Raiders, 1968; Rangeland Hercules, 1968; McGraw's Inheritance, 1968; The Bad Bunch, 1968; The Making of a Lawman, 1968; Goodnight's Dream, 1969; The Peacemakers, 1969; 44 Calibre Man, 1969; Gunsmoke Thunder, 1969; The Trouble Busters, 1969; From Hide and Horn, 1969; Cuchilo, 1969; The Small Texan, 1969; The Town Tamers, 1969; A Horse Called Mogollon, 1971; Hell in the Palo Duro, 1971; Go Back to Hell, 1972; To Arms! to Arms, in Dixie!, 1972; The South Will Rise Again, 1972; Trail, 1973; The Hide and Tallow Men, 1974; The Quest for Bowie's Blade, 1974; Beguinage, 1978; Beguinage Is Dead!, 1978; Set A-Foot, 1978; Viridian's Trail, 1978; The Gentle Giant, 1979; The Hooded Riders, 1980; Master of Triggernometry, 1981; White Indians, 1981; Old Moccasins on the Trail, 1981; Diamonds, Emeralds, Cards and Colts, 1986; No Finger on the Trigger, 1987. WACO SERIES: Sagebrush Sleuth, 1962; The Drifter, 1963; Waco Rides In, 1964; Hound Dog Man, 1967; Doc Leroy, M.D., 1977; Waco's Badge, 1981; Arizona Ranger, 1988. CIVIL WAR SERIES: The Fastest Gun in Texas, 1963; The Devil Gun, 1966; The Colt and the Sabre, 1966; Comanche, 1967; The Rebel Spy, 1968; The Bloody Border, 1969; Back to the Bloody Border, 1970 in US as Renegade; Kill Dusty Fog!, 1970; Under the Stars and Bars, 1970; You're in Command Now, Mr. Fog, 1973; The Big Gun, 1973; Best of J. T. Edson, 1973; Set Texas Back on Her Feet, 1973; A Matter of Honour, 1981; Decision for Dusty Fog, 1986; The Code of Dusty Fog, 1988; Lone Star Killers, 1990. CALAMITY JANE SERIES: The Bull Whip Breed, 1965; Trouble Trail, 1965; The Cow Thieves, 1965; The Big Hunt, 1967; Calamity Spells Trouble, 1968; Cold Deck, Hot Lead, 1969; White Stallion, Red Mare, 1970; The Remittance Kid, 1978; The Whip and the War Lance, 1979. ROCKABYE COUNTY SERIES: The Professional Killers, 1968; The Quarter Second Draw, 1969; The Deputies, 1969; Point of Contact, 1970; The Owlhoot, 1970; Run for the Border, 1971; Bad Hombre, 1971; The Sixteen Dollar Shooter, 1974; The Sheriff of Rockabye County, 1981; The Lawmen of Rockabye County, 1982. OLD DEVIL HARDIN SERIES: Get Urrea, 1975; Ole Devil and the Caplocks, 1976; Ole Devil and the Mule Train, 1976; Ole Devil at San Jacinto, 1977; Ole Devil's Hands and Feet, 1982. CAP FOG SERIES: Cap Fog, Texas Ranger, Meet Mr. J.G. Reeder, 1977; You're a Texas Ranger, Alvin Fog, 1979; Rapido Clint, 1980; The Justice of Company Z, 1981; The Return of Rapido Clint and Mr J.G. Reeder, 1984; Decision for Dusty Fog, 1987; Young Ole Devil, 1988. BUNDUKI SERIES: Bunduki and Dawn, 1975; Sacrifice for the Quagga God, 1975; Bunduki, 1975; Fearless Master of the Jungle, 1978. OTHER: Slaughter's Way, 1965; Slip Gun, 1971; Two Miles to the Border, 1972; Blonde Genius, 1973; J.T.'s Hundredth, 1979; J.T.'s Ladies, 1980; The Hide and Horn Saloon, 1983; Cut One, They All Bleed, 1983; Wanted! Belle Starr, 1983; Buffalo Are Coming, 1984; Is-A-Man, 1985; More J.T.'s Ladies, 1987; Mark Counter's Kin, 1989; Rapid Clint Strikes Back, 1989; Texas Kidnappers, 1996; Mississippi Raider, 1996; Cure the Texas Fever, 1996; Wedge Goes to Arizona, 1996; Arizona Range War, 1996; Arizona Gun Law, 1996.

Address: c/o Joanna Marston, Rosica Colin Ltd., 1 Clareville Grove Mews, London, GL SW7 5AH, England.

EDSON, Russell. American (born United States), b. 1935. **Genres:** Novels, Plays/Screenplays, Poetry, Essays, Novellas/Short Stories, Young Adult Fiction, Literary Criticism And History. **Career:** Poet, playwright and novelist. **Publications:** Appearances: Fable & Drawings, 1961; A Stone Is Nobody's: Fables and Drawings, 1961; The Boundary, 1964; The Very Thing That Happens: Fables and Drawings, 1964; The Brain Kitchen: Writings and Woodcuts, 1965; What a Man Can See, 1969; The Childhood of an Equestrian, 1973; The Clam Theater, 1973; A Roof with Some Clouds behind It, 1975; The Falling Sickness: A Book of Plays (plays), 1975; The Intuitive Journey and Other Works, 1976; The Reason Why the Closet-Man Is Never Sad, 1977; Edson's Mentality, 1977; The Traffic, 1978; The Wounded Breakfast: Ten Poems, 1978; With Sincerest Regrets, 1980; Wuck Wuck Wuck!, 1984; Gulping's Recital, (novel) 1984; The Wounded Breakfast: Ten Poems (full book, 60 prose poems), 1985; Tick Tock: Short Stories and Woodcut, 1992; The Song of Percival Peacock (novel), 1992; The Tunnel: Selected Poems, 1994; The Tormented Mirror, 2001; Rooster's Wife: Poems, 2005; See Jack, 2009. **Address:** Georges Borchardt Inc., 136 E 57th St., New York, NY 10022, U.S.A. **Online address:** russedson@earthlink.net

EDWARDS, Allen Jack. American (born United States), b. 1926. **Genres:** Psychology, Medicine/Health, Sciences. **Career:** University of Kansas, assistant professor, 1958-62, associate professor of education, 1962-63; Southern Illinois University, associate professor, 1963-65; University of Missouri, associate professor, professor of education, 1965-72; Southwest Missouri State University, professor of psychology, 1973-, Center for Gerontological Studies, director, now emeritus. Writer. **Publications:** (Co-author) Educational Psychology: The Teaching-Learning Process, 1968; Individual Mental Testing, vol. I: History and Theories, 1971, vol. II: Measurement, 1972; (ed. and contrib.) Selected Writings of David Wechser, 1974; Dementia, 1993; When Memory Fails: Helping the Alzheimer's and Dementia Patient, 1994; Psychology of Orientation: Time Awareness Across Life Stages and in Dementia, 2002. **Address:** Department of Psychology, Southwest Missouri State University, 901 S National Ave., Springfield, MO 65897, U.S.A.

EDWARDS, Anne. American (born United States), b. 1927. **Genres:** Novels, Romance/Historical, Children's Non-fiction, Autobiography/Memoirs, Biography, Documentaries/Reportage, Young Adult Fiction, Film, History, Theatre, Music. **Career:** Metro-Goldwyn-Mayer, junior writer, 1944; freelance film writer, 1950-54; freelance film and television writer, 1954-57. **Publications:** (Adaptor) A Child's Bible, 1967; The Survivors, 1968; The Bible for Young Readers: The Old Testament, 1968; Miklos Alexandrovitch Is Missing in UK as Alexandrovitch is Missing, 1970; Shadow of a Lion, 1971; Haunted Summer, 1972; The Hesitant Heart, 1974; Judy Garland: A Biography, 1975; Child of Night in UK as Ravenwings, 1975; (with S. Citron) The Inn and Us (reminiscences), 1976; The Great Houdini (juvenile), 1977; Vivien Leigh: A Biography, 1977; P.T. Barnum (juvenile), 1977; A Child's Bible in Colour: The Old Testament, 1978; Sonya: The Life of the Countess Tolstoy, 1981; The Road to Tara: The Life of Margaret Mitchell, 1983; Matriarch: Queen Mary and the House of Windsor, 1984; A Remarkable Woman: A Biography of Katherine Hepburn, 1985; Early Reagan: The Rise to Power, 1987; Shirley Temple: American Princess, 1988; The De Milles: An American Family, 1988; Royal Sisters: Queen Elizabeth and Princess Margaret, 1990; Wallis: The Novel, 1991; The Grimaldis of Monaco: Centuries of Scandal, Years of Grace, 1992; La Divina, 1994; Throne of Gold: The Lives of the Aga Khans, 1995; Streisand: A Biography, 1997; Ever After: Diana and the Life She Led, 2000; Katharine Hepburn: A Remarkable Woman, 2000; Maria Callas: An Intimate Biography, 2001; Callas: Her Life, Her Loves, Her Music, 2001; Reagans: Portrait of a Marriage, 2003; Leaving Home: A Hollywood Blacklisted Writer's Years Abroad, 2012. Contributor of articles to magazines. **Address:** International Creative Management Inc., 40 W 57th St., New York, NY 10019, U.S.A.

EDWARDS, Anne K. See EMMONS, Mary L.

EDWARDS, Brendan Frederick R. Canadian (born Canada), b. 1976. **Genres:** Intellectual History, Librarianship, Travel/Exploration, Local History/Rural Topics, Race Relations. **Career:** Writer, librarian and educator. **Publications:** (Ed. with E.H. Jones) Anson House: A Refuge and a Home, Trent University's History 475 Class, 2001; Paper Talk: A History of Libraries, Print Culture, and Aboriginal Peoples in Canada before 1960, 2005;

Slovakia-Culture Smart!: The Essential Guide to Customs & Culture, 2011. Contributor to books and journals. **Address:** ON , Canada. **Online address:** brendanfredwards@gmail.com

EDWARDS, Brent Hayes. American (born United States), b. 1968. **Genres:** Novels. **Career:** Rutgers University, assistant professor, 1997-2003, associate professor of English, 2003-, professor; New York Public Library, Dorothy and Lewis B. Cullman Center for Scholars and Writers, fellow, 2005-06; Columbia University, Louis Armstrong Visiting Professor of Jazz Studies, 2007, Department of English and Comparative Literature, professor; Social Text Journal, co-editor; Cornell University, senior fellow. **Publications:** The Practice of Diaspora: Literature, Translation and the Rise of Black Internationalism, 2003; (ed. with F.J. Griffin and R.G. O'Meally) Uptown Conversation: The New Jazz Studies, 2004; (ed., contrib. and intro.) The Souls of Black Folk, 2007; Epistrophies, 2011. **Address:** Department of English & Comparative Literature, Columbia University, 609 Philosophy Hall, 1150 Amsterdam Ave., PO Box 4927, New York, NY 10027, U.S.A. **Online address:** bhe2@columbia.edu

EDWARDS, Clive D. British (born England), b. 1947. **Genres:** Antiques/ Furnishings, Art/Art History, History, Business/Trade/Industry, Technology, Humanities, Homes/Gardens. **Career:** Perrings Furnishings, retail manager, 1965-85; Victoria and Albert Museum, staff, 1989-91; Loughborough University, lecturer, senior lecturer in art and design history, reader in art and design, 1991-2010, professor of design history. Writer. **Publications:** Victorian Furniture: Technology and Design, 1993; Twentieth-Century Furniture: Its Materials, Manufacture and Markets, 1994; Eighteenth-Century Furniture, 1996; Encyclopedia of Furniture-Making Materials, Trades and Techniques, 2000; Turning Houses into Homes: Retailing and Consumption of the Domestic Interior, 2003; Encyclopedia of Furnishing Textiles, Floor coverings and Home Furnishing Practices, 1200-1950, 2007; How to Read Pattern, 2009; Interior Design: A Critical Introduction, 2010. Contributor of articles to books and periodicals. **Address:** School of Arts, Loughborough University, Epinal Way, Loughborough, LE LE11 0QE, England. **Online address:** c.edwards@lboro.ac.uk

EDWARDS, David B. American (born United States) **Genres:** Documentaries/Reportage, History, Social Sciences, Anthropology/Ethnology. **Career:** Williams College, professor of anthropology, department chair, Afghan Media Project, director, W. Van Alan Clark '41 third century professor in the social sciences. Writer. **Publications:** Heroes of the Age: Moral Fault Lines on the Afghan Frontier, 1996; Before Taliban: Genealogies of the Afghan Jihad, 2002; Kabul Transit, 2006. Contributor to journals. **Address:** Department of Anthropology and Sociology, Williams College, Hollander Hall, 85 Mission Park Dr., Williamstown, MA 01267, U.S.A. **Online address:** david.b.edwards@williams.edu

EDWARDS, Frank B. Canadian (born Canada), b. 1952. **Genres:** Children's Fiction, Children's Non-fiction, How-to Books, History. **Career:** Canadian Geographic, assistant editor, 1975-78; Harrowsmith Magazine, associate editor, 1979-82; Equinox Magazine, executive editor, 1981-85; Camden House Books, publisher and editorial director, 1985-89; Pokeweed Press, principal, 1986- ; Bungalo Books, principal, 1986-2009; Hedgehog Productions, founder, president and communications consultant, 1989-; St. Lawrence College, instructor, 1995; Globe and Mail, freelance obituary writer, 2009-. **Publications:** FOR CHILDREN: Mortimer Mooner Stopped Taking a Bath!, 1990; Melody Mooner Stayed Up All Night, 1991; Snow: Learning for the Fun of it, 1992; (with L. Aziz) Close Up: Microscopic Photographs of Everyday Stuff, 1992; Grandma Mooner Lost Her Voice, 1992; (with Aziz) Ottawa: A Kid's Eye View, 1993; A Dog Called Dad, 1994; Mortimer Mooner Makes Lunch, 1995; Melody Mooner Takes Lessons, 1996; Downtown Lost & Found, 1997; The Zookeeper's Sleepers, 1997; Peek-a-boo at the Zoo, 1997; Snug as a Big Red Bug, 1999; A Crowded Ride in the Countryside, 1999; Nightgown Countdown, 1999; Robin Hood with Lots of Dogs: A Canine Condensation of Great Britain's Most Famous Tale, 1999; Treasure Island with Lots of Dogs, 1999; Frogger, 2000; Bug, 2002; The Life of Robert Munsch: A Juvenile Biography, 2009. FOR ADULTS: The Smiling Wilderness, 1984; (ed.) The Cottage Book: A Collection of Practical Advice for Lakeside Living, 1991, rev. ed., 1994; (with T. Carpenter) Kids, Computers, and You, 1995; Cultivating the Wilderness: The Parrott Family of Lennox & Addington County, 2005; A House Worthy of God: A Brief History of St. Patrick's Church Napa-

nee, 2007; Robert Munsch biography, 2009. **Address:** Pokeweed Press, 829 Norwest Rd., Ste. 337, Kingston, ON K7P 2N3, Canada. **Online address:** fedwards@hedgehogproductions.com

EDWARDS, Hank. *See* **BROOMALL, Robert W(alter).**

EDWARDS, Harvey. American/French (born France), b. 1929. **Genres:** Plays/Screenplays, Children's Non-fiction, Education, Recreation, Sports/ Fitness, Travel/Exploration. **Career:** Skiing Magazine, European editor; Ski Magazine, correspondent; Mountain Gazeyye, correspondent; Jewish Braille Institute, assistant to director, 1956-58; Edwards Films Inc., owner, filmmaker, director, 1981-. Writer. **Publications:** Scandinavia: The Challenge of Welfare, 1968; Lars Olav: A Norwegian Boy, 1969; Leise: A Danish Girl from Dragoer, 1970; France and the French, 1972; Skiing to Win, 1973; (with I. Spring) 100 Hikes in the Alps, 1979, (with V. Spring) 2nd ed., 1992. **Address:** Edwards Films Inc., 203 Center Rd., Eagle Bridge, NY 12057, U.S.A. **Online address:** harvey.edwards@edwardsfilms.com

EDWARDS, Jo. *See* **EDWARDS, Johanna.**

EDWARDS, Johanna. (Jo Edwards). American (born United States), b. 1978. **Genres:** Novels, Young Adult Fiction. **Career:** Daily Helmsman, arts and entertainment editor, 1999-2001; Blockbuster Video, staff, 2002; WYPL, Book Talk, producer, 2002-05; novelist, 2005-. Journalist. **Publications:** The Next Big Thing, 2005; Your Big Break, 2006; (with J. Kenner and S. Robar) Fendi, Ferragamo, & Fangs, 2007; (as Jo Edwards) Love Undercover, 2006; How to be Cool, 2007; (as Jo Edwards) Go Figure, 2007. **Address:** c/o Jenny Bent, Trident Media Group L.L.C., 41 Madison Ave., 36th Fl., New York, NY 10010-2257, U.S.A. **Online address:** johanna@johannaedwards.com

EDWARDS, June. *See* **FORRESTER, Helen.**

EDWARDS, (Kenneth) Martin. British (born England), b. 1955. **Genres:** Novels, Novellas/Short Stories, Mystery/Crime/Suspense, Law, Horror. **Career:** Booth and Co., trainee, 1978-80; Mace & Jones, solicitor, 1980-84, partner, 1984-2011; Weightmanss L.L.P., partner, 2011-. Writer. **Publications:** Understanding Computer Contracts, 1983; Understanding Dismissal Law, 1984; Managing Redundancies, 1986; (with E. Usher) Careers in the Law, 1988, 7th ed., 1995; Executive Survival, 1989, 2nd ed. as How to Get the Best Deal from Your Employer, 1991; Dismissal Law, 1991; Know-How for Employment Lawyers, FT Law and Tax, 1996; (with B. Knox) The Lazarus Widow, 1999; Urge to Kill, 2003. NOVELS: Take My Breath Away, 2002; Dancing for the Hangman, 2008. HARRY DEVLIN NOVELS: All the Lonely People, 1991; Suspicious Minds, 1992; I Remember You, 1993; Yesterday's Papers, 1994; Eve of Destruction, 1998; The Devil in Disguise, 1998; The First Cut Is the Deepest, 1999; Waterloo Sunset, 2008. LAKE DISTRICT MYSTERIES SERIES: The Coffin Trail, 2004; The Cipher Garden, 2005; The Arsenic Labyrinth, 2007; The Serpent Pool, 2010; The Hanging Wood, 2011. EDITOR: Northern Blood, 1992; Northern Blood 2, 1995; (with R. Church) Anglian Blood, 1995; Perfectly Criminal, 1996; Why Dunit?, 1997; Northern Blood 3, 1998; Past Crimes, 1998; Missing Persons, 1999; Scenes of Crime, 2000; Murder Squad, 2001; Crime in the City, 2002; Green for Danger, 2003; Mysterious Pleasures, 2003; Crime on the Move: The Official Anthology of the Crime Writers' Association, 2005; I.D: Crimes of Identity, 2006; (with S. Feder) The Trinity Cat and Other Mysteries, 2006. M.O.: Crimes of Practice, 2008; Original Sins, 2010; Guilty Consciences, 2011; Best Eaten Cold and Other Stories, 2011. Contributor to periodicals. **Address:** Watson Little Ltd., 12 Egbert St., London, GL NW1 8LJ, England. **Online address:** martinedwards10@btconnect.com

EDWARDS, Larry. American (born United States), b. 1957. **Genres:** Novels, Film, Mystery/Crime/Suspense, Music, Biography, Humor/Satire, Autobiography/Memoirs, Young Adult Fiction, Young Adult Fiction. **Career:** Relim Publishing, feature writer; Infonent Inc., entertainment editor. **Publications:** Blood on the Streets (fiction), 1989; Buster: A Legend in Laughter, 1994; Bela Lugosi: Master of the Macabre, 1997. Contributor to magazines. **Address:** 2554 Alemany Blvd., San Francisco, CA 94112, U.S.A.

EDWARDS, Laurie Elizabeth. American (born United States), b. 1980?. **Genres:** Medicine/Health. **Career:** Northeastern University, lecturer. Journalist and consultant. **Publications:** Life Disrupted: Getting Real about Chronic Illness in Your Twenties and Thirties, 2008. Contributor of articles to periodicals. **Address:** c/o Matthew Carnicelli, Trident Media Group, 41

Madison Ave., 36th Fl., New York, NY 10010, U.S.A. **Online address:** laurie.edwards@gmail.com

EDWARDS, Louis. American (born United States), b. 1962?. **Genres:** Novels, Romance/Historical. **Career:** Festival Productions Inc., vice president of marketing and public relations. Writer. **Publications:** NOVELS: Ten Seconds, 1991; N: A Romantic Mystery, 1997; Oscar Wilde Discovers America, 2003. Contributor to periodicals. **Address:** c/o Author Mail, Dutton, 375 Hudson St., New York, NY 10014, U.S.A.

EDWARDS, Michael. French/British (born England), b. 1938. **Genres:** Poetry, Art/Art History, Literary Criticism And History. **Career:** University of Warwick, Department of French, lecturer, 1965-, professor, through 1973, Department of English, professor, 1987-2002; University of Essex, Department of Literature, professor, 1977-87; University of Paris 12, associate professor, 1989-90; College de France, visiting professor, 1997, professor and European chair, 2000-01, Literary Creation in English, chair; Ecole Normale Superieure, visiting professor, 1998. Writer. **Publications:** La Thâbaâde de Racine, 1965; Eliot/Language, 1975; Towards a Christian Poetics, 1984; Poetry and Possibility, 1988; Of Making Many Books, 1990; Raymond Mason, 1994; Eloge de l'attente, 1996; De Poetica Christiana, 1997; Beckett ou le don des langues, 1998; Leâons de poâsie, 2001; Ombres de lune, 2001; Sur un vers d'Hamlet, 2001; Un monde même et autre, 2002; Shakespeare et la comâdie de l'âmerveillement, 2003; Terre de poâsie, 2003; Racine et Shakespeare, 2004; Shakespeare et l'oeuvre de la tragâdie, 2005; Le Gânie de la poâsie anglaise, 2006; De l'émerveillement, 2008; Shakespeare: le poète au théâtre, 2009; L'étrangereté, 2010; Le bonheur d'etre ici, 2011. POETRY: Commonplace, 1971; To Kindle the Starling, 1972; Where, 1975; The Ballad of Mobb Conroy, 1977; The Magic, Unquiet Body, 1985; Rivage Mobile, 2003; Paris demeure, 2008; 79 la racine de feu, 2009. EDITOR: French Poetry Now, 1975; (with M. Straus and G. Dego) Directions in Italian Poetry, 1975; Raymond Queneau, 1978; Words/Music, 1979; Languages, 1981. **Address:** College de France, 11 Pl. Marcelin Berthelot, 75231 Cedex 05, Paris, 75231, France. **Online address:** michael.edwards@college-de-france.fr

EDWARDS, Michael B. American (born United States) **Genres:** Mystery/Crime/Suspense, Novels, Young Adult Fiction. **Career:** Writer and advocate. **Publications:** Murder at the Panionic Games (mystery novel), 2002; Murder at the Festival of Apaturia, forthcoming. **Address:** c/o Author Mail, Academy Chicago Publishers, 4W, 363 W Erie St., Ste. 7E, Chicago, IL 60654, U.S.A. **Online address:** m.edwards157@btinternet.com

EDWARDS, Mickey Henry. American (born United States), b. 1937. **Genres:** Politics/Government, History, Intellectual History. **Career:** Newspaper reporter and editor, 1958-63; Oklahoma City University, instructor in law and journalism, 1976; Harvard University, John F. Kennedy School of Government, John Quincy Adams lecturer in legislative practice, 1993-2004; Princeton University, Woodrow Wilson School of Public and International Affairs, lecturer, 2004-; Aspen Institute, vice-president and director; Harvard Law School, visiting lecturer; Georgetown University, Public Policy Institute, visiting professor; Chicago Tribune, columnist; Los Angeles Times, columnist. **Publications:** Behind Enemy Lines: A Rebel in Congress Proposes a Bold New Politics for the 1980s, 1983; Financing America's Leadership: Protecting American Interests and Promoting American Values; Report of an Independent Task Force, 1997; (with M. Watkins and U. Thakrar) Winning the Influence Game: What Every Business Leader Should Know about Government, 2001; Reclaiming Conservatism: How a Great American Political Movement Got Lost-and How It Can Find Its Way Back, 2008. Contributor to periodicals. **Address:** Woodrow Wilson School of Public and International, Affairs, Princeton University, 120 Bendheim Hall, Princeton, NJ 08544, U.S.A. **Online address:** mickeye@princeton.edu

EDWARDS, P. D. (Peter David Edwards). Australian (born Australia), b. 1931. **Genres:** Literary Criticism And History, Young Adult Fiction, Romance/Historical. **Career:** University of Queensland, lecturer in English, 1954-58, 1961, professor of English, 1969-96, pro-vice-chancellor for humanities, 1985-90; University of Sydney, lecturer, senior lecturer in English, 1962-68, Writer. **Publications:** Anthony Trollope, 1968; (ed. with R.B. Joyce) Australia, 1968; Some Mid-Victorian Thrillers; The Sensation Novel, Its Friends and Its Foes, 1971; Anthony Trollope: His Art and Scope, 1978; (intro.) An Autobiography, 1980; (comp.) Edmund Yates, 1831-1894, 1980; Anthony Trollope's Son in Australia, 1982; (comp.) Frances Cashel Hoey, 1830-1908, 1982; Idyllic Realism from Mary Russell Mitford to Hardy, 1988;

(intro.) Framley Parsonage, 1989; (comp. with I.G. Sibley and M. Versteeg) Indexes to Fiction in Belgravia (1867-1899), 1989; (ed. and intro.) Harry Heathcote of Gangoil: A Tale of Australian Bushlife, 1992; (comp.) Edmund Yates Papers in The University of Queensland Library, 1993; (ed. and intro.) Aurora Floyd, 1996; Dickens's Young Men, 1997; (ed. and intro.) Rachel Ray, 2008; My Toy! My Toy! My Toy!, 2008. **Address:** Department of English, University of Queensland, Saint Lucia, Brisbane, QL 4072, Australia. **Online address:** p.edwards@uq.net.au

EDWARDS, Peter David. See **EDWARDS, P. D.**

EDWARDS, Philip (Walter). British (born England), b. 1923. **Genres:** Literary Criticism And History, Travel/Exploration, Biography, Autobiography/Memoirs, Essays, History. **Career:** University of Birmingham, lecturer in English, 1946-60; University of Dublin, Trinity College, professor of English literature, 1960-66; University of Michigan, visiting professor, 1964-65; University of Essex, professor, 1966-74; University of Liverpool, professor and King Alfred professor of English literature, 1974-90, now professor emeritus. Writer. **Publications:** Sir Walter Raleigh, 1953, 4th ed., 1978; Thomas Kyd and Early Elizabethan Tragedy, 1966; Shakespeare and the Confines of Art, 1968; Person and Office in Shakespeare's Plays, 1970; Nationalist Theatres: Shapkespeare and Yeats, 1976; Sir Walter Ralegh, 1976; Threshold of a Nation: A Study in English and Irish Drama, 1979; Shakespeare: A Writer's Progress, 1986; Last Voyages, 1988; The Story of the Voyage: Sea-Narratives in Eighteenth-Century England, 1994; Sea-Mark: The Metaphorical Voyage, 1997; Pathways to Anarchism, 1997; Pilgrimage and Literary Tradition, 2005. EDITOR: Thomas Kyd: The Spanish Tragedy, 1958; (with R.J. McHugh) Jonathan Swift, 1667-1967, 1967; The Spanish Tragedy, 1969; William Shakespeare, 1975; King Lear, 1975; Shakespeare, Pericles Prince of Tyre, 1976; (with C.A. Gibson) Plays and Poems of Philip Massinger, 1976; (with A. Muir) Aspects of Othello: Articles Reprinted from Shakespeare Survey, 1977; (with K. Muir) Aspects of Macbeth: Articles Reprinted from Shakespeare Survey, 1977; (with I. Ewbank and G.K. Hunter) Shakespeare's Styles: Essays in Honour of Kenneth Muir, 1980; Shakespeare, Hamlet, 1985; Hamlet, Prince of Denmark, 1985, rev. ed., 2003; The Journals of Captain Cook, 1999; Hunt for the Southern Continent, 2007. **Address:** University of Liverpool, Brownlow Hill, Liverpool, MS L69 3BX, England. **Online address:** pedwards@gilling.edi.co.uk

EDWARDS, Robert. British (born England), b. 1955. **Genres:** Biography, Military/Defense/Arms Control, History. **Career:** Writer and financial market analyst. **Publications:** Archie and the Listers: The Heroic Story of Archie Scott Brown and the Marque He Made Famous, 1995; Managing a Legend: Stirling Moss, Ken Gregory, and the British Racing Partnership, 1997; Aston Martin: Ever the Thoroughbred, 1999; The Art of Dexter Brown, 2001; Stirling Moss: The Authorised Biography, 2001; Haynes Classic Makes Series: Aston Martin, 2003; White Death: Russia's War on Finland, 1939-40, 2006 in US as The Winter War: Russia's Invasion of Finland, 1939-1940, 2008. Contributor to magazines and newspapers. **Address:** Andrew Lownie Literary Agency Ltd., 36 Great Smith St., London, GL SW1P 3BU, England.

EDWARDS, Sarah (Anne). American (born United States), b. 1943. **Genres:** Novels, Business/Trade/Industry, Economics, Marketing, Money/Finance. **Career:** Office of Economic Opportunity Regional Office, community representative, 1966-68; Department of Health, Education and Welfare, social services/parent involvement and resource specialist, 1968-73; University of Kansas Medical Center, Children's Rehabilitation Unit, Social Services Department, director of training, 1975-76; Cathexis Institute, co-director, 1976-77; CompuServe Information Service, Working from Home Forum, co-founder and manager, 1983-97; Business Radio Network, co-host, 1987-2001; CNBC, commentator, 1996-99; NPR Marketplace, commentator, 1996-97; Center for the New West, senior fellow; Pine Mountain Institute, co-founder and director, 2002-. Clinical social worker and writer. **Publications:** WITH P. EDWARDS: How to Make Money with Your Personal Computer, 1984; Working from Home: Everything You Need to Know about Living and Working Under the Same Roof, 1985, 5th ed., 1999; The Best Home Business for the 90s: The Inside Information You Need to Know to Select a Home-based Business That's Right for You, 1991, 3rd ed. as The Best Home Business for the 21st Century: The Information You Need to Know to Select a Home-based Business That's Right for You, 1999; (and with L.C. Douglas) Getting Business to Come to You: Everything You Need to Know to Do Your Own Advertising, Public Relations, Direct Mail and Sales Promotion and Attract All the Business You Can Handle, 1991, 2nd ed. as Getting Business to

Come to You: A Complete Do-It-Yourself Guide to Attracting All the Business You Can Enjoy, 1998; Making It on Your Own: Surviving and Thriving on the Ups and Downs of Being Your Own Boss, 1991, rev. ed., 1996; Making Money with Your Computer at Home, 1993, 2nd ed. as Making Money with Your Computer at Home: The Inside Information You Need to Know to Select and Operate a Full-Time, Part-Time, or Add-on Business That's Right for You, 1997, 3rd ed., 2005; Finding Your Perfect Work: The New Career Guide to Making a Living, Creating a Life, 1996; Secrets of Self-Employment: Surviving and Thriving on the Ups and Downs of Being Your Own Boss, 1996; (and with W. Zooi) Home Business You Can Buy: The Definitive Guide to Exploring Franchises, Multi-Level Marketing and Business Opportunities, 1997; (and with R. Benzel) Teaming Up: The Small-Business Guide to Collaborating with Others to Boost Your Earnings and Expand Your Horizons, 1997; (and with L. Rohrbough) Making Money in Cyberspace, 1998; (and with W. Zooi) Outfitting Your Home Business for Much Less, 2000; The Practical Dreamer's Handbook: Finding the Time, Money and Energy to Live Your Dreams, 2000; (and with P. Economy) Home-Based Business for Dummies, 2000, 3rd ed., 2010; Changing Directions without Losing Your Way: Managing the Six Stages of Change at Work and in Life, 2001; (and with M. Nemko) Cool Careers for Dummies, 2001; Write and Design Successful Sales Materials, 2001; (and with L.M. Roberts) The Entrepreneurial Parent: How to Earn Your Income at Home and Still Enjoy Your Family, Your Work and Your Life, 2002; (and with P. Economy) Why Aren't You Your Own Boss?: Leaping Over the Obstacles that Stand Between You and Your Dream, 2003; Best Home Business for People 50+: Opportunities for People Who Believe the Best is Yet to Be!, 2004; Middle-class Lifeboat: Careers and Life Choices for Navigating a Changing Economy, 2007; Middle Class Lifeboat: Three Safeguards to Secure Your Financial Future Now, 2008. **Address:** Pine Mountain Institute, 2624 Teakwood Ct., PO Box 6775, Pine Mountain Club, CA 93222-6775, U.S.A. **Online address:** sedwards@frazmtn.com

EDWARDS, Virginia. Canadian (born Canada), b. 1942. **Genres:** Psychiatry, Medicine/Health, Self Help. **Career:** University of Toronto, lecturer; Toronto East General Hospital, chief of child psychiatry. Writer. **Publications:** Stories of old St. Augustine, 1973; Depression and Bipolar Disorders: Everything You Need to Know, 2002. **Address:** 567 Rushton Rd., Toronto, ON M6C 2Y6, Canada.

EFIMOVA, Alla. American/Russian (born Russia), b. 1961. **Genres:** Art/Art History, Translations. **Career:** State University of New York College, instructor in foreign languages and literatures, 1990-91; University of Rochester, instructor in art history, 1991-92; University of California-Irvine, visiting lecturer in art history, 1995; University of California-Santa Cruz, lecturer in art history, 1996-, visiting assistant professor, 1996-98; Archive: Jewish Immigrant Culture, co-founder and vice president; University of California-Berkeley, Art Museum and Pacific Film Archive, associate curator, 1999-2004, Judah L. Magnes Museum, director and chief curator, 2003-10, The Magnes Collection of Jewish Art and Life, Jacques And Esther Reutliner director, 2010-. Writer. **Publications:** (Ed. and trans. with L. Manovich) Tekstura: Russian Essays on Visual Culture, 1993; (co-author) Layers: Contemporary Collage from St. Petersburg, Russia, 1999; Surviving Suprematism: Lazar Khidekel, 2005. Contributor of articles to books and journals. **Address:** Magnes Collection of Jewish Art and Life, Bancroft Library, University of California, Rm. 2121 Allston Way, PO Box 6300, Berkeley, CA 94720-6000, U.S.A. **Online address:** aefimova@library.berkeley.edu

EGAN, Desmond. Irish (born Ireland), b. 1936. **Genres:** Poetry, Translations. **Career:** Newbridge College, teacher, 1972-87; Era (literary magazine), editor and founder, 1974-84; writer, 1987-. **Publications:** POETRY: Midland, 1972; Leaves, 1974; Siege!: Monasterevin 22 October/7 November, 1976; Woodcutter, 1978; Athlone?, 1980; Seeing Double, 1983; Collected Poems, 1983; Poems for Peace, 1986; A Song for My Father, 1989; Peninsula: Poems of the Dingle Peninsula, 1992; Selected Poems, 1992; Snapdragon, 1992; In the Holocaust of Autumn, 1994; Poems for Eimear (sequence), 1994; Poems, 1995; Famine, 1997; Elegies, 1996; Music, 2000; Bronze Horseman: Revaluations, 2009. EDITOR: (with M. Hartnett) Choice: An Anthology of Irish Poetry Selected by the Poets Themselves with a Comment on their Choice, 1973, 2nd ed., 1979; James McKenna: A Celebration, 2002. TRANSLATOR: Medea, Euripides, 1991; Sophocles: Philoctetes, 1998. OTHERS: Terre et paix, 1988; The Death of Metaphor: Collected Prose, 1990; Desmond Egan, 1992; Prelude, 1999; The Hill of Allen, 2001; Outdoor Light: A Sequence In Memory of James McKenna, 2005; (with N. Hoare) James McKenna: A

Catalogue, 2005; Athlone, Athlone, 2010. Works appear in anthologies. Contributor to magazines. **Address:** Great Connell, Newbridge, KL 4, Ireland.

EGAN, Ferol. American (born United States), b. 1923. **Genres:** Novels, History, Biography, Military/Defense/Arms Control, Travel/Exploration. **Career:** Teacher of English, 1948-49, 1952-53; Yuba College, instructor in English, 1950-51; Stockton College, instructor in English and history, 1953-55; California College of Arts and Crafts, associate professor of humanities, 1956-61; University of California, science writer (biology), 1961-65; Imagery: American Journal of Cinematic Art, film critic, 1961-63; The American West, associate editor, 1970-72, contributing editor, 1972-; University of San Francisco, The Fromm Institute, professor of humanities, 1982-91. **Publications:** The El Dorado Trail: The Story of the Gold Rush Routes Across Mexico, 1970; Sand in a Whirlwind: The Paiute Indian War of 1860, 1972; Frémont: Explorer for a Restless Nation, 1977; The Taste of Time, 1977; Last Bonanza Kings: The Bourns of San Francisco, 1998. EDITOR: Incidents of Travel in New Mexico, 1969; A Sailor's Sketch of the Sacramento Valley in 1842, 1971; California, Land of Gold, or, Stay At Home and Work Hard, 1971; A Dangerous Journey, 1972; Overland Journey to Carson Valley and California, 1973; Across the Rockies with Fremont, 1975; (and intro.) With Frémont to California and the Southwest 1845-1849, 1975. Contributor of articles to newspapers. **Address:** 1199 Grizzly Peak Blvd., Berkeley, CA 94708-2149, U.S.A.

EGAN, Greg. Australian (born Australia), b. 1961. **Genres:** Novels, Novellas/Short Stories, Science Fiction/Fantasy, Young Adult Fiction. **Career:** Writer and computer programmer. **Publications:** NOVELS: An Unusual Angle, 1983; Quarantine, 1992; Permutation City, 1994; Distress, 1995; Diaspora, 1997; Teranesia, 1999; Schild's Ladder, 2002; Incandescence, 2008; Zendegi, 2010; Orthogonal, 2011. SHORT STORIES: Our Lady of Chernoble, 1995; Axiomatic, 1997; Luminous, 1998; Oceanic and Other Stories, 2000; Reasons to be Cheerful and Other Stories, 2003; Oceánico, 2005; Singleton and Other Stories, 2006; TAP and Other Stories, 2008; Dark Integers and Other Stories, 2008; Oceanic, 2009; Crystal Nights and Other Stories, 2009. Contributor of short stories to magazines. **Address:** c/o Peter Robinson, Curtis Brown Ltd., Haymarket House, 28-29 Haymarket, London, GL SW1Y 4SP, England. **Online address:** gregegan@netspace.net.au

EGAN, Jennifer. American (born United States), b. 1962. **Genres:** Novels, Novellas/Short Stories, Literary Criticism And History. **Career:** Freelance writer and journalist, 1991-. **Publications:** The Invisible Circus (novel), 1995; Emerald City and Other Stories (short stories), 1996; Look at Me (novel), 2001; The Keep, 2006; Visit From the Goon Squad, 2010. Contributor to periodicals. Works appear in anthologies. **Address:** c/o Amanda Urban, ICM, 40 W 57th St., 17th Fl., New York, NY 10019, U.S.A. **Online address:** jegan8@hotmail.com

EGAN, Ken. American (born United States), b. 1956. **Genres:** inspirational/Motivational Literature. **Career:** Middlebury College, visiting assistant professor of American literature, 1984-85; Rocky Mountain College, assistant professor, associate professor, professor of English, 1985-2002, faculty, 1995-96, Division of Arts and Humanities, chair, 1995-96, 2000-01; University of Athens, Fulbright lecturer, 1992; Comenius University, Fulbright lecturer, 1999; Drury University, professor of English and department chair, 2002-08. Writer. **Publications:** The Riven Home: Narrative Rivalry in the American Renaissance, 1997; (co-ed.) Writers under the Rims: A Yellowstone County Anthology, 2001; Hope and Dread in Montana Literature, 2003. Contributor to books. **Address:** Humanties Montana, 311 Brantly, Missoula, MT 59812, U.S.A. **Online address:** kegan@drury.edu

EGAN, Kieran. Canadian/Irish (born Ireland), b. 1942. **Genres:** Education, Literary Criticism And History, Reference. **Career:** Simon Fraser University, professor of education, 1972-; Government of Canada, CRC Secretariat, Canada research chair in education, 2001-08. Writer. **Publications:** The Tudor Peace, 1969; Structural Communication, 1976; Educational Development, 1979 as (intro. and foreword) Individual Development and the Curriculum, 1986; (with D.A. Nyberg) The Erosion of Education: Socialization and the Schools, 1981; Education and Psychology: Plato, Piaget and Scientific Psychology, 1983; Teaching as Story Telling: An Alternative Approach to Teaching and Curriculam in the Elementary School, 1986; Primary Understanding: Education in Early Childhood, 1988; Romantic Understanding: The Development of Rationality and Imagination, Ages Eight through Fifteen, 1990; Imagination in Teaching and Learning: The Middle School Years, 1992; The Educated Mind: How Cognitive Tools Shape Our Understanding, 1997; Children's Minds, Talking Rabbits and Clockwork Oranges: Essays on Education, 1999; Building My Zen Garden, 2000; Getting it Wrong from the Beginning: Our Progressivist Inheritance from Herbert Spencer, John Dewey and Jean Piaget, 2002; Imaginative Approach to Teaching, 2005; Teaching Literacy: Engaging the Imagination of New Readers and Writers, 2006; Future of Education: Reimagining our Schools from the Ground Up, 2008; Learning in Depth: A Simple Innovation that can Transform Schooling, 2010. EDITOR: (with K.A. Strike) Ethics and Educational Policy, 1978; (with S. de Castell and A. Luke) Literacy, Society and Schooling, 1986; (with D. Nadaner) Imagination and Education, 1988; (with H. McEwan) Narrative in Teaching, Learning and Research, 1995; (with M. Stout and K. Takaya) Teaching and Learning Outside the Box: Inspiring Imagination Across the Curriculum, 2007; (with K. Madej) Engaging Imagination and Developing Creativity in Education, 2010. **Address:** Department of Education, Simon Fraser University, 8888 University Dr., Burnaby, BC V5A 1S6, Canada. **Online address:** kieran_egan@sfu.ca

EGAN, Linda. American (born United States), b. 1945. **Genres:** Literary Criticism And History. **Career:** Spanish teacher, 1970-78; Santa Barbara City College, lecturer, 1974-83, instructor in Spanish and chair of journalism department, 1988-90; Santa Barbara News-Press, reporter, 1980-82, editorial page editor, 1983-88; Los Rios Community College District, public information manager, 1982-83; University of California, Department of Spanish and Portuguese, associate professor of Spanish, 1993-. **Publications:** Diosas, Demonios y Debate: Las Armas Metafísicas de Sor Juana, 1997; Carlos Monsiváis: Culture and Chronicle in Contemporary Mexico, 2001; (ed. with M.K. Long) Mexico Reading the United States, 2009. Contributor of articles to books and periodicals. **Address:** Department of Spanish and Portuguese, University of California, 707 Sproul Hall, 1 Shields Ave., Davis, CA 95616, U.S.A. **Online address:** ldegan@ucdavis.edu

EGAN, Ronald. (Ronald C. Egan). American (born United States), b. 1948. **Genres:** Literary Criticism And History, Translations. **Career:** Harvard University, faculty; Wellesley College, faculty; University of California, professor. Writer. **Publications:** The Literary Works of Ou-yang Hsiu (1007-72), 1984; Word, Image, and Deed in the Life of Su Shi, 1994; (ed. and trans.) Qian Zhongshu, Limited Views: Essays on Ideas and Letters, 1998; The Problem of Beauty: Aesthetic Thought and Pursuits in Northern Song Dynasty China, 2006. Contributor to journals. **Address:** Dept of East Asian Languages & Cultural Studies, University of California, Santa Barbara, CA 93106-9670, U.S.A. **Online address:** ronegan@eastasian.ucsb.edu

EGAN, Ronald C. See **EGAN, Ronald.**

EGAN, Tim. American (born United States), b. 1957. **Genres:** Children's Fiction, Illustrations, Humor/Satire. **Career:** Egan Design, art director; Recycled Paper Greetings, writer and illustrator. **Publications:** Friday Night at Hodges' Café, 1994; Chestnut Cove, 1995; Mile from Ellington Station, 2001; Serious Farm, 2003; Trial of Cardigan Jones, 2004; Roasted Peanuts, 2006. SELF-ILLUSTRATED FOR CHILDREN: Metropolitan Cow, 1996; Burnt Toast on Davenport Street, 1997; Distant Feathers, 1998; Blunder of the Rogues, 1999; Experiments of Doctor Vermin, 2002; Dodsworth in New York, 2007; Pink Refrigerator, 2007; Dodsworth in Paris, 2008; Dodsworth in London, 2009; Dodsworth in Rome, 2011. **Address:** 7453 Jordan Ave., Canoga Park, CA 91303, U.S.A. **Online address:** eganstudio@sbcglobal.com

EGAN, Timothy. American (born United States), b. 1954. **Genres:** Criminology/True Crime, Travel/Exploration, Young Adult Non-fiction, History. **Career:** New York Times, chief of seattle bureau, 1987-2008, correspondent, 1987-, national enterprise reporter. Writer. **Publications:** NONFICTION: Seattle, 1986; The Good Rain: Across Time and Terrain in the Pacific Northwest, 1990; Breaking Blue, 1992; Lasso the Wind: Away to the New West, 1998; Winemaker's Daughter: A Novel, 2004; Wild Seattle: A Celebration of the Natural Areas in and Around the City, 2004; Worst Hard Time: The Untold Story of Those who Survived the Great American Dust Bowl, 2006; (intro.) The photographs of Ben Shahn, 2008; Big Burn: Teddy Roosevelt and the Fire that Saved America, 2009. Contributor to periodicals. **Address:** New York Times, 220 30th Ave., PO Box 18375, Seattle, WA 98122, U.S.A.

EGBUNA, Obi (Benedict). American/Nigerian (born Nigeria), b. 1938. **Genres:** Novels, Plays/Screenplays, Race Relations, Novellas/Short Stories, Essays, Theology/Religion. **Career:** Bishop Shanahan College, teacher, 1955-56; Beaver College, teacher, 1967; ECBS TV, writer-in-residence

and director, 1973-76; University of Iowa, honorary fellow, 1976; Howard University, Department of African Studies, teacher, 1979-81, Department of German-Russian Studies, teacher, 1981-86, writer-in-residence, 1987; Pan-African Liberation Organization, founding member, 1991-. Essayist, critic, novelist and playwright. **Publications:** Wind Versus Polygamy (novel), 1964 as Elina, 1978; The Anthill, 1965; The Wind; The Murder of Nigeria, 1968; Daughters of the Sun and Other Stories, 1970; Destroy This Temple, 1971; Menace of the Hedgehog, 1973; The ABC of Black Power Thought, 1973; Emperor of the Sea and Other Stories, 1974; The Minister's Daughter (novel), 1975; Dem Say; Diary of a Homeless Prodigal (essays), 1976; The Hoe; Divinity; Black Candle for Christmas (short story), 1980; The Rape of Lysistrata (novel), 1980; The Madness of Didi (novel), 1980; The Dialectical Process in Modern African Literature: A Study in the Epistemology of Decolonization, 1986. **Address:** 3636 16th St. NW, Apt. B705, Washington, DC 20010, U.S.A.

EGELAND, Jan. Norwegian (born Norway), b. 1957. **Genres:** Politics/Government, Military/Defense/Arms Control. **Career:** Amnesty International, chairperson; Amnesty International, vice chairperson of the international executive committee; Norwegian Ministry of Foreign Affairs, secretary of state, 1990-97; United Nations, secretary-general's special advisor on Colombia, 1999-2002; Norwegian Red Cross, secretary general, 2002-03; United Nations, undersecretary-general for humanitarian affairs & emergency relief coordinator, 2003-06; Norwegian Institute of International Affairs, director, 2007; United Nations, secretary-general's special adviser on conflict, 2007. Writer. **Publications:** Humanitarian Initiative against Political "Disappearances": A Study of the Status and Potential of International Humanitarian and Human Rights Instruments, and the Role of the International Committee of the Red Cross, in Protecting against the Practice of Enforced or Involuntary "Disappearances,", 1982; Impotent Superpower'Potent Small State: Potentials and Limitations of Human Rights Objectives in the Foreign Policies of the United States and Norway, 1985; Menneskerettighetene Etter Revolusjonen: Nicaragua 1986, 1986; Third World Organizational Development: A Comparison of NGO Strategies, 1987; Det Nytter: Rapport Fra Frontlinjene, 2007; A Billion Lives: An Eyewitness Report from the Frontlines of Humanity, 2008. **Address:** Norwegian Institute of International Affairs, C.J. Hambros plass 2D, Pb. 8159 Dep, Oslo, 0033, Norway.

EGERTON, Douglas R. American (born United States), b. 1956. **Genres:** History, Essays. **Career:** Le Moyne College, associate professor, professor of history. Writer and historian. **Publications:** Charles Fenton Mercer and the Trial of National Conservatism, 1989; Gabriel's Rebellion: The Virginia Slave Conspiracies of 1800 and 1802, 1993; He Shall Go Out Free: The Lives of Denmark Vesey, 1999, rev. ed., 2004; Rebels, Reformers, & Revolutionaries: Collected Essays and Second Thoughts, 2002; (co-author) The Atlantic World: A History, 1400-1888, 2007; Death or Liberty: African Americans and Revolutionary America, 2009. Contributor to periodicals. **Address:** Department of History, Le Moyne College, 1419 Salt Springs Rd., Syracuse, NY 13214, U.S.A. **Online address:** egertodr@lemoyne.edu

EGGERS, Kerry. American (born United States), b. 1953. **Genres:** Sports/Fitness, Biography, Autobiography/Memoirs. **Career:** Oregonian, sports writer, 1975-2000; Portland Tribune, sportswriter, 2001-, sports columnist and sports reporter. **Publications:** Blazers Profiles, 1991; Against the World, 1992; Wherever You May Be: The Bill Schonely Story, 1999; (with C. Drexler) Clyde the Glide, 2004. **Address:** Portland Tribune, 6605 SE Lake Rd., Portland, OR 97222, U.S.A. **Online address:** keggers@portlandtribune.com

EGGINTON, Joyce. American/British (born England) **Genres:** Documentaries/Reportage, Criminology/True Crime, Politics/Government, History, Horror. **Career:** The Observer, New York correspondent, 1964-84; New York University, Graduate School of Journalism, adjunct professor of journalism, 1986-90. Full-time writer. **Publications:** Excursion to Russia, 1955; They Seek a Living, 1957; The Poisoning of Michigan, 1980, 2nd ed., 2009 in UK as Bitter Harvest, 1980; From Cradle to Grave: The Short Lives and Strange Deaths of Marybeth Tinning's Nine Children, 1989; Day of Fury: The Story of the Tragic Shootings That Forever Changed the Village of Winnetka, 1991 as Too Beautiful a Day to Die, 1992; Circle of Fire: Murder and Betrayal in the Swiss Nanny Case, 1994. Contributor of articles to periodicals. **Address:** Michigan State University Press, Manly Miles Bldg., 1405 S Harrison Rd., Ste. 25, East Lansing, MI 48823-5245, U.S.A. **Online address:** rejoyce@bigplanet.com

EGGINTON, William. American (born United States), b. 1969. **Genres:** Politics/Government. **Career:** Dartmouth College, assistant teacher of Spanish and French, 1988-91, Composition Center Writing, assistant, 1990-91; Centro Cooperativo de Idiomas, instructor in English, 1991-92; University of Minnesota, teaching assistant, 1992-94; Stanford University, teaching assistant, 1994-97, Writing and Critical Thinking, instructor, 1998-99; State University of New York, assistant professor, 1999-2004, associate professor of Romance languages and literatures, 2004-; Johns Hopkins University, professor of German and romance languages and literatures, 2006-, Graduate Studies, Spanish and Latin American Literature Section, director, 2006, Standing Committee on Study Abroad, chair, 2008, Department of German and Romance Languages and Literatures, chair, 2009-, Andrew W. Mellon professor in the humanities, 2010-. Writer. **Publications:** How the World Became a Stage: Presence, Theatricality, and the Question of Modernity, 2003; (trans.) Borges: The Passion of an Endless Quotation, 2003; (ed. with M. Sandbothe) The Pragmatic Turn in Philosophy: Contemporary Engagements between Analytic and Continental Thought, 2004; Perversity and Ethics, 2006; The Philosopher's Desire: Psychoanalysis, Interpretation, and Truth, 2007; A Wrinkle in History: Essays on Literature and Philosophy, 2007; (ed. with D.E. Johnson) Thinking with Borges, 2009; Theater of Truth: The Ideology of (Neo) Baroque Aesthetics, 2010; In Defense of Religious Moderation, 2011. **Address:** Department of German and Romance Languages, and Literatures, John Hopkins University, 470 Gilman Hall, 3400 N Charles St., Baltimore, MD 21218, U.S.A. **Online address:** egginton@jhu.edu

EGGLESTON, Larry G. American (born United States), b. 1937. **Genres:** Social Sciences, History, Military/Defense/Arms Control. **Career:** U.S. Department of Defense, contract specialist, contract negotiator, contracting officer, 1967-97; writer, 1997-. Historian. **Publications:** Getting Started in Government Contracting, 1998; Women in the Civil War: Extraordinary Stories of Soldiers, Spies, Nurses, Doctors, Crusaders, and Others, 2003; Porter County Lakes and Resorts, 2004. Contributor to periodicals. **Address:** Wanatah Historical Museum Society, 106 Sprunger Dr., Wanatah, IN 46390, U.S.A. **Online address:** leggleston@juno.com

EGIELSKI, Richard. American (born United States), b. 1952. **Genres:** Children's Fiction, Mythology/Folklore. **Career:** Illustrator, 1973-. Writer. **Publications:** SELF-ILLUSTRATED: Buz, 1995; The Gingerbread Boy, 1997; Jazper, 1998; Three magic Balls, 2000; Slim and Jim, 2001; Saint Francis and the Wolf, 2005; Captain Sky Blue, 2010; Sleepless Little Vampire. Illustrator of books by others. **Address:** 27 Amsterdam Rd., Milford, NJ 08848-1724, U.S.A. **Online address:** richard@richardegielski.com

EGLER, Claudio A. G. Brazilian (born Brazil), b. 1951. **Genres:** Economics, Technology, Geography, Education. **Career:** Federal University of Paraiba, professor of economic geography, 1978-87; Federal University of Rio de Janeiro, professor of economic geography, 1987-, deputy chief of department of geography; National Council of Technological and Scientific Development, consultant; Inter-American Institute for Agricultural Cooperation; Universidade Federal do Rio de Janeiro, Department of Geography, associate professor; Ecole Normale Superieure, visiting professor; Université de Lyon, visiting professor; Universite de Paris, visiting professor. Writer and consultant. **Publications:** (Co-author) Geographie et Ecologie de la Paraiba, 1980; (with B.K. Becker) Brazil: A New Regional Power in the World Economy, 1992; (co-author) Innovation Technogiques et Mutations Industrielles en Amerique Latine, 1993; (co-author) Redescobrindo o Brasil: 500 anos depois, 1998; (with O. de Carvalho) Alternativas de desenvolvimento para o Nordeste Semi-arido, 2003; (co-author) Expansão da Soja na pré-Amazônia Mato-grossense: Impactos Socioambientais, 2007. **Address:** Department of Geography, Federal University of Rio de Janeiro, Cidade Universitaria, Ilha do Fundao, Rio de Janeiro, 21941-590, Brazil. **Online address:** egler@ufrj.br

EGLI, Ida Rae. American (born United States), b. 1946. **Genres:** Literary Criticism And History, Adult Non-fiction, Novellas/Short Stories, Women's Studies And Issues, Military/Defense/Arms Control, Young Adult Fiction. **Career:** Santa Rosa Junior College, Department of English, instructor in English, 1985-, chair. Writer. **Publications:** (Ed.) No Rooms of Their Own: Women Writers of Early California, 1991; (ed. and intro.) Women of the Gold Rush: The New Penelope and Other Stories, 1998; Micra Poulakia: Little Birds, A Collection of Contemporary Greek Stories, 2003; Echoes from a Grecian Urn: A Tale of Women in War, 2006; Of Wisdom and War: Women

Trapped in Hitler's Greece, 2008. Contributor of articles to periodicals. **Address:** PO Box 125, The Sea Ranch, CA 95497-0125, U.S.A. **Online address:** info@idaraeegli.com

EGNAL, Marc. Canadian/American (born United States), b. 1943. **Genres:** History, Economics. **Career:** University of Wisconsin, teaching assistant, 1966-68; York University, lecturer, 1970-73, assistant professor, 1973-76, associate professor, 1976-97, professor of history, 1998-. Writer, historian, consultant and commentator. **Publications:** A Mighty Empire: The Origins of the American Revolution, 1988; Divergent Paths: How Culture and Institutions Have Shaped North American Growth, 1996; New World Economies: The Growth of the Thirteen Colonies and Early Canada, 1998; Clash of Extremes: The Economic Origins of the Civil War, 2009. Contributor to books, periodicals, newspapers and journals. **Address:** Department of History, York University, 2138 Vari Hall, 4700 Keele St., Toronto, ON M3J 1P3, Canada.

EHLE, John. American (born United States), b. 1925. **Genres:** Novels, Biography, Plays/Screenplays, History, Race Relations, Autobiography/Memoirs. **Career:** University of North Carolina, faculty, 1951-63, Communications Center, associate professor, 1952-65; New York University, visiting associate professor, 1957-58; Terry Sanford of North Carolina, special assistant, 1963-64; Ford Foundation, program officer, 1964-65; White House Group for Domestic Affairs, advisor, 1964-66. Writer. **Publications:** Move Over Mountain, 1957; The Survivor: The Story of Eddy Hukov, 1958; Kingstree Island, 1959; Shepherd of the Streets: The Story of the Reverend James A. Gusweller and His Crusade on the New York West Side, 1960; Lion on the Hearth, 1961; The Land Breakers, 1964; The Free Men, 1965; The Road, 1967; Time of Drums, 1970; The Journey of August King, 1971; The Cheeses and Wines of England and France, with Notes on Irish Whiskey, 1972; The Changing of the Guard: A Novel, 1974; The Winter People, 1982; Last One Home, 1984; Trail of Tears: The Rise and Fall of the Cherokee Nation, 1988; The Widow's Trial, 1989; Dr. Frank: Living with Frank Porter Graham, 1993. Contributor to periodicals. **Address:** 125 Westview Dr. NW, Winston-Salem, NC 27104, U.S.A.

EHLERT, Lois (Jane). American (born United States), b. 1934. **Genres:** Children's Fiction, Illustrations, Picture/Board Books. **Career:** Layton School of Art Junior School, teacher; John Higgs Studio, layout and production assistant; Jacobs-Keelan Studio, layout and design illustrator; freelance illustrator and designer, 1962-. Writer. **Publications:** SELF-ILLUSTRATED FOR CHILDREN: Growing Vegetable Soup, 1987; Planting a Rainbow, 1988; Color Zoo, 1989; Eating the Alphabet: Fruits and Vegetables from A to Z, 1989; Color Farm, 1990; Feathers for Lunch, 1990; Fish Eyes: A Book You Can Count On, 1990; Red Leaf, Yellow Leaf, 1991; Circus, 1992; Moon Rope: A Peruvian Folktale/Un lazo a la luna: una layenda peruana, 1992; Nuts to You!, 1993; Mole's Hill: A Woodland Tale, 1994; Snowballs, 1995; Under My Nose, 1996; Cuckoo: A Mexican Folktale/Cucu: Un cuento folklorico mexicano, 1997; Hands, 1997; Top Cat, 1998; Market Day: A Story Told with Folk Art, 2000; Waiting for Wings, 2001; In My World, 2002; Pie in the Sky, 2004; Leaf Man, 2005; Eating the Alphabet: Fruits and Vegetables from A to Z, 2006; Wag a Tail, 2007; Oodles of Animals, 2008; Boo to You!, 2009; Lots of Spots, 2010; Rrralph, 2011. **Address:** Children's Books, Harcourt Brace Inc., 525 B St., Ste. 1900, San Diego, CA 92101, U.S.A.

EHRENBERG, John. American (born United States), b. 1944. **Genres:** Politics/Government, History. **Career:** University of New Mexico, assistant professor of political science, 1972-77; St. John's University, assistant professor of political science, 1977-80; Long Island University, Department of Political Science, associate professor, 1980-85, professor of political science, 1985-, senior professor of political science, chair, Brooklyn Campus Faculty Senate, chair. Writer. **Publications:** The Dictatorship of the Proletariat: Marxism's Theory of Socialist Democracy, 1992; Proudhon and His Age, 1996; Civil Society: The Critical History of an Idea, 1999; Servants of Wealth: The Right's Assault on Economic Justice, 2006; (co-ed.) The Iraq Papers, 2010. Contributor of articles to journals. **Address:** Department of Political Science, Brooklyn Campus, Long Island University, H843, 1 University Plz., Brooklyn, NY 11201-8423, U.S.A. **Online address:** john.ehrenberg@liu.edu

EHRENBERG, Pamela. American (born United States), b. 1972?. **Genres:** Novels. **Career:** National Council for Accreditation of Teacher Education, consultant. Writer and educator. **Publications:** NOVELS: Ethan, Suspended, 2007; Tillmon County Fire, 2009. Contributor to periodicals. **Address:** Washington, DC , U.S.A. **Online address:** pmehrenberg@pamelaehrenberg.com

EHRENSPERGER, Kathy. Welsh (born Wales), b. 1956. **Genres:** Theology/Religion. **Career:** Swiss Reformed Church, minister, 1987; City Parish of Binningen-Bottmingen, senior minister and pastor, 1987-2004; University of Wales, School of Theology, Religious Studies and Islamic Studies, senior lecturer, program director for distance learning, Lampeter Center for Biblical Studies, director, 2004-. Writer. **Publications:** (Trans. with W. Stedman) K. Stendahl, Das Verm Achtnis des Paulus: Neues vom Romerbrief, 1996; That We May Be Mutually Encouraged: Feminism and the New Perspective in Pauline Studies, 2004; Paul and the Dynamics of Power: Communication and Interaction in the Early Christ-Movement, 2007; (ed. with J.B. Tucker) Reading Paul in Context: Explorations in Identity Formation, 2010. CONTRIBUTOR: Navigating Romans through Cultures: Challenging Readings by Charting a New Course, 2004; Romans: Shared Ground, Uncertain Borders, 2005; Reading Romans with Contemporary Philosophers and Theologians, 2007; Searching for Meaning: A Practical Guide to New Testament Interpretation, 2008. Contributor to periodicals and journals. **Address:** School of Theology, Religious Studies and, Islamic Studies, University of Wales, Sheikh Khalifa Bldg., Lampeter Campus, Ceredigion, SA48 7ED, Wales. **Online address:** k.ehrensperger@trinitysaintdavid.ac.uk

EHRET, Christopher. American (born United States), b. 1941. **Genres:** History, Language/Linguistics, Anthropology/Ethnology, Archaeology/Antiquities. **Career:** University of California, distinguished professor of history and linguistics. Writer. **Publications:** Southern Nilotic History: Linguistic Approaches to the Study of the Past, 1971; Ethiopians and East Africans: The Problem of Contacts, 1974; The Historical Reconstruction of Southern Cushitic Phonology and Vocabulary, 1980; (with M. Posnansky) The Archaeological and Linguistic Reconstruction of African History, 1982; Reconstructing Proto-Afroasiatic: Vowels, Tone, Consonants, and Vocabulary, 1995; An African Classical Age, 1998; A Historical-Comparative Reconstruction of Nilo-Saharan, 2001; The Civilizations of Africa: A History to 1800, 2002; Sudanic Civilization 2003; History and the Testimony of Language 2011. **Address:** Department of History, University of California, 7290 Bunche Hall, PO Box 951473, Los Angeles, CA 90095-1473, U.S.A. **Online address:** ehret@history.ucla.edu

EHRET, Terry. American (born United States), b. 1955. **Genres:** Poetry, Travel/Exploration. **Career:** Children's Health Council, tutor and researcher, 1975-77; High school teacher of English, psychology and art history, 1977, 1990; California Poets in the Schools, poet-teacher, 1990-; Santa Rosa Junior College, instructor in English, 1991-; Sonoma State University, lecturer in poetry, 1994-; San Francisco State University, lecturer, 1995-99; Sixteen Rivers Press, co-founder, 1999-. Writer. **Publications:** (With S. Gilmartin and S.H. Sibbet) Suspensions (poems), 1990; Lost Body (poems), 1992; Travel/How We Go on Living, 1995; Translations from the Human Language, 2001; Lucky Break, 2008; Night Sky Journey, 2011; Sleep Under Stone, forthcoming. Contributor to periodicals. **Address:** Santa Rosa Junior College, 680 Sonoma Mountain Pkwy., Petaluma, CA 94954-2522, U.S.A. **Online address:** terry@terryehret.com

EHRLER, Brenda. American (born United States), b. 1953. **Genres:** How-to Books, inspirational/Motivational Literature, Human Relations/Parenting, Self Help. **Career:** Williams Energy Services, budget and procedure assistant, 1991-93, budget and procedure specialist, 1993-96, senior coordination specialist, 1996-98; writer and motivational speaker, 1998-; Just Be Publishing Inc., owner. **Publications:** Learning to Be You: It's an Inside Job: Recovery and Healing for the Loved Ones of the Substance-Addicted, 1999. **Address:** Just Be Publishing Inc., PO Box 571176, Murray, UT 84157, U.S.A. **Online address:** bl_ehrler@att.net

EHRLICH, Amy. American (born United States), b. 1942. **Genres:** Children's Fiction, Young Adult Fiction, Young Adult Non-fiction, Biography, Autobiography/Memoirs, Literary Criticism And History. **Career:** Family Circle magazine, roving editor, 1975-77; Delacorte Press, senior editor, 1977-78; Dial Books for Young Readers, senior editor, 1978-82, executive editor, 1982-84; Candlewick Press, vice president, editor-in-chief, 1991-96, editor-at-large, 1996-; Ohio State University, Center for Continuing Medical Education, program specialist, 2005-, conference coordinator, program manager, Center for Personalized Health Care, program director. **Publications:** Zeek Silver Moon, 1972; (adapter) Wounded Knee: An Indian History of the American West, 1974; The Everyday Train, 1977; Leo, Zack and Emmie, 1981; Annie and the Kidnappers, 1982; Annie Finds a Home, 1982; Annie: The Storybook Based on the Movie, 1982; (adapter) Ewoks and the Lost Children, 1985; Bunnies All Day Long, 1985; (adapter) Random House Book of Fairy Tales, 1985; Bunnies on Their Own, 1986; Buck-Buck the Chicken, 1987; Leo, Zack and Emmie Together Again, 1987; Emma's New Pony, 1988; Where It Stops, Nobody Knows, 1988; The Story of Hanukkah, 1989; Lucy's Winter Tale, 1992; Parents in the Pigpen: Pigs in the Tub, 1993; The Dark Card, 1993; Maggie and Silky and Joe, 1994; Hurry Up, Mickey!, 1996; Kazam's Magic, 2001; Joyride, 2001, 2nd ed., 2008; Bravo, Kazam!, 2002; Rachel: The Story of Rachel Carson, 2003; Willa: The Story of Willa Cather, 2006; Baby Dragon, 2008; The Girl Who Wanted to Dance, 2009. RETELLER: Thumbelina, 1979, rev. ed., 2005; The Wild Swans, 1981; The Snow Queen, 1982, rev. ed., 2006; Cinderella, 1985; Rapunzel, 1989; Pome and Peel: A Venetian Tale, 1990; Wild Swans, 2008. OTHER: (ed. and intro.) When I Was Your Age: Original Stories about Growing Up, 1996, vol. II, 2003. **Address:** Center for Personalized Health Care, Ohio State University, 193V McCampbell Hall, 1581 Dodd Dr., Columbus, OH 43210, U.S.A. **Online address:** ehrlich.11@osu.edu

EHRLICH, Paul (Ralph). American (born United States), b. 1932. **Genres:** Biology, Environmental Sciences/Ecology. **Career:** Northern Insect Survey, field officer, 1951-52; University of Kansas, research assistant, 1952-54, associate investigator, 1956-57, research associate, 1957-59; Kansas University, fellow, 1954-66; Chicago Academy of Science, research associate, 1957-58; Stanford University, assistant professor, 1959-62, associate professor, 1962-66, professor of biological sciences, 1966-, director of biological science graduate study department, 1966-69, 1974-76, Bing professor of population studies, 1977-, Center for Conservation Biology, president; Behavioral Research Laboratories, consultant, 1963-67; McGraw-Hill Book Co., editor in population biology and consultant in biology, 1964-; University of Sydney, National Science Foundation fellow, 1965-66; Zero Population Growth, founder, 1969-70; National Broadcasting Co. (NBC), correspondent, 1989-92. Biologist. **Publications:** How to Know the Butterflies, 1961; (with R.W. Holm) The Process of Evolution, 1963, 2nd ed., 1974; (contrib.) Papers on Evolution, 1968; Principles of Modern Biology, 1968; The Population Bomb, 1968, rev. ed., 1975; (with R.L. Harriman) How to Be a Survivor, 1971; (commentary) Man and the Ecosphere, 1971; (ed. with J.P. Holdren) Global Ecology: Readings Toward a Rational Strategy for Man, 1971; (with A.H. Ehrlich and J.P. Holdren) Human Ecology: Problems and Solutions, 1973; (with R.W. Holm and M.E. Soulé) Introductory Biology, 1973; (with D.C. Pirages) Ark II: Social Response to Environmental Imperatives, 1973; (with R.W. Holm) Evolution, 1974; (co-author) Humanökologie: derMensch in Zentrum einer neuen Wissenschaft, 1975; (co-author) Biology and Society, 1976; Population, Resources, Environment Crisis: Where Do We Stand Now?, 1976; The Bomb, 1977; Ecoscience: Population, Resources, Environment, 1977; (with S.S. Feldman) The Race Bomb: Skin Color, Prejudice, and Intelligence, 1977; (co-author) Introduction to Insect Biology and Diversity, 1978; (co-author) Golden Door: International Migration, Mexico and the United States, 1979; (co-author) The Cold and the Dark: The World after Nuclear War, 1984; The Machinery of Nature, 1986; (with J. Roughgarden) The Science of Ecology, 1987; (ed. with J.P. Holdren) The Cassandra Conference: Resources and the Human Predicament, 1988; (co-author) The Birders Handbook: A Field Guide to the Natural History of North American Birds: Including all Species that Regularly Breed North of Mexico, 1988; (with R. Ornstein) New World, New Mind: Moving towards Conscious Evolution, 1989, rev. ed., 2000; (co-author) Birds in Jeopardy: The Imperiled and Extinct Birds of the United States and Canada including Hawaii and Puerto Rico, 1992; (co-ed.) Reconstruction of Fragmented Ecosystems: Global and Regional Perspectives, 1993; (co-author) The Birdwatchers Handbook: A Guide to the Natural History of the Birds of Britain and Europe: Including 516 Species that Regularly Breed in Europe and Adjacent Parts of the Middle East and North Africa, 1994; (co-author) The Stork and the Plow: The Equity Answer to the Human Dilemma, 1995; A World of Wounds, 1997; Human Natures: Genes, Cultures and the Human Prospect, 2000; (with A.Beattie) Wild Solutions: How Biodiversity is Money in the Bank, 2001; (co-ed.) Butterflies: Ecology and Evolution Taking Flight, 2003; (ed. with I. Hanski) On the Wings of Checkerspots: A Model System for Population Biology, 2004; (with R.E. Ornstein) Humanity on a Tightrope: Thoughts on Empathy, Family, and Big Changes for a Viable Future, 2010; (ed. with N.S. Sodhi) Conservation Biology for All, 2010. WITH A.H. EHRLICH: Population, Resources, Environment: Issues in Human Ecology, 1970, 2nd ed., 1972; The End of Affluence: A Blueprint for Your Future, 1974; Extinction: The Causes and Consequences of the Disappearance of Species, 1981; Earth, 1987; The Population Explosion, 1990; Healing the Planet: Strategies for Resolving the Environmental Crisis, 1991; Betrayal of Science and Reason: How Anti-Environmental Rhetoric Threatens Our Future, 1996; One with Nineveh: Politics, Consumption, and the Human Future, 2004; Dominant Animal: Human Evolution and the Environment, 2008. Contributor to books and periodicals. **Address:** Department of Biological Sciences, Stanford University, 409 Herrin, Gilbert Hall, PO Box 5020, Stanford, CA 94305-5020, U.S.A. **Online address:** pre@stanford.edu

EHRLICH, Tracy L. American (born United States), b. 1965. **Genres:** Adult Non-fiction, History, Architecture. **Career:** Dumbarton Oaks, junior fellow, 1993-94, fellow, 2000-01; Colgate University, assistant professor of art history; Columbia University, faculty; Vassar University, faculty; Rutgers University, faculty; Bard Graduate Center, faculty. Writer. **Publications:** Landscape and Identity in Early Modern Rome: Villa Culture at Frascati in the Borghese Era (nonfiction), 2002. **Address:** Department of Art History, Colgate University, 13 Oak Dr., Hamilton, NY 13346-1338, U.S.A.

EHRLICH, Uri. Israeli (born Israel), b. 1956. **Genres:** Theology/Religion, History. **Career:** Efrata Teachers College, lecturer, 1986-88; Shalom Hartman Institute for Advanced Jewish Studies, lecturer, 1987-91; David Yellin Teachers College, Department of History and Jewish Studies, lecturer, 1990-96; Ben-Gurion University, Department of History, assistant lecturer in Talmud and Jewish philosophy, 1993-95, lecturer, 1996-99, Goldstein-Goren Department of Jewish Thought, lecturer, 2000-01, senior lecturer, 2001-08, academic director, associate professor, 2009-; Israel Academy of Sciences and Humanities, Mifal Hatefila Project, director, 2003-. Writer. **Publications:** Darkhe ha-tefilah u-mashmáutan bi-teḳufat ha-Mishnah yeha-Talmud, 1993; Kol 'atsmotai Tomarnah, 1999. Contributor to journals. **Address:** Department of Jewish Thought, Ben-Gurion University, Rm. 552, Bldg. 72, PO Box 653, Beer-Sheva, 84105, Israel. **Online address:** ehrlich@bgu.ac.il

EHRMAN, Bart D. American (born United States), b. 1955. **Genres:** Theology/Religion, Adult Non-fiction. **Career:** Rutgers University, Department of Religion, lecturer at the rank of instructor, 1984-85, lecturer at the rank of assistant professor, 1985-88; Princeton Theological Seminary, instructor in New Testament Greek and exegesis, 1985; University of North Carolina, assistant professor, 1988-94, associate professor, 1994-99, director of graduate studies, 1996-99, Bowman and Gordon Gray professor, 1998-2001, professor of religious studies, 1999-, department chair, 2000-06, James A. Gray distinguished professor, 2003-; Duke University, visiting assistant professor, 1991, adjunct professor, 2000-. Writer. **Publications:** Didymus the Blind and the Text of the Gospels, 1986; (with G.D. Fee and M.W. Holmes) The Text of the Fourth Gospel in the Writings of Origen, 1992; The Orthodox Corruption of Scripture: The Effect of Early Christological Controversies on the Text of the New Testament, 1993; (ed. with M.W. Holmes) The Text of the New Testament in Contemporary Research: Essays on the Status Quaestionis, 1995; The New Testament: A Historical Introduction to the Early Christian Writings, 1997, 5th ed., 2012; The New Testament and Other Early Christian Writings: A Reader, 1998, 2nd ed., 2004; After the New Testament: A Reader in Early Christianity, 1999; Jesus, Apocalyptic Prophet of the New Millennium, 1999; Lost Christianities: The Battle for Scripture and the Faiths We Never Knew, 2003; (ed. and trans.) Apostolic Fathers, 2003; (ed.) Lost Scriptures: Books That Did Not Make it to the New Testament, 2003; Truth and Fiction in The Da Vinci Code: A Historian Reveals What We Really Know About Jesus, Mary Magdalene, and Constantine, 2004; Brief Introduction to the New Testament, 2004, 2nd ed., 2009; (with A.S. Jacobs) Christianity in Late Antiquity, 300-450 C.E.: A Reader, 2004; (with B.D. Ehrman) Text of the New Testament: Its Transmission, Corruption, and Restoration, 2005; Misquoting Jesus: The Story Behind Who Changed the Bible and Why, 2005; Studies in the Textual Criticism of the New Testament, 2006; Peter, Paul, and Mary Magdalene: The Followers of Jesus in History and Legend, 2006; The Lost Gospel of Judas Iscariot: Betrayer and Betrayed Reconsidered, 2006; God's Problem: How the Bible Fails to Answer Our Most Important Question-Why We Suffer, 2008; (contrib.) Gospel of Judas, 2008; Jesus, Interrupted: Revealing the Hidden Contradictions in the Bible (and Why We Don't Know about Them), 2009; Brief Introduction to the New Testament, 2009; (with D.B. Wallace) Reliability of the New Testament, 2011; Orthodox Corruption of Scripture: The Effect of Early Christological Controversies on the Text of the New Testament, 2011; Forged: Writing in the Name of God: Why the Bible's Authors are Not Who We Think They Are, 2011; (with Z. Plese) Apocryphal Gospels, 2011. **Address:** Department of Religious Studies, University of North Carolina, Saunders 117, PO Box 3225, Chapel Hill, NC 27599, U.S.A. **Online address:** behrman@email.unc.edu

EHRMAN, John. American (born United States), b. 1959. **Genres:** Politics/

Government, History, Humanities. **Career:** George Washington University, lecturer in history, 1992-. Writer. **Publications:** The Rise of Neoconservatism: Intellectuals and Foreign Affairs, 1945-1994, 1995; Eighties: America in the Age of Reagan, 2005; (with M.W. Flamm) Debating the Reagan Presidency, 2009. Contributor to periodicals. **Address:** c/o Carl Brandt, Brandt & Hochman Literary Agents Inc., 1501 Broadway, New York, NY 10036-5601, U.S.A.

EICHENGREEN, Barry J. American (born United States), b. 1952. **Genres:** Economics, Business/Trade/Industry. **Career:** Harvard University, assistant professor, associate professor, 1980-86; National Bureau of Economic Research, faculty research fellow, 1981-86, research associate, 1986-; Centre for Economic Policy Research, research fellow, 1984-; University of California, professor of economics, 1986-94, John L. Simpson professor of economics and professor of political science, 1994-99, George C. Pardee and Helen N. Pardee professor of economics and professor of political science, 1999-; International Monetary Fund, senior policy advisor, 1997-98; Kiel Institute of World Economics, international research fellow, 2001-. Writer. **Publications:** Sterling and the Tariff, 1929-32, 1981; (with A. Cairncross) Sterling in Decline: The Devaluations of 1931, 1949, and 1967, 1983, 2nd ed., 2003; (ed.) The Gold Standard in Theory and History, 1985; The Australian Recovery of the 1930s in International Comparative Perspective, 1985; (ed. with T.J. Hatton) Interwar Unemployment in International Perspective, 1988; (ed. with P.H. Lindert) The International Debt Crisis in Historical Perspective, 1989; (with R. Portes) Dealing with Debt: The 1930s and the 1980s, 1989; Elusive Stability: Essays in the History of International Finance, 1919-1939, 1990; (ed. with E. Aerts) Unemployment and Underemployment in Historical Perspective: Session B-9: Proceedings, Tenth International Economic History Congress, Leuven, August 1990, 1990; (ed.) Monetary Regime Transformations, 1992; (with T. Bayoumi) Shocking Aspects of European Monetary Unification, 1992; European Monetary Unification and the Regional Unemployment Problem, 1992; Golden Fetters: The Gold Standard and the Great Depression, 1919-1939, 1992; Should the Maastricht Treaty Be Saved?, 1992; (ed. with L. Ulman and W.T. Dickens) Labor and an Integrated Europe, 1993; (ed. with M.D. Bordo) A Retrospective on the Bretton Woods System: Lessons for International Monetary Reform, 1993; Reconstructing Europe's Trade and Payments: The European Payments Union, 1993; (ed. with J. Frieden) The Political Economy of European Monetary Unification, 1994, 2nd ed., 2001; (with T. Bayoumi) One Money or Many? Analyzing the Prospects for Monetary Unification in Various Parts of the World, 1994; Financing Infrastructure in Developing Countries: Lessons from the Railway Age, 1994; International Monetary Arrangements for the 21st Century, 1994; (ed.) Europe's Post-war Recovery, 1995; (ed. with J. Frieden and J. von Hagen) Monetary and Fiscal Policy in an Integrated Europe, 1995; (ed. with J. Frieden and J. von Hagen) Politics and Institutions in an Integrated Europe, 1995; (ed. with J.B. de Macedo and J. Reis) Currency Convertibility: The Gold Standard and Beyond, 1996; (co-ed.) Modern Perspectives on the Gold Standard, 1996; (ed.) The Reconstruction of the International Economy, 1945-1960, 1996; (with A. Fishlow) Contending with Capital Flows: What is Different about the 1990s?, 1996; Globalizing Capital: A History of the International Monetary System, 1996, 2nd ed., 2008; A More Perfect Union? The Logic of Economic Integration, 1996; European Monetary Unification: Theory, Practice, and Analysis, 1997; (co-author) Capital Account Liberalization: Theoretical and Practical Aspects, 1998; (co-author) Exit Strategies: Policy Options for Countries Seeking Greater Exchange Rate Flexibility, 1998; (ed. with J. Frieden) Forging an Integrated Europe, 1998; (co-author) Hedge Funds and Financial Market Dynamics, 1998; (ed.) Transatlantic Economic Relations in the Post-Cold War Era, 1998; (co-author) Transition Strategies and Nominal Anchors on the Road to Greater Exchange-Rate Flexibility, 1999; (with A. Mody) Lending Booms, Reserves, and the Sustainability of Short-Term Debts: Inferences from the Pricing of Syndicated Bank Loans, 1999; Toward a New International Financial Architecture: A Practical Post-Asia Agenda, 1999; Capitalizing on Globalization, 2002; Financial Crises: And What to Do about Them, 2002; Capital Flows and Crises, 2003; (ed. with D. Chung) The Korean Economy beyond the Crisis, 2004; Financial Development in Asia: The Way Forward, 2004; (ed. with R. Hausmann) Other People's Money: Debt Denomination and Financial Instability in Emerging Market Economies, 2005; (ed. with D. Chung) Toward an East Asian Exchange Rate Regime, 2007; The European Economy Since 1945: Coordinated Capitalism and Beyond, 2007; Global Imbalances and the Lessons of Bretton Woods, 2007; (ed. with C. Wyplosz and Y.C. Park) China, Asia, and the New World Economy, 2008; (ed. with C. Brown and M. Reich) Labor in the Era of Globalization, 2009; (with P. Gupta) The Two Waves of Service-sector

Growth, 2009; (ed. with D. Chung) Fostering Monetary & Financial Cooperation in East Asia, 2009; (with P. Gupta) The Service Sector as India's Road to Economic Growth?, 2010; (ed. with P. Gupta and R. Kumar) Emerging Giants: China and India in the World Economy, 2010; Exorbitant Privilege: The Decline of the Dollar and the Future of the International Monetary System, 2011. Contributor of articles to journals. **Address:** Department of Economics, University of California, 508-1 Evans Hall, PO Box 3880, Berkeley, CA 94720-3880, U.S.A. **Online address:** eichengr@econ.berkeley.edu

EICHLER, Selma. American (born United States) **Genres:** Mystery/Crime/Suspense, Novels, Young Adult Fiction. **Career:** Writer. **Publications:** DESIREE SHAPIRO MYSERY NOVELS: Murder Can Kill Your Social Life, 1994; Murder Can Ruin Your Looks, 1995; Murder Can Stunt Your Growth, 1996; Murder Can Wreck Your Reunion, 1997; Murder Can Spook Your Cat, 1998; Murder Can Singe Your Old Flame, 1999; Murder Can Spoil Your Appetite, 2000; Murder Can Upset Your Mother, 2001; Murder Can Cool Off Your Affair, 2002; Murder Can Rain on Your Shower, 2003; Murder Can Botch Up Your Birthday, 2004; Murder Can Mess Up Your Mascara, 2005; Murder Can Run Your Stockings, 2006; Murder Can Depress your Dachshund, 2007; Murder Can Crash Your Party, 2008. **Address:** c/o Stuart Krichevsky, Stuart Krichevsky Literary Agency Inc., 381 Park Ave. S, Ste. 428, New York, NY 10016, U.S.A. **Online address:** selma@selmaeichlerbooks.com

EICHORN, Rosemary D. American (born United States), b. 1943. **Genres:** Architecture, Design. **Career:** Educator and writer. **Publications:** The Art of Fabric Collage: An Easy Introduction to Creative Sewing, 2000. **Address:** c/o Author Mail, Taunton Press, 63 S Main St., PO Box 5506, Newtown, CT 06470-2355, U.S.A. **Online address:** rosemary@sewjourn.com

EICHSTAEDT, Peter H. American (born United States), b. 1947. **Genres:** History. **Career:** Institute for War and Peace Reporting (IWPR), Africa editor and news advisor; Santa Fe New Mexican, reporter. Journalist. **Publications:** If You Poison Us: Uranium and Native Americans, 1994; First Kill Your Family: Child Soldiers of Uganda and the Lord's Resistance Army, 2009. **Address:** Denver, CO , U.S.A. **Online address:** peter.eich@gmail.com

EICKHOFF, Diane. American (born United States) **Genres:** Biography, Social Sciences, Young Adult Non-fiction. **Career:** Editor and educator. **Publications:** Revolutionary Heart: The Life of Clarina Nichols and the Pioneering Crusade for Women's Rights, 2006. **Address:** Kansas City, MO , U.S.A. **Online address:** dequindaro@gmail.com

EICKHOFF, Randy Lee. American (born United States), b. 1945. **Genres:** Novels, Theatre, Young Adult Non-fiction, History. **Career:** Lincoln Star, reporter, columnist and journalist; University of Texas, English Graduate School, faculty. **Publications:** NOVELS: A Hand to Execute, 1987; The Gombeen Man, 1992; The Fourth Horseman, 1998; (with L.C. Lewis) Bowie, 1998; Fallon's Wake, 2000; Return to Ithaca: A Confessional Novel, 2001; The Destruction of the Inn, 2001; Then Came Christmas, 2002; He Stands Alone, 2002; And Not to Yield: A Novel of the Life and Times of Wild Bill Hickok, 2004; Quick and the Dead, 2005; Bill, forthcoming; Vietnam War, forthcoming. ULSTER CYCLE SERIES: The Raid, 1997; The Feast, 1999; The Sorrows, 2000; The Red Branch Tales, 2003; Beowulf, forthcoming. OTHER: Exiled: The Tigua Indians of Ysleta del Sur (nonfiction), 1996; (as R.L. Eickhoff) The Odyssey: A Modern Translation of Homer's Classic Tale, 2001; The Death Tales, 2004; Falstaff: A Comic Foil to Bolinbroke and The American Canon. Contributor to journals. **Address:** c/o Jacques de Spoelberch, J. de S. Associates Inc., 9 Shagbark Rd., Wilson Pt., South Norwalk, CT 06854, U.S.A. **Online address:** randyeickhoff@aol.com

EIDINOW, John. British (born England) **Genres:** Novels, Military/Defense/Arms Control, Biography. **Career:** British Broadcasting Co. (BBC), television director, producer and interviewer. Journalist. **Publications:** WITH D. EDMONDS: Wittgenstein's Poker: The Story of a Ten-Minute Argument Between Two Great Philosophers, 2001; Bobby Fischer Goes to War: How the Soviets Lost the Most Extraordinary Chess Match of All Time, 2004; Rousseau's Dog: Two Great Thinkers At War in the Age of Enlightenment, 2006. Contributor to periodicals. **Address:** c/o Jacqueline Korn, David Higham Associates Ltd., 5-8 Lower John St., Golden Sq., London, GL W1F 9HA, England.

EIDSE, Faith. American/Canadian (born Canada), b. 1955. **Genres:** Children's Fiction, Young Adult Non-fiction, Autobiography/Memoirs. **Career:** Carillon News, reporter and photographer, 1975-79; Virginia Gazette, reporter and photographer, 1980-84; Sun-Independent, editor, 1985-86; Tallahassee Democrat, community columnist, 1993-94; International Quarterly, managing editor, 1994; Florida State University, instructor in creative writing and multicultural literature, 1999-2000; Northwest Florida Water Management District, oral historian and public information specialist, 2000-. Writer. **Publications:** (With N. Sichel) Unrooted Childhoods: Memoirs of Growing up Global, 2004; (ed.) Voices of the Apalachicola, 2006. Contributor to books. **Address:** c/o Maria Massie, Lippincott Massie McQuilkin, 80 5th Ave., Ste. 1101, New York, NY 10011, U.S.A. **Online address:** faith_eidse@hotmail.com

EIDSON, Thomas. American (born United States), b. 1944?. **Genres:** Novels, Young Adult Fiction. **Career:** Hill & Knowlton (public relations) president and chief executive officer; Fidelity Investments, staff in public relations, executive vice-president and director of corporate affairs. Writer. **Publications:** St. Agnes' Stand, 1994; The Last Ride, 1995; All God's Children, 1996; Hannah's Gift, 1998; The Missing: A Novel, 2003; In This House, 2005; Souls of Angels: A Novel, 2007. **Address:** Dutton Publishers, Penguin Group USA, 375 Hudson St., New York, NY 10014-3657, U.S.A.

EIGENBROD, Renate. Canadian/German (born Germany), b. 1944?. **Genres:** Literary Criticism And History, Autobiography/Memoirs. **Career:** Lakehead University, Department of English, instructor; University of Manitoba, Department of Native Studies, associate professor, 2006-, graduate program chair, 2008-, department head, 2010-. **Publications:** (Ed. with J. Episkenew) Creating Community: A Roundtable on Canadian Aboriginal Literature, 2002; Travelling Knowledges: Positioning the Immigrant Reader of Aboriginal Literatures in Canada, 2005; (ed. with R. Hulan) Aboriginal Oral Traditions: Theory, Practice, Ethics, 2008; (ed. with Paul De Pasquale and Emma LaRocque) Across Cultures/Across Borders: Canadian Aboriginal and Native American Literatures, 2010; (ed. with N.J. Sinclair) The Canadian Journal of Native Studies 29.1&2, 2009. Contributor to books and journal articles. **Address:** Department of Native Studies, University of Manitoba, 204 Isbister Bldg., Winnipeg, MB R3T 2N2, Canada. **Online address:** eigenbro@cc.umanitoba.ca

EILBERG-SCHWARTZ, Howard. American (born United States), b. 1956. **Genres:** Theology/Religion, History, Anthropology/Ethnology, Politics/Government. **Career:** Indiana University, assistant professor of religious studies, 1986-89; Temple University, assistant professor of religious studies, 1989-90; Stanford University, assistant professor of religious studies, 1990-94; San Francisco State University, associate professor of religious studies and director of Jewish studies, 1994-95. Writer and consultant. **Publications:** The Human Will in Judaism: The Mishnah's Philosophy of Intention, 1986; The Savage in Judaism: An Anthropology of Israelite Religion and Ancient Judaism, 1990; (ed.) From Intercourse to Discourse: Control of Sexuality in Rabbinic Literature, 1992; (ed.) People of the Body: Jews and Judaism from an Embodied Perspective, 1992; God's Phallus and Other Problems for Men and Monotheism, 1994; (ed. with W. Doniger) Off with Her Head!: The Denial of Women's Identity in Myth, Religion, and Culture, 1995; Liberty in America's Founding Moment, 2011. **Address:** CA , U.S.A. **Online address:** hsaccount@yahoo.com

EILON, Samuel. British (born England), b. 1923. **Genres:** Administration/Management, Economics, Money/Finance, Technology, Adult Non-fiction, Business/Trade/Industry, Industrial Relations. **Career:** Palestine Electric Company Ltd., testing engineer, 1947-48; Imperial College of Science and Technology, research assistant and lecturer, 1952-57; Israel Institute of Technology, associate professor, 1957-59; Imperial College of Science and Technology, reader in production engineering, 1959-63; professor of industrial and management engineering, 1963-, head of department of management science, Center for Advanced Management, chairman, 1958-59, now professor emeritus; Israel Institute of Productivity, board director, 1958-59; Imperial College, Department of Management Science, head, 1963-87; OMEGA, International Journal of Management Science, chief editor, 1971-93. Writer. **Publications:** Industrial Engineering Tables, 1962; Elements of Production Planning and Control, 1962; (with J.R. King and R.I. Hall) Exercises in Industrial Management: A Series of Case Studies, 1966; (with J.R. King) Industrial Scheduling Abstracts (1950-1966), 1967; (with W. Lampkin) Inventory Control Abstracts (1953-1965), 1968; (with C.D.T. Watson-Gandy and N. Christofides) Distribution Management: Mathematical Modelling and Practical Analysis, 1971; Management Control, 1971, rev. ed., 1979; (ed. with T.R. Fowkes) Applications of Management Science in Banking and Finance, 1972; On the Corporate Ethos, 1973; (with B. Gold and J. Soesan) Applied Productivity Analysis for Industry, 1976; Aspects of Management, 1977, 2nd ed., 1979; The Art of Reckoning: Analysis of Performance Criteria 1984; Management Assertions and Aversions, 1985; (with B. Blackwell) The Global Challenge of Innovation, 1991; Management Practice and Mispractice, 1992; (ed.) Management Science: An Anthology, 1995; Management Strategies: A Critique of Theories and Practices, 1999. **Address:** 1 Meadway Close, London, GL NW11 7BA, England. **Online address:** sam@bensoftware.com

EINHORN, Barbara. British/New Zealander (born New Zealand), b. 1942. **Genres:** Politics/Government, Children's Non-fiction, Young Adult Non-fiction. **Career:** University of Sussex, Centre for Migration Research, lecturer and convenor, 1995-, professor of gender studies, now professor emeritus of gender studies, Department of Sociology, now professor emeritus of sociology; The European Journal of Women's Studies, associate editor. **Publications:** Der Roman in der DDR 1949-1969: Die Gestaltung d. Verhältnisses von Individuum u. Gesellschaft: E. Analyse d. Erzählstruktur, 1978; Living in Berlin, 1986; West Germany, 1988; West German Food and Drink, 1989; Cinderella Goes to Market: Citizenship, Gender, and Women's Movements in East Central Europe, 1993, new ed., 2002; (ed. with E.J. Yeo) Women and Market Societies: Crisis and Opportunity, 1995; (ed. with M. Kaldor and Z. Kavan) Citizenship and Democratic Control in Contemporary Europe, 1996; Citizenship in An Enlarging Europe: From Dream to Awakening, 2006; (with M. Evans) Religion, Gender, Politics: Questioning the Secular, 2011. **Address:** Centre for Migration Research, University of Sussex, Freeman Ctr., North Wing, Ground Fl., Sussex House, Brighton, ES BN1 9RH, England. **Online address:** b.einhorn@sussex.ac.uk

EINOLF, Christopher J. American (born United States), b. 1969. **Genres:** History. **Career:** Joint Voluntary Agency, field coordinator/senior caseworker, 1994-95; FACETS, program director, 1996-97; National Capital Area, Lutheran Social Services, asylum advocate, 1997-2001; Pennsylvania Immigrant Resource Center, Children's Advocacy and Assistance to Torture Survivors, director, 2001-03; University of Virginia, visiting lecturer, 2006-07; University of Richmond, visiting lecturer, 2007-08; DePaul University, School for Public Service, assistant professor, 2008-. Writer, historian and biographer. **Publications:** The Mercy Factory: Refugees and the American Asylum System, 2001; George Thomas: Virginian for the Union, 2007. Contributor to periodicals and journals. **Address:** School for Public Service, DePaul University, 1 E Jackson Blvd., Ste. 1250, Chicago, IL 60604, U.S.A. **Online address:** ceinolf@depaul.edu

EISEN, Adrienne. American (born United States), b. 1966?. **Genres:** Novels. **Career:** Boston University, faculty; Dartmouth Institute for Advanced Graduate Studies, speaker and panelist; Artcommotion.com, editor. **Publications:** Making Scenes, 2001. Contributor to periodicals. **Address:** c/o Author Mail, Eastgate Systems Inc., 134 Main St., Watertown, MA 02472-4416, U.S.A. **Online address:** adrienneeisen@earthlink.net

EISEN, Sydney. Canadian/Polish (born Poland), b. 1929. **Genres:** Education, History, Humanities, Intellectual History, Theology/Religion, Bibliography, Social Sciences, Reference, Reference. **Career:** Johns Hopkins University, Vincent fellow, 1951-55, Bissing fellow, 1953-54; Williams College, instructor, 1955-58, assistant professor, 1958-61; City College of the City University of New York, assistant professor, 1961-65; University of Toronto, visiting associate professor, 1965-66; York University, associate professor, 1965-68, professor of history and humanities, 1968-96, Department of History, chair, 1970-72, dean of faculty of arts, 1973-78, director of Centre for Jewish Studies, 1989-94, Vanier College, university professor, 1993-96, University emeritus professor, 1996-; National Humanities Faculty, faculty, 1972-85, president and chairman of board of directors, 1976-80; Institute for the History and Philosophy of Science, associate fellow, 1982-; Brandeis University, lecturer, 1985. Writer. **Publications:** (With M. Filler) The Human Adventure: Readings in World History, 2 vols., 1964; (with B.V. Lightman) Victorian Science and Religion: A Bibliography with Emphasis on Evolution, Belief and Unbelief, Comprised of Works Published from 1900-75, 1984; (intro.) Victorian Faith in Crisis, 1990. EDITOR: The West and The World, 1967-80; The Making of the Modern Age, 1987. Contributor to periodicals. **Address:** Division of Humanities, Faculty of Arts, York University, 254 Vanier College, 76 Winters Ln., Toronto, ON M3J 1P3, Canada. **Online address:** seisen@yorku.ca

EISENBERG, Deborah. American (born United States), b. 1945. **Genres:** Novellas/Short Stories, Plays/Screenplays. **Career:** The New York Review of Books, editorial assistant, 1973; University of Virginia, professor, 1994-, Fine Arts Creative Writing Program, master; Washington University in St. Louis, Hurst Professor, 1989, Visiting Hurst Professor; City College of New York, visiting professor, 1993-94; New York University, adjunct professor, 1995-96; University of Iowa, Iowa Writers' Workshop, faculty; Bomb Magazine, contributing editor. **Publications:** STORIES: Transactions in a Foreign Currency, 1986; Under the 82nd Airborne, 1992; The Stories (So Far) of Deborah Eisenberg, 1997; All Around Atlantis, 1997. PLAYS: Pastorale, 1982. OTHERS: Air, 24 Hours: Jennifer Bartlett (monograph), 1994; Little Fish, 2003; Twilight of the Superheroes, 2006; (intro.) Memoirs of an Anti-Semite: A Novel in Five Stories, 2008; Picador Shots, 2008; The Collected Stories of Deborah Eisenberg, 2010. Contributor to periodicals. **Address:** Department of English, University of Virginia, 219 Bryan Hall, PO Box 400121, Charlottesville, VA 22904-4121, U.S.A.

EISENBERG, Ellen M. American (born United States), b. 1962. **Genres:** History, Local History/Rural Topics. **Career:** Social Science Research Council, research assistant, 1988-89; Willamette University, assistant professor, 1990-95, associate professor, 1995-2001, professor of history, 2001-, Dwight and Margaret Lear professor of American history, 2003-; Oregon Women's Penitentiary, Holocaust educator, 1995-96. Writer. **Publications:** Jewish Agricultural Colonies in New Jersey, 1882-1920, 1995; First to Cry Down Injustice: Western Jews and Japanese Removal During WWII, 2008; (co-author) Jews of the Pacific Coast: Reinventing Community on America's Edge, 2009. Contributor to periodicals. **Address:** Department of History, College of Liberal Arts, Willamette University, Eaton 101, 900 State St., Salem, OR 97301, U.S.A. **Online address:** eeisenbe@willamette.edu

EISENBERG, John S. American (born United States), b. 1956. **Genres:** Autobiography/Memoirs, Sports/Fitness, Autobiography/Memoirs. **Career:** Baltimore Sun, sportswriter, 1988-2007. Journalist. **Publications:** The Longest Shot: Lil E. Tee and the Kentucky Derby, 1996; Cotton Bowl Days: Growing Up with Dallas and the Cowboys in the 1960s, 1997; From 33rd Street to Camden Yards: An Oral History of the Baltimore Orioles, 2001; Native Dancer: The Grey Ghost: Hero of a Golden Age, 2003; The Great Match Race: When North Met South in America's First Sports Spectacle, 2006; (with E. Prado) My Guy Barbaro: a Jockey's Journey Through Love, Triumph and Heartbreak with America's Favorite Horse, 2008; That First Season: How Vince Lombardi Took the Worst Team in the NFL and Set it on the Path to Glory, 2009. Contributor to magazines. **Address:** c/o Author Mail, Warner Books, 1271 Ave. of the Americas, New York, NY 10020, U.S.A. **Online address:** john.eisenberg@baltsun.com

EISENBERG, Jon B. American (born United States), b. 1953?. **Genres:** Law, Adult Non-fiction. **Career:** Farella, Braun & Martel L.L.P., litigation associate, through 1982; California Court of Appeal, First Appellate District, judicial staff attorney, 1982-96; Alameda County Bar Association, director, 1995-96; Horvitz and Levy L.L.P., counsel, 1996-; Hastings College of the Law, adjunct professor, Hastings Law Journal, associate editor; Eisenberg and Hancock L.L.P., partner. Writer. **Publications:** Remittitur in California Civil Appellate Practice, 2nd ed., 1985; Action Guide: Handling Civil Appeals, 1985; Using Terri: The Religious Right's Conspiracy to Take Away Our Rights, 2005. Contributor of articles to periodicals. **Address:** Eisenberg & Hancock L.L.P., 1970 Broadway, Ste. 1200, Oakland, CA 94612, U.S.A. **Online address:** jon@eandhlaw.com

EISENBERG, Nora. American (born United States), b. 1946. **Genres:** Novels, Autobiography/Memoirs, Young Adult Non-fiction. **Career:** Stanford University, faculty; Georgetown University, faculty; City University of New York, faculty and director of Faculty Fellowship Program for Emerging Scholars. Writer. **Publications:** NONFICTION WITH H.S. WIENER: The English Exercise Book, 1983; Stepping Stones: Skills for Basic Writers, 1985; (comp.) Great Writing: A Reader for Writers, 1987, 3rd ed., 2002; The American Values Reader, 1999; The Questioning Reader, 2001. NOVELS: The War at Home: A Memoir-Novel, 2002; Just the Way You Want Me: A Novel, 2003; When You Come Home: A Novel, 2008. **Address:** New York, NY , U.S.A. **Online address:** eisenbergha@lagcc.cuny.edu

EISENBERG, Robert. American (born United States), b. 1956. **Genres:** Documentaries/Reportage, Travel/Exploration. **Career:** Journalist. **Publications:** Boychiks in the Hood: Travels in the Hasidic Underground (nonfiction), 1995. **Address:** 1101 Harney St., Omaha, NE 68102-1829, U.S.A.

EISENHOWER, John S(heldon) D(oud). (Young Ike). American (born United States), b. 1922. **Genres:** History, Autobiography/Memoirs, Military/Defense/Arms Control. **Career:** U.S. Army, cadet, 1941-44, regular officer, 1944-63, reserve officer, 1963-, brigadier general, 1974-, now retired; U.S. Military Academy, instructor in English, 1948-51; White House, assistant staff secretary, 1958-61; U.S. ambassador to Belgium, 1969-71. Writer. **Publications:** The Bitter Woods: The Battle of the Bulge, 1944-1945, 1969; The Bitter Woods: The Dramatic Story, told at all Echelons, from Supreme Command to Squad Leader, of the Crisis that Shook the Western Coalition, 1969; Strictly Personal (memoir), 1974; (ed. and contrib.) Letters to Mamie, 1978; Allies: Pearl Harbor to D-Day, 1982; So Far from God: The U.S. War with Mexico, 1846-1848, 1989; Intervention! The United States and the Mexican Revolution, 1913-1917, 1993; Agent of Destiny: The Life and Times of General Winfield Scott, 1997; (with J.T. Eisenhower) Yanks: The Epic Story of the American Army in World War I, 2001; General Ike: A Personal Reminiscence, 2003; They Fought at Anzio, 2007; Zachary Taylor, 2008; (foreword) The Eisenhower Legacy: A Tribute to Ida Stover Eisenhower and David Jacob Eisenhower, 2010. **Address:** Free Press, 1230 Ave. of the Americas, New York, NY 10020, U.S.A.

EISENMAN, Stephen F. American (born United States), b. 1956. **Genres:** Art/Art History, Anthropology/Ethnology, History, Biography. **Career:** Clark Art Institute, assistant paintings conservator, 1979; Occidental College, Art History, assistant professor, 1983-88, associate professor, 1988-96, professor, 1996-, chair of department of art history, 1991-95, 1996-97; University of California, visiting graduate professor of art history, 1995; Northwestern University, Department of Art History, chair, 1998-2002, associate professor, 1998-, director of general studies, 2003-. Writer. **Publications:** Le Fantastique Reel: Graphic Works by Odilon Redon, 1990; The Temptation of Saint Redon: Biography, Ideology and Style in the Noirs of Odilon Redon, 1992; (ed. and contrib.) Nineteenth-Century Art: A Critical History, 1994, 2nd ed., 2002; Gauguin's Skirt, 1997; (with R.R. Brettell) Nineteenth Century Paintings in the Norton Simon Museum, 2006; Abu Ghraib Effect, 2007; (with C. Granof) Design in the Age of Darwin: From William Morris to Frank Lloyd Wright, 2008; Da Corot a Monet: La Sinfonia Della Natura, 2010; Nineteenth Century Art, 2011. **Address:** Department of Art History, Northwestern University, Kresge Hall, Rm. 3-400, 1880 Campus Dr., Evanston, IL 60208-2208, U.S.A. **Online address:** s-eisenman@northwestern.edu

EISENSON, Marc. American (born United States), b. 1943. **Genres:** Economics, Money/Finance, Self Help, Business/Trade/Industry. **Career:** Good Advice Press, partner, 1984-. Writer. **Publications:** Banker's Secret: Your Mortgage is a Great Investment, 1989; The Banker's Secret Credit Card Software, 1990; The Banker's Secret, 1990; The Banker's Secret Loan Software, 1992; (with A. Eisenson) The Peanut Butter and Jelly Game (juvenile), 1996; Stop Junk Mail Forever, 1997, rev. ed., 2001; (with G. Detweiler) Debt Consolidation 101, 1997; (with G. Detweiler and N. Castleman) Invest in Yourself: Six Secrets to a Rich Life, 1998; (with G. Detweiler and N. Castleman) Slash Your Debt: Save Money and Secure Your Future, 1999. **Address:** Good Advice Press, PO Box 78, Elizaville, NY 12523-0078, U.S.A. **Online address:** info@goodadvicepress.com

EISENSTADT, Martin. *See* GORLIN, Eitan.

EISENSTADT, Martin. *See* MIRVISH, Dan.

EISENSTAEDT, Jean. French (born France), b. 1940. **Genres:** Sciences, Adult Non-fiction, History, Physics, Astronomy. **Career:** Centre National de la Recherche Scientifique (CNRS), senior researcher. Writer. **Publications:** NONFICTION: (ed. with A.J. Kox) Studies in the History of General Relativity: Based on the Proceedings of the 2nd International Conference on the History of General Relativity, 1988; Einstein et la Relativite Generale: Les Chemins De l'Espace-temps, 2002; The Universe of General Relativity, 2005; Avant Einstein: Relativite, Lumiere, Gravitation, 2005; The Curious History of Relativity: How Einstein's Theory of Gravity was Lost and Found Again, 2006. **Address:** Observatoire de Paris, 61 Ave. de l'Observatoire, Paris, 75014, France. **Online address:** jean.eisenstaedt@obspm.fr

EISENSTEIN, Hester. American (born United States), b. 1940. **Genres:** Sociology, Women's Studies And Issues, History, Economics, Politics/Government. **Career:** Yale University, acting instructor, 1966-68, instructor, 1967-68, assistant professor of history, 1968-70; Columbia University, Barnard College, assistant professor of history and coordinator of experimental college, 1970-77, lecturer in experimental education, 1977-79, senior lecturer, 1977-79, Experimental Studies Program, coordinator, 1977-80; Office of the Director of Equal Opportunity in Public Employment, senior equal employment opportunity adviser, 1981-84, assistant director, 1984-85; State University of New York, visiting associate professor, 1988-89, visiting professor of women's studies, 1989-90, professor of American studies, 1990-96; City University of New York, Queens College, Department of Sociology, professor of sociology, 2000-, Women's Studies Program, director, 1996-2000. Writer. **Publications:** (Ed.) The Scholar and the Feminist (series), 1979-80; (ed. with A. Jardine) The Future of Difference, 1980; Contemporary Feminist Thought, 1983; Gender Shock: Practicing Feminism on Two Continents, 1991; Inside Agitators: Australian Femocrats and the State, 1996; Feminism Seduced: How Global Elites Use Women's Labor and Ideas to Exploit the World, 2009. Works appear in anthologies. Contributor of articles to journals. **Address:** Department of Sociology, Queens College, City University of New York, 252C Powdermaker Hall, 65-30 Kissena Blvd., Flushing, NY 11367-1575, U.S.A. **Online address:** hester_eisenstein@qc.edu

EISENSTEIN, Phyllis (Kleinstein). American (born United States), b. 1946. **Genres:** Science Fiction/Fantasy, Medicine/Health. **Career:** Michigan State University, teacher, 1983; Columbia College, teacher of science fiction/fantasy, 1979-80, 1989-, teacher of popular fiction writing, 1992-. Writer. **Publications:** Born to Exile, 1978; Sorcerer's Son, 1979; Shadow of Earth, 1979; In the Hands of Glory, 1981; The Crystal Palace, 1988; In the Red Lord's Reach, 1989; (ed. with A. Eisenstein) Stars My Destination, 1996; (with S.M. Scheiner) Overcoming the Pain of Inflammatory Arthritis, 1997; The Book of Elementals: The Saga of the Sorcerer's Son, 2003; (with A. Eisenstein) Night Lives: Nine Stories of the Dark Fantastic, 2003; The City in Stone, 2004. Works appear in anthologies. **Address:** 6208 N Campbell Ave., PO Box 59723, Chicago, IL 60659, U.S.A. **Online address:** phyllis@ripco.com

EISGRUBER, Christopher L(udwig). American (born United States), b. 1961. **Genres:** Adult Non-fiction, Politics/Government, Law, History. **Career:** New York University, School of Law, assistant professor, 1990-93, associate professor, 1993-95, professor of law, 1995-2001; Princeton University, Program in Law and Public Affairs, visiting research fellow, 2000-01, director, 2001-04, provost, 2004-, Woodrow Wilson School, Laurance S. Rockefeller professor of public affairs, 2001-, University Center for Human Values, faculty, 2001-, Department of Politics, associated faculty, 2001-, Program in Ethics and Public Affairs, acting director, 2002-03. Writer. **Publications:** Constitutional Self-Government, 2001; (ed. with A. Sajó) Global Justice and the Bulwarks of Localism: Human Rights in Context, 2005; The Next Justice: Repairing the Supreme Court Appointments Process, 2007; (with L.G. Sager) Religious Freedom and the Constitution, 2007. Contributor to books. **Address:** Office of the Provost, Princeton University, 4 Nassau Hall, Princeton, NJ 08544, U.S.A. **Online address:** eisgrube@princeton.edu

EISIMINGER, Sterling (Skip). American (born United States), b. 1941. **Genres:** Poetry, Humanities, Language/Linguistics, Essays, Art/Art History, Literary Criticism And History. **Career:** Clemson University, professor of English, 1968-, now professor emeritus. Writer. **Publications:** (With J. Idol) Why Can't They Write?, 1975; (co-author) Business in Literature, 1977; Wordspinner: Mind-Boggling Games for Word Lovers, 1991; Consequence of Error, 1991; (with J. Idol and R.K. Gollin) Prophetic Pictures: Nathaniel Hawthorne's Knowledge and Uses of the Visual Arts, 1991; The Consequence of Error and Other Language Essays, 1991; Nonprescription Medicine, 1995; Integration with Dignity, 2003; Felix Academicus: Tales of a Happy Academic, 2007. **Address:** Department of English, Clemson University, 808 Strode Twr., PO Box 345708, Clemson, SC 29634-0535, U.S.A. **Online address:** esterli@clemson.edu

EISLER, Barry. American (born United States), b. 1964?. **Genres:** Novels, Mystery/Crime/Suspense. **Career:** Hamada and Matsumoto, attorney; Matsushita Electric and Industrial Company Ltd., counsel; Central Intelligence Agency, directorate of operations; Silicon Valley, technology lawyer and executive. Writer. **Publications:** JOHN RAIN SERIES: Rain Fall, 2002; Hard Rain, 2003; Rain Storm, 2004; Killing Rain, 2005; The Last Assassin, 2006; Requiem for an Assassin, 2007; Fault Line, 2009; Inside Out: A Novel, 2010. **Address:** c/o Author Mail, Penguin Group Inc., 375 Hudson St., New York, NY 10014-3658, U.S.A. **Online address:** barry@barryeisler.com

EISLER, Benita. American (born United States), b. 1937. **Genres:** Biography, Young Adult Non-fiction, Art/Art History, Photography. **Career:** WNET-

TV, producer, 1975-78; Public Education Association, editor; Princeton University, lecturer in French. Photographer. **Publications:** (Ed. and intro.) The Lowell Offering: Writings by New England Mill Women, 1840-1845, 1978; Class Act: America's Last Dirty Secret, 1983; Private Lives: Men and Women of the Fifties, 1986; O'Keeffe and Stieglitz: An American Romance, 1991; Bryon: Child of Passion, Fool of Fame, 1999; Chopin's Funeral, 2003; Naked in the Marketplace: The Lives of George Sand, 2006. Contributor to books and periodicals. **Address:** Watkins Loomis Agency Inc., 133 E 35th St., PO Box 20925, New York, NY 10016-3886, U.S.A.

EISNER, Gisela. British/German (born Germany), b. 1925. **Genres:** Economics, History. **Career:** University of Southampton, researcher, 1946-48; Institute of Economic and Social Research, researcher, 1948-50; University of Manchester, researcher, 1951-56; Buxton College of Further Education, governor. Writer. **Publications:** Jamaica 1830-1930: A Study in Economic Growth, 1961. **Address:** 69 Macclesfield Rd., Buxton, DB SK17 9AG, England.

EISNER, Michael Alexander. American (born United States) **Genres:** Novels, Young Adult Fiction. **Career:** U.S. State Department, attorney, 1997; Morrison and Forester, attorney. Writer. **Publications:** The Crusader, 2001. **Address:** Doubleday, 1540 Broadway, New York, NY 10019, U.S.A.

EISNER, Peter (Norman). American (born United States), b. 1950. **Genres:** Writing/Journalism, Biography, History. **Career:** Register-Star, reporter, 1974-75; Poughkeepsie Journal, reporter, 1975-76; Associated Press (news service), newsman, 1978-79, correspondent in Brasilia, 1979-81, bureau chief in Caracas, 1982, news editor, 1982-83; Newsday, deputy foreign editor, 1984-85, senior foreign editor, 1985-89, senior correspondent, 1989-94; NewsCom, managing director, 1994-98; Center for Public Integrity, managing director, 1999-2001; Washington Post, staff writer, deputy foreign editor, 2003-. **Publications:** Death Beat: A Colombian Journalist's Life inside the Cocaine Wars, 1994; (with M. Noriega) America's Prisoner: The Memoirs of Manuel Noriega, 1997; The Freedom Line: The Brave Men and Women Who Rescued Allied Pilots from the Nazis during World War II, 2004; (with K. Royce) The Italian Letter: How the Bush Administration Used a Fake Letter to Build the Case for War in Iraq, 2007. Contributor to periodicals. **Address:** c/o Author Mail, William Morrow, 10 E 53rd St., 7th Fl., New York, NY 10022, U.S.A.

ELAD, Amikam. Israeli (born Israel), b. 1946. **Genres:** Theology/Religion, History, Architecture. **Career:** Hebrew University of Jerusalem, Department of Islamic and Middle Eastern History, senior lecturer, head, Institute of Asian and African Studies, director. Writer. **Publications:** Kavim le-hit-pathut ha-Tsava ha-'Avasi (be-meyuhad yehidot Ahel H'arasan ve-Alavn'a): 'im dagesh 'al tekufat Alamin ve-Almamun, 1986; Medieval Jerusalem and Islamic Worship: Holy Places, Ceremonies and Pilgrimage, 1995. Contributor to journals. **Address:** Department of Islamic and Middle East Studies, Hebrew University of Jerusalem, Mount Scopus, Jerusalem, 91905, Israel. **Online address:** amikam@h2.hum.huji.ac.il

ELAINE, Monika. See JACKSON, Monica.

ELAM, Jason. American (born United States), b. 1970. **Genres:** Criminology/True Crime, Horror, Mystery/Crime/Suspense. **Career:** Writer and American football placekicker. **Publications:** (With S. Yohn) Monday Night Jihad (Riley Covington Thriller series), 2007; (with S. Yohn) Blown Coverage (Riley Covington Thriller series), 2009; (with S. Yohn) Blackout, 2010; (with S. Yohn) Inside Threat, 2011. **Address:** c/o Matthew Yates, Yates & Yates L.L.P., 1100 Town & Country Rd., Ste. 1300, Orange, CA 92868, U.S.A.

ELBIRT, Paula M. (Paula Elbirt-Bender). American (born United States), b. 1954. **Genres:** Medicine/Health, Sports/Fitness, Human Relations/Parenting, Sciences. **Career:** MDS4KIDS, president, 1984-99; Drpaula.com Inc., medical director, 1997-2001; Children's Aid Society of New York, medical director, 2002-; Brooklyn Hospital, director of pediatric primary care education. Writer. **Publications:** (As Paula Elbirt-Bender with L.L. Small) A New Mother's Home Companion, 1993; (with S. Solin) The Seventeen Guide to Sex and Your Body, 1996; Dr. Paula's House Calls to Your Newborn: Birth Through Six Months, 2000; Dr. Paula's Good Nutrition Guide for Babies, Toddlers, and Preschoolers, 2001; (with L.L. Small) 365 Ways to Get Your

Child to Sleep, 2001; Ask Dr. Paula, 2002; (contrib.) Johnson's Mother and Baby, 2003. **Address:** 150 E 77th St., New York, NY 10075-1922, U.S.A. **Online address:** pelbirt@nac.net

ELBIRT-BENDER, Paula. See ELBIRT, Paula M.

ELBORN, Andrew. See CLEMENTS, Andrew.

ELBOROUGH, Travis. British (born England), b. 1973?. **Genres:** Young Adult Non-fiction, History. **Career:** Writer. **Publications:** The Bus We Loved: London's Affair with the Routemaster (nonfiction), 2005; The Long-Player Goodbye: The Album from Vinyl to iPod and Back Again (nonfiction), 2008 in US as The Vinyl Countdown: The Album from LP to iPod and Back Again, 2009; Wish You Were Here: England on Sea, 2010. Contributor to periodicals. **Address:** Granta Books, 12 Addison Ave., London, GL W11 4QR, England. **Online address:** travis1971@appleonline.net

ELBOZ, Stephen. British (born England), b. 1956?. **Genres:** Children's Fiction, Novels. **Career:** Writer and Educator. **Publications:** The House of Rats, 1991; The Games Board Map, 1993; Bottle Boy, 1994; The Byzantium Bazaar, 1996 as A Store of Secrets, 2000; Ghostlands, 1996; The Tower at Moonville, 1999; The Prisoner's Apprentice, 2006. TEMMI SERIES: Temmi and the Flying Bears, 1997; Temmi and the Frost Dragon, 2002. FOR YOUNG READERS: Captain Skywriter and Kid Wonder (stories), 1995; Kid Wonder and the Terrible Truth, 1999; Kid Wonder and the Half-Hearted Hero, 2000; Kid Wonder and the Sticky Skyscraper, 2000; (with D. Schulman) Clever Monkeys, 2007. KIT STIXBY SERIES: A Handful of Magic, 2000; A Land without Magic, 2001; A Wild Kind of Magic, 2001; An Ocean of Magic, 2003. Contributor to periodicals. **Address:** c/o Author Mail, Oxford University Press, Great Clarendon St., Oxford, OX OX2 6DP, England.

ELCOCK, Howard (James). British (born England), b. 1942. **Genres:** Public/Social Administration, History, Politics/Government. **Career:** University of Hull, lecturer, 1966-77, senior lecturer in politics, 1977-81; University of Northumbria, School of Government, head, 1981-87, professor of government, 1984-, now professor emeritus, honorary research fellow, 1997-; State University of New York College, visiting professor of political science, 1993-94. Writer. **Publications:** Administrative Justice, 1969; Portrait of a Decision: The Council of Four and the Treaty of Versailles, 1972; Political Behaviour, 1976; Strategic Planning Processes in Regional and Local Government, 1979; (with S. Haywood) The Buck Stops Where? Accountability and Control in the NHS, 1980; (ed.) What Sort of Society?: Economic and Social Policy in Modern Britain, 1982; Local Government: Politicians, Professionals, and the Public in Local Authorities, 1982, 3rd ed. as Local Government: Policy and Management in Local Authorities, 1994; (ed. with G. Jordan) Learning from Local Authority Budgeting, 1987; (with J. Fenwick and K. Harrop) The Public Domain in an English Region: Aspects of Adaptation and Change in Public Authorities, 1989; (with G. Jordon and A. Midwinter) Budgeting in Local Government: Managing the Margins, 1989; Change and Decay: Public Administration in the 1990s, 1991; (ed. with M. Keating) Remaking the Union: Devolution and British Politics in the 1990s, 1998; Political Leadership, 2001. **Address:** University of Northumbria, Ellison Pl., Newcastle upon Tyne, TW NE1 8ST, England. **Online address:** howard.elcock@unn.ac.uk

ELDER, Jo-Anne. Canadian (born Canada) **Genres:** Novels, Plays/Screenplays, Poetry, Translations, Theology/Religion. **Career:** Writer and translator. **Publications:** (Ed. with C. O'Connell) Voices and Echoes: Canadian Women's Spirituality, 1997; Postcards from Ex-Lovers, 2005. TRANSLATIONS: Elder and Cogswell, Rêves inachevés: Anthologie de pósie acadienne contemporaine (title means: 'Unfinished Dreams'), 1990; Contemporary Poetry of Acadie, 1990; énigmes et Anecdotes (title means: 'Enigmas and Anecdotes'), 1994; Donatien Gaudet, Dolores Breau: Portraits d'un peuple (title means: 'Portraits of a People'), 1996; Climats: pósie (title means: 'Climates: Poetry'), 1999; Livraison spéciale: L'héritage postal (title means: 'Special Delivery: Canada's Postal Heritage'), 2000; (with F. Cogswell) H. Chiasson, Conversations, 2001; G. Leblanc, Moncton Mantra (title means: 'Elder'), 2001; F. Enguehard, Tales from Dog Island: St. Pierre et Miquelon, 2002; L. Diamond, The Past at Our Feet, 2004; A. D'Alfonso, A Friday in August: A Novel, 2005; H. Chiasson, Lifedream: A Play, 2006; C. Forand, In the Claws of the Cat, 2006; H. Chiasson, Beatitudes, 2007; S.P. Thibodeau, Seul On Est (title means: 'One'), 2009. **Address:** c/o Author Mail, Broken Jaw Press Inc., PO Box 596, Sta. A, Fredericton, NB E3B 5A6, Canada.

ELDER, John. American (born United States), b. 1947. **Genres:** Literary Criticism And History, Environmental Sciences/Ecology, Natural History, Essays. **Career:** Middlebury College, professor of English and environmental studies, 1973-2010, professor emeritus, 2010-; Bread Loaf School of English, teacher, 1983-. Writer. **Publications:** Following the Brush: An American Encounter with Classical Japanese Culture, 1993; Imagining the Earth: Poetry and the Vision of Nature, 1985, 2nd ed., 1996; Reading the Mountains of Home, 1998; The Frog Run: Words and Wildness in the Vermont Woods, 2001; Pilgrimage to Vallombrosa: From Vermont to Italy in the Footsteps of George Perkins Marsh, 2006. EDITOR: (with R. Finch) The Norton Book of Nature Writing, 1990; (with S. Rockefeller) Spirit and Nature: Why the Environment Is a Religious Issue: An Interfaith Dialogue, 1992; (with H. Wong) The Family of Earth and Sky: Indigenous Tales of Nature from around the World, 1994; American Nature Writers, 1996; Return of the Wolf: Reflections on the Future of Wolves in the Northeast, 2000. **Address:** Library 351, Davis Family Library, Middlebury College, Middlebury, VT 05753, U.S.A. **Online address:** elder2348@gmail.com

ELDON, Kathy. American (born United States), b. 1946. **Genres:** Travel/Exploration, Food And Wine. **Career:** Creative Visions Foundation, founder and president; Msafiri Magazine, editor; Kenya Airways Magazine, editor; Creative Visions Productions, principal and film producer. Broadcaster, media consultant, speaker and freelance journalist. **Publications:** Kitchens and Cooking, 1972; The Story of Medicine, 1974; Tom-Tom to Television, 1976; (comp. with J. Kane and N. Swanborg) Nairobi, All You Need to Know, But Don't Know Who to Ask: A Guide for Visitors and Residents in Kenya, 1979; (with E. Mullan) Tastes of Kenya, 1981; Making Music in Kenya, 1981; Kathy Eldon's Eating Out Guide to Kenya, 1983; (contrib.) Specialities of the House from Kenya's Finest Restaurants, 1985; More Specialties of the House, 1987; (with A. Eldon) Safari Diary, 1988; Angel Catcher: A Journal of Loss and Remembrance, 1998; (with A. Eldon) Soul Catcher: A Journal to Help You Become Who You Really Are, 1999; (with A. Eldon) Love Catcher: A Journal to Bring More Love into Your Life, 2002. EDITOR: The Journey Is the Destination: The Journals of Dan Eldon, 1997; Dan Eldon: The Art of Life, 2000. **Address:** Creative Visions Foundation, 1223 Sunset Plaza Dr., Ste. B, West Hollywood, CA 90069, U.S.A. **Online address:** kathyeldon@aol.com

ELDRIDGE, Colin Clifford. Welsh/British (born England), b. 1942. **Genres:** History, Law. **Career:** University of Edinburgh, postdoctoral fellow, 1966-68; Nottingham University, tutor; University of Wales, Saint David's University College, Department of History, lecturer, 1968-75, senior lecturer in history, 1975-92, reader in history, 1992-99, professor of history, 1999, head, School of English, European Languages and Cultures, History, head; Trivium Journal, editor, 1984-2002; British Association of Canadian Studies, History Section, founding chairman, 1990-96; National Library of Wales, governor. Writer. **Publications:** England's Mission: The Imperial Idea in the Age of Gladstone and Disraeli, 1868-1880, 1973; Victorian Imperialism, 1978; The Zulu War: Origins, Course and Aftermath, 1996; Disraeli and the Rise of a New Imperialism, 1996; The Imperial Experience: From Carlyle to Forster, 1996. EDITOR: Essays in Honor of C.D. Chandaman, 1980; British Imperialism in the Nineteenth Century, 1984; From Rebellion to Patriation, 1989; Empire, Politics and Popular Culture, 1990; Kith and Kin: Canada, Britain, and the United States from the Revolution to the Cold War, 1997. Contributor of articles to journals. **Address:** Department of History, University of Wales, Lampeter, Ceredigion, SA48 7ED, Wales. **Online address:** c.eldridge@lamp.ac.uk

ELDRIDGE, John E. T. Scottish/British (born England), b. 1936. **Genres:** Sociology, Social Sciences, Military/Defense/Arms Control, Economics, Politics/Government, Anthropology/Ethnology. **Career:** University of York, lecturer and senior lecturer, 1964-69; University of Bradford, professor, 1969-72; University of Glasgow, professor of sociology, 1972-, now professor emeritus. Writer. **Publications:** Industrial Disputes: Essays in the Sociology of Industrial Relations, 1968; (ed.) Max Weber: The Interpretation of Social Reality, 1971; Sociology and Industrial Life, 1971; (with A.D. Crombie) Sociology of Organizations, 1974; (co-author) Bad News, 1976; (co-author) More Bad News, 1980; Recent British Sociology, 1980; C. Wright Mills, 1983; (co-author) War and Peace News, 1985; (with P. Cressey and J. MacInnes) Just Managing, 1985; (with P. Cressey and J. MacInnes) Industrial Society and Economic Crisis, 1991; (co-author) Targeting Moscow: Talking about Trident, 1991; (ed.) Getting the Message: News, Truth and Power, 1993; (with L. Eldridge) Raymond Williams: Making Corrections, 1994; (ed.) The Glasgow Media Group Reader: News Content, Language and Visuals, 1995; (with J.

Kitzinger and K. Williams) The Mass Media and Power in Modern Britain, 1997; (co-ed.) For Sociology: Legacies and Prospects, 2000. Contributor to journals. **Address:** Department of Sociology, School of Social and Political Sciences, University of Glasgow, Adam Smith Bldg., 40 Bute Gardens, Glasgow, G12 8RT, Scotland. **Online address:** john.eldridge@glasgow.ac.uk

ELDWORTH, R. *See* **PERRETT, Bryan.**

ELEGANT, Robert (Sampson). Italian/British/American (born United States), b. 1928. **Genres:** Novels, History, International Relations/Current Affairs, Language/Linguistics, Biography, Documentaries/Reportage, Adult Non-fiction, Young Adult Fiction, Young Adult Fiction. **Career:** Overseas News Agency, International News Service, journalist, war correspondent, 1951-53; Newsweek, South Asian correspondent and chief of New Delhi bureau, 1956-57, Southeast Asian correspondent and chief of Hong Kong bureau, 1958-61, Central European bureau chief, 1962-65; Los Angeles Times, chief of Hong Kong bureau, 1965-69, foreign affairs columnist, 1970-76; University of South Carolina, visiting professor, 1976; independent author, 1977-; Institute for Advanced Study, Berlin, fellow, 1993-94; Boston University, visiting professor, 1994-95; Harvard University, Fairbank Center for Chinese Studies, fellow. **Publications:** China's Red Masters: Political Biographies of the Chinese Communist Leaders in UK as China's Red Leaders, 1951; The Dragon's Seed: Peking and the Overseas Chinese, 1959; The Center of the World: Communism and the Mind of China, 1963, rev. ed., 1968; Mao's Great Revolution, 1971; Mao Vs. Chiang: The Battle for China 1925-1949, 1972; Hong Kong: The Great Cities, 1977; Pacific Destiny: Inside Asia Today (nonfiction), 1990; Shanghai, 2001. NOVELS: A Kind of Treason, 1966; The Seeking, 1969; Dynasty, 1977; Manchu, 1980; Mandarin, 1983; White Sun, Red Star, 1986 in US as From a Far Land, 1987; Bianca: A Novel of Venice, 1992, 2nd ed., 2000; The Everlasting Sorrow, 1994; The Big Brown Bears, 1995; Last Year in Hong Kong: A Love Story, 1997; Cry Peace, 2005. **Address:** Casalichiari, Torre Gentile, Todi, Perugia, 06059, Italy. **Online address:** relegant@yahoo.com

ELEGANT, Simon. American (born United States), b. 1960?. **Genres:** Novels, Young Adult Fiction, Autobiography/Memoirs. **Career:** Far Eastern Economic Review, arts and society editor. **Publications:** A Floating Life: The Adventures of Li Po, 1997. **Address:** c/o Author Mail, Ecco Press, HarperCollins Publishers, 10 E 53rd St., 7th Fl., New York, NY 10022, U.S.A.

EL-ENANY, Rasheed. British/Egyptian (born Egypt), b. 1949. **Genres:** Biography, History, Literary Criticism And History. **Career:** University of Exeter, Institute of Arab and Islamic Studies, professor and chair of modern Arabic literature, now professor emeritus. Writer and biographer. **Publications:** (Trans.) N. Mahfouz, Respected Sir, 1987; Naguib Mahfouz: The Pursuit of Meaning, 1993; Dirāsat al-makhtūtāt al-Islāmīyah: bayna i'tibārāt al-māddah wa-al-bashar: a'māl al-mu'tamar al-thānī li-Mu'assasat al-Furqān lil-Turāth al-Islāmī, Dīsambir 1993/Jumādá al-ākhirah 1414, 1997; Najīb Mahfūz: has ād al-qawl, 1997; Arab Representations of the Occident: East-West Encounters in Arabic Fiction, 2006; Istintāq al-nas sPTE: maqālāt fī al-s Istintāq al-nass: maqālāt fī al-sard al-'Arabī, 2006; Naguib Mahfouz: Egypt's Nobel Laureate, 2007 in US as Naguib Mahfouz: His Life and Times, 2008. **Address:** Institute of Arab and Islamic Studies, University of Exeter, Stocker Rd., Exeter, DN EX4 4ND, United Kingdom. **Online address:** r.el-enany@exeter.ac.uk

ELEY, Beverley. Australian (born Australia) **Genres:** Biography, Autobiography/Memoirs. **Career:** Angus and Robertson Bookshops, publicity and advertising manager; Cassell Australia Collier Macmillan, marketing manager; Australia Consumers Association, marketing manager and spokesperson; author, 1995-. **Publications:** Ion Idriess, 1995; The Book of David, 1996; Conversations with Alys, forthcoming. **Address:** HarperCollins Publishers, 10 E 53rd St., 7th Fl., New York, NY 10022-5244, U.S.A. **Online address:** beverleyskerry@aol.com

ELFERS, James E. American (born United States), b. 1963. **Genres:** Adult Non-fiction, Travel/Exploration, Sports/Fitness. **Career:** University of Delaware, Morris Library, library assistant, 1989-. Writer. **Publications:** The Tour to End All Tours: The Story of Major League Baseball's 1913-1914 World Tour, 2003. **Address:** Morris Library, University of Delaware, 181 S College Ave., Newark, DE 19717-5267, U.S.A. **Online address:** elfers@udel.edu

ELFSTROM, Gerard A. American (born United States), b. 1945. **Genres:** Ethics, Politics/Government, Adult Non-fiction. **Career:** Morris Brown College, assistant professor of philosophy and head of department, 1976-80; Emory University, visiting assistant professor of philosophy, 1981-84; Agnes Scott College, assistant professor of philosophy, 1985-88; Auburn University, assistant professor, 1988-92, associate professor of philosophy, 1992-97, professor, 1997-. Writer. **Publications:** (With N. Fotion) Military Ethics, 1986; Ethics for a Shrinking World, 1989; Moral Issues and Multinational Corporations, 1991; (with N. Fotion) Toleration, 1992; New Challenges for Political Philosophy, 1997; International Ethics: A Reference Handbook, 1998. Contributor of articles to periodicals. **Address:** Department of Philosophy, Auburn University, 6092 Haley Ctr., Auburn, AL 36849-5210, U.S.A. **Online address:** elfstga@auburn.edu

ELGIN, Suzette Haden. American (born United States), b. 1936. **Genres:** Science Fiction/Fantasy, Language/Linguistics, Self Help. **Career:** San Diego State University, assistant professor, 1972-, associate professor, professor, professor emeritus, 1980-; Linguistics and Science Fiction Newsletter, publisher, producer and writer, 1981-. **Publications:** The Communipaths, 1970; Furthest, 1971; At the Seventh Level, 1972; (with J.T. Grinder) Guide to Transformational Grammar: History, Theory, Practice, 1973; What is Linguistics?, 1973, 2nd ed., 1979; A Primer of Transformational Grammar for Rank Beginners, 1975; Pouring Down Words, 1975; Queé es la lingüística?, 1977; Star-Anchored, Star-Angered, 1979; The Gentle Art of Verbal Self-Defense, 1980; Communipath Worlds, 1980; Ozark Fantasy Trilogy, 3 vols., 1981; Grand Jubilee, 1981; Twelve Fair Kingdoms, 1981; And Then There'll Be Fireworks, 1981; More on the Gentle Art of Self-Defense, 1983; Native Tongue, 1984; Yonder Comes the Other End of Time, 1986; The Last Word on the Gentle Art of Self-Defense, 1987; Native Tongue II: The Judas Rose, 1987; Success with the Gentle Art of Verbal Self-Defense, 1989; Staying Well with the Gentle Art of Verbal Self-Defense, 1990; (with R. Haden) A Celebration of Ozark English, 1991; The Gentle Art of Written Self-Defense, 1993; Genderspeak: Men, Women, and the Gentle Art of Verbal Self-Defense, 1993; Native Tongue III: Earth Song, 1994; You Can't Say That to Me!, 1995; Business Speak, 1995; The Gentle Art of Communicating with Kids, 1996; Try to Feel It My Way: New Help for Touch Dominant People and Those Who Care about Them, 1997; How to Disagree without Being Disagreeable: Getting Your Point Across with the Gentle Art of Verbal Self-Defense, 1997; How to Turn the Other Cheek and Still Survive in Today's World, 1997; The Grandmother Principles, 1998; The Language Imperative, 2000; Language in Emergency Medicine, 2000; The Ozark Trilogy, 2000; Peacetalk 101, 2003; Murder & Mystery, 2007. **Address:** San Diego State University, 5500 Campanile Dr., San Diego, CA 92120, U.S.A. **Online address:** ocls@madisoncounty.net

EL-HAI, Jack. American (born United States) **Genres:** Sciences, History, Psychology. **Career:** Writer. **Publications:** NONFICTION: (contrib.) Minnesota Collects, 1992; Celebrating Tradition, Building the Future: Seventy-Five Years of Land o'Lakes, 1996; Memories of a Lifetime: Jostens, 1897-1997, 1998; Clean and Friendly for More Than 25 Years: The Super 8 Story, 1999; Lost Minnesota: Stories of Vanished Places, 2000; The Lobotomist: A Maverick Medical Genius and His Tragic Quest to Rid the World of Mental Illness, 2005; Services Rendered: The Story of Valley Proteins, 2009. Contributor to periodicals. **Address:** Laura Langlie Agency, 63 Wyckoff St., Brooklyn, NY 11201, U.S.A. **Online address:** jack@el-hai.com

ELIAS, Jason. American (born United States), b. 1947. **Genres:** Medicine/Health. **Career:** Tri State Institute for Traditional Chinese Acupuncture, teacher, 1984-88. Writer. **Publications:** (With K. Ketcham) In the House of the Moon: Reclaiming the Feminine Spirit of Healing, 1995; (with S.R. Masline) The A-Z Guide to Herbal Healing Remedies, 1995; (with K. Ketcham) Feminine Healing: A Woman's Guide to a Healthy Body, Mind, and Spirit, 1997; (with K. Ketcham) Chinese Medicine for Maximum Immunity, 1998; (with K. Ketcham) The Five Elements of Self-Healing: Using Chinese Medicine for Maximum Immunity, Wellness and Health, 1998; And Sometimes Y, 2010. Contributor to periodicals. **Address:** Integral Health Associates, 3 Paradies Ln., New Paltz, NY 12561, U.S.A. **Online address:** jasonforhealth@aol.com

ELIAS, Scott A. (Scott Armstrong Elias). British/American (born United States), b. 1953. **Genres:** Zoology, Earth Sciences, Sciences. **Career:** University of Bern, Geobotanical Institute, visiting scientist, 1981; University of Colorado, Institute of Arctic and Alpine Research, research associate, 1982-94, fellow, 1994-95; University of Alaska, visiting professor, 1991; University of London, Geography Department of Royal Holloway, lecturer, 2000-, professor of quaternary science, 2007-. Writer. **Publications:** Quaternary

Insects and Their Environments, 1994; Ice Age History of Alaskan National Parks, 1995; Ice Age Environments of National Parks in the Rocky Mountains, 1996; Ice-Age History of Southwestern National Parks, 1997; Rocky Mountains, 2002; (with J.F. Hoffecker) Human Ecology of Beringia, 2007; (ed.) Encyclopedia of Quaternary Science, 2007; Advances in Quaternary Entomology, 2009. **Address:** Department of Geography, Royal Holloway, University of London, Egham, SR TW20 0EX, England. **Online address:** s.elias@rhul.ac.uk

ELIAS, Scott Armstrong. See **ELIAS, Scott A.**

ELIAV, Yaron Z. American (born United States) **Genres:** Cultural/Ethnic Topics, Literary Criticism And History, Theology/Religion, Art/Art History. **Career:** Hebrew University, instructor, 1992-98, Institute of Advanced Studies, senior fellow, 2004-05; Princeton University, teaching assistant, 1995-96; New York University, Dorot teaching fellow, 1998-99; University of Michigan, Department of Near Eastern Studies, associate professor, Frankel assistant professor of rabbinic literature, 2000-06, associate professor of rabbinic literature and Jewish history of late antiquity, 2006-; Hebrew University, Institute of Advanced Studies, senior fellow, 2004-05. Writer. **Publications:** Sites, Institutions and Daily Life in Tiberias during the Talmudic Period: A Source Book, 1995; God's Mountain: The Temple Mount in Time, Place, and Memory, 2005; (and comp. with A. Knysh and R. Williams) Judaism, Christianity & Islam: A Sourcebook, 2005; (ed. with E.A. Friedland and S. Herbert) The Sculptural Environment of the Roman Near East: Reflections on Culture, Ideology, and Power, 2008; (ed. with A. Norich) Jewish Literatures and Cultures: Context and Intertext, 2008; A Jew in the Roman Bathhouse: Daily Life Encounters with Hellenism in Roman Palestine, forthcoming; A Jew in the Roman Bathhouse: The Poetics of Cultural Interaction in the Roman Mediterranean, forthcoming. Contributor of articles to periodicals and journals. **Address:** Department of Near Eastern Studies, University of Michigan, 4151 Thayer Academic Bldg., Ann Arbor, MI 48104-1608, U.S.A. **Online address:** yzeliav@umich.edu

ELIE, Lolis Eric. American (born United States), b. 1963. **Genres:** Essays, Adult Non-fiction. **Career:** Freelance journalist, 1986-; Atlanta Journal, staff writer, 1986-89; Callaloo, assistant managing editor, 1989-90; University of Virginia, instructor in English, 1989-90; Wynton Marsalis Enterprises Inc., road manager, 1991-93; The Times-Picayune, metro columnist, 1995-2009; HBO Series Treme, staff; CBS Sunday Morning, commentator. **Publications:** Smokestack Lightning: Adventures in the Heart of Barbecue Country, 1995; (ed.) Cornbread Nation Two: The United States of Barbecue, 2004. Contributor to periodicals. Works appear in anthology. **Address:** 3800 Howard Ave., PO Box 50160, New Orleans, LA 70150-0160, U.S.A. **Online address:** tpelie@aol.com

ELIE, Paul. American (born United States), b. 1965?. **Genres:** Adult Non-fiction, Humanities, Theology/Religion, History. **Career:** Farrar, Straus and Giroux, editor, 1993-; senior editor; Publishers Weekly, part-time copy editor; Columbia University, faculty. **Publications:** (Ed.) A Tremor of Bliss: Contemporary Writers on the Saints, 1994; The Life You Save May Be Your Own: An American Pilgrimage, 2003. Contributor to periodicals. **Address:** c/o Author Mail, Farrar, Straus and Giroux, 18 W 18th St., New York, NY 10011, U.S.A.

ELISHA, Ron. Australian/Israeli (born Israel), b. 1951. **Genres:** Children's Fiction, Plays/Screenplays, Young Adult Fiction, Anthropology/Ethnology. **Career:** General practitioner of medicine, 1977-. Writer. **Publications:** FOR CHILDREN: Pigtales, 1994; Too Big, 1997. PLAYS: In Duty Bound, 1983; Two, 1985; Einstein, 1986; The Levine Comedy, 1987; Safe House, 1989; Esterhaz, 1990; Pax Americana, 1990; Choice, 1994; The Goldberg Variations, 2000. Contributor to periodicals. **Address:** Sandy Wagner, 12/44A Bayswater Rd., Kings Cross, NW 2011, Australia. **Online address:** relisha@bigpond-net.au

ELIUM, Don. American (born United States), b. 1954. **Genres:** Human Relations/Parenting, Sports/Fitness. **Career:** Bank of America, trainer and consultant; American Telephone and Telegraph, trainer and consultant; Touchstone Counseling, therapist, 1985-; John F. Kennedy University, psychology faculty, 1986-; Los Medanos College, instructor, 1989-. Writer. **Publications:** WITH J. ELIUM: Raising a Son: Parents and the Making of a Healthy Man, 1992, 3rd ed., 2004; Raising a Daughter: The Awakening of a Healthy Woman, 1993, rev. ed., 2003; Raising a Family: Living on Planet Parenthood, 1997; Raising a Teenager: Teenager: Parents and the Nurturing of a Responsible Teen, 1999; Raising a Daughter: Parents and the Awakening of a Healthy Woman, 2003. **Address:** Touchstone Counseling, 140 Mayhew, Ste. 606, Pleasant Hill, CA 94523, U.S.A. **Online address:** don@donelium.com

ELIUM, Jeanne (Ann). American (born United States), b. 1947. **Genres:** Education, Human Relations/Parenting, Psychology, Young Adult Fiction. **Career:** Writer, 1965-; teacher, 1969-71; Planned Parenthood, patient educator, 1972-84; Ada County Volunteer Bureau, director, 1976; Stewards Group, founding member; John F. Kennedy University, instructor in child development. **Publications:** WITH D. ELIUM: Raising a Son: Parents and the Making of a Healthy Man, 1992, 3rd ed., 2004; Raising a Daughter: Parents and the Awakening of a Healthy Woman, 1994, rev. ed., 2003; Raising a Family: Living on Planet Parenthood, 1997; Raising a Teenager: Parents and the Nurturing of a Responsible Teen, 1999. Contributor to periodicals. **Address:** 2168 Norris Rd., Walnut Creek, CA 94596-5839, U.S.A. **Online address:** jeanne@jeanneelium.com

ELIZONDO, Virgil P. American (born United States), b. 1935. **Genres:** Cultural/Ethnic Topics. **Career:** Ordained Roman Catholic priest, 1965; Assumption Seminary, dean of students, 1969-; San Fernando Cathedral, rector; Mexican American Cultural Center, organiser, 1972-; University of Notre Dame, fellow, professor of pastoral and hispanic theology; Kellogg Institute, fellow; Institute for Latino Studies, fellow; y Sociales, founding member. Writer. **Publications:** A Search for Meaning in Life and Death, 1971 as The Human Quest: A Search for Meaning through Life and Death, 1978; Christianity and Culture: An Introduction to Pastoral Theology and Ministry for the Bicultural Community, 1975; Mestizaje: The Dialectic of Cultural Birth and the Gospel; A Study in the Intercultural Dimension of Evangelization, 3 vols., Mexican American Cultural Center, 1978; (with A. Erevia) Our Hispanic Pilgrimage, Mexican-American Cultural Center, 1980; La Morenita, evangelizadora de las Américas, 1981; Galilean Journey: The Mexican-American Promise, 1983, 8th ed., 2000. The Future is Mestizo: Life Where Cultures Meet, 1988, 6th ed., 2000; Guadalupe, Mother of the New Creation, 1997, 3rd ed., 1998; (with T.M. Matovina) Mestizo Worship: A Pastoral Approach to Liturgical Ministry, 1998; Retreat with Our Lady of Guadalupe and Juan Diego: Heeding the Call, 1998; (with T.M. Matovina) San Fernando Cathedral: Soul of the City, 1998; Beyond Borders: Writings of Virgilio Elizondo and Friends, 2000; (co-author) The Catholic Experience of Small Christian Communities, 2000; Galilean Journey: The Mexican-American Promise, 2000; Future is Mestizo: Life Where Cultures Meet, 2000; Virgen y madre: reflexiones biblicas sobre Maria de Nazaret, 2003; (with G. Espinosa and J. Miranda) Hispanic Churches in American Public life: Summary of Findings, 2003; God of Incredible Surprises: Jesus of Galilee, 2003; (with J.L. Gonzalez) Go and Do Likewise: Studies on Christian Faith and Social Action, 2006; (with J.L. Gonzalez) Who is My Neighbor?: Christian Faith and Social Action, 2006; Charity, 2008; Virgilio Elizondo: Spiritual Writings, 2010. EDITOR: (with N. Greinacher) Women in a Men's Church, 1980; (with N. Greinacher) Tensions between the Churches in the First World and the Third World, 1981; (with N. Greinacher) Churches in Socialist Societies of Eastern Europe, 1982; (with N. Greinacher) Church and Peace, 1983; (with C. Geffré and G. Gutiérrez) Difference Theologies, Common Responsibility: Babel or Pentecost?, 1984; (with Leonardo Boff) The People of God Amidst the Poor, 1984; (with N. Greinacher) The Transmission of the Faith to the Next Generation, 1984; (with L. Boff) Option for the Poor: Challenge to the Rich Countries, 1986; (with L. Boff) People of God Amidst the Poor, 1986; (with L. Boff) Convergences and Differences, 1988; (with L. Boff) 1492-1992: The Voice of the Victims, 1990; (with L. Boff) 1492-1992: The Voice of the Victims, 1990; Way of the Cross: The Passion of Christ in the Americas, 1992; (with Leonardo Boff) Any Room for Christ in Asia?, 1993; (with L. Boff and contrib.) Ecology and Poverty: Cry of the Earth, Cry of the Poor, 1995; (with S. Freyne) Pilgrimage, 1996; (with J.O. Beozzo) Return of the Plague, 1997; (with J. Sobrino) 2000: Reality and Hope, 1999; (with G. Espinosa and J. Miranda) Latino Religions and Civic Activism in the United States, 2005; (with A.F. Deck and T. Matovina) Treasure of Guadalupe, 2006. Contributor to periodicals. **Address:** Department of Theology, University of Notre Dame, 250 McKenna Hall, Notre Dame, IN 46556, U.S.A. **Online address:** elizondo.2@nd.edu

ELIZUR, Joel. Israeli (born Israel), b. 1952. **Genres:** Psychology, Psychiatry, Human Relations/Parenting, Medicine/Health, Social Sciences. **Career:** Kibbutz Child and Family Clinic, director of medical psychology, 1975-; Hebrew University of Jerusalem, Department of Psychology, professor, 1991-. Writer. **Publications:** (With S. Minuchin) Institutionalizing Madness: Fami-

lies, Therapy, and Society, 1989; Temunot ḥayim: sipuram shel mitmodedim, 2003. Contributor to periodicals. **Address:** Department of Psychology, Hebrew University of Jerusalem, Mt. Scopus, 91 905, Israel.

ELKELES, Simone. American (born United States), b. 1970. **Genres:** Novels. **Career:** Writer. **Publications:** How to Ruin a Summer Vacation, 2006; How to Ruin My Teenage Life, 2007; Leaving Paradise, 2007; How to Ruin Your Boyfriend's Reputation, 2009; Perfect Chemistry, 2009; Return to Paradise, 2010; Rules of Attraction, 2010. Contributor to periodicals. **Address:** c/o Flux, 2143 Wooddale Dr., Woodbury, MN 55125-2989, U.S.A. **Online address:** simone@simoneelkeles.net

ELKINS, Charlotte. American (born United States), b. 1948. **Genres:** Mystery/Crime/Suspense, Romance/Historical, Novels. **Career:** Artist, 1972-73; school teacher, 1974-76; M.H. DeYoung Museum, librarian of American art, 1980-81; writer, 1982-. **Publications:** MYSTERY NOVELS WITH A. ELKINS: A Wicked Slice, 1989; Rotten Lies, 1995; Nasty Breaks, 1997; On the Fringe, 2005. NOVELS: (with A. Elkins) Where Have All the Birdies Gone?, 2004; The Golf Mystery, 2007; (with A. Elkins) A Dangerous Talent, 2012. Works appear in anthologies. Contributor to books and periodicals. **Address:** c/o Nat Sobel, Sobel Weber Associates Inc., 146 E 19th St., New York, NY 10003-2404, U.S.A.

ELKINS, Dov Peretz. American (born United States), b. 1937. **Genres:** Education, Psychology, Theology/Religion. **Career:** Har Zion Temple, rabbi, 1966-70; Villanova University, Department of Theology, faculty, 1969-70; Temple Bethel, rabbi, 1972-76; Growth Associates, founder and director, 1976-; Park Synagogue, senior rabbi, 1987-92; Princeton NJ Jewish Center, rabbi, 1992-2005; Jewish Center of Princeton, rabbi emeritus, 2005-. Writer. **Publications:** (With A. Eisenberg) Worlds Lost and Found (biblical archaeology), 1964; So Young to Be a Rabbi, 1969; (with A. Eisenberg) Treasures from the Dust (biblical archaeology), 1972; A Tradition Reborn (sermons and essays), 1972; God's Warriors, Stories of Military Chaplains (children), 1974; Glad to Be Me, 1976; Humanizing Jewish Life, 1976; Teaching People to Love Themselves, 1977; Clarifying Jewish Values, 1977; Jewish Consciousness Raising, 1977; Loving My Jewishness, 1978; Self Concept Sourcebook, 1979; Experiential Programs for Jewish Groups, 1979; 12 Pathways to Feeling Better about Yourself, 1980; My 72 Friends, 1989; Prescription for a Long and Happy Life, 1993; Shepherd of Jerusalem: A Biography of Rabbi Abraham Isaac Kook, 1995; Jewish Guided Imagery: A How-To Book for Rabbis, Educators, and Group Leaders, 1996; (trans. with J. Elkins and S. Raz) Hasidic Wisdom, 1997; A Shabbat Reader, 1998; Forty Days of Transformation, 1999; Meditations for the Days of Awe, 1999; New and Old Prayers for the High Holy Days, 2000; Chicken Soup for the Jewish Soul, 2001; The Bible's Top 50 Ideas: The Essential Concepts Everyone Should Know, 2005. EDITOR: Rejoice with Jerusalem (reading and prayers), 1972; Loving My Jewishness: Jewish Self-Pride and Self-Esteem, 1978; Moments of Transcendence, vol. I: Rosh Hashanah, vol. II: Yom Kippur, 1992; A Shabbat Reader: Universe of Cosmic Joy, 1998; Forty Days of Transformation: Daily Reflections of Teshuvah for Spiritual Growth from Rosh Hodesh Elul to Yom Kippur, 1999; New and Old Prayers and Readings: For the High Holy Days, Shabbat, and Festive Occasions, 2000; Enveloped in Light: The Tallit Sourcebook, 2004; Yom Kippur Readings: Inspiration, Information, Contemplation, 2005; Rosh Hashanah Readings: Inspiration, Information, and Contemplation, 2006; Wisdom of Judaism: An Introduction to the Values of the Talmud, 2007; Jewish Stories from Heaven and Earth: Inspiring Tales to Nourish the Heart and Soul, 2008; Sidrah Sparks: Talking Torah at the Table with the Family, 2010. **Address:** Growth Associates, 22 Governors Ln., Princeton, NJ 08540, U.S.A. **Online address:** dpe@jewishgrowth.org

ELLENBECKER, Todd S. American (born United States), b. 1962. **Genres:** Medicine/Health, Sports/Fitness, Education. **Career:** Lincoln Institute for Athletic Medicine, staff physical therapist, 1986-89; Healthsouth Sports Medicine and Rehabilitation, clinical director of sports medicine and coordinator of clinical education, 1989-95; Physiotherapy Associates Scottsdale Sports Clinic, clinic director, national director of clinic research, 1995-; Rocky Mountain University, faculty, 1999-; University of Wisconsin-LaCrosse, adjunct clinical professor, 2001-; Association of Tennis Professionals, director of medical services, 2007-. Writer and consultant. **Publications:** The Elbow in Sport: Mechanism of Injury, Evaluation, and Treatment, 1996; (with P. Roetert) Complete Conditioning for Tennis, 1998; (ed.) Knee Ligament Rehabilitation, 2000; (with J.S. Davies) Closed Kinetic Chain Exercise, 2001; (ed. with P. Page) The Scientific and Clinical Application of Elastic Resistance,

2003; Clinical Examination of the Shoulder, 2004; (with P. Page) Strength Band Training, 2005, 2nd ed., 2011; (ed.) Shoulder Rehabilitation: Non-operative Treatment, 2006; (with E.P. Roetert) Complete Conditioning for Tennis, 2007; (with M.D. Carlo and C.D. Rosa) Effective Functional Progressions in Sport Rehabilitation, 2009. Contributor to books and journals. **Address:** Physiotherapy Associates, Scottsdale Sports Clinic, 9449 N 90th St., Ste. 100, Scottsdale, AZ 85258, U.S.A.

ELLENBERG, George B. American (born United States), b. 1958. **Genres:** History, Business/Trade/Industry. **Career:** University of West Florida, professor, 1994-, associate dean, 2007-, vice provost, 2010-; Naval War College, fleet professor. Writer. **Publications:** Mule South to Tractor South: Mules, Machines, and the Transformation of the Cotton South, 2007. **Address:** University of West Florida, Bldg. 10/212 Office of the Provost, 11000 University Pkwy., Pensacola, FL 32514, U.S.A. **Online address:** gellenberg@uwf.edu

ELLENBERG, Jordan S. American (born United States), b. 1971?. **Genres:** Novels, Young Adult Fiction. **Career:** Princeton University, instructor, 1998-2001, assistant professor, 2001-05; University of Wisconsin, assistant professor of mathematics, 2005-07, associate professor, 2007-11, professor, 2011-. Writer. **Publications:** The Grasshopper King, 2003. Contributor to journals and periodicals. **Address:** Department of Mathematics, University of Wisconsin, 323 Van Vleck Hall, 480 Lincoln Dr., Madison, WI 53706-1325, U.S.A. **Online address:** ellenber@math.wisc.edu

ELLENBLUM, Roni. *See* **ELLENBLUM, Ronnie.**

ELLENBLUM, Ronnie. (Roni Ellenblum). Israeli (born Israel), b. 1952?. **Genres:** History, Travel/Exploration. **Career:** Hebrew University of Jerusalem, assistant faculty member, 1986-88, 1989-91, teaching fellow, 1993-94, lecturer, 1994-97, senior lecturer, 1998-2004, associate professor, 2005-; Cambridge University, Clare Hall College, visiting fellow, 1998-99. Writer. **Publications:** (with A. Ramon) The Walls of Jerusalem: A Guide to the Ramparts Walking Tour, 1995; Frankish Rural Settlement in the Latin Kingdom of Jerusalem, 1998; (ed. with I. Shagrir and J. Riley-Smith) In Laudem Hierosolymitani: Studies in Crusades and Medieval Culture in Honour of Benjamin Z. Kedar, 2007; Crusader Castles and Modern Histories, 2007. **Address:** Department of Geography, Hebrew University of Jerusalem, Mount Scopus, 91905, Israel. **Online address:** msronni@mscc.huji.ac.il

ELLENBOGEN, Gustavo Gorriti. *See* **GORRITI, Gustavo.**

ELLENSON, David Harry. American (born United States), b. 1947?. **Genres:** Theology/Religion. **Career:** Ordained rabbi, 1977; Hebrew Union College-Jewish Institute of Religion, president & I.H. and Anna Grancell professor of Jewish religious thought; Shalom Hartman Institute of Jerusalem, fellow; Hebrew University, Institute of Advanced Studies, fellow & lecturer. Writer. **Publications:** Tradition in Transition: Orthodoxy, Halakhah and the Boundaries of Modern Jewish Identity, 1989; (co-author) VersOhnung in der judischen und christlichen Liturgie, 1990; Rabbi Esriel Hildesheimer and the Creation of a Modern Jewish Orthodoxy, 1990; Religious Pluralism and Modern Israel: Implications for Israel-Diaspora Relations, 1992; (ed. with S. Chyet) Bits of Honey: Essays for Samson H. Levey, 1993; Between Tradition and Culture: The Dialectics of Modern Jewish Religion and Identity, 1994; (with J.M. Harris) Parshanut ha-Mikra ve-hithavut ha-Ortodoksyah Ha-modernit, ha-Fakultah le-mada'e ha-ruah, 2002; After Emancipation: Jewish Religious Responses to Modernity, 2004; Wissenschaft des Judentums, Historical Consciousness and Jewish Faith: The Diverse Paths of Frankel, Auerbach and Halevy, 2004. **Address:** Hebrew Union College-Jewish Institute of Religion, 1 W 4th St., New York, NY 10012, U.S.A.

ELLER, Scott. *See* **SHEPARD, Jim.**

ELLERBECK, Rosemary. Also writes as Nicola Thorne, Katherine Yorke, Anna L'estrange. British/South African (born South Africa) **Genres:** Novels, Adult Non-fiction, Young Adult Fiction. **Career:** Editor, through 1976; full-time writer, 1976-; Milton House Books, editorial director. Publisher. **Publications:** AS NICOLA THORNE: The Girls, 1967; Bridie Climbing, 1969; In Love, 1973; A Woman Like Us, 1979; The Perfect Wife and Mother, 1980; The Daughters of the House, 1981; Sisters & Lovers, 1981; Cashmere, 1982; Where the Rivers Meet, 1982; Affairs of Love, 1984; The Askham Chronicles, 1898-1967: Never Such Innocence, 1985, Yesterday's Promises, 1986, Bright Morning, 1986, A Place in the Sun, 1987; Pride of Place, 1988; Cham-

pagne, 1989; Bird of Passage, 1990; The People of This Parish, 1991; The Rector's Daughter, 1992; Champagne Gold, 1992; A Wind in Summer, 1993; Silk, 1993; Profit and Loss, 1994; Trophy Wife, 1995; Repossession, 1996; Worlds Apart, 1996; Old Money, 1997; Rules of Engagement, 1997; In This Quiet Earth, 1998; The Good Samaritan, 1998; Past Love, 1998; Class Reunion, 1999; A Time of Hope, 1999; In Time of War, 2000; My Name Is Martha Brown, 2000; In Search of Martha Brown (nonfiction), 2000; The Broken Bough, 2001; The Blackbird's Song, 2001; A Friend of the Family, 2002; The Water's Edge, 2002; The Coppitts Green, 2003; Oh Happy Day!, 2003; The House by the Sea, 2004; Coppitt's Green, 2004; The Little Flowers, 2004; On a Day Like Today, 2010; The Holly Tree, 2010. OTHERS: Inclination to Murder, 1965; Hammersleigh, 1976; Rose, Rose Where Are You?, 1978; (as Anna L'estrange) Return to Wuthering Heights, 1978; Pride of Place, 1988; Silk: A Novel, 1993; Profit and Loss, 1994; and Trophy Wife, 1995. AS KATHERINE YORKE: The Enchantress, 1979; Falcon Gold, 1980; Lady of the Lakes, 1982; Woman's Place, 1983; The Pair Bond, 1984; Swift Flows the River, 1988; People of This Parish, 1991; Wind in Summer, 1991. **Address:** Juliet Burton Literary Agency, 2 Clifton Ave., London, GL W12 9DR, England. **Online address:** rosemary@ellerbeck01fsnet.co.uk

ELLINGHAM, Lewis. American (born United States), b. 1933. **Genres:** Poetry, Genealogy/Heraldry, Biography, History. **Career:** Writer. **Publications:** The Jefferson Airplane (poetry), 1967; (with E.J. Rose) The Heymanns of Kaltenholzhausen, 1995; The Ancestors of David Miller and Clarissa Moore, 1995; Ellingham Index in North America, 1998; (with K. Killian) Poet Be like God (biography), 1998; Two Coventry Shoemakers Become Indiana Farmers: The Descendants of William Ellingham & John Scotton, 2000; Birds and Other Poems, 2009. **Address:** Wesleyan University Press, 110 Mt. Vernon St., Middletown, CT 06459, U.S.A.

ELLINGSON, Stephen. American (born United States), b. 1962. **Genres:** Theology/Religion, Cultural/Ethnic Topics, History. **Career:** Pacific Lutheran Theological Seminary, assistant professor of sociology of religion; Hamilton College, associate professor of sociology. Writer. **Publications:** (co-author) Organizational Ethics in Health Care: Principles, Cases and Practical Solutions, 2001; (ed. with M.C. Green) Religion and Sexuality in Cross-cultural Perspective, 2002; (co-ed.) The Sexual Organization of the City, 2004; The Megachurch and the Mainline: Remaking Religious Tradition in the Twenty-first Century, 2007. **Address:** Hamilton College, 198 College Hill Rd., Clinton, NY 13323, U.S.A. **Online address:** sellings@hamilton.edu

ELLINGTON, Sara. American (born United States), b. 1969. **Genres:** Human Relations/Parenting, Sports/Fitness. **Career:** Hay House Radio, The Mommy Chronicles Show (radio talk show), co-host, 2005-06; Seko Air Freight, account executive. Writer. **Publications:** (With S. Triplett) The Mommy Chronicles: Conversations Sharing the Comedy and Drama of Pregnancy and New Motherhood, 2005; (with S. Triplett) The Must-Have Mom Manual: Two Mothers, Two Perspectives, One Book That Tells You Everything You Need to Know, 2009. Contributor to periodicals. **Address:** c/o Sharon Propson, The Random House Publishing Group, 1745 Broadway, New York, NY 10019, U.S.A. **Online address:** behnke@carolina.rr.com

ELLINGWOOD, Ken. American/Israeli (born Israel) **Genres:** Young Adult Fiction, Politics/Government. **Career:** Los Angeles Times, staff writer, 1992-, staff reporter and border correspondent, 1998-2002, bureau chief, 2002-03, Jerusalem Bureau, staff reporter, 2003-, Mexico City Bureau, editorial staff. Journalist. **Publications:** Hard Line: Life and Death on the U.S.-Mexico Border, 2004. **Address:** Foreign Bureau, Los Angeles Times, 202 W 1st St., Los Angeles, CA 90012-4105, U.S.A. **Online address:** ellingwood@latimes.com

ELLIOT, Alistair. British (born England), b. 1932. **Genres:** Poetry, Theatre, Translations, Literary Criticism And History. **Career:** English Children's Theatre, stage manager, 1957-59; Kensington Public Library, library assistant, 1959-61; University of Keele, assistant cataloging librarian, 1961-65; Pahlavi University Library, accessions librarian, 1965-67; University of Newcastle upon Tyne, special collections librarian, 1967-82; translator and writer, 1983-. **Publications:** POETRY: Air in the Wrong Place, 1968; Contentions, 1978; Kisses, 1978; Talking to Bede, 1982; Talking Back, 1982; On the Appian Way, 1984; My Country: Collected Poems, 1989; Turning the Stones, 1993; Facing Things, 1997; Roman Food Poems: A Modern Translation, 2003; Real Poems, 2008. TRANSLATOR: Euripides, Alcestis, 1965; Aristophanes, Peace, in Greek Comedy, 1965; Verlaine, Femmes/Hombres, Women/Men, 1979; H. Heine, The Lazarus Poems, 1979; French Love Poems, 1991;

Italian Landscape Poems, 1993; Euripides, Medea, 1993; Valéry, La Jeune Parque, 1997; Euripides, Phaethon, 2008. EDITOR: Poems by James I and Others, 1970; Lines on the Jordan, 1971; Virgil, The Georgics with John Dryden's Translation, 1981. OTHER: (comp. with J. Bagnall) Short-Title List of the Sandes Library, 1969. **Address:** c/o Nicki Stoddart, Peters Fraser & Dunlop Group Ltd., Drury House, 34-43 Russell St., London, GL WC2B 5HA, England. **Online address:** alistair.elliot@btinternet.com

ELLIOT, Bruce. See FIELD, Edward.

ELLIOTT, Anna. American (born United States), b. 1978. **Genres:** Novels. **Career:** Writer. **Publications:** Twilight of Avalon: A Novel of Trystan and Isolde, 2009; Dark Moon of Avalon: A Novel of Trystan and Isolde, 2011. **Address:** c/o Jacques de Spoelberch, J de S Associates Inc., 9 Shagbark Rd., South Norwalk, CT 06854, U.S.A. **Online address:** email@annaelliottbooks.com

ELLIOTT, Charles. (Charles W. Elliott). American (born United States), b. 1951. **Genres:** Biography, History, Novels, Young Adult Non-fiction. **Career:** Air France, accountant, 1975-80; Jean Cocteau Repertory Theatre, costume designer, 1977-80; Alta Plaza Bar, manager, 1980-90; Metro Bar, bartender, manager, 1991-. Writer. **Publications:** Princesse of Versailles: The Life of Marie Adelaide of Savoy, 1992; The Diamond Necklace, forthcoming. **Address:** Philip G. Spitzer Literary Agency, 788 9th Ave., New York, NY 10019, U.S.A.

ELLIOTT, Charles W. See ELLIOTT, Charles.

ELLIOTT, Clark A. American (born United States), b. 1941. **Genres:** History, Librarianship, Sciences, Biography, Reference, Technology, Engineering, Philosophy, Philosophy. **Career:** Simmons College, assistant professor of library science, 1969-71; Harvard University, associate curator for archives administration and research, 1971-97; History of Science in America: News and Views, founder and editor, 1980-87; Massachusetts Institute of Technology, Dibner Institute for the History of Science and Technology, Burndy Library, librarian, 1997-2000; American Academy of Arts and Sciences, consultant (archives and history), 2000-05. **Publications:** (Comp.) A Descriptive Guide to the Harvard University Archives, 1974; Biographical Dictionary of American Science: The Seventeenth through the Nineteenth Centuries, 1979; (comp.) Biographical Index to American Science, 1990; (ed. with M.W. Rossiter) Science at Harvard University: Historical Perspectives, 1992; History of Science in the United States: A Chronology and Research Guide, 1996; (ed. with P.G. Abiv-Am) Commemorative Practices in Science: Historical Perspectives on the Politics of Collective Memory, 1999; Thaddeus William Harris (1795-1856): Nature, Science and Society in the Life of an American Naturalist, 2008. **Address:** 105 Beech St., Ste. 2, Belmont, MA 02478, U.S.A. **Online address:** claelliott@earthlink.net

ELLIOTT, David. American (born United States), b. 1947?. **Genres:** Picture/Board Books, Children's Fiction, Graphic Novels, Children's Non-fiction. **Career:** Colby-Sawyer College, instructor, International Student Services, director, English Language and American Culture Program, director, faculty of creative writing. Writer. **Publications:** An Alphabet of Rotten Kids!, 1991; The Cool Crazy Crickets, 2000; The Cool Crazy Crickets to the Rescue!, 2001; The Transmogrification of Roscoe Wizzle, 2001; Hazel Nutt, Mad Scientist, 2003; Hazel Nutt, Alien Hunter, 2004; And Here's to You!, 2004; Evangeline Mudd and the Golden-haired Apes of the Ikkinasti Jungle, 2004; Evangeline Mudd and the Great Mink Escapade, 2006; One Little Chicken: A Counting Book, 2007; Jeremy Cabbage and the Living Museum of Human Oddballs and Quadruped Delights, 2008; Wuv Bunnies From Outers Pace, 2008; On the Farm, 2008; Knitty Kitty, 2008; What the Grizzly Knows, 2008; Finn Throws a Fit!, 2009; In the Wild, 2010; In the Sea, 2012. **Address:** Department of Humanities, Colby-Sawyer College, 541 Main St., New London, NH 03257, U.S.A. **Online address:** delliott@colby-sawyer.edu

ELLIOTT, Elaine M. American (born United States), b. 1931. **Genres:** Romance/Historical, Young Adult Fiction, Human Relations/Parenting. **Career:** Writer. **Publications:** Love's Sweet Fire, 1984; Daughter of the Reservation, 1998. Contributor to periodicals. **Address:** 377 Dominion View Rd., Colville, WA 99114-9250, U.S.A. **Online address:** jackpot@plix.com

ELLIOTT, Joey. See HOUK, Randy.

ELLIOTT, John Huxtable. British (born England), b. 1930. **Genres:** History. **Career:** Cambridge University, assistant lecturer, 1958-62, lecturer in history, 1962-67, University of London, King's College, professor of history, 1968-73; British Academy, fellow, 1972; School of Historical Studies, Institute for Advanced Study, professor, 1973-90; American Academy of Arts and Sciences, fellow, 1977; New York University, King Juan Carlos visiting professor, 1988; Oxford University, Regius professor of modern history, 1990-97, Regius professor emeritus of modern history; University of Warwick, visiting honorary professor, 2003-07; Oriel College, honorary fellow; Trinity College, honorary fellow, 1991. Writer. **Publications:** Imperial Spain, 1469-1716, 1963; The Revolt of the Catalans: A Study in the Decline of Spain (1598-1640), 1963; Europe Divided, 1559-1598, 1968, 2nd ed., 2000; The Old World and the New, 1492-1650, 1970; (with H.G. Koenigsberger) The Diversity of History, 1970; The Discovery of America and the Discovery of Man, 1972; El conde-duque de Olivares y la herencia de Felipe II, 1977; Memoriales y Cartas del Conde Duque de Olivares, 1978; (with J. Brown) A Palace for a King: The Buen Retiro and the Court of Philip IV, 1980, rev. ed., 2003; Richelieu and Olivares, 1984; Discurso de investidura de doctor honoris causa, 1984; The Count-Duke of Olivares: The Statesman in An Age of Decline, 1986; Spain and Its World, 1500-1700, 1989; The Hispanic World, 1991; National and Comparative History, 1991; El mundo hispánico: civilización e imperio: Europa y América: pasado y presente, 1991; The Spanish World: Civilization and Empire, Europe and the Americas, Past and Present, 1991; Lengua e imperio en la España de Felipe IV, 1994; Do the Americas have a Common History?: An Dddress, 1998; Empires of the Atlantic World: Britain and Spain in America, 1492-1830, 2006; Spain, Europe & The Wider World, 1500-1800, 2009. EDITOR: (with L. Brockliss) The World of the Favourite, 1999; (with J. Brown) The Sale of the Century, 2002; (with J. Arrieta) Forms of Union: The British and Spanish Monarchies in the Seventeenth and Eighteenth Centuries, 2009. Contributor to periodicals. **Address:** Oriel College, Oxford, OX OX1 4EW, England.

ELLIOTT, Kate. See RASMUSSEN, Alis A.

ELLIOTT, Marianne. British/Irish (born Ireland), b. 1948. **Genres:** History, Theology/Religion. **Career:** West London Institute of Higher Education, lecturer in history, 1975-77; University of Wales, University College, research fellow and lecturer in history, 1977-82; Iowa State University, honorary visiting professor of history, 1983; University of South Carolina, visiting professor of history, 1984; University of Liverpool, research fellow in history, 1984-87, Andrew Geddes and John Rankin professor of modern history, 1993-, honorary research fellow, Institute of Irish Studies, director, 1997-; Victoria University of Manchester, Simon senior research fellow, 1988-89; University of London, Birkbeck College, lecturer in history, 1991-93; Oxford University, Ford Lecturer, 2005. Writer. **Publications:** Partners in Revolution: The United Irishmen and France, 1982; Watchmen in Sion: The Protestant Idea of Liberty, 1985; (trans.) R.C. Cobb, The People's Armies, 1987; Wolfe Tone: Prophet of Irish Independence, 1989; (co-author) A Citizen's Inquiry: The Opsahl Report on Northern Ireland, 1993; The Catholics of Ulster: A History, 2000; (ed.) The Long Road to Peace in Northern Ireland: Peace Lectures from the Institute of Irish Studies at Liverpool University, 2002; Robert Emmet: The Making of a Legend, 2003; When God Took Sides: Religion and Identity in Ireland, 2009. Contributor of articles to books and journals. **Address:** Institute of Irish Studies, University of Liverpool, 1 Abercromby Sq., Liverpool, MS L69 7WY, England. **Online address:** melliott@liverpool.ac.uk

ELLIOTT, Melinda. American (born United States), b. 1947. **Genres:** History, Archaeology/Antiquities, Social Sciences, Humanities. **Career:** Journalist and writer. **Publications:** The School of American Research: A History: The First Eighty Years, 1987; (with R. Dillingham) Acoma and Laguna Pottery, 1992; Great Excavations: Tales of Early Southwestern Archaeology, 1888-1939, 1995. Contributor to periodicals. **Address:** c/o Maggie Duval, PO Box 515, Tesuque, NM 87574, U.S.A.

ELLIOTT, Odette. British (born England), b. 1939. **Genres:** Children's Fiction. **Career:** International Voluntary Service, secretary and assistant administrator of overseas work camp exchange scheme, 1980-83; University College London, secretary and administrator, 1984-87; Centre for Policy on Ageing, secretary and administrator, 1988-92; Horizon House Publications, secretary, 1993-. Writer. **Publications:** Under Sammy's Bed, 1989; Sammy Goes Flying, 1990, new ed., 2011; Sammy and the Telly, 1991; Sammy's Christmas Workshop, 1992; Nightingale News, 1996; My Big Brother JJ, 2009. **Address:** 35 Meyrick Rd., Willesden, London, GL NW10 2EL, England. **Online address:** odette.elliott@ntlworld.com

ELLIOTT, William. *See* **ELLIS, William E.**

ELLIS, Alec (Charles Owen). British (born England), b. 1932. **Genres:** Education, History, Librarianship. **Career:** Liverpool City Libraries, assistant librarian, 1949-61; St. Katharine's College of Education, librarian, 1961-64; Liverpool Polytechnic, School of Information Science and Technology, lecturer, 1965-68, senior lecturer, 1968-72, principal lecturer, 1972-78, School of Librarianship and Information Studies, head, 1978-88, deputy director of academic affairs, 1988-91; University of Liverpool, external examiner, 1968-71; University of Wales, external examiner, 1980-. Writer. **Publications:** How to Find Out about Children's Literature, 1966, 3rd ed., 1973; A History of Children's Reading and Literature, 1968; Library Services for Young People in England and Wales 1830-1970, 1971; Books in Victorian Elementary Schools, 1971; Public Libraries and the First World War, 1975; (ed.) The Parish of All Hallows Allerton, Allerton, 1876-1976, 1976; (ed. with M. Crouch) Chosen for Children: An Account of the Books Which Have been Awarded the Library Association Carnegie Medal, 1936-1975, 1977; Public Libraries at the Time of the Adams Report, 1979; Educating Our Masters: Influences on the Growth of Literacy in Victorian Working Class Children, 1985; Librarianship on the Mersey, 1987; The Parish of All Hallows Allerton: A History, 2000; The Bibby Family and All Hallows Church, Allerton, 2001. **Address:** Liverpool Polytechnic, Tithebarn St., Liverpool, MS L2 2ER, England.

ELLIS, Anita J. American (born United States) **Genres:** Art/Art History, History. **Career:** Cincinnati Art Museum, Curatorial Affairs, deputy director, 1974-. Curator and writer. **Publications:** Illusions in Glass: The Art of Christopher Ries, 1988; (co-author) Fine Art of Folk Art, 1990; Rookwood Pottery: The Glorious Gamble, 1992; Rookwood Pottery: The Glaze Lines, 1995; (contrib.) The Collections of the Cincinnati Art Museum, 2000; (contrib.) Treasures for a Queen: A Millennium Gift to Cincinnati, 2001; (co-writer) An Expression of the Community: Cincinnati Public Schools Legacy of Art and Architecture, 2001; The Ceramic Career of M. Louise McLaughlin, 2003; (contrib.) The Cincinnati Wing: The Story of Art in the Queen City, 2003; (co-writer) Rookwood and the American Indian: Masterpieces of Art Pottery from the James J. Gardner Collection, 2007. **Address:** Cincinnati Art Museum, 953 Eden Park Dr., Cincinnati, OH 45202, U.S.A. **Online address:** aellis@cincyart.org

ELLIS, Barbara W. American (born United States), b. 1953. **Genres:** Horticulture, Homes/Gardens, How-to Books, Animals/Pets, Botany, Crafts, Environmental Sciences/Ecology, Natural History, Natural History. **Career:** Fred C. Gloeckner Co., executive assistant, producer, editor of horticultural supply catalogs, 1978-79; American Horticultural Society, associate editor, 1980-83, publications director and editor, 1983-87; freelance writer and editor, 1987-88, 1994-; Rodale Press, editor of garden books, 1988-89, senior editor, 1989-93, managing editor, 1993-94. **Publications:** Attracting Birds and Butterflies, 1997; Easy Practical Pruning, 1997; How to Grow North America's Favorite Plants, 1998; Taylor's Guide to Growing North America's Favorite Plants, 1998; Taylor's Guide to Annuals, 1999; (with J. Benjamin and D.L. Martin) Rodale's Low-Maintenance Landscaping Techniques, 1999; The Complete Gardener's Dictionary, 2000; Taylor's Guide to Perennials, 2000; Taylor's Guide to Bulbs, 2001; Deckscaping, 2001; Deckscaping, 2002; 20 Plans for Colorful Shady Retreats, 2003; Covering Ground, 2007; The Veggie Gardener's Answer Book, 2008. EDITOR: Rodale's Illustrated Encyclopedia of Gardening and Landscaping Techniques, 1990, rev. ed., 2009; (with F.M. Bradley) Rodale's All-New Encyclopedia of Organic Gardening, 1992; (with F.M. Bradley) Organic Gardener's Handbook of Natural Insect and Disease Control, 1992; (with J. Benjamin) Rodale's No-Fail Flower Garden, 1994; Safe and Easy Lawn Care, 1997; Organic Pest and Disease Control, 1997; (with F.M. Bradley and D.L. Martin) Organic Gardener's Handbook of Natural Pest and Disease Control, 2009. Contributor to garden magazines. **Address:** 23161 Buck Neck Rd., Chestertown, MD 21620, U.S.A. **Online address:** bwe@fast.net

ELLIS, Bret Easton. American (born United States), b. 1964. **Genres:** Novels, Novellas/Short Stories, Literary Criticism And History. **Career:** Writer. **Publications:** Less Than Zero, 1985; The Rules of Attraction, 1987; American Psycho, 1990; The Informers, 1994; Glamorama, 1998; Lunar Park, 2005; Water from the Sun and Discovering Japan, 2006; Imperial Bedrooms, 2010. Contributor of articles to periodicals. **Address:** Knopf Publicity, 1745 Broadway, New York, NY 10019-4368, U.S.A.

ELLIS, David. American (born United States), b. 1967. **Genres:** Young Adult Fiction, Novels. **Career:** Writer and lawyer. **Publications:** Line of Vision, 2001; Life Sentence, 2003; Jury of One, 2004; In the Company of Liars, 2005; Eye of the Beholder, 2007; The Hidden Man, 2009; Breach of Trust, 2011; (with J. Patterson) Guilty Wives, 2012. **Address:** c/o Summer Smith, Penguin/Putnam Inc., 375 Hudson St., New York, NY 10014, U.S.A. **Online address:** dave@davidellis.com

ELLIS, Donald. (Donald G. Ellis). American (born United States), b. 1947?. **Genres:** Communications/Media, Young Adult Fiction, Young Adult Nonfiction. **Career:** Purdue University, faculty; Michigan State University, faculty; Communication Theory Journal, editor; University of Pennsylvania, Asch Center for the Study of Ethnopolitical Conflict, fellow; University of Hartford, professor of communications, Arts Sciences Humanities Center, director. **Publications:** Stylistic Analysis of Newspaper Portrayals of Hispanic Americans in Six Western U.S. Communities, 1981; (ed. with W.A. Donohue) Contemporary Issues in Language and Discourse Processes, 1986; (with B.A. Fisher) Small Group Decision Making: Communication and the Group Process, 3rd ed., 1990, 4th ed., 1994; From Language to Communication, 1992, 2nd ed., 1999; Crafting Society: Ethnicity Class and Communication Theory, 1999; Transforming Conflict: Communication and Ethnopolitical Conflict, 2006. **Address:** School of Communication, University of Hartford, E215 Harry Gray Ctr., 200 Bloomfield Ave., West Hartford, CT 06117-1599, U.S.A. **Online address:** dellis@hartford.edu

ELLIS, Donald G. *See* **ELLIS, Donald.**

ELLIS, Ella Thorp. American (born United States), b. 1928. **Genres:** Novels, Children's Fiction, Autobiography/Memoirs, Science Fiction/Fantasy. **Career:** Acalanes Adult School, teacher of English, 1971-76; University of California, extension instructor in creative writing, 1972-77, extension lecturer in longer fiction, 1987-94; San Francisco State University, lecturer in creative writing, 1974-80; University of Women's Studies, lecturer, 1981-85. Writer. **Publications:** Roam the Wild Country, 1967; Riptide, 1969; Celebrate the Morning, 1972; Where the Road Ends, 1974; Hallelujah (science fiction), 1976; Sleepwalker's Moon, 1980; Hugo and the Princess Nena, 1983; Swimming with the Whales, 1995; The Year of My Indian Prince, 2001; Dune Child, 2011. Works appear in anthologies. **Address:** c/o Patricia Myrer, McIntosh & Otis Inc., 353 Lexington Ave., Ste. 1500, New York, NY 10016-0900, U.S.A. **Online address:** ellathorpellis@hotmail.com

ELLIS, Evelyn. British (born England), b. 1948. **Genres:** Law, Race Relations. **Career:** University of Birmingham, lecturer, 1972-88, senior lecturer in law, 1988-93, reader in public law, 1993-96, professor of public law, 1996-, 2008, head, 2000, 2003, now professor emeritus; University of Western Australia, adjunct professor; King Edward VI Foundation, governor; Hereford Cathedral School, governor; Sytchampton First School, governor; Jersey Institute of Law, faculty. Writer and barrister. **Publications:** Sex Discrimination Law, 1988; European Community Sex Equality Law, 1991, 2nd ed. as EC Sex Equality Law, 1998; (with T. Tridimas) Public Law of the European Community, 1995; (ed.) The Principle of Proportionality in the Laws of Europe, 1999; EU Anti-Discrimination Law, 2005; (contrib.) Equality into Reality: Action for Diversity and Non-Discrimination in Iceland, 2012. **Address:** Birmingham Law School, University of Birmingham, Edgbaston, Birmingham, WM B15 2TT, England. **Online address:** e.d.ellis@bham.ac.uk

ELLIS, Gwen. American (born United States), b. 1938. **Genres:** Children's Fiction, Children's Non-fiction, Film, inspirational/Motivational Literature, Picture/Board Books, Theology/Religion. **Career:** Focus on Family, managing editor of books, 1991-95; Servant Publications, acquisitions editor, 1996-98; Zondervan, gift product director, 1998-99, children's acquisitions editor, 1999-; Seaside Creative Services Inc., founder, 2003-. **Publications:** Raising Kids on Purpose for the Fun of It, 1989; Finding Time for Family Fun, 1991; Finding Dollars for Family Fun: Creating Happy Memories on a Budget, 1993; Thriving as a Working Woman, 1995; 101 Ways to Make Money at Home, 1995; By His Pattern: A Devotional for Needlework Lovers, 1998; The Big Book of Family Fun, 1999; (with J.A. Janssen) Decorating on a Shoestring: You Can Create a Beautiful Home Without Spending a Fortune, 1999; Big Book of Family Fun, 2000; (with J.A. Janssen) Dress Like a Million Bucks Without Spending It!, 2003; Thriving as a Working Woman, 2005; Simply Fun for Families, 2005; The Read and Share Bible, 2007. **Address:** 2607 Gold Cv, Port Hueneme, CA 93041-1558, U.S.A. **Online address:** gwen@seasidecreativeservices.com

ELLIS, Gwynn Pennant. Welsh/British (born England) **Genres:** Chemistry, Sciences, Reference. **Career:** Monsanto Chemicals, research chemist, 1951-53; Imperial Chemical Industries, scientific officer, 1953-57; Fisons Pharmaceuticals, head of chemistry research, 1957-62; Progress in Medicinal Chemistry, founder and co-editor, 1961-; University of Wales, reader, 1962-89. **Publications:** Modern Textbook of Organic Chemistry, 1966; (with W.J. Criddle) Qualitative Organic Chemical Analysis, 1967; (ed.) Medicinal Chemistry Reviews, 1972; (with W.J. Criddle) Spectral and Chemical Characterisation of Organic Compounds, 1976, 3rd ed. 1990; (ed.) Chromenes, Chromanones and Chromones, 1977; (ed. with I.M. Lockhart) Chromans and Tocopherols, 1981; Synthesis of Fused Heterocycles, 1987. **Address:** 6 Ffordd Gwyndy, Penrhos Garnet, Bangor, GY LL57 2EX, Wales.

ELLIS, Harold. British (born England), b. 1926. **Genres:** Medicine/Health, Sciences. **Career:** University of Oxford, surgical tutor, 1959-61; Westminster Medical School, professor, 1961-89; Westminster Hospital, foundation chair of surgery, 1962-89; University of London, senior lecturer, professor of surgery, 1989, now professor emeritus, King's College London School of Medicine, Department of Anatomy and Human Sciences, professor; University of Cambridge, University Clinical Anatomist, 1989-93; Guy's Hospital, clinical anatomist, 1993; University of Cambridge, faculty, 1993. Writer. **Publications:** Clinical Anatomy: A Revision and Applied Anatomy for Clinical Students, 1966, (with V. Mahadevan) 12th ed., 2010; (with S. Feldman) Principles of Resuscitation, 1967, (with S. Feldman) 2nd ed., 1975; (with R.Y. Calne) Lecture Notes on General Surgery, 1968, (with R. Calne and C. Watson) 12th ed., 2011; History of the Bladder Stone, 1969; (with M. McLarty) Anatomy for Anaesthetists, 1969, (with S. Feldman and W.H. Griffiths) 8th ed., 2004; General Surgery for Nurses, 1976; Multiple Choice Questions on Lecture Notes on General Surgery, 1977; Intestinal Obstruction, 1982; Varicose Veins: How They Are Treated and What You Can Do to Help, 1982; Famous Operations, 1984; Maingot's Abdominal Operations, 1985, (with S.I. Schwartz and W.C. Husser) 9th ed., 1989; Spleen, 1988; Spot Diagnosis in General Surgery, 1990; Research in Medicine: A Guide to Writing A Thesis in The Medical Sciences, 1990; Human Cross-Sectional Anatomy: Atlas of Body Sections and CT Images, 1992; Surgical Case Histories from the Past; (with R. Savalgi) Clinical Anatomy for Laparoscopic and Thoracoscopic Surgery, 1996; Index of Differential Diagnosis, (ed. with M. Kinirons) 14th ed., 2005; Operations that Made History, 1996; Clinical Anatomy: A Revision and Applied Anatomy for Clinical Students, 1997, 11th ed., 2006; (ed.) French's Index of Surgical Differential Diagnosis, 1999; Applied Radiological Anatomy, 1999; (ed. with B.M. Logan and A.K. Dixon) Human Sectional Anatomy: Atlas of Body Sections, CT and MRI Images, 1999, (with B.M. Logan and A.K. Dixon) 3rd ed., 2007; (with G. Murrell and C. Huang) Research in Medicine: Planning a Project, Writing a Thesis, 1999; History of Surgery, 2001; Gray's Anatomy: The Anatomical Basis of Clinical Practice, 2005, (co-ed.) 39th ed., 2005; French's Index of Differential Diagnosis: An A-Z, 2005; (with A. Mitchell and P. Butler) Applied Radiological Anatomy for Medical Students, 2007; (with C. Watson) Surgery: Clinical Cases Uncovered, 2008; Cambridge Illustrated History of Surgery, 2009. **Address:** Department of Anatomy, Kings College, Strand, London, GL WC2R 2LS, England.

ELLIS, Jamellah. American (born United States) **Genres:** Novels, Young Adult Fiction. **Career:** Saul Ewing L.L.P., attorney, 2003-; U.S. District Court for the District of Maryland, judicial clerk; Arnold and Porter, attorney. Writer. **Publications:** That Faith, That Trust, That Love (novel), 2001. **Address:** Saul Ewing LLP, 100 S Charles St., Baltimore, MD 21201-2773, U.S.A. **Online address:** jamellahellis@msn.com

ELLIS, Jerry. American (born United States), b. 1947. **Genres:** Travel/Exploration, History, Essays. **Career:** Tanager Center, co-founder. Writer and educator. **Publications:** Walking the Trail: One Man's Journey along the Cherokee Trail of Tears, 1991; Bareback! One Man's Journey along the Pony Express Trail, 1993; Marching through Georgia: My Walk with Sherman, 1995; Walking the Trail: One Man's Journey Along the Cherokee Trail of Tears, 2001; On the Trail of the Pony Express, 2002; Walking to Canterbury: A Modern Journey through Chaucer's Medieval England, 2003. **Address:** 1714 Smith Gap Rd. NW, Fort Payne, AL 35968, U.S.A. **Online address:** tanager@peop.tds.net

ELLIS, Kate. British (born England), b. 1953. **Genres:** Mystery/Crime/Suspense, Novels, Young Adult Fiction. **Career:** Teacher, 1974-81; novelist,

1998-. **Publications:** WESLEY PETERSON CRIME NOVELS: The Merchant's House, 1998; The Armada Boy, 1999; An Unhallowed Grave, 1999; The Funeral Boat, 2000; The Bone Garden, 2001; A Painted Doom, 2002; The Skeleton Room, 2003; The Plague Maiden, 2004; A Cursed Inheritance, 2005; The Marriage Hearse, 2006; The Shining Skull, 2007; The Blood Pit, 2008; A Perfect Death, 2009; The Flesh Tailor, 2010; The Jackal Man, 2011. JOE PLANTAGENET SERIES: Seeking The Dead, 2008; Playing With Bones, 2009; Kissing the Demons, 2011. A LADY KATHERYN BULKELEY MYSTERY: The Devil's Priest, 2006. **Address:** Piatkus Books, Little, Brown Book Group, 100 Victoria Embankment, London, GL EC4Y 0DY, England. **Online address:** kateellis_bullock@ntlworld.com

ELLIS, Keith. British (born England), b. 1927?. **Genres:** Mathematics/Statistics, Money/Finance, Psychology, Young Adult Fiction, Humanities, Social Sciences. **Career:** John Bull, staff writer, 1950-60; freelance writer, 1960-. **Publications:** How to Make Money in Your Spare Time, 1967; The American Civil War, 1971; Warriors and Fighting Men, 1971; The Making of America, 1973; Man and Measurement, 1973; Man and Money, 1973; Prediction and Prophecy, 1973; Thomas Telford, Father of Civil Engineering, 1974; Thomas Edison, Genius of Electricity, 1974; Science and the Supernatural, 1974; Critical Approaches to Ruben Dario, 1975; Numberpower: In Nature, Art and Everyday Life, 1977; How to Cope with Insomnia, 1983; (intro.) Amerindian Elements in the Poetry of Rubén Dario: The Alter Ego as the Indigenous Other, 2008. **Address:** 3 Belmont Hill, St. Albans, HF AL1 1RD, England.

ELLIS, Mark (Karl). British/Indian (born India), b. 1945. **Genres:** Novels, Language/Linguistics, Mystery/Crime/Suspense, Education. **Career:** Regional Institute of English, lecturer in English, 1967-69; University of Tripoli, assistant lecturer in English, 1970-73; Asian Institute of Technology, assistant professor of English, 1973-78; Professional Language Services, course coordinator, 1978-80; LTS Training and Consulting, co-founder and senior partner, 1980-. Writer. **Publications:** Bannerman, 1973; A Fatal Charade, 1974; The Adoration of the Hanged Man, 1975; Survivors Beyond Babel, 1979; (co-author) Language Guide to the Economist, 1982; (co-author) Professional English, 1984; (co-author) Counterpoint, 4 vols., 1985; (with N. Driscoll) Socializing, 1987; (with P. Ellis) Shades of Meaning, 1988; Counterpoint Intensive, 1988; (co-author) Marathon vol. I, 1991, vol. II, 1993; (co-author) Pyramid, 1993; (co-author) Teaching Business English, 1994; Kiss in the Dark, 1997; Functional English, 2005. **Address:** LTS Training and Consulting, 5 Belvedere, Lansdown Rd., Bath, SM BA1 5ED, England. **Online address:** mark@printha.com

ELLIS, Markman. British (born England) **Genres:** History, Travel/Exploration, Business/Trade/Industry, Economics. **Career:** University of London, Queen Mary and Westfield College, professor of eighteenth-century studies. Writer. **Publications:** The Politics of Sentimentalism: Controversy and Polemic in the Sentimental Novel, 1758-1771, 1992 in US as The Politics of Sensibility: Race, Gender and Commerce in the Sentimental Novel, 1996; The History of Gothic Fiction, 2000; The Coffee House: A Cultural History, 2004; (ed. with B. Carey and S. Salih) Discourses of Slavery and Abolition: Britain and Its Colonies, 1760-1838, 2004; Eighteenth Century Coffee-House Culture, 2006; Tea and the Tea-Table in Eighteenth-Century England, 2010. Contributor to periodicals. **Address:** School of English & Drama, University of London, Mile End Rd., London, GL E1 4NS, England. **Online address:** m.ellis@qmul.ac.uk

ELLIS, Mary Relindes. American (born United States), b. 1960. **Genres:** Novels, History. **Career:** Writer. **Publications:** The Turtle Warrior, 2004; Geese, forthcoming. Works appear in anthologies. Contributor to periodicals. **Address:** c/o Marly Rusoff, Marly Rusoff & Associates, 811 Palmer Rd., Ste. AA, Bronxville, NY 10708-3344, U.S.A.

ELLIS, Peter Berresford. Also writes as Peter Tremayne, Peter MacAlan. British (born England), b. 1943. **Genres:** Novels, Mystery/Crime/Suspense, Horror, Young Adult Non-fiction. **Career:** Brighton Herald (weekly newspaper), junior reporter, 1960-62; Irish Post, deputy editor, 1970, coulumnist, 2000-08; Newsagent & Bookshop, editor, 1974-75; full-time writer, 1975-; Irish Democrat, columnist, 1987-2008; Celtic League, international chairman, 1988-90; The International Sister Fidelma Society, founder, 2001-. Historian. **Publications:** Wales-A Nation Again!, 1968; (with S.M. A'Ghobhainn) The Scottish Insurrection of 1820, 1970; (with S.M. A'Ghobhainn) The Problem of Language Revival, 1971; A History of the Irish Working Class, 1972; (ed. and intro.) J. Connolly: Selected Writings, 1973; The Cornish Language and

Its Literature, 1974; Hell or Connaught!: The Cromwellian Colonisation of Ireland, 1652-1660, 1975; The Boyne Water, 1976; The Great Fire of London, 1976; H. Rider Haggard: A Voice from the Infinite, 1978; Caesar's Invasion of Britain, 1978; A Voice from the Infinite: The Life of Sir Henry Rider Haggard, 1856-1925, 1978; MacBeth: High King of Scotland, 1040-57 AD, 1980; (with P. Williams) By Jove, Biggles!: The Life of Captain W.E. Johns, 1981 as Biggles!: The Life of Captain W.E. Johns, with J. Scholfield, 1993; The Liberty Tree (novel), 1982; The Last Adventurer: The Life of Talbot Mundy, 1879-1940, 1984; Celtic Inheritance, 1985; The Celtic Revolution, 1985; The Rising of the Moon, 1987; A Dictionary of Irish Mythology, 1987; The Celtic Empire, 1990; A Guide to Early Celtic Remains in Britain, 1991; (ed. and comp.) Beeston Castle, Cheshire, 1993; A Dictionary of Celtic Mythology, 1992; Celt and Saxon, 1993; The Celtic Dawn, 1993; (with R. Ellsworth) The Book of Deer, 1994; The Druids, 1995; Celtic Women, 1996; Celt and Greek, 1997; Celt and Roman, 1998; The Chronicles of the Celts, 1999; Erin's Blood Royal, 1999; Eyewitness to Irish History, 2004; The Celts: A History, 2004. AS PETER MacALAN: The Judas Battalion, 1983; Airship, 1984; The Confession, 1985; Kitchener's Gold, 1986; The Valkyrie Directive, 1987; The Doomsday Decree, 1988; Fireball, 1990; The Windsor Protocol, 1993. AS PETER TREMAYNE: The Hound of Frankenstein, 1977; Dracula Unborn, 1977 in US as Bloodright: A Memoir of Mircea, Son of Vlad Tepes of Wallachia, Also Known as Dracula, 1979; (ed. and intro.) Masters of Terror: William Hope Hodgson, vol. I, 1977; The Vengeance of She, 1978; The Revenge of Dracula, 1978; The Ants, 1979; The Curse of Loch Ness, 1979; (ed.) Irish Masters of Fantasy, 1979 as The Wondersmith and Other Tales, 1988; The Fires of Lan-Kern, 1978; Dracula, My Love, 1980; Zombie!, 1981; The Return of Raffles, 1981; The Morgow Rises!, 1982; The Destroyers of Lan-Kern, 1982; The Buccaneers of Lan-Kern, 1983; Snowbeast!, 1983; Raven of Destiny, 1984; Kiss of the Cobra, 1984; Swamp!, 1985; Angelus!, 1985; My Lady of Hy-Brasil and Other Stories, 1987; Nicor!, 1987; Trollnight!, 1987; Ravenmoon, 1988 in US as Bloodmist, 1988; Island of Shadows, 1991; Aisling and Other Irish Tales of Terror, 1992; Dracula Lives!, 1993; The Sister Fidelma Mysteries: Murder by Absolution, 1994; Shroud for the Archbishop, 1995; Suffer Little Children, 1995; The Subtle Serpent, 1996; (with P. Haining) The Un-Dead: The Legend of Bram Stoker and Dracula, 1997; The Spider's Web, 1997; Valley of the Shadow, 1998; The Monk Who Vanished, 1999; Act of Mercy, 1999; Hemlock at Vespers, 2000; Our Lady of Darkness, 2000; Smoke in the Wind, 2001; The Haunted Abbot, 2002; Badger's Moon, 2003; Whispers of the Dead, 2004; The Leper's Bell, 2004; Master of Souls, 2005; An Ensuing Evil and Others: Fourteen Historical Mystery Stories, 2005; Prayer for the Damned: A Mystery of Ancient Ireland, 2007; Dancing with Demons: A Mystery of Ancient Ireland, 2007; The Council of the Cursed: A Mystery of Ancient Ireland, 2008; The Dove of Death: A Mystery of Ancient Ireland, 2009; The Chalice of Blood, 2010; Behold a Pale Horse, 2011. Contributor to newspapers, periodicals and journals. **Address:** A. M. Heath & Company Ltd., 6 Warwick Ct., Holborn, London, GL WC1R 5DJ, England.

ELLIS, Ralph D. American (born United States) **Genres:** Philosophy, Law, Social Sciences, Politics/Government. **Career:** Clark Atlanta University, professor of philosophy; Consciousness and Emotion (academic journal), editor. Philosopher. **Publications:** An Ontology of Consciousness, 1986; (with C.S. Ellis) Theories of Criminal Justice: A Critical Reappraisal, 1989; Coherence and Verification in Ethics, 1992; Questioning Consciousness: The Interplay of Imagery, Cognition and Emotion in the Human Brain, 1995; Eros in a Narcissistic Culture: An Analysis Anchored in the Life-World, 1996; Just Results: Ethical Foundations for Policy Analysis, 1998; (with A. Bueno) Craft of Thinking: Logic, Scientific Method and the Pursuit of Truth, 1999, 2nd ed., 2004; (ed. with N. Newton) The Caldron of Consciousness: Motivation, Affect and Self-Organization: An Anthology, 1999; Love and the Abyss: An Essay on Finitude and Value, 2004; (ed. with N. Newton) Consciousness & Emotion: Agency, Conscious Choice and Selective Perception, 2004; Curious Emotions: Roots of Consciousness and Personality in Motivated Action, 2005; (with N. Fischer and J.B. Sauer) Foundations of Civic Engagement: Rethinking Social and Political Philosophy, 2006; (with N. Newton) How the Mind uses the Brain: To Move the Body and Image the Universe, 2010. **Address:** Department of Religion & Philosophy, Clark Atlanta University, Rm. 34, McPheeters-Dennis Hall, 223 James P. Brawley Dr. SW, Atlanta, GA 30314, U.S.A. **Online address:** rellis@cau.edu

ELLIS, Reuben J. American (born United States), b. 1955. **Genres:** Novels, Literary Criticism And History, Sports/Fitness, Recreation. **Career:** Teikyo Lorretto Heights University, assistant professor of English, 1991-94; Hope College, associate professor of English, 1994-99; Prescott College, associate professor of English, 1999-2007, professor, 2007-; Ellis Farms, co-owner and vice president, 2007-; Woodbury University, associate professor, Writer. **Publications:** (Ed. and intro.) Beyond Borders: The Selected Essays of Mary Austin, 1997; (ed. and intro.) Stories and Stone: Writing the Anasazi Homeland, 1997; Vertical Margins: Mountaineering and the Landscapes of Neoimperialism, 2001. **Address:** Prescott College, 301 Grove Ave., Prescott, AZ 86301, U.S.A. **Online address:** rellis@prescott.edu

ELLIS, Richard (J.). American/British (born England), b. 1960. **Genres:** History, Politics/Government, Social Sciences. **Career:** University of California, visiting lecturer in political science, 1989; Willamette University, Department of Political Science, assistant professor, 1990-95, associate professor, 1995-99, Mark O. Hatfield professor, 1999-. Writer. **Publications:** (With A. Wildavsky) Dilemmas of Presidential Leadership: From Washington Through Lincoln, 1989; (with M. Thompson and Wildavsky) Cultural Theory, 1990; American Political Cultures, 1993; (ed. with D.J. Coyle) Politics, Policy and Culture, 1994; Presidential Lightning Rods: The Politics of Blame Avoidance, 1994; (ed. with M. Thompson) Culture Matters: Essays in Honor of Aaron Wildavsky, 1997; The Dark Side of the Left: Illiberal Egalitarianism in America, 1998; (ed.) Speaking to the People: The Rhetorical Presidency in Historical Perspective, 1998; (ed.) Founding the American Presidency, 1999; Culture Wars by Other Means: Environmental Attitudes and Cultural Biases in the Pacific Northwest, 2000; Democratic Delusions: The Initiative Process in America, 2002; To the Flag: The Unlikely History of the Pledge of Allegiance, 2005; (ed. with M. Nelson) Debating the Presidency: Conflicting Perspectives on the American Executive, 2006, 2nd ed., 2010; Presidential Travel: The Journey from George Washington to George W. Bush, 2008; (ed.) Judging Executive Power: Sixteen Supreme Court Cases that Have Shaped the American Presidency, 2009; (ed. with M. Nelson) Debating Reform: Conflicting Perspectives on How to Fix the American Political System, 2010; The Development of the American Presidency, 2012. **Address:** Department of Political Science, Willamette University, 324 Smullin Hall, 900 State St., Salem, OR 97301, U.S.A. **Online address:** rellis@willamette.edu

ELLIS, Robert. American (born United States), b. 1954. **Genres:** Novels. **Career:** Writer, producer and director. **Publications:** Access to Power, 2001; The Dead Room, 2002; City of Fire, 2007; The Lost Witness, 2009; Murder Season, 2011. **Address:** Minotaur Books, 175 5th Ave., New York, NY 10010, U.S.A. **Online address:** robert@robertellis.net

ELLIS, Royston. (Richard Tresillian). British (born England), b. 1941. **Genres:** Novels, Romance/Historical, Poetry, Antiques/Furnishings, Business/Trade/Industry, Food And Wine, Travel/Exploration, Biography, Humor/Satire. **Career:** Freelance poet, 1956-61; Jersey News and Features Agency, assistant editor, 1961-63; Canary Island Sun, associate editor, 1963-66; Emerald Hillside Estates, project director and agent, 1966-74; Marquis of Bristol, attorney, 1966-74; Radio Dominica, producer and broadcaster, 1973-76; Dominica Broadcasting Services, director, 1976-78; Wordsman Ltd., editor, 1977-86, staff, 1996-97; freelance travel writer, 1986-; Explore Sri Lanka, editorial consultant, 1990-96, 2000-10; President's Office, staff, 1999-2001; Sunday Times, hotel and book reviewer, 2000-; Baros Resort, staff, 2010-. **Publications:** Jiving to Gyp: A Sequence of Poems, 1959; Drifting with Cliff Richard, 1959; Rave, 1960; Rainbow Walking Stick, 1961; The Big Beat Scene, 1961, rev. ed., 2010; The Shadows by Themselves, 1961; Rebel, 1962; The Seaman's Suitcase, 1963; Myself for Fame, 1964; (contrib.) Generation X, 1965; The Flesh Merchants, 1966; The Rush at the End, 1967; The Cherry Boy, 1967; The Small Business Institute Guide to Import/Export, 1976; Blood of the Bondmaster, 1977; (as Richard Tresillian) The Bondmaster, 1978; Bondmaster Breed, 1979; Fleur, 1979; Bondmaster Fury, 1982; The Bondmaster's Revenge, 1983; Bondmaster Buck, 1984; Master of Black River, 1984; Black River Affair, 1985; Black River Breed, 1985; (as Richard Tresillian) Bloodheart, 1986; Bloodheart Royal, 1986; Bloodheart Feud, 1987; Giselle, 1988; Guide to Mauritius, 1988, rev. ed., 2009; India by Rail, 1989, rev. ed., 1997; The Grand Hotel, 1991; Sri Lanka by Rail, 1994; (with G. Amarasinghe) Guide to Maldives, 1995, rev. ed., 2008; (with G. Amarasinghe) A Maldives Celebration, 1997; Seeing Sri Lanka by Train, 1997; History of the Bandarawela Hotel, 1998; History of the Tea Factory Hotel, 1998; (with J.R. Jones) Madagascar, 1999; A Man for All Islands (biography of H.E. Mamoon Abdul Gayoom), 1998; On Freedom's Wings, 1998; STO: On the Move, 1999; Trinidad, 1999; My Story: Toni the Maldive Lady, 1999; Sri Lanka: An Insight Guide, 2000, rev. ed., 2002; A Hero in Time, 2001; Sri Lanka: The Bradt Travel Guide, 2002, rev. ed., 2011; Maldives: An Insight Guide, 2002; The Sri Lanka Story, 2003; Full Moon, Maldives, 2003; The Growing Years, 2004; Twenty Years Uncovered, 2006; The Berlitz Pocket Guide to Maldives, 2007; Gone Man Squared, 2009; What Love Is: The Season of the Peacock, 2010; Sri Lanka Step By Step 2010; The Kurumba Story, 2012. **Address:** Horizon Cottage, Kaikawala Rd., Induruwa, 80510, Sri Lanka. **Online address:** royston@roystonellis.com

ELLIS, Sarah. Canadian (born Canada), b. 1952. **Genres:** Children's Fiction, Young Adult Fiction, Adult Non-fiction, Children's Non-fiction, Novels. **Career:** Toronto Public Library, librarian, 1975; Vancouver Public Library, children's librarian, 1976-81; North Vancouver District Library, children's librarian, 1981-; Vermont College of Fine Arts, faculty. Writer. **Publications:** CHILDREN'S FICTION: The Baby Project, 1986 in US as A Family Project, 1988; Next-Door Neighbours, 1989; Pick-Up Sticks, 1991; Out of the Blue, 1994; Next Stop, 2000; A Prairie as Wide as the Sea: The Immigrant Diary of Ivy Weatherall, 2001; Big Ben, 2001. YOUNG ADULT FICTION: Putting Up with Mitchell, 1989; Back of Beyond, 1996; Odd Man Out, 2006. OTHER: The Young Writers' Companion (children's non-fiction), 1999; From Reader to Writer (adult non-fiction), 2000; Several lives of Orphan Jack, 2003; (with D. Suzuki) Salmon Forest, 2003. **Address:** 4432 Walden St., Vancouver, BC V5V 3S3, Canada. **Online address:** andyspandy@telus.net

ELLIS, Steven G. Irish/British (born England), b. 1950. **Genres:** History. **Career:** Queen's University, Institute of Irish Studies, faculty; National University of Ireland, Department of History, assistant, 1976-77, junior lecturer, 1977-84, statutory lecturer, 1984-91, professor in history, 1991-, head, 2004-, School of Humanities, school head, 2007-. Writer. **Publications:** Tudor Ireland, 1985; Reform and Revival: English Government in Ireland, 1470-1534, 1986; Pale and the Far North: Government and Society in Two Early Tudor Borderlands, 1988; Tudor Frontiers and Noble Power: The Making of the British State, 1995; (ed. with S. Barber) Conquest and Union: Fashioning a British State, 1485-1725, 1995; Ireland in the Age of the Tudors, 1447-1603: English Expansion and the End of Gaelic Rule, 1998; (ed.) Empires and States in European Perspective, 2002; (ed. with R. Esser) Frontiers and the Writing of History, 1500-1850, 2006; The Making of the British Isles: The State of Britain and Ireland 1450-1660, 2007; (ed. with R. Esser, J. Berdah and M. Řezník) Frontiers, Regions and Identities in Europe, 2009. **Address:** Department of History, National University of Ireland, Rm. 411, University Rd., Galway, 1, Ireland. **Online address:** steven.ellis@nuigalway.ie

ELLIS, Trey. American (born United States), b. 1962?. **Genres:** Novels, Plays/Screenplays. **Career:** Columbia University, Graduate School of Film, assistant professor of screenwriting. Writer. **Publications:** Platitudes, 1988; Home Repairs, 1993; Right Here, Right Now, 1999; Bedtime Stories: Adventures in the Land of Single-Fatherhood, 2008. Contributor to periodicals. **Address:** School of the Arts, Columbia University, 513 Dodge Hall, PO Box 1808, New York, NY 10027, U.S.A. **Online address:** trey@treyellis.com

ELLIS, William E. (William Elliott). American (born United States), b. 1940. **Genres:** Novellas/Short Stories, History, Education. **Career:** High school teacher and coach, 1962-66; Lees Junior College, instructor in history, 1967-70; Eastern Kentucky University, professor of history, 1970-99, Oral History Center, director, university historian, 1999-, now professor emeritus; Kentucky Monthly, columnist. **Publications:** (With H.E. Everman and R.D. Sears) Madison County, 1985; A Man of Books and a Man of the People: E.Y. Mullins and the Crisis of Moderate Southern Baptist Leadership, 1985; Patrick Henry Callahan: Progressive Layman in the American South, 1989; River Bends and Meanders: Stories, Sketches, and Tales of Kentucky (fiction), 1992; Dog Days and Other Stories (fiction), 1996; Robert Worth Bingham and the Southern Mystique: From the Old South to the New South and Beyond, 1997; The Kentucky River, 2000; A History of Eastern Kentucky University: The School of Opportunity, 2005; A History of Education in Kentucky, 2011. **Address:** Department of History, Eastern Kentucky University, 521 Lancaster Ave., 323 Keith Bldg., Richmond, KY 40475, U.S.A. **Online address:** hisellis@acs.eku.edu

ELLISON, Elizabeth Stow. American (born United States), b. 1970?. **Genres:** Children's Fiction. **Career:** Teacher and writer. **Publications:** Flight, 2008. **Online address:** mailbox@elizabethstowellison.com

ELLISON, Harlan (Jay). (Paul Merchant). American (born United States), b. 1934. **Genres:** Novels, Novellas/Short Stories, Science Fiction/Fantasy,

Plays/Screenplays, Graphic Novels, Young Adult Non-fiction. **Career:** Writer, 1954-; Science Fiction Writers of America, co-founder, vice president, 1965-66; Rogue Magazine, editor, 1959-60; Regency Books, founder and editor, 1960-61; television series and movie scriptwriter, 1962-77; Los Angeles Free Press Newspaper, weekly columnist; Los Angeles Times, book critic, 1969-82; Michigan State University, Clarion Writers Workshops, instructor, 1969-77, 1984; Canadian Broadcasting Co. (CBC-TV), editorial commentator, 1972-78; Pyramid Books, creator and editor, 1973-77; Kilimanjaro Corp., president, 1979-; Columbia Broadcasting Systems Inc. (CBS-TV), creative consultant, writer and director, 1984-85; Cutter's World, creative consultant, writer and director, 1987-88. Lecturer. **Publications:** SCIENCE FICTION NOVELS: The Man with Nine Lives, 1959; Doomsman, 1967; (with E. Bryant) Phoenix without Ashes, 1975; The City on the Edge of Forever (novelization of TV play), 1977. SCIENCE FICTION SHORT STORIES: A Touch of Infinity, 1959; Paingod and Other Delusions, 1965, rev. ed., 1975; I Have No Mouth, and I Must Scream, 1967; From the Land of Fear, 1967; Love Ain't Nothing but Sex Misspelled, 1968; The Beast That Shouted Love at the Heart of the World, 1969; Over the Edge: Stories from Somewhere Else, 1970; (co-author) Partners in Wonder, 1971; Alone against Tomorrow, 1971 in UK as All the Sound of Fear, and The Time of the Eye, 2 vols., 1973-74; De Helden van de Highway, 1973; Approaching Oblivion, 1974; Ellison Wonderland, 1974; Deathbird Stories: A Pantheon of Modern Gods, 1975; No Doors, No Windows, 1975, rev. ed., 1991; Hoe Kan Ik Schreeuwen Zonder Mond, 1977; Strange Wine: Fifteen New Stories from the Nightside of the World, 1978; The Illustrated Harlan Ellison, 1978; The Fantasies of Harlan Ellison (omnibus), 1979; Shatterday, 1980; Stalking the Nightmare, 1982; The Essential Ellison: A 35 Year Retrospective, 1987, rev. ed. as The Essential Ellison: A 50-year Retrospective, 2001; Angry Candy, 1988; Footsteps, 1989; Dreams with Sharp Teeth (omnibus), 3 vols., 1989; Run for the Stars, 1991; Ensamvark, 1992; Mind Fields, 1994; Jokes without Punchlines, 1995; Slippage: Precariously Poised, Previously Uncollected Stories, 1997; Troublemakers: Stories, 2001. GRAPHIC NOVELS: Demon with a Glass Hand, 1986; Night and the Enemy, 1987; (with R. Corben) Vic and Blood, 1989; Harlan Ellison's Dream Corridor, 1995. SCIENCE FICTION PLAYS: The City on the Edge of Forever, 1967; (with I. Asimov) I, Robot, 1994. NOVELS: Rumble, 1958, rev. ed. as Web of the City, 1958; The Juvies, 1961; Rockabilly, 1961; All the Lies That Are My Life, 1989; Run for the Stars, 1991; Mefisto in Onyx, 1993. SHORT STORIES: The Deadly Streets, 1958; (as Paul Merchant) Sex Gang, 1959; Gentlemen Junkie and Other Stories of the Hung-up Generation, 1961, rev. ed., 1975; Children of the Streets, 1961; All the Sounds of Fear, 1973; The Time of the Eye, 1974. PLAYS: Harlan Ellison's Movie, 1991; Spider Kiss, 1991; (with K.J. Anderson) The Outer Limits: Armageddon Dreams, 2000. OTHERS: Memos from Purgatory: Two Journeys of our Times, 1961; The Glass Teat, 1970; The Other Glass Teat, 1975; Flop Sweat, 1977; The Book of Ellison, 1978; Sleepless Nights in the Procrustean Bed: Essays, 1984; An Edge in My Voice, 1985; Harlan Ellison's Watching, 1989; The Harlan Ellison Hornbook (essays), 1990; Edgeworks, 1996; (with I. Asimov) I, Robot: The Illustrated Screenplay, 2004; (intro.) Shadows of Death: Terrifying Tales, 2005; (with E. Gorman and R.W. Bailey) The Phantom Chronicles 2, 2009. EDITOR: Dangerous Visions, 1967; Nightshade and Damnations, 1968; Again, Dangerous Visions, 1972; J. Sutherland, Stormtrack, 1975; Autumn Angels, 1975; The Light at the End of the Universe, 1976; Islands, 1976; Involution Ocean, 1978; Medea: Harlan's World, 1985; (and intro.) The Thinking Machine, 2003. Contributor to periodicals. **Address:** The Harlan Ellison Recording Collection, PO Box 55548, Sherman Oaks, CA 91413-0548, U.S.A.

ELLISON, J. Audrey. *See* **ELLISON, Joan Audrey.**

ELLISON, Joan Audrey. Also writes as J. Audrey Ellison, Elspeth Robertson. British (born England), b. 1928?. **Genres:** Food And Wine, Translations, Music, Cultural/Ethnic Topics. **Career:** Microbiologist, 1948-50; Queen Elizabeth College, lecturer, 1950-54; Flour Advisory Bureau Ltd., Department of Nutrition and Home Economics, head, 1972-78; Royal Society of Health, secretary general, 1979-84; International Artists' Management, concert agent, 1987-. Writer. **Publications:** (As J. Audrey Ellison trans. and ed.) The Great Scandinavian Cook Book, 1966; (as Elspeth Robertson) The Findus Book of Fish Cookery, 1968; (trans. and ed.) E. Sverdrup, Norway's Delights, 1969; (co-author) Growing for the Kitchen, 1978; (ed.) In Memoriam: N.W.G.T., 1910-1978, 1978; The Colman Book of British Traditional Cooking, 1980; The Bread Book, 1987; Patisserie of Scandinavia, 1989; Baking Bread, 1995; (trans.) The Best of Scandinavian Cookery, 1997. **Address:**

International Artists' Management, 135 Stevenage Rd., Fulham, London, GL SW6 6PB, England. **Online address:** jaellison@btinternet.com

ELLISON, Joan Jarvis. American (born United States), b. 1948. **Genres:** Autobiography/Memoirs, Young Adult Non-fiction. **Career:** University of Texas, research associate, 1974-76; Freelance writer, 1980-; Pelican Rapids Public Library, president; Northcroft Wool, owner and operator. **Publications:** Shepherdess: Notes from the Field (nonfiction), 1995; The Faces of Change, 2005; From Sheep to Shawl: Stories and Patterns for Fiber Lovers, 2011; (with S. Williams) Many Cultures, One Community. **Address:** 20740 410th St., Pelican Rapids, MN 56572-7439, U.S.A. **Online address:** dellison@loretel.net

ELLORY, R. J. British (born England), b. 1965. **Genres:** Mystery/Crime/Suspense. **Career:** Novelist. **Publications:** Candlemoth, 2003; Ghostheart, 2004; A Quiet Vendetta, 2005; A City of Lies, 2006; A Quiet Belief in Angels, 2007; A Simple Act of Violence, 2008; The Anniversary Man, 2009. **Address:** c/o Euan Thorneycroft, A.M. Heath & Company Ltd., Warwick Ct., London, GL WC1R 5DJ, England.

ELLROY, James. American (born United States), b. 1948. **Genres:** Mystery/Crime/Suspense, Novels. **Career:** Writer. **Publications:** Brown's Requiem, 1981; Clandestine, 1982; Blood on the Moon, 1984; Because the Night, 1985; Killer on the Road, 1986; Suicide Hill, 1986; Silent Terror, 1986; The Black Dahlia, 1987; The Big Nowhere, 1988; L.A. Confidential, 1990; White Jazz, 1992; Hollywood Nocturnes, 1994; American Tabloid, 1995; My Dark Places: An L.A. Crime Memoir, 1996; L.A. Noir, 1998; Crimewave: Reportage and Fiction from the Underside of L.A., 1999; The Cold 6,000, 2001; (ed. with O. Penzler) The Best American Mystery Stories, 2002, 2002; Destination: Morgue!: L.A. Tales, 2004; (intro.) Dain Curse: The Glass Key, 2007; Blood's a Rover, 2009; (contrib.) Ed Ruscha, 2010; Hillker Curse: My Pursuit of Women, 2010; (ed. with O. Penzler) Best American Noir of the Century, 2010; The Hilliker Curse, 2010; Police Gazette, forthcoming. **Address:** c/o Nat Sobel, Sobel Weber Associates Inc., 146 E 19th St., New York, NY 10003-2404, U.S.A. **Online address:** richiegarcia@yahoo.com

ELLWOOD, Sheelagh (Margaret). British (born England), b. 1949. **Genres:** History, Politics/Government, Military/Defense/Arms Control, Social Sciences. **Career:** Freelance writer, 1975-88; Foreign and Commonwealth Office, principal research officer, 1988-94, assistant, 1994-, senior principal research officer, 1998-. **Publications:** Prietas las filas: Historia De Falange Española, 1933-1983, 1984; (co-author) España Bajo El Franquismo, 1986; Spanish Fascism in the Franco Era: Falange Española De Las Jons, 1936-76, 1987; The Spanish Civil War, 1991; Franco: Profiles in Power, 1994, 2nd ed., 2000. Contributor to books. **Address:** Foreign and Commonwealth Office, King Charles St., London, GL SW1A 2AH, England.

ELLYARD, David. Australian (born Australia), b. 1942?. **Genres:** Astronomy, Meteorology/Atmospheric Sciences, Technology, Sciences. **Career:** Physicist, 1965-67; science teacher, 1969-72; Australian Broadcasting Co., radio and television broadcaster, 1972-87, television weather reporter; New South Wales Department of Business and Regional Development, manager of industry development services; David Ellyard Communications, owner. Writer. **Publications:** (With S. Cockburn) Oliphant, the Life and Times of Sir Mark Oliphant, 1981; The Proud Arch, 1982; Quantum, 1986; Sky Watch, 1988, rev. ed., 1998; Astronomy of the Southern Sky, 1993; Droughts and Flooding Plains, 1994; (with W. Tirion) The Southern Sky Guide, 1993, 3rd ed., 2008; (ed.) Weather, 1996; Weatherwise, 1999; (co-ed.) Our Amazing Planet, 2001; Who Discovered What When, 2006; Great Inventions of our Time, 2007; Who Invented What When, 2007. **Address:** David Ellyard Communications, Royal Exchange, PO Box 1403, Sydney, NW 1225, Australia. **Online address:** david@davidellyard.com

ELMER, Robert. American (born United States), b. 1958. **Genres:** Novels, Novellas/Short Stories, Romance/Historical, Children's Fiction, Young Adult Fiction, Literary Criticism And History. **Career:** Reporter, 1980-81, 1985-87; Olympia News, reporter, 1981-82; Simpson College, director of admissions, 1981-83; assistant pastor, 1983-85; Westside Alliance Church, assistant pastor, 1983-84; Goldendale Sentinel, editor, 1985-87; Baron & Co., senior copywriter, 1988-; author and public speaker, 1994-. **Publications:** FOR CHILDREN: A Way Through the Sea, 1994; Beyond the River, 1994; Into the Flames, 1994; Far from the Storm, 1995; Chasing the Wind, 1996; A Light in the Castle, 1996; Follow the Star, 1997; Touch the Sky, 1997; Escape to

Murray River, 1997; Captive at Kangaroo Springs, 1997; Rescue at Boomerang Bend, 1998; Dingo Creek Challenge, 1998; Race to Wallaby Bay, 1998; Firestorm at Kookaburra Station, 1999; Koala Beach Outbreak, 1999; Panic at Emu Flat, 1999; Promise Breaker, 2000; Peace Rebel, 2000; Great Galaxy Goof, 2000; Zero-G Headache, 2000; Refugee Treasure, 2001; Brother Enemy, 2001; Wired Wonder Woof, 2001; Miko's Muzzy Mess, 2001; About-Face Space Race, 2001; Cosmic Camp Caper, 2001; Freedom Trap, 2002; The Super-Duper Blooper, 2002; Astro Ball Free-4-All, 2002; Mid-Air Zillionaire, 2002; Tow-Away Stowaway, 2002; True Betrayer, 2002; (with L. Strobel and R. Suggs) Case for Christ for Kids, 2010; (with L. Strobel and R. Suggs) Case for Faith for Kids, 2010; (with L. Strobel and R. Suggs) Case for a Creator for Kids, 2010. YOUTH NOVELS: Digital Disaster, 2004; Fudge Factor, 2004; Webjam, 2004; Spam Alert, 2004; Web Jam: The Incredible Adventures of the World Wide Websters, 2005; Spam Alert: The Incredible Adventures of the World Wide Websters, 2005; Trion Rising, 2008; Beyond Corista, 2009. FOR ADULTS: The Duet: A Novel, 2004; Wildflowers of Terezin, 2010. OTHERS: Practicing God's Presence: Brother Lawrence for Today's Reader, rev. ed., 2005; (ed. with M. Carroll) Eat My Martian Dust: Finding God Among Aliens, Droids and Mega Moons, 2005; Road Blog, 2005; Hack Attack, 2005; Celebrity: A Novel, 2005; Rediscovering Daily Graces: Classic Voices on the Transforming Power of the Sacraments, 2006; The Recital, 2006; Beetle Bunker, 2006; Candy Bombers, 2006; Smuggler's Treasure, 2006; (with L. Strobel) Off My Case for Kids: 12 Stories to Help You Defend Your Faith, 2006; Like Always: A Novel, 2007; Owling, 2008; Homespun Harvest, 2008; April's Hope, 2009; Prayers and Promises, 2009; A Time to Grow, 2010. **Address:** Water Brook Press, 2375 Telstar Dr., Ste. 160, Colorado Springs, CO 80920, U.S.A. **Online address:** elmerbooks@earthlink.net

EL-MOSLIMANY, Ann P(axton). American (born United States), b. 1937. **Genres:** Children's Fiction, Novels. **Career:** Teacher, 1959-83; Kuwait University, faculty, 1984-86; Seattle Central Community College, faculty, 1986-90; Palynological Consultants, Paleoecological Research, staff, 1987-; Islamic School of Seattle, principal and teacher, 1989-, director. Writer. **Publications:** Zaki's Ramadhan Fast, 1994. Contributor to journals. **Address:** Islamic School of Seattle, 720 25th Ave., Seattle, WA 98122-4902, U.S.A. **Online address:** annelmoslimany@yahoo.com

ELMSLIE, Kenward. Also writes as Lavinia Sanchez. American (born United States), b. 1929. **Genres:** Novels, Novellas/Short Stories, Plays/Screenplays, Poetry, Songs/Lyrics And Libretti, Young Adult Fiction. **Career:** Z Press, publisher and editor, 1972-; Z Magazine, publisher and editor, 1973; National Endowment for the Arts, composer, 1973-76. **Publications:** Pavilions, 1961; Power Plant Poems, 1967; The Champ, 1968; Album, 1969; Circus Nerves, 1971; Girl Machine, 1971; Motor Disturbance, 1971; City Junket (play), 1972; The Grass Harp (musical), 1972; The Orchid Stories, 1973; Penguin Modern Poets 24, 1974; (ed.) ZZZ, 1974; Tropicalism, 1975; The Alphabet Work, 1977; Communications Equipment, 1979; (ed.) Mobile Homes, 1979; Moving Right Along, 1980; Bimbo Dirt, 1982; 26 Bars: A Collaboration, 1987; Sung Sex, 1989; Paydirt, 1991; The Lavinia Sanchez Festschrift, 1992; Postcards on Parade (musical), 1993; Champ Dust, 1994; Bare Bones, 1995; Champ Dust Spinoff: Ten Collages, 1995; Routine Disruptions, 1998; Nite Soil, 2000; Cyberspace, 2000; Blast from the Past, 2000; Snippets, 2002; (with M. Kite) Spilled Beans, 2002; Agenda Melt, 2004; Lingoland (musical), 2005. Works appear in anthologies. Contributor to periodicals. **Address:** Poet Cor., Calais, VT 05648, U.S.A.

EL-OR, Tamar. Israeli (born Israel), b. 1955. **Genres:** Sociology, Anthropology/Ethnology. **Career:** Tel-Aviv University, research and teaching assistant, 1980-90; Hebrew University of Jerusalem, senior lecturer in sociology and anthropology, 1992-, Interdisciplinary Research Center in Jewish Studies, fellow, 2004-06; Hebrew University, professor of anthropology; University of Pennsylvania, The Center for Advanced Judaic Studies, fellow, 2003. Writer. **Publications:** Maśkilot u-vurot: Me-'olaman shel nashim ḥarediyot, 1992; Educated and Ignorant: Ultraorthodox Jewish Women and Their World, 1994; Be-Fesahha-ba: Nashim ve-oryanut ba-Tsiyonut ha-datit, 1998, trans. as Next Year I Will Know More: Literacy and Identity among Young Orthodox Women in Israel, 2002; Mahomet shemurim: Migdar ve-etniyut be-mahuzot ha-datveha-teshuvah, 2006; Reserved Seats: Ethnicity, Religion and Gender in Contempora, 2006. **Address:** Department of Sociology & Anthropology, Hebrew University of Jerusalem, Mount Scopus, Jerusalem, 91905, Israel. **Online address:** tamarelor@huji.ac.il

ELROD, P(at) N. American (born United States), b. 1954?. **Genres:** Science Fiction/Fantasy, Paranormal, Mystery/Crime/Suspense, Horror. **Career:** Writer, 1990-. **Publications:** THE VAMPIRE FILES SERIES: Bloodlist, 1990; Lifeblood, 1990; Bloodcircle, 1990; Art in the Blood, 1991; Fire in the Blood, 1991; Blood on the Water, 1992; A Chill in the Blood, 1998; Dark Sleep, 1999; Lady Crymsyn, 2000; Cold Streets, 2003; The Vampire Files, 2003, vol. IV, 2011; Dark Road Rising, 2009; The Devil You Know, forthcoming. THE JONATHAN BARRETT VAMPIRE SERIES: Red Death, 1993; Death and the Maiden, 1994; Death Masque, 1995; Dance of Death, 1996; Song in the Dark, 2005. RICHARD DUN SERIES; WITH NIGEL BENNETT: Keeper of the King, 1997; His Father's Son, 2001; Siege Perilous, 2004. OTHERS: Dark Sleep, 1996; The Wind Breathes Cold, 1996; (ed. with M.H. Greenberg) Time of the Vampires, 1996; I, Strahd: The War against Azalin, 2000; Quincey Morris, Vampire, 2001; (ed.) Dracula in London, 2001; The Adventures of Myhr, 2003; (ed. with R.L. Conrad) Stepping Through the Stargate: Science, Archaeology and the Military in Stargate SG-1, 2004; I, Strahd: The Memoirs of A Vampire, 2006; (ed.) My Big Fat Supernatural Wedding, 2006; (ed.) My Big Fat Supernatural Honeymoon, 2008; (ed.) Strange Brew, 2009; (ed.) Dark and Stormy Knights, 2010; (ed.) Hex Appeal, 2012. Contributor to books and periodicals. **Address:** c/o Lucienne Diver, Knight Literary Agency, 570 East Ave., Madison, GA 30650, U.S.A. **Online address:** mystikmerchant@sbdglobal.net

ELSE, Barbara. New Zealander (born New Zealand), b. 1947. **Genres:** Plays/Screenplays, Novels, Novellas/Short Stories, Young Adult Fiction, Humor/Satire. **Career:** TFS Literary Agency and Assessment Service, cofounder; University of Victoria, writer-in-residence, 1999. **Publications:** The Warrior Queen, 1995; Gingerbread Husbands, 1996; Skitterfoot Leaper, 1997; Eating Peacocks, 1998; Tricky Situations, 1999; Three Pretty Widows, 2000; (ed.) Grand Stands: New Zealand Writers on Being Grandparents, 2000; (ed.) Another 30 New Zealand Stories for Children, 2002; (ed.) 30 Weird & Wnderful New Zealand Stories, 2003; The Case of the Missing Kitchen, 2003; (ed.) Claws & Jaws 30 New Zealand Animal Stories, 2004; (ed.) Mischief and Mayhem, 2005; (ed.) Like Wallpaper-New Zealand Short Stories for Teenagers, 2005; (ed.) Hideous and Hilarious 30 New Zealand Historical Stories, 2006; (ed.) Dare and Double Dare 30 New Zealand Sporty Stories, 2007; Wild Latitudes, 2007; (ed.) Showtime!, 2008; The Travelling Restaurant, 2011. Contributor to periodicals. **Address:** TFS Literary Agency & Assessment Service, Park Ave., PO Box 46-031, Lower Hutt, 5044, New Zealand. **Online address:** barbara@elseware.co.nz

EL-SHAZLY, Nadia El-Sayed. Egyptian (born Egypt), b. 1936. **Genres:** International Relations/Current Affairs, Military/Defense/Arms Control, History. **Career:** Al-Mossawar (weekly magazine), trainee, 1956; Al-Ahram (daily newspaper), correspondent, 1957-58; Umm al-Bahariyah Society, founder, 1972, board director, 1972-80; United Seamen's Services-Egypt, founder, 1976, board director, 1976-88; Imhotep Society, founder, 1979, president, 1979-87. Writer. **Publications:** The Gulf Tanker War: Iran's and Iraq's Maritime Swordplay, 1998. Contributor to periodicals. **Address:** Zahra, 34 Ahmed Yehya St., Apt. 46, Zizinia, Alexandria, W5 2FS, Egypt. **Online address:** neselshazly@aol.com

ELSON, Jeffrey. *See* **NELSON, Ray.**

ELSON, R. E. Australian (born Australia), b. 1947. **Genres:** Politics/Government, History. **Career:** University of Queensland, professor. Writer and researcher. **Publications:** The Cultivation System and Agricultural Involution, 1978; Javanese Peasants and the Colonial Sugar Industry: Impact and Change in an East Java Residency, 1830-1940, 1984; (ed. and trans. with A. Kraal) C. Fasseur, The Politics of Colonial Exploitation: Java, the Dutch, and the Cultivation System, 1992; Village Java under the Cultivation System, 1830-1870, 1994; The End of the Peasantry in Southeast Asia: A Social and Economic History of Peasant Livelihood, 1800-1990s, 1997; Suharto: A Political Biography, 2001; (contrib.) Komentar & Pendapat Detik-detik Yang Menentukan: Jalan Panjang Indonesia Menuju Demokrasi Bacharuddin Jusuf Habibie, 2006; The Idea of Indonesia: A History, 2008. Contributor to books and periodicals. **Address:** University of Queensland, Rm. E334, 1 Forgan Smith Bldg., St. Lucia, Brisbane, QL 4072, Australia. **Online address:** r.elson@uq.edu.au

ELSON, R. N. *See* **NELSON, Ray.**

ELSTER, Kathi. American (born United States) **Genres:** Business/Trade/Industry, Human Relations/Parenting, Administration/Management. **Career:** Small Business Strategy Inc., founder and co-owner, 1986-; K Squared Enterprises, executive coach, president, management consultant. Writer. **Publications:** (With K. Crowley) Going Indie: Self-Employment, Freelance, and Tempting Opportunities, 1997; (with K. Crowley) Working with You Is Killing Me: Freeing Yourself from Emotional Traps at Work, 2006; (with K. Crowley) Working for You Isn't Working for Me: The Ultimate Guide to Managing Your Boss, 2009. **Address:** K Squared Enterprises, 119 W 23rd St., Ste. 1009, New York, NY 10011-2427, U.S.A. **Online address:** kathi@ksquaredenterprises.com

ELSY, (Winifred) Mary. British (born England) **Genres:** Children's Fiction, Travel/Exploration. **Career:** Teacher, 1947-51; freelance writer, 1951-57, 1968; Realist Film Unit, associate, 1957-58; Rediffusion Television, assistant to script writer, 1958-59; Fleetway Publications, sub-editor and caption writer, 1960-62; B.P.C. Publishing Ltd., writer and editorial assistant, 1963-64; Evans Brothers, sub-editor, 1965-66; Abelard Schuman Ltd., children's book editor, 1967-68; British Institute of Human Rights, secretary to director, 1979. **Publications:** Travels in Belgium and Luxembourg, 1966; Brittany and Normandy, 1974; (with J. Normandy) Travels in Normandy, 1988; (with J. Normandy) Travels in Brittany, 1988; Travels in Alsace and Lorraine, 1989; (with J. Normandy) Travels in Burgundy, 1989; Pedals and Petitticoats, 2005. Contributor to articals to magazines. **Address:** c/o Gerald Pollinger, Laurence Pollinger Ltd., 18 Maddox St., Mayfair, London, GL W1R OEU, England. **Online address:** melsy_trav_chnwtr@btopenworld.com

EL-TAHRI, Jihan. French/Lebanese (born Lebanon) **Genres:** Novels, History. **Career:** U.S. News & World Report, news correspondent, Tunis special correspondent; Reuters News Agency, news correspondent; Washington Post, Tunis special correspondent; The Financial Time, Tunis special correspondent; Sunday Times, Cairo correspondent. Journalist and film director. **Publications:** (With C. Boltanski) Les sept vies de Yasser Arafat, 1997; (with A. Bregman) Israël et les arabes: La guerre de cinquante ans, 1998, trans. as The Fifty Years' War: Israel and the Arabs, 1999. Contributor to periodicals. **Address:** Big Sister, 4 Rue lacepede, Paris, 75005, France.

ELTIS, Walter (Alfred). British/Czech (born Czech Republic), b. 1933. **Genres:** Economics, Money/Finance, Business/Trade/Industry. **Career:** Oxford University, lecturer in economics, 1963-86; Exeter College, fellow, 1963-88, emeritus fellow, 1988-; National Economic Development Office, economic consultant, 1963-66, economic director, 1986-88, director general, 1988-92; University of Toronto, visiting professor, 1976-77; Rowe & Pitman, economic and financial consultant, 1976-86; European University, visiting professor, 1979; consultant and bank credit analyst, 1983-88, 1995-; University of Reading, visiting professor, 1992-; Department of Trade and Industry, chief economic adviser to the president of the board of trade, 1992-95; Gresham College, Gresham professor of commerce; Wycliffe College, governor; University of Washington, visiting reader; Oxford Economic Papers, editor. **Publications:** Economic Growth: Analysis and Policy, 1966; Growth and Distribution, 1973; (with R.W. Bacon) Age of U.S. and U.K. Machinery, 1974; (with R. Bacon) Britain's Economic Problem: Too Few Producers, 1976, 2nd ed., 1978; The Classical Theory of Economic Growth, 1984, 2nd ed., 2000; Classical Economics, Public Expenditure, and Growth, 1993; (with R. Bacon) Britain's Economic Problem Revisited, 1996; (contrib.) Commerce and Government Considered in Their Mutual Relationship, 1997; Britain, Europe, and EMU, 2000; The Classical Theory of Money, 2012. EDITOR: (with M.F.G. Scott and J.N. Wolfe) Induction, Growth and Trade: Essays in Honour of Sir Roy Harrod, 1970; (with P.J.N. Sinclair) The Money Supply and the Exchange Rate, 1981; (with P. Sinclair) Keynes and Economic Policy: The Relevance of the General Theory After Fifty Years, 1990. Contributor to journals and newspapers. **Address:** Exeter College, Hele Rd., Exeter, DN EX4 4JS, England.

ELTON, Hugh. Canadian/British (born England), b. 1964. **Genres:** History, Archaeology/Antiquities. **Career:** Rice University, visiting assistant professor, 1993-94; Trinity College, visiting assistant professor, 1994-98; University of Connecticut, visiting lecturer, 1997-98; Florida International University, assistant professor, 1998-2001; British Institute at Ankara, director, 2001-06; Trent University, Department of Ancient History and Classics, associate professor, 2006-11, professor, 2011-, chair, 2007-10, acting dean of arts and science, 2010-12; King's College, Department of Classics, visiting research fellow, 2007-. Writer. **Publications:** (Ed. with J.F. Drinkwater and contrib.)

Fifth-Century Gaul: A Crisis of Identity?, 1992; Warfare in Roman Europe, A.D. 350-425, 1996; Frontiers of the Roman Empire, 1996; (intro.) The Roman Imperial Army of the First and Second Centuries A.D., 3rd ed., 1998. Contributor to books. **Address:** Department of Ancient History and Classics, Trent University, Champlain College K4, 1600 Westbank Dr., Peterborough, ON K9J 7B8, Canada. **Online address:** hughelton@trentu.ca

ELTRINGHAM, S(tewart) K(eith). British/Canadian (born Canada), b. 1929. **Genres:** Environmental Sciences/Ecology, Marine Sciences/Oceanography, Natural History, Zoology, Sciences, Young Adult Fiction, Young Adult Non-fiction. **Career:** Wildfowl Trust, aerial survey biologist, 1957-61; University of London, King's College, lecturer in zoology, 1962-67; Queen Elizabeth National Park, Nuffield unit of tropical ecology, director, 1966-71; Uganda Institute of Ecology, director, 1971-73; Uganda National Parks, chief research officer, 1971-73; Cambridge University, lecturer in applied biology, 1973-; African Journal of Ecology, associate editor. **Publications:** Life in Mud and Sand, 1971; The Ecology and Conservation of Large African Mammals, 1979; Elephants, 1982; Wildlife Resources and Economic Development, 1984; The Hippos: Natural History and Conservation 1999. EDITOR: (with E.G. Jones) Marine Borers, Fungi and Fouling Organisms of Wood, 1971; The Illustrated Encyclopedia of Elephants, 1991. Contributor to scientific journals. **Address:** Department of Zoology, University of Cambridge, Downing St., City Ctr., Cambridge, CB CB2 3EJ, England. **Online address:** ske1000@cam.ac.uk

ELUKIN, Jonathan. American (born United States), b. 1961. **Genres:** History, Humanities, Geography. **Career:** Trinity College, assistant professor, 1997-2003, associate professor, 2003-. Writer. **Publications:** Living Together, Living Apart: Rethinking Jewish-Christian Relations in the Middle Ages, 2007. Contributor of articles to periodicals. **Address:** Hartford, CT , U.S.A. **Online address:** jonathan.elukin@trincoll.edu

ELVENSTAR, Diane C. *See* **MEDVED, Diane.**

ELY, Christopher. American (born United States), b. 1963?. **Genres:** Adult Non-fiction. **Career:** Florida Atlantic University, assistant professor, associate professor of history; Harvard University, lecturer, Freshman Seminars Program, faculty; Lesley College, adjunct professor. Writer. **Publications:** This Meager Nature: Landscape and National Identity in Imperial Russia, 2002; (ed. with M. Bassin and M.K. Stockdale) Space, Place and Power in Modern Russia, 2010. **Address:** Office of Admissions, Harriet L. Wilkes Honors College, Florida Atlantic University, 5353 Parkside Dr., Jupiter, FL 33458, U.S.A. **Online address:** cely@fau.edu

ELY, David. (David E. Lilienthal). American (born United States), b. 1927. **Genres:** Novels, Novellas/Short Stories, Mystery/Crime/Suspense, Travel/Exploration. **Career:** United States Navy, staff, 1945-46; Saint Louis Post-Dispatch, reporter, 1949-50, 1952-54, 1955-56; Development and Resources Corp., administrative assistant, 1956-59. Writer. **Publications:** Trot, 1963; Seconds, 1963; The Tour, 1967; Time Out (short stories), 1968; Poor Devils, 1970; Walking Davis, 1972; Mr. Nicholas, 1974; Always Home: And Other Stories (short stories), 1991; A Journal of the Flood Year (novel), 1992. **Address:** PO Box 1387, East Dennis, MA 02641-1387, U.S.A.

ELY, Melvin Patrick. American (born United States), b. 1952. **Genres:** History, Cultural/Ethnic Topics. **Career:** Huguenot High School, teacher, 1973-75; Granby High School, teacher, 1975-76; University of Virginia, Carter G. Woodson Institute, postdoctoral fellow, 1985-86; Yale University, assistant professor, 1986-92, associate professor of history and Afro-American studies, 1992-95; College of William and Mary, associate professor, 1995-96, professor of history and black studies, 1996-, William R. Kenan Jr. professor of humanities; Hebrew University of Jerusalem, Fulbright professor of American studies, 1998-99. Writer. **Publications:** The Adventures of Amos 'n' Andy: A Social History of an American Phenomenon, 1991, 2nd ed., 2001; (trans with N. Zahavi-Ely) The Handicap Principle, 1999; Israel on the Appomattox: A Southern Experiment in Black Freedom from the 1790s through the Civil War, 2004. **Address:** Department of History, College of William and Mary, Blair 301, PO Box 8795, Williamsburg, VA 23187-8795, U.S.A. **Online address:** mpelyx@wm.edu

EMANUEL, James A(ndrew). French/American (born United States), b.

1921. **Genres:** Poetry, Songs/Lyrics And Libretti, Literary Criticism And History, Autobiography/Memoirs, Essays, Social Sciences, Biography, Humanities, Humanities. **Career:** Pre-Induction Section, Army and Air Force Induction Station, civilian chief, 1950-53; Harlem YWCA Business School, instructor, 1954-56; City College of New York, instructor, professor of English, 1957-84; University of Grenoble, Fulbright professor of American literature, 1968-69; University of Toulouse, visiting professor of English, 1971-73, 1979-81; University of Warsaw, Fulbright professor of American literature, 1975-76. Writer. **Publications:** POETRY: The Tree House and Other Poems, 1968; At Bay, 1969; Panther Man, 1970; Black Man Abroad: The Toulouse Poems, 1978; A Chisel in the Dark: Poems, Selected and New, 1980; A Poet's Mind, 1983; The Broken Bowl, New and Uncollected Poems, 1983; Deadly James and Other Poems, 1987; The Quagmire Effect, 1988; Whole Grain: Collected Poems, 1958-1989, 1990; Dela rage au coeur, 1992; (with G. Simons) Blues in Black and White, 1992. OTHER: Langston Hughes, 1967; (ed. with T.L. Gross) Dark Symphony: Negro Literature in America, 1968; (with M. Kantor and L. Osgood) How I Write 2, 1972; Reaching for Mumia: 16 Haiku, 1995; JAZZ from the Haiku King, 1999; The Force and the Reckoning, 2001. Contributor to periodicals. **Address:** PO Box 339, Paris, 75266, France. **Online address:** james@james-a-emanuel.com

EMBERLEY, Peter C. Canadian (born Canada), b. 1956. **Genres:** Education, Theology/Religion. **Career:** Carleton University, professor of political science and philosophy, 1984-, College of the Humanities, founding director, 1994. Writer. **Publications:** (Ed.) By Loving Our Own: George Grant and the Legacy of Lament, 1990; (trans. and ed. with B. Cooper) Faith and Political Philosophy: The Correspondence Between Leo Strauss and Eric Voegelin, 1934-1964, 1993; (with W.R. Newell) Bankrupt Education: The Decline of Liberal Education in Canada, 1994; Values Education and Technology: The Ideology of Dispossession, 1995; Zero Tolerance: Hot Button Politics in Canada's Universities, 1996; (ed. with A. Davis) Collected Works of George Grant, 2000; Divine Hunger: Canadians on Spiritual Walkabout, 2002. **Address:** Department of Political Science, Carleton University, D685 Loeb Bldg., 1125 Colonel By Dr., Ottawa, ON K1S 5B6, Canada. **Online address:** pemberle@magma.ca

EMECHETA, (Florence Onye) Buchi. British/Nigerian (born Nigeria), b. 1944. **Genres:** Novels, Sociology, Autobiography/Memoirs, Human Relations/Parenting, inspirational/Motivational Literature, Literary Criticism And History, Young Adult Non-fiction. **Career:** British Museum, library officer, 1965-69; Inner London Education Authority, youth worker and sociologist, 1969-76; writer, 1972-; Pennsylvania State University, visiting professor; University of California, visiting professor; Rutgers University, visiting professor; University of Illinois, visiting professor; University of Calabar, senior resident fellow and visiting professor of English, 1980-81; Ogwugwu Afor Publishing Co., proprietor, 1982-83; London University, fellow, 1986. **Publications:** In the Ditch, 1972; Second-class Citizen, 1974; The Bride Price: A Novel, 1976; The Slave Girl: A Novel, 1977; Titch the Cat, 1979; Joys of Motherhood: A Novel, 1979; Nowhere to Play, 1980; The Wrestling Match, 1980; The Moonlight Bride, 1980; (intro.) Our Own Freedom, 1981; Destination Biafra: A Novel, 1982; Naira Power, 1982; Double Yoke, 1982; Adah's Story: A Novel, 1983; The Rape of Shavi, 1984; Head above Water (autobiography), 1986; A Kind of Marriage 1986; Gwendolen, 1989 in US as The Family, 1990; Kehinde, 1994; The New Tribe, 2000. Contributor to journals. **Address:** 7 Briston Grove, Crouch End, London, GL N8 9EX, England.

EMERSON, Claudia. American (born United States), b. 1957. **Genres:** Poetry. **Career:** Chatham Hall (girls' boarding school), academic dean, 1996-98; University of Mary Washington, Mary Washington College, associate professor of English, 1998-, Arrington chair of poetry; Greensboro Review, poetry editor; Shenandoah, contributing editor; Lee University, faculty; Randolph-Macon Women's College, faculty. Poet and educator. **Publications:** Pharaoh, Pharaoh: Poems, 1997; Pinion: An Elegy, 2002; Late Wife: Poems, 2005; Figure Studies: Poems, 2008. **Address:** c/o Author Mail, Louisiana State University Press, PO Box 25053, Baton Rouge, LA 70894-5053, U.S.A.

EMERSON, Earl W. American (born United States), b. 1948. **Genres:** Mystery/Crime/Suspense, Novels, Young Adult Fiction, Literary Criticism And History. **Career:** Seattle Fire Department, lieutenant, 1978-. Writer. **Publications:** Fill the World with Phantoms, 1979; The Rainy City, 1985; Poverty Bay, 1985; Nervous Laughter, 1986; Fat Tuesday, 1987; Black Hearts and Slow Dancing, 1988; Deviant Behavior, 1988; Help Wanted: Orphans Preferred, 1990; Yellow Dog Party, 1991; Morons and Madmen, 1993; The

Portland Laugher, 1994; The Vanishing Smile, 1995; Going Crazy in Public, 1996; The Million-Dollar Tattoo, 1996; The Dead Horse Paint Company, 1997; Deception Pass, 1997; Catfish Café, 1998; Vertical Burn, 2002; Into the Inferno, 2003; Pyro, 2004; Smoke Room: A Novel of Suspense, 2005; Firetrap, 2006; Primal Threat, 2008; Cape Disappointment: A Novel, 2009. Contributor to periodicals. **Address:** Jane Rotrosen Agency, 318 E 51St St., New York, NY 10022, U.S.A. **Online address:** author@earlemerson.com

EMERSON, Isabelle Putnam. American (born United States), b. 1936?. **Genres:** Music, Dance/Ballet. **Career:** University of Nevada, professor emerita, Department of Music, chair; Columbia University, Saint Paul's Chapel, university organist and director of music, 1969-77. Educator, musician and writer. **Publications:** Twentieth-Century American Music for the Dance: A Bibliography, 1996; Five Centuries of Women Singers, 2005. **Address:** Department of Music, University of Nevada, 4505 S Maryland Pkwy., PO Box 455025, Las Vegas, NV 89154-5025, U.S.A. **Online address:** emerson@ccmail.nevada.edu

EMERSON, Jill. *See* BLOCK, Lawrence.

EMERSON, Ken. American (born United States), b. 1948. **Genres:** Music, Literary Criticism And History, Popular Culture, Autobiography/Memoirs, Ghost Writer, Adult Non-fiction. **Career:** Boston Phoenix, writer and editor, 1968-77; New York Times Magazine, editor, 1980-89; New York Newsday, editor, 1990-95; Edna McvConnell Clark Foundation, communications adviser, 2008-. **Publications:** NONFICTION: Doo-Dah!: Stephen Foster and the Rise of American Popular Culture, 1997; (with E.K. Zilkha) From Baghdad to Boardrooms: My Family's Odyssey: A Memoir, 1999; (with J. Mollenkopf) Rethinking the Urban Agenda: Reinvigorating the Liberal Tradition in New York City and Urban America, 2001; Always Magic in the Air: The Bomp and Brilliance of the Brill Building Era, 2005; (ed.) Stephen Foster & Co.: Lyrics of America's First Great Popular Songs, 2010. **Address:** The Edna McConnell Clark Foundation, 415 Madison Ave., 10th Fl., New York, NY 10017, U.S.A. **Online address:** emersonrk@aol.com

EMERSON, Michael O. American (born United States), b. 1965. **Genres:** Race Relations. **Career:** St. John's University, assistant professor of sociology, 1991-95; Bethel College, assistant professor, associate professor of sociology, 1995-99; Rice University, Department of Sociology, associate professor, 1999-2003, R.A. Tsanoff Professor of Public Affairs and Sociology, 2003-04, Allyn R. & Gladys M. Cline professor of sociology, Center on Race, Religion and Urban Life (CORRUL), founding director, 2005-, interim chair, 2007, Kinder Institute for Urban Research, co-director, 2010-, Hobby Center for the Study of Texas, faculty, 2010-; University of Notre Dame, professor of sociology and director of the DuBois Center for the Advanced Study of Religion and Race, 2004-05; Panel Study of American Religion and Ethnicity (PS-ARE), director. Writer. **Publications:** (Co-author) American Evangelicalism: Embattled and Thriving, 1998; (with C. Smith) Divided by Faith: Evangelical Religion and the Problem of Race in America, 2000; (ed. and contrib. with S.C. Monahan and W. Mirola) Sociology of Religion: A Reader, 2001; (with C. DeYoung, G. Yancey and K.C. Kim) United by Faith: The Multiracial Congregation as an Answer to the Problem of Race, 2003; (with B. Christerson and K.L. Edwards) Against All Odds: The Struggle for Racial Integration in Religious Organizations, 2005; (with R.M. Woo) People of the Dream: Multiracial Congregations in the United States, 2006; (with C. Smith and P. Snel) Passing the Plate: Why American Christians Don't Give Away More Money, 2008; (ed. with A.B. Pinn and C.F. Levander) Teaching and Studying the Americas: Cultural Influences from Colonialism to the Present, 2010 (with G. Yancey) Transcending Racial Barriers: Toward a Mutual Obligations Approach, 2011; (with W.A. Mirola and S.C. Monahan) Religion Matters: What Sociology Teaches us about Eeligion in our World, 2011. Contributor to books and periodicals. **Address:** Department of Sociology, Rice University, SH 380, 6100 S Main St., Houston, TX 77251-1892, U.S.A. **Online address:** moe@rice.edu

EMERSON, Thomas E. American (born United States), b. 1945. **Genres:** Anthropology/Ethnology, Archaeology/Antiquities. **Career:** Upper Mississippi Valley Archaeological Research Program, Orendorf Project, field director, 1973-74; Northeastern Archaeological Foundation, director, 1974-77; archaeological consultant, 1976-77, 1982-84; University of South Dakota, Lake Francis Case and Crow Creek Projects, field director, 1978-79; University of Illinois, FAI-270 Archaeological Mitigation Project, site director, 1979-82, Department of Anthropology, Illinois Transportation Archaeo-

logical Research Program, director and adjunct professor of anthropology, 1994-2009, Prairie Research Institute, Illinois State Archaeological Survey, director, 2010-; Illinois Historic Preservation Agency, chief archaeologist, 1984-94; Illinois Archaeological Survey, director, 1993-94. Writer. **Publications:** Mississippian Stone Images in Illinois, 1982; (with G.R. Milner and D.K. Jackson) The Florence Street Site, 1983; (with D.K. Jackson) The BBB Motor Site, 1984; (with D.K. Jackson) The Go-Kart North Site, 1984; (with D.K. Jackson) Emergent Mississippian and Early Mississippian Homesteads at the Marcus Site, 1987; Cahokia and the Archaeology of Power, 1997. EDITOR: (with K.B. Farnsworth) Early Woodland Archeology, 1986; (with R.B. Lewis) Cahokia and the Hinterlands: Middle Mississippian Cultures of the Midwest, 1991; (with J.A. Walthall) Calumet and Fleur-de-Lys: French and Indian Interaction in the Midcontinent, 1992; (with T.R. Pauketat) Cahokia: Domination and Ideology in the Mississippian World, 1997; Keeshin Farm Site and the Rock River Langford Tradition in Northern Illinois, 1999; (with D.L. McElrath and A.C. Fortier) Late Woodland Societies: Tradition and Transformation Across the Mid-Continent, 2000; (with R.B. Lewis) Cahokia and the Hinterlands: Middle Mississipian Cultures of the Midwest, 2000; (with D.L. McElrath and A.C. Fortier) Archaic Societies, 2009. Contributor to books and journals. **Address:** Illinois State Archaeological Survey, University of Illinois, 209 Nuclear Physics Lab, 23 E Stadium Dr., Champaign, IL 61820-6910, U.S.A. **Online address:** teee@illinois.edu

EMERY, Clayton. (Ian Hammell). American (born United States), b. 1953. **Genres:** Science Fiction/Fantasy, Young Adult Fiction, Novels, Mystery/Crime/Suspense. **Career:** Writer. **Publications:** MAGIC: THE GATHERING SERIES: Whispering Woods, 1995; Shattered Chains, 1995; Final Sacrifice, 1995. ARCANE AGE: NETHERIL TRILOGY: Sword Play, 1996; Dangerous Games, 1996; Mortal Consequences, 1997. SHADOW WORLD SERIES AS IAN HAMMELL: The Burning Goddess, 1994; Clock Strikes Sword, 1995; City of Assassins, 1995; Stormriders, 1996. OTHERS: (with E. Wajenberg) The 4D Funhouse, 1985; Tales of Robin Hood, 1988; Runesword: Outcasts, 1990; Card Master, 1997; The Secret World of Alex Mack: Father-Daughter Disaster!, 1997; Are You Afraid of the Dark? The Tale of the Campfire Vampires, 1997; Star of Cursrah, 1999; (co-author) Halls of Stormweather, 2000; Jedit, 2001; Johan, 2001; Robin Hood and The Beasts Of Sherwood, 2001; Hazezon, 2002; (with E.G. Wajenberg) Jumping the Jack, 2003; (contrib.) How to Write Killer Historical Mysteries, 2008; Mandrake and Murder, 2009; Royal Hunt, 2009; Pale Ghost, 2009. Contributor to books and periodicals. **Address:** 155 Grove Rd., Rye, NH 03870-2508, U.S.A. **Online address:** clayton@claytonemery.com

EMERY, Robert Firestone. American (born United States), b. 1927. **Genres:** Economics, History, Business/Trade/Industry, Money/Finance. **Career:** Federal Reserve System, economist, 1955-92; Southeastern University, adjunct professor, 1960-88, Department of Financial Administration, chairman, 1963-65, dean, 1965-68, professor emeritus of finance, 1988-; International economic consultant, 1992-. Writer. **Publications:** The Use of Interest Rate Policies as a Stimulus to Economic Growth, 1971; The Financial Institutions of Southeast Asia: A Country-by-Country Study, 1971; The Japanese Money Market, 1984; The Money Markets of Developing East Asia, 1991; The Bond Markets of Developing East Asia, 1997; Korean Economic Reform: Before and Since the 1997 Crisis, 2001. **Address:** 3421 Shepherd St., Chevy Chase, MD 20815, U.S.A.

EMERY, Robert J. American (born United States), b. 1941. **Genres:** Adult Non-fiction, Plays/Screenplays, Film. **Career:** Media Entertainment Inc., vice president and chief executive officer, 1977-, president. Writer, television producer and director. **Publications:** (Comp.) Directors: In Their Own Words, 1999; The Directors: Take One, 2002; The Directors: Take Two: In Their Own Words, 2002; The Directors: Take Three, 2003; The Directors: Take Four, 2003; In the Realm of Eden, 2008; Eden Destroyed, forthcoming; My Father's Sons, forthcoming. **Address:** c/o Author Mail, Allworth Press, 307 W 36th St., 11th Fl., New York, NY 10018, U.S.A. **Online address:** media8@verizon.net

EMERY, Tom. American (born United States), b. 1971. **Genres:** History, Biography, Autobiography/Memoirs, Humanities. **Career:** Blackburn College, sports information director, 1993-94, instructor in economics, 2000; Monterey Coal Co., journalist, 1994-95; Macoupin County Enquirer, reporter, 1994-96; History in Print, owner and general manager, 1997-. **Publications:** Richard Rowett: Thoroughbreds, Beagles, and the Civil War, 1997; The Other John Logan: Col. John Logan and the 32nd Illinois, 1998; 19th-Century

Echoes: The Carlinville City Cemetery, 2000, 2nd ed., 2003; The Beagle: Its Beginnings in America, 2001; The Memorable Month: Minor-League Baseball in Staunton, 2001; Hold the Fort: The Battle of Allatoona Pass, 2001; The Macoupin County Courthouse: Scandalous Symbol, 2002; Eddie: Lincoln's Forgotten Son, 2002; Gustave Loehr: Rotary's Forgotten Founder, 2003; Carlinville: The First Century, 2007. **Address:** 337 E 2nd S St., Carlinville, IL 62626, U.S.A. **Online address:** tomemery11@yahoo.com

EMMER, Michele. Italian (born Italy), b. 1945. **Genres:** Art/Art History, Mathematics/Statistics, Sciences, Theatre, Essays, Picture/Board Books, Architecture, Film, Film. **Career:** Università Ca' Foscari, professor, 1988-94; University of Rome, professor, 1994-. Writer and filmmaker. **Publications:** Bolle di sapone: un viaggio tra arte, scienza e fantasia, 1991; (ed.) The Visual Mind: Art and Mathematics, 1993; (ed.) Matematica e cultura 2000, 2000; (ed.) Matematica e cultura 2001, 2001; (ed. with M. Manaresi) Mathematics, Art, Technology, cinema, matematica, arte, 2002; (ed. with D. Schattschneider) M.C. Escher's Legacy: A Centennial Celebration, 2003; Mathland: From Flatland to Hypersurfaces, 2003; (ed.) The Visual Mind II, 2005; (ed.) Matematica e cultura 2005, 2005; Visibili armonie: Arte, cinema, teatro e matematica, 2006; (ed.) Math and Culture IV, 2006; (ed.) Math and Culture V, 2006; Bolle di sapone tra arte e matematica, premio Viareggio, 2009; Best Italian Essay 2010; (ed.) Matematica e cultura 2010, 2010; Numeri Immaginari, cinema e matematica, 2011; Il mio Harrys bar, 2011. **Address:** Department of Mathematics, University of Rome, Studio 101, Rome, 00185, Italy. **Online address:** emmer@mat.uniroma1.it

EMMERIJ, Louis (Johan). Dutch/American (born United States), b. 1934. **Genres:** Economics, International Relations/Current Affairs. **Career:** University of Paris, Institut d'Etudes Economiques et Sociales, associate, 1961-62; Organization for Economic Cooperation and Development, Directorate of Scientific Affairs, associate, 1962-70, Development Center, president, 1986-92; United Nations, International Labor Office, World Employment Program, director, 1971-76; Institute of Social Studies, rector, 1976-85; OECD Development Center, president, 1986-92; Inter-American Development Bank, special advisor to the president, 1993-99; The City University of New York, senior research fellow, 1999-2010; United Nations Intellectual History Project, project co-director, 1999-2010. Writer. **Publications:** Can the School Build a New Social Order?, 1974; (with J.A.E. Clobus) Volledige Werkgelegenheid Door Creatief Verlof: Naar een Maatschappij van de Vrije Keuze, 1978; Internationale Economische Herstructurering, 1982; Schade en Herstel: Een Sociaal-Democratisch Perspectief, 1984; (ed.) One World or Several?, 1989; (with A. Salam) Science, Technology, and Science Education in the Development of the South, 1989; (ed. with E. Iglesias) Restoring Financial Flows to Latin America, 1991; Nord-Sud: La Grenade Degoupillee, 1992; Limits to Competition, 1995; (with R. Jolly and T.G. Weiss) Ahead of the Curve?: UN Ideas and Global Challenges, 2001; (with R. Jolly and T.G. Weiss) UN Contributions to Development Thinking and Practice, 2004; Power of UN Ideas: Lessons from the First 60 years: A Summary of the Books and Findings From the United Nations Intellectual History Project, 2005; (with R. Jolly and T.G. Weiss) UN Ideas that Changed the World, 2009. CO-AUTHOR: The Mediterranean Regional Project: Spain, 1965; The Mediterranean Regional Project: Yugoslavia, 1965; Education, Human Resources, and Development in Argentina, 1967; Occupational and Educational Structure of the Labour Force and Levels of Economic Development, 2 vols., 1970; Employment, Growth, and Basic Needs: A One-World Problem, 1976; De Crisis te Lijf: Een Ander Sociaal-Democratisch Beleid, 1981; (comp. with J. Nunez del Arco) El desarrollo económico y social en los umbrales delsiglo XXI, 1998. CONTRIBUTOR: Econometric Models of Education, 1965; Alternative Educational Futures in the United States in Europe: Methods, Issues, and Policy Relevance, 1972; Development of Societies: The Next Twenty-Five Years, 1979; From the Old to a New Global Order, 1979; Unemployment in Western Countries, 1980; European Studies in Development, 1980; One World One Future: New International Strategies for Development, 1985; Trade in Transit, 1986; (ed.) Development Policies and the Crisis of the 1980's, 1987; The UN under Attack, 1988; Dimensions of Peace, 1988; Europe: Dimensions of Peace, 1988; Change: Threat or Opportunity for Human Progress? 1992; Economic Decision-making in a Changing World, 1993; Regime Transformations and Global Realignments: Indo-European Dialogues on the Post-Cold War, 1993; The World Economy Challenges of Globalization and Regionalization, 1996; The Aftermath of Real Existing Socialism in Eastern Europe, 1996; (ed. and contrib.) Economic and Social Development into the XXI Century, 1997. **Address:** The Graduate Center, The City University of New York, 365 5th Ave., Ste. 5203, New York, NY 10016, U.S.A. **Online address:** emmerij@netzero.net

EMMET, Alan. American (born United States), b. 1927. **Genres:** Novels, Homes/Gardens, Horticulture, History, Travel/Exploration, Young Adult Fiction. **Career:** Harvard University, Graduate School of Design, Graduate Program Historic Landscape Preservation, course assistant, 1978-81; Society for the Preservation of New England Antiquities, consultant, 1982-92; National Trust for Historic Preservation, consultant, 1993-94; full-time writer, 1994-. **Publications:** (Co-author) Cambridge, Massachusetts, the Changing of a Landscape, 1978; So Fine a Prospect: Historic New England Gardens, 1996; The Mr. and Mrs. Club, 2001. Contributor to periodicals. **Address:** 224 Concord Rd., Westford, MA 01886-4205, U.S.A.

EMMETT, Ayala. American/Israeli (born Israel), b. 1935. **Genres:** Anthropology/Ethnology, Novels, Young Adult Fiction. **Career:** Empire State College of the State University, mentor, 1981-83; University of Rochester, research associate, 1981-87, assistant professor, 1981-84, lecturer, 1984-87, assistant professor, 1987-94, associate professor of anthropology, 1994-, Seeds for College, founder; Haifa University, visiting professor, 1990; Sex Roles, associate editor. **Publications:** Our Sisters' Promised Land: Women's Peace Politics and the Israeli Palestinian Conflict, 1996; After the Disappearance, forthcoming. Contributor of articles to periodicals. **Address:** Department of Anthropology, University of Rochester, 437 Lattimore, Rochester, NY 14627, U.S.A. **Online address:** ayala.emmett@rochester.edu

EMMIS, Yetta. See MEKLER, Eva.

EMMONS, Henry. American (born United States) **Genres:** Psychiatry, Medicine/Health, Self Help. **Career:** St. Olaf Counseling Center, staff, 1997-; University of Minnesota, Center for Spirituality and Healing, adjunct faculty; Health Partners, clinical psychiatrist; Mind, Body, Spirit Clinic, clinical psychiatrist; Allina Medical Clinic, clinical psychiatrist; Inner Life of Healers Retreat, program leader. University of Rochester Medical Center, chief resident. Writer. **Publications:** (With R. Kranz) The Chemistry of Joy: A Three-Step Program for Overcoming Depression through Western Science and Eastern Wisdom, 2006; The Chemistry of Calm: A Powerful, Drug-free Plan to Quiet Your Fears and Overcome Your Anxiety, 2010. **Address:** Allina Medical Clinic-Northfield, 1400 Jefferson Rd., Northfield, MN 55057, U.S.A.

EMMONS, Mary L. (Anne K. Edwards). American (born United States), b. 1940. **Genres:** Novels, E-books, Autobiography/Memoirs. **Career:** Novelist. **Publications:** AS ANNE K. EDWARDS: Death on Delivery 2007; (with M. Calvani) Slippery Art of Book Reviewing, 2008; Jeremy and the Dragon 2008; The Last to Fall, 2009; Shadows Over Paradise, 2010; (ed.) How I Wrote My First Book, the Story Behind the Story, 2011. Contributor of articles to periodicals. **Address:** PO Box 3402, Gettysburg, PA 17325, U.S.A. **Online address:** marbob00@earthlink.net

EMMONS, Phillip. See LITTLE, Bentley.

EMMONS, Robert A. American (born United States), b. 1958. **Genres:** Adult Non-fiction, Medicine/Health, Psychology. **Career:** Michigan State University, assistant professor of psychology, 1986-88; Journal of Personality and Social Psychology, consulting editor, 1986-88; Journal of Personality, editorial board, 1987-91; University of California, assistant professor, 1988-90, associate professor, 1990-96, professor of psychology, 1996-; International Journal for the Psychology of Religion, editorial consultant, 1999-; Stanford University, teacher; Biola University, consultant; Rosemead School of Psychology, consultant; Institute for Research on Psychology and Spirituality, consultant, 2000-; Journal of Personality and Social Psychology-Personality and Individual Differences, associate editor, 2000-02; Journal of Positive Psychology, editor-in-chief, 2005-; Baylor University Institute for Studies of Religion, consultant, 2006-. **Publications:** NONFICTION: (ed. with S. Frank, R.A. Zucker and A.I. Rabin) Studying Persons and Lives, 1990; The Psychology of Ultimate Concerns: Motivation and Spirituality in Personality, 1999; (with J. Hill) Words of Gratitude for Mind, Body and Soul, 2001; (ed. with M.E. McCullough) The Psychology of Gratitude, 2004; (contrib.) The Handbook of the Psychology of Religion, 2005; (contrib.) Oxford Companion to the Affective Sciences; (contrib.) Encyclopedia of Positive Psychology, 2007; Thanks! How the New Science of Gratitude Can Make You Happier, 2007. Contributor of articles to books and journals. **Address:** Department of Psychology, University of California, Davis, CA 95616-8686, U.S.A. **Online address:** raemmons@ucdavis.edu

EMORY, Jerry. American (born United States), b. 1957. **Genres:** Young

Adult Non-fiction, Natural History, Travel/Exploration, History. **Career:** Golden Gate Audubon Society, executive director, 1979-81; Mono Lake Coalition, steward, 1981-85; Pacific Beat, for Pacific Discovery, columnist, California Academy of Sciences, staff, 1988-90. Writer. **Publications:** NON-FICTION FOR YOUNG ADULTS. GREENPATCH SERIES: Nightprowlers: Everyday Creatures under Every Night Sky, 1994; Dirty, Rotten, Dead? A Worm's Eye View of Death, Decomposition and Life, 1996. OTHER: San Francisco Bay Shoreline Guide, 1995; (with D. McConnell) Bay Area Backroads, 1999; The Monterey Bay Shoreline Guide, 1999. **Address:** 740 Summit Ave., Mill Valley, CA 94941, U.S.A. **Online address:** jemory@hooked.net

EMSHWILLER, Carol (Fries). American (born United States), b. 1921. **Genres:** Novels, Science Fiction/Fantasy, Westerns/Adventure, Novellas/Short Stories. **Career:** Clarion Science-Fiction Writing Workshop, teacher, 1972-73, 1978-79; New York University, adjunct associate professor in continuing education, 1974-2003; Science Fiction Bookstore Work Shop, organizer, 1975-76. Writer. **Publications:** Joy in Our Cause, 1974; Verging on the Pertinent (short stories), 1989; Start of the End of It All, 1990, rev. ed., 1991; Carmen Dog, 1990; Venus Rising, 1992; Ledoyt, 1995; Leaping Man Hill, 1999; The Mount, 2002; Report to the Men's Club and Other Stores, 2002; Mister Boots: A Fantasy Novel, 2005; I Live with You, 2005; The Secret City, 2007; In the Time of War & Master of the Road to Nowhere, 2011. Contributor to books. **Address:** 210 E 15th St., Apt. 12E, New York, NY 10003-3938, U.S.A. **Online address:** cemsh@aol.com

EMSLEY, Clive. British (born England), b. 1944. **Genres:** History. **Career:** Open University, professor of history, 1970-, International Center for Comparative Criminological Research, co-director and co-founder, 2003-09; Griffith University, visiting professor, 1983, 1996; University of Paris VIII, visiting professor, 1984-85; University of Calgary, visiting professor, 1988, 1990; University of Christchurch, visiting professor, 2003; Australian National University, visiting research fellow, 2004, Australian Centre for Excellence in Policing and Security, visiting fellow, 2010. Writer. **Publications:** (With G. Werskey) War in Our Own Day, 1973; (with U. Semin) Introduction to the Study of Revolutions and Some Interpretations of 1848, 1976; (intro.) North Riding Naval Recruits: The Quota Acts & the Quota Men, 1795-1797, 1978; British Society and the French Wars, 1793-1815, 1979; Policing and Its Context, 1750- 1870, 1984; Crime and Society in England, 1750- 1900, 1987, 4th ed., 2010; World War II and Its Consequences, 1990; The English Police: A Political and Social History, 1991, 2nd ed., 1996; The Longman Companion to Napoleonic Europe, 1993; Gendarmes and the State in Nineteenth-Century Europe, 1999; Britain and the French Revolution, 2000; Napoleon, Pearson 2003; Hard Men: Violence in England since 1750, 2005 as The English and Violence since 1750, 2006; Crime, Police and Penal Policy: European Experiences, 1750-1940, 2007; The Great British Bobby: A History of British Policing from the 18th century to the present, 2009; Crime and Society in Twentieth-Century England, 2011. EDITOR: Conflict and Stability in Europe, 1979; Essays in Comparative History: Economy, Politics and Society in Britain and America, 1850-1920, 1984; (with J. Walvin) Artisans, Peasants and Proletarians, 1760-1860: Essays Presented to Gwyn A. Williams, 1985; (with A. Marwick and W. Simpson) War, Peace and Social Change in Twentieth-Century Europe, 1989; (with B. Weinberger) Policing Western Europe: Politics, Professionalism and Public Order, 18501940, 1991; (with P. Robert) Geschichte Und Soziologie Des Verbrechens, 1991; (with L.A. Knafla) Crime History and Histories of Crime: Studies in the Historiography of Crime and Criminal Justice in Modern History, 1996; (with R. Bessel) Patterns of Provocation: Police and Public Disorder, 2000; (with A. Marwick and W. Simpson) Total War and Historical Change: Europe, 1914-1955, 2001; (with B. Godfrey and G. Dunstall) Comparative Histories of Crime, 2003; (with E. Johnson and P. Spierenburg) Social Control in Europe, 1800-2000, 2004; (with H. Shpayer-Makov) Police Detectives in History, 1750-1950, 2006. **Address:** Department of History, Open University, Walton Hall, Milton Keynes, BK MK7 6AA, England. **Online address:** c.emsley@open.ac.uk

EMSLEY, John. British (born England), b. 1938. **Genres:** Chemistry, Sciences, Criminology/True Crime, History. **Career:** University of London, King's College, lecturer, 1967-82, reader, 1982-90, Imperial College of Science and Technology, science writer-in-residence, 1990-97; University of Cambridge, Department of chemistry, science writer-in-residence, 1997-2002. **Publications:** The Inorganic Chemistry of the Non-Metals, 1971; The Chemistry of Phosphorus, 1976; (co-author) Complex Chemistry, 1984, (with D. Hall) The Elements, 1989, 3rd ed., 1998; The Consumer's Good Chemical Guide, 1994; Molecules at an Exhibition, 1998; Was It Something You Ate?, 1999; The 13th Element, 2000; The Shocking History of Phosphorus, 2000; Nature's Building Blocks, 2002; Vanity, Vitality, and Virility, 2004; Elements of Murder, 2005; Better Looking, Better Living, Better Loving, 2007; Molecules of Murder, 2008; A Healthy, Wealthy, Sustainable World, 2010. **Address:** Department of Chemistry, University of Cambridge, Lensfield Rd., Cambridge, CB2 1EW, England. **Online address:** johnemsley38@aol.com

ENCINIAS, Miguel. American (born United States), b. 1923. **Genres:** Cultural/Ethnic Topics, History, Translations, Literary Criticism And History. **Career:** Compania de Teatro and La Zarzuela de Albuquerque, founder. Writer and educator. **Publications:** (Ed. and trans. with A. Rodríguez and J.P. Sánchez) G.P. De Villagrá, Historia de la Nueva México, 1610, 1992; Two Lives for Oñate, 1997. **Address:** 1009 Green Valley Rd. NW, Albuquerque, NM 87107-6321, U.S.A.

ENDLICH, Lisa. American/British (born England), b. 1959. **Genres:** Novels, Business/Trade/Industry, Biography. **Career:** Goldman Sachs, currency trader and vice president, 1985-89. Writer. **Publications:** Goldman Sachs: The Culture of Success, 1999; Optical Illusions: Lucent and the Crash of Telecom, 2004; Be the Change, 2008. Contributor to periodicals. **Address:** c/o Author Mail, Simon Schuster Inc., 1230 Ave. of the Americas, New York, NY 10020, U.S.A.

ENER, Güner. Turkish (born Turkey), b. 1935. **Genres:** Novellas/Short Stories, Mystery/Crime/Suspense, History. **Career:** Yuekselis College, teacher of painting, 1968-69; Cem Yayinevi, illustrator of book covers, 1972-78; freelance painter, 1978-. Writer. **Publications:** Tired of September (stories), 1969; Blue of the Broken Glass (stories), 1972; The Bald-Headed Girl (children's stories), 1990; (trans.) Sister Shako and Kolo the Goat, 1994. Contributor to art magazines and newspapers. **Address:** ICBS/IBIS, Kvaesthusgade 3F, Copenhagen, 1251, Denmark.

ENG, David L. American (born United States), b. 1967?. **Genres:** Social Commentary, Social Sciences, Race Relations. **Career:** Columbia University, teacher of English and comparative literature; University of Pennsylvania, Department of English and Comparative Literature, professor, Penn English Program in London, director, 2010-. Writer. **Publications:** (Ed. with A.Y. Hom) &QA: Queer in Asian America, 1998; Racial Castration: Managing Masculinity in Asian America, 2001; (ed. with D. Kazanjian) Loss: The Politics of Mourning, 2003; The Feeling of Kinship: Queer Liberalism and the Racialization of Intimacy, 2010; (with J. Boston and A. Bradstock) Public Policy: Why Ethics Matters, 2010. **Address:** Department of English & Comparitive Literature, University of Pennsylvania, Fisher-Bennett Hall 212, 3340 Walnut St., Philadelphia, PA 19104-6273, U.S.A. **Online address:** deng@english.upenn.edu

ENGDAHL, Sylvia L(ouise). American (born United States), b. 1933. **Genres:** Science Fiction/Fantasy, Young Adult Fiction, Young Adult Nonfiction, Novels. **Career:** Teacher, 1955-56; System Development Corp., programmer and computer systems specialist, 1957-67; freelance writer, 1968-80; Connected Education Inc., faculty, 1985-97; freelance editor, 2004- . **Publications:** Enchantress from the Stars, 1970, new ed., 2001; Journey Between Worlds, 1970, rev. ed., 2006; The Far Side of Evil, 1971, rev. ed., 2003; This Star Shall Abide, 1972, new ed., 2010 in UK as Heritage of the Star, 1973; Beyond the Tomorrow Mountains, 1973; The Planet-Girded Suns: Man's View of Other Solar Systems, 1974; (with R. Roberson) The Subnuclear Zoo: New Discoveries in High Energy Physics, 1977; (with R. Roberson) Tool for Tomorrow: New Knowledge about Genes, 1979; Our World Is Earth, 1979; The Doors of the Universe, 1981; Children of the Star, 2000; Stewards of the Flame, 2007; Promise of the Flame, 2009. EDITOR: (with R. Roberson) Universe Ahead: Stories of the Future, 1975; Anywhere, Anywhere: Stories of Tomorrow, 1976; Extraterrestrial Life, 2005; Cloning, 2006; Genetic Engineering, 2006; Euthanasia, 2006; Artificial Intelligence, 2007; Online Social Networking, 2007; Religious Liberty, 2007; Free Speech, 2007; Blogs, 2008; Prescription Drugs, 2008; Domestic Wiretapping, 2008; Vaccines, 2008; Assisted Suicide, 2008; Medical Rights, 2008; War on Drugs, 2009; Right to Private Property, 2009; Amendments XVIII and XXI: Prohibition and Repeal, 2009; Amendment XIV: Equal Protection, 2009; Amendment XXVI: Lowering the Voting Age, 2009; Intellectual Property Rights, 2009; Cybercrime, 2009; Prisons, 2009; Animal Welfare, 2010; Mental Health, 2010; Amendment XXV: Presidential Disability and Succession, 2010; Meningitis, 2010; Fibromyalgia, 2010; War, 2010; Taxation, 2010; Welfare, 2010; Forensic Technology, 2010; The John F. Kennedy Assassination, 2010; The

Atomic Bombings of Hiroshima and Nagasaki, 2011; The Elderly, 2011; Patriotism, 2011; Sleep Disorders, 2011; Welfare, 2011; Free Press, 2011; Alternative Therapies, 2011; The Apollo 11 Moon Landing, 2011; Chronic Fatigue Syndrome, 2011. **Address:** 3088 Delta Pines Dr., Eugene, OR 97408-1616, U.S.A. **Online address:** sle@sylviaengdahl.com

ENGEL, Bernard F. American (born United States), b. 1921. **Genres:** Literary Criticism And History, History. **Career:** Newspaper reporter, 1946-48; University of Idaho, instructor in English, 1949-50; Oregon State College (now University), instructor in English, 1952-53; Consolidated Freightways, clerk, 1953-54; Sacramento State College, instructor in English, 1954-57; Michigan State University, Department of American Language, assistant professor, professor, 1957-89, chairman, 1967-77, professor emeritus, 1990-; University College Quarterly, associate editor, 1958-62, editor, 1962-67; University of Argentina, Fulbright lecturer in American literature, 1963. **Publications:** (Ed. and co-author) History of the 413th Infantry, 1946; Marianne Moore, 1964, rev. ed., 1989; (ed.) The Achievement of Richard Eberhart, 1968; Richard Eberhart, 1971; (ed. with P.W. Julius) A New Voice for a New People: Midwestern Poetry 1800-1910, 1985; (with J. Strandness) Closing Circles: Selected Poems, 1989. Contributor of articles to journals. **Address:** Department of American Thought and Language, Michigan State University, East Lansing, MI 48824, U.S.A.

ENGEL, Beverly. American (born United States), b. 1947. **Genres:** Psychology, Human Relations/Parenting. **Career:** Writer and psychotherapist. **Publications:** The Right to Innocence: Healing the Trauma of Childhood Sexual Abuse, 1989; The Emotionally Abused Woman: Overcoming Destructive Patterns and Reclaiming Yourself, 1990; Divorcing a Parent: Free Yourself from the Past and Live the Life You've Always Wanted, 1990; Partners in Recovery: How Mates, Lovers & Other Prosurvivors Can Learn to Support & Cope with Adult Survivors of Childhood Sexual Abuse, 1991; Encouragements for the Emotionally Abused Woman, 1993; Families in Recovery: Working Together to Heal the Damage of Childhood Sexual Abuse, 1994, 2nd ed., 2000; Raising Your Sexual Self-esteem: How to Feel Better about Your Sexuality and Yourself, 1995; Blessings from the Fall: Turning a Fall from Grace into a New Beginning, 1997; Beyond the Birds and the Bees: Fostering Your Child's Healthy Sexual Development, 1997; The Parenthood Decision: Deciding Whether You Are Ready and Willing to Become a Parent, 1998; Sensual Sex: Arousing Your Senses and Deepening the Passion in Your Relationship, 1999; Loving Him without Losing You: How to Stop Disappearing and Start Being Yourself, 2000; Women Circling the Earth: A Guide to Fostering Community, Healing, and Empowerment, 2000; The Power of Apology: Healing Steps to Transform All Your Relationships, 2001; The Emotionally Abusive Relationship: How to Stop Being Abused and How to Stop Abusing, 2002; Honor Your Anger: How Transforming Your Anger Style Can Change Your Life, 2004; Breaking the Cycle of Abuse: How to Move Beyond Your Past to Create an Abuse-free Future, 2005; Healing Your Emotional Self: A Powerful Program to Help You Raise Your Self-esteem, Quiet Your Inner Critic, and Overcome Your Shame, 2006; The Jekyll and Hyde Syndrome: What to Do If Someone in Your Life Has a Dual Personality? Or If You Do, 2007; The Nice Girl Syndrome: Stop Being Manipulated and Abused-and Start Standing Up for Yourself, 2008. **Address:** 225 Wild Plum, San Marcos, TX 78666, U.S.A. **Online address:** beverly@beverlyengel.com

ENGEL, Cindy. British/American (born United States) **Genres:** Animals/Pets, Sciences, Medicine/Health. **Career:** Open University, associate lecturer, lecturer in environmental sciences; Energy Arts, instructor. Writer, conservationist, animal researcher and biologist. **Publications:** Wild Health: How Animals Keep Themselves Well and What We Can Learn from Them, 2002. Contributor to periodicals. **Address:** Houghton Mifflin Co., 222 Berkeley St., Boston, MA 02116-3748, U.S.A. **Online address:** ce24@tutor.open.ac.uk

ENGEL, Howard. (F. X. Woolf). Canadian (born Canada), b. 1931. **Genres:** Novels, Criminology/True Crime, Mystery/Crime/Suspense, Plays/Screenplays, Novellas/Short Stories. **Career:** Teacher, 1955-56; Crime Writers of CA, CBC, freelance broadcaster, 1956-67, radio producer, 1967-68, executive producer, 1968-80, literary editor, 1980-85, co-founder, 1982, treasurer, 1982-85, editor of Fingerprints, 1985-86, chairman, 1986-87; full-time novelist, 1985-; Canadian Give the Gift of Literacy Foundation, director, 1992; International Association of Crime Writers, founding member; Crime Writers of Canada, founding member. **Publications:** NOVELS: The Suicide Murders, 1980; The Ransom Game, 1981; Murder Sees the Light, 1985; Murder on Location, 1985; (with J. Hamilton as F.X. Woolf) Murder in Space, 1985;

A City Called July, 1986; A Victim Must Be Found, 1988; The OTHER: The Whole Megillah (novella), 1992; (ed. with E. Wright) Criminal Shorts (short stories): Mysteries by Canadian Crime Writers, 1992; There Was An Old Woman, 1993; Lord High Executioner (nonfiction), 1996; A Child's Christmas in Scarborough, 1997; Behold the Lord High Executioner: An Unabashed Look at Hangmen, Headsmen and Their Kind, 1996; Getting Away with Murder, 1998; Murder in Montparnasse, 1999; Dead and Buried, 2001; Crimes of Passion: An Unblinking Look at Murderous Love, 2002; Cooperman Variations: A Benny Cooperman Mystery, 2002; Mr. Doyle & Dr. Bell: A Victorian Mystery, 2003; Memory Book, 2005; The Man Who Forgot How To Read, 2008; East of Suez: A Benny Cooperman Mystery, 2008. Contributor to periodicals. **Address:** Toronto, ON M5S 2L5, Canada. **Online address:** howard.engel@utoronto.ca

ENGEL, Jeffrey A. American (born United States) **Genres:** Politics/Government, Air/Space Topics, Military/Defense/Arms Control, History. **Career:** Harry S. Truman Presidential Library Institute, research fellow, 1999; Eisenhower Library, Eisenhower World Affairs Council, visiting research fellow, 1999; John F. Kennedy Presidential Library Foundation, dissertation research fellow, 1999; Temple University, Center for the Study of Force and Diplomacy, visiting fellow, 2000-01; Yale University, International Security Studies, Olin postdoctoral fellow, 2001-03, lecturer in history, 2002-03, visiting fellow, 2007; National Parks Service, Historic Resource Survey, Minuteman Missile National Historic Site, principal investigator, 2002-03; University of Pennsylvania, lecturer in history and international relations, 2003-04; Texas A&M University, assistant professor of history and public policy, 2004-09, associate professor of history and public policy, 2009-, Verlin and Howard Kruse '52 Founders professor, Evelyn and Ed F. Kruse '49 faculty fellow, 2006-, Scowcroft Institute for International Affairs, associate director, 2007-08, interim director, 2008-09, director of programming, 2009-. Writer. **Publications:** (Contrib.) Air Warfare: An International Encyclopedia, 2002; (contrib.) Facts on File Encyclopedia of American History, 2002; (contrib.) Europe since 1914, 2006; Cold War at 30, 000 Feet: The Anglo-American Fight for Aviation Supremacy, 2007; (contrib.) A Companion to International History, 1900-2001, 2007; (ed.) Local Consequences of the Global Cold War, 2007; (ed.) The China Diary of George H.W. Bush: The Making of a Global President, 2008; Seeking Monsters to Destroy: Language and War from Thomas Jefferson to George W. Bush, 2009; (ed. with M. Lawrence and A. Preston) The United States and the World: A History in Documents, 2009; (ed.) Fall of the Berlin Wall: The Revolutionary Legacy of 1989, 2009; (ed. with J.R. Cerami) Rethinking Leadership and Whole of Government National Security Reform: Problems, Progress and Prospects, 2010; When the World Seemed New: American Foreign Policy in the Age of George H.W. Bush, forthcoming. Contributor to journals. **Address:** Bush School of Government & Public Service, Texas A&M University, Allen Rm. 1080, 4220 TAMU, College Station, TX 77843-4220, U.S.A. **Online address:** jaengel@tamu.edu

ENGEL, Joel. American (born United States), b. 1952. **Genres:** Human Relations/Parenting, Film, Humanities. **Career:** Journalist; New York Times, entertainment writer; Los Angeles Times, staff writer, contributing editor. **Publications:** It's O.K. to Be Gifted or Talented!: A Parent/Child Manual, 1987; It's O.K. to Grow Up!: A Parent/Child Manual, 1987; (with J. Youngblood) Blood, 1988; (comp.) Addicted: Kids Talking about Drugs in Their Own Words, 1989; Rod Serling: The Dreams and Nightmares of Life in the Twilight Zone, 1989; (with C. Carroll) Surf-Dog Days and Bitchin' Nights, 1989; Gene Roddenberry: The Myth and the Man behind Star Trek, 1994; Screenwriters On Screen-Writing: The Best in the Business Discuss Their Craft, 1995; (with G. Foreman) By George: The Autobiography of George Foreman, 1995; (with J. Morris) The Oldest Rookie: Big-League Dreams from a Small-Town Guy, 2001; Oscar-winning Screenwriters on Screenwriting: The Award-winning Best in the Business Discuss Their Craft, 2002; (with E. Ware) By Duty Bound: Survival and Redemption in a Time of War, 2005; We've Got it Made in America: A Common Man's Salute to an Uncommon Country, 2006; (C.B. Jones) What Would Martin Say?, 2008. **Address:** c/o Author Mail, Hyperion Books, 77 W 66th St., 11th Fl., New York, NY 10023, U.S.A. **Online address:** joel.engel@latimes.com

ENGEL, Jonathan. American (born United States), b. 1964. **Genres:** Medicine/Health, History. **Career:** Healthcare Financing Administration Office of Legislation and Policy, research analyst, 1991-92; Seton Hall University, assistant professor, 1995-2001, associate professor, 2001-07, department chairman, 2003-05, professor, 2007-; Essex and Union Advisory Board for Health Planning, director of research 1996-98; Columbia University, Mailman School of Public Health, teacher; University of Massachusetts, School of Public Health, teacher; City University of New York, Baruch College, professor and associate dean, 2008-. Writer. **Publications:** Doctors and Reformers: Discussion and Debate over Health Policy, 1925-1950, 2002; The Epidemic: A Global History of AIDS, 2006; Poor People's Medicine: Medicaid and American Charity Care since 1965, 2006; American Therapy: The Rise of Psychotherapy in the United States, 2008. **Address:** School of Public Affairs, Baruch College, City University of New York, 135 E 22nd St., New York, NY 10010, U.S.A. **Online address:** jonathan.engel@baruch.cuny.edu

ENGEL, Margorie L(ouise). American (born United States), b. 1943. **Genres:** Business/Trade/Industry, How-to Books, Human Relations/Parenting, Law, Sociology, Young Adult Non-fiction. **Career:** Educational program developer, 1965-76; Fairfield University, public relations staff, 1976-78; Siebert Associates, partner, 1978-85; Hamilton-Forbes Associates, president, 1985-; Manhattanville College, professor, 1987-88; Northeastern University, Brudnick Center for the Study of Conflict and Violence, fellow, 1998-; Stepfamily Association of America, president and chief executive ofiider, 1998, chair of educational resources; Your Stepfamily Magazine, senior editorial adviser, 2002-; Investors Strategy Institute, founder and director; Children's Museum, director; Stepfamily Magazine, senior editorial advisor and financial columnist; U.S. Governor's Advisory Commission, commissioner; SAA Advisory Council, founder; Entrepreneurial Women's Network, faculty; Association for Corporate Growth, vice president; The Business Council of Fairfield County, president. Writer. **Publications:** A Guide to Mergers and Acquisitions, 1984; (with D.D. Gould) The Divorce Decisions Workbook: A Planning and Action Guide, 1992; (with D. Gould) Weddings for Complicated Families: The New Etiquette for Couples with Divorced Parents and Those Planning to Remarry, 1993, 2nd ed. as Weddings: A Family Affair, 1998; Divorce Help Sourcebook, 1994; (with J.D. Payne and M. Payne) The Canadian Divorce Decisions Workbook, 1994; Stepfamilies Business Decisions Booklet Series, 2001. Contributor to books and periodicals. **Address:** 25 Walnut St., Boston, MA 02108, U.S.A. **Online address:** engel@saafamilies.org

ENGEL, Michael S. American (born United States), b. 1971. **Genres:** Natural History, Zoology, Biology, Earth Sciences. **Career:** American Museum of Natural History, research scientist, 1998-2000, research associate, 2000-; Linnean Society of London, fellow, 2000; University of Kansas, Division of Entomology, Natural History Museum, curator-in-charge, 2000-01, 2007, assistant curator, 2000-05, associate curator, 2005-08, courtesy curator of invertebrate paleontology, 2006-, senior curator, 2008-; Department of Ecology and Evolutionary Biology, assistant professor, 2000-05, associate professor, 2005-08, professor and courtesy professor of geology, 2008-. Writer. **Publications:** (Ed. with B.A. Alexander) Proceedings of the Eickwort Memorial Symposium, 1997; (with D. Grimaldi) Evolution of the Insects, 2005; (with D.A. Grimaldi) Diverse Neuropterida in Cretaceous Amber, with Particular Reference to the Paleofauna of Myanmar (Insecta), 2008. **Address:** Division of Entomology, University of Kansas, Public Safety Bldg., 1501 Crestline Dr., Ste. 140, Lawrence, KS 66049-2811, U.S.A. **Online address:** msengel@ku.edu

ENGEL, Monroe. American (born United States), b. 1921. **Genres:** Novels, Literary Criticism And History, Young Adult Fiction. **Career:** Reynal & Hitchcock, editor, 1946-47; Viking Press, editor, 1947-51; Princeton University, lecturer, 1954-55; Harvard University, assistant professor of English, 1955-60, lecturer, senior lecturer, 1960-89. **Publications:** NOVELS: A Length of Rope, 1952; Maturity of Dickens, 1959; Visions of Nicholas Solon, 1959; Voyager Belsky, 1962; Fish, 1981; Statutes of Limitations, 1988. OTHER: (intro.) The Middle of the Journey, 1947; (ed.) The Uses of Literature, 1973. **Address:** c/o Candida Donadio, Russell & Volkening Inc., 50 W 29th St., Ste. 7E, New York, NY 10001, U.S.A. **Online address:** miengel@comcast.net

ENGEL, Richard. American (born United States), b. 1973. **Genres:** International Relations/Current Affairs, History, Adult Non-fiction. **Career:** WGBH-Boston radio, Middle East correspondent, 2001-03; American Broadcasting Corporation (ABC-TV), freelance journalist, correspondent, 2002-03; National Broadcasting Corporation (NBC-TV), staff correspondent, 2003-06, Middle East correspondent and Beirut bureau chief, 2006-, news chief foreign correspondent, 2008-; World, freelance reporter, Middle East correspondent;

British Broadcasing Corporation Radio, freelance reporter, Middle East correspondent; Public Radio Intl., freelance reporter, Middle East correspondent; WGBH Radio, freelance reporter; USA Today, freelance reporter; Reuters, freelance reporter; Jane's Defense Weekly, freelance reporter. **Publications:** A Fist in the Hornet's Nest: On the Ground in Baghdad Before, During and After the War, 2004; War Journal: My Five Years in Iraq, 2008. **Address:** c/o Richard Leibner, N.S. Bienstock Agency, 1740 Broadway, 24th Fl., New York, NY 10019, U.S.A.

ENGELBERG, Alan (D.). American (born United States), b. 1941. **Genres:** Novels, Young Adult Fiction, Science Fiction/Fantasy. **Career:** University of California, assistant clinical professor of medicine; Cedars-Sinai Health Associates, internist. Writer. **Publications:** Variant (novel), 1988. **Address:** 436 N Bedford Dr., Ste. 214, Beverly Hills, CA 90210, U.S.A.

ENGELHARD, Jack. American/French (born France), b. 1940. **Genres:** Novels, Plays/Screenplays, Adult Non-fiction. **Career:** Suburban Newspaper Group, reporter; Willingboro Suburban, editor; Burlington County Times, reporter and feature writer; Philadelphia Inquirer, humor columnist and racing reporter; Westinghouse Broadcasting, KYW Radio, editor in charge of newsroom. Freelance writer. **Publications:** The Horsemen (non-fiction), 1974; Indecent Proposal (novel), 1988; Deadly Deception, 1997; Escape from Mount Moriah: Memoirs of a Refugee Child's Triumph, 2001; The Days of the Bitter End, 2001; The Bathsheba Deadline, 2005; The Girls of Cincinnati, 2008; Slot Attendant, 2009; Escape From Mount Moriah: The Trials & Triumphs of a Kid in a New Homeland, 2011. **Address:** 419 Cherry Hill Blvd., Cherry Hill, NJ 08002, U.S.A. **Online address:** jack@jackengelhard.com

ENGELHARDT, H(ugo) Tristram. American (born United States), b. 1941. **Genres:** Ethics, Medicine/Health, Philosophy. **Career:** University of Texas Medical Branch, assistant professor, 1972-75, associate professor, 1975-77; Georgetown University, School of Foreign Service, faculty, 1977-78, professor of philosophy, professor of health and humanities, Rosemary Kennedy professor of the philosophy of medicine; Baylor College of Medicine, professor of community medicine, 1983-, professor of medical ethics and professor of obstetrics and gynecology, 1990-2001, professor emeritus, 2001-; Southern Methodist University, adjunct assistant professor, 1974-75, adjunct associate professor, 1976-77; Masters & Johnson Institute, board director, 1977-82; Javeriana University, visiting professor, 1981-; Institute of Religion, distinguished visiting professor, 1982, adjunct research fellow, 1983-2001; Rice University, professor, 1983-, visiting fellow, 1984-88; Centro Oncologico de Excelencia, consulting medical staff, 1987-94; University of Adelaide, M.S. McLeod visiting professor, 1987. Writer. **Publications:** Mind-Body, 1973; (trans. with R.M. Zaner) A. Schutz and T. Luckmann, The Structures of the Life-World, 1973; Philosophy and medicine, 1975; The Foundations of Bioethics, 1986, 2nd ed., 1996; (with B.A. Brody) Bioethics, 1987; (with H.Y.H. Cho, K. Hisatake and L.N. Hen) Baioeshikkusu no kiso, 1988; Bioethics and Secular Humanism, 1991; The Foundations of Christian Bioethics, 2000. EDITOR: (with S.F. Spicker) Evaluation and Explanation in the Biomedical Sciences, 1975; (with S.F. Spicker) Philosophical Dimensions of the Neuro-Medical Sciences, 1976; (with D. Callahan) Science, Ethics, and Medicine, 1976; (with S.F. Spicker) Philosophical Medical Ethics, 1977; (with D. Callahan) Knowledge, Value, and Belief, 1977; The Encyclopedia of Bioethics, 1978; (with D. Callahan) Morals, Science, and Sociality, 1978; Mental Health, 1978; Clinical Judgment, 1979; (with D. Callahan) Knowing and Valuing, 1980; Mental Illness, 1980; Concepts of Health and Disease, 1981; The Roots of Ethics, 1981; (with J.M. Healey and S.F. Spicker) The Law-Medicine Relation, 1981; (with W.B. Bondeson, S.F. Spicker and J.M. White) New Knowledge in the Biomedical Sciences, 1982; (co-ed.) Abortion and the Status of the Fetus, 1983, 2nd ed., 1984; (with S.F. Spicker and W.B. Bondeson) The Contraceptive Ethos, 1987; (with A.L. Caplan) Scientific Controversies, 1987; (with R.C. McMillan and S.F. Spicker) Euthanasia and the Newborn, 1987; (co-ed.) The Use of Human Beings in Research, 1988; (with C. Sachsse) Sicherheit und Freiheit, 1991; (with T. Pinkard) Hegel Reconsidered: Beyond Metaphysics and the Authoritian State, 1994; Philosophy of Medicine: Framing the Field, 2000; (with L.M. Rasmussen) Bioethics and Moral Content: National Traditions of Health Care Morality, 2002; (with M.J. Cherry) Allocating Scarce Medical Resources: Roman Catholic Perspectives, 2002; Global Bioethics: The Collapse of Consensus, 2006; (with F. Jotterand) Philosophy of Medicine Reborn: A Pellegrino Reader, 2008; (with J.R. Garrett) Innovation and the Pharmaceutical Industry: Critical Reflections on the Virtues of Profit, 2008. Works appear in anthologies. Contributor to journals. **Address:** Department of Philosophy, Rice University, Rm.

MS 14, 6100 S Main St., Houston, TX 77005-1892, U.S.A. **Online address:** htengelh@rice.edu

ENGELKE, Matthew Eric. British (born England), b. 1972. **Genres:** Theology/Religion. **Career:** London School of Economics and Political Science, lecturer; University of Virginia, instructor; University of Richmond, instructor; University of Zimbabwe, instructor. Writer. **Publications:** (Ed. with M. Tomlinson) The Limits of Meaning: Case Studies in the Anthropology of Christianity, 2006; A Problem of Presence: Beyond Scripture in an African Church, 2007; (ed.) The Objects of Evidence: Anthropological Approaches to the Production of Knowledge, 2009. Contributor of articles to books, periodicals and journals. **Address:** England. **Online address:** m.engelke@lse.ac.uk

ENGELL, James. American (born United States), b. 1951?. **Genres:** Education, Literary Criticism And History, Humanities, Environmental Sciences/Ecology, Sciences, Philosophy. **Career:** Harvard University, assistant professor, 1978-80, associate professor, 1980-82, Gurney professor of English literature, professor of comparative literarture, 1983-. Writer. **Publications:** The Creative Imagination: Enlightenment to Romanticism, 1981; Forming the Critical Mind: Dryden to Coleridge, 1989; Coleridge, The Early Family Letters, 1994; The Committed Word: Literature and Public Values, 1999; Saving Higher Education in the Age of Money, 2005. EDITOR: (with W.J. Bate) Samuel Taylor Coleridge, Biographia Literaria; or, Biographical Sketches of My Literary Life and Opinions, vol. II, 1983; Johnson and His Age, 1984; (with D. Perkins and contrib.) Teaching Literature: What is Needed Now, 1988; (co-ed.) Environment, An Interdisciplinary Anthology, 2008. **Address:** Department of English, Center for the Environment, Harvard University, 162 Barker Ctr., 12 Quincy St., Cambridge, MA 02138, U.S.A. **Online address:** jengell@fas.harvard.edu

ENGELSTEIN, Laura. American (born United States), b. 1946. **Genres:** History. **Career:** Yale University, Henry S. McNeil Professor of History; Cornell University, faculty; Princeton University, faculty. Writer. **Publications:** Moscow, 1905: Working- Class Organization and Political Conflict, 1982; The Keys to Happiness: Sex and the Search for Modernity in Fin-de-Siecle Russia, 1992; Castration and the Heavenly Kingdom: A Russian Folktale, 1999; (ed. with S. Sandler) Self and Story in Russian History, 2000; (co-author) Zhizn' ne imeet zhalosti: pis'ma 1922-1935 gg. synu Borisu Ivanovichu Nikolaevskomu iz Orenburga i Moskvy v Berlin i Parizh, 2005; Slavophile Empire: Imperial Russia's Illiberal Path, 2009. **Address:** Yale University, 246 Church St., New Haven, CT 06520-8321, U.S.A. **Online address:** laura.engelstein@yale.edu

ENGER, Leif. (L. L. Enger). American (born United States), b. 1961?. **Genres:** Novels, Young Adult Fiction. **Career:** Minnesota Public Radio, reporter and producer, 1984-2000; Minnesota State University, M.F.A. writing program, professor and director. **Publications:** NOVELS. Peace like a River, 2001; So Brave, Young, and Handsome, 2008. WITH L. ENGER AS L.L. ENGER: Comeback, 1990; Swing, 1991; Strike, 1992; Sacrifice, 1993; The Sinners' League: A Gun Pedersen Mystery, 1994; Undiscovered Country, 2008. **Address:** c/o Paul Cirone, Aaron M. Priest Literary Agency, 708 3rd Ave., 23rd Fl., New York, NY 10017-4103, U.S.A.

ENGER, L. L. See **ENGER, Leif.**

ENGERMAN, David C. (David Charles Engerman). American (born United States), b. 1966. **Genres:** Novels. **Career:** Brandeis University, assistant professor of history, associate professor of history, professor; Herbert Hoover Presidential Library, Packard fellow, 1994; Franklin D. Roosevelt Presidential Library, Winant fellow, 1995; Harvard University, Davis Center for Russian and Eurasian Studies, research associate, 2000-07; Organization of American Historians, distinguished lecturer, 2010. Writer and historian. **Publications:** (Ed. and intro.) The God That Failed, 2001; Modernization from the Other Shore: American Intellectuals and the Romance of Russian Development, 2003; (co-ed.) Staging Growth, 2003; Know Your Enemy: The Rise and Fall of America's Soviet Experts, 2009; The Second World's Third World, 2011. **Address:** Department of History, Brandeis University, 123 Olin-Sang, 415 South St., Waltham, MA 02454, U.S.A. **Online address:** engerman@brandeis.edu

ENGERMAN, David Charles. See **ENGERMAN, David C.**

ENGLADE, Ken(neth Francis). American (born United States), b. 1938. **Genres:** Criminology/True Crime, Mystery/Crime/Suspense, Adult Non-fiction. **Career:** LaFourche Comet (newspaper), reporter, 1960-63; United Press Intl., reporter, bureau manager, correspondent, 1963-77; freelance writer, 1977-79; Florida Times Union, Georgia capital correspondent, 1980-83; freelance writer, 1983-; U.S. Air Force and the Missile Defense Agency, public information officer. **Publications:** CRIME NONFICTION: Cellar of Horror, 1989; Murder in Boston, 1990; Beyond Reason: The True Story of a Shocking Double Murder, a Brilliant and Beautiful Virginia Socialite, and a Deadly Psychotic Obsession, 1990; Deadly Lessons, 1991; A Family Business, 1992; To Hatred Turned: A True Story of Love and Death in Texas, 1993; Hoffa, 1993; Blood Sister, 1994; Hot Blood: The Money, The Brach Heiress, and The Horse Murders, 1996; Beyond Reason, 2001. NOVELS IN TONY HILLERMAN'S FRONTIER, PEOPLE OF THE PLAINS SERIES: People of the Plains, 1996; The Tribes, 1996; The Soldiers, 1996; Battle Cry, 1997; Brothers in Blood (part of Tony Hillerman's Frontier series), 1998; Everybody's Best Friend, 1999; (with W. Camp) Comanche Trail (part of Tony Hillerman's Frontier series), 1999. **Address:** 3228 Renaissance Dr. SE, Rio Rancho, NM 87124-7934, U.S.A. **Online address:** kenglade@yahoo.com

ENGLAND, Chris. British (born England), b. 1961. **Genres:** Plays/Screenplays, Sports/Fitness, Travel/Exploration, Music. **Career:** Four Four Two, columnist, 1994-98. Director and playwright. **Publications:** (With A. Smith) An Evening with Gary Lineker (play), 1992; (with N. Hancock) What Didn't Happen Next, 1997; Balham to Bollywood, 2002; No More Buddha, Only Football, 2003; The Fun Factory, forthcoming. **Address:** 56 Ellison Rd., London, GL SW16 5BY, England.

ENGLE, Margarita. American (born United States), b. 1951. **Genres:** Novels, Children's Fiction, Young Adult Fiction, Poetry. **Career:** California State Polytechnic University, associate professor of agronomy, 1978-82. Writer. **Publications:** Singing to Cuba, 1993; Skywriting, 1995; Poet-Slave of Cuba: A Biography of Juan Francisco Manzano, 2006; The Surrender Tree, 2008; Tropical Secrets: Holocaust Refugees in Cuba, 2009; Summer Birds: The Butterflies of Maria Merian, 2010; Firefly Letters: A Suffragette's Journey to Cuba, 2010; Hurricane Dancers: The First Caribbean Pirate Shipwreck, 2011; Wild Book, 2012. Works appear in anthologies. Contributor to journals. **Address:** c/o Julie Castiglia, 1155 Camino Del Mar, Ste. 510, Del Mar, CA 92014, U.S.A. **Online address:** englefam@earthlink.net

ENGLEHART, Bob. American (born United States), b. 1945. **Genres:** Cartoons, Picture/Board Books. **Career:** Chicago Today, staff artist, 1966-72; Fort Wayne Journal Gazette, editorial cartoonist, 1972-75, freelance artist; Englehart and Associates, owner, 1972-75; Journal Herald, staff, editorial cartoonist, 1975-80; Hartford Courant, editorial cartoonist, 1980-. Writer. **Publications:** Never Let Facts Get in the Way of a Good Cartoon: Editorial Cartoons, 1979; A Distinguished Panel of Experts (cartoons), 1985. **Address:** The Hartford Courant, 285 Broad St., Hartford, CT 06115, U.S.A. **Online address:** benglehart@courant.com

ENGLEMAN, Paul. (Paul Francis). American (born United States), b. 1953. **Genres:** Mystery/Crime/Suspense, Young Adult Fiction, Novels. **Career:** Playboy Magazine, publicity manager, 1977-83, publicity director, 1984-85. Writer. **Publications:** Dead in Center Field, 1983; Catch a Fallen Angel, 1986; Murder-in-Law, 1987; Who Shot Longshot Sam?, 1989; (as Paul Francis with D. Clark) Murder on Tour, 1989; The Man with My Name, 1994; Left for Dead: A Mark Renzler Novel, 1996; The Man With My Cat, 2000. **Address:** c/o James Trupin, Jet Literary Associates Inc., 2570 Camino San Patricio, Santa Fe, NM 87505, U.S.A.

ENGLISH, Allan D. Canadian (born Canada), b. 1949. **Genres:** Novels, Young Adult Fiction. **Career:** Royal Military College of Canada, Department of Military Psychology and Leadership, lecturer, 1987-91, Department of History, lecturer, 1991-92, assistant professor, 1993-95, associate professor, 1996-99, instructor for directed reading courses, 1995-96, 1997-98, 1998-99, 2003-04; Queen's University, lecturer, 1993-94, adjunct assistant professor, 1994-2004, adjunct associate professor, 2004-; Canadian Forces Leadership Institute, senior research fellow, 2002-04; Canadian Forces College, faculty. Writer. **Publications:** The Cream of the Crop: Canadian Aircrew 1939-1945, 1996; The Changing Face of War: Learning from History, 1998; (co-author) Bian hua zhong de zhan zheng=The Changing Face of War, 2001; Understanding Military Culture: A Canadian Perspective, 2004; (ed.) Air Campaigns in the New World Order, 2004; (ed.) The Operational Art: Canadian Perspectives: Context and Concepts, 2005; (ed. with J.C. Taylor) The Operational Art: Canadian Perspectives: Health Service Support, 2006; (ed.) The

Operational Art: Canadian Perspectives: Leadership and Command, 2006; (with J. Westrop) Canadian Air Force Leadership and Command: The Human Dimension of Expeditionary Air Force Operations, 2007; (with R.G. and H.G. Coombs) Networked Operations and Transformation: Context and Canadian Contributions, 2007; Command and Control of Canadian Aerospace Forces: Conceptual Foundations, 2008; Effects-Based Approaches to Operations: Canadian Perspectives, 2008. Contributor to periodicals. **Address:** Department of History, Queens University, 129 Watson Hall, 49 Bader Ln., Kingston, ON K7L 3N6, Canada. **Online address:** kmg1@sympatico.ca

ENGLISH, Barbara (Anne). British/Scottish (born Scotland), b. 1933. **Genres:** History, Bibliography, Humanities. **Career:** National Register of Archives, archivist, 1958-62; Thomas Nelson & Sons Ltd., publisher, assistant editor, 1962-64; University of Hull, research fellow, 1979-82, lecturer, senior lecturer, reader, professor of history, 1982-, now professor emeritus. **Publications:** John Company's Last War in US as The War for a Persian Lady, 1971; The Lords of Holderness, 1086-1260: A Study in Feudal Society, 1979; (co-author) Beverley: An Archaeological and Architectural Study, 1982; (with J. Saville) Strict Settlement: A Guide for Historians, 1983; Yorkshire Enclosure Awards, 1985; (ed.) Domesday Book and the East Riding, 1986; The Great Landowners of East Yorkshire 1530-1910, 1990; Royal Historical Society's Annual Bibliography, 1992; (ed.) Yorkshire Hundred and Quo Warranto Rolls, 1996. Contributor to periodicals. **Address:** Department of History, University of Hull, Cottingham Rd., Hull, HU6 7RX, England.

ENGLISH, Beth Anne. American (born United States), b. 1973. **Genres:** Business/Trade/Industry. **Career:** College of William and Mary, faculty, 1998-2004; College of William and Mary, visiting assistant professor, 2000-01, 2003-04; Princeton University, Liechtenstein Institute on Self-Determination, publications and grants program manager, 2005-, Women in International Relations Program, director, 2005-; Temple University, adjunct assistant professor, 2006-10; H-Net: Humanities and Social Sciences Online, online editor; Journal of Southern History and Feminist Studies, manuscript referee; National Science Foundation, Science and Society Program, project proposal evaluator. Writer. **Publications:** A Common Thread: Labor, Politics and Capital Mobility in the Textile Industry, 2006. **Address:** Liechtenstein Institute on Self-determination, Woodrow Wilson School, Princeton University, 014 Bendheim Hall, Princeton, NJ 08544, U.S.A. **Online address:** baenglish@princeton.edu

ENGLISH, Camper. American (born United States) **Genres:** Sociology. **Career:** Freelance writer. **Publications:** Party Like a Rockstar: Even When You're Poor As Dirt, 2005. Contributor to books. **Address:** c/o Author Mail, Alyson Publications, 6922 Hollywood Blvd., Ste. 1000, Los Angeles, CA 90028-6130, U.S.A. **Online address:** alcademics@gmail.com

ENGLISH, Darby. American (born United States), b. 1974?. **Genres:** Young Adult Non-fiction, Art/Art History. **Career:** University of Chicago, assistant professor of art history. Writer. **Publications:** NONFICTION: (co-ed.) Kara Walker: Narratives of a Negress, 2003; How to See a Work of Art in Total Darkness, 2007. Contributor to books. **Address:** Department of Art History, Division of the Humanities, University of Chicago, 166 Cochrane Woods Art Ctr., 5540 S Greenwood Ave., Chicago, IL 60637-1506, U.S.A. **Online address:** denglish@uchicago.edu

ENGLISH, John A(lan). American/Canadian (born Canada), b. 1940. **Genres:** Military/Defense/Arms Control, History, Humanities. **Career:** Queen's University, visiting defense fellow, 1984-85, postdoctoral fellow and assistant professor, 1992-95, adjunct assistant professor, 1995-97; Canadian Land Forces Command and Staff College, directing staff instructor, 1985-86, 1988-90; International Institute for Strategic Studies, research associate, 1990-91; U.S. Naval War College, professor of strategy, 1997-. Writer. **Publications:** A Perspective on Infantry, 1981 as On Infantry, 1984, (with B.I. Gudmundsson) rev. ed., 1994; (ed. with J. Addicott and P.J. Kramers) The Mechanized Battlefield: A Tactical Analysis, 1985; The Canadian Army and the Normandy Campaign: A Study of Failure in High Command, 1991 as Failure in High Command: The Canadian Army and the Normandy Campaign, 1995; (contrib.) Canadian Military History, 1993; (contrib.) Military Heretics, 1993; Marching through Chaos: The Descent of Armies in Theory and Practice, 1996; (contrib.) The North Atlantic Triangle in a Changing World: Anglo-American-Canadian Relations, 1902-1956, 1996; (contrib.) The Operational Art, 1996; (with J.H. Allan) Peacekeeping, 1996; Lament for an Army: The Decline of Canadian Military Professionalism, 1998; Pat-

ton's Peers: The Forgotten Allied Field Army Commanders of the Western Front, 1944-45, 2009; Surrender Invites Death: Fighting the Waffen SS in Normandy, 2011. Contributor to books and periodicals. **Address:** Strategy and Policy Department, U.S. Naval War College, 686 Cushing Rd., Newport, RI 02841, U.S.A. **Online address:** englishj@nwc.navy.mil

ENGLISH, Lyn D. Australian (born Australia), b. 1953. **Genres:** Education, Mathematics/Statistics, Engineering, Sciences, Reference. **Career:** Classroom teacher at state primary schools in Queensland, 1974-78; Open Access Unit, mathematics curriculum co-ordinator, 1979-85; Queensland University of Technology, lecturer, 1982-88, senior lecturer, 1988-92, associate professor of mathematics education, 1992-2000, Centre for Mathematics and Science Education, assistant director, 1993-2004, professor of mathematics education, 2000-. Writer. **Publications:** (With A.R. Baturo) Sunshine Maths, Years 1-7, 1983-85; (co-author) Primary School Mathematics: Teaching Numeration, 1986; Primary School Mathematics: Teaching the Operations, 1986; Using Calculators in Primary Mathematics, 1986; (with G.S. Halford) Mathematics Education: Models and Processes, 1995; International Perspectives on Mathematics Education, 2000. EDITOR: Mathematical Reasoning: Analogies, Metaphors, and Images, 1997; (and contrib.) Mathematical Reasoning, Nature, Form and Development, 1999; (with S. Goodchild) Researching Mathematics Classrooms: A Critical Examination of Methodology, 2000; (co-ed.) Mathematical Thinking and Learning: Statistical Thinking and Learning 2000, 2000; Handbook of International Research in Mathematics Education, 2002, 2nd ed., 2008; Mathematical and Analogical Reasoning of Young Learners, 2004; (with B. Sriraman) Theories of Mathematics Education: Seeking New Frontiers, 2010. Contributor to books and professional journals. **Address:** Queensland University of Technology, S BLOCK Level 4 406, Kelvin Grove, Victoria Park Rd., Brisbane, QL 4059, Australia. **Online address:** l.english@qut.edu.au

ENGLISH, Richard Ludlow. Irish (born Ireland), b. 1963. **Genres:** Novels. **Career:** Queen's University, lecturer, 1990-95, reader, 1995-99, professor of politics, 1999-. Writer. **Publications:** (ed. with C. O'Malley) Prisoners: The Civil War Letters of Ernie O'Malley, 1991; History of Ireland, 1991; Radicals and the Republic: Socialist Republicanism in the Irish Free State, 1925-1937, 1994; (ed. with G. Walker) Unionism in Modern Ireland: New Perspectives on Politics and Culture, 1996; Ernie O'Malley: IRA Intellectual, 1998; (ed. with J.M. Skelly) Ideas Matter: Essays in Honour of Conor Cruise O'Brien, 1998; (ed. with C. Townshend) The State: Historical and Political Dimensions, 1999; (ed. with M. Kenny) Rethinking British Decline, 2000; Armed Struggle: The History of the IRA, 2003; Irish Freedom: The History of Nationalism in Ireland, 2007. **Address:** Queen's University, 21 University Sq., Ulster, BT7 1PA, Northern Ireland. **Online address:** r.english@qub.ac.uk

ENGLISH, Sharon. Canadian (born Canada), b. 1965. **Genres:** Language/Linguistics, Novellas/Short Stories, Young Adult Fiction. **Career:** University of Toronto, Innis College, Writing Centre, instructor in writing, 2000-, acting director, 2002-03, 2004-05, director, 2005-; Ryerson University, faculty, 2007-08; George Brown College, faculty, 2007-08. Writer. **Publications:** Uncomfortably Numb, 2002; Zero Gravity, 2006. Contributor to journals. **Address:** Writing Centre, Innis College, University of Toronto, 2 Sussex Ave., Toronto, ON M5S 1J5, Canada. **Online address:** sharon.english@utoronto.ca

ENGLISH, Thomas Joseph. See ENGLISH, T. J.

ENGLISH, T. J. (Thomas Joseph English). American (born United States), b. 1957. **Genres:** Criminology/True Crime. **Career:** Freelance journalist and writer. **Publications:** The Westies: Inside the Hell's Kitchen Irish Mob, 1990, as The Westies: Inside New York's Irish Mob, 2006; Born to Kill: America's Most Notorious Vietnamese Gang and the Changing Face of Organized Crime, 1995; Paddy Whacked: The Untold Story of the Irish-American Gangster, 2005; The Havana Mob: Gangsters, Gamblers, Showgirls and Revolutionaries in 1950s Cuba, 2007, as Havana Nocturne: How the Mob Owned Cuba-and Then Lost It to the Revolution, 2008. Contributor to periodicals. **Address:** c/o Nat Sobel, Sobel Weber Associates Inc., 146 E 19th St., New York, NY 10003, U.S.A. **Online address:** info@tj-english.com

ENGLUND, Steven. French (born France) **Genres:** Human Relations/Parenting, Romance/Historical, History. **Career:** Time Magazine, staff correspondent, 1968-74; University of California, lecturer in history, 1977-87; Commission for a National Agenda for the Eighties, staff, 1980-81; University de Paris-VIII, chargé de conference, 1985-87; l'école des Hautes études en Sciences Sociales, 1989-, visiting director of studies, 2007; World Economic Forum, contract writer, 1997-2000; freelance writer, 2000-; American University of Paris, Department of History, distinguished New York University professor, 2007-; New York University School of Law, John E. Sexton, Esq. Dean and contract writer; Loyola University, Father John Piderit S.J. president, contract writer. **Publications:** (With E.E. Ford) For the Love of Children: A Realistic Approach to Raising Your Child, 1977; (with E.E. Ford) Permanent Love: Practical Steps to a Lasting Relationship, 1979; (with L. Ceplair) The Inquisition in Hollywood: Politics in the Film Community, 1930-1960, 1980; Report of the President's Commission for a National Agenda for the Eighties, 1981; Man Slaughter, 1983; Grace of Monaco: An Interpretive Biography, 1984; Tamar & Amnon (ballet in three movements), 1984; (contrib.) Dictionnaire des oeuvres politiques, 2nd ed., 1989; (contrib.) Une histoire de la democratie en Europe, 1991; Napoleon: A Political Life, 2004. Contributor to periodicals. **Address:** American University of Paris, 11 rue Pierre Villey, Paris, 75007, France. **Online address:** amdgsle@aol.com

ENGS, Ruth C(lifford). American (born United States), b. 1939. **Genres:** History, Medicine/Health. **Career:** Dalhousie University, assistant professor, 1970; Indiana University, assistant professor, 1973-79, associate professor, 1980-92, professor of applied health science, 1992-2003, professor emeritus of applied health science, 2003-; University of Queensland, visiting professor, 1980. Writer. **Publications:** (With S.E. Barnes and M. Wantz) Health Games Students Play: Creative Strategies for Health Education, 1975; (with M. Wantz) Teaching Health Education in the Elementary School, 1978; Responsible Alcohol and Drug Use, 1979; Alcohol and Other Drugs: Self Responsibility, 1987; Clean Living Movements: American Cycles of Health Reform, 2000; The Progressive Era's Health Reform Movement: A Historical Dictionary, 2003; The Eugenics Movement: An Encyclopedia, 2005; Conversations in the Abbey: Senior Monks of Saint Meinrad Reflect on Their Lives, 2007. EDITOR: Controversies in the Addiction Field, 1990; Women: Alcohol and Other Drugs, 1990; Unseen Upton Sinclair: Nine Unpublished Stories, Essays and Other Works, 2009. Contributor to professional journals. **Address:** Department of Applied Health Science, Indiana University, Poplars 615, 400 E 7th St., Bloomington, IN 47405, U.S.A. **Online address:** engs@indiana.edu

ENGSTER, Daniel (Albert). American (born United States), b. 1965. **Genres:** Politics/Government. **Career:** Santa Fe Technical High School, history teacher, 1988-89; University of Chicago, lecturer, 1993-97; Tulane University, visiting assistant professor of political science, 1997-98; University of Texas, Department of Political Science and Geography, assistant professor of political science, 1998-2003, associate professor, 2003-. Writer. **Publications:** Divine Sovereignty: The Origins of Modern State Power, 2001; The Heart of Justice: Care Ethics and Political Theory, 2007; (ed. with T. Metz) Justice and the Family in Contemporary Political Thought, 2013; Justice and the Welfare State: A Comparative Normative Approach, forthcoming; (with A. Johnson) Legal Reasoning, Practical Logic, and LSAT Preparation, forthcoming. **Address:** Department of Political Science and Geography, University of Texas, MS 4.03.36, 1 UTSA Cir., San Antonio, TX 78249-0648, U.S.A. **Online address:** daniel.engster@utsa.edu

ENGSTROM, Elizabeth. American (born United States), b. 1951. **Genres:** Mystery/Crime/Suspense, inspirational/Motivational Literature, Novels, Novellas/Short Stories. **Career:** Writer, 1978-; Maui Writers Retreat, writing instructor, 1990-, Department of Continuing Education, director; Lane Community College, instructor, 1991-; Love and Mercy Ministries, founder and interfaith minister, 2010-; University of Phoenix, online instructor, 2011-. **Publications:** NOVELS: When Darkness Loves Us, 1985; Black Ambrosia, 1988; Lizzie Borden, 1990; Lizard Wine, 1995; Suspicions, 2002; Black Leather, 2003; The Northwoods Chronicles, 2008; York's Moon, 2011. SHORT STORIES: Nightmare Flower, 1992; The Alchemy of Love: A Collaborative Endeavor, 1998; (comp. with J. Tullius) The Maui Writers Conference Presents Word by Word: An Inspirational Look at the Craft of Writing, 2000; (ed.) Dead on Demand: The Best of Ghost Story Weekend, 2001; Mota 9: Addiction, 2009. Works appear in anthologies. Contributor to magazines and periodicals. **Address:** University of Phoenix, 3157 E Elwood St., Phoenix, AZ 85034, U.S.A. **Online address:** liz@elizabethengstrom.com

ENNALS, Peter. Canadian (born Canada), b. 1943. **Genres:** Architecture, Geography, Local History/Rural Topics. **Career:** Queen's University, lecturer in geography, 1972-74; Mount Allison University, Department of Geography, faculty, 1974-, head, 1986-97, 2003-06, professor emeritus, 2007-, dean of social science, 1992-97, vice-president for academics and research, 1998-2002;

Kwansei Gakuin University, visiting professor of Canadian studies, 1986-87, 1992. Writer. **Publications:** (Ed.) Canadian Maritimes: Images and Encounters, 1993; (with D.W. Holdsworth) Homeplace: The Making of the Canadian Dwelling Over Three Centuries, 1998. Contributor to journals. **Address:** Department of Geography, Mount Allison University, 144 Main St., Avard-Dixon, Sackville, NB E4L 1A7, Canada. **Online address:** pennals@cogeco.ca

ENNIS, Garth. American/Irish (born Ireland), b. 1970. **Genres:** Children's Fiction, Novels, Cartoons, Graphic Novels. **Career:** Comic book writer, 1990-; screenwriter, 2004-; Marvel Comics, editor-in-chief. **Publications:** True Faith, 1990; Judge Dredd: Democracy Now!, 1992; Judge Dredd: Tales of the Damned, 1993; Judge Dredd: Babes in Arms, 1995; Preacher, 1996; Preacher: Gone to Texas, 1996; Preacher Special: Saint of Killers, 1996; Preacher Special: The Story of You-Know-Who, 1996; Bloody Mary, 1996; Medieval Spawn Witchblade, 1997; Preacher: Until the End of the World, 1997; Preacher Special: The Good Old Boys, 1997; Preacher: Proud Americans, 1997; Hitman, 1997; Bloody Mary: Lady Liberty, 1997; Heartland, 1997; Unknown Soldier, 1998; Hitman: 10, 000 Bullets, 1998; Preacher Special: Cassidy, Blood and Whiskey, 1998; Preacher: Dixie Fried, 1998; Preacher: Ancient History, 1998; Preacher: War in the Sun, 1999; Preacher: Salvation, 1999; Hitman: Local Heroes, 1999; Hitman: The Ace of Killers, 2000; Preacher Special: Tall in the Saddle, 2000; Preacher: All Hell's A-Comin', 2000; Preacher, Dead or Alive: Covers by Glenn Fabry, 2000; The Worm: The Longest Comic Strip in the World, 2000; The Punisher Kills the Marvel Universe, 2000; Enemy Ace: War in Heaven, 2001; Darkness, vol. I, 2001; D-Day Dodgers, 2001; Preacher: Alamo, 2001; The Punisher: Welcome Back, Frank, 2001; Hitman: Who Dares Wins, 2001; Judge Dredd: Emerald Isle, 2002; Goddess, 2002; Nightingale, 2002; Screaming Eagles, 2002; Fury, 2002; Spider-Man's Tangled Web, vol. I, 2002; Just a Pilgrim: Garden of Eden, 2003; Judge Dredd: Muzak Killer, 2003; Garth Ennis' Dicks, vol. I, 2003; Alan Moore's The Courtyard, 2003; Judge Dredd: Innocents Abroad, 2003; The Reivers, 2003; Judge Dredd: Death Aid, Featuring Return of the King and Christmas with Attitude, 2003; Judge Dredd: Goodnight Kiss, Featuring the Marshal and Enter Jonni Kiss, 2003; Animal Farm, 2003; Star Wars Tales, vol. III, 2003; The Punisher: Streets of Laredo, 2003; Punisher, vol. II, 2003; The Punisher: Born, 2004; Punisher Max: In the Beginning, 2004; The Punisher: Confederacy of Dunces, 2004; The Punisher, 2004; Thor: Vikings, 2004; War Stories, vol. I, 2004; Judge Dredd: Judgment Day, 2004; The Pro, 2004; Pride and Joy, 2004; Adventures in the Rifle Brigade, 2004; The Punisher: Army of One, 2004; The Authority: Kev, 2005; Judge Dredd: Helter Skelter, 2005; Judge Dredd: Justice One, 2005; Constantine, 2005; The Punisher: Business as Usual, 2005; Punisher Max: Mother Russia, 2005; The Punisher: Full Auto, 2005; Boys, 2006; Preacher, vol. I: Gone to Texas, 2009, vol. II, 2010. JOHN CONSTANTINE, HELLBLAZER SERIES: GRAPHIC NOVELS: Hellblazer Special, 1993; Dangerous Habits, 1994; Fear and Loathing, 1997; Tainted Love, 1998; Damnation's Flame, 1999; Rake at the Gates of Hell, 2003; Son of Man, 2004; Rare Cuts, 2005. Works appear in anthologies. **Address:** DC Comics, 1700 Broadway, 7th Fl., New York, NY 10019-5905, U.S.A.

ENNULAT, Egbert M. American (born United States), b. 1929. **Genres:** Art/Art History, Music, Reference. **Career:** Methodist College, teacher, 1961; Oberlin College, instructor, 1963-64; College of Wooster, instructor, 1964-65; University of Georgia, assistant professor, 1965-72, associate professor, 1972-79, professor of music, 1979-2000, Josiah Meigs professor, 1994-2000, professor emeritus, 2000-; Yuonsei University, Fulbright lecturer, 1987; Sandy Beaver professor for excellence in teaching, 1988-91. Writer and musician. **Publications:** EDITOR: The Collected Works of Johann De Fossa, 1978. OTHER: Arnold Schoenberg Correspondence: A Collection of Translated and Annotated Letters with Guido Adler, Pablo Casals, Emanuel Feuermann and Olin Downes, 1991. Contributor to periodicals. **Address:** School of Music, University of Georgia, 250 River Rd., Athens, GA 30602, U.S.A. **Online address:** eennulat@uga.edu

ENO, Will. American (born United States), b. 1965?. **Genres:** Novels, Literary Criticism And History, Humanities. **Career:** Writer. **Publications:** Night Night, 2000; Tragedy: A Tragedy, 2001; The Flu Season, 2003; Thom Pain: Based on Nothing, 2004; Tough the Tough, 2005; The Flu Season, 2005; Oh, the Humanity: A Short Drama, 2005; The Flu Season and Other Plays, 2008; Oh, the Humanity and Other Good Intentions, 2008; Middletown,

2010. Contributor to periodicals. **Address:** Mark Christian Subias Agency, 331 W 57th St., Ste. 462, New York, NY 10019, U.S.A. **Online address:** e-fosnes@online.no

ENQUIST, Per Olov. Swedish (born Sweden), b. 1934. **Genres:** Novels, Novellas/Short Stories, Plays/Screenplays, Young Adult Fiction. **Career:** Uppsala Nya Tidning, literary and theater critic, 1960-63; newspaper columnist and TV debate moderator, 1965-76; Svenska Dagbladet, literary and theater critic, 1966-67; Expressen, literary and theater critic, 1967-; University of California, visiting professor, 1973. Writer. **Publications:** FICTION: Kristallögat (title means: 'The Crystal Eye'), 1961; Färdvägen (title means: 'The Route'), 1963; (with T. Ekbom and P. Husberg) Broderna Casey (title means: 'The Casey Brothers'), 1964; Magnetisörens femte vinter, 1967, trans. as Magnetist's Fifth Winter, 1989; Hess, 1968; Legionärerna, 1968; Sekonden: Roman, 1971; Berättelser från de inställda upprorens tid, 1974; Musikanternas uttåg, Roman, 1978, trans. as The March of the Musicians, 1993; (with A. Ehnmark) Doktor Mabuses nya testamente, 1982; Nedstörtad ängel: en kärleksroman, 1985; (with A. Ehnmark) Protagoras sats: på spaning efter det politiska förnuftet, 1987; Kapten Nemos bibliotek: Roman, 1991; Captain Nemo's Library, 1992; Kartritarna, 1992; Livläkarens besök: Roman, 1999, trans. as The Royal Physician's Visit, 2001. PLAYS: Tribadernas: ett skådespel från 1889, 1975, trans. as Night of the Tribades, 1978; (with A. Ehnmark) Chez nous: bilder från svenskt församlingsliv, 1976; (with A. Ehnmark) Mannen på trottoaren: förundersökning angående mordet på doktor Plehve, 1979; Till Fedra, 1980; Fran regnormarnas liv, 1981, trans. as The Rain Snakes; En triptyk, 1981; The Hour of the Lynx, 1990; Tre pjäser, 1994; Bildmakarna, 1998; Systrarna, 2000. OTHER: (ed.) Sextiotalskritik: en antologi (title means: 'Criticism of the Sixties: An Anthology'), 1966; De misstolkade legionärerna (nonfiction), 1970; Katedralen i München och andra berättelser, 1972; Nach den klassischen Höhepunkten, 1976; Strindberg-ett liv, 1984; Mannen i baten, 1985; Tva reportage om idrott, 1986; Hamsun: en fortælling (film script), 1996; Jakten på den förlorade själen, 1997; Lewis resa: Roman, 2001, trans. as Lewi's Journey, 2005; Book about Blanche and Marie, 2006; Three Cave Mountain, or: Grandfather and the Wolves, 2007; Ett annat liv, 2008. **Address:** Norstedts Forlag, Tryckerigatan 4, PO Box 2052, Stockholm, 103 12, Sweden.

ENSLIN, Theodore (Vernon). *See* Obituaries.

ENSLOW, Sam. American/Egyptian (born Egypt), b. 1946. **Genres:** Art/Art History, History, Archaeology/Antiquities, Travel/Exploration, Travel/Exploration. **Career:** ITT Sheraton Corp., manager, 1968-73; Green Retreat Nursery, owner and operator, 1974-80; Hotel Tequendama, international representative, 1979-86; La Ventana, general partner, 1980-90; Fort Lauderdale's Museum of Archaeology, coordinator, 1989; Northern Virginia Community College, coordinator, 1989. Writer and consultant. **Publications:** (With F. Smith and G. Graves) Romancing the Gold: Pre-Columbian Ceramics and Gold from Private Collections, 1986; The Art of Prehispanic Colombia: An Illustrated Cultural and Historical Survey, 1990; Lake of Dreams, 1997. Contributor to periodicals. **Address:** 5449 NE 5th Ave., Fort Lauderdale, FL 33334, U.S.A. **Online address:** a004915t@bc.setlin.org

ENSMINGER, Peter A. American (born United States), b. 1957?. **Genres:** Biology, Botany, Medicine/Health, Natural History, Sciences, Essays. **Career:** Syracuse University, research associate; Freiburg University, research associate; Cornell University, research associate, through 1994; science consultant and writer, 1994-99; Northeast Parallel Architectures Center, consultant and technical writer, 1999-. **Publications:** Life Under the Sun, 2001. Contributor of articles. **Address:** 256 Greenwood Pl., Syracuse, NY 13210, U.S.A. **Online address:** ensmingr@twcny.rr.com

ENSOR, Robert. American (born United States), b. 1922. **Genres:** Children's Fiction, Illustrations, Education, Young Adult Fiction. **Career:** Barnes Engineering Co., Field Research Special Instrument Section, head, 1952-85; Marshall Point Lighthouse Museum, director, 1990-98. Writer and engineer. **Publications:** SELF-ILLUSTRATED: Nellie, the Flying Instructor: As Narrated By Nellie, 1995. Illustrator of books by J. Scarpino and E. Ensor. **Address:** Marshall Point Rd., PO Box 247, Port Clyde, ME 04855-0247, U.S.A.

ENTINE, Jon. American/American (born United States), b. 1952. **Genres:** Sciences, Social Commentary, Popular Culture, Medicine/Health, Politics/Government, Business/Trade/Industry, Biology, Genealogy/Heraldry, Genealogy/Heraldry. **Career:** American Broadcasting Companies Inc. (ABC), ABC News, assignment editor and producer, 20/20, Primetime Live, writer and producer, 1974-83, 1991-93; National Broadcasting Company Inc. (NBC), NBC News, Nightly News, producer, senior producer of documentaries and specials, 1983-90; Ethical Corporation Magazine, columnist, 2000-; American Enterprise Institute for Public Policy Research, visiting fellow, 2002-; George Mason University Center for Health & Risk Communication/STATS, senior fellow; Genetic Literacy Project/GMU, executive director; ESG MediaMetrics, founder and executive director; New York University, lecturer; Columbia University, lecturer; University of Michigan, lecturer; Arizona State University, lecturer; Miami University, lecturer. Journalist. **Publications:** Taboo: Why Black Athletes Dominate Sports and Why We Are Afraid to Talk About It, 2000; (ed.) Pension Fund Politics: The Dangers of Socially Responsible Investing, 2005; (ed.) Let Them Eat Precaution: How Politics is Undermining the Genetic Revolution in Agriculture, 2006; Abraham's Children: Race, Identity, and the DNA of the Chosen People, 2007; No Crime but Prejudice: Fischer Homes, the Immigration Fiasco and Extra-judicial Prosecution, 2009; (ed.) Crop Chemophobia: Will Precaution Kill the Green Revolution?, 2011; Scared to Death: How Chemophobia Threatens Public Health, 2011. Contributor to periodicals. **Address:** ESG MediaMetrics, 6255 S Clippinger Dr., Cincinnati, OH 45243, U.S.A. **Online address:** jon@jonentine.com

ENYEART, James L. American (born United States), b. 1943. **Genres:** Photography, History. **Career:** Nelson Gallery of Art, staff photographer, 1965-66; Albrecht Gallery of Art, charter director, 1967-68; Missouri Western Junior College (now Missouri Western State College), instructor in drawing and design, 1967-68; University of Kansas, Helen Foresman Spencer Museum of Art, curator of photography, 1968-76, acting assistant director of photography, 1970-76; University of Kansas, lecturer, 1969-70, assistant professor, 1970-72, associate professor of art history, 1973-76; Friends of Photography, executive director, 1976-77; University of Arizona, Center for Creative Photography, director, 1977-89, professor of art, 1982-, professor of museum studies program; Kansas Arts Commission, commissioner, 1973-74; Friends of Photography, vice-president, 1978-81, director; Polaroid Corp., consultant, 1983-; George Eastman House, director, 1989-95; College of Santa Fe, Anne and John Marion Center for Photographic Arts, founding director, 1995-2002, Anne and John Marion professor emeritus, 2002-. Writer. **Publications:** (With T. Evans and L. Schwarm) No Mountains in the Way: Kansas Survey, NEA, 1976; Creative Camera, 1976; Francis Bruguière: His Photographs and His Life, 1977; (intro.) George Fiske, Yosemite Photographer, 1980; (foreword) Photography of the Fifties: An American Perspective, 1980; Jerry N. Uelsmann: Photographs from 1975-1979, 1980; (foreword) W. Eugene Smith: Master of the Photographic Essay, 1981; Jerry Uelsmann: 25 Years, A Retrospective, 1982; Aaron Siskind: Terrors and Pleasures 1931-1980, 1982; (intro.) Edge to Edge, 1982; Jerry N. Uelsmann: Twenty-five Years, A Retrospective, 1982; (with R.D. Monroe and P. Stoker) Three Classic American Photographs: Texts and Contexts, 1982; (co-author) Edward Weston Omnibus, 1984; Edward Weston's California Landscapes, 1984; (intro.) Judy Dater: 20 Years, 1986; (foreword) Andreas Feininger: A Retrospective, 1986; (intro.) Ansel Adams in Color, 1993; (intro.) Seeing the Unseen: Dr. Harold E. Edgerton and the Wonders of Strobe Alley, 1994; Tarnished Silver, 1996; Land, Sky and All That Is Within: Visionary Photographers in the Southeast, 1998; Jim Dine: Color Photographs, 1999; Harmony of Reflected Light: Photography of Arthur Wesley Dow, 2001; (co-author) Photographers, Writers and the American Scene, 2002; Lee Friedlander: Sticks & Stones: Architectural America, 2004; (with I. Sandler and D. Sylvester) Picturing Artists, 1950s-1960s, 2007; Willard Van Dyke: Changing the World through Photography and Film, 2008. EDITOR: Kansas Album, 1977; Dale Eldred: Sculpture Into Environment, 1978; Heinecken, 1980; (with N. Solomon) Writings of Henry Holmes Smith: Collected Writings 1935-1985, 1986; (co-ed.) Henry Holmes Smith: Collected Writings 1935-1985, 1986; Decade by Decade: Twentieth-Century American Photography from the Collection of the Center for Creative Photography, 1989. Contributor to books and periodicals. **Address:** Santa Fe University of Art and Design, 1600 Saint Michael's Dr., Santa Fe, NM 87505-7634, U.S.A. **Online address:** jenyeart@csf.edu

EOYANG, Eugene Chen. American (born United States), b. 1939. **Genres:** Literary Criticism And History, Translations, Language/Linguistics, Children's Non-fiction. **Career:** Doubleday and Co., editorial trainee, 1960-61; Anchor Books, editor, 1961-66; Indiana University, lecturer, 1969-71, assistant professor, 1971-74, associate professor, 1974-78, professor of comparative literature, 1978-2002, professor emeritus of comparative literature and of East Asian languages and cultures, 2003-, associate dean of research and graduate development, 1977-80, Department of East Asian Languages and

Cultures, chair, 1982-84, East Asian Summer Language Institute, resident and founding director, 1984-89; University of Illinois-Urbana-Champaign, visiting professor, 1987; Lingnan University, chair professor of English, 1996-2006, chair professor of humanities, 2006-07, chair professor of translation, 2007-08, director of general education, 2000-08, chair professor emeritus of English, humanities, translation, and general education, 2008-; Hong Kong Baptist University, visiting professor of translation, 2008-. **Publications:** The Transparent Eye: Translation, Chinese Literature, and Comparative Poetics, 1993; Coat of Many Colors: Reflections on Diversity by a Minority of One, 1995; Borrowed Plumage: Polemical Essays on Translation, 2003; Two-way Mirrors: Cross-cultural Studies in Glocalization, 2007; The Smile of a Crocodile: Rhymes for Chloe (and Kyle), 2008; The Promise and Premise of Creativity: Why Comparative Literature Matters, 2012. EDITOR: (trans. and intro.) Ai Qing: Selected Poems, 1982; (contrib.) Harper Collins World Reader, 1994; (co-ed.) Translating Chinese Literature, 1995. **Address:** Department of Comparative Literature, Indiana University, 914 Ballantine Hall, Bloomington, IN 47405, U.S.A. **Online address:** eoyang@ln.edu.hk

EPANOMITIS, Fotini. Australian (born Australia), b. 1969. **Genres:** Novels, Humor/Satire, Literary Criticism And History. **Career:** University of Canberra, writer-in-residence, 1996. Writer. **Publications:** The Mule's Foal, 1993. **Address:** Allen & Unwin, PO Box 8500, St. Leonards, Sydney, NW 1590, Australia.

EPHRON, Delia. (Delia Brock). American (born United States), b. 1944. **Genres:** Children's Fiction, Children's Non-fiction, Picture/Board Books. **Career:** New York Magazine, journalist, writer, 1975-78. **Publications:** How to Eat Like a Child and Other Lessons in not Being a Grown-up, 1978; Teenage Romance: Or How to Die of Embarrassment, 1981; Santa and Alex, 1983; Funny Sauce: Us, The Ex, the Ex's New Mate, the New Mate's Ex and the Kids, 1986; Do I Have to Say Hello?: Aunt Delia's Manners Quiz for Kids and Their Grownups, 1988; My Life and Nobody Else's, 1991; The Girl Who Changed the World, 1993; Hanging Up, 1995; Big City Eyes, 2000; Frannie in Pieces, 2007; The Girl with the Mermaid Hair, 2010. WITH L. BODGER: (as Delia Brock) The Adventurous Crocheter, 1972; (as Delia Brock) Gladrags, 1974; Crafts for All Seasons, 1980. **Address:** c/o Lynn Nesbit, Janklow & Nesbit Associates, 445 Park Ave., Fl 13, New York, NY 10022, U.S.A. **Online address:** frannieinpieces@aol.com

EPHRON, Nora. American (born United States), b. 1941. **Genres:** Novels, Plays/Screenplays, Literary Criticism And History, Young Adult Fiction, Humor/Satire. **Career:** New York Post, reporter, 1963-68; freelance journalist, 1968-72; Esquire Magazine, columnist and contributing editor, 1972-73, senior editor and columnist, 1974-76; New York Magazine, contributing editor, 1973-74. **Publications:** Wallflower at the Orgy, 1970; Crazy Salad Plus Nine, 1975; Scribble, Scribble: Notes on the Media (columns), 1978; Heartburn (novel), 1983; When Harry Met Sally, 1990; Nora Ephron Collected, 1991; Crazy Salad: Some Things about Women, 2000; Imaginary Friends, 2003; (contrib.) Scenes from the City: Filmmaking in New York, 1966-2006, 2006; I Feel Bad about My Neck: And Other Thoughts on Being a Woman, 2006; I Remember Nothing, and Other Reflections, 2010. **Address:** c/o Sam Cohn, International Creative Management, 825 8th Ave., New York, NY 10019, U.S.A.

EPPERSON, Michael. American (born United States) **Genres:** Physics, Adult Non-fiction, Philosophy, Science Fiction/Fantasy. **Career:** Santa Clara University, teaching assistant in biology, 1987-88; Brophy College Preparatory, teacher, 1990-93; Jesuit High School, history teacher, 1994, 1997; University of Chicago, faculty, 1995-97, resident head, 1998-2004, 2002-04, assistant director; Saint Ignatius College Preparatory, teacher, 1996-97; Lumen Christi Institute, program coordinator, 1998-2002, assistant director of program in science and religion, 2002-04; Loyola University, teacher, 2002-04; California State University, Philosophy Department, teacher, 2005-, research professor, 2007-, Center for Philosophy and the Natural Sciences, director and principal investigator, 2008-; MNIMI Foundation, co-director, Archangel Films, writer and producer. **Publications:** (Contrib.) Physics and Whitehead: Process, Quantum and Experience, 2003; Quantum Mechanics and the Philosophy of Alfred North Whitehead, 2004; (with D.R. Griffin and T. Eastman) Physics and Speculative Philosophy: The Rehabilitation of Metaphysics in 21st Century Science, forthcoming. Contributor of articles to books and periodicals. **Address:** Department of Philosophy, California State University-Sacramento, Rm. 3000, Mendocino Hall, 6000 J St., Sacramento, CA 95819-6033, U.S.A. **Online address:** epperson@csus.edu

EPPING, Charles. See **EPPING, Randy Charles.**

EPPING, Randy Charles. (Charles Epping). Swiss/American (born United States), b. 1952. **Genres:** Novels, Economics. **Career:** IFS Project Management AG, founder and manager, 1989-; Central Europe Foundation, president, 1999-; Swiss-based International Consulting Co., managing director. Financial consultant and writer. **Publications:** A Beginner's Guide to the World Economy: Seventy-one Basic Economic Concepts That Will Change the Way You See the World, 1992, 3rd ed. as A Beginner's Guide to the World Economy: Eighty-one Basic Economic Concepts That Will Change the Way You See the World, 2001; Trust (thriller novel), 2006; The Twenty-First-Century Economy: A Beginner's Guide; With 101 Easy-to-Learn Tools for Surviving and Thriving in the New Global Marketplace, 2009. Contributor to periodicals. **Address:** Greenleaf Book Group L.L.C., PO Box 91869, Austin, TX 78709, U.S.A.

EPPLE, Anne Orth. American (born United States), b. 1927. **Genres:** Children's Non-fiction, Crafts, Natural History, Botany, Sciences, Environmental Sciences/Ecology. **Career:** Bronx Zoo, assistant in education department and school lecturer, 1946-52. Writer. **Publications:** Nature Quiz Book, 1955; (comp. with L.E. Epple) Modern Science Quiz Book, 1958; The Beginning Knowledge Book of Ants, 1969; The Beginning Knowledge Book of Fossils, 1969; The Lookalikes, 1971; Nature Crafts, 1974; Something from Nothing Crafts, 1976; The Amphibians of New England, 1983; (with L.E. Epple) A Field Guide to the Plants of Arizona, 1995; Lilliputian Floral Designs, 2005; Plants of Arizona: A Field Guide, 2012. **Address:** Lenniger Literary Agency Inc., 437 5th Ave., New York, NY 10016, U.S.A. **Online address:** lepple@aol.com

EPPRIDGE, Bill Alfredo Eduardo. American/Argentine (born Argentina), b. 1938. **Genres:** Photography, History. **Career:** Life, staff photographer, 1964-72, photojournalist and reporter; Time, contract photographer, 1973-76, photojournalist and reporter; Sports Illustrated, contract photographer, 1976-89, staff photographer, 1998-2006, photojournalist and reporter; National Geographic, photojournalist and reporter; Fortune, photojournalist and reporter; People, photojournalist and reporter. **Publications:** (With R.R. Jones) Upland Passage, 1992; The Beatles! Backstage and Behind the Scenes, 2004; A Time It Was: Bobby Kennedy in the Sixties, 2008. Contributor to books. **Address:** ABRAMS, 115 W 18th St., 6th Fl., New York, NY 10011, U.S.A. **Online address:** bill@billeppridge.com

EPPS, Bradley S. (Brad). American (born United States), b. 1958. **Genres:** Literary Criticism And History, Sex. **Career:** Emory University, assistant professor, 1989-91; Harvard University, assistant professor, professor of Romance languages and literatures, 1991-, John L. Loeb professor of humanities, 1996-98, professor of studies in women, gender and sexuality, 2003-, chair of studies of women, gender and sexuality, Department of Romance Languages and Literatures, professor; University of Wisconsin, visiting professor, 1994. Writer. **Publications:** Significant Violence: Oppression and Resistance in the Narratives of Juan Goytisolo, 1970-1990, 1996; (ed. with Luis Fernández-Cifuentes) Spain Beyond Spain: Modernity, Literary History and National Identity, 2005; Passing Lines: Immigration and Sexuality; (ed. with Keja Valens and Bill Johnson) González, 2005; (ed. with Despina Kakoudaki) All About Almodávar: A Passion for Cinema Despina Kakoudaki, 2009; No todo se perdió en Cuba, forthcoming; Retos, riesgos, pautas y promesas de la teoría queer, forth coming. Contributor to books, catalogues, dictionaries and encyclopedias. Contributor of articles to periodicals. **Address:** Department of Romance Languages and Literatures, Harvard University, 327 Boylston Hall, Cambridge, MA 02138, U.S.A. **Online address:** bsepps@fas.harvard.edu

EPRILE, Tony. American/South African (born South Africa), b. 1955?. **Genres:** Novels, Novellas/Short Stories, Autobiography/Memoirs, Literary Criticism And History, Young Adult Fiction. **Career:** Skidmore College, faculty, 2003-04; Northwestern University, faculty; Bennington College, faculty; Lesley University, faculty; University of Iowa, Iowa Writers' Workshop, visiting faculty. Writer. **Publications:** Temporary Sojourner, and Other South African Stories, 1989; (with J.P. Gold) The Well-informed Patient's Guide to Coronary Bypass Surgery, 1990; The Persistence of Memory, 2004. Contributor of short stories and poetry to periodicals. **Address:** c/o Author Mail, W. W. Norton Inc., 500 5th Ave., New York, NY 10010-0002, U.S.A.

EPSTEIN, Barbara Leslie. American (born United States), b. 1944. **Genres:** Politics/Government. **Career:** University of California, professor. Writer.

Publications: The Politics of Domesticity: Women, Evangelism, and Temperance in Nineteenth-Century America, 1981; Political Protest and Cultural Revolution: Nonviolent Direct Action in the 1970s and 1980s, 1991; (ed. with M. Darnovsky and R. Flacks) Cultural Politics and Social Movements, 1995; The Minsk Ghetto, 1941-1943: Jewish Resistance and Soviet Internationalism, 2008. Contributor of articles to periodicals. **Address:** U.S.A. **Online address:** bepstein@nature.berkeley.edu

EPSTEIN, Catherine. (Catherine A. Epstein). American (born United States), b. 1962. **Genres:** History. **Career:** Stanford University, visiting lecturer, 1998-99; Mount Holyoke College, visiting assistant professor, 1999-2000; Amherst College, Department of history, assistant professor, 2000-, associate professor, chair of history. Writer. **Publications:** A Past Renewed: A Catalog of German-Speaking Refugee Historians in the United States after 1933, 1993; The Last Revolutionaries: German Communists and Their Century, 2003; Model Nazi: Arthur Greiser and the Occupation of Western Poland, 2010. Contributor to periodicals. **Address:** Department of History, Amherst College, 22 Chapin Hall, PO Box 2254, Amherst, MA 01002-5000, U.S.A. **Online address:** caepstein@amherst.edu

EPSTEIN, Catherine A. See **EPSTEIN, Catherine.**

EPSTEIN, Dan. American (born United States), b. 1966?. **Genres:** Cultural/Ethnic Topics. **Career:** Shockhound.com, managing editor. **Publications:** 20th Century Pop Culture, vol. I: The Early Years to 1949, vol. II: he 50s: America Tunes In, vol. III: The 60s: A Decade of Change, vol. IV: The 70s: Beyond Disco, vol. V: The 80s: The Decade of Plenty, vol. VI: The 90s: Without Boundaries, 2001; Big Hair and Plastic Grass: A Funky Ride through Baseball and America in the Swinging '70s, 2010. Contributor to periodicals. **Address:** CA , U.S.A. **Online address:** dpfde@earthlink.net

EPSTEIN, Eric Joseph. American (born United States), b. 1959. **Genres:** Environmental Sciences/Ecology, Biography, Geography, Reference. **Career:** Tri-County OIC, Loysville Secure Treatment Unit, lead instructor and adult basic education instructor, 1985-; State Correctional Institute-Camp Hill, lead instructor and adult basic education instructor, 1985-; Dauphin County Prison, lead instructor and adult basic education instructor, 1985-; Pennsylvania Department of Corrections, corrections officer, 1989; Pennsylvania State University, visiting assistant professor of humanities, 1992-99; EFMR Monitoring Group, founder, president, coordinator, 1992-; Rock The Capital (RTC), founder and coordinator, 2005-; Three Mile Island Alert Inc., chairman; Stray Winds Area Neighbors, chairman. Writer. **Publications:** (With P. Rosen) Dictionary of the Holocaust: Biography, Geography, and Terminology, 1997. **Address:** Rock The Capital, 4100 Hillsdale Rd., Harrisburg, PA 17112, U.S.A. **Online address:** epstein@efmr.org

EPSTEIN, Gene. American (born United States), b. 1944. **Genres:** Communications/Media, Economics, Business/Trade/Industry, Writing/Journalism. **Career:** New York Stock Exchange, chief economist; New School for Social Research, faculty; City University of New York, faculty; St. John's University, faculty; Barron's, economics editor, 1992-, columnist, 1993-. **Publications:** Econospinning: How to Read between the Lines When the Media Manipulate the Numbers, 2006. **Address:** Barron's, 1211 Ave. of the Americas, New York, NY 10036, U.S.A. **Online address:** gepstein@econospinning.com

EPSTEIN, Helen. American (born United States), b. 1961. **Genres:** Social Commentary, Trivia/Facts, Adult Non-fiction, Medicine/Health. **Career:** University of California, postdoctoral scientist, 1992; Case Western Reserve University, scientist conducting field research; Mulago Hospital, scientist conducting field research; Makerere University, Department of Biochemistry, lecturer, 1993-94; Chiron Corp., scientist conducting field research, 1993-95; Panos Institute, programme manager for acquired immunodeficiency syndrome (AIDS), 1995-97. Consultant and writer. **Publications:** The Invisible Cure: Africa, the West and the Fight against AIDS, 2007. Contributor to periodicals. **Address:** Farrar, Straus & Giroux, 19 Union Sq. W, New York, NY 10003, U.S.A. **Online address:** helenepstein@yahoo.com

EPSTEIN, James. (James A. Epstein). American (born United States), b. 1948. **Genres:** History. **Career:** Vanderbilt University, assistant professor, 1986-90, associate professor, 1990-95, professor of history and director of undergraduate studies, 1995-2009, distinguished professor of history, 2009; Journal of British Studies, co-editor, 2000-05. **Publications:** The Lion of Freedom: Feargus O'Connor and the Chartist Movement, 1832-1842, 1982;

(ed. with D. Thompson) The Chartist Experience: Studies in Working-Class Radicalism and Culture, 1830-60, 1982; (as James A. Epstein) Radical Expression: Political Language, Ritual, and Symbol in England, 1790-1850, 1994; In Practice: Studies in the Language and Culture of Popular Politics in Modern Britain, 2003; Scandal of Colonial Rule: Power and Subversion in the British Atlantic during the Age of Revolution, 2012. CONTRIBUTOR: Encyclopedia of Social History, 1993; Intellectuals and Public Life, 1996; Re-Reading the Constitution, 1996; Romantic Sociability: Social Networks and Literary Culture in Britain, 2002; At Home with the Empire: Metropolitan Culture and the Imperial World, 2006; Gender, Labour, War, and Empire: Essays on Modern Britain, 2008; The Peculiarities of Liberal Modernity in Imperial Britain, 2010. Contributor to periodicals and journals. **Address:** Department of History, Vanderbilt University, 2301 Vanderbilt Pl., VU Sta B, Ste. 351802, Nashville, TN 37235-1802, U.S.A. **Online address:** james.a.epstein@vanderbilt.edu

EPSTEIN, James A. See **EPSTEIN, James.**

EPSTEIN, Jennifer Cody. American (born United States) **Genres:** Novels, History, Biography. **Career:** Journalist. **Publications:** The Painter from Shanghai in UK as The Painter of Shanghai, 2008. Contributor to magazines and periodicals. **Address:** c/o Elizabeth Sheinkman, Curtis Brown Group Ltd., Haymarket House, 28-29 Haymarket, London, GL SW1Y 4SP, England. **Online address:** jennifer@jennifercodyepstein.com

EPSTEIN, Joseph. American (born United States), b. 1937. **Genres:** Social Commentary, Essays, Young Adult Fiction. **Career:** Northwestern University, visiting lecturer in literature and writing, lecturer, 1974-2002, now lecturer emeritus; American Scholar, editor, 1975-; The Weekly Standard, contributing editor. **Publications:** Divorced in America: Marriage in an Age of Possibility, 1974; Familiar Territory: Observations on American Life, 1979; Ambition: The Secret Passion, 1980; (ed. and intro.) Masters: Portraits of Great Teachers, 1981; The Middle of My Tether: Familiar Essays, 1983; Plausible Prejudices: Essays on American Writing, 1985; Once More around the Block: Familiar Essays, 1987; Partial Payments: Essays Arising from the Pleasures of Reading, 1989; A Line Out for a Walk: Familiar Essays, 1991; The Goldin Boys and Other Stories, 1992; With My Trousers Rolled, 1993; Pertinent Players, 1995; Life Sentences: Literary Essays, 1997; (ed.) The Norton Book of Personal Essays, 1997; (ed.) Portraits: A Gallery of Intellectuals, 1997; Anglophilia, American Style, 1997; Narcissus Leaves the Pool, 1999; Snobbery, 2002; Fabulous Small Jews (stories), 2003; Envy: The Seven Deadly Sins, 2003; Alexis De Tocqueville: Democracy's Guide, 2006; Friendship: An Exposé, 2006; In a Cardboard Belt! Essays Personal, Literary and Savage, 2007; (ed.) Literary Genius: 25 Classic Writers Who Define English & American Literature, 2007; Fred Astaire, 2008; The Love Song of A. Jerome Minkoff, 2010; Gossip, 2011. **Address:** Department of English, Weinberg College of Arts & Sciences, Northwestern University, University Hall 215, 1897 Sheridan Rd., Evanston, IL 60208, U.S.A. **Online address:** j-epstein@northwestern.edu

EPSTEIN, Lawrence J(effrey). American (born United States), b. 1946. **Genres:** Popular Culture. **Career:** Suffolk Community College, Department of English, professor, 1974-2008, assistant head, Humanities Division, chairperson, 1985-90; Suffolk Division of the American Jewish Congress, president, 1980-86; U.S. Congressman William Carney, district representative, 1982-86; Conversion to Judaism Resource Center, founder and president. Writer. **Publications:** Samuel Goldwyn, 1981; Zion's Call: Christian Contributions To The Origins And Development of Israel, 1984; A Treasury of Jewish Anecdotes, 1989; Jewish Inspirational Stories, 1991; The Theory and Practice of Welcoming Converts to Judaism: Jewish Universalism, 1992; A Treasury of Jewish Inspirational Stories, 1993; Conversion to Judaism: A Guidebook, 1994; (ed.) Readings on Conversion to Judaism, 1995; Questions and Answers on Conversion to Judaism, 1998; The Haunted Smile: The Story of Jewish Comedians in America, 2001; Mixed Nuts: America's Love Affair with Comedy Teams: From Burns and Allen to Belushi and Aykroyd, 2004; At The Edge Of A Dream: The Story Of Jewish Immigrants On New York's Lower East Side 1880-1920, 2007; Political Folk Music in America from its Origins to Bob Dylan, 2010; George Burns: An American Life, 2011. Contributor to periodicals. **Address:** Conversion to Judaism Resource Ctr., 74 Hauppauge Rd., Rm. 53, Commack, NY 11725, U.S.A.

EPSTEIN, Leslie (Donald). American (born United States), b. 1938. **Genres:** Novels, Novellas/Short Stories, Plays/Screenplays, Essays. **Career:**

Queens College of the City University of New York, lecturer, 1965-67, assistant professor, 1968-70, associate professor, 1970-75, professor of English, 1976-78; Boston University, Graduate Creative Writing Program, director, 1978-, professor; Tikkun, editorial board. Writer. **Publications:** NOVELS: P.D. Kimerakov, 1975; King of the Jews in UK as The Elder, 1979; Regina, 1982; Pinto and Sons, 1990; Pandaemonium, 1997; San Remo Drive, 2003; The Eighth Wonder of the World, 2006. OTHERS: Steinway Quintet Plus Four (stories), 1976; Stanley the Starfish, 1980; Goldkorn Tales (novellas), 1985, 2nd ed., 1986; Goldkorn Tales: Three Novellas, 1998; Ice Fire Water: A Leib Goldkorn Cocktail, 1999; Liebestod: Opera Buffa with Leib Goldkorn, 2012. **Address:** Department of English, Boston University, Rm. 214, 236 Bay State Rd., Boston, MA 02215, U.S.A. **Online address:** leslieep@bu.edu

EPSTEIN, Mikhail N. American/Russian (born Russia), b. 1950. **Genres:** Cultural/Ethnic Topics, Literary Criticism And History, Philosophy, Essays, inspirational/Motivational Literature, Language/Linguistics. **Career:** World Literature Institute of the Academy of Sciences of the U.S.S.R., researcher, 1973-78; Moscow Power Institute, All-Union Institute of Finance and Economics, lecturer, 1973-77; Moscow Bureau of Literary Education, lecturer, 1978-89; Interdisciplinary Image and Thought Association, director, 1986-88; Experimental Center of Creativity, Laboratory of Contemporary Culture, director, 1988-90; Wesleyan University, visiting professor, 1990; Emory University, assistant professor, 1990-95, associate professor, 1995-2000, Samuel Candler Dobbs professor of cultural theory and Russian literature, 2000-. Writer. **Publications:** Novoe v klassike, Derzhavin, Pushkin, Blok v sovremennom vospriiatii, 1982; Paradoksy novizny, 1988; Priroda, mir, tainik vselennoi, 1990; Tagebuch fur Olga: Chronik einer Vaterschaft, 1990; Relativistic Patterns in Totalitarian Thinking: An Inquiry into the Language of Soviet Ideology, 1991; Ottsóvstvo, 1992; Novoe sektantstvo: Tipyreligiozno-filosofskikh umonastroenii v Rossii, 1993; Velikaia Sov': Filosofsko-mifologicheskii ocherk, 1994; Vera i obraz: Reliogioznoebessoznatel'noe v russkoi kul'ture XX veka, 1994; Na granitsakh kul'tur: Rossiiskoe-amerikanskoe-sovetskoe, 1995; After the Future: The Paradoxes of Postmodernism and Contemporary Russian Culture, 1995; Bog detalie: Narodnaia dusha i chastnaia zhizn'v Rossii na iskhodeimperii, 1997, 2nd ed., 1998; (with A. Genis and S. Vladiv-Glover) Russian Postmodernism: New Perspectives on Post-Soviet Culture, 1999; (with E. Berry) Transcultural Experiments: Russian and American Models of Creative Communication, 1999; Postmodern v Rossii, 2000; Filosofiiavozmozhnogo, 2001; Cries in the New Wilderness: From the Files of the Moscow Institute of Atheism (fiction), 2002; Ottsovstvo: Metafizicheskiĭ dnevnik, 2003; Znak Probela: o budushchem gumanitarnykh nauk, 2004; Vsesse: v Dvukh Tomakh, 2005; Filosofiía tela, 2006; Slovo I Molchanie: Metafizika Russkoĭ Literatury, 2006; Velikaía sov', 2006; Amerossiía: Izbrannaía Ésseistika, 2007. Contributor to books and periodicals. **Address:** Department of Russian and East Asian Languages and, Cultures, Emory University, 1707 N Decatur Rd., Atlanta, GA 30322, U.S.A. **Online address:** russmne@emory.edu

EPSTEIN, Rachel S. American (born United States), b. 1941. **Genres:** Documentaries/Reportage, Business/Trade/Industry, Economics, Children's Fiction, Autobiography/Memoirs. **Career:** J.C. Penney and Company Inc., training writer, 1981-84; International Council of Shopping Centers, writer, 1984-94; New York Observer, shopping columnist, 1989-94; freelance writer, 1994-. **Publications:** (With N. Liebman) Biz Speak, 1986; Alternative Investments, 1988; Careers in the Investment World, 1988; Investment Banking, 1988; Investments and the Law, 1988; Careers in Health Care, 1989; Eating Habits and Disorders, 1990; Anne Frank, 1997; W.K. Kellogg: Generous Genius, 2000; Estee Lauder: Beauty Business Success, 2000; (co-author) A Shop of One's Own, 2002. **Address:** c/o Robin Straus, 229 E 79th St., New York, NY 10021, U.S.A. **Online address:** rachel.epstein@worldnet.att.net

EPSTEIN, Richard A(llen). American (born United States), b. 1943. **Genres:** Law. **Career:** University of Southern California, assistant professor of law, 1968-70, associate professor of law, 1970-73; University of California, School of Law, assistant professor, 1968-70, associate professor, 1970-73; University of Chicago, Law School, visiting associate professor, 1972-73, professor, 1973-82, James Parker Hall professor, 1982-88, James Parker Hall distinguished service professor of law, 1988-, now James Parker Hall distinguished service professor emeritus of law, senior lecturer, Medical School, Center for Clinical Medical Ethics, senior fellow, 1983-, interim dean, 2001-, faculty director for curriculum, Law and Economics Program, director; Journal of Law and Economics, editor, 1991-2001; Journal of Legal Studies, editor, 1981-91; New York University, School of Law, visiting

professor, 2007-10, Laurence A. Tisch professor of law; Hoover Institution, Peter and Kirstin Bedford senior fellow, 2000-. Writer. **Publications:** NONFICTION: (with C.O. Gregory and H. Kalven, Jr.) Cases and Materials on Torts, 1977, 9th ed., 2008; Modern Products Liability Law: A Legal Revolution, 1980; A Theory of Strict Liability: Toward a Reformulation of Tort Law, 1980; Supplement to Cases and Materials on the Law of Tort, 1981; Takings: Private Property and the Power of Eminent Domain, 1985; Torts: Adaptable to Fifth Edition of Epstein Casebook, 1991; Forbidden Grounds: The Case Against Employment Discrimination Laws, 1992; Bargaining with the State, 1993; Simple Rules for a Complex World, 1995; Mortal Peril: Our Inalienable Right to Health Care, 1997; Principles for a Free Society: Reconciling Individual Liberty with the Common Good, 1998; Torts, 1999; Skepticism and Freedom: A Modern Case for Classical Liberalism, 2003; Free Markets under Siege: Cartels, Politics, and Social Welfare, 2005; How Progressives Rewrote the Constitution, 2006; Overdose: How Excessive Government Regulation Stifles Pharmaceutical Innovation, 2006; Supreme Neglect: How to Revive Constitutional Protection for Private Property, 2008; The Case Against the Employee Free Choice Act, 2009. EDITOR: (with J. Paul) Labor Law and the Employment Market: Foundations and Applications, 1985; (with G.R. Stone and C.R. Sunstein) The Bill of Rights in the Modern State, 1992; (and intro.) Constitutional Protection of Private Property and Freedom of Contract, 2000; Private and Common Property, 2000; (and intro.) Modern Understandings of Liberty and Property, 2000; (and intro.) Classical Foundations of Liberty and Property, 2000; (and intro.) Contract-freedom and Restraint, 2000; (with C.R. Sunstein) Vote: Bush, Gore, and the Supreme Court, 2001; (with M.S. Greve) Competition Laws in Conflict: Antitrust Jurisdiction in the Global Economy, 2004; (with M.S. Greve) Federal Preemption: States' Powers, National Interests, 2007; Economics of Property Law, 2007; Free Markets under Siege: Cartels, Politics, and Social Welfare, 2008; Economics of Constitutional Law, 2009. Contributor to periodicals. **Address:** School of Law, New York University, Rm. 409A, 40 Washington Sq. S, New York, NY 10012, U.S.A. **Online address:** richard.epstein@nyu.edu

EPSTEIN, Robert M(orris). American (born United States), b. 1948. **Genres:** Military/Defense/Arms Control, History. **Career:** Teacher, 1973; Community College of Philadelphia, instructor in history, 1978-80; Drexel University, instructor, 1979; U.S. Army Command and General Staff College, School of Advanced Military Studies, associate professor, 1981-84, professor of history, 1984-2011; University of Kansas, adjunct professor, 1995-. Writer. **Publications:** Prince Eugene at War, 1809, 1984; Napoleon's Last Victory and the Emergence of Modern War, 1994. Contributor to books and journals. **Address:** Department of History, University of Kansas, 3650 Wescoe Hall, 1445 Jayhawk Blvd., Lawrence, KS 66045, U.S.A.

EPSTEIN, Seymour. American (born United States), b. 1917. **Genres:** Novels, Romance/Historical. **Career:** New School for Social Research, faculty; University of Denver, professor of contemporary literature and creative writing, 1968-, professor emeritus. Writer. **Publications:** Pillar of Salt, 1960; The Successor, 1961; Leah, 1964; A Penny for Charity, 1964; Caught in That Music, 1967; The Dream Museum, 1971; Looking for Fred Schmidt, 1973; Love Affair, 1979; A Special Destiny, 1986; September Faces, 1987; Light, 1989. Contributor to periodicals. **Address:** Henry Holt & Company Inc., 175 5th Ave., New York, NY 10010, U.S.A. **Online address:** contemplit@aol.com

EPSTEIN, Steven. American (born United States), b. 1961. **Genres:** Medicine/Health, Sciences, Politics/Government. **Career:** University of California-San Diego, Science Studies Program, postdoctoral fellow, 1993-94, director, 2006-08, faculty affiliate in science studies, critical gender studies, and ethnic studies, Department of Sociology, assistant professor, 1994-98, associate professor, 1998-2007, professor of sociology, 2007-09; Virginia Tech University, Nicholas Mullins lecturer in social studies of science and technology, 2006; University of Cincinnati, Charles Phelps Taft lecturer, 2009; Northwestern University, John C. Shaffer professor in the humanities and professor of sociology, 2009-, Center on Social Disparities and Health at the Institute for Policy Research, faculty associate, 2009-, Gender Studies Program, affiliate faculty, 2009-, Science in Human Culture Program, affiliate faculty, 2009-, director, 2010-12, Alice Kaplan Institute for the Humanities, faculty, 2009-, director of interdisciplinary graduate cluster in science studies, 2010-12. Writer and sociologist. **Publications:** (Co-author) Learning by Heart: AIDS and Schoolchildren in America's Communities, 1989; Impure Science: AIDS, Activism, and the Politics of Knowledge, 1996; Inclusion: The Politics of Difference in Medical Research, 2007. Contributor to periodicals and journals. **Address:** Department of Sociology, Northwestern University, Rm. 206, 1808 Chicago Ave., Evanston, IL 60208, U.S.A. **Online address:** s-epstein@northwestern.edu

EQUI, Elaine. American (born United States), b. 1953. **Genres:** Poetry. **Career:** Columbia College, writing instructor, 1983-89; The New School, poetry writing instructor, 1993; City University of New York, City College, writing instructor, 1995; Rutgers University, writing instructor, 1996-97; Conjunctions magazine, senior editor, 1998-2002. **Publications:** Federal Woman, 1978; Shrewcrazy: Poems, 1981; The Corners of the Mouth, 1986; Accessories, 1988; Surface Tension: Poems, 1989; Decoy: Poems, 1994; Voice-Over: Poems, 1998; Friendship with Things, 1998; The Cloud of Knowable Things: Poems, 2003; Ripple Effect: New and Selected Poems, 2007; Click and Clone, 2011. Works appear in anthologies. Contributor to periodicals. **Address:** New York, NY , U.S.A. **Online address:** eequi@aol.com

ERARD, Michael. American (born United States) **Genres:** Education. **Career:** FrameWorks Institute, senior researcher and metaphor designer; Texas Observer, contributing writer, 1998-. **Publications:** Um--Slips, Stumbles and Verbal Blunders and What They Mean, 2007; Babel No More: The Search for the World's Most Extraordinary Language Learners, 2012. Contributor to periodicals. **Address:** Austin, TX , U.S.A. **Online address:** author@umthebook.com

ERDRICH, Louise. American (born United States), b. 1954. **Genres:** Novels, Poetry, Novellas/Short Stories, Young Adult Fiction, Picture/Board Books. **Career:** North Dakota State Arts Council, visiting poet and teacher, 1977-78; Johns Hopkins University, writing instructor, 1978-79; Boston Indian Council, communications director, 1979-80; Circle, editor, 1979-80; Charles Merrill Co., textbook writer, 1980; Birchbark Books, owner. **Publications:** Imagination, 1980; Jacklight (poems), 1984; Love Medicine: A Novel, 1984; The Beet Queen: A Novel, 1986, 3rd ed., 1998; Tracks: A Novel, 1988, 2nd ed., 1989; Baptism of Desire (poems), 1989; (intro.) The Broken Cord: A Family's Ongoing Struggle with Fetal Alcohol Syndrome, 1989; (intro.) A Link with the River, 1989; (with M. Dorris) Route Two, 1990; (with M. Dorris) The Crown of Columbus, 1991; The Bingo Palace, 1994; (intro.) The Falcon: A Narrative of the Captivity and Adventures of John Tanner, 1994; The Blue Jay's Dance: A Birth Year, 1995; Tales of Burning Love, 1996; Grandmother's Pigeon, 1996; The Antelope Wife, 1998; The Birchbark House, 1999; The Last Report on the Miracles at Little No Horse, 2001; The Range Eternal, 2002; The Master Butcher's Singing Club, 2003; Original Fire: Selected and New Poems, 2003; Books and Islands in Ojibwe Country, 2003; Four Souls: A Novel, 2004; The Game of Silence, 2005; The Painted Drum, 2005; The Porcupine Year, 2008; The Plague of Doves, 2008; The Red Convertible: Selected and New Stories, 1978-2008, 2009; Shadow Tag: A Novel, 2010; Chickadee, 2012; The Round House, 2012. Contributor to periodicals. **Address:** The Wylie Agency, 250 W 57th St., Ste. 2114, New York, NY 10107-2199, U.S.A.

EREIRA, Alan. British (born England), b. 1943. **Genres:** Anthropology/Ethnology, History, Young Adult Fiction, Social Sciences. **Career:** British Broadcasting Corp., producer, 1965-96; Tairona Heritage Trust, founder, 1991-; Sunstone Films Ltd., director, 1992-. Writer. **Publications:** The People's England, 1981; The Invergordon Mutiny: A Narrative History of the Last Great Mutiny in the Royal Navy and How it Forced Britain off the Gold Standard in 1931, 1981; The Heart of the World, 1990 as The Elder Brothers: A Lost South American People and Their Message about the Fate of the Earth, 1992; (with T. Jones) Crusades, 1995; (with T. Jones) Terry Jones' Medieval Lives, 2004; (with T. Jones) Terry Jones' Barbarians, 2007. **Address:** Tairona Heritage Trust, 90 Summerlee Ave., London, GL N2 9QH, England.

ERHARD, Thomas A. *See* **ERHARD, Tom.**

ERHARD, Tom. (Thomas A. Erhard). American (born United States), b. 1923?. **Genres:** Novels, Plays/Screenplays, Literary Criticism And History. **Career:** Albuquerque Public Schools, information director, 1953-57; NMSU's literary magazine, faculty adviser; New Mexico State University, creative writing teacher, 1960-, professor of English and drama, 1960-91, professor emeritus, 1999-. Writer. **Publications:** For the Love of Pete, 1954; The High White Star, 1957; Rocket in His Pocket, 1960, 1964; The Electronovac Gasser, 1963; A Wild Fight for Spring, 1966; In Search of Leaders, 1967; Stress and Campus Response, 1968; The Agony and Promise, 1969; The Cataclysmic Loves of Cooper and Looper and Their Friend Who Was Squashed by a Moving Van, 1969; The Troubled Campus, 1970; Lynn Riggs: South-

western Playwright, 1970; The New Decade, 1971; 900 Plays: A Synopsis-History of American Theatre, 1978; Pomp and Circumstances, 1982; I Saved a Winter Just for You, 1984; A Merry Medieval Christmas, 1985; Laughing Once More, 1986. **Address:** New Mexico State University, PO Box 30001, Las Cruces, NM 88003-8001, U.S.A.

ERICKSON, Betty J(ean). American (born United States), b. 1923. **Genres:** Children's Fiction, Children's Non-fiction, Education. **Career:** Teacher, 1945-51, 1966-94; Stockton Unified School District, teacher, 1950-52; Prince William County Schools, teacher, reading specialist, reading recovery teacher, 1968-94; Springwoods Elementary School, reading specialist, 1994-2006. Writer. **Publications:** Oh, No, Sherman!, 1996; Play Ball, Sherman!, 1996; Use Your Beak, 1998; Big Bad Rex, 1998; Where's the Snow?, 1998; Look in My Book, 1998; Sherman, 1999; (reteller) The Little Rabbit Who Wanted Red Wings, 2000; In Search of Something Delicious, 2003; Why Do Worms Come up When It Rains?, 2003; Sherman's Lost and Found, 2004; Sherman in the Talent Show, 2004; A Special Invitation for Sherman, 2007; Sherman's Happy Walk, 2007; At the Post Office, 2007; Jamie the Lifeguard, 2008; Sherman's Shenanigans, 2008. Contributor to magazines. **Address:** 12191 Clipper Dr., Apt. A35, Woodbridge, VA 22192-2244, U.S.A. **Online address:** bettyeri@comcast.net

ERICKSON, Carolly. American (born United States), b. 1943. **Genres:** Biography, Novels, Young Adult Non-fiction, Young Adult Fiction. **Career:** Barnard College, lecturer in history, 1964-66; City University of New York, Brooklyn College, lecturer, 1965-66; San Fernando Valley State College (now California State University), instructor, 1966-67; Mills College, assistant professor, 1967-70; full-time writer, 1970-. **Publications:** (Ed. and intro.) The Records of Medieval Europe, 1971; The Medieval Vision, 1976; Bloody Mary, 1978; Civilization and Society in the West, 1978; Great Harry, 1980; The First Elizabeth, 1983; Mistress Anne: The Exceptional Life of Anne Boleyn, 1984; Our Tempestuous Day: A History of Regency, 1986; Bonnie Prince Charlie: A Biography, 1989; To the Scaffold: The Life of Marie Antoinette, 1991; Great Catherine, 1994; Her Little Majesty: The Life of Queen Victoria, 1997; Arc of the Arrow: Writing Your Spiritual Autobiography, 1998; Josephine: A Life of the Empress, 1999; Alexandra: The Last Tsarina, 2001; Lilibet: An Intimate Portrait of Elizabeth II, 2004; The Girl from Botany Bay, 2005; Hidden Diary of Marie Antoinette, 2005; The Last Wife of Henry VIII, 2006; Royal Panoply: Brief Lives of the English Monarchs, 2006; The Secret Life of Josephine: Napoleon's Bird of Paradise, 2007; The Tsarina's Daughter, 2008; The Memoirs of Mary Queen of Scots, 2009; Mary Queen of Scots: A Novel, 2010; Rival to the Queen, 2010; Favored Queen, 2011. Contributor of articles to periodicals. **Address:** St. Martin's Press, 175 5th Ave., New York, NY 10010-7703, U.S.A.

ERICKSON, Darlene (E.) Williams. American (born United States), b. 1941. **Genres:** Literary Criticism And History, Poetry. **Career:** Newark High School, teacher, 1977-84; Central Ohio Technical College, teacher, 1980-82, coordinator of gifted programs, 1984-89; Miami University, teaching fellow, 1985-86; Ashland-Otterbein College, adjunct professor, 1987-88; Ohio State University, instructor, 1988; Ohio Dominican University, professor, 1989-2010, Freshman Year Experience, chair, 1990-91, Department of English, chair, 1991-98. Writer. **Publications:** Illusion Is More Precise than Precision: The Poetry of Marianne Moore, 1992. Contributor to periodicals. **Address:** Ohio Dominican College, Rm. 226, Erskine Hall, 1216 Sunbury Rd., Columbus, OH 43219, U.S.A. **Online address:** ericksod@ohiodominican.edu

ERICKSON, Edward J. American (born United States), b. 1950?. **Genres:** History, Business/Trade/Industry, Economics, Military/Defense/Arms Control. **Career:** St. Lawrence University, assistant professor of military science, 1981-84; U.S. Army Corps, executive officer, 1992, Allied Land Forces, current operations coordinator, 1993-94, Plans and Emergency Operations, department head, 1995, international affairs advisor, 1995-97, lieutenant colonel, retired, 1997, 4th Infantry Division, political advisor, 2003; Norwich High School, dean of students, 1997-2004, social studies teacher, 1998-2003, 2005-07, 2008-09; International Research Associates, associate; Iraqi Ministry of Defense, Ministerial Training Center, professor of political science, 2007-08; Marine Corps University, associate professor of military history, 2009-. Writer. **Publications:** (Co-author) The Euphrates Triangle: Security Implications of the Southeastern Anatolia Project, 1999; Ordered to Die: A History of the Ottoman Army in the First World War, 2001; Defeat in Detail: The Ottoman Army in the Balkans, 1912-1913, 2003; Ottoman Army Effectiveness in World War I: A Comparative Study, 2007; (contrib.) By the Light of a Candle, 2009; (with M. Uyar) Military History of the Ottomans: From Osman to Atatürk, 2009; Gallipoli: The Ottoman Campaign, 2010. **Address:** Marine Corps University, 2076 South St., Quantico, VA 22134-5068, U.S.A. **Online address:** edward.erickson@usmc.mil

ERICKSON, Hal. American (born United States), b. 1950. **Genres:** Communications/Media, Film, Social Sciences. **Career:** Great American Children's Theatre, lecturer, 1978-84; writer, 1985-; Aldrich Chemical Co., customer service assistant, 1987-94; All-Music and Video Guide, contributing writer and editor, 1994-; Milwaukee Opera Co., Milwaukee Repertory Theater, actor. **Publications:** Syndicated Television: The First Forty Years, 1947-1987, 1989; Baseball in the Movies: A Comprehensive Reference, 1915-1991, 1992; Religious Radio and Television in the United States, 1921-1991: The Programs and Personalities, 1992; Television Cartoon Shows: An Illustrated Encyclopedia, 1949-1993, 1995, 2nd ed., 2005; Sid and Marty Krofft: A Critical Study of Saturday Morning Children's Television, 1969-1993, 1998; From Beautiful Downtown Burbank: A Critical History of Rowan and Martin's Laugh-In, 1968-1973, 1999; The Baseball Filmography 1915-2001, 2002; Encyclopedia of Television Law Shows: Factual and Fictional Series About Judges, Lawyers and the Courtroom, 1948-2008, 2009. Contributor to periodicals. **Address:** 6731 W Moltke Ave., Milwaukee, WI 53210, U.S.A. **Online address:** hle3@execpc.com

ERICKSON, Raymond (F.). American (born United States), b. 1941. **Genres:** Music. **Career:** Yale University, acting instructor in music, 1968-70, Pierson College, associate fellow, 1972-; International Business Machines (IBM), Systems Research Institute, research fellow, 1970-71; City University of New York, Queens College, Aaron Copland School of Music, assistant professor, 1971-75, associate professor, 1975-81, department head, 1978-81, professor of music, 1981-, founding director, 1981, dean of arts and humanities, 1993-2000; Aston Magna Foundation for Music and the Humanities Inc., academy director and lecturer, 1978-; State University of New York, Watson School of Engineering, adjunct professor, 1983-87. Writer. **Publications:** DARMS: A Reference Manual, 1976; (trans. and intro.) Musica Enchiriadis and Scolica Enchiriadis, 1995; (ed.) Schubert's Vienna: Viennese Culture in the Reign of Francis I (1792-1835), 1997; (ed.) The Worlds of Johann Sebastian Bach, 2009. Contributor of articles to books and journals. **Address:** Aaron Copland School of Music, Queens College, City University of New York, NMB 209, Rm. 203, 65-30 Kissena Blvd., Flushing, NY 11367, U.S.A. **Online address:** raymond.erickson@qc.cuny.edu

ERICKSON, Steve. American (born United States), b. 1950. **Genres:** Novels, Adult Non-fiction, inspirational/Motivational Literature, Literary Criticism And History, Social Sciences. **Career:** Freelance editor and writer, 1973-86; L.A. Weekly, arts and film editor, 1989-93; California Institute of the Arts, MFA writing faculty, 2000-; Los Angeles magazine, critic, 2001-; Black Clock, editor, 2004-. **Publications:** Days Between Stations, 1985; Rubicon Beach, 1986; Tours of the Black Clock, 1989; Leap Year, 1989; Arc d'X, 1993; Amnesiascope, 1996; American Nomad, 1997; The Sea Came in at Midnight, 1999; Our Ecstatic Days, 2005; Zeroville, 2007. Contributor to magazines. **Address:** Melanie Jackson Agency, 41 W 72nd St., Ste. 3F, New York, NY 10023, U.S.A. **Online address:** m.jackson@mjalit.com

ERICSON, David F. American (born United States), b. 1950. **Genres:** Politics/Government, Social Sciences. **Career:** Detroit News, copy editor, 1977-80; Oberlin College, Department of Government, instructor in political science, 1986-87; Washington University, Department of Political Science, visiting professor, 1987-89; University of Chicago, Department of Political Science, visiting professor, 1990-91; Wichita State University, Department of Political Science, assistant professor, 1992-98, associate professor, 1998-, chair, 2004-06; University at Albany, research associate professor, 2006-07, service associate professor, 2008-09; Princeton University, James Madison visiting fellow, 2007-08; George Mason University, term associate professor, 2009-. **Publications:** The Shaping of American Liberalism: The Debates Over Ratification, Nullification and Slavery, 1993; (ed. with L.B. Green) The Liberal Tradition in American Politics: Reassessing the Legacy of American Liberalism, 1999; The Debate Over Slavery: Antislavery and Proslavery Liberalism in Antebellum America, 2000; (ed.) The Politics of Inclusion and Exclusion: Identity Politics in Twenty-first Century America, 2011; Slavery in the American Republic: Developing the Federal Government, 1791-1861, 2011. Contributor to periodicals. **Address:** Department of Political Science, Wichita State University, 1845 Fairmount, PO Box 17, Wichita, KS 67260-0017, U.S.A. **Online address:** david.ericson@wichita.edu

ERIKSEN, Thomas Hylland. Norwegian (born Norway), b. 1962. **Genres:** Anthropology/Ethnology, History. **Career:** University of Oslo, PRIO-International Institute of Peace Research, senior research fellow, 1990-91, senior lecturer, 1991-95, professor, 1995-; EASA Newsletter, editor, 1992-94; Samtiden, editor, 1993-2001; Norwegian Journal of Anthropology, editor, 1993-97. **Publications:** Us and Them in Modern Societies: Ethnicity and Nationalism in Trinidad, Maritius, and Beyond, 1992; Common Denominators: Ethnicity, Nation-Building, and Compromise in Mauritius, 1998; (with F.S. Nielsen) A History of Anthropology, 2001; Tyranny of the Moment: Fast and Slow Time in the Information Age, 2001; Ethnicity and Nationalism: Anthropological Perspectives, 2002; Globalization: Studies in Anthropology, 2003; What Is Anthropology?, 2004; Engaging Anthropology: The Case for a Public Presence, 2005. **Address:** University of Oslo, PO Box 1091, Blindern, Oslo, 0317, Norway. **Online address:** t.h.eriksen@sai.uio.no

ERIKSON, Robert. Swedish (born Sweden), b. 1938. **Genres:** Sociology. **Career:** Stockholm University, assistant teacher, lecturer and reader, 1961-72, Department of Sociology, professor, 1982-, Swedish Institute for Social Research, senior research officer, 1973-81, acting professor in social policy, 1977, 1978, director, 1986-88; European Consortium for Sociological Research, president, 1990-97; Governmental Commission on Social Selection to Higher Education, head, 1991-93; Netherlands Institute for Advanced Study in the Humanities and Social Sciences, fellow, 1996-97; Swedish Council for Social Research, secretary general, 1997-2000; British Academy, corresponding fellow, 1998-; Luxembourg Income Study, president, 1998-; Royal Swedish Academy of Sciences, vice president, 2000-03; Swedish Council for Working Life and Social Research, secretary general, 2001-03; Nuffield College, honorary fellow, 2003-. Writer. **Publications:** (With J.H. Goldthorpe) The Constant Flux: A Study of Class Mobility in Industrial Societies, 1992. EDITOR: (with R. Åberg) Välfärd i förändring: levnadsvillkor i Sverige 1968-1981, 1984, trans. as Welfare in Transition: A Survey of Living Conditions in Sweden, 1968-1981, 1987; (co-ed.) The Scandinavian Model: Welfare States and Welfare Research, 1987; (co-ed.) Welfare Trends in the Scandinavian Countries, 1993; (with J.O. Jonsson) Can Education Be Equalized?: The Swedish Case in Comparative Perspective, 1996; (ed. with T. Smeeding and M. Jantii) Persistence, Privilege, and Parenting, 2011. **Address:** Swedish Institute for Social Research, Stockholm University, Universitetsvägen 10A, Stockholm, SE-106 91, Sweden. **Online address:** robert.erikson@sofi.su.se

ERIKSON, Steven. See LUNDIN, Steve.

ERIKSSON, Kjell. Swedish (born Sweden), b. 1953?. **Genres:** Translations, Science Fiction/Fantasy. **Career:** Writer and horticulturist. **Publications:** Den Upplyste Stigen, 1999; Prinsessan av Burundi, 2002; Das Steinbett, 2002; Nattskärran, 2003; Nattens Grymma Stjärnor, 2004; Mannen från Bergen, 2005; Öppen grav, 2009. **Address:** Leonhardt & Høier Literary Agency, Studiestræde 35A, Copenhagen, DK-1455, Denmark. **Online address:** kjelleman@swipnet.se

ERKKILA, Betsy. American (born United States), b. 1944. **Genres:** Cultural/Ethnic Topics, Gay And Lesbian Issues, Literary Criticism And History, Women's Studies And Issues, Biography, International Relations/Current Affairs, Politics/Government, Autobiography/Memoirs, Autobiography/Memoirs. **Career:** University of Amiens, American Studies, Fulbright lecturer, 1972-74; California State University, visiting assistant professor of English, 1974-80, London and Paris Travel-Study Program, director, 1977, 1978; University of Pennsylvania, assistant professor, 1980-86, associate professor, 1986-90, professor of English, 1990-, Walt Whitman Conference, director, 1992; Columbia University, adjunct associate professor, 1988; Princeton University, adjunct professor, 1990; Northwestern University, Henry Sanborn Noyes professor of literature, 1995-. Writer. **Publications:** Walt Whitman among the French: Poet and Myth, 1980; Whitman the Political Poet, 1989; The Wicked Sisters: Women Poets, Literary History, and Discord, 1992; Mixed Blood and Other Crosses: Rethinking Literature from the Revolution to the Culture Wars, 2005. EDITOR: (with J. Grossman) Breaking Bounds: Whitman and American Cultural Studies, 1996; Ezra Pound: The Contemporary Reviews, 2010; Walt Whitman's Songs of Male Intimacy and Love: Live Oak, with Moss and Calamus, 2010. **Address:** Department of English, Weinberg College of Arts & Sciences, Northwestern University, University Hall Rm. 408, 1897 Sheridan Rd., Evanston, IL 60208-2240, U.S.A. **Online address:** erkkila@northwestern.edu

ERLBACH, Arlene. (Max Taylor). American (born United States), b.

1948. **Genres:** Children's Fiction, Young Adult Fiction, Children's Nonfiction, Young Adult Non-fiction. **Career:** Young Author Program, director. Writer and educator. **Publications:** YOUNG ADULT NOVELS: Does Your Nose Get in the Way, Too?, 1987; Guys, Dating, and Other Disasters, 1987; Drop-Out Blues, 1988; Dial 555-Love, 1991; A Little More to Love, 1994. OTHERS: Dropout Blues, 1988; Blizzards, 1995; Forest Fires, 1995; Video Games, 1995. MIDDLE GRADE NOVELS AS MAX TAYLOR: The Halloween Hex, 1990; My Brother, the Droid, 1990; Short Circuit, 1990. CHILDREN'S NONFICTION: Hurricanes, 1993; Bicycles, 1994; Floods, 1994; Peanut Butter, 1994; Soda Pop, 1994; Tornadoes, 1994; The Best Friends Book: True Stories about Real Best Friends The Families Book: True Stories about Real Kids and the People they Live with and Love, 1996; Wonderful Wolves of the Wild, 1996; Happy Birthday Everywhere!, 1997; The Kids' Invention Book, 1997; Sidewalk Games around the World, 1997; Teddy Bears, 1997; My Pet Rat, 1998; The Kids' Business Book, 1998; The Kids' Volunteering Book, 1998; The Welfare System, 1998; Everything You Need to Know if Your Family is on Welfare, 1998; Bubble Gum, 1998; Kent State, 1998; Worth the Risk: True Stories about Risk Takers Plus How You Can be One, Too, 1999; T-Shirts, 1999; Happy New Year Everywhere!, 2000; Christmas, Celebrating Life, Giving and Kindness, 2001; Merry Christmas Everywhere!, 2002; Hanukkah: Celebrating the Holiday of Lights, 2002; The Middle School Survival Guide, 2003; (with H. Erlbach) Valentine's Day Crafts, 2004; (with H. Erlbach) Thanksgiving Day Crafts, 2005; (with H. Erlbach) Mother's Day Crafts, 2005. MIDDLE GRADE NOVEL: The Herbie Hummerston Homework Haters' Club, 1995. **Address:** c/o Lettie Lee, The Ann Elmo Agency Inc., 60 E 42nd St., New York, NY 10165, U.S.A. **Online address:** tbears48@comcast.net

ERLBAUM, Janice. American (born United States), b. 1969. **Genres:** Autobiography/Memoirs, Biography, Social Sciences. **Career:** POPsmear Magazine, editor-at-large; BUST Magazine, contributor, 1994-2007. **Publications:** Girlbomb: A Halfway Homeless Memoir, 2006; Have You Found Her: A Memoir, 2008; The Incredible True Love Story of Janice and Sam, forthcoming. Works appear in anthologies. Contributor to periodicals. **Address:** c/o Author Mail, Random House Inc., 1745 Broadway, New York, NY 10019, U.S.A. **Online address:** girlbomb@bway.net

ERLER, Mary C. (Mary Carpenter Erler). American (born United States) **Genres:** Literary Criticism And History, Poetry, Language/Linguistics, History, Bibliography. **Career:** University of Texas, instructor, 1966-67; Fordham University, instructor, professor of English, 1980-. Writer. **Publications:** (Ed. with M. Kowaleski) Women and Power in the Middle Ages, 1988; (co-ed.) Poems of Cupid, God of Love, 1991; (ed. as Mary Carpenter Erler) Robert Copland: Poems, 1993; Women, Reading, and Piety in Late Medieval England, 2002; (ed. with M. Kowaleski) Gendering the Master Narrative: Women and Power in the Middle Ages, 2003; Wynkyn De Worde: Father of Fleet Street, 3rd ed., 2003; (ed.) Records of Early English Drama: Ecclesiastical London, 2008. Contributor to journals. **Address:** Department of English, Fordham University, 441 E Fordham Rd., Bronx, NY 10458-5149, U.S.A. **Online address:** erler@fordham.edu

ERLER, Mary Carpenter. See ERLER, Mary C.

ERLICH, Reese W. American (born United States), b. 1947. **Genres:** History. **Career:** Ramparts (magazine), staff writer and research editor, 1963-75, part-time typist, reporter, 1968-69; Christian Science Monitor, freelancer, 1986; KQED-FM, media critic, 1988-99; San Francisco State University, faculty in journalism; California State University, faculty in journalism; University of California Berkeley Extension, faculty in journalism; Australian Broadcasting Corp., freelance reporter; Radio Deutsche Welle, freelance reporter; Latino USA, freelance reporter; National Public Radio, freelance reporter; Canadian Broadcasting Corp., freelance reporter; National Broadcasting Co., Monitor Radio, reporter; Common Ground, contract correspondent. **Publications:** (With N. Solomon) Target Iraq: What the News Media Didn't Tell You, 2003; The Iran Agenda: The Real Story of U.S. Policy and the Middle East Crisis, 2007; Dateline Havana: The Real Story of U.S. Policy and the Future of Cuba, 2009; Conversations with Terrorists, 2010. Contributor to books. **Address:** PO Box 19261, Oakland, CA 94619, U.S.A.

ERLINE, N. T. See RAGEN, Naomi.

ERLMANN, Veit. American/German (born Germany), b. 1951. **Genres:** Cultural/Ethnic Topics, Music, Theology/Religion, Politics/Government, Philosophy. **Career:** Université de Niamey, Institut de Recherches en Sciences Humaines, associate research fellow, 1979; University of Natal, assistant professor of ethnomusicology, 1981-85; University of the Witwatersrand, Department of Social Anthropology, visiting professor, 1986-87, African Studies Institute, senior research officer, 1986-87; Ethnographic Museum Berlin, Department of Ethnomusicology, assistant researcher, 1987-89; University of Frankfurt, Department of African Studies, visiting lecturer, 1988; University of Chicago, Department of Music, visiting associate professor, 1990-91; Free University, Department of Sociology, visiting professor, 1988, Department of Anthropology, Heisenberg fellow, 1991-96, visiting professor, 1993, adjunct professor, 1994-96; University of Texas, School of Music, professor of ethnomusicology and endowed chair of music history, 1997-, Deans fellow, 2003. Writer. **Publications:** Booku, Eine Literarisch-musikalische Gattung der Fulbe des Diamaré (Nordkamerun), 1979; Macht des Wortes: Preisgesang und Berufsmusiker beiden Fulbe des des Diamaré (Nordkamerun), 1980; Music and the Islamic Reform in the Early Sokoto Empire: Sources, Ideology, Effects, 1986; Girkaa: Une Cérémonie d'initiation au culte de Possession-bòorii des Hausa de la région de Maradi (Niger), 1989; African Stars: Studies in Black South African Performance, 1991; PopuläreMusik in Afrika, 1991; Nightsong: Performance, Power and Practice in South Africa, 1996; Music, Modernity and the Global Imagination: South Africa and the West, 1999; (ed.) Hearing Cultures: Essays on Sound, Listening, and Modernity, 2004; A Cultural History of the Ear, 2008; Reason and Resonance: A History of Modern Aurality, 2010. Contribuer to periodicals. **Address:** Butler School of Music, University of Texas, MBE 3.216, 1 University Sta. E3100, Austin, TX 78712-0435, U.S.A. **Online address:** erlmann@mail.utexas.edu

ERMATINGER, James W. American (born United States), b. 1959?. **Genres:** History, Intellectual History. **Career:** Earlham College, instructor in history, 1988; Wright State University, instructor in history, 1989; Kearney State College, instructor in history, 1989-91; University of Nebraska, assistant professor, professor of history, 1991-95; Lourdes College, professor of history, 1995-2001; Southeast Missouri State University, professor of history and chair of department, 2001-. Writer. **Publications:** The Economic Reforms of Diocletian, 1996; The Decline and Fall of the Roman Empire, 2004; Daily Life of Christians in Ancient Rome, 2007; Daily Life in the New Testament, 2008. Contributor to books and periodicals. **Address:** Department of History, Southeast Missouri State University, 1 University Plz., PO Box 2960, Cape Girardeau, MO 63701, U.S.A. **Online address:** jermatinger@semo.edu

ERNAUX, Annie. French (born France), b. 1940. **Genres:** Novels, Autobiography/Memoirs. **Career:** Haute-Savoie, secondary school teacher of French, 1966-77; Centre National d'Enseignement par Correspondence, professor, 1977-2000. French novelist and memoirist. **Publications:** Les armoires vides, 1974; Ce qu'ils disent ourien, 1977; La femme gelée, 1981; Laplace, 1983; Une femme, 1987; Cleaned Out, 1990; Passion Simple, 1991; Woman's Story, 1992; A Man's Place, 1993; Journal du dehors, 1993 trans. as Exteriors Seven Stories, 1996; A Frozen Woman, 1995; La Honte, 1997; Je ne sui passortie de ma nuit, 1997; Shame, 1998; I Remain in Darkness, 1999; événement, 2000; La vie extérieure: 1993-1999, 2000; Se Perdre, 2001; Happening, 2001; L'Óccupation, 2002; L'écriture commeun couteau, 2003; Simple Passion, 2003; (with M. Marie) Usage de la photo, 2005; The Possession, 2008; Les Années, 2008; Things Seen, 2010. **Address:** La Favola, 23 Allee des Lozeres, Cergy, 95000, France.

ERNEST, William. See MCKIBBEN, Bill.

ERNST, Carl W. American (born United States), b. 1950. **Genres:** Theology/Religion. **Career:** Pomona College, assistant professor, 1981-87, associate professor of religion, 1987-92, department head, 1991-92; EHESS, visiting lecturer, 1991, 2003; University of North Carolina, professor of religious studies, 1992-, department chair, 1995-2000, Zachary Smith professor, 2000-05, William R. Kenan Jr. distinguished professor, 2005-, Carolina Center for the Study of the Middle East and Muslim Civilizations, co-director, director; University of Seville, visiting lecturer, 2001; University of Malaya, visiting lecturer, 2005, 2010. Writer. **Publications:** Words of Ecstasy in Sufism, 1984; Eternal Garden: Mysticism, History and Politics at a South Asian Sufi Center, 1992, 2nd ed., 2004; (ed. with G.M. Smith) Manifestations of Sainthood in Islam, 1993; Rūzbihān Baqlī: Mystical Experience and the Rhetoric of Sainthood in Persian Sufism, 1996; (trans.) The Unveiling of Secrets: Diary of a Sufi Master, 1997; The Shambhala Guide to Sufism, 1997; (ed. and trans.) Teachings of Sufism, 1999; (with B.B. Lawrence) Sufi Martyrs of Love: Chishti Sufism in South Asia and Beyond, 2002; Following Muhammad: Rethinking Islam in the Contemporary World, 2003; Sufism: An Introduction to the Mystical Tradition of Islam, 2007; (ed. with R.C. Martin) Rethinking Islamic Studies: From Orientalism to Cosmopolitanism, 2010; (contrib. with A.S. Asani and K.K. Mumtaz) Sacred Spaces: A Journey with the Sufis of the Indus, 2010; How to Read the Qur'an, 2011; (ed. with B. Lawrence) Islamic Civilization and Muslim Networks Series, forthcoming. **Address:** Department of Religious Studies, University of North Carolina, 125 Saunders, PO Box 3225, Chapel Hill, NC 27599-3225, U.S.A. **Online address:** cernst@email.unc.edu

EROFEEV, Viktor V. Russian (born Russia), b. 1947. **Genres:** Novels, Social Sciences. **Career:** Gorky Institute of Literature, researcher, through 1992; writer, 1992-. **Publications:** Russian Beauty: A Novel, 1990; V labirinte prokliatykh voprosov, 1990; Zhizn s idiotom, 1991; Izbrannoe, ili, Karmannyi apokalipsis, 1993; Russkaia krasavitsa, 1994; (comp. and intro.) Penguin Book of New Russian Writing, 1995; Strashnyi sud, 1996; Muzhchiny, 1997; Russkie tsvety zla, 1997; Piat rek zhizni, 1998; Entsiklopediiarusskoi dushi, 1999; Bog X, 2001; EPS, 2002; Sharovaia Molniia: Malenkieesse, 2002; Roskosh, 2003; Khoroshii Stalin, 2004; Life With an Idiot, 2004; Profundis, 2006. **Address:** 9 1st Smolensky Ln., Moscow, 121099, Russia.

ERRE, Mike. American (born United States), b. 1971?. **Genres:** Theology/Religion, inspirational/Motivational Literature. **Career:** Rock Harbor Church, pastor of teaching, through 2010; Mariners Church, teaching pastor, 2010-. Writer. **Publications:** The Jesus of Suburbia: Have We Tamed the Son of God to Fit Our Lifestyle?, 2006; Why Guys need God, 2008; Death by Church: Rescuing Jesus from His Followers, Recapturing God's Hope for His People, 2009; Why the Bible Matters: Rediscovering Its Significance in an Age of Suspicion, 2010. **Address:** Rock Harbor Church, 3080 Airway, Ste. 100, Costa Mesa, CA 92626, U.S.A. **Online address:** merre@marinerschurch.org

ERRINGTON, Malcolm. See ERRINGTON, R. Malcolm.

ERRINGTON, R. Malcolm. Also writes as Malcolm Errington, Robert Malcolm Errington. German (born Germany) **Genres:** History. **Career:** Philipps-Universitat Marburg, professor of ancient history. Writer. **Publications:** Philopoemen, 1969; The Dawn of Empire: Rome's Rise to World Power, 1972; (as Malcolm Errington) Geschichte Makedoniens: Von Den Anfangen Bis Zum Untergang Des Konigreiches, 1986; A History of Macedonia, 1990; Zum Gedenken an Peter Herrmann 22.5.1927-22.11.2002, 2004; Roman Imperial Policy from Julian to Theodosius, 2006; A History of the Hellenistic World, 323-30 BC, 2008. Contributor to books. **Address:** Philipps-Universität Marburg, Biegenstrasse 10, Marburg, D- 35032, Germany. **Online address:** erringto@staff.uni-marburg.de

ERRINGTON, Robert Malcolm. See ERRINGTON, R. Malcolm.

ERSHLER, Phil. American (born United States) **Genres:** Novels, Travel/Exploration. **Career:** Writer, mountaineering guide and instructor. **Publications:** (With S. Ershler and R. Simons) Together on Top of the World: The Remarkable Story of the First Couple to Climb the Fabled Seven Summits: A Saga of Love and Courage (memoir), 2007. Contributor to periodicals. **Address:** International Mountain Guides, 31111 State Rte. 706 E, PO Box 246, Ashford, WA 98304-0246, U.S.A.

ERSHLER, Susan. American (born United States), b. 1956. **Genres:** Natural History, Travel/Exploration. **Career:** Qwest-U.S. West, sales staff; United Technologies, sales staff; FedEx-Kinko, sales staff; General Dynamics, sales staff; GTE-Verizon, sales staff, U.S. West Inc., sales staff. Mountain climber, speaker and writer. **Publications:** (With P. Ershler and R. Simons) Together on Top of the World: The Remarkable Story of the First Couple to Climb the Fabled Seven Summits: A Saga of Love and Courage (memoir), 2007. **Address:** Ershler International, 10536 NE 58th St., PO Box 3266, Kirkland, WA 98033, U.S.A. **Online address:** info@susanershler.com

ERSKINE, Kathryn. American/Dutch (born Netherlands) **Genres:** Novels, Children's Fiction, Young Adult Fiction, Business/Trade/Industry, Economics, Humor/Satire. **Career:** Writer and attorney. **Publications:** Quaking (novel), 2007; Mockingbird, 2010; Absolute Value of Mike, 2011. **Address:** VA , U.S.A. **Online address:** kathryn@kathrynerskine.com

ERTELT, Justin P. American (born United States), b. 1978. **Genres:** Business/Trade/Industry, Money/Finance, Economics. **Career:** Advanced Fire Protection, licensed fire sprinkler journeyman, 1997-; Just-in Time Publishing, president and chief executive officer, 2000-. Writer. **Publications:** Saving Your Way to Success, 2000, 2nd ed., 2003. **Address:** Just-in Time Publishing, PO Box 86-670, Fargo, ND 58107, U.S.A. **Online address:** justin@savingyourwaytosuccess.com

ERWIN, Douglas H. American (born United States), b. 1958. **Genres:** Earth Sciences, Social Sciences. **Career:** Michigan State University, Department of Geological Sciences, assistant professor, 1985-90, associate professor of geology, 1990; Smithsonian Institution, National Museum of Natural History, Department of Paleobiology, researcher, 1990-93, associate curator, 1990-93, curator of paleozoic invertebrates, 1993-, interim director, 2002-03, senior scientist, 2004-; International Geological Correlation Program, co-leader of project on biotic recoveries from mass extinctions, 1993-97; Santa Fe Institute, visiting professor, 2003-04, research professor, 2005-, chair of faculty, 2011-. Writer. **Publications:** The Great Paleozoic Crisis: Life and Death in the Permian, 1993; (with D.E.G. Briggs and F.J. Collier) The Fossils of the Burgess Shale, 1994; (J. Tong) Triassic Gastropods of the Southern Qinling Mountains, China, 2001; Extinction: How Life on Earth Nearly Ended 250 Million Years Ago, 2006; (with X.L. Zhang and D.G. Shu) Cambrian Naraoiids (Arthropoda): Morphology, Ontogeny, Systematics, and Evolutionary Relationships, 2007. EDITOR: (with R.L. Anstey) New Approaches to Speciation in the Fossil Record, 1995; (with D. Jablonski and J.H. Lipps) Evolutionary Paleobiology: In Honor of James W. Valentine, 1996. Contributor to books and journals. **Address:** Department of Paleobiology, National Museum of Natural History, Smithsonian Institution, MRC 121, 10th & Constitution NW, PO Box 37012, Washington, DC 20560-0121, U.S.A. **Online address:** erwind@si.edu

ERZEN, Tanya. American (born United States), b. 1972. **Genres:** Social Commentary, Adult Non-fiction, Theology/Religion. **Career:** Ohio State University, Department of Comparative Studies, assistant professor of comparative studies, associate professor. Writer. **Publications:** (Ed. with A. McArdle) Zero Tolerance: Quality of Life and the New Police Brutality in New York City, 2001; Straight to Jesus: Sexual and Christian Conversions in the Ex-Gay Movement, 2006. Contributor to periodicals. **Address:** Department of Comparative Studies, Ohio State University, 428 Hagerty Hall, 1775 College Rd., Columbus, OH 43210, U.S.A. **Online address:** erzen.2@osu.edu

ESCH, Ben. American (born United States), b. 1982?. **Genres:** Novels. **Career:** Writer. **Publications:** Sophomore Undercover (novel), 2009. **Address:** Los Angeles, CA , U.S.A. **Online address:** benjamin.esch@gmail.com

ESCKILSEN, Erik E. American (born United States) **Genres:** Novels, Sports/Fitness. **Career:** International Plaza Corp., curriculum developer and instructor, 1986-87; Entertainment Weekly, associate editor, 1993-95; Burlington College, adjunct instructor, 1997-2004; Champlain College, adjunct instructor, 1997-, Core Division, assistant professor, 2007-, Champlain View, editor, 2005-; Bowling Green State University, graduate teaching assistant, 2004-06, Mid-American Review, reviews editor, 2004-06. Journalist. **Publications:** The Last Mall Rat, 2003; Offsides: A Novel, 2004; The Outside Groove: A Novel, 2006. Contributor to periodicals. **Address:** Champlain College, Aiken 301, 251 S Willard St., Burlington, VT 05401-3907, U.S.A. **Online address:** esckilse@champlain.edu

ESDAILE, Charles J. British (born England), b. 1959. **Genres:** History, Military/Defense/Arms Control, Adult Non-fiction. **Career:** University of Liverpool, instructor in history, professor in history. Writer. **Publications:** NONFICTION: The Spanish Army in the Peninsular War, 1988; The Duke of Wellington and the Command of the Spanish Army, 1812-1814, 1990; The Wars of Napoleon, 1995; Spain in the Liberal Age: From Constitution to Civil War, 1808-1939, 2000; The French Wars, 1792- 1815, 2001; The Peninsular War: A New History, 2002; (ed.) Popular Resistance in the French Wars: Patriots, Partisans and Land-Pirates, 2004; Fighting Napoleon: Guerrillas, Bandits and Adventurers in Spain, 1808-1814, 2004; Napoleon's Wars: An International History, 1803-1815, 2007; (with J. Tusell) Época contemporánea, 1808-2004, 2007; Wellington en Espana. La Guerra de la Independencia, 2008; Peninsular Eye-Witnesses: The Experience of War in Spain and Portugal, 2008. Contributor to books. **Address:** School of History, University of Liverpool, 9 Abercromby Sq., Liverpool, MS L69 7WZ, England. **Online address:** epsom@liverpool.ac.uk

ESFANDIARI, Haleh. American/Iranian (born Iran), b. 1940. **Genres:** History, Women's Studies And Issues, Essays. **Career:** Women's Organization of Iran, journalist and deputy secretary general; Oxford University, instructor in Persian language; Princeton University, instructor in Persian language and culture, 1980-94; Woodrow Wilson International Center for Scholars, fellow, 1995-96, Middle East Program, director, 1996-. **Publications:** (Ed. with A.L. Udovitch) The Economic Dimensions of Middle Eastern History: Essays in Honor of Charles Issawi, 1990; Reconstructed Lives: Women and Iran's Islamic Revolution, 1997; My Prison, My Home: One Woman's Story of Captivity in Iran, 2009. Contributor of articles to journals. **Address:** Middle East Program, Woodrow Wilson Center, 1 Woodrow Wilson Plz., 1300 Pennsylvania Ave. NW, Washington, DC 20004-3027, U.S.A. **Online address:** halehesfandiari@halehesfandiari.net

ESHBAUGH-SOHA, Matthew. American (born United States), b. 1972. **Genres:** Trivia/Facts, Speech/Rhetoric. **Career:** Texas A&M University, graduate assistant, 1998-2001, graduate assistant lecturer, 2001-02, visiting assistant professor, 2002-03; George Washington University, visiting assistant professor, 2003-04; Texas Tech University, visiting assistant professor, 2004-05; University of North Texas, Department of Political Science, assistant professor, 2005-10, associate professor, 2010-. Writer. **Publications:** The President's Speeches: Beyond Going Public, 2006; (with J.S. Peake) Breaking Through the Noise: Presidential Leadership, Public Opinion, and the News Media, 2011. Contributor to journals and periodicals. **Address:** Department of Political Science, University of North Texas, 125 Wooten Hall, 1155 Union Cir., PO Box 305340, Denton, TX 76203-5017, U.S.A. **Online address:** mes@unt.edu

ESHLEMAN, Clayton. American (born United States), b. 1935. **Genres:** Poetry, Translations. **Career:** University of Maryland, instructor in English, 1961-62; Matsushita Electric Corp., instructor in English, 1962-64; New York University American Language Institute, instructor, 1966-68; Caterpillar Books, publisher, 1966-68; Caterpillar Magazine, editor, 1967-73, publisher, 1967-70; California Institute of the Arts, School of Critical Studies, faculty, 1970-72; American College, Paris, France, lecturer in American poetry, 1973-74; University of California Press, part-time staff, 1974-; University of California, Extension Division, instructor, 1974-, visiting lecturer, 1979-86; University of California-San Diego, visiting lecturer, 1979-86; University of California-Santa Barbara, visiting lecturer, 1979-86; California Institute of Technology, Dreyfuss Poet-In-Residence and lecturer in creative writing, 1979-84; Sulfur Magazine, founder and editor, 1981-2000; Eastern Michigan University, Department of English, professor, 1986-2003, professor emeritus, 2003-; Council of Literary Magazines and Presses, board director, 1987; University of Arizona, Poetry Center, poet-in-residence, 1992; Tennessee State University, writer-in-residence, 1999; Dalhousie University, writer-in-residence, 2001; State University of New York, writer-in-residence, 2001; Macalester College, writer-in-residence, 2002; Wichita State University, writer-in-residence, 2002; Lakewood (Ohio) Public Library, writer-in-residence, 2002; San Diego State University, writer-in-residence, 2002; University of Louisiana, writer-in-residence, 2002; University of Maine, writer-in-residence, 2002. **Publications:** Mexico and North, 1962; The Chavin Illumination, 1965; Lachrymae Mateo: 3 Poems for Christmas 1966, 1966; Walks, 1967; The Crocus Bud, 1967; Brother Stones, 1968; Cantaloups and Splendour, 1968; T'ai, 1969; The House of Okumura, 1969; Indiana: Poems, 1969; The House of Ibuki: A Poem, New York City, 14 March-30 Sept. 1967, 1969; The Yellow River Record, 1969; A Pitchblende, 1969; (ed.) A Caterpillar Anthology: A Selection of Poetry and Prose from Caterpillar Magazine, 1971; The Wand, 1971; Bearings, 1971; Altars, 1971; The Sanjo Bridge, 1972; Coils, 1973; Human Wedding, 1973; Aux Morts, 1974; Realignment, 1974; Portrait of Francis Bacon, 1975; The Gull Wall: Poems and Essays, 1975; Cogollo, 1976; The Woman Who Saw Through Paradise, 1976; Grotesca, 1977; Core Meander, 1977; What She Means, 1978; Nights we put the Rock Together, 1980; Our Lady of the Three-Pronged Devil, 1981; Hades in Manganese, 1981; Foetus Graffiti, 1981; Fracture, 1983; Visions of the Fathers of Lascaux, 1983; The Name Encanyoned River: Selected Poems1960-85, 1986; (ed.) The Parallel Voyages, 1987; Conductors of the Pit: Major Works by Rimbaud, Ballejo, Cesaire, Artaud and Holan, 1988; Antiphonal Swing: Selected Prose1962-1987, 1989; Novices: A Study of Poetic Apprenticeship, 1989, 2nd ed., 1996; Hotel Cro-Magnon, 1989; Under World Arrest, 1994; Nora's Roar, 1996; From Scratch, 1998; (contrib.) Ground, 1998; Erratics, 2000; A Cosmogonic Collage: Sections I, II, & V, 2000; Jisei, 2000; Companion Spider, 2001; Sweetheart, 2002; Juniper Fuse: Upper Paleolithic Imagination and the Construction of the Underworld, 2003; An Alchemist with One Eye on Fire, 2006; Reciprocal Distillations, 2007; Archaic Design, 2007; The

Grindstone of Rapport/A Clayton Eshleman Reader, 2008; Anticline, 2010. TRANSLATOR: P. Neruda, Residence on Earth, 1962; (with D. Kelly) A. Césaire, State of the Union 1966; C. Vallejo, Poemas Humanos Human Poems, 1968; (with J.R. Barcia) C. Vallejo, Spain, Take This Cup from Me, 1974; (with J.R. Barcia) César Vallejo: The Complete Posthumous Poetry, 1978; (with J.R. Barcia) C. Vallejo, Battles in Spain, 1978; (with N. Glass) Artaud, Four Texts, 1982; (with A. Smith) A. Césaire, The Collected Poetry, 1983; B. Bador, Sea-Urchin Harakiri, 1984; M. Deguy, Given Giving: Selected Poems of Michel Deguy, 1984; (with A. Smith) A. Césaire, Lost Body, 1986; (and intro.) B. Bador, Sea urchin harakiri, 1986; (with A. Smith) A. Césaire, Lyric and Dramatic Poetry1946-1982, 1990; C. Vallejo, Trilce, 1992; (with B. Bador) A. Artaud, Watch friends and Rack Screams, 1995; (and ed. with A. Smith) A. Césaire, Notebook of a Return to the Native Land, 2001; (ed. and intro.) Conductors of the Pit: Poetry Written in Extremis in Translation, 2005; (and ed.) C. Vallejo, The Complete Poetry, 2007; (and ed. with A.J. Arnold) A. Césaire, Solar Throat Slashed, 2011; B. Dao, Endure Poems, 2011; B. Bador, Curdled Skulls Poems, 2011. Contributor of poetry to books and periodicals. **Address:** Department of English, Eastern Michigan University, Hoyt-Ground Fl., Ypsilanti, MI 48197, U.S.A. **Online address:** spidermind@comcast.net

ESHUN, Ekow. British (born England), b. 1968. **Genres:** Novels. **Career:** Kiss FM radio, broadcaster, 1987-88; freelance journalist, 1990-93; The Face, assistant editor, 1993-96; Arena (magazine), editor, 1996-; Tank Magazine, editorial director, 1999-; Institute of Contemporary Arts, council member, 1999-2003, artistic director, 2005-; Bug Cultural Consultancy, director, 2000-04; University of Arts, governor, 2001-. **Publications:** Black Gold of the Sun: Searching for Home in England and Africa, 2005; Black Gold of the Sun: Searching for Home in Africa and Beyond, 2006. Contributor to periodicals. **Address:** Institute of Contemporary Arts, The Mall, London, GL SW1Y 5AH, England.

ESKEW, Glenn T. American (born United States), b. 1962. **Genres:** History, Race Relations, Theology/Religion. **Career:** E.B. Construction Corp., plumbing apprentice, 1978-83; Meridian Star, reporter, 1984-85; Georgia Historical Quarterly, editorial assistant, 1987-88; University of Georgia, graduate instructor, 1988-91; Albert Einstein Institution, fellow, 1991-93; Georgia State University, assistant professor of history, 1993-2000, tenured associate professor, 2001-, director of undergraduate studies. Writer. **Publications:** But for Birmingham: The Local and National Movements in the Civil Rights Struggle, 1997; (ed. with E.J. Cashin) Paternalism in a Southern City: Race, Religion and Gender in Augusta, Georgia, 2001; (ed.) Labor in the Modern South, 2001. Contributor of articles to books and periodicals. **Address:** Department of History, Georgia State University, 34 Peachtree St. NW, Ste. 2050, PO Box 4117, Atlanta, GA 30303, U.S.A. **Online address:** gteskew@gsu.edu

ESKILSON, Stephen John. American (born United States), b. 1964. **Genres:** Art/Art History. **Career:** Eastern Illinois University, associate professor of art history. Writer and art historian. **Publications:** (With J. Marquardt) Frames of Reference: Art, History, and the World, 2004; Graphic Design: A New History, 2007. **Address:** Eastern Illinois University, 1345 Doudna Fine Arts Ctr., Charleston, IL 61920, U.S.A. **Online address:** sjeskilson@eiu.edu

ESKRIDGE, Ann E. American (born United States), b. 1949. **Genres:** Novels, Plays/Screenplays, Literary Criticism And History. **Career:** Chicago Daily Defender, reporter, 1968-69; Oklahoma Daily, reporter, 1970; Oklahoma Journal, reporter, 1970; KWTV, reporter, 1970-71; WBEN-TV, reporter, 1971-72; WXYZ-TV, reporter, 1972-76; Lieutenant Governor of Michigan, executive assistant, 1978-79; Michigan State Treasurer, administrator, 1979-81; Statewide Nutrition Commission, administrator, 1982-83; Detroit Council President Erma Henderson, administrative assistant, 1983; Golightly Vocational Technical Center, instructor in mass media, 1983-90; freelance writer and teaching consultant, 1990-92, 1995-; Michigan Consolidated Gas Co., speech writer, 1992-96; Ameritech Grant, project manager, 1996-98; University of Detroit Mercy, Department of English, adjunct professor, 2000-, African American Studies Program, director, 2008-; Wayne State University, Department of Communications, adjunct professor, 2005-07, Wayne County Community College, adjunct professor, 2009; Emage Inc, president. **Publications:** The Sanctuary, 1994; Slave Uprisings and Runaways: Fighting for Freedom and the Underground Railroad, 2004. Contributor to periodicals. **Address:** Department of English, University of Detroit Mercy, 4001 W McNichols Rd, Detroit, MI 48221-3038, U.S.A. **Online address:** annesk@ameritech.net

ESKRIDGE, Kelley. American (born United States), b. 1960?. **Genres:** Novels, Young Adult Fiction, Gay And Lesbian Issues, E-books, Novellas/Short Stories, Science Fiction/Fantasy, Plays/Screenplays. **Career:** Clarion West Writers Workshop, board chair; Wizards of the Coast, vice president of project management. Writer. **Publications:** Solitaire, 2002; Dangerous Space, 2007. Works appear in anthologies. Contributor to periodicals. **Address:** c/o Shawna McCarthy, McCarthy Literary Agency, 7 Allen St., Rumson, NJ 07760, U.S.A. **Online address:** contact@kelleyeskridge.com

ESKRIDGE, William N(ichol). American (born United States), b. 1951. **Genres:** Law, Gay And Lesbian Issues. **Career:** U.S. District Court, law clerk to judge Edward Weinfeld, 1978-79; Shea & Gardner, associate, 1979-82; University of Virginia Law School, assistant professor, 1982-87; Georgetown University Law Center, associate professor, 1987-90, professor, 1990-98; New York University Law School, visiting professor, 1993, 2004; Harvard Law School, visiting professor, 1994; Stanford Law School, visiting professor, 1995; Yale Law School, visiting professor, 1995, John A Garver professor of jurisprudence, 1998-, deputy dean, 2001-02; University of Toronto, 1999, 2001; University of Vanderbilt, visiting professor, 2003; University of Columbia, visiting professor, 2003; University of Georgetown, professor of law, 2006; U.S. law schools, visiting professor. Writer. **Publications:** (With P.P. Frickey) Cases and Materials on Legislation: Statutes and the Creation of Public Policy, 1988, 4th ed., 2007; (with P. Frickey and D.A. Farber) Cases and Materials on Constitutional Law: Themes for the Constitution's Third Century, 1993, 4th ed., 2009; (with P. Frickey) Dynamic Statutory Interpretation, 1994; (contrib.) The Legal Process: Basic Problems in the Making and Application of Law, 1994; The Case for Same-Sex Marriage: From Sexual Liberty to Civilized Commitment, 1996; (with N. Hunter) Sexuality, Gender and the Law, 1997, 3rd ed., 2011; (with P.P. Frickey and E. Garrett) Legislation and Statutory Interpretation, 2000; Equality Practice: Civil Unions and the Future of Gay Rights, 2002; (with D.R. Spedale) Gay Marriage: For Better or For Worse?: What We've Learned from the Evidence, 2006; Dishonorable Passions: Sodomy Laws in America, 1861-2003, 2008; (with J. Ferejohn) American Constitutionalism and Our Republic of Statutes, 2010. EDITOR: A Dance along the Precipice: The Political and Economic Dimensions of the International Debt Problem, 1985; (with S. Levinson) Constitutional Stupidities, Constitutional Tragedies, 1998; Gaylaw: Challenging the Apartheid of the Closet, 1999; (with P.P. Frickey and E. Garrett) Statutory Interpretation Stories, 2011. **Address:** Yale Law School, Rm. 323, 127 Wall St., PO Box 208215, New Haven, CT 06520, U.S.A. **Online address:** william.eskridge@yale.edu

ESLER, Anthony James. American (born United States), b. 1934. **Genres:** Novels, History. **Career:** College of William and Mary, assistant professor, 1962-67, associate professor, 1967-72, professor of history, 1972-99; American Council of Learned Societies, research fellow, 1969-70. Writer. **Publications:** The Aspiring Mind of the Elizabethan Younger Generation, 1966; Bombs, Beards and Barricades: 150 Years of Youth in Revolt, 1971; The Blade of Castlemayne, 1974; Hellbane, 1975; Lord Libertine, 1976; Forbidden City, 1977; The Freebooters, 1979; Generational Studies: A Basic Bibliography, 1979; Babylon, 1980; Bastion, 1980; Generations in History: An Introduction to the Concept, 1982; The Generation Gap in Society and History: A Select Bibliography, 1984; The Human Venture: A World History, 1986, 5th ed., 2004; (co-author) A Survey of Western Civilization, 1987; The Western World: A History, 1994, 2nd ed., 1997; (co-author) Connections: A World History, 1997, 4th ed., 2007. EDITOR: The Youth Revolution: The Conflict of Generations in Modern History, 1974. **Address:** Department of History, College of William & Mary, PO Box 8795, Williamsburg, VA 23187-8795, U.S.A. **Online address:** Anthonyesler@aol.com

ESLER, Philip F. (Philip Francis Esler). Scottish (born Scotland), b. 1952?. **Genres:** Theology/Religion. **Career:** Saint Andrews University, Saint Mary's College, vice-principal for research, dean of faculty, professor of biblical criticism, 2005-09, principal, 2010-; U.K. Arts and Humanities Research Council, chief executive, 2005-09. Writer. **Publications:** (As Philip Francis Esler) Community and Gospel in Luke-Acts: The Social and Political Motivations of Lucan Theology, 1987; The First Christians in Their Social Worlds: Social-Scientific Approaches to New Testament Interpretation, 1994; (ed.) Modelling Early Christianity: Social-Scientific Studies of the New Testament in Its Context, 1995; Galatians, 1998; (ed.) Christianity for the Twenty-first Century, 1998; (ed.) The Early Christian World, 2000; Conflict and Identity in Romans: The Social Setting of Paul's Letter, 2003; (with J. Boyd) Visuality and Biblical Text: Interpreting Velázquez' Christ with Martha and Mary as a Test Case,

2004; New Testament Theology: Communion and Community, 2005; (ed.) Ancient Israel: The Old Testament in Its Social Context, 2006; (with R.A. Piper) Lazarus, Mary and Martha: Social-Scientific Approaches to the Gospel of John, 2006; Sex, Wives, and Warriors, 2011. CONTRIBUTOR: Ethnicity and the Bible, 1996; The Oxford Bible Commentary, 2001; The Social Setting of Jesus and the Gospels, 2002; Jesus in History, Culture, and Thought: An Encyclopedia, 2004; Iconography and the New Testament, 2005; The Nature of New Testament Theology, 2005; Prayer and Spirituality in the Early Church, 2006. Contributor to periodicals and journals. **Address:** St. Mary's College, The School of Divinity, University of St Andrews, South St., Saint Andrews, FF KY16 9JU, Scotland. **Online address:** pfe@st-andrews.ac.uk

ESLER, Philip Francis. See ESLER, Philip F.

ESPADA, Martín. American (born United States), b. 1957?. **Genres:** Poetry, Essays, Translations. **Career:** University of Massachusetts, Amherst, English professor. Writer. **Publications:** POETRY: The Immigrant Iceboy's Bolero, 1982; Trumpets From the Islands of Their Eviction, 1987; Rebellion is the Circle of a Lover's Hands, 1990; City of Coughing and Dead Radiators: Poems, 1993; (ed.) Poetry Like Bread: Poets of the Political Imagination From Curbstone Press, 1994, new ed., 2000; Imagine the Angels of Bread: Poems, 1996. OTHER: (trans. with C. Perez-Bustillo) The Blood that Keeps Singing: Selected Poems of Clemente Soto Velez, 1991; Trumpets from the Islands of their Eviction, 1994; (ed. and contrib.) El Coro: A Chorus of Latino and Latina Poetry, 1997; Zapata's Disciple (essays and poetry), 1998; A Mayan Astronomer in Hell's Kitchen: Poems, 2000; Alabanza: New and Selected Poems, 1982-2002, 2003; Republic of Poetry, 2006; Crucifixion in the Plaza De Armas: Poems, 2008; Tumba de Buenaventura Roig: Selected Poems, Poemas Selectos, 2008; Lover of a Subversive is also a Subversive: Essays and Commentaries, 2010; Trouble Ball: Poems, 2011. Contributor to periodicals. **Address:** Department of English, University of Massachusetts, 251 Bartlett Hall, Amherst, MA 01003, U.S.A. **Online address:** mespada@english.umass.edu

ESPAILLAT, Rhina P. American/British (born England), b. 1932. **Genres:** Novellas/Short Stories, Poetry, Essays, Young Adult Fiction. **Career:** New York City Public Schools, teacher, 1953-54; Jamaica High School, teacher, 1965-80; New York City, Board of Education, consultant, 1984-89. Writer. **Publications:** Lapsing to Grace: Poems and Drawings, 1992; Where Horizons Go, 1998; Rehearsing Absence, 2001; Troves of the Sea, 2002; (with L. Krisak) C.S. Beras, Trovas del mar, 2002; The Shadow I Dress In, 2004; Playing at Stillness, 2005; Agua de dos ríos: poemas, prosa y traducciones, 2006; (contrib.) Voces de la inmigración, 2007; Her Place in These Designs, 2008. CHAPBOOKS: Mundo y Palabra/The World and the Word, 2001; Rhina P. Espaillat: Greatest Hits, 1942-2001, 2003; The Story-Teller's Hour, 2004. Contributor to books. Works appear in anthologies. **Address:** 12 Charron Dr., Newburyport, MA 01950, U.S.A. **Online address:** espmosk@juno.com

ESPOSITO, Mary Ann. American (born United States), b. 1942. **Genres:** Food And Wine. **Career:** University of New Hampshire, instructor in Italian cooking, 1985-90; Public Broadcasting Service (PBS), Ciao Italia (televised cooking show), host and creator, 1989-; European Heritage Institute, lecturer, 1990-91; Mary Ann Esposito Inc., president, 1996-. Writer. **Publications:** COOKBOOKS: Ciao Italia: Traditional Italian Recipes from Family Kitchens, 1991; Nella Cucina: More Italian Cooking from the Host of Ciao Italia, 1993; Celebrations, Italian Style: Recipes and Menus for Special Occasions and Seasons of the Year, 1995; What You Knead, 1997; Easy Book of Yeast Dough, 1997; Mangia Pasta: Easy-to-make Recipes for Company and Every Day, 1998; Ciao Italia: Bringing Italy Home, 2001; Ciao Italia in Umbria: Recipes and Reflections from the Heart of Italy, 2002; Ciao Italia in Tuscany: Traditional Recipes from One of Italy's Most Famous Regions, 2003; Ciao Italia Pronto: 30-Minute Recipes from an Italian Kitchen, 2005; Ciao Italia Slow and Easy: Casseroles, Braises, Lasagne, and Stews From an Italian Kitchen, 2007; Ciao Italia Five-Ingredient Favorites: Quick and Delicious Recipes from an Italian Kitchen, 2009; Ciao Italia Family Classics, 2011. **Address:** Public Broadcasting Service, 2100 Crystal Dr., Arlington, VA 22202-3784, U.S.A. **Online address:** maryann@ciaoitalia.com

ESPOSITO, Phil(ip Anthony). Canadian (born Canada), b. 1942. **Genres:** Autobiography/Memoirs, Adult Non-fiction, Sports/Fitness. **Career:** Chicago Black Hawks, player, 1964-67; Boston Bruins, player, 1968-76; New York Rangers, player, 1976-81, general manager, 1986-89; Tampa Bay Lightning, president and general manager, 1992-99; Fox Sports Net, analyst, 1999-. Writer. **Publications:** (With T. Esposito and T. Moriarty) The Brothers Esposito, 1971; (with G. Eskenazi) Hockey Is My Life, 1972; (with T. Esposito and K. Walsh) We Can Teach You to Play Hockey, 1972; (with D. Dew) Phil Esposito's Winning Hockey for Beginners, 1976; Thunder and Lightning: A No-B.S. Hockey Memoir, 2003. Contributor to periodicals. **Address:** Triumph Books, 542 S Dearborn St., Ste. 750, Chicago, IL 60605, U.S.A.

ESSED, Philomena. Dutch (born Netherlands), b. 1955?. **Genres:** Race Relations. **Career:** University of Amsterdam, Womens Studies, student assistant, 1979-80, Center for Race and Ethnic Studies, junior researcher, 1985-89, lecturer, 1990-91, Institute for Development Research Amsterdam, researcher, 1992-93, Amsterdam Research Institute for Global Issues and Development Studies, co-director, 1993-2003, chair, senior researcher, 1994-96; Dutch National Institute, E-Quality: Gender and Ethnicity, co-founder, 1997-; University of California, visiting professor, 2001; Antioch University, professor of critical race, gender and leadership studies, 2005-; Utrecht University, Research Institute Culture and History, researcher. Writer. **Publications:** NONFICTION: Alledags Racisme, 1984, Everyday Racism: Reports from Women of Two Cultures, 1990; Understanding Everyday Racism: An Interdisciplinary Theory, 1991; Diversiteit: Vrouwen, Kleur en Cultuur, 1994, Diversity: Gender, Color, and Culture, 1996; (ed. with D.T. Goldberg) Race Critical Theories: Text and Context, 2002; (ed. with G. Frerks and J. Schrijvers) Refugees and the Transformation of Societies: Agency, Policies, Ethics, and Politics, 2004; (ed. with D.T. Goldberg and A. Kobayashi) A Companion to Gender Studies, 2005; Cloning Cultures, forthcoming; Humanizing Leadership, forthcoming. **Address:** Antioch University, 400 Corporate Pointe, Nieuwe Prinsengracht 130, Culver City, CA 90230, U.S.A. **Online address:** essed@phd.antioch.edu

ESSEX, Karen. American (born United States) **Genres:** Biography, Novels, Romance/Historical, Young Adult Fiction. **Career:** Blake Edwards Entertainment, vice president; Force Ten Productions, senior vice president. Writer. **Publications:** (With J.L. Swanson) Bettie Page: The Life of a Pin-up Legend, 1996; Kleopatra, 2001; Pharoah: Volume II of Kleopatra, 2002; Leonardo's Swans: A Novel, 2006; Stealing Athena, 2008; Dracula in Love: A Novel, 2010. Contributor to periodicals and magazines. **Address:** c/o Author Mail, Warner Books, 1271 Ave. of the Americas, New York, NY 10020, U.S.A.

ESSEX-CATER, Antony John. British (born England), b. 1923?. **Genres:** Medicine/Health, Mystery/Crime/Suspense. **Career:** Deputy Medical Officer of Health, 1961-68; Monmouthshire County Council, county medical officer, 1968-74; medical officer of health and consultant venereologist, 1974-88; National Association for Maternal and Child Welfare, chairman, 1976-88; National Association for Maternal and Child Welfare, vice president, 1988-. Writer. **Publications:** Synopsis of Public Health and Social Medicine, 1960, 3rd ed. as Manual of Public and Community Medicine, 1979. **Address:** Butterworth-Heinemann Ltd., Halley Ct., Oxford, OX OX2 8EJ, England.

ESTERBERG, Kristin G. American (born United States), b. 1960. **Genres:** Gay And Lesbian Issues, Sociology. **Career:** Houghton Mifflin Co., editorial assistant, associate editor, editor in college division, 1982-85; freelance editor, 1985-89; Cornell University, lecturer in sociology, human development, and family studies, 1990, 1991; University of Missouri, assistant professor, 1991-96, associate professor of sociology, 1996-97, director of women's studies, 1991-97; University of Massachusetts, assistant professor, 1997-2001, associate professor of sociology, 2001-08, department chair, 2002-04, associate provost and deputy provost, 2004-07; Salem State College, provost and academic vice president, 2009-, university's chief academic officer. **Publications:** Lesbian and Bisexual Identities: Constructing Communities, Constructing Selves, 1997; Qualitative Methods in Social Research, 2002. Contributor of articles to books and periodicals. **Address:** Salem State College, 352 Lafayette St., Salem, MA 01970, U.S.A. **Online address:** kesterberg@salemstate.edu

ESTERHAMMER, Angela. Swiss/Canadian (born Canada), b. 1961. **Genres:** Humanities, Literary Criticism And History. **Career:** University of Western Ontario, Department of English and Department of Modern Languages and Literatures, assistant professor, 1989-94, associate professor, 1994-2000, Department of Modern Languages and Literatures, professor, 2000-04, chair, 2000-04, Faculty of Arts and Humanities, acting dean, 2004-05, associate dean, 2005-06, distinguished university professor, 2005-07, adjunct distinguished university professor, 2007-; Freie Universität Berlin, visiting professor, 1996-98; University of Zürich, Department of English Literature, chair, 2007-, Ord. Professor. Writer. **Publications:** Creating States: Studies in the Performative Language of John Milton and William Blake,

1994; (trans. and intro.) R.M. Rilke, Two Stories of Prague, 1994; Romanticism and the Ideologies of Genre, 1994; (co-ed.) The Wordsworth Circle, 1994; (ed.) Philosophies of Genre, 1994; (with J.M. Wright) 1798 and Its Implications: Special Issue of European Romantic Review, 1999; The Romantic Performative: Language and Action in British and German Romanticism, 2000; (ed.) Romantic Poetry, 2002; Spontaneous Overflows and Revivifying Rays: Romanticism and the Discourse of Improvisation, 2004; Framing Contingency, 2004; (ed.) Northrop Frye on Milton and Blake, 2005; Romanticism and Improvisation, 1750-1850, 2008; (ed. with A.J. Dick) Spheres of Action: Speech and Performance in Romantic Culture, 2008; Identity and Community: Constructions, Deconstructions, Reconstructions, forthcoming. Contributor of articles to journals. **Address:** Department of English, University of Zurich, Englisches Seminar, 47 Plattenstrasse, Zurich, CH-8032, Switzerland. **Online address:** esterhammer@es.uzh.ch

ESTERHAZY, Peter. Hungarian (born Hungary), b. 1950. **Genres:** Novels, Theology/Religion, Young Adult Fiction. **Career:** Ministry of Metallurgy and Machine Industry, consultant, 1974-78; freelance writer, 1978-. **Publications:** Fancsikó és, Pinta, 1976, 2nd ed., 1981; Pápai Vizeken ne kalózkodj, 1977; Termelési-regény, 1979; Függö: Bevezetés a Szépirodalomba: Teljes, Gondozott Szöveg, 1981; Ki Szavatol a Lady Biztonságáért?: Bevezetés a szépirodalomba, 1982; Fuharosok: Regény, 1983; Daisy: Opera Semiseria egy Felvonásban, 1984; Kis Magyar Pornográfia: Bevezetés a Szépirodalomba, 1984; Szív Segédigéi: Bevezetés a Szépirodalomba, 1985; Bevezetés a Szépirodalomba, 1986; Kleine ungarische Pornographie, 1987; Fuhrleute: ein Roman, 1988; Kitömött hattyú: írások, 1988; Hrabal könyve, 1990; Hahn-Hahn grófnó Pillantása: Lefelé a Dunán, 1991; Esterházy-kalauz, 1991; Jegyzökönyv, 1993; Egy nö, 1993; Búcsúszimfónia: A Gabonakereskedö, 1994; írások, 1994; Nö, 1995; Kék Haris, 1996; She Loves Me, 1997; Harmonia Caelestis, 2000; Javított kiadás, 2002; (with K. Imre and N. Péter) Kalauz, 2003; Celestial Harmonies, 2004; Utazás a Tizenhatos mélyére, 2006; Rubens és a Nemeuklideszi Asszonyok, 2006; Semmi Müvészet, 2008; Lichterfeste, Schattenspiele, 2009; Not Art, 2010; Esti, 2010. **Address:** Hungarian Writers Federation, Bajza-utca 18, Budapest, H-1062, Hungary.

ESTES, Clarissa Pinkola. American (born United States), b. 1943. **Genres:** Songs/Lyrics And Libretti, Psychology, Women's Studies And Issues, Poetry. **Career:** Psychoanalyst in private practice, 1971-; Women in Transition Safe House, co-coordinator, 1973-75; C.G. Jung Center for Education and Research, executive director; Guadelupe Foundation, founder; Union Institute and University and Vermont College, trustee; Bloomsbury Review, contributing editor; Colorado Authors for Gay and Lesbian Equal Rights, co-founder and co-director; Authors Guild, director; Wake Forest Medical School, Maya Angelou Minority Health Foundation, director; The Bloomsbury Review, contributing editor; TheModerateVoice.com, deputy managing editor and columnist. Poet. **Publications:** Women Who Run with the Wolves: Myths and Stories of the Wild Woman Archetype, 1992; The Gift of Story: A Wise Tale about What Is Enough, 1993; The Faithful Gardener: A Wise Tale about That Which Can Never Die, 1995; (foreword) The Bloomsbury Review Booklover's Guide: A Collection of Tips, Techniques, Anecdotes, Controversies & Suggestions for the Home Library, 1996; Untie the Strong Woman: Ancient Blessed Mother in Modern Times, 2010; La Curandera: Healing in Two Worlds, 2011; La Pasionaria, The Bright Angel: The Collected Poetry of Clarissa Pinkola Estés, 2011; Warming the Stone Child: Myths & Stories on the Peculiar and Wondrous Powers of the Abandoned Child, 2011. Contributor to periodicals. **Address:** Ned Leavitt Agency, 70 Wooster St., Ste. 4F, New York, NY 10012, U.S.A.

ESTES, Daniel J(ohn). American (born United States), b. 1953?. **Genres:** Theology/Religion, Reference. **Career:** Dallas Theological Seminary, Lay Institute, instructor, 1977; Clintonville Baptist Church, assistant pastor, 1978-84, 1989-93; Cedarville University, assistant professor, 1984-90, associate professor, 1990-95, professor of Bible, 1995-2005, director of honors program, 1995-99, associate academic vice president, 2001-05, distinguished professor of Bible, 2005-, school of biblical and theological studies, dean; Linworth Baptist Church, assistant pastor, choir director. Writer. **Publications:** Learning and Living God's Word, 1993; (contrib.) God and Caesar, 1994; Hear, My Son: Wisdom and Pedagogy in Proverbs 1-9, 1997; Handbook on the Wisdom books and Psalms, 2005; (with D.C. Fredericks) Ecclesiastes and the Song of Songs, 2010. Contributor to books and periodicals. **Address:** Cedarville University, 251 N Main St., PO Box 601, Cedarville, OH 45314, U.S.A. **Online address:** estesd@cedarville.edu

ESTES, Steve. American (born United States), b. 1972?. **Genres:** History, Civil Liberties/Human Rights, Gay And Lesbian Issues, Social Sciences. **Career:** University of North Carolina, Southern Oral History Program, project coordinator, 1996-99, research and teaching assistant, 1996-99; Sunflower County Freedom Project, research coordinator and teacher, 1999-2000; American Youth Policy Forum, research associate, 1999-2001; Towson University, instructor, 2000-01; College of Charleston, visiting assistant professor, 2001-02; Sonoma State University, associate professor, 2002-. Historian, educator and writer. **Publications:** (Ed. with S. Jurich) Raising Academic Achievement, 2000; (ed. with S. Jurich and D. Walker) Raising Minority Academic Achievement, 2001; I Am a Man! Race, Manhood and the Civil Rights Movement, 2005; (contrib.) The Civil Rights Movement in American Memory, 2006; Ask & Tell: Gay and Lesbian Veterans Speak Out, 2007. Contributor to periodicals. **Address:** Department of History, Sonoma State University, 1801 E Cotati Ave., Rohnert Park, CA 94928, U.S.A. **Online address:** steve.estes@sonoma.edu

ESTES, William (Kaye). *See* Obituaries.

ESTEVEZ-ABE, Margarita. American (born United States), b. 1962. **Genres:** Business/Trade/Industry, Economics, Politics/Government. **Career:** University of Minnesota, assistant professor of political science, 1999-2001; Harvard University, associate professor of government, 2001-; Radcliffe Institute, Joy Foundation fellow, 2005-06; Keio University, research associate. Writer and political scientist. **Publications:** Welfare and Capitalism in Postwar Japan: Party, Bureaucracy, and Business, 2008. Contributor to books and periodicals. **Address:** East Asia Program, Maxwell School, Syracuse University, 346 Eggers Hall, Syracuse, NY 13244-1090, U.S.A.

ESTEY, Ralph H(oward). Canadian (born Canada), b. 1916. **Genres:** Agriculture/Forestry, Botany, History. **Career:** Wartime Emergency Training, teacher, 1942-43; University of Connecticut, botany teacher, 1956-57; McGill University, Department of Plant Science, assistant professor, 1957-61, associate professor, 1961-72, professor of mycology, history of plant pathology and nematology, 1972-82, department head, 1970-, professor emeritus, 1982-. Writer. **Publications:** Essays on the Early History of Plant Pathology and Mycology in Canada, 1994. **Address:** Department of Plant Science, McGill University, Macdonald Campus, 21 111 Lakeshore, Ste-Anne-de-Bellevue, Montreal, QC H9X 3V9, Canada. **Online address:** rhestey@videotron.ca

ESTLEMAN, Loren D. American (born United States), b. 1952. **Genres:** Mystery/Crime/Suspense, Westerns/Adventure, Novellas/Short Stories, inspirational/Motivational Literature, Novels. **Career:** Michigan Fed, cartoonist, 1967-70; Ypsilanti Press, reporter, 1973; Community Foto-News, editor-in-chief, 1975-76; Ann Arbor News, special writer, 1976-77; Dexter Leader, staff writer, 1977-80; Friends of the Dexter Library, instructor. **Publications:** The Oklahoma Punk, 1976 as Red Highway, 1988; Sherlock Holmes vs. Dracula: Or, The Adventure of the Sanguinary Count, 1978; The Hider, 1978; (ed.) Dr. Jekyll and Mr. Holmes, 1979; Aces & Eights, 1981, 2nd ed., 1985; The Wolfer, 1981; Mister St. John, 1983; This Old Bill, 1984; Gun Man, 1985; The Wister Trace: Classic Novels of the American Frontier, 1987; Bloody Season, 1988; Peeper, 1989, 2nd ed., 1991; The Best Western Stories of Loren D. Estleman, 1989; Western Story, 1989; (ed. with M.H. Greenberg) P.I. Files, 1990; Sudden Country, 1991; Crooked Way, 1993; The Judge, 1994; Billy Gashade, 1997; Journey of the Dead, 1998; The Rocky Mountain Moving Picture Association, 1999; White Desert, 2000; The Master Executioner, 2001; (ed. and intro.) American West: Twenty New Stories, 2001; Black Powder, White Smoke, 2002; (with J. Lescroart) Writing the Popular Novel: A Comprehensive Guide to Crafting Fiction That Sells, 2004; The Undertaker's Wife, 2005; The Adventures of Johnny Vermillion: A Novel, 2006; Amos Walker's Detroit, 2007; (with W.W. Johnstone, E. Kelton and L. L'Amour) Lost Trails, 2007; Gas City, 2008; The Branch and the Scaffold, 2008; Roy & Lillie: A Love Story, 2010; (contrib.) Law of the Gun, 2010; Valentino: Film Detective, 2011; Attitude and Other Stories of Suspense, forthcoming. VALENTINO MYSTERY: Frames, 2007; Alone, 2009. SHORT STORIES: People Who Kill, 1993; Director's Cut, 1998; Dark Lady Down, 1998; The Frankenstein Footage, 1998; The Man in the White Hat, 1999; Picture Palace, 2000; The Day Hollywood Stood Still, 2001; Greed, 2002; Bombshell, 2003; Shooting Big Ed, 2005; The Profane Angel, 2007; Garbo Writes, 2007; Wild Walls, 2007. AMOS WALKER SERIES: Motor City Blue, 1980; Angel Eyes, 1981, 2nd ed., 1984; The Midnight Man, 1982; The Glass Highway, 1983; Sugartown, 1984, 2nd ed., 1985; Every Brilliant Eye, 1986; Lady Yesterday, 1987; Downriver, 1988; General Murders, 1988; Silent Thunder, 1989; Sweet Women Lie, 1990; Never Street, 1996; The Witchfinder, 1998; The Hours of the Virgin, 1999; A Smile on the Face of the Tiger, 2000; Sinister Heights, 2002; Poison Blonde, 2003; Retro, 2004; Nicotine Kiss, 2006; American Detective, 2007; Amos Walker: The Complete Story Collection, 2010; The Left-handed Dollar, 2010; Infernal Angels, 2011; Burning Midnight, 2012. PETER MACKLIN SERIES: Kill Zone, 1984; Roses are Dead, 1985, 2nd ed., 1990; Any Man's Death, 1986; Something Borrowed, Something Black, 2002; Little Black Dress, 2005. DETROIT CRIME SERIES: Whiskey River, 1990; Motown, 1991; King of the Corner, 1992; Edsel, 1995; Stress, 1996; Jitterbug, 1998; Thunder City, 1999. PAGE MURDOCK SERIES: The High Rocks, 1979; Stamping Ground, 1980, 2nd ed., 1985; Murdock's Law, 1982; The Stranglers, 1984; City of Widows, 1994; Port Hazard, 2004; The Book of Murdock, 2010. Contributor to periodicals. **Address:** Tor/Forge, 175 5th Ave., New York, NY 10010, U.S.A.

ESTOW, Clara. American (born United States), b. 1945. **Genres:** History, Biography. **Career:** University of Massachusetts, instructor, 1968-71, assistant professor, 1974-82, associate professor, 1982-94, professor of Hispanic studies, 1994-2007, department head, 1989-92, Harbor Campus, department head, 1995-, director of Latin American studies program, 1995-98, Faculty Council, chair, 1999-2001, professor emerita, 2008; International Institute Foundation in Spain, secretary of executive committee. Writer. **Publications:** Pedro the Cruel of Castile, 1350-1369, 1995; La legitimacion de lo ilegitimo: Lopez de Ayala y la historiografia medieval, 2006. Contributor of articles to books and periodicals. **Address:** Department of Hispanic Studies, University of Massachusetts, 100 Morrissey Blvd., Boston, MA 02125-3300, U.S.A. **Online address:** clara.estow@umb.edu

ESTRADA, Rita Clay. Also writes as Tira Lacy, Rita Clay. American (born United States), b. 1941. **Genres:** Novels, Romance/Historical, Westerns/Adventure, Reference, Adult Non-fiction, Young Adult Fiction. **Career:** Romance Writers of America, president and co-founder; writer, 1980-. **Publications:** ROMANCE NOVELS: The Will and the Way, 1985; A Woman's Choice, 1985; The Best Things in Life, 1986; Something to Treasure, 1986; The Ivory Key, 1987; A Little Magic, 1987; Trust, 1988; Second to None, 1989; To Buy a Groom, 1990; The Lady Says No, 1991; Twice Loved, 1991; To Have and to Hold, 1992; One More Time, 1993; The Colonel's Daughter, 1993; Forms of Love, 1994; Conveniently Yours, 1994; The Twelve Gifts of Christmas, 1994; Interlude in Time, 1994; The Stormchaser, 1996; Love Me, Love My Bed, 1996; Wishes, 1997; Dreams, 1998; Everything about Him, 1999; Million Dollar Valentine, 2000; Bedazzled, 2002. ROMANCE NOVELS AS RITA CLAY: Wanderer's Dream, 1981; Sweet Eternity, 1981; Wise Folly, 1982; Yesterday's Dreams, 1982; Experiment in Love, 1983; Summer Song, 1983; Recapture the Love, 1984. ROMANCE NOVELS AS TIRA LACY: With Time and Tenderness, 1983; Only for Love, 1984. OTHER: Valentine Sampler, 1993; (ed. with R. Gallagher) Writing Romances: A Handbook, 1997; (with R. Gallagher) You Can Write a Romance!, 1999; Blissful (western), 2000; Too Wicked to Love (western), 2001. Contributor to periodicals. **Address:** Romance Writers of America, 14615 Benfer Rd., Houston, TX 77069, U.S.A. **Online address:** rcestrada1@juno.com

ESTRAIKH, Gennady. American/Russian (born Russia), b. 1952?. **Genres:** Reference. **Career:** New York University, associate professor of Hebrew and Judaic Studies, Rauch Associate Professor of Yiddish Studies. Writer. **Publications:** Moscow Purim Plays, 1993; Soviet Yiddish: Language Planning and Linguistic Development, 1999; Yiddish in the Contemporary World, 1999; (with M. Kruitikov) The Shtetl Image and Reality: Papers on the Second Mendel Friedman International Conference on Yiddish, 2000; (ed. with M. Krutikov) Yiddish and the Left: Papers of the Third Mendel Friedman International Conference on Yiddish, 2001; In Harness: Yiddish Writers' Romance with Communism, 2005; (ed. with J. Sherman) David Bergelson: From Modernism to Socialist Realism, 2007; Yiddish in the Cold War, 2008; (ed. with M. Krutikov) Yiddish in Weimar Berlin: At the Crossroads of Diaspora Politics and Culture, 2010. **Address:** New York University, Heyman Hall, 51 Washington Sq. S, New York, NY 10012-1075, U.S.A. **Online address:** ge293@nyu.edu

ESTRIN, Allen. American (born United States) **Genres:** Communications/Media, Novels. **Career:** American Film Institute, senior lecturer in screenwriting. Screenwriter and producer. **Publications:** Hollywood Professionals, vol. VI: Capra Cukor and Brown, 1980; Pocahontas II: Journey to a New World, 1998; (with J. Telushkin) Heaven's Witness (novel), 2nd ed., 2004. **Address:** American Film Institute, 2021 N Western Ave., Los Angeles, CA 90027-1657, U.S.A. **Online address:** aestrin@afifaculty.org

ESTY, Daniel C. American (born United States), b. 1959. **Genres:** Environmental Sciences/Ecology, Business/Trade/Industry, Social Sciences. **Career:** Arnold & Porter, attorney, 1986-89; U.S. Environmental Protection Agency, special assistant to the administrator, 1989-90, deputy chief of staff, 1990-91, deputy assistant administrator for policy, 1991-93; Peterson Institute for International Economics, deputy assistant administrator for policy, 1991-93, senior fellow, 1993-94; Yale University, associate professor of law, through 2001, Hill House professor of environmental law and policy, 1994, Center for Environmental Law and Policy, director, 1994-, School of Forestry and Environmental Studies, associate dean, 1998-2002, Yale World Fellows Program, director, 2001-07, Center for Business and Environment, director, 2006-; INSEAD, visiting professor, 2000-01; Journal of International Economic Law, editor; TechTurn, board director; Resources for the Future, trustee. Writer. **Publications:** Greening the GATT: Trade, Environment and the Future, Washington: Institute for International Economics, 1994; (ed. with S. Tay) Asian Dragons and Green Trade: Environment, Economics and International Law, 1996; (with M. Chertow) Thinking Ecologically: The Next Generation of Environmental Policy, 1997; (with A. Dua) Sustaining the Asia-Pacific Miracle: Environmental Protection and Economic Integration, 1997; (ed. with D. Geradin) Regulatory Co-petition in Regulatory Competition and Economic Integration: Comparative Perspectives, 2001; (ed. with P. Cornelius) Environmental Performance Measurement: The Global Report 2001-2002, 2002; (ed. with C. Deere) Greening the Americas: NAFTA's Lessons for Hemispheric Trade, 2002; (ed. with M. Ivanova) Revitalizing Global Environmental Governance: A Function-Driven Approach in Global Environmental Governance: Options & Opportunities, 2002; (with A. Winston) Green to Gold: How Smart Companies Use Environmental Strategy to Innovate, Create Value and Build Competitive Advantage, 2006. **Address:** Center for Environmental Law and Policy, Yale University, 301 Prospect St., New Haven, CT 06511, U.S.A. **Online address:** daniel.esty@yale.edu

ETERAZ, Ali. Pakistani (born Pakistan), b. 1980?. **Genres:** Autobiography/Memoirs. **Career:** Writer. **Publications:** Children of Dust: A Memoir, 2009. **Online address:** ae@alieteraz.com

ETERNO, John A. American (born United States), b. 1959?. **Genres:** Law. **Career:** New York Police Department, career police officer, 1983-2004, captain, now retired; Molloy College, Department of Criminal Justice, assistant professor, 2003-, associate professor, professor, chairperson, associate dean and director of graduate studies. Writer and consultant. **Publications:** Policing Within the Law: A Case Study of the New York City Police Department, 2003; (ed. with D.K. Das) Police Practices in Global Perspective, 2010. Contributor to books and periodicals. **Address:** Department of Criminal Justice, Molloy College, S108 Siena Hall, 1000 Hempstead Ave., PO Box 5002, Rockville Centre, NY 11571-5002, U.S.A. **Online address:** jeterno@molloy.edu

ETHERIDGE, Eric. American (born United States), b. 1957?. **Genres:** Social Sciences, Photography, Writing/Journalism. **Career:** Nation, assistant editor; Harper, journalist; Seven Days, city editor, 1989; Rolling Stone, senior features editor and political editor, 1990-94; New York Observer, executive editor, 1994-95; George, executive editor, 1995-96; Microsoft Network, New York Sidewalk Online City Guide, executive producer, 1996-99; MSN Entertainment, producer, 1998-99; Deja News Inc., vice president of programming, 1999-. Photographer. **Publications:** (Ed. with E. Shorris) While Someone Else Is Eating: Poets and Novelists on Reaganism, 1984; (with L.H. Lapham and M. Pollan) The Harper's Index Book, 1987; Beach of Peace: Portraits of the 1961 Mississippi Freedom Riders, 2008. **Address:** Atlas Publishing LP, PO Box 9994, Fayetteville, NC 28311, U.S.A. **Online address:** eetheridge@gmail.com

ETINGER, Almog. See ALMOG, Ruth.

ETLIN, Richard A. (Richard Allan Etlin). American (born United States), b. 1947. **Genres:** Architecture, Art/Art History, Environmental Sciences/Ecology, Social Sciences, Cultural/Ethnic Topics. **Career:** University of Kentucky, assistant professor of architectural history, 1975-81; Architectural Arts of Washington, founder and president, 1980-86; University of Maryland, assistant professor, 1981-83, associate professor, 1983-89, professor of architectural history, 1989-2000, Department of Art History and Archeology, affiliate professor, 1996-2000, Restoring Ancient Stabiae, founding director, 1998-2001, distinguished university professor, 2000-, Castellammare di Stabia Urban Revitalization Project, director, 2001-03; Humanistic Perspectives on the Fine Art, director and teacher, 1986-88; Harvard University, landscape architecture, board of senior fellow, 1999-2005; American Academy in Rome, fellow. Writer. **Publications:** The Architecture of Death: The Transformation of the Cemetery in Eighteenth-Century Paris, 1984; Modernism in Italian Architecture, 1890-1940, 1991; Frank Lloyd Wright and Le Corbusier: The Romantic Legacy, 1994; Symbolic Space: French Enlightenment Architecture and its Legacy, 1994; In Defense of Humanism: Value in the Arts and Letters, 1996. EDITOR: Nationalism in the Visual Arts, 1991; Modern Architecture and Cultural Identity, 1994-; Art, Culture, and Media under the Third Reich, 2002. **Address:** School of Architecture, Planning & Preservation, University of Maryland, Rm. 1207, Bldg. 145, College Park, MD 20742-1411, U.S.A. **Online address:** retlin@umd.edu

ETLIN, Richard Allan. See ETLIN, Richard A.

ETTER, Dave. American (born United States), b. 1928. **Genres:** Poetry, Travel/Exploration. **Career:** Northwestern University Press, editor, 1961-63; Encyclopaedia Britannica, editor and writer, 1964-73; Northern Illinois University Press, editor, 1974-80; freelance writer and editor, 1980-. **Publications:** Go Read the River, 1966; The Last Train to Prophetstown, 1968; Strawberries, 1970; (with J. Knoepfle and L. Mueller) Voyages to the Inland Sea, 1971; Crabtree's Woman, 1972; Well, You Needn't: The Thelonious Monk Poems, 1975; Bright Mississippi, 1975, 2nd ed., 1983; Central Standard Time: New and Selected Poems, 1978; Alliance, Illinois, 1978, new ed., 2005; Open to the Wind, 1978; Riding the Rock Island through Kansas, 1979; Cornfields, 1980; West of Chicago, 1981; Boondocks, 1982; Home State: A Prose Poem, 1985; Live at the Silver Dollar, 1985; Selected Poems, 1987; Midlanders, 1988; Electric Avenue, 1988; Carnival, 1990; (comp.) Sunflower County, 1994; I Want to Talk about You, 1995; How High the Moon, 1996; Next Time You See Me, 1997; The Essential Dave Etter, 2001; Greatest Hits 1960-2000, 2002; Looking for Sheena Easton, 2004; Dandelions, 2010. Contributor to books and periodicals. **Address:** 628 E Locust St., Lanark, IL 61046-1130, U.S.A.

ETTLINGER, Steve. American (born United States) **Genres:** Food And Wine, How-to Books, Education. **Career:** Magnum Photos, assistant bureau chief; GEO Magazine, associate picture editor, photo editor; The New School, faculty; The School of Visual Arts, faculty; Fordham University, Graduate Program in Public Communication, faculty; author, editor and book producer, 1985-; American Book Producers Association, president; Huffington Post, contributor; Ettlinger Editorial Projects, president. **Publications:** (With T. Philbin) The Complete Illustrated Guide to Everything Sold in Hardware Stores, 1988; (and ed. as Stephen R. Ettlinger) The Complete Illustrated Guide to Everything Sold in Garden Centers, 1990; The Kitchenware Book, 1992; (with C.D. Gardephe) Don't Pick Up the Baby or You'll Spoil the Child and Other Old Wives' Tales about Pregnancy and Parenting, 1993; (with C. Ajootian and T. Gannon) The Complete Illustrated Guide to Everything Sold in Marine Supply Stores, 1995; (with M. Falick) The Restaurant Lover's Companion: A Handbook for Deciphering the Mysteries of Ethnic Menus, 1995; (with M. Nachel) Beer for Dummies, 1996; The Complete Illustrated Guide to Everything Sold in Hardware Stores and Garden Centers, 2002; The Hardware Cyclopedia, 2003; The Pocket Guide to Nuts and Bolts, 2006; Twinkie, Deconstructed: My Journey to Discover How the Ingredients Found in Processed Foods Are Grown, Mined (Yes, Mined) and Manipulated into What America Eats, 2007. Contributor to periodicals. **Address:** c/o Liz Keenan, Penguin Group, 375 Hudson St., New York, NY 10014, U.S.A. **Online address:** steve@steveettlinger.com

ETZIONI, Amitai. American/German (born Germany), b. 1929. **Genres:** Sociology, Institutions/Organizations, History. **Career:** Columbia University, instructor to professor, 1958-59, assistant professor, 1959-61, associate professor, 1961-67, professor, 1967-80, Institute of War and Peace Studies, research associate, 1961-71, Bureau of Applied Social Research, senior staff, 1961-70, associate director, 1969-70, Department of Sociology, chairman, 1969-71; American Sociological Review, associate editor, 1964-68; Sociological Abstracts, associate editor, 1968-71; Center for Policy Research, director, 1968-; White House, senior advisor, 1979-80; George Washington University, The Elliott School of International Affairs, university professor, 1980-, professor of international affairs, Institute for Communitarian Policy Studies, founder and director, 1990-, The Communitarian Network, director, 1990-; Harvard University, Graduate School of Business, Thomas Henry Carroll Ford Foundation, visiting professor, 1987-89; International Society for the Advancement of Socio-Economics, founder, 1989-90. **Publications:** A Diary of a Commando Soldier, 1951; A Comparative Analysis of Complex Organizations, 1961, rev. ed., 1975; (ed.) Complex Organizations: A Sociological Reader, 1961, 3rd ed., 1980; The Hard Way to Peace: A New Strategy, 1962; Winning Without War, 1964; Modern Organizations, 1964; The Moon-Doggie: Domestic and International Implications of the Space Race, 1964; (ed. with E. Etzioni) Social Change: Sources, Patterns and Consequences, 1964; Political Unification: A Comparative Study of Leaders and Forces, 1965; Studies in Social Change, 1966; (ed.) International Political Communities, 1966; Alternative Ways to Democracy; the Example of Israel, 1966; The Active Society: A Theory of Societal and Political Processes, 1968; (ed.) Readings on Modern Organizations, 1969; (ed.) The Semi-Professions and Their Organization: Teachers, Nurses, Social Workers, 1969; (ed. with S. Heidt) Societal Guidance: A New Approach to Social Problems, 1969; (with C.O. Atkinson and I. Tinker) Post-Secondary Education and the Disadvantaged: A Policy Study, 1969; (ed. with P. Ehrensaft) Anatomies of America: Sociological Perspectives, 1969; (ed. with F.L. Dubow) Comparative Perspectives: Theories and Methods, 1970; (ed. with M. Wenglinsky) War and Its Prevention, 1970; (ed. with J.S. Coleman and J. Porter and contrib.) Macrosociology: Research and Theory, 1970; The Self-guiding Society, Based on the Active Society, 1971; Demonstration Democracy, 1971; (with R. Remp) Technological Shortcuts to Social Change, 1972; Genetic Fix: New Opportunities and Dangers for You, Your Child and the Nation, Macmillan, 1973, rev. ed. as Genetic Fix: The Next Technological Revolution, 1975; Moral Leadership in Government, 1976; Social Problems, 1976; (ed.) Policy Research, 1978; The Organizational Structure of the Kibbutz, 1980; (co-author) Perspectives on Productivity: A Global View, 1981; An Immodest Agenda: Rebuilding America before the Twenty-first Century, 1983; Capital Corruption: An Assault on American Democracy, 1984; (with E. Gross) Organizations in Society, 1985; The Moral Dimension, 1988; (ed.) Socio-Economics: Towards a New Synthesis, 1990; A Responsive Society: Collected Essays on Guiding Deliberate Social Change, 1991; The Spirit of Community: Rights, Responsibilities, 1993; Public Policy in a New Key, 1993; (comp.) Rights and the Common Good: The Communitarian Perspective, 1995; (ed.) New Communitarian Thinking: Persons, Virtues, Institutions and Communities, 1995; Macro Socio-economics: From Theory to Activism, 1996; The New Golden Rule: Community and Morality in a Democratic Society, 1997; (ed. with D.E. Carney) Repentance: A Comparative Perspective, 1997; (ed.) The Essential Communitarian Reader, 1998; The Limits of Privacy, 1999; (ed.) Civic Repentance, 1999; Martin Buber und die Kommunitarische Idee, 1999; Essays in Socio-economics, 1999; Third Way to a Good Society, 2000; Next: The Road to the Good Society, 2001. Political Unification Revisited: On Building Supranational Communities, 2001; The Monochrome Society, 2001; My Brother's Keeper: A Memoir and a Message, 2003; (ed. with D. Doherty) Voluntary Simplicity, 2003; (ed. with J.H. Marsh) Rights vs. Public Safety After 9/11, 2003; From Empire to Community: A New Approach to International Relations 2004; The Common Good, 2004; (ed. with J. Bloom) We Are What We Celebrate, 2004; (ed. with A. Volmert and E. Rothschild) The Communitarian Reader, 2004; How Patriotic is the Patriot Act?, 2004; (ed. with A. Bowditch) Public Intellectuals: An Endangered Species?, 2006; Security First: For a Muscular, Moral Foreign Policy, 2007; New Common Ground, 2009. Contributor to books, newspapers and journals. **Address:** Institute for Communitarian Policy Studies, Rm. 413, 1922 F St. NW, Washington, DC 20052-0042, U.S.A. **Online address:** etzioni@gwu.edu

EUBA, Femi. American/British/Nigerian (born Nigeria), b. 1942. **Genres:** Novels, Plays/Screenplays, Theatre, Novellas/Short Stories, Humanities, Third World, inspirational/Motivational Literature. **Career:** Ethel Walker School, researcher, 1973-75; University of Ibadan, lecturer, 1975-76; University of Ife, lecturer, 1976-80, senior lecturer, 1982-86; College of William and Mary, visiting professor, 1986-88; Louisiana State University, assistant professor, 1988-91, associate professor, 1991-96, professor, 1996-, Louise and Kenneth Kinney professor. Writer. **Publications:** Game, 1970; A Riddle of the Palms and Crocodiles, 1973; Archetypes, Imprecators and Victims of Fate: Origins and Developments of Satire in Black Drama, 1989; The Gulf: A Play in Two Parts, 1991; The Eye of Gabriel, a Full-Length Play, 2002; Dionysus of the Holocaust, a Play in Three Movements, 2003; Poetics of the Creative Process: An Organic Practicum to Playwriting, 2005. NOVEL: Camwood at Crossroads, 2007. Works appear in anthologies. Contributor to periodicals. **Address:** PO Box 1989, Baton Rouge, LA 70821, U.S.A. **Online address:** theuba@lsu.edu

EUCHNER, Charles C. American (born United States), b. 1960. **Genres:** Writing/Journalism, Urban Studies, Politics/Government, Communications/ Media. **Career:** Education Week, staff writer, 1982-84; Johns Hopkins University, teaching and research assistant, 1985-87; St. Mary's College of Maryland, instructor, 1989-90; College of the Holy Cross, assistant professor of political science, 1990-97; Boston Redevelopment Authority, director and coordinator, 1997-2000; Northeastern University, Center for Urban and Regional Policy, associate director, 1999-2000; Harvard University, John F. Kennedy School of Government, Rappaport Institute for Greater Boston, executive director, 2000-04; writer, 2004-; Yale University, Department of English, lecturer, 2007-10; The Writing Code, creator and principal, 2010-. **Publications:** (With J. Brinkman) The Umpire's Handbook, 1985, rev. ed., 1987; (with J.A. Maltese) Selecting the President: From Washington to Bush, 1991; Playing the Field: Why Sports Teams Move and Cities Fight to Keep Them, 1993; Extraordinary Politics: How Protest and Dissent Are Changing American Democracy, 1996; (ed. and contrib.) Governing Greater Boston: The Politics and Policy of Place, 2002; (ed. and contrib.) Governing Greater Boston: Serving the Needs of the Region's People, 2003; (with S.J. McGovern) Urban Policy Reconsidered: Dialogues on the Problems and Prospects of American Cities, 2003; The Last Nine Innings, 2006; Little League, Big Dreams: The Hope, The Hype and The Glory of the Greatest World Series Ever Played, 2006; Nobody Turn Me Around: A People's History of the 1963 March on Washington, 2010; The ABC's of Writing: A Practical Guide For Building Stories and Arguments, forthcoming. **Address:** Beacon Press, 25 Beacon St., Boston, MA 02108, U.S.A.

EUGENIDES, Jeffrey. American (born United States), b. 1960. **Genres:** Novels. **Career:** Princeton University, faculty, 2007, Peter B. Lewis Center for the Arts, professor of creative writing. Writer. **Publications:** NOVELS: The Virgin Suicides, 1993; Middlesex, 2002; The Marriage Plot, 2011. SHORT STORIES: Air Mail, 1997; The Speed of Sperm, 1997; Timeshare, 1999; Baster, 2000; The Ancient Myths, 2001; Early Music, 2005. OTHERS: PissIng Ink: 80 Pages from the Miriam Books, 2004; Thomas Demand, 2005; (intro.) Humboldt's Gift, 2008; (ed.) My Mistress's Sparrow is Dead, 2008. Contributor to periodicals. **Address:** Peter B. Lewis Center for the Arts, Princeton University, 185 Nassau St., Princeton, NJ 08544, U.S.A. **Online address:** jeugenid@princeton.edu

EUGSTER, Sandra Lee. American (born United States) **Genres:** Autobiography/Memoirs, Biography. **Career:** Independent Psychology Alliance, clinical psychologist. Writer. **Publications:** Notes from Nethers, 2007. **Address:** 313 Price Pl., Ste. 113, Madison, WI 53705, U.S.A. **Online address:** contact@independentpsych.com

EULA, Michael J(ames). American (born United States), b. 1957. **Genres:** History, Social Sciences, Law. **Career:** University of California, teaching assistant, associate, 1983-87, visiting assistant professor, 1991; California State University, visiting lecturer in history, 1988-89; Chapman University, visiting associate professor history and criminal justice, 1988-2002; El Camino College, instructor of history and American studies, 1989-91, assistant professor of history and American studies, 1991-95, associate professor of history and American studies, 1995-98, professor of history and American studies, 1998-2012, emeritus professor of history, 2012-; Riverside County, administrative law judge, 1999-; American College of Law, lecturer, 2000-01; St. Thomas University, School of Law, adjunct lecturer, 2002, lecturer in law, 2003. **Publications:** (Ed. and contrib. with A.J. Wrobel) American Ethnics and Minorities: Readings in Ethnic History, 1990; Between Peasant and Urban Villager: Italian-Americans of New Jersey and New York, 1880-1980: The Structures of Counter-Discourse, 1993. Contributor of articles to books and journals. **Address:** Department of History, El Camino College, 16007 Crenshaw Blvd., Torrance, CA 90506, U.S.A. **Online address:** meula@elcamino.edu

EVANGELISTI, Silvia. British/Italian (born Italy) **Genres:** Theology/Religion, Art/Art History, History, Cultural/Ethnic Topics. **Career:** University of East Anglia, lecturer in history. Writer. **Publications:** (With R. Barilli and B. Passamani) Romolo Romani, 1982; (with P. Marescalchi and M. Pinottini) Silvia Evangelisti, Fillia ELavanguardia Futurista Negli Anni del Fascismo, 1986; (ed. with C. Pozzati) Disegnata: Percorsi del Disegno Italiano dal 1945 ad Oggi, 1987; (ed.) Mario Pozzati, 1888-1947, 1987; (co-ed.) L Accademia di Bologna: Figure del Novecento: Bologna, Accademia di Belle Arti, 5 Settembre-10 Novembre 1988, 1988; (ed.) La Pinacoteca Civica di Pieve di Cento: Collezioni Comunali Del Novecento: Catalogo Generale, 1989; (ed.) Aldo Bandinelli (1897-1977), 1989; (with M. Corgnati and C. Cerritelli) Bargoni, Guarneri, Satta, 1991; (with P.G. Castagnoli and F. Gualdoni) Concetto

Pozzati: Antologica, 1991; Concetto Pozzati, 1993; Italiens de Paris: Campigli, De Chirico, De Pisis, Savinio, Tozzi, Severini, Magnelli, 1994; Nuns: A History of Convent Life, 1450-1700, 2007; (ed. with S. Cavallo) Domestic Institutional Interiors in Early Modern Europe, 2009; (ed. with S. Cavello) Faith and Religion in The Cultural History of Childhood and the Family, 2010. **Address:** University of East Anglia, 4.22 Arts Bldg., Norwich Research Pk., Norwich, NF NR4 7TJ, England. **Online address:** s.evangelisti@uea.ac.uk

EVANOVICH, Janet. (Steffie Hall). American (born United States), b. 1943. **Genres:** Mystery/Crime/Suspense, Romance/Historical, Novels. **Career:** Writer. **Publications:** DETECTIVE NOVELS STEPHANIE PLUM SERIES: One for the Money, 1994; Two for the Dough, 1996; Three to Get Deadly, 1997; Four to Score, 1998; High Five, 1999; Hot Six, 2000; Seven Up, 2001; Hard Eight, 2002; Visions of Sugar Plums, 2002; To the Nines, 2003; Ten Big Ones, 2004; Eleven on Top, 2005; Love Overboard, 2005; Twelve Sharp, 2006; Lean Mean Thirteen, 2007; (with S.J. Cannell) No Chance, 2007; Fearless Fourteen, 2008; Finger Lickin' Fifteen, 2009; Between the Plums, 2009; Sizzling Sixteen, 2010; Wicked Appetite, 2010; Smokin' Seventeen, 2011; Explosive Eighteen, 2011. ROMANCE NOVELS: The Grand Finale, 1988; Thanksgiving, 1988; Manhunt, 1988; Ivan Takes a Wife, 1989; Back to the Bedroom, 1989; Wife for Hire, 1990; Smitten, 1990; The Rocky Road to Romance, 1991; Naughty Neighbor, 1992; (with D. Kelly) Love in a Nutshell, 2012. METRO GIRL SERIES: Metro Girl, 2004. NOVELS AS STEFFI HALL: Hero at Large, 1987; Full House, 1989; Foul Play, 1989. NON-FICTION: (with I. Yalof) How I Write: Secrets of a Serial Fiction Writer, 2006. (with C. Hughes) MAX HOLT SERIES: Full Tilt, 2002; Full Speed, 2003; Full Blast, 2004; Full Bloom, 2005; Full Scoop, 2006. STEPHANIE PLUM BETWEEN-THE-NUMBERS NOVELS: Visions of Sugar Plums, 2002; Plum Lovin', 2007; Plum Lucky, 2008; Plum Spooky, 2009. ALEXANDRA BARNABY SERIES: Metro Girl, 2004; Motor Mouth, 2006; (with A. Evanovich and J. Jones) Troublemaker, 2010. CATE MADIGAN SERIES: (with L. Banks) Hot Stuff, 2007. **Address:** PO Box 2829, Naples, FL 34106, U.S.A. **Online address:** janet@evanovich.com

EVANS, Alan. British (born England), b. 1930. **Genres:** Novels, Children's Fiction, Young Adult Fiction. **Career:** Civil servant, 1951-; executive officer. Writer. **Publications:** The End of the Running, 1966; Mantrap, 1967; Bannon, 1968; Vicious Circle, 1970; The Big Deal, 1971; Running Scared (juvenile), 1975; Kidnap! (juvenile), 1977; Escape at the Devil's Gate (juvenile), 1978; Thunder at Dawn, 1978; Deed of Glory, 1984; Seek and Destroy, 1984 Dauntless, 1985; Ship of Force, 1986; Seek Out and Destroy, 1986; Audacity, 1987; Eagle at Taranto, 1987; Night Action, 1989; Orphans of the Storm, 1990; Sink or Capture, 1993; Sword at Sunrise, 1994. **Address:** c/o Murray Pollinger, 4 Garrick St., London, GL WC2E 9BH, England.

EVANS, Arthur V. American (born United States), b. 1956?. **Genres:** Natural History, Environmental Sciences/Ecology. **Career:** Natural History Museum, Insect Zoo, director, through 2000; Department of Conservation and Recreation, Virginia Natural Heritage Program, staff, through 2008; Smithsonian Institution, research associate; Virginia Museum of Natural History, research associate; National Public Radio, What's Bugging You? A Fond Look at the Animals We Love to Hate (radio show), host. Writer. **Publications:** (With C.L. Bellamy) An Inordinate Fondness for Beetles, 1996; (with J.N. Hogue) Introduction to California Beetles, 2004; Grzimek's Student Animal Life Resource: Insects and Spiders, 2005; Grzimek's Student Animal Life Resource: Crustaceans, Mollusks, and Segmented Worms, 2005; (with J.N. Hogue) Field Guide to Beetles of California, 2006; National Wildlife Federation Field Guide to Insects and Spiders & Related Species of North America, 2007; What's Bugging You? A Fond Look at the Animals We Love to Hate, 2008. Contributor of articles to journals. **Address:** Richmond, VA , U.S.A. **Online address:** arthurevans@verizon.net

EVANS, Ben. British (born England), b. 1976. **Genres:** Sciences, Astronomy, Technology. **Career:** Writer and educator. **Publications:** (With D.M. Harland) NASA's Voyager Missions: Exploring the Outer Solar System and Beyond, 2004; Space Shuttle Columbia: Her Missions and Crews, 2005; Space Shuttle Challenger: Ten Journeys into the Unknown, 2007; Escaping the Bonds of Earth: The Fifties and the Sixties, 2009. Contributor to periodicals. **Address:** Author Mail Springer, 233 Spring St., New York, NY 10013, U.S.A.

EVANS, Brendan. British (born England), b. 1944. **Genres:** Education, Politics/Government, History. **Career:** University of Huddersfield, School of Music and Humanities, dean, Academic Affairs, pro vice-chancellor, 1997-2007, now professor emeritus. Writer. **Publications:** Radical Adult Education: A Political Critique, 1987; The Politics of the Training Market: From Manpower Services Commission to Training and Enterprise Councils, 1992; From Salisbury to Major: Continuity and Change in Conservative Politics, 1996; Thatcherism and British Politics, 2000; (co-author) Sons and Daughters of Labour: A History and Recollection of the Labour Party Within the Historic Boundaries of the West Riding of Yorkshire, 2007. **Address:** Human and Health Sciences, University of Huddersfield, Queensgate, HHRG/03, Huddersfield, WY HD1 3DH, England. **Online address:** b.j.evans@hud.ac.uk

EVANS, Calvin (Donald). Canadian (born Canada), b. 1931. **Genres:** History, Bibliography, Philosophy. **Career:** Halifax Citadel Museum, secretary, 1954; United Church of Canada, minister, 1955-66; Memorial University of Newfoundland, cataloger, 1967-68, head of periodicals division at university library, 1968-73; University of Guelph, head of humanities and social sciences at university library, 1973-79; University of Alberta, assistant librarian for public services, 1979-83, assistant librarian for planning and personnel, 1983-84; McGill University, area librarian at Humanities and Social Sciences Library, 1984-93, branch services coordinator, 1993-. Writer. **Publications:** For Love of a Woman: The Evans Family and a Perspective on Shipbuilding in Newfoundland, 1992; Soren Kierkegaard Bibliographies: Remnants, 1944-1980 and the Multimedia, 1925-1991, 1993. Contributor to journals. **Address:** 13 Marine Dr., PO Box 569, Botwood, NL A0H 1E0, Canada.

EVANS, C. Wyatt. American (born United States) **Genres:** Biography, Autobiography/Memoirs, Military/Defense/Arms Control. **Career:** Drew University, Department of History, assistant professor, associate professor, Caspersen School of Graduate Studies, director of history and culture program; OAH Distinguished Lectureship Program, distinguished lecturer; Drew Review, faculty co-advisor, 2009-. Writer. **Publications:** The Legend of John Wilkes Booth: Myth, Memory, and a Mummy, 2004. Contributor to periodicals. **Address:** Department of History, Drew University, 21 Gilbert House, 36 Madison Ave., Madison, NJ 07940-1434, U.S.A. **Online address:** wevans@drew.edu

EVANS, Danny. American (born United States), b. 1957. **Genres:** Autobiography/Memoirs. **Career:** Sirius Satellite Radio, commentator; National Public Radio, commentator; SXSW 2007, commentator. Journalist. **Publications:** Rage against the Meshugenah: Why It Takes Balls to Go Nuts: A Memoir, 2009. Contributor to periodicals. **Address:** c/o Karen Gerwin, The Creative Culture, 47 E 19th St., 3rd Fl., New York, NY 10003, U.S.A. **Online address:** danny@dannyevansbooks.com

EVANS, D(avid) Ellis. British/Welsh (born Wales), b. 1930. **Genres:** Archaeology/Antiquities, Classics, Language/Linguistics, Literary Criticism And History, Essays. **Career:** University of Wales, University College of Swansea, assistant lecturer, 1957-60, lecturer, 1961-68, reader, 1968-74, professor of Welsh, 1974-78; The Bulletin of the Board of Celtic Studies, Language and Literature Section, editor, 1972-88, chief editor, 1989-93; University of Oxford, Jesus College, Jesus professor of Celtic, 1978-96, honorary fellow, 1996-, now professor emeritus; Studia Celtica, chief editor, 1994-95. **Publications:** Gaulish Personal Names: A Study of Some Continental Celtic Formations, 1967; (ed.) Cofiant Agricola, lywodraethwr Prydain, 1974; Gorchest y Celtiaid yn yr Hen Fyd: Darlith Agoriadol Athro'r Gymraeg a Draddodwyd yny Coleg ar Fawrth 4, 1975, 1975; The Labyrinth of Continental Celtic, 1981; Dursley and Cam, 1981; (ed. with J.G. Griffith and E.M. Jope) Proceedings of the Seventh International Congress of Celtic Studies Held at Oxford, from 10th to 15th July, 1983, 1986; (with R.B. Jones) Cofio'r Dafydd: Cymdeithas Dafydd ap Gwilym, 1886-1986, 1987; (contrib.) Hispano-Gallo-Brittonica: Essays in Honour of Professor D. Ellis Evans on the Occasion of His Sixty-Fifth Birthday, 1995. Contributor to journals. **Address:** University of Oxford, Jesus College, Turl St., Oxford, GL OX1 3DW, England.

EVANS, Douglas. American (born United States), b. 1953. **Genres:** Children's Fiction, Education, Novels. **Career:** Teacher, 1976-83; International School of Helsinki, teacher, 1983-84; American School of London, teacher of second grade, 1984-85; Orinda School District, teacher of second grade, 1987-97; full-time writer, 1998-. **Publications:** Classroom at the End of the Hall, 1996; So What Do You Do?, 1997; Apple Island, Or, The Truth about Teachers, 1998; Tales from W.T. Melon Elementary School, 1999; The Elevator Family, 2000; Math Rashes and Other Classroom Tales, 2000; Sylvia's

Garage, 2001; MVP: Magellan Voyage Project, 2004; Mouth Moths: More Classroom Tales, 2006. Contributor to magazines. **Address:** c/o George Nicholson, Sterling Lord Literistic Inc., 65 Bleecker St., New York, NY 10012, U.S.A. **Online address:** mvp@wtmelon.com

EVANS, Earlene Green. American (born United States), b. 1938. **Genres:** Education, Reference, Humor/Satire, History. **Career:** Elementary school teacher, 1964-74; library media specialist, 1974-97; Virginia State Senate, assistant page supervisor, 1998-99; auditor of testing standards for state of Virginia, 1999-; notary public. Writer. **Publications:** WITH M.M. BRANCH: (comp.) Hidden Skeletons and Other Funny Stories, 1995; A Step Beyond: Multimedia Activities for Learning American History, 1995; 3-D Displays for Libraries, Schools and Media Centers, 2000. Contributor to periodicals and newspapers. **Address:** 9024 Kinsale Cir., PO 15121, Richmond, VA 23228-2231, U.S.A. **Online address:** neenie59@aol.com

EVANS, Eric J(ohn). British (born England), b. 1945. **Genres:** History, Theology/Religion, Biography. **Career:** University of Stirling, lecturer in history, 1969-70; University of Lancaster, lecturer, 1971-80, senior lecturer, 1980-84, reader in modern British history, 1984-85, professor of social history, 1985-2005, professor emeritus, 2005-; Lancaster Pamphlets, joint editor, 1983-; Making of the Contemporary World, Routledge, joint editor, 1994-; Longman Advanced History, 1995-; Social History Society, chairman, 1991-98. **Publications:** Tillicountry: A Centenary History 1871-1971, 1971; The Contentious Tithe: The Tithe Problem and English Agriculture, 1976; (ed.) Social Policy, 1830-1914, 1978; (with J. Richards) A Social History of Britain in Postcards 1870-1930, 1980; The Forging of the Modern State: Early Industrial Britain, 1783-1870, 1983, 3rd ed., 2001; The Great Reform Act of 1832, 1983, 2nd ed., 1994; Political Parties in Britain 1783-1867, 1985; Britain Before the Reform Act: Politics and Society 1815-32, 1989, 2nd ed., 2008; (ed. with P. Summerfield) Technical Education and the State Since 1850: Historical and Contemporary Perspectives, 1990; Liberal Democracies, 1990; Sir Robert Peel: Statesmanship, Power and Party, 1991, 2nd ed., 2006; The Birth of Modern Britain, 1780-1914, 1997; Thatcher and Thatcherism, 1997, 2nd ed., 2004; (with A.G. Crosby) Tithes: Maps, Apportionments, and the 1836 Act: A Guide for Local Historians, 1997; William Pitt the Younger, 1999; Parliamentary Reform in Britain, c. 1770-1918, 1999; Shaping of Modern Britain: Identity, Industry and Empire, 1780-1914, 2011. **Address:** Department of History, University of Lancaster, Furness, B56, Bailrigg, Lancaster, LC LA1 4YG, England. **Online address:** e.evans@lancaster.ac.uk

EVANS, Frances Monet Carter. *See* **CARTER, Frances Monet.**

EVANS, Gareth John. Australian (born Australia), b. 1944. **Genres:** Politics/Government, Law, History. **Career:** Australian minister for foreign affairs and trade, 1988-96; Victoria senator, 1978-96; Australian Parliament, attorney general, 1983-84, minister for resources and energy, 1984-87, minister for transport and communications, 1987-88, foreign minister, 1988-96; Government of Canada, Intl. Commission on Intervention and State Sovereignty, co-chair, 2000-01; Intl. Crisis Group, president and chief executive officer, 2000-09, president emeritus, 2009-; Intl. Commission on Nuclear Nonproliferation and Disarmament, co-chair, 2008-; University of Melbourne, honorary professorial fellow, 2009-; Weapons of Mass Destruction Commission, commissioner. Writer, attorney and administrator. **Publications:** (Ed.) Labor and the Constitution, 1972-1975: Essays and Commentaries on the Constitutional Controversies of the Whitlam Years in Australian Government, 1977; (ed.) Law, Politics, and the Labor Movement, 1980; The Politics of Justice, 1981; (with J. McMillan and H. Storey) Australia's Constitution: Time for Change?, 1983; (with B. Grant) Australia's Foreign Relations in the World of the 1990s, 1991, 2nd ed., 1995; Cooperating for Peace: The Global Agenda for the 1990's and Beyond, 1993; (contrib.) Building International Community: Cooperating for Peace: Case Studies, 1994; The Responsibility to Protect: Ending Mass Atrocity Crimes Once and for All, 2008. FOREWORD: A Crisis of Expectations: UN Peacekeeping in the 1990s, 1995; The United Nations as a Dispute Settlement System, 1996; God, Oil and Country: Changing the Logic of War in Sudan, 2002; Bread and Stones: Leadership and the Struggle to Reform the United Nations World Food Programme, 2006; The United Nations, Peace, and Security, 2006; Humanitarian Intervention: War and Conflict in the Modern World, 2007; North Korea on the Brink: Struggle for Survival, 2008. CO-AUTHOR: Criminal Investigation: Report of the Australian Law Reform Commission, 1975; Preventing Deadly Conflict: Final Report of the Carnegie Commission on Preventing Deadly Conflict, 1997; The Responsibility to Protect: Report of the International Commission on Intervention and

State Sovereignty, 2001; A More Secure World: Our Shared Responsibility: Report of the Secretary-General's High Level Panel on Threats, Challenges, and Change, 2004; Weapons of Terror: Freeing the World of Nuclear, Biological, and Chemical Arms: Report of the Weapons of Mass Destruction Commission, 2006; Meeting Global Challenges: International Cooperation in the National Interest: Report of the International Task Force on Global Public Goods, 2006. Contributor to books. **Address:** International Commission on Nuclear, Nonproliferation and Disarmament, R.G. Casey Bldg., John McEwen Cres., Barton, AC 0221, Australia. **Online address:** ge@gevans.org

EVANS, Gary P. American (born United States), b. 1942. **Genres:** Music, Art/Art History. **Career:** Ferrum College, professor of music, 1978-, now retired. Writer. **Publications:** Music Inspired by Art: A Guide to Recordings, 2002. **Address:** 226 Arthur Cir., Ferrum, VA 24088-2505, U.S.A. **Online address:** gevans@ferrum.edu

EVANS, Greg. American (born United States), b. 1947. **Genres:** Cartoons, Humor/Satire, Children's Fiction, Illustrations, Graphic Novels. **Career:** Teacher, 1970-74. Writer. **Publications:** SELF-ILLUSTRATED: Meet Luann, 1986; Why Me?, 1986; Is It Friday Yet?, 1987; Who Invented Brothers Anyway?, 1989; School and Other Problems, 1989; Homework Is Ruining My Life, 1989; So Many Malls, So Little Money, 1990; Pizza Isn't Everything but It Comes Close, 1991; Dear Diary: The Following Is Top Secret, 1991; Will We Be Tested on This?, 1992; There's Nothing Worse than First Period P.E., 1992; If Confusion Were a Class I'd Get an A, 1992; School's OK if You Can Stand the Food, 1992; I'm Not Always Confused, I Just Look that Way, 1993; My Bedroom and Other Environmental Hazards, 1993; Sometimes, You Just Have to Make Your Own Rules, 1998; Luann-The Plunge, 1998; Passion! Betrayal! Outrage! Revenge!, 1999; Luann, Curves Ahead, 2003; Luann 2: Dates and Other Disasters, 2004; Luann 3: Sixteen Isn't Pretty, 2006; Luann 4: Seriously..., 2008. Contributor to books and periodicals. **Address:** United Media, 200 Madison Ave., New York, NY 10016, U.S.A. **Online address:** gregevans@gregevans.com.au

EVANS, Helen C. American (born United States) **Genres:** History, Essays, Art/Art History. **Career:** Metropolitan Museum of Art, curator of early Christian and Byzantine art. Writer. **Publications:** (Ed. with W.D. Wixom) The Glory of Byzantium: Art and Culture of the Middle Byzantine Era, A.D. 843-1261, 1997; (ed.) Byzantium: Faith and Power (1261-1557), 2004; Saint Catherine's Monastery, Sinai, Egypt: A Photographic Essay, 2004; (ed. with J.D. Alchermes and T.K. Thomas) Anathemata Heortika: Studies in Honor of Thomas F. Mathews, 2009. Contributor to periodicals. **Address:** Metropolitan Museum of Art, 1000 5th Ave., New York, NY 10028-0198, U.S.A.

EVANS, James Allan S. Canadian (born Canada), b. 1931. **Genres:** Classics, History, Writing/Journalism. **Career:** University of Western Ontario, Waterloo College, assistant professor of classics, 1955-60; University of Texas, assistant professor of classics, 1961-62; University of Toronto, visiting special lecturer, 1960-61; McMaster University, professor of history, 1962-72; University of British Columbia, professor of classics, 1972-96, head of department, 1986-93, post-doctoral fellow, professor emeritus, 1996-; Vergilius, editor, 1963-73; Commentator, literary editor, 1967-71; Studies in Medieval and Renaissance History, editor, 1978-; Association of Ancient Historians Newsletters, secretary and treasurer, 1979-82; University of Washington, visiting professor of history, 1997; American School of Classical Studies, Whitehead visiting professor, 1998-99; Thomas Day Seymour fellow; Simon Fraser University, visiting faculty, 1998; Yale University, Martin Kellogg fellow. **Publications:** Social and Economic History of an Egyptian Temple in Greco-Roman Egypt, 1961; Procopius, 1972; (ed.) Polis and Imperium: Studies in Honour of Edward Togo Salmon, 1974; Herodotus, 1982; Herodotus, Explorer of the Past: Three Essays, 1991; The Age of Justinian: The Circumstances of Imperial Power, 1996; The Empress Theodora, 2002; The Power Game in Byzantium, 2003; Arts and Humanities through the Eras: Ancient Greece and Rome, 2004; The Emperor Justinian and the Byzantine Empire, 2005; The Beginnings of History: Herodotus and the Persian Wars, 2006; Daily Life in the Hellenistic Age: From Alexander to Cleopatra, 2008; Power Game in Byzantium: Antonina and the Empress Theodora, 2011. **Address:** Department of Classical Studies, University of British Columbia, Rm. EOS-Main 313H, Vancouver, BC V6T 1W5, Canada. **Online address:** jevans@eos.ubc.ca

EVANS, James H. American (born United States), b. 1950?. **Genres:** Literary Criticism And History, Theology/Religion, Social Sciences. **Career:** Ordained Baptist minister, 1973; Southern Connecticut State College, student chaplain, 1974-75; Baptist church, associate pastor, 1975-79; Colgate Rochester Divinity School/Bexley Hall/Crozer Theological Seminary, lecturer, 1979, assistant professor, 1980-84, associate professor of theology and black church studies and Martin Luther King, Jr., Memorial Professor of Theology and Black Studies, 1984-88, Robert K. Davies Professor of Systematic Theology, Black Church Studies and Alternate Education Program, acting director, 1982, dean of black church studies, 1989, Ayer Lecturer, 1989, president, 1990-; Malcolm-King College, faculty, 1977; University of Rochester, adjunct assistant professor, 1983, visiting associate professor, 1988, adjunct associate professor, 1989-90; Princeton Theological Seminary, visiting professor, 1984-85; Colgate University, university professor of the humanities in philosophy and religion, 1990; Eastern Baptist Theological Seminary, Frank B. Mitchell Lecturer, 1991-; University of New Haven, Afro-American Historical Society, research assistant, 1975; St. Luke Tabernacle Community Church, founding pastor. Writer. **Publications:** Spiritual Empowerment in Afro-American Literature: Frederick Douglass, Booker T. Washington, Rebecca Jackson, Richard Wright, Toni Morrison, 1987; Black Theology: A Critical Assessment and Annotated Bibliography, 1987; We Have Been Believers: Faith, Freedom and Black Theology, 1992; We Have Been Believers: An African-American Systematic Theology, 1992, 2nd ed., 2012; We Shall all be Changed: Social Problems and Theological Renewal, 1997; Playing, 2010. Works appear in anthologies. Contributor of articles to journals. **Address:** Colgate Rochester Divinity School, Bexley Hall/Crozer Theological Seminary, 1100 S Goodman St., Rochester, NY 14620, U.S.A. **Online address:** jevansjr@rochester.rr.com

EVANS, Jimmie Ruth. See JAMES, (Darryl) Dean.

EVANS, Jon. Canadian (born Canada), b. 1973?. **Genres:** Graphic Novels, Novels, Science Fiction/Fantasy. **Career:** Writer. **Publications:** Dark Places, 2004 in UK as Trail of the Dead, 2004; The Blood Price, 2005; Invisible Armies, 2007; The Executor, 2010; Beasts of New York: A Children's Book for Grownups, 2011. **Address:** c/o Deborah Schneider, Gelfman Schneider Literary Agents Inc., 250 W 57th St., Ste. 2122, New York, NY 10107-2506, U.S.A. **Online address:** jon@rezendi.com

EVANS, Jonathan. See FREEMANTLE, Brian (Harry).

EVANS, Justin. American (born United States), b. 1971?. **Genres:** Novels, Ghost Writer, Mystery/Crime/Suspense, Romance/Historical. **Career:** New York Times, staff of advertising group, business strategist; The Nielsen Co., business strategist; The Pluck Corp., strategy executive. Writer. **Publications:** A Good and Happy Child, 2007; The White Devil, 2011. **Address:** c/o Diane Bartoli, Artists Literary Group, 27 W 20th St., 10th Fl., New York, NY 10011, U.S.A. **Online address:** justin@justinevans.com

EVANS, Liz. (Patricia Grey). British (born England) **Genres:** Novels, Mystery/Crime/Suspense, Young Adult Fiction, Horror. **Career:** BBC Radio, staff. Writer. **Publications:** NOVELS AS PATRICIA GREY: Balaclava Row, 1994; Junction Cut, 1994; Good Hope Station, 1997; Cutter's Wharf, 1998. GRACE SMITH MYSTERY SERIES: Who Killed Marilyn Monroe?, 1997; JFK Is Missing!, 1998; Don't Mess with Mrs. In-Between, 2000; Barking!, 2001; Sick As a Parrot, 2004; Cue the Easter Bunny, 2005. Works appear in anthologies. **Address:** c/o Author Mail, Orion Publishing Group, Orion House, 5 Upper Saint Martin's Ln., London, GL WC2H 9EA, England. **Online address:** feedback@Lizevans.net

EVANS, Martin. British (born England), b. 1964. **Genres:** Literary Criticism And History, Cultural/Ethnic Topics. **Career:** University of Portsmouth, professor of contemporary European history; British Academy, researcher. Writer. **Publications:** (Ed.) War and Memory in the Twentieth Century, 1997; (ed.) The Algerian War and the French Army: Experiences, Images, Testimonies, 2002; (ed.) Empire and Culture: The French Experience, 1830-1940, 2004; (with E. Godin) France, 1815-2003: Modern History for Modern Languages, 2004; (with J. Phillips) Algeria: Anger of the Dispossessed, 2007; Mémoires de la guerre d'Algérie, 2007; Algeria: The Undeclared War, 2011. **Address:** School of Languages and Area Studies, University of Portsmouth, Park Bldg., King Henry 1st St., Portsmouth, HM PO1 2DZ, England. **Online address:** martin.evans@port.ac.uk

EVANS, Mary Anna. American (born United States), b. 1961. **Genres:** Mystery/Crime/Suspense, Novels. **Career:** Writer, consultant, administrator and educator. **Publications:** Artifacts, 2003; Relics, 2005; Effigies, 2007; Findings, 2008; Floodgates, 2009; Strangers, 2010; Wounded Earth, 2011; (with F. Wallace) Mathematical Literacy in the Middle and Secondary Grades, 2011; Plunder, 2012. **Address:** 8321 SW 23rd Pl., Gainesville, FL 32607, U.S.A. **Online address:** maryannaevans@yahoo.com

EVANS, Michael. See EVANS, Mike.

EVANS, Michael Robert. American/German (born Germany), b. 1959?. **Genres:** Novels, Art/Art History. **Career:** Indiana University, Department of Journalism, associate professor of journalism and associate lecturer. Writer. **Publications:** The Layers of Magazine Editing, 2004; 68 Knots (novel), 2007; Isuma: Inuit Video Art, 2008; The Fast Runner: Filming the Legend of Atanarjuat, 2010. Contributor to books, periodicals and magazines. **Address:** c/o Rebecca Grose, SoCal Public Relations, 8130 La Mesa Blvd., Ste. 137, La Mesa, CA 91942, U.S.A.

EVANS, Mike. (Michael Evans). American (born United States), b. 1947. **Genres:** History, Novels, Politics/Government, Theology/Religion. **Career:** Jerusalem Prayer Team, founder. Christian evangelist and writer. **Publications:** Young Lions of Judah, 1974; Israel-Americas Key to Survival, 1981; Jerusalem D.C., 1984; The Return, 1986; Jerusalem Betrayed: Ancient Prophecy and Modern Conspiracy Collide in the Holy City, 1997; Religious Leaders of America, ed., 1999; The Jerusalem Scroll, 1999; Why Christians Should Support Israel, 2003; The Unanswered Prayers of Jesus, 2003; The Prayer of David: In Times of Trouble, 2003; God-wrestling: Like Jacob of Old, A Life-Changing Encounter with the Almighty, 2004; The American Prophecies: Ancient Scriptures Reveal Our Nation's Future, 2004; (with J.R. Corsi) Showdown with Nuclear Iran: Radical Islam's Messianic Mission to Destroy Israel and Cripple the United States, 2006; The Final Move Beyond Iraq, 2007. **Address:** PO Box 30000, Phoenix, AZ 85046, U.S.A. **Online address:** memi@jpteam.org

EVANS, Ray. See GILL, Anton.

EVANS, Richard. British (born England), b. 1964. **Genres:** Science Fiction/Fantasy, Novellas/Short Stories, Young Adult Fiction. **Career:** Freelance writer, 1995-. Science fiction novelist and musician. **Publications:** Machine Nation, 2002; Robophobia, 2004; Exilium, 2008. SHORT STORIES: (contrib.) Perverted by Language; Paint a Vulgar Picture, forthcoming. Contributor to periodicals. **Address:** c/o Author Mail, Writers Club Press, 5220 S 16th St., Ste. 200, Lincoln, NE 68512, U.S.A. **Online address:** info@richardevansonline.com

EVANS, Richard I(sadore). American (born United States), b. 1922. **Genres:** Psychology, Documentaries/Reportage, Education, Social Work. **Career:** University of Tennessee, visiting professor of psychology, 1947-48; Michigan State College (now University), faculty, 1948-50; University of Houston, Central Campus, professor of psychology, 1950-, Social Psychology/Behavioral Medicine Research and Graduate Training Group, director, 1979-, distinguished university professor of psychology, 1989-, Hugh Roy and Lillie Cranz Cullen distinguished university professor, Social Psychology Program, director, 1992. Writer. **Publications:** (With R.G. Smith and W.K. Colville) The University Faculty and Educational Television: Hostility, Resistance and Change: A Social Psychological Investigation in Depth, 1962; Conversations with Carl Jung and Reactions from Ernest Jones, 1964, rev. ed. as Jung on Elementary Psychology, 1976, as Dialogue with C.G. Jung, 1981; Dialogue with Erich Fromm, 1966; Dialogue with Erik Erikson, 1967; B.F. Skinner: The Man and His Ideas, 1968, as Dialogue with B.F. Skinner, 1981; (with P.K. Leppmann) Resistance to Innovation in Higher Education: A Social Psychological Exploration Focused on Television and the Establishment, 1968; Psychology and Arthur Miller, 1969; (with J. Bierer) Innovations in Social Psychiatry: A Social Psychological Perspective Through Dialogue, 1969; Gordon Allport, the Man and His Ideas, 1971, as Dialogue with Gordon Allport, 1981; Jean Piaget: The Man and His Ideas, 1973, as Dialogue with Jean Piaget, 1981; Carl Rogers: The Man and His Ideas, 1975, as Dialogue with Carl Rogers, 1981; Konrad Lorenz: The Man and His Ideas, 1975; The Making of Psychology, 1976; R.D. Laing, the Man and His Ideas, 1976, as Dialogue with R.D. Laing, 1981; Konrad Lorenz: Gespräche mit Richard Evans, ein Briefwechsel mit Donald Campbell undvier Essays, 1977; Albert Bandura: The Man and His Ideas, 1989. EDITOR: Journal of Social Issues, 1963; (with R.M. Rozelle) Social Psychology in Life, 1970, 2nd ed., 1973;

The Making of Social Psychology, 1980; (with W.J. Bukoski) Cost-Benefit/Cost-Effectiveness Research of Drug Abuse Prevention: Implications for Programming and Policy, 1998. **Address:** Department of Psychology, University of Houston, 214 Heyne Bldg., 3800 Calhoun Blvd., Houston, TX 77204-5341, U.S.A. **Online address:** rievans@uh.edu

EVANS, Richard J(ohn). British (born England), b. 1947. **Genres:** History, Medicine/Health, Politics/Government, Law, Civil Liberties/Human Rights, Urban Studies. **Career:** Stirling University, lecturer in history, 1972-76; University of East Anglia, lecturer, 1976-83, professor of European history, 1983-89; Columbia University, visiting associate professor of European history, 1980; University of London, Birkbeck College, professor of history, 1989-98, vice-master, 1993-98, acting master, 1997; Gonville and Caius College, fellow, 1998-2010; Cambridge University, professor of modern history, 1998-; Gresham College, visiting professor of history, 2006, 2008, Gresham professor of rhetoric, 2009-12; University of Cambridge, Regius professor of modern history, 2008-, fellow; University of Stirling, faculty; Wolfson College Cambridge, president, 2010-. Writer. **Publications:** The Feminist Movement in Germany, 1894-1933, 1976; The Feminists: Women's Emancipation Movements in Europe, America and Australasia, 1840-1920, 1977; Sozialdemokratie und Frauenemanzipation im Deutschen Kaiserreich, 1979; Comrades and Sisters: Feminism, Socialism and Pacifism in Europe, 1870-1945, 1987; Steam Cars, 1987; Rethinking German History: Nineteenth-Century Germany and the Origins of the Third Reich, 1987; Death in Hamburg: Society and Politics in the Cholera Years, 1830-1910, 1987; Kneipengespräche im Kaiserreich: Die Stimmungsberichte Der Hamburger Politischen Polizei 1892-1914, 1989; In Hitler's Shadow: West German Historians and the Attempt to Escape from the Nazi Past, 1989; Proletarians and Politics: Socialism, Protest and the Working Class in Germany Before the First World War, 1990; Rituals of Retribution: Capital Punishment in Germany 1600-1989, 1996; Rereading German History: From Unification to Reunification, 1800-1995, 1997; In Defence of History, 1997; Tales from the German Underworld: Crime and Punishment in the Nineteenth Century, 1998; In Defense of History, 1999; Lying about Hitler: History, Holocaust and the David Irving Trial, 2001; The Coming of the Third Reich, 2004; Third Reich in Power, 1933-1939, 2005; Third Reich in Power, 2006; The Third Reich at War, 2008; Cosmopolitan Islanders: British Historians and the European Continent, 2009. EDITOR: Society and Politics in Wilhelmine Germany, 1978; (with W.R. Lee) The German Family: Essays on the Social History of the Family in Nineteenth-and Twentieth-Century Germany, 1981; German Working Class, 1888-1933: The Politics of Everyday Life, 1982; (with W.R. Lee) German Peasantry: Conflict and Community in Rural Society from the Eighteenth to the Twentieth Centuries, 1985; (with D. Geary) The German Unemployed: Experiences and Consequences of Mass Unemployment from the Weimar Republic to the Third Reich, 1987; German Underworld: Deviants and Outcasts in German History, 1988; (with D. Blackbourn) The German Bourgeoisie: Essays on the Social History of the German Middle Class from the Late Eighteenth to the Early Twentieth Century, 1991. Contributor to periodicals. **Address:** The President's Lodge, Wolfson College, Barton Rd., Cambridge, CB CB3 9BB, England. **Online address:** rje36@cam.ac.uk

EVANS, Robert C. American (born United States), b. 1955. **Genres:** History, Literary Criticism And History. **Career:** Auburn University Montgomery, Department of English, instructor, 1982-84, assistant professor, 1984-86, associate professor, 1986-94, professor, 1994-, distinguished research professor, 1994-97, university alumni professor, 1997-2000, distinguished teaching and research professor, 2001-, interim department head. Writer. **Publications:** Ben Jonson and the Poetics of Patronage, 1989; Jonson, Lipsius and the Politics of Renaissance Stoicism, 1991; Jonson and the Contexts of His Time, 1994; Habits of Mind: Evidence and Effects of Ben Jonson's Reading, 1995; Close Readings: Analyses of Short Fiction, 2000, (co-author) 3rd ed., 2010; (intro.) An Collins, 2003; Culture and Society in Shakespeare's Day, 2012. EDITOR: (with B. Wiedemann) My Name Was Martha: A Renaissance Woman's Autobiographical Poem, 1993; (with A.C. Little) The Muses Females Are: Martha Moulsworth and Other Women Writers of the English Renaissance, 1995; (with A. Depas-Orange) The Birthday of My Self: Martha Moulsworth, Renaissance Poet, 1996; (with A.C. Little and B. Wiedemann) Short Fiction: A Critical Companion, 1997; (with R. Harp) Frank O'Connor: New Perspectives, 1998; (and comp.) Ben Jonson's Major Plays: Summaries of Modern Monographs, 2000; (and comp.) Kate Chopin's Short Fiction: A Critical Companion, 2001; (with R. Harp) Companion to Brian Friel, 2002; (and intro.) Alicia D'Anvers, 2003; (and comp.) Ambrose Bierce's An Occurrence at Owl Creek Bridge: An Annotated Critical Edition, 2003; (and in-

tro.) Eliza, 2003; (and intro.) Miscellaneous Short Poetry, 1641-1700, 2006; (and intro.) Jane Barker, 2009; Joy Luck Club, by Amy Tan, 2010; (with D.C. Solomon) American Novel, 2010; (with E.J. Sterling) Seventeenth-century Literature Handbook, 2010. Contributor to books and journals. **Address:** Department of English and Philosophy, Auburn University Montgomery, 341 Liberal Arts, 7400 E Dr., PO Box 2444023, Montgomery, AL 36117, U.S.A. **Online address:** revans@aum.edu

EVANS, Sara M(argaret). American (born United States), b. 1943. **Genres:** History, Politics/Government, Women's Studies And Issues, Social Sciences. **Career:** University of North Carolina, instructor in history, 1974, assistant professor of history, 1975-76; Duke University, instructor in history, 1974-75; University of Minnesota, Department of History, assistant professor, 1976-79, associate professor of history, 1979-89, professor of history, 1989-91, chair, 1991-94, regents professor, 2004-, now regents professor emeritus; Feminist Studies, editor; Journal of American History, consulting editor. **Publications:** Personal Politics: The Roots of Women's Liberation in the Civil Rights Movement and the New Left, 1979; (with H.C. Boyte) Free Spaces: The Sources of Democratic Change in America, 1986; (with B.J. Nelson) Wage Justice: Comparable Worth and the Paradox of Technocratic Reform, 1989; Born for Liberty: A History of Women in America, 1989; Tidal Wave: How Women Changed America at Century's End, 2003; (ed.) Journeys that Opened up the World: Women, Student Christian Movements and Social Justice, 1955-1975, 2003. **Address:** Department of History, University of Minnesota, 1110 Heller Hall, 271 19th Ave. S, Minneapolis, MN 55455, U.S.A. **Online address:** s-evan@umn.edu

EVANS, Sheila. American (born United States), b. 1934?. **Genres:** Novels. **Career:** Tokay High School, English teacher; The Space Between Journal, co-editor. Writer. **Publications:** Maggie's Rags, 1996; Northport: Stories of the Coast, 1998; Under the Camouflage: Revolving Wheels of Time Power a Mother-Daughter Relationship, 2001; Stanley California, 2003; The Widow's Husband, 2005. **Address:** c/o Author Mail, Permanent Press Publishing, 4170 Noyac Rd., Sag Harbor, NY 11963, U.S.A.

EVANS, Stephen. American (born United States), b. 1955. **Genres:** Novels. **Career:** Writer, playwright and computer analyst. **Publications:** The Marriage of True Minds (novel), 2008. **Address:** Silver Springs, MD , U.S.A. **Online address:** steve@writerseeksreader.com

EVANS, Stephen S(tewart). American (born United States), b. 1954?. **Genres:** History, Literary Criticism And History, Military/Defense/Arms Control, Social Sciences, Philosophy. **Career:** Marine Corps University, educational adviser, 1996-, lecturer, 1997-, University Press, acquisitions editor, 2010-, University Journal, acquisitions editor. **Publications:** The Heroic Poetry of Dark-Age Britain: An Introduction to Its Dating, Composition and Use as a Historical Source, 1996, rev. ed., 2000; The Lords of Battle: Image and Reality of the Comitatus in Dark Age Britain, 1997; (comp.) U.S. Marines and Irregular Warfare, 1898-2007: Anthology and Selected Bibliography, 2008. **Address:** 4 Wellington Dr., Stafford, VA 22554, U.S.A.

EVANS, Tammy. American (born United States), b. 1959. **Genres:** History, Civil Liberties/Human Rights, Mystery/Crime/Suspense. **Career:** Teacher, 1981-85; Bradenton Middle School, team leader and teacher, 1986-93; Martha B. King Middle School, language arts department chair, 1993-98; Braden River Middle School, language arts department chair, 1998-2000; University of South Florida, graduate teaching assistant, 1999-2004; University of South Florida, editorial assistant, 2001-03; Manatee School for the Arts, English department chair and curriculum coordinator, 2003-04; Manatee Community College, adjunct professor, 2004; Lakewood Ranch High School, teacher, 2004-; University of Miami, adjunct professor, 2004-; Braden River High School, language arts department chair, 2005-. **Publications:** The Silencing of Ruby McCollum: Race, Class and Gender in the South, 2006. Contributor to periodicals. **Address:** University of Miami, 5500 34th St. W, Bradenton, FL 34210, U.S.A. **Online address:** jevans19@tampabay.rr.com

EVANZZ, Karl. American (born United States), b. 1953. **Genres:** History, Biography, Autobiography/Memoirs, Romance/Historical. **Career:** Lowe, Mark & Moffett, law clerk, 1976-77; law clerk to Harry T. Alexander, 1977-81; Washington Post, on-line editor and staff researcher, 1980-; St. Louis Argus, Washington correspondent, 1981-83. **Publications:** The Judas Factor: The Plot to Kill Malcolm X, 1992; The Messenger: The Rise and Fall of Elijah Muhammad, 1999; I Am the Greatest: The Best Quotations from

Muhammad Ali, 2002. Contributor of articles to periodicals. **Address:** News Department, Washington Post, 1150 15th St. NW, 4th Fl., Washington, DC 20071, U.S.A. **Online address:** evanzzk@washpost.com

EVELEIGH, Victoria. British (born England), b. 1959?. **Genres:** Children's Fiction, Novellas/Short Stories, Animals/Pets. **Career:** Exmoor National Park Authority, staff; Tortoise Publishing, founder, 2001-. Writer. **Publications:** Katy's Exmoor: The Story of an Exmoor Pony, 2002; Katy's Exmoor Adventures: The Sequel to Katy's Exmoor, 2003; Katy's Exmoor Friends, 2005; The Exmoor Horn Sheep Colouring Book, 2007; Midnight On Lundy, 2008. **Address:** Tortoise Publishing, West Ilkerton Farm, Lynton, DN EX35 6QA, England.

EVENSON, B. K. See EVENSON, Brian.

EVENSON, Brian. (B. K. Evenson). American (born United States), b. 1966. **Genres:** Novellas/Short Stories, Novels, Horror, Mystery/Crime/Suspense, Science Fiction/Fantasy. **Career:** University of Washington, lecturer in English, 1990-93, assistant director of computer integrated class, 1991-93; Magic Realism, contributing editor, 1992-97; Brigham Young University, assistant professor of English, 1993-95; Oklahoma State University, assistant professor of English, 1995-99; Conjunctions magazine, senior editor, 1998-; University of Denver, associate professor of English, 1999-; Brown University, professor of English 2003-; Brown University, director of literary arts, 2005-. **Publications:** STORIES: Altmann's Tongue: Stories and a Novella, 1994; The Din of Celestial Birds, 1997; Prophets and Brothers, 1997; Contagion, 2000; Wavering Knife, 2004; Fugue State: Stories, 2009. NOVELS: Father of Lies, 1998; Dark Property: An Affliction, 2002; Open Curtain, 2006; Last Days, 2009; Baby Leg, 2009; Immobility, 2012; Windeye, 2012. OTHERS: Understanding Robert Coover, 2003; (trans.) Mountain R, 2004; (trans.) Electric Flesh, 2006; (trans.) Donogoo-Tonka, or, The Miracles of Science, 2009. AS B.K. EVENSON: Aliens: No Exit, 2008; Dead Space: Martyr, 2010. Contributor to periodicals. **Address:** Literary Arts Program, Brown University, 68 1/2 Brown St. Rm. 305, Providence, RI 02912, U.S.A. **Online address:** brian_evenson@brown.edu

EVERARD, Katherine. See VIDAL, Gore.

EVERDELL, William R(omeyn). American (born United States), b. 1941. **Genres:** Poetry, History, Intellectual History, Politics/Government, Sciences, Theology/Religion. **Career:** Lycee Arago, assistant in English, 1963-64; St. Ann's School, Department of History, chair, 1972-73, co-chair, 1975-84, Upper School, head, 1973-75, dean of humanities, 1984-, faculty; New York University, adjunct instructor, 1984-89; New York Times, contributor. Writer. **Publications:** (With M. MacKay) Rowboats to Rapid Transit, 1973; The End of Kings: A History of Republics and Republicans, 1983, 2nd ed., 2000; Christian Apologetics in France, 1730-1790: The Roots of Romantic Religion, 1987; The First Moderns: Profiles in the Origins of Twentieth-Century Thought, 1997. Contributor to periodicals. **Address:** St. Ann's School, 129 Pierrepont St., Brooklyn Heights, NY 11201, U.S.A. **Online address:** everdell@aol.com

EVERETT, Anna. American (born United States), b. 1954. **Genres:** Communications/Media, Race Relations. **Career:** University of California, professor of film and media studies; Screening Noir Online (internet newsletter), founder and managing editor. **Publications:** Returning the Gaze: A Genealogy of Black Film Criticism, 1909-1949, 2001; (ed. with J.T. Caldwell) New Media: Theories and Practices of Digitextuality, 2003; (ed.) Learning Race and Ethnicity: Youth and Digital Media, 2008; Digital Diaspora: A Race for Cyberspace, 2009. **Address:** Department of Film and Media Studies, University of California, 2433 Social Sciences and Media Studies Bldg., Santa Barbara, CA 93106-4010, U.S.A. **Online address:** everett@filmandmedia.ucsb.edu

EVERETT, Daniel L. (Daniel Leonard Everett). American (born United States), b. 1951. **Genres:** Language/Linguistics. **Career:** University of Campinas, assistant professor, 1983-86; University of Pittsburgh, Department of Linguistics, assistant professor, 1988-92, professor of linguistics and chair, 1992-; Journal of Amazonian Languages, editor, 1995; Bentley University, dean of arts and sciences; Illinois State University, Department of Languages, Literatures and Cultures, chair; University of Manchester, faculty. Writer, anthropologist and linguist. **Publications:** (As Daniel Leonard Everett) A l íingua pirahã e a teoria da sintaxe: descricao, perspectives e teoria, 1991; Why

There Are No Clitics: An Alternative Perspective on Pronominal Allomorphy, 1996; (with B. Kern) Wari: The Pacaas Novos Language of Western Brazil, 1997; Don't Sleep, There Are Snakes: Life and Language in the Amazonian Jungle, 2008; Language, 2011; (with J. Sakel) Linguistic Fieldwork, 2012. Contributor to magazines. **Address:** Department of Linguistics, University of Pittsburgh, 2816 Cathedral of Learning, Pittsburgh, PA 15260, U.S.A.

EVERETT, Daniel Leonard. See EVERETT, Daniel L.

EVERITT, James H. American (born United States) **Genres:** Horticulture, Natural History. **Career:** Kika De La Garza Agricultural Center, range scientist, 1974-, now retired. Author. **Publications:** (With R.I. Leonard and F.W. Judd) Woody Plants of the Lower Rio Grande Valley, Texas, 1991; (with D.L. Drawe) Trees, Shrubs and Cacti of South Texas, 1993, rev. ed., 2002; (ed.) Proceeding of the Sixteenth Biennial Workshop on Videographing Color Photography in Resource Assessment, 1997; (with D.L. Drawe and R.I. Lonard) Field Guide to the Broad-leaved Herbaceous Plants of South Texas: Used by Livestock and Wildlife, 1999; (with R.I. Leonard and C.R. Little) Weeds in South Texas and Northern Mexico: A Guide to Identification, 2007; (co-author) Grasses of South Texas: A Guide to Their Identification and Value, 2011. **Address:** Texas Tech University Press, 2903 4th St., Ste. 201, PO Box 41037, Lubbock, TX 79415, U.S.A. **Online address:** james.everitt@ars.usda.gov

EVERS, Larry. American (born United States), b. 1946. **Genres:** Anthropology/Ethnology, Cultural/Ethnic Topics, Mythology/Folklore, Translations, Poetry. **Career:** University of Chicago, Department of Anthropology, postdoctoral fellow, 1972-73; University of Arizona, Department of English, assistant professor, 1974-80, associate professor, 1980-86, professor of English, 1986-, head, director of graduate study, 1991-94, American Indian Studies, affiliated faculty. Writer. **Publications:** (Co-ed.) Native American Perspectives, 1978; (co-ed.) South Corner of Time: Hopi, Navajo, Papago, Yaqui Tribal Literature, 1980; (with F.S. Molina) Yaqui Deer Songs, Maso Bwikam: A Native American Poetry, 1987; (trans. with F.S. Molina) Wo'i bwikam: Coyote Songs: From the Yaqui Bow Leaders' Society, 1989; (ed. with O. Zepeda) Home Places: Contemporary Native American Writing from Sun Tracks, 1995; (ed. with B. Toelken) Native American Oral Traditions: Collaboration and Tradition, 2001. **Address:** Department of English, University of Arizona, Rm. 445, Modern Languages Bldg., 1423 E University Blvd., PO Box 210067, Tucson, AZ 85721-0067, U.S.A. **Online address:** levers@email.arizona.edu

EVERSZ, Robert (McLeod). American (born United States), b. 1954. **Genres:** Mystery/Crime/Suspense, Novels. **Career:** Earl Wilson and Associates (marketing consultants), vice president for operations, 1981-84; Robert Eversz and Associates (marketing consultants), consultant, 1984-88; writer, 1988-; Western Michigan University, visiting professor and writer-in-residence, 2006-08; University of California, Writers' Program, instructor, 2009-11. **Publications:** The Bottom Line Is Murder: A Viking Novel of Mystery and Suspense, 1988; False Profit, 1990; Gypsy Hearts, 1997. NINA ZERO SERIES: Shooting Elvis: Confessions of an Accidental Terrorist, 1996; Killing Paparazzi, 2002; Burning Garbo, 2003; Digging James Dean, 2005; Zero to the Bone, 2006. **Address:** 1008 Mercer Pl., Frederick, MD 21701, U.S.A. **Online address:** eversz@mac.com

EVEY, Stuart. American (born United States), b. 1933?. **Genres:** Young Adult Non-fiction. **Career:** Getty Oil, senior executive, vice president, 1978-; ESPN (television sports network), founding chairman, 1979-85. Writer, consultant and entrepreneur. **Publications:** (With I. Broughton) Creating an Empire: ESPN: The No-Holds-Barred Story of Power, Ego, Money, and Vision That Transformed a Culture, 2004. **Address:** Triumph Books, 542 S Dearborn St., Ste. 750, Chicago, IL 60605-1525, U.S.A. **Online address:** stuevey@comcast.net

EVIOTA, Elizabeth Uy. Filipino (born Philippines), b. 1946. **Genres:** Area Studies, Bibliography, History, Social Sciences, Sociology, Third World, Women's Studies And Issues, Literary Criticism And History, Literary Criticism And History. **Career:** Ateneo de Manila University, Institute of Philippine Culture, Women in Development Project, project director, 1976-79, School of Social Sciences, Department of Sociology and Anthropology, lecturer in sociology and anthropology, 1983-, Women's Studies Consortium, university representative, 1989-92; United Nations Children's Fund, Family Welfare, People's Participation, and Women in Development Division, research associate, 1980-81; Asian Development Bank, consultant on gender and development, 1987, 1991; Canadian International Development Agency,

1988, 1994-96; National Commission on the Role of Filipino Women, consultant, 1988-89; University of Sussex, Institute of Development Studies, visiting fellow, 1990; Economic Development Institute of the World Bank, consultant, 1991-93. Writer. **Publications:** Philippine Women and Development: An Annotated Bibliography, 1978; (comp. with R.G. Abad) Philippine Poor II: Philippine Poverty: An Annotated Bibliography, 1970-1983, 1985; (ed.) Sex and Gender in Philippine Society: A Discussion of Issues on the Relations between Women and Men, 1990; The Political Economy of Gender: Women and the Sexual Division of Labour in the Philippines, 1992. Works appear in anthologies. Contributor to journals and periodicals. **Address:** Department of Sociology and Anthropology, Ateneo de Manila University, Ricardo & Dr. Rosita Leong Hall, Ground Fl., Loyola Heights, PO Box 154, Quezon City, 1108, Philippines.

EWAN, Chris. British (born England), b. 1976?. **Genres:** Novels. **Career:** Writer. **Publications:** The Good Thief's Guide to Amsterdam (novel), 2007; The Good Thief's Guide to Paris (novel), 2008. **Address:** Sheil Land Associates, 52 Doughty St., London, WC1N 2LS, England. **Online address:** chrisewan@gmail.com

EWEN, Pamela Binnings. American (born United States), b. 1944. **Genres:** Novels. **Career:** Harris, Cook, Browning & Barker, law clerk, 1977-79; Kleberg, Dyer, Redford, & Weil, associate, 1979-80; Gulf Oil Corp., attorney, 1980-84; Baker & Botts L.L.P., associate, 1980-84, partner, 1988-2004; Inprint Inc., director; Tennessee Williams Festival, director; Northshore Literary Society, co-founder. Writer. **Publications:** Faith on Trial, 1999; Walk Back the Cat (novel), 2006; The Moon in the Mango Tree (novel), 2008. **Address:** Mandeville, LA , U.S.A. **Online address:** pamelaewen@bellsouth.net

EWING, Lynne. American (born United States) **Genres:** Novels, Adult Non-fiction, Natural History, Mystery/Crime/Suspense. **Career:** Writer. **Publications:** YOUNG-ADULT NOVELS: Drive-By, 1996; Party Girl, 1998. DAUGHTERS OF THE MOON SERIES: Goddess of the Night, 2000; Into the Cold Fire, 2000; Night Shade, 2001; The Secret Scroll, 2001; The Sacrifice, 2001; The Lost One, 2001; Moon Demon, 2002; Possession, 2002; The Choice, 2003; The Talisman, 2003; The Prophecy, 2004; The Becoming, 2004; The Final Eclipse, 2007. SONS OF THE DARK SERIES: Barbarian, 2004; Escape, 2004; Outcast, 2005; Night Sun, 2005. SISTERS OF ISIS SERIES: Enchantress, 2007; Divine One, 2007; The Summoning, 2007; The Haunting, 2008. **Address:** c/o Author Mail, Hyperion Books for Children, 114 5th Ave., New York, NY 10011-5604, U.S.A.

EYER, Diane E(lizabeth). American (born United States), b. 1944. **Genres:** History, Psychology, Sociology, Women's Studies And Issues, Science Fiction/Fantasy, Medicine/Health. **Career:** Institute of Pennsylvania Hospital, poetry therapist, 1971-73; Philadelphia Institute for Gestalt Therapy, counselor, 1971-75; University of Pennsylvania, teaching assistant, 1983-85, research assistant, 1984-87, lecturer, 1991-; Rutgers University, instructor, 1985-89; Temple University, instructor, 1986-87, assistant professor of psychology, 1994-. Writer. **Publications:** Mother-Infant Bonding: A Scientific Fiction, 1992; Motherguilt: How Our Culture Blames Mothers for What's Wrong with Society, 1996; (with K. Hirsh-Pasek and R. Golinhoff) Einstein Never Used Flash Cards: How Our Children Really Learn-And Why they Need to Play More and Memorize Less, 2003. Contributor to books and periodicals. **Address:** c/o Beth Vesel, Sanford J. Greenburger Associates, 55 5th Ave., New York, NY 10003, U.S.A. **Online address:** byereyer@voicenet.com

EYETSEMITAN, Frank E. American (born United States), b. 1955. **Genres:** Adult Non-fiction, Sociology, Gerontology/Senior Issues, Social Sciences. **Career:** McKendree College, professor of psychology, Division of Social Sciences, chair, 1991-. Writer and psychologist. **Publications:** (With J.T. Gire) Aging and Adult Development in the Developing World: Applying Western Theories and Concepts, 2003. **Address:** McKendree College, 701 College Rd., Lebanon, IL 62254-1291, U.S.A.

EYNON, Bob. See **EYNON, Robert.**

EYNON, Robert. (Bob Eynon). Welsh (born Wales), b. 1941?. **Genres:** Novellas/Short Stories, Westerns/Adventure. **Career:** The High School, language teacher, 1963-65; teacher of English, 1965-67; Peter Symond's School, language teacher, 1967-69; Girl's Grammar School, language teacher, 1968-72; University College, lecturer in education, 1972-84; Ibadan University,

visiting lecturer, 1975; Rhondda Borough Council, parks labourer, 1985-86; writer, 1987-. **Publications:** Bitter Waters, 1988; Texas Honour, 1988; Giangster Coll, 1989; Johnny One-Arm, 1989; Gunfight at Simeon's Ridge, 1991; Gun-Law Legacy, 1991; Sunset Reckoning, 1993; Crockett yn achub y dydd, 1995; Anderton Justice, 1997; Pecos Vengeance, 1998; Brothers till Death, 1999; Arizona Payback, 2001; Poison Valley, 2003; The Reluctant Lawman, 2005. **Address:** 5 Troedyrhiw Terr., Treorchy, MG CF42 6PG, Wales.

EYRE, Annette. See **WORBOYS, Anne.**

EYRE, Elizabeth. See **STAYNES, Jill.**

EYRE, Elizabeth. See **STOREY, Margaret.**

EYRE, Peter. American (born United States), b. 1942. **Genres:** Translations, Young Adult Fiction, Literary Criticism And History, History. **Career:** Actor, 1960-; director; Royal Shakespeare Co., staff; Old Vic Theatre, staff; Royal National Theatre, staff. Writer. **Publications:** (Trans. with T. Alexander) Klaus Mann, Siblings: The Children's Story, 1992; (adapted) Chère Maître: The Correspondence of Gustave Flaubert and George Sand, 2002. **Address:** c/o Antony Harwood, Curtis Brown, 162-168 Regent St., London, GL W1R 5TB, England.

EYSENCK, Michael (William). British (born England), b. 1944. **Genres:** Psychology. **Career:** University of London, Birkbeck College, lecturer, 1965-80, reader in psychology, 1981-87, Royal Holloway and Bedford New College, professor of psychology, 1987-, professor emeritus of psychology.; European Society of Cognitive Psychology, founding member; British Psychological Society, Cognitive Psychology Section, chairman, 1982-87. Writer. **Publications:** Human Memory: Theory, Research, and Individual Differences, 1977; (with H. Eysenck) Mindwatching: Why People Behave the Way They Do, 1981; Attention and Arousal: Cognition and Performance, 1982; A Handbook of Cognitive Psychology, 1984; (with H.J. Eysenck) Personality and Individual Differences, 1985; (with G. Cohen and M.E. Le Voi) Memory: A Cognitive Approach, 1986; (ed. with T.E. Richardson and D.W. Piper) Student Learning: Research in Education and Cognitive Psychology, 1987; (ed.) Cognitive Psychology: An International Review, 1990; Happiness: Facts and Myths, 1990; (co-author) Cognitive Psychology: A Student's Handbook, 1990, 6th ed., 2010; (ed.) Blackwell Dictionary of Cognitive Psychology, 1991; (with M. Weller) The Scientific Basis of Psychiatry, 1992; Anxiety: The Cognitive Perspective, 1992; (ed. with A. Gale) Handbook of Individual Differences: Biological Perspectives, 1992; Principles of Cognitive Psychology, 1993; Individual Differences: Normal and Abnormal, 1994; Perspectives on Psychology, 1994; Simply Psychology, 1996, 2nd ed., 2002; Anxiety and Cognition: A Unified Theory, 1997; Psychology: An Integrated Approach, 1998; (with C. Flanagan) Psychology for AS Level, 2000; Psychology: A Student's Handbook, 2000; (with C. Flanagan) Psychology for A2 Level, 2001; Psychology: An International Perspective, 2004; Fundamentals of Cognition, 2006, 2nd ed., 2011; (ed. with P. Buchwald and T. Ringeisen) Stress and Anxiety: Application to Life Span Development and Health Promotion, 2008; Fundamentals of Psychology, 2009; (with A. Baddeley and M. Anderson) Memory, 2009; (ed. with T. Maruszewski and M. Fajkowska) Personality from Biological, Cognitive, and Social Perspectves, 2010; (ed. with M. Fajkowska and T. Maruszewski) Personality, Cognition, and Emotion, 2011. **Address:** Department of Psychology, University of London, Rm. W344, Royal Holloway, Egham Hill, Egham, SR TW20 0EX, England. **Online address:** m.eysenck@rhul.ac.uk

EZELL, Lee. American (born United States), b. 1944. **Genres:** inspirational/ Motivational Literature, Regional/Urban Planning, Social Sciences, Theology/Religion. **Career:** Ezell Communications, director. Writer. **Publications:** The Cinderella Syndrome: Discovering God's Plan When Your Dreams Don't Come True, 1985; The Missing Piece: Finding God's Peace for Your Past, 1986; Private Obsessions, 1991; Pills for Parents in Pain, 1992; What Men Understand about Women, 1992; (with L. Gilbert) Iron Jane: It's Time for a Lasting, Loving Ceasefire in the Battle of the Sexes, 1994; Will the Real Me Please Stand Up!, 1995; Porcupine People: Learning to Love the Unlovable, 1998; Finding God When Life's Not Fair: Surviving Soul-Shakers and Aftershocks, 2001. Contributor to periodicals. **Address:** Ezell Communications, PO Box 80848, Rancho Santa Margarita, CA 92688, U.S.A. **Online address:** leeezell@aol.com

EZELL, Margaret J. M. American (born United States), b. 1955. **Genres:** Literary Criticism And History, Women's Studies And Issues, Economics. **Career:** Texas A&M University, professor of English, 1982-, distinguished professor of English, John Paul Abbott professor of liberal arts, Sara and John Lindsey chair of liberal arts, Interdisciplinary Group for History Literary Studies, fellow; Folger Shakespeare Library and Institute, visiting lecturer, 1991. Writer. **Publications:** The Patriarch's Wife: Literary Evidence and the History of the Family, 1987; Writing Women's Literary History, 1993; Social Authorship and the Advent of Print, 1999. EDITOR: The Poems and Prose of Mary, Lady Chudleigh, 1993; (with K. O'Keeffe) Cultural Artifacts and the Production of Meaning: The Page, the Body and the Image, 1994. Contributor to magazines. **Address:** Department of English, Texas A&M University, 243D Blocker Bldg., PO Box 4227, College Station, TX 77843, U.S.A. **Online address:** m-ezell@tamu.edu

EZRAHI, Yaron. Israeli (born Israel), b. 1940?. **Genres:** Communications/ Media, Cultural/Ethnic Topics, Politics/Government, Sciences, Technology, Engineering, History. **Career:** Hebrew University of Jerusalem, Department of Political Science, lecturer, 1972-77, senior lecturer, 1977-97, associate professor, 1997-98, Gersten Family Professor of Political Science, 1998-2008, professor emeritus, 2008-, Advanced Program for the History and Sociology of the Sciences, head; Stanford University, Center for Advanced Study in the Behavioral Sciences, fellow, 1978; Duke University, visiting professor, 1984-86; Harvard University, visiting professor, 1986, 1990; Israel Democracy Institute, senior fellow emeritus; Brown University, visiting professor, 2008; Pennsylvania University, visiting professor. Writer. **Publications:** NONFICTION: (ed. with E. Tal) Science Policy and Development: The Case of Israel, 1972; The Descent of Icarus: Science and the Transformation of Contemporary Democracy, 1990; (ed. with E. Mendelsohn and H. Segal) Technology, Pessimism, and Postmodernism, 1994; Rubber Bullets: Power and Conscience in Modern Israel, 1996; (with O. Ben-Shahar and R. Lal) Reformah ba-shidur ha-tsiburi: derakhim le-hitmodedut 'im ha-sakanot ha-orvot la-shidur ha-tsiburi ba-demokratyah ha-Yiśre'elit, 1997; (contrib.) After Rabin: New Art from Israel, 1998; Current Israeli Attitudes toward American Jews: Contexts, Problems, and Recommendations, 1999; (with M. kremnister) Yi'śra'el Likrat demokratyah hukatit: 'ekronot le-tikun Medinah u-mishtar, 2001; (with Z. Goshen and H. komaneshter) televizyah ha-rav-'arutsit be-Yiśra'el, 2001; (with Z. Goshen and S. Leshem) Ba'alut tsolevet-shelitah ve-taharut be-shuk ha-tikshoret ha-Yiśre'eli: hebetim kalkaliyim im u-mishpatiyim ve-hashlakhotehem 'al ha-demokratyah ha-Yiśre'elit, 2003. Contributor to periodicals. **Address:** Department of Political Science, Hebrew University of Jerusalem, Rm. 5327, Mt. Scopus, Jerusalem, 91905, Israel. **Online address:** yaron.ezrahi@huji.ac.il

F

FAAS, K. Ekbert. German (born Germany), b. 1938. **Genres:** Novels, Literary Criticism And History, Genealogy/Heraldry. **Career:** Goethe Institute, lecturer, 1961-64; University of Wuerzburg, assistant professor of English, 1965-68, privatdozent, 1971-72; York University, professor of humanities and English, 1976-; Winters College, fellow. **Publications:** (Ed. with M. Seletzky) Ted Hughes, Gedanken-Fuchs, 1971; Poesie als Psychogramm: Die dramat.-monolog. Vers-dichtung im viktorian. Zeitalter, 1974; Offene Formen in der modernen Kunst und Literatur: Zur Entstehungeiner neuen Ästhetik, 1975; (ed.) Towards a New American Poetics: Essays and Interviews: Charles Olson, Robert Duncan, Gary Snyder, Robert Creeley, Robert Bly, Allen Ginsberg, 1978; Ted Hughes: The Unaccommodated Universe: With Selected Critical Writings by Ted Hughes and Two Interviews, 1980; (ed. and foreword) Kenneth Rexroth: Excerpts from a Life, 1981; Young Robert Duncan: Portrait of the Poet as Homosexual in Society, 1983; Tragedy and After: Euripides, Shakespeare, Goethe, 1984; Shakespeare's Poetics, 1986; Retreat into the Mind: Victorian Poetry and the Rise of Psychiatry, 1988; (ed. with S. Reed) Irving Layton and Robert Creeley: The Complete Correspondence, 1990; Woyzeck's Head: A Novel, 1991; (with M. Trombacco) Robert Creeley: A Biography, 2001, rev. ed. 2005; The Genealogy of Aesthetics, 2002. FORTHCOMING: The Son; The Revolutionist; The Genealogy of Beauty. Contributor to literature journals. **Address:** Department of English, York University, 242 Winters College, Toronto, ON M3J 1P3, Canada. **Online address:** efmt@yorku.ca

FABER, Michel. Scottish/Dutch (born Netherlands), b. 1960. **Genres:** Novels, Children's Fiction, Novellas/Short Stories, Essays, Adult Non-fiction. **Career:** Nurse; Scotland on Sunday, reviewer, 2001-04; The Guardian, reviewer, 2003-; Sunday Herald, feature writer, 2004. **Publications:** Some Rain Must Fall (short stories), 1998; Under the Skin (novel), 2000; The Hundred and Ninety-Nine Steps (novella), 2001; (ed.) Shorts 4: The Macallan/Scotland on Sunday Short Story Collection, 2001; The Crimson Petal and the White (novel), 2002; The Courage Consort (novellas), 2002; The Fahrenheit Twins (short stories), 2005; Vanilla Bright Like Eminem (short stories), 2005; The Apple: New Crimson Petal Stories, 2006; The Fire Gospel, 2008; (co-author) Ox-Tales: Water, 2009. Works appear in anthologies. Contributor to magazines and periodicals. **Address:** Canongate Books Ltd., 14 High St., Edinburgh, LT EH1 1TE, Scotland. **Online address:** michelfaber@ablach.freeserve.co.uk

FABRICANT, Michael B. American (born United States), b. 1948. **Genres:** Adult Non-fiction, Social Work, Education. **Career:** Community Service Society, research associate, 1975-80; Hunter College, assistant professor, 1980-85, associate professor, 1985-88, professor of social work, 1988-, executive officer; City University of New York, treasurer of professional staff, 2006, consultant; American Red Cross, consultant; Henry Street Settlement, consultant; National Coalition for the Homeless, board director; Union County Legal Services, board director; Elizabeth Coalition to House the Homeless, board director; St. Joseph's Social Service Center, board director. Writer. **Publications:** Deinstitutionalizing Delinquent Youth, 1980; Juvenile Injustice: Dilemmas of the Family Court System, 1981; Juveniles in the Family Court, 1983; (with S. Burghardt) Working Under the Safety Net: Policy and Practice with the New American Poor, 1987; (with S. Burghardt) The Welfare State Crisis and the Transformation of Social Service Work, 1992; (with R. Fisher) Settlement Houses Under Seige: The Struggle to Sustain Community

Organizations in New York City, 2002; Organizing for Educational Justice: The Campaign for Public School Reform in the South Bronx, 2010; (with M. Fine) Charter Schools and The Corporate Makeover of Public Education: What's at Stake?, 2012; Besieged Social Services: Settlements at the Close of the 20th Century, forthcoming. **Address:** School of Social Work, City University of New York, Rm. 605, 129 E 79th St., New York, NJ 10021, U.S.A. **Online address:** mfabrica@hunter.cuny.edu

FABRIZIO, Timothy C(harles). American (born United States), b. 1948. **Genres:** Antiques/Furnishings, Music, Photography, Fash Ion/Costume. **Career:** National Pantomime Theater, actor and technician, 1968-71; Lift Bridge Book Shops, co-owner, 1972-84; Terra Firma Antiques and Phonophan, owner, 1985-; Phonophan.com, owner and webmaster, 1997-; Library of Congress, consultant in music machine and record acquisition. Writer. **Publications:** WITH G.F. PAUL: The Talking Machine: An Illustrated Compendium, 1877-1929, 1997, 2nd. ed., 2005; Antique Phonograph: Gadgets, Gizmos, and Gimmicks, 1999; Discovering Antique Phonographs, 2000; Phonographs with Flair: A Century of Style in Sound Reproduction, 2001; Antique Phonograph Advertising: An Illustrated History, 2002; Antique Phonograph Accessories and Contraptions, 2003; Phonographica: The Early History of Recorded Sound Observed, 2004; A World of Antique Phonographs, 2007. **Address:** Phonophan, PO Box 747, Henrietta, NY 14467-0747, U.S.A. **Online address:** phonophan@aol.com

FACEY-CROWTHER, David R. Canadian (born Canada), b. 1938. **Genres:** History, Military/Defense/Arms Control. **Career:** Memorial University of Newfoundland, professor of history, 1968-2003, Department head, 2001-03; Government of Newfoundland, Classification Appeal Board, chair, 1972-91, now emeritus; Atlantic Association of Historians, secretary-treasurer 1972-2002, president 2002-03. Writer. **Publications:** The New Brunswick Militia Commissioned Officers' List, 1787-1867, 1984; The New Brunswick Militia, 1787-1867, 1990; (ed. with D. Brinkley) The Atlantic Charter, 1994; Better than the Best: The Story of the Royal Newfoundland Regiment, 1795-1995, 1995; (ed.) Lieutenant Owen William Steele of the Newfoundland Regiment, 2002; (intro.) The Fighting Newfoundlander, 2006. **Address:** 1529 W Pender St., Apt. 1406, Vancouver, BC V6G 3J3, Canada. **Online address:** zg7006@shaw.ca

FADIMAN, Anne. American (born United States), b. 1953. **Genres:** Documentaries/Reportage, Literary Criticism And History, Essays. **Career:** Life Magazine, staff writer and editor, 1981-88; Library of Congress Magazine, founding editor, Civilization, editor-at-large and columnist, 1994-98; American Scholar, editor-in-chief, 1998-2004; Smith College, visiting lecturer in American studies, English and literature, 2000-02; Yale University, Department of English, Francis writer-in-residence, 2006-. **Publications:** The Spirit Catches You and You Fall Down: A Hmong Child, Her American Doctors, and the Collision of Two Cultures, 1997; Ex Libris: Confessions of a Common Reader, 1998; (ed. with R. Atwan) Best American Essays 2003, 2003; (ed.) Rereadings, 2005; At Large and at Small: Familiar Essays, 2007. Contributor to periodicals. **Address:** Farrar, Straus & Giroux, 18 W 18th St., Ste. 7, New York, New York, NY 10011-4675, U.S.A.

FAGAN, Brian Murray. American/British (born England), b. 1936. **Genres:**

Anthropology/Ethnology, Archaeology/Antiquities, History, Travel/Exploration. **Career:** British Institute in Eastern Africa, Bantu Studies Project, director; Livingstone Museum, keeper of prehistory, 1959-65; University of Illinois, visiting associate professor, 1965-66; University of California, associate professor, 1967-69, professor of anthropology, 1969-2004, now emeritus. Writer. **Publications:** Southern Africa during the Iron Age, 1966; (with S.G.H. Daniels and D.W. Phillipson) Iron Age Cultures in Zambia, vol. I, 1967, vol. II, 1969; (with F. Van Noten) The Hunter-Gatherers of Gwisho, 1971; In the Beginning, 1972, 12th ed., 2008; Men of the Earth, 1974, 13th ed. as People of the Earth, 2009; Elusive Treasure, 1977; Quest for the Past, 1978; Return to Babylon, 1979; World Prehistory, 1979, 8th ed., 2010; The Aztecs, 1984; Clash of Cultures, 1984, rev ed., 2002; The Adventure of Archaeology, 1985; Bareboating, 1985; Anchoring, 1985; The Great Journey, 1987; The Journey from Eden, 1991; Archaeology: A Brief Introduction, 1978, 10th ed., 2009; Ancient North America, 1991, 4th ed., 2005; Kingdoms of Gold, Kingdoms of Jade, 1992; Time Detectives, 1995; From Black Land to Fifth Son, 1998; Floods, Famines and Emperors, 1999, rev. ed., 2008; Ancient Lives, 2000, 4th ed., 2011; Cruising Guide to Central and Southern California, 2001; Little Ice Age, 2001; Before California, 2003; The Long Summer, 2004; The Rape of the Nile, rev ed., 2004; Chaco Canyon, 2005; Brief History of Archaeology: Classical Times to the Twenty-First Century, 2005; Writing Archaeology: Telling Stories about the Past, 2006, rev. ed., 2010; From Stonehenge to Samarkand: An Anthology of Archaeological Travel Writing, 2006; Fish on Friday: Feasting, Fasting and the Discovery of the New World, 2006; Return to Babylon: Travelers, Archaeologists and Monuments in Mesopotamia, 2007; People of the Earth: An Introduction to World Prehistory, 2007; Archaeology and You, 2007; Ancient Lives: An Introduction to Archaeology and Prehistory, 2007; Ancient Civilizations, 3rd ed., 2008; Great Warming: Climate Change and the Rise and Fall of Civilizations, 2008; Cro-Magnon: How the Ice Age Gave Birth to the First Modern Humans, 2010; First North Americans: An Archaeological Journey, 2011; Elixir: A History of Water and Humankind, 2011. EDITOR: Victoria Falls Handbook: A Handbook to the Victoria Falls, the Batoka Gorge and Part of the Upper Zambesi River, 1964; A Short History of Zambia: From the Earliest Times until A.D. 1900, 1966; The Oxford Companion to Archaeology, 1996; Eyewitness to Discovery, 1997; The Seventy Great Mysteries of the Ancient World: Unlocking the Secrets of Past Civilizations, 2001; The Seventy Great Inventions of the Ancient World, 2004; Discovery!: Unearthing the New Treasures of Archaeology, 2007. **Address:** Lindbriar Corporation, 170 Hot Springs Rd., Santa Barbara, CA 93108, U.S.A. **Online address:** brian@brianfagan.com

FAGAN, Louis J. American (born United States), b. 1971. **Genres:** Novels. **Career:** Listener, editorial assistant, 1995-96; State University of New York, adjunct instructor in English, 1997-. **Publications:** New Boots (novel), 1999. Contributor to periodicals. **Address:** 612 W 6th St., Jamestown, NY 14701-4717, U.S.A.

FAGAN, Thomas K(evin). American (born United States), b. 1943. **Genres:** Psychology. **Career:** Western Illinois University, assistant professor, associate professor of psychology, 1969-76, School Psychology Program, director, 1969-76; University of Memphis, associate professor, 1976-80, professor of psychology, 1980-, School Psychology Programs, coordinator, 1976-, director; National Association of School Psychologists, president, 1980-81, 1987-88; NASP Communique, editor, 1981-87; International School Psychologists Association, co-chair. **Publications:** School Psychology: Past, Present, and Future, 1994, 3rd ed., 2007; (ed. with G.R. VandenBos) Exploring Applied Psychology: Origins and Critical Analyses, 1993; (ed. with P.G. Warden) Historical Encyclopedia of School Psychology, 1996. **Address:** Department of Psychology, University of Memphis, 202 Psychology Bldg., Memphis, TN 38152-3230, U.S.A. **Online address:** tom-fagan@mail.psyc.memphis.edu

FAGGEN, Robert. American (born United States) **Genres:** Literary Criticism And History, Poetry, History. **Career:** Claremont McKenna College, faculty, 1988-94, associate professor of literature, 1994-2005, Barton Evans and H. Andrea Neves Professor of Literature and chair, 2005-, Family of Benjamin Z. Gould Center for Humanistic Studies, director; Claremont Graduate University, adjunct associate professor; The Paris Review, contributing editor. **Publications:** Robert Frost and the Challenge of Darwin, 1997; (ed.) Striving Towards Being: The Letters of Thomas Merton and Czeslaw Milosz, 1997; (ed. and intro.) Selected Poems, 1997; (ed. and intro.) Early Poems, 1998; (ed.) The Cambridge Companion to Robert Frost, 2001; (ed.) The Notebooks of Robert Frost, 2006; The Cambridge Introduction to Robert Frost, 2008. Contributor to books and periodicals. **Address:** Family of Benja-

min Z. Gould Center for Humanistic, Studies, Claremont McKenna College, 850 Columbia Ave., Claremont, CA 91711-6420, U.S.A. **Online address:** robert.faggen@cmc.edu

FAHEY, David (Allen). American (born United States), b. 1948. **Genres:** Art/Art History, Photography, Humor/Satire. **Career:** Compton College, instructor, 1974-84; G. Ray Hawkins Gallery, director, 1975-86; University of California, instructor and lecturer, 1982-84; University of Southern California, instructor, 1985; Hollywood Photographers Archive, co-founder, 1985-86; Fahey/Klein Gallery, co-owner and co-director, 1986-; Twelve Trees Press, Herb Ritts Pictures, project director, 1988. Writer. **Publications:** (With L. Rich) Masters of Starlight: Photographers in Hollywood, 1987. EDITOR: Not Fade Away: The Rock & Roll Photography of Jim Marshall, 1997; Private View: Photographs & Diary, 1998. **Address:** Fahey/Klein Gallery, 148 N La Brea Ave., Los Angeles, CA 91104, U.S.A.

FAHEY, David M(ichael). American (born United States), b. 1937. **Genres:** History. **Career:** Assumption College, instructor, 1963-65, assistant professor of history, 1965-66; University of Notre Dame, lecturer, 1965; Indiana University, assistant professor, 1966-69; Miami University, associate professor, 1969-82, professor of history, 1982-2006, part-time teacher, through 2010, now professor emeritus; Social History of Alcohol and Drugs: An Interdisciplinary Journal, editor-in-chief, 2003-04; Milestone Documents of World Religions, senior editor. **Publications:** (Co-author) The English Heritage (textbook), 1978; Temperance and Racism: John Bull, Johnny Reb and the Good Templars, 1996. EDITOR: The Collected Writings of Jessie Forsyth, 1988; The Black Lodge in White America: True Reformer Browne and His Economic Strategy, 1994; (with J.S. Blocker and I.R. Tyrrell) Alcohol and Temperance in Modern History: An International Encyclopedia, 2003; The Alabama, British Neutrality and the American Civil War by the Late Frank J. Merli, 2004; Women's Temperance Crusade in Oxford, Ohio: Including a Sketch of the Family of Dr. Alexander Guy (1800-1893), With Excerpts from the Memoir of William Evans Guy, 2010. Contributor to periodicals. **Address:** Department of History, Miami University, 279D Upham Hall, 100 Bishop Cir., 501 E High St., Oxford, OH 45056, U.S.A. **Online address:** faheydm@muohio.edu

FAHLMAN, Clyde. American (born United States), b. 1931. **Genres:** Humor/Satire, Business/Trade/Industry, Economics. **Career:** Pacific Northwest Bell, district manager for marketing, 1955-86; Portland Community College, adjunct faculty, 1986-. Writer. **Publications:** Laughing Nine to Five: The Quest for Humor in the Workplace, 1997. **Address:** Steelhead Press, 685 SW 84th Ave., Portland, OR 97225-6309, U.S.A. **Online address:** laff9to5@teleport.com

FAHN, Abraham. Israeli/Austrian (born Austria), b. 1916?. **Genres:** Botany. **Career:** Hebrew University of Jerusalem, faculty, 1945, instructor, 1949-52, lecturer, 1952-55, senior lecturer, 1955-60, associate professor, 1960-65, dean of the faculty of science, 1964-66, professor, 1965-76, pro-rector, 1969-70, Department of Botany, head, 1965-72, Otto Warburg professor, 1976-85, Otto Warburg professor emeritus of botany, 1985-; Cambridge University, visiting researcher, 1952-53; Harvard University, research fellow and Bullard fellow, 1956, visiting professor, 1981; University of Wisconsin, visiting Brittingham professor, 1972-73; International Society of Plant Morphologists, vice-president, 1995-99; International Academy of Wood Science, fellow. Writer. **Publications:** Anatomyah shel ha-te-maḥ, 1962; Tsimḥe ha-tarbut shel Yiśrael, me-et M. Zohari, 1967; Plant Anatomy, 1967, 4th ed. 1990; Secretory Tissues in Plants, 1979; (with E. Werker and P. Baas) Wood Anatomy and Identification of Trees and Shrubs from Israel and Adjacent Regions, 1986; (with D.F. Cutler) Xerophytes, 1992. **Address:** Department of Plant and Environmental Sciences, The Alexander Silberman Institute of Life Sciences, Hebrew University of Jerusalem, Edmond J. Safra Campus, Jerusalem, 91904, Israel. **Online address:** fahn@vms.huji.ac.il

FAHNESTOCK, Todd. American (born United States) **Genres:** Novels, Young Adult Fiction, Science Fiction/Fantasy, Reference. **Career:** Juvenile Diabetes Research Foundation, special events manager; Pikes Peak Writers' Conference, instructor, 2005. Writer. **Publications:** WITH G. CARWYN: Heir of Autumn (fantasy novel), 2006; Mistress of Winter, 2007; Queen of Oblivion, 2008. Contributor to periodicals. **Address:** Donald Maass Literary Agency, 121 W 27th St., Ste. 801, New York, NY 10001, U.S.A. **Online address:** todd@carwynfahnestock.com

FAHY, Thomas. American (born United States), b. 1972?. **Genres:** Novels, Mystery/Crime/Suspense, Horror, Young Adult Fiction, Literary Criticism And History, Popular Culture, Theatre. **Career:** Long Island University, associate professor of English and director of American studies; California Polytechnic University, visiting assistant professor; Loyola Marymount University, faculty; California State University, faculty. Writer. **Publications:** (Ed. with K. King and intro.) Peering behind the Curtain: Disability, Illness, and the Extraordinary Body in Contemporary Theater, 2002; Gabriel Garcia Marquez's Love in the Time of Cholera: A Reader's Guide, 2003; (ed. with K. King and intro.) Captive Audience: Prison and Captivity in Contemporary Theater, 2003; Night Visions (novel), 2004; (ed.) Considering Aaron Sorkin: Essays on the Politics, Poetics, and Sleight of Hand in the Films and Television Series, 2005; (ed.) Considering Alan Ball: Essays on Sexuality, Death, and America in the Television and Film Writings, 2006; Freak Shows and the Modern American Imagination: Constructing the Damaged Body from Willa Cather to Truman Capote, 2006; (ed.) Considering David Chase: Essays on The Rockford Files, Northern Exposure, and The Sopranos, 2007; The Unspoken (young adult novel), 2008; Sleepless (young adult novel), 2009; (ed.) The Philosophy of Horror, 2010; Staging Modern American Life: Popular Culture in the Experimental Theatre of Millay, Cummings, and Dos Passos, 2011. **Address:** Department of English, Long Island University, C. W. Post, 720 Northern Blvd., Brookville, NY 11548-1319, U.S.A. **Online address:** tom@thomasfahy.com

FAIG, Kenneth W(alter). American (born United States), b. 1948. **Genres:** Literary Criticism And History, Essays, Young Adult Fiction. **Career:** North American Co. for Life and Health Insurance, actuary, 1973-87; Allstate Life Insurance Co., actuary, 1987-89; Moshassuck Press, publisher, 1987-; Poly-Systems, actuary, 1989-. Writer. **Publications:** H.P. Lovecraft: His Life, His Work, 1979; The Parents of H.P. Lovecraft, 1990; Edward Francis Gamwell and His Family, 1991; (comp.) Early Historical Accounts of Foster, Rhode Island, 1993; Some of the Descendants of Asaph Phillips and Esther Whipple of Foster, Rhode Island, 1993; Corrections and Additions for Some of the Descendants of Asaph Phillips and Esther Whipple of Foster, Rhode Island, 1994; Tales of the Lovecraft Collectors, 1995; Going Home, 1995; (ed.) Susan's Obituary, 1996; (ed.) Criticism of Amateur Verse, 1998; The Coast of Bohemia, 2000; Big Heart: Remembering Robert Earl Hughes, 1926-1958, 2001; (with C.J. Docherty and A.L. Searles) Devonshire Ancestry of Howard Phillips Lovecraft, 2003; The Unknown Lovecraft, 2008; (ed. with S. Donnelly) Dead Houses & Other Works, 2008. **Address:** 2311 Swainwood Dr., Glenview, IL 60025, U.S.A. **Online address:** moshasuk@interaccess.com

FAIGEN, Anne G. American (born United States), b. 1930. **Genres:** Novels, Mystery/Crime/Suspense. **Career:** Writer and educator. **Publications:** Finding Her Way (young adult novel), 1997; Brave Salamander (young adult novel), 2005; New World Waiting (young adult novel), 2006; Frame Work (mystery novel), 2008; Out of Turns (mystery novel), 2009. **Address:** Pittsburgh, PA , U.S.A. **Online address:** marcnann@comcast.net

FAIGLEY, Lester. American (born United States), b. 1947?. **Genres:** Writing/Journalism, Technology, Speech/Rhetoric, Communications/Media. **Career:** University of Texas, Department of English, faculty, 1976-, professor of English, 1979-, Robert Adger Law and Thos. H. Law professor in humanities, Department of Rhetoric and Writing, founding director, 1993-2001, faculty, Concentration in Science, Technology, and Society, founding director, 1998-2000, Undergraduate Writing Center, director, 2002-06; National University of Singapore, senior fellow, 1986-87; Pennsylvania State University, visiting professor, 1990; Oxford University, Brasenose College, visiting professor, 1992. Writer. **Publications:** (With N.D. Kinghorn and T. Clemens) A Syntactic Approach to College Writing: An Analysis of Theory and Effect, 1981; (with S.P. Witte) Evaluating College Writing Programs, 1983; (co-author) Assessing Writers' Knowledge and Processes of Composing, 1985; Fragments of Rationality: Postmodernity and the Subject of Composition, 1992; The Longman Guide to the Web, 2000; (with J. Selzer) Good Reasons with Contemporary Arguments, 2001, 5th ed. as Good Reasons: Researching and Writing Effective Arguments, 2012; The Brief Penguin Handbook, 2003, 4th ed. as The Brief Penguin Handbook with Exercises, 2012; Penguin Handbook, 2003, 4th ed., 2012; (co-author) Picturing Texts, 2004; Writing: A Guide for College and Beyond, 2007, 3rd ed., 2012; The Little Penguin Handbook, 2007, 3rd ed., 2012; Backpack Writing, 2008, 3rd ed., 2011; (with J. Selzer) Little Argument, 2010. **Address:** Department of English, University of Texas, 216 Calhoun Hall, 1 University Sta. B5000, Austin, TX 78712-1164, U.S.A. **Online address:** faigley@uts.cc.utexas.edu

FAIGMAN, David L. American (born United States) **Genres:** Sciences, Law. **Career:** University of California at San Francisco, Hastings College of the Law, assistant professor, 1987-90, associate professor, 1990-93, professor of law, 1993-2006, Harry H. and Lillian H. Hastings research chair, 1997-98, distinguished professor of law, 2006-07, David L. Faigman, John F. Digardi distinguished professor of law, 2007-, Hastings Consortium on Law, Science, and Health Policy, director, 2009-; University of Arkansas, visiting professor, 1992; Universite D'Aix-Marseille, visiting professor, 1995; Universita Degli Studi di Trento, visiting professor, 1995, 1998; Universita Degli Studi di Allassandria, visiting professor, 2000. Writer. **Publications:** Modern Scientific Evidence: The Law and Science of Expert Testimony, 1997, 2nd ed., 2002; Legal Alchemy: The Use and Misuse of Science in the Law, 1999; (co-ed.) Science in the Law: Forensic Science Issues, 2002; (co-ed.) Science in the Law: Standards Statistics and Research Issues, 2002; (co-ed.) Science in the Law: Social and Behavioral Science Issues, 2002; The Evidence Map, 2003; Laboratory of Justice: The Supreme Courts 200-Year Struggle to Integrate Science and the Law, 2004; Constitutional Fictions: A Unified Theory of Constitutional Facts, 2008. **Address:** Hastings College of the Law, University of California, 200 McAllister St., San Francisco, CA 94102, U.S.A. **Online address:** faigmand@uchastings.edu

FAILING, Patricia. American (born United States), b. 1944. **Genres:** Art/Art History. **Career:** Arts News Magazine, associate editor, 1978-80, contributing editor, 1980-; Lewis and Clark College, lecturer in philosophy, 1985; Reed College, visiting associate professor, 1986; University of Washington, assistant professor, 1989-92, associate professor of art history, 1992-2000, professor, 2000, Division of Art History, chair, 1995-2000, 2003-06, School of Art, acting director, 2007-. **Publications:** Best-loved Art from American Museums, 1983; Doris Chase, Artist in Motion, with Videotape, 1991; Ted Katz: Recent Paintings, 1991; Howard Kottler: Face to Face, 1995. Contributor of articles to books and periodicals. **Address:** Department of History, School of Art, University of Washington, Rm. 311, Art Bldg., Seattle, WA 98195-3440, U.S.A. **Online address:** failing@u.washington.edu

FAIN, Michael. (Judith Michael). American (born United States), b. 1937?. **Genres:** Novels, Romance/Historical, Photography, Human Relations/Parenting. **Career:** National Aeronautics and Space Administration, engineer; JM Productions Ltd., owner. Writer and photographer. **Publications:** NOVELS AS JUDITH MICHAEL: Deceptions, 1982; Possessions, 1984; Private Affairs, 1986; Inheritance, 1988; Ruling Passion, 1989; Sleeping Beauty, 1991; Pot of Gold, 1993; A Tangled Web, 1994; Acts of Love, 1996; A Certain Smile, 1999; The Real Mother, 2005. Contributor to periodicals. **Address:** Jane Rotrosen Agency, 318 E 51st St., New York, NY 10022, U.S.A. **Online address:** mzf25@aol.com

FAIN, Sarah. American (born United States), b. 1971?. **Genres:** Novels, Young Adult Non-fiction. **Career:** AmeriCorps, Teach for America, English instructor. Writer and producer. **Publications:** (With E. Craft) Bass Ackwards and Belly Up (novel), 2006; (with E. Craft) Footfree and Fancyloose (novel), 2008. **Address:** Poppy Publishing, 237 Park Ave., New York, NY 10017, U.S.A. **Online address:** sarahfain@gmail.com

FAINARU, Steve. American (born United States) **Genres:** Sports/Fitness. **Career:** San Jose Mercury News, staff; Hartford Courant, staff; Boston Globe, New York bureau chief, Latin America bureau chief, investigative reporter, sportswriter; Washington Post, investigative reporter, 2000-10, Baghdad Bureau, foreign correspondent, 2004-07; The Bay Citizen, managing editor for news, 2010-, interim editor-in-chief. **Publications:** (With R. Sanchez) The Duke of Havana: Baseball, Cuba, and the Search for the American Dream, 2001; Big Boy Rules: America's Mercenaries Fighting in Iraq, 2008. Contributor of articles to periodicals. **Address:** The Bay Citizen, 126 Post St., Ste. 500, San Francisco, CA 94108, U.S.A.

FAINLIGHT, Ruth. British/American (born United States), b. 1931. **Genres:** Novellas/Short Stories, Poetry, Songs/Lyrics And Libretti, Translations, Literary Criticism And History, Young Adult Fiction. **Career:** Vanderbilt University, poet-in-residence, 1985, 1990. **Publications:** A Forecast, A Fable, 1958; Cages, 1966; (ed.) 18 Poems from 1966, 1967; To See the Matter Clearly, and Other Poems, 1968; (with A. Sillitoe and T. Hughes) Poems, 1971; Daylife and Nightlife: Stories, 1971; The Region's Violence, 1973; Twenty One Poems, 1973; Another Full Moon, 1976; Two Fire Poems, 1977; (with J. Rothchild) Leaves, 1977; The Function of Tears, 1979; Two Wind Poems, 1980; Sibyls and Others, 1980; Fifteen to Infinity, 1983; Climates,

1984; Selected Poems, 1987, rev. ed., 1997; Three Poems, 1988; The Knot, 1990; Sibyls: A Book of Poems, 1991; This Time of Year: A Collection of Poems, 1994; Dr. Clock's Last Case: And Other stories, 1994; Sugar-Paper Blue, 1997; (contrib.) Handbag: For Soprano, Clarinet in Bb, Bass Clarinet in Bb, Viola, Cello, and Double Bass, 2001; Burning Wire, 2002; Feathers: Eight Poems, 2002; Postcard from Tunisia, 2004; Moon Wheels, 2006; New and Collected Poems, 2010. TRANSLATOR: (with A. Sillitoe) L. de Vega, Fuenteovejuna (title means: 'All Citizens Are Soldiers'), 1969; S. de Mello Breyner Andresen, Navigacions, 1983; S. de Mello Breyner Andresen, Marine Rose, 1987; (and intro. with R.J. Littman) Sophocles, The Theban Plays: Oedipus the King, Oedipus at Colonus, Antigone, 2009; Works appear in anthologies. **Address:** 14 Ladbroke Terr., London, GL W11 3PG, England. **Online address:** ruthfainlight@writersartists.net

FAIR, David. American (born United States), b. 1952. **Genres:** Children's Fiction, Music. **Career:** Carroll County Public Library, librarian, 1977-. Writer. **Publications:** The Fabulous Four Skunks, 1996. **Address:** 1 Black Oak Ln., Westminster, MD 21157-5711, U.S.A.

FAIRBAIRN, Brett. Canadian (born Canada), b. 1959. **Genres:** Economics, History. **Career:** University of Saskatchewan, Department of History, assistant professor, professor, 1986-, director of graduate studies in history, 1996-99, Saskatchewan Archives Board, chairperson, 1997-99, Students' Union, president, director of centre for the study of cooperatives, 2000-04, head of department of history, 2004-, principal investigator of the largest research project ever undertaken on cooperatives, 2002-07, provost and vice president of academic, 2008-, adjunct professor of history, University Council, chair; Government of Saskatchewan, special adviser to department of post-secondary education, 1996, Saskatchewan Archives Board, chair, 1997-. Writer. **Publications:** Building a Dream: The Co-operative Retailing System in Western Canada, 1928-1988, 1989; (co-author) Co-operatives and Community Development: Economics in Social Perspective, 1991; (ed. with H.R. Baker and J.A. Draper) Dignity and Growth: Citizen Participation in Social Change, 1991; Meaning of Rochdale: The Rochdale Pioneers and the Co-operative Principles, 1994; Democracy in the Undemocratic State: The German Reichstag Elections of 1898 and 1903, 1997; (ed. with I. MacPherson and N. Russell) Canadian Cooperatives in the Year 2000: Memory, Mutual Aid and the Millennium, 2001; Living the Dream: Membership and Marketing in the Co-operative Retailing System, 2003; (ed. with N. Russell) Co-operative Membership and Globalization: New Directions in Research and Practice, 2004; Canada's Co-operative Province: Individualism and Mutualism in a Settler Society, 1905-2005: Reflections In Celebration off Saskatchewan's Centennial Year, 2005; Co-operative Heritage: Where We've Come From: Reflections on Co-operative History on the Occasion of Saskatchewan's Hundredth Anniversary, 2006. **Address:** Department of History, University of Saskatchewan, 208 College Bldg., 101 Diefenbaker Pl., Saskatoon, SK S7N 5B8, Canada. **Online address:** brett.fairbairn@usask.ca

FAIRBANKS, Nancy. *See* **HERNDON, Nancy.**

FAIRCHILD, B(ertram) H. American (born United States), b. 1942. **Genres:** Poetry, Literary Criticism And History. **Career:** C&W Machine Works, staff, through 1966; Hercules Inc., staff, 1966-67; Kearney State College, instructor, 1968-70; University of Tulsa, teaching fellow, 1970-73; Southwest Texas State University, assistant professor, 1973-76; Texas Woman's University, associate professor, 1976-83; California State University, professor, 1983-2005, professor emeritus, 2005-; Claremont Graduate University, faculty; University of North Texas, faculty. Poet. **Publications:** Such Holy Song: Music as Idea, Form and Image in the Poetry of William Blake (literary criticism), 1980; C&W Machine Works (chapbook), 1983; Flight (chapbook), 1985; The System of Which the Body Is One Part (chapbook), 1988. POETRY: Arrival of the Future, 1985, 2nd ed., 2000; The Art of the Lathe: Poems, 1998; Local Knowledge, 1991; Early Occult Memory Systems of the Lower Midwest, 2003; Usher, 2009. Contributor of articles to periodicals. **Address:** California State University, 5500 University Pkwy., San Bernardino, CA 92407, U.S.A. **Online address:** bhfairchil@aol.com

FAIRFIELD, John D. American (born United States), b. 1955. **Genres:** Urban Studies, History. **Career:** University of Rochester, lecturer in History, 1980, instructor, 1982-84; Wells College, lecturer in History, 1981, instructor, 1982-84; Rochester Institute of Technology, lecturer in history, 1982-83, instructor, 1982-84; Alfred University, instructor, 1982-84, lecturer in history, 1983-84; Xavier University, Department of History, assistant profes-

sor, 1984-90, associate professor of history, 1990-96, professor, 1996-, chair, Honors Programs, professor, Xavier's Institute for Politics and Public Life, academic director. Writer. **Publications:** The Mysteries of the Great City: The Politics of Urban Design, 1877-1937, 1993; Public and Its Possibilities: Triumphs and Tragedies in the American City, 2010. Contributor to journals. **Address:** Department of History, Xavier University, 609 Schott Hall, 3800 Victory Pkwy., PO Box 5161, Cincinnati, OH 45207, U.S.A. **Online address:** fairfiel@xavier.edu

FAIRFIELD, Paul. Canadian (born Canada), b. 1966. **Genres:** Philosophy, Education, Politics/Government, Social Sciences. **Career:** Symposium, editor, 2001-07; Queen's University, Department of Philosophy, adjunct assistant professor, 2002-, associate professor; International Institute for Hermeneutics, senior associate fellow. **Publications:** (With G.B. Madison and I. Harris) Is There a Canadian Philosophy? Reflections on the Canadian Identity, 2000; Moral Selfhood in the Liberal Tradition: The Politics of Individuality, 2000; Theorizing Praxis: Studies in Hermeneutical Pragmatism, 2000; Death and Life, 2001; The Ways of Power: Hermeneutics, Ethics and Social Criticism, 2002; Public/Private, 2005; Why Democracy?, 2008; Education After Dewey, 2009; (ed.) John Dewey and Continental Philosophy, 2010; (ed.) Education, Dialogue and Hermeneutics, 2010; Philosophical Hermeneutics Reinterpreted: Dialogues with Existentialism, Pragmatism, Critical Theory and Postmodernism, 2011. Contributor to books and periodicals. **Address:** Department of Philosophy, Queen's University, Watson Hall, Kingston, ON K7L 3N6, Canada. **Online address:** paulfairfield@hotmail.com

FAIRLEY, James S(tewart). American/Irish (born Ireland), b. 1940. **Genres:** Animals/Pets, Natural History, Zoology, Sciences, Education. **Career:** Queen's University, research fellow, 1966-68; National University of Ireland, University College, lecturer in zoology, 1968-91, associate professor, 1991-99, Department of Zoology, professor emeritus. Writer. **Publications:** Irish Wild Mammals: A Guide to the Literature, 1972, 2nd ed., 1992; An Irish Beast Book: A Natural History of Ireland's Furred Wildlife, 1975, 2nd ed., 1984; (ed.) The Experienced Huntsman, 1977; Irish Whales and Whaling, 1981; A Basket of Weasels: The Weasel Family of Ireland and Other Furred Irish Beasts: Bats, the Rabbit, Hares and Rodents, 2001. **Address:** 15 Luxor Gardens, Belfast, AT BT5 5NB, Northern Ireland.

FAIRMAN, Joan A(lexandra). American (born United States), b. 1935. **Genres:** Children's Fiction, Animals/Pets. **Career:** Curtis Publishing Co., executive secretary, 1953-70; Towers, Perrin, Forster and Crosby Inc., executive secretary, 1970-76, administrative assistant, 1976-. Writer. **Publications:** A Penny Saved, 1971. **Address:** Salem Harbour, Apt. C-2, 435 Olde Bridge Rd., Andalusia, PA 19020, U.S.A.

FAIRSTEIN, Linda A. American (born United States), b. 1947. **Genres:** Mystery/Crime/Suspense, Law, Novels, Young Adult Non-fiction. **Career:** New York County District Attorney's Office, staff, 1972-, Sex Crimes Prosecution Unit, chief, 1976-2002, Trial Division, deputy chief, 1981-2002; Mount Sinai Hospital, Friends of the Rape Crisis Intervention Program, board director, 1990-; New York Women's Agenda, board director, 1993-; Phoenix House Foundation, board director, 1994-; Choice Cares, board director, full-time writer and consultant, 2002-. **Publications:** Sexual Violence: Our War against Rape, 1993; Final Jeopardy, 1996; Likely to Die, 1997; Cold Hit, 1999; The Deadhouse, 2001; The Bone Vault, 2003; (co-author) I'd Kill for That, 2004; The Kills, 2004; Entombed, 2005; Death Dance, 2006; (with O. Penzler) The Best American Crime Reporting, 2007; Bad Blood, 2007; Killer Heat, 2008; Lethal Legacy, 2009; (ed.) Mystery Writers of America Presents The Prosecution Rests: New Stories about Courtrooms, Criminals, and the Law, 2009; Hell Gate, 2010; Silent Mercy, 2011. **Address:** Dutton Books, 375 Hudson St., New York, NY 10014-3657, U.S.A.

FAITH, Nicholas. British (born England), b. 1933?. **Genres:** Business/ Trade/Industry, Economics, Documentaries/Reportage. **Career:** The Economist, assistant editor, senior editor; Sunday Times, industrial editor, deputy business editor, business news editor, senior editor; Independent on Sunday, contributing editor; International Spirits Challenge, founder, chairman. **Publications:** The Infiltrators: The European Business Invasion of America, 1971; Money Matters, 1973; Wankel: The Curious Story behind the Revolutionary Engine, 1975 in UK as The Wankel Engine: The Story of the Revolutionary Rotary Engine, 1976; The Winemasters, 1978; Safety in Numbers: The Mysterious World of Swiss Banking, 1982; Victorian Vineyard: Chateau Loudenne and the Gilbeys, 1983; Sold: The Rise and Fall of the House of

Sotheby, 1985; Cognac, 1987; The Simon and Schuster Pocket Guide to Cognac and Other Brandies, 1987; The Story of Champagne: The History and Pleasures of the Most Celebrated of Wines, 1989; The World the Railways Made, 1990; Château Margaux, 1991, rev. ed., 2005; Château Beychevelle, 1991; Classic Trucks, 1995; Classic Ships: Romance and Reality, 1996; Black Box: The Air-Crash Detectives: Why Air Safety is No Accident, 1997; (with I. Wisniewski) Classic Vodka, 1997; Classic Trains, 1998; Crash: The Limits of Car Safety, 1998; Blaze: The Forensics of Fire, 2000; Classic Brandy, 2000; Derail: Why Trains Crash, 2001; A Very Different Country: A Typically English Revolution, 2002; Burgundy and Its Wines, 2002; Liquid Gold: The Story of Australian Wine and its Makers, 2002; Australia's Liquid Gold, 2003; Bronfmans: The Rise and Fall of the House of Seagram, 2006; The Winemakers of Bordeaux. **Address:** St. Martin's Press, 175 5th Ave., New York, NY 10010, U.S.A.

FALCK, Colin. British (born England), b. 1934. **Genres:** Poetry, Literary Criticism And History, Philosophy, Theology/Religion. **Career:** University of London, London School of Economics, lecturer in sociology, 1961-62, Chelsea College, lecturer in humanities, 1964-84; The Review, founder and co-editor, 1962, 1965-72; The New Review, poetry editor, 1974-78; Thurlow Road Poetry Workshop, acting chair, 1984-; Syracuse University, London Centre, adjunct lecturer of English literature, 1985-89; York College, associate professor in modern literature, 1989-99. **Publications:** The Garden in the Evening: Poems from the Spanish of Antonio Machado, 1964; Promises (poetry pamphlet), 1969; Backwards into the Smoke, 1973; In This Dark Light, 1978; Myth, Truth, and Literature: Towards a True Post-Modernism, 1989, 2nd ed., 1994; Memorabilia, 1992; Post-Modern Love: An Unreliable Narration (poems), 1997; American and British Verse in the Twentieth Century: The Poetry that Matters, 2003. EDITOR: (with I. Hamilton) Poems Since 1900: An Anthology of British and American Verse in the Twentieth Century, 1975; Robinson Jeffers: Selected Poems, 1987; (and intro.) Edna St. Vincent Millay: Selected Poems: The Centenary Edition, 1991. Contributor to journals. **Address:** John Johnson Ltd., Clerkenwell House, 45-47 Clerkenwell Green, London, GL EC1R OHT, England.

FALCO, Edward. American (born United States), b. 1948. **Genres:** Novels, Plays/Screenplays, Poetry, Novellas/Short Stories. **Career:** Syracuse University, instructor in English, 1979-84; Onondaga Community College, adjunct instructor in English, 1979-82; LeMoyne College, adjunct instructor in English, 1982-84; Virginia Polytechnic Institute and State University, instructor, 1984-88, assistant professor, 1988-90, associate professor of English, 1990-98, professor of English and creative writing, 1998-, MFA Program, director, creative writing committee, chair, 1989-. Writer. **Publications:** Concert in the Park of Culture (prose poems), 1984; Plato at Scratch Daniel's and Other Stories, 1990; Winter in Florida (novel), 1990; Sea Island, 1995; Acid, 1996; A Dream with Demons, 1997; Wolf Point, 2005; Sabbath Night in the Church of the Piranha, 2005; In the Park of Culture, 2005; Saint John of the Five Boroughs, 2009; Burning Man, 2011; The Family Corleone, 2012. **Address:** Department of English, Virginia Polytechnic Institute, Blacksburg, VA 24061-0112, U.S.A. **Online address:** efalco524@verizon.net

FALCON, Mark. (Eileen Marion Pickering). British (born England), b. 1940?. **Genres:** Novels, Young Adult Fiction, Westerns/Adventure. **Career:** Publisher and writer. **Publications:** NOVELS: Reluctant Outlaw, 1979; The Yellow Bandana, 1980; Lightning Hits Glory Town, 1980; The Outlaw's Woman, 2003; Outlaw's Loot, 2004; Kinsella's Revenge, 2004; Smoky Hill Trail, 2006; They Called Him Lightning, 2007; Lightning at the Hanging Tree, 2008. **Address:** 121 Highbury Grove, Clapham, BD MK41 6DU, England.

FALCONER, Delia. Australian (born Australia), b. 1966?. **Genres:** Novels, Novellas/Short Stories. **Career:** Writer, 1994-; Royal Melbourne Institute of Technology, creative writing teacher; University of Technology Sydney, faculty, 2004-, Creative Practices Group, senior lecturer, Arts and Social Sciences, faculty. **Publications:** The Service of Clouds (novel), 1998; Lost Thoughts of Soldiers, 2006; (ed.) Penguin Book of The Road, 2008; (ed.) Best Australian Stories, 2008. Contributor of articles to journals. **Address:** Creative Practices Group, University of Technology Sydney, Rm. CB03.04.49, 15 Broadway, Ultimo, NW 2007, Australia. **Online address:** delia.falconer@uts.edu.au

FALCONER, Helen. Irish/British (born England), b. 1958?. **Genres:** Novels, Young Adult Fiction, Mystery/Crime/Suspense. **Career:** Guardian Newspaper, book reviewer; journalist and writer. **Publications:** Primrose Hill,

1999; Sky High: A Novel, 2003. **Address:** c/o Author Mail, Persea Books, 853 Broadway, Ste. 601, New York, NY 10003, U.S.A.

FALCONER, Lee N. See **MAY, Julian.**

FALES-HILL, Susan. American/Italian (born Italy), b. 1962. **Genres:** Autobiography/Memoirs, Novels, Young Adult Non-fiction, History, Sciences. **Career:** Writer and television producer. **Publications:** Always Wear Joy: My Mother Bold and Beautiful, 2003; One Flight Up: A Novel, 2010; Im perfect bliss, 2012. Contributor to magazines. **Address:** c/o Author Mail, Harper-Collins Publishers, 10 E 53 St., 7th Fl., New York, NY 10022-5244, U.S.A. **Online address:** susanfaleshill@yahoo.com

FALK, Avner. Israeli (born Israel), b. 1943. **Genres:** History, Politics/Government, Psychiatry, Psychology, Biography, Geography. **Career:** Jerusalem Psychiatric Hostel and Halfway House, psychologist, 1966; Washington University Child Guidance Clinic, St. Louis, trainee, 1966-67; St. Louis State Hospital and Missouri Institute of Psychiatry, intern, 1967-68; Jewish Hospital of St. Louis, Department of Psychitary, intern, 1968-69; St. Louis Child Guidance Clinic, psychologist, 1970-71; Talbiyeh Mental Health Center, clinical psychologist, 1971-72; Sarah Herzog Mental Health Center, senior and supervising clinical psychologist, 1972-82; Kfar Shaul Mental Health Center, senior and supervising clinical psychologist, 1973-75; Etanim Mental Health Center, senior and supervising clinical psychologist, 1975-83; Hebrew University Medical School, clinical lecturer in psychiatry, 1976-79. Writer. **Publications:** Books: Moshe Dayan, halsh veha Agadah: Biographia Psychoanalytith, 1985; David Melech Yisrael: Biographia Psychoanalytith shel David Ben-Gurion, 1987; Herzl, King of the Jews: A Psychoanalytic Biography of Theodor Herzl, 1993; A Psychoanalytic History of the Jews, 1996; Fratricide in the Holy Land: A Psychoanalytic View of the Arab-Israeli Conflict, 2004; Napoleon Against Himself: A Psychobiography, 2005; Anti-Semitism: A History and Psychoanalysis of Contemporary Hatred, 2008; Islamic Terror: Conscious and Unconscious Motives, 2008; Franks and Saracens: Reality and Fantasy in the Crusades, 2010; The Riddle of Barack Obama: A Psychobiography, 2010. **Address:** 6 Caspi St., North Talpiot, Jerusalem, 93554, Israel. **Online address:** avner.falk@usa.net

FALK, Barbara J. Canadian (born Canada), b. 1962. **Genres:** Politics/Government, Institutions/Organizations, Economics, Social Commentary. **Career:** Ontario Women's Directorate, Pay Equity Project, policy analyst, 1985-87, executive assistant, 1987-88; Pay Equity Commission of Ontario, Policy and Research Branch, senior policy advisor, 1988-89; Seneca College, Human Resources Management, instructor, 1989-91; Cooperative Housing Federation of Toronto, president, 1989; George Brown College, instructor, 1989-91; Sony Music Entertainment (Canada) Inc., director of human resources, 1989-91; Government of Ontario, Compensation Policy Branch, director, 1991-95; York University, teacher of political science, 1998-2000; Humber College, professor, 2000-03; University of Toronto, Centre for European, Russian, and Eurasian Studies, fellow, 2000-06, lecturer in political science, 2003-; Canadian Forces College, Department of Defence Studies, associate professor, 2006-. Writer. **Publications:** The Dilemmas of Dissidence in East-Central Europe: Citizen Intellectuals and Philosopher Kings, 2003; Making Sense of Political Trials: Causes and Categories, 2008. Contributor of articles to periodicals. **Address:** Department of Defence Studies, Canadian Forces College, 215 Yonge Blvd., Toronto, ON M5M 3H9, Canada. **Online address:** falkb@sympatico.com

FALK, Candace. American (born United States), b. 1947. **Genres:** History, Politics/Government, Social Commentary, Women's Studies And Issues, Biography, Young Adult Non-fiction. **Career:** Woodlawn Mental Health Center, research associate, 1970-71; Stockton State College, instructor in methods of inquiry, 1971-72; Center for Social Research and Education, editor, 1972-79; Southeast Asia Resource Center, editor and research associate, 1976-79; University of California, Emma Goldman Papers Project, editor, director and Guggenheim fellow, 1980-. **Publications:** Love, Anarchy and Emma Goldman: A Biography, 1984, rev. ed., 1990; The Emma Goldman Papers (microfilm ed.), 1991; (with L. Roose and M.A. Dougherty) The Life and Times of Emma Goldman: A Curriculum for Middle and High School Students: Primary Historical Documents, 2nd ed., 1992; (ed.) Emma Goldman: A Guide to Her Life and Documentary Sources, 1995; Emma Goldman: Selections from the American Years-A Documentary Edition, 4 vols., 2002-05; Emma

Goldman: A Documentary History of the American Years, 2003. **Address:** The Emma Goldman Papers, University of California, 2241 Channing Way, Berkeley, CA 94704, U.S.A. **Online address:** emma@uclink.berkeley.edu

FALK, Dean. American (born United States), b. 1944. **Genres:** Sciences. **Career:** Rollins College, assistant professor of anthropology, 1976-77; Southern Illinois University, assistant professor of anthropology, 1977-79; Boston University, assistant professor of health sciences, 1979-80; University of Puerto Rico, School of Medicine, assistant and associate professor of anatomy, 1980-86; Caribbean Primate Research Center, Primate Skeletal Collection, curator, 1982-86; Purdue University, associate professor of anthropology, 1986-88; State University of New York, professor of anthropology, 1988-2001, adjunct professor of psychology, 1991-2001; New York University, visiting professor of anthropology, 1991-92; Journal of Human Evolution, associate editor, 1998-2000; Florida State University, Department of Anthropology, professor of anthropology, 2001-03, chair, 2002-08, Hale G. Smith professor of anthropology, 2003-. **Publications:** (With C.A. Reed) The Stature and Weight of Sterkfontein 14: A Gracile Australopithecine from Transvaal as Determined from the Innominate Bone, 1977; External Neuroanatomy of Old World Monkeys (Cercopithecoidea), 1978; (ed. with E. Armstrong) Primate Brain Evolution: Methods and Concepts, 1982; Evolution of the Brain and Cognition in Hominids, 1992; Braindance, 1992, rev. ed. as Braindance: New Discoveries about Human Origins and Brain Evolution, 2004; Primate Diversity, 2000; (ed. with K.R. Gibson) Evolutionary Anatomy of the Primate Cerebral Cortex, 2001; (with G.G. Gallup, Jr. and P. Keenan) The Face in the Mirror: The Search for the Origins of Consciousness, 2003; Finding Our Tongues: Mothers, Infants and the Origins of Language, 2009; The Fossil Chronicles: How Two Controversial Discoveries Changed Our View of Human Evolution, 2011. **Address:** Department of Anthropology, Florida State University, 1847 W Tennessee St., Tallahassee, FL 32306-7772, U.S.A. **Online address:** dfalk@fsu.edu

FALK, Lee. *See* **COPPER, Basil.**

FALK, Peter H(astings). American (born United States), b. 1950. **Genres:** Art/Art History. **Career:** Independent art historian, researcher and writer, 1976-; Sound View Press, publisher, 1985-2000; Falk Art Reference, publisher, 2001-; AskART, editor-in-chief, 2005. **Publications:** The Photographic Art Market, 1981; (ed.) Who Was Who in American Art, 3 vols., 1985-1999; (with P.J. Staiti) Minerva J. Chapman, 1986; American Artists Materials Suppliers Directory, 1987; (ed.) The Annual exhibition record of the Pennsylvania Academy of the Fine Arts, 1988; Dictionary of Signatures & Monograms of American Artists: From the Colonial Period to the Mid 20th Century, 1988; (ed.) The annual Exhibition Record of the Art Institute of Chicago, 1888-1950, 1990; (ed.) Annual Exhibition Record of the National Academy of Design, 1901-1950, 1990; Print price index, 1991; (ed.) The Biennial Exhibition Record of the Corcoran Gallery of Art, 1907-1967, 1991; (ed.) The Annual & Biennial Exhibition Record of the Whitney Museum of American Art, 1918-1989, 1991; (with A. Lewis) Annie Gooding Sykes: (1855-1931): An American Watercolorist Rediscovered, 1998; (ed.) F. Luis Mora: America's Annual Exhibition Record of the National Academy of Design: First Hispanic Master (1874-1940), 2008. **Address:** Hastings Art Management Services Inc., 70 Wall St., PO Box 833, Madison, CT 06443, U.S.A. **Online address:** peterfalk@comcast.net

FALK, Stanley Lawrence. American (born United States), b. 1927. **Genres:** History, International Relations/Current Affairs, Military/Defense/Arms Control, Adult Non-fiction. **Career:** U.S. Department of the Army, Office of Chief of Military History, military historian, 1949-54, 1959-62; American University, affiliated with bureau for social science research, 1954-56, Special Operations Research Office, consultant, 1963-; U.S. Department of Defense, joint chiefs of staff, affiliated with history section, 1956-59; Industrial College of the Armed Forces, associate professor of security affairs, 1962-70, professor of international relations, 1970-74; U.S. Air Force, chief historian, 1974-80; U.S. Army Center of Military History, deputy chief historian for Southeast Asia, 1980-; Historical Evaluation and Research Organization, associate, 1963-. Writer. **Publications:** Bataan: The March of Death, 1962, rev. ed., 1989; The International Arena, 1964; (with H.B. Yoshpe) Organization for National Security, 1965; Human Resources for National Strength, 1966; Decision at Leyte, 1966; The Liberation of the Philippines, 1971; (with T.W. Bauer) The National Security Structure, 1972; (with E.M. Gershater and G.L. Simpson) Defense Manpower, 1974; Bloodiest Victory: Palaus, 1974; Seventy Days to Singapore, 1975; Seventy Days to Singapore: The Malayan

Campaign, 1941-1942, 1975; (with H.J. Clem) The Environment of National Security, 1977; (contrib.) National Security Policy Formulation, 1977. EDITOR: The Reports of General MacArthur, 1966; The World in Ferment: Problem Areas for the United States, 1970; FOO: A Japanese-American Prisoner of the Rising Sun, 1993; (with W.M. Tsuneishi) MIS in the War against Japan: Personal Experiences Related at the 1993 MIS Capital Reunion, "The Nisei Veteran: An American Patriot", 1995. Contributor of articles to books and journals. **Address:** Department of Army, U.S. Army Ctr. of Military History, Fort Lesley J. McNair, Washington, DC 20314, U.S.A. **Online address:** stanfalk@verizon.net

FALK, Thomas H(einrich). American/German (born Germany), b. 1935. **Genres:** Literary Criticism And History, Young Adult Fiction. **Career:** University of Southern California, instructor in German, 1961-67; North Texas State University, instructor, 1964-65; Michigan State University, East Lansing, instructor, 1965-70, assistant professor, 1970-79, associate professor of German and interdisciplinary studies, 1979-92, associate professor emeritus, 1992-. Writer. **Publications:** Elias Canetti: A Critical Study, 1993. Contributor of articles journals. **Address:** Department of Linguistics and Germanic, Slavic, Asian and African Languages, Michigan State University, A-614 Wells Hall, East Lansing, MI 48824-1027, U.S.A. **Online address:** thfalk@san.rr.com

FALKINGHAM, Jane (Cecelia). British (born England), b. 1963. **Genres:** Demography, Economics, Social Sciences, Young Adult Non-fiction, Politics/Government. **Career:** City University, tutor in economics, 1985-86; London School of Economics and Political Science, research officer on the economics of retirement, 1986-88, Suntory Toyota International Centre for Economics and Related Disciplines, faculty, 1988-92, research fellow, 1991-93, lecturer in population studies, 1993-2002; University of Southampton, professor of demography and international social policy, 2002-, Faculty of Law, Arts and Social Sciences, associate dean, ESRC Centre for Population Change, director, Demography and International Social Policy, professor; Population Europe, chair. Writer. **Publications:** (With P. Johnson) Ageing and Economic Welfare, 1992; (with P. Johnson) Life-cycle Distributional Consequences of Pay-as-You-Go and Funded Pension Systems: A Microsimulation Modelling Analysis, 1993; (with A. Harding) Poverty Alleviation Versus Social Insurance Systems: A Comparison of Lifetime Redistribution, 1996. EDITOR: (with S. Baldwin and contrib.) Social Security and Social Change: New Challenges to Beveridge, 1994; (with J. Hills) The Dynamics of Welfare, 1994; (co-ed.) Household Welfare in Central Asia, 1997; Women and Gender Relations in Tajikistan, 2000; (with M. Mckee and J. Healy) Health Care in Central Asia, 2002. Works appear in anthologies. Contributor to journals. **Address:** School of Social Statistics, University of Southampton, University Rd., Southampton, SO17 1BJ, England. **Online address:** j.c.falkingham@soton.ac.uk

FALKNER, Brian. New Zealander (born New Zealand), b. 1962?. **Genres:** Novels. **Career:** Author. **Publications:** Henry and the Flea, 2003 in Australia as The Flea Thing, 2007; The Real Thing, 2004; The Super Freak, 2005; The Tomorrow Code, 2008; Brain Jack, 2009. **Address:** Auckland, New Zealand. **Online address:** brian@brianfalkner.co.nz

FALLA, Jonathan. Scottish/Jamaican (born Jamaica), b. 1954?. **Genres:** Novels, Literary Criticism And History, Young Adult Fiction. **Career:** Writer. **Publications:** Topokana Martyrs Day, 1983; True Love and Bartholomew: Rebels on the Burmese Border, 1991; The Hummingbird Tree, 1991; Down the Tubes, 1996; Diriamba!, 1997; Free Rope, 1998; Blue Poppies, 2002; Poor Mercy, 2005. **Address:** c/o The Agency, 24 Pottery Ln., Holland Pk., London, GL W11 4LZ, England.

FALLENBERG, Evan. Israeli/American (born United States), b. 1961. **Genres:** Novels. **Career:** Bar-Ilan University, Shaindy Rudoff Graduate Program in Creative Writing, instructor; MacDowell Colony, guest artist, 2002; Japanese Ministry of Education, staff. Writer and translator. **Publications:** NOVELS: (trans.) Batya Gur, Murder in Jerusalem: A Michael Ohayon Mystery, 2006; (trans.) Meir Shalev, A Pigeon and a Boy, 2007; (trans.) Alon Hilu, Death of a Monk, 2007; Light Fell, 2008; (trans.) Ron Leshem, Beaufort, 2008. **Address:** The Studio, PO Box 372, Bitan Aharon, 40294, Israel. **Online address:** evanfallenberg@gmail.com

FALLON, Ivan (Gregory). British/Irish (born Ireland), b. 1944. **Genres:** Business/Trade/Industry, Biography, Autobiography/Memoirs. **Career:** Irish Times, sub-editor, 1963-66; Thomson Newspapers, writer, 1966-67; Daily

Mirror, writer, 1967-68; Sunday Express, deputy city editor, 1967-70; Sunday Telegraph, city editor, 1979-84; Sunday Times, deputy editor, 1984-94; Independent News & Media, executive director, 1994-2002, director, 1995-, chief executive officer, 2002-; N. Brown P.L.C, director, 1994-; Independent News & Media (SA) Ltd., chief executive officer of South Africa, 1994-2002, director, 1995-, chief executive officer of Johannesburg, 1997-2002; ITouch P.L.C., chair, 2000-05; Truphone, director, 2006-; Verivox, chair, 2007-; Clear Channel Independent (Pty) Ltd., director. **Publications:** (With J.L. Srodes) Dream Maker: The Rise and Fall of John Z. DeLorean, 1983 in UK as De-Lorean: The Rise and Fall of a Dream-maker; (with C. Monckton) The Laker Story, 1984; (with J. Srodes) Takeovers, 1987; The Brothers: The Rise and Rise of Saatchi and Saatchi, 1988; Billionaire: The Life and Times of Sir James Goldsmith, 1991; Paperchase, 1993; Luck of O'Reilly: A Biography of Tony O'Reilly, 1994. **Address:** Independent News & Media (UK) Ltd., Independent House, London, GL E14 9RS, England.

FALLON, Jennifer. Australian (born Australia), b. 1959?. **Genres:** Novels, Science Fiction/Fantasy. **Career:** Anzac Hill Gymnastics Club, founder; ABC Radio 783, news reviewer. Writer. **Publications:** Medalon, 2000; Treason Keep, 2001; Harshini, 2001; The Lion of Senet, 2002; Eye of the Labyrinth, 2003; Lord of the Shadows, 2003; Treason Keep, 2004; Gods of Amyrantha, 2007; The Palace Of Impossible Dreams, 2008; The Immortal Prince, 2008; The Chaos Crystal, 2008; Gezeitenstern-Saga 04. Der Kristall des Chaos, 2010; The Chaos Crystal, 2011. HYTHRUN CHRONICLES: Wolfblade, 2006; Warrior, 2006; Warlord, 2007. FORTHCOMING: The Undivided; Dark Divide; Reunion. Contributor to periodicals. **Address:** Australian Literary Management, 2A Booth St., Balmain, AC 2041, Australia. **Online address:** info@jenniferfallon.com

FALLON, Linda. See **JONES, Linda Winstead.**

FALLON, Peter. Irish/German (born Germany), b. 1951. **Genres:** Poetry, Novellas/Short Stories, Literary Criticism And History, inspirational/Motivational Literature, Novels. **Career:** Gallery Press, founder, editor and publisher, 1970-; Deerfield Academy, poet-in-residence, 1976-77, 1996-97; O'Brien Press, fiction editor, 1979-. Poet, Writer, reader and lecturer. **Publications:** POETRY: Among the Walls, 1971; Co-incidence of Flesh, 1972; The First Affair, 1974; The Speaking Stones, 1978; Finding the Dead, 1978; Winter Work, 1983; The News and Weather, 1988; Eye to Eye, 1992; The Deerfield Stories, 1992; News of the World: Selected Poems, 1993; Tarry Flynn: A Play in Three Acts Based on the Novel By Patrick Kavanagh, 2004; (trans.) The Georgics of Virgil, 2004; Morning Glory, 2006; The Company of Horses, 2007; Airs and Angels, 2007; Ballynahinch Postcards, 2007. EDITOR: (intro.) The Poems of Emily Lawless, 1965; New and Selected Poems, 1976; A Farewell to English, 1978; (with D. O'Driscoll) The First Ten Years: Dublin Arts Festival Poetry, 1979; The Headgear of the Tribe: Selected Poems, 1979; (with S. Golden) Soft Day: A Miscellany of Contemporary Irish Writing, 1980; (with A. Carpenter) The Writers: A Sense of Ireland: New Work by 44 Irish Writers, 1980; After the Wake: Twenty One Prose Works including Previously Unpublished Material, 1981; The Port Wine Stain: Patrick Boyle's Short Stories, 1983; The Diviner: Brian Friel's Best Short Stories, 1983; (with P. Egan) Jimeen: Lucky Tree Books for Children, 1984; The Weaver's Grave, 1985; The Second Voyage, 1986; (with D. Mahon) The Penguin Book of Contemporary Irish Poetry, 1990; Selected and New Poems, 1994; Collected Poems, 2001; A Book of Strays, 2002; Collected, 2005; (with D. Lally and J. Fanning) Captivating Brightness: Ballynahinch, 2008; Chosen Lights: Poets on Poems by John Montague in Honour of His 80th Birthday, 2009. Contributor to books and periodicals. **Address:** Gallery Press, Loughcrew, Oldcastle, ME 14, Ireland. **Online address:** gallery@indigo.ie

FALLOWELL, Duncan (Richard). British (born England), b. 1948. **Genres:** Novels, Songs/Lyrics And Libretti, Travel/Exploration, Autobiography/Memoirs. **Career:** Writer. **Publications:** (Ed.) Drug Tales (stories), 1979; (with A. Ashley) April Ashley's Odyssey (memoir), 1982; Satyrday (novel), 1986; The Underbelly (novel), 1987; To Noto, or, London to Sicily in a Ford (travel) 1989; 20th Century Characters (profiles), 1994; One Hot Summer in St. Petersburg (travel) 1994; A History of Facelifting (novel), 2003; Going As Far As I Can: The Ultimate Travel Book, 2008; How To Disappear: A Memoir for Misfits, 2011. Contributor to periodicals. **Address:** Aitken Alexander Associates Ltd., 18-21 Cavaye Pl., London, GL SW10 9PT, England. **Online address:** human@duncanfallowell.com

FALLOWS, James Mackenzie. American (born United States), b. 1949.

Genres: Economics, Environmental Sciences/Ecology, Military/Defense/Arms Control, Politics/Government, Biography, Sciences. **Career:** Harvard Crimson, president, 1969; Washington Monthly, staff editor, 1972-74; freelance magazine writer, 1972-76; Texas Monthly, associate editor, 1974-76; President Jimmy Carter, chief speech writer, 1977-79; Atlantic (formerly Atlantic Monthly), Washington editor, 1979-86, Asian correspondent, 1986-90, editor, 1990-96, national correspondent, 1998-, national editor; National Public Radio, national commentator, 1987-; U.S. News & World Report, editor, 1996-98; University of California, teacher, 2000-01; Microsoft, software designer. **Publications:** The Water Lords, 1971; (with M.J. Green and D.R. Zwick) Who Runs Congress?, 1972; Warren G. Magnuson: Democratic Senator from Washington, 1972; (ed. with C. Peters) The System: The Five Branches of American Government, 1976; (ed. with C. Peters) Inside the System, 1976; Old Capital and a New President, 1979; National Defense, 1981; Human Capital: The Cultural Sources of America's Economic Decline: And Rebirth, 1988; More like Us: Making America Great Again, 1989; Japanese Education: What Can I Teach American Schools?, 1990; (with O. Ichirō, M. Nobuo and A.J. Hen) Nichi-Bei Kankei o Yomu, 1990; Looking at the Sun: The Rise of the New East Asian Economic and Political System, 1994; (coauthor) Journalism, 1996; Breaking the News: How the Media Undermine American Democracy, 1996; Free Flight: From Airline Hell to a New Age of Travel, 2001; Free Flight: Inventing the Future of Travel, 2002; Blind into Baghdad: America's War in Iraq, 2006; Postcards from Tomorrow Square: Reports from China, 2009; China Airborne, 2012. **Address:** The Atlantic, 77 N Washington St., Ste. 5, Boston, MA 02114-1908, U.S.A. **Online address:** jamesfallows@theatlantic.com

FALOLA, Toyin. American/Nigerian (born Nigeria), b. 1953. **Genres:** History, Area Studies. **Career:** Elementary schoolteacher, 1970-71; high school teacher, 1973; Government College, high school teacher, 1976-77; Public Service Commission of Oyo State, administrative officer, 1977; University of Ife (now Obafemi Awolowo University), lecturer, 1981-85, senior lecturer, 1985-88; Cambridge University, research fellow, 1988-89; Nigerian Institute of International Affairs, senior research fellow and coordinator, 1989; York University, professor of history, 1990-91; University of Texas, professor of African history, 1991-, Frances Higginbotham Nalle Centennial professor in history, 1999-, distinguished teaching professor; Australian National University, fellow, 1995; Smith College, Carter visiting professor, 1999; Nigerian Academy of Letters, fellow. Writer. **Publications:** (With B. Adediran) Islam and Christianity in West Africa, 1983; (co-author) Summary of West African History, 1983; The Political Economy of a Pre-Colonial African State: Ibadan, 1830-1900, 1984; (with D. Oguntomisin) The Military in Nineteenth-Century Yoruba Politics, 1984; (with J. Ihonvbere) The Rise and Fall of Nigeria's Second Republic, 1979-1984, 1985; Politics and Economy in Ibadan, 1893-1945, 1989; (co-author) A History of Nigeria, vol. I: Nigeria Before 1800, 1989, vol. II: Nigeria in the Nineteenth Century, 1991, vol. III: Nigeria in the Twentieth Century, 1992; Yoruba Historiography, African Studies Program, 1991; (co-author) The Military Factor in Nigeria, 1994; (with P. Williams) Religious Impact on the Nation State: The Nigerian Predicament, 1995; Development Planning and Decolonization in Nigeria, 1996; (with M.H. Kukah) Religious Militancy and Self-Assertion: Islam and Politics in Nigeria, 1996; Violence in Nigeria: The Crisis of Religious Politics and Secular Ideologies, 1998; Violence in Nigeria: The Crisis of Religious Politics and Secular Ideologies, 1998; History of Nigeria, 1999; Yoruba Gurus: Indigenous Production of Knowledge in Africa, 1999; (with A. O'Hear) Studies in the Nineteenth-Century Economic History of Nigeria, 1999; (with A. Adebayo) Culture, Politics & Money among the Yoruba, 2000; Nationalism and African Intellectuals, 2001; (with G.O. Oguntomisin) Yoruba Warlords of the Nineteenth Century, 2001; (with S.J. Salm) Culture and Customs of Ghana, 2002; Power of African Cultures, 2003; Economic Reforms and Modernization in Nigeria, 1945-1965, 2004; Mouth Sweeter than Salt: An African Memoir, 2004; (with A. Genova) Politics of the Global Oil Industry: An Introduction, 2005; Education and Trans-Atlantic Connections: The U.S. Side, 2006; (with V. Bahl) Scoundrels of Deferral: Poems to Redeem Reflection, 2006; (with A. Adesanya) Etches on Fresh Waters, 2008; (with A. Genova) Historical Dictionary of Nigeria, 2009; Colonialism and Violence in Nigeria, 2009; (with K. Essien) Culture and Customs of Sudan, 2009; (with A.O. Oyebade) Hot Spot: Sub-Saharan Africa, 2010; (with S. Aderinto) Nigeria, Nationalism and Writing History, 2010. EDITOR: (with S.A. Olanrewaju) Rural Development Problems in Nigeria, 1992; (and intro.) Pioneer, Patriot and Patriarch: Samuel Johnson and the Yoruba People, 1994; Tradition and Change in Africa: The Essays of J.F. Ade. Ajayi, 2000; Culture and Customs of Nigeria, 2001; African Politics in Postimperial Times: The Essays of Richard L. Sklar, 2001; (with C. Jennings)

Africanizing Knowledge: African Studies across the Disciplines, 2002; (with A. Jalloh) Black Business and Economic Power, 2002; (with B. Harlow) Palavers of African Literature: Essays in Honor of Bernth Lindfors, 2002; (E.S.A. Odhiambo) Challenges of History and Leadership in Africa: The Essays of Bethwell Allan Ogot, 2002; Ghana in Africa and the World: Essays in Honor of Adu Boahen, 2003; (with P.E. Lovejoy) Pawnship, Slavery and Colonialism in Africa, 2003; (with C. Jennings) Sources and Methods in African History: Spoken, Written, Unearthed, 2003; (with S.J. Salm) Nigerian Cities, 2004; (with S.J. Salm) Globalization and Urbanization in Africa, 2004; Teen Life in Africa, 2004; (with M.D. Childs) Yoruba Diaspora in the Atlantic World, 2004; Africa in the Twentieth Century: The Adu Boahen Reader, 2004; (with S.J. Salm) African Urban Spaces in Historical Perspective, 2005; Christianity and Social Change in Africa: Essays in Honor of J.D.Y. Peel, 2005; Dark Webs: Perspectives on Colonialism in Africa, 2005; (with A. Genova) Orisa: Yoruba Gods and Spiritual Identity in Africa and the Diaspora, 2005; (with S.J. Salm) Urbanization and African Cultures, 2005; Igbo History and Society: The Essays of Adiele Afigbo, 2005; Myth, History and Society: The Collected Works of Adiele Afigbo, 2005; Nigerian History, Politics and Affairs: The Collected Essays of Adiele Afigbo, 2005; (with M.M. Heaton) Endangered Bodies: Women, Children and Health in Africa, 2006; (with M.M. Heaton) Traditional and Modern Health Systems in Nigeria, 2006; (with A. Genova) Yorubá Identity and Power Politics, 2006; (with A. Genova) Yoruba in Transition: History, Values and Modernity, 2006; Igbo Art and Culture and Other Essays, 2006; Igbo Religion, Social Life and Other Essays, 2006; (with N. Afolabi) African Minorities in the New World, 2007; (with A. Ogundiran) Archaeology of Atlantic Africa and the African Diaspora, 2007; (with A. Warnock) Encyclopedia of the Middle Passage, 2007; (with M.M. Heaton) HIV/AIDS, Illness and African Well-Being, 2007; (with N. Afolabi) Human Cost of African Migrations, 2007; (with O.O. Okpeh) Population Movements, Conflicts and Displacements in Nigeria, 2007; Ifa: The Yoruba God of Divination in Nigeria and the United States, 2008; (with N. Afolabi and A.A. Adesanya) Migrations and Creative Expressions in Africa and the African Diaspora, 2008; (with K.D. Roberts) Atlantic World, 1450-2000, 2008; (with M.D. Childs) Changing Worlds of Atlantic Africa: Essays in Honor of Robin Law, 2008; (with A. Paddock) Emergent Themes and Methods in African Studies: Essays in Honor of Adiele E. Afigbo, 2008; (with A. Akínyemí) Emerging Perspectives on Akínwùmí iș òlá, 2008; (with M.M. Heaton) Health Knowledge and Belief Systems in Africa, 2008; (with S.M. Hassan) Power and Nationalism in Modern Africa: Essays in Honor of Don Ohadike, 2008; (with N. Afolabi) Trans-Atlantic Migration: The Paradoxes of Exile, 2008; (with A. Jalloh) United States and West Africa: Interactions and Relations, 2008; (with A. Akínyemí and J.E. Tishken) Sàngó in Africa and the African Diaspora, 2009; (with A. Usman) Movements, Borders and Identities in Africa, 2009; (with F. Ngom) Oral and Written Expressions of African Cultures, 2009; (with T. Akinyemi) Emerging Perspectives on Femi Osofisan, 2009; (with M.D. Childs) Changing Worlds of Atlantic Africa: Essays in Honor of Robin Law, 2009; (with A. Agwuele) Africans and the Politics of Popular Culture, 2009; (with W.J. Kalu and N. Wariboko) Christian Missions in Africa: Success, Ferment and Trauma, 2010; (with W.J. Kalu and N. Wariboko) Religions in Africa, 2010; (with W.J. Kalu and N. Wariboko) African Pentecostalism: Global Discourses, Migrations, Exchanges and Connections, 2010; (with H. Haar) Narrating War and Peace in Africa, 2010; (with R.C. Njoku) War and peace in Africa, 2010; (with F. Ngom) Facts, Fiction and African Creative Imaginations, 2010; (with B. House-Soremekun) Globalization and Sustainable Development in Africa, 2011; (with E. Brownell) Landscape and Environment in Colonial and Postcolonial Africa, 2011; (with A. Paddock) The Women's War of 1929, 2011; (with S.U. Fwatshak) Beyond Tradition, 2011; (with A. Oyebade) Yoruba Fiction, Orature and Culture, 2011; (with B. House-Soremekun) Gender, Sexuality and Mothering in Africa, 2011; (with A. Paddock) Environment and Economics in Nigeria, 2011; (with E. Brownell) Africa, Empire and Globalization, 2011; (with T. Fleming) Music, Performance and African Identities, 2012. EDITOR/CO-EDITOR and CONTRIBUTOR: Nigeria: Peoples, States and Culture, 1986; (with S.A. Olanrewaju) Transport Systems in Nigeria, 1986; A History of West Africa, 1987; Britain and Nigeria: Exploitation or Development?, 1987; (with J.O. Ihonvbere) Nigeria and the International Capitalist System, 1988; Obafemi Awolowo: The End of an Era?, 1988; Modern Nigeria: A Tribute to G.O. Olusanya, 1990; (with J. Olupona) Religion and Society in Nigeria: Historical and Comparative Perspectives, 1991; (with D. Ityavyar) The Political Economy of Health in Africa, 1991; (with R. Law) Warfare and Diplomacy in Pre-Colonial Nigeria, 1992; (with T.O. Pearce) Child Health in Nigeria: The Impact of a Depressed Economy, 1994; (with P.E. Lovejoy) Pawnship in Africa: Debt Bondage in Historical Perspective, 1994. FORTHCOMING: Daiogal-Sore. Contributor to books and journals. **Address:** Department of History, University of Texas, GAR 2.142, 1 University Sta., PO Box B7000, Austin, TX 78712, U.S.A. **Online address:** toyin.falola@mail.utexas.edu

FALSANI, Cathleen. American (born United States), b. 1970. **Genres:** Theology/Religion, Adult Non-fiction. **Career:** Chicago Sun-Times, religion writer and religion columnist, 2000-10, religion reporter, through 2007; Religion News Service, columnist; Sojourners Magazine, columnist and contributing editor; Duke University, Duke Divinity School, fellow, 2009; Brandeis University, Gralla fellow in Jewish studies. Journalist. **Publications:** The God Factor: Inside the Spiritual Lives of Public People, 2006; Sin Boldly: A Field Guide for Grace, 2008; The Dude Abides: The Gospel According to the Coen Brothers, 2009; The Thread, 2010; BELIEBER: Fame, Faith and the Heart of Justin Bieber, 2011. Contributor to periodicals. **Address:** c/o Chris Ferebee, Yates & Yates, 1100 Town & Country Rd., Ste. 1300, Orange, CA 92868, U.S.A. **Online address:** cfalsani@suntimes.com

FALUDI, Susan. American (born United States), b. 1959. **Genres:** Women's Studies And Issues, Civil Liberties/Human Rights. **Career:** New York Times, copy clerk, 1981-82; Miami Herald, reporter, 1983; Atlanta Constitution, reporter, 1984-85; West magazine, staff writer, 1985-89; Mercury News, reporter, 1986-88; Wall Street Journal, staff writer, 1990-92, affiliate, 1990-. **Publications:** Backlash: The Undeclared War against American Women, 1991; Stiffed: The Betrayal of the Modern Man, 1999; The Terror Dream: Fear and Fantasy in Post-9/11 America, 2007. Contributor of articles to periodicals. **Address:** c/o Melanie Jackson, 1 W 72nd St., Ste. 3F, New York, NY 10023, U.S.A.

FALZEDER, Ernst. (Ernst Michael Falzeder). Austrian (born Austria), b. 1955. **Genres:** Psychology. **Career:** University of Salzburg, Psychological Institute, assistant, 1979-85, lecturer, 1985-, assistant professor, 1986-87; Lebensberatung (Counseling Center), psychotherapist, 1985; University of Innsbruck, Psychological and Pedagogical Institutes, lecturer, 1985-; community improvement program, psychologist, 1986-87; Cornell Medical School, research associate, 1997-98. Writer. **Publications:** Die Sprachverwirrung und die Grundstorung: Die Untersuchungen S. Ferenczis und Michael Balints uber Entstehung und Auswirkungen fruher Objektbeziehungen, 1986; (ed. with A. Papst) Wie Psychoanalyse wirksam wird-Sepp Schindler zum 65, 1987; (ed. with E. Brabant and P.G. Deutsch) Sigmund Freud-Sandor Ferenczi, Correspondance, Tome I, 1908-1914, 1992; (ed. with A. Haynal) 100 Years of Psychoanalysis, 1994; (ed.) The Complete Correspondence of Sigmund Freud and Karl Abraham, 1907-1925, 2002; (with A. Haynal and P. Roazen) Dans les Secrets de la Psychanalyse et de Son Histoire, 2005; (with K. Abraham) Briefwechsel 1907-1925, 2009; Unterdess Halten wir Zusammen, 2010. Contributor of articles. **Address:** Department of Psychology, University of Innsbruck, Innrain, A-6020, Austria. **Online address:** falzeder@yahoo.com

FALZEDER, Ernst Michael. See FALZEDER, Ernst.

FAN, Nancy Yi. American/Chinese (born China), b. 1993. **Genres:** Young Adult Fiction, Children's Fiction, Animals/Pets, Science Fiction/Fantasy. **Career:** Writer. **Publications:** Swordbird (young adult novel), 2007; Sword Quest, 2008. **Address:** c/o Author Mail, HarperCollins Publishers, 10 E 53rd St., New York, NY 10022, U.S.A.

FANCHER, Jane S(uzanne). American (born United States), b. 1952. **Genres:** Science Fiction/Fantasy, Graphic Novels, Young Adult Fiction, Literary Criticism And History. **Career:** Warp Graphics, art assistant; Writer. **Publications:** GRAPHIC NOVELS: (adapted) The Gate of Ivrel: Claiming Rites, 1987; Gate of Ivrel: Fever Dreams, 1988. CANTRELL SERIES: Groundties, 1991; Uplink, 1992; Harmonies of the 'Net, 1992. OTHERS: Ring of Lightning, 1995; Ring of Intrigue, 1997; Ring of Destiny, 1999; Rings of Change: Alizant, forthcoming. Contributor to periodicals. **Address:** c/o DAW Publicity, 375 Hudson St., 3rd Fl., New York, NY 10014, U.S.A. **Online address:** fancher@cherryh.com

FANCHI, John R(ichard). American (born United States), b. 1952. **Genres:** Novels, Earth Sciences, Engineering, Mathematics/Statistics, Physics, Sciences. **Career:** Colorado School of Mines, professor of petroleum engineering; U.S. Department of Energy, BOAST and BOAST II Simulators, principal creator; Fanchi Enterprises, co-owner; Marathon Oil Co., senior engineer; Chevron Energy, senior engineer; Cities Service, staff; Getty Oil Inc., staff; Texas Christian University, Department of Engineering, professor of engineering, Matthews professor of petroleum engineering. Writer. **Publications:** Parametrized Relativistic Quantum Theory, 1993; Principles of Applied Reservoir Simulation, 1997, 3rd ed., 2006; Math Refresher for Scientists and Engineers, 1997, 3rd ed., 2006; Integrated Flow Modeling, 2000; Flashpoint: Sakhalin, 2001; Shared Earth Modeling, 2002; Energy: Technology and Directions for the Future, 2004; Energy in the 21st Century, 2005, (with C.J. Fanchi) 2nd ed., 2011; Integrated Reservoir Asset Management, 2010. Contributor to journals. **Address:** Department of Engineering, Texas Christian University, Tucker Technology Ctr., PO Box 298640, Fort Worth, TX 76129, U.S.A. **Online address:** j.r.fanchi@tcu.edu

FANCUTT, Walter. British (born England), b. 1911. **Genres:** History, Theology/Religion, Administration/Management. **Career:** Baptist minister, 1933-57; Southern Baptist Association, baptist minister and general secretary, 1934-57, president, 1950, 1984; Mission to Lepers, editorial secretary, 1957-69, editorial consultant, 1969-. Writer. **Publications:** Then Came Jesus, 1943; From Vision to Advance, 1951; Whitchurch Baptist Church 1652-1952, 1952; In This Will I Be Confident, 1957; Beyond the Bitter Sea, 1959; Present to Heal, 1963; Daily Remembrance: A Prayer Cycle for the Leprosy Mission, 1966; The Imprisoned Splendour: A Series of Devotional Studies Set in the Context of a Visit to Indian Leprosy Centres, 1972; The Southern Baptist Association, 1974; With Strange Surprise, 1974; The Luminous Cloud: A Series of Devotional Studies in Verse and Prose Set in the Context of a Visit to Indian Leprosy Centres, 1980; His Excellent Greatness, 1982; East Dene, 1982; With William Carey in Ryde, 1993. EDITOR: Kingsgate Pocket Poets, vol. IX, 1943; Escaped as a Bird, 1963. **Address:** 4 B St., Boniface Gardens, Ventnor, IW PO38 1NN, England.

FANDRICH, Ina Johanna. American/German (born Germany), b. 1957. **Genres:** History, Humanities. **Career:** Louisiana State University, assistant professor of religious studies. Writer. **Publications:** The Mysterious Voodoo Queen, Marie Laveaux: A Study of Powerful Female Leadership in Nineteenth-Century New Orleans, 2004. Contributor to books and periodicals. **Address:** Department of Philosophy and Religious Studies, Louisiana State University, 106 Coates Hall, Baton Rouge, LA 70803-3901, U.S.A.

FANE, Bron. *See* **FANTHORPE, R(obert) Lionel.**

FANÉS, Fèlix. Spanish (born Spain), b. 1948?. **Genres:** History. **Career:** Salvador Dali Museum, director of archives; Universitat Autònoma de Barcelona, professor of art history. Writer. **Publications:** La vaga de tramvies del 1951: una crònica de Barcelona, 1977; Cifesa, la antorcha de los éxitos, 1982; La germana fosca, 1988; El cas cifesa, vint anys de cine espanyol (1932-1951), 1989; (co-author) Dalí escriptor, 1990; (with D.G. Miracle) Dalí: felicitaciones de navidad=Christmas Cards=Weihnachtskarten: 1958-1976, 1992; (ed. with M. Aguer) Dalí: El pan, 1993; (ed. and intro.) Un diari, 1919-1920: Les meves impressions i records Intims, 1994; (ed.) Dalí joven, 1918-1930: Museo Nacional Centro de Arte Reina Sofia, del 18 de Octubre de 1994 al 16 de Enero de 1995, 1994; (ed.) L'alliberament dels dits: Obra catalana completa, 1995; (co-author) Cinema, art i pensament, 1999; Salvador Dalí: La construcción de la imagen 1925-1930, 1999; (ed. with J.M. Minguet) Homenatge a Joan Brossa: Doctor honoris causa per la UAB, 2000; La pintura y sus sombras: Cuatro estudios sobre salvador Dalí, 2004; La indiferència, 2006; Pere Portabella: Avantguarda, cinema, política, 2008; Diari de guerra, 2011. **Address:** Universitat Autònoma de Barcelona, Placa Civica, Gran Via de les Corts Catalanes, 585, Bellaterra, Barcelona, 08193, Spain.

FANNING, Diane Lynn. American (born United States), b. 1950. **Genres:** Novels, Mystery/Crime/Suspense, Novellas/Short Stories, Criminology/True Crime, Horror. **Career:** Writer. **Publications:** (Ed. with S.K. Flatau) Red Boots & Attitude: The Spirit of Texas Women Writers, 2002. FICTION: The Windwalkers (novel), 2000; Bite the Moon: A Molly Mullet Mystery (novel), 2007. LUCINDA PIERCE NOVELS: The Trophy Exchange, 2008; Punish the Deed, 2009; Mistaken Identity, 2010; Twisted Reason, 2011; False Front, 2012. TRUE CRIME: Through the Window, 2003; Into the Water: The Story of Serial Killer Richard Marc Evonitz, 2004; Written in Blood: A True Story of Murder and a Deadly 16-Year-Old Secret That Tore a Family Apart, 2005; Gone Forever: The True Story of Marriage, Betrayal and Murder, 2006; Baby Be Mine: The Shocking True Story of a Woman Accused of Murdering a Pregnant Woman to Steal Her Child, 2006; Under the Knife: A Beautiful Woman, a Phony Doctor and a Shocking Homicide, 2007; Out There: The In-Depth Story of the Astronaut Love Triangle Case That Shocked America, 2007; Pastor's Wife: The True Story of a Minister and the Shocking

Death that Divided a Family, 2008; A Poisoned Passion: The True Story of a Young Mother, Her War Hero Husband, the Marriage Ended in Murder, 2009; Mommy's Little Girl: Casey Anthony and Her Daughter Caylee's Tragic Fate, 2009; Her Deadly Web, 2012. **Address:** c/o Jane Dystel, Dystel and Goderich Literary Management, 1 Union Sq. W, Ste. 904, New York, NY 10003, U.S.A. **Online address:** diane@dianefanning.com

FANNING, Philip Ashley. American (born United States), b. 1935. **Genres:** Sciences, Biography, Theology/Religion, Reference. **Career:** W.H. Freeman and Co. (publisher), staff, 1957-77; Fannings Bookstore, staff, 1977-88. Writer. **Publications:** Mark Twain and Orion Clemens: Brothers, Partners, Strangers, 2003; Isaac Newton and the Transmutation of Alchemy: An Alternate View of the Scientific Revolution, 2009; Prometheus: The First Quantum Computer, forthcoming. Contributor to periodicals. **Address:** Michael Larsen and Elizabeth Pomada, 1029 Jones St., San Francisco, CA 94109, U.S.A. **Online address:** lindagail38@yahoo.com

FANTASKEY, Beth. American (born United States), b. 1965?. **Genres:** Science Fiction/Fantasy. **Career:** Susquehanna University, part-time English instructor. Writer. **Publications:** Jessica's Guide to Dating on the Dark Side, 2009; Jekel Loves Hyde, 2010. **Address:** Lewisburg, PA , U.S.A. **Online address:** bethfantaskey@yahoo.com

FANTE, Dan. American (born United States), b. 1944. **Genres:** Poetry, Novels, Mystery/Crime/Suspense. **Career:** Writer. **Publications:** POEMS: A Gin-Pissing-Raw-Meat-Dual-carburetor-V8-Son-of-a-Bitch from Los Angeles: Collected Poems, 1983-2002, 2002; (with T. Cumming and G. Hattersley) The Slab, 2004; Kissed by a Fat Waitress: New Poems, 2008. BRUNO DANTE SERIES: CRIME NOVELS: Chump Change, 1998; Mooch, 2000; Spitting off Tall Buildings, 2002; Corksucker: Cab Driver Stories from the L.A. Streets, 2005 in US as Short Dog: Cab Driver Stories from the L.A. Streets, 2006; 86'd, 2009. OTHER: Don Giovanni: A Play, 2006. **Address:** AZ , U.S.A. **Online address:** danfante@aol.com

FANTHORPE, R(obert) Lionel. Also writes as Leo Brett, Lee Barton, Victor La Salle, Thornton Bell, Bron Fane. British (born England), b. 1935. **Genres:** Novels, Novellas/Short Stories, Horror, Science Fiction/Fantasy, Plays/Screenplays, Poetry, Songs/Lyrics And Libretti, Children's Non-fiction, Criminology/True Crime, History, inspirational/Motivational Literature, Mythology/Folklore, Paranormal, Theology/Religion, Documentaries/Reportage. **Career:** Educator, 1963-69; Phoenix Timber Co., industrial training officer, 1969-72, chief training executive; Hellesdon High School, head of English, deputy head, 1972-79; Glyn Derw High School, headmaster, 1979-89; Anglican priest, 1988-; Scientific Study of Anomalous Phenomena Association, president; British UFO Research Association, president; Cardiff Academy, Media Studies, director. Writer. **Publications:** SCIENCE FICTION NOVELS: The Waiting World, 1958; Alien from the Stars, 1959; Hyperspace, 1959; Space-Borne, 1959; Fiends, 1959; Doomed World, 1960; Satellite, 1960; Asteroid Man, 1960; Out of the Darkness, 1960; Hand of Doom, 1960; Flame Mass, 1961; The Golden Chalice, 1961; Space Fury, 1962; Negative Minus, 1963; Neuron World, 1965; The Triple World, 1965; The Unconfined, 1965; The Watching World, 1966; (with P. Fanthorpe) The Black Lion, 1979. SCIENCE FICTION AS LEO BRETT: The Druid (stories), 1959; The Return (stories), 1959; Exit Humanity, 1960; The Microscopic Ones, 1960; Faceless Planet, 1960; March of the Robots, 1961; Wind Force, 1961; Black Infinity, 1961; Nightmare, 1962; Face in the Night, 1962; The Immortals, 1962; They Never Came Back, 1962; The Frozen Tomb (stories), 1962; The Forbidden, 1963; From Realms Beyond, 1963; The Alien Ones, 1963; Power Sphere, 1963; Phantom Crusader (stories), 1963. SCIENCE FICTION AS BRON FANE: Juggernaut, 1960 in US as Blue Juggernaut, 1965; Last Man on Earth, 1960; The Crawling Fiend (stories), 1960; Rodent Mutation, 1961; Storm God's Fury (stories), 1962; The Intruders, 1963; Somewhere Out There, 1963; The Thing from Sheol (stories), 1963; Softly by Moonlight, 1963; Unknown Destiny, 1964; Nemesis, 1964; Suspension, 1964; The Macabre Ones, 1964; U.F.O. 517, 1966. AS JOHN E. MULLER: The Ultimate Man, 1961; The Uninvited, 1961; Crimson Planet, 1961; The Venus Venture, 1961; Forbidden Planet, 1961; Return of Zeus, 1962; Perilous Galaxy, 1962; Uranium 235, 1962; The Man Who Conquered Time, 1962; Orbit One, 1962; The Eye of Karnak, 1962; Micro Infinity, 1962; Beyond Time, 1962; Infinity Machine, 1962; The Day the World Died, 1962; Vengeance of Siva, 1962; The X-Machine, 1962; Reactor XK9, 1963; Special Mission, 1963; Dark Continuum, 1964; Mark of the Beast, 1964; The Negative Ones, 1965; The Exorcists, 1965; The Man from Beyond, 1965; Beyond the Void, 1965; Spec-tre of Darkness, 1965; Out of the Night, 1965; Phenomena X, 1966; Survival Project, 1966. AS LIONEL ROBERTS: Dawn of the Mutants, 1959; Time Echo, 1959; Cyclops in the Sky, 1960; The In-World, 1960; The Face of X, 1960; The Last Valkyrie, 1961; The Synthetic Ones, 1961; Flame Goddess, 1961. AS PEL TORRO: Frozen Planet, 1960; World of the Gods, 1960; The Phantom Ones, 1961; Legion of the Lost, 1962; The Strange Ones, 1963; Galaxy 666, 1963; Formula 29X, 1963; Through the Barrier, 1963; The Timeless Ones, 1963; The Last Astronaut, 1963; The Face of Fear, 1963; The Return, 1964; Space No Barrier, 1964; Force 97X, 1965. AS KARL ZEIGFREID: Walk through To-Morrow, 1962; Android, 1962; Gods of Darkness, 1962; Atomic Nemesis, 1962; Zero Minus X, 1962; Escape to Infinity, 1963; Radar Alert, 1963; World of Tomorrow, 1963; The World That Never Was, 1963; Projection Infinity, 1964; No Way Back, 1964; Barrier 346, 1965; The Girl from Tomorrow, 1965. OTHERS: (as Victor La Salle) Menace from Mercury, John Spencer, 1954; (as Trebor Thorpe) Five Faces of Fear, 1960; (as Trebor Thorpe) Lightning World, 1960; (as Lee Barton) The Unseen, 1963; (as Neil Thanet) Beyond the Veil, 1964; (as Neil Thanet) The Man Who Came Back, 1964; (as Thornton Bell) Space Trap, 1964; (as Thornton Bell) Chaos, Badger Books, 1964; (as Erle Barton) The Planet Seekers, 1964; (as Lee Barton) The Shadow Man, 1966; (with W. H. Farrer) Spencer's Metric and Decimal Guide, 1970. SHORT STORY COLLECTIONS: (as Lionel Roberts) The Incredulist, 1954; Resurgam, 1957; Secret of the Snows, 1957; The Flight of the Valkyries, 1958; Watchers of the Forest, 1958; Call of the Werewolf, 1958; The Death Note, 1958; (as Lionel Roberts) Guardians of the Tomb, 1958; (as Lionel Roberts) The Golden Warrior, 1958; (as Trebor Thorpe) The Haunted Pool, 1958; (as Leo Brett) The Druid, 1959; (as Leo Brett) The Return, 1959; Mermaid Reef, 1959; The Ghost Rider, 1959; (as Bron Fane) The Crawling Fiend, 1960; The Man Who Couldn't Die, 1960; Werewolf at Large, 1960; Whirlwind of Death, 1960; (as Trebor Thorpe) Voodoo Hell Drums, 1961; Fingers of Darkness, 1961; Face in the Dark, 1961; Devil from the Depths, 1961; Centurion's Vengeance, 1961; The Grip of Fear, 1961; (as Leo Brett) The Frozen Tomb, 1962; (as Bron Fane) Storm God's Fury, 1962; Chariot of Apollo, 1962; Hell Has Wings, 1962; Graveyard of the Damned, 1962; The Darker Drink, 1962; Curse of the Totem, 1962; (as Leo Brett) Phantom Crusader, 1963; (as Bron Fane) The Thing from Sheol, 1963; Goddess of the Night, 1963; Twilight Ancestor, 1963; Sands of Eternity, 1963; (as Olaf Trent) Roman Twilight, 1963; (as Bron Fane) The Walking Shadow, 1964; (as Phil Nobel) The Hand from Gehenna, 1964; Moon Wolf, 1964; Avenging Goddess, 1964; Death Has Two Faces, 1964; The Shrouded Abbot, 1964; Bitter Reflection, 1964; Call of the Wild, 1965; Vision of the Damned, 1965; The Sealed Sarcophagus, 1965; Stranger in the Shadow, 1966; Curse of the Khan, 1966. WITH P.A. FANTHORPE: Spencer's Metric Conversion Tables, 1970; Spencer's Office Guide, 1971; Spencer's Metric and Decimal Companion, 1971; Spencer's Decimal Payroll Tables, 1971; The Black Lion, 1979; The Holy Grail Revealed, 1982; God in All Things, 1987; Thoughts and Prayers for Troubled Times, 1989; The Story of St. Francis, 1989; Secrets of Rennes-le-Chateau, 1992; The Oak Island Mystery: The Secret of the World's Greatest Treasure, 1995; The World's Most Mysterious People, 1998; The World's Most Mysterious Places, 1999; Mysteries of the Bible, 1999; The World's Most Mysterious Objects, 2002; The World's Most Mysterious Murders, 2003; Mysteries of Templar Treasure & the Holy Grail: Secrets of Rennes-le-Chateau, 2004; Mysteries and Secrets of the Templars: The Story behind the Da Vinci Code, 2005; Mysteries and Secrets of the Masons: the Story behind the Masonic Order, 2006; Mysteries and Secrets of Voodoo, Santeria and Obeah, 2008; (with P. Fanthorpe) Secrets of the World's Undiscovered Treasures, 2009; The Big Book of Mysteries, 2010; Satanism and Demonology 2011. **Address:** Rivendell, 48 Claude Rd., Roath, Cardiff, CF24 3QA, Wales. **Online address:** fanthorpe@aol.com

FANTONI, Barry (Ernest). Also writes as Sylvie Krin, E. J. Thribb. British (born England), b. 1940. **Genres:** Mystery/Crime/Suspense, Plays/Screenplays, Humor/Satire. **Career:** Private Eye Magazine, assistant editor, 1963-; Listener, cartoonist, 1968-; St. Martin's Review, editor, 1969-74; The Times Diary, art critic, 1973-77, cartoonist, 1983-89; Punch, record reviewer, 1976-77; Chelsea Arts Club, chairman, 1978-80; Woman, contributor, 1986-88; Plus, contributor, 1989-. **Publications:** (With R. Ingrams) Bible for Motorists, 1967; Tomorrow's Nicodemus, 1974; (with R. Ingrams as Sylvie Krin) Love in the Saddle, 1974; Private Eye Cartoons, 1975; (as E.J. Thribb and ed.) So Farewell Then and Other Poems, 1977; Mike Dime (crime novel), 1980; (as Sylvie Krin) Born to Be Queen, 1981; (with G. Melly) The Media Mob, 1981; Stickman (crime novel), 1982; (ed.) Colemanballs, 1982, 4th ed., 1988; Private Eye's Colemanballs, 1984; The Times Diary Cartoons, 1984; Barry Fantoni's Chinese Horoscopes, 1985; Barry Fantoni Cartoons, 1987;

The Royal Chinese Horoscopes, 1988; (as Sylvie Krin) Heir of Sorrows, 1988; Chinese Horoscopes, Love Signs, 1989; (with Ingrams and Hislop) The People's Prince, 1989; The Best of Barry Fantoni Cartoons, 1990; Complete Chinese Horoscopes, 1991; Colemanballs 6, 1992; Colemanballs 7, 1994; Colemanballs 8, 1996; Colemanballs 9, 1998; Modigliani, My Love (play), 1998; Colemanballs 10, 2000. **Address:** Peter Fraser & Dunlop, 5th Fl., The Chambers, Chelsea Harbour, Lots Rd., London, GL SW10 OXF, England. **Online address:** bazfan@lineone.net

FAQIH, Ahmed. (Ahmad Ibrāhīm al-Faqīh). British (born England), b. 1942. **Genres:** Novels, Plays/Screenplays, Theology/Religion. **Career:** Azure, editor-in-chief. **Publications:** Al-Sahrā' wa-ashjār al-naft, 1979; Kalimāt min Laylā Sulaymān, 1981; Gardens of the Night (trilogy of novels), 1995; Ghin-a Al-nuj-um: Al-masrah-iy-at, 1997; Khams khan-afis tuh-akimu al-shajarah: majm-uahqisas-iyah, 1997; Mar-ay-a V-in-isy-a: Majm-u at Qisas, 1997; Charles, Diana, and Me, and Other Stories, 1999; Valley of Ashes, 1999; (ed.) Libyan Stories: Twelve Short Stories from Libya, 2000; Gazelles and Other Plays, 2000; Who's Afraid of Agatha Christie? and Other Stories, 2000; Fi'rān bi-lā juhūr: safhah min kitāb al-jū, 2000; Tahaddiy-at asr Jad-id, Markaz al-Had-arah al-Arab-iyah, 2000; Thalāthūn qiṣ ṣ ah qaṣ īrah, 2002. **Address:** 5 Porchester Square Mews, The Colonnades, London, GL W2 6AT, England.

FAQIR, Fadia A.M. Jordanian/British (born England), b. 1956. **Genres:** Novels, Autobiography/Memoirs. **Career:** Garnet Publishing, senior editor, 1990-94; Exeter University, lecturer, 1990-92; University of California, creative writing instructor, 1993-96; Durham University, Centre for Middle Eastern and Islamic Studies, Project of Middle Eastern Women's Studies, lecturer and coordinator, 1994. **Publications:** Nisanit (novel), 1987; Pillars of Salt: A Novel, 1997; (ed. and trans. with S. Eber) In the House of Silence: Autobiographical Essays by Arab Women Writers, 1998; The Cry of the Dove in UK as My Name Is Salma (novel), 2007. Contributor to books. **Address:** St. Mary's College, Elvet Hill Rd., Durham, DH1 3LR, England.

FARA, Patricia. British (born England), b. 1948. **Genres:** Sciences, Information Science/Computers, History. **Career:** University of Cambridge, Department of History and Philosophy of Science, affiliated lecturer; Clare College, current senior tutor and director of studies in history and philosophy of science. Writer. **Publications:** NONFICTION: Computers: How They Work and What They Do, 1982; Magnetic England in the Eighteenth Century (thesis), 1993; (with S. Reid) The Usborne Book of Inventors, 1994; Instruments of Attraction (exhibition guide), 1996; Sympathetic Attractions: Magnetic Practices, Beliefs and Symbolism in Eighteenth-Century England, 1996; (ed. with P. Gathercole and R. Laskey) The Changing World, 1996; (ed. with K. Patterson) Memory, 1998; Newton: The Making of Genius, 2002; An Entertainment for Angels: Electricity in the Enlightenment, 2002; Sex, Botany and Empire: The Story of Carl Linnaeus and Joseph Banks, 2003; Pandora's Breeches: Women, Science and Power in the Enlightenment, 2004; Athene's Owl: A History of Women in Science, 2005; Scientists Anonymous: Great Stories of Women in Science, 2005; Fatal Attraction: Magnetic Mysteries of the Enlightenment, 2006; Science: A Four Thousand Year History, 2009. Contributor to periodicals. **Address:** Clare College, University of Cambridge, Cambridge, CB2 1TL, England. **Online address:** pf10006@cam.ac.uk

FARAGHER, John Mack. American (born United States), b. 1945. **Genres:** History, Biography. **Career:** Yale University, instructor in American studies, 1975-77, Arthur Unobskey professor of American history, 1993-, Howard R. Lamar Center, director, 2000-, chair, 2004-06, Whitney Humanities Center, fellow, 1994-97, director of graduate studies, 1999-2003; University of Hartford, assistant professor of history, 1977-78; Mount Holyoke College, assistant professor of history, 1978-83, associate professor of history, 1983-86, professor of history, 1986-93, department chair, 1988-91, American Studies Program, chair, 1982-83, 1985-87; University of Massachusetts, faculty, 1991-93. Writer. **Publications:** Women and Men on the Overland Trail, 1979, 2nd ed., 2001; Sugar Creek: Life on the Illinois Prairie, 1986; Daniel Boone: The Life and Legend of an American Pioneer, 1992; (co-author) Out of Many: A History of the American People, 1994, 6th ed., 2010; (with R.V. Hine) Frontiers, 2007. EDITOR: (with F. Howe) Women and Higher Education in American History: Essays from the Mount Holyoke College Sesquicentennial Symposia, 1988; The Encyclopedia of Colonial and Revolutionary America, 1990; The Encyclopedic Dictionary of American History, 4th ed., 1991; Rereading Frederick Jackson Turner: The Significance of the Frontier in American History, and Other Essays, 1994; The American Heritage Encyclopedia of American History, 1998; (with R.V. Hine) The American West: A New Interpretive

History, 2000; A Great and Noble Scheme: The Tragic Story of the Expulsion of the Acadians from Their American Homeland, 2005. Contributor to books and periodicals. **Address:** Department of History, Yale University, TC 31, WHC B04, PO Box 208324, New Haven, CT 06520-8323, U.S.A. **Online address:** john.faragher@yale.edu

FARAH, Douglas. American (born United States), b. 1957. **Genres:** Politics/Government. **Career:** United Press Intl., UPI bureau chief, 1980-87; freelance foreign correspondent and investigative reporter, 1987-; Washington Post, staff, 1990, staff correspondent for Central America and the Caribbean, 1992-97, international investigative reporter, 1997-2000, West Africa bureau chief, 2000-03, staff, through 2004; Consortium for the Study of Intelligence, researcher, 2004; Nine Eleven Finding Answers Foundation, senior investigator, 2005-; International Assessment and Strategy Center, senior fellow for financial investigations and transparency; IBI Consultants, president. Writer. **Publications:** Blood from Stones: The Secret Financial Network of Terror, 2004; (with R.H. Shultz and I.V. Lochard) Armed Groups: A Tier-One Security Priority, USAF Institute for National Security Studies, 2004; (with S. Braun) Merchant of Death: Money, Guns, Planes and the Man Who Makes War Possible, 2007. Contributor to periodicals and journals. **Address:** International Assessment and Strategy Center, 211 N Union St., Ste. 100, Alexandria, VA 22314, U.S.A. **Online address:** doug@douglasfarah.com

FARBER, Barry J. American (born United States), b. 1959. **Genres:** Business/Trade/Industry, Bibliography. **Career:** Ricoh Americas Corp., national sales training manager, 1986-90; Farber Training Systems Inc., president, 1990-; The Diamond Group, president, 1990-. Writer. **Publications:** (With J. Wycoff) Breakthrough Selling: Customer-Building Strategies from the Best in the Business, 1992; State of the Art Selling, 1994; Diamond in the Rough, 1995; Sales Secrets from Your Customers, 1995; Superstar Sales Secrets, 1995, rev. ed., 2003; Superstar Sales Manager's Secrets, 1995, rev. ed., 2003; Diamonds in the Rough, 1995; Diamonds Under Pressure: Five Steps to Turning Adversity into Success, 1998; Dive Right In: 101 Powerful Action Steps for Personal Achievement, 1999; Diamond Power: Gems of Wisdom from America's Greatest Marketer, 2004; Barry Farber's Guide to Handling Sales Objections, 2005; 12 Clichés of Selling and Why They Work. **Address:** Farber Training Systems Inc., 66 E Sherbrooke Pkwy., Livingston, NJ 07039, U.S.A. **Online address:** barryjfarber@erols.com

FARBER, Celia. American (born United States), b. 1965. **Genres:** Medicine/Health, History, Social Sciences, Sciences. **Career:** SPIN Magazine, research assistant. Journalist. **Publications:** Serious Adverse Events: An Uncensored History of AIDS, 2006. Contributor to periodicals. **Address:** Random House of Canada Ltd., 1 Toronto St., Ste. 300, Toronto, ON M5C 2V6, Canada. **Online address:** cifarber@aol.com

FARBER, Naomi. (Naomi B. Farber). American (born United States), b. 1956. **Genres:** Medicine/Health, Social Sciences, Sociology, Human Relations/Parenting. **Career:** Lakehead University, Department of Social Work, field instructor, 1980-82; University of Chicago, Social Policy Research Center, research assistant, 1983-85, School of Social Service Administration, teaching assistant, 1985-86; University of Wisconsin, Institute for Research on Poverty, associate professor, 1987-; Bryn Mawr College, Graduate School of Social Work and Social Research, assistant professor, 1991-98; University of South Carolina, College of Social Work, associate professor, 1998-, faculty associate of women's studies, 2003-, Doctoral Program, director, 2004-08. Writer. **Publications:** Adolescent Pregnancy: Policy and Prevention Services, 2003, (as Naomi B. Farber) 2nd ed., 2009. **Address:** College of Social Work, University of South Carolina, 327 Desaussure, Columbia, SC 29208, U.S.A. **Online address:** naomi.farber@sc.edu

FARBER, Naomi B. See **FARBER, Naomi.**

FARBMAN, Albert I. American (born United States), b. 1934. **Genres:** Biology, Medicine/Health, Sciences. **Career:** New York University, instructor in anatomy, 1962-64; Northwestern University, assistant professor, 1964-67, associate professor, 1967-72, professor of anatomy, 1972-81, professor of neurobiology and physiology, 1981-, now professor emeritus. Writer. **Publications:** Cell Biology of Olfaction, 1992. **Address:** Department of Neurobiology and Physiology, Northwestern University, 2205 Tech Dr., Hogan 2-160, Evanston, IL 60208, U.S.A. **Online address:** afarbman@northwestern.edu

FARCAU, Bruce W. See **GRACE, Alexander M.**

FARICY, Robert. (Robert Leo Faricy). American (born United States), b. 1926. **Genres:** Theology/Religion. **Career:** Catholic University of America, assistant professor of theology and spirituality, 1966-71; Gregorian University, professor, 1971-, now professor emeritus; Marquette University, now emeritus professor of spirituality. Writer, priest and theologian. **Publications:** Teilhard de Chardin's Theology of the Christian in the World, 1967; Building God's World, 1976; Spirituality for Religious Life, 1976; (with M. Flick and G. O'Collins) The Cross Today, 1978; Praying, 1979; Praying for Inner Healing, 1979; All Things in Christ: The Spirituality of Teilhard de Chardin, 1981; Christian Faith in My Everyday Life, 1981; The End of the Religious Life, 1983; Wind and Sea Obey Him, 1983; Seeking Jesus in Contemplation and Discernment, 1983; (with L. Rooney) Mary, Queen of Peace: Is Our Lady Appearing at Medjugorje?, 1984; (with L. Rooney) Medjugorje Unfolds, 1985 in US as Medjugorje Up Close, 1986; (with S. Blackborow) The Healing of the Religious Life, 1985; (with L. Rooney) The Contemplative Way of Prayer, 1986; (with R. Wicks) Contemplating Jesus, 1986; (with L. Rooney) Medjugorje Journal, 1988; The Lord's Dealing: The Primacy of the Feminine in Christian Spirituality, 1988; Wind and Sea Obey Him: Approaches to a Theology of Nature, 1988; (with L. Rooney) Lord Jesus, Teach Me to Pray, 1989; (with L. Rooney) Medjugorje Retreat, 1989; A Pilgrim's Journal, 1989; (with L. Pecoraio) Mary among Us, 1989; (with L. Rooney) Our Lady Comes to Scottsdale: Is It Authentic?, 1991; The Scottsdale Apparitions, 1992; (with L. Rooney) Return to God: The Scottsdale Message, 1993; Contemplative Way of Prayer: Deepening Your Life with God, 1993; Praying with Teilhard de Chardin, 1995; (with L. Rooney) Your Wounds I Will Heal, 1999; (with L. Rooney) Praying with Mary, 2002. **Address:** Marquette University, 1404 W Wisconsin Ave., Milwaukee, WI 53233-2238, U.S.A. **Online address:** bobfaricy@yahoo.com

FARICY, Robert Leo. See **FARICY, Robert.**

FARISH, Terry. American (born United States), b. 1947. **Genres:** Novels, Children's Fiction, Young Adult Fiction, Writing/Journalism. **Career:** Ralston Public Library, director, 1976-82; Leominster Public Library, head of children's services, 1986-90; Rivier College, faculty, 1993-99; Salt Institute for Documentary Studies, faculty, 2001-03; New Hampshire Humanities Council, literacy coordinator. **Publications:** Why I'm Already Blue (young adult novel), 1989; Shelter for a Seabird (young adult novel), 1990; Flower Shadows (novel), 1992; If the Tiger (novel), 1995; Talking in Animal (children's novel), 1996; A House in Earnest, 2000; The Cat Who Liked Potato Soup, 2003; The Good Braider, 2012. **Address:** Portsmouth, NH , U.S.A. **Online address:** spring@terryfarish.com

FARKAS, George. American (born United States), b. 1946. **Genres:** Economics, Business/Trade/Industry. **Career:** Yale University, Department of Sociology and the Institution for Social and Policy Studies, assistant professor, 1972-78; Abt Associates Inc., senior analyst, 1978-82; University of Texas, School of Social Sciences, Department of Sociology and Political Economy, associate professor, 1982-87, professor, 1982-2000, graduate program in political economy, program head, 1989-94, Center for Education and Social Policy, founder and director, 1993-2000; The Pennsylvania State University, professor of sociology, demography and education, 2000-08, Department of Sociology, director of graduate studies, 2004-08, Population Research Institute, Statistics Core, director, 2005-07; University of California, professor of education and sociology, 2008-, co-director, 2010-. Writer. **Publications:** (Ed. with E.W. Stromsdorfer) Evaluation Studies Review Annual, vol. V, 1980; (contrib.) The Youth Employment Problem: Its Nature, Causes, and Consequences, 1982; (with P. England) Households, Employment and Gender: A Social, Economic, and Demographic View, 1986; (ed. with England and contrib.) Industries, Firms and Jobs: Sociological and Economic Approaches, 1988; Human Capital or Cultural Capital?: Ethnicity and Poverty Groups in an Urban School District, 1996; (contrib.) Challenges for Work and Family in the Twenty-First Century, 1998. Contributor of articles to books and journals. **Address:** Department of Education, University of California, 2001 Berkeley Pl., Irvine, CA 92697-5500, U.S.A. **Online address:** gfarkas@pop.psu.edu

FARLAND, Dave. See **WOLVERTON, Dave.**

FARLAND, David. See **WOLVERTON, Dave.**

FARLEY, David. American (born United States), b. 1971. **Genres:** Travel/Exploration, Autobiography/Memoirs, Adult Non-fiction. **Career:** New York University, teacher; Gotham Writers' Workshop, teacher; BlackBook Magazine, nightlife editor; Gayot.com, New York City restaurant editor. **Publications:** (Ed. and contrib. with J. Sholl) Prague and the Czech Republic: True Stories (anthology of literary nonfiction), 2006; An Irreverent Curiosity: In Search of the Church's Strangest Relic in Italy's Oddest Town (travel memoir and narrative history), 2009. Contributor to books, magazines and periodicals. **Address:** New York, NY , U.S.A. **Online address:** david.farley@gmail.com

FARLEY, Margaret A. American (born United States), b. 1935. **Genres:** History, Medicine/Health, Essays. **Career:** Mercy College-Detroit, Department of Philosophy, faculty, 1962-67; University of Detroit, Department of Philosophy, visiting lecturer, 1966-67; Yale University, Divinity School, lecturer, 1971-72, assistant professor, 1972-74, associate professor, 1974-84, professor, 1984-, Gilbert L. Stark professor of Christian ethics, 1986-. Writer. **Publications:** Personal Commitments: Beginning, Keeping, Changing, 1986; (ed. with L.S. Cahill) Embodiment, Morality, and Medicine, 1995; (ed. with C.E. Curran and R.A. McCormick) Feminist Ethics and the Catholic Moral Tradition, 1996; (ed. with S. Jones) Liberating Eschatology: Essays in Honor of Letty M. Russell, 1999; Compassionate Respect: A Feminist Approach to Medical Ethics and Other Questions, 2002; Just Love: A Framework for Christian Sexual Ethics, 2006; A Just & True Love: Feminism at the Frontiers of Theological Ethics: Essays in Honor of Margaret A. Farley, 2007. Contributor to periodicals. **Address:** Divinity School, Yale University, 409 Prospect St., New Haven, CT 06511-2167, U.S.A. **Online address:** margaret.farley@yale.edu

FARLEY, Terri. American (born United States), b. 1950. **Genres:** Novellas/Short Stories, Novels. **Career:** Writer, journalist and teacher. **Publications:** PHANTOM STALLION SERIES: The Wild One, 2002; Mustang Moon, 2002; Dark Sunshine, 2002; The Renegade, 2003; Free Again, 2003; The Challenger, 2003; Desert Dancer, 2003; Golden Ghost, 2003; Gift Horse, 2003; Red Feather Filly, 2004; Untamed, 2004; Rain Dance, 2004; Heartbreak Bronco, 2004; Moonrise, 2005; Kidnapped Colt, 2005; The Wildest Heart, 2005; Mountain Mare, 2005; Firefly, 2005; Secret Star, 2006; Blue Wings, 2006; Dawn Runner, 2006; Wild Honey, 2006; Gypsy Gold, 2006; Run Away Home, 2006. WILD HORSE ISLAND SERIES: The Horse Charmer, 2007; The Shining Stallion, 2007; Wild Horse, 2007; Rain Forest Rose, 2007; Water Lily, 2008; Castaway Colt, 2008; Fire Maiden, 2008; Sea Shadow, 2008; Mist Walker, 2008; Snowfire, 2008; Faraway Filly, 2009; Galloping Gold, 2009. NOVELS: Seven Tears Into the Sea, 2005; Into the Green, 2009; On Borrowed Wings, 2009. OTHERS: (contrib.) Seaswept Rapture, 1992. **Address:** c/o Karen Solem, Spencerhill Agency, 24 Pk. Row, PO Box 374, Chatham, NY 12037, U.S.A. **Online address:** farleyterri@aol.com

FARLOW, James O(rville). American (born United States), b. 1951. **Genres:** Earth Sciences, Sciences, Geography. **Career:** Indiana University-Purdue University, Department of Geosciences, lecturer in geology, 1978-79, assistant professor, 1982-87, associate professor, 1987-90, professor of geology, 1990-; Hope College, assistant professor of geology, 1979-81; Texas Department of Parks and Wildlife, consultant, 1985-. Writer. **Publications:** (Intro.) Bones for Barnum: Adventures of a Dinosaur Hunter, 1985; A Guide to Lower Cretaceous Dinosaur Footprints and Tracksites of the Paluxy River Valley, Somervell County, Texas (guidebook), 1987; (ed.) Paleobiology of the Dinosaurs, 1989; On the Tracks of Dinosaurs: A Study of Dinosaur Footprints (children's book), 1991; The Dinosaurs of Dinosaur Valley State Park, Texas Department of Parks and Wildlife, 1993; (with R.E. Molnar) The Great Hunters: Meat-Eating Dinosaurs and Their World (children's book), 1995; (ed. with M.K. Brett-Surman and R.F. Walters) The Complete Dinosaur, 1997; Bringing Dinosaur Bones to Life: How do We know What Dinosaurs Were Like?, 2001; (ed. with M.K. Brett-Surman) Kyōryū Daihyakka Jiten, 2001; (co-author) Te Dinosaurs of the Heritage Museum of the Texas Hill Country, 2006; (co-author) Texas Giants, 2006; Contributor of articles to journals and magazines. **Address:** Department of Geosciences, Indiana University-Purdue University, SB-242, 2101 E Coliseum Blvd., Fort Wayne, IN 46805-1445, U.S.A. **Online address:** farlow@ipfw.edu

FARMAIAN, Sattareh Farman. American/Iranian (born Iran), b. 1921. **Genres:** Education, Social Work, Urban Studies, Women's Studies And Issues, Autobiography/Memoirs, Biography, Reference. **Career:** Cities Service Oil Co., consultant, 1951-54; United Nations, social welfare expert for Arab states, 1954-58; Community Welfare Centers of Iran, founder and executive director, 1958-79; Family Planning Association of Iran, founder, executive director and chairman, 1958-79; Tehran School of Social Work, founder and dean, 1958-79; Researcher for Tehran University, faculty of social sciences,

1958-79; adviser to United Nations, 1969-79; County of Los Angeles, Department of Social Services, children's services worker, 1980-92; United Way of Los Angeles, consultant for social welfare planning on priorities, 1980-. Writer. **Publications:** The Social Problems of Urbanization in Iraq, 1958; Children's Needs, 1960; County Profile of Iranian Family Planning and Social Welfare, 1965; Children and Teachers, 1966; Prostitution Problems in the City of Tehran, 1969; Pīrāmūn-i rū spī garī dar shahr-i Tihrān, 1970; Traditional Division of Work Between the Sexes, a Source of Inequality: Research Symposium on Women and Decision Making: A Social Policy Priority, 1976; On the Other Side of the China Wall, 1977; (with D. Munker) Daughter of Persia: A Woman's Journey from Her Father's Harem through the Islamic Revolution, 1992; Dar ā nsū -yi dī vār-i Chī n: guzā rishī az yak safar-i 33 rū zah bihkishvar-i Chī n, 1997; Pīshgāmān-i madadkārī-i ijtimadar īrān, 2008. Contributor of articles to periodicals. **Address:** 10687 Wilkins Ave., Ste. 4, Los Angeles, CA 90024, U.S.A. **Online address:** sattareh@earthlink.net

FARMELO, Graham. American (born United States), b. 1953. **Genres:** Sciences. **Career:** Science Museum, head of science communication; Northeastern University, associate professor of physics. Theoretical physicist, consultant and writer. **Publications:** (Co-author) Discovering Physics, Unit 13: The Beginnings of Modern Atomic Physics, 1982; (co-author) Physics of Matter, Unit 2-3, 1986; (co-author) Macroscopic Descriptions of Matter, 1986; (co-author) Here and Now: Contemporary Science and Technology in Museums and Science Centres; Proceedings of a Conference Held at the Science Museum, London, 21-23 November 1996, 1997; (ed.) It Must Be Beautiful: Great Equations of Modern Science, 2002; (with D. Chittenden and B.V. Lewenstein) Creating Connections: Museums and the Public Understanding of Current Research, 2004; The Strangest Man: The Hidden Life of Paul Dirac, Mystic of the Atom, 2009 in UK as The Strangest Man: The Hidden Life of Paul Dirac, Quantum Genius, 2009. **Address:** Department of Physics, Northeastern University, 111 Dana Research Ctr., 110 Forsyth St., Boston, MA 02115, U.S.A.

FARMER, Jared. American (born United States), b. 1974. **Genres:** History. **Career:** State University of New York at Stony Brook, assistant professor and affiliate to consortium for interdisciplinary environmental research, 2007-. Writer. **Publications:** Glen Canyon Dammed: Inventing Lake Powell and the Canyon Country, 1999; On Zion's Mount: Mormons, Indians, and the American Landscape, 2008. **Address:** Department of History, State University of New York at Stony Brook, Social and Behavioral Sciences Bldg., 3rd Fl., Stony Brook, NY 11794-4348, U.S.A. **Online address:** jared.farmer@stonybrook.edu

FARMER, Jerrilyn. American (born United States), b. 1953. **Genres:** Novels, Mystery/Crime/Suspense, Women's Studies And Issues. **Career:** Writer and novelist. **Publications:** MADELINE BEAN NOVELS: Sympathy for the Devil, 1998; Immaculate Reception, 1999; Killer Wedding: A Madeline Bean Catering Mystery, 2000; Dim Sum Dead, 2001; Mumbo Gumbo: A Madeline Bean Novel, 2003; Perfect Sax: A Madeline Bean Novel, 2004; The Flaming Luau of Death: A Madeline Bean Novel, 2005. OTHER: (with J. Rivers) Murder at the Academy Awards: A Red Carpet Murder Mystery, 2009. **Address:** William Morrow, 10 E 53rd St., 11th Fl., New York, NY 10022, U.S.A. **Online address:** jerrilyn@earthlink.net

FARMER, John J. American (born United States), b. 1957. **Genres:** Criminology/True Crime. **Career:** New Jersey Supreme Court, Associate Justice Alan B. Handler, law clerk; Riker, litigation associate; Danzig, litigation associate; Scherer, litigation associate; Hyland & Peretti LLP, litigation associate; Office of the U.S. Attorney in Newark, federal prosecutor; Administration of New Jersey Governor Christine Todd Whitman, assistant counsel, deputy chief counsel, chief counsel, 1994; New Jersey Office of Emergency Management, supervisor, 1999-2001; State of New Jersey, attorney general, 1999-2002; New Jersey Domestic Preparedness Task Force, chair; 9/11 Commission, senior counsel and team leader, 2003-04; K&L Gates (law firm), partner; Arseneault, Whipple, Farmer, Fassett and Azzarello, LLP, founding partner, 2007-09; Rutgers School of Law, adjunct professor, dean, 2009-; New Jersey Institute for Social Justice, president. Writer. **Publications:** Overview, Highlights, and Action Steps of the Final Report of the State Police Review Team, 1999; (with L.Z. Celentano) Computer Crime: A Joint Report, 2000; The Ground Truth: The Untold Story of America under Attack on 9/11, 2009. Contributor to periodicals. **Address:** Rutgers School of Law-Newark, 123 Washington St., Newark, NJ 07102, U.S.A. **Online address:** jfarmer@kinoy.rutgers.edu

FARMER, Nancy. American (born United States), b. 1941. **Genres:** Children's Fiction. **Career:** University of California, lab technician, 1969-72; Loxton, Hunting and Associates, chemist and entomologist, 1972-74; University of Zimbabwe, lab technician and entomologist, 1975-78; freelance scientist and writer in Harare, 1978-88; Stanford University Medical School, lab technician, 1991-92; freelance writer, 1992-. **Publications:** The Mirror, 1987; Lorelei: The Story of a Bad Cat, 1987; Tsitsi's Skirt (picture book), 1988; The Ear, the Eye and the Arm, 1990; Tapiwa's Uncle, 1993; Do You Know Me, 1993; The Warm Place, 1995; Runnery Granary, 1996; A Girl Named Disaster, 1996; Casey Jones's Fireman: The Story of Sim Webb, 1998; The House of the Scorpion, 2002; Sea of Trolls, 2004; Clever Ali, 2006; Land of the Silver Apples, 2007; The Islands of the Blessed, 2009. Works appear in anthology. Contributor to periodicals. **Address:** c/o Michelle Fadlalla, Simon & Schuster, 1230 Ave. of the Americas, New York, NY 10020, U.S.A.

FARMER, Penelope (Jane). British (born England), b. 1939. **Genres:** Novels, Children's Fiction, Young Adult Fiction, Translations, Adult Non-fiction. **Career:** London County Council Education Department, teacher, 1961-63, sociological researcher, 1985-90. Writer. **Publications:** FOR ADULTS: Standing in the Shadow, 1984; Away from Home, 1987; Eve: Her Story, 1988; Glasshouses, 1988; Snakes and Ladders, 1993; Penelope: A Novel, 1996. FOR CHILDREN: Daedalus and Icarus, 1971; Serpent's Teeth: The Story of Cadmus, 1971; (contrib.) The Story of Persephone, 1972; Heracles, 1975; August the Fourth, 1975; The Coal Train, 1977; The Runaway Train, 1980. FOR YOUNG ADULTS: The China People, 1960; The Summer Birds, 1962; The Magic Stone, 1964; Saturday Shillings, 1965; The Sea Gull, 1966; Emma in Winter, 1966; Charlotte Sometimes, 1969; The Dragonfly Summer, 1971; A Castle of Bone, 1972; William and Mary: A Story, 1974; Year King, 1977; Thicker than Water, 1989; Stone Croc, 1991. OTHERS: (comp. and ed.) Beginnings: Creation Myths of the World, 1978; (trans. with A. Oz) A. Oz, Soumchi, 1995; (and ed.) Two, or, The Book of Twins and Doubles, 1996; (ed.) Sisters: An Anthology, 1999; (and ed.) The Virago Book of Grandmothers: An Autobiographical Anthology, 2000. Contributor to journals. **Address:** New York Review Books, 435 Hudson St., Ste. 300, New York, NY 10014, U.S.A.

FARMER, Roger E. A. American (born United States), b. 1955. **Genres:** Economics, History. **Career:** University of Toronto, lecturer, 1980-82, assistant professor, 1982-83; University of Pennsylvania, assistant professor, 1983-88; University of California, Department of Economics, associate professor, 1988-91, professor, 1991-2010, chair, 2009-, distinguished professor of economics, 2010-, vice chair for graduate affairs, 2006-09; Macroeconomic Dynamics, associate editor, 1997-; European University Institute, professor, 1998-2000; Federal Reserve Bank of Atlanta, consultant, 2006-; Journal of Economic Growth, associate editor; Journal of Public Economic Theory, associate editor; European Central Bank, consultant; Reserve Bank of Australia, consultant; Bank of England, consultant. **Publications:** (Co-ed.) Monetary Policy in Our Times, 1985, 2nd ed., 1999; The Macroeconomics of Self-fulfilling Prophecies, 1993, 2nd ed., 1999; Macroeconomics, 1999, 2nd ed., 2002; (ed. and contrib.) Macroeconomics in the Small and the Large: Essays on Microfoundations, Macroeconomic Applications and Economic History in Honor of Axel Leijonhufvud, 2009; Expectations, Employment and Prices, 2010; How the Economy Works: Confidence, Crashes and Self-fulfilling Prophecies, 2010. OTHERS: (with D.F. Waggoner and T. Zha) Indeterminacy in a Forward Looking Regime Switching Model, 2006; Shooting the Auctioneer, 2006; (with A. Beyer and J. Henry) Factor Analysis in a Model with Rational Expectations, 2007; Aggregate Demand and Supply, 2007; (with D.F. Waggoner and T. Zha) Understanding the New-Keynesian Model When Monetary Policy Switches Regimes, 2007; Fiscal Policy Can Reduce Unemployment: But There Is a Less Costly and More Effective Alternative, 2009. Contributor to books and periodicals. **Address:** Department of Economics, University of California, PO Box 951477, Los Angeles, CA 90095-1477, U.S.A. **Online address:** rfarmer@econ.ucla.edu

FARMILOE, Dorothy. Canadian (born Canada), b. 1920. **Genres:** Poetry, Adult Non-fiction, Writing/Journalism, Novels. **Career:** Long Point Lodge, owner and operator, 1955-63; St. Clair College, teacher of English, 1969-78; Sesame Press, founding member and publisher; Mainline Magazine, founding member; Elk Lake Explorer, publisher, 1979-. Writer. **Publications:** POETRY: The Lost Island and Other Poems, 1966; (co-author) 21 x 3, 1967; Poems for Apartment-dwellers, 1970; Winter Orange Mood, 1972; Blue is the Colour of Death, 1973; Elk Lake Diary: Poems, 1976; Adrenalin of Weather, 1978; Words for My Weeping Daughter, 1980; Elk Lake Lore and Legend,

1984; Dragons and Dinosaurs and Other Poems, 1988; Mothers and Daughters: Poems New and Selected, 1997; Cobalt in Retrospect and Rhyme, 2003. OTHERS: (ed. and contrib.) Contraverse, 1971; And Some in Fire, 1974; Creative Communication, 1974; Creative Communication for Business Students, 1977; How to Write a Better Anything: The Creative Writer's Handbook, 1979; Isabella Valancy Crawford: The Life and the Legends, 1983; Legend of Jack Munro: A Portrait of a Canadian Hero, 1994; Elk Lake: Lore and Legend, 1999. Contributor of articles to journals. **Address:** PO Box 94, Elk Lake, ON P0J 1G0, Canada.

FARNSWORTH, Clyde. (Clyde Henri Farnsworth). American (born United States), b. 1931. **Genres:** International Relations/Current Affairs, Young Adult Fiction, History, Economics, Literary Criticism And History. **Career:** New York Times, Washington and foreign correspondent. Writer and reporter. **Publications:** No Money Down, 1963; (as Clyde H. Farnsworth) Out of This Nettle: A History of Postwar Europe, 1974; Shadow Wars (fiction), 1998. Contributor to periodicals. **Address:** 3207 Macomb St., Washington, DC 20008, U.S.A. **Online address:** clydefarnsworth@chesapeake.net

FARNSWORTH, Clyde Henri. See **FARNSWORTH, Clyde.**

FARNSWORTH, Stephen J(ames). American (born United States), b. 1961. **Genres:** Politics/Government. **Career:** Kansas City Star and Times, staff reporter, 1985-90; Fairchild News Service, national economics correspondent, 1990-93; Center for the Study of Responsive Law, researcher, 1993-94; Georgetown University, lecturer in political science, 1994-95; Mary Washington College, senior lecturer, 1995, instructor, 1996-97, assistant professor, 1997-, associate professor of political science; George Mason University, Department of Communication, assistant professor. Writer. **Publications:** (With S.R. Lichter) The Nightly News Nightmare: Network Television's Coverage of U.S. Presidential Elections, 1988-2000, 2003, 3rd ed. as Nightly News Nightmare: Media Coverage of U.S. Presidential Elections, 2010; Political Support in a Frustrated America, 2003; (with S.R. Lichter) Mediated Presidency: Television News and Presidential Governance, 2006; Spinner in Chief: How Presidents Sell Their Policies and Themselves, 2009. Contributor to periodicals. **Address:** Department of Communication, George Mason University, 149 Science & Technology II, 4400 University Dr., MSN 3D6, Fairfax, VA 22030, U.S.A. **Online address:** sfarnswo@mwc.edu

FAROGHI, Suraiya. (Suraiya Faroqhi). German (born Germany), b. 1941. **Genres:** History, Crafts. **Career:** Ludwig Maximilians University, professor of Middle Eastern and Turkish studies, 1988-2008, professor emeritus, 2008-, Institut für Den Nahen und Mittleren Osten, director, 2002-08; University of the Bosporus, visiting faculty, 1998, 2001; University of Minnesota, Union Pacific visiting professor, 1998; Charles University, visiting faculty, 2000-01; Wissenschaftskolleg, fellow, 2001-02; Bilgi University, professor. Writer. **Publications:** AS SURAIYA FAROQHI: Bektaschi-Orden in Anatolien, 1981; Towns and Townsmen of Ottoman Anatolia: Trade, Crafts, and Food Production in an Urban Setting, 1520-1650, 1984; Peasants, Dervishes, and Traders in the Ottoman Empire, 1986; Men of Modest Substance: House Owners and House Property in Seventeenth-Century Ankara and Kayseri, 1987; Herrscher über Mekka: die Geschichte der Pilgerfahrt, 1990; (ed. with H. Berktay) New Approaches to State and Peasant in Ottoman History, 1992; Kultur und Alltag im Osmanischen Reich, 1995; Coping with the State: Political Conflict and Crime in the Ottoman Empire, 1550-1720 (collected articles), 1995; Making a Living in the Ottoman Lands, 1480 to 1820 (collected articles), 1995; Pilgrims and Sultans, 1996; Approaching Ottoman History: An Introduction to the Sources, 1999; Geschichte des Osmanischen Reiches, 2000; Subjects of the Sultan, 2000, new ed., 2005; (ed. with F. Adanir) Ottomans and the Balkans, 2002; Stories of Ottoman Men and Women: Establishing Status, Establishing Control (collected articles), 2002; (ed. with C.K. Neumann) Illuminated Table, the Prosperous House, 2003; (ed. with C.K. Neumann) Ottoman Costumes, 2004; Ottoman Empire and the World Around It, 2004; (ed. with R. Deguilhem) Crafts and Craftsmen of the Middle East, 2005; (ed.) Later Ottoman Empire, 1603-1839, 2006; Another Mirror for Princes, 2008; (with G. Veinstein) Merchants in the Ottoman Empire, 2008; Artisans of Empire, 2009; (ed. with K. Fleet) Ottoman Empire as a World Power, 1453-1603, 2012. Contributor to books. **Address:** University of Munich, Geschwister-Scholl-Platz 1, Munich, 80539, Germany. **Online address:** sfaroqhi@bilgi.edu.tr

FARON, Fay. American (born United States), b. 1949. **Genres:** Criminology/True Crime, Reference, Social Sciences, Psychology, Reference, Writing/

Journalism. **Career:** Rat Dog Dick Detective Agency, owner, 1982-; Creighton-Morgan Publishing Group, owner, 1987-; Elder Angels, founder, 1997. Writer. **Publications:** The Instant National Locator Guide, 1991; A Private Eye's Guide to Collecting a Bad Debt, 1991; Missing Persons: A Writer's Guide to Finding the Lost, the Abducted and the Escaped, 1997; Congames, 1998; Rip-Off: A Writer's Guide to Crimes of Deception, 1998; Lily Kills Her Client, forthcoming. **Address:** Rat Dog Dick Detective Agency, 500 Pelican Ave., Ste. 209, New Orleans, LA 70114, U.S.A. **Online address:** ratdog@sprintmail.com

FAROOKI, Roopa. British/Pakistani (born Pakistan), b. 1974?. **Genres:** Novels. **Career:** JWT, staff; Saatchi & Saatchi Co., staff. Full-time writer, 2004. **Publications:** Bitter Sweets (novel), 2007; Corner Shop (novel), 2008; Ways Things Look to Me, 2009. **Address:** Gillon Aitken Associates, 18-21 Cavaye Pl., London, SW10 9PT, England.

FAROQHI, Suraiya. See **FAROGHI, Suraiya.**

FARQUHAR, Mary Ann. Australian/Chinese (born China), b. 1949?. **Genres:** Bibliography, Art/Art History, Film. **Career:** Griffith University, Department of International Business and Asian Studies, associate professor, professor, professor emeritus. Writer. **Publications:** Children's Literature in China: From Lu Xun to Mao Zedong, 1999; (with C. Berry) China on Screen: Cinema and Nation, 2006; (ed. with Y. Zhang) Chinese Film Stars, 2010. Contributor to books and periodicals. **Address:** Department of International Business and Asian, Studies, Griffith University, 170 Kessels Rd., Nathan Campus, Nathan, QL 4111, Australia. **Online address:** m.farquhar@griffith.edu.au

FARR, Diana. See **PULLEIN-THOMPSON, Diana.**

FARR, Diane. American (born United States) **Genres:** Romance/Historical, Young Adult Fiction, Humor/Satire, Novels, Novellas/Short Stories. **Career:** Writer. **Publications:** ROMANCE NOVELS: Fair Game, 1999; The Nobody, 1999; Falling for Chloe, 2000; Once upon a Christmas, 2000; (co-author) A Regency Christmas Eve: Five Stories, 2000; Duel of Hearts, 2002; The Fortune Hunter, 2002; Under the Wishing Star, 2003; Under a Lucky Star, 2004. YOUNG ADULT: Wicked Cool, 2010. OTHER: Dashing Through the Snow, 2011. **Address:** c/o Irene Goodman, Irene Goodman Literary Agency, 27 W 24th St., Ste. 700B, New York, NY 10010, U.S.A. **Online address:** dianefarr@aol.com

FARR, James R. American (born United States), b. 1950?. **Genres:** History. **Career:** University of Tennessee, assistant professor of history, 1983-88; Purdue University, Department of History, assistant professor, 1988-90, associate professor, 1990-95, professor, 1995-2009, Germaine Seelye Oesterle professor of history, 2009-. Writer. **Publications:** Hands of Honor: Artisans and Their World in Dijon, 1550-1650, 1988; Authority and Sexuality in Early Modern Burgundy (1550-1730), 1995; Artisans in Europe, 1300- 1914, 2000; A Tale of Two Murders: Passion and Power in Seventeenth-Century France, 2005. Contributor to periodicals. **Address:** Purdue University, University Hall, UNIV 311, 672 Oval Dr., West Lafayette, IN 47907-2087, U.S.A. **Online address:** jrfarr@purdue.edu

FARR, Jory. American (born United States), b. 1952. **Genres:** Music, History, Literary Criticism And History. **Career:** Press-Enterprise, popular culture critic and columnist, 1987-. **Publications:** Moguls and Madmen: The Pursuit of Power in Popular Music, 1994; Rites of Rhythm: The Music of Cuba, 2003. **Address:** Ken Sherman & Associates, 9507 Santa Monica Blvd., Beverly Hills, CA 90210, U.S.A.

FARR, Thomas F. American (born United States), b. 1948. **Genres:** Theology/Religion. **Career:** Witherspoon Institute, senior fellow, International Religious Freedom, chair; Georgetown University, Edmund A. Walsh School of Foreign Service, visiting professor and senior fellow, Berkeley Center for Religion, Peace and World Affairs, Program on Religion and U.S. Foreign Policy, director; U.S. Foreign Service, American diplomat; U.S. Department of State, Office of International Religious Freedom, first director; Christian Solidarity Worldwide-USA, board vice chair; Review of Faith and International Affairs, contributing editor. **Publications:** World of Faith and Freedom: Why International Religious Liberty Is Vital to American National Security, 2008. Contributor to books and periodicals. **Address:** Falls Church, VA , U.S.A. **Online address:** tff8@georgetown.edu

FARRAR, Ronald T(ruman). American (born United States), b. 1935. **Genres:** Communications/Media, Biography, Essays, Advertising/Public Relations, Law, Education. **Career:** Arkansas Democrat, reporter, 1957; Paragould Daily Press, news editor, 1958; Arkansas Gazette, reporter, 1958-60; Trumann Democrat, editor-manager, 1960-61; Daily Iowan, circulation manager, 1961-62; Indiana University, lecturer, associate professor of journalism, 1964-70; Southern Methodist University, associate professor of journalism and chairman of department, 1970-73; University of Mississippi, professor of journalism and chairman of department, 1973-77; University of Kentucky, School of Journalism, director, 1977-86; University of South Carolina, School of Journalism and Mass Communications, Reynolds-Faunt professor of journalism, 1986, interim dean, now distinguished professor emeritus. **Publications:** Reluctant Servant: The Story of Charles G. Ross, 1969; (ed. with J.D. Stevens) Mass Media and the National Experience; Essays in Communications History, 1971; College 101, 1984, rev. ed. as College 101: Making the Most of Your Freshman Year, 1988; Mass Communication: An Introduction to the Field, 1988, 2nd ed., 1996; (with J.F. Worthington) The Ultimate College Survival Guide, 1995, 4th ed., 1998; Creed for My Profession: Walter Williams, Journalist to the World, 1998; (with R.L. Moore and E.L. Collins) Advertising and Public Relations Law, 1998. Contributor to journals. **Address:** School of Journalism and Mass Communications, University of South Carolina, Main St., Columbia, SC 29201-4258, U.S.A.

FARRELL, David. See **SMITH, Frederick E(screet).**

FARRELL, David M. Irish (born Ireland), b. 1960. **Genres:** Politics/Government. **Career:** Dublin Institute of Technology, lecturer, 1986-87; University College, lecturer, 1987-88, Professor in politics; University of Manchester, lecturer, 1988-89; University of Wales-Cardiff, lecturer 1989-90; University of Manchester, head of social sciences, Jean Monnet lecturer, 1991-97, Senior Jean Monnet lecturer, 1997-2000, Jean Monnet professor in European politics, 2000-; Oxford University Press, co-editor. **Publications:** Comparing Electoral Systems, 1997; Electoral Systems: A Comparative Introduction, 2001, 2nd ed., 2011; (with I. McAllister) Australian Electoral System: Origins, Variations, and Consequences, 2006; (with R. Scully) Representing Europe's Citizens?, 2007. EDITOR: (with S. Bowler) Electoral Strategies and Political Marketing, 1992; (with D. Broughton, D. Denver and C. Rallings) British Elections and Parties Yearbook, 1994, 1995; (co-ed.) British Elections and Parties Yearbook, 1995, 1996; (with J. Fisher, D. Broughton and D. Denver) British Elections and Parties Yearbook, 1996, 1996; (with S. Bowler and R.S. Katz) Party Discipline and Parliamentary Government, 1999; (with R. Schmitt-Beck) Do Political Campaigns Matter? Campaign Effects in Elections and Referendums, 2002; (with P. Webb and I. Holliday) Political Parties in Advanced Industrial Democracies, 2002; Political Parties and Political Systems, 2005; (co-ed.) Non-party Actors in Electoral Politics, 2008; Contributor to books and journals. **Address:** 16 North Rd., Glossop, SK13 7AS, England. **Online address:** david.farrell@man.ac.uk

FARRELL, Mike Joseph. American (born United States), b. 1939. **Genres:** Autobiography/Memoirs, Humor/Satire. **Career:** Death Penalty Focus, president, 1994; Screen Actors Guild, vice president, 2002-05; Farrell/Minoff productions, partner. Writer and actor. **Publications:** Just Call Me Mike: A Journey to Actor and Activist (memoir), 2007; Of Mule and Man (memoir), 2009. Contributor to books, newspapers and magazines. **Address:** Innovative Artists, 1505 10th St., Santa Monica, CA 90401, U.S.A. **Online address:** mfocontact@gmail.com

FARRELL, Richard. American (born United States), b. 1957?. **Genres:** Autobiography/Memoirs. **Career:** University of Massachusetts, adjunct professor of English; Maryann De, co-director and co-producer. Writer. **Publications:** (With P. Nee and M. Blythe) A Criminal & an Irishman: The Inside Story of the Boston Mob-IRA Connection, 2006; What's Left of Us: A Memoir of Addiction, 2009. Contributor to periodicals. **Address:** Milford, NH , U.S.A. **Online address:** richardafarrell@comcast.net

FARRELL, S. L. See **LEIGH, Stephen.**

FARRELL, Warren (Thomas). American (born United States), b. 1943. **Genres:** Business/Trade/Industry, How-to Books, Human Relations/Parenting, Women's Studies And Issues, Politics/Government, Psychology, Sex, Sociology, Women's Studies And Issues, History, Law. **Career:** Fordham University, lecturer, 1970; New Jersey State College, instructor, 1970; Rutgers University, lecturer, 1971-73; American University, lecturer, 1973-74;

Georgetown University, lecturer, 1973-75; California School of Professional Psychology, professor, 1978-79; San Diego State University, professor, 1979-80; University of California, adjunct assistant professor, 1986-88; City University of New York, adjunct assistant professor; Midland Park High School, student body president. Author and consultant. **Publications:** The Liberated Man: Beyond Masculinity; Freeing Men and their Relationships with Women, 1974; Why Men Are the Way They Are: The Male-Female Dynamic, 1986; The Myth of Male Power: Why Men Are the Disposable Sex-Fated for War, Programmed for Work, Divorced from Emotion, 1993; (contrib.) Ultimate Answering Machine Message Book, 1997; Women Can't Hear What Men Don't Say: Destroying Myths, Creating Love, 1999; Father and Child Reunion: How to Bring the Dads We Need to the Children We Love, 2001; The Pay Paradox: What Women Aren't Told about Why Men Earn More, 2004; Why Men Earn More: The Startling Truth behind the Pay Gap and What Women Can Do about It, 2005; (with S. Svoboda and J.P. Sterba) Does Feminism Discriminate Against Men?: A Debate, 2008; (with J. Gray) The Boy Crisis, forthcoming. Contributor of articles to periodicals, journals and books. **Address:** 24 Marsh Dr., Mill Valley, CA 94941, U.S.A. **Online address:** warren@warrenfarrell.com

FARRELL-BECK, Jane. American (born United States) **Genres:** Fash Ion/Costume, History. **Career:** Iowa State University, professor of textiles and clothing, now professor emeritus of apparel, educational studies and hospitality management. Writer. **Publications:** (With B. Payne and G. Winakor) The History of Costume from Ancient Mesopotamia through the Twentieth Century, 2nd ed., 1992; (with C. Gau) Uplift: The Bra in America, 2002; (with J. Parsons) Twentieth Century Dress in the United States, 2006. Contributor to periodicals. **Address:** Textiles and Clothing Program, Iowa State University, 1072 LeBaron, Ames, IA 50011-1120, U.S.A. **Online address:** jfarrell@iastate.edu

FARRER-HALLS, Gill. British (born England), b. 1958. **Genres:** Theology/Religion, Sports/Fitness, Self Help. **Career:** Meridian Trust, Buddhist Film and Video Archive, administrator and videotape producer, 1991-98, freelance producer, production manager. Writer and educator. **Publications:** The World of the Dalai Lama: An Inside Look at His Life, His People, and His Vision, 1998; Handbook of Buddhist Wisdom, 1999; The Illustrated Encyclopedia of Buddhist Wisdom, 2000; Meditations & Rituals Using Aromatherapy Oils, 2001; Creating Calm: Meditations in Daily Life, 2002; The Feminine Face of Buddhism, 2002; (ed.) Women on the Buddhist Path, 2002; A Gift of Positive Thinking, 2004; Face Creams, Hair Rinses and Body Lotions: Recipes for Natural Beauty, 2004; A Gift of Awakening, 2004; A Gift of Happiness, 2004; Gift of Inner Peace, 2004; Soap and Scent: Recipes for Natural Beauty, 2004; The Aromatherapy Bible: The Definitive Guide to Using Essential Oils, 2005; The Buddha Book, 2005; Natural Beauty Recipe Book: How to Make Your Own Organic Cosmetics and Beauty Products, 2006; Spiritual Spa: Create a Private Sanctuary to Refresh Body and Spirit, 2006. **Address:** Elizabeth Puttick Literary Agency, 46 Brookfield Mansions, Highgate W Hill, London, GL N6 6AT, England.

FARRINGTON, David P. British (born England), b. 1944. **Genres:** Criminology/True Crime, Psychiatry, Psychology. **Career:** Cambridge University, Institute of Criminology, staff, 1969-, research officer, 1969-70, senior research officer, 1970-74, assistant director of research, 1974-76, university lecturer in criminology, 1976-88, reader in psychological criminology, 1988-92, professor of psychological criminology, 1992-, acting director, 1993, 1995, M.Phil. Course in Criminology, director, 1975-78, Cambridge Study in Delinquent Development, director, 1982-, data protection officer, 1986-, Ph.D. Programme, director, 2005-06, 2010-11; Pembroke College, Studies in Social Sciences, director, 1972-76; Selwyn College, director, 1974-76; Darwin College, fellow, 1980-83; University of Pittsburgh, Western Psychiatric Institute, adjunct professor; Criminal Behavior and Mental Health, co-editor. **Publications:** (With D.J. West) Who Becomes Delinquent?: Second Report of the Cambridge Study in Delinquent Development, 1973; (with D.J. West) The Delinquent Way of Life: Third Report of the Cambridge Study in Delinquent Development, 1977; Wiley Series on Current Research in Forensic Psychiatry and Psychology, 1982; (with L. Ohlin and J.Q. Wilson) Understanding and Controlling Crime: Toward a New Research Strategy, 1986; (with M. Tonry and L.E. Ohlin) Human Development and Criminal Behavior: New Ways of Advancing Knowledge, 1991; (with P.A. Langan) Crime and Justice in the United States and in England and Wales, 1998; (co-author) Antisocial Behavior and Mental Health Problems, 1998; (with E.G. Cohn and R.A. Wright) Evaluating Criminology and Criminal Justice, 1998; (co-author) Evaluation

of Two Intensive Regimes for Young Offenders, 2002; (with R. Loeber and D. Petechuk) Child Delinquency: Early Intervention and Prevention, 2003; (with B.C. Welsh) Saving Children from a Life of Crime: Early Risk Factors and Effective Interventions, 2007; (with A.R. Piquero and A. Blumstein) Key Issues in Criminal Career Research: New Analyses of the Cambridge Study in Delinquent Development, 2007; (with B.C. Welsh) Förbättrad utomhusbelysning och brottsprevention: en systematisk forskningsgenomgång, 2007; (with T.H. Bennett and K.R. Holloway) Grannsamverkans effekter på brottsligheten: en systematisk forskningsgenomgång, 2008; (with D. Jolliffe) Mentorskaps inverkan på återfall i brott, 2008; (with B.C. Welsh) Making Public Places Safer: Surveillance and Crime Prevention, 2009; (with D. Jolliffe) Effectiveness of Interventions with Adult Male Violent Offenders, 2009; (with B.C. Welsh and S.J. O'Dell) Effectiveness of Public Area Surveillance for Crime Prevention, 2010; (with R. Loeber) Young Homicide Offenders and Victims, 2011. EDITOR: (with K. Hawkins and S. Lloyd-Bostock) Psychology, Law and Legal Processes, 1979; (with J. Gunn) Abnormal Offenders, Delinquency and the Criminal Justice System, 1982; (with J. Gunn) Reactions to Crime: The Public, the Police, Courts, and Prisons, 1985; (with J. Gunn) Aggression and Dangerousness, 1985; (with R. Tarling) Prediction in Criminology, 1985; (with S. Walklate) Offenders and Victims, 1992; (with R.J. Sampson and P.O.H. Wikstrom) Integrating Individual and Ecological Aspects of Crime, 1993; Psychological Explanations of Crime, 1994; (with M. Tonry) Building a Safer Society: Strategic Approaches to Crime Prevention, 1995; (with A. Raine, P.A. Brennan and S.A. Mednick) Biosocial Bases of Violence, 1997; (with R. Loeber) Serious & Violent Juvenile Offenders: Risk Factors And Successful Interventions, 1998; (with B.C. Welsh and L.W. Sherman) Costs and Benefits of Preventing Crime, 2001; (with R. Loeber) Child Delinquents, 2001; (with G.A. Bernfeld and A.W. Leschied) Offender Rehabilitation in Practice: Implementing and Evaluating Effective Programs, 2001; (with C.R. Hollin and M. McMurran) Sex and Violence, 2001; (co-ed.) Evidence-Based Crime Prevention, 2002; (with J.W. Coid) Early Prevention Of Adult Antisocial Behavior, 2003; (with P.A. Langan and M. Tonry) Cross-national Studies In Crime And Justice, 2004; Integrated Developmental & Life-Course Theories Of Offending, 2005; (with M. Tonry) Crime and Punishment In Western Countries, 1980/1999, 2005; (with A. Perry and C. McDougall) Reducing Crime: The Effectiveness of Criminal Justice Intervention, 2006; (with B.C. Welsh) Preventing Crime: What Works for Children, Offenders, Victims, and Places, 2006; (with B.C. Welsh) The Oxford Handbook of Crime Prevention, 2011; (with A. Bottoms and F. Lösel) Young Adult Offenders, 2012; (with R. Loeber) From Juvenile Delinquency to Adult Crime, 2012. **Address:** Institute of Criminology, University of Cambridge, Rm. 2.3, 7 West Rd., Sidgwick Ave., Cambridge, CB CB3 9DT, England. **Online address:** dpfl@cam.ac.uk

FARRIS, William Wayne. American (born United States), b. 1951. **Genres:** History, Social Sciences, Politics/Government, Local History/Rural Topics. **Career:** Harvard University, instructor, 1980-81; University of Tennessee, assistant professor, 1981-88, associate professor, 1988-94, professor, 1994-; Hawaii University, Department of History, professor and Sen chair, Soshitsu Sen professor of traditional Japanese culture and history, Sen Soshitsu XV distinguished professor of traditional Japanese history and culture, Sen Soshitsu XV chair of traditional Japanese history and culture, Soshitsu Sen XV distinguished chair of traditional Japanese culture and history. Writer. **Publications:** Population, Disease, and Land in Early Japan, 645-900, 1985; Heavenly Warriors: The Evolution of Japan's Military, 500-1300, 1992; (ed.) What's Cooking in Politics Book II, 1995; Sacred Texts and Buried Treasures: Issues in the Historical Archaeology of Ancient Japan, 1998; Japan's Medieval Population: Famine, Fertility, And Warfare in a Transformative Age, 2006; Japan to 1600: A Social and Economic History, 2009; Daily Life and Demographics in Ancient Japan, 2009. **Address:** Department of History, Hawaii University, B412 Sakamaki Hall, 2530 Dole St., Honolulu, HI 96822-2283, U.S.A. **Online address:** wfarris@hawaii.edu

FARTHING-KNIGHT, Catherine. Australian (born Australia), b. 1933. **Genres:** Autobiography/Memoirs, Children's Fiction, Picture/Board Books, Young Adult Fiction. **Career:** Papua New Guinea, girl guide leader, 1967-84, district commissioner, 1967-71; Spastic Society, pianist, 1972-86; Villa Maria School for the Blind, pianist, 1994-96. Painter and poet. Writer. **Publications:** Days with Gran, 1995. **Address:** 34 College St., Hawthorn, VI 3122, Australia.

FARUQUE, Cathleen Jo. American (born United States) **Genres:** Social Work, Education, Social Commentary, Literary Criticism And History. **Career:** St. Joseph's Children's Home, cottage supervisor, 1982-83; Community Counseling Center, case manager of day treatment programs, 1983-87; San Diego County Human Services-Adult Protective Services, clinical social work intern, 1989-90; Home Start Inc., administrative social work intern, 1990-91; Mission de la Casa Rehabilitation Center, director of social services, 1991-92; Community Services Agency, director of senior programs, 1992-97; Family Service Association of San Jose, consultant, 1997; Winona State University, assistant professor, 1997-2003, associate professor of social work, 2003-, director of social work program, 1998-2004, director of field education, 2004-09, professor and department chair, 2009-; Master's Institute, teacher of adult education classes, 1993-97, instructor, 1997; San Jose State University, instructor, 1996-97; San Jose County Social Services advisory board county commissioner, 1995-97. Writer. **Publications:** Migration of Hmong to the Midwestern United States, 2003; The Invisible People: Poverty and Resiliency in the Dhaka Slums, 2008; (with M. Samad and T. Hill) The Invisible People of Bangladesh: Reflections of Poverty, 2009. **Address:** Department of Social Work, Winona State University, Minne Hall 228, PO Box 5838, Winona, MN 55987, U.S.A. **Online address:** cfaruque@winona.edu

FARWELL, Edith F. American (born United States), b. 1960. **Genres:** Communications/Media. **Career:** Solar Cookers Intl., board director, 1990-97; Association for Progressive Communications, executive director, 1991-. Writer. **Publications:** (As Edie Farwell with A.H. Maiden) The Tibetan Art of Parenting, 1997; Women@Internet, 1999. **Address:** Association for Progressive Communications, Torney Ave., Presidio Bldg. 1012, PO Box 29904, San Francisco, CA 94129, U.S.A. **Online address:** efarwell@igc.apc.org

FASCHING, Darrell J. American (born United States), b. 1944. **Genres:** Ethics, Theology/Religion, History. **Career:** University of Minnesota, faculty, 1968-69; Syracuse University, faculty, 1971-75, assistant dean of Hendricks Chapel, 1975-80; LeMoyne College, assistant professor of religious studies, 1980-82; University of South Florida, assistant professor of religious studies, 1982-85, assistant professor of medical ethics, 1983-, director of graduate religious studies, 1984-89, associate professor of religious studies, 1985-89, professor of religious studies, 1989-, associate dean, arts and sciences, 1991-93, Department of Religious Studies, chair, 1993-98, College of Education, professor of special education, 1996-; Oxford University, International Holocaust Conference, principal investigator, 2000-01.Writer. **Publications:** The Thought of Jacques Ellul: A Systematic Exposition, 1981; (ed.) The Jewish People in Christian Preaching, 1984; Narrative Theology after Auschwitz: From Alienation to Ethics, 1992; The Ethical Challenge of Auschwitz and Hiroshima: Apocalypse or Utopia?, 1993; The Coming of the Millennium: Good News for the Whole Human Race, 1996; (with D. de Chant) Comparative Religious Ethics: A Narrative Approach, 2001. WITH J. ESPOSITO AND T. LEWIS: World Religions Today, 2002, 3rd ed., 2009; Religion & Globalization: World Religions in Historical Perspective, 2008; Religions of the West Today, 2009; Religions of Asia Today, 2009. Works appear in anthologies. Contributor to journals. **Address:** Departmentof Religious Studies, University of South Florida, Cooper Hall 309, 4202 E Fowler Ave., Tampa, FL 33620-5550, U.S.A. **Online address:** fasching@cas.usf.edu

FASCHINGER, Lilian. Austrian (born Austria), b. 1950. **Genres:** Novels, Novellas/Short Stories, Poetry. **Career:** Novelist and poet. **Publications:** NOVELS: Die Neue Scheherazade, 1985; Lustspiel: Ein Roman, 1989; Magdalena Süenderin, 1995; Magdalena the Sinner: A Novel, 1997; Woman with Three Aeroplanes, 1998; Wiener Passion, 1999; Paarweise: Acht Pariser Episoden, 2002; Stadt der Verlierer, 2007. SHORT STORIES: Frau mit drei Flugzeugen, 1993. POETRY: Ortsfremd: Gedichte, 1994. **Address:** HarperCollins Publishers Ltd., 2 Bloor St E, 20th Fl., Toronto, ON M4W 1A8, Canada.

FASOLT, Constantin. American/German (born Germany), b. 1951. **Genres:** History. **Career:** Columbia University, preceptor in History, 1979-81, lecturer in history, 1981-83; University of Chicago, Department of History and the College, assistant professor, 1983-90, associate professor, 1990-98, professor of history, 1999-2007, Karl J. Weintraub professor, 2007-, History of Western Civilization Program, chair, 1989-95, Master of the Social Sciences Collegiate Division, deputy dean of division of the social sciences, associate dean of colleges, 2005-08; University of Virginia, visiting professor of history, 1999-2000; University of Notre Dame, visiting professor of history, 2002-03; State University of New York, lecturer; Saint Mary's College, lecturer; Hillsdale College, lecturer; University of Heidelberg, lecturer. Writer. **Publications:** Council and Hierarchy: The Political Thought of William Durant the Younger, 1991; Visions of Order in the Canonists and Civilians, 1995; Blindsided by the Evidence, 2000; The Limits of History, 2004; (ed. and trans.) Hermann Conring's New Discourse on the Roman-German Emperor, 2005. Works appear in anthologies. Contributor of articles to journals. **Address:** Department of History, University of Chicago, 1126 E 59th St., PO Box 73, Chicago, IL 60637, U.S.A. **Online address:** icon@uchicago.edu

FASSETT, John D. American (born United States), b. 1926. **Genres:** History, Autobiography/Memoirs, Biography, Law. **Career:** United States Supreme Court, law clerk, 1954-55; Wiggin and Dana, partner, 1954-73; Yale University, lecturer, 1955-56; United Illuminating Co., chief executive officer, president, chairman, 1973-85, director; New Haven Chamber of Commerce, chair, 1979-81; Connecticut Public Expenditure Council, chair, 1979-81; New England Council, director; Quinnipiac Council, Boy Scouts of America, director; Visiting Nurses Association, director. Writer. **Publications:** United Illuminating: History of an Electric Company, 1990; (contrib.) The Supreme Court Justices: Illustrated Biographies, 1789-1993, 1993; New Deal Justice: The Life of Stanley Reed of Kentucky (biography), 1994. Contributor to periodicals. **Address:** 2600 Croasdaile Farm Pkwy., Apt. 354, Durham, NC 27705, U.S.A. **Online address:** jdfass@highstream.net

FASSIN, Didier. American (born United States), b. 1955. **Genres:** Social Sciences. **Career:** National Institute for Health Research, junior researcher, 1984-86; Hospital Pitie-Salpetriere, assistant professor in infectious diseases and public health, 1987-89; French Institute for Research in the Andes, senior researcher, 1989-91; University of Paris Nord, assistant professor, 1991-97, professor, 1997-2009; ecole des Hautes etudes en Science Sociales, director of studies, 1999-; Medecins Sans Frontieres, administrator, 1999-2001, vice president, 2001-03; Comite Medical pour les Exiles, president, 2005-; Institut de Recherche Interdisciplinaire sur les Enjeux Sociaux, founding director, 2007-; Institute for Advanced Study, James D. Wolfensohn professor, 2009-; Medical Anthropology Quarterly, editor. **Publications:** Pouvoir et maladie en Afrique: anthropologie sociale dans la banlieue de Dakar, 1992; Antropologia y salud en comunidades indigenas: manual de capacitacion para promotores campesinos de salud, 1992; L'espace politique de la santé: essai de genealogie, 1996; Quand les corps se souviennent: experiences et politiques du SIDA en Afrique du Sud, 2006; (with R. Rechtman) L'empire du traumatisme: enquête sur la condition de victime, 2007. EDITOR: (with A.C. Defossez and M. Viveros) Mujeres de los Andes: condiciones de vida y salud, 1992; (with A. Morice and C. Quiminal) Les lois de l'inhospitabilité: les politiques de l'immigration à l'épreuve des sans- papiers, 1997; (with J. Dozon) Les enjeux politiques de la santé: études sénégalaises, équatoriennes et fran aises, 2000; (with J. Dozon) Critique de la santé publique: une approche anthropologique, 2001; Afflictions: l'Afrique du Sud, de l'apartheid au SIDA, 2004; (with D. Memmi) Le gouvernement des corps, 2004; (with P. Bourdelais) Les constructions de l'intolérable: études d'anthropologie et d'histoire sur les frontieres de l'espace moral, 2005; (with E. Fassin) De la question sociale à la question raciale? représenter la société fran aise, 2006; (with A. Bensa) Les politiques de l'enquête: épreuves ethnographiques, 2008; (with M. Pandolf) Contemporary States of Emergency: The Politics of Military and Humanitarian Interventions, 2010. Contributor to periodicals. **Address:** Institute for Advanced Study, Einstein Dr., Princeton, NJ 08540, U.S.A. **Online address:** dfassin@ehess.fr

FASSMANN, Heinz. Austrian/German (born Germany), b. 1955. **Genres:** Demography, Geography. **Career:** Austrian Academy of Sciences, researcher, 1981-92, Institute for Urban and Regional Research, managing director, 1992-96, deputy executive director, 2002-05, executive director, 2006-, Commission for Migration and Integration Studies, chairman, 2004-07; Technical University, professor of applied geography, 1996-2000; University of Vienna, university professor of applied geography, 2000-, Faculty of Geosciences, geography and astronomy, vice-dean, 2004-06, dean, 2006-08, Human Resources Development and International Relations, vice rector, 2011-; Lousiana State University, Fulbright professor, 2005. Writer. **Publications:** (With E. Lichtenberger) Gastarbeiter: Leben in Zwei Gesellschaften, 1984; (with H. Fassmann and D. Mühlgassner) Stadtentwicklung und dynamische Faktorialökologie, 1987; (co-author) Migration und Arbeitsmarkt, 1988; (co-author) Standort Burgenland: Probleme und Entwicklungschancender Peripherie, 1990; (co-author) Erhöhte Mobilität: dieStruktur des österreichischen Arbeitsmarktes 1990: Datenband, 1991; (with P. Findl and R. Münz) Auswirkungen der internationalen Wanderungen auf österreich: Szenarien zur regionalen Bevölkerungsentwicklung, 1991-2031, des Instituts für Demographieder österreichischen Akademie der Wissenschaften, 1991; Einwanderungsland österreich?: Gastarbeiter, Flüchtlinge, Immigranten, 1992; (co-author) Festschrift zum 60. Geburtstag von O.Universitäts professor Dr. Bruno Backé,

1992; (co-author) Haushaltsentwicklung, Wohnbau und Wohnungsbedarf in österreich, 1961-2031: Analysen, Szenarien und Prognosen zur Entwicklung von Lebensformen und Wohnversorgung, 1992; (ed. with R. Münz) European Migration in the Late Twentieth Century: Historical Patterns, Actual Trends and Social Implications, 1994. UNTRANSLATED WORKS: (with R.Mçnz) Märkte in Bewegung, 1995; (with R. Münz) Einwanderungsland österreich?: Historische Migrationsmuster, aktuelle Trends und politische Massnahmen, 1995; (with J. Kohlbacher and U. Reeger) Die neue Zuwanderung aus Ostmitteleuropa: Eine Empirische Analyse amBeispiel der Polen in österreich, 1995; (with R. Holzmann and R. Neck) Ostöffnung: Wirtschaftliche Folgen für österreich, 1996; Die Rückkehr der Regionen: Beitrage zur regionalen Transformation Ostmitteleuropas, 1997; (with C. Hintermann) Migrations potential Ostmitteleuropa: Struktur und Motivation Potentieller Migranten aus Polen, der Slowakei, Tschechien und Ungarn, 1997; (with H. Matuschak and E. Menasse) Abgrenzen, Ausgrenzen, Aufnehmen: Empirische Befunde zu Fremdenfeinslichkeit und Integration, 1999; (with P. Meusburger) Arbeitsmarkt Geographie, 1997; (ed. with J. Kohlbacher and U. Reeger) Zuwanderung und Segregation: Europäische Metropolen im Vergleich, 2002; (co-author) österreichischer Migrationsund Integrationsbericht: Demographische Entwicklungen - Sozioökonomische Strukturen-Rechtliche Rahmenbedingungen, 2003; (with J. Kohlbacher and U. Reeger) Polen in Wien: Entwicklung, Strukturmerkmale und Interaktionsmuster, 2004; (ed. with U. Reeger and W. Sievers) Statistics and Reality, 2009; Wien, 2009; (with H. Uhl and W. Müller-Funk) Kulturen der Differenz, 2009; (ed. with M. Haller and D. Lane) Migration and mobility in Europe, 2009. **Address:** Institute of Geography and Regional Research, University of Vienna, 7/5/A522, Universitätsstr. 7, Wien, A-1010, Austria. **Online address:** heinz.fassmann@univie.ac.at

FATCHEN, Max. Australian (born Australia), b. 1920. **Genres:** Novellas/Short Stories, Children's Fiction, Poetry, Literary Criticism And History. **Career:** Adelaide News and Sunday Mail, journalist, 1946-55; The Advertiser, journalist, 1955-84, literary editor, 1971-81, special writer, 1981-84, columnist. **Publications:** POETRY: Driver and Trains, 1963; Keepers and Lighthouses, 1963; The Plumber, 1963; The Electrician, 1963; The Transport Driver, 1965; The Carpenter, 1965; Peculia Australia: Verses, 1965; Just Fancy, Mr. Fatchen! A Collection of Verse, Prose and Fate's Cruel Blows, 1967; Songs for My Dog and Other People (nonsense verse), 1980; Wry Rhymes for Troublesome Times, 1983; A Paddock of Poems, 1987; A Pocketful of Rhymes, 1989; A Country Christmas, 1990; The Country Mail is Coming: Poems from Down Under, 1990; Tea for Three, 1994; Peculiar Rhymes and Lunatic Lines, 1995; Australia at the Beach, 1999; Terrible Troy, 2000; The Very Long Nose of Jonathan Jones, 2000. FICTION: The River Kings, 1966; Conquest of the River, 1970; The Spirit Wind, 1973; Chase through the Night, 1977; The Time Wave, 1979; Closer to the Stars, 1981; Had Yer Jabs?, 1987; Pass Me a Poem, 1989. OTHER: Forever Fatchen, 1983; Had Yer Jabs (short stories), 1987; A Country Christmas, 1990; Mostly Max, 1995. **Address:** The Advertiser, 31 Waymouth St., Adelaide, SA 5000, Australia.

FATE, Robert. (Robert Fate Bealmear). American (born United States), b. 1935?. **Genres:** Novels, Horror. **Career:** Writer. **Publications:** Baby Shark, 2006; Baby Shark's Beaumont Blues, 2007; Baby Shark's High Plains Redemption, 2008; Baby Shark's Jugglers at the Border, 2009. Contributor to periodicals. **Address:** 2032 Balmer Dr., Los Angeles, CA 90039, U.S.A. **Online address:** robert-fate@sbcglobal.net

FATSIS, Stefan. American (born United States), b. 1963?. **Genres:** Sports/Fitness. **Career:** Associated Press, reporter; Wall Street Journal, sports writer, On Sports, columnist, 1995-; National Public Radio, radio host, 1997-; ESPN, writer and color commentator. **Publications:** Wild and Outside: How a Renegade Minor League Revived the Spirit of Baseball in America's Heartland, 1995; Word Freak: Heartbreak, Triumph, Genius, and Obsession in the World of Competitive Scrabble Players, 2001; A Few Seconds of Panic: A 5-Foot-8, 170-Pound, 43-Year-Old Sportswriter Plays in the NFL, 2008. Contributor to books and periodicals. **Address:** Washington, DC , U.S.A. **Online address:** stefan@stefanfatsis.com

FAULKNER, Charles Herman. American (born United States), b. 1937. **Genres:** Anthropology/Ethnology, Archaeology/Antiquities. **Career:** St. Lawrence University, instructor of sociology and anthropology, 1963-64; University of Tennessee, College of Arts and Sciences, Department of Anthropology, assistant professor, 1964-71, associate professor, 1971-76, professor of anthropology, 1976-, now professor emeritus, distinguished professor of humanities, 1999-. Writer. **Publications:** An Archaeological Survey of Marshall County, 1961; (with J.B. Graham) Highway Salvage in the Nickajack Reservoir, 1966; (with J.B. Graham) Westmoreland-Barber Site (40Mi-11) Nickajack Reservoir, Season II, 1966; The Old Stone Fort: Exploring an Archaeological Mystery, 1968; The Late Prehistoric Occupation of Northwestern Indiana, 1972; Introductory Report of the Normandy Reservoir Salvage Project, 1972; (with C.R. McCollough) Excavation of the Higgs and Doughty Sites: I-75 Salvage Archaeology, 1973; (with C.K. Buckles) Glimpses of Southern Appalachian Folk Culture: Papers in Memory of Norbert F. Riedl, 1978; (with G.W. Kline and G.D. Crites) The McFarland Project: Early Middle Woodland Settlement and Subsistence in the Upper Duck River Valley in Tennessee, 1982; Ramseys at Swan Pond: The Archaeology and History of an East Tennessee Farm, 2008. EDITOR: Archaeological Investigations in the Tims Ford Reservoir, Tennessee, 1966, 1968; (with C.R. McCollough) Report of the Normandy Archaeological Project, 1978; (with C.R. McCollough) 1974 Excavations at the Ewell III Site (40CF118), Jernigan II Site (40CF37) and the Parks Site (40CF5), 1982; (with C.R. McCollough) 1975 Excavations at the Eoff I Site (40CF32), Aaron Shelton Site (40CF69), and the Duke I Site (40CF97), 1982; The Prehistoric Native American Art of Mud Glyph Cave, 1986; The Bat Creek Stone, 1992; (with A. Young) Proceedings of the Tenth Symposium on Ohio Valley Urban and Historic Archaeology, 1993; Rock Art of the Eastern Woodlands, 1996. Contributor to journals. **Address:** Department of Anthropology, College of Arts & Sciences, University of Tennessee, 250 S Stadium Hall, Knoxville, TN 37996-0720, U.S.A. **Online address:** cfaulkne@utk.edu

FAULKNER, Colleen. (Hunter Morgan). American (born United States), b. 1962?. **Genres:** Romance/Historical, Novellas/Short Stories. **Career:** Writer. **Publications:** Forbidden Caress, 1987; Raging Desire, 1987; Snowfire, 1988; Traitor's Caress, 1989; Passion's Savage Moon, 1989; Temptation's Tender Kiss, 1990; Love's Sweet Bounty, 1991; Patriot's Passion, 1991; Savage Surrender, 1992; Sweet Deception, 1992; Flames of Love, 1993; Forever His, 1993; (co-author) Spellbound Kisses (novella), 1993; Captive, 1994; (co-author) To Love and to Honor (novella), 1995; O'Brian's Bride, 1995; (co-author) A Christmas Embrace (novella), 1995; (co-author) After Midnight (novella), 1995; Destined to Be Mine, 1996; (co-author) Deck the Halls (novella), 1996; To Love a Dark Stranger, 1997; Fire Dancer, 1997; Angel in My Arms, 1998; Once More, 1998; If You Were Mine, 1999; (with H. Howell and J.E. French) Castle Magic (novella), 1999; Highland Bride, 2000; Marrying Owen, 2000; Taming Ben, 2000; Tempting Zack, 2000; Maggie's Baby, 2000; Highland Lady, 2001; Highland Lord, 2002; (with A. Basso and D. Raleigh) Only with a Rogue (novella), 2002; A Shocking Request, 2002; Barefoot and Pregnant?, 2004; AS HUNTER MORGAN: The Other Twin, 2003; She'll Never Live, 2004; She'll Never Know, 2004; She'll Never Tell, 2004; What She Can't See, 2005; Unspoken Fear, 2006; Are You Scared Yet?, 2007. **Address:** c/o Evan Marshall, The Evan Marshall Literary Agency, 6 Tristam Pl., Pine Brook, NJ 07058-9445, U.S.A. **Online address:** hunter@huntermorgannovels.com

FAULKNER, Howard J. American (born United States), b. 1945. **Genres:** Autobiography/Memoirs, Biography, Psychiatry, Psychology. **Career:** Washburn University, instructor, 1972-73, assistant professor, 1973-78, associate professor, 1981-82, professor of American literature, 1982-2010, chair, 2006-10, professor emeritus of English, 2010-; University of Skopje, Fulbright professor, 1979-80; University of Metz, visiting professor, 1987-88; Sofia University, Fulbright professor, 1995-96; Moulay Ismail University, Fulbright professor, 2003-04. Writer. **Publications:** (Ed. with V. Pruitt) The Selected Correspondence of Karl A. Menninger, 1919-1945, 1988; (ed. with V. Pruitt and intro.) The Selected Correspondence of Karl A. Menninger, 1946-1965, 1995; (ed. with V. Pruitt and intro.) Dear Dr. Menninger: Women's Voices from the Thirties, 1997; The Rules of the Game: An Introductory English Grammar, 2001; (ed. with V. Pruitt) For Dear Life and Selected Short Stories, 2003; Contradiction and Compromise: An Introduction to American Culture, 2004. Contributor to journals. **Address:** Department of English, Washburn University, 1700 SW College Ave., Topeka, KS 66621, U.S.A. **Online address:** howard.faulkner@washburn.edu

FAULKNER, Mary. American (born United States) **Genres:** Adult Nonfiction, Medicine/Health, Human Relations/Parenting. **Career:** Institute of Integrative Healing Arts, director; Loyola University, adjunct faculty; Tennessee State University, adjunct faculty; Recovering, founding editor, 1986, executive editor. **Publications:** (With G. Kelly and P. Turley) Your Guide to Irish Law, 1993; The Eleven-Minute Attitude Adjustment, 1998; (with R.T. O'Gorman) The Complete Idiots Guide to Understanding Catholicism, 2000,

3rd ed., 2006; (with B. O'Gorman) El Catolicismo, 2001; The Complete Idiots Guide to Womens Spirituality, 2002; Supreme Authority: Understanding Power in the Catholic Church, 2003; Easy Does It Recovery Pack: Affirmation Cards Meditation Book and Journal, 2004; Easy Does It Dating Guide: For People in Recovery, 2004; My Parents Betrayed Me, 2006; Elana's Dream, 2006; Easy Does it Relationship Guide: For People in Recovery, 2007; Flame Lily, 2007; Women's Spirituality, 2011. **Address:** Linda Roghaar Literary Agency, 113 High Point Dr., Amherst, MA 01002, U.S.A.

FAUNCE, John. American (born United States), b. 1949. **Genres:** Novels, History. **Career:** Writer, producer and director. **Publications:** Lucrezia Borgia: A Novel, 2003. **Address:** c/o Albert Zuckerman, Writers House, 21 W 26th St., New York, NY 10010, U.S.A. **Online address:** johnfaunce@lucreziaborgia.com

FAURE, Michael G. Dutch/Belgian (born Belgium), b. 1958. **Genres:** Environmental Sciences/Ecology, Law, Economics. **Career:** Van Goethem law firm, attorney at law, 1982-; Ministry of Justice School of Criminology, lecturer of environmental law, 1988-90; Leiden University, senior lecturer, 1988-90, senior lecturer, 1990-91; Maastricht University, full-time professor, 1991-2008, Maastricht European Institute for Transnational Legal Research, academic director, 1991, part-time professor of comparative and international environmental law, 2008-; Ius Commune Research School, academic director, 1995-; ECTIL (European Centre of Tort and Insurance Law), academic director, 1999-; Erasmus University, part-time professor of comparative private law and economics, 2008-; University of Pennsylvania, Law School, visiting professor of law, 2009-. Writer. **Publications:** (With R. van den Bergh) Objectieve aansprakelijkheid, verplichteverzekering en veiligheidsregulering, 1989; (ed. with J.C. Oudijk and D. Schaffmeister) Zorgen Van Heden: opstellen over het milieustrafrecht in theorie en praktijk, 1991; Umweltrecht in Belgien: strafrecht imspannungsfeld von zivil-und verwaltungsrecht, 1992; De strafrechtelijketoerekening van milieudelicten, 1992; De strafrechtelijke toerekening vanmilieudelicten, 1992; (co-ed.) Regulation of Professions: A Law and Economics Approach to the Regulation of Attorneys and Physicians in the U.S., Belgium, the Netherlands, Germany and the U.K., 1993; Aansprakelijkheidvoor het nucleaire risico, 1993; (ed. with J. Vervaele and A. Weale) Environmental Standards in the European Union in an Interdisciplinary Framework, 1994; Enforcement Issues for Environmental Legislation in Developing Countries, 1995; (ed. with K. Deketelaere) Ius Commune EnMilieurecht: Actualia in het milieurecht in Belgié en Nederland, 1997; (ed. with K. Schwarz) De strafrechtelijke en civielrechtelijke aansprakelijkheid van de rechtspersoon en zijn bestuurders, 1998; (co-ed.) Geluidhinder veroorzaakt door vliegtuigen, 1998; (co-ed.) Grensoverschrijdende milieuproblemen: uitdagingen voor de nationale eninternationale rechtsorde, 1998; (with M. Visser) De strafrechtelijke bescherming van het leefmilieu in Belgié, Duitsland en Nederland: Modellen van strafbaarstelling en hun bewijsrechtelijke implicaties, 1999; (ed. with K. Deketelaere) Environmental Law in the United Kingdom and Belgium from a Comparative Perspective, 1999; (ed. with G. Heine) Environmental Criminal Law in the European Union: Documentation of the Main Provisions with Introductions, 2000; (ed. with A. Akkermans and T. Hartlief) Proportionele aansprakelijkheid, 2000; (ed. with H. Koziol) Cases on Medical Malpractice in a Comparative Perspective, 2001; (ed. with T. de Roos and M. Visser) Herziening van het commune milieustrafrecht, 2001; (co-ed.) Towards a European Ius Commune in Legal Education and Research: Proceedings of the Conference Held at the Occasion of the 20th Anniversary of the Maastricht Faculty of Law, 2002; (ed. with C.A. Schwarz) Milieuaansprakelijkheid: Recente ontwikkelingen in eenondernemingsrechtelijk kader, 2002; (with T. Hartlief) Nieuwe risico's envragen van aansprakelijkheid en verzekering, 2002; (ed. with J. Neethling) Aansprakelijkheid, risico en onderneming: Europese en Zuid-Afrikaanseperspectieven, 2003; (ed.) Deterrence, Insurability, and Compensation in Environmental Liability: Future Developments in the European Union, 2003; (ed. with J. Gupta and A. Nentjes) Climate Change and the Kyoto Protocol: The Role of Institutions and Instruments to Control Global Change, 2003; (ed. with J. Gupta and A. Nentjes) Climate Change and the Kyoto Protocol: The Role of Institutions and Instruments to Control Global Change, 2003; (with M. Pâques) La protection de l'environnement au coeur du système juridique international et du droit interne, 2003; (with G. Skogh) The Economic Analysis of Environmental Policy and Law: AnIntroduction, 2003; (with T. Hartlief) Insurance and Expanding Systemic Risks, 2003; (co-ed.) Liability for and Insurability of Biomedical Research with Human Subjects in a Comparative Perspective, 2004; (co-ed.) No-Fault Compensation in the Health Care Sector, 2004; (ed. with N.J. Vig) Green Giants? Environmental Policies of the United States and the European

Union, 2004; (ed. with G. Heine) Criminal Enforcement of Environmental Law in the European Union, 2005; (with C.A.R. Moerland) Griffierechten: Een vergelijkende beschrijving van griffierechten-envergelijkbare stelsels in een aantal landen van de Europese Unie, 2006; (ed. with T. Hartlief) Financial Compensation for Victims of Catastrophes: A Comparative Legal Approach, 2006; (ed. with N. Niessen) Environmental Law in Development: Lessons from the Indonesian Experience, 2006; (ed. with J. Hu) Prevention and Compensation of Marine Pollution Damage: Recent Developments in Europe, China and the U.S., 2006; (ed. with T. Hartlief) Financiële voorzieningen na rampen in het buitenland, 2006; (ed. with W.H. van Boom) Shifts in Compensation between Private and Public Systems, 2007; (ed. with T. Eger and Z. Naigen) Economic Analysis of Law in China, 2007; (ed. with A. Verheij) Shifts in Compensation for Environmental Damage, 2007; (ed. with S. Ying) China and International Environmental Liability: Legal Remedies for Transboundary Pollution, 2008; (ed. with F. Stephen) Essays in the Law and Economics of Regulation: In Honour of Anthony Ogus, 2008; (ed.) Tort Law and Economics, 2009; (ed.) The Impact of Behavioural Law and Economics on Accident Law, 2009; (with C. Cauffman and T. Hartlief) Harmonisatie van het consumenten contractenrecht in Europa, 2009; (co-author) Evaluatie tuchtrechtelijke handhaving, 2009; (ed. with H. Lixin and S. Hongjun) Maritime Pollution Liability and Policy, 2010; (co-author) Milieuaansprakelijkheid goed geregeld?, 2010; (ed. with A.V.D. Walt) Globalization and Private Law, 2010; (ed. with D.A. Farber) Disaster Law, 2010; (ed. with M. Peeters) Climate Change Liability, 2011. **Address:** Maastricht European Institute, Maastricht University, Bouillonstraat 3, Rm. 2.108, PO Box 616, Maastricht, NL-6200 MD, Netherlands. **Online address:** michael.faure@facburfdr.unimaas.nl

FAUSETT, David. (David John Fausett). New Zealander (born New Zealand), b. 1950. **Genres:** Literary Criticism And History, History, Language/ Linguistics, Translations, Travel/Exploration. **Career:** Writer. **Publications:** Writing the New World: Imaginary Voyages and Utopias of the Great Southern Land, 1993; The Strange Surprizing Sources of Robinson Crusoe, 1994; Images of the Antipodes in the Eighteenth Century: A Study in Stereotyping, 1995. EDITOR: (and trans.) G. de Foigny, The Southern Land, Known, 1993; The Mighty Kingdom of Krinke Kesmes, 1994. **Address:** 4 Wilding Ave., Epsom, Auckland, 3, New Zealand.

FAUSETT, David John. See **FAUSETT, David.**

FAUST, Christa. American (born United States), b. 1969. **Genres:** Novels, Mystery/Crime/Suspense, Sex, Novellas/Short Stories. **Career:** Writer. **Publications:** Control Freak, 1998; Hoodtown, 2004; (with P.Z. Brite) Triads, 2004; (contrib.) A Nightmare on Elm Street: Dreamspawn, 2005; (contrib.) Twilight Zone: Burned/One Night at Mercy, 2005; Snakes on a Plane, 2006; (contrib.) Final Destination III, 2006; (contrib.) Friday the 13th, 2006; Money Shot, 2008; Hunt Beyond the Frozen Fire, 2010; Choke Hold, 2011. Contributor to books and periodicals. **Address:** 2658 Griffith Park Blvd., Ste. 297, Los Angeles, CA 90039, U.S.A. **Online address:** faust@christafaust.com

FAUST, Irvin. American (born United States), b. 1924. **Genres:** Novels, Novellas/Short Stories, Young Adult Fiction. **Career:** Manhattanville Junior High School, teacher, 1949-53; Lynbrook High School, guidance counselor, 1956-60; Garden City High School, Guidance and Counseling, director, 1960-, now retired; New School for Social Research, teacher, 1975; Swarthmore College, teacher, 1976; City College of the City University of New York, teacher, 1977. Writer. **Publications:** Entering Angel's World, 1963; Roar Lion Roar, 1965; The Steagle, 1966; The File on Stanley Patton Buchta, 1970; Willy Remembers, 1971; Foreign Devils, 1973; A Star in the Family, 1975; Newsreel, 1980; The Year of the Hot Jock, 1985; Jim Dandy, 1994. Contributor to magazine. **Address:** c/o Gloria Loomis, Watkins Loomis Agency Inc., 150 E 35th St., Ste. 530, New York, NY 10016, U.S.A.

FAUST, Jeff. American (born United States), b. 1966. **Genres:** Sports/Fitness, Young Adult Non-fiction, Travel/Exploration, Technology, Science Fiction/Fantasy, Mathematics/Statistics. **Career:** Manpower Temporary Services, office worker, 1988-96; Toycrafter, press operator, 1996-; Classic Adventures, tour leader, 1992-94. Writer. **Publications:** SELF-ILLUSTRATED: Greenberg's American Flyer Track Plans and Operating Instructions, 1989. OTHERS: Rochester by Bike, 1992; Mountain Bike! New Hampshire: A Guide to the Classic Trails, 1998. **Address:** 55 Oakland St., Rochester, NY 14620, U.S.A. **Online address:** jeff_faust@rbcbbs.win.net

FAUST, John R. American (born United States), b. 1930. **Genres:** International Relations/Current Affairs, Politics/Government. **Career:** University of Southwestern Louisiana, assistant professor of political science, 1960-62; Illinois Wesleyan University, associate professor of political science, 1962-66; Eastern Illinois University, visiting associate professor, 1963-65, associate professor, professor of political science, 1966-, now professor emeritus; Institute of Developmental Administration, visiting professor, 1993; Sino-American Relations, consultant, 1988-. Writer. **Publications:** (With J.F. Kornberg) China in World Politics, 1995, 2nd ed., 2004. Contributor to journals and books. **Address:** Department of Political Science, Eastern Illinois University, 600 Lincoln Ave., Charleston, IL 61920-3099, U.S.A.

FAUSTO-STERLING, Anne. American (born United States), b. 1944. **Genres:** Biology. **Career:** Brown University, research associate, 1970-71, assistant professor of medical science, 1971-76, associate professor of medical science, 1977-86, professor of biology and gender studies, 1986-, Nancy Duke Lewis professor of biology and gender studies, Science and Technology Studies, chair; University of Amsterdam, visiting professor, 1986; SUNY, distinguished visiting professor, 1987; University of Cincinnati, visiting professor, 1989; Cornell University, Department of Social Studies of Science and Technology, visiting consultant, 1992; Mount Holyoke College, Henry R. Luce professor of gender and science, 1992; Radcliffe College, visiting professor of women's studies, 1998; Stanford Humanities Center Marta Sutton Weeks, distinguished visitor, 2003. Writer. **Publications:** Myths of Gender: Biological Theories about Women and Men, 1985, 2nd ed., 1992; Sexing the Body: Gender Politics and the Construction of Sexuality, 2000; Cuerpos sexuados Editorial Melusina: Barcelona Spain, 2006. Contributor to journals. **Address:** Division of Biology and Medicine, Brown University, PO Box G-160J, Providence, RI 02912, U.S.A. **Online address:** anne_fausto-sterling@brown.edu

FAVORITE, Eileen. American (born United States), b. 1964. **Genres:** Novels, Literary Criticism And History. **Career:** School of the Art Institute of Chicago, teaching assistant, faculty, 1998. Writer. **Publications:** The Heroines (novel), 2008. Contributor of articles to periodicals. **Address:** School of the Art Institute of Chicago, 27 S Wabash Ave., Chicago, IL 60603, U.S.A.

FAVREAU, Jon. American (born United States), b. 1966. **Genres:** Business/Trade/Industry, Plays/Screenplays, Humor/Satire. **Career:** Writer and director. **Publications:** Swingers, 1996. **Address:** Endeavor Agency L.L.C., 9701 Wilshire Blvd., 10th Fl., Beverly Hills, CA 90212-2010, U.S.A.

FAWCETT, Quinn. See YARBRO, Chelsea Quinn.

FAWCETT, Tina. British (born England) **Genres:** Natural History, Sciences, Earth Sciences, Meteorology/Atmospheric Sciences. **Career:** University of Oxford, Environmental Change Institute, researcher, 1996-, senior researcher, Centre for the Environment, Personal Carbon Trading and Equity, researcher. Writer. **Publications:** DECADE: Domestic Equipment and Carbon Dioxide Emissions: 2MtC, Two Million Tonnes of Carbon, 1997; (with H. Griffin) Country Pictures: Supporting Material for Lower Carbon Futures, 2000; (with B. Boardman and K.B. Lane) Lower Carbon Futures for European Households, 2000; (with B. Boardman) Competition for the Poor: Liberalisation of Electricity Supply and Fuel Poverty: Lessons from Great Britain and Northern Ireland, 2002; (with A. Hurst and B. Boardman) Carbon U.K., 2002; Investigating Carbon Rationing as a Policy for Reducing Carbon Emissions from UK Household Energy Use, 2005; (with S.C. Rajan and M. Hillman) The Suicidal Planet: How to Prevent Global Climate Catastrophe, 2007; Housing Market Transformation, 2009. **Address:** Environmental Change Institute, Oxford University, Center for the Environment, South Parks Rd., Oxford, OX OX1 3QY, England. **Online address:** tina.fawcett@eci.ox.ac.uk

FAWKES, Richard. See CHARRETTE, Robert N.

FAY, Jim. American (born United States), b. 1934. **Genres:** Education, How-to Books, Human Relations/Parenting, Sports/Fitness. **Career:** School Consultant Services Inc., president, founder; Cline-Fay Institute Inc., co-founder, president and chief executive officer; The Love and Logic Institute, co-founder. Writer. **Publications:** Who Says You're So Great?, 1982; Principally Speaking, 1985; (with F.W. Cline) Parenting with Love and Logic: Teaching Children Responsibility, 1990, rev. ed., 2006; (with F.W. Cline) Parenting Teens with Love and Logic: Preparing Adolescents for Responsible Adulthood, 1992, rev. ed., 2006; Parenting Solutions, 1993; Tickets to Success: Techniques to Lead Children to Responsible Decision-Making, 1994;

I've Got What It Takes!, 1994; Helicopters, Drill Sergeants and Consultants: Parenting Styles and the Messages they Send, 1994; (with F.W. Cline) Grandparenting with Love and Logic: Practical Solutions to Today's Grandparenting Challenges, 1994; Taking Control of the Classroom with Love and Logic, 1994; (with D. Funk) Teaching with Love and Logic: Taking Control of the Classroom, 1995; (with F.W. Cline) The Love and Logic Journal: Tenth Anniversary Collection, 1995; (with C. Fay) Love and Logic Magic for Early Childhood: Practical Parenting from Birth, 2000; (with F.W. Cline) The Pearls of Love and Logic for Parents and Teachers, 2000; Meeting the Challenge: Using Love and Logic to Help Children Develop Attention and Behavior Skills, 2000; (with C. Fay) Love and Logic Magic When Kids Leave You Speechless Disruptions, 2000; (ed. with C. Fay) Love and Logicisms: Wise Words About Kids, 2001; (ed. with C. Fay) Love and Logic Teacher-isms: Wise Words for Teachers, 2002; Tales of Successes With Kids: From Parents and Educators Who Use Love and Logic, 2003; How to Discipline Kids Without Losing Their Love and Respect: An Introduction to Love and Logic, 2004; (with C. Fay and F.W. Cline) More Ideas About Parenting with Less Stress: Journal Collection Years 2000 to 2005, 2005; Salamander is Not a Fish!: A Positive Schoolwide Discipline Plan Without the Loopholes, 2005; (with C. Fay and F.W. Cline) Taking the Stress Out of Raising Great Kids: Journal Collection Years 1995 to 2000, 2005; ABC's of Raising an Entitled Child: How to Make Monsters out of Miracles, 2005; (with D.L. Billings) From Innocence to Entitlement: A Love and Logic Cure for the Tragedy of Entitlement, 2005; (with K. Leatherman) Millionaire Babies or Bankrupt Brats?: Love and Logic Solutions to Teaching Kids about Money, 2008; (with K. Leatherman) Love and Logic Money-isms: Wise Words about Raising Money-smart Kids, 2009; (with C. Fay) Love and Logic Powder Room Reader, 2009. **Address:** Cline-Fay Institute Inc., 2207 Jackson St., Golden, CO 80401-2317, U.S.A.

FAYER, Steve. American (born United States), b. 1935. **Genres:** Novels, Novellas/Short Stories, Plays/Screenplays, Civil Liberties/Human Rights, History, Race Relations, Documentaries/Reportage, Politics/Government, Biography, Film. **Career:** Screen and television writer, 1977-. Consultant. **Publications:** (Comp. with H. Hampton and S. Flynn) Voices of Freedom: An Oral History of the Civil Rights Movement from the 1950s through the 1980s, 1990. NOVELLAS/SHORT STORIES: Hassins Ridge, 2001; Inside The Barn Are My Aunt Golda's Clothes, 2001; Parricide, 2001; Anabel's Decameron, 2002; The Hi-Flyer, 2002; Herman's Window, 2003; MacNamara's Ghost, 2003; The Vision of Mr. Brand, 2003; The Settlement, 2004; Beans At The Gee Whiz Cafe, 2005; Jonathan's Quest, 2007; Sea Dogs, 2007; The Uncertainty of Mountain Time, 2007; Mawtin's March, 2008; Calliope, 2009; Rhoda, 2009; The Rock, 2009; The White Boy's Dream, 2009; Sleepy Willie, 2010; Matt Cahill Tells All, 2011. Contributor to periodicals. **Address:** 189 Bay State Rd., Boston, MA 02215, U.S.A. **Online address:** fayersteve@aol.com

FAZIO, Michael W. American (born United States), b. 1943?. **Genres:** Architecture, History. **Career:** Kent State University, School of Architecture and Environmental Design, assistant professor, associate professor, 1970-74; Mississippi State University, College of Architecture, Art and Design, associate professor, professor, 1974-2005, School of Architecture, acting dean, 1986-87, School of Architecture, acting associate dean, 1996-98, 2001-03, director of the graduate program, 1995-2001, emeritus professor of architecture, 2005-. Writer. **Publications:** The Architecture of Mentor, Ohio: A Guide to Historic Buildings, 1973; Order and Image in the American Small Town, 1981; Change and Tradition in the American Small Town, 1983; (with M. Moffett and L. Wodehouse) Buildings across Time: An Introduction to World Architecture, 2004; (with M. Moffett and L. Wodehouse) A World History of Architecture, 2004; (with P.A. Snadon) The Domestic Architecture of Benjamin Henry Latrobe, 2006; Landscape of Transformations: Architecture and Birmingham, Alabama, 2010. **Address:** College of Architecture, Art and Design, Mississippi State University, 126 Giles Hall, Barr Ave., Mississippi, MS 39762, U.S.A. **Online address:** mfazio@caad.msstate.edu

FEARNLEY-WHITTINGSTALL, Jane. British (born England), b. 1939. **Genres:** Botany, Cultural/Ethnic Topics, History, Homes/Gardens, Horticulture, How-to Books, Human Relations/Parenting. **Career:** Writer and broadcaster. **Publications:** Rose Gardens: Their History and Design, 1989; Historic Gardens, 1990; Ivies, 1992; Jane Fearnley-Whittingstall's Gardening Made Easy, 1995; Gardening Made Easy: A Step-by-Step Guide to Planning, Preparing, Planting, Maintaining, and Enjoying your Garden, 1995; Jane Fearnley-Whittingstall's Garden Plants Made Easy, 1996; Garden Plants Made Easy: 500 Plants Which Give the Best Value in Your Garden, 1997;

Peonies: The Imperial Flower, 1999; The Garden: An English Love Affair, 2002; The Good Granny Guide, 2005, The Good Granny Companion, 2006; The Good Granny Cookbook, 2007; The Ministry of Food, 2010; For Better for Worse, 2010. Contributor to newspapers and periodicals. **Address:** Merlin Haven House, Wotton-under-Edge, GC GL12 7BA, England. **Online address:** fearnley.whittingstall@virgin.net

FEAVER, William (Andrew). British (born England), b. 1942. **Genres:** Art/Art History. **Career:** The Listener, art critic, 1970-74; University of Newcastle-upon-Tyne, James Knott Research Fellow, 1971-73; Financial Times, art critic, 1973-74; Sunday Times Magazine, art adviser, 1973-75; The Observer, art critic, 1975-98. Writer, curator and broadcaster. **Publications:** The Art of John Martin, 1975; When We Were Young: Two Centuries of Children's Book Illustration, 1977; (intro.) Masters of Caricature: From Hogarth and Gillray to Scarfe and Levine, 1981; Pitmen Painters: The Ashington Group 1934-1984, 1988; Lucian Freud, 2002; James Boswell: Unofficial War Artist, 2007; (contrib.) Mirror & the Mask: Portraiture in the Age of Picasso, 2007; (contrib.) Espejo y la Máscara: El Retrato En El Siglo De Picasso, 2007; Frank Auerbach, 2009. Contributor to magazines. **Address:** Rogers, Coleridge & White Ltd., 20 Powis Mews, London, GL W11 1JN, England.

FEBOS, Melissa. American (born United States), b. 1980. **Genres:** Autobiography/Memoirs. **Career:** Baccalaureate School for Global Education, instructor, 2006-07; State University of New York, Purchase College, lecturer, 2007-; Sponsors for Educational Opportunity, instructor, 2007-08; Gotham Writers' Workshop, faculty, 2008-; Hofstra University, lecturer, 2008-09; Prospect Writes, founder, 2009-; New York University, lecturer, 2009-. Writer. **Publications:** Whip Smart (memoir), 2010. Contributor to periodicals. **Address:** Brooklyn, NY , U.S.A. **Online address:** melissafebos@gmail.com

FEDDER, Norman Joseph. American (born United States), b. 1934. **Genres:** Plays/Screenplays, Literary Criticism And History, Theatre. **Career:** Baruch College, lecturer in English, 1957-58; Long Island University, lecturer in English, 1957-58; College of New Jersey (formerly Trenton State College), assistant professor of English, 1960-61; Indiana State College (now Indiana University of Pennsylvania), associate professor of English, 1961-64; Florida Atlantic University, associate professor of English, 1964-67; University of Arizona, associate professor of drama, 1967-70; Kansas State University, associate professor of theatre, 1970-80, professor of theatre, 1980-89, university distinguished professor of theatre, 1989-99, university distinguished professor emeritus of theatre, 1999-; Nova Southeastern University, professor, 2002-, Interdisciplinary Arts Program, associate director, 2002-. Writer. **Publications:** The New Playwright and the University Theatre, 1964; The Influence of D. H. Lawrence on Tennessee Williams, 1966; All the Nonsense about Rules for Playwriting, 1976; The Matter with Kansas-A Statewide Model of Dramatic Art in the Religious Community, 1976; Tennessee Williams Dramatic Technique, 1977; The Betrayal-a Play in One Act, 1978; American Jewish Theatre, 1979; Beyond Absurdity and Sociopolitics-The Religious Theatre Movement in the Seventies, 1979; Unstiffening Those Stiffnecked People-Creative Drama and the Bible, 1985; Face to Face-Dramatizing Moses, 1991; Facing Sudden Success-Philip Roth and Zuckerman Unbound, 1992; Dramatizing the Torah-Plays about Moses, 1992; Arthur Miller and the Holocaust, 2003; Shimon Wincelberg and the Holocaust, 2003. **Address:** 7966B Lexington Club Blvd., Delray Beach, FL 33446-3939, U.S.A. **Online address:** fedder@ksu.edu

FEDER, Bernard. American (born United States), b. 1924. **Genres:** History, Medicine/Health, Sciences, Social Sciences, Politics/Government. **Career:** Social studies teacher, 1949-66; C.W. Post College, adjunct assistant professor, 1959-65; Adelphi Suffolk College, lecturer, 1962-65; New York University, lecturer, 1965-66; Hofstra University, assistant professor, 1966-69, associate professor of education 1969-70; University of Sarasota, professor of education, 1975-90. Writer. **Publications:** Viewpoints USA, 1967; Viewpoints in World History, 1968, rev. ed., 1973; The Process of American Government, 1972; Bucking the System: Politics of Dissent, 1973; The Price of Maintaining Poverty: Politics of Welfare, 1973; A Matter of Life and Breath, 1973; Walking the Straight Line: Politics of Drug Control, 1973; Policeman and Citizen: Politics of Law and Order, 1973; Then and Now: Cases in the American Experience, 1974; Conscience versus Law, 1975; Our Nation of Immigrants, 1976; The Complete Guide to Taking Tests, 1979; (with E. Feder) The Expressive Arts Therapies, 1981; (ed.) Medguide, 1984; (co-author) The Savvy Patient: How to Be an Active Participant in Your Medical Care, 1990; (with E. Feder) The Art and Science of Evaluation in the Arts Therapies,

1998; Cleopatra's Nose: Historical Accidents That Helped Shape Our World, forthcoming. Contributor to periodicals and journals. **Address:** 21 NW 101 Ct., Gainesville, FL 32607, U.S.A. **Online address:** federb@atlantic.net

FEDER, Chris Welles. American (born United States), b. 1938. **Genres:** Poetry, Education, Autobiography/Memoirs. **Career:** Encyclopaedia Britannica, foreign language editor, 1964-68; Ludi Education Inc., managing editor, 1968-73; freelance writer, 1974-; educational consultant. **Publications:** (With S. Margulies) Developing Everyday Reading Skills, 1988; (with S. Margulies) Century 21 Reading Program, 1989; (with G. Sesso) New York City Story, Then and Now (for children), 1991, rev. ed., 1999; Brain Quest (Grades 1-7), 1992, rev. ed., 1999; Brain Quest (Preschool), 1993, rev. ed., 2005; Brain Quest (Kindergarten), 1993, rev. ed., 1999; Brain Quest for Threes (Ages 3-4), 1994, rev. ed., 1999; My First Brain Quest (Ages 2-3), 1994, rev. ed., 1999; The Movie Director: Dramatic Monologues and Poems, 2002; Brain Quest Black History, 2005; Brain Quest Presidents, 2005; Brain Quest Hispanic America: Ages 9-12, 850 Questions, 850 Answers about People, Places, Culture & Language, 2005; In My Father's Shadow: A Daughter Remembers Orson Welles, 2009; The Movie Director's Daughter, forthcoming. Works appear in anthologies. Contributor to magazines. **Address:** c/o Raines & Raines, 103 Kenyon Rd., Medusa, NY 12120-1404, U.S.A.

FEDER, Martin E(lliott). American (born United States), b. 1951. **Genres:** Biology. **Career:** University of Chicago, Department of Anatomy, postdoctoral fellow, 1977-78, assistant professorial lecturer in biology, 1977-78, assistant professor, 1979-85, associate professor, 1985-88, professor of organismal biology and anatomy, 1989-, Division of The Biological Sciences, associate dean, 1988-91, Biological Sciences Collegiate Division, master, 1988-91, Division of The Biological Sciences and The Pritzker School of Medicine, faculty dean of academic affairs, 2004-; Silliman University, Department of Biology, visiting research professor, 1978. Writer. **Publications:** (Ed. with G.V. Lander) Predator-Prey Relationships: Perspectives and Approaches from the Study of Lower Vertebrates, 1986; (co-ed.) New Directions in Ecological Physiology, 1987; (with W.W. Burggren) Environmental Physiology of the Amphibians, 1992. Contributor to journals. **Address:** Department of Organismal Biology and Anatomy, University of Chicago, Rm. 201, Anatomy Bldg., 1027 E 57th St., Chicago, IL 60637-1508, U.S.A. **Online address:** m-feder@uchicago.edu

FEDERICO, Giovanni. Italian (born Italy), b. 1954. **Genres:** Young Adult Non-fiction, Economics, History, Translations. **Career:** University of Pisa, Department of Modern and Contemporary History, researcher and life fellow, 1983-2002, professor of economic history, 2002-; European University Institute, J. Monnet fellow, 1989-90, Department of History and Civilization, professor, 2002-10, senior research fellow, 2010-, ERC Project, director; University of London, Institute for Historical Research, visiting professor, 1994-95. Writer. **Publications:** NONFICTION: The Economic Development of Italy since 1870, 1994; Il filo d'oro: industria mondiale della seta dalla restaurazione alla grande crisi, 1994, trans. as An Economic History of the Silk Industry, 1830-1930, 1997; (ed. with J. Foreman-Peck) European Industrial Policy: The Twentieth-Century Experience, 1999; (with J. Cohen) The Growth of the Italian Economy, 1820-1960, 2001; Feeding the World: An Economic History of Agriculture, 1800-2000, 2005; Breve storia economica dell'agricoltura, 2009. Contributor to books and periodicals. **Address:** Department of History and Civilization, European University Institute, Villa Schifanoi, Via Boccaccio 121, Florence, 50133, Italy. **Online address:** giovanni.federico@eui.eu

FEDERICO, Meg. Canadian (born Canada), b. 1956?. **Genres:** Autobiography/Memoirs. **Career:** Freelance writer. **Publications:** Welcome to the Departure Lounge: Adventures in Mothering Mother, 2009. Contributor to periodicals. **Address:** Halifax, NS , Canada. **Online address:** megfederico@gmail.com

FEDOROFF, Nina (V.). American (born United States), b. 1942. **Genres:** Sciences, Medicine/Health, Food And Wine, Genealogy/Heraldry. **Career:** Biological Abstracts, Translational Bureau, assistant manager, 1962-63; freelance translator, 1963-66; Syracuse Symphony Orchestra, flutist, 1964-66; University of California, acting assistant professor of biology, 1972-74; Carnegie Institution of Washington, staff scientist, 1975-; Johns Hopkins University, professor of biology, 1979-; Pennsylvania State University, faculty, 1995-, Biotechnology Institute, director, 1995-2002, Huck Institutes of Life Sciences, founding director, Willaman professor of life science, Department of Biology, Evan Pugh professor, 2002-, Verne M Willaman chair of life sciences; US Secretary of State, science and technology adviser, 2007-10. Writer. **Publications:** (Ed. with D. Botstein) The Dynamic Genome: Barbara McClintock's Ideas in the Century of Genetics, 1992; (ed. with J.E. Cohen) Colloquium on Plants and Population: Is There Time?, 1999; (with N.M. Brown) Mendel in the Kitchen: A Scientist's View of Genetically Modified Foods, 2004. Works appear in anthologies. Contributor of articles to journals and periodicals. **Address:** Biotechnology Institute, Pennsylvania State University, 219 Wartik Laboratory, 417 Old Main, University Park, PA 16802-5301, U.S.A. **Online address:** nvfl@psu.edu

FEELEY, Gregory. American (born United States), b. 1955. **Genres:** Novels, Science Fiction/Fantasy, Food And Wine. **Career:** Writer. **Publications:** The Oxygen Barons (science fiction), 1990; Arabian Wine, 2005. **Address:** Richard Curtis Associates, 171 E 74th St., 2nd Fl., New York, NY 10021-3221, U.S.A.

FEELEY, Malcolm M(cCollum). American (born United States), b. 1942. **Genres:** Law. **Career:** New York University, Department of Politics, instructor, assistant professor, 1968-72; Russell Sage Foundation, fellow in law and social science, 1972-74; Yale Law School, Institution for Social and Policy Studies, lecturer, 1974-77; University of Wisconsin, Department of Political Science, assistant professor, 1977-, professor, through 1984; University of California, School of Law, visiting professor, 1982-83, professor, 1984-, Center for the Study of Law and Society, director of the campus, 1987-92, Claire Sanders Clements Dean's chair professor of law, 1994-; Hebrew University, visiting professor, 1992-94, 1997, 1999, 2001, 2005, 2010, UC Study Center, director, 1992-94, Institute of Advanced Studies, fellow, 1993-94; Center for the Advanced Study in Behavioral Sciences, fellow, 2001-02; Kobe University, visiting professor; Princeton University, visiting professor, Law and Public Affairs Program, fellow, 2008-09, Woodrow Wilson School, visiting professor. Writer. **Publications:** The Process is the Punishment: Handling Cases in a Lower Court, 1979; (with A. Sarat) The Policy Dilemma: Federal Crime Policy and the Law Enforcement Assistance Administration, 1980; Court Reform on Trial, 1983; (with S. Krislov) Casebook in Constitutional Law, 1985; (with Krislov) Constitutional Law, 1985, 2nd ed., 1990; (with J. Kaplan and J.H. Skolnick) Criminal Justice: Introductory Cases and Materials, 1991, 6th ed., 2005; (with E. Rubin) Judicial Policy Making and the Modern State, 1998; (with S. Miyazawa) The Japanese Adversary System in Context, 2002; (with E. Rubin) Federalism: Political Identity and Tragic Compromise, 2008. EDITOR: (with R. Hill) Affirmative School Integration, 1968; (with T.L. Becker) The Impact of Supreme Court Decisions, 1973; (with R. Tomasic) Neighborhood Justice, 1982; (with H.N. Scheiber) Power Divided: Essays on the Theory and Practice of Federalism, 1989; (co-ed.) Fighting for Political Freedom: Comparative Studies of the Legal Complex and Political Liberalism, 2007. Contributor to books and journals. **Address:** School of Law, University of California, 2240 Piedmont Ave., Berkeley, CA 94720-7200, U.S.A. **Online address:** mfeeley@law.berkeley.edu

FEENEY, Don J(oseph). American (born United States), b. 1948. **Genres:** Psychology, Medicine/Health, Self Help. **Career:** Champaign Council on Alcoholism, clinical director, 1976-79; Tri-County Mental Health Center, psychologist, 1980-82; Christ Hospital, psychologist with alcohol treatment program, 1982-; Psychological Consulting Services, consultant, 1985-, chief executive officer, 1998-, clinical psychologist and executive director. Writer. **Publications:** Entrancing Relationships: Exploring the Hypnotic Framework of Addictive Relationships, 1999; Motifs: The Transformative Creation of Self, 2001; Creating Cultural Motifs Against Terrorism: Empowering Acceptance of Our Uniqueness, 2003. Contributor to journals and periodicals. **Address:** Psychological Consulting Services, 6900 Main St., Ste. 54, Downers Grove, IL 60516, U.S.A.

FEHLBAUM, Beth. American (born United States), b. 1966. **Genres:** Novels. **Career:** Author and educator. **Publications:** Courage in Patience (young adult novel), 2008. **Address:** TX , U.S.A. **Online address:** beth@bethfehlbaum.com

FEHLER, Gene. American (born United States), b. 1940. **Genres:** Poetry, Sports/Fitness, Novels, Children's Fiction, Young Adult Fiction, Adult Nonfiction. **Career:** Kishwaukee College, English teacher and writer-in-residence, 1969-80; Park College, teacher; Austin Community College, teacher; Auburn University, Athens Academy, teacher. **Publications:** Center Field Grasses: Poems from Baseball, 1991; I Hit the Ball! Baseball Poems for the Young, 1996; Tales from Baseball's Golden Age, 2000; Let the Poems Begin!

A Poet's Guide to Writing Poetry, 2000; Dancing on the Basepaths: Baseball Poetry and Verse, 2001; More Tales from Baseball's Golden Age, 2002; (with R. Harrison) Goblin Giggles: A Ghastly Lift-the-Flap Book, 2005; Beanball, 2008; Change-Up: Baseball Poems, 2009; Never Blame the Umpire, 2010; Forced Out, 2012. Works appear in anthologies. Contributor to periodicals. **Address:** 106 Laurel Ln., Seneca, SC 29678, U.S.A. **Online address:** fehler@nctv.com

FEHRENBACH, T(heodore) R(eed). (Thomas Freeman). American (born United States), b. 1925. **Genres:** History, Military/Defense/Arms Control, Money/Finance. **Career:** Royal Poinciana Corp., president, 1971-93; Texas Historical Commission, chairman, 1987-91. Writer. **Publications:** Battle of Anzio, 1962; U.S. Marines in Action, 1962; (as Thomas Freeman) Crisis in Cuba, 1963; This Kind of War, 1963; Swiss Banks, 1966; Crossroads in Korea, 1966; The Gnomes of Zurich, 1966; This Kind of Peace, 1966; Sillok Hanguk chŏnjaeng, 1967; F.D.R.'s Undeclared War, 1967; Lone Star, a History of Texas and the Texans, 1968; Greatness to Spare, 1968; The United Nations in War and Peace, 1968; Fight for Korea, 1969; Fire and Blood, 1973; Comanches, 1974; (co-author) The San Antonio Story, 1978; Seven Keys to Texas, 1983; Texas: A Salute from Above, 1985; (with D. Crowley & S. Siegel) Lone Star: The Story of Texas, 2003; (foreword) San Antonio Portrait, 2005; The Anglos (novel), forthcoming; World Without End, forthcoming. Contributor of articles to periodicals. **Address:** Richard Curtis Associates Inc., 171 East 74th St., 2nd Fl., New York, NY 10021-3221, U.S.A.

FEIFER, George. American (born United States), b. 1934. **Genres:** History, International Relations/Current Affairs, Novels, Biography, Autobiography/Memoirs. **Career:** CBS News, news writer, 1964; freelance writer and lecturer, 1965-; Dartmouth College, Summer School, instructor in Soviet studies, 1988. **Publications:** NONFICTION: Justice in Moscow, 1964; The Challenge of Change, 1967; Message from Moscow, 1969; Russia Close-Up, 1973 in US as Our Motherland, and Other Ventures in Russian Reportage, 1974; (with B. Rosen and B. Rosen) The Destined Hour: The Hostage Crisis and One Family's Ordeal, 1982; Tennozan: The Battle of Okinawa and the Atomic Bomb, 1992; (comp.) Divorce: An Oral Portrait, 1995; Red Files, 2000; The Battle of Okinawa: The Blood and the Bomb, 2001; Breaking Open Japan: Commodore Perry, Lord Abe, and American Imperialism in 1853, 2006. NOVELS: The Girl from Petrovka, 1971; Moscow Farewell, 1976. OTHERS: (with D. Burg) Solzhenitsyn (biography), 1972; (with V. Panov) To Dance (autobiography), 1978. Works appear in anthologies. Contributor to books and periodicals. **Address:** 48 Cross Brook Rd., Roxbury, CT 06783-1211, U.S.A. **Online address:** gfeifer@worldnet.att.net

FEIFFER, Jules. American (born United States), b. 1929. **Genres:** Novels, Novellas/Short Stories, Plays/Screenplays, Humor/Satire, Cartoons, Young Adult Fiction, Children's Fiction, Autobiography/Memoirs, Illustrations, Young Adult Fiction. **Career:** Freelance cartoonist, 1951-; Village Voice, cartoonist, 1956-97; Yale University, School of Drama, faculty, 1972-73; Northwestern University, adjunct professor of writing, 1996; Columbia University, National Arts Journalism Program, senior fellow, 1997; Stony Brook Southampton College, adjunct professor of writing, 1999-. Writer. **Publications:** Sick, Sick, Sick, 1958; Passionella and Other Stories, 1959; The Explainers, 1960, Boy, Girl, Boy, Girl, 1961; Hold Me!, 1963; Feiffer's Album, 1963; Harry, the Rat with Women: A Novel, 1963; Garçon, Fille, Garçon, Fille, 1964; The Unexpurgated Memoirs of Bernard Mergendeiler, 1965; The Great Comic Book Heroes, 1965; The Penguin Feiffer, 1966; Feiffer on Civil Rights, 1966; Feiffer's Marriage Manual, 1967; Little Murders, 1968; Feiffer's People: Sketches And Observations, 1969; Was Getekend, 1970; The White House Murder Case: A Play in Two Acts & Dick and Jane: A One-Act Play, 1970; Pictures at a Prosecution: Drawings and Text from the Chicago Conspiracy Trial, 1971; Feiffer on Nixon: The Cartoon Presidency, 1974; (with I. Horovitz) VD Blues, 1974; Knock, Knock: A Play, 1976; Hold Me!: An Entertainment, 1977; Ackroyd: A Novel, 1977; Tantrum, 1979; Popeye, 1980; Jules Feiffer's America: From Eisenhower to Reagan, 1982; (with W. Eisner and W. Wood) Outer Space Spirit, 1952, 1983; Marriage Is an Invasion of Privacy and Other Dangerous Views, 1984; (intro.) The Complete E.C. Segar Popeye, 1984; Feiffer's Children: Including Munro, 1986; Ronald Reagan in Movie America, 1988; Elliot Loves, 1989; The Complete Color Terry and the Pirates, 1990; The Feiffer, Collected Works, vol. I-IV, 1989-92; (with H. Foote, M. Norman and N. Shange) Selected from Contemporary American Plays: An Anthology, 1990. FOR CHILDREN: A Barrel of Laughs, a Vale of Tears, 1995; Meanwhile?, 1997; (foreword) 5 Novels: Alan Mendelsohn, the Boy from Mars, 1997; The Snarkout Boys and the Avocado of Death, 1997; I Lost My Bear, 1998; Bark, George, 1999; I'm Not Bobby!, 2001; By the Side of the Road, 2002; The House across the Street, 2002; The Daddy Mountain, 2004; A Bad Friend, 2005; A Room With A Zoo, 2005; Henry, The Dog With No Tail, 2007; Backing into Forward: A Memoir, 2010; Slaves of Spiegel; The Last Guru. SELF-ILLUSTRATED: Man in the Ceiling, 1993. Illustrator of books by others. **Address:** Universal Press Syndicate, 4520 Main St., Ste. 700, Kansas City, MO 64111-7701, U.S.A. **Online address:** julesfeiffer@gmail.com

FEIFFER, Kate. American (born United States), b. 1964?. **Genres:** Children's Fiction, Human Relations/Parenting, Animals/Pets, Picture/Board Books, Documentaries/Reportage. **Career:** Freelance writer, 1998-; J.B. Pictures, picture researcher and editor; Public Broadcasting Service, Frontline, associate producer; WHDH-TV, political producer; Reallife (news program), producer. **Publications:** Double Pink, 2005; Henry, the Dog with No Tail, 2007; President Pennybaker, 2008; My Mom Is Trying to Ruin My Life, 2009; The Problem with the Puddles, 2009; Which Puppy?, 2009; The Wild Wild Inside: A View from Mommy's Tummy, 2010; But I Wanted a Baby Brother!; 2010; My Side of the Car, 2011. **Address:** Oak Bluffs, MA, U.S.A. **Online address:** kfeiffer@comcast.net

FEIGON, Lee. American (born United States), b. 1945. **Genres:** International Relations/Current Affairs, Biography, History. **Career:** Colby College, professor of history, 1976-, East Asian Studies, director, 1978-, chair; University of Chicago, Center for East Asian Studies, research associate; Northwestern University, Kellogg School of Management, adjunct professor; Censea Inc., chief executive officer; The Wall Street Journal, writer; Barron's, writer; Nation, writer; The Chicago Tribune, writer; The Atlantic, writer; The Boston Globe, writer; Council of Independent Colleges, Woodrow Wilson visiting fellow. Director and producer. **Publications:** Chen Duxiu: Founder of the Chinese Communist Party, 1983; China Rising: The Meaning of Tiananmen, 1990; Demystifying Tibet: Unlocking the Secrets of the Land of the Snows, 1996; Mao: A Reinterpretation, 2002. **Address:** Ivan R. Dee, Publisher, 4501 Forbes Blvd., Ste. 200, Lanham, MD 20706, U.S.A.

FEILEN, John. *See* **MAY, Julian.**

FEILER, Bruce. (Bruce S. Feiler). American (born United States), b. 1964. **Genres:** Documentaries/Reportage, Theology/Religion, Photography, Reference. **Career:** Teacher, 1987-88; Kyodo News Service, reporter, 1988-89; writer, 1991-; National Public Radio, correspondent. **Publications:** Learning to Bow: An American Teacher in a Japanese School, 1991; (as Bruce S. Feiler) Learning to Bow: Inside the Heart of Japan, 1991; Looking for Class: Days and Nights at Oxford and Cambridge, 1993; Under the Big Top: A Season with the Circus, 1995; Dreaming Out Loud: Garth Brooks, Wynonna Judd, Wade Hayes, and the Changing Face of Nashville, 1998; Walking the Bible: A Journey by Land through the Five Books of Moses, 2001; Abraham: A Journey to the Heart of Three Faiths, 2002; Walking the Bible: An Illustrated Journey for Kids through the Greatest Stories Ever Told, 2004; Walking the Bible: A Photographic Journey, 2005; Where God Was Born: A Journey by Land to the Roots of Religion, 2005; America's Prophet: Moses and the American Story, 2009; Council of Dads: My Daughters, My Illness, and the Men Who Could be Me, 2010. Contributor to periodicals. **Address:** c/o Author Mail, William Morrow/HarperCollins Publishers, 10 E 53rd St., New York, NY 10022-5244, U.S.A.

FEILER, Bruce S. *See* **FEILER, Bruce.**

FEIN, Richard J. American (born United States), b. 1929. **Genres:** Poetry, Literary Criticism And History, Translations. **Career:** New York City Department of Welfare, counselor, 1954-56; City University of New York, Hunter College, instructor in English, 1958-60; Fairleigh Dickinson University, instructor in English, 1960-61; University of Puerto Rico, assistant professor of English, 1961-63; State University of New York, assistant professor, 1961-63, associate professor, 1963-65, professor of English, 1965-, now professor emeritus; University of Madras, American literature, Fulbright lecturer, 1971-72. Writer. **Publications:** Robert Lowell, 1970, 2nd ed., 1979; The Dance of Leah: Discovering Yiddish in America, 1986; (trans., ed. and intro.) Selected Poems of Yankev Glatshteyn, 1987; Kafka's Ear, 1990; At the Turkish Bath, 1994; To Move into the House, 1996; Ice Like Morsels, 1999; I Think of Our Lives, 2002; Mother Tongue, 2004; Reversion, 2006; (trans. and ed.) With

Everything We've Got: A Personal Anthology of Yiddish Poetry, 2008. **Address:** Department of English, State University of New York, 1 Hawk Dr., New Paltz, NY 12561, U.S.A. **Online address:** richard_fein@yahoo.com

FEINBERG, Barbara. American (born United States) **Genres:** Mystery/Crime/Suspense, Biography, Autobiography/Memoirs. **Career:** Story Shop (children's writing and arts program), creator and operator. Writer. **Publications:** Welcome to Lizard Motel: Children Stories and the Mystery of Making Things Up, 2004; Welcome to Lizard Motel: Protecting the Imaginative Lives of Children, 2005. **Address:** Trident Media Group L.L.C., 41 Madison Ave., 36th Fl., New York, NY 10010, U.S.A.

FEINBERG, Margaret. American (born United States), b. 1976?. **Genres:** Theology/Religion. **Career:** Author. **Publications:** God Whispers: Learning to Hear His Voice, 2002; Simple Acts of Faith: Heartwarming Stories of One Life Touching Another, 2003; (contrib.) Simple Acts of Friendship: Heartwarming Stories of One Friend Blessing Another, 2004; Twentysomething: Surviving and Thriving in the Real World, 2004; (with L. Oines) How to Be a Grownup: 247 Lab-Tested Strategies for Conquering the World, 2005; Just Married, 2005; Redefining Life: My Career, 2005; Redefining Life: My Relationships: A Navstudy Featuring the Message Remix, 2005; Simple Prayers of Hope, 2005; What the Heck Am I Going to Do with My Life?, 2005; (with N.N. Gillespie) Five-Star Living on a Two-Star Budget, 2006; Redefining Life: For Women: A Navstudy Featuring the Message Remix, 2006; The Organic God, 2007; Overcoming Fear, 2007; The Sacred Echo: Hearing God's Voice in Every Area of Your Life, 2008; Scouting the Divine, 2009; Making the Most of Your Resources, 2009; Over the Top, 2010; Hungry for God, 2011. Contributor to periodicals. **Address:** Transparent Faith, PO Box 441, Morrison, CO 80465, U.S.A.

FEINBERG, Richard. American (born United States) **Genres:** Anthropology/Ethnology, Language/Linguistics, Adult Non-fiction, History. **Career:** Roosevelt University, instructor, 1974-; Kent State University, assistant professor, 1974-80, associate professor, 1980-86, professor of cultural anthropology, 1986-, acting coordinator of American studies program, 1980-81, Kent Research Group, president, 1997-98, faculty senate, chair, 1997-98; East-West Center, research associate, 1991-; Solomon Islands Development Trust, research associate, 2000-. Writer. **Publications:** Social Structure of Anuta Island, 1973; The Anutan Language Reconsidered: Lexican and Grammar of a Polynesian Outlier, vol. II, 1977; Social Change in a Navajo Community, 1978; Anutan Concepts of Disease: A Polynesian Study (monograph), 1979; Anuta: Social Structure of a Polynesian Island, 1981; Polynesian Seafaring and Navigation: Ocean Travel in Anutan Culture and Society, 1988; Oral History of a Polynesian Outlier: Texts and Translations from Anuta, Solomon Islands, 1993; Oral Traditions of Anuta: A Polynesian Outlier in the Solomon Islands, 1998; Anuta: Polynesian Lifeways for the 21st Century, 2004; Cultural and Social Change: An Anthropological Perspective, forthcoming. EDITOR: (and contrib.) Tempest in a Tea House: American Attitudes toward Breast-Feeding, 1980; (and comp. with S. Win) ASAO Bibliography, 1991; (and contrib.) Seafaring in the Contemporary Pacific Islands: Studies in Continuity and Change, 1995; (with K.A. Watson-Gegeo and contrib.) Leadership and Change in the Western Pacific: Essays in Honor of Sir Raymond Firth (monograph), 1996; (with M. Ottenheimer) The Cultural Analysis of Kinship: The Legacy of David M. Schneider, 2001. Contributor to books and periodicals. **Address:** Department of Anthropology, Kent State University, 231 Lowry, Kent, OH 44242-0001, U.S.A. **Online address:** rfeinber@kent.edu

FEINBERG, Rosa Castro. American (born United States), b. 1939. **Genres:** Language/Linguistics, Education. **Career:** Gadsden County Public Schools, teacher, 1960-61; Leon County Public Schools, teacher, 1961-63; Dade County Public Schools, high school English teacher and debate coach, 1963-64; junior high school teacher of Spanish, 1964-75; University of Miami, Desegregation Assistance Center, staff, 1975-90, research professor of educational and psychological studies, 1988-90; National Origin Desegregation Assistance Center, assistant director, 1975-76, associate director, 1977-80, director, 1980-90, Bilingual Education Training Program for Administrators, director, 1983-87, Institute for Cultural Innovation, director, 1986-90, research professor of educational and psychological studies, 1988-90; Agency for International Development, 1978-82; Dade County Housing Finance Authority, commissioner, 1984-86; Coalition for Quality Education in Dade County, honorary co-chair, 1989-95, Florida International University, visiting associate professor, 1990-92, associate professor, 1992-2002, adjunct professor, 2003; University of Chicago, Joyce lecturer, 1991. Writer. **Publications:** (Ed.

with L.A. Valverde and E.M. Marquez) Educating English-speaking Hispanics, 1980; Bilingual Education: A Reference Handbook, 2002. Contributor of articles to books and periodicals. **Address:** c/o Author Mail, ABC-CLIO, 130 Cremona Dr., PO Box 1911, Santa Barbara, CA 93117, U.S.A. **Online address:** rcastro@fiu.edu

FEINSTEIN, David. American (born United States), b. 1946. **Genres:** Psychology, Medicine/Health. **Career:** Johns Hopkins University, School of Medicine, instructor in psychiatry, 1973-75; San Diego Mental Health Services, senior clinical psychologist, 1976-83; Inner source/Energy Medicine Institute, executive director, 1983-. Writer. **Publications:** (With P.E. Mayo) Rituals for Living and Dying, 1990; (with D. Eden) Energy Medicine, 1999; Energy Psychology Interactive, 2003; (with D. Eden and G. Craig) The Promise of Energy Psychology, 2005; (with S. Krippner) Personal Mythology, 2007; (with D. Eden) Energy Medicine for Women, 2008; Ethics Handbook for Energy Healing Practitioners, 2011. **Address:** 777 E Main St., Ashland, OR 97520, U.S.A. **Online address:** df777@earthlink.net

FEINSTEIN, Edward. American (born United States), b. 1954?. **Genres:** Adult Non-fiction, Theology/Religion. **Career:** Solomon Schechter Academy, founding director, 1982; Congregation Shearith Israel, associate rabbi; Camp Ramah, executive director, 1990-93; Valley Beth Shalom, rabbi, 1993-2005, senior rabbi, 2005-; American Jewish University (formerly University of Judaism), Ziegler Rabbinical School, lecturer; Wexner Heritage Foundation, faculty; Whizen Institute on the Family, faculty; Shalom Hartman Institute, Wexner Heritage Program, faculty; Jewish Journal of Los Angeles, columnist and contributing editor. **Publications:** Tough Questions Jews Ask: A Young Adult's Guide to Building a Jewish Life, 2003; (ed.) Jews and Judaism in the 21st Century: Human Responsibility, The Presence of God and the Future of the Covenant, 2007. **Address:** Valley Beth Shalom, 15739 Ventura Blvd., Encino, CA 91436-2903, U.S.A. **Online address:** efeinstein@vbs.org

FEINSTEIN, Elaine. British (born England), b. 1930. **Genres:** Novels, Novellas/Short Stories, Poetry, Biography, Translations, Adult Non-fiction. **Career:** Cambridge University Press, editorial staff, 1960-62; Bishop's Stortford Training College, lecturer in English, 1963-66; University of Essex, assistant lecturer in literature, 1967-70; writer, 1980-; British Council, writer-in-residence. **Publications:** POETRY: In a Green Eye, 1966; The Magic Apple Tree, 1971; At the Edge, 1972; The Celebrants and Other Poems, 1973; Some Unease and Angels: Selected Poems, 1977, 2nd ed., 1982; The Feast of Euridice, 1981; Badlands, 1986; City Music, 1990; Selected Poems, 1994; Daylight, 1997; Gold, 2000. NOVELS: The Circle, 1970; The Amberstone Exit, 1972; The Glass Alembic, 1973 in US as The Crystal Garden, 1974; The Children of the Rose, 1974; The Ecstasy of Dr. Miriam Garner, 1976; The Shadow Master, 1978; The Border, 1984; Mother's Girl, 1988; All You Need, 1991; The Survivors, 1991; Loving Brecht, 1992; Dreamers, 1994; Lady Chatterley's Confession, 1995; Dark Inheritance, 2001. OTHER: (ed.) Selected Poems of John Clare, 1968; (trans.) The Selected Poems of Marina Tsvetayeva, 1971, 5th ed., 1999; Matters of Chance (short stories), 1972; (comp. and trans.) Three Russian Poets: Margarita Aliger, Yunna Mortiz and Bella Akhmadulina, 1979; (ed. with F. Weldon) New Stories Four, 1979; The Silent Areas: Short Stories, 1980; Bessie Smith, 1986; A Captive Lion: The Life of Marina Tsvetayeva, 1987; (trans. with A.W. Bouis) N. Turbina, First Draft: Poems, 1988; (ed.) P.E.N. New Poetry II, 1988; Marina Tsvetayeva, 1989; Lawrence and the Women: The Intimate Life of D.H. Lawrence in UK as Lawrence's Women: The Intimate Life of D.H. Lawrence, 1993; Pushkin, 1998 in US as Pushkin: A Biography, 1999; (ed.) After Pushkin: Versions: The Poems: Alexander Sergeevich Pushkin By Contemporary Poets, 1999; Ted Hughes: The Life of a Poet, 2001; Collected Poems and Translations, 2002; Anna of all the Russias: The Life of Anna Akhmatova, 2007; Talking to the Dead, 2007; The Russian Jerusalem, 2008; (trans. and intro.) M. Tsvetaeva, Bride of Ice: New Selected Poems, 2009; Cities, 2010. Contributor to periodicals. **Address:** c/o Gil Coleridge, Rogers, Coleridge & White Ltd., 20 Powis Mews, London, GL W11 1JN, England. **Online address:** elaine.feinstein@gmail.com

FEINSTEIN, John. American (born United States), b. 1956. **Genres:** Sports/Fitness, Mystery/Crime/Suspense, Novels, Young Adult Non-fiction. **Career:** Washington Post, sports writer, 1977-88, 1992-; Sports Illustrated, sportswriter, 1988-90; The National, staff writer, 1990-91; Washington Post Sunday Magazine, contract columnist; National Public Radio, commentator; ESPN, commentator. **Publications:** A Season on the Brink: A Year with Bob Knight and the Indiana Hoosiers, 1986; A Season Inside: One Year in College Basketball, 1988; Forever's Team, 1990, rev. ed., 1991; Hard Courts: Real Life on the Professional Tennis Tours, 1991; Running Mates, 1992; Play Ball: The Life and Troubled Times of Major League Baseball, 1993; Good Walk Spoiled: Days and Nightson the PGA Tour, 1995; Winter Games: A Mystery, 1995; Civil War, Army vs. Navy: A Year Inside College Football's Purest Rivalry, 1996; (ed.) The Best American Sports Writing 1996, 1997; First Coming: Tiger Woods, Master or Martyr?, 1998; A March to Madness: The View from the Floor in the Atlantic Coast Conference, 1998; The Majors: In Pursuit of Golf's Holy Grail, 1999; The Last Amateurs: Playing for Glory and Honor in Division I College Basketball, 2000, rev. ed., 2001; The Punch: One Night, Two Lives and the Fight That Changed Basketball Forever, 2002; Open: Inside the Ropes at Bethpage Black, 2003; (with R. Auerbach) Let Me Tell You a Story: A Lifetime in the Game, 2004; Caddy for Life: The Bruce Edwards Story, 2004, rev. ed., 2005; Next Man Up: A Year Behind the Lines in Today's NFL, 2005; Last Shot: A Final Four Mystery, 2005; Last Dance: Behind the Scenes at the Final Four, 2006; Vanishing Act: Mystery at the U.S. Open, 2006; Cover-up, 2007; Tales from Q School: Inside Golf's Fifth Major, 2007; Living on the Black: Two Pitchers, Two Teams, One Season to Remember, 2008; Change-up: Mystery at the World Series, 2009; (with R. Mediate) Are You Kidding Me?, 2009; Moment of Glory: The Year Underdogs Ruled Golf, 2010; The Rivalry: Mystery at the Army-Navy Game, 2010; One on One, 2011; Best Seat in the House, 2011; Portable Palmer, 2011; Rush for the Gold: Mystery at the Olympic Games, 2012; The Classic Palmer, 2012. Contributor to periodicals. **Address:** 9200 Town Gate Ln., Bethesda, MD 20817, U.S.A. **Online address:** john@feinsteinonthebrink.com

FEINSTEIN, Sascha. American (born United States), b. 1963. **Genres:** Poetry, Bibliography, Literary Criticism And History, Essays. **Career:** Indiana University, assistant instructor, 1986-91, associate instructor, 1991-94, part-time instructor, 1994-95; Indiana University-Purdue University, associate instructor, 1991-94; Lycoming College, assistant professor to associate professor, 1995-2000, co-director of creative writing program, 1996-, professor of English; Brilliant Corners, editor, 1996-. **Publications:** POETRY: Summerhouse Piano (poetry chapbook), 1989; Christmas Eve (poetry chapbook), 1994; Blues Knowledge of Departure (poetry chapbook), 1997; Misterioso, 2000. ANTHOLOGIES: (ed. with Y. Komunyakaa) The Jazz Poetry Anthology, 1991, vol. II, 1996; (ed. with D. Rife) Jazz Fiction Anthology, 2009; (ed. with K. Sloane) Keystone Korner: Portrait of a Jazz Club, 2011. CRITICAL STUDIES: Jazz Poetry: From the 1920s to the Present, 1997; A Bibliographic Guide to Jazz Poetry, 1998; Ask Me Now: Conversations on Jazz & Literature, 2007. ESSAY: Black Pearls: Improvisations on a Lost Year, 2008. Contributor to books, journals and periodicals. **Address:** Department of English, Lycoming College, 700 College Pl., Williamsport, PA 17701-5192, U.S.A. **Online address:** feinstein@lycoming.edu

FEIRING, Alice. American (born United States), b. 1956?. **Genres:** Food And Wine. **Career:** Time Magazine, wine and travel columnist. **Publications:** The Battle for Wine and Love: Or How I Saved the World from Parkerization, 2008; (with S. Nestor) Living with Wine: Passionate Collectors, Sophisticated Cellars, and Other Rooms for Entertaining, Enjoying, and Imbibing; 2009; Naked Wine: Letting Grapes Do What Comes Naturally, 2011. Contributor to newspapers. **Address:** Perseus Books Group, 11 Cambridge Ctr., Cambridge, MA 02142, U.S.A. **Online address:** barola@alicefeiring.com

FEIS, William B. American (born United States), b. 1963?. **Genres:** History, Biography, Humanities. **Career:** The Ohio State University, graduate teaching associate, 1989-93, graduate research associate, 1994-96; Buena Vista University, assistant professor of history, 1996-2002, associate professor of history, 2002-07, professor of history, 2007-; North & South Magazine, associate and contributing editor, 1997-. **Publications:** Grants Secret Service: The Intelligence War from Belmont to Appomattox, 2002; The Worst Angels of Our Nature: Guerrilla Warfare in the American Civil War, 2008. Contributor to books and periodicals. **Address:** Department of History, Buena Vista University, Dixon-Eilers 202C, Storm Lake, CT 50588, U.S.A. **Online address:** feis@bvu.edu

FEIST, Raymond E(lias). American (born United States), b. 1945. **Genres:** Science Fiction/Fantasy, Novels. **Career:** Writer. **Publications:** FANTASY NOVELS: RIFTWAR SERIES: Magician: Apprentice, 1982; Magician: Master, 1982; Silverthorn, 1985; A Darkness at Sethanon, 1986; Prince of the Blood, 1989; The King's Buccaneer, 1992. EMPIRE SERIES: (with J. Wurts) Daughter of the Empire, 1987; (with J. Wurts) Servant of the Empire, 1990; (with J. Wurts) Mistress of the Empire, 1992. THE SERPENTWAR SAGA: Shadow of a Dark Queen, 1994; Rise of a Merchant Prince, 1995; Rage of a

Demon King, 1997; Shards of a Broken Crown, 1998. RIFTWAR LEGACY: Krondor, The Betrayal, 1998; (intro.) Return to Krondor: Prima's Official Strategy Guide, 1998; Krondor, the Assassins, 1999; Krondor, Tear of the Gods, 2000. OTHER NOVELS: Faerie Tale, 1988; Talon of the Silver Hawk, 2003; King of Foxes, 2004; Exile's Return, 2005; (with W.R. Forstchen) Honoured Enemy, 2006; (with J. Rosenberg) Murder in LaMut, 2007. DARK-WAR SERIES: Flight of the Nighthawks, 2006; Into a Dark Realm, 2007; Wrath of a Mad God, 2008. DEMONWAR SAGA: Rides a Dread Legion, 2009; At the Gates of Darkness, 2010; A Kingdom Besieged, 2011; A Crown Imperilled, 2012. FORTHCOMING: Jigsaw Lady; Atlas of Midkemia; Magician's End; Return of the Demon King; Krondor the Crawler; Krondor the Dark Mage. **Address:** Bantam Doubleday Dell Publishing Group Inc., 1540 Broadway, New York, NY 10036, U.S.A.

FEITH, Douglas J. (Douglas Jay Feith). American (born United States), b. 1953. **Genres:** Military/Defense/Arms Control, History, Law. **Career:** Fried, Frank, Harris, Shriver and Kampelman, associate, 1978-81; United States Government, National Security Council, Mid-East specialist, 1981-82; United States Department of Defense, special counsel to assistant secretary for international security, 1982-84, deputy assistant secretary of defense for negotiations policy, 1984-86, undersecretary of defense for policy, 2001-05; Feith & Zell P.C., managing partner, 1986-2001; Georgetown University, Edmund A. Walsh School of Foreign Service, professor and distinguished practitioner of national security policy, 2005-08; Hudson Institute, Center for National Security Strategies, senior fellow and director. Writer. **Publications:** (Co-ed.) Israel's Legitimacy in Law and History, 1993; War and Decision: Inside the Pentagon at the Dawn of the War on Terrorism, 2008. Contributor to books and periodicals. **Address:** Center for National Security Strategies, Hudson Institute, Inc, 1015 15th St., NW 6th Fl., Washington, DC 20005, U.S.A. **Online address:** djf35@georgetown.edu

FEITH, Douglas Jay. *See* FEITH, Douglas J.

FEIYU ZHU, Bi. *See* BI, Feiyu.

FELD, Ellen F. American (born United States), b. 1961. **Genres:** Children's Fiction, Animals/Pets. **Career:** Amherst College, Department of Physics, faculty, 1988; Willow Bend Publishing, publisher; Feathered Quill Book Reviews, book reviewer. Writer. **Publications:** Blackjack: A Morgan Horse, 2001; Frosty: The Adventures of a Morgan Horse, 2003; Rusty: The High-Flying Morgan Horse, 2004; Robin: The Lovable Morgan Horse, 2005; Shadow: The Curious Morgan Horse, 2006; Annie: The Mysterious Morgan Horse, 2007; Rimfire: The Barrel Racing Morgan Horse, 2009. **Address:** Willow Bend Publishing, PO Box 304, Goshen, MA 01032, U.S.A. **Online address:** effeld@willowbendpublishing.com

FELDER, David W. American (born United States), b. 1945. **Genres:** Philosophy, Business/Trade/Industry. **Career:** Wayne State University, Department of Philosophy, teaching fellow, 1967-69; Florida State University, Department of Philosophy, university fellow, 1970-71; Florida Agricultural and Mechanical University, Interdisciplinary Studies, instructor, 1971-76, Department of Philosophy, assistant professor, 1976-80, associate professor, 1981-87, professor, 1987-, adjunct professor in peace studies, 1992-. Writer. **Publications:** The Best Investment: Land in a Loving Community, 1983; How to Work for Peace, 1991; From Conflict to Consensus: An Introduction to Logic, 1996; Environmental Conflicts: Role-play Peacegames, 2010; Family Conflicts: Role-play Peacegames, 2010; Courtroom Conflicts: Role-play Peacegames, 2010; Multicultural and Racial Conflicts: Role-play Peacegames, 2010; Middle East Conflicts: Role-play Peacegames, 2010; Divorce Conflicts: Role-play Peacegames, 2010; Camp David Accords: Role-play Peacegame, 2010; Breaking Up: Role-play Peacegame, 2010; Conservation and Indian Rights: Role-play Peacegame, 2010; Civil Court: Role-play Peacegame, 2010; Criminal Court Plea Bargain: Role-play Peacegame, 2010; Development Issues: Role-play Peacegame, 2010; Deciding Where to Retire: Role-play Peacegame, 2010; Divorce Court: Role-play Peacegame, 2010; Divorce Conflicts: Role-play Peacegames, 2010; Election 2000: Role-play Peacegame, 2010; Israel & Syria: Role-play Peacegame, 2010; Obamas Mideast Diplomacy: Role-play Peacegame, 2010; Rehabilitation Center: Role-play Peacegame, 2010; Rehabilitation Hospital: Role-play Peacegame, 2010; Raising Biracial Children: Role-play Peacegame, 2010; River Cleanup: Role-play Peacegame, 2010; Same Sex Equal Partners: Role-play Peacegame, 2010; Relocation Conflict: Role-play Peacegame, 2010; Sexual Harassment: Role-play Peacegame, 2010; She Wants Her Share: Role-play Peacegame,

2010; Selenium Contamination: Role-play Peacegame, 2010; Spinal Center: Role-play Peacegame, 2010; Star Wars Controversies: Role-play Peacegame, 2010; Single Moms Boyfriend: Role-play Peacegame, 2010; They Work at the Same Place: Role-play Peacegame, 2010; Training Center: Role-play Peacegame, 2010; The Test Ban Treaty: Role-play Peacegame, 2010; Visiting Divorced Dad: Role-play Peacegame, 2010; Affair With Lovers Daughter: Role-play Peacegame, 2010; Balkan Conflicts: Role-play Peacegame, 2010; Unmarried and Pregnant: Role-play Peacegame, 2010. **Address:** Florida Agricultural And Mechanical University, 406 Tucker Hall, Tallahassee, FL 32307, U.S.A. **Online address:** felderdave@aol.com

FELDER, Deborah G. American (born United States) **Genres:** Novels, Women's Studies And Issues, History, Literary Criticism And History, Poetry. **Career:** Scholastic publishing Co., editor. **Publications:** The Kids' World Almanac of Animals and Pets, 1989; The Kids' World Almanac of History, 1991; (adapter) The Three Musketeers, 1994; (adapter) Anne of Green Gables, 1994; Jim Carrey Comic Ace, 1995; The 100 Most Influential Women of All Time: A Ranking Past and Present, 1996; Changing Times: The Story of a Tennessee Walking Horse and the Girl Who Proves Grown-ups Don't Always Know Best, 1996; Ride of Courage: The Story of a Spirited Arabian Horse and the Daring Girl Who Rides Him, 1996; Pretty Lady of Saratoga: The Story of a Spirited Thoroughbred a Determined Girl and the Race of a Lifetime, 1997; (with C. Hubbard) Christmas in Silver Lake: The Story of a Dependable Clydesdale and the Immigrant Girl Who Turns to Her for Comfort, 1997; A Century of Women: The Most Influential Events in Twentieth-Century Womens History, 1999; (with D. Rosen) Fifty Jewish Women Who Changed the World, 2003; A Bookshelf of Our Own: Works That Changed Womens Lives, 2005. **Address:** c/o Author Mail, Random House, 1745 Broadway, 3rd Fl., New York, NY 10019-4368, U.S.A.

FELDHERR, Andrew. American (born United States), b. 1963?. **Genres:** Literary Criticism And History, Poetry. **Career:** Dartmouth College, visiting assistant professor, 1991-92, assistant professor, 1992-96; Columbia University, visiting assistant professor, 1996-97; Princeton University, Department of Classics, assistant professor, 1997-2004, associate professor, 2004-08, professor of classics, 2008-. Writer. **Publications:** Spectacle and Society in Livy's History, 1998; (intro.) Catullus: Poems, 1998; (ed.) The Cambridge Companion to the Roman Historians, 2009; Playing Gods: Ovid's Metamorphoses and the Politics of Fiction, 2010; (ed. with G. Hardy) The Oxford History of Historical Writing, vol. I: Beginnings to AD 600, 2011. Contributor to periodicals. **Address:** Department of Classics, Princeton University, 164 E Pyne Bldg., Princeton, NJ 08544-5264, U.S.A. **Online address:** feldherr@princeton.edu

FELDMAN, Daniel L(ee). American (born United States), b. 1949. **Genres:** Politics/Government, Law, Public/Social Administration. **Career:** Olwine, Connelly, Chase, O'Donnell and Weyher (law firm), associate, 1973-74; executive assistant to Congresswoman Elizabeth Holtzman, 1974-77; New York State Assembly, counsel to a subcommittee, 1977-78, counsel to committee, 1979-80, 45th Assembly District, assemblyman, 1981-98, Committee on Correction, chair, 1987-98; City University of New York, John Jay College of Criminal Justice, adjunct professor, 1977-79, associate professor, 2010-; Oxford University, visiting professor, 1982, 1990; Long Island University, adjunct professor, 1982-86; New York University, adjunct professor, 1985-89; Holy Cross College, visiting professor, 1987-88; Brooklyn Law School, adjunct professor, 1990-94; Baruch College, adjunct professor, 1995-98; New York State's Department of Law, Legal Policy and Program Development, assistant deputy attorney general, 1999-2005; Fordham Law School, adjunct professor of law, 2003-07; State-Federal Judicial Council, advisor, 2004-; New York State Trial Lawyers Association, executive director and general counsel; New York State Office of the Comptroller, special counsel for law and policy, 2007-10. Writer. **Publications:** Reforming Government: Winning Strategies Against Waste, Corruption and Mismanagement, 1981; The Logic of American Government: Applying the Constitution to the Contemporary World, 1990; New York Criminal Law, 1996; (with G. Benjamin) Tales from the Sausage Factory: Making Laws in New York State, 2010. Contributor to journals. **Address:** John Jay College of Criminal Justice, 445 West 59 St., New York, NY 10019, U.S.A. **Online address:** dan.feldman1@gmail.com

FELDMAN, David Lewis. American (born United States), b. 1951. **Genres:** Environmental Sciences/Ecology. **Career:** University of Missouri, instructor in comparative politics, 1978; Water Resources Planning Program, Department of Natural Resources, resource planner, 1978; Central Methodist College, instructor, 1979-80; West Virginia State College, Department of Political Science, assistant professor, 1980-82; Moorhead State University, Department of Political Science, associate professor, 1982-88, acting chair, 1987-88; Oak Ridge National Lab, policy analyst, 1988-93; University of Tennessee, Forum for Applied Research and Public Policy, senior editor, 1988-93, Environment and Resources Center, senior research scientist, 1993-2003, Department of Political Science and Graduate Program in Environmental Policy, lecturer, 1993-2003, Southeast Water Policy Initiative, director, 2001, Initiate to Improve Teaching, Research and Service, president, 2001, professor and head, 2003-07, UTS Graduate Program in Environmental Policy, head; American Water Resources Association, president, 2004-05; University of California, School of Social Ecology, Department of Planning, Policy and Design, professor and chair, 2007-, Urban Water Research Center, faculty associate, professor of political science, 2007-, W.O.S. professor of political science, 2007-. **Publications:** Water Resources Management: In Search of an Environmental Ethic, 1991; (ed.) Global Climate Change and Public Policy, 1994; (ed.) The Energy Crisis: Unresolved Issues and Enduring Legacies, 1996; (ed. with R.S. de Suplee and D. Skaar) Evaluation of Fecal Coliform Concentrations Along Selected Reaches of the Upper Smith River, 2003; Water Policy for Sustainable Development, 2007; (with I. Blokov) Civil Society Since the End of Communism: Politics, Environmental Policy and Russias Post-1991 Experience, forthcoming. Contributor to books. **Address:** Department of Planning, Policy and Design, School of Social Ecology, University of California, 202B Social Ecology I, 5300 Social and Behavioral Sciences Gateway, Irvine, CA 92697-7075, U.S.A. **Online address:** feldmand@uci.edu

FELDMAN, Ellen. American (born United States), b. 1941?. **Genres:** Novels. **Career:** Writer. **Publications:** NOVELS: A.k.a. Katherine Walden, 1982; Conjugal Rites, 1986; Looking for Love, 1990; Too Close for Comfort, 1994; Rearview Mirror, 1996; God Bless the Child, 1998; Lucy, 2003; The Boy Who Loved Anne Frank, 2005; Scottsboro, 2008. Contributor of articles to books, newspapers and magazines. **Address:** NY , U.S.A. **Online address:** ellen@ellenfeldman.com

FELDMAN, Gayle. American (born United States), b. 1951. **Genres:** Autobiography/Memoirs, Human Relations/Parenting, Psychology, Medicine/ Health. **Career:** Publishers Weekly, book news editor, 1989-95, contributing editor, 1996-2008; The Bookseller, correspondent, 1999-. **Publications:** You Don't Have to Be Your Mother, 1994; Best and Worst of Times: The Changing Business of Trade Books, 1975-2002, 2003. **Address:** c/o Eric Simonoff, William Morris Endeavor Agency, 1325 Ave. of the Americas, New York, NY 10019, U.S.A. **Online address:** feldmang@aol.com

FELDMAN, Irving (Mordecai). American (born United States), b. 1928. **Genres:** Poetry. **Career:** University of Puerto Rico, member of faculty, 1954-56; University of Lyons, faculty, 1957-58; Kenyon College, faculty, 1958-64; State University of New York at Buffalo, faculty, distinguished professor of English, 1964-2004, distinguished professor emeritus of English, 2004-, now professor emeritus. Writer. **Publications:** Works and Days and Other Poems, 1961; The Pripet Marshes and Other Poems, 1965; Magic Paper and Other Poems, 1970; Lost Originals, 1972; Leaping Clear and Other Poems, 1976; New and Selected Poems, 1979; Teach Me, Dear Sister, 1983; All of Us Here, 1986; The Life and Letters, 1994; Beautiful False Things, 2000; Collected Poems 1954-2004, 2004. **Address:** Department of English, State University of New York, 306 Clemens Hall, State University Plz., 353 Broadway, Buffalo, NY 14260, U.S.A. **Online address:** feldman@buffalo.edu

FELDMAN, Lynne B. Canadian (born Canada), b. 1956. **Genres:** Business/Trade/Industry, Cultural/Ethnic Topics, History, Race Relations, Travel/ Exploration, Biography, Philosophy, Economics, Economics. **Career:** Gage Publishing Co., editor, 1986-88; freelance writer and researcher, 1988-. **Publications:** A Sense of Place: Birmingham's Black Middle-Class Community, 1890-1930, 1999. WITH J.N. INGHAM: Contemporary American Business Leaders, 1990; African American Business Leaders: A Biographical History, 1992; African-American Business Leaders: A Biographical Dictionary, 1994. Contributor to books. **Address:** 90 Farnham Ave., Toronto, ON M4V 1H4, Canada. **Online address:** lynfeling@yahoo.com

FELDMAN, Noah (R.). American (born United States), b. 1970?. **Genres:** Administration/Management, History, Social Commentary, Adult Non-fiction. **Career:** Department of State, Consulate General Jerusalem, economic officer, 1992; Oxford University, tutor, 1994; Yale University, visiting lecturer, 1996; U.S. Court of Appeals for the D.C. Circuit, law clerk, 1997-98; Har-

vard University, Society of Fellows, junior fellow, 1998-2001; U.S. Supreme Court, law clerk; New York University School of Law, assistant professor, 2001-04, associate professor of law, 2004-05, Center on Law and Security, faculty co-director, 2004-07, Cecelia Goetz professor of law, 2006-07; NYU Oxford Institute, director; New America Foundation, adjunct fellow, 2002-05; New York Times, contributing writer, 2005-; Council on Foreign Relations, adjunct senior fellow, 2006-; Harvard Law School, visiting associate professor of law, 2005, professor of law, 2007-, Bemis Professor of Law, 2007-. Writer. **Publications:** After Jihad: America and the Struggle for Islamic Democracy, 2003, 2nd ed., 2004; What We Owe Iraq: War and the Ethics of Nation Building, 2004; Divided by God: Americas Church-State Problem and What We Should Do about It, 2005, rev. ed., 2006; The Fall and Rise of the Islamic State, 2008; Scorpions: The Battles and Triumphs of FDRs Great Supreme Court Justices, 2010. Contributor to periodicals. **Address:** c/o Author Mail, Farrar, Straus & Giroux, 19 Union Sq. W, New York, NY 10003, U.S.A. **Online address:** noah.feldman@nyu.edu

FELDMAN, Richard Jay. American (born United States), b. 1952. **Genres:** Autobiography/Memoirs. **Career:** U.S. Department of Commerce, special assistant, 1982-94; constable and auxiliary police officer, 1984-87; National Rifle Association, political director, 1984-87; Coalition of Americans to Protect Sports, executive director, 1987-; Save Our Sports, director, 1998. Writer. **Publications:** Ricochet: Confessions of a Gun Lobbyist (autobiography), 2008. **Address:** Coalition of Americans to Protect Sports, 200 Castlewood Dr., North Palm Beach, FL 33408-5666, U.S.A.

FELDMANN, Doug. American (born United States), b. 1970?. **Genres:** Sports/Fitness. **Career:** Libertyville High School, teacher, 1992-95; Rockford Eisenhower Middle School, teacher, 1992-95; DeKalb Public Schools, teacher, 1992-95; Indiana University, associate instructor, 1995-98; Southern Illinois University, assistant professor, 1998-2002; Franklin College, assistant professor, 2002-03; University of Southern Mississippi, assistant professor, 2003-05; Northern Kentucky University, College of Education and Human Services, assistant professor, 2005-08, associate professor, 2008-; Midwestern Educational Research Association, president. Writer. **Publications:** Dizzy and the Gas House Gang: The 1934 Saint Louis Cardinals and Depression-Era Baseball, 2000; Fleeter Than Birds: The 1985 St. Louis Cardinals and Small Ball's Last Hurrah, 2002; Curriculum and the American Rural School, 2003; September Streak: The 1935 Chicago Cubs Chase the Pennant, 2003; Miracle Collapse: The 1969 Chicago Cubs, 2006; El Birdos: The 1967 and 1968 St. Louis Cardinals, 2007; The 1976 Cincinnati Reds, 2008; St. Louis Cardinals Past and Present, 2009; Gibson's Last Stand, forthcoming, A Season Too Short, forthcoming. **Address:** College of Education and Human Services, Northern Kentucky University, Highland Heights, KY 41099, U.S.A. **Online address:** feldmannd1@nku.edu

FELICIANO, Hector. Puerto Rican (born Puerto Rico), b. 1952?. **Genres:** History, Documentaries/Reportage, Education. **Career:** World Media Network (newspaper syndicate), editor-in-chief; Washington Post, journalist; Los Angeles Times, journalist. **Publications:** NONFICTION: (co-author) New York, 1988; (trans.) The Lost Museum: The Nazi Conspiracy to Steal the World's Greatest Works of Art, 1995; The Great Culture Robbery: The Plunder of Jewish-Owned Art, 1998. Contributor to periodicals. **Address:** Basic Books, 10 E 53rd St., New York, NY 10022, U.S.A.

FELINTO (BARBOSA DE LIMA), Marilene. Brazilian (born Brazil), b. 1957. **Genres:** Novels, Novellas/Short Stories, History. **Career:** College of Journalism, assistant professor of Portuguese language, 1983-87; Folha de Sao Paulo, journalist, 1989-; University of California, visiting writer, 1992; Haus der Kulturen der Welt, visiting lecturer, 1994. **Publications:** As Mulheres de Tijucopapo (novel), 1982, trans. as The Women of Tijucopapo, 1994; Outros Herois e Este Graciliano (nonfiction), 1983; Graciliano Ramos, 1983; O Lago Encantado de Grongonzo (novel), 1987; Postcard (stories), 1991; Natural History, 1995; Jornalisticamente incorreto, 2000; Obsceno Abandono: Amor e perda, 2002. Works appear in anthologies. **Address:** Secret Admins, Al Barao de Limeira 425, Sao Paulo, SP 01290-001, Brazil.

FELIX, Antonia. American (born United States) **Genres:** Sciences, Natural History, Children's Non-fiction. **Career:** Writer and opera singer. **Publications:** Wild about Harry: The Illustrated Biography of Harry Connick, Jr., 1995; Christie Todd Whitman: People's Choice, 1996; Prayers and Meditations for Children, 1997; (with S. Christian) Can It Really Rain Frogs?: The World's Strangest Weather Events, 1997; (with S. Christian) Shake, Rattle, and Roll: The World's Most Amazing Volcanoes, Earthquakes, and Other Forces, 1997; (with S. Christian) Is There a Dinosaur in Your Backyard?: The World's Most Fascinating Fossils, Rocks, and Minerals, 1998; (with S. Christian) What Makes the Grand Canyon Grand?: The World's Most Awe-Inspiring Natural Wonders, 1998; Christmas in America, 1999; Andrea Bocelli: A Celebration, 2000; (comp.) The Post's New York, 2001; Silent Soul: The Miracles and Mysteries of Audrey Santo, 2001; Laura: America's First Lady, First Mother, 2002; Condi: The Condoleezza Rice Story, 2002, rev. ed., 2005; Wesley K. Clark: A Biography, 2004; (with J. DeBlois) Some Kind of Genius: The Extraordinary Journey of Musical Savant Tony DeBlois, 2005; Sonia Sotomayor, 2010. EDITOR: A Charlie Brown Christmas: The Making of a Tradition, 2000; (with L. Sunshine) Pearl Harbor: The Movie and the Moment, 2001; Windtalkers, 2002. **Address:** c/o Paul Fedorko, Trident Media Group, 41 Madison Ave., 36th Fl., 175 5th Ave., New York, NY 10010, U.S.A. **Online address:** antonia@antoniafelix.com

FELL, Alison. British/Scottish (born Scotland), b. 1944. **Genres:** Novels, Poetry, Young Adult Fiction, Natural History, Social Sciences. **Career:** Welfare State Theatre, co-founder, 1970; Women's Street Theatre, co-founder, 1971; Underground Press, journalist, 1971-75; Spare Rib, fiction editor, 1975-79; London Borough of Brent, C. Day Lewis fellow, 1978; writer, 1979-; London Borough of Walthamstow, writer-in-residence, 1981-82; New South Wales Institute of Technology, writer-in-residence, 1986; University of East Anglia, writing fellow, 1998; University College, Royal Literary Fund fellow, 2002; University of Middlesex, research fellow, 2003. **Publications:** NOVELS: The Grey Dancer, 1981; Every Move You Make, 1984; Kisses for Mayakovsky, 1984; The Bad Box, 1987; The Crystal Owl, 1988; The Shining Mountain, 1989; Mer de Glace, 1991; The Pillow Boy of the Lady Onogoro, 1994; The Mistress of Lilliput, or, The Pursuit, 1999; Tricks of the Light, 2003. POETRY: Dionysus Day (prose poem), 1992; Dreams, Like Heretics, 1997; Lightyear, 2005. OTHERS: (ed.) Hard Feelings: Fiction and Poetry from Spare Rib, 1979; (ed.) The Seven Deadly Sins, 1988; (ed.) The Seven Cardinal Virtues, 1990; (ed.) Serious Hysterics, 1992; Dreams Like Heretics, 1997. Works appear in anthologies. Contributor to books and periodicals. **Address:** c/o Tony Peake, Peake Associates, 14 Grafton Cres., London, GL NW1 8SL, England.

FELL, Dafydd. British (born England), b. 1970. **Genres:** Local History/Rural Topics, Adult Non-fiction, Politics/Government. **Career:** University of London, School of Oriental and African Studies, Centre of Taiwan Studies (formerly the Taiwan Studies Programme), coordinator, 2003-06, deputy director, 2006-, Centre for Financial and Management Studies, lecturer of Taiwan studies, Department of Politics and International Studies, lecturer of Taiwan studies, senior lecturer in Taiwan studies, Department of Financial and Management Studies, senior lecturer in Taiwan studies. Writer. **Publications:** Party Platform Change and the Democratic Evolution in Taiwan, 1991-2001, 2003, rev. ed. as Party Politics in Taiwan: Party Change and the Democratic Evolution of Taiwan, 1991-2004, 2005; (ed. with H. Klöter and C. Bi-Yu) What Has Changed?: Taiwan before and after the Change in Ruling Parties, 2006; (ed.) Modern Politics of Taiwan, 2008; (ed.) The Politics of Modern Taiwan, 2008; Government and Politics in Taiwan, 2011. Contributor to journals. **Address:** Department of Politics and International Studies, School of Oriental and African Studies, University of London, Rm. 201, Thornhaugh St., Russell Sq., London, GL WC1H 0XG, England. **Online address:** df2@soas.ac.uk

FELSKE, Coerte V. W. American (born United States), b. 1960?. **Genres:** Horror, Novels, Literary Criticism And History. **Career:** Writer. **Publications:** The Shallow Man, 1995; Word, 1998; The Millennium Girl, 1999; Supergirl, 2001. Contributor to periodicals. **Address:** The Dolce Vita Press, 200 E 66th St., New York, NY 10065, U.S.A.

FELSTEIN, Ivor. Also writes as Philip McCann. British/Scottish (born Scotland), b. 1933. **Genres:** Novellas/Short Stories, Medicine/Health, Psychology, Sex, Social Sciences. **Career:** Kingston Group Hospitals, medical registrar, 1960-63; Bolton District General Hospital, physician in geriatrics, 1963-98; Bolton Evening News, medical columnist, 1966-70; British Journal of Sexual Medicine, consulting editor, 1973-86; Liverpool Echo, medical columnist, 1974-76; Reed Publications, book reviewer. **Publications:** Later Life: Geriatrics Today and Tomorrow, 1969; Sex and the Longer Life, 1970; Snakes and Ladders: Medical and Social Aspects of Modern Management, 1971; A Change of Face and Figure, 1971; Living to Be a Hundred, 1973; Sex in Later Life, 1973; (with J. Mitson and M. Barnard) The Medical Short-

hand Typist, 1974; Sexual Pollution: The Fall and Rise of Venereal Diseases, 1974; Looking at Retirement, 1977; (co-author) B.M.A. Book of Executive Health, 1979; Sex in Later Life, 1980; (co-author) Well Being, 1982; Understanding Sexual Medicine, 1986; (co-author) Foot Health, 1989; (co-author) Care of the Elderly, 1995. Contributor to periodicals. **Address:** Flat 2 Tower Grange, New Hall Rd., Salford, LC MN 4EL, England. **Online address:** ivor@felstein1826.freeserve.co.uk

FELSTINER, Mary Lowenthal. American (born United States), b. 1941. **Genres:** History, Mystery/Crime/Suspense, Women's Studies And Issues, Humanities, Medicine/Health. **Career:** Stanford University, lecturer in history, 1970-72, visiting professor, 1997, 1999, 2007-10; Sonoma State College, lecturer, 1971-72; San Francisco State University, faculty, 1972, assistant professor, 1973-76, associate professor, 1976-81, professor of history, 1981-2006, emeritus professor of history, 2006-; Yale University, visiting lecturer, 1990; University of California at Santa Cruz, visiting professor, 1998. Writer. **Publications:** (Co-ed. and contrib.) Chanzeaux: A Village in Anjou, 1966; To Paint Her Life: Charlotte Salomon in the Nazi Era, 1994; Metsayeret et hayehah, 2003; Out of Joint: A Private & Public Story of Arthritis, 2005. Contributor to periodicals. **Address:** Department of History, San Francisco State University, SCI 265, 1600 Holloway Ave., San Francisco, CA 94132, U.S.A. **Online address:** mf@sfsu.edu

FELTON, R. Todd. American (born United States), b. 1969. **Genres:** Local History/Rural Topics, Literary Criticism And History, Travel/Exploration, Transportation. **Career:** Writer, editor, educator, automotive traveler and columnist. **Publications:** A Journey into the Transcendentalists' New England, 2006; A Journey into Ireland's Literary Revival, 2007; Walking Boston: 36 Tours Through Beantown's Cobblestone Streets, Historic Districts, Ivory Towers and New Waterfront, 2008; A Journey into the England of the Lake Poets, forthcoming. **Address:** Wilderness Press, c/o Keen Communications, 2204 1st Ave., S, Ste 102, Birmingham, AL 35233, U.S.A. **Online address:** rtfelton@earthlink.net

FELTS, Susannah. American (born United States), b. 1973. **Genres:** Novels. **Career:** School of the Art Institute of Chicago, adjunct assistant professor of English and creative writing, 2000-06; Health Magazine, associate editor. **Publications:** This Will Go down on Your Permanent Record, 2008. **Address:** Birmingham, AL , U.S.A. **Online address:** susannah.felts@gmail.com

FENBY, Jonathan. British (born England), b. 1942. **Genres:** History. **Career:** Reuters Ltd., Reuters World Service, correspondent and editor, 1963-77; Economist, senior correspondent, 1982-86; Independent, home editor and assistant editor, 1986-88; Guardian, deputy editor, 1988-93; Observer, editor, 1993-95; South China Morning Post, editor, 1995-97; Sunday Morning Post, editor, 1995-97; Trusted Sources U.K. Ltd., co-founder, 2006-, China Team, managing director; Earlywarning.com, editor; University of London, School of Oriental and African Studies, research associate. **Publications:** (With L. Chester) Fall of the House of Beaverbrook, 1979; Piracy and the Public: Forgery, Theft, and Exploitation, 1983; International News Services, 1986; France on the Brink, 1999; Dealing with the Dragon: A Year in the New Hong Kong, 2000; Generalissimo: Chiang Kai-shek and the China He Lost, 2003; Chiang Kai Shek: China's Generalissimo and the Nation He Lost, 2004; Sinking of the Lancastria: The Twentieth Century's Deadliest Naval Disaster and How Churchill Made it Disappear, 2005 in UK as Sinking of the Lancastria: Britain's Greatest Maritime Disaster and Churchill's Cover-Up, 2005; (contrib.) North Korea, 2006; Alliance: The Inside Story of How Roosevelt, Stalin and Churchill Won One War and Began Another, 2006; (ed.) Seventy Wonders of China, 2007; Penguin History of Modern China: The Fall and Rise of a Great Power, 1850-2008, 2008; Modern China: The Fall and Rise of a Great Power, 1850 to the Present, 2008; The General: Charles de Gaulle and The France He Saved, 2010. **Address:** Trusted Sources UK Ltd., 9 Orange St., London, GL WC2H 7EA, England. **Online address:** jtf@trustedsources.co.uk

FENDRICH, James Max. American (born United States), b. 1938. **Genres:** Sociology. **Career:** Florida State University, assistant professor, 1965-68, associate professor, 1968-74, professor, 1974-2003, professor emeritus, 2003-. Writer. **Publications:** (With L.M. Killian and C.U. Smith) Leadership in American Society: A Case Study of Black Leadership, 1969; Ideal Citizens: The Legacy of the Civil Rights Movement, 1993. Contributor to periodicals. **Address:** Department of Sociology, Florida State University, 526 Bellamy Bldg., 600 W College Ave., Tallahassee, FL 32306-2270, U.S.A. **Online address:** jimfendrich@comcast.net

FENLON, Iain. British (born England), b. 1948. **Genres:** Essays. **Career:** University of Birmingham, Hayward Research Fellow, 1974-75; Villa i Tatti (Harvard Center for Italian Renaissance Studies), 1975-76; King's College, junior research fellow, senior research fellow, 1976-83; Cambridge University, lecturer, 1979-96, reader, 1996-; Wellesley College, visiting faculty, 1978-79; Harvard University, visiting faculty, 1984-85; British School in Rome, visiting faculty, 1985; Centre de Musique Ancienne, visiting faculty, 1988-89; école Normale Supérieure, visiting faculty, 1998-99; University of Bologna, visiting faculty, 2000-01. Musicologist and writer. **Publications:** Catalogue of the Printed Music and Music Manuscripts before 1801 in the Music Library of the University of Birmingham Barber Institute of Fine Arts, 1976; Catalogue of the Printed Music and Music Manuscripts Before 1801 in the Music Library of the University of Birmingham Barber Institute of Fine Arts, 1976; Music and Patronage in Sixteenth-Century Mantua, vol. I, 1980, vol. II, 1982; The Winchester Anthology: A Facsimile of British Library Additional Manuscript 60577, 1981; (with J. Haar) The Italian Madrigal in the Early Sixteenth Century: Sources and Interpretation, 1988; (with P.N. Miller) The Song of the Soul: Understanding Poppea, 1992; Music, Print and Culture in Early Sixteenth-Century Italy: The Panizzi Lectures, 1994, 1995; Giaches De Wert: Letters and Documents, 1999; (with P.D. Col) Le Istitutioni Harmoniche: Venezia, 1561, 1999; (with P.D. Vecchia) Venezia 1501: Petrucci e la Stampa Musicale: Catalogo Della Mostra, 2001; Music and Culture in Late Renaissance Italy (essays), 2002; (with F. Piperno) Studi Marenziani, 2003; The Ceremonial City: History, Memory and Myth in Renaissance Venice, 2007; Piazza San Marco, 2009. EDITOR: Early Music History: Studies in Medieval and Early Modern Music, 29 vols., 1981-2009; Music in Medieval and Early Modern Europe: Patronage, Sources, and Texts, 1981; Cambridge Music Manuscripts, 900-1700, 1982; The Renaissance: From the 1470s to the End of the 16th Century, 1989; (with V. Rumbold) A Short-Title Catalogue of Music Printed before 1825 in the Fitzwilliam Museum, Cambridge, 1992; (and contrib. with T. Carter) Con Che Soavità: Studies in Italian Opera, Song, and Dance, 1580-1740, 1995. **Address:** Faculty of Music, University of Cambridge, 11 West Rd., Cambridge, CB CB3 9DP, England. **Online address:** iaf100@cam.ac.uk

FENN, Donna. American (born United States) **Genres:** Business/Trade/Industry, Economics. **Career:** Inc. Magazine, writer, 1983-88, contributing editor, 1992-; Associated Press, correspondent, 1988-92; BNET/CBSi, blogger, 2010-. Business writer. **Publications:** (Ed. with C. Trueblood) Hazards of Walking and Other Memos from Your Bureaucrats, 1982; Alpha Dogs: How Your Small Business Can Become a Leader of the Pack, 2005; Upstarts!: How GenY Entrepreneurs are Rocking the World of Business and 8 Ways You Can Profit from Their Success, 2009. **Address:** c/o Esmond Harmsworth, Zachary Shuster Harmsworth, 525 Boylston St., Boston, MA 02116, U.S.A. **Online address:** dmfenn1@gmail.com

FENNELLY, Beth Ann. American (born United States), b. 1971. **Genres:** Poetry, Novels. **Career:** Slezka Univerzítna, visiting instructor, 1993-94; University of Arkansas, Department of English, graduate teaching assistant, 1994-98, Creative Writing Program, assistant, 1996-98, University of Arkansas Press, marketing intern, 1995; University of Wisconsin, Department of English, Diane Middlebrook fellow, 1998-99; Knox College, Department of English, assistant professor of English, 1999-2002, Creative Writing Program, associate director, 2001-02; University of Mississippi, Department of English, assistant professor, 2002-07, associate professor of English, 2007-, M.F.A. Pprogram in Creative Writing, director. Writer. **Publications:** A Different Kind of Hunger, 1998; Open House, 2002; Tender Hooks, 2004; Great with Child, 2006; Unmentionables, 2008. Contributor to periodicals. **Address:** Department of English, University of Mississippi, 104 W Bondurant Hall, PO Box 1848, University, MS 38677-1848, U.S.A. **Online address:** bafennel@olemiss.edu

FENNER, Frank John. See Obituaries.

FENNER, Roger T(heedham). British (born England), b. 1943. **Genres:** Engineering, Technology, Sciences. **Career:** Imperial Chemical Industries Ltd., Plastics Division, technical officer, 1965-68; University of London, Imperial College, lecturer, 1968-79, reader, 1979-91, professor of engineering computation, 1991-. Writer. **Publications:** Extruder Screw Design, 1970; Computing for Engineers, 1974; Finite Element Methods for Engineers, 1975; Principles of Polymer Processing, 1979; Engineering Elasticity, 1986; Mechanics of Solids, 1989; Finite Element Methods for Engineers, 1996. **Address:** Depart-

ment of Mechanical Engineering, Imperial College, Exhibition Rd., London, GL SW7 2AZ, England. **Online address:** r.fenner@imperial.ac.uk

FENSKE, Jennifer Manske. American (born United States) **Genres:** Novels, Literary Criticism And History. **Career:** Reporter and consultant. **Publications:** Toss the Bride, 2006; The Wide Smiles of Girls, 2009. Contributor to periodicals. **Address:** c/o Ryann Gastwirth, St. Martin's Press, 175 5th Ave., New York, NY 10010-7703, U.S.A. **Online address:** jennifer@jennifermanskefenske.com

FENTEN, D. X. American (born United States), b. 1932. **Genres:** Information Science/Computers, Homes/Gardens, Literary Criticism And History. **Career:** Progressive Grocer (magazine), associate editor, 1965-70; Syosset High School, teacher of creative writing, journalism, modern communications and cinematography, 1970-; Weekend Gardener, author and columnist, 1974-; Newsday Newspaper, garden editor, 1978-91; Grumman Aircraft Engineering Corp., staff; Perfection on Long Island Inc., staff; McGraw-Hill Book Co., staff. **Publications:** Better Photography for Amateurs, 1960; Electric Eye Still Camera Photography, 1961; Flower and Garden Photography, 1966; Aviation Careers: Jobs in the Air and on the Ground, 1969; Plants for Pots: Projects for Indoor Gardeners, 1969; Harvesting the Sea, 1970; Sea Careers: Jobs on the Waterways of the World, 1970; The Clear and Simple Gardening Guide, 1971; Making of a Police Officer, 1972; (with B. Fenton) The Organic Grow It, Cook It, Preserve It Guidebook, 1972; Ins and Outs of Gardening, 1972; Gardening Naturally, 1973; Ms. M.D., 1973; (with B. Fenton) Natural Foods, 1974; (with B. Fenton) The Concise Guide to Natural Foods, 1974; Indoor Gardening: A First Book, 1974; Ms. Attorney, 1974; The Concise Guide to Volunteer Work, 1975; Strange Differences, 1975; TV and Radio Careers, 1976; The Weekend Gardener, 1976; Greenhousing for Purple Thumbs, 1976; (with B. Fenton) Careers in the Sports Industry, 1977; The Children's Complete How Does Your Garden Grow Guide to Plants and Planting, 1977; Ms. Architect, 1977; (with B. Fenton) Tourism and Hospitality Careers Unlimited, 1978; (with B. Fenton) Behind the Television Scenes, 1980; (with B. Fenton) Behind the Sports Scene, 1980; (with B. Fenton) Behind the Radio Scene, 1980; (with B. Fenton) Behind the Newspaper Scene, 1980; (with B. Fenton) Behind the Circus Scene, 1980; Easy to Make House Plants, 1981; (with B. Fenton) The Team Behind the Great Parades, 1981. SELF-ILLUSTRATED: Greenhorn's Guide to Gardening, 1969. **Address:** 27 Bowdon Rd., Greenlawn, NY 11740, U.S.A.

FENTON, Alexander. Scottish/British (born England), b. 1929. **Genres:** Anthropology/Ethnology, Adult Non-fiction, Food And Wine, Social Commentary, Cultural/Ethnic Topics, History, Politics/Government. **Career:** Scottish National Dictionary, senior assistant editor, 1955-59; University of Edinburgh, lecturer, 1958-60, 1974-80, professor of Scottish ethnology and director of school of scottish studies, 1990-, now professor emeritus; National Museum of Antiquities of Scotland, assistant keeper, 1959-75, deputy keeper, 1975-78, director, 1978-85; National Museums of Scotland, research director, 1985-89; European Ethnological Research Center, director, 1989-, chief executive officer. **Publications:** The Various Names of Shetland, 1973, 2nd ed., 1977; Scottish Country Life, 1976, rev. ed. as Country Life in Scotland, 2007; The Island Blackhouse: A Guide to the Blackhouse at 42 Arnol, Lewis, 1978; The Northern Isles: Orkney and Shetland, 1978, rev. ed., 1997; Continuity and Change in the Building Tradition of Northern Scotland, 1979; (with B.D. Walker) The Rural Architecture of Scotland, 1981; (trans.) If all the World Were a Blackbird: Poems, 1985; The Shape of the Past, 2 vols., 1985-86; Wirds an' wark 'e seasons roon on an Aberdeenshire Farm, 1987; Country Life in Scotland: Our Rural Past, 1987; The Turra Coo: A Legal Episode in the Popular Culture of North-East Scotland, 1989; Scottish Country Life, 1989; On Your Bike: 13 Years of Travelling Curators, 1990; Craiters or 20 Buchan Tales, 1995; Buchan Words and Ways, 2005; Food of the Scots, 2007. EDITOR AND CONTRIBUTOR: (with A. Gailey) The Spade in Northern and Atlantic Europe, 1970; (with J. Podolak and H. Rasmussen) Land Transport in Europe, 1973; (with B.D. Walker and G. Stell) Building Construction in Scotland, 1976; (with H. Palsson) The Northern and Western Isles in the Viking World, 1984; (with G. Stell) Loads and Roads in Scotland and Beyond, 1984; (with E. Kisban) Food in Change, 1986; (with J. Myrdal) Food and Drink and Travelling Accessories: Essays in Honour of Goesta Berg, 1988; (with M.R. Schärer) Food and Material Culture: Proceedings of the Fourth Symposium of the International Commission for Research into European Food History, 1998; (and comp. with J. Beech) Glenesk: The History and Culture of An Angus Community, 2000; Order and Disorder: The Health Implications of Eating and Drinking in the Nineteenth and Twentieth Centuries: Proceedings of the Fifth Symposium of the International Commission for Research into European Food History, Aberdeen 1997, 2000. Contributor to books and periodicals. **Address:** European Ethnological Research Ctr., National Museums of Scotland, Queen St., Edinburgh, EH2 1JF, Scotland. **Online address:** a.fenton@nms.ac.uk

FENTON, Julia. *See* **FENTON, Robert L.**

FENTON, Kate. (Kathryn Stacey). British (born England), b. 1954. **Genres:** Novels, Young Adult Fiction. **Career:** Yorkshire Theatre Co., touring musical director, 1974-76; House of Commons, researcher and secretary, 1977-78; British Broadcasting Corp. (BBC-Radio), researcher, producer of radio features, 1978-85; writer, 1985-. **Publications:** NOVELS: (as Kathryn Stacey) Song of My Heart, 1989; The Colours of Snow, 1990; (as Kathryn Stacey) The Governess, 1992; Dancing to the Pipers, 1993; Lions and Liquorice, 1995 in US as Vanity and Vexation: A Novel of Pride and Prejudice, 2004; Balancing on Air, 1996; Too Many Godmothers, 2000; Picking Up, 2002. **Address:** Thomas Dunne Books, 175 5th Ave., New York, NY 10010, U.S.A. **Online address:** office@katefenton.com

FENTON, Margaret. American (born United States), b. 1970?. **Genres:** Novels. **Career:** Writer. **Publications:** Little Lamb Lost, 2009. **Address:** Montgomery, AL , U.S.A. **Online address:** margaret@margaretfenton.com

FENTON, M(elville) Brockett. Canadian/Guyanese (born Guyana), b. 1943. **Genres:** Biology, Natural History, Sciences, Animals/Pets. **Career:** Royal Ontario Museum, Department of Mammology, research associate, 1969-; Carleton University, assistant professor, 1969-81, professor of biology, 1981-86; Rockefeller University, visiting associate professor, 1976; Cornell University, visiting professor, 1985-86; York University, professor of biology, 1986-, head of department, 1986-94, associate vice president for research, 1995-; University of Western Ontario, Department of Biology, chair, 2003-08, acting chair, 2008-09, professor. Writer. **Publications:** (With R.L. Peterson) Variation in the Bats of the Genus Harpyionycteris, With the Description of a New Race, 1970; Population Studies of Myotis Lucifugus (Chiroptera: Vespertilionidae) in Ontario, 1970; Observations on the Biology of Some Rhodesian Bats, Including a Key to the Chiroptera of Rhodesia, 1975; Just Bats, 1983; Communication in the Chiroptera, 1985; (ed. with P. Racey and J.M.V. Rayner) Recent Advances in the Study of Bats, 1987; Bats, 1992, rev. ed., 2001; The Bat: Wings in the Night Sky, 1998; (ed. with T.H. Kunz) Bat Ecology, 2003. Contributor to journals and periodicals. **Address:** Department of Biology, University of Western Ontario, 104 Collip Biological & Geological Sciences Bldg., London, ON N6A 5B7, Canada. **Online address:** bfenton@uwo.ca

FENTON, Peter. American (born United States), b. 1949?. **Genres:** Novels, Biography, Photography. **Career:** National Enquirer, tabloid reporter; Secrets Exchange, editor. **Publications:** I Forgot to Wear Underwear on a Glass-Bottom Boat: Real People, True Secrets, 1997; Truth or Tabloid? (novelty), 2003; Eyeing the Flash: The Education of a Carnival Con Artist (memoir), 2005. Contributor to periodicals. **Address:** c/o Author Mail, Simon & Schuster, 1230 Ave. of the Americans, New York, NY 10020, U.S.A.

FENTON, Robert L. (Julia Fenton). American (born United States), b. 1929. **Genres:** Novels, Romance/Historical. **Career:** Fenton Entertainment Group Inc, president; Marygrove College, adjunct professor. Writer. **Publications:** NOVELS AS JULIA FENTON: Black Tie Only, 1990; Blue Orchids, 1992; Royal Invitation, 1995; Three Wise Men, 2008. **Address:** Fenton Entertainment Group, 31800 Northwestern Hwy., Ste. 204, Farmington Hills, MI 48334-1664, U.S.A. **Online address:** fenent@msn.com

FERBER, Brenda Aaronson. American (born United States), b. 1967. **Genres:** Children's Fiction, Sports/Fitness. **Career:** Leo Burnett advertising agency, staff. Writer. **Publications:** Julia's Kitchen, 2006; Jemma Hartman, Camper Extraordinaire, 2009; The Yuckiest, Stinkiest, Best Valentine's Day Ever, 2011; Zoey Maloney, forthcoming. **Address:** Farrar Straus Giroux Books for Young Readers, 175 5th Ave., New York, NY 10010, U.S.A. **Online address:** brenda_ferber@mail.vresp.com

FERBER, Richard A. American (born United States), b. 1944?. **Genres:** Medicine/Health. **Career:** Children's Hospital, Center for Pediatric Sleep Disorders, director; Harvard Medical School, associate professor of neurology. Pediatrician and writer. **Publications:** Solve Your Child's Sleep Problems,

1985, rev. ed., 2006; (ed. with M. Kryger) Principles and Practice of Sleep Medicine in the Child, 1995; (ed. with S. Sheldon and M. Kryger) Principles and Practice of Pediatric Sleep Medicine, 2005. **Address:** Ctr. for Pediatric Sleep Disorders, Children's Hospital Boston, 9 Hope Ave., Waltham, MA 02453, U.S.A.

FERDER, Fran. American (born United States) **Genres:** Theology/Religion, Psychology, Communications/Media, Self Help, Sports/Fitness, Novels. **Career:** Seattle University, School of Theology and Ministry, part-time faculty, adjunct faculty, 1989-; Therapy and Renewal Associates, co-director; Quixote Center, staff. Clinical psychologist, author, speaker and workshop leader. **Publications:** Called to Break Bread?: A Psychological Investigation of 100 Women Who Feel Called to Priesthood in the Catholic Church, 1978; Word Made Flesh: Scripture, Psychology and Human Communication, 1986; (with J. Heagle) Partnership: Women and Men in Ministry, 1989; (with J. Heagle) Your Sexual Self: Pathway to Authentic Intimacy, 1992; (with J. Heagle) Tender Fires: The Spiritual Promise of Sexuality, 2002; Enter the Story: Biblical Metaphors for Our Lives, 2010; Justice Rising: A New Vision of Biblical Peace Making, 2010; Enter the Feast: Biblical Stories as Metaphors for Human Life, 2010. Contributor to books. **Address:** School of Theology & Ministry, Seattle University, 901 12th Ave., PO Box 222000, Seattle, WA 98122-1090, U.S.A.

FERGUS, Maureen. Canadian (born Canada), b. 1967. **Genres:** Young Adult Fiction. **Career:** Red River College, lecturer in marketing technology. Freelance writer. **Publications:** Exploits of a Reluctant (But Extremely Goodlooking) Hero, 2007. Contributor of articles to magazines and periodicals. **Address:** Kids Can Press Ltd., 25 Dockside Dr., Toronto, ON M5A 0B5, Canada. **Online address:** mfergus@mts.net

FERGUSON, Alane. American (born United States), b. 1957. **Genres:** Children's Fiction, Young Adult Fiction, Novels, Mystery/Crime/Suspense. **Career:** Writer. **Publications:** NOVELS: That New Pet!, 1986; Show Me the Evidence, 1989; Cricket and the Crackerbox Kid, 1990; The Practical Joke War, 1991; Overkill, 1992; Stardust, 1993; Poison, 1994; A Tumbleweed Christmas, 1995; (with E. Conford and L. Wardlaw) See You in September, 1995; Secrets, 1997. MYSTERY SOLVERS SERIES: WITH MOTHER, GLORIA SKURZYNSKI: Mystery of the Spooky Shadow, 1996; Mystery of the Fire in the Sky, 1997; Mystery of the Haunted Silver Mine, 1997; Mystery of the Vanishing Creatures, 1997. NATIONAL PARK MYSTERY SERIES: WITH GLORIA SKURZYNSKI; FOR YOUNG ADULTS: Wolf Stalker, 1997; Rage of Fire, 1998; Cliff Hanger, 1999; Deadly Waters, 1999; The Hunted, 2000; Ghost Horses, 2001; Over the Edge, 2001; Valley of Death, 2001; Running Scared, 2002; Out of the Deep, 2002; Escape from Fear, 2002; Buried Alive, 2003; Night of the Black Bear, 2007; (with G. Skurzynski) Hunted: A Mystery in Glacier National Park, 2007. FORENSIC MYSTRIES: Christopher Killer: A Forensic Mystery, 2006; Angel of Death: A Forensic Mystery, 2006; The Circle of Blood, 2008; Dying Breath, 2009. Contributor to periodicals. **Address:** 1460 Conifer Trl., Elizabeth, CO 80107, U.S.A. **Online address:** aferguson@alaneferguson.com

FERGUSON, Andrew. American (born United States), b. 1956?. **Genres:** Novels. **Career:** Weekly Standard, senior editor; Washingtonian magazine, senior writer; Time magazine, contributing editor; President George H.W. Bush, speechwriter. **Publications:** Fools Names, Fools Faces, 1996; Land of Lincoln: Adventures in Abes America, 2007; Crazy U: One Dads Adventures in Getting His Kid into College, 2011. Contributor to periodicals. **Address:** The Weekly Standard, 1150 17th St. NW, Ste. 505, Washington, DC 20036, U.S.A. **Online address:** ferguson@andrewfergusonbooks.com

FERGUSON, Brad. American (born United States), b. 1953?. **Genres:** Science Fiction/Fantasy, Novels, Novellas/Short Stories. **Career:** Columbia Broadcasting System (CBS), Radio News, journalist, writer, editor and producer, 1982-90; freelance writer, 1986-; Science Fiction and Fantasy Writers of America, eastern regional director, 1999-2002. **Publications:** Crisis on Centaurus, 1986; The World Next Door, 1990; A Flag Full of Stars, 1991; The Last Stand, 1995; (with K. Ferguson) The Haunted Starship, 1997. Contributor to periodicals. Works appear in anthologies. **Address:** Pocket Books, 1230 Ave. of the Americas, 11th Fl., New York, NY 10020-1513, U.S.A. **Online address:** thirteen@fred.net

FERGUSON, Everett. American (born United States), b. 1933. **Genres:** Theology/Religion, History, Reference. **Career:** Northeastern Christian Junior College, dean, 1959-62; Abilene Christian University, associate professor, 1962-98, emeritus professor, 1969-, director of graduate study in religion, 1970-; The Second Century, editor, 1981-92; Journal of Early Christian Studies, co-editor, 1993-99. **Publications:** Church History: Early and Medieval, 1966; Church History: Reformation and Modern, 1967; The New Testament Church, 1968; Early Christians Speak, 1971, 3rd ed. as Early Christians Speak: Faith and Life in the First Three Centuries, 1999; A Cappella Music in the Public Worship of the Church, 1972; (with A.J. Malherbe) Gregory of Nyssa: The Life of Moses, 1978; Demonology of the Early Christian World, 1984; Acts of Apostles: The Message of the New Testament, 1986; (with J.P. Lewis and E. West) Instrumental Music Issue, 1987; Backgrounds of Early Christianity, 1987, 3rd ed., 2003; Everlasting Kingdom: The Kingdom of God in Scripture and in Our Lives, 1989; (ed.) Encyclopedia of Early Christianity, 1990, 2nd ed., 1998; (ed. with D.L. Balch and W.A. Meeks) Greeks, Romans, and Christians: Essays in Honor of Abraham J. Malherbe, 1990; Church of Christ: A Biblical Ecclesiology for Today, 1996; (co-ed.) Early Church in Its Context: Essays in Honor of Everett Ferguson, 1998; Women in the Church, 2003; (comp.) Inheriting Wisdom: Readings for Today from Ancient Christian Writers, 2004; Church History, vol. I: From Christ to Pre-Reformation: The Rise and Growth of the Church in Its Cultural, Intellectual, and Political Context, 2005; Baptism in the Early Church: History, Theology, and Liturgy in the First Five Centuries, 2009. EDITOR AND AUTHOR OF INTRODUCTION: Conversion, Catechumenate, and Baptism in the Early Church, 1992; Acts of Piety in the Early Church, 1993; The Bible in the Early Church, 1993; Christian Life: Ethics, Morality, and Discipline in the Early Church, 1993; Church and State in the Early Church, 1993; Church, Ministry and Organization in the Early Church Era, 1993; Doctrines of God and Christ in the Early Church, 1993; Doctrines of Human Nature, Sin, and Salvation in the Early Church, 1993; Early Christianity and Judaism, 1993; The Early Church and Greco-Roman Thought, 1993; Literature of the Early Church, 1993; Missions and Regional Characteristics of the Early Church, 1993; Orthodoxy, Heresy, and Schism in Early Christianity, 1993; Personalities of the Early Church, 1993; Worship in Early Christianity, 1993; Christianity and Society: The Social World of Early Christianity, 1999; Christianity in Relation to Jews, Greeks, and Romans, 1999; Doctrinal Diversity: Varieties of Early Christianity, 1999; Forms of Devotion: Conversion, Worship, Spirituality, and Asceticism, 1999; History, Hope, Human Language and Christian Reality, 1999; Norms of Faith and Life, 1999. **Address:** Abilene Christian University, 1600 Campus Ct., Abilene, TX 79699, U.S.A. **Online address:** eferguson29@cox.net

FERGUSON, Gary. American (born United States), b. 1956. **Genres:** Natural History, Environmental Sciences/Ecology, Travel/Exploration, Adult Non-fiction, Illustrations. **Career:** U.S. Forest Service at Sawtooth National Recreation Area, interpretive naturalist. Author, naturalist and public speaker. **Publications:** SELF-ILLUSTRATED: Folklore of Medicinal Plants and Herbs, 1970. OTHERS: Freewheeling: Bicycling the Open Road, 1984; Walks of California, 1987; (with H. Wolinsky) The Heart Attack Recovery Handbook, 1988; Walks of the Rockies, 1988; Walks of the Pacific Northwest, 1991; Rocky Mountain Walks, 1993; Walking down the Wild: A Journey Through the Yellowstone Rockies, 1993; (with K. Wall) Lights of Passage: Rituals and Rites of Passage for the Problems and Pleasures of Modern Life, 1994; New England Walks, 1995; Northwest Walks, 1995; Yellowstone Wolves, 1996; Spirits of the Wild: The World's Great Nature Myths, 1996; The Sylvan Path: A Journey through America's Forests, 1997 as Through the Woods: A Journey through America's Forests, 1998; (with K. Wall) Rites of Passage: Celebrating Life's Changes, 1998; Shouting at the Sky: Troubled Teens and the Promise of the Wild, 1999; (with J. Clayton and M.B. Keilty) Guide to America's Outdoors: Southern Rockies, 2001; Hawk's Rest: A Season in the Remote Heart of Yellowstone, 2003; The Great Divide: The Rocky Mountains in the American Mind, 2003; (with D.W. Smith) Decade of the Wolf: Returning the Wild to Yellowstone, 2005; (contrib.) America's Parks, 2006; Nature's Keeper, 2012; The Carry Home, forthcoming. Contributor to magazines and newspapers. **Address:** c/o Anita Anderson, 1161 Rhode Island St., San Francisco, CA 94107, U.S.A. **Online address:** ferguson@wildwords.net

FERGUSON, Gillian. See HEAL, Gillian.

FERGUSON, Kathy E. American (born United States), b. 1950. **Genres:** Women's Studies And Issues, Politics/Government. **Career:** State University of New York, Department of Political Science and Women's Studies Program, adjunct professor, 1979-85; Siena College, Department of Political Science, head, 1983-85, Women and Minority Studies, coordinator, 1984-85; Institute

for Advanced Studies, visiting professor, 1985; University of Hawaii, Department of Political Science and Women's Studies, visiting professor, 1985-87, professor, 1992-, department chair, 1994-97, Summer Institute for Semiotics and Structural Studies, faculty, 1991, Women's Studies Program, director, 2001-05; University of Goteborg, Peace and Development Studies, visiting professor, 2000. Writer. **Publications:** Self, Society, and Womankind: The Dialectic of Liberation, 1980; The Feminist Case against Bureaucracy, 1984; The Man Question: Visions of Subjectivity in Feminist Theory, 1993; Kibbutz Journal: Reflections on Gender, Race and Militarism in Israel, 1995; (with P. Turnbull) Oh, Say Can You See? The Semiotics of the Military in Hawai'i, 1999; (ed. with M. Mironesco) Gender and Globalization in Asia and the Pacific: Method, Practice, Theory, 2008; A Resource Guide About Dyslexia for People in Hawai'i, 2008; Emma Goldman: Political Thinking in the Streets, 2011. **Address:** Department of Political Science and, Women's Studies Program, University of Hawaii, 640 Saunders Hall, Honolulu, HI 96822, U.S.A. **Online address:** kferguso@hawaii.edu

FERGUSON, Kitty. American (born United States), b. 1941. **Genres:** Novels, Adult Non-fiction. **Career:** Community Presbyterian Church, music director, 1974-77; Chester Ensemble, music director and founder, 1975-80; Brookside Community Church, music director, 1977-82; Liberty Corner Presbyterian Church, music director, 1982-86; Episcopal Diocese of Newark, John Elbridge Hines lecturer in science and religion, 1994; St. Peter's Episcopal Church, St. Peter's Kothapallimitta Companionship, coordinator, 2000. Writer. **Publications:** Black Holes in Spacetime, 1991; Stephen Hawking: Quest for a Theory of the Universe, 1991; Steven Hawking: Quest for a Theory of Everything, 1992; The Fire in the Equations, 1994 in US as The Fire in the Equations: Science, Religion, and The Search for God, 1995; Prisons of Light: Black Holes, 1996; Measuring the Universe: Our Historic Quest to Chart the Horizons of Space and Time, 1999; Tycho and Kepler: The Unlikely Partnership That Forever Changed Our Understanding of the Heavens, 2002; The Nobleman and His Housedog: Tycho Brahe and Johannes Kepler: The Strange Partnership that Revolutionised Science, 2002; Music of Pythagoras: How an Ancient Brotherhood Cracked the Code of the Universe and Lit the Path from Antiquity to Outer Space, 2008; Stephen Hawking: An Unfettered Mind, 2012. **Address:** c/o Rita Rosenkranz, Rita Rosenkranz Literary Agency, 440 W End Ave., Ste. 15D, New York, NY 10024-5358, U.S.A. **Online address:** contact@kitty-ferguson.com

FERGUSON, Mark W. J. British/Irish (born Ireland), b. 1955. **Genres:** Biology, Medicine/Health, Natural History, Zoology. **Career:** Queen's University of Belfast, lecturer in anatomy, 1978-84; University of Southern California, research fellow, 1981; Victoria University of Manchester, professor of biological sciences, 1984-, Department of Cell and Structural Biology, head, 1986-92, School of Biological Sciences, dean, 1994-96; Renovo Group plc., co-founder, 2000-, chief executve officer; International Union for the Conservation of Nature, vice-chair; Craniofacial Society of Great Britain and Ireland, president; Royal College of Surgeons in Ireland, fellow; Zoological Society, fellow. Writer. **Publications:** (Ed.) The Structure, Development and Evolution of Reptiles, 1984; (co-author) Alligators and Crocodiles: An Illustrated Encyclopedic Account by International Experts, 1990; (with A. Huddart) Cleft Lip and Palate: Long Term Results and Future Prospects, 1991. EDITOR: (with D.C. Deeming) Egg Incubation: Its Effects on Embryonic Development in Birds and Reptiles, 1992; (co-ed.) Gray's Anatomy, 38th ed., 1996; (with M.F. Teaford and M.M. Smith) Development, Function and Evolution of Teeth, 2000. **Address:** Faculty of Life Sciences, University of Manchester, 3.239 Stopford Bldg., Oxford Rd., Manchester, GM M13 9PT, England. **Online address:** mark.w.ferguson@manchester.ac.uk

FERGUSON, R. Brian. American (born United States), b. 1951. **Genres:** Anthropology/Ethnology, Bibliography. **Career:** Drew University, lecturer, 1977; City University of New York, Hunter College, lecturer, 1980, John Jay College of Criminal Justice, lecturer, 1982-83; Rutgers University, instructor, 1983-85, assistant professor, 1985-91, associate professor, 1991-99, professor of anthropology, 1999-. Writer. **Publications:** (With L.E. Farragher) The Anthropology of War: A Bibliography, 1988; Yanomami Warfare: A Political History, 1995. EDITOR: Warfare, Culture, and Environment, 1984; (with N.L. Whitehead) War in the Tribal Zone: Expanding States and Indigenous Warfare, 1992; The State, Identity and Violence: Political Disintegration in the Post Cold War World, 2003. Contributor of articles to books, journals and magazines. **Address:** Department of Sociology & Anthropology, Rutgers

University, Rm. 619, Hill Hall, Newark, NJ 07102-1897, U.S.A. **Online address:** bfergusn@andromeda.rutgers.edu

FERGUSON, Robert (Thomas). British (born England), b. 1948. **Genres:** Biography, History, Novels, Plays/Screenplays, Translations. **Career:** Writer. **Publications:** Best Radio Drama 1984, 1985; Best Radio Drama 1986, 1987; Enigma: The Life of Knut Hamsun, 1987; Henry Miller: A Life, 1991; Henrik Ibsen: A New Biography, 1996; (trans.) Knut Hamsun, Tales of Love and Loss, 1997; Dr. Ibsens Gjengangere (play) 1999; Siste kjaerlighet (novel), 2002; The Short Sharp Life of T.E. Hulme, 2002; (novel) Fleetwood, 2004; Respekt (play), 2005; (trans.) Said About Ibsen, 2006; (History) The Hammer and the Cross: A New History of the Vikings, 2009; (trans.) Knut Hamsun, The Ring Is Closed, 2010. **Address:** Trudvangveien 25, Oslo, 0363, Norway. **Online address:** r-ferguson@hotmail.com

FERGUSON, Ron. Scottish (born Scotland), b. 1939. **Genres:** Novels, Sports/Fitness, Technology, Theology/Religion, Autobiography/Memoirs, Biography, History, Young Adult Fiction, Young Adult Fiction. **Career:** Church of Scotland, minister; Iona Abbey, deputy warden, 1980-81; Iona Community, leader, 1981-88; writer, 1988-; St. Magnus Cathedral, minister, 1990-2001; The Herald, columnist. Journalist. **Publications:** The Writing on the Wall, 1978; Geoff: The Life of Geoffrey M. Shaw: A Biography, 1979; Grace and Dysentery, 1986; Chasing the Wild Goose: The Story of the Iona Community, 1988, rev. ed., 1998; George MacLeod: Founder of the Iona Community, 1990; Black Diamonds and the Blue Brazil, 1993; Technology at the Cross Roads, 1994; Love Your Crooked Neighbor, 1999; Donald Dewar Ate My Hamster!, 1999; Hitler was a Vegetarian, 2001; Fear and Loathing in Lochgelly, 2002; The Reluctant Reformation of Clarence McGonigall, 2003; George Mackay Brown: The Wound and the Gift, 2011. **Address:** Vinbreck, Orphir, OK KW17 2RE, Scotland. **Online address:** ronferguson@clara.co.uk

FERGUSON, Sarah (Margaret). British (born England), b. 1959. **Genres:** Children's Fiction, Children's Non-fiction, Novels, Picture/Board Books. **Career:** Writer, 1973-; Children in Crisis (humanitarian group), founder, 1993; Sarah Foundation, chief executive officer, 2006-. **Publications:** AS SARAH, DUCHESS OF YORK: Budgie the Little Helicopter, 1989; Budgie at Bendick's Point, 1989; Budgie Goes to Sea, 1991; Budgie and the Blizzard, 1991; (with B. Stoney) Victoria and Albert: Life at Osborne House, 1991; The Adventures of Budgie (children's fiction), 1992; Travels with Queen Victoria, 1993; Bright Lights, 1996; The Royal Switch, 1996; (with J. Coplon) My Story, 1996; Budgie and Pippa Count to Ten!, 1996; Budgie to the Rescue, 1996; Budgie's Book of Colors, 1996; Budgie's Busy Day, 1996; Dieting with the Duchess: Secrets & Sensible Advice for a Great Body, 1998; Dining with the Duchess: Making Everyday Meals a Special Occasion, 1998; Win the Weight Game: Successful Strategies for Living Well, 2000; Reinventing Yourself with the Duchess of York: Inspiring Stories and Strategies for Changing Your Weight and Your Life, 2001; Little Red, 2003; Moments: Reflections in Words and Pictures, 2003; Energy Breakthrough: Jump-start Your Weight Loss and Feel Great, 2003; What I Know Now: Simple Lessons Learned the Hard Way, 2003; Little Red's Christmas Story, 2004; Energy Secrets: The Ultimate Well Being Plan, 2005; Little Red's Summer Adventure, 2006; Hartmoor, 2008; Little Red to the Rescue, 2008; (foreword) Eating Disorders: A Guide for Families and Children, 2008; Tea for Ruby, 2008; Little Red's Autumn Adventure, 2009; Michael and His New Baby Brother, 2010; Every Mother's Heart, 2010; Ashley Learns About Strangers, 2010; Emily's First Day of School, 2010; Matthew and the Bullies, 2010; Jacob Goes to the Doctor and Sophie Visits the Dentist, 2011; Molly Makes Friends, 2011; Olivia Says Goodbye to Grandpa, 2011; When Katie's Parents Separated, 2011; Zach Gets Some Exercise, 2011; Finding Sarah: A Duchess's Journey to Find Herself, 2011; Get Well Soon, Adam, 2011; Lauren's Moving Day, 2011; Healthy Food for Dylan, 2011; Ballerina Rosie, 2012. Contributor to books and periodicals. **Address:** Department of Publicity, Simon & Schuster Inc., 1230 Ave. of the Americas, 11th Fl., New York, NY 10020-1586, U.S.A.

FERGUSON, Will. Canadian (born Canada), b. 1964. **Genres:** Adult Non-fiction, Novels, Autobiography/Memoirs, Young Adult Fiction, Travel/Exploration, Humor/Satire. **Career:** Writer and syndicated columnist. **Publications:** Why I Hate Canadians, 1997; The Hitchhiker's Guide to Japan, 1997; Hokkaido Highway Blues: Hitchhiking Japan, 1998 in US as Hitching Rides with Buddha, 2005; I Was A Teenage Katima-Victim: A Canadian Odyssey, 1998; Bastards & Boneheads: Canada's Glorious Leaders, Past and Present, 1999; (with T. Dickerson and B. Spencer) The Girlfriend's Guide to Hockey, 1999, new ed., 2007; Canadian History for Dummies, 2000, 2nd ed., 2005;

Generica: A Novel, 2001; (with I. Ferguson) How to Be A Canadian: Even If You Already Are One, 2001; Happiness, 2001; Beauty Tips from Moose Jaw: Travels in Search of Canada, 2004; (ed. and intro.) The Penguin Anthology of Canadian Humour, 2006; Spanish Fly, 2007; Beyond Belfast, 2009; Coal Dust Kisses: A Christmas Memoir, 2010; Canadian Pie, 2011. **Address:** Penguin Canada, 90 Eglinton Ave. E, Ste. 700, Toronto, ON M4P 2Y3, Canada.

FERLING, John E. American (born United States), b. 1940. **Genres:** History, Bibliography, Biography, Military/Defense/Arms Control. **Career:** Morehead State University, assistant professor of history, 1965-68; West Chester State University, associate professor of history, 1970-71; University of West Georgia, Department of History, professor of history, 1971-2004, professor emeritus, 2004-. Writer and historian. **Publications:** The Loyalist Mind: Joseph Galloway and the American Revolution, 1977; A Wilderness of Miseries: War and Warriors in Early America, 1980; The First of Men: A Life of George Washington, 1988; (ed.) World Turned Upside Down: The American Victory in the War of Independence, 1988; John Adams: A Life, 1992; Struggle for a Continent: The Wars of Early America, 1993; (comp.) John Adams: A Bibliography, 1994; Setting the World Ablaze: Washington, Adams, Jefferson, and the American Revolution, 2000; A Leap in the Dark: The Struggle to Create the American Republic, 2003; Adams vs. Jefferson: The Tumultuous Election of 1800, 2004; Almost a Miracle: The American Victory in the War of Independence, 2007; The Ascent of George Washington: The Hidden Political Genius of an American Icon, 2009; Independence: The Struggle to Set America Free, 2011. Contributor to periodicals. **Address:** Department of History, University of West Georgia, 3200 Technology Learning Ctr., Carrollton, GA 30118, U.S.A. **Online address:** jferling@westga.edu

FERLINGHETTI, Lawrence. American (born United States), b. 1919. **Genres:** Novels, Plays/Screenplays, Poetry, Art/Art History, Translations, History, Young Adult Fiction. **Career:** City Lights Pocket Bookshop (now City Lights Books), co-owner and co-founder, 1953-, City Lights Publishing, founder, publisher and editor, 1955-; Time Magazine, staff. **Publications:** Pictures of the Gone World, 1955, 2nd ed., 1995; A Coney Island of the Mind, 1958; (trans.) J. Prevert, Selections from Paroles, 1958; Tentative Description of a Dinner Given to Promote the Impeachment of President Eisenhower, 1958; (ed.) Beatitude Anthology, 1960; Her (novel), 1960; One Thousand Fearful Words for Fidel Castro, 1961; Berlin, 1961; Starting from San Francisco: Poems, 1961; (with J. Spicer) Dear Ferlinghetti, 1962; Unfair Arguments with Existence: Seven Plays for a New Theatre, 1963; (with G. Corso and A. Ginsberg) Penguin Modern Poets 5, 1963; Thoughts to a Concerto of Telemann, 1963; Routines (play and short pieces), 1964; Where Is Vietnam?, 1965; An Eye on the World: Selected Poems, 1967; Ord om Vietnam, 1967; After the Cries of the Birds, 1967; Moscow in the Wilderness, Segovia in the Snow, 1967; Reverie Smoking Grass, 1968; Two Scavengers in a Truck, Two Beautiful People in a Mercedes, 1968; (ed.) Hunk of Skin, 1969; (ed.) Panic Grass, 1969; The Secret Meaning of Things, 1969; Tyrannus Nix?, 1969; The Mexican Night: Travel Journal, 1970; Back roads to far towns after Bashō, 1970; Back Roads to Far Places, 1971; Love Is No Stone on the Moon, 1971; Illustrated Wilfred Funk, 1971; World Awash with Fascism & Fear, 1971; Open Eye, Open Heart, 1973; (ed.) City Lights Anthology, 1974; Director of Alienation, 1976; Who Are We Now?, 1976; Political Pamphlet, 1976; Howl of the Censor, 1976; Northwest Ecology, 1978; Landscapes of Living and Dying, 1979; (with N.J. Peters) Literary San Francisco, 1980; Mule Mountain Dreams, 1980; Endless Life: Selected Poems, 1981; A Trip to Italy and France, 1981; The Populist Manifestos, 1981; Leaves of Life, 1983; Seven Days in Nicaragua Libre, 1984; Over all the Obscene Boundaries: European Poems and Transitions, 1984; Antipoems: New and Selected, 1985; (trans. with F. Valente) P.P. Pasolini, Roman Poems, 1986; Inside the Trojan Horse, 1987; Love in the Days of Rage (novel), 1988; Wild Dreams of a New Beginning, 1988; When I Look at Pictures (poems and paintings), 1990; These Are My Rivers: New and Selected Poems, 1955-1993, 1993; The Canticle of Jack Kerouac, 1993; A Buddha in the Woodpile, 1993; The Cool Eye, 1993; (ed.) City Lights Pocket Poets Anthology, 1995; A Far Rockaway of the Heart: New Poems, 1997; (contrib.) Don't Let that Horse, 1998; What is Poetry?, 2000; Luna Park Del Cuore, 2000; How to Paint Sunlight, 2001; San Francisco Poems, 2001; Life Studies, Life Stories: Drawings, 2003; (with S. Peek) Back Roads to Far Places after Basho, 2003; Americus: Book I, 2004; At La Puerta Escondida, 2005; Mr. Ferlinghetti's Poem, 2006; Poetry as Insurgent Art, 2007. Contributor to books and periodicals. **Address:** City Lights Books, 261 Columbus Ave. at Broadway, San Francisco, CA 94133-4519, U.S.A.

FERLITA, Ernest. (Ernest (Charles) Ferlita). American (born United States),

b. 1927. **Genres:** Plays/Screenplays, Songs/Lyrics And Libretti, Film, Theatre, Theology/Religion, Translations. **Career:** Jesuit priest, 1962-; Loyola University, professor of drama and speech, 1969-, now professor emeritus, chairman, 1970-88. Writer. **Publications:** The Theatre of Pilgrimage, 1971; (with J.R. May) Film Odyssey, 1976; The Way of the River, 1977; (with J.R. May) The Parables of Lina Wertmuller, 1977; (trans.) The Spiritual Marriage of the Shepherd Peter and the Mexican Church, 1977; Quetzal, 1979; (co-author) Religion in Film, 1982; Gospel Journey: Forty Meditations Drawn from the Life of Christ, 1983; Introduction to Poems of Gerard Manley Hopkins, 1986; The Uttermost Mark: The Dramatic Criticism of Gerard Manley Hopkins, 1990; Performance: Hopkins' Sine Qua Non (essay), 1991; The Paths of Life: Cycle A, 1992; Cycle B, 1993; Cycle C, 1994; A Third Remove: Hopkins and St. Patrick (essay), 1996; The Road to Bethlehem: The Use of the Imagination in the Spiritual Exercises (essay), 1997; The Playwright as Theologian Confronting Evil (essay), 1997; Advent/Christmas Season, 1999; In the light of the Lord: Weekday Reflections for Lent and Easter, 2003. **Address:** Jesuit Community, Loyola University, 6363 St. Charles Ave., PO Box 214, New Orleans, LA 70118-6153, U.S.A. **Online address:** ferlita@loyno.edu

FERLITA, Ernest (Charles). *See* FERLITA, Ernest.

FERMI, Rachel. American (born United States), b. 1964. **Genres:** Photography. **Career:** Camden County College, assistant professor of photography, 1990-; Pasadena City College, instructor. Writer. **Publications:** (With E. Samra) Picturing the Bomb: Photographs from the Secret World of the Manhattan Project, 1995. **Address:** Pasadena City College, Visual Arts & Media Studies - T102, 1570 E Colorado Blvd., Pasadena, CA 91106, U.S.A. **Online address:** rf215@uswest.net

FERMINE, Maxence. French (born France), b. 1968. **Genres:** Poetry, Novels. **Career:** Alps Magazine, reporter, 2010-. Author and poet. **Publications:** Le Violon Noir, 1999; Neige, 1999; L'apiculteur, 2000; (with O. Besson) Sagesses et malices de Confucius, le roi sans royaume, 2001; Opium, 2002; Il violino nero, 2003; Billiard Blues: suivi de Jazz blanc et Poker, 2003; Tango massaï, 2005; Labyrinthe du temps, 2006; Tombeau d'étoiles, 2007; Les Carnets de Guerre de Victorien Mars: Roman, 2008; Le Papillon de Siam: Roman, 2010; Rhum Caraibes, 2011. **Address:** c/o Author Mail, Atria Books, Simon and Schuster, 1230 Ave. of the Americas, New York, NY 10020, U.S.A.

FERMOR, Patrick (Michael) Leigh. *See* Obituaries.

FERNÁNDEZ-ARMESTO, Felipe (Fermin Ricardo). British (born England), b. 1950. **Genres:** History, Travel/Exploration, Biography. **Career:** University College, part-time lecturer, 1975-76; Charter House, Surrey, master, 1976-81; Warwick University, Coventry, visiting lecturer, 1981-82; Oxford University, St. Antony's College, fellow and director of Iberian studies, 1981-90, faculty of modern history, 1983-2005; University of Warwick, lecturer, 1982-83, visiting senior lecturer, 1984-86, visiting professor, 1990-91; Brown University, National Endowment for the Humanities Summer Institute, visiting professor, 1992; John Carter Brown Library, Andrew W. Mellon senior visiting research fellow, 1997-98; Queen Mary, University of London, professor of history and geography, 2000-05, professor of global environmental history, 2003-05, Institute of Historical Research, director, 2003-05, visiting professor, 2005-09; Tufts University, Prince of Asturias professor, 2005-09; University of Notre Dame, Department of History, William P. Reynolds professor of history, 2009-. Writer. **Publications:** Columbus and the Conquest of the Impossible, 1974, rev. ed., 2000; Ferdinand and Isabella, 1975; Sadat and His Statecraft, 1982; The Canary Islands After the Conquest: The Making of a Clonial Society in the Early Sixteenth Century, 1982; Before Columbus: Exploration and Colonization from the Mediterranean to the Atlantic, 1229-1492, 1987; Spanish Armada: The Experience of War in 1588, 1988; Colombus, 1991; (intro.) Edward Gibbon's Atlas of the World, 1991; (ed.) The Times Atlas of World Exploration: 3000 Years of Exploring, Explorers and Map making, 1991; Barcelona: A Thousand Years of the City's Past, 1992; Antes de Colón: Exploración y colonización desde el Mediterraneo hacia el Atlántico, 1229-1492, 1993; (ed.) The Times Guide to the Peoples of Europe, 1994; (co-author) Canarias e Inglaterra através de la historia, 1995; (ed.) European Opportunity, 1995; Millennium: A History of the Last Thousand Years, 1995; (ed.) Global Opportunity, 1995; Truth: A History, 1997; (with D. Wilson) Reformations: A Radical Interpretation of Christianity and the World, 1500-2000, 1997; Religion, 1997; Truth: A History and a Guide for the Perplexed, 1999; Civilizations: Culture, Ambition and the Transformation of Nature, 2001; Near a Thousand Tables: A History of Food, 2002; Food: A

History, 2002; Americas: A Hemispheric History, 2003; Americas: The History of a Hemisphere, 2003; (ed. with L. Blussé) Shifting Communities and Identity Formation in Early Modern Asia, 2003; (contrib.) World of Myths, 2003; Ideas that Changed the World, 2003; Humankind: A Brief History, 2004; So You Think You're Human?: A Brief History of Humankind, 2004; Pathfinders: A Global History of Exploration, 2006; Amerigo: The Man Who Gave His Name to America, 2007; The World: A History, 2007; The World: A Brief History, 2008; (ed. with J. Muldoon) Internal Colonization in Medieval Europe, 2008; (ed. with J. Muldoon) The Medieval Frontiers of Latin Christendom: Expansion, Contraction, Continuity, 2008; 1492: The Year the Four Corners of the Earth Collided, 2009; World: A History: Combined Volume, 2010; Columbus on Himself, 2010; (with M. Restall) Conquistadors: A Very Short Introduction, 2011. Contributor to periodicals and journals. **Address:** c/o Bruce Hunter, 5-8 Lower John St., Golden Sq., London, GL W1F 9HA, England. **Online address:** felipe.fernandez-armesto@nd.edu

FERNANDEZ-SHAW, Carlos M(anuel). Spanish (born Spain), b. 1924. **Genres:** Cultural/Ethnic Topics, Music, History, Adult Non-fiction. **Career:** University of Madrid, assistant lecturer in public international law, 1949-51; Institute of Spanish Culture, Department of Cultural Exchange, head, 1956-58; Spanish Diplomatic Service, Ministry of Foreign Affairs, 1949-51; Department of Institutions and Publications, Cultural Affairs Division, assistant secretary of Madrid, 1970-73, ambassador to Paraguay, 1973-81; inspector general, 1983-85. Writer. **Publications:** Presencia Española en los Estados Unidos, 1972, 3rd ed., 1992; The Spanish Contributions to the Independence of the U.S.A., 1976; Ventura y tribulaciones de un padre recién Estrenado, 1976; Los Estados Independientes de Norteamérica, 1977; El Primer Consul de Espana en Australia: Antonio Arrom, 1988; La Florida Contemporánea: Siglos XIX y XX, 1992; El arpa en el contexto musical del Paraguay, 1992; Hispanic Presence in North America from 1492 to Today, 1991; Espana y Australia: Cinco Siglos de Historia, 2000; España y Australia: Quinientos años de relaciones, 2001. **Address:** Claudio Coello 60, Madrid, 28001, Spain.

FERNER, Mike. American (born United States), b. 1951?. **Genres:** Novels. **Career:** Journalist and writer. **Publications:** Inside the Red Zone: A Veteran for Peace Reports from Iraq, 2006. **Address:** Greenwood Publishing Group Inc., 88 Post Rd. W, Westport, CT 06880-4208, U.S.A. **Online address:** info@mikeferner.org

FERNYHOUGH, Charles. British (born England), b. 1968. **Genres:** Novels. **Career:** Durham University, Department of Psychology, developmental psychologist, part-time, lecturer, 1999-2001, 2002-07, senior lecturer, 2007-10, reader, 2010-, Wolfson Research Institute, fellow, 2008-, Centre for Medical Humanitie, affiliate, 2009-; Staffordshire University, lecturer, 1994-97; University of East Anglia, faculty; Newcastle University, faculty. Writer. **Publications:** The Auctioneer (novel), 1999; (ed. with P. Lloyd) Lev Vygotsky: Critical Assessments, 1999; The Baby in the Mirror: A Child's World from Birth to Three, 2008 in US as A Thousand Days of Wonder: A Scientist's Chronicle of His Daughter's Developing Mind, 2009; (ed. with A. Winsler and I. Montero) Private Speech, Executive Functioning and the Development of Verbal Self-regulation, 2009. Works appear in anthologies. Contributor to journals. **Address:** David Grossman Literary Agency Ltd.,, 118b Holland Park Ave., London, GL W11 4UA, England. **Online address:** author@charlesfernyhough.com

FERRARA, Nadia. Canadian (born Canada), b. 1967. **Genres:** Psychology. **Career:** McGill University, adjunct professor of anthropology; Government of Canada, staff, 2003-, Sustainable Development Division, Department of Indian and Northern Affairs, manager, senior policy manager; Jewish General Hospital, researcher. Writer and anthropologist. **Publications:** Emotional Expression among Cree Indians: The Role of Pictorial Representations in the Assessment of Psychological Mindedness, 1999; Healing through Art: Ritualized Space and Cree Identity, 2004. **Address:** McGill University, Rm. 718, Leacock Bldg., 845 Sherbrooke St. W, Montreal, QC H3A 2T7, Canada. **Online address:** ferraran@ainc-inac.gc.ca

FERRARI, Mark J. American (born United States), b. 1956. **Genres:** Novels. **Career:** Writer, artist and illustrator. **Publications:** The Book of Joby, 2007. **Address:** Tor Books, 175 5th Ave., New York, NY 10010, U.S.A. **Online address:** mferrari@mcn.org

FERRARI, R(onald) L(eslie). British (born England), b. 1930. **Genres:** Engineering, Sciences. **Career:** GEC Ltd., Hirst Research Centre, research officer, 1956-65; Cambridge University, lecturer in engineering, 1965-90, Trinity College, fellow of engineering and director of studies in engineering, 1966-; Cornell University, visiting professor, 1964-65; McGill University, visiting professor, 1972-73; Netherhall School, governor, 1986-90. Writer. **Publications:** (Ed. with A.K. Jonscher) Problems in Physical Electronics, 1973; Introduction to Electromagnetic Fields, 1975; (with P.P. Silvester) Finite Elements for Electrical Engineers, 1983, 3rd ed., 1996. **Address:** Trinity College, Cambridge University, Cambridge, CB CB2 1TQ, England. **Online address:** rlf1@cam.ac.uk

FERRARIS, Zoë. American (born United States), b. 1970?. **Genres:** Novels. **Career:** Writer, educator and proofreader. **Publications:** Finding Nouf (novel), 2008 in UK as The Night of the Mi'raj, 2008. **Address:** c/o Julie Barer, 270 Lafayette St., Ste. 1504, New York, NY 10012-3327, U.S.A. **Online address:** contact@zoeferraris.com

FERRARO, Barbara. American (born United States), b. 1943. **Genres:** Women's Studies And Issues, Adult Non-fiction. **Career:** Parish minister and teacher, 1966-81; Covenant House, co-director, 1981-. Writer. **Publications:** The Inside Stories: Thirteen Valiant Women Challenging the Church, 1987; (with P. Hussey and J. O'Reilly) No Turning Back: Two Nuns' Battle with the Vatican over Women's Right to Choose, 1990. **Address:** Covenant House, 600 Shrewsbury St., Charleston, WV 25301-1211, U.S.A. **Online address:** bferraro@wvcovenanthouse.org

FERRARO, Susan (Lyons). American (born United States), b. 1946. **Genres:** Romance/Historical, Literary Criticism And History, Young Adult Fiction. **Career:** New York Daily News, staff writer; State University of New York College, teacher in literature and journalism; Marymount College, teacher; College of New Rochelle, teacher. **Publications:** Remembrance of Things Fast, 1990; Responsible Writing, 1994; Sweet Talk: The Language of Love, 1995. Contributor to periodicals. Works appear in anthologies. **Address:** c/o Molly Friedrich, Aaron M. Priest Literary Agency, 708 3rd Ave., 23rd Fl., New York, NY 10017-4201, U.S.A.

FERRÉ, Frederick. American/German (born Germany), b. 1933. **Genres:** Philosophy, Theology/Religion. **Career:** Oberlin College, faculty, 1950-51; Vanderbilt University, visiting assistant professor of philosophy, 1958-59, College of Arts and Sciences, visiting professor of philosophy, 1977-78, School of Engineering, visiting professor of technology and public policy; Mount Holyoke College, assistant professor of religion, 1959-62; Dickinson College, associate professor of philosophy, 1962-67, professor of philosophy, 1967-70, Charles A. Dana professor of philosophy, 1970-80; Southern Methodist University, Graduate Council for the Humanities, visiting associate professor of philosophy and fellow, 1964-65; Purdue University, Eli Lily Visiting Professor of Science, Theology and Human Values, 1974-75; University of Georgia, Department of Philosophy and Religion, professor and head, 1980-84, Department of Philosophy, professor of philosophy and head, 1984-88, Faculty of Environmental Ethics, chair, 1984-91, research professor of philosophy, 1988-98, professor emeritus of philosophy, 1998-. Writer. **Publications:** Language, Logic, and God, 1961; (with K. Bendall) Exploring the Logic of Faith: A Dialogue on the Relation of Modern Philosophy to Christian Faith, 1962; (ed.) William Paley's Natural Theology, 1963; Basic Modern Philosophy of Religion, 1967; (ed., trans. and intro.) Auguste Comte, Introduction to Positive Philosophy, 1970; Shaping the Future: Resources for the Post-Modern World, 1976; (ed. with J.J. Kockelmans and J.E. Smith) The Challenge of Religion: Contemporary Readings in Philosophy of Religion, 1982; (ed. with R.H. Mataragnon) God and Global Justice: Religion and Poverty in an Unequal World, 1985; Philosophy of Technology, 1988; (ed.) Concepts of Nature and God: Resources for College and University Teaching: Philosophy Curriculum Workshop Papers Developed at the 1987 NEH Summer Institute on Concepts of Nature and God, 1989; Hellfire and Lightning Rods: Liberating Science, Technology and Religion, 1993; (ed. with P. Hartel) Ethics and Environmental Policy: Theory Meets Practice, 1994; Being and Value: Toward a Constructive Postmodern Metaphysics, 1996; Knowing and Value: Toward a Constructive Postmodern Epistemology, 1998; Living and Value: Toward a Constructive Postmodern Ethics, 2001. CONTRIBUTOR: Masterpieces of Christian Literature, vol. II, 1963; America and the Future of Theology, 1967; Philosophical Resources for Christian Thought, 1968; Science and Religion: New Perspective on the Dialogue, 1968; Philosophy and Religion: Some Contemporary Perspectives, 1968; New Essays on Religious Language, 1969; Earth Might Be Fair: Reflections on Ethics, Religion and Ecology, 1972; Dictionary of the History of Ideas, 1973; The

Centrality of Science and Absolute Values, 1975; The Nature of Scientific Discovery: A Symposium Commemorating the 500-Anniversary of the Birth of Nicolaus Copernicus, 1975; Philosophy and Contemporary Issues, 1976; Marriage-Divorce: A Humanistic Perspective, 1978; The Early College in Theory and Practice, 1978; The Humanities and the Energy Issue, 1980; The Philosophy of Brand Blanshared, 1980; Experience, Reason and God, 1980; Metaphor and Religion: Theolinguistics 2, 1983; Physics and the Ultimate Significance of Time, 1986; Religion and Environmental Crisis, 1986; The Encyclopedia of Religion, 1987; Religion and Philosophy in the United States of America, 1987; God in Language, 1987; Erinnern um Neues Zu Sagen, Die Bedeutung der Metapher fuer die religioese Sprache, 1988; The Reenchantment of Science, 1988; Human Ecology: Research and Applications, 1988; Spirituality and Society: Postmodern Visions, 1988; Christian Spirituality, 1988; Life World and Technology, 1990; Broad and Narrow Interpretations of Philosophy of Technology, 1990; Individuality and Cooperative Action, 1991; L'Etica Nelle Politiche Ambientali, 1991; Contemporary Classics in Philosophy of Religion, 1991; A New Handbook of Christian theology, 1992; Prospects for Natural Theology, 1992; Great Thinkers of the Western World, 1992; Empirical Theology: A Handbook, 1992; The Bill of Rights: Bicentennial Reflections, 1993; Ethics and Environmental Policies, 1993; Principles of Conservation Biology, 1994; Science, Technology and Religious Ideas, 1994; Agricultural Ethics: Issues for the 21st Century, 1994; Etica Ambientale: Teoria e Pratica, 1994; Philosophy and the Natural Environment, 1994; Philosophy, Humanity and Ecology, 1994; The Social Power of Ideas, 1995; Religious Experience and Ecological Responsibility, 1996; A Companion to Philosophy of Religion, 1997; Environmental Ethics and the Global Marketplace, 1998; New Europe: Transformation and Environmental Issues, 1998; Dictionary of Literary Biography: British Philosophers, 1500-1799, 2001; On Human Nature: Anthropological, Biological and Philosophical Foundations, 2002; Encyclopedia of Global Environmental Change, 2002; Personalism Revisited: Its Proponents and Critics, 2002; Food for Thought: The Debate Over Eating Meat, 2004; Philosophy of Religion for a New Century, Essays in Honor of Eugene Thomas Long, 2004; Whitehead's Philosophy: Points of Connection, 2004; The Quest for Liberation and Reconciliation: Essays in Honor of J. Deotis Roberts, 2005; Nature, Truth and Value: Exploring the Thinking of Frederick Ferre, 2005; Researching with Whitehead: System and Adventure, 2008. **Address:** Department of Philosophy, University of Georgia, 107 Peabody Hall, Athens, GA 30602-1627, U.S.A. **Online address:** fferre@uga.edu

FERRE, John P. American (born United States), b. 1956. **Genres:** Communications/Media, Ethics, Theology/Religion. **Career:** Purdue University Calumet, visiting instructor in English and philosophy, 1979-80; University of Louisville, assistant professor, 1985-90, associate professor, 1990-98, professor of communication, 1998-, associate dean of arts and sciences, 2004-. Writer. **Publications:** Merrill Guide to the Research Paper, 1983; A Social Gospel for Millions: The Religious Bestsellers of Charles Sheldon, Charles Gordon, and Harold Bell Wright, 1988; (with S.C. Willihnganz) Public Relations and Ethics: A Bibliography, 1991; (with C.G. Christians and P.M. Fackler) Good News: Social Ethics and the Press, 1993. EDITOR: (with S.E. Pauley) Rhetorical Patterns: An Anthology of Contemporary Essays, 1981; (and contrib.) Channels of Belief: Religion and American Commercial Television, 1990. Work appear in anthologies. Contributor of articles to professional journals. **Address:** Department of Communication, University of Louisville, Louisville, KY 40292, U.S.A. **Online address:** ferre@louisville.edu

FERREE, Myra Marx. American (born United States), b. 1949. **Genres:** Sociology, Women's Studies And Issues. **Career:** Harvard University, consultant, 1973-74; Boston College, senior research associate, 1975-76; Tufts University, lecturer, 1976; University of Connecticut, assistant professor, associate professor, 1976-87, director, 1985-87, professor, 1987-91, professor of sociology and women's studies, 1991-2000; University of Wisconsin-Madison, professor of sociology, 2000-, European Union Center, director, 2002-03, Center for German and European Studies, director, 2004-08, 2009-11, Martindale-Bascom professor of sociology, 2006-. Writer. **Publications:** (With J. Gugler) Participation of Women in the Urban Labor Force and in Rural-Urban Migration in India, 1984; (with B.B. Hess) Controversy and Coalition: The New Feminist Movement, 1985, 3rd ed., 2000; (ed. with B.B. Hess) Analyzing Gender: A Handbook of Social Science Research, 1987; (ed. with P.Y. Martin) Feminist Organizations: Harvest of the New Women's Movement, 1995; (ed. with J. Lorber, B.B. Hess) Revisioning Gender, 1999; (co-author) Shaping Abortion Discourse: Democracy and the Public Sphere in Germany and the United States, 2002; (ed. with A.M. Tripp) Global Feminism: Transnational Women's Activism, Organizing, and Human Rights, 2006. **Address:** Department of Sociology, University of Wisconsin, 7103 Social Sciences Bldg., 1180 Observatory Dr., Madison, WI 53706, U.S.A. **Online address:** mferree@ssc.wisc.edu

FERREIRO, Alberto. American/Mexican (born Mexico), b. 1952. **Genres:** Bibliography, History, Essays. **Career:** Seattle Pacific University, professor of European history, 1986-; University of Sacramento, adjunct professor, 2006-; Anuario de Historia de la Iglesia, associate editor, reviewer; Indice Histórico Espanol, abstractor; Journal of Early Christian Studies, reviewer; Religious and Theological Abstracts, abstractor; Medieval Sermon Studies, associate editor, reviewer. **Publications:** The Visigoths in Gaul and Spain, A.D. 418-711: A Bibliography, 1988; (ed.) The Devil, Heresy, and Witchcraft in the Middle Ages: Essays in Honor of Jeffrey B. Russell, 1998; (ed.) The Visigoths: Studies in Culture and Society, 1999; (ed.) The Twelve Prophets, 2003; Simon Magus in Patristic, Medieval, and Early Modern Traditions, 2005; The Visigoths in Gaul and Iberia: A Supplemental Bibliography, 1984-2003, 2006; The Visigoths in Gaul and Iberia: A Supplemental Bibliography, 2004-2006, 2008. Contributor of articles to books and journals. **Address:** Department of History, Seattle Pacific University, 3307 3rd Ave. W, Seattle, WA 98119-1997, U.S.A. **Online address:** beto@spu.edu

FERREIRO, Carmen. (Carmen Ferreiro-Esteban). Spanish (born Spain), b. 1958. **Genres:** Young Adult Fiction, Science Fiction/Fantasy, Novels, Children's Fiction, Young Adult Non-fiction, Sciences, Biology, Medicine/Health, Medicine/Health. **Career:** University of California, Department of Animal Sciences, postdoctoral researcher, 1986-88, Department of Plant Pathology, researcher, 1988-90; Consejo Superior de Investigaciones Científicas, postdoctoral researcher, 1990-93; freelance writer and translator, 1999-. **Publications:** Heroin, 2003; Ritalin and Other Methylphenidate-containing Drugs, 2004; Mad Cow Disease (Bovine Spongiform Encephalopathies), 2005; Lung Cancer, 2007; (as Carmen Ferreiro-Esteban) Two Moon Princess, 2007; The King in the Stone, forthcoming. Contributor of articles to periodicals. **Address:** 315 Hedgerow Ln., Doylestown, PA 18901, U.S.A. **Online address:** carmenferreiro@aol.com

FERREIRO, Larrie D. American (born United States), b. 1958. **Genres:** Military/Defense/Arms Control, Technology, History, Adult Non-fiction, Engineering, Sciences. **Career:** Office of Naval Research, scientist; U.S. Coast Guard, risk systems engineer; U.S. Navy, naval architect; Catholic University of America, adjunct lecturer in systems engineering; Defense Acquisition University, professor of systems engineering and science and technology management. Writer and historian. **Publications:** The Technology of the Ships of Trafalgar, 2006; Ships and Science: The Birth of Naval Architecture in the Scientific Revolution, 1600-1800, 2007; Measure of the Earth: The Enlightenment Expedition that Reshaped Our World, 2011. Contributor to books. **Address:** Fairfax Station, VA , U.S.A. **Online address:** larrie.ferreiro@gmail.com

FERREIRO-ESTEBAN, Carmen. *See* **FERREIRO, Carmen.**

FERRELL, Carolyn. American (born United States), b. 1962. **Genres:** Novels, Literary Criticism And History, Young Adult Fiction. **Career:** Linsey Abram's Magazine, associate editor, 1993-94; Sarah Lawrence College, undergraduate faculty, 1996-; National Endowment for the Arts, literature fellow, 2004. **Publications:** Don't Erase Me: Stories, 1997. Contributor to periodicals. **Address:** Department of Writing/Fiction, Sarah Lawrence College, 1 Mead Way, Bronxville, NY 10708, U.S.A.

FERRELL, Jeff. American (born United States), b. 1954. **Genres:** Criminology/True Crime, Popular Culture, Sociology, Urban Studies, Adult Non-fiction. **Career:** University of Texas, instructor in sociology, 1979-82; Regis University, assistant professor, 1982-88, associate professor of sociology, 1988-95; Northern Arizona University, associate professor, 1995-97, professor of criminal justice, 1997-2001; Southern Methodist University, visiting professor of sociology, 2002-03; Texas Christian University, associate professor, 2003-05, professor of criminal justice, 2005-08, Department of Sociology and Anthropology, professor of sociology, 2008-; Crime, Media, Culture: An International Journal, founding editor, 2005-09, associate editor, 2010-; University of Kent, visiting professor of criminology, 2006-. **Publications:** NONFICTION: Crimes of Style: Urban Graffiti and the Politics of Criminality, 1993; (ed. with C.R. Sanders) Cultural Criminology, 1995; (ed. with M.S. Hamm) Ethnography at the Edge: Crime, Deviance, and Field Research,

1998; (ed. with N. Websdale) Making Trouble: Cultural Constructions of Crime, Deviance, and Control, 1999; Tearing Down the Streets: Adventures in Urban Anarchy, 2001, rev. ed., 2002; (co-ed.) Cultural Criminology Unleashed, 2004; Empire of Scrounge: Inside the Urban Underground of Dumpster Diving, Trash Picking, and Street Scavenging, 2006; (with K. Hayward and J. Young) Cultural Criminology: An Invitation, 2008; (ed. with K. Hayward) Cultural Criminology: Theories of Crime, 2011. Contributor to books and periodicals. **Address:** Department of Sociology & Anthropology, Texas Christian University, 2855 Main Dr., PO Box 298710, Fort Worth, TX 76109, U.S.A. **Online address:** j.ferrell@tcu.edu

FERRELL, John S. American (born United States) **Genres:** Information Science/Computers, Law. **Career:** Carr & Ferrell L.L.P., founding partner, Intellectual Property Practice Group, chair. Writer. **Publications:** Protecting Your Techknowledgy: The Entrepreneurs Guide to Patents, 2003; Inventors Notebook: The Perfect Place to Store Your Great Ideas, 2004; Patent Pro Se: The Entrepreneurs Guide to Filing Your Own Provisional Patent Application, 2004; Ferrell on Patents: Basic FAQs, 2005; Unfair Advantage: Five Strategies for Monopolizing Markets, forthcoming. **Address:** Carr & Ferrell L.L.P., 120 Constitution Dr., Menlo Park, CA 94025, U.S.A. **Online address:** jsferrell@carrferrell.com

FERRELL, Monica. American/Indian (born India), b. 1975?. **Genres:** Poetry. **Career:** Poet and novelist. **Publications:** The Answer Is Always Yes, 2008; Beasts for the Chase: Poems, 2008. **Address:** c/o Amanda Urban, International Creative Management, 825 8th Ave., New York, NY 10019-7416, U.S.A. **Online address:** monica@monicaferrell.com

FERRER, Elizabeth. American (born United States), b. 1955. **Genres:** Art/Art History, Young Adult Non-fiction, Photography. **Career:** South Street Seaport Museum, exhibitions coordinator, 1980-82; Brooklyn Educational and Cultural Alliance, research and educational programs director, 1982-83; Pictogram (contemporary art gallery), founder and director, 1984-86; Columbia University, curatorial consultant and administrator, 1987-89; America's Society, curator and exhibitions coordinator, 1989-94, director of visual arts department and curator of art gallery, 1994-97; Austin Museum of Art, director, 1997-2001; Independent curator, writer and consultant, 2001-07; BRIC Arts & Media, director of contemporary art, 2007-. Writer. **Publications:** (Co-ed.) Wifredo Lam: Works on Paper, 1992; A Shadow Born of Earth: New Photography in Mexico, 1993; (ed. with W. Rasmussen and F. Bercht) Latin American Artists of the Twentieth Century, 1993; (co-ed.) Space of Time: Contemporary Art in the Americas, 1993; (foreword) C. Puerto, A Selective Bibliography on Twentieth-Century Latin American Women Artists, 1996; (with O. Debroise and E. Poniatowska) The True Poetry: The Art of Maria Izquierdo, 1997; Ricardo Mazal: From Reality to Abstraction, 2004; Lola Alvarez Bravo, 2006; Realidades Refractadas: al otro lado de la lente, 2008; (with Y. Andrade) A través del cristal, 2008; American Voices: Chicano, Cuban and Puerto Rican Photography, forthcoming. Contributor of articles to periodicals. **Address:** BRIC Arts Media Bklyn, 647 Fulton St., Brooklyn, NY 11217, U.S.A. **Online address:** elizabeth_ferrer@yahoo.com

FERRIÈRES, Madeleine. French (born France) **Genres:** History, Food And Wine, Technology, Engineering, Sciences. **Career:** University of Avignon, professor of social history. Writer. **Publications:** Histoire des Peurs Alimentaires: du Moyen Âge à l'aube du XXe Siècle, 2002; Le Bien des Pauvres: La Consommation Populaire en Avignon, 1600-1800, 2004; Sacred Cow, Mad Cow: A History of Food Fears, 2006; Nourritures Canailles, 2007. **Address:** Université d'Avignon, 74 rue Louis Pasteur, Avignon, 84029, France.

FERRIGNO, Robert. American (born United States), b. 1947. **Genres:** Novels, Criminology/True Crime, Young Adult Fiction. **Career:** Orange County Register, feature writer, through 1988; California State University, instructor in journalism. **Publications:** NOVELS: The Horse Latitudes, 1990; The Cheshire Moon, 1993; Dead Man's Dance, 1995; Dead Silent, 1996; Heartbreaker, 1999; Visible Man, 2001; Flinch, 2001; Scavenger Hunt, 2003; Wake Up, 2004; Prayers for the Assassin: A Novel, 2006; Sins of the Assassin: A Novel, 2008; Heart of the Assassin: A Novel, 2009. Contributor to periodicals. **Address:** PO Box 934, Kirkland, WA 98083, U.S.A. **Online address:** talktorobert@comcast.net

FERRIS, Jean. American (born United States), b. 1939. **Genres:** Young Adult Fiction, Novels, How-to Books, Humor/Satire. **Career:** Veterans Administration Hospital, clinical audiologist, 1962-63, San Diego Speech and

Hearing Association, clinical audiologist, 1963-64; freelance writer, 1977-. **Publications:** YOUNG ADULT FICTION: Amen, Moses Gardenia, 1983; The Stainless Steel Rule, 1986; Invincible Summer, 1987; Looking for Home, 1989; Across the Grain, 1990; Relative Strangers, 1993; Signs of Life, 1995; All That Glitters, 1996; Into the Wind, 1996; Song of the Sea, 1996; Weather the Storm, 1996; Bad, 1998; Love among the Walnuts, 1998; Eight Seconds, 2000; Of Sound Mind, 2001; Once upon a Marigold, 2002; Much Ado About Grubstake, 2006; Underground, 2007; Twice Upon a Marigold, 2008; Taking Pictures, forthcoming; Music from the Moon, forthcoming; Why My Mother Is Green, forthcoming. **Address:** Farrar, Straus & Giroux, 175 5th Ave., Ste. 500, New York, NY 10010, U.S.A.

FERRIS, Jeri Chase. American (born United States), b. 1937. **Genres:** Children's Non-fiction, Biography, Adult Non-fiction, History. **Career:** Los Angeles Unified School District, teacher, 1967-93. Writer. **Publications:** Go Free or Die: A Story about Harriet Tubman, 1988; Walking the Road to Freedom: A Story about Sojourner Truth, 1988; What Are You Figuring Now?: A Story about Benjamin Banneker, 1988; What Do You Mean?: A Story about Noah Webster, 1988; Arctic Explorer: The Story of Matthew Henson, 1989; Native American Doctor: The Story of Susan LaFlesche Picotte, 1991; What I Had Was Singing: The Story of Marian Anderson, 1994; Thomas Jefferson: Father of Liberty, 1998; With Open Hands: A Story about Biddy Mason, 1999; Remember the Ladies: A Story about Abigail Adams, 2001; Demanding Justice: A Story about Mary Ann Shadd Cary, 2003; Noah Webster and His Words, 2012. Contributor to periodicals. **Address:** Lerner Publications, 241 1st Ave. N, Minneapolis, MN 55401, U.S.A. **Online address:** jchaseferris@sbcglobal.net

FERRIS, John (Stephen). British (born England), b. 1937. **Genres:** Environmental Sciences/Ecology, Social Sciences, Urban Studies, Sciences. **Career:** British Home Office, administrative officer, 1963-69; University of Nottingham, School of Sociology and Social Policy, lecturer in social studies, 1972-, associate lecturer and research associate; University of Bielefeld, research associate, 1988. Writer. **Publications:** Participation in Urban Planning- the Barnsbury Case: A Study of Environmental Improvement in London, 1972; Best Snakes for Kids: Proven and Tested by Mom and I, 2010. EDITOR: (with D. Whynes and P. Bean) In Defence of Welfare, 1985; (with R. Page) Social Policy in Transition: Anglo-German Perspectives, 1992; British Army and Signals Intelligence during the First World War, 1992; Realism in Green Politics: Social Movements and Ecological Reform in Germany, 1993; (with J. Machacek) The European City in the Nineteenth Century, 1995; (with M. Morris, C. Norman and J. Sempik and contrib.) People, Land and Sustainability, 2000; (with A. Thrush) The House of Commons, 1604-1629, 2010. Works appears in anthologies. Contributor to periodicals. **Address:** School of Social Studies, University of Nottingham, University Pk., Nottingham, NG7 2RD, England. **Online address:** john.ferris4@ntlworld.com

FERRIS, Joshua. American (born United States), b. 1974. **Genres:** Novels, Young Adult Fiction. **Career:** Davis Harrison Dion, advertising staff, 1998; Draft Worldwide, staff. Writer. **Publications:** Then We Came to the End: A Novel, 2007; The Unnamed: A Novel, 2010. Contributor to periodicals. Works appear in anthologies. **Address:** c/o Julie Barer, Barer Literary L.L.C., 270 Lafayette St., New York, NY 10012, U.S.A. **Online address:** ferris.joshua@gmail.com

FERRIS, Marcie Cohen. American (born United States) **Genres:** Food And Wine, Popular Culture, History, Social Sciences. **Career:** The Natchez Jewish Experience (documentary film), producer, 1995; University of North Carolina, assistant professor in American studies, 2004-, Carolina Center for Jewish Studies, Department of American Studies, associate professor and associate director, department coordinator, 2008-; Norlands Living History Center, administrator and educator; Colonial Williamsburg, administrator and educator; Plimoth Plantation, administrator and educator; Museum of Southern Jewish Experience, administrator and educator; University of Mississippi, Center for Public Service and Continuing Education, administrator and educator, Southern Foodways Alliance, president; Weaving Women's Words Oral History Project, Jewish Women's Archive, administrator. Writer. **Publications:** (Contrib.) Shalom Y'all: Images of Jewish Life in the American South, 2002; (contrib.) Cornbread Nation 1: The Best of Southern Food Writing, 2002; (contrib.) American Jewish Women: An Historical Reader from Colonial Times to the Present, 2002; (contrib.) Cornbread Nation 2: The Best of Southern Food Writing, 2004; Matzoh Ball Gumbo: Culinary Tales of the Jewish South, 2005; (ed. with M.I. Greenberg) Jewish Roots in Southern Soil: A New

History, 2006; The Edible South: Food and History in an American Region, forthcoming. Contributor to periodicals. **Address:** Department of American Studies, Carolina Center for Jewish Studies, University of North Carolina, 20 Greenlaw Hall, PO Box 3520, Chapel Hill, NC 27599-3520, U.S.A. **Online address:** ferrism@email.unc.edu

FERRIS, Paul. Welsh (born Wales), b. 1929. **Genres:** Novels, Plays/Screenplays, Medicine/Health, Biography, Young Adult Fiction, Young Adult Non-fiction. **Career:** Observer (Sunday newspaper), assistant in foreign news service, 1953, radio columnist, 1954-, news editor, 1962. **Publications:** A Changed Man, 1958; The City, 1960; Then We Fall, 1960; The Church of England, 1962; A Family Affair, 1963; The Doctors, 1965; The Destroyer, 1965; The Nameless: Abortion in Britain Today, 1966; The Dam, 1967; Men and Money: Financial Europe Today, 1968 in US as The Money Men of Europe, 1969; The House of Northcliffe: The Harmsworths of Fleet Street, 1971; The New Militants: Crisis in the Trade Unions, 1972; Very Personal Problems: A Novel, 1973; The Cure: A Novel, 1974; The Detective: A Novel, 1976; High Places, 1976; Dylan Thomas, 1977; Talk to Me about England, 1979; Richard Burton, 1981; A Distant Country: A Novel, 1983; Gentlemen of Fortune: The World's Merchant and Investment Bankers, 1984; The Master Bankers: Controlling the World Finances, 1984; (ed.) Collected Letters of Dylan Thomas, 1985, rev. ed., 2000; Sir Huge: The Life of Huw Weldon, 1990; Sex and the British: A Twentieth Century History, 1993; The Divining Heart, 1995; Children of Dust, 1995; Caitlin: The Life of Caitlin Thomas, 1995; Dr. Freud, a Life, 1998; Infidelity, 1999; Dylan Thomas: The Biography, 1999; Cora Crane, 2003; Gower in History: Myth, People, Landscape, 2009. **Address:** Curtis Brown Group Ltd., Haymarket House, 28-29 Haymarket, London, GL SW1Y 45P, England.

FERRIS, Timothy. American/Irish (born Ireland), b. 1944. **Genres:** Astronomy, Sciences, Writing/Journalism, Politics/Government, Physics. **Career:** United Press Intl., reporter, 1967-69; New York Post, reporter, 1969-71; Rolling Stone Magazine, reporter and editor, 1971-73, contributing editor, 1973-80; City University of New York, Brooklyn College, professor of English, 1974-82; NASA Voyager Interstellar Record, producer, 1977; University of Southern California, professor of journalism, 1982-85; University of California, professor of journalism, 1986-2001, professor emeritus, 2001-; Public Broadcasting Service, MacNeil-Lehrer News Hour, essayist, 1992-95. **Publications:** The Red Limit: The Search for the Edge of the Universe, 1977, rev. ed., 1983; Galaxies, 1980; (with C. Zecca) Spaceshots: The Beauty of Nature beyond Earth, 1984; (with B. Porter) The Practice of Journalism: A Guide to Reporting and Writing the News, 1988; Coming of Age in the Milky Way, 1988; (ed.) World Treasury of Physics, Astronomy and Mathematics, 1991; The Mind's Sky: Human Intelligence in a Cosmic Context, 1992; The Universe and Eye: Making Sense of the New Science, 1993; The Whole Shebang: A State-of-the-Universe(s) Report, 1997; Life Beyond Earth, 1999; Life beyond Earth, 2000; (ed.) Best American Science Writing, 2001; (intro.) Celestial Nights: Visions of an Ancient Land: Photographs from Israel and the Sinai, 2001; Seeing in the Dark: How Backyard Stargazers are Probing Deep Space and Guarding Earth from Interplanetary Peril, 2002; The Science of Liberty, 2010. **Address:** ClockDrive Productions, 97 Telegraph Hill Blvd., San Francisco, CA 94133, U.S.A. **Online address:** tf@timothyferris.com

FERRIS, William (R.). American (born United States), b. 1942. **Genres:** Local History/Rural Topics, Cultural/Ethnic Topics, Mythology/Folklore, Bibliography, Songs/Lyrics And Libretti, Music. **Career:** Jackson State University, assistant professor of English, 1970-72; Yale University, associate professor of American and Afro-American studies, 1972-79; Center for Southern Folklore, co-founder and president, 1972-84; The Blues (documentary), Mississippi Authority for Educational Television, producer and host, 1972; University of Mississippi, professor of anthropology and director of Center for the Study of Southern Culture, 1979-97; Stanford University, Stanford Humanities Center, visiting fellow, 1989-90; National Endowment for the Humanities, chairman, 1997-; University of North Carolina, Department of History, professor, Joel Williamson eminent professor, Center for the Study of the American South, senior associate director, adjunct professor in the folklore curriculum. Writer. **Publications:** Blues from the Delta, 1970, rev. ed., 1978; Mississippi Black Folklore: A Research Bibliography and Discography, 1971; Black Prose Narrative from the Mississippi Delta, 1974; Images of the South: Visits with Eudora Welty and Walker Evans, 1978; Local Color: A Sense of Place in Folk Art, 1982; Ray Lum: Mule Trader and Storyteller, 1992; You Live and Learn, Then You Die and Forget It All: Ray Lum's Tales of Horses, Mules and Men, 1992; Give My Poor Heart Ease: Voices of the

Mississippi Blues, 2010. EDITOR: Afro-American Folk Arts and Crafts, vol. II, 1978, rev. ed., 1983; (with S. Hart) Folk Music and Modern Sound, 1982; (with C.R. Wilson) Encyclopedia of Southern Culture, 1989. **Address:** The Wendy Weil Agency Inc., 232 Madison Ave., Ste. 1300, New York, NY 10016, U.S.A.

FERRITER, Diarmaid. Irish (born Ireland), b. 1972?. **Genres:** Politics/ Government, Psychology, History. **Career:** University College Dublin, lecturer in modern Irish history, 1996-98, professor of modern Irish history, 2008-; St. Patrick's College, Department of History, instructor, senior lecturer in Irish history, 1999-2008. Writer. **Publications:** A Nation of Extremes: The Pioneers of Twentieth-Century Ireland, 1999; Lovers of Liberty?: Local Government in Twentieth-Century Ireland, 2001; (with C. Tólbín) The Irish Famine: A Documentary, 2001; The Transformation of Ireland, 1900-2000, 2004; What If?: Alternative Views of Twentieth-century Ireland, 2006; Judging Dev: A Reassessment of the Life and Legacy of Eamon de Valera, 2007; Occasions of Sin: Sex and Society in Modern Ireland, 2009. Contributor to periodicals. **Address:** School of History and Archives, University College Dublin, K112 Newman Bldg., Belfield, DU 4, Ireland. **Online address:** diarmaid.ferriter@ucd.ie

FERTIG, Beth. American (born United States), b. 1966. **Genres:** Reference. **Career:** WNYC Radio, senior reporter, staff, 1995-; Monitor Radio Network, intern. **Publications:** Why Cant U Teach Me 2 Read? Three Students and a Mayor Put Our Schools to the Test, 2009. **Address:** New York, NY , U.S.A. **Online address:** mail@bethfertig.com

FESHBACH, Murray. American (born United States), b. 1929. **Genres:** Environmental Sciences/Ecology, Medicine/Health, Demography, History. **Career:** National Bureau of Economic Research Inc., staff, 1955-56; U.S. Bureau of the Census, Foreign Demographic Analysis Division, analyst, 1957-67, chief, 1967-79; Woodrow Wilson International Center for Scholars, fellow, 1979-80; Kennan Institute, fellow, 1979-80; Georgetown University, Center for Population Research, professorial lecturer in demography, 1981-84, research professor of demography, 1984-2000, research professor emeritus, 2000-; Columbia University, adjunct professor, 1983-85; North Atlantic Treaty Organization (NATO), Office of the Secretary General, Sovietologist-in-residence, 1986-87; American University, lecturer; George Washington University, lecturer; Institute of East-West Security Studies, 1992, lecturer; Foreign Policy Research Institute, lecturer, 1992. Consultant and writer. **Publications:** The Soviet Statistical System, 1960; (with C. Davis) Rising Infant Mortality in the U.S.S.R. in the 1970's, 1980; (with L.E. Nolting) Statistics on Research and Development Employment in the U.S.S.R, 1981; Compendium of Soviet Health Statistics, 1985; Soviet Population Policy Debate: Actors and Issues, 1986; (with A. Friendly, Jr.) Ecocide in the USSR: Health and Nature Under Siege, 1992; Ecological Disaster: Cleaning Up The Hidden Legacy of The Soviet Regime, 1995; Russia's Health and Demographic Crises: Policy Implications and Consequences, 2003. EDITOR: National Security Issues in the USSR, 1987; (in-chief) Environmental and Health Atlas of Russia, 1995. **Address:** Woodrow Wilson International Center for Scholars, International Trade Center, Ronald Reagan Bldg., 1 Woodrow Wilson Plz., 1300 Pennsylvania Ave. NW, Washington, DC 20004-3027, U.S.A. **Online address:** murray.feshbach@wilsoncenter.org

FESSENDEN, Tracy. American (born United States), b. 1961. **Genres:** Young Adult Non-fiction, Literary Criticism And History, Theology/Religion. **Career:** Millsaps College, assistant professor, 1992-94; Arizona State University, Department of Religious Studies, assistant professor, 1994-2000, associate professor, 2000-. Writer. **Publications:** (Ed. with N.F. Radel and M.J. Zaborowska) The Puritan Origins of American Sex: Religion, Sexuality and National Identity in American Literature (nonfiction), 2001; Culture and Redemption: Religion, the Secular and American Literature (nonfiction), 2007. Contributor to books and periodicals. **Address:** Department of Religious Studies, Arizona State University, PO Box 874302, Tempe, AZ 85287-3104, U.S.A. **Online address:** tracyf@asu.edu

FESSLER, Ann. American (born United States), b. 1949?. **Genres:** Adult Non-fiction, Women's Studies And Issues, History, Sociology, Social Work, Ethics, Social Commentary. **Career:** Webster University, faculty and assistant director for media studies program, 1975-79; University of Arizona, teaching assistantship, 1979-81; Tyler School of Art, visiting artist, 1981-82; Maryland Institute, Photography Department, faculty, 1982-93, acting chairperson and acting director of graduate photography program, 1985-86; Rhode Is-

land School of Design, Graduate Program in Photography, director, 1993-96, 2007-11, head of photography department, 1993-98, professor, 1993-; Wexner Center for the Arts, resident; Banff Center for the Arts, resident; Nexus Press, resident; Visual Studies Workshop Press, resident. **Publications:** The Girls Who Went Away: The Hidden History of Women Who Surrendered Children for Adoption in the Decades before Roe v. Wade, 2006. **Address:** Department of Photography, Rhode Island School of Design, 2 College St., Providence, RI 02903, U.S.A. **Online address:** afessler@risd.edu

FETHERSTON, Drew. American (born United States) **Genres:** Documentaries/Reportage, Business/Trade/Industry, History, Engineering, Technology, Sciences. **Career:** Newsday, staff writer and columnist; Wall Street Journal, reporter. **Publications:** The Chunnel: The Amazing Story of the Undersea Crossing of the English Channel, 1997; Greed and Its Rewards, 2000. Contributor to periodicals. **Address:** Red Rock Press, 331 W 57th St., Ste. 175, New York, NY 10019, U.S.A. **Online address:** fetherst@newsday.com

FETTERS, Thomas T. American (born United States), b. 1938. **Genres:** Children's Fiction, Transportation, Architecture, History, Humanities, Technology. **Career:** Crown Cork and Seal Co., consultant in packaging performance, 1961-. Writer. **Publications:** (With P.W. Swanson, Jr.) Piedmont and Northern: The Great Electric System of the South, 1974; Palmetto Traction: Electric Railways of South Carolina, 1978; Logging Railroads of South Carolina, 1990; The Lustron Home: The History of a Postwar Prefabricated Housing Experiment, 2001; Logging Railroads of the Blue Ridge and Smoky Mountains, 2007; The Charleston & Hamburg: A South Carolina Railroad and an American Legacy, 2008. Contributor to perioidcals. **Address:** Mcfarland and Company Inc., 960 McFarland, NC Hwy. 88 W, PO Box 611, Jefferson, NC 28640, U.S.A. **Online address:** tfetters@attbi.com

FEUERSTEIN, Georg. American/German (born Germany), b. 1947. **Genres:** Cultural/Ethnic Topics, Philosophy, Social Commentary, Theology/ Religion, Translations, Psychology, Essays, Politics/Government, Politics/ Government. **Career:** University of Durham, Yoga Research Centre, director, 1975-80; Dawn Horse Press, editorial director, 1981-86; Integral Publishing, director, 1986-; California Center for Jean Gebser Studies, co-director, 1986-; Healing Buddha Foundation, co-director, 1994-99; Yoga Research and Education Center, founder, director and president, 1996-2003; Yoga World, editor, 1997-2001; International Journal of Yoga Therapy, editor, 1999-; Traditional Yoga Studies, owner. **Publications:** Yoga: Sein Wesen und Werden, 1969; (with J. Miller) Reappraisal of Yoga: Essays in Indian Philosophy, 1969 as Yoga and Beyond: Essays in Indian Philosophy, 1972; The Essence of Yoga: A Contribution to the Psychohistory of Indian Civilisation, 1974, rev. ed. as Wholeness or Transcendence?, 1992; The Bhagavad-Gita: Its Philosophy and Cultural Setting, 1974 as The Bhagavad-Gītā: An Introduction, 1983; Textbook on Yoga, 1975; Essence of Yoga: A Contribution to the Psychohistory of Indian Civilization, 1976; Yoga-sūtra of Patañjali: An Exercise in the Methodology of Textual Analysis, 1979; The Yoga-sūtra of Patañjali: A New Translation and Commentary, 1979; The Bhagavad-Gita: A Critical Rendering, 1980; The Philosophy of Classical Yoga, 1980; (comp., intro. and ed. with T. Koontz and D. Dykstra) Adept: Selections From Talks and Essays By Da Free John on the Nature and Function of the Enlightened Teacher, 1983; (comp., intro. and ed.) Easy Death: Talks and Essays on the Inherent and Ultimate Transcendence of Death and Everything Else, 1983; (comp., intro. and ed.) Look at the Sunlight on the Water: Educating Children for a Life of Self-Transcending Love and Happiness: An Introduction, 1983; (ed.) Humor Suddenly Returns: Essays on the Spiritual Teaching of Master Da Free John: A Scholarly Tribute, 1984; (comp., intro. and ed.) Transmission of Doubt: Talks and Essays on the Transcendence of Scientific Materialism Through Radical Understanding, 1984; Structures of Consciousness: The Genius of Jean Gebser, 1987; Yoga: The Technology of Ecstasy, 1989; (ed.) Enlightened Sexuality: Essays On Body-Positive Spirituality, 1989; Jean Gebser: What Color Is Your Consciousness?, 1989; Encyclopedic Dictionary of Yoga, 1990, rev. ed. as The Shambhala Encyclopedia of Yoga, 1997; Holy Madness: The Shock Tactics and Radical Teachings of Crazy-Wise Adepts, Holy Fools, and Rascal Gurus, 1991, rev. ed. as Holy Madness: Spirituality, Crazy-Wise Teachers, and Enlightenment, 2006; Sacred Paths: Essays on Wisdom, Love and Mystical Realization, 1991; Wholeness or Transcendence?: Ancient Lessons for the Emerging Global Civilization, 1992; Sacred Sexuality: Living the Vision of the Erotic Spirit, 1992; (ed. with T. Feuerstein) Voices on the Threshold of Tomorrow: 145 Views of the New Millennium, 1993; (ed. with S. Bodian) Living Yoga: A Comprehensive Guide For Daily Life, 1993; The Mystery of Light: The Life and Teaching of Omraam Mikhael Aivanhov, 1994; Spirituality by the Numbers, 1994; (with S. Kak and D. Frawley) In Search of the Cradle of Civilization: New Light on Ancient India, 1995, 2nd ed., 2001; The Shambhala Guide to Yoga, 1996; Lucid Waking: Mindfulness and the Spiritual Potential of Humanity, 1997; (trans. and ed.) Teachings of Yoga, 1997; Tantra: The Path of Ecstasy, 1998; Essence of Yoga: Essays on the Development of Yogic Philosophy from the Vedas to Modern Times, 1998; Yoga Tradition: Its History, Literature, Philosophy and Practice, 1998; (with L. Payne) Yoga for Dummies, 1999, 2nd ed., 2010; Yoga Gems, 2002; Sacred Sexuality: The Erotic Spirit in the World's Great Religions, 2003; Deeper Dimension of Yoga: Theory and Practice, 2003; Little Book for Lovers, 2006; Yoga Morality: Ancient Teachings at a Time of Global Crisis, 2007; Aha!Reflections on the Meaning of Everything, 2007; (with B. Feuerstein) Green Yoga, 2007; Traditional Yoga Studies, 2007; Green Dharma, 2008; Encyclopedia of Yoga and Tantra, 2011; (with B. Feuerstein) The Bhagavad-Gita: A New Translation, 2011; Esoteric Philosophy of Hatha-Yoga, forthcoming. Contributor to periodicals. Works appear in anthologies. **Address:** Traditional Yoga Studies, 35 Jacklin Cir., Milpitas, CA 95035-3530, U.S.A. **Online address:** mail@yrec.org

FEUERWERKER, Albert. American (born United States), b. 1927. **Genres:** History, Economics. **Career:** University of Toronto, lecturer in history, 1955-58; Harvard University, Center for East Asian Studies, research fellow, 1958-60; University of Michigan, associate professor, 1959-63, professor of history, 1963-86, A.M. and H.P. Bentley professor of history, 1986-96, A.M. and H.P. Bentley professor emeritus of history, 1996-, Center for Chinese Studies, director, 1961-67, 1974-84; Chinese Materials and Research Aids Service Center, chairman and president, 1964-74; Ecole des Hautes Etudes en Sciences Sociales, director, 1981; Harvard University, lecturer on contemporary Chinese affairs; Stanford University, lecturer on contemporary Chinese affairs. Writer. **Publications:** China's Early Industrialization, 1958; (with S. Cheng) Chinese Communist Studies of Modern Chinese History, 1961; Chinese Economy, 1912-1949, 1968; Rebellion in Nineteenth-Century China, 1975; State and Society in Eighteenth-Century China: The Ch'ing Empire in Its Glory, 1976; The Foreign Establishment in China in the Early Twentieth Century, 1976; Economic Trends in the Republic of China, 1912-1949, 1977; The Chinese Economy, 1870-1911, 1978; Studies in the Economic History of Late Imperial China, 1995; The Chinese Economy, 1870-1949, 1995. EDITOR AND CONTRIBUTOR: Modern China, 1964; (with R. Murphey and M.C. Wright) Approaches to Modern Chinese History, 1967; History in Communist China, 1968; Chinese Social and Economic History from the Song to 1900, 1982; (with J.K. Fairbank) Cambridge History of China, vol. XIII, 1986. Contributor to books and journals. **Address:** Department of History, University of Michigan, 1029 Tisch Hall, 435 S State St., Ann Arbor, MI 48109-1003, U.S.A. **Online address:** afeuer@umich.edu

FEURER, Rosemary. American (born United States) **Genres:** Social Sciences. **Career:** Northern Illinois University, associate professor of history. Academic, historian and writer. **Publications:** Radical Unionism in the Midwest, 1900-1950, 2006. Contributor to books and periodicals. **Address:** Department of History, Northern Illinois University, Zulauf Hall 715, DeKalb, IL 60115-2854, U.S.A. **Online address:** rfeurer@niu.edu

FFORDE, Jasper. Welsh/British (born England), b. 1961. **Genres:** Novels, Young Adult Fiction. **Career:** Writer. **Publications:** THURSDAY NEXT SERIES: The Eyre Affair, 2001; Lost in a Good Book, 2002; Thursday Next in Lost in a Good Bok: A Novel, 2003; Thursday Next in the Well of Lost Plots: A Novel, 2004; Thursday Next in Something Rotten: A Novel, 2004; Thursday Next: First Among Sequels, 2007. NURSERY CRIME SERIES: The Big Over Easy: A Nursery Crime, 2005; The Fourth Bear, 2006. SHADES OF GREY: Shades of Grey: The Road to High Saffron, 2010. OTHERS: The Well of Lost Plots, 2003; The Last Dragonslayer, 2010; One of Our Thursdays is Missing, 2011; The Song of the Quarkbeast, 2011. Contributor of stories to periodicals. **Address:** Janklow & Nesbit UK Ltd., 29 Adam & Eve Mews, London, GL W8 6UG, England. **Online address:** email@jasperfforde.com

FFORDE, Katie. British (born England), b. 1952. **Genres:** Romance/Historical, Novels, Young Adult Fiction. **Career:** Writer. **Publications:** The Rose Revived, 1996; Stately Pursuits, 1997; Wild Designs, 1997; Life Skills, 1999; Thyme Out, 2000 in US as Second Thyme Around, 2001; Artistic Licence, 2002; Highland Fling, 2002; Paradise Fields, 2003; Restoring Grace, 2004; Bidding for Love, 2007; Practically Perfect, 2006; Going Dutch, 2007;

Wedding Season, 2008; Love Letters, 2009; Living Dangerously, 2009; A Perfect Proposal, 2010. **Address:** c/o Sarah Molloy, A.M. Heath and Co., 79 St. Martin's Ln., London, GL WC2N 4AA, England. **Online address:** katie@katiefforde.com

FIALKA, John J. American (born United States), b. 1938. **Genres:** Documentaries/Reportage, Economics, Technology, Military/Defense/Arms Control, Theology/Religion, Bibliography, History. **Career:** Baltimore Sun, reporter, 1965-76; Washington Star, reporter, 1967-81; Wall Street Journal, national security reporter, 1981-97, energy and environment reporter, 1997; Support Our Aging Religious Inc., co-founder, 1986-. Writer. **Publications:** Hotel Warriors: Covering the Gulf War, 1992; War by Other Means: Economic Espionage in America, 1997; Sisters: Catholic Nuns and the Making of America, 2003. Contributor to periodicals. **Address:** Hecker Center for Ministry, Support Our Aging Religious Inc., 3025 4th St NE, Washington, DC 20017-2145, U.S.A. **Online address:** john.fialka@wsj.com

FIALLOS, Rosario. (Rosario Aguilar). American (born United States), b. 1938. **Genres:** Novels, Novellas/Short Stories, Literary Criticism And History, Biography. **Career:** Writer. **Publications:** NOVELS: Primavera Sonámbula, 1964; Quince Barrotes de Izquierda a Derecha, 1965; Rosa Sarmiento (biographical novel), 1968; Aquel Mar sin Fondo ni Playa, 1970; Las Doce y Veintinueve, 1975; 7 Relatos Sobre el Amor y la Guerra, 1986; La Niña Blanca y los Pájaros sin Pies (historical novel), 1992; El Guerrillero, rev. ed., 1999; La Promesante, 2001; Rubén Darío y su Vigencia en el Siglo XXI, 2003. SHORT STORIES: Lucãa, 1982; Sonia, 1986; Siete Relatos sobre el Amor y la Guerra, 1986; El mar estaba calmo, 1994; Margarita Maradiaba, 1995; El Regreso, 1997; Lost Chronicles of Terra Firma, 1997. BIOGRAPHY: Soledad: tú eres el enlace, 1995. **Address:** PO Box 162, León, 00107, Nicaragua. **Online address:** agfia@ibw.com.ni

FICERA, Kim (M.). American (born United States), b. 1959. **Genres:** Novels, Young Adult Fiction. **Career:** Freelance writer and consultant, 1982-; New Mass Media, developer, writer and researcher, 1996-99, manager and web manager, 1996-03, web site production artist, 1999-2000; After Ellen, contributing writer; Benchmark Education, copy editor, 2004-05; MTV Network, columnist, 2005-08; Corktease Wine Country Gear, owner, 2010-; Autodesk, corporate communications and technical writer, 2011-. **Publications:** Sex, Lies and Stereotypes: An Unconventional Life Uncensored, 2003. Contributor to periodicals. **Address:** c/o John Talbot, The John Talbot Agency Inc., 540 W Boston Post Rd., PO Box 266, Mamaroneck, NY 10543-3437, U.S.A. **Online address:** kim@kimficera.com

FICKETT, David C. American (born United States), b. 1958?. **Genres:** Novels, Young Adult Fiction, Science Fiction/Fantasy. **Career:** Writer. **Publications:** Nectar, 2002. Contributor to periodicals. **Address:** c/o Author Mail, Forge Books, 175 5th Ave., New York, NY 10010, U.S.A.

FIDO, Martin (Austin). American/British (born England), b. 1939. **Genres:** Bibliography, Criminology/True Crime, Biography. **Career:** Balliol College, junior research fellow in English, through 1966; University of Leeds, lecturer in English, 1966-73; Michigan State University, visiting associate professor, University of West Indies, reader in English, Department of English and Linguistics, head, 1973-83; Hoevec Investors Ltd., actor, 1981-83; broadcaster, guide-lecturer, courier and writer, 1983-; Boston University, senior lecturer, 2001-. **Publications:** NONFICTION: Charles Dickens, 1968; Charles Dickens: An Authentic Account of His Life and Times, 1973; Oscar Wilde, 1973; Rudyard Kipling, 1974; Shakespeare, 1978; Oscar Wilde: An Illustrated Biography, 1985; Shakespeare, 1985; The Crimes, Detection, and Death of Jack the Ripper, 1987; Bodysnatchers: A History of the Resurrectionists, 1742-1832, 1988; Murders after Midnight, 1990; Murder Guide to London, 1990; (with K. Skinner) The Peasenhall Murder, 1990; (with P. Begg and K. Skinner) The Jack the Ripper A to Z, 1992; The Chronicle of Crime: The Infamous Felons of Modern History and Their Hideous Crimes, 1993; Deadly Jealousy, 1993; (with P. Begg) Great Crimes and Trials of the Twentieth Century, 1994; Twentieth Century Murder, 1995; (with K. Fido) The World's Worst Medical Mistakes, 1996; (with K. Fido) Our Family, 1997; The World of Charles Dickens, 1997; World of Sherlock Holmes: The Facts and Fiction behind the World's Greatest Detective, 1998; World of Agatha Christie: The Facts and Fiction behind the World's Greatest Crime Writer, 1999. PLAYS: Let's Go Bajan!, 1983. AUDIOTAPES, WRITER AND READER: Silence of the Lambs: The True Stories, 1992; Guilty or Insane?, 1992; The Kennedys, 1992; On the Trail of Jack the Ripper, 1992; Son of Sam, 1992; Hell Hath No

Fury, 1992; 10 Rillington Place, 1993; Shady Ladies and Wicked Women, 1993; The Yorkshire Ripper, 1993; The Krays, 1993; Classic Murders, 1994; The Manson Family, 1994, reissued as A Passion for Killing, 1995; The Truth about Jack the Ripper, 1994; Serial Killers, 1995; The Mob, 1996; Who Killed JFK?, 1996; Cults that Kill, 1996. Contributor of reviews to periodicals. **Address:** Boston University Arts & Sciences, Rm 301L, 730 Commonwealth Ave., Boston, MA 02215, U.S.A. **Online address:** fido@bu.edu

FIEDLER, Fred E(dward). American/Austrian (born Austria), b. 1922. **Genres:** Administration/Management, Psychology, Business/Trade/Industry. **Career:** University of Chicago, research associate and instructor, 1950-51; University of Illinois, assistant professor, 1951-55, associate professor, 1955-59, professor of psychology, 1960-69, Group Effectiveness Research Laboratory, director, 1953-69; University of Washington, professor of psychology and professor of management and organization, 1969-, now professor emeritus of psychology and professor emeritus of management and organization. Writer. **Publications:** Leader Attitudes and Group Effectiveness, 1958; (with E.B. Hutchins and J.S. Dodge) Quasi-Therapeutic Relations in Small College and Military Groups, 1959; (with E.P. Godfrey and D.M. Hall) Boards, Management and Company Success, 1959; Contingency Model of Leadership Effectiveness, 1963; (with S.M. Nealey) Second-Level Management: A Review and Analysis, 1966; A Theory of Leadership Effectiveness, 1967; (with M.M. Chemers) Leadership and Effective Management, 1974; (with M.M. Chemers and L. Mahar) Improving Leadership Effectiveness: The Leader Match Concept, 1976, 2nd ed., 1984; (ed. with B. King and S. Streufert) Managerial Control and Organizational Democracy, 1978; (coauthor) People, Management, and Productivity: Featuring Io Enterprises, a Microcomputer Simulation, 1986; (with J.E. Garcia) New Approaches to Effective Leadership: Cognitive Resources and Organizational Performance, 1987; Leadership Experience and Leadership Performance, 1994; (co-author) The Estate Recovery Notification: Implementation Plan, Washington State Department of Social and Health Services, 1999. CONTRIBUTOR: Psychotherapy: Theory and Research, 1953; Person Perception and Interpersonal Behavior, 1958; Group Dynamics, 2nd ed., 1960, 3rd ed., 1968; Advances in Experimental Social Psychology, 1964; Basic Studies in Social Psychology, 1965; Problems in Social Psychology, 1966; Kleingruppenforschung und Gruppe im Sport, 1966; Studies in Personnel and Industrial Psychology, 1967; Contemporary Management: Issues and Viewpoints, 1974. Contributor of articles to journals. **Address:** Department of Psychology, University of Washington, PO Box 351525, Seattle, WA 98195-1525, U.S.A. **Online address:** fiedler@u.washington.edu

FIELD, D. M. See GRANT, Neil.

FIELD, Dorothy. Canadian/American (born United States), b. 1944. **Genres:** Plays/Screenplays, Poetry, Children's Non-fiction, Women's Studies And Issues. **Career:** Freelance artist and writer. **Publications:** FOR CHILDREN: In the Street of the Temple Cloth Printers, 1996. OTHERS: Meditations at the Edge: Paper and Spirit, 1996; (with C.G. Chudley) Between Gardens, 1999; Leaving the Narrow Place (poetry), 2004; Paper and Threshold: the Paradox of Spiritual Connection in Asian Cultures, 2007; Wearing My People Like a Shawl, 2008; The Blackbird Must Be, 2010. **Address:** 1560 Gladstone, Victoria, BC V8R 1S5, Canada. **Online address:** dotter@seaside.net

FIELD, Edward. (Bruce Elliot). American (born United States), b. 1924. **Genres:** Novels, Poetry, Translations, Travel/Exploration, Romance/Historical, Film, Children's Non-fiction, Autobiography/Memoirs, Autobiography/Memoirs. **Career:** Eckerd College, poet-in-residence; Hofstra University, YM-YWHA Poetry Center, lecturer; Sarah Lawrence College, faculty. **Publications:** POEMS: Stand Up, Friend, with Me, 1963; Variety Photoplays, 1967; (ed. and trans.) Songs and Stories of the Netsilik Eskimos, 1967, rev. ed. as Eskimo Songs and Stories, 1973, rev. ed. as Magic Words, 1998; Sweet Gwendolyn and the Countess, 1975; A Full Heart, 1977; Stars in My Eyes, 1978; New and Selected Poems from the Book of My Life, 1987; Counting Myself Lucky, Selected Poems, 1963-1992, 1992; A Frieze for a Temple of Love, 1998; (ed.) Dancing with a Tiger: Poems 1941-1998, 2003; After the Fall: Poems Old and New, 2007. FICTION: (with N. Derrick) The Potency Clinic, 1978; (with N. Derrick) Die Potenz Klinik, 1982; (with N. Derrick) Village, 1982 as The Villagers, 1999, rev. ed., 2009; (with N. Derrick) The Office, 1987. OTHERS: (ed.) A Geography of Poets (anthology), 1979; (ed.) Head of a Sad Angel: Stories, 1953-1966, 1990; (ed. and comp. with G. Locklin and C. Stetler) A New Geography of Poets, 1992; (ed. and foreword) Looking for Genet: Literary Essays and Reviews, 1992; The Man Who Would Marry Susan Sontag and Other Intimate Literary Portraits of the Bohemian Era, 2005; Kabuli Days: Travels in Old Afghanistan, 2008. **Address:** 463 West St., Ste. A323, New York, NY 10014, U.S.A. **Online address:** fieldinski@yahoo.com

FIELD, Genevieve. American (born United States), b. 1970?. **Genres:** Documentaries/Reportage, Art/Art History, Young Adult Fiction, Sex, Essays. **Career:** Connie Clausen & Associates, literary agent; Cader Books, editor; Melcher Media, MTV Books, executive editor; Nerve (online magazine), cofounder and executive editor, 1997-; Glamour, features director; Gothamist, sex and sensibility editor; Cookie, contributing writer. **Publications:** MTV's Road Rules, Road Trips, 1996; (ed. with R. Griscom) Nerve: Literate Smut: Fiction, Essays, and Photographs from Some of Today's Most Provocative Writers and Artists, 1998; (ed.) Smart Sex, 1998; (and ed.) Nerve: The New Nude, 2000; (ed. with J. Murnighan) Full Frontal Fiction: The Best of Nerve.com, 2000; Robert Maxwell: Photographs, 2000; (ed.) Sex and Sensibility: 28 True Romances from the Lives of Single Women, 2005. **Address:** Pocket Books, Simon & Schuster Inc., 1230 Ave. of the Americas, 11th Fl., New York, NY 10020-1513, U.S.A. **Online address:** genevieve@nerve.com

FIELD, Mark G(eorge). American (born United States), b. 1923. **Genres:** Medicine/Health, Sociology, Social Commentary, History. **Career:** Beth Israel Hospital, associate director of medical care study, 1955-57; Joint Commission on Mental Illness and Health, research associate, 1957-59; Harvard University, Department of Social Relations, lecturer, 1957-61, Russian Research Center, associate, 1959-61, 1963-, Davis Center for Russian and Eurasian Studies, fellow, associate, 1962-, adjunct professor, 1988-, Medical School, lecturer in sociology and consultant, 1971-72, School of Public Health, consultant, 1971-72, visiting lecturer on health services administration, 1972-; University of Illinois, associate professor of sociology, 1961-62; Boston University, professor of sociology, 1962-, now professor emeritus; Arthur D. Little Inc., consultant, 1962-63, 1966-67; Massachusetts General Hospital, Department of Psychiatry, assistant sociologist, senior sociologist, 1964-, program on technology and society, research associate, 1966-67; World Health Organization, consultant, 1969; Children Hospital, Family and Child Health Division, research associate, 1972-74. Writer. **Publications:** Social Change in Russia: The Importance of the Historical Background in Understanding the Russian Social System and the Mechanisms of Social Change, 1948; The Soviet Doctor: A Case Study of the Professional in Soviet Society, 1952; Organization of Medical Services in the Soviet Union, 1954; The Medical Profession in Soviet Society: A Study in Bureaucratization and Control, 1955; Some Problems Of Soviet Medical Practice: A Sociological Approach, 1955; (co-author) Report of Medical Visit to the USSR, Aug. 30-Sept. 8, 1956, 1956; The Re-legalization of Abortion in Soviet Russia, 1956; Doctor and Patient in Soviet Russia, 1957; The Social Environment and Its Effect on the Soviet Scientist, 1959; (co-author) Social Approaches to Mental Patient Care, 1964; Soviet Socialized Medicine: An Introduction, 1967; Technology, Medicine and Society: Effectiveness, Differentiation and Depersonalization, 1968; Child Psychiatry in the Soviet Union, 1972; (co-author) Evaluating Health Program Impact: The U.S.-Yugoslav Cooperative Research Effort, 1974; Soviet Infant Mortality: A Mystery Story, 1986; (with A. D'Houtaud) La santé: Approche Sociologique De Ses Représentations Et De Ses Fonctions Dans La Société, 1989; Soviet Health Problems and the Convergence Hypothesis, 1991; Soviet Medicine before and after the Fall, 1992; Post-Communist Medicine: Morbidity, Mortality and the Deteriorating Health Situation, 1994; The Health Crisis in the Former Soviet Union: A Report from the Post-War Zone, 1995; (with A. D'Houtaud) Representations of Health: A Neglected Dimension, 1995; (with A. D'Houtaud) Cultural Images of Health: A Neglected Dimension, 1995; Turf Battles on Medicine Avenue, 1996; (co-author) Russia: Socioeconomic Dimensions of the Gender Gap in Mortality in Challenging Inequities in Health: From Ethics to Action, 2001; The Soviet Legacy: The Past as Prologue, 2002. EDITOR: The Social Consequences of Modernization in Communist Societies, 1976; Success and Crisis in National Health Systems: A Comparitive Approach, 1989; (with M. Rosenthal and I. Butler) The Political Dynamics of Physician Manpower Policy, 1990; (with J.L. Twigg) Russia's Torn Safety Nets: Health and Social Welfare During the Transition, 2000. Contributor to books. **Address:** Department of Sociology, Boston University, 96 Cummington St., Boston, MA 02215, U.S.A. **Online address:** mfield@fas.harvard.edu

FIELD, Ophelia. British/Australian (born Australia), b. 1971?. **Genres:** Autobiography/Memoirs, History. **Career:** European Council on Refugees and Exiles (ECRE), policy analyst and advocate, through 1998; Human Rights

Watch, policy analyst; Sunday Telegraph, books consultant. Writer. **Publications:** The Favourite: Sarah, Duchess of Marlborough, 2002; Sarah Churchill, Duchess of Marlborough: The Queen's Favourite, 2003; The Kit-Cat Club: Friends Who Imagined a Nation, 2008. Contributor to periodicals. **Address:** c/o Lizzy Kremer, David Higham Associates, 5-8 Lower John St., Golden Square, GL W1F 9HA, England.

FIELD, Thalia. American (born United States), b. 1966?. **Genres:** Poetry, Songs/Lyrics And Libretti, Novels. **Career:** Conjunctions, editor, 1995, senior editor, 1996-99; Teachers and Writers Collaborative, Theater for a New Audience, instructor; Bard College, instructor; Naropa University, instructor, Summer Writing Program, teacher; Brown University, associate professor of literary arts. Writer. **Publications:** Point and Line, 2000; Incarnate: Story Material, 2004; ULULU, 2007; Bird Lovers, Backyard, 2010; (with A. Lang) A Prank of Georges, 2010; Experimental Animals, forthcoming. Contributor to periodicals. **Address:** Brown University, Rm. 301, 68 1/2 Brown St., 45 Prospect St., PO Box 1923, Providence, RI 02906, U.S.A. **Online address:** thalia_field@brown.edu

FIELDHOUSE, David K(enneth). British/Indian (born India), b. 1925. **Genres:** History, Third World, Humanities, Politics/Government. **Career:** Haileybury College, history master, 1950-52; University of Canterbury, lecturer in modern history, 1953-57; Oxford University, Beit lecturer in Commonwealth history, 1958-81; Nuffield College, fellow, 1966-81; Cambridge University, Vere Harmsworth professor of imperial and naval history, 1981-92, now professor emeritus; Jesus College, fellow, 1981-92. Writer. **Publications:** The Colonial Empires: A Comparative Survey from the Eighteenth Century, 1966; (comp.) The Theory of Capitalist Imperialism, 1967; Economics and Empire, 1830-1914, 1973, rev. ed., 1984; Empires Coloniaux à partir du XVIIIe siècle, 1973; Unilever Overseas: The Anatomy of a Multinational, 1895-1965, 1978; Colonialism, 1870-1945: An Introduction, 1981; Select Documents of the Constitutional History of the British Empire and Commonwealth: The Foundations of a Colonial System of Government, 1985; Black Africa 1945-80: Economic Decolonization and Arrested Development, 1986; The Dependent Empire and Ireland, 1840-1900: Advance and Retreat in Representative Self-Government, 1991; Merchant Capital and Economic Decolonization: The United Africa Company, 1929-1987, 1994; The West and the Third World: Trade, Colonialism, Dependence and Development, 1999. EDITOR: Oxford and the Idea of Commonwealth, 1982; The Modern Plantation in the Third World, 1984; The Empire of the Bretaignes, 1175-1688: Foundations of a Colonial System of Government, 1985; Classical Period of the First Britain Empire, 1689-1783: Select Documents of the Constitutional History, 1985; Imperial Reconstruction, 1763-1840: The Evolution of Alternative Systems of Colonial Government, 1987; Settler Self-Government, 1840-1900: The Development of Representative and Responsible Government, 1990; Managing the Business of Empire: Essays in Honour of David Fieldhouse, 1998; Kurds, Arabs and Britons, 2001; Western Imperialism in the Middle East 1914-1958, 2006. **Address:** Jesus College, Cambridge, CB CB5 8BL, England. **Online address:** dkf1000@cam.ac.uk

FIELDING, Helen. British (born England), b. 1958. **Genres:** Novels, Humor/Satire, Young Adult Fiction. **Career:** BBC-TV, producer, 1979-89; freelance writer, 1989-; Sunday Times, journalist and columnist; The Telegraph, journalist and columnist; London Independent, journalist, columnist, 1995-97, 2005-. **Publications:** (With S. Bell and R. Curtis) Who's Had Who, In Association with Berk's Rogerage: An Historical Rogister Containing Official Lay Lines of History from the Beginning of Time to the Present Day, 1987 as Who's Had Who: An Historical Rogister Containing Official Lay Lines of History from the Beginning of Time to the Present Day, 1990; Cause Celeb (novel), 1994; Bridget Jones's Diary (novel), 1996; Bridget Jones: The Edge of Reason, 2000; Bridget Jones's Guide to Life, 2001; Helen Fielding's Bridget Jones's Diary: A Reader's Guide, 2002; Olivia Joules and the Overactive Imagination, 2003. Contributor to magazines. **Address:** The Independent, 191 Marsh Wall, Canary Wharf, London, GL E14 9RS, England.

FIELDING, Nigel G(oodwin). American/British (born England), b. 1950. **Genres:** Criminology/True Crime, Law, Sociology, Economics, Politics/Government, Social Sciences. **Career:** Metropolitan Police College, lecturer in law, 1972-73; Lewes Technical College, part-time lecturer in sociology, 1973-77; Ealing College of Higher Education, lecturer in criminology, 1977-78; University of Surrey, lecturer in criminology, 1978-89, senior lecturer in sociology, 1989-93, reader in sociology, 1993-95, professor of sociology, 1995-, associate dean; Institute of Social Research, director, 1996-; Univer-

sity of Bremen, distinguished international visiting professor, 1999-. Writer and consultant. **Publications:** The National Front, 1981; The Probation Practice, 1984; (with J.L. Fielding) Linking Data: The Articulation of Qualitative and Quantitative Methods in Social Research, 1986; Joining Forces: Police Training, Socialization and Occupational Competence, 1988; Actions and Structure: Research Methods and Social Theory, 1988; Investigating Child Sexual Abuse, 1990; The Police and Social Conflict: Rhetoric and Reality, 1991, 2nd ed., 2005; (ed. with R.M. Lee) Using Computers in Qualitative Research, 1991; (with C. Kemp and C. Norris) Negotiating Nothing: Police Decision-making in Disputes, 1992; Community Policing, 1995; (with R.M. Lee) Computer Analysis and Qualitative Research, 1998; (ed. with A. Clarke and R. Witt) The Economic Dimensions of Crime, 2000; (ed. with M. Schreier) Qualitative and Quantitative Research: Conjunctions and Divergences, 2001; (ed.) Interviewing, 2003; (ed.) Questionnaires, 2004; Courting Violence: Offences Against the Person Cases in Court, 2006; (ed. with R.M. Lee and G. Blank) SAGE Handbook of Online Research Methods, 2008. **Address:** Department of Sociology, University of Surrey, 22 AD 03, Guildford, SR GU2 7XH, England. **Online address:** n.fielding@surrey.ac.uk

FIELDING, Raymond. American (born United States), b. 1931. **Genres:** Plays/Screenplays, Film, Technology, History. **Career:** University of California, lecturer, 1957-61, assistant professor, 1961-65, associate professor, 1965-66; University of Southern California, visiting lecturer, 1960, visiting assistant professor, 1961, visiting director of cinema studies, 1980-81; New York University, visiting associate professor and director of motion picture workshop, 1965; University of Iowa, associate professor, 1966-69; Temple University, professor of communications, 1969-78; American Film Institute, trustee, 1973-79; University of Houston, professor, 1978-90, School of Communications, director, 1985-90; Francis Coppola Co., Zoetrope Studios, director of research and development, 1980-81; Florida State University, College of Motion Picture, Television and Recording Arts, dean, 1990-2003, dean emeritus, 2003-. Writer. **Publications:** (Ed.) The Wills of the Presidents, 1958; The Technique of Special Effects Cinematography, 1965, 3rd ed., 1972; (ed.) A Technological History of Motion Pictures and Television: An Anthology from the Pages of the Journal of the Society of Motion Picture and Television Engineers, 1967; (intro.) Motion Pictures from the Library of Congress Paper Print Collection, 1894-1912, 1967; The American Newsreel, 1911-1967, 1972, 2nd ed., 2007; (contrib.) Guidebook to Film, 1972; (contrib.) The American Cinema, 1974; The March of Time, 1935-51, 1978; A Bibliography of Theses and Dissertations on the Subject of Film, 1916-1979, 1979; (contrib.) Sound and the Cinema, 1980; The Technique of Special Effects Cinematography, 4th ed., 1985. **Address:** College of Moving Picture Arts, Florida State University, University Ctr. 3100A, Tallahassee, FL 32306-2350, U.S.A. **Online address:** rayrfielding@aol.com

FIELDS, Hillary. American (born United States) **Genres:** Romance/Historical. **Career:** Writer. **Publications:** HISTORICAL ROMANCES: The Maiden's Revenge, 2000; Marrying Jezebel, 2000; Heart of a Lion, 2001. OTHER: A Belly Full of Empty, forthcoming. Contributor to periodicals. **Address:** St. Martin's Press, 175 5th Ave., New York, NY 10010-7703, U.S.A.

FIELDS, Jennie. American (born United States), b. 1953. **Genres:** Novels, Psychology. **Career:** Foote, Cone, and Belding, copywriter, 1977-79; Needham, Harper, and Steers, senior copywriter, 1979-81; Young and Rubicam (advertising agency), senior vice-president, 1982-85, senior vice-president and creative director, 1989-93; Leo Burnett, senior copywriter, 1986-89; Lowe and Partners, senior vice-president and creative director, 1993-95; Bozell Advertising, group creative director, 1995-99; Robert A. Becker, senior vice president and creative director, 1999-2002; Euro RSCG Life, creative director, 1999-2001, senior vice president, 1999-2002; Chelsea, senior vice president, 1999-2002; McCann-Erickson Inc., senior vice-president and group creative director, 2003-09, McCann Worldgroup, senior vice-president and group creative director, 2003-09. Writer. **Publications:** Lily Beach, 1993; Crossing Brooklyn Ferry, 1997; The Middle Ages, 2002; The Age of Ecstasy, 2012. Contributor to periodicals. **Address:** c/o Lisa Bankoff, International Creative Management Inc., 730 5th Ave., New York, NY 10019, U.S.A. **Online address:** lilybeach@gmail.com

FIELDS, Terri. (Terri Susan Fields). American (born United States), b. 1948?. **Genres:** Young Adult Fiction, Young Adult Non-fiction, Novels, Picture/Board Books. **Career:** Sunnyslope High School, teacher. Writer. **Publications:** NOVELS AS T.S. FIELDS: Danger in the Desert, 1997; Missing in the Mountains, 1999. NONFICTION: Help Your Child Make the Most of

School: An Award-winning Teacher Reveals How Much You Can Matter in Your Child's Education, 1987; How to Help Your Child Make the Most of School, 1987. FOR CHILDREN: Fourth Graders Don't Believe in Witches, 1989; The Day the Fifth Grade Disappeared, 1992; Bug Off!, 1995; Fifth-grade Frankenstein, 1996; After the Death of Anna Gonzales (young adult novel in verse), 2002; Counting Arizona's Treasures, 2003; Holdup (young adult novel), 2007; Burro's Tortillas, 2007; My Father's Son (young adult novel), 2008. **Address:** Roaring Brook Press, 175 5th Ave., New York, NY 10010-7703, U.S.A. **Online address:** authorterrifields@yahoo.com

FIELDS, Terri Susan. *See* **FIELDS, Terri.**

FIENBERG, Anna. Australian/British (born England), b. 1956. **Genres:** Children's Fiction, Young Adult Fiction. **Career:** School Magazine, staff, 1980-90, editor, 1988-90. Writer, educator and consultant. **Publications:** CHILDREN'S FICTION: Billy Bear and the Wild Winter, 1988; The Champion, 1988; Wiggy and Boa, 1990, as Pirate Trouble for Wiggy and Boa, 1996; The Nine Lives of Balthazar, 1989; The Magnificent Nose and Other Marvels, 1991; Ariel, Zed and the Secret of Life, 1992; The Hottest Boy Who Ever Lived, 1995; Madeline the Mermaid and Other Fishy Tales, 1995; Power to Burn, 1995; Dead Sailors Don't Bite, 1996; The Doll's Secret, 1997; Minton Goes Flying, 1998; Minton Goes Sailing, 1998; Minton Goes Driving, 1999; Minton Goes Trucking, 1999; Minton Goes Under, 2000; Minton Goes Home, 2000; Tashi and the Dancing Shoes, 2001; The Big, Big, Big Book of Tashi, 2001; Joseph, 2001; The Witch in the Lake, 2001; Horrendo's Curse, 2003. WITH B. FIENBERG: Tashi, 1995; Tashi and the Giants, 1995; Tashi and the Ghosts, 1997; Tashi and the Demons, 1999; Tashi and the Genie, 1997; Tashi and the Baba Yaga, 1998; Tashi and the Big Stinker, 2000; Tashi and the Haunted House, 2002; Tashi and the Royal Tomb, 2003; Tashi Lost in the City, 2004; There Once was a Boy Called Tashi, 2004; The 2nd Big Big Book of Tashi, 2006; Tashi and the Baba Yaga, 2006; Tashi and the Forbidden Room, 2006; Tashi and the Stolen Bus, 2007; Number 8, 2007; Tashi and the Mixed-up Monster, 2007; The Amazing Tashi Activity Book, 2009; Tashi and the Golem, 2010; Great Big Enormous Book of Tashi, 2010; Madeline The Mermaid, 2010. OTHERS: Eddie, 1988; (reteller) The World of May Gibbs, 1997; Borrowed Light, 1999. **Address:** Allen & Unwin Pty Ltd., PO Box 8500, St Leonards, NW 1590, Australia. **Online address:** afienberg@bigpond.com

FIENNES, Ranulph. British (born England), b. 1944. **Genres:** Military/Defense/Arms Control, Travel/Exploration, Autobiography/Memoirs. **Career:** Occidental Petroleum Corp., executive consultant, 1984-90. Writer and British adventurer. **Publications:** A Talent for Trouble, 1970; Ice Fall in Norway, 1972; The Headless Valley, 1973; Where Soldiers Fear to Tread, 1975; Hell on Ice, 1979; To the Ends of the Earth: The Transglobe Expedition, The First Pole-to-Pole Circumnavigation of the Globe, 1983; (with V. Fiennes) Bothie, the Polar Dog: The Dog Who Went to Both Poles with the Transglobe Expedition, 1984; Living Dangerously: An Autobiography, 1987; The Feather Men, 1991; Atlantis of the Sands: The Search for the Lost City of Ubar, 1992; Mind Over Matter: The Epic Crossing of the Antarctic Continent, 1993; The Sett, 1996; Fit for Life, 1998; Beyond the Limits: The Lessons Learned From a Lifetime's Adventures, 2000; Secret Hunters, 2001; Captain Scott, 2003; Race to the Pole: Tragedy, Heroism and Scott's Antarctic Quest, 2004; Mad Bad & Dangerous To Know: The Autobiography, 2007; (foreword) Extremer Running, 2007; Mad Dogs and Englishmen, 2010; My Heroes, 2011. Contributor to books and periodicals. **Address:** Ed Victor Ltd., 6 Bayley St., Bedford Sq., London, GL WC1B 3HB, England.

FIENUP-RIORDAN, Ann. American (born United States), b. 1948. **Genres:** History, Anthropology/Ethnology, Film. **Career:** University of Alaska, instructor in anthropology, 1973-74, assistant professor of anthropology, 1983-84; Mud Inc., owner and operator, 1974; Nelson Island School of Design, researcher and publication designer, 1975; Alaska State Council on the Arts, instructor, 1978; Yukon Kuskokwim Health Corp., interviewer and research consultant, 1978-80; Alaska Pacific University, assistant professor of social science, 1980-83; U.S. Department of the Interior, Minerals Management Service, Yukon Delta specialist, 1986-88; Yupiit Nation, consulting anthropologist, 1988-89; Anchorage Museum of History and Art, curator of exhibition, 1994-96; Nelson Island Oral History Project, consulting humanist; Arctic Anthropology, associate editor, 1994-96; National Museum of Natural History, Arctic Studies Center, research associate. **Publications:** Maraiurivik Nunakauiami, 1975; Shape Up with Baby: Exercise Games for the New Parent and Child, 1980; The Nelson Island Eskimo, 1983; (ed. and intro.) The Yup'ik Eskimos as Described in the Travel Journals and Ethnographic Ac-

counts of John and Edith Kilbuck, 1885-1900, 1988; Eskimo Essays, 1990; The Real People and the Children of Thunder, 1991; Boundaries and Passages, 1994; Freeze Frame: Alaska Eskimos in the Movies, 1995; (ed.) Agayuliyararput, 1996; The Living Tradition of Yup'ik Masks, 1996; (ed.) Where the Echo Began: And Other Oral Traditions from Southwestern Alaska, 2000; (co-author) Hunting Tradition in a Changing World, 2000; (ed.) Stories for Future Generations: The Oratory of Yup'ik Paul John, 2003; Qulirat Qanemcit-Llu Kinguvarcimalriit, 2003; Taprarmiuni Kassiyulriit, 2004; (ed.) Stebbins Dance Festival, 2004; (ed.) Yupiit qanruyutait, 2005; (ed.) Ciuliamta akluit/Things of Our Ancestors: Yup'ik Elders Explore the Jacobsen Collection at the Ethnologisches Museum Berlin, 2005; Wise Words of the Yup'ik People, 2005; Yup'ik Elders at the Ethnologisches Museum Berlin, 2005; Yup'ik Words of Wisdom, 2005; Yuungnaqpiallerput: Masterworks of Yup'ik Science and Survival, 2007; (ed. with L.D. Kaplan) Words of the Real People: Alaska Native Literature in Translation, 2007; Way We Genuinely Live, 2007; (ed.) Paitarkiutenka: My Legacy to You, 2008; (with J.H. Barker and T.A. John) Yupiit yuraryarait, 2010; Qaluyaarmiuni Nunamtenek Qanemciput, 2011. Contributor of articles to journals, books and magazines. **Address:** Calista Elders Council, 9951 Prospect Dr., Anchorage, AK 99507-5905, U.S.A. **Online address:** riordan@alaska.net

FIERSTEIN, Harvey (Forbes). American (born United States), b. 1954. **Genres:** Plays/Screenplays. **Career:** Actor and writer. **Publications:** In Search of the Cobra Jewels, 1975; Freaky Pussy, 1976; Flatbush Tosca, 1977; Cannibals Just Don't Know No Better, 1978; Torch Song Trilogy, 1981; La Cage aux Folles, 1983; Forget Him, 1984; Safe Sex, 1987; Spookhouse, 1987; Harvey Fierstein's Safe Sex, 1987; HBO Showcase of Tidy Endings, 1988; (co-author) Legs Diamond, 1988; White Dove and Other Fairy Tales, 1996; Common Ground, 2000; The Sissy Duckling, 2002; (foreword) Out Plays, 2008. **Address:** RF Entertainment Inc., 29 Haines Rd., Bedford Hills, NY 10507, U.S.A. **Online address:** ron@rfent.com

FIFIELD, Christopher G(eorge). British (born England), b. 1945. **Genres:** Music, Biography, Photography. **Career:** Glyndebourne Festival Opera, music staff, 1971-72, 1977-86; University College London, director of music, 1980-90; Lambeth Orchestra, music director, 1982-; Jubilate Choir, conductor, 1988-2001; Northampton Symphony Orchestra, conductor, 1990-96; Central Festival Opera, music director, 1990-96; Reigate and Redhill Choral Society, conductor, 1992-96. Writer. **Publications:** Max Bruch: His Life and Works, 1988, 2nd ed., 2005; (contrib.) Wagner in Performance, 1990; True Artist and True Friend: A Biography of Hans Richter, 1993; Bruckner, 1999; (ed.) Letters and Diaries of Kathleen Ferrier, 2003; Ibbs and Tillett: The Rise and Fall of a Musical Empire, 2005; (ed.) Letters and Diaries of Kathleen Ferrier, 2005. Contributor to journals. **Address:** 80 Wolfington Rd., London, GL SE27 0RQ, England. **Online address:** christopherfifield@ntlworld.com

FIGES, Eva. British/German (born Germany), b. 1932. **Genres:** Novels, Novellas/Short Stories, Literary Criticism And History, Women's Studies And Issues, Writing/Journalism, Autobiography/Memoirs, Adult Non-fiction, Young Adult Non-fiction, Picture/Board Books, Translations. **Career:** Longmans, Green & Company Ltd., editor, 1955-57; Weidenfeld & Nicolson Ltd., editor, 1962-63; Blackie & Son Ltd., editor, 1964-67; writer, 1967-; Macmillan Women Writers Series, co-editor, 1987-; Queen Mary's College, fellow, 1990; Westfield College, fellow, 1990. **Publications:** Equinox, 1966; Modern Choice 2, 1966; The Musicians of Bremen, 1967; Winter Journey, 1967; The Banger, 1968; Konek Landing, 1969; Patriarchal Attitudes in UK as Patriarchal Attitudes: Women in Society, 1970; Scribble Sam: A Story, 1971; B, 1972; Days, 1974; Tragedy and Social Evolution, 1976; Nelly's Version, 1977; Little Eden: A Child at War, 1978; Waking, 1981; Sex and Subterfuge: Women Novelists to 1850, 1982; Light, 1983; The Seven Ages, 1986; Ghosts, 1988; The Tree of Knowledge, 1990; The Tenancy, 1993; (ed. and intro.) Women's Letters in Wartime: 1450-1945, 1993; The Knot, 1996; Tales of Innocence and Experience, 2003; Journey To Nowhere: One Woman Looks for the Promised Land, 2008. TRANSLATOR: The Gadarene Club, 1960; The Old Car, 1967; He and I and the Elephants, 1967; Little Fadettes, 1967; A Family Failure, 1970; The Deathbringer, 1971. Works appear in anthologies. Contributor to journals. **Address:** Rogers, Coleridge & White Ltd., 20 Powis Mews, London, GL W11 1JN, England.

FIGES, Kate. British (born England), b. 1957?. **Genres:** Women's Studies And Issues, Young Adult Fiction. **Career:** Mail on Sunday, You Magazine, books editor, 1996; Pandora Press, staff; Cosmopolitan Magazine, fiction editor. **Publications:** Because of Her Sex: The Myth of Equality for Women in

Britain, 1994; (with J. Zimmerman) Life after Birth: What Even Your Friends Won't Tell You about Motherhood, 2001, rev. ed., 2008; Baby and You: The Real Life Guide to Birth And Babies, 2002; The Terrible Teens: What Every Parent Needs to Know, 2002; What About Me?, 2004; What About Me, Too?, 2006; The Big Fat Bitch Book for Grown-up Girls, 2007; Couples: The Truth, 2010. EDITOR: The Best of Cosmopolitan Fiction, 1991; The Cosmopolitan Book of Short Stories, 1995; (and intro.) The Penguin Book of International Women's Stories, 1996; Childhood (anthology), 1998. Contributor to newspapers. **Address:** The Guardian, 90 York Way, Kings Pl., London, GL N1 9GU, England. **Online address:** kate.figes@wyld.demon.co.uk

FIGES, Orlando (G.). British (born England), b. 1959. **Genres:** History, Humanities. **Career:** Trinity College, fellow, lecturer in history, 1984-99; Cambridge University, university lecturer in history, 1987-99, director of studies in history, 1988-98; Birkbeck College, professor of history, 1999-. Writer. **Publications:** (Trans. and contrib.) V.P. Danilov, Rural Russia Under the New Regime, 1988; Peasant Russia, Civil War: The Volga Countryside in Revolution, 1917-1921, 1989, rev. ed., 2001; A People's Tragedy: The Russian Revolution, 1891-1924, 1997; (with B. Kolonitskii) Interpreting the Russian Revolution: The Language and Symbols of 1917, 1999; Natasha's Dance: A Cultural History of Russia, 2002; The Whisperers: Private Life in Stalin's Russia, 2007; Crimean War: A History, 2010; Just Send Me Word: A True Story of Love and Survival in the Gulag, 2012. Contributor to books and periodicals. **Address:** Department of History, Birkbeck College, University of London, 403 Rm., 28 Russell Sq., Bloomsbury, GL WC1B 5DQ, England. **Online address:** ogf1000@cam.ac.uk

FIGIEL, Sia. American Samoan (born American Samoa), b. 1967?. **Genres:** Essays, Novels, Poetry, Literary Criticism And History. **Career:** Institucio de les Lletres Catalanes, writer-in-residence; University of the South Pacific, Pacific Writing Forum, artist-in-residence; University of Technology, artist-in-residence; University of Hawaii, East West Center, Center for Pacific Islands Studies, writer-in-residence. Journalist. **Publications:** NOVELS: Where We Once Belonged, 1996; They Who Do Not Grieve, 1999. POETRY: The Girl in the Moon Circle, 1996; To a Young Artist in Contemplation: Poetry and Prose, 1998. Contributor to periodicals. **Address:** c/o Author Mail, Pasifika Press, 283 Karangahape Rd., Auckland, 1010, New Zealand.

FIGLEY, Marty Rhodes. American (born United States), b. 1948?. **Genres:** Biography, Theology/Religion, History, Picture/Board Books, Children's Fiction. **Career:** Writer. **Publications:** The Story of Zacchaeus, 1995; Mary and Martha, 1995; Noah's Wife, 1996; Lydia, 1996; The School Children's Blizzard, 2003; Saving the Liberty Bell, 2004; Washington is Burning, 2005; Prisoner for Liberty, 2008; The Night the Chimneys Fell, 2009; John Greenwood's Journey to Bunker Hill, 2011; President Lincoln, Willie Kettels, and the Telegraph Machine, 2011; Clara Morgan and the Oregon Trail Adventure, 2011; The Prison-Ship Adventures of James Forten, Revolutionary War Captive; The Prairie Adventures of Sarah and Annie, Blizzard Survivors, 2011; Who was William Penn? And Other Questions About The Founding Of Pennsylvania, 2012; Emily and Carlo, 2012. **Address:** 3913 Keith Pl., Annandale, VA 22003, U.S.A. **Online address:** marty@martyrhodesfigley.com

FIGUEIRA, Thomas J. American (born United States), b. 1948. **Genres:** Classics, History, Archaeology/Antiquities, Language/Linguistics. **Career:** Stanford University, acting assistant professor, 1977-78; Dickinson College, assistant professor, 1978-79; Rutgers University, assistant professor, 1979-85, associate professor, 1985-90, professor of classics and ancient history, 1991-99, professor (II) of classics and ancient history, 1999-, Douglass Residential College, fellow, 1982-89, Department of Classics and Archaeology, advisor, 1987-89, Livingston College, fellow, 1989-2007, Department of Classical Studies, graduate director, 1990-93; University of Wales, Institute of Classics and Ancient History, honorary fellow, 2003-; National Institute of Ancient Greek History, fellow, 2005-. Writer. **Publications:** Aegina, Society and Politics, 1981; (ed. with G. Nagy) Theognis of Megara, 1985; Athens and Aigina in the Age of Imperial Colonization, 1991; Excursions in Epichoric History, 1993; The Power of Money, 1998; Wisdom of the Ancients: Enduring Business Lessons from Alexander the Great, Julius Caesar, and the Illustrious Leaders of Ancient Greece and Rome, 2001; (ed.) Spartan Society, 2004; Archaic Restorations, forthcoming; Sinews of Empire: Thucydides and the Tribute of the Athenian Allies, forthcoming; Helotage: The Political Economy of Sparta, forthcoming. Contributor to books and journals. **Address:** Depart-

ment of Classics, Rutgers University, 131 George St., New Brunswick, NJ 08903-1414, U.S.A. **Online address:** figueira@rci.rutgers.edu

FIKES, Jay C(ourtney). American/Turkish (born Turkey), b. 1951. **Genres:** Anthropology/Ethnology, Social Sciences, Theology/Religion, Biography, Autobiography/Memoirs. **Career:** Palomar Community College, Pala Indian Reservation, bilingual tutor in chemistry, 1974; Allan Hancock Community College, Vandenberg Air Force Base Center, instructor in anthropology, 1975-76; University of Michigan, teaching assistant, 1976-79; U.S. International University, adjunct professor of anthropology, 1985; Marmara University, instructor of social science research methods, 1985-87; freelance researcher and writer, 1988-89; Highlands University, adjunct professor of anthropology, 1989; Smithsonian Institution, post-doctoral anthropology fellow, 1991-92, 1995; Institute of Intercultural Issues, president, 1993-98; Yeditepe University, professor of anthropology, 1999-. Writer. **Publications:** (With N. Nix) Step inside the Sacred Circle: Aboriginal American Animal Allegories, 1989; Carlos Castaneda: Academic Opportunism and the Psychedelic Sixties, 1993; (reteller and intro.) Reuben Snake, Your Humble Serpent: Indian Visionary and Activist, 1996; Huichol Indian Ceremonial Cycle, 1997; (ed. with P.C. Weigand and A.G. de Weigand) La Mitología de los Huicholes, 1998; (with J.G. Mercado) The Man Who Ate Honey, 2003; (ed. with P.C. Weigand and A.G. de Weigand) Huichol Mythology, 2004; Unknown Huichol: Shamans and Immortals, Allies against Chaos, 2010; How Sun and Fire Came to the Huichol, forthcoming. Contributor of articles to books and periodicals. **Address:** Department of Anthropology, Yeditepe University, 26 Ağustos Yerleşimi, Ataşehir, İstanbul, 34755, Turkey. **Online address:** cfikes@yeditepe.edu.tr

FILDERMAN, Diane E(lizabeth). American (born United States), b. 1959. **Genres:** Children's Fiction, Humor/Satire. **Career:** Children's book author. **Publications:** Mickey Steals the Show, 1995. **Address:** 10664 Quarterstaff Rd., Columbia, MD 21044, U.S.A.

FILES, Gemma. Canadian/British (born England), b. 1968?. **Genres:** Literary Criticism And History, Young Adult Fiction. **Career:** Eye Weekly, entertainment periodical, film critic; FearZone.com, columnist. Trebas Institute, instructor of screenwriting. **Publications:** FICTION: Kissing Carrion (stories), 2003; The Worm in Every Heart (stories), 2006; A Book of Tongues (Hexslinger series), 2010; A Rope of Thorns (Hexslinger series), 2011. Contributor to periodicals. **Address:** Toronto, ON , Canada. **Online address:** gfiles@interlog.com

FILES, Meg. American (born United States), b. 1946?. **Genres:** Novellas/Short Stories, Poetry. **Career:** Pima Community College, faculty, 1987-, director of writing lab, 1988-, Department of English and Journalism, chair, Pima Writers' Workshop, director; Ohio State University, creative writing, writer-in-residence; University of Arizona, creative writing; University of Maryland, creative writing; Colorado Mountain College, creative writing; Writer's Voice Project, creative writing. **Publications:** Meridian 144, 1991; Home Is the Hunter: And Other Stories, 1996; Write From Life: Turning Your Personal Experiences into Compelling Stories, 2002; Lasting: Poems On Aging, 2005; Love Hunter and other Poems, 2006. Contributor to periodicals. **Address:** Department of English-Journalism, Pima Community College, WC J 103, 4905 E Broadway Blvd., Tucson, AZ 85709-1010, U.S.A. **Online address:** mfiles@pima.edu

FILEY, Mike. Canadian (born Canada), b. 1941?. **Genres:** Travel/Exploration, History, Transportation. **Career:** Ontario Water Resources Commission (now the Ontario Ministry of the Environment), staff; Toronto Sunday Sun, columnist; freelance writer, 1970-; CFRB, staff. **Publications:** A Toronto Album: Glimpses of the City That Was, 1970, 2nd ed., 2001; Toronto: Reflections of the Past, 1972; Toronto: The Way We Were: A Collection of Photos & Stories About North America's Greatest City, 1974; Trillium and Toronto Island, 1976; Toronto City Life: Old and New, 1979; Not a One-Horse Town: 125 Years of Toronto and Its Streetcars, 1986; Like No Other in the World: The Story of Toronto's Sky Dome, 1989; Mount Pleasant Cemetery: An Illustrated Guide, 1990, rev. ed., 1999; From Horse Power to Horsepower, 1993; Toronto Sketches; More Toronto Sketches, 1993; Toronto Sketches 3: The Way We Were, 1994; Toronto Sketches 4: The Way We Were, 1995; The TTC Story: The First Seventy-Five Years, 1996; I Remember Sunnyside: The Rise and Fall of a Magical Era, 1996; Discover & Explore Toronto's Waterfront: A Walker's, Jogger's, Cyclist's, Boater's Guide to Toronto's Lakeside Sites and History, 1998; Toronto Sketches 6: The Way We Were, 2000; Toronto Album 2: More Glimpses of the City That Was, 2002; Toronto Sketches 7, 2003;

Toronto Sketches 8, 2004; Toronto Sketches 9, 2006; Toronto: The Way We Were, 2008; Toronto Sketches 10, 2010. Contributor to periodicals. **Address:** The Toronto Sunday Sun, 333 King St. E, Toronto, ON M5A 3X5, Canada. **Online address:** mike.filey@sympatico.ca

FILIPACCHI, Amanda. American/French (born France), b. 1967. **Genres:** Novels. **Career:** Novelist, 1993-. **Publications:** Nude Men, 1993; Vapor: A Novel, 1999; Love Creeps, 2005. Works appears in anthologies. **Address:** c/o Melanie Jackson, 250 W 57th St., Ste. 1119, New York, NY 10107, U.S.A. **Online address:** amandafilipa@gmail.com

FILKINS, Dexter. (Dexter Price Filkins). American (born United States), b. 1961. **Genres:** History, Military/Defense/Arms Control. **Career:** Miami Herald, reporter, 1986-95; Los Angeles Times, reporter, 1995-97, New Delhi bureau chief, 1997-2000; New York Times, foreign correspondent, 2000-; Harvard University, Carr Center for Human Rights Policy, fellow, 2007, 2008. **Publications:** The Forever War, 2008. **Address:** New York Times, 229 W 43rd St., New York, NY 10036-3913, U.S.A. **Online address:** info@dexterfilkins.net

FILKINS, Dexter Price. See FILKINS, Dexter.

FILKINS, Peter. American (born United States), b. 1958. **Genres:** Poetry, Translations, Novels. **Career:** Parnassus: Poetry in Review, assistant editor, 1981-83; University of Vienna, Fulbright fellow, 1983-85; Schottengymnasium, teaching assistant, 1984-85; North Adams State College, Department of English, adjunct instructor, 1986, 1988-89; Hiram College, Department of English, visiting instructor, 1986-87; Williams College, instructor, 1990-93, 1996; Bard College, Division of Languages and Literature, associate professor, 1988-, visiting professor of literature, 2007; Yaddo Artists Colony, artist-in-residence, 1989, coordinator of poetry fiction series, 1990-; Millay Colony for the Arts, artist-in-residence, 1993; MacDowell Colony, artist-in-residence, 1997. **Publications:** TRANSLATOR: I. Bachmann, Songs in Flight: The Collected Poems of Ingeborg Bachmann, 1994; (and foreword) A. Hotschnig, Leonardo's Hands, 1999; I. Bachmann, The Book of Franza & Requiem for Fanny Goldmann, 1999; H.G. Adler, Journey: A Novel, 2008; H.G. Adler, Panorama: A Novel, 2010. OTHERS: What She Knew (poems), 1998; After Homer (poems), 2002. Contributor to periodicals. **Address:** Bard College, Hall College Ctr., 2nd Fl., 84 Alford Rd., Simon's Rock, Great Barrington, MA 01230-1978, U.S.A. **Online address:** pfilkins@simons-rock.edu

FINCH, Annie (Ridley Crane). American (born United States), b. 1956. **Genres:** Plays/Screenplays, Poetry, Songs/Lyrics And Libretti, Literary Criticism And History. **Career:** Natural History, editorial assistant, 1981-82; Sequoia, general editor and poetry editor, 1987-91; Magic Theatre, assistant to literary manager, 1989-90; New College of San Francisco, Graduate Poetics Program, faculty, lecturer in poetry writing, 1991-92; University of Northern Iowa, poet-in-residence, director of creative writing and assistant professor of English, 1992-95; Broadview Press, reviewer, 1995-; University of Michigan Press, reviewer, 1995-; WOM-PO (national listserve devoted to the discussion of women's poetry), founder and co-ordinator, 1997-; Oxford University Press, reviewer, 1998-; Miami University, assistant professor of English, 1995-99, associate professor of English and creative writing, 1999-2004; Elon College, poet-in-residence, 2000; Bluffton College, poet-in-residence, 2000; University of Southern Maine, professor and director, Stone Coast MFA in Creative Writing, director, 2004-; Modern Language Association, reviewer. **Publications:** POETRY: The Encyclopedia of Scotland, 1982; The Furious Sun in Her Mane (song cycle), 1994; Catching the Mermother, 1995; Eve, 1997; Season Poems, 2001; Calendars, 2003; Home Birth, 2004; The Encyclopedia of Scotland, 2004; (trans.) The Complete Poems of Louise Lebe, 2005; Among the Goddesses, 2010. CRITICISM: The Ghost of Meter: Culture and Prosody in American Free Verse, 1993; The Body of Poetry, 2005, A Poet's Craft, 2011, A Poet's Ear, 2011. LIBRETTI: A Captive Spirit, 1999; Merina, 2003. EDITOR/CO-EDITOR: (and contrib.) A Formal Feeling Comes: Poems in Form by Contemporary Women, 1994; After New Formalism (essays), 1999; Carolyn Kizer: Perspectives on Her Life and Work, 2001; An Exaltation of Forms: Contemporary Poets Celebrate the Diversity of Their Art, 2002. Work appears in anthologies. Contributor to books to articles and periodicals. **Address:** Stonecoast MFA, University of Southern Maine, 222 Deering Ave., PO Box 9300, Portland, ME 04102, U.S.A. **Online address:** afinch@usm.maine.edu

FINCH, Caleb E(llicott). American/British (born England), b. 1939.

Genres: Gerontology/Senior Issues, Zoology, Sciences, Psychology. **Career:** Cornell University, School of Medicine, assistant professor of anatomy, 1970-72; University of Southern California, assistant professor, 1972-75, associate professor, 1975-78, professor of gerontology and biological sciences, 1978-, ARCO and William F. Kieschnick professor of neurobiology of aging, 1985-, adjunct professor of neurology, physiology, biophysics, 1984-89, university distinguished professor, 1989-, Research Institute of Ethel Percy Andrus Gerontology Center, associate director for neurogerontology, 1984-89, Alzheimers' Disease Research Center, founding principal investigator and co-director, Gerontology Research Institute, director, Departments of Molecular Biology and Neurobiology, founding member; California Institute of Technology, visiting associate, 1983-84; Johns Hopkins University, lecturer, 1987; University of Maryland, lecturer, 1987; Mount Sinai School of Medicine of the City University of New York, Wellcome Foundation, visiting professor, 1987; Directors of National Institute on Aging Alzheimer's Centers, president, 1988-90; University of Kansas, Kathleen Osborn memorial lecturer, 1991; University of South Florida, David B. Tyler memorial lecturer, 1992; Los Angeles Department of Veteran Affairs, Sigiloff memorial lecturer, 1992. Writer. **Publications:** Cellular Activities During Ageing in Mammals, 1969; Longevity, Senescence and the Genome, 1990; (with R.E. Ricklefs) Aging: A Natural History, 1995; (with T.B.L. Kirkwood) Chance, Development and Aging, 2000; The Biology of Human Longevity: Inflammation, Nutrition and Aging in the Evolution of Lifespans, 2007. EDITOR: (with L. Hayflick and contrib.) Handbook of the Biology of Aging, 1977, 2nd ed. (with E.L. Schneider), 1985; (with A.C. Adelman and D. Gibson and contrib.) Development of the Rodent as a Model for Aging, vol. II, 1978; (with J.A. Behnke and G.B. Moment) The Biology of Aging, 1978; (with D.E. Potter and A.D. Kenny and contrib.) Parkinson's Disease, vol. II: Aging and Neuroendocrine Relationships, 1978; (with A. Cherkin, N. Kharasch, T. Makinodan and contrib.) Aging, vol. VIII: Physiology and the Cell Biology of Aging, 1979; Parkinson's Disease-II: Aging and Neuroendocrine Relationships, 1979; (with P. Davies and contrib.) Molecular Neuropathology of Aging, 1987; (with P. Davies and contrib.) Molecular Approaches to the Neuropathology of Aging, 1987; (with P. Davies and contrib.) The Molecular Biology of Alzheimer's Disease, 1988; (co-ed.) NIH Workshop on Alternate Animal Models for Research on Aging, 1989; (with T.E. Johnson) The Molecular Biology of Aging: Proceedings of a UCLA Colloquium held at Santa Fe, New Mexico, March 4-10, 1989, 1990; (with M.R. Rose) Genetics of Aging, Genetica, 1993; (with M.R. Rose) Genetics and Evolution of Aging, 1994; (with C. Maddox) Encyclopedia of Aging, 1995; (with K.W. Wachter) Between Zeus and the Salmon: The Biodemography of Longevity, 1997; Clusterin in Normal Brain Functions and during Neurodegeneration, 1999; (with J.W. Vaupel and K. Kinsella) Cells and Surveys: Should Biological Measures Be Included in Social Science Research?, 2001; (with Y. Christen and J.M. Robin) Brain and Longevity, 2003. Works appear in anthologies. Contributor to periodicals. **Address:** Ethel Percy Andrus Gerontology Center, University of Southern California, Rm. GER 336, 3715 McClintock Ave., Los Angeles, CA 90089-0191, U.S.A. **Online address:** cefinch@usc.edu

FINCH, Charles. (Charles B. Finch). American (born United States), b. 1980?. **Genres:** Young Adult Fiction, Novels, Mystery/Crime/Suspense. **Career:** Writer. **Publications:** (As Charles B. Finch) CHARLES LENOX MYSTERIES SERIES: A Beautiful Blue Death, 2007; The September Society, 2008; The Fleet Street Murders, 2009; A Stranger in Mayfair, 2010. **Address:** Minotaur Books, 175 5th Ave., 18th Fl., New York, NY 10010-7703, U.S.A. **Online address:** charles@charles-finch.com

FINCH, Charles B. See FINCH, Charles.

FINCH, Christopher. American/British (born England), b. 1939?. **Genres:** Art/Art History, Film, Biography, Essays. **Career:** Walker Art Center, associate curator, curator, 1968-69. Writer. **Publications:** Peter Phillips, 1967; Pop Art: Object and Image, 1968; Image As Language: Aspects of British Art, 1950-1968, 1968; Patrick Caulfield (art), 1971; The Art of Walt Disney: From Mickey Mouse to the Magic Kingdoms, 1973, rev. ed. 2004; Rainbow: The Stormy Life of Judy Garland, 1975; Norman Rockwell's America, 1976; (intro.) Fifty Norman Rockwell Favorites, 1977; Walt Disney's America, 1978; (intro.) 102 Favorite Paintings by Norman Rockwell, 1978; (with L. Rosenkrantz) Gone Hollywood, 1979; (intro.) 332 Magazine Covers, 1979; Norman Rockwell, 1980; Of Muppets and Men, 1981; The Making of The Dark Crystal: Creating a Unique Film, 1983; Special Effects: Creating Movie Magic, 1984; American Watercolors, 1986; Twentieth-Century Water Colours, 1988; Beer: A Connoisseur's Guide to the World's Best, 1989; Nineteenth-Century

Watercolors, 1991; (with C.S. Finch) Highways to Heaven: The Auto Biography of America, 1992; Jim Henson: The Works: The Art, the Magic, the Imagination, 1993; The Art of the Lion King, 1994; (with W.S. Griffiths) America's Best Beers, 1994; (with S. Griffiths) Famous Chefs (and Other Characters) Cook with Beer, 1996; (with L. Rosenkrantz) Sotheby's Guide to Animation Art, 1998; Disney's Winnie the Pooh: A Celebration of the Silly Old Bear, 2000; In the Market: The Illustrated History of the Financial Markets, 2001; Chuck Close: Work, 2007; Joseph Raffael, 2007; Chuck Close: Life, 2010. Contributor to periodicals. **Address:** c/o Author Mail, Abbeville Press, 116 W 23rd St., Ste. 500, New York, NY 10011, U.S.A. **Online address:** info@christopher-finch.com

FINCH, Matthew. *See* **FINK, Merton.**

FINCH, Merton. *See* **FINK, Merton.**

FINCH, Peter. Welsh (born Wales), b. 1947?. **Genres:** Poetry, Language/Linguistics, Literary Criticism And History, Travel/Exploration, History. **Career:** Second Aeon Publishers, editor, 1966-; Arts Council of Wales, Oriel Bookshop, manager, 1973-98; Yr Academi Gymreig, treasurer, 1978-81; Academi, Welsh National Literature Promotion Agency Chief Executive, 1998-2010; Literature Wales , chief executive, 2011. **Publications:** (With S. Morris) Wanted, 1968; Pieces of the Universe, 1969; Cycle of the Suns, 1970; Beyond the Silence, 1970; An Alteration in the Way I Breathe, 1970; (with J.W. Rushton) The Edge of Tomorrow, 1971; The End of the Vision, 1971; Whitesung, 1972; Blats, 1973; Anatarktika, 1973; Trowch Eich Radio Ymlaen, 1977; How to Learn Welsh, 1978; Connecting Tubes, 1980; Blues and Heartbreakers, 1981; Big Band Dance Music, 1981; Collected Visual Poetry 1930-50, 1981; Between 35 and 42, 1982; Dances Interdites, 1983; Some Music and a Little War, 1984; On Criticism, 1985; How to Publish Your Poetry, 1985; Reds in the Bed, 1986; Selected Poems, 1987; How to Publish Yourself, 1988; Peter's Leeks, 1988; The Cheng Man Ching Variation, 1990; Publish Yourself: Not too Difficult after All, 1990; Make, 1990; Poems for Ghosts, 1991; Five Hundred Cobbings, 1993; The Poetry Business, 1994; The Spell, 1995; Useful, 1997; Antibodies, 1997; Dauber, 1997; Food, 2001; Real Cardiff, 2002; Vizet-Water, 2003; Real Cardiff Two, 2005; The Welsh Poems, 2006; New and Selected Poems, 2007; Real Wales, 2008; Real Cardiff Three, 2009; Zen Cymru, 2010. EDITOR: Storm of Bloods, 1970; For Jack Kerouac, 1970; Blats, 1972; Typewriter Poems, 1973; (with M. Stephens) The Green Horse, 1978; (with G. Davies) The Big Book of Cardiff, 2006. **Address:** 19 Southminister Rd., Cardiff, CF23 5AT, Wales. **Online address:** peter@peterfinch.co.uk

FINCH, Robert (Charles). American (born United States), b. 1943. **Genres:** Essays, Natural History. **Career:** Oregon State University, instructor in English, 1969-71; Cape Cod Community College, part-time instructor, 1972-74, 1995; The Cape Naturalist, editor, 1973-82; Brewster Conservation Commission, co-chair, 1980-87; Cape Cod Museum of Natural History, director of publications, 1982-86; Brewster Land Acquisition Commission, co-chair, 1984-87; Emerson College, part-time instructor, 1995; Friends of the Cape Cod National Seashore, director, 1995-96; Williams College, professor. **Publications:** Common Ground: A Naturalist's Cape Cod (essays), 1981; The Primal Place, 1983; Outlands: Journeys to the Outer Edges of Cape Cod (essays), 1986; (ed.) On Nature: Essays on Nature, Landscape, and Natural History, 1987; (ed. with J. Elder) The Norton Book of Nature Writing, 1990; The Cape Itself, 1991; Cape Cod National Seashore Handbook, 1992; (ed.) A Place Apart: A Cape Cod Reader, 1993; Cape Cod: Its Natural and Cultural History: A Guide to Cape Cod National Seashore, Massachusetts, 1993; Smithsonian Guides to Natural America, vol. I: The Mid-Atlantic States: The Mid-Atlantic States: Pennsylvania, New York, New Jersey, 1996, vol. II: Southern New England, Massachusetts, Connecticut, and Rhode Island, 1996; Death of a Hornet, and Other Cape Cod Essays, 2000; (ed. with J. Elder) Nature Writing: The Tradition in English, 2002; Special Places: On Cape Cod and the Islands, 2003; Introduction to Acoustics, 2004; Primal Place, 2006; Iambics of Newfoundland: Notes from an Unknown Shore, 2007. Contributor to periodicals. Works appear in anthologies. **Address:** Counterpoint, 1010 Wisconsin Ave., Ste. 650, Washington, DC 20007, U.S.A.

FINCHLER, Judy. American (born United States), b. 1943. **Genres:** Children's Fiction, History. **Career:** Schoolteacher, 1964-67; supplemental instructor, 1977-81; Paterson Board of Education, teacher, 1981-86, teacher-librarian, 1986-2004, now retired. Writer. **Publications:** Miss Malarkey Doesn't Live in Room 10, 1995; Miss Malarkey Won't Be in Today, 2000; Testing Miss Malarkey, 2000; You're a Good Sport, Miss Malarkey, 2002; (with K. O'Mailey) Miss Malarkey's Field Trip, 2004; (with K. O'Mailey) Miss Malarkey Leaves No Reader Behind, 2006; (with K. O'Mailey) Congratulations, Miss Malarkey!, 2009. **Address:** 23 Trouville Dr., Parsippany, NJ 07054, U.S.A. **Online address:** judyfinchler@optonline.net

FINDLAY, Alison. British (born England), b. 1963. **Genres:** Theology/Religion, Theatre. **Career:** Lancaster University, professor, Shakespeare Programme, director. Writer. **Publications:** Illegitimate Power: Bastards in Renaissance Drama, 1994; A Feminist Perspective on Renaissance Drama, 1999; (with S. Hodgson-Wright and G. Williams) Women and Dramatic Production, 1550-1900, 2000; (ed. with R. Dutton and R. Wilson) Theatre and Religion: Lancastrian Shakespeare, 2003; (ed. with R. Dutton and R. Wilson) Region, Religion and Patronage: Lancastrian Shakespeare, 2003; Playing Spaces in Early Women's Drama, 2006; Women in Shakespeare: A Dictionary, 2010; Much Ado About Nothing, 2011. Contributor to periodicals. **Address:** Department of English & Creative Writing, Bowland College, Lancaster University, Lancaster, LC LA1 4UD, England. **Online address:** a.g.findlay@lancaster.ac.uk

FINE, Anne. British (born England), b. 1947. **Genres:** Novels, Children's Fiction, Young Adult Fiction, Children's Non-fiction, Young Adult Non-fiction, Picture/Board Books. **Career:** Cardinal Wiseman Girls' Secondary School, English teacher, 1968-70; Saughton Jail, teacher, 1971-72; freelance writer, 1973-. **Publications:** CHILDREN'S FICTION: The Summer-house Loon, 1978; The Other, Darker Ned, 1979; The Stone Menagerie, 1980; Round behind the Ice-House, 1981; The Granny Project, 1983; Scaredy-Cat, 1985; Anneli the Art Hater, 1986; Alias Madame Doubtfire, 1987; Crummy Mummy and Me, 1988; A Pack of Liars, 1988; My War with Goggle Eyes, 1989; Bill's New Frock, 1989; Stranger Danger, 1989; The Country Pancake, 1989; A Sudden Puff of Glittering Smoke, 1989; Bill's New Frock, 1989; A Sudden Swirl of Icy Wind, 1990; Only a Show, 1990; The Country Pancake, 1990, new ed. as Saving Miss Mirabelle, 2007; Design a Pram, 1991; A Sudden Glow of Gold, 1991; Poor Monty, 1991; The Worst Child I Ever Had, 1991; The Book of the Banshee, 1991; The Angel of Nitshill Road, 1992; Flour Babies, 1992; Same Old Story Every Year, 1992; The Chicken Gave It to Me, 1992; The Haunting of Pip Parker, 1992; Press Play, 1994; The Diary of a Killer Cat, 1994; Step by Wicked Step, 1995; Celebrity Chicken, 1995; How to Write Really Badly, 1996; The Tulip Touch, 1996; Keep It in the Family, 1996; Jennifer's Diary, 1996; Countdown, 1996; Care of Henry, 1996; Telling Liddy, 1998; Loudmouth Louis, 1998; (reteller) The Twelve Dancing Princesses, 1998; Telling Tales: An Interview with Anne Fine, 1999; Charm School, 1999; Roll Over Roly, 1999; Bad Dreams, 2000; Ruggles, 2001; Very Different: And Other Stories, 2001; Notso Hotso, 2001; (ed.) A Shame to Miss 1, 2001; (ed.) A Shame to Miss 2, 2002; (ed.) A Shame to Miss 3, 2002; Up on Cloud Nine, 2002; The Jamie and Angus Stories, 2002; The More the Merrier in US as The True Story of Christmas, 2003; The Return of the Killer Cat, 2003; (co-author) Meetings with the Minister: Five Chidren's Authors on the National Literacy Strategy, 2003; Nag Club, 2004; Frozen Billy, 2004; Diary of a Killer Cat, 2006; The Road of Bones, 2006; Countdown, 2006; It Moved!, 2006; Jamie and Angus Together, 2007; Jennifer's Diary, 2007; Ivan the Terrible, 2007; The Killer Cat Strikes Back, 2007; The Killer Cat's Birthday Bash, 2008; Jamie and Angus Forever, 2009; The Killer Cat's Christmas, 2009; Eating Things on Sticks, 2009; Under a Silver Moon, 2010; Friday Surprise, 2010; Where is Strawberry Moshi?: Moshi Moshi Kawaii, 2010; The Devil Walks, 2011; Trouble in Toadpool, 2012; Big Red Balloon, 2012; Hole in the Road, 2012. ADULT FICTION: The Killjoy, 1986; Taking the Devil's Advice, 1990; In Cold Domain, 1994; All Bones and Lies, 2001; Fly in the Ointment, 2008; Our Precious Lulu, 2009. OTHERS: How to Cross the Road and Not Turn Into a Pizza, 2002; Raking the Ashes, 2005; (co-author) Shining On: A Collection of Stories in Aid of the Teen Cancer Trust, 2006; On the Summer-House Steps, 2006; (with M. Morpurgo and J. Wilson) Three for Tea: Tasty Tales for You And Me, 2006. Contributor to periodicals. **Address:** David Higham Associates Ltd., 5-8 Lower John St., Golden Sq., London, GL W1F 9HA, England.

FINE, Doris Landau. American/German (born Germany), b. 1949. **Genres:** Education, History, Young Adult Non-fiction, Social Sciences. **Career:** Columbia Point Health Center, physical therapist, 1971-73; Kinderschool of United Cerebral Palsy, staff, 1973-75; Eunice Kennedy Shriver Center, assistant director of physical therapy, 1975-77; University of Massachusetts, adjunct faculty, 1979-80; Waltham Public Schools, Waltham, physical therapist, 1980-82; Wheelock College, instructor, 1984; Northeastern University, lecturer in physical therapy, 1985-88; Youville Hospital, staff, 1988-90; Education Development Center Inc., training specialist, 1992-93, consultant, 1995-; Boston University, Sargent College of Allied Health Professionals, lecturer, 1993-96; Kids Are People Elementary School, physical therapist and staff trainer. Writer. **Publications:** When Leadership Fails: Desegregation and Demoralization in the San Francisco Schools, 1986; (with K. Blenk) Making School Inclusion Work: A Guide to Everyday Practices, 1995. Contributor of articles to journals. **Address:** Education Development Center Inc., 55 Chapel St., Newton, MA 02458, U.S.A.

FINE, Jerramy Sage. American (born United States), b. 1977?. **Genres:** Autobiography/Memoirs. **Career:** Author. **Publications:** Someday My Prince Will Come: True Adventures of a Wannabe Princess (memoir), 2008. **Address:** London, GL , England. **Online address:** info@jerramyfine.com

FINE, Jonathan. Canadian (born Canada), b. 1949. **Genres:** Language/Linguistics, Art/Art History, Medicine/Health. **Career:** Hebrew University of Jerusalem, Center for Applied Linguistics, visiting senior lecturer in English, 1983-85; St. Joseph's Hospital, McMaster Psychiatric Unit, research associate, 1978-80; Ontario Institute for Studies in Education, research officer in applied psychology, 1979-80; Educational Testing Service, collaborator and consultant, 1980-81; University of Medicine and Dentistry of New Jersey, Rutgers Medical School, instructor in psychiatry, 1981-82; Tel Aviv University, visiting senior lecturer in linguistics, 1983; Bar-Ilan University, senior lecturer, 1983-94, coordinator of linguistics, 1986-91, Department of English, head, 1991-93, chairman, 1991-93, coordinator of undergraduate program in linguistics, 1993-, associate professor of English, 1994-2005, professor, 2005-; Department of Psychiatry, visiting scientist, 1996-97; University of Toronto, visiting lecturer, 1996; Hospital for Sick Children, visiting scientist, 1989-90, 1996-97. Writer. **Publications:** How Language Works: Cohesion in Normal and Nonstandard Communication, 1994; (with B.A. Lewin and L. Young) Expository Discourse: A Genre-Based Approach to Social Science Research Texts, 2001; Language in Psychiatry: A Handbook for Clinical Practice, 2006. EDITOR: (with R.O. Freedle) Developmental Issues in Discourse, 1983; Second Language Discourse, 1988. Contributor to books and journals. **Address:** Department of English, Bar-Ilan University, SAL 404, Rm. 201, Ramat-Gan, 52900, Israel. **Online address:** finejo@mail.biu.ac.il

FINE, Marshall. American (born United States), b. 1950. **Genres:** Film, Biography. **Career:** Clarion Ledger, entertainment editor/film, theater and music critic, 1977; Argus Leader, entertainment editor/film, theater and music critic, 1978-83; Times-Union, entertainment writer/film, theater and music critic, 1983-86; Marin Independent Journal, entertainment writer/film and theater critic, 1986-87; Gannett Westchester Newspapers, entertainment writer and film critic, 1987-; National Critics Institute's Eugene O'Neill Theater Center, faculty, 1988-89, 2001-02; New York film Critics Circle, chairman, 1992, 2002, 2006; Jacob Burns Film Center, Journal NewsFilm Club, creator, 2001-04, host/producer, 2001-; Flo Fox's Dicthology, documentary short film, director, 2002; Star Magazine, film/television critic; Cigar Aficionado magazine, contributing editor; Emelin Theater, Emelin Film Club, creator, producer and hosts, 2005; Huffington Post, film/TV critic. **Publications:** Bloody Sam: The Life and Films of Sam Peckinpah, 1991; Harvey Keitel: The Art of Darkness, 1998; (with A. Carolla and M. Fine) Dr. Drew and Adam Book: A Survival Guide to Life and Love, 1998; Accidental Genius: How John Cassavetes Invented American Independent Film, 2005. Contributor to newspapers and periodicals. **Address:** c/o David Vigliano, David Vigliano Agency Ltd., 386 Park Ave. S, New York, NY 10016, U.S.A.

FINE, Richard. American (born United States), b. 1951. **Genres:** Writing/Journalism, Young Adult Fiction. **Career:** Virginia Commonwealth University, American Studies Program, coordinator, 1979-, assistant professor, 1979-86, Department of English, assistant, 1984-85, 1986-87, associate professor, 1986-96, associate chair, 1989-94, chair, 1994-2000, professor of English, 1997-, Glasgow Artists and Writers Workshop, director, 1994-, acting director of composition and rhetoric; Université de Caen, Fulbright junior lecturer in American studies and American literature, 1981-82, Institut d'Anglais, visiting professor, 1987-88; Université de Pau et des pays de l'Adour, visiting professor, 2000-01. Writer. **Publications:** Hollywood and the Profession of Authorship, 1928-1940, 1985; James M. Cain and the American Authors' Authority, 1992; West of Eden: Writers in Hollywood, 1928-1940, 1993. Contributor to journals. **Address:** Department of English, Virginia Com-

monwealth University, 302A Anderson House, 913 W Franklin St., PO Box 842005, Richmond, VA 23284-2005, U.S.A. **Online address:** rfine@vcu.edu

FINELLO, Dominick. (Domnick Louis Finello). American (born United States), b. 1944. **Genres:** Literary Criticism And History, Bibliography, Reference, Young Adult Fiction. **Career:** Rider University, Department of Foreign Languages and Literatures, professor of Spanish, now professor emeritus. Writer. **Publications:** (Ed. as Dominick L. Finello with R.T. Rodriguez) Cornada: Drama en un prólogo, Dos Actos y un epílogo, 1975; (with D.B. Drake) Analytical and Bibliographical Guide to Criticism on Don Quixote (1790-1893), 1987; Pastoral Themes and Forms in Cervantes' Fiction, 1994; Cervantes: Social and Literary Polemics, 1998; (co-ed.) A Celebration of Brooklyn Hispanism: Hispanic Literature from Don Quijote to Today, 2004; Evolution of the Pastoral Novel in Early Modern Spain, 2008. **Address:** Rider University, 2083 Lawrenceville Rd., Lawrenceville, NJ 08648, U.S.A. **Online address:** finello@rider.edu

FINELLO, Domnick Louis. *See* **FINELLO, Dominick.**

FINEMAN, Martha Albertson. American (born United States), b. 1943. **Genres:** Law, Women's Studies And Issues, Human Relations/Parenting, Gay And Lesbian Issues, Institutions/Organizations, Politics/Government, Popular Culture, Social Commentary, Social Commentary. **Career:** U.S. Court of Appeals (7th Circuit), law clerk, 1975-76; University of Wisconsin Law School, assistant professor, associate professor, 1976-86, professor, 1987-91; Feminism and Legal Theory Project, founding director, 1984-; Columbia University School of Law, Maurice T. Moore professor, 1991-99; Cornell University School of Law, Dorothea S. Clarke professor of feminist Jurisprudence, 1999-2004; Emory Law School, Robert W. Woodruff professor of law, 2004-, Vulnerability and The Human Condition Initiative, director. Writer. **Publications:** The Illusion of Equality: The Rhetoric and Reality of Divorce Reform, 1991; The Neutered Mother, the Sexual Family and Other Twentieth Century Tragedies, 1995; The Autonomy Myth: A Theory of Dependency, 2004; The Vulnerable Subject: Anchoring Equality in the Human Condition, 2011. EDITOR: (with N.S. Thomadsen) At the Boundaries of Law: Feminism and Legal Theory, 1991; (with R. Mykitiuk) The Public Nature of Private Violence: The Discovery of Domestic Abuse, 1994; (with I. Karpin) Mothers in Law: Feminist Theory and the Legal Regulation of Motherhood, 1995; (with M.T. McCluskey) Feminism, Media, and the Law, 1997; (with T. Dougherty) Feminism Confronts Homo Economicus: Gender, Law, and Society, 2005; (with J. Jackson and A. Romero) Feminist and Queer Legal Theories: Intimate Encounters, Uncomfortable Conversations, 2009; (with K. Worthington) What Is Right For Children?: The Competing Paradigms Religion and International Human, 2009; Transcending the Boundaries of Law: Generations of Feminism and Legal Theory, 2010. Contributor to books to periodicals and journals. **Address:** Emory University Law School, Gambrell Hall, 1301 Clifton Rd., Atlanta, GA 30322, U.S.A. **Online address:** mfineman@law.emory.edu

FINGLETON, Eamonn. Japanese/Irish (born Ireland), b. 1948. **Genres:** Business/Trade/Industry, Economics, Money/Finance, Politics/Government, History, Social Sciences. **Career:** Financial Times, personal finance editor, 1978-79; Now! Magazine, deputy business editor, 1979-81; Forbes, associate editor, 1981-83; Merrill Lynch Market Letter, senior financial editor, 1983-84; Euromoney, East Asia editor, 1985-87, deputy editor, 1987-89; Freelance writer and public speaker, 1989-. **Publications:** Making the Most of Your Money, 1977; (with T. Tickell) The Penguin Money Book, 1981; Blindside: Why Japan Is Still on Track to Overtake the U.S. By the Year 2000, 1995; In Praise of Hard Industries: Why Manufacturing, Not the Information Economy, is the Key to Future Prosperity, 1999; Unsustainable: How Economic Dogma is Destroying American Prosperity, 2003; In the Jaws of the Dragon: America's Fate in the Coming Era of Chinese Hegemony, 2008. Contributor to periodicals. **Address:** Aoyama NK Bldg. 2F, 4-3-24 Minami Aoyama, Minato-ku, Tokyo, 107-0062, Japan. **Online address:** efingleton@gmail.com

FINK, Carole (Kapiloff). American (born United States), b. 1940. **Genres:** History, Biography, Politics/Government. **Career:** Connecticut College, instructor in history, 1964-65; Albertus Magnus College, lecturer in history, 1966-67; Canisius College, assistant professor of history, 1968-71; State University of New York, assistant professor of history, 1971-78; University of North Carolina, professor of history, 1978-91; Loyola College, Cardin chair in the humanities, 1987-88; Ohio State University, Department of History, professor of history, 1991-, humanities distinguished professor of history, Mershon Center for International Security Studies, associate; United States

Holocaust Memorial Museum, The Center for Advanced Holocaust Studies, Charles H. Revson Foundation fellow, 2003-04. Writer. **Publications:** The Genoa Conference: European Diplomacy, 1921-1922, 1984; (ed. with I.V. Hull and M. Knox) German Nationalism and the European Response, 1890-1945, 1985; (trans. and intro.) M. Bloch, Memoirs of War, 1914-15, 1988, 2nd ed., 1989; Marc Bloch: A Life in History, 1989; (ed. with A. Frohn and J. Heideking) Genoa, Rapallo, and European Reconstruction in 1922, 1991; (ed. with C. Baechler) L'établissement des frontières en Europe après les deux guerres mondiales, 1996; (ed. with P. Gassert and D. Junker) 1968, The World Transformed, 1998; Jews and Minority Rights during and after World War 1, 1999; (ed. with A. Fleury and L. Jílek) Droits de l'homme en Europe depuis 1945=Human Rights in Europe since 1945, 2003; Defending the Rights of Others: The Great Powers, the Jews, and International Minority Protection, 1878-1938, 2004; (ed. with F. Hadler and T. Schramm) 1956: European and Global Perspectives, 2006; (ed. with B. Schaefer) Ostpolitik, 1969-1974: European and Global Responses, 2008; Research on the Polish Minorities Treaty of June, 1919, forthcoming. **Address:** Department of History, Ohio State University, 214 Dulles Hall, 230 W 17th Ave., Columbus, OH 43210-1367, U.S.A. **Online address:** fink.24@osu.edu

FINK, Deborah. American (born United States), b. 1944. **Genres:** Anthropology/Ethnology, Local History/Rural Topics, Women's Studies And Issues, Social Commentary. **Career:** Grinnell College, visiting professor, 1980; Iowa State University, visiting professor, 1980-81, 1983; University of Iowa, visiting professor, 1984-85. Writer and anthropologist. **Publications:** Open Country, Iowa: Rural Women, Tradition and Change, 1986; Agrarian Women: Wives and Mothers in Rural Nebraska, 1880-1940, 1992; Cutting into the Meatpacking Line: Workers and Change in the Rural Midwest, 1998. Contributor to periodicals. **Address:** 222 S Russell, Ames, IA 50010, U.S.A. **Online address:** fink27@gmail.com

FINK, Karl J. American (born United States), b. 1942. **Genres:** Language/Linguistics, Intellectual History, Literary Criticism And History, Sciences, History, Biography. **Career:** Texas Lutheran College, instructor in German, 1966-67; Luther College, instructor in German, 1967-69; University of Illinois, visiting assistant professor of German, 1974-77; Southern Illinois University, visiting assistant professor of German, 1977-78; University of Kentucky, assistant professor of German, 1978-82; St. Olaf College, professor of German, 1982-, department chair. Writer. **Publications:** Goethe's History of Science, 1991. EDITOR: (with J.W. Marchand) The Quest for the New Science: Language And Thought In Eighteenth-Century Science, 1979; (with M.L. Baeumer) Goethe as a Critic Of Literature, 1984; (with H. Rowland) The Eighteenth Century German Book Review, 1995. **Address:** Department of German, St. Olaf College, Old Main, Rm. 34A, Tomson Hall 340, 1520 St. Olaf Ave., Northfield, MN 55057, U.S.A. **Online address:** kjfink@stolaf.edu

FINK, Leon. American (born United States), b. 1948. **Genres:** Politics/Government, Social Sciences, History, Bibliography, Essays, Business/Trade/Industry, Economics. **Career:** City College of New York, Department of history, lecturer, 1972-74; University of Munich, Amerika-Institute, senior Fulbright lecturer, 1983-84; University of North Carolina, Department of History, assistant professor, 1977-85, associate professor, 1985-90, professor, 1990-2000, Zachary Smith professor, 1995-97; University of Illinois, Department of History, distinguished professor, 2000-. Writer. **Publications:** Workingmens Democracy: The Knights of Labor and American Politics, 1983; (with B. Greenberg) Upheaval in the Quiet Zone: The History of Hospital Workers Local 1199, 1989, 2nd ed. as Upheaval in the Quiet Zone: 1199SEIU and the Politics of Health Care Unionism, 2009; Major Problems in the Gilded Age and the Progressive Era: Documents And Essays, 1993, 2nd ed., 2001; In Search of the Working Class: Essays in American Labor History and Political Culture, 1994; (ed. with S.T. Leonard and D.M. Reid) Intellectuals and Public Life: Between Radicalism and Reform, 1996; Progressive Intellectuals and the Dilemmas of Democratic Commitment, 1997; The Maya of Morganton: Work And Community In The Nuevo New South, 2003; Sweatshops at Sea: Merchant Seamen in the Worlds First Globalized Industry, from 1812 to the Present, 2011; (ed.) Workers Across the Americas: The Transnational Turn in Labor History, 2011. Contributors to periodicals. **Address:** Department of History, University of Illinois, 601 S Morgan St., 913 University Hall, Chicago, IL 60607-7109, U.S.A. **Online address:** leonfink@uic.edu

FINK, Merton. Also writes as Merton Finch, Matthew Finch. British (born England), b. 1921. **Genres:** Novels, Romance/Historical, Education, Humor/Satire, Medicine/Health, Young Adult Fiction. **Career:** National Health Service, dental surgeon, 1952-; Bath Literary Society, deputy chairman. Writer. **Publications:** AS MATTHEW FINCH: Dentist in the Chair, 1955; Teething Troubles, 1956; The Third Set, 1957; Hang Your Hat on a Pension, 1958; The Empire Builder, 1959; Snakes and Ladders, 1960; Solo Fiddle, 1961; Beauty Bazaar, 1962; The Match Breakers, 1963; Five are the Symbols, 1964; Jones in a Rainbow, 1965; Chew This Over: The Life of a Dentist, 1965; The Succubus, 1966; Eye with Mascara, 1967; A Fox Called Flavius, 1974; (with B. Tidy) Open Wide. AS MERTON FINCH: Simon Bar Cochba: Rebellion in Judea, 1969. **Address:** Quill Cottage, 27 Harbutts, Bathampton, Bath, SM BA2 6TA, England.

FINK, Mitchell. American (born United States) **Genres:** History, Biography. **Career:** Record World, editor, 1970-; Los Angeles Herald Examiner, music columnist, 1978-, reporter for entertainment, politics, investigative reporting, sports and hard news and gossip columnist, 1987-89; KTTV Fox Entertainment News, staff; People, Insider, columnist and creator, 1990-98; CNN's Showbiz Today, contributor; New York Daily News, gossip columnist and column creator, 1998-2002. Journalist. **Publications:** (Ed.) Off the Record: An Oral History of Popular Music, 1988; (with L. Mathias) Never Forget: An Oral History of September 11, 2001, 2002; The Last Days of Dead Celebrities, 2006; Classic Papers in Critical Care, 2008; Change of Heart: A Black Man, A White Woman, A Heart Transplant and A True Love Story, 2012. **Address:** Open Books Press, Pen & Publish Inc., 4735 S SR 446, Bloomington, IN 47401, U.S.A. **Online address:** mitchell@mitchellfink.com

FINK, Sheri. American (born United States) **Genres:** Biography, Humanities, Adult Non-fiction, Medicine/Health. **Career:** Physicians for Human Rights, researcher, 1990; Students Against Genocide, founder and activist, 1993-98; International Medical Corps, physician, 2003-; The World (radio program), correspondent, 2004-; ProPublica (nonprofit news organization), reporter, 2008-; Tulane University, faculty; Harvard University, faculty, Harvard Humanitarian Initiative, senior fellow; Harvard School of Public Health, visiting scientist, Francois-Xavier Bagnoud Center for Health and Human Rights, fellow; New School for Social Research, faculty; Kaiser Family Foundation, Kaiser media fellow, 2007-08; Center for Balkan Development, board director. Writer. **Publications:** (Contrib.) This Time We Knew: Western Responses to Genocide in Bosnia, 1996; War Hospital: A True Story of Surgery and Survival, 2003. Contributor to periodicals. **Address:** ProPublica Inc., 1 Exchange Plz., 55 Broadway, 23rd Fl., New York, NY 10006, U.S.A. **Online address:** sheri.fink@propublica.org

FINKEL, Alvin. Canadian (born Canada), b. 1949. **Genres:** Business/Trade/Industry, History, Social Sciences. **Career:** Queen's University, Department of History, visiting lecturer, 1975-76; University of Alberta, sessional lecturer, 1976-78; Athabasca University, assistant professor, 1978-81, associate professor, 1981-86, professor of history, 1986-. Writer. **Publications:** Business and Social Reform in the Thirties, 1979; The Social Credit Phenomenon in Alberta, 1989; (with M. Conrad and C. Jaenen) History of the Canadian Peoples, vol. I: Origins to 1867, (with M. Conrad) vol. II: 1867 to the Present, 2nd ed., 1997, 3rd ed., 2001; (with C. Leibovitz) In Our Time: The Chamberlain-Hitler Collusion, 1997; Our Lives: Canada after 1945, 1997; (with C. Leibovitz) In Our Time: The Chamberlain-Hitler Collusion, 1998; (with M. Conrad) Canada: A National History, 2003; History of Canadian Social Policy, 2006; (ed. with S. Carter and P. Fortna) West and Beyond: New Perspectives on an Imagined Region, 2010. **Address:** Department of History, Athabasca University, 1 University Dr., Athabasca, AB T9S 3A3, Canada. **Online address:** alvinf@athabascau.ca

FINKEL, Caroline. (Caroline Fiona Finkel). British/Scottish (born Scotland) **Genres:** History, Archaeology/Antiquities, Adult Non-fiction, History. **Career:** London University, Imperial College of Science and Technology, Seismology Section of the Department of Engineering, research assistant, 1985-; Akkerman Fortress Project, co-director; The University of Edinburgh, honorary fellow. Writer and historian. **Publications:** NONFICTION: The Administration of Warfare: The Ottoman Military Campaigns in Hungary, 1593-1606, 1988; (with N.N. Ambraseys) The Seismicity of Turkey and Adjacent Areas: A Historical Review, 1500- 1800, 1995; Osman's Dream: The Story of the Ottoman Empire, 1300-1923, 2005; (with G. McLean) Infidel Images: Portraits of Europeans in Ottoman Manuscript, forthcoming. **Address:** School of History, Classics and Archaeology, University of Edinburgh, Doorway 4, Teviot Pl., Edinburgh, EH8 9AG, England. **Online address:** carolinefinkel@yahoo.co.uk

FINKEL, Caroline Fiona. *See* **FINKEL, Caroline.**

FINKEL, David. American (born United States), b. 1955. **Genres:** History. **Career:** Washington Post, writer and editor. **Publications:** The Good Soldiers, 2009. **Address:** Silver Springs, MD , U.S.A. **Online address:** davidfinkel@thegoodsoldiers.com

FINKEL, Madelon Lubin. American (born United States), b. 1949. **Genres:** Medicine/Health, Politics/Government. **Career:** Columbia University, School of Public Health, staff associate, 1974-75; New York City Department of Health, Department of Biostats, consultant, 1975-77; Cornell University, Weill Medical College, research associate, 1977-82, professor of clinical public health, 1982-, Office of Global Health Education, director, 2004-; Second Opinion Consulting, president and chief executive officer, 1986-93; MedSearch Network, vice president, 1991-99; State University of New York, adjunct professor of research, 1996-99; Health Care Analytics LLC, managing director, 1997-99; University of Sydney, visiting professor, 2004; Mobil Oil Corp., consultant; Amalgamated Meat Cutters, consultant; New York City Board of Education, consultant; American Council on Science and Health, consultant; Wyeth Pharmaceuticals, consultant; National Public Radio, commentator. Epidemiologist, educator, and author. **Publications:** Health Care Cost Management: A Basic Guide, 1985; (ed.) Surgical Care in the United States: A Policy Perspective, 1988; Understanding the Mammography Controversy: Science, Politics, and Breast Cancer Screening, 2005; Truth, Lies, and Public Health: How We Are Affected When Science and Politics Collide, 2007. WITH H.S. RUCHLIN: (and with E.G. McCarthy) Second Opinion Elective Surgery, 1981; Retiree Health Care: A Ticking Time Bomb, 1988; The Health Care Benefits of Retirees, 1991. Contributor of articles to journals. **Address:** Weill Medical College, Cornell University, 1300 York Ave., New York, NY 10065-4805, U.S.A.

FINKELSTEIN, Adrian. American (born United States) **Genres:** Psychology, Medicine/Health, Sports/Fitness. **Career:** University of Health Sciences, Chicago Medical School, assistant professor of psychiatry, 1972-75; Mount Sinai Medical Center, Psychiatric Department, chief of outpatient psychiatry, 1972-75; Rush Medical School and University, assistant professor of psychiatry, 1975-90; University of California, clinical assistant professor of psychiatry, 1990-, professor; Malibu Holistic Health Center, psychiatrist; Cedars Sinai Medical Center, technical staff. Writer. **Publications:** A Psychiatrist's Search for G-d: Back to G-d: Finding Joy in Divine Union, 1996; Your Past Lives and the Healing Process: A Psychiatrist Looks at Reincarnation and Spiritual Healing, 1996; Marilyn Monroe Returns: The Healing of a Soul, 2006. **Address:** Malibu Holistic Health Center, 22837 Pacific Coast Hwy., Ste. B, Malibu, CA 90265, U.S.A. **Online address:** afinkelstein@pastlives.com

FINKELSTEIN, Max W. Canadian (born Canada), b. 1952. **Genres:** Adult Non-fiction, Travel/Exploration. **Career:** Canadian Wildlife Service, head of interpretive section and creator of exhibits; Canadian Parks Service, senior interpretive writer, 1983-89; Canadian Heritage Rivers System, secretary and treasurer, communications officer, senior writer, park planner, 1989-, marketing and communications officer, spokesman. **Publications:** Canoeing a Continent: On the Trail of Alexander Mackenzie, 2002; (with J. Stone) Paddling the Boreal Forest: Rediscovering A.P. Low, 2004. Contributor to books and periodicals. **Address:** Canadian Heritage Rivers System, Parks Canada, 25 Eddy St., Gatineau, QC K1A 0M5, Canada. **Online address:** max_finkelstein@pch.gc.ca

FINKELSTEIN, Stan N. American (born United States) **Genres:** Medicine/Health, Economics. **Career:** Massachusetts Institute of Technology (MIT), Engineering Systems Division, senior research scientist, 1975-, Harvard-MIT Division of Health Sciences and Technology, senior research scientist, 1975-; Harvard Medical School, Department of Health Care Policy, associate professor. Writer and consultant. **Publications:** (With A.W. Drake and H.M. Sapolsky) The American Blood Supply, 1982; (with P. Temin) Reasonable Rx: Solving the Drug Price Crisis, 2008. **Address:** Massachusetts Institute of Technology, Bldg. E40-251, 77 Massachusetts Ave., Cambridge, MA 02139-4301, U.S.A. **Online address:** snf@mit.edu

FINKENSTAEDT, Rose L. H. French/American (born United States), b. 1927. **Genres:** Race Relations, Social Sciences. **Career:** Writer. **Publications:** Face-to-Face: Blacks in America: White Perceptions and Black Re-

alities, 1994. Contributor of articles to journals and periodicals. **Address:** 22 Quai de Bethune, Paris, 75004, France.

FINKLE, Derek. Canadian/American (born United States), b. 1968?. **Genres:** Documentaries/Reportage, Adult Non-fiction, Criminology/True Crime. **Career:** Saturday Night, features editor, 2002; Toro Magazine, editor, 2002-07, editor-in-chief; Canadian Writers Group, founder. **Publications:** No Claim to Mercy: Elizabeth Bain and Robert Baltovich, A Suburban Mystery (nonfiction), 1998; No Claim to Mercy: The Controversial Case for Murder Against Robert Baltovich, 2004. Contributor to periodicals. **Address:** Canadian Writers Group, 536 Eastern Ave., Toronto, ON M4M 1C7, Canada. **Online address:** derek.finkle@sympatico.ca

FINLAN, Stephen. American (born United States), b. 1952. **Genres:** Theology/Religion. **Career:** Fordham University, professor of theology, 1998-2011; Drew University, professor of theology, 1998-2011; Seton Hall University, professor of theology, 1998-2011; University of Durham, professor of theology, 1998-2011; Mathewson Street United Methodist Church, pastor. **Publications:** The Background and Content of Paul's Cultic Atonement Metaphors, 2004; Problems with Atonement: The Origins of and Controversy about, the Atonement Doctrine, 2005; (ed. with V. Kharlamov) Theosis: Deification in Christian Theology, 2006; Options on Atonement in Christian Thought, 2007; The Apostle Paul and the Pauline Tradition, 2008; The Family Metaphor in Jesus' Teaching: Gospel and Ethics, 2009. **Address:** Mathewson Street UMC, 134 Mathewson St., Providence, RI 02903, U.S.A. **Online address:** sfinlan@yahoo.co.uk

FINLAY, Peter (Warren). (D. B. C. Pierre). British/Australian (born Australia), b. 1961. **Genres:** Novels, Literary Criticism And History, Young Adult Fiction, Humanities. **Career:** Cartoonist, graphic designer, photographer, filmmaker and writer. **Publications:** NOVEL AS D.B.C. PIERRE: Vernon God Little: A Twenty-first-Century Comedy in the Presence of Death, 2003; Vernon God Little, 2004; Ludmila's Broken English, 2006; Lights Out in Wonderland, 2010. Contributor to periodicals. **Address:** c/o Author Mail, Faber & Faber Ltd., 3 Queen Sq., London, GL WC1N 3AU, England.

FINLAY, Richard J(ason). British/Scottish (born Scotland), b. 1962. **Genres:** Politics/Government, Area Studies, History. **Career:** University of Strathclyde, Department of History, lecturer, professor, head. Writer. **Publications:** Independent and Free: Scottish Politics and the Origins of the Scottish National Party, 1918-1945, 1994; A Partnership for Good?: Scottish Politics and the Union, 1880, 1997; (with E.J. Cowan and W. Paul) Scotland since 1688: Struggle for a Nation, 2000; Modern Scotland: 1914-2000, 2004. EDITOR: (with D. Broon and M. Lynch) Scottish National Identity through the Ages, 1995; (with T.M. Devine) Scotland in the Twentieth Century, 1996; (with D. Broun and M. Lynch) Image and Identity: The Making and Re-making of Scotland through the Ages, 1998; (with E.J. Cowan) Scottish History: The Power of the Past, 2002; (with A. Murdoch, E.J. Cowan and W. Paul) The Scottish Nation: Identity and History: Essays in Honour of William Ferguson, 2007. Contributor to books and journals. **Address:** Department of History, University of Strathclyde, 16 Richmond St., Glasgow, G1 1XQ, Scotland. **Online address:** richard.finlay@strath.ac.uk

FINLAYSON, Iain (Thorburn). Welsh/Scottish (born Scotland), b. 1945. **Genres:** Fash Ion/Costume, Biography, Cultural/Ethnic Topics, Literary Criticism And History, Local History/Rural Topics, Novellas/Short Stories, Reference. **Career:** Home Office, civil servant, 1970-74; writer, 1974-. **Publications:** Winston Churchill, 1980; The Moth and the Candle, 1984; The Sixth Continent, 1986 in UK as Writers in Romney Marsh, 1987; The Scots, 1987; (contrib.) Denim: An American Legend, 1990; Tangier: City of the Dream, 1992; Browning: A Private Life, 2004. Contributor to newspapers and magazines. **Address:** c/o Deborah Rogers, Rogers, Coleridge & White Ltd., 20 Powis Mews, London, GL W11 1JN, England.

FINLEY, Glenna. (Glenna Finley Witte). American (born United States), b. 1925. **Genres:** Romance/Historical, Young Adult Fiction, Novels. **Career:** KEVR-Radio, announcer, 1941-42; NBC International Division, producer, 1945-47; March of Time Newsreel Series, film librarian, 1947-48; Time Inc., news bureau staff, 1948-49; freelance writer, 1957-. **Publications:** Death Strikes Out, 1957; Career Wife, 1964; A Tycoon for Ann, 1964; Nurse Pro Tem, 1967; Young Lions, 1968; Journey to Love, 1970; Love's Hidden Fire, 1971; Treasure of the Heart, 1971; Love Lies North, 1972; Bridal Affair, 1972; Kiss a Stranger, 1972; Love in Danger, 1973; When Love Speaks,

1973; The Romantic Spirit, 1973; Surrender My Love, 1974; A Promising Affair, 1974; Love's Magic Spell, 1974; The Reluctant Maiden, 1975; The Captured Heart, 1975; Holiday for Love, 1976; Love for a Rogue, 1976; Storm of Desire, 1977; Dare to Love, 1977; To Catch a Bride, 1977; Master of Love, 1978; Beware My Heart, 1978; The Marriage Merger, 1978; Wildfire of Love, 1979; Timed for Love, 1979; Love's Temptation, 1979; Stateroom for Two, 1980; Doubleday Romance Library, 1980; Affairs of Love, 1980; Midnight Encounter, 1981; Return Engagement, 1981; One Way to Love, 1982; Taken by Storm, 1982; A Business Affair, 1983; Wanted for Love, 1983; A Weekend for Love, 1984; Love's Waiting Game, 1985; A Touch of Love, 1985; Diamonds for My Love, 1986; Secret of Love, 1987; The Marrying Kind, 1989; Island Rendezvous, 1990; Stowaway for Love, 1992; The Temporary Bride, 1993. **Address:** Ann Elmo Agency Inc., 305 7th Ave., Ste. 1101, New York, NY 10165, U.S.A.

FINLEY, Karen. American (born United States), b. 1956?. **Genres:** Plays/Screenplays, Autobiography/Memoirs, Humor/Satire. **Career:** Performance artist, 1980-; National Endowment for the Arts, head. Writer. **Publications:** Shock Treatment, 1990; Enough is Enough: Weekly Meditations for Living Dysfunctionally (aphorisms), 1993; Living It Up: Humorous Adventures in Hyperdomesticity, 1996; Pooh Unplugged-An Unauthorized Memoir, 1999; A Different Kind of Intimacy: The Collected Writings of Karen Finley, 2000; (ed.) Aroused: A Collection of Erotic Writing, 2001; George & Martha, 2006; The Reality Shows, 2011. **Address:** City Lights Books Inc., 261 Columbus Ave., San Francisco, CA 94133, U.S.A.

FINLEY, Michael. (Mike Finley). American (born United States), b. 1950. **Genres:** Business/Trade/Industry, Technology, Autobiography/Memoirs, Information Science/Computers, Poetry, E-books, Animals/Pets, Biography, Biography. **Career:** University of Minnesota-Twin Cities, editor, 1973-78; Worthington Daily Globe, editor, 1978-80; On the Edge (writing and consulting business), owner, 1980-. **Publications:** Techno-Crazed: The Businessperson's Guide to Controlling Technology-Before it Controls You, 1995; (with H. Robbins) Why Teams Don't Work: What Went Wrong and How to Make it Right, 1995; (with H. Robbins) Why Change Doesn't Work: Why Initiatives Go Wrong and How to Try Again-and Succeed, 1996; (with H. Robbins) Transcompetition: Moving beyond Competition and Collaboration, 1998; (with H. Robbins) New Why Teams Don't Work: What Goes Wrong and How to Make It Right, 2000; (with H. Robbins) Accidental Leader: What to do When You're Suddenly in Charge, 2004; The Orchard, 2009. AS MIKE FINLEY: Lucky You, 1976; The Movie Under the Blindfold, 1978; The Beagles of Arkansas, 1978. **Address:** 1841 Dayton Ave., St. Paul, MN 55104-6013, U.S.A. **Online address:** mfinley@mfinley.com

FINLEY, Mike. See **FINLEY, Michael.**

FINLEY, Mitch. American (born United States), b. 1945. **Genres:** Human Relations/Parenting, Theology/Religion. **Career:** Roman Catholic Diocese of Spokane, Family Life Office, director, 1977-82; freelance writer, 1982-. **Publications:** (With K. Finley) Christian Families in the Real World: Reflections on a Spirituality for the Domestic Church, 1984; Catholic Spiritual Classics: Introductions to Twelve Classics of Christian Spirituality, 1987; (with C.C. Barbeau) The Father of the Family: A Christian Perspective, 1990; Time Capsules of the Church, 1990; Your Family in Focus: Appreciating What You have, Making it Even Better, 1993; Everybody Has a Guardian Angel: And Other Lasting Lessons I Learned in Catholic School, 1993; Catholic Is Wonderful!, 1994; Heavenly Helpers: St. Anthony and St. Jude: Amazing Stories of Answered Prayers, 1994; Season of Promises: Praying through Advent with Julian of Norwich, Thomas à Kempis, Caryll Houselander, Thomas Merton, Brother Lawrence, Max Picard, 1995; Whispers of Love: Inspiring Encounters with Deceased Relatives and Friends, 1995, rev. ed. as Whispers of God's Love: Touching the Lives of Loved Ones after Death, 2004; The Gospel Truth: Living for Real in an Unreal World, 1995; Season of New Beginnings: Praying Through Lent with Saint Augustine of Hippo, Dorothy Day, Vincent van Gogh, Saint Teresa of Avila, John Henry Newman, Flannery O'Connor, 1996; The Joy of Being Catholic, 1996; (with K. Finley) Building Christian Families, 1996; 101 Ways to Nourish Your Soul, 1996; The Seeker's Guide to Being Catholic, 1997; Let's Begin with Prayer: 130 Prayers for Junior and Senior High Schools, 1997; Surprising Mary: Meditations and Prayers on the Mother of Jesus, 1997; The Seeker's Guide to the Christian Story, 1997; The Joy of Being a Eucharistic Minister, 1998; For Men Only: Strategies for Living Catholic, 1998; (intro.) Saints Speak to You Today: 365 Daily Remainders, 1999; Catholic Virtues: Seven Pillars of a Good Life, 1999; Prayer for

People Who Think Too Much: A Guide to Everyday, Anywhere Prayer from the World's Faith Traditions, 1999; Your Are My Beloved: Meditations on God's Steadfast Love, 1999; The Ten Commandments: Timeless Challenges for Today, 2000; The Seeker's Guide to Saints, 2000; Your One-Stop Guide to Mary, 2000; The Joy of Being a Lector, 2000; Saint Anthony and Saint Jude: True Stories of Heavenly Help, 2001; What Faith Is Not, 2001; The Seven Gifts of the Holy Spirit, 2001; Corporal and Spiritual Works of Mercy: Living Christian Love and Compassion, 2003; It's Not the Same without You: Coming Home to the Catholic Church, 2003; 101 Ways to Happiness: Nourishing Body, Mind and Soul, 2005; Key Moments in Church History: A Concise Introduction to the Catholic Church, 2005; The Heart and Soul of Imitating Christ: A Fresh Look at the Thomas à Kempis Classic, 2006; Rosary Handbook: A Guide for Newcomers, Old-Timers and Those In Between, 2007; The Patron Saints Handbook, 2010. Contributor to journals. **Address:** The Word Among Us, 9639 Dr. Perry Rd., Ste. 126, Ijamsville, MD 21754, U.S.A. **Online address:** fivestrbanjo@aol.com

FINLEY, Randy. American (born United States), b. 1954. **Genres:** History, Social Sciences. **Career:** Ashdown Public Schools, high school History teacher, 1976-88; DeKalb College, assistant professor of history, 1992-; Smithsonian Institution, pre-doctoral fellow, 1992; Georgia Perimeter College, associate professor of history, professor of history. Writer. **Publications:** From Slavery to Uncertain Freedom (monograph): The Freedmen's Bureau in Arkansas, 1865-1869, 1996; (ed. with T.A. DeBlack) Southern Elite and Social Change: Essays in Honor of Willard B. Gatewood, Jr., 2002. **Address:** Department of Social Science, Georgia Perimeter College-Dunwoody Campus, NE 2212, 2101 Womack Rd., Dunwoody, GA 30338-4435, U.S.A. **Online address:** rfinley@gpc.edu

FINLEY, Robert. Canadian (born Canada), b. 1957. **Genres:** Literary Criticism And History, Humor/Satire. **Career:** Université Canadienne en France, lecturer, 1989-94; Université Sainte-Anne, associate professor of literature and creative writing, 1994-, adjunct professor of English; University of Calgary, Markin-Flanagan Writer-in-Residence, 2004; Memorial University, Department of English Language and Literature, associate professor. **Publications:** The Accidental Indies, 2000; (co-author) A Ragged Pen: Essays on Poetry & Memory, 2006. Contributor of articles to periodicals. **Address:** Department of English Language and Literature, Memorial University, Rm. AA3003, Arts and Administration Bldg., St. John's, NL A1C 5S7, Canada. **Online address:** rfinley@mun.ca

FINN, Margot C. American (born United States), b. 1960. **Genres:** History, Economics. **Career:** Journal of British Studies, editor, 1997-2001; Emory University, assistant professor, 1989-94, associate professor of history, 1994-; Warwick University, professor of history, head of department, 2006-09, Institute of Advanced Study, founding director, 2007-09; Royal History Society, vice president, 2010-12; Development and Widening Participation, pro-vice chancellor, 2011-. Writer. **Publications:** After Chartism: Class and Nation in English Radical Politics, 1848-1874, 1993; When the Other is Another Other: British Orientalism in an East African Context, 1999; The Character of Credit: Personal Debt in English Culture, 1740-1914, 2003; (ed. with J.B. Taylor and M. Lobban) Legitimacy and Illegitimacy in Law, Literature and History, 2010. **Address:** Department of History, Warwick University, H010 Humanities Bldg., Coventry, WM CV4 7AL, England. **Online address:** m.c.finn@warwick.ac.uk

FINN, R(alph) L(eslie). See Obituaries.

FINN, Richard. (Richard Damian Finn). British (born England), b. 1963. **Genres:** History, Theology/Religion. **Career:** Regent's Park College, Centre for Christianity and Culture, lecturer; Melbourne College of Divinity, lecturer; University of Leicester, chaplain; Cambridge University, Fisher House, assistant chaplain; Oxford University, Blackfriars Hall, regent, 2004-, Centre for Animal Ethics, advisor. Writer, Dominican priest and academic. **Publications:** Almsgiving in the Later Roman Empire: Christian Promotion and Practice (313-450), 2006; Asceticism in the Graeco-Roman World, 2009. **Address:** Blackfriars Hall, Oxford University, 64 St. Giles, Oxford, OX OX1 3LY, England.

FINN, Richard Damian. See **FINN, Richard.**

FINNEGAN, Lisa. American (born United States) **Genres:** Communications/Media, Writing/Journalism. **Career:** Port Jefferson Record, reporter;

Saratogian, reporter; Press Enterprise, reporter; States News Service, reporter; Occupational Hazards, editor and staff writer; Fordham University, associate director of public affairs for media relations. Freelance journalist. **Publications:** No Questions Asked: News Coverage since 9/11, 2006. **Address:** Fordham University, Rose Hill Campus, Bronx, NY 10458, U.S.A. **Online address:** writer@noquestionsasked.org

FINNEGAN, Terrence J. American (born United States), b. 1952?. **Genres:** Adult Non-fiction, History, Military/Defense/Arms Control. **Career:** United States Air Force, Reserves, officer, now retired; National Guard Bureau, defense contractor. Writer. **Publications:** Shooting the Front: Allied Aerial Reconnaissance and Photographic Interpretation on the Western Front-World War I, 2006; Shooting the Front: Allied Aerial Reconnaissance in the Great War, 2011. **Address:** National Defense Intelligence College Press, Bolling Air Force Base, Washington, DC 20340-5100, U.S.A. **Online address:** tfinnegan@juno.com

FINNEGAN, William (Patrick). American (born United States), b. 1952. **Genres:** Race Relations, Adult Non-fiction, Civil Liberties/Human Rights, Politics/Government, Third World, Writing/Journalism, Military/Defense/Arms Control, History, Social Sciences. **Career:** Grassy Park High School, English teacher, 1980; New Yorker, contributor, 1984-, staff writer, 1987-. **Publications:** Crossing the Line: A Year in the Land of Apartheid, 1986; Dateline Soweto: Travels with Black South African Reporters, 1988; A Complicated War: The Harrowing of Mozambique, 1992; Cold New World: Growing Up in a Harder Country, 1998. Contributor to books and periodicals. **Address:** c/o Amanda Urban, International Creative Management, 730 5th Ave., New York, NY 10019, U.S.A.

FINNEY, Ernest J. American (born United States) **Genres:** Novels, Novellas/Short Stories, Literary Criticism And History, Young Adult Fiction. **Career:** Writer. **Publications:** NOVELS: Winterchill, 1989; Lady with the Alligator Purse, 1992; Words of My Roaring, 1993; California Time, 1998. STORIES: Birds Landing, 1986; Flights in the Heavenlies, 1996; Sequoia Gardens: California Stories, 2010. Contributor to periodicals. **Address:** PO Box 4416, Visalia, CA 93278, U.S.A.

FINNIS, Jane. British (born England) **Genres:** Novels. **Career:** BBC Radio, freelance broadcaster. Writer. **Publications:** MYSTERY NOVELS: Get Out or Die, 2004; A Bitter Chill, 2005; Death Cuts both Ways, 2005; Buried Too Deep, 2008; Danger in the Wind, 2011. Works appear in anthologies. **Address:** Poisoned Pen Press, 6962 E 1st Ave., Ste. 103, Scottsdale, AZ 85251, U.S.A. **Online address:** janefinnis@ukf.net

FINNIS, John M(itchell). American/Australian (born Australia), b. 1940. **Genres:** Philosophy, Ethics, Law, Theology/Religion, Social Sciences. **Career:** University of California, associate in law, 1965-66; University College, fellow and praelector in jurisprudence, 1966-; Oxford University, lecturer in law, 1967-72, reader in commonwealth and U.S. law, 1972-89, professor of law and legal philosophy, 1989-; University of Malawi, professor of law and head of department, 1976-78; Linacre Centre for Healthcare Ethics, governor, 1981-2007, vice chairman, 1987-85, 2002-07; British Academy, fellow, 1990; Boston College Law School, Huber distinguished visiting professor, 1993-94; University of Notre Dame, Biolchini professor of law, 1995-, Department of Philosophy, adjunct professor. Writer. **Publications:** (Contrib.) The Rights and Wrongs of Abortion, 1971; Natural Law and Natural Rights, 1980, 2nd. Ed., 2011; Fundamentals of Ethics, Georgetown University Press, 1983. (with J.M. Boyle, Jr. and G. Grisez) Nuclear Deterrence, Morality and Realism, 1987; Moral Absolutes: Tradition, Revision and Truth, 1991; (ed.) Natural Law, 2 vols., 1991; Aquinas: Moral, Political, and Legal Theory, 1998; (co-ed.) Derecho a la vida, 1998; Human Rights and Common Good, 2011; Philosophy of Law, 2011; Reason in Action, 2011; Religion and Public Reasons, 2011; Intention and Identity, 2011. Contributor to periodicals. **Address:** Law School, University of Notre Dame, 2117 Eck Hall of Law, PO Box 780, Notre Dame, IN 46556, U.S.A. **Online address:** john.m.finnis.1@nd.edu

FINSTAD, Suzanne. (Suzanne Elaine Finstad). American (born United States), b. 1955. **Genres:** Mystery/Crime/Suspense, Adult Non-fiction, Film, Genealogy/Heraldry, International Relations/Current Affairs, Law, Music, Theatre, Biography, Documentaries/Reportage, Autobiography/Memoirs, Art/Art History. **Career:** Butler and Binion, legal assistant, 1976-78, law clerk, 1978-80, trial attorney, 1980-82; writer and legal consultant, 1982-. **Publications:** Heir Not Apparent, 1984; Ulterior Motives: The Killing and

Dark Legacy of Tycoon Henry Kyle, 1987; Dancing near the Flame, 1990; Sleeping with the Devil, 1991; (collaborator) Queen Noor Memoirs, 1994; Child Bride: The Untold Story of Priscilla Beaulieu Presley, 1997; Natasha: The Biography of Natalie Wood, 2001; Warren Beatty: A Private Man, 2005. Contributor to magazines. **Address:** c/o Michael Carlisle, William Morris Agency, 1350 Ave. of the Americas, New York, NY 10019, U.S.A.

FINSTAD, Suzanne Elaine. See FINSTAD, Suzanne.

FINTUSHEL, Noelle. See OXENHANDLER, Noelle.

FIORETOS, Aris. Swedish (born Sweden), b. 1960?. **Genres:** Novels. **Career:** Swedish Embassy, counsellor of culture, 2003-07. Writer. **Publications:** (ed.) Word Traces: Readings of Paul Celan, 1994; Vanitasrutinerna, 1998; (ed.) The Solid Letter: Readings of Friedrich Holderlin, 1999; The Gray Book, 1999; Stockholm Noir, 2000; (with C. Schreier and M. Gisbourne) Are You Talking to Me? Sprichst du mit mir?, 2004; The Truth about Sascha Knisch: A Novel, 2006; Berlin uber und unter der Erde: Alfred Grenander, die U-Bahn und die Kultur der Metropolo, 2006. **Address:** Stockholm, Sweden. **Online address:** information@arisfioretos.com

FIRESTONE, Reuven. American (born United States), b. 1952. **Genres:** Theology/Religion, History. **Career:** Ordained rabbi, 1982; Union American Hebrew Congregations, director of college education department, 1982-87; Hebrew Union College-New York, lecturer, 1985-87; Drew University, lecturer, 1986-87; Boston University, assistant professor, 1987-92, academic director of the study abroad program, 1988-92; Congregation B'nai Torah, rabbi, 1988; Hebrew Union College-Los Angeles, associate professor, 1993-97, professor, 1997-, Edgar J. Magnin School of Graduate Studies, director, 1997-2005; University of Southern California, Jerome Louchheim School of Undergraduate Jewish Studies, director, 1997-2005. Writer. **Publications:** Journeys in Holy Lands: The Evolution of the Abraham-Ishmael Legends in Islamic Exegesis, 1990; Jihad: The Origin of Holy War in Islam, 1999; Children of Abraham: An Introduction to Judaism for Muslims, 2001; (with L. Swidler and K. Duran) Trialogue: Jews, Christians, and Muslims in Dialogue, 2007; An Introduction to Islam for Jews, 2008; Who Are the Real Chosen People? The Meaning of Chosenness in Judaism, Christianity, and Islam, 2008. Contributor to books and periodicals. **Address:** Hebron Union College, 3077 University Ave., Los Angeles, CA 90007, U.S.A.

FIRKATIAN, Mari A. American (born United States), b. 1949. **Genres:** Biography, History, Food And Wine, Biography, Human Relations/Parenting, Travel/Exploration, Women's Studies And Issues. **Career:** Slavic and East European Journal, assistant editor, 1983-84; Auburn University, instructor in history, 1987-96; Baltic Trade Co., vice-president, 1991-96; American University, assistant professor of history, 1992-94; University of Hartford, instructor in history, 1996-, assistant professor of history, associate professor of history, 2001. Writer. **Publications:** The Forest Traveler: Georgi Stoikov Rakovski and Bulgarian Nationalism, 1996; Diplomats and Dreamers: The Stancioff Family in Bulgarian History, 2008; Diplomati, Mechtateli, Patrioti Bulgaria i Evropa prez pogleda na semeistvo Stanchovi, 2009. Contributor of articles to periodicals. **Address:** Department of Humanities, University of Hartford, 322 Hillyer Hall, 200 Bloomfield Ave., West Hartford, CT 06117-1599, U.S.A. **Online address:** firkatian@hartford.edu

FIROUZ, Anahita (Homa). American/Iranian (born Iran), b. 1953. **Genres:** Novels, Young Adult Fiction, Romance/Historical. **Career:** University of Pittsburgh, instructor in contemporary fiction, 2003. Writer. **Publications:** In the Walled Gardens, 2002. **Address:** c/o Author Mail, Little Brown & Co., 1271 Ave. of the Americas, New York, NY 10020, U.S.A.

FIRSCHING, Ferdinand Henry. See FIRSCHING, F. Henry.

FIRSCHING, F. Henry. (Ferdinand Henry Firsching). American (born United States), b. 1923. **Genres:** Sciences, Theology/Religion. **Career:** Diamond Alkali, senior research chemist, 1955-58; University of Georgia, assistant professor of chemistry, 1958-63; Southern Illinois University, professor of chemistry, 1963-92, now professor emeritus. Writer. **Publications:** The God Hypothesis: A Scientist Looks at Religion, 1997; The Most Intriguing Story Ever Told: A Summary of Scientific Studies about How We Got Here, 2002. Contributor to journals. **Address:** Department of Chemistry, Southern Illinois University Edwardsville, Science Bldg., PO Box 1652, Edwardsville, IL 62026-1652, U.S.A. **Online address:** ffirsch@siue.edu

FIRST, Philip. *See* **WILLIAMSON, Philip G.**

FISCHEL, Jack R. American (born United States), b. 1937?. **Genres:** History. **Career:** Millersville University, professor, 1965-2004, emeritus professor, 2004-; Messiah College, visiting professor of the humanities, 2004-. Writer. **Publications:** (Co-ed.) Jewish American History and Culture: An Encyclopedia, 1992; The Holocaust, 1998; Historical Dictionary of the Holocaust, 1999; The Religious Impact of the Holocaust, 2004; (ed.) Encyclopedia of Jewish-American Popular Culture, 2008. Contributor of articles to periodicals. **Address:** 3704 Little Mac Dr., Landisville, PA 17538, U.S.A. **Online address:** jackiefischel@aol.com

FISCHEL, William A. American (born United States), b. 1945. **Genres:** Economics, Law, Urban Studies, Business/Trade/Industry. **Career:** Dartmouth College, assistant professor, 1973-79, associate professor, 1979-85, vice chair, 1986-91, 1996-98, department chair, 2002-02, Hale chair, 2002-, professor of economics, 1985-, Patricia F. and William B. Hale 1944 professor in arts and sciences 2002-10, Robert C. 1925 and Hilda Hardy professor of legal studies, 2010-; University of California-Davis, visiting associate professor of economics, 1980-81; Vermont Law School, adjunct professor, 1984-91; University of California-Santa Barbara, visiting professor of economics, 1985-86, visiting researcher in economics, 2005-06; University of California-Berkeley, School of Law, Olin fellow in law and economics, 1991-92; George Mason University School of Law, Law and Economics Center, instructor, 1995-98; Lincoln Institute of Land Policy, faculty associate, 1997-2006, board director, 2006-10; University of Washington, Graduate School of Public Affairs, visiting professor, 1998-99. Writer. **Publications:** The Economics of Zoning Laws: A Property Rights Approach to American Land Use Controls, 1985; Do Growth Controls Matter?: A Review of Empirical Evidence on the Effectiveness and Efficiency of Local Government Land Use Regulation, 1989; Regulatory Takings: Law, Economics, and Politics, 1995; The Homevoter Hypothesis: How Home Values Influence Local Government Taxation, School Finance, and Land-Use Policies, 2001; (ed.) The Tiebout Model at Fifty: Essays in Public Economics in Honor of Wallace Oates, 2006; Making the Grade: The Economic Evolution of American School Districts, 2009. **Address:** Department of Economics, Dartmouth College, Rm. 324, 6106 Rockefeller Hall, Hanover, NH 03755-3514, U.S.A. **Online address:** fischel@dartmouth.edu

FISCHER, Debbie Reed. American (born United States), b. 1967?. **Genres:** Novels. **Career:** Writer and educator. **Publications:** YOUNG ADULT NOVELS: Braless in Wonderland, 2008; Swimming with the Sharks, 2008. **Address:** c/o Steven Chudney, The Chudney Agency, 72 N State Rd., Ste. 501, Briarcliff Manor, NY 10510, U.S.A. **Online address:** info@debbiereedfischer.com

FISCHER, Dennis. American/German (born Germany), b. 1960. **Genres:** Film, Horror, Reference. **Career:** Spotlight Cable, assistant traffic controller, 1982-83; Hollywood Reporter, assistant editor, 1984-85; high school teacher, 1985-. **Publications:** Horror Film Directors, 1931 to 1990, 1991; Science Fiction Film Directors, 1895-1998, 2000. **Address:** 6820 Alondra Blvd., Paramount, CA 90723, U.S.A.

FISCHER, Klaus P. German (born Germany), b. 1942. **Genres:** History, Humanities. **Career:** Fort Lewis College, instructor in European history, 1968-69; Chapman College, adjunct professor of history and philosophy, 1973-; Salier-Gymnasium, exchange teacher, 1973; U.S. International University, adjunct professor, 1978; Vandenberg Air Force Base, director of school, 1978-90; Allan Hancock College, professor of philosophy and history, 1990-, Department of Social Science, chairperson, 1994. Writer. **Publications:** Der Mensch als Geheimnís: die Anthropologie Karl Rahners, 1974; Zufalloder Fügung?, 1977; History and Prophecy: Oswald Spengler and the Decline of the West, 1977; (with H. Schiedermair) Die Sache mit dem Teufel: Teufelsglaube und Besessenheit zwischen Wahn und Wirklichkeit, 1980; Gotteserfahrung: Mystagogie in der Theologie Karl Rahners und in der Theologie der Befreiung, 1986; Nazi Germany: A New History, 1995; The History of an Obsession: German Judeophobia and the Holocaust, 1998; America in White, Black, and Gray: The Stormy 1960s, 2006; Hitler and America, 2011. Con-

tributor to journals. **Address:** Department of Social Science, Allan Hancock College, C-304 Bldg., 800 S College Dr., Santa Maria, CA 93454, U.S.A. **Online address:** kfischer@hancockcollege.edu

FISCHER, Lucy Rose. American (born United States), b. 1944. **Genres:** Gerontology/Senior Issues, Human Relations/Parenting, Medicine/Health, Psychology, Sociology, Young Adult Fiction. **Career:** University of Minnesota, assistant professor of sociology, 1979-87; Saint Olaf College, associate professor, 1987-89; Wilder Research Center, senior research scientist, 1989-92; Health Partners Research Foundation, senior investigator, 1992-2002; Midwest Council for Social Research on Aging, newsletter editor; Healthy Outcomes, editor; Lucy Rose Designs, owner. **Publications:** Linked Lives: Adult Daughters and Their Mothers, 1986; (co-author) The Provision of Home Health Care Services through Health Maintenance Organizations, 1988; (with D.P. Mueller, P.W. Cooper and R.A. Chase) Older Minnesotans: What Do They Need? How Do They Contribute?, 1989; Minnesota Age-In-Place Project: The On-Site Coordinator Study, 1992; (with K. Schaffer) Older Volunteers: Time and Talent, 1993; I'm New at Being Old, 2010. Contributor to periodicals. **Address:** Lucy Rose Designs, 2320 Parklands Rd., St. Louis Park, MN 55416, U.S.A. **Online address:** lucy.r.fischer@healthpartners.com

FISCHER, Lynn. American (born United States), b. 1943. **Genres:** Food And Wine, Gerontology/Senior Issues, How-to Books, Medicine/Health, Psychology, Sports/Fitness. **Career:** Fox Television, medical anchor and host, 1984-86; Discovery Channel, The Low Cholesterol Gourmet, host, 1991-95; Public Broadcasting Service, Lynn Fischer's Healthy Indulgences, host, 1995-96; Michaels Media, Fat Free and Healthy, host, 1995-96; Healthy Living, staff, president; March of Dimes, National Capital Area Chapter, board director; Washington Symphony Orchestra, board director. Writer. **Publications:** (With W.V. Brown) Fischer/Brown low Cholesterol Gourmet: The Healthy Heart Guide, 1988; The Quick Low Cholesterol Gourmet, 1992; Healthy Indulgences: Enjoy the Good Life and Food Food with The Low-Cholesterol Gourmet, 1995; Fabulous Fat-Free Cooking: More Than 225 Dishes-All Delicious, All Nutritious, All With Less than 1 Gram of Fat!, 1997; The Better Sex Diet, 1996; (with C.A. Rinzler) Healthy Eating On-the-go for Dummies, 1997; Lowfat Cooking for Dummies, 1997; Quick & Healthy for Dummies, 2000. **Address:** 175 E 96th St., New York, NY 10001, U.S.A. **Online address:** lowfatlife@aol.com

FISCHER, R. J. *See* **FLUKE, Joanne.**

FISCHER, Steven R. New Zealander/American (born United States), b. 1947?. **Genres:** Novels, Humanities, Social Sciences. **Career:** Institute of Polynesian Languages and Literatures, director. Writer. **Publications:** The Dream in the Middle High German Epic: Introduction to the Study of the Dream as a Literary Device to the Younger Contemporaries of Gottfried and Wolfram, 1978; Evidence for Hellenic Dialect in the Phaistos Disk, 1988; The Complete Medieval Dreambook: A Multilingual, Alphabetical Somnia Danielis Collation, 1989; Das Somniarium: Ein mittelalterisches Traumbuch, 1989; (ed.) Easter Island Studies: Contributions to the History of Rapanui in Memory of William T. Mulloy, 1993; Rongorongo: The Easter Island Script: History, Traditions, Texts, 1997; Glyphbreaker, 1997; (with H.G.A. Hughes) William Pascoe Crook, Samuel Greatheed, and Tima'u Te'ite'i, An Essay toward a Dictionary and Grammar of the Lesser-Australian Language, according to the Dialect Used at the Marquesas (1799), 1998; A History of Language, 1999; (ed. with Wolfgang B. Sperlich) Leo Pasifika: Proceedings of the Fourth International Conference on Oceanic Linguistics: Niue Island (South Pacific), 5th-9th July 1999, 2000; (ed.) Possessive Markers in Central Pacific Languages, 2000; A History of Writing, 2001; A History of the Pacific Islands, 2002; A History of Reading, 2003; Island at the End of the World: The Turbulent History of Easter Island, 2005. **Address:** Institute of Polynesian Languages & Literatures, Wellesley St., PO Box 6965, Auckland, 0110, New Zealand.

FISCHER, Tibor. British (born England), b. 1959. **Genres:** Novels, Young Adult Fiction, Novellas/Short Stories. **Career:** Daily Telegraph, correspondent, 1988-90; freelance journalist and novelist, 1992-. **Publications:** Under the Frog in US as Under the Frog: A Black Comedy, 1992; The Thought Gang, 1994; The Collector Collector, 1997; Don't Read This Book if You're Stupid, 2000; I Like Being Killed: Stories, 2000; Voyage to the End of the Room (novel), 2003; Good to be God, 2008. Contributor to periodicals. **Ad-**

dress: c/o Stephanie Cabot, William Morris Agency, 52-53 Poland St., London, GL W1F 7LX, England.

FISCHEROVÁ, Daniela. Czech (born Czech Republic), b. 1948. **Genres:** Plays/Screenplays, Literary Criticism And History. **Career:** Orbis Publishing, editor, 1973-74; Prague Broadcasting, staff; Literary Academy of Josef Skvorecky, lecturer of creative field writing. **Publications:** Povídánís li ou, 1978; Neúplné zatmení, 1983; Hodina mezi psem a vlkem: Soudní pze Frantizka Villona, 1984; Báj, 1987; Princezna T, 1988; Náhlé nestestí, 1993; Andelsky smích, 1993; Fantomima, 1993; Prst, který se nikdy nedotkne, 1995; Přísudek je v této větě podmět, 1996; Velká vterina: rozhlasové hry, 1997; Duhová jiskra, 1998; Jiskra ve senehu, 1999; Fingers Pointing Somewhere Else, 2000. **Address:** c/o Author Mail, Catbird Press, 16 Windsor Rd., North Haven, CT 06473, U.S.A. **Online address:** info@danielafischerova.cz

FISCHETTI, Mark. American (born United States) **Genres:** Adult Nonfiction, Business/Trade/Industry, Sciences, Medicine/Health, Economics. **Career:** Family Business, editor; IEEE Spectrum, managing editor; Harvard Business Review, editor; Issues in Science and Technology Journal, editor; Scientific American, science writer and contributing editor; The New York Times, editor; Smithsonian Magazine, editor; Fast Company Magazine, editor; Omni Magazine, editor; MIT Technology Review Magazine, editor; Forbes Magazine, editor; Sports Illustrated Magazine, editor. **Publications:** (Ed.) The Family Business Management Handbook, 1996; (with T. Berners-Lee) Weaving the Web: The Original Design and Ultimate Destiny of the World Wide Web by Its Inventor, 1999; Building Strong Family Teams, 1999; (ed.) Financial Management of Your Family Company, 2000; (with E. Levy) The New Killer Diseases: How the Alarming Evolution of Mutant Germs Threatens Us All, 2003. Contributor to periodicals. **Address:** Scientific American Inc., 415 Madison Ave., New York, NY 10017-1111, U.S.A.

FISCHKIN, Barbara. American (born United States) **Genres:** Novels, History, Sociology. **Career:** Newsday, staff writer; New York University, journalism professor; Adelphi University, journalism professor; Writers on Autism, founder. **Publications:** Muddy Cup: A Dominican Family Comes of Age in a New America, 1997; Exclusive: Reporters in Love ... and War, 2005; Confidential Sources: A Novel, 2006. Contributor to periodicals. **Address:** The Literary Group Intl., 14 Penn Plz., Ste. 925, New York, NY 10122, U.S.A. **Online address:** barbara@barbarafischkin.com

FISCHLER, Alan. American (born United States), b. 1952. **Genres:** Literary Criticism And History. **Career:** PTN Publishing Corp., associate editor, 1973; Genesee Community College, instructor in English and journalism, 1975-77; Eisenhower College, visiting instructor in rhetoric, 1977-78; Nazareth College of Rochester, instructor in English, 1977-81; Rochester Institute of Technology, faculty and chairman of humanities and international studies, 1981-84; Hartman Materials Handling Systems, manager of technical communications, 1984-86; Rochester Institute of Technology, visiting assistant professor of language, literature and communication, 1987-88; Le Moyne College, assistant professor, 1988-91, associate professor, 1991-97, professor of English, 1997-, director of communication program, 1995-2001; Rochester Gilbert and Sullivan Co., founder and director. **Publications:** Modified Rapture: Comedy in W.S. Gilbert's Savoy Operas, 1991. Contributor to magazines and newspapers. Works appear in anthologies. **Address:** Department of English, Le Moyne College, Rm. 312, Reilly Hall, 1419 Salt Springs Rd., Le Moyne Hts., Syracuse, NY 13214, U.S.A. **Online address:** fischlab@lemoyne.edu

FISDEL, Steven A. American (born United States) **Genres:** History, Humanities, Self Help, Theology/Religion. **Career:** Hebrew Academy of Northwest Indiana, teacher, 1975-80; Temple Chai, educational director, 1982-85; Berlitz School of Languages, translator and instructor, 1983-86; Katriel Enterprises, proprietor, 1988-; Beth Israel, congregational rabbi, 1992-97; Foothill College, instructor in history and religion, 1994-; Chochmat HaLev Institute for Jewish Learning, instructor in Kabbalah and rabbinic studies, 1995-2009; B'nai Torah, congregational rabbi, 1997-; Esalen Institute, instructor, 1997-2005; Center for Jewish Mystical Studies, founder and director, 2004-. Writer. **Publications:** The Practice of Kabbalah: Meditation in Judaism, 1996; The Dead Sea Scrolls: Understanding Their Spiritual Message, 1997. Contributor to books and periodicals. **Address:** Center for Jewish Mystical Studies, 1126 Marin Ave., Ste. 2, Albany, CA 94706-2027, U.S.A. **Online address:** rabbifisdel@classicalkabbalist.org

FISH, Charles (K.). American (born United States), b. 1936. **Genres:** Lo-cal History/Rural Topics, Agriculture/Forestry, Photography, Social Commentary, Autobiography/Memoirs, Literary Criticism And History. **Career:** Princeton University, instructor, assistant professor of English, 1963-68; Windham College, associate professor of English, 1968-76, academic dean, 1969-71; Vermont Council, Humanities and Public Issues, program development consultant, assistant director for the state, 1976-77; Martocci and Henry Real Estate Inc., sales manager, 1982-87, principal broker, 1982-89, director of policy and operations, 1987-89; Western New England College, associate professor of English, 1989-2001, School of Arts and Sciences, acting dean, 1990-91, Department of English and Humanities, chair, 1998-2001, associate professor emeritus of English, 2002-. Writer. **Publications:** In Good Hands: The Keeping of a Family Farm, 1995; Blue Ribbons and Burlesque: A Book of Country Fairs, 1998; In the Land of the Wild Onion: Travels Along Vermont's Winooski River, 2006. Contributor to journals. **Address:** East Dummerston, VT 05346, U.S.A. **Online address:** cfish05346@yahoo.com

FISH, Joe. See WILLIAMSON, Philip G.

FISH, Stanley E(ugene). American (born United States), b. 1938. **Genres:** Law, Literary Criticism And History, History, Poetry. **Career:** University of California, instructor, 1962-63, assistant professor, 1963-67, associate professor, 1967-69, professor of English, 1969-74; Washington University, visiting assistant professor, 1967; State University of New York, Liguistics Institute, visiting professor, 1971; Johns Hopkins University, Department of English and Humanities, visiting professor, 1971, professor, 1974-78, William Kenan Jr. professor, 1978-85, chairman, 1983-85; University of Southern California, Leonard S. Bing visiting professor, 1973-74; University of Maryland, Law School, adjunct professor, 1976-85; Columbia University, visiting professor, 1983-84; Duke University, Department of English, chairman, 1986-92, arts and sciences professor of English and professor of law, 1985-98, associate vice provost, 1993-98, Duke University Press, executive director, 1993-98; University of Illinois, College of Liberal Arts and Sciences, distinguished professor of English, criminal justice and political science, 1999-2005, dean, 1999-2004, dean emeritus, 2004-05; John Marshall Law School, distinguished visiting professor, 2000-02; Florida International University, professor of law and Davidson-Kahn distinguished university professor, 2005-. Writer. **Publications:** John Skelton's Poetry, 1965; Surprised by Sin: The Reader in Paradise Lost, 1967, 2nd ed., 1998; (ed.) Seventeenth-century Prose: Modern Essays in Criticism, 1971; Self-Consuming Artifacts: The Experience of Seventeenth-Century Literature, 1972; The Living Temple: George Herbert and Catechizing, 1978; Is There a Text in This Class? The Authority of Interpretive Communities, 1980; Doing What Comes Naturally: Change, Rhetoric, and the Practice of Theory in Literary and Legal Studies, 1989; There's No Such Thing as Free Speech and It's a Good Thing, Too, 1994; Professional Correctness, 1995; The Trouble with Principle, 1999; How Milton Works, 2001; Milton in the Age of Fish: Essays on Authorship, Text, and Terrorism, 2006; Save the World on Your Own Time, 2008; The Fugitive in Flight: Faith, Liberalism, and Law in a Classic TV Show, 2010; How to Write a Sentence: And How to Read One, 2011. **Address:** College of Law, Florida International University, University Park Campus, Rafael Diaz-Balart Hall, Miami, FL 33199, U.S.A. **Online address:** stanley.fish@fiu.edu

FISHBACK, Mary. American (born United States), b. 1954. **Genres:** Genealogy/Heraldry, History, Travel/Exploration. **Career:** Loudoun Hospital Center, nurse and phlebotomist, 1973-89; Northern Virginia Hospice, nurse, 1980-87; Graydon Manor, nurse and phlebotomist, 1989-99; Thomas Balch Library Commission, chair, 1994-99; Town of Leesburg, library assistant, 2000-; Book Center, coordinator. Writer. **Publications:** Loudoun County: 250 Years of Towns and Villages, 1999; Loudoun County: People and Places, 2000; (co-author) Middleburg Cemeteries, Loudoun County, Virginia, 2000; Loudon County: A Family Album, 2001; Loudoun County: Family Traditions, 2001; Northern Virginia's Equestrian Heritage, 2002; Leesburg, 2003. Contributor to periodicals. **Address:** Town of Leesburg, 25 W Market St., Leesburg, VA 20176-2901, U.S.A. **Online address:** mfishback@leesburgva.gov

FISHBACK, Price V(anmeter). American (born United States), b. 1955. **Genres:** Economics, History, Business/Trade/Industry, Politics/Government. **Career:** University of Washington, teaching assistant, 1977-82; Weyerhaeuser Co., economic researcher and forecaster, 1979-80; University of Georgia, temporary assistant professor, 1982-83, assistant professor, 1983-87, associate professor of economics, 1987-91; University of Texas, visiting professor, 1987-89; University of Arizona, associate professor of economics, 1990-93, professor of economics, 1993-, Frank and Clara Kramer professor of economics, 1999-2010, Thomas R. Brown professor of economics, 2010-; National Bureau of Economic Research, research economist, 1993-94, research associate, 1994-; Southern Economic Journal, associate editor, 2001-06; TIAA-CREF Institute, fellow, 2005-; Journal of Economic History, co-editor. **Publications:** Soft Coal, Hard Choices: The Economic Welfare of Bituminous Coal Miners, 1890-1930, 1992; (with S.E. Kantor) Prelude to the Welfare State: The Origins of Workers' Compensation, 2000; (ed. with E. Zajac and G. Libecap) Public Choice Essays in Honor of a Maverick Scholar: Gordon Tullock, 2000; (co-author) Government and the American Economy: A New History, 2007. Contributor of articles to journals. **Address:** Department of Economics, University of Arizona, 401GG McClelland Hall, 1130 E Helen St., PO Box 210108, Tucson, AZ 85721-0050, U.S.A. **Online address:** pfishback@eller.arizona.edu

FISHBURN, Angela Mary. British (born England), b. 1933?. **Genres:** Crafts, Homes/Gardens. **Career:** Writer. **Publications:** Lampshades: Technique and Design, 1974; Making Lampshades, 1975; Making Lampshades: Lampshades Technique and design, 1977; The Batsford Book of Soft Furnishings, 1978; The Complete Home Guide to Making Pillows, Draperies, Lampshades, Quilts, and Slipcovers, 1978; Curtains and Window Treatments, 1982; Batsford Book of Home Furnishings, 1982; Batsford Book of Lampshades, 1984; Creating Your Own Soft Furnishings: A Practical Guide to Ideas and Techniques, 1986; Soft Furnishings for the Bedroom, 1988. **Address:** Anova Books Group Ltd., Old Magistrates Ct., 10 Southcombe St., London, GL W14 0RA, England.

FISHER, Allen. British (born England), b. 1944. **Genres:** Poetry, Art/Art History. **Career:** Aloes Books, co-publisher, 1972-; Spanner, publisher, 1974-, editor; New London Pride, co-publisher, 1975-81; Hereford College of Art, head of academic affairs; Roehampton University, head of art; Manchester Metropolitan University, English Research Institute, professor of poetry and art, head of contemporary art, now emeritus professor of poetry and art. **Publications:** Thomas Net's Tree-Birst, 1971; Before Ideas, Ideas, 1971; Spaces for Winter Solstice (Blueprint), 1972; Sicily, 1973; Place, 1974; Long Shout to Kernewek, 1975; 5 Plages 'shun, 1975; Paxton's Beacon, 1976; Gripping the Rail, 1976; Der Verolene Operation, 1976; Stane, 1977; Fire-Place (with Hearth-Work by Pierre Joris), 1977; Self-Portraits, Pink 149, 1977; Doing, 1977; Samuel Matthews, 1977; Docking, 1978; London Blight, 1978; Convergences, in Place, of the Play, 1978; Becoming, 1978; The Apocalyptic Sonnets, 1978; Intermediate Spirit Receiver, 1980; Hooks (Taken Out of Place 32), 1980; Eros, Father, Pattern, 1980; Imbrications, 1981; Unpolished Mirrors, 1981; The Art of Flight VI-IX, 1982; Poetry for Schools, Including Black Light, Shorting-Out, and Other Poems, 1982; Bending Windows, 1982; Defamiliarising, 1983; African Boog, 1983; Banda, 1983; Brixton Fractals, 1985; Buzzards and Bees, 1987; Camel Walk, 1988; Stepping Out, 1989; Convalescence, 1992; (with B. Catling and B. Griffiths) Future Exiles, 1992; Dispossession and Cure, 1994; Scram, 1994; Fizz, 1994; Breadboard, 1994; Civic Crime, 1994; Emergent Manner, 1999; Topological Shovel, 1999; Ring Shout, 2000; Sojourns, 2001; Gravity, 2004; Entanglement, 2004; Place, 2005; Stroll & Strut Step, 2005; Singularity Stereo, 2006; Leans, 2007; Proposals, 2010; Assemblage & Empathy: American Literature and Art 1950-1969, 2012. **Address:** English Research Institute, Manchester Metropolitan University, Geoffrey Manton Bldg., Rosamond St. W, Manchester, LC M15 6LL, England. **Online address:** allenfisherstudio@me.com

FISHER, Angela. British/Australian (born Australia), b. 1947. **Genres:** Anthropology/Ethnology, Third World, Photography, Art/Art History, Photography. **Career:** Social worker, 1968-70; traditional jewelry researcher, 1970-77; jewelry designer, 1970-77, 1984-; photographer and writer, 1977-. **Publications:** Africa Adorned, 1984; (with C. Beckwith) African Ark: People and Ancient Cultures of Ethiopia and the Horn of Africa, 1990; (with C. Beckwith) African Ceremonies, 1999; (with C. Beckwith) Passages: Photographs in Africa, 2000; (with C. Beckwith) Faces of Africa: Thirty Years of Photography, 2004; (with C. Beckwith) Dinka: Legendary Cattle Keepers of Sudan, 2008. **Address:** African Ceremonies Inc., 42 Belsize Ave., Belsize Pk., London, GL NW3 4AH, England. **Online address:** africanceremonies@btinternet.com

FISHER, Catherine. Welsh (born Wales), b. 1957?. **Genres:** Novels, Picture/Board Books. **Career:** University of Glamorgan, visiting professor of children's literature, lecturer in creative writing. Writer. **Publications:** SNOW-WALKER SERIES: The Snow-Walker's Son, 1993; The Empty Hand, 1995; The Soul Thieves, 1996; The Snow-Walker Trilogy, 2003. BOOK OF THE CROW SERIES: The Relic Master, 1998; The Interrex, 1999; Flain's Coro-

net, 2000; The Margrave, 2001. ORACLE SERIES: The Oracle, 2003; The Archon, 2004; The Scarab, 2005. ORACLE PROPHECIES: The Oracle Betrayed, 2004; The Sphere of Secrets, 2005. INCARCERON SERIES: Incarceron, 2007; Sapphique, 2008. RELIC MASTER SERIES: The Dark City, 2011; The Lost Heiress, 2011; The Hidden Coronet, 2011. NOVELS: The Conjuror's Game, 1990; Fintan's Tower, 1991; Saint Tarvel's Bell, 1992; The Candleman, 1994; Belin's Hill, 1997; The Lammas Field, 1999; Darkwater Hall, 2000; Corbenic, 2002; The Glass Tower: Three Doorsways to the Otherworld, 2004; Darkhenge, 2005; The Pickpocket's Ghost, 2008; Crown of Acorns, 2010; The Magic Thief, 2010. POEMS: Immrama, 1988; The Unexplored Ocean, 1994; Altered States, 1999. OTHERS: (with K. Henkes and N. Warburton) Magical Mystery Stories, 1999; The Dark Water Hall, 2000; Folklore, 2003; The Weather Dress, 2005; Day of the Scarab, 2006; Darkwater, 2012. Works appear in anthologies. **Address:** c/o Lesley Pollinger, Pollinger Ltd., 9 Staple Inn, Holborn, GL WC1V 7QH, England.

FISHER, Clive. American (born United States), b. 1960?. **Genres:** Biography, Autobiography/Memoirs. **Career:** New York Public Library, Cullman fellow, 2006-07. Freelance journalist and critic. **Publications:** Noel Coward, 1992; Cyril Connolly: The Life and Times of England's Most Controversial Literary Critic, 1996; Hart Crane: A Life, 2002. Contributor to periodicals. **Address:** c/o Bill Hamilton, A.M. Heath and Company Ltd., 6 Warwick Ct., Holborn, London, GL WC1R 5DJ, England.

FISHER, Dana R. American (born United States), b. 1971?. **Genres:** Politics/Government, Economics, Sciences. **Career:** Columbia University, Department of Sociology, assistant professor, 2002-07, associate professor, 2007-, Institute for Social and Economic Research and Policy, Environmental Stewardship Project, director; University of Maryland, Department of Sociology, associate professor. Writer. **Publications:** National Governance and the Global Climate Change Regime, 2004; Activism, Inc.: How the Outsourcing of Grassroots Campaigns is Strangling Progressive Politics in America, 2006. Contributor to books and journals. **Address:** Department of Sociology, University of Maryland, 3133 Art-Sociology, College Park, MD 20742, U.S.A. **Online address:** drfisher@umd.edu

FISHER, David E. American (born United States), b. 1932. **Genres:** Novels, Plays/Screenplays, Sciences, History. **Career:** Oak Ridge National Laboratory, physicist, 1957-58; Brookhaven National Laboratory, chemist, 1958-60; Cornell University, assistant professor of applied physics, 1960-66; University of Miami, professor of geochemistry, 1966-, professor of cosmo chemistry. Writer. **Publications:** A Courtesy Not to Bleed, 1970; Crisis, 1971; Compartments, 1972; A Fearful Symmetry, 1974; The Last Flying Tiger, 1976; The Creation of the Universe, 1977; The Creation of Atoms and Stars, 1979; The Ideas of Einstein, 1980; The Man You Sleep With, 1981; Variation on a Theme, 1981; Katie's Terror, 1982; Grace for the Dead, 1985; The Third Experiment: Is There Life on Mars?, 1985; The Birth of the Earth: A Wanderlied through Space, Time and the Human Imagination, 1987; A Race on the Edge of Time: Radar-The Decisive Weapon of World War II, 1988; The Origin and Evolution of Our Own Particular Universe, 1988; (with R. Albertazzie) Hostage One, 1989; Fire and Ice: The Greenhouse Effect, Ozone Depletion and Nuclear Winter, 1990; Across the Top of the World: To the North Pole by Sled, Balloon, Airplane and Nuclear Icebreaker, 1992; The Wrong Man, 1993; The Scariest Place on Earth: Eye to Eye with Hurricanes, 1994; (with M.J. Fisher) Tube: The Invention of Television, 1996; A Brief History of Life on Other Worlds, 1997; (with M.J. Fisher) Strangers in the Night: A Brief History of Life on Other Worlds, 1998; (ed.) Hurricanes, 2004; Summer Bright and Terrible: Winston Churchill, Lord Dowding, Radar and the Impossible Triumph of the Battle of Britain, 2005; Much Ado About (practically) Nothing: A History of the Noble Gases, 2010. **Address:** PO Box 291, East Orleans, MA 02643, U.S.A. **Online address:** dfisher@miami.edu

FISHER, Donald M. American (born United States), b. 1967?. **Genres:** Sports/Fitness, History. **Career:** State University of New York, Niagara County Community College, assistant professor of history, professor. Writer. **Publications:** Lacrosse: A History of the Game, 2002. **Address:** Department of History, Niagara County Community College, State University of New York, 3111 Saunders Settlement Rd., Sanborn, NY 14132, U.S.A. **Online address:** fisher@niagaracc.suny.edu

FISHER, Ernest F. American (born United States), b. 1918. **Genres:** Military/Defense/Arms Control, History, Social Sciences. **Career:** U.S. Army, Center of Military History, staff, 1960-83; University of Virginia, Northern

Virginia Center, part-time instructor in history, 1960-70. Writer. **Publications:** Cassino to the Alps, 1977; Guardians of the Republic: A History of the Noncommissioned Officer Corps of the U.S. Army, 1994. Contributor to periodicals. **Address:** 1701 N Kent St., Ste. 402, Arlington, VA 22209-2121, U.S.A.

FISHER, Franklin M. American (born United States), b. 1934. **Genres:** Economics. **Career:** Harvard University, teaching fellow, 1956-57, Society of Fellows, junior fellow, 1957-59, Department of Economics, visiting professor, 1981-82; University of Chicago, assistant professor of economics, 1959-60; Massachusetts Institute of Technology, assistant professor, 1960-62, associate professor, 1962-65, professor of economics, 1965-2004, Jane Berkowitz Carlton and Dennis William Carlton professor of microeconomics, 2000-04, Jane Berkowitz Carlton and Dennis William Carlton professor emeritus of microeconomics, 2004-; Netherlands School of Economics, Econometric Institute, national science foundation postdoctoral fellow, 1962-63; Review of Economic Studies, American editor, 1965-68; Journal of the American Statistical Association, associate editor, 1965-68; London School of Economics, Ford Foundation faculty research fellow in economics, 1966-67; Hebrew University, Ford Foundation faculty research fellow in economics, 1966-67, visiting professor, 1967, 1973, 1985; CRA International Inc., consultant and director, 1967-; Econometrica, editor, 1968-77; Tel Aviv University, visiting professor, 1973, 1977-81; Econometric Society, vice president, 1977-78, president, 1979; University of Illinois, David Kinley Lecturer, 1978; National Bureau of Economic Research, research associate, 1980-89, director, 1989-; Hillel Council of Greater Boston, vice president, 1981-86; Boston Friends of Peace Now, president, 1985-87; American Friends of Peace Now, chair, 1985-89; University of Cincinnati, Taft lecturer, 1993; American Jewish Congress, president, 1993-95; New Israel Fund, president, 1996-99; Americans for Peace Now, chair, 2006-09. **Publications:** A Priori Information and Time Series Analysis, 1962; (with C. Kaysen) A Study in Econometrics: The Demand for Electricity in the United States, 1962; (with A. Ando and H.A. Simon) Essays on the Structure of Social Science Models, 1963; Supply and Costs in the U.S. Petroleum Industry, 1964; The Identification Problem in Econometrics, 1966; (with K. Shell) The Economic Theory of Price Indices, 1972; (with J.J. McGowan and J.E. Greenwood) Folded, Spindled, and Mutilated, 1983; (with R.B. Mancke and J.W. McKie) IBM and the U.S. Data Processing Industry, 1983; Disequilibrium Foundations of Equilibrium Economics, 1983; (ed.) Antitrust and Regulation: Essays in Memory of John J. McGowan, 1985; (with K. Shell) The Economic Theory of Production Price Indexes, 1997; (with K. Shell) Economic Analysis of Production Price Indexes, 1998; (co-author) Did Microsoft Harm Consumers?, 2000; (co-author) Liquid Assets: An Economic Approach for Water Management and Conflict Resolution in the Middle East and Beyond, 2005. **Address:** Department of Economics, Massachusetts Institute of Technology, Rm. E52-243F, 50 Memorial Dr., Cambridge, MA 02142-1347, U.S.A. **Online address:** ffisher@mit.edu

FISHER, Jessica. American (born United States), b. 1976?. **Genres:** Poetry, Young Adult Fiction. **Career:** University of California, Holloway postdoctoral fellow in poetry and poetics. Poet. **Publications:** (Ed. with R. Hass) The Addison Street Anthology: Berkeley's Poetry Walk, 2004; Frail-Craft, 2007. Contributor to periodicals. **Address:** Department of English, University California, 322 Wheeler Hall, Berkeley, CA 94720, U.S.A. **Online address:** jmfisher@berkeley.edu

FISHER, Julieta Dias. American/Kenyan (born Kenya), b. 1947. **Genres:** Librarianship, Social Sciences, Reference. **Career:** American Security and Trust Co., bank teller, 1968-69; International Bank for Reconstruction and Development (now World Bank), records assistant and classifier, 1969-71; Southwest Citizens Organization for Poverty Elimination, director of glassboro area center, 1973-74; McCowan Memorial Library, senior library clerk, 1977-83, assistant director, 1983-87; Rowan University, Schaub Curriculum Lab, librarian, 1987; Washington Township School District, school librarian; Wedgewood Elementary School, librarian and media specialist, 1987-89; Orchard Valley Middle School, librarian and media specialist, 1989-97; Washington Township High School, librarian and media specialist, 1997-; Camden County College, reference librarian, 2000-03. Writer. **Publications:** (With A.M. Hill) Tooting Your Own Horn: Web-Based Public Relations for the Twenty-First Century Librarian, 2002; (ed. and contrib.) Ready to Present, 2004. Contributor to periodicals. **Address:** Washington Township High School, 509 Hurffville-Crosskeys Rd., Sewell, NJ 08080, U.S.A. **Online address:** jfisher@wtps.org

FISHER, Leonard Everett. American (born United States), b. 1924. **Genres:** Children's Fiction, Young Adult Fiction, Children's Non-fiction, Mythology/Folklore, Young Adult Non-fiction, Illustrations. **Career:** Yale Art School, graduate teaching fellow, 1949-50; Whitney School of Art, dean, 1951-53; Paier College of Art, faculty, 1966-78, professor of fine arts and dean of academic affairs, 1978-82, academic dean emeritus, 1982-, visiting professor, 1982-87; Westport-Weston Arts Council, founding member, director, 1969-76, vice president, 1972-73, president, 1973-74, chair, 1975-76; Westport Public Library, vice president, 1985-86, president, 1986-89. Writer, artist and consultant. **Publications:** SELF-ILLUSTRATED: Pushers, Spads, Jennies and Jets: A Book: Airplanes, 1961; Pumpers, Boilers, Hooks and Ladders: A Book: Fire Engines, 1961; The Silversmiths, 1964; The Glassmakers, 1964; The Wigmakers, 1965; The Printers, 1965; The Papermakers, 1965; The Hatters, 1965; The Tanners, 1966; The Cabinetmakers, 1966; The Weavers, 1966; The Schoolmasters, 1967; The Shoemakers, 1967; The Doctors, 1968; The Peddlers, 1968; The Limners: America's Earliest Portrait Painters, 1969; The Potters, 1969; The Architects, 1970; Picture Book of Revolutionary War Heroes, 1970; Two if by Sea, 1970; The Shipbuilders, 1971; The Death of Evening Star: The Diary of a Young New England Whaler, 1972; The Homemakers, 1973; The Warlock of Westfall, 1974; Across the Sea from Galway, 1975; Sweeney's Ghost, 1975; The Blacksmiths, 1976; Letters from Italy, 1977; Alphabet Art: Thirteen ABCs from Around the World, 1978; The Factories, 1979; The Railroads, 1979; The Sports, 1980; A Russian Farewell, 1980; The Hospitals, 1980; The Seven Days of Creation, 1981; The Newspapers, 1981; The Unions, 1982; Number Art: Thirteen 123s From Around the World, 1982; The Schools, 1983; Star Signs, 1983; Symbol Art: Thirteen (Square)s, (Circle)s, (Triangle)s From Around the World, 1985; Calendar Art: Thirteen Days, Weeks, Months, and Years From Around the World, 1987; Theseus and the Minotaur, 1988; Jason and the Golden Fleece, 1990; Cyclops, 1991; David and Goliath, 1993; Stars and Stripes: Our National Flag, 1993; Moses, 1995. OTHERS: Head Full of Hats, 1962; (with M.M. Fisher) But Not Our Daddy, 1962; The Art Experience: Oil Painting, 15th-19th Centuries, 1973; The Liberty Book, 1974; Noonan: A Novel About Baseball, ESP, and Time Warps, 1978; Storm at the Jetty, 1980; Boxes! Boxes!, 1984; The Olympians: Great Gods and Goddesses of Ancient Greece, 1984; The Statue of Liberty, 1985; Masterpieces of American Painting, 1985; The Great Wall of China, 1986; Ellis Island: Gateway to the New World, 1986; Look Around: A Book About Shapes, 1986; Remington and Russell, 1986; The Tower of London, 1987; The Alamo, 1987; Monticello, 1988; Pyramid of the Sun, Pyramid of the Moon, 1988; The White House, 1989; The Wailing Wall, 1989; The Oregon Trail, 1990; Prince Henry the Navigator, 1990; The ABC Exhibit, 1991; Sailboat Lost, 1991; Galileo, 1992; Tracks Across America: The Story of the American Railroad, 1825-1900: With Photographs, Maps, and Drawings, 1992; Gutenberg, 1993; Marie Curie, 1994; Kinderdike, 1994; Gandhi, 1995; Niagara Falls: Nature's Wonder, 1996; William Tell, 1996; Anasazi, 1997; The Jetty Chronicles, 1997; Gods and Goddesses of Ancient Egypt, 1997; To Bigotry, No Sanction: The Story of the Oldest Synagogue in America, 1998; Alexander Graham Bell, 1999; Gods and Goddesses of the Ancient Maya, 1999; Sky, Sea, the Jetty, and Me, 2001; Gods and Goddesses of the Ancient Norse, 2001; The Gods and Goddesses of Ancient China, 2003. Illustrator of books by others. **Address:** 7 Twin Bridge Acres Rd., Westport, CT 06880-1028, U.S.A. **Online address:** l.e.fisher@sbcglobal.net

FISHER, Louis. American (born United States), b. 1934. **Genres:** Politics/Government. **Career:** Dow Chemical Co., sales representative, 1959-60; Miles-Samuelson (advertising agency), writer, 1960-62; Plastics Technology (magazine), assistant editor, 1962-63; Queens College, assistant professor of political science, 1967-70; Library of Congress, analyst, 1970-74, specialist, 1974-88, Congressional Research Service, Separation of Powers, senior specialist, 1998-; American University, professor of political science and law, 1975-77; Georgetown University, professor of political science and law, 1976-77; Indiana University, professor of political science and law, 1987; Johns Hopkins University, professor of political science and law, 1989; College of William and Mary, School of Law, professor of political science and law, 1990-92; Catholic University, professor of political science and law, 1990-96. **Publications:** President and Congress: Power and Policy, 1972; Presidential Spending Power, 1975; The Constitution Between Friends: Congress, the President and the Law, 1978; The Politics of Shared Power: Congress and the Executive, 1981, 4th ed., 1998; Constitutional Conflicts between Congress and the President, 1985, 5th ed., 2007; Constitutional Dialogues: Interpretation as Political Process, 1988; American Constitutional Law, 1990, 9th ed. (with K.J. Harriger), 2011; (with N. Devins) Political Dynamics of Constitutional Law, 1992, 5th ed., 2011; (ed. with L.W. Levy) Encyclopedia of the American Presidency, 1994; Constitutional Rights: Civil Rights and Civil Liberties, 1995; Constitutional Structures: Separated Powers and Federalism, 1995; Presidential War Power, 1995, 2nd ed., 2004; Congressional Abdication on War and Spending, 2000; Religious Liberty in America: Political Safeguards, 2002; Congressional Protection of Religious Liberty, 1003; House Appropriations Process, 1789-1993, 2003; Military Tribunals, 2003; Nazi Saboteurs on Trial: A Military Tribunal & American Law, 2003, 2nd ed., 2005; The Politics of Executive Privilege, 2004; (with L. Fisher) Democratic Constitution, 2004; Military Tribunals and Presidential Power: American Revolution to the War on Terrorism, 2005; (with J. Elsea) Suspected Terrorists and What to Do with Them, 2006; In the Name of National Security: Unchecked Presidential Power and the Reynolds Case, 2006; Constitution and 9/11: Recurring Threats to America's Freedoms, 2008; War Power: Original and Contemporary, 2009; Supreme Court and Congress: Rival Interpretations, 2009; On Appreciating Congress: the People's Branch, 2010; Defending Congress and the Constitution, 2011. **Address:** Library of Congress, 101 Independence Ave. SE, Washington, DC 20540-5240, U.S.A. **Online address:** lfisher@crs.loc.gov

FISHER, Marshall Jon. American (born United States), b. 1963. **Genres:** Documentaries/Reportage, Sports/Fitness, Recreation, Young Adult Non-fiction, Children's Non-fiction, Technology, Engineering, Sciences, Social Sciences. **Career:** Writer. **Publications:** The Ozone Layer, 1992; (with D.E. Fisher) Tube: The Invention of Television, 1996; (with D.E. Fisher) Strangers in the Night: A Brief History of Life on Other Worlds, 1998; (with D.E. Fisher) Mysteries of Lost Empires, 2000; Terrible Splendor: Three Extraordinary Men, a World Poised for War, and the Greatest Tennis Match Ever Played, 2009. **Address:** Counterpoint Press, 2117 4th St., Ste. D, Berkeley, CA 94710, U.S.A. **Online address:** mjfisher@usa.net

FISHER, Marvin. American (born United States), b. 1927. **Genres:** History, Literary Criticism And History, Young Adult Fiction. **Career:** Wayne State University, instructor in English, 1951-52; General Motors Institute, instructor in English, 1952-53; University of Minnesota, instructor in English, 1953-58; Arizona State University, assistant professor, 1960-66, associate professor, 1960-66, professor of English, 1966, chairman of department, 1977-83, now professor emeritus of English; Aristotelian University, visiting professor of American civilization, 1961-63; University of Oslo, visiting professor of American civilization, 1966-67; University of California, visiting professor of American studies and acting chairman of department, 1969-70. Writer. **Publications:** Workshops in the Wilderness: The European Response to American Industrialization 1830-1860, 1967; (contrib.) The American Culture, 1968; (contrib.) Americana Norvegica, 1968; (contrib.) American Dreams, American Nightmares, 1970; Going Under: Melville's Short Fiction and the American 1850's, 1977; Continuities: Essays and Ideas in American Literature, 1986; Herman Melville: Life, Work and Criticism, 1988. Contributor to books. **Address:** Department of English, Arizona State University, Rm. 542, 851 S Cady Mall, PO Box 874302, Tempe, AZ 85287-0302, U.S.A.

FISHER, Nikki. *See* STRACHAN, Ian.

FISHER, Paul. American (born United States), b. 1960. **Genres:** Art/Art History. **Career:** Wellesley College, assistant professor American studies, professor of American literature. Writer. **Publications:** Artful Itineraries: European Art and American Careers in High Culture, 1865-1920, 2000; House of Wits: An Intimate Portrait of the James Family, 2008. Contributor to periodicals. **Address:** Department of English, Wellesley College, 103 Founders Hall, 106 Central St., Wellesley, MA 02481-8203, U.S.A. **Online address:** pfisher@wellesley.edu

FISHER, Ralph Talcott. American (born United States), b. 1920. **Genres:** History, Politics/Government, Social Commentary. **Career:** Yale University, instructor, 1952-55, assistant professor of history, 1955-58; University of Illinois, associate professor, 1958-60, professor of history, 1960, now professor emeritus, Russian, East European, and Eurasian Center, founder, 1960-, Summer Research Lab, founder. **Publications:** The New England Seminar on the Soviet Union and Eastern Europe, 1955; Pattern for Soviet Youth: A Study of the Congresses of the Komsomol, 1918-1954, 1959; (ed. with G. Vernadsky) Dictionary of Russian Historical Terms from the Eleventh Century to 1917, 1970; (co-ed.) A Source Book for Russian History from Early Times to 1917, 1972. **Address:** Russian, East European, and Eurasian Center, College of Liberal Arts and Sciences, University of Illinois, 104 Intl Studies Bldg., 910 S 5th St., PO BOX 487, Champaign, IL 61820-6216, U.S.A. **Online address:** r-fisher@illinois.edu

FISHER, Robert E. American (born United States), b. 1940. **Genres:** Art/Art History, Technology, Engineering, Architecture, Literary Criticism And History. **Career:** University of Redlands, professor of art history and head of department, 1971-72; Waseda University, resident director for year-in-Japan program, 1974-75, director of program for study in Japan, 1988-90; Korean Cultural Service, cultural adviser, 1980-86. Writer. **Publications:** Mystics and Mandalas: Bronzes and Paintings of Tibet and Nepal, 1974; Buddhist Art and Architecture, 1993; Art of Tibet, 1997. CONTRIBUTOR: Royal Patrons and Great Temple Art, 1988; Art and Architecture of Ancient Kashmir, 1989; The World of Jade, 1992. Contributor to periodicals. **Address:** PO Box 2556, Carmel, CA 93921-2556, U.S.A.

FISHER, Robin Gaby. American (born United States), b. 1953?. **Genres:** Biography, Autobiography/Memoirs, Sociology, Mystery/Crime/Suspense. **Career:** Courier-News, reporter, 1986-94; Star-Ledger, feature writer, 1994-; Rutgers University, faculty of journalism. **Publications:** After the Fire: A True Story of Friendship and Survival, 2008; (with M. O'McCarthy and R.W. Straley) Boys of the Dark: A Story of Betrayal and Redemption in the Deep South, 2010; (with A.J. Guglielmo) Woman Who Wasn't There: The True Story of an Incredible Deception, 2012. **Address:** The Star-Ledger, 1 Star Ledger Plz., Newark, NJ 07102, U.S.A. **Online address:** robin@robingabyfisher.com

FISHER, Roger (Dummer). American (born United States), b. 1922. **Genres:** International Relations/Current Affairs. **Career:** Bar of Massachusetts, attorney, 1948; Economic Cooperation Administration, assistant, 1948-49; Bar of Washington, attorney, 1950; Covington and Burling, attorney, 1950-56; Bar of U.S. Supreme Court, attorney, 1956; U.S. Department of Justice, assistant to the solicitor general, 1956-58; Harvard University, lecturer, 1958-60, professor, 1960-76, Samuel Williston professor of law, 1976; Harvard Negotiation Project, director, 1980-, Samuel Williston professor emeritus of law, 1992-; U.S. Department of Defense, consultant on international security affairs, 1962-68; The Advocates, TV series, originator and executive editor, 1969-70; Public Interest Communication Services Inc., director, 1976-; Overseas Development Council, director, 1977-; International Peace Academy, director, 1977-; Conflict Management Inc., senior consultant, director, 1984-. **Publications:** (With R.A. Flake and W.T. Burke) Essays on Intervention, 1964, (ed.) International Conflict and Behavioral Science, 1964; International Conflict for Beginners, 1969 in UK as Basic Negotiating Strategy, 1971; (with C. Wolf and A. Geyer) Is America Becoming Militarized?, 1971; Dear Israelis, Dear Arabs, 1972; Points of Choice, 1978; Improving Compliance with International Law, 1981; (with W. Ury) Getting to Yes, 1981, 3rd ed., 2011; (co-author) Negotiation: Materials Prepared for a Continuing Legal Education Videotape Presentation held in Various Locations throughout British Columbia, January and February, 1986, 1986; (with S. Brown) Getting Together, 1988; (with E. Kopelman and A.K. Schneider) Beyond Machiavelli: Tools for Coping with Conflict, 1994; (with D. Ertal) Getting Ready to Negotiate: The Getting to Yes Workbook, 1995; (with A.K. Schneider) Coping with International Conflict: A Systematic Approach to Influence in International Negotiation, 1997; Getting It Done: How to Lead When You're Not in Charge, 1998; (with D.L Shapiro) Beyond Reason: Using Emotions as You Negotiate, 2005. **Address:** Harvard University, Law School, Pound 525, Cambridge, MA 02138, U.S.A. **Online address:** rfisher@law.harvard.edu

FISHER, Roy. British (born England), b. 1930. **Genres:** Poetry, inspirational/Motivational Literature. **Career:** School and college teacher, 1953-63; Dudley College of Education, lecturer, senior lecturer, 1958-63; Bordesley College of Education, Department of English and Drama, principal lecturer, head, 1963-71; University of Keele, Department of American Studies, faculty, 1972-82, now retired; Freelance writer and musician, 1982-. **Publications:** City, 1961; Then Hallucinations: City 2, 1962; The Ship's Orchestra, 1966; Ten Interiors with Various Figures, 1967; The Memorial Fountain, 1967; Collected Poems 1968: The Ghost of a Paper Bag, 1969; Titles, 1969; (with T. Phillips) Correspondence, 1970; Matrix, 1971; (with Phillips) Metamorphoses, 1971; The Cut Pages, 1971; (with D. Greaves) Also There, 1972; (with R. King) Bluebeard's Castle, 1972; (with I. Tyson) Cultures, 1975; (co-author) Widening Circles: Five Black Country Poets, 1976; (with R. King) Neighbours!, 1976; 19 Poems and an Interview, 1976; Barnardine's Reply, 1977; The Thing about Joe Sullivan: Poems, 1971-77, 1978; Scenes from the Alphabet, 1978; Comedies, 1979; Poems 1955-80, 1980; Talks for Words, 1980;

Consolidated Comedies, 1981; (with R. King) The Half-Year Letters: An Alphabet Book, 1983; Turning the Prism, 1985; A Furnace, 1986; (with R. King) The Left-Handed Punch, 1986; (with P. Lester) A Birmingham Dialogue, 1986; Poems 1955-86, 1988; Poems, 1955-1987, 1988; Top Down Bottom Up, 1990; (with T. Pickard) Birmingham's What I Think With (film), 1991; (with R. King) Anansi Company: A Collection of Thirteen Hand-Made Wire and Card Rod-Puppets Animated in Colour and Verse, 1992; Birmingham River, 1994; It Follows That, 1994; The Dow Low Drop: New and Selected Poems, 1996; (with I. Tyson) Roller, 1999; Interviews through Time and Selected Prose, 2000; (with R. King) Tabernacle, 2000; Long and the Short of It: Poems 1955-2005, 2005; Standard Midland, 2010. Contributor of articles to periodicals. **Address:** Four Ways, Earl Sterndale, Buxton, DB SK17 0EP, England. **Online address:** mad.litt@btinternet.com

FISHER, Stephen L(ynn). American (born United States), b. 1944. **Genres:** Politics/Government, Local History/Rural Topics, Social Sciences. **Career:** Tulane University, faculty, 1970-71; Emory and Henry College, faculty, 1971-2006, Hawthorne Professor of Political Science, head of department, 1972-77, 1979-80, 1982-85, Public Policy and Community Service, program director, Appalachian Center for Community Service, director, 1995-2006. Writer and consultant. **Publications:** The Minor Parties of the Federal Republic of Germany: Toward a Comparative Theory of Minor Parties, 1974; (ed.) A Landless People in a Rural Region: A Reader on Land Ownership and Property Taxation, 1979; (ed. and contrib.) Fighting Back in Appalachia: Traditions of Resistance and Change, 1993; (co-ed. and contrib.) Transforming Places: Lessons from Appalachia, 2012. Works appear in anthologies. Contributor of articles to journals, magazines and newspapers. **Address:** PO Box 992, Emory, VA 24327-0992, U.S.A. **Online address:** slfisher44@embarqmail.com

FISHER-WIRTH, Ann W. (Ann Carolyn Welpton). American (born United States), b. 1947. **Genres:** Poetry, Environmental Sciences/Ecology, Literary Criticism And History, Autobiography/Memoirs. **Career:** International School of Liege, teacher, 1968-71; University of Virginia, assistant professor of English, 1981-88; University of Mississippi, professor of English, 1988, Environmental Studies, director; University of Fribourg, Fulbright senior lecturer, 1994-95; Uppsala University, Fulbright distinguished chair in American studies, 2002-03. Writer. **Publications:** William Carlos Williams and Autobiography: The Woods of His Own Nature, 1989. POETRY: Blue Window, 2003; Corvus, 2003; The Trinket Poems, 2003; Five Terraces, 2005; Walking Wu-Wei's Scroll, 2005; Carta Marina, 2009; Slide Shows, 2009; Dream Cabinet, 2012. **Address:** Department of English, University of Mississippi, Bondurant C212, PO Box 1848, University, MS 38677-1848, U.S.A. **Online address:** afwirth@olemiss.edu

FISHGALL, Gary. American (born United States) **Genres:** Biography, Autobiography/Memoirs, Art/Art History. **Career:** Writer and director. **Publications:** Against Type: The Biography of Burt Lancaster, 1995; Pieces of Time: The Life of James Stewart, 1997; Gregory Peck: A Biography, 2002; Gonna Do Great Things: The Life of Sammy Davis Jr., 2003. **Address:** Simon & Schuster Inc., 1230 Ave. of the Americas, New York, NY 10020, U.S.A.

FISHKIN, Shelley Fisher. American (born United States), b. 1950. **Genres:** Literary Criticism And History, Humanities, Race Relations, Popular Culture, Theatre, Essays, Humor/Satire, Animals/Pets, Women's Studies And Issues. **Career:** Yale University, visiting lecturer in American Studies, 1981-84; University of Texas, senior lecturer, 1985-89, associate professor, 1989-93, professor of American studies, 1993-, professor of American studies and English, 1994-2003; Charlotte Perkins Gilman Society, co-founder and executive director, 1990-; Stanford University, professor of English, 2003-, Joseph S. Atha Professor of Humanities, Program in American Studies, director, 2003, Clayman Institute Faculty, research fellow, 2010-11. Writer. **Publications:** From Fact to Fiction: Journalism & Imaginative Writing in America, 1985; Was Huck Black?: Mark Twain and African-American Voices, 1993; Lighting Out for the Territory: Reflections on Mark Twain and American Culture, 1997. EDITOR: (with E. Hedges) Listening to Silences: New Essays in Feminist Criticism, 1994; (with J. Rubin-Dorsky) People of the Book: Thirty Scholars Reflect on Their Jewish Identity, 1996; Oxford Mark Twain, 1996; (with D. Bradley) The Encyclopedia of Civil Rights in America, 1997; The Oxford Historical Guide to Mark Twain, 2002; Is He Dead?: (and foreword) A Comedy in Three Acts, 2003; Mark Twain at the Turn of the Century, 1890-1910, 2005; (and intro. with D, Bradley) Sport of the Gods: And Other Essential Writings, 2005; Anthology of American Literature, 9th ed., 2006, 10th ed., 2011; Feminist Engagements: Forays into American Literature and Cul-

ture, 2009; Mark Twain's Book of Animals, 2009; (afterword and intro.) Mark Twain's Book of Animals, 2010; The Mark Twain Anthology: Great Writers on his Life and Works, 2010. Works appear in anthologies. Contributor to books and periodicals. **Address:** Department of English, Stanford University, Rm. 201, 460-420 Bldg., 450 Serra Mall, Stanford, CA 94305-2087, U.S.A. **Online address:** sfishkin@stanford.edu

FISHLOCK, Trevor. British (born England), b. 1941. **Genres:** Travel/Exploration, Documentaries/Reportage. **Career:** Portsmouth Evening News, staff, 1957-62; Freelance News Agency, reporter, 1962-68; London Times, staff correspondent, 1968-78, 1980-86; World Press Institute, fellow, 1977-78; Daily Telegraph, roving foreign correspondent, 1986-89, 1991-, Moscow correspondent, 1989-91; Sunday Telegraph, roving foreign correspondent, 1991-93; The Times, staff correspondent. **Publications:** Wales and the Welsh, 1972; Talking of Wales, 1976; Discovering Britain: Wales, 1979; Americans and Nothing Else, 1980; Gandhi's Children, 1983; India File, 1983, new ed., 1987; Indira Gandhi, 1986; The State of America, 1986; Out of Red Darkness: Reports From the Collapsing Soviet Empire, 1992; My Foreign Country: Trevor Fishlock's Britain, 1997; Wild Tracks, 1998; Cobra Road: An Indian Journey, 1999; More Wild Tracks, 2000; Conquerors of Time: Exploration and Invention in the Age of Daring, 2004; In this Place: The National Library of Wales, 2007; Senedd, 2010; Pembrokeshire, 2011. **Address:** Daily Telegraph, 1 Canada Sq., Canary Wharf, London, GL E14 5DT, England.

FISHMAN, Aryei. Israeli/Polish (born Poland), b. 1922. **Genres:** Theology/Religion, Sociology, Social Sciences. **Career:** Kibbutz Yavne, affiliate, 1946-47; Jewish Agency, affiliate, 1950; Bar-Ilan University, associate professor of sociology, 1969-, associate professor emeritus of sociology, 1976, Department of Sociology and Anthropology, faculty. Writer. **Publications:** (Ed.) The Religious Kibbutz Movement, 1957; (contrib.) The Perennial Quest, 1984; Ben dat le-ide'ologyah: Yahadut u-modernizatsyah ba-ḳibuts ha-dati, 1990; Judaism and Modernization on the Religious Kibbutz, 1992; Judaism and Collective Life: Self and Community in the Religious Kibbutz, 2002. **Address:** 3 Pinsker St., Jerusalem, 92228, Israel.

FISHMAN, Cathy Goldberg. American (born United States), b. 1951. **Genres:** Picture/Board Books, Theology/Religion, Children's Non-fiction. **Career:** Teacher, 1973-75. Writer. **Publications:** On Rosh Hashanah and Yom Kippur, 1997; On Passover, 1997; On Hanukkah, 1998; On Purim, 2000; On Shabbat, 2001; Soup, 2002; Car Wash Kid, 2003; On Sukkot and Simchat Torah, 2005; Passover, 2006; When Jackie and Hank Met, 2012. **Address:** Marshall Cavendish Childrens Books, 99 White Plains Rd., Tarrytown, NY 10591, U.S.A. **Online address:** catfishg@groupz.net

FISHMAN, Charles N. American (born United States), b. 1961. **Genres:** Business/Trade/Industry, Economics, Sciences, Environmental Sciences/Ecology, Politics/Government, Social Sciences. **Career:** Washington Post, journalist; Orlando Sentinel Sunday Magazine, editor; News & Observer, assistant managing editor; Fast Co. magazine, senior writer, 1996-. **Publications:** The Wal-Mart Effect: How the World's Most Powerful Company Really Works-and How It's Transforming the American Economy, 2006; The Big Thirst: A Tour of the Bitter Fights, Breathtaking Beauty, Relentless Innovation, and Big Business Driving the New Era of High-Stakes Water, 2011. **Address:** c/o Maggie Sivon, Penguin Group Inc., Library Marketing Dept, 375 Hudson St., New York, NY 10014, U.S.A. **Online address:** cnfish@mindspring.com

FISHMAN, David E. American (born United States), b. 1957?. **Genres:** Theology/Religion. **Career:** Brandeis University, instructor; Russian State University, instructor, Project Judaica, director; Jewish Theological Seminary of America, professor of Jewish history and department chair, Judaica Project, director; YIVO Institute for Jewish Research, senior research associate; Bar Ilan University, faculty; Yeshiva University, faculty; Hebrew University, Institute of Advanced Studies, fellow; University of Pennsylvania, Center for Advanced Judaic Studies, fellow; Bernard Revel Graduate School of Jewish Studies, faculty. Writer. **Publications:** (Co-ed.) Guide to Jewish Collections in Moscow Museums, Libraries and the Former Communist Party Archives, 1984; Russia's First Modern Jews: The Jews of Shklov, 1995; Shayṭlekh Aroysgerisn Fun Fayer: Dos Oprateven Yidishe Ḳultur-oystres in yilne, 1996; (ed. with B.L. Visotzky) From Mesopotamia to Modernity: Ten Introductions to Jewish History and Literature, 1999; (intro. with D. Abramowicz) Farshyundene geshṭalṭn, 1999; (with Vysotski) Ot Avraama do sovremennosti, 2002; (with V.N. Kuzelenkov and M.S. Kupovetsii) Dokumenty Po Istorii

I Kulture Evreev V Trofeinykh Kollektsiiakh Rossiĭskogo Gosudarstvennogo Voennogo Arkhiva: Putevoditel, 2005; The Rise of Modern Yiddish Culture, 2005; (ed.) Yiddish Drashos and Writings, 2009; (with L. Katsis and M. Kaspina) Idish, 2009. **Address:** The Jewish Theological Seminary of America, Brush 411, 3080 Broadway, New York, NY 10027, U.S.A. **Online address:** dafishman@jtsa.edu

FISHMAN, Katharine Davis. American (born United States), b. 1937. **Genres:** Cultural/Ethnic Topics, Dance/Ballet, Education, Psychiatry, Psychology, Social Sciences, Essays. **Career:** Vogue, copywriter, 1958-60; Mademoiselle, assistant travel editor, 1960-63; freelance writer, 1964-; American Society of Journalists and Authors, staff, 1982-, executive vice president, 1989-90, president, 1990-91, Writers Emergency Assistance Fund, chair, 2000-03, trustee, 2003-; Authors Guild, staff, 1982-. **Publications:** The Computer Establishment, 1981; Behind the One-Way Mirror: Psychotherapy and Children, 1995; Attitude!: Eight Young Dancers Come of Age at the Ailey School, 2004. Contributor to periodicals. **Address:** Barnes & Noble Booksellers Inc., 122 5th Ave., Ste. 2, New York, NY 10011, U.S.A. **Online address:** kdfishman@attitudethebook.com

FISHMAN, Lisa. American/Canadian (born Canada), b. 1966. **Genres:** Poetry, Humanities. **Career:** Beloit College, assistant professor of English, 1998-; Chicago Arts Program, writer-in-residence; Columbia College, MFA in Creative Writing-Poetry Programs, director and associate professor of English. **Publications:** The Deep Heart's Core Is a Suitcase (poems), 1996; Dear, Read (poems), 2002; KabbaLoom, 2007; The Happiness Experiment, 2007; The Holy Spirit does not Deal in Synonimes: A Transcription of Elizabeth Barrett Browning's Marginalia in Her Greek and Hebrew Bibles, 2008; Lining, 2009; Current, 2010; Flower Cart, 2011. **Address:** Department of English, Columbia College, Rm. 520, 33 E Congress, 600 S Michigan Ave., Chicago, IL 60605-1900, U.S.A. **Online address:** lfishman@colum.edu

FISHMAN, Steve. American (born United States), b. 1955. **Genres:** Business/Trade/Industry, Sciences, Medicine/Health, Children's Fiction, Westerns/Adventure. **Career:** Norwich Bulletin, journalist; Miami Herald, journalist; Newsweek, journalist; United Press Intl., editor; Christian Science Monitor, stringer; Associated Press, stringer; Newsweek, stringer. **Publications:** A Bomb in the Brain: A Heroic Tale of Science, Surgery, and Survival, 1988; Karaoke Nation, or, How I Spent a Year in Search of Glamour, Fulfillment, and a Million Dollars, 2003; Ralphie the Gopher, 2006. Contributor to periodicals. **Address:** c/o Author Mail, Free Press, Simon & Schuster, 1230 Ave. of the Americas, New York, NY 10020, U.S.A.

FISHMAN, Sylvia Barack. American (born United States), b. 1942?. **Genres:** Young Adult Fiction. **Career:** Brandeis University, associate professor of contemporary Jewry, American Jewish sociology, professor of contemporary Jewish life, department chair, Hadassah-Brandeis Institute, co-director, Cohen Center for Modern Jewish Studies, faculty, affiliate. Writer. **Publications:** (Co-author) Intermarriage and American Jews Today, 1990; (ed. with L.I. Sternberg and G.A. Tobin) Changing Jewish Life: Service Delivery and Planning in the 1990s, 1991; (ed. and intro.) Follow My Footprints: Changing Images of Women in American Jewish Fiction, 1992; A Breath of Life: Feminism in the American Jewish Community, 1993; More than Chemistry: The Romantic Choices of American Jews, 1995; Negotiating Both Sides of the Hyphen: Coalescence Compartmentalization and American-Jewish Values, 1996; Real Americans: The Evolving Identities of American Jews, 1996; I of the Beholder: Jews and Gender in Film and Popular Culture, 1998; From Skala to Ramat Gan: An Educational Journey, 1998; (with T. Belzer) The Status of Jewish Women's Studies in the United States and Canada, 1998; Jewish Life and American Culture, 2000; Jewish and Something Else: A Study of Mixed-Marriage Families, 2001; Relatively Speaking: Constructing Identity in Jewish and Mixed Married Families, 2002; Double or Nothing? Jewish Families and Mixed Marriage, 2004; Way into the Varieties of Jewishness, 2007. **Address:** Department of Sociology, Brandeis University, 210 Lown, 415 South St., PO Box 054, Waltham, MA 02453, U.S.A. **Online address:** fishman@brandeis.edu

FISK, Milton. American (born United States), b. 1932. **Genres:** Ethics, Philosophy, Sociology. **Career:** University of Notre Dame, instructor, assistant professor, 1957-63; Yale University, assistant professor, 1963-66; Indiana University, associate professor, professor, 1966-97, professor emeritus, 1997-. **Publications:** Modern formal logic, 1964; Nature and Necessity, 1973; Ethics and Society: A Marxist Interpretation of Value, 1980; The State and Justice:

An Essay in Political Theory, 1989; (ed.) Justice, 1993; Toward a Healthy Society: The Morality and Politics of American Health Care Reform, 2000; (ed. with A. Anton and N. Holmstrom) Not for Sale: A Defense of Public Goods, 2001; Bienes publicos y justicia radical, 2004. **Address:** 3984 E Brighton Crest, Bloomington, IN 47401, U.S.A. **Online address:** fiskm@indiana.edu

FISK, Pauline. British (born England), b. 1948. **Genres:** Children's Fiction, Young Adult Fiction, Novels, Novellas/Short Stories, Literary Criticism And History. **Career:** Writer. **Publications:** The Southern Hill (stories), 1972. NOVELS: Midnight Blue, 1990; Telling the Sea, 1992; Tyger Pool, 1994; The Beast of Whixall Moss, 1997; The Candle House, 1999; Sabrina Fludde, 2001 in US as The Secret of Sabrina Fludde, 2002; The Red Judge, 2005; The Mrs. Merridge Project, 2005; Mad Dog Moonlight, 2009; Flying for Frankie, 2009; In the Trees, 2010. Contributor to periodicals. **Address:** Laura Cecil Agency, 17 Alwyne Villas, London, GL N1 2HG, England.

FISKE, Robert H(artwell). American (born United States), b. 1948. **Genres:** Writing/Journalism, Literary Criticism And History, Reference. **Career:** The Vocabula Review, editor and publisher, 1999-; Vocabula Communications Co., owner. **Publications:** Guide to Concise Writing, 1990; Thesaurus of Alternatives to Worn-Out Words and Phrases, 1994; The Writer's Digest Dictionary of Concise Writing, 1996; (ed. with R.M. Hilliard) Strangers and Pilgrims, 2000; The Dimwit's Dictionary, 2002; (ed.) Vocabula Bound: Outbursts, Insights, Explanations and Oddities, 2004; 101 Wordy Phrases, 2005; 101 Foolish Phrases, 2005; 101 Elegant Paragraphs, 2005; The Dictionary of Concise Writing, 2006; The Dictionary of Disagreeable English, 2006; Silence, Language and Society: A Guide to Style and Grammar, Grace and Compassion, 2008; Speaking of Silence (or Agnes and Otto), 2008; (ed.) Vocabula Bound 1: Outbursts, Insights, Explanations and Oddities, 2008; (and ed.) Vocabula Bound 2: Our Wresting, Writhing Tongue, 2008; Poem, Revised: 54 Poems, Revisions, Discussions, 2008; The Best Words: More Than 200 of the Most Excellent, Most Desirable, Most Suitable, Most Satisfying Words, 2011. **Address:** Vocabula Communications Co., PO Box 611, Andover, MA 01810, U.S.A. **Online address:** editor@vocabula.com

FISKE, Sharon. See HILL, Pamela.

FISS, Owen M(itchell). American (born United States), b. 1938. **Genres:** Law, Essays. **Career:** United States Court of Appeals, Second Circuit, law clerk, 1964-65; Supreme Court of the United States, law clerk, 1965-66; United States Department of Justice, Civil Rights Division, special assistant, 1966-68, Office of Planning and Coordination, acting director, 1967-68; University of Chicago, associate professor, 1968-71, professor of law, 1971-74; U.S. President's Commission, consultant, 1970; Yale University, Law School, professor of law, 1974-82, Alexander M. Bickel professor of public law, 1982-92, Sterling professor of law, 1992-, now Sterling professor emeritus of law and professorial lecturer in law. Writer. **Publications:** Injunctions: Teaching Materials, 1971, (with D. Rendleman) 2nd ed., 1984; (co-author) Affirmative Action: The Answer to Discrimination?: An AEI Round Table Held on May 28, 1975, At the American Enterprise Institute for Public Policy Research, Washington, D.C., 1976; Civil Rights Injunction, 1978; (with R.M. Cover) The Structure of Procedure, 1979; (with P.J. Bergan and C.W. McCurdy) Fields and the Law: Essays, 1986; (with R.M. Cover and J. Resnik) Procedure, 1988; (ed. with R.M. Cover and J. Resnik) Federal Procedural System: A Rule and Statutory Source Book, 1988; Troubled Beginnings of the Modern State, 1888-1910, 1993; Liberalism Divided: Freedom of Speech and The Many Uses of State Power, 1996; The Irony of Free Speech, 1996; A Community of Equals: The Constitutional Protection of New Americans, 1999; A Way Out: America's Ghettos and the Legacy of Racism, 2003; (with J. Resnik) Adjudication and Its Alternatives: An Introduction to Procedure, 2003; The Law as It Could Be, 2003. Contributor to journals and magazines. **Address:** Law School, Yale University, PO Box 208215, New Haven, CT 06520, U.S.A. **Online address:** owen.fiss@yale.edu

FISTER, Barbara. (Barbara Ruth Fister). American (born United States), b. 1954?. **Genres:** Novels, Literary Criticism And History. **Career:** Gustavus Adolphus College, academic librarian. Writer. **Publications:** Third World Women's Literatures: A Dictionary and Guide to Materials in English, 1995; (contrib.) Research and Documentation in the Electronic Age, 1998, 4th ed., 2006; On Edge (novel), 2002; In the Wind (novel), 2008. **Address:** Gustavus Adolphus College, 800 W College Ave., Saint Peter, MN 56082-1485, U.S.A. **Online address:** bfister@hickorytech.net

FISTER, Barbara Ruth. *See* FISTER, Barbara.

FITCH, David E. American (born United States), b. 1956?. **Genres:** Theology/Religion, Philosophy, Institutions/Organizations. **Career:** Northern Baptist Theological Seminary, adjunct professor, Betty R. Lindner chair of evangelical theology, M.A. program in Missional Church Ministry, director; Life on the Vine Christian Community, pastor; Up/ Rooted, co-founder. Writer. **Publications:** The Great Giveaway: Reclaiming the Mission of the Church from Big Business, Parachurch Organizations, Psychotherapy, Consumer Capitalism and Other Modern Maladies, 2005; End of Evangelicalism?: Discerning a New Faithfulness for Mission: Towards an Evangelical Political Theology, 2011. Contributor of articles to journals. **Address:** Northern Baptist Theological Seminary, 660 E Butterfield Rd., Lombard, IL 60148, U.S.A. **Online address:** fitchest@gmail.com

FITCH, Noel Riley. American (born United States), b. 1937. **Genres:** Literary Criticism And History, Travel/Exploration, Biography. **Career:** Moscow Junior High School, teacher of language arts, 1959-62; Moscow Senior High School, teacher of English, 1962-63; Washington State University, teaching assistant, 1963-66, instructor, 1967-68; Eastern Nazarene College, assistant professor, 1966-67, 1968-71; California State University, associate professor, 1976-78; Point Loma College, professor of literature, 1971-87, Department of Literature and Modern Languages, chair, 1982-85; University of Southern California, professional, 1986-, now retired; American University of Paris, lecturer, 1987-, now retired; Professional Biographers Group, co-founder, 1993. **Publications:** Sylvia Beach and the Lost Generation: A History of Literary Paris in the Twenties and Thirties, 1983; (ed. with R.W. Etulain) Faith and Imagination: Essays on Evangelicals and Literature, 1985; Hemingway in Paris: Parisian Walks for the Literary Traveller, 1989; Literary Cafés of Paris, 1989; (author of intro.) In Transition: A Paris Anthology, 1990; Walks in Hemingway's Paris: A Guide to Paris for the Literary Traveler, 1990; Anaïs: The Erotic Life of Anais Nin, 1993; Appetite for Life: The Biography of Julia Child, 1997; The Grand Literary Cafés of Europe, 2006; (with R. Tulka) Paris Café: The Sélect Crowd, 2007. Contributor of articles to journals. **Address:** c/o Kris Dahl, International Creative Management, 40 W 57th St., Ste. 1711, New York, NY 10019, U.S.A. **Online address:** noelriley@aol.com

FITCH, Sheree. Canadian (born Canada), b. 1956. **Genres:** Poetry, Young Adult Fiction, Children's Fiction, Plays/Screenplays. **Career:** Performance poet; actress. Writer. **Publications:** POETRY FOR CHILDREN: Toes in My Nose, And Other Poems, 1987; Sleeping Dragons All Around, (prose), 1989; Merry-Go-Day, 1991; There Were Monkeys in My Kitchen!, 1992; I am Small, 1994; Mabel Murple, 1995; If You Could Wear My Sneakers!: Poems, 1997; There's a Mouse in My House, 1998; The Hullabaloo Bugaboo Day, 1998; The Other Author, Arthur, 1999; No Two Snowflakes, 2001; One More Step, 2002; Pocket Rocks, 2004; Peek-a-Little Boo, 2005; If I Had a Million Onions, 2005; The Gravesavers, 2005; Birthday Party Pandamonium, 2006; Big Bad Bertha, 2007; (with L. Swartz) The Poetry Experience, 2008; Kisses Kisses Baby-O!, 2008; Pluto's Ghost, 2010; Mabel Murple, 2010; Sun-Day, Moon-Day, Some Day Dreams, forthcoming. PLAYS: Light a Little Candle, 1996; Rummabubba, Lid-Maker of the Snufflewogs, 1997; The Monkeys are Back and We're Out of Bananas, 1998; The Hullabaloo Bugaboo Day, 1998. POETRY FOR ADULTS: In This House Are Many Women, 1996; Kiss the Joy as It Flies, 2008. Contributor to periodicals. **Address:** c/o Writer's Federation of Nova Scotia, 1113 Marginal Rd., Halifax, NS B3H 4P7, Canada. **Online address:** sheree.fitch@starpower.net

FITCH, Stona. American (born United States), b. 1961?. **Genres:** Novels. **Career:** Daily Princetonian, chair; Anchorage Daily News, writer; Miami Herald, reporter; Concord Free Press, founder, 2008-. **Publications:** Strategies for Success: A Novel, 1992; Senseless, 2001; Printer's Devil, 2009; Give + Take, 2010. **Address:** c/o Michelle Lapautre, 6 rue Jean Carries, Paris, 75007, France. **Online address:** stona7@aol.com

FITES, Philip. (Philip E. Fites). Canadian/American (born United States), b. 1946. **Genres:** Information Science/Computers, Communications/Media. **Career:** Computer programmer, 1966-67; University of Alberta, assistant analyst, 1967-70; Northwestern Utilities Ltd., programmer and analyst, 1971-72; City of Edmonton, analytical services officer, 1975-77; Computer Sciences Canada, customer consultant and financial products specialist, 1977-78; Noram Timesharing Development Ltd., owner, director and officer, 1978-79; Fites and Kulpa (consultants), partner, 1978-79; Fites and Associates Management Consultants Ltd., owner, 1979-; Northern Alberta Institute

of Technology, instructor, 1984-85; Computer Career Institute, curriculum development coordinator, 1986; DPMA Canada ACFOR, ambassador, 1986-89; Canadian Advisory Council on Information Technology Security, secretary, 1994-95; International Information Security Systems Security Certification Consortium, founding member, 1989, president and chairman of board of directors, 1989-90; Special Interest Group for Computer Security, president, 1990-92; AEPOS Technologies, senior information security consultant, 1996-98; Ontario Power Generation, senior information technology security advisor, 1999-2000; JAWZ Inc., senior security consultant, 2000-; Athabasca University, teacher; Aurora College, Thebacha campus, teacher. Writer. **Publications:** (With P. Johnson and M. Kratz) The Computer Virus Crisis, 1989, 2nd ed., 1992; (with M.P.J. Kratz and A.F. Brebner) Control and Security of Computer Information Systems, 1989; (with M.P.J. Kratz) Information Systems Security: A Practitioner's Reference, 1993. Contributor to periodicals. **Address:** 200 Baseline Rd., Ottawa, ON K2C 0A2, Canada. **Online address:** fites@sympatico.ca

FITES, Philip E. *See* FITES, Philip.

FITTEN, Marc. American (born United States), b. 1974?. **Genres:** Novels. **Career:** Writer and editor. **Publications:** Valeria's Last Stand: A Novel, 2009. Contributor to periodicals. **Address:** Atlanta, GA , U.S.A. **Online address:** marc@marcfitten.com

FITTER, Chris. American/British (born England), b. 1955. **Genres:** Cultural/Ethnic Topics, History, Poetry, Literary Criticism And History. **Career:** Fairleigh Dickinson University, Wroxton College, adjunct professor of English, 1983-85; University of Mississippi, assistant professor of English, 1988-94; Rutgers University, assistant professor of English, 1994-98, associate professor 1998-. Writer. **Publications:** Poetry, Space, Landscape: Toward a New Theory (cultural history), 1995; Radical Shakespeare, 2007. Contributor to books and periodicals. **Address:** Department of English, Rutgers University, 482 Armitage Hall, Camden, NJ 08102, U.S.A. **Online address:** fitter@camden.rutgers.edu

FITZGERALD, Astrid. American/Swiss (born Switzerland), b. 1938. **Genres:** Novels, Young Adult Fiction, Art/Art History, Philosophy, Travel/Exploration, Theology/Religion. **Career:** Freelance fine artist, 1965-. Writer. **Publications:** (Comp. and ed.) An Artist's Book of Inspiration: A Collection of Thoughts on Art, Artists and Creativity, 1996; Being Consciousness Bliss: A Seeker's Guide, 2001; Winter Break: A Luminous Journey into Wisdom and Love: A Novel, 2008. Contributor to periodicals. **Address:** 118 Lower Granite Rd., Kerhonkson, NY 12446, U.S.A. **Online address:** astrid@bestweb.net

FITZGERALD, Carol. American (born United States), b. 1942. **Genres:** Bibliography, History, Biography. **Career:** Broward County Commission, commission aide, 1978-2001; Broward County Library System, administrative coordinator for the director, 2001-03; Florida Center for the Book, literary resources coordinator, 2003-05, retired, 2005. Writer. **Publications:** The Rivers of America: A Descriptive Bibliography, 2 vols., 2001; Series Americana: Post Depression-Era Regional Literature, 1938-1980, A Descriptive Bibliography, 2 vols., 2009. **Address:** 2100 S Ocean Ln., Apt. 706, Fort Lauderdale, FL 33316, U.S.A. **Online address:** riversgal@aol.com

FITZGERALD, Cathy. American (born United States) **Genres:** Social Work, Autobiography/Memoirs, Biography, Business/Trade/Industry, Economics. **Career:** Retirement Living from A to Z, co-owner. Writer and educator. **Publications:** (With J. Cullinane) The New Retirement: The Ultimate Guide to the Rest of Your Life, 2004, rev. ed., 2007. **Address:** c/o Author Mail, Rodale Press, 733 3rd Ave., 15th Fl., New York, NY 10017-3293, U.S.A. **Online address:** cathyfitz@gmail.com

FITZGERALD, Conor. Italian/British (born England), b. 1964?. **Genres:** Novels. **Career:** Makeperfect (translation agency), co-founder; Scuola Superiore per I Traduttori e Interpreti, translator and instructor. Writer. **Publications:** The Dogs of Rome: A Commissario Alec Blume Novel, 2010. Contributor to books. **Address:** Rome, Italy. **Online address:** alec@alecblume.com

FITZGERALD, Mary Anne. South African (born South Africa), b. 1945?. **Genres:** Documentaries/Reportage, History, Social Sciences. **Career:** Morgan, Orr and Associates, public relations consultant; freelance foreign correspondent. Writer. **Publications:** Nomad: Journeys from Samburu, 1993; My Warrior Son, 1998; Throwing the Stick Forward: The Impact of War on

Southern Sudanese Women, 2002. Contributor to periodicals. **Address:** c/o Michael Joseph Ltd., 27 Wright's Ln., London, GL W8 5TZ, England.

FITZGERALD, Michael W(illiam). American (born United States), b. 1956. **Genres:** History, Intellectual History, Social Sciences. **Career:** St. Olaf College, assistant professor, 1986-93, associate professor, 1993-2001, professor of history, 2001-, American Racial and Multicultural Studies, director, Africa and the Americas Concentration, director; University of Virginia, Carter G. Woodson Center for Afro-American and African History, fellow, 1988; Carleton College, visiting professor, 1989, 1995. Writer. **Publications:** The Union League and Movement in the Deep South: Politics and Agricultural Change during Reconstruction, 1989; Urban Emancipation: Popular Politics in Reconstruction Mobile, 1860-1890, 2002; Splendid Failure: Postwar Reconstruction in the American South, 2007. **Address:** Department of History, St. Olaf College, Holland Hall 532, 1520 St. Olaf Ave., Northfield, MN 55057, U.S.A. **Online address:** fitz@stolaf.edu

FITZGERALD, William. British (born England), b. 1952. **Genres:** History, Poetry, Literary Criticism And History, Young Adult Fiction. **Career:** Caius College, university lecturer in classics; University of Cambridge, university lecturer in classics; University of San Diego, Department of Literature, professor. Writer. **Publications:** Agonistic Poetry: The Pindaric Mode in Pindar, Horace, Holderlin, and the English Ode, 1987; Catullan Provocations: Lyric Poetry and the Drama of Position, 1995; Slavery and the Roman Literary Imagination, 2000; Martial: The World of the Epigram, 2007; (ed. with E. Gowers) Ennius Perennis: The Annals and Beyond, 2007. Contributor to periodicals. **Address:** Department of Classics, Gonville & Caius College, Trinity St., Cambridge, CB CB2 1TA, England.

FITZGERALD-HOYT, Mary. American (born United States), b. 1955. **Genres:** History, Biography, Literary Criticism And History. **Career:** Siena College, professor. Writer. **Publications:** William Trevor: Re-imagining Ireland, 2003. Contributor to periodicals and journals. **Address:** Siena College, 515 Loudon Rd., Loudonville, NY 12211-1462, U.S.A.

FITZMAURICE, Gabriel. Irish (born Ireland), b. 1952. **Genres:** Poetry, Literary Criticism And History, Translations, Essays. **Career:** Irish Department of Education, school teacher, 1972-; Writer's Week, chair, 1982-85, 1991-92, literary advisor. Writer. **Publications:** POETRY: Rainsong, 1984; Road to the Horizon, 1987; Nocht, 1989; Dancing Through, 1990; The Father's Part, 1992; The Space Between: New and Selected Poems 1984-1992, 1993; Ag Siobshiul Chun An Rince, 1995; The Village Sings, 1996; Giolla na n-Amhran: Danta 1988-1998, 1998; A Wrenboy's Carnival: Poems 1980-2000, 2000; I and the Village, 2002; The Boghole Boys, 2005; Really Rotten Rhymes, 2007; Essential Gabriel Fitzmaurice, 2008. POETRY FOR CHILDREN: The Moving Stair, 1989, rev. ed., 1993; Nach Iontach Mar Ata, 1994; But Dad!, 1995; Puppy and the Sausage, 1998; Dear Grandad, 2001; A Giant Never Dies, 2002; The Oopsy Kid, 2003; Don't Squash Fluffy, 2004; I'm Proud to Be Me, 2005. OTHERS: Kerry on My Mind (essays), 1999; Beat the Goatskin till the Goat Cries: Notes from a Kerry Village, 2006; Twenty One Sonnets, 2007; In Praise of Football, 2009; G.F. Woz Ere, 2009; Do Teachers Go to the Toilet?, 2010. TRANSLATOR: M. Hartnett, Airtneide, The Purge, 1989; Poems I Wish I'd Written, 1996; G. Rosenstock, The Rhino's Specs, 2003; Poems from the Irish: Collected Translations, 2004; B. Long, Ventry Calling, 2005. EDITOR: (with D. Kiberd) An Crann Faoi Bhlath/The Flowering Tree, 1991; Between the Hills and Sea, 1991; Con Greaney, Traditional Singer, 1991; Homecoming/An Bealach'na Bhaile, 1993; Irish Poetry Now, 1993; Kerry through Its Writers, 1993; The Listowel Literary Phenomenon: North Kerry Writers, 1994; (with R. Dunbar) Rusty Nails and Astronauts, 1999; (with A. Cronin and J. Looney) The Boro and The Cross, 2000; The Kerry Anthology, 2000; Come All Good Men & True, 2004; The World of Bryan Mac Mahon, 2005; The World of Bryan MacMahon, 2005. **Address:** Kennys Bookshop & Art Galleries, Liosbán Retail Pk., Tuam Rd., Galway, 1-24, Ireland.

FITZPATRICK, Becca. American (born United States), b. 1979?. **Genres:** Novels. **Career:** Novelist and educator. **Publications:** HUSH, HUSH YOUNG-ADULT NOVEL SERIES: Hush, Hush, 2009; Crescendo, 2010; Untitled, 2011. **Address:** c/o Catherine Drayton, InkWell Management, 521 5th Ave., 26th Fl., New York, NY 10175, U.S.A. **Online address:** becca@beccafitzpatrick.com

FITZPATRICK, David. Irish/Australian (born Australia), b. 1948. **Genres:**

History, Literary Criticism And History. **Career:** Oxford University, Nuffield College, research fellow, 1975-77; University of Melbourne, research fellow, 1977-79; Trinity College, lecturer, 1979-93, fellow, 1982-, associate professor, 1993-2000, professor of modern history, 2000-; University of Aberdeen, Research Institute of Irish and Scottish Studies, honorary professor, 2000-05. Writer. **Publications:** Politics and Irish Life, 1913-1921: Provincial Experience of War and Revolution, 1977, rev. ed., 1998; Irish Emigration, 1801-1921, 1984, rev. ed., 1989; (ed.) Ireland and the First World War, 1986; Visible Immigrants: Neglected Sources for the History of Australian Immigration, 1989; (ed.) Revolution?: Ireland 1917-1923, 1990; (ed.) Home or Away?: Immigrants in Colonial Australia: Visible Immigrants, Three, 1992; (with D. Lindsay) Records of the Irish Famine: A Guide to Local Archives, 1840-1855, 1993; Oceans of Consolation: Personal Accounts of Irish Migration to Australia, 1994; The Two Irelands, 1912-1939, 1998; Harry Boland's Irish Revolution, 2003; (ed.) The Feds: An Account of the Federated Dublin Voluntary Hospitals, 1961-2005, 2006; Solitary and Wild: Frederick MacNeice and the Salvation of Ireland, 2010. **Address:** Department of History, Trinity College, Dublin, 2, Ireland. **Online address:** david.fitzpatrick@tcd.ie

FITZPATRICK, Deanne. Canadian (born Canada) **Genres:** Crafts, Art/Art History. **Career:** Fiber artist and writer. **Publications:** Hook Me a Story: The History and Method of Rug Hooking in Atlantic Canada, 1999; Hooking Mats and Rugs: 33 New Designs from An Old Tradition, 2008. Contributor to periodicals. **Address:** RR 5, Amherst, NS B4H 3Y3, Canada. **Online address:** info@hookingrugs.com

FITZPATRICK, Flo. American (born United States) **Genres:** Novels. **Career:** Novelist and choreographer. **Publications:** Ghost of a Chance, 2004; Sweet Dreams, 2005; Hot Stuff, 2005; Haunting Melody, 2007; It's a Marvelous Night for a Moondance, 2010; Melody's Follies, 2010. **Address:** TX, U.S.A. **Online address:** flogently@flofitzpatrick.com

FITZPATRICK, Frank. American (born United States) **Genres:** Sports/Fitness. **Career:** Philadelphia Inquirer, Inquirer Sports Department, sportswriter, 1980-. **Publications:** NONFICTION: And the Walls Came Tumbling Down: Kentucky, Texas Western, and the Game That Changed American Sports, 1999; You Can't Lose 'em All: The Year the Phillies Finally Won the World Series, 2001; The Lion in Autumn: A Season with Joe Paterno and Penn State Football, 2005; Pride of the Lions: The Biography of Joe Paterno, 2011. Contributor to periodicals. **Address:** Philadelphia Inquirer, PO Box 8263, Philadelphia, PA 19101, U.S.A. **Online address:** ffitzpatrick@phillynews.com

FITZPATRICK, Mary Anne. American (born United States), b. 1949. **Genres:** Communications/Media, Human Relations/Parenting, Psychology, Adult Non-fiction. **Career:** O'Hara High School, social studies teacher, 1971-72; Emerson College, debate coach and instructor, 1972-73; West Virginia University, teaching assistant in educational psychology, 1973-74; University of Wisconsin-Milwaukee, assistant professor of communications, 1976-78; University of Wisconsin-Madison, assistant professor, 1978-81, associate professor, 1981-84, professor of communications, 1984-2005, now professor emeritus, Center for Communication Research, director, 1980-, department head, 1993-, Vilas Associate in Social Science, 1989-91, College of Letters & Science, deputy dean; University of Texas, visiting professor, 1983; University of Nebraska, visiting professor, 1984; New Mexico State University, distinguished visiting professor, 1987; George Washington University, visiting professor, 1987-88; University of California, visiting professor, 1988; University of Iowa, visiting professor, 1990; University of Kansas, visiting professor, 1992; University of South Carolina, College of Arts and Science, founding dean, 2005-, Carolina Educational Foundation distinguished professor of psychology, chief academic and operating officer; International Communication Association, fellow, 1993, president. Writer. **Publications:** Between Husbands and Wives: Communication in Marriage, 1988; (with P. Noller) Communication in Family Relationships, 1993. EDITOR and CONTRIBUTOR: (with P. Noller) Perspectives on Marital Interaction (monograph), 1988; (with T. Edgar and V. Freimuth) AIDS: A Communication Perspective, 1992; (with A.I. Vangelisti) Explaining Family Interactions, 1995; (ed. with A.L. Vangelisti and H.T. Reis) Stability and Change in Relationships, 2002. Work appears in anthologies. Contributor of articles to journals. **Address:** College of Arts & Science, University of South Carolina, Rm. 251, Gambrell Hall, Columbia, SC 29208, U.S.A. **Online address:** fitzpatm@mailbox.sc.edu

FITZPATRICK, Sheila Mary. Australian (born Australia), b. 1941. **Genres:** History, Autobiography/Memoirs, Politics/Government. **Career:** School of

Slavonic and Eastern European Studies, research fellow, 1969-71; London School of Economics and Political Science, research fellow, 1971-72; University of Texas, Slavic Department, lecturer, 1972-73, professor of history, 1981-, Oliver H. Radkey professor of history, 1987-89; St. Johns University, associate professor of history, 1974-75; Columbia University, assistant professor, 1975-, associate professor of history, through 1980; University of Chicago, professor of history, Bernadotte E. Schmitt distinguished service professor of history, 1990; Wissenschaftskolleg-Berlin, fellow, 2008-09. **Publications:** The Commissariat of Enlightenment: Soviet Organization of Education and the Arts under Lunacharsky, October 1917-1921, 1970; (ed.) Cultural Revolution in Russia, 1928-1931, 1978; Education and Social Mobility in the Soviet Union, 1921-1934, 1979; The Russian Revolution, 1982, 3rd ed., 2008; Culture et revolution, 1989; (ed. with L. Viola) A Researcher's Guide to Sources on Soviet Social History in the 1930s, 1990; (co-ed.) Russia in the Era of NEP: Explorations in Soviet Society and Culture, 1991; The Cultural Front: Power and Culture in Revolutionary Russia, 1992; Stalin's Peasants: Resistance and Survival in the Russian Village after Collectivization, 1994; (ed. with R. Gellately) Accusatory Practices: Denunciation in Modern European History, 1789-1989, 1997; (ed.) Everyday Stalinism: Ordinary Life in Extraordinary Times, Soviet Russia in the 1930s, 1999; Stalinism: New Directions, 2000; (ed. with Y. Slezkine) In the Shadow of Revolution: Life Stories of Russian Women from 1917 to the Second World War, 2000; Tear Off the Masks! Identity and Imposture in Twentieth-Century Russia, 2005; (ed. with S. Macintyre and contrib.) Against the Grain: Brian Fitzpatrick and Manning Clark in Australian Politics and History, 2007; (ed. with C. Rasmussen) Political Tourists: Travellers from Australia to the Soviet Union in the 1920s-1940s, 2008; (ed. with M. Geyer) Beyond Totalitarianism: Stalinism and Nazism Compare, 2009; My Father's Daughter: Memories of an Australian Childhood, 2010. **Address:** Department of History, University of Chicago, 1126 E 59th St., PO Box 30, Chicago, IL 60637, U.S.A. **Online address:** sf13@uchicago.edu

FITZPATRICK, Tony. American (born United States), b. 1949. **Genres:** Environmental Sciences/Ecology, Natural History, Economics, Novels. **Career:** Teacher, 1972-73; University of Illinois, agriculture writer and editor, 1980-87; Washington University, science editor, 1987, senior science editor. **Publications:** Signals From the Heartland, 1993. Contributor to periodicals. **Address:** Washington University, 1 Brookings Dr., PO Box 1089, St. Louis, MO 63130-4862, U.S.A. **Online address:** tony_fitzpatrick@wustl.edu

FITZPATRICK, Vincent (dePaul). American (born United States), b. 1950. **Genres:** Biography, Literary Criticism And History, Autobiography/Memoirs, Literary Criticism And History, Politics/Government. **Career:** Enoch Pratt Free Library, H.L. Mencken Collection, assistant curator, 1980-. Writer. **Publications:** (Contrib.) Three Hundred Years of German Immigrants in North America, 1982; H.L.M., The Mencken Bibliography: A Second Ten-Year Supplement, 1972-1981, 1986; (contrib.) Critical Essays on H.L. Mencken, 1987; H.L. Mencken, 1989; (contrib.) American Literary Magazines: The Twentieth Century, 1990; (contrib.) Maryland: Unity in Diversity, Essays on Maryland Life and Culture, 1990; (with M.B. Ruscica and C.H. Fitzpatrick) The Complete Sentence Workout Book With Readings, 5th ed., 2004; (ed. with F. Hobson and B. Jacobs) Thirty-five Years of Newspaper Work: A Memoir, 1994; Gerald W. Johnson: From Southern Liberal to National Conscience, 2002. Contributor to magazines and newspapers. **Address:** Department of Humanities, Enoch Pratt Free Library, 400 Cathedral St., Baltimore, MD 21201-4484, U.S.A.

FITZROY, Charles (Patrick Hugh). British (born England), b. 1957. **Genres:** Travel/Exploration, History. **Career:** Fine Art Travel Ltd., director, 1984-; Robert Holden Ltd., director, 1984-. Writer. **Publications:** Italy: A Grand Tour for the Modern Traveller, 1991; Italy Revealed, 1994; (ed. with K. Harry) Grafton Regis: The History of a Northamptonshire Village, 2000; Return of the King: The Restoration of Charles II, 2007; Renaissance Florence on 5 Florins a Day, 2010. **Address:** Fine Art Travel Ltd., 13 Old Burlington St., London, GL W1S 3AJ, England. **Online address:** charles@finearttravel.co.uk

FITZSIMONS, Cecilia (A. L.). British (born England), b. 1952. **Genres:** Animals/Pets, Children's Non-fiction, Illustrations, Picture/Board Books, Earth Sciences, Environmental Sciences/Ecology, Geography, How-to Books, Marine Sciences/Oceanography, Medicine/Health, Natural History, Sciences, Travel/Exploration, Zoology, Young Adult Fiction. **Career:** Author and illustrator. **Publications:** My First Birds, 1985; My First Butterflies, 1985; (with

E. Lawrence) An Instant Guide to Trees, 1985; My First Fishes and Other Waterlife, 1987; My First Insects, Spiders and Crawlers, 1987; (ed.) The Modern Ark: The Endangered Wildlife of Our Planet, 1989; Seashore Life of North America, 1989; In the Field, 1990; In the Playground, 1990; In the Woods, 1990; At the Seaside, 1990; Sainsbury's Book of the Sea, 1991; Rivers and Ponds, 1992; The Seashore, 1992; Trees and Woodlands, 1992; Animals in Danger, 1993; Sainsbury's Book of Birds, 1994; Clever Clogs, Wild Animals, 1994; Sainsbury's Animals of the World, 1995 in US as Animals of the World, 1996; Step-by-Step 50 Nature Projects for Kids, 1995; Animal Habitats, 1996; Animal Lives, 1996; Creatures of the Past, 1996; Water Life, 1996; (with M. Elliot and P. Boase) 100 Things for Kids to Make and Do, 1996; Fruit, 1996; Vegetables and Herbs, 1997; Cereals, Nuts & Spices, 1997; Dairy Foods & Drinks, 1997; Sainsbury's Book of Dangerous Animals, 1997; Birds of Prey, 1997; Horses and Ponies of the World, 1998; Wildlife Explorer, 1998; The Giant Book of Bugs, 1998; (with E. Lawrence) An Instant Guide to Trees: Nearly 200 of the Most Common North American Trees Described and Illustrated in Full Color, 1999; Small Pets, 1999; The Wildlife of Valderrama, 1999; A Day in Donana, 1999; I Didn't Know That: Wolves Howl at the Moon, 2000; I Didn't Know That: Giant Pandas Eat All Day, 2000; Dinosaurs, 2000; Giant Pandas Eat All Day Long, 2000; Animal Friends, 2001; (with E. Fejer) An Instant Guide to Rocks & Minerals: The Most Familiar Rocks and Minerals of North America Described and Illustrated in Full Color, 2001; (with H. Gee and S. McCormick) Fossils: The Most Common Plant and Animal Fossils of Europe Described and Illustrated in Colour, 2002; An Instant Guide to Seashore Life: The Plants and Animals of the North American Seashore Described and Illustrated in Full Color, 2003; (with H. Gee and S. McCormick) British & European Fossils, 2008. WITH P. FOREY: An Instant Guide to Mammals: The Most Familiar Species of North American Mammals Described and Illustrated in Color, 1986; An Instant Guide to Wildflowers: The Most Familiar Species of North American Wildflowers Described and Illustrated in Color, 1986; An Instant Guide to Butterflies: The Most Familiar Species of North American Butterflies Described and Illustrated in Full Color, 1987; Instant Guide to Edible Plants: The Most Familiar Edible Wild Plants of North America Described and Illustrated in Full Color, 1997; An Instant Guide to Reptiles & Amphibians: The Most Familiar Species of North American Reptiles and Amphibians Described and Illustrated in Full Color, 1997; An Instant Guide to Wildflowers: The Most Familiar Species of North American Wildflowers Described And Illustrated In Full Color, 1997; An Instant Guide to Stars & Planets: The Sky at Night Described and Illustrated in Full Color, 1999; An Instant Guide to Insects: The Most Familiar Species of North American Insects Described and Illustrated in Full Color, 1999; An Instant Guide to Seashells: The Most Familiar Species of North American Seashells Described and Illustrated in Full Color, 2000. SELF-ILLUSTRATED: An Instant Guide to Small Pets: A Complete Guide to the Wide Range of Small Pets, from the Most Common to the Exotic, Described and Illustrated in Full Color, 2000. Illustrator of books by others. Contributor to books. **Address:** Woodstock Lodge, 25 Hazelgrove, Clanfield, Waterlooville, HM P08 0LE, England. **Online address:** fitz.art@btopenworld.com

FIX, Michael. (Michael E. Fix). American (born United States), b. 1950. **Genres:** Politics/Government, Urban Studies, Business/Trade/Industry, Economics, Agriculture/Forestry. **Career:** Rockefeller Foundation, consultant, 1986-88; Urban Institute, senior research associate, 1983-94, director of program on immigrant policy, 1992-98, principal research associate, 1994-2005, director of immigration studies, 1998-2004; Migration Policy Institute, senior vice president and director of studies, 2005-, National Center on Immigrant Integration Policy, co-director; Institute for the Study of Labor (IZA), Bonn, research fellow. Writer. **Publications:** The Impact of Selected Federal Actions on Municipal Outlays: A Study Prepared for the Use of the Joint Economic Committee, Congress of the United States, 1979; (with G.C. Eads) Relief or Reform? Reagans Regulatory Dilemma, 1984; (ed. with G.C. Eads) Reagan Regulatory Strategy: An Assessment, 1984; (ed. with D.A. Kenyon) Coping with Mandates: What are the Alternatives?, 1990; (with P.T. Hill) Enforcing Employer Sanctions: Challenges and Strategies, 1990; Remedying IRCA-related Discrimination: Modest Proposals, 1990; (ed.) The Paper Curtain: Employer Sanctions Implementation, Impact, and Reform, 1991; (with M.A. Turner and R.J. Struyk) Opportunities Denied, Opportunities Diminished: Racial Discrimination in Hiring, 1991; (ed. with R.J. Struyk) Clear and Convincing: Measurement of Discrimination in America, 1993; (with W. Zimmermann) Educating Immigrant Children: Chapter1 in the Changing City, 1993; (co-author) Immigration and Immigrants: Setting the Record Straight, 1994; (with J.E. Taylor and P.L. Martin) Poverty Amid Prosperity: Immigration and the Changing Face of Rural California, 1997; (with P. Martin and J.E. Taylor)

The New Rural Poverty: Agriculture and Immigration in California, 2006; (ed.) Securing the Future: U.S. Immigrant Integration Policy: A Reader, 2007; (with J. Batalova and J. Murray) Measures of Change: The Demography and Literacy of Adolescent English Learners: A Report to the Carnegie Corporation of New York, 2007; (ed.) Immigrants and Welfare: The Impact of Welfare Reform on America's Newcomers, 2010; (contrib.) Tamunhwa sahoe Miguk ŭi iminja tonghap chŏngchaek=America immigrant integration policy, 2010. **Address:** National Center on Immigrant Integration Policy, Migration Policy Institute, 1400 16th St. NW, Ste. 300, Washington, DC 20036, U.S.A. **Online address:** mfix@migrationpolicy.org

FIX, Michael E. *See* **FIX, Michael.**

FLACK, Jerry D(avid). American (born United States), b. 1943. **Genres:** Education, Biography, History. **Career:** Teacher, 1965-80, academic specialist for English, 1972-75, academic specialist for gifted/talented education, 1978-79; Purdue University, instructor in education, 1982; University of Southern Maine, instructor, 1982; University of Colorado, associate professor of gifted and talented education, 1983-, professor of gifted children, now professor emeritus; National Association for Gifted Children, board director. Writer. **Publications:** Once Upon a Time: Creative Problem Solving through Fairy Tales, 1985; Hey! It's My Future, 1986; Using Today's Headlines to Create Tomorrow's Lifetimes, 1986; Inventing, Inventions, and Inventors: A Teaching Resource Book, 1989; Mystery and Detection: Thinking and Problem Solving with the Sleuths, 1990; Lives of Promise: Studies in Biography and Family History, 1992; TalentEd: Strategies for Developing the Talent in Every Learner, 1993; Odysseys: Personal Discoveries, 1993; Voyages: Extending Horizons, 1993; Distinations: Grand Visions, 1993; From the Land of Enchantment: Creative Teaching with Fairy Tales, 1997. Contributor of articles to journals. **Address:** School of Education, University of Colorado, 1420 Austin Bluffs Pkwy., PO Box 7150, Colorado Springs, CO 80933-7150, U.S.A. **Online address:** jflack@ix.netcom.com

FLAHERTY, Alice W. American (born United States), b. 1963. **Genres:** Medicine/Health, Psychiatry, Adult Non-fiction, Writing/Journalism, Children's Fiction. **Career:** Massachusetts General Hospital, chief resident, 1997-98, attending physician, 1998-, Movement Disorders Fellowship, director, 2004-; Harvard Medical School, associate professor of neurology and psychiatry, 2011-. Writer and neurologist. **Publications:** The Massachusetts General Hospital Handbook of Neurology, 2000, 2nd ed., 2007; The Midnight Disease: The Drive to Write, Writer's Block and the Creative Brain, 2004; The Luck of the Loch Ness Monster: A Tale of Picky Eating, 2007; Acting Sick, forthcoming; Playing Doctor, forthcoming. **Address:** Neurology Associates, Massachusetts General Hospital, 15 Parkman St., Boston, MA 02114-3117, U.S.A. **Online address:** aflaherty@partners.org

FLAHERTY, Liz. American (born United States), b. 1950. **Genres:** Romance/Historical, Novels, Young Adult Fiction. **Career:** Writer. **Publications:** Always Annie (romance fiction), 1999; Because of Joe (fiction), 2003; The Debutante's Second Chance (novel), 2007; Home to Singing Trees, 2010. Contributor to periodicals. **Address:** c/o Jill Grosjean, Jill Grosjean Literary Agency, 1390 Millstone Rd., Sag Harbor, NY 11963, U.S.A. **Online address:** flaherty@netusa1.net

FLAHERTY, Michael G. American (born United States), b. 1952. **Genres:** Sociology. **Career:** Eckerd College, Department of Sociology, assistant professor, 1980-87, associate professor, 1987-92, professor of sociology, 1992-; University of South Florida, Department of Sociology, professor, 1997-. Writer. **Publications:** A Watched Pot: How We Experience Time, 1999; The Textures of Time: Agency and Temporal Experience, 2011. EDITOR (with C. Ellis): Investigating Subjectivity: Research on Lived Experience, 1992; Social Perspectives on Emotions, vol. III, 1995. Contributor to sociology journals. **Address:** Department of Sociology, Eckerd College, SHC 113, 4200 54th Ave. S, St. Petersburg, FL 33711, U.S.A. **Online address:** flahermg@eckerd.edu

FLAM, Jack D(onald). American (born United States), b. 1940. **Genres:** Art/Art History, History. **Career:** Rutgers University, instructor in art, 1963-66; University of Florida, assistant professor, 1966-69, associate professor of art, 1969-72; City University of New York, Brooklyn College, associate professor, 1975-80, professor, 1980-90, distinguished professor of art and art history, 1991-2010, distinguished professor emeritus, 2010-; Wall Street Journal, art critic, 1984-92; Dedalus Foundation, president, 2002-. Writer. **Publi-**

cations: (Ed.) Matisse on Art, 1973, rev. ed., 1995; Zoltan Gorency (novel), 1974; Bread and Butter (novel), 1977; (with J. Cowart, D. Fourcade and J.H. Neff) Henri Matisse Paper Cut Outs, 1978; (with D. Ashton) Robert Motherwell, 1981; Matisse: The Man and His Art, 1869-1918, 1986; (ed.) Matisse: A Retrospective, 1988; Motherwell, 1991; Richard Diebenkorn: Ocean Park, 1992; Matisse: The Dance, 1993; (with D. Shapiro) Western Artists/African Art, 1994; (ed.) Robert Smithson: The Collected Writings, 1996; Judith Rothschild: An Artist's Search, 1998; Les peintures de Picasso: Un theatre mental, 1998; (co-author) New York Collects: Drawings and Watercolors, 1900-1950, 1999; The Modern Drawing, 1999; Matisse in the Cone Collection, 2001; Matisse and Picasso: The Story of Their Rivalry and Friendship, 2003; Primitivism and Twentieth-Century Art: A Documentary History, 2003; Matisse and Picasso: The Story of Their Rivalry and Friendship, 2003; Manet: Un bar aux Folies-Bergre ou l'abysse du miroir, 2005; Matisse in Transition: Around Laurette, 2006; (with K. Rogers and T. Clifford) Robert Motherwell Paintings and Collages: A Catalogue Raisonné, 1941-1991, 2012. CONTRIBUTOR: The Paine Webber Art Collection, 1995; Powerful Expressions: Recent American Drawings, 1996; Matisse, His Art and His Textiles: The Fabric of Dreams, 2004; Matisse-Derain, Collioure 1905, un été fauve, 2005; Traces du sacré, 2008; Pierre Bonnard: The Late Still Lifes and Interiors, 2009. Contributor to periodicals. **Address:** Georges Borchardt Inc., 136 E 57th St., New York, NY 10022, U.S.A. **Online address:** jackflam@aol.com

FLAMHAFT, Ziva. American/Israeli (born Israel), b. 1944?. **Genres:** International Relations/Current Affairs, Politics/Government, History. **Career:** Office of the Prime Minister of Israel, Department of Special Affairs, public relations assistant and office manager, 1964-69; Government of Israel, staff, 1969-73; Hunter College of the City, adjunct lecturer, 1984; City University of New York, Queens College, Department of Political Science, adjunct lecturer, 1985-92, adjunct assistant professor, 1992-94, substitute instructor, 1994-96, instructor, 1996-, Departmental Program on International Relations and Conflict Resolution, director. Writer. **Publications:** Israel on the Road to Peace: Accepting the Unacceptable, 1996; (contrib.) Israel in the Nineties, 1996; Iron Breaks Too: Israeli Women Talk about War, Bereavement, and Peace, forthcoming. Contributor to newspapers. **Address:** Department of Political Science, Queens College, City University of New York, 200D Powdermaker Hall, 65-30 Kissena Blvd., Flushing, NY 11367, U.S.A. **Online address:** ziva.flamhaft@qc.cuny.edu

FLAMINI, Roland. American (born United States) **Genres:** Biography, Film, Translations, Young Adult Non-fiction, Theology/Religion. **Career:** Time Magazine, foreign correspondent and world section editor, 1968-94; writer, 1975-; United Press Intl., chief international correspondent, 2000-06; CQ Weekly, foreign policy columnist; Town and Country Magazine, contributor; Architectural Digest, contributor; WashingtonLife, contributor. **Publications:** NONFICTION: Scarlett, Rhett and a Cast of Thousands: The Filming of Gone with the Wind, 1975; Pope, Premier, President: The Cold War Summit That Never Was, 1980; Ava: A Biography, 1983; Ten Years at Number 10: Images of a Decade in Office, 1989; Sovereign: Elizabeth II and the Windsor Dynasty, 1991; Thalberg: The Last Tycoon and the World of M-G-M, 1994; Passport Germany: Your Pocket Guide to German Business, Customs Scarlett, Rhe and Etiquette, 1997; (trans.) Parallel Empires: The Vatican and the United States-Two Centuries of Alliance and Conflict, 2009. Contributor to periodicals. **Address:** Congressional Quarterly Inc., 1255 22nd St. NW, Washington, DC 20037-1217, U.S.A. **Online address:** iscribble3@hotmail.com

FLAMM, Michael W. American (born United States), b. 1964. **Genres:** Civil Liberties/Human Rights, Criminology/True Crime, Adult Non-fiction. **Career:** Rumson-Fair Haven High School, history teacher, 1986-89; Scarsdale High School, history teacher, 1989-91; Columbia University, teaching assistant, 1992-96; Ohio Wesleyan University, Department Of History, assistant professor, 1998-2003, associate professor, 2003-08, professor, 2008-; Columbia University and Georgetown University, Gilder Lehrman Institute of American History, faculty instructor, 2000-. Writer. **Publications:** Law and Order: Street Crime, Civil Unrest, and the Crisis of Liberalism in the 1960s, 2005; (with D. Steigerwald) Debating the 1960s: Liberal, Conservative, and Radical Perspectives, 2008; (with M.W. Flamm) Debating the Reagan Presidency, 2009; (co-author) The Chicago Handbook for Teachers: A Practical Guide to the College Classroom, 2nd ed., forthcoming; In the Heat of the Summer: Racial Unrest in New York, 1964, forthcoming; (with D. Steigerwald) American History II: 1865 to the Present, forthcoming. Contributor to journals. **Address:** Department of History, Ohio Wesleyan University, 61

S Sandusky St., Elliott 114, Delaware, OH 43015, U.S.A. **Online address:** mwflamm@owu.edu

FLAMMING, Douglas. (James Douglas Flamming). American (born United States), b. 1959. **Genres:** History. **Career:** Vanderbilt University, teaching assistant, 1982-84, head teaching assistant, 1984-86; American Textile History Museum, Sullivan fellow, 1986; Virginia Polytechnic Institute and State University, visiting assistant professor of history, 1987-88; California Institute of Technology, assistant professor, 1988-94, associate professor of history, 1994-97; Huntington Library, Haynes fellow, 1996; Georgia Institute of Technology, associate professor, 1997-2006, Center for the Study of Southern Industrialization, director, 1997-2003, Undergraduate Studies of the School of History, Technology and Society, director, 2003-06, professor of history, 2006-; Museum of Rural Life, historical consultant. Writer and academic. **Publications:** Creating the Modern South: Millhands and Managers in Dalton, Georgia, 1884-1984, 1992; Bound for Freedom: Black Los Angeles in Jim Crow America, 2005; African Americans in the West, 2009. Contributor to periodicals and journals. **Address:** School of History, Technology and Science, Georgia Institute of Technology, Rm. 118, Old Civil Engineering Bldg., Atlanta, GA 30332, U.S.A. **Online address:** doug.flamming@hts.gatech.edu

FLAMMING, James Douglas. *See* **FLAMMING, Douglas.**

FLANAGAN, Erin. American (born United States), b. 1971?. **Genres:** Novels, Young Adult Fiction. **Career:** Wright State University, Department of English, assistant professor, associate professor. Writer. **Publications:** Angel by My Side: Lily's Story, 1995; Angel by My Side: Grace's Story, 1995; Till the Leaves Change, 1996; The Usual Mistakes, 2005. Contributor of articles to periodicals. **Address:** Department of English, Wright State University, 463 Millett Hall, Dayton, OH 45435, U.S.A. **Online address:** erin.flanagan@wright.edu

FLANDERS, Judith. Canadian (born Canada), b. 1959?. **Genres:** History, Dance/Ballet, Art/Art History. **Career:** Evening Standard, dance critic, 2003-04; TLS, dance critic, 2005-; Buckingham University, senior research fellow, 2011-. Freelance arts journalist. **Publications:** A Circle of Sisters: Alice Kipling, Georgina Burne-Jones, Agnes Poynter, and Louisa Baldwin, 2001; The Victorian House: Domestic Life from Childbirth to Deathbed, 2003 in US as Inside the Victorian Home: A Portrait of Domestic Life in Victorian England, 2004; Consuming Passions: Leisure and Pleasure in Victorian Britain, 2006; The Invention of Murder, 2011. **Address:** A M Heath & Company Ltd., 6 Warwick Ct., Holborn, London, GL WC1R 5DJ, England. **Online address:** judithflanders@hotmail.com

FLANDERS, Laura. American/British (born England), b. 1961. **Genres:** Politics/Government, Social Sciences. **Career:** Air America Radio, Radionation, host; GRITtv, host. Writer. **Publications:** Real Majority Media Minority: The Costs of Sidelining Women in Reporting, 1997; Bushwomen: Tales of a Cynical Species, 2004; (ed.) The W Effect: Bush's War on Women, 2004; Blue Grit: True Democrats Take Back Politics from the Politicians, 2007; (co-author) The Contenders, 2008; (ed.) At the Tea Party, 2010. Contributor to periodicals. **Address:** Feminist Press, 365 5th Ave., Ste. 5406, New York, NY 10016, U.S.A. **Online address:** laura@lauraflanders.com

FLANDERS, Rebecca. *See* **BALL, Donna Rochelle.**

FLANNERY, Tim(othy Fridtjof). Australian (born Australia), b. 1956. **Genres:** Environmental Sciences/Ecology, Zoology. **Career:** Museum of Victoria, staff; Australian Museum, principal research scientist, 1985-98, director; Harvard University, chair of Australian studies, 1998-99; South Australian Museum, director; Premier's Science Council, chairman; University of Adelaide, professor; Macquarie University, professor, chair, 2007-; Copenhagen Climate Council, chairman; Australian Wildlife Conservancy, director. Writer. **Publications:** (With M. Archer and G. Grigg) The Kangaroo, 1985; (with P. Kendall) Australia's Vanishing Mammals, 1990; Mammals of New Guinea, 1990, rev. ed., 1995; The Future Eaters: An Ecological History of the Australasian Lands and People, 1994; (with P. Schouten) Possums of the World: A Monograph of the Phalangeroidea, 1994; Mammals of the South-West Pacific and Moluccan Islands, 1995; (with R. Martin, A. Szalay and P. Schouten) Tree Kangaroos, 1996; Throwim 'Way Leg, 1998; (with P. Schouten) A Gap in Nature, 2001; The Eternal Frontier: An Ecological History of North America in 5 Acts, 2001; (with J. Long, M. Archer and S. Hand) Prehistoric Mammals of Australia and New Guinea, 2002; Beautiful Lies:

Population and Environment in Australia, 2003; (with P. Schouten) Astonishing Animals, 2004; Country, 2004; Weather Makers: How Man is Changing the Climate and What it Means for Life on Earth, 2005; Adelaide: Nature of a City: The Ecology of a Dynamic City from 1836 to 2036, 2005; Country: A Continent, a Scientist & a Kangaroo, 2005; Explorer's Notebook: Essays on Life, History and Climate, 2007; Chasing Kangaroos: A Continent, a Scientist, and a Search for the World's Most Extraordinary Creature, 2007; Now or Never: A Sustainable Future for Australia?, 2009; Now or Never: Why We Must Act now to End Climate Change and Create a Sustainable Future, 2009; We are the Weather Makers: The History of Climate Change, 2009. EDITOR: 1788 Watkin Tench, 1996; (intro.) Life and Adventures, 1776-1801, 1997; The Explorers, 1998; Life and Adventures of John Nicol, Mariner, 1999; (intro.) Terra Australis: The Journals of Matthew Flinders, 2000; (intro.) The Birth of Sydney, 2000; (intro.) Two Classic Tales of Australian Exploration, 2000; The Life and Adventures of William Buckley, 2002; The Birth of Melbourne, 2002; Sailing Alone around the World, 2003; 1788: Comprising a Narrative of the Expedition to Botany Bay and a Complete Account of the Settlement at Port Jackson, 2009. Contributor to periodicals. **Address:** The South Australian Museum, North Terr., Adelaide, SA 5000, Australia. **Online address:** komar.vera@saugov.sa.gov.au

FLASTE, Richard (Alfred). American (born United States), b. 1942. **Genres:** Food And Wine, Adult Non-fiction, Food And Wine, Autobiography/Memoirs, Law. **Career:** New York Times, science and health editor, parent-child columnist, reporter, 1973-76, assistant style editor, 1976-80, deputy director of science news, 1980-82, director of science news, 1982-, science associate editor; Allure Magazine, contributing editor. **Publications:** NON-FICTION: (with D.N. Flaste and E. Rodman) The New York Times Guide to Children's Entertainment: In New York, New Jersey and Connecticut, 1976; (with P. Franey) Pierre Franey's Kitchen, 1982; (with P. Franey) Pierre Franey's Low-Calorie Gourmet, 1984; (co-author) The New York Times Guide to the Return of Halley's Comet, 1985; (with P. Franey) The New York Times 60-Minute Gourmet's Low Calorie Cooking, 1989; The New York Times Book of Science Literacy: What Everyone Needs to Know From Newton to the Knuckleball, 1991; (with P. Franey) Pierre Franey's Cooking in America, 1992; (co-author) Medicine's Great Journey: One Hundred Years of Healing, 1992; (with P. Franey) Pierre Franey's Cooking in France, 1994; (with P. Franey and B. Miller) A Chef's Tale: A Memoir of Food, France and America, 1994; (with J.E. Brody) Jane Brody's Good Seafood Book, 1994; (with E.L. Deci) Why We Do What We Do: The Dynamics of Personal Autonomy, 1995; (with L. Abramson) The Defence Is Ready: Life in the Trenches of Criminal Law, 1997; (as Rick Flaste with J. Lahey) My Bread: The Revolutionary No-work, No-knead Method, 2009. Contributor to periodicals. **Address:** New York Times, 229 W 43rd St., New York, NY 10036-3959, U.S.A.

FLATH, Carol (Apollonio). (Carol Apollonio). American/British (born England), b. 1955. **Genres:** Language/Linguistics, Literary Criticism And History, Translations, Novels. **Career:** Duke University, instructor, 1980-83, lecturer, 1985-89, assistant professor, 1989-95, associate professor of the practice of Slavics, 1995-, professor; University of Virginia, instructor, 1982; North Carolina State University, lecturer in Japanese, 1987-88; American Association of Teachers of Slavic and East European, president, 1989-90. Writer. **Publications:** (Co-author) S mesta v kar'er: Leaping into Russian: A Systematic Introduction to Contemporary Russian Grammar, 1993; Dostoevsky's Secrets: Reading against the Grain, 2009; (ed.) New Russian Dostoevsky: Readings for the Twenty-first Century, 2010. TRANSLATED FROM JAPANESE: S. Kizaki, The Phoenix Tree and Other Stories, 1990; S. Kizaki, The Sunken Temple (novel), 1993. TRANSLATED FROM RUSSIAN: (ed. with T. Lahusen, V. Garros and N. Korbanevskaya) Intimacy and Terror: Soviet Diaries of the 1930s, 1995; Labor Camp Socialism: The Gulag in the Soviet Totalitarian System, 2000. Contributor of articles to periodicals. **Address:** Department of Slavic & Eurasian Studies, Duke University, 310 Languages Bldg., PO Box 90259, Durham, NC 27708-0259, U.S.A. **Online address:** flath@duke.edu

FLAYHART, William Henry. American (born United States), b. 1944. **Genres:** History, Adult Non-fiction, Transportation, Travel/Exploration. **Career:** Delaware State University, Department of History and Politial Science, assistant professor, 1970-73, associate professor, 1973-75, professor, 1974-2005, chair, 1993-2000, professor emeritus of history and political science, 2005-; University of Leiden, visiting professor, 1994-95; Netherlands Maritime Museum, visiting lecturer. Writer. **Publications:** (With J.H. Shaum Jr.) Majesty at Sea: The Four-Stackers, 1981; (with R.W. Warwick) QE2, 1985; Counterpoint to Trafalgar: The Anglo-Russian Invasion of Naples, 1805-

1806, 1992, rev. ed., 2004; The American Line, 1871-1902, 2000; Perils of the Atlantic: Steamship Disasters, 1850 to the Present, 2003; Disaster at Sea, 150 Years of Maritime Disasters, 1850-2000, 2005; The Inman Life of Liverpool, forthcoming; Biography of Lt. General Sir James Henry Craig, forthcoming. **Address:** W. W. Norton & Company Inc., 500 5th Ave., New York, NY 10110, U.S.A. **Online address:** wflayhar@desu.edu

FLEESON, Lucinda. American (born United States), b. 1950. **Genres:** Autobiography/Memoirs. **Career:** Philadelphia Inquirer, staff reporter, 1980-95; University of Maryland, Philip Merrill College of Journalism, Hubert Humphrey Fellowship Program, director, 2002-, instructor in journalism, 2002-. Journalist, memoirist and administrator. **Publications:** Waking Up in Eden: In Pursuit of an Impassioned Life on an Imperiled Island (memoir), 2009. Contributor to newspapers and periodicals. **Address:** Washington, DC , U.S.A. **Online address:** lucinda@wakingupineden.com

FLEETWOOD, Hugh. See FLEETWOOD, Hugh (Nigel).

FLEETWOOD, Hugh (Nigel). (Hugh Fleetwood). British (born England), b. 1944. **Genres:** Novels, Plays/Screenplays, Novellas/Short Stories, Young Adult Non-fiction, Literary Criticism And History. **Career:** Writer, 1972-. **Publications:** NOVELS: A Painter of Flowers, 1972; The Girl Who Passed for Normal, 1973; Foreign Affairs, 1973; A Conditional Sentence, 1974; A Picture of Innocence, 1975; The Order of Death, 1976; An Artist and a Magician, 1977; Roman Magic, 1978; The Beast, 1979; The Godmother, 1979; The Redeemer, 1979; A Young Fair God, 1982; Paradise, 1986; The Past, 1987; The Witch, 1989; The Mercy Killer, 1990; Brothers, 1999; The Dark Paintings, 2006; A Casualty of War, 2008. OTHER: Fictional Lives (stories), 1980; A Dance to the Glory of God (stories), 1983; (with E. de Concini and R. Faenza) Corrupt, 1984; A Dangerous Place (nonfiction), 1985; The Man Who Went Down with His Ship (stories), 1988. **Address:** Flat 3, 10 Carlingford Rd., London, GL NW3 1RX, England. **Online address:** h.n.fleetwood@btinternet.com

FLEISCHER, Ari. Also writes as Lawrence Ari Fleischer. American (born United States), b. 1960. **Genres:** Novels. **Career:** Jon Fossel, press secretary, 1982; Congressman Norman Lent, press secretary; U.S. Senator Pete Domenici, member of staff; President George H.W. Bush, deputy communications director, 1992; lobbying firm, owner, 1992-94; U.S. House of Representatives, press secretary, 1994-99; Elizabeth Dole for President campaign, communications director, 1999; White House, press secretary, 2000-03; Ari Fleischer Communications (media consulting firm), owner, 2004. **Publications:** Taking Heat: The President the Press and My Years in the White House, 2005. **Address:** c/o Author Mail, William Morrow Co., 10 E 53 St., 7th Fl., New York, NY 10022-5244, U.S.A.

FLEISCHER, Lawrence Ari. See FLEISCHER, Ari.

FLEISCHMAN, Paul. American (born United States), b. 1952. **Genres:** Novellas/Short Stories, Children's Fiction, Young Adult Fiction, inspirational/Motivational Literature, Literary Criticism And History. **Career:** Writer. **Publications:** The Birthday Tree, 1979; The Half-a-Moon Inn, 1980; Graven Images: Three Stories, 1982; Animal Hedge, 1983; Finzel the Farsighted, 1983; Path of the Pale Horse, 1983; Phoebe Danger, Detective, in the Case of the Two-Minute Cough, 1983; Coming-and-Going Men: Four Tales of Itinerants, 1985; I Am Phoenix: Poems for Two Voices, 1985; Rear-view Mirrors, 1986; Rondo in C, 1988; Joyful Noise: Poems for Two Voices, 1988; Saturnalia, 1990; Shadow Play: Story, 1990; The Borning Room, 1991; Time Train, 1991; Townsend's Warbler, 1992; Bull Run, 1993; Copier Creations: Using Copy Machines to Make Decals, Silhouettes, Flip Books, Films, and Much More, 1993; A Fate Totally Worse than Death, 1995; Dateline: Troy, 1996, rev. ed., 2006; Ghosts' Grace: A Poem of Praise for Four Voices, 1996; Seedfolks, 1997, rev. ed., 2004; Whirligig, 1998; Weslandia, 1999; Mind's Eye, 1999; (ed.) Cannibal in the Mirror, 2000; Big Talk: Poems for Four Voices, 2000; Lost!: A Story in String, 2000; Seek, 2001; Breakout, 2003; (with K. Hawkes) Sidewalk Circus, 2004; Zap, 2005; Glass Slipper, Gold Sandal: A Worldwide Cinderella, 2007; Dunderheads, 2009; Dunderheads Behind Bars, 2012. Contributor to periodicals. **Address:** PO Box 646, Aromas, CA 95004-0646, U.S.A.

FLEISCHMAN, Paul R. American (born United States), b. 1945. **Genres:** Essays, Medicine/Health, inspirational/Motivational Literature, Psychiatry, Theology/Religion. **Career:** Yale University School of Medicine, psychiatry residency, 1971-74, chief resident in psychiatry, 1973-74, clinical faculty, supervisor of psychotherapy, and seminar leader in psychiatry and religion; University of Kansas Medical School, Williamson lecturer in religion and medicine; Amherst College, lecturer; Smith College, lecturer; Hampshire College, lecturer; University of Massachusetts, lecturer. Writer. **Publications:** Therapeutic Action of Vipassana Meditation (essays), 1986; Why I Sit, 1986; Healing Zone: Religious Issues in Psychotherapy, 1989; The Healing Spirit, 1990, rev. ed., 1994; Healing the Healer and the Experience of Impermanence (essays), 1991; Spiritual Aspects of Psychiatric Practice, 1993; Cultivating Inner Peace, 1997; (with F.D. Fleischman) Karma & Chaos: New and Collected Essays on Vipassana Meditation, 1999; You Can Never Speak Up Too Often for the Love of All Things, 2001; The Buddha Taught Nonviolence, Not Pacifism, 2002; Cultivating Inner Peace: Exploring the Psychology, Wisdom, and Poetry of Gandhi, Thoreau, the Buddha, and Others, 2004; Ancient Path: Public Talks on Vipassana Meditation, 2009. Contributor to periodicals. **Address:** 1394 S East St., Amherst, MA 01002, U.S.A.

FLEISCHNER, Jennifer. American (born United States), b. 1956. **Genres:** Children's Non-fiction, Literary Criticism And History, Young Adult Non-fiction, Biography. **Career:** Dover Publications Inc., publicity director, 1977-78; State University of New York, lecturer, 1986-88, affiliated faculty in women's studies, 1988-, assistant professor, 1988-96, Diversity lecturer, 1995, associate professor of English and director of undergraduate studies, 1996-2002, director of honors program, 1997-99; College of Mount St. Vincent, visiting assistant professor, 1989-90; Hartwick College, Babcock Lecturer, 1992; Harvard University, Andrew W. Mellon faculty fellow in Afro-American studies, 1993-94; Macmillan Publishing Company Inc., managing editor, 1993; Adelphi University, professor of English and chair, 2002-; Knox College, Lincoln Studies Institute, board director; Abraham Lincoln Association, board director. **Publications:** FOR ADULTS: Book Group Guide to the Work of Barbara Kingsolver, 1994; Book Group Guide to the Work of Louise Erdrich, 1995; Book Group Guide to the Work of Doris Lessing, 1995; Mastering Slavery: Memory, Family and Identity in Women's Slave Narratives, 1996; Mrs. Lincoln and Mrs. Keckly: The Remarkable Story of the Friendship between a First Lady and a Former Slave, 2003; Nobody's Boy, 2006. EDITOR and CONTRIBUTOR: The American Experience, 1990; Scholastic Encyclopedia of American Presidents, 1994; (with S.O. Weisser) Feminist Nightmares: Women at Odds, Feminism and the Problem of Sisterhood, 1994. FOR YOUNG READERS: The Inuits: People of the Arctic, 1995; The Dred Scott Case: Testing the Right to Live Free, 1996; I Was Born a Slave: The Life of Harriet Jacobs as Told in Her Own Words, 1997. OTHERS: The Apaches: People of the Southwest, 1994; (ed. and intro.) Incidents in the Life of a Slave Girl: Written by Herself, 2010. Contributor of articles to books and magazines. **Address:** Department of English, Adelphi University, Rm 201, Harvey Hall, PO Box 701, Garden City, NY 11530-0701, U.S.A. **Online address:** fleischner@adelphi.edu

FLEISHER, Paul. American (born United States), b. 1948. **Genres:** Children's Non-fiction, Education, Natural History, Young Adult Non-fiction, Essays, Marine Sciences/Oceanography, Meteorology/Atmospheric Sciences, Sciences, Sciences, Writing/Journalism, Animals/Pets, Biology, Astronomy. **Career:** Teacher, 1970-72, 1975-78; Richmond Public Schools, teacher in programs for gifted, 1978-2005; Virginia Commonwealth University, adjunct faculty, 1981-86, 2006-; Johns Hopkins University, Center for Talented Youth, adjunct faculty, 1989-90; University of Richmond, Adult Continuing Studies, instructor, 1998-; Richmond Peace Education Center, assistant to the director, 2006-. Writer. **Publications:** Secrets of the Universe, 1987; Understanding the Vocabulary of the Nuclear Arms Race, 1988; Write Now!, 1989; Tanglers, 1991; (with P. Keeler) Looking Inside (juvenile), 1991; Changing Our World: A Handbook for Young Activists, 1993; Ecology A-Z, 1993; Our Oceans: Experiments and Activities in Marine Science, 1995; Life Cycles of a Dozen Diverse Creatures, 1996; Brain Food: Games That Teach Kids to Think, 1997; Tanglers Too, 1998; Ice Cream Treats: The Inside Scoop, 2000; Gorilla, 2000; Ants, 2002; 21st Century Writing, 2003. WEBS OF LIFE SERIES: Tide Pool, Coral Reef, Saguaro Cactus, Oak Tree, 1997; Salt Marsh, Pond, Alpine Meadow, Mountain Stream, 1998; The Big Bang, 2005; Evolution, 2005; Parasites, 2006; Brainbuilders, 2006. FOOD WEBS SERIES: Desert, Forest, Grasslands, Ocean, Ponds and Lakes, Tundra, 2007; Early Bird Astronomy, Neptune, Venus, 2009. WEATHERWISE SERIES: Gases, Pressure and Wind, 2010; Vapor, Rain and Snow, 2010; Lightning, Hurricanes and Blizzards, 2010; Predicting the Weather, 2010. Contributor to magazines.

Address: 2781 Beowulf Ct., Richmond, VA 23231, U.S.A. **Online address:** pfleishe@earthlink.net

FLEISHMAN, Avrom. (Avrom Hirsch Fleishman). American (born United States), b. 1933. **Genres:** Film, Literary Criticism And History, Social Commentary, Young Adult Non-fiction. **Career:** Industrial Design, associate editor, 1956-58; Printers' Ink, associate editor, 1958; Columbia University, instructor in English, 1958-59; Hofstra University, instructor in English, 1960-63; University of Minnesota, assistant professor, 1963-66; Michigan State University, assistant professor, 1966-67; Johns Hopkins University, associate professor, 1968-70, professor of English, 1970-99, professor emeritus, 1999-. **Publications:** A Reading of Mansfield Park: An Essay in Critical Synthesis, 1967; Conrad's Politics: Community and Anarchy in the Fiction of Joseph Conrad, 1967; The English Historical Novel: Walter Scott to Virginia Woolf, 1971; Virginia Woolf: A Critical Reading, 1975; Fiction and the Ways of Knowing: Essays on British Novels, 1978; Figures of Autobiography: The Language of Self-Writing in Victorian and Modern England, 1983; Narrated Films: Storytelling Situations in Cinema History, 1992; The Condition of English: Literary Studies in a Changing Culture, 1998; New Class Culture: How an Emergent Class Is Transforming America's Culture, 2002; George Eliot's Intellectual Life, 2010. **Address:** Department of English, Johns Hopkins University, 1102A Dell House, 3400 N Charles St., Baltimore, MD 21218, U.S.A.

FLEISHMAN, Avrom Hirsch. *See* **FLEISHMAN, Avrom.**

FLEISHMAN, Lazar. American/Ukranian (born Ukraine), b. 1944. **Genres:** Literary Criticism And History, Essays. **Career:** Hebrew University, research fellow, 1974-77, senior lecturer, 1974-81, associate professor of comparative literature and Slavic studies, 1981-85; University of California, visiting associate professor, 1978-79, visiting professor, 1980-81; University of Texas, visiting professor, 1981-82; Stanford University, professor of Slavic languages and literature, 1985-, chair of department, 1991-94, Europe Center Research, affiliate; Columbia University, Russian Institute, senior research fellow, 1985. Writer. **Publications:** Stat'i o Pasternake (essays on Pasternak), 1977; Boris Pasternak v dvadtsatye gody, 1980; (ed. with R. Hughes and O. Raevsky) Russkii Berlin, 1921-1923, 1983; Boris Pasternak v tridtsatye gody, 1984; Poetry and Revolution in Russia, 1905-1930: An Exhibition of Books and Manuscripts, 1989; Boris Pasternak: The Poet and His Politics, 1990; Materialy po istorii russkoi i sovetskoi kul'tury: Iz arkhiva Guverovskogo Instituta, 1992; (with H.B. Harder S. Dorzweiler) Boris Pasternak's Lehrjahre, 1996; (with I. Abyzov and B. Ravdin) Russkaia pechat' v Rige (Russian Press in Riga, vol. I-V), 1997; (ed.) Poetry and Revolution: Boris Pasternak's My Sister Life, 1999; V krugu Zhivago: Pasternakovskii sbornik, 2000; V tiskakh provokatsii: Operatsiia Trest i russkaia zazubezhnaia pechat', 2003; (ed.) Eternity's Hostage: Selected Papers from the Stanford International Conference on Boris Pasternak, May, 2004: Boris Pasternak i literaturnoe dvizhenie 1930-kh godov, 2006; (ed. with H. McLean) Century's Perspective: Essays on Russian literature in Honor of Olga Raevsky Hughes and Robert P. Hughes, 2006; In Honor of Evgeny Pasternak and Elena Pasternak, 2006; (co-ed.) Real Life of Pierre Delalande: Studies in Russian and Comparative Literature to Honor Alexander Dolinin, 2007; (co-ed.) Russian Literature and the West: A Tribute for David M. Bethea, 2008; (co-ed.) Sankirtos: Studies in Russian and Eastern European Literature, Society and Culture: In Honour of Tomas Venclova, 2008; Ot Pushkina k Pasternaku: Izbrannye raboty po poetike I istorii russkoi literatury; (ed.) The Life of Boris Pasternak's Doctor Zhivago, 2009; Vstrecha russkoi emigratsii s Doktorom Zhivago: Boris Pasternak I kholodnaia voina, 2009; (ed.) Mandelstam, 2010. **Address:** Department of Slavic Languages and Literatures, Stanford University, Bldg. 40, Rm. 42L, Encina Hall, 616 Serra St., Stanford, CA 94305, U.S.A. **Online address:** lazar.fleishman@stanford.edu

FLEISSNER, Robert F. Also writes as Archibald Harris. American (born United States), b. 1932. **Genres:** Literary Criticism And History. **Career:** Spring Hill College, instructor in English, speech and drama, 1958-59; Ohio State University, assistant instructor in English, 1960-61; City College of the City University of New York, lecturer in English, 1962-64; Dominican College, assistant professor of English, 1964-66; University of New Mexico, instructor in English, 1966-67; Central State University, assistant professor, 1967-, associate professor of English, professor, now professor emeritus, chair. Writer. **Publications:** Dickens and Shakespeare: A Study in Histrionic Contrasts, 1965; Resolved to Love: The 1592 Edition of Henry Constable's Diana, 1980; The Prince and the Professor: The Wittenberg Connection in Marlowe, Shakespeare, Goethe and Frost: A Hamlet/Faust(us) Analogy, 1986;

Ascending the Prufrockian Stair: Studies in a Dissociated Sensibility, 1988; A Rose by Another Name: A Survey of Literary Flora From Shakespeare to Eco, 1989; Shakespeare and the Matter of the Crux: Textual, Topical, Onomastic, Authorial and Other Puzzlements, 1991; T.S. Eliot and the Heritage of Africa: The Magus and The Moor as Metaphor, 1992; Frost's Road Taken, 1996; (ed.) E.M. Fleissner, The Magic Key, 1999; Sources, Meaning and Influences of Coleridge's Kubla Khan, 2000; Names, Titles and Characters by Literary Writers, 2001; The Master Sleuth on the Trail of Edwin Drood, 2002; Shakespearean and Other Literary Investigations with the Master Sleuth (and Conan Doyle), 2003; Shakespeare and Africa, 2005; Shakespearean Puzzles, 2008. **Address:** Department of Humanities, Central State University, 1400 Brush Row Rd., PO Box 1004, Wilberforce, OH 45384, U.S.A.

FLEM, Lydia. Belgian (born Belgium), b. 1952. **Genres:** Psychology, Self Help, Biography, History, Romance/Historical. **Career:** Author. **Publications:** La vie quotidienne de Freud et ses patients, 1986; L'homme Freud, 1991; Casanova, ou, L'exercise du bonheur, 1995; La Voix des amants, 2002; Freud The Man: An Intellectual Biography, 2003; Comment j'aividé la maison de mes parents, 2004; Panique, 2005; Lettres d'amour enhéritage, 2006; The Final Reminder: How I Emptied My Parents' House, 2007. **Address:** Farrar Straus & Giroux, 19 Union Sq. W, New York, NY 10003, U.S.A.

FLEM-ATH, Rand. Canadian (born Canada), b. 1949?. **Genres:** Archaeology/Antiquities, Mystery/Crime/Suspense, Social Sciences. **Career:** Researcher, librarian and writer. **Publications:** (With R. Flem-Ath) When the Sky Fell: In Search of Atlantis, 1995, rev. ed., 2009; Field of Thunder: A Thriller, 1997; (with C. Wilson) The Atlantis Blueprint: Unlocking the Ancient Mysteries of a Long Lost Civilization, 2000. **Address:** c/o Author Mail, Delacorte Press, Bantam Dell Publishing Group, 1540 Broadway, Ste. 9E, New York, NY 10036, U.S.A. **Online address:** oncetherewasaway@hotmail.com

FLEMING, Alice (Carew Mulcahey). American (born United States), b. 1928. **Genres:** Children's Fiction, Children's Non-fiction, Social Commentary, Poetry, Medicine/Health. **Career:** Writer. **Publications:** The Key to New York, 1960; Wheels, 1960; A Son of Liberty, 1961; Doctors in Petticoats, 1964; A Complete Guide to the Accredited Correspondence Schools, 1964; Great Women Teachers, 1965; The Senator from Maine: Margaret Chase Smith, 1969; Alice Freeman Palmer: Pioneer College President, 1970; Reporters at War, 1970; General's Lady: The Life of Julia Grant, 1971; Highways into History, 1971; Pioneers in Print: Adventures in Courage, 1971; Ida Tarbell: First of the Muckrakers, 1971; Psychiatry: What's It All About?, 1972; Nine Months: An Intelligent Woman's Guide to Pregnancy, 1972; The Moviemakers, 1973; Trials That Made Headlines, 1974; Contraception, Abortion, Pregnancy, 1974; New on the Beat: Women Power in the Police Force, 1975; Alcohol: The Delightful Poison, 1975; Something for Nothing: A History of Gambling, 1978; The Mysteries of ESP, 1980; What to Say When You Don't Know What to Say, 1982; Welcome to Grossville, 1985; The King of Prussia and a Peanut Butter Sandwich, 1988; George Washington Wasn't Always Old, 1991; What, Me Worry? How to Hang in When Your Problems Stress You Out, 1992; P.T. Barnum: The World's Greatest Showman, 1993; A Century of Service: A History of the Auxiliary of Saint Vincents Hospital and Medical Center, 1997; Frederick Douglass: From Slave to Statesman, 2004; Martin Luther King, Jr.: The Voice of Civil Rights, 2008. EDITOR: Hosannah the Home Run! Poems About Sports, 1972; America Is Not All Traffic Lights, 1976. **Address:** Raines & Raines, 103 Kenyon Rd., Medusa, NY 12120-1404, U.S.A.

FLEMING, Anne. British (born England), b. 1928. **Genres:** Mystery/Crime/Suspense, Literary Criticism And History, Medicine/Health, Novels, Adult Non-fiction, Young Adult Fiction. **Career:** Old Forge Press, founder; Byron Journal, editorial staff; freelance writer, 1984-. **Publications:** NONFICTION: Bright Darkness: The Poetry of Lord Byron Presented in the Context of His Life and Times, 1984; In Search of Byron in England and Scotland, 1988; The Myth of the Bad Lord Byron, 1998. EDITOR: (comp.) The Desert and the Marketplace: Writings, Letters, Journals, 1995. CRIME NOVELS: There Goes Charlie, 1990; Sophie Is Gone, 1994; Death and Deconstruction, 1995; This Means Mischief, 1996. OTHER: (comp.) Relaxation for Concentration, Stress Management, and Pain Control Using the Fleming Method, 1997. Contributor of articles to periodicals. **Address:** St. Martin's Press, 175 5th Ave., New York, NY 10010, U.S.A.

FLEMING, Candace. American (born United States), b. 1962. **Genres:** Children's Fiction, Novels, Young Adult Fiction, Biography, Picture/Board

Books, Romance/Historical. **Career:** Writer, 1990-; Harper College, adjunct professor of liberal arts, 1997-. **Publications:** Professor Fergus Fahrenheit and His Wonderful Weather Machine, 1994; Women of the Lights, 1996; Madame La Grande and Her So High, to the Sky, Uproarious Pompadour, 1996; Gabriella's Song, 1997; Westward Ho, Carlotta!, 1998; The Hatmaker's Sign: A Story by Benjamin Franklin, 1998; When Agnes Caws, 1999; A Big Cheese for the White House: The True Tale of a Tremendous Cheddar, 1999; Who Invited You?, 2001; Muncha! Muncha! Muncha!, 2002; Ben Franklin's Almanac: Being a True Account of the Good Gentlemen's Life, 2003; Boxes for Katje, 2003; Smile, Lily!, 2004; Gator Gumbo: A Spicy-Hot Tale, 2004; This Is the Baby, 2004; Our Eleanor: A Scrapbook Look at Eleanor Roosevelt's Remarkable Life, 2005; Sunny Boy!: The Life and Times of a Tortoise, 2005; Lowji Discovers America, 2005; Fabled Fourth Graders of Aesop Elementary School, 2007; Tippy-Tippy-Tippy-Hide!, 2007; Nam! Nam! Nam!, 2007; Lincolns: A Scrapbook Look at Abraham and Mary, 2008; Great and Only Barnum: The Tremendous, Stupendous Life of Showman P.T. Barnum, 2009; Imogene's Last Stand, 2009; Fabled Fifth Graders of Aesop Elementary School, 2010; Seven Hungry Babies, 2010; Clever Jack Takes the Cake, 2010; Amelia Lost: The Life and Disappearance of Amelia Earhart, 2011; Oh, No!, 2011; On the Day I Died, 2012. Contributor to periodicals and magazines. **Address:** 415 E Golf Rd., Arlington Heights, IL 60005, U.S.A. **Online address:** cf@candacefleming.com

FLEMING, Cardine. *See* **MATHER, Anne.**

FLEMING, Caroline. *See* **MATHER, Anne.**

FLEMING, Jacky. British (born England), b. 1955. **Genres:** Women's Studies And Issues, Cartoons, Humor/Satire. **Career:** Writer and cartoonist. **Publications:** Be a Bloody Train Driver, 1991; Never Give Up, 1992; Falling in Love, 1993; Dear Katie, 1994; Hello Boys, 1996; Demented, 2004. Contributor to periodicals. **Address:** PO Box 162, Leeds, WY LS4 2XF, England. **Online address:** jackyfleming1@hotmail.com

FLEMING, James E. American (born United States), b. 1954. **Genres:** Politics/Government, History, Law. **Career:** Brookings Institution, research fellow in government studies, 1981-82; Cravath, Swaine & Moore, attorney, 1986-91; Fordham University, School of Law, associate professor, 1991-98, professor of law, 1998-2006, Leonard F. Manning distinguished professor of law, 2006-07; Harvard University, Center for Ethics and Professions, faculty fellow in ethics, 1999-2000; Boston University, School of Law, professor of law, 2007-, associate dean for research and intellectual life, 2010-. Writer. **Publications:** (With W.F. Murphy and W.F. Harris II) American Constitutional Interpretation, 1986, (with W.F. Murphy, S.A. Barber and S. Macedo) 4th ed., 2008; Securing Constitutional Democracy: The Case of Autonomy, 2006; (with S.A. Barber) Constitutional Interpretation: The Basic Questions, 2007; (ed.) Getting to the Rule of Law, 2011; Nomos LII, 2012; (with L. C. McClain) Rights, Responsibilities and Virtues, forthcoming; Fidelity to our Imperfect Constitution, forthcoming. Contributor to periodicals and journals. **Address:** School of Law, Boston University, Rm. 1070A, 765 Commonwealth Ave., Boston, MA 02215, U.S.A. **Online address:** jfleming@bu.edu

FLEMING, James Rodger. American (born United States), b. 1949. **Genres:** History, Sciences, Meteorology/Atmospheric Sciences, Technology, Bibliography, Earth Sciences, Environmental Sciences/Ecology. **Career:** National Center for Atmospheric Research, research meteorologist, 1973; University of Washington, research meteorologist, 1973-74; American Meteorological Society, historical consultant, 1987-88; Colby College, professor of science, technology and society, 1988-; Smithsonian National Air and Space Museum, Lindberg Chair, 2005-06. Writer. **Publications:** Meteorology in America, 1800-1870, 1990; Historical Perspectives on Climate Change, 1998; The Callendar Effect, 2007; Fixing the Sky: The Checkered History of Weather and Climate Control, 2010. EDITOR: Guide to Historical Resources in the Atmospheric Sciences, 1989; (with H.A. Gemery) Science, Technology, and the Environment: Multidisciplinary Perspectives, 1994; (with R.E. Goodman) International Bibliography of Meteorology: From the Beginning of Printing to 1889. 4 vols., 1994; Historical Essays on Meteorology, 1919-1995, 1996; Weathering the Storm: Sverre Petterssen, the D-day Forecast and the Rise of Modern Meteorology, 2001; (with V. Jankovic and D.R. Coen) Intimate Universality: Local and Global Themes in the History of Weather and Climate, 2006; (with J.T. Fleming) The Papers of Guy Stewart Callendar, 2007; Climate Change and Anthropogenic Greenhouse Warming: A Selection of Key Articles, 1824-1995, with Interpretive Essays, 2008; (with R.D. Launius and D.H. DeVorkin) Globalizing Polar Science: Reconsidering the International Polar and Geophysical Years, 2010; (with V. Jankovic) Osiris, vol. XXVI: Klima, 2011. Contributor to books and journals. **Address:** Science, Technology, and Society Program, Colby College, 5881 Mayflower Hill, Waterville, ME 04901-8858, U.S.A. **Online address:** jfleming@colby.edu

FLEMING, Justin. Australian (born Australia), b. 1953. **Genres:** Documentaries/Reportage, Adult Non-fiction, Plays/Screenplays. **Career:** The Australian Writers' Guild, vice-president; Office of the Attorney General, judge's associate, 1974-79; Office of the Commonwealth Crown Solicitor, legal officer, 1979-80; New South Wales Supreme Court, barrister, 1980-92; Irish Supreme Court, barrister, 1980-92. Writer. **Publications:** PLAYS: Hammer, 1981; Barbarism to Verdict: A History of the Common Law, 1994; Burnt Piano and Other Plays, 1999; Paris Studio, 2001; Coup d'Etat & Other Plays, 2003. OTHERS: All That Brothers Should Be, 1997; The Vision Splendid: A History of Carroll & O'Dea, 1999; The Crest of the Wave, 2003; The Wave Rolls On: Waverley College Old Boys' Union 1908-2008, 2009; Burnt Piano, 2010; Stage Lines, 2011. **Address:** c/o Barbara Hogenson, Barbara Hogenson Agency, 165 W End Ave., Ste. 19C, New York, NY 10023, U.S.A. **Online address:** justin@fleming.net

FLEMING, Kate. British (born England), b. 1946. **Genres:** Biography, Autobiography/Memoirs, Photography. **Career:** Writer. **Publications:** The Churchills, 1975; Celia Johnson, 1991. Contributor to periodicals. **Address:** c/o Andrew Hewson, 45/47 Clerkenwell Green, London, GL EC1R 0EB, England.

FLEMING, Keith. American (born United States), b. 1960?. **Genres:** Young Adult Non-fiction, Biography, Autobiography/Memoirs, Literary Criticism And History. **Career:** Chicago Literary Review, editor. **Publications:** The Boy with a Thorn in His Side: A Memoir, 2000; Original Youth: The Real Story of Edmund White's Boyhood, 2003. **Address:** c/o Author Mail, HarperCollins Publishers, 10 E 53rd St., 7th Fl., New York, NY 10022, U.S.A.

FLEMING, Robert E. American (born United States), b. 1936. **Genres:** Literary Criticism And History, Young Adult Fiction, History. **Career:** Teacher, 1959-60, 1960-64; University of New Mexico, assistant professor, 1967-71, associate professor, 1971-76, professor of English, 1976-, now emeritus, College of Arts and Sciences, associate dean, 1988-; National Endowment for the Humanities, New Mexico Humanities Council, lecturer, 1978, 1980, 1985; Minority Voices, associate editor, 1979-83; American Poetry, associate editor, 1983-86; American Literary Realism, co-editor, 1986-; Gorky Institute, lecturer; Moscow State University, lecturer; Kuban State University, lecturer, 1993; Ernest Hemingway Foundation, director, 1993-. **Publications:** Willard Motley, 1978; James Weldon Johnson and Arma Wendell Bontemps: A Reference Guide, 1978; Sinclair Lewis: A Reference Guide, 1980; Charles F. Lummis, 1981; James Weldon Johnson, 1987; The Face in the Mirror: Hemingway's Writers, 1994; (ed.) Hemingway and the Natural World, 1999; (ed. with R. Lewis) Under Kilimanjaro, 2005. Contributor of articles and reviews to academic journals. **Address:** Department of English Language & Literature, University of New Mexico, Humanities 217, Albuquerque, NM 87131, U.S.A.

FLEMING, Sally. *See* **WALKER, Sally M(acArt).**

FLEMING, Stephen. *See* **ARNOLD, Guy.**

FLEMING, Thomas. American (born United States), b. 1927. **Genres:** Novels, History, Biography, Autobiography/Memoirs, Military/Defense/Arms Control, Young Adult Fiction. **Career:** Yonker's Herald Statesman, reporter, 1951; Reader's Digest, assistant, 1951-52; Oursler Estate, literary executor, 1952-54; Cosmopolitan Magazine, associate editor, 1954-58, executive editor, 1958-61; Fulltime writer, 1961-; Society of Magazine Writers, president, 1967-68; American Revolution Round Table, chairman, 1970-81; PEN, American Center, president, 1971-73. **Publications:** HISTORY: Now We are Enemies: The Story of Bunker Hill, 1960; Beat the Last Drum, 1963; One Small Candle, 1964; West Point: The Man and Times of the U.S. Military Academy, 1969; The Forgotten Victory, 1973; 1776: Year of Illusions, 1975; New Jersey, 1977; The First Stroke, 1978; The Living Land of Lincoln, 1980; Downright Fighting: The Story of Cowpens, 1989; Liberty!: The American Revolution, 1997; Lights along the Way, 1999; Duel: Alexander Hamilton, Aaron Burr and the Future of America, 1999; The New Dealer's War: FDR and the War within World War II, 2001; The Louisiana Purchase, 2003; The Illusion of Victory: America in World War I, 2003; Mysteries of My Father: An Irish-American Memoir, 2005. NOVELS: All Good Men, 1961; The God of Love, 1963; King of the Hill, 1966; A Cry of Whiteness, 1967; Romans, Countrymen, Lovers, 1969; The Sandbox Tree, 1970; The Good Shepherd, 1974; Liberty Tavern, 1976; Rulers of the City, 1977; Promises to Keep, 1978; A Passionate Girl, 1979; The Officers' Wives, 1981; Dreams of Glory, 1983; The Spoils of War, 1984; Time and Tide, 1987; Over There, 1992; Loyalties: A Novel of World War II, 1994; Remember the Morning, 1997; The Wages of Fame, 1998; Hours of Gladness, 1999; When This Cruel War Is Over, 2001; Conquerors of the Sky, 2003; A Passionate Girl, 2004; The Secret Trial of Robert E. Lee, 2006; West Point Blue and Grey, 2006; The Perils of Peace: America's Struggle for Survival after Yorktown, 2007. BIOGRAPHY: First in Their Hearts, 1967; The Man from Monticello, 1969; The Man Who Dared the Lightning, 1971. EDITOR: Affectionately Yours, George Washington, 1967; Benjamin Franklin: A Biography in His Own Words, 1972. YOUNG ADULT HISTORY: Battle of Yorktown, 1968; The Golden Door: The Story of American Immigration, 1970; Give Me Liberty: Black Valor in the Revolutionary War, 1971; Thomas Jefferson, 1971; Band of Brothers: West Point in the Civil War, 1988; Behind the Headlines: The Story of American Newspapers, 1989; Harry S. Truman, President, 1993; Washington's Secret War: The Hidden History of Valley Forge, 2005; Everybody's Revolution, 2006; (with S.E. Ambrose, C. Carr and V. Hanson) The Cold War: A Military History, 2006; Way of the Pilgrims, 2009; Intimate Lives of the Founding Fathers, 2009; Irish American Chronicle, 2009. Contributor of articles to magazines. **Address:** 315 E 72nd St., New York, NY 10021-4625, U.S.A. **Online address:** tflem37048@aol.com

FLEMING, Virginia (Edwards). American (born United States), b. 1923. **Genres:** Poetry, Children's Fiction, Young Adult Fiction, Songs/Lyrics And Libretti. **Career:** First Presbyterian Church, nursery school teacher, 1973-83, deacon, 1976-80. Writer. **Publications:** So Tender the Spirit (poetry), 1985; Wellspring (poetry), 1986; Be Good to Eddie Lee, 1993; Red Wolf Howling, forthcoming; Summer Visitors, forthcoming. Work appears in anthologies. **Address:** 516 McKinley Ave., Pitman, NJ 08071-1864, U.S.A. **Online address:** nutool@juno.com

FLENLEY, John (Roger). New Zealander/British (born England), b. 1936. **Genres:** Geography, Adult Non-fiction, Sciences, Natural History, Earth Sciences, Environmental Sciences/Ecology, Essays. **Career:** University of Hull, reader in geography; Massey University, professor of geography, 1989-, now professor emeritus. Writer. **Publications:** (Ed.) The Water Relations of Malesian Forests: Being the Transactions of the First Aberdeen-Hull Symposium on Malesian Ecology, 1971; The Equatorial Rain Forest: A Geological History, 1979; (ed. with J. Neale) The Quaternary in Britain: Essays Reviews and Original Work on the Quaternary Published in Honour of Lewis Penny on His Retirement, 1981; Biogeography, 1986; (ed. with T.R.R. Johnston) Aspects of Environmental Change, 1991; (with P. Bahn) Easter Island Earth Island, 1992, 2nd ed. as The Enigmas of Easter Island: Island on the Edge, 2003; (ed. with M.B. Bush) Tropical Rainforest Responses to Climatic Change, 2007. Contributor to periodicals. **Address:** Massey University, Palmerston North Campus, PO Box 11 222, Palmerston North, 4442, New Zealand. **Online address:** j.flenley@massey.ac.nz

FLESCHER, Irwin. American (born United States), b. 1926. **Genres:** Human Relations/Parenting, Psychology, Education. **Career:** New York State Department of Labor, placement counselor, 1952-55; Bureau of Child Guidance, staff psychologist, 1955-58; East Williston Public Schools, school and research psychologist, 1960-; Psychological Services Institute, clinical associate, 1967-; Long Island University, adjunct associate professor, 1971-74. Writer. **Publications:** Ocular-manual laterality and perceptual rotation of literal symbols, 1962; Children in the Learning Factory: The Search for a Humanizing Teacher, 1972; Wearing Thin: Rhymes from the Diet Jungle, 2001. Contributor of articles to journals. **Address:** 225 Locust Ln., Roslyn Heights, NY 11577, U.S.A.

FLETCHER, Christine. (Christine Marie Fletcher). American (born United States), b. 1964. **Genres:** Novels, Young Adult Fiction. **Career:** Writer, veterinarian and educator. **Publications:** Tallulah Falls, 2006; Ten Cents a Dance, 2008. **Address:** c/o Deb Shapiro, Bloomsbury Children's Books, 175 5th Ave., New York, NY 10010, U.S.A. **Online address:** chris@christinefletcherbooks.com

FLETCHER, Christine Marie. *See* **FLETCHER, Christine.**

FLETCHER, George P. American (born United States), b. 1939. **Genres:** Law, Politics/Government. **Career:** University of California, law professor, 1969-83; Columbia Law School, faculty, 1983-, Cardozo professor of jurisprudence. Writer. **Publications:** Rethinking Criminal Law, 1978; (ed. with A. Eser) Rechtfertigung und Entschuldigung: Rechtsvergleichende Perspektiven, 1987; A Crime of Self-Defense: Bernhard Goetz and the Law on Trial, 1988; Loyalty: An Essay on the Morality of Relationships, 1993; With Justice for Some: Victims' Rights in Criminal Trials, 1995; Basic Concepts of Legal Thought, 1996; Basic Concepts of Criminal Law, 1998; Rethinking Criminal Law, 2000; Our Secret Constitution: How Lincoln Redefined American Democracy, 2001; Romantics at War: Glory and Guilt in the Age of Terrorism, 2002; (with S. Sheppard) American Law in a Global Context: The Basics, 2005; The Grammar of Criminal Law: American, Comparative, and International, 2007; Tort Liability for Human Rights Abuses, 2008; (with J.D. Ohlin) Defending Humanity: When Force Is Justified and Why, 2008; The Bond: A Novel, 2009. **Address:** Columbia Law School, 435 W 116th St., PO Box 4004, New York, NY 10027-7297, U.S.A. **Online address:** fletch@law.columbia.edu

FLETCHER, Joel L. American (born United States), b. 1935. **Genres:** Biography, History. **Career:** Council on International Educational Exchange, staff; City University of New York, faculty; Fletcher/Copenhaver Fine Art, co-owner, 1992-. Writer. **Publications:** Louisiana Education since Colonial Days, 1948; The Acadians in Louisiana Today, 1959; Ken and Thelma: The Story of a Confederacy of Dunces, 2005. Contributor of articles to periodicals. **Address:** Fletcher/Copenhaver Fine Art, PO Box 1038, Fredericksburg, VA 22402-1038, U.S.A. **Online address:** info@fc-fineart.com

FLETCHER, John Walter James. British (born England), b. 1937. **Genres:** Humanities, Literary Criticism And History, Translations. **Career:** University of Toulouse, lecturer in English, 1961-64; University of Durham, lecturer in French, 1964-66; University of East Anglia, lecturer in French, 1966-68, reader in French, 1968-69, professor of European and comparative literature, 1969-98, pro-vice-chancellor, 1974-79; Calder & Boyars, Critical Appraisals Series, editor, 1974-79; University of Kent, honorary senior research fellow, 1998-; University of East Anglia, now professor emeritus of French and comparative literature. Writer. **Publications:** The Novels of Samuel Beckett, 1964, 2nd ed., 1970; (comp.) Russia: Past, Present and Future, 1967; Samuel Beckett's Art, 1967; A Critical Commentary on Flaubert's Trois Contes, 1968; New Directions in Literature: Critical Approaches to a Contemporary Phenomenon, 1968; Die Kunst des Samuel Beckett, 1969; (with R. Federman) Samuel Beckett: His Works and His Critics, an Essay in Bibliography, 1970; (with J. Spurling) Beckett: A Study of His Plays, 1972, 2nd ed., 1978; Claude Simon and Fiction Now, 1975; (with B.S. Fletcher) A Student's Guide to the Plays of Samuel Beckett, 1978, 2nd ed., 1985; Novel and Reader, 1980; Alain Robbe-Grillet, 1983; (with J. Spurling) Beckett the Playwright, 1985; (contrib.) Encounters with Iris Murdoch, 1988; (contrib.) Abjection, Melancholia and Love, 1990; (with C. Bove) Iris Murdoch: A Descriptive Primary and Annotated Secondary Bibliography, 1994; Samuel Beckett: A Faber Critical Guide, 2000; About Beckett: The Playwright and the Work, 2003, 2nd ed., 2006. EDITOR: (with B. Fletcher) Samuel Beckett: Fin de partie, 1970; Samuel Beckett: Waiting for Godot, 1971; Forces in Modern French Drama: Studies in Variations on the Permitted Lie, 1972; (with J. Calder) The Nouveau Roman Reader, 1986. TRANSLATOR: (with B. Fletcher) C. Simon, The Georgics, 1989; (with B. Fletcher) J.C. Favez, The Red Cross and the Holocaust, 1999; J.P. Boule, Herve Guibert, Voices of the Self, 1999. **Address:** School of European Culture and Languages, University of Kent, Cornwallis Bldg., Canterbury, KT CT2 7NF, England. **Online address:** j.w.j.fletcher@kent.ac.uk

FLETCHER, Michael A. American (born United States) **Genres:** Novels, Biography, Autobiography/Memoirs. **Career:** Baltimore Sun, reporter, through 1995; Washington Post, national race relations reporter, 1995-, White House correspondent. Biographer. **Publications:** Leadership Transitions for Growth: Growing Exceptional Churches in the 21st Century, 2003; Building Successful Relationships, 2004; Overcoming Barriers to Growth: Proven Strategies for Taking Your Church to the Next Level, 2006; (with K. Merida) Supreme Discomfort: The Divided Soul of Clarence Thomas, 2007. **Address:** Washington Post, 1150 15th St. NW, Washington, DC 20071, U.S.A.

FLETCHER, Ralph. American (born United States), b. 1953. **Genres:** Children's Fiction, Poetry, Education, Crafts, Writing/Journalism, Young Adult Non-fiction. **Career:** Educational consultant, 1985-; author, 1990-. **Publications:** CHILDREN FICTION: Fig Pudding, 1995; Spider Boy, 1997; Flying Solo, 1998; Tommy Trouble and the Magic Marble, 2000; The Circus Surprise, 2001; Uncle Daddy, 2001. CHILDREN NONFICTION: A Writer's Notebook: Unlocking the Writer within You, 1996; Live Writing: Breathing Life into Your Words, 1999; How Writers Work: Finding a Process That Works for You, 2000; Poetry Matters: Writing a Poem from the Inside Out, 2002; Pyrotechnics on the Page: Playful Craft that Sparks Writing, 2010; Also Known as Rowan Pohi, 2011. POETRY: Magic Nest: Fertility Poems, 1980; Water Planet: Poems about Water, 1991; Am Wings: Poems about Love, 1994; Ordinary Things: Poems from a Walk in Early Spring, 1997; Twilight Comes Twice, 1997; Buried Alive: The Elements of Love, 1996; Room Enough for Love, 1998; Relatively Speaking: Poems about Family, 1999; Grandpa Never Lies, 2000; Have You Been to the Beach Lately?, 2001; Hello, Harvest Moon, 2003; Writing Kind of Day: Poems for Young Poets, 2005. OTHERS: Walking Trees: Teaching Teachers in the New York City Schools, 1991 as Trees: Portraits of Teachers and Children in the Culture of Schools, 1995; What a Writer Needs, 1993; Breathing In, Breathing Out: Keeping a Writer's Notebook, 1996; (with J. Portalupi) Craft Lessons: Teaching Writing K-8, 1998, 2nd ed., 2007; (with J. Portalupi) Nonfiction Craft Lessons: Teaching Information Writing K-8, 2001; (with J. Portalupi) Writing Workshop: The Essential Guide, 2001; (ed. with J. Portalupi) Teaching the Qualities of Writing: Ideas, Design, Language, Presentation, 2004; Marshfield Dreams: When I was a Kid, 2005; (with J. Portalupi) Lessons for the Writer's Notebook, 2005; Boy Writers: Reclaiming Their Voices, 2006; Reflections, 2006; Moving Day, 2006; The One O' Clock Chop, 2007; How to Write Your Life Story, 2007; The Sandman, 2008; Mentor Author, Mentor Texts: Short Texts, Craft Notes and Practical Classroom Uses, 2011; Guy-write: What Every Guy Writer Needs to Know, 2012. Contributor to periodicals. **Address:** c/o Ronnie Ann Herman, Herman Agency, 350 Central Pk. W, New York, NY 10025, U.S.A. **Online address:** fletcher17@earthlink.net

FLETCHER, Susan. British (born England), b. 1979?. **Genres:** Novels, Literary Criticism And History, Young Adult Fiction. **Career:** Writer. **Publications:** Eve Green, 2004; Oystercatchers, 2006; Corrag, 2010; Witch Light, 2010; The Highland Witch, 2011. Contributor to periodicals. **Address:** W. W. Norton & Company Inc., 500 5th Ave., New York, NY 10110-0002, U.S.A.

FLETCHER, Susan (Clemens). American (born United States), b. 1951. **Genres:** Children's Fiction, Novels. **Career:** Campbell-Mithun, media buyer, 1974-77, advertising copywriter, 1977-79; Portland Community College, lecturer, 1988-90; Vermont College, instructor in writing for children, 2000-04. Writer. **Publications:** Dragon's Milk (fantasy), 1989; The Stuttgart Nanny Mafia (novel), 1991; Flight of the Dragon Kyn (fantasy), 1993; The Sign of the Dove (fantasy), 1996; Shadow Spinner (novel), 1998; Walk across the Sea (novel), 2001; Alphabet of Dreams, 2006; Dadblamed Union Army Cow, 2007; Ancient, Strange, and Lovely (fantasy) 2010. Contributor to periodicals. **Address:** c/o Emilie Jacobson, Curtis Brown Ltd., 10 Astor Pl., New York, NY 10003, U.S.A. **Online address:** susanfletcher@centurytel.net

FLEURANT, Gerdès. American/Haitian (born United States), b. 1939. **Genres:** Mythology/Folklore, Music, Education, Race Relations, Sociology, Popular Culture, Cultural/Ethnic Topics, Humanities, Theology/Religion. **Career:** Salem State College, professor of sociology, 1971-93; Wellesley College, associate professor of music, 1993-, chairperson of department and director of multicultural planning and policy, 1993-, professor emeritus, 2005-. Writer. **Publications:** Dancing Spirits: Rhythms and Rituals of Haitian Vodun, the Rada Rite, 1996; (intro.) Vodou: Visions and Voices of Haiti, 1998. **Address:** Department of Music, Wellesley College, 106 Central St., Wellesley, MA 02481, U.S.A. **Online address:** gfleurant@wellesley.edu

FLICKENGER, Rob. American/Romanian (born Romania) **Genres:** Communications/Media, Information Science/Computers. **Career:** NDA, Unix administrator, 1998-2000; O'Reilly and Associates, internet systems administrator, 2000-02; freelance writer and editor, 2003-; NoCat.net, co-founder. **Publications:** Building Wireless Community Networks: Implementing the Wireless Web, 2002, 2nd ed., 2003; Linux Server Hacks: 100 Industrial-Strength Tips and Tools, 2003; Wireless Hacks: 100 Industrial-Strength Tips and Tools, 2003, (with R. Weeks) 2nd ed., 2006; Trucos Redes Inalambricas, 2004. Contributor of articles to periodicals. **Address:** c/o Author Mail, O'Reilly Books, 1005 Gravenstein Hwy. N, Sebastopol, CA 95472, U.S.A. **Online address:** rob@oreillynet.com

FLIEGER, Verlyn. American (born United States), b. 1933. **Genres:** Young Adult Fiction, Literary Criticism And History. **Career:** Brazilian-American Cultural Institute, instructor in English, 1965-66; Catholic University, graduate assistant in English, 1971-76; University of Maryland, Department of English, instructor, 1976-77, lecturer, 1977-78, assistant professor, 1978-84, associate professor, 1984-97, professor, 1998-. Writer. **Publications:** Splintered Light: Logos and Language in Tolkien's World, 1983, 2nd. ed., 2002; A Question of Time: J.R.R. Tolkien's Road to Faërie, 1997; (ed. with C.F. Hostetter) Tolkien's Legendarium: Essays on The History of Middle Earth, 2000; Pig Tale, 2002; (ed.) Smith of Wootton Major, 2005; Interrupted Music: The Making of Tolkien's Mythology, 2005; (with D.A. Anderson) Tolkien on Fairy Stories, 2008; Green Suns and Faerie: Essays on Tolkien, 2012. **Address:** Department of English, University of Maryland, 3219 Tawes Hall, College Park, MD 20742, U.S.A. **Online address:** verlynf@umd.edu

FLIER, Michael S. American (born United States), b. 1941. **Genres:** Cultural/Ethnic Topics, Language/Linguistics, Literary Criticism And History. **Career:** University of California, Department of Slavic languages and literatures, assistant professor, 1968-73, associate professor, 1973-79, professor, 1979-91, chairman, 1978-84, 1987-89, Harvard University, Oleksandr Potebnja professor of Ukrainian philology, 1991-, Department of Linguistics, chairman, 1994-98, Department of Slavic Languages and Literatures, chairman, 1999-, Harvard Ukrainian Research Institute, director, 2004-, Davis Center for Russian and Eurasian Studies, faculty associate, visiting professor. Writer. **Publications:** Aspects of Nominal Determination in Old Church Slavic, 1974; Say It in Russian, 1982. EDITOR: Slavic Forum: Essays in Linguistics and Literature, 1974; American Contributions to the Ninth International Congress of Slavists 1983, vol. I: Linguistics, 1983; (with H. Birnbaum) Medieval Russian Culture, 1984, (with D. Rowland) vol. II, 1994; (with R.D. Brecht) Issues in Russian Morphosyntax, 1985; (with A. Timberlake) The Scope of Slavic Aspect, 1985; (with D.S. Worth) Slavic Linguistics, Poetics, Cultural History, 1985; (with S. Karlinsky) Language, Literature, Linguistics: In Honor of Francis J. Whitfield, 1987; (with R.P. Hughes) For SK: In Celebration of the Life and Career of Simon Karlinsky, 1994; (with H. Birnbaum) The Language and Verse of Russia: In Honor of Dean S. Worth, 1995; Ukrainian Philogy and Linguistics, 1996; (with H. Andersen) Old Church Slavic Reader, 2004. **Address:** Department of Slavic Languages and Literatures, Harvard University, 368 Barker Ctr., 12 Quincy St., Cambridge, MA 02138, U.S.A. **Online address:** flier@fas.harvard.edu

FLINDERS, Neil J. American (born United States), b. 1934. **Genres:** Education, Human Relations/Parenting, Speech/Rhetoric, Theology/Religion, Self Help, Philosophy, Adult Non-fiction. **Career:** Church of Jesus Christ of Latter-day Saints, missionary teacher, 1954-56, Department of Education, teacher of theology and supervisor of seminary teacher training, 1960-, Department of Seminaries, director of research and evaluation, 1969-75, Institute of Religion, director of research and evaluation, 1969-75, Long Range Planning Church Educational System, director of research, 1969-79; Brigham Young University, consultant and trainer in human relations, 1963-, professor of education psychology, 1979-95, now associate professor emeritus of educational leadership and foundation; Weber State College, consultant and trainer in human relations, 1963-. Writer. **Publications:** Personal Communications: How to Understand and Be Understood, 1966; Leadership and Human Relations: A Handbook for Parents, Teachers and Executives, 1969; Continue in Prayer, 1975; Moral Perspective and Educational Practice, 1979; A Piece of Cowardice, 1982; My Decision: An Act of Faith or A Piece of Cowardice, 1984; Teach the Children: An Agency Approach to Education, 1990. **Address:** PO Box 215, Nauvoo, IL 62354, U.S.A.

FLINN, Alex. American (born United States), b. 1966. **Genres:** Novels, Romance/Historical. **Career:** Miami-Dade State Attorney's Office, intern. Writer. **Publications:** Breathing Underwater, 2001; Breaking Point, 2002; Nothing to Lose (novel), 2004; Fade to Black, 2005; Diva, 2006; Beastly, 2007; A Kiss in Time, 2009; Cloaked, 2011; Bewitching, 2012. **Address:** c/o Author Mail, HarperCollins Publishers, 10 E 53rd St., New York, NY 10022, U.S.A. **Online address:** alixwrites@aol.com

FLINN, Caryl. American (born United States), b. 1957. **Genres:** Art/Art History. **Career:** University of Arizona, professor of women's studies. Writer. **Publications:** Strains of Utopia: Gender, Nostalgia and Hollywood Film Music, 1992; Music and Cinema, 2000; The New German Cinema: Music,

History and the Matter of Style, 2004; Brass Diva: The Life and Legends of Ethel Merman, 2007. **Address:** Department of Women's Studies, University of Arizona, 925 N Tyndall Ave., PO Box 210438, Tucson, AZ 85721-0438, U.S.A. **Online address:** cflinn@email.arizona.edu

FLINN, Kathleen. American (born United States) **Genres:** Food And Wine, Travel/Exploration, Autobiography/Memoirs, Crafts. **Career:** Microsoft, Sidewalk.com, founding restaurant editor, 1990-99; Internet Underground, founding editor, 1995-96; MSN.co.uk, editorial director, 1999-2003. Journalist. **Publications:** (Ed.) Seattle Sidewalk Offline Restaurant Guide: The Most Comprehensive Guide to Dining in Seattle, 1997; The Sharper Your Knife, the Less You Cry: Love, Learning and Tears at the World's Most Famous Cooking School, 2007; Kitchen Counter Cooking School: How a Few Simple Lessons Transformed Nine Culinary Novices into Fearless Home Cooks, 2011. Contributor to periodicals. **Address:** Writing Loft, Richard Hugo House, 1634 11th Ave., Seattle, WA 98122, U.S.A. **Online address:** kat@kathleenflinn.com

FLINN, Kelly. American (born United States), b. 1970. **Genres:** Autobiography/Memoirs, Biography, History. **Career:** Air Force Academy, assistant. Writer. **Publications:** Proud to Be: My Life, the Air Force, the Controversy, 1997. Contributor to periodicals. **Address:** Random House Inc., 1745 Broadway, New York, NY 10019-4368, U.S.A. **Online address:** kjfdefense@aol.com

FLINT, Anthony. American (born United States), b. 1962?. **Genres:** Business/Trade/Industry, Politics/Government. **Career:** Boston Globe, reporter; Harvard University, Loeb fellow, 2000-01; Office for Commonwealth Development, education director, 2005-06; Lincoln Institute of Land Policy (urban planning think tank), publics affairs manager. **Publications:** This Land: The Battle over Sprawl and the Future of America, 2006; Wrestling with Moses: How Jane Jacobs Took on New York's Master Builder and Transformed the American City, 2009. Contributor to books and periodicals. **Online address:** anthonyflint@anthonyflint.net

FLINT, James. Also writes as Cooper James. British (born England), b. 1968. **Genres:** Novels. **Career:** Times of India, general reporter, 1988; Independent, researcher and journalist, 1994-95; Wired magazine, section editor and staff writer, 1995-97, Mute, internet editor, 1995, founding member, 1995-2002; freelance writer, 1997-; Telegraph Media Group, editor of digital arts and features, 2006-; Telegraph Earth, head of digital development, 2007-; Telegraph TV, general manager; Telegraph Newspaper, editor. **Publications:** NOVELS: Habitus, 1998; 52 Ways to Magic America, 2000; The Book of Ash, 2004. SHORT STORIES: Douce Apocalypse, 2004. OTHERS: The truth about fiction, 2007. Contributor to periodicals. **Address:** c/o Jonny Geller, Curtis Brown, Haymarket House, 28-29 Haymarket, London, GL SW17 4SP, England. **Online address:** flint@bigfoot.com

FLINT, John Edgar. Canadian (born Canada), b. 1930. **Genres:** History, Third World, Biography, Reference, Travel/Exploration. **Career:** University of London, King's College, assistant lecturer, 1954-56, lecturer, 1956-63, reader in history, 1963-67; University of Nigeria, Department of History, professor and head, 1963-64; Government of Nigeria, British adviser, 1963-64; Dalhousie University, Department of History, professor of history, 1967-92, head, 1968-, professor emeritus, 1992-. Writer. **Publications:** Sir George Goldie and the Making of Nigeria, 1960; (ed.) Mary Kingsley: A Reassessment, 1963; (ed.) Travels in West Africa, 1964; (ed.) West African Studies, 1965; Nigeria and Ghana, 1966; Books on the British Empire and Commonwealth, 1968; (ed. with G. Williams) Perspectives of Empire: Essays Presented to Gerald S. Graham, 1973; Cecil Rhodes, 1974; (ed.) Cambridge History of Africa, vol. V: 1790-1870, 1977; British West Africa: The Origins of Deconolisation, 1938-1943, 1980. Contributor of articles to Journals. **Address:** Department of History, Dalhousie University, Rm. 115, Marion McCain Bldg., 6135 University Ave., 1459 Oxford St., Halifax, NS B3H 4R2, Canada. **Online address:** jflint@chat.carleton.ca

FLINT, Richard. American (born United States), b. 1946. **Genres:** Architecture. **Career:** Center for Desert Archaeology, research associate; Documents of the Coronado Expedition Project, co-director; University of New Mexico, Latin American and Iberian Institute, research associate professor. Writer and historian. **Publications:** A Pocket Guide to Chaco Canyon Architecture, 1987; Chacoesque: Chaco-Like Great Pueblo Architecture outside Chaco Canyon, 1989; Great Cruelties Have Been Reported: The 1544 Investigation of the Coronado Expedition, 2002; No Settlement, No Conquest: A History of the Coronado Entrada, 2008. SELF-ILLUSTRATED: A Field Guide to Mesa Verde Architecture--Chapin Mesa, Wetherill Mesa, Ute Mountain Tribal Park, 1991. EDITED S.C. FLINT: The Coronado Expedition to Tierra Nueva: The 1540-1542 Route across the Southwest, 1997; The Coronado Expedition: From the Distance of 460 Years, 2003; Documents of the Coronado Expedition, 1539-1542: They Were Not Familiar with His Majesty, nor Did They Wish to Be His Subjects, 2005. **Address:** Center for Desert Archaeology, 300 N Ash Aly, Tucson, AZ 85701, U.S.A. **Online address:** center@cdarc.org

FLINT, Shamini Mahadevan. Singaporean/Malaysian (born Malaysia), b. 1969. **Genres:** Criminology/True Crime. **Career:** Sunbear Publishing, owner and publisher; National University of Singapore, instructor. Writer and attorney. **Publications:** Sasha's Travel Stories, 2004; Jungle Blues, 2005; Turtle Takes a Trip, 2006; Criminal Minds, 2008; An Elephant in the Room, 2008; Partytime, Artwork by Mariann Johansen-Ellis, 2008; The Seeds of Time, 2008; Snake Rattle & Roll, Artwork by Mariann Johansen-Ellis, 2008; A T-Rex Ate My Homework, 2008; What Color Were the Dinosaurs?, 2008; Ten, 2009; Sleep Tight, 2010; INSPECTOR SINGH SERIES; MYSTERY NOVELS: Inspector Singh Investigates: A Most Peculiar Malaysian Murder, 2009; Inspector Singh Investigates: A Bali Conspiracy Most Foul, 2009; Inspector Singh Investigates: Singapore School of Villainy, 2010; Inspector Singh Investigates: A Deadly Cambodian Crime Spree, 2011. Contributor to periodicals. **Address:** Singapore. **Online address:** shamini@shaminiflint.com

FLITTER, Marc. American (born United States) **Genres:** Autobiography/Memoirs. **Career:** University of New Mexico, Department of Surgery, clinical assistant professor; Hamot Medical Center, chief of neurosurgery; San Juan Regional Medical Center, neurosurgeon, 2001-. Writer. **Publications:** Judith's Pavilion: The Haunting Memories of a Neurosurgeon (memoirs), 1997. Contributor to periodicals. **Address:** San Juan Regional Medical Ctr., 4 Corners Neurological Services, 555 S Schwartz Ave., Farmington, NM 87401-5955, U.S.A. **Online address:** mflitter@sjrmc.net

FLOCA, Brian. American (born United States) **Genres:** Children's Non-fiction, Children's Fiction. **Career:** Author and illustrator. **Publications:** SELF-ILLUSTRATED: The Frightful Story of Harry Walfish, 1997; Five Trucks, 1999; Dinosaurs at the Ends of the Earth: The Story of the Central Asiatic Expeditions, 2000; The Racecar Alphabet, 2003; Up in the Air: The Story of the Wright Brothers, 2003; Lightship, 2007; Moonshot: The Flight of Apollo 11, 2009. **Address:** Scholastic Inc., 557 Broadway, New York, NY 10012, U.S.A. **Online address:** brian@brianfloca.com

FLOCK, Elizabeth. American (born United States) **Genres:** Novels, Young Adult Fiction. **Career:** Vanity Fair, editorial assistant; San Francisco Cable News Station, news anchor and reporter; National Broadcasting Corp., news writer; Columbia Broadcasting System News, correspondent; Time Magazine, reporter, journalist; People Magazine, reporter, journalist. Writer. **Publications:** But Inside I'm Screaming, 2003; Me & Emma, 2005; Everything Must Go, 2007; Sleepwalking In Daylight, 2009. **Address:** c/o Larry Kirshbaum, LJK Literary Management, 708 3rd Ave., Ste. 1600, New York, NY 10017, U.S.A. **Online address:** lizflock@aol.com

FLOEGSTAD, Kjartan. (Kjartan Villum). Norwegian (born Norway), b. 1944. **Genres:** Poetry, Novels, Translations, Adult Non-fiction. **Career:** Writer, 1968-. **Publications:** POETRY: Valfart, 1968; Seremoniar, 1968; Dikt og spelmannmusikk 1968-1993, 1993; Pablo Neruda: Kapteinens vers, 2003. NONFICTION: Den hemmelege jubel, 1970; Loven vest for Pecos, og andre essays om populoer kunst og kulturindustri, 1981; Ordlyden, 1983; Tyrannosaurus Text, 1988; Portrett av eit magisk liv: Poeten Claes Gill, 1988; Arbeidets lys, 1990; Pampa Union: Latinamerikanske reiser, 1994; Dei ytterste ting N'dvendighetsartiklar, 1998; Eld og vatn Nordmenn i Sor-Amerika, 1999; Evig varer lengst, 2000; Sudamericana, 2000; Osloprosessen, 2000; Shanghai Ekspress, 2001; Hotell Tropical, 2003; Brennbart, 2004; Snohetta: hus som vil meg hysa, 2004; Gi lyd: Tekstar 1968-2008, 2008; Grense Jakobselv: Roman, 2009. NOVELS: Fangliner, 1972; Rasmus, 1974; (as Kjartan Villum) Doeden ikke heller, 1975; (as Villum) Ein for alle, 1976; Dalen Portland, 1977; Fyr og flamme, 1980; U3, 1983; Det 7. klima: Salim Mahmood i Media Thule, 1986; Kron og mynt, 1998; Kniven på strupen, 1991; Fimbul, 1994; Paradis På Jord, 2002; Grand Manila, 2006. TRANSLATIONS: J.T. Ungerer, De tre roevarane, 1973; Litteratur i revolusjonen: Dikt fra Cuba, 1973; P. Neruda, Dikt i utval (Selected Poetry), 1973. OTHERS: Dollar Road, 1989; Ved Roma port, 1994; (with H. Flor) Gunnar Torvund, 1998; (contrib.)

Tore Hansen, 2010. **Address:** c/o Gyldendal Norsk Forlag, St. Olavs Plass, PO Box 6860, Oslo, 0130, Norway.

FLOKOS, Nicholas. American (born United States), b. 1930?. **Genres:** Romance/Historical, Literary Criticism And History. **Career:** University of Pittsburgh, writing instructor. **Publications:** Nike: A Romance, 1998. Contributor to periodicals. **Address:** c/o Joseph Regal, Russell and Volkening Inc., 50 W 29th St., Ste. 7E, New York, NY 10001, U.S.A.

FLOOD, Joe. American (born United States), b. 1981. **Genres:** Information Science/Computers. **Career:** Journalist and author of nonfiction. **Publications:** The Fires: How a Computer Formula, Big Ideas and the Best of Intentions Burned Down New York City and Determined the Future of Cities, 2010. **Address:** New York, NY , U.S.A. **Online address:** joe.flood@gmail.com

FLOOD, (Nancy) Bo. American (born United States), b. 1945. **Genres:** Medicine/Health, Psychology, Adult Non-fiction. **Career:** Center for Retarded Children, teacher and therapist, 1968; University of Hawaii, assistant professor of psychology, 1971-72; University of Minnesota, assistant professor of psychology, 1972-74; Colorado Mountain College, instructor in psychology, 1974-95; Sopris Mental Health Center, staff psychologist, 1974-81; Northern Marianas College, instructor in psychology, 1989-91, instructor and counselor in education, arts and humanities, 1995-, director of programs for persons with disabilities, 1995-97; University of Guam, instructor, 1995-2001; Navajo Diné Community College, instructor, 2001-; Northern Arizona University, instructor, 2002-; Kaplan University, instructor, 2007-. Writer. **Publications:** Working Together against World Hunger, 1994; (with L. Lafferty) Born Early: A Premature Baby's Story for Children, 1995; From the Mouth of the Monster Eel: Stories from Micronesia, 1996; I'll Go to School If..., 1997; (with M. Nuckols) The Counseling Handbook: Practical Strategies to Help Children with Common Problems, 1998; (with B.E. Strong and W. Flood) Pacific Island Legends: Tales from Micronesia, Melanesia, Polynesia, and Australia, 1999; Marianas Island Legends: Myth and Magic, 2001; (with B.E. Strong and W.Flood) Micronesian Legends: History and Culture, 2002; The Navajo Year: Walk through Many Seasons, 2006; Sand to Stone and Back Again, 2009; Warriors in the Crossfire, 2010; The Hogan That Great-grandfather Built, 2010; No Name Baby, 2012. Contributor to periodicals. **Address:** 4339 4 Mile Rd., Glenwood Springs, CO 81601, U.S.A. **Online address:** wflood@hotmail.com

FLOOD, Pansie Hart. American (born United States), b. 1964. **Genres:** Children's Fiction, Illustrations, Social Sciences. **Career:** Bertie County Schools, school health educator, 1986-87; Wake County Schools, middle school and high school teacher, 1987-88; Pitt County Schools, middle school teacher, 1988-. Writer. **Publications:** Sylvia and Miz Lula Maye, 2001; Secret Holes, 2003; It's Test Day, Tiger Turcotte, 2004; Sometimey Friend, 2005; Tiger's Trouble with Donut Head, 2005; Tiger Turcotte Takes on the Know-It-All, 2005. **Address:** PO Box 20614, Greenville, NC 27858, U.S.A. **Online address:** floodpan@embarqmail.com

FLORA, Joseph M(artin). American (born United States), b. 1934. **Genres:** Literary Criticism And History. **Career:** University of Michigan, instructor in English, 1961-62; University of North Carolina, instructor, 1962-64, assistant professor, 1964-67, associate professor, 1967-77, professor of English, 1977-2010, acting department chair, 1980-81, department chair, 1980-91, professor emeritus, 2010-, Graduate School, assistant dean, 1967-72, associate dean, 1977-78, Center for the Study of the American South, acting director, 2008-09; Duke University, University of North Carolina Cooperative Program in Humanities, assistant, 1963-67; University of New Mexico, visiting professor, 1976, 1996. Writer. **Publications:** Vardis Fisher, 1965; William Ernest Henley, 1970; Frederick Manfred, 1974; Hemingway's Nick Adams, 1982; Ernest Hemingway: A Study of the Short Fiction, 1989; Vardis Fisher: Centennial Essays, 2000; The Companion to Southern Literature, 2002. EDITOR: The Cream of the Jest, 1975; (co-ed.) Southern Writers: A Biographical Dictionary, 1979; The English Short Story 1880-1945: A Critical History, 1985; (with R. Bain) Fifty Southern Writers Before 1900: A Bio-Biographical Source Book, 1987; (with R. Bain) Fifty Southern Writers After 1900: A Bio-Bibliographical Source Book, 1987; Contemporary Novelists of the South, 1993; (with R. Bain) Contemporary Fiction Writers of the South: A Bio-Bibliographical Source Book, 1993; (with R. Bain) Contemporary Poets, Dramatists, Essayists of the South: A Bio-Bibliographical Sourcebook, 1993; Rediscovering Vardis Fisher: Centennial Essays, 2000; (with L.H. MacKethan) The Companion to Southern Literature: Themes, Genres, Places, People, Movements and Motifs, 2002; (co-ed.) Southern Writers: A New Biographical Dictionary, 2006; Reading Hemingway's Men Without Women, 2008. **Address:** Department of English and Comparative Literature, University of North Carolina, Greenlaw Hall, CB Ste. 3520, Chapel Hill, NC 27599-3520, U.S.A. **Online address:** jflora@email.unc.edu

FLORBY, Gunilla. Swedish (born Sweden), b. 1943. **Genres:** Literary Criticism And History, Social Sciences. **Career:** Lund University, professor of English, through 2002; University of Göteborg, professor of English literature, 2002-. Writer. **Publications:** The Painful Passage to Virtue: A Study of George Chapman's The Tragedy of Bussy D'Ambois and The Revenge of Bussy D'Ambois, 1982; The Margin Speaks: A Study of Margaret Laurence and Robert Kroetsch from a Post-Colonial Point of View, 1997; Echoing Texts: George Chapman's Conspiracy and Tragedy of Charles Duke of Byron, 2004; (ed. with K. Aijmer) Lines and Traces: Papers Presented to Lennart Björk on the Occasion of His 70th Birthday, 2006; (ed. with M. Shackleton and K. Suhonen) Canada: Images of a Post/national Society, 2009. Contributor to periodicals. **Address:** Department of English, University of Gothenburg, PO Box 200, Gothenburg, 405 30, Sweden. **Online address:** gunilla.florby@eng.gu.se

FLORES-GALBIS, Enrique. American/Cuban (born Cuba), b. 1952?. **Genres:** Mystery/Crime/Suspense, History, Novels. **Career:** Visual Arts Center of New Jersey, faculty; Parsons School of Design, faculty; Morris Museum, teacher; Montclair Museum, teacher; Metropolitan Museum, lecturer. Portrait, landscape painter and writer. **Publications:** Raining Sardines, 2007; Sugar in the Rain, 2008; 90 Miles to Havana, 2010. **Address:** Stimola Literary Studio, 306 Chase Ct., Edgewater, NJ 07020, U.S.A. **Online address:** efg@efgportraits.com

FLORES HABITO, Ruben Leodegario. See **HABITO, Ruben L.F.**

FLORIDA, Richard (L.). Canadian/American (born United States), b. 1957. **Genres:** Business/Trade/Industry, Economics, Social Sciences, Sciences. **Career:** Rutgers University, Center for Urban Policy Research, research associate, 1980-83; State University of New York, Department of Environmental Design and Planning, lecturer, 1983-93; Ohio State University, Department of City and Regional Planning, instructor, 1984-85, assistant professor, 1985-87, director of undergraduate program, 1985-87; Carnegie-Mellon University, H. John Heinz III School of Public Policy and Management, associate professor of management and public policy, 1987-90, associate professor of management and public policy, 1990-94, professor of management and public policy, 1994-98, Heinz professor of regional economic development, 1996-2004, Center for Economic Development, director, 1993-98, Software Industry Center, director, 2001-05; Harvard University, John F. Kennedy School of Government, visiting professor, 1995-96; Brookings Institution, non-residential fellow, 2004-07; George Mason University, Hirst professor of public policy, 2004-07; Gallup Organization, senior scientist, 2005-07; University of Toronto, Rotman School of Management, professor of business and creativity, 2007-, Martin Prosperity Institute, director, 2007-; The Atlantic Magazine, senior editor, 2011-; Creative Class Group, founder. **Publications:** (Ed.) Housing and the New Financial Markets, 1986; (with M. Kenney) The Breakthrough Illusion: Corporate America's Failure to Move from Innovation to Mass Production, 1990; (with M. Kenney) Beyond Mass Production: The Japanese System and Its Transfer to the United States, 1993; (ed. with L.M. Branscomb and F. Kodama) Industrializing Knowledge: University-Industry Linkages in Japan and the United States, 1999; The Rise of the Creative Class: And How It's Transforming Work, Leisure, Community and Everyday Life, 2004; (ed. with M. Kenney) Locating Global Advantage: Industry Dynamics in the International Economy, 2004; Flight of the Creative Class: The New Global Competition for Talent, 2005; Cities and the Creative Class, 2005; Who's Your City?: How the Creative Economy is Making Where to Live the Most Important Decision of Your Life, 2008; The Great Reset: How New Ways of Living and Working Drive Post-Crash Prosperity, 2010. Contributor to journals, books and periodicals. **Address:** Rotman School of Management, University of Toronto, 105 St. George St., Toronto, ON M5S 3E6, Canada. **Online address:** florida@rotman.utoronto.ca

FLORINE, Hans E. American (born United States), b. 1964. **Genres:** Sports/Fitness, Recreation. **Career:** Parker Seals, production manager, 1988-90; Touchstone Climbing, marketing executive, 2000-; TranSystems

Corp., administrator, 2007-. Writer and photographer. **Publications:** (With B. Wright) Climb On!: Skills for More Efficient Climbing, 2002, 2nd ed. as Speed Climbing!: How to Climb Faster and Better, 2004. **Address:** TranSystems Corp., 180 Grand Ave., Ste. 400, Oakland, CA 94612-3715, U.S.A. **Online address:** hans@hansflorine.com

FLORITA, Kira. American (born United States), b. 1957. **Genres:** Biography, Music, Autobiography/Memoirs. **Career:** Hastings/Western Merchandising, vice president of accounting, 1980-89; Mercury Records, vice president of catalog and marketing, 1990-2001; Lost Highway, vice president of marketing, 2001-02; Country Music Hall of Fame, director of special projects, 2002-; Leadership Music Inc., executive director. Writer. **Publications:** (With C. Escott) Hank Williams: Snapshots from the Lost Highway, 2001. **Address:** Leadership Music Inc., PO Box 158010, Nashville, TN 37215, U.S.A. **Online address:** kira@leadershipmusic.org

FLORY, David A. American (born United States), b. 1939. **Genres:** History, Literary Criticism And History. **Career:** Rutgers University, assistant professor, 1970-75; Opera Theater, artistic director, 1979-81; Middlesex County Cultural and Heritage Commission, public information officer, 1983-89; Purdue University, assistant professor, associate professor of Spanish and Portuguese, 1989-, professor, now professor emeritus, Language Placement Examination, director. Writer. **Publications:** El Conde lucanor: Don Juan Manuel en su contexto histórico, 1995; Marian Representations in the Miracle Tales of Thirteenth-Century Spain and France, 2000. **Address:** School of Languages and Cultures, Purdue University, SC 146G, 640 Oval Dr., West Lafayette, IN 47907-2039, U.S.A. **Online address:** daflory@purdue.edu

FLOWERS, Pam. American (born United States), b. 1946?. **Genres:** Autobiography/Memoirs. **Career:** Respiratory therapist, adventurer, speaker and writer. **Publications:** Hug a Husky, 1996; (with A. Dixon) Alone across the Arctic: One Woman's Epic Journey by Dog Team, 2001; (with A. Dixon) Big-Enough Anna: The Little Sled Dog Who Braved the Arctic, 2003; Douggie: The Playful Pup Who Became a Sled Dog Hero, 2008; (with B. Farnsworth) Ellie's Long Walk: The True Story of Two Friends on the Appalachian Trail, 2011. Contributor to periodicals. **Address:** Pam Flowers Expeditions, PO Box 874924, Wasilla, AK 99687, U.S.A. **Online address:** pam@pamflowers.com

FLOWERS, Ronald B(ruce). American (born United States), b. 1935. **Genres:** Law, Theology/Religion. **Career:** Texas Christian University, Department of Religion-Studies, assistant professor, 1966-73, associate professor, 1973-84, professor of religion, 1984-, department head, 1990-99, John F. Weatherly professor of religion, 1998-2003, now John F. Weatherly emeritus professor of religion; American Academy of Religion, Section on the History of Christianity, chair, 1980-81, Southwest section, president, 1988-89; Southwest Commission on Religion Studies, vice president, 1981-82. Writer. **Publications:** (With R.T. Miller) Toward Benevolent Neutrality: Church, State, and the Supreme Court, 1977, 5th ed., 1996; Religion in Strange Times: The 1960s and 1970s, 1984; That Godless Court?: Supreme Court Decisions on Church-State Relationships, 1994, 2nd ed., 2005; To Defend the Constitution: Religion, Conscientious Objection, Naturalization, and the Supreme Court, 2003; (with M. Rogers and S.K. Green) Religious Freedom and the Supreme Court, 2008. Contributor to books. **Address:** Department of Religion, Texas Christian University, 2800 S University Dr., Fort Worth, TX 76129, U.S.A. **Online address:** r.flowers@tcu.edu

FLOWERS, Sarah. American (born United States), b. 1952. **Genres:** Air/Space Topics, Children's Non-fiction, History. **Career:** Santa Clara County Library, librarian, 1991-93, adult program librarian, 1995-98, community librarian, 1998-2003, deputy county librarian, 2003-08; Los Gatos Public Library, young adult librarian, 1993-95; Young Adult Library Services, editor, 2009-; freelance writer, editor and library consultant, 2009-. **Publications:** The Reformation, 1996; Sports in America, 1996; Age of Exploration, 1999; Space Exploration: A Pro/Con Issue, 2000; Young Adults Deserve the Best: YALSA's Competencies in Action, 2011. **Address:** Santa Clara County Library, 14600 Winchester Blvd., Los Gatos, CA 95032-1817, U.S.A. **Online address:** sarah.flowers@lib.sccgov.org

FLOYD, John E(arl). Canadian (born Canada), b. 1937. **Genres:** Economics, Money/Finance, Mathematics/Statistics. **Career:** University of Washington, Department of Economics, assistant professor, 1962-66, associate professor, 1966-70, professor, 1970-71; University of Toronto, professor emeritus of economics, 1970-; City University of New York, Graduate Center,

visiting professor, 1973-74; Australian National University, visiting fellow, 1987. **Publications:** Endogenous Technology and Population in a Theory of Economic Growth, 1972; (co-author) Microsets, 1981; On the Canadian Dollar, 1985; World Monetary Equilibrium: International Monetary Theory in an Historical-Institutional Context, 1985; (with T.J.O. Dick) Canada and the Gold Standard: Balance-of-Payments Adjustment, 1871-1913, 1992; Interest Rates, Exchange Rates and World Monetary Policy, 2010; Interest Rates, Exchange Rates and World Monetary Policy, forthcoming. Works appear in books. Contributor to journals. **Address:** Department of Economics, University of Toronto, 150 St. George St., Toronto, ON M5S 3G7, Canada. **Online address:** floyd@chass.utoronto.ca

FLOYD, Nancy. American (born United States), b. 1956?. **Genres:** Photography, Art/Art History. **Career:** Georgia State University, Ernest G. Welch School of Art and Design, associate professor of photography, 1996-. Writer. **Publications:** She's Got a Gun, 2008. **Address:** Ernest G. Welch School of Art and Design, Georgia State University, 50 Decatur St., PO Box 4107, Atlanta, GA 30303-2924, U.S.A. **Online address:** nancy@gsu.edu

FLUEHR-LOBBAN, Carolyn. American (born United States), b. 1945. **Genres:** Anthropology/Ethnology, Area Studies, Social Sciences, Law. **Career:** Rhode Island College, Department of Anthropology, assistant professor, 1972-78, associate professor, 1978-84, professor of anthropology, 1984-, now professor emeritus. Writer and anthropologist. **Publications:** Law and Anthropology in the Sudan: An Analysis of Homicide Cases in Sudan, 1972; (contrib.) Three Studies on National Integration in the Arab World, 1974; Islamic Law and Society in the Sudan, 1986; (ed.) International Perspectives on Marxist Anthropology, 1989; Modern Egypt And its Heritage, 1990; (ed.) Ethics and the Profession of Anthropology: Dialogue for a New Era, 1991, 2nd ed. as Ethics and the Profession of Anthropology: Dialogue for Ethically Conscious Practice, 2003; (with R.A. Lobban, Jr. and J.O. Voll) Historical Dictionary of the Sudan, 2nd ed., 1992, (with R.A. Lobban, Jr. and R.S. Kramer) 3rd ed., 2002; Islamic Society in Practice, 1994, 2nd ed. as Islamic Societies in Practice, 2004; (ed.) Against Islamic Extremism: The Writings of Muhammad Sa'id al-'Ashmawy, 1998; (ed. with K. Rhodes) Race and Identity in the Nile Valley, 2004; (ed. with J.M. Billson) Female Well-being: Toward a Global Theory of Social Change, 2005; Race and Racism: An Introduction, 2005. Contributor to journals. **Address:** Department of Anthropology, Rhode Island College, Gaige Hall, 600 Mount Pleasant Ave., Providence, RI 02908, U.S.A. **Online address:** cfluehr@ric.edu

FLUKE, Joanne. Also writes as Kathryn Kirkwood, R. J. Fischer, Chris Hunter, Gina Jackson, Jo Gibson. American (born United States), b. 1943?. **Genres:** Novels, Mystery/Crime/Suspense, Romance/Historical, Young Adult Fiction. **Career:** Writer. **Publications:** NOVELS: The Stepchild, 1980; The Other Child, 1983; Winter Chill, 1984; Cold Judgment, 1985; Vengeance is Mine, 1986; Video Kill, 1989; Final Appeal, 1989; Dead Giveaway, 1990; Fatal Identity, 1993; Deadly Memories, 1995. HANNAH SWENSON MYSTERIES: Chocolate Chip Cookie Murder, 2000; Strawberry Shortcake Murder, 2001; Blueberry Muffin Murder, 2002; Lemon Meringue Pie Murder, 2003; Fudge Cupcake Murder, 2004; Sugar Cookie Murder, 2004; Peach Cobbler Murder, 2005; Cherry Cheesecake Murder, 2006; Key Lime Pie Murder: A Hannah Swensen Mystery with Recipes, 2007; Candy Cane Murder: A Hannah Swensen Mystery with Recipes, 2007; Carrot Cake Murder: A Hannah Swensen Mystery with Recipes, 2008. AS JOHN FISCHER: High Stakes, 1986; Station Break, 1987. AS CHRIS HUNTER: (ed.) Dispute Resolution in the PRC, 1995; Eyes, 1996; Eight Lives Down, 2008. ROMANCES AS GINA JACKSON: Caitlyn's Cowboy, 1999; Cookies and Kisses 2000. ROMANCES AS KATHRYN KIRKWOOD: A Match for Melissa, 1998; A Season for Samantha, 1999; Winter Kittens, 1999; A Husband for Holly, 1999; A Valentine for Vanessa, 2000; A Townhouse for Tessa, 2001. YOUNG ADULT NOVELS AS JO GIBSON: (ed.) Partnering for Profit in the New Russia, 1993; The Dead Girl, 1993; The Crush, 1994; The Crush II, 1994; Slay Bells, 1994; My Bloody Valentine, 1995; The Seance, 1996; Wicked, 1996; Dance of Death, 1996. HUMOR AS R.J. FISCHER: Baby's Guide to Raising Mom, 1997; Doggy Do's and Don'ts, 1997; Where Would I Be without You, Mom?, 1998. OTHERS: Plum Pudding Murder, 2009; Cream Puff Murder, 2009; (with L. Levine and L. Meier) Gingerbread Cookie Murder, 2010; Apple Turnover Murder, 2010; Joanne Fluke's Lake Eden Cookbook, 2011; Devil's Food Cake Murder, 2011; Cinnamon Roll Murder, 2012. Contributor to books. **Address:** c/o Author Mail, Kensington Publishing Corp., 119 W 40th St., New York, NY 10018, U.S.A. **Online address:** gr8clues@aol.com

FLYNN, Elizabeth A. American (born United States), b. 1944. **Genres:** Education, Bibliography, Essays. **Career:** Ohio State University, teaching assistant, 1967-69, 1970-71, 1974-76, lecturer, 1977, instructor in English, 1978-79; University of Duesseldorf, teaching assistant, 1974; Antioch College, assistant professor, 1978-79; Michigan Technological University, assistant professor, 1979-83, associate professor, 1983-91, Institute for Research on Language and Learning, director, 1985-93, department head, 1987-89, professor of humanities, 1991-, director of liberal arts, 2003-04, Graduate Program in Rhetoric and Technical Communication, director, 2006-10, professor of reading and composition; University of Calgary, visiting instructor, 1987. Writer. **Publications:** (With C.F. Donaldson) Alternative Careers for Ph.D.s in the Humanities: A Selected Bibliography, 1982; (ed. with P.P. Schweickart and contrib.) Gender and Reading: Essays on Readers, Texts and Contexts, 1986; (ed. with J.L. Schilb and J. Clifford) Constellations: A Contextual Reader for Writers, 1992; Feminism beyond Modernism, 2002; (ed. with P.P. Schweickart and intro.) Reading Sites: Social Difference and Reader Response, 2004; (with P. Sotirin and A. Brady) Feminist Rhetorical Resilience, 2012. **Address:** Departement of Humanities, Michigan Technological University, 1400 Townsend Dr., Houghton, MI 49931-1295, U.S.A. **Online address:** eflynn@mtu.edu

FLYNN, James Robert. New Zealander/American (born United States), b. 1934. **Genres:** Philosophy, Politics/Government, Psychology, Social Sciences. **Career:** Eastern Kentucky University, assistant professor of political science, 1957-61; Congress of Racial Equality, Madison County (KY), chairman, 1960-61; Wisconsin State University, assistant professor of political science, 1961-62; Lake Forest College, assistant professor of political science, 1962-63; University of Canterbury, lecturer, senior lecturer, 1963-67; University of Otago, Department of Politics, professor and head, 1967-96, professor emeritus, 1996-. Writer. **Publications:** (Contrib.) Sixth form Seminar: Three Addresses Delivered at Nelson & Invercargill, 1966; American Politics: A Radical View, 1967; The Negro Revolt, 1969; Humanism and Ideology, 1973; Race, IQ, and Jensen, 1980; Asian Americans: Achievement beyond IQ, 1991; How to Defend Humane Ideals: Substitutes for Objectivity, 2000; What is Intelligence?: Beyond the Flynn Effect, 2007; Where Have All the Liberals Gone?: Race, Class, and Ideals in America, 2008; Torchlight List: Around the World in 200 Books, 2010. Contributor of articles to journals. **Address:** Department of Politics, University of Otago, Rm. G03, PO Box 56, Dunedin, 9054, New Zealand. **Online address:** jim.flynn@otago.ac.nz

FLYNN, Joseph. American (born United States), b. 1951?. **Genres:** Film, Novels. **Career:** Foote, Cone & Belding, copywriter; J. Walter Thompson, copywriter; Doyle, Dane, Bernbach, copywriter; Ogilvy & Mather, copywriter; McCann-Erickson, copywriter. **Publications:** The Concrete Inquisition, 1993; Digger, 1997; (co-author) Naked Came the Farmer, 1998; The Next President, 2000; Hot Type, 2005; Gasoline, Texas, 2007; Farewell Performance, 2007; The President's Henchman, 2009; The Hangman's Companion, 2010; Round Robin, 2011; Blood Street Punx, 2011; Nailed, 2011; One False Step, 2011; Still Coming, 2011; The K Street Killer, 2011. **Address:** c/o Author Mail, Bantam Books, 1745 Broadway, New York, NY 10019, U.S.A. **Online address:** mail@josephflynn.com

FLYNN, Katie. *See* **TURNER, Judith.**

FLYNN, Kevin. American (born United States), b. 1957?. **Genres:** Mystery/Crime/Suspense, Autobiography/Memoirs, Biography. **Career:** District of Columbia, assistant attorney. Writer. **Publications:** Relentless Pursuit: A True Story of Family, Murder, and the Prosecutor Who Wouldn't Quit, 2007. **Address:** G.P. Putnam's Sons, 375 Hudson St., New York, NY 10014-3658, U.S.A. **Online address:** relentless.p@gmail.com

FLYNN, Laura M. American (born United States), b. 1966. **Genres:** Novels, Autobiography/Memoirs. **Career:** University of Minnesota, instructor in editing. Writer. **Publications:** (Ed.) Eyes of the Heart: Seeking a Path for the Poor in the Age of Globalization, 2000; Swallow the Ocean, 2008. **Address:** Lippincott Massie McQuilkin, 80 5th Ave., Ste. 1101, New York, NY 10011, U.S.A. **Online address:** lauramflynn@gmail.com

FLYNN, Nancy L. American (born United States), b. 1956. **Genres:** Administration/Management, Business/Trade/Industry, Law. **Career:** The ePolicy Institute, founder and executive director; Write to Business, founder. Ohio State University, School of Journalism, Department of English, adjunct writing instructor. Consultant, writer and speaker. **Publications:** (With T. Flynn)

Writing Effective E-mail: Improving Your Electronic Communication, 1998, rev. ed., 2003; The 100,000 Dollar Writer: How to Make a Six-Figure Income As a Freelance Business Writer, 2000; The e-Policy Handbook: Designing and Implementing Effective E-Mail, Internet and Software Policies, 2001; (with R. Kahn) E-Mail Rules: A Business Guide to Managing Policies, Security and Legal Issues for E-Mail and Digital Communication, 2003; Networking for Success: The Art of Establishing Personal Contacts, 2003; Instant Messaging Rules: A Business Guide to Managing Policies, Security and Legal Issues for Safe IM Communication, 2004; Blog Rules: A Business Guide to Managing Policy, Public Relations, and Legal Issues, 2006; E-mail Management: 50 Tips for Keeping Your Inbox Under Control, 2007; E-Policy Handbook: Rules and Best Practices to Safely Manage your Company's E-mail, Blogs, Social Networking and Other Electronic Communication Tools, 2009. Contributor to periodicals. **Address:** Write to Business, 2300 Walhaven Ct., Ste. 100A, Columbus, OH 43220, U.S.A. **Online address:** nancy@epolicyinstitute.com

FLYNN, Pat. Australian (born Australia), b. 1968?. **Genres:** Children's Fiction. **Career:** Writer and educator. **Publications:** To the Light, 2005; The Mal Rider, 2006; The Tuckshop Kid, 2006; The Line Formation, 2006 as Out of His League, 2008; The Adventures of Danny: Beeware, 2007; The Adventures of Danny: Treeified, 2007; The Adventures of Danny: Snowidea, 2008; Don't Kiss Girls, 2008; Get Rich Quick, 2009; How to Get Dumped, 2009; The Toilet Kid, 2009; The Trophy Kid, 2010. ALEX JACKSON SERIES: Grommet, 2001; SWA, 2002; Closing Out, 2003; Dropping In, 2004. Contributor to periodicals. **Address:** Australia. **Online address:** author@patflynnwriter.com

FLYNN, Robert (Lopez). American (born United States), b. 1932. **Genres:** Novellas/Short Stories, Humor/Satire, Theology/Religion, Autobiography/Memoirs, E-books. **Career:** Gardner-Webb College, instructor, 1957-59; Baylor University, assistant professor, 1959-63; Trinity University, professor, now professor emeritus; novelist-in-residence, 1963-2001. **Publications:** North to Yesterday, 1967; In the House of the Lord, 1969; The Sounds of Rescue, The Signs of Hope, 1970; And Holy Is His Name, 1983; Seasonal Rain and Other Stories, 1986; Wanderer Springs, 1987; A Personal War in Vietnam, 1989; When I Was Just Your Age, 1992; The Last Klick, 1994; Living with the Hyenas, 1995; (with D. Klepper) The Devils Tiger, 2000; Tie-Fast Country, 2001; Growing up a Sullen Baptist, 2001; Paul Baker and the Integration of Abilities, 2002; Slouching toward Zion, 2004; Burying the Farm: A Memoir of Chillicothe, Texas, 2008; Echoes of Glory, 2009; Jade: Outlaw, 2010. **Address:** 101 Cliffside Dr., Shavano Park, TX 78231-1510, U.S.A. **Online address:** rlflynn@earthlink.net

FLYNN, Thomas R. American (born United States), b. 1936. **Genres:** History, Philosophy. **Career:** Ordained Roman Catholic priest, 1961; Carroll College, instructor, 1962-66, assistant professor, 1970-71, 1976-78; Columbia University, preceptor, 1968-70; Catholic University of America, assistant professor, 1971-75; Emory University, assistant professor, 1978-82, associate professor, 1982-86, professor, 1987-88, Samuel Candler Dobbs professor of philosophy, 1988-, Fox Center for Humanistic Inquiry, faculty fellow, 2006-07; Villanova University, visiting professor, 1995. Writer, academician and philosopher. **Publications:** Sartre and Marxist Existentialism: The Test Case of Collective Responsibility, 1984; (ed. with D. Judovitz) Dialectic and Narrative, 1993; Sartre, Foucault, and Historical Reason, vol. I: Toward an Existentialist Theory of History, 1997, vol. II: A Post-structuralist Mapping of History, 2005; (ed. with D. Carr and R.A. Makkreel) The Ethics of History, 2004; (ed. with P. Kampits and E. Vogt) Über Sartre: Perspektiven und Kritiken, 2005; Existentialism: A Very Short Introduction, 2006. Contributor to periodicals and journals. **Address:** Department of Philosophy, Emory University, 561 S Kilgo Cir., 214 Bowden Hall, Atlanta, GA 30322-1120, U.S.A. **Online address:** tflynn@emory.edu

FLYNT, Mike. American (born United States), b. 1948. **Genres:** Biography, Sports/Fitness. **Career:** Powerbase Fitness, manager. Physical trainer, coach and author. **Publications:** (With D. Yaeger) The Senior, 2008. **Address:** Franklin, TN , U.S.A. **Online address:** mike@mikeflynt.com

FLYVBJERG, Bent. Danish (born Denmark), b. 1952. **Genres:** Design, Business/Trade/Industry. **Career:** Aalborg University, Department of Development and Planning, professor and research director, Geography Program, founder, 2001, Program in Planning and Environment, co-founder, Research Program on Mega Projects, founding director, 1979-2009; Delft University of Technology, Infrastructure Policy and Planning, chairman, 2006-09; European University Institute, visiting fellow; University of Oxford, St. Anne's

College, Saïd Business School, BT professor, BT Centre for Major Programme Management, director, professorial fellow. Writer. **Publications:** Demokrati, magt og bymilj ø: hvem bestemmer I bypolitik og -planlaing, et case studium, 1985; Miljø, trafik og demokrati: Miljømassige og sociale konsekvenser af planlaing for et bedre bycenter i Aalborg: etimplementerings studie om baredygtige bycentre, 1989; Rationality and Power: Democracy in Practice, 1998; Making Social Science Matter: Why Social Inquiry Fails and How It Can Succeed Again, 2001; (with N. Bruzelius and W. Rothengatter) Mega Projects and Risk: An Anatomy of Ambition, 2003; Policy and Planning for Large Infrastructure Projects: Problems, Causes, Cures, 2005; (ed. with H. Priemus and B.V. Wee) Decision-Making On Mega-Projects: Cost-Benefit Analysis, Planning and Innovation, 2008; (ed. with T. Landman and S. Schram) Real Social Science: Applied Phronesis, 2012. Contributor to periodicals. **Address:** Saïd Business School, St Anne's College, University of Oxford, Park End St., Oxford, OX1 1HP, United Kingdom. **Online address:** bent.flyvbjerg@sbs.ox.ac.uk

FODEN, Giles. British (born England), b. 1967. **Genres:** Novels, History, Military/Defense/Arms Control, Young Adult Fiction. **Career:** Media Week Magazine, journalist; Times Literary Supplement, assistant editor, 1993-97; Guardian, deputy literary editor, 1996-2006; Condé Nast Traveller, review editor; University of East Anglia, professor of creative writing; University of London, fellow in creative and performing arts. **Publications:** The Last King of Scotland, 1998; Ladysmith, 1999; Zanzibar, 2002; Mimi and Toutou Go Forth: The Bizarre Battle of Lake Tanganyika, 2004; Mimi and Toutou's Big Adventure: The Bizarre Battle of Lake Tanganyika, 2005; Turbulence: A Novel of the Atmosphere, 2009. Contributor to periodicals. **Address:** School of Literature and Creative Writing, Faculty of Arts and Humanities, University of East Anglia, Norwich, NF NR4 7TJ, England. **Online address:** g.foden@uea.ac.uk

FOEGE, Alec. American (born United States) **Genres:** Novellas/Short Stories. **Career:** Fortune Small Business, contributing writer. **Publications:** Confusion Is Next: The Sonic Youth Story, 1994; The Empire God Built: Inside Pat Robertson's Media Machine, 1996; Right of the Dial: The Rise of Clear Channel and the Fall of Commercial Radio, 2008. Contributor to periodicals. **Address:** CT , U.S.A. **Online address:** alec@alecfoege.com

FOER, Franklin. American (born United States) **Genres:** Industrial Relations, Politics/Government. **Career:** New York Magazine, editor; New Republic, editor, 2006-10, senior editor, editor-at-large. **Publications:** How Soccer Explains the World: An Unlikely Theory of Globalization, 2004; How Football Explains the World: An Unlikely Theory of Globalization, 2005; (co-author) Election 2008: A Voter's Guide, 2007. **Address:** c/o Author Mail, HarperCollins Publishers, 10 E 53rd St., 7th Fl., New York, NY 10022-5244, U.S.A.

FOER, Jonathan Safran. American (born United States), b. 1977. **Genres:** Novels, Ghost Writer. **Career:** Writer and educator. **Publications:** (Ed.) A Convergence of Birds: Original Fiction and Poetry Inspired by the Work of Joseph Cornell, 2001; The Unabridged Pocketbook of Lightning, 2005; (ed.) New American Haggadah, 2012. NOVELS: Everything Is Illuminated, 2002; Extremely Loud & Incredibly Close, 2005; Eating Animals, 2009; Tree of Codes, 2010. Contributor to magazines and periodicals. **Address:** c/o Nicole Aragi, 245 8th Ave., PO Box 134, New York, NY 10011-1607, U.S.A.

FOERSTEL, Herbert N. American (born United States), b. 1933. **Genres:** Writing/Journalism, Communications/Media. **Career:** Towson State University, fine arts librarian, 1959-66; University of Maryland, science librarian, 1967-79, Engineering and Physical Sciences Library, head and head of branch libraries, 1979-96, now retired; George Washington University, National Security Archive, board director, 1988-. Writer. **Publications:** Surveillance in the Stacks: The FBI's Library Awareness Program, 1991; Secret Science: Federal Control of American Science and Technology, 1993; Banned in the U.S.A.: A Reference Guide to Book Censorship in Schools and Public Libraries, 1994, rev. ed., 2002; (with K. Foerstel) Climbing the Hill: Gender Conflict in Congress, 1996; Free Expression and Censorship in America, 1997; Banned in the Media: A Reference Guide to Censorship in the Press, Motion Pictures, Broadcasting, and the Internet, 1998; Freedom of Information and the Right to Know: The Origins and Applications of the Freedom of Information Act, 1999; From Watergate to Monicagate: Ten Controversies in Modern Journalism and Media, 2001; Refuge of a Scoundrel: The Patriot Act in Libraries, 2004; Killing the Messenger: Journalists at Risk in Modern Warfare,

2006; The Patriot Act: A Documentary and Reference Guide, 2008; Toxic mix?: A Handbook of Science and Politics, 2010. Contributor of articles to periodicals. **Address:** National Security Archive, George Washington University, Gelman Library, Ste. 701, 2130 H St. NW, Washington, DC 20037, U.S.A. **Online address:** foerstel@aol.com

FOERSTEL, Karen. American (born United States), b. 1965. **Genres:** Women's Studies And Issues, Biography, Politics/Government. **Career:** Roll Call, reporter, 1989-95; Congressional Quarterly, reporter, 1995-96, 1998-, political affairs correspondent; New York Post, congressional correspondent, 1996-98; The Nature Conservancy, media specialist and senior writer; Blue Ventures, public relations officer and communications manager. **Publications:** (With H.N. Foerstel) Climbing the Hill: Gender Conflict in Congress, 1996; Biographical Dictionary of Congressional Women, 1999. **Address:** Greenwood Publishing Group Inc., 88 Post Rd. W, PO Box 5007, Westport, CT 06881, U.S.A. **Online address:** karen@blueventures.org

FOERSTNER, Abigail M. American (born United States), b. 1949. **Genres:** Autobiography/Memoirs, Biography. **Career:** Northwestern University, Medill School of Journalism, lecturer, 2002-; Chicago Tribune, staff reporter; North Shore Magazine, columnist. Journalist and educator. **Publications:** Picturing Utopia: Bertha Shambaugh and the Amana Photographers, 2000; James Van Allen: The First Eight Billion Miles, 2007. Contributor of articles to periodicals. **Address:** Medill School of Journalism, Northwestern University, 1845 Sheridan Rd., Evanston, IL 60208-2101, U.S.A. **Online address:** a-foerstner@northwestern.edu

FOGEL, Robert William. American (born United States), b. 1926. **Genres:** Business/Trade/Industry, Economics, History. **Career:** Johns Hopkins University, instructor, 1958-59; University of Rochester, assistant professor, 1960-64, professor, 1968-75, Gilbert lecturer, 1984; Ford Foundation, visiting research professor, 1963-64, associate professor, 1964-65; University of Chicago, Booth School of Business, associate professor, 1964-65, professor, 1965-75, professor, 1981-, Charles R. Walgreen Professor of American Institutions, 1981-, Walgreen Foundation, director, 1981-, Center for Population Economics, director, 1981-; National Academy of Science, staff, 1973; Harvard University, Taussig Research Professor, 1973-74, professor, 1975-81; Cambridge University, American History and Institutions, Pitt Professor, 1975-76; Texas A&M University, centennial professor, 1976; University of Illinois, Kinley Lecturer, 1977; Economic History Association, president, 1977-78; National Bureau of Economic Research, research associate, 1978-, Program on the Development of the American Economy, director, 1978-91; University of California, Snyder Lecturer, 1979; Social Science History Association, president, 1980-81; University of Iowa, Ida Beam Lecturer, 1982; Center for Economic Policy Research, research fellow, 1984-89; Queen's University, Mackintosh Lecturer, 1987; Yale University, Simon Kuznets Memorial Lecturer, 1992; Gettysburg College, Fortenbaugh Memorial Lecturer, 1994; American Council of Learned Societies, Charles Homer Haskins Lecturer, 1996; Cambridge University, Ellen McArthur Lecturer, 1996; Whitehall, Nestlé Lecturer, 1997; American Economic Association, president, 1998; NBER Program on Cohort Studies, co-director, 1998-; University of London, Hayes-Robinson Lecturer, 2000; Louisiana State University-Baton Rouge, Fleming Lecturer, 2001; Xiamen University, honorary professor, 2001; Colorado College, W.P. Carey Nobel Laureate in Economics Lecturer, 2001; University of Iowa, College of Law, Murray Lecturer, 2001; University of California-Berkeley, Hitchcock Professor, 2004; Capital Normal University, honorary professor, 2005; Chongqing University, honorary professor, 2005. Writer. **Publications:** The Union Pacific Railroad: A Case in Premature Enterprise, 1960; Railroads and American Economic Growth: Essays in Econometric History, 1964; Neue Wirtschaftsgeschichte: Forschungsergebnisse und Methoden, 1970; (ed. with S.L. Engerman) The Reinterpretation of American Economic History, 1971; (ed. with W.O. Aydelotte and A.G. Bogue) The Dimensions of Quantitative Research in History, 1972; (with S.L. Engerman) Time on the Cross: The Economics of American Negro Slavery, 1974; Railroads and American Economic Growth: Essays in Econometric History, 1974; Ten Lectures on the New Economic History, 1977; (co-ed.) Aging: Stability and Change in the Family, 1981; Trends in Nutrition, Labor Welfare, and Labor Productivity, 1982; (with G.R. Elton) Which Road to the Past? 1983; Long-Term Changes in Nutrition and the Standard of Living, 1986; Without Consent or Contract: The Rise and Fall of American Slavery, 1989; Without Consent or Contract: The Rise and Fall of American Slavery: Evidence and Methods, 1992; (contrib.) Strategic Factors in Nineteenth Century American Economic History, 1992; Without Consent or Contract: The Rise and Fall of

American Slavery: Markets and Production: Technical Papers, vol. I, 1992, vol. II: Conditions of Slave Life and the Transition to Freedom: Technical Papers, 1992; The Conquest of High Mortality and Hunger in Europe and America: Timing and Mechanisms, 1993; The Quest for the Moral Problem of Slavery: An Historiographic Odyssey, 1994; The Fourth Great Awakening & the Future of Egalitarianism, 2000; The Slavery Debates, 1952-1990: A Retrospective, 2003; The Escape from Hunger and Premature Death, 1700-2100: Europe, America and the Third World, 2004; (with R. Floud, B. Harris and S.C. Hong) The Changing Body: Health, Nutrition and Human Development in the Western World since 1700, forthcoming; Enid and Bob: An American Odyssey, forthcoming; (with E.M. Fogel) Simon Kuznets and the Empirical Tradition in Economics, forthcoming; (with E.M. Fogel and M. Guglielmo) The Transformation of Economics, 1914-1980: Interviews with Economists, forthcoming. **Address:** Booth School of Business, University of Chicago, 5807 S Woodlawn Ave., Chicago, IL 60637, U.S.A. **Online address:** rwf@cpe.uchicago.edu

FOGELMARK, Staffan. (Staffan J.H. Fogelmark). Swedish (born Sweden), b. 1939. **Genres:** Classics, Bibliography. **Career:** University of Lund, reader in Greek, 1972-85, acting professor, 1976, 1978, 1986, lecturer in Greek, 1985-96; University of Edinburgh, Charles Gordon Mackay lecturer, 1979; University of Gothenburg, professor of Greek, 1997-2004, emeritus professor, 2004-. Writer. **Publications:** Studies in Pindar with Particular Reference to Paean VI and Nemean VII, 1972; Chrysaigis: IG XII, v, 611, 1975; Flemish and Related Panel-Stamped Bindings: Evidence and Principles, 1990. Contributor of articles to journals. **Address:** Center for Languages & Literature, Lund University, Helgonabacken 12, PO Box 201, Lund, SE-221 00, Sweden. **Online address:** staffan.fogelmark@klass.gu.se

FOGELMARK, Staffan J.H. *See* **FOGELMARK, Staffan.**

FOGLE, Jeanne. American (born United States), b. 1949. **Genres:** History, Documentaries/Reportage. **Career:** A Tour de Force Inc., owner, 1984-; Smithsonian Institution, Resident Associate Program, tour leader and lecturer, 1985-; Northern Virginia Community College, adjunct professor of Washington history and regional tour guiding and tour managing, 1990-. Writer. **Publications:** Two Hundred Years: Stories of the Nation's Capital, 1991; Proximity to Power: Neighbors to the Presidents Near Lafayette Square, 1999; Encyclopedia Britannica: Washington, DC City Article, 2001; Washington, D.C.: A Pictorial Celebration, 2005; A Neighborhood Guide to Washington, D.C.'s Hidden History, 2009. **Address:** A Tour de Force Inc., PO Box 2782, Washington, DC 20013-2782, U.S.A. **Online address:** tdforce@aol.com

FOGTDAL, Peter H. American/Danish (born Denmark), b. 1956. **Genres:** Novels. **Career:** Portland State University, visiting instructor. Writer. **Publications:** The Tsar's Dwarf (novel), 2008. **Address:** Foreign Languages and Literatures, Liberal Arts & Sciences, Portland State University, PO Box 751, Portland, OR 97207, U.S.A. **Online address:** phf@pdx.edu

FOISTER, Susan Rosemary. British (born England), b. 1954. **Genres:** Art/ Art History. **Career:** National Gallery, curator & director of collections. Writer. **Publications:** Holbein and His English Patrons, 1981; (co-author) The National Portrait Gallery Collection, 1988; Cardinal Newman 1801-90, 1990; (with J. Dunkerton, D. Gordon and N. Penny) Giotto to Dürer: Early Renaissance Painting in the National Gallery, 1994; (ed. with H. Colvin) Anthonis van den Wyngaerde, The Panorama of London circa 1544, 1996; (ed. with S. Nash) Robert Campin: New Directions in Scholarship, 1996; (with R. Jones and O. Meslay) Young Gainsborough (exhibition book), 1997; (with A. Roy and M. Wyld) Holbein's Ambassadors, 1997; (with J. Dunkerton and N. Penny) Dürer to Veronese: Sixteenth-Century Paintings in the National Gallery, 1999; (ed. with Sue Jones and D. Cool) Investigating Jan Van Eyck, 2000; (co-author) Lucas Cranach: Glaube, Mythologie und Moderne: Ausstellung Des Bucerius Kunst Forums: Eine Ausstellung Des Bucerius Kunst Forums, 2003; Holbein and England, 2004; Dürer and the Virgin in the Garden, 2004; Art of Light: German Renaissance Stained Glass, 2007. **Address:** National Gallery London, Trafalgar Sq., London, GL WC2N 5DN, England.

FOLBRE, Nancy. American (born United States) **Genres:** Economics. **Career:** Bowdoin College, assistant professor of economics, 1980-83; Center for Popular Economics, staff economist, 1980-; New School for Social Research, assistant professor of economics, 1983-85; Royal Swedish Academy of Science, Beijer Institute, Zimbabwe Energy Planning Project, consultant, 1983; University of Massachusetts, associate professor of economics, 1984-

91, professor of economics, 1991-, Department of Economics, chair, 2003-04; American University, visiting associate professor, 1991; University of Wisconsin, Eugene Havens Center, visiting lecturer, 1991; International Labour Office, consultant, 1992; MacArthur Research Network on the Family and the Economy, co-chair, 1997-2003; Dancing Monkey Project, co-founder and chief executive officer, 1998-; Australian National University, Research School of Social Sciences, Social and Political Theory Program, adjunct professor, 2003-07; Feminist Economics, associate editor. Writer and consultant. **Publications:** A Field Guide to the U.S. Economy, 1988; (co-ed.) Issues in Contemporary Economics, vol. IV: Women's Work in the World Economy, 1991; (ed.) Women's Work in the World Economy, 1993; Who Pays for the Kids?: Gender and the Structures of Constraint, 1994; (with the Center for Popular Economics) A Field Guide to the U.S. Economy, 1987, rev. ed. as The New Field Guide to the U.S. Economy: A Compact and Irreverent Guide to Economic Life in America, 1995, as The Ultimate Field Guide to the U.S. Economy: A Compact and Irreverent Guide to Economic Life in America, 2000, rev. ed., 2006; (ed.) The Economics of the Family, 1996; (with R. Albelda and the Center for Popular Economics) The War on the Poor: A Defense Manual, 1996; De la différence des sexes en économie politique, 1997; The Invisible Heart: Economics and Family Values, 2001; (ed. with M. Bittman) Family Time: The Social Organization of Care, 2004; (co-ed.) Warm Hands in a Cold Age: Gender and Aging, 2006; Valuing Children: Rethinking the Economics of the Family, 2008; Greed, Lust & Gender: A History of Economic Ideas, 2009; Saving State U: Why We Must Fix Public Higher Education, 2010. Contributor to periodicals. **Address:** Department of Economics, University of Massachusetts, 836 Thompson Hall, Amherst, MA 01003, U.S.A. **Online address:** folbre@econs.umass.edu

FOLDVARY, Fred E. American (born United States), b. 1946. **Genres:** Economics, Politics/Government, Philosophy. **Career:** Federal Reserve Bank, programmer analyst, 1978-81; American Topical Association, editor, 1981-87; Latvian University of Agriculture, associate professor of economics, 1992-93; Mary Washington College, instructor, 1994; Virginia Polytechnic Institute and State University, visiting assistant professor of economics, 1994-95; Santa Clara University, Civil Society Institute, co-director, lecturer in economics, 1998-; The Independent Institute, research fellow; The Foundation for the Defense of Democracies, academic fellow; California State University, faculty; John F. Kennedy University, faculty; American Institute for Economic Research, EconJournalWatch Journal, co-editor and associate editor; The Progress Report Journal, commentator and senior editor. **Publications:** The Soul of Liberty, 1980; Natural Rights, 1985; Public Goods and Private Communities, 1994; (ed. and contrib.) Beyond Neoclassical Economics: Heterodox Approaches to Economic Theory, 1996; Dictionary of Free Market Economics, 1998; (ed. with D.B. Klein) The Half-Life of Policy Rationales: How New Technology Affects Old Policy Issues, 2003; The Depression of 2008, 2007. Contributor to books and journals. **Address:** Department of Economics, Santa Clara University, Rm. 300, Lucas Hall, 500 El Camino Real, Santa Clara, CA 95053, U.S.A. **Online address:** ffoldvary@scu.edu

FOLEY, Denise (M.). American (born United States), b. 1950. **Genres:** Medicine/Health, Adult Non-fiction, Sports/Fitness. **Career:** Montgomery Publishing, editor and reporter, 1974-77; Bucks County Courier Times, reporter and columnist, 1977-83; Prevention (magazine), senior editor, 1983-86; Children (magazine), Emmaus, managing editor, 1986-89; freelance writer, 1989-; Temple University, instructor in writing, 1990-; Chapman University, adjunct faculty; Agora Publishing, consulting editor, 1995-97; www.irishphiladelphia.com, writer, editor and co-owner, 2005-; Publication Services of America, deputy editor, 2007-09. **Publications:** (With E.Nechas) What Do I Do Now?, 1992; (with Nechas) Women's Encyclopedia of Health and Emotional Healing: Top Women Doctors Share Their Unique Self-Help Advice on Your Body, Your Feelings and Yours Life, 1993; Guía Médica De Remedios Caseros Para Niños: Cientos DeMétodos y Tips Aprobados Por Los Médicos Para Cuidar a Su Hijo, Desde Alergias y Mordeduras De Animales Hasta Dolor Dental y Adicciónа La Televisiońn, trans. as The Doctors Book of Home Remedies for Children: From Allergies and Animal Bites to Toothache and TV Addiction: Hundreds of Doctor-Proven Techniques and Tips to Care For Your Kid, 1994; (with Nechas) Unequal Treatment: What You Don't Know about How Women Are Mistreated by the Medical Community, 1994. Contributor to periodicals. **Address:** c/o Connie Clausen, Apt. 16 H, 250 E 87th St., New York, NY 10128, U.S.A. **Online address:** dfoley@chapman.edu

FOLEY, Gaelen. American (born United States) **Genres:** Romance/Historical, Novels. **Career:** Ballantine Random House, senior editor. **Publications:**

HISTORICAL ROMANCE: ASCENSION TRILOGY: The Pirate Prince, 1998; Princess, 1999; Prince Charming, 2000. KNIGHT MISCELLANY FAMILY SERIES: The Duke, 2000; Lord of Fire, 2002; Lord of Ice, 2002; Lady of Desire, 2003; Devil Takes a Bride, 2004; One Night of Sin, 2005; His Wicked Kiss, 2006. SPICE TRILOGY: Her Only Desire, 2007; Her Secret Fantasy, 2007; Her Every Pleasure, 2008. INFERNO CLUB SERIES: My Wicked Marquess, 2009; My Dangerous Duke, 2010; My Irresistible Earl, 2011. **Address:** 4017 Washington Rd., PO Box 320, McMurray, PA 15317, U.S.A. **Online address:** gaelenfoley@aol.com

FOLEY, Jack. American (born United States), b. 1940. **Genres:** Poetry, Biography. **Career:** KPFA-FM, host and executive producer-in-charge of poetry program, 1988-; Poetry USA, editor-in-chief, 1990-95; Poetry Flash, contributing editor, 1992-. Poet. **Publications:** POETRY: Letters/Lights-Words for Adelle, 1987; Gershwin, 1991; Adrift, 1993; Exiles, 1996; Advice to the Lovelorn, 1998; New Poetry from California: Dead/Requiem, 1998; Saint James, 1998; O Powerful Western Star, 2000; Some Songs by Georges Brassens, 2001; Greatest Hits 1974-2003, 2004; The Dancer & the Dance: A Book of Distinctions, 2008; Visions & Affiliations: A California Literary Time Line, 2011. OTHER: Inciting Joy (monograph), 1993; O Her Blackness Sparkles! The Life and Times of the Batman Art Gallery, 1960-65, 1995; (ed.) The Fallen Western Star Wars: A Debate About Literary California, 2001; (ed.) All: A James Broughton Reader, 2007. Contributor to journals. Work appear in anthologies. **Address:** 2569 Maxwell Ave., Oakland, CA 94601, U.S.A. **Online address:** jasfoley@aol.com

FOLEY, (Mary) Louise Munro. American/Canadian (born Canada), b. 1933. **Genres:** Novels, Mystery/Crime/Suspense, Children's Fiction, Young Adult Fiction, Plays/Screenplays, Social Work, Theology/Religion, Writing/Journalism, Writing/Journalism. **Career:** CHOK Radio, copy editor, 1953-54; CJSP Radio, copy editor, 1954-56; KLIX-TV, copy editor, 1956-58; KGMS Radio, copy editor, 1958-60; California State University, Institute for Human Service Management, editor of publications, 1975-80, Extension Program, lecturer, School of Social Work, editor. **Publications:** The Caper Club, 1969; No Talking, 1970; Sammy's Sister, 1970; A Job for Joey, 1970; Somebody Stole Second, 1972; Tackle 22, 1978; The Train of Terror, 1982; The Sinister Studies of KESP-TV, 1983; The Lost Tribe, 1983; The Mystery of the Highland Crest, 1984; The Mystery of Echo Lodge, 1985; Danger at Anchor Mine, 1985; Forest of Fear, 1986; The Mardi Gras Mystery, 1987; Mystery of the Sacred Stones, 1988; Australia: Find the Flying Foxes!, 1988; The Cobra Connection, 1989; Thief! said the Cat, 1992; Blood! said the Cat, 1992; Poison! said the Cat, 1992; In Search of the Hidden Statue, 1993; Moving Target, 1993; Stolen Affections, 1995; Ghost Train, 1995; Running into Trouble, 1996; My Substitute Teacher's Gone Batty, 1996; The Bird-Brained Fiasco, 1996; The Phoney-Baloney Professor, 1996; The Catnap Cat-Astrophe, 1996; Ordinary Sinners, 2003. EDITOR: Stand Close to the Door, 1976; Women in Skilled Labor, 1980. **Address:** Tom Doherty Associates Inc., 175 5th Ave., New York, NY 10010, U.S.A.

FOLEY, Mick. American (born United States), b. 1965. **Genres:** Autobiography/Memoirs, Poetry, Young Adult Non-fiction, Picture/Board Books, Novels. **Career:** Writer. **Publications:** Mankind, Have a Nice Day! A Tale of Blood and Sweatsocks, 1999; Mick Foley's Christmas Chaos, 2000; Foley is Good: ... and the Real World is Faker than Wrestling, 2001; Mick Foley's Halloween Hijinx, 2001; Tietam Brown: A Novel, 2003; Tales from Wrescal Lane, 2004; Scooter: A Novel, 2005; The Hardcore Diaries, 2007; Countdown to Lockdown: A Hardcore Journal, 2010. **Address:** Luke Janklow, Janklow & Nesbit Associates, 445 Park Ave., New York, NY 10022-2606, U.S.A.

FOLEY, Robert T. (Robert Thomas Foley). British (born England), b. 1969. **Genres:** History, Intellectual History. **Career:** King's College London, senior lecturer in defense studies; Defense Academy of the United Kingdom, lecturer; University of Liverpool, senior lecturer in modern military history, School of History Board of Studies, chair, deputy head of history and director of postgraduate research. Writer, academic and historian. **Publications:** Link Attrition: Its Theory and Application in German Strategy, 1880-1916, 1999; (ed.) (as Robert Thomas Foley) Alfred Von Schlieffen's Military Writings, 2003; (as Robert Thomas Foley) German Strategy and the Path to Verdun: Erich Von Falkenhayn and the Development of Attrition, 1870-1916, 2005; (ed. with H.M. Cartney) The Somme: An Eyewitness History, 2006. Contributor to periodicals and books. **Address:** School of History, University of Liverpool, 9 Abercromby Sq., Liverpool, MS L69 7WZ, England. **Online address:** robert.foley@liverpool.ac.uk

FOLEY, Robert Thomas. *See* **FOLEY, Robert T.**

FOLGARAIT, Leonard. American (born United States), b. 1950. **Genres:** Art/Art History. **Career:** Vanderbilt University, professor of history of art, director of graduate studies and chair. Writer. **Publications:** So Far from Heaven: David Alfaro Siqueiros's The March of Humanity and Mexican Revolutionary Politics, 1987; Mural Painting and Social Revolution in Mexico, 1920-1940: Art of the New Order, 1998; Seeing Mexico Photographed, 2008; Mexican Muralism: A Critical History, forthcoming. Contributor to art periodicals. **Address:** Department of History of Art, Vanderbilt University, 113 Cohen Hall, 1221 21st Ave. S, Nashville, TN 37203, U.S.A. **Online address:** leonard.folgarait@vanderbilt.edu

FOLI, Karen J. American (born United States), b. 1959?. **Genres:** Novels. **Career:** Purdue University, School of Nursing, assistant professor. Writer. **Publications:** Like Sound through Water: A Mother's Journey through Auditory Processing Disorder, 2002; (with J.R. Thompson) The Post-Adoption Blues: Overcoming the Unforeseen Challenges of Adoption, 2004; (with L.A. Jason and B.D. Olson) Rescued Lives: The Oxford House Approach to Substance Abuse, 2007. **Address:** c/o Jodie Rhodes, Jodie Rhodes Literary Agency, 8840 Villa La Jolla Dr., Ste. 315, La Jolla, CA 92037, U.S.A. **Online address:** karenfoli@bluemarble.net

FOLK, Thomas C. American (born United States), b. 1955. **Genres:** Literary Criticism And History, Art/Art History. **Career:** Rutgers University, associate professor, professor; curator. Writer. **Publications:** The Pennsylvania School of Landscape Painting: An Original American Impressionism, 1984; Edward Redfield: First Master of the Twentieth Century Landscape, 1987; The Pennsylvania Impressionists, 1997; (with C.I. Oaklander) Charles F. Ramsey: Father of New Hope Modernism, 2003. **Address:** 14 Pheasant Hill Dr., PO Box 501, Far Hills, NJ 07931, U.S.A. **Online address:** drtomfolk@aol.com

FOLKS, Jeffrey Jay. American (born United States), b. 1948. **Genres:** Poetry, Literary Criticism And History, History. **Career:** Indiana University, associate instructor, 1970-72; lecturer in English, 1975-76; Tennessee Wesleyan College, instructor, 1976-79, assistant professor, 1979-82, associate professor, 1982-85, professor of English, 1985-; University of Skopje, senior Fulbright lecturer, 1986-87; Sofia University, senior Fulbright lecturer, 1994-95. Writer. **Publications:** (Trans. with M. Holton and C. Simic and ed. and intro.) M. Jovanovski, Faceless Men and Other Macedonian Stories, 1992; Essays on Robert Drake, 1992; Southern Writers and the Machine: Faulkner to Percy, 1993; The First of September: Poems, 1993; (ed. with D. Madden) Remembering James Agee, 1997; (ed. with J.A. Perkins) Southern Writers at Century's End, 1997; (ed. with N.S. Folks) The World is Our Home: Society and Culture in Contemporary Southern Writing, 2000; From Richard Wright to Toni Morrison: Ethics in Modern and Postmodern American Narrative, 2001; In a Time of Disorder: Form and Meaning in Southern Fiction From Poe to O'Connor, 2003; Damaged Lives: Southern & Caribbean Narrative from Faulkner to Naipaul, 2005; Heartland of the Imagination: Conservative Values in American Literature from Poe to O'Connor to Haruf, 2012. **Address:** McFarland & Co., 960 NC Hwy. 88 W, PO Box 611, Jefferson, NC 28640, U.S.A. **Online address:** jjfolks@usa.net

FOLLETT, CB. American (born United States), b. 1936. **Genres:** Poetry. **Career:** Arctos Press, owner, publisher and editor, 1997-; Peaceable Kingdom, founder, owner, business manager and designer, 1973-94; Cunningham & Walsh, copy editor and proofreader; McCann Erickson, copy editor and proofreader; International Business Relations, copy editor and proofreader; Stanford University, copy editor and proofreader; Attic Theater Co., board director; Urban School, president; University High School, founding board director; De Young Museum Art School and Auxiliary, president. **Publications:** The Latitudes of Their Going, 1993; Gathering the Mountains, 1995; Bull Kelp, 1995; Nightmare Fish, 1997; Arms, 1997; Vallon-Pont'Arc, 1998; Visible Bones, 1998; At the Turning of the Light, 2001; Runaway Girl, 2007; Hold and Release, 2007; A Cat Who Falls from a Tree Branch Will Always Claim He Meant To, 2008; Poems for Red Canyons, 2009; And Freddie Was My Darling, 2009; One Bird Falling: Poems, 2011. EDITOR: Beside the Sleeping Maiden: Poets of Marin, 1997; Grrrr: A Collection of Poems about Bears, 2000; (with S. Terris) Runes: A Review of Poetry, 2002. Works appear in anthologies. Contributor to magazines. **Address:** Arctos Press, PO Box 401, Sausalito, CA 94966, U.S.A. **Online address:** runes@aol.com

FOLLETT, Ken(neth Martin). Also writes as Zachary Stone, Simon Myles,

Bernard L. Ross, Martin Martinsen. British/Welsh (born Wales), b. 1949. **Genres:** Mystery/Crime/Suspense, Young Adult Fiction, Novels, Mystery/Crime/Suspense. **Career:** South Wales Echo, trainee journalist and rock music columnist, 1970-73; Evening News, reporter, 1973-74; Everest Books Ltd., editorial director, 1974-76, deputy managing director, 1976-77; writer, 1977-; University College, fellow, 1995. **Publications:** NOVELS: The Shakeout, 1975; The Bear Raid, 1976; The Secret of Kellerman's Studio (juvenile), 1976 as Mystery Hideout, 1990; Eye of the Needle in UK as Storm Island, 1978; Triple, 1979; The Key to Rebecca, 1980; The Man from St. Petersburg, 1982; On Wings of Eagles, 1983; Lie Down with Lions, 1986; The Pillars of the Earth, 1989; Night over Water, 1991; A Dangerous Fortune, 1993; Pillars of the Almighty, 1994; A Place Called Freedom, 1995; The Third Twin: A Novel, 1996; The Hammer of Eden, 1998; Code to Zero, 2000; Jackdaws, 2001; Hornet Flight, 2002; Whiteout, 2004; World Without End, 2007; Fall of Giants, 2010; Winter of the World, 2012. OTHERS: (as Simon Myles) The Big Black, 1974; (as Simon Myles) The Big Needle, 1974 in US as The Big Apple, 1975; (as Simon Myles) The Big Hit, 1975; (as Martin Marinsen) The Power Twins and the Worm Puzzle: A Science Fantasy for Young People, 1976 as Power Twins, 1990; (as Bernard L. Ross) Amok: King of Legend, 1976; (as Zachary Stone) The Modigliani Scandal, 1976; (as Zachary Stone) Paper Money, 1977; (with R.L. Maurice) The Heist of the Century, 1978 as The Gentlemen of 16 July: A Work of Narrative Nonfiction, 1978; (as Bernard L. Ross) Capricorn One, 1978; Under the Streets of Nice: The Bank Heist of the Century, 1986. Contributor to periodicals. **Address:** PO Box 4, Knebworth, HF SG3 6UT, England.

FOLLY, Martin H(arold). British (born England), b. 1957. **Genres:** History, Biography, Young Adult Fiction. **Career:** Brunel University, senior lecturer in American and international history, 1989-. Writer. **Publications:** People in History (juvenile), 1988; Churchill, Whitehall and the Soviet Union, 1940-45, 2000; United States and World War II: The Awakening Giant, 2002; Palgrave Concise Historical Atlas of the Second World War, 2004; (with N. Palmer) Historical Dictionary of U.S. Diplomacy from World War I through World War II, 2010. Contributor to periodicals. **Address:** Department of Politics and History, Brunel University, 110 Marie Jahoda Bldg., London, GL UB8 3PH, England. **Online address:** martin.folly@brunel.ac.uk

FOLSOM, Allan (R.). American (born United States), b. 1941. **Genres:** Novels, Literary Criticism And History. **Career:** Writer. **Publications:** The Day After Tomorrow (novel), 1994; Day of Confession, 1998; The Exile, 2004; The Machiavelli Covenant, 2006; The Hadrian Memorandum, 2009. Contributor to periodicals. **Address:** Aaron M. Priest Literary Agency, 708 3rd Ave., 23rd Fl., New York, NY 10017-4201, U.S.A.

FOLSTER, David. Canadian (born Canada), b. 1937. **Genres:** Agriculture/Forestry, Film, Geography, History, Essays, Business/Trade/Industry. **Career:** Daily Gleaner, reporter and sports editor, 1960; Sprague Electric Co., technical writer, 1961-66; full-time writer, 1967-. **Publications:** (Ed.) On with the Dance: A New Brunswick Memoir, 1935-1960, 1986; The Great Trees of New Brunswick, 1987; The Chocolate Ganongs of St. Stephen, 1990; Ganong: A Sweet History of Chocolate, 2006. Contributor to periodicals. **Address:** PO Box 21017, Fredericton, NB E3B 7A3, Canada. **Online address:** treehouse@fundy.net

FOMBRUN, Charles J. American/Haitian (born Haiti), b. 1954. **Genres:** Administration/Management, Business/Trade/Industry, Economics. **Career:** Columbia University, instructor in management, 1978-79; University of Pennsylvania, Wharton School, lecturer, 1979-80, assistant professor of management, 1980-84; New York University, visiting associate professor, 1984-86, associate professor, 1986-91, professor of management, 1991-2003, research professor, 1992-2003, professor emeritus of management, 2003-; Reputation Institute, co-founder and chief executive officer, 1997-. Writer. **Publications:** (With N.M. Tichy and M.A. Devanna) Strategic Human Resource Management, 1984; Turning Points: Creating Strategic Change in Corporations, 1992; (ed. with Tichy and McGill and contrib.) Corporate Citizenship, 1994; Good as Gold: How Companies Build, Sustain and Defend Their Reputations, 1994; Leading Corporate Change: How the World's Foremost Companies are Launching Revolutionary Change, 1994; Reputation: Realizing Value from the Corporate Image, 1996; (with M.D. Nevins) The Advice Business: Essential Tools and Models for Management Consulting, 2004; Fame and Fortune: How Successful Companies Build Winning Reputations, 2004. (with C.B.M. van Riel) Essentials of Corporate Communication: Implementing Practices for Effective Reputation Management, 2007. Works appear in anthologies. Contributor of articles to journals and newspapers. **Address:** Reputation Institute, 55 Broad St., New York, NY 10004, U.S.A. **Online address:** cfombrun@reputationinstitute.com

FONAGY, Peter. British/Hungarian (born Hungary), b. 1952. **Genres:** Psychology. **Career:** Royal Free Hospital, probationer clinical psychologist, 1976-78, honorary senior clinical psychologist and lecturer, 1981-85; North East Thames Regional Authority, trainee clinical psychologist, 1977-80; University College London, lecturer, 1977-87, senior lecturer, 1988-92, Freud memorial professor of psychoanalysis, 1992-, Centre for Health in Society, founding member, Sub-Department of Clinical Health Psychology, director, 1995-2007, Department of Research, head, 2008-, Mental Health and Wellbeing Theme, interim program director, 2010-, Department of Health, interim clinical lead, 2011-; London Clinic of Psychoanalysis, staff, 1982-85; Anna Freud Centre, consultant to research, coordinator of research, 1986-89, director of research, 1989-2003, chief executive officer, 2003-; Hebrew University, Sigmund Freud Centre, visiting professor, 1993; University of Haifa, Department of Psychology, visiting professor, 1993; Kansas University, adjunct professor, 1995-2002; Menninger Clinic, Child and Family Center, coordinator, 1995-2003; The Karl Menninger School of Psychiatry and Mental Health Sciences, Marie & Scott S. Smith chair in child development, 1999-2003; Baylor College of Medicine, adjunct professor, 2003-; Yale University, School of Medicine, clinical professor of psychiatry, 2005-, Joint Seminar on Contemporary British Art, initiator. Consultant and writer. **Publications:** (With A. Higgitt) Personality Theory and Clinical Practice, 1984; (with Higgitt and M. Lader) The Natural History of Tolerance to the Benzodiazepines, 1988; Attachment Theory and Psychoanalysis, 2001; What Works for Whom?: A Critical Review of Treatments for Children and Adolescents, 2002; (with A.W. Bateman) Psychotherapy for Borderline Personality Disorder: Mentalization-Based Treatment, 2004; (with A. Roth) What Works for Whom?: A Critical Review of Psychotherapy Research, 1996, 2nd ed., 2005; (with A.W. Bateman) Mentalization-Based Treatment for Borderline Personality Disorder: A Practical Guide, 2006; (with J.G. Allen and A.W. Bateman) Mentalizing in Clinical Practice, 2008. EDITOR: (with E.S. Person) Freud's On Narcissism: An Introduction, 1991; (with E.S. Person and A. Hagelin) On Freud's Observations on Transference-Love, 1993; (with E.S. Person and S.A. Figueira) On Freud's Creative Writers and Day-Dreaming, 1995; (with A. Cooper and R. Wallerstein) The Theory of Psychoanalytic Practice, 1994; (with J. Sandler) Recovered Memories of Abuse: True or False?, 1997; (with A.M. Cooper and R.S. Wallerstein) Psychoanalysis on the Move: The Work of Joseph Sandler, 1999; (co-ed.) Affect Regulation, Mentalization and the Development of the Self, 2002; (with J.G. Allen) Handbook of Mentalization-Based Treatment, 2006; (with G. Baruch and D. Robins) Reaching the Hard to Reach: Evidence-Based Funding Priorities for Intervention and Research, 2007; (with L. Mayes and M. Target) Developmental Science and Psychoanalysis: Integration and Innovation, 2007; (with C. Sharp and I. Goodyer) Social Cognition and Developmental Psychopathology, 2008; (with J.F. Clarkin and G.O. Gabbard) Psychodynamic Psychotherapy for Personality Disorders: A Clinical Handbook, 2010; (with A.W. Bateman) Handbook of Mentalizing in Mental Health Practice, 2012. Works appears in anthologies. Contributor of articles to journals. **Address:** Psychoanalysis Unit, Sub-Department of Clinical Psychology, University College London, Rm. TP542, Chandler House, 1-19 Torrington Pl., London, GL WC1E 6BT, England. **Online address:** p.fonagy@ucl.ac.uk

FONDA, Peter. American (born United States), b. 1939. **Genres:** Plays/Screenplays, Novels, Autobiography/Memoirs. **Career:** Writer. **Publications:** Don't Tell Dad: A Memoir, 1998. **Address:** Indian Hills Ranch, Rte. 38G, PO Box 2040, Livingston, MT 59047, U.S.A.

FONE, Byrne R. S. American (born United States), b. 1936. **Genres:** Literary Criticism And History, Gay And Lesbian Issues, Romance/Historical, Novels, Language/Linguistics. **Career:** New York University, Department of English, assistant, 1960-63, instructor, 1964-65; Queens College, lecturer, 1963-64; City University of New York, City College, faculty, 1965-68, assistant professor, 1968-, professor of English, now professor emeritus of English. Writer. **Publications:** (With G. Marcelle) Boswell's Life of Johnson, and Other Works, 1966; (with G. Marcelle) Melville's Moby Dick and Other Works, 1966; (ed. and intro.) An Apology for the Life of Colley Cibber, with an Historical View of the State During His Own Time, 1968; Colley Cibber's Love's Last Shift, 1968; Love's Last Shift and Sentimental Comedy, 1969; The Augustan Translators, 1974; History of English Literature, 1974; (ed.) Hidden Heritage, History and the Gay Imagination: An Anthology, 1981; Masculine Landscapes: Walt Whitman and the Homoerotic Text, 1992; A Road to Stonewall: Male Homosexuality and Homophobia in England and America Literature, 1750-1969, 1995; (ed.) The Columbia Anthology of Gay Literature: Readings from Western Antiquity to the Present Day, 1998; Homophobia: A History, 2000; Historic Hudson: An Architectural Portrait, 2005. Contributor to periodicals. **Address:** Department of English, City College, City University of New York, Rm. 6/219, North Academic Bldg., 160 Convent Ave., New York, NY 10031-9101, U.S.A. **Online address:** byrnefone@wanadoo.fr

FONER, Eric. American (born United States), b. 1943. **Genres:** History, Race Relations, Politics/Government. **Career:** Columbia University, assistant professor of history, 1969-73, professor of history, 1982-88, Dewitt Clinton professor of history, 1988-, Society of American Historians, president, 2006; City University of New York, City College and Graduate Center, associate professor of history, 1973-82; Cambridge University, Pitt professor of American history and institutions, 1980-81; Moscow State University, Fulbright professor of American history, 1990; Oxford University, Harmsworth professor of American history, 1993-94. **Publications:** America's Black Past: A Reader in Afro-American History, 1970; Free Soil, Free Labor, Free Men: The Ideology of the Republican Party before the Civil War, 1970; Nat Turner, 1971; Tom Paine and Revolutionary America, 1976; Politics and Ideology in the Age of the Civil War, 1980; Nothing but Freedom: Emancipation and its Legacy, 1983; Reconstruction: America's Unfinished Revolution, 1863-1877, 1988; A Short History of Reconstruction, 1863-1877, 1988; (with O. Mahoney) A House Divided: America in the Age of Lincoln, 1990; The Tocsin of Freedom: The Black Leadership of Radical Reconstruction, 1992; Half Slave and Half Free: The Roots of Civil War, 1992; Freedom's Lawmakers: A Directory of Black Officeholders During Reconstruction, 1993, rev. ed., 1996; Slavery and Freedom in Nineteenth-Century America, 1994; (with O. Mahoney) America's Reconstruction: People and Politics after the Civil War, 1995; Slavery, the Civil War and Reconstruction, 1997; The Story of American Freedom, 1998; Who Owns History?: Rethinking the Past in a Changing World, 2002; Idea of Freedom in the American Century, 2003; Give Me Liberty!: An American History, 2004, 3rd ed., 2012; Forever Free: The Story of Emancipation and Reconstruction, 2005; The Fiery Trial: Abraham Lincoln and American Slavery, 2010; (with R. Follett and W. Johnson) Slavery's Ghost, 2011. EDITOR: Divided Left: American Radicalism, 1900-1975, 1978; World of the Worker: Labor in Twentieth-Century America, 1980; Spreading the American Dream: American Economic and Cultural Expansion, 1890-1945, 1982; Incorporation of America: Culture and Society in the Gilded Age, 1982; Pillars of the Republic: Common Schools and American Society, 1780-1860, 1983; Struggle for Black Equality, 1954-1992, 1983; American Revolution, 1985; Standing at the Crossroads: Southern Life since 1900, 1986; Artisans into Workers: Labor in Nineteenth-Century America, 1989; Liberty and Power: The Politics of Jacksonian America, 1990; New American History, 1990, rev. ed., 1997; (with J.A. Garraty) Reader's Companion to American History, 1991; Divided Lives: American Women in the Twentieth Century, 1992; Brief History of American Sports, 1993; Green Revolution: The American Environmental Movement, 1962-1992, 1993; American Populism: A Social History, 1877-1898, 1993; Long, Bitter Trail: Andrew Jackson and the Indian, 1993; Prisoners Without Trial: Japanese Americans in World War II, 1993; Age of Great Dreams: America in the 1960s, 1994; Specter of Communism: The United States and the Origins of the Cold War, 1917-1953, 1994; (co-ed.) The Thaddeus Stevens Papers: Guide and Indexes to the Microfilm Edition, 1994; Holy Warriors: The Abolitionists and American Slavery, 1996; (ed.) American Reformers, 1815-1860, 1997; (ed. with L. Garafola) Dance for a City: Fifty Years of the New York City Ballet, 1999; American Colonies, 2001; Voices of Freedom: A Documentary History, 2004, 3rd ed., 2011; (with M. Marable) Herbert Aptheker on Race and Democracy: A Reader, 2006; Our Lincoln: New Perspectives on Lincoln and His World, 2008; (with L. McGirr) American History Now, 2011. Contributor to periodicals. **Address:** Department of History, Columbia University, 620 Fayerweather Hall, 116th St. and Broadway, PO Box 2522, New York, NY 10027, U.S.A. **Online address:** ef17@columbia.edu

FONES-WOLF, Elizabeth. (Elizabeth A. Fones-Wolf). American (born United States), b. 1954?. **Genres:** Civil Liberties/Human Rights, Economics. **Career:** University of Illinois Press, associate editor; West Virginia University, Eberly College of Arts and Sciences, Department of History, professor and chair. **Publications:** Selling Free Enterprise: The Business Assault on Labor and Liberalism, 1945-60, 1994; Waves of Opposition: Labor and the Struggle for Democratic Radio, 2006. Contributor to periodicals. **Address:**

Department of History, Eberly College of Arts and Sciences, West Virginia University, 221F Woodburn Hall, PO Box 6303, Morgantown, WV 26506-6303, U.S.A. **Online address:** elizabet.fones-wolf@mail.wvu.edu

FONES-WOLF, Elizabeth A. See **FONES-WOLF, Elizabeth.**

FONG, Bobby. American (born United States), b. 1950. **Genres:** Literary Criticism And History, Theology/Religion, Social Sciences, Education. **Career:** Berea College, instructor to associate professor of English, 1978-89; Hope College, professor of English, 1989-95, dean for arts and humanities, 1989-94; Hamilton College, professor of English, 1995-2001, dean of faculty, 1995-2000; Butler University, president, 2001-. Writer. **Publications:** (Contrib.) Faculty Assessment of Student Learning, 1988; (contrib.)Contemporary Critical Theory and the Teaching of Literature, 1990; (ed. with D.A. Hoekema) Christianity and Culture in the Crossfire, 1997; (contrib.) The Cambridge Companion to Oscar Wilde, 1997; (ed. with K. Beckson) The Oxford English Text Edition of the Complete Works of Oscar Wilde, 1998, 2nd ed., 2001; (ed.) The Complete Works of Oscar Wilde, 2001. **Address:** Office of the President, Butler University, 4600 Sunset Ave., Indianapolis, IN 46208, U.S.A. **Online address:** bfong@butler.edu

FONROBERT, Charlotte Elisheva. American/German (born Germany), b. 1965. **Genres:** Theology/Religion, Women's Studies And Issues, Language/Linguistics, Philosophy, Sports/Fitness. **Career:** University of Washington, lecturer, 1994-95; Syracuse University, acting assistant professor of religion, 1995-96; University of Judaism, assistant professor of Talmud, 1996-2000; Stanford University, assistant professor of religious studies, 2000-06, associate professor of religious studies, 2006-. Writer. **Publications:** Menstrual Purity: Rabbinic and Christian Reconstructions of Biblical Gender, 2000; (ed. and intro. with V. Shemtov) Jewish Conceptions and Practice of Space, 2005; (ed. and intro. with M.S. Jaffee) Cambridge Companion to Rabbinic Literature, 2006; (ed. with A. Engel) From Cult To Culture: Fragments Towards A Critique Of Historical Reason, 2010; Replacing the Nation: Judaism, Diaspora and the Neighborhood, forthcoming. Contributor to periodicals. **Address:** Department of Religious Studies, Stanford University, Rm. 71B Main Quad, Bldg. 70, Stanford, CA 94305-2165, U.S.A. **Online address:** fonrober@stanford.edu

FONSECA, James W(illiam). American (born United States), b. 1947. **Genres:** Demography, Social Sciences, Geography, Education. **Career:** George Mason University, associate professor of geography, 1973-, acting dean of graduate school, 1988-90, Prince William Institute, director, 1992-; Ohio University, interim dean of regional higher education, dean and professor of geography, 1998-. Writer. **Publications:** (Ed.) Virginia Geographer, 1980-87; The Urban Rank-Size Hierarchy (monograph), 1988; (with A.C. Andrews) The Atlas of American Higher Education, 1993; (with A.C. Andrews) The Atlas of American Society, 1995. Contributor to journals. **Address:** Department of Geography, Ohio University, 104 Elson Hall, Zanesville Campus, 1425 Newark Rd., Zanesville, OH 43701, U.S.A. **Online address:** fonseca@ohio.edu

FONT, Andreu Carranza. See **CARRANZA, Andreu.**

FONTAINE, Carole R. American (born United States), b. 1950. **Genres:** Theology/Religion, Education. **Career:** University of North Carolina, lecturer, 1979; Duke Divinity School, lecturer, 1979; Andover Newton Theological School, professor, 1979-, artist-in-residence, 1995-97; Boston College, adjunct faculty, 1982; Greenheart Studio, founder and artist, 1990. Writer. **Publications:** Traditional Sayings in the Old Testament: A Contextual Study, 1982; (ed. with A. Brenner) Wisdom and Psalms, 1998; (ed. with A. Brenner) A Feminist Companion to Reading the Bible: Approaches, Methods and Strategies, 2001; Smooth Words: Women, Proverbs, and Performance in Biblical Wisdom, 2002; With Eyes of Flesh: The Bible, Gender, and Human Rights, 2008. **Address:** Andover Newton Theological School, 210 Herrick Rd., Newton Center, MA 02459, U.S.A. **Online address:** cfontaine@ants.edu

FONTANEL, Béatrice. French/Moroccan (born Morocco), b. 1957. **Genres:** Fash Ion/Costume, History, Art/Art History, Young Adult Non-fiction, Animals/Pets. **Career:** Bayard-Presse, journalist, 1981-88; Gallimard Jeunesse (book publisher), editor, 1990-96; Herve de la Martiniere (publisher), writer, 1996-. **Publications:** Cats, Big and Little, 1991; The Penguin, a Funny Bird, 1992; Support and Seduction: The History of the Corsets and Bras, 1997; Babies: History, Art and Folklore, 1997; Babies Celebrated, 1998; Monsters:

The Book of the Ugliest Animals, 1998; Monsters: The World's Most Incredible Animals, 2000; L'éternel féminin: une histoire ducorps intim, 2001; (with D. Wolfromm) Quand les artistes peignaient l'histoire de France: de Vercingétorix à 1918, 2002; Gustave Taloche, roi de la bagarre, 2005; éloge des nuages, 2005; Daily Life in Art, 2006; (with D. Wolfromm) Petite Histoire du Préservatif, 2009. **Address:** 15 rue Littre, Paris, 75006, France. **Online address:** beatrice.fontanel@wanadoo.fr

FONTANELLA, John J. American (born United States), b. 1945. **Genres:** Sciences, Physics. **Career:** United States Naval Academy, Physics Department, officer instructor, 1971-74, assistant professor, 1974-78, associate professor, 1978-84, professor of physics, 1984-, now professor emeritus. Writer. **Publications:** The Physics of Basketball, 2006. Contributor to books and journals. **Address:** Physics Department, United States Naval Academy, Rm. 043, Chauvenet Hall, 572C Holloway Rd., Annapolis, MD 21402, U.S.A. **Online address:** fontanel@comcast.net

FONTES, Manuel D(a Costa). American/Portuguese (born Portugal), b. 1945. **Genres:** Literary Criticism And History, Language/Linguistics, Humanities, Mythology/Folklore. **Career:** Stanford University, lecturer, 1972-73; University of California, teaching assistant, 1973-75; Kent State University, assistant professor, 1975-79, associate professor, 1979-85, professor of Spanish and Portuguese, 1985-2007, professor emeritus, 2007-. Writer. **Publications:** Romanceiro Português do Canadá, 1979; Romanceiro Português dos Estados Unidos, vol. I: Nova Inglaterra, 1980, vol. II: Califórnia, 1983; Romanceiro da Ilha de São Jorge, 1983; Romanceiro da Provincia de Trás-os-Montes (Distrito de Bragança), 2 vols., 1987; Portuguese and Brazilian Balladry: A Thematic and Bibliographic Index, 2 vols., 1997; (ed. with S.G. Armistead) Cancioneiro Tradicional de Trás-os-Montes, 1998; Folklore and Literature: Studies in the Portuguese, Brazilian, Sephardic, and Hispanic Oral Traditions, 2000; Art of Subversion in Inquisitorial Spain: Rojas and Delicado, 2005; (co-ed.) Entra mayo y sale abril: Medieval Spanish Literary and Folklore Studies in Memory of Harriet Goldberg, 2005. Contributor to periodicals. **Address:** Department of Modern & Classical Language Studies, Kent State University, 304D Satterfield Hall, Kent, OH 44242, U.S.A. **Online address:** mfontes@kent.edu

FONTES, Montserrat. (Jessie Lattimore). American (born United States), b. 1940. **Genres:** Novels, Literary Criticism And History, Humanities, Science Fiction/Fantasy. **Career:** Markham Junior High School, teacher of English, 1968-72; University High School, teacher of English and journalism, 1973-; John Marshall High School, teacher, 1978-. Writer. **Publications:** (As Jessie Lattimore with N. Dresser) High Contrast, 1988; First Confession (novel), 1991; Dreams of the Centaur, 1996; The General's Widow, forthcoming. Contributor to periodicals. **Address:** 915 Osceola St., Glendale, CA 91205-3820, U.S.A. **Online address:** montserratfontes@hotmail.com

FONTES, Ron. American (born United States), b. 1952. **Genres:** Graphic Novels, Mythology/Folklore, Popular Culture, Trivia/Facts, Cartoons, Biography, History, Novels, Novels. **Career:** Creative Corp., designer, 1971-73; McDonald and Associates Advertising, designer, 1978-80; Western Publishing, designer and staff artist for Whitman Comics line, 1980-81; Marvel Comics, production supervisor of special projects, 1981-85; Sonic Publishing, co-founder, 2004. Writer. **Publications:** WITH J. KORMAN: My Friend Fang, 1992; The Ghost Who Couldn't Boo, 1994; The Grumpy Easter Bunny, 1995; Beware of dog!, 1998; Babe, Pig in the City, 1998; Mushu's Story, 1998; How the Leopard Got Its Spots: Three Tales from around the World, 1999; How the Turtle Got Its Shell, 2000; How the Camel Got It's Hump, 2001. DISNEY'S AMERICAN FRONTIER SERIES WITH J. KORMAN: Davy Crockett at the Alamo, 1991; Davy Crockett and the Creek Indians, 1991; Davy Crockett and the Highwaymen, 1992; Calamity Jane at Fort Sanders, 1992; Annie Oakley in the Wild West Extravaganza!, 1993; Wild Bill Hickok versus the Rebel Raiders, 1993; Davy Crockett Meets Death Hug, 1993. BIKER MICE FROM MARS SERIES WITH J. KORMAN: Hands off My Bike!, 1994; The Masked Motorcyclist, 1994. NONFICTION WITH J. FONTES: Abraham Lincoln: Lawyer, Leader, Legend, 2001; George Washington: Soldier, Hero, President, 2001; Rescue Mission, 2001; Battle in the Arena, 2002; Brazil, 2003; China, 2003; France, 2003; India, 2003; Ireland, 2003; Israel, 2003; Italy, 2003; Kenya, 2003; Mexico, 2003; Russia, 2003; Delaware, the First State, 2003; North Dakota, the Peace Garden State, 2003; West Virginia, the Mountain State, 2003; Wyoming, the Equality State, 2003; Proteins, 2005; Rachel Carson, 2005. GRAPHIC NOVELS: (ed. with J. Fontes) Captain Fortune, 1994; (with N. Wunderman) Earth Invasion, 2003; Tales of the Termi-

nal Diner, 2004; (with J. Fontes) The Batsons, 2005; (with J. Fontes) 2006; Bloodlust, 2006; (with J. Fontes) Wooden Sword/Rudis Princeps: Vesuvius; Via Appia; Arena, 3 vols., 2006; (with J. Fontes) Atalanta: The Race against Destiny, 2007; (with J. Fontes) Sunjata: Warrior King of Mali: A West African Legend, 2007; (with J. Fontes) Itchy Mitch, 2007; (with J. Fontes) Demeter and Persephone: Spring Held Hostage, 2007; (with J. Fontes) Captured by Pirates, 2007; (with J. Fontes) The Trojan Horse: The Fall of Troy, 2007; (with J. Fontes) The Fifth Musketeer, 2012. WINDMILL TOP SECRET GRAPHICA MYSTERY CASEBOOKS WITH J. FONTES: Atlantis, 2009; Bermuda Triangle, 2009; Bigfoot, 2009; Ghosts, 2009; The Loch Ness Monster, 2009; UFOs and Alien Encounters, 2009; Vampires, 2009; Werewolves, 2009. OTHERS: Walt Disney Pictures Presents: Dinosaur Joke Book, 2000; Rango: The Movie Storybook, 2011. NOVELS: The Rocketeer, 1991; Mars Attacks!, 1996; (with J. Korman-Fontes and D.M. Wieger) Wild America, 1997; (with J. Fontes) Rango: The Novel, 2011; (with J. Fontes) Arthur Christmas, 2011. **Address:** PO Box 585, Readfield, ME 04355-0585, U.S.A. **Online address:** critter@gwi.net

FOON, Dennis. Canadian/American (born United States), b. 1951. **Genres:** Children's Fiction, Young Adult Fiction, Plays/Screenplays, Children's Nonfiction, Novels. **Career:** University of British Columbia, Centre for Continuing Education, instructor in playwriting, 1974-79; Green Thumb Theatre for Young People, co-founder and artistic director, 1975-88; International Association of Theatres for Children and Youth, vice-president, 1979-82; Young People's Theatre, playwright-in-residence, 1983-84. **Publications:** PLAYS FOR CHILDREN: The Last Days of Paul Bunyan, 1978; The Windigo, 1978; Heracles, 1978; Raft Baby, 1978; New Canadian Kid, 1982; The Hunchback of Notre Dame, 1983; Trummi Kaput, 1983; Skin, 1988; Liars, 1988; Invisible Kids, 1989; War, 1995; Chasing the Money, 2000, Mirror Game, 1992; Seesaw, 1993; Kindness, 2009; RICK, 2011. OTHERS FOR CHILDREN: (with Knight) Am I the Only One?: A Young People's Book about Sex Abuse (non-fiction), 1985; The Short Tree and the Bird That Could Not Sing, 1986. NOVELS: Double or Nothing, 2000; Freewalker (science fiction), 2001; Skud, 2002; The Dirt Eaters (science fiction), 2003; The Keeper's Shadow, 2006. **Address:** Annick Press, 119 W Pender St., Ste. 205, Vancouver, BC V6B 1S5, Canada. **Online address:** contact@dennisfoon.com

FOOS, Laurie. American (born United States), b. 1966. **Genres:** Novels. **Career:** Fisher College, adjunct instructor, 1993-; Lesley University, Low Residency MFA Program, teacher; Sewanee Writers Conference, fellow, 1997; Wesleyan Writers Conference, fellow, 1997; Novel Workshop, faculty, 2000. Writer. **Publications:** Ex Utero (novel), 1995, rev. ed., 1996; Portrait of the Walrus by a Young Artist: A Novel about Art, Bowling, Pizza, Sex, and Hair Spray, 1997, rev. ed., 1998; Twinship, 1999; Bingo Under the Crucifix: A Novel, 2002; Before Elvis There Was Nothing, 2005. Works appear in anthologies. Contributor to periodicals. **Address:** Coffee House Press, 79 13th Ave. NE, Minneapolis, MN 55413, U.S.A. **Online address:** laurie@lauriefoos.com

FOOT, David. British (born England), b. 1929. **Genres:** Biography, Sports/Fitness, Autobiography/Memoirs, Social Sciences. **Career:** Western Gazette, journalist, 1946-55; Bristol Evening World, journalist, 1955-62; freelance journalist, 1962-; television and radio journalist; sports reporter; Melody Maker, music reviewer; Wisden Cricket Monthly, columnist; Wisden Cricketer, columnist. **Publications:** EDITOR: The Hand That Bowled Bradman, 1973; Ladies' Mile, 1977; Gardening My Way, 1978. OTHERS: (with V. Richards) Viv Richards, 1979; From Grace to Botham, 1980; Harold Gimblett: Tormented Genius of Cricket, 1982; Zed, 1983; (with R. Cousins) Skateaway, 1984; Cricket's Unholy Trinity, 1985; Sunshine, Sixes and Cider, a History of the Somerset County Cricket Club, 1986; Hungry Fighters of the West, 1988; 40 Years On: Story of Lord's Taverners, 1990; Country Reporter, 1990; Beyond Bat and Ball, 1993; Wally Hammond, the Reasons Why, 1996; Fragments of Idolatry, 2001; (with D. Shepherd) Shep, 2001; Footsteps from East Coker, 2010. Contributor to periodicals. **Address:** 20 Downs Cote View, Westbury-on-Trym, Bristol, SM BS9 3TU, England. **Online address:** footydavid@hotmail.com

FOOT, John. British (born England), b. 1964. **Genres:** Politics/Government, Cultural/Ethnic Topics, Social Sciences. **Career:** University College London, Department of Italian, professor of modern Italian history. Writer and filmmaker. **Publications:** Milan since the Miracle: City, Culture, and Identity, 2001; (ed. with J. Dickie and F.M. Snowden) Disastro! Disasters in Italy since 1860: Culture, Politics, Society, 2002; Modern Italy, 2003; (ed. with R. Lumley) Italian Cityscapes: Culture and Urban Change in Contemporary Italy, 2004; Winning at All Costs: A Scandalous History of Italian Soccer, 2007; Italy's Divided Memory, 2009. **Address:** Department of Italian, University College London, Gower St., London, GL WC1E 6BT, England. **Online address:** j.foot@ucl.ac.uk

FOOT, Michael Richard Daniell. (M. R. D. Foot). British (born England), b. 1919. **Genres:** Art/Art History, History, International Relations/Current Affairs, Biography, Politics/Government, Military/Defense/Arms Control. **Career:** Oxford University, resident senior in research and teaching, 1947-59, researcher, 1959-67; Manchester University, professor of modern history, 1967-73; European Discussion Centre, deputy chairman, 1973-75; historian, 1975-. Writer. **Publications:** AS M.R.D. FOOT: (with J.L. Hammond) Gladstone and Liberalism, 1952; British Foreign Policy since 1898, 1956; Men in Uniform; Military Manpower in Modern Industrial Societies, 1961; SOE in France: An Account of the Work of the British Special Operations Executive in France, 1940-1944, 1966, new ed., 2004; Resistance: An Analysis of European Resistance to Nazism 1940-1945, 1976; Six Faces of Courage, 1978, rev. ed. as Six Faces of Courage: Secret Agents Against Nazi Tyranny, 2003; (with J.M. Langley) MI9: Escape and Evasion, 1939-1945, 1979; SOE: An Outline History Of the Special Operations Executive, 1940-46, 1985, new ed., 1999; Art and War: Twentieth Century Warfare as Depicted by War Artists, 1990; SOE in the Low Countries, 2001; Memories of an S.O.E. Historian, 2008; (foreword) Report on Experience, 2010. EDITOR: Gladstone Diaries, vol. I-II: 1825-1839, 1968, (with H.C.G. Matthew) vol. III-IV: 1840-1855, 1975; War and Society; Historical Essays in Honour and Memory of J.R. Western, 1928-1971, 1973; Holland at War against Hitler: Anglo-Dutch Relations, 1940-1945, 1990; (with I.C.B. Dear) Oxford Companion to the Second World War, 1995; Oxford Companion to World War II, 1995; Secret Lives, 2002. **Address:** Martins Cottage, Nuthampstead, Royston, HF SG8 8ND, England.

FOOT, Mirjam M(ichaela). American/British/Dutch (born Netherlands), b. 1941. **Genres:** Art/Art History, Bibliography, Business/Trade/Industry. **Career:** British Library, curator of rare books, 1965-85, head of acquisitions and Western European collections, 1985-90, director of collections and preservation, 1990-99; University College London, professor of library and archive studies, 2000, now professor emeritus; Rare Book School, faculty. Writer. **Publications:** (Comp. with J. Backhouse and J. Barr) William Caxton: An Exhibition to Commemorate the Quincentenary of the Introduction of Printing into England: British Library Reference Division, 24 September 1976-31 January 1977, 1976; Collection of Book Bindings, 1979; The Henry Davis Gift: Studies in the History of Bookbinding, vol. I, 1978, vol. II, 1983; Pictorial Bookbindings, 1986; (with H. Nixon) The History of Decorative Bookbinding in England, rev. ed., 1992; Studies in the History of Bookbinding, 1993; The History of Bookbinding as a Mirror of Society, 1998; (ed.) For the Love of Bookbinding: Studies in Bookbinding History Presented to Mirjam Foot, 2000; Eloquent Witnesses: Bookbindings and their History, 2004; Decorated Bindings in Marsh's Library, Dublin, 2004; Bookbinders at Work: Their Roles and Methods, 2006. Contributor to journals. **Address:** Rare Book School, Alderman Library, 160 McCormick Rd., Charlottesville, VA 22904-4103, U.S.A. **Online address:** m.foot@ucl.ac.uk

FOOT, M. R. D. See **FOOT, Michael Richard Daniell.**

FOOTE, David. American (born United States), b. 1960?. **Genres:** History, Theology/Religion, Social Sciences. **Career:** University of California, lecturer, 1998-2000; Mississippi State University, assistant professor, 2000-04; University of St. Thomas, Department of History, assistant professor, 2005-, associate professor. Historian and writer. **Publications:** Lordship, Reform and the Development of Civil Society in Medieval Italy: The Bishopric of Orvieto, 1100-1250, 2004. Contributor to periodicals. **Address:** Department of History, University of St. Thomas, Mail JRC 432, 2115 Summit Ave., Saint Paul, MN 55105-1078, U.S.A. **Online address:** dnfoote@stthomas.edu

FOOTITT, Hilary. British (born England), b. 1948. **Genres:** History, Politics/Government, Women's Studies And Issues. **Career:** Cambridgeshire College of Arts and Technology, lecturer in French studies, 1972-89, head of languages, 1988-89; University of Westminster, head of languages, 1990-; University of Reading, Department of Modern Languages and European Studies, professor, senior research fellow, project supervisor. Writer. **Publications:** (With J. Simmonds) France, 1943-1945, 1988; Women, Europe and the New Languages of Politics, 2002; War and Liberation in France: Living with

the Liberators, 2004; France: The Long Liberation, 2007; Europe Re-written: New Perspectives on the Social Reconstruction of Britain, France and Germany After 1945, 2007. **Address:** University of Reading, Rm. 222, HumSS Bldg., PO Box 217, Whiteknights, BR RG6 6AH, United Kingdom. **Online address:** h.a.foot@reading.ac.uk

FORAN, John. American (born United States), b. 1955. **Genres:** Adult Nonfiction, Social Commentary, Politics/Government. **Career:** University of California, Program in Latin American and Iberian Studies, director, 1995-99, professor of sociology, 1988-, Department of Sociology, vice chair, 2002-03, director of undergraduate studies, 2003-06; Smith College, visiting professor of sociology and Latin American studies, 2000-02; University of London, visiting professor of sociology, 2009-10. Writer. **Publications:** Fragile Resistance: Social Transformation in Iran from 1500 to the Revolution, 1993; (ed.) A Century of Revolution: Social Movements in Iran, 1994; (ed.) Theorizing Revolutions, 1997; (ed. with K.K. Bhavnani and P.A. Kurian) Feminist Futures: Re-Imagining Women, Culture and Development, 2003; (ed.) The Future of Revolutions: Rethinking Radical Change in the Age of Globalization, 2003; Taking Power: On the Origins of Third World Revolutions, 2005; (ed. with D. Lane and A. Zivkovic) Revolution in the Making of the Modern World: Social Identities, Globalization and Modernity, 2007. Contributor to various journals. **Address:** Department of Sociology, University of California, 102 San Roque Rd., Santa Barbara, CA 93105, U.S.A. **Online address:** foran@soc.ucsb.edu

FORBES, Anna. (Anna Shipley Forbes). American (born United States), b. 1954. **Genres:** Medicine/Health, Children's Fiction. **Career:** Planned Parenthood of Southeastern Pennsylvania, family planning counselor, 1978-81, public affairs coordinator, 1981-82; National Abortion Rights Action League, regional coordinator, 1981-83; American Civil Liberties Union of Pennsylvania, development associate, 1983-85; Philadelphia AIDS Task Force, support services coordinator, 1985-86; Action AIDS, co-founder, 1986, director of community relations, 1988-90; Philadelphia Department of Public Health, public information and policy consultant in AIDS Activities Coordinating Office, 1990-94; Pennsylvania State HIV Planning Council, Regional delegate, 1991-96; independent consultant on AIDS and women's health policy, 1994-; Encampment for Citizenship, director, 1997-. Writer. **Publications:** What Is AIDS?, 1996; Where Did AIDS Come From?, 1996; Living in a World with AIDS, 1996; Myths and Facts about AIDS, 1996; What You Can Do about AIDS, 1996; Kids with AIDS, 1996; Heroes against AIDS, 1996; When Someone You Know Has AIDS, 1996. Contributor to magazines. **Address:** 2430 Avon Rd., Ardmore, PA 19003, U.S.A. **Online address:** aforbes@critpath.org

FORBES, Anna Shipley. See **FORBES, Anna.**

FORBES, Bruce David. American (born United States), b. 1948. **Genres:** History. **Career:** Morningside College, professor, 1978-, Department of Religious Studies, chair; Augsburg College, Weekend College, adjunct professor; United Methodist Church, ordained minister. Writer. **Publications:** (Ed. with J.H. Mahan) Religion and Popular Culture in America, 2000; Rapture, Revelation, and the End Times: Exploring the Left Behind Series, 2004; Christmas: A Candid History, 2007. **Address:** Minneapolis, MN , U.S.A. **Online address:** forbes@morningside.edu

FORBES, Camille F. American (born United States) **Genres:** Novellas/Short Stories, Biography, Autobiography/Memoirs, Cultural/Ethnic Topics. **Career:** University of California, Department of Literature, African American Literature and Culture, assistant professor. Writer and historian. **Publications:** Introducing Bert Williams: Burnt Cork, Broadway, and the Story of America's First Black Star, 2008. Contributor to journals. **Address:** University of California, Department of Literature, 9500 Gilman Dr., PO Box 0410, La Jolla, CA 92093, U.S.A. **Online address:** camille@camillefforbes.com

FORCE, Marie Sullivan. American (born United States), b. 1966?. **Genres:** Novels, Romance/Historical. **Career:** Writer. **Publications:** Line of Scrimmage (novel), 2008; Same Time Sunday (novel), 2009; Love at First Flight: One Round Trip that Would Change Everything, 2009. **Address:** Sourcebooks, Inc., 1935 Brookdale Rd., Ste. 139, Naperville, IL 60563, U.S.A. **Online address:** mforce@cox.net

FORCHÉ, Carolyn (Louise). American (born United States), b. 1950. **Genres:** Poetry. **Career:** Michigan State University, visiting lecturer in poetry, 1974; San Diego State University, visiting lecturer, 1975, assistant professor, 1976-78; University of Virginia, journalist and human rights, 1978-80; visiting lecturer, 1979, visiting associate professor, 1982-83; University of Arkansas, assistant professor, 1980, associate professor, 1981; New York University, visiting writer, 1983, 1985; Vassar College, visiting writer, 1984, Columbia University, 1984-85; State University of New York, writer-in-residence, 1985; University of Minnesota, visiting associate professor, 1985; Georgetown University, Department of English, associate professor, 1994-, professor, Lannan visiting professor of poetry, Lannan Foundation endowed chair in poetry. **Publications:** (With M.J. Soltlow and M. Massre) Women in American Labor History, 1825-1935, 1972; Gathering the Tribes, 1976; Undisclosed No. 24, 1977; (with P. Wheaton) History and Motivations of U.S Involvement in the Control of the Peasant Movement in El Salvador: The Role of AIFLD in the Agrarian Reform Process, 1970-1980, 1980; (ed.) Women and War in El Salvador, 1980; The Country Between Us, 1981; (trans.) Flowers from the Volcano, 1982; The Colonel, 1982; El Salvador: Work of Thirty Photographers, 1983; (trans with W. Kulik) The Selected Poems of Robert Desnos, 1991; (ed. and intro.) Against Forgetting: Twentieth-Century Poetry of Witness, 1993; The Angel of History, 1994; Colors Come from God-Just Like Me!, 1995; (with R. Carvajal and S. Horne) Lani Maestro, 1996; (trans.) Saudade/Sorrow, 1999; (ed. with P. Gerard) Writing Creative Nonfiction: Instruction and Insights from Teachers of the Associated Writing Programs, 2001; (trans. and ed. with M. Akash) Unfortunately, It was Paradise: Selected Poems, 2003; Blue Hour, 2003; (ed. with J. Reidel) Arrival, 2009; The Horse on Our Balcony, 2010; A Book of Essays, forthcoming; In the Lateness of the World, forthcoming. **Address:** Department of English, George Mason University, 404 New N 4400 University Dr., PO Box 3E4, Fairfax, VA 22030-4444, U.S.A. **Online address:** clf39@georgetown.edu

FORD, Barbara. American (born United States), b. 1934?. **Genres:** Children's Fiction, Animals/Pets, Food And Wine, Medicine/Health, History. **Career:** Freelance writer, 1970-; Institute of Children's Literature, instructor, 1988-; American Museum of Natural History, writer. **Publications:** FOR CHILDREN: Can Invertebrates Learn?, 1972; How Birds Learn to Sing, 1975; Katydids: The Singing Insects, 1976; Animals That Use Tools, 1978; (with R.R. Keiper) The Island Ponies: An Environmental Study of Their Life on Assateague, 1979; Why Does a Turtle Live Longer Than a Dog? A Report on Animal Longevity, 1980; Black Bear: The Spirit of the Wilderness, 1981; Alligators, Raccoons and Other Survivors: The Wildlife of the Future, 1981; The Elevator, 1982; (with D.C. Switzer) Underwater Dig: The Excavation of a Revolutionary War Privateer, 1982; Keeping Things Cool: The Story of Refrigeration and Air Conditioning, 1986; Wildlife Rescue, 1987; The Automobile, 1987; St. Louis, 1989; Walt Disney: A Biography, 1989; The Eagles' Child, 1990; Howard Carter: Searching for King Tut, 1995; Most Wonderful Movie in the World, 1996; The Creature in Crestwood Park, 1996; Paul Revere: Rider for the Revolution, 1997. ADULT: Future Food: Alternate Protein for the Year 2000, 1978. **Address:** Pleasant Valley Rd., Mendham, NJ 07945, U.S.A.

FORD, Brian John. British (born England), b. 1939. **Genres:** Biology, Physics, Sciences, Sex, Adult Non-fiction, Anthropology/Ethnology, Environmental Sciences/Ecology, Biography, Biography. **Career:** Medical Research Council of Wales, junior research assistant, 1958-59; research scientist, writer, television host, research biologist and broadcaster, 1961-; British Broadcasting Corp., radio science broadcaster, 1962-, Where Are You Taking Us Television Program, chairperson, 1974, Science Now Weekly Program, founder and presenter, 1975-76, Computer Challenge Game Show, host, 1986-87; Newport College of Art and Design, lecturer in science and art, 1965-66; Independent Television, science broadcaster, 1966-; Foreign and Commonwealth Office, British Council Division, visiting lecturer, 1978, 2007; Channel 4 Television, Food for Thought Program, presenter, 1984-85; Cardiff University, fellow; Open University, royal literary fellow, 1999-2002; University of Leicester, visiting professor, 2006-09; University of Cambridge, Gonville and Caius College, associate, 2007-. **Publications:** German Secret Weapons: Blueprint for Mars, 1969; Microbiology and Food, 1970; Allied Secret Weapons, the War of Science, 1971; Nonscience or How to Rule the World (satire), 1971; The Optical Microscope Manual: Past and Present Uses and Techniques, 1973; Earth Watchers, 1973; Revealing Lens: Mankind and the Microscope, 1973; Microbe Power: Tomorrow's Revolution, 1976; Patterns of Sex: The Mating Urge and Our Sexual Future, 1980; Cult of the Expert (satire), 1982; 101 Questions about Science, 1983; 101 More Questions about Science, 1984; Single Lens, the Story of the Simple Microscope, 1984; Compute!: How? Where? Why? Do you Really Need To?, 1985; The Food

Book, 1986; The Human Body, 1990; Leeuwenhoek Legacy, 1990; Images of Science: A History of Scientific Illustration, 1993; The First Encyclopedia of Science, 1993; New Quiz Book, 1994; BSE The Facts, 1996; Sensitive Souls: Senses and Communication in Plants, Animals and Microbes, 1999, new ed., 2002; Genes: The Fight for Life, 1999; The Secret Language of Life, 2000; The Future of Food, 2000; Czujace Istoty, zmysly i emocje roslin, zwierzat i mikroorganizmow, 2000; Morgen nur noch Junk Food?, 2001; Nel piatto, salute, sicurezza e futuro del cibo, 2001; Defnuddio'r Microsgop Digidol, 2002; Using the Digital Microscope, 2003; El futuro de los alimentos, Perspectivas de futuro, 2003; Maisto ateitis, 2004; Secret Weapons, Technology, Science and the Race to win WWII, 2011; Meat, the Secret Story of our Greatest Addiction, 2012. EDITOR: Science Diary, 1967, 13th ed., 1979; Walking in Britain, 1988; Institute of Biology: The First 50 Years, 2000; GM Crops: The Scientists Speak, 2002; The Second Mouse Gets the Cheese, Proverbs and Their Uses, 2005; A History of the The King's School, Peterborough, 2005. CO-AUTHOR: The Recovery, Removal and Reconstruction of Human Skeletal Remains, 1970; History of English-Speaking Peoples, 1971; The Cardiff Book, 1973; Viral Pollution of the Environment, 1983; Sex and Your Health, 1985; Yours Truly: True Life Stories from the Good and the Great, 1990; (with J. Brown and R. Brown) Our Bodies, 1990. **Address:** University of Leicester, University Rd., Leicester, LE LE1 7RH, England. **Online address:** mail@brianjford.com

FORD, Carolyn (Mott). American (born United States), b. 1938. **Genres:** Children's Fiction, Poetry, Picture/Board Books, Literary Criticism And History. **Career:** Writer. **Publications:** Nothing in the Mailbox, 1996. Works appear in anthologies. Contributor of articles to periodicals. **Address:** 548 Ocean Blvd., Ste. 20, Long Branch, NJ 07740, U.S.A.

FORD, Darnella D. American (born United States), b. 1967?. **Genres:** Novels. **Career:** Sun City, newspaper intern, 1983-88; Young Mentors Program, founder, 2003. Writer and spoken-word artist. **Publications:** NOVELS: Rising, 2003; Crave, 2004; Choke, 2006; Naked Love, 2007; Finding Me, 2009. **Address:** Andrew Stuart Agency, 260 W 52nd St., Ste. 24C, New York, NY 10010, U.S.A. **Online address:** info@darnella.com

FORD, Glyn. British (born England), b. 1950. **Genres:** Technology, Sciences. **Career:** Manchester University, Department of Science and Technology Policy, senior research fellow, 1974-84; University of Tokyo, visiting professor, 1983; Tameside Local Council, local councilor, 1979-85; European Parliament, Globalisation Intergroup, secretary, Sports Intergroup, vice president; European Parliament Labour Party, leader, 1989-93. Writer. **Publications:** (With C. Niblett and L. Walker) The Future for Ocean Technology, 1987; Report Drawn Up on Behalf of the Committee of Inquiry into Racism and Xenophobia on the Findings of the Committee of Inquiry, 1991; Fascist Europe: The Rise of Racism and Xenophobia, 1992; (co-author) Changing States: A Labour for Europe, 1996; Making European Progress, 2002; (with S. Kwon) North Korea on the Brink: Struggle for Survival, 2008; (with T. Yun) Pyŏrang kkŭt e sŏn Pukhan, 2009. **Address:** Pluto Press, 345 Archway Rd., London, GL N6 5AA, England. **Online address:** mep@glynford.eu

FORD, G. M. American (born United States), b. 1945. **Genres:** Mystery/Crime/Suspense, Novels, Ghost Writer, Young Adult Fiction. **Career:** Rogue Community College, instructor, 1972-85; City University, communications instructor, 1986-92. Writer. **Publications:** LEO WATERMAN MYSTERY SERIES: Who in Hell Is Wanda Fuca?: A Leo Waterman Mystery, 1995; Cast in Stone: A Leo Waterman Mystery, 1996; The Bums Rush: A Leo Waterman Mystery, 1997; Slow Burn: A Leo Waterman Mystery, 1998; The Last Ditch, 1999; The Deader the Better: A Leo Waterman Mystery, 2000. FRANK CORSO MYSTERY SERIES: Fury, 2001; Black River, 2002; A Blind Eye, 2003; Red Tide, 2004; No Mans Land, 2005; Blown Away, 2006. OTHER: The Nameless Night in UK as Identity, 2008. **Address:** c/o Author Mail, HarperCollins Publishers, 10 E 53rd St., New York, NY 10022, U.S.A. **Online address:** jxxf@eskimo.com

FORD, Herbert (Paul). American (born United States), b. 1927. **Genres:** History, Biography. **Career:** Seventh-Day Adventist Church, director of mass communications of western headquarters, 1954-63; The Voice of Prophecy, public relations director and editor, 1969-74; Pacific Union College, professor of journalism, 1974-81, 1982-89, professor emeritus of journalism, 1989-; Adventist Health/West, director of corporate communications, 1981-82; Pitcairn Islands Study Center, director, 1989-. **Publications:** Wind High, Sand Deep, 1965; Flee the Captor, 1966; No Guns on Their Shoulders, 1968;

Crimson Coats and Kimonos: The Story of the Japanese Choral Arts Society, 1968; Affair of the Heart, 1970; Rudo: The Reckless Russian, 1970; Man Alive, 1971; For the Love of China, 1971; Pitcairn, 1972; The Miscellany of Pitcairn's Island, 1980; Island of Tears: John I. Tay and the Story of Pitcairn, 1989; Pitcairn: Port of Call, 1996; Pitcairn Island as a Port of Call, 2011. **Address:** Pacific Union College, Pitcairn Islands Study Ctr., 1 Angwin Ave., Angwin, CA 94508, U.S.A. **Online address:** hford@puc.edu

FORD, Jamie Mark. American (born United States), b. 1968. **Genres:** Novels. **Career:** Writer and advertising art director. **Publications:** Hotel on the Corner of Bitter and Sweet: A Novel, 2009. Contributor to books, journals and periodicals. **Address:** c/o Kristin Nelson, Nelson Literary Agency, 1732 Wazee St., Ste. 207, Denver, CO 80202, U.S.A.

FORD, Jennifer. American (born United States) **Genres:** Literary Criticism And History, Young Adult Fiction. **Career:** Writer. **Publications:** Coleridge on Dreaming: Romanticism, Dreams and the Medical Imagination, 1998. Contributor to books and periodicals. **Address:** c/o Author Mail, Cambridge University Press, Edinburgh Bldg., Shaftesbury Rd., Cambridge, CB CB2 2RU, England.

FORD, Jerome W. See **FORD, Jerry.**

FORD, Jerry. (Jerome W. Ford). American (born United States), b. 1949. **Genres:** Recreation, Children's Fiction. **Career:** Scottsdale Progress, sports reporter, 1971-77; Arizona Daily Sun, sports reporter, 1977-79; Logan Herald and Journal, entertainment/news reporter, 1979-84; Decatur Herald Review, news editor, 1984-88; Holland Sentinel, managing editor, 1988-90. **Publications:** The Grand Slam Collection: Have Fun Collecting Baseball Cards, 1992. **Address:** c/o Jerry Ford, Lerner Publications Co., 1251 Washington Ave. N., Minneapolis, MN 55401-1036, U.S.A.

FORD, John C. American (born United States), b. 1971?. **Genres:** Young Adult Fiction. **Career:** Author and attorney. **Publications:** The Morgue and Me, 2009. **Address:** c/o Sara Crowe, Harvey Klinger Inc., 300 W 55th St., Ste. 11V, New York, NY 10019, U.S.A. **Online address:** john@johncfordbooks.com

FORD, Katie. American (born United States), b. 1975. **Genres:** Poetry. **Career:** Coffey Communications, writing intern and editorial aide, 1997-98, staff writer and medical journalist, 1998; Harvard Vanguard Medical Associates, research assistant, 1998-99; University of Iowa, instructor in writing, 2002; Kirkwood Community College, adjunct faculty, 2002; New Orleans Review, poetry editor, 2005-09, contributing editor; Loyola University, assistant professor of creative writing, 2003-; Reed College, faculty; Franklin & Marshall College, assistant professor of English. **Publications:** Deposition, 2002; Storm, 2006; Colosseum: Poems, 2008. **Address:** Department of English, Franklin & Marshall College, 308A KEI, 415 Harrisburg Ave., PO Box 3003, Lancaster, PA 17604-3003, U.S.A. **Online address:** katie.ford@fandm.edu

FORD, Kirk. See **SPENCE, William John Duncan.**

FORD, Marjorie Leet. American (born United States), b. 1947?. **Genres:** Novels. **Career:** Writer and producer. **Publications:** (With L. Hinrichs and N. Zurek) Cactus: A Prickly Portrait of a Desert Eccentric, 1995; Do Try To Speak As We Do: The Diary of an American Au Pair (novel), 2001 in UK as The Diary of an American Au Pair, 2001; People in the Park, 2003. Contributor to periodicals. **Address:** c/o Author Mail, St. Martin's Press, 175 5th Ave., New York, NY 10010-7703, U.S.A. **Online address:** leetford@ricochet.net

FORD, Melissa Mathison. See **MATHISON, Melissa.**

FORD, Michael Curtis. American (born United States), b. 1960?. **Genres:** Novels, Young Adult Fiction, History, Romance/Historical. **Career:** Author, translator, consultant and musician. **Publications:** NOVELS: The Ten Thousand: A Novel of Ancient Greece, 2001; Gods and Legions, 2002; The Last King: Rome's Greatest Enemy, 2004; The Sword of Attila: A Novel of the Last Years of Rome, 2005; The Fall of Rome: A Novel of a World Lost, 2007. Contributor to periodicals. **Address:** c/o Author Mail, St. Martin's Press, 175 5th Ave., New York, NY 10010, U.S.A. **Online address:** michaelford@michaelcurtisford.com

FORD, Michael Thomas. American (born United States), b. 1968?. **Genres:** Novels, Adult Non-fiction, Gay And Lesbian Issues, Young Adult Fiction. **Career:** Novelist and columnist. **Publications:** NONFICTION: One Hundred Questions and Answers about AIDS: A Guide for Young People, 1992; The Voices of AIDS: Twelve Unforgettable People Talk about How AIDS Has Changed Their Lives, 1995; The World out There: Becoming Part of the Lesbian and Gay Community, 1996; Outspoken: Role Models from the Lesbian and Gay Community, 1998; Alec Baldwin Doesn't Love Me and Other Trials of My Queer Life, 1998; That's Mr. Faggot to You: Further Trials from My Queer Life, 1999; Paths of Faith: Conversations about Religion and Spirituality, 2000; It's Not Mean If It's True: More Trials from My Queer Life, 2000; The Little Book of Neuroses: Ongoing Trials from My Queer Life, 2001; Looking for It, 2004; Ultimate Gay Sex, 2004; Path of the Green Man: Gay Men, Wicca and Living a Magical Life, 2005; Full Circle, 2005; Tangled Sheets: Tales of Erotica, 2005; Suicide Notes, 2008. FICTION: The Dollhouse That Time Forgot, 1998; (co-author) Masters of Midnight, 2003; Last Summer, 2003; My Big Fat Queer Life: The Best of Michael Thomas Ford, 2003; (co-author) Midnight Thirsts, 2004; Changing Tides, 2007; What We Remember, 2009; The Road Home, 2010; Jane Bites Back: A Novel, 2010; Z, 2010; Jane Goes Batty, 2011. **Address:** Mitchell Waters, Curtis Brown Ltd., 10 Astor Pl., New York, NY 10003, U.S.A. **Online address:** mike@michaelthomasford.com

FORD, Richard Thompson. American (born United States), b. 1966?. **Genres:** Law. **Career:** City of Cambridge, housing policy consultant, 1990-91; Stanford Law School, associate professor, 1994-99, professor of law, 1999-, Justin M. Roach, faculty scholar, 2003-04, George E. Osborne professor of law, 2004-; Morrison & Foerster, litigation associate; Harvard Law School, Reginald Lewis Fellow; Housing Authority of the City and County of San Francisco, commissioner, 199798; Columbia Law School, visiting professor of law, 2000. Writer and law educator. **Publications:** (ed. with N. Blomley and D. Delaney) The Legal Geographies Reader: Law, Power and Space, 2001; (with G.E. Frug and D.J. Barron) Local Government Law, 2001; Racial Culture: A Critique, 2005; The Race Card: How Bluffing about Bias Makes Race Relations Worse, 2008. Contributor to periodicals. **Address:** Stanford Law School, Crown Quadrangle, 559 Nathan Abbott Way, Stanford, CA 94305-8610, U.S.A. **Online address:** rford@stanford.edu

FORD, Susan. American (born United States), b. 1957. **Genres:** Mystery/Crime/Suspense, Novels, Young Adult Fiction. **Career:** Associated Press, photojournalist; Newsweek, photojournalist; Money Magazine, photojournalist; Ladies Home Journal, photojournalist; Topeka Capital-Journal, photojournalist; The Omaha Sun, photojournalist; Betty Ford Center, director, 1992-, chairman, 2005. Photographer and writer. **Publications:** (With L. Hayden) Double Exposure: A First Daughter Mystery, 2002; (with L. Hayden) Sharp Focus: A First Daughter Mystery, 2003. Contributor to magazines. **Address:** c/o Author Mail, Thomas Dunne Books, Saint Martin Press, 175 5th Ave., New York, NY 10010, U.S.A.

FORDE, Catherine. Scottish/British (born England), b. 1961?. **Genres:** Children's Fiction, Novels. **Career:** Collins (publisher), lexicographer. Writer. **Publications:** NOVELS: Think Me Back, 2001; The Finding, 2002; Fat Boy Swim, 2003; Exit Oz, 2004; Skarrs, 2004; The Drowning Pond, 2005; I See You Baby, 2005; L-L-L-Loser, 2006; Firestarter, 2006; Tug of War, 2007; Sugarcoated, 2008; Dead Men Don't Talk, 2009; Bad Wedding, 2009; Fifteen Minute Bob, 2010; Empty, 2010; Let's Do It!, 2011; Slippy, 2012. **Address:** c/o Author Mail, Egmont Books, 239 High St., Kensington, GL W8 6SA, England. **Online address:** info@catherineforde.co.uk

FORDER, Anthony. British (born England), b. 1925?. **Genres:** Public/Social Administration, Social Work, Adult Non-fiction. **Career:** London Probation Service, probation officer, 1953-59; London School of Economics, lecturer, 1959-63; Oppenheimer College of Social Service, senior lecturer; University of Zambia, senior lecturer, 1963-66; Liverpool University, lecturer in social administration, 1966-70; Millbank College of Commerce, Department of Applied Social Studies, head, 1971-72; Liverpool Polytechnic, principal lecturer, 1972-76, Department of Social Work, head, 1976-84. Writer. **Publications:** Social Casework and Administration, 1966, 2nd ed., 1968; (ed.) Penelope Hall's Social Services of England and Wales, 1969, (ed. with J. Mays and O. Keidan) 10th ed., 1983; Concepts in Social Administration: A Framework for Analysis, 1974; (co-author) Theories of Welfare, 1984; (ed.) Working with Parents of Handicapped Children, 1985. **Address:** 26 Eric Rd., Wallasey, MS CH44 5RQ, England.

FOREMAN, Amanda. American/British (born England), b. 1968?. **Genres:** Biography, Social Sciences, History. **Career:** Lady Margaret Hall, researcher, 1991-. Writer. **Publications:** (Foreword) Gender in Eighteenth Century England, 1997; Georgiana, Duchess of Devonshire (biography), 1998; Georgiana's World, 2001; (foreword) The Sylph, 2001; (foreword) Madame de Pompadour, 2001; (foreword) What Might Have Been, 2005; (foreword) George IV, 2007; The Duchess, 2008; Our American Cousins, 2009; A World on Fire: An Epic History of Two Nations Divided, 2010; A World on Fire: Britian's Crucial Role in the American Civil War, 2011. Contributor of articles to newspapers. **Address:** The Wylie Agency, 250 W 57th, Ste. 2114, New York, NY 10107, U.S.A.

FOREMAN, George. American (born United States), b. 1949. **Genres:** Autobiography/Memoirs, inspirational/Motivational Literature, Adult Non-fiction, Food And Wine, Business/Trade/Industry. **Career:** George Foreman Youth and Community Center, founder, 1984. Writer. **Publications:** (With J. Engel) By George: The Autobiography of George Foreman, 1995; (C. Calbom) George Foreman's Knock-out-the-Fat Barbeque and Grilling Cookbook, 1996; (with C. Merydith) George Foreman's Big George Rotisserie Cookbook, 1999; (with B. Witt) George Foreman's Big Book of Grilling, Barbecue and Rotisserie: More than Seventy-five Recipes for Family and Friends, 2000; (foreword) And the Fans Roared: The Sports Broadcasts That Kept Us on the Edge of Our Seats, 2000; (with C. Merydith) The George Foreman Lean Mean Fat-reducing Grilling Machine Cookbook, 2000; (with L. Kulman) George Foreman's Guide to Life: How to Get up off the Canvas When Life Knocks You Down, 2002; The George Foreman Lean Mean Contact Roasting Machine Recipe Book, 2002; 50 Great George Foreman Recipes!: Lean mean Fat Reducing Grilling Machine, 2003; (with C. Merydith) The Next Grilleration: Great Grilling Recipes, 2004; (with K. Kellinger) George Foreman's Indoor Grilling Made Easy, 2004; The George Foreman Next Grilleration G5 Cookbook: Inviting & Delicious Recipes for Grilling, Baking, Waffles, Sandwiches & More!, 2005; (with F. Manushkin) Let George Do It!, 2005; (with K. Abraham) God in My Corner, 2007; (with J. Lund) Going the Extra Smile: Discovering the Life-Changing Power of a Positive Outlook, 2007; (with M. Davis) Fatherhood By George: Hard-Won Advice on Being a Dad, 2008; (with K. Abraham) Knockout Entrepreneur: A Champion's Secrets to Success, Happiness and Significance, 2009. **Address:** c/o Author Mail, Simon & Schuster, 1230 Ave. of the Americas, New York, NY 10020, U.S.A. **Online address:** george@biggeorge.com

FOREMAN, Lelia M. *See* **FOREMAN, Lelia Rose.**

FOREMAN, Lelia Rose. (Lelia M. Foreman). American (born United States), b. 1952. **Genres:** Science Fiction/Fantasy. **Career:** Children's Orthopedic Hospital, medical technician, 1974. **Publications:** Shatterworld, 1995. Work represented in anthologies. **Address:** 7318 Michigan St., Vancouver, WA 98664-1324, U.S.A.

FOREMAN, Michael. British (born England), b. 1938. **Genres:** Children's Fiction, Young Adult Fiction, Illustrations, Novellas/Short Stories. **Career:** Ambit, art director, 1960-; St. Martin's School of Art, lecturer, 1963-66; Playboy Magazine, art director, 1965; King Magazine, art director, 1966-67; London College of Printing, lecturer, 1966-68; Royal College of Art, lecturer, 1967-70; Central School of Art, lecturer, 1971-72; London School of Printing, lecturer. Writer. **Publications:** (With J. Charters) The General, 1961; The Perfect Present, 1967; The Two Giants, 1967; The Great Sleigh Robbery, 1968; Horatio, 1970; Moose, 1971; Dinosaurs and All That Rubbish, 1972; War and Peas, 1974; Private Zoo, 1975; All the King's Horses, 1976; Panda's Puzzle, and His Voyage of Discovery, 1977; Winter's Tales, 1979; Trick a Tracker, 1981; Panda and the Odd Lion, 1981; Land of Dreams, 1982; Panda and the Bunyips, 1984; Cat and Canary, 1984; Panda and the Bushfire, 1986; Ben's Baby, 1987; (with D. Pelham) Worms Wiggle, 1988; The Angel and the Wild Animal, 1988; One World, 1989; War Boy: A Country Childhood, 1989; (ed.) Michael Foreman's World of Fairy Tales, 1990; (ed.) Mother Goose, 1991; Jack's Fantastic Voyage, 1992; (with R. Seaver) The Boy Who Sailed with Columbus, 1992; War Game, 1993; Grandfather's Pencil and the Room of Stories, 1993; After the War was Over, 1995; Look! Look!, 1997; Angel and the Box of Time, 1997; Jack's Big Race, 1998; Chicken Licken, 1998; Panda, 1999; Little Red Hen, 1999; Rock-a-Doodle-Do, 2000; Michael Foreman's Christmas Treasury, 2000; Memories of Childhood, 2000; Cat in the Manger, 2000; Saving Sinbad!, 2002; (ed.) Michael Foreman's Playtime Rhymes, 2002; Wonder Goal!, 2002; Trip to Dinosaur Time, 2003; Hello, World, 2003; Cat on the Hill, 2003; (reteller) Classic Fairy Tales, 2005; Can't Catch Me!,

2005; Mida's Story: A Sketchbook of Hopes and Dreams, 2006; Norman's Ark, 2006; Mia's Story: A Sketchbook of Hopes and Dreams, 2006; Fox Tale, 2006; The Littlest Dinosaur, 2008; (with J. Foreman) Say Hello, 2008; A Child's Garden: A Story of Hope, 2009; The Littlest Dinosaur's Big Adventure, 2009; Fortunately, Unfortunately, 2011. SELF-ILLUSTRATED: Ben's Box: A Pop-up Fantasy, 1986; Dad! I Can't Sleep, 1994; Surprise! Surprise!, 1995; Seal Surfer, 1996; The Little Reindeer, 1996; Friends, 2012. Illustrator of books by others. **Address:** Andersen Press USA, 1251 Washington Ave. N, Minneapolis, MN 55401, U.S.A.

FOREMAN, Richard. American (born United States), b. 1937. **Genres:** Plays/Screenplays, Novels, Young Adult Fiction. **Career:** Ontological-Hysteric Theater (nonprofit institution), founder and artistic director, 1968-; artistic director, 1973-85; Order of Arts and Letters of France, officer, 2004. Writer. **Publications:** Plays and Manifestos, 1976; Reverberation Machines: The Later Plays and Essays, 1985; Love & Science: Selected Music-Theatre Texts, 1991; Unbalancing Acts: Foundations for a Theater, 1992; My Head Was a Sledgehammer: Six Plays, 1995; (contrib.) The Theatre of Images, 1996; No-Body (novel), 1997; Paradise Hotel and Other Plays, 2001; Bad Boy Nietzsche! and Other Plays, 2005; (contrib.) Life of Galileo, 2008. **Address:** 152 Wooster St., New York, NY 10012-5330, U.S.A.

FOREST, Jim. Dutch/American (born United States), b. 1941. **Genres:** Children's Fiction, Biography. **Career:** The Catholic Worker, managing editor; U.S. Weather Bureau, staff, 1960; The Staten Island Advance, reporter, 1964; Reconciliation Intl., editor, Fellowship Magazine (magazine of Fellowship of Reconciliation), editor, Fellowship of Reconciliation, publication director, 1973; International Fellowship of Reconciliation, head staff, 1977, general secretary, 1977-88; New York Theological Seminary, faculty; College of New Rochelle, faculty; Ecumenical Institute, faculty, 1985; Orthodox Peace Fellowship, international secretary, In Communion, editor; Peace Media Service, editor. **Publications:** (Ed. with T.C. Cornell) A Penny a Copy: Readings from the Catholic Worker, 1968; Thomas Merton, A Pictorial Biography, 1980; Units in Woodworking, 1981; Thomas Merton's Struggle with Peacemaking, 1986; Love is the Measure: A Biography of Dorothy Day, 1986, rev. ed., 1994; Making Friends of Enemies: Reflections on the Teachings of Jesus in UK as Making Enemies Friends, 1987; Pilgrim to the Russian Church: An American Journalist Encounters a Vibrant Religious Faith in the Soviet Union in UK as Finding God Among the Russians, 1988; (with N. Forest) Four Days in February: The Story of the Nonviolent Overthrow of the Marcos Regime, 1988; The Tale of the Turnip, 1989; Religion in the New Russia: The Impact of Perestroika on Soviet Religious Life in Soviet Union in UK as Free at Last?, 1990; Living With Wisdom: A Life of Thomas Merton, 1991, rev. ed., 2008; The Whale's Tale, 1992; Praying With Icons, 1997, rev. ed., 2008; The Ladder of the Beatitudes, 1999; Confession: Doorway to Forgiveness, 2002; (intro.) Mother Maria Skobtsova: Essential Writings, 2002; The Resurrection of the Church in Albania: Voices of Orthodox Christians, 2002; The Wormwood File: E-mail from Hell, 2004; Silent as a Stone: Mother Maria of Paris and the Trash Can Rescue, 2007; The Road to Emmaus: Pilgrimage as a Way of Life, 2007; All is Grace: A Biography of Dorothy Day, 2011; Saint George & the Dragon, 2011; (ed. with H. Bos) For the Peace from Above: An Orthodox Resource Book on War, Peace and Nationalism, 2011. **Address:** Peace Media Service, Kanisstraat 5, Alkmaar, 1811 GJ, Netherlands. **Online address:** jhforest@cs.com

FORKER, Charles R(ush). American (born United States), b. 1927. **Genres:** Plays/Screenplays, Poetry, Literary Criticism And History, Theatre, Bibliography. **Career:** Harvard University, teaching fellow, 1955-57; University of Wisconsin, instructor in English, 1957-59; Indiana University, instructor, 1959-61, assistant professor, 1961-65, associate professor, 1965-68, professor of English, 1968-92, professor emeritus, 1992-; University of Michigan, visiting professor, 1969-70; Dartmouth College, visiting professor, 1982-83; Concordia University, visiting professor, 1989. Writer. **Publications:** (With D.G. Calder) Edward Phillips's History of the Literature of England and Scotland: A Translation from the Compendiosa Enumeratio Poetarum with an Introduction and Commentary (monograph), 1973; (comp. with J. Candido) Henry V: An Annotated Bibliography, 1983; Skull beneath the Skin: The Achievement of John Webster, 1986; Fancy's Images: Contexts, Settings, and Perspectives in Shakespeare and His Contemporaries, 1990. EDITOR: The Cardinal, 1964; Henry V, 1971; Visions and Voices of the New Midwest, 1978; Edward the Second, 1994; Richard II: The Critical Tradition, 1998; Richard the Second, 2002; The Troublesome Reign of John, King of England, 2011. Contributor of articles to journals. **Address:** Department of English, Indiana University,

442 Ballantine Hall, 1020 E Kirkwood Ave., Bloomington, IN 47405-7103, U.S.A. **Online address:** forker@indiana.edu

FORMAN, Richard T. T. American (born United States), b. 1935. **Genres:** Environmental Sciences/Ecology, Sciences. **Career:** Escuela Agricola Panamericana, instructor, 1962-63; University of Wisconsin, assistant professor, 1963-66; Rutgers University, professor and director of Hutcheson memorial forest center, 1966-84; Centre National de la Recherche Scientifique, researcher, 1977-78; Harvard University, PAES professor of landscape ecology, 1984-; Cambridge University, Clare Hall, fellow; Institute of Applied Ecology, Academia Sinica, honorary professor; University of Melbourne, Miegunyah fellow; Australian National University, CRES Fellow; Inner Mongolia University, honorary professor. Writer. **Publications:** (Ed.) Pine Barrens: Ecosystem and Landscape, 1979; (with M. Godron) Landscape Ecology, 1986; (ed.) Changing Landscapes: An Ecological Perspective, 1990; Land Mosaics: The Ecology of Landscapes and Regions, 1995; (with W.E. Dramstad and J.D. Olson) Landscape Ecology Principles in Landscape Architecture and Land-Use Planning, 1996; (co-author) Road Ecology: Science and Solutions, 2003; Land Mosaic for the Greater Barcelona Region, 2004; Urban Regions: Ecology and Planning Beyond the City, 2008. Contributor to periodicals. **Address:** Graduate School of Design, Harvard University, 48 Quincy St., Cambridge, MA 02138, U.S.A. **Online address:** rforman@gsd.harvard.edu

FORMAN, Robert K. C. American (born United States), b. 1947. **Genres:** Theology/Religion. **Career:** Vassar College, faculty, 1987-89; City University of New York, Hunter College, assistant professor, associate professor of religious studies, 1989-; professor of comparative religions; The Forge Institute, founder and chief executive officer; Journal of Consciousness Studies, founder and executive editor. **Publications:** Meister Eckhart: Mystic as Theologian, 1992; Mysticism, Mind, Consciousness, 1999; (with C. Davison) Grassroots Spirituality: What It Is, Why It Is Here, Where It Is Going, 2004; Enlightenment Ain't What It's Cracked Up To Be: A Journey of Discovery, Snow and Jazz in the Soul, 2011. EDITOR: The Problem of Pure Consciousness, 1990; Religions of the World, 3rd ed., 1993; Religions of Asia, 1993; The Innate Capacity: Mysticism, Psychology, and Philosophy, 1998; (with J. Andresen) Cognitive Models and Spiritual Maps: Interdisciplinary Explorations of Religious Experience, 2002. **Address:** The Forge Institute, 383 Broadway, Hastings on Hudson, NY 10706, U.S.A. **Online address:** forman@theforge.org

FORMAN, Steven M. American (born United States), b. 1942?. **Genres:** Novels. **Career:** Forman Industries, founder and CEO, 1970-. Writer. **Publications:** Boca Knights (novel), 2009; Boca Mournings (novel), 2010; Boca Daze, 2011. Contributor to periodicals. **Address:** c/o Kyle Avery, 175 5th Ave., New York, NY 10010, U.S.A. **Online address:** steve@formanindustries.com

FORMENT, Carlos A. American (born United States) **Genres:** History. **Career:** New School for Social Research, associate professor of sociology; Centro de Investigacion y Documentacion de la Vida PUblica, director. Writer. **Publications:** Democracy in Latin America, 1760-1900: Volume 1, Civic Selfhood and Public Life in Mexico and Peru, 2003. **Address:** New School for Social Research, 65 5th Ave., New York, NY 10003, U.S.A. **Online address:** formentc@newschool.edu

FORNÉS, Maria Irene. American/Cuban (born Cuba), b. 1930. **Genres:** Plays/Screenplays, Young Adult Non-fiction, inspirational/Motivational Literature. **Career:** Playwright, 1960-; New York Theatre Strategy, co-founder, 1972; New York's Signature Theatre, artist-in-residence, 1999. Director and textile designer. **Publications:** The Office, 1965; The Successful Life of 3: A Skit for Vaudeville, 1966; Dr. Kheal, 1968; A Vietnamese Wedding, 1971; Fefu and Her Friends, 1978; Mud, 1983; The Conduct of Life, 1985; Cold Air, 1985; (co-author) Orchards: Stories, 1986; (contrib.) Lovers and Keepers, 1987; Promenade and Other Plays, 1987; And What of the Night, 1989; (co-author) Teatro: 5 Autores Cubanos, 1995; The Danube, 1998; Abingdon Square, 2000; Letters from Cuba and Other Plays, 2007; What of the Night?: Selected Plays, 2008. **Address:** c/o Morgan Jenness, Abrams Artists Agency, 275 7th Ave., 26th Fl., New York, NY 10001-6708, U.S.A.

FORNI, P(ier) M(assimo). American/Italian (born Italy), b. 1951. **Genres:** Literary Criticism And History, Poetry, Young Adult Fiction, Translations. **Career:** Istituto Gonzaga, instructor, 1976-78; University of California, Center for Medieval and Renaissance Studies, research assistant, 1980-81; lecturer in Italian, 1981-82; University of Pittsburgh, assistant professor of

Italian, 1983-85; Johns Hopkins University, assistant professor, 1985-90, associate professor, 1990-95, professor of Italian literature, 1995-, Johns Hopkins Civility Project, co-founder and co-director, 1997-. Writer. **Publications:** Stemmi: poesie, 1977; Grandi leggende cavalleresche, 1978; (trans.) P. Fisk, La Collina degli Agrifogli (translation of Midnight Blue), 1991; Forme Complesse nel Decameron, 1992; Adventures in Speech: Rhetoric and Narration in Boccaccio's Decameron, 1996; Hotel Pace dei Monti (poems), 1996; Choosing Civility: The Twenty-five Rules of Considerate Conduct, 2002; Civility Solution, 2008. EDITOR: (with G. Cavallini) Il Legame Musaico: Saggi di Letteratura Italiana, 1984; Ninfale Fiesolano, 1991; (co-ed.) Forma e Parola: Studi in Memoria di Fredi Chiappelli, 1992; I Fioretti di San Francesco, 1993; (with R. Bragantini) Lessico Critico Decameroniano, 1993. **Address:** Department of Romance Languages & Literatures, Johns Hopkins University, 422 Gilman, 3400 N Charles St., Baltimore, MD 21218, U.S.A. **Online address:** forni@jhu.edu

FORREST, Alan. (Alan I. Forrest). British (born England), b. 1945?. **Genres:** History, Military/Defense/Arms Control, Essays, Reference. **Career:** University of York, professor of modern history, Centre for Eighteenth Century Studies, director; International Commission on the History of the French Revolution, president. Writer. **Publications:** Society and Politics in Revolutionary Bordeaux, 1975; The French Revolution and the Poor, 1981; Conscripts and Deserters: The Army and French Society during the Revolution and Empire, 1989; The Soldiers of the French Revolution, 1990; (ed. with P. Jones) Reshaping France: Town, Country and Region during the French Revolution, 1991; The French Revolution, 1995; The Revolution in Provincial France: Aquitaine, 1789-1799, 1996; Napoleon's Men: The Soldiers of the Revolution and Empire, 2002; Paris, the Provinces and the French Revolution, 2004; (ed. with M. Crook and W. Doyle) Enlightenment and Revolution: Essays in Honour of Norman Hampson, 2004; (ed. with P.G. Dwyer) Napoleon and His Empire: Europe, 1804-1814, 2007; (ed. with R. Blaufarb and K. Hagemann) War, Culture and Society, 1750-1850, 2008; (ed. with P.H. Wilson) Bee and the Eagle: Napoleonic France and the End of the Holy Roman Empire, 1806, 2009; Legacy of the French Revolutionary Wars: The Nation-in-arms in French Republican Memory, 2009; (ed. with K. Hagemann and J. Randell) Soldiers, Citizens and Civilians: Experiences and Perceptions of the Revolutionary and Napoleonic Wars, 1790-1820, 2009. Contributor to journals. **Address:** Centre for Eighteenth Century Studies, University of York, The King's Manor, KG/70, Exhibition Sq., York, NY YO1 7EP, England. **Online address:** aif1@york.ac.uk

FORREST, Alan I. See **FORREST, Alan.**

FORREST, Christopher. American (born United States), b. 1971?. **Genres:** Novels, Young Adult Fiction, Mystery/Crime/Suspense. **Career:** Bowman George Scheb & Toale, lawyer. Writer. **Publications:** The Genesis Code (novel), 2007. **Address:** Forge Books, 175 5th Ave., New York, NY 10010, U.S.A. **Online address:** cdflaw@yahoo.com

FORREST, Katherine V(irginia). American/Canadian (born Canada), b. 1939. **Genres:** Novels, Novellas/Short Stories, Mystery/Crime/Suspense, Science Fiction/Fantasy. **Career:** Spinsters Ink, editor, staff, editorial supervisor; Naiad Press, senior fiction editor, 1984-94; Lambda Literary Foundation, president. Writer. **Publications:** CRIME FICTION: Amateur City, 1984; Murder at the Nightwood Bar, 1987; (ed.) Yellowthroat, 1988; The Beverly Malibu, 1989; Murder by Tradition, 1991; (ed. with B. Grier) The Erotic Naiad: Love Stories by Naiad Press Authors, 1992; (ed. with B. Grier) The Romantic Naiad: Love Stories by Naiad Press Authors, 1993; (ed. with B. Grier) The Mysterious Naiad: Love Stories by Naiad Press Authors, 1994; Liberty Square, 1996; Apparition Alley: A Kate Delafield Mystery, 1997; Sleeping Bones: A Kate Delafield Mystery, 1999. NOVELS: Curious Wine, 1983; Daughters of a Coral Dawn, 1984; An Emergence of Green, 1986; Dreams and Swords (short stories), 1987; Flashpoint, 1994; Daughters of an Amber Noon, 2002; Hancock Park: A Kate Delafield Mystery, 2004; Daughters of an Emerald Dusk, 2005; (ed.) Lesbian Pulp Fiction: The Sexually Intrepid World of Lesbian Paperback Novels, 1950-1965, 2005; (ed.) Women of Mystery: An Anthology, 2006; All in the Seasoning, 2006. **Address:** Lambda Literary Foundation, PO Box 1957, Old Chelsea Sta., New York, NY 10113, U.S.A. **Online address:** kvforrest@ad.com

FORRESTER, Duncan B(aillie). Scottish (born Scotland), b. 1933. **Genres:** Ethics, Theology/Religion, Adult Non-fiction. **Career:** University of Edinburgh, part-time assistant in politics, 1957-58, professor and chair of Christian ethics and practical theology, 1978-2000, Centre for Theology and Public Issues, founder, director, 1984-2000, New College, principal, 1986-96, dean of faculty of divinity, 1996-2000, professor of theology and public issues, 2000-01, professor emeritus, 2001-, honorary fellow, School of Social and Political Science, professor of divinity, now professor emeritus of divinity; Hillside Church Edinburgh, St. James Mission, assistant minister and leader, 1960-61; Madras Christian College, lecturer, professor of politics, 1962-70; Church of South India, ordained presbyter, 1962; University of Sussex, School of African and Asian Studies, chaplain and lecturer in politics and religious studies, 1970-78. Writer. **Publications:** Caste and Christianity, 1980; (with J.I.H. McDonald and G. Tellini) Encounter with God: An Introduction to Christian Worship and Practice, 1983, 2nd ed., 2004; (ed. with D.M. Murray) Studies in the History of Worship in Scotland, 1983, 2nd ed., 1996; Christianity and the Future of Welfare, 1985; (ed. with A. Elliott) The Scottish Churches and the Political Process Today, 1986; Theology and Politics, 1988; (ed. and contrib.) Just Sharing: A Christian Approach to the Distribution of Wealth, Income, and Benefits, 1988; (co-ed.) Worship Now, Book 2, 1989; Beliefs, Values, and Policies: Conviction Politics in a Secular Age, 1989; (ed. and contrib.) Theology and Practice, 1990; The True Church and Morality: Reflections on Ecclesiology and Ethics, 1997; Christian Justice and Public Policy, 1997; Truthful Action: Explorations in Practical Theology, 2000; On Human Worth: A Christian Vindication of Equality, 2001; Apocalypse Now?: Reflections on Faith in a Time of Terror, 2005; Theological Fragments: Explorations in Unsystematic Theology, 2005; Forrester on Christian Ethics and Practical Theology: Collected Writings on Christianity, India, and the Social Order, 2010. Contributor to books. **Address:** New College, University of Edinburgh, The Mound Pl., Edinburgh, EH1 2LU, Scotland. **Online address:** d.forrester@ed.ac.uk

FORRESTER, Helen. Also writes as J. Rana, June Edwards, June Bhatia. Canadian/British (born England), b. 1919. **Genres:** Novels, Autobiography/Memoirs, Social Sciences. **Career:** Writer, 1953-. **Publications:** Alien There is None, 1959; The Latchkey Kid, 1971; Twopence to Cross the Mersey, 1974; (as June Edwards) Most Precious Employee, 1976; Minerva's Stepchild, 1979; (ed.) Anthology 80, 1979; Liverpool Daisy, 1979; By the Waters of Liverpool, 1981; Liverpool Miss, 1982; Three Women of Liverpool, 1984; Thursday's Child, 1985; Lime Street at Two, 1985; The Moneylenders of Shahpur, 1987; Yes, Mama, 1987; The Lemon Tree, 1990; The Liverpool Basque, 1993; Mourning Doves, 1996; Madame Barbara, 1999; A Cuppa Tea and an Aspirin, 2003. Contributor to magazine. **Address:** The Writers' Union of Canada, 40 Wellington St. E, 3rd Fl., Toronto, ON M5E 1C7, Canada.

FORRESTER, John. British (born England), b. 1949. **Genres:** Psychiatry, History, Psychology. **Career:** Psychoanalysis and History Journal, editor-in-chief; Cambridge University, lecturer in history and philosophy of science, 1984-, professor, head of department. **Publications:** Language and the Origins of Psychoanalysis, 1980; (trans. with S. Tomaselli) Jacques Lacan, The Seminars of Jacques Lacan: Freud's Writings on Technique 1953-1954, 1988; The Seductions of Psychoanalysis: Freud, Lacan, and Derrida, 1990; (with L. Appignanesi) Freud's Women, 1992; Dispatches from the Freud Wars: Psychoanalysis and Its Passions, 1997; Truth Games: Lies, Money, and Psychoanalysis, 1997. Contributor to periodicals. **Address:** Department of History and Philosophy of Science, University of Cambridge, Free School Ln., Cambridge, GL CB2 3RH, England.

FORRESTER, Michael A. British/Scottish (born Scotland), b. 1953. **Genres:** Psychology. **Career:** Loughborough University of Technology, research associate, 1986-87; University of Kent, lecturer, 1987-94, senior lecturer in psychology, 1995-, reader in psychology. Writer. **Publications:** The Development of Young Children's Social-Cognitive Skills, 1992; Psychology of Language: A Critical Introduction, 1996; Psychology of the Image, 2000; (ed. with H. Gardner) Analysing Interactions in Childhood: Insights from Conversation Analysis, 2010; (ed.) Doing Qualitative research in Psychology: A Practical Guide, 2010. **Address:** School of Psychology, Keynes College, University of Kent, A3.11 Keynes, Canterbury, KT CT2 7NP, England. **Online address:** m.a.forrester@kent.ac.uk

FORRESTER, Sandra. American (born United States), b. 1949. **Genres:** Young Adult Fiction, Novels, Children's Fiction. **Career:** Department of the Army, occupational analyst, 1974-85, management analyst, 1985-92; National Institute of Environmental Health Sciences, management analyst, 1992-. Writer. **Publications:** Sound the Jubilee (young adult novel), 1995; My Home Is over Jordan, 1997; Dust from Old Bones, 1999; Wheel of the Moon, 2000.

BEATRICE BAILEY SERIES: The Everyday Witch, 2002; The Witches of Sea-Dragon Bay, 2003; The Witches of Friar's Lantern, 2003; The Witches of Winged-Horse Mountain, 2004; The Witches of Bailiwick, 2005; The Witches of Widdershins Academy, 2007; Leo and the Lesser Lion, 2009. **Address:** Barbara Kouts Literary Agency, PO Box 558, Bellport, NY 11713, U.S.A.

FORRESTER, Sibelan. American (born United States), b. 1961. **Genres:** Poetry, Language/Linguistics, Literary Criticism And History, Translations. **Career:** Oberlin College, assistant professor of Russian, 1989-94; Swarthmore College, assistant professor, 1994-98, associate professor of Russian, 1998-2007, professor of Russian, 2008-. Writer and translator. **Publications:** (Ed. with P. Chester) Engendering Slavic Literature, 1996; (trans. with C. Hawkesworth) I. Vrkljan, The Silk, the Shears, and Marina, or, About Biography, 1999; (ed. with M.J. Zaborowska and E. Gapova) Over the Wall/after the Fall: Post-Communist Cultures Through an East-West Gaze, 2004; (ed. with T. Newlin) Towards a Classless Society: Studies in Literature, History, and Politics in Honor of Thompson Bradley, 2004; (trans.) E. Ignatova, Diving Bell: Poems, 2006. **Address:** Department of Modern Languages and Literatures, Swarthmore College, Kohlberg 340, 500 College Ave., Swarthmore, PA 19081, U.S.A. **Online address:** sforres1@swarthmore.edu

FORRET, Jeff. (Jeffrey P. Forret). American (born United States), b. 1972?. **Genres:** History, Race Relations, Adult Non-fiction. **Career:** Lamar University, Department of History, history professor and graduate director. Writer. **Publications:** Race Relations at the Margins: Slaves and Poor Whites in the Antebellum Southern Countryside (nonfiction), 2006; Slavery in the United States (nonfiction), 2012. Contributor to journals. **Address:** U.S.A. **Online address:** jeffrey.forret@lamar.edu

FORRET, Jeffrey P. See **FORRET, Jeff.**

FORSBERG, Tuomas. Finnish (born Finland), b. 1967. **Genres:** History. **Career:** Ministry of Defense, principal secretary of the planning board on defense information, 1987-90; Finnish Institute of International Affairs, researcher, 1990-92, Academy of Finland, research associate, 1992-95, researcher, 1997-98, acting director, 1998-2001, senior researcher and head of program, 2001-02; Ulkopolitiikka: The Finnish Journal of Foreign Policy, editor-in-chief, 1998-2001; University of Helsinki, docent, 2000-, Centre of Excellence in Global Governance Research, professor of international relations and world politics, 2004-; University of Lapland, docent, 2001-; George C. Marshall European Center for Security Studies, professor of Western European security studies, 2002-04; UniversitÉ Libre de Bruxelles, visiting professor, 2005. Writer and academic. **Publications:** (with P. Visuri) Saksa ja Suomi: pohjoismainen Näkökulma Saksan kysymykseen, 1992; Johdatus Suomen ulkopolitiikkaan: kylmästä sodasta uuteen maailmanjärjestykseen, 1993; (co-ed.) Ikuinen Viipuri: ajankuvia Seitsemältä vuosisadalta, 1993; (ed.) Contested Territory: Border Disputes at the Edge of the Former Soviet Empire, 1995; (co-author) Foreign Policy of the Communists, 1999; Nato-kirja, 2002; (with G.P. Herd) Divided West: European Security and the Transatlantic Relationship, 2006. **Address:** Centre of Excellence in Global Governance Research, University of Helsinki, P O Box 4 (Yliopistonkatu 3), Helsinki, 00014, Finland. **Online address:** tuomas.forsberg@helsinki.fi

FORSDYKE, Donald R. Canadian (born Canada) **Genres:** Sciences. **Career:** Queen's University, School of Medicine, Department of Biomedical and Molecular Sciences, professor. Writer. **Publications:** Tomorrow's Cures Today?: How to Reform the Health Research System, 2000; The Origin of Species, Revisited: A Victorian Who Anticipated Modern Developments in Darwin's Theory, 2001; Evolutionary Bioinformatics, 2006, 2nd ed., 2011; (with A.G. Cock) Treasure Your Exceptions: The Science and Life of William Bateson, 2008. Contributor of articles to journals. **Address:** Department of Biomedical and Molecular Sciences, Queen's University, Rm. 253, Botterell Hall, 18 Stuart St., Kingston, ON K7L 3N6, Canada. **Online address:** forsdyke@queensu.ca

FORSTENZER, Thomas R. French/American (born United States), b. 1944. **Genres:** History, Literary Criticism And History, Social Sciences. **Career:** Rutgers University, professor of history, 1970-80; UNESCO, consultant, 1980-83, staff, Executive Office of the Director-General, executive officer, 1984-. Writer. **Publications:** Youth in the 1980's, 1979; French Provincial Police and the Fall of the Second Republic: Social Fear and Counter Revolution, 1981; (contrib.) Nova Pàgina, 1994; (as Tom Forstenzer with F. Mayor) The New Page, 1995. **Address:** UNESCO, 7 place de Fontenoy, Paris, 75352, France.

FORSTER, Marc R. American (born United States), b. 1959. **Genres:** History. **Career:** Harvard University, lecturer in history, 1989-90; Connecticut College, Department of History, assistant professor, 1990-95, associate professor, 1995-, professor, Henry B. Plant professor of history, chair, 2001-06; Ecole des Hautes Etudes en Sciences Sociales, visiting professor. Writer. **Publications:** The Counter-Reformation in the Villages: Religion and Reform in the Bishopric of Speyer, 1560-1720, 1992; Catholic Revival in the Age of the Baroque: Religious Identity in Southwest Germany, 1550-1750, 2001; (ed. with B.J. Kaplan) Piety and Family in Early Modern Europe: Essays in Honour of Steven Ozment, 2005; Catholic Germany from the Reformation to the Enlightenment, 2007. **Address:** Department of History, Connecticut College, 270 Mohegan Ave., PO Box 5497, New London, CT 06320, U.S.A. **Online address:** mrfor@conncoll.edu

FORSTER, Margaret. British (born England), b. 1938. **Genres:** Novels, Biography, Young Adult Non-fiction, Young Adult Fiction, History. **Career:** Barnsbury Girls' School, teacher, 1961-63; novelist, biographer and freelance literary critic, 1963-; Evening Standard, literary critic, 1977-80. **Publications:** Dames' Delight, A Novel, 1964; Bogeyman: A Novel, 1965; Georgy Girl, A Novel, 1965; Travels of Maudie Tipstaff, 1967; Park, 1968; Miss Owen-Owen is at Home, 1969 in UK as Miss Owen-Owen, 1969; Fenella Phizackerley, 1970; Mr. Bone's Retreat, 1971; Rash Adventurer: The Rise and Fall of Charles Edward Stuart, 1973; Seduction of Mrs. Pendlebury, 1974; (ed.) William Makepeace Thackeray: Memoirs of a Victorian Gentleman, 1978 in US as Memoirs of a Victorian Gentleman, 1979; Bride of Lowther Fell: A Romance, 1980; Marital Rites, 1981; (ed. and intro.) Drawn from Life: The Journalism of William Makepeace Thackeray, 1984; Significant Sisters: The Grassroots of Active Feminism, 1839-1939, 1984, rev. ed., 1986; Private Papers, 1986; Elizabeth Barrett Browning: The Life and Loves of a Poet, 1988; (intro.) Elizabeth Barrett Browning: Selected Poems, 1988; Elizabeth Barrett Browning: A Biography, 1989; Have the Men Had Enough?, 1989; Lady's Maid, 1990; The Battle for Christabel, 1991; Daphne du Maurier: The Secret Life of the Renowned Storyteller, 1993; Mothers' Boys, 1994; Hidden Lives: A Family Memoir, 1995; Shadow Baby, 1996; Rich Desserts and Captain's Thin: A Family and Their Times, 1831-1931, 1997; Memory Box, 1999; Precious Lives, 2000; Good Wives?: Mary, Fanny, Jennie & Me, 1845-2001, 2001; Diary of an Ordinary Woman 1914-1995, 2003; Mother Can You Hear Me?, 2004; Is There Anything You Want?, 2005; Keeping the World Away: A Novel, 2006; Over, 2007; Isa & May, 2010. **Address:** Sayle Literary Agency, 8b King's Parade, Cambridge, CB CB2 1SJ, England.

FORSTER, Michelanne. New Zealander/American (born United States), b. 1953. **Genres:** Children's Fiction. **Career:** Television script writer, editor and director for television, 1980-; TVNZ, studio and film director, 1982, After School, director, 1983-, producer, 1988-89; New Zealand Broadcasting School, Christchurch Polytechnic Institute of Technology, instructor in television production, 1998-; University of Canterbury, writer-in-residence, 1995; Rangi Ruru Girls School, writer-in-residence, 2001; Writers' Studio Programme for Playmarket, owner; University of Auckland, teacher. **Publications:** Rodney the Rat and the Sunken Treasure, 1983; The Four-legged Prince, 1985; Rodney the Rat and the Sneaky Weasel Gang, 1985; Rodney Rat and the Space Creatures, 1989; Daughters of Heaven, 1992; When It's Over: New Zealanders Talk about Their Experiences of Separation and Divorce, 1998. **Address:** New Zealand Broadcasting School, Christchurch Polytechnic Institute, PO Box 540, Christchurch, 8140, New Zealand. **Online address:** forsterm@cpitac.nz

FORSYTH, Frederick. British (born England), b. 1938. **Genres:** Novels, Novellas/Short Stories, Mystery/Crime/Suspense, Young Adult Non-fiction, Horror, Literary Criticism And History. **Career:** King's Lynn, reporter, 1958-61; Reuters News Agency, reporter, 1961-63, bureau chief, 1963-64; British Broadcasting Corp. (BBC), reporter, 1965-66, assistant diplomatic correspondent, 1967-68; freelance journalist, 1968-69; Eastern Daily Press, reporter, 1985-61. **Publications:** The Biafra Story: The Making of an African Legend (non-fiction), 1969; The Day of the Jackal, 1971; The Odessa File, 1972; The Dogs of War, 1974; The Shepherd, 1975; The Devil's Alternative, 1979; Forsyth's Three, 1980 as Three Complete Novels, 1981; No Comebacks: Collected Short Stories, 1982; Emeka (biography), 1982, 2nd ed., 1993; The Four Novels (contains The Day of the Jackal, The Odessa File, The Dogs of War and The Devil's Alternative), 1982; The Fourth Protocol, 1984; The Negotiator, 1989; Chacal, 1990; Deceiver, 1991; (ed. and intro.) Great Flying Stories, 1991; The Fist of God, 1994; I Remember: Reflections on Fishing in

Childhood, 1995; Icon, 1996; The Phantom of Manhattan, 1999; The Veteran: Five Heart-stopping Stories, 2001; Veteran and Other Stories, 2001; Day of the Jackal, 2002; Avenger, 2003; (foreword) VE Day: A Day to Remember: A Celebration of Reminiscences Sixty Years On, 2005; The Afghan, 2006; (foreword) Latin Today: Hodie Latina, 2007; The Cobra, 2010. Contributor of articles to journals. **Address:** Bantam Books, 62-63 Uxbridge Rd., London, GL W5 5SA, England.

FORSYTH, Kate. (Kate Humphrey). Australian (born Australia), b. 1966. **Genres:** Science Fiction/Fantasy, Children's Fiction, Young Adult Fiction, Novels, Poetry, History, Mythology/Folklore, Literary Criticism And History, Literary Criticism And History. **Career:** Writer. **Publications:** THE WITCHES OF EILEANAN SERIES: Dragonclaw, 1997 in US as The Witches of Eileannan, 1998; The Pool of Two Moons, 1998; The Cursed Towers, 1999; The Forbidden Land, 2000; The Skull of the World, 2001; The Fathomless Caves, 2002. RHIANNON'S RIDE SERIES: The Tower of Ravens, 2004; The Shining City, 2005; The Heart of Stars, 2006. THE CHAIN OF CHARM SERIES: The Gypsy Crown, 2006; The Silver Horse, 2006; The Herb of Grace, 2007; The Cat's Eye Shell, 2007; The Lightning Bolt, 2007; The Butterfly in Amber, 2007. CHILDREN'S NOVELS: The Starthorn Tree, 2002; Dragon Gold, 2005; Wishing For Trouble, 2006; Sea Magic: Ben and Tim's Magical Misadventures, 2008; The Puzzle Ring, 2009; The Wildkin's Curse, 2010. OTHERS: (as Kate Humphrey) Full Fathom Five, 2003; Radiance (poetry), 2005; I Am, 2007. **Address:** Curtis Brown Australia, Level 1, 2 Boundary St., Paddington, NW 2021, Australia. **Online address:** kforsyth@ozemail.com.au

FORSYTH, Michael. British (born England), b. 1951. **Genres:** Architecture, History, Art/Art History, Philosophy, Homes/Gardens. **Career:** Arthur Erickson, architect, 1976-79; Forsyth Chartered Architects, director, 1979-2002; University of Bristol, lecturer in architecture, 1979-84, research fellow in Drama, 1984-90; special lecturer in theatre architecture, 1990-98; Friends of the Victoria Art Gallery, chairman, 1995-2000; University of Bath, director of studies, 1998-, lecturer; University College Dublin, external examiner, 2006-08. Writer. **Publications:** Buildings for Music: The Architect, the Musician and the Listener from the Seventeenth Century to the Present Day, 1985; Auditoria: Designing for the Performing Arts, 1987; Bath: Pevsner Architectural Guide, 2003; Architectural Conservation: Philosophy and Practice, forthcoming. EDITOR: Historic Building Conservation III: Materials and Skills, 2005; Historic Building Conservation II: Structure and Construction, 2004; Historic Building Conservation I: Understanding Conservation, 2005; Understanding Historic Building Conservation, 2007; Structures & Construction in Historic Building Conservation, 2007; Materials & Skills for Historic Building Conservation, 2007; (with L. White) Interior Finishes and Fittings for Historic Building Conservation, 2011. Contributor to periodicals. **Address:** Department of Architecture and Civil Engineering, University of Bath, 6 E 2.21, Claverton Campus, Bath, SM BA2 7AY, England. **Online address:** m.forsyth@bath.ac.uk

FORSYTH, Phyllis Young. Canadian/American (born United States), b. 1944. **Genres:** Classics, History. **Career:** University of Waterloo, Department of Classical Studies, professor of classical studies, 1969-2002, distinguished professor emeritus, 2002-, chair, Department of Anthropology, chair. Writer. **Publications:** Atlantis: The Making of Myth, 1980; The Poems of Catullus: A Teaching Text, 1986; (ed. with H.V. Bender) Catullus: Student Text, 1996; Thera in the Bronze Age, 1997; (ed. with H.V. Bender) Catullus for the AP: A Supplement: Student Text, 2004. Contributor of articles to journals. **Address:** Department of Classical Studies, University of Waterloo, 200 University Ave. W, Waterloo, ON N2L 3G1, Canada. **Online address:** forsyth@watarts.uwaterloo.ca

FORT, Ilene Susan. American (born United States), b. 1949. **Genres:** Art/Art History, History. **Career:** H.W. Wilson Co., Reader's Guide to Periodical Literature, indexer, 1971-73; Worldwide Books, editor, 1975-79; Los Angeles County Museum of Art, assistant curator, 1983-87, associate curator, 1987-93, curator, 1993-. **Publications:** Flag Paintings of Child Hassam, 1988; (with M. Quick) American Art: A Catalogue of the Los Angeles County Museum of Art, 1991; Paintings of California, 1993; Childe Hassam's New York, 1993; The Figure in American Sculpture: A Question of Modernity, 1995; (with T. Abram) American Paintings in Southern California Collections: From Gilbert Stuart to Georgia O'Keeffe, 1996; Jacques Schnier, Art Deco and Beyond: Sixty Years of Sculpture, 1998; (with S. Barron and S. Bernstein) Made in

California: Art, Image, and Identity, 1900-2000, 2000; (ed. with S. Barron and S. Bernstein) Reading California: Art, Image, and Identity, 1990-2000, 2000; Sargent and Italy, 2003; (ed.) Manly Pursuits: Writings on the Sporting Images of Thomas Eakins, 2011; (co-author) Rodin and America, 2011; (with T. Arcq and T. Geis) In Wonderland: The Surealist Adventures of Women Artists in Mexico and the United States, 2012. Contributor to journals. **Address:** Los Angeles County Museum of Art, 5905 Wilshire Blvd., Los Angeles, CA 90036, U.S.A. **Online address:** ifort@lacma.org

FORTE, Maurizio. American/Italian (born Italy), b. 1961. **Genres:** Archaeology/Antiquities, Social Sciences. **Career:** Bologna University, laurea in ancient history, 1985-; ICARUS Project, tutor; University of California, School of Social Sciences, professor; National Research Council, researcher. Writer and archeologist. **Publications:** Le terrecotte ornamentali dei templi lumensi: Catalogo delle terrecotte architettoniche a stampo conservate al Museo archeologico nazionale di Firenze, 1991; (with P. von Eles) La Pianura Bolognese nel Villanviano: Insediamenti Della Prima etá del ferro, 1994; (ed. with A. Siliotti) Virtual Archeology: Re-Creating Ancient Worlds, 1997; (ed. with J.A. Barcelo and D.H. Sanders) Virtual Reality in Archaeology, 2000; (ed. with S.Campana) Remote Sensing in Archaeology: XI Ciclo di lezioni sulla ricercaapplicata in archeologia, Certosa di Pontignano (Siena), 6-11, dicembre 1999, 2001; (ed. with P.R. Williams) Reconstruction of Archaeological Landscapes Through Digital Technologies: Proceedings of the 1st Italy-United States Workshop, 2003; (ed. with S. Campana) From Space to Place: 2nd International Conference on Remote Sensing in Archaeology, 2006; (ed. with S. Campana and C. Liuzza) Space, Time, Place, 2010; (ed.) Cyber-Archaeology, 2010. **Address:** School of Social Sciences, Humanities and Arts, University of California, 5200 N Lake Rd., PO Box 2039, Merced, CA 95344, U.S.A. **Online address:** mforte@ucmerced.edu

FORTES (DE LEFF), Jacqueline. Mexican (born Mexico), b. 1952. **Genres:** Psychology, Sciences, Social Sciences. **Career:** Universidad Nacional Autonoma de Mexico, assistant professor, 1973-74, associate researcher, 1980-84, professor of psychology, 1984-; Instituto de la Familia, professor, 1983-, family therapist and senior supervisor, 1991-, vice-president and chief of teaching programs, 1991-93, president and researcher, 1993-; Clinic of Psychological Services, family therapist and supervisor, 1984-89; National Institute of Cardiology, family therapist and supervisor of trainees, 1990-91. Writer. **Publications:** (With L. Lomnitz) La Formacion del Cientifico en Mexico: Adquiriendo una nueva Identidad, 1991. Contributor to books and periodicals. **Address:** Hegel 120-204, Mexico City, DF 11570, Mexico. **Online address:** jfortes@prodigy.net.mx

FORTEY, Richard. British (born England), b. 1946. **Genres:** Natural History, Earth Sciences, Adult Non-fiction, Sciences. **Career:** Natural History Museum, research fellow, 1970-73, senior science officer, 1973-77, principal scientific officer and merit researcher, 1978-86, research scientist, merit researcher invertebrate palaeo, senior paleontologist, 1991-2006; University of Oxford, visiting professor of paleobiology; University of Bristol, Institute for Advanced Studies, Collier professor in public understanding of science and technology, 2002. Writer. **Publications:** Fossils: The Key to the Past, 1982, 3rd ed., 2002; The Dinosaurs' Alphabet, 1990; The Hidden Landscape: A Journey in to the Geological Past, 1993; Life: An Unauthorized Biography, 1997 in US as Life: A Natural History of the First Four Billion Years of Life on Earth, 1998; (ed. with R.H. Thomas) Arthropod Relationships, 1998; Trilobite! Eyewitness to Evolution, 2000; The Earth: An Intimate History, 2004; Dry Storeroom No. 1: The Secret Life of the Natural History Museum, 2008; Fossils, 2009; Survivors: The Animals and Plants that Time has Left Behind, 2011. **Address:** Natural History Museum, Cromwell Rd., London, GL SW7 5BDF, England. **Online address:** raf@nhm.ac.uk

FORTNA, Virginia Page. American (born United States), b. 1969?. **Genres:** Social Sciences. **Career:** Henry L. Stimson Center, research assistant, 1990-92; Columbia University, assistant professor, 1999-2005, associate professor of international relations, 2005-. Writer. **Publications:** Peace Time: Cease-Fire Agreements and the Durability of Peace, 2004; Does Peacekeeping Work? Shaping Belligerents' Choices after Civil War, 2007. Contributor of articles to books, periodicals and journals. **Address:** Department of Political Science, Columbia University, 1326 International Affairs Bldg., PO Box 3347, New York, NY 10027, U.S.A. **Online address:** vpf4@columbia.edu

FOSS, Sonja K. American (born United States), b. 1950. **Genres:** Adult Non-fiction. **Career:** Northwestern University, Department of Communication Studies, teaching assistant, 1974-76; Banta West (book manufacturer), customer service representative, 1976-77; Virginia Polytechnic Institute and State University, assistant professor, 1977-78; Norfolk State University, instructor, 1978-80; University of Denver, Department of Speech Communication, assistant professor, 1980-86, associate professor, 1986, senior research associate, 1996-97; University of Georgia, visiting professor, 1985; University of Oregon, Department of Speech, director of graduate studies and assistant professor, 1986-88, associate professor, 1988-89, director of speech fundamentals course; St. Louis University, visiting associate professor, 1989-90; Ohio State University, associate professor, 1990-96, coordinator, 1991-93, director of presentational speaking course, 1992-, chair, 1992-94, Undergraduate Studies, chair, 1995-; University of Colorado, Department of Communication, chair, 1997-2003, professor, 1997-, director of graduate studies, 2006-07, research professor. Writer. **Publications:** (Comp.) Rhetorical Criticism: Exploration & Practice, 1988, 4th ed., 2009; (contrib.) Women Communicating: Studies of Women's Talk, 1988; (contrib.) Research on Women's Communication: Alternative Perspectives in Theory and Method, 1989; (contrib.) Essays to Commemorate the 75th Anniversary of The Speech Communication Association, 1990; (contrib.) Rhetorical Movement: Studies in Honor of Leland M. Griffin, 1993; (co-ed.) Cultural Identity in the West, 2004; (co-ed.) The New Face of Arts Leadership in the West, 2006. CO-AUTHOR: (comp.) Contemporary Perspectives on Rhetoric, 1985, 3rd ed., 2002; (with K.A. Foss) Women Speak: The Eloquence of Women's Lives, 1991; (with K.A. Foss) Inviting Transformation: Presentational Speaking for a Changing World, 1994, 2nd ed., 2003; (with K.A. Foss and C.L. Griffin) Feminist Rhetorical Theories, 1999; (ed. with K.A. Foss and R. Trapp) Readings in Contemporary Rhetoric, 2002; (with K.A. Foss) Inviting Transformation: Presentational Speaking for a Changing World, 2003; (ed. with K.A. Foss and C.L. Griffin) Readings in Feminist Rhetorical Theory, 2004; (with W. Waters) Destination Dissertation: A Traveler's Guide to a Done Dissertation, 2007. **Address:** Department of Communication, University of Colorado, 102J Plz., PO Box 173364, Denver, CO 80217-3364, U.S.A. **Online address:** sonja.foss@cudenver.edu

FOSTER, Alan Dean. American (born United States), b. 1946. **Genres:** Novellas/Short Stories, Science Fiction/Fantasy, Novels, Young Adult Non-fiction, Graphic Novels, Romance/Historical. **Career:** Writer, 1968-; Headlines Ink Agency, head copywriter, 1970-71; University of California, Los Angeles City College, instructor of English and film, 1971-76; Los Angeles City College, instructor of English and film, 1972-76; City of Prescott Planning and Zoning Commission, vice chairperson, 1986-87; Northern Arizona University, adjunct faculty, 1991-. **Publications:** SCIENCE FICTION NOVELS: The Man Who Used the Universe, 1983; The I Inside, 1984; Slipt, 1984; Shadowkeep, 1984; Into the Out Of, 1986; Glory Lane, 1987; Malendipity, 1987; To the Vanishing Point, 1988; Quozl, 1989; Cyber Way, 1990; Cat-a-Lyst, 1991; Codgerspace, 1992; Chorus Skating, 1994; Greenthieves, 1994; (with E. Barcel and G. Santos) Premio UPC 1993, 1994; (with E.F. Russell) Design for Great-Day, 1995; Life-Form, 1995; Parallelities, 1995; The Dig, 1995; Dinotopia Lost, 1996; Mad Amos, 1996; (with J.C. Christensen and R. St. James) Voyage of the Basset, 1996; Jed the Dead, 1996; The Hand of Dinotopia, 1999; Into the Thinking Kingdoms, 1999; A Triumph of Souls, 2000; (co-author) Inner Visions: The Art of Ron Walotsky, 2000; Kingdoms of Light, 2001; Interlopers, 2001; The Mocking Program, 2002; The Chronicles of Riddick, 2004; Sagramanda: A Novel of Near-future India, 2006. COMMONWEALTH SERIES: The Tar-Aiym Krang, 1972; Bloodhype, 1973; Icerigger, 1974; Midworld, 1975; Orphan Star, 1977; The End of the Matter, 1977; Mission to Moulokin, 1979; Cachalot, 1980; Nor Crystal Tears, 1982; Flinx of the Commonwealth, 1982; For Love of Mother-Not, 1983; Voyage to the City of the Dead, 1984; Sentenced to Prism, 1985; The Deluge Drivers, 1987; Flinx in Flux, 1988; Mid-Flinx, 1995; The Howling Stones: A Novel of the Commonwealth, 1997; Reunion: A Pip & Flinx Novel, 2001; Drowning World: A Novel of the Commonwealth, 2003; Flinx's Folly: A Pip & Flinx Novel, 2003; Sliding Scales: A Pip & Flinx Novel, 2004; Running from the Deity, 2005; Trouble Magnet: A Pip & Flinx Adventure, 2006; Quofum, 2008. FOUNDING OF THE COMMONWEALTH SERIES: Phylogenesis, 1999; Dirge, 2000; Diuturnity's Dawn, 2002. SPELLSINGER SERIES FANTASY NOVELS: Spellsinger, 1981; Spellsinger at the Gate, 1983; The Hour of the Gate, 1984; The Day of the Dissonance, 1984; The Moment of the Magician, 1984; Season of the Spellsong, 1984; The Paths of the Perambulator, 1985; The Time of the Transference, 1986; Spellsinger's Scherzo, 1987; Son of Spellsinger, 1993; Chorus Skating, 1994. JOURNEYS OF THE CATHECHIST SERIES: Carnivores of Light and Darkness, 1998; Into the Thinking Kingdoms, 1999; A Triumph of Souls, 2000. STAR TREK SERIES: Star Trek

Log One, 1974; Star Trek Log Two, 1974; Star Trek Log Three, 1975; Star Trek Log Four, 1975; Star Trek Log Five, 1975; Star Trek Log Six, 1976; Star Trek Log Seven, 1976; Star Trek Log Eight, 1976; Star Trek Log Nine, 1977; With Friends like These ..., 1977; Star Trek Log Ten, 1978; Who Needs Enemies?, 1984; The Metrognome and Other Stories, 1990; Star Trek Logs One, Two, and Three, 1992; Star Trek Logs Four, Five and Six, 1993; Star Trek Logs Seven, Eight and Nine, 1993; Montezuma Strip (stories), 1995; Star Trek, the Animated Series, 2006; Star Trek: A Novel, 2009; Star Trek: Refugees, 2010. THE DAMNED SERIES: A Call to Arms, 1991; The False Mirror, 1992; The Spoils of War, 1993. TAKEN TRILOGY: Lost and Found: A Novel, 2004; The Light-years Beneath My Feet, 2005; The Candle of Distant Earth, 2006. NOVELS: Luana, 1974; Dark Star, 1974; Star Wars: From the Adventures of Luke Skywalker, 1976; Splinter of the Mind's Eye: From the Adventures of Luke Skywalker, 1978; Star Trek-The Motion Picture, 1979; Alien, 1979; The Black Hole, 1980; Clash of the Titans, 1981; Outland, 1981; The Thing, 1982; Krull, 1983; The Last Starfighter, 1984; Starman, 1984; Pale Rider, 1985; Aliens, 1986; Alien Nation, 1988; Alien 3, 1991; Star Wars, the Approaching Storm, 2002; Transformers: Ghosts of Yesterday, 2007; Revenge of the Fallen, 2009; The Veiled Threat, 2009. OTHERS: Horror on the Beach: A Tale in the Cthulhu Mythos, 1978; (ed.) Animated Features and Silly Symphonies, 1980; (ed.) The Best of Eric Frank Russell, 2nd ed., 1986; Maori (historical novel), 1988; (ed. with M.H. Greenberg) Smart Dragons, Foolish Elves, 1991; (ed.) Betcha Can't Read Just One, 1993; Sir Charles Barkley and the Referee Murders, 1993; Mad Amos, 1996; Primal Shadows (suspense), 2001; Impossible Places, 2002; (ed.) Short Stories from Small Islands: Tales Shared in Palau, 2005; Patrimony, 2007; Exceptions to Reality, 2008; Flinx Transcendent, 2009; The Human Blend, 2010; Untold Adventures, 2011, Body, Inc., 2012. Works appear in anthologies. Contributor to magazines. **Address:** Thranx Inc., PO Box 12757, Prescott, AZ 86304-2757, U.S.A. **Online address:** adf@alandeanfoster.com

FOSTER, Brooke Lea. American (born United States) **Genres:** Human Relations/Parenting, Humanities, Social Sciences. **Career:** Washingtonian, staff writer, senior writer. **Publications:** Feeling Them Fall, 2006; The Way They Were: Dealing with Your Parents' Divorce after a Lifetime of Marriage, 2006; (with N.I. Bernstein) There When He Needs You: How to Be an Available, Involved and Emotionally Connected Father to Your Son, 2008. Contributor to periodicals. **Address:** c/o Author Mail, Three Rivers Press, 1745 Broadway, New York, NY 10019, U.S.A. **Online address:** bfoster@washingtonian.com

FOSTER, Cecil (A.). Canadian/Barbadian (born Barbados), b. 1954. **Genres:** Race Relations, Novels. **Career:** Caribbean News Agency, senior reporter and editor, 1975-77; Barbados Advocate News, reporter and columnist, 1977-79; Toronto Star, reporter, 1979-82; Contrast, editor, 1979-82; Transportation Business Management, editor, 1982-83; Globe and Mail, reporter, 1983-89; Financial Post, senior editor, 1989-; Ontario's Ministry of Culture, advisor; University of Guelph, professor of sociology and anthropology. **Publications:** Distorted Mirror: Canada's Racist Face, 1991; No Man in the House (novel), 1991; Sleep On, Beloved (novel), 1995; Caribana, the Greatest Celebration, 1995; Slammin? Tar: A Novel, 1998; Island Wings: A Memoir, 1998; Dry Bone Memories, 2001; Where Race Does Not Matter: The New Spirit of Modernity, 2004; Blackness and Modernity: The Colour of Humanity and the Quest for Freedom, 2007. Contributor of articles to periodicals. **Address:** Department of Sociology and Anthropology, University of Guelph, 6th Fl, MacKinnon Bldg., Guelph, ON N1G 2W1, Canada. **Online address:** cfoster@uoguelph.ca

FOSTER, David Manning. Australian (born Australia), b. 1944. **Genres:** Novels, Poetry, Novellas/Short Stories. **Career:** U.S. Public Health Service, research fellow, 1970-71; University of Sydney, Medical School, Department of Medicine, research officer, 1972-. Writer. **Publications:** North, South, West: Three Novellas, 1973; The Pure Land, 1974; The Fleeing Atalanta, 1975; Escape to Reality, 1977; (with D.K. Lyall) The Empathy Experiment, 1977; Moonlite, 1981; Dog Rock: A Postal Pastoral, 1985; Adventures of Christian Rosy Cross, 1986; Testostero, 1987; Hitting the Wall: Two Novellas, 1989; Mates of Mars, 1991; (ed. and intro.) Self Portraits, 1991; A Slab of Fosters, 1994; Plumbum: The Ultimate Heavy Metal Experience, 1995; The Glade within the Grove, 1996; The Pale Blue Crochet Coathanger Cover, 1996; (co-author) Crossing the Blue Mountains: Journeys through Two Centuries from Naturalist Charles Darwin to Novelist David Foster, 1997; The Ballad of Erinungarah, 1997; In the New Country, 1999; Studs and Nogs: Essays 1987-98, 1999; (with G. Foster) A Year of Slow Food, 2002; The Land Where Stories End: As Narrated By The Angel Depicted In Madonna con

Bambino e due angeli by Filippo Lippi, 2003; Sons of the Rumour, 2009. **Address:** Curtis Brown Aus Pty Ltd., PO Box 19, Paddington, NW 2021, Australia.

FOSTER, David William. American (born United States), b. 1940. **Genres:** Literary Criticism And History, Bibliography. **Career:** University of Washington, research associate, instructor and teaching assistant in Spanish, 1961-64; University of Missouri, assistant professor of Spanish, 1964-66; Arizona State University, Department of Languages and Literatures, assistant professor, 1966-68, associate professor, 1968-70, professor of Spanish, 1970-, Regents' professor of Spanish and women's studies, Department of Languages and Literatures, chair, 1997-2001; Universidad Nacional de la Plata, Fulbright professor, 1967; Universidad Catolica de Chile, inter-American development bank professor of linguistics, 1975; Rocky Mountain Review of Language and Literature, editor, 1980-84; University of California, visiting professor of Spanish, 1989; Universidad Nacional de Rio Cuarto, Fulbright professor of American literature, 2003; Universidad Nacional de Crdoba, Fulbright professor of American literature, 2003. **Publications:** (Co-author) Research on Language Teaching, 1962; Forms of the Novel in the Work of Camilo Jose Cela, 1967; Myth of Paraguay in the Fiction of Augusto Roa Bastos, 1969; (with V.R. Foster) Manual of Hispanic Bibliography, 1970; (with V.R. Foster) A Research Guide to Argentine Literature, 1970; A Bibliography of the Works of Jorge Luis Borges, 1971; Christian Allegory in Early Hispanic Poetry, 1971; The Marques de Santillana, 1971; (with G.L. Bower) Haiku in Western Languages, 1972; Early Spanish Ballad, 1972; Unamuno and the Novel as Expressionist Conceit, 1973; (with V.R. Foster) Modern Latin American Literature, 1975; Currents in the Contemporary Argentine Novel, 1975; Twentieth Century Spanish-American Novel: A Bibliography, 1975; (with H.J. Becco) La Nueva Narrativa Hisposmericana: Bibliograffa, 1976; Chilean Literature: A Working Bibliography, 1978; Augusto Roa Bastos, 1978; Studies in the Contemporary Spanish American Short Story, 1979; Mexican Literature: A Bibliography of Secondary Sources, 1981, 2nd ed., 1992; Peruvian Literature: A Bibliography of Secondary Sources, 1981; (with R. Reis) A Dictionary of Contemporary Brazilian Authors, 1982; Para Una Lectura Semiotica Del Ensayo Latinoamericano, 1983; Jorge Luis Borges: An Annotated Primary and Secondary Bibliography, 1984; Estudios Sobre Teatro Mexicano Contemporaneo: Semiologia De La Competencia Teatral, 1984; Cuban Literature, 1984; Alternate Voices in the Contemporary Latin American Narrative, 1985; The Argentine Teatro-Independiente, 1930-1955, 1986; Social Realism in the Argentine Narrative, 1986; Handbook of Latin American Literature, 1987; From Mafalda to Los Super machos, 1989; The Argentine Generation of 1880, 1990; (with W. Rela) Brazilian Literature: A Research Bibliography, 1990; Gay and Lesbian Themes in Latin American Writing, 1991; Contemporary Argentine Cinema, 1992; Cultural Diversity in Latin American Literature, 1994; Latin American Writers on Gay and Lesbian Themes: A Bio-Critical Sourcebook, 1994; Violence in Argentine Literature, 1995; (with D. Altamiranda, G. Geirola and C. de Urioste) Literatura Espanola: Una Antologia, 1995; Sexual Textualities, 1997; Espacio Escenicoy Lenguaje, 1998; Buenos Aires: Perspective on the City and Cultural Production, 1998; A Funny Dirty Little War, 1998; (with M.F. Lockhart and D.B. Lockhart) Culture and Customs of Argentina, 1998; (with D. Altamiranda and C. de Urioste) The Writer's Reference Guide to Spanish, 1999; Gender and Society in Contemporary Brazilian Cinema, 1999; Produccion Cultural e Identidades Homoeroticas, 1999; Mexico City and Contemporary Mexican Filmmaking, 2002; Queer Issues in Contemporary Latin American Cinema, 2003; (trans.) R.B. Bretaña, Night Watch, 2004; Ambiente nuestro: Chicano/Latino Homoerotic Writing, 2006; Urban Photography in Argentina: Nine Artists of the Post-Dictatorship Era, 2007. EDITOR: A Dictionary of Contemporary Latin American Authors, 1975; Sourcebook of Hispanic Culture in the United States, 1982; Marques de Santillana: Poesia (selection), 1982; (with F.A. Rosales) Hispanics and the Humanities in the Southwest, 1983; The Redemocratization of Argentine Culture, 1983; Handbook of Latin-American Literature, 1987, 2nd ed., 1992; Beyond: An International Research Symposium, 1989; Literatura Hispanoamericana: Una Antologia, 1994; Latin-American Writers on Gay and Lesbian Themes: A Bio-Critical Sourcebook, 1994; Mexican Literature: A History, 1994; (with Reis) Bodies and Biases: Sexualities in Hispanic Cultures and Literatures, 1996; Literatura Chicana, 1965-1995: An Anthology in Spanish, English, and Calo, 1997; (with D. Altamiranda) Twentieth-Century Spanish-American Literature since 1960, 1997; (with D. Altamiranda) From Romanticism to Modernismo in Latin America, 1997; (with D. Altamiranda) Writers of the Spanish Colonial Period, 1997; (with D. Altamiranda) Theoretical Debates in Spanish-American Literature, 1997; Chicano/Latino Homoerotic Identities, 1999; Spanish

Writers on Gay and Lesbian Themes: A Bio-Critical Sourcebook, 1999; (with C.M. Tompkins) Notable Twentieth-Century Latin American Women: A Biographical Dictionary, 2000; (with D. Altamiranda and C. de Urioste) Spanish Literature: Current Debates on Hispanism, 2000; (with D. Altamiranda and de Urioste) Spanish Literature: From Origins to 1700, 2000; (with D. Altamiranda and C. de Urioste) Spanish Literature: 1700 to the Present, 2000; (with J.R. Kelly) Bibliography in Literature, Folklore, Language, and Linguistics: Essays on the Status of the Field, 2003; Latin American Jewish Cultural Production, 2009; Sao Paulo: Perspectives on the City and Cultural Production, 2011. **Address:** School of International Letters and Cultures, Arizona State University, Rm. 422C, Language & Literature Bldg., Tempe, AZ 85287-0202, U.S.A. **Online address:** david.foster@asu.edu

FOSTER, Edward Halsey. American (born United States), b. 1942. **Genres:** Poetry, Literary Criticism And History, Essays. **Career:** Stevens Institute of Technology, assistant professor, 1970-75, associate professor, 1975-84, professor of English and American literature, 1985-, director of programs in the humanities and social sciences, 2002-, associate dean for administration, 2007-; Haceteppe University, Fulbright lecturer, 1978-79; University of Istanbul, visiting Fulbright professor, 1985-86; Drew University, Graduate School of English, visiting professor, 1991, 1992, 1994, 1996; Talisman House Publishers, president, 1993-; Beykent University, visiting professor, 2001; Greenfield Distribution Inc., president; Russian and American Cultural Exchange Program, co-director. Writer. **Publications:** Catherine Maria Sedgwick, 1974; The Civilized Wilderness: Backgrounds to American Romantic Literature, 1817-1860, 1975; Josiah Gregg and Lewis H. Garrard, 1977; Susan and Anna Warner, 1978; Cummington Poems, 1982; Richard Brautigan, 1983; William Saroyan, 1984; Jack Spicer, 1991; William Saroyan: A Study of the Short Fiction, 1991; Understanding the Beats, 1992; The Space between Her Bed and Clock (poems), 1993; Understanding the Black Mountain Poets, 1994; Postmodern Poetry: The Talisman Interviews, 1994; Code of the West: A Memoir of Ted Berrigan, 1994; The Understanding (poems), 1994; All Acts Are Simply Acts, 1995; Adrian as Song, 1996; Boy in the Key of E, 1998; Answerable to None: Berrigan, Bronk, and the American Real, 1999; The Angelus Bell, 2001; Mahrem: Things Men Should do for Men: A Suite for O, 2002; What He Ought to Know: New and Selected Poems, 2006; A History of the Common Scale, 2008; Febra Alba: Poeme Alese, 2009; Beginning of Sorrows, 2009. EDITOR: (with G.W. Clark) Hoboken: A Collection of Essays, 1976; (with D. Mesyats) The New Freedoms, 1994; (co-ed.) Primary Trouble: An Anthology of Contemporary American Poetry, 1996; The White Tomb: Selected Poems of Stuart Merrill, 1999; Decadents, Symbolists, and Aesthetes in America: fin-de-siècle American Poetry: An Anthology, 2000; Poetry and Poetics in a New Millenium: Interviews with Clark Coolidge and others, 2000; (with J. Donahue) The World in Time and Space, 2002; (ed. with C. Firan and P.D. Mugur) Born in Utopia: An Anthology of Modern and Contemporary Romanian poetry, 2006. OTHER: Adalet Agaoglu, Yazsonu (title means: 'Summer's End'), 2008. Contributor to periodicals. **Address:** Stevens Institute of Technology, 331 Morton, 1 Castle Point, Hoboken, NJ 07030, U.S.A. **Online address:** efoster@stevens.edu

FOSTER, Frances Smith. American (born United States), b. 1944. **Genres:** History, Literary Criticism And History, Women's Studies And Issues. **Career:** Cass Technical H.S., teacher in English, 1966-68; University of Southern California, teaching assistant in English, 1969-70; California State University, lecturer in English, 1970-71, Office of New Programs and Development, coordinator of special projects, 1979-80; University of California, Third College Writing Program, instructor, 1971-72, professor of literature, 1988-94; San Diego State University, assistant professor of Afro-American studies, 1971-72, assistant professor, associate professor of English and comparative literature, 1976-79, professor of English and comparative literature, 1979-82, Department of Afro-American Studies, chair, 1972-74, faculty coordinator, 1975-76, College of Arts and Letters, assistant dean, 1976-79, College of Arts and Letters Academic Advising Center, director, 1976-79; Pacific Coast Philology, managing editor, 1981-84; California State University, administrative fellow, 1983-84; Emory University, Department of English, professor of English, 1994-96, emeritus professor of English, 1996-, Charles Howard Candler professor of English and Women's Studies, chair, 2005-08, strategic plan coordinator for race and difference initiative, 2005-06, Emory Institute for Women's Studies, director, 1999-2002. **Publications:** Witnessing Slavery: The Development of Ante-Bellum Slave Narratives, 1979, 2nd ed., 1994; Written by Herself: Literary Production by African American Women, 1746-1892, 1993; Till Death or Distance Do Us Part: Love and Marriage in Antebellum African America, 2010. EDITOR: (and intro.) A Brighter Com-

ing Day: A Frances Ellen Watkins Harper Reader, 1990; Minnie's Sacrifice: Sowing and Reaping: Trial and Triumph: Three Rediscovered Novels, 1994; (with W.L. Andrews and T. Harris) Oxford Companion to African American Literature, 1997; Behind the Scenes: Formerly a Slave, but more Recently Modiste and a Friend to Mrs. Lincoln, or, Thirty Years a Slave and Four years in the White House, 2001; (with W.L. Andrews and T. Harris) The Concise Oxford Companion to African American Literature, 2001; (with N.Y. McKay) Incidents in the Life of a Slave Girl: Contexts, Criticism, 2001; Love & Marriage in Early African America, 2007; (with S.M. James and B.G. Sheftall) Still Brave: The Evolution of Black Women's Studies, 2009. Contributor to periodicals. **Address:** Department of English, Emory University, N 302 Callaway Ctr., 537 Kilgo Cir., 1380 Oxford Rd. NE, Atlanta, GA 30322, U.S.A. **Online address:** ffoster@emory.edu

FOSTER, Hal. American (born United States), b. 1955. **Genres:** Novels. **Career:** Cornell University, faculty; Princeton University, professor; art historian and editor. Writer. **Publications:** (Ed.) The Anti-Aesthetic: Essays on Postmodern Culture, 1983; Recodings: Art, Spectacle, Cultural Politics, 1985; Compulsive Beauty, 1993; The Return of the Real: The Avant-Garde at the End of the Century, 1996; (ed. with G. Hughes) Richard Serra, 2000; Design and Crime and Other Diatribes, 2002; (with R. Krauss, Y.A. Bois and B.H.D. Buchloh) Art since 1900: Modernism, Antimodernism, Postmodernism, 2004; Prosthetic Gods, 2004; (ed. with M. Francis) Pop, 2005; The Art-Architecture Complex, 2011; The First Pop Age: Painting and Subjectivity in the Art of Hamilton, Lichtenstein, Warhol, Richter and Ruscha, 2012. Contributor to periodicals. **Address:** Princeton University, 105 & 314 McCormick Hall, Princeton, NJ 08544, U.S.A. **Online address:** hfoster@princeton.edu

FOSTER, Iris. See **POSNER, Richard.**

FOSTER, Jeanne. See **WILLIAMS, Jeanne.**

FOSTER, Joanne Reckler. American (born United States), b. 1941. **Genres:** Autobiography/Memoirs, Biography. **Career:** Rocky Mountain News, assistant, assistant city editor, general assignment reporter, 1963-67; National Observer, staff writer, 1967-69; Washington Post, reporter, 1969; freelance writer, editor and proofreader, 1978-. **Publications:** (With D.D. Dempsey) The Captain's a Woman: Tales of a Merchant Mariner (memoir), 1998. **Address:** 2380 Mosquito Point Rd., White Stone, VA 22578-2917, U.S.A. **Online address:** whitetop@crosslink.net

FOSTER, John Bellamy. American (born United States), b. 1953. **Genres:** Economics, History, Sociology. **Career:** York University, Department of Political Science, faculty, 1976, teaching assistant, 1977-79, Bethune College, fellow, 1978-86, Social Science Division, teaching assistant, 1979-80, 1982-84; Evergreen State College, faculty, 1985; University of Oregon, visiting assistant professor, 1985-86, assistant professor, 1986-91, associate professor of sociology, 1991-99, professor, 2000-; Monthly Review Foundation, associate, 1988-, director, 1988-, president, 2002-; Organization & Environment, co-editor, 1996-2001, critical essay editor, archives editor, 2002-; Monthly Review, acting co-editor, 2000-01, co-editor, 2001-05, editor, 2006-; The World Forum for Alternatives/Forum Mondial Des Alternatives, vice president, 2010-; University of Wisconsin-Madison, visiting lecturer; University of Lancaster, visiting lecturer; Universidad Autonoma Metropolitana-Itzapalapa, visiting lecturer; Menlo College, visiting lecturer; St. Mary's University, visiting lecturer; Halifax University, visiting lecturer; University of Nova Scotia, visiting lecturer. **Publications:** (Ed. with H. Szlajfer and contrib.) The Faltering Economy: The Problem of Accumulation Under Monopoly Capitalism, 1984; The Theory of Monopoly Capitalism: An Elaboration of Marxian Political Economy, 1986; The Vulnerable Planet: A Short Economic History of the Environment, 1994; (ed. and intro.) E. Fischer, How to Read Karl Marx, 1996; (ed. with E.M. Wood) In Defense of History: Marxism and the Postmodern Agenda, 1997; (ed. with R. McChesney and E.M. Wood) Capitalism and the Information Age: The Political Economy of the Global Communication Revolution, 1998; Marx's Ecology: Materialism and Nature, 2000; (ed. with F. Magdoff and F. Buttel) Hungry for Profit: The Agribusiness Threat to Farmers, Food and the Environment, 2000; Ecology Against Capitalism, 2002; (ed. with R.W. McChesney) Pox Americana: Exposing the American Empire, 2002; Emperyalizm in Yeniden Kesfi, trans. as Imperialism Rediscovered 2005; Naked Imperialism: America's Pursuit of Global Dominance, 2006; (with B. Clark and R. York) The Critique of Intelligent Design: From Antiquity to the Present, 2008; Ecological Revolution: Making Peace With the Planet, 2009; (with F. Magdoff) Great Financial Crisis:

Causes and Consequences, 2009; (with B. Clark and R. York) Ecological Rift: Capitalism's War on the Earth, 2010; What Every Environmentalist Needs to Know About Capitalism: A Citizen's Guide to Capitalism and the Environment, 2011; Communications and Monopoly Capital, forthcoming. Contributor to periodicals. **Address:** Department of Sociology, University of Oregon, 628 PLC, 736 Prince Lucien Campbell, 1415 Kincaid, Eugene, OR 97403, U.S.A. **Online address:** jfoster@uoregon.edu

FOSTER, John Wilson. Irish (born Ireland), b. 1944?. **Genres:** Botany, History, Cultural/Ethnic Topics. **Career:** University of British Columbia, assistant professor, 1974-, professor of English, through 2002, professor emeritus, 2002-; Queen's University, Institute of Irish Studies, senior research fellow, 1986-87, honorary research fellow; National University of Ireland, visiting professor, 2001, Arts Faculty, visiting fellow, 2006; University of Ulster, Academy for Irish Cultural Heritages, Leverhulme visiting professor, 2004-05; University of Toronto, Armstrong visiting professor, 2005. Freelance writer and literary critic. **Publications:** Forces and Themes in Ulster Fiction, 1974; Fictions of the Irish Literary Revival: A Changeling Art, 1987; Colonial Consequences: Essays in Irish Literature and Culture, 1991; The Achievement of Seamus Heaney, 1995; The Titanic Complex: A Cultural Manifest, 1996; Recoveries: Neglected Episodes in Irish Cultural History, 1860-1912, 2002; The Age of Titanic: Cross-Currents in Anglo-American Culture, 2002; Irish Novels, 1890-1940: New Bearings in Culture and Fiction, 2008; Between Shadows: Modern Irish Writing and Culture, 2009; (contrib.) Words of the Grey Wind, 2009. EDITOR: (with G. Dawe) The Poet's Place: Ulster Literature and Society: Essays in Honour of John Hewitt, 1907-87, 1991; The Idea of the Union: Statements and Critiques in Support of the Union of Great Britain & Northern Ireland, 1995; (with H.C.G. Chesney) Nature in Ireland: A Scientific and Cultural History, 1997; The Titanic Reader, 2000; The Cambridge Companion to the Irish Novel, 2006. Contributor to periodicals. **Address:** Department of English, University of British Columbia, 397-1873 East Mall, Vancouver, BC V6T 1Z1, Canada. **Online address:** j.foster@qub.ac.uk

FOSTER, Ken. American (born United States), b. 1964. **Genres:** Autobiography/Memoirs, Young Adult Fiction, Novellas/Short Stories. **Career:** William Morrow (publisher), publicist; North Carolina School of the Arts, instructor; Northeastern University, instructor; New School University, writing instructor. Writer. **Publications:** SHORT STORIES: (ed.) The KGB Bar Reader, 1998; The Kind I'm Likely to Get, 1999; Dog Culture: Writers on the Character of Canines, 2002; The Dogs Who Found Me: What I've Learned from Pets Who Were Left Behind, 2006; Dogs I Have Met: And the People they Found, 2008. Contributor to periodicals. **Address:** PO Box 3780, New Orleans, LA 70177-3780, U.S.A. **Online address:** dogswhofoundme@gmail.com

FOSTER, Kennedy. American (born United States), b. 1944. **Genres:** Young Adult Fiction. **Career:** Walla Walla Community College, instructor in writing and English as a second language, 1988-. Writer. **Publications:** All Roads Lead Me Back to You, 2009. **Address:** Walla Walla, WA , U.S.A. **Online address:** kennedyfoster@ymail.com

FOSTER, Linda Nemec. American (born United States), b. 1950. **Genres:** Poetry. **Career:** Center for Environmental Study, social demographer, 1971-74; Jones and Laughlin Steel Corp., clerk, 1974-77; Michigan Council for the Arts, teacher of poetry and writing, 1980-2002; Ferris State University, lecturer in writing, 1984; Urban Institute for Contemporary Arts, director of literature programming, 1989-96; Aquinas College, Contemporary Writers Series, founder and program coordinator, 1997-, professor of English, 1999. **Publications:** POETRY: A History of the Body, 1987; A Modern Fairy Tale: The Baba Yaga Poems, 1992; Trying to Balance the Heart, 1993; Living in the Fire Nest, 1996; Contemplating the Heavens, 2001; Amber Necklace from Gdansk, 2006; Listen to the Landscape, 2006; Ten Songs from Bulgaria, 2008; Talking Diamonds, 2009. Contributor to periodicals. **Address:** c/o Marianne Swierenga, New Issues Poetry & Prose, Western Michigan University, 1903 W Michigan Ave., Kalamazoo, MI 49008-5463, U.S.A. **Online address:** mfapwgrr9@aol.com

FOSTER, L. L. See **FOSTER, Lori L.**

FOSTER, Lori L. (L. L. Foster). American (born United States), b. 1958. **Genres:** Romance/Historical, Novels. **Career:** Writer. **Publications:** Impetuous, 1996; Scandalized!, 1997; Outrageous, 1997; Fantasy, 1998; (co-author) Charmed, 1999; Sizzle!, 1999; Taken!, 1999; Tantalizing, 1999; (with J.A. Krentz) The Private Eye/Beguiled, 1999; Little Miss Innocent?, 1999; Mar-

ried to the Boss, 2000; (co-author) All I Want for Christmas, 2000; (with S. Forster, K. Randell and M. Shayne) Sinful, 2000; In Too Deep, 2000; (co-author) All through the Night, 2000; Say Yes, 2001; (co-author) Hot and Bothered, 2001; Annie Get Your Guy/Messing around with Max, 2001; Sex Appeal: Heat, 2001; Never Too Much, 2002; Too Much Temptation: A Novel about Erotic Temptation (Brava Brothers series), 2002; Heat of the Night, 2002; Riley, 2003; (with D. Kauffman and J. Shalvis) Men of Courage, 2003; Unexpected, 2003; (with L. Lael and C. Neggers) Under His Skin: Three Sizzling Tales of Romance, 2003; (co-author) Jingle Bell Rock, 2003; (co-author) Perfect for the Beach, 2003; Scandalous, 2004; (with K. Rolofson and C. Burnes) The Truth about Cats Dogs, 2004; (with J.E. Leto) Lip Service, 2004; (with L. Monroe and D. Castell) Star Quality, 2005; (co-author) Unzipped: Tantalizing Playmates: His Every Fantasy, 2005; (co-author) The Night before Christmas, 2005; (with D. Kauffman and J. Shalvis) Men of Courage II, 2005; Judes Law (Law Books series), 2006; Murphys Law (Law Books series), 2006; (with G. Bruce and J. Maynard) A Very Merry Christmas, 2006; (with C. Phillips and J. Cruise) Santa, Baby, 2006; Causing Havoc (SBC Fightersseries), 2007; Simon Says (SBC Fighters series), 2007; PRP Truth or Dare, 2007; The Write Ingredients: Recipes from Your Favorite Authors (nonfiction), 2007. WINSTON BROTHERS SERIES: Wild, 2002; Say No to Joe?, 2003; Just A Hint Clint, 2004; The Secret Life of Bryan, 2004; When Bruce Met Cyn..., 2004; Jamie, 2005; Wildly Winston, 2006. BAD BOYS OMNIBUS SERIES: (with J. Denison and D. Kauffman) I Love Bad Boys: Indulge Me/Naughty by Night/And When They Were Bad, 2002; (with J. Denison and S. McKenna) I Brake for Bad Boys: Drive Me Wild/Something Wilde/Touch Me, 2002; (with J. Denison and N. Warren) Bad Boys to Go: Bringing Up Baby/Wilde One/Going after Adam, 2003; (with D. Kauffman and N. Warren) Bad Boys on Board: My House, My Rules/Going Down?/Fast Ride, 2003; (with E. McCarthy and M. Leigh) Bad Boys in Black Tie: Good with His Hands/Miss Extreme Congeniality/Last Call, 2004; (with E. McCarthy and A. Garvey) Bad Boys of Summer: Luscious/Its about Time/Wish You Were Here, 2006; (with E. McCarthy and H. Dimon) When Good Things Happen to Bad Boys: Playing Doctor/Lady of the Lake/Hardhats and Silk Stockings, 2006. P.I. MEN TO THE RESCUE SERIES: Wanton, 2000; Caught in the Act, Mr. November, 2001; Treat Her Right, 2001; Fallen Angels: Beguiled/Wanton/Uncovered, 2004; Out of the Light, Into the Shadow, 2009. BUCK-HORN BROTHERS SERIES: Gabe, 2000; Sawyer, 2000; Jordan, 2001; Morgan, 2001; Casey, 2002; Forever and Always: Gabe/Jordan, 2002; Once and Again: Sawyer/Morgan, 2002. AS L.L. FOSTER: Awakening, 2007; Acceptance, 2008; Servant: The Kindred, 2009. OTHERS: Enticing, 2007; Heartbreakers, 2008; Caught!, 2008; Hard to Handle, 2008; Double the Pleasure, 2008; ?Power of Love, 2008; Tails of Love, 2009; My Man, Michael, 2009; Bodyguard, 2009; Yule Be Mine, 2009; Tempted, 2010; Unbelievable, 2010; The Gift of Love, 2010; Back in Black, 2010; Bewitched, 2010; Watson Brothers, 2010; The Guy Next Door, 2011; When You Dare, 2011; The Promise of Love, 2011; Trace of Fever, 2011; Savor the Danger, 2011; Luring Lucy, 2011; A Perfect Storm, 2012. **Address:** PO Box 854, Ross, OH 45061, U.S.A. **Online address:** l.l.foster@fuse.net

FOSTER, Mark. American (born United States), b. 1961?. **Genres:** History. **Career:** Writer. **Publications:** Whale Port: A History of Tuckanucket, 2007. **Address:** Somerville, MA , U.S.A. **Online address:** mark@fosterartandbooks.com

FOSTER, M(ichael) A(nthony). American (born United States), b. 1939. **Genres:** Science Fiction/Fantasy, Poetry, Novellas/Short Stories, Literary Criticism And History. **Career:** Writer. **Publications:** POETRY: Shards from Byzantium, 1969; The Vaseline Dreams of Hundifer Soames, 1970. SCIENCE FICTION: The Warriors of Dawn, 1975; The Gameplayers of Zan, 1977; The Day of the Klesh, 1979; Waves, 1980; The Morphodite, 1981; (contrib.) New Voices 4, 1981; Transformer, 1983; Dreams, 1984; (contrib.) New Voices 5, 1984; Preserver, 1985; Owl Time, 1985. **Address:** 5409 Amberhill Dr., Greensboro, NC 27405, U.S.A.

FOSTER, Nora R(akestraw). American (born United States), b. 1947. **Genres:** Marine Sciences/Oceanography, Sciences, Environmental Sciences/Ecology. **Career:** University of Alaska Museum, co-ordinator of aquatic collection, 1980-97, research associate, now retired; Hidden Hill Friends Center, board director, 1984-90; Association for Women in Science, Alaska chapter president, 1993-94; Western Society of Malacologists, president, 1994-95; NRF Taxonomic Services, zoologist, 1998-; Interior Alaska Land Trust, president. Writer. **Publications:** Intertidal Bivalves: A Guide to the Common Marine Bivalves of Alaska, 1991; Database on the Marine Invertebrate Macrofauna of Prince William Sound: An Addition to the University of Alaska Museum's ARCTOS Network, 2004. **Address:** NRF Taxonomic Services, 2998 Gold Hill Rd., Fairbanks, AK 99709, U.S.A. **Online address:** fyaqua@uaf.edu

FOSTER, Raymond E. American (born United States), b. 1959. **Genres:** Law, Adult Non-fiction. **Career:** Los Angeles Police Department, police officer, 1980-88, sergeant, 1988-97, lieutenant, 1997-2003; Hi Tech Criminal Justice, owner and editor, 2003-; Connection House, board chair, 2003-; Union Institute and University, faculty advisor and instructor, 2004-; California State University, instructor, 2004-. Boy Scouts of America, assistant scoutmaster, assistant cubmaster. **Publications:** Police Technology, 2005; (foreword) Technology and Law Enforcement: From Gumshoe to Gamma Rays, 2007; (with A.J. Harvey) Leadership: Texas Hold 'Em Style, 2007; (with J. O'Keefe) NYPD to LAPD: An Introduction to Policing, 2009. Contributor to periodicals. **Address:** Hi Tech Criminal Justice, 1034 W Arrow Hwy., Ste. D, PO Box 122, San Dimas, CA 91773, U.S.A. **Online address:** editor@police-writers.com

FOSTER, Richard. British (born England), b. 1946?. **Genres:** Art/Art History, Architecture, Biography, Theology/Religion, Social Sciences. **Career:** British Broadcasting Corp. (BBC), television producer, 1970-72. Writer. **Publications:** Discovering English Churches: A Beginner's Guide to the Story of the Parish Church from before the Conquest to the Gothic Revival, 1981; (with P. Tudor-Craig) The Secret Life of Paintings, 1986; The Parish Churches of Britain, 1988; Patterns of Thought: The Hidden Meaning of the Great Pavement of Westminster Abbey, 1991; William Morris: Broken Dreams, 1995. Contributor to magazines. **Address:** c/o Rachel Calder, Tessa Sayle Agency, 11 Jubilee Pl., London, GL SW3 3TE, England.

FOSTER, Sesshu. American (born United States), b. 1957. **Genres:** Novels, Poetry, Literary Criticism And History, Young Adult Fiction. **Career:** Francisco Bravo Medical Magnet High School, composition and literature instructor, 1985-; University of Iowa, teacher of writing; California Institute of the Arts, teacher of writing; University of California, teacher of writing; Jack Kerouac School, Summer Writing Program, teacher of writing. Writer. **Publications:** (Ed. with N. Quinonez and M. Clinton) Invocation L.A: Urban Multicultural Poetry, 1989; City Terrace: Field Manual, 1996; Atomik Aztex, 2005; World Ball Notebook, 2008. Contributor to journals. Works appear in anthologies. **Address:** c/o Author Mail, City Lights Books, San Francisco, CA 94133, U.S.A.

FOSTER, Steven. American (born United States), b. 1957. **Genres:** Photography, Medicine/Health, Biology. **Career:** Organic Herb Growers and Producers Coop, founding board director, 1978-80; Santa Cruz County Community Gardens, board director, 1979; Herb Garden Project, director, 1979; Well-Being, botanical editor, 1979-82; Herb News, review editor, 1980-82; Ozark Resources Center, Ozark Beneficial Plant Project, research director, 1983-87; Izard Ozark Native Seeds, proprietor, 1983-88; HerbalGram, contributing editor, 1985-89, associate editor, 1989-; Business of Herbs, associate editor, 1985-; Herb Business Bulletin, editor, 1986-88; Eureka Springs, writer and consultant, 1987-; Clear Spring School, vice president of board director, 1988-91; Botanical and Herb Reviews, editor, 1989-; Herb Quarterly, contributing editor, 1989; Bestways, contributing editor, 1989; Journal of Herbs, Spices, and Medicinal Plants, associate editor, 1991; Steven Foster Group Inc., founder. **Publications:** Herbal Bounty: The Gentle Art of Herb Culture, 1984; East-West Botanicals: Comparisons of Medicinal Plants Disjunct Between Eastern Asia and Eastern North America, 1986; (with J.A. Duke) A Field Guide to Medicinal Plants: Eastern and Central America, 1990; Echinacea: Nature's Immune Enhancer, 1991; (with Y. Chongxi) Herbal Emissaries: Bringing Chinese Herbs to the West, 1992; Herbal Renaissance: Growing, Using & Understanding Herbs In The Modern World, 1993; (with R. Caras) A Field Guide to Venomous Animals and Poisonous Plants of North America, North of Mexico, 1994; Forest Pharmacy: Medicinal Plants in American Forests, 1995; Herbs for Your Health: A Handy Guide for Knowing and Using 50 Common Herbs, 1996; (with A.Y. Leung) Encyclopedia of Common Natural Ingredients Used in Food, Drugs, and Cosmetics, 1996; 101 Medicinal Herbs: An Illustrated Guide, 1998; (with V.E. Tyler) Tyler's Honest Herbal: A Sensible Guide to the Use of Herbs and Related Remedies, 1999; Steven Foster's Guide to Herbal Dosages: How Much? How Often? What Not to Take, Handy Reference Chart, 1999; (with L.B. White) Herbal Drugstore: The Best Natural Alternatives to Over-the-Counter and Prescription Medicines!, 2000; (with J.A. Duke) Field Guide to Medicinal Plants and Herbs of Eastern and Central North America, 2000; (with C. Hobbs) Field Guide to Western Medicinal Plants and Herbs, 2002; A Desk Reference to Nature's Medicine, 2006; Herbal Pearls: Traditional Chinese Folk Wisdom, 2008; (with T.L. Dog, R.L. Johnson and D. Kiefer) National Geographic Guide to Medicinal Herbs: The World's Most Effective Healing Plants, 2010. **Address:** Steven Foster Group Inc., PO Box 191, Eureka Springs, AR 72632, U.S.A. **Online address:** sfoster@stevenfoster.com

FOSTER, Thomas C. American (born United States) **Genres:** Literary Criticism And History. **Career:** Michigan State University, graduate assistant, 1975-80, instructor, 1980-81, assistant professor of American thought and language, 1981-82, 1983-87; Kalamazoo College, assistant professor of English, 1982-83; University of Michigan, Department of English, assistant professor, 1987-93, associate professor, 1993-2001, professor of English, 2001-, Master of Arts in English Language and Literature (MA) Program, director, 2007-. Writer. **Publications:** Form and Society in Modern Literature, 1988; Seamus Heaney, 1989; Understanding John Fowles, 1994; (ed. with C. Siegel and E.E. Berry) Bodies of Writing, Bodies in Performance, 1996; (ed.) Online Casebook on At Swim-Two-Birds, 2002; How to Read Literature Like a Professor: A Lively and Entertaining Guide to Reading between the Lines, 2003; How to Read Novels Like a Professor, 2008; Twenty-five Books that Shaped America, 2011; A Song of Their Own: Contemporary Irish Poetry and the English Lyric Tradition, forthcoming; Novel Possibilities: Further Adventures in the Art of Reading, forthcoming. **Address:** Department of English, University of Michigan, 303 E Kearsley St., Flint, MI 48502, U.S.A. **Online address:** tfos@umflint.edu

FOSTER, (William) Lawrence. American (born United States), b. 1947. **Genres:** Sex, Theology/Religion, History. **Career:** Antioch College, lecturer, 1966-69; Roosevelt University, instructor in American social history, 1976-77; Georgia Institute of Technology, assistant professor, 1977-82, associate professor of American history, 1982-96, professor, 1996-; University of Sydney, Fulbright professor, 1985; Antioch Outdoor Education Center, lecturer; Chicago Historical Society, lecturer; Field Museum of Natural History, lecturer; History of the British Empire, lecturer. Writer. **Publications:** Religion and Sexuality: Three American Communal Experiments of the Nineteenth Century, 1981, rev. ed. as Religion and Sexuality: The Shakers, the Mormons and the Oneida Community, 1984; (contrib.) Engineering the New South: Georgia Tech, 1885-1985, 1985; (contrib.) Uncivil Religion: Interreligious Hostility in America, 1987; (contrib.) Religion and Society in the American West: Historical Essays, 1987; (contrib.) The Disappointed: Millerism and Millenarianism in the Nineteenth Century, 1987; Women, Family, and Utopia: Communal Experiments of the Shakers, the Oneida Community, and the Mormons, 1991; (ed. and intro.) Free Love in Utopia: John Humphrey Noyes and the Origin of the Oneida Community, 2001. Contributor to books and periodicals. **Address:** School of History, Technology and Society, Georgia Institute of Technology, Rm. 121, Old Civil Engineering Bldg., Atlanta, GA 30332-0345, U.S.A. **Online address:** lawrence.foster@hts.gatech.edu

FOTOPOULOS, Takis. British/Greek (born Greece), b. 1940. **Genres:** Economics, Environmental Sciences/Ecology, Philosophy, Politics/Government, Social Sciences, Young Adult Non-fiction. **Career:** University of North London, lecturer, 1969-72, senior lecturer in economics, 1973-89; Polytechnic of North London, senior lecturer in economics; Society and Nature, editor, 1992-98; Democracy and Nature, writer and editor, 1999-2003; International Journal of Inclusive Democracy, writer and editor, 2004-; Inclusive Democracy Movement, founder; Athens Daily Eleftherotypia, columnist. **Publications:** Dependent Development, 1985; The War in the Gulf, 1991; Neophileleuthere Synainese kai he krise tes Oikonomias Anaptyxes, 1993; The New World Order and Greece, 1997; Towards an Inclusive Democracy, 1997; Periektike Demokratia, 1999; Drugs: An Alternative Approach, 1999; The New Order in the Balkans, 1999; Religion, Autonomy, Democracy, 2000; From Athenian Democracy to Inclusive Democracy, 2000; Globalisation, Left and Inclusive Democracy, 2002; Polemos kata tes Tromokratias: He Genikeumene Epithese tōn Elit, 2003; Chomsky's Capitalism, 2004; The Multi-dimensional Crisis and Inclusive Democracy, 2004; Inclusive Democracy-10 Years Afterwards, 2008. Contributor to books and periodicals. **Address:** 20 Woodberry Way, London, GL N12 0HG, England. **Online address:** takis@fotopoulos1.fsnet.co.uk

FOULKES, (Albert) Peter. British (born England), b. 1936. **Genres:** Literary Criticism And History, Travel/Exploration, Young Adult Fiction. **Career:** University of Mississippi, assistant professor of German, 1961-63; University of Illinois, assistant professor of German, 1963-65; Stanford University, assistant professor, 1965-67, associate professor, 1967-72, associate dean of humanities and sciences, 1970-72, professor of German studies, 1972-77; University of Constance, Alexander von Humboldt senior research fellow in linguistics, 1972-74; University of Stirling, reader in German, 1974-77; University of Mainz, visiting professor of comparative literature, 1976; University of Wales, professor of German and head of department, 1977-90; Institute of Linguists, vice president, 1990-99. Writer. **Publications:** The Reluctant Pessimist: A Study of Franz Kafka, 1967; The Search for Literary Meaning: A Semiotic Approach to the Problem of Interpretaion in Education, 1975; Literature and Propaganda, 1983. EDITOR: (with E. Lohner) Deutsche Novellen von Tieck bis Hauptmann. 1969; (with E. Lohner) Dasdeutsche Drama von Kleist bis Hauptmann, 1973; The Uses of Criticism, 1976; (co-ed.) Essays in Literary Semantics, 1978; Die Judenbuche, 1989; Tales from French Catalonia, 2001. **Address:** Clara, Prades, 66500, France.

FOULKES, Richard (George). British (born England), b. 1944. **Genres:** Theatre, History. **Career:** University of Birmingham, administrator, 1967-73; University of Leicester, lecturer, 1973-98, reader, 1998-, professor of theatre history, School of English, head, 2004-08, emeritus professor of theatre history; Northampton Repertory Players, director, 1990-96, vice-chair, 1992-, chairman, 1995-96; Society for Theatre Research, chairman. Writer. **Publications:** The Shakespeare Tercentenary of 1864, 1984; The Calverts: Actors of Some Importance, 1992; Repertory at the Royal: Sixty-Five Years of Theatre in Northampton, 1992; Church and Stage in Victorian England, 1997; Performing Shakespeare in the Age of Empire, 2002; Theatre, 2002; Lewis Carroll and the Victorian Stage: Theatricals in a Quiet Life, 2005. EDITOR: Shakespeare and the Victorian Stage, 1986; British Theatre in the 1890's: Essays on Drama and the Stage, 1992; Scenes from Provincial Stages, 1994; Henry Irving: A Re-Evaluation of the Pre-Eminent Victorian Actor Manager, 2008. Contributor to journals. **Address:** Department of English, University of Leicester, University Rd., Leicester, LE1 7RH, England. **Online address:** rf24@le.ac.uk

FOURIE, Corlia. South African (born South Africa), b. 1944. **Genres:** Children's Fiction, Novellas/Short Stories, Mythology/Folklore, Children's Non-fiction. **Career:** Die Burger, journalist; Sarie, journalist; Rooi Rose, fiction editor; Journalist and writer, 1965-. **Publications:** Marianne en die leeu in die pophuis, 1982; Moeders en dogters, 1985; Leuens, 1985; En die son skyn in Suid-Afrika, 1985; Die volstruisie watgraag wou vlieg, 1986; Die meisie wat soos 'n bottervoël sing; Tintinyane, the Girl Who Sang like a Magic Bird, 1990; Jakkalsstreke, 1991; Liefde en geweld (short stories), 1992; Ganekwane and the Green Dragon, 1992; (comp.) Vrou-mens: Verhale deur vroue oor vroue, 1992; Die deurmekaardier, 1993; Sê (short stories), 1994; Die towersak (The Magic Pouch), 1995; Die oop deur, 1996; Nolito en die wonderwater, 1997; Die wit vlinder, 1993; (comp.) Want die lewe is goed: keur uit die werk van Mikro, 2003; Stories met stertjies, 2007; (comp.) Ware liefde: bekende Suid-Afrikaanse paartjies, 2008; Remember: South Africans in Love, 2008; Heleen en die heks met die hoofpyn, 2008; Alle paaie lei deur die strand, 2008. **Address:** Rooi Rose, Howard Pl. 7450, Caxton Bldg., Old Millweg, 36 Ndabeni, PO Box 260, Cape Town, 7405, South Africa.

FOURNIER, Marcel. Canadian (born Canada), b. 1945. **Genres:** Politics/Government, Bibliography, Communications/Media, History. **Career:** University of Montreal, professor; Durkheim Studies, editor; Sociologie et Sociétés, editor. **Publications:** Rawdon: 175 Ans d'histoire, 1974; Guide Bibliographique Joliette-Lanaudière: Livres et Journaux, 1847-1976, 1976; La Représentation Parlementaire de la Région de Joliette, 1791-1976, 1977; Communisme et Anticommunisme au Québec, 1920-1950, 1979; Entre l'école et l'usine: La Formation Professionnelle des Jeunes Travailleurs, 1980; L'entré dans la Modernité: Science, Culture, et Société au Québec, 1986; Les Générations d'artistes, 1986; (with Y. Gingras and O. Keel) Sciences & Médecine au Québec: Perspectives Sociohistoriques, 1987; Les Européens au Canada: Des Origines 1765 (hors France), 1989; (ed. with M. Lamont) Cultivating Differences: Symbolic Boundaries and the Making of Inequality, 1992; Marcel Mauss, 1994; L'espace Public de la Science, ou, La Visibilité Sociale des Scientifiques: Rapport Présenté au Conseil de la Science et de la Technologie, 1995; (comp.) Ecrits Politiques, 1997; (with P. Besnard) Lettres Marcel Mauss, 1998; Musique, Enjeux Sociaux, et Défis Méthodologiques: Perspectives Comparés Québec, France, Cuba, 2006; (ed. with A. Sales) Knowledge, Communication and Creativity, 2007; Emile

Durkheim, 1858-1917, 2007. **Address:** Department of Sociology, Université de Montréal, PO Box 6128, Sta. Centre-ville, Montreal, QC H3C 3J7, Canada. **Online address:** marcel.fournier@umontreal.ca

FOUST, J'aimé L. American (born United States), b. 1955. **Genres:** inspirational/Motivational Literature, Librarianship, Education. **Career:** Queensbury High School, social studies teacher, 1985-91, librarian, 1991-, school library media specialist, Queensbury Middle School, administrative intern. Writer. **Publications:** Dewey Need to Get Organized?: A Time Management and Organization Guide for School Librarians, 2002. **Address:** Queensbury High School, 409 Aviation Rd., Queensbury, NY 12804, U.S.A. **Online address:** jfoust@queensburyschool.org

FOUST, Jeff. American (born United States), b. 1971. **Genres:** Information Science/Computers, Technology. **Career:** Coola Inc., web developer, 1999-2001; Futron Corp., space industry analyst, 2001-, senior analyst and project manager; The Space Review, publisher, 2003-. Writer. **Publications:** (With D. Kerven and J. Zakour) HTML 3 How-To: The Definitive HTML 3 Problem-Solver, 1996; (with D. Kerven and J. Zakour) HTML 3.2 How-To, 1997; (with D. Kerven and J. Zakour) HTML 4 How-To: The Definitive HTML 4 Problem-Solver, 1997; Astronomer's Computer Companion, 2000. Contributor to periodicals. **Address:** Futron Corp., 7315 Wisconsin Ave., Ste. 900W, 555 DeHaro St., Bethesda, MD 20814, U.S.A. **Online address:** jeff@jfoust.com

FOWERS, Blaine J. American (born United States), b. 1956. **Genres:** Psychology, Social Sciences, Medicine/Health. **Career:** University of Texas at Austin, Counseling and Psychological Service Center, counselor, 1984-85; State University of New York, University Counseling Service, counseling psychology intern, 1985-86; Falkirk Hospital, staff psychologist, 1986-87; University of New Mexico, Department of Counseling and Family Studies, assistant professor, 1987-90, director of training, 1990; Family Center for Counseling and Education, clinical director, 1988-90; University of Miami, Department of Educational and Psychological Studies, assistant professor, 1990-95, associate professor, 1995-2003, director of training, 1997-2005, acting chairperson, 1998, professor, 2003-, chairperson, 2005-09. Writer. **Publications:** (With F.C. Richardson and C.B. Guignon) Re-Envisioning Psychology: Moral Dimensions of Theory and Practice, 1999; Beyond the Myth of Marital Happiness: How Embracing the Virtues of Loyalty, Generosity, Justice, and Courage Can Strengthen Your Relationship, 2000; Virtue and Psychology: Pursuing Excellence in Ordinary Practices, 2005. Contributor to books and periodicals. **Address:** Department of Educational and Psych Studies, School of Education, University of Miami, 319-D Merrick Bldg., PO Box 248065, Coral Gables, FL 33124-2040, U.S.A. **Online address:** bfowers@miami.edu

FOWLER, Alastair (David Shaw). Scottish (born Scotland), b. 1930. **Genres:** Poetry, Literary Criticism And History, Education. **Career:** Oxford University, Queen's College, junior research fellow, 1955-59, Brasenose College, fellow and tutor in English, 1962-71; Indiana University, visiting instructor, 1957-58; University of Wales, University College of Swansea, lecturer in renaissance literature, 1959-61; University of Virginia, visiting professor, 1969, 1979, 1980-90, professor of English, 1990-97; University of Edinburgh, Regius professor of rhetoric and English literature, 1972-84, Regius professor emeritus of rhetoric and English literature, 1984-, university fellow, 1985-87; Princeton University, Council of the Humanities, visiting fellow, 1974; Longman Annotated Anthologies of English Verse, general editor, 1977-80. **Publications:** Spenser and the Numbers of Time, 1964; Triumphal Forms: Structural Patterns in Elizabethan Poetry, 1970; Seventeen (poetry), 1971; Readers of Literature, 1972; Conceitful Thought: The Interpretation of English Renaissance Poems, 1975; Catacomb Suburb, 1976; Edmund Spenser, 1977; Spenser, 1978; From the Domain of Arnheim, 1982; Kinds of Literature: An Introduction to the Theory of Genres and Modes, 1982; A History of English Literature, 1987, rev. ed., 1989; (comp.) The Country House Poem: A Cabinet of Seventeenth-Century Estate Poems and Related Items, 1994; Metaphysical Lyrics and Poems of the Seventeenth Century: Donne to Butler, 1995; Time's Purpled Masquers: Stars and the Afterlife in Renaissance English Literature, 1996; Renaissance Realism: Narrative Images in Literature and Art, 2003; How to Write, 2006. EDITOR: (and trans.) Richard Wills, De Re Poetica, 1958; Spenser's Images of Life, 1967; (with J. Carey) The Poems of John Milton, 1968; Silent Poetry: Essays in Numerological Analysis, 1970; (with I.C. Butler) Topics in Criticism: An Ordered Set of Positions in Literary Theory, 1971; Paradise Lost, 1971, 2nd ed., 2007; The New Oxford

Book of Seventeenth Century Verse, 1991. Contributor to journals. **Address:** School of Literatures, Languages & Cultures, University of Edinburgh, 19 & 27 George Sq., Edinburgh, EH8 9LD, Scotland.

FOWLER, Christopher. British (born England), b. 1953. **Genres:** Novels, Novellas/Short Stories, Humor/Satire, Plays/Screenplays, Mystery/Crime/Suspense. **Career:** Creative Partnership (film marketing firm), founder and creative director, 1979-. Writer. **Publications:** Seventy-seven Clocks, 2005; White Corridor, 2007; Old Devil Moon, 2007; The Victoria Vanishes, 2008; Bryant and May on the Loose: A Peculiar Crimes Unit Mystery, 2009; Paperboy, 2009; Bryant and May off the Rails: A Peculiar Crimes Unit Mystery, 2010; The Curse of Snakes: Hellion, 2010; Bryant & May and the Memory of Blood, 2011; Memory of Blood: A Peculiar Crimes Unit Mystery, 2012. HUMOR: How to Impersonate Famous People, 1985; The Ultimate Party Book: The Illustrated Guide to Social Intercourse, 1987. NOVELS: Roofworld, 1988; Rune, 1991; Red Bride, 1992; Darkest Day, 1993; Spanky, 1994; Psychoville, 1995; Disturbia, 1997; (with J. Bolton) Menz Insana (graphic novel), 1997; Soho Black, 1998; Calabash, 2000; Breathe: Everyone Has to Do It, 2004. STORIES: City Jitters 1(anthology), 1986, rev. ed., 1992; City Jitters 2 (anthology), 1988; More City Jitters, 1988; The Bureau of Lost Souls, 1989; Sharper Knives, 1992; Flesh Wounds, 1995; Personal Demons, 1998; Uncut, 1999; The Devil in Me, 2001; P Demonized, 2003; Full Dark House, 2003; The Water Room, 2005; Ten Second Staircase: A Bryant and May Mystery, 2006. Contributor to periodicals. **Address:** Creative Partnership, 13 Bateman St., London, GL W1V 5TB, England. **Online address:** chris@cfowler.demon.co.uk

FOWLER, Connie May. American (born United States), b. 1960. **Genres:** Novels, Mystery/Crime/Suspense, Young Adult Fiction, Autobiography/Memoirs. **Career:** Women with Wings, founder, director, 1997-2003; Rollins College, Irving Bachellor professor of creative writing, 2003-07; Spalding University, professor of creative writing. Novelist. **Publications:** Sugar Cage, 1992; River of Hidden Dreams, 1994; Before Women Had Wings, 1996; Remembering Blue, 2000; When Katie Wakes: A Memoir, 2002; Problem with Murmur Lee: A Novel, 2005; The Problem with Murmur Lee, 2006; How Clarissa Burden Learned to Fly, 2010. Contributor to periodicals. Works appear in anthology. **Address:** Joy Harris Literary Agency Inc., 156 5th Ave., Ste. 617, New York, NY 10010-7002, U.S.A. **Online address:** conniemayhome@aol.com

FOWLER, Don D. American (born United States), b. 1936. **Genres:** Anthropology/Ethnology, History, Photography. **Career:** Glen Canyon Project, staff archaeologist, 1957-62; University of Nevada, instructor, 1964-65, assistant professor, 1965-67, associate research professor, 1968-71, research professor of anthropology, 1971-78, Human Systems Center of Desert Research Institute, executive director, 1968-71, Social Sciences Center, Desert Research Institute, executive director, 1971-78, Mamie Kleberg professor of anthropology and historic preservation, 1978-2005, emeritus, Department of Anthropology, chairperson, 1990-; Archaeological Research Project, director, 1966-; Northwestern Anthropological Research Notes, associate editor, 1966-71; American Society for Ethnohistory, book review editor, 1967-71; Smithsonian Institution, visiting postdoctoral fellow, 1967-68, research associate, 1970-2004; American Antiquity, assistant editor, 1970-75; Society for American Archaeology, president, 1985-87; Sundance Archaeological Research Fund program, director, 1994-2001; American Anthropological Association, fellow; Southwestern Anthropological Association, anthropology associate. Writer. **Publications:** Archeological Survey in Eastern Nevada, 1966, 1968; (with C.S. Fowler and R.C. Euler) John Wesley Powell and the Anthropology of the Canyon Country, 1969; In a Sacred Manner We Live: Edward S. Curtis's Photographs of North American Indians, 1972; (with J.F. Matley) Material Culture of the Numa: The John Wesley Powell Collection, 1867-1880, 1979; Western Photographs of John K. Hillers: Myself in the Water, 1989; A Laboratory for Anthropology: Science and Romanticism in American Southwest, 1846-1930, 2000; (with N.J. Parezo) Anthropology Goes to the Fair: The 1904 Louisiana Purchase Exposition, 2000; (foreword) Men Met Along the Trail: Adventures in Archaeology, 2009; The Glen Canyon Country: A Personal Memoir, 2010. EDITOR/CO-EDITOR: Down the Colorado: John Wesley Powell's Diary of the First Trip through the Grand Canyon, 1969; (with C.S. Fowler) Anthropology of the Numa, 1971; Photographed All the Best Scenery: Jack Hiller's Diary of the Powell Expedition, 1972; Great Basin Cultural Ecology: A Symposium, 1972; (with C.J. Condie) Anthropology of the Desert West: Essays in Honor of Jesse P. Jennings, 1986; (with D.J. Meltzer and J.A. Sabloff) American Archaeology Past & Future: A Celebration

of the Society for American Archaeology, 1935-1985, 1986; (with C. Irwin-Williams) Regional Conferences: Summary Report, 1986; H. Stansbury's Exploration of the Valley of the Great Salt Lake, 1988; (with D.L. Hardesty) Others Knowing Others: Perspectives on Ethnographic Careers, 1994; (with D.R. Wilcox) Philadelphia and the Development of Americanist Archaeology, 2003; (with L.S. Cordell) Southwest Archaeology in the Twentieth Century, 2005; (with C.S. Fowler) Great Basin: People and Place in Ancient Times, 2008; Cleaving an Unknown World: The Powell Expeditions and the Scientific Exploration of the Colorado Plateau, 2011. Contributor to periodicals. **Address:** University of Nevada, Reno, NV 89557, U.S.A.

FOWLER, Earlene. American (born United States), b. 1954. **Genres:** Mystery/Crime/Suspense, Novels, Literary Criticism And History. **Career:** Writer, 1994-. **Publications:** Fool's Puzzle, 1994; Irish Chain, 1995; Kansas Troubles, 1996; Goose in the Pond, 1997; Dove in the Window, 1998; (co-author) Murder on Route 66, 1999; Mariner's Compass, 1999; Seven Sisters, 2000; Arkansas Traveler, 2001; Steps to the Altar, 2002; Sunshine and Shadow, 2003; Broken Dishes, 2004; Benni Harper Quilt Album, 2004; Delectable Mountains, 2005; The Saddlemaker's Wife, 2006; Tumbling Blocks, 2007; Love Mercy, 2009; State Fair, 2010; Spider Web, 2011. **Address:** c/o Ellen Geiger, Curtis Brown Ltd., 10 Astor Pl., New York, NY 10003, U.S.A. **Online address:** earlenefowler@earlenefowler.com

FOWLER, Gene. American (born United States), b. 1931. **Genres:** Poetry, Adult Non-fiction, Social Sciences, Literary Criticism And History. **Career:** Writer, 1963-; University of Wisconsin, poet-in-residence and workshop director, 1970. **Publications:** Field Studies, 1965; Quarter Tones, 1966; Shaman Songs, 1967; Her Majesty's Ship, 1969; Fires, 1972, rev. ed. as Fires: Selected Poems, 1963-1976, 1975; Vivisection, 1975; Felon's Journal, 1975; Return of the Shaman, 1981; The Makings (criticism), 1981; Waking the Poet: Acquiring the Deep Seated Crafts Usually Called Talents, 1981; The Quiet Poems, 1982. **Address:** 1432 Spruce St., Berkeley, CA 94709, U.S.A. **Online address:** acorioso@earthlink.net

FOWLER, James H. American (born United States), b. 1970. **Genres:** Sciences. **Career:** University of California, assistant professor, 2003-06, associate professor, 2006-, Center for Wireless and Population Health Systems affiliate, 2009-, School of Medicine, Division of Social Sciences, professor of medical genetics and political science. Writer. **Publications:** (With O. Smirnov) Mandates, Parties and Voters: How Elections Shape the Future, 2007; Connected: The Surprising Power of Our Social Networks and How They Shape Our Lives, 2009. Contributors to books, periodicals and journals. **Address:** Department of Political Science, University of California, Social Science Bldg. 383, Ste. 0521, La Jolla, CA 92093-0521, U.S.A. **Online address:** jhfowler@ucsd.edu

FOWLER, Loretta. American (born United States), b. 1944. **Genres:** History, Politics/Government. **Career:** University of Oklahoma, Department of Anthropology, professor, now professor emeritus. Writer. **Publications:** Arapahoe Politics, 1851-1978: Symbols in Crises of Authority, 1982; Shared Symbols, Contested Meanings: Gros Ventre Culture and History, 1778-1984, 1987; The Arapaho, 1989; Tribal Sovereignty and the Historical Imagination: Cheyenne-Arapaho Politics, 2002; The Columbia Guide to American Indians of the Great Plains, 2003; (ed. with D.M. Cobb) Beyond Red Power: American Indian Politics and Activism since 1900, 2007; Wives and Husbands: Gender and Age in Southern Arapaho History, 2010. **Address:** Department of Anthropology, University of Oklahoma, Rm. 330, 455 W Lindsey, Dale Hall, 521 Twr., 332 Cate Center Dr., 3rd Fl., Norman, OK 73019, U.S.A. **Online address:** lfowler@ou.edu

FOWLER, Ruth. American/British (born England), b. 1979. **Genres:** Autobiography/Memoirs. **Career:** Writer and educator. **Publications:** No Man's Land: A Memoir, 2008. Contributor to periodicals. **Address:** U.S.A. **Online address:** info@ruthfowler.co.uk

FOWLER, Virginia C. American (born United States), b. 1948. **Genres:** Literary Criticism And History, Poetry. **Career:** Virginia Tech, College of Liberal Arts and Human Sciences, Department of English, assistant professor, 1977-83, associate professor, 1983-96, professor of English, 1996-, director of graduate studies, 1985-91, director of literature, language and culture; Indiana University, visiting professor of English, 1996. Writer. **Publications:**

Henry James's American Girl: The Embroidery on the Canvas, 1984; Nikki Giovanni, 1992; (ed.) Conversations with Nikki Giovanni, 1992; Gloria Naylor: In Search of Sanctuary, 1996; Collected Poetry of Nikki Giovanni, 1968-1998, 2003. Works appear in anthologies. Contributor of articles to journals and books. **Address:** Department of English, College of Liberal Arts and Human Sciences, Virginia Tech, 323 Shanks Hall, Blacksburg, VA 24061-0112, U.S.A. **Online address:** vfowler@vt.edu

FOWLKES, Diane L(owe). American (born United States), b. 1939. **Genres:** Politics/Government, Women's Studies And Issues, Adult Non-fiction. **Career:** Georgia State University, assistant professor, 1973-80, associate professor, 1980-92, professor, 1992-98, professor emeritus of political science, 1998-2007, interim director of women's studies, 1990-94, Women's Studies Institute, founding director, 1995-98, retired; Diable Stable Inc., president; Women's Policy Group/Women's Policy Education Fund, vice president, 1992-. Writer. **Publications:** How Feminist Theory Reconstructs American Government and Politics, 1983; (ed. with C.S. McClure) Feminist Visions: Toward a Transformation of the Liberal Arts Curriculum, 1984; White Political Women: Paths from Privilege to Empowerment, 1992. Contributor to journals. **Address:** PO Box 3806, Ocala, FL 34478-3806, U.S.A. **Online address:** sophieatsgii@aol.com

FOX, Andrew Jay. American (born United States), b. 1964. **Genres:** Young Adult Fiction. **Career:** Sagamore Children's Center, administrative intern, 1988-90; Hillel Jewish Students Center, faculty, 1990-91; Louisiana Office of Public Health, Commodity Supplemental Food Program, manager, 1991-; New Year Coalition, co-founder. Writer. **Publications:** Fat White Vampire Blues, 2003; Bride of the Fat White Vampire, 2004; The Good Humor Man: Or, Calorie 3501, 2009. **Address:** c/o Author Mail, Random House, 1745 Broadway, New York, NY 10019, U.S.A. **Online address:** andrewfox@andrewfoxbooks.com

FOX, Barry. American (born United States) **Genres:** How-to Books, Biography, Ghost Writer, Autobiography/Memoirs, Business/Trade/Industry, Film, History, Medicine/Health, Medicine/Health. **Career:** Author. **Publications:** Foods to Heal By: An A-to-Z Guide to Medicinal Foods and Their Curative Properties, 1996; To Your Health: The Healing Power of Alcohol, 1997; (with J. Theodosakis and B. Adderly) The Arthritis Cure: The Medical Miracle that Can Halt, Reverse, and May Even Cure Osteoarthritis, 1997; (with J. Theodosakis and B. Adderly) Maximizing the Arthritis Cure: A Step-by-Step Program to Faster, Stronger Healing during Any Stage of the Cure, 1998; (with G. Mirkin) The 20/30 Fat and Fiber Diet Plan, 1998; (with S. Schimmel) Cancer Talk: Voices of Hope and Endurance from The Group Room, the Worlds Largest Cancer Support Group, 1999; (with G. Reaven and T. Kristen) Syndrome X: Overcoming the Silent Killer that Can Give You a Heart Attack, 2000; (with A. Mauskop) What Your Doctor May Not Tell You about Migraines: The Breakthrough Program that Can Help End Your Pain, 2001; Patents: A Guide, 2003; (with F. Vagnini) The Side Effects Bible: The Dietary Solution to Unwanted Side Effects of Common Medications, 2005; (with R. Hoffman) Alternative Cures That Really Work: For The Savvy Health Consumer-A Must-Have Guide to More Than 100 Food Remedies, Herbs, Supplements, and Healing Techniques, 2006; (with G.T. Grossberg) Essential Herb-drug-vitamin Interaction Guide: The Safe Way to Use Medications and Supplements Together, 2007. WITH A. FOX: DLPA to End Chronic Pain and Depression, 1985; Wake Up! Youre Alive: MDs Prescription for Healthier Living through Positive Thinking, 1988; Immune for Life: Live Longer and Better by Strengthening Your Doctor Within, 1989; Making Miracles: Inspiring Mind-Methods to Supercharge Your Emotions and Rejuvenate Your Health, 1989; Beyond Positive Thinking: Putting Your Thoughts into Action, 1991; 14-Day Miracle Plan: Inspiring Mind Methods to Supercharge Your Emotions and Rejuvenate Your Health, 1991; The Healthy Prostate: A Doctors Comprehensive Program for Preventing and Treating Common Problems, 1996; Alternative Healing, 1996; Boost Your Immune System Now!: Live Longer and Better by Strengthening Your Doctor Within, 1997. WITH N. TAYLOR: (and with R. Delorm) Diana and Dodi: A Love Story, 1998; Arthritis for Dummies, 2000, (with J. Yazdany) 2nd ed., 2007; (and with M. Houston) What Your Doctor May Not Tell You about Hypertension: The Revolutionary Nutrition and Lifestyle Program to Help Fight High Blood Pressure, 2003. Contributor of articles to periodicals. **Address:** 23679 Calabasas Rd., Ste. 223, Calabasas, CA 91302, U.S.A. **Online address:** barry@barryfox.us

FOX, Bryanna. See **WOODS, Janet.**

FOX, Connie. See **FOX, Hugh (Bernard).**

FOX, Faulkner. American (born United States) **Genres:** Adult Non-fiction, Biography, Autobiography/Memoirs. **Career:** State of Virginia, special assistant to the secretary of human resources, 1986-87; National Abortion Rights Action League (NARAL) director, 1992-94; University of Texas, poetry instructor; Duke University, creative writing instructor, 2002-, lecturing fellow. Writer. **Publications:** Dispatches from a Not-So-Perfect Life; or How I Learned to Love the House the Man the Child, 2003. Contributor to periodicals. **Address:** Department of English, Duke University, 303A Allen Bldg., PO Box 90015, Durham, NC 27708-0563, U.S.A. **Online address:** faulkner@faulknerfox.com

FOX, Frank. American/Polish (born Poland), b. 1923. **Genres:** History, Translations, Animals/Pets. **Career:** Temple University, teacher, 1963-67; West Chester University, professor, 1967-89, now professor emeritus in East European history; Writer and translator, 1989-; University of Delaware, lecturer; St. Joseph's University, lecturer; Gene Autry Museum, consultant. **Publications:** (Ed. and trans.) C. Perechodnik, Am I a Murderer? Testament of a Jewish Ghetto Policeman (memoir), 1996; Polish Posters: Combat on Paper, 1960-1990 (exhibit catalog), 1996; God's Eye: Aerial Photography and the Katyn Forest Massacre, 1999; Zoos in Wartime, forthcoming. Contributor to periodicals. Work appears in anthologies. **Address:** Department of History, West Chester University, 500 Main Hall, West Chester, PA 19383, U.S.A. **Online address:** fischele@aol.com

FOX, Helen. American/British (born England), b. 1962?. **Genres:** Science Fiction/Fantasy, Young Adult Fiction, Literary Criticism And History. **Career:** Marketing executive, actress, teacher and writer. **Publications:** Eager, 2004; Eager's Nephew, 2006; Eager and the Mermaid, 2007. Contributor to periodicals. **Address:** c/o Author Mail, Wendy Lamb Books, 1745 Broadway, New York, NY 10019, U.S.A.

FOX, Hugh (Bernard). (Connie Fox). American (born United States), b. 1932. **Genres:** Novels, Plays/Screenplays, Poetry, Literary Criticism And History, Autobiography/Memoirs. **Career:** Loyola University (now Loyola Marymount University), professor of American literature, 1958-68; University of Hermosillo, Fulbright professor, 1961; University Catolica, Institute Pedagogico, Smith-Mundt professor of American studies, 1964-66; Michigan State University, Department of American Thought and Language, professor, 1968-99, professor emeritus, 1999-; Federal University of Santa Catarina, Fulbright professor, 1978-80. Writer. **Publications:** 40 Poems, 1966; A Night with Hugh Fox, 1966; Eye into Now, 1967; Soul Catcher Songs, 1967; Apotheosis of Olde Towne, 1968; Henry James, 1968; Permeable Man, 1969; (with S. Schott) Ghost Dance; Portfolio I, 1968; Open Letter to a Closed System, 1969; Countdown of an Empty Streetcar, 1969; Charles Bukowski, 1969; Mind Shaft, 1969; Son of Camelot Meets the Wolfman, 1969; (with A. Cortina) Ghost Dance: Portfolio II, 1970; Ecological Suicide Bus, 1970; (with E.A. Vigo) Handbook against Gorgons, 1971; (with G. Deisler) The Industrial Ablution, 1971; Paralytic Grandpa Dream Secretions, 1971; The Omega Scriptures, 1971; Icehouse, 1971; Kansas City Westport Mantras, 1971; Survival Handbook, 1972; Just, 1972; Caliban and Ariel, 1972; Peeple, 1973-74; Gods of the Cataclysm, 1975; The Face of Guy Lombardo, 1976; Huaca, 1977; First Fire, 1978; Mom-Honeymoon, 1978; Leviathan: An Indian Ocean Whale Journal, 1981; The Guernica Cycle: The Year Franco Died, 1982; Lyn Lifshin: A Critical Study, 1985; Guernica Cycle: Spanish Diaries 1975-76, 1985; Papa Funk (chapbook), 1986; The Mythological Foundations of the Epic Genre, 1989; F. Richard (Dick) Thomas' 50th Birthday (poetry), 1991; Jamais Vu (poetry), 1991; The Sacred Cave (poetry collection), 1992; Entre Nous (poetry), 1992; Shaman, 1993; (ed. with S. Cornish) The Ghost Dance Anthology: 25 Years of Poetry from Ghost Dance, 1968-1993, 1994; Other Kinds of Scores, 1994; The Last Summer (novel), 1995; The Living Underground: The Prose Anthology, 1995; Stairway to the Sun (anthology), 1995; Hugh Fox: The Greatest Hits (poetry), 2002; Boston: A Long Poem, 2002; The Book of Ancient Revelations, 2004; Our Gang: The Last Act, 2005; Home of the Gods, 2005; Way, Way Off the Road, 2006; Defiance: Pensees Rouges et Noirs, 2007; Peace/La Pai: Ballades et Contes en quête de Vérité, 2008. AS CONNIE FOX: Blood Cocoon, 1980; The Dream of the Black Topaze Chamber (poetry), 1983; Oma, 1985; Babushka: A Poem-cycle, 1985; Nachthymnen, 1986; 10/170, 1986; Ten to the One Hundred Seventieth Power, 1986; Babicka, 1986; Skull Worship (poetry), 1988; Noria, 1988; Our Lady of Laussel (poetry), 1991. EDITOR: The Living Underground, 1973; The Diamond Eye, 1975; (and intro.) First Fire: Central and South American

Indian Poetry, 1978. Contributor of articles to periodicals. **Address:** Department of Writing, Rhetoric and American Cultures, Michigan State University, 235 Bessey Hall, East Lansing, MI 48824-1033, U.S.A. **Online address:** hughfox@aol.com

FOX, Jo. (Joanne Clare Fox). British (born England), b. 1973. **Genres:** History, Film. **Career:** Durham University, Department of History, senior lecturer in history, professor. Writer. **Publications:** Filming Women in the Third Reich, 2000; Film Propaganda in Britain and Nazi Germany: World War II Cinema, 2007. Works appear in anthologies. **Address:** Department of History, Durham University, 43 North Bailey, Durham, DU DH1 3EX, England. **Online address:** j.c.fox@durham.ac.uk

FOX, Joanne Clare. See **FOX, Jo.**

FOX, John O. American (born United States), b. 1938. **Genres:** Money/Finance, Adult Non-fiction. **Career:** Arent, Fox, Kintner, Plotkin & Kahn, associate, 1964-68; Sherman, Fox, Meehan & Canton, founding and managing partner, 1968-84, counsel, 1984-2000; Catholic University, Law School, adjunct professor of law, 1978-83; Mount Holyoke College, visiting lecturer, 1985-, visiting professor. Writer. **Publications:** If Americans Really Understood the Income Tax: Uncovering Our Most Expensive Ignorance, 2001; 10 Tax Questions the Candidates Don't Want to Ask, 2004; (co-author) Business, Financial & Estate Mediation, forthcoming. **Address:** Mount Holyoke College, 50 College St., South Hadley, MA 01075, U.S.A. **Online address:** johno.fox@comcast.net

FOX, Les. American (born United States), b. 1947. **Genres:** Novels, Young Adult Non-fiction, Food And Wine. **Career:** Writer and publisher, 1996-. **Publications:** WITH S. FOX: Silver Dollar Fortune Telling, 1986; Return to Sender: The Secret Son of Elvis Presley; A Novel, 1996; The Beanie Baby Handbook, 1997; (with J. Long) The Beanie Baby Cookbook, 1998; Washington Deceased, forthcoming; When the Cookie Crumbles, forthcoming; City Prey, forthcoming; January Fever, forthcoming. **Address:** West Highland Publishing Company Inc., PO Box 36, Midland Park, NJ 07432-0036, U.S.A.

FOX, Louisa. See **KROLL, Virginia L(ouise).**

FOX, Margalit. American (born United States), b. 1961. **Genres:** Adult Non-fiction, Education. **Career:** New York Times, New York Times Book Review, editor, 1994-2004, reporter, staff writer, 2004-. **Publications:** Talking Hands: What Sign Language Reveals about the Mind, 2007. Contributor to books and periodicals. **Address:** c/o Katinka Matson, Brockman Inc., 5 E 59th St., New York, NY 10022-1027, U.S.A. **Online address:** author@talkinghandsbook.com

FOX, Mem. Australian (born Australia), b. 1946. **Genres:** Children's Fiction, Adult Non-fiction. **Career:** Dominican school, drama teacher, 1970-72; South Australian College of Advanced Education, lecturer, 1973-86, senior lecturer in drama, 1987-; Flinders University, associate professor in literacy studies Writer. **Publications:** FOR CHILDREN: Possum Magic, 1983; Wilfrid Gordon McDonald Partridge, 1984; A Cat Called Kite, 1985, rev. ed., 2008; Sail Away, 1986; Arabella: The Smallest Girl in the World, 1986; Just Like That, 1986; Hattie and the Fox, 1987; Koala Lou, 1988; With Love, at Christmas, 1988; Night Noises, 1989; Guess What?, 1990; Shoes from Grandpa, 1990; Time for Bed, 1993; Sophie, 1994; Tough Boris, 1994; Wombat Divine, 1995; Guillermo Jorge Manuel Jose, 1995; A Bedtime Story, 1996; Great Scott!, 1996; Boo to a Goose, 1996; Feathers and Fools, 1996; The Straight Line Wonder, 1996; Zoo-Looking, 1996; Whoever You Are, 1997; Because of the Bloomers, 1998; Sleepy Bears, 1999; Harriet, You'll Drive Me Wild, 2000; Reading Magic: Why Reading Aloud to Our Children Will Change Their Lives Forever, 2001; The Magic Hat, 2002; Noammehapeś zikhronot, 2002; Where's the Green Sheep?, 2004; Hunwick's Egg, 2005; Fairy, Fairy Quite Contrary, 2005; A Particular Cow, 2006; Where the Giant Sleeps, 2007; Ten Little Fingers and Ten Little Toes, 2008; (with S. Jenkins) Hello Baby, 2009; Goblin and the Empty Chair, 2009; Two Little Monkeys, 2010; The Night Goblin, forthcoming. FOR ADULTS: How to Teach Drama to Infants Without Really Crying, 1984 in US as Teaching Drama to Young Children, 1987; Mem's the Word, 1990; Memories: An Autobiography, 1992; Dear Mem Fox, I've Read All Your Books Even the Pathetic Ones: And Other Incidents in the Life of a Children's Book Author, 1992; Mem Fox Reads, 1993; Articles of Faith, 1993; (with L. Wilkinson) English Essentials: The Wouldn't-Be-Without-It Handbook on Writing Well, 1993; Radical Reflections: Passionate

Opinions on Teaching, Learning and Living, 1993. OTHERS: Let's Count Goats!, 2010; Giraffe in the Bath, 2010; (with R. Harvey) The Little Dragon, 2011; Tell Me About Your Day Today, 2012. Contributor to periodicals. **Address:** Jenny Darling & Associates Pty Ltd., PO Box 413, Toorak, VI 3142, Australia.

FOX, M(ichael) W. British (born England), b. 1937. **Genres:** Children's Fiction, Agriculture/Forestry, Animals/Pets, Children's Non-fiction, Environmental Sciences/Ecology, Fash Ion/Costume, Food And Wine, Natural History, Philosophy. **Career:** State Research Hospital, medical research associate, 1964-67; Washington University, assistant professor, 1967-69, associate professor of psychology, 1969-76; Humane Society of the United States, Institute for the Study of Animal Problems, director, 1976-87, scientific director, 1980-87, Center for Respect of Life and Environment, director, 1988-90, Bioethics and Farm Animal Protection, vice president, 1988-97. Writer. **Publications:** Canine Behavior, 1965; Canine Pediatrics, 1966; Integrative Development of Brain and Behavior in the Dog, 1971; Behaviour of Wolves, Dogs and Related Canids, 1971; Understanding Your Dog, 1972; Understanding Your Cat, 1974; Concepts in Ethology: Animal and Human Behavior, 1974; Ramu and Chennai, Brothers of the Wild, 1975; Between Animal and Man, 1976; What Is Your Dog Saying, 1976; What Is Your Cat Saying, 1977; Wild Dogs Three, 1977; Dog: Its Domestication and Behavior, 1978; Understanding Your Pet, 1978; One Earth One Mind, 1980; Returning to Eden: Animal Rights and Human Responsibilities, 1980; The Soul of the Wolf, 1980; The Touchlings, 1981; How To Be Your Pet's Best Friend, 1981; Dr. Michael Fox's Massage Program for Cats and Dogs, 1980; Love Is a Happy Cat, 1982; Farm Animal Welfare and the Human Diet, 1983; The Healing Touch, 1983; Farm Animals: Husbandry, Behavior and Veterinary Practice, 1984; The Whistling Hunters, 1984; The Animal Doctor's Answer Book, 1984; Agricide: The Hidden Crisis that Affects Us All, 1986; Laboratory Animal Husbandry, 1986; The New Eden, 1989; (with N.E. Wiswall) Hidden Costs of Beef, 1989; St. Francis of Assisi, Animals, and Nature, 1989; Inhumane Society: The American Way of Exploiting Animals, 1990; Superdog: Raising the Perfect Canine Companion, 1990; Supercat: Raising the Perfect Feline Companion, 1990; You Can Save the Animals: 50 Things to Do Right Now, 1991; Animals Have Rights Too, 1991; Superpigs and Wondercorn: The Brave New World of Biotechnology and Where It All May Lead, 1992; The Boundless Circle: Caring for Creatures and Creation, 1996; Eating with Conscience: The Bioethics of Food, 1997; Beyond Evolution: The Genetically Altered Future of Plants, Animals, the Earth-Humans, 1999; Bringing Life to Ethics: Global Bioethics for a Humane Society, 2001; Killer Foods: When Scientists Manipulate Genes, Better is not Always Best, 2004; Cat Body, Cat Mind: Exploring your Cat's Consciousness and Total Well-Being, 2007; (with E. Hodgkins and M.E. Smart) Not Fit for a Dog!: The Truth about Manufactured Dog and Cat Food, 2008; Healing Animals And The Vision of One Health, 2011; Animals and Nature First, 2011. FOR CHILDREN-FICTION: The Wolf, 1973; Vixie, The Story of a Little Fox, 1973; Sundance Coyote; Whitepaws: A Coyote-Dog, 1979; Dr. Fox's Fables: Lessons from Nature, 1980; The Way of the Dolphin, 1981. EDITOR: Abnormal Behavior in Animals, 1968; The Wild Canids, 1974; On the Fifth Day: Animal Rights and Human Obligations, 1978; (with L.D. Mickley) Advances in Animal Welfare Science, 1984. **Address:** 2135 Indiana Ave. N, Minneapolis, MN 55422, U.S.A. **Online address:** ipan@erols.com

FOX, Paula. American (born United States), b. 1923. **Genres:** Novels, Children's Fiction, Young Adult Fiction, History, Autobiography/Memoirs, Animals/Pets, Education. **Career:** Ethical Culture School, teacher; University of Pennsylvania, professor of English literature, 1963-, visiting lecturer. Writer. **Publications:** NOVELS FOR ADULTS: Poor George, 1967; Desperate Characters, 1970; The Western Coast, 1972; The Widow's Children, 1976; A Servant's Tale, 1984; The God of Nightmares, 1990; News from the World: Stories and Essays, 2011. NOVELS FOR CHILDREN: Maurice's Room, 1966; A Likely Place, 1967; How Many Miles to Babylon?, 1967; The Stone-faced Boy, 1968; Dear Prosper, 1968; Portrait of Ivan, 1969; The King's Falcon, 1969; Hungry Fred, 1969; Blowfish Live in the Sea, 1970; Good Ethan, 1973; The Slave Dancer, 1973; The Little Swineherd and Other Tales, 1979; A Place Apart, 1980; One-eyed Cat, 1984; (intro.) Tell Me That You Love Me, Junie Moon, 1984; The Moonlight Man, 1986; Lily and the Lost Boy, 1987; The Village by the Sea, 1988; In a Place of Danger, 1989; Monkey Island, 1991; Western Wind, 1993; Amzat and His Brothers: Three Italian Tales, 1993; The Eagle Kite, 1995; Radiance Descending, 1997; Western Coast, 2001; Traces, 2008. OTHERS: Borrowed Finery: A Memoir, 2001; The Coldest Winter:

A Stringer in Liberated Europe, 2005. Contributor to periodicals. **Address:** c/o Robert Lescher, Lescher & Lescher Ltd., 346 E 84th St., New York, NY 10028, U.S.A.

FOX, Richard Allan. American (born United States), b. 1943. **Genres:** Anthropology/Ethnology, Archaeology/Antiquities, History. **Career:** University of North Dakota, instructor in anthropology, 1977-78, associate research archaeologist, 1977-82, research archaeologist, 1988-90, assistant professor of anthropology, 1988-91; Old Sun College, instructor in education, 1983-85; University of Calgary, instructor in archaeology, 1988; University of South Dakota, assistant professor, 1991-93, associate professor of anthropology, 1994-, director of archaeology laboratory, 1991-. Writer. **Publications:** Archaeological and Historical Studies in the Vicinity of the Proposed Coyote Station Electrical Generation Plant Site near Beulah, North Dakota, 1976; (co-author) Grass, Tipis and Black Gold, 1976; (with D.D. Scott) Archaeological Insights into the Custer Battle: An Assessment of the 1984 Field Season, 1987; (co-author) Archaeological Perspectives on the Battle of the Little Big Horn, 1989; Archaeology, History and Custer's Last Battle: The Little Big Horn Reexamined, 1993; Archaeological Investigations and National Register Testing at 14LV114 and 14LV118, Fort Leavenworth, Kansas, 2000. Contributor to books and journals. **Address:** Department of Anthropology, University of South Dakota, 301 E Hall, 414 E Clark St., Vermillion, SD 57069, U.S.A. **Online address:** rfox@usd.edu

FOX, Richard L. (Richard Logan Fox). American (born United States), b. 1967. **Genres:** Women's Studies And Issues. **Career:** Loyola Marymount University, associate professor of political science, department chair; Union College, associate professor, Department of Political Science, chair; Rutgers University, visiting professor. Writer. **Publications:** Gender Dynamics in Congressional Elections, 1997; (with R.W.V. Sickel) Tabloid Justice: Criminal Justice in an Age of Media Frenzy, 2001, 2nd ed., 2007; (with J.L. Lawless) It Takes a Candidate: Why Women Don't Run for Office, 2005, rev. ed., 2010; (ed. with S.J. Carroll) Gender and Elections: Shaping the Future of American Politics, 2006, 2nd ed., 2010; (ed. with J. Ramos) IPolitics: Citizens, Elections, and Governing in the New Media Era, 2011. Contributor to journals. **Address:** Department of Political Science, Loyola Marymount University, University Hall 4129, Ste. 4600, Los Angeles, CA 90045, U.S.A. **Online address:** richard.fox@lmu.edu

FOX, Richard Logan. See **FOX, Richard L.**

FOX, Robert. British (born England), b. 1938. **Genres:** History, Sciences. **Career:** University of Lancaster, lecturer, 1966-72, senior lecturer, 1972-75, reader, 1975-87, professor of history of science, 1987-2006; The British Journal for the History of Science, editor, 1971-77; British Society for the History of Science, president, 1980-82; French National Centre for Scientific Research, Center for Research in History of Science and Technology, director, 1986-88; Science Museum, assistant director, 1988; Division of History of Science of the International Union of History and Philosophy of Science, president, 1994-97; International Union of History and Philosophy of Science, president, 1996-97; European Society for the History of Science, president, 2004-06; University of Oxford, professor of the history of science, retired, 2006, Linacre College, emeritus fellow; Notes and Records of the Royal Society, editor, 2007-. **Publications:** The Caloric Theory of Gases from Lavoisier to Regnault, 1971; (co-author) The Patronage of Science in the Nineteenth Century, 1976; The Culture of Science in France, 1700-1900, 1992; Science, Industry and the Social Order in Post-Revolutionary France, 1995; (with C.C. Gillispie and I. Grattan-Guinness) Pierre-Simon Laplace, 1749-1827, 1997; (A. Guagnini) Laboratories, Workshops and Sites, 1999. EDITOR: Reflexions sur la puissance motrice du feu, 1978; (with G. Weisz) The Organization of Science and Technology in France 1808-1914, 1980; (and trans.) S. Carnot, Reflexions on the Motive Power of Fire, 1986; (with A. Guagnini) Education, Technology, and Industrial Performance in Europe, 1850-1939, 1993; Technological Change, 1996; (with A. Turner) Luxury Trades and Consumerism in Ancien Regime Paris, 1998; (with A. Nieto-Galan) Natural Dyestuffs and Industrial Culture in Europe, 1750-1880, 1999; An Elizabethan Man of Science, 2000; Thomas Harriot: an Elizabethan Man of Science, 2000; (with G. Gooday) Physics in Oxford, 1839-1939, 2005. **Address:** The Royal Society, 6-9 Carlton House Terr., London, SW1Y 5AG, England. **Online address:** robert.fox@history.ox.ac.uk

FOX, Robin. American/British (born England), b. 1934. **Genres:** Anthropology/Ethnology, Sciences, Literary Criticism And History. **Career:** Harvard University, Fulbright fellow, Chester Hastings Arnold fellow in contemporary civilization, 1957; University of Exeter, lecturer in sociology, 1959-62; University of London, London School of Economics and Political Science, lecturer in social anthropology, 1962-67, Malinowski Memorial Lecturer, 1967; Rutgers University, chair, professor of anthropology, 1967-84, university professor of social theory, 1984-; University of Georgia, distinguished visiting lecturer, 1972; Oxford University, visiting professor of anthropology, 1973-74; University of New Mexico, Byron Harvey III Lecturer, 1975; Haverford College, William Pyle Phillips lecturer, 1976; University of Paris VI, Ecole des Hautes Etudes en Sciences Sociales and Maison des Sciences de l'Homme, director of associate studies, 1979-80; Universidad de los Andes, visiting professor, 1981-82; University of California, visiting professor, 1982; Smith College, Neal B. De Nood memorial lecturer, 1982; St. John's College, visiting professor, 1982-83; University of Notre Dame, inaugural lecturer, 1983; University of Virginia, lecturer, 1988. Writer. **Publications:** The Keresan Bridge: A Problem in Pueblo Ethnography, 1967; Kinship and Marriage: An Anthropoligical Perspective, 1967; (with L. Tiger) The Imperial Animal, 1971, rev. ed., 1998; Encounter with Anthropology, 1973, 2nd ed., 1991; (ed. and contrib.) Biosocial Anthropology, 1975; The Tory Islanders: A People of the Celtic Fringe, 1978, rev. ed., 1995; The Red Lamp of Incest: An Inquiry into the Origins of Mind and Society, 1980; (ed. and contrib. with J. Mehler) Neonate Cognition: Beyond the Blooming Buzzing Confusion, 1985; The Violent Imagination, 1989; The Search for Society: Quest for a Biosocial Science and Morality, 1989; Reproduction and Succession: Studies in Anthropology, Law, and Society, 1993; The Challenge of Anthropology: Old Encounters and New Excursions, 1994; Conjectures and Confrontations: Science, Evolution, Social Concern, 1997; The Passionate Mind: Sources of Destruction and Creativity, 2000; Participant Observer: Memoir of a Transatlantic Life, 2004; The Tribal Imagination: Civilization and the Savage Mind, 2011. Contributor to magazine and newspapers. **Address:** Department of Anthropology, Rutgers University, Ruth Adams Bldg., Douglass Campus, New Brunswick, NJ 08903-0270, U.S.A. **Online address:** rfox@rci.rutgers.edu

FOX, Roy F. American (born United States), b. 1948. **Genres:** Communications/Media, Social Sciences, Technology, Reference. **Career:** Boise State University, associate professor of English, 1978-91, director of writing, 1980-91, English Language and Literature Center, director of technology, 1987-91; University of Missouri, Department of Learning, Teaching and Curriculum, associate professor, professor, 1991-, chair, Missouri Writing Project, director, 1991-, Maxine Christopher Shutz lecturer, 1996, William T. Kemper fellow, 1998; MPI Media Group, consultant; Idaho Supreme Court, consultant; Idaho Department of Vocational Rehabilitation, consultant. Writer. **Publications:** (Ed.) Images in Language, Media and Mind, 1994; Technical Communication: Problems and Solutions, 1994; Harvesting Minds: How TV Commercials Control Kids, 1996; (ed.) Up Drafts: Case Studies in Teacher Renewal, 2000; Media Speak: Three American Voices, 2001; The Debate Book, 2009. Contributor to professional journals. **Address:** Department of Learning, Teaching & Curriculum, University of Missouri, 211C Townsend Hall, Columbia, MO 65211, U.S.A. **Online address:** foxr@missouri.edu

FOX, Sarah. American (born United States), b. 1966. **Genres:** Poetry, Writing/Journalism. **Career:** Center for Visionary Poetics, co-founder; Fuori Editions, publisher. Writer and educator. **Publications:** Because Why: Poems, 2006. Contributor of articles to periodicals. **Address:** Fuori Editions, 1809 5th St. NE, Minneapolis, MN 55418-4401, U.S.A. **Online address:** segf@aol.com

FOX, Ted. American (born United States), b. 1954. **Genres:** Music, Photography. **Career:** Freelance writer; Audio, senior editor. **Publications:** Showtime at the Apollo, 1983, rev. ed., 2003; In the Groove: The People Behind the Music, 1986. **Address:** Mill Road Enterprises, 287 Mill Rd., PO Box 561, Rhinebeck, NY 12572, U.S.A.

FOX, William L. American (born United States), b. 1953. **Genres:** History, Theology/Religion, Social Sciences, Photography. **Career:** Universalist National Memorial Church, senior minister, 1979-88, 1993-98, emeritus senior minister; senior minister of Congregational church, 1988-92; Claremont School of Theology, adjunct professor in church history, 1990-92; Howard University, School of Divinity, adjunct professor, 1992-99; Montgomery College, associate professor of philosophy and history, 1993-95; Goucher College, director of foundation relations, 1999-2000, acting associate dean for graduate and professional programs, 2000-01, acting director of institutional research, 2000-01, special assistant, 1999-2003, lecturer in history, 2000-03, acting vice-president, 2001-03; Culver-Stockton College, senior lecturer in history, philosophy and religion, president, 2003-09; St. Lawrence University, president, 2009-, senior lecturer in history. Writer. **Publications:** Willard L. Sperry: The Quandaries of a Liberal Protestant Mind, 1914-1939, 1991; Lodge of the Double-Headed Eagle: Two Centuries of Scottish Rite Freemasonry in America's Southern Jurisdiction, 1997; Valley of the Craftsmen: A Pictorial History, Scottish Rite Freemasonary in America's Southern Jurisdiction 1801-2001, 2001. **Address:** St. Lawrence University, Vilas Hall, 23 Romoda Dr., Canton, NY 13617, U.S.A. **Online address:** wfox@stlawu.edu

FOXMAN, Abraham H. American/Polish (born Poland), b. 1940?. **Genres:** History, Social Sciences. **Career:** Anti-Defamation League, staff, 1965-, national director, 1987-. Writer. **Publications:** (Intro.) Heroes of the Holocaust, 1993; Never Again? The Threat of the New Anti-Semitism, 2003; The Deadliest Lies: The Israel Lobby and the Myth of Jewish Control, 2007. **Address:** Anti-Defamation League, PO Box 96226, Washington, DC 20090-6226, U.S.A.

FOXWORTHY, Jeff. American (born United States), b. 1958. **Genres:** Humor/Satire. **Career:** IBM Corp., staff, 1979-84. Recording artist, comedian, author, 1984-. **Publications:** HUMOR: You Might Be a Redneck If..., 1989; Hick is Chic: A Guide to Etiquette for the Grossly Unsophisticated, 1990; Hick is Chic, 1990; Red Ain't Dead: 150 More Ways to Tell If You're a Redneck, 1991; Check Your Neck: More of You Might Be a Redneck If..., 1992; (with V. Henley) You're Not a Kid Anymore When..., 1993; (with V. Henley) Games Rednecks Play, 1994; Redneck Classic: The Best of Jeff Foxworthy, 1995; No Shirt. No Shoes, No Problem, 1996; Those People: Humorous Drawings, 1996; (with B.J. Foxworthy) Foxworthy Down-Home Cookbook: No Arugula, No Paté, No Problem!, 1997; Final Helping of You Might be a Redneck If-, 1999; You Might be a Redneck If-this is the Biggest Book You've Ever Read, 2004; There's No Place like a Mobile Home for the Holidays, 2004; Redneck Grill, 2005; Redneck Extreme Mobile Home Makeover, 2005; Red is the Color of My True Love's Neck, 2005; Jeff Foxworthy's Redneck Dictionary: Words You Thought You Knew the Meaning of, 2005; No Redneck Left Behind: Facing the Real World after Getting' Your Diploma, 2006; Jeff Foxworthy's Redneck Dictionary II: More Words You Thought You Knew the Meaning Of, 2006; Redneck Doesn't Fall Far From the Tree, 2006; How Many Women Does It Take to Change a Redneck?, 2006; (co-author) Jeff Foxworthy's Redneck Dictionary III: Learning to Talk more Gooder Fastly, 2007; (with B. Hartt) How to Really Stink at Golf, 2008; Dirt On My Shirt, 2008; Silly Street, 2009; How to Really Stink at Work, 2009; Hide!!!, 2010. **Address:** Creative Artists Agency, 162 5th Ave., 6th Fl., New York, CA 10010, U.S.A.

FOXX, Daniel. American (born United States) **Genres:** Biography, Autobiography/Memoirs, Humor/Satire, History. **Career:** Arizona State Legislature, legislative aide; Glendale Community College, adjunct professor of history; East Carolina University, faculty; Ottawa University, associate professor of history, 1982-, professor of history, now professor emeritus. **Publications:** I Only Laugh When It Hurts, 1995; (with E.W. Davison) Nathan Bedford Forrest: In Search of the Enigma, 2007. Contributor to journals. **Address:** Ottawa University, Phoenix Campus, 10020 N 25th Ave., Phoenix, AZ 85021-0637, U.S.A. **Online address:** foxxdan@ottawa.edu

FOY, George. See **FOY, George Michelsen.**

FOY, George Michelsen. Also writes as George Foy, G. F. Michelsen. American/French (born France), b. 1952?. **Genres:** Novels, Sciences, Essays, Adult Non-fiction, Travel/Exploration. **Career:** Writer, 1983-: New York University, adjunct professor, creative writing, 1998-; Cape Cod Register, reporter; Cape Cod Times, editor; International Herald Tribune, editor; Business Week, editor. **Publications:** Zero Decibels: The Quest for Absolute Silence, 2010. AS G.F. MICHELSEN: Hard Bottom, 2001; The Art and Practice of Explosion, 2003; Mettle: A Novel, 2007; To Sleep with Ghosts: A Novel of Africa, 1992. AS GEORGE FOY: Music in Stone: Great Sculpture Gardens of the World, 1984; Asia Rip, 1984; Coaster, 1986; Challenge, 1988; Blues for Nansen (Germany), 1993; The Shift, 1996; Contraband, 1997; (with S. Lawrence) The Memory of Fire: A Novel, 2000; The Last Harbor: A Novel, 2001. Contributor of articles to magazines and newspapers. **Address:** c/o Harold Matson Inc., 276 5th Ave., New York, NY 10001, U.S.A. **Online address:** gf27@nyu.edu

FOYSTER, Elizabeth A. British (born England), b. 1968. **Genres:** Human Relations/Parenting. **Career:** University of Cambridge, Clare College, part-time lecturer in history, director of studies. Writer and historian. **Publications:** Manhood in Early Modern England: Honour, Sex and Marriage, 1999; Marital Violence: An English Family History, 1660-1875, 2005; The Family in Early Modern England, 2007; History of Everyday Life in Scotland, 1600 to 1800, 2010; Cultural History of Childhood and Family, 2010. Contributor of articles to journals. **Address:** Clare College, Cambridge University, Trinity Ln., Cambridge, CB CB2 1TL, England. **Online address:** eaf21@cam.ac.uk

FOYT, Victoria. American (born United States) **Genres:** Young Adult Fiction, Novels, Film. **Career:** Novelist. **Publications:** The Virtual Life of Lexie Diamond, 2007; Saving Eden: The Plight of the Pearls, 2011. Contributor of articles to periodicals. **Address:** Sand Dollar Press, 1301 Montana Ave., Ste. C, Santa Monica, CA 90403, U.S.A. **Online address:** victoriaweb@mac.com

FRACIS, Sohrab Homi. American/Indian (born India), b. 1958. **Genres:** Science Fiction/Fantasy, Young Adult Fiction. **Career:** University of North Florida, adjunct instructor of English, 1993-2003; State Street Review, fiction and poetry editor, 1994-2001; Kalliope, proofreader, 1998-. **Publications:** Ticket to Minto: Stories of India and America, 2001; Fahrschein bis Minto: Erzahlungen aus Indien und Amerika, 2006. **Address:** University of Iowa Press, 119 West Park Rd., Iowa City, IA 52242, U.S.A. **Online address:** sfracis@att.net

FRADER, Laura Levine. American (born United States), b. 1945?. **Genres:** History, Agriculture/Forestry, Business/Trade/Industry. **Career:** Oakland University, assistant professor, 1978-79; Northeastern University, Department of History, assistant professor, 1979-86, associate professor, 1986-2004, professor and chair, 2004-; Harvard University, senior associate, 1992. Writer, historian and researcher. **Publications:** (With L.A. Loubere, J. Sagnes and R. Pech) The Vine Remembers: French Vignerons Recall Their Past, 1985; Peasants and Protest: Agricultural Workers, Politics, and Unions in the Aude, 1850-1914, 1991; (ed. with S.O. Rose) Gender and Class in Modern Europe, 1996; (ed. with H. Chapman) Race in France: Interdisciplinary Perspectives on the Politics of Difference, 2004; The Industrial Revolution: A History in Documents, 2006; Breadwinners and Citizens: Gender in the Making of the French Social Model, 2008. Contributor of articles to books, periodicals and journals. **Address:** U.S.A. **Online address:** lfrader@neu.edu

FRADIN, Judith (Bernette) Bloom. American (born United States), b. 1945. **Genres:** Biography, Photography, Social Sciences, Geography. **Career:** Teacher, 1967-75, 1982-90; Northeastern Illinois University, writing instructor, 1975-82; photo researcher, 1985-; writer, 1990-; Luther Burbank Elementary School, author-in-residence; Southwest Evanston Associated Residents, president. **Publications:** FROM SEA TO SHINING SEA SERIES WITH D.B. FRADIN: Montana, 1992; New Mexico, 1993; Missouri, 1994; Arkansas, 1994; Delaware, 1994; Connecticut, 1994; Indiana, 1994; Maryland, 1994; North Dakota, 1994; Washington, 1994; West Virginia, 1994; Wyoming, 1994; Minnesota, 1995; Louisiana, 1995; Kansas, 1995; Mississippi, 1995; Nevada, 1995; Puerto Rico, 1995; Oklahoma, 1995; Oregon, 1995; Rhode Island, 1995; South Dakota, 1995. OTHERS WITH D.B. FRADIN: Ida B. Wells: Mother of the Civil Rights Movement, 2000; Who was Sacagawea?, 2002; Fight On!: Mary Church Terrell's Battle for Integration, 2003; The Power of One: Daisy Bates and the Little Rock Nine, 2004; 5000 Miles to Freedom: Ellen and William Craft's Flight from Slavery, 2006; Jane Addams: Champion of Democracy, 2006; Volcanoes, 2007; Hurricanes, 2007; Lewis and Clark Expedition, 2008; Earthquakes: Witness to Disaster, 2008; Droughts, 2008; Tsunamis, 2008; Salem Witch Trials, 2009; Hurricane Katrina, 2010; Investing, 2010; Saving, 2010; Spending, 2010; Borrowing, 2010; Earning, 2010; Volcano!, 2010; Tornado!, 2011; Irish Potato Famine, 2012; Zora!, 2012; Stolen Into Slavery, 2012. Contributor to periodicals. **Address:** 2121 Dobson, Evanston, IL 60202, U.S.A. **Online address:** yudiff@aol.com

FRAENKEL, Jack R. American (born United States), b. 1932. **Genres:** Criminology/True Crime, Education, Social Sciences, Reference. **Career:** Teacher in public schools in San Francisco, Pacifica, 1959-64; San Francisco State University, associate professor, 1966-71, professor of interdisciplinary studies in education, 1971-; Teachers Corps, Taba Curriculum Development Project in Social Studies, associate director, 1966-69; National Science Foundation, consultant, 1966-67; National Defense Education Act Institute on Teaching Disadvantaged Children, coordinator, 1968; World Law Fund, consultant, 1968-71; American Institutes for Research, consultant, 1969-

; University of California Medical Center, consultant, 1969-70; National Competency-Based Educational Research and Development Project, associate director, 1970-71; Wadsworth Publishing Co., consulting editor, 1973-76; Children's Book Council, consultant, 1973-. **Publications:** Emerging Africa: An Introduction to the History, Geography, Peoples, and Current Problems of the Multi-National African Continent on Its Way from Colonialism to Independence, 1965; The Rim of Asia-Japan and Southeast Asia: An Introduction to the Geography, Peoples, History, Cultures and Problems of the Mainland and Island Countries of East Asia, 1965; The U.S. War with Spain 1898: Was Expansionism Justified?, 1969; (ed. with R.E. Gross and W. McPhie) Teaching the Social Studies: What, Why and How, 1969; Crime and Criminals: What Can We Do about Them?, 1970, 2nd ed., 1977; Inquiry into Crucial American Problems, 16 vols., 1970-73, 2nd ed., 1976; (with H. Taba, A. McNaughton and M. Durkin) Teacher's Handbook to Elementary Social Studies, 1971; Helping Students Think and Value: Strategies for Teaching the Social Studies, 1972, 2nd ed., 1980; (with B. Reardon and M. Carter) Peacekeeping: Problems and Possibilities, 1973; (ed.) Inquiry into World Cultures, 6 vols., 1974-76; (with B. Reardon and M. Carter) The Struggle for Human Rights: A Question of Values, 1975; Crucial Issues in American Government, 15 vols., 1975-77; (ed. with C. Ubbelohde and contrib.) Values of the American Heritage: Challenges, Case Studies, and Teaching Strategies, 1976; How to Teach About Values: An Analytic Approach, 1977; (co-author) Decision-Making in American Government, 1977; (co-author) Civics-Government and Citizenship, 1983; Toward Improving Research in Social Studies Education, 1988; (with N.E. Wallen) How to Design and Evaluate Research in Education, 1990, 8th ed., 2011; (with N.E. Wallen) Educational Research: A Guide to the Process, 1991, 2nd ed., 2001; (with E.I. Sawin and N.E. Wallen) Visual Statistics: A Conceptual Primer, 1999. Contributor to books. **Address:** College of Education, San Francisco State University, 522 Burk Hall, 1600 Holloway Ave., San Francisco, CA 94132, U.S.A. **Online address:** jrf@sfsu.edu

FRAISER, Jim. American (born United States), b. 1954. **Genres:** Novels, History, Adult Non-fiction, Art/Art History. **Career:** Down South Magazine, columnist, 1988; University of Mississippi and Mississippi University for Women, paralegal instructor, 1990-93; Mississippi Office of the Attorney General Civil Litigation Division, special assistant attorney general, 1995-; Jackson Business Journal, contributing editor. **Publications:** M Is for Mississippi: An Irreverent Guide to the Magnolia State, 1990; Shadow Seed (novel), 1997; For the Love of the Game: The Holy Wars of Millsaps College and Mississippi College Football, 2000; Mississippi River Country Tales: A Celebration of 500 Years of Deep South History, 2001; The Majesty of the Mississippi Delta, 2002; The French Quarter of New Orleans, 2003; The Majesty of Eastern Mississippi and the Coast, 2004; Vanished Mississippi Gulf Coast, 2006; Whiskey with Chaser: The John Clements Novels, 2007; The Garden District of New Orleans, 2012; Majesty of Mobile, 2012. **Address:** Pelican Publishing Co., 1000 Burmaster St., Gretna, LA 70053-2246, U.S.A. **Online address:** cfrais@cs.com

FRAJLICH(-ZAJAC), Anna. American/Polish (born Poland), b. 1942. **Genres:** Poetry, Literary Criticism And History, Language/Linguistics. **Career:** Magazine for the Blind, associate editor, 1965-69; State University of New York, instructor in Polish, 1970-71; Kimbell Research Institute, research assistant in epidemiology, 1971-75; New York University, instructor in Polish, 1977; Radio Free Europe, freelance writer, broadcaster and interviewer, 1977-81; Columbia University, Department of Slavic Languages, lecturer, 1982-93, adjunct assistant professor, 1993-98, adjunct associate professor, 1998-99, lecturer in Polish, 1999-2005; senior lecturer in Polish, 2005-. **Publications:** POETRY: Aby wiatr namalować, 1976; Tylko ziemia, 1979; Indian Summer, 1982; Ktory las, 1986; Drzewo za oknem, 1991; Ogrodem I ogrodzeniem, 1993; Jeszcze w drodze, 1994; W słońcu listopada, 2000; Znów szuka mnie wiatr, 2001; Le vent, a nouveau me cherche, 2003. OTHERS: Living Language: Fast and Easy Polish (booklet), 1992; (ed.) Between Lvov, New York, and Ulysses' Ithaca: Józef Wittlin: Poet, Essayist, Novelist, 2001; The Legacy of Ancient Rome in the Russian Silver Age, 2007; (with F. Bromberg and W. Zajac) Po Marcu: Wiedeń, Rzym, Nowy Jork, 2008. Works appear in anthologies. Contributor to books and magazines. **Address:** Department of Slavic Languages, Columbia University, 704 Hamilton Hall, PO Box 2840, New York, NY 10027, U.S.A. **Online address:** af38@columbia.edu

FRAKES, George Edward. American (born United States), b. 1932. **Genres:** Environmental Sciences/Ecology, History, Race Relations. **Career:** Sequoia High School, teacher, 1958-; Santa Barbara City College, instructor in history, 1962-65, assistant professor, 1967-69, associate professor,

1969-71, professor of history and geography, 1973-94, emeritus professor of history and geography, 1994-, Department of History, chairman, 1971-73, 1986-87, Social Science Division, chairman, 1973-76, Instructors Association, president; University of California, supervisor of student teachers, 1965-66. Writer. **Publications:** (With A. DeConde) Instructor's Manual for Patterns in American History, 1968; Laboratory for Liberty, 1970; (with W.R. Adams) From Columbus to Aquarius: An Interpretive History, 2 vols., 1976; A Teacher's Life, 2002. EDITOR: (with C. Solberg) Pollution Papers, 1971; (with C. Solberg) Minorities in California History, 1971. Contributor to journals. **Address:** Department of History, Santa Barbara City College, 721 Cliff Dr., Santa Barbara, CA 93109-2394, U.S.A. **Online address:** gefsb@aol.com

FRAKES, William B. American (born United States), b. 1952. **Genres:** Information Science/Computers, Mathematics/Statistics. **Career:** American Telephone and Telegraph Bell Laboratories, technical staff, 1982-87, distinguished technical staff, 1987, Intelligent Systems Research Group, supervisor, 1987-89; Rutgers University, Computer Science Department, adjunct faculty, 1986-87; Columbia University, Computer Science Department, adjunct faculty, 1988-89; Software Productivity Consortium, manager of software reuse research, 1989-92; Virginia Polytechnic Institute and State University, Northern Virginia Graduate Center, computer science department director, 1992-98, associate professor, 1992-; Software Engineering Guild, president, 1992-; Universidad Carlos III de Madrid, Department of Computer Science, distinguished visiting professor, 1999, 2001; University of Calgary, Department of Electrical and Computer Engineering, distinguished visiting researcher, 1999. Writer. **Publications:** (With C.J. Fox and B.A. Nejmeh) Software Engineering in the UNIX/C Environment, 1991. EDITOR: (with R. Baeza-Yates) Information Retrieval: Data Structures & Algorithms, 1992; (with R. Prieto-Díaz) Advances in Software Reuse: Selected Papers from the Second International Workshop on Software Reusability: Proceedings, March 24-26, 1993, 1993; Third International Conference on Software Reuse: Advances in Software Reusability: Proceedings, November 1-4, 1994, 1994; Software Reuse: Advances in Software Reusability: 6th International Conference, ICSR-6, Vienna, Austria, June 27-29, 2000: Proceedings, 2000. Contributor to journals and books. **Address:** Computer Science Department, Virginia Polytechnic Inst and State Univ, Rm. 302 Northern Virginia Center, 7054 Haycock Rd., Falls Church, VA 22043-2311, U.S.A. **Online address:** frakes@cs.vt.edu

FRALEY, Tobin. American (born United States), b. 1951. **Genres:** Art/Art History, Photography, Natural History, Children's Fiction. **Career:** Writer. **Publications:** The Carousel Animal, 1983; (with C. Bialkowski) Carousels: The Myth, the Magic, and the Memories, 1991; The Great American Carousel: A Century of Master Craftsmanship, 1994; A Humbug Christmas (children's book), 1998; Carousel Animals: Artistry in Motion, 2002; 36 Acres: A Portrait of the Reed-Turner Woodland, 2010. Contributor to periodicals. **Address:** Woodland Grove Gallery, 215 Robert Coffin Rd., Long Grove, IL 60047, U.S.A. **Online address:** tobin@humbugs.com

FRAME, J. Davidson. American (born United States), b. 1947. **Genres:** Administration/Management, inspirational/Motivational Literature, Adult Non-fiction, Institutions/Organizations, Business/Trade/Industry, Economics. **Career:** Computer Horizons Inc., vice-president, 1973-79; George Washington University, professor, 1979-98, chairman of management science department, 1988-89, International Center for Project Management Excellence, director, 1995-98; Project Management Institute, director of certification, 1990-96, director of education services, 1996-98, fellow, 2004-; University of Management and Technology, academic dean, 1998-; Yankee Clipper Group, vice president. Writer. **Publications:** International Business and Global Technology, 1983; Managing Projects in Organizations: How to Make the Best Use of Time, Techniques, and People, 1987, 3rd ed., 2003; The New Project Management: Tools for an Age of Rapid Change, Corporate Re-engineering, and Other Business Realities, 1994, 2nd ed. as The New Project Management: Tools for an Age of Rapid Change, Complexity, and Other Business Realities, 2002; (with T. Block) The Project Office, 1997; Project Management Competence: Building Key Skills for Individuals, Teams, and Organizations, 1999; Managing Risk in Organizations: A Guide for Managers, 2003; Project Finance: Tools and Techniques, 2003. **Address:** University of Management and Technology, 1901 N Fort Myer Dr., Ste. 700, Arlington, VA 22209-1609, U.S.A. **Online address:** davidson.frame@umtweb.edu

FRAME, Ronald. Scottish (born Scotland), b. 1953. **Genres:** Novels, Novellas/Short Stories, Plays/Screenplays, Young Adult Fiction. **Career:** Writer,

1981-; Edinburgh International Book Festival, Saltire lecturer, 2001. **Publications:** Winter Journey: A Novel, 1984; Watching Mrs. Gordon and Other Stories, 1985; A Long Weekend With Marcel Proust: Seven Stories and A Novel, 1986; Sandmouth People, 1987; A Woman of Judah: A Novel and Fifteen Stories, 1987; Paris, 1987; Penelope's Hat, 1989; Bluette, 1990; Underwood and After, 1992; Mask and Shadow, 1992; Walking My Mistress in Deauville: A Novella and Nine Stories, 1992; The Sun on The Wall: Three Novels, 1994; Lantern Bearers: A Novel, 2001; Permanent Violet, 2002; Time in Carnbeg: Short Stories, 2004; Unwritten Secrets, 2010. Contributor to periodicals. Works appear in anthologies. **Address:** Blake Friedmann Literary Agency, 122 Arlington Rd., London, GL NW1 7HP, England. **Online address:** ronald.frame@waitrose.com

FRANCAVIGLIA, Richard V. American (born United States), b. 1943. **Genres:** History, Cultural/Ethnic Topics, Natural History. **Career:** Southeastern Arizona Governments Organization, manager of regional and environmental planning programs, 1979-83; Ohio State Government, deputy state historic preservation officer, 1984-88; Ohio Historical Society, director of the Local History Office, 1988-91; University of Texas, professor of history, director of the Center for Greater Southwestern Studies and the History of Cartography, 1991-. Writer and historian. **Publications:** (ed. with H.A. Edmonson) Railroad Station Planbook, 1977; The Mormon Landscape: Existence, Creation and Perception of a Unique Image in the American West, 1978; Mining Town Trolleys: A History of Arizona's Warren-Bisbee Railway, 1983; Hard Places: Reading the Landscape of America's Historic Mining Districts, 1991; (ed. with D. Narrett) Essays on the Changing Images of the Southwest, 1994; The Shape of Texas: Maps as Metaphors, 1995; Main Street Revisited: Time, Space and Image Building in Small-Town America, 1996; From Sail to Steam: Four Centuries of Texas Maritime History, 1500-1900, 1998; The Cast Iron Forest: A Natural and Cultural History of the North American Cross Timbers, 2000; (ed. with D.W. Richmond) Dueling Eagles: Reinterpreting the U.S.Mexican War, 1846- 1848, 2000; Believing in Place: A Spiritual Geography of the Great Basin, 2003; Mapping and Imagination in the Great Basin: A Cartographic History, 2005; (ed. with J. Rodnitzky) Lights, Camera, History: Portraying the Past in Film, 2007; (ed. with R.R. Treviño) Catholicism in the American West: A Rosary of Hidden Voices, 2007; Over the Range: A History of the Promontory Summit Route of the Pacific, 2008; (with D. Buisseret and G. Saxon) Historic Texas from the Air, 2009. **Address:** Ctr for Greater SW Studies/History of Cartography, University of Texas, PO Box 19497, Arlington, TX 76019-0497, U.S.A.

FRANCE, Linda. British (born England), b. 1958. **Genres:** Poetry, Self Help. **Career:** Workers' Educational Association, tutor, 1985-95; University of Newcastle upon Tyne, Centre for Continuing Education and School of English, tutor, 1987-, Newcastle Centre for Literary Arts, creative writing teacher, Moorbank Botanic Garden, Leverhulme artist-in-residence; Arvon Foundation, tutor; Queen's Hall Arts Centre, literature adviser. Writer. **Publications:** Acts of Love, 1990; Red, 1992; (ed.) Sixty Women Poets, 1993; (with B. Aris) Acknowledged Land, 1994; The Gentleness of the Very Tall, 1994; (ed.) Sauce, 1994; Diamonds in Your Pockets, 1996; Storyville, 1997; The Simultaneous Dress, 2002; I am Frida Kahlo, 2002; Aerogramme, 2004; Wild, 2004; The Toast of the Kit Cat Club: A Life of Lady Mary Wortley Montagu in Eleven Chapters, 2005; Book of Days, 2009; You are Her, 2010. **Address:** School of English Literature,, Language and Linguistics, Newcastle University, Percy Bldg., Newcastle upon Tyne, NE1 7RU, England. **Online address:** linda.france@ncl.ac.uk

FRANCE, Miranda. British (born England), b. 1966. **Genres:** Travel/Exploration, Translations, Reference. **Career:** Freelance journalist, 1989-93, 1995-; University of Edinburgh, part-time teacher of Spanish literature, 1992-93. **Publications:** Bad Times in Buenos Aires (travel book), 1999; Don Quixote's Delusions: Travels in Castilian Spain, 2002; (trans.) P. Kaufmann, Lake, 2007; (trans.) C. Piñeiro, Thursday Night Widows, 2009; (trans.) A. Manguel, All Men are Liars, 2010; Hill Farm, 2011. Contributor to magazines and newspapers. **Address:** c/o Derek Johns, A.P. Watt Ltd., 20 John St., London, GL WC1N 2DR, England.

FRANCE, R(ichard) T(homas). Welsh/Irish (born Ireland), b. 1938. **Genres:** Theology/Religion. **Career:** University of Ife, lecturer in biblical studies, 1969-73; Tyndale House, librarian, 1973-76, research fellow, 1977-78, warden, 1978-81; Trinity Evangelical Divinity School, visiting professor, 1975; Ahmadu Bello University, senior lecturer in religious studies, 1976-77; Cambridge University, faculty of divinity, 1979-81; London Bible College,

senior lecturer in New Testament, 1981-88, Department of Biblical Studies, head, 1982-88, vice-principal, 1983-88; Wycliffe Hall, principal, 1989-95; Oxford University, chairperson of faculty of theology, 1994-95; St. James' Cathedral, honorary canon, 1994-; University of Wales, honorary research fellow, 2004-; Bangor University, honorary research fellow. Writer. **Publications:** The Living God, 1970; Jesus and the Old Testament, 1971; (comp. with A.R. Millard and G.N. Stanton and ed.) A Bibliographical Guide to New Testament Research, 1974; I Came to Set the Earth on Fire: A Portrait of Jesus, 1975; The Man They Crucified, 1975, rev. ed. as Jesus the Radical, 1989; Gospel according to Matthew: An Introduction and Commentary, 1985; The Evidence for Jesus, 1986; Matthew: Evangelist and Teacher, 1989; Divine Government, 1990; Jesus in a Divided Society, 1993; Mark: The People's Bible Commentary, 1996; Women in the Church's Ministry, 1997; (with P. Jenson) Translating the Bible, 1997; The Gospel of Mark, 1998; A Slippery Slope? The Ordination of Women and Homosexual Practice, 2000; Timothy, Titus and Hebrews, 2007; Gospel of Matthew, 2007. EDITOR: (with D. Wenham and contrib.) Gospel Perspectives, vol. I, 1980, vol. II, 1981, vol. III, 1983; (with D. Wenham) Studies in Midrash and Historiography, 1983; (with A.E. McGrath) Evangelical Anglicans, 1993. Contributor to books and periodicals. **Address:** Ty'n-y-'Twll, Llangelynin, Llwyngwril, GY LL37 2QL, Wales.

FRANCESCHINI, Remo. American (born United States), b. 1932. **Genres:** Criminology/True Crime, Biography, Autobiography/Memoirs, Social Sciences. **Career:** New York Police Department, commander of detectives, 1957-91; St. John's University, adjunct professor of criminal justice. **Publications:** A Matter of Honor: One Cop's Lifelong Pursuit of John Gotti and the Mob, Simon and Schuster, 1993. **Address:** 6276 Spyglass Dr., West Palm Beach, FL 33412, U.S.A.

FRANCIA, Peter L. American (born United States), b. 1974. **Genres:** Politics/Government, Economics, Social Sciences. **Career:** University of Maryland, Center for American Politics and Citizenship, faculty research assistant, 2000-01, assistant research scientist, 2001-04, Department Of Political Science, assistant professor, 2004-08, associate professor, 2008-. Writer. **Publications:** (Co-author) The Financiers of Congressional Elections: Investors, Ideologues and Intimates, 2003; The Future of Organized Labor in American Politics, 2006; (with J.C. Baumgartner) Conventional Wisdom and American Elections: Exploding Myths, Exploring Misconceptions, 2008, 2nd ed., 2010; (ed. with D.Z. Strolovitch and B.A. Loomis) Guide to Interest Groups and Lobbying in the United States, 2011. Contributor to professional journals. **Address:** Department of Political Science, East Carolina University, Brewster A-119, Greenville, NC 27858, U.S.A. **Online address:** franciap@ecu.edu

FRANCIS, Clare. (Clare Mary Francis). British (born England), b. 1946. **Genres:** Novels, Travel/Exploration, Autobiography/Memoirs, Mystery/Crime/Suspense, Young Adult Non-fiction, Young Adult Fiction. **Career:** Beecham Products Ltd., marketing staff, 1968-70; Robertsons Foods Ltd., product manager, 1970-73; writer, 1973-; The University of Manchester Institute of Science and Technology, honorary fellow; Society of Authors, chairman, 1997-99; British Broadcasting Corp., hostess; Action for ME, president and trustee; University College London, fellow. **Publications:** Woman Alone: Sailing Solo across the Atlantic, 1977; Come Hell or High Water, 1977; Come Wind or Weather, 1978; The Commanding Sea, 1981; Night Sky, 1983; Red Crystal, 1985; Wolf Winter, 1987; Requiem, 1991 in US as The Killing Winds, 1992; Deceit, 1993; Betrayal, 1995; (ed. with O. Upton) A Feast of Stories, 1996; A Dark Devotion, 1997; Keep Me Close, 1999; A Death Divided, 2001; Homeland, 2004; Unforgotten, 2008. **Address:** c/o John Johnson, Johnson & Alcock Ltd., Clerkenwell House, 45-47 Clerkenwell Green, London, GL EC1R 0HT, England.

FRANCIS, Clare Mary. See **FRANCIS, Clare.**

FRANCIS, David J. (David John Francis). British (born England), b. 1965. **Genres:** Economics, Regional/Urban Planning. **Career:** University of Bradford, Department of Peace Studies, Africa Centre for Peace and Conflict Studies, director, professor & personal research chair. Writer. **Publications:** The Politics of Economic Regionalism: Sierra Leone in ECOWAS, 2001; (ed.) Civil Militia: Africa's Intractable Security Menace?, 2005; (co-author) Dangers of Co-Deployment: UN Co-Operative Peacekeeping in Africa, 2005; Uniting Africa: Building Regional Peace and Security Systems, 2006. **Ad-**

dress: Africa Ctr. for Peace & Conflict Studies, Department of Peace Studies, University of Bradford, Pemberton Bldg., Bradford, WY BD7 1DP, England. **Online address:** d.j.francis@bradford.ac.uk

FRANCIS, David John. *See* **FRANCIS, David J.**

FRANCIS, Diana Pharaoh. American (born United States) **Genres:** Novels. **Career:** University of Montana-Western, associate professor, professor of English. Academic and writer. **Publications:** PATH SERIES: Path of Fate, 2003; Path of Honor, 2004; Path of Blood, 2006. CROSSPOINTE SERIES: The Cipher, 2007; The Black Ship, 2008. Contributor of articles to journals. **Address:** Department of English, University of Montana-Western, 710 S Atlantic, Dillon, MT 59725, U.S.A. **Online address:** dfp@dianapfrancis.com

FRANCIS, Diane (Marie). Canadian/American (born United States), b. 1946. **Genres:** Business/Trade/Industry, Politics/Government, Advertising/Public Relations, Economics, Criminology/True Crime, Demography, Money/Finance, Technology, Technology, Sociology. **Career:** Canadian Business, contributing editor, 1979-81; Quest, columnist, 1981-83; Toronto Star, reporter and financial columnist, 1981-87; Canadian Broadcasting Corp., CBC-Radio, commentator, 1985-95; Maclean's, columnist, 1987-98; Toronto Sun, columnist, 1987-98; Financial Post, editor, 1991-98, editor-at-large, 1998-; Canadian Foundation for AIDS Research, director; CARE Canada, director; Aurizon Mines Ltd., director, 2007-; Ryerson University, Ted Rogers School of Management, visiting professor, 2008-; Toronto Symphony Orchestra, director, 2008-. **Publications:** Controlling Interest: Who Owns Canada?, 1986; Contrepreneurs, 1988; The Diane Francis Inside Guide to Canada's 50 Best Stocks, 1990; A Matter of Survival: Canada in the 21st Century, 1993; Underground Nation: The Secret Economy and the Future of Canada, 1994; Fighting for Canada, 1996; Bre-X: The Inside Story, 1997; Immigration: The Economic Case, 2002; Who Owns Canada Now, 2008. **Address:** National Post, 300-1450 Don Mills Rd., Don Mills, ON M3B 3R5, Canada. **Online address:** dfrancis@nationalpost.com

FRANCIS, Dorothy Brenner. Also writes as Pat Alden, Pat Louis, Ellen Goforth, Sue Alden. American (born United States), b. 1926. **Genres:** Mystery/Crime/Suspense, Romance/Historical, Children's Fiction, Adult Non-fiction. **Career:** Band and vocal instructor, 1948-52, 1961-62; Methodist junior high school, trumpet and director; Institute of Children's Literature, correspondence teacher; Marshalltown Tuesday Music Club, president. Writer. **Publications:** Adventure at Riverton Zoo, 1966; Mystery of the Forgotten Map, 1968; Laugh at the Evil Eye, 1970; Another Kind of Beauty, 1970; Hawaiian Interlude, 1970; Studio Affair, 1972; Blue Ribbon for Marni, 1973; Nurse on Assignment, 1973; Nurse under Fire, 1973; Murder in Hawaii, 1973; Nurse in the Caribbean, 1974; Golden Girl, 1974; Nurse of the Keys, 1974; Nurse at Spirit Lake, 1975; Keys to Love, 1975; Legacy of Merton Manor, 1976; Nurse at Playland Park, 1976; (as Sue Alden) The Magnificent Challenge, 1976; Two against the Arctic, 1976; The Flint Hills Foal, 1976; (as Sue Alden) Nurse of St. John, 1977; Piggy Bank Minds, 1977; Run of the Sea Witch, 1978; The Boy with the Blue Ears, 1979; Shoplifting: The Crime Everybody Pays For, 1980; (as Ellen Goforth) Path of Desire, 1980; New Boy in Town, 1981; Special Girl, 1981; (as Ellen Goforth) A New Dawn, 1982; Say Please, 1982; Captain Morgana Mason, 1982; (as Pat Louis) Treasure of the Heart, 1982; Ghost of Graydon Place, 1982; A Secret Place, 1982; A Blink of the Mind, 1982; Just Friends, 1983; Promises and Turtle Shells, 1984; The Warning, 1984; The Magic Circle, 1984; Kiss Me Kit, 1984; Bid for Romance, 1985; Write On, 1986; Stop Thief!, 1986; The Tomorrow Star, 1986; Fellow Your Heart, 1986; Computer Crime, 1987; The Right Kind of Girl, 1987; Vonnie and Monique, 1987; Suicide: The Preventable Tragedy, 1989; Drift Bottles in History and Folklore, 1990; Metal Detecting for Treasure, 1992; Survival at Big Shark Key, 1999; The Toy Deer of the Florida Keys, 1999; Bigfoot in New York City?, 1999; Case of the Bad-Luck Bike Ride across Iowa, 2001; The Case of the Missing Emeralds, 2001; Cody Smith and the Holiday Mysteries, 2001; The Case of the Vanishing Cat, 2001; The Jayhawk Horse Mystery, 2001; The Case of the Disappearing Kidnapper, 2001; Sharks!, 2001; The American Alligator, 2001; Dolphins, 2001; Sea Turtles, 2001; Borderland Horse, 2001; Loess Hills Forever, 2002; Clara Barton, 2002; Our Transportation Systems, 2002; Courage on the Oregon Trail, 2003; Conch Shell Murder, 2003; Pier Pressure, 2005; Cold-Case Killer: A Keely Moreno Mystery, 2007; Eden Palms Murder: A Key West Mystery, 2008; Killer in Control: A Key West Mystery, 2011. Contributor to periodicals. **Address:** 1505 Brentwood Terr., Marshalltown, IA 50158, U.S.A. **Online address:** rdfran@attglobal.net

FRANCIS, H(erbert) E(dward). American/Spanish (born Spain), b. 1924. **Genres:** Novellas/Short Stories, Literary Criticism And History, Translations, History. **Career:** Pennsylvania State University, instructor in English and Spanish, 1950-52; University of Tennessee, instructor in English, 1952-56; Northern Illinois University, instructor in English, 1956-58; Emory University, assistant professor of English, 1958-66; Fulbright lecturer, 1964, 1965-66, 1970; University of Alabama, associate professor, professor of English, writer-in-residence, 1966, now professor emeritus. Writer. **Publications:** Toda la gente que nunca tuve, 1966; Cinco millas hasta diciembre (y) Comolos peces, comos los pajaros, como la hierba, 1966; The Itinerary of Beggars, 1973; Had, 1976; Naming Things, 1980; (contrib.) Pushcart Prize, 1980; A Disturbance of Gulls and Other Stories, 1983; The Healing of the Body and Other Stories, 1992; (trans.) Animal World: Stories, 1996; The Sudden Trees, 1999; Goya, Are You with Me Now?, 2000; The Invisible Country, 2003; I'll Never Leave You: Stories, 2004. Works appear in anthologies. Contributor to periodicals. **Address:** Department of English, University of Alabama, 301 Sparkman Dr., Huntsville, AL 35899, U.S.A.

FRANCIS, James A. American (born United States), b. 1954. **Genres:** Classics, Theology/Religion. **Career:** St. John's University, N.E.H. Christian Humanism Project, assistant director, 1978-81, instructor in liberal studies, 1980-81; Duke University, lecturer in early Christian asceticism and monasticism, 1985; Rollins College, visiting assistant professor of classics, 1991-95, interim director of the program in classics, 1993-95; University of Kentucky, assistant professor of classics, 1995-2000, Department of Modern and Classical Languages, Literatures and Cultures, associate professor, 2000-, Division of Classic, director, 2005-; Lexington Theological Seminary, adjunct professor of church history, 2003. Writer. **Publications:** (Trans. with C.V. Franklin and I. Havener) Early Monastic Rules: The Rules of the Fathers and the Regula Orientalis, 1982; Subversive Virtue: Asceticism and Authority in the Second-Century Pagan World, 1995. Contributor to books and journals. **Address:** Division of Classics, University of Kentucky, Patterson Office Twr. 1055, Lexington, KY 40506, U.S.A. **Online address:** j.francis@uky.edu

FRANCIS, Lesley Lee. American (born United States), b. 1931. **Genres:** Literary Criticism And History, Poetry, History. **Career:** Sweet Briar College, assistant professor of Spanish, 1960-62; St. Edward's University, assistant professor, 1966-69, associate professor of Spanish, 1969-74; Escuela de la Tahona, owner and director, 1968-73, 1983-88; Universities in Virginia, faculty; American Association of University Professors, associate secretary; Montgomery College, professional staff; Shenandoah University, faculty. Writer. **Publications:** The Frost Family's Adventure in Poetry: Sheer Morning Gladness at the Brim, 1994; Robert Frost: An Adventure in Poetry, 1900-1918, 2004. Contributor of articles to periodicals. **Address:** Shenandoah University, 1460 University Dr., Winchester, VA 22601-5100, U.S.A. **Online address:** lfrancis@erols.com

FRANCIS, Mark. New Zealander (born New Zealand), b. 1944. **Genres:** History. **Career:** University of Canterbury, senior lecturer in political science, associate professor in political science, professor of political science, Diplomacy Programme, coordinator, MLIP, coordinator. Historian and writer. **Publications:** (Ed.) The Viennese Enlightenment, 1985; Governors and Settlers: Images of Authority in the British Colonies, 1820-60, 1992; (with J. Morrow) A History of English Political Thought in the Nineteenth Century, 1994; Herbert Spencer and the Invention of Modern Life, 2007; (ed. with J. Tully) In the Public Interest: Essays in Honour of Professor Keith Jackson, 2009. Contributor to journals. **Address:** Department of Political Science, University of Canterbury, 618 English Bldg., PO Box 4800, Christchurch, 4800, New Zealand. **Online address:** mark.francis@canterbury.ac.nz

FRANCIS, Matthew (Charles). Welsh/British (born England), b. 1956. **Genres:** Novels, Poetry. **Career:** Hampshire County Council, computer programmer, 1983-85; Metier Ltd., technical writer, 1985-86; Powell Duffryn Systems Ltd., technical writer, 1986-87; freelance technical writer, 1987-94; Southampton University, research student, 1994-98; freelance teacher of creative writing, 1998-99; University of Glamorgan, lecturer in creative writing, 1999-; Aberystwyth University, Department of English and Creative Writing, reader-in-creative writing. **Publications:** Whom (novel), 1989; Blizzard (poems), 1996; David Copperfield: A Play, 1999; Dragons (poems), 2001; (ed.) New Collected Poems, 2004; (ed.) Where the People Are: Language and Community in the Poetry of W.S. Graham, 2004; Whereabouts, 2005;

Mandeville, 2008; Singing a Man to Death, 2012. **Address:** Department of English & Creative Writing, Aberystwyth University, Rm. D65, Hugh Owen Bldg., Aberystwyth, SY23 3DY, Wales. **Online address:** mwf@aber.ac.uk

FRANCIS, Paul. *See* **ENGLEMAN, Paul.**

FRANCIS, Richard. British (born England), b. 1945. **Genres:** Novels, Intellectual History, Area Studies. **Career:** Harvard University, fellow, 1970-72; Manchester University, professor of creative writing, 1972-99; Tripoli University, lecturer in English, 1976-77; University of Missouri, visiting professor of American literature and creative writing, 1987-88; Bath Spa University, professor of creative writing, 1999-2009. Writer. **Publications:** Blackpool Vanishes (novel), 1979; Daggerman (novel), 1980; The Enormous Dwarf (novel), 1982; The Whispering Gallery (novel), 1984; Swansong (novel), 1986; The Land Where Lost Things Go (novel), 1990; Taking Apart the Poco Poco (novel), 1995; Transcendental Utopias: Individual and Community at Brook Farm, Fruitlands and Walden, 1997; (ed.) I, Claudius and Claudius the God, 1998; Fat Hen (novel), 1999; Ann the Word: The Story of Ann Lee, Female Messiah, Mother of the Shakers, the Woman Clothed with the Sun, 2000; Prospect Hill (novel), 2003; Judge Sewall's Apology: The Salem Witch Trials and the Forming of an American Conscience, 2005; The Old Spring (novel), 2010; Fruitlands: The Alcott Family and Their Search for Utopia, 2010. **Address:** c/o Caroline Dawnay, United Agents, 12-26 Lexington St., London, GL W1F 0LE, England. **Online address:** rfrancis22@hotmail.com

FRANCIS, R(ichard) A. British (born England) **Genres:** History, Literary Criticism And History, Biography, Autobiography/Memoirs, Politics/Government, Adult Non-fiction. **Career:** University of Nottingham, Department of French, professor of eighteenth-century French literature. Writer. **Publications:** Romain Rolland and Gandhi Correspondence: Letters, Diary, Extracts, Articles, etc, 1976; The Abbé Prévost: 1697-1763, 1990; Manon Lescaut, 1993; The Abbé Prévost's First-Person Narrators, 1993; Romain Rolland, 1999; L'Abbé Prévost au tournant du siécle: Studies on Voltaire and the Eighteenth Century, 2000. **Address:** Department of French and Francophone Studies, University of Nottingham, University Pk., Nottingham, NT NG7 2RD, England. **Online address:** richard.francis@nottingham.ac.uk

FRANCISCO, Nia. American (born United States), b. 1952. **Genres:** Poetry, Cultural/Ethnic Topics, Young Adult Fiction, History, Literary Criticism And History. **Career:** Navajo Community College, instructor, 1976-78; Navajo Tribe Division of Education, faculty, 1977-79; Chinle Unified School District, staff, 1979-80; Navajo Academy, instructor, 1981-83. Writer. **Publications:** (Co-author) The Sacred: Ways of Knowledge Sources of Life, 1977; Blue Horses for Navajo Women, 1988; Carried Away by the Black River, 1994. Works appear in anthologies. **Address:** PO Box 794, Navajo, NM 87328, U.S.A.

FRANCO, Betsy. American (born United States), b. 1947?. **Genres:** Young Adult Fiction, Young Adult Non-fiction. **Career:** Writer. **Publications:** (With M. Verne) The Emperor was my Neighbor in Japan, 1986; Japan, 1993; Mexico, 1993; Russia, 1993; India, 1994; Nigeria, 1994; China, 1994; Brazil, 1995; South Korea, 1995; Italy, 1995; (with M. Verne) Quiet Elegance: Japan through the Eyes of Nine American Artists, 1997; Sorting All Sorts of Socks, 1997; Counting Caterpillars and Other Math Poems, 1998; Fourscore and 7, 1999; Grandpa's Quilt, 1999; Write and Read Math Story Books, 1999; Unfolding Mathematics with Unit Origami, 1999; Shells, 2000; Why the Frog Has Big Eyes, 2000; Caring, Sharing and Getting Along, 2000; Thematic Poetry: On the Farm, 2000; Twenty Marvelous Math Tales, 2000; Thematic Poetry: Neighborhoods and Communities, 2000; Thematic Poetry: Creepy Crawlies, 2000; 201 Thematic Riddle Poems to Build Literacy, 2000; Thematic Poetry: All About Me!, 2000; The Tortoise Who Bragged: A Chinese Tale with Trigrams, 2000; My Pinkie Finger, 2001; Instant Poetry Frames for Primary Poets, 2001; Fifteen Wonderful Writing Prompt Mini-Books, 2001; Clever Calculator Cat, 2001; Funny Fairy Tale Math, 2001; Thematic Poetry: Transportation, 2001; Clever Calculations about Cats and Other Cool Creatures (teacher resource book), 2001; Adding Alligators and Other Easy-to-Read Math Stories, 2001; Five-Minute Math Problem of the Day for Young Learners, 2001; 12 Genre Mini-Books, 2002; Instant Math Practice Pages for Homework or Anytime!, 2002; Six Silly Seals and Other Read Aloud Story Skits, 2002; Amazing Animals, 2002; Pocket Poetry Mini Books, 2002; Silly Sally, 2002; Jake's Cake Mistake, 2002; (with C. Jellison and J. Kaufman) 2002; (with D. Dauler) Math in Motion: Wiggle, Gallop and Leap with Numbers, 2002; Many Ways to 100, 2002; A Bat Named Pat,

2002; Subtraction Fun, 2002; Time to Estimate, 2002; Marvelous Math Word Problem Mini Books, 2002; What's Zero?, 2002; Going to Grandma's Farm, 2003; Word Families: Guess Me Poems and Puzzles, 2003; Mathematickles!, 2003; Amoeba Hop, 2003; Alphabet: Guess-Me Poems and Puzzles, 2003; Counting Our Way to the 100th Day!: 100 Poems and 100 Pictures to Celebrate the 100th Day of School, 2004; Conversations with a Poet: Inviting Poetry into K-12 Classrooms, 2005; Birdsongs: A Backwards Counting Book, 2006; Math Poetry: Linking Language and Math in a Fresh Way, 2006; Summer Beat, 2007; Curious Collection of Cats, 2008; Bees, Snails & Peacock Tails, 2008; Instant Poetry Frames: Neighborhood & Community, 2008; Pond Circle, 2009; Zero is the Sound of Snowflakes, 2009; Messing Around on the Monkey Bars and Other School Poems for Two Voices, 2009; Metamorphosis: Junior Year, 2009; Pond Cycle, 2009; Zero is The Sound of Snowflakes, 2009; Curious Collection of Cats, 2009; Zero is the Leaves on the Tree, 2009; Double Play, 2011; Dazzling Display of Dogs, 2011. EDITOR: You Hear Me?: Poems and Writing by Teenage Boys, 2000; Things I Have to Tell You: Poems and Writing by Teenage Girls, 2001; (with A.P. Ochoa and T.L. Gourdine) Night is Gone, Day Is Still Coming: Stories and Poems by American Indian Teenagers and Young Adults, 2003; Falling Hard: 100 Love Poems by Teenagers, 2008. **Address:** PO Box 60487, Palo Alto, CA 94306, U.S.A. **Online address:** francobe@aol.com

FRANCO, Dean J. American (born United States), b. 1968. **Genres:** Literary Criticism And History, Writing/Journalism, Theology/Religion, History. **Career:** University of Southern California, assistant lecturer, 1995-98; California State University, part-time instructor, 1995-2001; Wake Forest University, assistant professor, 2001-07, associate professor of English, 2007-, Department of English, associate chair, 2010-, Wake Forest Humanities Institute, co-founder. Writer. **Publications:** Ethnic American Literature: Comparing Chicano, Jewish, and African American Writing, 2006; Race, Rights, and Recognition: Jewish American Literature since 1969, 2012. Contributor of articles to books and journals. **Address:** Department of English, Wake Forest University, C-208, Tribble Hall, PO Box 7387, Reynolda Sta., Winston-Salem, NC 27109-7387, U.S.A. **Online address:** francodj@wfu.edu

FRANEY, Ros(alind). British (born England) **Genres:** Novels, Social Commentary, Documentaries/Reportage, Law, Social Sciences. **Career:** IPC Magazines, journalist, 1972-74; UNICEF, information officer, 1974-75; Shelter, journalist, 1977-82; Yorkshire Television, researcher, 1985-89, producer/director of documentaries, 1990-97; freelance executive producer, 1997-98, 2001-03; Channel 4 TV, deputy commissioning editor, 1998-2000; Mentorn TV, executive producer, 2003-. **Publications:** Poor Law: The Mass Arrest of Homeless Claimants in Oxford, 1983; Cry Baby (novel), 1987; (with G. McKee) Time Bomb: Irish Bombers, English Justice and the Guildford Four, 1988. **Address:** Mentorn, 43 Whitfield St., London, GL W1T 4HA, England.

FRANK, Charles R(aphael). Czech/American (born United States), b. 1937. **Genres:** Economics, International Relations/Current Affairs. **Career:** Makerere University College, lecturer, 1963-65; East African Institute of Social Research, research fellow, 1963-65; Yale University, assistant professor of economics, 1965-67; U.S. Agency for International Development, consultant, 1966-; Princeton University, associate professor, 1967-70, professor of economics and international affairs, 1970-74, Woodrow Wilson School, Research Program in Economic Development, associate director, 1967-69, director, 1969-72; World Bank, consultant, 1969-; United Nations Economic Commission for Asia and the Far East, consultant, 1969; Brookings Institution, senior fellow, 1972-74; U.S. Department of State, chief economist, policy planning staff, 1974-77, State of District Columbia, deputy assistant secretary, 1974-78; Salomon Brothers Inc., vice president, 1978-87; Frank and Company Inc., president and chief executive officer, 1987-88; G.E. Capital Corp., vice president, 1988-97; European Bank for Reconstruction and Development, vice president, 1997-; Central European Media Enterprises (CME), director, 2001-09, 2010-, interim chief financial officer, 2009-10; U.S. Department of State, deputy assistant secretary and chief economist. Writer. **Publications:** The Sugar Industry in East Africa: An Analysis of Some Problems and Policy Questions Relating to the Expansion of the Sugar Industry in a Developing Economy, 1965; (with B. van Arkadie) Economic Accounting and Development Planning, 1966, rev. ed., 1969; Employment and Economic Growth in Nigeria, 1967; Production Theory and Indivisible Commodities, 1969; Debt and Terms of Aid, 1970; Statistics and Econometrics, 1971; (co-author) Assisting Developing Countries, 1972; Adjustment Assistance: American Jobs and Trade with the Developing Countries, 1973; Foreign Trade Regimes and Economic Development: The Case of Korea, 1975; (with S. Levinson) Foreign Trade and Domestic Aid, 1977; (ed. with R. Webb) Income Distribution and Growth in the Less-Developed Countries, 1977; (with M.A. Soto and C.A. Sevilla) Guatemala, 1982; (with M.A. Soto and C.A. Sevilla) Integración económica y empleo en la industria centroamericana, 1983; (with K.S. Kim and L.E. Westphal) South Korea, 1985. **Address:** Central European Media Enterprises Ltd., Krizeneckeho nam. 1078/5, Praha, 152 00, Czech Republic.

FRANK, Dana. American (born United States) **Genres:** Novels, Young Adult Fiction. **Career:** State University of New York, visiting lecturer, 1987-88; University of Missouri, assistant professor of history, 1988-91; University of California, professor of history, 1991-, Department of Community Studies, faculty, Department of Latin American and Latino Studies, faculty. Writer. **Publications:** Purchasing Power: Consumer Organizing, Gender, and the Seattle Labor Movement, 1919- 1929, 1994; Buy American: The Untold Story of Economic Nationalism, 1999; (with H. Zinn and R.D.G. Kelley) Three Strikes: Miners, Musicians, Salesgirls, and the Fighting Spirit of Labor's Last Century, 2001; Bananeras: Women Transforming the Banana Unions of Latin America, 2005; Local Girl Makes History: Exploring Northern California's Kitsch Monuments, 2007.Contributor to books. **Address:** Department of History, University of California, 539, Humanities 1, 1156 High St., Santa Cruz, CA 95064, U.S.A. **Online address:** dlfrank@ucsc.edu

FRANK, Dorothea Benton. American (born United States) **Genres:** Travel/ Exploration, Novels, Romance/Historical. **Career:** Writer and lawyer. **Publications:** Sullivan's Island: A Lowcountry Tale, 2000; Plantation: A Lowcountry Tale, 2001; Isle of Palms: A Lowcountry Tale, 2003; Shem Creek: A Lowcountry Tale, 2004; Pawleys Island: A Lowcountry Tale, 2005; Full of Grace, 2006; The Land of Mango Sunsets, 2007; The Christmas Pearl, 2007; Bulls Island, 2008; Return to Sullivan's Island, 2009; Lowcountry Summer, 2010; Folly Beach, 2011; Porch Lights, 2012. Contributor to periodicals. **Address:** c/o Author Mail, William Morrow & Co., 10 E 53rd St., New York, NY 10022, U.S.A. **Online address:** dot@dotfrank.com

FRANK, E(mily) R. American (born United States), b. 1967?. **Genres:** Novels, Literary Criticism And History. **Career:** Writer, psychotherapist and consultant. **Publications:** Life Is Funny, 2000; America, 2002; Friction, 2003; Wave, 2005; Wrecked, 2005; (contrib.) Rush Hour. Contributor to periodicals. **Address:** Charlotte Sheedy Literary Agency, 65 Bleecker St., New York, NY 10012, U.S.A.

FRANK, Frederick S. American (born United States), b. 1935. **Genres:** Horror, Romance/Historical, Writing/Journalism, Bibliography, Adult Non-fiction. **Career:** Teacher, 1959-60; Boston University, assistant professor of English, 1964-70; Allegheny College, professor of English, 1970-, now professor emeritus. Writer. **Publications:** Guide to the Gothic: An Annotated Bibliography of Criticism, 1984; The First Gothics: A Critical Guide to the English Gothic Novel, 1987; Gothic Fiction: A Masterlist of Twentieth Century Criticism and Research, 1988; (ed.) Montague Summers: A Bibliographical Portrait, 1988; Through the Pale Door: A Guide to and through the American Gothic, 1990; Guide to the Gothic II, 1995; (with A. Magistrale) The Poe Encyclopedia, 1997; (ed. with S.M. Conger, G. O'Dea and J. Yocum) Iconoclastic Departures, 1997; (ed. with D.H. Thomson and J.G. Voller) Gothic Writers: A Critical and Bibliographical Guide, 2002; (ed.) The Castle of Otranto: A Gothic Story, 2003; Guide to the Gothic III: An Annotated Bibliography of Criticism, 1994-2003, 2005; (ed.) The Origins of the Modern Study of Gothic Drama, Together with a Re-Edition of Gothic Drama from Walpole to Shelley (1947), 2006; (ed. with D.L. Hoeveler) Narrative of Arthur Gordon Pym of Nantucket, 2010. Works appear in anthologies. **Address:** Department of English, Allegheny College, 520 N Main St., PO Box 24, Meadville, PA 16335-1312, U.S.A. **Online address:** ffrank@toolcity.net

FRANK, Jacquelyn. American (born United States), b. 1968?. **Genres:** Young Adult Non-fiction, Sex. **Career:** Writer and educator. **Publications:** NIGHTWALKERS SERIES: Jacob, 2006; Gideon, 2007; Elijah, 2008; Damien, 2008; Noah, 2008; Adam, 2011. SHADOWDWELLERS SERIES: Ecstasy, 2009; Rapture, 2009; Pleasure, 2009; SINGLE TITLE SERIES: Drink of Me, 2010; Bid, 2010. THE GATHERER SERIES: Stealing Kathryn, 2010; Hunting Julian, 2010. THE THREE WORLDS: Seduce Me In Dreams, 2011; Seduce Me In Flames, 2011. Works appear in Anthologies. **Address:** Ballantine Books, 1745 Broadway, New York, NY 10019, U.S.A. **Online address:** jackifrankwrites@gmail.com

FRANK, Joan. American (born United States), b. 1949?. **Genres:** Essays, Novels, Novellas/Short Stories. **Career:** San Francisco State University, Department of Consumer and Family Studies/Dietetics, lecturer. Writer. **Publications:** Desperate Women Need to Talk to You (essays), 1994; Boys Keep Being Born (short stories), 2001; Miss Kansas City: A Novel, 2006; The Great Far Away, 2007; In Envy Country, 2010. Works appear in anthologies. Contributor to periodicals. **Address:** Department of Consumer and, Family Studies/Dietetics, San Francisco State University, 307 Burk Hall, 1600 Holloway Ave., San Francisco, CA 94132-4161, U.S.A. **Online address:** jfrank@sfsu.edu

FRANK, J. Suzanne. Also writes as Chloe Green, Chloe Green. American (born United States), b. 1967. **Genres:** Novellas/Short Stories, Mystery/ Crime/Suspense, Romance/Historical. **Career:** Writer. **Publications:** Reflections in the Nile, 1997; Shadows on the Aegean, 1998; Sunrise on the Mediterranean, 1999; Twilight in Babylon, 2002. AS CHLOE GREEN: Going Out in Style, 2000; Designed to Die, 2001; Fashion Victim, 2002. Works appear in anthologies. **Address:** c/o David Smith, DHS Literary, 2528 Elm St., Ste. 350, Dallas, TX 75226, U.S.A. **Online address:** susan@ofearna.us

FRANK, Katherine. American (born United States), b. 1968. **Genres:** Music, Dance/Ballet, Gay And Lesbian Issues, Humor/Satire. **Career:** Sweet Briar College, faculty, 1998-2000; Randolph-Macon Women's College, adjunct assistant professor, 2000; College of the Atlantic, adjunct faculty, professor of anthropology, 2001-; University of Wisconsin, Department of Sociology, honorary research fellow. Writer. **Publications:** G-strings and Sympathy: Strip Club Regulars and Male Desire, 2002; (ed. with R.D. Egan and M.L. Johnson) Flesh for Fantasy: Producing and Consuming Exotic Dance, 2006. **Address:** College of the Atlantic, 105 Eden St., Bar Harbor, ME 04609, U.S.A. **Online address:** katherinefrank@mac.com

FRANK, Leonard. See KING, Roger (Frank Graham).

FRANK, Nathaniel. American (born United States), b. 1971?. **Genres:** Military/Defense/Arms Control, Gay And Lesbian Issues. **Career:** New School University, faculty; University of California-Santa Barbara, Palm Center, senior research fellow; New York University, adjunct professor of history. Writer. **Publications:** Unfriendly Fire: How the Gay Ban Undermines the Military and Weakens America, 2009. Contributor to periodicals. **Address:** Palm Center, University of California, Santa Barbara, CA 93106, U.S.A. **Online address:** frank@palmcenter.ucsb.edu

FRANK, Robert. American (born United States), b. 1968. **Genres:** Adult Non-fiction, Social Sciences, Economics. **Career:** Wall Street Journal, senior special writer. **Publications:** Richistan: A Journey through the American Wealth Boom and the Lives of the New Rich, 2007; Who Repo'd my Jet, 2011. **Address:** The Wall Street Journal, 1211 Ave. of the Americas, New York, NY 10036, U.S.A. **Online address:** robert.frank@wsj.com

FRANK, Robert H. American (born United States), b. 1945. **Genres:** Economics, Money/Finance. **Career:** Cornell University, 1972-78, associate professor, 1979-85, professor of economics, 1986-91, Goldwin Smith professor of economics, ethics, and public policy, 1991-2001, S.C. Cornell Johnson Graduate School of Management, professor, 1990-, H.J. Louis professor of management, 2002-; Civil Aeronautics Board, chief economist, 1978-80. Writer. **Publications:** TEXTBOOKS: Microeconomics and Behavior, 1991, 8th ed., 2010; (with B.S. Bernanke) Principles of Economics, 2001, 4th ed., 2009; (with B.S. Bernanke) Principles of Microeconomics, 2001, 4th ed., 2009; (with B.S. Bernanke) Principles of Macroeconomics, 2001, 4th ed., 2009; (with B.S. Bernanke and L.D. Johnston) Principles of Macroeconomics: Brief Edition, 2009. GENERAL-INTEREST ECONOMICS: (with R.T. Freeman) Distributional Consequences of Direct Foreign Investment, 1978; Choosing the Right Pond: Human Behavior and the Quest for Status, 1986; Passions within Reason: The Strategic Role of the Emotions, 1988; (with P.J. Cook) The Winner-Take-All Society: How More and More Americans Compete for Ever Fewer and Bigger Prizes, Encouraging Economic Waste, Income Inequality, and an Impoverished Cultural Life, 1995; Luxury Fever: Why Money Fails to Satisfy in an Era of Excess, 1999 as Luxury Fever: Money and Happiness in an Era of Excess, 2000 as Luxury Fever: Weighing the Cost of Excess, 2010; What Price the Moral High Ground? Ethical Dilemmas in Competitive Environments, 2004, 2nd ed. as What Price the Moral High Ground? How to Succeed without Selling Your Soul, 2010; The Economic Naturalist: In Search of Explanations for Everyday Enigmas, 2007; Falling

Behind: How Rising Inequality Harms the Middle Class, 2007; The Economic Naturalist's Field Guide: Common Sense Principles for Troubled Times, 2009. Works appear in anthologies. Contributor of articles to books. **Address:** Johnson Graduate School of Management, Cornell University, 327 Sage Hall, Ithaca, NY 14853-6201, U.S.A. **Online address:** rhf3@cornell.edu

FRANKE, William. American (born United States), b. 1956. **Genres:** Literary Criticism And History. **Career:** Vanderbilt University, professor of comparative literature and religious studies. Writer. **Publications:** Dante's Interpretive Journey, 1996; On What Cannot Be Said: Apophatic Discourses in Philosophy, Religion, Literature, and the Arts, vol. I: Classic Formulations, vol. II: Modern and Contemporary Transformations, 2007; Poetry and Apocalypse: Theological Disclosures of Poetic Language, 2009. FORTHCOMING: A Philosophy of the Unsayable; Dante and the Sense of Transgression: The Trespass of the Sign; The Veil of Eternity: Language and Transcendence in Dante's Paradiso; Philosophical Hermeneutics and the Literary Form of Revelation; The Revelation of Imagination: From Homer and the Bible through Virgil and Augustine to Dante; Infinite Figures: Proposals for a New Theoretical Rhetoric; Postmodern Theologics: Critical Theory in the Wake of the Death of God. Contributor of articles to books and journals. **Address:** Department of French and Italian, Vanderbilt University, PO Box 1709, Sta. B 351709, Nashville, TN 37235, U.S.A. **Online address:** william.franke@vanderbilt.edu

FRANKEL, Alona. Israeli/Polish (born Poland), b. 1937. **Genres:** Children's Fiction, Autobiography/Memoirs, Illustrations, Picture/Board Books, Children's Non-fiction. **Career:** Graphic designer and illustrator, 1955-; author and illustrator of children's books, 1975-. **Publications:** FOR CHILDREN: SELF-ILLUSTRATED: (and trans.) Once upon a Potty, 1975, vol. I: His, 1975, vol. I: Hers, 1978, vol. III: Boy, 2002, vol. IV: Girl, 2002; The Family of Tiny White Elephants, 1978; The Goodnight Book, 1979; Let's Go from Head to Toe, 1979; Tiyul Aher, 1979; Angela, the Little Devil, 1979; One, Two, Three, What Can a Mushroom Be, 1980; Sefer al Gamadim, Pitriyot u-mah od, 1980; Sefer Ha-hagim, 1980; Sefer Ha-okhel, 1980; A Book to Eat By, 1980; Sipur Meha-hayim, 1981; A True Story, 1981; Sefer Ha-Yareah, 1983; The Clothes We Wear, 1983; The Moon Book, 1983; The Book of Numbers, 1983; The Book of Letters, 1983; The Princess of Dreams, 1984; Ba'alat Hahalomot, 1984; A Fairy Tale, 1985; Ha-Sefinah Veha-i, 1985; There Is No One Like Mother, 1985; The Ship and the Island, 1985; Mi Bacinica y yo, 1986; The Princess and the Caterpillar, 1987; A Lullaby, 1987; One Day (a book of numbers), 1990; Sefer Ha-nimusim, 1990; From Armadillo to Octopus (a book of the Hebrew alphabet), 1990; The Book of Manners, 1990; I Want My Mother, 1990; A Book to Babysit By, 1991; Ha-Sefer Ha-gadol Shel O. Hilel, 1992; Yofi shel Tsava, 1993; Shabat Ba-Boker, O, Az Ma Ani Eese Ha-Yom, 1999; Prudence's Baby-sitter Book, 2000; Prudence's Book of Food, 2000; Prudence's Get Well Book, 2000; Prudence's Good Night Book, 2000; Joshua's Counting Book, 2000; Joshua's Book of Manners, 2000; Joshua's Book of Clothes, 2000; Moon and the Stars, 2000; On Grandparents Farm, 2001; Ma Ani Rotze Lihiot Kshe Ehie Gadol, 2003; Yaldah, 2004; Ha-Daiesa Shel Savta, 2006; Savta Shel Naftali Bishla Dayesa, 2007; Lama Le-Naftali Korim Naftali, 2009; Na'arah, 2009. Contributor to periodicals. Illustrator of books by others. **Address:** Child Matters, 155 Beech St., Boston, MA 02131-2714, U.S.A. **Online address:** yalda@alonafrankel.com

FRANKEL, Ellen. American (born United States), b. 1951. **Genres:** Novellas/Short Stories, Children's Fiction, Mythology/Folklore, Theology/Religion, Art/Art History, Homes/Gardens. **Career:** Franklin and Marshall College, literature and writing, teacher, 1977-79; Drexel University, literature and writing, teacher, 1979-80; Lancaster and Lebanon County Schools, creative writing, teacher, 1979-85; Millersville University, teacher of literature, writing and linguistics, 1981; freelance writer, 1981-89; Lancaster Jewish Day School, Judaic Principal, 1988-89; B'nai B'rith Book Club, editor, 1990. **Publications:** Choosing to Be Chosen (stories for children), 1985; George Washington and the Constitution, 1987; The Classic Tales: 4, 000 Years of Jewish Lore, 1989; (with B.P. Teutsch) The Encyclopedia of Jewish Symbols, 1992; (with S. Levine) Tell It like It Is: Tough Choices for Today's Teens, 1995; (with A.M. Morris) Bathroom Styles, 1995; The Five Books of Miriam: A Woman's Commentary on the Torah, 1996; (ed.) The Jewish Spirit: A Celebration in Stories and Art, 1997; (adaptor) The Illustrated Hebrew Bible: 75 Selected Stories, 1999; (ed. with F.D. Miller, Jr. and J. Paul) Natural Law and Modern Moral Philosophy, 2000; Beyond a Shadow of a Diet: The Therapist's Guide to Treating Compulsive Eating, 2004; Diet Survivor's Handbook: 60 Lessons in Eating, Acceptance, and Self-care, 2006; Beyond Measure: A Memoir about Short Stature and Inner Growth, 2006; (ed.) Folktales of

the Jews, 2006; (with M. Kaufman) Design Ideas for Decorative Concrete & Stone, 2006; (reteller) JPS Illustrated Children's Bible, 2009. **Address:** Jewish Publication Society, 2100 Arch St., 2nd Fl., Philadelphia, PA 19103, U.S.A. **Online address:** efrankel@juwishpub.org

FRANKEL, Glenn. American (born United States), b. 1949. **Genres:** International Relations/Current Affairs, Young Adult Non-fiction. **Career:** Richmond Mercury, reporter, 1973; Washington Post, bureau chief, 1979-82, Southern Africa, bureau chief, 1983-86, Jerusalem, bureau chief, 1986-89, London, bureau chief, 1989-92; Stanford University, Department of Communication, visiting hearst professional-in-residence, Lorry I. Lokey visiting professor; University of Texas, College of Communication, School of Journalism, director, G.B. Dealey regents professor in journalism. Journalist and writer. **Publications:** Beyond the Promised Land: Jews and Arabs on the Hard Road to a New Israel, 1994; Rivonia's Children: Three Families and the Cost of Conscience in White South Africa, 1999. Contributor to periodicals. **Address:** College of Communication, School of Journalism, University of Texas, PO Box Z, Austin, TX 78713-8926, U.S.A. **Online address:** glenn.frankel@austin.utexas.edu

FRANKEL, Sandor. American (born United States), b. 1943. **Genres:** Law, Novels, Criminology/True Crime. **Career:** United States District of Columbia, assistant attorney, 1968-71; Frankel & Abrams, managing partner. Writer. **Publications:** Beyond a Reasonable Doubt, 1971; (with W. Mews) The Aleph Solution, 1978; (with R.S. Fink) How To Defend Yourself Against the IRS, 1985; (with R.S. Fink) You Can Protect Yourself from the IRS, 1987, rev. ed. as You Can Protect Yourself from the IRS: The Year-Round Insider's Guide to Taxes, 1988. **Address:** Frankel & Abrams, Rm. 3330, 230 Park Ave., New York, NY 10169-3331, U.S.A.

FRANKEL, Valerie. American (born United States), b. 1965. **Genres:** Novels, Adult Non-fiction, Young Adult Non-fiction. **Career:** New York Woman, researcher, 1987-89; Mademoiselle, associate editor, 1990-95, articles editor, 1993-99. **Publications:** A Deadline for Murder, 1991; Murder on Wheels, 1992; Prime Time for Murder: A Wanda Mallory Mystery, 1994; (with E. Tien) The Heartbreak Handbook: How to Survive the Worst 24 Hours of Your Life and Move On, 1994; A Body to Die For, 1995; (with E. Tien) The I Hate My Job Handbook: How to Deal with Hell at Work, 1996; (with E. Tien) Prime-Time Style: The Ultimate TV Guide to Fashion Hits and Misses, 1996; Smart vs. Pretty, 2000; The Accidental Virgin, 2003; The Not-So-Perfect Man, 2004; (with S. Mullen) The Best You'll Ever Have: What Every Woman Should Know about Getting and Giving Knock-Your-Socks-Off Sex, 2005; The Girlfriend Curse, 2005; Fringe Girl: The Revolution Starts Now, 2006; Hex and the Single Girl, 2006; Fringe Girl in Love, 2007; I Take This Man, 2007; Henry Potty and the Deathly Paper Shortage: An Unauthorized Harry Potter Parody, 2008; Fringe Benefits, 2008; American Fringe, 2008; Thin is the New Happy, 2008; (with J. Rivers) Men are Stupid... and They like Big Boobs: A Woman's Guide to Beauty Through Plastic Surgery, 2009; From Girl to Goddess: The Heroine's Journey through Myth and Legend, 2010; It's Hard Not to Hate You, 2011; Four of a Kind, 2012. Contributor to books and periodicals. **Address:** c/o Nancy Yost, Nancy Yost Literary Agency, 350 7th Ave., Ste. 2003, New York, NY 10001, U.S.A. **Online address:** valfrankel@aol.com

FRANKFURTER, David Thomas Munro. American (born United States), b. 1961. **Genres:** Young Adult Non-fiction. **Career:** Planned Parenthood of Mid-Michigan, director, 1989-90; College of Charleston, assistant professor of religious studies, 1990-95; University of New Hampshire, assistant professor, 1995-98, associate professor, 1998-2002, professor of history & religious studies, 2002. Writer. **Publications:** NONFICTION: Elijah in Upper Egypt: The Apocalypse of Elijah and Early Egyptian Christianity, 1993; (ed.) Pilgrimage and Holy Space in Late Antique Egypt, 1998; Religion in Roman Egypt: Assimilation and Resistance, 1998; Evil Incarnate: Rumors of Demonic Conspiracy and Ritual Abuse in History, 2006. Contributor to books. **Address:** Department of History, University of New Hampshire, 436 Horton Social Science Ctr., Durham, NH 03824, U.S.A. **Online address:** davidtf@unh.edu

FRANKL, Razelle. American (born United States), b. 1932. **Genres:** Theology/Religion, Institutions/Organizations, Communications/Media. **Career:** League of Women Voters, president, 1967-68; Drexel University, instructor, 1972-73; Philadelphia '76 Inc. (bicentennial corporation), coordinator for health programs, 1973-74; Glassboro State College, adjunct member of faculty, 1974-77, 1981-82, assistant professor, 1982-88, associate professor of management, 1988-95, professor of organizational behavior, 1988-, coordinator of human resources management, 1982-88; Rowan University, professor of management, 1983-2000, professor emeritus, 2000-. Writer. **Publications:** Televangelism: The Marketing of Popular Religion, 1987. Contributor to books and periodicals. **Address:** Department of Management, Rowan University, 201 Mullica Hill Rd., Glassboro, NJ 08028, U.S.A. **Online address:** frankl@rowan.edu

FRANKLAND, (Anthony) Noble. British (born England), b. 1922. **Genres:** History, Military/Defense/Arms Control, Biography. **Career:** Air Historical Branch, narrator, 1948-51, Cabinet Office, official military historian, 1951-60; Royal Institute of International Affairs, deputy director of studies, 1956-60; Imperial War Museum, director, 1960-82; Trinity College, Lees Knowles lecturer, 1963; University of London, King's College, Military Archives Center, trustee, 1963-82; H.M.S. Belfast Trust, trustee, 1971-78, vice chair, 1972-78, director, 1978-82; Air Museum, director, 1976-82; Thames Television, advisor. Writer. **Publications:** (Ed.) Documents on International Affairs, 1956; Crown of Tragedy: Nicholas II, 1960 in US as Imperial Tragedy: Nicholas II, Last of the Tsars, 1961; (with C. Webster) The Strategic Air Offensive Against Germany, 1939-1945, vol. IV, 1961; The Bombing Offensive Against Germany: Outlines and Perspectives, 1965; Bomber Offensive: The Devastation of Europe, 1970; (ed. with C. Dowling) The Politics and Strategy of the Second World War, vol. VIII, 1974-78; (ed. with C. Dowling) Decisive Battles of the Twentieth Century: Land-Sea-Air, 1976; Prince Henry, Duke of Gloucester, 1980; (ed.) The Encyclopedia of Twentieth Century Warfare, 1989; Witness of a Century: The Life and Times of Prince Arthur Duke of Connaught, 1850-1942, 1993; History at War: The Campaigns of an Historian, 1998; The Unseen War, 2007; Belling's War, 2008. Contributor to journals. **Address:** 26-27 Riverview Terr., Abingdon, OX OX14 5AE, England.

FRANKLET, Duane. American (born United States), b. 1963. **Genres:** Information Science/Computers, Young Adult Fiction. **Career:** Writer, 1985-; Data Tracking Associates, president and partner, 1992-. **Publications:** Bad Memory, 1997; Stalking the Beast, 2005; Section 18, forthcoming. Contributor to periodicals. **Address:** Data Tracking Associates, 4200 Montrose Blvd., Ste. 300, Houston, TX 77006-5443, U.S.A. **Online address:** dfranklet@uh.edu

FRANKLIN, Allan (David). American (born United States), b. 1938. **Genres:** Sciences, History, Philosophy. **Career:** Princeton University, research associate, 1965-66, instructor, 1966-67; University of Colorado, assistant professor, 1967-73, associate professor, 1973-82, professor of physics, 1982-, associate chair; City University of New York, visiting professor and lecturer, 1974-75; University of Campinas, visiting professor and lecturer, 1982; University of London, visiting professor and lecturer, 1982-92. Writer. **Publications:** The Principle of Inertia in the Middle Ages, 1976; The Neglect of Experiment, 1986; Experiment, Right or Wrong, 1990; The Rise and Fall of the Fifth Force: Discovery, Pursuit, and Justification in Modern Physics, 1993; Can That Be Right? Essays on Experiment, Evidence, and Science, 1999; Are There Really Neutrinos?: An Evidential History, 2000; Selectivity and Discord: Two Problems of Experiment, 2002; No Easy Answers: Science and the Pursuit of Knowledge, 2005; (co-author) Ending the Mendel-Fisher Controversy, 2008. Contributor to journals. **Address:** Department of Physics, University of Colorado, Rm. F-627, 2000 Colorado Ave., PO Box 390, Boulder, CO 80309-0390, U.S.A. **Online address:** allan.franklin@colorado.edu

FRANKLIN, Caroline. Welsh/British (born England), b. 1949. **Genres:** Literary Criticism And History, Essays. **Career:** School teacher in Yorkshire, 1972-84; Trinity College, senior lecturer, 1989-94; University of Swansea, senior lecturer in English, 1995-, professor of English, 2004-; Women's Writing, associate editor. **Publications:** Byron's Heroines, 1992; (ed. with P. Garside) British Women Novelists, 1750-1850, 1992; The Wanderings of Warwick, 1992; Emmeline, 1992; The History of Cornelia, 1992; (ed. with P. Garside) The Romantics: Women Novelists, 1995; (ed.) The Romantics: Women Poets, 1770-1830, 1996; The Plays of Lord Byron: Critical Essays, 1997; Romanticism and Colonialism: Writing and Empire 1780-1830, 1998; (ed. and intro.) British Romantic Poets, 1998; (intro.) British Romantic Poets, 1998; Byron: A Literary Life, 2000; Political Economy, Taxation, Poor Laws and Paupers, 2001; (comp. with E.J. Clery and P. Garside.) Authorship, Commerce, and the Public: Scenes of Writing, 1750-1850, 2002; The Plays of Lord Byron: Critical Essays, 2003; Mary Wollstonecraft: A Literary Life, 2004; Women, Gender and Enlightenment, 2005; Byron, 2006; (ed.) Women's Travel Writing, 1750-1850, 2006; Byron, Routledge Guide, 2007; (ed.)

Longman Anthology of Gothic Verse, 2010; (ed.) The Wellesley Series IV: Nineteenth-Century Sources in the Humanities and Social Sciences. Works appear in anthologies. **Address:** Department of English Language and Literature, University of Swansea, Rm. 210, Keir Hardie Bldg., Singleton Pk., Swansea, WG SA2 8PP, Wales. **Online address:** c.franklin@swansea.ac.uk

FRANKLIN, Cheryl J. American (born United States), b. 1955. **Genres:** Science Fiction/Fantasy, Novels, Young Adult Fiction. **Career:** Rockwell International Corp., communications systems analyst, 1976-; Boeing, communications systems analyst, 1976-2001. Writer. **Publications:** Fire Get, 1987; Fire Lord, 1989; The Light in Exile, 1989; Fire Crossing, 1991; The Inquisitor, 1992; Sable, Shadow, and Ice, 1994; Ghost Shadow, 1996. **Address:** Rockwell International Corp., 3370 Miraloma Ave., PO Box 3105, Anaheim, CA 92803-3105, U.S.A.

FRANKLIN, Daniel P. American (born United States), b. 1954. **Genres:** Politics/Government, Social Commentary, Administration/Management, Film, Literary Criticism And History. **Career:** Colgate University, chief executive, 1985-2006, assistant professor of political science, 1985-91, representative of political science department, 1988-90; St. Edwards University, chief executive, 1985-2006; Georgia State University, chief executive, 1985-2006, associate professor of political science, 1991-, university senate, 1992-, Presidential Scholars Program, director, 1997, Georgia State Legislature, lobbyist, 1997-99. Writer. **Publications:** Extraordinary Measures: The Exercise of Prerogative Powers in the United States, 1991; Making Ends Meet: Congressional Budgeting in the Age of Deficits, 1993; (ed. with M. Baun) Political Culture and Constitutionalism: A Comparative Approach, 1995; Politics and Film: The Political Culture of Film in the United States, 2006. **Address:** Department of Political Science, Georgia State University, 1038 General Classroom Bldg., 38 Peachtree Center Ave., Ste. 1005, PO Box 4069, Atlanta, GA 30303-2514, U.S.A. **Online address:** dpfranklin@gsu.edu

FRANKLIN, David Byrd. American (born United States), b. 1951. **Genres:** Anthropology/Ethnology, History, Biography, Autobiography/Memoirs. **Career:** Young Harris College, professor of history and anthropology, 1979-, chairperson of social and behavioral studies, 1985-. Writer. **Publications:** The Scottish Regency of the Earl of Arran: A Study in the Failure of Anglo-Scottish Relations, 1995. **Address:** Young Harris College, 1 College St., PO Box 68, Young Harris, GA 30582-4137, U.S.A. **Online address:** davidf@yhc.edu

FRANKLIN, James L(ee). American (born United States), b. 1947. **Genres:** Classics, Art/Art History, History, Social Sciences. **Career:** Columbia University, Barnard College, assistant professor of classical studies, 1975-76; Wellesley College, assistant professor of classical studies, 1976-77; University of Michigan, visiting assistant professor of classical studies, 1977-80; Indiana University, Department of Classical Studies, assistant professor, 1981-84, associate professor, 1984-93, professor, 1993-, Hope School of Art, adjunct professor history of art, 2009-; Intercollegiate Center for Classical Studies in Rome, A.W. Mellon professor-in-charge, 1994-95, professor-in-charge, 1997-98; College of Charleston, lecturer; University of Massachusetts, lecturer; Clemson University, lecturer; University of Southern California, lecturer; Howard University, lecturer; University of Florida, lecturer; public speaker. Writer. **Publications:** Pompeii: The Casa del marinaio and Its History, 1990; Pompeii: The Buried City, 1995; Pompeis Difficile Est: Studies in the Political Life of Imperial Pompeii, 2001. Contributor of articles. **Address:** Department of Classical Studies, Indiana University Bloomington, Rm. 550, Ballantine Hall, 1020 E Kirkwood Ave., Bloomington, IN 47405-7103, U.S.A. **Online address:** franklin@indiana.edu

FRANKLIN, Jane (Morgan). American (born United States), b. 1934. **Genres:** History, Politics/Government, Military/Defense/Arms Control, Humanities. **Career:** Tobacco worker, 1942-51; Bailey Library, part-time librarian, 1948-51; United Nations, public information representative, 1955-56; freelance typist, proofreader, editor, researcher and writer, 1959-71; Grossman, Ackerman and Peters (law firm), legal secretary, 1973-74; WPOP, news writer, 1974-75; freelance editor and indexer, 1977-79; Center for Cuban Studies, staff, 1980-81; Cuba Update, researcher and writer, 1981-83, co-editor, 1984-90, contributing editor, 1990-2002. **Publications:** Cuban Foreign Relations: A Chronology, 1959-1982, 1984; (ed. with M.E. Gettleman, H.B. Franklin and M. Young) Vietnam and America: A Documented History, 1985; A Chronology of U.S.-Panama Relations in the U.S. Invasion of Panama: The Truth behind Operation Just Cause, 1991; The Cuban Revolution and the United States: A Chronological History, 1992; Cuba and the United States: A

Chronological History, 1997. Contributor of articles to periodicals and magazines. **Address:** Ocean Press, 511 Ave. of the Americas, Ste. 96, New York, NJ 10011-8436, U.S.A. **Online address:** jbfranklins@compuserve.com

FRANKLIN, Linda Campbell. Also writes as Barkinglips McFarland, Ninda Dumont. American (born United States), b. 1941. **Genres:** Antiques/Furnishings, Design, Technology, Bibliography, Illustrations, Reference, Poetry, Essays, Essays. **Career:** Editor and illustrator, 1970-76; Tree Communications Inc., editor, 1976-81, senior editor, 1981-84; The Ephemera News Quarterly, editor, 1981-83; Show Forth Bimonthly, editor, 1983-84; Kitchen Collectibles News bimonthly, editor and publisher, 1984-86. **Publications:** From Hearth to Cookstove, 1976, rev. ed., 1979; Antiques and Collectibles: A Bibliography of Works in English, 1978; Our Old Fashioned Country Diary, 1980, 17th ed., 1996; Library Display Ideas, 1980; 300 Years of Kitchen Collectibles, 1981, 5th ed., 2003; Breads and Biscuits, 1981; Our Christmas Book, 1981; Classroom Display Ideas, 1982; Display and Publicity Ideas for Libraries, 1985; The Official from Hearth to Cookstove: An American Domestic History of Gadgets and Utensils Made or Used in America from 1700 to 1930, 3rd ed., 1985; 300 Years of Housecleaning Collectibles, 1992; (ed.) My Heart 2 Heart Diary, 1994; Heart 2 Heart Scraps and Scribbles, 1995; Heart 2 Heart Diary: Blue Dog, 1996; Heart 2 Heart Scraps and Pockets, 1997; Heart 2 Heart Travel Diary, 1998; Heart 2 Heart Girlfriends' Book, 1999; Girlfriends' Address Book, 1999; Girlfriends' Stationery, 2000; Big Crush, 2002; My Secrets, 2002; Pass-Note Diary, 2003. **Address:** MD , U.S.A. **Online address:** barktok@mindspring.com

FRANKLIN, Michael J(ohn). Welsh (born Wales), b. 1949. **Genres:** Biography, Literary Criticism And History. **Career:** Worcester Girls' Grammar School, English teacher, 1974-83; University of Birmingham, extra-mural lecturer, 1982-83; University of Wales, University College, extra-mural lecturer in continuing education, 1989-, part-time lecturer in English, 1992-95; Trinity College, part-time lecturer, 1994-95; St. John's Comprehensive School, Department of English, head. Writer. **Publications:** Sir William Jones: A Critical Biography, 1995; (ed.) Sir William Jones: Selected Poetical and Prose Works, 1995; (ed.) Representing India: Indian Culture and Imperial Control in Eighteenth-Century British Orientalist Discourse, 2000; (ed.) Romantic Representations of British India, 2006; (ed. and intro.) Hartly House, Calcutta, 2007. Contributor to books and periodicals. **Address:** School of Arts and English, Swansea University, Singleton Pk., Swansea, WG SA2 8PP, Wales. **Online address:** m.j.franklin@swansea.ac.uk

FRANKLIN, Richard Langdon. (R. L. Franklin). Australian (born Australia), b. 1925?. **Genres:** Philosophy. **Career:** University of Western Australia, lecturer, 1956-67; University of New England, professor, 1968-86, emeritus professor of philosophy, 1986-. Writer. **Publications:** AS R.L. FRANKLIN: Freewill and Determinism: A Study of Rival Conceptions of Man, 1968; Can Philosophers Reach the Truth?, 1969; New Horizons: Reflections on the Future of Religion and Science, 1986; The Search for Understanding, 1995. **Address:** Department of Philosophy, University of New England, Armidale, NW 2351, Australia.

FRANKLIN, R. L. *See* **FRANKLIN, Richard Langdon.**

FRANKLIN, Robert M(ichael). American (born United States), b. 1954. **Genres:** Cultural/Ethnic Topics, Theology/Religion, Social Sciences, Young Adult Non-fiction. **Career:** Saint Paul Church of God in Christ, assistant pastor, 1978-84; University of Chicago, Divinity School, instructor in religion and psychological studies, ethics and director of field education, 1981-83; Harvard University, Divinity School, associate director of ministerial studies, 1984-85, visiting lecturer, 1986-88, visiting professor, 2003; Colgate Rochester/Bexley/Crozer Divinity School, assistant professor and dean of black church studies, 1985-89; Emory University, Candler School of Theology, assistant professor, 1989-91, associate professor of ethics and society, 1991-, director of black church studies, 1989-, presidential distinguished professor of social ethics, 2003-; Interdenominational Theological Center, president, 1997-2002; Morehouse College, president, 2007-; Emory University School of Law, Center for the Study of Law and Religion, senior fellow. Writer. **Publications:** Liberating Visions: Human Fulfillment and Social Justice in African-American Thought, 1990; Another Day's Journey, 1997; (co-author) From Culture Wars to Common Ground: Religion and the American Family Debate, 2001; Crisis in the Village: Restoring Hope in African American Communities, 2007. Contributor of articles to periodicals. **Address:** More-

house College, 830 Westview Dr., Atlanta, GA 30314, U.S.A. **Online address:** rfranklin@morehouse.edu

FRANKLIN, Samuel Harvey. New Zealander/British (born England), b. 1928?. **Genres:** Geography, Sociology. **Career:** Victoria University of Wellington, faculty, 1951-67, Department of Geography, professor, 1967-, professor emeritus. Writer. **Publications:** The European Peasantry, The Final Phase, 1969; Rural Societies, 1971; Trade, Growth, and Anxiety: New Zealand beyond the Welfare State, 1978; Cul de Sac: The Question of New Zealand's Future, 1985; Inferior Goods: Consumption, Social Change, and Industrial Restructuring in 20th Century, forthcoming. **Address:** Department of Geography, Victoria University of Wellington, PO Box 600, Wellington, 6140, New Zealand. **Online address:** harvey.franklin@vuw.ac.nz

FRANKLIN, Yelena. American (born United States), b. 1945. **Genres:** Mystery/Crime/Suspense, Young Adult Fiction. **Career:** Michigan Bell Telephone Co., editor, manager, writer, director and producer, 1973-88; Editorial Services, partner, 1989-93; Video Monitoring Services, general manager, 1993-94; Masco Corp., public relations manager, 1994-95. **Publications:** A Bowl of Sour Cherries, 1998; Second Hand Murder, 2001; Piranha Times, 2008. **Address:** c/o Author Mail, White Pine Press, PO Box 236, Buffalo, NY 14201-0236, U.S.A. **Online address:** yelenavf@aol.com

FRANTZEN, Allen J. American (born United States), b. 1947. **Genres:** Gay And Lesbian Issues, Intellectual History, Literary Criticism And History, Poetry. **Career:** Oberlin College, assistant professor of English, 1976-78; Loyola University of Chicago, assistant professor, 1978-83, associate professor, 1983-88, Graduate Programs in English, director, 1984-88, professor of English, 1988-, Loyola Community Literacy Center, founding director, director, 1992-2005, College of Arts and Sciences, master teacher, 1997-98. Writer. **Publications:** The Literature of Penance in Anglo-Saxon England, 1983; King Alfred, 1986; Desire for Origins: New Languages, Old English, and Teaching the Tradition, 1990; Speaking Two Languages: Traditional Disciplines and Contemporary Theory in Medieval Studies, 1991; Troilus and Criseyde: The Poem and the Frame, 1993; (ed. with D. Moffat) Work of Work: Servitude, Slavery, and Labor in Medieval England, 1994; (ed. with J.D. Niles) Anglo-Saxonism and the Construction of Social Identity, 1997; Before the Closet: Same-Sex Love from Beowulf to Angels in America, 1998; Bloody Good: Chivalry, Sacrifice, and the Great War, 2004; (ed. with J. Hines) Caeldmon's Hymn and Material Culture in the World of Bede: Six Essays, 2007; Anglo-Saxon Keywords: A Modular Approach to Early English Culture, forthcoming; Food Networks: Eating and Identity in Anglo-Saxon England, forthcoming; (co-ed.) Teaching Beowulf in the Twenty-First Century, forthcoming. **Address:** Department of English, Loyola University of Chicago, 6525 N Sheridan Rd., Chicago, IL 60626-5385, U.S.A. **Online address:** afrantz@luc.edu

FRANTZICH, Stephen E. American (born United States), b. 1944. **Genres:** Politics/Government, Social Commentary, Technology. **Career:** Denison University, assistant professor of political science, 1971-73; Hamilton College, assistant professor of political science, 1973-77; U.S. Naval Academy, professor of political science and department head, 1977-. Writer. **Publications:** Storming Washington: An Intern's Guide to National Government, 1977, 2nd ed., 1986; Computers in Congress: The Politics of Information, 1982; Write Your Congressman: Constituent Communications and Representation, 1986; Political Parties in the Technological Age, 1989; (with S. Percy) American Government: The Political Game, 1994, 2nd ed., 1996; (with S. Schier) Congress: Games and Strategies, 1995, (with S. Berube) 4th ed., 2010; (with J. Sullivan) The C-Span Revolution, 1996; Citizen Democracy: Political Activists in a Cynical Age, 1999, 3rd ed., 2008; Cyberage Politics 101: Mobility, Technology and Democracy, 2002; Founding Father: How C-SPAN's Brian Lamb Changed Politics in America, 2008; (with H.R. Ernst) Political Science Toolbox: A Research Companion to American Government, 2009; The Conversations of Democracy: Linking Citizens to American Government, 2010. **Address:** Department of Political Science, U.S. Naval Academy, 589 McNair Rd., Annapolis, MD 21402, U.S.A. **Online address:** frantzic@usna.edu

FRANZONI, David (H.). American (born United States), b. 1947. **Genres:** Plays/Screenplays. **Career:** Screenwriter. **Publications:** Jumpin' Jack Flash, 1986; Amistad, 1997; (with J. Logan) Gladiator, 1999; (with F. Thompson) King Arthur, 2004. **Address:** c/o Leslie Barnes, Creative Artists Agency L.L.C., 2000 Ave. of the Stars, Los Angeles, CA 90067, U.S.A.

FRAPPIER-MAZUR, Lucienne. American/French (born France), b. 1932. **Genres:** Literary Criticism And History, Adult Non-fiction, Young Adult Fiction, Translations. **Career:** University of Pennsylvania, assistant professor, 1962-71, associate professor, 1971-79, professor of French, 1979-96, associate director of French Institute, 1995-96, professor emeritus, 1996-; University of California, visiting professor, 1987; Yale University, visiting professor, 1989; University Paris VII, visiting professor, 1991. Writer. **Publications:** L'Expression métaphorique dans La Comédie humaine: Domaine Socialet Physiologique, 1976; (ed. and intro.) La Comedie humaine, 1977; Sade etl'ecriture de l'orgie: Pouvoir et parodie dans L'Histoire de Juliette, 1991, trans. as Writing the Orgy: Power and Parody in Sade, 1996; (co-ed.) Autobiography, Historiography, Rhetoric: A Festschrift in Honor of Frank Paul Bowman, 1994; Corps/Décors, 1999; (with J.M. Roulin) érotique balzacienne, 2001. Contributor to books and periodicals. **Address:** Department of Romance Languages, University of Pennsylvania, 521 Williams Hall, 255 S 36th St., Philadelphia, PA 19104-6305, U.S.A. **Online address:** frappier@sas.upenn.edu

FRASCA, Ralph. American (born United States), b. 1962. **Genres:** Military/Defense/Arms Control. **Career:** Belmont Abbey College, coordinator and professor of mass communication, 2007; Regional and Media Interest Group, head. Writer. **Publications:** The Rise and Fall of the Saturday Globe, 1992; The Mexican-American War: American Wars and the Media in Primary Documents, 2005; Benjamin Franklin's Printing Network: Disseminating Virtue in Early America, 2006. **Address:** Belmont Abbey College, 100 Belmont-Mt. Holly Rd., Belmont, NC 28012, U.S.A. **Online address:** ralphfrasca@bac.edu

FRASER, Anthea. Also writes as Lorna Cameron, Vanessa Graham. British (born England), b. 1930?. **Genres:** Novels, Mystery/Crime/Suspense. **Career:** Crime Writers' Association, secretary, 1986-96. Writer. **Publications:** Designs of Annabelle, 1971; In the Balance, 1973; (as Vanessa Graham) Second Time Around, 1974; Laura Possessed, 1974, rev. ed., 2001; Home through the Dark, 1974, rev. ed., 2001; Whistler's Lane, 1975, rev. ed., 1997; (as Vanessa Graham) The Summer Season, 1975; Breath of Brimstone, 1977; Presence of Mind, 1978; (as Vanessa Graham) Time on Trial, 1979; Island-in-Waiting, 1979; The Stone, 1980; (as Lorna Cameron) Summer in France, 1981; (as Vanessa Graham) The Stand-In, 1983; A Shroud for Delilah, 1986; A Necessary End, 1985; Pretty Maids All in a Row, 1987; Death Speaks Softly, 1987; The Nine Bright Shiners, 1988; Six Proud Walkers, 1988; (as Vanessa Graham) Such Men Are Dangerous, 1988; The April Rainers, 1989; Symbols at Your Door, 1990; The Lily-White Boys, 1991, as I'll Sing You Two-O, 1996; Three, Three the Rivals, 1992 in US, 1995; The Gospel Makers, 1994; The Seven Stars, 1995; The Macbeth Prophecy, 1995; One Is One and All Alone, 1996 in US, 1998; Motive for Murder, 1997; The Ten Commandments, 1997; Dangerous Deception, 1998; Eleven That Went to Heaven, 1999; The Twelve Apostles, 1999; Past Shadows, 2001; Fathers and Daughters, 2002; Brought to Book, 2003; Jigsaw, 2004; Person or Persons Unknown, 2005; A Family Concern, 2006; Rogue in Porcelain, 2007; Next Door to Murder, 2008; Thicker Than Water, 2009; Unfinished Portrait, 2010; Shifting Sands, 2011; A Question of Idenity, 2012. Contributor to periodicals. Works Appear in anthologies. **Address:** Juliet Burton Literary Agency, 2 Clifton Ave., London, GL W12 9DR, England.

FRASER, Antonia. British (born England), b. 1932. **Genres:** Mystery/Crime/Suspense, Children's Fiction, History, Biography, Translations, Autobiography/Memoirs, Novels, Young Adult Non-fiction, Young Adult Non-fiction. **Career:** Writer, 1954-; Weidenfeld & Nicolson, general editor, 1974-75. **Publications:** NOVELS: King Arthur and the Knights of the Round Table, 1954; Robin Hood, 1955; (trans. as Antonia Pakenham) Martyrs in China, 1956; (as Antonia Pakenham) Robin Hood (juvenile), 1957; (trans.) Dior by Dior: The Autobiography of Christian Dior, 1957, rev. ed., 2007; Dolls, 1963; Sixteenth-Century Scotland 1972; Mary Queen of Scots, 1969, new ed., 1994; Mary Queen of Scots and the Historians, 1974; King James, VI of Scotland, I of England, 1974; (co-author) More Women of Mystery, 1994; Obsession: Library Edition, 2006. JEMIMA SHORE MYSTERY SERIES: Quiet as a Nun, 1977; The Wild Island, 1978; A Splash of Red, 1981; Cool Repentance, 1982; Oxford Blood, 1985; Jemima Shore's First Case, 1986; Your Royal Hostage, 1987; The Cavalier Case, 1990; Jemima Shore at the Sunny Grave and Other Stories, 1991; Political Death, 1994; Marie Antoinette: The Journey, 2001; Tartan Tragedy, 2006. EDITOR: The Lives of the Kings and Queens of England, 1975; Scottish Love Poems: A Personal Anthology, 1975; Love Letters, 1976; Heroes & Heroines, 1980; (and intro.) Oxford and Ox-

fordshire in Verse, 1982; The Pleasure of Reading, 1992; Middle Ages, 2000; The Stuarts, 2000; The Wars of the Roses, 2000; The Houses of Hanover and Saxe-Coburg-Gotha, 2000; The House of Windsor, 2000; The Tudors, 2000; (and intro.) Agnes Strickland's Lives of the Queens of England, 2011. NON-FICTION: History of Toys, 1966; Cromwell, the Lord Protector, 1973; King Charles II in US as Royal Charles: Charles II and the Restoration, 1979; The Weaker Vessel: Woman's Lot in Seventeenth Century England, 1984; Boadicea's Chariot: The Warrior Queens, 1988; Cromwell: Our Chief of Men, 1988; (comp.) Love Letters: An Illustrated Anthology, 1989; The Six Wives of Henry VIII, 1992; Wives of Henry VIII, 1992; The Gunpowder Plot: Terror and Faith in 1605 in US as Faith and Treason: The Story of the Gunpowder Plot, 1996; The Battle of the Boyne: Irish Tragedy 1690, 2005; La Conspiracion De La Polvora, 2006; Love and Louis XIV: The Women in the Life of the Sun King, 2006; Las Seis Esposas De Enrique VIII/ the Wives of Henry VIII, 2007. OTHERS: Must You Go?: My Life with Harold Pinter, 2010; Elizabeth 1, 2010. **Address:** Curtis Brown Group Ltd., Haymarket House, 28-29 Haymarket, London, GL SW1Y 4SP, England.

FRASER, Conon. New Zealander/British (born England), b. 1930. **Genres:** Children's Fiction, Children's Non-fiction, Environmental Sciences/Ecology, Geography, History, Homes/Gardens, Travel/Exploration. **Career:** Writer, producer and director. **Publications:** CHILDREN'S FICTION: Dead Man's Cave, 1954; The Green Dragon, 1955; Shadow of Danger, 1956; The Underground Explorers, 1957; The Underground River, 1959; The Scoter Island Adventure, 1959; Lim of Hong Kong, 1960; Oyster Catcher Bay, 1962; Brave Rescue, 1964. OTHER: With Captain Cook in New Zealand (children's non-fiction), 1963; Looking at New Zealand, 1969; (with B. Matthews) Gardens of New Zealand, 1975; Beyond the Roaring Forties: New Zealand's Subantarctic Islands, 1986; (co-ed.) Enderby Settlement Diaries (history), 2000. **Address:** 39A Henry Hill Rd., Taupo, 3330, New Zealand.

FRASER, Evan David Gaviller. See **FRASER, Evan D. G.**

FRASER, Evan D. G. (Evan David Gaviller Fraser). British (born England), b. 1973?. **Genres:** Anthropology/Ethnology, Social Sciences. **Career:** University of Leeds, School of Earth and Environment, Sustainability Research Institute, lecturer, 2003-07, senior lecturer, 2007-. Writer. **Publications:** (with A. Rimas) Beef: The Untold Story of How Milk, Meat and Muscle Shaped the World, 2008; (with A. Rimas) Scraps after the Feast: The Past and Future of the Global Food Crisis, 2010. Contributor to books, periodicals and journals. **Address:** Sustainability Research Institute, School of Earth and Environment, University of Leeds, Leeds, LS2 9JT, England. **Online address:** evan@env.leeds.ac.uk

FRASER, George (C.). American (born United States), b. 1945. **Genres:** Business/Trade/Industry, Economics. **Career:** Procter & Gamble, unit marketing manager, 1972-84; United Way Services, director of marketing and communications, 1984-87; Ford Motor Co., minority dealership development program trainee, 1987-89; Success Source Inc., president and publisher, 1988-; FraserNet Inc., founding chairman and chief executive officer; Phoenix Village Academy, chairman; PowerNetworking Conference, founder and executive producer. Writer. **Publications:** Success Runs in Our Race: The Complete Guide to Effective Networking in the African-American Community, 1994, rev. ed. as Success Runs in Our Race: The Complete Guide to Effective Networking in the Black Community, 2004; Race for Success: The Ten Best Business Opportunities for Blacks in America, 1998; Click: Ten Truths for Building Extraordinary Relationships, 2008. Contributor to periodicals. **Address:** Frasernet Inc., 2940 Noble Rd., Ste. 203, Cleveland, OH 44121, U.S.A. **Online address:** gfraser@frasernet.com

FRASER, Gordon. French/Scottish (born Scotland), b. 1943. **Genres:** Sciences. **Career:** IPC Business Press, journalist, 1970-72; Rutherford Laboratory, information and press officer, 1975-77; CERN, editor and writer, 1977-2002; CERN Courier, editor, 1982-2002; Cambridge University Press, editor-in-chief, 2001-. Educator. **Publications:** (With E. Lillestøl and I. Sellevåg) Search for Infinity, 1995; The Quark Machines, 1997; (ed.) The Particle Century, 1998; Antimatter, 2000; (ed.) The New Physics for the Twenty-First Century, 2006; Cosmic Anger-Abdus Salam, the First Muslim Nobel Scientist, 2008. **Address:** Les Feuillantines, 241 rue de Lausanne, Divonne-les-Bains, 01220, France. **Online address:** gordon.fraser@orange.fr

FRASER, Harry. British (born England), b. 1937?. **Genres:** Crafts, How-to Books, Technology, Engineering, Industrial Relations, Sciences, Art/Art

History. **Career:** Twyfords Ltd., production manager, 1959-62; Armitage-Shanks Ltd., manager, 1962-65; Wengers Ltd., divisional manager, 1965-66; Podmore and Sons Ltd., staff, 1966-73; Harry Fraser Ltd., managing director, 1973-77; Potclay Kilns Ltd., director, 1976-, joint managing director, 1983-96, managing director, 1996-. Writer and educator. **Publications:** Kilns and Kiln Firing for the Craft Potter, 1969; Glazes for the Craft Potter, 1973; Electric Kilns, 1974; Electric Kilns and Firing, 1978; Ceramic Faults and Their Remedies, 1986; Electric Kilns: A User's Manual, 1994. Contributor to journals. **Address:** Potclays Ltd., Brickkiln Ln., Etruria, Stoke-on-Trent, ST ST4 7BP, England.

FRASER, Jane. *See* **PILCHER, Rosamunde.**

FRASER, Kathleen. American (born United States), b. 1935. **Genres:** Poetry, Essays, Women's Studies And Issues. **Career:** Mademoiselle Magazine, editorial associate; University of Iowa, Writers Workshop, visiting professor, 1969-71; Reed College, writer-in-residence, 1971-72; San Francisco State University, Poetry Center, director, 1972-75, American Poetry Archive, founder, 1974, associate professor, 1975-78, professor of creative writing, 1978-92; HOW(ever), publisher and editor, 1983-91. **Publications:** Change of Address and Other Poems, 1966; Stilts, Somersaults and Headstands: Game Poems Based on a Painting by Peter Breughel (juvenile), 1968; In Defiance of the Rains, 1969; (with M.F. Levy) Adam's World: San Francisco, 1971; Little Notes to You, from Lucas Street, 1972; What I Want, 1973; Magritte Series, 1978; New Shoes, 1978; Each Next (narratives), 1980; Something (even human voices) in the Foreground, a Lake, 1984; Boundayr, 1987; Notes Preceding Trust, 1987; When New Time Folds Up, 1993; Wing, 1995; Il Cuore: The Heart: Selected Poems, 1970-1995, 1997; Translating the Unspeakable: Poetry and the Innovative Necessity, 2000; 20th Century, 2000; Discrete Categories Forced into Coupling, 2004; Ii Ss, 2011. **Address:** 1936 Leavenworth St., San Francisco, CA 94133, U.S.A. **Online address:** kfraser@sfsu.edu

FRASER, Laura (Jane). American (born United States), b. 1961. **Genres:** Adult Non-fiction, Biography, Romance/Historical. **Career:** Freelance writer, 1982-94; University of California, Graduate School of Journalism, instructor; Good Housekeeping Magazine, contributing editor; Health and More Magazine, contributing editor. Writer. **Publications:** The Animal Rights Handbook: Everyday Ways to Save Animal Lives, 1990; Losing It: America's Obsession with Weight and the Industry That Feeds on It, 1997, as Losing It: False Hopes and Fat Profits in the Diet Industry, 1998; An Italian Affair, 2001; War on Choice: The Right-Wing Attack on Women's Rights and How to Fight Back, 2004; All Over the Map, 2010. Works appear in anthologies. Contributor to periodicals. **Address:** c/o Author Mail, Pantheon Books, 1540 Broadway St., New York, NY 10036, U.S.A. **Online address:** laura@laurafraser.com

FRASER, Margot. American (born United States), b. 1936. **Genres:** Novels, Novellas/Short Stories. **Career:** El Burro, editor, 1957-58; Juvenile Probation Department of San Diego County, probation officer, 1958-68; Serra Reference Center, reference librarian, 1969-70; U.S. International University, reference librarian, 1970-72; Innisfree Books, owner and manager, 1972-82. Writer. **Publications:** The Laying Out of Gussie Hoot (novel), 1990; Hardship (novella), 1993. **Address:** Southern Methodist University Press, PO Box 415, Dallas, TX 75275, U.S.A.

FRASER, Mary Ann. American (born United States), b. 1959. **Genres:** Children's Fiction, Children's Non-fiction, Illustrations, Science Fiction/Fantasy. **Career:** Graphic artist, 1982-90; fine artist, 1983-. Writer. **Publications:** SELF-ILLUSTRATED: On Top of the World: The Conquest of Mount Everest, 1991; Ten Mile Day and the Building of the Transcontinental Railroad, 1993; One Giant Leap, 1993; In Search of the Grand Canyon: Down the River with John Wesley Powell, 1994; Sanctuary, the Story of Three Arch Rocks, 1994. OTHERS: Forest Fire!, 1996; A Mission for the People: The Story of La Purisima, 1997; Where Are The Night Animals?, 1998; Vicksburg: The Battle That, 1999; I.Q. Goes to School, 2002; How Animal Babies Stay Safe, 2002; I.Q., It's Time, 2003; I.Q. Goes to the Library, 2003; I.Q. Gets Fit, 2007; Mermaid Sister, 2008; Pet Shop Lullaby, 2009; Pet Shop Follies, 2010; Heebie Jeebie Jamboree, 2011. Illustrator of books for children by others. **Address:** Barbara Kouts, 249 S Country Rd., Brookhaven, NY 11719, U.S.A. **Online address:** fraserde@fraserdecopainting.com

FRASER, Nicholas C(ampbell). British (born England), b. 1956. **Genres:** Natural History. **Career:** University of Aberdeen, Geology Museum, assis-

tant curator of paleontology, 1979-81; Cambridge University, Girton College, fellow, 1985-90; Virginia Museum of Natural History, curator of vertebrate paleontology, 1990-2008, director of research and collections, 2004-08; Virginia Polytechnic Institute and State University, adjunct professor of geology, 1993-; National Museums Scotland, keeper of natural sciences, 2008-, Department Natural sciences, head. Writer. **Publications:** (Ed. with H. Sues) In the Shadow of the Dinosaurs: Early Mesozoic Tetrapods, 1994; (with D. Henderson) The Dawn of the Dinosaurs: Life in the Triassic, 2006; (with H. Sues) Triassic Life on Land: the Great Transition, 2010. Contributor of articles to books. **Address:** National Museums Scotland, Chambers St., Edinburgh, LT EH1 1JF, Scotland. **Online address:** nick.fraser@nms.ac.uk

FRASER, Rebecca. American (born United States) **Genres:** Biography, Children's Fiction, History, Novels. **Career:** Researcher and journalist. **Publications:** The Brontës: Charlotte Brontë and Her Family, 1988; A Peoples History of Britain, 2003; The Story of Britain: From the Romans to the Present: A Narrative History, 2005. Contributor to periodicals. **Address:** W.W. Norton Co., 500 5th Ave., New York, NY 10110, U.S.A.

FRASER, Robert (H.). British (born England), b. 1947. **Genres:** Plays/Screenplays, Literary Criticism And History. **Career:** University of Cape Coast, lecturer in English, 1970-74; University of Leeds, lecturer in English, 1974-78; University of London, Royal Holloway and Bedford New College, research associate, 1986-91, School of Advanced Study, research fellow, 1997-99; University of Kuwait, visiting professor, 1988; University of Sao Paulo, visiting professor, 1990; Cambridge University, Trinity College, lecturer in English, 1991-93, director of studies in English, 1992-93; Open University, senior research fellow, 1999-, professor of English. Writer. **Publications:** The Novels of Ayi Kwei Armah, 1980; West African Poetry: A Critical History, 1986; The Making of The Golden Bough: The Origins and Growth of an Argument, 1990, rev. ed., 2001; Sir James Frazer and the Literary Imagination, 1990; Proust and the Victorians: The Lamp of Memory, 1993; Victorian Quest Romance: Stevenson, Haggard, Kipling and Conan Doyle, 1998; Lifting the Sentence: The Poetics of Postcolonial Fiction, 1999; The Chameleon Poet: A Life of George Barker, 2002; Ben Okri: Towards the Invisible City, 2002; Book History through Postcolonial Eyes: Rewriting the Script, 2008. EDITOR: The Collected Poems of George Barker, 1987; (intro.) Sir J. Frazer: The Golden Bough, A New Abridgement from the Second and Third Editions, 1994; The Selected Poems of George Barker, 1995; (with M. Hammond) Books without Borders, 2008. Contributor to periodicals. **Address:** Open University, Walton Hall, PO Box 197, Milton Keynes, MK7 6AA, England. **Online address:** r.fraser@open.ac.uk

FRASER, Ronald (Angus). German (born Germany), b. 1930. **Genres:** History, Area Studies, Autobiography/Memoirs, Humanities. **Career:** Reuters News Agency, foreign correspondent, 1952-57; New Left Review, editor. **Publications:** (Ed.) Work: Twenty Personal Accounts, vol. I, 1968, vol. II, 1969; In Hiding: The Life of Manuel Cortes, 1972; Tajos: The Story of a Village on the Costa del Sol, 1973 in UK as The Pueblo: A Mountain Village on the Costa del Sol, 1973; Blood of Spain: An Oral History of the Spanish Civil War, 1979 in UK as Blood of Spain: The Experience of Civil War, 1936-1939, 1979; (with P. Broue and P. Vilar) Metodologia historica de la guerra y revolucion espanolas, 1980; In Search of a Past: The Rearing of an English Gentleman, 1933-1945, 1984 in UK as In Search of a Past: The Manor House, Amnersfield, 1933-1945, 1984; (co-author) 1968: A Student Generation in Revolt, 1988; Napoleon's Cursed War: Spanish Popular Resistance in the Peninsular War, 1808-1814, 2008. **Address:** Tessa Sayle Agency, 11 Jubilee Pl., London, GL SW3, England.

FRASER, Russell A(lfred). American (born United States), b. 1927. **Genres:** Literary Criticism And History. **Career:** University of California, instructor in English, 1950; British Museum, researcher, 1951-52; Cambridge University Library, researcher, 1951-52; Bodleian Library, researcher, 1951-52; Duke University, instructor, 1952-55, assistant professor of English, 1955-56; Princeton University, assistant professor, 1956-61, associate professor of English, 1961-65, Graduate School, associate dean, 1962-65, Institute for Advanced Study, resident, 1976; Free University of Berlin, lecturer, 1965; Charles University of Prague, lecturer, 1965; National University of Hungary, lecturer, 1965; Vanderbilt University, Department of English, professor and chairman, 1965-68; University of Michigan, Austin Warren professor of English, 1968-95, Department of English Language and Literature, chairman, 1968-73, Austin Warren professor emeritus, 1995-. Writer. **Publications:** The Court of Virtue, 1962; Shakespeare's Poetics in Relation to King Lear, 1962;

Tragedy of King Lear (criticism), 1963; The War Against Poetry, 1970; An Essential Shakespeare, Nine Plays and the Sonnets, 1972; The Dark Ages & the Age of Gold, 1973; The Language of Adam, 1977; A Mingled Yarn: The Life of R.P. Blackmur, 1981; The Three Romes, 1985; Young Shakespeare, 1988; Shakespeare: The Later Years, 1992; Singing Masters: Poets in English, 1500 to the Present, 1999; Moderns Worth Keeping, 2005; Shakespeare: A Life in Art, 2008; Three Romes: Moscow, Constantinople and Rome, 2009; From China to Peru: A Memoir of Trave, 2009. EDITOR: (intro.) The Court of Venus, 1955; (with N.C. Rabkin) Drama of the English Renaissance, 1976; Selected Writings of Oscar Wilde, 1969; All's Well That Ends Well, 1985. **Address:** Department of English Language and Literature, University of Michigan, 3187 Angell Hall, 435 S State St., Ann Arbor, MI 48109-1003, U.S.A. **Online address:** rafraser@umich.edu

FRASER, Sarah E. (Sarah Elizabeth Fraser). American (born United States), b. 1960?. **Genres:** Popular Culture, Art/Art History, Politics/Government. **Career:** University of California, lecturer, 1988-95, visiting professor, 1994-95; Northwestern University, Department of Art History, associate professor, 1996-, chairman, 2003, 2004-07, director of graduate studies, 2000-03; Stanford University, instructor, 1996, visiting professor, 2000; Dunhuang Project, director, 1999-2004; école Pratique des Hautes études, directrice d'études, 1999-2000; Ruprecht-Karls-Universität Heidelberg, visiting professor, 2007. Writer. **Publications:** (Ed.) Merit, Opulence and the Buddhist Network of Wealth: Essays on Buddhist Material Culture, 2003; Performing the Visual: The Practice of Buddhist Wall Painting in China and Central Asia, 618-960, 2004. Contributor to journals and periodicals. **Address:** Department of Art History, Northwestern University, Rm. 3-400, Kresge Centennial Hall, 1880 Campus Dr., Evanston, IL 60208-2208, U.S.A. **Online address:** s-fraser2@northwestern.edu

FRASER, Sarah Elizabeth. See **FRASER, Sarah E.**

FRASER, W. Hamish. Scottish (born Scotland), b. 1941. **Genres:** History, Industrial Relations, Urban Studies. **Career:** University of Strathclyde, Department of History, lecturer, 1966-75, senior lecturer in history, 1975-, reader, 1987-96, professor in history, 1996-2003, professor emeritus, 2003-. Writer. **Publications:** Trade Unions and Society: The Struggle for Acceptance, 1850-1880, 1974; (ed. with J.T. Ward) Workers and Employers: Documents on Trade Unions and Industrial Relations in Britain since the Eighteenth Century, 1980; The Coming of the Mass Market, 1850-1914, 1981; Conflict and Class: Scottish Workers, 1700-1838, 1988; People and Society in Scotland 1830-1914, 1990; (ed. with I. Maver) Glasgow, vol. II: 1830-1912, 1996; Alexander Campbell and the Search for Socialism, 1996; A History of British Trade Unionism, 1700-1998, 1999; Scottish Popular Politics: From Radicalism to Labour, 2000; (ed. with C.H. Lee) Aberdeen, 1800-2000: A New History, 2000; (ed.) British Trade Unions, 1707-1918, 2007. **Address:** Department of History, University of Strathclyde, McCance Bldg., 16 Richmond St., Glasgow, G1 1XQ, Scotland. **Online address:** w.h.fraser@strath.ac.uk

FRASER, Wynnette (McFaddin). American (born United States), b. 1925. **Genres:** Children's Fiction, Mystery/Crime/Suspense, Education, Young Adult Fiction. **Career:** Shaw Air Base, staff; Darlington County Department of Social Services, caseworker. Writer. **Publications:** CHILDREN'S MYSTERY-ADVENTURE BOOKS: Mystery on Mirror Mountain, 1989; Courage on Mirror Mountain, 1989; Mystery at Deepwood Bay, 1992; Invasion on Mirror Mountain, 1994. Contributor to periodicals. **Address:** 212 W Smith Ave., Darlington, SC 29532, U.S.A.

FRASIER, Anne. See **WEIR, Theresa.**

FRASSETTO, Michael. American (born United States), b. 1961. **Genres:** History, Theology/Religion, Adult Non-fiction, Autobiography/Memoirs. **Career:** Widener University, instructor in history, 1989-90; La Grange College, assistant professor of history, 1990-98; Encyclopedia Britannica, religion editor, 1999-, associate editor; University College of Benedictine University, adjunct instructor, 2000-; University of Delaware, Department of History, adjunct faculty. Writer. **Publications:** (Ed.) Medieval Purity and Piety: Essays on Medieval Clerical Celibacy and Religious Reform, 1998; Perceptions of the Other: (ed. with D.R. Blanks) Western Views of Islam in Medieval and Early Modern Europe, 1999; Medieval Germany: An Encyclopedia, 2001; (ed.) The Year 1000: Religious and Social Response to the Turning of the First Millennium, 2002; Encyclopedia of Barbarian Europe: Society in Transformation, 2003; Lives of the Heretics, 2006; (ed.) Heresy and the Persecuting

Society in the Middle Ages: Essays on the Work of R.I. Moore, 2006; (ed. with D. Blanks and A. Livingstone) Medieval Monks and Their World: Ideas and Realities: Studies in Honor of Richard E. Sullivan, 2006; (ed.) Christian Attitudes toward the Jews in the Middle Ages: A Casebook, 2007; Great Medieval Heretics: Five Centuries of Religious Dissent, 2008; (intro.) Birth of Britain, 2009. Contributor of periodicals. **Address:** Department of History, University of Delaware, 236 John Munroe Hall, 46 W Delaware Ave., Newark, DE 19716-2547, U.S.A. **Online address:** mfrasset@eb.com

FRATIANNI, Michele. American/Italian (born Italy), b. 1941. **Genres:** Economics, Business/Trade/Industry. **Career:** Indiana University, Business Economics and Public Policy, assistant professor, 1971-75, associate professor, 1975-76, professor, 1979-93, AMOCO faculty fellow, 1993-97, chair, 1997-2006, W. George Pinnell professor of business economics, 1998-2006, CIBER Eminent faculty fellow; President's Council of Economic Advisers, senior staff economist, 1981-82, now emeritus; Catholic University, visiting professor of economics, 1985-86; Indiana Center for Global Business, fellow, 1989; University of Brescia, faculty, 2002-08; Universita Politecnica delle Marche, professor of economics, 2006-. Writer. **Publications:** (With G. La Malfa and B. Trezza) Economia Italiana 1974-75, 1975; Inflazione, produzione e Politica Economica in Italia, 1975; (with J.C. Pattison) Organizzazioni economiche internazionali, 1977; (with P. DeGrauwe and M. Nabli) Money, Output and Exchange Rates: The European Experience, 1985; (with J. von Hagen) German Dominance in the EMS: Evidence from Interest Rates, 1989; (with J. von Hagen) Asymmetries and the Realignments in the EMS, 1989; (with J. von Hagen) On the Road to EMU, 1990; (with J. Pattison) International Institutions and the Market for Information, 1990; (with J. von Hagen) Public Choice Aspects of European Monetary Unification, 1990; (with J. von Hagen) Policy Coordination in the EMS with Stochastic & Structural Asymmetries, 1990; (with J. von Hagen) Monetary and Fiscal Policy in a European Monetary Union: Some Public Choice Considerations, 1990; (with F. Spinelli) Storia monetaria d'Italia: l'evoluzione del sistema monetario e bancario, 1991; (with J. von Hagen and C. Waller) Maastricht Way to EMU, 1992; (with J. von Hagen) The European Monetary System and European Monetary Union, 1992; (with D. Salvatore) Monetary Policy in Eveloped Economies, 1993; (with F. Spinelli) The Monetary History of Italy, 1997; (with F. Spinelli) Storia monetaria d'Italia: lira e politica monetaria dall'unita all'Unione europea, 2001. EDITOR: (with T. Peeters) One Money for Europe, 1978; (with C. Wihlborg and T.D. Willett) Financial Regulation and Monetary Arrangements after 1992, 1991; (with D. Salvatore) Handbook of Monetary Policy, 1992; (with J. von Hagen and D. Salvatore) Macroeconomic Policy in open Economies, 1992; Mismatch Explanations of European Unemployment: A Critical Evaluation, 1998; (with D. Salvatore and P. Savona) Ideas for the Future of the International Monetary System, 1999; (with P. Savona and J. Kirton) Governing Global Finance, 2002; (with P. Savona and J.J. Kirton) Sustaining Global Growth and Development: G7 and IMF Governance, 2003; New Perspectives on Global Governance: Why America Needs the G8, 2005; Regional Economic Integration, 2006; (with P. Savona and J.J. Kirton) Financing Development: The G8 and UN Contribution, 2007; (with P. Savona and J.J. Kirton) Corporate, Public and Global Governance: The G8 Contribution, 2007; (ed. with P. Alessandrini and A. Zazzaro) Changing Geography of Banking and Finance, 2009. Contributor to periodicals. **Address:** Kelley School of Business, Indiana University, Bloomington, IN 47405, U.S.A. **Online address:** fratiann@indiana.edu

FRATKIN, Elliot. (Elliot M. Fratkin). American (born United States), b. 1948. **Genres:** Anthropology/Ethnology, Cultural/Ethnic Topics, Medicine/Health, Economics. **Career:** University of Nairobi, Institute of African Studies, research associate, 1974-76, 1985-86; University of Maryland, instructor of sociology and anthropology, 1979-85; Duke University, visiting assistant professor, 1987-89; North Carolina State University, Department of Anthropology and Sociology, visiting instructor, 1987; Pennsylvania State University, Department of Anthropology, assistant professor, 1989-94; Smith College, Department of Anthropology, assistant professor, 1994-97, associate professor, 1997-2002, professor, 2002-, chair of department of anthropology, co-director, African studies program. Writer. **Publications:** Why Elephant is an Old Woman: Animal Symbolism in Samburu, 1974; (as Elliot M. Fratkin) Herbal Medicine and Concepts of Disease in Samburu, 1975; Surviving Drought & Development: Ariaal Pastoralists of Northern Kenya, 1991; (ed. with K.A. Galvin and E.A. Roth) African Pastoralist Systems: An Integrated Approach, 1994; (as Elliot M. Fratkin) Ariaal Pastoralists of Kenya: Surviving Drought and Development in Africa's Arid Lands, 1998; (with D.G. Bates) (as Elliot M. Fratkin) Cultural Anthropology, 2nd ed., 1999, 3rd ed., 2003;

Social, Health and Economic Consequences of the Pastorl Sendentraization in Marsabit District, 2004; Ariaal Pastoralist of Kenya: Studying Pastoralism, Drought and Development in Africa's Arid Lands, 2004; (ed. with E.A. Roth) As Pastoralists Settle: Social, Health and Economic Consequences of Pastoral Sedentarization in Marsabit District, Kenya, 2004; (ed. with K. Ikeya) Pastoralists and their Neighbors in Asia and Africa, 2005; (as Elliot M. Fratkin) Laibon, 2011. **Address:** Department of Anthropology, Smith College, 204 Wright Hall, 7 Elm St., Northampton, MA 01063-6304, U.S.A. **Online address:** efratkin@smith.edu

FRATKIN, Elliot M. *See* **FRATKIN, Elliot.**

FRATTI, Mario. American/Italian (born Italy), b. 1927. **Genres:** Plays/Screenplays, Poetry. **Career:** Rubelli publishers, translator, 1953-63; Sipario, drama critic, 1963-66; drama critic, 1963-73; Columbia University, professor, 1967; Adelphi College, professor, 1967-68; City University of New York, Hunter College, professor, 1967-97, now emeritus; America Today, drama critic, 1986-. Writer. **Publications:** Il Ritorno, 1961 in US and UK as The Return, 1965; Il Suicidio, 1962 in UK as The Suicide, 1972; La Gabbia, 1963 in US as The Cage, 1972; The Academy, 1963; Le Vedova Bianca, 1963 in US as Mafia, 1971; Le Telefonata, 1965 in US as The Gift, 1972; I Frigoriferi, 1965 in US as The Refrigerators, 1972; Eleonora Duse, 1967; Il Ponte, 1967 in US as The Bridge, 1972; The Victim, 1968; Four Plays, 1972; Six Passionate Women, 1972; Races: Six New Plays, 1972; Birthday, 1978; Scene americane: atti unici per gli anni Ottanta, 1979; American Scenes, 2 vols., 1980; Nine, 1982; Mario Fratti (biography), 1983; Young Wife, Mothers and Daughters, Three Beds, 1984; Paganini, 1985; Lovers, 1985; A.I.D.S., 1986; 500: A Musical about Columbus, 1988; Friends, 1989; Porno, 1990; Family, 1992; Leningrad Euthanasia, 1993; Beata, the Pope's Daughter, 1994; Sacrifice, 1995; Jurors, 1996; L'Imboscata, 2000 in US as The Ambush; Erotic Adventures in Venice, 2001; Puccini: Passion and Music, 2002; Blindness, 2003; Terrorist, 2003; November 2004, 2004; Five Musicals (Puccini, Paganini, Seducers, Refrigerators, Madame Senator), 2004; Three Sisters and a Priest, 2006; Twenty-eight Unpredictable Plays, 2007; Twenty-one Plays in Italian, 2007; Garibaldi, 2007; Unpredicable Plays, 2007; Thirsty: Explaining Sarah Kane, 2008; Lovers, 2010; Dead Man's Bluff, 2010; Thirst, 2010; Sister, 2010; Brooklyn, 2010; Class Struggle, 2010; Trio, 2010; Quartet, 2011. **Address:** c/o Susan Schulman, 454 W 44th St., New York, NY 10036, U.S.A. **Online address:** mario@mariofratti.com

FRAUSTINO, Lisa Rowe. (Lisa Meunier). American (born United States), b. 1961. **Genres:** Children's Non-fiction, Plays/Screenplays, Picture/Board Books, Children's Fiction, Young Adult Fiction, Poetry. **Career:** National Education Corp., editor, 1985-86; The Legal Studies Forum, copy editor, 1985-87; University of Scranton, Department of English, adjunct faculty, 1985-90; Dick Jones Communications, associate editor, 1989-91; Institute of Children's Literature, instructor, 1989-94; Binghamton University, doctoral teaching assistant, 1990-93; Wyoming Seminary Preparatory School, faculty, 1995-2002; Hollins College, visiting associate professor, 1995-; Western Maryland College, visiting associate professor, 1999; Eastern Connecticut State University, Department of English, assistant professor, 2002-06, associate professor, 2006-, professor of children's and young adult literature. Writer. **Publications:** FOR CHILDREN: Grass and Sky, 1994; Ash, 1995; (ed.) Dirty Laundry: Stories about Family Secrets, 1998; The Hickory Chair, 2000; (ed.) Soul Searching: Thirteen Stories About Faith and Belief, 2002; (ed.) Don't Cramp My Style: Stories about that Time of the Month, 2004; I Walk In Dread: The Diary of Deliverance Trembley, Witness to the Salem Witch Trials, 2004; The Hole in the Wall, 2010; (as Lisa Meunier) Hitching to Istanbul, 2010. Contributor to magazines and periodicals. **Address:** Department of English, Eastern Connecticut State University, 83 Windham St., Willimantic, CT 06226, U.S.A. **Online address:** fraustinol@easternct.edu

FRAVEL, M. Taylor. American (born United States), b. 1971. **Genres:** International Relations/Current Affairs, History. **Career:** Harvard University, John M. Olin Institute for Strategic Studies, postdoctoral fellow, 2003-04; Massachusetts Institute of Technology, assistant professor, 2004-08, Cecil and Ida Green Career Development associate professor of political science, 2008-; National Bureau of Asian Research and Woodrow Wilson International Center, National Asia Research Program, research associate, 2010-. Writer. **Publications:** Strong Borders, Secure Nation: Cooperation and Conflict in China's Territorial Disputes, 2008. Contributor to books and journals. **Address:** Department of Political Science, Massachusetts Institute of Technol-

ogy, E38-632, 77 Massachusetts Ave., Cambridge, MA 02139, U.S.A. **Online address:** fravel@mit.edu

FRAYN, Michael. British (born England), b. 1933. **Genres:** Novels, Plays/Screenplays, Humor/Satire, Translations, Young Adult Fiction, Travel/Exploration, Essays, Novels, Novels. **Career:** Guardian, general-assignment reporter, 1957-59; Miscellany, columnist, 1959-62; The Observer, columnist, 1962-68. **Publications:** COLLECTED COLUMNS/ESSAYS: The Day of the Dog, 1962; The Book of Fub, 1963; On the Outskirts, 1964; At Bay in Gear Street, 1967; Constructions, 1974; The Original Michael Frayn, 1983; Speak After the Beep: Studies in the Art of Communicating with Inanimate and Semi-inanimate Objects, 1997; The Additional Michael Frayn, 2000; Alarms and Excursions: More Plays than One, 2000; The Human Touch: Our Part in the Creation of a Universe, 2006. NOVELS: Never Put Off to Gomorrah, 1964; The Tin Men, 1965; The Russian Interpreter, 1966; Towards the End of the Morning, 1967 in US as Against Entropy, 1967; Zwei Briten in Moskau Roman, 1968; A Very Private Life, 1968; Sweet Dreams, 1973; Noises Off: A Play in 3 Acts, 1982; Devash Pere, 1985; The Trick of It, 1989; A Landing on the Sun, 1991; Now You Know, 1993; Headlong, 1999; (with D. Burke) Celia's Secret: An Investigation, 2000 in US as The Copenhagen Papers: An Intrigue, 2001; Spies, 2002. PLAYS: The Two of Us: Four One-Act Plays for Two Players, 1970; The Sandboy, 1971; Alphabetical Order, 1976; Clouds, 1976; Donkeys' Years, 1977; Balmoral, 1978; Make and Break, 1980; Noises Off: A Play in Three Acts, 1982; Benefactors: A Play in Two Acts, 1984; Plays: One (collection), 1985; Clockwise, 1986; Look Look, 1990; Listen to This: 21 Short Plays and Sketches, 1990; Audience: A Play in One-act, 1991; Plays: Two, 1992; Here: A Play in Two Acts, 1994; La belle Vivette, 1995; Now You Know: A Play in 2 Acts, 1995; Copenhagen, 1999; Plays: Three, 2000; Alarms and Excursions: More Plays than One, 2000; Democracy: A Play, 2004. TRANSLATIONS: (intro.) The Cherry Orchard: A Comedy in Four Acts, 1978; (intro.) The Fruits of Enlightenment, 1979; (intro.) Three Sisters: A Drama in Four Acts, 1983. OTHERS: (ed.) The Best of Beachcomber, 1963; (ed. with B. Gascoigne) Timothy: The Drawings and Cartoons of Timothy Birdsall, 1964; Constructions, 1974; (co-author) Great Railway Journeys of the World, 1981; Remember Me?, 1997; The Crimson Hotel; and Audience, 2007; Afterlife, 2008; Stage Directions, 2008; Travels with a Typewriter: A Reporter at Large, 2009; My Father's Fortune: A Life, 2010; Frayn Plays, 2010; Skios, 2012. Works appear in anthologies. Contributor to periodicals. **Address:** Greene & Heaton Ltd., 37 Goldhawk Rd., London, GL W12 8QQ, England.

FRAZEE, Randy. American (born United States), b. 1961. **Genres:** Theology/Religion, inspirational/Motivational Literature. **Career:** Pantego Bible Church, senior pastor, 1990-2005; Willow Creek Community Church, teaching pastor, 2005-08; Oak Hills Church, senior minister, 2008-. Writer. **Publications:** (With L.E. Schaller) The Comeback Congregation: New Life for a Troubled Ministry, 1995; The Connecting Church: Beyond Small Groups to Authentic Community, 2001; Making Room for Life: Trading Chaotic Lifestyles for Connected Relationships, 2003, The Christian Life Profile Assessment Tool: Workbook, 2005; (with D. Willard) Renovation of the Heart: Putting on the Character of Christ, 2005; (with R. Frazee) Real Simplicity: Making Room for Life, 2011; (with M. Lucado and K.D. Hill) Story for Children: A Storybook Bible, 2011; Heart of the Story: Tracing God's Big Idea Through Every Story in the Bible, 2011. **Address:** c/o Author Mail, Zondervan, 5300 Patterson Ave. SE, Grand Rapids, MI 49512-9512, U.S.A. **Online address:** randy@pantego.org

FRAZER, Gail. (Margaret Frazer). American (born United States), b. 1946. **Genres:** Novels, Mystery/Crime/Suspense, Literary Criticism And History. **Career:** Writer. **Publications:** SISTER FREVISSE MYSTERY NOVELS: UNDER PSEUDONYM MARGARET FRAZER: The Novice's Tale, 1992; The Servant's Tale, 1993; The Outlaw's Tale, 1994; The Bishop's Tale, 1994; The Boy's Tale, 1995; The Murderer's Tale, 1996; The Prioress's Tale, 1997; The Maiden's Tale, 1998; The Reeve's Tale, 1999; The Squire's Tale, 2000; The Clerk's Tale, 2002; The Bastard's Tale, 2003; The Hunter's Tale, 2004; A Play of Isaac, 2004; The Widow's Tale, 2005; A Play of Dux Moraud, 2005; The Sempster's Tale, 2006; A Play of Knaves, 2006; The Traitor's Tale, 2007; A Play of Lords, 2007; The Apostate's Tale, 2008; The Prioress Tale, 2009; A Play of Treachery., 2009; A Play of Piety, 2010; Play of Heresy, 2011. **Address:** c/o Nancy Yost, Lowenstein Associates, 121 W 27th St., Ste. 601, New York, NY 10001, U.S.A. **Online address:** fenyx3204@aol.com

FRAZER, Margaret. *See* **FRAZER, Gail.**

FRAZER, Megan. American (born United States), b. 1977?. **Genres:** Young Adult Fiction. **Career:** Librarian and author. **Publications:** Secrets of Truth & Beauty, 2009. **Address:** Poland, ME , U.S.A. **Online address:** megan@meganfrazer.com

FRAZER, Timothy C. American (born United States), b. 1941. **Genres:** Language/Linguistics. **Career:** Millikin University, instructor in English, 1969-71; Western Illinois University, assistant professor, 1972-76, associate professor, 1976-81, professor of English, 1981-2002, professor emeritus, 2002-, coordinator of writing program, 1982-83; Lincoln Land Community College, ESL instructor, 2003-05; College of Saint Mary Magdalen, adjunct tutor, 2006-. Writer. **Publications:** Midland Illinois Dialect Patterns, 1987; (ed.) Heartland English: Variation and Transition in the American Midwest, 1993. Works appear in anthologies. Contributor of articles to journals. **Address:** College of Saint Mary Magdalen, 511 Kearsarge Mountain Rd., Warner, NH 03278-4012, U.S.A. **Online address:** tcf@macomb.com

FRAZIER, Alison Knowles. American (born United States) **Genres:** History. **Career:** Dartmouth College, visiting assistant professor, 1995-96; University of Texas, assistant professor, 1996-2004, associate professor of history, 2004-. Writer. **Publications:** Possible Lives: Authors and Saints in Renaissance Italy, 2005. **Address:** TX , U.S.A. **Online address:** akfrazier@mail.utexas.edu

FRAZIER, Charles (Robinson). American (born United States), b. 1950. **Genres:** Novels, Travel/Exploration, Military/Defense/Arms Control, Young Adult Fiction, Literary Criticism And History. **Career:** University of Colorado, instructor in early American literature, professor of English; North Carolina State University, professor of English; freelance writer, 1990-. **Publications:** (With R.W. Ingram) Developing Communications Skills for the Accounting Profession, 1980; (with D. Seacrest) Adventuring in the Andes: The Sierra Club Guide to Peru, Bolivia, the Amazon Basin and the Galapagos, 1985; Cold Mountain (novel), 1997; Thirteen Moons, 2006; Nightwoods: A Novel, 2011. **Address:** Darhansoff & Verrill Literary Agents, 236 W 26th St., Ste. 802, New York, NY 10001-6736, U.S.A.

FRAZIER, Donald S(haw). American (born United States), b. 1965. **Genres:** History, Travel/Exploration. **Career:** Six Flags Over Texas, games and attractions staff, 1981-82; Star-Telegram, staff writer, 1983-87; Citizen Journal, writer, 1983-87; National Football League, freelance production assistant, 1983-84; National Basketball League, freelance production assistant, 1983-84; Major League Baseball, freelance production assistant, 1983-84; NCAA, freelance production assistant, 1983-84; General Dynamics Corp., technical publications analyst, 1987-88; Tarrant County Junior College, adjunct instructor, 1991; Texas Christian University, research assistant, 1988-90, graduate teaching assistant, 1990-92, visiting assistant professor of history, 1992-93; McMurry University, Department of History, assistant professor, 1993-97, associate professor, 1997-2001, professor, 2002-, chair, 1997-2002, The Grady McWhiney Research Foundation, executive director, 1997-2006, president and chief executive officer, 2006-; Longwood College, Francis B. Simpkins memorial lecturer, 1997. **Publications:** Blood & Treasure: Confederate Empire in the Southwest, 1995; (with R.W. Sledge) Snapshots in Time: Readings in American History, 1995; Cottonclads!: The Battle of Galveston and the Defense of the Texas Coast, 1996; (ed.) The United States and Mexico at War: Nineteenth-Century Expansionism and Conflict, 1998; (with R.F. Pace) Frontier Texas: History of a Borderland to 1880, 2004; (with R.F. Pace and R.P. Wettemann, Jr.) The Texas You Expect: The Story of Buffalo Gap Historic Village, 2006; (with R.F. Pace) Abilene Historic Landmarks: An Illustrated Tour, 2008; Fire in the Cane Field: The Federal Invasion of Louisiana and Texas, January 1861-January 1863, 2009; (ed.) Loving: The Civil War Letters of Gus Ball, 23rd Texas Cavalry and McMahan's Texas Battery, 2009; (ed. with A. Hillhouse) Love and War: The Civil War Letters and Medicinal Book of Augustus V. Ball, 2010; Thunder across the Swamp: The Fight for the Lower Mississippi, February 1863-May 1863, 2010; Blood on the Bayou: Tom Greens Texans and the Defense of Louisiana and Texas, 2011; Death at the Landing: The Contest for the Red River and the Collapse of Confederate Louisiana, 2012; Americans at War, 1861-1865: The Struggle for Southern Independence, forthcoming. **Address:** Department of History, McMurry University, 203 Old Main, 1400 Sayles Blvd., PO Box 638, Abilene, TX 79605, U.S.A. **Online address:** dfrazier@mcm.edu

FRAZIER, Kit. American (born United States), b. 1965. **Genres:** Novels. **Career:** Journalist. **Publications:** Scoop: A Cauley MacKinnon Novel, 2006; Dead Copy: A Cauley MacKinnon Novel, 2007. **Address:** Midnight Ink, 2143 Wooddale Dr., Woodbury, MN 55125-2989, U.S.A. **Online address:** kitfrazier@yahoo.com

FRAZIER, Lessie Jo. American (born United States), b. 1966. **Genres:** Politics/Government, History. **Career:** University of Indiana, adjunct assistant professor of history, anthropology, and cultural studies. Writer. **Publications:** (Ed. with R. Montoya and J. Hurtig) Gender's Place: Feminist Anthropologies of Latin America, 2002; Salt in the Sand: Memory, Violence, and the Nation-State in Chile, 1890 to the Present, 2007; (ed. with D. Cohen) Gender and Sexuality in 1968: Transformative Politics in the Cultural Imagination, 2009. **Address:** U.S.A. **Online address:** frazierl@indiana.edu

FRAZIER, Shirley George. American (born United States), b. 1982. **Genres:** Business/Trade/Industry, How-to Books, Marketing. **Career:** Sweet Survival L.L.C./GiftBasketBusiness.com, president, 1989-. Author and professional speaker. **Publications:** How to Start a Home-Based Gift Basket Business, 1998, 5th ed., 2010; The Gift Basket Design Book, 2004, 2nd ed. 2008; Marketing Strategies for the Home-Based Business: Solutions You Can Use Today, 2008. **Address:** Sweet Survival L.L.C., PO Box 91, Paramus, NJ 07653-0091, U.S.A. **Online address:** survival@sweetsurvival.com

FRAZIER, Sundee T. American (born United States), b. 1968?. **Genres:** Novels, Young Adult Non-fiction, Theology/Religion, Young Adult Fiction. **Career:** Writer. **Publications:** (Ed. with G.A. Yancey and S.W. Yancey) JUST DON'T MARRY ONE: Interracial Dating, Marriage, and Parenting, 2002; Check All That Apply: Finding Wholeness as a Multiracial Person, 2002; Worship, His Love Endures Forever: Eight Studies for Individuals or Groups, 2004; Brendan Buckley's Universe and Everything in It (for children), 2007; The Girls, 2008; The Other Half of My Heart (for children), 2010; Brendan Buckley's Sixth-grade Experiment, 2012. Works appear in anthologies. Contributor to books. **Address:** Random House, Inc., 1745 Broadway, New York, WA 10019, U.S.A. **Online address:** sundeefrazier@yahoo.com

FREADMAN, Richard. Australian (born Australia), b. 1951. **Genres:** Philosophy, Autobiography/Memoirs. **Career:** La Trobe University, professor; University of Sussex, professor; Lingnan University, professor; University of Western Australia, instructor. Writer. **Publications:** Eliot, James, and the Fictional Self: A Study in Character and Narration, 1986; (with L. Reinhardt) On Literary Theory and Philosophy, 1991; (with S. Miller) Re- thinking Theory: A Critique of Contemporary Literary Theory and an Alternative Account, 1992; (ed. with J. Adamson and D. Parker) Renegotiating Ethics in Literature, Philosophy, and Theory, 1998; Threads of Life: Autobiography and the Will, 2001; Shadow of Doubt: My Father and Myself, 2003; This Crazy Thing a Life: Australian Jewish Autobiography, 2007. Contributor to periodicals. **Online address:** r.freadman@latrobe.edu.au

FRECCERO, Carla. American (born United States), b. 1956?. **Genres:** Genealogy/Heraldry, Cultural/Ethnic Topics, Humanities. **Career:** University of California, Department of Literature, professor and chair. Writer. **Publications:** Father Figures: Genealogy and Narrative Structure in Rabelais, 1991; (ed. with L. Fradenburg) Premodern Sexualities, 1995; Popular Culture: An Introduction, 1999; Queer/Early/Modern, 2006. Contributor to books and periodicals. **Address:** Division of Humanities, University of California, Humanities 1 Ste. 503, 1156 High St., Santa Cruz, CA 95064-1077, U.S.A. **Online address:** freccero@ucsc.edu

FREDA, Joseph. American (born United States), b. 1951. **Genres:** Novels. **Career:** University of New Hampshire, instructor, 1977-81; Digital Equipment Corp., senior software writer, editor and system manager, 1981-84; Tegra Inc., communications manager, 1984-88, product manager, 1988-92, manager of creative services, 1992-94; Prepress Solutions, creative director, 1994-99; freelance writer, 1995-; Freda and Flaherty Creative, co-owner, principal, 1999-. **Publications:** NOVELS: Suburban Guerrillas, 1995; The Patience of Rivers, 2003. Contributor to journals. **Address:** c/o Gail Hochman, Brandt & Hochman Literary Agents, 1501 Broadway, New York, NY 10036-5601, U.S.A. **Online address:** joe@joefreda.com

FREDERICK, David C. American (born United States), b. 1961. **Genres:** Law. **Career:** U.S. Court of Appeals, Ninth Circuit, law clerk, 1989-91; Supreme Court, law clerk, 1991-92; Shearman and Sterling, attorney, 1992-95; U.S. Department of Justice, counselor, 1995-96, assistant, 1996-2001; Everybody Wins Inc., general counsel and director, 1995-97; First Presbyterian Church, elder, 1996-; Kellogg, Huber, Hansen, Todd, Evans and Figel,

P.L.L.C., partner. Writer. **Publications:** Rugged Justice: The Ninth Circuit Court of Appeals and the American West, 1891-1941, 1994; Supreme Court and Appellate Advocacy: Mastering Oral Argument, 2003, 2nd ed., 2010; The Art of Oral Advocacy, 2003, 2nd ed., 2011. Contributor to journals. **Address:** Kellogg, Huber, Hansen, Todd,, Evans and Figel, P.L.L.C., Sumner Sq., 1615 M St. NW, Ste. 400, Washington, DC 20036, U.S.A. **Online address:** dfrederick@khhte.com

FREDERICK, Jim. American (born United States), b. 1971. **Genres:** History. **Career:** Money Magazine, senior editor; Time Magazine, Tokyo bureau chief, 2002-06, senior editor-London, 2006-08, executive editor; Time.com Website, managing editor. Journalist. **Publications:** (With C.R. Jenkins) The Reluctant Communist: My Desertion, Court-Martial, and Forty-year Imprisonment in North Korea, 2008; Black Hearts: One Platoon's Plunge into Madness in the Triangle of Death, 2010. Contributor to periodicals. **Address:** New York, NY , U.S.A. **Online address:** jim@jimfrederick.com

FREEBORN, Richard (Harry). British/Welsh (born Wales), b. 1926?. **Genres:** Novels, Novellas/Short Stories, History, Literary Criticism And History, Translations, Reference. **Career:** Oxford University, Brasenose College, university lecturer in Russian, Hulme Lecturer in Russian, 1954-64; University of California, visiting professor, 1964-65; University of Manchester, Sir William Mather chair of Russian studies and Sir William Mather professor of Russian studies, 1965-67; University of London, professor, 1967-88, professor emeritus of Russian literature, 1988-. Writer. **Publications:** LITERARY CRITICISM: Turgenev: A Study, 1960; The Rise of the Russian Novel: Studies in the Russian Novel from Eugene Onegin to War and Peace, 1973; The Russian Revolutionary Novel: Turgenev to Pasternak, 1982; Dostoevsky, 2003; Furious Vissarion: Belinskii's Struggle for Literature, Love and Ideas, 2003. OTHER: Turgenev: The Novelist's Novelist, a Study 1960; A Short History of Modern Russia, 1966. NOVELS: Two Ways of Life, 1962; The Emigration of Sergey Ivanovich, 1963; Russian Roulette, 1979; The Russian Crucifix: A Victorian Mystery, 1987. TRANSLATOR: (and ed.) I. Turgenev, Sketches from a Hunter's Album, 1967; I. Turgenev, Home of the Gentry, 1970; I. Turgenev, Rudin, 1974; Love and Death: Six Stories by Ivan Turgenev, 1983; (and intro.) I. Turgenev, First Love and Other Stories, 1989; (and ed. and intro.) I. Turgenev, Fathers and Sons, 1991; (and ed.) I. Turgenev, A Month in the Country, 1991; (and intro.) F. Dostoevsky, An Accidental Family, 1994. EDITOR: Russian Literary Attitudes from Pushkin to Solzhenitsyn, 1976; (with C.A. Ward and R.R. Milner-Gulland) Russian and Slavic Literature to 1917, vol. I, 1976; (with J. Grayson) Ideology in Russian Literature, 1990; (and intro.) Anton Chekhov: The Steppe and Other Stories, 1991; (and intro.) Ivan Goncharov: Oblomov, 1992; Encyclopedia of the Novel, 1998; Reference Guide to Russian Literature, 1998; The Cambridge Companion to Tolstoy, 2002. Contributor to books. **Address:** School of Slavonic and East European Studies, University of London, 16 Taviton St., London, GL WC1H 0BW, England.

FREED, Anne O. American (born United States), b. 1917. **Genres:** Education, Gerontology/Senior Issues, Social Work, Autobiography/Memoirs, History, Psychology. **Career:** War Relocation Authority, assistant social science analyst, 1943-44; Eastern Pennsylvania Psychiatric Institute for Social Work, Children's Unit, assistant director, 1960-64, 1973-83; Boston University, adjunct professor of social work, 1964-93, adjunct lecturer, 1965-82, director of spring institute; Boston College, lecturer, professor of social work, 1964-83, adjunct associate and adjunct professor, 1982-2000; Smith College, School for Social Work, assistant professor, 1965-70, School for Social Work in International Program, adjunct faculty, 2000-; Family Service Association of Greater Boston, board director, 1972, director of professional services and director of clinical services; Jewish Vocational Counseling, board director, 1973-74; Consumer Credit Counseling, board director, 1978-83; Brookline Council on Aging, board director, 1984-; Sofia University, teacher, 1989; Center for the Study of Democracy, board director, 1990-; New Bulgarian University, teacher, 1992-93; Massachusetts Mental Health Center, Geriatric Unit, coordinator. Writer. **Publications:** (Ed. with D. Blau) Mental Health in The Nursing Home: An Educational Approach For Staff, 1979; The Changing Worlds of Older Women in Japan, Knowledge, Ideas, and Trends, 1993; (with R. Freed) Fulbrighters in Retirement: Networking with Bulgarians Keeps Us Engaged, 2008. Contributor of articles to journals. **Address:** 133 Del Pond Dr., Canton, MA 02021-2753, U.S.A. **Online address:** freedar@comcast.net

FREED, Curt R(ichard). American (born United States), b. 1943. **Genres:** Medicine/Health, Sciences. **Career:** Los Angeles County Harbor General

Hospital, intern, resident, 1969-71; Massachusetts General Hospital, resident, 1971-72; University of California, research fellow in clinical pharmacology, 1972-75; University of Colorado Health Sciences Center, staff, 1975-, assistant professor, 1975-81, associate professor, 1981-87, professor of medicine and pharmacology, 1987-, Neural Transplantation Program for Parkinson's Disease, director, 1988-, Division of Clinical Pharmacology and Toxicology, head, 1993-, National Parkinson Foundation Center of Excellence, director, 1995-2000, Neuroscience Program, director, 1997-2002; Parkinson's Center, director, 1997. Writer. **Publications:** (With S. LeVay) Healing the Brain: A Doctor's Controversial Quest for a Cell Therapy to Cure Parkinson's Disease, 2002. Contributor to periodicals. **Address:** Department of Pharmacology, Health Sciences Center, University of Colorado, CB C-237, 4200 E 9th Ave., Denver, CO 80262, U.S.A. **Online address:** curt.freed@uchsc.edu

FREED, Lynn. American/South African (born South Africa), b. 1945. **Genres:** Novels, Novellas/Short Stories, Travel/Exploration, Autobiography/ Memoirs, Essays, Humor/Satire. **Career:** University of California, professor of English, 1975-; Columbia University, WIT fellow. Writer. **Publications:** Heart Change, 1982, rev. ed. as Friends of the Family, 2000; Home Ground: A Novel, 1986; The Bungalow, 1993; The Mirror: A Novel, 1997; House of Women: A Novel, 2002; The Curse of the Appropriate Man, 2004; Reading, Writing and Leaving Home: Life on the Page, 2005; Servants Quarters, 2009. Contributor to periodicals. Works appear in anthologies. **Address:** Department of English, University of California, Rm. 253 Voorhies, 1 Shields Ave., Davis, CA 95616, U.S.A. **Online address:** lrfreed@ucdavis.edu

FREEDLAND, Michael. British (born England), b. 1934. **Genres:** Biography, Autobiography/Memoirs. **Career:** Luton News, journalist, 1951-60; Daily Sketch, journalist, 1960-61; British Broadcasting Corp., executive producer and presenter, 1971-. Writer. **Publications:** Jolson in UK as Al Jolson, 1972, rev. ed., 1985; Irving Berlin, 1974, rev. ed. as A Salute to Irving Berlin, 1986; James Cagney, 1974, as Cagney, 1975; Fred Astaire, 1976; Sophie: The Story of Sophie Tucker, 1976; Jerome Kern, 1978; The Two Lives of Errol Flynn in UK as Errol Flynn, 1978; Gregory Peck: A Biography, 1980; (with Morecambe and Wise) There's No Answer to That!: An Autobiography, 1981; Maurice Chevalier, 1981; Peter O'toole: A Biography, 1983; The Warner Brothers, 1983; So Lets Hear the Applause: The Story of the Jewish Entertainer, 1984; Dino: The Dean Martin Story, 1984; Jack Lemmon, 1985; Katharine Hepburn, 1985; The Secret Life of Danny Kaye, 1985; Jolie, 1985; Shirley MacLaine, 1986; Linda Evans, 1986; The Goldwyn Touch: A Biography of Sam Goldwyn, 1986; Jane Fonda, 1987; Leonard Bernstein, 1987; Liza with a Z, 1988, rev. ed., 2003; (with W. Scharf) Composed and Conducted, 1988; Dustin, 1989; Kenneth Williams, 1990; Andre Previn, 1991; Sean Connery, 1994, rev. ed., 2004; Music Man: The Story of Frank Simon, 1994; All the Way: A Biography of Frank Sinatra, 1997; Michael Caine, 1999; Bing Crosby, 1999; Bob Hope, 1999; Doris Day: The Illustrated Biography, 2000; Some Like It Cool, 2002; Confessions of a Serial Biographer, 2005; (with B. Paskin) Witch Hunt in Hollywood, McCarthyism's War on Tinseltown, 2007; (with B. Paskin) Hollywood On Trial: McCarthyisms War Against the Movies, 2007; Jolson: The Story of Al Jolson, 2007; The Men Who Made Hollywood, the Story of the Movie Moguls, 2009; Judy Garland, 2010. **Address:** Bays Hill Lodge, Barnet Ln., Elstree, HF WD6 3QU, England. **Online address:** michaelfreedland@boltblue.com

FREEDMAN, Adam. American (born United States) **Genres:** Novellas/ Short Stories. **Career:** Buenos Aires Herald, editor and columnist, 1998-99; New York Law Journal, Legal Lingo columnist; Vocabula Review, columnist. Attorney. **Publications:** Elated by Details: Award-winning Short Stories, 2003; The Party of the First Part: The Curious World of Legalese, 2007. Contributor of articles to periodicals. **Address:** Henry Holt and Company Inc., 175 5th Ave., New York, NY 10010, U.S.A. **Online address:** adamjfreedman@yahoo.com

FREEDMAN, Anne. (Anne Ellen Freedman). American (born United States), b. 1938. **Genres:** Politics/Government, Literary Criticism And History. **Career:** Bunting Institute, research associate, 1964-66; Wheaton College, instructor in political science, 1964-65; Saint Xavier College, instructor in political science, 1965-66; Roosevelt University, professor of political science and public administration, 1966-97, chair of political science department, 1970-73, head of graduate program, 1973-, acting chair, 1983-84, professor emeritus, through 2006; Journal of Voluntary Action Research, associate editor, 1971-85; Radcliffe Institute, researcher and writer; Colorado Mountain College, trustee, 2005-. Consultant. **Publications:** (With C. Smith) Voluntary

Associations: Perceptions on Literature, 1972; The Planned Society, 1972; (as Anne E. Freedman with P.E. Freedman) The Psychology of Political Control: Comprising Dialogues Between a Modern Prince and His Tutor on the Application of Basic Psychological Principles to the Realm of Politics, 1975; Patronage: An American Tradition, 1994. Contributor of articles to books and professional journals. **Address:** Colorado Mountain College, 831 Grand Ave., Glenwood Springs, CO 81601, U.S.A.

FREEDMAN, Anne Ellen. *See* **FREEDMAN, Anne.**

FREEDMAN, David H. American (born United States), b. 1954. **Genres:** Technology, Information Science/Computers. **Career:** New York Times Inc., contributing editor. Journalist. **Publications:** Brainmakers: How Scientists Are Moving beyond Computers to Create a Rival to the Human Brain, 1994; At Large: The Strange Case of the World's Biggest Internet Invasion, 1997; Corps Business: The 30 Management Principles of the U.S. Marines, 2000; (with E. Abrahamson) A Perfect Mess: The Hidden Benefits of Disorder: How Crammed Closets, Cluttered Offices, and On-the-Fly Planning Make the World a Better Place, 2006; Wrong: Why Experts Keep Failing Us-and How to Know When Not to Trust Them: Scientists, Finance Wizards, Doctors, Relationship Gurus, Celebrity CEOs, High-powered Consultants, Health Officials, and More, 2010. Contributor to magazines and newspapers. **Address:** U.S.A. **Online address:** dhfreedman@gmail.com

FREEDMAN, Eric. American (born United States), b. 1949. **Genres:** Business/Trade/Industry, Communications/Media, History, Law, Politics/Government, Recreation. **Career:** Knickerbocker News, reporter, 1976-84; New York Law Journal, Albany correspondent, 1977-84; Colorado State University, journalist-in-residence, 1983; Detroit News, reporter with Capitol Bureau, 1984-95; Michigan State University, School of Journalism, assistant professor of journalism, 1995-, associate professor of journalism, International Studies and Programs, assistant dean, Capital News Service School, director. Writer. **Publications:** Guns of the West, 1967; Espace Libre, 1970; On the Water, Michigan: Your Comprehensive Guide to Water Recreation in the Great Lake State, 1992; Pioneering Michigan, 1992; Michigan Free: Your Comprehensive Guide to Free Travel, Recreation and Entertainment Opportunities, 1993; Great Lakes, Great National Forests: A Recreational Guide to The National Forests of Michigan, Minnesota, Wisconsin, Illinois, Indiana, Ohio, Pennsylvania and New York, 1995; (with E. Hoffman) What to Study: 101 Fields in a Flash, 1997; How to Transfer to the College of Your Choice, 2002; (ed. with E. Hoffman) John F. Kennedy in His Own Words, 2005; African Americans in Congress: A Documentary History, 2008; Bibliographie des oeuvres publiées de Benjamin Fondane: 1912-2008, 2009; (ed. with R. Shafer) After the Czars and Commissars: Journalism in Authoritarian Post-Soviet Central Asia, 2011. Contributor to periodicals. **Address:** Michigan State University, Rm. 345 Communication Arts and Sciences Bldg., 209 International Ctr., East Lansing, MI 48824-1035, U.S.A. **Online address:** freedma5@msu.edu

FREEDMAN, Jeff. American (born United States), b. 1953. **Genres:** Children's Fiction, Novels, Young Adult Fiction. **Career:** Intel, senior software engineer, 1988-90; Cypress Semiconductor, senior software engineer, 1990-. Writer. **Publications:** (With D. McFarling) The Magic Dishpan of Oz, 1995; A Cure for a Cat, forthcoming. **Address:** Cypress Semiconductor, 9125 SW Gemini Dr., Ste. 200, Beaverton, OR 97008, U.S.A.

FREEDMAN, Jonathan. American (born United States), b. 1954. **Genres:** Cultural/Ethnic Topics. **Career:** Yale University, assistant professor, 1985-89, associate professor, 1989-90; University of Michigan, assistant professor, 1991-98, professor, 1999-, Frankel Center for Jewish Studies, faculty associate; Bread Loaf School of English, instructor, 1987-91, 1998-2000; California Institute of Technology, visiting professor, 1998-99; Oxford University, visiting professor of American Literature, 2002. Writer. **Publications:** Professions of Taste: Henry James, British Aestheticism and Commodity Culture, 1990; The Temple of Culture: Assimilation and Anti-Semitism in Literary Anglo-America, 2000; Klezmer America: Jewishness, Ethnicity, Modernity, 2008. EDITOR: Oscar Wilde: A Collection of Critical Essays, 1996; The Cambridge Companion to Henry James, 1998; (with R. Millington) Hitchcock's America, 1999; (with S. Blair) Jewish in America, 2004. Contributor of articles to journals and books. **Address:** Department of English Language and Literature, University of Michigan, 3187 Angell Hall, Ann Arbor, MI 48109, U.S.A. **Online address:** zoid@umich.edu

FREEDMAN, Jonathan B. *See* **FREEDMAN, Jonathan (Borwick).**

FREEDMAN, Jonathan (Borwick). (Jonathan B. Freedman). American (born United States), b. 1950. **Genres:** Documentaries/Reportage, Essays, Adult Non-fiction, Education, Politics/Government. **Career:** Sao Paulo and Rio de Janeiro, associated press reporter, 1974-75; The Tribune, editorial writer, 1981-90; Copley News Service, syndicated columnist, 1987-89; Schools of the Future Commission, board director, 1987; Public Broadcasting System, moderator, 1988; Los Angeles Times, freelance opinion and editorial writer, 1990-91; New York Times, freelance opinion and editorial writer, 1990-91; San Diego State University, visiting lecturer, 1990-. **Publications:** SELF-ILLUSTRATED: The Man Who'd Bounce the World: A Story, 1979. OTHERS: The Pulitzer Prizes, vol. I, 1987; The Editorials and Essays of Jonathan Freedman, 1988; From Cradle to Grave: The Human Face of Poverty in America, 1993; (as Jonathan B. Freedman) Wall of Fame, 2000. Contributor of articles to periodicals. **Address:** c/o Charlotte Sheedy, 65 Bleeker St., New York, NY 10012, U.S.A. **Online address:** jfreedman@att.net

FREEDMAN, Lawrence (David). British (born England), b. 1948. **Genres:** Military/Defense/Arms Control. **Career:** York University, teaching assistant, 1971-72; Nuffield College, research fellow, 1974-75; International Institute for Strategic Studies, research associate, 1975-76; Royal Institute for International Affairs, research fellow, 1976-78, head of policy studies, 1978-82; King's College, Department of War Studies, professor, 1982-, department head, 1992-97, Board of War Studies, chair, 1997-; Center for Defence Studies, honorary director, 1990-2001, vice-principal (research), 2003-; Falklands Campaign, offical historian, 1997; British Academy, fellow. Writer. **Publications:** U.S. Intelligence and the Soviet Strategic Threat, 1977, 2nd ed., 1986; The Price of Peace, 1978; Arms Production in the United Kingdom: Problems and Prospects, 1978; The West and the Modernization of China, 1979; Britain and Nuclear Weapons, 1981; The Evolution of Nuclear Strategy, 1981, 3rd ed., 2003; Atlas of Global Strategy, 1985; Arms Control: Management or Reform?, 1986; Terrorism and International Order, 1986; Strategic Defence in the Nuclear Age, 1987; Britain and the Falklands War, 1988; (with M. Navias and N. Wheeler) Independence in Concert, 1989; The South Atlantic Crisis of 1982, 1989; (with V. Gamba-Stonehouse) Signals of War: The Falklands Conflict of 1982, 1990; (with E. Karsh) The Gulf Conflict, 1990-1991: Diplomacy and War in the New World, 1993; Military Intervention in European Conflicts, 1994; The Revolution in Strategic Affairs, 1998; The Politics of British Defence, 1979-1998, 1999; Kennedy's Wars, 2000; Cold War: A Military History, 2001; Deterrence, 2004; Transformation of Strategic Affairs, 2006; Choice of Enemies: America Confronts the Middle East, 2008. EDITOR: The Troubled Alliance: Atlantic Relations in the 1980s, 1983; (with P. Bobbitt and G.F. Treverton) U.S. Nuclear Strategy, 1989; Europe Transformed, 1990; Military Power in Europe: Essays in Memory of Jonathan Alford, 1990; (with J. Saunders) Population Change and European Security, 1991; (with M. Clarke) Britain in the World, 1991; (with P. Hayes and R. O'Neill) War, Strategy and International Politics: Essays in Honour of Sir Michael Howard, 1992; War, 1994; Strategic Coercion, 1998; Superterrorism: Policy Responses, 2002. Contributor to periodicals. **Address:** Department of War Studies, King's College, James Clerk Maxwell Bldg., 57 Waterloo Rd., London, GL SE1 8WA, England. **Online address:** lawrence.freedman@kcl.ac.uk

FREEDMAN, Luba. Israeli (born Israel), b. 1953. **Genres:** Art/Art History. **Career:** Hebrew University of Jerusalem, instructor, 1985-86, teaching fellow, 1987-89, lecturer, 1992-96, senior lecturer in the history of art, 1996-2003, associate professor, 2003-11, professor; Folger Shakespeare Library, junior fellow, 1990. Writer and art historian. **Publications:** The Classical Pastoral in the Visual Arts, 1989; Titian's Independent Self-Portraits, 1990; Titian's Portraits through Aretino's Lens, 1995; (with G. Huber-Rebenich) Wege zum Mythos, 2001; The Revival of the Olympian Gods in Renaissance Art, 2003; Classical Myths in Italian Renaissance Painting, 2011. Contributor to periodicals. **Address:** Department of the History of Art, Hebrew University of Jerusalem, Mount Scopus, Jerusalem, 91905, Israel. **Online address:** lubafre@mscc.huji.ac.il

FREEDMAN, Michael R. American (born United States), b. 1952. **Genres:** Psychology, Medicine/Health. **Career:** University of Colorado, Raimy Psychology Clinic, therapist, 1982-83; Wardenberg Student Health Center, therapist, 1983-84; Boulder County Mental Health Center, Cedar House, primary therapist, 1984-85; University of Colorado, clinical intern, 1985-86, Health Sciences Center, instructor in psychology and assistant clinical professor of psychiatry, 1987-, clinical instructor, 1991-; National Jewish Center for Immunology and Respiratory Medicine, staff psychologist, 1986-88, chief of adult clinical psychology, 1988-91. Writer. **Publications:** Living Well with

Asthma, 1998. Contributor of articles to journals and magazines. **Address:** 2027 11th St., Boulder, CO 80302-5101, U.S.A.

FREEDMAN, Russell (Bruce). American (born United States), b. 1929. **Genres:** Children's Non-fiction, Animals/Pets, Military/Defense/Arms Control, Biography, Adult Non-fiction, History. **Career:** Associated Press, reporter and editor, 1953-56; J. Walter Thompson Co., publicity writer, 1956-60; Columbia University Press, Columbia Encyclopedia, associate staff, 1961-63; freelance writer, 1961-; Crowell-Collier Educational Corp., editor, 1964-65; New School for Social Research, writing workshop instructor, 1969-86. **Publications:** NONFICTION FOR YOUNG READERS: Teenagers Who Made History, 1961; 2000 Years of Space Travel, 1963; Jules Verne, 1965; Thomas Alva Edison: A Concise Biography, 1966; Scouting with Baden-Powell, 1967; (with J.E. Morriss) How Animals Learn, 1969; (with J.E. Morriss) Animal Instincts, 1970; Animal Architects, 1971; (with J.E. Morriss) The Brains of Animals and Man, 1972; The First Days of Life, 1974; Growing Up Wild: How Young Animals Survive, 1975; Animal Fathers, 1976; Animal Games, 1976; Hanging On: How Animals Carry Their Young, 1977; How Birds Fly, 1977; Getting Born, 1978; How Animals Defend Their Young, 1978; Immigrant Kids, 1980; They Lived with the Dinosaurs, 1980; Tooth and Claw: A Look at Animal Weapons, 1980; Animal Superstars: Biggest, Strongest, Fastest, Smartest, 1981; Farm Babies, 1981; When Winter Comes, 1981; Can Bears Predict Earthquakes?: Unsolved Mysteries of Animal Behavior, 1982; Killer Fish, 1982; Killer Snakes, 1982; Children of the Wild West, 1983; Dinosaurs and Their Young, 1983; Rattlesnakes, 1984; Cowboys of the Wild West, 1985; Sharks, 1985; Indian Chiefs, 1987; Lincoln: A Photobiography, 1987; Buffalo Hunt, 1988; Franklin Delano Roosevelt, 1990; The Wright Brothers: How They Invented the Airplane, 1991; An Indian Winter, 1992; Eleanor Roosevelt: A Life of Discovery, 1993; Kids at Work: Lewis Hine and the Crusade against Child Labor, 1994; The Life and Death of Crazy Horse, 1996; Out of Darkness: The Story of Louis Braille, 1997; Martha Graham, A Dancer's Life, 1998; Babe Didrikson Zaharias: The Making of a Champion, 1999; Give Me Liberty: The Story of the Declaration of Independence, 2000; In the Days of the Vaqueros: America's First True Cowboys, 2001; Confucius: The Golden Rule, 2002; In Defense of Liberty: The Story of America's Bill of Rights, 2003; The Voice That Challenged a Nation: Marian Anderson and the Struggle for Equal Rights, 2004. OTHERS: Holiday House: The First Fifty Years (adult), 1985; Children of the Great Depression, 2005; Adventures of Marco Polo, 2006; Freedom Walkers: The Story of the Montgomery Bus Boycott, 2006; Who was First?: Discovering the Americas, 2007; Washington at Valley Forge, 2008; The War to End All Wars: World War I, 2010; Lafayette and the American Revolution, 2010; The Boston Tea Party, 2011; Abraham Lincoln and Frederick Douglass, 2012. **Address:** 280 Riverside Dr., New York, NY 10025-9010, U.S.A.

FREEDMAN, Sarah Warshauer. American (born United States), b. 1946. **Genres:** Education, Communications/Media, Language/Linguistics, Adult Non-fiction. **Career:** Philadelphia School District, Overbrook High School, English teacher, 1967-68; Lower Merion High School, English teacher, 1968-69; University of North Carolina, instructor in English, 1970-71; Stanford University, instructor in English and linguistics, 1972-76; San Francisco State University, English Department, assistant professor, 1977-79, associate professor, 1979-81; University of California, School of Education, assistant professor, 1981-83, associate professor, 1983-89, professor, 1989-, English Single Subject Credential Program, faculty director, 1998-, Berkeley Human Rights Center, senior fellow, 2000-; National Center for the Study of Writing and Literacy, director, 1985-96; Universitat Autonoma de Barcelona, visiting researcher; University of Zimbabwe, visiting researcher. Writer. **Publications:** NONFICTION: (ed.) The Acquisition of Written Language: Response and Revision, 1985; (with C. Greenleaf and M. Sperling) Response to Student Writing, 1987; Exchanging Writing, Exchanging Cultures: Lessons in School Reform from the United States and Great Britain, 1994; (co-author) Inside City Schools: Investigating Literacy in Multicultural Classrooms, 1999; (ed. with A.F. Ball) Bakhtinian Perspectives on Language, Literacy and Learning, 2004. Contributor to books and periodicals. **Address:** School of Education, University of California, 5523 Tolman Hall, Berkeley, CA 94720, U.S.A. **Online address:** freedman@socrates.berkeley.edu

FREEDMAN, Stan. See COLLINSON, Alan S.

FREEHLING, William W(ilhartz). American (born United States), b. 1935. **Genres:** History, Military/Defense/Arms Control, Social Sciences. **Career:** University of California, Woodrow Wilson Fellow, 1961-63; Harvard Uni-

versity, instructor in history, 1963-64; University of Michigan, assistant professor, 1964-67, associate professor, 1967-70, professor of history, 1970-72; Johns Hopkins University, professor of history, 1972-91; State University of New York, Thomas B. Lockwood professor of history, 1991-94; Virginia Foundation for the Humanities, senior fellow; University of Kentucky, professor of history, Otis A. Singletary chair in humanities, 1994, Singletary professor of the humanities, Singletary professor emeritus of the humanities. Writer. **Publications:** Prelude to the Civil War: The Nullification Controversy in South Carolina, 1816-1836, 1966; (ed.) The Prelude to Civil War, 1966; Nullification Era: A Documentary Record, 1967; (ed.) Slavery and Freedom, 1982; The Road to Disunion, vol. I: Secessionists at Bay, 1776-1854, 1990, vol. II: Secessionists Triumphant, 1854-1861, 2007; (ed. with C.M. Simpson) Secession Debated: Georgia's Showdown in 1860, 1992; The Reintegration of American History: Slavery and the Civil War, 1994; (contrib.) A Place Not Forgotten: Landscapes of the South from the Morris Museum of Art, 1999; The South Versus The South: How Anti-Confederate Southerners Shaped the Course of the Civil War, 2001; (ed. with C.M. Simpson) Showdown in Virginia: The 1861 Convention and the Fate of the Union, 2010. **Address:** Department of History, University of Kentucky, 1715 Patterson Office Twr., Lexington, KY 40506-0027, U.S.A. **Online address:** wwfree0@uky.edu

FREEMAN, Anne Hobson. American (born United States), b. 1934. **Genres:** Novellas/Short Stories, Biography, Novels. **Career:** Writer, 1956-; International News Service, reporter, 1957; Virginia Museum of Fine Arts, editor, 1959-66; University of Virginia, lecturer in English, 1973-88; Hunton and Williams (law firm), firm historian, 1984-88. **Publications:** The Style of a Law Firm: Eight Gentlemen from Virginia, 1989; A Hand Well Played: The Life of Jim Wheat, Jr., 1994; (ed.) Learning to Fly: A Writer's Memoir, 2007. Works appear in anthologies. Contributor of articles to periodicals. **Address:** 314 Oyster Shell Ln., Callao, VA 22435-2016, U.S.A. **Online address:** ahfreeman@aol.com

FREEMAN, Barbara M. Canadian (born Canada), b. 1947. **Genres:** History, Women's Studies And Issues, Writing/Journalism, Gay And Lesbian Issues. **Career:** Evening Telegram, general news reporter, 1967-68; Canadian Broadcasting Corp., television current affairs researcher, reporter and editor, 1969-70, radio and TV general news reporter and editor, 1972-74, television general news reporter, radio education and community affairs reporter and editor, 1974-78; British Broadcasting Corp., sub editor for external radio services, 1970; Stratford and Newham Express, police and municipal affairs reporter, 1971-72; KEY Radio, municipal affairs reporter, news reader and editor, 1978-80; Carleton University, School of Journalism and Communications, instructor, 1980-89, assistant professor of journalism, 1989-98, associate professor, 1998-2010, adjunct research professor, 2010-. Writer. **Publications:** Kit's Kingdom: The Journalism of Kathleen Blake Coleman, 1989; The Satellite Sex: The Media and Women's Issues in English Canada, 1966-71, 2001; Beyond Bylines: Media Workers and Women's Rights in Canada, 2011. **Address:** School of Journalism and Communications, Carleton University, 346 St. Patrick's Bldg., 1125 Colonel By Dr., Ottawa, ON K1S 5B6, Canada. **Online address:** barbara_freeman@carleton.ca

FREEMAN, Castle (William). American (born United States), b. 1944. **Genres:** Novels, Novellas/Short Stories, Essays, Young Adult Fiction, Literary Criticism And History. **Career:** Franklin Institute, technical writer, 1970-72; Stephen Greene Press, editor, 1976-80; Old Farmer's Almanac, Farmer's Calendar (column), author, 1981-; Country Journal, copy editor, 1981-87; freelance writer and editor, 1987-. **Publications:** The Bride of Ambrose (stories), 1987; Spring Snow (essays), 1995; Judgment Hill (novel), 1997; My Life and Adventures (novel), 2002; Stitch in Time: Townshend, Vermont, 1753-2003, 2003; Go with Me: A Novel, 2008; All That I Have: A Novel, 2009. Contributor of articles to periodicals. **Address:** c/o Christina Ward, Christina Ward Literary Agency, PO Box 515, North Scituate, MA 02060-0515, U.S.A.

FREEMAN, Charles Wellman. Also writes as Chas W. Freeman, Limin Fu. American (born United States), b. 1943. **Genres:** International Relations/Current Affairs. **Career:** U.S. Department of State, foreign service officer, 1965, vice consultant, 1966-67, cultural affairs officer, 1967-68, principal Chinese interpreter, 1971-74, economic and commercial officer, 1971-74, deputy director, 1975-76, director of public programs, 1976-77, director of plans and management, 1976-77; Harvard University, Harvard Law School, East Asian Legal Studies, visiting fellow, 1974-75; U.S. Information Agency, director of program coordination and development, 1978, member of China normalization working group, 1978-79, acting and deputy U.S. coordinator for refugee affairs, 1979, director of Chinese affairs, 1979-81, deputy chief of mission at U.S. embassies, 1981-86, principal deputy assistant secretary of state for African affairs, 1986-89, U.S. ambassador to Saudi Arabia, 1989-92, assistant secretary of defense for international security affairs, 1993-94; Institute for National Strategic Studies, distinguished visiting fellow, 1992-93; Atlantic Council, director, 1994-; U.S. Institute of Peace, distinguished fellow, 1994-; Fleishman-Hillard, member of international advisory board, 1995-; Projects International Associates Inc., chairperson of board of directors, 1995-. Writer. **Publications:** Cooking Western in China (bilingual cookbook), 1986; The Diplomat's Dictionary, 1994, 2nd ed., 2010; Arts of Power: Statecraft and Diplomacy, 1997; (contrib.) Green Dragons: The Politics of Climate Change in Asia: A Report of the CSIS Asian Regionalism Initiative, 2010; (contrib.) Asia's Response to Climate Change and Natural Disasters: Implications for an Evolving Regional Architecture, 2010. **Address:** Projects International Inc., 1800 K St. NW, Ste. 1018, Washington, DC 20006, U.S.A.

FREEMAN, Chas W. *See* **FREEMAN, Charles Wellman.**

FREEMAN, Daniel E(van). American (born United States), b. 1959. **Genres:** History, Humanities, Music, Theatre. **Career:** University of Illinois, visiting assistant professor, 1987, 1995; University of Southern California, lecturer, 1988-91; University of Minnesota, lecturer, 1991-; Smithsonian Institution, resident associate, 2002-. Writer. **Publications:** Two Keyboard Concertos, 1991; The Opera Theater of Count Franz Anton von Sporck in Prague, 1992; Josef Myslivecek, Il Boemo, 2009; Mozart in Prague, forthcoming. Contributor to periodicals. **Address:** 6032 Sheridan Ave. S, Minneapolis, MN 55410, U.S.A. **Online address:** freem005@umn.edu

FREEMAN, Garry. American/British (born England), b. 1955. **Genres:** Art/Art History, Music. **Career:** St. Bede's Grammar School, history teacher, 2000-, curriculum support coordinator, 2001-; Carl Palmer Drum Circle and Masterclass, organizer and host, 2004. Writer and educator. **Publications:** The Bootleg Guide: Classic Bootlegs of the 1960s and 1970s, An Annotated Discography, 2003. Contributor to periodicals. **Address:** c/o Author Mail, Scarecrow Press, 4501 Forbes Blvd., Ste. 200, Lanham, MD 20706-4346, U.S.A.

FREEMAN, Gillian. Also writes as Eliot George. British (born England), b. 1929. **Genres:** Novels, Plays/Screenplays, Children's Non-fiction, Literary Criticism And History, Sociology, Young Adult Fiction. **Career:** C.J. Lytle Ltd., copywriter, 1951-52; London County Council, teacher, 1952-53; North London Observer, reporter, 1953; Louis Golding, literary secretary, 1953-55; author, 1955-. **Publications:** The Liberty Man, 1955; Fall of Innocence, 1956; Jack Would Be a Gentleman, 1959; The Story of Albert Einstein, 1960; (as Eliot George) The Leather Boys, 1961; The Campaign, 1963; The Leader, 1965; The Undergrowth of Literature, 1967; Pursuit (play), 1969; The Alabaster Egg, 1970; Marriage Machine: A Novel, 1975; The Schoolgirl Ethic: The Life and Work of Angela Brazil, 1976; Nazi Lady: The Diaries of Elisabeth von Stahlenberg, 1933-1948, 1978; The Confessions of Elisabeth von S: The Story of a Young Woman's Rise and Fall in Nazi Society, 1978; An Easter Egg Hunt, 1981; (as Elaine Jackson) Lovechild, 1984; (ed. with J. Glassborow) Atlas of the United States, 1986; Mayerling (film, ballet scenarios), 1978; Isadora, 1981; (with E. Thorpe) Ballet Genius, 1988; Termination Rock, 1989; His Mistress's Voice, 1999; But Nobody Lives in Bloomsbury, 2006. **Address:** Rochelle Stevens & Co., 2 Terretts Pl., Upper St., Upper St., London, GL N1 1QZ, England.

FREEMAN, Harry M. American (born United States), b. 1943. **Genres:** Environmental Sciences/Ecology, Sciences, Technology, Engineering, Education, Economics. **Career:** U.S. Environmental Protection Agency, staff, 1968-, Office of Research and Development, senior staff engineer; National Risk Management Research Laboratory, Pollution Prevention Research Branch, chief; University of New Orleans, Louisiana Environmental Leadership Pollution Prevention Program, director, Urban Waste Management and Research Center, senior research associate. Writer. **Publications:** Innovative Thermal Hazardous Organic Waste Treatment Processes, 1985; Innovative Thermal Processes for Treating Hazardous Wastes, 1986; (ed.) Incinerating Hazardous Wastes, 1988; (ed.) Standard Handbook of Hazardous Waste Treatment and Disposal, 1989, 2nd ed., 1998; (ed.) Hazardous Waste Minimization, 1990; (ed.) Physical/Chemical Processes, 1990; (ed.) Thermal Processes, 1990; (ed.) Industrial Pollution Prevention Handbook, 1995; (ed. with E.F. Harris) Hazardous Waste Remediation: Innovative Treatment Tech-

nologies, 1995; (ed. with Z. Puskas and R. Olbina) Cleaner Technologies and Cleaner Products for Sustainable Development, 1995. **Address:** University of New Orleans, 2000 Lakeshore Dr., New Orleans, LA 70148-2212, U.S.A. **Online address:** hmfce@uno.edu

FREEMAN, Jo. American (born United States), b. 1945. **Genres:** Politics/Government, History, Women's Studies And Issues, Sociology, Autobiography/Memoirs, Social Sciences, Humanities, Young Adult Non-fiction, Young Adult Non-fiction. **Career:** West Side Torch community newspaper, co-editor and photographer, 1967; Modern Hospital, assistant editor, 1967-68; McCarthy for President campaign, national staff, 1968; University of Chicago, research associate, 1968-70; lecturer in political science, 1971; State University of New York College, assistant professor of American studies, 1973-74; State University of New York College, assistant professor of political science, 1974-77; Employment and Training Administration, Broookings fellow, Department of Labor, staff, 1977-78; Cranston for President campaign, associate political director, 1983-84; Kings County, assistant district attorney, 1985-86; New York State Assembly, associate counsel, office of the speaker, 1987-88. **Publications:** The Politics of Women's Liberation: A Case Study of an Emerging Social Movement and Its Relation to the Policy Process, 1973; A Room at a Time: How Women Entered Party Politics, 2000; At Berkeley in the Sixties: The Education of An Activist, 1961-1965, 2004; We Will Be Heard: Women's Struggles for Political Power in the United States, 2008. EDITOR: Women: A Feminist Perspective, 1975, 5th ed., 1995; Social Movements of the Sixties and Seventies, 1983; (with V. Johnson) Waves of Protest: Social Movements Since the Sixties, 1999. Contributor to publications. **Address:** 410 E 8th St., Brooklyn, NY 11218, U.S.A. **Online address:** joreen@jofreeman.com

FREEMAN, Joshua B. (Joshua Benjamin Freeman). American (born United States), b. 1949. **Genres:** History, Organized Labor. **Career:** State University of New York College, instructor, 1981-, assistant professor of history, through 1985; City University of New York, Queen College, Graduate Center, Department of history, associate professor, 1998-2001, professor, 2001-, executive officer; Columbia University, assistant professor, 1987-91, associate professor of history, 1991-98; New Labor Forum, editor; International Labor and Working-Class History, editor. **Publications:** In Transit: The Transport Workers Union in NYC, 1989, rev. ed., 2001; (co-author) Who Built America? Working People and the Nation's Economy, Politics, Culture, and Society, vol. II, 1992. 2nd ed., 2000; (ed. with S. Fraser) Audacious Democracy: Labor, Intellectuals, and the Social Renewal of America, 1997; Working-Class New York: Life and Labor since World War II, 2000. **Address:** Deparment of History, Queens College, City University of New York, Powdermaker 352-Y, 65-30 Kissena Blvd, Flushing, NY 11367, U.S.A. **Online address:** jfreeman@gc.cuny.edu

FREEMAN, Joshua Benjamin. *See* **FREEMAN, Joshua B.**

FREEMAN, Linda Gay. *See* **HOLEMAN, Linda.**

FREEMAN, Marcia S. American (born United States), b. 1937. **Genres:** Children's Fiction, Children's Non-fiction, Writing/Journalism, Adult Non-fiction, Reference. **Career:** High school science teacher, 1961-62; elementary school teacher, 1976-85; presenter of writing education in-service training to elementary and middle-school teachers, 1987-2006; Friends of Gulf Gate Library, president, 1996-98. Writer. **Publications:** Building a Writing Community: A Practical Guide, 1995, rev. ed., 2003; Push and Pull, 1997; Listen to This: Developing an Ear for Expository, 1997; Catfish and Spaghetti, 1998; Wetlands, 1998; Pandas, 1998; Black Bear, 1998; Brown Bear, 1998; Pine Trees, 1998; Maple Trees, 1998; Palm Trees, 1998; Oak Trees, 1998; Ambulance, 1998; Watching the Weather, 1998; A Bird's-Eye View, 1998; Where Do You Live?, 1998; Using Nature's Gifts, 1998; Coast to Coast, 1998; Going to the City, 1998; Young Geographers, 1998; Teaching the Youngest Writers: A Practical Guide, 1998; Fire Boats, 1999; Giant Pandas, 1999; Fire Engine, 1999; Polar Bear, 1999; Police Car, 1999; Non-Fiction Writing Strategies Using Science Big Books as Models, 2000; Gift, 2002; Everything Under the Sun, 2004; You Are A Scientist, 2004; Animal Lives, 2005; (with R.M. Chappell and L.K. Mitten) Models for Teaching Writing-Craft Target Skills, 2005, 2nd ed., 2010; Science in the City, 2006; Seasons of the Year: Everything Science, 2005; What Plant is This?, 2005; Work Book, 2005; Crafting Comparison Papers, 2006; Going Up?, 2006; Ciencia en la ciudad, 2006; Sube o baja/Going up, 2006; Rourke's World of Science Encyclopedia, 2008; 1, 2, 3, ádelante!: un libro para aprendera contra, 2008; 1, 2, 3... Go!: A Book About Counting, 2008; á comollegamos a diez?: datos numericos/What Makes Ten?:

Number Facts, 2008; Unadocena de primos: aprendamos sobre el numero 12, 2008; A Dozen Cousins: Exploring the Number 12, 2008; Mas helado: palabras para comparacionesmatematicas, 2008; More Ice Cream: Words For Math Comparisons, 2008; Multiplicar con los dedos: la regla del nueve, 2008; Multiply By Hand: The Nines Facts, 2008; My sister Is In 3rd Grade: Putting Numbers In Order, 2008; What Makes Ten?: Number Facts, 2008; How Muscles and Bones Hold You Up: A Book About Models, 2008; (co-author) Descubre el mundo de las ciencias enciclopedia, 2010. Contributor of articles to magazines. **Address:** 4668 Sweetmeadow Cir., Sarasota, FL 34238, U.S.A. **Online address:** mikeandmarcy@compuserve.com

FREEMAN, Martha. American (born United States), b. 1956. **Genres:** Children's Fiction, Young Adult Fiction, Novels. **Career:** Freelance reporter and editor, 1980-95. **Publications:** Paths Less Travelled: Dispatches from the Front Lines of Exploration, 1988; Stink Bomb Mom, 1996; The Year My Parents Ruined My Life, 1997; The Polyester Grandpa, 1998; Fourth Grade Weirdo, 1999; The Trouble with Cats, 2000; The Spy Wore Shades, 2001; The Trouble with Babies, 2002; Who Is Stealing the Twelve Days of Christmas?, 2003; Who Stole Halloween, 2005; Mrs. Wow Never Wanted a Cow, 2006; 1,000 Reasons Never to Kiss a Boy, 2007; The Trouble with Twins, 2007; Who Stole Uncle Sam?, 2008; Who Stole Grandma's Million-dollar Pumpkin Pie?, 2009; The Case of the Rock 'n' Roll Dog, 2010; Case of the Diamond Dog Collar, 2011; The Case of the Ruby Slippers, 2012; The Case of the Piggy Bank Thief, 2012. **Address:** Holiday House, 425 Madison Ave., New York, NY 10017, U.S.A. **Online address:** martha@marthafreeman.com

FREEMAN, Michael. (Michael J. Freeman). British (born England), b. 1950. **Genres:** History, Geography, Young Adult Non-fiction. **Career:** University of Oxford, Mansfield College, supernumerary fellow and lecturer in human geography, senior research fellow in human geography; Regent's Park College, lecturer. Writer. **Publications:** A Perspective on the Geography of English Internal Trade during the Industrial Revolution: The Trading Economy of the Textile District of the Yorkshire West Riding circa 1800, 1982; (ed. with D.H. Aldcroft) Transport in the Industrial Revolution, 1983; (with D.H. Aldcroft) The Atlas of British Railway History, 1985; (with T. Mason) Atlas of Nazi Germany, 1987, 2nd ed. as Atlas of Nazi Germany: A Political, Economic and Social Anatomy of the Third Reich, 1995; (ed. with D.H. Aldcroft) Transport in Victorian Britain, 1988; (with D. Aldcroft) Atlas of the World Economy, 1991; Railways and the Victorian Imagination, 1999; (contrib.) The Penguin Atlas of British and Irish History, 2001; Victorians and the Prehistoric: Tracks to a Lost World, 2004; (ed. with M. Beaumont) The Railway and Modernity: Time, Space and the Machine Ensemble, 2007. Contributor to journals. **Address:** Mansfield College, Oxford University, Oxford, OX OX1 3TF, England. **Online address:** michael.freeman@mansfield.ox.ac.uk

FREEMAN, Michael J. See FREEMAN, Michael.

FREEMAN, Philip. American (born United States), b. 1961. **Genres:** Novels, Biography, History, Women's Studies And Issues, Military/Defense/Arms Control, Translations. **Career:** Boston University, postdoctoral fellow, 1994-97; Washington University, assistant professor of classics, 1997-2004, Robert S. Brookings Residential College, faculty fellow, 1999-2004; Luther College, Department of Classics, associate professor, 2004-, professor, head, 2005-, Orlando W. Qualley chair of classical languages, 2007-; Michigan State University, faculty of Irish history. Writer. **Publications:** The Galatian Language: A Comprehensive Survey of the Language of the Ancient Celts in Greco-Roman Asia Minor, 2001; Ireland and the Classical World, 2001; War, Women, and Druids: Eyewitness Reports and Early Accounts of the Ancient Celts, 2002; St. Patrick of Ireland: A Biography, 2004; The Philosopher and the Druids: A Journey among the Ancient Celts, 2006; Julius Caesar, 2008; A Transcription of the Latin Writings of St. Patrick from Seven Medieval Manuscripts, 2008; Lecture Notes: A Professor's Inside Guide to College Success, 2010; Alexander the Great, 2011; Oh My Gods, 2012; (trans. and intro.) Q.T. Cicero, How to Win an Election, 2012; Heroes of Olympus, 2012. Contributor to books and journals. **Address:** Department of Classics, Luther College, 700 College Dr., Decorah, IA 52101-1041, U.S.A. **Online address:** freeph01@luther.edu

FREEMAN, Thomas. See FEHRENBACH, T(heodore) R(eed).

FREEMANTLE, Brian (Harry). Also writes as John Maxwell, Jonathan Evans, Richard Gant, Harry Asher, Andre Hart. British (born England), b. 1936. **Genres:** Mystery/Crime/Suspense, Plays/Screenplays, Novels, Young Adult Fiction. **Career:** New Milton Advertiser, reporter, 1953-58; Bristol Evening World, reporter, 1958; London Evening News, reporter, 1959-61; Daily Express, reporter, 1961-63; Daily Express, assistant foreign editor, 1963-69; Daily Sketch, foreign editor, 1969-71; Daily Mail, staff, 1971-75; writer, 1975-. **Publications:** The Touchables, 1968; Goodbye to an Old Friend, 1973; Face Me When You Walk Away, 1974; The Man Who Wanted Tomorrow, 1975; The November Man, 1976; Charlie Muffin, 1977; Clap Hands, Here Comes Charlie in US as Here Comes Charlie M, 1978; The Inscrutable Charlie Muffin, 1979; Charlie Muffin, U.S.A, 1980; Charlie Muffin's Uncle Sam, 1980; Madrigal for Charlie Muffin, 1981; Deakin's War, 1982; KGB (non-fiction), 1982; CIA (non-fiction), 1983; Vietnam Legacy, 1984; The Lost American, 1984; The Kremlin Kiss, 1984; Rules of Engagement, 1984; The Fix (non-fiction), 1985; The Fifth Day of Every Month, 1986; The Blind Run, 1986; The Steal (non-fiction), 1986; See Charlie Run, 1987; The Bearpit, 1988; Betrayals, 1989; Comrade Charlie, 1989; The Run Around, 1989; O'Farrell's Law, 1990; The Factory, 1990; Little Grey Mice, 1991; The Button Man, 1992; Charlie's Apprentice, 1993; No Time for Heroes, 1994; The Octopus (non-fiction), 1995; Charlie's Chance, 1996; Charlie's Choice: The First Charlie Muffin Omnibus, 1997; The Kremlin Conspiracy, 1997; Bomb Grade, 1997; Gold, 1988; The Predators, 1998; Mind/Reader, 1998; The Iron Cage, 1999; Washington White, 1999; Hell's Paradise, 2001; Dead Men Living, 2000; Kings of Many Castles: A Charlie Muffin Thriller, 2002; Ice Age, 2002; The Watchmen, 2002; Ice Age, 2002; Two Women, Triple Cross, 2003; Triple Cross, 2004; The Holmes Inheritance: Dead End, 2004; The Holmes Factor, 2005; To Save a Son, 2006; Time to Kill, 2006; The Namedropper, 2007; Red Star Rising, 2010. AS HARRY ASHER: The Profiler, 1997; The Predadots, 1998. AS JONATHAN EVANS: Misfire, 1980; The Midas Men, 1981; At Any Price, 1982; Chairman of the Board, 1982; Monopoly, 1984; Kremlin Correction, 1984; The Laundryman, 1985 in US as Dirty White, 1986. AS RICHARD GANT: Ian Fleming: The Man with the Golden Pen, 1966; Sean Connery: Gilt-Edged Bond, 1967. AS ANDRE HART: A Mind to Kill, 1998; The Return, 1999. AS JOHN MAXWELL: H.M.S. Bounty, 1977; The Mary Celeste, 1979. AS JACK WINCHESTER: The Solitary Man, 1980; Deaken's War, 1982; The Choice of Eddie Franks, 1987. **Address:** Jonathan Clowes Ltd., 10 Iron Bridge House, Bridge Approach, London, GL NW1 8BD, England.

FREESE, Barbara. American (born United States), b. 1960?. **Genres:** Adult Non-fiction, History. **Career:** State of Michigan, assistant district attorney; State of Minnesota, assistant attorney general; Union of Concerned Scientists, consultant, senior policy analyst and attorney. Writer. **Publications:** Coal: A Human History, 2003; (with S. Clemmer and A. Nogee) Coal Power in a Warming World: A Sensible Transition to Cleaner Energy Options, 2008. **Address:** Union of Concerned Scientists, 2 Brattle Sq., Cambridge, MA 02138-3780, U.S.A. **Online address:** barbarafreese@comcast.net

FREESE, Mathias B(alogh). American (born United States), b. 1940. **Genres:** Novels. **Career:** Teacher, 1962-69, 1972-74; Board of Cooperative Educational Services, curriculum writer, 1969-72; Half Hollow Hills High School East, teacher and administrator of alternative high school, 1974-95; Middle Country Center for Psychotherapy, clinical social worker, 1979-82; Center for Counseling Services, clinical social worker and senior therapist, 1987-90. Writer. **Publications:** NOVELS: I, 1997; The I Tetralogy, 2005; I Am Not, forthcoming. OTHERS: Down to a Sunless Sea, 2007. Contributor of stories and articles to periodicals. **Address:** 10 E Camino De Diana, Green Valley, AZ 85614, U.S.A. **Online address:** ifreese@hotmail.com

FREEZE, Gregory L. American (born United States), b. 1945. **Genres:** History. **Career:** Harvard University, Davis Center for Russian Studies, research associate, 1972-; Brandeis University, assistant professor, 1972-77, associate professor, 1977-83, professor of history, 1983-, head of department, 1990-96, Victor and Gwendolyn Beinfield professor of history, Graduate School of Arts and Sciences, dean, 2006-10. Writer. **Publications:** The Russian Levites: Parish Clergy in the Eighteenth Century, 1977; Parish Clergy in Nineteenth-Century Russia: Crisis, Reform, Counter-Reform, 1983; (trans.) I.S. Belliustin, A Description of the Clergy in Rural Russia: The Memoir of a Nineteenth-Century Parish Priest, 1985; From Supplication to Revolution: A Documentary Social History of Imperial Russia, 1988. EDITOR: (and trans.) The Battle for Oil: The Economics and Politics of International Corporate Conflict over Petroleum, 1860-1930, 1990; Geschichte der Russischen Kirche, vol. II, 1991; Kratkii Putevoditel, 1993; (and contrib.) Russia: A History, 1997, 3rd ed., 2009; Pariahs, Partners, Predators: German-Soviet Relations, 1922-1941, 1997. Contributor to books and journals. **Address:** Department of History,

Brandeis University, 108 Mandel Ctr., Waltham, MA 02454-9110, U.S.A. **Online address:** freeze@brandeis.edu

FREGA, Donnalee. American (born United States), b. 1956. **Genres:** Literary Criticism And History, Biography, Photography. **Career:** University of North Carolina, assistant professor of English, 1990-96. Writer. **Publications:** Speaking in Hunger: Gender, Discourse, and Consumption in Richardson's Clarissa, 1998; Women of Illusion: A Circus Family's Story, 2001; Walking the Wire: Telling a Circus Family's Story, forthcoming; Letters to Ian, forthcoming. Contributor to periodicals. **Address:** 7020 Calais Dr., Durham, NC 27712-9624, U.S.A. **Online address:** fregad@wilmington.net

FREIDBERG, Susanne. American (born United States) **Genres:** Popular Culture. **Career:** Institute for Food and Development Policy, intern in publicity and development, 1988-89; University of California, Department Of Geography, teaching assistant, 1989-95, City And Regional Planning Department, manuscript editor, 1995-96, lecturer and postdoctoral fellow, 1996-97; Encarta Africana, Africa editor, 1997-98; Dartmouth College, assistant professor, 1998-2004, associate professor of geography, 2004-10, professor of geography, 2010-; Radcliffe Institute for Advanced Studies, Bunting fellow, 2000-01; Harvard University, W.E.B. Du Bois Institute, nonresident fellow, 2005-; Dartmouth College, professor of geography, 2010-. Writer. **Publications:** French Beans and Food Scares: Culture and Commerce in an Anxious Age, 2004; Fresh: A Perishable History, 2009. Contributor to periodicals. **Address:** Department of Geography, Dartmouth College, 6017 Fairchild Hall, Hanover, NH 03755, U.S.A. **Online address:** freidberg@dartmouth.edu

FREINKEL, Susan Elizabeth. American (born United States), b. 1957?. **Genres:** Natural History. **Career:** Wichita Eagle-Beacon, reporter; Recorder and American Lawyer, reporter, 1989-98; Health magazine, staff journalist, 1998-2000. Freelance writer, 2000-. **Publications:** (with S.R. Smith) Adjusting the Balance: Federal Policy and Victim Services, 1988; American Chestnut: The Life, Death and Rebirth of a Perfect Tree, 2007. Contributor of articles to periodicals. **Address:** San Francisco, CA , U.S.A. **Online address:** freinkel@mindspring.com

FREIREICH, Valerie J. American (born United States), b. 1952. **Genres:** Novels, Novellas/Short Stories, Science Fiction/Fantasy. **Career:** Lawyer, 1977-84; Chuhak and Tecson P.C., partner, principal. Writer. **Publications:** SCIENCE FICTION NOVELS: Becoming Human, 1994; Testament, 1994; Beacon, 1996. (with M.H. Greenberg) Sisters in Fantasy 2, 1996; Vashti and God, 1996; Imposter, 1997; The Broken Man, forthcoming. Contributor to periodicals. **Address:** c/o Merrilee Heifetz, Writer's House Inc., 21 W 26th St., New York, NY 10010, U.S.A. **Online address:** vfreireich@chuhak.com

FREIRICH, Roy. American (born United States) **Genres:** Young Adult Fiction, Literary Criticism And History. **Career:** Screenwriter and songwriter. **Publications:** Winged Creatures, 2008. Contributor to periodicals. **Address:** Malibu, CA , U.S.A.

FREITAS, Donna. American (born United States), b. 1972?. **Genres:** Young Adult Fiction, Young Adult Non-fiction, Theology/Religion. **Career:** Georgetown University, chaplain-in-residence, 2000-01; St. John's College High School, dean of student life and director of peer ministry, 2000-01; Marymount University, lecturer, 2001; New York University, community development educator, 2002-03; St. Johns University, lecturer, 2002; Saint Michael's College, assistant professor, 2003-07; Education Sector, senior fellow, 2005-; Boston University, visiting research faculty, 2007, assistant professor of religion. Author and theologian. **Publications:** FICTION: The Possibilities of Sainthood, 2008. NONFICTION: (with J. King) Save the Date: A Spirituality of Dating, Love, Dinner and the Divine, 2003; Becoming a Goddess of Inner Poise: Spirituality for the Bridget Jones in All of Us, 2005; (with J. King) Killing the Imposter God: Philip Pullman's Spiritual Imagination in His Dark Materials, 2007; Sex and the Soul: Juggling Sexuality, Spirituality, Romance and Religion on America's College Campuses, 2008. Contributor to periodicals and Journals. **Address:** Department of Religion, Boston University, 147 Bay State Rd., Ste. 506, Boston, MA 02215, U.S.A. **Online address:** freitas@bu.edu

FREKE, Timothy. British (born England), b. 1959?. **Genres:** Philosophy. **Career:** Author, philosopher and composer. **Publications:** Lao Tzu's Tao Te Ching, 1995; Exotic Massage for Lovers, 1996; Heaven: An Illustrated History of the Higher Realms, 1996; (with P. Gandy) The Hermetica: The

Lost Wisdom of the Pharaohs, 1997; Zen Wisdom: Daily Teachings from the Zen Masters, 1997; (with P. Gandy) The Complete Guide to World Mysticism, 1998; (with P. Gandy) The Wisdom of the Pagan Philosophers, 1998; The Wisdom of the Christian Mystics, 1998; The Wisdom of the Hindu Gurus, 1998; The Wisdom of the Sufi Sages, 1998; The Wisdom of the Tibetan Lamas, 1998; The Wisdom of the Zen Masters, 1998; The Illustrated Book of Sacred Scriptures, 1998; The Way of the Desert, 1998; The Way of the Sea, 1999; Zen Made Easy: An Introduction to the Basics of the Ancient Art of Zen, 1999; Shamanic Wisdomkeepers: Shamanism in the Modern World, 1999; Taoist Wisdom: Daily Teachings from the Taoist Sages, 1999; (with P. Gandy) The Jesus Mysteries: Was the Original Jesus a Pagan God?, 2000; The Encyclopedia of Spirituality: Information and Inspiration to Transform Your Life, 2000; Rumi Wisdom: Daily Teachings from the Great Sufi Master, 2000; (with P. Gandy) Jesus and the Lost Goddess: The Secret Teaching of the Original Christians, 2001; Heart of Islam, 2002; In the Light of Death: Spiritual Insight to Help you Live with Death and Bereavement, 2002; (with P. Gandy) Laughing Jesus: Religious Lies and Gnostic Wisdom, 2005; (with P. Gandy) Gospel of the Second Coming: Jesus is Back and this He's Funny!, 2007; Lucid Living: A Book You Can Read in One Hour that Will Turn Your World Inside Out, 2008; How Long is Now?: A Journey to Enlightenment ... and Beyond, 2009. **Address:** Susan Mears Literary Agency, Flowersent, 75 New Broadway, London, GL W5 5AL, England. **Online address:** tim@timothyfreke.com

FRELINGHUYSEN, Alice Cooney. American (born United States), b. 1954. **Genres:** Art/Art History, Homes/Gardens, Architecture. **Career:** Metropolitan Museum of Art, Department of American Decorative Arts, assistant curator, 1980-87, associate curator, 1987-94, Anthony W. and Lulu C. Wang curator, 1994-; Frelinghuysen Foundation, director; Shelburne (VT) Museum, director; Visiting Nurse Service of New York, director. Writer and art historian. **Publications:** American Porcelain, 1770-1920, 1989; Splendid Legacy: The Havemeyer Collection, 1993; American Art Pottery: Selections from the Charles Hosmer Morse Museum of American Art, 1995; Louis Comfort Tiffany at the Metropolitan Museum, 1998; (co-author) The Lamps of Louis Comfort Tiffany, 2005; Louis Comfort Tiffany and Laurelton Hall: An Artist's Country Estate, 2006. **Address:** Metropolitan Museum of Art, 1000 5th Ave., New York, NY 10028-0198, U.S.A.

FREMGEN, James Morgan. American (born United States), b. 1933. **Genres:** Administration/Management, Money/Finance, Economics, Business/Trade/Industry. **Career:** Indiana University, lecturer in accounting, 1959-61; University of Notre Dame, assistant professor, 1961-64, associate professor of accounting, 1964-65; Naval Postgraduate School (NPS), associate professor, 1965-69, professor of accounting, 1969-2000, professor emeritus, 2000-. Writer. **Publications:** Managerial Cost Analysis, 1966, rev. ed. as Accounting for Managerial Analysis, 1972, 3rd ed., 1976; (with S.S. Liao) The Allocation of Corporate Indirect Costs, 1981. Contributor to journals. **Address:** Naval Postgraduate School, 1 University Cir., Monterey, CA 93943-5000, U.S.A.

FRENCH, Albert. American (born United States), b. 1943. **Genres:** Novels, Autobiography/Memoirs, Biography, History. **Career:** U.S. Marine Corps, staff, 1963-67; Pittsburgh Post-Gazette, photojournalist, 1971-83; Pittsburgh Preview Magazine, co-founder, publisher, 1980-88. Writer. **Publications:** NOVELS: Billy, 1993; Holly, 1995; I Can't Wait on God, 1998. OTHER: Patches of Fire: A Story of War and Redemption (autobiography), 1996; Cinder, 2007. **Address:** c/o Anchor Books, Doubleday & Company Inc., 1540 Broadway, New York, NY 10036-4094, U.S.A.

FRENCH, Antonia. *See* **KUREISHI, Hanif.**

FRENCH, David. British (born England), b. 1954?. **Genres:** Military/Defense/Arms Control, Economics. **Career:** University College London, Department of History, professor, now professor emeritus. Writer. **Publications:** British Economic and Strategic Planning, 1905-1915, 1982; British Strategy & War Aims, 1914-1916, 1986; Britain and NATO: Past, Present, and Future, 1990; The British Way in Warfare, 1688-2000, 1990; The Strategy of the Lloyd George Coalition, 1916-1918, 1995; (ed. with M. Dockrill) Strategy and Intelligence: British Policy during the First World War, 1996; Raising Churchill's Army: The British Army and the War against Germany, 1919-1945, 2000; (ed. with B.H. Reid) The British General Staff: Reform and Innovation c. 1890-1939, 2002; Military Identities: The Regimental System, the British Army, and the British People, c. 1870-2000, 2005; The British Way in Counter-Insurgency, 1945-1967, 2011; Army, Empire and Cold War: British Military Policy, c. 1945-1970, forthcoming. **Address:** Department of History, University College London, Rm. B21, 24 Gordon Sq., Gower St., London, GL WC1E 6BT, England. **Online address:** d.french@ucl.ac.uk

FRENCH, Fiona. British (born England), b. 1944. **Genres:** Children's Fiction, Illustrations, Children's Non-fiction. **Career:** Long Grove Psychiatric Hospital, childrens art therapy teacher, 1967-69; Bridget Riley, assistant, 1967-72; Wimbledon School of Art, design teacher, 1970-71; Leicester and Brighton Polytechnics, design teacher, 1973-74. Writer. **Publications:** SELF-ILLUSTRATED: Jack of Hearts, 1970; Huni, 1971; The Blue Bird, 1972; Star Child, 1979; The Princess and the Musician, 1981; John Barleycorn, 1982; Maid of the Wood, 1985; Snow White in New York, 1986; Song of the Nightingale, 1987; Cinderella, 1987; The Magic Vase, 1991; Miss Mouse Gets Married, 1996. OTHERS: Un-Fairy Tales, 1966; King Tree, 1973; City of Gold, 1974; Aio the Rainmaker, 1975; Matteo, 1976; Hunt the Thimble, 1978; Future Story, 1984; Rise and Shine!, 1989; Anancy and Mr. Dry-Bone, 1991; King Of Another Country, 1993; Little Inchkin, 1994; Lord of the Animals: A Miwok Indian Creation Myth, 1997; (with D. Newby) Jamil's Clever Cat, 1999, 3rd ed., 2006; (ed.) Bethlehem: With Words from the Authorized Version of the King James Bible, 2001; (ed.) Easter: With Words from the King James Bible, 2002; (ed.) Paradise, 2004. Illustrator of books by others. **Address:** Deepings The St., Little Barningham, Norwich, NF NR11 7AG, England. **Online address:** f.french@londonmet.ac.uk

FRENCH, Francis. American/British (born England), b. 1970?. **Genres:** Novels, Sciences, Technology, Young Adult Fiction, Biography, Autobiography/Memoirs. **Career:** Reuben H. Fleet Science Center, education programs coordinator; Sally Ride Science, director of events; San Diego Air and Space Museum, director of education. Writer. **Publications:** (With C. Burgess) Into That Silent Sea: Trailblazers of the Space Era, 1961-1965, 2007; (with C. Burgess) In the Shadow of the Moon: A Challenging Journey to Tranquility, 1965-1969, 2007; (with A. Worden) Falling to Earth: An Apollo 15 Astronaut's Journey, 2011. **Address:** San Diego Air & Space Museum, 2001 Pan American Plz., Balboa Pk., San Diego, CA 92101-1636, U.S.A.

FRENCH, Howard W. American (born United States), b. 1957. **Genres:** History, Local History/Rural Topics. **Career:** Self-employed translator, 1979-80; University of Ivory Coast, assistant professor of English, 1980-82; Washington Post, stringer, 1981-86; New York Times, metropolitan reporter, 1986-90, correspondent, 1990, bureau chief, 1990-. Journalist and writer. **Publications:** A Continent for the Taking: The Tragedy and Hope of Africa, 2004. **Address:** New York Times, 229 W 43rd St., New York, NY 10036, U.S.A.

FRENCH, Judith E. American (born United States) **Genres:** Romance/Historical, Mystery/Crime/Suspense, Novels. **Career:** Writer. **Publications:** ROMANCE NOVELS: Tender Fortune, 1986; Starfire, 1987; By Love Alone, 1987; Bold Surrender, 1988; Windsong, 1988; Scarlet Ribbons, 1989; Lovestorm, 1990; Moonfeather, 1990; Highland Moon, 1991; Moon Dancer, 1992; Fortune's Mistress, 1993; Fortune's Flame, 1993; Fortune's Bride, 1994; Fierce Loving, 1994; Shawnee Moon, 1995; McKenna's Bride, 1995; Sundancer's Woman, 1996; Fire Hawk's Bride, 1997; Rachel's Choice, 1998; (with H. Howell and C. Faulkner) Castle Magic (collection), 1999; Morgan's Woman, 1999; The Irish Rogue, 2000; The Taming of Shaw MacCade, 2001; Falcon's Angel, 2002; (with D. Jordan and J. Wilson) Wedded Bliss (collection), 2003; At Risk, 2005; Blood Sport, 2008. ALEXANDER THE GREAT TRILOGY ROMANCE NOVELS: The Conqueror, 2003; The Barbarian, 2004; The Warrior, 2005. TAWES BAY SERIES: Blood Kin, 2006; Blood Ties, 2007. OTHER: (with S. Cameron, L.L. Miller and A. Stuart) To Love and to Honor, 1993. Contributer to periodicals. **Address:** c/o Author Mail, Dorchester Publishing, 200 Madison Ave., Ste. 2000, New York, NY 10016, U.S.A. **Online address:** jefnovels@judithefrench.com

FRENCH, Linda. (Linda Mariz). American (born United States), b. 1948. **Genres:** Mystery/Crime/Suspense, Novels, Young Adult Fiction, Literary Criticism And History, Mystery/Crime/Suspense. **Career:** Whatcom Community College, instructor in western civilization, 1972-73; Western Washington University, faculty, 1979-81. Writer. **Publications:** MYSTERIES:

Talking Rain, 1998; Coffee to Die For, 1999; Steeped in Murder, 1999. MYSTERIES AS LINDA MARIZ: Body English, 1992; Snake Dance, 1992. **Address:** Ruth Cohen Inc., PO Box 7627, Menlo Park, CA 94025-7627, U.S.A.

FRENCH, Nicci. *See* **FRENCH, Sean.**

FRENCH, Patrick. British (born England), b. 1966. **Genres:** History, Biography, Literary Criticism And History. **Career:** Free Tibet Campaign, director and co-founder, 1996-99. Writer. **Publications:** Younghusband: The Last Great Imperial Adventurer (biography), 1994; Liberty or Death: India's Journey to Independence and Division (history), 1997; Tibet, Tibet: A Personal History of a Lost Land, 2003; World is What It Is: The Authorized Biography of V.S. Naipaul, 2008; India, 2010. Contributor of articles for newspapers and periodicals. **Address:** c/o Author Mail, HarperCollins Publishers, 10 E 53rd St., 7th Fl., New York, NY 10022, U.S.A.

FRENCH, Philip (Neville). British (born England), b. 1933. **Genres:** Film, Literary Criticism And History, History, Music. **Career:** Bristol Evening Post, journalist, 1958-59; BBC Radio, senior talks and documentary producer, 1959-90; University of Texas, visiting professor, 1972; The Observer, film critic, 1978-, chief film critic; The Times, deputy film critic. **Publications:** (Ed. with M. Sissons) The Age of Austerity 1945-51, 1963, rev. ed., 1976; The Novelist as Innovator, 1966; (co-author) Films of Jean-Luc Godard, 1967; The Movie Moguls, 1969; Westerns: Aspects of a Movie Genre, 1973, rev. ed., 1977; Three Honest Men: Edmund Wilson, F.R. Leavis, and Lionel Trilling: A Critical Mosaic, 1980; The Third Dimension: Voices from Radio 3, 1983; Ariel at Bay: Reflections on Broadcasting and the Arts: A Festschrift for Philip French, 1990; (ed. with D. Rossell) Press Observed and Projected, 1991; (ed.) Malle on Malle, 1993; (ed. with K. Wlaschin) The Faber Book of Movie Verse, 1993; (with K. French) Wild Strawberries, 1995; (with K. French) Cult Movies, 2000; (with J. Petley) Censoring the Moving Image, 2007; I Found It at the Movies, 2011. **Address:** The Observer, Kings Pl., 90 York Way, London, GL N1 9GU, England. **Online address:** philip.french@observer.co.uk

FRENCH, Scot. American (born United States), b. 1959. **Genres:** Education. **Career:** University of Virginia, Corcoran Department of History, assistant professor, 2001-, adjunct assistant professor of history, research associate professor, Carter G. Woodson Institute for African American and African Studies, associate director, 1997-2006, Virginia Center for Digital History, director, 2006-10, Center for the Study of Local Knowledge, co-director. Writer. **Publications:** The Rebellious Slave: Nat Turner in American Memory, 2004; (with C. Barton and P. Flora) Booker T. Washington Elementary School and Segregated Education in Virginia, 2007. Contributor to books and journals. **Address:** Corcoran Department of History, University of Virginia, 102 Minor Hall, 1540 Jefferson Park Ave., PO Box 400180, Charlottesville, VA 22903-3246, U.S.A. **Online address:** sfrench@virginia.edu

FRENCH, Sean. (Nicci French). British (born England), b. 1959. **Genres:** Novels, Trivia/Facts, Recreation, Film, Children's Fiction, Young Adult Fiction. **Career:** British Vogue, theater critic, 1981-86; Sunday Times, deputy literary editor, 1981-86; New Society, deputy editor, 1986-88; Marie Claire, film critic, 1987-91; New Statesman (magazine), columnist, 1987-2000; Observer, Journalist. Writer. **Publications:** (Ed.) Fatherhood, 1992; (with K. French and P. French) The French Brothers' Wild and Crazy Film Quiz Book, 1992; The Imaginary Monkey, 1993; Patrick Hamilton: A Life, 1993; Bardot, 1994; Dreamer of Dreams, 1995; The Terminator, 1996; Jane Fonda, 1997; (ed.) The Faber Book of Writers on Writers, 1999. AS NICCI FRENCH: The Memory Game, 1997; The Safe House, 1998; Killing Me Softly: A Novel of Obsession, 1999; Beneath the Skin, 2000; The Red Room, 2001; Land of the Living, 2003; Secret Smile, 2003; Start from Here, 2004; Catch Me When I Fall, 2006; Until It's Over, 2008; Losing You, 2008; What to Do When Someone Dies, 2009; The Other Side of the Door, 2010; Complicit, 2009; Blue Monday, 2011. **Address:** 54 Lady Somerset Rd., London, GL NW5 1TU, England. **Online address:** seanicci@dircon.co.uk

FRENCH, Tana. Irish/American (born United States), b. 1973?. **Genres:** Novels. **Career:** PurpleHeart Theatre Co., liaison officer. Writer and actress. **Publications:** In the Woods (novel), 2007; The Likeness, 2008; Faithful Place, 2010; Broken Harbor, 2012. Contributor to periodicals. **Address:** Darley Anderson Agency, Estelle House, 11 Eustace Rd., London, GL SW6 1JB, England.

FRENCH, Vivian. Also writes as Louis Catt, Louis Catt. British/Scottish (born Scotland) **Genres:** Novels, Children's Fiction, Mystery/Crime/Suspense. **Career:** University of the West of England, visiting lecturer. Guardian and writer. **Publications:** Tottie Pigs Special Birthday, 1990; Tottie Pigs Noisy Christmas, 1990; It's a Go to the Park Day, 1991; One Ballerina Two, 1991; Baker Ben, 1991; Doctor Elsie, 1991; Christmas Mouse, 1992; Tillie McGillies Fantastical Chair, 1992; A Christmas Carol, 1992; Mary Poggs and the Sunshine, 1993; Once upon a Time, 1993; Jacksons Juniors, 1993; Ian and the Stripy Bath Plug, 1993; Why the Sea Is Salt, 1993; Mandy and the Purple Spotted Hanky, 1993; Kevin and the Invisible Safety Pin, 1993; Kim and the Sooper Glooper Torch, 1993; Under the Moon, 1993; Caterpillar Caterpillar, 1993; Hedgehogs Don't Eat Hamburgers, 1993; Little Ghost, 1994; The Apple Trees, 1994; The Little Red Hen and the Sly Fox, 1994; Princess Primrose, 1994; Little Tiger Goes Shopping, 1994; The Hedgehogs and the Big Bag, 1994; Fat Ginger and the Awful Aliens, 1994; Warren and the Flying Football, 1994; Spider Watching, 1994; Buster and the Bike Burglar, 1994; Mervyn and the Hopping Hat, 1994; Robbie and the Amazing Presents, 1994; Please Princess Primrose, 1994; Painter Bear, 1995; The Thistle Princess and Other Stories, 1995; A Walker Treasury: Magical Stories, 1995; Sea Dog Williams and the Frozen North, 1995; Olivers Vegetables, 1995; Morris the Mouse Hunter, 1995; Morris in the Apple Tree, 1995; Captain Jennifer Jellyfish Jones, 1995; First Mate Mutt and the Wind Machine Mutiny, 1995; Jolly Roger and the Underwater Treasure, 1995; A Song for Little Toad, 1995; Lazy Jack, 1995; Squeaky Cleaners in a Tip!, 1996; The Christmas Kitten, 1996; Morris and the Cat Flap, 1996; Squeaky Cleaners in a Hole!, 1996; Once upon a Picnic, 1996; Squeaky Cleaners in a Stew!, 1996; Bob the Dog, 1996; Little Tiger Finds a Friend, 1996; Molly in the Middle, 1996; Squeaky Cleaners in a Muddle!, 1996; Oh No Anna!, 1997; Zenobia and Mouse, 1997; Peter and the Ghost, 1997; A Christmas Star Called Hannah, 1997; Aesops Funky Fables, 1997; Guinea Pigs on the Go, 1997; Kelly and the Crime Club, 1997; Sleepover on Friday the Thirteenth, 1998; Sleepover on Friday the Thirteenth, 1998; Kick Back, 1998; Olivers Fruit Salad, 1998; The Thistle Princess, 1998; The Boy Who Walked on Water and Other Stories, 1998; I Spy ABC, 1998; Iggy Pigs Party, 1998; Write around the World: The Story of How and Why We Learnt to Write, 1998; Whale Journey, 1998; Iggy Pigs Big Bad Wolf Trouble, 1998; Lullaby Lion, 1998; Not Again Anna!, 1998; Iggy Pigs Skippy Day, 1998; Sleepover Girls Go Detective, 1999; Rainbow House, 1999; Tiger and the Temper Tantrum, 1999; Space Dog Visits Planet Earth, 1999; Space Dog to the Rescue, 1999; Space Dog Meets Space Cat, 1999; Big Fat Hen and the Red Rooster, 1999; Space Dog Finds Treasure, 1999; Tiger and the New Baby, 1999; The Snow Dragon, 1999; Iggy Pigs Snow Day, 1999; Iggy Pigs Shopping Day, 1999; Mrs Hippos Pizza Parlour, 1999; Iggy Pigs Dark Night, 1999; Iggy Pig at the Seaside, 1999; The Story of Christmas, 1999; Big Fat Hen and the Hairy Goat, 1999; Farmer Duck, 2000; The Three Billy Goats Gruff, 2000; Growing Frogs, 2000; The Gingerbread Boy, 2000; Were Going on a Bear Hunt, 2000; Falling Awake, 2000; This Is the Bear, 2000; Space Dog, 2000; Noahs Ark and Other Bible Stories, 2000; Little Rabbit Foo Foo, 2000; Swallow Journey, 2000; Space Dog and the Space Egg, 2000; The Kingfisher Book of Fairy Tales, 2000; Space Dog Goes to Planet Purrgo, 2000; Lets Go Anna!, 2000; Funky Tales, 2000; From Zero to Ten: The Story of Numbers, 2000; Mean Green Machine, 2001; Five Little Ducks, 2001; Ladybird Ladybird, 2001; Olivers Milk Shake, 2001; Big Bad Bug, 2001; Singing to the Sun and Other Magical Tales, 2001; Guinea Pigs Go to Sea, 2001; The Three Little Pigs, 2001; One Fat Cat, 2001; The Tiger and the Jackal: A Traditional Indian Tale, 2001; Jack and the Beanstalk, 2001; A Present for Mom, 2002; Baby Baby, 2002; Paying for It and Other Stories, 2002; Survivor and Other Stories, 2002; To Mum with Love, 2002; Wicked Chickens, 2003; Morris the Mouse Hunter, 2003; T. Rex, 2004; I Love You, Grandpa, 2004; Bert and the Burglar, 2004; Bill Bird's New Boots, 2004; I Wish I Was an Alien, 2005; Brian the Giant, 2005; Buck and His Truck, 2005; The Cat in the Coat, 2005; Pig in Love, 2005; Meet the Mammoth!, 2005; A Cat in a Coat, 2005; Sharp Sheep, 2005; The Magic Bedtime Storybook, 2005; Princess Charlotte and the Birthday Ball, 2005; Princess Alice and the Magical Mirror, 2005; Princess Sophia and the Sparkling Surprise, 2005; Princess Emily and the Beautiful Fairy, 2005; Henny Penny, 2006; Ellie and Elvis, 2006; Detective Dan, 2006; Princess Charlotte and the Enchanted Rose, 2006; Princess Katie and the Silver Pony, 2007; Princess Daisy and the Dazzling Dragon, 2007; Princess Emily and the Substitute Fairy, 2007; Princess Daisy and the Magical Merry-go-round, 2007; Princess Alice and the Glass Slipper, 2007; Princess Katie and the Silver Pony, 2007; Princess Katie and the Mixed Up Potion, 2007; Princess Emily and the Wishing Star, 2007; Singing To the Sun, 2008; Winter Wonderland, 2008; Robe of Skulls, 2008; Princess Olivia and the Velvet Cape, 2008; Princess Lauren and the Diamond Necklace, 2008; Princess Georgia and the Shimmering Pearl, 2008; Princess Jessica and the Best-Friend Bracelet, 2008; Princess Amy and the Forgetting Dust, 2008; Princess Sarah and the Silver Swan, 2009; Princess Lucy and the Runaway Puppy, 2009; Princess Isabella and the Snow-White Unicorn, 2009; Princess Hannah and the Little Black Kitten, 2009; Princess Grace and the Golden Nightingale, 2009; Princess Ellie and the Enchanted Fawn, 2009; Bag of Bones: the Second Tale From the Five Kingdoms, 2009; Princess Abigail and the Baby Panda, 2009; Heart of Glass: the Third Tale From the Five Kingdoms, 2010; Polly's Pink Pajamas, 2010; Yucky Worms, 2010; The Flight of Dragons: The Fourth Tales from the Five Kingdoms, 2011. SLEEPOVER CLUB SERIES: Sleepover on Friday the Thirteenth, 1998; Sleepover Girls Go Camping, 1999; Sleepover Girls at Camp, 2002. Contributor to periodicals. **Address:** 6 Wellington Pl., Leith, EH6 7EQ, England.

FRERE, S(heppard) S(underland). British (born England), b. 1916. **Genres:** Archaeology/Antiquities, History. **Career:** Epsom College, master, 1938-40; Lancing College, master, 1945-54; Canterbury Excavations, director, 1946-60; University of Manchester, lecturer in archaeology, 1954-55; Verulamium Excavations, director, 1955-61; University of London, Institute of Archaeology, reader, 1955-66, professor of archaeology of the Roman provinces, 1955-66; Oxford University, All Souls College, archaeology of the Roman empire, professor and fellow, 1966-83, emeritus fellow, 1983-; Royal Archaeological Institute, president, 1978-81. Writer. **Publications:** (Ed.) Problems of the Iron Age in Southern Britain, 1961; Britannia: A History of Roman Britain, 1967, 4th ed., 1999; (contrib.) Britannia Romana, 1971; Some Inscriptions from Roman Britain, 2nd ed., 1971; Verulamium Excavations, 3 vols., 1972-84; Excavations on the Roman and Medieval Defences of Canterbury, 1982; Excavations at Canterbury, vol. VII, 1987; (with J.K. St. Joseph) Roman Britain from the Air, 1983; (with F.A. Lepper) Trajan's Column: A New Edition of the Cichorius Plates, 1988; (with J.J. Wilkes) Strageath: Excavations within the Roman Fort, 1973-1986, 1989; Romanitas, 2006. **Address:** All Souls College, Oxford University, 27 High St., City Ctr., Oxford, OX OX1 4AL, England.

FREUD, Esther. British (born England), b. 1963. **Genres:** Novels, Plays/Screenplays. **Career:** Norfolk Broads (a women's theater company), co-founder. Writer. **Publications:** NOVELS: Hideous Kinky, 1992; Peerless Flats, 1993; Meeting Bilal, 1996; Gaglow, 1997; Summer at Gaglow, 1998; The Wild, 2000; The Sea House, 2003; Love Falls, 2007; Lucky Break, 2010. COLLECTION: (co-author) Ox-Tales: Water, 2009. Contributor to periodicals. **Address:** A. P. Watt Ltd., 20 John St., London, GL WC1N 2DR, England.

FREUD, Sophie. American/Austrian (born Austria), b. 1924. **Genres:** Autobiography/Memoirs, Novels, Psychology. **Career:** Simmons College, professor of social work, 1978-92, now professor emeritus of social work; Harvard University Extension, lecturer. Writer. **Publications:** My Three Mothers and Other Passions, 1988; (and ed.) Living in the Shadow of the Freud Family, 2007. Contributor of articles to periodicals. **Address:** School of Social Work, Simmons College, 51 Commonwealth Ave., Boston, MA 02116-2323, U.S.A. **Online address:** sophief@att.net

FREUDENBERGER, Herman. American/German (born Germany), b. 1922. **Genres:** Economics, Translations. **Career:** School of Insurance, lecturer, 1955-56; Rutgers University, lecturer, 1958-59; Brooklyn College, instructor in history, 1956-58, 1959-60; Montana State University, assistant professor of history, 1960-62; Tulane University, Department of Economics, associate professor, 1962-66, chairman, 1966-70, professor of economics, 1966-92, now professor emeritus; Vienna University of Economics and Business, visiting professor. Writer. **Publications:** The Waldstein Woolen Mill: Noble Entrepreneurship in Eighteenth-Century Bohemia, 1963; (contrib.) Wirtschafts-und-sozialgeschichtliche Problemeder fruehen Industrialisierung, 1968; (with G. Mensch) Von der Provinzstadt zur Industrieregion, 1975; The Industrialization of a Central European City: Brno and the Fine Woollen Industry in the 18th Century, 1977; (trans. and ed. with E. Larking) A Redemptorist Missionary in Ireland 1851-1854: Memoirs by Joseph Prost, 1998; Lost Momentum: Austrian Economic Development 1750s-1830s, 2003. Contributor to journals. **Address:** Department of Economics, Tulane University, 206 Tilton Hall, 6823 St. Charles Ave., New Orleans, LA 70118, U.S.A. **Online address:** hfreudeats@tulane.edu

FREUDENHEIM, Ellen. American (born United States) **Genres:** Money/Finance, Social Work, Politics/Government, Travel/Exploration, Young Adult

Non-fiction. **Career:** New Yorkers Against Gun Violence (NYAGV), co-founder, 1993. Researcher and freelance writer. **Publications:** The Executive Bride: A Ten-Week Wedding Planner, 1985; (with D.P. Wiener) Brooklyn: Where to Go What to Do How to Get There, 1991; Healthspeak: A Complete Dictionary of America's Healthcare System, 1996; Brooklyn: A Soup-to-Nuts Guide to Sites, Neighborhoods, and Restaurants, 1999; Looking Forward: An Optimists Guide to Retirement, 2004; Brooklyn: The Ultimate Guide to New York's Most Happening Borough, 3rd ed., 2004; Queens: What to Do, Where to Go in New York's Undiscovered Borough, 2006. **Address:** Wendy Sherman Associates, 450 7th Ave., Ste. 3004, New York, NY 10123, U.S.A.

FREUDENTHAL, Gad. Israeli (born Israel), b. 1944. **Genres:** Physics, Sciences, History, Theology/Religion, Cultural/Ethnic Topics. **Career:** Centre National de la Recherche Scientifique, Institute for the History of Science, director of research, 1982-, senior research fellow, 2005; Center for the History of Arabic and Medieval Science and Philosophy, researcher. Writer. **Publications:** Aristotle's Theory of Material Substance: Heat and Pneuma, Form and Soul, 1995; Torah et Science: Perspectives Historiques et Théoriques: études Offertes à Charles Touati, 2001; Science in the Medieval Hebrew and Arabic Traditions, 2005. EDITOR: Etudes sur Helene Metzger/Studies on Helene Metzger, 1990; (intro.) Scientific Growth: Essays On The Social Organization and Ethos of Science, 1991; Studies on Gersonides: A Fourteenth-Century Jewish Philosopher-Scientist, 1992; (intro.) Jewish Responses to AIDS, 1998; Science in Medieval Jewish Cultures, 2011. **Address:** Centre National de la Recherche Scientifique, Institut d'histoire des Sciences, 3, rue Michel-Ange, Paris, 75794, France. **Online address:** freudent@msh-paris.fr

FREUND, Diane. *See* Obituaries.

FREUND, Thatcher. American (born United States), b. 1955. **Genres:** Antiques/Furnishings. **Career:** Teacher, 1979; Howard, Prim, paralegal, 1979-82; New England Monthly, staff writer, 1986-89, editor. **Publications:** Objects of Desire: The Lives of Antiques and Those Who Pursue Them, 1994. **Address:** 704 E Franklin St., Chapel Hill, NC 27514-3823, U.S.A. **Online address:** thatcherfreund@hotmail.com

FREUNDEL, Barry. American (born United States) **Genres:** Theology/Religion. **Career:** Rabbi, 1990-; Baltimore Hebrew University, assistant professor of rabbinics; University of Maryland, adjunct instructor; Georgetown University, adjunct professor of law; George Washington University, adjunct lecturer; Ethics Review Board of the National Institute of Aging of the National Institutes of Health, consultant. Writer. **Publications:** Contemporary Orthodox Judaism's Response to Modernity, 2004. Contributor to journals. **Address:** Baltimore Hebrew University, 5800 Park Heights Ave., Baltimore, MD 21215, U.S.A. **Online address:** bfreundel@bhu.edu

FREWER, Glyn. (Mervyn Lewis). British (born England), b. 1931. **Genres:** Mystery/Crime/Suspense, Children's Fiction, Plays/Screenplays, Novels, Young Adult Fiction. **Career:** British Council, student officer, 1955; Spottiswoode Ltd., trainee copywriter, 1955-57, copywriter, 1957-; D'Arcy-Mac-Manus & Masius, staff, 1961-, creative controller, 1965-74, associate director, 1974-. **Publications:** Adventure in Forgotten Valley, 1962, rev. ed., 1964; Adventure in the Barren Lands, 1964, rev. ed., 1966; The Last of the Wispies, 1965; The Token of Elkin, 1970; Crossroad, 1970; (as Mervyn Lewis) Death of Gold, 1970; The Square Peg, 1972; The Raid, 1976; The Trackers, 1976; Tyto: The Odyssey of an Owl, 1977; Bryn of Brockle Hanger, 1980; Fox, 1984; The Call of the Raven, 1987. **Address:** Bolt & Watson Ltd., Cedar House, High St., Ripley, OX GU23 6AE, England.

FREY, James N. American (born United States), b. 1943. **Genres:** Novels, Literary Criticism And History, Biography, Young Adult Non-fiction. **Career:** Author and educator. **Publications:** The Last Patriot, 1984; The Armageddon Game, 1985; The Elixir, 1986; The Long Way to Die, 1987; U.S.S.A., 1987; How to Write a Damn Good Novel, 1987; Circle of Death, 1988; A Killing in Dreamland, 1988; Came a Dead Cat, 1991; Winter of the Wolves, 1992; How to Write a Damn Good Novel, II: Advanced Techniques for Dramatic Storytelling, 1994; The Key: How to Write Damn Good Fiction Using the Power of Myth, 2000; How to Write a Damn Good Mystery: A Practical Step-by-Step Guide from Inspiration to Finished Manuscript, 2004; Gift of the White Light: The Strange and Wonderful Story of Annette Martin, Psychic, 2008; How to Write a Damn Good Thriller: A Step-by-step Guide for Novelists and Screenwriters, 2010. Contributor to periodicals. **Address:** PO Box 7427, Berkeley, CA 94707, U.S.A. **Online address:** jnfrey@jamesnfrey.com

FREY, Julia (Bloch). American (born United States), b. 1943. **Genres:** Poetry, Art/Art History, Literary Criticism And History, Biography, Humanities, International Relations/Current Affairs, Language/Linguistics, Popular Culture, Social Commentary, Writing/Journalism, Education, Cultural/Ethnic Topics, Adult Non-fiction, Humor/Satire, Autobiography/Memoirs, Translations, Essays, Novels. **Career:** Brown University, instructor in French, 1972-73; University of Paris, lecturer, 1974-75; Yale University, lecturer in French, 1975-76; University of Colorado, professor of French, 1976-2001; University of San Diego, Law School, Paris Institute of International and Comparative Law, professor, 1979-89; writer and curator, 2002-. **Publications:** Toulouse-Lautrec: A Life (biography), 1994; Balcony View: A 9/11 Diary (non-fiction memoir), 2011. Contributor of articles to books and periodicals. **Address:** 16 rue Mabillon, Paris, 75006, France. **Online address:** noletjb@gmail.com

FREY, Linda (Sue). American (born United States), b. 1947?. **Genres:** History. **Career:** Denison University, visiting lecturer in history, 1971; University of Montana, assistant professor, 1971-76, associate professor, 1976-82, professor of European History, 1982-; Ohio State University, visiting professor, 1986; U.S. Military Academy, visiting professor, 1996-97, McDermott chair, 2000-01. Writer. **Publications:** WITH M. FREY: (trans. with R. Zylawy) Les Dieux Ont So if, 1978; (ed. with J.C. Rule) Observations from The Hague and Utrecht: William Harrison's Letters to Henry Watkins, 1711-1712, 1979; (ed. with J. Schneider) Women in Western European History, 1982; A Question of Empire: Leopold I and the War of Spanish Succession, 1701-1705, 1983; Frederick I: The Man and His Times, 1984; (with J. Schneider) Women in Western European History, 1984; (with J. Schneider) Women in Western European History, 1986; Societies in Upheaval: Insurrections in France, Hungary, and Spain in the Early Eighteenth Century, 1987; (ed.) The Treaties of the War of the Spanish Succession, 1995; The History of Diplomatic Immunity, 1999; The French Revolution, 2004; (ed.) Daily Lives of Civilians in Wartime Europe, 1618-1900, 2007. Contributor of articles to books and journals. **Address:** Department of History, University of Montana, Rm. LA 252, 32 Campus Dr., PO Box 6264, Missoula, MT 59812, U.S.A. **Online address:** linda.frey@umontana.edu

FREY, Marsha L. American (born United States) **Genres:** History, Bibliography, Area Studies, Literary Criticism And History, Social Sciences. **Career:** Ohio State University, teaching associate, 1970-71, lecturer, 1971-72; University of Oregon, visiting assistant professor, 1972-73; Kansas State University, assistant professor, 1973-79, associate professor, 1980-84, professor of history, 1984-, MASUA Honors lecturer, 1988-89; United States Military Academy, professor of history, 2000-01. Writer. **Publications:** WITH L. FREY: (trans. with R. Zylawy) A. France, Les Dieux Ont Soif, 1978; (ed. with J.C. Rule) Observations from the Hague and Utrecht: William Henry Harrison's Letters to Henry Watkins, 1711-1712, 1979; Societies in Upheaval: Insurrections in France, Hungary and Spain in the Early Eighteenth Century, 1987; The Treaties of the War of the Spanish Succession: An Historical and Critical Dictionary, 1995; The History of Diplomatic Immunity, 1999; French Revolution, 2004; (ed.) Daily Lives of Civilians in Wartime Europe, 1618-1900, 2007. COMPILER WITH L. FREY AND J. SCHNEIDER: (and ed.) Women in Western European History: A Select Chronological, Geographical, and Topical Bibliography from Antiquity to the French Revolution, 1982; (and ed.) Women in Western European History: A Select Chronological, Geographical and Topical Bibliography: The Nineteenth and Twentieth Centuries, 1984; (and ed.) Women in Western European History. First Supplement: A Select Chronological, Geographical and Topical Bibliography, 1986. Contributor of articles to books and journals. **Address:** Department of History, Kansas State University, 204 Eisenhower Hall, Manhattan, KS 66506-1002, U.S.A. **Online address:** mfrey@ksu.edu

FREY, Stephen W. American (born United States), b. 1960?. **Genres:** Money/Finance. **Career:** Westdeutsche Landesbank, vice-president of corporate finance; J.P. Morgan and Co., Department of Mergers and Acquisitions, staff; Westham Capital Partners, managing director. Writer. **Publications:** The Takeover, 1995; The Vulture Fund, 1996; Inner Sanctum, 1997; Legacy, 1998; Insider, 1999; Trust Fund, 2001; Day Trader, 2002; Silent Partner, 2003; Shadow Account, 2004; Chairman: A Novel, 2005; Protégé, 2006; Power Broker: A Novel, 2006; Fourth Order, 2007; The Successor, 2007; Forced Out, 2008; Hell's Gate, 2009; Heaven's Fury, 2010; Stephen Fury, 2010. **Address:** Westdeutsche Landesbank, 1211 Ave. of the Americas, 24th Fl., New York, NY 10036-8701, U.S.A. **Online address:** sfrey@westhamcapital.com

FREYD, Jennifer J.(Joy). American (born United States), b. 1957. **Genres:** Psychology. **Career:** Cornell University, assistant professor of psychology, 1983-87; University of Oregon, associate professor, 1987-92, professor of psychology, 1992-; Center for Advanced Study in the Behavioral Sciences, fellow, 1989-90; John Simon Guggenheim Memorial Foundation, fellow, 1989-90; American Association for the Advancement of Science, fellow, 1992; Aslan Counseling Center, counselor, 1992; Association for Psychological Science, fellow, 1994; Microsoft Corp., psychology editorial advisor, 1995; American Psychological Association, fellow, 1996; Journal of Trauma and Dissociation, co-editor, 2005, editor, 2006-; International Society for the Study of Trauma and Dissociation, fellow, 2009. **Publications:** Betrayal Trauma: The Logic of Forgetting Childhood Abuse, 1996; (with A.P. DePrince) Trauma and Cognitive Science: A Meeting of Minds, Science and Human Experience, 2001. Contributor to books and periodicals. **Address:** Department of Psychology, University of Oregon, 1227 Straub Hall, Eugene, OR 97403-1227, U.S.A. **Online address:** jjf@uoregon.edu

FREYDONT, Shelley. American (born United States), b. 1949. **Genres:** Mystery/Crime/Suspense, Novels, Romance/Historical, Young Adult Fiction. **Career:** California State University, professor, 1974-76; Louis Falco Dance Co., dancer, 1977-79; Twyla Tharp Dance, dancer 1979-85; American Ballroom Theater, 1986-90; dancer. Consultant and writer. **Publications:** LINDY HAGGERTY MYSTERY NOVELS: Backstage Murder, 1999; High Seas Murder, 2000; Midsummer Murder, 2001; Halloween Murder, 2002; A Merry Little Murder, 2004. KATIE McDONALD MYSTERY NOVELS: The Sudoku Murder, 2007; Sudden Death Sudoku, 2008; Serial Killer Sudoku, 2009; Beach Colors, fothcoming; A Fatal Fall, forthcoming. **Address:** 370 Ponfield Pl., Ridgewood, NJ 07450, U.S.A. **Online address:** sfreydont@aol.com

FREYER, Tony (Allan). American (born United States), b. 1947. **Genres:** Law, Economics, History, Biography, Politics/Government, Business/Trade/Industry, Reference. **Career:** Indiana University, lecturer in law, 1974-75, Bicentennial of the Constitution lecturer, 1984; University of Arkansas, assistant professor, 1976-80, associate professor of history, 1980-81; University of Alabama, associate professor, 1985-86, professor of history and law, 1986-90, University research professor, u990-; Harvard University, Harvard Business School, Harvard-Newcomen Postdoctoral Fellow, 1975-76, Charles Warren Center, fellow, 1981-82; Vanderbilt University, Martin Luther King, Jr. lecturer, 1991; University of Warsaw, Fulbright distinguished chair in American studies, 2000. Writer. **Publications:** Forums of Order: The Federal Courts and Business in American History, 1979; Harmony & Dissonance: The Swift and Erie Cases in American Federalism, 1981; The Little Rock Crisis: A Constitutional Interpretation, 1984; The Constitution Resisted and School Desegregation, 1985; (ed.) Justice Hugo L. Black and Modern America, 1990; Hugo L. Black and the Dilemma of American Liberalism, 1990, 2nd ed., 2008; Regulating Big Business: Antitrust in Great Britain and America, 1880-1990, 1992; Producers versus Capitalists: Constitutional Conflict in Antebellum America, 1994; (with T. Dixon) Discretion and Dependence: A History of the Alabama Federal Courts, 1994; (ed.) A Frank Johnson Reader, 1994; (with T. Dixon) Democracy and Judicial Independence: A History of the Federal Courts of Alabama, 1820-1994, 1995; (ed.) Defending Constitutional Rights, 2001; Antitrust and Global Capitalism, 1930-2004, 2006; Little Rock on Trial: Cooper v. Aaron and School Desegregation, 2007; (with L.M. Campbell) Freedom's Conditions in the U.S.-Canadian Borderlands in the Age of Emancipation, 2010; Rights Defied, forthcoming; American Praxis, forthcoming. Contributor of articles to journals. **Address:** School of Law, University of Alabama, PO Box 870382, Tuscaloosa, AL 35487-0382, U.S.A. **Online address:** tfreyer@law.ua.edu

FREZZA, Robert (A.). American (born United States), b. 1956. **Genres:** Science Fiction/Fantasy, Mystery/Crime/Suspense, Military/Defense/Arms Control, Young Adult Fiction. **Career:** U.S. Army Claims Service, Claims and Recovery Division, deputy chief of personnel, 1985-93; writer, 1993-. **Publications:** A Small Colonial War, 1989; McLendon's Syndrome, 1993; Fire in a Faraway Place, 1994; Cain's Land, 1995; The VMR Theory, 1996; The Black Hats, forthcoming. Contributor of books. **Address:** 8133 Turn Loop Rd., Glen Burnie, MD 21061-1110, U.S.A. **Online address:** rfrezza@juno.com

FRICCHIONE, Gregory. (Gregory Lewis Fricchione). American (born United States) **Genres:** Medicine/Health, Adult Non-fiction. **Career:** New York University-Bellevue Hospital Center, resident and chief resident in psychiatry; Massachusetts General Hospital, Psychopharmacology Unit, psy-

chiatrist, 1982-83, Cardiac Rehabilitation Unit, project psychiatrist and physician, 1982-83, fellow in consultation psychiatry and psychosomatic medicine, associate chief of psychiatry, 2002-; State University of New York, Health Science Center, Psychiatry Consultation Division, director; Harvard Medical School, associate professor of psychiatry, 1983-, professor of psychiatry, Brigham and Women's Hospital, director of the medical psychiatry service, 1993-2000, Carter Center Mental Health Program, director, 2000-02, Division of Psychiatry and Medicine, director, 2002-, Division of International Psychiatry, director, 2002-09, senior scientist, 2009-, Benson-Henry Institute for Mind Body Medicine, director; Auckland Hospital, visiting senior lecturer and psychiatric consultant, 1987-88; Mind-Body Medical Institute, Beth Israel-Deaconess Medical Center, director of research, 1998-2000. Writer. **Publications:** (With W. Ting) The Heart-Mind Connection: How Emotions Contribute to Heart Disease and What to Do About It, 2006; (as Gregory L. Fricchione) Compassion and Healing in Medicine and Society: On the Nature and Use of Attachment Solutions to Separation Challenges, 2011. Contributor to journals. **Address:** Department of Psychiatry, Massachusetts General Hospital, 55 Fruit St., Boston, MA 02114, U.S.A. **Online address:** gfricchione@partners.org

FRICCHIONE, Gregory Lewis. *See* **FRICCHIONE, Gregory.**

FRICK, Carole Collier. American (born United States) **Genres:** Fash Ion/Costume, History, Social Sciences, Design. **Career:** Southern Illinois University, Department of Historical Studies, associate professor and graduate advisor, professor and graduate director, chair of department. Writer and historian. **Publications:** Dressing Renaissance Florence: Families, Fortunes, & Fine Clothing, 2002; (contrib.) Italian Women Artists: from Renaissance to Baroque. Contributor to books and periodicals. **Address:** College of Arts & Sciences, Southern Illinois University, PO Box 1608, Edwardsville, IL 62026, U.S.A. **Online address:** cfrick@siue.edu

FRICKER, Christophe E. German (born Germany), b. 1978. **Genres:** Translations, Essays. **Career:** Duke University, lecturer; Junge Oper Rhein-Main, translator-in-residence, 2004-06, Markets & Management Studies, visiting assistant professor; Oxford University, faculty, 2004-06. Writer. **Publications:** (Ed. with J. Bonin) Dunkeldeutschland: zehn Jahre deutsche Einheit inihrer Provinz, 2000; (ed. with M.R. Goldschmidt) "Unser Ganzes Geheimnis Liegt im Du": Wolf van Cassel, 1946-1994, 2001; (ed. with J. Curran) Schiller's "On Grace and Dignity" in Its Cultural Context: Essays and a New Translation, 2005; (ed. with B. Pieger) Friedrich Hölderlin Zu Seiner Dichtung, 2005; (ed. and trans.) Living Together: Die Amerikanischen Dichter Edgar Bowers, Dick Davis und Timothy Steele, 2006; (trans.) S.A. Cooper, Augustine for Armchair Theologians, 2007; (ed. and intro.) Friedrich Gundolf, Friedrich Wolters: Ein Briefwechsel Aus Dem Kreis Um Stefan George, 2009; Stefan George: Gedichte für dic, 2011. Contributor to journals. **Address:** Department of Germanic Languages & Literature, Duke University, 111A Old Chemistry Bldg., Durham, NC 27708, U.S.A. **Online address:** cefl5@duke.edu

FRICKER, Mary. American (born United States), b. 1940. **Genres:** Business/Trade/Industry, Young Adult Non-fiction. **Career:** Russian River News, reporter and news editor, 1982-83; Press Democrat, editorial assistant, 1985-86, editorial writer, 1986-90, business reporter and copy editor, 1990-92, assistant business editor, 1992-; Stringer and consultant, 1989; College of William and Mary, assistant public relations director; Serendip Carpet Co., owner. **Publications:** (With S. Pizzo and P. Muolo) Inside Job: The Looting of America's Savings and Loans, McGraw, 1989. **Address:** c/o Denise Marcil, Literary Agency Inc., 685 W End Ave., New York, NY 10025-6819, U.S.A.

FRIED, Dennis F. American (born United States), b. 1946. **Genres:** Humor/Satire, History, Essays, Animals/Pets. **Career:** Eiffel Press, publisher and president, 1999-. Writer. **Publications:** A Tongue in the Sink: The Harrowing Adventures of a Baby Boomer Childhood, 2004; More Memoirs of a Papillon: Diary of a Mad Dog, 2005. **Address:** Eiffel Press, 431 Oak Point Rd., PO Box 339, Osprey, FL 34229-9265, U.S.A. **Online address:** eiffelpress@comcast.net

FRIED, Robert L. American (born United States) **Genres:** Education, Food And Wine, Sex. **Career:** University of Hartford, associate professor of educational leadership; Northeastern University, associate professor of education. Writer. **Publications:** The Passionate Teacher: A Practical Guide, 1995; The Passionate Learner: How Teachers and Parents Can Help Children Reclaim the Joy of Discovery, 2001; The Skeptical Visionary: A Seymour Sarason Education Reader, 2003; The Game of School: Why We All Play It, How It Hurts Kids, and What It Will Take to Change It, 2005; Great Food, Great Sex: The Three Food Factors for Sexual Fitness, 2006. Contributor to periodicals. **Address:** School of Education, Northeastern University, 50 Nightingale Hall, 39 Lake Hall, 360 Huntington Ave., Boston, MA 02115, U.S.A. **Online address:** r.fried@neu.edu

FRIEDBERG, Maurice. American/Polish (born Poland), b. 1929. **Genres:** International Relations/Current Affairs, Literary Criticism And History, Translations, History, Language/Linguistics. **Career:** City University of New York, Brooklyn College, instructor, 1951, Hunter College, Russian Division, associate professor of Russian and chairman, 1955-65; Harvard University, Russian Research Center, associate, 1953; Middlebury College, Russian Summer School, instructor, 1960, 1961; Columbia University, visiting assistant professor of Russian literature, 1961-62; Hebrew University of Jerusalem, Fulbright professor of Russian literature, 1965-66; Indiana University, professor of Slavic languages and literatures, 1966-75, Russian and East European Institute, director, 1967-71; University of Illinois, professor of Slavic languages and literatures and department head, 1975-2000, professor emeritus of Slavic languages and literatures, 2000-, Center for Advanced Study, associate; Ecole des Hautes Etudes en Sciences Sociales, director d'etudes associe, 1984-85; National Endowment for the Humanities, Summer Institute, director. Writer. **Publications:** Russian Classics in Soviet Jackets, 1962; Party and the Poet in the U.S.S.R., 1963; The Jew in Post-Stalin Soviet Literature, 1970; (co-author) Encyclopedia Judaica, 16 vols., 1971-72; Why They Left: A Survey of Soviet Jewish Emigrants, 1972; American Literature through the Filter of Recent Soviet Publishing and Criticism, 1976; A Decade of Euphoria: Western Literature in Post-Stalin Russia, 1954-64, 1977; Reading for the Masses: Popular Soviet Fiction, 1976-80, 1981; Russian Culture in the 1980s, 1985; How Things were Done in Odessa: Cultural and Intellectual Pursuits in a Soviet City, 1991; Literary Translation in Russia: A Cultural History, 1997. EDITOR: (and intro.) A Bilingual Collection of Russian Short Stories, 1964, (and trans. with R.A. Maguire) vol. II, 1965; The Young Lenin, 1972; (with H. Isham) Soviet Society Under Gorbachev: Current Trends and the Prospects for Reform, 1987; (with M.T. Choldin) The Red Pencil: Artists, Scholars, and Censors in the U.S.S.R., 1989. **Address:** Department of Slavic Languages and Literatures, University of Illinois, MC-173, 2090 Foreign Languages Bldg., 707 S Mathews St., Urbana, IL 61801, U.S.A. **Online address:** friedbrg@illinois.edu

FRIEDEBERG-SEELEY, Frank (J. B.). American/British (born England), b. 1912. **Genres:** Literary Criticism And History, Essays, Education. **Career:** Oxford University, part-time assistant lecturer, 1935-36; University of London, School of Slavonic and East European Studies, lecturer, 1943-57; University of Nottingham, senior lecturer and head of department of Slavonic studies, 1957-67; Columbia University, visiting professor of Russian literature, 1963-64; University of Pennsylvania, professor of Russian literature, 1967-71; State University of New York, professor of Russian literature, 1971-82, professor of comparative literature and chair of department of Slavic studies. Writer. **Publications:** (Trans. with J. Barnes) Leone Ebreo: The Philosophy of Love, 1937; (with S. Konovalov) Russian Prose Reader: Nineteenth Century Authors, 1945; (with H. Rapp) The Gateway Russian Course, 1963; Turgenev: A Reading of His Fiction, 1991; From the Heyday of the Superfluous Man to Chekhov: Essays on 19th Century Russian Literature, 1994; Saviour or Superman?: Old and New Essays on Tolstoy and Dostoevsky, 1999. Contributor to journals. **Address:** 404 Watters Crossing Ct., Allen, TX 75013, U.S.A.

FRIEDEN, Jeffry. American (born United States), b. 1953. **Genres:** Money/Finance, Politics/Government, Social Commentary, Economics, Institutions/Organizations, History. **Career:** University of California, Department of Political Science, staff, 1983-95; Harvard University, Department of Government, professor, 1995-. Writer. **Publications:** Banking on the World: The Politics of American International Finance, 1987; (ed. with D.A. Lake) International Political Economy: Perspectives on Global Power and Wealth, 1987, (with J.L. Broz and D.A. Lake) 5th ed., 2010; (co-author) Post Imperialism: International Capitalism and Development in the Late Twentieth Century, 1987; (co-ed.) Crisis in Central America: Regional Dynamics and U.S. Policy in the 1980s, 1988; Debt, Development and Democracy: Modern Political Economy and Latin America, 1965-1985, 1991; Studies in International Finance: Private Interest and Public Policy in the International Political Economy, 1993; (ed. with B. Eichengreen) The Political Economy of European

Monetary Unification, 1994, 2nd ed., 2001; (ed. with B. Eichengreen and J. von Hagen) Monetary and Fiscal Policy in an Integrated Europe, 1995; (ed. with B. Eichengreen and J. von Hagen) Politics and Institutions in an Integrated Europe, 1995; (ed. with D. Gros and E. Jones) The New Political Economy of European Monetary Unification, 1998; (ed. with B. Eichengreen) Forging an Integrated Europe, 1998; (ed. with E. Jones and F. Torres) Joining Europe's Monetary Club: The Challenge for Smaller Member States, 1998; (ed. with M. Pastor and M. Tomz) Modern Political Economy and Latin America: Theory and Policy, 2000; (ed. with E. Stein) The Currency Game: Exchange Rate Politics in Latin America, 2001; Global Capitalism: Its Fall and Rise in the Twentieth Century, 2006; (with D.A. Lake and K.A. Schultz) World Politics: Interests, Interactions and Institutions, 2010; (with M. D. Chinn) Lost Decades: The Making of America's Debt Crisis and the Long Recovery, 2011. **Address:** Department of Government, Harvard University, 211 CGIS Knafel Bldg., 1737 Cambridge St., Cambridge, MA 02138, U.S.A. **Online address:** jfrieden@harvard.edu

FRIEDENBERG, Robert V. (Robert Victor Friedenberg). American (born United States), b. 1943. **Genres:** Communications/Media. **Career:** Miami University, professor of communication, 1970-. Consultant and writer. **Publications:** (With J.S. Trent) Political Campaign Communication: Principles and Practices, 1983, 7th ed. 2011; Hear O' Israel: The History of American Jewish Preaching, 1654-1970, 1989; Theodore Roosevelt and the Rhetoric of Militant Decency, 1990; (ed.) Rhetorical Studies of National Political Debates, 1960-1988, 1990; Communication Consultants in Political Campaigns: Ballot Box Warriors, 1997; Notable Speeches in Contemporary Political Campaigns, 2002; George W. Bush's Rhetorical War on Terrorism: Year One, forthcoming. **Address:** Department of Communication, Miami University, 120 Williams Hall, 1601 University Blvd., Hamilton, OH 45011, U.S.A. **Online address:** friederv@muohio.edu

FRIEDENBERG, Robert Victor. See **FRIEDENBERG, Robert V.**

FRIEDL, Erika (Loeffler). American/Austrian (born Austria), b. 1940. **Genres:** Anthropology/Ethnology. **Career:** University of Chicago, Oriental Institute, research associate, 1964-65; Western Michigan University, instructor, 1968-69, assistant professor, 1971-78, associate professor, 1978-85, professor of anthropology, 1985-, Women's Studies Program, director, 1986-87, now professor emeritus; University of Michigan, lecturer; Franklin and Marshall College, lecturer; Harvard University, lecturer. Writer. **Publications:** Träger medialer Begabung im Hindukusch und Karakorum, 1966; Women of Deh Koh: Lives in an Iranian Village, 1989; (ed. with M. Afkhami) In the Eye of the Storm: Women in Post-Revolutionary Iran, 1994; (ed. with M. Afkhami) Muslim Women and the Politics of Participation: Implementing the Beijing Platform, 1997; Children of Deh Koh: Young Life in an Iranian Village, 1997; (ed. with M.E. Hegland) Ethnographic Fieldwork in Iran, 2004; Tales from a Persian Tribe: A Monograph, 2007. Contributor to periodicals. **Address:** Department of Anthropology, Western Michigan University, 1005 Moore Hall, Kalamazoo, MI 49008, U.S.A.

FRIEDLAND, Martin L(awrence). Canadian (born Canada), b. 1932. **Genres:** Law, Criminology/True Crime, History, Autobiography/Memoirs. **Career:** Osgoode Hall Law School, assistant professor of law, associate professor of law, 1961-65; University of Toronto, Faculty of Law, associate professor, 1965-68, professor of law, 1968-98, dean, 1972-79, university professor, 1985-98, professor of law emeritus and university professor emeritus, 1998-; Hebrew University, visiting professor, 1979; Tel Aviv University, visiting professor, 1979; Massey College, senior fellow, 1985-; Canadian Institute for Advanced Research, fellow, 1986-98; Writer. **Publications:** Detention before Trial: A Study of Criminal Cases Tried in the Toronto Magistrates' Courts, 1965; Cases and Materials on Criminal Law and Procedure, 2nd ed., 1968, 8th ed., 1997; Double Jeopardy, 1969; (ed.) Courts and Trials: A Multidisciplinary Approach, 1975; (with P.E.S. Jewett and L.J. Jewett) Access to the Law: A Study Conducted for the Law Reform Commission of Canada, 1975; National Security: The Legal Dimensions, 1979; The Trials of Israel Lipski: A True Story of a Victorian Murder in the East End of London, 1984; A Century of Criminal Justice: Perspectives on the Development of Canadian Law, 1984; The Case of Valentine Shortis: A True Story of Crime and Politics in Canada, 1986; (with S. Jackson and C. Pilkey) Report of the Task Force on Inflation Protection for Employment Pension Plans, 1988; (with S. Jackson and C. Pilkey) Research Studies, 1988; (ed.) Sanctions and Rewards in the Legal System: A Multidisciplinary Approach, 1989; Securing Compliance: Seven Case Studies, 1990; (with M. Trebilcock and K. Roach)

Regulating Traffic Safety, 1990; (ed.) Rough Justice: Essays on Crime in Literature, 1991; The Death of Old Man Rice: A True Story of Criminal Justice in America, 1994; A Place Apart: Judicial Independence and Accountability in Canada, 1995; Controlling Misconduct in the Military: A Study Prepared for the Commission of Inquiry into the Deployment of Canadian Forces to Somalia, 1996; The University of Toronto: A History, 2002; My Life in Crime and Other Academic Adventures, 2007. Contributer to periodicals. **Address:** Faculty of Law, University of Toronto, 78 Queen's Pk., Toronto, ON M5S 2C5, Canada. **Online address:** m.friedland@utoronto.ca

FRIEDLAND, William H(erbert). American (born United States), b. 1923. **Genres:** Agriculture/Forestry, Food And Wine, Industrial Relations, History. **Career:** Cornell University, assistant professor, 1961-64, associate professor, 1964-69; University of California, professor, 1969-91, acting dean of social sciences, 1988-90, professor emeritus of community studies and sociology, 1991-. Writer. **Publications:** Unions and Industrial Relations in Underdeveloped Countries, 1963; Unions, Labor and Industrial Relations in Africa, an Annotated Bibliography, 1965; Vuta Kamba: The Development of Trade Unions in Tanganyika, 1969; (with I.L. Horowitz) The Knowledge Factory, 1971; (with D. Nelkin) Migrant Agricultural Workers in America's Northeast, 1971; (with A.E. Barton and R.J. Thomas) Manufacturing Green Gold: Capital, Labor, and Technology in the Lettuce Industry, 1981; (co-author) Revolutionary Theory, 1982. EDITOR: (with C.G. Rosberg, Jr.) African Socialism, 1964; (with F. Buttel, L. Busch and A. Rudy) Toward a New Political Economy of Agriculture, 1991; (with A. Bonnano, L. Busch, L. Gouveia and E. Mingione) From Columbus to Conagra: The Globalization of Agriculture and Food, 1994. **Address:** University of California, College 8, 323, Santa Cruz, CA 95064, U.S.A. **Online address:** friedla@ucsc.edu

FRIEDLANDER, Henry (Egon). American/German (born Germany), b. 1930. **Genres:** History, Local History/Rural Topics, Law. **Career:** American History Association, War Document Project, staff, 1957-58; Louisiana State University, instructor in history, 1958-64; McMaster University, assistant professor, 1964-67; University of Missouri, assistant professor, 1967-70; City College, assistant professor of history, 1970-72, assistant professor of Jewish studies, 1972-75; City University of New York, Brooklyn College, professor of history in Judaic studies, 1975-2001, professor emeritus of history in Judaic studies, 2001-; United States Holocaust Memorial Museum, senior Ruth Meltzer fellow. Writer. **Publications:** (Ed. with G. Schwab) Detente in Historical Perspective: The First SUNY Conference on History and Politics, 1975; (ed. with S. Milton) The Holocaust: Ideology, Bureaucracy and Genocide-The San Jose Papers, 1980; (co-author) Jewish Immigrants of the Nazi Period in the U.S.A., 1981; (ed. with S. Milton) Archives of the Holocaust: An International Collection of Selected Documents, 1989; The German Revolution of 1918, 1992; The Origins of Nazi Genocide: From Euthanasia to the Final Solution, 1995; (with H. Langbein) People in Auschwitz, 2004; (ed. with N. Stoltzfus) Nazi Crimes and the Law, 2008. Contributor to periodicals. **Address:** Department of Judaic Studies, Brooklyn College, City University of New York, 3111 James Hall, 2900 Bedford Ave., Brooklyn, NY 11210-2850, U.S.A.

FRIEDLANDER, Michael W. American/South African (born South Africa), b. 1928. **Genres:** Physics, Astronomy, Sciences. **Career:** University of Cape Town, junior lecturer in physics, 1951-52; University of Bristol, research associate in physics, 1954-56; Washington University, assistant professor, 1956-61, associate professor, 1961-67, professor of physics, 1967-, professor emeritus, Department of Music, interim chairman, 1984-86; Imperial College of Science and Technology, visiting professor, 1962-63, 1971, Faculty of Arts and Sciences Faculty Council, chairman, University Senate Council, chairman; American Association of University Professors, vice-president; Encyclopedia Britannica, consultant. Writer. **Publications:** The Conduct of Science, 1972; Astronomy, from Stonehenge to Quasars, 1985; Cosmic Rays, 1989; At the Fringes of Science, 1995; A Thin Cosmic Rain: Particles from Outer Space, 2000. Contributor to journals. **Address:** Department of Physics, Washington University, 251 Compton, CB 1105, 1 Brookings Dr., St. Louis, MO 63130-4899, U.S.A.

FRIEDLANDER, Shems. Egyptian/American (born United States) **Genres:** Art/Art History, Poetry, Adult Non-fiction. **Career:** Parsons School of Design, professor of editorial communication, advertising and design, 1987-88; American University, lecturer, 1992-, senior lecturer in journalism and mass communication, 1994-, Apple Center for Graphic Communications, founding director, 1994-, Department of Journalism, professor, The Photographic Gal-

lery, director; Look, designer and art director. Writer and visual artist. **Publications:** (Contrib.) The Whirling Dervishes, Being an Account of the Sufi Order Known as the Mevlevis and Its Founder the Poet and Mystic Mevlana Jalalu'ddin Rumi, 1975; (with A.S. Muzaffereddin) Ninety-Nine Names of Allah: The Beautiful Names, 1978; When You Hear Hoofbeats, Think of a Zebra: Talks on Sufism, 1987; Sunlight, Poems, and Other Words, 1997; Rumi: The Hidden Treasure, 2001; Rumi and the Whirling Dervishes: Being an Account of the Sufi Order Known as the Mevlevis and Its Founder the Poet and Mystic Mevlana Jalalu'ddin Rumi, 2003. **Address:** The Photographic Gallery, American University, American University in Cairo Ave., PO Box 74, New Cairo, 11835, Egypt. **Online address:** shems_f@aucegypt.edu

FRIEDMAN, Aimee. American (born United States), b. 1979?. **Genres:** Young Adult Fiction, Novels, Romance/Historical. **Career:** Children's book author. **Publications:** YOUNG-ADULT NOVELS: South Beach, 2005; A Novel Idea, 2005; French Kiss, 2005; (with H. Abbott, M. de la Cruz and N. Malkin) Mistletoe, 2006; Breaking Up: A Fashion High Graphic Novel, 2007; Hollywood Hills, 2007; The Year My Sister Got Lucky, 2008; Sea Change, 2009. Work appears in anthologies. **Address:** Scholastic Inc., 557 Broadway, New York, NY 10012, U.S.A. **Online address:** aimee@aimeefriedmanbooks.com

FRIEDMAN, Alan Warren. American (born United States), b. 1939. **Genres:** Literary Criticism And History. **Career:** University of Texas, Department of English, instructor, 1964-66, assistant professor, 1966-69, associate professor, 1969-76, professor of English, 1976-, Faculty Senate, chair, 1987-89. Writer. **Publications:** Lawrence Durrell and the Alexandria Quartet: Art for Love's Sake, 1970; Multivalance: The Moral Quality of Form in the Modern Novel, 1978; William Faulkner, 1984; Fictional Death and the Modernist Enterprise, 1995; Party Pieces: Oral Storytelling and Social Performance in Joyce and Beckett, 2007. EDITOR: Forms of Modern British Fiction: A Symposium, 1975; (ed. with C. Rossman) Mario Vargas Llosa: Critical Essays, 1978; Critical Essays on Lawrence Durrell, 1987; (with C. Rossman and D. Sherzer) Beckett Translating/Translating Beckett, 1987; (with E. Carton) Situating College English: Lessons from an American University, 1996; Beckett in Black and Red: The Translations for Nancy Cunard's Negro Anthology, 2000. **Address:** Department of English, University of Texas, Parlin 108, 1 University Sta. B5000, Austin, TX 78712, U.S.A. **Online address:** friedman@mail.utexas.edu

FRIEDMAN, Andrew. American (born United States), b. 1967?. **Genres:** Food And Wine, Autobiography/Memoirs. **Career:** Writer, 1997-. **Publications:** (With A. Portale) Alfred Portale's 12 Seasons Cookbook, 2000; Chef on a Shoestring: More Than 120 Delicious, Easy-on-the-Budget Recipes from America's Best Chefs, 2001; (with S. Marchetto and S. Haas) Da Silvano Cookbook: Simple Secrets From New York's Favorite Italian Restaurant, 2001; (with T. Valenti) Welcome to My Kitchen: A New York Chef Shares His Robust Recipes and Secret Techniques, 2002; (with T. Valenti) Tom Valenti's Soups, Stews, and One-Pot Meals: 125 Home Recipes from the Chef-owner of New York City's Quest and 'Cesca, 2003; (with P. Luongo and M. Pulini) La Mia Cucina Toscana: A Tuscan Cooks in America, 2003; (with L. Tourondel) Go Fish: Fresh Ideas for American Seafood, 2004; (with B. Telepan) Inspired by Ingredients: Market Menus and Family Favorites from a Three-Star Chef, 2004; (with A. Portale) Alfred Portale Simple Pleasures: Home Cooking from Gotham Bar and Grill's Acclaimed Chef, 2004; (with M. Lomonaco) Nightly Specials: 125 Recipes for Spontanious, Creative Cooking at Home, 2004; (with D. Walzog) The New American Steakhouse Cookbook: It's Not Just Meat and Potatoes Anymore, 2005; (with T. Brennan) Artisanal Cooking: A Chef Shares His Passion for Handcrafting Great Meals at Home, 2005; (ed. with K. Witherspoon) Don't Try This At Home: Kitchen Disasters and Memorable Mishaps from the World's Greatest Cooks and Chefs, 2005; (with J. Bradley) The Red Cat Cookbook: 125 Recipes from New York City's Favorite Neighborhood Restaurant, 2006; (with W. Scheib) White House Chef: The Clintons, The Bushes, The Inaugurations, The State Dinners, The Picnics, The Family Meals and Everything in Between, 2007; (with W. Scheib) White House Chef: Eleven Years, Two Presidents, One Kitchen, 2007; (with D. Waltuck) Chanterelle: The Story and Recipes of a Restaurant Classic, 2008; (with M. Bernstein) Cuisine a Latina: Fresh Tastes and a World of Flavors from Michy's Miami Kitchen, 2008; (with T. Valenti) You Don't Have to be Diabetic to Love this Cookbook, 2009; Knives at Dawn: The American Quest for Culinary Glory at the Legendary Bocuse d'Or Competition, 2009; (with P. Luongo) Dirty Dishes: A Restaurateur's Story of Passion, Pain, and Pasta,

2009. **Address:** c/o Author Mail, Wiley Publishing, 111 River St., 5th Fl., Hoboken, NJ 07030, U.S.A.

FRIEDMAN, Barry E. American (born United States), b. 1958. **Genres:** Law, Politics/Government. **Career:** University of Alabama, professor; Davis, Polk & Wardwell, lawyer; Georgetown University, Law Center, adjunct professor; Vanderbilt University, School of Law, professor, 1986-99; New York University, School of Law, faculty, 1999-, Jacob D. Fuchsberg Professor of Law and vice dean, Furman Academic Scholars Program, founder and co-director. Writer. **Publications:** (Ed. with S.B. Burbank) Judicial Independence at the Crossroads: An Interdisciplinary Approach, 2002; The Will of the People: How Public Opinion Has Influenced the Supreme Court and Shaped the Meaning of the Constitution, 2009. **Address:** School of Law, New York University, 40 Washington Sq. S, New York, NY 10012, U.S.A. **Online address:** barry.friedman@nyu.edu

FRIEDMAN, Benjamin M. American (born United States), b. 1944. **Genres:** Economics. **Career:** Federal Reserve Bank of New York, research assistant, 1968; Federal Reserve Bank of Boston, staff consultant, 1968-69, consultant to the president, 1969-71; Federal Reserve Board, Division of Research and Statistics, assistant, 1969; Morgan Stanley and Co., economist, 1971-72; Harvard University, Department of Economics, assistant professor, 1972-76, associate professor, 1976-80, professor of economics, 1980-89, William Joseph Maier professor of political economy, 1989-, chair, 1991-94. Writer. **Publications:** Economic Stabilization Policy: Methods in Optimization, 1975; (ed.) New Challenges to the Role of Profit, 1978; Monetary Policy in the United States: Design and Implementation, 1981; (ed.) Changing Roles of Debt and Equity in Financing U.S. Capital Formation, 1982; (ed.) Corporate capital structures in the United States, 1985; (ed.) Financing Corporate Capital Formation, 1986; Day of Reckoning: The Consequences of American Economic Policy under Reagan and After, 1988; Implications of Increasing Corporate Indebtedness for Monetary Policy, 1990; (ed. with F.H. Hahn) Handbook of Monetary Economics, 1990; (ed. and intro.) Should the United States Privatize Social Security?, 1990; (with J. Agell and M. Persson) Does Debt Management Matter?, 1992; (ed. and intro.) Inequality in America: What Role For Human Capital Policies?, 1999; Risks and Impediments to U.S. Economic Expansion, 2003; The Moral Consequences of Economic Growth, 2005; (ed. and intro.) Offshoring of American Jobs: What Response from U.S. Economic Policy?, 2009; (ed. and intro.) Reforming U.S. Financial Markets: Reflections Before and Beyond Dodd-Frank, 2011. Contributor to periodicals. **Address:** Department of Economics, Harvard University, 127 Littauer Ctr., 12 Holyoke St., Cambridge, MA 02138-5014, U.S.A. **Online address:** bfriedman@harvard.edu

FRIEDMAN, Bonnie. American (born United States), b. 1958?. **Genres:** Adult Non-fiction. **Career:** University of Iowa, Department of English, teaching assistant, 1984-87; Dartmouth College, Department of English, lecturer, 1988-89; Drew University, Department of English, adjunct lecturer, 2003; New York University, Department of Creative Writing, adjunct instructor, 2003-08; University of North Texas, Department of English, assistant professor, 2008-. Writer. **Publications:** Writing Past Dark: Envy, Fear, Distraction and Other Dilemmas in the Writer's Life, 1993; The Thief of Happiness: The Story of an Extraordinary Psychotherapy, 2002; Brooklyn Spiritual, forthcoming. Works appear in anthologies and textbooks. Contributor to newspapers and magazines. **Address:** c/o Malaga Baldi, Baldi Agency, 19C, 233 W 99th St., New York, NY 10025, U.S.A. **Online address:** bonitafriedman@gmail.com

FRIEDMAN, Brandon. American (born United States), b. 1978. **Genres:** Military/Defense/Arms Control. **Career:** Vote Vets.org, vice chairman & editor; U.S. Army 101st Airborne Division, infantry officer; Individual Ready Reserve, captain. **Publications:** The War I Always Wanted: The Illusion of Glory and the Reality of War: A Screaming Eagle in Afghanistan and Iraq, 2007. Contributor to books and periodicals. **Address:** Dallas, TX , U.S.A. **Online address:** brandon@brandonrfriedman.com

FRIEDMAN, Bruce Jay. American (born United States), b. 1930. **Genres:** Novels, Novellas/Short Stories, Plays/Screenplays, Essays, Young Adult Fiction. **Career:** Magazine Management Co., publishers, editorial director, 1954-66. Novelist. **Publications:** Stern, 1962; Far from the City of Class and Other Stories, 1963; Mother's Kisses, 1964; (ed.) Black Humor, 1965; 23 Pat O'Brian Movies, 1966; A Change of Plan, 1966; Black Angels, 1966; Scuba Duba: A Tense Comedy, 1967; The Dick, 1970; Steambath (play), 1971; About Harry Towns, 1974; The Lonely Guy's Book of Life, 1978; Let's Hear It for a Beautiful Guy, 1984; Tokyo Woes, 1985; The Current Climate, 1989; The Slightly Older Guy, 1995; The Collected Short Fiction of Bruce Jay Friedman, 1995; (co-author) Hampton Shorts, 1996; A Father's Kisses, 1996; Even the Rhinos Were Nymphos (essays), 2000; Violencia, 2001; Lonely Guy, and, the Slightly Older Guy, 2001; Sexual Pensées, 2006; Three Balconies: Stories and a Novella, 2008. **Address:** 252 7th Ave., New York, NY 10001-7326, U.S.A.

FRIEDMAN, C(elia) S. American (born United States), b. 1957. **Genres:** Science Fiction/Fantasy, Young Adult Fiction, Novels. **Career:** Shenandoah University, faculty. Writer and designer. **Publications:** In Conquest Born, 1987; The Madness Season, 1990; This Alien Shore, 1998; The Erciyes Fragments, 1999; The Wilding, 2004; Feast of Souls, 2007; The Wings of Wrath, 2008; Legacy of Kings, 2011. COLDFIRE TRILOGY: Black Sun Rising, 1991; When True Night Falls, 1993; Crown of Shadows, 1995. **Address:** c/o Author Mail, DAW Books, 375 Hudson St., New York, NY 10014-3657, U.S.A. **Online address:** csfstuff@comcast.net

FRIEDMAN, Debra. Canadian (born Canada), b. 1955. **Genres:** Children's Non-fiction, Photography, Crafts. **Career:** Art photographer, 1980-; Village Square, liaison and marketing director. Writer. **Publications:** Picture This: Fun Photography and Crafts, 2003. **Address:** 18 Langford Ave., Toronto, ON M4J 3E3, Canada. **Online address:** debra.friedman@sympatico.ca

FRIEDMAN, George. American/Hungarian (born Hungary), b. 1949. **Genres:** Military/Defense/Arms Control, Politics/Government, Adult Non-fiction. **Career:** Dickinson College, professor of political science, 1974-92; American University, adjunct professor-in-residence, 1992-94; Louisiana State University, Center for Geopolitical Studies, founder and director, 1994-96; G.P.A. Strategic Forecasting Group (now Stratfor), founder, 1996-, chief intelligence officer, financial overseer, chief executive officer, chairman and director; Tulane University, adjunct professor, 1996. Writer. **Publications:** The Political Philosophy of the Frankfurt School, 1981; (with M. LeBard) The Coming War with Japan, 1991; (with M. Friedman) The Future of War: Power, Technology and American World Dominance in the Twenty-first Century, 1996; (co-author) The Intelligence Edge: How to Profit in the Information Age, 1997; America's Secret War: Inside the Hidden Worldwide Struggle between America and Its Enemies, 2004; The Next 100 Years: A Forecast for the 21st Century, 2009; The Next Decade, 2011. **Address:** Stratfor Global Intelligence, 221 W 6th St., Ste. 400, Austin, TX 78701, U.S.A. **Online address:** gfriedman@stratfor.com

FRIEDMAN, Kinky. American (born United States), b. 1944. **Genres:** Mystery/Crime/Suspense, Novels, Young Adult Fiction. **Career:** Peace Corps, staff, 1966-68; King Arthur & the Carrots Band, singer; Kinky Friedman and The Texas Jewboys Band, singer; Texas Monthly, columnist. **Publications:** KINKY FRIEDMAN MYSTERY SERIES: Greenwich Killing Time, 1986; A Case of Lone Star, 1987; When the Cat's Away, 1988; Frequent Flyer, 1989; Musical Chairs, 1991; The Kinky Friedman Crime Club, 1992 in US as Three Complete Mysteries, 1993; Elvis, Jesus and Coca-Cola, 1993; Armadillos and Old Lace, 1994; God Bless John Wayne, 1995; The Love Song of J. Edgar Hoover, 1996; Roadkill, 1997; Blast from the Past, 1998; Spanking Watson: A Novel, 1999; (with M. McGovern) Eat, Drink and Be Kinky: A Feast of Wit and Fabulous Recipes for Fans of Kinky Friedman, 1999; The Mile High Club, 2000; Steppin' on a Rainbow, 2001; Kinky Friedman's Guide to Texas Etiquette Or, How To Get to Heaven or Hell Without Going through Dallas-Fort Worth, 2001; Meanwhile Back at the Ranch, 2002; Kill Two Birds and Get Stoned, 2003; Great Psychedelic Armadillo Picnic: A Walk in Austin, 2004; Prisoner of Vandam Street: A Novel, 2004; 'Scuse Me While I Whip this Out: Reflections on Country Singers, Presidents and Other Troublemakers, 2004; Ten Little New Yorkers: A Novel, 2005. OTHERS: More Kinky Friedman: Musical Chairs/Frequent Flyer/Elvis, Jesus and Coca Cola, 1993; Texas Hold 'em: How I Was Born in a Manger, Died in the Saddle and Came Back as a Horny Toad, 2005; The Christmas Pig: A Fable, 2006; Cowboy Logic: The Wit and Wisdom of Kinky Friedman (and Some of His Friends); 2006; You Can Lead a Politician to Water, But You Can't Make Him Think: Ten Commandments for Texas Politics, 2007; What Would Kinky Do?: How to Unscrew a Screwed-up World, 2008; Kinky's Celebrity Pet Files, 2009; Heroes of a Texas Childhood, 2009. Contributor to periodicals. **Address:** c/o Esther Newberg, International Creative Management, 730 5th Ave., New York, NY 10019, U.S.A.

FRIEDMAN, Lawrence M. American (born United States), b. 1930. **Genres:** Education, Law. **Career:** D'Ancona, Pflaum, Wyatt, and Riskind, staff, 1955-57; St. Louis University Law School, assistant professor of law, 1957-60, associate professor of law, 1960-61; University of Wisconsin Law School, associate professor of law, 1961-65, professor of law, 1965-68; Stanford University School of Law, visiting professor of law, 1966-67, professor of law, 1968-75, Marion Rice Kirkwood professor of law, 1976-, professor of political science, professor of history; Center for Advanced Study in the Behavioral Sciences, fellow, 1974-; Law and Society Association, president, 1979-81; American Society for Legal History, vice president, 1987-89, president, 1990-92, honorary fellow, 1997; International Sociological Association, Research Committee on the Sociology of Law, director, 1990-95; University of London, University College, Faculty of Laws, honorary professor, 2001-. Writer. **Publications:** Contract Law in America, 1965; Government and Slum Housing: A Century of Frustration, 1968; (with S. Macaulay) Law and the Behavioral Sciences, 1969, 2nd ed., 1977; A History of American Law, 1973, 3rd ed., 2005; The Legal System: A Social Science Perspective, 1975; Law and Society: An Introduction, 1977; (with R.V. Percival) The Roots of Justice: Crime and Punishment in Alameda County, California, 1870-1910, 1981; American Law, 1984, 2nd ed., 1998; Total Justice, 1985; Your Time Will Come, 1984; Introduccion al derecho norte americano, 1988; The Republic of Choice, 1990; Crime and Punishment in American History, 1993; (with G. Fisher) Crime Conundrum: Essays on Criminal Justice, 1997; The Horizontal Society, 1999; Law in America: A Short History, 2002; American Law in the 20th Century, 2002; Private Lives: Families, Individuals, and the Law, 2004; Guarding Life's Dark Secrets: Legal and Social Controls over Reputation, Propriety, and Privacy, 2007; (with S. Macaulay and E. Mertz) Law in Action: A Socio-Legal Reader, 2007; Dead Hands: A Social History of Wills, Trusts, and Inheritance Law, 2009; (with R. Perez-Perdomo and M. Gomez) Law in Many Societies, 2011; (with J. Grossman) Inside the Castle: Law and the Family in 20th Century America, 2011. EDITOR: (with H.N. Scheiber) American Law and the Constitutional Order, 1978; (with J.H. Merryman and D.S. Clark) Law and Social Change in Mediterranean Europe and Latin America, 1979; (with S. Macaulay and J. Stookey) Law and Society: Readings on the Social Study of Law, 1995; (with H.N. Scheiber) Legal Culture and the Legal Profession, 1996; (with R. Pérez-Perdomo) Legal Culture in the Age of Globalization: Latin America and Latin Europe, 2003; (ed. with H.F. Fierro and R.P. Perdomo) Culturas juridicas latinas de Europa y America en tiempos de globalizacion, 2003. **Address:** School of Law, Stanford University, 559 Nathan Abbott Way, Stanford, CA 94305-8602, U.S.A. **Online address:** lmf@stanford.edu

FRIEDMAN, Lawrence S(amuel). American (born United States), b. 1936. **Genres:** Literary Criticism And History, Biography. **Career:** Stephens College, instructor in Humanities, 1965; Indiana University-Purdue University, assistant professor, associate professor, professor, 1965-, now professor emeritus of English; Warsaw University, visiting professor, 1979-81. Writer. **Publications:** Understanding Isaac Bashevis Singer, 1988; Understanding Cynthia Ozick, 1991; William Golding, 1993; The Cinema of Martin Scorsese, 1997. Contributor to books and periodicals. **Address:** Department of English and Linguistics, Indiana University-Purdue University, 2101 E Coliseum Blvd., Fort Wayne, IN 46805-1499, U.S.A. **Online address:** ljfriedm@indiana.edu

FRIEDMAN, Matthew. Canadian/American (born United States), b. 1940. **Genres:** Writing/Journalism, Business/Trade/Industry. **Career:** InternetWeek, associate editor; Concordia University, Department of Journalism, lecturer. **Publications:** Fuzzy Logic: Dispatches from the Information Revolution, 1997; (with M. Blanshay) Understanding B2B, 2001. Contributor of articles to newspapers and periodicals. **Address:** Vehicule Press, PO Box 125, Pl. du Parc Sta., Montreal, QC H2X 4A3, Canada. **Online address:** mwf@total.net

FRIEDMAN, Norman. American (born United States), b. 1925. **Genres:** Poetry, Literary Criticism And History, Psychology, History. **Career:** Harvard University, teaching fellow, 1950-52; University of Connecticut, Department of English, instructor, 1952-57, assistant professor, 1957-61, associate professor of English, 1961-63; City University of New York, Queens College, associate professor, 1963-67, professor of English, 1968-88, professor emeritus, 1988-, Gestalt Therapy Center of Queens, director, 1984-, Gestalt Center for Psychotherapy and Training, academic director, 1996-2000, executive co-director, 2000-03, academic consultant, 2003-, academic dean emeritus; New School for Social Research, faculty, 1964-66, Fulbright lecturer in France, 1966-67; E.E. Cummings Society, coordinator, editor. **Publications:**

E.E. Cummings: The Art of His Poetry, 1960; (with C.A. McLaughlin) Poetry: An Introduction to Its Form and Art, 1961, rev. ed., 1963; (with C.A. McLaughlin) Logic, Rhetoric, and Style, 1963; E.E. Cummings: The Growth of a Writer, 1964; E.E. Cummings: A Collection of Critical Essays, 1972; Form and Meaning in Fiction, 1975; The Magic Badge: Poems 1953-1984, 1984; The Intrusions of Love: Poems, 1992; (Re)Valuing Cummings: Further Essays on the Poet, 1962-1993, 1996; Seapower and Space: Navies in the Missile Age, 2000; Naval Firepower: Battleship Guns and Gunnery in the Dreadnought Era, 2007; British Destroyers: From Earliest Days to the Second World War, 2009; Naval Weapons of World War One: Guns, Torpedoes, Mines and Asw Weapons of All Nations, 2011. CONTRIBUTOR: New Voices 2: American Writing Today, 1955; The National Poetry Anthology 1958, 1958; Lyrics of Love: Best New Love Poems, 1963, 1963; Best Poems of 1963: Borestone Mountain Poetry Awards, 1964, 1964; Best Poems of 1966: Borestone Mountain Poetry Awards, 1967; May My Words Feed Others, 1974; Passage IV, 1978. Contributor to books. **Address:** Gestalt Therapy Center of Queens, 33-54 164th St., Flushing, NY 11358-1442, U.S.A. **Online address:** nfriedman18@aol.com

FRIEDMAN, Paul (Alan). American (born United States), b. 1937. **Genres:** Novels, Novellas/Short Stories, Medicine/Health. **Career:** University of Wisconsin, instructor, 1964-66, assistant professor, 1966-68; University of Illinois, assistant professor, 1968-71, associate professor of English, 1971-, professor, now professor emeritus. Writer. **Publications:** STORIES: And If Defeated Allege Fraud, 1971; Serious Trouble, 1986; (with D.L. Hayes and M.A. Lloyd) Cardiac Pacing and Defibrillation: A Clinical Approach, 2000, (ed. with D.L. Hayes) 2nd ed. as Cardiac Pacing, Defibrillation and Resynchronization: A Clinical Approach, 2008. **Address:** Department of English, University of Illinois, English 300, 608 S Wright St., Urbana, IL 61801, U.S.A. **Online address:** pfriedma@illinois.edu

FRIEDMAN, Philip (J.). American (born United States), b. 1944. **Genres:** Novels, Plays/Screenplays, Young Adult Non-fiction, Literary Criticism And History. **Career:** The High Frontier Co., general partner and chief executive officer, 1979-84; Sovereign International Inc., president and chief executive officer, 1988-89; Learning in Focus Inc., director, 1993-; MaxiVision Cinema Technology, senior vice president and general counsel, 1998-2003. Writer. **Publications:** Rage, 1972; Termination Order: A Novel, 1979; Act of Love, Act of War, 1979; (with G. Eisen) Pilates Method of Physical and Mental Conditioning, 1980; Reasonable Doubt: A Novel, 1990; Inadmissable Evidence: A Novel, 1992; Grand Jury: A Novel, 1996; No Higher Law, 1999; (with G. Eisen) Pilates Method of Physical and Mental Conditioning, 2005. Contributor to periodicals. **Address:** c/o Michael Rudell, Franklin, Weinrib, Rudell and Vassallo, 488 Madison Ave., New York, NY 10022, U.S.A.

FRIEDMAN, Rebecca. American (born United States), b. 1968. **Genres:** History. **Career:** Harvard University, research assistant, 1991-92; University of Michigan, Michigan Feminist Studies, editor, 1993-94; Center for Jewish History, intern, 1995; University of Maryland, Department of History, instructor, 1998-99; Florida International University, Department of History/Humanities Program, assistant professor, 2000-06, associate professor, 2006-, Women's Studies Center, assistant director, 2005-06, Department of History, director of European studies program, 2006-, Miami-Florida European Union Center of Excellence, co-director. Writer. **Publications:** (Contrib.) The Encyclopedia of the Russian Women's Movement, 2001; (ed. with B.E. Clemens and D. Healey) Russian Masculinities in History and Culture, 2002; Masculinity, Autocracy and the Russian University, 1804-1863, 2005; (ed. with M. Thiel) European Identity and Culture: Narratives of Transnational Belongings, 2011; Domestic Interiors and Modern Imaginings: A Cultural History of the Russian Home, forthcoming. Contributor to journals. **Address:** European Studies, Florida International University, SIPA 507, Modesto A. Maidique Campus, 11200 SW 8th St., Miami, FL 33199, U.S.A. **Online address:** rebecca.friedman@fiu.edu

FRIEDMAN, Ron. (Ronald M. Friedman). American (born United States), b. 1943. **Genres:** Law, Novels. **Career:** Writer and real estate attorney. **Publications:** (With B.N. Henszey) Real Estate Law, 1979, 5th ed., 2006; Pennsylvania Guide to Real Estate Licensing Examinations for Salespersons and Brokers, 1981; (with B.N. Henszey) Protecting Your Sales Commission: Professional Liability in Real Estate, 1982; Pennsylvania Landlord-Tenant Law and Practice, 1988, 3rd ed., 2001; And Nothing But the Truth (novel), 1995; (ed.) Ladner Pennsylvania Real Estate Law, 5th ed., 2006. **Address:** PO Box 10362, State College, PA 16805, U.S.A.

FRIEDMAN, Ronald M. *See* **FRIEDMAN, Ron.**

FRIEDMAN, Ronald S(amuel). American (born United States), b. 1962. **Genres:** Chemistry. **Career:** Harvard University, teaching assistant, 1984-85; Harvard-Smithsonian Center for Astrophysics, research assistant, 1984-89; University of Minnesota, postdoctoral research associate, 1989-91; Indiana University-Purdue University, Department of Chemistry, assistant professor, 1991-97, associate professor, 1997-2004, professor of chemistry and chair, 2004-. Writer. **Publications:** (With P.W. Atkins) Molecular Quantum Mechanics, 3rd ed., 1996, 5th ed., 2010; (with P.W. Atkins) Solutions Manual for Molecular Quantum Mechanics, 3rd ed., 1997; (with P. Atkins and J. de Paula) Quanta, Matter, and Change, 2009. Contributor to books and journals. **Address:** Department of Chemistry, Indiana University-Purdue University, Rm. 496, Science Bldg., 2101 E Coliseum Blvd., Fort Wayne, IN 46805-1499, U.S.A. **Online address:** friedmar@ipfw.edu

FRIEDMAN, Rosemary. Also writes as Rosemary Tibber, Robert Tibber. British (born England), b. 1929. **Genres:** Novels, Plays/Screenplays, Young Adult Fiction. **Career:** Writer. **Publications:** NOVELS: The Life Situation, 1977; The Long Hot Summer, 1980; Proofs of Affection, 1982; A Loving Mistress, 1983; Rose of Jericho, 1984; A Second Wife, 1986; To Live in Peace, 1987; An Eligible Man, 1989; Golden Boy, 1994; Vintage, 1996; The Writing Game, 1999; Intensive Care, 2001; Paris Summer, 2004; (comp.) Writer's Commonplace Book, 2006; Life is a Joke: A Writer's Memoir, 2010. AS ROBERT TIBBER: No White Coat, 1957; Love on My List, 1959; We All Fall Down, 1960; Patients of a Saint, 1961; The Fraternity, 1963; The Commonplace Day, 1964; Aristide, 1966; The General Practice, 1967; (contrib.) Confrontations with Judaism (symposium), 1967. AS ROSEMARY TIBBER: Practice Makes Perfect, 1969. OTHERS: Aristide (juvenile), 1966; Aristide in Paris (juvenile), 1987. **Address:** 3 Cambridge Gate, Apt. 5, Regent's Pk., London, GL NW1 4JX, England. **Online address:** rosemaryfriedman@hotmail.com

FRIEDMAN, Stewart D. American (born United States), b. 1952?. **Genres:** Business/Trade/Industry, Psychology. **Career:** Dartmouth Medical School, psychotherapist, 1975-78; State University of New York, counseling psychologist, 1978-80; University of Pennsylvania, Wharton School of Business, 1984-, practice professor of management, director of academic affairs, undergraduate division, 1991-92, Wharton Work/Life Integration Project, founding director, 1991-, Wharton Leadership Program, founding director, 1992-99; Ford Motor Co., Leadership Development Center, director, 1999-2001. Writer. **Publications:** Leadership Succession Systems and Corporate Performance, 1985; Leadership Succession, 1987; (ed. with J. DeGroot and P.M. Christensen) Integrating Work and Life: The Wharton Resource Guide, 1998; (with J.H. Greenhaus) Work and Family-llies or Enemies? What Happens When Business Professionals Confront Life Choices, 2000; Total Leadership: Be a Better Leader, Have a Richer Life, 2008. **Address:** Wharton School, University of Pennsylvania, 3620 Locust Walk, Philadelphia, PA 19104, U.S.A. **Online address:** friedman@wharton.upenn.edu

FRIEDMAN, Thomas L(oren). American (born United States), b. 1953. **Genres:** International Relations/Current Affairs, History, Geography. **Career:** Ball bearing Co., vice president; United Press Intl., staff correspondent, 1978-79, middle east correspondent, 1979-81; New York Times, financial reporter, 1981-82, Beirut bureau chief, 1982-84, Jerusalem bureau chief, 1984-89, chief diplomatic correspondent, 1989-92, chief white house correspondent, 1992-94, international economics correspondent, 1994-95, foreign affairs columnist, 1995-; Harvard University, visiting lecturer, 2000, 2005; Brandeis University, trustee, 2004-. Writer. **Publications:** (Intro.) War Torn, 1984; From Beirut to Jerusalem, 1989; (with R. Rhodes) Writing in an Era of Conflict, 1990; The Lexus and the Olive Tree, 1999, rev. ed., 2000; Longitudes and Attitudes: Exploring the World After September 11, 2002; The World is Flat: A Brief History of the Twenty-First Century, 2005, rev. ed., 2007; Hot, Flat and Crowded: Why We Need a Green Revolution and How It Can Renew America, 2008; (with M. Mandelbaum) That Used to be Us: How America Fell Behind in the World it Invented and How We Can Come Back, 2011. Contributor to magazines and periodicals. **Address:** New York Times, 1627 1st St. NW, Washington, DC 20006, U.S.A. **Online address:** publicity@picadorusa.com

FRIEDMANN, Daniel. Israeli (born Israel), b. 1936. **Genres:** Adult Nonfiction. **Career:** Supreme Court of Israel, law clerk, 1959-61; Hebrew University of Jerusalem, instructor, 1966-68; Tel Aviv University, senior lecturer,

1968-70, associate professor, 1970-73, professor of law, 1973-, dean of law faculty, 1974-78, Cegla Institute for Comparative and Private International Law, founding member and director, 1986-91, College of Management, founding member, Law School, dean, 1990-97, Danielle Rubinstein chair of comparative private law, 2000; Harvard University Law School, visiting professor, 1978-79; Queen Mary College, W.G. Hart visiting professor, 1982-83; University of Pennsylvania, visiting professor, 1986-87; Fordham University, visiting professor, 2002-03. Writer. **Publications:** Dine a'śiyat osher ve-lo ba-mishpat, 1970, 2nd ed., 1998; The Effect of Foreign Law on the Law of Israel, 1975; Sefer Lovenberg, 1987; Rules for Free International Trade in Services: A Symposium, 1990; ḥozim, 1991; Conflict Resolution in International Trade: A Symposium, 1993; Dine ḥiyuvim-helek kelali, 1994; Good Faith and Fault in Contracts, 1995; Ha-ratsaḥta ve-gam yarashta: Mishpat, musar ve-hevrah be-sipure ha-Mikra, 2000; Human Rights in Private Law, 2001; To Kill and Take Possession: Law, Morality, and Society in Biblical Stories, 2002; (with A. Barak) Sefer Menasheh Shayah, 2006; Dat ve-din, 2009. **Address:** Tel Aviv University, Rm. 430, Minkoff Bldg., PO Box 39040, Ramat Aviv, 69978, Israel. **Online address:** frie@post.tau.ac.il

FRIEDMANN, Patty. American (born United States), b. 1946. **Genres:** Novels, Novellas/Short Stories, Humor/Satire, E-books, Young Adult Fiction. **Career:** Writer. **Publications:** Too Smart to Be Rich: On Being a Yuffie (humor), 1987. NOVELS: The Exact Image of Mother, 1991; Eleanor Rushing, 1999; Odds, 2000; Secondhand Smoke, 2002; Side Effects: A New Orleans Love Story, 2005; A Little Bit Ruined, 2007; Taken Away, 2010. Contributor to journals, magazines and newspapers. **Address:** 8330 Sycamore Pl., New Orleans, LA 70118, U.S.A. **Online address:** afreelunch@aol.com

FRIEDMANN, Yohanan. Israeli (born Israel), b. 1936. **Genres:** History, Theology/Religion. **Career:** Hebrew University, Institute of Asian Studies and African Studies, chair, 1975-78, Graduate School, chair, 1980-83, dean of humanities, 1985-88, Department of Arabic Language and Literature, chair, 2002-04, now Max Schloessinger professor emeritus of Islamic studies; Israel Academy of Sciences and Humanities, Division of Humanities, chair, 2007-. Writer. **Publications:** Shaykh Ahmad Sirhindi: An Outline of His Thought and a Study of His Image in the Eyes of Posterity, 1971; Islam in Asia, 1984; Ha-Nevuah be-mahashevet ha-tenuah ha-Ahmadit be-Islam, 1984; Prophecy Continuous: Aspects of Ahmadi Religious Thought and Its Medieval Background, 1989; The Naqshbandis and Awrangzeb: A Reconsideration, 1990; Husain Ahmad Madani, 1992; (trans.) The History of Tabari: The Battle of al-Qadisiyya and the Conquest of Syria and Palestine, 1992; Jam iyyat al-ùlama-'i Hind, 1995; Ahmadiyya, 1995, vol. I, 2003; The Messianic Claim of Ghulam Ahmad, 1998; Classification of Unbelievers in Sunni Muslim Law and Tradition, 1998; Conditions of Conversion in Early Islam, 2000; Messianismus im Islam, vol. V, 2003; Chiliasmus im Islam, vol. II, 2003; Tolerance and Coercion in Islam: Interfaith Relations in the Muslim Tradition, 2003. **Address:** Institute of Asian and African Studies, Hebrew University of Jerusalem, Jerusalem, 91905, Israel. **Online address:** msyfried@mscc.huji.ac.il

FRIEDRICH, Paul. American (born United States), b. 1927. **Genres:** Poetry, Anthropology/Ethnology, Language/Linguistics, Humanities. **Career:** Yale University, research assistant, 1952-55; University of Connecticut, instructor in anthropology and sociology, 1956-57; Harvard University, instructor in anthropology, 1957-58; University of Pennsylvania, assistant professor of anthropology and linguistics, 1959-62; University of Chicago, associate professor, 1962-67, professor of anthropology and linguistics, 1967-, Graham School, professor, 1998-, Department of Slavic Languages and Literatures, associate, now professor emeritus of anthropology. Writer. **Publications:** (With R. Burling) The Cross-Cultural Study of Semantic Structure: Final Report, 1964; On the Meaning of the Tarascan Suffixes of Space, 1969; Proto-Indo-European Trees, 1970; Agrarian Revolt in a Mexican Village, 1970; The Tarascan Suffixes of Locative Space: Meaning and Morphotactics, 1971; Phonology of Tarascan, 1975; Proto-Indo-European Syntax, 1975; Neighboring Leaves Ride This Wind, 1976; The Meaning of Aphrodite, 1978; Language, Context and the Imagination, 1979; Bastard Moons, 1979; (with J. Greenberg and D. Hymes) On Linguistic Anthropology, 1980; Redwing, 1982; The Language Parallax: Linguistic Relativism and Poetic Indeterminacy, 1986; The Princes of Naranja: An Essay in Anthrohistorical Method, 1986; (co-ed.) Russia and Eurasia/China, 1994; Music in Russian Poetry, 1998; The Gita within Walden, 2008. **Address:** Department of Anthropology, University of Chicago, 5836 Haskell Hall, S Greenwood Ave., 1126 E 59th St., Chicago, IL 60637, U.S.A.

FRIEL, Brian. Irish (born Ireland), b. 1929. **Genres:** Novels, Novellas/Short Stories, Plays/Screenplays, Literary Criticism And History, Music. **Career:** Teacher, 1950-60; writer, 1960-; Tyrone Guthrie Theatre, observer, 1963; Field Day Theatre Co., co-founder, 1980. **Publications:** A Saucer of Larks (stories), 1962; Philadelphia, Here I Come!, 1965; The Gold in the Sea: Stories, 1966; Mr. Sing-Meines-Herzens-Freude, 1966; Loves of Cass McGuire, 1967; Lovers, 1968; Crystal and Fox, 1970; The Mundy Scheme, 1970; The Gentle Island, 1973; The Freedom of the City, 1974; Living Quarters, 1978; (and intro.) Enemy Within, 1979; Selected Stories, 1979; Aristocrats: A Play in Three Acts, 1980; Faith Healer: A Drama, 1980; Anton Chekhov's Three Sisters: A Translation, 1981; Translations, 1981; Communication Cord, 1983; The Diviner, 1983; (ed. and intro.) The Last of the Name, 1986; Fathers and Sons: After the Novel by Ivan Turgenev, 1987; Making History, 1989; Volunteers, 1989; Dancing at Lughnasa: A Play, 1990; (with C. Macklin) London Vertigo: Based on a Play The True Born Irishman, or, The Irish Fine Lady, 1990; Month in the Country: After Turgenev, 1992; Wonderful Tennessee, 1993; Molly Sweeney, 1994; Traduzioni e Altri Drammi, 1996; Give Me Your Answer, Do!, 1997; Uncle Vanya, 1998; Plays Two, 1999; The Yalta Game: After Chekhov, 2001; Three Plays After, 2002; Performances, 2003; The Home Place, 2005; Hedda Gabler: After Ibsen, 2008; Henrik Ibsen's Hedda Gabler, 2008; (co-author) Dramaty Irlandzkie, 2011. Contributor to periodicals. **Address:** International Creative Management, 730 5th Ave., New York, NY 10019, U.S.A.

FRIEND, Craig Thompson. American (born United States), b. 1961. **Genres:** Adult Non-fiction, History, Regional/Urban Planning. **Career:** Georgetown College, assistant professor of history, 1995-99; University of Central Florida, assistant professor, associate professor of history, 1999-2005; North Carolina State University, associate professor and director of public history, 2005-, Chass distinguished graduate professor. Cultural and historic resource surveyor. Writer. **Publications:** (Ed. and contrib..) The Buzzel about Kentuck: Settling the Promised Land, 1999; (contrib.) The Human Tradition in Antebellum America, 2000; (ed. with L. Glover and contrib.) Southern Manhood: Perspectives on Masculinity in the Old South, 2004; Along the Maysville Road: The Early American Republic in the Trans-Appalachian West, 2005; (ed.) Southern Masculinity: Perspectives on Manhood in the South Since Reconstruction, 2009; (ed. with A. Jabour) Family Values in the Old South, 2010; Kentucke's Frontiers, 2010. Contributor to periodicals. **Address:** Department of History, North Carolina State University, 368 Withers Hall, PO Box 8108, Raleigh, NC 27695-8108, U.S.A. **Online address:** craig_friend@ncsu.edu

FRIEND, Dorie. See FRIEND, Theodore (Wood).

FRIEND, Theodore (Wood). (Dorie Friend). American (born United States), b. 1931. **Genres:** Novels, History, Young Adult Fiction. **Career:** State University of New York, assistant professor, 1959-, professor of history, through 1973; Swarthmore College, president, 1973-82; Philadelphia Committee on Foreign Relations, chairman, 1986-2000, emeritus; Meritor Financial Group, director, 1975-; Eisenhower Exchange Fellowships Inc., trustee, 1982-, president, 1984-96, now emeritus; Westmoreland Coal Sales Co., director, 1986-; Foreign Policy Research Institute, senior fellow, 1997-; Metanexus Institute, director; Johns Hopkins University, School of Advanced International Studies, C.V. Starr distinguished visiting professor, 2004-; Harry S. Truman Scholarship Foundation, chair. Writer. **Publications:** Between Two Empires: The Ordeal of the Philippines, 1965; (ed.) Philippine Polity: A Japanese View, 1967; (as Dorie Friend) Family Laundry: A Novel, 1986; The Blue-Eyed Enemy: Japan against the West in Java and Luzon, 1942-1945, 1988; Indonesian Destinies, 2003. **Address:** Foreign Policy Research Institute, 1528 Walnut St., Ste. 610, Philadelphia, PA 19102, U.S.A.

FRIENDLY, Alfred. American (born United States), b. 1938. **Genres:** Documentaries/Reportage, Writing/Journalism, Environmental Sciences/Ecology. **Career:** Newsweek, journalist, 1962-66, writer, 1974-76, correspondent, bureau chief; New York Times, journalist, 1966-71, correspondent; associate White House press secretary, 1980. **Publications:** (Ed. with E. Yankelevich) Alarm and Hope, 1978; (with M. Feshbach) Ecocide in the USSR: Health and Nature under Siege, 1992; (ed.) Operation ANADYR: U.S. and Soviet Generals Recount the Cuban Missile Crisis, 1994. **Address:** Random House, 57-63 Uxbridge Rd., London, GL W5 5SA, England.

FRIESEN, Bernice (Sarah Anne). Canadian (born Canada), b. 1966. **Genres:** Children's Fiction, Novellas/Short Stories, Poetry. **Career:** Saska-toon Correctional Center, art teacher, 1985; University of Saskatchewan, lab assistant, 1986-87; A.K.A. Gallery, 26 and Under: Young Saskatoon Artists, project coordinator, 1987; Y.W.C.A., art class instructor, 1988; Mendel Art Gallery, Clue Into Art, instructor, 1989, instructor of children's color class, 1993; Estevan National Exhibition Centre, art educator, 1990-91; Ballet de les Americas(a folk dance troupe), costume designer, 1991; Valley Action Industries, junior group home operator, 1992-93; Saskatchewan Writers Guild, board director, secretary, 1994-95; freelance writer, 1995-. **Publications:** The Seasons Are Horses (Fiction), 1995; Sex, Death and Naked Men (poems): Bernice Friesen, 1998; Book of Beasts, 2007. Works appear in anthologies. Contributor to periodicals. **Address:** Thistledown Press, 633 Main St., Saskatoon, SK S7H 0J8, Canada. **Online address:** bernicefriesen@bernicefriesen.com

FRIESEN, Jonathan. American (born United States), b. 1967?. **Genres:** Novels. **Career:** Author and educator. **Publications:** Jerk, California, 2008; Rush, 2010; The Last Martin, 2011. **Address:** PO Box 59, Mora, MN 55051, U.S.A.

FRIGSTAD, David B. American (born United States), b. 1954. **Genres:** Marketing, Economics, Administration/Management. **Career:** Market Intelligence Research Co., founder, 1980-93; Frost & Sullivan, chairperson, 1993-. Writer. **Publications:** Venture Capital Proposal Package, 1989; Market Research in High Technology, 1993; Customer Engineering: Cutting-edge Selling Strategies, 1995; Know Your Market: How to do Low-cost Marketing Research, 1995; Market Engineering in Health Care, 1996; Competitor Engineering, 1996; Market Research and Forecasting in Healthcare Industries, 1996. **Address:** Frost & Sullivan, 7550 Interstate 10 W, Ste. 400, San Antonio, TX 78229-5616, U.S.A.

FRIMANSSON, Inger. Swedish (born Sweden), b. 1944. **Genres:** Young Adult Fiction, Mystery/Crime/Suspense, Horror. **Career:** Journalist. (With A. Bakk) Trots Allt: Samtal Med Föräldrar till Utvecklingsstörda, 1976; 16 kvinnor berättar, 1977; Dubbelsängen, 1984; Den Förtrollade Prinsen, 1986; Den Nya Omsorgslagen, 1986; Tills hon hittar något eget, 1987; Djuret under tummarna, 1989; Mannen med barnvagnen, 1990; Jag kan också gå på vattnet, 1991; Handdockan, 1992; Mannen som flö över bergen, 1993; Skräpsommaren, 1993; Soldaternas dotter, 1995; Kärlek, trohet, vänskap, hat, 1995; Stilla under regnbågsytan, 1995; Där Inne Vilar ögat: Noveller, 1996; Fruktar jag intetont, 1997; God Natt Min älskade, 1998; Mannen Med Oxhjärtat, 1999; Elden, 1999; Katten Som Inte Dog, 2000; Mord i Midsommartid, 2000; Ett Mycket Bättre Liv, 2001; Midvintermord, 2001; De Nakna Kvinnornas ö, 2002; Bebådelsedag, 2003; Mörkerspår, 2003; Ge mig en drink, jag är rädd!, 2003; Inga livstecken, 2004; Svarta diamanter, 2004; Noveller för Värdens, 2004; Skuggan I vattnet, 2005; Mord i juletid, 2005; Ligga som ett O, 2007; Good Night, My Darling, 2007; The Shadow in the Water, 2008; Island of the Naked Women, 2009; Råttfångerskan, 2009; Hitta Jeppe. Contributor to periodicals. **Publications:** WRITINGS: (with A. Bakk) Trots Allt: Samtal Med Föräldrar till Utvecklingsstörda, 1976; 16 kvinnor berättar, 1977; Dubbelsängen, 1984; Den Förtrollade Prinsen, 1986; Den Nya Omsorgslagen, 1986; Tills hon hittar något eget, 1987; Djuret under tummarna, 1989; Mannen med barnvagnen, 1990; Jag kan också gå på vattnet, 1991; Handdockan, 1992; Mannen som flö över bergen, 1993; Skräpsommaren, 1993; Soldaternas dotter, 1995; Kärlek, trohet, vänskap, hat, 1995; Stilla under regnbågsytan, 1995; Där Inne Vilar ögat: Noveller, 1996; Fruktar jag intetont, 1997; God Natt Min älskade, 1998; Mannen Med Oxhjärtat, 1999; Elden, 1999; Katten Som Inte Dog, 2000; Mord i Midsommartid, 2000; Ett Mycket Bättre Liv, 2001; Midvintermord, 2001; De Nakna Kvinnornas ö, 2002; Bebådelsedag, 2003; Mörkerspår, 2003; Ge mig en drink, jag är rädd!, 2003; Inga livstecken, 2004; Svarta diamanter, 2004; Noveller för Värdens, 2004; Skuggan I vattnet, 2005; Mord i juletid, 2005; Ligga som ett O, 2007; Good Night, My Darling, 2007; The Shadow in the Water, 2008; Island of the Naked Women, 2009; Råttfångerskan, 2009; Hitta Jeppe. **Address:** Salomonsson Agency, Stora Nygatan 20, Stockholm, 11127, Sweden. **Online address:** inger@frimansson.se

FRISBIE, Charlotte J(ohnson). American (born United States), b. 1940. **Genres:** Anthropology/Ethnology, Biography, Autobiography/Memoirs, Women's Studies And Issues, Theology/Religion, Social Sciences. **Career:** Anna State Hospital, social worker, 1968-70, coordinator of aftercare program, 1970; Southern Illinois University, assistant professor, 1970-73, associate professor, 1973-77, professor of anthropology, 1977-98, professor emeritus, 1999-, chairperson of anthropology program, 1973-75, 1985-87, 1992-96; Society for Ethnomusicology, president and co-founder, 1982; Laurentian University, distinguished lecturer, 1993; Smithsonian Institution, consultant; National Park Service, consultant. Writer. **Publications:** Kinaaldá: A Study of the Navaho Girl's Puberty Ceremony, 1967; Music and Dance Research of Southwestern United States Indians: Past Trends, Present Activities and Suggestions for Future Research, 1977; (ed. with D.P. McAllester) Navajo Blessingway Singer: The Autobiography of Frank Mitchell 1881-1867, 1978, rev. ed., 2003; (ed.) Southwestern Indian Ritual Drama, 1980, rev. ed., 1989; (ed. with D.M. Brugge) Navajo Religion and Culture: Selected Views: Papers in Honor of Leland C. Wyman, 1982; (ed.) Explorations in Ethnomusicology: Essays in Honor of David P. McAllester, 1986; Navajo Medicine Bundles or Jish: Acquisition, Transmission and Disposition in the Past and Present, 1987; (ed.) Tall Woman: The Life Story of Rose Mitchell, a Navajo Woman, c. 1874-1977, 2001. Contributor of articles to books and periodicals. **Address:** Department of Anthropology, Southern Illinois University, Rm. 2202, Rendleman Hall, PO Box 1451, Edwardsville, IL 62026-1451, U.S.A. **Online address:** cfrisbie@siue.edu

FRISBY, Terence. British (born England), b. 1932. **Genres:** Plays/Screenplays, Autobiography/Memoirs, Novels, History. **Career:** Actor, director and producer, 1957-. Writer. **Publications:** The Subtopians, 1964; There's a Girl in my Soup: A Comedy in Three Acts, 1966; There's a Girl in my Soup, 1970; The Bandwagon, 1970; It's All Right if I Do It, 1977; Seaside Postcard, 1978; Just Remember Two Things: It's Not Fair and Don't Be Late, 1989; Rough Justice, 1994; Outrageous Fortune (autobiography), 1998; Funny about Love, 2002; Kisses on a Postcard, 2009. **Address:** c/o Harvey Unna, 14 Beaumont Mews, Marylebone High St., London, GL W1, England. **Online address:** terence@tfrisby.wanadoo.co.uk

FRISCH, Walter. American (born United States), b. 1951. **Genres:** Music, History, Documentaries/Reportage. **Career:** Columbia University, professor, 1982-, H. Harold Gumm/Harry and Albert Von Tilzer professor of music, director of graduate studies, 2010-11, department chair; University of New Hampshire, American Brahms Society, president, 1983-93. Writer. **Publications:** Brahms and the Principle of Developing Variation, 1984; (ed.) Schubert: Critical and Analytical Studies, 1986; (ed.) Brahms and His World, 1990; The Early Works of Arnold Schoenberg, 1893-1908, 1993; Brahms: The Four Symphonies, 1996; (ed.) Schoenberg and His World, 1999; German Modernism: Music and the Arts, 2005. **Address:** Department of Music, Columbia University, 613 Dodge Hall, 2960 Broadway, PO BOx 1820, New York, NY 10027, U.S.A. **Online address:** wf8@columbia.edu

FRIST, William H. American (born United States), b. 1952. **Genres:** Medicine/Health, Politics/Government, Sciences, Biography, Autobiography/Memoirs. **Career:** Massachusetts General Hospital, resident in surgery, 1978-83, research fellow in surgery, 1983, chief resident in cardiothoracic surgery, 1984-85; Southampton General Hospital, senior registrar in cardiothoracic surgery, 1983; Stanford University, Cardiac Transplant Service, senior fellow and chief resident in cardiovascular surgery, 1985-86; Nashville Veterans Administration Hospital, staff surgeon, 1986-93; Vanderbilt University, assistant professor of cardiac and thoracic surgery, 1986-93, director of heart and heart-lung transplantation and surgical director of Vanderbilt Multi-Organ Transplant Center, 1989-93, distinguished university professor of business and medicine; Nashville Veterans Administration Hospital, staff surgeon, 1986-93; National Kidney Foundation of Middle Tennessee, vice president, 1991-92; U.S. Senator, 1995-2007, U.S. Senate Majority Leader, 2003-07; Congressional Heart and Stroke Coalition, founder and co-chairman; Senate Republican Medicare Working Group, chairman, 1995-96; Alliance for Health Reform, vice chairman, 1997-. Writer. **Publications:** Transplant: A Heart Surgeon's Account of the Life-and-Death Dramas of the New Medicine, 1989; (ed. with J.H. Helderman) Grand Rounds in Transplantation, 1995; (with J.L. Annis, Jr.) Tennessee Senators, 1911-2001: Portraits of Leadership in a Century of Change, 1999; (as Bill Frist) When Every Moment Counts: What You Need to Know about Bioterrorism from the Senate's Only Doctor, 2002; Cuando No hay Tiempo Que Perder: elúnico médico del Senado Revela Todo lo Que hay que Saber Sobre el Bioterrorismo, 2002; (with S. Wilson) Good People Beget Good People: A Genealogy of the Frist family, 2003; Tobacco Use and Public Health: Federal Efforts to Prevent and Reduce Tobacco use Among Youth: Report to the Honorable Bill Frist, U.S. Senate, 2003; A Heart to Serve: The Passion to Bring Health, Hope and Healing, 2009. Works appear in anthologies. **Address:** Vanderbilt Owen Graduate School of Management, 401 21st Ave., Nashville, TN 37203, U.S.A. **Online address:** senator_frist@frist.senate.gov

FRITCHLEY, Alma. British (born England), b. 1954?. **Genres:** Mystery/ Crime/Suspense, Novels, Young Adult Fiction, Criminology/True Crime. **Career:** Author. **Publications:** LETTY CAMPBELL MYSTERY SERIES: Chicken Run, 1997; Chicken Feed, 1998; Chicken Out, 1999; Chicken Shack, 2000. **Address:** c/o Author Mail, Womens Press, 27 Goodge St., London, GL W1T 2LD, England.

FRITH, David (Edward John). British (born England), b. 1937. **Genres:** Autobiography/Memoirs, Sports/Fitness, Biography, History. **Career:** The Cricketer, editor, 1972-78; Wisden Cricket Monthly, founding editor, 1979-96. **Publications:** My Dear Victorious Stod: A Biography of A.E. Stoddart, 1970; The Archie Jackson Story: A Biography, 1974; The Fast Men: A 200 Year Cavalcade of Speed Bowlers, 1975, rev. ed., 1977; (ed.) Cricket Gallery: Fifty Profiles of Famous Players from The Cricketer, 1976; England versus Australia: A Pictorial History of the Test Matches since 1877, 1977, rev. ed., 1981; (with G. Chappell) Ashes '77, 1977; The Golden Age of Cricket, 1890-1914, 1978; The Ashes '79, 1979; (ed. with M. Tyler) The Illustrated History of Test Cricket, 1979; The Slow Men, 1984; (with G. Wright) Cricket's Golden Summer, 1985; England versus Australia Test Match Records, 1877-1985, 1986; Pageant of Cricket, 1987; Guildford Jubilee, 1938-1988, 1988; By His Own Hand, 1990; Popular Music, 1992; Stoddy's Mission: The First Great Test Series, 1894-1895, 1994; Silence of the Heart: Cricket Suicides, 2001; Bodyline Autopsy: The Full Story of the Most Sensational Test Cricket Series: Australia v. England 1932-33, 2002; Ross Gregory Story, 2003; Battle Renewed: The Ashes Regained 2006-2007, 2007; (with G. Haigh) Inside Story: Unlocking Australian Cricket's Archives, 2007; Frith on Cricket, 2010. **Address:** 6 Beech Ln., Guildown, Guildford, SR GU2 5ES, England.

FRITH, Katherine Toland. American (born United States), b. 1946. **Genres:** Advertising/Public Relations, Communications/Media. **Career:** N.W. Ayer & Son, 1969-71; J. Walter Thompson Inc., copywriter, 1971-73; Grey Advertising, copywriter, 1973-74; Pima County Board of Supervisors, public relations, 1977-79; Institute of Technology Mara, Fulbright professor, 1987-88; Iowa State University, assistant professor, 1983-86, associate professor, 1986-88; Institute Technology Bandung, Fulbright senior lecturer, 1993; Pennsylvania State University, associate professor, 1988-99, Advertising Program, chair, 1989-92, 1994-99; Nanyang Technological University, associate professor, 1998-2007; Southern Illinois University, School of Journalism, associate professor, 2008-, professor. **Publications:** (Ed.) Advertising in Asia: Communication, Culture, and Consumption, 1996; Undressing the Ad: Reading Culture in Advertising, 1997; (ed. with K. Karan) Commercializing Women: Images of Asian Women in the Media, 2008; (with B. Mueller) Advertising and Societies: Global Issues, 2003, 2nd ed., 2010. **Address:** School of Journalism, Southern Illonois University, 1230 Communications Bldg., 1100 Lincoln Dr., PO Box 6066, Carbondale, IL 62901, U.S.A. **Online address:** kfrith@siu.edu

FRITSCH, Albert J(oseph). American (born United States), b. 1933. **Genres:** Environmental Sciences/Ecology, Ethics, Recreation, Theology/Religion, Self Help. **Career:** Entered Society of Jesus (S.J.; Jesuits), staff, 1956, ordained Roman Catholic priest, 1967; University of Texas, research associate, 1969-70; Center for the Study of Responsive Law, technical consultant, 1970-71; Center for Science in the Public Interest, co-founder and director, 1971-77; Earth Healing, director; Technical Information Project, president, 1974-, Appalachian Coalition, 1978-, Sun-rep, 1980-; Appalachia-Science in the Public Interest, director, 1977-2002, Solar Lobby, president of board of directors, 1980-; Santa Clara University, Bannon chair, 1996; Marquette University, Wade chair, 1998; Good Shepherd Catholic Church, sacramental minister, 2003-04; St. Elizabeth Church, parish priest, 2004-; Research Policy Institute, director; Center for the Study of Commercialism, director; Environmental Resource Assessment Service, director; Kentuckians for Nursing Home Reform, director. Writer. **Publications:** A Theology of the Earth, 1972; Gasoline, 1972; (with J.W. Egan) Big Oil: A Citizens Factbook on the Major Oil Companies, 1973; (with B. Hogan and S. Guhl) How Aerosol Sprays Can Affect Your Safety and Health, 1973; (with B.I. Castleman) Asbestos and You, 1973; The Contrasumers: A Citizens Guide to Resource Conservation, 1974; (with Castleman) Lifestyle Index, 1974; (ed.) Shale Oil: An Environmental Critique, 1974; (with R. Gitomer) Major Oil: What Citizens Should Know About the Eight Major Oil Companies, 1974; (with L.W. Dujack and D.A. Jimerman) Energy and Food: Energy Used in Production, Processing, Delivery, and Marketing of Selected Food Items, 1975, rev. ed., 1977; (ed.) A Citizens Oil Factbook: What Every Citizen Should Know About the Eighteen Largest Oil Companies, 1975; (ed.) Solar Energy: One Way to Citizen Control, 1976; 99 Ways to a Simple Lifestyle, 1977; (with D. Darcey, G. McMohan and E. Burns) Strip Mine Blasting, 1977; (co-ed.) Household

Pollutants Guide, 1978; (with J. Nardt) Harlan County Flood Report, 1978; (with M. Morgan) Citizens Blasting Handbook, 1978; (with J. Clemens and F. Kazemek) Citizens Coal Haul Handbook, 1978; Toxic Substances and Trade Secrecy, 1978; (with R. Schemel) Citizens Resource Handbook, 1979; Toxic Substances: Decisions and Values, 1979-80; (with McMahon, Okagaki and W. Millerd) Environmental Ethics: Choices for Concerned Citizens, 1980; Green Space, 1982; Appalachia: A Meditation, 1986; Renew the Face of the Earth, 1987; Earthen Vessels, 1990; (with A. Ladavaia-Cox) Eco-Church; An Action Manual, 1992; Down to Earth Spirituality, 1992; Out of the Waste Land, 1994; Religion in Ecology: Scientists Speak, 1998; Spirituality of Gardening, 2000; Ecotourism in Appalachia: Marketing the Mountains, 2004; (with A.H. Pucell and M.B. Davis) Critical Hour: Three Mile Island, the Nuclear Legacy and National Securtiy, 2004; (with P. Gallimore) Healing Appalachia: Sustainable Living through Appropriate Technology, 2007; Water Sounds: Reminiscenses: North Americas Missionary, 2010; (with W.E. Brunner) Mountain Moments, 2010. Contributor to periodicals. **Address:** St. Elizabeth of Hungary Church, 316 5th St., Ravenna, KY 40472-1312, U.S.A. **Online address:** alfritsch@earthhealing.info.com

FRITTS, Mary Bahr. American (born United States), b. 1946. **Genres:** Children's Fiction, Young Adult Fiction, Children's Non-fiction, History, Literary Criticism And History, Writing/Journalism, Young Adult Non-fiction, Humor/Satire, Humor/Satire. **Career:** Minnesota Department of Corrections, library trainee, 1968-69; Presbyterian Medical Center, medical librarian, 1969-70, registrar, 1971-74; Cobb County Public Library, library assistant, 1981-84; Pikes Peak Library District, Penrose Reference Library, information and reference technician, 1990-97; New Writers Magazine, columnist, 1991-94; Five Owls, children's book reviewer, 1993-99. **Publications:** The Memory Box, 1992; Jabberyacky, 1996; Jordi's Run, 1997; If Nathan Were Here, 2000; My Brother Loved Snowflakes: The Story of Wilson A. Bentley, the Snowflake Man, 2002. Contributor to books and periodicals. **Address:** 807 Hercules Pl., Colorado Springs, CO 80906-1130, U.S.A.

FRITZ, Jean. American/Chinese (born China), b. 1915. **Genres:** Children's Fiction, Children's Non-fiction, History, Mystery/Crime/Suspense, Young Adult Non-fiction, Novels, Literary Criticism And History, Adult Non-fiction, Adult Non-fiction. **Career:** Silver Burdett Co., research assistant, 1937-41; Dobbs Ferry Library, children's librarian, 1955-57; Jean Fritz Writers Workshops, founder, instructor, 1962-70; Board of Cooperative Educational Service, teacher, 1971-73; Appalachian State University, faculty, 1980-82. Writer. **Publications:** Bunny Hopwell's First Spring, 1954; Help Mr. Willy Nilly, 1954; Fish Head, 1954; Hurrah for Jonathan!, 1955; 121 Pudding Street, 1955; Growing Up, 1956; The Late Spring, 1957; The Cabin Faced West, 1958; (with T. Clute) Champion Dog, Prince Tom, 1958; The Animals of Doctor Schweitzer, 1958; How to Read a Rabbit, 1959; Brady, 1960; Tap, Tap Lion, 1, 2, 3, 1962; San Francisco, 1962; I, Adam, 1963; Magic to Burn, 1964; Surprise Party, 1965; The Train, 1965; Early Thunder, 1967; George Washington's Breakfast, 1969; Cast for a Revolution: Some American Friends and Enemies, 1728-1814, 1972; And Then What Happened, Paul Revere?, 1973; Why Don't You Get a Horse, Sam Adams?, 1974; Where was Patrick Henry on the 29th of May?, 1975; Who's that Stopping on Plymouth Rock?, 1975; Will You Sign Here, John Hancook?, 1976; What's the Big Idea, Ben Franklin?, 1976; The Secret Diary of Jeb and Abigail: Growing up in America, 1776-83, 1976; Can't You Make Them Behave, King George?, 1977; Brendan the Navigator: A History Mystery About the Discovery Of America, 1979; Stonewall, 1979; Where Do You Think You're Going, Christopher Columbus?, 1980; The Man Who Loved Books, 1981; Traitor: The Case of Benedict Arnold, 1981; Back to Early Cape Cod, 1981; The Good Giants and the Bad Pukwudgies, 1982; Homesick: My Own Story, 1982; The Double Life of Pocahontas, 1983; China Homecoming, 1985; Make Way for Sam Houston!, 1986; Shh! We're Writing the Constitution, 1987; China's Long March: 6, 000 Miles of Danger, 1988; The Great Little Madison, 1989; (co-author) Worlds of Childhood: The Art and Craft of Writing for Children, 1990; Bully for You, Teddy Roosevelt!, 1991; George Washington's Mother, 1992; (co-author) The World in 1492, 1992; Surprising Myself, 1992; The Great Adventure of Christopher Columbus: A Pop-up Book, 1992; Just a Few Words, Mr. Lincoln: The Story of the Gettysburg Address, 1993; Around the World in a Hundred Years: From Henry the Navigator to Magellan, 1994; Harriet Beecher Stowe and the Beecher Preachers, 1994; You want Women to Vote, Lizzie Stanton?, 1995; Why Not, Lafayette?, 1999; Leonardo's Horse, 2001; Lost Colony of Roanoke, 2004; (intro.) Buffalo Knife, 2004; (intro.) Flaming Arrows, 2004; (intro.) Perilous Road, 2004; Who's Saying What in Jamestown, Thomas Savage?, 2007; Alexander Hamilton: The Outsider, 2011. Contributor of periodi-

cals. **Address:** Gina Maccoby Literary Agency, 1123 Broadway, Ste. 1010, New York, NY 10010-2007, U.S.A. **Online address:** jfritz60@aol.com

FRITZ, Robert. American (born United States), b. 1943. **Genres:** inspirational/Motivational Literature, Medicine/Health, Business/Trade/Industry. **Career:** Robert Fritz Inc., founder; DMA, founder; Technologies for Creating, founder; Innovation Associates, co-founder. Writer and consultant. **Publications:** The Path of Least Resistance: Principles for Creating What You Want to Create, 1984, rev. ed., The Path of Least Resistance: Learning to Become the Creative Force in Your Own Life, 1989; Creating, 1991; Corporate Tides: The Inescapable Laws of Organizational Structure, 1996; The Path of Least Resistance for Managers: Designing Organizations to Succeed, 1999; Your Life as Art, 2003; (with B. Bodaken) The Managerial Moment of Truth: The Essential Step in Helping People Improve Performance, 2006; Elements: The Writings of Robert Fritz, 2007. **Address:** Robert Fritz Inc., PO Box 189, Newfane, VT 05345, U.S.A. **Online address:** seminars@robertfritz.com

FRITZ, Stephen G. American (born United States), b. 1949. **Genres:** History, Military/Defense/Arms Control. **Career:** East Tennessee State University, professor of history. Writer and historian. **Publications:** Frontsoldaten: The German Soldier in World War II, 1995; Endkampf: Soldiers, Civilians and the Death of the Third Reich, 2004; Ostkrieg: Hitlers War of Extermination In The East, 2011. Contributor to periodicals. **Address:** Department of History, East Tennessee State University, 204 Rogers Stout Hall, PO Box 70672, Johnson City, TN 37614-1709, U.S.A. **Online address:** fritzs@etsu.edu

FRITZE, Ronald H. American (born United States), b. 1951. **Genres:** History, Institutions/Organizations, Mythology/Folklore, Adult Non-fiction. **Career:** Louisiana State University, research assistant and research associate, 1979-92, instructor in history, 1981-82; Rice University, Fondren Library, librarian, 1982-84; Houston Community College, instructor, 1983-84; Lamar University, assistant professor, 1984-89, associate professor, 1989-95, professor, 1995-96, university professor of history, 1996-2001; Lamar Journal of the Humanities, business manager, 1986-88; University of Central Arkansas, professor of history and department chair, 2001-05; Athens State University, College of Arts and Sciences, dean, 2005-. Writer and historian. **Publications:** (Contrib.) Protestantism and the National Church in Sixteenth-Century England, 1987; (with B.E. Coutts and L.A. Vyhnanek) Reference Sources in History: An Introductory Guide, 1990, 2nd ed., 2004; (with R. Roberts and J.S. Olson) Reflections on Western Civilization: A Reader, 1991; (ed. with G. Elton and W. Sutton) Historical Dictionary of Tudor England, 1485-1603, 1991; Legend and Lore of the Americas before 1492: An Encyclopedia of Visitors, Explorers, and Immigrants, 1993; (with J.S. Olson and R.W. Roberts) Reflections on World Civilization: A Reader, 1993; (ed. with W.B. Robison and W. Sutton) Historical Dictionary of Stuart England, 1603-1689, 1996; Travel Legend and Lore: An Encyclopedia, 1998; (ed. with W.B. Robison) Historical Dictionary of Late Medieval England, 1272-1485, 2002; New Worlds: The Great Voyages of Discovery, 1400-1600, 2002; Invented Knowledge: False History, Fake Science and Pseudo-Religions, 2009; The Twilight Zone of History, forthcoming. Contributor to books and periodicals. **Address:** College of Arts and Sciences, Athens State University, Rm. 204, Naylor Hall, 300 N Beaty St., Athens, AL 35611, U.S.A. **Online address:** ron.fritze@athens.edu

FRITZELL, Peter A(lgren). American (born United States), b. 1940. **Genres:** Poetry, Intellectual History, Literary Criticism And History, Essays, Writing/Journalism, Humanities. **Career:** Lawrence University, assistant professor, 1966-73, associate professor, 1973-83, chair of department, 1973-77, 1987-90, professor of English, 1983-2003, Patricia Hamar Boldt professor of liberal studies, 1989-2003, professor emeritus, 2003-, London Study Center, director, 1977-78; Stanford University, visiting professor, 1968, 1974, 1977; University of Wisconsin-Green Bay, lecturer, 1974. Writer. **Publications:** Nature Writing and America: Essays upon a Cultural Type, 1990. Contributor of articles to books and periodicals. **Address:** Department of English, Lawrence University, PO Box 599, Appleton, WI 54912-0599, U.S.A. **Online address:** fritzelp@lawrence.edu

FRITZER, Penelope Joan. American (born United States), b. 1949. **Genres:** Communications/Media. **Career:** Social worker, 1975-76; University of Miami, teaching assistant and instructor, 1977-80; Broward Community College, teacher of English, 1982-84; Broward County School System, teacher, 1985-93; Florida Atlantic University, assistant professor, 1993-99, associate professor, 1999-2004, campus coordinator and assistant to the chair, 1997-2003, graduate faculty (level B), 1997-, graduate faculty (level A), 2002-, assistant to associate dean, 2001-03, graduate coordinator, 2003-04, professor, 2004-, interim department chair, 2005-06, department chair, 2006-07. Writer. **Publications:** Jane Austen and Eighteenth-century Courtesy Books, 1997; Ethnicity and Gender in the Barsetshire Novels of Angela Thirkell, 1999; (with B. Bland) Merry Wives and Others: A History of Domestic Humor Writing, 2002; Social Studies Content for Elementary and Middle School Teachers, 2002, (with E.A. Brewer) 2nd ed., 2009; (with V. Bristor) Science Content for Elementary and Middle School Teachers, 2004; (with B. Ridener) Mathematics Content for Elementary and Middle School Teachers, 2004; (ed.) Character and Concept in the Barsetshire Novels of Angela Thirkell, 2005; Aesthetics and Nostalgia in the Barsetshire Novels of Angela Thirkell, 2009. **Address:** Florida Atlantic University, Rm. ES221, 2912 College Ave., Davie, OH 33314, U.S.A. **Online address:** fritzer@fau.edu

FRITZSCHE, Peter. American (born United States), b. 1959. **Genres:** History. **Career:** University of Illinois, Department of History, assistant professor, 1987-91, associate professor, 1991-95, professor of history, 1995-. Writer. **Publications:** Die politische Kultur Italiens, 1987; Rehearsals for Fascism: Populism and Political Mobilization in Weimar Germany, 1990; A Nation of Fliers: German Aviation and the Popular Imagination, 1992; (with K. Hewitt) Berlinwalks, 1994; Reading Berlin 1900, 1996; Germans into Nazis, 1998; Stranded in the Present: Modern Rime and the Melancholy of History, 2004; Ordnungen in der Krise: zur politischen Kulturgeschichte Deutschlands 1900-1933, 2007; (intro.) Nietzsche and the Death of God: Selected Writings, 2007; Life and Death in the Third Reich, 2008; Turbulent World of Franz Göll: An Ordinary Berliner Writes the Twentieth Century, 2011. EDITOR: (with C.C. Stewart) Imagining the Twentieth Century, 1997; (with A. Confino) The Work of Memory: New Directions in the Study of German Society and Culture, 2002. **Address:** Department of History, University of Illinois, Rm. 300A, Gregory Hall, 810 S Wright St., Urbana, IL 61801, U.S.A. **Online address:** pfritzsc@illinois.edu

FROHNEN, Bruce (P.). American (born United States), b. 1962. **Genres:** Law, Philosophy, Politics/Government, History, Social Sciences. **Career:** National Federation of Independent Business, legislative assistant, 1983-85; Reed College, visiting assistant professor of political studies, 1988-89; Cornell College, visiting assistant professor of political studies, 1989-90; Heritage Foundation, Henry Salvatori Center, adjunct fellow, 1991-93; Oglethorpe University, instructor in political science, 1992-93; Office of United States Senator Spencer Abraham, legislative aide, 1995-2000; Ave Maria School of Law, assistant professor of law, 2001-08; Earhart Foundation, secretary and director, 2004-05; Russell Kirk Center for Cultural Renewal, senior fellow, 2000-; Ohio Northern University, College of Law, visiting associate professor, 2008-09, associate professor of law, 2010-; Liberty Fund Inc., senior fellow; Emory University, faculty; Catholic University of America, faculty. Writer. **Publications:** Virtue and the Promise of Conservatism: The Legacy of Burke and Tocqueville, 1993; The New Communitarians and the Crisis of Modern Liberalism, 1996; (ed. with G.W. Carey) Community and Tradition: Conservative Perspectives on the American Experience, 1998; (ed. and contrib.) The Anti-Federalists: Selected Writings and Speeches, 1999; (ed.) The American Republic, 2002; (ed. with J. Beer and J.O. Nelson) American Conservatism: An Encyclopedia, 2006; (ed. with K. Grasso) Defending the Republic: Constitutional Morality in a Time of Crisis; Essays in Honor of George W. Carey, 2008; (ed. with K.L. Grasso) Rethinking Rights: Historical, Political, and Philosophical Perspectives, 2008; (ed.) American Nation: Primary Sources, 2008. Works appear in anthologies. Contributor to journals. **Address:** College of Law, Ohio Northern University, Rm. 189 Tilton Hall, 525 S Main St., Ada, OH 45810, U.S.A. **Online address:** b-frohnen@onu.edu

FROHOFF, Toni. American (born United States), b. 1963. **Genres:** Animals/Pets. **Career:** TerraMar Research, co-founder and director of research, POD Group (Protect Our Dolphins), founder. Writer. **Publications:** (Ed. with B. Peterson) Between Species: Celebrating the Dolphin-Human Bond, 2003; (with K. Dudzinski) Dolphin Mysteries: Unlocking the Secrets of Communication, 2008. Contributor to books. **Address:** Seattle, WA , U.S.A. **Online address:** info@terramarresearch.org

FROME, Michael. American (born United States), b. 1920. **Genres:** Environmental Sciences/Ecology, Natural History. **Career:** Washington Post, news reporter, 1945-46; American Automobile Association, travel editor, 1947-57; American Forests, columnist, 1959, 1966-71; Changing Times, columnist, 1959-81; Women's Day, columnist, 1961-82; Field and Stream, conservation editor and columnist, 1968-74; Defenders of Wildlife Magazine, columnist, 1975-94; Los Angeles Times, columnist, 1977-81; University of Vermont, visiting professor, 1978; Pinchot Institute for Conservation Studies, author-in-residence, 1981-82; University of Idaho, College of Forestry, visiting associate professor, 1982-86; Western Washington University, Huxley College of Environmental Studies, visiting professor, 1987. Writer. **Publications:** Better Vacations for Your Money, 1959, 2nd ed., 1960; Washington: A Modern Guide to the Nation's Capital, 1960; Whose Woods These Are, 1962; 1001 Ways to Enjoy Your Car, 1962; Vacations, U.S.A., 1966; Strangers in High Places, 1966, 3rd ed., 1994; Virginia, 1966, 3rd ed., 1971; Rand McNally National Park Guide, 1967, 29th ed., 1995; (with O.L. Freeman) The National Forests of America, Country Beautiful Corp., 1968; Kodak Guide: America's National Parks, 1969; The Varmints: Our Unwanted Wildlife, 1969; Kodak Guide to Colonial America, 1970; The Forest Service, 1971, 2nd ed., 1984; National Park Guide, 1971; Battle for the Wilderness, 1974, 3rd ed., 1997; (with D. Muench) The National Parks, 1977; Hosteling USA: The Official American Youth Hostels Handbook, 1981, 2nd ed., 1983; Promised Land: Adventures and Encounters in Wild America, 1985, 2nd ed., 1994; (ed.) Issues in Wilderness Management, 1985; America's Favorite National Parks, 1985, 3rd ed., 1989; Conscience of a Conservationist: Selected Essays, 1989; (with D. Muench) Uncommon Places: A Celebration of Appalachian Trail Country, 1991; Regreening the National Parks, 1992; Our Great Treasures: America's National Parks, 1992; Chronicling the West: Thirty Years of Environmental Writing, 1996; Green Ink: An Introduction to Environmental Journalism, 1998; Greenspeak: Fifty Years of Environmental Muckraking and Advocacy, 2002; Rebel on the Road: And Why I was Never Neutral, 2007. **Address:** 638 N Powers St., Port Washington, WI 53074-1633, U.S.A. **Online address:** mfrome@aol.com

FROMM, Pete. American (born United States), b. 1958. **Genres:** Novels, Novellas/Short Stories, Adult Non-fiction, Film. **Career:** Lake Mead National Recreation Area, lifeguard supervisor, 1978-81; Grand Teton National Park, supervisory river ranger, 1982-87; Big Bend National Park, river ranger, 1985; freelance writer, 1989-. **Publications:** STORIES: The Tall Uncut, 1992; King of the Mountain, 1994; Dry Rain, 1997; Blood Knot, 1998; Night Swimming, 1999. NOVELS: Monkey Tag, 1994; How All This Started, 2000; As Cool As I Am, 2003. OTHER: Indian Creek Chronicles: A Winter in the Wilderness, 1993. Contributor to periodicals and journals. **Address:** 316 Daly Ave., Missoula, MT 59801, U.S.A. **Online address:** petefromm@msn.com

FROMMEL, Christoph Lvitpold. Italian/German (born Germany), b. 1933. **Genres:** Architecture, Photography, History. **Career:** Bibliotheca Hertziana, teaching assistant, 1959-67, director, 1980-2001; University of Bonn, professor, 1968-80; University La Sapienta, professor, 2002-. Writer. **Publications:** Die Farnesia und Peruzzis Architektonisches Freuhwerk, 1961; Der reomische Palastban der Hockrenaissance, 1973; Michelangelo und Tommaso deCavalieri, 1979; Der Palazzo Venezia in Rom, 1982; The Architectural Drawings of Antonio de Sangallo the Younger and His Circle, vol. I, 1993, vol. II, 2000, vol. III, 2004; (with A. Esch) Arte, committenza ed economiacaa Roma e nelle corti del Rinascimento: 1420-1530: atti del convegnointernazionale, Roma 24-27 ottobre 1990, 1995; (with S. Schutze) Pietro daCortona: atti del convegno internazionale Roma-Firenze, 12-15 novembre 1997, 1998; (with I. Lauterbach and K. Endemann) Die Landshuter Stadtresidenz: Architektur und Ausstattung, 1998; (with R. Bosel) Borromini: e luniverso barocco, 2000; (with R. Bosel) Borromini: Architektim barocken Rom, 2000; (with E. Sladek) Francesco Borromini: atti delconvegno internazionale, 2000; Bramante milanese e l'architettura del Rinascimento lombardo, 2002; Palazzo Caffarelli Vidoni, 2002; Architettura alla corte papale nel Rinascimento, 2003; Vignola e I Farnese: atti delconvegno internazionale Piacenza 18-20 Aprile 2002, 2003; Renaissance Architecture, 2004; Baldassarre Peruzzi, 1481-1539, 2005; Limmagine di Cristo dall Acheropita alla mano dartista: dal tardo medioevo alletà barocca, 2006; Architettura ecommittenza da Alberti a Bramante, 2006; The Architecture of the Italian Renaissance, 2007; (contrib.) Lantica Basilica di San Lorenzo in Damaso: indagini archeologiche nel Palazzo della Cancelleria, 1988-1993, 2009. **Address:** Bibliotheca Hertziana, Via Gregoriana 28, Rome, I-00147, Italy. **Online address:** cfrommel@libero.it

FROMMER, Benjamin. American (born United States), b. 1969. **Genres:** History. **Career:** The Fighter (documentary film), consultant, 1999; Northwestern University, assistant professor, 1999-2005, associate professor, 2005-, professor of history, 2005-, director of graduate studies, 2005-, director of European studies, 2006-; Wayne V. Jones research professor in history, 2010-;

Weinberg College of Arts and Sciences, Department of Slavic Languages and Literatures, faculty; Central and Southeastern Europe Study Group, co-director. Writer. **Publications:** (Contrib.) Redrawing Nations: Ethnic Cleansing in East Central Europe, 2001; (contrib.) Constructing Nationalities in East Central Europe, 2004; National Cleansing: Retribution against Nazi Collaborators in Postwar Czechoslovakia, 2005; (contrib.) Gender and War in 20th Century Eastern Europe, 2006; The Road to Theresienstadt: The Persecution of Bohemian and Moravian Jews, 1938-1945, forthcoming. Contributor of articles to journals and books. **Address:** Department of History, Northwestern University, Rm. 409, 1800 Sherman Ave., Ste. 106, Evanston, IL 60201, U.S.A. **Online address:** b-frommer@northwestern.edu

FROST, David (Paradine). British (born England), b. 1939. **Genres:** Social Commentary, Humor/Satire, Adult Non-fiction. **Career:** London Weekend Television, founder; David Paradine Ltd., founder, chairman and chief executive, 1966-; Equity Enterprises, joint deputy chairman, 1973-; TV-AM, founding director, 1983; Varsity, editor; Footlights Drama Society, secretary; Motor Neurone Disease Association, vice-president; Alzheimer's Research Trust, vice-president; East Anglia's Children's Hospices, vice-president; Elton John AIDS Foundation, vice-president; Associated-Rediffusion TV, trainee; British Broadcasting Corp., staff. Television performer, producer, actor and writer. **Publications:** (Ed. with N. Sherrin) That was the Week That Was, 1963; How to Live under Labour, or at Least Have as Much Chance as Anybody Else, 1964; Talking with Frost, 1967; To England with Love, 1967; (with A. Jay) English, 1967; The Presidential Debate, 1968; The Americans, 1970; The Bluffer's Guide, 1971; An Evening with David Frost, 1971; Billy Graham talks with David Frost, 1971; Whitlam and Frost, 1974; I Gave Them a Sword: Behind the Scenes of the Nixon Interviews, 1978; I Could Have Kicked Myself, 1982; World's Worst Decisions, 1983; Who Wants to Be a Millionaire?, 1983; Millionaires, Multimillionaires and Really Rich People, 1984; (with M. Shea) The Mid-Atlantic Companion, How to Misunderstand Americans as much as They Misunderstand Us, 1986; (with M. Shea) The Rich Tide: Men, Women, Ideas and Their Transatlantic Impact, 1986; The World's Shortest Books, 1987; U.S. News & World Report Presents The Next President, 1988; David Frost: An Autobiography-Part One from Congregation to Audiences, 1993; Billy Graham: Personal Thoughts of a Public Man, 1997; (with B. Zelnick) Frost/Nixon: Behind the Scenes of the Nixon Interviews, 2007. **Address:** David Paradine Ltd., 5 St Mary Abbots Pl., London, GL W8 6LS, England.

FROST, Diane. British (born England), b. 1962?. **Genres:** History, Race Relations, Sociology, Economics. **Career:** University of Liverpool, Department of Economic and Social History, research fellow, 1991-94, lecturer in sociology, 2002-; University of Central Lancashire, senior lecturer race and ethnic studies, 1994-2002. Writer. **Publications:** (Ed.) Ethnic Labour and British Imperial Trade: A History of Ethnic Seafarers in the UK, 1995; Work and Community among West African Migrant Workers since the Nineteenth Century, 1999; (ed. with T. Zack-Williams and A. Thomas) Africa in Crisis: New Challenges and Possibilities, 2002. **Address:** School of Sociology and Social Policy, The University of Liverpool, Eleanor Rathbone Bldg., Bedford St. S, Liverpool, MS L69 7ZA, England. **Online address:** dfrost@liverpool.ac.uk

FROST, Elizabeth. See **FROST-KNAPPMAN, L. Elizabeth.**

FROST, Ellen L. American (born United States), b. 1945. **Genres:** History. **Career:** U.S. Senate, legislative assistant, 1971-74; United States Treasury Department, staff, 1974-77; United States Department of Defense, deputy assistant secretary of defense for economic and technology affairs, 1977-81; Office of the United States Trade Representative, counselor to the U.S. trade representative, 1993-95; National Defense University, adjunct research fellow; Institute for International Economics, visiting fellow. Writer. **Publications:** For Richer, For Poorer: The New U.S.-Japan Relationship, 1987; (ed. with R.L. Kugler) The Global Century: Globalization and National Security, 2 vols., 2001; (with S.J. Flanagan and R.L. Kugler) Challenges of the Global Century: Report of the Project on Globalization and National Security, 2001; Asia's New Regionalism, 2008; India's Role in East Asia: Lessons from Cultural and Historical Linkages, 2009. **Address:** U.S.A. **Online address:** ellefrost@earthlink.net

FROST, Helen. American (born United States), b. 1949. **Genres:** Children's Fiction, Adult Non-fiction, Poetry, Children's Non-fiction. **Career:** Indiana University, Kilquhanity House School (boarding school), teacher; Purdue, instructor; Fort Wayne Dance Collective, staff of interdisciplinary program,

1995-2006. Author. **Publications:** Season of Dead Water, 1990; Skin of a Fish, Bones of a Bird: Poems, 1993; Bird Nests, 1999; Baby Birds, 1999; Bird Families, 1999; Butterfly Eggs, 1999; Caterpillars, 1999; Butterfly Colors, 1999; Monarch Butterflies, 1999; Your Teeth, 1999; Going to the Dentist, 1999; Food for Healthy Teeth, 1999; Brushing Well, 1999; The Fruit Group, 2000; Eating Right, 2000; The Vegetable Group, 2000; The Dairy Group, 2000; Fats, Oils and Sweets, 2000; Drinking Water, 2000; The Grain Group, 2000; The Meat and Protein Group, 2000; Keeping Water Clean, 2000; The Water Cycle, 2000; Water as a Solid, 2000; Water as a Liquid, 2000; Water as a Gas, 2000; We Need Water, 2000; Memorial Day, 2000; Independence Day, 2000; Martin Luther King, Jr., Day, 2000; Presidents' Day, 2000; Your Senses, 2000; Smelling, 2000; Touching, 2000; Tasting, 2000; Seeing, 2000; Hearing, 2000; Feeling Sad, 2001; Feeling Angry, 2001; Feeling Scared, 2001; Feeling Happy, 2001; The Circulatory System, 2001; The Respiratory System, 2001; The Nervous System, 2001; The Muscular System, 2001; The Skeletal System, 2001; The Digestive System, 2001; What Are Inclined Planes?, 2001; What Are Levers?, 2001; What Are Screws?, 2001; What Are Wedges?, 2001; What Are Wheels and Axles?, 2001; What Are Pulleys?, 2001; When I Whisper, Nobody Listens: Helping Young People Write about Difficult Issues, 2001; Cats, 2001; Fish, 2001; Hamsters, 2001; Dogs, 2001; Rabbits, 2001; Birds, 2001; Praying Mantises, 2001; Walkingsticks, 2001; Water Bugs, 2001; Moths, 2001; Wasps, 2001; Cicadas, 2001; Jaguars, 2002; Boa Constrictors, 2002; Gorillas, 2002; Tree Frogs, 2002; Tarantulas, 2002; Parrots, 2002; A Look at France, 2002; A Look at Kenya, 2002; A Look at Russia, 2002; German Immigrants, 1820-1920, 2002; A Look at Japan, 2002; A Look at Canada, 2002; A Look at Australia, 2002; A Look at Mexico, 2002; A Look at Egypt, 2003; A Look at Cuba, 2003; A Look at Germany, 2003; A Look at Vietnam, 2003; Lemurs, 2003; Chimpanzees, 2003; Leaf-cutting Ants, 2003; Tigers, 2003; Russian Immigrants, 1860-1949, 2003; John F. Kennedy, 2003; Sojourner Truth, 2003; Betsy Ross, 2003; Let's Meet Jackie Robinson, 2004; Let's Meet Booker T. Washington, 2004; Let's Meed Ida B. Wells-Barnett, 2004; Ice, 2004; Fog, 2004; Snow, 2004; Wind, 2004; Triceratops, 2004; Sabertooth Cat, 2004; We Need Plumbers, 2004; Woolly Mammoth, 2005; We Need School Bus Drivers, 2005; We Need Pharmacists, 2005; Allosaurus, 2005; Stegosaurus, 2005; We Need Auto Mechanics, 2005; Tyrannosaurus Rex, 2005; Braid, 2006; Estegosaurio, 2006; Mamut lanudo, 2006; Tigre dientes de sable, 2006; Triceratops, 2006; Alosaurio, 2007; Caribou, 2007; Puffins, 2007; Snowy Owls, 2007; Tiranosaurio Rex, 2007; Diamond Willow, 2008; Monarch and Milkweed, 2008. POLAR ANIMALS SERIES JUVENILE NONFICTION: Snowy Owls, 2007; Puffins, 2007; Caribou, 2007; Arctic Hares, 2007. JUVENILE FICTION: Keesha's House, 2003; Spinning through the Universe: A Novel in Poems from Room 214, 2004; The Braid, 2006; Diamond Willow, 2008; Crossing Stones, 2009; Hidden, 2011. FOR ADULTS: (ed.) Season of Dead Water, 1990; Skin of a Fish, Bones of a Bird: Poems, 1993; (ed.) Why Darkness Seems So Light: Young People Speak Out about Violence, 1998; When I Whistle, Nobody Listens: Helping Young People Write about Difficult Issues, 2001. **Address:** 6108 Old Brook Dr., Fort Wayne, IN 46835-2438, U.S.A. **Online address:** info@helenfrost.net

FROST, Jo. British (born England), b. 1970. **Genres:** Human Relations/ Parenting, Literary Criticism And History. **Career:** Writer. **Publications:** Supernanny: How to Get the Best from Your Children, 2005; Ask Supernanny: What Every Parent Wants to Know, 2006; Jo Frost's Confident Baby Care, 2008. **Address:** c/o Jacqueline Harris, 1325 Ave. of the Americas, New York, NY 10019-6026, U.S.A.

FROST, Karolyn Smardz. Canadian (born Canada) **Genres:** History, Social Sciences, Biography. **Career:** York University, postdoctoral fellow, 2004-05. Writer. **Publications:** (Ed. with S.J. Smith) The Archaeology Education Handbook: Sharing the Past with Kids, 2000; (with A. Shadd and A. Cooper) The Underground Railroad: Next Stop, Toronto!, 2002; I've Got a Home in Glory Land: A Lost Tale of the Underground Railroad, 2007; (ed.) Ontario's African-Canadian Heritage: Collected Writings by Fred Landon, 1918-1967, 2009. Contributor to periodicals. **Address:** Dundurn Press, 3 Church St., Ste. 500, Toronto, ON M5E 1M2, Canada.

FROST, Linda. American (born United States) **Genres:** Adult Non-fiction. **Career:** University of Alabama, associate professor of English, 1993-, Honors Program, associate director, 2004-; Eastern Kentucky University, Honors Program, director, 2008-. Poet. **Publications:** (Contrib.) Generations: Academic Feminists in Dialogue, 1997; (contrib.) Rhetoric in an Antifoundational World: Language, Culture, and Pedagogy, 1998; (contrib.) Blue Pencils and Hidden Hands: Women Editing Periodicals, 1830-1910, 2004; Never One Nation: Freaks, Savages, and Whiteness in U.S. Popular Culture, 1850-1877, 2005; (ed.) Conjoined Twins in Black and White: The Lives of Millie-Christine McKoy and Daisy and Violet Hilton, 2009; Happy Birthday Kansas!: A Sampler Quilt Celebrating 150 Years on the Prairie, 2011. Contributor to books and periodicals. **Address:** Honors Program, Eastern Kentucky University, 521 Lancaster Ave., Richmond, KY 40475-3100, U.S.A. **Online address:** linda.frost@eku.edu

FROST, Mark C. (Eric Bowman). American (born United States), b. 1953. **Genres:** Plays/Screenplays, Novels, Humor/Satire, Young Adult Fiction. **Career:** Writer, producer and director. **Publications:** NOVELS: The List of Seven, 1993; The Six Messiahs, 1995; (as Eric Bowman) Before I Wake, 1997; The Second Objective, 2007. OTHERS: (with D. Lynch and R.S. Wurman) Welcome to Twin Peaks: An Access Guide to the Town, 1991; Greatest Game Ever Played: Harry Vardon, Francis Ouimet, and the Birth of Modern Golf, 2002; Grand Slam: Bobby Jones, America and the Story of Golf, 2004; Match: The Day the Game of Golf Changed Forever, 2007; Game Six: Cincinnati, Boston, and the 1975 World Series: The Triumph of America's Pastime, 2009; Paladin Protocol, 2012. Contributor to periodicals. **Address:** William Morrow & Company Inc., 1350 Ave. of the Americas, New York, NY 10019-4702, U.S.A.

FROST, P. R. See RADFORD, Irene.

FROST, Scott. American (born United States) **Genres:** Novels, Young Adult Non-fiction. **Career:** Writer. **Publications:** The Autobiography of F.B.I. Special Agent Dale Cooper: My Life, My Tapes, 1991; Run the Risk, 2004; Never Fear, 2006; Point of No Return, 2008; Don't Look Back, 2009; Wait for Dark, 2010; One Last Chance, 2012. Contributor to periodicals. **Address:** G. P. Putnams Sons, 375 Hudson St., New York, NY 10014-3658, U.S.A.

FROST, Shelley. American (born United States), b. 1960. **Genres:** Sports/Fitness, Adult Non-fiction, Animals/Pets, Young Adult Fiction. **Career:** Peninsula Humane Society, public relations officer, 1988-89; Pets in Need, manager, 1989-94; HEN, judge of essay contest, 1990-; CAPE, founder, 1993-2000; Frosting on the Cake Productions, director and video producer, 1994-; San Carlos Children's Theater, drama instructor. Writer. **Publications:** (With A. Troussieux) Throw like a Girl: Discovering the Body, Mind and Spirit of the Athlete in You!, 2000; Animals in the News, 2003; Your Adopted Dog: Everything You Need to Know About Rescuing and Caring for a Best Friend in Need, 2007. Contributor to periodicals. **Address:** Andrea Brown Literary Agency, 1076 Eagle Dr., Salinas, CA 93905, U.S.A. **Online address:** videofrosting@aol.com

FROST, Stanley Brice. Canadian/British (born England), b. 1913. **Genres:** Poetry, History, Theology/Religion, Literary Criticism And History. **Career:** Ordained methodist minister, 1939; Methodist Churches, pastor, 1939-49; Staffordshire, pastor, 1942-49; Didsbury College, Old Testament Languages and Literature, chair, 1949-56, special lecturer in Hebrew, 1952-56; McGill University, professor of Old Testament, 1956-74, professor emeritus, 2004-, dean of faculty of divinity, 1957-63, dean of faculty of graduate studies and research, 1963-69, vice-principal of university, 1969-74, History of McGill Project, director, 1974-. Writer. **Publications:** Die Autoritätslehre in den Werken John Wesleys, 1938; The Pattern of Methodism, 1948; Old Testament Apocalyptic, Its Origins and Growth, 1952; The Beginning of the Promise, Eight Lectures on the Book of Genesis, 1960; Patriarchs and Prophets, 1963; (contrib.) The Bible in Modern Scholarship, 1965; (contrib.) Horizons of Theological Education, 1966; Standing and Understanding: A Re-appraisal of the Christian Faith, 1969; (contrib.) The Interpreter's One-Volume Commentary, 1971; (contrib.) A Light Unto My Path, 1974; McGill University for the Advancement of Learning, 1980; The Man in the Ivory Tower: F. Cyril James of McGill, 1991; James McGill of Montreal, 1995. POETRY: Something for My Friends, 1993; Days of Grace and Favour, 1994; Drawn at a Venture, 1996; Memoranda: Moments for Recollection, 1999; A Tale of Two Books, 2000; Millennial Melange, 2001; Autumn Harvest: Selected Poems, 2003. Contributor to journals. **Address:** McGill University, 845 Sherbrooke St. W, Montreal, QC H3A 2T5, Canada.

FROST-KNAPPMAN, L. Elizabeth. (Elizabeth Frost). American (born United States), b. 1943. **Genres:** Women's Studies And Issues, Law, Young Adult Non-fiction, History. **Career:** William Collins and Sons, editor, 1967-69; Natural History Press, editor, 1970-71; Doubleday and Comapny Inc., editor, senior nonfiction editor, 1972-80; William Morrow and Company Inc.,

senior nonfiction editor, 1980-82; New England Publishing Associates Inc., founder and vice-president, 1983-2007. **Publications:** (With D. Shrager) The Quotable Lawyer, 1986; (ed.) Bully Pulpit: Quotations from America's Presidents, 1988; (with K.C. DuPont) Women's Suffrage in America: An Eyewitness History, 1992, rev. ed., 2005; (ed.) The World Almanac of Presidential Quotations, 1993; (with S. Kurian) The ABC-CLIO Companion to Women's Progress in America, 1994; (with K.C. DuPont) Women's Rights on Trial: 101 Historic Trials from Anne Hutchinson to the Virginia Military Institute Cadets, 1997; (ed. with E.W. Knappman and L. Paddock) Courtroom Drama: 120 of the World's Most Notable Trials, 1998. **Address:** New England Publishing Associates Inc., PO Box 361, Chester, CT 06412, U.S.A. **Online address:** nepa@nepa.com

FROUD, Brian. British (born England), b. 1947?. **Genres:** Young Adult Fiction, Illustrations, Humor/Satire. **Career:** Writer and illustrator. **Publications:** (Intro.) The Land of Froud, 1977; (with A. Lee) Faeries, 1978; The Faeries Pop-Up Book, 1980; Goblins, 1983; The Goblins of Labyrinth, 1986; (with T. Jones) The Goblin Companion, 1996; (with T. Jones) Strange Stains and Mysterious Smells: Quentin Cottington's Journal of Faery Research, 1996; Good Faeries, 1998; The Faeries' Oracle, 2000; (with A. Berk) The Runes of Elfland: Visions and Stories from the Faerie Alphabet, 2003; The World of the Dark Crystal, 2003; Brian Froud's World of Faerie, 2007; (with W. Froud) Trolls, 2012. Illustrator of books by others. Contributor to periodicals. **Address:** c/o Author Mail, Harry N. Abrams Inc., 115 W 18th St., 6th Fl., New York, NY 10011, U.S.A.

FRUEH, Joanna. American (born United States), b. 1948. **Genres:** Humanities, Sex, Adult Non-fiction, Art/Art History, Fash Ion/Costume, inspirational/Motivational Literature, Philosophy, Self Help, Theatre, Women's Studies And Issues, Autobiography/Memoirs, Essays, Biography. **Career:** Columbia College, instructor, 1978-80; University of Illinois, adjunct assistant professor, 1980; Oberlin College, assistant professor, 1981-83; University of Arizona, visiting assistant professor, 1983-84, 1988, assistant professor, 1984-85, Joseph Gross Gallery, director, 1984-85, School of Art, professor of practice, 2007-; University of Missouri, adjunct assistant professor, 1986; Union Graduate School, adjunct professor, 1987-89; Southern Illinois University, visiting assistant professor, 1988; Rochester Institute of Technology, visiting assistant professor, 1989-90; University of Nevada, assistant professor, 1990-91, associate professor, 1992-96; professor of art history, 1997-2006; professor emeritus, 2007-. Writer and artist. **Publications:** Brumas, 1982; (ed. with A. Raven and C.L. Langer) Feminist Art Criticism: An Anthology, 1988; (contrib.) Hannah Wilke: A Retrospective, 1989; (ed. with C.L. Langer and A. Raven) New Feminist Criticism: Art, Identity, Action, 1994; Erotic Faculties, 1996; (ed. with L. Fierstein and J. Stein) Picturing the Modern Amazon, 2000; Monster/Beauty: Building the Body of Love, 2001; Swooning Beauty: A Memoir of Pleasure, 2006; Clairvoyance (For Those in the Desert): Performance Pieces, 1979-2004, 2008; The Glamour of Being Real, 2011. **Address:** School of Art, University of Arizona, Rm. 101D, 1031 N Olive Rd., J. Gross Gallery, PO Box 210002, Tucson, AZ 85721-0007, U.S.A. **Online address:** aphrodite@joannafrueh.com

FRUIN, W. Mark. American (born United States), b. 1943. **Genres:** Business/Trade/Industry, Administration/Management. **Career:** University of British Columbia, lecturer, 1970-71, Hong Kong Bank professor of Asian research, 1992-97, Institute of Asian Research, director, 1992-96, Hong Kong Bank of Canada professor, 1992-97, Hong Kong Bank chair, 1992-; California State University, Department of History, assistant professor, associate professor, professor, 1972-88; Harvard University, Harvard Graduate School, postdoctoral fellow and senior research associate, 1979-81, Harvard Business School, Business History Review, faculty, 1987-2007; National University of Singapore, professor of economic history, 1982-83; Osaka University, visiting professor, 1984-85; European Institute of Business Administration, professor of strategy and management, 1988-92; University of California, visiting professor, 1991-92; International Institute of Economic Studies-Japan, faculty, 1992-2000; University of Michigan, School of Business, Corporate Strategy, visiting professor, 1996-98; Institute of International Studies, fellow, 1996-98; San Jose State University, visiting professor, 1998-99, professor of strategy, 1999-; Monterey Institute of International Studies Strategy, visiting and adjunct professor, 1998-2001; Cardiff Business School, Asia Pacific Business Review, teacher, 2002-03; University of San Francisco, Journal of Asia Business Studies, faculty, 2005-. Writer. **Publications:** Kikkoman: Company, Clan, and Community, 1983; The Japanese Enterprise System: Competitive Strategies and Cooperative Structures, 1992; Knowledge Works:

Managing Intellectual Capital at Toshiba, 1997; (ed.) Networks, Markets and Pacific Rim: Studies in Strategy, 1998; (ed. with J.K. Liker and P.S. Adler) Remade in America: Transplanting and Transforming Japanese Management Systems, 1999. **Address:** College of Business, San Jose State University, BT 665, 1 Washington Sq., San Jose, CA 95192-0066, U.S.A. **Online address:** fruin_m@cob.sjsu.edu

FRUM, David. American/Canadian (born Canada), b. 1960. **Genres:** Mystery/Crime/Suspense, Politics/Government. **Career:** Yale University, visiting lecturer, 1986; American Enterprise Institute, associate editor, 1988-; Wall Street Journal, editor, 1989-92; Forbes magazine, columnist, 1992-94; Manhattan Institute for Public Policy Research, senior fellow, 1994-2000; Rudolph Giuliani's presidential campaign, senior foreign policy advisor, 2007-; Federalist Society, president; National Public Radio, commentator. **Publications:** Dead Right, 1994; What's Right: The New Conservative Majority and the Remaking of America, 1996; How We got Here: The 70's, the Decade that Brought You Modern Life (for Better or Worse), 2000; (with R. Pete) End to Evil: How to Win the War on Terror, 2003; The Right Man: An Inside Account of the Bush White House, 2003; The Right Man: The Surprise Presidency of George W. Bush, 2003, as The Right Man: An Inside Account of the Bush White House, 2005; Comeback: Conservatism that Can Win Again, 2008. Contributor of articles to periodicals and newspapers. **Address:** 3111 Foxhall Rd. NW, Washington, DC 20016, U.S.A. **Online address:** dfrum@aei.org

FRY, Andrew C. American (born United States), b. 1956. **Genres:** Sports/Fitness. **Career:** Sweep Left Health Club, owner and operator, 1979-85; National Strength and Conditioning Association, strength and conditioning specialist, 1985, editorial assistant, 1986-88; U.S. Weightlifting Federation, weightlifting coach, 1988, U.S. Olympic Training Center, research technician; University of Connecticut, Human Performance Laboratory, research coordinator, 1988-89, Medical Center, Osteoporosis Center, research assistant, 1989; Ohio University, instructor in anatomy and physiology, 1992-94; University of Memphis, human movement sciences and education, associate professor, 1994-, professor, Exercise Biochemistry Laboratory, director. **Publications:** Overtraining in Sport, 1998. Contributor of articles to journals. **Address:** Department of Health and Sport Sciences, University of Memphis, 135 Roane Field House Memphis, PO Box 526223, Memphis, TN 38152, U.S.A. **Online address:** afry@memphis.edu

FRY, Joseph A. American (born United States), b. 1947?. **Genres:** Business/Trade/Industry. **Career:** University of Nevada, professor of history, distinguished professor, 1975-. Writer. **Publications:** Henry S. Sanford: Diplomacy and Business in Nineteenth-Century America, 1982; John Tyler Morgan and the Search for Southern Autonomy, 1992; Dixie Looks Abroad: The South and U.S. Foreign Relations, 1789-1973, 2002; Debating Vietnam: Fulbright, Stennis, and Their Senate Hearings, 2006. **Address:** History Department, University of Nevada, 4505 Maryland Pkwy., PO Box 455020, Las Vegas, NV 89154-5020, U.S.A. **Online address:** joseph.fry@unlv.edu

FRY, Virginia Lynn. American (born United States), b. 1952. **Genres:** Medicine/Health, Psychology, Self Help, Art/Art History, Young Adult Non-fiction. **Career:** Hospice and Palliative Care Council of Vermont, executive director, 1985-, newsletter editor; Central Vermont Home Health and Hospice, bereavement coordinator; University of Vermont, adjunct faculty; Woodbury College, teacher; national public speaker and workshop presenter; Vermont Department of Social Rehabilitative Services and Vermont Department of Education, consultant. Writer. **Publications:** Arts-in-Hospice, 1990; Part of Me Died, Too: Stories of Creative Survival Among Bereaved Children and Teenagers, 1995. **Address:** Hospice and Palliative Care Council of Vermont, 10 Main St., Montpelier, VT 05602, U.S.A. **Online address:** vlfbc4@yahoo.com

FRY, William Finley. American (born United States), b. 1924. **Genres:** Poetry, Food And Wine, History, Literary Criticism And History, Psychiatry, Sciences, Cartoons, Humor/Satire, Humor/Satire. **Career:** University of California, clinical assistant, 1953-56; Palo Alto Medical Research Foundation. research assistant, 1953-62; Stanford University, clinical instructor, 1958-62, associate clinical professor, 1959-, assistant clinical professor, 1963-, associate professor, professor, now professor emeritus; Mental Research Institute, director of education, 1962-67; Wayne State University Press, Humor in Life and Letters, advisory editor; International Gelotology Institute, director. Psychiatrist, consultant and writer. **Publications:** Sweet Madness: A Study of Humor, 1963; (with M. Allen) Make 'Em Laugh: Life Studies of Comedy

Writers, 1976 as Life Studies of Comedy Writers: Creating Humor, 1998; (ed. with W.A. Salameh) Handbook of Humor and Therapy, 1987; (ed. with W.A. Salameh) Advances in Humor and Psychotherapy, 1993; The Seasons (poems), 1999; (ed. with W. Salameh) Humor and Wellness in Clinical Intervention, 2001; Sweet Madness: A Study of Humor, 2010. Contributor to journals. **Address:** Stanford University, School of Medicine, Rm. LK3C02291, Campus Dr., Li Ka Shing Bldg., 3rd Fl., Stanford, CA 94305-5101, U.S.A. **Online address:** frywf@yahoo.com

FRYD, Vivien Green. American (born United States), b. 1952. **Genres:** Art/Art History, Literary Criticism And History. **Career:** Pittsburg State University, instructor, 1978; University of Wisconsin-Madison, College of Letters and Science Student Academic Affairs, assistant to the associate dean, 1981-84; Arizona State University, visiting assistant professor, 1984-85; Vanderbilt University, assistant professor of history of art, 1985-92, associate professor of history of art, 1992-2003, professor of history of art, 2003-, Department of the History of Art, vice chair, 2008-09, chair, 2009-. Writer. **Publications:** Art and Empire: The Politics of Ethnicity in the United States Capitol, 1815-1860, 1992; Art and the Crisis of Marriage: Edward Hopper and Georgia O'Keeffe, 2003; Feminist Art and Sexual Trauma: Ending the Silence in Contemporary American Art, 2007; The Ghosting of Sexual Violence, Rape, and Incest in Nineteenth-Century American Art, forthcoming. Works appear in anthologies. **Address:** Department of History of Art, Vanderbilt University, 103 Cohen Memorial Hall, 230 Appleton Pl., PO Box 0274, Nashville, TN 37203-5721, U.S.A. **Online address:** vivien.g.fryd@vanderbilt.edu

FRYE, Marilyn. American (born United States), b. 1941?. **Genres:** Women's Studies And Issues, Philosophy, Adult Non-fiction, Social Sciences, Essays. **Career:** University of Pittsburgh, Department of Philosophy, faculty; Michigan State University, faculty, 1974-, Phi Beta Kappa Romanell Lecturer, university distinguished professor, associate dean of graduate studies, Phi Beta Kappa's Romanell professor in philosophy, 2007-08, professor emeritus, 2008-. Writer. **Publications:** Some Reflections on Separatism and Power, 1981; The Politics of Reality: Essays in Feminist Theory, 1983; Willful Virgin: Essays in Feminism, 1976-1992, 1992; (ed. with S.L. Hoagland) Feminist Interpretations of Mary Daly, 2000. Contributor to journals and periodicals. Works appear in anthologies. **Address:** Department of Philosophy, College of Arts and Letters, Michigan State University, 503 S Kedzie Hall, East Lansing, MI 48824-1032, U.S.A. **Online address:** fryem@msu.edu

FRYER, Jonathan. British (born England), b. 1950. **Genres:** History, Theology/Religion, Third World, Biography. **Career:** Reuters, journalist and correspondent, 1973-74; University of Nairobi, School of Journalism, visiting lecturer, 1976; Joint Task Force on Development Issues, executive secretary, 1978-; World Council of Churches, consultant, 1979-82; Earthscan Features, editor, 1986-87; Liberal Intl., chairman, 1989-92; Government of the United Kingdom, honorary consul, 1990-; University of London, School of Oriental and African Studies, part-time lecturer, 1993-; City University, faculty; British Broadcasting Corp., broadcaster; Public Affairs Intl., consultant; Canadian Broadcasting Corp., Mutual Network, interviewer; Belgische Radio en Televisie, interviewer. **Publications:** The Great Wall of China, 1975; Isherwood: A Biography of Christopher Isherwood, 1977; (ed.) China Education and the West, 1978; (contrib.) Brussels Seen by Naïf Artists, 1979; L'aide Alimentaire, Un marché De Dupes, 1982; (ed. and intro.) George Fox and the Children of the Light, 1991; Eye of the Camera: A Life of Christopher Isherwood, 1993; Dylan: The Nine Lives of Dylan Thomas, 1993; (with S. Bradford and J. Pearson) The Silwells, 1994; Soho in the Fifties and Sixties, 1998; André & Oscar: The Literary Friendship of André Gide and Oscar Wilde, 1998; Robbie Ross: Oscar Wilde's Devoted Friend, 2000; Wilde, 2005; Fuelling Kuwait's Development, 2007. **Address:** School of Oriental and African Studies, University of London, Thornhaugh St., Russell Sq., London, GL WC1H 0XG, England. **Online address:** jf10@soas.ac.uk

FRYKENBERG, Robert E(ric). American/Indian (born India), b. 1930. **Genres:** History. **Career:** University of Chicago, visiting assistant professor, 1961-62; South Asia Microform Project, founder and director, 1962-68; University of Wisconsin, assistant professor, 1962-67, associate professor, 1967-71, Department of South Asian Studies, chairman, 1970-73, Center for South Asian Studies, director, 1970-73, Departments of History and South Asian Studies, professor, 1971-97, emeritus professor, 1997-, Pew Research Advancement Project, director, 1994-2000. Writer. **Publications:** Guntur District 1788-1848: A History of Local Influence and Central Authority in South India, 1965; Today's World in Focus: India, 1968; History and Belief: The Foundations of Historical Understanding, 1996; Christianity in India: From Beginnings to the Present, 2008. EDITOR: Land Control and Social Structure in Indian History, 1969; India's Imperial Tradition, 1976; Land Tenure and Peasants in South Asia, 1979; (with P. Kolenda) Studies of South India, 1985; Delhi through the Ages: Essays on Urban Culture and Society, 1986, 1993; (co-ed.) Christians, Cultural Interactions and India's Religious Traditions, 2002; (ed.) Christians and Missionaries in India: Cross-Cultural Communication Since 1500, with Special Reference to Caste, Conversion and Colonialism, 2003; (ed.) India and the Indianness of Christianity, 2009. **Address:** Department of History, University of Wisconsin, 4134 Humanities Bldg., Madison, WI 53706, U.S.A. **Online address:** frykenberg@macc.wisc.edu

FU, Limin. See **FREEMAN, Charles Wellman.**

FUCHS, Marek. American (born United States), b. 1967. **Genres:** Criminology/True Crime. **Career:** Manhattan College, professor of journalism. Writer. **Publications:** A Cold-blooded Business: Adultery, Murder and a Killer's Path from the Bible Belt to the Boardroom, 2009. Contributor to magazines. **Address:** Westchester County, NY , U.S.A. **Online address:** info@marekfuchs.com

FUCHS, Michael Stephen. British (born England), b. 1970. **Genres:** Novels, Young Adult Fiction. **Career:** Virginia Institute of Government, coordinator of Internet services; Security First Technologies, webmaster; Stanford University Medical Center, manager of web development team; Netfish Technologies, webmaster, program manager for the wireless division, performed training, consulting and presales support functions in the Global Services group; Independent consultant and contractor, 2001-. Writer. **Publications:** The Manuscript (novel), 2006; Pandora's Sisters (novel), 2007; D-Boys, forthcoming. **Address:** Pan Books, 158-162 Fulham Rd., London, SW10 9PR, England. **Online address:** fuchs@michaelfuchs.org

FUCHS, Miriam. American (born United States), b. 1949. **Genres:** Literary Criticism And History, Language/Linguistics, History, Reference. **Career:** York College of the City University of New York, adjunct lecturer, 1973-76; State University of New York, adjunct lecturer, 1974-79, adjunct assistant professor, 1979-86; Elizabeth Seton College, assistant professor, 1978-81, associate professor of English, 1981-87, department head, 1981-85; University of Hawaii, visiting assistant professor, 1986-87, assistant professor, 1987-93, associate professor of English, 1993, professor of English, director of honors program in English, 1991-95, Biographical Research Center, vice-president, 1997-. Writer. **Publications:** (Ed. and intro. with E.G. Friedman) Breaking the Sequence: Women's Experimental Fiction, 1989; (ed.) Marguerite Young, Our Darling: Tributes and Essays, 1994; (co-author) Focus on Grammar: An Intermediate Course for Reference and Practice, 1994; The Text is Myself: Women's Life Writing and Catastrophe, 2003; (ed. with C. Howes) Teaching Life Writing Texts, 2008. Works appear in anthologies. Contributor of articles to journals and magazines. **Address:** Department of English, University of Hawaii at Manoa, 325 Henke, 1733 Donaghho Rd., Honolulu, HI 96822, U.S.A. **Online address:** miriam@hawaii.edu

FUCHS, Rachel G(innis). American (born United States), b. 1939. **Genres:** History, Social Commentary, Humanities, Urban Studies, Women's Studies And Issues, Social Sciences. **Career:** Indiana University, visiting assistant professor, 1980-81; Purdue University, Women's Resource Office, director, 1981-83; Arizona State University, School of History Philosophy, Religious Studies, assistant professor, 1983-89, associate professor, 1989-93, professor, 1993-2006, distinguished foundation professor of history, 2006-, regents professor of history, 2011-, associate chair, 1998-2003, Institute for Humanities Research, undergraduate director, interim director; Pacific Coast Branch of the American Historical Association, president, 2008. Writer. **Publications:** Abandoned Children: Foundlings and Child Welfare in Nineteenth-Century France, 1984; Poor and Pregnant in Paris: Strategies for Survival in the Nineteenth Century, 1992; (with E.A. Accampo and M.L. Stewart) Gender and the Politics of Social Reform in France, 1870-1914, 1995; (with V.E. Thompson) Women in Nineteenth-Century Europe, 2005; Gender and Poverty in Nineteenth-Century Europe, 2005; Contested Paternity: Constructing Families in Modern France, 2008. **Address:** Department of History, Arizona State University, PO Box 874302, Tempe, AZ 85287-4302, U.S.A. **Online address:** rfuchs@asu.edu

FUDGE, Erica. British (born England), b. 1968. **Genres:** Humanities, Cultural/Ethnic Topics, Philosophy, History, Animals/Pets. **Career:** Middlesex University, reader in literary and cultural studies; British Animal Studies Network, director; Humanities of Society and Animals, associate editor; University of Strathclyde, professor. Writer. **Publications:** (Ed. with R. Gilbert and S. Wiseman) At the Borders of the Human: Beasts, Bodies, and Natural Philosophy in the Early Modern Period, 1999; Perceiving Animals: Humans and Beasts in Early Modern English Culture, 2000; (ed. and contrib.) Renaissance Beasts: Of Animals, Humans, and Other Wonderful Creatures, 2004; Brutal Reasoning: Animals, Rationality, and Humanity in Early Modern England, 2006; Pets, 2008. Contributor to books and periodicals. **Address:** University of Strathclyde, 7.28 Livingston Twr., 16 Richmond St., Glasgow, G1 1XQ, Scotland. **Online address:** e.fudge@mdx.ac.uk

FUEGI, John. American/British (born England), b. 1936. **Genres:** Literary Criticism And History, Biography, Documentaries/Reportage, Film, History, Photography. **Career:** Free University, lecturer in American literature, 1965-67; University of Wisconsin, assistant professor, 1967-69, associate professor, 1969-72, professor of comparative literature, 1972-76; International Brecht Society, founder, 1970; University of Maryland, professor, 1976-86, Research Center for Arts and Humanities, director, 1986-88, Comparative Literature Program, director, 1994-; The Visual Press, academic director, 1988-90; Flare Films, president; Kingston University, visiting professor; University of Wisconsin, faculty; Harvard University, faculty; Wesleyan University, faculty. Writer. **Publications:** The Essential Brecht, 1972; Bertolt Brecht: Chaos, According to Plan, 1987; Brecht and Company: Sex, Politics and the Making of the Modern Drama, 1994; Brecht & Co., 1997. **Address:** Department of History, University of Maryland, 2115 Francis Scott Key Hall, College Park, MD 20742, U.S.A. **Online address:** jf36@umail.umd.edu

FUESS, Harald. German/British (born England) **Genres:** Human Relations/Parenting, Sociology. **Career:** Harvard University, staff; University of Duisburg-Essen, visiting professor; Sophia University, associate professor for modern Japanese history; Columbia University, visiting lecturer; University of Tokyo, visiting lecturer; Oxford University, visiting lecturer; German National Institute for Japanese Studies, research fellow; Boston Consulting Group, financial service consultant; Sheffield University, School of East Asian Studies, lecturer in business and Japanese history; White Rose East Asia Centre, director of postgraduate studies; Heidelberg University, professor for cultural economic history, Centre for East Asian Studies, faculty, Department of History, faculty. Writer. **Publications:** (Ed. with H. Meyer-Ohle) Japanstudien 9: Consumer and Service in the 1990s, 1997; (ed.) The Japanese Empire in East Asia and Its Postwar Legacy, 1998; Divorce in Japan: Family, Gender, and the State, 1600-2000, 2004; Corporate Capitalism and Consumer Culture: A Transnational History of Beer in Japan, 2012; The Republic of Commerce: Consular Courts and Conflict-Resolution in East Asia, 2015. Works appear in anthologies. **Address:** Heidelberg University, Karl Jaspers Ctr., Vobstrabe 2, 4400 Bldg., Heidelberg, 69115, Germany. **Online address:** fuess@asia-europe.uni-heidelberg.de

FUGARD, Athol. American/South African (born South Africa), b. 1932. **Genres:** Novels, Plays/Screenplays, Autobiography/Memoirs, Novellas/Short Stories. **Career:** Playwright, 1959-; Serpent Players, co-founder and director, 1963-; The Space (experimental theatre), co-founder, 1972; University of California, Department of Theatre and Dance, adjunct professor of playwriting, acting, and directing, now professor emeritus; Indiana University, Class of 1963 Wells Scholar Professor. Writer. **Publications:** Blood Knot, 1963; Hello and Goodbye: A Play in Two Acts, 1966; People are Living There, 1970; Coat, 1971; Boesman and Lena, 1971; Statements, 1974; Three Port Elizabeth Plays, 1974; Sizwe Banzi is Dead: And The Island, 1976; Dimetos and Two Early Plays, 1977; (with R. Devenish) Guest: An Episode in the Life of Eugène Marais, 1977; Tsotsi: A Novel, 1980; Lesson From Aloes, 1981; Marigolds in August, 1982; Master Harold: And the Boys, 1982; Notebooks, 1960-1977, 1983; Road to Mecca, 1986; Selected Plays, 1987; Place with the Pigs: A Personal Parable, 1988; My Children! My Africa!, 1990; Blood Knot, and other Plays, 1991; Hera Nemirdibû, 1991; Playland and Other Words, 1992; Township Plays, 1993; Cousins: A Memoir, 1994; My Life: And, Valley Song, 1996; Valley Song, 1996; The Captain's Tiger: A Memoir for the Stage, 1999; Sorrows and Rejoicings, 2002; Exits And Entrances, 2005; Karoo and Other Stories, 2005; Victory, 2009; The Train Driver, 2010. **Address:** c/o Samuel Liff, William Morris Agency Inc., 1325 Ave. of the Americas, New York, NY 10019-6026, U.S.A.

FUGARD, Lisa. American/South African (born South Africa), b. 1961?.

Genres: Novels, Politics/Government, Race Relations. **Career:** Writer. **Publications:** Skinner's Drift: A Novel, 2006. Contributor to periodicals. **Address:** Molly Dorozenski, Scribner Publicity Department, Simon & Schuster Inc., 1230 Ave. of the Americas, New York, NY 10020, U.S.A. **Online address:** lisa@lisafugard.com

FUJIMURA, Joan H. American (born United States) **Genres:** Anthropology/Ethnology, Sciences. **Career:** Harvard University, assistant professor of anthropology, 1988-93; Stanford University, associate professor of anthropology, 1993-, Henry R. Luce professor in biotechnology and society, professor of sociology; University of California, faculty. Writer. **Publications:** (Ed. with A.E. Clarke) The Right Tools for the Job: At Work in Twentieth-Century Life Sciences, 1992; Crafting Science: A Sociohistory of the Quest for the Genetics of Cancer, 1996. **Address:** Department of Anthropology, Stanford University, 450 Serra Mall, Stanford, CA 94305, U.S.A. **Online address:** fujimura@leland.stanford.edu

FUKUDA, Haruko. British/Japanese (born Japan), b. 1946. **Genres:** Economics, Third World, Young Adult Fiction, Business/Trade/Industry. **Career:** Trade Policy Research Centre, research officer, 1968-70; Overseas Development Institute, research officer, 1970-71; International Bank for Reconstruction and Development, Economics Department, research officer, 1971-72; Vickers da Costa and Comapany Ltd., economist, 1972-74; James Capel and Co., staff, 1974-88, partner, 1980-88; Foreign and Colonial Investment Trust plc, director, 1988-; Nikko Europe, board director, 1988-94, vice chairman, 1994-98; Lazard Brothers and Company Ltd., senior adviser, 1999-; World Gold Council, chief executive, 1999-; Japan Society, joint chairman; Mitsubishi Trust Oxford Foundation, trustee. Writer. **Publications:** Britain in Europe: Impact on the Third World, 1973; Japan and World Trade: The Years Ahead, 1974; Britain and Japan, 1859-1991; Themes and Personalities, 1991. Contributor to periodicals. **Address:** 4 St. James, Wissington, London, SW1A 1NP, England.

FUKUI, Isamu Carter. American (born United States), b. 1990. **Genres:** Novels. **Career:** Writer. **Publications:** YOUNG ADULT NOVELS: Truancy, 2008; Truancy Origins, 2009. **Address:** c/o Matt Bialer, Sanford Greenburger Associates Inc., 55 5th Ave., New York, NY 10003, U.S.A.

FUKUYAMA, Francis. American (born United States), b. 1952. **Genres:** Third World, Politics/Government, History. **Career:** Pan Heuristics Inc., consultant, 1978-79; RAND Corp., associate social scientist, 1979-81, consultant, 1990-94, senior social scientist, 1995-96; U.S. Department of State, staff, 1981-82, 1989-90; University of California, visiting lecturer in political science, 1986, 1989; George Mason University, Omer L. and Nancy Hirst professor, 1996-2001; Johns Hopkins University, dean of faculty, 2002-05, Bernard L. Schwartz professor of international political economy and director of the international development program, 2005-, SAIS Foreign Policy Institute, senior fellow. Writer. **Publications:** Soviet Threats to Intervene in the Middle East, 1956-73, 1980; Soviet Union and Iraq Since 1968, 1980; Escalation in the Middle East and Persian Gulf, 1984; Moscows Post-Brezhnev Reassessment of the Third World, 1986; (ed. with A. Korbonski) The Soviet Union and the Third World: The Last Three Decades, 1987; Soviet Civil-Military Relations and the Power Projection Mission, 1987; (with S. Bruckner and S. Stoecker) Soviet Political Perspectives on Power Projection, 1987; Gorbachev and the New Soviet Agenda in the Third World, 1989; A Look at The End of History?, 1990; The End of History and the Last Man, 1992; Estado & Mercado: delenfrentamiento a la armonización, 1993; U.S.-Japan Security Relationship After the Cold War, 1993; Trust: The Social Virtues and the Creation of Prosperity, 1995; (with P. Breuer and D. Chandler) Transit: Passagen globaler Kooperation: Passages of Global Cooperation, 1997; (with A.N. Shulsky) Virtual Corporation and Army Organization, 1997; The Great Disruption: Human Nature and the Reconstitution of Social Order, 1999; (with C.S. Wagner, R. Schum and D. Pelletiere) Information and Biological Revolutions: Global Governance Challenges: Summary of a Study Group, 2000; Our Posthuman Future: Consequences of the Biotechnology Revolution, 2002; State-Building: Governance and World Orderin the 21st century, 2004; (ed.) Nation-building: Beyond Afghanistan and Iraq, 2006; America at the Crossroads: Democracy, Power, and the Neoconservative Legacy, 2006; After the Neocons: America at the Crossroads, 2006; La brecha entre América Latina y Estados Unidos: Determinantes políticos e institucionales del desarrollo económico, 2006; (ed.) Blindside: How to Anticipate Forcing Events and Wild Cards in Global Politics, 2007; (ed. with K.E. Calder) East

Asian Multi lateralism: Prospects for Regional Stability, 2008; (ed.) Falling Behind: Explaining the Development Gap between Latin America and the United States, 2008; (ed. with N. Birdsall) New Ideas on Development after the Financial Crisis, 2011; The Origins of Political Order: from Prehuman Times to the French Revolution, 2011. Contributor to periodicals. **Address:** Nitze Sch of Advanced Intl Studies, Johns Hopkins University, Rm. 733, 1717Massachusetts Ave. NW, Washington, DC 20036, U.S.A. **Online address:** f.fukuyama@jhu.edu

FULANI, Lenora (Branch). American (born United States), b. 1950. **Genres:** Politics/Government. **Career:** New York Institute for Social Therapy, associate; East Side Center for Short Term Psychotherapy, psychotherapist; All-Stars Talent Show Network, founder, 1981-; National Alliance Party, founder; Unified Independent Party, co-founder. Psychologist, psychotherapist and writer. **Publications:** Independent Black leadership in America: Minister Louis Farrakhan, Dr. Lenora B. Fulani, Reverend Al Sharpton, 1990; The Making of a Fringe Candidate, 1992. EDITOR: The Politics of Race and Gender in Therapy, 1988; The Psychopathology of Everyday Racism and Sexism, 1988. Contributor to books and periodicals. **Address:** Committee for a Unified Independent Party, 225 Broadway, Ste. 2010, New York, NY 10007-3001, U.S.A. **Online address:** lenora@fulani.org

FULCHER, James. British (born England), b. 1942. **Genres:** Sociology. **Career:** University of Leicester, lecturer, 1966-, senior lecturer in sociology, reader in education; International Language Testing Association, vice president, 2005, president, 2006; Language Testing, co-editor; Assessing Writing, editor; TOEFL Research Committee, chair. **Publications:** Labour Movements, Employers, and the State: Conflict and Cooperation in Britain and Sweden, 1991; (with J. Scott) Sociology, 1999, 4th ed., 2011; Capitalism: A Very Short Introduction, 2004. Contributor of articles to journals. **Address:** Department of Sociology, University of Leicester, Attenborough 410, University Rd., Leicester, LE1 7RH, England. **Online address:** gf39@le.ac.uk

FULDA, Jennette. American (born United States), b. 1980?. **Genres:** Autobiography/Memoirs. **Career:** Writer. **Publications:** Half-Assed: A Weight-Loss Memoir, 2008. **Address:** Indianapolis, IN , U.S.A. **Online address:** halfofme@pastaqueen.com

FULGHUM, Robert (L.). American (born United States), b. 1937. **Genres:** Essays, Novels, Adult Non-fiction, Education. **Career:** Unitarian Churches, parish minister; Lakeside School, staff; Rock-Bottom Remainders, founding member. Writer. **Publications:** All I Really Need To Know I Learned In Kindergarten: Uncommon Thoughts On Common Things, 1988; It Was On Fire When I Lay Down On It, 1989; All I Really Need To Know I Learned In Kindergarten: The Essay That Became A Classic, 1990; Mermaids Stand By The King Of The Sea, 1991; Uh-Oh, 1991; Maybe (Maybe Not): Second Thoughts From A Secret Life, 1993; It All Started In Kindergarten: Unforgettable Stories For Listening And Conversation, 1994; From Beginning To End: The Rituals Of Our Lives, 1995; True Love, 1997; Three By Fulghum: The Boxed Set, 1997; Words I Wish I Wrote: A Collection of Writing That Inspired My Ideas, 1997; All I Really Need to Know I Learned in Kindergarten: Reconsidered, Revised & Expanded with Twenty-five New Essays, 2003; What On Earth Have I Done?: Stories, Observations and Affirmations, 2007; Third Wish, 2009; Drž mě pevně, miluj mě zlehka, 2011. **Address:** Villard Books, 201 E 50th St., New York, NY 10022-7703, U.S.A.

FULLAN, Michael G. Canadian (born Canada), b. 1940. **Genres:** Education, Administration/Management, Business/Trade/Industry. **Career:** University of Toronto, dean of the faculty of education, 1998-2003, Ontario Institute for Studies in Education, professor emeritus and dean. Writer, education consultant, researcher and policy advisor. **Publications:** (With J.J. Loubser) Industrial Conversion and Workers' Attitudes to Change in Different Industries, 1969; (contrib.) Thornlea: A Case Study of an Innovative Secondary School, 1972; (with G. Eastabrook) School and Community: Principals and Community Schools in Ontario, 1978; (with P. Park, K. Drope and C. Willis) Curriculum Implementation: A Resource Booklet, 1981; The Meaning of Educational Change, 1982; (with S.E. Anderson and E.E. Newton) Support Systems for Implementing Curriculum in School Boards, 1986; (co-author) The Supervisory Officer in Ontario: Current Practice and Recommendations for the Future, 1987; (co-author) Teacher Education in Ontario: Current Practice and Options for the Future, 1987, new ed., 1990; What's Worth Fighting for in the Principalship? Strategies for Taking Charge in the Elementary School Principalship, 1988; (with S. Stiegelbauer) The New Meaning of Educational Change, 1991, 4th ed., 2007; (with A. Hargreaves) What's Worth Fighting For? Working Together for Your School, 1991; (ed. with A. Hargreaves) Teacher Development and Educational Change, 1992; (ed. with A. Hargreaves) Understanding Teacher Development, 1992; Successful School Improvement: The Implementation Perspective and Beyond, 1992; Change Forces, 1993; (with A. Hargreaves) What's Worth Fighting for in Your School?, 1996; What's Worth Fighting for in the Principalship?, 1997, 2nd ed., 2008; (ed.) The Challenge of School Change: A Collection of Articles, 1997; (with A. Hargreaves) What's Worth Fighting for Out There?, 1998; (co-author) The Rise & Stall of Teacher Education Reform, 1998; Change Forces: The Sequel, 1999; Leading in a Culture of Change: Personal Action Guide and Workbook, 2001; (ed. with E. Polyzoi and J.P. Anchan) Change Forces in Post-Communist Eastern Europe: Education in Transition, 2003; The Moral Imperative of School Leadership, 2003; Change Forces with a Vengeance, 2003; (with A.C. Ballew) Personal Action Guide and Workbook, 2004; Leadership & Sustainability: System Thinkers in Action, 2005; Facilitator's Guide: The Moral Imperative of School Leadership, 2005; (ed.) Fundamental Change, 2005; Turnaround Leadership, 2006; (with C. Germain) Learning Places: A Field Guide for Improving the Context of Schooling, 2006; (with P. Hill and C. Crévola) Breakthrough, 2006; Facilitator's Guide: Leadership & Sustainability: System Thinkers in Action, 2006; (ed. with A. Hargreaves) Change Wars, 2008; The Six Secrets of Change: What the Best Leaders Do to Help Their Organizations Survive and Thrive, 2008; (ed.) The Challenge of Change: Start School Improvement Now!, 2009; (with L. Sharratt) Realization: The Change Imperative for Deepening District-wide Reform, 2009; (with G. Scott) Turnaround Leadership for Higher Education, 2009. **Address:** Ontario Institute for Studies in Education, University of Toronto, 252 Bloor St. W, Toronto, ON M5S 1V6, Canada. **Online address:** changeforces@oise.toronto.ca

FULLER, Charles. American (born United States), b. 1939. **Genres:** Plays/Screenplays, inspirational/Motivational Literature, Novels. **Career:** Afro-American Arts Theatre, co-founder, 1967-, co-director, through 1971; WIP-Radio, The Black Experience Program, writer and director, 1970-71; Temple University, professor of African-American studies, through 1993. **Publications:** The Rise, 1969; Zooman and the Sign, 1982; A Soldier's Play, 1982; Snatch: The Adventures of David and Me in Old New York, 2010. **Address:** c/o Author Mail, Creative Artists Agency, 2000 Ave. of the Stars, Los Angeles, CA 90067, U.S.A.

FULLER, Jack (William). American (born United States), b. 1946. **Genres:** Novels, Sciences, Education. **Career:** Chicago Tribune, reporter, 1973-75, Washington correspondent, 1977-78, editorial writer, 1978-79, deputy editorial page editor, 1979-82, editorial page editor, 1982-87, executive editor, 1987-89, editor, 1989-93, president and publisher, 1993-97; U.S. Department of Justice, special assistant, 1975-76; Tribune Publishing Co., president, 1997-2004; freelance writer, 2004-. **Publications:** Convergence, 1982, 2nd ed., 1991; Fragments, 1984; Mass, 1985; Our Fathers' Shadows, 1987; Legends' End, 1990; News Values: Ideas for an Information Age, 1996; The Best of Jackson Payne: A Novel, 2000; Abbeville, 2008; What is Happening to News: The Information Explosion and the Crisis in Journalism, 2010. Contributor to periodicals. **Address:** The University of Chicago Press, 1427 E 60th St., Chicago, IL 60637, U.S.A.

FULLER, John (Leopold). British (born England), b. 1937. **Genres:** Novels, Novellas/Short Stories, Plays/Screenplays, Poetry, Literary Criticism And History. **Career:** State University of New York, visiting lecturer, 1962-63; Manchester University, assistant lecturer, 1963-66; Magdalen College, fellow, 1966-2002, emeritus fellow, 2002-; Sycamore Press, publisher. Writer. **Publications:** Fairground Music, 1961; The Tree That Walked, 1967; Herod Do Your Worst (play), 1967; The Art of Love, 1968; The Labours of Hercules: A Sonnet Sequence, 1969; Three London Songs, 1969; Annotations of Giant's Town, 1970; The Wreck, 1970; Half a Fortnight, 1970; A Reader's Guide to W.H. Auden, 1970; The Spider Monkey Uncle King (play), 1971; Cannibals and Missionaries, 1972; Boys in a Pie, 1972; Fox-Trot (libretto), 1972; The Sonnet, 1972; Hut Groups, 1973; (with A. Mitchell and P. Levi) Penguin Modern Poets 22, 1973; Epistles to Several Persons, 1973; Poems and Epistles, 1974; Squeaking Crust, 1974; The Queen in the Golden Tree (libretto), 1974; The Mountain in the Sea, 1975; The Last Bid, 1975; Carving Trifles, 1976; Bel and the Dragon, 1977; The Wilderness, 1977; Lies and Secrets, 1979; The Illusionists, 1980; The Extraordinary Wood Mill and Other Stories, 1980; The

January Divan, 1980; The Ship of Sounds, 1981; Waiting for the Music, 1982; The Beautiful Inventions, 1983; Come Aboard and Sail Away (for children), 1983; The Adventures of Speedfall (stories), 1985; Selected Poems 1954-82, 1985; (with J. Fenton) Partingtime Hall (poems), 1987; The Grey among the Green (poems), 1988; The Mechanical Body, 1991; The Worm and the Star (stories), 1993; Stones and Fires (poems), 1996; Collected Poems, 1996; W.H. Auden: A Commentary, 1998; W.H. Auden: A Selection by John Fuller, 2000; Now and for a Time (poems), 2002; Ghosts (poems) 2004; The Space of Joy (poems), 2006; Song & Dance (poems), 2008; Alexander Pope: A Selection by John Fuller (2008); The Shell Hymn Book (poems), 2009; Pebble & I (poems), 2010; (with D. Hurn) Writing the Picture (photographs and poems), 2010; (with N. LeFanu) Dream Hunter (opera), 2010; Who is Ozymandias? And Other Puzzles in Poetry (criticism), 2011. NOVELS: Flying to Nowhere, 1983; Tell It Me Again, 1988; The Burning Boys, 1989; Look Twice, 1991; A Skin Diary, 1997; The Memoirs of Laetitia Horsepole, 2001; Flawed Angel, 2005. EDITOR: Light Blue Dark Blue, 1960; Oxford Poetry, 1960, 1960; Poetry Supplement, 1962; (with H. Pinter and P. Redgrove) New Poems 1967, 1968; Poetry Supplement, 1970; Nemo's Almanac, 17 vols., 1971-87; The Dramatic Works by John Gay; Poets in Hand (for children), 1985; Chatto Book of Love Poetry, 1990; The Oxford Book of Sonnets, 2000; W. H. Auden: poems selected by John Fuller, 2000; Alexander Pope: Poems Selected by John Fuller, 2008. **Address:** United Agents Ltd., 12-26 Lexington St., London, GL W1F 0LE, England. **Online address:** john.fuller@magd.ox.ac.uk

FULLER, Mary Lou. American (born United States), b. 1929. **Genres:** Women's Studies And Issues, Autobiography/Memoirs, Humor/Satire, Gay And Lesbian Issues, Education. **Career:** First Pennsylvania Banking and Trust, assistant director of training, 1946-61; Guaranty Bank and Trust, assistant director of training, 1961-63; John Hancock Inn, manager; Fitzwilliam Inn, owner, 1963-73; National Grange assistant director of training, 1975-80; University of New Hampshire, business manager for student dining, 1980-89; KALM Publishing, partner, 1989-. Writer. **Publications:** A Horse in the Ladies' Room, 1997; Where Lame Donkeys Lie, 1998; On the Wings of a Unicorn, 1999; (ed. with G.W. Olsen) Home-School Relations: Working Successfully with Parents and Families, 1998, 4th ed. as Home and School Relations: Teachers and Parents Working Together, 2012; Sisters by Heart: Partners in Aging, 2001; (with T.G. Jones) Teaching Hispanic Children, 2003. **Address:** 149 E Side Dr., Ste. 135, Concord, NH 03301, U.S.A. **Online address:** uniqueyankee@aol.com

FULLER, Sophie. British (born England), b. 1961. **Genres:** Music, Bibliography, History. **Career:** London Veena Music Group, flautist, 1984-85; Sidcup Adult Education Institute, teacher, 1989; Women in Music Archive and Information Service, project coordinator, 1992-96; Ithaca College, London Center, staff, 1993-94; University of Southampton, faculty, 1993-96; University of Reading, lecturer in music, 1995-, director of teaching and learning music; London News Talk Radio, classical music correspondent, 1995; Old Royal Naval College, Trinity Laban Conservatoire of Music and Dance, MMus course leader. Writer. **Publications:** Islanders and The Fisher of Men, 1984; Reclaiming the Muse: A Select Bibliography of English-Language Writing on Women and Music, 1991; The Pandora Guide to Women Composers: Britain and the United States 1629-Present, 1994; The Women in Music Classical Repertoire Guide: Orchestral Music, 1996; (ed. with L. Whitesell) Queer Episodes in Music and Modern Identity, 2002; (ed. with N. Losseff) The Idea of Music in Victorian Fiction, 2004. **Address:** Trinity Laban Conservatoire of Music and Dance, Old Royal Naval College, King Charles Ct., Greenwich, London, GL SE10 9JF, England. **Online address:** s.fuller@trinitylaban.ac.uk

FULLER, Steve William. British/American (born United States), b. 1959. **Genres:** Philosophy, Sciences, Sociology, Speech/Rhetoric. **Career:** University of Pittsburgh, teaching fellow in history and philosophy of science, 1982-85, associate professor in the rhetoric of science, 1993-94; University of Colorado, assistant professor of philosophy, 1985-88; Virginia Polytechnic Institute and State University, assistant professor, 1988-92, associate professor of science and technology studies, 1992-94; University of Durham, professor of sociology and social policy, 1994-99; University of Warwick, professor of sociology, 1999-, Auguste Comte chair in social epistemology, 2011. Writer. **Publications:** Social Epistemology, 1988, 2nd ed., 2002; (ed.) The Cognitive Turn: Sociological and Psychological Perspectives On Science, 1989; Philosophy of Science and Its Discontents, 1989, 2nd ed., 1993; Philosophy, Rhetoric and the End of Knowledge: The Coming of Science and Technology Studies, 1993, 2nd ed., 2004; (ed. with T. Brante and W. Lynch) Controversial Science: From Content to Contention, 1993; (ed. with W.R. Sadish) The

Social Psychology of Science, 1994; Science, 1997; The Governance of Science: Ideology and the Future of the Open Society, 2000; Thomas Kuhn: A Philosophical History for Our Times, 2000; Knowledge Management Foundations, 2002; Kuhn vs. Popper: The Struggle for the Soul of Science, 2003; The Intellectual, 2005; The Philosophy of Science and Technology Studies, 2006; The New Sociological Imagination, 2006; The Knowledge Book: Key Concepts in Philosophy, Science and Culture, 2007; Science vs. Religion?, 2007, New Frontiers in Science and Technology Studies, 2007; Dissent over Descent, 2008; The Sociology of Intellectual Life, 2009; Science: The Art of Living, 2010; Humanity 2.0, 2011. Contributor to journals and newspapers. **Address:** Department of Sociology, University of Warwick, Rm. 2.23, Ramphal Bldg., Gibbet Hill Rd., Coventry, WM CV4 7AL, England. **Online address:** s.w.fuller@warwick.ac.uk

FULLERTON, Alma. Canadian (born Canada), b. 1969. **Genres:** Novels, Children's Non-fiction. **Career:** Writer. **Publications:** NOVELS: In the Garage, 2006; Walking on Glass, 2007; Libertad, 2008; Burn, 2010. **Address:** Cormorant Books Inc., 215 Spadina Ave., Ste. 230, Toronto, ON M5T 2C7, Canada. **Online address:** almafullerton@almafullerton.com

FULLERTON, Gail. Also writes as Gail J. Putney, Gail Putney Fullerton. American (born United States), b. 1927. **Genres:** Human Relations/Parenting, Sociology, Social Sciences. **Career:** Drake University, lecturer in sociology, 1955-57; Florida State University, assistant professor of sociology, 1957-59; San Jose State University, assistant professor, 1963-68, associate professor, 1968-72, dean of graduate studies and research, 1972-76, professor of sociology, 1972-91, executive vice-president, 1977-78, president, 1978-91. Writer. **Publications:** (As Gail J. Putney with S. Putney) Normal Neurosis, 1964; The Adjusted American, 1966; Survival in Marriage, 1972, 2nd ed., 1977. **Address:** c/o Gerard McCauley, 159 W 53rd St., Ste. 27-A, New York, NY 10019-6068, U.S.A.

FULLERTON, Gail Putney. See FULLERTON, Gail.

FULTON, Joe B. American (born United States), b. 1962. **Genres:** Race Relations, Theology/Religion, History. **Career:** Dalton College, assistant professor; Baylor University, Department of English, professor. Writer. **Publications:** Mark Twain's Ethical Realism: The Aesthetics of Race, Class and Gender, 1997; Mark Twain in the Margins: The Quarry Farm Marginalia and a Connecticut Yankee in King Arthur's Court, 2000; The Reverend Mark Twain: Theological Burlesque, Form, and Content, 2006; Reconstruction of Mark Twain: How a Confederate Bushwhacker Became the Lincoln of Our Literature, 2010. Contributor of articles to journals. **Address:** Department of English, Baylor University, Rm. 209, Carroll Science Bldg., 1 Bear Pl., Ste. 97404, Waco, TX 76798-7404, U.S.A. **Online address:** joe_fulton@baylor.edu

FULTZ, James R. (Jay Fultz). American (born United States), b. 1936. **Genres:** Biography, Essays. **Career:** Northwest Missouri State College, teacher of English composition and literature, 1965-66; Eastern College, teacher of English composition and literature, 1966-67; South Dakota State University, instructor in English, 1967-70; Library of Congress, Maude Hammond Fling Fellow, 1974; University of Nebraska-Lincoln, Maude Hammond Fling Fellow, 1974, instructor in English, 1975-82; University of Nebraska Press, editorial associate, 1984-87, Bison Books, editor, 1987-98; freelance editor and writer, 1998-. **Publications:** In Search of Donna Reed, 1998. Contributor to periodicals. **Address:** 1024 S 28th St., Parsons, KS 67357, U.S.A. **Online address:** jay@cpol.net

FULTZ, Jay. See FULTZ, James R.

FUMENTO, Rocco. American (born United States), b. 1923. **Genres:** Novels, Film, Young Adult Fiction, History. **Career:** University of Illinois, faculty, 1952-, associate professor of English, 1964-, now professor emeritus in English, film and creative writing. Writer. **Publications:** Devil by the Tail, 1954; Tree of Dark Reflection, 1962; A Decent Girl Always Goes to Mass on Sunday, 2002; A Lesser Saint, 2006. EDITOR: Introduction to the Short Story, 1962; (and intro.) 42nd Street, 1980; (with T. Williams) Jack London's The Sea Wolf, 1998. **Address:** 1100 Main St., Dalton, MA 01226-2202, U.S.A. **Online address:** rfumento@webtv.net

FUMIZUKI, Kou. American (born United States) **Genres:** Children's Fiction, Novels, Literary Criticism And History. **Career:** Illustrator and writer.

Publications: Ai Yori Aoshi, 17 vols., 2007. Contributor to periodicals. **Address:** c/o Author Mail, TokyoPop, 5900 Wilshire Blvd., Ste. 2000, Los Angeles, CA 90036-5020, U.S.A.

FUNAKAWA, Atsushi. Japanese (born Japan), b. 1956. **Genres:** Administration/Management, Business/Trade/Industry. **Career:** Toshiba, sales coordinator, 1980-82; American Life Insurance Co., section chief, 1983-90; Clarke Consulting Group, intercultural business specialist, 1992-94; Globis Corp., program director for organizational learning, 1995-; Geonexus Communications, staff. Writer. **Publications:** Transcultural Management: A New Approach for Global Organizations, 1997. Contributor to periodicals. **Address:** Globis Corp., Kojimachi G. N. Yasuda Bldg., Ste. 2F, 3-6-5 Kojimachi, Chiyoda ku, Tokyo, 102, Japan. **Online address:** funakawa@globis.co.jp

FUNDERBURG, Lise. (Lise Kristin Funderburg). American (born United States), b. 1959. **Genres:** Autobiography/Memoirs, Race Relations, Music. **Career:** Cable Publications, executive editor; University of Pennsylvania, journalist and teacher of creative writing; Rutgers University, journalist and teacher of creative writing. **Publications:** Black, White, Other: Biracial Americans Talk about Race and Identity, 1994; The Color Purple: A Memory Book of the Broadway Musical, 2006; Pig Candy: Taking My Father South, Taking My Father Home, 2008. Contributor to magazines. **Address:** c/o Geri Thoma, Elaine Markson Literary Agency, 44 Greenwich Ave., New York, NY 10011-8347, U.S.A. **Online address:** lf@lisefunderburg.com

FUNDERBURG, Lise Kristin. See FUNDERBURG, Lise.

FUNK, Liz. American (born United States), b. 1988?. **Genres:** Social Sciences. **Career:** Columbia University, instructor. Journalist, public speaker and writing coach. **Publications:** Supergirls Speak Out: Inside the Secret Crisis of Overachieving Girls, 2009. Contributor to periodicals. **Address:** Wendy Sherman Associates, 27 W 24th St., Ste. 700B, New York, NY 10010, U.S.A. **Online address:** liz.funk@gmail.com

FUNK, Tom. American (born United States), b. 1965. **Genres:** Business/Trade/Industry, Technology. **Career:** Timberline Interactive (a Web development and online marketing consultancy), vice president of client services; Vermont Teddy Bear Co., web manager; Calyx & Corolla, web manager; PajamaGram, web manager; Overlook Press, staff. Writer. **Publications:** Web 2.0 and Beyond: Understanding the New Online Business Models, Trends and Technologies, 2009. **Address:** Bristol, VT , U.S.A. **Online address:** tfunk@timberlineinteractive.com

FUNKHOUSER, Erica. American (born United States), b. 1949. **Genres:** Plays/Screenplays, Poetry. **Career:** Cambridge Historical Commission, writer, 1974-77; Boston University, Metropolitan College, part-time teacher, 1976-87; Salem State College, part-time teacher, 1976-87; North Shore Community College, part-time teacher, 1976-87; Revels Inc., scriptwriter, 1986-; Lesley College, adjunct lecturer in adult degree program, 1987-; Massachusetts Institute of Technology, poet and lecturer, 1998-, University of Massachusetts-Dartmouth, lecturer. **Publications:** (Ed. with D. Dimancescu and R. Stephenson) This is Boston: A Walking Guide to Boston and Cambridge, 1974; Natural Affinities (poems), 1983; Sure Shot and Other Poems, 1992; The Actual World (poetry), 1997; (contrib.) Lewis & Clark, 1997; Pursuit (poetry), 2002; Earthly, 2008. Contributor to magazines. **Address:** University of Massachusetts, PWHS, 14N-221C, 285 Old Westport Rd., North Dartmouth, MA 02747-2300, U.S.A. **Online address:** ericaf@mit.edu

FURDELL, Elizabeth Lane. American (born United States), b. 1944. **Genres:** Medicine/Health, History, Humanities. **Career:** University of Great Falls, assistant professor, associate professor, 1971-83, faculty president, 1981-83; University of North Florida, professor of history, 1983-, distinguished professor, 2002; University of London, Institute for Historical Research, research associate, 1983, 1985, 1987, 1989, 1991; The Sally Corp., historical consultant; Writer. **Publications:** (With W.J. Furdell) Great Falls: A Pictorial History, 1987; (contrib.) The Historical Dictionary of Stuart England, 1996; (contrib.) The Historical Dictionary of the British Empire, 1996; James Welwood: Physician to the Glorious Revolution, 1998; The Royal Doctors, 1485-1714: Medical Personnel at the Tudor and Stuart Courts, 2001; Publishing and Medicine in Early Modern England, 2002; The Oxford Dictionary of National Biography, 2004; (ed.) Textual Healing: Essays on Medieval and Early Modern Medicine, 2005; Fatal Thirst: Diabetes in Britain until Insulin,

2008. **Address:** Department of History, University of North Florida, 1 UNF Dr., Jacksonville, FL 32224-7699, U.S.A. **Online address:** efurdell@unf.edu

FUREY, Leo. Canadian (born Canada) **Genres:** Novels. **Career:** Newfoundland and Labrador Film Development Corp., executive director. Writer. **Publications:** The Long Run: A Novel, 2004. **Address:** Anne McDermid & Associates Ltd., 83 Willcocks St., Toronto, ON M5S 1C9, Canada.

FURIA, Philip (G.). American (born United States), b. 1943. **Genres:** Biography, Music, History. **Career:** University of Minnesota, assistant professor, 1970-76, associate professor, 1976-84, professor of English, 1984-96, director of undergraduate studies in English, 1977-80, chairman of individualized degree programs, 1980-82, assistant chairman of department, 1983-86, College of Liberal Arts, associate dean; University of East Anglia, visiting exchange professor, 1976-77; University of Graz, Fulbright professor, 1982-83; Metropolitan State University, College of Arts and Sciences, dean, 1995; University of North Carolina, chair of department of English, 1996-99, director of film studies, 2000-02, chair of department of creative writing, 2004-, professor. Writer. **Publications:** Pound's Cantos Declassified, 1984; The Poets of Tin Pan Alley: A History of America's Great Lyricists, 1990; Ira Gershwin: The Art of the Lyricist, 1996; Irving Berlin: A Life in Song, 1998; (ed.) American Song Lyricists, 1920-1960, 2002; Skylark: The Life and Times of Johnny Mercer, 2003; (with M. Lasser) America's Songs: The Stories Behind the Songs of Broadway, Hollywood and Tin Pan Alley, 2006; (with L. Patterson) Songs of Hollywood, 2010. **Address:** Department of Creative Writing, University of North Carolina, 1232 Kenan Hall, 601 S College Rd., Wilmington, NC 28403-5938, U.S.A. **Online address:** furiap@uncw.edu

FURINO, Antonio. American/Italian (born Italy), b. 1931. **Genres:** Economics, Education, Information Science/Computers, Medicine/Health, Politics/Government, Social Sciences. **Career:** University of Texas Health Science Center, owner, director, 1966, Development through Applied Science, director, 1966-, professor of economics, 1985-, senior research fellow, 1986-, Center for Health Economics and Policy, director, 1987-, professor, 1990, Regional Center for Health Workforce Studies, Innovation Creativity, Capital Institute, director, 2001-, associate director, 2006-. Writer. **Publications:** Grassroots Entrepreneurship in the Health Arena: Technology for Communities at the Crossroads, 2003. EDITOR: Cooperation and Competition in the Global Economy: Issues and Strategies, 1988; (with B.S. Fogel and G.L. Gottlieb) Mental Health Policy for Older Americans: Protecting Minds at Risk, 1990; Health Policy and the Hispanic, 1992. **Address:** University of Texas Health Science Center, 7703 Floyd Curl Dr., San Antonio, TX 78229, U.S.A. **Online address:** furino@uthscsa.edu

FURNISH, Victor Paul. American (born United States), b. 1931. **Genres:** Theology/Religion, Ethics. **Career:** United Methodist Church, ordained minister, 1955; Southern Methodist University, Perkins School of Theology, instructor, 1959-60, assistant professor, 1960-65, associate professor, 1965-71, professor, 1971-83, university distinguished professor of New Testament, 1983-2000, distinguished professor emeritus of New Testament, 2000-; Abingdon New Testament Commentaries, general editor, 1996-. **Publications:** Theology and Ethics in Paul, 1968; The Love Command in the New Testament, 1972; (with J.H. Snow) Easter: Series A, 1975; (ed. with K. Crim and L. Bailey) The Interpreter's Dictionary of the Bible: Supplementary Volume, 1976; The Moral Teaching of Paul: Selected Issues, 1979, 3rd ed., 2009; (ed. with L. Bailey) Interpreting Biblical Texts, 1981, vol. VIII, 1987; Homosexuality, in Search of a Christian Understanding: Biblical, Theological-Ethical and Pastoral Care Perspectives, 1981; (with R.L. Thulin) Pentecost 3: Series A, 1981; (ed. with T.E. Fretheim and L.R. Bailey, Sr.) Deuteronomic History, 1983; (ed. with R.E. Murphy and L.R. Bailey, Sr.) Wisdom Literature and Psalms, 1983; (ed. with L.E. Keck and L.R. Bailey, Sr.) The Pauline Letters, 1984; (trans. and intro.) II Corinthians, 1984; Lent: Series A, 1986; Jesus According to Paul, 1993; (ed.) Sexuality Debate in North American Churches, 1988-1995: Controversies, Unresolved Issues, Future Prospects, 1995; (ed. with E.H. Lovering, Jr.) Theology and Ethics in Paul and His Interpreters: Essays in Honor of Victor Paul Furnish, 1996; The Theology of the First Letter to the Corinthians, 1999; 1 Thessalonians, 2 Thessalonians, 2007. **Address:** Abingdon Press, 201 8th Ave. S, PO Box 801, Nashville, TN 37202-0801, U.S.A.

FURNISS, Graham (Lytton). British (born England), b. 1949. **Genres:** Area Studies, Language/Linguistics, Literary Criticism And History. **Career:** Bayero University, part-time lecturer in Nigerian languages, 1973-74; Uni-

versity of Maiduguri, lecturer in languages and linguistics, 1977-79; University of London, School of Oriental and African Studies, lecturer, 1979-89, senior lecturer, 1990-96, reader in Hausa cultural studies, 1996-99, Centre of African Studies, chairperson, 1989-93, dean of languages, 1995-97, professor of African-language literature, 1999-, dean of the faculty of languages and cultures, 2002-04, pro-director of SOAS 2008-. Writer. **Publications:** Second Level Hausa: Grammar in Action, 1991; Ideology in Practice: Hausa Poetry as Exposition of Values and Viewpoints, 1995; Poetry, Prose, and Popular Culture in Hausa, 1996; Orality: The Power of the Spoken Word, 2004; (co-author) Bibliography of Hausa Popular Fiction 1987-2002, 2004. EDITOR: Writings on Hausa Grammar: The Collected Papers of F.W. Parsons, 1982; (with P.J. Jaggar and contrib.) Studies in Hausa Language and Linguistics, 1988; African Languages and Cultures, 2 vols., 1988-89; (with R. Fardon and contrib.) African Languages, Development, and the State, 1994; (with L. Gunner) Power, Marginality, and African Oral Literature, 1995; (with R. Fardon) African Broadcast Cultures: Radio in Transition, 2000. Contributor to books and periodicals. **Address:** Department of African Languages and Cultures, School of Oriental & African Studies, University of London, Thornhaugh St., Russell Sq., London, GL WC1E 7HP, England. **Online address:** gf1@soas.ac.uk

FURUBOTN, Eirik G. American (born United States), b. 1923. **Genres:** Economics, Business/Trade/Industry, History. **Career:** Rice Institute (now Rice University), instructor in economics, 1949-51; Wesleyan University, instructor in economics, 1953-55; Rensselaer Polytechnic Institute, instructor in economics, 1955-58; Lafayette College, assistant professor of economics, 1958-60; Emory University, associate professor of economics, 1960-63; State University of New York, professor of economics, 1963-67, chair of department, 1966-67; Tulane University, visiting associate professor, 1964-65; Texas A&M University, professor of economics, 1967-82, Private Enterprise Research Center, research fellow, 1996-; University of Texas, visiting professor, 1981-82, James L. West professor of economics, 1982-96, research associate; University of Saarland, visiting professor, 1985, Center for the Study of the New Institutional Economics, co-director, 1986-, honorary professor of economics; University of Konstanz, visiting research professor, 1986. Writer. **Publications:** (With R.B. Ekelund and W.P. Gramm) The Evolution of Modern Demand Theory (essays), 1972; The Economics of Industrial Democracy: An Analysis of Labor Participation in the Management of Business Firms, 1979; (with R. Richter) Institutions and Economic Theory, 1997, 2nd ed., 2005. EDITOR AND CONTRIBUTOR: (with S.A. Pejovich) The Economics of Property Rights, 1974; (with R. Richter) Some Views on Hospital Finance, 1988; (with R. Richter) The Economics and Law of Banking Regulation, 1990; (with R. Richter) The New Institutional Economics: A Collection of Articles from the Journal of Institutional and Theoretical Economics, 1991. Contributor to economic journals. **Address:** 750 N Rosemary Dr., Bryan, TX 77802, U.S.A.

FURUTANI, Dale. American (born United States), b. 1946. **Genres:** Mystery/Crime/Suspense, Novels, Horror. **Career:** Yamaha Motorcycles, parts marketing manager; Nissan Motor Corporation USA, director of information technology; Edmunds.com, chief information officer. Writer. **Publications:** MYSTERY NOVELS: Death In Little Tokyo: A Ken Tanaka Mystery, 1996; Toyotomi Blades: A Ken Tanaka Mystery, 1997; Death At The Crossroads: A Samurai Mystery, 1998; Jade Palace Vendetta: A Samurai Mystery, 1999; Kill the Shogun: A Samurai Mystery, 2000; Blood on the Pacific Rim, forthcoming. Contributor of articles to periodicals. **Address:** c/o Neeti Madan, Sterling Lord Literistic Inc., 65 Bleecker St., New York, NY 10012, U.S.A. **Online address:** dfurutani@aol.com

FUSILLI, Jim. American (born United States), b. 1954?. **Genres:** Novels, Mystery/Crime/Suspense, Animals/Pets. **Career:** Wall Street Journal, music critic, 1983-; Boston Globe, mystery fiction critic, 2002-03; St. Peter's College, school newspaper and radio staff; National Public Radio, music critic; State University of New York, visiting professor, 2005-. Writer. **Publications:** Closing Time, 2001; A Well-known Secret, 2002; Tribeca Blues, 2003; Hard Hard City, 2004; The Beach Boys Pet Sounds, 2005; The Chopin Manuscript, 2007; Marley Z and the Bloodstained Violin, 2008. **Address:** c/o Author Mail, Penguin Putnam, 375 Hudson St., New York, NY 10014-3658, U.S.A. **Online address:** jimfusillibooks@aol.com

FUSSELL, Bob. *See* **FUSSELL, E. Robert.**

FUSSELL, E. Robert. (Bob Fussell). American (born United States), b.

1942. **Genres:** Novels, Young Adult Fiction, History. **Career:** Secondary school teacher, 1966-68; E. Robert Fussell P.C. (law office), owner and president, 1972-; Genesee County Chamber of Commerce, director, 1974-78, president, 1976; LeRoy Village trustee, staff, 1992-, deputy-mayor, 1997-; Ingham University Press, owner and president, 1998-. Writer. **Publications:** Human-itis B: Family at War (fiction), 2000; (as Bob Fussel) My Great Life, 2005; (ed.) Unbridled Cowboy, 2008. **Address:** 46 Wolcott St., Ste. 1, LeRoy, NY 14482, U.S.A. **Online address:** info@erobertfussell.com

FUSSELL, Paul. American (born United States), b. 1924. **Genres:** Literary Criticism And History, Social Commentary, Travel/Exploration, Adult Nonfiction. **Career:** Connecticut College, instructor in English, 1951-54; Rutgers University, assistant professor, 1955-59, associate professor, 1959-64, professor of English, 1964-76, John DeWitt professor of English literature, 1976-83; University of Heidelberg, Fulbright lecturer, 1957-58; American University, lecturer, 1965-; University of Pennsylvania, Donald T. Regan professor of English literature, 1983-94, Donald T. Regan professor emeritus of English literature, 1994-; King's College, visiting professor, 1990-92. Writer. **Publications:** Theory of Prosody in Eighteenth-Century England, 1954; (co-author) The Presence of Walt Whitman, 1962; The Rhetorical World of Augustan Humanism, 1965; Poetic Meter and Poetic Form, 1965, rev. ed. 1979; Samuel Johnson and the Life of Writing, 1971; The Great War and Modern Memory, 1975; Abroad: British Literary Traveling between the Wars, 1980; The Boy Scout Handbook and Other Observations, 1982; Class: A Guide through the American Status System, 1983 in UK as Caste Marks: Style and Status in the USA, 1984; Thank God for the Atom Bomb and Other Essays, 1988; Wartime: Understanding and Behavior in the Second World War, 1989; (intro.) Middle Parts of Fortune, 1990; BAD or, the Dumbing of America, 1991; The Anti-egotist: Kingsley Amis, Man of Letters, 1994; Doing Battle: The Making of a Skeptic, 1996; Uniforms: Why We are What We Wear, 2002; The Boys' Crusade: The American Infantry in Northwestern Europe, 1944-

1945, 2003; (intro.) The Gallery, 2004; (intro.) The Road to Roxiana, 2007. EDITOR: (co-ed.) Eighteenth-century English Literature, 1969; (intro.) English Augustan Poetry, 1972; The Ordeal of Alfred M. Hale, 1975; Siegfried Sassoon's Long Journey: Selections from the Sherston Memoirs, 1983; The Norton Book of Travel, 1987; The Norton Book of Modern War, 1991; The Bloody Game: An Anthology of Modern War, 1992. Contributor to periodicals. **Address:** Department of English, University of Pennsylvania, Rm. 127, Fisher-Bennett Hall, 3340 Walnut St., Philadelphia, PA 19104-6273, U.S.A. **Online address:** behrfuss@aol.com

FUTCHER, Jane P. American (born United States), b. 1947. **Genres:** Novels, Adult Non-fiction, Gay And Lesbian Issues, Medicine/Health, Young Adult Fiction, Travel/Exploration. **Career:** Philadelphia Public School System, substitute teacher, 1972-73; Harper & Row Media, staff project editor, producer and writer, 1973-77; Guidance Associates, scriptwriter, 1977-80; World College West, adjunct faculty and writing tutor, 1990-92; Marin Independent Journal, reporter, 1995-2004. Writer. **Publications:** NOVELS: Crush, 1981; Promise Not to Tell, 1991; Dream Lover, 1997. NONFICTION: Marin: The Place, the People, 1981. Contributor of articles to periodicals. **Address:** 235 Shelvin Rd., Novato, CA 94947, U.S.A. **Online address:** jfutcher@aol.com

FUTTERMAN, Enid (Susan). American (born United States), b. 1943. **Genres:** Novels, Plays/Screenplays, Songs/Lyrics And Libretti, Writing/Journalism. **Career:** Grey Advertising Co., copywriter and lyricist, 1964-76; lyricist and librettist, 1976-; author and photographer, 1995-; Our Town Magazine, co-editor, publisher, writer. **Publications:** Bittersweet Journey: A Modestly Erotic Novel of Love, Longing and Chocolate, 1998. **Address:** 661 Rte. 23, PO Box 158, Craryville, NY 12521, U.S.A. **Online address:** enidfutterman@bittersweetjourney.com

FYFIELD, Frances. See **HEGARTY, Frances.**

G

GAARD, Greta. (Greta Claire Gaard). American (born United States), b. 1960. **Genres:** Environmental Sciences/Ecology, Gay And Lesbian Issues, Literary Criticism And History, Women's Studies And Issues, Politics/Government, Adult Non-fiction. **Career:** University of Minnesota, instructor in English and women's studies, 1980-89, assistant professor of writing and women's studies, 1989-94, associate professor of writing and women's studies, 1994-97; Inver Hills Community College, instructor in English, 1985; Hamline University, instructor in introductory composition, 1986; Augsburg College, instructor in English, 1986-87; Washington University, associate professor, 1997-2002; University of Wisconsin, assistant professor, associate professor, 2005-; Metropolitan State University, community faculty in women's studies. Writer. **Publications:** EDITOR: Ecofeminism: Women, Animals, Nature, 1993; (with P.D. Murphy) Ecofeminist Literary Criticism: Theory, Interpretation, Pedagogy, 1998. OTHERS: Ecological Politics: Ecofeminist and the Greens, 1998; The Nature of Home: Taking Root In a Place, 2007. Contributor to books. **Address:** Department of English, University of Wisconsin, 410 S 3rd St., 256 Kleinpell Fine Arts, River Falls, MN 54022-5001, U.S.A. **Online address:** greta.gaard@uwrf.edu

GAARD, Greta Claire. *See* GAARD, Greta.

GABBARD, David A. American (born United States) **Genres:** Education, Philosophy, Reference. **Career:** Eastern Montana College, educator, 1991-94; East Carolina University, Department of Curriculum and Instruction, assistant professor, 1995-98, associate professor, 1998-2003, professor, 2003-, Marxian Analysis of Society, program area coordinator, Special Interest Group of the American Educational Research Association, program area coordinator. Writer. **Publications:** Silencing Ivan Illich: A Foucauldian Analysis of Intellectual Exclusion, 1993. EDITOR: Knowledge and Power in the Global Economy: Politics and the Rhetoric of School Reform, 2000, 2nd ed. as Knowledge & Power in the Global Economy: The Effects of School Reform in a Neoliberal/Neoconservative Age, 2007; (with K.J. Saltman and intro.) Education As Enforcement: The Militarization and Corporatization of Schools, 2003; (with E.W. Ross) Defending Public Schools: Education Under the Security State, 2004; (with A. Beaulieu) Michel Foucault and Power Today: International Multidisciplinary Studies in the History of the Present, 2006. Contributor to periodicals. **Address:** Department of Curriculum & Instruction, College of Education, East Carolina University, 304 Speight, Greenville, NC 27858, U.S.A. **Online address:** gabbardd@ecu.edu

GABBAY, Tom. American (born United States), b. 1953. **Genres:** Novels, Plays/Screenplays, Mystery/Crime/Suspense. **Career:** National Broadcasting Corp., director of children's programming, 1985-87, director of comedy programming, 1987-90, director of European production division, 1990-93. Writer and producer. **Publications:** The Berlin Conspiracy (thriller novel), 2006; Lisbon Crossing, 2007; Tehran Conviction, 2009. **Address:** Dystel & Goderich Literary Agency, 1 Union Sq. West, Ste. 903, New York, NY 10003, U.S.A. **Online address:** info@tomgabbay.com

GABBERT, Wolfgang. German (born Germany), b. 1957. **Genres:** History, Philosophy. **Career:** University of Hanover, Institute for Sociology and Social Psychology, scientific assistant, 1990-94, professor of sociology, 2002-; Free University of Berlin, Latin America Institute, research associate, 1995-2002. Writer. **Publications:** Creoles-Afroamerikaner Im Karibischen Tiefland Von Nicaragua, 1992; Becoming Maya: Ethnicity and Social Inequality in Yucatan since 1500, 2004. **Address:** Institute for Sociology, Gottfried Wilhelm Leibniz University of Hanover, Schneiderberg 50, Hanover, 30167, Germany. **Online address:** w.gabbert@ish.uni-hannover.de

GABHART, Ann Houchin. American (born United States), b. 1947. **Genres:** Romance/Historical, Children's Fiction, Young Adult Fiction, inspirational/Motivational Literature, Theology/Religion. **Career:** Writer. **Publications:** HISTORICAL ROMANCE NOVELS: A Forbidden Yearning, 1978; A Heart Divided, 1980. FOR YOUNG ADULTS: A Chance Hero, 1985; The Look of Eagles, 1986; The Gifting, 1987; A Kindred Spirit, 1987; Only in Sunshine, 1988; Wish Come True, 1988; For Sheila, 1991; Bridge to Courage, 1993; Secrets To Tell, 1994; Angels at the Crossroads, 2006; Orchard of Hope, 2007; Outsider, 2008; Summer of Joy, 2008; Believer, 2009; Seeker: A Novel, 2010; Angel Sister: A Novel, 2011; Blessed: A Novel, 2011; The Gifted, 2012; Words Spoken True, 2012. FOR CHILDREN: Discovery at Coyote Point, 1989; Two of a Kind, 1992; The Scent of Lilacs, 2005. **Address:** Baker Publishing Group, 6030 East Fulton Rd., Ada, MI 49301, U.S.A. **Online address:** anngabhart@bellsouth.net

GABLER, Hans Walter. German (born Germany), b. 1938. **Genres:** Literary Criticism And History, Bibliography. **Career:** University of Munich, Shakespeare Librarian, 1965-68, assistant professor, 1970-81, professor of English literature and editorial scholarship, 1981-2003, professor emeritus of English, 2003-; University of Virginia, visiting professor, 1975; University of London, School of Advanced Study, Institute of English Studies, senior research fellow, 2007-. Writer. **Publications:** Zur Funktion Dramatischer und Literarischer Parodie im Elisabethanischen Drama: Beiträge zur Interpretation Ausgewählter Dramen aus dem Werk Lylys, Marlowes und Greenes und dem Frühwerk Shakespeares, 1966; Geschmack und Gesellschaft: Rhetorische und Sozialgeschichtliche Aspekte der Früehaufkläererischen Geschmackskategorie, 1982; (co-author) Schrift, Text, Edition: Hans Walter Gabler zum 65 Geburtstag, 2003; Rocky Road to Ulysses, 2005. EDITOR: (and intro.) English Renaissance Studies in German, 1945-1967, A Check-list of German, Austrian, and Swiss Academic Theses, Monographs, and Book Publications on English Language and Literature, 1500-1650, 1970; (with W. Hettche and intro.) A Portrait of the Artist as a Young Man: A Facsimile of the Final Holograph Manuscript, 1977, rev. ed., 1993; (with W. Hettche and intro.) Dubliners: A Facsimile of Drafts & Manuscripts, 1978; (intro.) Notes, Criticism, Translations & Miscellaneous Writings: A Facsimile of Manuscripts & Typescripts, 1979; (with W. Steppe and C. Melchior) Ulysses, 1984; (with W. Steppe) A Handlist to James Joyce's Ulysses: A Complete Alphabetical Index to the Critical Reading Text, 1985; (with G. Bornstein and G.B. Pierce) Contemporary German Editorial Theory, 1995; (with W. Hettche) A Portrait of the Artist as a Young Man: Authoritative Text, Backgrounds And Contexts, Criticism, 2007. Contributor to periodicals. **Address:** Department of English, University of Munich, 3 Schellingstrasse, Munich, D-80799, Germany. **Online address:** gabler@anglistik.uni-muenchen.de

GABLIK, Suzi. British/American (born United States), b. 1934. **Genres:** Art/Art History, Biography, Autobiography/Memoirs. **Career:** Writer, artist and educator. **Publications:** (With J. Russell) Pop Art Redefined, 2nd ed. as

Pop Art: Hayward Gallery, 1969; Magritte, 1970; Progress in Art, 1976; Has Modernism Failed?, 1984, 2nd ed., 2004; Ann McCoy (essay), 1989; The Reenchantment of Art, 1991; Conversations before the End of Time, 1995; Living the Magical Life: An Oracular Adventure, 2002. **Address:** 3271 Deer Run Rd., Blacksburg, VA 24060, U.S.A.

GABOR, Andrea (Anna Gisela). American (born United States) **Genres:** Intellectual History, Biography, Autobiography/Memoirs, Business/Trade/Industry, Economics, Industrial Relations, Sociology, Women's Studies And Issues, Women's Studies And Issues. **Career:** Architectural Record, assistant editor, 1981-82; Business Week, associate editor, 1982-85; U.S. News & World Report, associate editor, 1985-88, senior editor, 1988-91; Columbia University, adjunct instructor, 1994-2002; City University of New York, Baruch College, Weissman School of Arts and Sciences, adjunct lecturer, 1997-99, assistant professor, 1999-2005, associate professor, 2005-08, Bloomberg Professor, 2008-. **Publications:** The Man Who Discovered Quality: How W. Edwards Deming Brought the Quality Revolution to America: The Stories of Ford, Xerox, and GM, 1990; Einstein's Wife: Work and Marriage in the Lives of Five Great Twentieth-Century Women, 1995; The Capitalist Philosophers: The Geniuses of Modern Business-Their Lives, Times, and Ideas, 1999. **Address:** Weissman School of Arts & Sciences, Baruch College, 7-259 Vertical Campus, 1 Bernard Baruch Way, 55 Lexington at 24th St., New York, NY 10010, U.S.A. **Online address:** andrea.gabor@baruch.cuny.edu

GABOR, Thomas. Canadian/Hungarian (born Hungary), b. 1952. **Genres:** Criminology/True Crime, Sociology, Social Sciences, Politics/Government. **Career:** Douglas Psychiatric Hospital, Montreal, child care worker, 1973-74; University of Ottawa, research assistant, 1976, lecturer, 1981-83, assistant professor, 1983-86, associate professor, 1986-90, professor of criminology, 1990-; Thomas Gabor L.L.C., president. Writer. **Publications:** Prediction of Criminal Behaviour, 1986; Armed Robbery, 1987; Everybody Does It: Crime by the Public, 1994; Basics of Criminology, 2009. Contributor to books and journals. **Address:** Department of Criminology, University of Ottawa, Rm. 304, 34-36 Stewart Bldg., 25 University St., Ottawa, ON K1N 6N5, Canada. **Online address:** tgabor@cyberus.ca

GABRIEL, Adriana. *See* BUCCIERI, Lisa Rojany.

GABRIEL, Jüri (Evald). British/Estonian (born Estonia), b. 1940. **Genres:** Travel/Exploration, Antiques/Furnishings, Communications/Media. **Career:** Associated Rediffusion Television (programme contractors), cameraman, 1963-65; Thames and Hudson Ltd., editor, publisher, 1965-67; writer, photographer and translator, 1967-; Dedalus, chairman, publisher, 1984-; Copyright Licensing Agency, chairman, 1988-89; Adrian Knowles Associates, associate; Morley College, creative writing teacher. **Publications:** Victoriana, 1969; Victorian Furniture and Furnishings, 1971; (with L. Hemmant) Europa: Gastronomic Guide to Europe, vol. III, 1971; (ed.) Rand McNally/RAC Guide to British and Continental Camping and Caravanning Sites, 1974-81; Unqualified Success: Comprehensive Guide to Jobs for School Leavers, 1984, rev. ed. 1986. SELF-ILLUSTRATED: Thinking About Television, 1973. **Address:** 35 Camberwell Grove, London, GL SE5 8JA, England.

GABRIEL, Michael P. American (born United States), b. 1962. **Genres:** Biography, History. **Career:** University of Pittsburgh, instructor in history, 1992, 1993-94; Kutztown University, instructor, 1994-96, assistant professor, 1996-2001, associate professor, 2001-04, department chair, 2002-, professor of history, 2004-. Writer. **Publications:** Major General Richard Montgomery: The Making of an American Hero, 2002; (ed.) Québec during the American Invasion, 1775-1776: The Journal of François Baby, Gabriel Taschereau, and Jenkin Williams, 2005. Contributor to books and periodicals. **Address:** Department of History, Kutztown University, 146 Lytle Hall, Kutztown, PA 19530, U.S.A. **Online address:** gabriel@kutztown.edu

GABRIEL, Richard A(lan). American (born United States), b. 1942. **Genres:** Politics/Government, Psychology, History. **Career:** U.S. Army, staff, now retired; St. Anselm's College, professor of political science; Royal Military College of Canada, Department of History and War Studies, distinguished professor; Canadian Forces College, Department of Defence Studies, distinguished professor; Marine Corps University, visiting chair in military ethics; U.S. Army War College, professor of history and politics, Department of National Security and Strategy, director of advanced courses; University of New Hampshire, faculty; University of Massachusetts, faculty; Daniel Webster College, adjunct professor of humanities and ethics. Writer. **Publica-**

tions: Ethnic Voting in Primary Elections: The Irish and Italians of Providence, Rhode Island, 1969; Ethnic Attitudes and Political Behavior in City and Suburb: The Irish and Italians of Rhode Island, 1969, as The Irish and Italians: Ethnics in City and Suburb, 1980; The Political Machine in Rhode Island, 1970; (with P.L. Savage) The Ethnicity Attribute: Persistence and Change in an Urban and Suburban Environment, 1973; (with Savage) What Voters Think about Politics and Why: A Case Study of Political Ethos in a New England City, 1973; The Ethnic Factor in the Urban Polity, 1973; Program Evaluation: A Social Science Approach, 1975; (with Savage) Crisis in Command: Mismanagement in the Army, 1978; The New Red Legions, vol. I: A Survey Data Source Book, vol. II: An Attitudinal Portrait of the Soviet Soldier, 1980; To Serve with Honor: A Treatise on Military Ethics and the Way of the Soldier, 1982; The Antagonists: A Comparative Combat Assessment of the Soviet and American Soldier, 1984; (comp.) The Mind of the Soviet Fighting Man: A Quantitative Survey of Soviet Soldiers, Sailors, and Airmen, 1984; Operation Peace for Galilee: The Israeli-PLO War in Lebanon, 1984; Military Incompetence: Why the American Military Doesn't Win, 1985; Soviet Military Psychiatry: The Theory and Practice of Coping with Battle Stress, 1986; No More Heroes: Madness and Psychiatry in War, 1987; The Painful Field: The Psychiatric Dimension of Modern War, 1988; The Culture of War: Invention and Early Development, 1990; (with K.S. Metz) From Sumer to Rome: The Military Capabilities of Ancient Armies, 1991; (with Metz) A History of Military Medicine, vol. I: From Ancient Times to the Middle Ages, vol. II: From the Renaissance through Modern Times, 1992; (with K.S. Metz) A Short History of War: The Evolution of Warfare and Weapons, 1992; (with D.W. Boose, Jr.) The Great Battles of Antiquity: A Strategic and Tactical Guide to Great Battles That Shaped the Development of War, 1994; Great Captains of Antiquity, 2001; The Great Armies of Antiquity, 2002; Gods of Our Fathers: The Memory of Egypt in Judaism and Christianity, 2002; The Military History of Ancient Israel, 2003; Subotai the Valiant: Genghis Khan's Greatest General, 2004; Empires at War: A Chronological Encyclopedia, 2005; Genghis Khan's Greatest General: Subotai the Valiant, 2006; Muhammad: Islam's First Great General, 2007; Warrior's way: A Treatise on Military Ethics, 2007; The Ancient World, 2007; Scipio Africanus: Rome's Greatest General, 2008; Thutmose III: A Military Biography of Egypt's Greatest Warrior King, 2009; Philip II of Macedonia: Greater than Alexander, 2010; Hannibal: The Military Biography of Rome's Greatest Enemy, 2011; Man and Wound in the Ancient World, 2012. EDITOR: (with S.H. Cohen) The Environment: Critical Factors in Strategy Development, 1973; Antagonists in the Middle East: A Combat Assessment (part of Fighting Armies series), 1983; NATO and the Warsaw Pact: A Combat Assessment (part of Fighting Armies series), 1983; Nonaligned, Third World and Other Ground Armies: A Combat Assessment (part of Fighting Armies series), 1983; Military Psychiatry: A Comparative Perspective, 1986; Battle Atlas of Ancient Military History, 2008. Contributor to periodicals. **Address:** Daniel Webster College, 20 University Dr., Nashua, NH 03063, U.S.A.

GABRIEL, Theodore P. C. British/Indian (born India), b. 1935. **Genres:** Theology/Religion, History, Social Sciences. **Career:** University of Gloucestershire, lecturer in theology and religious studies, senior lecturer in theology and religious studies, through 2000, lecturer emeritus, 2000-, honorary research fellow. Writer. **Publications:** Lakshadweep, History, Religion and Society, 1989; Hindu-Muslim Relations in North Malabar, 1498-1947, 1996; Christian-Muslim Relations: A Case Study of Sarawak, East Malaysia, 1996; (ed.) Islam in the Contemporary World, 2000; Hindu and Muslim Inter-Religious Relations in Malaysia, 2000; (ed. with C. Partridge) Mysticisms East and West: Studies in Medieval Experience, 2003; (co-ed.) Islam and the West Post, 2004; Christian Citizens in an Islamic State: The Pakistan Experience, 2007; (with R. Geaves) Isms: Understanding Religion, 2007; Playing God: Belief and Ritual in the Muttappan Cult of North Malabar, 2010; (co-ed.) Islam and the Veil, 2011. Contributor to books and periodicals. **Address:** Department of Humanities, University of Gloucestershire, Francis Close Hall, Swindon Rd., Cheltenham, GC GL50 4AZ, England. **Online address:** tgabriel@glos.ac.uk

GABRIELE, Lisa. Canadian (born Canada) **Genres:** Novels. **Career:** Canadian Broadcasting Corp., director/producer, senior producer, writer, reporter, radio researcher; LifeSize Television (television production Co.), executive producer; History Channel, producer; Life Network, producer; Slice TV, producer. **Publications:** Tempting Faith DiNapoli, 2002; Starlite Variety, 2008; The Almost Archer Sisters, 2008. Contributor to periodicals. Works appear in anthologies. **Address:** c/o Author Mail, Helen Heller Agency, 4-216 Heath St. W, Toronto, ON M5P 1N7, Canada.

GABRIELI, Christopher. American (born United States), b. 1960?. **Genres:** Education, Human Relations/Parenting, Administration/Management. **Career:** Bessemer Venture Partners, senior partner in biotechnology; Gabrieli Medical Information Systems, co-founder, president and chairman; Ironwood Capital Ltd., managing director; Harvard Graduate School of Education, part-time lecturer. Writer. **Publications:** (With W. Goldstein) Time to Learn: How a New School Schedule Is Making Smarter Kids, Happier Parents, and Safer Neighborhoods, 2008. **Address:** Ironwood Capital Ltd., 1 Beacon St., 34th Fl., Boston, MA 02108, U.S.A. **Online address:** chrisandwarren@timeandlearning.org

GABRIEL (LOVING), Kathryn (Ann). American (born United States), b. 1955. **Genres:** Anthropology/Ethnology, Archaeology/Antiquities, History, Local History/Rural Topics, Mythology/Folklore, Travel/Exploration, Theology/Religion. **Career:** Writer. **Publications:** Roads to Center Place: A Cultural Atlas to Chaco Canyon and the Anasazi, 1991; (ed. and comp.) Marietta Wetherill: Reflections on Life with the Navajos in Chaco Canyon, 1992; Gambler Way: Indian Gaming in Mythology, History, and Archaeology in North America, 1996; Country Towns of New Mexico, 1996; (with R. Jones) Dinosaurs On-line: A Guide to the Best Dinosaur Sites on the Internet, 2000. Contributor to periodicals. **Address:** NM , U.S.A.

GACKENBACH, Jayne. Canadian/American (born United States), b. 1946. **Genres:** Psychology. **Career:** Virginia Commonwealth University, part-time instructor, 1976-78; John Tyler Community College, part-time instructor, 1977-78; Clarion State College, assistant professor of psychology, 1978-80; University of Northern Iowa, assistant professor, associate professor of psychology, 1980-89; Lucidity Association, managing director, 1981-93; Wartburg College, part-time instructor, 1982; Athabasca University, part-time instructor in psychology and communication, 1989-; University of Alberta, part-time instructor in psychology and communication, 1989-; Northern Alberta Institute of Technology, part-time instructor in psychology and communication, 1989-; Augustana University College, part-time instructor in psychology and communication, 1989-; Grant MacEwan College, instructor in psychology and communication, 1992-; Saybrook Institute, part-time instructor, 1995, adjunct faculty; Blue Quills Native College, part-time instructor; Maskwachees Cultural College, part-time instructor; Yellowhead Tribal Council, part-time instructor; Grant MacEwan College, Department of Psychology and Sociology, professor, part-time instructor, 1992-2002, instructor, 2002-. Writer. **Publications:** (With J. Bosveld) Control Your Dreams, 1989; The Traditional Death of Crow Woman, 1996. EDITOR: Sleep and Dreams: A Sourcebook, 1987; (with S.P. LaBerge and contrib.) Conscious Mind, Sleeping Brain: Perspectives on Lucid Dreaming, 1988; (with A. Sheikh and contrib.) Dream Images: A Call to Mental Arms, 1991; (contrib.) Psychology and the Internet: Intrapersonal, Interpersonal and Transpersonal Implications, 1998, 2nd ed., 2007; (with J.F. Gillispie) Cyber Rules: What You Really Need to Know About the Internet, 2007. Contributor to books and journals. **Address:** Department of Psychology and Sociology, Grant MacEwan College, Rm. 6-323H, 10700-104 Ave., Edmonton, AB T5J 4S2, Canada. **Online address:** gackenbachj@macewan.ca

GADDIS, John Michael. *See* **GADDIS, Michael.**

GADDIS, Michael. (John Michael Gaddis). American (born United States), b. 1970. **Genres:** Theology/Religion. **Career:** Syracuse University, assistant professor, 1999-2005, associate professor of history, 2005-, director of undergraduate studies, 2001-. Writer. **Publications:** There Is No Crime for Those Who Have Christ: Religious Violence in the Christian Roman Empire, 2005; (trans. with R. Price) The Acts of the Council of Chalcedon, 2005. **Address:** Syracuse University, 313A Maxwell Hall, Syracuse, NY 13244-1090, U.S.A. **Online address:** jmgaddis@maxwell.syr.edu

GADDIS-ROSE, Marilyn. American (born United States), b. 1930. **Genres:** Biography, Translations. **Career:** State University of New York, distinguished service professor of comparative literature, Translation Research and Instruction Program, co-director, 1968-; Translation Perspectives, managing editor, 1984-; American Translators Association, editor, 1987-98. **Publications:** Julian Green, 1971; Jack B. Yeats, 1972; Katharine Tynan, 1973; (ed.) Translation in the Humanities, 1977; (ed.) Translation Spectrum: Essays in Theory and Practice, 1980; (ed.) Translations, Works, Words-Old, New: A Folio of Poetry Translations, 1984; (ed. with A. Otis) Varied Forms, Similar Balances, Poetic Expanses: A Folio of Poetry and Poetic Prose Translations, 1985; Translation and Literary Criticism, 1997. TRANSLATOR: V. de l'Isle-Adam,

Axel, 1971; V. de l'Isle-Adam, Eve of the Future Eden, 1981; L. Colet, Lui: A View of Him, 1986; J. Green, Adrienne Mesurat, 1991; C.A. Sainte-Beuve, Volupte: The Sensual Man, 1995. **Address:** Department of Comparative Literature, State University of New York, 1508 Library Twr., Binghamton, NY 13902-6000, U.S.A. **Online addreSS:** mgrose@binghamton.edu

GADNEY, Reg. British (born England), b. 1941. **Genres:** Plays/Screenplays, Art/Art History, History, Mystery/Crime/Suspense, Young Adult Non-fiction, Novels. **Career:** London Magazine, regular contributor, 1964-96; Massachusetts Institute of Technology, School of Architecture and Planning, instructor in architecture and research fellow, 1966-67; National Film Theatre, deputy controller, 1967-68; Royal College of Art, senior tutor and fellow, 1968-78, part-time tutor, 1970, pro-rector, 1978-83; American Arts Documentation Centre, consultant; full-time writer, 1984-. **Publications:** MYSTERY NOVELS: Drawn Blanc, 1970; Somewhere in England, 1971; Seduction of a Tall Man, 1972; Something Worth Fighting For, 1974; Victoria in UK as The Last Hours Before Dawn, 1975; The Cage in UK as The Champagne Marxist, 1977; Kennedy, 1983; Cry Hungary!: Uprising 1956, 1986; Nightshade, 1987; Just When We Are Safest, 1995; Gone to Nagasaki, 1995; The Achilles Heel, 1996; Happy Christmas Lucy Smith, 1996; Mother, Son and Holy Ghost, 1998; Strange Police, 2000; The Scholar of Extortion, 2003; Immaculate Deception, 2006; The Woman in Silk, 2011. ART BOOKS: Constable and His World, 1976; (contrib.) John Constable R.A., 1776-1837: A Catalogue of Drawings and Watercolours, With a Selection of Mezzotints by David Lucas After Constable for English Landscape Scenery, in the Fitzwilliam Museum, Cambridge, 1976. Contributor to magazines. **Address:** International Creative Management Ltd., Oxford House, 76 Oxford St., London, GL W1D 1BS, England.

GADOL, Peter. (Peter Daniel Gadol). American (born United States), b. 1964. **Genres:** Novels, Mystery/Crime/Suspense, Young Adult Fiction. **Career:** California Institute of the Arts, faculty; University of California, faculty; Otis College of Art and Design, Graduate Writing Program, assistant chair, associate professor, 2005-. Writer. **Publications:** NOVELS: Coyote, 1990; The Mystery Roast, 1993; Closer to the Sun, 1996; The Long Rain, 1997; Light at Dusk, 2000; Silver Lake, 2009; American Modern, forthcoming. Contributor to periodicals. **Address:** Otis College of Art and Design, 9045 Lincoln Blvd., Los Angeles, CA 90045, U.S.A. **Online address:** pgadol@otis.edu

GADOL, Peter Daniel. *See* **GADOL, Peter.**

GAETZ, Dayle Campbell. Canadian (born Canada), b. 1947. **Genres:** Children's Fiction, Young Adult Fiction, Children's Non-fiction, Novels. **Career:** British Columbia Tel-Communications, draftsperson; School District No. 64, teacher on call; freelance writer and journalist, 1998-. **Publications:** FICTION FOR CHILDREN: Grandfather Heron Finds a Friend, 1986; A Sea Lion Called Salena, 1994; The Mystery at Eagle Lake, 1995; Night of the Aliens, 1995; Alien Rescue, 1997; The Case of the Belly-up Fish, 1998; Mystery from History, 2001; Barkerville Gold, 2004; Alberta Alibi, 2005; Sea Dog, 2006; Crossbow, 2007. FOR YOUNG ADULTS: Spoiled Rotten, 1991; Tell Me the Truth, 1992; Heather, Come Back, 1993; The Golden Rose, 1996; Living Freight, 1998; No Problem, 2003. NONFICTION: The Whale Project, 1994; Discover Salt Springs: Funky Facts and Awesome Activities for Kids of All Ages, 2000; Something Suspicious in Saskatchewan, 2006. **Address:** 3970 S Island Hwy., Campbell River, BC V9H 1L9, Canada. **Online address:** dgaetz@saltspring.com

GAGE, Eleni N. American/Greek (born Greece), b. 1974. **Genres:** Travel/Exploration, Mythology/Folklore, Autobiography/Memoirs, Novels, Adult Non-fiction. **Career:** Allure Magazine, staff writer, 1996-2001; Elle Magazine, staff writer, 1996-2001; InStyle Magazine, staff writer, 1996-2001; People Magazine, beauty editor, 2004-06; Columbia University, writing instructor, 2008-10. **Publications:** North of Ithaka: A Journey Home through a Family's Extraordinary Past, 2005; Other Waters, 2012. **Address:** c/o Stephanie Abou, Foundry Literary and Media, 33 W 17th St., New York, NY 10011, U.S.A. **Online address:** eleni_gage@yahoo.com

GAGE, Leighton D. American (born United States), b. 1942?. **Genres:** Young Adult Non-fiction. **Career:** Lions Festival, jury member; Clio Awards, jury member; New York Film Festival, jury member; One Show of the Art Director's Club, jury member. Writer. **Publications:** (with C. Meyer) O Filme Publicitário (title means: 'The Advertising Film'), 1991; Blood of the Wicked, 2008; Buried Strangers, 2009; Dying Gasp, 2010. **Address:** J de S Associates, 9 Shagbark Rd., Wilson Pt., South Norwalk, CT 06854, U.S.A. **Online address:** leighton@leightongage.com

GAGE, S. R. Canadian/American (born United States), b. 1945. **Career:** United Steelworkers of America, District 6, staff, 1975-79; McMaster University, Labour Studies Program, assistant director, 1979-82; freelance writer and researcher, 1982-. **Publications:** (With L. Whiteson) The Liveable City: The Architecture and Neighbourhoods of Toronto, 1982; A Few Rustic Huts: Ranger Cabins and Logging Camp Buildings of Algonquin Park, 1985; A Walk on the Canol Road: Exploring the First Major Northern Pipeline, 1990; Forgotten Places in the North, 2001. **Address:** Mosaic Press, PO Box 1032, Oakville, ON L6J 5E9, Canada.

GAGLIANI, W. D. *See* **GAGLIANI, William.**

GAGLIANI, William. (W. D. Gagliani). American (born United States), b. 1962?. **Genres:** Novels, Horror, Mystery/Crime/Suspense. **Career:** University of Wisconsin, creative writing and composition teacher, 1985-88; Marquette University, Raynor Memorial Libraries, stacks supervisor, 1988-. Writer. **Publications:** AS W.D. GAGLIANI: Wilbur Smith's When the Lion Feeds, 1964; Wolf's Trap, 2003; (with D. Benton) Mood Elevator, 2007; Wolf's Gambit, 2009; Wolf's Bluff, 2010; Savage Nights, 2010. **Address:** c/o Jack Byrne, Sternig & Byrne Literary Agency, 2370 S 107th St., Apt. 4, Milwaukee, WI 53227-2036, U.S.A. **Online address:** wdg@williamdgagliani.com

GAGLIANO, Anthony. American (born United States), b. 1955. **Genres:** Adult Non-fiction, Mystery/Crime/Suspense, Literary Criticism And History. **Career:** Freelance writer and teacher. **Publications:** Preventative Fitness 101: A Pocket Guide to Health and Longevity, 2003; Straits of Fortune, 2007. Contributor to periodicals. **Address:** Miami, FL , U.S.A. **Online address:** anthony@anthonygaglianobooks.com

GAGLIANO, Eugene M. American (born United States), b. 1946. **Genres:** Children's Fiction, Picture/Board Books, Young Adult Fiction, Novellas/Short Stories, Poetry. **Career:** Elementary school teacher, 1969-2003; author and speaker, 2003-. **Publications:** Secret of the Black Widow, 2002; Inside the Clown, 2003; C Is for Cowboy: A Wyoming Alphabet, 2003; Falling Stars, 2004; Prairie Parcels, 2005; Four Wheels West, a Wyoming Number Book, 2006; V is for Venus Flytrap: A Plant Alphabet, 2009; My Teacher Dances on the Desk, 2009; Little Wyoming, 2010; Dee and the Mammoth, 2011; The Magic Box, 2011. **Address:** 20 Hillside Dr., Buffalo, WY 82834, U.S.A. **Online address:** eugene.gagliano@gmail.com

GAGLIANO, Frank. American (born United States), b. 1931. **Genres:** Novels, Plays/Screenplays. **Career:** Royal Shakespeare Co., playwright-in-residence, 1967-69; Florida State University, assistant professor of drama, playwright-in-residence, Contemporary Playwright's Center, director, 1969-73; University of Texas, lecturer in playwriting, E.P. Conkle Workshop for Playwrights, director, 1973-74; University of Rhode Island, distinguished visiting alumni professor, 1975; West Virginia University, Benedum professor of theatre, 1974-, Benedum professor of playwriting, 1976-, now retired; Carnegie-Mellon University, New Plays, artistic director, 1987-98; University of Michigan, Festival of New Works, artistic director, 1999-2001. **Publications:** Conerico Was Here to Stay, 1964; Frank Gagliano's City Scene, 1965; The City Scene (2 Plays), 1966; Night of the Dunce, 1967; Father Uxbridge Wants to Mary, 1968; The Hide-and-Seek Odyssey of Madeleine Gimple, 1970; The Prince of Peasantmania, 1970; Big Sur, 1971; In the Voodoo Parlour of Marie Laveau, 1974; The Commedia World of Lafcadio B., 1974; The Total Immersion of Madelaine Favorini, 1981; San Ysidro (dramatic cantata), 1985; From the Bodoni County Songbook Anthology, 1986, 1987; Anton's Leap (novel), 1988; Hanna: A Run on Odyssey, 1990-92; The Farewell Concert of Irene and Vernon Palazzo, 1995; And the Angels Sing, 1996; Piano Bar, 1998. **Address:** c/o Gilbert Parker, Curtis Brown Ltd, 575 Madison Ave., New York, NY 10022, U.S.A. **Online address:** frank.gagliano@mail.wvu.edu

GAGNÉ, Marcel. American (born United States) **Genres:** Information Science/Computers, Technology. **Career:** Salmar Consulting Inc. (computer consulting firm), co-owner; Transversions, co-owner, co-editor, co-publisher. **Publications:** Linux System Administration: A Users Guide, 2002; Moving to the Linux Business Desktop, 2005; Moving to Linux: Kiss the Blue Screen of Death Goodbye!, 2006; Moving to Free Software, 2007; Moving to Ubuntu Linux, 2007. **Address:** c/o Author Mail, Addison-Wesley Publishing Company, 75 Arlington St., Ste. 300, Boston, MA 02116, U.S.A.

GAGNON, Michelle. American (born United States), b. 1971. **Genres:** Novels, Mystery/Crime/Suspense, Young Adult Fiction. **Career:** Writer. **Publications:** KELLY JONES MYSTERY NOVELS: The Tunnels, 2007; Boneyard, 2008; The Gatekeeper, 2009; Kidnap & Ransom, 2010. **Address:** Levine Greenberg Literary Agency, 307 7th Ave., Ste. 2407, New York, NY 10001, U.S.A. **Online address:** michelle@michellegagnon.com

GAIDUK, Ilya V(alerievich). American/Russian (born Russia), b. 1961. **Genres:** Military/Defense/Arms Control, History. **Career:** Teacher, 1984-87; Russian Academy of Sciences, Institute of World History, junior research fellow, 1990-97, senior research fellow, 1997-, Cold War Studies Center, coordinator, 1995-99, Woodrow Wilson Center, senior research fellow; Moscow State Linguistic University, senior lecturer, 1997-99. Writer. **Publications:** The Soviet Union and the Vietnam War, 1996; Great Confrontation: Europe and Islam Through the Centuries, 2003; Confronting Vietnam: Soviet Policy Toward the Indochina Conflict, 1954-1963, 2003. Contributor to books and periodicals. **Address:** Russian Academy of Sciences, Woodrow Wilson Center, 1 Woodrow Wilson Plz., 1300 Pennsylvania Ave. NW, Washington, DC 20004, U.S.A. **Online address:** ilya.gaiduk@wilsoncenter.org

GAILLARD, Frye. American (born United States), b. 1946. **Genres:** Novels, History, Music, Sports/Fitness, Writing/Journalism, Autobiography/Memoirs. **Career:** Race Relations Reporter, managing editor and staff writer, 1970-72; Charlotte Observer, staff writer, editorial writer and southern editor, 1972-90; Queens College, Charlotte, writer-in-residence, 1981, instructor in nonfiction writing, 1990-99; writer, 1990-; Novello Festival Press, founding editor, 2000-; Creative Loafing (alternative newspaper), columnist; University of Southern Alabama, writer-in-residence, 2005-; Light Factory Photographic Arts Center, board director; University of South Alabama, writer-in-residence. **Publications:** Watermelon Wine: The Spirit of Country Music, 1978; Race, Rock, and Religion, 1982; (with D. Jackson and D. Sturkey) The Catawba River, 1983; (with R. Maschal and E. Williams) Becoming Truly Free: 300 Years of Black History in the Carolinas, 1985; The Unfinished Presidency: Essays on Jimmy Carter, 1986; The Dream Long Deferred, 1988, 3rd ed., 2006; The Secret Diary of Mikhail Gorbachev (novel), 1990, 3rd ed., 2006; (with N.B. Gaillard) Southern Voices: Profiles and Other Stories, 1991; (with K. Petty) Kyle at 200 M.P.H: A Sizzling Season in the Petty/NASCAR Dynasty, 1993; Lessons from the Big House: One Family's Passage through the History of the South, 1994; If I Were a Carpenter: 20 Years of Habitat for Humanity, 1996; The Heart of Dixie: Southern Rebels, Renegades and Heroes, 1996; (with R. Gaillard) The Way We See It, 1995; (with N. Gaillard and T. Gaillard) Mobile and the Eastern Shore, 1997; Voices from the Attic, 1997; As Long as the Waters Flow: Native Americans in the South and East, 1998; (with B. Baldwin) The 521 All-Stars: A Championship Story of Baseball and Community, 1999; (ed. with A. Rogers and R. Inman) No Hiding Place: Uncovering The Legacy Of Charlotte-Area Writers: An Anthology, 1999; (with M. Farbman) Spacechimp: NASA's Ape in Space, 2000; The Greensboro Four: Civil Rights Pioneers, 2001; Cradle of Freedom: Alabama and the Movement That Changed America, 2004; Prophet From Plains: Jimmy Carter and His Legacy, 2007; With Music And Justice For All: Some Southerners and Their Passions, 2008; (with S. Hagler and P. Denniston) In the Path of the Storms: Bayou La Batre, Coden, and the Alabama Coast, 2008; (with J. Lindsay and J.D. Neefe) Alabama's Civil Rights Trail: An Illustrated Guide to the Cradle of Freedom, 2009. **Address:** c/o Sally Hill McMillan, Sally Hill Mcmillan and Associates Inc., 429 E Kingston Ave., Charlotte, NC 28203, U.S.A. **Online address:** wfg2346@gmail.com

GAILLY, Christian. French (born France), b. 1943. **Genres:** Novels, Novellas/Short Stories, Mystery/Crime/Suspense. **Career:** Novelist and jazz saxophonist. **Publications:** Dit-il, 1987; K. 622, 1989; L'air, 1991; Dring, 1991; Les fleurs, 1993; Be-bop, 1995; Lincident, 1996; Les évadés, 1997; La passion de Martin Fissel-Brandt, 1998; Nuage rouge, 2000; Un soir au club, 2001; The Passion of Martin Fissel-Brandt, 2002; Evening At The Club, 2003; Dernier amour, 2004; Red Haze=Nuage Rouge, 2005; Les oubliés, 2007; Lily Et Braine, 2010. **Address:** c/o Author Mail, University of Nebraska Press, 1111 Lincoln Mall, Lincoln, NE 68588-0630, U.S.A.

GAIMAN, Neil (Richard). British (born England), b. 1960. **Genres:** Science Fiction/Fantasy, Novels. **Career:** Freelance journalist, 1983-87. Writer,

1987-. **Publications:** (With K. Newman) Ghastly beyond Belief, 1985; Don't Panic-The Hitchhiker's Guide to the Galaxy Companion, 1987; Violent Cases, 1987, 3rd ed., 1997; (with T. Pratchett) Good Omens: The Nice and Accurate Prophecies of Agnes Nutter, Witch, 1990; Breakthrough, 1990; Sandman: The Doll's House, 1990; Black Orchid, 1991; Miracleman: The Golden Age, 1992; Signal to Noise, 1992; Angels and Visitations, 1993; The Books of Magic, 1993; Mr. Punch, 1994; Last Temptation, 1994; Death Talks About Life, 1994; (with D. McKean) The Tragical Comedy or Comical Tragedy of Mr. Punch, 1994; Death: The High Cost of Living, 1994; (with G. Capullo) Angela, 1995; Warning: Contains Language, 1995; Neverwhere, 1996; (with D. Mckean) The Day I Swapped My Dad for Two Goldfish (for children), 1996; The Compleat Alice Cooper: Incorporating the Three Acts of Alice Cooper: The Last Temptation, 1996; Stardust: Being a Romance within the Realms Of Faerie, 1997; Death: The Time of Your life, 1997; Elric, 1998; Smoke and Mirrors, 1998; Midnight Days, 1999; The Quotable Sandman: Memorable Lines from the Acclaimed Series, 2000; Only the End of the World Again, 2000; Green Lantern/Superman: Legend of the Green Flame, 2000; American Gods, 2001; Bento, 2001; Harlequin Valentine, 2001; (with G. Wolfe) A Walking Tour of the Shambles, 2002; Coraline, 2002; Adventures in the Dream Trade, 2002; Two Plays for Voices, 2002; The Sandman: Endless Nights, 2003; The Matrix Comics, 2003; The Wolves in the Walls, 2003; 1602, 2004; A Screenplay, 2004; (intro.) Selected Poems and Tales, 2004; Creatures of the Night, 2004; (with D. Matuszak) Melinda, 2004; (D. McKean) The Alchemy of Mirrormask, 2005; Mirror Mask, 2005; Anansi Boys, 2005; Fragile Things, 2006; M is for Magic, 2007; Eternals, 2007; (with M. Reaves) Interworld, 2007; The Graveyard Book, 2008; Neil Gaiman on His Work and Career: A Conversation with Bill Baker, 2008; The Dangerous Alphabet, 2008; The Complete Death, 2008; Coraline, 2008; Blueberry Girl, 2009; Crazy Hair, 2009; (foreword) Vampire Archives: the Most Complete Volume of Vampire Tales Ever Published, 2009; Absolute Death, 2009; Batman Whatever Happened to the Caped Crusader?: With Other Tales of the Dark Knight, 2009; Odd and the Frost Giants, 2009; (intro.) Hope-in-the-Mist: The Extraordinary Career and Mysterious life of Hope Mirrlees, 2009; Instructions, 2010; Sandman: A Game of You, 2011. EDITOR: (with K. Newman) Ghastly Beyond Belief, 1985; (with S. Jones) Now We Are Sick, 1991; (with A. Stewart) Temps, 1991; (with A. Stewart) Euro Temps, 1992; (with E. Kramer) The Sandman: Book of Dreams, 1996; (with A. Sarrantonio) Stories: All New Tales, 2010; (and intro.) Best American Comics 2010, 2010. **Address:** c/o Merrilee Heifetz, Writers House Inc., 21 W 26th St., New York, NY 10010, U.S.A.

GAINES, Jane (Marie). American (born United States), b. 1946?. **Genres:** Plays/Screenplays, Art/Art History, Film. **Career:** Northwestern University, Radio/TV/Film Department, instructor, 1980; Duke University, assistant professor, 1982-91, associate professor, 1991-2001, professor of literature and English, 2001-, founder and director of program in film and video, 1986-2004, Women Film Pioneers Project, chair, 1994, Duke in Los Angeles Program, founder, 1995; University of Iowa, visiting assistant professor, 1990; University of Washington, Andrew A. Hilen lecturer, 1990; Vassar College, Luce distinguished professor, 1993-94; University of Southern California, School of Cinema-Television, 1995, director of program, 2000; Columbia University, Film Division, School of the Arts, visiting professor, 2007-08. Writer. **Publications:** EDITOR: (with C. Herzog) Fabrications: Costume and the Female Body, 1990; Classical Hollywood Narrative: The Paradigm Wars, 1992; (with M. Renov) Collecting Visible Evidence, 1999; (with P. Bowser and C. Musser) Oscar Micheaux and His Circle: African-American Filmmaking and Race Cinema of the Silent Era (exhibition catalogue), 2001; (with F. Casetti and V. Re) Dall'inizio alla fine: teorie del cinema in prospettiva: Film-Forum/2009, 2010. OTHERS: Contested Culture: The Image, the Voice and the Law, 1991, 2nd ed., forthcoming; (with K. Mercer) Competing Glances: Reading Robert Mapplethorpe, 1992; Fire and Desire: Mixed-Race Movies in the Silent Era, 2001; (contrib.) Alice Guy Blaché: Cinema Pioneer, 2009; The Fantasy of Creating Fantasies, forthcoming; Fictions and Histories: Women Film Pioneers, forthcoming. Contributor of articles to books and periodicals. **Address:** Duke University, 104 Crowell Hall, PO Box 90670, Durham, NC 27708, U.S.A. **Online address:** jmgaines@duke.edu

GAINES, Thomas A. American (born United States), b. 1923. **Genres:** Architecture, Art/Art History, Cultural/Ethnic Topics, Economics, History, Humanities. **Career:** Casas de Costa Rica, president, 1950-77; Latin American Investment Council, president, 1952-55; New York Times, critic; Places Magazine, critic; Historic Preservation Magazine, critic; The Washington Post, critic; Boston Globe Magazine, critic; Modern Community Developers,

staff, 1965-70. Writer. **Publications:** Profits with Progress: Latin America's Bright Investment Future, 1954; The Campus as a Work of Art, 1991; 15 Pinnacles-History's Glorious Golden Ages, 2002; Parsnippets: Clippings from the Tall Grass. Contributor of articles to magazines. **Address:** 77 Edwards Rd., Hampton, CT 06247, U.S.A. **Online address:** kaytom77@earthlink.net

GAITHER, Carl C. American (born United States), b. 1944. **Genres:** Language/Linguistics, Sciences, Technology, Biology, Botany, Zoology, Natural History, Astronomy, Physics. **Career:** University of Southwest Louisiana, teacher of remedial mathematics, 1983-85; McNeese State University, teacher of mathematics and statistics, 1985-86; Aviation Test Board, civilian mathematical statistician, 1987-88; Aviation Test Directorate, civilian engineering psychologist, 1988-90, civilian operations research analyst, 1990-95; mathematics teacher, 1992-; freelance writer, 1995-; Louisiana State Penitentiary, hospital administrator; Texas Department of Corrections, research assistant. Writer. **Publications:** WITH A.E. CAVAZOS-GAITHER: (ed.) Statistically Speaking: A Dictionary of Quotations, 1996; (ed.) Physically Speaking: A Dictionary of Quotations on Physics and Astronomy, 1997; (ed.) Mathematically Speaking: A Dictionary of Quotations, 1998; Engineeringly Speaking: A Dictionary of Quotations, 1998; (ed.) Practically Speaking: A Dictionary of Quotations on Engineering, Technology, and Architecture, 1998; (ed.) Medically Speaking: A Dictionary of Quotations on Dentistry, Medicine, and Nursing, 1999; (ed.) Scientifically Speaking: A Dictionary of Quotations, 2000; (ed.) Naturally Speaking: A Dictionary of Quotations on Biology, Botany, Nature and Zoology, 2001; (ed.) Chemically Speaking: A Dictionary of Quotations, 2002; (ed.) Astronomically Speaking: A Dictionary of Quotations on Astronomy and Physics, 2003; (ed.) The Gaither's Dictionary of Scientific Quotations, 2008. **Address:** 502 Weiss Dr., Killeen, TX 76542-2662, U.S.A. **Online address:** cgaither@n-link.com

GAL, Laszlo. Canadian/Hungarian (born Hungary), b. 1933. **Genres:** Children's Fiction, Illustrations, Theology/Religion. **Career:** Globe & Mail, artist of political portraits, 1956; Eaton's (department store), layout artist, 1957; Canadian Broadcasting Co. (CBC), graphic designer, 1958-65, 1977-; Arnoldo Mondadori Editore, illustrator, 1965-69; freelance illustrator, 1969-77. Educator and author. **Publications:** SELF-ILLUSTRATED FOR CHILDREN: Sziklaévek: hátrahagyott versek 1969-1975, 1983; Nagy utazás, 1986; Prince Ivan and the Firebird, 1991; East of the Sun and West of the Moon, 1993; Merlin's Castle, 1995; Csak a szépre: Budapesti élet-képek az 1950-60-as évekböl, 2005. Illustrator of books by others. Contributor to periodicals. **Address:** Canadian Broadcasting Co., PO Box 500, Sta A, Toronto, ON M5W 1E6, Canada.

GALANES, Philip. American (born United States), b. 1963. **Genres:** Novels. **Career:** Yale Law Journal, senior editor, 1991-; Yale Journal of Law and the Humanities, senior editor, 1991; American School, teacher; New York Times, news assistant; Debevoise & Plimpton, mergers and acquisitions attorney, 1991-94; Paul, Weiss, Rifkind, Wharton & Garrison, entertainment attorney, 1994-96; Golden Books Family Entertainment, general counsel, 1996-98, vice president of legal affairs and chief operating officer, 1998-2001. **Publications:** Father's Day, 2004; Emma's Table: A Novel, 2008; Social Qs: How to Survive the Quirks, Quandaries, and Quagmires of Today, 2011. **Address:** 1 Union Sq. W 810, New York, NY 10003, U.S.A. **Online address:** pg@philipgalanes.com

GALANG, M. Evelina. American (born United States), b. 1961. **Genres:** Novellas/Short Stories, Adult Non-fiction. **Career:** University of Wisconsin, University Theatre for Children and Young People, staff of ensemble, 1982-86; WMTV Channel 15, program creator, director, writer of promotions and public service announcements, production worker, program editor, 1982-86, creator, developer and producer of 1986 children's special, By Kids, For Kids; Children's Theater of Madison, ensemble staff and teacher of creative dramatics for children, 1985-86; Sedelmaier Films, Chicago Story, GKO Productions, Finerty Films, Dix and Associates, Ebel Productions and Genesis (all film production houses), script and continuity supervisor, 1986-; Women in the Director's Chair, public relations, 1987-88; Menomenee Boys and Girls Club, teacher of creative dramatics for children, 1988-90; Colorado Review, assistant manager, production coordinator, 1991-92; Guild Literary Complex, volunteer coordinator, supervisor and planner of multicultural literary events and workshops in poetry, fiction and music; Colorado State University, instructor in composition and creative writing, 1992-94, graduate reader, 1993-94; Old Dominion University, visiting assistant professor of creative writing in fiction, 1994-; Miami University, associate professor and director of creative writing, 1994-. **Publications:** Her Wild American Self (short fiction), 1996; (ed.) Screaming Monkeys, 2003; One Tribe, 2006; Lolas' House: Women Living with War, Stories of Surviving Filipina Comfort Women of World War II, forthcoming; Angel de la Luna, forthcoming; Smooches, forthcoming; Beautiful Sorrow, Beautiful Sky, forthcoming. Contributor of articles to periodicals. **Address:** Department of English, University of Miami, PO Box 248145, Coral Gables, FL 33124, U.S.A. **Online address:** mevelinag@yahoo.com

GALANT, Debra. American (born United States) **Genres:** Novels, Young Adult Fiction. **Career:** New York Times, Jersey columnist, 1998-2003; Barista.net, founder and writer, 2004-. **Publications:** (With Reha and A. Sokolow) Defying the Tide: An Account of Authentic Compassion during the Holocaust, 2003; Rattled, 2006; Fear and Yoga in New Jersey, 2008; Cars From A Marriage, 2010. **Address:** Lisa Bankoff, ICM Literary, 825 8th Ave., New York, NY 10019, U.S.A. **Online address:** debra@debragalant.com

GALASSO, Vincenzo. Italian (born Italy), b. 1967. **Genres:** Politics/Government, Social Sciences. **Career:** University of California, teaching assistant and lecturer, 1992-95; University of Carlos III, assistant professor of economics, 1996-2000; Universitá degli Studi di Napoli Federico II, lecturer, 1997-98; Centre for Economic Policy Research, research affiliate, 1997-; Boconi University, associate professor of economics, 2002-, IGIER research fellow, 2002-; European Commission, DG ECFIN visiting fellow, 2002; European Journal of Political Economy, associate editor, 2003-; OECD, external consultant, 2005-06. Writer. **Publications:** (Ed. with T. Boeri, M. Castanheira and R. Faini) Structural Reforms without Prejudices, 2006; The Political Future of Social Security in Aging Societies, 2006; (with T. Boeri) Contro I Giovani: Come L'Italia Sta Tradendo Le Nuove Generazioni, 2007. Contributor to periodicals and journals. **Address:** Bocconi University, Via Salasco 5, Milan, 20136, Italy.

GALA (Y VELASCO), Antonio. Spanish (born Spain), b. 1936. **Genres:** Plays/Screenplays, Poetry, Essays, Translations, Young Adult Fiction, Novels. **Career:** Writer and educator. **Publications:** (Trans.) P. Claudel, El zapato de raso, 1965; Noviembre y un poco de yerba (title means: 'November and a Bit of Grass'), 1967; Anillos para una dama (title means: 'A Ring for a Lady'), 1973; Suerte, campeón!, 1973; Lascítaras colgadas de los árboles (title means: 'Zithers Hung in the Trees'), 1974; 4 conmemoraciones, 1976; Petra Regalada, 1980; La vieja señorita del Paraíso, 1981; Obras escogidas, 1981; El cementerio de los pájaros (title means: 'The Bird Cemetery'), 1982; El cementerio de los pájaros, 1982; Trilogía de la libertad, 1983; Paisaje andaluz con figuras, 1984; Samarkanda, 1985; Paisaje con figuras, 2nd ed., 1985; El hotelito (title means: 'The Little Family Manor'), 1985; (with E. Jiménez) El sombrero de trespicos, 1986; Seneca, o el beneficio de la duda, 1987; Carmen Carmen, 1988; Cristóbal Colón, 1989; Los bellos durmientes, 1994; Si las piedras hablaran, 1995; Troneras, 1993-1996, 1996; El don de la palabra, 1996; Las afueras de Dios, 1999; Plays, 1999; Cinco Conmemoraciones, 1999; Teatro musical, 2000; Los verdes campos del Edén, 1964; La Alhambra: entre el cielo y la tierra=Between Heaven and Earth, 2001; Inés Desabrochada, 2003. NOVELS: El manuscritocarmesí (title means: 'The Crimson Manuscript'), 1990; La pasiónturca, 1993; Más allá del jardín, 1995; Si las piedrashablaran, 1995; La regla de tres, 1996; Café cantante, 1997; Elcorazón tardío, 1998; Las manzanas del viernes, 1999. POETRY: Enemigo íntimo, 1960; Testamento Andaluz, 1998; El águilabicéfala: Textos de amor, 1993; Poemas de amor, 1997; Cuaderno de Amor (anthology), 2001. OTHERS: Córdoba para vivir, 1965; Cantar del Santiago paratodos, 1974; Vicente Vela (criticism), 1975; Los buenos dias perdidos, 1977; Texto y pretexto, 1977; Teatro de hoy, teatro de mañana, 1978; Charlas con Troylo (title means: 'Conversations with Troylo'), 1981, rev. ed. as Charlas con Troylo y desde entonces, 1998; En propia mano (essays), 1983; Cuaderno de la dama de otoño (essays), 1985; Dedicado a Tobías (essays), 1988; Guía de los vinos españoles/Spanish Wines Guide (nonfiction), 1990; La soledad sonora (essays), 1991; (co-author) Pobreza, desarrollo y medio ambiente, 1992; La truhana, 1992; LaGranada de los nazaríes, 1992; Proas y troneras, 1993; Córdoba de Gala, 1993; A quien va conmigo (essays), 1994; Andaluz, 1994; Carta a los herederos, 1995; El don de lapalabra, 1996; La casa sosegada, 1998; Andalucía eterna, 1998; Ahora hablaré de mí (autobiography), 2000; Sobre la vida y el escenario (biography), 2001; Teatro de la historia, 2001; El imposible olvido, 2001; Losinvitados al jardín, 2002; (co-author) I [love] NY, 2002; Dueño de la Herida, 2003; Texto y Pretexto, 1973-1978, 2005; Poema de Tobías Desangelado, 2005; Granada de los Nazaríes, 2006; Pedestal de las Estatuas, 2007; Papeles de Agua, 2008. **Address:** c/o Coreo Autor, Editorial Planeta, Córega 273-277, Barcelona, 08008, Spain.

GALBRAITH, Kathryn O(sebold). American (born United States), b. 1945. **Genres:** Novels, Children's Fiction, Young Adult Fiction, Picture/Board Books. **Career:** Seattle Public Library, children's librarian, 1970-71; Fordham University, Lincoln Center, business librarian, 1971-74; New City Rand Institute, librarian, 1974-75; Family Service Association of America, librarian, 1975-79; Tacoma Philharmonic, director, 1982-; University of Washington, teacher. Writer. **Publications:** PICTURE BOOKS: Spots Are Special!, 1976; Katie Did!, 1982; Waiting for Jennifer, 1987; Laura Charlotte, 1990; Look! Snow!, 1992. CHAPTER BOOKS: Roommates, 1990; Roommates and Rachel, 1991; Roommates Again, 1994; Holding onto Sunday, 1995. NOVELS: Come Spring, 1979; Something Suspicious, 1985. OTHERS: Traveling Babies, 2006; Boo, Bunny!, 2008; One Shy Bunny, One Dark Night, 2008; Arbor Day Square, 2010; Planting the Wild Garden, 2011. **Address:** Houghton Mifflin Harcourt, 222 Berkeley St., Boston, MA 02116, U.S.A. **Online address:** sorkgalbraith@msn.com

GALDIKAS, Birute. (Birute Marija Filomena Galdikas). Canadian/German (born Germany), b. 1946. **Genres:** Zoology, Biology. **Career:** Simon Fraser University, professor; Universitas Nasional in Jakarta, professor extraordinaire.; University of British Columbia, professor; Jakarta National University, professor. Writer. **Publications:** NONFICTION: (as Birute Marija Filomena Galdikas) Adaptasi orangutan di Suaka Tanjung Puting, Kalimantan Tengah, 1984; (as Birute M.F. Galdikas) Reflections of Eden: My Years with the Orangutans of Borneo, 1995; (co-ed.) The Neglected Ape, 1996; (as Birute M.F. Galdikas with N. Briggs) Orangutan Odyssey, 1999; (co-ed.) All Apes Great and Small, 2001; (as Birute Mary Galdikas) Great Ape Odyssey, 2005. **Address:** c/o Author Mail, Harry N. Abrams Inc., 115 W 18th St., New York, NY 10011, U.S.A.

GALDIKAS, Birute Marija Filomena. See **GALDIKAS, Birute.**

GALDORISI, George V(ictor). American (born United States), b. 1948?. **Genres:** Law, Novels, Young Adult Fiction. **Career:** Space and Naval Warfare Systems Center, senior adviser, Decision Support Group, director; Naval War College, Center for Advanced Research, fellow; SPAWAR Systems Center Pacific, Corporate Strategy Group, director. Writer. **Publications:** (With D. Bandow and M.C. Jarman) The United States and the 1982 Law of the Sea Convention: The Cases Pro and Con, 1994; (with K.R. Vienna) Beyond the Law of the Sea: New Directions for U.S. Oceans Policy, 1997; Coronado Conspiracy (novel), 1998; Alert Seven (novel), 1999; For Duty and Honor, 2000. Contributor to periodicals. **Address:** 1061 Pine St., Coronado, CA 92118-2418, U.S.A.

GALE, Fredric G. American (born United States), b. 1933. **Genres:** Writing/Journalism, Law. **Career:** State University of New York, visiting lecturer, 1992; University of Arkansas, assistant professor of English, associate professor of rhetoric, 1992-. Writer. **Publications:** (With J.M. Moxley) Writing the Winning Brief: Strategies for Effective Memoranda, Briefs, Client Letters and Other Legal Documents, 1992; (with J.M. Moxley) Teaching Legal Writing: A Modern, Case-Study Approach, 1993; Political Literacy: Rhetoric, Ideology and the Possibility of Justice, 1994; (ed. with P. Sipiora and J.L. Kinneavy) Ethical Issues in Teaching Writing, 1999; (ed. with P. Sipiora and J.L. Kinneavy) Ethical Issues in College Writing, 1999; (ed. with X.L. Gale) (Re)visioning Composition Textbooks: Conflicts of Culture, Ideology and Pedagogy, 1999. **Address:** Department of Rhetoric, University of Arkansas, Little Rock, AR 72204, U.S.A.

GALE, Monica R(achel). Irish/British (born England), b. 1966. **Genres:** Classics, Poetry. **Career:** University of Newcastle, lecturer in Latin, 1991; Sir James Knott research fellow, 1992-93; University of Keele, faculty, 1992; University of London, lecturer in classics, 1993-99; University of Dublin, Trinity College Dublin, School of Histories and Humanities, Department of Classics, lecturer in classics, 1998-, associate professor. Writer. **Publications:** Myth and Poetry in Lucretius, 1994; Virgil on the Nature of Things: The Georgics, Lucretius and the Didactic Tradition, 2000; Lucretius and the Didactic Epic, 2001; (ed.) Latin Epic and Didactic Poetry: Genre, Tradition and Individuality, 2004; (ed.) Lucretius, 2007; (ed. and trans.) Lucretius: De Rerum Natura V, 2009; (ed. with J.H.D. Scourfield) Texts and Violence in the Roman World, forthcoming. **Address:** School of Histories and Humanities, Trinity College Dublin, University of Dublin, College Green, Dublin, DU 2, Ireland. **Online address:** mrgale@tcd.ie

GALEF, David. American (born United States), b. 1959. **Genres:** Novels,

Novellas/Short Stories, Children's Fiction, Poetry, Language/Linguistics. Career: Overseas Training Center, English teacher, 1981-82; Stanley H. Kaplan Educational Centers, teacher of English and mathematics, 1983-85; Columbia University, teacher of logic and rhetoric, 1986-88, preceptor in literature and humanities, 1988-89; University of Mississippi, assistant professor of English, 1989-95, assistant director of graduate studies in English, 1993-95, associate professor, 1995-2002, MFA program administrator, 2001-, professor of English, 2002-08; Montclair State University, professor. Writer. Publications: Even Monkeys Fall from Trees, and Other Japanese Proverbs, 1987; The Supporting Cast: A Study of Flat and Minor Characters, 1993; (ed.) Second Thoughts: A Focus on Rereading (anthology), 1998; (and trans.) Even A Stone Buddha Can Talk: The Wit and Wisdom of Japanese Proverbs, 2000; Laugh Track (short stories), 2002; (ed. with B. Weinhouse) 20 over 40: Stories from the Middle of Everything, 2006; Flaws, 2007; A Man of Ideas and Other Stories, 2007; Lists, 2007; (trans. and comp.) Japanese Proverbs: Wit and Wisdom, 2012. NOVELS: Flesh, 1995; Turning Japanese, 1998; How to Cope with Suburban Stress, 2006. JUVENILE: The Little Red Bicycle, 1988; Tracks, 1996. Address: Department of English, Montclair State University, Rm. 409, Dickson Hall, Montclair, NJ 07043, U.S.A. Online address: galefd@mail.montclair.edu

GALENORN, Yasmine. American (born United States), b. 1961. **Genres:** Natural History, Medicine/Health. **Career:** Writer. **Publications:** Trancing the Witch's Wheel: A Guide to Magickal Meditation, 1997; Embracing the Moon: A Witch's Guide to Ritual Spellcraft and Shadow Work, 1998; Dancing with the Sun: Celebrating the Seasons of Life, 1999; Tarot Journeys: Adventures in Self-Transformation, 1999; Crafting the Body Divine: Ritual, Movement and Body Art, 2001; Meditations on the Wheel of the Year, 2002; Magical Meditations: Guided Imagery for the Pagan Path, 2003; Sexual Ecstasy & the Divine: The Passion & Pain of Our Bodies, 2003; Totem Magic: Dance of the Shape-Shifter, 2004; Night Huntress, 2009; Demon Mistress, 2009; (co-author) Never After, 2010; Bone Magic, 2010; (co-author) Inked, 2010; (contrib.) Songs of Love & Death, 2010; (with I. Andrews, A. James and J.C. Stein) Hexed, 2011; Night Veil, 2011; Night Seeker, 2012. CHINTZ 'N' CHINA SERIES NOVELS: Ghost of a Chance, 2003; Legend of the Jade Dragon, 2004; Murder under a Mystic Moon, 2005; A Harvest of Bones, 2005; One Hex of a Wedding, 2006. BATH AND BODY SERIES AS INDIA INK: Scent to Her Grave, 2005; A Blush with Death, 2006; Glossed and Found, 2007; Dragon Wytch, 2008. SISTERS OF THE MOON SERIES NOVELS: Witchling, 2006; Changeling, 2007; Darkling, 2007. **Address:** c/o Erin Galloway, Berkley Publishing, 375 Hudson St., New York, NY 10014, U.S.A. **Online address:** mgoodbern@aol.com

GALEOTTI, Mark. American/British (born England), b. 1965. **Genres:** History, Criminology/True Crime, Politics/Government, International Relations/Current Affairs, Technology, Engineering. **Career:** University of Keele, lecturer in international history, 1991-96, senior lecturer in international history, 1997-, head of department, Organised Russian & Eurasian Crime Research Unit, director, 1997-; Foreign and Commonwealth Office, senior research fellow, 1996-97; School of Criminal Justice, visiting professor of public security, 2005-06; Rutgers University, visiting professor of public security; New York University, Center for Global Affairs, academic chair, director, clinical full professor of global affairs. Writer. **Publications:** Eurosource, the Eurotheatre Sourcebook for Cyberpunk: Everything the Cyberpunk Player Wants to Know About the Europe of the Future, 1991; The Age of Anxiety, 1995; Afghanistan: The Soviet Union's Last War, 1995; The Kremlin's Agenda, 1995; Cross-border Crime and the Former Soviet Union, 1995; Unstable Russia, 1996; Gorbachev and His Revolution, 1997; Criminal Russia, 1999, 4th ed., 2003; (ed. with I.M. Synge) Putin's Russia, 2002; Russian and Post-Soviet Organized Crime, 2002; (ed.) Global Crime Today, 2005; (ed.) Organized Crime in History, 2008; (ed.) Politics of Security in Modern Russia, 2009. **Address:** Center for Global Affairs, New York University, Rm. 414, 15 Barclay St., New York, NY 10128, U.S.A. **Online address:** hia15@keele.ac.uk

GALGANO, Robert C. American (born United States), b. 1970?. **Genres:** Young Adult Fiction, History. **Career:** University of Richmond, adjunct instructor of history; James Madison University, instructor; College of William and Mary, instructor. Writer, archaeologist and historian. **Publications:** Feast of Souls: Indians and Spaniards in the Seventeenth-Century Missions of Florida and New Mexico, 2005. **Address:** Department of History, University of Richmond, 218 Ryland Hall, 28 Westhampton Way, Richmond, VA 23173, U.S.A. **Online address:** rgalgano@richmond.edu

GALINSKY, Gotthard Karl. See **GALINSKY, Karl.**

GALINSKY, Karl. (Gotthard Karl Galinsky). American (born United States), b. 1942. **Genres:** Classics, Poetry. **Career:** Princeton University, instructor of classics, 1965-66; University of Texas, assistant professor, 1966-68, associate professor, 1968-72, professor of classics, 1972-, chair, 1974-90, James R. Daugherty, Jr. centennial professor of classics, 1984-85, Robert M. Armstrong centennial professor of classics, 1985-91, Floyd A. Cailloux centennial professor of classics, 1991-, distinguished teaching professor, 1999-; Tulane University, visiting Mellon professor of humanities, 1995; Universidad Nacional de La Plata, visiting professor, 1997; Johannes-Gutenberg Universität, visiting professor, 1998; Ruhr-Universität, research professor, 2009-. Writer. **Publications:** Aeneas, Sicily and Rome, 1969; The Herakles Theme, 1972; Ovid's Metamorphoses, 1975; Classical and Modern Interactions, 1992; Augustan Culture, 1996. EDITOR: (with F.W. Lenz) Albii Tibulli aliorumque carminum libri tres, 1971; Perspectives of Roman Poetry, 1974; The Interpretation of Roman Poetry: Empiricism or Hermeneutics?, 1992; The Cambridge Companion to the Age of Augustus, 2005. Contributor to journals. **Address:** Department of Classics, University of Texas, Rm. 215 Waggener Hall, 1 University Sta., PO Box C 3400, Austin, TX 78712-0308, U.S.A. **Online address:** galinsky@mail.utexas.edu

GALISON, Peter (Louis). American (born United States), b. 1955. **Genres:** Philosophy, History. **Career:** Stanford University, assistant professor, 1982-85, associate professor, 1985-90, professor of philosophy of physics and co-chair of history of science program, 1990-92; Princeton University, visiting assistant professor, 1985, Center for Advanced Study in Behavioral Science, fellow, 1989-90, chair of program, 1990-92; Boston University, Center of the Philosophy and History of Science, director, 1993-96; Harvard University, Department of the History of Science, chair, 1993-97, Mallinckrodt professor of the history of science, 1994-, Joseph Pellegrino University Professor, Department of Physics, Mallinckrodt professor of the history of science, 1994-, Joseph Pellegrino university professor, Collection of Historical Scientific Instruments, director. Writer. **Publications:** How Experiments End, 1987; Image and Logic: A Material Culture of Microphysics, 1997; Einstein's Clocks and Poincaré's Maps: Empires of Time, 2003; (with L. Daston) Objectivity, 2007. EDITOR: (with B. Hevly) Big Science: The Growth of Large-scale Research, 1992; (with D.J. Stump) The Disunity of Science: Boundaries, Contexts, and Power, 1996; (with C.A. Jones) Picturing Science, Producing Art, 1998; (with E. Thompson) The Architecture of Science, 1999; (with A. Roland) Atmospheric Flight in the Twentieth Century, 2000; (and intro. with M. Gordin and D. Kaiser) Science and Society: The History of Modern Physical Science in the Twentieth Century, 2001; (with S.R. Graubard and E. Mendelsohn) Science in Culture, 2001; (with M. Biagioli) Scientific Authorship: Credit and Intellectual Property in Science, 2003; (with G. Holton and S.S. Schweber) Einstein for the 21st Century: His Legacy in Science, Art, and Modern Culture, 2008. **Address:** Department of the History of Science, Harvard University, 371 Science Ctr., 1 Oxford St., Cambridge, MA 02138, U.S.A. **Online address:** galison@fas.harvard.edu

GALL, Henderson Alexander. See **GALL, Sandy.**

GALL, Lothar. German (born Germany), b. 1936. **Genres:** History, Adult Non-fiction. **Career:** University of Giessen, professor, 1968; Free University of Berlin, professor, 1972; Oxford University, visiting professor, 1972-73; University of Frankfurt, professor of contemporary history, 1975-, chair of medieval and modern history, 1975-2004; Historical Journal, editor, 1975-; Historical Commission of Frankfurt, chairperson, Historical Commission of the Bavarian Academy of Science, chairperson, 1994-2012. **Publications:** Bismarck: der weisse Revolutionaer, 1980; Bankier Hermann Josef Abs: Eine Biographie, 2004 as Banker Hermann Josef Abs: A Biography, 2004. UNTRANSLATED WORKS: Benjamin Constant: Seine Politische Ideenwelt und der deutsche Vormaerz, 1963; Liberalismus als regierende Partei: das Grossherzogtum Baden zwischen Restauration und Reichsgruendung, 1968; Dokumente Zur Reichsgrundung, 1972; Fragen an die deutsche Geschichte: Ideen, Kraefte, Entscheidungen von 1800 bis zur Gegenwart: historische Ausstellung im Reichstagsgebaude in Berlin, 1974, 20th ed., 2000; Europa auf dem Weg in die Moderne, 1850-1890, 1984, 4th ed., 2004; Buergertum in Deutschland, 1989; (with K.H. Juergens) Bismarck: Lebensbilder, 1990; Von der staendischen zur buergerlichen Gesellschaft, 1993; Germania, eine deutsche Marianne?, 1993; (co-author) Die Deutsche Bank, 1870-1995, 1995; Buergertum, liberale Bewegung und Nation. Ausgewaehlte Aufsaetze, 1996; Otto von Bismarck und Wilhelm II: Repraesentanten eines Epochenwechsels?,

2000; Krupp: Der Aufstieg eines Industrieimperiums, 2000; Neuerscheinungen zur Geschichte des 20. Jahrhunderts, 2001; Otto von Bismarck und die Parteien, 2001; Krupp im 20. Jahrhundert: die Geschichte des Unternehmens vom Ersten Weltkrieg bis zur Gruendung der Stiftung, 2002; Regierung, Parlament und Oeffentlichkeit im Zeitalter Bismarcks: Politikstile im Wandel, 2003; Historie und Leben: der Historiker als Wissenschaftler und Zeitgenosse: Festschrift fuer Lothar Gall zum 70. Geburtstag, 2006; Bismarcks Mitarbeiter, 2009; Walther Rathenau: Portrait einer Epoche, 2009; Wilhelm von Humboldt, 2011. EDITOR: Liberalismus, 1976; O. von Bismarck, Die Grossen Reden, 1981; (with R. Koch) Der Europaeische Liberalismus im 19. Jahrhundert: Texte zu seiner Entwicklung, 1981; (co-ed.) Enzyklopaedie deutscher Geschichte, 1988; Stadt und Buergertum im 19. Jahrhundert, 1990; Vom alten zum neuen Buergertum: Die mitteleuropaeische Stadt im Umbruch, 1780-1820, 1991; Neuerscheinungen zur Geschichte des 20. Jahrhunderts, 1992, rev. ed., 2001; Stadt und Buergertum im Uebergang von der traditionalen zur modernen Gesellschaft, 1993; (with D. Langewiesche) Liberalismus und Region: Zur Geschichte des deutschen Liberalismus im 19. Jahrhundert, 1995; Frankfurter Gesellschaft fuer Handel, Industrie, und Wissenschaft: Casino-Gesellschaft von 1802, 1995; Die Grossen Deutschen unserer Epoche, 1995; Burgerkultur im 19. Jahrhundert: Bildung, Kunst und Lebenswelt, 1996; Buergertum und buergerlich-liberale Bewegung in Mitteleuropa seit dem 18. Jahrhundert, 1997; 1848: Aufbruch zur Freiheit: Eine Ausstellung des Deutschen Historischen Museums und der Schirn Kunsthalle Frankfurt zum 150 jaehrigen Jubilaeum der Revolution von 1848/49: 18. Mai bis 18. September 1998 in der Schirn Kunsthalle Frankfurt, 1998; Unternehmen im Nationalsozialismus, 1998; (with U. Lappenkueper) Fuer deutsche Geschichts- und Quellenforschung: 150 Jahre Historische Kommission bei der Bayerischen Akademie der Wissenschaften, 1998; (with M. Pohl) Die Eisenbahn in Deutschland: Von den Anfaengen bis zur Gegenwart, 1999; Das Jahrtausend im Spiegel der Jahrhundertwenden, 1999; Quelleneditionen und kein Ende?: Symposium der Monumenta Germaniae Historica und der Historischen Kommission bei der Bayerischen Akademie der Wissenschaften, Muenchen, 22./23. Mai 1998, 1999. **Address:** Department of History, University of Frankfurt, Rm. 3515, Grueneburgplatz 1, Frankfurt, 60629, Germany. **Online address:** l.gall@em.uni-frankfurt.de

GALL, Pete. American (born United States), b. 1971. **Genres:** Biography, Autobiography/Memoirs. **Career:** Freelance writer, public speaker and consultant. **Publications:** My Beautiful Idol, 2008; Learning My Name, 2009. **Address:** Indianapolis, IN , U.S.A. **Online address:** stopstaring@petegall.com

GALL, Sandy. (Henderson Alexander Gall). British/Malaysian (born Malaysia), b. 1927. **Genres:** Travel/Exploration, Writing/Journalism, Documentaries/Reportage, History, Social Sciences, Reference. **Career:** Reuters News Agency, foreign correspondent, 1953-63; Independent Television News, correspondent, television journalist, 1963-92, retired, 1992; University of Aberdeen, rector, 1978-81; freelance writer and broadcaster, 1993-. **Publications:** Gold Scoop (novel), 1977; Chasing the Dragon (novel), 1981; Don't Worry about the Money Now, 1983; Behind Russian Lines: An Afghan Journal, 1983; Afghanistan: Agony of a Nation, 1988; Salang (novel), 1989; George Adamson, Lord of the Lions, 1991; News from the Front: A Television Reporter's Life, 1994; The Bushmen of Southern Africa: Slaughter of the Innocent, 2001. **Address:** Doubleton Oast House, Penshurst, Tonbridge, KT TN11 8JA, England. **Online address:** sgaa@btinternet.com

GALLAGHER, Gary W(illiam). American (born United States), b. 1950. **Genres:** History, Essays. **Career:** National Archives and Records Administration, Lyndon Baines Johnson Library, archivist, 1977-86; Pennsylvania State University, assistant professor, 1986-89, associate professor, 1989-91, professor of history, 1991-98, head of department, 1991-95; University of Texas, visiting lecturer, 1986, George W. Littlefield lecturer, 1995-96; Penn State/Mont Alto Annual Conferences on the Civil War, academic coordinator, 1987-; University of Virginia, professor of history, 1998-99, John L. Nau III professor in the history of the American Civil War, 1999-; Association for the Preservation of Civil War Sites, founder. Writer. **Publications:** (Ed. and contrib.): Essays on Southern History: Written in Honor of Barnes F. Lathrop, General Libraries, 1980; Stephen Dodson Ramseur: Lees Gallant General, 1985; (ed.) Fighting for the Confederacy: The Personal Recollections of General Edward Porter Alexander, 1989; Antietam: Essays on the 1862 Maryland Campaign, 1989; Struggle for the Shenandoah: Essays on the 1864 Valley Campaign, 1991; The First Day at Gettysburg: Essays on Confederate and Union Leadership, 1992; The Second Day at Gettysburg: Essays on Confederate and Union Leadership, 1993; The Third Day at Gettysburg

and Beyond, 1994; (intro.) Jeb Stuart, 1994; The Fredericksburg Campaign: Decision on the Rappahannock, 1995; Jubal A. Early, The Lost Cause, and Civil War History: A Persistent Legacy, 1995; (contrib.) The Battle of Chancellorsville, 1995; Lee the Soldier, 1996; Chancellorsville: The Battle and Its Aftermath, 1996; The Wilderness Campaign, 1997; The Confederate War: How Popular Will, Nationalism, and Military Strategy Could Not Stave Off Defeat, 1997; The Spotsylvania Campaign, 1998; Lee and His Generals in War and Memory, 1998; (ed.) The Antietam Campaign, 1999; Three Days at Gettysburg: Essays on Confederate and Union Leadership, 1999; (ed. with A.T. Nolan) The Myth of the Lost Cause and Civil War History, 2000; Lee & His Army in Confederate History, 2001; The American Civil War: The War in the East, 1861-May 1863, 2001; (with M.E. Wagner and P. Finkelman) The Library of Congress Civil War Desk Reference, 2002; The Richmond Campaign of 1862: The Peninsula and the Seven Days, 2002; (ed.) The Shenandoah Valley Campaign of 1862, 2003; (ed. with J.T. Glatthaar) Leaders of the Lost Cause, 2004; (ed.) The Shenandoah Valley Campaign of 1864, 2006; (ed. with E.L. Ayers and A.J. Torget) Crucible of the Civil War: Virginia From Secession to Commemoration, 2006; Causes Won, Lost, and Forgotten: How Hollywood and Popular Art Shape What We know About the Civil War, 2008; (ed.) Two Witnesses at Gettysburg: The Personal Accounts of Whitelaw Reid and A.J.L. Fremantle, 2009; (ed. with J. Waugh) Wars Within a War: Controversy and Conflict Over the American Civil War, 2009; (foreword) The Civil War: A History, 2010; (with R. ONeill) The Civil War: Bull Run and Other Eastern Battles, 1861-May-1863, 2011; The Union War, 2011; (ed. with R.A. Shelden) A Political Nation, 2012. Works appear in anthologies. Contributor to periodicals. **Address:** Department of History, University of Virginia, 423 Nau Hall-South Lawn, Charlottesville, VA 22904, U.S.A. **Online address:** gallagher@virginia.edu

GALLAGHER, Kathleen. Canadian (born Canada), b. 1965?. **Genres:** Plays/Screenplays, Education, Gay And Lesbian Issues, Popular Culture, Race Relations, Theatre, Urban Studies, Women's Studies And Issues, Women's Studies And Issues. **Career:** St. Joseph's College, teacher of dramatic arts, French, and English, 1989-99; Brock University, Department of Film Studies, Visual and Dramatic Arts, instructor of drama education, 1998-99; University of Toronto, Ontario Institute for Studies in Education, Department of Curriculum, Teaching and Learning, assistant professor, 1999-2004, Canada Research Chair, 2004-, associate professor, 2004-09, professor, 2009-, Centre for Urban Schooling, academic director, 2005-; Tarragon Theatre, educational consultant, 1999-; Nightwood Theatre, director, 2000-. Writer. **Publications:** Drama Education in the Lives of Girls: Imagining Possibilities, 2000; (ed. with K. Gallagher and D. Booth) How Theatre Educates: Convergences and Counterpoints with Artists, Scholars, and Advocates, 2003; The Theatre of Urban: Youth and Schooling in Dangerous Times, 2007; The Methodological Dilemma: Creative, Critical, and Collaborative Approaches to Qualitative Research, 2008. Contributor of articles to books to periodicals. **Address:** Department of Curriculum Teaching & Learning, Ontario Institute for Studies in Education, University of Toronto, 252 Bloor St. W, Toronto, ON M5S 1V6, Canada. **Online address:** kgallagher@oise.utoronto.ca

GALLAGHER, Katie. See ALLEN, Sarah Addison.

GALLAGHER, Liz. American (born United States), b. 1978. **Genres:** Novels, Young Adult Fiction, Education. **Career:** Red Tricycle, editor; Highlights for Children, editorial intern; Montessori school, assistant. **Publications:** The Opposite of Invisible, 2008; My Not-So-Still Life, 2011. **Address:** c/o Rosemary Stimola, Stimola Literary Studio L.L.C., 306 Chase Ct., Edgewater, NJ 07020, U.S.A. **Online address:** liz@lizgallagher.com

GALLAGHER, Mary Elizabeth. American (born United States), b. 1969. **Genres:** Politics/Government, Economics. **Career:** Overseas Training Center, English language instructor, 1991-93; Foreign Affairs College, instructor, 1996-97; Washington Post, translator, 1996-97; University of Michigan, Department Of Political Science, assistant professor, 2000-, associate professor, 2008-, Center for Chinese Studies, faculty associate, 2000-, director, 2008-Center for Japanese Studies, faculty associate, 2001-, Institute of Labor and Industrial Relations, faculty associate, Institute of Social Research, Center for Comparative Political Studies, faculty, 2004-. Writer. **Publications:** Contagious Capitalism: Globalization and the Politics of Labor in China, 2005; (ed. with S. Kuruvilla and C.K. Lee) From Iron Rice Bowl to Informalization: Markets, Workers, and the State in a Changing China, 2011; (ed. with M.Y.K. Woo) Chinese Justice: Civil Dispute Resolution in Contemporary China, 2011. Contributor to periodicals. **Address:** Political Science Department, University of Michigan, 5700 Haven Hall, 505 S State St., Ann Arbor, MI 48109-1045, U.S.A. **Online address:** metg@umich.edu

GALLAGHER, Patricia C. American (born United States), b. 1957. **Genres:** Business/Trade/Industry, Crafts, Education, How-to Books, Medicine/Health, Recreation, Economics, Young Adult Fiction, Young Adult Fiction. **Career:** Writer and publishing consultant. **Publications:** Child Care and You: A Comprehensive Guide to Organizing a Profitable Home Based Child Care Business, 1987; So You Want to Open a Day Care Center: A Basic How to Do It Guide, 1987; Robin's Play and Learn Book: Creative Activities for Preschoolers, 1987; Robin's Play and Learn Book: How to Entertain Children at Home or in Preschool, 1988; Start Your Own At-Home Child Care Business, 1989; (comp.) For All the Write Reasons: Forty Successful Authors, Publishers, Agents and Writers Tell You How to Get Your Book Published, 1991; Raising Happy Kids on a Reasonable Budget, 1993. **Address:** PO Box 555, Worcester, PA 19490, U.S.A.

GALLAGHER, Shaun. American (born United States), b. 1948. **Genres:** Young Adult Non-fiction, Psychology. **Career:** Villanova University, adjunct instructor, 1977-81; Institut Supérieur de Philosophie, visiting researcher, 1979-80; Gwynedd-Mercy College, assistant professor, 1980-81; Canisius College, assistant professor, 1981-86, associate professor, 1986-93, professor, 1993-2003, Cognitive Science Program, director, 1996-2003; University of Central Florida, Department of Philosophy, professor, 2003-, chair of department, 2003-05, Cognitive Science Program, director, 2003-05, 2010-, Institute of Simulation and Training, senior research faculty, 2008-, Ph.D. Program in Texts and Technology, graduate faculty, 2008-; University of Memphis, Moss professor of excellence in philosophy, 2011-; University of Aarhus, visiting professor; University of Hertfordshire, research professor. Writer. **Publications:** NONFICTION: (ed. with T.W. Busch) Merleau-Ponty, Hermeneutics and Postmodernism, 1992; Hermeneutics and Education, 1992; (ed.) Hegel, History, and Interpretation, 1997; The Inordinance of Time, 1998; (ed. with J. Shear) Models of the Self, 1999; How the Body Shapes the Mind, 2005; (ed. with S. Pockett and W.P. Banks) Does Consciousness Cause Behavior?, 2006; Brainstorming: Views and Interviews on the Mind, 2008; (ed.) Oxford Handbook of the Self, 2011; (with D. Zahavi) Phenomenological Mind, 2012. Contributor of articles to journals. **Address:** Department of Philosophy, University of Central Florida, 411 Colbourn Hall, Bldg. PSY0220, 4000 Central Florida Blvd., Orlando, FL 32816-1352, U.S.A. **Online address:** gallaghr@mail.ucf.edu

GALLAGHER, Stephen. Also writes as John Lydecker, Stephen Couper. British (born England), b. 1954. **Genres:** Mystery/Crime/Suspense, Horror, Plays/Screenplays, Art/Art History, Novels. **Career:** Yorkshire Television, Department of Documentaries, researcher, 1975; Granada Television, transmission controller, 1975-80; Piccadilly Radio, radio scriptwriter, 1977-80; British Broadcasting Corp., television scriptwriter, 1978-80; full-time freelance writer, 1980-; Writers' Guild of Great Britain, northern chair; NBC, lead writer, 2008; ABC, co-executive producer, 2009. **Publications:** FICTION: The Last Rose of Summer (adaptation of radio serial), 1978, rev. ed. (as Stephen Couper) Dying of Paradise, 1982; Saturn 3, 1980; (as John Lydecker) Silver Dream Racer, 1980; Warrior's Gate, 1982; Chimera, 1982; (as Stephen Couper) The Ice Belt, 1983; Terminus, 1983; Follower, 1984; Valley of Lights, 1987; Oktober, 1988; Down River, 1989; Rain, 1990; Dark Visions (3-author collection), 1990; The Boat House, 1991; Nightmare, with Angel, 1992; Red, Red Robin, 1995; Journeyman: The Art of Chris Moore (nonfiction), 2000; White Bizango, 2002; Out of His Mind, 2004; The Spirit Box, 2005; The Painted Bride, 2006; The Kingdom of Bones: A Novel, 2007; Plots and Misadventures, 2007; The Suicide Hour, 2010; Bedlam Detective: A Novel, 2012. **Address:** The Agency Ltd., 24 Pottery Ln., Holland Pk., London, GL W11 4LZ, England.

GALLAGHER, Susan VanZanten. American (born United States), b. 1955. **Genres:** Literary Criticism And History, Social Sciences, Young Adult Fiction, Language/Linguistics, Humanities. **Career:** Covenant College, assistant professor of English, 1982-86; Calvin College, assistant professor, 1986-87, associate professor, 1987-91, professor of English, 1991-93; Seattle Pacific University, professor of English, 1993-, director of University scholars. Writer. **Publications:** (With R. Lundin) Literature through the Eyes of Faith, 1989; A Story of South Africa: J. M. Coetzee's Fiction in Context, 1991; (ed.) Postcolonial Literature and The Biblical Call to Justice, 1994; (ed. with M.D. Walhout) Literature and the Renewal of the Public Sphere, 2000; Truth and Reconciliation: The Confessional Mode in South African Literature, 2002.

Contributor to periodicals. Work appears in anthologies. **Address:** Department of English, Seattle Pacific University, 3307 3rd Ave. W, Seattle, WA 98119-1997, U.S.A. **Online address:** gallaghe@spu.edu

GALLAGHER, Tess. Also writes as Tess Bond. American (born United States), b. 1943. **Genres:** Novellas/Short Stories, Poetry, Film, Travel/Exploration, Essays. **Career:** St. Lawrence University, faculty, 1974-75; Kirkland College, faculty, 1975-77; University of Montana, faculty, 1977-78; University of Arizona, faculty, 1979-80; Syracuse University, professor, 1980-90; Willamette University, instructor, 1981; Whitman College, visiting Arnold professor, 1996-97; Bucknell University, Stadler Poetry Center, poet-in-residence. Writer. **Publications:** Stepping Outside, 1974; Instructions to the Double, 1976; On Your Own, 1978; Under Stars, 1978; Portable Kisses, 1978; Death of the Horses by Fire, 1984; Willingly, 1984; A Concert of Tenses: Essays on Poetry, 1986; The Lover of Horses, 1986; Amplitude: New and Selected Poems, 1987; Moon-Crossing Bridge, 1992; Portable Kisses, 1992; I Stop Writing the Poem, 1992; Valentine Elegies, 1993; Portable Kisses Expanded, 1993; My Black Horse, 1995; At the Owl Woman Saloon, 1997; Soul Barnacles, Ten More Years with Ray, 2000; Dear Ghosts, 2006; Words Like Distant Rain, 2006; (with J. Gray) Barnacle Soup, and Other Stories from the West of Ireland, 2007; Man from Kinvara, 2009; Midnight Lantern: New and Selected Poems, 2011. Contributor to periodicals. **Address:** c/o Amanda Urban, ICM, 40 W 57th St., New York, NY 10019, U.S.A.

GALLAGHER, Tom. British/Scottish (born Scotland), b. 1954. **Genres:** History, Sociology, Bibliography, Adult Non-fiction. **Career:** University of Bradford, professor of ethnic conflict and peace, M.A. admissions tutor, research unit for South-East-European Studies, chair, 2005-; National Endowment for Democracy, fellow, 2008. Writer. **Publications:** Dictatorial Portugal, 1926-1974: A Bibliography, 1979; (ed. with J. O'Connell) Contemporary Irish Studies, 1983; Portugal: A Twentieth-Century Interpretation, 1983; Edinburgh Divided: John Cormack and No Popery in the 1930s, 1987; Glasgow, the Uneasy Peace: Religious Tension in Modern Scotland, 1819-1914, 1987; (ed. with A.M. Williams) Southern European Socialism: Parties, Elections, and the Challenge of Government, 1989; (ed. with G. Walker) Sermons and Battle Hymns: Protestant Popular Culture in Modern Scotland, 1990; (ed.) Nationalism in the Nineties, 1991; Romania after Ceausescu: The Politics of Intolerance, 1995; Democracy and Nationalism in Romania, 1989-1998, 1999; (ed. with G. Pridham) Experimenting with Democracy: Regime Change in the Balkans, 2000; Outcast Europe: The Balkans, 1789-1989, from the Ottomans to Milosevic, 2001; The Balkans after the Cold War: From Tyranny to Tragedy, 2003; Modern Romania: The End of Communism, the Failure of Democratic Reform, and the Theft of a Nation, 2005; Theft of a Nation: Romania since Communism, 2005; The Balkans in the New Millennium: In the Shadow of War and Peace, 2005; Romania and the European Union: How the Weak Vanquished the Strong, 2009; Illusion of Freedom: Scotland Under Nationalism, 2009. Contributor to journals. **Address:** University of Bradford, Richmond Rd., Bradford, WY BD7 1DP, England. **Online address:** t.g.gallagher@bradford.ac.uk

GALLAGHER, Winifred. American (born United States) **Genres:** Novels, inspirational/Motivational Literature, Theology/Religion, Psychology. **Career:** American Health, psychology editor. Journalist. **Publications:** The Power of Place: How Our Surroundings Shape Our Thoughts Emotions and Actions, 1993; I.D: How Heredity and Experience Make You Who You Are, 1996; Just the Way You Are: How Heredity and Experience Create the Individual, 1997; Working on God, 1999; Spiritual Genius: The Mastery of Lifes Meaning, 2001; It's in the Bag: What Purses Reveal-and Conceal, 1st ed., 2006; House Thinking: A Room-by-Room Look at How We Live, 1st ed., 2006; Rapt: Attention and the Focused Life, 2009; New: Understanding Our Need for Novelty and Change, 2011. **Address:** c/o Kristine Dahl, International Creative Management, 730 5th Ave., New York, NY 10019, U.S.A. **Online address:** winigallagher@aol.com

GALLAHER, (William) Rhea. (Judith Gould). American (born United States), b. 1945. **Genres:** Novels, Young Adult Fiction, Travel/Exploration. **Career:** English teacher, 1965-66; Biomedical Information Corp., editor and writer, 1975-76; freelance editor, 1976-82; writer, 1979-. **Publications:** NOVELS AS JUDITH GOULD WITH N.P. BIENES: Sins, 1982; Love-Makers, 1985; Dazzle, 1989; Never Too Rich, 1990; Texas Born, 1992; Forever, 1992; Too Damn Rich, 1993; Second Love, 1997; Till the End of Time, 1998; Rhapsody, 1999; Time to Say Good-Bye, 2000; A Moment In Time, 2001; The Best Is Yet to Come, 2002; The Greek Villa, 2003; Parisian Affair, 2004; Dreamboat, 2005; Secret Heiress, 2006, Greek Winds of Fury, 2008. OTHERS: (with R. Koretsky) Brew Cuisine: Cooking with Beer, 1989; The World Who's Who of Women, 1997. **Address:** Dutton Publicity, 375 Hudson St., New York, NY 10014-3658, U.S.A. **Online address:** judithgould001@yahoo.com

GALLANT, Jennie. *See* **SMITH, Joan Gerarda.**

GALLANT, Roy Arthur. American (born United States), b. 1924. **Genres:** Astronomy, Biology, Chemistry, Children's Non-fiction, Earth Sciences, Environmental Sciences/Ecology, Zoology, Biography, Biography, Natural History. **Career:** Retailing Daily, Boy's Life, reporter and staff writer, 1949-51; Scholastic Teacher, managing editor, 1953-56; Doubleday and Company Inc., author-in-residence, 1956-58; Columbia University, Teachers College, instructor, 1958; Aldus Books Ltd., executive editor, 1959-62; Natural History Press, editor-in-chief, 1962-65; Hackley School, lecturer in astronomy, 1969-70; American Museum of Natural History, Hayden Planetarium, faculty, 1972-79; University of Maine, associate professor, 1975-76; Rangeley Highlander, owner, publisher and editor, 1977-78; University of Southern Maine, professor of English, 1980-2000, professor emeritus, 2001-, Southworth Planetarium, director, 1980-2000, director emeritus, 2000-; WCSH-TV, science commentator, 1985-86. **Publications:** Exploring the Moon, 1955, rev. ed., 1966; Exploring Mars, 1956, rev. ed., 1968; Exploring the Universe, 1956, rev. ed., 1968; Exploring the Weather, 1957, rev. ed., 1969; Exploring the Sun, 1958; Exploring the Planets, 1958; Exploring Chemistry, 1958; Man's Reach into Space, 1959; The Nature of the Weather; 1959; Exploring under the Earth, 1960; Antarctic, 1962; The ABC's of Astronomy, 1963; The ABC's of Chemistry, 1963; (with C.J. Schuberth) Discovering Rocks and Minerals, 1967; Man Must Speak: The Story of Language and How We Use It, 1969; Me and My Bones, 1971; Man's Reach for the Stars, 1971; Man the Measurer, 1972; Charles Darwin: The Making of a Scientist, 1972; Explorers of the Atom, 1973; (with R.A. Suthers) Biology: The Behavioral View, 1973; Astrology: Sense or Nonsense?, 1974; How Life Began: Creation Versus Evolution, 1975, rev. ed. as Beyond Earth: The Search For Extraterrestrial Life, 1977; Beyond Earth, 1977; Earth: The Making of A Planet, 1997; Fires in the Sky, 1978; Earth's Changing Climate, 1979; The Constellations, How They Came to Be, 1979, rev. ed., 1991; You and Your Memory, 1980; The National Geographic Atlas of Our Universe, 1980, rev. ed., 1986; Memory: How It Works and How to Improve It, 1980; (with I. Asimov) Ginn Science Program (grades 4-8), 1981; The Planets, Exploring The Solar System, 1982; Once around the Galaxy, 1982; 101 Questions and Answers About the Universe, 1984; Lost Cities, 1985; Fossils, 1985; Ice Ages, 1985; Macmillan Book of Astronomy, 1986; Our Restless Earth, 1986; From Living Cells to Dinosaurs, 1986; TheRise of Mammals, 1986; Private Lives of the Stars, 1986; Rainbows, Mirages and Sundogs: The Sky as a Source of Wonder, 1987; When the Sun Dies, 1989; Ancient Indians, 1989; Before The Sun Dies: The Story of Evolution, 1989; Ancients Indians, 1989; The Peopling of Planet Earth: Human Population Growth Through the Ages, 1990; Earth's Vanishing Forests, 1991; A Young Person's Guide to Science: Ideas That Change the World, 1993; The Day the Sky Split Apart, 1995; Sand Dunes, 1997; Geysers: When Earth Roars, 1997; Planet Earth, 1997; Limestone Caves, 1998; Sand on the Move: The Story of Dunes, 1998; Glaciers, 1999; Early Humans, 2000; The Ever Changing Atom, 2000; Earth's Place in Space, 2000; Dance of the Continents, 2000; The Life Stories of Stars, 2000; Comets, Asteroids and Meteorites, 2001; The Origins of Life, 2001; Minerals, 2001; Rocks, 2001; Space Stations, 2001; Stars, 2001; The Planets, 2001; Water, 2001; The Treasure of Inheritance, 2002; Biodiversity, 2002; Earth's Restless Crust, 2002; Earth's Natural Resources, 2002; Earth's Water, 2002; Earth's Atmosphere, 2002; Earth's Structure and Composition, 2002; Earth's History, 2002; Meteorite Hunter: The Search for Siberian Meteorite Craters, 2002; Atmosphere: Sea of Air, 2003; History: Journey Through Time, 2003; Plates: Restless Earth, 2003; Resources: Nature's Riches, 2003; Structure: Exploring Earth's Interior, 2003; Wonders of Biodiversity, 2003; Water: Our Precious Resource, 2003. EDITOR: (with Fisher and J. Huxley) Nature, 1960; (with F. Debenham) Discovery and Exploration, 1960; (with F. Manley) Geography, 1961; (with G.E.R. Deacon) Seas, Maps and Men, 1963; (with H. Garnott) Treasures of Yesterday, 1964; (with T.F. Gaskell) World beneath the Oceans, 1964; (with C.A. Ronan) Man Probes the Universe, 1964; (with R. Clark) Explorers of the World, 1964; (with McElroy) Foundations of Biology, 1968; (with C.E. Swartz) Measure and Find Out 1-3, 1969; Charting the Universe, 1969; The Universe in Motion, 1969; Gravitation, 1969; The Message of Starlight, 1969; The Life Story of a Star, 1969; Galaxies and the Universe, 1969. Contributor to books and magazines. **Address:** Southworth Planetarium, University of Southern Maine, PO Box 9300, Portland, ME 04104-9300, U.S.A. **Online address:** rgal@megalink.net

GALLANT, Stephen I. American (born United States), b. 1946. **Genres:** Biology, Sciences. **Career:** Northeastern University, associate professor, 1983-90; HNC Inc., senior scientist, 1990-93; Belmont Research Inc., senior scientist, 1993-; Xchange Inc., director of analytic services. **Publications:** Neural Network Learning and Expert Systems, 1993. Contributor to journals. **Address:** Belmont Research Inc., 84 Sherman St., Cambridge, MA 02140-3261, U.S.A.

GALLARDO, Evelyn. American (born United States), b. 1948. **Genres:** Animals/Pets, Children's Non-fiction, How-to Books, Biography, Photography. **Career:** Writer and wild life photographer, 1988-; Educational Travel Services, instructor, 1989-. **Publications:** Among the Orangutans: The Biruté Galdikas Story, 1993; (contrib.) Endangered Wildlife, 1993; How to Promote Your Children's Book: A Survival Guide, 1997, 2nd ed., 2000. Contributor to books and magazines. **Address:** Primate Productions, 2208 The Strand, Ste. B, PO Box 3038, Manhattan Beach, CA 90266-4449, U.S.A. **Online address:** evegal22@aol.com

GALLAS, John (Edward). New Zealander (born New Zealand), b. 1950. **Genres:** Poetry, Children's Fiction, Art/Art History, Photography. **Career:** University of Otago, assistant lecturer in English, 1975; University of Liverpool, archivist, 1977-78; Cizakca Lisesi, teacher in English, 1980; Robert Smyth School, teacher in English, 1981-87; Akademi, teacher in English, 1988; Student Support Service, teacher of students with special needs, 1989-. Writer. **Publications:** POETRY: Practical Anarchy, 1989; Flying Carpets over Filbert Street, 1993; Grrrrr, 1997; Resistance Is Futile, 1999; The Song Atlas: A Book of World Poetry, 2003; Ballad of Robin Hood and the Deer, 2003; The Ballad of Santo Caserio, 2003; Star City: Including The Coalville Divan and Excellent Men, 2004; The Book with Twelve Tales, 2008; Forty Lies, 2010. **Address:** c/o Clare Pearson, Eddison Pearson Ltd., 22 Upper Grosvenor St., 3rd Fl., London, GL W1X 9PB, England. **Online address:** john.gallas@ntlworld.com

GALLAS, Karen. American (born United States), b. 1949. **Genres:** Language/Linguistics. **Career:** School teacher, 1972-79, 1985-87; Bridgewater State College, demonstration teacher, 1979-80; University of Maine, assistant professor, 1981-85, professor of education; Lesley College, faculty, 1983-93; Lawrence School, elementary teacher, 1987-; Brookline Public Schools, elementary teacher, 1987-; Galef Institute, consultant; Wheelock College, faculty. Writer. **Publications:** The Languages of Learning: How Children Talk, Write, Dance, Draw and Sing Their Understanding of the World, 1994; Talking Their Way into Science: Hearing Children's Questions and Theories, Responding with Curricula, 1995; Sometimes I Can Be Anything: Power, Gender, and Identity in a Primary Classroom, 1998; Imagination and Literacy: A Teacher's Search for the Heart of Learning, 2003. **Address:** Lawrence School, 27 Francis St., Brookline, MA 02446-6699, U.S.A.

GALLAWAY, Morgana Bridget. American (born United States), b. 1983. **Genres:** Novels. **Career:** Writer. **Publications:** The Nightingale, 2009. **Address:** c/o Daniel Lazar, Writers House, 21 W 26th St., New York, NY 10010, U.S.A. **Online address:** contact@morganagallaway.com

GALLENKAMP, Charles (Benton). American (born United States), b. 1930. **Genres:** Young Adult Fiction, Archaeology/Antiquities, Children's Non-fiction, History, Biography, Autobiography/Memoirs. **Career:** University of New Mexico, Museum of Anthropology, assistant director, 1948-51; Houston Museum of Natural History, research associate in anthropology, 1952-56; Houston Museum of Natural Science, assistant curator of anthropology, 1957-62; Interam Foundation, Maya Research Fund, director, 1957-62; writer, 1959-; Janus Gallery, director, 1970-78; School of American Research, research associate, 1976-98; Albuquerque Museum, exhibition coordinator, 1981-87; American Art Gallery, owner. **Publications:** The Pueblo Indians in Story, Song and Dance (juvenile), 1955; Maya: The Riddle and Rediscovery of a Lost Civilization 1959, 3rd ed., 1987; Finding Out about the Maya (juvenile), 1963; (with C. Meyer) The Mystery of the Ancient Maya, 1985; (ed. with R.E. Johnson) Maya: Treasures of an Ancient Civilization, 1985; (with C. Meyer) Mystery of the Ancient Maya, 1995; (with M.J. Novacek) Dragon Hunter: Roy Chapman Andrews and the Central Asiatic Expeditions, 2001. **Address:** c/o Owen Laster, William Morris Agency, 1325 Ave. of the Americas, New York, NY 10019, U.S.A.

GALLEYMORE, Frances. British (born England), b. 1946?. **Genres:** Novels, Novellas/Short Stories. **Career:** Novelist and screenwriter. **Publications:** The Orange Tree, 1970; Ground Wave Sailing, 1975; Dangerous Relations, 1994; Lifemask, 1995; Safe, 1996; Widow Maker, 1999; Veritas: Finding The Goddess, 2011. **Address:** Orion House, Orion Publishing Group Ltd., 5 Upper St., Martins Ln., London, GL WC2H 9EA, England.

GALLHOFER, Irmtraud N(ora). Spanish/Austrian (born Austria), b. 1945. **Genres:** Politics/Government. **Career:** University of Amsterdam, Department of Romance Languages and Literature, research assistant, 1969-70, senior researcher, 2001-06; Free University of Amsterdam, Department of Education, research assistant in education, 1978-79; Sociometric Research Foundation, managing director, 1984-93, faculty, 1983; University of Essex, Summerschool of the European Consortium for Political Research, teacher, 1985-90; National Science Foundation, senior researcher, 1997-2001; Ramon Llull University, senior researcher, 2006-09; Universitat Pompeu Fabra, senior researcher, 2009-. Writer. **Publications:** (With J.Z. Namenwirth and K. Niemöller) Reader on Text-Analysis, 1978. WITH W.E. SARIS: Foreign Policy Decision-Making: A Qualitative and Quantitative Analysis of Political Argumentation, 1996; Collective Choice Processes: A Qualitative and Quantitative Analysis of Foreign Policy Decision-Making, 1997; Design, Evaluation, and Analysis of Questionnaires for Survey Research, 2007. EDITOR AND CONTRIBUTOR: (with M. Melman and W.E. Saris) Different Text-Analysis Procedures for the Study of Decision-Making, 1986; (with W.E. Saris) Sociometric Research, 2 vols., 1988. Contributor to books and periodicals. **Address:** Universitat Pompeu Fabra, 10-12 Plaça de la Mercè, Barcelona, E-08002, Spain. **Online address:** irmtraud.gallhofer@gmail.com

GALLI, Richard. American (born United States) **Genres:** Politics/Government, Law, Novels, History, Military/Defense/Arms Control. **Career:** Providence Journal, reporter and photographer; Adler Pollock & Sheehan, partner. Lawyer. **Publications:** Rescuing Jeffrey (memoir), 2000; Of Rice and Men: A Novel of Vietnam, 2006. **Address:** 224 Cindyann Dr., East Greenwich, RI 02818, U.S.A. **Online address:** richard@gallilaw.com

GALLIGAN, John. American (born United States) **Genres:** Plays/Screenplays, Human Relations/Parenting, Mystery/Crime/Suspense. **Career:** Madison Area Technical College, instructor in English. Writer. **Publications:** NOVELS: Red Sky, Red Dragonfly, 2001; The Nail Knot, 2003; The Blood Knot, 2005; The Clinch Knot, 2008; The Wind Knot, 2011. OTHER: Oh Brother! Said the Mother of Tony Pepperoni (juvenile), 2003. **Address:** Madison Area Technical College, Rm. D241, 211 N. Carroll St., Madison, WI 53703, U.S.A. **Online address:** jgalligan@matcmadison.edu

GALLIMORE, Paul. American (born United States), b. 1947?. **Genres:** How-to Books, Medicine/Health, Architecture, Technology. **Career:** Earth Healing (an environmental education organization), environmental resource assessment service coordinator; Long Branch Environmental Education Center, founder and executive director, 1974-; Southwestern Community College, faculty; Blanton's Junior College, faculty; University of North Carolina, faculty; environmental activist; Center for Renewable Resources, board director; Solar Lobby, National Recycling Coalition, board director; Southern Unity Network for Renewable Energy Projects, board director; North Carolina Coalition for Renewable Energy Resources, board director; North Carolina Solar Energy Association, board director; Carolina Farm Stewardship Association, board director. Consultant and writer. **Publications:** (With A. Fritsch) Healing Appalachia: Sustainable Living through Appropriate Technology, 2007. **Address:** Long Branch Environmental Education Center, Big Sandy Mush Creek, PO Box 369, Leicester, NC 28748, U.S.A. **Online address:** paulg@main.nc.us

GALLO, Gina. American (born United States), b. 1954. **Genres:** Criminology/True Crime, Autobiography/Memoirs, Essays, Humor/Satire, Mystery/Crime/Suspense, Popular Culture, Social Commentary. **Career:** Chicago Department of Mental Health, clinical therapist, 1976-79; Chicago Police Department, police officer, 1982-98; NYCOP Online Magazine, writer. **Publications:** Crime Scenes, 2000; Armed and Dangerous: Memoirs of a Chicago Policewoman, 2001. Works appear in anthologies. Contributor to periodicals. **Address:** c/o Michael Congdon, Don Congdon Associates, 156 5th Ave., Ste. 625, New York, NY 10010-7002, U.S.A. **Online address:** swornsecrets@hotmail.com

GALLO, Patrick J. American (born United States), b. 1937. **Genres:** History, Cultural/Ethnic Topics, Essays, Humanities. **Career:** Teaneck High School, teacher of American history, 1968-; New York University, adjunct professor of political science; NEH fellow, 1986, 1993. Writer. **Publications:** Ethnic Alienation: The Italian Americans, 1974; (ed.) Patterns of American Foreign Policy, 1974; (ed.) The Urban Experience of Italian Americans, 1977; India's Image of the International System, 1980; Swords and Plowshares: The United States and Disarmament, 1898-1979, 1980; Old Bread, New Wine: A Portrait of the Italian-Americans, 1981; The American Paradox: Politics and Justice in America, 1999; Enemies: Mussolini and the Antifascists, 2002; For Love and Country: The Italian Resistance, 2003; (ed.) Pius XII, the Holocaust, and the Revisionists: Essays, 2006. Contributor to periodicals. **Address:** Teaneck High School, 100 Elizabeth Ave., Teaneck, NJ 07666-4713, U.S.A.

GALLO, Rubén. American/Mexican (born Mexico), b. 1969. **Genres:** Humanities, Literary Criticism And History, Essays, Art/Art History. **Career:** Cornell University, faculty; University of Toronto, faculty; Princeton University, Department of Spanish and Portuguese Languages and Cultures, professor of Spanish and Portuguese languages and cultures, 2002-, Program in Latin American Studies, director, 2008-. Writer. **Publications:** (Ed.) The Mexico City Reader, 2004; New Tendencies in Mexican Art: The 1990s, 2004; México D.F.: Lecturas Para Paseantes, 2005; Mexican Modernity: The Avant-garde and the Technological Revolution, 2005; (with I. Padilla) Heterodoxos Mexicanos: Una Antología Dialogada, 2006; Freud's Mexico: Into the Wilds of Psychoanalysis, 2010; Proust's Latin Americans, forthcoming. **Address:** Department of Spanish and Portuguese Languages and, Cultures, Princeton University, 337 E Pyne Bldg., Princeton, NJ 08544-5264, U.S.A. **Online address:** gallo@princeton.edu

GALLOWAY, Janice. British/Scottish (born Scotland), b. 1956. **Genres:** Novels, Novellas/Short Stories, Adult Non-fiction. **Career:** Teacher of English, 1980-90; British Library, research fellow, 1999; Glasgow University, tutor, 2002-03; Scotland on Sunday, classical music correspondent; BBC Radios 3 and 4, music reviewer; Faber and Faber's innovative Faber Academy, faculty. Writer. **Publications:** NOVELS: The Trick is to Keep Breathing, 1990; Foreign Parts, 1994; Clara, 2002. STORIES: Blood, 1991; Where You Find It, 1996; Boy Book See, 2002; Collected Stories, 2009. EDITOR: (with H. Whyte) The Day I Met the Queen Mother, (fiction anthology), 1990; (with H. Whyte) Scream If You Want to Go Faster, 1991; (with M. Sinclair) Meantime: Looking Forward to the New Millennium, (fiction anthology), 1991; (with H. Whyte) New Writing Scotland 9, 1991; (with H. Whyte) Pig Squealing, 1992; Secrets: New Scottish Writing, 2005. OTHER: (with A. Bevan) Pipelines, 2000; Monster (libretto), 2002; This is Not About Me, 2008. Contributor to periodicals. **Address:** c/o Derek Johns, A.P. Watt Ltd., 20 John St., London, GL WC1N 2DR, England. **Online address:** janice@galloway.1to1.org

GALLOWAY, Kara. See CAIL, Carol.

GALLOWAY, Terry. American/German (born Germany), b. 1950. **Genres:** Autobiography/Memoirs. **Career:** Actual Lives Theater Troupe (for disabled adults), founder; Mickee Faust Alternative Performance Club, co-founder; Esther's Follies, co-founder; California Institute of the Arts, visiting artist; Florida State University, visiting artist; University of Texas at Austin, visiting artist. Writer, theatrical director, and performance artist. **Publications:** Mean Little Deaf Queer: A Memoir, 2009. Contributor to books and periodicals. Works appear in anthologies. **Address:** Austin, TX , U.S.A. **Online address:** tlgalloway@aol.com

GALSTON, William A. American (born United States), b. 1946. **Genres:** Politics/Government, Law, History. **Career:** University of Texas, associate professor, professor of government; University of Maryland, professor of public policy, 1998-2005, Saul I. Stern professor of civic engagement, Institute for Philosophy and Public Policy, director, 1995-2006, Center for Information and Research on Civic Learning and Engagement, director; Clinton Administration, deputy assistant for domestic policy, 1993-95; National Commission on Civic Renewal, executive director; Democratic Leadership Council, senior advisor; Brookings Institution, visiting fellow, senior fellow and Ezra K. Zilkha chair in governance studies, 2006-; Roosevelt Center for American Policy Studies, director of economic and social programs. Writer. **Publications:** Kant and the Problem of History, 1975; Justice and the Human Good, 1980; (with J.C. Obert) Down-Down-Down-on the Farm: The Farm Financial Crisis, a Background Paper, 1985; A Tough Row to Hoe: The 1985 Farm Bill and Beyond, 1985; (with M.J. Rovner) Southern Voices/Southern

Views: A Report on Focus Groups Conducted by the Roosevelt Center for American Policy Studies, 1987; (with M.J. Rovner) One Year to Go: Citizen Attitudes in Iowa and New Hampshire: A Report on Focus Groups Conducted by the Roosevelt Center for American Policy Studies, 1987; Liberal Purposes: Goods, Virtues, and Diversity in the Liberal State, 1991; (ed. with J.W. Chapman) Virtue, 1992; (with K.J. Baehler) Rural Development in the United States: Connecting Theory, Practice, and Possibilities, 1995; Liberal Pluralism: The Implications of Value Pluralism for Political Theory and Practice, 2002; Public Matters: Essays on Politics, Policy and Religion, 2005; The Practice of Liberal Pluralism, 2005; (co-author) Democracy at Risk: How Political Choices Undermine Citizen Participation, and What We Can Do About It, 2005; (ed. with P.H. Hoffenberg) Poverty and Morality: Religious and Secular Perspectives, 2010. Contributor of articles to periodicals. **Address:** Brookings Institution, 1775 Massachusetts Ave. NW, Washington, DC 20036, U.S.A.

GALT, George. Canadian (born Canada), b. 1948. **Genres:** Novels, Poetry, Essays, Travel/Exploration, Romance/Historical. **Career:** Saturday Night, associate editor, book reviews editor; freelance writer. **Publications:** Love Poems, 1974; Trailing Pythagoras, 1982; Whistlestop: A Journey across Canada, 1987; Scribes and Scoundrels (novel), 1997. EDITOR: The Purdy-Woodcock Letters: Selected Correspondence, 1964-1984, 1988; The Saturday Night Traveller (essays), 1990; The Thinking Heart: Best Canadian Essays, 1991. Contributor of essays to magazines. **Address:** Quadrant Editions, Montreal, QC H3G 1M8, Canada.

GALVIN, Brendan. American (born United States), b. 1938. **Genres:** Poetry, Novellas/Short Stories, Literary Criticism And History. **Career:** Northeastern University, instructor in English, 1963-65; Slippery Rock State College, assistant professor of English, 1968-69; Central Connecticut State University, assistant professor, 1969-74, associate professor, 1974-80, professor of English, 1980-, professor emeritus; Connecticut Writers Conference, founder and director; Connecticut College, visiting writer, 1975-76; Wesleyan-Suffield Writer-Reader Conference, affiliate, 1977-78; Martha's Vineyard Poetry Seminar, 1986; University of Alabama, Coal Royalty visiting chair in creative writing, 1993; East Carolina University, professor of English and Whichard distinguished chair in the humanities; Hollins College, Wyndham Robertson writer-in-residence; Loyola University, visiting writer; Western Carolina University, poet-in-residence. **Publications:** POETRY: The Narrow Land, 1971; The Salt Farm, 1972; No Time for Good Reasons, 1974; The Minutes No One Owns, 1977; Atlantic Flyway: Poems, 1980; Winter Oysters: Poems, 1983; A Birder's Dozen, 1984; Seals in the Inner Harbor, 1985; Raising Irish Walls, 1989; Wampanoag Traveler: Being, in Letters, the Life and Times of Loranzo Newcomb, American and Natural Historian: A Poem, 1989; Great Blue: New and Selected Poems, 1990; Outer Life: The Poetry of Brendan Galvin, 1991; Saints in Their Ox-Hide Boat: A Poem, 1992; Early Returns, 1992; Sky and Island Light: Poem, 1996; Hotel Malabar: A Narrative Poem, 1998; The Strength of a Named Thing: Poem, 1999; Place Keepers: Poems, 2003; Habitat: New and Selected Poems, 1965-2005, 2005; Ocean Effects: Poems, 2007; Whirl is King: Poems from a Life List, 2008. Contributor to periodicals. **Address:** Department of English, East Carolina University, 1002 Bate Bldg., Greenville, NC 27858-4353, U.S.A. **Online address:** galvinb@mail.ecu.edu

GALVIN, Matthew R(eppert). American (born United States), b. 1950. **Genres:** Medicine/Health, Children's Non-fiction, Psychiatry, Psychology, Young Adult Fiction, Young Adult Non-fiction. **Career:** Indiana University, Medical Center, fellow in child psychiatry, 1982-84, assistant professor, 1984-89, clinical assistant professor, 1990-92, 1993-95, clinical associate professor of psychiatry, 1995-; Larue Carter Hospital, staff psychiatrist, 1984-88, Youth Service, acting director, 1988-90; Indiana University Hospitals, staff psychiatrist, 1984-, Psychiatric Services for Children and Adolescents, assistant director, 1991-98; Riley Child Psychiatric Services, staff child adolescent psychiatrist, 1990-, Child Adolescent Psychiatric Inpatient Program, medical director, 1991-98; St. Vincent's Hospital, staff psychiatrist, 1993-97, 2001-; Methodist Hospital, staff psychiatrist, 1995-; Pleasant Run Inc., child psychiatrist, 1998-2001; Children's Bureau Inc., consultant, 2001-; Indiana School for the Blind, staff, 2003-; Meridian Youth Psychiatric Center P.C., consultant; Conscience Works, editorial staff. **Publications:** Ignatius Finds Help: A Story about Psychotherapy for Children, 1988; Otto Learns about His Medicine: A Story about Medication for Hyperactive Children, 1988, 3rd ed. as Otto Learns about His Medicine: A Story about Medication for Children with ADHD, 2001; Robby Really Transforms: A Story about Grown-ups Helping Children, 1988; Clouds and Clocks: A Story for Children Who Soil, 1989, 2nd

ed., 2007; (with R. Collins) Sometimes Y: A Story for Families with Gender Identity Issues, 1992; (with B. Stilwell) The Conscience Celebration, 1998; (with B.M. Stilwell and S.M. Kopta) Right vs. Wrong: Raising a Child with a Conscience, 2000; (with M. Gaffney and B. Stilwell) Rachel and the Seven Bridges of Conscience-Berg, 2002; The Otters of Conscience-Berg, 2005; Carlotta Learns about Her Medicine, 2005. Contributor to books and journals. **Address:** Meridian Youth Psychiatric Center P.C., 210 E 91st St., Ste. C, Indianapolis, IN 46420, U.S.A. **Online address:** mrgalvin@stvincent.org

GAMBETTA, Diego. British/Italian (born Italy), b. 1952. **Genres:** Criminology/True Crime, Sociology, Politics/Government, Social Sciences. **Career:** University of Turin, Institute of Sociology, researcher, 1976-77; Regional Administration of the Piemonte, research officer, 1978-79, 1982-84; Cambridge University, King's College, junior research fellow, 1984-88, senior research fellow, 1988-91; Oxford University, lecturer, 1991-93, reader in sociology, 1993-, Saint Anne's College, fellow, 1991-, university reader in sociology, 1995-, All Souls College, fellow, 1995-2003, professor of sociology in recognition of distinction, 2002, Nuffield College, professor of sociology and official fellow, 2003-; University of Chicago, visiting professor, 1994-95; Columbia University, Italian Academy for Advanced Studies, inaugural fellow, 1996-97; Stanford University, Center for Advanced Study in the Behavioral Sciences, fellow, 1998; British Academy, research reader, 2000-02. Writer. **Publications:** (With L. Ricolfi) Il Compromesso Difficile: Forme di Rappresentanza Erapporti di Classe dal Centrosinistra al Compromesso Storico, 1978; (co-author) L'offerta di lavoro giovanile in Piemonte, 1981; Were They Pushed or Did They Jump?: Individual Decision Mechanisms in Education, 1987, rev. ed., 1996; (ed. and contrib.) Trust: Making and Breaking Cooperative Relations, 1988; La Mafia Siciliana: Un'industria Della Protezione Privata, 1992, trans. as The Sicilian Mafia: The Business of Private Protection, 1993; (with S. Warner) La Retorica della Riforma: Finedel Sistema Proporzionale in Italia, 1994; Crimes and Signs: Cracking the Codes of the Underworld, 2004; (ed.) Making Sense of Suicide Missions, 2005; (with H. Hamill) Streetwise: How Taxi Drivers Establish Their Customers' Trustworthiness, 2005; People's Trust: The Design of a Survey-Based Experiment, 2006; Codes of The Underworld: How Criminals Communicate, 2009. Contributor to periodicals. Works appear in anthologies. **Address:** Department of Sociology, Nuffield College, University of Oxford, New Rd., Oxford, OX OX1 1NF, England. **Online address:** diego.gambetta@nuffield.oxford.ac.uk

GAMBLE, Ed. American (born United States), b. 1943. **Genres:** Social Commentary, Cartoons. **Career:** Nashville Banner, editorial cartoonist, 1972-80; Florida Times-Union, editorial cartoonist, 1980-. Reporter. **Publications:** A Peek at the Great Society, 1965; (co-author) A Cartoon History of the Reagan Years, 1988; You Get Two for the Price of One, 1995. Contributor to magazines. Works appear in anthologies. **Address:** Florida Times-Union, 1 Riverside Ave., Jacksonville, FL 32202, U.S.A. **Online address:** ed.gamble@jacksonville.com

GAMBLE, Terry. American (born United States) **Genres:** Dance/Ballet, Novels, Human Relations/Parenting, Young Adult Fiction. **Career:** Writer. **Publications:** The Water Dancers (novel), 2003; Good Family, 2005. **Address:** c/o Author Mail, HarperCollins Publishers Inc., 10 E 53rd St., 7th Fl., New York, NY 10022-5244, U.S.A. **Online address:** terry@terrygamble.com

GAMMEL, Irene. Canadian (born Canada), b. 1959. **Genres:** Literary Criticism And History, Sex. **Career:** McMaster University, lecturer in English and comparative literature, 1992-93; University of Prince Edward Island, assistant professor, 1993-97, associate professor, 1997-2000, professor of English, 2000-04, Womens Studies Program, director; Friedrich-Schiller-Universität (Canadian studies), visiting professor, 2001; Ryerson University, professor of English, modern literature and culture, Canada research chair, 2005-; Canadian Comparative Literature Association, vice-president, president; L.M. Montgomery Institute, co-chair. Writer. **Publications:** Sexualizing Power in Naturalism: Theodore Dreiser and Frederick Philip Grove, 1994; Baroness Elsa: Gender, Dada, and Everyday Modernity: A Cultural Biography, 2002; Looking for Anne of Green Gables: The Story of L.M. Montgomery and her Literary Classic, 2008; Looking for Anne: How Lucy Maud Montgomery Dreamed Up a Literary Classic, 2008. EDITOR: (with E. Epperly) L.M. Montgomery and Canadian Culture, 1999; Confessional Politics: Women's Sexual Self-Representations in Life Writing and Popular Media, 1999; Making Avonlea: L.M. Montgomery and Popular Culture, 2002; Intimate Life of L.M. Montgomery, 2005. Contributor of articles to journals. **Address:** Department of English, Ryerson University, Rm. JOR 528, 350 Victoria St., Toronto, ON M5B 2K3, Canada. **Online address:** gammel@ryerson.ca

GAMMER, Moshe. Israeli/Russian (born Russia), b. 1950. **Genres:** Area Studies, Human Relations/Parenting, International Relations/Current Affairs, Social Sciences, Politics/Government. **Career:** Tel Aviv University, School of Overseas Students, teacher, 1989, external teacher, 1989-93, Dayan Center for Middle Eastern and African Studies, Dayan fellow, 1990-91, Cummings Center for Russian and East European Studies, postdoctoral fellow, 1990-92, Department of Middle Eastern and African history, visiting lecturer, 1993-94, senior lecturer, 1994-2007, associate professor, 2007, associated fellow; Open University, tutor, 1989-90, 1991-93; Bar Ilan University, Department of General History, visiting lecturer, 1990-91; Hadera Menashe College, Middle Eastern History department, staff, Program of Middle Eastern History, director of program, 1996-97; Hebrew University, Institute of Advanced Studies, fellow, 1999-2000. Writer. **Publications:** Lgude poalim be-Mitsrayim bitekfat Sadat, 1979; (ed.) The Political Negotiations between Israel and Egypt, September, 1978-March, 1979: Main Documents, 1979; (contrib.) Arab Relations in the Middle East: The Road to Realignment, 1979; (ed.) The Normalization of Relations between Israel and Egypt, April, 1979-October, 1980: Main Documents, 1981; (ed.) The Autonomy Negotiations, April, 1979-October, 1980: Main Documents, 1981; (contrib.) The North Caucasus Barrier: The Russian Advance toward the Muslim World, 1992; Muslim Resistance to the Tsar: Shamil and the Conquest of Chechnia and Daghestan, 1994; (contrib.) Muslim Eurasia: Tradition and Change, 1995; (contrib.) The Russian Conquest of the Caucasus, 1997; (ed. with J. Kostiner and M. Shemesh) Political Thought and Political History: Studies in Memory of Elie Kedourie, 2003; (ed.) State and Society in the Second and Third Worlds: Comparative and Case Studies from Africa, Eurasia, Latin America, and the Middle East, 2004; (ed.) The Caspian: A Re-emerging Region, 2004; The Lone Wolf and the Bear: Three Centuries of Chechen Defiance of Russian Power, 2005; (ed. with D.J. Wasserstein) Daghestan and the World of Islam, 2006; (ed.) Ethnonationalism, Islam and the State in the Caucasus: Post-Soviet Disorder, 2007; (ed. with I. Baldauf and T. Loy) Bukharan Jews in the 20th Century: History, Experience and Narration, 2008; (ed.) Islam and Sufism in Daghestan, 2009. Works appear in anthologies. Contributor of articles to periodicals. **Address:** Department of Middle Eastern and African History, Tel Aviv University, PO Box 39040, Tel Aviv, 69978, Israel. **Online address:** gammer@post.tau.ac.il

GAMSON, Joshua. See GAMSON, Joshua (Paul).

GAMSON, Joshua (Paul). (Joshua Gamson). American (born United States), b. 1962. **Genres:** Sociology, Popular Culture, Gay And Lesbian Issues, Social Commentary, Cultural/Ethnic Topics, Biography, Adult Non-fiction, History, History. **Career:** University of California, instructor and lecturer in sociology, 1992-93; Yale University, assistant professor, 1993-98, Program on Non-Profit Organizations, fellow, 1994, associate professor of sociology, 1998-2002; University of San Francisco, associate professor of sociology, 2002-05, professor of sociology, 2005-. Writer. **Publications:** Ethnography Unbound: Power and Resistance in the Modern Metropolis, 1991 (co-author); Claims to Fame: Celebrity in Contemporary America, 1994; Freaks Talk Back: Tabloid Talk Shows and Sexual Nonconformity, 1998; The Fabulous Sylvester: The Legend, The Music, The Seventies in San Francisco, 2005. Contributor to books and periodicals. **Address:** Department of Sociology, University of San Francisco, KA 259, 2130 Fulton St., PO Box 208265, San Francisco, CA 94117-1080, U.S.A. **Online address:** gamson@usfca.edu

GAMSON, William A(nthony). American (born United States), b. 1934. **Genres:** Politics/Government, Social Sciences, Sociology, Art/Art History. **Career:** Harvard University, research associate in social psychology, 1959-62; University of Michigan, assistant professor, 1962-64, Center for Research on Conflict Resolution, 1962-71, associate professor, 1964-66, professor of sociology, 1966-82, chairman of department, 1974-78, research sociologist; Harvard University, visiting lecturer, 1968-69; Hebrew University of Jerusalem, visiting professor, 1969, 1972-73; Boston College, professor of sociology, 1982-. Writer. **Publications:** Power and Discontent, 1968; SIMSOC: Simulated Society, 1969, 5th ed., 2000; (with A. Modigliani) Untangling the Cold War: A Strategy for Testing Rival Theories, 1971; (with A. Modigliani) Conceptions of Social Life: A Text-Reader for Social Psychology, 1974; The Strategy of Social Protest, 1975, 2nd ed., 1990; (with B. Fireman and S. Rytina) Encounters with Unjust Authority, 1982; What's News: A Game Simulation of TV News, 1984; Talking Politics, 1992; (co-author) Shaping Abortion Discourse: Democracy and the Public Sphere in Germany and the

United States, 2002. Contributor to books. **Address:** Department of Sociology, Boston College, 140 Commonwealth Ave., Chestnut Hill, MA 02467, U.S.A. **Online address:** gamson@bc.edu

GAMST, Frederick Charles. American (born United States), b. 1936. **Genres:** Anthropology/Ethnology. **Career:** Rice University, instructor, 1966-67, assistant professor, 1967-71, Lovett College, associate, 1967-75, associate professor, 1971-75; University of Massachusetts, associate provost for graduate studies, 1978-83, professor of anthropology, 1975-, chairman of department, 1975-78, now professor emeritus. Writer. **Publications:** Travel and Research in Northwestern Ethiopia, Notes for Anthropologists and Other Field Workers in Ethiopia No. 2, 1965; The Qemant: A Pagan-Hebraic Peasantry of Ethiopia, 1969; Peasants in Complex Society, 1974; (ed.) Studies in Cultural Anthropology, 1975; (ed. with E. Norbeck) Ideas of Culture, 1976; The Hoghead: An Industrial Ethnology of the Locomotive Engineer, 1980; Highballing with Flimsies: Working under Train Orders on the Espee's Coast Line, 1990; (ed.) Letters from the United States of North America on Internal Improvements, Steam Navigation, Banking, Written by Francis Chevalier de Gerstner in 1839, 1990; (ed.) Meanings of Work: Considerations for the 21st Century, 1995; Early American Railroads; Franz Anton Ritter Von Gerstners Die innern Communicationen (1842-1843), vol. II, 1997. **Address:** Department of Anthropology, University of Massachusetts, Harbor Campus, Boston, MA 02125-3393, U.S.A. **Online address:** fcgamst@aol.com

GANAS, Monica. American (born United States), b. 1950?. **Genres:** Cultural/Ethnic Topics. **Career:** Azusa Pacific University, Department of theater, film, and television, cochair and professor of communication studies; Azusa Renaissance Project, codirector. Writer and actor. **Publications:** Under the Influence: California's Intoxicating Spiritual and Cultural Impact on America, 2010. Contributor to periodicals and journals. **Online address:** mganas@apu.edu

GANDER, Forrest. American (born United States), b. 1956. **Genres:** Poetry, Translations, Novels. **Career:** Rhode Island School of Design, special lecturer, 1984-86; Providence College, assistant professor, 1988-92, associate professor, 1993-95, professor of English literature, 1996-99; Harvard University, Briggs-Copeland Poet, 1999-2001; Brown University, professor of English and comparative literature, 2001-10, Adele Kellenberg Seaver professor of literary arts and comparative literature, 2010-. Writer. **Publications:** Rush to the Lake, 1988; Eggplants and Lotus Root, 1991; (ed. and trans.) Mouth to Mouth: Poems by 12 Contemporary Mexican Women, 1993; Lynchburg, 1993; Deeds of Utmost Kindness, 1994; Science and Steepleflower, 1998; Torn Awake, 2001; (trans.) No Shelter: The Selected Poems of Pura Lopez-Colome, 2002; (trans. with K. Johnson) Immanent Visitor: Selected Poems of Jaime Saez, 2002; Twelve X 12.00, 2003; The Blue Rock Collection, 2005; Sound of Summer Running, 2005; Faithful Existence, 2005; Eye Against Eye, 2005; (ed.) Connecting Lines: New Poems from Mexico, 2006; (trans. and intro.) J. Saenz, The Night, 2007; (trans.) Firefly Under the Tongue, 2008; As a Friend, 2008; (trans.) Spectacle & Pigsty by Kiwao Nomura, 2011; Core Samples from the World, 2011; (trans.) P. Lopez-Colome, Watchword, 2011; (with J. Kinsella) Redstart, A Collaborative EcoPoetics, 2012; (trans.) Fungus Skull Eye Wing: Selected Poems of Alfonso D'Aquino, 2013. **Address:** Department of Comparative Literature, Brown University, PO Box 1923, Providence, RI 02912-1923, U.S.A. **Online address:** forrest_gander@brown.edu

GANDT, Robert. (Robert L. Gandt). American (born United States), b. 1939?. **Genres:** Military/Defense/Arms Control, Novels, Air/Space Topics, Adult Non-fiction, Literary Criticism And History. **Career:** Pan American World Airways, pilot and airline captain, 1965-91; Redhawk Aerobatic Team, founder and pilot, 1985-; Delta Air Lines, airline captain and international line check airman, 1991-; Intrepid Sea, Air and Space Museum, president; Intrepid Fallen Heroes Fund, president; flight instructor; weapons test pilot; crop duster; airshow pilot and performer. Writer. **Publications:** Season of Storms: The Siege of Hongkong, 1941, 1982; China Clipper: The Age of the Great Flying Boats, 1991; Skygods: The Fall of Pan Am, 1995; Bogeys and Bandits: The Making of a Fighter Pilot, 1997; Fly Low, Fly Fast: Inside the Reno Air Races, 1999; With Hostile Intent, 2001; Acts of Vengeance, 2002; Black Star, 2003; Shadows of War, 2004; The Killing Sky, 2005; Black Star Rising, 2007; (with B. White) Intrepid: The Epic Story of America's Most Legendary Warship, 2008; Twilight Warriors: The Deadliest Naval Battle of World War II and the Men Who Fought It, 2010. Contributor to periodicals. **Address:** c/o Author Mail, Penguin Putnam/Viking, 375 Hudson St., New York, NY 10014, U.S.A.

GANDT, Robert L. *See* **GANDT, Robert.**

GANEK, Danielle. American (born United States), b. 1965?. **Genres:** Novels, Children's Fiction. **Career:** Woman's Day, staff; Mademoiselle, staff; Galeries Lafayette, creative director. Writer. **Publications:** Lulu Meets God and Doubts Him, 2007; The Summer We Read Gatsby, 2010. **Address:** Penguin Group Inc., Library Marketing Dept, 375 Hudson St., New York, NY 10014, U.S.A. **Online address:** danielle@danielleganek.com

GANESAN, Indira. American/Indian (born India), b. 1960?. **Genres:** Novels, Young Adult Fiction. **Career:** Many Mountains Moving Literary Magazine, fiction editor, 2007-; Long Island University, Southampton College, instructor; Lesley University, instructor; Naropa University, Jack Kerouac School of Disembodied Poetics, faculty. Writer. **Publications:** NOVELS: The Journey, 1990; Inheritance, 1998; Finding Her Way Home, forthcoming. **Address:** Jack Kerouac School of Disembodied Poetics, Naropa University, 2130 Arapahoe Ave., Boulder, CO 80302-6602, U.S.A. **Online address:** igaresan@southampton.livnet.edu

GANGEMI, Joseph G. (J. G. Passarella). American (born United States), b. 1970?. **Genres:** Novels, Plays/Screenplays, Literary Criticism And History. **Career:** Screenplay writer and novelist, 1998-. **Publications:** (As J.G. Passarella with J. Passarella) Wither: A Novel, 1999; Inamorata: A Novel, 2004. Work appears in anthologies. Contributor to periodicals. **Address:** c/o Theresa Pk., Sanford J. Greenburger & Associates, 55 5th Ave., New York, NY 10003, U.S.A. **Online address:** joegangemi@comcast.net

GANJI, Akbar. Iranian (born Iran), b. 1960. **Genres:** Politics/Government, History. **Career:** Journalist and political activist. **Publications:** Tarik'khanah-'i ashba: Asib'shinasi-i guzar bih dawlat-i dimukratik-i tawsi'ah'gara, 1999; Talaqqi-i fashisti az din va hkumat, 2000; Naqdi bara-yi tamam-i fusul: Guft va gu-yi Akbar Ganji ba 'Abd Allah Nuri: Bih payvast-i matn-i istizah-i Abd Allah Nuri dar Majlis-i panjum, 2000; Alijanab-i surkhpush va 'alijanaban-i khakistari: Asib'shinasi-i guzar bih dawlat-i dimukratik-i tawsi'ah'gara, 2000; Islahgari-i mi'maranah: Asib'shinasi-i guzar bih dawlat-i dimukratik-i tawsi'ah'gara, 2000; The Road to Democracy in Iran, 2008. **Address:** Iran. **Online address:** contact@akbarganji.org

GANNETT, Ruth Stiles. American (born United States), b. 1923. **Genres:** Children's Fiction, Science Fiction/Fantasy. **Career:** Boston City Hospital, medical technician; Massachusetts Institute of Technology, radar research technician; Children's Book Council, staff. Writer. **Publications:** My Father's Dragon, 1948; The Wonderful House-Boat-Train, 1949; Elmer and the Dragon, 1950; The Dragons of Blueland, 1951; Katie and the Sad Noise, 1961; Three Tales of My Father's Dragon, 1998; (intro.) The Book of Dragons, 2009. **Address:** 8513 Rte. 277, Trumansburg, NY 14886, U.S.A.

GANNON, Martin John. American (born United States), b. 1934?. **Genres:** Administration/Management, Business/Trade/Industry. **Career:** Columbia University, Graduate School of Business, assistant, 1966; University of Maryland, College of Business and Management, Robert H. Smith School of Business, Center for Global Business, lecturer of management and organizational behavior, 1968-69, assistant professor, 1969-71, associate professor, 1971-74, professor of management, 1974-2003, acting associate dean for academic affairs, 1978-79, director, 1998-2003, professor emeritus, 2003-, Maryland Business School, Faculty of Management and Organization, professor and chairperson, 1977-78, 1979-81, IMPACT Certificate Program, academic director, 1997-2003, College Park Scholars Program in Business, Society and the Economy, director, 1998-2001; Center for the Study of Higher Education and Work, senior research Fulbright professor, 1981-82; Thammasat University, John F. Kennedy Foundation/Fulbright professor, 1988; California State University, College of Business Administration, professor of strategy and cross-cultural management, 2003-. Writer and consultant. **Publications:** Management: An Organizational Perspective, 1977; Management: An Integrated Framework, 1977, 2nd ed., 1982; Organizational Behavior, 1979; (co-author) Strategic Management Skills, 1986; Management: Managing for Results, 1988; (with K.G. Smith and C.M. Grimm) The Dynamics of Competitive Strategy, 1992; (co-author) Understanding Global Cultures, 1994, (with R. Pillai) 4th ed. as Understanding Global Cultures: Metaphorical Journeys through 29 Nations, Clusters of Nations, Continents, and Diversity, 2010; (co-author) Managing without Traditional Methods, 1996; (with S.J. Carroll, Jr.) Ethical Dimensions of International Management, 1997; Working across Cultures, 2001; Paradoxes of Culture and Globalization, 2008. EDITOR: (with C. Anderson) Readings in Management, 1977; Cultural Metaphors: Readings, Research Translations, and Commentary, 2001; (with K.L. Newman) The Blackwell Handbook of Cross-Cultural Management, 2001. Contributor of articles to books and periodicals, journals and magazines. **Address:** College of Business Administration, California State University, Rm. 343, Markstein Hall, 333 S Twin Oaks Valley Rd., San Marcos, CA 92096-0001, U.S.A. **Online address:** mgannon@csusm.edu

GANNON, Steve. American (born United States), b. 1944. **Genres:** Novels, Young Adult Fiction. **Career:** Writer, engineer and doctor of dental surgery. **Publications:** A Song for the Asking, 1997. **Address:** 106 Southern Comfort Rd., PO Box 722, Ketchum, ID 83340, U.S.A. **Online address:** sgannon@sunvalley.net

GANS, Chaim. Israeli (born Israel), b. 1948. **Genres:** Law, Social Sciences, Politics/Government, Reference. **Career:** Writer, 1971-76; Tel Aviv University, Department of Philosophy, teaching assistant, 1973-76, lecturer, senior lecturer, associate professor, 1981-2001, full professor, 2001-, Law Review, editor, 1987-88, Israeli Minerva Center for Human Rights, director, 2000-; South Sinai Development Authority, legal advisor, 1974-76. **Publications:** Philosophical Anarchism and Political Disobedience, 1992; The Limits of Nationalism, 2002; Me-Rikhard Vagner 'ad zekhut ha-shivah, 2006; From Richard Wagner to the Palestinian Right of Return: Philosophical Analysis of Israeli Public Affairs, 2006; (ed. with E. Benvenisti and S. Hanafi) Israel and the Palestinian refugees, 2007; A Just Zionism: On The Morality of the Jewish State, 2008. Contributor to newspapers. **Address:** Faculty of Law, Tel Aviv University, Ramat Aviv, Rm. 438, Trubowicz - Law Bldg., Tel Aviv, 69978, Israel. **Online address:** gansch@post.tau.ac.il

GANS, Eric L. American (born United States), b. 1941. **Genres:** Literary Criticism And History, Humanities, Film, Anthropology/Ethnology. **Career:** State University of New York, instructor in French, 1965-67; Indiana University, Department of French and Italian, assistant professor, 1967-69; University of California, assistant professor, 1969-73, associate professor, 1973-76, chairman of department, 1974-77, 1981-86, 2002-03, professor of French, 1976-. Writer. **Publications:** The Discovery of Illusion: Flaubert's Early Works 1835-1837, 1971; Un pari contre l'histoire: les premieres nouvelles de Merimee, 1972; Musset et le drame tragique, 1974; Le paradoxe de Phedre, 1975; Essais d'esthetique paradoxale, 1977; The Origin of Language: A Formal Theory of Representation, 1981; The End of Culture: Toward a Generative Anthropology, 1985; Madame Bovary: The End of Romance, 1989; Science and Faith: The Anthropology of Revelation, 1990; Originary Thinking, 1993; Signs of Paradox, 1997; The Scenic Imagination from Hobbes to the Present Day, 2007; Carole Landis: A Most Beautiful Girl, 2008; A New Way of Thinking: Religion, Philosophy, Art, 2011. **Address:** Department of French, University of California, 212 Royce Hall, Los Angeles, CA 90095-1550, U.S.A. **Online address:** gans@humnet.ucla.edu

GANS, Herbert J. American/German (born Germany), b. 1927. **Genres:** Sociology, Politics/Government, Social Sciences. **Career:** American Society of Planning Officials, research assistant, 1950; Chicago Housing Authority, assistant planner, 1950-51; P.A.C.E. Associates, chief research planner, 1951-52; U.S. Housing and Home Finance Agency, Division of Slum Clearance, field representative, 1952-53; University of Pennsylvania, Institute for Urban Studies, research associate, 1953-57, Department of City Planning, lecturer, 1956-57, assistant professor of city planning, 1958-61, Department of Sociology, lecturer; Columbia University, Teachers College, associate professor of sociology and education, 1964-66, Institute for Urban Studies, research associate, 1964-65, Center for Urban Education, staff, 1965-66, senior staff sociologist, 1966-69, adjunct professor of sociology and education, 1966-69; professor of sociology and Ford Foundation urban chair, 1971-85, Robert S. Lynd professor of sociology, 1985-2007, R S Lynd Professor Emeritus and special lecturer, 2007-; Center for Urban Education, research associate, 1965-66, senior staff sociologist, 1966-69; American Sociological Association, president; Massachusetts Institute of Technology, professor of sociology and planning, 1969-71, Massachusetts Institute of Technology-Harvard University Joint Center for Urban Studies, faculty associate, 1969-71; Center for Policy Research, senior research associate, 1971-80. Writer. **Publications:** The Urban Villagers: Groups and Class in the Life of Italian-Americans, 1962, rev. ed., 1982; The Levittowners: Ways of Life and Politics in a New Suburban Community, 1967, 2nd ed., 1982; People and Plans: Essays on Urban Problems and Solutions, 1968, rev. ed. as People, Plans and Policies: Essays on Poverty, Racism and Other National Urban Problems, 1991; The

Uses of Television and Their Educational Implications, 1968; More Equality, 1973; Popular Culture and High Culture: An Analysis and Evaluation of Taste, 1975, rev. ed., 1999; Deciding What's News: A Study of CBS Evening News, NBC Nightly News, Newsweek and Time, 1979; Sociologie en gebouwde omgeving, 1982; Middle American Individualism: The Future of Liberal Democracy, 1988; People, Plans and Policies: Essays on Poverty, Racism and other National Urban Problems, 1991; The War against the Poor: The Underclass and Antipoverty Policy, 1995; Making Sense of America: Sociological Analyses and Essays, 1999; Democracy and the News, 2003; Imagining America in 2033: How the Country Put Itself Together after Bush, 2008. EDITOR: On the Making of Americans: Essays in Honor of David Riesman, 1979; Sociology in America, 1990. Contributor of articles to magazines and journals. **Address:** Department of Sociology, Columbia University, 605 Knox Hall,606 W 122nd St., PO Box 9649, New York, NY 10027, U.S.A. **Online address:** hjg1@columbia.edu

GANSKY, Alton. American (born United States), b. 1953. **Genres:** Mystery/Crime/Suspense, Novels, Adult Non-fiction, Novels. **Career:** High Desert Baptist Church, senior pastor, 1989-; Gansky Communications, founder, 1992-; author, 1996-. **Publications:** NOVELS: By My Hands, 1996; Through My Eyes, 1997; The Prodigy: A Novel of Suspense, 2001; Incumbent, 2004; Director's Cut, 2005; Another Dies, 2005; Finder's Fee, 2007; Crime Scene Jerusalem, 2007. NONFICTION: Uncovering God's Mysterious Ways, 2003; Uncovering the Bible's Greatest Mysteries, 2002; (with J.V. Diest) Secrets God Kept, 2005; 40 Days: Encountering Jesus between the Resurrection and Ascension, 2007; The Indispensable Guide to Practically Everything: Jesus, 2010. THRILLERS: Tarnished Image, 1998; Terminal Justice, 1998; Marked for Mercy, 1998; A Ship Possessed, 1999; A Small Dose of Murder, 1999; Vanished, 2000; Distant Memory, 2000; Dark Moon, 2002; A Treasure Deep, 2004; The Incumbent, 2004; Out of Time, 2003; Beneath the Ice, 2004; Before Submerged, 2005; The Secrets God Kept, 2005; Before Another Dies, 2005; Angel, 2007; Zero-G, 2007; Enoch, 2008; (with R. Cornuke) Bell Messenger, 2008; Jesus, 2009; (with J. Struecker) Certain Jeopardy, 2009; (with R. Cornuke) The Pravda Messenger: A Novel, 2009; (with B. Fleet) Solomon Secret: 7 Principles of Financial Success from King Solomon, History's Wealthiest Man, 2009; (with A. Gansky) Blaze of Glory, 2010. OTHERS: (with M. Hitchcock) The Mayan Apocalypse, 2010; A Conversation with God: If You Could Ask God Anything What Would It Be?, 2011; (with J. Struecker) Fallen Angel, 2011; (with R.J. Jeffrey) The Scroll, 2011; (with J. Struecker) Hide and Seek, 2012; (with M. Hitchcock) Digital Winter, 2012. **Address:** Gansky Communications, 9983 Rose Dr., Hesperia, CA 92345-0220, U.S.A. **Online address:** alton@altongansky.com

GANSLER, Jacques Singleton. American (born United States), b. 1934. **Genres:** Military/Defense/Arms Control, Business/Trade/Industry, Politics/Government, Social Sciences. **Career:** Raytheon Corp., engineering manager, 1956-62; Singer Corp., program manager, 1962-70; Intl. Telephone and Telegraph, vice-president, 1970-72; U.S. Department of Defense, deputy assistant secretary, 1972-77; TASC, senior vice-president, 1977-97; Under Secretary of Defense for Acquisition, Technology and Logistics, staff, 1997-2001; University of Maryland, School of Public Affairs, faculty, 2001-, professor, Roger C. Lipitz chair, Center for Public Policy and Private Enterprise, vice-president for research. Writer. **Publications:** The Defense Industry, 1980; Affording Defense, 1989; Defense Conversion: Transforming the Arsenal of Democracy, 1995; (contrib.) Missile Defense in Asia, 2003; (ed. with H. Binnendijk) Information Assurance: Trends in Vulnerabilities, Threats, and Technologies, 2004; Democracy's Arsenal: Creating a Twenty-First-Century Defense Industry, 2011. **Address:** Center for Public Policy and Private Enterprise, School of Public Policy, University of Maryland, 4139 Van Munching Hall, College Park, MD 20742, U.S.A. **Online address:** jgansler@umd.edu

GANSON, Barbara. (Bárbara Ganson de Rivas). American (born United States), b. 1953. **Genres:** Air/Space Topics. **Career:** National Archives and Library of Congress, research assistant, 1982-85; University of Texas, Department of History, teaching assistant, 1987-90, 1991-93; Florida Atlantic University, Dorothy F. Schmidt College of Arts and Letters, Department of History, assistant professor, 1994-99, associate professor of history, 1999-; Gustavus McLeod's Round the World Pole to Pole World Aviation Record Attempt and the Korea Aerospace Research Institute, curriculum director, 2002-. Writer. **Publications:** (As Bárbara Ganson de Rivas) Consecuencias demográficas y sociales de la Guerra de la Triple Alianza, 1985; The Guaraní under Spanish Rule in the Río de la Plata, 2003. Contributor to periodicals. **Address:** Department of History, Dorothy F. Schmidt College of Arts and

Letters, Florida Atlantic University, 2912 College Ave., Davie, FL 33314-7714, U.S.A. **Online address:** bganson@fau.edu

GANT, Richard. See FREEMANTLE, Brian (Harry).

GANTNER, Neilma. See SIDNEY, Neilma.

GANTSCHEV, Ivan. German (born Germany), b. 1925. **Genres:** Children's Fiction, Illustrations, Animals/Pets, Young Adult Fiction. **Career:** Freelance artist, through 1966, 1989-; J. Walter Thompson (advertising agency), illustrator, 1968-. Writer. **Publications:** SELF-ILLUSTRATED FOR CHILDREN: Journey of the Storks, 1983; Noah & the Ark & the Animals, 1984; The Christmas Train, 1984; Walk under the Rainbow, 1985; Otto the Bear, 1986; Iwan Ganchefu ehon gengaten 1989, 1989; Three Kings: A Christmas Tale, 1990; Good Morning, Good Night, 1991; The Christmas Story by Father Christmas, 1992; The Christmas Teddy Bear, 1994; Libby's Journey, 1995; Where the Moon Lives, 1998; Rabbit and the Bear: A Christmas Tale, 2007. OTHERS: The Volcano, 1981; Moon Lake, 1981; Weihnachtszug, 1982; Rumprump, 1984; Two Islands, 1985; The Train to Grandma's, 1987; Santa's Favorite Story, 1988; Where Is Mr. Mole?, 1989; The Art of Ivan Gantschev, 1994. **Address:** Bettinastrasse 33, Frankfurt, 6000, Germany.

GANZ, Marshall. American (born United States), b. 1943. **Genres:** History, Young Adult Non-fiction. **Career:** Civil rights worker, 1964; United Farm Workers, director of organizing, 1965-81; Harvard University, Kennedy School of Government, lecturer, 2000-. Writer. **Publications:** (with T. Skocpol and A. Liazos) What a Mighty Power We Can Be: African American Fraternal Groups and the Struggle for Racial Equality, 2006 . Why David Sometimes Wins: Leadership, Organization and Strategy in the California Farm Worker Movement, 2009. Contributor to books and periodicals. **Address:** John F. Kennedy School of Government, 79 JFK St., PO Box 143, Cambridge, MA 02138, U.S.A. **Online address:** marshall_ganz@ksg.harvard.edu

GÄNZL, Kurt (Friedrich). New Zealander (born New Zealand), b. 1946. **Genres:** Plays/Screenplays, Songs/Lyrics And Libretti, Music, Theatre, Reference, Biography, Autobiography/Memoirs, Dance/Ballet, Dance/Ballet. **Career:** New Zealand Opera Co., basso soloist, 1968; vocalist, 1968-75; writer, 1976-; Talent Artists Ltd., theatrical agent and casting director, 1978-89. **Publications:** British Musical Theatre, 2 vols., 1986; (with A. Lamb) Gänzl's Book of the Musical Theatre, 1988; The Complete Aspects of Love, 1990; The Blackwell Guide to the Musical Theatre on Record, 1990; The Encyclopaedia of the Musical Theatre, 2 vols., 1994, 2nd ed., 3 vols., 2001; Gänzl's Book of the Broadway Musical, 1995; Musicals in US as Song and Dance, 1995, 2nd ed., 2001; The Musical: A Concise History, 1997; Lydia Thompson, Queen of Burlesque, 2002; William B Gill, from the Goldfields to Broadway, 2002; Emily Soldene: In Search of a Singer, 2 vols., 2006. Contributor to periodicals. **Address:** Talent Artists Ltd., 59 Sydner Rd., London, GL N16 7UF, England. **Online address:** ganzl@xtra.co.nz

GAO, Minglu. American (born United States), b. 1949. **Genres:** Antiques/Furnishings, Art/Art History. **Career:** State University of New York, assistant professor of art history; State University of New York, University at Buffalo, assistant professor of art history, affiliated faculty; University of Pittsburgh, research professor; Cafa Art Museum, curator and critic; Sichuan Fine Art Institute, Department of Art History, chair and professor for distinguished service. Writer. **Publications:** Zhongguo dang dai mei shu shi, 1985-1986, 1991; (ed. with J. Andrews) Fragmented Memory: The Chinese Avant-Garde in Exile, 1993; (ed.) Inside Out: New Chinese Art, 1998; A Century's Utopia: Chinese Avant-Garde Art, 2000; Chinese Maximalism, 2003; Wall: Reshaping Contemporary Chinese Art, 2005; Total Modernity and the Avant-Garde in Twentieth-Century Chinese Art, 2011. **Address:** Henry Clay Frick Department of History of Art and, Architecture, University of Pittsburgh, Rm. 213, Frick Fine Arts Bldg., Pittsburgh, PA 15260-7610, U.S.A. **Online address:** minglu@pitt.edu

GAPOSCHKIN, M. Cecilia. American (born United States), b. 1970. **Genres:** History. **Career:** Darmouth College, assistant dean of faculty for pre-major advising and adjunct assistant professor of history. Writer. **Publications:** The Making of Saint Louis: Kingship, Sanctity, and Crusade in the Later Middle Ages, 2008. Contributor to books and journals. **Address:** Dartmouth College, 305 Carpenter Hall, Hanover, NH 03655, U.S.A. **Online address:** cecilia.gaposchkin@dartmouth.edu

GAPPAH, Petina. Swiss/Zimbabwean (born Zimbabwe), b. 1971. **Genres:** Young Adult Fiction, Novels. **Career:** World Trade Organization, staff lawyer, 1999-2002; ACWL, counsel, 2002-. Writer. **Publications:** An Elegy for Easterly: Stories, 2009; The Book of Memory, 2012. **Address:** Faber and Faber Ltd., Bloomsbury House, 74-77 Great Russell St., London, GL WC1B 3DA, England. **Online address:** petina.gappah@bluewin.ch

GARAUDY, Roger. French (born France), b. 1913. **Genres:** Philosophy, Young Adult Non-fiction. **Career:** Institut international pour le dialogue des civilizations, Department of Tarn to Two Constitutive Assemblies, deputy, 1945-46; teacher, 1958-59; First National Assembly, affiliated, 1946-51; Department of Seine, deputy, 1956-58; National Assembly, vice president, 1956-58; senator, 1959-62; Centre d'Etudes et de Recherches Marxistes, director, 1960-70; Clermond-Ferrand, master lecturer of letters, 1962-65; Poitiers, Department of Literature, professor, 1965-72. Writer. **Publications:** NON-FICTION: L'Eglise, le communisme et les chretiens, 1939; Fundamentos del anticomunismo, 1940; Communisme et l'homme, 1943; Le Communisme et la morale, 1945; Antee: Journal de Daniel Chenier, 1946; Comunismo, la cultura y la moral, 1947; Les Sources francaises du socialisme scientifique, 1948; Marxisme et la personne humaine, 1949; Grammaire de la liberte, 1950; La Theorie materialiste de la connaissance, 1953; La Liberte, 1955; (co-author) Mesaventures de l'anti-marxisme: Les Malheurs de M. Merleau-Ponty, 1956; Humanisme marxiste: Cinq essais polemiques, 1957; Perspectives de l'homme: Existentialisme, pensee catholique, marxisme, 1959; Questions a Jean-Paul Sartre, precedees d'une lettre ouverte, 1960; L'Itineraire d'Aragon: Du Surrealisme au monde reel, 1961; Dieu est mort: Etude sur Hegel, 1962; Qu'estce que la morale marxiste?, 1963; D'Un Realisme sans rivages: Picasso, Saint-John Perse, Kafka, 1963; Karl Marx, 1964; Femmes du XXe siecle, 1965; De L'Anatheme du dialogue: Un Marxistes adresse au Concile, 1965; Marxisme du XXe siecle, 1966; La Pensee de Hegel, 1966; Le Probleme chinois, 1967; (with G.M.M. Cottier) Chretiens et marxistes, 1967; Lenine, 1968; (comp.) La Liberte en sursis, 1968: Avec des textes traduits du tcheque, de Alexandre Dubcek, Ota Sik, Radovan Richta, Frantisek Chamalik, 1968; (with Q. Lauer) A Christian-Communist Dialogue, 1968; Peut-on etre communiste aujourd'hui!, 1968; Pour un realisme du xxe siecle: Dialogue posthume avec Fernand Leger, 1968; Pour un modele francais du socialisme, 1968; Grand tournant du socialisme, 1969; Aktualität des Marzschen Denkens, 1969; Ganze Wahrheit, 1970; (trans.) Marxism in the Twentieth Century, 1970; (comp.) Toute la Verite, 1970; Esthetique et invention du futur, 1971; Reconquete de l'espoir, 1971; L'Alternative, 1972; Danser sa vie, 1973; ästhetik und Erfindung der Zukunft, 1973; (with R. Bellman and J. Wilkinson) Dynamic Programming of Human Systems: A Social and Historical Analysis, 1973; Soixante Oeuvres qui annoncerent le futur: Sept Siecles de peinture occidentale, 1974; Alternative Future: A Vision of Christian Marxism, 1974; 60 uvres qui annoncèrent le futur: 7 siécles de peinture occidentale, 1974; Ludmila Tcherina: Erotisme et mystique, 1975; Parole d'homme, 1975; (E. Balducci) Cristianesimo Come Liberazione, 1975; Karl Marx, The Evolution of his Thought, 1976; Le Projet espérance, 1976; Clovekova beseda, 1977; Le Marxisme, 1977; Pour un dialogue des civilisations: l'Occident est un accident, 1977; Pensée de Hegel, 1977; Qui ditesvous que je suis: Roman, 1978; Comment l'homme devint humain, 1978; Appel aux vivants, 1979; Il est encore temps de vivre: voici comment, 1980; L'Islam habite notre avenir, 1981; Pour L'Avenement de la femme, 1981; Promesses de l'Islam, 1981; The Case of Israel, 1983; Affaire Israël, 1983; (co-author) Estructura y organización de los servicios sociales, 1983; Mosquée, miroir de l'Islam The Mosque, Mirror of Islam, 1985; Biographie du XXe siècle, 1985; La Palestine, terre des messages divins, 1986; Milaff Isräil: diräsah lil-Sihyünīyah al-siyäsīyah, 1986; L'Islam en Occident: Cordoue, une capitale de l'esprit, 1987; Poesía vivida: Don Quijote, 1989; An 2000 moins 10: Ou allons-nous, 1990; Integrismes, 1990; Rūjīh Ghārūdī: min alilhäd ilá al-īmän, 1990; Les Fossoyeurs: Un Nouvel Appel aux vivants, 1992; Avons-nous besoin de Dieu, 1993; Souvienstoi!: brève histoire de l'Union Soviétique, 1994; Vers une guerre de religion: le débat du siècle, 1995; Mythes fondateurs de la politique israélienne, 1996; Mythical Foundations of Israeli Policy, 1997; Kashf alhaqä iq al-tārīkhīyah, 1997; Mes témoins, 1997; Founding Myths of the Israeli Policy, 1997; états-Unis, avant-garde de la décadence: comment préparer le XXIe siècle, 1997; Procès du sionisme israélien, 1998; (with J. Vergè) Procès de la liberté, 1998; Avenir, mode d'emploi, 1998; Mon tour du siècle en solitaire: mémoires, 1999; Qirä ah fī fikr ulamä al istirätījīyah. Järūdīyundhiruwayuhadhdhir, 2001; Founding Myths of Modern Israel, 2000; Terrorisme Occidental, 2004. **Address:** 69 rue de Sucy, Chennevieres-sur-Marne, Marne, 94430, France.

GARB, Tamar. British/German (born Germany), b. 1956?. **Genres:** Art/Art History. **Career:** Courtauld Institute, lecturer, 1988; University College, lecturer in art history, 1989-95, reader, 1995-2001, professor, 2001-, Durning Lawrence professor, head of department. Writer. **Publications:** Women Impressionists, 1986; (with K. Adler) Berthe Morisot (monograph), 1987; Sisters of the Brush: Women's Artistic Culture in Late Nineteenth-Century Paris, 1994; (ed. with L. Nochlin) The Jew in the Text: Modernity and the Construction of Identity, 1995; (with D. Semin and D. Kuspit) Christian Boltanski, 1997; Bodies of Modernity: Figure and Flesh in fin de siecle France, 1998; (ed.) On Installation, 2002; Painted Face: Potraits of Women in France, 1814-1914, 2007; Vivienne Koorland: Reisemalheurs, 2007; Body in Time: Figures of Femininity in Late Nineteenth-Century France, 2008; (contrib.) Home Lands, Land Marks: Contemporary Art From South Africa, 2008; (ed.) Gauguin: Maker of Myth, 2010. **Address:** Department of History of Art, University College, 20-21 Gordon Sq., London, GL WC1H 0AG, England. **Online address:** t.garb@ucl.ac.uk

GARBER, Anne. American/Canadian (born Canada), b. 1956. **Genres:** Food And Wine, Travel/Exploration, Homes/Gardens, Horticulture, How-to Books, Institutions/Organizations, Marketing, Social Commentary, Social Commentary. **Career:** Toronto Stock Exchange, deputy supervisor, 1968-70; Recent Developments, chief executive officer, 1972-; Dunsky Advertising Ltd., account group supervisor, 1973-76; Asta Productions, head film writer, 1977-82; Canadian Broadcasting Corporation-TV, Program Consumers Report, commentator, 1983; Vancouver Sun Newspaper, children's book reviewer, 1983-88, BCTV-TV News, consumer commentator, 1984; CVOR-Radio, Dave Barrett Show, producer and host, 1984-89; CKVU-TV, consumer commentator, 1986-89; Vancouver film commissioner, 1987-88; Office of the Mayor of Vancouver, communications officer, 1987-88; Associated Producers Bureau, executive director, 1988-; The Province Newspaper, featured columnist, 1988-, restaurant critic, 1990-; Serious Publishing, editor-in-chief, 1991-; Telus Multimedia, national food and book editor, 1998-2001; Canadian Association of Food and Travel Journalists, executive director, 2001-; Evalu8.org Media Inc., managing director, 2002-, content editor and food editor; Food Today Magazine, assignment editor, 2002-; International Association of Food and Travel Journalists, chief executive officer, 2004-; Culver City News, contributing editor, 2005-. **Publications:** The Vancouver Super Shopper, 1982, 4th ed., 1986; (with J. Crawford) Rise and Shine Vancouver, 1990; Vancouver Out to Lunch, 1990; Shopping the World, 1991; Cheap Eats, 1991, (with J.T.D. Keyes) 2nd ed., 1998; The Serious Shopper's Guide to Vancouver, 1992; (with J.T.D. Keyes) Victoria's Best Bargains, 1994; (with L. Gannon) Vancouver's Best Bargains, 1995; (with J.T.D. Keyes and L. Gannon) Exploring Ethnic Vancouver, 1995; (with J.T.D. Keyes) Vancouver's Cheap Eats, 1997; British Columbia Vacation Planner, 2005. Contributor to magazines and newspapers. **Address:** Evalu8.org Media Inc., PO Box 3796, Blaine, WA 98231-3796, U.S.A. **Online address:** foodtoday.magazine@gmail.com

GARBER, Eric. *See* HOLLERAN, Andrew.

GARBER, Marjorie. American (born United States), b. 1944. **Genres:** Literary Criticism And History. **Career:** Yale University, assistant professor of English, 1969-75, associate professor of English, 1975-79; Haverford College, professor of English, 1979-81; Harvard University, professor of English, 1981-95, Graduate Studies in English, director, 1981-, Humanities Center in the Faculty of the Arts and Sciences, director, 1986-2005, Harvard faculty of Arts and Sciences, associate dean, 1990-2001, William R. Kenan, Jr. professor of English, 1995-2004, Consortium of Humanities Centers and Institutes, chair, 1998-, Department of Visual and Environmental Studies, chair, 2001-10, Carpenter Center for the Visual Arts, director, 2001-10, Center for Literary and Cultural Studies, director, William R. Kenan Jr. professor of English and of visual and environmental studies, 2004-, Program in Dramatic Arts, chair; Trustee of the English Institute, chair, 1986; Dartmouth College, visiting professor of comparative literature, 1987; Consortium of Humanities Centers and Institutes, president, 2001-07, president emerita; American Council of Learned Societies, director. Writer. **Publications:** Dream in Shakespeare: From Metaphor to Metamorphosis, 1974; Coming of Age in Shakespeare, 1981; Shakespeare's Ghost Writers: Literature as Uncanny Causality, 1987; Vested Interests: Cross Dressing and Cultural Anxiety, 1992; Vice Versa: Bisexuality and the Eroticism of Everyday Life, 1995 as Bisexuality and the Eroticism of Everyday Life, 2000; Dog Love, 1996; Symptoms of Culture, 1998; (co-author) The Lives of Animals, 1999; Sex and Real Estate: Why We Love Houses, 2000; Academic Instincts, 2001; A Manifesto for Literary Studies, 2003; Quotation Marks, 2003; Shakespeare after All, 2004; Profiling Shakespeare, 2008; Patronizing the Arts, 2008; Shakespeare and Modern

Culture, 2008; Shakespeare's Ghost Writers: Literature as Uncanny Causality, 2010; Use and Abuse of Literature, 2011. EDITOR: Cannibals, Witches and Divorce: Estranging the Renaissance, 1987; (with J. Matlock and R.L. Walkowitz) Media Spectacles, 1993; (with R.L. Walkowitz) Secret Agents, The Rosenberg Case, McCarthyism, and Fifties America, 1995; (with P.B. Franklin and R.L. Walkowitz) Field Work: Sites in Literary and Cultural Studies, 1996; (with R.L. Walkowitz) One Nation Under God?: Religion and American Culture, 1999; (with R.L. Walkowitz and B. Hanssen) The Turn to Ethics, 2000; (with N.J. Vickers) The Medusa Reader, 2003. **Address:** Department of English, Harvard University, 12 Quincy St., Cambridge, MA 02138, U.S.A.

GARBER, Zev. American (born United States), b. 1941. **Genres:** Education, Essays. **Career:** Los Angeles Valley College, professor of Jewish studies, 1970-2007, emeritus chairman and director of Jewish studies, 2007-; University of California, visiting professor of religious studies, 1983-94; Case Western Reserve University, Rosenthal fellow, 2005; Shofar, co-editor, Studies in Shoah, editor-in-chief, Shofar Supplements, founder and editor. **Publications:** Teaching Hebrew Language and Literature at the College Level, 1991; Shoah: The Paradigmatic Genocide: Essays in Exegesis and Eisegesis, 1994; (co-author) Post-Shoah Dialogues: Re-Thinking Our Texts Together, 2004; (with B. Zuckerman) Double Takes: Thinking and Rethinking Issues of Modern Judaism, 2004. EDITOR: Methodology in the Academic Teaching of Judaism, 1986; (with A. Berger and R. Libowitz) Methodology in the Academic Teaching of the Holocaust, 1988; Perspectives on Zionism, 1994; What Kind of God?: Essays in Honor of Richard L. Rubenstein, 1995; Peace, in Deed: Essays in Honor of Harry James Cargas, 1998; Academic Approaches to Teaching Jewish Studies, 2000; Mel Gibson's Passion, The Film, the Controversy, and Its Implications, 2006; Casden Annual 6: The Impact of the Holocaust in America, 2009; Maven in Blue Jeans: Festschrift in Honor of Zev Garber, 2009; Jesus in the Context of Judaism, 2010; The Jewish Jesus: Revelation, Reflection, Reclamation, 2011. Contributor to books and periodicals. **Address:** Los Angeles Valley College, 5800 Fulton Ave., Valley Glen, CA 91401, U.S.A. **Online address:** zevgarber@juno.com

GARBERA, Katherine. American (born United States) **Genres:** Novels, Young Adult Fiction, Romance/Historical, Sex. **Career:** Writer. **Publications:** The Bachelor Next Door, 1997; Miranda's Outlaw, 1998; Overnight Cinderella, 2001; Some Kind of Incredible, 2001; Cinderella's Convenient Husband, 2002; The Tycoon's Temptation, 2002; Tycoon for Auction, 2003; Cinderella's Christmas Affair, 2003; Cinderella's Millionaire, 2003; In Bed with Beauty, 2003; Sin City Wedding, 2004; Operation: Second Chance, 2004; One Hot Weekend, 2004; Night Life, 2004; Let It Ride, 2004; Exposed: Athena Force, 2004; Mistress Minded, 2004; Her Baby's Father, 2004; Rock Me All Night, 2005; (with N. Singh) Desert Warrior, 2005; (co-author) The Night before Christmas (novella), 2005; The Amazon Strain, 2005; (with E. Rose) A Passionate Proposal, 2005; Their Million-Dollar Night, 2006; His Wedding-Night Wager, 2006; Her High-Stakes Affair, 2006; The Once-a-Mistress Wife, 2006; Exclusive, 2006; Body Heat, 2006; The Ultimate Romantic Challenge, 2006; Make-Believe Mistress, 2007; Six-Month Mistress, 2007; High-Society Mistress, 2007; Legends and Lies, 2007; Sex with a Stranger, 2007; Bare Witness, 2008; Bare Facts, 2008; The Greek Tycoon's Secret Heir, 2008; The Spanish Aristocrat's Woman, 2008; The Wealthy Frenchman's Proposition, 2008; Baby Witness, 2008; Moretti Heir, 2009; The Moretti Arrangement, 2009; The Moretti Seduction, 2009; Bare Nerve, 2009; Mercenary: The Savage Seven, 2009; Taming the Texas Tycoon, 2009; Master of Fortune, 2010; Scandalizing the CEO, 2010; His Royal Prize, 2010; The Pirate, 2010; Reunited...With Child, 2011; Seducing His Opposition, 2011; Taming the VIP Playboy, 2011. **Address:** The Knight Agency Inc., 570 East Ave., Madison, GA 30650, U.S.A. **Online address:** kathy@katherinegarbera.com

GARBUS, Cassandra. American (born United States), b. 1966. **Genres:** Novels, Young Adult Fiction, Literary Criticism And History. **Career:** Musician and writer. **Publications:** Solo Variations, 1998. **Address:** 255 W 108th St., New York, NY 10025, U.S.A. **Online address:** cass139207@aol.com

GARBUS, Martin. American (born United States), b. 1934. **Genres:** Law, Autobiography/Memoirs. **Career:** Columbia University, Center on Social Welfare Policy and Law, co-director, 1966, director, 1968; American Civil Liberties Union, associate director, 1969; Yale University, lecturer in law, 1974, adjunct professor; Frankfurt, Garbus, Klein and Selz, law partner, 1977-2003; Davis & Gilbert L.L.P., law partner, 2003-; Tsinghau University, lecturer, 2004; Harvard University Law School, lecturer; Stanford Law School,

lecturer. Writer. **Publications:** Ready for the Defense, 1971; Constitutional Litigation, 1975, 1975; Traitors and Heroes: A Lawyer's Memoir, 1987; (with S. Cohen) Tough Talk: How I Fought for Writers, Comics, Bigots, and the American Way, 1998; Courting Disaster: The Supreme Court and the Unmaking of American Law, 2002; The Next 25 Years: The New Supreme Court and What It Means for Americans, 2007; The Ten Techniques of Torture, 2009; China's Legal System, 2010. Contributor to newspapers and journals. **Address:** Davis & Gilbert L.L.P., 1740 Broadway, New York, NY 10019, U.S.A. **Online address:** mgarbus@evw.com

GARCEAU, Dee. (Dee Garceau-Hagen). American (born United States), b. 1955. **Genres:** History, Women's Studies And Issues, Social Sciences, Biography. **Career:** Canyonlands Field Institute, program coordinator and director of desert writer's workshop, 1986-89; University of Montana, visiting instructor in history, 1991-95; Rhodes College, assistant professor, associate professor of history, 1995-. Writer and film producer. **Publications:** The Important Things of Life: Women, Work and Family in Sweetwater County, 1880-1929, 1995; (ed. with M. Basso and L. McCall) Across the Great Divide: Cultures of Manhood in the American West, 2001; (ed.) Portraits of Women in the American West, 2005; Mormon Women at Winter Quarters: Women's Experiences on the North American Plains, 2007; (foreword) Bound Like Grass: A Memoir from the Western High Plains, 2010. Contributor to books. **Address:** Department of History, Rhodes College, 206 Buckman Hall, 2000 N Pkwy., Memphis, TN 38122, U.S.A. **Online address:** garceau@rhodes.edu

GARCEAU-HAGEN, Dee. See **GARCEAU, Dee.**

GARCÍA, Cristina. American/Cuban (born Cuba), b. 1958. **Genres:** Novels. **Career:** The New York Times, staff; Time Magazine, reporter and researcher, 1983-85, correspondent, 1985-90, bureau chief, 1987-88; University of California-Riverside, visiting associate professor, 2001-03; University of California-Los Angeles, visiting associate professor, 2003-04, 2005-06; Mills College, distinguished visiting writer, 2005-09; Centrum Writers' Exchange, artistic director, 2008-10; University of Nevada, Department of Creative Writing, visiting professor and Black Mountain Institute teaching fellow, 2009-10; Texas Tech University, professor of creative writing. Writer. **Publications:** Dreaming in Cuban, 1992; Cars of Cuba, 1995; Agüero sisters, 1997; Hermanas Agüero, 1997; Soñar en Cubano, 1998; Cubanisimo!: The Vintage Book of Contemporary Cuban Literature, 2003; Caída del cielo, 2003; Monkey Hunting, 2003; (ed. and intro.) Bordering Fires: The Vintage Book of Contemporary Mexican and Chicano, 2006; Handbook to Luck, 2007; (ed. and intro.) Voces sin fronteras: antología Vintage Español de literatura mexicana y chicana contempornea, 2007; I Wanna be Your Shoebox, 2008; Dog Who Loved the Moon, 2008; The Lady Matador's Hotel, 2010; The Lesser Tragedy of Death, 2010; Dreams of Significant Girls, 2011. **Address:** c/o Ellen Levine, Trident Media Group, 41 Madison Ave., 36th Fl., New York, NY 10010-2257, U.S.A. **Online address:** pinkhydrangea@hotmail.com

GARCIA, Diana. American (born United States), b. 1960?. **Genres:** Novels, Young Adult Fiction, Romance/Historical. **Career:** Writer and computer analyst. **Publications:** NOVELS: Love Lessons/Lecciones Lmorosas, 1999; Help Wanted/Aviso Oportuno, 2000; Stardust, 2001. **Address:** 2004 E Irvington Rd., Ste. 205, Tucson, AZ 85714-1809, U.S.A. **Online address:** dianagar1@aol.com

GARCIA, J. Malcolm. American (born United States), b. 1957. **Genres:** Biography, Autobiography/Memoirs. **Career:** Kansas City Star, reporter, 2001-07. **Publications:** The Khaarijee: A Chronicle of Friendship and War in Kabul, 2009. Contributor to periodicals. Works appear in anthologies. **Address:** Lippincott Massie McQuilkin, 27 W 20th St., Ste. 305, New York, NY 10011, U.S.A.

GARCÍA, Laura Gallego. Spanish (born Spain), b. 1977. **Genres:** History, Science Fiction/Fantasy. **Career:** Novelist. **Publications:** Finis mundi, 1999; El valle de los lobos, 2000; El cartero de lossūenos, 2001; Las hijas de Tara, 2002; La maldición del maestro, 2002; La leyenda del rey errante, 2002; Dónde está Alba?, 2003; La llamada de los muertos, 2003; Mandrágora, 2003; Elcoleccionista de relojes extraordinares, 2004; Alas de fuego, 2004; Memorias de Idhún: la resistencia, 2004; La hija de la noche, 2004; Feris, el elfo, 2004; Memorias de Idhún: Tríada, 2005; Max ya nohace reír, 2005; Alba tiene una amiga muy especial, 2005; Un fantasmaen apuros, 2005; The Legend of the Wandering King, 2005; The Valley of the Wolves, 2006; La emperatriz de los etéreos, 2007; Dos velas para el diablo/Two Candles for the

Devil, 2008; Memorias de Idhún. Panteón, 2009. **Address:** 76 Apartado de Correos, Alboraya, Valencia, 46120, Spain.

GARCIA, Luis M. Australian/Cuban (born Cuba), b. 1959?. **Genres:** Biography, History. **Career:** Journalist and public relations executive. **Publications:** (With K. Chikarovski) Chika, 2004; Child of the Revolution: Growing Up in Castro's Cuba, 2006. **Address:** Allen & Unwin, 83 Alexander St., Crows Nest, NW 2065, Australia. **Online address:** luismgarcia2006@hotmail.com

GARCIA-AGUILERA, Carolina. American/Cuban (born Cuba), b. 1949. **Genres:** Mystery/Crime/Suspense, Novels. **Career:** C&J Investigations, president, 1986-; novelist, 1995-. **Publications:** LUPE SOLANO MYSTERY NOVELS: Bloody Waters, 1996; Bloody Shame, 1997; Bloody Secrets, 1998; A Miracle in Paradise, 1999; Havana Heat, 2000; Bitter Sugar, 2001. NOVELS: One Hot Summer, 2002; Luck of the Draw, 2003; Bloody Twist, 2010. Works appear in anthologies. **Address:** 1030 14th St., Miami Beach, FL 33139, U.S.A. **Online address:** 4cubans@bellsouth.net

GARCÍA-CASTAÑÓN, Santiago. Spanish (born Spain), b. 1959. **Genres:** Novels, Poetry, Language/Linguistics, Literary Criticism And History, Translations. **Career:** Illinois Wesleyan University, instructor in Spanish, 1989-90, assistant professor, 1990-92; University of Georgia, assistant professor, 1992-97; University of Oviedo, associate professor, 1996-98; Georgia College and State University, associate professor, 1998-2003, professor of Spanish, 2003-07; Western Carolina University, Department of Modern Foreign Languages, professor of Spanish, 2007-, department head. Writer. **Publications:** Sangre, Valor y Fortuna (critical edition), 1990; Tiempos Imperfectos (poetry), 1994; Entre las Sombras (poetry), 1996; Por su rey y por su Dama (critical edition), 1997; (co-trans.) Theories of Literary Realism, 1997; Diccionario de Epónimos del Español, 2001; Lo que Queda (poetry), 2002; Verdadera Relación de la Grandeza del Reino de China (critical edition), 2002; El Castillo de los Halcones (novel), 2004; (ed. and intro.) Poesía Selecta de Francisco Bances Candamo, 2004; Rota Memoria, 2006; Vida y Fabulosas Aventuras de Pedro Menéndez de Avilés, 2006. **Address:** Department of Modern Languages, Western Carolina University, McKee 122, Cullowhee, NC 28723, U.S.A. **Online address:** sgarcia@email.wcu.edu

GARCIA Y ROBERTSON, R(odrigo). American (born United States), b. 1949?. **Genres:** Novels, Novellas/Short Stories, Science Fiction/Fantasy. **Career:** University of California, faculty; Villanova University, faculty. Writer. **Publications:** The Spiral Dance (novel), 1991; The Virgin and the Dinosaur, 1996; American Woman (novel), 1998; The Moon Maid and Other Fantastic Adventures (short stories), 1998; Knight Errant, 2001; Lady Robyn, 2003; White Rose, 2004; Firebird, 2006. Contributor of short stories. **Address:** c/o Author Mail, Forge, 175 5th Ave., New York, NY 10010, U.S.A.

GARDAM, Jane. British (born England), b. 1928. **Genres:** Novels, Novellas/Short Stories, Children's Fiction, Adult Non-fiction, Young Adult Fiction, Young Adult Non-fiction. **Career:** Hospital Libraries, red cross travelling librarian, 1951; Weldon Ladies Journal, sub-editor, 1952-53; Time and Tide, assistant literary editor, 1952-54. **Publications:** JUVENILE FICTION: A Few Fair Days (short stories), 1971; A Long Way from Verona (novel), 1971; The Summer after the Funeral (novel), 1973; Bilgewater, 1976; God on the Rocks (novel), 1978; Bridget and William (novel), 1981; The Hollow Land (short stories), 1981; Horse, 1982; Kit, 1983; Kit in Boots, 1986; Swan, 1987; Through the Doll's House Door, 1987; Going into a Dark House (short stories), 1994; (with M. Fedden) The Green Man, 1998; The Flight of the Maidens, 2000. ADULT FICTION: Black Faces, White Faces (short stories), 1975; Pineapple Bay Hotel, 1976; The Sidmouth Letters (short stories), 1980; The Pangs of Love and Other Stories, 1983; Crusoe's Daughter (novel), 1985; Showing the Flag (short stories), 1989; The Queen of the Tambourine, 1991; (with W. Trevor and R. Tremain) Trio: Three Stories from Cheltenham, 1993; Black Woolly Pony, 1993; The Iron Coast (non-fiction), 1994; Animal Stories, 1995; Magical Stories, 1995; Stories for Five-Year-Olds, 1995; Stories for Six-Year-Olds, 1995; Faith Fox: A Nativity (novel), 1996; Tufty Bear, 1996; Missing the Midnight (short stories), 1997; The Kit Stories, 1998; Old Filth (novel), 2004; The People on Privilege Hill and Other Stories, 2007; Showing the Flag, 2009; The Man in the Wooden Hat, 2009. Works appear in anthologies. Contributor to books and magazines. **Address:** David Higham Associates Ltd., 5-8 Lower John St., Golden Sq., London, GL W1F 9HA, England.

GARDAPHÉ, Fred L(ouis). American (born United States), b. 1952. **Genres:** Novellas/Short Stories, Plays/Screenplays, Cultural/Ethnic Topics, Literary Criticism And History, Writing/Journalism. **Career:** City Stoop Press, founding co-editor, 1978-79; Columbia College, associate professor of English, 1978-89, professor of English, 1989-98; Wilton House, Senior Citizens Writing Program, founder and director, Prologue High School, president, 1989-98; State University of New York, professor of Italian American studies, 1998-2008; City University of New York, Queens College, John D. Calandra Italian American Institute, Department of English, distinguished professor of English and Italian American studies, 2008-. **Publications:** Italian Signs, American Streets: The Evolution of Italian American Narrative, 1996; Dagoes Read: Tradition and the Italian American Writer, 1996; Moustache Pete Is Dead!: Ewiva Baffo Pietro!, 1997, 2nd ed. as Moustache Pete Is Dead: Evviva Baffo Pietro! The Fra Noi Columns 1985-1988, 2010; Leaving Little Italy: Essaying Italian American Culture, 2004; From Wiseguys to Wise Men: Masculinities and the Italian American Gangster, 2006; Introducing Italian Americana: Generalities on Literature and Film: A Bilingual Forum, 2006. EDITOR AND CONTRIBUTOR: (with A.J. Tamburri and P.A. Giordano) From the Margin: Writings in Italian Americana, 1991, rev. ed., 2000. EDITOR: Italian-American Ways, 1989; (with D. Candeloro and P.A. Giordano) Italian Ethnics: Their Languages, Literature and Lives: Proceedings of the 20th Annual Conference of the American Italian Historical Association, Chicago, Illinois, November 11-13, 1987, 1990; New Chicago Stories, 1991; (with D. Ashyk and A.J. Tamburri) Shades of Black & White, 1999; Importato dall'Italia, 2009; (with W.J. Connell) Anti-Italianism: Essays on A Prejudice, 2010; The Art of Reading Italian Americana, 2011; (with D. Candeloro) Reconstructing Italians in Chicago, 2011. **Address:** John D. Calandra Italian American Institute, Queens College, City University of New York, Klapper 535, 25 W 43rd St., Ste. 1700, New York, NY 10036, U.S.A. **Online address:** fred.gardaphe@qc.cuny.edu

GARDELL, Mattias. Swedish (born Sweden), b. 1959. **Genres:** Cultural/Ethnic Topics. **Career:** University of Stockholm, associate professor of religious history; Uppsala University, Nathan Soderblom professor, Nathan Soderblom chair of comparative religion, 2006. Writer. **Publications:** Countdown to Armageddon: Minister Farrakhan and the Nation of Islam in the Latter Days, 1996 in US as In the Name of Elijah Muhammad: Louis Farrakhan and the Nation of Islam, 1996; The New Romantics: A Swedish Expert on Right-Wing Extremism Says that Racist Odinism is the Radical Religion of the Future, 2001; Gods of the Blood: The Pagan Revival and White Separatism, 2003; Vad ar Rasism?, 2005; Bin Ladin I våra hjärtan: globaliseringen och framväxten av politisk islam, 2005; Tortyrens återkomst, 2008; Islamofobi, 2010. **Address:** Department of Theology, Uppsala University, Thunbergsvagen 3 B, Engelska Parken, PO Box 511, Uppsala, 751 20, Sweden. **Online address:** mattias.gardell@teol.uu.se

GARDELLA, Robert (P.). Tanzanian (born Tanzania, United Republic of), b. 1943. **Genres:** History, Humanities. **Career:** U.S. Merchant Marine Academy, professor of humanities, 1977-, professor emeritus of humanities. Writer. **Publications:** Harvesting Mountains: Fujian and the China Tea Trade, 1757-1937, 1994; (co-ed.) Chinese Business History: Interpretive Trends and Priorities for the Future, 1998; (co-ed.) Contract and Property in Early Modern China, 2004. Contributor to journals. **Address:** Department of Humanities, U.S. Merchant Marine Academy, 300 Steamboat Rd., Kings Point, NY 11024-1699, U.S.A. **Online address:** gardella@usmma.edu

GARDELLA, Tricia. American (born United States), b. 1944. **Genres:** Picture/Board Books, Children's Fiction. **Career:** Writer. **Publications:** PICTURE BOOKS: Just Like My Dad, 1993; Casey's New Hat, 1997; Blackberry Booties, 2000. **Address:** 8931 Montezuma Rd., Jamestown, CA 95327, U.S.A. **Online address:** trigar@mlode.com

GARDEN, Edward (James Clarke). British/Scottish (born Scotland), b. 1930. **Genres:** Music. **Career:** Clifton College, music staff, 1954-57; Loretto, director of music, 1957-66; University of Glasgow, lecturer, 1966-70, senior lecturer in music and organist, 1970-75; University of Sheffield, professor and chairman of music, 1975-93, dean of the faculty of arts, 1988-90. Composer, organist and writer. **Publications:** Balakirev: A Critical Study of His Life and Music, 1967; Tchaikovsky, 1973, 2nd ed., 1993; Tschaikowsky: Leben und Werk, 1986; (ed.) Correspondence Between Tchaikovsky and Nadezhda von Meck, 1876-1878, 1993; (ed. with N. Gotteri and intro.) To My Best Friend: Correspondence Between Tchaikovsky and Nadezhda von Meck, 1876-1878, 1993. Contributor to periodicals. **Address:** 91 Millhouses Ln., Sheffield, S72 HD, England.

GARDEN, Nancy. American (born United States), b. 1938. **Genres:** Novels, Children's Fiction, Children's Non-fiction, Young Adult Fiction. **Career:** Junior Scholastic, contributing editor, 1969-70; American Observer, contributing editor, 1970-72; Houghton Mifflin Co., associate editor, 1972, assistant editor, 1973, editor, 1974-76; Lambda Book Report, contributing editor, 1991-2000. Speaker and educator. **Publications:** Berlin: City Split in Two, 1971; What Happened in Marston, 1971; The Loners, 1972; Vampires, 1973; Werewolves, 1973; Witches, 1975; Devils and Demons, 1976; Fun with Forecasting Weather, 1977; Fours Crossing, 1981; The Kid's Code and Cipher Book, 1981; Maria's Mountain, 1981; Annie on My Mind, 1982; Watersmeet, 1983; Prisoner of Vampires, 1984; Peace, O River, 1986; The Door Between, 1987; Mystery of the Night Raiders, 1987; Mystery of the Midnight Menace, 1988; Mystery of the Secret Marks, 1989; Lark in the Morning, 1991; My Sister, the Vampire, 1992; Mystery of the Kidnapped Kidnapper, 1994; Mystery of the Watchful Witches, 1995; My Brother, the Werewolf, 1995; Dove and Sword: A Novel of Joan of Arc, 1995; Good Moon Rising, 1996; The Year They Burned the Books, 1999; Holly's Secret, 2000; The Secret of Smith's Hill (serial novel), 1999; Meeting Melanie, 2002; Nora and Liz, 2002; The Case of the Stolen Scarab: A Candlestone Inn Mystery, 2002; Molly's Family, 2004; Endgame, 2006; Hear Us Out!: Lesbian and Gay Stories of Struggle, Progress and Hope, 1950 to the Present, 2007; The Case of the Vanishing Valuables: A Candlestone Inn Mystery, 2010. Contributor to books and periodicals. **Address:** McIntosh & Otis Inc., 353 Lexington Ave., New York, NY 10016, U.S.A. **Online address:** nancygarden@aol.com

GARDINER, Jeremy. German (born Germany), b. 1957. **Genres:** Photography. **Career:** Massachusetts Institute of Technology, Harkness fellow, 1984-85; Pratt Institute, assistant professor of computer graphics, 1986-93; Charlex, paintbox artist, 1987-88; School of Visual Arts, visiting professor, 1988; New World School of the Arts, senior associate professor, 1993-; CyberArts Productions, president; University of London, Birkbeck College, professor, AHRC funded project, senior research fellow; Victoria and Albert Museum, senior research fellow; Thames Valley University, faculty. Writer. **Publications:** Digital Photo Illustration, 1994; (ed. with N. Lambert and F. Franco) CAT Symposium 2010: Ideas Before Their Time: Proceedings, 2010. Works appear in anthologies. **Address:** Faculty of the Arts, Thames Valley University, St. Mary's Rd., Ealing, GL W5 5RF, England. **Online address:** mail@jeremygardiner.co.uk

GARDINER, Judith Kegan. American (born United States), b. 1941. **Genres:** Literary Criticism And History, Women's Studies And Issues. **Career:** Fisk University, assistant professor, 1968-69; University of Illinois, assistant professor, 1969-76, associate professor, 1976-88, professor of English and women's studies, 1988-, Women's Studies Program, acting director, 1978-80, director of graduate studies, 1994-96, 2000-02, Center for Research on Women and Gender, interim director, 2002-04; Newberry Library, research associate, 1986-87; Feminist Studies Journal, senior editor, 1989-. **Publications:** Craftsmanship in Context: The Development of Ben Jonson's Poetry, 1975; Rhys, Stead, Lessing, and the Politics of Empathy, 1989. EDITOR: Provoking Agents, 1995; Masculinity Studies and Feminist Theory, 2002; The International Encyclopedia of Men and Masculinities, 2007. CONTRIBUTOR: Changing Subjects: The Making of Feminist Literary Criticism, 1993; Rereading Aphra Behn: History, Theory, and Criticism, 1993; Privileging Gender in Early Modern Britain, 1993; Psychoanalytic Sociology, 1993; The Oxford Companion to Women's Writing in the United States, 1995; The Emergence of Quaker Writing: Dissenting Literature in Seventeenth-Century England, 1995; Men Doing Feminism, 1998; Feminisms at a Millennium, 2000; Women's Studies on Its Own, 2002; The Freud Encyclopedia: Theory, Therapy, and Culture, 2002; Sage Handbook on Men and Masculinities, 2004; A Companion to the British and Irish Novel 1945-2000, 2005; Doris Lessing: Border Crossings, 2009. Contributor to books and journals. **Address:** Department of English, University of Illinois, MC 162, 601 S Morgan St., Ste. 1810, Chicago, IL 60607-7120, U.S.A. **Online address:** gardiner@uic.edu

GARDINER, Meg. American (born United States), b. 1957. **Genres:** Novels. **Career:** University of California, writing program, instructor. Writer. **Publications:** EVAN DELANEY SERIES MYSTERY NOVELS: China Lake, 2002; Mission Canyon, 2002; Jericho Point, 2004; Crosscut, 2005; Kill Chain, 2006. JO BECKETT SERIES MYSTERY NOVELS: The Dirty Secrets Club, 2008; The Memory Collector, 2009; Liar's Lullaby, 2010; Nightmare Thief, 2011; Ransom River, 2012. **Address:** 375 Hudson St., New York, NY 10014-3657, U.S.A. **Online address:** meg@meggardiner.com

GARDNER, Craig Shaw. (Peter Garrison). American (born United States), b. 1949. **Genres:** Science Fiction/Fantasy, Novels, Novellas/Short Stories. **Career:** Writer. **Publications:** EBENEZUM SERIES: A Malady of Magics, 1985; A Multitude of Monsters, 1986; A Night in the Netherhells, 1987; The Exploits of Ebenezum, 1987. WUNTVOR SERIES: A Difficulty with Dwarves, 1987; An Excess of Enchantment, 1988; A Disagreement with Death, 1989; The Wanderings of Wuntvor, 1989. CINEVERSE SERIES: Slaves of the Volcano God, 1989; Bride of the Slime Monster, 1990; Revenge of the Fluffy Bunnies, 1990; Cineverse Cycle, 1992. ARABIAN NIGHTS SERIES: The Other Sinbad, 1991; A Bad Day for Ali Baba, 1991; Scheherazade's Night Out, 1992; The Last Arabian Night, 1993. DRAGON CIRCLE SERIES: Dragon Sleeping, 1994; Dragon Waking, 1995; Dragon Burning, 1996. NOVELS: The Lost Boys, 1987; Wishbringer, 1988; Back to the Future, vol. II: A Novel, 1989; Batman, 1989; The Batman Murders, 1990; Back to the Future, vol. III: A Novel, 1990; Batman Returns, 1992; (with M. Costello) The Seventh Guest, 1995; Buffy the Vampire Slayer: Return to Chaos, 1998; Spiderman-Wanted: Dead or Alive, 1998; Leprechauns, 1999; Jason and the Argonauts, 2000. OTHERS: The Little Purple Book of Peculiar Stories, 2005; (with J. Alexander and D. Bishop) The Phantom Chronicles: New Tales of the Ghost Who Walks!, 2007. AS PETER GARRISON: The Changeling War, 1999; The Sorcerer's Gun, 1999; The Magic Dead, 2000. **Address:** c/o Jennifer Jackson, Donald Maass Literary Agency, 121 W 27th St., Ste. 801, New York, NY 10001-6262, U.S.A. **Online address:** csgcsgcsg@aol.com

GARDNER, James A. American (born United States), b. 1959?. **Genres:** Public/Social Administration, Law. **Career:** United States Department of Commerce, economist, 1980-81; United States Department of Justice, Civil Division, lawyer, 1984-88; College of William and Mary, Marshall-Wythe School of Law, visiting professor of law, 1988-2001; Western New England College, School of Law, assistant professor, 1988-91, associate professor, 1991-93, professor of law, 1993-2001; New York Civil Liberties Union, co-operating attorney, 1992-96; State University of New York, University at Buffalo, School of Law, professor of law, 2001-, Joseph W. Belluck and Laura L. Aswad professor of civil justice, 2005-, SUNY distinguished professor, 2011-, Edwin F. Jaeckle Center for State and Local Democracy, director, 2005-, vice dean for academic affairs, 2007-, Jaeckle Center for Law and Democracy, director. Writer. **Publications:** Legal Argument: The Structure and Language of Effective Advocacy, 1993; (ed. and intro.) State Expansion of Federal Constitutional Liberties: Individual Rights in a Dual Constitutional System, 1999; Interpreting State Constitutions: A Jurisprudence of Function in a Federal System, 2005; What are Campaigns For?: The Role of Persuasion in Electoral Law and Politics, 2009; (ed. with J. Rossi) New Frontiers of State Constitutional Law: Dual Enforcement of Norms, 2010. Contributor of articles to journals. **Address:** Law School, University at Buffalo, State University of New York, 514 John Lord O'Brian Hall, North Campus, Buffalo, NY 14260-1100, U.S.A. **Online address:** jgard@buffalo.edu

GARDNER, Jeremy. See GARDNER, Jerome.

GARDNER, Jerome. Also writes as John Gilchrist, Jeremy Gardner, Paul Tully, Elizabeth Gardner Weddington. British/American (born United States), b. 1932. **Genres:** Novels, Westerns/Adventure, Novellas/Short Stories, Young Adult Fiction. **Career:** Writer. **Publications:** NOVELS AS JEREMY GARDNER: Summer Palace, 1960. WESTERNS: Trail Out of Leavenworth, 1970; Pistolero, 1971; Frenchman's Brand, 1972; Heist at Apache Pass, 1972; The Mossyhorns, 1972; Lucky Cowpoke, 1973; Wagon to Hangtown, 1973; Huntsville Break, 1973; Travelling Judge, 1974; The All-Show Sheriff, 1974; Wilderness Saloon, 1974; Gunman's Holiday, 1975; Dilemma at Dripspring, 1976; The Underhand Mail, 1976; Two-Bit Town, 1977; The Old-timers, 1979; Confession at Dripspring, 1982; The Jayhawk Legacy, 1983; The Bounty Scalper, 1983; Medicine Show Doc, 1983; Judgment in the Territory, 1983; The Hangman and the Ladies' League, 1984; The Blood-Tie, 1984; The Hangman's Apprentice, 1985; The Pitchman Healer, 1985; The Rawhide Redeemer, 1986; The Tumbleweed Twosome, 1986; Get Maledon!, 1986; The Parker Ransom, 1987; The Hanging Week, 1987; Double on Death Row, 1988; The Owlhoot Convention, 1988; Wide Open Town, 1990; Date with a Noose, 1990; Maledon Calls the Shots, 1990; A Tale of Three Bullets, 1990; The Quick Hanging, 1991; The Wishbook Wife, 1992; The High-Toned Hellion, 1992; Hot Gun, 1992; The Saloonwoman, 1995; Fort Smith Posse, 1995. NOVELS AS JOHN GILCHRIST: Birdbrain, 1975; Out North, 1975; Lifeline, 1975; The English Corridor, 1976; The Engendering, 1978. NOVELS AS PAUL TULLY: The Horsing Blacksmith, 1985; The Bond Jumper, 1987; The Jehovahs' Jailbreak, 1987; The Strychnine Stand-Off, 1988; Night-

Hawk, 1991. **Address:** Robert Hale Ltd., Clerkenwell House, 45-47 Clerkenwell Green, London, GL EC1R OHT, England.

GARDNER, Katy. British (born England), b. 1964. **Genres:** Travel/Exploration, Anthropology/Ethnology. **Career:** Overseas Development Administration, assistant social development advisor; University of Kent, lecturer, 1991-93; Sussex University, professor of social anthropology, 1993-. Novelist and anthropologist. **Publications:** Songs at the River's Edge: Stories from a Bangladeshi Village, 1991; Global Migrants, Local Lives: Travel and Transformation in Rural Bangladesh, 1995; (with D. Lewis) Anthropology, Development, and the Post-modern Challenge, 1996; Age, Narrative, and Migration: The Life Course and Life Histories of Bengali Elders in London, 2002; Losing Gemma, 2002; The Mermaid's Purse, 2003; (ed. with F. Osella) Migration, Modernity, and Social Transformation in South Asia, 2004; Hidden, 2006; Faker, 2009. **Address:** Brighton, ES , England. **Online address:** k.gardner@sussex.ac.uk

GARDNER, Leonard. American (born United States), b. 1934?. **Genres:** Novels, Plays/Screenplays. **Career:** Writer. **Publications:** Fat City (novel), 1969; (ed.) Stolen Pleasures: Selected Stories of Gina Berriault, 2011. Contributor to journals and periodicals. **Address:** c/o Author Mail, University of California Press, 2120 Berkeley Way, Berkeley, CA 94720, U.S.A.

GARDNER, Lyn. British (born England) **Genres:** Science Fiction/Fantasy. **Career:** Independent, reporter; City Limits (publishing co-operative), founding member & editor of theatre section; Guardian, theater critic. Journalist. **Publications:** Into the Woods, 2006. **Address:** Guardian, 119 Farringdon Rd., London, EC1R 3ER, England. **Online address:** lyn.gardner@guardian.co.uk

GARDNER, Mark L(ee). American (born United States), b. 1960. **Genres:** History, Music, Travel/Exploration. **Career:** National Park Service, seasonal park ranger and living history interpreter, 1981-86; Colorado Historical Society, historic site administrator, 1987-91; independent historian, writer and consultant, 1991-. **Publications:** Santa Fe Trail: National Historic Trail, 1993; Elbert County: Window to the Past, 1993; Fort Bowie National Historic Site, 1994; Little Bighorn Battlefield National Monument, 1996; Bent's Old Fort National Historic Site, 1998; In the Shadow of Pikes Peak: An Illustrated History of Colorado Springs, 1999; Wagons for the Santa Fe Trade: Wheeled Vehicles and Their Makers, 1822-1880, 2000; Washita Battlefield National Historic Site, 2002; George Armstrong Custer: A Biography, 2005; Fort Union National Monument, 2005; Biography: Geronimo, 2006; (intro.) Southwestern Journals of Zebulon Pike, 1806-1807, 2006; To Hell on a Fast Horse, 2010. EDITOR: The Mexican Road: Trade, Travel, and Confrontation on the Santa Fe Trail, 1989; Brothers on the Santa Fe and Chihuahua Trails: Edward James Glasgow and William Henry Glasgow, 1846-1848, 1993; (with M. Simmons) The Mexican War Correspondence of Richard Smith Elliott, 1997. Contributor of articles to periodicals. **Address:** PO Box 879, Cascade, CO 80809-0879, U.S.A. **Online address:** markgardner@songofthewest.com

GARDNER, Michael R. American (born United States), b. 1942. **Genres:** Biography, Politics/Government, History, Social Sciences. **Career:** Bracewell and Patterson (law firm), partner, 1977-82; Akin, Gump, Strauss, Hauer and Feld (law firm), partner, 1982-89; United States Ambassador to the International Telecommunication Union (ITU) Plenipotentiary Conference, staff, 1982; United States Telecommunications Training Institute (USTTI), founder and pro bono chair, 1982-; The Law Offices of Michael R. Gardner, communications policy lawyer, 1990-; College of Georgetown University, adjunct professor, 1992-2000; Pennsylvania Avenue Development Corporation of Washington, board of directors; International Cultural Trace Center Commission, board of directors. Attorney and writer. **Publications:** Harry Truman and Civil Rights: Moral Courage and Political Risks, 2002. Contributor to periodicals. **Address:** c/o Author Mail, Southern Illinois University Press, 1915 University Press Dr., PO Box 6806, Carbondale, IL 62902-4323, U.S.A.

GARDNER, Robert. American (born United States), b. 1929. **Genres:** Children's Non-fiction, Criminology/True Crime, History, Sciences, Sports/Fitness, Technology, Young Adult Non-fiction, Environmental Sciences/Ecology, Environmental Sciences/Ecology. **Career:** American Cyanamid, Atomic Energy Division, staff, 1951-52; Salisbury School, science teacher, 1952-89, head of department, 1959-89, Salisbury Summer School, director of admissions, 1976-87; Education Development Center, staff, 1963-64, 1966-68; writer and consultant on science education, 1989-. **Publications:** JUVENILE NONFICTION: (with D. Webster) Shadow Science, 1976; Magic through

Science, 1978; (with D. Webster) Moving Right Along: A Book of Science Experiments and Puzzlers about Motion, 1978; (with H.E. Flanagan) Basic Lacrosse Strategy: An Introduction for Young Players, 1979; This Is the Way It Works: A Collection of Machines, 1980; Space: Frontier of the Future, 1980; Save That Energy, 1981; Kitchen Chemistry: Science Experiments to Do at Home, 1982; Water, the Life Sustaining Resource, 1982; The Whale Watchers' Guide, 1984; (with C.S. Brockway and S.F. Howe) Allyn and Bacon General Science, 1985; Science around the House, 1985; The Young Athlete's Manual, 1985; (with D. Webster) Science in Your Backyard, 1987; Projects in Space Science, 1988; (with D. Shortelle) The Future and the Past: Life 100 Years from Now and 100 Years Ago, 1989; Celebrating Earth Day: A Sourcebook of Activities and Experiments, 1992; Crime Lab 101: Experimenting with Crime Detection, 1992; Robert Gardner's Favorite Science Experiments, 1992; (with D. Shortelle) The Forgotten Players: The Story of Black Baseball in America, 1993; Robert Gardner's Challenging Science Experiments, 1993; (with E.A. Shore) Math in Science and Nature: Finding Patterns in the World Around Us, 1994; Math & Society: Reading Life in Numbers, 1995; Where on Earth am I?, 1996; Make an Interactive Science Museum: Hands-on Exhibits, 1996; (with D. Shortelle) From Talking Drums to the Internet: An Encyclopedia of Communications Technology, 1997; Science Project Ideas about Trees, 1997; Science Project Ideas about the Sun, 1997; Science Project Ideas about the Moon, 1997; Science Project Ideas about Rain, 1997; (with D. Webster) Science Project Ideas about Animal Behavior, 1997; Science Project Ideas about Air, 1997; What's So Super about the Supernatural?, 1998; Science Fair Projects-Planning, Presenting, Succeeding, 1999; Human Evolution, 1999; Science Projects about Kitchen Chemistry, 1999; Science Projects about Math, 1999; Science Projects about Physics in the Home, 1999; Science Projects about Plants, 1999; Science Projects about the Environment and Ecology, 1999; Science Projects about the Physics of Toys and Games, 2000; Science Projects about the Science Behind Magic, 2000; Science Projects about the Physics of Sports, 2000; Science Projects about Sound, 2000; Science Projects about Solids, Liquids and Gases, 2000; Science Projects about Methods of Measuring, 2000; Health Science Projects about Your Senses, 2000; Health Science Projects about Heredity, 2001; Health Science Projects about Anatomy and Physiology, 2001; (with N. Anthony) The Bombing of Pearl Harbor in American History, 2001; Science Project Ideas in the House, rev. ed., 2002; Science Project Ideas about Space Science, rev. ed., 2002; Science Project Ideas about Kitchen Chemistry, rev. ed., 2002; (with B.G. Conklin) Health Science Projects about Sports Performance, 2002; (with B.G. Conklin) Health Science Projects about Psychology, 2002; Health Science Projects about Nutrition, 2002; (with B.G. Conklin and D. Shortelle) Encyclopedia of Forensic Science: A Compendium of Detective Fact and Fiction, 2002; Sound Projects with a Music Lab You Can Build, 2008; Physics Projects with a Light Box You Can Build, 2008; Meteorology Projects with a Weather Station You Can Build, 2008; Chemistry Projects with a Laboratory You Can Build, 2008; Astronomy Projects with an Observatory You Can Build, 2008; Easy Genius Science Projects with Weather: Great Experiments and Ideas, 2009; (with D. Webster, K.G. Rainis and B.G. Conklin) Ace Your Animal Science Project: Great Science Fair Ideas, 2009; (with T.R. Rybolt, L.M. Rybolt and B.G. Conklin) Ace Your Science Project About the Senses: Great Science Fair Ideas, 2009; (with M. Goodstein) Ace Your Space Science Project: Great Science Fair Ideas, 2009; (with P.J. Perry and S. Tocci) Ace Your Ecology and Environmental Science Project: Great Science Fair Ideas, 2009; (with M. Goodstein and B.G. Conklin) Ace Your Sports Science Project: Great Science Fair Ideas, 2009; (with P.J. Perry) Ace Your Plant Science Project: Great Science Fair Ideas, 2009; Easy Genius Science Projects with the Human Body: Great Experiments and Ideas, 2009; Easy Genius Science Projects with Light: Great Experiments and Ideas, 2009; Easy Genius Science Projects with Electricity and Magnetism: Great Experiments and Ideas, 2009; Easy Genius Science Projects with Chemistry: Great Experiments and Ideas, 2009; Ace Your Science Project using Chemistry Magic and Toys: Great Science Fair Ideas, 2009; (with D. Shortelle) Slam Dunk! Science Projects with Basketball, 2010; (with B.G. Conklin) Ace Your Human Biology Science Project: Great Science Fair Ideas, 2010; (with S. Tocci and K.G. Rainis) Ace Your Chemistry Science Project: Great Science Fair Ideas, 2010; (with S. Tocci and T.R. Rybolt) Ace Your Food Science Project: Great Science Fair Ideas, 2010; (with S. Tocci) Ace Your Weather Science Project: Great Science Fair Ideas, 2010; (with B.G. Conklin and S. Tocci) Ace Your Exercise and Nutrition Science Project: Great Science Fair Ideas, 2010; (with M. Goodstein) Ace Your Forces and Motion Science Project: Great Science Fair Ideas, 2010; (with M. Goodstein and T.R. Rybolt) Ace Your Physical Science Project: Great Science Fair Ideas, 2010; Ace Your Math and Measuring Science Project: Great Science Fair Ideas, 2010; Whose

Fingerprints are These?: Crime-Solving Science Projects, 2011; Who Forged this Document?: Crime-solving Science Projects, 2011; Who Can Solve the Crime?: Science Projects using Detective Skills, 2011; Atoms And Molecules Experiments Using Ice, Salt, Marbles and More: One Hour or Less Science Experiments, 2012; Solids, Liquids and Gases Experiments Using Water, Air, Marbles and More: One Hour or Less Science Experiments, 2012; Energy Experiments Using Ice Cubes, Springs, Magnets and More: One Hour or Less Science Experiments, 2012; Electricity and Magnetism Experiments Using Batteries, Bulbs, Wires and More: One Hour or Less Science Experiments, 2012; Human Body Experiments Using Fingerprints, Hair, Muscles and More: One Hour or Less Science Experiments, 2013; Simple Machine Experiments Using Seesaws, Wheels, Pulleys and More: One Hour or Less Science Experiments, 2013. EXPERIMENTAL SCIENCE SERIES: Ideas for Science Projects, 1986; More Ideas for Science Projects, 1989; Famous Experiments You Can Do, 1990; (with E. Kemer) Making and Using Scientific Models, 1993. GETTING STARTED IN SCIENCE SERIES: Experiments with Balloons, 1995; Experiments with Bubbles, 1995; Experiments with Light and Mirrors, 1995; Experiments with Motion, 1995. PROJECTS FOR YOUNG SCIENTISTS SERIES: Energy Projects for Young Scientists, 1987, (with R.C. Adams) rev. ed., 2002. FIRST BOOK SERIES: Science Experiments, 1988. VENTURE SERIES: Science and Sports, 1988; Experimenting with Illusions, 1990; Experimenting with Inventions, 1990; Experimenting with Light, 1991; Experimenting with Sound, 1991; Experimenting with Energy Conservation, 1992; Experimenting with Water, 1993; Experimenting with Science in Sports, 1993; Experimenting with Time, 1995. INVESTIGATE AND DISCOVER SERIES: Light, 1991; Forces and Machines, 1991; Electricity, 1993; (with E. Kemer) Temperature and Heat, 1993. SCIENCE PROJECTS SERIES: Science Projects about the Human Body, 1993; Science Projects about Chemistry, 1994; Science Projects about Electricity and Magnets, 1994; Science Projects about Light, 1994; (with E. Kemer) Science Projects about Temperature and Heat, 1994; (with D. Webster) Science Projects about Weather, 1994; Super-Sized Science Projects with Volume: How Much Space Does it Take Up?, 2003; Split-Second Science Projects with Speed: How Fast Does it Go?, 2003; Really Hot Science Projects with Temperature: How Hot is It? How Cold is It?, 2003; It's About Time! Science Projects: How Long Does it Take?, 2003; Heavy-Duty Science Projects with Weight: How Much Does it Weigh?, 2003; Far-Out Science Projects with Height and Depth: How High is Up? How Low is Down?, 2003; Science Fair Projects about the Properties of Matter Using Marbles, Water, Balloons, and More, 2004; Light, Sound, and Waves Science Fair Projects: Using Sunglasses, Guitars, CDs, and Other Stuff, 2004; Forces and Motion Science Fair Projects: Using Water Balloons, Pulleys, and Other Stuff, 2004; Electricity and Magnetism Science Fair Projects using Batteries, Balloons, and Other Hair-Raising Stuff, 2004; (with B.G. Conklin) Chemistry Science Fair Projects Using French Fries, Gumdrops, Soap, and Other Organic Stuff, 2004; Chemistry Science Fair Projects using Acids, Bases, Metals, Salts, and Inorganic Stuff, 2004; Bicycle Science Projects: Physics on Wheels, 2004; Weather Science Fair Projects: Using Sunlight, Rainbows, Ice Cubes, and More, 2005; Planet Earth Science Fair Projects: Using the Moon, Stars, Beach Balls, Frisbees, and Other Far-Out Stuff, 2005; Genetics and Evolution Science Fair Projects using Skeletons, Cereal, Earthworms, and More, 2005; Sizzling Science Projects with Heat and Energy, 2006; Sensational Science Projects with Simple Machines, 2006; Melting, Freezing, and Boiling Science Projects with Matter, 2006; Jazzy Science Projects with Sound and Music, 2006; Energizing Science Projects with Electricity and Magnetism, 2006; Dazzling Science Projects with Light and Color, 2006; Wild Science Projects about Earth's Weather, 2008; Super Science Projects about Earth's Soil and Water, 2008; Stellar Science Projects about Earth's Sky, 2008; Smashing Science Projects about Earth's Rocks and Minerals, 2008; Forensic Science Projects with a Crime Lab You Can Build, 2008; Far-Out Science Projects about Earth's Sun and Moon, 2008; Earth-Shaking Science Projects about Planet Earth, 2008; (with E. Kemer) Easy Genius Science Projects with Temperature and Heat: Great Experiments and Ideas, 2009; Forces and Motion Science Fair Projects, Revised and Expanded using the Scientific Method, 2010; Light, Sound, and Waves Science Fair Projects, Revised and Expanded using the Scientific Method, 2010; Chemistry Science Fair Projects using Inorganic Stuff, Revised and Expanded using the Scientific Method, 2010; (with B.G. Conklin) Organic Chemistry Science Fair Projects, Revised and Expanded using the Scientific Method, 2010; Weather Science Fair Projects, Revised and Expanded using the Scientific Method, 2010; Planet Earth Science Fair Projects, Revised and Expanded using the Scientific Method, 2010; Genetics and Evolution Science Fair Projects, Revised and Expanded using the Scientific Method, 2010; Electricity and Magnetism Science Fair Projects, Revised and Expanded using the Scien-

tific Method, 2010; Science Fair Projects about the Properties of Matter, Revised and Expanded using the Scientific Method, 2010; Whose Bones are These?: Crime-solving Science Projects, 2011; Soil: Green Science Projects for a Sustainable Planet, 2011; Water: Green Science Projects for a Sustainable Planet, 2011; Energy: Green Science Projects about Solar, Wind, and Water Power, 2011; Recycle: Green Science Projects for a Sustainable Planet, 2011; Air: Green Science Projects for a Sustainable Planet, 2011; Earth's Cycles: Great Science Projects about the Water Cycle, Photosynthesis, and More, 2011. YESTERDAY'S SCIENCE, TODAY'S TECHNOLOGY SERIES: Architecture, 1994; Communication, 1994; Electricity and Magnetism, 1994; Optics, 1994; Space, 1994; Transportation, 1994. Contributor of articles to periodicals. **Address:** 275 Seagull Ln., PO Box 256, North Eastham, MA 02651-0256, U.S.A.

GARDNER, (Robert) Brian. British (born England), b. 1931. **Genres:** History, Biography, Mystery/Crime/Suspense, Literary Criticism And History. **Career:** Western Mail, feature writer, 1956-57; Sunday Times, reporter, 1957; Sunday Express, feature writer, 1957-61; Daily Sketch, television critic, 1963-64. **Publications:** The Big Push, A portrait of the Battle of the Somme, 1963; German East: The Story of the First World War in the East Africa, 1963; The Wasted Hour, the Tragedy of 1945, 1963; On to Kilimanjaro, 1963; The Year That Changed the World: 1945, 1964; Allenby, 1965; (ed. and intro.) Up the Line to Death: The War Poets, 1914-1918, 1965, 2nd ed., 1978; Allenby of Arabia, 1966; The War Poets, 1939-1945, 1966; (intro. and contrib.) The Terrible Rain: The War Poets, 1939-1945, 1966, rev. ed., 1993; Mafeking: A Victorian Legend, 1966; The Quest for Timbuctoo, 1968; Big Push: The Somme 1916, 1968; (anthologist) Churchill in His Time: A Study in a Reputation 1939-1945, 1968; The Lion's Cage, 1969; Rhodes and the Siege of Kimberley, 1969; Churchill In Power: As Seen By His Contemporaries, 1970; The African Dream, 1970; The East India Company: A History, 1971; The Public Schools: An Historical Survey, 1973; (with M. Davey) Systems Performance: Student Course Guide, 1982; East India Company, 1990; European Agriculture: Policies, Production and Trade, 1997; Tales Reborn in Blood, 2000. **Address:** Brandt & Brandt, 101 Park Ave., New York, NY 10017, U.S.A.

GARDNER, Robert W(ayne). American (born United States), b. 1940. **Genres:** Demography, Cultural/Ethnic Topics. **Career:** East-West Population Institute, research associate, assistant director, 1971-92; demographic consultant, 1992-. Writer. **Publications:** (With E.C. Nordyke) Demographic Situation in Hawaii, 1974; (with C.B. Park and E.C. Nordyke) Life Tables by Ethnic Group for Hawaii, 1920-1970, 1979; Nutritional Analysis System: A Physician's Manual for Evaluation of Therapeutic Diets with Special Emphasis On The Rotary Diversified Diet, 1980; (ed. with G.F. De Jong) Migration Decision Making: Multidisciplinary Approaches to Microlevel Studies in Developed and Developing Countries, 1981; (with J.A. Palmore) Measuring Mortality, Fertility, and Natural Increase: A Self-Teaching Guide to Elementary Measures, 1983, 5th ed., 1994; (with P. Wright) Ethnicity, Birthplace, and Achievement: The Changing Hawaii Mosaic, 1983; (with E.C. Nordyke and K.C. Lee) Profile of Hawaii's Elderly Population, 1984; Life Tables by Ethnic Group for Hawaii, 1980, 1984; Asian Americans: Growth, Change and Diversity, 1985; (with H.R. Barringer and M.J. Levin) Asians and Pacific Islanders in the United States, 1993. **Address:** 8 Noble St., Brunswick, ME 04011, U.S.A.

GARDNER, Sandra. American (born United States), b. 1940. **Genres:** Novels, Writing/Journalism, Young Adult Non-fiction, Social Sciences. **Career:** Author, 1981-; New York Times, columnist and social issues writer for New Jersey weekly section, 1981-86, 1991-93; public relations writer, 1986-96; health care specialist, 1986-; health writer and editor, 1997-2000. **Publications:** English Teacher's Companion, 1975; Southeast Asia, 1976; Mini-Mysteries, vol. II, 1976; Six Who Dared, 1981; Street Gangs, 1983; Teenage Suicide, 1985, (with G. Rosenberg) rev. ed., 1990; Street Gangs in America, 1992; (adapted with Lewis) More Solv-A-Crime, 1997. **Address:** 16 Cedar Way, Woodstock, NY 12498, U.S.A.

GARDNER, Ted. *See* **GARDNER, Theodore Roosevelt.**

GARDNER, Theodore Roosevelt. (Ted Gardner). American (born United States), b. 1934. **Genres:** Novels, Mystery/Crime/Suspense, Romance/Historical, Children's Fiction, Environmental Sciences/Ecology, Homes/Gardens, Humor/Satire, Art/Art History, Art/Art History. **Career:** Writer. **Publications:** (As T. Gardner) Off the Wall: The Newspaper Columns of Ted Gardner, 1993; Something Nice to See (children's book), 1994; Lotusland:

A Photographic Odyssey, 1995; Flip Side: A Novel of Suspense, 1997; Give Gravity a Chance: A Love Story, 1998; Nature's Kaleidoscope, 1998; (as T. Gardner) Wit's End (essays), 1999; The Hermitage Santa Barbara at 20, 2010. NOVELS: The Paper Dynasty, 1990; The Real Sleeper: A Love Story, 1995; Flipside: A Novel of Suspense, 1997; He's Back, 2000; All Lost Time: A Novel of Baby Fever, 2002, Momma Baby & Judgie: A Memoir, 2004; Voyage to Oblivion, 2007. **Address:** Allen A. Knoll Publishers, 200 W Victoria St., Santa Barbara, CA 93101-3627, U.S.A.

GARDNER, Tom. American (born United States), b. 1968. **Genres:** Economics, Money/Finance. **Career:** Smart Money magazine, columnist, 1996-97; The Motley Fool, co-chairman, co-founder and chief executive officer. Investment advisor, newspaper columnist and writer. **Publications:** WITH D. GARDNER: The Motley Fool Investment Guide: How the Fool Beats Wall Street's Wise Men and How You Can Too, 1996; The Motley Fool Investment Workbook, 1998, rev. ed., 2003; You Have More Than You Think: The Motley Fool Guide to Investing What You Have, 1998; (with D. Berger) The Motley Fool U.K. Investment Guide, 1998; The Motley Fool's Rule Breakers, Rule Makers: The Foolish Guide to Picking Stocks, 1999; The Motley Fool Investment Guide: How the Fool Beats Wall Street's Wise Men and How You Can Too, 2001; The Motley Fool's What to Do with Your Money Now: Ten Steps to Staying Up in a Down Market, 2002; The Motley Fool Investment Guide for Teens: Eight Steps to Having More Money Than Your Parents Ever Dreamed Of, 2002; (co-author) The Motley Fool Personal Finance Workbook: A Foolproof Guide to Organizing Your Cash and Building Wealth, 2003; The Motley Fool's Money after 40: Building Wealth for a Better Life, 2004; Motley Fool Million Dollar Portfolio: How to Build and Grow a Panic-Proof Investment Portfolio, 2009. **Address:** The Motley Fool, 123 N Pitt, 4th Fl., Alexandria, VA 22314, U.S.A. **Online address:** tomg@fool.com

GARDON, Anne. (Justine Saint-Laurent). Canadian/French (born France), b. 1948. **Genres:** Novels, Food And Wine, Photography, Natural History. **Career:** Writer and photographer. **Publications:** La cuisine des champs, 1994; La cuisine, naturellement, 1995; Délices en conserve, 1996; Le congélateur de gourmet, 1997; The Wild Food Gourmet: Fresh and Savory Food from Nature, 1998; Preserving for All Seasons, 1999; Comfort Food Fast: Easy and Elegant Food that Soothes the Soul, 2001; The Gourmet's Garden: Cooking With Edible Flowers, Herbs and Berries, 2004; Les Francs-Juges, forthcoming. EDITOR: Le gourmet au jardin, 2000. AS JUSTINE SAINT-LAURENT: Chantage No. 5 (novel), 2003. Contributor to periodicals. **Address:** 129 Rang Sainte-Marie, Saint-Chrysostome, QC J0S 1R0, Canada. **Online address:** agardon@dsuper.net

GARELICK, Rhonda K. American (born United States), b. 1962?. **Genres:** Art/Art History. **Career:** Yale University, faculty; University of Colorado, assistant professor; Columbia University, faculty; Connecticut College, faculty; University of Nebraska, professor of English, Hixson-Lied School of Fine and Performing Arts, professor of English, Interdisciplinary Arts Symposium, founder and director. Writer. **Publications:** Rising Star: Dandyism, Gender, and Performance in the Fin de Siècle, 1998; (contrib.) Chanel, 2005; Electric Salome: Loie Fuller's Performance of Modernism, 2007; (ed. with J.D. Veneciano) Fabulous Harlequin: Orlan and the Patchwork Self, 2010. Contributor to periodicals. **Address:** Department of English, University of Nebraska, 355 Andrews Hall, Lincoln, NE 68588-0333, U.S.A. **Online address:** rgarelick2@unlnotes.unl.edu

GARFIELD, Brian (F. W.). Also writes as Bennett Garland, Drew Mallory, Jonas Ward, John Ives, Alex Hawk. American (born United States), b. 1939. **Genres:** Mystery/Crime/Suspense, Romance/Historical, Westerns/Adventure, Plays/Screenplays, Film, History. **Career:** Western Writers of America Inc., vice-president, 1965-66; president, 1966-67; director, 1967-68; Shan Productions Company Inc. (motion picture productions), president, 1974-96; Mystery Writers of America Inc., director, 1974-84, president, 1983. Writer. **Publications:** Range Justice, 1960; The Arizonans, 1961; The Lawbringers, 1962; Trail Drive, 1962; Vultures in the Sun, 1963; Apache Canyon, 1963; The Vanquished, 1964; The Last Bridge, 1966; The Thousand-Mile War, 1969, rev. ed., 1996; Valley of the Shadow, 1970; The Villiers Touch, 1970; Slip-hammer, 1970; The Hit, 1970; What of Terry Conniston?, 1971; Sweeny's Honour, 1971; Gun Down, 1971 as the Last Hard Men, 1976; Deep Cover, 1971; Relentless, 1972; Line of Succession, 1972; Death Wish, 1972; Tripwire, 1973; (with D.W. Westlake) Gangway, 1973; Kolchak's Gold, 1974; The Threepersons Hunt, 1974; The Romanov Succession, 1974; Hopscotch, 1975; Death Sentence, 1975; Recoil, 1977; Wild Times, 1978; The Paladin,

1979; Checkpoint Charlie, 1981; Western Films: A Complete Guide, 1982; Suspended Sentences, 1983; Necessity, 1984; Manifest Destiny, 1989; The Hit and the Marksman, 2003; Hopscotch, 2004; The Meinertzhagen Mystery: The Life and Legend of a Colossal Fraud, 2007. EDITOR: War Whoop and Battle Cry, 1968; I Witness, 1978; The Crime of My Life: Favorite Stories by Presidents of the Mystery Writers of America, 1983. AS BENNETT GARLAND: Seven Brave Men, 1962; (with T.V. Olsen) High Storm, 1963; The Last Outlaw, 1964; Rio Chama, 1969. AS ALEX HAWK: Savage Guns, 1968. AS JOHN IVES: Fear in a Handful of Dust, 1978; The Marchand Woman, 1979. AS DREW MALLORY: Target Manhattan, 1975. AS FRANK O'BRIAN: The Rimfire Murders, 1962; Bugle and Spur, 1966; Act of Piracy, 1975. AS JONAS WARD: Buchanan's Gun, 1968. AS BRIAN WYNNE: Mr. Sixgun, 1964; The Night It Rained Bullets, 1965; The Bravos, 1966; The Proud Riders, 1967; A Badge for a Badman, 1967; Brand of the Gun, 1968; Gundown, 1969; Big Country, Big Men, 1969. AS FRANK WYNNE: Massacre Basin, 1961; The Big Snow, 1962; Arizona Rider, 1962; Dragoon Pass, 1963; Rio Concho, 1964; Rails West, 1964; Lynch Law Canyon, 1965; The Wolf Pack, 1966; Call Me Hazard, 1966; The Lusty Breed, 1966. **Address:** 115 W California Blvd., Ste. 404, Pasadena, CA 91105, U.S.A. **Online address:** briagar@aol.com

GARFINKLE, David. American (born United States), b. 1958. **Genres:** Air/Space Topics. **Career:** Washington University, research associate, 1985-87; University of Florida, research associate, 1987-89; University of California, research associate, 1989-91; Oakland University, assistant professor, 1991-95, associate professor, 1995-2000, professor of physics, 2000-; University of Guelph, professor, Perimeter Institute for Theoretical Physics, associate, 2003-04; Matters of Gravity, editor. **Publications:** (With R. Garfinkle) Three Steps to the Universe: From the Sun to Black Holes to the Mystery of Dark Matter, 2008. **Address:** MI , U.S.A. **Online address:** garfinkl@oakland.edu

GARFUNKEL, Trudy. American (born United States), b. 1944. **Genres:** Dance/Ballet, Food And Wine, Theology/Religion, Young Adult Non-fiction, Theatre, Biography. **Career:** Dial Press, publicity-advertising manager, 1967-82; Garland Communications, director, 1982-; City Ballet's Information Committee, chair. Writer. **Publications:** On Wings of Joy: The Story of Ballet from the 16th Century to Today, 1994, 2nd ed., 2002; Letter to the World: The Life and Dances of Martha Graham, 1995; Start Exploring Ballet, 1996; The Kosher Companion: A Guide to Food, Cooking, Shopping and Services, 1997; Kosher for Everybody: The Complete Guide to Understanding, Shopping, Cooking and Eating the Kosher Way, 2004. Contributor to books. **Address:** Curtis Associates, 171 E 74th St., New York, NY 10021, U.S.A. **Online address:** trudygpr@aol.com

GARGAN, Edward A. American (born United States), b. 1950. **Genres:** Area Studies, Local History/Rural Topics. **Career:** New York Times, bureau chief, 1985-89, 1991-99; Newsday, Asia bureau chief, 2000-05; Global Post, China correspondent. Journalist. **Publications:** China's Fate: A People's Turbulent Struggle with Reform and Repression, 1980-1990, 1991; The River's Tale: A Year on the Mekong, 2002. Contributor to periodicals. **Address:** GlobalPost, The Pilot House, Lewis Wharf, Boston, MA 02110, U.S.A. **Online address:** edgargan@hotmail.com

GARLAND, Alex. British (born England), b. 1970?. **Genres:** Novels, Young Adult Fiction. **Career:** Fiction writer. **Publications:** The Beach (novel), 1997; The Tesseract, 1999; The Weekenders: Travels in the Heart of Africa, 2001; The Coma, 2004; Sunshine, 2007. Contributor to periodicals. **Address:** Putnam Publishing Group Inc., 375 Hudson St., New York, NY 10014-3657, U.S.A.

GARLAND, Bennett. See **GARFIELD, Brian (F. W.).**

GARLAND, David. See **MILES, Keith.**

GARLAND, Mark (A.). American (born United States), b. 1953. **Genres:** Novels, Young Adult Fiction. **Career:** Service manager, 1978-. Writer. **Publications:** NOVELS: (with C.G. McGraw): Dorella, 1992; Demon Blade, 1994; Frost, 2000. OTHERS: (with C.G. McGraw) Ghost of a Chance, 1996; (with M.J. Friedman) Saratoga, 1996; Sword of the Prophets, 1997; Trial by Error, 1997; Rescue Party, 1999. Contributor of books. **Address:** 1016 Cadillac St., Syracuse, NY 13208-1916, U.S.A.

GARLAND, Max. American (born United States), b. 1954. **Genres:** Novels,

Poetry, Literary Criticism And History. **Career:** University of Iowa, Elderhostel Program, creative writing instructor, 1988-92, Iowa Summer Writing Festival, instructor, 1990-; University of Wisconsin-Madison, visiting lecturer in creative writing, 1990-96, poetry fellow, 1990-91; University of Wisconsin-Eau Claire, Department of English, assistant professor, professor, 1996-. Writer. **Publications:** The Postal Confessions (poems), 1995; Apparition, 1999; Hunger Wide as Heaven, 2006. Works appear in anthologies. Contributor of articles to periodicals. **Address:** Department of English, University of Wisconisn, Rm. 405, Hibbard Humanities Hall, 105 Garfield Ave., Eau Claire, WI 54702-4004, U.S.A. **Online address:** garlanm@uwec.edu

GARMAISE, Freda. American/British (born England), b. 1928. **Genres:** Novels, Writing/Journalism, Humor/Satire. **Career:** Montreal Star, humor columnist, 1974-79; Eurowoman Syndicate, American correspondent, 1980; Canadian Broadcasting Corp., New York entertainment reporter, 1980, reporter and commentator, 1982-90; British Broadcasting Corp., reporter and commentator, 1982-90. Writer. **Publications:** Love Bites (comic novel), 1981; Tough Girls Don't Knit and Other Tales of Stylish Subversion, 1990. Contributor to periodicals. **Address:** c/o Liz Darhansoff, 1220 Park Ave., Ste. 13B, New York, NY 10128-1733, U.S.A. **Online address:** garm4@aol.com

GARMENDIA, Joseba Irazu. *See* ATXAGA, Bernardo.

GARNEAU, Michel. Canadian (born Canada), b. 1939. **Genres:** Plays/Screenplays, Translations. **Career:** Writer, 1958-; Canadian Broadcasting Corp., television announcer and scriptwriter, 1960-68; Les Cailloux, singer; freelance broadcaster, 1967-68; National Theatre School of Canada, associate director, 1982-88. **Publications:** Eau de pluie, 1958; Langage, 1962; (co-author) Le Pays, 1963; Vous pouvez m'acheter pour 69 ct., 1972; Blues des elections, 1972; l'Animalhumain, 1972; Moments, 1973; J'aime la littérature, elle est utile, 1974; Politique, 1974; Sur le matelas, 1974; La Chanson d'amour de cul, 1974; Quatre à quatre, 1974; Strauss et Pesant (et Rosa), 1974; Plus belle île, 1975; Les Petits Chevals amoureux (poetry), 1977; Abries, desabriees, suivi de L'Usage du coeur dans le domaine reel, 1979; Elégie au génocide des nasopodes, 1979; Poésies complètes, 1955-87 (poetry collection), 1988; Le phénix de neige (poetry), 1992; Une pelletée de nuages, 1999; Corde de bran de scie: poèmes, 2002; Discrète parade d'éléphants: poèmes, 2004; (with F. Durand) Critures, 2007; (trans.) L. Cohen, Book of Longing, 2007; Poèmes du traducteur, 2008; Chevaux approximatifs, 2010. **Address:** VLB éditeur, 1010 rue de la Gauchetière ESt., Montreal, QC H2L 2N5, Canada.

GARNER, Alan. British (born England), b. 1934. **Genres:** Novels, Science Fiction/Fantasy, Children's Fiction, Plays/Screenplays, Songs/Lyrics And Libretti, Mythology/Folklore, Documentaries/Reportage, Essays, Essays, Picture/Board Books, Young Adult Non-fiction. **Career:** Writer. **Publications:** STONE BOOK SERIES: The Stone Book, 1976; Granny Reardun, 1977; Tom Fobble's Day, 1977; The Aimer Gate, 1978. NOVELS: Elidor, 1965; The Old Man of Mow, 1966; The Owl Service, 1967; Smith, 1969; Red Shift, 1973; The Breadhorse, 1975; The Golden Brothers, 1976; The Girl of the Golden Gate, 1979; Lad of the Gad, 1980; Once Upon A Time, 1993; Strandloper, 1996; The Well of the Wind, 1998; Thursbitch, 2003; The Weirdstone of Brisingamen: A Tale of Alderley, 2006; The Moon of Gomrath: A Tale of Alderley, 2006; Complete Folk Tales, 2011. OMNIBUS: Alan Garner Omnibus, 1976. COLLECTIONS: The Guizer: A Book of Fools, 1975; The Stone Book Quartet, 1978; Alan Garner's Fairy Tales of Gold, 1979; Alan Garner's Book of British Fairy Tales, 1984; A Bag of Moonshine, 1986; Fairytales of Gold, 1989. CHAPBOOKS: Holly from the Bongs: A Nativity Play, 1966; Princess and the Golden Mane, 1979; Three Golden Heads of the Well, 1979; Jack and the Beanstalk, 1992; The Little Red Hen, 1997; Grey Wolf, Prince Jack and the Firebird, 1998. NON FICTION: The Voice That Thunders, 1997. **Address:** The Harvill Press, Random House, 20 Vauxhall Bridge Rd., London, GL SW1V 2SA, England.

GARNER, Gretchen. American (born United States), b. 1939. **Genres:** Photography. **Career:** New Art Examiner Magazine, photography editor, 1975-77; Columbia College, visiting instructor, 1978, 1982; Illinois Institute of Technology, Institute of Design, visiting instructor, 1979; Saint Xavier College, Department of Art, instructor, assistant professor, associate professor, SXC Gallery, director, 1979-81, chair, 1982-84; Grand Valley State University, School of Communications, assistant professor, associate professor of communications, Calder Art Gallery, director, 1987-89; University of Connecticut, Department of Art, professor, 1989-94, department head, 1989-92; Moore College of Art and Design, academic dean, 1994-97; Ohio State Uni-

versity, visiting artist and adjunct professor, 2003-07. Writer. **Publications:** An Art History of Ephemera: Gretchen Garner's Catalog, 1982; Reclaiming Paradise: American Women Photograph the Land, Tweed Museum of Art, 1987; Six Ideas in Photography: A Celebration of Photography's Sesquicentennial, 1989; Disappearing Witness: Change in Twentieth-Century American Photography, 2003. **Address:** 1181 Haddon Rd., Columbus, OH 43209, U.S.A. **Online address:** gretchengarner@sbcglobal.net

GARNER, Helen. Australian (born Australia), b. 1942. **Genres:** Novels, Novellas/Short Stories, Plays/Screenplays, Essays, Film, Women's Studies And Issues, Adult Non-fiction. **Career:** Werribee High School, teacher, 1966-67; Upfield High School, teacher, 1968-69; Fitzroy High School, teacher, 1971-72; Digger, freelance journalist, 1973; The Age, feature writer, 1981-; National Times, Melbourne theater critic, 1982-83; Griffith University, writer-in-residence, 1983; University of Western Australia, writer-in-residence, 1984; New York University, Graduate Creative Writing Program, visiting professor, 1993. **Publications:** Childern's Bach, 1984; (with S. Clarke) Our Homes, Our Selves: A Report of an International Conference on Women and Housing, 1988; (with L. Jones and B. Burstall) La Mama, the Story of a Theatre, 1988; The Last Days of Chez Nous and Two Friends, 1992; The First Stone: Some Questions about Sex and Power (non-fiction), 1995; True Stories: Selected Non-Fiction, 1996; (contrib.) And the Winner Is: Eighteen Winning Stories from Eltham's Alan Marshall Award, 1997; The Feel of Steel (essays), 2001; Joe Cinque's Consolation, 2004. NOVELS: Monkey Grip, 1977; (with J. Giles) Moving Out, 1983; The Children's Bach, 1984; Cosmo Cosmolino, 1992; The Spare Room, 2008. STORIES: Honour & Other People's Children: Two Stories (novellas), 1980; Postcards from Surfers, 1985; My Hard Heart, 1998. Contributor to periodicals. **Address:** Barbara Mobbs, PO Box 126, Edgecliff, NW 2027, Australia.

GARNER, John S. American (born United States), b. 1945. **Genres:** Architecture, History, Social Sciences. **Career:** Society for the Preservation of New England Antiquities, preservationist, 1971-73; Boston University, lecturer in urban affairs, 1973-74; preservation consultant, 1974-; Texas A&M University, assistant professor, 1974-77, associate professor, 1977-81; University of Illinois, School of Architecture, associate professor, 1981-87, professor, 1987-, now emeritus. Writer. **Publications:** The Model Company Town: Urban Design through Private Enterprise in Nineteenth-Century New England, 1984; (comp. and ed.) Main and Market Streets, Mount Carroll, Illinois: A University of Illinois Case Study in Recording Historic Buildings, 1986; (ed.) The Midwest in American Architecture, 1991; (ed.) The Company Town: Architecture and Society in the Early Industrial Age, 1992. **Address:** Department of History & Preservation, School of Architecture, University of Illinois, 304 Architecture, M/C 621, 611 Lorado Taft Dr., Champaign, IL 61820, U.S.A. **Online address:** jsgarner@illinois.edu

GARNET, A. H. *See* SLOTE, Alfred.

GARNETT, Gale Zoë. Canadian/New Zealander (born New Zealand), b. 1942. **Genres:** Novels, Plays/Screenplays, Young Adult Fiction, Romance/Historical. **Career:** Actor, director and writer. **Publications:** Visible Amazement: A Novel, 1999; Transient Dancing, 2003; Room Tone, 2007; Savage Adoration: A Novel, 2009. Contributor to book and periodicals. **Address:** c/o Jackie Kaiser, Westwood Creative Artists, 94 Harbord St., Toronto, ON M5S 1G6, Canada.

GARNETT, Richard (Duncan Carey). British (born England), b. 1923. **Genres:** Children's Fiction, Biography, Translations, Autobiography/Memoirs, History, Reference, Economics. **Career:** Rupert Hart-Davis Ltd., production manager, 1951-59, director, 1954-66; Adlard Coles Ltd., director, 1963-66; Macmillan-London, editor, 1966-82, director, 1972-82; Macmillan Publishers, director, 1982-87. **Publications:** The Silver Kingdom, 1956 in US as The Undersea Treasure, 1960; The White Dragon, 1963; Jack of Dover, 1966; Constance Garnett: A Heroic Life, 1991; Rupert Hart-Davis Limited: A Brief History with a Checklist of Publications, 2004. EDITOR: Goldsmith: Selected Works, 1950; (with R. Grenfell) Joyce, 1980; Sylvia and David: The Townsend Warner/Garnett Letters, 1994. TRANSLATOR: R. Gruss, The Art of the Aqualung, 1955; B. Heuvelmans, On the Track of the Unknown Animals, 1958; B. Heuvelmans, In the Wake of the Sea-Serpents, 1968. **Address:** Hilton Hall, Hilton, Huntingdon, CB PE28 9NE, England.

GARNHAM, Trevor. British (born England), b. 1947. **Genres:** Architecture, Art/Art History. **Career:** University of Kingston, senior lecturer in architecture, 1988-. Writer. **Publications:** The Oxford Museum, 1992; Melsetter House, 1993; St. Andrew's Church, Roker, Edward Prior, 1995; (coauthor) Encounters Between Here and There, 2001; (with B. Dunlop) Lines on the Landscape, Circles from the Sky: Monuments of Neolithic Orkney, 2004; (with R. Thomas) The Environments of Architecture: Environmental Design in Context, 2007. **Address:** School of Architecture, University of Kingston, Knights Pk., Kingston, SR KT1 2QJ, England. **Online address:** t.garnham@kingston.ac.uk

GARRARD, Graeme. Welsh/Canadian (born Canada), b. 1965. **Genres:** Social Commentary, History, Philosophy. **Career:** Cardiff University, lecturer in European studies, 1995-2006, senior lecturer, 2006-, Political Theory Masters Programme, co-director; Harvard University, Center for European Studies, visiting fellow, 2000; Dartmouth College, visiting associate professor, 2000-01; Williams College, visiting associate professor, 2002-01, American of Paris University, visiting associate professor, 2004. Writer and educator. **Publications:** Rousseau's Counter-Enlightenment, 2003; Counter-Enlightenment: From the Eighteenth-Century to the Present, 2005; Politics and the New Science of Human Nature, forthcoming. Contributor to periodicals. **Address:** Cardiff School of European Studies, Cardiff University, Rm. 1.24, 65-68 Park Pl., Cardiff, SG CF10 3YQ, Wales. **Online address:** garrard@cardiff.ac.uk

GARRARD, John (Gordon). American (born United States), b. 1934. **Genres:** Literary Criticism And History, Biography. **Career:** Carleton University, lecturer in Russian language and literature, 1958-62; Dartmouth College, assistant professor, 1964-69, associate professor of Russian literature, 1969-71; St. Antony's College, associate fellow, 1967-68; Indiana University, visiting associate professor, 1970-71; University of Virginia, professor of Russian literature, 1971-84, Department of Slavic Languages and Literature, chair, 1971-76, Center for Russian and East European Studies, director, 1972-83; University of Arizona, professor of Russian studies, 1984-, Institute for the Study of the Soviet Union and Eastern Europe, director, 1985-87, Department of Russian and Slavic Studies, head, 1985-88; Columbia University, visiting research fellow; Hoover Institution, visiting research fellow; Oxford University, visiting research fellow; Centre for Hebrew and Jewish Studies, visiting research fellow. Writer. **Publications:** Mixhail Chulkov: An Introduction to His Prose and Verse, 1970; Mikhail Lermontov, 1982; (with A. Corning) Soviet Reader: Data from SIP, 1987; (with C. Garrard) Inside the Soviet Writers' Union, 1990; (with C. Garrard) The Bones of Berdichev: The Life and Fate of Vasily Grossman, 1996; (with C. Garrard) Russian Orthodoxy Resurgent: Faith and Power in the New Russia, 2008. EDITOR: Vladimir Tendryakov, Three Novellas, 1967; The Eighteenth Century in Russia, 1973; The Russian Novel from Pushkin to Pasternak, 1983; (with C. Garrard) World War II and the Soviet People, 1993. Contributor to books and journals. **Address:** Learning Services, University of Arizona, PO Box 210105, Tucson, AZ 85721-0105, U.S.A. **Online address:** okcoh@email.arizona.edu

GARRATT, James E. Canadian (born Canada), b. 1954. **Genres:** Environmental Sciences/Ecology, Natural History. **Career:** Save the Rouge Valley System, chairman; Federation of Ontario Naturalists, board directors; Friends of Altona Forest and Petticoat Creek, founding director; Scanlon Creek Outdoor Education Centre, environmental instructor; Kortright Center for Conservation, staff. Writer. **Publications:** The Rouge River Valley: An Urban Wilderness, 2000; Northen Euphoria, forthcoming; Scarborough Bluffs: Another Urban Wilderness, forthcoming; Oak Ridges Moraine: Life on the Edge, forthcoming. Contributor to periodicals. **Address:** 32 Greendowns Dr., Scarborough, ON M1M 2G7, Canada. **Online address:** jamesegarratt@gmail.com

GARRETT, Laurie. American (born United States), b. 1951. **Genres:** Medicine/Health, Social Sciences. **Career:** Freelance journalist, 1979; National Public Radio, freelance reporter, 1980-88, science correspondent; British Broadcasting Corp., freelance reporter, 1980-88; American Broadcasting Co., freelance reporter, 1980-88; Canadian Broadcasting Corp., freelance reporter, 1980-88; Pacifica News Service, freelance reporter, 1980-88; Newsday, science correspondent and medical and science writer, 1988-2005; Harvard School of Public Health, visiting fellow, 1992-93; University of California, visiting fellow, 1997; Council on Foreign Relations, senior fellow for global health, 2004-; KPFA Radio Station, science reporter. **Publications:** The Coming Plague: Newly Emerging Diseases in a World Out of Balance, 1994; Microbes versus Mankind: The Coming Plague, 1996; (contrib.) A Field Guide For Science Writers, 1997; Betrayal of Trust: The Collapse of Global Public Health, 2000. Contributor of articles to books and periodicals. **Address:**

Council on Foreign Relations, The Harold Pratt House, 58 E 68th St., New York, NY 10065, U.S.A. **Online address:** zliberman@cfr.org

GARRETT, Leslie. Canadian (born Canada), b. 1964. **Genres:** Children's Non-fiction, Biography, Adult Non-fiction, Sciences. **Career:** Freelance writer, editor and columnist. **Publications:** Superkids: Young Heroes in Action, 1997; Record Breakers: True Stories of This Century's Amazing Kids, 2000; Superkids Too!: More Young Heroes in Action, 2001; The Story of Muhammad Ali, 2002; The Push and Pull Playground, 2003; The Dictionary of Forces and Energy, 2003; David Suzuki: Lamour De La Nature, 2004; Tom Longboat: Coureur De Fonds, 2004; Helen Keller: A Photographic Story of a Life, 2004; Push and Pull, 2005; Earth Smart, 2006; The Virtuous Consumer: Your Essential Shopping Guide for a Better, Kinder, Healthier World, 2007. **Address:** Dorling Kindersley Publishing, 375 Hudson St., New York, NY 10014, U.S.A. **Online address:** leslie@virtuousconsumer.com

GARRETT, Martin. British (born England) **Genres:** Literary Criticism And History, History, Humanities. **Career:** Oxford University, tutor and lecturer. Writer. **Publications:** A Diamond, Though Set in Horn: Philip Massinger's Attitude to Spectacle, 1984; (ed.) Massinger: The Critical Heritage, 1991; Greece: A Literary Companion, 1994; (ed.) Sidney: The Critical Heritage, 1996; Browning Chronology: Elizabeth Barrett and Robert Browning, 1998; Traveller's Literary Companion to Italy, 1999; (ed.) Elizabeth Barrett Browning and Robert Browning: Interviews and Recollections, 2000; George Gordon, Lord Byron, 2000; Venice: A Cultural and Literary Companion, 2000; Elizabeth Barrett Browning and Robert Browning, 2001; A Mary Shelley Chronology, 2002; Mary Shelley, 2002; Cambridge: A Cultural and Literary History, 2004; Provence: A Cultural History, 2006; Palgrave Literary Dictionary of Byron, 2010; Loire: A Cultural History, 2011. Contributor to periodicals. **Address:** c/o Author Mail, Interlink Publishing, 46 Crosby St., Northampton, MA 01060-1804, U.S.A.

GARRETT, Susan. American (born United States), b. 1931. **Genres:** Medicine/Health, Photography. **Career:** York Hospital, administrator, 1978-82; University of Michigan, Medical School, associate administrator, 1983-84; Martha Jefferson Hospital, vice-president, 1984-87; Hospice of the Piedmont, president, 1988-90; Coalition for Mentally Disabled Citizens of Virginia, co-chair person, 1989-92. Writer. **Publications:** Taking Care of Our Own: A Year in the Life of a Small Hospital, 1994; Miles to Go: Aging in Rural Virginia, 1998; Quick-Eyed Love: Photography and Memory, 2005. **Address:** c/o Jane Gelfman, Gelfman-Schneider, 250 W 57th St., Ste. 2515, New York, NY 10107, U.S.A.

GARRETTSON, Charles Lloyd. American (born United States), b. 1953. **Genres:** Politics/Government, History. **Career:** Muhlenberg College, visiting professor, 1990-93, assistant director of admissions, 1993-94. Lehigh Valley Young Democrats, president; Allentown Board of Ethics, president. **Publications:** Hubert M. Humphrey: The Politics of Joy, 1993. **Address:** 717 E High St., Pottstown, PA 19464-5770, U.S.A.

GARRIS, Mick. American (born United States), b. 1951. **Genres:** Plays/Screenplays, Humor/Satire. **Career:** Screenwriter, director and producer. **Publications:** Hocus Pocus, 1993. Contributor of articles to magazines. Works appear in anthologies. **Address:** c/o John Levan, Creative Artists Agency, 9830 Wilshire Blvd., Beverly Hills, CA 90212-1825, U.S.A.

GARRISON, Bruce. American (born United States), b. 1950. **Genres:** Communications/Media, Writing/Journalism, Autobiography/Memoirs, Reference, Information Science/Computers. **Career:** East Texas State University, professor, 1975-77; Marquette University, professor, 1977-81; University of Miami, School of Communication, professor of journalism and photography, 1981-; Shanghai International Studies University, faculty, 2004-05. Writer. **Publications:** (With M. Sabljak) Sports Reporting, 1985, 2nd ed., 1993; Professional Feature Writing, 1989, 5th ed., 2010; Professional News Writing, 1990; (with M.B. Salwen) Latin American Journalism, 1991; Advanced Reporting: Skills for the Professional, 1992; Professional News Reporting, 1992; Computer-Assisted Reporting, 1995, 2nd ed., 1998; Successful Strategies for Computer-Assisted Reporting, 1996; (ed. with M.B. Salwen and P.D. Driscoll) Online News and the Public, 2005. **Address:** School of Communication, University of Miami, 2009 Frances L. Wolfson Bldg., 5100 Brunson Dr., Coral Gables, FL 33146, U.S.A. **Online address:** bruce@miami.edu

GARRISON, Daniel H. American (born United States), b. 1937. **Genres:**

Literary Criticism And History, Intellectual History, Medicine/Health, Young Adult Non-fiction, Psychology. **Career:** Latin teacher, 1959-60; West Virginia University, instructor in classics and Spanish, 1962-63; University of California, acting instructor in comparative literature, 1963-66; Northwestern University, assistant professor, 1966-73, associate professor of classics, 1973-95, professor of classics, 1995-, master of Jones, 2000-03, University Faculty Senate, secretary, Weinberg College of Arts and Sciences, secretary, Undergraduate Academic Conduct Committee, chair, Lang Classical Studies, editor. **Publications:** Mild Frenzy: A Reading of the Hellenistic Love Epigram, 1978; The Language of Virgil: An Introduction to the Poetry of the Aeneid, 1984, rev. ed., 1993; Who's Who in Wodehouse, 1987, rev. ed., 1989; How to Write an A Paper in an Emergency, rev. ed., 1987; The Student's Catullus, 1989, (ed.) 3rd ed., 2004; (ed.) Epodes and Odes, 1991; Sexual Culture in Ancient Greece, 2000; Andreas Vesalius' De humani corporis fabrica, 2012. **Address:** Department of Classics, Northwestern University, Kresge Hall 1-540, 1880 Campus Dr., Evanston, IL 60208-2200, U.S.A. **Online address:** d-garrison@northwestern.edu

GARRISON, David Lee. American (born United States), b. 1945. **Genres:** Literary Criticism And History, Translations, Poetry. **Career:** Landon School, Spanish teacher, 1968-71; Johns Hopkins University, graduate assistant, 1971-74; Indiana University, visiting professor, 1975-76; Washington College, visiting professor, 1977; University of Kansas, visiting professor, 1978-79; Wright State University, professor of Spanish and Portuguese, 1979-2009, professor emeritus, 2009-. Writer. **Publications:** CRITIC: Gongora and the Pyramus and This be Myth from Ovid to Shakespeare, 1994. EDITOR: (with T. Hermsen) O Taste and See: Food Poems, 1998. TRANSLATOR: A Bird of Paper: Poems of Vicente Aleixandre, 1982; Poems of Jose Bergamin (1895-1983): Echoes of a Distant Sea, 1991; Certain Chance: Poems of Pedro Salinas, 2000. POEMS: Inside the Sound of Rain, 1997; Sweeping the Cemetery: New and Selected Poems, 2007. **Address:** 206 E Dixon Ave., Dayton, OH 45419-3544, U.S.A. **Online address:** david.garrison@wright.edu

GARRISON, Deborah (Gottlieb). American (born United States), b. 1965. **Genres:** Poetry, Young Adult Fiction. **Career:** New Yorker, editorial staff, senior nonfiction editor, 1986-98; Alfred A. Knopf Inc., poetry editor; Pantheon Books, senior editor. **Publications:** A Working Girl Can't Win and Other Poems, 1998; The Second Child: Poems, 2007. Contributor to periodicals. **Address:** Random House Inc., 1745 Broadway, New York, NY 10019, U.S.A.

GARRISON, J. Ritchie. American (born United States), b. 1951. **Genres:** History, Homes/Gardens, Architecture, Cultural/Ethnic Topics. **Career:** Historic Deerfield Inc., director of education, 1976-85; University of Delaware, assistant professor of history, 1985-91, Office of Advanced Studies, associate professor, 1991-, associate director of museum studies program, Winterthur Program-American Material Culture, director, professor of history. **Publications:** (Ed. with B.L. Herman and B.M. Ward) After Ratification: Material Life in Delaware, 1789-1820, 1988; Landscape and Material Life in Franklin County, Massachusetts, 1770-1860, 1991; (ed. with A.S. Martin) American Material Culture: The Shape of the Field, 1997; Two Carpenters: Architecture and Building in Early New England, 1799-1859, 2006. **Address:** Department of History, University of Delaware, 203 Mechanical Hall, 46 W Delaware Ave., Newark, DE 19716-2547, U.S.A. **Online address:** jrg@udel.edu

GARRISON, Peter. See **GARDNER, Craig Shaw.**

GARRISON, Philip. American (born United States), b. 1942. **Genres:** Essays, Poetry, Novellas/Short Stories. **Career:** University of Texas, instructor, 1965-67; Central Washington University, Department of English, professor of English, 1967-2007, professor emeritus, 2007-; APOYO, co-founder and president, 1995-. Writer, translator and community activist. **Publications:** ESSAY COLLECTIONS: Augury, 1991; Waiting for the Earth to Turn Over, 1996; Because I Don't Have Wings: Stories of Mexican Immigrant Life, 2006. POETRY: The Deer Paintings, 1969; A Woman and Certain Women, 1971; Lipstick, 1974; Lime Tree Notes, 1975; (contrib.) Between Fire and Love: Contemporary Peruvian Writing, 1980; Away Awhile, 1985; (contrib.) Mexico: A Traveler's Literary Companion, 2006. OTHER: The Permit that Never Expires: Migrant Tales from the Ozark Hills and the Mexican Highlands, 2009. Contributor to periodicals. **Address:** Department of English, Central Washington University, 224 Hertz Hall, 400 E University Way, Ellensburg, WA 98926-7558, U.S.A. **Online address:** garrison@cwu.edu

GARROW, David J. American (born United States), b. 1953. **Genres:** Civil Liberties/Human Rights, Politics/Government, Race Relations. **Career:** Duke University, instructor, 1978-79; University of North Carolina, assistant professor of political science, 1980-84; City University of New York, College and the Graduate Center, associate professor, 1984-87, professor of political science, 1987-91; Virginia Center for Humanities, visiting fellow, 1991; Cooper Union, visiting distinguished professor of history, 1992-93; College of William and Mary, James Pinckney Harrison professor of history, 1994-95; American University, distinguished historian-in-residence, 1995-96; Emory University School of Law, Presidential distinguished professor, 1997-2005; Homerton College, University of Cambridge, senior research fellow, 2005-11; University of Pittsburgh School of Law, research professor of history and law, 2011-. Writer. **Publications:** Protest at Selma: Martin Luther King, Jr. and the Voting Rights Act of 1965, 1978; FBI and Martin Luther King, Jr.: From Solo: To Memphis, 1981; Bearing the Cross: Martin Luther King, Jr. and the Southern Christian Leadership Conference, 1986; Liberty and Sexuality: The Right to Privacy and the Making of Roe v. Wade, 1994. EDITOR: (and foreword) Montgomery Bus Boycott and the Women Started It: The Memoir of Jo Ann Gibson Robinson, 1987; Eyes on the Prize: Civil Rights Reader, 1987, rev. ed., 1991; (and intro.) Atlanta, Georgia, 1960-61: Sit-ins and Student Activism, 1989; (and intro.) Birmingham, Alabama, 1956-63: The Black Struggle for Civil Rights, 1989; (and intro.) Martin Luther King, Jr.: Civil Rights Leader, 1989; (and intro.) St. Augustine, Florida, 1963-64: Mass Protest and Racial Violence, 1989; (and intro.) Walking City: The Montgomery Bus Boycott, 1955-1956, 1989; (and intro.) We Shall Overcome: The Civil Rights Movement in the United States in the 1950s and 1960s, 1989; (and intro.) Chicago 1966: Open Housing Marches, Summit Negotiations and Operation Breadbasket, 1989; (and foreword and afterword with D.J. Hutchinson) Forgotten Memoir of John Knox: A Year in the Life of a Supreme Court Clerk in FDR's Washington, 2002. **Address:** University of Pittsburgh School of Law, 3900 Forbes Ave., Pittsburgh, PA 15260, U.S.A. **Online address:** garrow@pitt.edu

GARRY, Patrick M. American (born United States) **Genres:** Young Adult Fiction. **Career:** University of South Dakota, professor of law, 2003-; University of Utah, visiting professor, 2005; George Washington University, visiting professor, 2006, 2007. Writer. **Publications:** NONFICTION: The American Vision of a Free Press: An Historical and Constitutional Revisionist View of the Press as a Marketplace of Ideas, 1990; Liberalism and American Identity, 1992; An American Paradox: Censorship in a Nation of Free Speech, 1993; Scrambling for Protection: The New Media and the First Amendment, 1994; A Nation of Adversaries: How the Litigation Explosion is Reshaping America, 1997; Cultural Whiplash: The Unforeseen Consequences of America's Crusade against Racial Discrimination, 2006; Rediscovering a Lost Freedom: The First Amendment Right to Censor Unwanted Speech, 2006; Wrestling with God: The Courts' Tortuous Treatment of Religion, 2006; An Entrenched Legacy: How the New Deal Constitutional Revolution Continues to Shape the Role of the Supreme Court, 2008; Conservatism Redefined: A Creed for the Poor and Disadvantaged, 2010. FICTION: Suicidal Tendencies, 2006; In the Shadow of War, 2006; Saving Faith, 2007; Contagion, 2007; The Prisoner, 2007; A Bridge Back, 2008; A Bomb Shelter Romance, 2008; The Price of Guilt, 2011. **Address:** School of Law, University of South Dakota, 414 E Clark St., Vermillion, SD 57069, U.S.A. **Online address:** pgarry@usd.edu

GARTEN, Helen A. American (born United States), b. 1953. **Genres:** Money/Finance, Law, Business/Trade/Industry, Administration/Management. **Career:** Sullivan and Cromwell, lawyer, 1979-83; Debevoise and Plimpton, lawyer, 1983-84; Rutgers University, School of Law, faculty, 1984-, professor of law, 1990-; Harvard Law Review, editor. **Publications:** Why Bank Regulation Failed: Designing a Bank Regulatory Strategy for the 1990s, 1991; U.S. Financial Regulation and the Level Playing Field, 2001. Contributor to books and journals. **Address:** School of Law, Rutgers University, 123 Washington St., Newark, NJ 07102-3026, U.S.A. **Online address:** hgarten@kinoy.rutgers.edu

GARTEN, Jeffrey E. American (born United States), b. 1946. **Genres:** Business/Trade/Industry. **Career:** Blackstone Group, managing director; Lehman Brothers, managing director; U.S. Government, undersecretary of commerce for international trade, 1993-95; Yale University, School of Management, dean, 1995-2005, Juan Trippe professor in the practice of international trade, finance and business; Eliot Group, founder; Newsweek Intl., columnist. **Publications:** A Cold Peace: America, Japan, Germany, and the Struggle for Supremacy, 1992; (with R.H. Brown) U.S. Industrial Outlook 1994: Forecasts for Selected Manufacturing and Service Industries, 1994; The Big Ten: The

Big Emerging Markets and How They Will Change Our Lives, 1997; (ed. and intro.) World View: Global Strategies for the New Economy, 2000; The Mind of the CEO, 2001; The Politics of Fortune: A New Agenda for Business Leaders, 2002. Contributor to periodicals. **Address:** Yale School of Management, Yale University, 135 Prospect St., PO Box 208200, New Haven, CT 06511-3729, U.S.A. **Online address:** jeffrey.garten@yale.edu

GARTHOFF, Raymond L(eonard). American/Egyptian (born Egypt), b. 1929. **Genres:** History, International Relations/Current Affairs, Military/Defense/Arms Control, Autobiography/Memoirs, Young Adult Non-fiction, Politics/Government. **Career:** RAND Corp. (non-profit research), Social Science Division, soviet affairs analyst, 1950-57; U.S. Department of the Army, foreign affairs adviser, 1957-61; U.S. Department of State, Soviet Bloc Political-Military Affairs, special assistant, 1961-67; U.S. Mission to NATO, counselor, 1968-70, U.S. SALT Delegation, senior state department adviser, 1969-72, Bureau of Political-Military Affairs, deputy director, 1970-73, senior foreign service inspector, 1974-77, U.S. ambassador to Bulgaria, 1977-79; Brookings Institution, senior fellow, 1980-94; George Washington University, Institute for Sino-Soviet Studies, professorial lecturer, 1963-64; Johns Hopkins University, School for Advanced International Studies, professorial lecturer, 1963-67. Writer. **Publications:** Soviet Military Doctrine, 1953; How Russia Makes War, 1954; Significant Features of Soviet Military Doctrine, 1954; Soviet Strategy in the Nuclear Age, 1958, rev. ed., 1962; The Soviet Image of Future War, 1959; Soviet Military Policy: A Historical Analysis, 1966; Perspectives on the Strategic Balance: A Staff Paper, 1983; Intelligence Assessment and Policymaking: A Decision Point in the Kennedy Administration: A Staff Paper, 1984; Détente and Confrontation: American-Soviet Relations from Nixon to Reagan, 1985, rev. ed., 1994; Policy versus the Law: The Reinterpretation of the ABM Treaty, 1987; Reflections on the Cuban Missile Crisis, 1987, rev. ed., 1989; Deterrence and the Revolution in Soviet Military Doctrine, 1990; Assessing the Adversary: Estimates by the Eisenhower Administration of Soviet Intentions and Capabilities, 1991; The Great Transition: American-Soviet Relations and the End of the Cold War, 1994; A Journey through the Cold War: A Memoir of Containment and Coexistence, 2001; Svidetelstva za studenata voĭna: poslanikŭt na SASHT Reĭmŭnd Gartkhof za bŭlgaro-amerikanskite otnosheniia: nepublikuvani spomeni i dokumenti, 2002; (foreword) First Domino, 2004. EDITOR: (and trans.) G. Pokrovsky, Science and Technology in Contemporary War, 1959; (and trans.) V.D. Sokolovsky, Military Strategy, 1963; Sino-Soviet Military Relations, 1966. Contributor to journals. **Address:** 2128 Bancroft Pl. NW, Washington, DC 20008-4020, U.S.A.

GARTNER, Scott Sigmund. American (born United States), b. 1963. **Genres:** History, Military/Defense/Arms Control. **Career:** The Georgia Bureau of Investigation, intern, 1985; The Federal Bureau of Investigation, honors intern, 1986; The National Institute of Justice, Social Science Program, specialist in drugs, alcohol and crime section, 1987; University of California-Davis, Department of Political Science, acting assistant professor, 1991-92, assistant professor, 1992-97, associate professor, 1997-2007, professor of political science, 2007-, International Relations Program, director, 2009-; University of California-San Diego, visiting research fellow, 1995-97; University of Illinois, lecturer, 1997; Stanford University, lecturer, 1998; The University of Iowa, visiting associate professor, 2002; University of Canterbury, visiting associate professor, 2003. Writer. **Publications:** Strategic Assessment in War, 1997, rev. ed., 1999; (co-author) Historical Statistics of the United States, 2006; (ed. with J. Bercovitch) International Conflict Mediation: New Approaches and Findings, 2009. Contributor of articles to periodicals. **Address:** Department of Political Science, University of California, 682 Kerr Hall, 1 Shields Ave., Davis, CA 95616-8682, U.S.A. **Online address:** ssgartner@ucdavis.edu

GARTON ASH, Timothy. (Timothy John Garton Ash). American/British (born England), b. 1955. **Genres:** History, International Relations/Current Affairs, Politics/Government, Autobiography/Memoirs, Essays. **Career:** Woodrow Wilson International Center for Scholars, fellow, 1986-87; University of Oxford, professor; Saint Antony's College, fellow, 1990-, professor of European Studies, European Studies Centre, director, 2001-06, Isaiah Berlin professorial fellow; Hoover Institution, faculty, senior fellow, 2000; Royal Society of Literature, fellow; Royal Historical Society, fellow; Royal Society of Arts, fellow; Berlin-Brandenburg Academy of Sciences, corresponding fellow; Times, editorial writer of central European affairs; Spectator, foreign editor; Independent, columnist. **Publications:** The Polish Revolution: Solidarity, 1983; The Uses of Adversity: Essays on the Fate of Central Europe, 1989; The

Magic Lantern: The Revolution of '89 Witnessed in Warsaw, Budapest, Berlin and Prague, 1990 in UK as We the People, 1990; In Europe's Name: Germany and the Divided Continent, 1993; (ed.) Freedom for Publishing, Publishing for Freedom: The Central and East European Publishing Project, 1995; The File: A Personal History, 1997; History of the Present: Essays, Sketches and Despatches from Europe in the 1990s, 2000; Wächst zusammen, was zusammengehört?, 2001; Free World: America, Europe and the Surprising Future of the West, 2004; Facts Are Subversive: Political Writing from a Decade Without a Name, 2009; (ed. with A. Roberts) Civil Resistance and Power Politics: The Experience of Non-Violent Action from Gandhi to the Present, 2009. **Address:** c/o George Borchardt, 136 East 57th St., New York, NY 10022, U.S.A.

GARTON ASH, Timothy John. *See* **GARTON ASH, Timothy.**

GARVER, John W. American (born United States), b. 1946. **Genres:** History, Military/Defense/Arms Control. **Career:** U.S. Army, staff, 1969-70; University of Colorado, teaching assistant, 1973-75; University of Maryland, Overseas Program, instructor, 1977; Oakland University, instructor, 1979-80; University of Nevada, assistant professor, 1981-92; Inter-University Program, language and research fellow, 1982-83; Lindblad Travel Co., sinologist, 1983; Pomona College, liaison representative, 1983; Eastern Michigan University, lecturer, 1984-85; Georgia Institute of Technology, School of Social Sciences, assistant professor, 1985-90, Sam Nunn School of International Affairs, associate professor, 1990-93, professor, 1993-, director of program for East Asia study abroad. Writer. **Publications:** China's Decision for Rapprochement with the United States, 1968-1971, 1982; Chinese-Soviet Relations, 1937-1945: The Diplomacy of Chinese Nationalism, 1988; Foreign Relations of the People's Republic of China, 1993; Face Off: China, the United States, and Taiwan's Democratization, 1997; The Sino-American Alliance: Nationalist China and American Cold War Strategy in Asia, 1997; Protracted Contest: Sino-Indian Rivalry in the Twentieth Century, 2001; China and Iran: Ancient Partners in a Post-imperial World, 2006; (with J.B. Alterman) The Vital Triangle: China, the United States, and the Middle East, 2008; China's Anti-encirclement Struggle, 2010; (ed. with R. Ash and P.B. Prime) Taiwan's Democracy: Economic and Political Challenges, 2011. **Address:** Sam Nunn School of International Affairs, Georgia Institute of Technology, Rm. 140, 781 Marietta St. NW, Atlanta, GA 30332-0610, U.S.A. **Online address:** john.garver@inta.gatech.edu

GARVER, Newton. American (born United States), b. 1928. **Genres:** Philosophy, Literary Criticism And History, Social Sciences. **Career:** National College of Choueifat, senior English master, 1954-56; Cornell University, instructor, 1956-57; University of Minnesota, instructor, 1958-61; State University of New York, lecturer, 1961-66, associate professor, 1966-71, professor of philosophy, 1971-91, distinguished service professor, 1991-, now professor emeritus distinguished service; Oakwood School, president, 1973-75, 1977-79; Alternatives to Violence Project, vice-president, 1992-93. Writer. **Publications:** Jesus, Jefferson and the Task of Friends, 1983; (intro. and ed. with P.H. Hare) Naturalism and Rationality, 1986; (ed. with J.B. Brady) Justice, Law and Violence, 1991; (with S.C. Lee) Derrida and Wittgenstein, 1994; This Complicated Form of Life: Essays on Wittgenstein, 1994; (with E.H. Reitan) Nonviolence and Community: Reflections on the Alternatives to Violence Project, 1995; Wittgenstein and Approaches to Clarity, 2006; Limits to Power: Some Friendly Reminders, 2006. **Address:** Department of Philosophy, State University of New York, 135 Park Hall, Buffalo, NY 14260-4150, U.S.A. **Online address:** garver@acsu.buffalo.edu

GARVEY, John H. American (born United States), b. 1948. **Genres:** Law. **Career:** Morrison & Foerster, litigation associate, 1975-76; University of Kentucky, Wendell Cherry professor of law, 1976-94, university research professor, 1989-90; U.S. Department of Justice, assistant, 1981-84; University of Michigan, visiting professor, 1985-86; University of Notre Dame, professor of law, 1994-99; Boston College Law School, acting dean, dean, 1998-2010, director of public affairs; The Catholic University of America, president, 2010-. Writer. **Publications:** (Ed. with T.A. Aleinikoff) Modern Constitutional Theory: A Reader, 1989, 5th ed., 2004; (ed. with F.F. Schauer) The First Amendment: A Reader, 1992, 2nd ed., 1996; What Are Freedoms For?, 1996; (with M.W. McConnell and T.C. Berg) Religion and the Constitution, 2002, 3rd ed., 2011; (ed. with L.S. Cahill and T.F. Kennedy) Sexuality and the U.S. Catholic Church: Crisis and Renewal, 2006. **Address:** Boston College Law School, M305, Stuart House, 885 Centre St., Newton, MA 02459, U.S.A. **Online address:** john.garvey.1@bc.edu

GARWOOD, Julie. (Emily Chase). American (born United States), b. 1946. Genres: Mystery/Crime/Suspense, Romance/Historical, Young Adult Fiction, Novels, Novellas/Short Stories, History, Horror. Career: Writer. Publications: HISTORICAL ROMANCE NOVELS: Gentle Warrior, 1985; Rebellious Desire, 1986; Honor's Splendor, 1987; The Lion's Lady, 1988; The Bride, 1989; Guardian Angel, 1990; The Gift, 1991; The Prize, 1991; The Secret, 1992; Castles, 1993; Saving Grace, 1993; Prince Charming, 1994; For the Roses, 1995; The Wedding, 1996; Come the Spring, 1997; The Clayborne Brides, 1997; Ransom, 1999; Shadow Music: A Novel, 2007; Fire and Ice, 2008; Sizzle: A Novel, 2009; The Ideal Man, 2011. CLAYBORNES' BRIDES: One Pink Rose, 1997; One White Rose, 1997; One Red Rose, 1997. CONTEMPORARY SUSPENSE NOVELS: Heartbreaker, 2000; Mercy, 2001; Killjoy, 2002; Murder List, 2004; Slow Burn: A Novel, 2005; Shadow Dance: A Novel, 2007. FOR YOUNG ADULTS: A Girl Named Summer, 1986; (as Emily Chase) What's a Girl to Do, 1985. Address: PO Box 7574, Leawood, KS 66211, U.S.A.

GASAWAY, Laura N. American (born United States), b. 1945. Genres: Law, Librarianship. Career: University of Houston, law librarian, assistant professor of law, 1973-75; University of Oklahoma, director, professor of law, 1975-84; University of North Carolina, director, professor of law, 1985-2006, associate dean for academic affairs, 2006-10, professor of law, 2010-. Writer. Publications: (With J.L. Hoover and D.M. Warden) American Indian Legal Materials: A Union List, 1980; (with M. Murphy) Legal Protection for Computer Programs, 1980; Equal Pay for Equal Work: Women in Special Libraries, 1981; (with B.S. Johnson and J.M. Murray) Law Library Management During Fiscal Austerity, 1992; (with S.K. Winant) Librarians and Copyright: A Guide to Copyright in the 1990s, 1994; (ed. with M.G. Chiorazzi) Law Librarianship: Historical Perspectives, 1996; Growing Pains: Adapting Copyright to Libraries, Education, and Society, 1997; Get Copyright Right: The Best of Copyright Corner From Sla's Information Outlook, 2006. Address: 24 Brown Bear, Chapel Hill, NC 27517, U.S.A. Online address: laura_gasaway@unc.edu

GASCHNITZ, Michael K. Canadian (born Canada) Genres: Sports/Fitness, History, Biography. Career: Writer. Publications: Professional Sports Statistics: A North American Team-by-team and Major Non-team Events, Year-by-Year Reference, 1876 through 1996, 1997; The Edmonton Oilers, 2002; Statistical Encyclopedia of North American Professional Sports: All Major League Teams and Major Non-team Events Year by Year, 1876 through 2006, 2008. Address: 59 Westview Cres., Spruce Grove, AB T7X 1K9, Canada.

GASCOIGNE, Bamber. British (born England), b. 1935. Genres: Novels, History, Literary Criticism And History, Theatre, Art/Art History. Career: Spectator, drama critic, 1961-63; Observer, drama critic, 1963-64; Granada TV, University Challenge, chairman, 1962-87; BBC2-TV, presenter, 1988-89; Historyworld, chairman. Writer. Publications: Twentieth Century Drama, 1962; World Theatre, 1968; The Great Moghuls, 1971; Murgatreud's Empire, 1972; Treasures and Dynasties of China, 1973; The Heyday, 1973; Ticker Khan, 1974; (intro.) Castles of Britain, 1975; The Christians, 1977; Images of Richmond, 1978; Images of Twickenham, 1981; Why the Rope Went Tight, 1981; Fearless Freddie's Magic Wish (and Sunken Treasure), 1982; Quest for the Golden Hare, 1983; Cod Streuth, 1987; How to Identify Prints, 1986, 2nd ed., 2004; Encyclopedia of Britain, 1993; Milestones in Colour Printing, 1997; World History: A Narrative Encyclopedia (e-book), 2001; Brief History of the Great Moghuls, 2002; Christianity: A History, 2003; Dynasties of China: A History, 2003. Address: 1 St. Helena Terr., Friars Ln., Richmond, TW9 1NR, England. Online address: bamber@historyworld.net

GASCOIGNE, John. Australian/British (born England), b. 1951. Genres: Education, History, Theology/Religion, Philosophy, Politics/Government, Cultural/Ethnic Topics, Biography. Career: University of Papua New Guinea, lecturer in history, 1977-78; University of New South Wales, School of History and Philosophy, tutor, 1980-84, lecturer, 1984-89, senior lecturer in history, 1989-96, associate professor, 1996-2002, Scientia professor, 2002-. Writer. Publications: Cambridge in the Age of the Enlightenment: Science, Religion and Politics from the Restoration to the French Revolution, 1989; Joseph Banks and the English Enlightenment: Useful Knowledge and Polite Culture, 1994; Science in the Service of Empire: Joseph Banks, the British State and the Uses of Science in the Age of Revolution, 1998; Science, Politics and Universities of Europe, 1600-1800, 1998; The Enlightenment and the Origins of European Australia, 2002; Captain Cook: Voyager between Worlds, 2007; Science, Philosophy and Religion in the Age of the Enlighten-

ment: British and Global Contexts, 2010; (ed. with H.M. Carey) Church and State in Old and New Worlds, 2011. Address: School of History and Philosophy, University of New South Wales, Rm. 368, Morven Brown Bldg., Sydney, NW 2052, Australia. Online address: j.gascoigne@unsw.edu.au

GASH, Jonathan. Also writes as Graham Gaunt. British (born England), b. 1933. Genres: Mystery/Crime/Suspense, Young Adult Fiction, Novels. Career: University of Hong Kong, Division of Clinical Pathology, lecturer and head, 1965-68; University of London, Faculty of Medicine, microbiologist and head of bacteriology, 1971-88; physician and consultant on infectious diseases, 1988-. Writer. Publications: Member of Parliament, 1974; Terminus, 1976; The Judas Pair, 1977; Gold by Gemini, 1978; The Grail Tree, 1979; Spend Game, 1981; The Vatican Rip: A Lovejoy Narrative, 1981; (as Graham Gaunt) The Incomer, 1981; The Sleepers of Erin: A Lovejoy Novel of Suspense, 1983; The Gondola Scam, 1984; Firefly Gadroon: A Lovejoy Novel of Suspense, 1984; Pearlhanger, 1985; Tartan Sell, 1986; Tartan Ringers: A Lovejoy Narrative, 1986; Moonspender: A Lovejoy Novel of Suspense, 1987; Jade Woman, 1989; The Very Last Gambado, 1990; The Great California Game, 1991; The Lies of Fair Ladies, 1991; Paid and Loving Eyes, 1993; Paid in Loving Eyes, 1992; The Sin Within Her Smile, 1994; The Grace in Older Women, 1995; The Possessions of a Lady, 1996; Different Women Dancing, 1997; The Rich and the Profane: A Lovejoy Novel, 1998; Prey Dancing: A Dr. Clare Burtonall Mystery, 1998; A Rag, A Bone and A Hank of Hair: The Twenty-First Lovejoy Novel, 2000; Die Dancing, 2000; Every Last Cent, 2001; Bone Dancing, 2002; Ten Word Game, 2004; The Year of the Woman, 2004; Finding Davey, 2005; Blood Dancing, 2006; Bad Girl Magdalene, 2007; Faces in the Pool: A Lovejoy Mystery, 2009. Address: Silver Willows, Chapel Ln., W. Bergholt, Colchester, EX CO6 3EF, England.

GASKELL, Ivan. (Ivan George Alexander De Wend Gaskell). American/British (born England), b. 1955. Genres: Art/Art History, History, Politics/Government. Career: University of London, Warburg Institute, research fellow and academic curatorial assistant, 1980-83; Cambridge University, Wolfson College, Speelman Fellow and faculty of architecture and history of art, 1983-91, Cambridge Studies in Philosophy and Arts, editor, 1988-2000; Thyssen-Bornemisza Foundation, consultant, 1987-91; Cambridge Darkroom Gallery, chair, 1989-91; Harvard University, Fogg Art Museum, curator of paintings and sculpture, 1991-, Harvard Art Museum, Margaret S. Winthrop curator, senior lecturer of fine arts, 1991-2002, senior lecturer on history, 2002-; Yishushi Yanjiu, editor, 2000-; Journal of the History of Ideas, editor, 1997-2006. Writer. Publications: Seventeenth Century Dutch and Flemish Painting, 1990; (ed. with S. Kemal) Language of Art History, 1991; Offbeat Collection of Dutch and Flemish Paintings, 1993; (ed. with S. Kemal) Landscape, Natural Beauty and the Arts, 1993; (ed. with S. Kemal) Explanation and Value in the Arts, 1993; (ed.) Canopy: A Work for Voice and Light in Harvard Yard, 1997; (ed. with S. Kemal and D.W. Conway) Nietzsche, Philosophy and the Arts, 1998; (with M. Jonker) Vermeer Studies, 1998; (ed. with H. Lie) Sketches in Clay for Projects by Gian Lorenzo Bernini: Theoretical, Technical and Case Studies, 1999; (ed. with S. Kemal) Performance and Authenticity in the Arts, 1999; (ed. with S. Kemal) Politics and Aesthetics in the Arts, 2000; Vermeer's Wager: Speculations on Art History, Theory and Art Museums, 2000. Contributor to journals. Address: Department of History, Harvard University, Rm. L-25, Robinson Hall, 35 Quincy St., Cambridge, MA 02138, U.S.A. Online address: ivan_gaskell@harvard.edu

GASKELL, Ivan George Alexander De Wend. See GASKELL, Ivan.

GASKELL, Jane. British (born England), b. 1941. Genres: Novels. Career: Daily Express, feature writer; Daily Mail, feature writer, 1965-84. Publications: Strange Evil, 1957; King's Daughter, 1958; Attic Summer, 1958, new ed., 1969; The Serpent, 1963; The Shiny Narrow Grin, 1964; The Fabulous Heroine, 1965; Atlan, 1965; The City, 1966; All Neat in Black Stockings, 1966; A Sweet Sweet Summer, 1969; Summer Coming, 1972; Some Summer Lands, 1977; The Dragon, 1977; Sun Bubble, 1990; Secondary Schools in Canada: The National Report of the Exemplary Schools Project, 1995. Address: The Sharland Organisation Ltd., The Manor House, Manor St., Raunds, NH NN9 6JW, England.

GASKELL, Whitney. (Piper Banks). American (born United States), b. 1972?. Genres: Novels. Career: Writer and lawyer. Publications: NOVELS: Pushing 30, 2003; True Love (and Other Lies), 2004; She, Myself & I, 2005; Testing Kate, 2006; Mommy Tracked, 2007; Good Luck, 2008. YOUNG ADULT

NOVELS AS PIPER BANKS: Geek High, 2007; Geek Abroad, 2008. **Address:** Stuart, FL , U.S.A. **Online address:** whitney@whitneygaskell.com

GASKILL, Malcolm. British (born England), b. 1967?. **Genres:** Novels, Young Adult Non-fiction. **Career:** Keele University, lecturer, 1993-94; Queen's University, lecturer, 1994-95; Anglia Ruskin University, lecturer, 1995-99; University of Cambridge, Churchill College, lecturer, fellow and director of studies in history, 1999; University of East Angelia, reader in early modern history, professor; Royal Historical Society, fellow. Writer. **Publications:** NONFICTION: Reporting Murder: Fiction in the Archives in Early Modern England, 1998; Crime and Mentalities in Early Modern England, 2000; Hellish Nell: The Last of Britain's Witches, 2001; Witchfinders: A Seventeenth-Century English Tragedy, 2005; Witchcraft: A Very Short Introduction, 2010. OTHER: The Matthew Hopkins Trials, 2003. **Address:** School Of History, University of East Anglia, 4.26, Arts Bldg., Norwich, NF NR4 7TJ, England. **Online address:** m.gaskill@uea.ac.uk

GASKIN, J. C. A. (John Charles Addison Gaskin). Irish/British (born England), b. 1936. **Genres:** Novellas/Short Stories, Classics, Philosophy, Mystery/Crime/Suspense, Theology/Religion. **Career:** Royal Bank of Scotland, accountant, 1960-62; University of Dublin, Trinity College, lecturer, 1965-78, fellow, 1978-, professor of philosophy, 1982-94, professor of naturalistic philosophy, 1994-98, Department of Philosophy, head, 1995-98; Hatfield College, tutor, 1997-. Writer. **Publications:** Hume's Philosophy of Religion, 1978, rev. ed., 1988; The Quest for Eternity: An Outline of the Philosophy of Religion, 1984; (ed.) Varieties of Unbelief from Epicurus to Sartre, 1989; (ed.) The Epicurean Philosophers, 1994; (ed. and intro.) The Elements of Law, Natural and Politic: vol. I, Human Nature, vol. II, De corpore politico: With Three Lives, 1994; (ed. and intro.) Leviathan, 1996; (ed. and intro.) Principal Writings on Religion Including Dialogues Concerning Natural Religion, 1998; The Dark Companion, Ghost Stories, 2001; Principle Writings on Religion, Including Dialogues Concerning Natural Religion and the Natural History of Religion, 2008. **Address:** Department of Philosophy, Trinity College, University of Dublin, Dublin, 2, Ireland.

GASKIN, John Charles Addison. See GASKIN, J. C. A.

GASKINS, Richard H. American (born United States), b. 1946. **Genres:** Environmental Sciences/Ecology, Law, Sciences. **Career:** Bryn Mawr College, associate professor and dean of social work, 1975-87; University of Chicago, associate professor, 1987-91; New School for Social Research, associate dean of graduate faculty, 1992-94; Brandeis University, professor of legal studies, 1994-, Joseph M. Proskauer professor of law and social welfare, director of legal studies program, Proskauer chair in law and social welfare. Writer. **Publications:** Environmental Accidents: Personal Injury and Public Responsibility, 1989; Burdens of Proof in Modern Discourse, 1992. **Address:** Department on American Studies, Brandeis University, Brown 313, 415 S St., Waltham, MA 02453, U.S.A. **Online address:** gaskins@brandeis.edu

GASS, Thomas Edward. American (born United States) **Genres:** Politics/Government, Medicine/Health, Sciences. **Career:** Educator and writer. **Publications:** Nobody's Home: Candid Reflections of a Nursing Home Aide, 2004. Contributor to periodicals. **Address:** Cornell University Press, 512 E State St., Ithaca, NY 14850, U.S.A.

GASS, William (Howard). American (born United States), b. 1924. **Genres:** Novels, Literary Criticism And History, Novellas/Short Stories, Essays, Young Adult Non-fiction, Young Adult Fiction. **Career:** College of Wooster, instructor in philosophy, 1950-54; Purdue University, assistant professor, 1954-60, associate professor, 1960-66, professor of philosophy, 1966-69; University of Illinois, visiting lecturer in English and philosophy, 1958-59; Washington University, professor of philosophy, 1969-78, David May distinguished university professor in the humanities, 1979-99, David May distinguished university professor emeritus, 2000-, International Writers Center, founder and director, 1990-2000. Writer. **Publications:** FICTION: Omensetter's Luck: A Novel, 1966; In the Heart of the Heart of the Country and Other Stories, 1968; Willie Masters' Lonesome Wife, 1968; The First Winter of My Married Life, 1979; Culp, 1985; The Tunnel, 1995; Cartesian Sonata and Other Novellas, 1998. NON-FICTION: Fiction and Figures of Life, 1970; (intro.) The Geographical History of America, 1973; On Being Blue: A Philosophical Inquiry, 1975; The World Within the Word: Essays, 1978; (with P. Eisenman) Peter Eisenman's House VI: The Client's Response, 1980; The Habitations of the Word: Essays, 1985; Words about the Nature of Things,

1985; A Temple of Texts: Fifty Literary Pillars: An Exhibition to Inaugurate the International Writers Center, 1991; Finding A Form: Essays, 1996; (contrib.) Catherine Wagner: Art and Science, Investigating Matter, 1996; (contrib.) Sabina Ott: Everywhere There is Somewhere, November 7, 1997 - January 3, 1998, 1997; (contrib.) The Dual Muse: The Writer as Artist, The Artist as Writer, 1997; Reading Rilke: Reflections On The Problems Of Translation, 1999; (with N. Lebowitz and G. Early) 3 Essays: Reflections On the American Century, 2000; A Defense of the Book, 2001; Tests of Time, 2002; (afterword) Praise of Folly, 2003. EDITOR: (with L. Cuoco) The Writer in Politics, 1996; The (with L. Cuoco) Writer and Religion, 2000; (with L. Cuoco) Literary St. Louis: A Guide, 2000. OTHERS: (intro.) The Anatomy of Melancholy, 2001; Conversations with William H. Gass, 2003; Life Sentences, 2012; Middle C, forthcoming. Contributor to periodicals. **Address:** International Creative Management, 730 5th Ave., New York, NY 10019, U.S.A. **Online address:** iwl@artsci.wustl.edu

GASSENHEIMER, Linda. American (born United States), b. 1942. **Genres:** Food And Wine, Medicine/Health. **Career:** CuisinEase, founder and manager, 1977-86; Gardner's Markets, executive director for food and public relations, 1987-. Writer. **Publications:** French Cuisine, 1984; Simply Sauces, 1984; Keys Cuisine: Flavors of the Florida Keys, 1992; Dinner in Minutes, 1993; Vegetarian Dinner in Minutes: 75 Recipes for Quick and Easy Everyday Meals, 1997; Low-Carb Meals in Minutes, 2000; More Low-Carb Meals in Minutes: A Three-Stage Plan for Keeping It Off, 2003; Mix 'n Match Meals in Minutes for People with Diabetes, 2003, 2nd ed., 2007; Good-Carb Meals in Minutes: A Three-Stage Plan to Permanent Weight Loss, 2005; Good-Carb Diet for Life, 2005; Prevention's Fit and Fast Meals in Minutes, 2006; The Portion Plan: How to Eat the Foods You Love & Still Lose Weight, 2007; The Flavors of the Florida Keys, 2010; Fast and Flavorful, 2011. **Address:** Miami Herald, 1 Herald Plz., Miami, FL 33134, U.S.A. **Online address:** linda@dinnerinminutes.com

GASSER, Urs. Swiss (born Switzerland), b. 1972. **Genres:** Information Science/Computers, Technology. **Career:** TEAG Advisors Ltd., part-time legal advisor, 1996-99; Webopera GmbH, part-time legal counsel, 1996-99; University of St. Gallen, Institute for European, Business and Comparative Law, research assistant, 1996-2000, assistant and dean of the law faculty, 1998, Research Center for Information Law, executive manager, 2001-05, associate professor of law, faculty director, 2006-; Law Office of Gründler and Nef, intern, 2001, associate, 2002; Harvard Law School, visiting researcher, 2003-04; Principles on Free Expression and Privacy Initiative, advisor, 2007-; Gruter Institute for Law and Behavioral Research, research fellow, 2008-; U.S. Internet Safety Technical Task Force, advisor, 2008-; Harvard University, Berkman Center for Internet and Society, executive director, 2009-. Writer. **Publications:** (Co-author) Informationsrecht in e-Umgebungen, 2002; (with J. Palfrey) Born Digital: Understanding the First Generation of Digital Natives, 2008. Works appear in anthologies. Contributor to periodicals. **Address:** Research Center for Information Law, University of St. Gallen, Bodanstrasse 1, St. Gallen, CH-9000, Switzerland. **Online address:** ugasser@cyber.law.harvard.edu

GASTIL, John (Webster). American (born United States), b. 1967. **Genres:** Politics/Government, Social Sciences. **Career:** University of New Mexico, Institute for Public Policy, research manager, 1994-97; University of Washington, School of Communication, adjunct professor, 1998-2002, Department of Political Science, adjunct professor, 1999-, Department of Speech Communication, assistant professor, 1998-2001, associate professor, 2001-07, associate chair, 2006-08, professor, 2007-11; Penn State University, Department of Communication Arts and Sciences, professor and head, 2011-. Writer. **Publications:** Democracy in Small Groups: Participation, Decision Making, and Communication, 1993; By Popular Demand: Revitalizing Representative Democracy Through Deliberative Elections, 2000; (ed. with P. Levine) The Deliberative Democracy Handbook: Strategies for Effective Civic Engagement in the Twenty-first Century, 2005; Political Communication and Deliberation, 2008; Group in Society, 2009; (co-author) The Jury and Democracy: How Jury Deliberation Promotes Civic Engagement and Political Participation, 2010. **Address:** Department of Communication Arts and Sciences, Penn State University, 240H Sparks Bldg., 417 Old Main, University Park, PA 16802, U.S.A. **Online address:** jgastil@psu.edu

GASTON, Diane. Also writes as Diane Perkins. American (born United States), b. 1948. **Genres:** Novels, Romance/Historical, Young Adult Fiction. **Career:** Novelist and mental health therapist. **Publications:** The Mysterious Miss M, 2004; (as Diane Perkins) The Improper Wife, 2004; (as Diane Perkins) The Marriage Bargain, 2005; A Reputable Rake, 2006; The Wagering Widow, 2006; (with E. Rolls and D. Hale) Mistletoe Kisses, 2006; Innocence and Impropriety, 2007; The Vanishing Viscountess, 2007; Scandalizing The Ton, 2008; (with D. Marlowe and A. McCabe) Diamonds Of Welbourne Manor, 2009; (contrib.) Pleasurably Undone!, 2010; Valiant Soldier, Beautiful Enemy, 2011; Three Soldiers: Gallant Officer, Forbidden Lady, 2009; Chivalrous Captain, Rebel Mistress, 2011; Regency Improprieties, 2011. **Address:** PO Box 523131, Springfield, VA 22152, U.S.A. **Online address:** diane@dianegaston.com

GASTON, Patricia S. American (born United States), b. 1946. **Genres:** Poetry, Literary Criticism And History. **Career:** Jefferson State Junior College, instructor in English department, 1972-75; Lawson State Community College, instructor, 1975-76; Jefferson County Community Schools, site coordinator, 1976-77; Stetson University, instructor, 1984-86; University of Florida, instructor, 1986-87; Santa Fe Community College, adjunct, 1986-87; Auburn University, instructor in English department, 1987-92, editor of English department newsletter, 1989-92; West Virginia University, Department of English, assistant professor, professor, 1992-. **Publications:** Prefacing the Waverly Prefaces: A Reading of Sir Walter Scott, 1992. Contributor to books and periodicals. **Address:** Department of English, West Virginia University, 300 Campus Dr., Parkersburg, WV 26104, U.S.A. **Online address:** patricia.gaston@mail.wvu.edu

GAT, Azar. Israeli (born Israel), b. 1959. **Genres:** Military/Defense/Arms Control, Politics/Government, History. **Career:** Tel Aviv University, Department of Political Science, lecturer, 1987-91, senior lecturer, 1991-, chair, 1999-2003, Executive Master's Program in Diplomacy and Security, founder and head; Ohio State University, Mershon Center for International Security Studies, visiting fellow; Georgetown University, Goldman visiting Israeli professor; Stanford University, Hoover Institution, Koret distinguished Israeli fellow; University of Freiburg, Alexander Von Humboldt fellow. Writer. **Publications:** The Origins of Military Thought from the Enlightenment to Clausewitz, 1989; The Development of Military Thought: The Nineteenth Century, 1992; Fascist and Liberal Visions of War: Fuller, Liddell Hart, Douhet and Other Modernists, 1998; British Armour Theory and the Rise of the Panzer Arm: Revising the Revisionists, 2000; Meorot ha-maashavah ha-tsevaitha-modernit, 2000; A History of Military Thought: From the Enlightenment to the Cold War, 2001; (ed. with Z. Maoz) War in a Changing World, 2001; Hitpatut ha-maashavah ha-tsevait ba-meah ha-esrim: Fuler, Lidle Har, Dueh i-modernisim aerim, 2002; War in Human Civilization, 2006; Victorious and Vulnerable: Why Democracy Won in the 20th Century and how It is Still Imperiled, 2009. **Address:** Department of Political Science, Tel Aviv University, Rm. 507, Ramat Aviv, Ste. 507, Tel Aviv, 69978, Israel. **Online address:** azargat@post.tau.ac.il

GATCH, Milton McC. American (born United States), b. 1932. **Genres:** Librarianship, Literary Criticism And History, Theology/Religion. **Career:** Wooster School, master in Latin and acting chaplain, 1963-64; Shimer College, chaplain, 1964-66, chairman of humanities faculty, 1966-67; Northern Illinois University, associate professor of English and acting director of graduate studies, 1967-68; University of Missouri, associate professor, professor of English, 1968-78, chairman of department, 1971-75; Union Theological Seminary, professor of church history, 1978-98, academic dean, 1978-90, provost, 1986-90, professor emeritus, 1998-, Burke Library, director, 1991-98; Columbia University, adjunct professor of religion, 1982-98. Writer and photographer. **Publications:** Death: Meaning and Mortality in Christian Thought and Contemporary Culture, 1969; Loyalties and Traditions: Man and His World in Old English Literature, 1971; Preaching and Theology in Anglo-Saxon England: Aelfric and Wulfstan, 1977; (ed. with C.T. Berkhout) Anglo-Saxon Scholarship: The First Three Centuries, 1982; Eschatology and Christian Nurture (collected essays), 2000; The Yeats Family and the Book, Circa 1900: Catalogue of an Exhibition at the Grolier Club, 2000; The Library of Leander van Ess and the Earliest American Collections of Reformation Pamphlets, 2007. FORTHCOMING: The Social and Documentary History of Indulgences in the Fifteenth and Sixteenth Centuries; Sammlung und Verzeichniss: Catalogue of Manuscripts, 1823, Sold by Leander van Ess to Sir Thomas Phillipps; Philip Gatch (1751-1834) and Gatch Family History. Contributor of articles to journals. **Address:** 105 E 29th St., New York, NY 10016, U.S.A. **Online address:** mac@miltongatch.us

GATELEY, Edwina. British (born England), b. 1943. **Genres:** Novels, inspirational/Motivational Literature, Theology/Religion, History. **Career:** Missionary worker, 1964-68; Volunteer Missionary Movement, founder, 1969-; Genesis House, founder, 1983. Writer and public speaker. **Publications:** OTHERS: I Hear a Seed Growing, 1990; A Warm, Moist, Salty God: Women Journeying towards Wisdom, 1993; God Goes on Vacation, 1994; There Was No Path, So I Trod One: Poems, 1996; Psalms of a Laywoman, 1998; God Goes to Church, 1999; Growing into God, 2000; (with J. Hammond-Clarke) Whispers: Conversations with Edwina Gateley, 2000; Soul Sisters: Women in Scripture Speak to Women Today, 2002; In God's Womb, 2009; (with S. Mattucci) Mothers, Sisters, Daughters, 2012. SELF-ILLUSTRATED: A Mystical Heart: 52 Weeks in the Presence of God, 1998; God Goes to School, 2009. **Address:** 229 Eagle Point Blvd., Erie, PA 16511, U.S.A. **Online address:** edwinagateley@aol.com

GATENBY, Greg. Canadian (born Canada), b. 1950. **Genres:** Poetry, Literary Criticism And History, Social Sciences, Geography, Young Adult Non-fiction. **Career:** McClelland & Stewart, editor, 1973-75; Harbourfront Reading Series, artistic director, 1975-; Harbourfront International Festival of Authors, founder and artistic director, 1980-; League of Canadian Poets, honorary lifetime member, 1991; PEN Canadian Centre, founding member, PEN World Congress, principal organizer; Writers Development Trust, director; Writers Union of Canada, member. **Publications:** Rondeaus for Erica, 1976; Adrienne's Blessing, 1976; The Brown Stealer, 1977; The Salmon Country, 1978; Growing Still, 1981; The Wild is Always There: Canada Through the Eyes of Foreign Writers, 1993; Toronto: A Literary Guide, 1999; Canada Through The Eyes Of Foreign Writers, forthcoming.; Belles Lettres: Famous Authors in Vintage Postcards, forthcoming; Spadina, forthcoming; Grandeur: Canadians And World War One, forthcoming; Illustrated Guide to the Canadians in WWI, forthcoming. EDITOR: 52 Pickup, 1976; Whale Sound: An Anthology of Poems About Whales and Dolphins, 1977; Contemporary Canadian Poets, 1980; Whales Art, 1981; Whales: A Celebration, 1983; The Definitive Notes, 1991; The Very Richness of That Past, 1995. Contributor to periodicals. **Address:** The Writers Union of Canada, 90 Richmond St. E, Ste. 200, Toronto, ON M5C 1P1, Canada.

GATES, Barbara T(imm). American (born United States), b. 1936. **Genres:** History, Intellectual History, Literary Criticism And History, Natural History, Illustrations, Psychology, Reference. **Career:** Widener College, lecturer in English, 1965-67; University of Delaware, assistant professor of English, 1971-76, associate professor of English, 1976-88, professor of English, 1988-94, London Program, director, 1988, director of women's studies, 1992, alumni distinguished professor of English and women's studies, 1994-; Monash University, exchange professor, 1983, 1990; University of California-Davis, visiting professor, 1986. Writer. **Publications:** Victorian Suicide: Mad Crimes and Sad Histories, 1988; (comp.) Critical Essays on Charlotte Bronte, 1990; Kindred Nature: Victorian and Edwardian Women Embrace the Living World, 1998. EDITOR: (and intro.) Journal of Emily Shore, 1991; (with A.B. Shteir) Natural Eloquence: Women Reinscribe Science, 1997; In Nature's Name: An Anthology of Women's Writing and Art, 1780-1930, 2002; (intro.) The Fairy-land of Science, 2003; (intro.) Wild Nature Won By Kindness and More About Wild Nature, forthcoming. **Address:** Department of English, University of Delaware, 212 Memorial Hall, Newark, DE 19716, U.S.A. **Online address:** bgates@udel.edu

GATES, David. American (born United States), b. 1947. **Genres:** Novels, Novellas/Short Stories, Natural History, Literary Criticism And History. **Career:** Bennington College, Graduate Writing Program, teacher; University of Virginia, Department of English, lecturer, 1975-77; Harvard University, instructor, 1977; Newsweek, Correspondence Department, general editor, senior editor, 1979-; Pratt Institute, visiting writer. **Publications:** NOVELS: Jernigan, 1991; Preston Falls, 1998; The Wonders of the Invisible World (stories), 1999. OTHERS: (ed. and intro.) Labor Days: An Anthology of Fiction About Work, 2004. Contributor to periodicals. **Address:** Newsweek, 251 W 57th St., New York, NY 10019-1802, U.S.A.

GATES, Henry Louis. American (born United States), b. 1950. **Genres:** Literary Criticism And History, Bibliography, Race Relations, Autobiography/Memoirs. **Career:** Anglican Mission Hospital, general anesthetist, 1970-71; John D. Rockefeller Gubernatorial Campaign, director of student affairs, 1971, director of research, 1972; Time, London Bureau, staff correspondent, 1973-75; Yale University, lecturer, 1976-79, assistant professor, 1979-84, associate professor of English and Afro-American studies, 1984-85, director of undergraduate Afro-American studies, 1976-79; Cornell University, professor of English, comparative literature and African studies, 1985-88, W.E.B. DuBois professor of literature, 1988-90; Virginia Commonwealth University, visiting professor, 1987-; Duke University, John Spencer Bassett professor of English and literature, 1989-91; Harvard University, W.E.B. DuBois professor of the humanities, 1991-2006, professor of English and American literature and language, 1991-, chair of Afro-American studies, 1991-2006, W.E.B. Du Bois Institute for African and African American Research, director, 1991-, Alphonse Fletcher University Professor, 2006-; Oxford African American Studies Center, editor-in-chief; TheRoot.com, editor-in-chief. **Publications:** Figures in Black: Words, Signs and the Racial Self, 1987; The Signifying Monkey: Towards a Theory of Afro-American Literary Criticism, 1988; Loose Canons: Notes on the Culture Wars, 1992; Colored People: A Memoir, 1994; Speaking of Race, Speaking of Sex: Hate Speech, Civil Rights and Civil Liberties, 1995; (with C. West) The Future of the Race, 1996; Thirteen Ways of Looking at a Black Man, 1997; Wonders of the African World, 1999; (with C. West) The African-American Century: How Black Americans Have Shaped Our Country, 2000; Come Sunday: Photographs by Thomas Roma, 2002; Back to Africa, 2002; The Trials of Phillis Wheatley: America's First Black Poet and Her Encounters with the Founding Fathers, 2003; America behind the Color Line: Dialogues with African Americans, 2004; Finding Oprah's Roots: Finding Your Own, 2007; (intro.) Life & Loves of Mr. Jiveass Nigger: A Novel, 2008; (foreword) Lyle Ashton Harris, Excessive Exposure: The Complete Chocolate Portraits, 2008; In Search of Our Roots: How 19 Extraordinary African Americans Reclaimed Their Past, 2009; Faces of America: How 12 Extraordinary People Discovered their Pasts, 2010; Tradition and the Black Atlantic, 2010. EDITOR: Black Is the Color of the Cosmos: Charles T. Davis's Essays on Afro-American Literature and Culture, 1942-1981, 1982; (and intro.) Our Nig; or Sketches from the Life of a Free Black, 1983; Black Literature and Literary Theory, 1984; (with C.T. Davis) The Slave's Narrative: Texts and Contexts, 1986; (with J. Gibbs and K.H. Katrak) Wole Soyinka: A Bibliography of Primary and Secondary Sources, 1986; (intro.) Race, Writing and Difference, 1986; (and intro.) The Classic Slave Narratives, 1987; In the House of Oshugbo: A Collection of Essays on Wole Soyinka, 1988; The Oxford-Schomburg Library of Nineteenth-Century Black Women Writers, 1988; The Souls of Black Folk, 1989; The Autobiography of an Ex-Coloured Man, 1989; Three Classic African-American Novels, 1990; Their Eyes Were Watching God, 1990; Jonah's Gourd Vine, 1990; Tell My Horse, 1990; Mules and Men, 1990; Reading Black, Reading Feminist: A Critical Anthology, 1990; Voodoo Gods of Haiti, 1991; The Schomburg Library of Nineteenth-Century Black Women Writers, 1991; (with R.K. Burkett and N.H. Burkett) Black Biography, 1790-1950: A Cumulative Index, 1991; (with G. Bass) Mulebone: A Comedy of Negro Life, 1991; Bearing Witness: Selections from African-American Autobiography in the Twentieth Century, 1991; The Amistad Chronology of African-American History from 1445-1990, 1993; Frederick Douglass: Autobiographies, 1994; The Complete Stories of Zora Neale Hurston, 1995; (with N.Y. McKay) The Norton Anthology of African-American Literature, 1996, 2nd ed., 2004; Ann Petry: Critical Perspectives Past and Present, 1997; Chinua Achebe: Critical Perspectives Past and Present, 1997; Harriet A. Jacobs: Critical Perspectives Past and Present, 1997; Ralph Ellison: Critical Perspectives Past and Present, 1997; Wole Soyinka: Critical Perspectives Past and Present, 1997; Frederick Douglass: Critical Perspectives Past and Present, 1997; The Essential Soyinka: A Reader, 1998; (with W.L. Andrews) Pioneers of the Black Atlantic: Five Slave Narratives from the Enlightenment, 1772-1815, 1998; (with M. Diedrich and C. Pedersen) Black Imagination and the Middle Passage, 1999; (with W.L. Andrews) The Civitas Anthology of African American Slave Narratives, 1999; Wonders of the African World, 1999; Slave Narratives, 2000; Harvard Guide to African-American History, 2001; Schomburg Library of Nineteenth-Century Black Women Writers, 2002; The Bondwoman's Narrative, 2002; In the House of Oshugbo: Critical Essays on Wole Soyinka, 2003; (with E.B. Higginbotham) African American Lives, 2004; (with G.A. Jarrett) The New Negro: Readings on Race, Representation and African American Culture, 1892-1938, 2007; (and intro. with H. Robbins) The Annotated Uncle Tom's Cabin, 2007; (with E.B. Higginbotham) African American National Biography, 2008, 2nd ed., 2012; God's Trombones: Seven Negro Sermons in Verse, 2008; (with E.B. Higginbotham) Harlem Renaissance Lives from the African American National Biography, 2009; (with D. Yacovone and intro.) Lincoln on Race and Slavery, 2009; (with J. Burton) Call and Response, 2010; (with D. Bindman) Image of the Black in Western Art, 2010; (with H. Robbins) Iola Leroy, or, Shadows Uplifted, 2010; (co-ed.) Oxford Handbook of African American Citizenship, 2011; Black in Latin America, 2011; Life Upon These Shores: Looking at African American History, 1513-2008, 2011; (with E.K. Akyeampong) Dictionary of African Biography, 2012. EDITOR WITH K.A.

APPIAH: Gloria Naylor: Critical Perspectives Past and Present, 1993; Alice Walker: Critical Perspectives Past and Present, 1993; Langston Hughes: Critical Perspectives Past and Present, 1993; Richard Wright: Critical Perspectives Past and Present, 1993; Toni Morrison: Critical Perspectives Past and Present, 1993; Zora Neale Hurston: Critical Perspectives Past and Present, 1993; The Dictionary of Global Culture, 1995; Identities, 1995; Africana: The Encyclopedia of the African and African American Experience, 2003, 2nd ed., 2005; Transition 96, 2004; Transition 97/98, 2004; Encyclopedia of Africa, 2010. Contributor to periodicals and journals. **Address:** Department of African and African American Studies, Harvard University, Rm. 3R, 104 Mount Auburn St., Cambridge, MA 02138-5019, U.S.A. **Online address:** gates@harvard.edu

GATES, Marilyn. Canadian/British (born England), b. 1944. **Genres:** Sociology, Anthropology/Ethnology. **Career:** Simon Fraser University, Department of Sociology and Anthropology, associate professor of anthropology and associate faculty in Latin American studies, 1974-, professor emeritus of anthropology and adjunct professor. Writer. **Publications:** In Default: Peasants, the Debt Crisis, and the Agricultural Challenge in Mexico, 1993. **Address:** Department of Sociology and Anthropology, Simon Fraser University, 8888 University Dr., Burnaby, BC V5A 1S6, Canada. **Online address:** gates@sfu.ca

GATES, Ronda. American (born United States), b. 1940. **Genres:** Medicine/Health, Sports/Fitness. **Career:** Lifestyles by Ronda Gates, president, 1978-; Systems Fitness, corporate fitness instructor; Oregon Governor's Council on Health, Fitness, and Sports, co-chair. Writer. **Publications:** (With V. Parker) The Lowfat Lifestyle, 7 vols., 1984-90; Nutrition Nuggets and More/Changes, 1990; (with C. Bailey) Smart Eating: Choosing Wisely, Living Lean, 1996; (with F.I. Katch and V.L. Katch) The Scale Companion: How to Find Your Ideal Body Weight, 1998; (with B. Whipple) Smart Women, Strong Bones, 2000; (with E. Harms) Beauty, More than Skin Deep, 2000; (with B. Whipple) Outwitting Osteoporosis: The Smart Woman's Guide to Bone Health, 2003. Contributor to periodicals. **Address:** Lifestyles by Ronda Gates, 1378 Casada Ct, Leisure World, Mesa, AZ 85206, U.S.A. **Online address:** ronda@rondagates.com

GATHORNE-HARDY, Jonathan. (Sylvia Thornton). British/Scottish (born Scotland), b. 1933. **Genres:** Novels, Novellas/Short Stories, Children's Fiction, Plays/Screenplays, History, Social Commentary, Autobiography/Memoirs, Biography, Biography. **Career:** Educator and advertising copy-writer, 1960-75; writer, 1960-. **Publications:** One Foot in the Clouds, 1961; Jane's Adventures in and Out of the Book, 1966; Chameleon, 1967; Jane's Adventures On the Island of Peeg, 1968; The Office, 1970; The Rise and Fall of the British Nanny, 1972 in US as The Unnatural History of the Nanny, 1973; Operation Peeg, 1974; Jane's Adventures in a Balloon, 1975; The Airship Ladyship Adventure, 1977; The Public School Phenomenon, 1977 in US as The Old School Tie, 1978; The Terrible Kidnapping of Cyril Bonhamy, 1978; Love, Sex, Marriage and Divorce in US as Sex, Love, Marriage and Divorce, 1981; Cyril Bonhamy Versus Madam Big, 1981; The Centre of the Universe Is 18 Baedekerstrasse (short stories), 1981; Cyril Bonhamy and the Great Father Christmas Robbery, 1981; (as Sylvia Thornton) The Man from the Sea, 1982; Cyril Bonhamy and the Great Drain Robbery, 1983; Doctors, 1984; Cyril Bonhamy and Operation Ping, 1985; The City Beneath the Skin (novel), 1986; Cyril of the Apes, 1987; The Munros' New House, 1987; The Tunnel Party, 1989; Gerald Brenan: The Interior Castle (biography), 1992; The Twin Detectives (children's fiction), 1995; Particle Theory (novel), 1996; Alfred C. Kinsey: Sex the Measure of All Things (biography), 1998; (intro.) Kinsey (film and source book), 2004; Half an Arch (autobiography), 2004. Contributor to periodicals. **Address:** c/o Curtis Brown, 162-8, Regent St., London, GL W1R 5TA, England. **Online address:** jonnygathorne@freenet.co.uk

GATI, Charles. American/Hungarian (born Hungary), b. 1934. **Genres:** Politics/Government, Social Sciences. **Career:** Union College, instructor in political science, 1963-65, assistant professor, 1965-68, associate professor, 1969-74, professor, 1974-94, founder and director of program in comparative communist studies, 1970-71, 1972-74, Department of Political Science, chair, 1975-78; University of Kansas, visiting professor, 1968-69; Columbia University, Research Institute on International Change, visiting lecturer, 1972, visiting associate professor, 1972-74; Harriman Institute for Advanced Study of the Soviet Union, visiting professor, 1975-86, Research Institute on International Change, director of East Europe project, 1984-85; U.S. Department of State, policy planning Staff, senior adviser; John Hopkins University, senior adjunct professor of Russian and Eurasian studies, professorial lecturer in Russian and Eurasian studies, Foreign Policy Institute, fellow, 1994-; Interinvest, senior vice president, 1994-2000. Writer. **Publications:** (With T.T. Gati) The Debate over Détente, Foreign Policy Association 1977; Eastern Europe and the World, 1978; Hungary and the Soviet Bloc, 1986; The Bloc That Failed: Soviet-East European Relations in Transition, 1990; Failed Illusions: Moscow, Washington, Budapest, and the 1956 Hungarian Revolt, 2006. EDITOR AND CONTRIBUTOR: The Politics of Modernization in Eastern Europe: Testing the Soviet Model, 1974; Caging the Bear: Containment and the Cold War, 1974; (with P. Berton) Symposium on the Comparative Study of Communist Foreign Policies, 1975; The International Politics of Eastern Europe, 1976; (with J.F. Triska) Blue-Collar Workers in Eastern Europe, 1981. Contributor to books and periodicals. **Address:** Paul H. Nitze School of Advanced Intl. Studies, John Hopkins University, Rome 518, 1619 Massachusetts Ave., Washington, DC 20036-1983, U.S.A. **Online address:** cgati@jhu.edu

GATISS, Mark. British (born England), b. 1966. **Genres:** Young Adult Fiction, Mystery/Crime/Suspense. **Career:** Writer. **Publications:** James Whale: A Biography, or, The Would-Be Gentleman, 1995; (with D. Miller) They Came from Outer Space! Alien Encounters in the Movies, 1995; (with J. Dyson) The Essex Files: To Basildon and Beyond (novel), 1997; (with J. Dyson, S. Pemberton and R. Shearsmith) The League of Gentlemen Scripts and That, 2003. DR. WHO: NEW ADVENTURES SERIES: Nightshade, 1992; St Anthony's Fire, 1994. DR. WHO: THIRD DOCTOR SERIES: Last of the Gadarene, 2000. DR. WHO SERIES: The Roundheads, 1997. LUCIFER BOX SERIES: The Vesuvius Club: A Bit of Fluff, 2004; The Devil in Amber, 2007; Black Butterfly, 2008. **Address:** Simon & Schuster Inc., 1230 Ave. of the Americas, 11th Fl., New York, NY 10020, U.S.A.

GATOS, Stephanie. *See* KATZ, Steve.

GATTEY, Charles Neilson. British (born England), b. 1921. **Genres:** Novels, Romance/Historical, Plays/Screenplays, Social Commentary, Biography, Animals/Pets, Autobiography/Memoirs, Art/Art History, Art/Art History. **Career:** Society of Civil Service Authors (now Society of Civil & Public Service Writers), president, 1980-2005, publicity officer. Writer and educator. **Publications:** The Bloomer Girls, 1967; Gauguin's Astonishing Grandmother: Biography of Flora Tristan, 1970; A Bird of Curious Plumage, 1971; The Incredible Mrs. Van der Elst, 1972; They Saw Tomorrow: Seers and Sorcerers from Delphi Till Today, 1977; Queens of Song, 1979; The Elephant That Swallowed a Nightingale, 1981; Peacocks on the Podium, 1982; Great Dining Disasters, 1984; Foie Gras and Trumpets, 1984; Farmer George's Black Sheep, 1985; Excess in Food, Drink and Sex, 1986; Visionaries and Seers, 1988; In Bed with an Elephant, 1989; Luisa Tetrazzini: A Tiger at the Tailor's, 1989; Prophecy and Prediction in the Twentieth Century, 1989; Luisa Tetrazzini: The Florentine Nightingale, 1995; Crowning Glory: Merits of the Monarchy, 2002. WITH J. LAWRENCE: The White Falcon, 1952; Queen's Night, 1953; The Birth of Elizabeth, 1954; Queen of a Thousand Dresses, 1955. WITH Z. BRAMLEY-MOORE: The Eleventh Hour, 1952; In the Maze, 1953; Tidings of Canute, 1954; A Spell of Virtue, 1955; The Birth of the Bloomer, 1955; Mightier than the Sword, 1955; Mrs. Adams and Eve, 1955; Treasure from France, 1956; Man in a Million, 1956; Farewell, Pots and Pans, 1956; True Love or The Bloomer, 1958; By a Hand Unknown, 1958; Life with Alfredo, 1958; The Cloak of Courage, 1959; The Landlady's Brother, 1959; The Colour of Anger, 1963; Fair Cops, 1965; The King Who Could not Stay the Tide, 1971. **Address:** The Garrick Club, 15 Garrick St., London, GL WC2E 9AY, England.

GATTI, Anne. Irish (born Ireland), b. 1952. **Genres:** Young Adult Fiction, Young Adult Non-fiction, Music, Children's Fiction. **Career:** Collins Harvill, editorial assistant, 1976-78; Reader's Digest, researcher, 1978-80; Eaglemoss Publications, editor, 1980-81; freelance writer and editor, 1984-. **Publications:** OTHER: Stepping Out (youth information handbook), 1985. EDITOR: Tales for the Telling: Irish Folk and Fairy Stories, 1986; Land of the Long White Cloud: Maori Myths, 1989; Tales from the African Plains, 1994; The Magic Flute, 1997. NONFICTION: Isabella Bird Bishop (biography), 1988. **Address:** 17 Boltons Ln., Pyrford, Woking, SR GU22 8, England. **Online address:** anniegatti@aol.com

GAU, Colleen. American (born United States) **Genres:** Novels, Fashion/Costume. **Career:** CPR Tex Inc., president; Iowa State University, professor of textiles and clothing. Writer. **Publications:** (With J. Farrell-Beck) Uplift: The Bra in America, 2002. Contributor of articles to periodicals. **Address:** c/o Author Mail, University of Pennsylvania Press, 3905 Spruce St., Philadelphia, PA 19104-4112, U.S.A.

GAUBATZ, Kathlyn Taylor. American (born United States), b. 1957. **Genres:** Criminology/True Crime, Adult Non-fiction. **Career:** Brandeis University, National Institute for Sentencing Alternatives, assistant director, 1980-81; New England Coalition Against Prisons, coordinator, 1981-82; Compass Community Services, counselor, 1989-90; Homeless Family Program, coordinator and case manager, 1990-91; CCR Family Center, program director, 1991-94; Market Street Counseling Center, program director, 1991-94, executive director, 1994-. Writer. **Publications:** Crime in the Public Mind, 1995. **Address:** Compass Community Services, 942 Market St., 6th Fl., San Francisco, CA 94102, U.S.A.

GAUBATZ, Kurt Taylor. American (born United States), b. 1957. **Genres:** Politics/Government, Civil Liberties/Human Rights, International Relations/Current Affairs, Military/Defense/Arms Control, Social Sciences. **Career:** Fletcher School, John Moors Cabot fellow, 1980-81; Stanford University, assistant professor, 1990-99, international relations field convener, 1990-93, Susan Louise Dyer Peace fellow, 1996-97; Old Dominion University, Department of Political Science, director of graduate studies, 1993-94, Graduate Program in International Studies, associate professor, associate director, 2000-01, director, 2001-04; Hoover Institution, Susan Louise Dyer Peace fellow, 1996-97; Oxford University, Nuffield College, John G. Winant lecturer in American foreign policy, 1999-2000; Virginia Modeling, Analysis and Simulation Center, faculty associate, faculty senate, 2005-. Writer. **Publications:** Elections and War: The Electoral Incentive in the Democratic Politics of War and Peace, 1999. Contributor to books and periodicals. **Address:** Graduate Program in International Studies, Old Dominion University, 7030 Batten Arts & Letters, Norfolk, VA 23529-0086, U.S.A. **Online address:** kgaubatz@odu.edu

GAUCH, Patricia Lee. American (born United States), b. 1934. **Genres:** Children's Fiction, Young Adult Fiction, Natural History, Young Adult Fiction, Novels, Picture/Board Books. **Career:** Louisville Courier-Journal, reporter, 1957-59; Coward-McCann and Geoghegan/ Putnam, publisher writer, 1969-; Gill-St. Berhards School, teacher, 1972-83; Drew University, part-time professor; Rutgers University, part-time professor; Philomel Books, vice president and editorial director, 1985-. Writer. **Publications:** FICTION FOR CHILDREN: My Old Tree, 1970; A Secret House, 1970; Christina Katerina and the Box, 1971; Aaron and the Green Mountain Boys, 1972; Grandpa and Me, 1972; Christina Katerina and the First Annual Grand Ballet, 1973; This Time, Tempe Wick?, 1974, rev. ed., 2003; Thunder at Gettysburg, 1975, rev. ed., 1990; The Impossible Major Rogers, 1977, rev. ed., 2006; Once upon a Dinkelsbuhl, 1977; Schuett, 1977; On to Widecombe Fair, 1978; The Little Friar Who Flew, 1980; Christina Katerina and the Time She Quit the Family, 1987; (with S. Ichikawa) Dance, Tanya, 1989; Christina Katerina and the Great Bear Train, 1990; Bravo, Tanya, 1992; Uncle Magic, 1992; Noah, 1994; Tanya and Emily in a Dance for Two, 1994; Christina Katerina and Fats Watson and the Great Neighborhood War, 1996; Tanya Steps Out, 1996; Tanya and the Magic Wardrobe, 1997; Poppy's Puppets, 1999; Presenting Tanya, the Ugly Duckling, 1999; Tanya Treasury, 2002, Tanya and the Red Shoes, 2002; (ed.) G is for Goat, 2003; (ed.) Graves Family, 2003; The Knitting of Elizabeth Amelia, 2005; Impossible Major Rogers, 2006. YOUNG ADULT NOVELS: The Green of Me, 1978; Fridays, 1979; Kate Alone, 1980; Morelli's Game, Putnam, 1981; Night Talks, 1983; The Year the Summer Died, 1985. Contributor to periodicals. **Address:** c/o Dorothy Marinko, McIntosh & Otis Inc., 18 E 41st St., New York, NY 10014, U.S.A.

GAUDÉ, Laurent. French (born France), b. 1972. **Genres:** History, Novels, Literary Criticism And History. **Career:** Writer. **Publications:** NOVELS: Cris, 2001; La mort du roi Tsongor, 2002, trans. as The Death of King Tsongor, 2003; Le soleil des Scorta, trans. as The Scortas' Sun, 2004; Onysos the Wild, 2005; The House of Scorta, 2005; Death of an Ancient King, 2007. PLAYS: Pluie de cendres, 2001; Combats de possédés (title means: Battle of Will), 2002; Cendres sur les mains, 2002; Eldorado, 2006; Dans la nuit Mozambique et autres récits, 2007; Je suis le chien pitié, 2009. Contributor to periodicals. **Address:** c/o Author Mail, MacAdam/Cage Publishing, 155 Sansome St., Ste. 550, San Francisco, CA 94104-3615, U.S.A.

GAUDET, Marcia. (Mary Marcia Gendron Gaudet). American (born United States), b. 1943?. **Genres:** Mythology/Folklore, Essays. **Career:** University of Louisiana, professor, Center for Cultural & Eco-Tourism, research fellow.

Educator and author of nonfiction. **Publications:** Tales from the Levee: The Folklore of St. John the Baptist Parish, 1984; (with C. Wooton) Porch Talk with Ernest Gaines: Conversations on the Writer's Craft, 1990; (ed. with J.C. McDonald) Mardi Gras, Gumbo, and Zydeco: Readings in Louisiana Culture, 2003; Carville: Remembering Leprosy in America, 2004; (ed. with R. Young) Mozart and Leadbelly: Stories and Essays, 2005. Works appear in anthologies. Contributor of articles to periodicals. **Address:** Department of English, University of Louisiana, PO Box 44691, Lafayette, LA 70504-4691, U.S.A. **Online address:** mgaudet@louisiana.edu

GAUDET, Mary Marcia Gendron. *See* GAUDET, Marcia.

GAUKROGER, Stephen. Australian (born Australia), b. 1950. **Genres:** History, Intellectual History, Language/Linguistics, Philosophy, Essays, Biography. **Career:** Cambridge University, research fellow, 1977-78; University of Melbourne, Department of History and Philosophy of Science, research fellow, 1978-80; University of Sydney, professor of history of philosophy and history of science, 1981-; University of Aberdeen, professor of philosophy, chair; Australasian Society for the History of Philosophy, president, 1993-99; Australasian Association for the History, Philosophy and Social Studies of Science, president, 1995-97; International Society for Intellectual History, president. Writer. **Publications:** Explanatory Structures: A Study of Concepts of Explanation in Early Physics and Philosophy, 1978; (ed.) Descartes: Philosophy, Mathematics and Physics, 1980; Cartesian Logic: An Essay on Descartes's Conception of Inference, 1989; (trans. and author of intro.) Antoine Arnauld, On True and False Ideas, 1990; (ed.) The Uses of Antiquity: The Scientific Revolution and the Classical Tradition, 1991; Descartes: An Intellectual Biography, 1995; The Genealogy of Knowledge: Analytical Essays in the History of Philosophy and Science, 1997; (ed.) The Soft Underbelly of Reason: The Passions in the Seventeenth Century, 1998; (trans. and ed.) Rene Descartes, The World and Other Writings, 1998; (ed. with J. Schuster and J. Sutton) Descartes' Natural Philosophy, 2000; Francis Bacon and the Transformation of Early-Modern Philosophy, 2001; Descartes' System of Natural Philosophy, 2002; The Emergence of a Scientific Culture: Science and the Shaping of Modernity, 1210-1685, 2006; (ed.) The Blackwell Guide to Descartes' Meditations, 2006; (ed. with C. Condren and I. Hunter) The Philosopher in Early Modern Europe: The Nature of a Contested Identity, 2006; Collapse of Mechanism and the Rise of Sensibility: Science and the Shaping of Modernity, 1680-1760, 2010. **Address:** Department of Philosophy, University of Sydney, Main Quad A14, Sydney, NW 2006, Australia. **Online address:** stephen.gaukroger@arts.usyd.edu.au

GAULD, Alan (Ogilvie). British (born England), b. 1932. **Genres:** Psychology, Paranormal, Philosophy, History. **Career:** Cambridge University, Emmanuel College, research fellow, 1958-62; University of Nottingham, lecturer, reader in psychology, 1962-96, now retired. Writer. **Publications:** The Founders of Psychical Research, 1968; (with J.D. Shotter) Human Action and Its Psychological Investigation, 1977; (with A.D. Cornell) Poltergeists, 1979; Mediumship and Survival: A Century of Investigation, 1982; A History of Hypnotism, 1992; Learn To Program Using Python, 2001; (with E.F. Kelly and E.W. Kelly) Irreducible Mind, 2007. **Address:** Braeside, Park Ave., Plumtree Pk., Keyworth, Nottingham, NT NG12 5LU, England. **Online address:** alangauld@yahoo.co.uk

GAULDIE, Enid Elizabeth. Scottish/British (born England), b. 1928. **Genres:** Architecture, Business/Trade/Industry, Local History/Rural Topics, History, Novellas/Short Stories, Novels. **Career:** University of Saint Andrews, librarian, 1948; University of Dundee, Department of Modern History, faculty, 1966-71, research historian; Duncan of Jordanstone College of Art, Department of Town Planning, visiting lecturer, board governor; writer, 1969-. **Publications:** (Ed.) The Dundee Textile Industry, 1790-1985: From the Papers of Peter Carmichael of Arthurstone, 1969; (co-author) Dundee and Its Textile Industry, 1850-1914, 1969; Cruel Habitations: A History of Working Class Housing, 1780-1918, 1974; The Scottish Country Miller 1700-1900: A History of Water-powered Meal Milling in Scotland, 1981; The Quarries and the Feus, 1981; One Artful and Ambitious Individual: Alexander Riddoch, 1989; Flights of Angels: History Today, 1992; The Bonnets of Bonnie Dundee, 1993; Spinning and Weaving, 1995. Contributor to periodicals. **Address:** Waterside, Invergowrie, Dundee, DD2 5DP, Scotland.

GAULT, Peter. Canadian (born Canada), b. 1958. **Genres:** Novels, Young Adult Fiction, Psychology, Literary Criticism And History. **Career:** Writer. **Publications:** Goldenrod, 1988; Knucklehead: A Journey Out of the Mind,

1995. Contributor to periodicals. **Address:** 40 High Park Ave., Ste. 1912, Toronto, ON M6P 2S1, Canada.

GAUNT, Carole O'Malley. American (born United States), b. 1946?. **Genres:** Autobiography/Memoirs. **Career:** Author. **Publications:** Hungry Hill: A Memoir, 2007. **Address:** c/o Author Mail, University of Massachusetts Press, 671 N Pleasant St., PO Box 429, East Experiment Sta., Amherst, MA 01003, U.S.A. **Online address:** carolegaunt@gmail.com

GAUNT, Graham. *See* GASH, Jonathan.

GAUNT, Kyra D. American (born United States) **Genres:** Plays/Screenplays, Sociology, Music, Social Sciences. **Career:** University of Michigan, instructor, 1991-92, 1994; Washtenaw Community College, instructor, 1995; Tufts University, instructor, 1996; University of Virginia, assistant professor, 1996-2002; New York University, assistant professor, 2002-06; City University, Baruch College, Department of Fine and Performing Arts, associate professor, 2006-; Kyraocity, Development Co., chief executive officer. Writer and ethnomusicologist. **Publications:** The Games Black Girls Play: Learning the Ropes from Double-Dutch to Hip-Hop, 2006. Contributor of articles to journals and books. **Address:** Department of Fine & Performing Arts, Baruch College, New York, NY 10010, U.S.A. **Online address:** kyra_gaunt@baruch.cuny.edu

GAUVREAU, Michael. Canadian (born Canada), b. 1956?. **Genres:** Theology/Religion. **Career:** McMaster University, professor. Writer. **Publications:** The Evangelical Century: College and Creed in English Canada from the Great Revival to the Great Depression, 1991; (with N. Christie) A Full-Orbed Christianity: The Protestant Churches and Social Welfare in Canada, 1900-1940, 1996; The Catholic Origins of Quebec's Quiet Revolution, 1931-1970, 2005. EDITOR: (with N. Christie) Cultures of Citizenship in Post-war Canada, 1940-1955, 2003; (with N. Christie) Mapping the Margins: The Family and Social Discipline in Canada, 1700-1975, 2004; (with O. Hubert) The Churches and Social Order in Nineteenth-and Twentieth-Century Canada, 2006. **Address:** Department of History, McMaster University, Chester New Hall 619, 1280 Main St. W, Hamilton, ON L8S 4L9, Canada. **Online address:** mgauvrea@mcmaster.ca

GAVRONSKY, Serge. American/French (born France), b. 1932. **Genres:** Novels, Poetry, History, Translations, Young Adult Fiction, Literary Criticism And History. **Career:** Columbia University, Barnard College, lecturer, 1960-63, instructor, 1963-65, assistant professor, 1965-69, associate professor, 1969-74, professor of French, 1974-, Olin professor of French, 1994-99, department chair, 1975-2001, now professor emeritus. Writer. **Publications:** The French Liberal Opposition and the American Civil War, 1968; Culture/Ecriture, essais critiques, 1983; The German Friend (novel), 1984; Ecrire l'homme, essais critiques, 1986; The Name of the Father (novel), 1993; Louis Zukofsky, l'homme/poete, 1993; (trans. and intro.) Toward a New Poetics: Contemporary Writing in France, 1994; (trans.) J. Mansour, Screams, 1995; (ed. and intro.) L. Kaplan, Six Contemporary French Women Poets, 1997; Mallarmé spectral, 1998; Andorthe, 2007; Sudden Death Of-, 2008; (trans. and intro.) Essential Poems and Writings of Joyce Mansour, 2008. POETRY: Lectures et compte rendu, 1973; Meme-la suivi de Geste (poetry), 1992; L'interminable Discussion, 1996; L'obscur d'ici, 1998; France d'hier/Yesterday's France, 1999; Sixty Six for Starters, 2002; Temps mort, 2002; Une toute autre histoire, 2002. EDITOR: (trans.) Poems and Texts, 1969; (with J. Blanchard) Littérature française: le milieu et le moment, 1972; (with J-M. Blanchard) Le Moyen Age, 1974; (and trans. With P. Terry) Modern French Poetry, 1975; (and trans.) F. Ponge, The Sun Placed in the Abyss and Other Texts, 1977; (and trans.) Francis Ponge: The Power of Language, 1979; (and trans.) Ten Poems, Dix Poemes de Francis Ponge, 1983; (and trans.) J. Mansour, Dechirures/Torn Apart, 1999; (and trans.) L. Zukofsky, A-8 a A-11, 2001. **Address:** Department of French, Barnard College, Columbia University, 320 Milbank Hall, New York, NY 10027, U.S.A. **Online address:** sgavronsky@barnard.edu

GAWLYTA, Eva-Maria. *See* WESSELL, Eva.

GAWRYCH, George. American (born United States), b. 1950. **Genres:** History, Military/Defense/Arms Control. **Career:** Baylor University, professor of history. Writer. **Publications:** Key to the Sinai: The Battles for Abu Ageila in the 1956 and 1967 Arab-Israeli Wars, 1990; The 1973 Arab-Israeli War: The Albatross of Decisive Victory, 1996; The Albatross of Decisive Victory: War and Policy between Egypt and Israel in the 1967 and 1973 Arab-Israeli Wars, 2000; (with R.F. Baumann and W.E. Kretchik) Armed Peacekeepers in Bosnia, 2004; The Crescent and the Eagle: Ottoman Rule, Islam and the Albanians, 1874-1913, 2006. **Address:** Department of History, Baylor University, Tidwell Bible Bldg., 2nd Fl., Waco, TX 78798, U.S.A. **Online address:** george_gawrych@baylor.edu

GAY, John H. American (born United States), b. 1928. **Genres:** Young Adult Fiction, Anthropology/Ethnology, Area Studies, Social Sciences, History. **Career:** Cuttington University College, dean of instruction, 1958-60, chair of social science division, 1958-68, 1970-73; UN Development Programme, rural sociologist, 1973-74; UN Food and Agriculture Organization, rural sociologist, 1975-77; Ministry of Agriculture, social analyst of planning unit, 1977-79; National University of Lesotho, senior lecturer, 1979-80, Fulbright lecturer, 1979-82; Transformation Resource Centre, team staff, 1986-92; Sechaba Consultants, consultant, 1992-2001, now retired. Writer. **Publications:** (With M. Cole) The New Mathematics and an Old Culture, 1967; (with W. Welmers) Mathematics and Logic in the Kpelle Language, 1971; (co-author) The Cultural Context of Learning and Thinking, 1971; Red Dust on the Green Leaves, 1973; The Brightening Shadow, 1980; (ed. with B. Lloyd) Universals of Human Thought: Some African Evidence, 1981; (with A. Blair) Growing up in Lesotho, 1981; Lectures on Missiology, 1983; Social and Economic Aspects of the Catholic Relief Services Food and Nutrition Program in Lesotho, 1985; (co-author) The Situation of Women and Children in Lesotho, 1991; (co-author) Poverty in Lesotho, 1991, rev. ed., 2000; (with D. Gill) Health in Lesotho, 1993; (with D. Hall and D. Gill) Lesotho's Long Journey, 1995; Citizen Perceptions of Democracy, Governance, and Political Crisis in Lesotho, 2000; Public Attitudes Towards Democracy, Politics and Development in Lesotho, 2000; Long Day's Anger, 2004; Africa: A Dream Deferred, 2004; (ed. and comp.) Best of Work for Justice: Articles from the Newsletter of the Transformation Resource Centre Lesotho, 1983-2004, 2006. **Address:** 59 Fenno St., Cambridge, MA 02138-6717, U.S.A. **Online address:** judyjohngay@comcast.net

GAY, Kathlyn R. American (born United States), b. 1930. **Genres:** Young Adult Non-fiction, Sciences, Communications/Media, Environmental Sciences/Ecology, History, Social Commentary, Sociology, Women's Studies And Issues, Reference, Biography, Reference, Military/Defense/Arms Control. **Career:** Church World Service, Christian Rural Overseas Program, editor and public relations writer, 1962-66; Juhl Advertising Agency, publicity and public relations writer, 1966; freelance writer, 1966-; Americana Healthcare Center, community relations director, 1976-79; Elkhart Area Career Center, instructor in creative writing, 1970-73. **Publications:** Girl Pilot, 1966; Money Isn't Everything: The Story of Economics at Work, 1967; Meet the Mayor of Your City, 1967; Meet Your Governor, 1968; Beth Speaks Out, 1968; Careers in Social Service, 1969; Where the People Are: Cities and Their Future, 1969; The Germans Helped Build America, 1971; Proud Heritage on Parade, 1972; Core English: English for Speakers of Other Languages, 1972; A Family Is for Living: The Changing Family in a Changing World, 1972; Our Working World, 1973; Body Talk, 1974; Be a Smart Shopper, 1974; (with B.E. Barnes) The River Flows Backward, 1975; What's in a Name?, 1975; Care and Share: Teenagers and Volunteerism, 1977; Look Mom! No Words!, 1977; (with M. Gay) Get Hooked on Vegetables, 1978; (co-author) English around the World, 1979; (with M. Gay) Eating What Grows Naturally, 1980; (with B.E. Barnes) Your Fight Has Just Begun, 1980; (with B.E. Barnes) Beginner's Guide to Better Boxing, 1980; (co-author) I Like English, 1981; English for a Changing World, 1981; Boxes and More Boxes, 1981; (co-author) Family Living, 1982, 3rd ed., 1988; Junkyards, 1982; Acid Rain, 1983; Cities under Stress, 1985; Ergonomics: Making Products and Places Fit People, 1986; Crisis in Education: Will the United States Be Ready for the Year 2000?, 1986; The Rainbow Effect: Interracial Families, 1987; Changing Families: Meeting Today's Challenges, 1988; Science in Ancient Greece, 1988; Silent Killers: Radon and Other Hazards, 1988; Bigotry, 1989; Ozone, 1989; Adoption and Foster Care, 1990; They Don't Wash Their Socks!: Sports Superstitions, 1990; Water Pollution, 1990; Cleaning Nature Naturally, 1991; Air Pollution, 1991; Garbage and Recycling, 1991; Day Care: Looking for Answers, 1992; Church and State: Government and Religion in the United States, 1992; Global Garbage: Exporting Trash and Toxic Waste, 1992; Caution! This May Be an Advertisement: Teen Guide to Advertising, 1992; Caretakers of the Earth, 1993; The Right to Die: Public Controversy, Private Matter, 1993; Getting Your Message Across, 1993; Breast Implants: Making Safe Choices, 1993;

Pregnancy: Private Decisions, 1994; Rainforests of the World, 1994, 2nd ed., 2001; The New Power of Women in Politics, 1994; Pollution and the Powerless: The Environmental Justice Movement, 1994; I Am Who I Am: Speaking Out about Multiracial Identity, 1995; Keep the Buttered Side Up: Food Superstitions from around the World, 1995; (with M. Gay) Encyclopedia of North American Eating and Drinking Traditions, Customs and Rituals, 1995; Rights and Respect: What You Need to Know about Gender Bias and Sexual Harassment, 1995; World War I, 1995; World War II, 1995; War of 1812, 1995; Spanish-American War, 1995; Revolutionary War, 1995; Civil War, 1995; Korean War, 1996; Persian Gulf War, 1996; Vietnam War, 1996; (with M. Gay) Heores of Conscience: A Biographical Dictionary, 1996; Saving the Environment: Debating the Costs, 1996; (with D. Gay) The Not-So-Minor Leagues, 1996; (with M. Gay) The Information Superhighway, 1966; Communes and Cults, 1997; Militias: Armed and Dangerous, 1997; Neo-Nazis: A Growing Threat, 1997; (with M. Gay) Emma Goldman, 1997; (with M. Gay) After the Shooting Stops: The Aftermath of War, 1998; Who's Running the Nation?: How Corporate Power Threatens Democracy, 1998; Child Labor: A Global Crisis, 1998; (with M.K. Gay) Encyclopedia of Political Anarchy, 1999; Leaving Cuba: From Operation Pedro Pan to Elian, 2000; Silent Death: The Threat of Chemical and Biological Terrorism, 2001; (with C. Whittington) Body Marks: Tattooing, Piercing, and Scarification, 2002; (with S. McGarrahan) Epilepsy: The Ultimate Teen Guide, 2002; The Encyclopedia of Women's Health Issues, 2002; Eating Disorders: Anorexia, Bulimia, and Binge Eating, 2003; Cultural Diversity: Conflicts and Challenges, 2003; Abortion: Understanding the Debate, 2004; Volunteering: The Ultimate Teen Guide, 2004; Death and Dying A-Z, 2004; Religion and Spirituality in America: The Ultimate Teen Guide, 2006; Mother Jones, 2006; Am I Fat?: The Obesity Issue For Teens, 2006; African-American Holidays, Festivals, and Celebrations: The History, Customs, and Symbols Associated With Both Traditional and Contemporary Religious and Secular Events Observed By Americans of African Descent, 2007; Superfood or Superthreat: The Issue of Genetically Engineered Food, 2008; Military and Teens: The Ultimate Teen Guide, 2008; Mao Zedong's China, 2008; Chinese Nationalist Revolution, 2009; Aftermath of the Russian Revolution, 2009; Scoop on What to Eat: What You Should Know about Diet and Nutrition, 2009; Body Image and Appearance: The Ultimate Teen Guide, 2009; Aftermath of the Chinese Nationalist Revolution, 2009; Body Image & Appearance: The Ultimate Teen Guide, 2009; American Dissidents: An Encyclopedia of Activists, Subversives, and Prisoners of Conscience, 2011; Living Green: The Ultimate Teen Guide, 2012; Food: The New Gold, 2012. Contributor of articles to books and periodicals. **Address:** 11633 Bayonet Ln., New Port Richey, FL 34654-1601, U.S.A. **Online address:** kgay@microd.com

GAY, Marie Louise. Canadian (born Canada), b. 1952. **Genres:** Children's Fiction, Plays/Screenplays, Illustrations, Picture/Board Books, Cartoons, Young Adult Fiction, Graphic Novels, Children's Non-fiction, Children's Non-fiction. **Career:** Editorial illustrator of Canadian and American magazines, 1972-87; Perspectives and Decormag, graphic designer, 1974-76; La Courte Echelle, art director, 1980; University of Quebec, lecturer in illustration, 1981-89; Ahuntsic College, visiting lecturer in illustration, 1984-85; designer of children's clothing, 1985-; author and set designer of plays and films, 1989. **Publications:** FOR CHILDREN: SELF-ILLUSTRATED PICTURE BOOKS: De zăro àÿminuit (title means: 'From Zero to Midnight'), 1981; La soeur de Robert (title means: 'Robert's Sister'), 1983; Mon Potager, 1985, trans. as The Garden, 1985; Voyage au Clair de Lune, 1986, trans. as Moonbeam on a Cat's Ear, 1986, rev. ed., 1992; Magie d'un jour de pluie, 1986, trans. as Rainy Day Magic, 1987; Angèle et l'ours polaire, 1988, trans. as Angel and the Polar Bear, 1988; Le Cirque de Charlie Chou, 1989, trans. as Fat Charlie's Circus, 1989; Willy Nilly, 1990; Mademoiselle Moon, 1992; Lapin bleu, 1993, trans. as Rabbit Blue, 1993; Mimi-la-Nuit, 1994, trans. as Midnight Mimi, 1994; Qui a peur de Loulou?: Théâtre, 1994; The Three Little Pigs, 1994; Rumpelstiltskin, 1997; Stella, Star of the Sea, 1999; Princesse Pistache, 1999; Le Jardin de Babel: Théâtre, 1999; On My Island, 2000; Yuck, a Love Story, 2000; Stella, Queen of the Snow, 2000; Stella, Princess of the Sky, 2004; What Are You Doing Sam, 2006; Caramba, 2006; Travels With My Family, 2006; When Stella Was Very, Very Small, 2009. DROLE D'éCOLE SERIES: SELF-ILLUSTRATED BOARD BOOKS: Rond comme ton visage, 1984; Blanccomme neige, 1984; Petit et grand, 1984; Un léopard dans mon placard, 1984. OTHER: (contrib.) La Vache et d'autres animaux (nonfiction), 1982; (contrib.) The Last Piece of Sky, 1993; (with D. Gillmor) The Fabulous

Song, 1996; (with S. Musgrave) Dreams are More Real than Bathtubs, 1998; Good Night Sam, 2003; Good Morning Sam, 2003. Illustrator of books by others. Contributor to books and periodicals. **Address:** Groundwood Books, 110 Spadina Ave., Ste. 801, Toronto, ON M5V 2K4, Canada.

GAY, Peter. American/German (born Germany), b. 1923. **Genres:** History, Intellectual History, Theology/Religion, Translations. **Career:** Columbia University, instructor, assistant professor of government, 1947-56, associate professor, 1956-62, professor of political science, 1948-55, professor of history, 1955-69; Yale University, professor of comparative and intellectual European history, 1969-93, Durfee professor of history, 1970-84, Sterling professor of history, 1984-93, Sterling professor of history emeritus, 1993-; New York Public Library, Center for Scholars and Writers, director, 1997-2003. Writer. **Publications:** The Dilemma of Democratic Socialism: Edward Bernstein's Challenge to Marx, 1952; Voltaire's Politics: The Poet as Realist, 1959; (trans. and ed.) Candide, 1963; The Party of Humanity: Essays in the French Enlightenment, 1964; (ed. and intro.) John Locke on Education, 1964; A Loss of Mastery: Puritan Historians in Colonial America, 1966; The Enlightenment, vol. I: The Rise of Modern Paganism, 1966, vol. II: The Science of Freedom, 1969; Deism: An Anthology, 1968; Weimar Culture: The Outsider as Insider, 1968; The Bridge of Criticism: Dialogues on the Enlightenment, 1970; (ed.) Eighteenth Century Studies, 1972; (with R.K. Webb) Modern Europe, 1972; (ed. with G.A. Garraty) History of the World, 1972; (ed. with G.A. Garraty) The Columbia History of the World, 1972; (ed. with G.J. Cavanaugh) Historians at Work, 1972; Style in History, 1974; Art and Act: On Causes in History-Manet, Gropius, Mondrian, 1976; (contrib.) A View of a Decade, Museum of Contemporary Art, Chicago, Illinois, September 10 through November 10, 1977, 1977; Freud, Jews and Other Germans, 1978; The Bourgeois Experience: Victoria to Freud, vol. I: Education of the Senses, 1984, vol. II: The Tender Passion, 1986, vol. III: The Cultivation of Hatred, 1993, vol. IV: The Naked Heart, 1995, vol. V: Pleasure Wars, 1998; Freud for Historians, 1985; A Godless Jew: Freud, Atheism, and the Making of Psychoanalysis, 1987; Freud: A Life in Our Time, 1988; (ed.) A Freud Reader, 1989; Reading Freud: Explorations and Entertainments, 1990; My German Question: Growing up in Nazi Berlin, 1998; Mozart, 1999; Moritz Frölich-Morris Gay: A German Refugee in the United States, 1999; (contrib.) Enlightenment, Passion, Modernity, 2000; Schnitzler's Century: The Making of Middle-Class Culture, 1815-1914, 2002; Savage Reprisals: Bleak House, Madame Bovary, Buddenbrooks, 2002; Freud: A Life for Our Time, 2006; Modernism: The Lure of Heresy: From Baudelaire to Beckett and Beyond, 2008. Contributor of articles to periodicals. **Address:** Department of History, Yale University, Hall of Graduate Studies, 320 York St., PO Box 208324, New Haven, CT 06511, U.S.A.

GAYLE, Stephanie. American (born United States), b. 1975. **Genres:** Young Adult Fiction, Novels, Literary Criticism And History. **Career:** Writer. **Publications:** My Summer of Southern Discomfort, 2007. Contributor to periodicals. **Address:** William Morrow Publishers, 10 E 53rd St., New York, NY 10022-5244, U.S.A. **Online address:** stephgayle@gmail.com

GAYLIN, Alison. (Alison Sloane Gaylin). American (born United States) **Genres:** Novels, Mystery/Crime/Suspense. **Career:** In Touch Weekly Magazine, writer. Journalist. **Publications:** SAMANTHA LEIFFER SERIES: You Kill Me, 2005; Hide Your Eyes, 2005. NOVELS: Trashed, 2007; Heartless, 2008; And She Was, 2012. **Address:** c/o Kristina Anderson, Penguin Group, 375 Hudson St., New York, NY 10014-3658, U.S.A. **Online address:** info@alisongaylin.com

GAYLIN, Alison Sloane. See **GAYLIN, Alison.**

GAYLIN, Willard. American (born United States), b. 1925. **Genres:** Civil Liberties/Human Rights, Criminology/True Crime, Ethics, Law, Psychiatry, Psychology. **Career:** Cleveland City Hospital, intern, 1951-52; Veterans Administration Hospital, resident in psychiatry, 1952-54; Columbia University, Psychoanalytic School, faculty, 1956-, adjunct professor of psychiatry and law, 1970, clinical professor of psychiatry, 1972-; Institute of Society, Ethics and the Life Sciences, Hastings Center, co-founder and president, 1996-93, chairman, through 1994, board director; Union Theological Seminary, adjunct professor of psychiatry; Planned Parenthood Federation of America, board of directors. Writer and consultant. **Publications:** (With H. Hendrin and A. Carr) Psychoanalysis and Social Research, 1965; The Meaning of Despair, 1968, 2nd ed. as Psychodynamic Understanding of Depression, 1984; In the Service of Their Country: War Resisters in Prison, 1970; (with R. Veatch and C.

Morgan) The Teaching of Medical Ethics, 1973; Partial Justice, 1975; (with J. Meister and R. Neville) Operating on the Mind, 1975; Caring, 1976; (co-author) Doing Good, 1978; Feelings: Our Vital Signs, 1979; The Killing of Bonnie Garland, 1982; The Rage Within, 1984; Rediscovering Love, 1986; Adam and Eve and Pinocchio, 1990; The Male Ego, 1992; (with B. Jennings) The Perversion of Autonomy, 1996, rev. ed., 2003; Talk is not Enough: How Psychotherapy Works, 2001; Hatred: The Descent into Terror, 2002. EDITOR: (with C. Morgan and R. Veatch) The Teaching of Medical Ethics, 1973; Operating on the Mind: The Psychosurgery Conflict, 1975; (with R. Macklin) Mental Retardation and Sterilization: A Problem of Competency and Paternalism, 1981; (co-ed.) Violence and the Politics of Research, 1981; (with R. Macklin) Who Speaks for the Child?, 1982; (with R. Macklin and T. Murray) Feeling Good and Doing Better: Ethics and Nontherapeutic Drug Use, 1984; (with E. Person) Passionate Attachments, 1988. Contributor to periodicals. **Address:** Hastings Ctr., 21 Malcolm Gordon Rd., Garrison, NY 10524-4125, U.S.A. **Online address:** willgaylin@aol.com

GAZE, R(aymond) Michael. (R. M. Gaze). Scottish/British (born England), b. 1927. **Genres:** Biology, Medicine/Health. **Career:** University of Edinburgh, Department of Physiology, lecturer, 1955-62, reader, 1966-70, Division of Developmental Biology, head, 1970-83, deputy director, 1977-83, Medical Research Council Neural Development and Regeneration Group, head, 1984-92. Writer. **Publications:** The Formation of Nerve Connections, 1970; (co-ed.) Growth and the Development of Pattern, 1981. **Address:** Institute Cell Animal Biology, Ashworth Lab W Mains Rd., Edinburgh, EH9 3JT, Scotland. **Online address:** mikegaze@talk21.com

GAZE, R. M. See **GAZE, R(aymond) Michael.**

GAZETAS, Aristides. Canadian/American (born United States), b. 1930. **Genres:** Art/Art History, Education, Film, Theatre, Social Sciences. **Career:** National Theatre School, Design Program, chair, 1968-72; University of Calgary, associate professor of drama and stage designer, 1972-76; Southern Alberta Institute of Technology, Art History Program, chair, 1976-80; University of Lethbridge, Department of Theater, cinematic arts development officer, 1980-83; University of British Columbia, lecturer and associate professor of theater and film, 1988-93. Writer. **Publications:** An Introduction to World Cinema, 2000, 2nd ed., 2008; Imagining Selves: The Politics of Representation, Film Narratives, and Adult Education, 2000. **Address:** 42-5840 Dover Cres., Richmond, BC V7C 5P4, Canada. **Online address:** agazetas@axionet.com

GEACH, Christine. Also writes as Christine Wilson, Elizabeth Dawson, Anne Lowing. British (born England), b. 1930. **Genres:** Romance/Historical, Novels, Literary Criticism And History. **Career:** Radiographer, 1954-56; freelance writer. **Publications:** AS ELIZABETH DAWSON: Isle of Dreams, 1975; Wine in a Crystal Goblet, 1974; The Bending Reed, 1976. AS ANNE LOWING: Masked Ball, 1966; The Denbigh Affair, 1967; Black Midnight, 1968; Yasmin, 1969; Shadow on the Wind, 1970; The Gossamer Thread, 1972; Melyonen, 1972; The Captain's Pawn, 1974; The Napoleon Ring, 1975; The Branch and the Briar, 1976; Copper Moon, 1979; Girl in the Shadows, 1984. AS CHRISTINE WILSON: Broken Vows, 1966; Trial of Love, 1966; A Husband for Charlotte, 1967; A Deeper Love, 1967; Love's True Face, 1967; The Doubting Heart, 1967; Nurse Emma in Love, 1968; Dr. Mary's Dilemma, 1968; The Driven Clouds, 1969; Watch for Me by Moonlight, 1969; The Gift of Happy Rain, 1969; Is This My Island?, 1970; The Lonely Tower, 1970; This Nearly Was Mine, 1971; Some Other Spring, 1973; The Man Beyond Price, 1974; Where Is Tomorrow?, 1979; The Man in the Blue Car, 1978; A Garland of Whispers, 1978; Proud Swells the Tide, 1979; The Light in the Window, 1980; Football Dreams, 1982. **Address:** Blue Waters, 6 Seaview Dr., Wembury, Plymouth, DN PL9 0JR, England.

GEAR, W. Michael. American (born United States), b. 1955. **Genres:** Westerns/Adventure, Novels. **Career:** Western Wyoming College, field archaeologist, 1979-81; Metcalf-Zier Archaeologists Inc., archaeologist, 1981; Pronghorn Anthropological Association, owner and principal investigator, 1982-84; Wind River Archaeological Consultants, owner and principal investigator, 1988-2000. Writer. **Publications:** WAY OF SPIDER: The Warriors of Spider, 1988; The Way of Spider, 1988; The Web of Spider, 1989. FIRST NORTH AMERICAN SERIES WITH K. GEAR: People of the Wolf, 1990; People of the Fire, 1990; People of the Earth, 1992; People of the River, 1992; People of the Sea, 1993; People of the Lakes, 1994; People of the Lightning, 1995; People of the Silence, 1996; People of the Mist, 1997; People of the

Masks, 1998; People of the Owl: A Novel of Prehistoric North America, 2003; People of the Raven, 2004; People of the Moon, 2005; People of the Nightland, 2007; People of the Weeping Eye, 2008; People of the Thunder, 2009; (with K. Gear) Children of the Dawnland, 2009; People of the Longhouse, 2010; Searing Wind, 2012; Broken Land, 2012; Summoning God, 2012. FORBIDDEN BORDERS SERIES: Requiem for the Conqueror, 1991; Relic of Empire, 1992; Countermeasures, 1993. ANASAZI MYSTERIES WITH K. GEAR: The Visitant, 1999; The Summoning God, 2000; Bone Walker, 2001. NOVELS: Long Ride Home, 1988; The Big Horn Legacy, 1988; The Artifact, 1990; Starstrike, 1990; The Morning River, 1996; Coyote Summer, 1997; (with K. Gear) Dark Inheritance, 2001; (with K. Gear) Raising Abel, 2002; The Athena Factor, 2005; (with K. Gear) The Betrayal: The Lost Life of Jesus, 2008. OTHERS: Coming of the Storm, 2010; Fire the Sky, 2010; (with K. Gear) Dawn Country: A People of the Longhouse Novel, 2011; Comes a Green Sky, forthcoming; People of the Thunder, forthcoming. **Address:** c/o Owen Laster, William Morris Literary Agency, 1325 Ave. of the Americas, New York, NY 10019, U.S.A. **Online address:** wmgear1@aol.com

GEARY, David C(yril). American (born United States), b. 1957. **Genres:** Psychology, Sciences, Biology, Business/Trade/Industry. **Career:** University of Texas, visiting assistant professor of psychology, 1986-87; University of Missouri-Rolla, assistant professor of psychology, 1987-89; University of Missouri-Columbia, assistant professor, 1989-93, adjunct associate professor of anthropology, 1994-, associate professor, 1993-96, professor of psychological sciences, 1996-, department chair, 2002-05, Curators' professor, 2005-, Thomas Jefferson professor, 2009-11. Writer. **Publications:** Children's Mathematical Development: Research and Practical Applications, 1994; Male, Female: The Evolution of Human Sex Differences, 1998, 2nd ed., 2010; The Origin of the Mind: Evolution of Brain, Cognition and General Intelligence, 2005; Sex Differences: Summarizing More Than a Century of Scientific Research, 2008. **Address:** Department of Psychological Sciences, University of Missouri, 210 McAlester Hall, Columbia, MO 65211-2500, U.S.A. **Online address:** gearyd@missouri.edu

GEARY, Joseph. (Patrick Lynch). American/British (born England), b. 1958?. **Genres:** Art/Art History, Novels, Mystery/Crime/Suspense, Science Fiction/Fantasy. **Career:** Writer. **Publications:** Spiral (novel), 2003; Mirror, 2004. AS PATRICK LYNCH WITH P. SINGTON: The Annunciation, 1993; The Immaculate Conception, 1994; Carriers, 1995; Omega, 1997; The Policy, 1999; Figure of 8, 2000. AS PATRICK LYNCH: From the Cave to the City, 1959; (with B. Sewell) The Story of Ancient Egypt, 1961; Man and Nature, 1963. Contributor to periodicals. **Address:** c/o Author Mail, Pantheon Publicity, 1745 Broadway, New York, NY 10019, U.S.A.

GEARY, Patricia (Carol). American (born United States), b. 1951. **Genres:** Novels, Science Fiction/Fantasy. **Career:** Orange Coast Community College, instructor, 1976-81; Irvine Valley College, instructor, 1978-81; Louisiana State University, assistant professor, 1981-87; Radcliffe College, Bunting Institute, Carnegie Mellon fellow, 1983-85; University of California, visiting assistant professor, 1986-87; University of Redlands, assistant professor, 1987, creative writing professor; Harvard University, Bunting Fellow. Writer. **Publications:** NOVELS: Living in Ether: A Novel, 1982; Strange Toys, 1987; The Other Canyon, 2002; Guru Cigarettes, 2005. Contributor to periodicals. **Address:** Department of English, University of Redlands, 103 Holt, 1200 E Colton Ave., Redlands, CA 92374-3720, U.S.A. **Online address:** patricia_geary@redlands.edu

GEAVES, Ron. See GEAVES, Ronald Allan.

GEAVES, Ronald Allan. (Ron Geaves). British (born England) **Genres:** Theology/Religion, Biography. **Career:** University of Chester, professor of the study of religion, 2002-07; Liverpool Hope University, professor of comparative study of religion, 2007-. Writer. **Publications:** AS RON GEAVES: Sectarian Influences in British Islam, 1996; Sufis of Britain: An Exploration of Muslim Identity, 2000; Continuum Glossary of Religious Terms, 2002; (ed.) Islam and the West Post 9/11, 2004; Aspects of Islam, 2005; Key Words in Buddhism, 2006; Key Words in Religious Studies, 2006; Key Words in Judaism, 2006; Key Words in Islam, 2006; Key Words in Hinduism, 2006; Key Words in Christianity, 2006; (with T. Gabriel) Isms: Understanding Religion, 2006; (with G.D.Chryssides) Study of Religion: An Introduction to Key Ideas and Methods, 2007; Saivism in the Diaspora: Contemporary Forms of Skanda Worship, 2007; (ed. with M. Dressler and G. Klinkhammer) Sufis in Western Society: Global Networking and Locality, 2008; Islam in Victorian

Britain: The Life and Times of Abdullah Quilliam, 2010; Islam Today, 2010. **Address:** Department of Theology & Religious Studies, Liverpool Hope University, Hope Pk., Liverpool, MS L16 9JD, England. **Online address:** geavesr@hope.ac.uk

GEBHARDT, James F(rederick). American (born United States), b. 1948. **Genres:** Translations, Military/Defense/Arms Control, History. **Career:** U.S. Army, career officer, 1966-69, 1974-92; Cubic Applications Inc., computer simulation specialist, 1992-. Writer. **Publications:** Leavenworth Papers No. 17: The Petsamo-Kirkenes Operation: Soviet Breakthrough and Pursuit in the Arctic, October, 1944, 1990; (trans.) Blood on the Shores, 1993; (trans.) The Official Makarov 9mm Pistol Manual, 1995; (ed. and trans.) D. Loza, Commanding the Red Army's Sherman Tanks: The World War II Memoirs of Hero of the Soviet Union, Dmitriy Loza, 1996; (ed. and trans.) Dmitriy Loza, Fighting for the Soviet Motherland: Recollections From the Eastern Front Hero of the Soviet Union, 1998; The Road to Abu Ghraib: U.S. Army Detainee Doctrine and Experience, 2005; Eyes Behind the Lines: U.S. Army Long-range Reconnaissance and Surveillance Units, 2005; (trans.) Dragons on Bird Wings: The Combat History of the 812th Fighter Regiment, 2006. **Address:** 1509 Jackson Ct., Leavenworth, KS 66048, U.S.A. **Online address:** kargeb@aol.com

GECAN, Michael. American (born United States) **Genres:** Administration/Management, Politics/Government. **Career:** Industrial Areas Foundation, community organizer, director; East Brooklyn Congregations, lead organizer; United Power for Action and Justice, executive director. Writer. **Publications:** (Ed.) Seen through Our Eyes, 1972; Going Public: An Inside Story of Disrupting Politics as Usual, 2002; Going Public: An Organizer's Guide to Citizen Action, 2004; After America's Midlife Crisis, 2009. **Address:** c/o Author Mail, Beacon Press, 25 Beacon St., Boston, MA 02108-2824, U.S.A.

GEDDES, Gary. Canadian (born Canada), b. 1940. **Genres:** Novellas/Short Stories, Poetry, Archaeology/Antiquities, Travel/Exploration, Essays, Translations. **Career:** University of Toronto, faculty, 1965-70; York University, instructor in English, 1966-67; Ryerson Polytechnic Institute, instructor in English, 1966-69; Trent University, visiting assistant professor, 1969; Carleton University, lecturer, 1971-72; University of Victoria, lecturer, 1972-74; University of British Columbia, British Columbia Institute of Technology, lecturer in English, 1974-76, Green College, writer-in-residence; University of Alberta, writer-in-residence, 1976, visiting associate professor, 1977; Concordia University, visiting associate professor, 1978-87, writer-in-residence, 1979, professor of English, 1987-98; Western Washington University, distinguished professor of Canadian culture, 1998-2001; Douglas and McIntyre, Studies in Canadian Literature Series, general editor; University of Ottawa, writer-in-residence, 2004. **Publications:** POETRY: Rivers Inlet, 1971; Poems, 1972; Snakeroot, 1973; Letter of the Master of Horse, 1973; War and Other Measures, 1976; The Acid Test, 1981; The Terracotta Army, 1984; Changes of State, 1986; Hong Kong Poems, 1987; No Easy Exit/Salida difícil, 1989; Light of Burning Towers: Poems New and Selected, 1990; Girl by the Water, 1993; The Perfect Cold Warrior, 1995; Active Trading: Selected Poems 1970-1995, 1996; Flying Blind, 1998; Skaldance, 2004. OTHER: Conrad's Later Novels, 1980; (co-author) Chinada: Memoirs of the Gang of Seven, 1982; (co-trans.) I Didn't Notice the Mountain Growing Dark, 1985; The Unsettling of the West (stories), 1986; Letters from Managua (essays), 1990; Sailing Home: A Journey through Time, Place and Memory, 2001; Kingdom of Ten Thousand Things, 2005; Falsework, 2007; Kingdom of Ten Thousand Things: An Impossible Journey from Kabul to Chiapas, 2007; Out of the Ordinary: Politics, Poetry and Narrative, 2009; Swimming Ginger, 2010. EDITOR: 20th-century Poetry and Poetics, 1969, 2nd ed., 1973; (with P. Bruce) 15 Canadian Poets, 1970, 4th ed. as 15 Canadian Poets X 3, 2001; Skookum Wawa: Writings of the Canadian Northwest, 1975; Divided We Stand, 1977; The Inner Ear: An Anthology of New Canadian Poets, 1982; (and intro.) Vancouver: Soul of a City, 1986; (with H. Hazelton) Companeros: An Anthology of Writings about Latin America, 1990; The Art of Short Fiction: An International Anthology, 1993. Contributor to periodicals. **Address:** 975 Seaside Dr., RR 2, Sooke, BC V0S 1N0, Canada. **Online address:** gedworks@islandnet.com

GEDGE, Pauline (Alice). Canadian/New Zealander (born New Zealand), b. 1945. **Genres:** Science Fiction/Fantasy, Novels. **Career:** Writer. **Publications:** FICTION: Child of the Morning, 1977; The Eagle and the Raven, 1978; Stargate, 1982; The Twelfth Transforming, 1984; Mirage, 1990; Scroll of Saqqara, 1990; Covenant, 1992; House of Dreams, 1994; Lady of the Reeds, 1995; House of Illusions, 1997; The Oasis, 1999; The Hippopotamus

Marsh, 2000; The Horus Road, 2000; The Twice Born, 2008; Seer of Egypt, 2008; The King's Man, 2011. Contributor to periodicals. **Address:** c/o Bella Pomer, The Bella Pomer Agency, 355 St. Clair Ave. W, Ste. 801, Toronto, ON M5P 1N5, Canada.

GEDIMAN, Helen K. American (born United States), b. 1931. **Genres:** Psychology, Psychiatry, Medicine/Health. **Career:** New York Freudian Society, faculty and training and supervisory analyst, 1971-; New York University, clinical professor of psychology, 1973-, clinical consultant and supervisor. Writer. **Publications:** (Co-author) Ego Functions in Schizophrenics, Neurotics, and Normals: A Systematic Study of Conceptual, Diagnostic, and Therapeutic Aspects, 1973; Fantasies of Love and Death in Life and Art: A Psychoanalytic Study of the Normal and the Pathological, 1995; (with J.S. Lieberman) Many Faces of Deceit: Omissions, Lies, and Disguise in Psychotherapy, 1996. Contributor to journals. **Address:** New York University, 240 Greene St., 3rd Fl., New York, NY 10003-6675, U.S.A. **Online address:** hgediman@compuserve.com

GEDMIN, Jeffrey (N.). Czech/American (born United States), b. 1958. **Genres:** Politics/Government, History, Social Commentary. **Career:** Georgetown University, adjunct professor, 1985-; New Atlantic Initiative, executive director, 1996-2001; Aspen Institute Berlin, director, 2001-07; Radio Free Europe/Radio Liberty, director, 2007-, president and chief executive officer, 2007-11; Legatum Institute, president and chief executive officer, 2011-. Writer. **Publications:** The Hidden Hand: Gorbachev and the Collapse of East Germany, 1992; (ed.) The Germans: Portrait of a New Nation, 1995; (ed.) European Integration and American Interests: What the New Europe Really Means for the United States, 1997; (ed.) A Single European Currency?, 1997. Contributor of articles to journals and magazines. **Address:** Legatum Institute, 11 Charles St., Mayfair, GL W1J 5DW, United Kingdom. **Online address:** jgedmin@aei.org

GEE, Darien. See KING, Mia Hsu.

GEE, Maggie (Mary). British (born England), b. 1948. **Genres:** Novels, Science Fiction/Fantasy, Sciences, Art/Art History, Literary Criticism And History, Writing/Journalism. **Career:** Elsevier International Press, editor, 1972-74; Wolverhampton Polytechnic, research assistant, 1975-79; Sussex University, visiting fellow, 1986-; Northern Arts, writer-in-residence, 1996. **Publications:** Dying in Other Words, 1981; (ed.) Anthology of Writing against War: For Life on Earth, 1982; The Burning Book, 1983; Light Years, 1985; Grace, 1989; Where Are the Snows, 1991 as Christopher and Alexandra, 1992; Lost Children, 1994; How May I Speak in My Own Voice? Language and the Forbidden, 1996; The Ice People, 1998; The White Family, 2002; The Flood, 2004; My Cleaner, 2005; The Blue, 2006; (ed. with B. Evaristo) NW15, 2007; My Driver, 2009; My Animal Life, 2010. Contributor to periodicals. **Address:** Society of Authors, 84 Drayton Gardens, London, GL SW10 9SB, England.

GEE, Maurice (Gough). New Zealander (born New Zealand), b. 1931. **Genres:** Novels, Novellas/Short Stories, Children's Fiction. **Career:** Teacher, 1955-57; Alexander Turnbull Library, assistant librarian, 1967-69; Napier Public Library, city librarian, 1970-72; Teachers College Library, deputy librarian, 1974-75; writer, 1976-; Victoria University of Wellington, writing fellow. **Publications:** Landfall, 1955; The Big Season, 1962; A Special Flower, 1965; In My Father's Den, 1972; A Glorious Morning, Comrade: Stories, 1975; Games of Choice, 1976; Plumb, 1978; Nelson Central School: A History, 1978; Under the Mountain, 1979; The World around the Corner, 1980; Meg, 1981; The Halfmen of O, 1982; Sole Survivor, 1983; The Priests of Ferris, 1984; Motherstone, 1985; Collected Stories, 1986; Prowlers, 1987; The Champion, 1989; The Burning Boy, 1990; Going West, 1992; The Fire-Raiser, 1992; Crime Story, 1994; The Fat Man, 1994; Loving Ways, 1996; Live Bodies, 1998; Orchard Street, 1998; Hostel Girl, 1999; Ellie and the Shadow Man, 2001; The Scornful Moon: A Moralist's Tale, 2003; Blindsight: A Novel, 2005; Salt, 2007; Gool, 2008; Access Road, 2009; Limping Man, 2010. **Address:** 41 Chelmsford St., Ngaio, New Wellington, 9, New Zealand.

GEE, Shirley. British (born England), b. 1932. **Genres:** Plays/Screenplays, Young Adult Fiction. **Career:** Stage and television actress, 1952-66; playwright and screen writer. **Publications:** Never in My Lifetime, 1987; Ask for the Moon, 1988; Warrior, 1991. **Address:** David Higham Associates, 5-8 Lower John St., Golden Sq., London, GL W1F 9HA, England.

GEE, Sophie. American/Australian (born Australia), b. 1974. **Genres:** Nov-

els, History. **Career:** Princeton University, assistant professor of English, 2002-, associate professor, director of undergraduate studies; University College London, visiting lecturer. Writer. **Publications:** The Scandal of the Season (novel), 2007; Making Waste: Leftovers and the Eighteenth-Century Imagination, 2010. **Address:** Department of English, Princeton University, 49 McCosh Hall, Princeton, NJ 08544-1014, U.S.A. **Online address:** sgee@princeton.edu

GEER, Charlie. Spanish/American (born United States), b. 1970?. **Genres:** Human Relations/Parenting, Humor/Satire, Young Adult Fiction. **Career:** University of Charleston, visiting instructor; Crazyhorse, assistant editor; College of Charleston, instructor, professor, visiting professor; Crazyhorse, assistant editor. **Publications:** Outbound: The Curious Secession of Latter-Day Charleston, 2005. Contributor to periodicals. **Address:** River City Publishing, 1719 Mulberry St., Montgomery, AL 36106, U.S.A. **Online address:** geerc@cofc.edu

GEHMAN, Mary W. American (born United States), b. 1923. **Genres:** Children's Fiction, Literary Criticism And History. **Career:** Gehmans Mennonite School, elementary teacher, 1954-57, 1976-79; Cocalico School District, teacher, 1979-83. Writer. **Publications:** Abdi and the Elephants, 1995. Contributor to periodicals. **Address:** 111 Witmer Rd., Reinholds, PA 17569, U.S.A.

GEHRIG, Klaus. Canadian/German (born Germany), b. 1946. **Genres:** Novels, Travel/Exploration, Sports/Fitness, Recreation, Reference. **Career:** Writer. **Publications:** Taking a Little Sailing Ship: A View of the World from a Thirty-Foot Schooner, 1991; The Eyes of the Roof, 2001. Contributor to periodicals. **Address:** Gehrig Studio, 2270 Windsor Rd., Hwy. 14, Chester, NS B0J 1J0, Canada. **Online address:** gehrig_k@hotmail.com

GEHRING, Wes D(avid). American (born United States), b. 1950. **Genres:** Film, Biography, Autobiography/Memoirs. **Career:** Ball State University, professor of telecommunications, 1978-; USA Today Magazine, associate media editor. **Publications:** Leo McCarey and the Comic Anti-Hero in American Film, 1980; Charlie Chaplin's World of Comedy, 1980; Charlie Chaplin: A Bio-Bibliography, 1983; Screwball Comedy: Defining a Film Genre, 1983; W.C. Fields, A Bio-Bibliography, 1984; Screwball Comedy: A Genre of Madcap Romance, 1986; The Marx Brothers: A Bio-Bibliography, 1987; (ed.) Handbook of American Film Genres, 1988; Laurel and Hardy: A Bio-Bibliography, 1990; Mr. B or Comforting Thoughts about the Bison: A Critical Biography of Robert Benchley, 1992; Groucho and W.C. Fields: Huckster Comedians, 1994; Populism and the Capra Legacy, 1995; American Dark Comedy: Beyond Satire, 1996; Dark Humor: Beyond Satire, 1996; Personality Comedians as Genre: Selected Players, 1997; Parody as Film Genre: Never Give a Saga an Even Break, 1999; Seeing Red...The Skelton in Hollywood's Closet, 2001; Film Classics Reclassified: A Shocking Spoof of Cinema, 2001; World of Comedy: Five Takes on Funny, 2001; Romantic vs Screwball Comedy: Charting the Difference, 2002; Carole Lombard: The Hoosier Tornado, 2003; Irene Dunne: The First Lady of Hollywood, 2003; Mr. Deeds Goes to Yankee Stadium, 2004; Leo McCarey: From Marx to McCarthy, 2005; James Dean: Rebel With a Cause, 2005; Joe E. Brown: Film Comedian and Baseball Buffoon, 2006; Film Clowns of the Depression: Twelve Defining Comic Performances, 2007; Red Skelton: The Mask Behind the Mask, 2008; Steve McQueen: The Great Escape, 2009; Forties Film Funnymen: The Decade's Great Comedians at Work in the Shadow of War, 2010; Robert Wise, 2011. Works appears in anthologies. Contributor of essays to periodicals. **Address:** Department of Telecommunications, Ball State University, Ball Communication Bldg. 201E, 2000 W University Ave., Muncie, IN 47306, U.S.A. **Online address:** wesgehring@bsu.edu

GEISERT, Arthur (Frederick). American (born United States), b. 1941. **Genres:** Children's Fiction, Animals/Pets. **Career:** Concordia College, art teacher. Writer. **Publications:** SELF-ILLUSTRATED FOR CHILDREN: The Orange Scarf, 1970; Pa's Balloon and Other Pig Tales, 1984; Alphabet Book, 1985; Pigs from A to Z, 1986; The Ark, 1988; Oink, 1991; Aesop and Company, 1991; Pigs from 1 to 10, 1992; Oink Oink, 1993; After the Flood, 1994; Haystack, 1995; Roman Numerals I to MM, 1996; The Etcher's Studio, 1997; Prairie Town, 1998; River Town, 1999; Mountain Town, 2000; Desert Town, 2001; Nursery Crimes, 2001; The Giant Ball of String, 2002; Mystery, 2003; Pigaroons, 2004; Lights Out, 2005; Oops, 2006; Hogwash, 2008;

Country Road ABC: An Illustrated Journey Through America's Farmland, 2010. Contributor to periodicals. **Address:** PO Box 113, Bernard, IL 52032, U.S.A. **Online address:** geisert@galenalink.net

GEISMAR, Ludwig Leo. American/German (born Germany), b. 1921. **Genres:** Sociology. **Career:** Ministry of Social Welfare, coordinator of social research, 1954-56; Family Centered Project, research director, 1956-59; Rutgers, The State University of New Jersey, Graduate School of Social Work, Department of Sociology, associate professor, 1959-62, professor of social work and sociology, 1962-74, distinguished professor of social work and sociology, 1974-91, distinguished professor emeritus of social work and sociology, 1992-, Social Work Research Center, director; University of Melbourne, visiting professor and director of a cross-national family study, 1975-76. Writer. **Publications:** Community Organization in Israel, 1955; Family Centered Project, 1957; (with B. Ayres) Families in Trouble, 1958; (with Ayres) Patterns of Change in Problem Families, 1959; (with B. Ayres) Measuring Family Functioning, 1960; (with M.A. La Sorte) Understanding the Multi-Problem Family: A Conceptual Analysis and Exploration in Early Identification, 1964; Report on a Check List Survey, 1967; (with J. Krisberg) The Forgotten Neighborhood: Site of an Early Skirmish in the War on Poverty, 1967; Preventive Intervention in Social Work, 1969; Family and Community Functioning, 1971, 2nd ed., 1980; (co-author) Early Supports for Family Life, 1972; 555 Families: A Social Psychological Study of Young Families in Transition, 1973; (with S. Geismar) Families in an Urban Mold, 1979; (ed. with M. Dinerman) A Quarter-Century of Social Work Education, 1984; (with K. Wood) Family and Delinquency: Resocializing the Young Offender, 1986; (with K.M. Wood) Families at Risk: Treating the Multiproblem Family, 1989; (with M. Camasso) The Family Functioning Scale, 1993; In the Shadow of the Holocaust: Events and Ideologies Confronting an Immigrant to the United States, 2005. Contributor to journals. **Address:** Graduate School of Social Work, Rutgers, The State University of New Jersey, 26 Nichol Ave., New Brunswick, NJ 08901, U.S.A. **Online address:** geismar@rci.rutgers.edu

GEIST, Bill. (William E. Geist). American (born United States), b. 1945. **Genres:** Writing/Journalism, Essays, Sports/Fitness, Adult Non-fiction. **Career:** The Chicago Tribune, reporter and columnist, 1972-80; New York Times, columnist, 1980-87; CBS News, commentator and feature reporter, 1987-, Sunday Morning, correspondent, 1987-; 60 Minutes II, columnist, 2003-04. **Publications:** AS WILLIAM GEIST: Toward a Safe and Sane Halloween and Other Tales of Suburbia (essays), 1985 as The Zucchini Plague and Other Tales of Suburbia, 1987. AS WILLIAM E. GEIST: City Slickers, 1987; About New York, 1987. AS BILL GEIST: Little League Confidential: One Coach's Completely Unauthorized Tale of Survival (nonfiction), 1992; Monster Trucks & Hair-in-a-Can: Who Says America Doesn't Make Anything Anymore?, 1994; Big Five-Oh!: Fearing, Facing and Fighting Fifty, 1997; Fore! Play: The Last American Male to Take Up Golf, 2001; Way Off the Road: Discovering the Peculiar Charms of Small-Town America, 2007. **Address:** CBS News, CBS Broadcasting Inc., 51 W 52nd St., New York, NY 10019-6165, U.S.A.

GEIST, William E. See **GEIST, Bill.**

GEKOSKI, R. A. See **GEKOSKI, Rick.**

GEKOSKI, Rick. Also writes as R. A. Gekoski. American (born United States) **Genres:** inspirational/Motivational Literature, Bibliography, Autobiography/Memoirs, Biography. **Career:** R.A. Gekoski Booksellers, founder and owner, 1982-; BBC Radio 4, presenter; University of Warwick, senior lecturer in English. Writer. **Publications:** Conrad: The Moral World of the Novelist, 1978; (with P.A. Grogan) William Golding: A Bibliography 1934-1993, 1994; Staying Up: A Fan behind the Scenes in the Premiership, 1998; Nabokov's Butterfly and Other Stories of Great Authors and Rare Books in UK as Tolkien's Gown and Other Stories of Great Authors and Rare Books, 2004; Outside of a Dog: A Bibliomemoir, 2009. Contributor to periodicals. **Address:** Pied Bull Yard, 15A Bloomsbury Sq., London, GL WC1A 2LP, England. **Online address:** rick@gekoski.com

GELB, Jeff. American (born United States) **Genres:** Horror, Novels, Young Adult Fiction. **Career:** Educator and writer. **Publications:** EDITOR-HOT BLOOD ANTHOLOGY SERIES: (with L. Friend) Hot Blood: Tales of Erotic Horror, 1989; (with M. Garrett) Hotter Blood: More Tales of Erotic Horror, 1991; (with M. Garrett) Hottest Blood, 1993; (with M. Garrett) Deadly after Dark, 1994; (with M. Garrett) Seeds of Fear, 1995; (with M. Garrett) Stranger by Night, 1995; (with M. Garrett) Fear the Fever, 1996; (with M. Garrett) Kiss and Kill, 1997; (with M. Garrett) Hot Blood: Crimes of Passion, 1997; (with M. Garrett) Hot Blood X, 1998; (with M. Garrett) Hot Blood XI: Fatal Attractions, 2003; Strange Bedfellows, 2004; Dark Delicacies, 2005; Dark Delicacies 2, 2007; (with M. Garrett) Dark Passions: Hot Blood, 2007. EDITOR-FLESH AND BLOOD ANTHOLOGY SERIES: (with M.A. Collins) Flesh and Blood: Erotic Tales of Crime and Passion, 2001; (with M.A. Collins) Flesh and Blood: Dark Desires: Tales of Crime and Passion, 2002; (with M.A. Collins) Flesh and Blood: Guilty As Sin: Erotic Tales of Crime and Passion, 2003. OTHER: Specters, 1988; (ed.) Shock Rock (anthology), 1992; (ed.) Shock Rock II (anthology), 1994; (ed.) Fear Itself (anthology), 1995. **Address:** c/o Author Mail, Mysterious Press, Warner Books, 1271 Ave. of the Americas, New York, NY 10020, U.S.A.

GELB, Michael J. American (born United States), b. 1952. **Genres:** Education, How-to Books, Reference. **Career:** High Performance Learning, founder and president, 1982-; Conscious Capitalism Institute, director of creativity and innovation leadership. Writer, speaker and consultant. **Publications:** Body Learning: An Introduction to the Alexander Technique, 1981; Present Yourself! Captivate Your Audience with Great Presentation Skills: Transforming Fear, Knowing Your Audience, Setting the Stage, Making Them Remember, 1988; (with T. Buzan) Lessons from the Art of Juggling: How to Achieve Your Full Potential in Business, Learning and Life, 1994; Thinking for a Change: Discovering the Power to Create, Communicate and Lead, 1995; (with R. Keene) Samurai Chess: Mastering Strategic Thinking Through the Martial Art of the Mind, 1997; How to Think Like Leonardo da Vinci: Seven Steps to Genius Every Day, 1998; The How to Think Like Leonardo da Vinci Workbook: Your Personal Companion to How to Think like Leonardo da Vinci, 1999; Discover Your Genius: Ten Secrets to Break through Thinking from History's Most Revolutionary Minds, 2002; More Balls Than Hands: Juggling Your Way to Success by Learning to Love Your Mistakes, 2003; Da Vinci Decoded: Discovering the Spiritual Secrets of Leonardo's Seven Principles, 2004; (with S.M. Caldicott) Innovate Like Edison: The Success System of Americas Greatest Inventor, 2007; Wine Drinking for Inspired Thinking: Uncork Your Creative Juices, 2010; Brain Power: Improve Your Mind as You Age, 2012. Contributor to periodicals. **Address:** c/o Muriel Nellis, 3543 Albemarle St. NW, Washington, NM 20008, U.S.A. **Online address:** michael@michaelgelb.com

GELBER, Yoav. Israeli (born Israel), b. 1943. **Genres:** History. **Career:** Israel Defense Forces (IDF), career officer, 1961-74, Agranat State Commission of Inquiry, academic and military assistant, 1973-75; Ben-Gurion University, instructor in Jewish history, 1975-77; University of Haifa, Department of Land of Israel Studies, associate professor, 1983- 87, professor, 1987-, chair, 1999-2001, Strochlitz Institute for Research and Study of the Holocaust, head, 1985-95; Herzl Institute for Research and Study of Zionism, head, 1987, School of history, chair, 2000-02; Seminario Rabinico Latinoamericano, visiting professor, 1993; Knox College, 1996. Writer. **Publications:** IN HEBREW: Toldot ha- hitnadvut, 1979; Ha-hitnadvut la-tsava ha-Briti be-Milhemet ha-'Olam ha-Sheniyah, 1984; Lamah perku et ha-Palmah: ha-koah ha-tseva'i ba-ma'avar mi-yishuv li-medinah, 1986; Gar'in le-tsava 'Ivri sadir: terumatam shel yots'e ha-Tsava ha-Briti la-hakamat Tsahal, 1986; Meha-ma'avak neged ha-Britim le-Milhemet ha-'Atsma'ut: yom 'iyun, 1989; Metsadah: ha-haganah 'al Erets-Yisra'el be-Milhemet ha-'olam hasheniyah, 1990; Moledet hadashah: 'aliyat Yehude merkaz Eropah u-kelitatam, 1933-1948, 1990; (ed.) Bene keshet: me'ah shenot ma'avak, hamishim shenot Tsahal, 1998; Komemiyut ve-Nakbah: Yisra'el, ha-Falestinim u-medinot 'Arav, 1948, 2004; Historyah, zikaron ve- ta'amulah: ha-distsiplinah ha-historit ba-'olam uva-arets, 2007. IN ENGLISH: The Emergence of a Jewish Army: The Veterans of the British Army in the IDF, 1986; Why the Palmach Was Disbanded? The Jewish Military Force in the Transition from a Yishuv to a State, 1947-1949, 1986; (ed. with C. Wardi and A. Cohen) Comprehending the Holocaust: Historical and Literary Research, 1988; Masada: The Defense of Palestine in the Second World War, 1990; A New Homeland: The Immigration from Central Europe and Its Absorption in Eretz Israel, 1933- 1948, 1990; (ed. with A. Cohen, Y. Cochavi and C. Alpert) Dapim: Studies on the Shoah, 1991; (ed. with A. Cohen and Y. Cochavi) The Shoah and the War, 1992; Jewish-Transjordanian Relations, 1921-48, 1997; Palestine, 1948: War, Escape, and the Emergence of the Palestinian Refugee Problem, 2001; Israeli-Jordanian Dialogue, 1948-1953: Cooperation, Conspiracy, or Collusion?, 2004; Independence versus Nakbah: The Arab-Israeli War of 1948, 2004. THE HISTORY OF ISRAELI INTELLIGENCE SERIES: The History of Israeli Intelligence, vol. I: Growing a Fleur-de-Lis: The Intelligence Services of the Jewish Yishuv in Palestine, 1918-1947, 1992, vol. II: Budding a Fleur-de-Lis: Israeli Intelligence in the War of Independence, 1947-1949, 2001. JEWISH PALESTINIAN VOLUNTEERING IN THE BRITISH ARMY DURING THE SECOND WORLD WAR SERIES: Jewish Palestinian Volunteering in the British Army during the Second World War, vol. I: Volunteering and Its Role in the Zionist Party, 1939-1942, 1979, vol. II: The Struggle for a Jewish Army, 1981, vol. III: The Standard Bearers The Mission of the Volunteers to the Jewish People, 1983, vol. IV: Jewish Volunteers in British Units, 1984. OTHER: (with W. Goldstern) Vertreibung und Emigration deutschsprachiger Ingenieure nach Palastina, 1933-1945, 1988. **Address:** The Inter-disciplinary Center, Kanfei Nesharim St., PO Box 167, Herzliya, 46150, Israel. **Online address:** ygelber@idc.ac.il

GELDARD, Richard G. American (born United States), b. 1935. **Genres:** Literary Criticism And History, Travel/Exploration, Essays. **Career:** Collegiate School, head, 1979-85; Yeshiva University, teacher of philosophy, 1985-94; Pacifica Graduate Institute, faculty of Greek mystery religions; University of Philosophical Research, professor; writer, 1996-. **Publications:** A Traveler's Key to Ancient Greece: A Guide to the Sacred Places of Ancient Greece, 1989; Esoteric Emerson: The Spiritual Teachings of Ralph Waldo Emerson, 1993; (ed. and intro.) Vision of Emerson, 1995; God in Concord, 1999; The Find At Ephesus, 2000; Remembering Heraclitus, 2000; Spiritual Teachings of Ralph Waldo Emerson, 2001; The Olympic Ideal, 2004; (ed. and intro.) Essential Transcendentalists, 2005; (trans.) Parmenides and The Way of Truth, 2007; Listening to Emerson, 2008; Anaxagoras and Universal Mind, 2008; Emerson and the Dream of America: Finding Our Way to a New and Exceptional Age, 2010. **Address:** 650 W End Ave., New York, NY 10025-7355, U.S.A. **Online address:** richgeldard@gmail.com

GELDENHUYS, Deon. (Tom Barnard). South African (born South Africa), b. 1950. **Genres:** International Relations/Current Affairs, Politics/Government. **Career:** University of Stellenbosch, Department of Politics, faculty; South African Institute of International Affairs, researcher; Rand Afrikaans University, faculty of humanities, 1981-, Department of Politics, lecturer, professor of politics, 1985-; Political Science Association, president, 1989-91. Writer. **Publications:** South Africa's Search for Security Since the Second World War, 1978; (ed.) Sanctions Against South Africa, 1979; (ed.) Role of Multinational Corporations in South Africa, 1979; International Attitudes on the Recognition of Transkei, 1979; Neutral Option and Sub-Continental Solidarity, 1979; (ed.) South African Labour Scene in the 1980s: Discussions of the Study Group on Multinational Corporations, 1980; Constellation of Southern African States and the Southern African Development Coordination Council, 1981; (with W. Gutteridge) Instability and Conflict in Southern Africa, 1983; The Diplomacy of Isolation: South African Foreign Policy Making, 1984; Internasionale isolasie: Suid-Afrika in vergelykende perspektief, 1985; Die groepsgebod in P.W. Botha se politieke oortuigings, 1987; Isolated States: A Comparative Analysis, 1990; (as Tom Barnard) South Africa 1994-2004: A Popular History, 1991; South Africa and the China Question: A Case for Dual Recognition, 1995; Foreign Political Engagement: Remaking States in the Post-Cold War World, 1998; Deviant Conduct in World Politics, 2004; Contested States in World Politics, 2009. **Address:** Department of Politics & Governance, University of Johannesburg, C-Ring 707, Kingsway Campus, PO Box 524, Auckland Park, 2006, South Africa. **Online address:** deong@uj.ac.za

GELDERMAN, Carol (Wettlaufer). American (born United States), b. 1939. **Genres:** Adult Non-fiction, Theatre, Writing/Journalism, Biography, Essays. **Career:** Louisiana State University, assistant professor of English, 1972-75; University of New Orleans, associate professor, 1975-80, professor, 1980-88, research professor, 1988-93, distinguished professor of English, 1993-2009, now professor emeritus, Creative Writing Workshop, faculty. Writer. **Publications:** George Fitzmaurice (literary criticism), 1979; Henry Ford: The Wayward Capitalist, 1981; Better Writing for Professionals, 1984; Mary McCarthy: A Life, 1989; (ed.) Conversations with Mary McCarthy, 1991; Better Business Writing, 1992; Louis Auchincloss, A Writer's Life, 1993, rev. ed., 2007; All the Presidents' Words: The Bully Pulpit and the Creation of the Virtual Presidency, 1997; A Free Man of Color and His Hotel: Race, Reconstruction, and the Role of the Federal Government, 2012. Contributor to journals and magazines. **Address:** Department of English, University of New Orleans, 261 Liberal Arts Bldg., 2000 Lakeshore Dr., New Orleans, LA 70148, U.S.A. **Online address:** cgelderm@uno.edu

GELEK, Ngawang. (Gelek Rimpoche). Tibetan/American (born United States), b. 1939. **Genres:** Area Studies, Literary Criticism And History, inspirational/Motivational Literature, Philosophy, Psychology, Theology/Religion. **Career:** Tibetan Incarnate Lama and Intl., lecturer; Case Western Reserve University, instructor; University of Michigan, research consultant; Jewel Heart, instructor, president and founder, 1988-. Writer. **Publications:** (With M.C. Goldstein) A History of Modern Tibet, 1918-1951: The Demise of the Lamaist State, 1989; (with M.C. Goldstein and L. Phuntshog) Essentials of Modern Literary Tibetan: A Reading Course and Reference Grammar, 1991; (as R.N. Gehlek) Good Life, Good Death: Tibetan Wisdom on Reincarnation, 2001; Tara Box with Brenda Rosen, 2004. **Address:** Jewel Heart, 1129 Oak Valley Dr., Ann Arbor, MI 48108, U.S.A. **Online address:** gelek@jewelheart.org

GELERNTER, David (Hillel). American (born United States), b. 1955?. **Genres:** Information Science/Computers, History, Politics/Government, Theology/Religion. **Career:** Scientific Computing Associates, consultant. Yale University, Department of Computer Science, associate professor, now professor. Writer. **Publications:** (With N. Carriero) How to Write Parallel Programs: A First Course, 1990; (with S. Jagannathan) Programming Linguistics, 1990; (ed. with A. Nicolau and D. Padua) Languages and Compilers for Parallel Computing, 1990; Mirror Worlds, or The Day Software Puts the Universe in a Shoebox: How It Will Happen and What It Will Mean, 1991; The Muse in the Machine: Computerizing the Poetry of Human Thought, 1994; 1939, The Lost World of the Fair, 1995; Drawing Life: Surviving the Unabomber, 1997; The Aesthetics of Computing, 1998; Machine Beauty: Elegance and the Heart of Technology, 1999; Americanism: The Fourth Great Western Religion, 2007; Judaism: A Way of Being, 2009. Contributor to periodicals. **Address:** Yale University, 107 A.K. Watson Hall, 51 Prospect St., New Haven, CT 06511, U.S.A. **Online address:** david.gelernter@yale.edu

GELLATELY, Robert. American/Canadian (born Canada), b. 1943?. **Genres:** History, Politics/Government, Social Sciences, Law. **Career:** Clark University, Strassler professor in Holocaust history, 1998-2003; Florida State University, faculty, 2003-, Earl Ray Beck professor of history, 2003-; Cornell University, faculty; University of Western Ontario, Huron College, faculty; Oxford University, Bertelsmann visiting professor of twentieth century Jewish politics and history, 2004-05. Writer. **Publications:** The Politics of Economic Despair: Shopkeepers and German Politics, 1890-1914, 1974; The Gestapo and German Society: Enforcing Racial Policy, 1933-1945, 1990; (ed. with S. Fitzpatrick) Accusatory Practices: Denunciation in Modern European History, 1789-1989, 1997; Backing Hitler: Consent and Coercion in Nazi Germany, 2001; (ed. with N. Stoltzfus) Social Outsiders in Nazi Germany, 2001; (ed. with B. Kiernan) The Specter of Genocide: Mass Murder in Historical Perspective, 2003; (ed. and intro.) The Nuremberg Interviews: An American Psychiatrist's Conversations with Defendants and Witnesses, 2004; Lenin, Stalin and Hitler: The Age of Social Catastrophe, 2007. **Address:** Department of History, Florida State University, 401 Bellamy Bldg., PO Box 3062200, Tallahassee, FL 32306-2200, U.S.A. **Online address:** rgellate@fsu.edu

GELLER, Jaclyn. American (born United States), b. 1963. **Genres:** Sociology, Social Sciences, Cultural/Ethnic Topics. **Career:** New York University, instructor, 1997-; Barnard College, instructor, 2001-; Central Connecticut State University, assistant professor, 2004-10, associate professor of English literature, 2010-. Writer. **Publications:** Here Comes the Bride: Women, Weddings, and the Marriage Mystique, 2001. Contributor to books and periodicals. **Address:** Department of English, Central Connecticut State University, 303 Willard Hall, 1615 Stanley St., New Britain, CT 06050-4010, U.S.A. **Online address:** jqg2039@nyu.edu

GELLER, Jay Howard. American (born United States), b. 1972?. **Genres:** Theology/Religion, History, Social Sciences. **Career:** Albertus Magnus College, adjunct professor, 2001; Southern Connecticut State University, adjunct professor, 2001; University of Tulsa, assistant professor, 2002-07, associate professor of history, 2007-10, Program in Judaic Studies, director; Case Western Reserve University, associate professor of history, 2011-, Samuel Rosenthal professor of Judaic studies, 2011-. Writer. **Publications:** Jews in Post-Holocaust Germany, 1945-1953, 2005. Works appear in anthologies. Contributor of articles to journals. **Address:** Department of History, University of Tulsa, 800 S Tucker Dr., Tulsa, OK 74104-9700, U.S.A. **Online address:** jay-geller@utulsa.edu

GELLES, Edith B. American (born United States), b. 1936?. **Genres:** History. **Career:** Writer, historian and educator. **Publications:** (Ed. and intro.) For Instruction and Research: A Century of Library Collections at Stanford: An Exhibition Catalogue Issued on the Occasion of Stanford University's Centennial, 1991; Portia: The World of Abigail Adams, 1995; (ed. and intro.) First Thoughts: Life and Letters of Abigail Adams, 1998; Abigail Adams: A Writing Life, 2002; The Letters of Abigaill Levy Franks, 1733-1748, 2004; Abigail & John: Portrait of a Marriage, 2009. **Address:** 10 E 53rd St., New York, NY 10022, U.S.A. **Online address:** gelles@stanford.edu

GELLIS, Roberta (Leah Jacobs). Also writes as Priscilla Hamilton, Leah Jacobs, Max Daniels. American (born United States), b. 1927. **Genres:** Novellas/Short Stories, Mystery/Crime/Suspense, Romance/Historical, Science Fiction/Fantasy, Adult Non-fiction, Young Adult Fiction. **Career:** Foster D. Snell Inc., chemist, 1947-53; FMcGraw-Hill Book Co., editor, 1953-56; Macmillan Co., editor, 1956-58; New York University, teaching assistant in English, 1956-58; Academic Press, editor, 1956-70; Hudson Laboratories, microbiologist, 1961-63; freelance author, 1964-. **Publications:** (As Max Daniels) Passport to Terror, 1960; Knight's Honor, 1964; Bond of Blood, 1965; (as Leah Jacobs) The Psychiatrist's Wife, 1966; Sing Witch, Sing Death, 1975; The Dragon and the Rose, 1977; The Sword and the Swan, 1977; (as Max Daniels) Space Guardian (science fiction), 1978; (as Max Daniels) Offworld! (science fiction), 1979; (as Priscilla Hamilton) Love Token, 1979; A Tapestry of Dreams, 1985; The Rope Dancer, 1986; Fires of Winter, 1987; Masques of Gold, 1988; A Delicate Balance, 1993; Dazzling Brightness, 1994; Shimmering Splendor, 1995; Irish Magic: Four Tales of Rand Enchantment from Four Acclaimed Authors, 1995; Enchanted Fire, 1996; How to Write Historical Fiction, 1998; A Bull God, 2000; Thrice Bound, 2001; Lucrezia Borgia and the Mother of Poisons, 2003; (with M. Lackey) This Scepter'd Isle, 2004; Overstars Mail: Imperial Challenge, 2004; Ill Met By Moonlight, 2005; (with M. Lackey) By Slanderous Tongues, 2007; (with M. Lackey) And Less than Kind, 2008. THE ROSELYNDE CHRONICLES: Roselynde, 1978; Alinor, 1978; Joanna, 1978; Gilliane, 1979; Rhiannon, 1982; Sybelle, 1983; Desiree, 2004. HEIRESS SERIES: The English Heiress, 1980, The Cornish Heiress, 1981; The Kent Heiress, 1982, Fortune's Bride, 1983; A Woman's Estate, 1984. ROYAL DYNASTY SERIES: Siren Song, 1981; Winter Song, 1982; Fire Song, 1984; A Silver Mirror, 1989. MAGDALENE LA BATARD MYSTERY SERIES: Mortal Bane, 1999; A Personal Devil, 2001; Bone of Contention, 2002; Chains of Folly: A Magdalene la Batarde Mystery, 2006. Contributor to books. **Address:** PO Box 67, Lafayette, IN 47902, U.S.A. **Online address:** robertagellis@juno.com

GELLMAN, Marc. American (born United States) **Genres:** Theology/Religion, inspirational/Motivational Literature, History, Children's Fiction. **Career:** Temple Beth Torah, senior rabbi, 1981-; Beth Torah Synagogue, rabbi; The God Squad (syndicated interfaith program), Faith and Values/VISN cable network, cohost; Hebrew Union College, faculty; Northwestern University of Chicago, professor of English; Antioch College, faculty; Amherst College, lecturer; Princeton University, lecturer. Writer. **Publications:** FOR CHILDREN: Does God Have a Big Toe? Stories about Stories in the Bible, 1989; (with T. Hartman) Where Does God Live?, 1991; (with T. Hartman) How Do You Spell God? Answers to the Big Questions from Around the World, 1995; God's Mailbox: More Stories about Stories in the Bible, 1996; Always Wear Clean Underwear!: And Other Ways Parents Say I Love You, 1997; Lost and Found: A Kid's Book for Living through Loss, 1999; (with T. Hartman) Religion for Dummies, 2002; (with T. Hartman) Bad Stuff in the News: A Guide to Handling the Headlines, 2002; And God Cried, Too: A Kid's Book of Healing and Hope, 2002; Someday You'll Thank Me for This!, 2007. Contributor of book reviews to periodicals. **Address:** Temple Beth Torah, 35 Bagatelle Rd., Melville, NY 11747, U.S.A.

GELL-MANN, Murray. American (born United States), b. 1929. **Genres:** Physics, Sciences. **Career:** University of Illinois, research associate, 1951, 1953; University of Chicago, instructor, 1952-53, assistant professor, 1953-54, associate professor, 1954-55; Columbia University, visiting professor, 1954; California Institute of Technology, associate professor, 1955-56, professor, 1956-67, Robert Andrews Millikan professor, 1967-93, Robert Andrews Millikan professor emeritus, 1993-; Rand Corp., consultant, 1956-; Los Alamos Scientific Laboratory, consultant, 1956-; College de France and University of Paris, visiting professor, 1959-60; Massachusetts Institute of Technology, visiting professor, 1963; Churchill College, overseas fellow, 1966; Institute for Defense Analyses, consultant, 1961-70; CERN, visiting professor, 1971-72, 1979-80; John D. & Catherine T. MacArthur Foundation,

director, 1979-2002; Los Alamos National Lab, laboratory fellow, 1982; Santa Fe Institute, professor and distinguished fellow, 1993-; University of New Mexico, visiting professor, 1995-. **Publications:** Lectures on Weak Interactions of Strongly Interacting Particles, 1961; (with Y. Ne'eman) The Eightfold Way: A Review with a Collection of Reprints, 1964; (with K. Wilson) Broken Scale Invariance and the Light Cone, 1971; (ed. with J.A. Hawkins) Evolution of Human Languages: Proceedings of the Workshop on the Evolution of Human Languages, Held August, 1989 in Santa Fe, New Mexico, 1992; (ed. with G.J. Gumerman) Understanding Complexity in the Prehistoric Southwest, 1994; The Quark and the Jaguar: Adventures in the Simple and the Complex, 1994; (ed. with C. Tsallis) Nonextensive Entropy: Interdisciplinary Applications, 2003. **Address:** Santa Fe Institute, 1399 Hyde Park Rd., Santa Fe, NM 87501-8943, U.S.A. **Online address:** mgm@santafe.edu

GELPI, Albert. American (born United States), b. 1931. **Genres:** Literary Criticism And History, Biography, Autobiography/Memoirs, Politics/Government, Young Adult Fiction. **Career:** Harvard University, assistant professor of English, 1962-67; Stanford University, Department of English, associate professor, 1968-75, professor of English, 1975-78, William Robertson Coe professor of American literature, 1978-99, professor emeritus, 1999-, associate dean of graduate studies, chairman; Cambridge Studies in American Literature and Culture, founding editor. **Publications:** Emily Dickinson: The Mind of the Poet, 1965; The Tenth Muse: The Psyche of the American Poet, 1975; A Coherent Splendor: The American Poetic Renaissance 1910-1950, 1987; Living in Time: The Poetry of C. Day Lewis, 1998. EDITOR: (and intro.) The Poet in America: 1650 to Present, 1973; (with B.C. Gelpi) Adrienne Rich's Poetry: Texts of the Poems: The Poet on Her Work: Reviews and Criticism, 1975 as Adrienne Rich's Poetry and Prose: Poems, Prose, Reviews, and Criticism, 1993; Wallace Stevens: The Poetics of Modernism, 1985; (and intro.) Denise Levertov: Selected Criticism, 1993; (and afterword) The Blood of the Poet: Selected Poems of William Everson, 1994; (and intro.) The Wild God of the World: An Anthology of Robinson Jeffers, 2003; (and intro.) Dark God of Eros: A William Everson Reader, 2003; (with R.J. Bertholf) The Letters of Robert Duncan and Denise Levertov, 2004; (with R.J. Bertholf) Robert Duncan and Denise Levertov: The Poetry Of Politics, The Politics Of Poetry, 2006; Postmodernism and Neoromanticism: American Poetry since 1950, forthcoming. Contributor to periodicals. **Address:** Department of English, Stanford University, Bldg. 460, Margaret Jacks Hall, Stanford, CA 94305-2087, U.S.A. **Online address:** agelpi@stanford.edu

GELTMAKER, Ty. American (born United States), b. 1952. **Genres:** History, Novellas/Short Stories, Documentaries/Reportage, Psychology. **Career:** Peoria Journal Star, reporter and copy editor, 1972-73; Rome Daily American, copy editor, feature writer and page layout technician, 1976-77; teacher, 1976-78; International Daily News (Rome), editor, political writer, page layout technician and typesetter, 1977-79; United Press Intl. (NYC), editor international and foreign desks, 1979-81; freelance writer and editor, 1981-; Cerritos Community College, history instructor, 1989; California Institute of the Arts, history and literature instructor, 1993-95, 2002-04; University of Southern California, Italian history and literature instructor, 1994-2001, visiting lecturer in Italian, 2001; City University of New York, Bronx Community College, adjunct assistant professor of history, 1996-97. **Publications:** Tired of Living: Suicide in Italy from National Unification to World War I, 1860-1915, 2002. Contributor to books and periodicals. **Address:** 1400 N Coronado St., Los Angeles, CA 90026, U.S.A. **Online address:** echobamboo@sbcglobal.net

GELVIN, James L. American (born United States), b. 1951. **Genres:** History. **Career:** University of California, Department of History, assistant profesor, 1995-99, associate professor, 1999-2005, professor, 2005-; American University of Beirut, Sheikh Zayed visiting professor of Islamic studies, 2002-03. Writer. **Publications:** Divided Loyalties: Nationalism and Mass Politics in Syria at the Close of Empire, 1998; (contrib.) The Invention of Religion: Rethinking Belief and Politics in History, 2002; (contrib.) The Waking Dream of T.E. Lawrence: Essays on His Life, Literature and Legacy, 2002; The Israel-Palestine Conflict: One Hundred Years of War, 2005, 2nd ed., 2007; The Modern Middle East: A History, 2005, 3rd ed., 2011, Arab Uprisings: What Everyone Needs to Know, 2012; From Modernization to Globalization: The United States, the Middle East, and the World Economy in the Twentieth Century, forthcoming; (co-ed.) Circuits and Networks: Islam and Islamic Communities in the First Age of Globalization, forthcoming. Contributor to journals. **Address:** Department of History, University of California, 7377 Bunche Hall, PO Box 951473, Los Angeles, CA 90095-1473, U.S.A. **Online address:** gelvin@history.ucla.edu

GEMMELL, Jim. American (born United States), b. 1965?. **Genres:** Technology, Information Science/Computers. **Career:** Microsoft Research, senior researcher. Writer and computer engineer. **Publications:** (With G. Bell) Total Recall: How the E-memory Revolution Will Change Everything, 2009. Contributor of articles to journals. **Address:** c/o James A. Levine, Levine Greenberg Literary Agency Inc., 307 7th Ave., Ste. 2407, New York, NY 10001, U.S.A. **Online address:** jgemmell@microsoft.com

GEMUNDEN, Gerd. American/German (born Germany), b. 1959. **Genres:** Film, History, Social Sciences, Art/Art History, Humanities. **Career:** Dartmouth College, department chair, 2002-08, Ted and Helen Geisel third century professor in the humanities, Sherman Fairchild professor of the humanities. Writer. **Publications:** Hermeneutische Wende: Disziplin und Sprachlosigkeit nach 1800, 1990; Wim Wenders: Einstellungen, 1993; (ed. with R.F. Cook) The Cinema of Wim Wenders: Image, Narrative and the Postmodern Condition, 1997; Framed Visions: Popular Culture, Americanization and the Contemporary German and Austrian, Imagination, 1998; (ed. with C.G. Calloway and S. Zantop) Germans and Indians: Fantasies, Encounters, Projections, 2002; Filmemacher mit Akzent: Billy Wilder in Hollywood, 2006; (ed. with M.R. Desjardins) Dietrich Icon, 2007; A Foreign Affair: Billy Wilder's American Films, 2008. **Address:** Department of German Studies, Dartmouth College, 330 Dartmouth Hall, Hanover, NH 03755-3511, U.S.A. **Online address:** gerd.gemunden@dartmouth.edu

GENASI, Chris. British (born England), b. 1962?. **Genres:** Business/Trade/Industry, Law, Politics/Government, Philosophy. **Career:** Countrywide Porter Novelli, associate director, 1985-92; Ketchum, associate director, 1992-96; Countrywide Communications, associate director, 1996-98; Weber Shandwick Intl., Corporate Division, chief executive and global director of strategy, 1996-2003; Chartered Institute of Public Relations (CIPR), president, 2004-05; Eloqui Public Relations, chief executive officer and founding partner, 2004-07; Nestle, staff; Unilever, staff; Toyota, staff; Visa, staff; European Corporate Practice, chief executive; APCO Worldwide, director. Writer and consultant. **Publications:** Winning Reputations: How to Be Your Own Spin Doctor, 2002; (with T. Bills) Creative Business: Achieving Your Goals through Creative Thinking and Action, 2003. **Address:** Eloqui Public Relations, Victory House, 99-101 Regent St., London, GL W1B 4EZ, England. **Online address:** cgenasi@eloquipr.co.uk

GENESSE, Paul. American (born United States), b. 1973?. **Genres:** Novels. **Career:** Nurse and writer. **Publications:** The Golden Cord, 2008. Contributor to books. **Address:** South Jordan, UT , U.S.A. **Online address:** pgenesse@msn.com

GENIESSE, Jane Fletcher. American (born United States), b. 1936. **Genres:** Novels, Biography. **Career:** New York Times, reporter, 1978-82; Boston Traveler, reporter; freelance writer, 1982-; Random House Inc., editor. **Publications:** The Riches of Life (novel), 1976; Passionate Nomad: The Life of Freya Stark (biography), 1999; American Priestess: The Extraordinary Story of Anna Spafford and the American Colony in Jerusalem, 2008. Contributor to magazines. **Address:** Modern Library, Random House Inc., 1745 Broadway, 18th Fl., New York, NY 10019, U.S.A.

GENINI, Ronald. American (born United States), b. 1946. **Genres:** Film. **Career:** Central Unified School District, history teacher, 1970-; California Department Education, Golden State Exam Committee, director, 1989-92. Writer. **Publications:** (With R, Hutchinson) Romualdo Pacheco: A Californio in Two Eras, 1985; (with T. Bond) Darn Right Its Butch, 1994; Theda Bara: A Biography of the Silent Screen Vamp, with a Filmography, 1996. Contributor of articles to periodicals. **Address:** Central High School, East Campus, 3535 N Cornelia Ave., Fresno, CA 93722, U.S.A. **Online address:** r_genini@yahoo.com

GENTILE, John S(amuel). American (born United States), b. 1956. **Genres:** Theatre, Speech/Rhetoric, Literary Criticism And History, Young Adult Fiction, History. **Career:** University of Northern Iowa, instructor in interpretation, 1984-85; Kennesaw State College, assistant professor, 1985-90, associate professor of communication and performance studies, 1990-, artistic director of the performance series, 1985-, Department of Theatre and Performance Studies, professor and chair. Writer. **Publications:** Cast of One: One-Person Shows from the Chautauqua Platform to the Broadway Stage, 1989. Contributor to periodicals. **Address:** Department of Theatre & Performance Studies, Kennesaw State University, 1000 Chastain Rd., Kennesaw,

GA 30144, U.S.A. **Online address:** jgentile@kennesaw.edu

GENTILE, Olivia. American (born United States), b. 1974. **Genres:** Natural History, Travel/Exploration, Autobiography/Memoirs. **Career:** Rutland Herald, reporter, 1996-99; Hartford Courant, staff, 1999-2001. Writer. **Publications:** (With N. Boutin) The Budget Guide to France 1995 (Let's Go), 1994; Life List: A Woman's Quest for the World's Most Amazing Birds, 2009. Contributor to periodicals. **Address:** c/o Priscilla Gilman, Janklow & Nesbit Associates, 445 Park Ave., New York, NY 10022-2606, U.S.A. **Online address:** lifelistthebook@gmail.com

GENTLE, Mary. (Roxanne Morgan). British (born England), b. 1956. **Genres:** Science Fiction/Fantasy, Children's Fiction, Novels. **Career:** Writer, 1979-. Movie projectionist. **Publications:** NOVELS: A Hawk in Silver, 1977; Golden Witchbreed, 1983; Ancient Light, 1989; Moon at Midday, 1989; Scholars and Soldiers, 1989; Rats and Gargoyles, 1990; The Architecture of Desire, 1991; Grunts!: A Fantasy with Attitude, 1995; Ash: A Secret History, 1999; The Wild Machines, 2000; (with S.M. Stirling, W.J. Williams and H. Turtledove) Worlds that Weren't, 2005; Sundial in a Grave 1610, 2005; Ilario, the Lion's Eye, 2006; Ilario: The Stone Golem, 2006; The Kingdom of the Two Sicilies, 2009. AS ROXANNE MORGAN: Who Dare Sins, 1995; Dares, 1995; Sinner Takes All, 1997; Bets, 1997; A Game of Masks, 1999; Degrees of Desire, 2001; Maximum Exposure, 2004. OTHERS: (ed. with R. Kaveney) Villains!, 1992; (ed. with R. Kaveney and N. Gaiman) The Weerde, 1992; Left to His Own Devices, 1994. **Address:** HarperCollins Publishers, 77-85 Fulham Palace Rd., Hammersmith, London, GL W6 8JB, England.

GENTLEMAN, David. British (born England), b. 1930. **Genres:** Children's Fiction, Adult Non-fiction, Architecture, Art/Art History, Design, Travel/Exploration, Documentaries/Reportage, Illustrations, Illustrations. **Career:** Royal College of Art, School of Graphic Design, instructor, 1953-55; freelance designer, illustrator and painter, 1955-; Royal designer for industry, staff, 1970; Royal Army Education Corps, education sergeant; Royal College of Art, junior tutor. **Publications:** Bridges on the Backs: A Series of Drawings, 1961; The Shell Book of Roads, 1964; Fenella in France, 1964; Fenella in Spain, 1964; Fenella in Greece, 1964; Fenella in Ireland, 1964; Fenella in the South of France, 1967; Design in Miniature, 1972; Everyday Architecture in Towns, 1975; Everyday Architecture in the Country, 1975; Everyday Architecture at the Seaside, 1975; Everyday Industrial Architecture, 1975; A Cross for Queen Eleanor: The Story of the Building of the Mediaeval Charing Cross, the Subject of the Decorations of the Northern Line Platforms of the New Charing Cross Underground Station, 1979; David Gentleman's Britain, 1982; (contrib.) Art and Graphics, 1983; David Gentleman's London, 1985; A Special Relationship, 1987; David Gentleman's Coastline, 1988; David Gentleman's Paris, 1991; (ed.) The Crooked Scythe, 1993; David Gentleman's India, 1994; (contrib.) Inwards Where all the Battle is: A Selection of Alun Lewis's Writings from India, 1997; David Gentleman's Italy, 1997; David Gentleman's Paris, 2000; Art Work, 2002; David Gentleman's India, 2004. **Address:** Faber and Faber Ltd., 74-77 Great Russell St., London, GL WC1B 3DA, England. **Online address:** d@gentleman.demon.co.uk

GENTRY, Christine. American (born United States), b. 1954?. **Genres:** Mystery/Crime/Suspense, Young Adult Fiction, Young Adult Non-fiction, Novels. **Career:** Waldenbooks, bookseller and assistant manager; Brush Puppies Mobile Pet Grooming, founder. Freelance writer, 1979-. **Publications:** When Dogs Run Wild: The Sociology of Feral Dogs and Wildlife, 1983; (with S. Gibson-Downs) Encyclopedia of Trekkie Memorabilia: Identification and Value Guide, 1988; When Spirits Walk, 1988; (with S.G. Downs) Greenbergs Guide to Star Trek Collectibles, 1991; (with S.G. Downs) Motorcycle Toys: Identification Values: Antique and Contemporary, 1995; Mesozoic Murder, 2003; Carnosaur Crimes, 2005. Contributor to periodicals. **Address:** Poisoned Pen Press, 6962 E 1st Ave., Ste. 103, Scottsdale, AZ 85251, U.S.A. **Online address:** christine@gentrybooks.com

GENTRY, Curt. American (born United States), b. 1931. **Genres:** Science Fiction/Fantasy, History, Biography, Young Adult Fiction, Criminology/True Crime, Technology, Social Sciences, Adult Non-fiction, Adult Non-fiction. **Career:** Part-time reporter, 1947-50; Paul Elder Books, Mail Order Department, head, 1954-57; Tro Harper Books, manager, 1957-61; freelance writer, 1961-. **Publications:** The Dolphin Guide to San Francisco and the Bay Area: Present and Past, 1962, (with T. Horton) rev. ed., 1982; (with R. Gump) Jade Stone of Heaven, 1962; The Madams of San Francisco: An Irreverent History of the City by the Golden Gate, 1964; (with J.M. Browning) John M.

Browning: American Gunmaker, A Illustrated Biography of the Man and His Guns, 1964, rev. ed., 1994; The Vulnerable Americans, 1966; Frame-Up: The Incredible Case of Tom Mooney and Warren Billings, 1967; The Killer Mountains: A Search for the Legendary Lost Dutchman Mine, 1968; The Last Days of the Late, Great State of California, 1968; (with F.G. Powers) Operation Overflight: The U-2 Spy Pilot Tells His Story for the First Time, 1970; (ed.) A Kind of Loving, 1970; (with E.R. Murphy Jr.) Second in Command, The Uncensored Account of the Capture of the Spy Ship Pueblo, 1971; (with V. Bugliosi) Helter Skelter: The True Story of the Manson Murders, 1974 in UK as The Manson Murders, 1975; J. Edgar Hoover: The Man and the Secrets, 1991; Vegas, 2005. **Address:** c/o Irving S. Feffer, 609 N Alta, Beverly Hills, CA 90210, U.S.A.

GENYA, Monica. Kenyan (born Kenya) **Genres:** Adult Non-fiction, Literary Criticism And History, Young Adult Fiction. **Career:** Writer. **Publications:** Links of a Chain, 1996; The Other Side of Love, 2004; The Wrong Kind of Girl, 2004. **Address:** c/o East African Educational Publishers Ltd., PO Box 45314, Nairobi, 00100, Kenya.

GEOFFREY, Iqbal. *See* JAFREE, Mohammed Jawaid Iqbal.

GEORGE, Alice L. American (born United States), b. 1952. **Genres:** History, Local History/Rural Topics, Intellectual History, Politics/Government, Reference. **Career:** Detroit Free Press, assistant; Philadelphia Daily News, deputy managing editor. **Publications:** Awaiting Armageddon: How Americans Faced the Cuban Missile Crisis, 2003; Old City Philadelphia: Cradle of American Democracy, 2003; Challenge and Change: History of the Jews in America, 2004; Philadelphia: A Pictorial Celebration, 2006; (with J.C. Stoner) The Social History of the United States: The 1950s, 2008; (with L.S. Watts and S. Beekman) The Social History of the United States: 1920s, 2008. **Address:** 440 S Broad St., Ste. 1509, Philadelphia, PA 19146, U.S.A. **Online address:** letter1962@aol.com

GEORGE, Alice Rose. American (born United States), b. 1944. **Genres:** Poetry, Photography, Art/Art History. **Career:** Time Magazine, assistant photographic editor, 1968-79; GEO, photography editor, 1979-82; Fortune, photography editor, 1982-; JGS Foundation Inc., curator; Damiani, representative. Consultant. **Publications:** Ceiling of the World (poetry), 1995. EDITOR: (with A. Heyman and E. Hoffman) Flesh and Blood: Photographers' Images of Their Own Families, 1992; (with A. Harris) A New Life: Stories and Photographs from the Suburban South, 1997; Twenty-five and Under: Photographers, 1997; (with L. Marks) Hope: Photographs (exhibition catalogue), 1998; (co-ed.) Here is New York: A Democracy of Photographs, 2001. Contributor to periodicals. **Address:** c/o Author Mail, W.W. Norton, 500 5th Ave., New York, NY 10010, U.S.A.

GEORGE, Barbara. *See* KATZ, Bobbi.

GEORGE, David (John). Welsh (born Wales), b. 1948. **Genres:** Literary Criticism And History, History, Art/Art History. **Career:** University College of Swansea, lecturer in Spanish, 1972-, professor of Hispanic studies, 2004-, now professor emeritus. Writer. **Publications:** From Pierrot to Harlequin: Valle-Inclan, Lorca and the Commedia Dell'arte in Hispanic Literature, 1890-1935, 1994; The History of the Commedia dell'arte in Modern Hispanic Literature with Special Attention to the Work of García Lorca, 1995; (trans.) K. Chatten, Sugar Dollies, 1996; (trans. with X.R. Rosell and J. London) S. Belbel, After the Rain, 1996. EDITOR/CO-EDITOR: (with D. Gagen) La guerra civil espanola: Arte y violencia, 1990; (with C.J. Gossip and contrib.) Studies in the Commedia Dell'arte, 1993; (contrib.) Contemporary Catalan Drama, 1994; The Theatre in Madrid and Barcelona, 1892-1936: Rivals or Collaborators?, 2002; Sergi Belbel and Catalan Theatre: Text, Performance and Identity, 2010. Works appear in anthologies. Contributor of articles to journals. **Address:** Department of Hispanic Studies, University College of Swansea, Singleton Pk., Swansea, WG SA2 8PP, Wales. **Online address:** d.j.george@swansea.ac.uk

GEORGE, Eliot. *See* FREEMAN, Gillian.

GEORGE, Elizabeth. American (born United States), b. 1949. **Genres:** Mystery/Crime/Suspense, Novels. **Career:** Mater Dei High School, English teacher, 1974-75; El Toro High School, English teacher, 1975-87; Coastline Community College, creative writing teacher, 1988-91; Irvine Valley College, creative writing teacher, 1989; University of California, teacher of creative writing, 1990; University of British Columbia, visiting professor; Oxford University, Exeter College, visiting professor. Maui Writer's Retreat, creative writing instructor. Writer. **Publications:** A Great Deliverance, 1989; Payment in Blood, 1989; Well-Schooled in Murder, 1990; A Suitable Vengeance, 1991; For the Sake of Elena, 1992; Missing Joseph, 1993; Playing for the Ashes, 1994; In the Presence of the Enemy, 1996; Deception on His Mind, 1997; In Pursuit of The Proper Sinner, 1999; A Traitor to Memory, 2001; A Place of Hiding, 2002; I, Richard, 2002; Write Away: One Novelist's Approach to Fiction and the Writing Life, 2004; (ed.) A Moment on the Edge: 100 Years of Crime Stories by Women, 2004; With No One as Witness, 2005; What Came Before He Shot Her, 2006; Careless in Red, 2008; (ed.) Two of the Deadliest, 2009; This Body of Death: A Novel, 2010. Works appear in anthologies. **Address:** c/o Robert Gottlieb, Trident Media Group L.L.C., 41 Madison Ave., Fl. 36, New York, NY 10010, U.S.A.

GEORGE, Emily. *See* KATZ, Bobbi.

GEORGE, Jean Craighead. American (born United States), b. 1919. **Genres:** Children's Fiction, Young Adult Fiction, Children's Non-fiction, Natural History, Food And Wine, Animals/Pets. **Career:** International News Service, reporter, 1942-44; Washington Post, reporter, 1943-46; Artist Pageant Magazine, reporter, 1946-47; Newspaper Enterprise Association, artist, reporter, 1946-47; teacher, 1960-68; Reader's Digest, staff writer, 1969-74, roving editor, 1974-82. **Publications:** WITH J.L. GEORGE: Vulpes the Red Fox, 1948; Vision the Mink, 1949; Masked Prowler: The Story of a Raccoon, 1950; Meph, The Pet Skunk, 1952; Bubo the Great Horned Owl, 1954; Dipper of Copper Creek, 1956. OTHER: The Hole in the Tree, 1957; Snow Tracks, 1958; My Side of the Mountain, 1959; The Summer of the Falcon, 1962; Red Robin Fly Up!, 1963; Gull Number 737, 1964; Hold Zero, 1966; Spring Comes to the Ocean, 1965; The Thirteen Moons (The Moon of the Owls, Bears, Salamander, Chicadee, Monarch, Butterfly, Fox Pups, Wild Pigs, Mountain Lion, Deer, Alligator, Wolves, Winter Bird, and Mole), 13 vols., 1967-69, new ed., 1991-93; Coyote in Manhattan, 1968; Beastly Inventions: A Surprising Investigation into How Smart Animals Really Are in UK as Animals Can Do Anything, 1970; All Upon a Stone, 1971; Who Really Killed Cock Robin?, 1971; Julie of the Wolves, 1972; Everglades Wild Guide, 1972; All upon a Sidewalk, 1974; Hook a Fish, Catch a Mountain, 1975; Going to the Sun, 1976; The Wentletrap Trap, 1977; The American Walk Book: An Illustrated Guide To The Country's Major Historic and Natural Walking Trails From New England To The Pacific Coast, 1977; The Wounded Wolf, 1978; River Rats, Inc., 1979; The Cry Of The Crow: A Novel, 1980; Journey Inward (autobiography), 1982; The Wild Wild Cookbook: A Guide For Young Wild-Food Foragers, 1982; The Grizzly Bear with the Golden Ears, 1982; The Wild, Wild Cookbook: A Guide for Young Foragers, 1982; Exploring The Out-Of-Doors, 1983; The Talking Earth, 1983; One Day (One Day in the Desert, Alpine Tundra, Prairie, Woods, Tropical Rain Forest), 5 vols., 1983-90; How to Talk to Your Animals, 1985; How to Talk to Your Cat, 1985; How to Talk to Your Dog, 1986; Water Sky, 1987; Shark Beneath the Reef, 1988; One Day in the Woods (children's musical), 1989; On the Far Side of the Mountain, 1990; The Missing Gator of Gumbo Limbo: An Ecological Mystery, 1992; (ed.) The Big Book for Our Planet, 1993; The Fire Bug Connection, 1993; The First Thanksgiving, 1993; Dear Rebecca, Winter is Here, 1993; The Everglades Field Guide, 1994; Animals Who Have Won Our Hearts, 1994; Julie, 1994; There's An Owl in the Shower, 1995; Everglades, 1995; To Climb a Waterfall, 1995; Acorn Pancakes, Dandelion Salad, and 38 Other Wild Recipes, 1995; The Tarantula in My Purse: And 172 Other Wild Pets, 1996; The Case of the Missing Cutthroats: A Ecological Mystery, 1996; Look to the North: A Wolf Pup Diary, 1997; Arctic Son, 1997; Julie's Wolf Pack, 1997; Giraffe Trouble, 1998; Gorilla Gang, 1998; Dear Katie, the Volcano Is a Girl, 1998; Elephant Walk, 1998; Rhino Romp, 1998; Morning, Noon, and Night, 1999; Frightful's Mountain, 1999; Snow Bear, 1999; Incredible Animal Adventures, 1999; Nutik, the Wolf Pup, 2000; Autumn Moon, 2001; Winter Moon, 2001; Nutik and Amaroq Play Ball, 2001; Cliffhanger, 2002; Spring Moon, 2002; Summer Moon, 2002; Frightful's Daughter, 2002; Tree Castle Island, 2002; Firestorm, 2003; Charlie's Raven, 2004; Snowboard Twist, 2004; Luck, 2006; Frightful's Daughter Meets The Baron Weasel, 2007; The Wolves are Back, 2008; Goose And Duck, 2008; Last Polar Bear, 2009; Cats of Roxville Station, 2009; Pocket Guide to the Outdoors, 2009; (with M.T. Cimarusti) The Buffalo Are Back, 2010; Galapagos George, 2013; Special Gift for Grammy, 2013. **Address:** 20 William St., Chappaqua, NY 10514-3114, U.S.A. **Online address:** jeangeorge1@verizon.net

GEORGE, Judith W(ordsworth). Scottish/British (born England), b. 1940.

Genres: Literary Criticism And History, Education. **Career:** Open University, deputy director, honorary senior research fellow. Consultant and writer. **Publications:** Venantius Fortunatus: A Latin Poet in Merovingian Gaul, 1992; Venantius Fortunatus: Personal and Political Poems, 1995; (co-author) Distance Education in Norway and Scotland: Experiences and Reflections, 1996; (with J. Cowan) A Handbook of Techniques for Formative Evaluation: Mapping the Student's Learning Experience, 1999. **Address:** Open University, 10 Drumsheugh Gardens, Edinburgh, EH3 7QJ, Scotland. **Online address:** j.w.george@open.ac.uk

GEORGE, Kathleen Elizabeth. American (born United States), b. 1943. **Genres:** Novels, Theatre. **Career:** University of Pittsburgh, assistant instructor in theatre arts, 1964-66, associate professor, 1976-2001, professor of theatre, 2001-, director; Carlow College, assistant professor of speech and theatre arts, 1968-76; Semester-at-Sea, academic dean, 1987. Writer. **Publications:** Rhythm in Drama, 1980; Playwriting: The First Workshop, 1994; The Man in the Buick and Other Stories (short stories), 1999; Winter's Tales: Reflections on the Novelistic Stage, 2005. NOVELS: Taken, 2001; Fallen, 2004; Afterimage, 2007; Odds, 2009; Hideout, 2011. Contributor of magazines. **Address:** Department of Theatre Arts, University of Pittsburgh, 1617 Cathedral of Learning, Pittsburgh, PA 15260-6299, U.S.A. **Online address:** kathy@kathleengeorgebooks.com

GEORGE, Lindsay Barrett. American/Spanish (born Spain), b. 1952. **Genres:** Children's Fiction, Illustrations, Children's Non-fiction. **Career:** Fine art printer, 1978-81; mechanical artist, 1981-84; author and illustrator, 1985-; educator, 1989-. **Publications:** SELF-ILLUSTRATED FOR CHILDREN: William and Boomer, 1987; (with W.T. George) Beaver at Long Pond, 1988; In the Snow: Who's Been Here?, 1995; In the Woods: Who's Been Here?, 1995; Around the Pond: Who's Been Here?, 1996; Around the World: Who's Been Here?, 1999; My Bunny and Me, 2001; Inside Mouse, Outside Mouse, 2004; Secret, 2005; In the Garden: Who's Been Here?, 2006; Alfred Digs, 2008; Maggie's Ball, 2010; A Nose for Acorns, 2011; That Pup!, 2011. Illustrator of books by W.T. George and C. Huck. **Address:** c/o Author Mail, HarperCollins Publishers, 10 E 53rd St., 18th Fl., New York, NY 10022, U.S.A. **Online address:** lindsaybarrettgeorge@msn.com

GEORGE, Margaret. American (born United States), b. 1943?. **Genres:** Novels, Autobiography/Memoirs. **Career:** National Institutes of Health, science writer, 1966-70; Washington University, news writer, 1970-72; freelance writer, 1973-. **Publications:** The Autobiography of Henry VIII: With Notes by His Fool, Will Somers, 1986; Mary Queen of Scotland and the Isles, 1992; The Memoirs of Cleopatra, 1997; Mary, Called Magdalene, 2002; Helen of Troy, 2006 in France as Helene de Troie: La Prisonniere de Sparte, 2007; (with C.J. Murphy) Lucille Lost, 2006; Elizabeth I, 2011. Contributor to periodicals. **Address:** c/o Jacques de Spoelberch, J de S Associates, 9 Shagbark Rd., Wilson Pt., South Norwalk, CT 06854, U.S.A.

GEORGE, Robert P. American (born United States), b. 1955. **Genres:** Novels, Law, Politics/Government, Theology/Religion. **Career:** New College, lecturer, 1982-85; Robinson & McElwee, of counsel, 1990-; Princeton University, assistant professor, associate professor, professor, 1986-99, McCormick professor of jurisprudence, 1999-, McCormick chair in jurisprudence, American Ideals and Institutions, James Madison Program, founding director, 2000-, Program in Law and Public Affairs, faculty associate. Writer. **Publications:** Making Men Moral: Civil Liberties and Public Morality, 1993; In Defense of Natural Law, 1999; The Clash of Orthodoxies: Law, Religion, and Morality in Crisis, 2001; Para hacer mejores a los hombres, 2002; (with P. Lee) Body-Self Dualism in Contemporary Ethics and Politics, 2008; (with C. Tollefsen) Embryo: A Defense of Human Life, 2008, 2nd ed., 2011; (with S. Girgis and R.T. Anderson) What is Marriage?, 2012. EDITOR: Natural Law Theory: Contemporary Essays, 1992; The Autonomy of Law: Essays on Legal Positivism, 1996; Natural Law, Liberalism, and Morality: Contemporary Essays, 1996; Natural Law and Moral Inquiry: Ethics, Metaphysics, and Politics in the Work of Germain Grisez, 1998; Great Cases in Constitutional Law, 2000; (with C. Wolfe) Natural Law and Public Reason, 2000; (with S.A. Barber) Constitutional Politics: Essays on Constitution Making, Maintenance, and Change, 2001; Natural Law, 2003; (with J.B. Elshtain) The Meaning of Marriage: Family, State, Market, and Morals, 2006. **Address:** James Madison Program, Princeton University, 83 Prospect Ave., Princeton, NJ 08540-5210, U.S.A. **Online address:** rgeorge@princeton.edu

GEORGE, Rose. British (born England), b. 1969?. **Genres:** Sciences, Phi-

losophy. **Career:** Writer and editor, 1994-. **Publications:** A Life Removed: Hunting for Refuge in the Modern World, 2004; The Big Necessity: The Unmentionable World of Human Waste and Why It Matters, 2008 **Address:** Leeds, WY , England. **Online address:** rose@rosegeorge.com

GEORGE, Rosemary. British (born England), b. 1950?. **Genres:** Novels, Food And Wine. **Career:** Freelance wine journalist; wine merchant, 1972-81; wine writer, 1981-. **Publications:** The Wines of Chablis and the Yonne, 1984; (with P. Hyman and M. Hyman) Webster's Wine Tours-France, 1988; The Simon & Schuster Pocket Wine Label Decoder, 1989; The Mitchell Beazley Pocket Guide to Decoding Wine Labels, 1989; French Country Wines, 1990; Chianti and the Wines of Tuscany, 1990; Lateral Wine-Tasting, 1992; (ed. with C. Austin) The Which? Wine Guide, 1992; (ed. with F. Prial and M. Edwards) The Companion to Wine, 1992; The Wines of New Zealand, 1996; The Wines of the South of France: From Banyuls to Raphaël, 2001; Treading Grapes: Walking through the Vineyards of Tuscany, 2004; (with J. Arkell) Wine, 2005. Contributor to periodicals. **Address:** c/o Author Mail, Bantam Dell Publishing Group, 1745 Broadway, New York, NY 10019-4368, U.S.A.

GEORGE, Sally. *See* ORR, Wendy.

GEORGE, Terry. Irish (born Ireland), b. 1952. **Genres:** Film. **Career:** Writer, director and producer. **Publications:** (With J. Sheridan) In the Name of the Father, 1993; (with J. Sheridan) Some Mother's Son, 1996; (with J. Sheridan) The Boxer, 1997; A Bright Shining Lie, 1998; Hart's War, 2002; (with K. Pearson) Hotel Rwanda: Bringing The True Story of an African Hero to Film, 2004; (contrib.) Never Again, Again, Again...: Genocide: Armenia, The Holocaust, Cambodia, Rwanda, Bosnia and Herzegovina, Darfur, 2007. **Address:** Metro-Goldwyn-Mayer Inc., 10250 Constellation Blvd., Los Angeles, CA 90067-6421, U.S.A.

GEORGE BLOOMFIELD, Susanne K. American (born United States), b. 1947. **Genres:** Local History/Rural Topics, Biography, Literary Criticism And History, Women's Studies And Issues, Cultural/Ethnic Topics, History, Novellas/Short Stories, Cultural/Ethnic Topics, History. **Career:** Axtell Community Schools, teacher of English and French, 1968-73; University of Nebraska, lecturer, 1979-87; assistant professor, 1988-92, associate professor, 1992-97, professor, 1997-; Nebraska Book Festival, chair. Writer. **Publications:** The Adventures of the Woman Homesteader: The Life and Letters of Elinore Pruitt Stewart, 1992; (co-ed.) The Platte River: An Atlas of the Big Bend Region, 1993; (ed.) Wellsprings: A Collection of Poems by Six Nebraska Poets, 1995; Kate M. Cleary: A Literary Biography with Selected Works, 1997; A Prairie Mosaic: An Atlas of Central Nebraska's Land, Nature, and Culture, 2000; A Presidential Visit, 2002; Absolutely No Manners: On Having the Audacity to Write Biography. Monograph, 2003; Impertinences: Selected Editorials of Elia W. Peattie, A Journalist in the Gilded Age, 2005; From the Beginning: A Century of Excellence at the University of Nebraska at Kearney, 2005; (ed. with E.M. Reed) Adventures in the West: Stories Young Readers, 2007. Contributor of articles to journals. **Address:** Department of English, University of Nebraska, 109D Thomas Hall, Kearney, NE 68849-1320, U.S.A. **Online address:** bloomfields@unk.edu

GEORGI-FINDLAY, Brigitte. German (born Germany), b. 1956. **Genres:** Cultural/Ethnic Topics, History, Translations, Women's Studies And Issues, Politics/Government. **Career:** Free University of Berlin, John F. Kennedy Institute, assistant professor of American literature, 1988-95; University of Bremen, associate professor of American studies, 1995-97; University of Dresden, professor of North American studies, 1997-. **Publications:** Indianer in Der amerikanischen Literatur: Das weisse Rassenverstandnis bis 1900 und die indianische Selbstdarstellung ab 1833: Versuch einer Gegenuberstellung, 1982; Tradition und Moderne in Der Zeitgenossischen Indianischen Literatur der USA: N. Scott Momadays Roman House Made of Dawn, 1986; (ed.) America Seen from the Outside: Topics, Models, and Achievements of American Studies in the Federal Republic of Germany: Proceedings of a Symposium held at the John F. Kennedy-Institut fur Nordamerikastudien, December 1-4, 1988, 1990; The Frontiers of Women's Writing: Women's Narratives and the Rhetoric of Westward Expansion, 1996; (ed. with H. Mohr) Millennial Perspectives: Lifeworlds and Utopias, 2003. **Address:** Institut fuer Anglistik/Amerikanistik, Fakulta ur Sprach, Lit und Kulturwissenschaften, Technische Universitaet Dresden, Zeunerstrasse 1c, R 317, Dresden, D-01062, Germany. **Online address:** gfindlay@rcs.urz.tu-dresden.de

GERAGHTY, Paul. British/South African (born South Africa), b. 1959.

Genres: Novels, Children's Fiction, Young Adult Fiction, Picture/Board Books, Illustrations. **Career:** Writer, illustrator, educator and musician. **Publications:** OTHERS: (with J. Bush) Giraffe Who Got in a Knot, 1987. NOVELS: Pig, 1988; Tina Come Home, 1992. FOR CHILDREN: SELF-ILLUSTRATED: Over the Steamy Swamp, 1988; The Great Knitting Needle Hunt, 1989; What On Earth Was That?, 1990; Look Out, Patrick!, 1990; Slobcat, 1991; Stop That Noise!, 1992; The Great Green Forest, 1992; Monty's Journey, 1992; The Hunter, 1994; Solo, 1995; Simplified Dictionary of Modern Fijian, 1996; The Wonderful Journey, 1999; Tortuga, 2000; The Hoppameleon, 2001; Dinosaur in Danger, 2004; Rotten and Rascal, 2006; Help Me!, 2010. Illustrator of books by others. **Address:** 42 Dukes Ave., New Malden, SR KT3 4HN, England. **Online address:** info@paulgeraghty.net

GERARD, Charley. American (born United States), b. 1950. **Genres:** Cultural/Ethnic Topics, Music, Race Relations. **Career:** Gerard and Sarzin Publishing Co., editor, 1991-. Composer and saxophonist. **Publications:** Jazz Riffs for Flute, Saxophone, Trumpet and Other Treble Instruments, 1976; Improvising Jazz Sax, 1978; Sonny Rollins, 1980; (with M. Sheller) Salsa! The Rhythm of Latin Music, 1989, rev. ed., 1998; Jazz in Black and White: Race, Culture and Identity in the Jazz Community, 1998; Music from Cuba: Mongo Santamaria, Chocolate Armenteros, and Cuban Musicians in the United States, 2001. EDITOR: Originals and Standards, 1991; Straight Ahead Jazz Fakebook, 1993. **Address:** 99 Gold St., Ste. 1L, Brooklyn, NY 11201, U.S.A. **Online address:** cgerard@pipeline.com

GERARD, Philip. American (born United States), b. 1955. **Genres:** Novels, Plays/Screenplays, Writing/Journalism, Adult Non-fiction, Young Adult Fiction. **Career:** Arizona State University, visiting assistant professor of English, 1981-82, writer-in-residence, 1983-86; Lake Forest College, assistant professor of English, 1986-89; University of North Carolina, associate professor of English, 1989-99, acting director of professional and creative writing, 1990-91, director, 1991-98, professor of creative writing 1999-, chair; North Carolina Humanities, managing editor, 1993-94. **Publications:** NOVELS: Hatteras Light, 1986; Cape Fear Rising, 1994; Desert Kill, 1994. NONFICTION: Brilliant Passage: A Schooning Memoir, 1989; Creative Nonfiction: Researching and Crafting Stories of Real Life, 1996; Writing a Book That Makes a Difference, 2000; (ed. with C. Forché) Writing Creative Nonfiction, 2001; Secret Soldiers: The Story of World War II's Heroic Army of Deception, 2002. Contributor to periodicals. **Address:** Department of Creative Writing, University of North Carolina, Kenan Hall 1208, 601 S College Rd., Wilmington, NC 28409, U.S.A. **Online address:** pg@philipgerard.com

GERAS, Adèle (Daphne Weston). British/Israeli (born Israel), b. 1944. **Genres:** Novellas/Short Stories, Children's Fiction, Poetry. **Career:** Fairfield High School, French teacher, 1968-71; writer, 1976-. **Publications:** FOR CHILDREN: Tea at Mrs. Manderby's, 1976; Apricots at Midnight and Other Stories from a Patchwork Quilt, 1982; Beyond the Cross Stitch Mountains, 1977; The Girls in the Velvet Frame, 1979; The Painted Garden, 1979; A Thousand Yards of Sea, 1981; The Rug That Grew, 1981; The Green behind the Glass, 1982 in US as Snapshots of Paradise: Love Stories, 1984; Other Echoes, 1982; The Christmas Cat, 1983; Voyage, 1983; Letters of Fire and Other Unsettling Stories, 1984; Happy Endings, 1986; Little Elephant's Moon, 1986; Ritchie's Rabbit, 1986; Finding Annabel, 1987; Fishpie for Flamingoes, 1987; The Fantora Family Files, 1988; Pink Medicine, 1988; The Strange Bird, 1988; The Coronation Picnic, 1989; The Tower Room, 1990; My Grandmother's Stories, 1990; A Lane to the Land of the Dead, 1994; Beauty and the Beast and Other Stories, 1996; (ed.) A Treasury of Jewish Stories, 1996; The Little Swan, 1997; Louisa's Secret, 1997; Louisa in the Wings, 1997; Louisa and Phoebe, 1997; From Lullaby to Lullaby, 1997; Blossom's Revenge, 1997; Picasso Perkins, 1997; Callie's Kitten, 1998; Doll's House, 1998; Geejay the Hero, 1998; Swan Lake, 2000; The Wedding Present, 2001; Sleep tight, Ginger Kitten, 2001; The Firebird, 2001; Louisa on Screen, 2001; Good Luck, Louisa!, 2001; My Wishes for You, 2002; Coppelia, 2002; Ballet Class, 2003; Happy Ever After, 2005. FOR ADULTS: (with P. Stainer) Up on the Roof (poetry), 1987; The Glittering River, 1990; Nina's Magic, 1990; A Magic Birthday, 1992; Yesterday, 1992; Watching the Roses, 1992; Pictures of the Night, 1993; Golden Windows, 1993; The Fantora Family Photographs, 1993; A Candle in the Dark, 1995; Silent Snow Secret Snow, 1998; Lights, Camera, Action!, 2000; Giselle, 2000; The Nutcracker, 2000; Sleeping Beauty, 2000; Troy, 2001; The Curtain Call, 2001; A Taste of Winter: A Story About Hanukkah, 2002; My Wishes for You, 2002; Rebecca's Passover, 2003; Facing the Light, 2003; Ballet Class, 2003; Hester's Story, 2004; Time for Ballet, 2004; Lizzie's Wish, 2004; Ithaka, 2005; Made In Heaven, 2006; A

Hidden Life, 2007; Cecily's Portrait, 2007; Cleopatra: Discover the World of Cleopatra Through the Diary of Her Handmaiden, Nefret, 2007; Little Ballet Star, 2008; Dido, 2009. OTHERS: Golden Windows and other Stories of Jerusalem, 1993; The Fabulous Fantoras, vol. I: Family Files, 1998, vol. II: Family Photographs, 1999; The Cats of Cuckoo Square, 2003. **Address:** David Fickling Books, 31 Beaumont St., Oxford, OX OX1 2NP, England. **Online address:** adele@adelegeras.com

GERAS, Norman (Myron). Zimbabwean (born Zimbabwe), b. 1943. **Genres:** Politics/Government, Essays. **Career:** University of Manchester, lecturer, 1967-84, senior lecturer, 1984-90, reader in government, 1990-94, professor, 1995-2003, professor emeritus, 2003-. **Publications:** The Legacy of Rosa Luxemburg, 1976; Masas, partido y revolucion, 1980; Marx and Human Nature: Refutation of a Legend, 1983; Literature of Revolution, 1986; Discourses of Extremity: Radical Ethics and Post-Marxist Extravagances, 1990; Solidarity in the Conversation of Humankind: The Ungroundable Liberalism of Richard Rorty, 1995; Ashes '97: Two Views from the Boundary, 1997; The Contract of Mutual Indifference, 1998; (ed. with R. Wokler) Enlightenment and Modernity, 1999; Men of Waugh: Ashes 2001, 2002; Crimes Against Humanity: Birth of a Concept, 2011. **Address:** School of Social Science, University of Manchester, Oxford Rd., Manchester, GM M13 9PL, England. **Online address:** norman.geras@manchester.ac.uk

GERASSI, John. American/French (born France), b. 1931. **Genres:** History, Politics/Government, Biography, Theology/Religion. **Career:** Time Magazine, Latin American editor, 1957-61; New York Times, correspondent, 1961-62; freelance writer, 1962-63; Newsweek Magazine, Latin American editor, 1963-71; San Francisco State College (now San Francisco State University), instructor; University of Paris, instructor; City University of New York, Queens College, The Graduate Center, instructor in political science, professor of political science. **Publications:** The Great Fear: The Reconquest of Latin America by Latin Americans, 1963 as The Great Fear in Latin America, 1965; The Boys of Boise: Furor, Vice and Folly in an American Society, 1966, rev. ed., 2002; North Vietnam: A Documentary, 1968; Fidel Castro: A Biography, 1973; (with F. Browning) The American Way of Crime, 1980; The Premature Antifascists: North American Volunteers in the Spanish Civil War, 1936-1939, 1986; Jean-Paul Sartre: Hated Conscience of His Century, 1989. EDITOR: (and intro.) Venceremos: The Speeches and Writings of Ernesto Che Guevara, 1968; (with I.L. Horowitz and J. de Castro) Latin American Radicalism: A Documentary Report on Left and Nationalist Movements, 1969; (and intro.) The Coming of the New International, 1971; (and intro.) Towards Revolution, 1971; (and intro.) Revolutionary Priest: The Complete Writings and Messages of Camilo Torres, 1971; (and trans.) Talking with Sartre, 2009. **Address:** Department of Political Science, Queens College, 200R Powdermaker Hall, 65-30 Kissena Blvd., Flushing, NY 11367-1575, U.S.A. **Online address:** jgerassi@qc.cuny.edu

GERBER, Douglas E. Canadian (born Canada), b. 1933. **Genres:** Classics, Literary Criticism And History, Bibliography. **Career:** University of Toronto, University College, lecturer in Greek, 1958-59; University of Western Ontario, lecturer, 1959-60, assistant professor, 1960-64, associate professor, 1964-69, professor, 1969-77, William Sherwood Fox professor of classics, 1977-, now professor emeritus. Writer. **Publications:** A Bibliography of Pindar, 1513-1966, 1969; Emendations in Pindar, 1513-1972, 1974; Pindar's Olympian One: A Commentary, 1982; Lexicon in Bacchylidem, 1984; Pindar, Nemean Six: A Commentary, 1999; A Commentary on Pindar Olympian Nine, 2002. EDITOR: (and intro.) Euterpe: An Anthology of Early Greek Lyric, Elegiac and Iambic Poetry, 1970; Greek Poetry and Philosophy: Studies in Honour of Leonard Woodbury, 1984; (co-author) Pindare: huit exposés suivis dediscussions, 1985; A Companion to the Greek Lyric Poets, 1997; (and trans.) Greek Iambic Poetry: From the Seventh to the Fifth Centuries BC, 1999; (and trans.) Greek Elegiac Poetry: From the Seventh to the Fifth Centuries BC, 1999. Contributor to journals. **Address:** Department of Classical Studies, Talbot College, University of Western Ontario, Rm. 423, London, ON N6A 3K7, Canada. **Online address:** degerber@uwo.ca

GERBER, Merrill Joan. American (born United States), b. 1938. **Genres:** Novels, Novellas/Short Stories, Children's Fiction, Autobiography/Memoirs, Essays, inspirational/Motivational Literature, Young Adult Fiction. **Career:** Pasadena City College, creative writing lecturer, 1980-89; California Institute of Technology, creative writing lecturer, 1989-; Houghton Mifflin Co., editor; University of California, teacher; University of Florida, teacher. Writer. **Publications:** Stop Here, My Friend, 1965; An Antique Man, 1967; Now

Molly Knows, 1974; The Lady with the Moving Parts: A Novel, 1978; Please Don't Kiss Me Now, 1981; Name a Star for Me: A Novel, 1983; Honeymoon: Stories, 1985; I'm Kissing as Fast as I Can, 1985; The Summer of My Indian Prince, 1986; Also Known as Sadzia! The Belly Dancer!, 1987; Marry Me Tomorrow, 1987; Even Pretty Girls Cry at Night, 1988; I'd Rather Think about Robby, 1989; King of the World, 1989; Handsome as Anything, 1990; Chattering Man: Stories and a Novella, 1991; The Kingdom of Brooklyn, 1992; This Old Heart of Mine: The Best of Merrill Joan Gerber's Redbook Stories, 1993; Old Mother, Little Cat: A Writer's Reflections on Her Kitten, Her Aged Mother and Life (memoir), 1995; Anna in Chains, 1998; Anna in the Afterlife (novel), 2002; Botticelli Blue Skies: An American in Florence (memoir), 2002; Gut Feelings: A Writer's Truths and Minute Inventions (essays), 2003; Glimmering Girls: A Novel of the Fifties, 2005; This Is a Voice from Your Past: New and Selected Stories, 2005; Victory Gardens of Brooklyn: A Novel, 2007. Contributor of articles to periodicals and magazines. **Address:** 542 Santa Anita Ct., Sierra Madre, CA 91024-2623, U.S.A. **Online address:** mjgerber@its.caltech.edu

GERBER, Michael E. American (born United States), b. 1936. **Genres:** Business/Trade/Industry, Mythology/Folklore. **Career:** E-Myth Worldwide, founder and chief executive officer; Chief Dreamer Enterprises Inc., founder and chief executive officer; Michael E. Gerber Companies Inc., founder. Writer. **Publications:** E-Myth, Why Most Businesses Don't Work and What to do About It, 1986; The Power Point, 1991; The E-Myth Revisited: Why Most Small Businesses Don't Work and What to Do about It, 1995; The E-Myth Manager: Why Management Doesn't Work and What to Do about It, 1998; The E-Myth Contractor: Why Most Contractors' Businesses Don't Work and What to Do about It, 2002; The E-Myth Physician: Why Most Medical Practices Don't Work and What to Do about It, 2003; E-Myth Mastery: The Seven Essential Disciplines for Building a World Class Company, 2005; Awakening The Entrepreneur Within: How Ordinary People Can Create Extraordinary Companies, 2008; E-myth Enterprise: How to Turn a Great Idea into a Thriving Business, 2009; (with R. Armstrong and S.M. Fisch) The E-Myth Attorney: Why Most Legal Practices Don't Work and What to do About It, 2010; The Most Successful Small Business in the World: The Ten Principles, 2010; (with M.D. Root) E-Myth Accountant: Why Most Accounting Practices Don't Work and What to do About It, 2011. **Address:** Michael E. Gerber Companies Inc., PO Box 131195, Carlsbad, CA 92013, U.S.A. **Online address:** michael@inthedreamingroom.com

GERDES, Eckhard. American (born United States), b. 1959. **Genres:** Novels, Novellas/Short Stories. **Career:** Bookcase, sales clerk, 1978-80; Waldenbooks, assistant manager, 1981-82; Bob's News Emporium, manager, 1983-84; Chicago-Main News, co-manager, 1985-87; University of Dubuque, news assistant in university relations, 1987-88; Bookworks, trade book buyer, 1990-92; Barnes and Noble Books, department supervisor, 1992-94; Roosevelt University, instructor in English, 1994-; Hardy Freeman and Associates, executive assistant, 1994-; The Journal of Experimental Fiction, editor; Triton College, adjunct faculty. **Publications:** NOVELS: The Million-Year Centipede: or Liquid Structures, 1976; Aspic Interregencies, 1978; Systems of Flux, 1980; The Intersection of Two Loops, 1985; Hugh Moore, 1987; Truly Fine Citizen, 1989; Citizen Reclaimed, 1990; Ring in a River, 1994; Cistern Tawdry, 2002; Przewalkski's Horse, 2005; My Landlady the Lobotomist, 2008. OTHER: Projections (novella), 1986. Contributor of articles to periodicals. **Address:** Department of English, Triton College, 2000 5th Ave., River Grove, IL 60171, U.S.A. **Online address:** eckhard@experimentalfiction.com

GERDY, John R. American (born United States), b. 1957. **Genres:** Education, Social Commentary, Sports/Fitness, History. **Career:** Youth Sports Programming, director, 1980-82; National Collegiate Athletic Association, legislative assistant, 1986-89; The National Review of Athletics, associate editor, 1993-95; University of Rhode Island, Institute for International Sport, sports ethics fellow, 1994; Ohio University, Masters Program in Sports Administration, visiting professor, 1995-; Music For Everyone, founder and president, 2005-; University of Memphis, College Sports Research Institute, executive board, 2007-. **Publications:** The Successful College Athletic Program: The New Standard, 1997; (ed.) Sports in School: The Future of an Institution, 2000; Sports: The All-American Addiction, 2002; Air Ball: American Education's Failed Experiment with Elite Athletics, 2006. **Address:** 409 Sickman Mill Rd., Conestoga, PA 17516, U.S.A. **Online address:** jrg331234@aol.com

GERGES, Fawaz A. American/Lebanese (born Lebanon), b. 1958?. **Genres:** Politics/Government. **Career:** Sarah Lawrence College, Middle East Studies,

International Affairs and Middle Eastern Studies, professor and Christian A. Johnson chair, 1994-; American Broadcasting Co. (ABC), senior analyst and commentator, 2000-06; National Public Radio (NPR), commentator; Princeton University, research fellow; University of Oxford, faculty; Harvard University, faculty; Columbia University, faculty; London School of Economics and Political Science, professor of Middle East politics and international relations, Contemporary Middle East, emirates chair, Middle East Centre, inaugural director. Writer. **Publications:** NONFICTION: The Superpowers and the Middle East: Regional and International Politics, 1955-1967, 1994; America and Political Islam: Clash of Cultures or Clash of Interests?, 1999; The Far Enemy: Why Jihad Went Global, 2005, 2nd ed., 2009; Journey of the Jihadist: Inside Muslim Militancy, 2006; (foreword) A Brief History of Pakistan, 2009; (foreword) A Brief History of Saudi Arabia, 2nd ed., 2010; Obama and the Greater Middle East, 2011; The Rise and Fall of Al-Qaeda, 2011; The Making of the Arab World: The Legacy of Militarism; The New Jihadists, forthcoming. **Address:** Sarah Lawrence College, 1 Mead Way, Bronxville, NY 10708, U.S.A. **Online address:** fgerges@slc.edu

GERHARDS, Jürgen. German (born Germany), b. 1955?. **Genres:** Politics/Government, Cultural/Ethnic Topics, History. **Career:** Social Science Center, senior researcher, 1988-94; University of Leipzig, professor, 1994-2004; Free University of Berlin, professor, 2004-. Writer. **Publications:** Wahrheit und Ideologie: Eine kritische Einfuhrung in die Systemtheorie von Niklas Luhmann, 1984; Soziologie der Emotionen: Fragestellungen, Systematik und Perspektiven, 1988; (with B. Schmidt) Intime Kommunikation: Eine empirische Studie über Wege der Annaherung und Hindernisse fur Safer Sex, 1992; Neue Konfliktlinien in der Mobilisierung öffentlicher Meinung: Eine Fallstudie, 1993; Soziologie der Kunst: Produzenten, Vermittler und Rezipienten, 1997; (with F. Neidhardt and D. Rucht) Zwischen Palaver und Diskurs: Strukturen öffentlicher Meinungsbildung am Beispiel der deutschen Diskussion zur Abtreibung, 1998; (co-ed.) Eigenwilligkeit und Rationalität sozialer Prozesse: Festschrift zum 65. Geburtstag von Friedhelm Neidhardt, 1999; (with J. Rossel) Interessen und Ideen im Konflikt um das Wahlrecht: Eine kultursoziologische Analyse der parlamentarischen Debatten über das Dreiklassenwahlrecht in Preussen, 1999; Die Vermessung kultureller Unterschiede: USA und Deutschland im Vergleich, 2000; (co-ed.) Shaping Abortion Discourse: Democracy and the Public Sphere in Germany and the United States, 2002; Die Moderne und ihre Vornamen: Eine Einladung in die Kultursoziologie, 2003, trans. as The Name Game: Cultural Modernization & First Names, 2005; (with M. Holscher) Kulturelle Unterschiede in der Europäischen Union: Ein Vergleich zwischen Mitgliedsländern, Beitrittskandidaten und der Türkei, 2005, trans. as Cultural Overstretch: The Enlargement of the European Union and the Cultural Differences between Old and New Member States and Turkey, 2007; (with M.S. Schafer) Die Herstellung Einer Offentlichen Hegemonie: Humangenomforschung in der Deutschen und Der US-amerikanischen Presse, 2006. Contributor of articles to journals. **Address:** Institut fur Soziologie, Freie University of Berlin, Garystr. 55, Berlin, 14195, Germany. **Online address:** j.gerhards@fu-berlin.de

GERHARDT, Michael E. American (born United States), b. 1947. **Genres:** Novels. **Career:** Procter & Gamble, brand assistant, 1972-74; Hanes Corp., brand manager, 1974-78; AAMCO, director of marketing, 1979-80; Franklin Mint, vice president for marketing, 1980-85; Impact Marketing Inc., owner, 1985-; Impact Ratings Inc., vice president. Writer. **Publications:** Presidential Powers, 1999; The Lincoln Affairs, 2003. **Address:** Impact Press, 3 N Line Rd., Newtown Square, PA 19073-4328, U.S.A. **Online address:** megerhardt@aol.com

GERHART, Ann. American (born United States) **Genres:** Biography. **Career:** Daily News, columnist, 1984-95; Washington Post, Style Section, columnist, 1995-, veteran reporter; Glamour Magazine, contributing editor, 2004-. Journalist. **Publications:** The Perfect Wife: The Life and Choices of Laura Bush, 2004. **Address:** Washington Post, 1150 15th St. NW, Washington, DC 20071-0001, U.S.A. **Online address:** gerharta@washpost.com

GERLACH, Don R. American (born United States), b. 1932. **Genres:** History, Biography, Military/Defense/Arms Control, Autobiography/Memoirs. **Career:** University of Maryland, Far East Division, instructor, 1958-59; University of Nebraska, instructor, 1961-62; University of Akron, assistant professor, 1962-65, associate professor, 1965-72, professor of history, 1972-94, professor emeritus, 1994-; Holyrood Seminary, instructor in history, 1983-94. Writer. **Publications:** Philip Schuyler and the American Revolution in New York 1733-1777, 1964; Philip Schuyler and the Growth of New York, 1733-

1804, 1968; Twenty Years of the Promotion of Literature: The Regents of the University of the State of New York 1784-1804, 1974; Proud Patriot: Philip Schuyler and the War of Independence 1775-1783, 1987. Contributor to history journals. **Address:** Department of History, University of Akron, Akron, OH 45404, U.S.A.

GERLACH, Douglas. American (born United States), b. 1963. **Genres:** Money/Finance. **Career:** National Association of Investors Corp., co-creator, consulting editor, board director, 1995-2004, vice president and secretary; Investorama.com (Web site), founder, editor-in-chief, 1995-2001, president; First Albany Corp., internet business analyst, 1997-98; ArmchairMillionaire. com (Web site), senior editor, 1998; ICLUBcentral Inc., board director, product manager and president. Writer and consultant. **Publications:** Investor's Web Guide: Tools and Strategies for Building Your Portfolio, 1997; The Complete Idiot's Guide to Online Investing, 1998, 2nd ed., 2000; (with T. McFeat and J. Gravelle) The Complete Idiot's Guide to Online Investing for Canadians, 1999; (with L. Schiff) The Armchair Millionaire: Build and Protect an Extraordinary Portfolio, Even on an Ordinary Income, by Following One Commonsense Investing Strategy, 2001; (with A. McQuade) Investment Clubs for Dummies, 2002; (with L. Epstein) The Pocket Idiot's Guide to Direct Stock Investing, 2010. Contributor to magazines and periodicals. **Address:** ICLUBcentral Inc., 711 W 13 Mile Rd., Madison Heights, MI 48071, U.S.A. **Online address:** gerlach@yahoo.com

GERLACH, Larry R(euben). American (born United States), b. 1941. **Genres:** Area Studies, History, Sports/Fitness, History, Humanities, Local History/Rural Topics. **Career:** University of Utah, assistant professor, 1968-, professor of history, 1977-, College of Humanities, associate dean, 1982-83, Department of History, chair, 1983-88; College of William and Mary, visiting assistant professor, 1970-71; Utah Humanities Center, director, 1988-90. Writer. **Publications:** Historical Studies and Documents Research Foundation (Salt Lake City), 1973; Road to Revolution, 1975; William Franklin, New Jersey's Last Royal Governor, 1975; Prologue to Independence: New Jersey in the Coming of the American Revolution, 1976; Connecticut Congressman: Samuel Huntington, 1731-1796, 1976; The Men in Blue: Conversations with Umpires, 1980; Blazing Crosses in Zion: The Ku Klux Klan in Utah, 1982; (with C.B. von Schmidt) Dining in-Salt Lake City: Cookbook, 1985; The Olympic Games: Ancient to Modern, 2002. EDITOR: The American Revolution: New York as a Case Study, 1972; Documents Illustrative of the American Revolution, 1763-1788, 1973; New Jersey in the American Revolution, 1763-1783: A Documentary History, 1975; We Hold These Truths: Fundamental Testaments of the American Revolution, 1976; Legacies of the American Revolution, 1978; Winter Olympics: From Chamonix to Salt Lake, 2004. **Address:** Department of History, University of Utah, Rm. 310, Carolyn Tanner Irish Humanities Bldg., 215 S Central Campus Dr., Salt Lake City, UT 84112, U.S.A. **Online address:** larry.gerlach@utah.edu

GERMAN, Bill. American (born United States), b. 1962?. **Genres:** Autobiography/Memoirs. **Career:** Rolling Stones, Beggars Banquet, founder, 1978-96. Writer. **Publications:** (With R. Wood) Ron Wood: The Works, 1987; Under Their Thumb: How a Nice Boy from Brooklyn Got Mixed Up with the Rolling Stones (and Lived to Tell about It) (memoir), 2009. **Address:** Beggars Banquet, PO Box 813, New York, NY 10024, U.S.A. **Online address:** undertheirthumb@usa.net

GERNET, Jacques. French (born France), b. 1921. **Genres:** History, Theology/Religion, Translations, Sciences, Philosophy. **Career:** Ecole Pratique des Hautes Etudes, professor of economic and social sciences, director, 1955-76; University of Paris, professor of Chinese language and civilization, 1957-74; College de France, professor, chair in social and intellectual history of China, 1975-92. Writer. **Publications:** Entretiens Du maître de dhŷana Chen-houei du Ho-taö (668-760), 1949; Aspects économiques du Bouddhisme dans la Société chinoise du Ve au Xe siècle, 1956; Vie Quotidienne en Chine, à la Veille de l'invasion Mongole 1250-1276, 1959; Daily Life in China on the Eve of the Mongol Invasion (1250-1276), 1962; Ancient China from the Beginnings to the Empire, 1968; Le Monde chinois, 1972, trans. as A History of Chinese Civilization, 2nd ed., 1996; Chine Ancienne: Des Origines à l'Empire, 1977; Nan Song She hui Sheng huo Shi, 1982; A History of Chinese Civilization, 1982, rev. ed., 1996; Chine et Christianisme: Action et Reaction, 1982, trans. as China and the Christian Impact: A Conflict of Cultures, 1985; L'intelligence de la Chine: lesocial et le mental, 1994; Aspects économiques du Buddhism dans la societechinoise du Ve au Xe siecle, trans. as Buddhism in Chinese Society: An Economic History from the Fifth to the Tenth Centuries, 1995;

Zhongguo Shehui Shi, 1995; En Suivant la Voie Royale: Mélanges offerts en hommageà Leon Vandermeersch, 1997; Zhongguo 5-10 shi ji de si yuan jing ji, 2004; Raison des Choses: essai sur la philosophie de Wang Fuzhi, 1619-1692, 2005; Société et pensée chinoises aux XVIe et XVIIesiècles: Résumés des cours et séminaires au collège de France: Chaire d'histoire intellectuelle et sociale de la Chine, 1975-1992, 2007. Contributor to periodicals. **Address:** College de France, 75231 Paris Cedex 05, 11 place Marcelin-Berthelot, Paris, 75005, France. **Online address:** gernet@ext.jussieu.fr

GERONIMUS, Dennis. American (born United States), b. 1972. **Genres:** Biography, Autobiography/Memoirs, Art/Art History. **Career:** New York University, Department of Art History, assistant professor of Italian renaissance art, associate professor of art history. Writer. **Publications:** Piero di Cosimo: Visions Beautiful and Strange, 2006. Contributor to periodicals. **Address:** Department of Art History, New York University, Silver 303, 100 Washington Sq. E, New York, NY 10003, U.S.A. **Online address:** dennis.geronimus@nyu.edu

GERRARD, A. J. *See* **GERRARD, John.**

GERRARD, John. (A. J. Gerrard). British (born England), b. 1944. **Genres:** Earth Sciences, Social Sciences, Geography. **Career:** University of Birmingham, Department of Geography, lecturer, 1969-89, senior lecturer, 1989-97, reader, 1997-, honorary senior research fellow. Writer. **Publications:** Soils and Landforms, 1981; The Book of Plymouth, 1982; (as A.J. Gerrard) Rocks and Landforms, 1988; Mountain Environments: An Examination of the Physical Geography of Mountains, 1990; Soil Geomorphology: An Integration of Pedology and Geomorphology, 1992; Fundamentals of Soils, 2000; Encyclopedia of Geomorphology, forthcoming. EDITOR: Applied Geomorphology, 1984; Alluvial Soils, 1987; (as A.J. Gerrard) Managing a Conurbation: Birmingham and Its Region, 1996. **Address:** Department of Geography, University of Birmingham, GES 332, Birmingham, B15 2TT, England. **Online address:** a.j.w.gerrard@bham.ac.uk

GERRARD, Michael B. American (born United States), b. 1951. **Genres:** Environmental Sciences/Ecology, Law, Adult Non-fiction. **Career:** Council on the Environment of New York, policy analyst, 1973-75; Natural Resources Defense Council, legal intern, 1976-78; Office of Mayor, deputy director, 1982; Metropolitan Transportation Authority, special counsel, 1983; Berle, Kass & Case, environmental lawyer, 1978-94, associate, 1978-81, 1984-85, partner, 1985-94; Environmental Law in New York newsletter, editor, 1989-; New York University School of Law, adjunct professor of law, 1992; Arnold & Porter, partner, 1994-2008, managing partner, 2007-08, senior counsel, 2009-; Yale School of Forestry and Environmental Studies, lecturer, 1997-99; Columbia Law School, lecturer, 1992-2008, Andrew Sabin professor of professional practice, 2009-, New Center for Climate Change Law, director. Writer. **Publications:** Transportation Policy and the New York Environment, 1974; (with H. Gershinowitz) Energy and the New York City Environment, 1974; Economics of Pollution: A Bibliography, 1979; (with D.A. Ruzow and P. Weinberg) Environmental Impact Review in New York, 1990; (ed.) The Environmental Law Practice Guide, 8 vols., 1992; Whose Backyard, Whose Risk: Fear and Fairness in Toxic and Nuclear Waste Siting, 1994; (ed.) Brownfields Law and Practice: The Cleanup and Redevelopment of Contaminated Land, 1998; (ed.) The Law of Environmental Justice: Theories and Procedures to Address Disproportionate Risks, 1999; (with J.M. Gross) Amending CERCLA: The Post-SARA Amendments to the Comprehensive Environmental Response, Compensation, and Liability Act, 2006; (ed.) Global Climate Change and U.S. Law, 2007; (ed. with J.C. Howe and F.R. Fucci) Law of Green Buildings, 2010; (ed.) Law of Clean Energy, 2011. **Address:** Columbia Law School, Rm. 517, Jerome Greene Hall, 435 W 116th St., New York, NY 10027-7237, U.S.A. **Online address:** michael.gerrard@law.columbia.edu

GERRIG, Richard J. American (born United States), b. 1959. **Genres:** Psychology, Literary Criticism And History, Medicine/Health. **Career:** Yale University, assistant professor, 1984-90, associate professor of psychology, 1990-94; Stanford University, visiting assistant professor, 1989; State University of New York, associate professor of psychology, 1994-, professor of psychology. Writer. **Publications:** Experiencing Narrative Worlds: On the Psychological Activities of Reading, 1993; (ed.) The Psychology of Survivor: Overanalyze, Overemote, Overcompensate: Leading Psychologists Take an Unauthorized Look at The Most Elaborate Psychological Experiment Ever ConductedSurvivor!, 2007; (with P.G. Zimbardo) Psychology and Life, 19th ed., 2010. Contributor of articles to books and journals. **Address:** Department of Psychology, State Univeristy of New York, Rm. B-201, Stony Brook, NY 11794-2500, U.S.A. **Online address:** richard.gerrig@stonybrook.edu

GERRISH, B. A. *See* **GERRISH, Brian Albert.**

GERRISH, Brian Albert. (B. A. Gerrish). American/British (born England), b. 1931. **Genres:** Theology/Religion, History, Essays. **Career:** West End Presbyterian Church, assistant minister, 1956-58; Union Theological Seminary, tutor in philosophy of religion, 1957-58, distinguished service professor, 1996-2002; McCormick Theological Seminary, instructor, 1958-59, assistant professor, 1959-63, associate professor of church history, 1963-65; University of Chicago, Guggenheim fellow, Divinity School, associate professor, 1965-68, professor, 1968-85, John Nuveen professor, 1985-96, John Nuveen professor emeritus, 1996-; Journal of Religion, co-editor, 1972-85; American Society of Church History, president, 1979. **Publications:** Grace and Reason: A Study in the Theology of Luther, 1962; Tradition and the Modern World: Reformed Theology in the Nineteenth Century, 1978; The Old Protestantism and the New: Essays on the Reformation Heritage, 1982; A Prince of the Church: Schleiermacher and the Beginnings of Modern Theology, 1984; Grace and Gratitude: The Eucharistic Theology of John Calvin, 1993; Continuing the Reformation: Essays on Modern Religious Thought, 1993; Saving and Secular Faith: An Invitation to Systematic Theology, 1999; The Pilgrim Road: Sermons on Christian Life, 2000; Thinking with the Church: Essays in Historical Theology, 2010. EDITOR: The Faith of Christendom: A Source Book of Creeds and Confessions, 1963; Reformers in Profile, 1967; (co-ed.) Westminster Dictionary of Church History, 1971; (with R. Benedetto) Reformatio Perennis: Essays on Calvin and the Reformation in Honor of Ford Lewis Battles, 1981; Reformed Theology for the Third Christian Millennium: The 2001 Sprunt Lectures, 2003. **Address:** The University of Chicago, 5801 S Ellis Ave., Chicago, IL 60637, U.S.A.

GERRITSEN, Terry. *See* **GERRITSEN, Tess.**

GERRITSEN, Tess. (Terry Gerritsen). American (born United States), b. 1953. **Genres:** Mystery/Crime/Suspense, Romance/Historical, Plays/Screenplays. **Career:** Writer. **Publications:** ROMANTIC SUSPENSE NOVELS: Adventure's Mistress, 1985; Call after Midnight, 1987; Never Say Die, 1990; Under the Knife, 1990; Whistle Blower, 1992; Presumed Guilty, 1993; (as Terry Gerritsen) Peggy Sue Got Murdered, 1994; In Their Footsteps, 1994; Thief of Hearts, 1995; Keeper of the Bride, 1996. JANE RIZZOLI CRIME THRILLERS: The Surgeon, 2001; The Apprentice, 2002; The Sinner, 2003; Body Double, 2004; Vanish, 2005; The Mephisto Club, 2006; The Keepsake in UK as Keeping the Dead, 2008; Ice Cold in UK as The Killing Place, 2010; The Silent Girl, 2011. MEDICAL THRILLERS: Harvest, 1996; Life Support, 1997; Bloodstream, 1998; Gravity, 1999; The Bone Garden, 2007. **Address:** c/o Meg Ruley, Jane Rotrosen Agency, 318 E 51st St., New York, NY 10022, U.S.A. **Online address:** jogerrit@aol.com

GERSHONI, Israel. Israeli (born Israel), b. 1946. **Genres:** History. **Career:** Israel Oriental Society, secretary, 1970-73; University of Haifa, Department of the History of the Middle Eastern Countries, instructor and lecturer, 1976-78; Tel Aviv University, Department of Middle Eastern and African History, lecturer, 1978-82, senior lecturer, 1982-87, Aranne School of History, Middle Eastern Graduate Studies, advisor, 1984-86, Overseas Student Program, instructor, 1985-, associate professor, 1987-95, professor, 1994-; Hebrew University of Jerusalem, Institute for Advanced Studies, fellow, 1981-82, staff, 2005-06; University of Pennsylvania, research fellow, 1995-96; National Humanities Center, fellow, 2004-05; Oxford University, Saint Antony's College, Middle East Centre, senior associate, 1989-90. Writer. **Publications:** Major Trends in the Evolution of the Egyptian National Self-image, 1900-1950, 1977; Mitsrayim ben yihud le-ahdut: ha-hipuś ahar zehut le'umit, 1919-1948, 1979; Emergence of pan-Arabism in Egypt, 1981; (with J.P. Jankowski) Egypt, Islam and the Arabs: The Search for Egyptian Nationhood, 1900-1930, 1986; (with J.P. Jankowski) Redefining the Egyptian Nation, 1930-1945, 1995; (ed. with J.P. Jankowski) Rethinking Nationalism in the Arab Middle East, 1997; Or ba-tsel: Mitsrayim yeha-Fashizm, 1922-1937, 1999; (ed. with Y. Elman) Transmitting Jewish Traditions: Orality, Textuality, and Cultural Diffusion, 2000; (ed. with H. Erich) The Nile: Histories, Cultures, Myths, 2000; (ed. with H. Erdem and U. Wokock) Histories of the Modern Middle East: New Directions, 2002; (with J. Jankowski) Commemorating the Nation: Collective Memory, Public Commemoration, and National Identity in Twentieth-century Egypt, 2004; Piramidah la-umah: hantsahah, zikaron u-le'umiyut be-Mitsrayim ba-me'ah ha-esrim, 2006; (A. Singer and Y.H. Er-

dem) Middle East Historiographies: Narrating the Twentieth Century, 2006; (ed. with M. Hatina) Narrating the Nile: Politics, Cultures, Identities, 2008; (with J. Jankowski) Confronting Fascism in Egypt, 2010. **Address:** Department of Middle Eastern & African History, Tel Aviv University, Ramat Aviv, Tel Aviv, 69978, Israel. **Online address:** gershon@post.tau.ac.il

GERSHOW, Miriam. American (born United States), b. 1970. **Genres:** Novels, Literary Criticism And History. **Career:** University of Wisconsin, faculty; Johns Hopkins University, faculty; University of Oregon, writing instructor, associate director. Writer. **Publications:** The Local News: A Novel, 2009. Works appear in anthologies. Contributor to journals and periodicals. **Address:** c/o Emily Forland, The Wendy Weil Agency, 232 Madison Ave., Ste. 1300, New York, NY 10016, U.S.A.

GERSHTEN, Donna M. American (born United States), b. 1953. **Genres:** Novels, Young Adult Fiction, Literary Criticism And History. **Career:** Writer. **Publications:** Kissing the Virgin's Mouth, 2001. Contributor of articles to journals. **Address:** c/o Author Mail, HarperCollins, 10 E 53rd St., 7th Fl., New York, NY 10023, U.S.A.

GERSHUNY, Grace. American (born United States), b. 1950. **Genres:** Agriculture/Forestry, Homes/Gardens, Earth Sciences, Horticulture. **Career:** Rural Education Center, horticultural director, 1982; Northeast Organic and Sustainable Farmers Network, organic certification field inspector and trainer, 1984-, program developer, 1989-91; GAIA Services, proprietor, consultant, speaker, writer and educator, 1985-; Institute for Social Ecology, instructor, 1985-2004; Burlington College, Faculty, 1994-99; Sterling College, Sustainable Agriculture, adjunct faculty, 2003. **Publications:** The Soul of Soil: A Guide to Ecological Soil Management, 1983, 4th ed. (with J. Smillie), 1999; (ed. with D.L. Martin) The Rodale Book of Composting, 1992; Start with the Soil: The Organic Gardener's Guide to Improving Soil for Higher Yields, More Beautiful Flowers and a Healthy, Easy-Care Garden, 1993; Compost, Vermicompost and Compost Tea: Feeding the Soil on the Organic Farm, 2011. Contributor to magazines. **Address:** GAIA Services, 1417 Joe's Brook Rd., St. Johnsbury, VT 05819, U.S.A. **Online address:** graceg@kingcon.com

GERSON, Kathleen. American (born United States), b. 1947. **Genres:** Sociology, Business/Trade/Industry, Economics. **Career:** University of California-Berkeley, Department of Sociology, Survey Research Center, research assistant, 1972-73, Institute of Industrial Relations, research assistant, 1973-76, Institute of Urban and Regional Development, research specialist, 1975-77; Stanford University, Program on Urban Studies, instructor, 1979; New York University, assistant professor, 1980-87, associate professor of sociology, 1988-94, 1990-96, full professor of sociology, 1995-, Undergraduate Studies in Sociology, director, 1990-96, Department of Sociology, chair, 2000-03, collegiate professor, 2010-; Stanford University, Center for Advanced Studies in the Behavioral Sciences, fellow, 2011-12. Writer. **Publications:** (Co-author) Networks and Places: Social Relations in the Urban Setting, 1977; Hard Choices: How Women Decide about Work, Career and Motherhood, 1985; No Man's Land: Men's Changing Commitments to Family and Work, 1993; Time Divide: Work, Family and Gender Inequality, 2004; The Unfinished Revolution: How a New Generation is Reshaping Family, Work, and Gender in America, 2010. Contributor to journals and periodicals. **Address:** Department of Sociology, New York University, Rm. 4128, 295 Lafayette St., 4th Fl., New York, NY 10012-9604, U.S.A. **Online address:** kathleen.gerson@nyu.edu

GERSON, Lloyd P. (L. P. Gerson). Canadian/American (born United States), b. 1948. **Genres:** Novels, Biography, Translations. **Career:** University of Toronto, Department of Philosophy, lecturer, 1974-75, assistant professor, 1975-79, associate professor, 1979-80, professor of philosophy, 1990-; International Society for Neoplatonic Studies, board director, 2004-; Journal of the History of Philosophy, board director, 2007-. Writer and philosopher. **Publications:** NONFICTION: (co-author) Hamartia, 1983; God and Greek Philosophy: Studies in the Early History of Natural Theology, 1990; Plotinus, 1994; (foreword) Neoplatonism, 1995; Knowing Persons: A Study in Plato, 2003; Aristotle and Other Platonists, 2005; Ancient Epistemology, 2009. TRANSLATOR: (with H.G. Apostle) Aristotle, Selected Works, 1982, 3rd ed., 1991; (with H.G. Apostle) Aristotle's Politics, 1986; (and intro. with B. Inwood) Hellenistic Philosophy: Introductory Readings, 1988, 2nd ed., 1997; (and ed. with B. Inwood) The Epicurus Reader: Selected Writings and Testimonia, 1994; (and intro. with B. Inwood) Stoics Reader: Selected Writings and Testimonia, 2008. EDITOR: Graceful Reason: Essays in Ancient and Medieval Philosophy Presented to Joseph Owens, on the Occasion of his Seventy-fifth Birthday and the Fiftieth Anniversary of His Ordination, 1983; The Cambridge Companion to Plotinus, 1996; Aristotle: Critical Assessments, 4 vols., 1999; (with J. Dillon) Neoplatonic Philosophy: Introductory Readings, 2004; (and intro.) Aristotle's Gradations of Being in Metaphysics E-Z, 2007; Cambridge History of philosophy in Late Antiquity, 2010; The Morality of Nations: An Aristotelian Approach; Blackwell's Readings in Ancient Philosophy, forthcoming. Contributor to books and journals. **Address:** Department of Philosophy, University of Toronto, Rm. 423, 170 St. George St., Toronto, ON M5R 2M8, Canada. **Online address:** lloyd.gerson@utoronto.ca

GERSON, L. P. See **GERSON, Lloyd P.**

GERSON, Michael J. (Michael John Gerson). American (born United States), b. 1964. **Genres:** Politics/Government, Social Sciences. **Career:** Bob Dole Presidential Campaign, speech writer, 1996; U.S. News and World Reports, senior editor, 1997-99; Bush-Cheney Presidential Campaign, speech writer and senior policy advisor, 1999-2000; George W. Bush White House, deputy assistant to the president and director of presidential speech writing, 2001-02, assistant to the president for speech writing and policy advisor, 2002-05, assistant to the president for policy and strategic planning, 2005-06; Council on Foreign Relations, Roger Hertog Senior Fellow, 2006-; Washington Post, syndicated columnist, 2007-; Heritage Foundation, senior policy advisor. Journalist. **Publications:** Heroic Conservatism: Why Republicans Need to Embrace America's Ideals (and Why They Deserve to Fail If They Don't), 2007. Contributor to magazines. **Address:** Council on Foreign Relations, 1779 Massachusetts Ave. NW, Washington, DC 20036-2109, U.S.A.

GERSON, Michael John. See **GERSON, Michael J.**

GERSTEIN, Daniel M. American (born United States), b. 1958. **Genres:** Information Science/Computers, Military/Defense/Arms Control. **Career:** American University, School of International Service, adjunct lecturer. Writer. **Publications:** Securing America's Future: National Strategy in the Information Age, 2005; Leading at the Speed of Light: New Strategies for U.S. Security in the Information Age, 2006; (with P.M. Smith) Assignment: Pentagon: How to Excel in a Bureaucracy, 4th ed., 2007; Bioterror in the 21st Century: Emerging Threats in a New Global Environment, 2009. **Address:** Naval Institute Press, 291 Wood Rd., Annapolis, MD 21402, U.S.A. **Online address:** gerstein@american.edu

GERSTEN, Alexandra. See **GERSTEN-VASSILAROS, Alexandra.**

GERSTENBERGER, Erhard S. German (born Germany), b. 1932. **Genres:** Theology/Religion, History. **Career:** Yale University, instructor, assistant professor, 1962-64; Escola Superior de Teologia, professor of Old Testament, 1975-81; pastor, 1965-75; University of Marburg, professor of Old Testament, 1985-. Writer. **Publications:** Wesen und Herkunft des Apodiktischen Rechts, 1965; Psalmen in der Sprache Unserer Zeit: Der Psalter u. d. Klagelieder, 1972; (with W. Schrage) Leiden, 1977; Der Bittende Mensch: Bittritual u. Klagelied d. Einzelnen im Alten Testament, 1980; Jahwe, ein Patriarchaler Gott?: Traditionelles Gottesbild und Feministische Theologie, 1988; Psalms: A Form-Critical Commentary, vol. I: With an Introduction to Cultic Poetry, 1988, vol. II: And Lamentations, 2001; Theologien im Alten Testament: Pluralität und Synkretismus Alttestamentlichen Gottesglaubens, 2001; Israel in der Perserzeit: 5. und 4. Jahrhundert v. Chr., 2005; (contrib.) Wer knackt den Code, 2009. **Address:** University of Marburg, Lahntor 3, Marburg, D-35032, Germany. **Online address:** gersterh@staff.uni-marburg.de

GERSTEN-VASSILAROS, Alexandra. (Alexandra Gersten). American (born United States) **Genres:** Plays/Screenplays, Novels, Romance/Historical. **Career:** Writer. **Publications:** (As Alexandra Gersten) My Thing of Love: A Comic Drama, 1992; (with T. Rebeck) Omnium Gatherum, 2003; The Argument, 2005. Contributor to periodicals. **Address:** International Creative Management Inc., 40 W 57th St., New York, NY 10019, U.S.A.

GERSTLER, Amy. American (born United States), b. 1956. **Genres:** Poetry, Novels. **Career:** California Institute of Technology, faculty; University of Southern California, faculty; University of Utah, faculty; Antioch University, faculty; Pitzer College, faculty; Bennington College, Bennington Writing Seminars Program, faculty; California Institute for the Arts, faculty; University of California, visiting professor of creative writing, 1996; Art Center College of Design, faculty; Beyond Baroque, assistant director. Writer. **Publications:** POETRY: Yonder, 1981; Christy's Alpine Inn, 1982; White Marriage/

Recovery, 1984; Early Heaven, 1984; The True Bride, 1986; Bitter Angel, 1990; Nerve Storm, 1993; Crown of Weeds, 1997; Medicine, 2000. OTHERS: Martine's Mouth (fiction), 1985; Primitive Man (fiction), 1987; (with A. Smith) Past Lives (artists book), 1989; Ghost Girl, 2004; (with C.S. Eliel and L. Pittman) Lee Mullican: An Abundant Harvest of Sun, 2005; Dearest Creature, 2009. Contributor to periodicals. **Address:** Bennington College, 1 College Dr., Bennington, VT 05201, U.S.A.

GERSTMANN, Evan. American (born United States) **Genres:** Gay And Lesbian Issues, Social Sciences, Sex. **Career:** Loyola Marymount University, Loyola Law School, Professor of Law and Political Science, 1996-, Department of Political Science, assistant professor of political science, associate professor, 1996-, chair, 2005-11, professor, 2007-, professor of law, 2011-. Writer. **Publications:** The Constitutional Underclass: Gays, Lesbians and the Failure of Class-Based Equal Protection, 1999; Same-Sex Marriage and the Constitution, 2004, 2nd ed., 2008; Academic Freedom at the Dawn of a New Century: How Terrorism, Governments, and Culture Wars Impact Free Speech at Universities, 2006. **Address:** Department of Political Science, Loyola Marymount University, 4125 University Hall, 1 LMU Dr., Ste. 4600, Los Angeles, CA 90045, U.S.A. **Online address:** egerstma@lmu.edu

GERTEIS, Joseph. American (born United States), b. 1970. **Genres:** Social Sciences. **Career:** University of Minnesota, associate professor of sociology, American Mosaic Project, co-director; American Journal of Sociology, consulting editor. **Publications:** (Co-ed.) Contemporary Sociological Theory, 2002, 2nd ed., 2007; (co-ed.) Classical Sociological Theory, 2002, 2nd ed., 2007; Class and the Color Line: Interracial Class Coalition in the Knights of Labor and the Populist Movement, 2007. Contributor to journals. **Address:** Department of Sociology, University of Minnesota, 909 Social Sciences Hall, 267 19th Ave. S, Minneapolis, MN 55455, U.S.A.

GERTRIDGE, Allison. Canadian (born Canada), b. 1967. **Genres:** Children's Non-fiction, Young Adult Non-fiction, Sports/Fitness, Recreation. **Career:** Scholastic Canada Ltd., editor, 1989-93; writer, 1993-. **Publications:** Animals by Alphabet, 1991; Skating Superstars, 1994, rev. ed., 1996; Meet Canadian Authors and Illustrators: 60 Creators of childrens books, 1994, rev. ed., 2001; Skating Superstars II, 1997; Trim a Tree, 2000. **Address:** Scholastic Canada Ltd., 175 Hillmount Rd., Markham, ON L6C 1Z7, Canada. **Online address:** allison.gertridge@rogers.com

GERVAIS, (George) Paul. Italian/American (born United States), b. 1946. **Genres:** Biography, Illustrations, Novels, Horticulture. **Career:** Writer. **Publications:** SELF-ILLUSTRATED: A Garden in Lucca: Finding Paradise in Tuscany, 2000. OTHERS: Extraordinary People, 1991; Gar-an-guli, 1999; Thoughts That Come in Words, 2006; Un Giardino a Lucca, 2008. **Address:** Irene Skolnick Literary Agency, 22 W 23rd St., 5th Fl., Ste. 307, New York, NY 10010, U.S.A. **Online address:** vlmassei@lunet.it

GERVAIS, Ricky. British (born England), b. 1961. **Genres:** Young Adult Fiction. **Career:** The 11 O'Clock Show, actor, 1998; Meet Ricky Gervais, host, writer, director, 2000; The Office, British Broadcasting Corp. (BBC), co-creator, co-director, actor, 2001-03; Dog Eat Dog, actor, 2001; Legend of the Lost Tribe, actor, 2002; Comic Relief, actor, 2003; The Big Hair Do, actor, 2003; Valiant, voice work, 2005; Extras, co-creator, co-director, actor, 2005-07; For Your Consideration, actor, 2006; Night at the Museum, actor, 2006; Stardust, actor, 2007; Ghost Town, actor, 2008. Actor, writer and broadcaster. **Publications:** Flanimals, 2004; More Flanimals, 2006. TELEVISION SERIES-WITH OTHERS: The 11 O'Clock Show, 1998; Bruiser, 2000; Meet Ricky Gervais, 2000; The Sketch Show, 2001; (with S. Merchant) The Office, 2001; Stromberg, 2004; (with S. Merchant) Extras, 2005; Le Bureau, 2006; Kelsey Grammer Presents: The Sketch Show, 2005; Ricky Gervais Meets, 2006. TELEVISION SPECIALS AND EPISODES: Golden Years, 1999; Ricky Gervais Live: Animals, 2003; Ricky Gervais Live 2: Politics, 2004; Homer Simpson: This Is Your Wife, The Simpsons, 2006; Ricky Gervais Live 3: 2007; Ricky Gervais: Out of England: The Stand-Up Special, 2008. **Address:** Plumplard Productions, 38 Pickwick House, London, SE16 4UT, England.

GERZINA, Gretchen Holbrook. American (born United States), b. 1950. **Genres:** Biography, Novels. **Career:** Stanford University, Center for Teaching and Learning, assistant director, 1984-85; professor of English, 1985-; State University of New York at Albany, lecturer, 1985-86; Skidmore College, assistant professor of English, 1986-89; Princeton University, humanities fellow, 1989-90; Vassar College, assistant professor of English, 1989-, associate dean of the faculty; Columbia University, Barnard College, professor of English and director of African American studies, through 2005; Dartmouth College, Kathe Tappe Vernon professor in biography, 2005-, Department of English, chair, 2006-; University of Exeter, honorary visiting professor; Oxford University, George Eastman visiting professor, Balliol College, fellow, Eastman professor. Writer. **Publications:** Carrington: A Life, in England as Carrington: A Life of Dora Carrington, 1893-1932, 1989; Black London: Life before Emancipation, in England as Black England: Life before Emancipation, 1996; (ed.) Black Victorians-Black Victoriana, 2003; Frances Hodgson Burnett: The Unexpected Life of the Author of The Secret Garden, 2004; (ed.) The Secret Garden: Authoritative Text, Backgrounds and Contexts, Frances Hodgson Burnett in the Press, Criticism, 2005; (ed. and intro.) Annotated Secret Garden, 2007; Mr. and Mrs. Prince: How an Extraordinary 18th-Century Family Moved out of Slavery and Into Legend, 2008; A Room of their Own: The Bloomsbury Artists in American Collections, 2008. Contributor to periodicals. **Address:** c/o Kent Holland, Plesser Holland Associates, 20 W 22nd St., Ste. 903, New York, NY 10010, U.S.A. **Online address:** gretchen.h.gerzina@dartmouth.edu

GERZON, Robert. American (born United States), b. 1946?. **Genres:** Self Help, Psychology, Young Adult Fiction. **Career:** Conscious & Creative Living, owner; Psychotherapist, educator and author. **Publications:** Finding Serenity in an Age of Anxiety, 1997. **Address:** Conscious & Creative Living, 77 Bolton St., Concord, MA 01742, U.S.A.

GESCH, Roy (George). American (born United States), b. 1920. **Genres:** Theology/Religion, Travel/Exploration, Adult Non-fiction. **Career:** Lutheran clergyman, 1944-; pastor, 1944-70; Lutheran Churches, area counselor, 1949-50, 1953-60, 1964-68; St. Paul's Lutheran Church, pastor, 1970-75; Messengers of Christ, Lutheran Bible Translators Inc., director of public relations, 1975-76, executive director, 1976-84, associate director, 1984-86. Writer. **Publications:** (Contrib.) Of Such Is the Kingdom, 1964; (contrib.) Advertising with God, 1965; On Active Duty: Meditations for the Serviceman, 1967; A Husband Prays, 1968; A Wife Prays, 1968; Parents Pray, 1968; God's World through Young Eyes, 1969; Help! I'm in College, 1969, rev. ed., 1976; Man at Prayer, 1970; Lord of the Young Crowd, 1971; (with J. Nelesen) And Yet the Church Goes On!, 1972; (with D. Gesch) Discover Europe: A Guide to the Unique and Exceptional, 1973; And Yet the Church Goes On!, 1974; Service Prayer Book, 1981; Confirmed in Christ, 1983, rev. ed., 1997; To Love and to Cherish, 1985; Made for Each Other: Devotions for Newly Married Couples, 1987; Silver Reflections, 1989. **Address:** Lutheran Bible Translators Inc., PO Box 5566, Orange, CA 92863-5566, U.S.A. **Online address:** royndot@cox.net

GESLER, Wilbert M. American/Indian (born India), b. 1941. **Genres:** Geography, Medicine/Health. **Career:** Robert College for Girls, instructor in mathematics, 1965-68; Pennsylvania State University, Behrend Campus, instructor in mathematics, 1968-69; University of Malawi, Bunda College of Agriculture, lecturer in mathematics, 1969-71; Carolina Population Center, research assistant, 1973-75; University of Lagos, Institute of Child Health, research fellow, 1976-77; University of North Carolina, instructor in geography, 1978, assistant professor, 1982-87, associate professor of geography, 1987-, professor of geography, director of graduate studies, 1988-, now professor emeritus; Rutgers University, assistant professor of geography, 1978-81; University of London, Queen Mary, visiting professor. Writer. **Publications:** Health Care in Developing Countries, 1984; (with M.S. Meade and J.W. Florin) Medical Geography, 1988; The Cultural Geography of Health Care, 1991; (ed. with T. Ricketts) Health in Rural North America: The Geography of Health Care Services and Delivery, 1992; (ed. with D.J. Rabiner and G.H. DeFriese) Rural Health and Aging Research: Theory, Methods, and Practical Applications, 1998; (ed. with R.A. Kearns) Putting Health into Place: Landscape, Identity, and Well-Being, 1998; (ed. with R.J. Gordon and B.C. Nienstedt) Alternative Therapies: Expanding Options in Health Care, 1998; (ed. with D.P. Albert and B. Levergood) Spatial Analysis, GIS and Remote Sensing Applications in the Health Sciences, 2000; (with R.A. Kearns) Culture/Place/Health, 2002; Healing Places, 2003; (with N. Dines, V. Cattell and S. Curtis) Public Spaces, Social Relations and Well-being in East London, 2006. Works appear in anthologies. Contributor to journals. **Address:** Department of Geography, University of North Carolina, 323 Saunders Hall, PO Box 3220, Chapel Hill, NC 27599, U.S.A. **Online address:** wgesler@email.unc.edu

GESNER, Carol. American/Spanish (born Spain), b. 1922. **Genres:** Poetry, Literary Criticism And History, Young Adult Fiction. **Career:** Berea College, instructor, 1954-56, assistant professor, 1956-61, associate professor, 1961-67, professor, 1967-87, professor emeritus of English, 1987-. Writer. **Publications:** The Crystal Spectrum (poetry), 1964; Shakespeare and the Greek Romance: A Study of Origins, 1970; Plymouth Exploration, 1976; Plymouth and the Palimpsest: A View from Berea Ridge, 2002. Contributor of articles to periodicals. **Address:** Department of English, Berea College, Draper 201B, PO Box 1893, Berea, KY 40404, U.S.A.

GESSEL, Van C. American (born United States), b. 1950. **Genres:** Literary Criticism And History, Biography, Translations, Autobiography/Memoirs, Young Adult Fiction. **Career:** Columbia University, assistant professor, 1979-80; University of Notre Dame, assistant professor of Japanese, 1980-82; University of California, Department of Japanese, assistant professor, 1982-89, associate professor, 1989-90; Brigham Young University, associate professor, 1989-94, professor of Japanese, 1994-, Department of Asian and Near Eastern Languages, chair, 1992-97, College of Humanities, dean, 1997-. Writer. **Publications:** (Ed. with T. Matsumoto) The Shōwa Anthology: Modern Japanese Short Stories, vol. I: 1929-1961, vol. II: 1961-1984, 1986; The Sting of Life: Four Contemporary Japanese Novelists, 1989; Three Modern Novelists: Soseki, Tanizaki, Kawabata, 1993; (co-author) Ibunka to no deai: Nihon bunka o yominaosu, 1995; (ed.) Japanese Fiction Writers, 1868-1945, 1997; Japanese Fiction Writers since World War II, 1997; (ed. with J.T. Rimer) Columbia Anthology of Modern Japanese Literature, vol. I, 2005, vol. II, 2007; (ed. with R.L. Neilson) Taking the Gospel to the Japanese, 1901-2001, 2006; (trans.) Final Martyrs, 2009. TRANSLATOR OF BOOKS BY S. ENDO: When I Whistle, 1979; Stained Glass Elegies, 1984; Scandal, 1988; The Final Martyrs, 1993; Deep River, 1995; The Samurai, 1997; Five by Endo, 2000. **Address:** College of Humanities, Brigham Young University, 3075 JFSB, Provo, UT 84602, U.S.A. **Online address:** van_gessel@byu.edu

GESSNER, Lynne. (Merle Clark). American/Cuban (born Cuba), b. 1919. **Genres:** Children's Fiction, Novellas/Short Stories, Young Adult Fiction, History. **Career:** Educator and writer. **Publications:** Trading Post Girl, 1968; Lightning Slinger, 1968; (as Merle Clark) Ramrod, 1969; Bonnie's Guatemala Adventure, 1970; (contrib.) Baleful Beasts and Eerie Creatures, 1976; Navajo Slave, 1976; Yamadan, 1976; Malcolm Yucca Seed, 1977, 2nd ed., 1993; To See a Witch, 1978; Danny, 1979; Edge of Darkness, 1979; Brother to the Navajo, 1979. Contributor of articles to journals. **Address:** 6507 E Holly St., Scottsdale, AZ 85257, U.S.A.

GESTON, Mark S(ymington). American (born United States), b. 1946. **Genres:** Science Fiction/Fantasy, Novels. **Career:** Eberle, Berlin, Kading, Turnbow & McKlveen, associate, 1971-77, partner, 1977-2003; The Cabin, A Literary Center for Idaho, director, 2008-011; Stoel Rives LLP, attorney. Writer. **Publications:** Lords of the Starship, 1967; Out of the Mouth of the Dragon, 1969; The Day Star, 1972; The Siege of Wonder, 1976; Mirror to the Sky, 1992. Works appear in anthologies. Contributor to periodicals. **Address:** Stoel Rives L.L.P., 101 S Capitol Blvd., Ste. 1900, Boise, ID 83702-7705, U.S.A. **Online address:** msgeston@stoel.com

GETIS, Victoria. American (born United States), b. 1966. **Genres:** History, Law, Politics/Government. **Career:** Mount Holyoke College, visiting lecturer, 1997; University of Massachusetts, curriculum design associate, Center for Computer-Based Instructional Technology, senior research fellow, 1999-; Ohio State University, Digital Union, director. Writer. **Publications:** Muddy Boots and Ragged Aprons: Images of Working-Class Detroit, 1900-1930 (pictorial history), 1997; The Juvenile Court and the Progressives, 2000. Contributor to periodicals. **Address:** Center for Computer-Based Instructional Technology, University of Massachusetts, 140 Governors Dr., Amherst, MA 01002, U.S.A. **Online address:** vgetis@cs.umass.edu

GETLER, Warren. American (born United States) **Genres:** Novels, History. **Career:** International Herald Tribune, Frankfurt correspondent, 1984; Foreign Affairs, associate editor, 1990; The Wall Street Journal, reporter, 1992; Discovery Channel, senior writer, 1995; Bloomberg News, editor-at-large, 2002; Bertelsmann Foundation, director, 2010. **Publications:** (With B. Brewer) Shadow of the Sentinel: One Man's Quest to Find the Hidden Treasure of the Confederacy, 2003. **Address:** Bertelsmann Foundation, 1101 New York Ave. NW, Ste. 901, Washington, DC 20005, U.S.A.

GETMAN, Julius (G.). American (born United States), b. 1931. **Genres:** Education, Organized Labor. **Career:** National Labor Relations Board, attorney, 1959-61; Indiana University, associate professor, 1963-67, professor of law, 1967-76; Banaras Hindu University, visiting professor, 1967-68; Indian Law Institute, visiting professor, 1967-68; University of Chicago, visiting professor, 1970-71; Stanford University, professor of law, 1976-77; Yale University, professor of law, 1978, William K. Townsend professor of law, 1978-86; Connecticut State Police Union, chief negotiator, 1978-82; American Association of University Professors, general counsel, 1980-82, president; University of Texas, Earl E. Sheffield regents professor of law, 1986-; Boston College, Richard Huber distinguished visiting professor, 1991-92. Writer. **Publications:** (With S.B. Goldberg and J.B. Herman) Union Representation Elections: Law and Reality, 1976; Labor Relations: Law, Practice, and Policy, 1978, (with J.D. Blackburn) 2nd ed., 1983; (co-author) Casebook: Employment Discrimination BNA, 1979; (with B.B. Pogrebin) Labor Relations: The Basic Processes, Law and Practice, 1988; (co-author) Employee Rights in a Changing Economy: The Issue of Replacement Workers, 1991; In the Company of Scholars: The Struggle for the Soul of Higher Education, 1992; The Betrayal of Local 14, 1998; (with B.B. Pogrebin and D.L. Gregory) Labor Management Relations and the Law, 1999; (ed. with R. Marshall) Future of Labor Unions: Organized Labor in the 21st Century, 2004; Strike!, 2006; Restoring the Power of Unions: It Takes a Movement, 2010. **Address:** School of Law, University of Texas, 727 E Dean Keeton St., PO Box Z, Austin, TX 78705, U.S.A. **Online address:** jgetman@law.utexas.edu

GETSY, David J. (David John Getsy). American (born United States), b. 1973. **Genres:** Art/Art History, Sex. **Career:** Yale University, Paul Mellon Centre for Studies in British Art, postdoctoral fellow, 2002; Dartmouth College, Leslie Center for the Humanities, Mellon postdoctoral fellow, 2002-04; University of Texas, Harry Ransom Humanities Research Center, research fellow, 2003; Dartmouth College, Digital Media, Leslie Center for the Humanities, faculty, 2003; Harvard University, J. Paul Getty postdoctoral fellow in the History of Art and the Humanities, 2004-05; School of the Art Institute of Chicago, assistant professor, 2005-08, director of the Graduate Program in modern and contemporary art history, theory and criticism, 2006-09, associate professor and Goldabelle McComb Finn distinguished chair in art history, 2008-11, director of undergraduate programs in art history, theory and criticism, 2010-, Goldabelle McComb Finn distinguished professor of art history, 2011-; Indiana University, Everett Helm visiting fellow, 2006; William Andrews Clark Memorial Library, research fellow; University of California, Center for Seventeenth- and Eighteenth-Century Studies, research fellow, 2008; University of York, visiting professor, 2010. Historian, critic and writer. **Publications:** (Ed.) Sculpture and the Pursuit of a Modern Ideal in Britain, 1880-1930, 2004; Body Doubles: Sculpture in Britain, 1877-1905, 2004; Rodin: Sex and The Making of Modern Sculpture, 2010; (ed.) From Diversion to Subversion: Games, Play, and Twentieth-Century Art, 2011. Contributor to periodicals and journals. **Address:** Department of Art History, Theory & Criticism, Art Institute of Chicago, 112 S Michigan Ave., Chicago, IL 60603, U.S.A. **Online address:** dgetsy@saic.edu

GETSY, David John. See **GETSY, David J.**

GETTY, Sarah Sovereign. American (born United States), b. 1943. **Genres:** Poetry. **Career:** Rhode Island College, assistant professor, 1969-76; New England Foundation for Humanities, project director, 1988-92, program officer, 1992-94, executive director, 1994-96; University of Massachusetts, associate director for corporate and foundation relations, 1998-99; Wheelock College, grants officer, 1999-2003. Poet. **Publications:** The Land of Milk and Honey (poems), 1996; Bring Me Her Heart (poems), 2005. Contributor of articles to periodicals and journals. **Address:** Bedford, MA , U.S.A. **Online address:** sg@sarahgetty.net

GETZ, Christine S. (Christine Suzanne Getz). American (born United States), b. 1957?. **Genres:** Music, History. **Career:** University of Iowa, associate professor of musicology. Writer. **Publications:** Music in the Collective Experience in Sixteenth-Century Milan, 2005. Contributor to journals. **Address:** School of Music, University of Iowa, 1006 Voxman Music Bldg., Iowa City, IA 52242-1795, U.S.A. **Online address:** christine-getz@uiowa.edu

GETZ, Christine Suzanne. See **GETZ, Christine S.**

GETZ, David. American (born United States), b. 1957. **Genres:** Novels, Adult Non-fiction, Technology, History. **Career:** New York City Board of Education, teacher, 1984-, principal. Writer. **Publications:** FICTION: Thin Air, 1990; Almost Famous, 1992. NONFICTION: Frozen Man, 1994; Life on Mars, 1997, rev. ed., 2004; Frozen Girl, 1998; Moonwalkers, 2003. OTHER: Floating Home (picture book), 1997; Purple Death: The Mysterious Flu of 1918, 2000. Contributor to periodicals. **Address:** East Side Middle School, 331 E 91st St., New York, NY 10128, U.S.A.

GETZ, Marshall J(ay). American (born United States), b. 1957. **Genres:** Biography, Medicine/Health, Politics/Government, History, Autobiography/Memoirs. **Career:** Maryknoll Convent School, college advisor, 1991-99, Department of History, department head, 1993-99; University of Houston, CUST graduate assistant instructor, 2004-05; Houston Community College, psychology and history instructor, 2004-11. Writer. **Publications:** Subhas Chandra Bose: A Biography, 2002; The Ice Pick of Oblivion: Moniz, Freeman and the Development of Psychosurgery, 2009. **Address:** PO Box 19159, Houston, TX 77224-9159, U.S.A. **Online address:** marshallgetz@aol.com

GETZ, Trevor R. American (born United States) **Genres:** Social Sciences, History. **Career:** University of New Orleans, assistant professor, 2000-02; San Francisco State University, assistant professor of African history, 2002-07, associate professor of history, 2007-, professor, General Education, director, Academic Senate, vice-chair. Historian and writer. **Publications:** Slavery and Reform in West Africa: Toward Emancipation in Nineteenth-Century Senegal and the Gold Coast, 2004; (with R.J. Hoffman and J. Rodriguez) Exchanges: A Global History Reader, 2009; African History Reader: Interdisciplinary Readings in African History, 2009; (with H.S. Salter) Modern Imperialism and Colonialism: A Global Perspective, 2010. (with L. Clarke) Abina and the Important Men: A Graphic History, 2011; (with H.S. Salter) Modern Imperialism and Colonialism: A Global Perspective, 2011; (with E.B. Garcia) African Histories: New Sources and New Techniques for Studying African Pasts, 2012. Contributor to periodicals. **Address:** Department of History, San Francisco State University, Science 220, 1600 Holloway Ave., San Francisco, CA 94132, U.S.A. **Online address:** tgetz@sfsu.edu

GEVISSER, Mark. South African (born South Africa), b. 1964?. **Genres:** Politics/Government, Education. **Career:** Johannesburg Sunday Times, journalist; University of Pretoria, writer-in-residence; Trace, founder and associate. Political analyst and curator. **Publications:** (Ed. with E. Cameron) Defiant Desire: Gay and Lesbian Lives in South Africa, 1995; Portraits of Power: Profiles in a Changing South Africa, 1996; (with M. Morris) Manifesto on Values, Education and Democracy, 2001; Thabo Mbeki: The Dream Deferred, 2007 in US as A Legacy of Liberation: Thabo Mbeki and the Future of the South African Dream, 2009. Contributor to periodicals. **Address:** University of Pretoria, PO Box X20, Hatfield, 0028, South Africa. **Online address:** admin@markgevisser.com

GEWERTZ, Deborah B. American (born United States), b. 1948. **Genres:** Anthropology/Ethnology, History, Social Sciences. **Career:** Amherst College, faculty, 1977-, G. Henry Whitcomb professor of anthropology; Australian National University, visiting faculty; Ecole Des Hautes Etudes, visiting faculty; University of Auckland, visiting faculty. Writer. **Publications:** Sepik River Societies: A Historical Ethnography of the Chambri and their Neighbors, 1983; (with F.K. Errington) Cultural Alternatives and a Feminist Anthropology: An Analysis of Culturally Constructed Gender Interests in Papua New Guinea, 1987; (with F.K. Errington) Twisted Histories, Altered Contexts: Representing the Chambri in a World System, 1991; (with F.K. Errington) Articulating Change in the Last Unknown, 1995; (with F.K. Errington) Emerging Class in Papua New Guinea: The Telling of Difference, 1999; (with F.K. Errington) Yali's Question: Sugar, Culture, and History, 2004; (with F.K. Errington) Cheap Meat: The Global Omnivore's Dilemma in the Pacific Islands, 2010. EDITOR AND CONTRIBUTOR: (with E. Schieffelin) History and Ethnography in New Guinea, 1985; Myths of Matriarchy Reconsidered, 1988. Works appear in anthologies. Contributor of articles to journals. **Address:** Department of Anthropology-Sociology, Amherst College, 203C Morgan Hall, PO Box AC 2226, Amherst, MA 01002-5000, U.S.A. **Online address:** dbgewertz@amherst.edu

GEYER, Georgie Anne. American (born United States), b. 1935. **Genres:** Area Studies, Education, Geography, History, International Relations/Current Affairs, Autobiography/Memoirs, Biography. **Career:** Chicago Daily News, society desk reporter, 1959-60, general assignment reporter, 1960-64, foreign correspondent, 1964-75; Los Angeles Times Syndicate, syndicated columnist, 1975-80; Syracuse University, Lyle M. Spencer professor of journalism, 1976; Universal Press Syndicate, syndicated columnist, 1980-; American University, trustee, 1981-86. **Publications:** The New Latins: Fateful Change in South and Central America, 1970; The New 100 Years War, 1972; The Young Russians, 1975; Buying the Night Flight: The Autobiography of a Woman Foreign Correspondent, 1983, rev. ed., 1996; Guerrilla Prince: The Untold Story of Fidel Castro, 1991, 3rd ed., 2001; Waiting for Winter to End: An Extraordinary Journey through Soviet Central Asia, 1994; Americans No More: The Death of Citizenship, 1996; Who Killed the Foreign Correspondent?, 1996; Tunisia: A Journey through the Country That Works, 2002; When Cats Reigned like Kings: On the Trail of the Sacred Cats, 2004; Predicting the Unthinkable, Anticipating the Impossible: From the Fall of the Berlin Wall to America in the New Century, 2011. **Address:** Universal Press Syndicate, 1130 Walnut St., Kansas City, MO 64106-2109, U.S.A. **Online address:** gigi_geyer@juno.com

GEYMAN, John P. American (born United States), b. 1931. **Genres:** Air/Space Topics, Medicine/Health. **Career:** University of Utah, College of Medicine, Division of Family Practice, associate professor, chairman, 1971-72; University of California, School of Medicine, Department of Family Practice, professor, vice-chairman, 1972-76; Journal of Family Practice, editor, 1974-90; University of Washington, School of Medicine, Department of Family Medicine, professor, chairman, 1976-90, professor emeritus, 1993-; Journal of American Board of Family Practice, editor, 1990-2003. **Publications:** The Modern Family Doctor and Changing Medical Practice, 1971; Content of Family Practice, 1976; Family Practice in the Medical School, 1977; Research in Family Practice, 1978; (ed.) Preventive Medicine in Family Practice, 1979; Profile of the Residency-Trained Family Physician, 1980; Family Practice: Foundation of Changing Health Care, 1980, 2nd ed., 1985; (ed. with R.H. Layton and G.M. Rosen) Behavioral Science in Family Practice, 1980; (ed.) Funding of Patient Care, Education and Research in Family Practice, 1981; Family Practice: An International Perspective in Developed Countries, 1982; (co-author) The Family Practice Drug Handbook, 1990; (co-ed.) Evidence-Based Clinical Practice: Concepts and Approaches, 2000; (ed. with T.E. Norris and L.G. Hart) Textbook of Rural Medicine, 2000; Flight as a Lifetime Passion: Adventures, Misadventures, and Lessons, 2000; Health Care in America: Can Our Ailing System Be Healed?, 2001; Corporate Transformation of Health Care; Can the Public Interest Still Be Served?, 2004; Falling through the Safety Net: Americans without Health Insurance, 2005; Shredding the Social Contract: The Privatization of Medicare, 2006; The Cancer Generation: Baby Boomers Facing a Perfect Storm, 2009; Hijacked: The Road to Single Payer in the Aftermath of Stolen Health Care Reform, 2010; Breaking Point: How the Primary Care Crisis Endangers the LIves of Americans, 2011. **Address:** 615 Harrison St., Friday Harbor, WA 98250, U.S.A. **Online address:** jgeyman@u.washington.edu

GHAHRAMANI, Zarah. Iranian/Australian (born Australia), b. 1981?. **Genres:** Novels. **Career:** Writer. **Publications:** (with R. Hillman) My Life as a Traitor (memoir), 2008. **Address:** Melbourne, VI , Australia.

GHAREEB, Edmund. American (born United States) **Genres:** History, Politics/Government, Social Sciences. **Career:** George Washington University, adjunct professor of history; Georgetown University, faculty; University of Virginia, faculty; McGill University, faculty; American University, School of International Service, adjunct professor of Middle East history and politics. Writer. **Publications:** (Ed. with N. Aruri) Enemy of the Sun, 1970; Al-Harakah al-qawmīyah al-Kurdīyah, 1973; (ed.) Split Vision: Arab Portrayal in the American Media, 1977, rev. ed., 1983; The Kurdish Question in Iraq, 1981; War in the Gulf 1990-91: The Iraq-Kuwait Conflict and Its Implications, 1997; Al-Watan al-Arabī fī al-siyāsah al-Amrīkīyah, 2002; Historical Dictionary of Iraq, 2004; Refugees from Iraq: Their History, Culture and Background, 2008. **Address:** School of International Service, American University, Hurst 210, 4400 Massachusetts Ave., NW, Washington, DC 20016-8071, U.S.A. **Online address:** ghareeb@american.edu

GHAZVINIAN, John. American (born United States), b. 1974. **Genres:** History, Politics/Government. **Career:** University of Pennsylvania, instructor in critical writing program, senior fellow and lecturer, through 2009. Writer. **Publications:** Untapped: The Scramble for Africa's Oil, 2007; Children of the Revolution: Iran and America from the Mayflower to the Mullahs, forthcoming. Contributor to periodicals. **Address:** Anderson Literary Management, 12 W 19 St., 2nd Fl., New York, NY 10011, U.S.A. **Online address:** john_ghazvinian@yahoo.com

GHERMAN, Beverly. American (born United States), b. 1934. **Genres:** Biography, Children's Non-fiction, Natural History, Autobiography/Memoirs. **Career:** University of California, medical researcher, 1956-58; San Francisco School System, teacher's aide, 1967-74; Kaiser Permanente, medical researcher, 1975; Jewish Community Library, library assistant, 1976-80. Writer. **Publications:** Georgia O'Keeffe: The Wideness and Wonder of Her World, 1986; Agnes De Mille: Dancing off the Earth, 1990; Sandra Day O'Connor: Justice for All, 1991; E.B. White: Some Writer!, 1992; The Mysterious Rays of Dr. Röentgen, 1994; Robert Louis Stevenson: Teller of Tales, 1996; Norman Rockwell: Storyteller with a Brush, 2000; Ansel Adams: America's Photographer, 2002; Jimmy Carter, 2004; First Son and President: A Story About John Quincy Adams, 2006; Anne Morrow Lindbergh: Between the Sea and the Stars, 2008; Sparky: The Life and Art of Charles Schulz, 2010. Contributor to periodicals. **Address:** c/o Author Mail, Simon & Schuster Inc., 1230 Ave. of the Americas, 10th Fl., New York, NY 10020-1513, U.S.A.

GHIGLIONE, Loren. American (born United States), b. 1941. **Genres:** Biography, Reference, History. **Career:** Worcester County Newspapers, owner and president, 1969-95; Southbridge Evening News, owner and editor, 1969-95; Freedom Forum Newseum, consultant, 1995-96; Emory University, James M. Cox Jr. professor of journalism, journalism program director, 1996-99; University of Southern California, Annenberg School of Journalism, director, 1999-2001; Northwestern University, Medill School, professor and dean, 2001-06, Richard A. Schwarzlose professor of media ethics, 2007-10, Medill professor, 2010-; writer, 2010-. **Publications:** The American Journalist: Paradox of the Press, 1990; CBS's Don Hollenbeck: An Honest Reporter in the Age of McCarthyism, 2008. EDITOR: Evaluating the Press, New England Daily Newspaper Survey, 1973; Improving Newswriting: The Best of the Bulletin of the American Society of Newspapers Editors, 1982; Gentlemen of the Press: Profiles of American Newspaper Editors, 1984; The Buying and Selling of America's Newspapers, 1984; (with J. Rodell and M. Rodell) Rodell Revisited: Selected Writings of Fred Rodell, 1994; (intro.) Radio's Revolution: Don Hollenbeck's CBS Views the Press, 2008. **Address:** Northwestern University, Medill School, 1870 Campus Dr., Evanston, IL 60208-2170, U.S.A. **Online address:** ghiglion@northwestern.edu

GHILARDUCCI, Teresa. American (born United States), b. 1957. **Genres:** Economics, Organized Labor, Women's Studies And Issues, Business/Trade/Industry. **Career:** University of Notre Dame, assistant professor of economics, 1983-91, associate professor of economics, 1991-2005, professor, 2005-, New School for Social Research, Irene and Bernard L. Schwartz professor of economic policy analysis, Irene and Bernard L. Schwartz chair, Schwartz Center for Economic Policy Analysis, director; Indiana Public Employees Retirement Fund, trustee, 1997-2002. Writer. **Publications:** Pensions and Collective Bargaining: Toward a Comprehensive Retirement Income Security Policy, 1985; Labor's Capital: The Economics and Politics of Private Pensions, 1992; Portable Pension Plans for Casual Labor Markets, 1995; (ed.) What You Need to Know about the Economics of Growing Old: A Provocative Reference Guide to the Economics of Aging, 2004; (ed. with V.D. Ooms, J.L. Palmer and C. Hill) In Search of Retirement Security: The Changing Mix of Social Insurance, Employee Benefits and Individual Responsibility, 2005; (ed. with J. Turner) Work Options for Older Americans, 2007; (ed. with C.E. Weller) Employee Pensions: Policies, Problems and Possibilities, 2007; When I'm Sixty-Four: The Plot against Pensions and the Plan to Save Them, 2008. Works appear in anthologies. Contributor to journals. **Address:** Schwartz Center for Economic Policy Analysis, New School for Social Research, University of Notre Dame, 6 E 16th St., 11th Fl., New York, NY 10003, U.S.A. **Online address:** ghilardt@newschool.edu

GHIRARDI, G. C. Italian (born Italy), b. 1935. **Genres:** Sciences, Physics, Intellectual History. **Career:** University of Parma, assistant professor, 1962-76; University of Trieste, assistant professor, 1962-76, professor of quantum mechanics, 1976-, Institute of Theoretical Physics, director, 1981-85, Department of Theoretical Physics, director, 1985-91, 1993-99; Consorzio per l'incremento degli Studi e Ricerche in Fisica, director, 1990-, president, 1993-; International School for Advanced Studies, Interdisciplinary Laboratory Trieste, faculty, 1991-97. Writer. **Publications:** (With A.O. Barut and P. Codero) Crossing Symmetry in the 0 (4, 2) Formulation of the Dirac Theory, International Atomic Energy Agency, 1968; (with L. Fonda) Symmetry Principles in Quantum Physics, 1970; (co-author) The Stochastic Interpretation of Quantum Mechanics: A Critical Review, 1978; (ed. with G. Denardo and T. Weber) Group Theoretical Methods in Physics, 1984; (co-author) Unified Dynamics for Microscopic and Macroscopic Systems, 1986; (ed. with G. Corsi and M.L.D. Chiara) Bridging the Gap: Philosophy, Mathematics, and Physics, 1993; Un'occhiata alle carte di Dio: Gli interrogativi che la scienza moderna pone all'uomo, 1997; Sneaking a Look at God's Cards, 2003. **Address:** Abdus Salam Internat'l Ctr for Theoretical Phys, MB Rm. 210, Strada Costiera 11, Trieste, 34151, Italy. **Online address:** ghirardi@ictp.it

GHOSE, Indira. Swiss/German (born Germany) **Genres:** Women's Studies And Issues, History. **Career:** Free University of Berlin, lecturer of English, 1995-2006; University of Fribourg, chair of English literature, 2007-, professor. Writer. **Publications:** (Ed.) Memsahibs Abroad: Writings by Women Travellers in Nineteenth Century India, 1998; Women Travellers in Colonial India: The Power of the Female Gaze, 1998; (ed. and intro. with S. Mills) Wanderings of a Pilgrim in Search of the Picturesque, 2001; Shakespeare and Laughter: A Cultural History, 2008; (ed. with D. Renevey) Construction of Textual Identity in Medieval and Early Modern Literature, 2009. **Address:** Department of English, University of Fribourg, MIS 2221, Ave. de l'Europe 20, Fribourg, CH - 1700, Switzerland. **Online address:** indira.ghose@unifr.ch

GHOSE, Zulfikar. British/American (born United States), b. 1935?. **Genres:** Novels, Poetry, Literary Criticism And History, Autobiography/Memoirs. **Career:** The Observer, cricket correspondent, 1960-65; London, school teacher, 1963-69; University of Texas, professor of English, 1969-2007. Writer. **Publications:** (With B.S. Johnson) Statement Against Corpses, 1964; The Loss of India (verse), 1964; Confessions of a Native-Alien, 1965; The Contradictions, 1966; The Murder of Aziz Khan (novel), 1967; Jets from Orange (verse), 1967; The Incredible Brazilian, Book 1 (novel), 1972; The Violent West (verse), 1972; (with G. Ewart and B.S. Johnson) Penguin Modern Poets 25, 1974; Crump's Terms (novel), 1975; The Beautiful Empire (novel), 1975; Hamlet, Prufrock, and Language, 1978; A Different World (novel), 1978; Hulme's Investigations into the Bogart Scipt (novel), 1981; A New History of Torments (novel), 1982; The Fiction of Reality (criticism), 1983; Don Bueno (novel), 1983; A Memory of Asia (poetry), 1984; Figures of Enchantment (novel), 1986; Selected Poems (poetry), 1991; The Triple Mirror of the Self (novel), 1992; Shakespeare's Mortal Knowledge (criticism), 1993; Veronica and the Gongora Passion (short fiction), 1998; Beckett's Company (essays), 2009; 50 Poems (poetry), 2010; In the Ring of Pure Light (Lectures on Language and Literature), 2011. **Address:** Department of English, University of Texas, 1 Univ Sta. B5000, PAR 20, Austin, TX 78712-1164, U.S.A. **Online address:** zulfji@mail.utexas.edu

GHOSH, Amitav. American/Indian (born India), b. 1956. **Genres:** Sociology, Novels. **Career:** Centre for Social Sciences, visiting fellow, 1982-83; Delhi University, Department of Sociology, research associate, 1983-87, lecturer, 1987; University of Virginia, Department of Literature and Anthropology, faculty, 1988; Columbia University, South Asia Centre, visiting professor, 1989; University of Pennsylvania, Department of Anthropology, visiting professor, 1989; Centre for Studies in Social Science, fellow, 1990-92; American University in Cairo, distinguished visiting professor, 1994; Columbia University, Department of Anthropology, visiting professor, 1994-97; Queens College, Department of Comparative Literature, distinguished professor, 1999-2003; Harvard University, Department of English, visiting professor, 2004-. Writer. **Publications:** Relations of Envy in an Egyptian Village, 1985; Bisvabidyara ananda-prangane Rabindranatha, 1986; The Circle of Reason, 1986; The Shadow Lines, 1988; (trans.) Slave of Ms. H. 6, 1990; In an Antique Land, 1992; Calcutta Chromosome (novel), 1997; Dancing In Cambodia At Large In Burma, 1998; Countdown, 1999; The Glass Palace: A Novel, 2001; The Imam and the Indian: Prose Pieces, 2002; Hungry Tide, 2004; Incendiary Circumstances: A Chronicle of the Turmoil of Our Times, 2005; Sea of Poppies, 2008; River of Smoke, 2011. **Address:** Harvard Book Review, Harvard University, 59 Shepard St., PO Box 176, Cambridge, MA 02138, U.S.A. **Online address:** amitav@amitavghosh.com

GHOSH, Arun Kumar. Indian (born India), b. 1930. **Genres:** Economics, Money/Finance, Administration/Management, Agriculture/Forestry. **Career:** Burdwan Town School, assistant teacher, 1950-51; University of Calcutta, Department of Economics, postgraduate research fellow, 1952-55, examiner and scrutineer of intermediate and bachelor examinations, 1955-74, Department of Economics, research assistant in industrial finance, 1956-66; Seth Anandaram Jaipuria College, lecturer in economics and commerce, 1955-56; Institute of Cost and Works Accountants of India, part-time tutor, 1965-70, assistant director of research, 1970-85, part-time lecturer, 1971-72, assistant director of examinations, 1985-; Indian Institute of Management Calcutta, visiting professor, 1973; International Institute of Management Sciences, faculty,

1984-, chairman of examinations committee, 1984-86. Writer. **Publications:** Fiscal Problem of Growth with Stability, 1959; Fiscal Policy and Economic Growth: A Cross-Section Study, vol. I: 1962, vol. II: 1963; Monetary Policy of the Reserve Bank of India, 1964; Inflation and Price Control, 1975; Cost Accounting in Commercial Banking Industry, 1979; Management Accountants' Role in Monitoring Bank Financing, 1982; Introduction to Cost Accounting in Commercial Banking Industry, 1983; Fiscal Policy, Stability and Growth Experience and Problems of the Underdeveloped Economies, 1929-39 and 1945-65, 1990; Cost Accounting and Farm Product Costing, 1991. **Address:** Institute of Cost and Works Accountants of India, 12 Sudder St., Calcutta, WB 700 016, India.

GHOSH, Durba. American (born United States), b. 1967. **Genres:** History. **Career:** University of California, visiting lecturer, 1999; Amherst College, Five College Fellow, 1999-2000; Harvard University, lecturer, 2000-01; Wellesley College, Andrew Mellon Teaching Fellow, 2001-03; Mount Holyoke College, assistant professor, 2003-05; Cornell University, assistant professor of history, 2005-. Writer and historian. **Publications:** (ed. with D. Kennedy) Decentring Empire: Britain, India, and the Transcolonial World, 2006; Sex and the Family in Colonial India: The Making of Empire, 2006. Contributor to books, periodicals and journals. **Address:** Institute for the Social Sciences, Cornell University, 364 McGraw Hall, Ithaca, NY 14853, U.S.A. **Online address:** dg256@cornell.edu

GIAMO, Benedict. American (born United States), b. 1954. **Genres:** Sociology. **Career:** University of Notre Dame, visiting assistant professor, 1990-91, assistant professor, 1991-97, director, 1991-93, associate professor of American studies, 1997-, department chair, 2000-06; Doshisha University, visiting professor of American studies, 1993-95; Central Connecticut State University, visiting assistant professor, 1989-90. Writer. **Publications:** On the Bowery: Confronting Homelessness in American Society, 1989; (ed. with J. Grunberg) Beyond Homelessness: Frames of Reference, 1992; The Homeless of Ironweed: Blossoms on the Crag, 1996; Kerouac, the Word and the Way: Prose Artist as Spiritual Quester, 2000; The Jack of Jacks: Kerouac and American Football, 2010; Homeless come Home, 2011. **Address:** Department of American Studies, University of Notre Dame, 168 Decio Faculty Hall, Notre Dame, IN 46556, U.S.A. **Online address:** bgiamo@nd.edu

GIAMPIERI-DEUTSCH, Patrizia. Austrian/Italian (born Italy) **Genres:** Philosophy, Ethics, Psychology, Sciences, Biology, History. **Career:** University of Trieste, Institute of Philosophy, lecturer of ethics, 1986-93, visiting professor of theoretical philosophy, 1988-89; Institute of German Studies, visiting professor of German language and literature, 1989-90; University of Vienna (Austria), lecturer of ethics and contemporary philosophy, 1992-2000, assistant professor, 1997-98; Hertha-Firnberg position, 1999-2002, assistant professor, 2003-07, professor, 2007-; University of Torino, Faculty of Psychology, PhD Program Clinical and Interpersonal Relationships Psychology, visiting professor, 2007-. Writer. **Publications:** (Ed. with E. Brabant and E. Falzeder) Sigmund Freud/Sandor Ferenczi, Correspondance, 3 vols., 1992-2000; Sigmund Freud/Sandor Ferenczi, Briefwechsel, 3 vols., 1993-2005; The Correspondence of Sigmund Freud and Sandor Ferenczi, 3 vols., 1994-2000; (ed. with A. Bokay and P.L. Rudnytsky) Ferenczi's Turn in Psychoanalysis, 1996; Die Rezeption der oesterreichischen Philosophie in Italien, 1996; (co-author) Brueder, zur Sonne, zur Freiheit! Mythen und Legenden uber das Revolutionaere, 1997; (ed.) Psychoanalyse im Dialog der Wissenschaften Europaeische Perspektiven, vol. I, 2002; (ed.) Psychoanalyse im Dialog der Wissenschaften. Anglo-amerikanische Perspektiven, vol. II, 2004; (ed.) Psychoanalysis as an Empirical, Interdisciplinary Science: Collected Papers on Contemporary Psychoanalytic Research, 2005; Geist, Gehirn, Verhalten Sigmund Freud und die modernen Wissenschaften, 2009; (ed. with F. Barth and H.D. Klein) Sensory Perception-Mind and Matter, 2010. **Address:** Oelzeltgasse 1/3, Universitaetsstrasse 7, Vienna, A-1030, Austria. **Online address:** patrizia.giampieri-deutsch@univie.ac.at

GIANAKARIS, Constantine John. American (born United States), b. 1934. **Genres:** Literary Criticism And History, Essays. **Career:** University of Wisconsin, College of Letters and Science, assistant, 1958-60; Illinois State University, associate professor of English, 1961-66; Western Michigan University, associate professor, 1966-72, College of Arts and Sciences, associate dean, 1979-82, professor of English and theatre, 1972-2004, professor emeritus, 2004-; Kalamazoo Gazette, music and theater reviewer; Comparative Drama, co-editor. **Publications:** Plutarch, 1970; Peter Shaffer: A Casebook, 1991; Peter Shaffer, 1992. EDITOR: Antony and Cleopatra, 1969; Foundations of Drama, 1975; The Drama of the Middle Ages: Comparative and Critical Essays, 1982; Drama in the Twentieth Century: Comparative and Critical Essays, 1984; (ed. with C. Davidson and J.H. Stroupe and intro.) Drama in the Renaissance: Comparative and Critical Essays, 1986. Contributor to journals. **Address:** Department of English, Western Michigan University, Sprau Twr., 6th Fl., 1201 Oliver St., Kalamazoo, MI 49008-3805, U.S.A. **Online address:** gianakaris@wmich.edu

GIANCANA, Sam. American (born United States), b. 1954?. **Genres:** Mystery/Crime/Suspense, Biography, Autobiography/Memoirs. **Career:** Writer. **Publications:** (With C. Giancana) Double Cross: The Explosive, Inside Story of the Mobster Who Controlled America, 1992; (with B. Giancana) 30 Seconds, 1998; (with M. Corbitt) Double Deal: The Inside Story of Murder, Unbridled Corruption, and the Cop Who Was a Mobster, 2003; (with S.M. Burnstein) Family Affair: Treachery, Greed & Betrayal in the Chicago Mafia, 2010. Contributor to periodicals. **Address:** c/o Author Mail, William Morrow, HarperCollins Inc., 10 E 53rd St., 7th Fl., New York, NY 10022, U.S.A.

GIANGRECO, D. M. American (born United States), b. 1952?. **Genres:** Civil Liberties/Human Rights. **Career:** Military Review, editor. **Publications:** Roosevelt de Gaulle and the Posts: Franco-American War Relations Viewed through Their Effects on the French Postal System 1942-1944, 1985; (with R.B. Griffin) Airbridge to Berlin: The Berlin Crisis of 1948: Origins and Aftermath, 1988; War in Korea 1950-1953, 1990; (with T. Griswold) Delta, America's Elite Counter Terrorist Force, 1992, 2nd ed., 2005; Stealth Fighter Pilot, 1993; (ed. with K. Moore) Dear Harry: Truman's Mail Room, 1945-1953 The Truman Administration through Correspondence with "Everyday Americans", 1999; (contrib.) U.S. Special Forces: Airborne Rangers, Delta & U.S. Navy SEALs, 1999; (with K. Moore) Eyewitness D-Day: Firsthand Accounts from the Landing at Normandy to the Liberation of Paris, 2004; (with D.L. Gilmore) Eyewitness Vietnam: Firsthand Accounts from Operation Rolling Thunder to the Saigon, 2006; Eyewitness Pacific Theater: Firsthand Accounts of the War in the Pacific from Pearl Harbor to the Atomic Bombs, 2008; Hell to Pay: Operation Downfall and the Invasion of Japan, 1945-47, 2009; Soldier from Independence: A Military Biography of Harry Truman, 2009; Eyewitness March Against Hitler, forthcoming. Contributor to periodicals. **Address:** U.S. Army Command and General Staff College, 1 Reynolds Ave., Fort Leavenworth, KS 66027-1352, U.S.A.

GIARDINELLI, Mempo. Argentine (born Argentina), b. 1947. **Genres:** Novels, Novellas/Short Stories, Essays. **Career:** Universidad Iberoamericana, professor, 1977-84; Puro Cuento (literary journal), founder and director, 1986; Wellesley College, visiting professor, 1986; University of Virginia, visiting professor, 1988, 1997, 2002, 2006; University of Louisville, visiting professor, 1988, 1989; Universidad Nacionál del Nordeste, visiting professor, 1989-94, honorary professor, 1996-; Gettysburg College, visiting professor, 1998; Florida State University, visiting professor, 1999; Universidad del Norte, honorary professor, 1999; Fundación Mempo Giardinelli, founder and affiliate. Writer. **Publications:** NOVELS: La revolución en bicicleta, 1980; El cielo con las manos, 1981; Por que prohibieron el circo?, 1983; Luna caliente, 1983; Que Solos se Quedan los Muertos, 1985; Santo Oficio de la Memoria, 1991; Imposible Equilibrio, 1995; (ed.) Cuento argentino Contemporaneo, 1996; Breve Antologia de Cuentos, 1996; El Decimo Infierno, 1999; Final de Novela en Patagonia, 2000; Textos Violentos, 2001; Diatriba Por la Patria, 2002; Cuestiones Interiores, 2003; Visitas Despues de Hora, 2003; (with J.L. Bernetti) Mexico, el exilio que hemos vivido, 2003; Luminoso Amarillo y Otros Cuentos, 2007; Soñario, 2008; Dos Nouvelles, 2009; 9 Historias de Amor, 2009. SHORT STORIES: Vidas Ejemplares, 1982; La Entrevista, 1986; Cuentos: Antologia Personal, 1987; Carlitos Dancing Bar y otros Cuentos, 1992; Carlito's Dancing Bar, 1993; (comp. with G. Gliemmo) Venus de papel, 1993; El Castigo de Dios, 1993; Cuentos Completos, 1999; Gente Rara, 2005; Prosas: Una Antología Personal, 2005; Estación Coghlan y Otros Cuentos, 2005. ESSAYS: El genero Negro, 1984; Asi se Escribe un Cuento, 1992; El Pais de Las Maravillas, 1998; Los Argentinos y sus Intelectuales, 2004; Volver a leer, 2006. Contributor to newspapers and magazines. **Address:** Jose Maria Paz 355, H3500CCG Resistencia, Chaco, Argentina, Resistencia, H3500CCG, Argentina. **Online address:** fmg2005@fundamgiardinelli.org.ar

GIBB, Camilla. Canadian/British (born England) **Genres:** Novels, Young Adult Fiction. **Career:** University of Toronto, post-doctoral research fellow, Jack McClelland writer-in-residence, 2006, Department of English, Creative Writing Program, adjunct faculty; University of Alberta, writer-in-residence;

University of Guelph, Graduate Creative Writing Program, adjunct faculty. Writer. **Publications:** NOVELS: Mouthing the Words, 2001; The Petty Details of So-and-So's Life, 2002; Sweetness in the Belly, 2006; The Beauty of Humanity Movement, 2010. Contributor to periodicals. Works appear in anthologies. **Address:** Anne McDermid & Associates Ltd., 64 Bloem Ave., Toronto, ON M6E 1S1, Canada. **Online address:** camilla.gibb@utoronto.ca

GIBB, Lorna. British/Scottish (born Scotland) **Genres:** History, Biography, Travel/Exploration. **Career:** Helsinki University, lecturer; Sheffield University, Department of English Language and Linguistics, lecturer, Centre for English Cultural Tradition, lecturer; University of Essex, visiting fellow; Middlesex University, EAP lecturer. Writer. **Publications:** Lady Hester: Queen of the East (biography), 2005. **Address:** c/o James Gill, PFD, Drury House, 34-43 Russell St., London, GL WC2B 5HA, England. **Online address:** lornagibb@lornagibb.com

GIBB, Robert. American (born United States), b. 1946. **Genres:** Poetry, Literary Criticism And History, Young Adult Fiction. **Career:** Cedar Crest College, faculty, 1978-87; Yarrow, contributing editor, 1981-83; Lehigh University, faculty, 1987; East Stroudsburg University, faculty, 1987-90; Mount Union College, faculty, 1990-93; Carnegie Mellon University, faculty, 1994-95; University of Pittsburgh, faculty, 1997-. **Publications:** Whale Songs, 1976, 2nd ed., 1979; The Margins, 1979; The Names of the Earth in Summer, 1983; The Winter House, 1984; Entering Time, 1986; A Geography of Common Names, 1987; Momentary Days, 1989; Fugue for a Late Snow, 1993; The Origins of Evening, 1997; Burning World: Poems, 2004; World Over Water: Poems, 2007; What the Heart Can Bear: Selected and Uncollected Poems, 1979-1993, 2009; Sheet Music: Poems, 2012; The Empty Loom, 2012. Contributor to periodicals. Works appear in anthologies. **Address:** 5036 Revenue St., Homestead, PA 15120-1227, U.S.A. **Online address:** rngibb@earthlink.net

GIBBON, Sean. American (born United States) **Genres:** Autobiography/ Memoirs, Art/Art History, Literary Criticism And History. **Career:** Vermont Magazine, managing editor. **Publications:** Gone Phising, 1957; Run like an Antelope: On the Road with Phish, 2001. Contributor to magazines and newspapers. **Address:** c/o Author Mail, St. Martin Press, 175 5th Ave., New York, NY 10010, U.S.A.

GIBBONS, Alan. British (born England), b. 1953. **Genres:** Novels, Young Adult Non-fiction. **Career:** Writer and educator. **Publications:** JUVENILE FICTION: Our Peculiar Neighbour, 1990; Pig, 1990; Whose Side Are You On?, 1991; The Jaws of the Dragon, 1991; Dagger in the Sky, 1992; S.O.S. Save Our Santa, 1992; Chicken, 1994; Grandad's Ears, 1994; Hattie Hates Hats, 1994; Not Yeti, 1994; Ganging Up, 1995; The Climbing Boys, 1995; City of Fire, 1995; Playing with Fire, 1996; When My Ship Came In, 1996; Street of Tall People, 1996; A Fight to Belong, 1999; Julie and Me Michael Owen Makes Three, 2001; Julie and Me: Treble Trouble, 2002; The Cold Heart of Summer, 2002; The Edge, 2002; Deathriders, 2003; Caught in the Crossfire, 2003; The Dark Beneath, 2003; The Lost Boys' Appreciation Society, 2004; The Defender, 2004; Hold On, 2005; Blood Pressure, 2005; The Greatest, 2006; The Number Seven Shirt, 2008; Night Hunger, 2008; Charles Darwin: Discover the World of Darwin through the Diary of a Ship's Boy, 2008. TOTAL FOOTBALL SERIES: Some You Win, 1997; Under Pressure, 1997; Divided We Fall, 1998; Injury Time, 1998; Last Man Standing, 1998; Power Play, 1998; Twin Strikers, 1999; Final Countdown, 1999. LEGENDEER TRILOGY: Shadow of the Minotaur, 2000; Vampyr Legion, 2000; Warriors of the Raven, 2001. LOST SOULS SERIES: Rise of the Blood Moon, 2006; Setting of a Cruel Sun, 2006. HELL'S UNDERGROUND SERIES: Scared to Death, 2007; The Demon Assassin, 2008; Renegade, 2009; Witch Breed, 2010; The Dying Photo, 2010; An Act of Love 2011. Contributor to periodicals. **Address:** Liverpool, MS , England. **Online address:** contact@alangibbons.com

GIBBONS, Anne R. American (born United States), b. 1947. **Genres:** Environmental Sciences/Ecology, Animals/Pets, Sciences, Natural History. **Career:** ARG Editorial Services, proprietor, 1983-. Writer. **Publications:** (With W. Gibbons) Ecoviews: Snakes, Snails, and Environmental Tales, 1998. **Address:** 14 Hillcrest, Tuscaloosa, AL 35401-5922, U.S.A. **Online address:** argedit@comcast.net

GIBBONS, Gail (Gretchen). American (born United States), b. 1944. **Genres:** Children's Fiction, Children's Non-fiction, Illustrations, Animals/Pets, Natural History, Sports/Fitness. **Career:** WCIA-Television, artist, 1967-69; WMAQ-TV, promotions and animation artist, 1969; Bob Howe Agency, staff artist, 1969-70; WNBC-Television, House of Animation, staff artist, 1970-76; freelance writer and illustrator of children's books, 1975-; United Press Intl., freelance artist, 1977-88. **Publications:** SELF-ILLUSTRATED FOR CHILDREN NONFICTION: Things to Make and Do for Halloween, 1976; Things to Make and Do for Columbus Day, 1977; Things to Make and Do for Your Birthday, 1978; Clocks and How They Go, 1979; Lock and Keys, 1980; The Too-Great Bread Bake Book, 1980; Trucks, 1981; Christmas Time, 1982; The Post Office Book: Mail and How It Moves, 1982; Tool Book, 1982; Boat Book, 1983; New Road!, 1983; Sun Up, Sun Down, 1983; Thanksgiving Day, 1983; Department Store, 1984; Fire! Fire!, 1984; Halloween, 1984; The Seasons of Arnold's Apple Tree, 1984; Tunnels, 1984; Check It Out, 1985; Fill It Up!, 1985; The Milk Makers, 1985; Playgrounds, 1985; Lights! Camera! Action!, 1985; Flying, 1986; From Path to Highway: The Story of the Boston Post Road, 1986; Happy Birthday!, 1986; Up Goes the Skyscraper!, 1986; Valentine's Day, 1986; Deadline!, 1987; Dinosaurs, 1987; Trains, 1987; Weather Forecasting, 1987; Zoo, 1987; Farming, 1988; Prehistoric Animals, 1988; Sunken Treasure, 1988; Catch the Wind!, 1989; Easter, 1989; Marge's Diner, 1989; Monarch Butterfly, 1989; Beacons of Light, 1990; How a House Is Built, 1990; Weather Words and What They Mean, 1990; From Seed to Plant, 1991; The Puffins Are Back!, 1991; Whales, 1991; The Great St. Lawrence Seaway, 1992; Recycle!, 1992; Say Woof, 1992; Sharks, 1992; Stargazers, 1992; Caves and Caverns, 1993; Frogs, 1993; Pirates: Robbers of the High Seas, 1993; The Planets, 1993, 3rd ed., 2008; Puff-Flash-Bang!, 1993; Spiders, 1993; Christmas on an Island, 1994; Country Fair, 1994; Emergency!, 1994; Nature's Green Umbrella, 1994; St. Patrick's Day, 1994; Wolves, 1994; Bicycle Book, 1995; Knights in Shining Armor, 1995; Planet Earth/Inside Out, 1995; The Reasons for Seasons, 1995; Sea Turtles, 1995; Cats, 1996; Deserts, 1996; Dogs, 1996; Music Maker, 1996; Click!, 1997; Gulls...Gulls...Gulls..., 1997; The Honey Makers, 1997; The Moon Book, 1997; Paper, Paper Everywhere, 1997; Marshes and Swamps, 1998; Soaring with the Wind, 1998; Yippee-Yay!, 1998; Rabbits, Rabbits and More Rabbits, 2000; Apples, 2000; My Baseball Book, 2000; My Soccer Book, 2000; My Football Book, 2000; My Basketball Book, 2000; Ducks!, 2001; Polar Bears, 2001; Behold...the Unicorns!, 2001; The Berry Book, 2002; Halloween Is..., 2002; Giant Pandas, 2002; Tell Me, Tree, 2002; Chicks and Chickens, 2003; Christmas Is..., 2003; Horses!, 2003; Grizzly Bears, 2003; The Quilting Bee, 2004; Mummies, Pyramids and Pharaohs, 2004; Thanksgiving Is..., 2004; Owls, 2005; From Sheep to Sweater, 2005; Surrounded by Sea: Life on a New England Fishing Island, 2005; Dinosaur Discoveries, 2005; Ice Cream: The Full Scoop, 2006; The Vegetables We Eat, 2007; Snakes, 2007; Groundhog Day!, 2007; Galaxies, Galaxies!, 2007; Coral Reefs, 2007; Elephants of Africa, 2008; Dinosaurs!, 2008; Corn, 2008; Tornadoes!, 2009; Hurricanes!, 2009; Alligators and Crocodiles, 2010; Gorillas, 2010; It's Snowing!, 2011. FICTION: Willy and His Wheel Wagon, 1975; Salvador and Mister Sam, 1975; The Missing Maple Syrup Sap Mystery, 1979; The Magnificent Morris Mouse Clubhouse, 1981. Illustrator of books by J. Yolen, J. Cole. **Address:** Goose Green Maple Syrup Co., 1 Goose Green St., Corinth, VT 05039, U.S.A.

GIBBONS, Reginald. American (born United States), b. 1947. **Genres:** Novels, Novellas/Short Stories, Poetry, Literary Criticism And History, Social Sciences, Sociology, History. **Career:** Princeton University, lecturer in creative writing, 1976-80; Northwestern University, professor of English, classics, Spanish and Portuguese, 1981-; Warren Wilson College, MFA Program for Writers, core faculty, 1989-; Guild Complex, co-founder and board director, 1989-. Writer. **Publications:** William Goyen: A Study of the Short Fiction, 1991; Five Pears or Peaches: Stories, 1991; Sweetbitter: A Novel, 1994; Slow Trains Overhead, 2010. TRANSLATOR: (ed.) Selected Poems of Luis Cernuda, 1977; (with A.L. Geist) Guillen on Guillen, 1979; Bakkhai/Euripides, 2001; (with C. Segal) Antigone/Sophokles, 2003. POETRY: Roofs Voices Roads, 1979; The Ruined Motel, 1981; Saints, 1986; Maybe It Was So, 1991; Sparrow: New and Selected Poems, 1997; Homage to Longshot O'Leary: Poems, 1999; It's Time, 2002; In the Warhouse, 2004; Fern-Texts, 2005; Creatures of a Day, 2008; Selected Poems, 2008. EDITOR: The Poet's Work, 1979; (with G. Graff) Criticism in the University, 1985; The Writer in Our World, 1986; Had I a Hundred Mouths: New & Selected Stories, 1947-1983, 1986; New Writing from Mexico, 1992; (with T. Des Pres) Thomas McGrath: Life and the Poem, 1992; (author of afterword) Half a Look of Cain: A Fantastical Narrative, 1994; TriQuarterly New Writers, 1996; The House of Breath, 1999. Contributor to periodicals. **Address:** Department of Eng-

lish, Northwestern University, University Hall, Rm. 404, 1897 Sheridan Rd., Evanston, IL 60208, U.S.A. **Online address:** rgibbons@northwestern.edu

GIBBS, A. M. *See* **GIBBS, Anthony Matthews.**

GIBBS, Anthony Matthews. Also writes as A. M. Gibbs. Australian (born Australia), b. 1933. **Genres:** History, Humanities, Intellectual History, Literary Criticism And History, Biography, Poetry, Plays/Screenplays. **Career:** Australian Academy of the Humanities, fellow, 1982-, editor, 1988-93, vice-president, 1988-89; University of Adelaide, lecturer in English, 1960-66, Southern Review, editor, 1963-64; University of Leeds, lecturer, 1966-69; University of Newcastle, professor of English and head of the department, 1969-75; Macquarie University, Department of English, professor, 1975-98, chair, professor emeritus, 1998-; University Senate, School of English, head. **Publications:** Shaw, 1969; (ed.) Sir William Davenant: The Shorter Poems, and Songs from the Plays and Shaw, 1969; The Shorter Poems, and Songs from the Plays and Masques, 1972; Art and Action in Hamlet, 1977; The Art and Mind of Shaw, 1983; (ed.) Shaw: Interviews and Recollections, 1990; (ed.) The Relevance of the Humanities, 1990; Bernard Shaw: Man and Superman and Saint Joan: A Casebook, 1992; Heartbreak House: Preludes of Apocalypse, 1994; (ed.) Masks of Time: Drama and Its Contexts, 1994; A Bernard Shaw Chronology, 2001; Bernard Shaw: A Life, 2005. **Address:** Department of English, Macquarie University, 2113 N Ryde, Sydney, NW 2109, Australia. **Online address:** gibbston@gmail.com

GIBBS, David N. American (born United States), b. 1958. **Genres:** Politics/Government. **Career:** U.S. Department of Commerce, foreign affairs assistant, Foreign Fisheries Analysis Division, Africa/Middle East desk head, 1981-82; University of Wisconsin, MacArthur postdoctoral fellow, 1989-90; University of Arizona, assistant professor of political science, 1990-96, associate professor of political science, 1996-2003, associate professor of history and political science, 2003-10, professor of history and government, 2010-; Udall Center for Studies in Public Policy, Udall research fellow, 1998. Writer. **Publications:** The Political Economy of Third World Intervention: Mines, Money and U.S. Policy in the Congo Crisis, 1991; First Do No Harm: Humanitarian Intervention and the Destruction of Yugoslavia, 2009. Works appear in anthologies. Contributor to journals, periodicals and newspapers. **Address:** Department of History, University of Arizona, Rm. 227, Social Sciences, 1145 E S Campus Dr., Tucson, AZ 85721, U.S.A. **Online address:** dgibbs@arizona.edu

GIBBS, Tyson. American (born United States), b. 1951. **Genres:** Anthropology/Ethnology, Social Sciences, Sports/Fitness, Reference. **Career:** Dartmouth College, assistant museum curator and School of Medicine, computer programmer, 1971-73; Baylor College of Medicine, Institute of Clinical Toxicology, data clerk, 1974-75; North Central Florida Community Mental Health Center, research assistant, 1975-76, research coordinator, 1976-78; University of South Carolina, instructor, 1980-81, assistant professor of preventive medicine and adjunct assistant professor of anthropology, 1981-83; Meharry Medical College, assistant professor of preventive dentistry and Center on Aging, associate director, 1983-87; Georgia State University, assistant professor of anthropology, 1991-92; West Georgia College, associate professor of sociology, 1992-93; Emory University, Geriatric Center, assistant professor of clinical medicine, 1993-94; University of North Texas, assistant professor, 1995-97, associate professor of anthropology, 1998-, chair. Writer. **Publications:** (With P. Gibbs) Horsman Dolls, 1985, rev. ed., 1988; (with P. Gibbs) The Collector's Encyclopedia of Black Dolls, 1987, rev. ed., 1990; (with P. Gibbs) Black Collectibles Sold in America, 1987, rev. ed., 2000; Ethnic Health Collections in the United States: A Guide to Repositories, 1995; A Guide to Ethnic Health Collections in the United States, 1996; (with A. Frishkey) Guide to Resources in Ethnic Studies on Minority Populations, 2000; African Americans at Snee Farm Plantation, Mount Pleasant, South Carolina, 2006; (ed. with S.G. Lurie) Health-seeking Behavior in Ethnic Populations, 2007. Contributor to books and journals. **Address:** Department of Anthropology, University of North Texas, Chilton Hall, 330Q, 1155 Union Cir., PO Box 310409, Denton, TX 76203-5017, U.S.A. **Online address:** tgibbs@pacs.unt.edu

GIBRAN, Daniel K. American/Guyanese (born Guyana), b. 1945. **Genres:** Military/Defense/Arms Control, History, Humanities. **Career:** Planning Institute of Jamaica, senior political economist, 1987-90; Shaw University, assistant professor, associate professor, 1991-96; Tennessee State University, professor of political science, 1996-. Writer. **Publications:** The Exclusion of Black Soldiers From The Medal of Honor, 1997; The Falklands War: Britain

Versus the Past in The South Atlantic, 1997; Leadership and Courage: A Brief History of the All-Black 92nd Infantry Division and The Italian Campaign in World War II, 2001. **Address:** Department of History, Tennessee State University, 209 Crouch Hall, 3500 John Merritt Blvd., Nashville, TN 37209, U.S.A. **Online address:** dgibran@tnstate.edu

GIBSON, Alan. American (born United States), b. 1961?. **Genres:** Intellectual History, Law, Politics/Government, Adult Non-fiction, Humanities. **Career:** California State University, Department of Political Science, professor, 2001-. Writer, historian and political scientist. **Publications:** Interpreting the Founding: Guide to the Enduring Debates over the Origins and Foundations of the American Republic, 2006, 2nd ed., 2009; Understanding the Founding: The Crucial Questions, 2007, 2nd ed., 2010. **Address:** Department of Political Science, California State University, 719 Butte Hall, 400 W 1st St., Chico, CA 95929-0455, U.S.A. **Online address:** agibson@csuchico.edu

GIBSON, A(lex) J. S. British/Singaporean (born Singapore), b. 1958. **Genres:** History, Military/Defense/Arms Control, Economics. **Career:** University of Exeter, lecturer in historical geography, 1989-; University of Plymouth, Centre for Health and Social Care Interdisciplinary Innovation and Research, innovation and research fellow. Writer. **Publications:** (With G. Whittington) The Military Survey of Scotland, 1747-1755: A Critique, 1986; (with T.C. Smout) Prices, Food, and Wages in Scotland, 1550-1780, 1995. **Address:** University of Plymouth, Roland Levinsky Bldg., Drake Circus, Plymouth, DN PL4 8AA, England. **Online address:** alex.gibson@plymouth.ac.uk

GIBSON, Ann Eden. American (born United States), b. 1944. **Genres:** Art/Art History, Philosophy. **Career:** Kent State University, adjunct instructor in studio art, 1969-72; Akron State University, adjunct instructor, 1970-72; Art Institute of Pittsburgh, studio instructor in design and drawing, 1972-75; Point Park College, assistant professor of art history and studio art, 1975-79; University of Pittsburgh, adjunct instructor in art history, 1979; University of Delaware, adjunct instructor in art history, 1980-81, professor of art history, 1998, chairperson of department, 1998-2003, now professor emeritus; Yale University, lecturer, 1982-84, assistant professor, 1984-87, associate professor of art history, 1987-90, Morse fellow, 1987-88, senior faculty fellow, 1990-91; State University of New York, associate professor of art history, 1991-98, acting department head, 1993-94, associate director of Humanities Institute, 1995-98; Walker Art Center, Mack lecturer, 1996; Rhodes College, Moss lecturer, 1997; Tulane University, Sandra Garrard memorial lecturer, 1998; Studio Museum of Harlem, curator, 1998. Writer. **Publications:** Issues in Abstract Expressionism: The Artist-Run Periodicals, 1990; Abstract Expressionism: Other Politics, 1997; (with M. Scala) Judith Godwin: Style and Grace, 1997; (with D. Veneciano) Norman Lewis: The Black Paintings, 1946-1977, 1998. Contributor to books and periodicals. **Address:** Department of Art History, University of Delaware, 206 Mechanical Hall, Newark, DE 19716, U.S.A. **Online address:** agibson@udel.edu

GIBSON, Chris. Australian (born Australia), b. 1973?. **Genres:** Adult Non-fiction, Popular Culture, Social Sciences, Geography. **Career:** University of New South Wales, faculty, Industrial Relations Research Centre, associate; University of Sydney, faculty; University of Western Sydney, faculty; Geographical Society of New South Wales, councilor; University of Wollongong, associate professor of human geography, 2005-, professor of human geography; ARC Cultural Research Network, node convenor; IAG Cultural Geography Study Group, deputy convenor. Writer. **Publications:** (With J. Connell) Sound Tracks: Popular Music, Identity and Place, 2003; (with P.D. Hall) Deadly Sounds, Deadly Places: Contemporary Aboriginal Music in Australia, 2004; (with J. Connell) Music and Tourism: On the Road Again, 2005; (ed. with J. Connell) Festival Places: Revitalising Rural Australia, 2011. Contributor to periodicals. **Address:** University of Wollongong, Rm. 41.G08, Wollongong, NW 2522, Australia. **Online address:** cgibson@uow.edu.au

GIBSON, Ian. Spanish/Irish (born Ireland), b. 1939?. **Genres:** History, Biography, Education, Reference. **Career:** Queen's University, lecturer in Spanish, 1962-68; London University, reader, lecturer in Spanish, 1970. Writer. **Publications:** Represión nacionalista de Granada en 1936 y la muerte de Federico García Lorca, 1971; The English Vice: Beating, Sex and Shame in Victorian England and After, 1978; Assassination of Federico García Lorca, 1979; En busca de José Antonio, 1980; Un irlandés en España: Diario de un año, 1981; La noche en quemataron a Calvo Sotelo, 1982; Paracuellos: Como fue, 1983; Federico García Lorca, vol. I, 1985, vol. II, 1987, trans. as Federico Garcia Lorca: A Life, 1989; Queipo de Llano, 1986; En Grana-

da, su Granada, 1989; Federico Garcia Lorca, 1989; Fire in the Blood: The New Spain, 1992; Lorca's Granada: A Practical Guide, 1992; Salvador Dalí, 1994; The Shameful Life of Salvador Dalí, 1998; Lorca, Dalí, 1999; Garcí, 2001; The Erotomaniac: The Secret Life of Henry Spencer Ashbee, 2001; Viento del sur: Memorias apócrifas de un ingléssalvado por España, 2001; Yo, Rubén Darío: Memoriaspóstumas de un rey de la Poesía, 2002; Cela, el hombre que quisoganar, 2003; Ligero de equipaje: La vida de Antonio Machado, 2006; Elhombre que detuvo a García Lorca: Ramón Ruiz Alonso y la muertedel poeta, 2007; Cuatro poetas en guerra, 2007; Hombre que detuvo a García Lorca: Ramón Ruiz Alonso y la muerte del poeta, 2007; Fosa de Lorca: crónica de un despropósito, 2010. **Address:** Faber and Faber Ltd. Publishers, 3 Queen Sq., London, GL WC1N 3AU, England. **Online address:** ian.gibson@dti.gsi.gov.uk

GIBSON, Jo. *See* FLUKE, Joanne.

GIBSON, Margaret. American (born United States), b. 1944. **Genres:** Poetry, Biography. **Career:** Madison College, instructor in English, 1967-68; Virginia Commonwealth University, instructor in English, 1968-70, instructor in MFA program, 1988-89, 1991; George Mason University, assistant professor of English, 1970-75; writer, 1975-; Connecticut College, lecturer, 1976-77; Phillips Academy, writer-in-residence, 1984-87; University of Connecticut, visiting professor of English, 1993-, now professor emeritus of English. **Publications:** POETRY: Lunes: Poems, 1973; (ed. with R. McCann) Landscape and Distance: Contemporary Poets from Virginia, 1975; On the Cutting Edge, 1976; Signs: Poems, 1979; Long Walks in the Afternoon: Poems, 1982; Memories of the Future: The Daybooks of Tina Modotti: Poems, 1986; Out in the Open: Poems, 1989; The Vigil: A Poem in Four Voices, 1993; Earth Elegy: New and Selected Poems, 1997; Icon and Evidence: Poems, 2001; Autumn Grasses: Poems, 2003; One Body: Poems, 2007; The Prodigal Daughter: Reclaiming an Unfinished Childhood, 2008; Second Nature, 2010. Contributor to periodicals. **Address:** Department of English, University of Connecticut, 215 Glenbrook Rd., Ste. 4025, Storrs, CT 06269-4025, U.S.A.

GIBSON, Marley. (Kate Harmon). American (born United States), b. 1966?. **Genres:** Horror. **Career:** Writer, 2001-; paranormal investigator, 2007-. **Publications:** (With C. Murphey) Christmas Miracles, 2009; (with P. Burns and D. Schrader) The Other Side: A Teen's Guide to Ghost Hunting and the Paranormal, 2009. GHOST HUNTRESS SERIES: The Awakening, 2009; The Guidance, 2009; The Reason, 2010; The Counseling, 2010. SORORITY 101 SERIES AS KATE HARMON: The Formal, 2008; The New Sisters, 2008; Zeta or Omega!, 2008. **Address:** c/o Deidre Knight, Knight Agency, 570 East Ave., Madison, GA 30650, U.S.A. **Online address:** marley@excite-lite.com

GIBSON, Mary Ellis. American (born United States), b. 1952?. **Genres:** Literary Criticism And History. **Career:** University of North Carolina, Department of English, professor of English, 1978-; Virginia Commonwealth University, Victorians Institute Journal, co-editor. **Publications:** History and the Prism of Art: Browning's Poetic Experiments, 1987; Epic Reinvented: Ezra Pound and the Victorians, 1995; Indian Angles: English Verse in Colonial India from Jones to Tagore, 2011. EDITOR: New Stories by Southern Women, 1989; Homeplaces: Stories of the South by Women Writers, 1991; Critical Essays on Robert Browning, 1992. **Address:** Department of English, University of North Carolina, 3115 Moore Humanities and Research, Administration Bldg., 1111 Spring Garden St., Greensboro, NC 27412, U.S.A. **Online address:** megibson@uncg.edu

GIBSON, Miles. British (born England), b. 1947. **Genres:** Novels, Children's Fiction, Young Adult Fiction, Poetry. **Career:** J. Walter Thompson, copywriter, 1968-72; free-lance writer, 1972-; The Panty Liners, lead vocalist. **Publications:** The Guilty Bystander, 1970; Permanent Damage, 1973; The Sandman, 1984; Dancing with Mermaids, 1985; Vinegar Soup, 1987; Hotel Plenti, 1987; Fascinated, 1993; Say Hello to the Buffalo (poems for children), 1994; The Prisoner of Meadow Bank, 1995; Kingdom Swann, 1998; Mr Romance, 2002; Little Archie (children's fiction), 2004; Einstein (novel), 2004; Whoops-There Goes Joe, 2006. Contributor to magazines. **Address:** c/o Jonathan Clowes, Jonathan Clowes Ltd., 10 Iron Bridge House, Bridge Approach, London, GL NW1 8BD, England.

GIBSON, Robert. (Robert Donald Davidson Gibson). British (born England), b. 1927. **Genres:** Literary Criticism And History, Biography, History.

Career: University of St. Andrews, assistant lecturer, 1954-55; University of Dundee, Queen's College, lecturer, 1955-58; Aberdeen University, lecturer, 1958-61; Queen's University, professor of French and department chair, 1961-65; University of Kent, sub-dean of faculty of humanities, 1961-72, professor of French, 1965-94, department chair, 1965-, now retired, Rutherford College, deputy master, 1966-71. Writer. **Publications:** The Quest of Alain-Fournier, 1953; Roger Martin du Gard, 1961; (comp.) Modern French Poets on Poetry, 1961; The Land without a Name, 1975; Alain-Fournier: Le Grand Meaulnes, 1986; Annals of Ashdon, 1988; Best of Enemies, 1995, new ed., 2004; The End of Youth: The Life and Work of Alain Fournier, 2005. EDITOR: Brouart et Le Desordre, 1962; Provinciales, 1965; Le Grand Meaulnes, 1968; Studies in French Fiction in Honour of Vivienne Mylne, 1988. **Address:** Thalassa, Cliff Rd., Sidmouth, DN EX10 8JN, England.

GIBSON, Robert Donald Davidson. *See* **GIBSON, Robert.**

GIBSON, Shimon. Israeli/British (born England), b. 1959?. **Genres:** Theology/Religion. **Career:** Palestine Exploration Fund, cataloger, 1989-95; Israel Antiquities Authority, Research and Scientific Reports Department, department head, 1995-99; W.F. Albright Institute of Archaeological Research, senior associate fellow; University of North Carolina, adjunct professor of archaeology; Bulletin of the Anglo-Israel Archaeological Society, editor; Dig Mount Zion, director. Archaeologist. **Publications:** (With D.M. Jacobson) Below the Temple Mount in Jerusalem: A Sourcebook on the Cisterns, Subterranean Chambers and Conduits of the Haram Al-Sharīf, 1996; (ed. with A. Negev) Archaeological Encyclopedia of the Holy Land, 2001, rev. ed., 2003; Jerusalem in Original Photographs, 1850-1920, 2003; The Cave of John the Baptist: The Stunning Archaeological Discovery That Has Redefined Christian History, 2004; (ed.) The Illustrated Dictionary & Concordance of the Bible, 2005; (contrib.) Flights into Biblical Archaeology, 2007; The Final Days of Jesus: The Archaeological Evidence, 2009. **Address:** Dig Mount Zion, PO Box 4405, Jerusalem, 91043, Israel.

GIBSON, Tanya Egan. American (born United States), b. 1967. **Genres:** Novels. **Career:** Writer. **Publications:** How to Buy a Love of Reading: A Novel (young adult novel), 2009. **Address:** Marin County, CA , U.S.A. **Online address:** tanya@tanyaegangibson.com

GIBSON, Thomas. American (born United States), b. 1956. **Genres:** Popular Culture, Theology/Religion, History, Anthropology/Ethnology. **Career:** Manchester University, faculty; Cambridge University, faculty; University of Rochester, Department of Anthropology, chair, 1995-2001, 2005-08, professor; Cornell University, Southeast Asia Program, visiting fellow, 2001-02. Writer and anthropologist. **Publications:** Sacrifice and Sharing in the Philippine Highlands: Religion and Society among the Buid of Mindoro, 1986; And the Sun Pursued the Moon: Symbolic Knowledge and Traditional Authority among the Makassar, 2005; Islamic Narrative and Authority in Southeast Asia: From the 16th to the 21st Century, 2007. **Address:** Department of Anthropology, University of Rochester, Lattimore 439, Rochester, NY 14627-0161, U.S.A. **Online address:** thomas.gibson@rochester.edu

GIBSON, Walter Samuel. American (born United States), b. 1932. **Genres:** Art/Art History, Bibliography, Architecture. **Career:** Case Western Reserve University, assistant professor, 1966-71, acting chairman, 1970-71, associate professor, 1971-78, chairman, 1971-79, Mellon professor of the humanities, 1978-97, Andrew W. Mellon professor emeritus of humanities; Guggenheim fellow, 1978; Williams College, Clark visiting professor of art history, 1989, 1992. Writer. **Publications:** Hieronymus Bosch, 1973; The Paintings of Cornelis Engebrechtsz, 1977; Bruegel, 1977; Hieronymus Bosch: An Annotated Bibliography, 1983; Mirror of the Earth: The World Landscape in Sixteenth-Century Flemish Painting, 1989; Pieter Bruegel the Elder: Two Studies, 1991; In Detail: New Studies of Northern Renaissance Art in Honor of Walter S. Gibson, 1998; Pleasant Places: The Rustic Landscape from Bruegel to Ruisdael, 2000; Pieter Bruegel and the Art of Laughter, 2006; Figures of Speech: Picturing Proverbs in Renaissance Netherlands, 2010. Contributor of articles to journals. **Address:** 938 Mason Hill Rd. N, Pownal, VT 05261-9767, U.S.A. **Online address:** wsgibson@together.net

GIDDENS, Anthony. British (born England), b. 1938. **Genres:** Social Work. **Career:** University of Leicester, lecturer in sociology, 1961-70; Simon Fraser University, visiting assistant professor, 1967-68; University of California, visiting assistant professor, 1968-69; King's College, lecturer in sociology, 1970-84, reader in sociology, 1984-86, professor of sociology, 1986-97, fellow;

Polity Press Ltd., chairman and director, 1985-; Blackwell-Polity Ltd., director, 1985-; Centre for Social Research, chairman and director, 1989-; Boston University, visiting professor; Harvard University, visiting professor; New York University, visiting professor; University of California-Berkele, visiting professor; La Trobe University, visiting professor; Indiana University, visiting professor; University of British Columbia, visiting professor; University of Melbourne, visiting professor; University of California-Santa Barbara, visiting professor; London School of Economics, director, 1997-2003, professor emeritus; Institute for Public Policy Research, trustee; American Academy of Science, fellow; Chinese Academy of Social Sciences, fellow. Writer. **Publications:** Sociology of Suicide: A Selection of Readings, 1971; (ed., trans. and intro.) Selected Writings, 1972; Politics and Sociology in the Thought of Max Weber, 1972; Class Structure of the Advanced Societies, 1973; (ed. and intro.) Positivism and Sociology, 1974; (with P. Stanworth) Elites and Power in British Society, 1974; New Rules of Sociological Method: A Positive Critique of Interpretative Sociologies, 1976; Studies in Social and Political Theory, 1977; Durkheim, 1978; Emile Durkheim, 1979; Central Problems in Social Theory: Action, Structure, and Contradiction in Social Analysis, 1979; The Class Structure of the Advanced Societies, 1981; A Contemporary Critique of Historical Materialism, 1981; Sociology, a Brief but Critical Introduction, 1982; Profiles and Critiques in Social Theory, 1982; (ed. with G. Mackenzie) Social Class and the Division of Labour: Essays in Honour of Ilya Neustadt, 1982; (ed. with D. Held) Classes, Power, and Conflict: Classical and Contemporary Debates, 1982; The Constitution of Society: Outline of the Theory of Structuration, 1984; (ed. and intro.) Durkheim on Politics and the State, 1986; Social Theory Today, 1987; Sociology, A Brief but Critical Introduction, 1987; Social Theory and Modern Sociology, 1987; The Consequences of Modernity, 1990; Modernity and Self-Identity: Self and Society in the Late Modern Age, 1991; Introduction to Sociology, 1991, 7th ed., 2009; Readings and Study Guide: Introduction of Sociology, 1991; (ed.) Human Societies: An Introductory Reader in Sociology, 1992; The Transformation of Intimacy: Sexuality, Love and Eroticism in Modern Societies, 1992; New Rules of Sociological Method: A Positive Critique of Interpretative Sociologies, 1993; The Giddens Reader, 1993; (with U. Beck and S. Lash) Reflexive Modernization: Politics, Tradition and Aesthetics in the Modern Social Order, 1994; Beyond Left and Right: The Future of Radical Politics, 1994; Politics, Sociology and Social Theory: Encounters with Classical and Contemporary Social Thought, 1995; A Contemporary Critique of Historical Materialism, 1995; In Defence of Sociology: Essays, Interpertations, and Rejoinders, 1996; Sociology, 1997; (with C. Pierson) Conversations with Anthony Giddens: Making Sense of Modernity, 1998; Third Way: The Renewal of Social Democracy, 1999; (ed. with W. Hutton) Global Capitalism, 2000; (ed. with W. Hutton) On the Edge: Living with Global Capitalism, 2000; Runaway World: How Globalization is Reshaping our Lives, 2000; Third Way and Its Critics, 2000; (ed.) Global Third Way Debate, 2001; Where Now for New Labour?, 2002; (ed.) Progressive Manifesto: New Ideas for the Centre-Left, 2003; Quan qiu hua yu di san tiao lu: Jidengsi zai Taiwan, 2005; (ed. with P. Diamond and R. Liddle) Global Europe, Social Europe, 2006; (with M. Duneier and R.P. Appelbaum) Essentials of Sociology, 2006, 3rd ed., 2010; Europe in the Global Age, 2007; Over to You, Mr. Brown: How Labour Can Win Again, 2008; Politics of Climate Change, 2009. Contributor to periodicals. **Address:** London School of Economics and Political Science, Houghton St., London, GL WC2A 2AE, England.

GIEBEL, Christoph. American (born United States) **Genres:** Politics/Government, History, Autobiography/Memoirs. **Career:** Mississippi State University, Department of History, assistant professor, 1996-98; University of Washington, Department of History, assistant professor, associate professor, 1998-, Henry M. Jackson School of International Studies, assistant professor, associate professor, 1998-; Political Asylum Research and Documentation Service (PARDS), consultant, 1999-. Writer. **Publications:** (With B. Kuster and H. von Werkverzeichnis) Heinrich Giebel, 1865-1951, 2001; Imagined Ancestries of Vietnamese Communism: Ton Duc Thang and the Politics of History and Memory, 2004. Contributor to books. **Address:** Department of History, University of Washington, 315 Smith Rd., PO Box 353560, Seattle, WA 98195-3560, U.S.A. **Online address:** giebel@u.washington.edu

GIENOW-HECHT, Jessica C. E. American/German (born Germany), b. 1964. **Genres:** History. **Career:** University of Bielefeld, postdoctoral fellow in history, 1995-96; Martin-Luther-University, Center for U.S. Studies, deputy director, 1996-99; Harvard University, Center for European Studies, John F. Kennedy fellow, 1999-2000, Charles Warren Center for Studies in American History, fellow, 2000-02, lecturer in history and literature program, 2002-, visiting fellow; Universities of Virginia, faculty; University of Cologne, professor of international history; Johann Wolfgang Goethe-University, Heisenberg fellow. Writer. **Publications:** Transmission Impossible: American Journalism as Cultural Diplomacy in Postwar Germany, 1945-1955, 1999; (ed. with F. Schumacher) Culture and International History, 2003; (ed.) Decentering America, 2007; Sound Diplomacy: Music and Emotions in Transatlantic relations, 1850-1920, 2009; (ed.) Emotions in American History, 2010; (ed. with M.C. Donfried) Searching for a Cultural Diplomacy, 2010. Contributor to periodicals. **Address:** Charles Warren Center for, Studies in American History, Harvard University, Emerson Hall, 4th Fl., Cambridge, MA 02138, U.S.A. **Online address:** gienow@fas.harvard.edu

GIER, Scott G. American (born United States), b. 1948?. **Genres:** Science Fiction/Fantasy, Literary Criticism And History. **Career:** Writer. **Publications:** Genellan: Planetfall, 1995; Genellan: In the Shadow of the Moon, 1996; Genellan: First Victory, 1997; Genellan: Earth Siege, 2005; Daystar, 2007. **Address:** c/o Kristin Lindstrom, Lindstrom Literary Management L.L.C., 871 N Greenbrier St., Arlington, NY 22205-1220, U.S.A. **Online address:** scott@genellan.com

GIESBERT, Franz-Olivier. French/American (born United States), b. 1949. **Genres:** Biography, Novels. **Career:** Le Nouvel Observateur, journalist, 1971-85, reporter, correspondent, head of policy, editor-in-chief, 1985-88; Le Figaro, managing editor, editor-in-chief, 1988-2000, publisher, 1999-2000; Louvre, director, 2000; Le Point, publishing director, 2000-. **Publications:** Fran çois Mitterrand: ou, la tentation de l'histoire (biography), 1977; (with P. Mauroy and L. Rioux) Héritiers de l'avenir, 1977; Monsieur Adrien, 1982; Jacques Chirac (biography), 1987; Le Prsident (biography of Charles de Gaulle), 1990; L'affreux, 1992; La fin d'une époque, 1993; La souille, 1995; François Mitterrand: une vie (biography), 1996; Le sieur Dieu, 1998; Mort d'un berger, 2002; L'abatteur, 2003; L'Américain (memoir), 2004; Héros du 6 juin: le débarquement de 1944, 2004; Tragédie du président: scènes de la vie politique, 1986-2006, 2006; Immortel, 2007; Huitième prophète, ou, Les aventures extraordinaires d'Amros le Celte, 2008; Lessiveur, 2009; Très grand amour, 2009; Monsieur le président, 2011. **Address:** c/o Author Mail, éditions Gallimard, 5 rue Gaston-Gallimard, Paris, 75328, France.

GIFALDI, David. American (born United States), b. 1950. **Genres:** Children's Fiction, Young Adult Fiction, Sports/Fitness. **Career:** Bellingham School District, teacher, 1980-83; Vancouver School District, teacher, 1985-; Vermont College, faculty. Writer. **Publications:** NOVELS: One Thing for Sure, 1986; Yours Till Forever, 1989; Gregory, Maw and the Mean One, 1992; Toby Scudder, Ultimate Warrior, 1993; Ben, King of the River, 2001. OTHER: The Boy Who Spoke Colors (An Original Folktale), 1993; Rearranging and Other Stories (short stories), 1998; Toby Sudder, King of the School, 2005; Listening for Crickets, 2008. Contributor to periodicals. **Address:** Albert Whitman & Co., 6340 Oakton St., Morton Grove, IL 60053-2723, U.S.A. **Online address:** dg@davidgifaldi.com

GIFFORD, Barry (Colby). American (born United States), b. 1946. **Genres:** Novels, Novellas/Short Stories, Poetry, Autobiography/Memoirs, Biography, Essays, Graphic Novels. **Career:** Black Lizard Books (publisher of noir fiction), co-founder and editor, through 1989. **Publications:** POETRY: The Blood of the Parade, 1967; Coyote Tantras, 1973; Persimmons, 1976; The Boy You Have Always Loved, 1976; A Quinzaine in Return for a Portrait of Mary Sun, 1977; Horse Hauling Timber out of Hokkaido Forest, 1978; Lives of the French Impressionist Painters, 1978; Snail Hut, 1978; Beautiful Phantoms, 1981; Ghosts No Horse Can Carry, 1989; Flaubert at Key West, 1997; Replies to Wang Wei, 2001; Las cuatro reinas, 2001; Back in America, 2004. STORIES: A Boy's Novel, 1973; Francis Goes to the Seashore, 1982; The Wild Life of Sailor and Lula (novellas), 1996; My Last Martini, 2000; American Falls: The Collected Short Stories, 2002; Do the Blind Dream?, 2004. ESSAYS: Kerouac's Town, 1973, rev. ed., 1977; Out of the Past: Adventures in Film Noir, 2001. OTHER: (trans.) Selected Poems of Francis Jammes, 1976; My Mother's People, 1976; (ed.) The Portable Curtis: Selected Writings of Edward S. Curtis, 1976; Living in Advance, 1976; (ed. and intro.) As Ever: The Collected Correspondence of Allen Ginsberg and Neal Cassady, 1977; (with L. Lee) Jack's Book: An Oral Biography of Jack Kerouac, 1978; (with L. Lee) Saroyan: A Biography, 1984; A Day at the Races, 1988; The Devil Thumbs a Ride and Other Unforgettable Films, 1988; Giotto's Circle, 1988; New Mysteries of Paris, 1991; Hotel Room Trilogy (plays), 1995; Hot Rod, 1997; (with D. Lynch) Lost Highway, 1997; Bordertown, 1998; The Rooster Trapped in the Reptile Room, 2003; Brando Rides Alone: A Reconsideration

of the Film One-eyed Jacks, 2004; The Stars Above Veracruz, 2006; Memories from a Sinking Ship, 2007; The Cavalry Charges: Writings on Books, Film and Music, 2007; The Imagination of the Heart, 2009; Sailor & Lula: The Complete Novels, 2010; Sad Stories of the Death of Kings, 2010; Un Education Americaine, 2010. MEMOIRS: The Neighborhood of Baseball, 1981; A Good Man to Know: A Semi-Documentary Fictional Memoir, 1992; The Phantom Father, 1997; Imagining Paradise, 2012. NOVELS: Landscape with Traveler, 1980; Port Tropique, 1980; An Unfortunate Woman, 1984; Wild at Heart: The Story of Sailor and Lula, 1990; Sailor's Holiday, 1991; Sultan's of Africa, 1991; Consuelo's Kiss, 1991; Night People, 1992; Bad Day for the Leopard Man, 1992; Arise and Walk, 1994; Baby Cat-Face, 1995; Perdita Durango, 1996 as Graphic Novel, 1995; Baby Cat-Face, 1995; Wyoming, 2000; The Sinaloa Story, 2005. Contributor to periodicals. **Address:** Curtis Brown Ltd., 10 Astor Pl., New York, NY 10003, U.S.A.

GIFFORD, Clive. British (born England), b. 1966?. **Genres:** Sports/Fitness, Biography, Geography. **Career:** Usborne (publisher), senior editor; Mikro-Leisure (computer games company), founder and owner. Journalist. **Publications:** FOR CHILDREN; The Usborne Book of Planes and Helicopters, 1993; Racing Cars, 1993; The Usborne Book of Cutaway Planes, 1995; The Usborne Book of Juggling, 1995; The Really Useless Spy School, 1996; Uncle Alf and the Time Travel Detectives, 1996; The Cosmic Toaster, 1996; Mindmaster (based on an original idea by Tony Allen), 1996; Time Warp Virus, 1996; The Flask of Doom, 1996; Tactics, 1997; Football, 1998; Cycling, 1998; Swimming, 1998; Media, 1999 in US as Media and Communications, 1999; Basketball, 1999; How the Future Began: Machines, 1999; Golf, 2000; (with A. Wilson) The Kingfisher Encyclopedia of the Future, 2000; Juggling, 2000; Athletics, 2000; Room Makeover, 2000; Cricket, 2000; Quiz Kids, 2000; Live on Mars, 2000 in US as How to Live on Mars, 2001; How the Future Began: Everyday Life, 2000; How to Build a Robot, 2000; How to Meet Aliens, 2001; Yuk! The Gruesome File of Foul Facts, 2001; The Kingfisher Facts and Records Book of Space, 2001; The Water Puppets: A Story from Vietnam, 2001 in US as The Water Puppets: A Story from the War in Vietnam, 2002; The Kingfisher Young People's Book of Living Worlds, 2002 in UK as The Kingfisher Book of Living Worlds, 2002; So You Think You Know The Lord of the Rings?, 2002; World War I, 2002; World War II: True Stories, 2002; Geography: Over 2, 000 Questions and Answers, 2002; Refugees, 2002; Soccer: The Ultimate Guide to the Beautiful Game, 2002 in UK as Football: The Ultimate Guide to the Beautiful Game, 2002; The Kingfisher Geography Encyclopedia, 2003; Racism, 2003; Drugs and Sports, 2003; So You Think You Know David Beckham?, 2003; So You Think You Know Harry Potter?, 2003; Robots, 2003; So You Think You Know the Simpsons?, 2003; Euthanasia, 2004; A World-Class Sprinter, 2004; Diary of a Kickboxing Freak, 2004; The Arms Trade, 2004; So You Think You Know Lemony Snicket?, 2004; So You Think You Know Premier League Football?, 2004; So You Think You Know the '80s?, 2004; So You Think You Know the '60s?, 2004; So You Think You Know TV Soaps?, 2004; So You Think You Know London?, 2004; The Fair of Fear?, 2004; Pants Attack!, 2004; Ratman and the Big Cat, 2004; A Big Hit for Kit, 2004; There's a Slug in My Mug, 2004; Food Technology, 2004; Spies, 2004; Summer Olympics: The Definite Guide to the World's Greatest Sports Celebration, 2004 in UK as Olympics: The Definite Guide to the Greatest Sports Celebration in the World, 2004; Sustainable Development, 2004; The Concise Geography Encyclopedia, 2005; Flooding and Drought, 2005; (with J. Harrison and E.V. Zandt) The Kingfisher Student Atlas of North America, 2005; Materials, 2005; Bus Stop Bob, 2005; The Phony Phantom Gopher, 2005; Soccer Skills, 2005 in UK as Football Skills, 2005; Space Exploration, 2005; Mountain Biking, 2005; Skateboarding, 2005; Espionage and Disinformation, 2005; The Vietnam War, 2005; Advertising and Marketing: Developing the Marketplace, 2005; So You Think You Know Test Cricket?, 2005; So You Think You Know Narnia?, 2005; So You Think You Know The Da Vinci Code?, 2005; So You Think You Know Roald Dahl?, 2005; So You Think You Know Dr. Who?, 2005; Weathering and Erosion, 2005; Waste, 2006; Pollution, 2006; Skateboarding, 2006; Fantastic Football, 2006; Snowboarding, 2006; Crimebusters, 2006; So You Think You Know James Bond?, 2006; So You Think You Know Man Utd.?, 2006; Rugby, 2006; Football, 2006; (co-author) The Kingfisher Science Encyclopedia, 2006; Energy, 2006; Racing: The Ultimate Motorsports Encyclopedia, 2006 in UK as The Kingfisher Motorsports Encyclopedia, 2006; Track Athletics, 2006; Striker, 2006; The Kingfisher Soccer Encyclopedia, 2006 in UK as The Kingfisher Football Encyclopedia, 2006; Violence on the Screen, 2006; So You Think You Know His Dark Materials?, 2006; So You Think You Know Discworld?, 2006; So You Think You Know the World Cup?, 2006; Gangs, 2006; Badminton, 2007; Tennis, 2007; Netball, 2007; Millionaires, 2007; Goalkeeper, 2007; Snowboarding, 2007; Tomb Hunters, 2007; Honda, 2007; So You Think You Know Shakespeare?, 2007; Linked Lives: Ten Explorers Who Changed the World, 2008; Linked Lives: Ten Leaders Who Changed the World, 2008; Cricket, 2008; (with M. Goldsmith and S. Callery) Explore, 2008; Track and Field, 2009; Basketball, 2009; Ducati, 2009; Soccer, 2009. OTHERS: Making the Most of Your Dragon 32, 1983; Dynamic Games for Your ORIC, 1983; Dynamic Games for Your Amstrad, 1984; Adventures for Your ZX Spectrum, 1984; (with T. Hartnell) The Amstrad Programmer's Guide, 1985; The Script, Marillion: An Illustrated Biography, 1987. Works appear in anthologies. Contributor to periodicals. **Address:** Manchester, GM , England. **Online address:** clivegiff@aol.com

GIFFORD, James J. American (born United States), b. 1946. **Genres:** Film, Gay And Lesbian Issues, Literary Criticism And History, Social Sciences, Theatre. **Career:** Mohawk Valley Community College, professor of humanities, professor emeritus, 1972-. Writer. **Publications:** Dayneford's Library: American Homosexual Writing, 1900-1913, 1995; (ed.) Imre: A Memorandum, 2002; (ed.) Glances Backward: An Anthology of American Homosexual Writing 1830-1920, 2007. Works appear in anthologies. **Address:** Mohawk Valley Community College, 1101 Sherman Dr., Utica, NY 13501, U.S.A. **Online address:** jgifford@mvcc.edu

GIFFORD, Peggy. American (born United States), b. 1952?. **Genres:** Children's Fiction, Poetry, Humor/Satire. **Career:** Writer. **Publications:** FOR CHILDREN: Moxy Maxwell Does Not Love Stuart Little, 2008; Moxy Maxwell Does Not Love Writing Thank-You Notes, 2008; Moxy Maxwell Does Not Love Practice the Piano: But She Does Love to Be in Recitals, 2009. OTHER: Clean and Disappointed (poetry), 1984. **Address:** c/o Ginger Knowlton, Curtis Brown Ltd., 10 Astor Pl., New York, NY 10003, U.S.A. **Online address:** Chester167@aol.com

GIFFORD, Rebecca. American (born United States), b. 1971. **Genres:** Medicine/Health. **Career:** Writer. **Publications:** Cancer Happens: Coming of Age with Cancer, 2003. **Address:** Joelle Delbourgo Associates Inc., 101 Park St., 3rd Fl., Montclair, NJ 07042, U.S.A. **Online address:** giffordrebecca@gmail.com

GIFFORD, Rob. British (born England) **Genres:** Adult Non-fiction, Area Studies, Travel/Exploration. **Career:** British Broadcasting Corp., World Service, staff; National Public Radio, WGBH-Boston, staff through 1990, foreign correspondent-Beijing, 1999-2005, London bureau chief, 2005-. Journalist. **Publications:** China Road: A Journey into the Future of a Rising Power, 2007. **Address:** National Public Radio, 635 Massachusetts Ave. NW, Washington, DC 20001-3740, U.S.A.

GIGLIO, James N. American (born United States), b. 1939. **Genres:** History, Bibliography, Biography, Social Sciences. **Career:** M. O'Neil Co., assistant buyer, 1964-65; Southwest Missouri State University, professor of history, 1968-, university fellow in research, 1999-2001, professor, 2000-, distinguished professor of history, professor emeritus, 2006-; Missouri Conference on History, coordinator, 1972; Mid-America Conference on History, originator and coordinator, 1977-79, 1987. Writer. **Publications:** H.M. Daugherty and the Politics of Expediency, 1978; (with G.G. Thielen) Truman in Cartoon and Caricature, 1984, new ed., 2001; The Presidency of John F. Kennedy, 1991, 2nd ed., 2006; (comp.) John F. Kennedy: A Bibliography, 1995; Musial: From Stash to Stan the Man, 2001; (with S.G. Rabe) Debating the Kennedy Presidency, 2003. Works appear in anthologies. Contributor of articles to journals. **Address:** Department of History, Southwest Missouri State University, 427 Strong Hall, 901 S National Ave., Springfield, MO 65804-0089, U.S.A. **Online address:** jng89of@mail.smsu.edu

GIKOW, Jacqueline. American (born United States), b. 1947?. **Genres:** Crafts, How-to Books, Design. **Career:** Hahn Shoes, assistant director of visual merchandising, 1980-82; Trenton State College (now The College of New Jersey), assistant professor of art, 1983-89; Rolex Watch USA, director visual merchandising, 1991-94, design manager, 1991-96; Colgate-Palmolive, industrial designer, 1998-2001; Jacqueline Gikow and Associates, editor and art director, 2002-, owner, 2004-; Chelsea Rainbow, owner, 2010-. **Publications:** Graphic Illustration in Black and White, 1991; Polymer Clay: Creating Functional and Decorative Objects, 2001. **Address:** Chelsea Rainbow, 202 W 24th St., Ste. 903, New York, NY 10011, U.S.A. **Online address:** jgikow@verizon.net

GIL, David Georg. American/Austrian (born Austria), b. 1924. **Genres:** Social Sciences, Social Work. **Career:** Jewish Community Council for Palestine, Department of Social Welfare, counselor and teacher, 1943-45; Government of Palestine, Department of Social Welfare, probation officer, 1945-48; Ministry of Social Welfare, senior probation officer, 1950-51, assistant director, 1951-53, chief supervisor, 1955-57; Hebrew University, lecturer, 1955-57; Jewish Family Service, family counselor and family life educator, 1957-59; Association for Jewish Children, supervisor and research associate, 1959-63; Massachusetts Society for the Prevention of Cruelty to Children, director of research, 1963-64; Brandeis University, Florence Heller Graduate School for Advanced Studies in Social Work, assistant professor, 1964-66, associate professor, 1966-69, professor of social policy, 1969-, now professor emeritus, Social Policy Study Program, director, 1969-73, Center for Social Change (Practice and Theory), director, 1983-2002; Washington University, visiting professor, 1975-2001; Boston University, School of Social Work, Division of Continuing Education, faculty, 1972; Harvard University, faculty, 1973; Tufts University, adjunct professor of sociology, 1973-77; McGill University, visiting professor, 1977; University of Nebraska, visiting professor, 1978-79; Smith College, lecturer, 1979-81; Association for Humanist Sociology, president, 1981-82; American Orthopsychiatric Association, board director, 1990-93. Writer and consultant. **Publications:** Violence Against Children: Physical Child Abuse in the United States, 1970; Unravelling Social Policy, Theory, Analysis, and Political Action towards Social Equality, 1973, 5th ed., 1992; The Challenge of Social Equality, 1976; Beyond the Jungle, 1979; (contrib.) In die Emigration, 1988; Confronting Injustice and Oppression, 1998; Perspectives on Social Justice, 2004. EDITOR: Child Abuse and Violence, 1979; (with E.A. Gil) Toward Social and Economic Justice, 1985; (with E.A. Gil) The Future of Work, 1987. Contributor to journals. **Address:** Heller School for Social Policy and Management, Brandeis University, 108 Heller, 415 South St., PO Box 035, Waltham, MA 02454-9110, U.S.A. **Online address:** gil@brandeis.edu

GIL, Moshe. Israeli/Polish (born Poland), b. 1921. **Genres:** History, Humanities. **Career:** Tel Aviv University, Chaim Rosenberg School of Jewish Studies, associate professor, 1974-80, professor, 1980-, now emeritus, dean of humanities, 1986-89. Writer. **Publications:** (Contrib.) Yalkut Shirim, 1965; (intro.) Documents of the Jewish Pious Foundations, 1976; The Tustaris, 1981; Erets Yiśra'el ba teḳufah ha Muslemit ha rishonah (634 1099), 1983; (co-author) Meḥḳarim be mada'e ha-Yahadut, 1986; A History of Palestine, 634 1099, 1992; Bem malkhut Yishma'el bi teḳufat ha ge'onim, 1997; (with E. Flaisher) Yehudah ha-Leyi u-vene ḥugo: 55 téudot min ha-Genizah, 2001; Jews in Islamic Countries in the Middle Ages, 2004; Related Worlds: Studies in Jewish and Arab Ancient and Early Medieval History, 2004; Veha-Roma i az Ba-Arets, 2008. **Address:** Tel Aviv University, Carter Bldg., PO Box 39040, Tel Aviv, 69978, Israel.

GILB, Dagoberto. American (born United States), b. 1950?. **Genres:** Novels. **Career:** Los Angeles County, certified journeyman carpenter, 1976-91; University of Texas, Department of English, visiting fiction writer, 1988; University of Arizona, Department of English, creative writing program, visiting writer, 1992; University of Wyoming, Department of English, visiting writer, 1994; Texas State University, Creative Writing, Master of Fine Arts Program, professor, tenured professor; University of Houston, writer-in-residence; Centro Victoria: Center for Mexican American Literature and Culture, executive director; Vassar College, visiting writer; California State University, visiting writer. **Publications:** Winners on the Pass Line, 1985; The Magic of Blood, 1993; The Last Known Residence of Mickey Acuña, 1994; Woodcuts of Women, 2001; Gritos, 2003; (ed.) Hecho en Tejas: An Anthology of Texas-Mexican Literature, 2006; The Flowers, 2008. Works appear in anthologies. Contributor to magazines. **Address:** Department of English, Texas State University, M21 Flowers Hall, 601 University Dr., San Marcos, TX 78666-4685, U.S.A. **Online address:** dg16@txstate.edu

GILBERT, Alan (Graham). British (born England), b. 1944. **Genres:** Area Studies, Geography, Regional/Urban Planning, Urban Studies, Politics/Government, Social Sciences. **Career:** University College London, Institute of Latin American Studies, fellow, 1969-70, lecturer in economic geography, 1970-85, reader in geography, 1985-90, professor of geography, 1990-2010, now emeritus professor; Developing Areas Research Group, Institute of British Geographers, founding secretary, 1970-77, chair, 1985-87; Society for Latin American Studies, chair, 1985-87. Writer. **Publications:** Latin American Development: A Geographical Perspective, 1974; (with J. Gugler) Cities, Poverty and Development: Urbanization in the Third World, 1982, 2nd ed.,

1992; (with P.M. Ward) Housing, the State and the Poor: Policy and Practice in Three Latin American Cities, 1985; (with P. Healey) The Political Economy of Land: Urban Development in an Oil Economy, 1985; Latin America, 1990; (with A. Varley) Landlord and Tenant: Housing the Poor in Urban Mexico, 1991; In Search of a Home: Rental and Shared Housing in Latin America, 1993; The Latin American City, 1994, 2nd ed., 1998; Rental Housing: An Essential Option for the Urban Poor in Developing Countries, 2003; (with M.T. Garces) Bogotá: Progreso, Gobernabilidad y Pobreza, 2008; Población y Urbanización, 2010. EDITOR: Development Planning and Spatial Structure, 1976; (with R. Ramírez and J.E. Hardoy) Urbanization in Contemporary Latin America: Critical Approaches to the Analysis of Urban Issues, 1982; Housing and Land in Urban Mexico, 1989; The Mega-city in Latin America, 1996; A Policy Guide to Rental Housing in Developing Countries, 2011. **Address:** Department of Geography, University College London, Pearson Bldg., Gower St., 26 Bedford Way, London, GL WC1E 6BT, England. **Online address:** a.gilbert@geog.ucl.ac.uk

GILBERT, Alma M. American/Mexican (born Mexico), b. 1937. **Genres:** Art/Art History, Picture/Board Books, Adult Non-fiction, Literary Criticism And History, Photography. **Career:** Children's Asthma Research Center, head of clinical laboratory, 1967-70; La Galeria, director, 1970-78; Maxfield Parrish Museum, director, 1978-85; Alma Gilbert Galleries, director, 1986-93; Cornish Colony Museum, director, 1998-; Alma Gilbert Inc., director. Writer. **Publications:** The Make Believe World of Maxfield Parrish and Sue Lewin, 1990; Maxfield Parrish: The Masterworks, 1992, 3rd ed., 2001; The Make Believe World of Maxfield Parrish, 1994; (intro.) Maxfield Parrish, the Poster Book, 1994; (comp.) Maxfield Parrish: A Treasury of Art and Children's Literature, 1995; Mechanic Who Loved to Paint: The Other Side of Maxfield Parrish, 1995; Maxfield Parrish: The Landscapes, 1998; (with J.B. Tankard) Place of Beauty: The Artists and Gardens of the Cornish Colony, 2000; (contrib.) Maxfield Parrish: Master of Make-Believe, 2005. **Address:** Alma Gilbert Inc., PO Box 63, Plainfield, NH 03781-0063, U.S.A. **Online address:** agilbert@best.com

GILBERT, Barbara Snow. American (born United States), b. 1954. **Genres:** Novels, Young Adult Fiction. **Career:** Attorney, 1980-; U.S. District Court, law clerk, 2001-. Writer. **Publications:** Stone Water, 1996; Broken Chords, 1998; Paper Trail, 2000. Contributor to periodicals. **Address:** 1121 Fenwick Pl., Oklahoma City, OK 73116, U.S.A. **Online address:** hbsa.gilbert@worldnet.att.net

GILBERT, Bil. American (born United States), b. 1927. **Genres:** Natural History, History, Animals/Pets, Environmental Sciences/Ecology, Earth Sciences. **Career:** American Society of Crows and Ravens, founder; Corvi Chronicle, contributor; New Yorker, writer; The New York Times, writer; Smithsonian, writer. Historian and naturalist. **Publications:** Bears in the Ladie's Room and Other Beastly Pursuits, 1966; How Animals Communicate (juvenile), 1966; The Weasels: A Sensible Look at a Family of Predators (juvenile), 1970; Chulo, 1973 as Chulo: A Year among the Coatimundis, 1984; The Trailblazers, 1973; Westering Man: The Life of Joseph Walker, 1983; In God's Countries, 1984; Our Nature, 1986; God Gave us This Country: Tekamthi and the First American Civil War, 1989; Natural Coincidence: The Trip from Kalamazoo, 2004. Contributor of articles to magazines. **Address:** The American Society of Crows & Ravens, Kaw Valley Roost, PO Box 1423, Lawrence, KS 66044-8423, U.S.A.

GILBERT, Elizabeth. American (born United States), b. 1969. **Genres:** Novellas/Short Stories, Biography, History, Young Adult Non-fiction. **Career:** Journalist. **Publications:** Pilgrims, 1997; Stern Men, 2000; The Last American Man, 2002; Eat, Pray, Love: One Woman's Search for Everything across Italy, India and Indonesia, 2006; Committed: A Skeptic Makes Peace with Marriage, 2010. Contributor to magazines. **Address:** Houghton Mifflin Harcourt, 222 Berkeley St., Boston, MA 02116, U.S.A.

GILBERT, Frances. See **COLLINGS, Gillian.**

GILBERT, Glenn G(ordon). American (born United States), b. 1936. **Genres:** Language/Linguistics, Essays. **Career:** University of Texas, instructor, 1963-65, assistant professor of Germanic languages, 1965-70; University of Marburg, Fulbright lecturer in linguistics, 1966-67; Southern Illinois University, associate professor, 1970-75, professor of linguistics, 1975-87, 1989-, chair of the linguistics department, 1987-89, 1999-2002, now professor emeritus; University of Mainz, Fulbright lecturer in linguistics, 1973-74;

Journal of Pidgin and Creole Languages, founder and editor, 1986-2001. **Publications:** Linguistic Atlas of Texas German, 1972; (contrib.) Studies in Contact Linguistics: Essays in Honor of Glenn G. Gilbert, 2006. EDITOR: Texas Studies in Bilingualism: Spanish, French, German, Czech, Polish, Sorbian and Norwegian in the Southwest, with a Concluding Chapter on Code-Switching and Modes of Speaking in American Swedish, 1970; (intro.) The German Language in America: A Symposium, 1971; (with J.Ornstein) Problems in Applied Educational Sociolinguistics: Readings on Language and Culture Problems of United States Ethnic Groups, 1974; Pidgin and Creole Languages: Selected Essays of Hugo Schuchardt, 1980; Pidgin and Creole Languages: Essays in Memory of John E. Reinecke, 1987; Pidgin and Creole Linguistics in the Twenty-First Century, 2002. **Address:** Department of Linguistics, Southern Illinois University Carbondale, 1220 Douglas Dr., Carbondale, IL 62901-4517, U.S.A. **Online address:** ggilbert@siu.edu

GILBERT, Harriett. British (born England), b. 1948. **Genres:** Novels, Communications/Media, Sex, Self Help, Romance/Historical, Literary Criticism And History, Medicine/Health, Travel/Exploration, Travel/Exploration. **Career:** City Limits, literary editor, 1981-83; New Statesman, literary editor, 1983-88; BBC World Service, Meridian Books, presenter, 1991-2003, The Word, presenter, 2003-; City University of London, Department of Journalism, lecturer, 1992-2004, director of MA program in creative writing, 2004-08. **Publications:** I Know Where I've Been, 1972; Hotels with Empty Rooms, 1973; An Offence against the Persons, 1974; Given the Ammunition, 1976; Tide Race, 1977; Running Away: A Novel, 1979; The Riding Mistress, 1983; A Women's History of Sex, 1987; (ed.) The Sexual Imagination from Acker to Zola: A Feminist Companion, 1993; (ed.) Fetishes, Florentine Girdles and Other Explorations into the Sexual Imagination, 1994; (with T. Holmes and S. Adams) Writing for Journalists, 1999, 2nd ed., 2008. **Address:** 1 Regency Mews, London, GL SW9 6UR, England. **Online address:** h.s.gilbert@city.ac.uk

GILBERT, John Raphael. British (born England), b. 1926. **Genres:** Adult Non-fiction, Art/Art History, Environmental Sciences/Ecology, History, Homes/Gardens, Natural History, Travel/Exploration, Zoology, Biography, Translations, Young Adult Fiction, Theology/Religion. **Career:** Marston & Co., publisher, 1947-50; J.C. Gilbert Ltd., staff, 1950-59; Paul Hamlyn Group, managing editor, 1960-68; freelance author and editor, 1968-. **Publications:** Modern World Book of Animals, 1947; Cats, Cats, Cats, Cats, Cats, Cats, 1961; Famous Jewish Lives, 1970; Myths and Legends of Ancient Rome, 1970; Pirates and Buccaneers, 1971; Highwaymen and Outlaws, 1971; Charting the Vast Pacific, 1971, as Pacific Voyages, 1973; National Costumes of the World, 1972; Eastern Islands, Southern Seas, 1973; Miracles of Nature, 1975; Nature's Wonders of Forests and Lowlands (juvenile), 1975; Nature's Wonders of Oceans and Mountains (juvenile), 1975; Buccaneers and Pirates, 1975 as The Golden Book of Buccaneers, 1976; (ed.) Beautiful Cats and Kittens: The World's Familiar Breeds and Helpful Hintson Cat Care, 1975; Knights of the Crusades, 1978; Vikings, 1978; Prehistoric Man, 1979; Les Vikings (title means: 'Vikings'), 1979; Dinosaurs Discovered, 1981; The Conquistadors (juvenile), 1982; Macdonald Encyclopedia of House Plants, 1986; Theory and Use of Colour, 1986; Macdonald Encyclopedia of Roses, 1987; Gardens of Britain, 1987; Trekking, USA, 1989; Trekking, Europe, 1990; Macdonald Encyclopedia of Herbs and Spices, 1990; Macdonald Encyclopedia of Bonsai, 1990; Macdonald Encyclopedia of Saltwater Fishes, 1994; Macdonald Encyclopedia of Climbing Plants, 1994; Prague Castle, 1994; Sevres Pottery, 1996; Caravaggio, 1998; Bosch, 1998; Leonardo da Vinci, 1999; Velasquez, 1999; Tortoises and Turtles, 2001; Sharks, 2001. TRANSLATOR: World of Wildlife, 10 vols., 1974; M. Rosci, The Hidden Leonardo, 1978; Leonardo da Vinci, 1978; G. Lotti and P. Radice, La Scala, 1979; A.V. Taglianti, The World of Mammals, 1979; Macdonald Encyclopedia of Trees, 1983; Macdonald Encyclopedia of Butterflies and Moths, 1988; Decorating Chinese Porcelain, 1994. **Address:** 28 Lyndale Ave., London, GL NW2 2QA, England.

GILBERT, Martin. (Martin John Gilbert). British (born England), b. 1936. **Genres:** History, Biography, Theology/Religion. **Career:** Merton College, fellow of governing body, 1962-95, honorary fellow, 1995-; research assistant to Randolph S. Churchill on official life of Winston Churchill, 1962-67; University of South Carolina, visiting professor, 1965; University of Tel Aviv, visiting professor, 1979-80; University of Jerusalem, visiting professor, 1980; Hebrew University of Jerusalem, governor, 1980-; Hillsdale College, lecturer, distinguished fellow, 2002-; University of Western Ontario, Department of History, professor, 2006-07. Writer. **Publications:** (With R. Gott) The Appeasers, 1963; Britain and Germany between the Wars, 1964; The European

Powers 1900-1945; Plough My Own Furrow: The Life of Lord Allen of Hurtwood, 1965; Servant of India: A Study of Imperial Rule 1905-1910, 1966; The Roots of Appeasement, 1966; Recent History Atlas 1860-1960, 1966; Winston Churchill (for young people), 1966; (ed.) Churchill, 1967; (ed.) A Century of Conflict, 1850-1950: Essays Presented to A.J.P. Taylor, 1967; Lloyd George, 1968; British History Atlas, 1968; American History Atlas, 1968; Jewish History Atlas, 1969; First World War Atlas, 1970; Winston S. Churchill (biography), vols. III-VIII, 1971-88; Russian History Atlas, 1972; Sir Horace Rumbold: Portrait of a Diplomat, 1869-1941, 1973; The Coming of War in 1939, 1973; Churchill: Photographic Portrait, 1974; The Arab-Israel Conflict: Its History in Maps, 1974; Churchill and Zionism, 1974; The Dent Atlas of the Arab-Israeli Conflict, 1974, 9th ed. as The Routledge Atlas of the Arab-Israeli Conflict, 2008; The Jews in Arab Lands: Their History in Maps, 1975; Jerusalem Illustrated History Atlas, 1977, 3rd ed., 1994; Exile and Return: The Struggle for a Jewish Homeland, 1978; Final Journey: The Fate of the Jews in Nazi Europe, 1979; Children's Illustrated Bible Atlas, 1979; Auschwitz and the Allies, 1981; Churchill's Political Philosophy, 1981; Churchill: The Wilderness Years, 1981; Atlas of the Holocaust, 1982; The Macmillan Atlas of the Holocaust, 1982; The Jews of Hope: The Plight of Soviet Jewry Today, 1984; The Holocaust in Retrospect: After 40 Years: First Annual Guest Lecture, 1984; Soviet Jewry in Crisis, 1984; Jerusalem: Rebirth of a City 1838-1898, 1985; Shcharansky: Hero of Our Time, 1986; Aṭlas ha-Shoʾah, 1986; The Holocaust: The Jewish Tragedy, 1987; Never Despair: Winston S. Churchill, 1945-1965, 1988; Second World War: A Complete History, 1989; (ed. and intro.) The Jews of St. Petersburg: Excursions Through a Noble Past, 1989; (ed. with intro.) Surviving the Holocaust: The Kovno Ghetto Diary, 1990; Churchill: A Life, 1991; Atlas of Russian History, 2nd ed., 1993; Atlas of Jewish History, 1993; First World War, 1994; The Routledge Atlas of the First World War, 2nd ed., 1994, 3rd ed., 2008; In Search of Churchill, 1994; Atlas of World War I, 2nd ed., 1994; Jerusalem: Past and Future, 1994; The Day the War Ended, 1995; Jerusalem in the Twentieth Century, 1996; The Boys, 1997; (ed. and intro.) Winston Churchill and Emery Reves, 1997; Holocaust Journey, 1997; A History of the 20th Century, vol. I, 1997, vol. II, 1998, vol. III, 1999; Never Again: A History of the Holocaust, 2000; Israel: A History, 1998; Holocaust Writing and Research Since 1945, 2001; History of the Twentieth Century, 2001; From the Ends of the Earth: The Jews in the Twentieth Century, 2001; Dearest Auntie Fori: 4000 Years of Jewish History, 2001; Letters to Auntie Fori: 5,000 Years of Jewish History and Faith, 2002; The Righteous: The Unsung Heroes of the Holocaust, 2002; (comp.) Churchill at War: His Finest Hour in Photographs, 1940-1945, 2003; D-Day, 2004; Winston Churchill's War Leadership, 2004; (contrib.) Churchill and the Great Republic, 2004; Continue to Pester, Nag and Bite: Churchill's War Leadership, 2004; (intro.) Holocaust Memoir Digest: Survivors' Published Memoirs with Study Guide and Maps, 2004; Churchill and America, 2005; (foreword) The Phases of Jewish History, 2005; Kristallnacht, Prelude to Destruction, 2006; The Somme: Heroism and Horror in the First World War, 2006; Roman's Journey: A Memoir of Survival, 2007; Churchill and the Jews: A Lifelong Friendship, 2007; The Routledge Atlas of British History, 4th ed., 2007; The Routledge Atlas of Russian History, 4th ed., 2007; The Routledge Atlas of the Second World War, 2008, 2nd ed., 2009; The Routledge Historical Atlas of Jerusalem, 4th ed., 2008; The Routledge Atlas of American History, 3rd ed., 1993, 6th ed., 2009; The Routledge Atlas of the Holocaust, 4th ed., 2009; The Routledge Atlas of Jewish History, 6th ed., 2003, 8th ed., 2010. **Address:** Merton College, Oxford University, Merton St., Oxford, OX OX1 4JD, England.

GILBERT, Martin John. *See* **GILBERT, Martin.**

GILBERT, Mary. *See* **DEFREES, Madeline.**

GILBERT, Ruth. New Zealander (born New Zealand), b. 1917?. **Genres:** Poetry, Autobiography/Memoirs. **Career:** Physiotherapist, 1938-46; New Zealand P.E.N., president. Writer. **Publications:** Lazarus and Other Poems, 1949; The Sunlit Hour, 1955; The Luthier, 1966; Collected Poems, 1984; Early Poems, 1938-1944, 1988; Breathings: Poems, 1992; Dream, Black Night's Child, 1993; Gongyla Remembers: Poems, 1994; Complete Early Poems, 1938-1944: With Six Later Pieces, 1994; Complete Sappho Poems of Ruth Gilbert, 1998; (ed. with D. Bolt) Selected Poems 1941-1998, 2008. **Address:** 23 Teece Dr., Motueka, 7120, New Zealand.

GILBERT, Sandra M(ortola). American (born United States), b. 1936.

Genres: Novellas/Short Stories, Poetry, Literary Criticism And History, Women's Studies And Issues, Autobiography/Memoirs, Novels, Politics/Government, Social Sciences, Social Sciences. **Career:** City University of New York, Queens College, lecturer in English, 1963-64, 1965-66; Sacramento State College (now California State University), lecturer in English, 1967-68; California State College (now California State University), assistant professor of English, 1968-71; St. Mary's College, lecturer in English, 1972, visiting lecturer; Indiana University, associate professor of English, 1973-75; University of California, Department of English, associate professor, 1975-80, professor, distinguished professor, 1989-, now distinguished professor emeritus; Princeton University, professor of English, 1985-89, Charles Barnwell Strout Class of 1923 Professor, 1989. Writer. **Publications:** Shakespeare's Twelfth Night, 1964; Two Novels by E.M. Forster, 1965; D.H. Lawrence's Sons and Lovers, 1965; The Poetry of W.B. Yeats, 1965; Two Novels by Virginia Woolf, 1966; Virginia Woolf's Mrs. Dalloway, and To the lighthouse, 1966; Acts of Attention: The Poems of D.H. Lawrence, 1972, 2nd ed., 1990; (with S. Gubar) The Madwoman in the Attic: The Woman Writer and the Nineteenth-century Literary Imagination, 1979, 2nd ed., 2000; (comp. with S. Gubar) The Norton Anthology of Literature by Women: The Tradition in English, 1985, 3rd ed., 2007; (with S. Gubar) No Man's Land: The Place of the Woman Writer in the 20th Century, 1988; Wrongful Death: A Medical Tragedy, 1995; (with S. Gubar) Masterpiece Theatre: An Academic Melodrama, 1995; On Burning Ground: Thirty Years of Thinking about Poetry, 2009; Rereading Women: Thirty Years of Exploring Our Literary Traditions, 2011; Aftermath: Poems, 2011. POETRY: In the Fourth World, 1979; The Summer Kitchen, 1983; Emily's Bread, 1984; Blood Pressure, 1988; Ghost Volcano, 1995; (with S. Gubar and D. O'Hehir) Mothersongs: Poems For, By, and About Mothers, 1995; Kissing the Bread: New and Selected Poems, 1969-1999, 2000; The Italian Collection: Poems of Heritage, 2003; Belongings, 2005; Death's Door: Modern Dying and the Ways We Grieve, 2006. EDITOR: (and intro. with S. Gubar) Shakespeare's Sisters: Feminist Essays on Women Poets, 1979; (and intro.) The Awakening and Selected Stories, 1984; (with S. Gubar) The Female Imagination and the Modernist Aesthetic, 1986; Orlando, 1993; (with W. Barker) The House is Made of Poetry: The Art of Ruth Stone, 1996; (and intro.) Inventions of Farewell: A Book of Elegies, 2001; (with S. Gubar) Feminist Literary Theory and Criticism: A Norton Reader, 2007. Works appear in anthologies. Contributor to periodicals and journals. **Address:** Department of English, University of California, Voorhies Hall, 1 Shields Ave., Davis, CT 95616-5270, U.S.A. **Online address:** sgilbert@ucdavis.edu

GILBERT, Sheri L. American (born United States) **Genres:** Young Adult Fiction, Children's Fiction. **Career:** Writer. **Publications:** The Legacy of Gloria Russell, 2004. **Address:** c/o Author Mail, Knopf Publishing Group, Random House, 299 Park Ave., New York, NY 10171-0002, U.S.A. **Online address:** sherilgilbert@qwest.net

GILBERT, Suzie. American (born United States), b. 1956. **Genres:** Environmental Sciences/Ecology, Autobiography/Memoirs. **Career:** Flyaway Inc., founder. Writer. **Publications:** Hawk Hill, 1996; Flyaway: How A Wild Bird Rehabber Sought Adventure and Found Her Wings, 2009. Contributor to periodicals. **Address:** Flyaway Inc., 241 Rt. 403, Garrison, NY 10524, U.S.A. **Online address:** gilbert@highlands.com

GILBERT, Tom. American (born United States), b. 1955. **Genres:** Biography, Sports/Fitness, Business/Trade/Industry, Art/Art History. **Career:** Variety, copy editor, 1984-85, assistant managing editor, 1985-89, managing editor, 1989-91, slot editor, 1991-93; writer, 1993-; Crossmap, feature writer. **Publications:** Roberto Clemente, 1991; Lee Trevino, 1992; (with C.S. Sanders) Desilu: The Story of Lucille Ball and Desi Arnaz, 1993; Pete Rose, 1995; Elysian Fields: The Birth of Baseball, 1995; Baseball and the Color Line, 1995; Superstars and Monopoly Wars: Nineteenth-Century Major-League Baseball, 1995; The Soaring Twenties: Babe Ruth and the Home-Run Decade, 1996; The Good Old Days: Baseball in The 1930s, 1996; Dead Ball: Major League Baseball Before Babe Ruth, 1996; Baseball at War: World War II and the Fall of the Color Line, 1997; Damn Yankees: Casey, Whitey, Yogi and the Mick, 1997. **Address:** 5700 Wilshire Blvd., Ste. 120, Los Angeles, CA 90036, U.S.A. **Online address:** tom@livingthesolution.com

GILBERT, W(illiam) Stephen. British (born England), b. 1947. **Genres:** Novels, Plays/Screenplays, Literary Criticism And History, Biography, History, Communications/Media. **Career:** Freelance writer. **Publications:** Private Means, 1986; Spiked, 1991; The Movie Superchallenge (quiz book),

1992; Fight and Kick and Bite: The Life and Work of Dennis Potter, 1995 in US as The Life and Work of Dennis Potter, 1998. Contributor to magazines and newspapers. **Address:** c/o Tony Peake, Peake Associates, 14 Grafton Cres., PO Box 66726, London, GL NW5 9FE, England. **Online address:** wsteg@macunlimited.net

GILCHRIST, Ellen. American (born United States), b. 1935. **Genres:** Novels, Novellas/Short Stories, Poetry, Essays, Biography. **Career:** Vieux Carre Courier, contributing editor, 1976-79; National Public Radio, commentator, 1984-85; University of Arkansas, visiting associate professor, visiting professor, 2000, Creative Writing Programs, associate professor of creative writing, 2001-. Writer. **Publications:** NOVELS: The Annunciation, 1983; The Anna Papers, 1988; Net of Jewels, 1992; Anabasis: A Journey to the Interior, 1994; Starcarbon: A Meditation on Love, 1994; Sarah Conley, 1997; Dangerous Age, 2008. POETRY: The Land Surveyor's Daughter, 1979; Riding Out the Tropical Depression, 1986. STORIES: In the Land of Dreamy Dreams, 1981; Victory over Japan, 1984; Drunk with Love, 1986; Two Stories: Some Blue Hills at Sundown and The Man Who Kicked Cancer's Ass, 1988; Light Can Be Both Wave and Particle, 1989; I Cannot Get You Close Enough (novellas), 1990; The Age of Miracles, 1995; Rhoda: A Life in Stories, 1995; The Courts of Love: A Novella and Stories, 1996; Nora Jane and Company, 1997; Flights of Angels, 1998; The Cabal and Other Stories, 1999; Collected Stories, 2000; I, Rhoda Manning, Go Hunting with My Daddy & Other Stories, 2002; The Writing Life, 2005; Nora Jane: A Life in Stories, 2005. OTHERS: Muppets, No. 1-5, 1984-86; Falling Through Space: The Journals of Ellen Gilchrist, 1987; Muppets: Foggy Mountain Breakdown, 1988; (contrib.) Bitch in the House: 26 Women Tell the Truth about Sex, Solitude, Work, Motherhood, and Marriage (essays), 2002. Contributor to magazines and journals. **Address:** c/o Author Mail, Warner Books, 1271 Ave. of the Americas, New York, NY 10020-1300, U.S.A. **Online address:** egilchr@uark.edu

GILCHRIST, John. See GARDNER, Jerome.

GILCHRIST, Roberta. British/Canadian (born Canada), b. 1965. **Genres:** Archaeology/Antiquities, Women's Studies And Issues, Theology/Religion, History. **Career:** University of East Anglia, lecturer, 1990-95; Museum of London Archaeology Services, academic advisor, 1991; Channel Four, Down to Earth, TV presenter, 1991-92; Norwich Cathedral, archaeologist, 1993-2005; University of Reading, Department of Archaeology, professor of archaeology, 1996-; World Archaeology, editor, 1997-2006. **Publications:** (Ed. with H. Mytum) The Archaeology of Rural Monasteries, 1989; (with M. Oliva) Religious Women in Medieval East Anglia, 1993; (ed. with H. Mytum) Advances in Monastic Archaeology: Conference on Urban Monasteries, 1993; Gender and Material Culture: The Archaeology of Religious Women, 1994; Contemplation and Action: The Other Monasticism, 1995; Gender and Archaeology: Contesting the Past, 1999; (ed. with D. Gaimster) The Archaeology of Reformation, 1480-1580: Papers Given at the Archaeology of Reformation Conference, February 2001, Hosted Jointly by Society for Medieval Archaeology, Society for Post-Medieval Archaeology, 2003; Norwich Cathedral Close: The Evolution of the English Cathedral Landscape, 2005; (with B. Sloane) Requiem: The Medieval Monastic Cemetery in Britain, 2005; (ed. with A. Reynolds) Reflections: 50 Years of Medieval Archaeology, 1957-2007, 2009. Contributor of articles to journals. **Address:** Department of Archaeology, University of Reading, Whiteknights, PO Box 227, Reading, BR RG6 6AB, England. **Online address:** r.l.gilchrist@reading.ac.uk

GILDEA, Robert. British (born England), b. 1952. **Genres:** History. **Career:** University of London, Kings College, lecturer in history, 1978-79; Oxford University, Merton College, tutor in modern history, 1979-, reader in modern history, 1996-, professor of modern history; Worcester College, fellow. Writer. **Publications:** Education in Provincial France, 1800-1914: A Study of Three Departments, 1983; Barricades and Borders: Europe, 1800-1914, 1987, 3rd ed., 2003; France, 1870-1914, 1988, 2nd ed., 1996; The Past in French History, 1994; France since 1945, 1996, 2nd ed., 2002; Marianne in Chains: In Search of the German Occupation, 1940-1945, 2002 in US as Marianne in Chains: Everyday Life in the French Heartland Under the German Occupation, 2003; Marianne in Chains: Daily Life in the Heart of France During the German Occupation, 2004; Surviving Hitler and Mussolini: Daily Life in Occupied Europe, 2007; (ed. with A. Simonin) Writing Contemporary History, 2008; Children of the Revolution: The French, 1799-1914, 2008. Contributor to periodicals. **Address:** Merton College, Oxford University, George St., Oxford, OX OX1 4JD, England. **Online address:** robert.gildea@merton.ox.ac.uk

GILDEA, William. American (born United States), b. 1939. **Genres:** Sports/Fitness, Young Adult Fiction. **Career:** Washington Post, columnist, journalist, 1965-. **Publications:** (With K. Turan) Future is Now, George Allen, Pro Football's Most Controversial Coach, 1972; (L. Brown) I'll always Get Up, 1973; (with W. Gildea and K. Turan) I'd Rather Be Wright; Memoirs of an Itinerant Tackle, 1974; (with C. Jennison) Fighting Irish, 1976; When the Colts Belonged to Baltimore: A Father and a Son, a Team and a Time, 1994; Where the Game Matters Most: A Last Championship Season in Indiana High School Basketball, 1997. **Address:** Washington Post, 1150 15th St. NW, Washington, DC 20071, U.S.A.

GILDEN, Mel. American (born United States), b. 1947?. **Genres:** Children's Fiction, Young Adult Fiction, Novels, Horror. **Career:** Writer. **Publications:** The Return of Captain Conquer, 1986; Pokey to the Rescue, 1987; RV and the Haunted Garage, 1987; Harry Newberry and the Raiders of the Red Drink, 1989; Outer Space and All That Junk, 1989; Star Trek: The Next Generation: Boogeymen, 1991; Hawaiian Aliens, 1991; The Planetoid of Amazement, 1991; Which Way to the Beach?, 1992; No Secrets, 1992; Star Trek: The Starship Trap, 1993; The Pumpkins of Time (sequel to Outer Space and All That Junk), 1994; (with T. Pedersen) Pet, 1994; The Jungle Book: A Novelization, 1994; My Brother Blubb, 1994; Blubb and the Chocolate Treasure, 1995; Blubb and the Amazing Morphing Machine, 1996; Cardassian Imps, 1997; NASCAR Racers: How They Work, 2000; NASCAR Racers: Official Owner's Manual, 2000; Spy Fox the Official Spy Manual, 2001; Spy Fox's Spy-tacular Adventure No. 1, 2001; Chain Reaction, 2001; Britney Spears is a Three-Headed Alien, 2001; Dangerous Hardboiled Magicians, forthcoming. FIFTH GRADE MONSTERS SERIES: JUVENILE FICTION: M Is for Monster, 1987; Born to Howl, 1987; The Pet of Frankenstein, 1988; Z Is for Zombie, 1988; Monster Mashers, 1989; Things That Go Bark in the Park, 1989; Yuckers!, 1989; The Monster in Creeps Head Bay, 1990; How to Be a Vampire in One Easy Lesson, 1990; Island of the Weird, 1990; Werewolf, Come Home, 1990; Monster Boy, 1991; Troll Patrol, 1991; The Secret of Dinosaur Bog, 1991. ZOOT MARLOWE SERIES: Surfing Samurai Robots, 1988; Hawaiian U.F.O. Aliens, 1991; Tubular Android Superheroes, 1991. BEVERLY HILLS 90210 SERIES: Beverly Hills 90210, 1991; More than Words: A Novelization, 1993; Graduation Day, 1994. CYBERSURFERS SERIES WITH TED PEDERSEN: Pirates on the Internet, 1995; Cyberspace Cowboy, 1995; Ghost on the Net, 1996; Cybercops & Flame Wars, 1996. SHORT FICTION: What About Us Girls?, 1971; What's the Matter with Herbie?, 1973; Everybody Loves: In a Circular Motion, 1973; A Lamed Wufnik, 1975; The Ice Cream Golem, 1976; The Perambulator, 1977; The Green Dog, 1978; Special Effects, 1979; Deadline, 1981; Small Miracles, 1982; The Ghost in the Machine, 1995; The Adventure of the Forgotten Umbrella, 2003. **Address:** Pocket Books, Simon & Schuster Inc., 1230 Ave. of the Americas, New York, NY 10020, U.S.A. **Online address:** melg@earthlink.net

GILDNER, Gary. American (born United States), b. 1938. **Genres:** Novels, Autobiography/Memoirs, Novellas/Short Stories, Poetry, Human Relations/Parenting, Literary Criticism And History. **Career:** Wayne State University, Department of University Relations, writer, 1961-62; Northern Michigan University, instructor in English, 1963-66; Drake University, associate professor of English, 1966-91, emeritus professor of English, 1991-; Reed College, visiting professor and writer-in-residence, 1983-85; Michigan State University, visiting professor, 1987; University of Warsaw, senior Fulbright lecturer, 1987-88; Davidson College, McGee Professor of Writing, 1992; Safarik University, senior Fulbright lecturer, 1992-93; Seattle University, distinguished visiting writer-in-residence, 2002. **Publications:** POETRY: First Practice, 1969; Digging for Indians, 1971; Eight Poems, 1973; Nails, 1975; Letters from Vicksburg: Poems, 1977; The Runner and Other Poems, 1978; Jabón: Poems, 1981; Blue Like the Heavens: New and Selected Poems, 1984; Clackamas, 1991; The Swing, 1996; The Bunker in the Parsley Fields: Poems, 1997; The Birthday Party, 2000. OTHERS: (ed. with J. Gildner) Out of This World: Poems from the Hawkeye State, 1975; The Crush, 1983; The Second Bridge: A Novel, 1987; A Week in South Dakota: Stories, 1987; The Warsaw Sparks, 1990; Pavol Hudak, The Poet, Is Talking, 1996; My Grandfather's Book: Generations of An American Family, 2002; Somewhere Geese are Flying: New and Selected Stories, 2004; Cleaning a Rainbow: Poems, 2007. Contributor to periodicals. **Address:** Drake University, 2507 University Ave., Des Moines, IA 50311-4505, U.S.A.

GILENS, Martin. American (born United States) **Genres:** Politics/Government, Social Sciences, Race Relations. **Career:** Yale University, Department of Political Science, assistant professor, 1992-97, associate professor, 1998-2000, director of undergraduate studies, 1995-98; University of California, Department of Political Science, associate professor, 2000-03, Institute for Social Science Research, associate director, 2000-03; Princeton University, Department of Politics, associate professor of politics, 2003-. Writer. **Publications:** (Contrib.) Perception and Prejudice: Race and Politics in the United States, 1988; Why Americans Hate Welfare: Race, Media and the Politics of Anti-Poverty Policy, 1999. Contributor to books and journals. **Address:** Department of Politics, Princeton University, 213 Robertson Hall, Princeton, NJ 08544-1012, U.S.A. **Online address:** mgilens@princeton.edu

GILES, Frank (Thomas Robertson). British (born England), b. 1919. **Genres:** Politics/Government, Writing/Journalism, Autobiography/Memoirs. **Career:** Painshill Park Trust, chair; British Institute, board governor; British Diplomatic Service, private secretary, 1945-46; Times, assistant correspondent, 1947-50, chief correspondent, 1950-60; Sunday Times, foreign editor, 1961-77, deputy editor, 1967-81, editor, 1981-83; Times Newspapers Ltd., director, 1981-85. **Publications:** Toughen Up! A Boy's Guide to Better Physical Fitness, 1963; A Prince of Journalists: The Life and Times of Henri Stefan Opper De Blowitz, 1974; Sundry Times (autobiography), 1986; The Locust Years: The Story of the Fourth French Republic, 1946-1958, 1991; (ed.) Corfu: The Garden Isle, 1994; Napoleon Bonaparte: England's Prisoner, 2001. Contributor to periodicals. **Address:** 42 Blomfield Rd., London, GL W9 2PF, England.

GILES, Gail. American (born United States) **Genres:** Young Adult Fiction, Children's Fiction, Poetry. **Career:** Writer and teacher. **Publications:** Breath of the Dragon, 1997; Shattering Glass, 2002; Dead Girls Don't Write Letters, 2003; Playing in Traffic, 2004; What happened to Cass McBride?, 2006; Right Behind You, 2007; Dark Song, 2010. **Address:** c/o Scott Treimel, Scott Treimel NY, 434 Lafayette St., New York, NY 10003, U.S.A. **Online address:** gail@gailgiles.com

GILES, Paul. British (born England), b. 1957. **Genres:** Literary Criticism And History, Language/Linguistics, History. **Career:** University of Staffordshire, lecturer in English, 1985-87; Portland State University, assistant professor, 1987-92, associate professor of English, 1992-94; University of Nottingham, lecturer in American Studies, 1994-97, reader, 1997-99; University of Cambridge, Fitzwilliam College, fellow, 1999-2002, lecturer in American literature, 1999-2002; University of Oxford, reader in American literature, 2002-06, Linacre College, fellow, 2002-, Rothermere American Institute, director, 2003-08, professor of American literature, 2006-; International American Studies Association, president, 2005-07; Comparative American Studies, associate editor. **Publications:** Hart Crane: The Contexts of The Bridge, 1986; American Catholic Arts and Fictions: Culture, Ideology, Aesthetics, 1992; Transatlantic Insurrections: British Culture and the Formation of American Literature, 1730-1860, 2001; Virtual Americas: Transnational Fictions and the Transatlantic Imaginary, 2002; Atlantic Republic: The American Tradition in English Literature, 2006; The Global Remapping of American Literature, 2010. Contributor of articles and reviews to academic journals. **Address:** Faculty of English, Oxford University, Saint Cross Bldg., Manor Rd., Oxford, OX OX1 3UQ, England. **Online address:** paul.giles@rai.ox.ac.uk

GILES, Robert Hartmann. American (born United States), b. 1933. **Genres:** Communications/Media, Writing/Journalism, Business/Trade/Industry. **Career:** Newport News Daily Press, reporter, 1957-58; Akron Beacon Journal, reporter, 1958-63, editorial writer, 1963-65, city editor, 1966-68, metropolitan editor, 1968-70, managing editor, 1970-73, executive editor, 1973-76; Harvard University, Nieman Fellow, 1965-66, Nieman Foundation for Journalism, curator, 2000-11; University of Kansas, School of Journalism, special lecturer, 1976-77; Times-Union, executive editor, editor, 1977-86; Democrat & Chronicle, executive editor, editor, 1977-86; Gannett Newspapers, executive editor, 1977-81, editor, 1981-86; Detroit News, vice-president and executive editor, 1986-89, editor and publisher, 1989-97; The New York Times, staff. **Publications:** (Ed.) Editors and Stress: A Report to APME on Stress and How It Affects the Lives of Newspaper Editors, 1982; Newsroom Management: A Guide to Theory and Practice, 1987; (contrib.) Jonesboro: Were the Media Fair?, 1998; (contrib.) Workplace: The Business Beat of the Future, 2000. EDITOR WITH R.W. SNYDER: Covering the Courts: Free Press, Fair Trials & Journalistic Performance, 1999; What's Fair?: The Problem of Equity in Journalism, 1999; What's Next?: Problems & Prospects of Journalism, 2000; 1968: Year of Media Decision, 2001; (and with L. DeLisle) Covering

China, 2001; (and with L. DeLisle) Profiles in Journalistic Courage, 2001; (and with L. DeLisle) Reporting the Post-Communist Revolution, 2001. **Address:** 27 Beverly Rd., Grosse Pointe Farms, MI 48236-3705, U.S.A. **Online address:** bob_giles@harvard.edu

GILKES, Cheryl Townsend. American (born United States), b. 1947. **Genres:** Race Relations, Social Sciences, Theology/Religion, Women's Studies And Issues, Sociology. **Career:** Boston University, assistant professor of sociology, 1978-87; Union Baptist Church, assistant pastor for special projects, 1982-; Colby College, professor of African-American studies and sociology, 1987-, John D. and Catherine T. MacArthur professor of sociology and African-American studies, African American Studies Program, director. Writer. **Publications:** If It Wasn't for the Women...: Black Women's Experience and Womanist Culture in Church and Community, 2001; Lots of Small Pieces: African-American Women and Their Community Work, forthcoming; That Blessed Book: The Bible and the African-American Cultural Imagination, forthcoming. Contributor to books and periodicals. **Address:** Dept. of Sociology & African-American Studies, Colby College, 4000 Mayflower Hill, Waterville, ME 04901, U.S.A.

GILL, A. A. British/Scottish (born Scotland), b. 1954. **Genres:** Novels, Young Adult Non-fiction, Travel/Exploration, Essays, Literary Criticism And History, Art/Art History. **Career:** Sunday Times, restaurant reviewer and television critic, restaurant critic, 1993-; Vanity Fair Magazine, restaurant reviewer. Writer. **Publications:** Sap Rising, 1996; The Ivy: The Restaurant and Its Recipes, 1997; Starcrossed, 1999; Le Caprice, 1999; A.A. Gill Is Away, 2002; Connoisseur with A.A. Gill, 2005; The Angry Island: Hunting the English, 2005; Previous Convictions: Assignments from Here and There, 2006; Table Talk: Sweet and Sour, Salt and Bitter, 2007; Breakfast at the Wolseley, 2008; Paper View: The Best of The Sunday Times Television Reviews, 2008; AA Gill is Further Away, 2011; AA Gill On America, 2012. **Address:** Sunday Times, 3 Thomas More Sq, London, GL E98 1XY, England.

GILL, Anton. (Ray Evans). British (born England), b. 1948. **Genres:** Mystery/Crime/Suspense, History, Writing/Journalism, Biography. **Career:** Royal Court Theatre, English Stage Co., assistant director, 1972-74; Arts Council of Great Britain, drama officer, 1976-78; British Broadcasting Corp., producer, 1976, senior drama producer, 1978-81; Norddeutscher Rundfunk, director of radio plays, 1981-82; TV-AM Ltd., journalist/producer, 1982-84; Writer, 1984-. **Publications:** Mad About the Boy: The Life and Times of Boy George and Culture Club, 1985; Martin Allen is Missing, 1985; How to Be Oxbridge, 1986; Croquet, 1988; The Journey Back from Hell: An Oral History, Conversations with Concentration Camp Survivors, 1988; Berlin to Bucharest, 1990; A Dance between Flames: Berlin 1919-1939, 1993; A Honourable Defeat: The German Resistance to Hitler, 1994; Ruling Passions, 1995; The Hanging Gale, 1995; The Devil's Mariner: A Life of William Dampier, 1997; The Last Talons of the Eagle, 1998; Peggy Guggenheim, the Life, 2001; Il Gigante, 2002; (with A. West) Extinct, 2002; The Great Escape, 2002; Ancient Egyptians, 2003; Art Lover: A Biography of Peggy Guggenheim, 2003; The Egyptians: The Kingdom of the Pharaohs Brought to Life, 2003; Trace Your Family History Back to The Tudors, 2006; Empire's Children, 2007; Gateway of the Gods: The Rise and Fall of Babylon, 2008; The Sacred Scroll, 2011; We Built the Titanic, 2011. EGYPTIAN MYSTERY TRILOGIES: City of the Horizon, 1991; City of the Dead, 1993; City of Dreams, 1994. **Address:** Mark Lucas Law Ltd., 14 Vernon St., London, GL W14 0RJ, England. **Online address:** anton@antongill.u-net.com

GILL, David Macinnis. American (born United States), b. 1963. **Genres:** Science Fiction/Fantasy, Biography. **Career:** Brainerd High School, teacher; Chattanooga School for the Arts and Sciences, teacher; Ohio University, assistant professor; University of North Carolina, associate professor. Writer. **Publications:** Graham Salisbury: Island Boy (biography), 2005; Soul Enchilada, 2009; Black Hole Sun, 2010. Contributor to periodicals. **Address:** Wilmington, NC , U.S.A. **Online address:** thunderchikin@me.com

GILL, Elizabeth. *See* **HANKIN, Elizabeth Rosemary.**

GILL, Gillian. *See* **GILL, Gillian C(atherine).**

GILL, Gillian C(atherine). (Gillian Gill). American/Welsh (born Wales), b. 1942. **Genres:** Women's Studies And Issues, Biography, Translations, History. **Career:** Northeastern University, assistant professor of French, 1970-81; Wellesley College, professor, 1970-81; Yale University, professor, 1970-81;

Harvard University, professor of literature; Yale University, Women's Studies Program, director, Jonathan Edwards College, resident fellow. Writer. **Publications:** AS GILLIAN GILL: Agatha Christie: The Woman and Her Mysteries, 1990; Mary Baker Eddy, 1998; (ed.) The Dead Good Time Capsule Book, 1999; Nightingales: The Extraordinary Upbringing and Curious Life of Miss Florence Nightingale, 2004; We Two: Victoria and Albert: Rulers, Partners, Rivals, 2009. TRANSLATOR: L. Irigaray, Speculum of the Other Woman, 1984; Marine Lover/of Friedrich Nietzsche, 1991; Sexes and Genealogies, 1993; (with C. Burke) An Ethics of Sexual Difference, 1993; L. Frappier-Mazur, Sade Writes the Orgy, 1995. Contributor to periodicals. **Address:** Harvard University, 208 Emerson Hall, Cambridge, MA 02138, U.S.A.

GILL, Graeme J(oseph). Australian (born Australia), b. 1947. **Genres:** Politics/Government. **Career:** University of Tasmania, tutor, 1976-77, lecturer, 1978-81; University of Sydney, lecturer, senior lecturer, 1981-88, associate professor, 1988-90, chair, 1990, professor of government and public administration and Australian professorial fellow (APF), 1990-, faculty of Economics, associate dean, deputy chair of the academic board, acting pro vice-chancellor (Research), School of Economics and Political Science, head; London School of Economics, visiting fellow; Moscow State University, visiting fellow; St Petersburg University, visiting fellow; Oxford University, visiting fellow; Cambridge University, visiting fellow; European University Institute, visiting fellow; Academy of the Social Sciences, fellow; Contemporary Europe Research Centre, principle fellow. Writer. **Publications:** Peasants and Government in the Russian Revolution, 1979; Soviet Union Under Gorbachev, 1985; Twentieth-Century Russia, 1987, 2nd ed., 1994; (ed.) The Rules of the Communist Party of the Soviet Union, 1988; Stalinism, 1990, 2nd ed., 1998; The Origins of the Stalinist Political System, 1990; (with S. White and D. Slider) The Politics of Transition: Shaping a Post-Soviet Future, 1993; The Collapse of a Single-Party System: The Disintegration of CPSU, 1995; (with R. Pitty) Power in the Party: The Organization of Power and Central-Republican Relations in the CPSU, 1997; (ed.) Elites and Leadership in Russian Politics: Selected Papers from the Fifth World Congress of Central and East European Studies, Warsaw, 1995, 1998; The Dynamics of Democratization: Elites, Civil Society and The Transition Process, 2000; (with R.D. Markwick) Russia's Stillborn Democracy?: From Gorbachev to Yeltsin, 2000; Democracy and Post-Communism, 2002; The Nature and Development of the Modern State, 2003; (ed.) Politics in the Russian Regions, 2007; Bourgeoisie, State and Democracy: Russia, Britain, France, Germany and the USA, 2008; Symbols and Legitimacy in Soviet Politics, 2011; (ed. with J. Young) Routledge Handbook of Russian Politics and Society, 2011. **Address:** School of Social and Political Sciences, University of Sydney, Rm. M283, H04-Merewether Bldg., Sydney, NW 2006, Australia. **Online address:** g.gill@econ.usyd.edu.au

GILL, Lakshmi. (Myrna Lakshmi Gill). Canadian/Filipino (born Philippines), b. 1943. **Genres:** Poetry, Novels, Young Adult Fiction. **Career:** Notre Dame University of Nelson, instructor; Mount Allison University, Department, instructor; University of Victoria, instructor; University of British Columbia, English Language Institute, instructor. Writer. **Publications:** AS MYRNA LAKSHMI GILL: POETRY: During Rain, I Plant Chrysanthemums, 1966; Mind-Walls: Poems, 1970; First Clearing: An Immigrant's Tour of Life, 1972; Novena to St. Jude Thaddeus, 1979; Bayang Magilu, 1980; Portraits: Main and Hastings, 1980. OTHERS: Rape of the Spirit, 1962; The Third Infinitive (fiction), 1993; Returning the Empties: Selected Poems, 1960s-1990s, 1998. **Address:** c/o Author Mail, Tsar Press, PO Box 6996, Sta. A, Toronto, ON M5W 1X7, Canada.

GILL, LaVerne McCain. American (born United States), b. 1947. **Genres:** Cultural/Ethnic Topics, Ethics, Politics/Government, Theology/Religion, Women's Studies And Issues, Reference. **Career:** Webster United Church of Christ, pastor, minister; Chautauqua United Church of Christ Society Inc., administrator; Life Transformation Foundation Inc., founder and president. Writer and television producer. **Publications:** African American Women in Congress, 1997; Daughters of Dignity: African Biblical Women and the Virtues of Black Womanhood, 2000; My Mother Prayed for Me: Faith Journaling for African American Women, 2000; Vashti's Victory and Other Biblical Women Resisting Injustice, 2003. **Address:** c/o Natasha Kern, A Kern Agency, PO Box 2908, Portland, OR 97208, U.S.A. **Online address:** igill@ic.net

GILL, Myrna Lakshmi. See **GILL, Lakshmi.**

GILL, Peter. British/Welsh (born Wales), b. 1939. **Genres:** Plays/Screen-

plays. **Career:** Royal Court, assistant director, 1964-, associate director, 1970-; Riverside Studios, artistic director, 1976-80; National Theatre, associate director, 1980-97, director; National Theatre Studio, founding director, 1984. Writer. **Publications:** The Sleeper's Den, 1965; Over Gardens Out, 1970; Small Change, 1976; Small Change, and Kick for Touch, 1985; Mean Tears, 1987; The Cherry Orchard, 1995; The Look Across the Eyes (short story), 1997; Cardiff East, 1997; Certain Young Men, 1999; The Seagull by Anton Chekhov, 2000; The York Realist, 2001; Peter Gill Plays: 1, 2001; Eclipse, 2001; Original Sin, 2002; Plays One, 2002; Apprenticeship, 2008; Another Door Closed, 2009. **Address:** National Theatre, South Bank, London, GL SE1 9PX, England.

GILL, Sam D. American (born United States), b. 1943. **Genres:** Cultural/Ethnic Topics, Theology/Religion, Humanities, Dance/Ballet. **Career:** The Coleman Co., research analyst, 1964-67; University of Chicago, systems analyst, 1967-73; Oklahoma State University, visiting assistant professor of humanities and religion, 1974-75; Arizona State University, Department of Religious Studies, assistant professor, 1975-80, associate professor of religious studies, 1980-83, Native American Religions Program, administrator, 1975-78; University of Colorado, visiting professor, 1981-82, Department of Religious Studies, professor of religious studies, 1983-, director of graduate studies, 1984-87, 1990-91, 1993-97, director of undergraduate studies, 2003-07; Journal of Ritual Studies, consulting editor; Journal of Religion and American Culture, consulting editor; Mythosphere: A Journal for Image, Myth, and Symbol, consulting editor. **Publications:** Songs of Life: An Introduction to Navajo Religious Culture, 1979; Sacred Words: A Study of Navajo Religion and Prayer, 1981; Beyond The Primitive: The Religions of Nonliterate Peoples, 1982; Native American Religions: An Introduction, 1982, 2nd ed., 2005; Native American Traditions: Sources and Interpretations, 1983; Mother Earth: An American Story, 1987; Native American Religious Action: A Performance Approach to Religion, 1987; (with I.F. Sullivan) Dictionary of Native American Mythology, 1992; Storytracking: Texts, Stories and Histories in Central Australia, 1998. Contributor of articles to journals. **Address:** Department of Religious Studies, University of Colorado, 288 Eaton Humanities, PO Box 292, Boulder, CO 80309-0292, U.S.A. **Online address:** sam.gill@colorado.edu

GILL, Walter. American (born United States), b. 1937. **Genres:** Education, Reference. **Career:** Teacher, 1962-72; Millersville University, assistant professor of education, 1994-. Writer. **Publications:** Issues in African American Education, 1991; A Common Sense Guide to Non-Traditional Urban Education, 1998; The Urban Chameleon, forthcoming; Models, Methods and Media, forthcoming. Contributor of articles to periodicals. **Address:** School of Education, Millersville University, PO Box 1002, Millersville, PA 17551-0302, U.S.A.

GILLER, Marc D. American (born United States), b. 1968?. **Genres:** Novels. **Career:** Florida law firm, information systems manager. Writer. **Publications:** Hammerjack: A Novel, 2005; Prodigal: A Novel, 2006; Star Trek, 2010. Contributor to periodicals. **Address:** c/o. Kimberley Cameron & Associates, 1550 Tiburon Blvd., Ste. 704, Tiburon, CA 94920, U.S.A.

GILLES, D. B. American (born United States), b. 1947. **Genres:** Plays/Screenplays, Art/Art History, Humor/Satire. **Career:** Columbia University, instructor in film; New York University, Gallatin School of Individualized Study, part-time faculty, Tisch School of the Arts, teacher. Writer. **Publications:** PLAYS: The Girl Who Loved the Beatles: A Play in One Act, 1974; The Legendary Stardust Boys: A Play in Two Acts, 1981; Men's Singles: A Comedy in Two Acts, 1986, rev. ed., 2005; Cash Flow, 1989. OTHERS: The Screenwriter Within: How to Turn the Movie in Your Head into a Salable Screenplay, 2000; (with S. Woodbury) W: The First 100 Days: A White House Journal, 2001; The Portable Film School: Everything You'd Learn in Film School (without Ever Going to Class), 2005; You're Funny!: Turn Your Sense of Humor into a Lucrative New Career, 2011. **Address:** Tisch School of the Arts, New York University, Rm. 1122, 721 Broadway, New York, NY 10003-6807, U.S.A. **Online address:** dbgillescript@gmail.com

GILLESPIE, Angus Kress. American (born United States), b. 1942. **Genres:** Urban Studies, Architecture, History, Cultural/Ethnic Topics, Mythology/Folklore, Military/Defense/Arms Control, Marine Sciences/Oceanography, Anthropology/Ethnology, Anthropology/Ethnology, History, Biography. **Career:** Rutgers University, instructor in American studies, 1973-75, assistant professor, 1975-81, associate professor, 1981-2000, professor of American studies, 2000-. Writer. **Publications:** (Contrib.) Natural and Cultural Resources of the New Jersey Pine Barrens, 1979; Folklorist of the Coal Fields: The Life and Work of George Korson, 1980; (ed.) Foodways in the United States: The Matrix of Regional and Ethnic Identity, 1984; (ed. and contrib. with J. Mechling) American Wildlife in Symbol and Story, 1987; (contrib.) Time out of Time, 1987; (with M.A. Rockland) Looking for America on the New Jersey Turnpike, 1989; Twin Towers: The Life of New York City's World Trade Center, 1999, 2nd ed., 2002; (ed. with D. Wilson) Rooted in American Soil: Food Lore of Popular Fruits and Vegetables, 1999; The Lore of America's Coal Miners: A Fresh Look at the George Korson Collection, 2004 September 20, 2004; Crossing Under the Hudson: The Story of the Holland and Lincoln Tunnels, 2011. **Address:** Department of American Studies, Rutgers University, 131 George St., New Brunswick, NJ 08901-1414, U.S.A. **Online address:** agillespie@amst.rutgers.edu

GILLESPIE, Carol Ann. American (born United States), b. 1951. **Genres:** Geography. **Career:** Substitute teacher, 1990-91; Seneca Valley School District, substitute teacher, 1996-99; Grove City College, adjunct instructor, 1998-2002; Pennsylvania Geographic Alliance, teacher consultant, 1999; Butler County Community College-Cranberry Township, part-time adjunct instructor, 1999-2001; Chatham College, adjunct instructor, 1999-2001; Educational Testing Service, AP reader, 2001-08, test developer, 2001-10, AP leader, 2006-11; Texas State University, adjunct instructor, 2002-03, Gilbert M. Grosvenor Center for Geographic Education, doctoral assistant, 2002-03; University of Pittsburgh, adjunct instructor, 2004-05; Butler County Community College-New Castle, adjunct instructor, 2005-06; Community College of Allegheny County, Fund for the Improvement of Postsecondary Education (FIPSE), grant project co-ordinator, 2005-08; Slippery Rock University, instructor, 2006-09; Pennsylvania Alliance for Geographic Education, on-line instructor, 2007-, My Wonderful World Public Engagement Program, coordinator, 2007-10; Pennsylvania Homeschoolers Association, on-line instructor, 2007-; National Geographic Society, My Wonderful World Public Engagement Program, coordinator, 2007-10; University of Phoenix, Axia College, on-line instructor, 2010-; National Aviary, grant writer, 2011-. **Publications:** New Zealand, 2002; Bahrain, 2002; Ethiopia, 2003; Mountain Mists: Appalachian Folkways of West Virginia, 2009. **Address:** National Aviary, Allegheny Commons W, 700 Arch St., Pittsburgh, PA 15212, U.S.A. **Online address:** cagillespie@zoominternet.net

GILLESPIE, Diane Filby. American (born United States), b. 1943. **Genres:** Literary Criticism And History, Essays, Novels. **Career:** University of Minnesota-Twin Cities, instructor in English, 1966-67; Stephens College, instructor in literature and writing, 1967-69; University of Alberta, lecturer in English, 1973-74; Washington State University, assistant professor, 1975-80, associate professor, 1980-89, professor of English, 1989-2001, professor emeritus, 2001-; Modernist Studies, associate editor, 1976-82. **Publications:** The Sisters' Arts: The Writing and Painting of Virginia Woolf and Vanessa Bell, 1988. EDITOR: (with E. Steele) Julia Duckworth Stephen: Stories for Children, Essays for Adults, 1987; The Multiple Muses of Virginia Woolf, 1993; Roger Fry: A Biography by Virginia Woolf, 1995; (with L. Hankins) Virginia Woolf and the Arts: Selected Papers from the Sixth Annual Conference on Virginia Woolf, 1997; (with D. Birrer) Diana of Dobson's: A Romantic Comedy in Four Acts, 2003; (intro.) The Library of Leonard and Virginia Woolf: A Short-Title Catalog, 2004. Contributor to periodicals. **Address:** Department of English, Washington State University, PO Box 645020, Pullman, WA 99164-5020, U.S.A.

GILLESPIE, Gerald (Ernest Paul). American (born United States), b. 1933. **Genres:** Literary Criticism And History, Language/Linguistics, Translations, Romance/Historical. **Career:** University of Southern California, assistant professor of German and comparative literature, 1961-65; State University of New York, associate professor, 1965-66, professor of German, 1966-69, professor of comparative literature, 1966-74, Department of German, chair, 1969-71, Center for Translation and Intercultural Communication, director, 1973-74; University of Pennsylvania, visiting professor, 1969; New York University, visiting professor, 1970; Stanford University, School of Humanities & Sciences, Division of Literatures, Cultures and Languages, professor of German studies and comparative literature, 1974-99, emeritus professor, 1999-; University of Minnesota, visiting professor, 1978; Cambridge University, visiting fellow, 1979; International Comparative Literature Association, secretary-general, 1979-85, vice president, president, 1979-88, 1994-97. Writer. **Publications:** Daniel Casper von Lohenstein's Historical Tragedies, 1965; German Grammar, College Level, 1966; German Baroque Poetry,

1971; Ouzhou Xiaoshuo De Yanhua, 1987; Garden and Labyrinth of Time: Studies in Renaissance and Baroque Literature, 1988; Proust, Mann, Joyce in the Modernist Context, 2003, 2nd ed., 2010; By Way of Comparison: Reflections on the Theory and Practice of Comparative Literature, 2004; Echoland: Readings from Humanism to Postmodernism, 2006. EDITOR: (and trans.) Die Nachtwachen des Bonaventura, 1971; (and trans.) The Night Watches of Bonaventura, 1972; (and trans.) L. Tieck, Der gestiefelte Kater, 1974; (and trans.) Puss-in-Boots, 1974; (and trans. with A. Zahareas) R.M. del Valle-Inclan, Luces de Bohemia, Bohemian Lights, 1976; (with E. Lohner) Herkommen und Erneuerung: Essays fur Oskar Seidlin, 1976; (with G. Spellerberg) Studien zum Werk D.C. von Lohenstein, 1983; Litterature comparee/litterature mondiale, 1990; German Theater Before 1750, 1992; Romantic Drama, 1994; Visions in History, 1995; (with A. Lorant) Powers of Narration, 1995; (with R.A. Prier) Narrative Ironies, 1997; (with R.G. Cohn) Mallarmé in the Twentieth Century, 1998; (with S.P. Sondrup and V. Nemoianu) Nonfictional Romantic Prose: Expanding Borders, 2004; (with M. Engel and B. Dieterle) Romantic Prose Fiction, 2008. Contributor to journals. **Address:** School of Humanities & Sciences, Stanford University, 450 Serra Mall, Stanford, CA 94305-2030, U.S.A.

GILLESPIE, Hollis. American (born United States), b. 1962?. **Genres:** Novellas/Short Stories. **Career:** Writer and columnist. **Publications:** Bleachy-Haired Honky Bitch: Tales from a Bad Neighborhood, 2004; Confessions of a Recovering Slut and Other Love Stories, 2005; Trailer Trashed: My Dubious Efforts toward Upward Mobility, 2008. **Address:** Atlanta, GA , U.S.A. **Online address:** hollisthewriter@gmail.com

GILLESPIE, J(ohn) David. American (born United States), b. 1944. **Genres:** Politics/Government, History, Civil Liberties/Human Rights. **Career:** Davidson Community College, instructor in history and political science, 1967-70; Samford University, assistant professor of political science, 1973-78, associate professor, 1978-79; Presbyterian College, associate professor of political science, 1979-88, professor to Charles A. Dana professor, 1988-2006, department chair, 1985-88, 1990-91, vice president for academic affairs, 1997-2005, professor emeritus, 2007-; College of Charleston, adjunct professor, 2007-. **Publications:** Australian Journal of Politics and History, 1977; Policy Studies Journal, 1979; Phylon, 1979; Employment and Labor Relations Policy, 1980; Journal of Palestine Studies, 1985; Politics at the Periphery: Third Parties in Two-Party America, 1993; Reader's Guide to American History, 1997; Encyclopedia of the Democratic Party and Encyclopedia of the Republican Party, 1997; Journal of Political Science, 1998; Inter-Ethnic Relations in Estonia, 1988-1998, 1999; Encyclopedia of Third Parties in America, 2000; (Contrib.) Oxford Encyclopedia of the Modern World, 1750-Present, 2008; Challengers to Duopoly: Why Third Parties Matter in American Two-Party Politics, 2012. **Address:** Department of Political Science, College of Charleston, 66 George St., Charleston, SC 29424, U.S.A. **Online address:** jdavidgi@gmail.com

GILLESPIE, Raymond. British/Irish (born Ireland), b. 1955?. **Genres:** Social Sciences. **Career:** Civil Service, administrative officer, 1982-89, assistant principal, 1989-91; Maynooth College, lecturer in history, 1991-95, senior lecturer, 1995-; National University of Ireland, professor in modern history. Writer. **Publications:** Colonial Ulster: The Settlement of East Ulster, 1600-1641, 1985; Conspiracy: Ulster Plots and Plotters in 1615, 1987; Devoted People: Belief and Religion in Early Modern Ireland, 1997; (with B. Cunningham) Stories from Gaelic Ireland: Microhistories from the Sixteenth-Century Irish Annals, 2003; Reading Ireland: Print, Reading and Social Change in Early Modern Ireland, 2005; Seventeenth-Century Ireland: Making Ireland Modern, 2006; (with R. Refausse) The Medieval Manuscripts of Christ Church Cathedral, Dublin, 2006; (with S.A. Royle) Belfast c. 1600 to c. 1900: The Making of the Modern City, 2007; Early Belfast: The Origins and Growth of an Ulster Town to 1750, 2007. EDITOR: (with C. Brady) Natives and Newcomers: Essays on the Making of Irish Colonial Society, 1534-1641, 1986; (with G. Moran) A Various Country: Essays in Mayo History, 1500-1900, 1987; (with H. O'Sullivan) The Borderlands: Essays on the History of the Ulster-Leinster Border, 1989; (with G. Moran) Longford: Essays in County History, 1989; (with B.P. Kennedy) Ireland: Art into History, 1994; Cavan: Essays on the History of an Irish County, 1995, 2nd ed., 2004; The Proctor's Accounts of Peter Lewis, 1564-1565, 1996; Chapter Act Book of Christ Church Dublin, 1574-1634, 1996; (with G. Moran) Galway: History & Society, 1996; The First Chapter Act Book of Christ Church Cathedral, Dublin, 1574- 1634, 1997; (with M. Hill) Doing Irish Local History: Pursuit and Practice, 1998; (with A.J. Fletcher) Irish Preaching, 700-1700, 2001; (with P. Clark) Two Capitals: London and Dublin, 1500-1840, 2001; The

Vestry Records of the Parish of St. John the Evangelist, Dublin, 1595-1658, 2002; (with W.G. Neely) The Laity and the Church of Ireland, 1000-2000: All Sorts and Conditions, 2002; Scholar Bishop: The Recollections and Diary of Narcissus Marsh, 1638-1696, 2003; The Remaking of Modern Ireland, 1750-1950: Beckett Prize Essays in Irish History, 2004; The Vestry Records of the Parishes of St. Catherine and St. James, Dublin, 1657-1692, 2004; (with A. Hadfield) The Irish Book in English, 1550-1800, 2005; (with A. Simms and H.B. Clarke) Avril Thomas, Derry-Londonderry, 2005; (with E. FitzPatrick) The Parish in Medieval and Early Modern Ireland: Community, Territory and Building, 2006; (with M. Fanning) Print Culture and Intellectual Life in Ireland, 1660-1941: Essays in Honour of Michael Adams, 2006; (with J. Crawford) St Patrick's Cathedral, Dublin: A History, 2009. Contributor to books. **Address:** Department of History, National University of Ireland, Rm. 50, Rhetoric House, South Campus, Maynooth, 4, Ireland. **Online address:** raymond.gillespie@nuim.ie

GILLETT, Grant (Randall). New Zealander (born New Zealand), b. 1950. **Genres:** Philosophy, Medicine/Health, Psychology. **Career:** Resident and lecturer in neurosurgery, 1977-83; Oxford University, Magdalen College, fellow, 1985, fellow in philosophy, 1986-88; University of Otago, Bioethics Centre, Division of Health Sciences, associate professor of medical ethics and consultant neurosurgeon, 1988-, honorary lecturer in philosophy. Writer. **Publications:** (Ed. with A. Peacocke) Persons and Personality: A Contemporary Inquiry, 1987; Reasonable Care, 1989; Representation, Meaning and Thought, 1992; Practical Medical Ethics, 1992; The Mind and Its Discontents, 1994; (with R. Harre) The Discursive Mind, 1994; (ed. with K.W.M. Fulford and J.M. Soskice) Medicine and Moral Reasoning, 1994; The Mind and Its Discontents: An Essay in Discursive Psychiatry, 1999, 2nd ed., 2009; (with J. McMillan) Consciousness and Intentionality, 2001; (with A. Campbell and G. Jones) Medical Ethics, 2001, 4th ed., 2005; Bioethics in the Clinic: Hippocratic Reflections, 2004; Subjectivity and Being Somebody: Human Identity and Neuroethics, 2008. **Address:** Bioethics Research Centre, University of Otago, PO Box 56, Dunedin, 9054, New Zealand. **Online address:** grant.gillett@stonebow.otago.ac.nz

GILLETT, Margaret. Canadian/Australian (born Australia), b. 1930?. **Genres:** Novels, Education, Women's Studies And Issues, Autobiography/Memoirs, Biography. **Career:** New South Wales Education Department, teacher, 1951-53; Commonwealth Office of Education, education officer, 1954-57; Dalhousie University, assistant professor, 1961-62; Haile Selassie I University, registrar, 1962-65; McGill University, associate professor, 1965-67, professor, 1967-82, Macdonald professor of education, 1982-94, William C. Macdonald emeritus professor in education, 1994-, History and Philosophy of Education Department, chair, 1966-68, Social Foundations of Education Department, chair, 1979-80, Centre for Research and Teaching on Women, founding director, 1988, McGill Journal of Education, editor, 1966-77. **Publications:** A History of Education: Thought and Practice, 1966; (with M. Kehoe) The Laurel and the Poppy: A Novel About the Life of Francis Thompson, 1859-1907, 1967; Readings in the History of Education, 1969; Educational Technology: Toward Demystification, 1973; (with J.A. Laska) Foundation Studies in Education: Justifications and New Directions, A Source Book, 1973; We Walked Very Warily: A History of Women at McGill, 1981; Dear Grace: A Romance of History, 1986; Traf: A History of Trafalgar School for Girls, 2000. EDITOR: (with E.A. Grozier) Plot Outlines of 101 Best Novels, 1962; (with K. Sibbald) A Fair Shake: Autobiographical Essays by McGill Women, 1984; (and contrib. with A. Beer) Aspects of Education, 1991; (with A. Beer) Our Own Agendas: Autobiographical Essays by Women Associated with McGill University, 1995. **Address:** Department of Integrated Studies in Education, McGill University, Rm. 244, Education Bldg., 3700 McTavish St., Montreal, QC H3A 1Y2, Canada. **Online address:** margaret.gillett@mcgill.ca

GILLETTE, J(an) Lynett. American (born United States), b. 1946. **Genres:** Natural History, Animals/Pets, Science Fiction/Fantasy. **Career:** National Museum of History, Smithsonian Institution, Department of Physical Anthropology, technician and research assistant, 1972-74; oil exploration geologist, 1981-83; Ruth Hall Museum of Paleontology, curator of paleontology, 1986-97; Southwest Paleontology Foundation, president, 1987-92. Writer. **Publications:** Dinosaur Diary: My Triassic Homeland, 1988; The Search for Seismosaurus: The World's Longest Dinosaur, 1994; Dinosaur Ghosts: The Mystery of Coelophysis, 1997. **Address:** Dial Books, 375 Hudson St., New York, NY 10014-3658, U.S.A.

GILLEY, Sheridan (Wayne). British/Australian (born Australia), b. 1945. **Genres:** History, Theology/Religion, Biography. **Career:** University of St. Andrews, lecturer in ecclesiastical history, 1971-78; University of Durham, lecturer, 1978-82, senior lecturer in theology, 1982-94, reader in theology, 1994-2002, now emeritus reader, 2002-; writer, 1994-. **Publications:** Newman and His Age (biography), 1991, new ed., 2003. EDITOR: (with R. Swift) The Irish in the Victorian City, 1985; (with R. Swift) The Irish in Britain, 1815-1939, 1989; Religion, State, and Ethnic Groups, 1992; (with W.J. Sheils) A History of Religion in Britain, 1994; (with R. Swift) The Irish in Victorian Britain: The Local Dimension, 1999; Victorian Churches and Churchmen: Essays Presented to Vincent Alan McClelland, 2005; (with B. Stanley) World Christianities, c. 1815-1914, 2005. Contributor to periodicals. **Address:** Department of Theology, University of Durham, Abbey House, Palace Green, DU DH1 3RS, England.

GILLIES, David. Canadian/Indian (born India), b. 1952. **Genres:** Politics/Government. **Career:** Northeast London Probation Service, probation officer, 1979-83; International Centre for Human Rights and Democratic Development, policy adviser, 1991-94; Aga Khan Foundation, manager of policy and research, 1995-97; Canadian International Development Agency, governance adviser, 1998-; North-South Institute, executive interchange. Writer. **Publications:** (With G.J. Schmitz) Challenge of Democratic Development: Sustaining Democratization in Developing Societies, 1992; Between Principle and Practice: Human Rights in North-South Relations, 1996; (ed.) Strategies of Public Engagement: Shaping a Canadian Agenda for International Cooperation, 1997; Managing for Growth and Change, forthcoming. **Address:** Canadian International Development Agency, 200 Promenade du Portage, Gatineau, QC K1R 7X7, Canada. **Online address:** marie.cocking@sympatico.ca

GILLIES, Isabel Boyer. American (born United States), b. 1970. **Genres:** Autobiography/Memoirs. **Career:** Writer. **Publications:** Happens Every Day: An All-Too-True Story (memoir), 2009; A Year And Six Seconds: A Love Story, 2011. **Address:** c/o Bill Clegg, William Morris Agency, 1325 Ave. of the Americas, New York, NY 10019, U.S.A. **Online address:** isabel@isabelgillies.com

GILLIES, Valerie. (Valerie Simmons). Scottish/Canadian (born Canada), b. 1948. **Genres:** Poetry, Songs/Lyrics And Libretti, Adult Non-fiction, Literary Criticism And History. **Career:** Boroughmuir High School, writer-in-residence, 1978; Edinburgh Academy, writer-in-residence, 1983; Duncan of Jordanstone College of Art, writer-in-residence, 1988-90; Dundee District Libraries, writer-in-residence, 1988-90; Mid and East Lothian, writer-in-residence, 1991-93; University of Edinburgh, writer-in-residence, 1995-97, fellow in creative writing, 2003-. Writer. **Publications:** Trio: New Poets from Edinburgh, 1971; Each Bright Eye: Selected Poems, 1976; Bed of Stone, 1984; Leopardi: A Scottish Quair, 1987; Tweed Journey, 1989; The Chanter's Tune, 1990; The Ringing Rock, 1995; Men and Beasts, 2000; The Lightning Tree, 2002; The Spring Teller, 2009. Work appear in anthologies. Contributor to magazines. **Address:** Luath Press, 543/2 Castlehill, The Royal Mile, Edinburgh, EH1 2ND, Scotland. **Online address:** info@valeriegillies.com

GILLIGAN, Carol. American (born United States), b. 1936. **Genres:** Psychology, Women's Studies And Issues, Social Sciences. **Career:** University of Chicago, lecturer, 1965-66; Harvard University, lecturer on general education, 1967-69, lecturer, 1968-70, assistant professor, 1971-78, associate professor, 1978-86, professor, 1986-97, tutor in social relations, 1969-70, Harvard Graduate School of Education, Patricia Albjerg professor, 1997-2002; Princeton University, Christian Gauss Seminars in Criticism, lecturer, 1982; Rutgers University, Blanche, Edith and Irving Laurie New Jersey chair in women's studies, 1986-87; Michigan State University, Henry A. Murray lecture in personality, 1988; Spencer Foundation, senior research fellow, 1989-93; University of Cambridge, Pitt professor, 1992-93, Jesus College, visiting Bye fellow, 2003-05, fellow, 2004-; British Academy, visiting professor, 2005; New York University, university professor, 2002-. Writer. **Publications:** In a Different Voice: Psychological Theory and Women's Development, 1982; (with L.M. Brown) Meeting at the Crossroads: Women's Psychology and Girl's Development, 1992; (with J.M. Taylor and A.M. Sullivan) Between Voice and Silence: Women and Girls, Race and Relationship, 1995; Birth of Pleasure, 2002; Kyra: A Novel, 2008; (with D.A.J. Richards) Deepening Darkness: Patriarchy, Resistance and Democracy's Future, 2009; Joining the Resistance, 2011. EDITOR: (with J.V. Ward, J.M. Taylor and B. Bardige) Mapping the Moral Domain: A Contribution of Women's Thinking to Psychological Theory and Education, 1988; (with N.P. Lyons and T.J.

Hanmer) Making Connections: The Relational Worlds of Adolescent Girls at Emma Willard School, 1989; (with A.G. Rogers and D.L. Tolman) Women, Girls & Psychotherapy: Reframing Resistance, 1991. Contributor to periodicals. **Address:** School of Law, New York University, Rm. 511, Vanderbilt Hall, 40 Washington Sq. S, New York, NY 10012, U.S.A. **Online address:** carol.gilligan@nyu.edu

GILLIGAN, James F. American (born United States), b. 1935. **Genres:** Criminology/True Crime, Law, Medicine/Health. **Career:** Harvard Medical School, Department of Psychiatry, faculty; Medical School's Institute of Law and Psychiatry, director; Regional Adolescent Programs of the Departments of Mental Health and Youth Services, senior psychiatric consultant; University of Chicago, intern, 1965-66; Harvard University, Massachusetts Mental Health Center, resident in psychiatry, 1966-69, instructor, 1969-94, lecturer in psychiatry, 1994-, Erikson lecturer, 1991, supervising psychiatrist for psychiatric residency training program, 1969-77; McLean Hospital, Institute of Law and Psychiatry, director, 1977-80; Bridgewater State Hospital, deputy medical director, 1977, medical director, 1977-80, Center for the Study of Violence, medical director, 1991-92; Prison Mental Health Service, clinical director, 1981-91; Institute for Psychoanalysis, Esther Schour Zetland lecturer, 1992; University of Pennsylvania, visiting professor of psychiatry and social policy; New York University, School of Law, adjunct professor of law, School of Arts and Science, collegiate professor, School of Medicine, clinical professor of psychiatry; Cambridge University, Clare Hall, visiting fellow. Writer. **Publications:** Violence: Our Deadly Epidemic and Its Causes, 1996 as Violence: Reflections on a National Epidemic, 1997; The Future of the Prison: Reform or Replacement?, 1998; Violence: Reflections on a Western Epidemic, 1999; Violence in California Prisons: A Proposal for Research into Patterns and Cures, 2000; Preventing Violence: An Agenda for the Coming Century, 2001; (ed. with J. Devine and K.A. Miczek) Youth Violence: Scientific Approaches to Prevention, 2004. Contributor to books. **Address:** School of Law, New York University, 40 Washington Sq. S, New York, NY 10012-1005, U.S.A. **Online address:** james.gilligan@nyu.edu

GILLILAND, Alexis A(rnaldus). American (born United States), b. 1931. **Genres:** Science Fiction/Fantasy, Cartoons, Humor/Satire, Young Adult Non-fiction, Graphic Novels. **Career:** National Bureau of Standards, thermochemist, 1956-67; Federal Supply Service, chemist and specification writer, 1967-82; freelance writer and cartoonist, 1982-. **Publications:** NOVELS: The Revolution from Rosinante, 1981; Long Shot for Rosinante, 1981; The Pirates of Rosinante, 1982; The End of the Empire, 1983; Wizenbeak, 1986; The Shadow Shaia, 1990; The Lord of the Troll-Bats, 1992. CARTOONS: The Iron Law of Bureaucracy, 1979; Who Says Paranoia Isn't In Anymore, 1984; The Waltzing Wizard, 1989. **Address:** 4030 8th St. S, Arlington, VA 22204, U.S.A. **Online address:** leeandalexis@hotmail.com

GILLIS, Chester. American (born United States), b. 1951. **Genres:** Theology/Religion. **Career:** Drew University, assistant professor of philosophy of religion, 1987-88; Georgetown University, Department of Theology, assistant professor of theology, 1988-94, associate professor of theology, 1994-2000, chair, 2001-06, professor, 2001-, Doctor of Liberal Studies Program, director, 2006-08, Amaturo chair of Catholic studies, 2007-09, Berkley Center for Religion, Peace, and World Affairs, senior fellow, 2007-, Program on the Church and Interreligious Dialogue, founding director, 2007-, Berkley Center Undergraduate Fellows Program, faculty mentor, 2008, Georgetown College, interim dean, 2008-09, dean, 2009-; Smithsonian Institution, Resident Associates Program, lecturer. Writer. **Publications:** A Question of Final Belief: John Hick's Pluralistic Theory of Salvation, 1989; Pluralism: A New Paradigm for Theology, 1993; Roman Catholicism in America, 1999; Catholic Faith in America, 2003; (ed.) Political Papacy: John Paul II, Benedict XVI and Their Influence, 2006. Contributor to books and journals. **Address:** Georgetown University, 108 White Gravenor, 37th and O Streets NW, Washington, DC 20057, U.S.A. **Online address:** gillisc@georgetown.edu

GILLMAN, Abigail. American (born United States), b. 1964?. **Genres:** Theology/Religion. **Career:** Boston University, associate professor and division head of German and Hebrew. Writer. **Publications:** Viennese Jewish Modernism: Freud, Hofmannsthal, Beer-Hofmann and Schnitzler, 2009. **Address:** U.S.A. **Online address:** agillman@bu.edu

GILLMAN, Peter (Charles). British (born England), b. 1942. **Genres:** Communications/Media, Writing/Journalism, Biography, Documentaries/Reportage, Sports/Fitness, History, Autobiography/Memoirs. **Career:** Town,

assistant editor, 1964-65; Daily Telegraph, staff writer, 1965-66; freelance writer, 1966-69, 1983-; Radio Times, features editor, 1969-71; Sunday Times, staff writer, co-editor and correspondent, 1971-83; Editorial Training Consultants, training consultant. **Publications:** (With D. Haston) Direttissima: The Eiger Assault, 1966 in UK as Eiger Direct, 1966; (with E. Davenport and P. Eddy) The Plumbat Affair, 1978; Fitness on Foot: Climbing and Walking for Pleasure, 1978; (with P. Eddy and J. Connell) Siege!, 1980; (with L. Gillman) Collar the Lot!: How Britain Interned and Expelled Its Wartime Refugees, 1980; (with M. Linklater and P. Eddy) War in the Falklands in UK as The Falklands War, 1982; (with S. Peniston) Library Automation: A Current Review, 1984; (with L. Gillman) Alias David Bowie: A Biography, 1986; The Duty Men, 1987; In Balance: Twenty Years of Mountaineering Journalism, 1989; (ed.) Text Retrieval: Information First: Proceedings of the Institute of Information Scientists 1990 Text Retrieval Conference, London, October 1990, 1991; (ed.) Everest: The Best Writing and Pictures from Seventy Years of Human Endeavor, 1993; Everest: Eighty Years of Triumph and Tragedy, 2000; (with L.Gillman) The Wildest Dream: Biography of George Mallory in UK as The Wildest Dream: Mallory, His Life and Conflicting Passions, 2000. **Address:** 21 Warminster Rd., London, GL SE25 4DL, England. **Online address:** petergillman@clara.co.uk

GILLMEISTER, Heiner. German (born Germany), b. 1939. **Genres:** Literary Criticism And History, History, Language/Linguistics, Popular Culture, Sports/Fitness, Biography, Mystery/Crime/Suspense. **Career:** University of Bonn, lecturer, 1968-71, senior lecturer, 1971-2004; Kolnische Rundschau, theater critic, 1970-86; Dusseldorf University, deputy chair of English-language history and medieval literature, 1980-81; German Sports University, lecturer in sports history, 1980. Writer. **Publications:** Chaucer und die Via Regia, 1972; Chaucer's Conversion: Allegorical Thought in Medieval Literature, 1984; Aufschlag fur Walter von der Vogelweide. Tennis seit dem Mittelalter, 1986; Kulturgeschichte des Tennis, 1990, rev. ed. as Tennis: A Cultural History, 1997; (co-author) Der Rheinische Merlin: Text, Ubersetzung der Merlinund Luthild-Fragmente, 1991; Service. Kleine Geschichte der englischen Sprache, 1993, rev. ed. as Second Service, 2002; Olympisches Tennis. Die Geschichte der olympischen Tennisturniere (1896-1992), 1993; (ed.) In bester Gesellschaft: John Pius Boland-Reisetagebuch des Olympiasiegers aus dem Jahre 1896, trans. as In Good Company: John Pius Boland-The Diary of an Olympic Champion (Athens 1896), 2004; 100 Jahre Golf in Deutschland, vol. I, 2007; (ed.) From Bonn to Athens, Single and Return. The Diary of John Pius Boland, Olympic Champion, Athens 1896, 2008. Contributor to books and periodicals. **Address:** Department of English, American & Celtic Studies, University of Bonn, Regina-Pacis-Weg 5, Bonn, D-53113, Germany. **Online address:** h.gillmeister@uni-bonn.de

GILLON, Adam. American (born United States), b. 1921. **Genres:** Novels, Plays/Screenplays, Poetry, Film, Literary Criticism And History, Translations. **Career:** Acadia University, Department of English, professor of English, head, 1957-62; State University of New York-New Paltz, faculty, 1962-, professor of English and comparative literature, now professor emeritus; Twayne Publishers Inc., Polish Series, editor, 1963-72; Conradiana, regional editor, 1968-72; The Joseph Conrad Society of America, founder, 1974; Joseph Conrad Today, founding and senior editor, 1975-95; Haifa University, professor of English, 1979-84. **Publications:** The Eternal Solitary: A Study of Joseph Conrad, 1960; A Cup of Fury (novel), 1962; Selected Poems and Translations, 1962; (trans.) The Wrecked Life, 1963; In the Manner of Haiku, 1967; (and trans.) J. Tuwim, The Dancing Socrates and Other Poems, 1968; Daily New and Old: Poems in the Manner of Haiku, 1971; Strange Mutations, 1973; Summer Morn' Winter Weather (poems), 1975; Conrad and Shakespeare and Other Essays, 1976; Joseph Conrad, 1982; The Withered Leaf: A Medley of Haiku and Senryu, 1982; Jared (novel), 1989; Joseph Conrad: Comparative Essays, 1994. EDITOR: (trans. and contrib.) Introduction to Modern Polish Literature, 1964; (trans. and contrib.) Poems of the Ghetto: A Testament of Lost Men, 1969; (and trans.) Israeli Literature, 1970; An Anthology of French Romantic and Parnassian Poetry, 1982. **Address:** 490 State Rte. 299 W, New Paltz, NY 12561, U.S.A. **Online address:** conradfilm@aol.com

GILLON, Steven M. American (born United States), b. 1956. **Genres:** History, Politics/Government, Popular Culture, Biography. **Career:** University of Oklahoma, Carol E. Young professor, 1997-2004, Honors College, dean, 1997-2004; History Channel, resident historian, History Center, host, 1998-2002; Yale University, associate professor of history, faculty; Oxford University, lecturer in modern history. Writer. **Publications:** Politics and Vision: The ADA and American Liberalism, 1947-1985, 1987; The Democrats' Dilemma:

Walter F. Mondale and the Liberal Legacy, 1992; America during the Cold War, 1993; That's Not What We Meant to Do: Reform and Its Unintended Consequences in Twentieth-Century America, 2000; The American Experiment: A History of the United States, 2002; The American Paradox: A History of the United States since 1945, 2003; Boomer Nation: The Largest and Richest Generation Ever and How It Changed America, 2004; Ten Days that Unexpectedly Changed America, 2006; The Pact: Bill Clinton, Newt Gingrich and the Rivalry that Defined a Generation, 2008; Kennedy Assassination-24 Hours After: Lyndon B. Johnson's Pivotal First Day as President, 2009. **Address:** Honors College, University of Oklahoma, David L. Boren Hall, 1300 Asp Ave., Norman, OK 73019, U.S.A. **Online address:** smgillon@ou.edu

GILMAN, Andrew D. American (born United States), b. 1951. **Genres:** Communications/Media, inspirational/Motivational Literature, Language/Linguistics, Education. **Career:** Attorney in general practice, 1980-; Comm Core Consulting Group, president and chief executive officer, 1985-. Writer. **Publications:** (With K. Berg) Get to the Point: How to Say What You Mean and Get What You Want, 1989, 2nd ed., 1995. Contributor to journals and periodicals. **Address:** c/o Chris Tomasino, R.L.R. Associates, 7 W 51st St., New York, NY 10019, U.S.A. **Online address:** agilman@commcoreconsulting.com

GILMAN, Felix. British (born England), b. 1974?. **Genres:** Novels. **Career:** Law clerk, writer and attorney. **Publications:** International Spectrum Auction Handbook: Policies for Licensing Radio Spectrum in Nations around the World, 2000; Thunderer (fantasy novel), 2008; Gears of the City, 2009. **Address:** c/o Howard Morhaim, Howard Morhaim Literary Agency, 30 Pierrepont St., Brooklyn, NY 11201, U.S.A. **Online address:** felix@felixgilman.com

GILMAN, George G. Also writes as Thomas H. Stone, Joseph Hedges, Terry Harknett, William Terry, Charles R. Pine. British (born England), b. 1936. **Genres:** Mystery/Crime/Suspense, Westerns/Adventure, Travel/Exploration, Ghost Writer, Novels, Horror, Criminology/True Crime. **Career:** Reuters News Agency, copyboy, 1952; Newspapers Features Ltd., feature writer, 1952-54, editor, 1958-61; Reuters Comtelburo, typist, 1956-57; 20th-Century Fox, exploitation assistant, 1957-58; National Newsagent, features editor, 1958-71; reporter, 1961-72; Writer, 1971-. **Publications:** WESTERNS EDGE SERIES: The Loner, 1972; Ten Thousand Dollars, American in US as Ten Grand, 1972; Apache Death, 1972; Killer's Breed, 1972; Blood on Silver, 1972; The Blue, the Grey, and the Red in US as Red River, 1973; California Killing, 1973 in US as California Kill, 1974; Seven Out of Hell in US as Hell's Seven, 1973; Bloody Summer, 1973; Vengeance Is Black, 1973 in US as Black Vengeance, 1974; Sioux Uprising, 1974; The Biggest Bounty in US as Death's Bounty, 1974; A Town Called Hate, 1974 in US as The Hated, 1975; The Big Gold, 1974 in US as Tiger's Gold, 1975; Blood Run in US as Paradise Loses, 1975; The Final Shot, 1975; Vengeance Valley, 1975; Ten Tombstones to Texas, 1975 in US as Ten Tombstones, 1976; Ashes and Dust, 1976; Sullivan's Law, 1976; Rhapsody in Red, 1976; Slaughter Road, 1977; Echoes of War, 1977; The Day Democracy Died, 1977 in US as Slaughterday, 1978; Violence Trail, 1978; Savage Dawn, 1978; Eve of Evil, 1978; The Living, the Dying and the Dead, 1978; Waiting for a Train in US as Towering Nightmare, 1979; The Guilty Ones, 1979; The Frightened Gun, 1979; The Hated, 1979 in US as Red Fury, 1980; A Ride in the Sun, 1980; Death Deal, 1980; Two of a Kind: Edge Meets Steele, 1980; Town on Trial, 1981; Vengeance at Ventura, 1981; Massacre Mission, 1981; The Prisoners, 1981; Montana Melodrama, 1982; Matching Pair: Edge Meets Adam Steele, 1982; The Killing Claim, 1982; Bloody Sunrise, 1982; Arapaho Revenge, 1983; House on the Range, 1983; The Godforsaken, 1982; Edge Meets Steele No. 3 Double Action, 1984; Edge: The Blind Side, 1984; The Moving Cage, 1984; School for Slaughter, 1985; Revenge Ride, 1985; Shadow of the Gallows, 1985; A Time for Killing, 1986; Brutal Border, 1986; Hitting Paydirt, 1986; Backshot, 1987; Uneasy Riders, 1987; Doom Town, 1987; Dying Is Forever, 1987; The Desperadoes, 1988; Terror Town, 1988; The Breed Woman, 1989; The Rifle, 1989. ADAM STEELE SERIES: The Violent Peace, 1974 in US as Rebels and Assassins Die Hard, 1975; The Bounty Hunter, 1974; Hell's Junction, 1974; Valley of Blood, 1975; Gun Run, 1975; The Killing Art, 1975; Cross-Fire, 1975; Comanche Carnage, 1976; Badge in the Dust, 1976; The Losers, 1976; Lynch Town, 1976; Death Trail, 1977; Bloody Border, 1977; Delta Duel, 1977; River of Death, 1977; Nightmare at Noon, 1978; Satan's Daughters, 1978; The Hard Way, 1978; The Tarnished Star, 1979; Wanted for Murder, 1979; Wagons East, 1979; The Big Game, 1979; Fort Despair, 1979; Manhunt, 1980; Steele's War: The Woman, The Preacher, The Storekeeper, The Stranger, 4 vols., 1980-81; The Big Prize, 1981; The Killer Mountains,

1982; The Cheaters, 1982; The Wrong Man, 1982; The Valley of the Shadow, 1983; The Runaway, 1983; Stranger in a Strange Town, 1983; The Hellraisers, 1984; Canyon of Death, 1985; High Stakes, 1985; Rough Justice, 1985; The Sunset Ride, 1986; The Killing Strain, 1986; The Big Gunfight, 1987; The Hunted, 1987; Code of the West, 1987; The Outcasts, 1987; The Return, 1988; Trouble in Paradise, 1988; Going Back, 1989; The Long Shadow, 1989. THE UNDERTAKER SERIES: Black as Death, 1981; Destined to Die, 1981; Funeral by the Sea, 1981; Three Graves to a Showdown, 1982; Back from the Dead, 1982; Death in the Desert, 1982. AS WILLIAM TERRY, NOVELIZATIONS OF SCREENPLAYS: Once a Copper, 1965; A Town Called Bastard, 1971; Hannie Caulder, 1971; The Weekend Game, 1971; Red Sun, 1972. AS CHARLES R. PIKE: The Killing Trail, 1974; Double Cross, 1974; The Hungry Gun, 1975. AS WILLIAM M. JAMES, APACHE SERIES: The First Death, 1974; Duel to the Death, 1974; Fort Treachery, 1975; Sonora Slaughter, 1976; Blood on the Tracks, 1977; All Blood Is Red, 1977; The Best Man, 1979; Blood Rising, 1979; Born to Die, 1979; Slow Dying, 1980; Blood Brother, 1980; Blood Wedding, 1981; Border Killing, 1982; Times Past, 1983; Hanging, 1983; Death Valley, 1983; Death Ride, 1983; Debt of Blood, 1984. CROWN SERIES AS TERRY HARKNETT: The Sweet and Sour Kill, 1970; Macao Mayhem, 1974; Bamboo Shoot-out, 1975. CRIME NOVELS AS TERRY HARKNETT: The Benevolent Blackmailer, 1962; The Scratch on the Surface, 1962; Invitation to a Funeral, 1963; Dead Little Rich Girl, 1963; The Evil Money, 1964; The Man Who Did Not Die, 1964; Death of an Aunt, 1967; The Two-Way Frame, 1967; The Softciver Kill, 1971; Promotion Tour, 1972; Upmarket Affair, 1973; (with P. Haining) The Hero, 1973. AS THOMAS H. STONE: Dead Set, 1972; One Horse Race, 1972; A Stopover for Murder, 1973; Black Death, 1973; Squeeze Play, 1973. AS JOSEPH HEDGES: Funeral Rites, 1973; Arms for Oblivion, 1973; The Chinese Coffin, 1974; The Gold-Plated Hearse, 1974; The Rainbow-Coloured Shroud, 1974; Corpse on Ice, 1975; The Mile-Deep Grave, 1975. OTHER: (as William Pine) The Protectors, 1967; (as Jane Harmon) W.I.T.C.H., 1971; (as Frank Chandler) A Fistful of Dollars, 1972; The Caribbean, 1972; The Balearic Islands, 1972. **Address:** Spring Acre, Springhead Rd., Uplyme, Lyme Regis, DS DT7 3RJ, England. **Online address:** terry.harknett@btinternet.com

GILMAN, Keith. American (born United States), b. 1960?. **Genres:** Mystery/Crime/Suspense. **Career:** Police officer, 1993-. Writer. **Publications:** Father's Day, 2009. **Address:** Clarks Summit, PA , U.S.A. **Online address:** keith@keithgilman.com

GILMAN, Owen W(inslow). (M. Thrice). American (born United States), b. 1947. **Genres:** Novels, Film, Literary Criticism And History, Humor/Satire, Young Adult Fiction, Bibliography, Essays. **Career:** University of Maine at Farmington, instructor, 1975-76; St. Joseph's University, college council, chair, 1993-94; teaching and learning Center, director, 1995-97; Department of English, professor, chairman, 1997-2006, Writing Studies Program, director, 2002-. Writer. **Publications:** (Ed. with L. Smith) America Rediscovered: Critical Essays on Literature and Film of the Vietnam War, 1990; Vietnam, Chaos, and the Dark Art of Improvisation, in Inventing Vietnam: The War in Film and Television, 1991; Vietnam and John Winthrop's Vision of Community, in Fourteen Landing Zones: Approaches to Vietnam War Literature, 1991; Vietnam and the Southern Imagination, 1992; Barry Hannah, in Contemporary Fiction Writers of the South, Bio-Bibliographical Sourcebook, 1993; The Spanish-American War, World War I, World War II, Korean War, Vietnam War, all in Companion to Southern Literature, 2002; (ed. with P. Rollins) The South, in History and Film, 2004. Contributor to journals. **Address:** Department of English, St. Joseph's University, Merion Hall 115, Philadelphia, PA 19131, U.S.A. **Online address:** ogilman@sju.edu

GILMORE, David D. American (born United States), b. 1943. **Genres:** Anthropology/Ethnology, Psychology, Social Sciences. **Career:** University of Pennsylvania, lecturer in anthropology, 1975-76; Rutgers University, lecturer in anthropology, 1976; University of Iowa, assistant professor of anthropology, 1976-77; State University of New York, Stony Brook University, faculty, assistant professor, 1977-80, associate professor, 1980-86, professor of anthropology and head of department, 1986-; Covington Fabrics Corp., board director. Writer. **Publications:** The People of the Plain: Class and Community in Lower Andalusia, 1980; Aggression and the Community: Paradoxes of Andalusian Culture, 1987; (ed.) Honor and Shame and the Unity of the Mediterranean, 1987; (comp. with S.C. Rogers and M. Clegg) Directory of Europeanist Anthropologists in North America, 1987; Manhood in the Making: Cultural Concepts of Masculinity, 1990; Carnival and Culture: Sex, Symbol and Status in Spain, 1998; Misogyny: The Male Malady, 2001; Monsters:

Evil Beings, Mythical Beasts and All Manner of Imaginary Terrors, 2003. Contributor to books. **Address:** Department of Anthropology, Stony Brook University, State University of New York, Circle Rd., SBS Bld., 5th Fl., Stony Brook, NY 11794-4364, U.S.A. **Online address:** david.gilmore@sunysb.edu

GILMORE, Dewitt. (Relentless Aaron). American (born United States), b. 1965?. **Genres:** Young Adult Non-fiction. **Career:** Relentless Content (publishing house), founder and publisher; Superstar (magazine), publisher. Writer. **Publications:** AS RELENTLESS AARON: Rappers 'R in Danger, 2000; Push, 2003; The Last Kingpin, 2004; Platinum Dolls, 2004; Triple Threat, 2004; I Did It! You Can Too!! (nonfiction), 2004; Seems Like You're Ready, 2005; Sugar Daddy, 2005; Topless, 2005; Live & Die in Harlem, 2005; Extra Marital Affairs, 2006; Derelict, 2007; Lady First, 2007; Single with Benefits, 2008; Burning Desire, 2009; Bumrush, 2010. **Address:** Macmillan, 175 5th Ave., New York, NY 10010, U.S.A. **Online address:** relentless@relentlessaaron.com

GILMORE, Glenda Elizabeth. American (born United States), b. 1949. **Genres:** Novels, History, Politics/Government, Young Adult Fiction. **Career:** Queens College, assistant professor, 1992-94; Yale University, professor, 1994-2001; Peter V. and C. Vann Woodward professor of history, 2001-, National Humanities Center, John Hope Franklin senior fellow, 2006-07, African American Studies, chair, 2008-09. Writer. **Publications:** Gender and Jim Crow: Women and the Politics of White Supremacy in North Carolina, 1896- 1920, 1996; (ed. with J. Dailey and B. Simon) Jumpin' Jim Crow: Southern Politics from Civil War to Civil Rights, 2000; (ed. and intro.) Who Were the Progressives? Readings, 2002; Defying Dixie: The Radical Roots of Civil Rights, 1919-1950, 2008. **Address:** Department of History, Yale University, PO Box 208324, New Haven, CT 06520-8324, U.S.A. **Online address:** glenda.gilmore@yale.edu

GILMORE, John. American (born United States), b. 1935. **Genres:** Criminology/True Crime, Novels, Autobiography/Memoirs, Plays/Screenplays. **Career:** Actor; director of films; Antioch College, teacher of writing, head; London Express News and Feature Service, writer and journalist, 1972-78. **Publications:** Eyetooth, 1962; Dark Obsession, 1963; Strange Fire, 1963; Hot Spot, 1968; Night Shark, 1969; The Tucson Murders, 1967; Overpass Blues, 1967; City of Suicide, 1970; The Garbage People, 1971, rev. ed. as The Garbage People: The Trip to Helter-Skelter and Beyond with Charlie Manson and the Family, 1995; The Real James Dean, 1975; Severed: The True Story of the Black Dahlia Murder, 1994; Wrecked Lives: Fame, Sex & Hollywood, 1994; Cold Blooded, 1996; Laid Bare, 1997; Live Fast-Die Young: Remembering the Short Life of James Dean, 1997; Fetish Blond (novel), 1999; You Can't Sleep in a Car in Hollywood, 1999; Manson, 2000; Hollywood Boulevard, 2004; Crazy Streak, 2006; Inside Marilyn Monroe, 2007. Contributor to periodicals. **Address:** c/o Richard Curtis, 156 E 52nd St., New York, NY 10022, U.S.A. **Online address:** gilmore@johngilmore.com

GILMORE, Kate. American (born United States), b. 1931. **Genres:** Horticulture, Children's Fiction, History, Science Fiction/Fantasy. **Career:** Writer, 1983-; Arboretal Artifacts, co-director and craftsman, 1989-. **Publications:** Of Griffins and Graffiti, 1986; Remembrance of the Sun, 1986; Enter Three Witches, 1991; Jason and the Bard, 1993; The Exchange Student, 1999. **Address:** Metropolis Ensemble, 421 W 24th St., Ste. 4C, PO Box 1315, New York, NY 10011, U.S.A. **Online address:** gilmore.kate@gmail.com

GILMORE, Rachna. (Rachna Mara). Canadian (born Canada), b. 1953?. **Genres:** Children's Fiction, Novellas/Short Stories, Young Adult Fiction, Novels, Picture/Board Books. **Career:** Writer. **Publications:** FOR CHILDREN: My Mother Is Weird, 1988; When-I-was-a-Little-Girl, 1989, 2nd ed., 2006; Jane's Loud Mouth, 1990; Aunt Fred Is a Witch, 1991; Lights for Gita, 1994; A Friend Like Zilla, 1995; Roses for Gita, 1996; Wild Rilla, 1997; A Gift for Gita, 1998; A Screaming Kind of Day, 1999; Fangs and Me, 1999; Ellen's Terrible TV Troubles, 1999; Mina's Spring of Colors, 2000; A Group of One, 2001; The Sower of Tales, 2005; Grandpa's Clock, 2006; Making Grizzle Grow, 2007; The Trouble With Dilly, 2009; Catching Time, 2010; That Boy Red, 2011; The Flute, 2011. FOR ADULTS AS RACHNA MARA: Of Customs and Excise, 1991. **Address:** Ottawa, ON , Canada. **Online address:** rachnagilmore@hotmail.com

GILMORE, Ruth Wilson. American (born United States), b. 1950. **Genres:** History. **Career:** City University of New York, professor of geography; University of Southern California, Department of American Studies and Ethnic-ity, associate professor and chair; Critical Resistance, California Prison Moratorium Project, founding member; Central California Environmental Justice Network, president. Writer. **Publications:** Golden Gulag: Prisons, Surplus, Crisis, and Opposition in Globalizing California, 2007. Contributor to books. **Address:** U.S.A. **Online address:** rwgilmor@email.usc.edu

GILMORE, Susan Gregg. American (born United States), b. 1961?. **Genres:** Novels. **Career:** Free Press, staff member, columnist; Smithsonian Institution, secretary. **Publications:** Looking for Salvation at the Dairy Queen (novel), 2008. Contributor to periodicals. **Address:** Braun Associates, Inc., 151 W 19th St., 4th Fl., New York, NY 10011, U.S.A.

GILMOUR, David. Scottish/British (born England), b. 1952. **Genres:** Novels, Local History/Rural Topics, Travel/Exploration, Biography. **Career:** Middle East Intl., deputy editor and contributing editor, 1978-85; St. Antony's College, fellow, 1996-97. **Publications:** Dispossessed: The Ordeal of the Palestinians, 1917-1980, 1980; Lebanon: The Fractured Country, 1983; The Transformation of Spain: From Franco to the Constitutional Monarchy, 1985; The Glass Bottom Boat: Fish Managers at Work, 1987; The Hungry Generations, 1991; Cities of Spain, 1992; The Pursuit of Italy: A History of a Land, Its Regions and Their Peoples, 2011. BIOGRAPHIES: The Last Leopard: A Life of Giuseppe di Lampedusa, 1988 in UK as The last Leopard: A Life of Giuseppe Tomasi di Lampedusa, 2007; Curzon, 1994 in US as Curzon: Imperial Statesman, 2003; The Long Recessional: The Imperial Life of Rudyard Kipling, 2002; Ruling Caste: Imperial Lives in the Victorian Raj, 2006. EDITOR: (and intro.) The French and Their Revolution, 1998; (and intro.) Paris and Elsewhere, 1998. Contributor to periodicals. **Address:** Aitken, Stone and Wylie, 29 Fernshaw Rd., London, GL SW10 0TG, England.

GILMOUR, David. Canadian (born Canada), b. 1949. **Genres:** Novels, Young Adult Fiction, Autobiography/Memoirs, Human Relations/Parenting. **Career:** Toronto Film Festival, managing editor, 1979-83; Canadian Broadcasting Corp., The Journal, film critic, 1986-97; University of Toronto, Victoria College, Pelham Edgar professor of literary studies, 2007-. **Publications:** NOVELS: Back on Tuesday, 1986, rev. ed., 2006; How Boys See Girls, 1991; An Affair With The Moon, 1993; Lost Between Houses, 1999; Sparrow Nights, 2001; A Perfect Night to Go to China, 2005; The Film Club. 2007; The Perfect Order of Things, 2011. OTHER: Glass Bottom Boat (nonfiction), 1986. **Address:** Victoria College, 73 Queen's Park Crescent, Toronto, ON M5S 1K7, Canada. **Online address:** gilmourd@hosers.com

GILMOUR, John C. American (born United States), b. 1939. **Genres:** Philosophy, Art/Art History. **Career:** Hofstra University, instructor, assistant professor of philosophy, 1963-68; Norwich University, assistant professor of philosophy, 1968-70; Alfred University, College of Liberal Arts and Sciences, assistant professor, associate professor, 1970-81, professor of philosophy, 1981-91, Margaret and Barbara Hagar professor in the humanities, 1991-96, Kruson distinguished professor of philosophy, 1996-2001, Kruson distinguished professor emeritus of philosophy, 2001-. Writer. **Publications:** Picturing the World, 1986; Fire on the Earth: Anselm Kiefer and the Postmodern World, 1990. Contributor of articles to journals. **Address:** College of Liberal Arts and Sciences, Division of Human Studies, Alfred University, 1 Saxon Dr., Alfred, NY 14802-1205, U.S.A. **Online address:** gilmourj@midcoast.com

GILMOUR, Michael J. Canadian (born Canada), b. 1967. **Genres:** Literary Criticism And History, Theology/Religion, Music. **Career:** Providence College, sessional instructor, 1994-95, faculty, 1998-, associate professor of New Testament and English literature; McGill University, sessional instructor, 1998; University of Manitoba, sessional instructor, 2001-04; Booth College, sessional instructor, 2004-; St. John's College, sessional instructor, 2007-. Writer. **Publications:** The Significance of Parallels between 2 Peter and Other Early Christian Literature, 2002; Tangled Up in the Bible: Bob Dylan and Scripture, 2004; (ed.) Call Me the Seeker: Listening to Religion in Popular Music, 2005; Gods and Guitars: Seeking The Sacred in Post-1960s Popular Music, 2009; Gospel According to Bob Dylan: The Old, Old Story for Modern Times, 2011. Contributor of articles to periodicals. **Address:** Providence College, Department of College Academics, 10 College Cres., Otterburne, MB R0A 1G0, Canada. **Online address:** michael.gilmour@prov.ca

GILPIN, Geoff. American (born United States), b. 1953. **Genres:** Sociology, Autobiography/Memoirs, Education. **Career:** Software Resource Publications Inc., co-owner, 1994-98. Writer and consultant. **Publications:** Ada: A Guided Tour and Tutorial, 1985; The Maharishi Effect: A Personal Journey through the Movement That Transformed American Spirituality, 2006. **Address:** Penguin Group Inc., 375 Hudson St., New York, NY 10014-3657, U.S.A. **Online address:** geoff@geoffgilpin.com

GILREATH, Shannon. American (born United States), b. 1977. **Genres:** Gay And Lesbian Issues, Politics/Government, Law, Sex. **Career:** Wake Forest University, Law School, American Law Program, International Graduate Programs, assistant director of master of laws, 2003-, Divinity School, associate professor of law, 2004-, adjunct professor of law, 2004-08, adjunct professor of women's and gender studies, 2005-, Undergraduate Women's and Gender Studies Program, instructor, fellow, 2008-, professor of interdisciplinary study, 2008-. Writer and attorney. **Publications:** Sexual Politics: The Gay Person in America Today, 2006; Sexual Identity Law in Context: Cases and Materials, 2007, 2nd ed., 2011; The End of Straight Supremacy: Realizing Gay Liberation, 2012. **Address:** School of Law, Wake Forest University, 2214 Worrell Professional Ctr., 1834 Wake Forest Rd., PO Box 7206, Winston-Salem, NC 27109, U.S.A. **Online address:** gilreasd@law.wfu.edu

GILROY, Frank D(aniel). American (born United States), b. 1925. **Genres:** Novels, Plays/Screenplays, Film. **Career:** Dramatists Guild, president, 1969-71. Playwright, film director and producer. **Publications:** PLAYS: The Middle World, 1949; Who'll Save the Plowboy?: Drama in Two Acts, 1962; The Subject Was Roses, 1962; That Summer-That Fall, & Far Rockaway, 1967; The Only Game in Town, 1968; Present Tense: Four Plays, 1972; Last Licks, 1979; The Next Contestant: A Drama in One Act, 1979; Dreams of Glory: A Play in One Act, 1980; Real to Reel, 1987; Match Point, 1990; Give the Bishop My Faint Regards, 1992; A Way with Words: Five One Act Plays, 1993; I Wake Up Screening!: Everything You Need to Know about Making Independent Films Including a Thousand Reasons Not To (non-fiction), 1993; Fore, 1993; Any Given Day: A Drama, 1994; The Golf Ball, 1999; Contact with the Enemy, 1999; Getting In: And, Contact with the Enemy, 2000; Frank D. Gilroy, 2000; Inspector Ohm, 2001. OTHERS: About Those Roses: Or, How Not to Do a Play and Succeed, and the Text of the Subject was Roses, 1956; (with R.C. Gilroy) Little Ego (for children), 1970; From Noon Till Three: The Possibly True and Certainly Tragic Story of an Outlaw and a Lady Whose Love Knew no Bounds, 1973; (with R. Rouse) The Fastest Gun Alive, 1981; (with D.J. Cohen) The Gig, 2000. NOVELS: Private, 1970; From Noon till Three: The Possibly True and Certainly Tragic Story of an Outlaw and a Lady Whose Love Knew No Bounds, 1973 in UK as For Want of a Horse, 1975; Writing for Love and Money: Outtakes from a Life on Spec: The Early Years, 2007. **Address:** Dramatists Guild of America, 1501 Broadway, Ste. 710, New York, NY 10036, U.S.A.

GILSDORF, Ethan. American (born United States), b. 1970?. **Genres:** Sports/Fitness. **Career:** Boston Globe, book and film critic; Grub Street, writing instructor, Young Adult Writers Program, co-founder; Emerson College, writing instructor; Media Bistro, writing instructor. Writer. **Publications:** Fantasy Freaks and Gaming Geeks: An Epic Quest for Reality among Role Players, Online Gamers, and Other Dwellers of Imaginary Realms, 2009. Contributor to periodicals. **Address:** c/o Sorche Fairbank, Fairbank Literary Representation, 199 Mount Auburn St., Ste. 1, Cambridge, MA 02138, U.S.A.

GILSON, Chris. See **GILSON, Christopher C.**

GILSON, Christopher C. (Chris Gilson). American (born United States) **Genres:** Business/Trade/Industry, Novels, Marketing, Romance/Historical, Young Adult Fiction. **Career:** Writer. **Publications:** (With H.W. Berkman) Consumer Behavior: Concepts and Strategies, 1978, 3rd ed., 1986; (with L.C. Cawley and W.R. Schmidt) How to Market Your Law Practice, 1979; (with H.W. Berkman) Advertising Concepts and Strategies, 1980, 2nd ed., 1987; (with L. Cawley and R. Schmidt) Consumer Revenge, 1981; (as Chris Gilson) Dare to Be Square, 1988; (as Chris Gilson) Crazy for Cornelia (novel), 2000. **Address:** c/o Author Mail, Warner Books, 1271 Ave. of the Americas, New York, NY 10020, U.S.A. **Online address:** chris@chrisgilson.com

GILSON, Simon A. British (born England) **Genres:** Literary Criticism And History. **Career:** University of Leeds, lecturer in Italian, 1998-99; University of Warwick, associate professor of Italian, 1999-; University of Oxford, staff; University of Birmingham, staff; Keio University, staff. Writer. **Publications:** Medieval Optics and Theories of Light in the Works of Dante, 2000; (ed. with P. Antonello) Science and Literature in Italian Culture from Dante to Calvino: A Festschrift for Patrick Boyde, 2004; Dante and Renaissance Florence, 2005.

Address: Department of Italian, University of Warwick, Coventry, CV4 7AL, England. **Online address:** s.gilson@warwick.ac.uk

GILSTRAP, John. American (born United States), b. 1957?. **Genres:** Mystery/Crime/Suspense, Plays/Screenplays, Novels, Young Adult Non-fiction, History. **Career:** Fairfax County, Burke Volunteer Fire Department, staff. Novelist. **Publications:** NOVELS: Nathan's Run, 1996; At All Costs, 1998; Even Steven, 2000; Scott Free, 2003; No Mercy, 2009; Hostage Zero, 2010. NON-FICTION: (with K. Muse) Six Minutes To Freedom, 2006; Threat Warning, 2011. **Address:** c/o Anne Hawkins, John Hawkins & Associates, 71 W 23rd St., Ste. 1600, New York, NY 10010, U.S.A. **Online address:** john@johngilstrap.com

GIMBLETT, Richard H. (Richard Howard Gimblett). Canadian (born Canada), b. 1956?. **Genres:** Military/Defense/Arms Control, Adult Non-fiction. **Career:** Royal Military College, military staff, 1985-87; HMCS Preserver, Combat Officer, 1988-89; Range Safety Officer, gunnery instructor, 1990; HMCS Protecteur, combat officer, 1990-91; Directorate of Access to Information and Privacy, staff officer, 1994-97; DHH, historian, 1998-99; Chief of Maritime Staff, staff officer, 1999; Canadian Navy, command historian, staff advisor; Dalhousie University, research fellow; Canadian Nautical Research Society, president; Maritime Strategy, analyst, directorate, 2000-01; Queen's University, adjunct professor of history; independent researcher, analyst and writer, 2001-05; Canadian Forces College, visiting faculty; Canadian Navy, command historian, 2006-. **Publications:** (With J.H. Morin) Operation Friction, 1990-1991: The Canadian Forces in the Persian Gulf, 1997; Operation Apollo: The Golden Age of the Canadian Navy in the War against Terrorism, 2004; (ed. and contrib. with M. Whitby and P. Haydon) The Admirals: Canada's Senior Naval Leadership in the Twentieth Century, 2006; (with A. Brown) In the Footsteps of the Canadian Corps: Canada's First World War 1914-1918, 2006; (with A. English and H. Coombs) Networked Operations and Transformation: Context and Canadian Contributions, 2006; (ed. with R.O. Mayne) People, Policy and Progammes: Proceedings of the 7th Maritime Command (MARCOM) Historical Conference (2005), 2008; (ed.) The Naval Service of Canada, 1910-2010: The Centennial Story, 2009; (with A. Brown) In the Footsteps of the First Canadian Army: Northwest Europe 1943-1945, 2009. **Address:** National Defence Headquarters, 101 Colonel By Dr., Ottawa, ON K1A 0K2, Canada. **Online address:** richard.gimblett@sympatico.ca

GIMBLETT, Richard Howard. See **GIMBLETT, Richard H.**

GIMFERRER, Pere. Spanish (born Spain), b. 1945. **Genres:** Novels, Translations. **Career:** Editorial Seix Barral (publishing company), staff, 1970, director, 1981-; Real Academy Española, academician, 1985-; Ediciones 62 (publishing company), poetry advisor. Writer. **Publications:** IN CATALAN EXCEPT AS NOTED: Mensaje del tetarca, 1963; Arde el mar, 1966; Tres poemas, 1967; La muerte en Beverly Hills, 1968; (trans.) J. Brossa, Teatro: Oro y sal, el gancho, Novela, 1968; Antología de la poesía modernista, 1969; Poemas, 1962-1969, 1969; (trans.) S. Beckett, Molloy, 1969; Els miralls, 1970; Treinta años de litertura, 1971; Hora foscant, 1972; La clau del foc, 1973; La poesía de J.V. Foix, 1973; Foc cec, 1973; (with A. Tàpies) Antoni Tàpies i l'esperit català, 1974; (with A. Tàpies) Tàpies: indagacions i presències, 1974; L'espai desert, 1977; (intro.) Juan Goytisolo, Obras completas, 1977; (with M. Ernst) Max Ernst: o la dissolució de la identitat, 1977; (with J. Miró) Miró y su mundo, 1978; (intro.) Ausias March, 1978; Radicalidades, 1978; (with J. Miró) Miró, colpir sense nafrar, 1978; Poesía, 1970-1977, 1978; Imágenes y recuerdos, 1910-1920: la pérdida del reino, 1979; Lecturas de Octavio Paz, 1980; (ed.) J. Brossa, Antología poética: 1941-1978, 1980; (with J. Goytisolo) Juan Goytisolo, 1981; (trans.) R. Llull, Obra escogida, 1981; Mirall, espai, aparicions: poesía, 1970-1980, 1981; Dietari, 1979-1980, 1981; Antología de la poesía modernista, 1981; (with G. Sansone) Curial y Gielfa, 1982; Segon dietari, 1980-1982, Apariciones y otras poemas, 1982; Octavio Paz, 1982; Fortuny, 1983; (intro.) El cuento de invierno; La tempestad, 1983; (with J.V. Foix) Antología poética, 1984; (with F. Ayala) Pefil de Vicente Aleixandre: discursso leido el dia 15 de diciembre de 1985 en el acto de su recepción pública, 1985; Los raros, 1985; Cine y literatura, 1985; (intro.) Magritte, 1986; (intro.) Ramon del Valle-Inclan, Sonata de primavera; sonata de estío; memoiras del Marqués de Bradomin, 1988; (co-author) El jardí dels guerrers, 1988; Giorgio de Chirico, 1988; El vendaval, 1988; Toulouse-Lautrec, 1991; (with J. Navarro) La llum/La luz, 1992; (with J. Noguero) Valències, 1971-1993, 1993; Pere Gimferrer: una poética del instante, 1993; Las raíces de Miró, 1993; (with J.M. Castellet) Dietari complet, 1994; Obra Catalana complete, vol. I: Poesia, vol. II: Dietari complete, 1979-1980, vol. III: Dietari complete, 1980-1982, vol. IV: Figures d'art, vol. V: Assaigs crítics, 1995; (with M. Rodoreda) Espejo roto, 1995; (with J. Jorda) Itinerario de un escritor, 1996; Noche en el ritz, 1996; Mascarada, 1996; L'obrador del poeta, 1996; Literatura catalana i periodisme, 1996; (with A. Gala) Poemas de amor, 1997; 24 poemas, 1997; Piedra de sol (lecture on O. Paz), 1998; L'agent provocador, 1998; (with S. Espriu) Sinònims i antònims de la llengua catalana, 1998; (author of prologue) Poesies i altres escrits, 1998; (ed.) P. Neruda, Poemas, 1998; (with T. Moix) Chulas y famosas, o bien, la venganza de Eróstrato, 1999; Los raros, 1999; Antología poètica, 1999; Memorias y palabras: cartas a Pere Gimferrer, 1966-1997, 1999; (with D. Alcoba) Cinco decadas de literatura internacional, 1999; (author of prologue) Maria-Mercè Marçal, Raó del cos, 2000; (author of prologue) Jose Maria Fonoliosa, 2000; (with L.G. Jambrina) Marea solar, marea lunar (poetry in Spanish and Catalan), 2000; (with J. Barella) Poemas, 1962-1969: poesía castellana completa, 2000; El diamant dins l'aigua, 2001; (co-author) La revolta poètica de Joan Brossa, 2003; Rimbaud y nosotros, 2005; Amor en vilo, 2006; Interludio azul, 2006; Tornado, 2008. OTHERS: Rapsodia, 2011. **Address:** Editorial Seix Barral, Diagonal 662-664, Barcelona, 08034, Spain.

GINDORF (PROF. DR.), Rolf. German (born Germany), b. 1939. **Genres:** Sex, Psychology, Sociology, Gay And Lesbian Issues. **Career:** International Businessman: Heinrich Schulte Industrieausruestungen Co., staff, 1959-71, president, 1965-71; Deutsche Gesellschaft fuer Sozialwissenschaftliche Sexualforschung (DGSS), founding president, 1971-78, vice-president, 1978-2004, honorary president, 2004-; Institut fuer Lebens und Sexualberatung, director and research and clinical sexologist, 1978-; Shanghai Sex Research Center, scientific adviser. Writer. **Publications:** IN ENGLISH TRANSLATION: (with E.J. Haeberle) Sexology Today, 1993; (ed. with Haeberle and contrib.) Bisexualitaeten, 1994; (ed. with E.J. Haeberle) Bisexualities: The Ideology and Practice of Sexual Contact with Both Men and Women, 1998. CO-EDITOR: IN GERMAN: Beitraege zur Sozialwissenschaftlichen Sexualforschung, 1979; Schriftenreihe Sozialwissenschaftliche Sexualforschung, 1986; (with J.C. Aigner and contrib.) Von der Last der Lust: Sexualität zwischen Liberalisierung und Entfremdung, 1986; (with E.J. Haeberle and contrib.) Sexualität als Sozialer Tatbestand: Theoretische und empirische Beiträge zu einer Soziologie der Sexualitäten, 1986; (with E.J. Haeberle and contrib.) Sexualitäten in unserer Gesellschaft, 1989; Sexualitaeten in unserer Gesellschaft: Beitraege zur Geschichte, Theorie und Empirie, 1989; (with E.J. Haeberle) Sexualwissenschaft und Sexualpolitik: Spannungsverhältnisse in Europa, Amerika und Asien, 1992; (with E.J. Haeberle) Sexualwissenschaft Heute, 1992. Contributor to journals and periodicals. **Address:** Deutsche Gesellschaft fuer Sozialwissenschaftliche, Sexualforschung, 20 Gerresheimer St., Duesseldorf, D-40211, Germany. **Online address:** rolf.gindorf@sexologie.org

GINSBERG, Blaze. American (born United States), b. 1987?. **Genres:** Autobiography/Memoirs. **Career:** Author. **Publications:** Episodes: My Life as I See It (autobiography), 2009. **Address:** San Diego, CA , U.S.A. **Online address:** blaze@blazeginsberg.com

GINSBORG, Paul (Anthony). Italian/British (born England), b. 1945?. **Genres:** Politics/Government, History, Social Sciences. **Career:** University of Florence, Department of Historical and Geographical Studies, professor of contemporary European history, 1992-; Churchill College, faculty and research fellow; University of Turin, visiting professor; University of Siena, visiting professor. Writer. **Publications:** The Politics of Lenin (pamphlet), 1974; Daniele Manin and the Venetian Revolution of 1848-49, 1979; Storia d'Italia dal dopoguerra a oggi: società e politica, 1943-1988, 1989, trans. as A History of Contemporary Italy: Society and Politics, 1943-1988, 1990; (ed. with J.A. Davis) Society and Politics in the Age of the Risorgimento: Essays in Honour of Denis Mack Smith, 1991; (ed.) Stato dell'Italia, 1994; L'Italia del tempo presente: famiglia, società civile, stato, 1980-1996, 1998, trans. as Italy and Its Discontents: Family, Civil Society, State, 1980-2001, 2001; (ed. with F. Ramella) Un'Italia minore: Famiglia, istruzione e tradizioni civiche in Valdelsa, 1999; Silvio Berlusconi: Television, Power and Patrimony, 2004, new ed., 2005; Tempo di cambiare: Politica e potere della vita quotidiana, 2004; Politics of Everyday Life: Making Choices, Changing Lives, 2005; Democrazia che non c'è, 2006; Democracy: Crisis and Renewal, 2008; Salviamo l'Italia, 2010; (ed. with E. Asquer) Berlusconismo, 2011. Contributor to periodicals. **Address:** Department of Geography, University of Florence, Via S. Gallo, Florence, 10-50129, Italy. **Online address:** paulanthony.ginsborg@unifi.it

GINSBURG, Faye D(iana). American (born United States), b. 1952. **Genres:** Sex, Women's Studies And Issues, Film. **Career:** WCCO-TV, associate documentary producer, 1981-83; New York University, professor of anthropology and director of program in culture and media, 1986-, Graduate Program in Culture and Media, director, Center for Religion and Media, co-director, 1992-, Center of Culture and History, director, 1992-, David B. Kriser professor of anthropology; New School for Social Research, visiting assistant professor of anthropology, 1985-86. Writer. **Publications:** Contested Lives: The Abortion Debate in an American Community, 1989; (ed. with A.L. Tsing) Uncertain Terms: Negotiating Gender in American Culture, 1990; (ed. with R. Rapp) Conceiving the New World Order: The Global Politics of Reproduction, 1995; (co-ed.) 9/11 and After, A Virtual Case Book, 2002; (ed. with L.A. Lughod and B. Larkin) Media Worlds: Anthropology on New Terrain, 2002; Mediating Culture: Indigenous Media in a Digital Age, forthcoming. **Address:** Department of Anthropology, New York University, 25 Waverly Pl., New York, NY 10003, U.S.A. **Online address:** faye.ginsburg@nyu.edu

GINSBURG, Mark B. American (born United States), b. 1949. **Genres:** Education, Philosophy, Young Adult Non-fiction, Social Sciences, Education. **Career:** University of Aston, lecturer, 1976-78; University of Houston, assistant professor, 1979-82, associate professor, 1982-87; University of Pittsburgh, Administrative and Policy Studies and Sociology, associate professor, 1987-89, professor, 1989-, Institute for International Studies in Education, director, 1987-93, 1996-; Pittsburgh Peace Institute, board director, 1989-97, co-chair, 1991-93; Alliance for Progressive Action, board director, 1992-. Writer. **Publications:** The Role of the Middle School Teacher, 1977; Contradictions in Teacher Education and Society, 1988; Understanding Educational Reform in Global Context: Economy, Ideology, and the State, 1991; (ed.) The Politics of Educator's Work and Lives, 1995; (ed. with B. Lindsay) The Political Dimension in Teacher Education: Comparative Perspectives on Policy Formation, Socialization, and Society, 1995; (co-ed.) Cuba in the Special Period: Cuban Perspectives, 1997; (ed. with J.M. Gorostiaga) Limitations and Possibilities of Dialogue among Researchers, Policy Makers, and Practitioners, 2003. **Address:** Institute for International Studies in Education, University of Pittsburgh, 5K01 Posvar Hall, 5H38 Forbes Quadrangle, Pittsburgh, PA 15260, U.S.A. **Online address:** mbg@pitt.edu

GINZBERG, Lori D. American (born United States), b. 1957. **Genres:** Women's Studies And Issues, Politics/Government, History. **Career:** Yale University, Frederick Douglass Papers, research assistant, 1979, teaching assistant/acting instructor, 1979-84; University of Rhode Island, visiting instructor, 1985; Pennsylvania State University, faculty, 1987-, assistant professor, professor, graduate officer of the Women's Studies Program, 2002-. Writer. **Publications:** Women and the Work of Benevolence: Morality, Politics, and Class in the Nineteenth-Century United States, 1990; Women in Antebellum Reform, 2000; Untidy Origins: A Story of Woman's Rights in Antebellum New York, 2005. Contributor to books and periodicals. **Address:** Pennsylvania State University, 108 Weaver Bldg., University Park, PA 16802, U.S.A. **Online address:** ldg1@psu.edu

GINZBURG, Carlo. American/Italian (born Italy), b. 1939?. **Genres:** History, Social Sciences. **Career:** University of Rome, assistant in modern Italian history, 1960; Warburg Institute, visiting fellow, 1964; University of Bologna, professor of modern history, 1970-; University of California, professor of Italian Renaissance studies, Franklin D. Murphy professor of Italian Renaissance Studies, now professor emeritus; Princeton University, visiting professor, 1973; Harvard University, Center for Italian Renaissance Studies, visiting fellow; Princeton Institute for Advanced Study, visiting fellow, 1975, 1986; Columbia University, Italian Academy for Advanced Studies in America, fellow in residence, 1998; Getty Center and at école Pratique des Hautes études, visiting fellow. Writer. **Publications:** I benandanti: Stregoneria e culti agrari tra cinquecento e seicento, 1966 as The Night Battles: Witchcraft and Agrarian Cults in the Sixteenth and Seventeenth Centuries, 1983; Il nicodemismo: Simulazione e dissimulazionereligiosa nell'Europa del '500, 1970; Costituti di don Pietro Manelfi, 1970; Benandanti, Stregoneria e culti agrari tra Cinquecento e Seicento, 1972; (with A. Prosperi) Giochi di pazienza: Un seminario sul Beneficio di Cristo, 1975; Formaggio e i vermi: Il cosmo di un mugnaio del '500, 1976; Cheese and the Worms: The Cosmos of a Sixteenth-century Miller, 1980; Indagini su Piero: il Battesimo, il Ciclo di Arezzo, la Flagellazione di Urbino, 1982; Erkundungen über Piero: Piero della Francesca, ein Malerder frü Renaissance, 1983; Enigma of Piero: Piero della Francesca: The Baptism, the Arezzo Cycle, the Flagellation, 1985; Miti, emblemi, spie: Morfologia e storia, 1986; Storia notturna: Una decifrazione del sabba, 1989; Clues, Myths, and the Historical Method, 1989; Ecstasies:

Deciphering the Witches' Sabbath, 1991; Giudice e lo storico: Considerazioni in margine al processo Sofri, 1991; The Night Battles: Witchcraft & Agrarian Cults in the Sixteenth & Seventeenth Centuries, 1992; (with A. Natoli) Registro: Carcere politico di Civitavecchia, 1941-1943, 1994; Indagini su Piero: Il Battesimo, il ciclo di Arezzo, la Flagellazione di Urbino, 1994; Discusión sobre la historia, 1995; Occhiacci di legno: Noveriflessioni sulla distanza, 1998; Venus von Giorgione, 1998; Judge and the Historian: Marginal Notes on a Late Twentieth-century Miscarriage of Justice, 1999; History, Rhetoric, and Proof, 1999; Enigma of Piero: Pierodella Francesca, 2000; Rapporti di forza: Storia, retorica, prova, 2000; Wooden Eyes: Nine Reflections on Distance, 2001; (with V. Foa) Dialogo, 2003; Conversazioni per Alberto Gajano, 2005; Un Seul teémoin, 2007; (ed.) Lettere a Ludovica, 2008; Paura, Reverenza, Terrore: Rileggere Hobbes Oggi, 2008; Vivre le sens, 2008; (intro.) Episodes: A Memorybook, 2010. Contributor to periodicals. **Address:** Department of History, University of California, Los Angeles, 6265 Bunche Hall, PO Box 951473, Los Angeles, CA 90095-1473, U.S.A. **Online address:** ginzburg@history.ucla.edu

GIOIA, (Michael) Dana. American (born United States), b. 1950. **Genres:** Novellas/Short Stories, Poetry, Songs/Lyrics And Libretti, Literary Criticism And History, Translations. **Career:** General Foods Corp., manager of new business development, 1977-87, marketing manager, 1988-89, vice-president, 1990-92; West Chester Poetry Conference, co-director, 1995-2002; Teaching Poetry Conference, co-director, 2000-02; Pomfret School, visiting fellow, 2008-09; University of Southern California, Thornton School of Music, adjunct professor of musicology, Judge Widney professor of poetry and public culture, 2010-. Writer. **Publications:** (Co-ed.) Sequoia: Twentieth Anniversary Issue: Poetry, 1956-1976, 1976; Summer: Poems, 1983; (ed. and intro.) Ceremony and Other Stories, 1984; (intro.) Two Prose Sketches, 1984; (ed. with W.J. Smith) Poems From Italy, 1985; (ed. with A. Reid) The Printed Poem: The Poem as Print, 1985; Daily Horoscope: Poems, 1986; Journeys in Sunlight, 1986; (trans. and intro.) Mottetti: Poems of Love: The Motets of Eugenio Montale, 1990; (trans.) Eugenio Montale's Motteti: Poem's of Love, 1990; (ed. with M. Palma) New Italian Poets, 1991; Gods of Winter: Poems, 1991; Can Poetry Matter?: Essays on Poetry and American Culture, 1992, 10th ed., 2002; Formal Introductions, 1994; (with X.J. Kennedy) An Introduction to Poetry, 1994, 13th ed., 2010; (trans.) Seneca, The Madness of Hercules, 1995; (comp. with X.J. Kennedy) Literature: An Introduction to Fiction, Poetry and Drama, 1995, 12th ed., 2011; (comp. with X.J. Kennedy) Introduction to Fiction, 1995, 9th ed., 2005; (ed. with W. Logan) Certain Solitudes: On the Poetry of Donald Justice, 1997; Ce bun poezia?: Doua eseuri despre poezia si cultura Americana, 1998; (comp. with R.S. Gwynn) Longman Anthology of Short Fiction: Stories and Authors in Context, 2001; (librettist) Nosferatu: An Opera Libretto, 2001; Interrogations at Noon: Poems, 2001; (ed. with R.S.Gwynn) Longman Masters of Short Fiction, 2002; Selected Short Stories of Weldon Kees, 2002; (with S.Timberg) The Misread City, 2003; Barrier of a Common Language: An American Looks at Contemporary British Poetry, 2003; (ed.) 100 Great Poets of the English Language, 2004; Disappearing Ink: Poetry at the End of Print Culture, 2004; Everyone Sang: Four Songs for Baritone and Piano, 2004; (co-ed.) Twentieth-Century American Poetics: Poets on the Art of Poetry, 2004; (co-ed.) Twentieth-Century AmericanPoetry, 2004; (contrib.) My California: Journeys by Great Writers, 2004; (co-ed.) California Poetry: From the Gold Rush to the Present, 2004; (co-author) Handbook of Literary Terms: Literature, Language, Theory, 2005; (ed. with X.J. Kennedy) Backpack Literature: An Introduction to Fiction, Poetry, and Drama, 2006, 4th ed., 2012; (ed. with R.S. Gwynn) Art of the Short Story, 2006; (with X.J. Kennedy and M. Bauerlein) Longman Dictionary of Literary Terms: Vocabulary for the Informed Reader, 2006; God only Knows: For Soprano and Piano, 2008; (intro.) Operation Homecoming: Iraq, Afghanistan, and the Home Front, in the Words of U.S. Troops and Their Families, 2008; (ed. with X.J. Kennedy and N. Revoyr) Literature for life, 2013. WITH X.J. KENNEDY: Literature: An Introduction to Fiction, Poetry, Drama, and Writing, 2007; Introduction to Fiction, 2007; (with M. Bauerlein) Handbook of Literary Terms: Literature, Language, Theory, 2009. Contributor to periodicals. **Address:** Thornton School of Music, University of Southern California, 355K Taper, Los Angeles, CA 90089-0851, U.S.A. **Online address:** dana.gioia@usc.edu

GIORELLO, Sibella. American (born United States), b. 1963?. **Genres:** Novels. **Career:** Richmond Times-Dispatch, features writer, 1989-. **Publications:** RALEIGH HARMON SERIES: The Stones Cry Out, 2007; The Rivers Run Dry, 2009; The Clouds Roll Away, 2010; Mountains Bow Down, 2011. **Address:** Thomas Nelson Inc., PO Box 141000, Nashville, TN 37214, U.S.A. **Online address:** sibella@sibellagiorello.com

GIOVAGNOLI, Melissa (E.). American (born United States), b. 1955. **Genres:** Business/Trade/Industry, Reference. **Career:** Networlding.com, president, 1986-; Closerlook.com, consultant; EnvisionaBetterWorld.org, co-founder. Writer. **Publications:** (With J. Moss) The Chicago Entrepreneurs Sourcebook: Your Complete Guide to Starting Smart, Finding Resources for Growth & Creating Your Survival Network, 1992; Make Your Connections Count!: The Six-Step System to Build Your Mega Network, 1995; Lee and Saralee Rosenberg's 50 Fabulous Places to Raise Your Family, 1996, 3rd ed., 2006; Angels in the Workplace: Stories and Strategies to Create a New World of Work, 1997; (with D. Whitney) 75 Cage Rattling Questions to Change the Way You Work: Shake-Em-Up Questions to Open Meetings, Ignite Discussion, and Spark Creativity, 1997; (with J.K. Conlon) The Power of Two: How Companies of All Sizes Can Build Alliance Networks that Generate Business Opportunities, 1998; Networlding: Building Relationships and Opportunities for Success, 2000; (with S. Benton) Wisdom Network: An 8-Step Process for Identifying, Sharing, and Leveraging Individual Expertise, 2006. **Address:** 222 N Columbus 4902, Chicago, IL 60607, U.S.A. **Online address:** megnetwork@aol.com

GIOVANNI, Nikki. American (born United States), b. 1943. **Genres:** Children's Fiction, Poetry, Race Relations, Biography, Essays, inspirational/Motivational Literature, Young Adult Fiction. **Career:** Rutgers University, Livingston College, associate professor of English, 1968-72; Encore Magazine, editorial consultant; Ohio State University, visiting professor of English, 1984; College of Mount St. Joseph, professor of creative writing, 1985-87; Virginia Tech, professor of English, 1987-99, Gloria D. Smith professor of black studies, 1997-99, university distinguished professor, 1999-; Texas Christian University, visiting professor in humanities, 1991; University of Oregon, Martin Luther King, Jr. visiting professor, 1992; University of Minnesota, Hill visiting professor, 1993; Indiana University, visiting professor, 1995; Fisk University, visiting distinguished professor, 2007. Writer. **Publications:** POETRY: Black Feeling, Black Talk, 1968, 3rd ed., 1970; Black Judgment, 1968; Re: Creation, 1970; Poem of Angela Yvonne Davis, 1970; My House, 1972; The Women and the Men, 1975; Cotton Candy on a Rainy Day, 1978; Those Who Ride the Night Winds, 1982; The Selected Poems of Nikki Giovanni, 1968-1995, 1996; Love Poems, 1997; Blues: For All the Changes: New Poems, 1999; Quilting the Black-eyed Pea: Poems and Not Quite Poems, 2002; The Collected Poetry of Nikki Giovanni: 1968-1998, 2003; Acolytes, 2007; Bicycles: Love Poems, 2009. CHILDREN'S POETRY: Spin a Soft Black Song: Poems for Children, 1971, rev. ed., 1985; Ego Tripping and Other Poems for Young People, 1974, 2nd ed., 1993; Vacation Time: Poems for Children, 1980; Knoxville, Tennessee, 1994; The Genie in the Jar, 1996; The Sun is So Quiet, 1996; The Girls in the Circle, 2004; Rosa, 2005; The Grasshopper's Song, 2008; Lincoln and Douglass: An American Friendship, 2008. PROSE: Gemini: An Extended Autobiographical Statement on My First Twenty-Five Years of Being a Black Poet, 1971; A Dialogue: James Baldwin and Nikki Giovanni, 1973; (with M. Walker) A Poetic Equation: Conversations between Nikki Giovanni and Margaret Walker, 1974, rev. ed., 1983; Sacred Cows and Other Edibles, 1988; Racism 101, 1994; Prosaic Soul of Nikki Giovanni, 2003; On My Journey Now: Looking At African-American History through the Spirituals, 2007; Jimmy Grasshopper Versus the Ants, 2007; Jimmy Grasshopper versus the Ants, 2008; Grasshopper and the Ants, forthcoming. EDITOR: Night Comes Softly: An Anthology of Black Female Voices, 1970; (with C. Dennison) Appalachian Elders, 1992; Grand Mothers: Poems, Reminiscences, and Short Stories about the Keepers of Our Traditions, 1994; Shimmy Shimmy Shimmy Like My Sister Kate: Looking At The Harlem Renaissance Through Poems, 1996; Grand Fathers: Reminiscences, Poems, Recipes and Photos of the Keepers of Our Traditions, 1999; (with M. Scott, W. Perdomo and T. Medina) Hip Hop Speaks to Children: A Celebration of Poetry with a Beat, 2008. Works appear in anthologies. Contributor to periodicals. **Address:** Department of English, Virginia Polytechnic Inst & State Univ, 323 Shanks Hall, Blacksburg, VA 24061, U.S.A. **Online address:** ngiovann@vt.edu

GIOVINO, Andrea. American (born United States) **Genres:** Criminology/True Crime, Adult Non-fiction, Autobiography/Memoirs, Biography. **Career:** Writer. **Publications:** (With G. Brozek) Divorced From The Mob: My

Journey From Organized Crime to Independent Woman, 2004. **Address:** c/o Blanca Oliviery, Avalon Publishing Group, 245 W 17th St., 11th Fl., New York, NY 10011-5300, U.S.A.

GIPI. Italian (born Italy), b. 1963?. **Genres:** Children's Fiction, Novels, History, Graphic Novels. **Career:** Writer and illustrator of comics, 1992-; Santa Maria Video, founder, 2000-; Fine Arts Academies, teacher. Producer and director. **Publications:** GRAPHIC NOVELS: The Innocents, 2005; They Found the Car, 2006; Garage Band, 2007; Notes for a War Story, 2007. Contributor to periodicals. **Address:** First Second Books, 175 5th Ave., New York, NY 10010, U.S.A. **Online address:** giannigipi@gmail.com

GIPSON, Carolyn R. (Carolyn Renee Gipson). American (born United States), b. 1944. **Genres:** Economics, Biography, Sciences, Reference, Business/Trade/Industry. **Career:** University of Michigan, assistant professor of English, 1971-76; U.S. Senate, legislative counsel, 1979-81; attorney, 1983-89; Foreign Trading Services, consultant, 1990-. Writer. **Publications:** The McGraw-Hill Dictionary of International Trade and Finance, 1993; Portraits of American Presidents: A Multimedia Adventure through American History, 1994. Contributor to periodicals. **Address:** Bk Nelson Inc., 84 Woodland Rd., Pleasantville, NY 10570, U.S.A.

GIPSON, Carolyn Renee. See GIPSON, Carolyn R.

GIRI, Ananta K. See GIRI, Ananta Kumar.

GIRI, Ananta Kumar. (Ananta K. Giri). Indian (born India), b. 1965. **Genres:** Law, Business/Trade/Industry, Education, Administration/Management. **Career:** Jamia Millia Islamia, lecturer in sociology, 1992; G.B. Pant Social Science Institute, lecturer in anthropology, 1992-93; Indian Institute of Management, Ravi Matthai Center for Educational Innovations, visiting professor, 1993-94; Madras Institute of Development Studies, assistant professor, 1995-2001, associate professor, 2001-; Aalborg University, Research Center on Development and International Relations, visiting associate professor, 2004-05; Punjab University, visiting professor, 2006. Writer and academic. **Publications:** Well-Being of Institutions: Problematic Justice and the Challenge of Transformation, 1997; Literature and the Tapashya of Transformation: A Glimpse into the Creative Worlds of Chittaranjan Das, 1998; Global Transformations: Postmodernity and Beyond, 1998; Rethinking Civil Society, 1998; Values, Ethics, and Business: Challenges for Education and Management, 1998; Gandhi, Tagore, and New Ethics of Argumentation, 2000; (with P.Q. van Ufford) Reconstituting Development as a Shared Responsibility: Ethics, aesthetics, and a Creative Shaping of Human Possibilities, 2000; Rule of Law and Indian Society: Colonial Encounters, Post-colonial Experiments, and Beyond, 2001; (ed.) Rethinking Social Transformation: Criticism and Creativity at the Turn of the Millennium, 2001; Spiritual Cultivation for a Secular Society, 2002; A School for the Subject: The Vision and Experiments of Integral Education, 2002; Building in the Margins of Shacks: The Vision and Projects of Habitat for Humanity, 2002; Conversations and Transformations: Toward a New Ethics of Self and Society, 2002; (ed. with P.Q. van Ufford) A Moral Critique of Development: In Search of Global Responsibilities, 2003; (ed. with A. van Harskamp and O. Salemink) The Development of Religion, the Religion of Development, 2004; (ed.) Creative Social Research: Rethinking Theories and Methods, 2004; Srasta, Sastra O Saskrunti, 2004; Bagalara Tila Chihna, 2004; Reflections and Mobilizations: Dialogues with Movements and Voluntary Organizations, 2005; Creative Social Research: Rethinking Theories and Methods and the Calling of an Ontological Epistemology of Participation, 2005; Hrudayara Sehi Akhi Duiti, 2007; Self-Development and Social Transformations? The Vision and Practice of the Self-Study Mobilization of Swadhyaya, 2008; (ed.) The Modern Prince and the Modern Sage: Transforming Power and Freedom, 2009. **Address:** Madras Institute of Development Studies, 79 2nd Main Rd., Gandhinagar, Adyar, Chennai, TN 600 020, India. **Online address:** aumkrishna@yahoo.com

GIRLING, John (Lawrence Scott). Australian/British (born England), b. 1926. **Genres:** International Relations/Current Affairs, Politics/Government, Third World, History, Social Sciences, Business/Trade/Industry. **Career:** Foreign Office, research staff, 1951-66; Australian National University, Research School of Pacific Studies, researcher, 1966-, senior research fellow, 1966-69; fellow in international relations, 1969-78; senior fellow, 1978-; Research School of Pacific Studies, researcher, 1966. Writer. **Publications:** People's War: Conditions and Consequences in China and South East Asia, 1969; Cambodia and the Sihanouk Myths, 1971; America and the Third World: Rev-

olution and Intervention, 1980; The Bureaucratic Polity in Modernizing Societies: Similarities, Differences and Prospects in the ASEAN Region, 1981; Thailand: Society and Politics, 1981; The State in the Third World, 1982; Capital and Power: Political Economy and Social Transformation, 1987; (ed.) Human Rights in the Asia-Pacific Region, 1991; Myths and Politics in Western Societies: Evaluating the Crisis of Modernity in the United States, Germany and Great Britain, 1993; Interpreting Development: Capitalism, Democracy and The Middle Class in Thailand, 1996; Corruption, Capitalism and Democracy, 1997; France: Political and Social Change, 1998; Social Movements and Symbolic Power: Radicalism, Reform and the Trail of Democracy in France, 2004; Emotion and Reason in Social Change: Insights from Fiction, 2006. **Address:** 33 rue Achille Viadieu, Apt. 33, Toulouse, 31400, France. **Online address:** john.nina.girling@wanadoo.fr

GIROUARD, Mark. British (born England), b. 1931. **Genres:** Art/Art History, Architecture. **Career:** Country Life, staff writer, 1958-66; Architectural Review, staff writer, 1971-75; Oxford University, Slade professor of fine art, 1975-76; architectural historian, 1976-; Columbia University, George Lurcy visiting professor, 1987; Society of Antiquaries, fellow; Royal Institute of British Architects, fellow; Victorian Society, founding member. **Publications:** Robert Smythson and the Architecture of the Elizabethan Era, 1967; The Victorian Country House, 1971, rev. ed., 1985; Victorian Pubs, 1975; (co-author) Spirit of the Age (based on the television series), 1975; Sweetness and Light: The Queen Anne Movement, 1860-1900, 1977; Life in the English Country House: A Social and Architectural History, 1978; Historic Houses of Britain, 1979; Alfred Waterhouse and the Natural History Museum, 1981; The Return to Camelot: Chivalry and the English Gentleman, 1981; Robert Smythson and the Elizabethan Country House, 1983; John Piper's Stowe, 1983; Cities & People: A Social and Architectural History, 1985; A Country House Companion, 1987; Hardwick Hall, 1989; The English Town: A History of Urban Life, 1990; Town and Country, 1992; Windsor: The Most Romantic Castle, 1993; Big Jim: The Life and Work of James Stirling, 1998; Life in the French Country House, 2000; Elizabethan Architecture: Its Rise and Fall, 1540-1640, 2009. Contributor to periodicals. **Address:** 35 Colville Rd., London, GL W11 2BT, England.

GIROUX, E. X. See SHANNON, Doris.

GISH, Robert F. (Robert Franklin Gish). American (born United States), b. 1940. **Genres:** Novels, Novellas/Short Stories, Literary Criticism And History, Autobiography/Memoirs, Popular Culture, Literary Criticism And History, Music, History, History. **Career:** University of Northern Iowa, professor of English language and literature, 1967-91, professor emeritus, 1991-; California Polytechnic State University, director of ethnic studies and professor of English, 1991-2001; University of New Mexico, instructor, Osher Lifelong Learning Institute, faculty; Jazz Improve Magazine, columnist. Jazz musician, guitarist and vocalist. **Publications:** Hamlin Garland: The Far West, 1976; Paul Horgan, 1983; Frontier's End: The Life and Literature of Harvey Fergusson, 1988; William Carlos Williams: The Short Fiction, 1989; Songs of My Hunter Heart: A Western Kinship, 1992; (as Robert Franklin Gish) First Horses: Stories of the New West, 1993; (reteller as Robert Franklin Gish) Retold Native American Myths, 1994; (as Robert Franklin Gish) When Coyote Howls: A Lavaland Fable, 1994; (as Robert Franklin Gish) Nueva Granada: Paul Horgan and the Southwest, 1995; (as Robert Franklin Gish) Bad Boys and Black Sheep: Fateful Tales from the West, 1996; (as Robert Franklin Gish) Beyond Bounds: Cross-Cultural Essays on Anglo, American Indian, and Chicano Literature, 1996; (as Robert Franklin Gish) Beautiful Swift Fox: Erna Fergusson and the Modern Southwest, 1996; (as Robert Franklin Gish) Dreams of Quivira: Stories in Search of the Golden West, 1998; West Bound: Stories of Providence, 2005. Contributor to magazines. **Address:** Department of Languages and Literatures, University of Northern Iowa, 1227 W 27th St., Cedar Falls, IA 50614, U.S.A. **Online address:** bob.gish@gmail.com

GISH, Robert Franklin. See GISH, Robert F.

GITLIN, Todd. American (born United States), b. 1943. **Genres:** Novels, Communications/Media, Politics/Government, Sociology, Writing/Journalism. **Career:** San Francisco Express Times, writer, 1968-69; San Jose State College, lecturer, 1970-76; University of California at Santa Cruz, lecturer, 1974-77; University of California at Berkeley, assistant professor, 1978-83, associate professor, 1983-87, professor of sociology and director of Mass Communications Program, 1987-92; New York University, professor of culture, journalism and sociology, 1995-2002; Columbia University, professor of journalism and sociology, 2002-, chair, Ph.D. program in communications, 2008- **Publications:** (With N. Hollander) Uptown: Poor Whites in Chicago, 1970; Busy Being Born (poetry), 1974; The Whole World Is Watching: Mass Media in the Making and Unmaking of the New Left, 1980; Inside Prime Time, 1983; The Sixties: Years of Hope, Days of Rage, 1987; The Murder of Albert Einstein, 1992; The Twilight of Common Dreams: Why America is Wracked by Culture Wars, 1995; Sacrifice, 1999; Media Unlimited: How the Torrent of Images and Sounds Overwhelms Our Lives, 2002; Letters to a Young Activist, 2003; The Intellectuals and the Flag, 2004; The Bulldozer and the Big Tent: Blind Republicans, Lame Democrats, and the Recovery of American Ideals, 2007; (with L. Leibovitz) The Chosen Peoples: America, Israel, and the Ordeals of Divine Election, 2010; Undying, 2011. EDITOR: Campfires of Resistance: Poetry from the Movement, 1971; Watching Television, 1987. **Address:** Graduate School of Journalism, Columbia University, 2950 Broadway, Rm. 201F, New York, NY 10027, U.S.A. **Online address:** tg2058@columbia.edu

GITTER, Elisabeth. American (born United States), b. 1945. **Genres:** Biography, Young Adult Non-fiction, Autobiography/Memoirs, History. **Career:** John Jay College of Criminal Justice, professor of English, now professor emeritus of English. Writer. **Publications:** The Imprisoned Guest: Samuel Howe and Laura Bridgman, the Original Deaf-Blind Girl, 2001. Contributor to periodicals. **Address:** Department of English, John Jay College of Criminal Justice, 899 10th Ave., New York, NY 10019, U.S.A. **Online address:** egitter@jjay.cuny.edu

GITTLIN, Adam. American (born United States), b. 1972?. **Genres:** Novels. **Career:** Writer. **Publications:** The Men Downstairs, 2003; The Deal (novel), 2008. **Address:** New York, NY , U.S.A. **Online address:** agittlin@gittlin.com

GIZIOWSKI, Richard (John). American (born United States), b. 1946. **Genres:** History, Military/Defense/Arms Control. **Career:** Auburn public schools, teacher, 1971-98; Military History Journal, book reviewer. Writer. **Publications:** The Enigma of General Blaskowitz, 1996; The Battle of the Falaise Gap and Hitler's Generals, forthcoming. **Address:** 14 Circle Dr., Dudley, MA 01571-3469, U.S.A. **Online address:** eagle_1@onemain.com

GIZZI, Peter. American (born United States), b. 1959. **Genres:** Poetry. **Career:** O-blek: A Journal of Language Arts, co-founder, co-editor and publisher, 1987-93; Brown University, teaching fellow, 1990-91, Department of English, visiting assistant professor, 1993-94; State University of New York-Buffalo, teaching fellow, 1991-93; University of California, assistant professor, 1995-99, Department of Literature, associate professor, 1999-2001; Naropa Institute, visiting faculty, 1998, 2007; University of Massachusetts, M.F.A. Program in Creative Writing, associate professor, 2001-05, professor, 2005-; Cambridge University, Judith E Wilson visiting fellow in poetry, 2011. **Publications:** POETRY: Creeley Madrigal, 1991; Music for Films, 1992; Periplum, or, I the Blaze, 1992; Hours of the Book, 1994; Ledger Domain, 1995; New Picnic Time, 1995; Artificial Heart, 1998; Add This to the House, 1999; Chateau If, 2000; Revival, 2002; Fin Amor, 2002; Some Values of Landscape and Weather, 2003; Outernationale, 2007; Pinocchio's Gnosis, 2011; History is Made at Night, 2011; Ode: Salute to the New York School 1950-1970, 2011; Threshold Songs, 2011. OTHERS: Exact Change Yearbook, 1995; (ed. and afterword) The House That Jack Built: The Collected Lectures of Jack Spicer, 1998; (ed.) My Vocabulary Did This to Me: The Collected Poetry of Jack Spicer, 2008. **Address:** University of Massachusetts, 487 Bartlett Hall, Amherst, MA 01003, U.S.A. **Online address:** gizzi@hfa.umass.edu

GJELTEN, Tom. American (born United States), b. 1948. **Genres:** Biography, Writing/Journalism. **Career:** National Public Radio (NPR), labor and education reporter, 1982-86, Latin America correspondent, 1986-90; University of Chicago, William Benton fellow, 1989-90; Berlin as Central Europe correspondent, 1990-94; U.S. diplomacy and military affairs correspondent, from the State Department and the Pentagon, 1994-2003; intelligence and other national security issues correspondent, 2003-; Washington Week news program, PBS television, regular panelist. Writer. **Publications:** Sarajevo Daily: A City and Its Newspaper under Siege, 1995; Professionalism in War Reporting: A Correspondent's View, 1998; (contrib.) Sarajevo Self-portrait: The View from Inside, 2000; Bacardi and the Long Fight for Cuba: The Biography of a Cause, 2008. **Address:** NPR, 635 Massachusetts Ave. NW, Washington, DC 20001, U.S.A.

GLADSTONE, Arthur M. Also writes as Cilla Whitmore, Margaret SeBastian, Lisabet Norcross, Cilla Whitmore. American (born United States), b. 1921?. **Genres:** Romance/Historical. **Career:** American Cyanamid, research chemist, 1947-48; Pittsburgh Coke and Chemical, research supervisor, 1948-53; Nopco Chemical, chief chemist and product manager, 1953-59; Hercules, Inc., director of proposal team, 1961-67; Product Development consultant, 1969-73; writer, 1973-. **Publications:** AS MARGARET SEBASTIAN: The Honorable Miss Clarendon, 1975; Meg Miller, 1976; Bow Street Gentleman, 1977; Bow Street Brangle, 1977; Miss Letty, 1977; My Lord Rakehell, 1977; Lord Orlando's Protegee, 1977; The Young Lady from Alton-St. Pancras, 1977; That Savage Yankee Squire!, 1978; The Poor Relation, 1978; Lord Dedringham's Divorce, 1978; The Courtship of Colonel Crowne, 1978; Her Knight on a Barge, 1979; The Awakening of Lord Dalby, 1979; Dilemma in Duet, 1979; Byway to Love, 1980; The Plight of Pamela Pollworth, 1980; Miss Keating's Temptation, 1981; A Keeper for Lord Linford, 1982. AS MAGGIE GLADSTONE: The Scandalous Lady, 1978; The Fortunate Belle, 1978; The Love Duel, 1978; The Reluctant Debutante, 1979; The Impudent Widow, 1979; The Love Tangle, 1980; The Lady's Masquerade, 1980; The Reluctant Protegee, 1980; A Lesson in Love, 1981. AS LISABET NORCROSS: Masquerade of Love, 1978; Heiress to Love, 1978; My Lady Scapegrace, 1979. AS CILLA WHITMORE: The Lady and the Rogue, 1978; Manner of a Lady, 1979; His Lordship's Landlady, 1979; Mansion for a Lady, 1980. **Address:** 323 Logtrac Rd., Stanardsville, VA 22973, U.S.A. **Online address:** amgladstone@hotmail.com

GLADWELL, Malcolm. American/British (born England), b. 1963. **Genres:** Young Adult Non-fiction, Psychology, Self Help. **Career:** Washington Post, reporter, science writer, New York city bureau chief, 1987-96; New Yorker Magazine, staff writer, science writer, 1996-. **Publications:** The Tipping Point: How Little Things Can Make a Big Difference, 2000; Blink: The Power of Thinking without Thinking, 2005; Outliers: The Story of Success, 2008; What the Dog Saw and Other Adventures, 2009. Contributor of articles to books. **Address:** Little Brown and Co., 1271 Ave. of the Americas, New York, NY 10020, U.S.A. **Online address:** contact@gladwell.com

GLAHE, Fred R. American (born United States), b. 1934. **Genres:** Economics, Politics/Government, Sciences. **Career:** General Motors Corp., Allison Division, engineer, 1957-61; Battelle Memorial Institute, research economist, 1964-65; University of Colorado, Department of Economics, assistant professor, 1965-68, associate professor, 1968-73, professor of economics, 1973-, now professor emeritus. Writer. **Publications:** Empirical Study of the Foreign-exchange Market, 1967; (ed. with J.M. Dowling) Readings in Econometric Theory, 1970; (contrib.) Collected Papers, 1971; Macroeconomics: Theory and Policy, 1973, 3rd ed., 1985; Implications of Regional Development in the Middle East for U.S. Trade, Capital Flows, and Balance of Payments, 1977; (with D.R. Lee) Microeconomics: Theory and Applications, 1981, 2nd ed., 1989; (with J.P. Cochran) The Hayek-Keynes Debate: Lessons for Current Business Cycle Research, 1999; The Drama: The Keynes-Hayek Debate on the Nature and Causes of the Business Cycle, 1999. EDITOR: (with M. Dowling) Reading in Econometric Theory, 1970; Collected Paper of Kenneth E. Boulding: Economics, vol. I-II, 1971; (with W.F. Owen) Guide to Graduate Study in Economics and Agricultural Economics, 3rd ed., 1975; (and intro.) Adam Smith and the Wealth of Nations, 1978; (with J.R. Peden) The American Family and the State, 1986; Keynes's The General Theory of Employment, Interest, and Money: A Concordance, 1991; Adam Smith's An Inquiry into the Nature and Causes of the Wealth of Nations: A Concordance, 1993. **Address:** Department of Economics, University of Colorado, Rm. 212, Economics Bldg., PO Box 256, Boulder, CO 80309-0256, U.S.A. **Online address:** fred.glahe@colorado.edu

GLAISTER, Lesley (G.). British (born England), b. 1956. **Genres:** Novels, Young Adult Fiction, Romance/Historical, Sociology, Psychology, Mystery/Crime/Suspense. **Career:** Parsons Cross College, teacher of adult education courses, 1982-; University of Sheffield, Loxley College, tutor, 1992-93; The Arvan Foundation, tutor, 1992-93; Sheffield Hallam University, teacher of creative writing, 1994-; Cheltenham Literature Festival, writer-in-residence, 2001-02; University of Edinburgh, writer-in-residence; University of St Andrews, faculty; Royal Society of Literature, fellow. **Publications:** NOVELS: Honour Thy Father, 1990; Trick or Treat, 1991; Digging to Australia, 1993; Limestone and Clay, 1993; Partial Eclipse, 1994; The Private Parts of Women, 1996; Easy Peasy, 1997; Sheer Blue Bliss, 1999; Now You See Me, 2001; As

Far as You Can Go, 2004; (ed.) Are You She?, 2004; Nina Todd Has Gone, 2007; Chosen, 2010. Contributor to periodicals. **Address:** Sheffield Hallam University, City Campus, Howard St., Sheffield, S1 1WB, England.

GLANCY, Diane. American (born United States), b. 1941. **Genres:** Novels, Novellas/Short Stories, Plays/Screenplays, Poetry, Essays, Adult Non-fiction, Film. **Career:** State Arts Council of Oklahoma, artist-in-residence, 1980-86; Macalester College, Department of English, visiting lecturer, 1988-89, assistant professor of English, 1989-95, associate professor of English, 1995-2001, professor of English, 2001-09; Kenyon College, visiting Richard Thomas professor of creative writing, 2008-09. Writer. **Publications:** POETRY: Brown Wolf Leaves the Res and Other Poems, 1984; One Age in a Dream, 1986; Offering, 1988; Iron Woman, 1990; Lone Dog's Winter Count, 1991; Asylum in the Grasslands, 1998; The Relief of America, 2000; The Shadow's Horse, 2003; Primer of the Obsolete, 2004; The Dance Partner, 2005; Rooms, 2005; Reason for Crows: A Story of Kateri Tekakwitha, 2009; Stories of the Driven World, 2010. STORIES: Trigger Dance, 1990; Firesticks, 1993; Monkey Secret, 1995; The Voice That Was in Travel, 1999. ESSAYS: Claiming Breath, 1992; The West Pole, 1997; The Cold-and-Hungrer Dance, 1998; In-between Places, 2005. NOVELS: Pushing the Bear, 1996; The Only Piece of Furniture in the House, 1996; Flutie, 1998; Fuller Man, 1999; The Man Who Heard the Land, 2001; The Mask Maker, 2002; Designs of the Night Sky, 2002; Stone Heart: A Novel of Sacajawea, 2003. OTHER: Drystalks of the Moon, 1981; War Cries, 1997; (ed. with M. Nowak) Visit Teepee Town: Native Writings After the Detours, 1999. **Address:** Shawnee Mission, KS , U.S.A. **Online address:** glancy@macalester.edu

GLANCY, Jennifer A. American (born United States), b. 1960. **Genres:** Theology/Religion. **Career:** Union Theological Seminary, instructor of biblical Greek, 1988; Le Moyne College, Department of Religious Studies, assistant professor, 1990-95, associate professor, 1995-99, Integral Honors Program, director, 1996-2000, professor, 1999-, chair, 2005-08; L Ecole Biblique et Archaeologique Francaise, Catholic Biblical Association Visiting Professor, 2004; University of Richmond, Department of Religion, George and Sallie Cutchins Camp Professor of Bible. Writer. **Publications:** (Co-author) Introduction to the Study of Religion Orbis, 1998; Slavery in Early Christianity, 2002; Corporal Knowledge: Early Christian Bodies, 2010; Slavery As Moral Problem: In The Early Church And Today, 2011. Contributor to journals. **Address:** Le Moyne College, 1419 Salt Springs Rd., Syracuse, NY 13214, U.S.A. **Online address:** glancy@lemoyne.edu

GLANCY, Ruth F(ergusson). British/Canadian (born Canada), b. 1948. **Genres:** Literary Criticism And History, Bibliography, Novels, Young Adult Fiction, Reference, Education. **Career:** University of Bristol, tutor in literature, 1976-80; University of Alberta, sessional lecturer, 1980-88, lecturer in English, 1990-92; Concordia University College, associate professor of English, 1990-, professor. Writer. **Publications:** Dickens's Christmas Books, Christmas Stories and Other Short Fiction: An Annotated Bibliography, 1985; A Tale of Two Cities: Dickens's Revolutionary Novel, 1991; A Tale of Two Cities: An Annotated Bibliography, 1993; Student Companion to Dickens, 1999; Thematic Guide to British Poetry, 2002; Charles Dicken's A Tale Two Cities: A Sourcebook, 2006. EDITOR: (and intro.) Dickens's Christmas Books, 1988; Dickens's Christmas Stories, 1996. Contributor of articles to journals. **Address:** Department of English, Concordia University College, Rm. HA324, 7128 Ada Blvd., Highlands Campus, Edmonton, AB T5B 4E4, Canada. **Online address:** ruth.glancy@concordia.ab.ca

GLANTZ, David M. American (born United States), b. 1942. **Genres:** History, Military/Defense/Arms Control. **Career:** U.S. Military Academy, instructor, assistant professor of modern European history, 1969-73; U.S. Army, Office of the Chief of Staff for Intelligence, intelligence analyst, 1977-79; U.S. Army Command and General Staff College, faculty and deputy director of Combat Studies Institute; 1979-83; U.S. Army War College, Center for Land Warfare, faculty and director of Soviet Studies, 1983-86; Combined Arms Center, director of research and deputy director of Soviet Army Studies Office, 1986-90, acting director, 1990, Foreign Military Studies Office, director, 1991-; The Journal of Slavic Military Studies, editor. **Publications:** August Storm: The Soviet 1945 Strategic Offensive in Manchuria, 1983; August Storm: Soviet Tactical and Operational Combat in Manchuria, 1945, 1983; The Soviet Airborne Experience, 1984; Soviet Military Deception in the Second World War, 1989; The Role of Intelligence in Soviet Military Strategy in World War II, 1990; Soviet Military Intelligence in War, 1990; Soviet Military Operational Art, 1990; From the Don to the Dnepr, 1990; The Soviet Con-

duct of Tactical Maneuver, 1991; The Military Strategy of the Soviet Union, 1917-1990, 1991; Soviet Airborne Forces, 1993; When Titans Clashed, 1995; Stumbling Colossus, 1998; Kharkov, May 1942, 1998; Marshal Zhukov's Greatest Defeat, 1999; The Battle of Kursk, 1999; The Battle for Kursk: The Soviet General Staff Study, 1999; Barbarossa, 2001; Belorussia 1944, 2001; The Battle for L'vov, July 1944, 2002; The Battle for Leningrad 1941-1944, 2002; The Soviet Strategic Offensive in Manchuria, 1945, 2003; Soviet Operational and Tactical Combat in Manchuria, 2003; Colossus Reborn, 2003; Red Storm Over the Balkans, 2006; To the Gates of Stalingrad, vol. I, 2009; Armageddon in Stalingrad, vol. II, 2009; Barbarossa Derailed: The Battle for Smolensk, 10 July-10 September 1941, 2 vols., 2010. **Address:** 805 Forbes Rd., Carlisle, PA 17013, U.S.A. **Online address:** rzhev@aol.com

GLANTZ, Kalman. American (born United States), b. 1937. **Genres:** Administration/Management, Psychology, Medicine/Health. **Career:** Campaign Research Associates (political and economic issues development firm), founder and director, 1975-80; Lesley College, professor of economics and social science, 1977-85; Massachusetts Institute of Technology, visiting scientist, 1996-; Virtual Reality Therapies Inc., clinical director, 1996-; Brighton-Allston Mental Health Center, psychotherapist; Tri-City Mental Health and Retardation Center, psychotherapist. Writer. **Publications:** (With J.K. Pearce) Exiles from Eden: Psychotherapy From an Evolutionary Perspective, 1989; (with J.G. Bernhard) Staying Human in the Organization: Our Biological Heritage and the Workplace, 1992. Contributor to periodicals. **Address:** 12 Kinnaird St., Cambridge, MA 02139-3733, U.S.A. **Online address:** kalman.glantz@gmail.com

GLANVILLE, Brian (Lester). British (born England), b. 1931. **Genres:** Novels, Children's Fiction, Plays/Screenplays, Sports/Fitness, Novellas/ Short Stories, Literary Criticism And History. **Career:** Bodley Head Ltd., literary adviser, 1958-62; Sunday Times Newspaper, sports columnist and chief football writer, 1958-92, football writer, 1998-; The People, sports columnist, 1992-96; The Times, sports columnist, 1996-98. **Publications:** (With C. Bastin) Cliff Bastin Remembers, 1950; The Reluctant Dictator, 1952; Henry Sows the Wind, 1954; Soccer Nemesis, 1955; Along the Arno, 1956; The Bankrupts, 1958; (with J. Weinstein) World Cup, 1958; After Rome, Africa, 1959; Soccer round the Globe, 1959; A Bad Streak and Other Stories, 1961; Diamond, 1962; (ed.) The Footballer's Companion, 1962; The Director's Wife and Other Stories, 1963; Goalkeepers Are Crazy, 1964; The Rise of Gerry Logan, 1965; The King of Hackney Marshes and Other Stories, 1965; Know about Football, 1965; A Second Home, 1965; A Roman Marriage, 1966; The Artist Type, 1967; People in Sport, 1967; Soccer: The History of the Game, Its Players and Its Strategy, 1968; The Olympian, 1969; A Betting Man and Other Stories, 1969; Soccer: A Panorama, 1969; A Cry of Crickets, 1970; Puffin Book of Football, 1970; Goalkeepers Are Different (children's fiction), 1972; The Financiers, 1972; Money is love, 1972; Brian Glanville's Book of World Football, 1972; World Football Handbook, 1972; The Sunday Times History of the World Cup in US as History of the Soccer World Cup, 1973; The Thing He Loves and Other Stories, 1973; The Comic, 1974, rev. ed., 2003; The Dying of the Light, 1976; A Bad Lot, 1977; Target Man (children's novel), 1978; A History of Soccer in US as A Book of Soccer, 1979; Never Look Back, 1980; Kevin Keegan, 1981; A Visit to the Villa (play), 1981; (with K. Whitney) The British Challenge, 1984; Love Is Not Love and Other Stories, 1985; Kissing America, 1985; (ed.) The Joy of Football, 1986; The Catacomb, 1988; The Story of the World Cup, 1993; Football Memories, 1999; Dictators, 2001; The Real Arsenal: From Chapman to Wenger: The Unofficial Story, 2009. **Address:** John Farquharson Ltd., 162-168 Regent St., London, GL W1R 5TB, England.

GLANVILLE, Doug. American (born United States), b. 1970. **Genres:** Sports/Fitness. **Career:** Chicago Cubs, baseball player, 1996-97; Philadelphia Phillies, baseball player, 1998-2001, 2004; Texas Rangers, baseball player, 2003; New York Times, op-ed columnist; GK Alliance L.L.C. (real estate development firm), founder; ESPN, baseball analyst. Writer. **Publications:** The Game from Where I Stand: A Ballplayer's Inside View, 2010. **Address:** U.S.A. **Online address:** doug@dougglanville.com

GLASBERG, Davita Silfen. American/German (born Germany), b. 1951. **Genres:** Sociology, Social Work. **Career:** City University of New York, Brooklyn College, Department of Sociology, adjunct lecturer, 1975-76; University of New York, Department of Sociology, instructor, 1978-83; Southern Illinois University, Department of sociology, assistant professor, 1983-88; University of Connecticut, Department of Sociology, assistant professor,

1988-91, associate professor, 1991-97, professor, 1997-, department head sociology, 2004-11, Graduate Studies in Sociology and University Human Rights Minor Program, director, 2004-05, College of Liberal Arts and Sciences, associate dean of social sciences and undergraduate education, 2011-. Writer. **Publications:** The Power of Collective Purse Strings: The Effect of Bank Hegemony on Corporations and the State, 1989; (with K. Neubeck) Sociology: A Critical Approach, 1996; (with D. Skidmore) Corporate Welfare Policy and the Welfare State: Bank Deregulation and the Savings and Loan Bailout, 1997; (with K.J. Neubeck) Sociology: Diversity, Conflict and Change, 2005; (with K.J. Neubeck and M.A. Neubeck) Social Problems, 2007. (with D. Shannon) Political Sociology: Oppression, Resistance and the State, 2011; (ed. with W.T. Armaline and B. Purkayastha) Human Rights In Our Own Backyard: Injustice and Resistance in the United States, 2011. **Address:** Department of Sociology, University of Connecticut, 220 Manchester Hall, Ste. 2068, Storrs, CT 06269-2068, U.S.A. **Online address:** davita.glasberg@uconn.edu

GLASCO, Michael. American (born United States), b. 1945. **Genres:** Novels. **Career:** Southern Methodist University, photography instructor, 1969-71; Commercial Photography Studio, owner and operator, 1971-94; writer, 1995-. **Publications:** Angels in Tesuque: A Novel, 1995. **Address:** 710 Scenic Ranch Cir., Fairview, TX 75069-1912, U.S.A.

GLASER, James M. American (born United States), b. 1960. **Genres:** Politics/Government, History. **Career:** Supreme Court of the United States, Office of the Administrative Assistant to the Chief Justice of the United States, research assistant, 1983-84; University of California, data consultant, 1985-90; Tufts University, Department of Political Science, assistant professor of political science, 1991-97, associate professor of political science, 1997-2005, department chair, 1999-2003, professor of political science, 2005-, dean of undergraduate education for arts, sciences and engineering, 2003-10, dean of academic affairs for arts and sciences, 2010-. Writer. **Publications:** Race, Campaign Politics, and the Realignment in the South, 1996; The Hand of the Past in Contemporary Southern Politics, 2005. Contributor to journals. **Address:** Registrar's Office, Tufts University, Dowling Hall, Medford, MA 02155, U.S.A. **Online address:** jglaser@tufts.edu

GLASER, Michael S. American (born United States), b. 1943. **Genres:** Poetry. **Career:** Kent State University, teaching fellow, 1966-70; St. Mary's College of Maryland, assistant professor, 1970-74, associate professor, 1974-82, professor, 1982-2008, professor emeritus, 2008-, Oxford Program, director, 1980-2002, Arts and Letters Division, chair, 1979-81, 2001-04, Department of English, chair, 1996-; Institute of Humanistic Education, chair, 1974-85; Festival of Poets and Poetry/Literary Festival, co-founder and director, 1980-2004. Writer and speaker. **Publications:** (Ed.) The Cooke Book: A Seasoning of Poets (poetry anthology), 1987; A Lover's Eye, 1989, 2nd ed., 1991; In the Men's Room and Other Poems (poetry chapbook), 1996; (ed.) Weavings 2000: The Maryland Millennial Anthology, 2000; Greatest Hits, 2001; Being a Father, 2004; Fire Before the Hands (chapbook), 2008; Remembering Eden (chapbook), 2008; Disrupting Consensus, 2010. **Address:** St. Mary College of Maryland, Goodpaster Hall, Saint Marys City, MD 20686-3001, U.S.A. **Online address:** msglaser@smcm.edu

GLASER, William Arnold. American (born United States), b. 1925. **Genres:** Social Sciences, Education. **Career:** Michigan State University, instructor, 1952-55, assistant professor, 1955-56; Columbia University, research assistant, 1956-58, senior research associate in sociology and political science, 1958-82; New School for Social Research, professor, 1982-; Council of Social Science Data Archives, executive director. Writer. **Publications:** (Co-ed.) Readings in Social Science, 1956; Three Papers on the Integrated Bar, 1960; (ed. with W.N. McPhee) Public Opinion and Congressional Elections, 1962; (ed. with D.L. Sills) The Government of Associations: Selections From the Behavioral Sciences, 1966; Sheltered Employment of the Disabled, 1966; Pre-Trial Discovery and the Adversary System, 1968; Social Settings and Medical Organization: A Cross-National Study of the Hospital, 1970; Paying the Doctor, 1970; The Brain Drain: Emigration and Return: Findings of a UNITAR Multinational Comparative Survey of Professional Personnel of Developing Countries who Study Abroad, 1978; Health Insurance Bargaining: Foreign Lessons for Americans, 1978; (ed. with W.N. McPhee) Public Opinion and Congressional Elections, 1981; Paying the Hospital: The Organization, Dynamics and Effects of Differing Financial Arrangements, 1987; Health Insurance in Practice: International Variations in Financing, Benefits and Problems, 1991; Teacher Unions and Policy Making, 1992; The Role of

Education Associations in Health and Other Public Policy: Cross-National Comparisons, 1993. **Address:** Graduate School of Management, New School for Social Research, 66 5th Ave., New York, NY 10011, U.S.A.

GLASMEIER, Amy (K.). American (born United States), b. 1955. **Genres:** Business/Trade/Industry, Economics. **Career:** Pennsylvania State University, assistant professor of community studies, 1985-86, associate professor, 1992-95, professor of geography and regional planning, 1995-, E. Willard Miller professor of economic geography, acting department head, 1995-96, Institute for Policy Research and Evaluation, senior research associate, 1992-95, senior scientist, 1995-, Center for Trade, Technology and Economic Growth, director, 1997-99, Center for Regional Research and Industrial Studies, director, 1999-, Center for Policy Research on Energy, Environment and Community Well-being, director, 2007-, Rural Policy Research Institute, Rural Poverty Research Center, research affiliate, 2004-, Center for Economic and Community Development, faculty affiliate, 2004-; University of Texas-Austin, assistant professor, 1986-90, associate professor of community and regional planning, 1990-91; University of Michigan, special lecturer, 1990; Appalachian Regional Commission; University of Oslo, visiting professor, 2000; Environmental Inquiry Minor, director, 2003-; Regional Studies, editor, 2002-05; Economic Geography, editor, 2003-08; University of New Hampshire, Carsey Institute for Families and Communities, 2005-06; Regions, Economy, Society, founding editor, 2006; Massachusetts Institute of Technology, Department of Urban Studies and Planning, department head and professor of geography and regional planning, 2009-. **Publications:** (With A.R. Markusen) Case against Boomtown Impact Aid, 1980; (with M.B. Teitz and D. Svensson) Small Business and Employment Growth in California, 1981; (with A.R. Markusen) Socio-Economic Impacts of the Proposed MX Missile Project, 1981; (with P. Hall and A.R. Markusen) Recent Evidence on High-Technology industries' Spatial Tendencies: A Preliminary Investigation, 1983; Regional Planning and Economic Development: A Bibliography, 1983; High Technology Industries in the Mid-1970s: The Distribution of Industries and Employment, 1984; (with A.R. Markusen and P. Hall) High-Tech America: The What, How, Where, and Why of the Sunrise Industries, 1986; (with G. Borchard) The Role of Services and Rural Economic Growth: A Bibliography, 1990; The High-Tech Potential: Economic Development in Rural America, 1991; (with A. Kays and J. Thompson) When Low Wages Aren't Enough Anymore: Prospects for Remote Branch Plant Regions in the International Economy, 1993; (with M. Howland) From Combines to Computers: Rural Services and Development in the Age of Information Technology, 1995; (with A. Kays, J.W. Thompson and R. Gurwitt) Branch Plants and Rural Development in the Age of Globalization, 1995; Global and Local Challenges to Theory, Practice, and Teaching in Economic Geography, 1998; (with L. Wood) On Hold: Telecommunications in Rural America, 2000; Manufacturing Time: Global Competition in the Watch Industry, 1795-2000, 2000; (with C. Nelson and J.W. Thompson) Jane Addams Resource Corporation: A Case Study of a Sectoral Employment Development Approach, 2000; Atlas of Poverty in America: One Nation, Pulling Apart, 1960-2003, 2006. Contributor of articles to books and journals. **Address:** Department of Urban Studies and Planning, Massachusetts Institute of Technology, 77 Massachusetts Ave., Cambridge, MA 02139, U.S.A. **Online address:** akg1@ems.psu.edu

GLASS, Charles. American/British (born England), b. 1951. **Genres:** Novellas/Short Stories, Area Studies, Civil Liberties/Human Rights, Film, Politics/Government, Theatre, Documentaries/Reportage, Essays, Essays. **Career:** American Broadcasting Companies Inc, news journalist, 1973-, correspondent, chief Middle East correspondent, 1983-93; freelance writer, 1993-; Cable News Network, overseas and investigative correspondent, 1999-2001; Times Magazine, overseas and investigative correspondent, 1999-2001; Charles Glass Books, founder, 2011-; The Observer, correspondent; The Spectator, correspondent; Frontline Club, editor; Newsweek magazine, correspondent. **Publications:** Tribes with Flags: A Dangerous Passage through the Chaos of the Middle East, 1990; Money for Old Rope: Disorderly Compositions, 1992; The Northern Front, 2006; The Tribes Triumphant, 2006; Americans in Paris: Life and Death under Nazi Occupation, 1940-1944, 2009 in US as Americans in Paris: Life and Death under Nazi Occupation, 2010. Contributor to periodicals. **Address:** PO Box 8308, London, GL W11 2WX, England. **Online address:** charles.glass@abc.com

GLASS, Dee Dee. See Obituaries.

GLASS, Leopold. See **PASCOE, Bruce.**

GLASS, Leslie. American (born United States) **Genres:** Novels, Mystery/Crime/Suspense. **Career:** New York Magazine, columnist; Reach Out Recovery Foundation, founder; crime and mystery writer. **Publications:** NOVELS: Getting Away With It, 1976; Modern Love, 1983; The Changing of Kings: Memories of Burma, 1934-1949, 1985; Survivors, 1989; To Do no Harm, 1992; For Love and Money: A Novel of Stocks and Robbers, 2005. MYSTERIES: Burning Time, 1993; Hanging Time, 1995; Loving Time, 1996; Judging Time, 1998; Stealing Time, 1999; Tracking Time, 2000; Natural Suspect, 2001; Silent Bride, 2002; Over His Dead Body, 2003; Killing Gift, 2003; Clean Kill, 2005. OTHERS: On The Edge, 1990; Sleeper, 2009. Contributor to periodicals.. **Address:** c/o Dutton, Penguin Group, 375 Hudson St., 5th Fl., New York, NY 10014, U.S.A. **Online address:** leslie@authorleslieglass.com

GLASS, Rodge. Scottish/British (born England), b. 1978?. **Genres:** Novels. **Career:** Herald, writer; Strathclyde University, writer-in-residence and creative writing teacher, 2008-. **Publications:** (With J. Polley and G. Turnbull) The Storey's Story: Memories, Stories, Poems, Images, 2004; No Fireworks (novel), 2005; Alasdair Gray: A Secretary's Biography, 2008; Hope for Newborns (novel), 2008. Contributor to magazines. **Address:** Strathclyde University, 16 Richmond St., Glasgow, G1 1XQ, Scotland. **Online address:** rodgeglass@hotmail.com

GLASSBERG, David. American (born United States), b. 1954?. **Genres:** History, Social Sciences, Photography, Politics/Government. **Career:** University of Massachusetts, Department of History, professor, chair. Writer. **Publications:** American Historical Pageantry: The Uses of Tradition in the Early Twentieth Century, 1990; Sense of History: The Place of the Past in American Life, 2001. Contributor to periodicals. **Address:** Deparment of History, University of Massachusetts, Herter Hall 608, Amherst, MA 01003, U.S.A. **Online address:** glassberg@history.umass.edu

GLASSER, Ira. (Ira Saul Glasser). American (born United States), b. 1938. **Genres:** Civil Liberties/Human Rights, Sociology, History. **Career:** City University of New York, Queens College, lecturer in mathematics, 1960-62; Sarah Lawrence College, faculty, 1962-65; Current Magazine, associate editor, 1962-63, editor, 1963-67; New York Civil Liberties Union, associate director, 1967-70, executive director, 1970-78; St. Vincent's Hospital Community Advisory Board, chair, 1970-72; American Civil Liberties Union, executive director, 1978-2001; University of Illinois, faculty; Drug Policy Alliance, chair and president. Writer. **Publications:** (With W. Gaylin, S. Marcus and D.J. Rothman) Doing Good: The Limits of Benevolence, 1978; Visions of Liberty: The Bill of Rights for All Americans, 1991. Works appear in anthologies. Contributor to magazines. **Address:** Drug Policy Alliance, 70 W 36th St., 16th Fl., New York, NY 10018, U.S.A.

GLASSER, Ira Saul. See **GLASSER, Ira.**

GLASSIE, Henry. American (born United States), b. 1941. **Genres:** Mythology/Folklore, Art/Art History, History, Architecture. **Career:** Pennsylvania Historical and Museum Commission, director of the ethnic culture survey and state folklorist, 1967-69; Pennsylvania State University, assistant professor of American studies, 1969-70; Indiana University, assistant professor of folklore, 1970-72, associate professor of folklore, 1972-76, adjunct professor, Folklore Institute, assistant director, 1973-76, co-chairman, 1989-90, college professor of folklore, 1988-, co-director of Turkish studies, 1988-, Near Eastern Languages and Cultures, acting chairman, 2000-01, now adjunct professor emeritus, Department of Folklore and Ethnomusicology, now professor emeritus; University of Pennsylvania, professor of folklore and American civilization, 1976-88, Department of Folklore and Folklife, chairman, 1976-80, graduate chairman, 1985-87, undergraduate chairman, 1987-88, adjunct faculty in architecture. Writer. **Publications:** (With M.E. Leach) A Guide for Collectors of Oral Traditions and Folk Cultural Material in Pennsylvania, 1968; (ed. with Austin and A. Fife) Forms Upon the Frontier: Folklife and Folk Arts in the United States, 1969; Pattern in the Material Folk Culture of the Eastern United States, 1969; (with J.F. Szwed and E.D. Ives) Folksongs and Their Makers, 1970; All Silver and No Brass: An Irish Christmas Mumming, 1975, rev. ed., 1989; Folk Housing in Middle Virginia: A Structural Analysis of Historic Artifacts, 1975; (with L. nda Dégh and F. Oinas) Folklore Today: A Festschrift for Richard M. Dorson, 1976; William Houck, Maker of Pounded Ash Adirondack Pack Baskets, 1980; Irish Folk History: Texts from the North, 1982, 2nd ed., 1998; Passing the Time in Ballymenone: Cul-

ture and History of an Ulster Community, 1982, 2nd ed., 1995; (ed.) Irish Folktales, 1985; The Spirit of Folk Art: The Girard Collection at the Museum of International Folk Art, 1989; Turkish Traditional Art Today, 1993; Art and Life in Bangladesh, 1997; Material Culture, 1999; The Potter's Art, 1999; (with F. Mahmud) Contemporary Traditional Art of Bangladesh, 2000; Vernacular Architecture, 2000; The Stars of Ballymenone, 2006; (ed. with F. Mahmud) Living Traditions, 2007; Prince Twins Seven-Seven: His Art, His Life in Nigeria, His Exile in America, 2010; (contrib.) The Individual and Tradition: Folkloristic Perspectives, 2011; (with T. Takahara) Lions of Clay: The Tradition of Figurative Ceramics in Contemporary Japan, forthcoming. **Address:** Department of Near Eastern Languages and Cultures, Indiana University, 506 N Fess 205, 219 Goodbody Hall, 1011 E 3rd St., Bloomington, IN 47405-7005, U.S.A. **Online address:** glassieh@indiana.edu

GLASSMAN, Bruce. American (born United States), b. 1961. **Genres:** Young Adult Fiction, Adult Non-fiction, Biography, Children's Fiction. **Career:** Blackbirch Press Inc., publisher, 1985-. Writer. **Publications:** YOUNG ADULTS FICTION: The Marathon Race Mystery, 1985; Midnight Fridge, 1998. NONFICTION: The Crash of '29 and the New Deal, 1986; Everything You Need to Know about Step-Families, 1988; Everything You Need to Know about Growing up Male, 1991, rev. ed., 1995; New York: Gateway to the New World, 1991; Zoolidays, 2007; Responsibility, 2008; Trustworthiness, 2008; Fairness, 2008; Citizenship, 2008; Respect, 2008; Caring, 2008. BIOGRAPHY: J. Paul Getty: Oil Billionaire, 1989; Mikhail Baryshnikov, 1990; Arthur Miller, 1990; Wilma Mankiller: Chief of the Cherokee Nation, 1992; John Lennon and Paul McCartney: Their Magic and their Music, 1995. OTHERS: (ed.) Macmillan Visual Almanac, 1996; (ed.) New View Almanac: The First all-Visual Resource of Vital Facts and Statistics!, 1996, 3rd ed., 2003. **Address:** Blackbirch Press, 260 Amity Rd., PO Box Box 3573, Woodbridge, CT 06525, U.S.A. **Online address:** bruce.glassman@ga6.com

GLASSMAN, Jonathon P. (Jonathon Philip Glassman). American (born United States), b. 1956?. **Genres:** History. **Career:** Duke University, visiting assistant professor of history, 1988-89; Northwestern University, Evanston, associate professor of history, 1989-, director of graduate studies, associate chair. Writer. **Publications:** Feasts and Riot: Revelry, Rebellion and Popular Consciousness on the Swahili Coast, 1856-1888, 1995; War of Words, War of Stones: Racial Thought and Violence in Colonial Zanzibar, 2011. **Address:** Department of History, Northwestern University, Rm. 316, Harris Hall, 1881 Sheridan Rd., Ste. 202, Evanston, IL 60208-2220, U.S.A. **Online address:** j-glassman@northwestern.edu

GLASSMAN, Jonathon Philip. See **GLASSMAN, Jonathon P.**

GLASSMAN, Ronald M. American (born United States), b. 1937. **Genres:** History, Sociology, Politics/Government. **Career:** City University of New York, Queens College, assistant professor of sociology, 1965-68, Herbert H. Lehman College, assistant professor of sociology, 1973-78; Connecticut College, assistant professor of sociology, 1968-71; New School for Social Research, visiting professor of sociology, 1976-78; New York University, New School for Social Research, adjunct assistant professor, 1995; William Paterson College, College of Humanities and Social Sciences, professor of sociology. Writer. **Publications:** The Political History of Latin America, 1969; Democracy and Despotism in Primitive Societies, 2 vols., 1986; Democracy and Equality, 1989; (with M. Green) A Democracy Agenda for the Year 2000, 1989; China in Transition, 1991; (with W. Swatos, Jr. and P. Kivisto) For Democracy, 1993; The Middle Class and Democracy in Socio-Historical Perspective, 1995; The New Middle Class and Democracy in Global Perspective, 1997; Caring Capitalism: A New Middle Class Base for the Welfare State, 2000; (with W.H. Swatos and B.J. Denison) Social Problems in Global Perspective, 2004. EDITOR/CO-EDITOR: (with A.J. Vidich) Conflict and Control: The Challenge to Legitimacy of Modern Governments, 1979; (with V. Murvar) Max Weber's Political Sociology, 1984; (with R.J. Antonio) A Weber-Marx Dialogue, 1985; (with W.H. Swatus, Jr.) Charisma, History and Social Structure, 1985; (with W.H. Swatos and P.L. Rosen) Bureaucracy against Democracy and Socialism, 1987; (with H. Etzkowitz) The Renascence of Sociological Theory, 1991. **Address:** Department of Sociology & Anthropology, William Paterson College, 300 Pompton Rd., New York, NY 10025, U.S.A. **Online address:** glassmanr@wpunj.edu

GLATT, John. British (born England), b. 1952. **Genres:** Biography, Mystery/Crime/Suspense, Literary Criticism And History, Novels, Autobiography/Memoirs, Criminology/True Crime. **Career:** News Ltd., staff, 1981.

Freelance journalist and writer. **Publications:** Rage and Roll: Bill Graham and the Selling of Rock, 1993; Lost in Hollywood: The Fast Times and Short Life of River Phoenix, 1995; The Chieftains: The Authorized Biography, 1997; The Royal House of Monaco, 1998; For I Have Sinned, 1998; Evil Twins, 1999; Cradle of Death, 2000; Blind Passion: A True Story of Seduction, Obsession and Murder, 2000; Internet Slavemaster, 2001; Cries in the Desert, 2002; Twisted: The Secret Desires and Bizarre Double Life of Dr. Richard Sharpe, 2003; Deadly American Beauty: A True Story of Passion, Adultery and Murder, 2004; One Deadly Night: A State Trooper, Triple Homicide and a Search for Justice, 2005; Depraved, 2005; Never Leave Me: An Obsessive Husband, an Unfaithful Wife, A Brutal Murder, 2006; The Doctor's Wife: A True Story of Marriage, Deception and Two Gruesome Deaths, 2007; Forgive Me, Father: A True Story of a Priest, a Nun, and a Brutal Murder, 2008; To Have and to Kill: Nurse Melanie McGuire, an Illicit Affair and the Gruesome Murder of her Husband, 2008; Secrets in the Cellar: A True Story of the Austrian Incest Case that Shocked the World, 2009; Playing With Fire: The True Story of a Nurse, Her Husband, and a Marriage Turned Fatal, 2010; Lost and Found, 2010. **Address:** c/o Peter Miller, PMA Literary & Film Management Inc., 45 W 21st St., PO Box 1817, New York, NY 10010, U.S.A.

GLATT, Lisa. American (born United States), b. 1963?. **Genres:** Novels, Poetry, Children's Fiction, Young Adult Fiction. **Career:** California State University, Department of English, faculty, 1992-, lecturer in English, lecturer, 2000-, assistant professor of English, Master of Arts in English Program, faculty; University of California, Writer's Exchange Program, instructor. Writer. **Publications:** Monsters and Other Lovers, 1996; Shelter, 1999; (with D. Hernandez) A Merciful Bed, 2001; A Girl Becomes a Comma like That: A Novel, 2004; The Apple's Bruise: Stories, 2005; (with S. Greenberg) Abigail Iris: The One And Only, 2009; (with S. Greenberg) Abigail Iris: The Pet Project, 2010. **Address:** Department of English, California State University, 317 MHB, 1250 Bellflower Blvd., Long Beach, CA 90840, U.S.A. **Online address:** lglatt@csulb.edu

GLATTHAAR, Joseph T(homas). American (born United States), b. 1957. **Genres:** History, Military/Defense/Arms Control, Humanities. **Career:** University of Wisconsin, lecturer, 1983; U.S. Army Command and General Staff College, visiting assistant professor, 1984-85; University of Houston, assistant professor, 1985-89, associate professor, 1989-92, graduate program director, 1987-89, department chair, 1990-92, professor of history, 1992-; U.S. Army Military History Institute, Harold K. Johnson visiting professor, 1991-92; University of North Carolina, Department of History, Stephenson distinguished professor. Writer. **Publications:** The March to the Sea and Beyond: Sherman's Troops in the Savannah and Carolinas Campaigns, 1985; Forged in Battle: The Civil War Alliance of Black Soldiers and White Officers, 1990; Partners in Command: The Relationships between Leaders in the Civil War, 1994; The Civil War's Black Soldiers, 1996; (ed.) Confederate Military Manuscripts, 1996; The Civil War in the West, 1863-1865, 2001; (ed. with G.W. Gallagher) Leaders of the Lost Cause: New Perspectives on The Confederate High Command, 2004; (with J.K. Martin) Forgotten Allies: The Oneida Indians and the American Revolution, 2006; General Lee's Army: From Victory to Collapse, 2008; Soldiering in the Army of Northern Virginia: A Statistical Portrait of the Men Who Served Under Robert E. Lee, 2011; (with R. O'Neill) The Civil War: Sherman's Capture of Atlanta and Other Western Battles, 1863-1865, 2011. Contributor to books and periodicals. **Address:** Department of History, University of North Carolina, Hamilton Hall CB, Ste. 3195, Chapel Hill, NC 27599-3195, U.S.A. **Online address:** jtg@unc.edu

GLAZER, Ellen Sarasohn. Also writes as Ellen Jean Tepper. American (born United States), b. 1947. **Genres:** Young Adult Fiction, Environmental Sciences/Ecology, Human Relations/Parenting, Psychology, Social Work, Women's Studies And Issues. **Career:** Mount Auburn Hospital, clinical worker, 1974-90; Harry and Lillian Cowan Foundation, board director, 1981-; Our Child Classes, instructor, 1984-88; Newton Girls Soccer League, coach, 1987-92; Newton Girls Softball League, coach, 1987-92; IVF-America, staff psychologist, 1990-91; New England Memorial Hospital, Fertility Center, program counselor, 1991-98; New England Medical Center, Department of Reproductive Medicine, 2000-; Act of Love Adoptions, consultant, 2000-; Boston Regional Center for Reproductive Medicine, staff. Writer. **Publications:** (With S.L. Cooper) Without Child: Experiencing and Resolving Infertility, 1988; The Long-Awaited Stork: A Guide for Parents after Infertility, 1990, rev. ed., 1998; When is Enough, Enough?, 1991; (with S.L. Cooper) Beyond Infertility: New Paths to Parenthood, 1994; (with S.L. Cooper) Choosing Assisted Reproduction: Social, Emotional and Ethical Considerations, 1998; (ed.) Ex-periencing Infertility: Stories to Inform and Inspire, 1998; (with E.W. Sterling) Having Your Baby Through Egg Donation, 2005. Contributor of books to periodicals. **Address:** 55 Farlow Rd., Newton, MA 02458, U.S.A. **Online address:** eglazer@gis.net

GLAZER, Melissa. *See* **MYERS, Tim.**

GLAZER, Nathan. American (born United States), b. 1923. **Genres:** Race Relations, Sociology, Urban Studies. **Career:** Commentary Magazine, editor, 1944-53; Doubleday Anchor Books, editor and editorial advisor, 1954-57; University of California, instructor in sociology, 1957-58, professor of sociology, 1963-69; Random House, editorial adviser, 1958-62; Bennington College, instructor in sociology, 1958-59; Smith College, instructor in sociology, 1959-60; Housing and Home Finance Agency, urban sociologist, 1962-63; Harvard University, professor of education and social structure, 1969-93, professor emeritus, 1993-; The Public Interest, co-editor, 1973-. **Publications:** (With D. Riesman and R. Denney) The Lonely Crowd, 1950; (with D. Riesman) Faces in the Crowd, 1952; American Judaism, 1957, 2nd ed., 1989; The Social Basis of American Communism, 1961; (with D.P. Moynihan) Beyond the Melting Pot, 1963; (co-author) Characteristics of American Jews, 1965; Remembering the Answers, 1970; Affirmative Discrimination: Ethnic Inequality and Public Policy, 1975; Ethnic Dilemmas 1964-1982, 1983; (with R. Ueda) Ethnic Groups in History Textbooks, 1983; New Perspectives in American Jewish Sociology, 1987; The Limits of Social Policy, 1988; New Immigration: A Challenge to American Society, 1988; We are all Multiculturalists Now, 1997; (with D. Riesman and R. Denney) Lonely Crowd: A Study of the Changing American Character, 2001; From a Cause to a Style: Modernist Architecture's Encounter with the American City, 2007. EDITOR: (with D. McEntire) Studies in Housing and Minority Groups, 1960; (and intro.) Cities in Trouble, 1970; (co-ed.) Perspectives on Soviet Jewry, 1971; (with D.P. Moynihan) Ethnicity: Theory and Experience, 1975; (with I. Kristol) American Commonwealth, 1976, 1976; (with W. Gorham) The Urban Predicament, 1976; (with K. Young) Ethnic Pluralism and Public Policy: Achieving Equality in the United States and Britain, 1983; Public Interest on Education, 1984; Public Interest on Crime and Punishment, 1984; Clamor at the Gates: The New American Immigration, 1985; (with M. Lilla) The Public Face of Architecture, 1987; (with S.R. Glazer) Conflicting Images: India and the United States, 1990; (with S.A. Thernstrom and R.T. Gill) Our Changing Population, 1992; (with J.D. Montgomery) Sovereignty under Challenge: How Governments Respond, 2002; (with C.R. Field) National Mall: Rethinking Washington's Monumental Core, 2008. **Address:** Graduate School of Education, Harvard University, Appian Way, Cambridge, MA 02138, U.S.A. **Online address:** nglazer@fas.harvard.edu

GLAZIER, Stephen D. American (born United States), b. 1949. **Genres:** Anthropology/Ethnology, Archaeology/Antiquities, Theology/Religion, Travel/Exploration, Social Sciences, Psychiatry, Mythology/Folklore, History, History. **Career:** University of Connecticut, lecturer, 1979-81; Trinity College, visiting assistant professor, 1981-82; Connecticut College, visiting assistant professor, 1982-83; Wayland Baptist University, associate professor, 1983-86; Westmont College, associate professor, 1986-88; University of Nebraska-Kearney, Department of Sociology, associate professor, 1988-94, professor, 1994-, head of department, 1988-91, 2007-08; University of Nebraska-Lincoln, Department of Anthropology, professor and graduate faculty fellow in anthropology, 2000-12, adjunct professor of anthropology. Writer. **Publications:** Spiritual Baptist Music of Trinidad, 1980; Marchin' the Pilgrims Home: Leadership and Decision-Making in an Afro-Caribbean Faith, 1983, rev. ed. as Marchin' the Pilgrims Home: A Study of the Spiritual Baptists of Trinidad, 1991. CONTRIBUTOR: Prophetic Religions and Politics, 1986; Sacred Journeys: The Anthropology of Pilgrimage, 1992; When They Read What We Write: The Politics of Ethnography, 1993; Religion and the Social Order, 1996; New Trends and Developments in African Religions, 1998; Religion, Diaspora, and Cultural Identity: A Reader in the Anglophone Caribbean, 1999; Anthropology and Theology: Gods, Icons, and Godtalk, 1999; (with L. Jones) The Encyclopedia of Religion, 2nd ed., 2005; Rastafari: A Universal Philosophy for the Third Millenium, 2006; The Encyclopedia of Anthropology, 2006; Sango in Africa and the African Diaspora, 2009; (Leslie G. Desmangles and Joseph M. Murphy) Understanding the Contemporary Caribbean, 2009; (with M. Hallin) 21st Century Anthropology, 2010; Cambridge History of Religions in America, 2010. EDITOR: Perspectives on Pentecostalism: Case Studies from the Caribbean and Latin America, 1980; (and intro.) Caribbean Ethnicity Revisited, 1985; Anthropology of Religion: A Handbook, 1997; The Encyclopedia of African and African-American Religions, 2001; (with A. Buckser) Anthropology of Religious Conversion, 2003; (with C.A. Flowerday) Selected Readings in the Anthropology of Religion: Theoretical and Methodological Essays, 2003. Contributor to books and periodicals. **Address:** Department of Anthropology, University of Nebraska, 810 Oldfather Hall, PO Box 880368, Lincoln, NE 68588-0368, U.S.A. **Online address:** glaziers@unk.edu

GLEASON, Katherine (A.). American (born United States), b. 1960. **Genres:** Children's Non-fiction, Crafts, Self Help, Theology/Religion. **Career:** Greenroom Enterprises, production associate, 1987-88; Michael Rowan Group, associate, 1988-90; WomaNews, contributing editor, 1989-91; Lingua Franca, managing editor, 1991-92; Lucas/Evans Books Inc., projects coordinator, 1992-94. Writer. **Publications:** Origami Ornaments, 1995; Flying Origami, 1996; Scary Origami, 1996; Native American Art, 1996; Native American Literature, 1997; Clay Pots: A Native American Craft Kit, 1997; Leap Frog Origami, 1997; Kirigami Christmas Tree, 1998; Paper Magic: The Art of Origami, 1998; (with D. Zimmermann) The Complete Idiot's Guide to Wicca and Witchcraft, 2000, 3rd ed., 2006; (with G.C. Feldman) Releasing the Goddess Within, 2003; Ancient World: A Chapter Book, 2003; The Intuitive Arts on Money: Using Astrology, Tarot, and Your Psychic Intuition to See Your Future, 2003; Awesome Science: A Chapter Book, 2004; (co-author) Complete Idiot's Guide to Psychic Awareness, 2nd ed., 2004; Friendship Origami, 2004; Social Lives of Animals: A Chapter Book, 2005; Ancient Egyptian Culture, 2005; Native American Culture, 2005; Masterpieces in 3-C: M.C. Escher and the Art of Illusion, 2005; Playing for Real, 2006; (with C. Nichols) Ripley's Virtual Odditorium, 2006; Amazing Geo-gami, 2007. CRAFT KITS WITH INSTRUCTIONS: Egyptian Treasure Box, 1997; Frame Your Friends: Make Your Own Mini Photo Frames, 1998; Christmas Origami, 2003; Geo-gami, 2006; Amazing Geo-gami, 2007. **Address:** 199 E 7th St., Ste. 2D, New York, NY 10009, U.S.A. **Online address:** katherine.gleason@gmail.com

GLEAVE, John T. British (born England), b. 1917?. **Genres:** Geography, Social Sciences. **Career:** Ipswich, assistant education officer, 1947-48; University of Leeds, director of extramural classes and courses, 1962-69, director of special courses, 1969-82. Writer. **Publications:** Geography for Uganda Schools, 2 vols., 1958; (ed.) World Atlas for Uganda Schools, 1960; Visual Geography of East Africa, 1966; Introducing Geography, Uganda: Civics for East African Schools, 1960; (co-author) Uganda Our Homeland. **Address:** Fulwith Close, Harrogate, NY HG2 8HP, England.

GLEDHILL, John. British (born England), b. 1949. **Genres:** Anthropology/Ethnology, Social Sciences. **Career:** University of London, lecturer, 1976-88, senior lecturer, 1988-93, reader in anthropology, 1993-96, Institute of Latin American Studies, associate fellow, 1990-96; University of Manchester, professor of social anthropology, 1996-2000, head, 1997-2001, Max Gluckman professor of social anthropology, 2000-, Latin American and Caribbean Studies Centre, director; Association of Social Anthropologists of the U.K. and Commonwealth, chair, 2005-09; International Union of Anthropological and Ethnological Sciences (IUAES), vice president, 2009, 17th IUAES World Congress, organiser; Center for Latin American and Caribbean Studies (CLACS), co-director; Critique of Anthropology, managing editor. **Publications:** (Ed. with B. Bender and M.T. Larsen) State and Society: The Emergence and Development of Social Hierarchy and Political Centralization, 1988; Casi Nada: A Study of Agrarian Reform in the Homeland of Cardenismo, 1991, rev. ed. as Casi nada: capitalismo, estado y los campesinos de Guaracha, 1993; Power and Its Disguises: Anthropological Perspectives on Politics, 1994, 2nd ed., 2000; Neoliberalism, Transnationalization, and Rural Poverty: A Case Study of Michoacán, Mexico, 1995; El Poder y Sus Distraces: perspectives antiopologicas de la politica, 2000; Cultura y Desafio en Ostula, 2004; (ed.) Corporate Scandal: Global Corporatism against Society, 2004. Contributor of books to periodicals. **Address:** School of Social Sciences, University of Manchester, Roscoe Bldg., Oxford Rd., Manchester, M13 9PL, England. **Online address:** john.gledhill@manchester.ac.uk

GLEES, Anthony. British (born England), b. 1948. **Genres:** History, International Relations/Current Affairs, Politics/Government, Military/Defense/Arms Control. **Career:** St. Antony's College, associate, senior associate; University of Warwick, lecturer in history, 1973-75; Brunel University, lecturer in government, 1975-, senior lecturer and director of European studies, 1988-89, professor of contemporary history, 2003-, Brunel Centre for Intelligence and Security Studies, director; British Broadcasting Corp., head of current affairs, 1987-88; University of Buckingham, professor of politics, Centre for Security and Intelligence Studies (BUCSIS), director. Writer. **Publications:**

Exile Politics During the Second World War: The German Social Democrats in Britain, 1982; The Secrets of the Service: A Story of Soviet Subversion of Western Intelligence, 1987; Reinventing Germany: German Political Development since 1945, 1996; The Stasi Files: East Germany's Secret Operations against Britain, 2003; (with C. Pope) When Students Turn to Terror: Terrorist And Extremist Activity on British Campuses, 2005. Contributor to books and periodicals. **Address:** Centre for Security and Intelligence Studies, University of Buckingham, Hunter St., Buckingham, BK MK18 1EG, England. **Online address:** anthony.glees@buckingham.ac.uk

GLEESON, Libby. Australian (born Australia), b. 1950. **Genres:** Children's Fiction, Picture/Board Books, Reference. **Career:** Writer and educator. **Publications:** Eleanor, Elizabeth, 1984; I Am Susannah, 1987; One Sunday, 1988; Dodger, 1990; The Great Big Scary Dog, 1991; Uncle David, 1992; Hurry Up!, 1992; Where's Mum?, 1993; Mum Goes to Work, 1993; Love Me, Love Me Not, 1993; Sleeptime, 1993; Walking to School, 1994; Great Big Scary Dog, 1994; Skating on Sand, 1994; The Princess and the Perfect Dish, 1995; Hannah Plus One, 1996; The Queen of the Universe, 1997; Refuge, 1998; The Great Bear, 1999; Hannah and the Tomorrow Room, 1999; Writing Hannah: On Writing for Children, 1999; Dear Writer, 2000; Shutting the Chooks In, 2000; An Ordinary Day, 2001; The Rum Rebellion: The Diary of David Bellamy, 2001; Making Picture Books, 2003; Cuddle Time, 2004; Hannah the Famous, 2004; Amy & Louis, 2006; Ray's Olympics, 2006; Clancy's Long Walk, 2007; Half a World Away, 2007; Happy Birthday X3, 2007; Writing Like a Writer 2007; Mahtab's Story, 2008; Clancy & Millie and the Very Fine House, 2009; I am Thomas 2011; Look a Book, 2011. **Address:** 11 Oxford St., Petersham, NW 2049, Australia. **Online address:** libbygleeson@yahoo.com

GLEICK, Peter H. American (born United States), b. 1956. **Genres:** Marine Sciences/Oceanography, Sciences, Technology. **Career:** University of California, Lawrence Berkeley National Laboratory, research and teaching assistant, 1978-81, Energy and Resources Group, research associate, 1983-86, post-doctoral staff, 1986-88; Office of the Governor of California, deputy assistant, 1980-82; Pacific Institute for Studies in Development, Environment, and Security, president and co-founder, 1987-, board director, 1988-; Environmental Science and Policy Institute, board director, 1991-97; International Water Resources Association, board director, 1997-2000; American Geophysical Union, Global Environmental Change Focus Group, vice chair, 2006-08. Writer. **Publications:** Water and Conflict, 1992; (ed.) Water in Crisis: A Guide to the World's Fresh Water Resources, 1993; The World's Water 1998-1999, vol. I: The Biennial Report on Freshwater Resources, 1998, vol. II: The World's Water 2000-2001, 2000, (co-author) vol. III: The World's Water 2002-2003, 2002, (co-author) vol. IV: The World's Water 2004-2005, 2004, (co-author) vol. V: The World's Water 2006-2007, 2006, (co-author) vol. VI: The World's Water 2008-2009, 2008, (co-author) vol. VII: The World's Water, 2011; Bottled and Sold: The Story Behind Our Obsession with Bottled Water, 2010. **Address:** Pacific Institute for Studies in Development, Environment, and Security, 654 13th St., Preservation Pk., Oakland, CA 94612, U.S.A. **Online address:** pgleick@pipeline.com

GLEITER, Jan. American (born United States), b. 1947?. **Genres:** Children's Fiction, Novels, Biography, Poetry, Literary Criticism And History. **Career:** Writer. **Publications:** NOVELS: Lie Down with Dogs, 1996; A House by the Side of the Road, 1998. FOR CHILDREN: Color Rhymes: Teddies (poems), 1985; Shape Rhymes, 1985; Picture Rhymes, 1985; Seaside Adventure, 1987; Tell the Time, 1987. BIOGRAPHIES: (with K. Thompson) Paul Bunyan and Babe the Blue Ox, 1985; (with K. Thompson) Pocahontas, 1985; (with K. Thompson) Daniel Boone, 1985; (with K. Thompson) Annie Oakley, 1987; (with K. Thompson) Casey Jones, 1987; (with K. Thompson) Christopher Columbus, 1987; (with K. Thompson) Johnny Appleseed, 1987; (with K. Thompson) Kit Carson, 1987; (with K. Thompson) Molly Pitcher, 1987; (with K. Thompson) Paul Revere, 1987; (with K. Thompson) Sacagawea, 1987; (with K. Thompson) Booker T. Washington, 1988; (with K. Thompson) David Farragut, 1988; (with K. Thompson) Elizabeth Cady Stanton, 1988; (with K. Thompson) Jack London, 1988; (with K. Thompson) Jane Addams, 1988; (with K. Thompson) John James Audubon, 1988; (with K. Thompson) Matthew Henson, 1988; (with K. Thompson) Sam Houston, 1988; (with K. Thompson) Sequoya, 1988; (with K. Thompson) Diego Rivera, 1989; (with K. Thompson) Hernando de Soto, 1989; (with K. Thompson) Jose Marti, 1989; (with K. Thompson) Juníper Serra, 1989; (with K. Thompson) Luis Muñoz Marín, 1989; (with K. Thompson) Miguel Hidalgo y Costilla, 1989; (with K. Thompson) Simón Bolívar, 1989; Benito Juárez, 1990; First Biographies, 1995, 2nd ed., 2002. ADAPTATIONS: (with K.

Thompson) The Legend of Sleepy Hollow, 1985; Great Expectations, 1989; Ivanhoe, 1989. **Address:** St. Martin's Press, Rm. 1715, 175 5th Ave., New York, NY 10010-7703, U.S.A.

GLEN, Frank Grenfell. New Zealander (born New Zealand), b. 1933. **Genres:** History, Military/Defense/Arms Control, Theology/Religion, Autobiography/Memoirs, Biography, Travel/Exploration. **Career:** Presbyterian Church of New Zealand, ordained minister, 1958; City of Otautau, minister, 1958-60; New Zealand Territorial Army, chaplain, 1962-70; Far West Mission and Flying Padre, superintendent, 1968-70; Royal Australian Air Force, senior chaplain, 1970-76; New Zealand Department of Justice, 1976-84; police chaplain, 1983-97; Presbyterian Support Services, chaplain, 1985-86; Thames Union Parish, chaplain, 1986-91; Australian Institute History and Arts, fellow, 1986; New Zealand Journal of Military History, editor, 1998-2002. **Publications:** Methodism in Southland, 1956; Methodist in Auckland during Maori Wars, 1860-64, 1958; Methodism in the Coal Field of Southland, 1960; Holy Joe's People: A Person in Fiordland, 1968, 3rd ed., 1975; Fly High Reach Far, 1971; Study of the Chaplain's Role and Religion in the R.A.A.F., 1973; Bush in Our Yard, 1980; For Glory and a Farm, 1984; Church Leaders and the First Taranaki War, 1860-61, 1992; New Zealand Army Chaplains at War, 1997; Bowler of Gallipoli Witness to the ANZAC Legend, 2004. **Address:** 32 Ti Rakau Dr., Woolston, Christchurch, 1, New Zealand.

GLEN, Paul (Michael). American (born United States), b. 1965. **Genres:** Administration/Management, Technology, Business/Trade/Industry. **Career:** SEI Information Technology, consultant, 1988-95, regional manager, 1995-99; C2 Consulting, founder, 1999-; University of Southern California, Marshall School of Business, adjunct faculty; Loyola Marymount University, adjunct faculty; Developing Technical Leaders Program, director; Leading Geeks Co., chief executive officer. Writer, consultant and speaker. **Publications:** Healing Client Relationships: A Professional's Guide to Managing Client Conflict, 2001; Leading Geeks: How to Manage and Lead People Who Deliver Technology, 2003. **Address:** Leading Geeks Co., 3253 Malcolm Ave., Los Angeles, CA 90034-4408, U.S.A. **Online address:** info@paulglen.com

GLENDENING, John. American (born United States), b. 1948. **Genres:** Literary Criticism And History, Travel/Exploration, Romance/Historical. **Career:** University of Montana, professor of English. Writer. **Publications:** The High Road: Romantic Tourism, Scotland, and Literature, 1720-1820, 1997; The Evolutionary Imagination in Late-Victorian Novels: An Entangled Bank, 2007. Contributor to journals. **Address:** Department of English, University of Montana, LA 133, Missoula, MT 59812, U.S.A. **Online address:** john.glendening@mso.umt.edu

GLENDINNING, Miles. Scottish/British (born England), b. 1956. **Genres:** Architecture, Autobiography/Memoirs. **Career:** RCAHMS (National Monuments Record), Threatened Buildings Survey, manager, 1978-, head of architecture, through 2005; University of Edinburgh, honorary fellow in social policy, 1993-, Edinburgh College of Art, Scottish Centre for Conservation Studies, director, reader in architectural conservation. Writer. **Publications:** Preservation: Dawn of the Living Dead, 1986; Tenements and Towers, 1990; (with S. Muthesius) Tower Block: Modern Public Housing in England, Scotland, Wales, and Northern Ireland, 1994; (with R. MacInnes and A. MacKechnie) A History of Scottish Architecture from the Renaissance to the Present Day, 1996; Rebuilding Scotland, 1997; (with R. MacInnes and A. MacKechnie) Building a Nation, 1999; (with D. Page) Clone City, 1999; (ed. with D. Watters) Home Builders: Mactaggart & Mickel and the Scottish Housebuilding Industry, 1999; (with A. MacKechnie) Scottish Architecture, 2004; The Architecture of Scottish Government: From Kingship to Parliamentary Democracy, 2004; The Last Icons: Architecture Beyond Modernism, 2004; (with D. Watters) Little Houses: The National Trust for Scotland's Improvement Programme for Small Homes, 2006; Modern Architect: The Life and Times of Robert Matthew, 2008. **Address:** Edinburgh College of Art, 74 Lauriston Pl., Edinburgh, EH3 9DF, Scotland. **Online address:** m.glendinning@eca.ac.uk

GLENDOWER, Rose. See HARRIS, Marion (Rose).

GLENER, Doug. American (born United States) **Genres:** History, inspirational/Motivational Literature. **Career:** Porter Henry & Co., staff writer; Rubenstein Public Relations, creative director and senior writer; writer, 1989-; Catalyst Creative Services, founder, 1992-; Dharma Foundation, board director; Brookline Arts Center, community advisor. **Publications:** (With S. Komagiri) Wisdom's Blossoms: Tales of the Saints of India, 2002. Contributor to periodicals. **Address:** Catalyst Creative Services, 283 Countryhaven Rd., Encinitas, CA 92024, U.S.A. **Online address:** doug.glener@sbcglobal.net

GLENN, Cheryl. American (born United States) **Genres:** Humanities, Classics, Communications/Media, Education, Women's Studies And Issues, Writing/Journalism. **Career:** High school, English teacher, 1972-75; teacher and consultant, 1977-85; Oregon State University, assistant professor, 1989-94, associate professor of English, 1994-97, College of Liberal Arts Center for Teaching Excellence, director, 1996-97, Elizabeth P. Ritchie distinguished professor, 1996, Center for the Humanities, faculty fellow, 1993; National Endowment for the Humanities, review panelist, 1993, 1997-98, 2000; Pennsylvania State University, associate professor of English, 1997-, liberal arts research professor of English and women studies, Center for Democratic Deliberation, co-director; Millikin University, visiting professor, 1997; Washington State University, speaker; Ball State University, speaker; Inaugural Biennial Institute, Rhetoric Society of America, co-director, 2005. Writer. **Publications:** (With A. Lunsford and R. Connors) St. Martin's Handbook, 1989; (with R.J. Connors) The St. Martin's Guide to Teaching Writing, 1989, 6th ed., 2008; (contrib.) Popular Literacies, 1996; Rhetoric Retold: Regendering the Tradition from Antiquity through the Renaissance, 1997; (contrib.) Listening to Their Voices: Essays on the Rhetorical Activities of Historical Women, 1997; St. Martin's Reader, 1999; (with R.J. Connors) New St. Martin's Guide to Teaching Writing, 1999; (with L. Gray) Writer's Harbrace Handbook, 2001, 5th ed., 2011; Making Sense: A New Rhetorical Reader, 2002, 3rd ed., 2010; Unspoken: A Rhetoric of Silence, 2004; (with M. Lyday and W. Sharer) Rhetorical Education in America; 2004; Making Sense: A Real-World Rhetorical Reader, 2005; Harbrace Guide to Writing: Class Test Booklet, 2008, 2nd ed., 2012; Harbrace Essentials, 2010; (co-author) The Hodges' Harbrace Handbook, 17th ed., 2010; (with L. Gray) The Essential Harbrace Handbook, 2010; (ed. with K. Ratcliffe) Silence and Listening as Rhetorical Arts, 2011; (with L. Gray) Harbrace Essentials with Resources for Multilingual Writers, 2013. Contributor of articles to journals. **Address:** Department of English, Pennsylvania State University, 223 S Burrowes Bldg., University Park, PA 16802, U.S.A. **Online address:** cjg6@psu.edu

GLENN, Evelyn Nakano. American (born United States), b. 1940. **Genres:** Women's Studies And Issues, Social Sciences. **Career:** Abt Associates, senior researcher, 1970-71; Boston University, lecturer, 1971-72, assistant professor of sociology, 1972-84; Florida State University, associate professor of sociology, 1984-86; State University, professor of sociology, 1986-90; University of California, Department of Ethnic Studies, professor of ethnic studies, 1990-, Department of Gender and Women's Studies, professor, 1990-, chair, 1993-95, Beatrice Bain Research Group, director, 2000-02, Center for Race and Gender, founding director, 2001-; Harvard University, Extension Division, lecturer, 1971-73, Radcliffe Institute, research affiliate, 1974; University of Hawaii, visiting assistant professor, 1983. Writer. **Publications:** Issei, Nisei, War Bride: Three Generations of Japanese American Women in Domestic Service, 1986; Hidden Aspects of Women's Work, 1987; (ed. with G. Chang and L.R. Forcey) Mothering: Ideology, Experience, and Agency, 1994; Unequal Freedom: How Race and Gender Shaped American Citizenship and Labor, 2002; (ed.) Shades of Difference: Why Skin Color Matters, 2009; Forced to Care: Coercion and Caregiving in America, 2010. Contributor to books and periodicals. **Address:** Department of Gender & Women's Studies, University of California, 610 Barrows Hall, Berkeley, CA 94720-1070, U.S.A. **Online address:** englenn@berkeley.edu

GLENN, Jason Kahn. American (born United States), b. 1967?. **Genres:** History, Politics/Government. **Career:** Syracuse University, department of history, visiting assistant professor, 1997-98; University of Southern California, department of history, assistant professor, 1998-2004, associate professor, 2004-; Huntington Library, Mellon Foundation Seminar in the Humanities, instructor, 2002. Writer. **Publications:** Politics and History in the Tenth Century: The Work and World of Richer of Reims, 2004. Contributor to journals. Works appear in anthologies. **Address:** Department of History, University of Southern California, Los Angeles, CA 90089-0034, U.S.A. **Online address:** jkglenn@usc.edu

GLENN, Mel. American/Swiss (born Switzerland), b. 1943. **Genres:** Children's Fiction, Young Adult Fiction, Poetry, Novels, Literary Criticism And History. **Career:** Public Junior High School, teacher in English, 1967-70;

Abraham Lincoln High School, teacher in English, 1970-2001, retired, 2001; writer, 1980-. **Publications:** YOUNG ADULT POETRY: Class Dismissed!: High School Poems, 1982; Class Dismissed II: More High School Poems, 1986; Back to Class, 1988; My Friend's Got This Problem, Mr. Candler, 1991; Who Killed Mr. Chippendale?: A Mystery in Poems, 1996; The Taking of Room 114: A Hostage Drama in Poems, 1997; Jump Ball: A Basketball Season in Poems, 1997; Foreign Exchange: A Mystery in Poems, 1999; Split Image: A Story in Poems, 2000. YOUNG ADULT FICTION NOVEL: One Order to Go, 1984. CHILDREN'S FICTION: Play-by-Play, 1986; Squeeze Play: A Baseball Story, 1989. **Address:** c/o Rosemary Brosnan, HarperCollins Children's Books, 1350 Ave. of the Americas, New York, NY 10019-4702, U.S.A. **Online address:** author114@aol.com

GLENN, Patricia Brown. American (born United States), b. 1953. **Genres:** Architecture, Art/Art History, Children's Fiction. **Career:** Landmarks Commission, research historian, 1978-79; Historic Kansas City Foundation, survey coordinator and architectural historian, 1979-81, director of research and education, 1981-83, director, 1992-94; Ottawa University, adjunct faculty, 1981-83; consultant, 1983-; University of Missouri, adjunct faculty, 1983, 1985-90. Writer. **Publications:** Under Every Roof: A Kid's Style and Field Guide to the Architecture of American Houses, 1993; From the Ground Up: Architects at Work in America, 1996; Discover America's Favorite Architects, 1996. Contributor to periodicals. **Address:** 6336 Ensley Ln., Shawnee Mission, KS 66208-1930, U.S.A.

GLENN, Richard A. American (born United States), b. 1968. **Genres:** Sociology, Law. **Career:** Millersville University, Department Government and Political Affairs, professor and chair. Writer. **Publications:** Right to Privacy: Rights and Liberties under the Law, 2003; (with O.H. Stephens) Unreasonable Searches and Seizures: Rights and Liberties under the Law, 2006. **Address:** Department Government and Political Affairs, Millersville University, Rm. 101, Fulton House, 1 S George St., PO Box 1002, Millersville, PA 17551-0302, U.S.A. **Online address:** richard.glenn@millersville.edu

GLENN, Sharlee Mullins. American (born United States), b. 1960. **Genres:** Novels. **Career:** Brigham Young University, adjunct faculty, 1989-97. Freelance writer. **Publications:** Circle Dance: A Novel, 1998; One in a Billion, 2000; Keeping Up With Roo, 2004; Just What Mama Needs, 2008. Contributor to periodicals. **Address:** c/o Author Mail, G. P. Putnam's Sons, 375 Hudson St., New York, NY 10014-3657, U.S.A. **Online address:** sharleeglenn@gmail.com

GLENNON, Karen M. American (born United States), b. 1946. **Genres:** Children's Fiction, Poetry, Young Adult Fiction. **Career:** The Book Shop, school liaison, 1991-93; West Junior High School, teacher, 1993-96; Nampa Senior High School, teacher, 1996-2000. Writer and educator. **Publications:** Miss Eva and the Red Balloon, 1990; The Kite War, forthcoming. **Address:** PO Box 6177, Boise, ID 83707-6177, U.S.A. **Online address:** ps6813@aol.com

GLENNON, Robert Jerome. American (born United States), b. 1944. **Genres:** Law, Social Sciences. **Career:** Brandeis University, Department of History of American Civilization, Crown fellow, 1970-73; Wayne State University, Law School, associate professor of law, 1973-77, professor of law, 1977-85; University of Illinois, College of Law, visiting associate professor of law, 1975; University of Minnesota, Law School, visiting professor of law, 1980; University of Arizona, College of Law, visiting professor of law, professor of law, 1985-97, Morris K. Udall professor of law and public policy, 1997-; University of Puerto Rico, School of Law, visiting professor, 1998; Mesa Refuge, writer-in-residence, 2004; Property and Environmental Research Center, Julian Simon fellow, 2006. Writer and lawyer. **Publications:** The Iconoclast as Reformer: Jerome Frank's Impact on American Law, 1985; Water Follies: Groundwater Pumping and the Fate of America's Fresh Waters, 2002; Unquenchable: America's Water Crisis and What to Do about It, 2009. Contributor to books and journals. **Address:** James E. Rogers College of Law, University of Arizona, PO Box 210176, Tucson, AZ 85721-0176, U.S.A. **Online address:** glennon@law.arizona.edu

GLICK, Bernard R. Canadian (born Canada), b. 1945. **Genres:** Biology, Technology, Sciences. **Career:** University of Toronto, postdoctoral fellow and research associate, 1974-78; National Research Council, research associate, 1978-79; Bio Logicals Inc., Molecular Genetics and Biochemistry

Group, group leader, 1979-82; University of Waterloo, associate professor, 1982-89, professor of biology, 1989-, professor of chemical engineering, 1992-, Department of Biology, chair, 2002-08. Consultant and writer. **Publications:** (With J.J. Pasternak) Molecular Biotechnology: Principles and Applications of Recombinant DNA, 1994, (with J.J. Pasternak and C.L. Patten) 4th ed., 2010; (co-author) Biochemical and Genetic Mechanisms Used by Plant Growth-Promoting Bacteria, 1999. EDITOR: (co-ed.) Biomass Conversion Technologies, 1987; (with J.E. Thompson) Methods in Plant Molecular Biology and Biotechnology, 1993. Contributor of articles to journals. **Address:** Department of Biology, University of Waterloo, B2 356C, 200 University Ave. W, Waterloo, ON N2L 3G1, Canada. **Online address:** glick@sciborg.uwaterloo.ca

GLICKMAN, James (A.). American (born United States), b. 1948. **Genres:** Novels, Novellas/Short Stories. **Career:** University of Arizona, Law School, instructor, 1972; Community College of Rhode Island, professor of English, 1972-, co-chair; Radcliffe Seminars, faculty, 1985-88. Writer. **Publications:** Sounding the Waters (novel), 1996. Contributor to periodicals, journals and magazines. **Address:** Writers House, 21 W 26th St., New York, NY 10010, U.S.A. **Online address:** jglickman@ccri.edu

GLICKMAN, Norman J. American (born United States), b. 1942. **Genres:** Economics, Social Sciences, Urban Studies. **Career:** National Industrial Conference Board Inc., economist, 1963-65; City University of New York, research fellow, 1964-65; City College, lecturer in economics, 1965; Hofstra University, lecturer in economics, 1966; Regional Science Research Institute, research fellow, 1967, research associate, 1969-71; University of Pennsylvania, teaching fellow, 1966, Department of City and Regional Planning, lecturer, 1969-70, assistant professor of city and regional planning, 1970-75, associate professor of city and regional planning and regional science, 1975-76, 1977-81, Department of Regional Science, associate professor of regional science, 1981-82, professor of regional science, 1982-83, Urban Studies Program, director and founder, 1970-74, visiting professor, 2003-; University of Haifa, Fulbright-Hays senior lecturer, 1972-73; Abt Associates Inc., consultant, 1976, 1979-80; RAND Corp., consultant, 1980-81; Netherlands Institute for Advanced Studies, fellow, 1981-82; University of Texas, Lyndon B. Johnson School of Public Affairs, Mike Hogg professor of urban policy and professor of economics, 1983-89, visiting professor, 2006-07; University of Iowa, Ida Beam visiting professor, 1984; University of Cambridge, Department of Land Economy, Vivian Stewart visiting fellow, 1984; Instituto Tecnologico y de Estudios Superiores de Monterrey, distinguished Fulbright professor, 1985-87; Rutgers University, Edward J. Bloustein School of Planning and Public Policy, professor of planning, 1989-2000, university professor, 2000-, State of New Jersey professor of urban planning, Center for Urban Policy Research, director, 1989-2000; University College London, The Bartlett School, visiting professor, 1998. Writer. **Publications:** Econometric Analysis of Regional Systems: Explorations in Model Building and Policy Analysis, 1977; The Growth and Management of the Japanese Urban System, 1979; (with S.S. Jacobs) HUD and the Cities: The Urban Impacts of HUD's Programs, 1979; (ed.) The Urban Impacts of Federal Policies, 1980; (ed. with F.G. Adams) Modeling the Multiregional Economic System: Perspectives for the Eighties, 1980; Emerging Urban Policies in a Slow-Growth Economy: Conservative Initiatives and Progressive Responses, 1981; (ed. with D.A. Hicks) Transition to the 21st Century: Prospect and Policies for Economic and Urban-Regional Transformation, 1983; (with R. Marshall) Choices for American Industry, 1987; (with D.P. Woodward) Regional Patterns of Manufacturing Foreign Direct Investment in the United States: A Report, 1987; (with D.P. Woodward) The New Competitors: How Foreign Investors Are Changing the U.S. Economy, 1989. Contributor to periodicals and newspapers. **Address:** Rutgers University, Rm. 360, Civic Square Bldg., 33 Livingston Ave., Ste. 400, New Brunswick, NJ 08901-1982, U.S.A. **Online address:** glickman@rutgers.edu

GLISERMAN, Martin. American (born United States), b. 1945. **Genres:** Literary Criticism And History, Language/Linguistics, Psychology, Education, Novels, Humanities. **Career:** Rutgers University, associate professor of English, 1971-; American Imago, editor-in-chief, 1987-2002, now editor emeritus; psychoanalyst, 1987-. **Publications:** Psychoanalysis, Language, and the Body of the Text, 1996. **Address:** Department of English, Rutgers University, Rm. 209, Murray Hall, College Ave., 510 George St., New Brunswick, NJ 08901-1167, U.S.A. **Online address:** martin.gliserman@rutgers.edu

GLISSON, J(ake) T. American (born United States), b. 1927. **Genres:** Novels, Plays/Screenplays, History. **Career:** Motivation Systems and Jaake' Creations, chief executive officer; Steinmetz Studio, photographer, 1950; New-man Lynde Advertising Agency, artist and illustrator, 1951; Advertising Trade Services of New York, artist and illustrator, 1952; All Florida, art director, 1954; Cape Haze Marine Laboratory, artist, 1955; Chemical Corps College, illustrator, 1956; National Mobile Home Dealers and Owners Association Magazine, chief executive officer and art director, 1957; Social and Visitors Guides, chief executive officer and art director, 1964; Florida State Museum, art director, designer and producer, 1968; Wild Wald Center, art director and conceptual artist, 1983. **Publications:** The Creek, 1993. **Address:** PO Box O, Evinston, FL 32633, U.S.A. **Online address:** jt31527@aol.com

GLIXON, Jonathan Emmanuel. American (born United States), b. 1952. **Genres:** Music, Humor/Satire, Art/Art History. **Career:** University of Washington, School of Music, acting assistant professor, 1979-80; University of Kentucky, School of Music, assistant professor, associate graduate faculty, 1983-88; graduate faculty, 1988, associate professor, 1988-2004, Musicology Division, coordinator, 1989-94, director of graduate studies in music, 1990-94, professor, 2004-, university research professor, 2008-09, provost's distinguished service professor, 2010-; National Endowment for the Humanities, fellow, 1997-98, 2004-05. Writer. **Publications:** Honoring God and the City: Music at the Venetian Confraternities, 1260-1807, 2003; (with B.L. Glixon) Inventing the Business of Opera: The Impresario and His World in Seventeenth-Century Venice, 2005. **Address:** School of Music, University of Kentucky, 105 Fine Arts Bldg., Lexington, KY 40506-0022, U.S.A. **Online address:** jonathan.glixon@uky.edu

GLOAG, Julian. French/British (born England), b. 1930. **Genres:** Novels, Plays/Screenplays, Literary Criticism And History. **Career:** Chamber's Encyclopaedia, researcher, 1954-56; Ronald Press, assistant editor, 1956-59; freelance writer, 1959-61, 1963-; Hawthorn Books, editor, 1961-63. **Publications:** (Ed.) The American Nation: A Short History of the United States (nonfiction), 1955; Our Mother's House, 1963; A Sentence of Life: A Novel, 1966; Maundy, 1969; A Woman of Character: A Novel, 1973; Sleeping Dogs Lie, 1980; Lost and Found, 1981; Blood for Blood, 1985; Only Yesterday, 1987; Love as a Foreign Language, 1991; Le passeur de la nuit, 1996; Chambre d'ombre, 1996. Contributor to periodicals. **Address:** Georges Borchardt Inc., 136 E 57th St., New York, NY 10022, U.S.A.

GLOCK, Allison. American (born United States) **Genres:** Autobiography/Memoirs, History, Biography. **Career:** ESPN, senior staff writer. **Publications:** Beauty before Comfort: A Memoir, 2003; (with C. Aiken) Learning to Sing: Hearing the Music in Your Life, 2004. Contributor to periodicals. **Address:** c/o Author Mail, Alfred A. Knopf Publicity, 1745 Broadway, New York, NY 10019, U.S.A.

GLOSS, Molly. American (born United States), b. 1944. **Genres:** Novels, Science Fiction/Fantasy, Young Adult Fiction. **Career:** Teacher, 1966-67; Consolidated Freightways, correspondence clerk, 1967-70; freelance writer, 1980-; Portland State University, faculty; Pacific University, Low-Residency MFA in Writing Program, visiting professor. **Publications:** NOVELS: Outside the Gates, 1986; The Jump-Off Creek, 1989; The Dazzle of Day, 1997; Wild Life: A Novel, 2000; The Hearts of Horses, 2007. OTHER: (intro.) A Homesteader's Portfolio, 1993. Work appears in anthologies. **Address:** Wendy Weil Agency, 232 Madison Ave., Ste. 1300, New York, NY 10016, U.S.A. **Online address:** molly@mollygloss.com

GLOSSOP, Ronald J. American (born United States), b. 1933. **Genres:** Philosophy, Politics/Government, Social Sciences, Law. **Career:** Boise State University, instructor in philosophy, 1960-61; Portland State University, instructor, 1961-63, assistant professor of philosophy, 1963-65; Southern Illinois University, Department of Philosophy, coordinator of peace studies, assistant professor, 1965-68, associate professor, 1968-73, professor of philosophical studies, 1973-98, emeritus professor, 1998-. Writer. **Publications:** Philosophy: An Introduction to Its Problems and Vocabulary, 1974; Confronting War: An Examination of Humanity's Most Pressing Problem, 1983, 4th ed., 2001; World Federation?: A Critical Analysis of Federal World Government, 1993. Works appear in anthologies. Contributor to journals and periodicals. **Address:** Department of Philosophy, College of Arts and Sciences, Southern Illinois University, Rm. 3212, Peck Hall, PO Box 1433, Edwardsville, IL 62026-1433, U.S.A. **Online address:** rglosso@siue.edu

GLOVER, Douglas. Canadian (born Canada), b. 1948. **Genres:** Novels, Novellas/Short Stories, Literary Criticism And History, History. **Career:**

University of New Brunswick, lecturer of philosophy, 1971-72, writer-in-residence, 1987-88; reporter and editor, 1972-79; Star-Phoenix, copy editor, 1979; University of Lethbridge, writer-in-residence, 1988; St. Thomas University, writer-in-residence, 1992-; State University of New York, New York State Writers Institute, writer-in-residence, 1992-, lecturer in English, 1996-2000; Skidmore College, Department of English, lecturer, 1992-93, visiting writer-in-residence, 1998-2000, visiting professor in English, 2000-01; The Book Show, radio host, 1994-96; Vermont College, MFA in Writing Program, faculty, assistant faculty director, 1994-; Colgate University, visiting professor of English, 1995; Utah State University, writer-in-residence, 1997-; Davidson College, McGee professor of writing, 2005-. **Publications:** STORIES: The Mad River and Other Stories, 1981; Dog Attempts to Drown Man in Saskatoon, 1985; A Guide to Animal Behaviour, 1991; 16 Categories of Desire: Stories, 2000. NOVELS: Precious, 1984; The South Will Rise at Noon, 1988; The Life and Times of Captain N., 1993; Elle, 2003; Seize sortes de désir: Nouvelles. OTHER: (ed.) Best Canadian Stories, 1996-2002; Notes Home from a Prodigal Son (essays), 1999; Bad News of the Heart, 2003; The Enamoured Knight, 2004; (ed.) Acquainted with Absence: Selected Poems, 2009. **Address:** PO Box 2282, Wilton, NY 12831, U.S.A. **Online address:** bigiduz@davidson.edu

GLOVER, Jane. British (born England), b. 1949. **Genres:** Novels. **Career:** St. Hugh's College, junior research fellow, 1973-75, lecturer in music, 1976-84, senior research fellow 1982-91; St. Anne's College, lecturer in music, 1976-80; Pembroke College, lecturer in music, 1979-84; Glyndebourne Touring Opera, music director, 1981-85; London Choral Society, principal conductor, 1983-; London Mozart Players, artistic director, 1984-91; Huddersfield Choral Society, principal conductor, 1989-96; Chicago's Music of the Baroque, music director, 2002-; Royal College of Music, fellow. Writer. **Publications:** Cavalli, 1978; Mozart's Women: His Family, His Friends, His Music, 2005. **Address:** c/o Peter Bloor, Askonas Holt Ltd., Lonsdale Chambers, 27 Chancery Ln., London, GL WC2A 1PF, England.

GLOVER, Judith. British (born England), b. 1943. **Genres:** Romance/Historical, Food And Wine, History, Language/Linguistics, Local History/Rural Topics, Area Studies. **Career:** Wolverhampton Express and Star, reporter, 1960-62; freelance writer, 1962-. **Publications:** The Place Names of Sussex, 1974; (intro.) Batsford Colour Book of Sussex, 1975; The Place Names of Kent, 1976; (intro.) Batsford Colour Book of Kent, 1976; (with A. Kersting) Sussex in Photographs, 1976; Drink Your Own Garden, 1979; The Stallion Man, 1982; Sisters and Brothers, 1984; To Everything a Season, 1986; Birds in a Gilded Cage, 1987; The Imagination of the Heart, 1990; Tiger Lilies, 1991; Mirabelle, 1992; Minerva Lane, 1993; Pride of Place, 1995; Sussex Place-Names, 1997. **Address:** 27 Brook Ln., Great Easton, Market Harborough, LE16 8SJ, England. **Online address:** gravelpatch@aol.com

GLOVER, Lorri. American (born United States), b. 1967?. **Genres:** History. **Career:** Institute for Southern Studies, research fellow, 1996; Otterbein College, assistant professor, 1996-97; University of Tennessee, assistant professor, 1997-2002, associate professor, 2002-08, professor of history, 2008-, College of Arts and Sciences, Lindsey Young professor, 2008-09. Writer and historian. **Publications:** All Our Relations: Blood Ties and Emotional Bonds among the Early South Carolina Gentry, 2000; (ed. with C.T. Friend) Southern Manhood: Perspectives on Masculinity in the Old South, 2004; Southern Sons: Becoming Men in the New Nation, 2007; (with D.B. Smith) The Shipwreck That Saved Jamestown: The Sea Venture Castaways and the Fate of America, 2008. Contributor to periodicals and journals. **Address:** Department of History, University of Tennessee, 2622 Dunford Hall, Knoxville, TN 37996-4065, U.S.A. **Online address:** lglover@utk.edu

GLUCKMAN, Janet. See **BERLINER-GLUCKMAN, Janet.**

GLUCKSMANN, André. French (born France), b. 1937. **Genres:** Novels, Politics/Government, Social Sciences. **Career:** Philosopher and writer. **Publications:** Le discours de la guerre (title means: 'The Discourse of War'), 1967, as Le discours de la guerre, précédé de, Europe 2004, 1979; Stratégie de la révolution, introduction, 1968; Violence on the Screen: A Report on Research into the Effects on Young People of Scenes of Violence in Films and Television, 1971; Lacuisinière et le mangeur d'hommes; essai sur les rapports entrel'état, le marxisme et les camps de concentration (title means: 'The Cook and the Devourer of Men: An Essay on the Relationships between the State, Marxism and the Concentration Camps'), 1975; Les Maîtrespenseurs, 1977; Cynisme et passion (title means: 'Cynicism and Passion'), 1981; La force du vertige (title means: 'The Force of Vertigo'), 1983; LeBétise, 1985; (with T. Wolton) Silence, on tue (title means: 'Quiet, One Is Killing'), 1986; Descartes, c'est la France (title means: 'Descartes, That's France'), 1987; Debakel einer Utopie, 1990; Le XIe commandement (title means: 'The Eleventh Commandment'), 1992; La fêlure du monde: éthique et SIDA (title means: 'The Wound of the World: Ethics and AIDS'), 1994; De Gaulleòu es tu? (title means: 'De Gaulle, Where Are You?'), 1995; Le bien etle mal: letters immorales d'Allemagne et de France (title means: 'Good and Evil: Immoral Letters from Germany and France'), 1997; Le bien et le mal: Letters imorales d'Allemagne et de France, 1997; La troisièmemort de Dieu (title means: 'The Third Death of God'), 2000; Doestoïevski à Manhattan (title means: 'Dostoevsky in Manhattan'), 2002; L'Ouest contre ouest (title means: 'The West versus the West'), 2003; Open Wound: Chechnya 1994 to 2003, 2003; Tchétchénie: la guerre jusqu'au dernier, 2003; Le discours de la haine, 2004; Une rage d'enfant, 2006; (co-author) Hommage à Anna Politkovskaïa, 2007; (with R. Glucksmann) Mai 68 expliquéà Nicolas Sarkozy, 2008; Les deux chemins de la philosophie, 2009; (with N. Bacharan, A.M. Mindel and A.Maddeb) La plus belle histoire de la liberté, 2009; République, la pantoufle et les petits lapins, 2011. **Address:** c/o Author Mail, Plon-Perrin, 76, rue Bonaparte, Paris, 75006, France.

GLUT, Don(ald) F. (Don(ald) Frank Glut). American (born United States), b. 1944. **Genres:** Novels, Art/Art History, Film, Literary Criticism And History, Earth Sciences, Regional/Urban Planning, Ghost Writer, Horror, Horror. **Career:** Assistant copywriter, 1965-71; part-time writer, 1966-; Castle of Frankenstein, contributing editor, 1969-71; Marvel Comic Group, Monsters of the Movies magazine, associate editor, 1974-; Frontline Entertainment, president. **Publications:** Frankenstein Lives Again (novels), 1971; Terror of Frankenstein and Sequels, 1971; (with J. Harmon) The Great Movie Serials: Their Sound and Fury, 1972; True Vampires of History, 1972; The Dinosaur Dictionary, 1972, rev. ed. as The New Dinosaur Dictionary, 1982; The Frankenstein Legend: A Tribute to Mary Shelley and Boris Karloff, 1973; Bugged! (science fiction), 1974; The Dracula Book, 1974; (with J. Harmon) Great Television Heroes, 1975; Spawn (novel), 1976; Bones of Frankenstein, 1977; Frankenstein Meets Dracula, 1977; Classic Movie Monsters, 1978; The Empire Strikes Back (novel), 1980; The Dinosaur Scrapbook, 1980; (with S. Massey) Dinosaurs, Mammoths, and Cavemen: The Art of Charles R. Knight, 1982; The Frankenstein Catalog, 1984; The Star Wars Trilogy, 1987; New Credits: Discover Dinosaurs, 1991; Amazing Dinosaurs, 1993; The Dinosaur Society Dinosaur Encyclopedia, 1993; Dinosaur Movies, 1993; Dinosaur Tracks: vol. I, 1994; Hollywood Goes Ape!, 1995; Dinosaur Valley Girls, 1996; Before LaBrea, 1997; Dinosaurs: The Encyclopedia, 1997; Carbon Dates: A Day by Day Almanac of Paleo Anniversaries and Dino Events, 1999; Chomper, 2000; Jurassic Classics, 2001; The Frankenstein Archive, 2002; True Werewolves of History, 2004; I was a Teenage Movie Maker: The Book, 2007; Brother Blood, 2010. Contributor to books. **Address:** Frontline Entertainment Inc., 2805 N Keystone St., Burbank, CA 91504-1604, U.S.A. **Online address:** pres@frontlinefilms.com

GLUT, Don(ald) Frank. See GLUT, Don(ald) F.

GLUZBERG-ZINIK See Zinik, Zinovy.

GLYER, Diana Pavlac. American (born United States), b. 1956. **Genres:** Literary Criticism And History. **Career:** Azusa Pacific University, Department of English, professor. Writer. **Publications:** (Ed. with D.L. Weeks) The Liberal Arts in Higher Education: Challenging Assumptions, Exploring Possibilities, 1998; The Company They Keep: C. S. Lewis and J. R. R. Tolkien as Writers in Community, 2007. Contributor to books and periodicals. **Address:** Department of English, Azusa Pacific University, PO Box 7000, Azusa, CA 91702-7000, U.S.A. **Online address:** dglyer@apu.edu

GLYNN, Alan. Irish (born Ireland), b. 1960?. **Genres:** Novels, Criminology/True Crime. **Career:** EFL teacher. Writer. **Publications:** The Dark Fields, 2001 as Limitless, 2011; Winterland, 2010; Bloodland, 2011. **Address:** c/o Author Mail, Bloomsbury USA, 175 5th Ave., Fl. 8, New York, NY 10010, U.S.A.

GMELCH, George. American (born United States), b. 1944. **Genres:** Anthropology/Ethnology. **Career:** Memorial University of Newfoundland, Institute of Social and Economic Research, research fellow, 1971-73; McGill University, assistant professor of anthropology, 1973-75; State University of New

York, Albany, assistant professor of anthropology, 1975-81; National University of Ireland, visiting senior research fellow, 1978-79; University College of Dublin, visiting research fellow, 1978-; Leicester Polytechnic, Union College, visiting senior research fellow, 1980-81, associate professor, 1981-92, Union College Roger Thayer Stone professor of anthropology, 1991-98, chair, 1991-98, professor, 1991-; New Mexico State University, visiting professor, 1988; University of Alaska, visiting professor, 1989; University of San Francisco, professor of anthropology and director of anthropology program, 2007-, Cultural Anthropology, co-director. Writer. **Publications:** Irish Tinkers: The Urbanization of an Itinerant People, 1977, 2nd ed., 1985; (with B. Kroup) To Shorten the Road: Traveller Folk Tales from Ireland, 1978; (contrib.) In Wicklow, West Kerry and Connemara, 1980; (with J. Cowell) Where They Lived in Dublin, 1980; Resource Use of Glacier Bay National Preserve, 1982; (ed. with W.P. Zenner) Urban Life: Readings in Urban Anthropology Abroad and Back Home, 1988, 5th ed., 2010; Double Passage: The Lives of Caribbean Migrants, 1992; (with S.B. Gmelch) The Parish behind God's Back: The Changing Culture of Rural Barbados, 1997; In the Ballpark: The Working Lives of Baseball People, 1998; The Ballplayers: Inside the Life of Professional Baseball, 2000; Inside Pitch: Life in Professional Baseball, 2001; Behind the Smile: The Working Lives of Caribbean Tourism, 2003, 2nd ed., 2012; (ed.) Baseball Without Borders: The International Pastime, 2006; Baseball without Borders: The International Pastime, 2008, Taking the Good Life: Wine Tourism in the Napa Valley, 2011; (with S.B. Gmelch) Tasting the Good Life, 2011. Contributor to journals. **Address:** Department of Sociology, University of San Francisco, 2130 Fulton St., San Francisco, CA 94117, U.S.A. **Online address:** gjgmelch@usfca.edu

GMELCH, Sharon (Bohn). American/Panamanian (born Panama), b. 1947. **Genres:** Anthropology/Ethnology, Area Studies, Cultural/Ethnic Topics, Women's Studies And Issues, Biography. **Career:** State University of New York, adjunct assistant professor of anthropology, 1975-; Union College, Department of Anthropology, visiting assistant and associate professor, 1976-, professor, 1981-; Leicester Polytechnic, visiting research fellow, 1980-81; O'Brien Press, editor, 1980-. **Publications:** Tinkers and Travellers, 1975; (ed.) Irish Life and Traditions, 1979; Nan: The Life of an Irish Travelling Woman, 1986; (with G. Gmelch) The Parish behind God's Back: Life in Rural Barbados, 1997; (with M.H. Stoffer and J.L. Yetzer) Gender on Campus: Issues for College Women, 1998; (ed.) Tourists and Tourism, 2004, 2nd ed., 2010; Tlingit Encounter with Photography, 2008; (with G. Gmelch) Tasting the Good Life: Wine Tourism in the Napa Valley, 2011. **Address:** Department of Anthropology, Union College, 807 Union St., Schenectady, NY 12308, U.S.A. **Online address:** gmelchs@union.edu

GOBBELL, John J. American (born United States), b. 1937. **Genres:** Novels. **Career:** KPMG Peat Marwick, consultant, 1967-70; Angeles Corp., director of personnel, 1970-73; Boyden Associates Inc., vice-president of branch, 1973-83; USC Commerce Associates, president, 1977; Gobbell Co., founder, managing director, 1983-; Orange County Fictionaires (reading group), president, 1996; Newport Harbor Nautical Museum, president, 2002; USC Catholic Center, director of development. Writer. **Publications:** NOVELS: The Brutus Lie, 1991; The Last Lieutenant, 1995; A Code for Tomorrow, 1999; When Duty Whispers Low, 2002; The Neptune Strategy, 2004; A Call to Colors: A Novel of the Leyte Gulf, 2006. **Address:** The Gobbell Co., 1601 Dove St., Ste. 145, Newport Beach, CA 92660, U.S.A. **Online address:** jgobbell@johnjgobbell.com

GOBLE, Alan. British (born England), b. 1938. **Genres:** Film, Bibliography, Music. **Career:** Department of Trade and Industry, assistant official receiver, now retired. Writer. **Publications:** (Ed.) The International Film Index, 1895-1990, vol. I: Film Titles, 1991, vol. II: Directors' Filmography and Indexes, 1996; The Complete Index to British Sound Films since 1928, 1999; The Complete Index to Literary Sources in Film, 1999. **Address:** 7 Raphael Rd., Hove, ES BN3 5QP, England. **Online address:** alangoble@citwf.com

GOBLE, Paul. American/British (born England), b. 1933. **Genres:** Children's Fiction, Young Adult Fiction, Children's Non-fiction, Mythology/Folklore, Young Adult Non-fiction, Illustrations, Classics. **Career:** Freelance industrial designer, 1960-68; Central School of Arts and Design, visiting lecturer, 1960-68; Ravensbourne College of Art and Design, senior lecturer, 1968-77; author and illustrator, 1969-. **Publications:** SELF-ILLUSTRATED FOR CHILDREN: (with D. Goble) Red Hawk's Account of Custer's Last Battle, 1969; (with D. Goble) Brave Eagle's Account of the Fetterman Fight, 21 December 1866, 1972 in UK as The Hundred in the Hands; (with D.

Goble) Lone Bull's Horse Raid, 1973; (with D. Goble) The Friendly Wolf, 1974, rev. ed. as Dream Wolf, 1990; The Girl Who Loved Wild Horses, 1978; The Gift of the Sacred Dog, 1980; Star Boy, 1982; Buffalo Woman, 1984; The Great Race of the Birds and Animals, 1985; Death of the Iron Horse, 1987; Her Seven Brothers, 1988; Iktomi and the Boulder: A Plains Indian Story, 1988; Beyond the Ridge, 1989; Iktomi and the Berries, 1989; Iktomi and the Ducks, 1990; I Sing for the Animals, 1991; Iktomi and the Buffalo Skull, 1991; Crow Chief, 1992; Love Flute, 1992; The Lost Children: The Boys Who were Neglected, 1993; Adopted by the Eagles: A Plains Indian Story of Friendship and Treachery, 1994; Iktomi and the Buzzard, 1994; Hau Kola-Hello Friend (autobiography for children), 1994; Remaking the Earth: A Creation Story from the Great Plains of North America, 1996; The Return of the Buffaloes: A Plains Indian Story about Famine and Renewal of the Earth, 1996; The Legend of the White Buffalo Woman, 1998; La niña que amaba los caballos salvajes, 1998; Iktomi and the Coyote, 1998; Iktomi Loses His Eyes: A Plains Indian Story, 1999; Paul Goble Gallery: 3 Native American Stories, 1999; Storm Maker's Tipi, 2001; Mystic Horse, 2003; Song of Creation, 2004; All Our Relatives, 2005; Tipi: Home of the Nomadic Buffalo Hunters, 2007; Boy & His Mud Horses: & Other Stories from the Tipi, 2010; Woman Who Lived with Wolves & other Stories from the Tipi, 2011. OTHERS: (co-author) The Art of Paul Goble, Author-Illustrator, 1995; Earth Made New: Plains Indian Stories of Creation, 2009. **Address:** 1803 9th St., Rapid City, SD 57701, U.S.A.

GOBODO-MADIKIZELA, Pumla. South African (born South Africa), b. 1955?. **Genres:** Civil Liberties/Human Rights, History. **Career:** University of Transkei, instructor, lecturer, 1986-88; senior lecturer, 1989-92; Unilever Ethics Centre, adjunct professor; University of Natal, adjunct professor; University of Cape Town, associate professor of psychology, 2003-; Brandeis University, Brandeis Ethics Center, Coexistence Program, faculty affiliate; Harvard University, faculty; Wellesley College, faculty; Tufts University, faculty. Writer. **Publications:** A Human Being Died That Night: A South African Story of Forgiveness, 2003, as A Human Being Died That Night: A South African Woman Confronts the Legacy of Apartheid, 2004; Women Contributions to South Africa Truth and Reconciliation Commission, 2005; (co-author) Critical Psychology in Africa, 2006; (with C.V. der Merwe) Narrating Our Healing: Perspectives on Working through Trauma, 2007; (ed. with C.V. der Merwe) Memory, Narrative and Forgiveness: Perspectives on the Unfinished Journeys of the Past, 2009. Contributor to periodicals and journals. **Address:** Department of Psychology, University of Cape Town, Rm. 4.09, Humanities Graduate Bldg., Rondebosch, Cape Town, 7700, South Africa. **Online address:** pumla.gobodo-madikizela@uct.ac.za

GOCHFELD, Michael. American (born United States), b. 1940. **Genres:** Environmental Sciences/Ecology, Medicine/Health. **Career:** Columbia University, School of Public Health, research associate, 1969-75; Rockefeller University, postdoctoral research fellow, 1975-77; New Jersey Department of Health, director of occupational and environmental medicine, 1978-80; University of Medicine and Dentistry of New Jersey, Robert Wood Johnson Medical School, Department of Environmental and Occupational Medicine, professor, 1980-, Occupational and Environmental Residency Program, director, 1980-. Writer. **Publications:** (Co-author) Environmental Risk and the Press, 1986; (with E.A. Favata) Hazardous Waste Workers, 1990; (with J. Burger) The Black Skimmer: Social Dynamics of a Colonial Species, 1990; (with J. Burger) The Common Tern: Breeding Biology and Social Behavior, 1991, rev. ed., 1999; (with J. Burger) Butterflies of New Jersey: A Guide to Their Status, Distribution, Conservation, and Appreciation, 1997; (with J. Burger) Twenty-five Nature Spectacles in New Jersey, 2000; (with J. Burger) M. Lead in Young Herring Gulls: Paradoxical Effects of Exercise on Tissue Concentrations, 2003; (co-author) Occupational Heath Services at then U.S. Department of Energy Weapon Sites, 2003; (with J. Burger) Amchitka Independent Assessment Science Plan, 2003. EDITOR: (with C. Witmer) The Chromium Problem, 1991; (with J. Burger and D.N. Nettleship) Seabirds on Islands: Threats, Case Studies and Action Plans, 1994; (with E.A. Emmet, A.L. Frank and S.M. Hessl) Yearbook of Occupational and Environmental Medicine, Annually, 1994; (with S. Brooks) Environmental Medicine, 1995; (with W.F. Martin) Protecting Personnel at Hazardous Waste Sites, 2000; (with J.K. Syers) Environmental Cadmium in the Food Chain: Sources, Pathways, and Risks, 2002. Contributor to journals and magazines. **Address:** Robert Wood Johnson Medical School, University of Medicine and Dentistry of New Jersey, Rm. 206, EOHSI Bldg., 675 Hoes Ln., Piscataway, NJ 08854-8020, U.S.A. **Online address:** gochfeld@eohsi.rutgers.edu

GODBOLD, E(dward) Stanly. American (born United States), b. 1942. **Genres:** History, Biography, Children's Non-fiction, Autobiography/Memoirs, Social Sciences. **Career:** University of Tennessee, assistant professor of history, 1969-70; Valdosta State College, assistant professor of history, 1970-77; Mississippi State University, associate professor of history, through 1977, professor emeritus, 2003-. Writer. **Publications:** Ellen Glasgow and the Woman Within, 1972; (co-ed.) Essays in Southern History in Honor of Robert H. Woody, 1974; (with R.H. Woody) Christopher Gadsden and the American Revolution, 1982; (with M.U. Russell) Confederate Colonel and Cherokee Chief: The Life of William Holland Thomas, 1990; Jimmy and Rosalynn Carter: The Georgia Years, 1924-1974, 2010; Jimmy Carter: A Biography, forthcoming. **Address:** Department of History, Mississippi State University, 214 Allen Hall, Mississippi State, MS 39762, U.S.A. **Online address:** esg@ra.msstate.edu

GODBOUT, Jacques. Canadian (born Canada), b. 1933. **Genres:** Poetry, Novels, Essays, Young Adult Fiction, Young Adult Non-fiction, Translations, Novellas/Short Stories. **Career:** University of Addis Ababa, assistant professor of French, 1954-57; National Film Board of Canada, filmmaker, 1957-; Liberte, co-founder, 1959; University of Montreal, lecturer, 1969; University of California, lecturer, 1985. Writer. **Publications:** Carton-pate (poetry), 1956; Les Paves secs, 1958; C'est la chaude loi des hommes (poetry), 1960; L'Aquarium (novel), 1962; (ed. with J.R. Colombo) Poésie/Poetry 64, 1963; Le Couteau sur la table (novel), 1965; Salut Galarneau! Roman (novel), 1967; Knife on the Table, 1968; (with J.R. Colombo) Le Grande Muraille de Chine, 1969; D'Amour, P.Q. (novel), 1972; (with P. Turgeon) L'Interview: texte radiophonique, 1973; Le Réformiste: textes tranquilles, 1975; L'Isle au dragon: Roman, 1976; Dragon Island, 1978; Les Têtes à Papineau: Roman, 1981; Le Murmure marchand: 1976-1984, 1984; Souvenirs Shop: Poèmes et prose 1956-1980, 1984; Une Histoire Américaine: Roman, 1986; American Story, 1988; (with L. Plamondon) Un Coeur de Rockeur, 1988; L'Ecran de bonheur (essay), 1990; L'écrivain de province: Journal, 1981-1990, 1991; Le Temps des Galarneau (novel): Roman, 1993; Golden Galarneaus, 1995; écran du bonheur: essais, 1985-1990, 1995; Une Lecon de chasse (short story), 1997; D'ile en ile (correspondence), 1996; Idée de pays, 1998; Buffet: dialogue sur le Québec à l'an 2000, 1998; Opération Rimbaud: roman, 1999; Concièrge du Panthéon: roman, 2006; Opération Rimbaud, 2008; Autos Biographie, 2008. Contributor to magazines. Works appear in anthologies. **Address:** 815 Pratt, Outremont, Montreal, QC H2V 2T7, Canada.

GODDARD, Hugh (P.). British (born England), b. 1953. **Genres:** Theology/Religion, History. **Career:** College of St. Paul and St. Mary, lecturer in Islamic studies, 1981-84; University of Nottingham, Department of Theology and Religious Studies, lecturer in Islamic theology, 1984-, professor of Christian-Muslim relations, 2004-; Nottingham Christian-Muslim Forum, secretary, 1990-94; University of Edinburgh, Islamic and Middle Eastern Studies, professor, The Alwaleed Bin Talal Centre for the Study of Islam in the Contemporary World, director. Writer. **Publications:** Christians and Muslims: From Double Standards to Mutual Understanding, 1995; Muslim Perceptions of Christianity, 1996; History of Christian-Muslim Relations, 2000; A History of Middle-Eastern Theologies, 2003; A Reader in Christian-Muslim Relations, 2004. **Address:** Islamic and Middle Eastern Studies, University of Edinburgh, 19 George Sq., Edinburgh, BR EH8 9LD, Scotland. **Online address:** hugh.goddard@ed.ac.uk

GODDARD, Robert (William). British (born England), b. 1954. **Genres:** Novels, Mystery/Crime/Suspense, Young Adult Fiction. **Career:** Devon County Council, educational administrator, 1978-87; writer, 1987-. **Publications:** NOVELS: The Little Jester Who Couldn't Laugh, 1967; Past Caring, 1986; In Pale Battalions 1988; Painting the Darkness, 1989; Debt of Dishonour, 1991; Take no Farewell, 1991; Hand in Glove, 1992; Closed Circle, 1993; Borrowed Time, 1995; Beyond Recall, 1998; Caught in the Light, 1999; Set in Stone, 1999; Sea Change, 2000; Dying to Tell, 2001; Days without Number, 2003; Play to the End, 2006; Name To A Face, 2007; Sight Unseen, 2007; Found Wanting, 2008; Past Caring, 2008; Name to a Face, 2009; Long Time Coming, 2010; Found Wanting, 2011; Blood Count, 2011. HARRY BARNETT MYSTERY SERIES: Into the Blue, 1990; Out of the Sun, 1996; Never Go Back, 2007. **Address:** PFD, Drury House, 34-43 Russell St., London, GL WC2B 5HA, England.

GODDARD, Tariq. British (born England), b. 1975?. **Genres:** Novels, Military/Defense/Arms Control. **Career:** Writer. **Publications:** Homage to a Firing Squad, 2002; Dynamo, 2003; The Morning Rides Behind Us, 2005;

The Picture of Contented New Wealth, 2009; The Message, 2011; War Pigs, forthcoming. **Address:** c/o Author Mail, Sceptre, 338 Euston Rd., London, GL NW1 3BH, England.

GODDEN, Geoffrey Arthur. British (born England), b. 1929?. **Genres:** Antiques/Furnishings, Art/Art History, Crafts. **Career:** Godden of Worthing Ltd., managing director, 1970-. Writer. **Publications:** Victorian Porcelain, 1961; Victorian Pottery, 1962; An Introductory Handbook to British China Marks of the Nineteenth Century, 1962; British Pottery and Porcelain, 1780-1850, 1964; Encyclopaedia of British Pottery and Porcelain Marks, 1964; Antique China and Glass under Pounds, 1966; An Illustrated Encyclopedia of British Pottery and Porcelain, 1966, 2nd ed., 1980; The Handbook of British Pottery and Porcelain Marks, 1968; Minton Pottery and Porcelain of the First Period, 1793-1850, 1968; The Illustrated Guide to Lowestoft Porcelain, 1969, 2nd ed., 1985; Caughley and Worcester Porcelains 1775-1800, 1969; Coalport and Coalbrookdale Porcelains, 1970; Stevengraphs and Other Victorian Silk Pictures, 1971; (ed.) Pencillings by the Way: A Constitutional Voyage Round the World: 1870 & 1871, 1971; The Illustrated Guide To Mason's Patent Ironstone China: The Related Wares; Stone China, New Stone, Granite China, and their Manufacturers, 1971; Jewitt's Ceramic Art of Great Britain 1800-1900, 1972; The Illustrated Guide to Ridgway porcelains, 1972; British Porcelain: An Illustrated Guide, 1974; British Pottery: An Illustrated Guide, 1974; An Introduction to English Blue & White Porcelains, 1974; Godden's Guide to English Porcelain, 1978; Oriental Export Market Porcelain and its Influence on European Wares, 1979; Godden's Guide to Mason's China and the Ironstone Wares, 1980, rev. ed., 1993; Chamberlain-Worcester Porcelain, 1982; (and ed.) Staffordshire Porcelain, 1983; English China, 1985; Ridgway Porcelains, 1985; Eighteenth-Century English Porcelain: A Selection from the Godden Reference Collection, 1985; Encyclopaedia of British Porcelain Manufacturers, 1988; (with T.A. Lockett) Davenport: China, Earthenware, Glass, 1989; The Concise Guide to British Pottery and Porcelain, 1990; (with M. Gibson) Collecting Lustreware, 1991; (ed. and foreword) Encyclopaedia of British Art Pottery, 1870-1920, 1991; Godden's Guide to European Porcelain, 1994; Collecting Picture Postcards, 1996; New Handbook of British Pottery and Porcelain Marks, 1999; Godden's Guide to Ironstone, 1999; Godden's New Guide to English Porcelain, 2004; Godden's Guide to English Blue and White Porcelain, 2004; New Hall Porcelains, 2004. **Address:** 3 The Sq., Findon, WS BN14 0TE, England.

GODFREY, Donald G. American/Canadian (born Canada) **Genres:** Communications/Media, Writing/Journalism. **Career:** KOET-Television, producer, director and local news anchor, 1966-68; KSVN-Radio, news director, 1966-68; Weber State University, KWCR-FM, station manager, 1967-68; University of Oregon, KWAX-FM, station manager, 1968-69; KEZI-Television, news reporter, 1968-69; KIRO-Television, production sound engineer, 1969-81; University of Washington, faculty associate, 1969-72, lecturer, 1972-75, assistant professor of communication, 1976-81, KCMU-FM, faculty director, 1971-81, News and magazine Program, faculty supervisor, 1972-81; University of Arizona, associate professor of radio and television studies, 1981-83; Southern Utah University, associate professor of communication and coordinator of telecommunications, 1983-86; Corporate Communications Media, consultant, 1985-; Philippine Imports, corporate communications director, 1986-87; Arizona State University, weekly student news magazine, faculty director, 1989-96, Walter Cronkite School of Journalism and Telecommunications, assistant professor, 1988-91, associate professor, 1991-95, professor of telecommunication, 1995-, production concentration coordinator, 2000-05, PhD Program, director, 2008-11, professor; Journal of Broadcasting and Electronic Media, editor, 2003-08. **Publications:** (Comp.) Reruns on File: A Guide to Electronic Media Archives, 1992; (with F. Leigh) Historical Dictionary of American Radio, 1998; Philo T. Farnsworth: The Father of Television, 2001; (with F.A. Leigh and J.E. Craft) Electronic Media, 2001; Philo T. Farnsworth: The Father of Television, 2001; EDITOR: A Directory of Broadcast Archives, 1983; (with B.Y. Card) The Diaries of Charles Ora Card: The Canadian Years, 1886-1903, 1993; (with M.D. Murray) Television in America: Local Station History from Across the Nation, 1997; (with M.D. Murray) Television in America: Pioneering Stations, 1997; (with F.A. Leigh) Historical Dictionary of American Radio, 1998; (with J. Craft and F. Leigh) American Electronic Media: Television, Cable, Radio and the Future, 2000; Methods of Historical Analysis in Electronic Media, 2006; (with K.W. Godfrey) The Diaries of Charles Ora Card: The Utah Years, 1871-1886, 2006; (ed. with R.S. Martineau-McCarty) An Uncommon Common Pioneer: The Journals of James Henry Martineau, 1828-1918, 2008. Contributor of articles to journals. **Address:** Cronkite School of Journalism & Mass Communica-

tion, Arizona State University, Rm. 467, 555 N Central Ave., Phoenix, AZ 85004, U.S.A. **Online address:** don.godfrey@asu.edu

GODFREY, Neale S. American (born United States), b. 1951?. **Genres:** Money/Finance, Young Adult Non-fiction, Young Adult Fiction, Economics, How-to Books, Business/Trade/Industry. **Career:** Chase Manhattan Bank, banker, 1972-85; First Women's Bank of New York, president, 1985-88; First Children's Bank, founder, 1988-; Children's Financial Network Inc., founder, 1988-, chairman; United Nations Agency for International Women's Rights, director; American Bankers Association, financial literacy advocate; White House Task Force, staff; Governor's Task Force, staff; The New York Board of Trade, director; UNICEF, director; University of Charleston, director; Young President's Organization, director. Writer. **Publications:** The Kids' Money Book, 1991; (with C. Edwards) Money Doesn't Grow on Trees: A Parent's Guide to Raising Financially Responsible Children, 1994; Why Money was Invented, 1995; (with T. Richards) A Penny Saved: Using Money to Teach Your Child the Way the World Works, 1995; Here's the Scoop!: Follow an Ice-cream Cone around the World, 1995; From Cradle to College (And Everything in Between): A Parent's Guide to Financing Your Child's Life, 1996; A Money Adventure: Earning, Saving, Spending, Sharing, 1996; (with T. Richards) Making Change: A Woman's Guide to Designing Her Financial Future, 1997; Ultimate Kids Money Book, 1998; (with T. Richards) Mom, Inc.: Taking Your Work Skills Home, 1999; (with R. Godfrey) The Teen Code: How to Talk to Us about Sex, Drugs and Everything Else: Teenagers Reveal What Works Best, 2004; (with T. Richards) Life Inc: The Ultimate Career Guide for Young People, 2007. **Address:** Children's Financial Network Inc., 31 Twin Brooks Trl., Chester, NJ 07930-2820, U.S.A. **Online address:** neale@childrensfinancialnetwork.com

GODFREY-JUNE, Jean. American (born United States), b. 1964. **Genres:** Fash Ion/Costume. **Career:** Elle, beauty and fitness director, 1993; beautyscene.com, editor-in-chief; Lucky, beauty editor. Beauty editor and writer. **Publications:** Free Gift with Purchase: My Improbable Career in Magazines and Makeup, 2006. **Address:** Upper Grandview, NY , U.S.A.

GODIN, Seth. See **GODIN, Seth Warren.**

GODIN, Seth Warren. (Seth Godin). American (born United States), b. 1960. **Genres:** Novels. **Career:** Spinnaker Software, brand manager, 1983-86; Skeibo Press Inc., founding manager, 1986-89; Seth Godin Productions, founder, 1986-; Yoyodyne Entertainment (later acquired by Yahoo!), founder & CEO, 1995-98; Squidoo LLC, founder, 1996; Yahoo, Inc.!, vice president of direct marketing, 1998-99; Gridworks/Science Methods Inc., 1988; Media Syndicate, consultant 1987; International Center for Creative Thinking, consultant, 1989. **Publications:** (with C. Conley) Business Rules of Thumb, 1987; (Creator) Show Me Language Books: French, 1990; (Creator) Show Me Language Books: German, 1990; (Creator) Show Me Language Books: Italian, 1990; (Creator) Show Me Language Books: Russian, 1990; (Creator) Show Me Language Books: Spanish, 1990; (Creator) Show Me Language Books: Japanese, 1991; (ed.) Quick Lit: Plots, Themes, Characters, and Sample Essays for the Most Assigned Books in English and Literature Courses'Written by Students for Students, 1992; Foolproof DOS, 1993; Foolproof Lotus 1-2- 3, 1993; Foolproof Windows, 1993; Foolproof WordPerfect, 1993; The Internet White Pages, 1994; E-Mail Addresses of the Rich & Famous, 1994; (with J.C. Levinson) The Guerrilla Marketing Handbook, 1994; (ed.) Best of the Net, 1995; Emarketing, 1995; Presenting Digital Cash, 1995; Wisdom, Inc., 1995; (with J.C. Levinson) Guerrilla Marketing for the Home-Based Business, 1995; (Compiler) The Encyclopedia of Fictional People: The Most Important Characters of the 20th Century, 1996; (Compiler) The Official Rules of Life: For Those of You Who Thought You'd Mastered Life's Little Instructions and Learned Everything You Needed to Know, 1996; Point & Click Business Builder, 1996; Point & Click Investor, 1996; Point & Click Jobfinder, 1996; If You're Clueless about Mutual Funds and Want to Know More, 1997; If You're Clueless about Retirement Planning and Want to Know More, 1997; If You're Clueless about Saving Money and Want to Know More, 1997; If You're Clueless about the Stock Market and Want to Know More, 1997, 2nd ed., 2001; Get What You Deserve! How to Guerrilla Market Yourself, 1997; If You're Clueless about Insurance and Want to Know More, 1998; If You're Clueless about Selling and Want to Know More, 1998; If You're Clueless about Starting Your Own Business and Want to Know More, 1998; (with W. Hall) The Totally Terrific $10,000 Trivia Challenge, 1998; (ed.) The America Online Insider's Guide to Finding Information Online, 1998; (ed.) America Online's Guide to Personal Computing, 1998; The Bootstrapper's

Bible: How to Start and Build a Business with a Great Idea and (Almost) No Money, 1998; (with P. Lim) If You're Clueless about Accounting and Finance and Want to Know More, 1998; (with J. Parmalee) If You're Clueless about Financial Planning and Want to Know More, 1998; (with B. Burns) If You're Clueless about Getting a Great Job and Want to Know More, 1998; Permission Marketing: Turning Strangers into Friends, and Friends into Customers, 1999; Unleashing the Ideavirus: Stop Marketing at People! Turn Your Ideas into Epidemics by Helping Your Customers Do the Marketing for You, 2001; The Big Red Fez: How to Make Any Web Site Better, 2002; Survival Is Not Enough: Zooming, Evolution, and the Future of Your Company, 2002; Purple Cow: Transform Your Business by Being Remarkable, 2003; Free Prize Inside: The Next Big Marketing Idea, 2004; (ed.) The Big Moo: Stop Trying to Be Perfect and Start Being Remarkable, 2005; All Marketers Are Liars: The Power of Telling Authentic Stories in a Low-Trust World, 2005; Small Is the New Big: And 183 Other Riffs, Rants, and Remarkable Business Ideas, 2006; The Dip: A Little Book That Teaches You When to Quit (and When to Stick), 2007; Meatball Sundae: Is Your Marketing out of Sync?, 2007; Tribes: We Need You to Lead Us, 2008. **Address:** Hastings-on-Hudson, NY , U.S.A. **Online address:** seth@sethgodin.com

GODKIN, Celia (Marilyn). Canadian/British (born England), b. 1948. **Genres:** Children's Non-fiction, Environmental Sciences/Ecology, Illustrations, Picture/Board Books. **Career:** University of Toronto, instructor in natural science illustration, 1981-82, assistant professor, 1987-99, department program supervisor, 1988-89, instructor for school of continuing studies, 1988-2005, associate professor of biomedical communications, 1999-2005; Network for Learning, instructor, 1985; Royal Ontario Museum, instructor, 1985-90; Ministry of the Environment, biological consultant, 1985-86; St. Lawrence College, studio arts instructor, 2005-10; Ottawa Experimental Farm, studio arts instructor, 2005-06; Haliburton School of the Arts, studio arts instructor, 2006-07. Writer and Illustrator. **Publications:** Wolf Island, 1989; Ladybug Garden, 1995; Sea Otter Inlet, 1997; Flying Lessons, 1999; When the Giant Stirred, 2002; Fire!: The Renewal of A Forest, 2006; Hurricane!, 2008. **Address:** 10 James St., Mod 6 Comp 12, Frankville, ON K0E 1H0, Canada. **Online address:** celiagodkin@ripnet.com

GODSHALK, C. S. American (born United States) **Genres:** Novels, Young Adult Fiction. **Career:** Children's Cancer Hospital, staff. Freelance journalist. **Publications:** Kalimantaan, 1998. Works appear in anthologies. **Address:** Henry Holt & Co., 115 W 18th St., 6th Fl., New York, NY 10011, U.S.A.

GODSON, Roy (S.). American (born United States), b. 1942. **Genres:** Organized Labor, History, International Relations/Current Affairs, Politics/Government. **Career:** Carnegie Mellon University, instructor, 1967-69; World Affairs Councils of Pittsburgh, educational director, 1967-69; Georgetown University, assistant professor, professor, now professor emeritus, International Labor Program, director; American Histadrut Cultural Exchange Institute, director, 1973-; FRONT LASH, director, 1973-; National Strategy Information Center, president, 1993-; Trends in Organized Crime, founding editor. **Publications:** American Labor and European Politics: The AFL as a Transnational Force, 1976; The Kremlin and Labor: A Study in National Security Policy, 1977; (with S. Haseler) Eurocommunism: Implications for East and West, 1978; (ed.) Intelligence Requirements for the 1980s, 7 vols., 1979-86; (with E.W. Lefever) The CIA and the American Ethic: An Unfinished Debate, 1979; (with R.H. Schultz) Dezinformatsia: Active Measures in Soviet Strategy, 1984; (ed.) Comparing Foreign Intelligence: The U.S. and the U.S.S.R., the U.K. and the Third World, 1988; (ed.) Intelligence Requirements for the 1990s: Collection, Analysis, Counterintelligence and Covert Action, 1989; (ed. with R.H. Schultz and T. Greenwood) Security Studies for the 1990s, 1993; (ed. with E.R. May and G. Schmitt) U.S. Intelligence at the Crossroads: Agendas for Reform, 1995; (ed. with R.H. Shultz and G.H. Quester) Security Studies for the Twenty-first Century, 1997; (ed. with J. Bailey) Organized Crime and Democratic Governability: Mexico and the U.S. Mexican Borderlands, 2000; Dirty Tricks or Trump Cards: U.S. Covert Action and Counterintelligence, 2000, rev. ed., 2001; (ed. with J.J. Wirtz) Strategic Denial and Deception: The Twenty-first-century Challenge, 2002; (ed.) Menace to Society: Political-Criminal Collaboration around the World, 2003. Contributor to periodicals. **Address:** Department of Government, Georgetown University, 37th and O St. NW 674 ICC, 674 ICC, Washington, DC 20057, U.S.A. **Online address:** godsonr@georgetown.edu

GODWIN, Gail (Kathleen). American (born United States), b. 1937.

Genres: Novels, Novellas/Short Stories, Literary Criticism And History, Social Sciences, Music, Young Adult Non-fiction. **Career:** Miami Herald, reporter, 1959-60; U.S. Travel Service, consultant, 1962-65; Saturday Evening Post, research, 1966; University of Iowa, instructor, 1967-70, Writers Workshop, lecturer, 1972-73; University of Illinois, Center for Advanced Studies, instructor and fellow, 1971-72; Vassar College, lecturer, 1975; Columbia University, lecturer, 1978, 1981. **Publications:** The Perfectionists, 1970; Glass People, 1972; The Odd Woman, 1974; Dream Children (short stories), 1976; Violet Clay, 1978; A Mother and Two Daughters, 1982; Mr. Bedford and the Muses, 1983; The Finishing School, 1985; A Southern Family, 1987; Father Melancholy's Daughter, 1991; The Good Husband, 1994; Evensong, 1999; (intro.) Woodstock Landscapes: Photographs, 2000; Heart: A Personal Journey through Its Myths and Meanings, 2001; Evenings at Five, 2003; Queen of the Underworld: A Novel, 2006; Making of a Writer: Journals, 1961-1963, 2006, vol. II, 2011; Red Nun: A Novel, 2009; Unfinished Desires: A Novel, 2009. Contributor to books and periodicals. **Address:** PO Box 946, Woodstock, NY 12498, U.S.A. **Online address:** gail@gailgodwin.com

GODWIN, Parke. (Kate Hawks). American (born United States), b. 1929. **Genres:** Novels, Science Fiction/Fantasy, History, Literary Criticism And History, Romance/Historical. **Career:** Writer. **Publications:** NOVELS: Darker Places, 1971; A Memory of Lions, 1983; A Truce with Time (A Love Story with Occasional Ghosts), 1988; Return to Nottingham: A Novel, 1993; Limbo Search, 1995; The Tower of Beowulf, 1995; Lord of Sunset (historical), 1998; Night You Could Hear Forever, 1999; (as Kate Hawks) The Lovers: The Legend of Trystan and Yseult, 1999; (as Kate Hawks) Watch by Moonlight, 2001; The Power of Friendship, 2005. SOLITUDE TRILOGY (with M. Kaye): The Masters of Solitude, 1978; Wintermind, 1982. ARTHURIAN SERIES: Firelord, 1980; Beloved Exile, 1984; The Last Rainbow, 1985. COLD BLUE LIGHT SERIES (with M. Kaye): A Cold Blue Light, 1983. SNAKE OIL WARS SERIES: Waiting for the Galactic Bus, 1988; The Snake Oil Wars: Or Scheherazade Ginsberg Strikes Again, 1989; The Snake Oil Variations, 1989. SHERWOOD SERIES: Sherwood, 1991; Robin and the King, 1993. OTHER: Unsigned Original, 1975; The Fire When It Comes (novella and short stories), 1984; A Matter of Taste, 1984; (ed.) Invitation to Camelot: An Arthurian Anthology of Short Stories (short stories), 1988; A Spell for Annalise, 1993; (co-author) Go Not Gently, 2006. **Address:** Writers House, 21 W 26th St., New York, CA 10010, U.S.A.

GODWIN, Rebecca T. American (born United States), b. 1950. **Genres:** Novels, Novellas/Short Stories, Essays. **Career:** Georgetown Steel Corp., secretary, 1968-80; Bumpy Thompson Realty, broker and partner, 1980-87; Higginbotham and Associates, writer, 1988-92; Bennington College, writer, 1992-2002, Bennington magazine, editor and writer, 1994-2002, Bennington Writing Workshops, teacher, 1995, MFA Writing Program, teacher, 2002-, faculty, 2002-, Plain China (Literary Magazine), faculty editor, 2009-; Wildacres Writing Workshop, teacher, 1996. **Publications:** NOVELS: Private Parts, 1992; Keeper of the House, 1994. Contributor of short stories and essays to periodicals. **Address:** Bennington College, 1 College Dr., Bennington, VT 05201, U.S.A. **Online address:** rgodwin@bennington.edu

GODWIN, Robert. Canadian/British (born England), b. 1958?. **Genres:** Air/Space Topics, Astronomy, Sciences. **Career:** The Orient Express, founder, 1981; music management and production, 1983-95; writer, 1984-; Griffin Music, founder, 1985; Collector's Guide Publishing, founder, 1987. **Publications:** The Illustrated Led Zeppelin Collection, 1984; The Illustrated Collectors Guide to Kate Bush, 1991; The Illustrated Collectors Guide to Hawkwind, 1993; (comp.) The Illustrated Collectors Guide to Led Zeppelin, 1994; Led Zeppelin: The Press Reports, 1997; The Making of Led Zeppelin IV, 1998; Space Toys of the Sixties, 1999; (ed.) Apollo 12: The NASA Mission Reports, 1999; (ed.) Friendship 7: The First Flight of John Glenn: The NASA Mission Reports, 1999; (ed.) Apollo 11: The NASA Mission Reports, 1999; (ed.) Apollo 9: The NASA Mission Reports, 1999; (ed.) Apollo 13: The NASA Mission Reports, 2000; (ed.) Apollo 8: The NASA Mission Reports, 2000; (ed.) X-15: The NASA Mission Reports, 2000; (ed.) Mars: The NASA Mission Reports, 2000; (ed.) Gemini 6: The NASA Mission Reports, 2000; (ed.) Apollo 10: The NASA Mission Reports, 2000; (ed.) Apollo 14: The NASA Mission Reports, 2000; (ed.) Apollo 7: The NASA Mission Reports, 2000; (ed.) Gemini 7: The NASA Mission Reports, 2000; (ed.) Freedom 7: The NASA Mission Reports, 2001; Rocket and Space Corporation Energia: The Legacy of S.P. Korolev, 2001; (ed.) Apollo 15: The NASA Mission Reports, 2001; (ed.) Space Shuttle: STS Flights 1-5 Including Approach and Landing Tests: The NASA Mission Reports, 2001; (ed.) Apollo 16: The NASA Mission Reports, 2002; (ed.) Apollo 17: The NASA Mission Reports, 2002; (ed.) Sigma 7: The Six Orbits of Walter M. Shirra: The NASA Mission Reports, 2003; (ed.) Dyna-Soar: Hypersonic Strategic Weapons System, 2003; The Rocket Team, 2003; The REAL Space Cowboys, 2004; Edisons Conquest of Mars, 2004; (ed.) Mars: The NASA Mission Reports, vol. II, 2004; Saturn 5: The Complete Test and Construction Records: The NASA Mission Reports, 2005; Project Apollo: The Test Program, 2005; (ed.) Deep Space: The NASA Mission Reports, 2005; First Men on the Moon: Apollo 11, 2006; Russian Spacecraft, 2006; Project Apollo: Exploring the Moon, 2006; Space Shuttle Fact Archive, 2007; Space Race, 2007; Around the World in 65 Days with George Griffith, 2008. **Address:** c/o Author Mail, Collectors Guide Publishing Inc., 1440 Grahams Ln., Ste. 2, Burlington, ON L7S 1W3, Canada.

GOEDECKE, Christopher (John). American (born United States), b. 1951. **Genres:** Recreation, Sports/Fitness, Children's Fiction. **Career:** International School of Judo and Karate, senior staff instructor, 1972-75; Wind School, karate headmaster and director, 1975-; Wind Warrior Company Inc., president, 1975-; Reader's Rendezvous, co-director, 1989-91. Writer. **Publications:** The Grand Master Game, 1980; A Guide to the Martial Arts of New Jersey, 1984; The Wind Warrior: The Training of a Karate Champion, 1992; Smart Moves: A Kid's Guide to Self-Defense, 1995; The Soul Polisher's Apprentice: A Martial Kumite About Personal Evolution, 2007. **Address:** Wind School, 16 Braidburn Way, Morristown, NJ 07960, U.S.A. **Online address:** windschool@earthlink.net

GOEHLERT, Robert. (Robert U. Goehlert). American (born United States), b. 1948. **Genres:** Bibliography, Reference, Politics/Government. **Career:** Indiana University, Political Science Data Archive and Computing Library, archivist, 1971-72, College of Arts and Sciences, assistant instructor, 1973, Department of Political Science, research and editorial assistant, 1973-74, instructor, 1975-, School of Library and Information Science, adjunct associate professor, 1985-; University Library, School of Library and Information Science, instructor, assistant to librarian for economics and political science, 1973-74, subject specialist for political science, economics and criminal justice, 1974-, assistant head of subject and area librarians, 1974-, Interlibrary Services, acting head, 1985-86; Honor's Division, assistant instructor, 1974; Commonwealth of Australia Parliamentary Library, visiting librarian, 1984; Australian National University's Menzies Library, visiting librarian, 1984. **Publications:** NONFICTION WITH F.S. MARTIN: The Parliament of Great Britain: A Bibliography, 1982; Policy Analysis and Management: A Bibliography, 1984; The Presidency: A Research Guide, 1984; The American Presidents: A Bibliography, 1988; The U.S. Supreme Court: A Bibliography, 1990; How to Research the Supreme Court, 1992; The United States Congress: An Annotated Bibliography 1980-93, 1994; (with J. Sayre) Members of Congress: A Bibliography, 1996; How to Research Congress, 1996; How to Research the Presidency, 1996; Political Science Journal of Information, 1997; American Government and Politics: A Guide to Books for Teachers, 1997. OTHERS: (with T.J. Michalak) Works of Kenneth E. Boulding: A Bibliography, 1974; Soviet Administrative Practices: A Bibliography, 1975; (ed. with T.J. Michalak) Bibliography Index: Reform of Local Government Structures in the United States 1945-1971, 1976; Presidential Campaigns: A Cartoon History 1789-1976, 1977; City and Regional Planning: A Bibliography of Journal Literature, 1945-1975, 1978; Bibliography of Reference Tools in Economics, 1979; Congress and Law-Making: Researching the Legislative Process, 1979; Local Government: A Selected Bibliography of Journal Literature, 1979; Reference Tools in Political Science, 1979; Research Resources in Criminology, 1979; Resources for the Study of British Politics, 1979; Municipal Government: A Selected Bibliography of Journal Literature, 1979; Directory of Librarians and Information Specialists in Political Science, 1979; (comp. with P.C. Baker and E. Ostrom) Metropolitan Reform: An Annotated Bibliography, 1979; (with E.R. Hoffmeister) CIA, a Bibliography, 1980; European Parliament, 1980; Reference Sources for the Study of Soviet Politics, 1980; West European Studies, 1980; Coalition Theory and Formation, 1981; Decision Making, Theories and Models, 1981; Planning and Implementation of Social Programs, 1981; Economic Decision Making, 1981; Evaluation of Social Programs, 1981; Political Attitudes: A Bibliography, 1981; Political Behavior, 1981; Political Decision Making, 1981; Political Psychology, 1981; Political Socialization, 1981; Public Goods and Expenditures, 1981; Public Opinion Research, 1981; Reapportionment and Redistricting, 1981; Research Methodologies in Political Science, 1981; Teaching Political Science, 1981; Welfare State and Welfare Economics, 1981; Voting Research and Modeling, 1981; Anarchism, 1982; Federal Elections, 1982; Political Leadership, 1982; Guide to Soviet Politics, 1982; (with J.R. Sayre) The United States

Congress: A Bibliography, 1982; John Stuart Mill, 1982; Political Representation, 1982; Political Parties in the United States, 1982; Writings of Kenneth Boulding: A Bibliography, 1982; Policy Studies on Development: A Selected Bibliography, 1983; Policy Studies on Service Delivery: A Selected Bibliography, 1983; Policy Studies on Taxation: A Selected Bibliography, 1983; Policy Studies on Science: A Selected Bibliography, 1983; Policy Studies on Research and Development: A Selected Bibliography, 1983; Policy Studies on Industrial Development: A Selected Bibliography, 1984; Urban Economics: A Selected Bibliography, 1984; Economic Modeling: A Selected Bibliography, 1984; Economic Transfers: A Selected Bibliography, 1984; Economic Behavior: A Selected Bibliography, 1984; Economic Externalities: A Selected Bibliography, 1984; Economic Indicators: A Selected Bibliography, 1984; Economic Inequality: A Selected Bibliography, 1984; Fiscal Policy: A Selected Bibliography, 1984; Human Resource Economics: A Selected Bibliography, 1984; Human Rights Policy: A Selected Bibliography, 1984; Institutional Economics: A Selected Bibliography, 1984; Keynesian Economics: A Selected Bibliography, 1984; Macroeconomic Policy: A Selected Bibliography, 1984; Managing the Legislative Workload: Lessons from the United States, 1984; Manpower Economics: A Selected Bibliography, 1984; Market Economics: A Selected Bibliography, 1984; Mathematical Economics: A Selected Bibliography, 1984; Minority Policy Studies: A Selected Bibliography, 1984; Organizational Economics: A Selected Bibliography, 1984; Policy Forecasting: A Selected Bibliography, 1984; Concepts of Political and Social Authority: A Selected Bibliography, 1984; Political and Social Advertising: A Selected Bibliography, 1984; Policy Studies on International Economics: A Selected Bibliography, 1984; (with F.W. Musto) State Legislatures: A Bibliography, 1985; Political Modernization: A Selected Bibliography, 1985; Political Change and Development: A Selected Bibliography, 1985; Political Communication and Information: A Selected Bibliography, 1985; Political Control: A Selected Bibliography, 1985; Political Corruption: A Selected Bibliography, 1985; Political Forecasting: A Selected Bibliography, 1985; (with E.R. Hoffmeister) The Department of State and American Diplomacy: A Bibliography, 1986; The People's Republic of China: Social Science Reference Sources, 1986; Basic Research Resources in Economics, 1986; Basic Research Resources in Political Science, 1986; (with N. Gunderson) Government Regulation of Business: An Information Sourcebook, 1987; Criminal Investigation: A Selected Bibliography, 1987; Administration of Criminal Justice: A Selected Bibliography, 1987; The Parliament of Australia: A Bibliography, 1988; (comp. with with H. Reynolds) The Executive Branch of the U.S. Government: A Bibliography, 1988; Chinese Communes: A Selected Bibliography, 1988; Chinese Communism: A Selected Bibliography, 1988; The Chinese Communist Party: A Selected Bibliography, 1988; The Chinese Cultural Revolution: A Selected Bibliography, 1988; Urbanism in China: A Selected Bibliography, 1988; Congress and Law-making: Researching the Legislative Process, 1989; Chinese Politics: A Selected Bibliography, 1989; Entrepreneurship: A Selected Bibliography of Books, 1989; The Parliament of Canada: A Select Bibliography, 1990; The Parliament of New Zealand: A Select Bibliography, 1990; (with M. Shaaban) The European Community: Basic Resources, 1991; The Parliament of India: A Selected Bibliography, 1991; (with M. Shaaban) UN Documentation: A Basic Guide, 1992; (with A.C. Stamatoples) The Chinese Economy: A Bibliography of Works in English, 1995; (with F.S. Martin) CQ's Resource Guide to Modern Elections: An Annotated Bibliography, 1960-1996, 2000; (with F.S. Martin) How to Research Elections, 2000; (with M. Shaaban) The European Union: Basic Resources, 2004. Works appear in anthologies. Contributor to periodicals. **Address:** School of Library & Information Science, Indiana University, Rm. E860, Main Library, 1320 E 10th St., LI 011, Bloomington, IN 47405-3907, U.S.A. **Online address:** goehlert@indiana.edu

GOEHLERT, Robert U. See **GOEHLERT, Robert.**

GOEMANS, Hein E. American/Dutch (born Netherlands), b. 1957. **Genres:** Politics/Government, Military/Defense/Arms Control. **Career:** Duke University, assistant professor of political science, 1996-2003; University of Rochester, Department of Political Science, assistant professor, 2004-10, associate professor, 2010-. Writer. **Publications:** War and Punishment: The Causes of War Termination and the First World War, 2000; (with G. Chiozza) Leaders and International Conflict, 2011. Contributor to periodicals. **Address:** Department of Political Science, University of Rochester, 320 Harkness Hall, Rochester, NY 14627-0146, U.S.A. **Online address:** hgoemans@mail.rochester.edu

GOERING, Joseph. Canadian (born Canada), b. 1947. **Genres:** Literary Criticism And History. **Career:** University of Toronto, St. Michael's College, St. George Campus, Department of History, professor. Writer. **Publications:** (Ed. with F.A.C. Mantello) Templum Dei, 1984; William De Montibus (c. 1140-1213): The Schools and the Literature of Pastoral Care, 1992; (ed. with F. Guardiani) Medievalism: The Future of the Past, 2000; (ed. with E.A. Mackie) Editing Robert Grosseteste: Papers Given at the Thirty-sixth Annual Conference on Editorial Problems, 2003; (ed. with J.D. McAuliffe and B.D. Walfish) With Reverence for the Word: Medieval Scriptural Exegesis in Judaism, Christianity, and Islam, 2003; An Introduction to Medieval Christian Biblical Interpretation, 2003; The Virgin and the Grail: Origins of a Legend, 2005; (ed. with F. Guardiani and G. Silano) Limina: Thresholds and Borders: Proceedings of a St. Michael's College Symposium, 28 February-1 March 2003, 2005; (ed. with F. Guardiani and G. Silano) Rule Makers and Rule Breakers: Proceedings of a St. Michael's College Symposium, 1-2 October 2004, 2006; (ed. with F. Guardiani and G. Silano) Weapons of Mass Instruction, 2008; Pastoralia: The Latin Literature of Pastoral Care in Thirteenth Century England, forthcoming. **Address:** Department of History, University of Toronto, Rm. 120, Odette Hall, 100 St. George St., Toronto, ON M5S 3G3, Canada. **Online address:** goering@chass.utoronto.ca

GOERLER, Raimund E. American (born United States), b. 1948. **Genres:** History. **Career:** Western Reserve Historical Society, manuscript specialist, 1976-78; Ohio State University, associate professor, 1997-2009, professor, 2000-11, university archivist, 1978-, chief archivist, 1990-, assistant director of libraries, 2000-; Kent State University, adjunct assistant professor, 1991-. Writer. **Publications:** (With G.A. Fry and F.W. Hebbard) The Ohio State University and Its College of Optometry: A Photographic History, 1993; (with T. Chute) The Ohio State University Trivia Book, 2007; The Ohio State University: An Illustrated History, 2011. EDITOR: The Tom L. Johnson Papers in the Library of the Western Reserve Historical Society, 1976; From History to Pre-History: Archivists Face the Future: Essays in Honor of the 25th Anniversary of the Society of Ohio Archivists, 1994; To the Pole: The Diary and Notebook of Richard E. Byrd, 1925-1927, 1998. Contributor of articles to journals. **Address:** University Archives, Ohio State University, 5815 Ackerman, Ackerman Rd., Columbus, OH 43202, U.S.A. **Online address:** goerler.1@osu.edu

GOERNER, Sally J. American (born United States), b. 1952. **Genres:** Environmental Sciences/Ecology, Information Science/Computers, Adult Nonfiction, Intellectual History, Physics, Sciences, Social Sciences, Technology, Technology. **Career:** NCR Corp., systems programmer, 1975-79; Asyst Design Services, co-founder, 1976, business systems consultant, 1976-79; Adaptronics, senior software engineer, 1979-81; Data General Corp., senior technical communications specialist, 1986-92; Triangle Center for the Study of Complex Systems, director and consultant, 1992-; Integral Science Institute, director, co-founder and president, 1999-. Writer. **Publications:** Chaos and the Evolving Ecological Universe, 1993; Complexity and the Web World, 1996; Life After the Clockwork Universe, 1996; After the Clockwork Universe: The Emerging Science and Culture of Integral Society, 1999; The Coming Great Change in Education, 2006; Sustainability as the Cutting Edge of Great Change, 2007. Contributor to journals and books. **Address:** Integral Science Institute, 374 Wesley Ct., Chapel Hill, NC 27516, U.S.A. **Online address:** sgoerner@mindspring.com

GOETHE, Ann. American (born United States), b. 1945. **Genres:** Novels, Plays/Screenplays, Songs/Lyrics And Libretti, Essays, Literary Criticism And History, Young Adult Fiction. **Career:** Blacksburg New School, founder, 1971. Writer. **Publications:** Midnight Lemonade (novel), 1993. Contributor to periodicals. **Address:** c/o Sandra Dijkstra, 1155 Camino, Del Mar, CA 92014, U.S.A. **Online address:** agoette@usit.net

GOFF, Barbara. (Barbara E. Goff). British (born England), b. 1958. **Genres:** History, Women's Studies And Issues, Theology/Religion. **Career:** Cambridge University, King's College, research fellow, 1986-90; University of Texas, Department of Classics, assistant professor, 1991-98, associate professor, 1998-; University of Reading, Department of Classics, professor, head, coordinator of B.A. Program. Writer. **Publications:** (As Barbara E. Goff) The Noose of Words: Readings of Desire, Violence, and Language in Euripides' Hippolytos, 1990; (ed. and intro.) History, Tragedy, Theory: Dialogues on Athenian Drama, 1995; Citizen Bacchae: Women's Ritual Practice in Ancient Greece, 2004; (ed.) Classics and Colonialism, 2005; (with M. Simpson) Crossroads in the Black Aegean: Oedipus, Antigone, and Dramas of the African Diaspora, 2007. **Address:** Department of Classics, University of Reading, Whiteknights, PO Box 217, Reading, BR RG6 6AH, England. **Online address:** b.e.goff@reading.ac.uk

GOFF, Barbara E. See **GOFF, Barbara.**

GOFF, M(adison) Lee. American (born United States), b. 1944. **Genres:** Criminology/True Crime. **Career:** B.P. Bishop Museum, Diptera Section, research assistant, 1964-66, Acarology Section, research assistant, 1968-71, acarologist, 1977-83, research associate in entomology, 1994-97; Hawaii Volcanoes National Park, International Biological Program Field Station, site manager, 1971; California State University, teaching assistant and research assistant, 1971-74; Kaiser Hospital, clinical laboratory assistant, 1974; University of Hawaii, teaching assistant, 1974-77, professor of entomology, 1983-2001, professor emeritus, 2001-, Entomology Museum, curator, 1993-, chair of entomology graduate field, 1994-98; State of Hawaii, Natural Area Reserves System Commission, commissioner and chair of commission, 1986-93; Acarological Society of America, president, 1991; American Academy of Forensic Sciences, Pathology/Biology Section, Discipline Assessment Task Force, chair of forensic entomology working group, 1993-96, secretary, 1995-96, chair, 1996-97; American Board of Forensic Entomology, board chair, 1996-99; Chaminade University of Honolulu, Forensic Sciences Program, director, 2001-, professor of forensic sciences. Writer. **Publications:** A Fly for the Prosecution: How Insect Evidence Helps Solve Crimes, 2000. Contributor to books and journals. **Address:** Forensic Sciences Program, Chaminade University of Honolulu, Rm. 5, Henry Hall, 3140 Waialae Ave., Honolulu, HI 96816-1510, U.S.A. **Online address:** lgoff@chaminade.edu

GOFF, Martyn. British (born England), b. 1923. **Genres:** Novels, History, Music, Sociology. **Career:** National Book League, director, 1970-86; Book Trust, chief executive, 1986-88, vice president, 2000-; Henry Sotheran Ltd., executive chairman. Writer. **Publications:** The Plaster Fabric, 1956; A Short Guide to Long Play: How to Enjoy Music On and Off The Record, 1957; A Season with Mammon, 1957; A Further Guide to Long Play, 1958; A Sort of Peace, 1959; Long Playing Collecting, 1960; The Youngest Director, 1961; Red on the Door, 1963; Flint Inheritance, 1965; Indecent Assault, 1967; Why Conform?, 1969; (intro.) Victorian and Edwardian Surrey from Old Photographs, 1972; Record Choice, 1974; The Royal Pavilion, Brighton, 1976; The Liberation of Rupert Bannister, 1977; Tar and Cement (novel), 1988; (ed. and intro.) Prize Writing: An Original Collection of Writings by Past Winners to Celebrate 21 Years of the Booker Prize, 1989; (ed.) The Best Winners of the Booker Prize, 1991. **Address:** A. M. Heath & Company Ltd., 6 Warwick Ct., Holborn, London, GL WC1R 5DJ, England.

GOFORTH, Ellen. See **FRANCIS, Dorothy Brenner.**

GOH, Evelyn. British (born England) **Genres:** Social Sciences. **Career:** University of Oxford, St. Anne's College, university lecturer in international relations, 2006-, Centre for Intl. Studies, research associate; University of London, reader in international studies. Writer. **Publications:** Singapore Island Map, 1999; Constructing the U.S. Rapprochement with China, 1961-1974: From Red Menace to Tacit Ally, 2004; Meeting the China Challenge: The U.S. in Southeast Asian Regional Security Strategies, 2005; (ed. with A. Acharya) Reassessing Security Cooperation in the Asia-Pacific: Competition, Congruence and Transformation, 2007; Developing the Mekong: Regionalism and Regional Security in China-Southeast Asian Relations, 2007. **Address:** Department of Politics & International Relations, St. Anne's College, University of Oxford, Manor Rd. Bldg., Manor Rd., Oxford, OX OX1 3UQ, England. **Online address:** evelyn.goh@st-annes.ox.ac.uk

GOIN, Peter. American (born United States), b. 1951. **Genres:** Photography. **Career:** University of Nevada, foundation professor of art in photography and videography, 1984-. Writer and photographer. **Publications:** Tracing the Line: A Photographic Survey of the Mexican-American Border, 1987; Nuclear Landscapes, 1991; Stopping Time: A Rephotographic Survey of Lake Tahoe, 1992; (ed.) Arid Waters: Photographs from the Water in the West Project, 1992; Humanature, 1996; (co-author) Atlas of the New West: Portrait of a Changing Region, 1997; (with R. Dawson and M. Webb) A Doubtful River, 2000; (with C.E. Raymond) Changing Mines in America, 2004; (with P.F. Starrs) Black Rock, 2005; Lake Tahoe, 2005; Nevada Rock Art, 2009; South Lake Tahoe Then and Now, 2010; (with P.F. Starrs) Field Guide to California Agriculture, 2010; Lake Tahoe A Maritime History, 2012. **Address:** University of Nevada, 1664 N Virginia St., Reno, NV 89557, U.S.A. **Online address:** pgoin@unr.edu

GOIN, Suzanne. American (born United States), b. 1966. **Genres:** Food And Wine, Medicine/Health. **Career:** Pain Adore et Fantasie, staff; Patisserie

Christian Pottier, staff; Olives, sous chef, 1993; Alloro, executive chef, 1994-96; Campanile, executive chef, 1997-98; Lucques, owner, 1998-; A.O.C., owner, 2002-; The Hungry Cat, owner, 2005-. Writer. **Publications:** (With T. Gelber) Sunday Suppers at Lucques: Seasonal Recipes from Market to Table (cookbook), 2005. **Address:** Lucques, 8474 Melrose Ave., West Hollywood, CA 90069, U.S.A. **Online address:** suzanne@lucques.com

GOING, Kelly L. American (born United States), b. 1973. **Genres:** Young Adult Fiction, Novels, Young Adult Non-fiction. **Career:** Writer. **Publications:** Fat Kid Rules the World, 2003; The Liberation of Gabriel King, 2005; Saint Iggy, 2006; The Garden of Eve, 2007; Writing & Selling the Young Adult Novel, 2008; King of the Screwups, 2009; (co-author) No Such Thing as the Real World, 2009; Cold Black Stone, 2010; Dog in Charge, 2012. Contributor to periodicals. **Address:** G. P. Putnam's Sons, 375 Hudson St., New York, NY 10014-3657, U.S.A. **Online address:** kl@klgoing.com

GOINGBACK, Owl. American (born United States), b. 1959. **Genres:** Novels, Young Adult Fiction, Ghost Writer, Mystery/Crime/Suspense. **Career:** Jim's Place, owner and manager, 1981-86; writer, 1987-. **Publications:** Confederacy of the Dead, 1993; Quest to Riverworld, 1993; The Book of Breed Kings, 1995; Excalibur, 1995; Phantoms of the Night, 1996; Crota: A Novel, 1996; Shaman Moon (novel), 1997; The Gift, 1997; Eagle Feathers, 1997; Darker Than Night, 1999; Evil Whispers, 2001; Breed, 2002. Works appear in anthologies. Contributor to books and magazines. **Address:** PO Box 5080, Winter Park, FL 32793-5080, U.S.A. **Online address:** o.goingback@yahoo.com

GOLANT, Stephen M(yles). American (born United States), b. 1945. **Genres:** Gerontology/Senior Issues. **Career:** University of Chicago, Department of Geography and the College, assistant professor, 1972-79, Department of Behavioral Sciences, assistant professor, 1974-77, associate professor, 1979-80; University of Guelph, Harshman lecturer, 1974; University of Florida, associate professor, 1980-84, professor of geography, adjunct professor of urban and regional planning, 1984-, Department of Geography, chair, 1982-88, Center for Gerontological Studies, faculty associate, 1980-; American Association of Retired Persons, consultant; U.S. Administration on Aging, consultant; Gerontological Planning Associates, consultant. Writer. **Publications:** (With I. Burton) Avoidance-Response to the Risk Environment, 1969; (with I. Burton) Meaning of a Hazard-Application of the Semantic Differential, 1969; The Residential Location and Spatial Behavior of the Elderly, 1972; (comp.) Location and Environment of Elderly Population, 1979; A Place to Grow Old: The Meaning of Environment in Old Age, 1984; Housing America's Elderly: Many Possibilities, Few Choices, 1992; (ed. and contrib.) The Columbia Retirement Handbook, 1994; Smart Housing, 1994; (with J. Hyde) Assisted Living Residence: A Vision for the Future, 2008. Contributor of books to articles. **Address:** Department of Geography, University of Florida, 3117 Turlington Hall, PO Box 117315, Gainesville, FL 32611, U.S.A. **Online address:** golant@geog.ufl.edu

GOLAY, Michael. American (born United States), b. 1951. **Genres:** History, Military/Defense/Arms Control. **Career:** The Exonian, faculty adviser; journalist, 1978-93; freelance writer and editor, 1993-; Phillips Exeter Academy, part-time faculty, 2000-04, instructor in history, 2004-, McConnell Hall, affiliate. **Publications:** The Civil War, 1992, rev. ed., 2011; To Gettysburg and Beyond, 1994; The Spanish-American War, 1995, rev. ed., 2010; The Black Experience During Reconstruction, 1996; Reconstruction and Reaction: The Emancipation of Slaves, 1861-1913, 1996; Where America Stands 1997, 1997; A Ruined Land, 1999; (with A.N. Fargnoli) William Faulkner A to Z: The Essential Reference to His Life and Work, 2002; (with J.S. Bowman) North American Exploration: America's March to the Pacific, 2003; (with A.N. Fargnoli and R.W. Hamblin) Critical Companion to William Faulkner, 2008. **Address:** Phillips Exeter Academy, 20 Main St., Exeter, NH 03833-2460, U.S.A. **Online address:** mgolay@exeter.edu

GOLCZEWSKI, James A. American (born United States), b. 1945. **Genres:** Gerontology/Senior Issues, Medicine/Health, Social Sciences. **Career:** ITT Communications Division, electronics engineer, 1969-73; Litton Industries, Airtron Division, materials engineer, 1974-79; University of Alabama, research fellow, 1980-82; University of Pennsylvania, Wistar Institute, fellow, 1982-83; Norwich University, assistant professor of physics, 1983-84; Passaic County Community College, adjunct teacher of biology and nutrition, 1984-85; University of Medicine and Dentistry of New Jersey, research associate, 1985-86; Rutgers University, research fellow, 1986-88; Medical Specialties

and Devices, senior scientist, 1989-92; University of Medicine and Dentistry of New Jersey, research specialist, 1993-96; freelance medical writer, 1996-. **Publications:** Aging: Strategies for Maintaining Good Health and Extending Life, 1998. Contributor to scientific journals. **Address:** 45 Ridge Rd., Roseland, NJ 07068, U.S.A. **Online address:** jigo@erols.com

GOLD, August. American (born United States), b. 1955. **Genres:** Young Adult Fiction, Theology/Religion. **Career:** Interfaith minister, 1989-; Sacred Center New York, co-founder, 2001-11, senior minister and spiritual director; Weekly Radio Program, host. Writer, broadcaster and public speaker. **Publications:** FOR YOUNGER READERS: (with M.J. Perlman) Where Does God Live?, 2001; Does God Hear My Prayer?, 2005; Does God Forgive Me?, 2006. OTHERS: (with J. Fotinos) The Prayer Chest: A Novel about Receiving All of Life's Riches, 2007; (with J. Fotinos) Think and Grow Rich Workbook, 2009; Thank You, God, for Everything, 2009; (with J. Fotinos) Little Daily Wisdom: 365 Inspiring Bible Verses to Change your Life, 2010; (with J. Fotinos) Prayer Partners: How Praying with Someone can Multiply your Blessings: Includes the 90-Day Prayer Partner Experience!, 2010; (with N. Hill and J. Fotinos) Think and Grow Rich Every Day: 365 Days of Success, 2010; (with N. Hill and J. Fotinos) The Think and Grow Rich Success Journal, 2010; (with J. Fotinos) Prayer Chest: A Tale about the Power of Faith, Community, and Love, 2011; (with N. Hill and J. Fotinos) Think and Grow Rich: The Master Mind Volume, 2011. **Address:** New World Library, 14 Pamaron Way, Novato, CA 94949, U.S.A.

GOLD, Bernice. Canadian (born Canada) **Genres:** Children's Fiction, Young Adult Fiction, History, Horror. **Career:** CBC Radio, freelance broadcaster; McGill-Montreal Children's Hospital Learning Center, teacher. Writer. **Publications:** My Four Lions, 1999; Strange School, Secret Wish, 2001; FORTHCOMING: This Horse of a Different Color; Take Me With You; Millie's War; Amy's Fortune. **Address:** Annick Press, 15 Patricia Ave., Toronto, ON M2M 1H9, Canada. **Online address:** agold@videotron.ca

GOLD, Dore. Israeli/American (born United States), b. 1953?. **Genres:** International Relations/Current Affairs, Adult Non-fiction, Military/Defense/Arms Control. **Career:** Advisor to Israeli Prime Minister Ariel Sharon; Jaffee Center for Strategic Defense Studies, Tel-Aviv University, director, U.S. foreign and development policy project, senior research associate, 1985-96; Prime Minister Benjamin Netanyahu, foreign policy advisor, 1996-97; United Nations, permanent representative of Israel, 1997-99; Jerusalem Center for Public Affairs, president, 2000-; University of Tel-Aviv, Dayan Center for Near East Studies, faculty; Israeli delegation at the Wye River negotiations, faculty, 1998; foreign policy expert. Writer. **Publications:** SDI: The U.S. Strategic Defense Initiative and the Implications of Israel's Participation, 1985; Yozmat Shults, 1988; America, the Gulf and Israel: CENTCOM (Central Command) and Emerging U.S. Regional Security Policies in the Mideast, 1988; Ma'amadah shel Yiśra'el be-Artsot ha-Berit ye-tahalikh ha-shalom, 1990; (ed.) Arms Control in the Middle East, 1991; Israel as an American NonNATO Ally: Parameters of Defense Industrial Cooperation in a Post-Cold War Relationship, 1992; U.S. Policy toward Israel's Qualitative Edge, 1992; After the American Elections: Preparing for Change in U.S.A.-Israel Relations: A Jaffee Center for Strategic Studies Working Group Report, 1993; U.S. Forces on the Golan Heights and Israeli-Syrian Security Arrangements, 1994; Jerusalem, Jaffee Center for Strategic Studies, 1995; ha-Ma'arakhah ha-diplomaṭit ʻal Yerushalayim, 2001; Hatred's Kingdom: How Saudi Arabia Supports the New Global Terrorism, 2003; Tower of Babble: How the United Nations Has Fueled Global Chaos, 2004; The Fight for Jerusalem: Radical Islam, the West and the Future of the Holy City, 2007; Iran, Hizbullah, Hamas and the Global Jihad: A New Conflict Paradigm for the West, 2007; (with J.D. Halevi) The UN Gaza Report: A Substantive Critique, 2009; The Rise of Nuclear Iran: How Tehran Defies the West, 2009; Contributor to periodicals. **Address:** Jerusalem Center for Public Affairs, 13 Tel Hai St., Jerusalem, 92107, Israel. **Online address:** jcpa@netvision.net.il

GOLD, Hazel. American (born United States), b. 1953. **Genres:** Literary Criticism And History, Cultural/Ethnic Topics, Language/Linguistics, Humanities. **Career:** University of Pennsylvania, lecturer in Spanish, 1976-80; Columbia University, assistant professor of Spanish, 1980-85; Northwestern University, assistant professor of Spanish, 1985-92; Emory University, Department of Spanish and Portuguese, associate professor of Spanish, 1992-, chair, 2000-03, 2009-, Tam Institute for Jewish Studies, associate professor and interim director, 2006; University of California, visiting professor, 1998. Writer. **Publications:** The Reframing of Realism: Galdós and the Discourses of the Nineteenth-Century Spanish Novel, 1993. Contributor of articles to journals and books. **Address:** Department of Spanish and Portuguese, Emory University, S514 Callaway Memorial Ctr., 537 Kilgo Cir., Atlanta, GA 30322-0001, U.S.A. **Online address:** hgold@emory.edu

GOLD, Herbert. American (born United States), b. 1924. **Genres:** Novels, Novellas/Short Stories, Autobiography/Memoirs, Essays. **Career:** Western Reserve University (now Case Western Reserve University), lecturer in philosophy and literature, 1951-53; Wayne State University, English Department, faculty, 1954-56; Cornell University, visiting professor, 1958; University of California, visiting professor, 1963, 1968, regents professor, 1973; Harvard University, visiting professor, 1964; Ohio University, McGuffey lecturer in English, 1971; University of California-Davis, visiting professor, 1974-79, 1985. Writer. **Publications:** Birth of a Hero: A Novel, 1951; The Prospect Before Us, 1954; The Man Who Was Not With It: A Novel, 1956 as The Wild Life, 1957; (with R.V. Cassill and J.B. Hall) 15 x 3 (short stories), 1957; (contrib.) Twelve Original Essays on Great American Novels, 1958; The Optimist: A Novel, 1959; Fiction of the Fifties: A Decade of American Writing: Stories, 1959; Therefore Be Bold: A Novel, 1960; Love and Like (short stories), 1960; Stories of Modern America, 1961; The Age of Happy Problems (essays), 1962; Salt: A Novel, 1963; The Man Who Was Not With It, 1965; The Fathers: A Novel in the Form of a Memoir, 1966; The Great American Jackpot, 1969; Biafra Goodbye, 1970; The Magic Will: Stories and Essays of a Decade, 1971, 2nd ed., 2002; My Last Two Thousand Years (autobiography), 1972; The Young Prince and the Magic Cone, 1973; Swiftie the Magician: A Novel, 1974; Waiting for Cordelia, 1977; Slave Trade: A Novel, 1979; He/She: A Novel, 1980; A Walk on the West Side: California on the Brink, 1981; Family: A Novel in the Form of a Memoir, 1981; True Love, 1982; Mister White Eyes: A Novel, 1984; Stories of Misbegotten Love, 1985; Lovers and Cohorts: Twenty-Seven Stories, 1986; A Girl of Forty, 1986; Dreaming: A Novel, 1988; Travels in San Francisco (memoirs), 1990; Best Nightmare on Earth: A Life in Haiti (autobiography), 1991, new ed., 2001; Bohemia: Where Art, Angst, Love & Strong Coffee Meet, 1993; She Took My Arm as if She Loved Me (novel), 1997; Daughter Mine (novel), 2000; The Age of Happy Problems, 2002; Still Alive!: A Temporary Condition, 2008. EDITOR: Fiction of the Fifties: A Decade of American Writing: Stories, 1959; (with D.L. Stevenson) Stories of Modern America, 1961, rev. ed., 1963; First Person Singular: Essays for the Sixties, 1963. **Address:** Axios Press, PO Box 118, Mount Jackson, VA 22842, U.S.A.

GOLD, Janet N(owakowski). American (born United States), b. 1948. **Genres:** Literary Criticism And History, Travel/Exploration, Women's Studies And Issues, Biography, Poetry. **Career:** Teacher, 1971-82; Centro Internacional de Idiomas, instructor in English, 1973; University of Massachusetts, teaching assistant, 1984-88; Bates College, instructor in Spanish language and literature, 1989-91; Louisiana State University, assistant professor of Spanish language and Latin American literature, 1991-95; University of New Hampshire, assistant professor of Spanish, 1995-2001, associate professor 2001-08, professor 2008-. Writer. **Publications:** Clementina Suarez: Her Life and Poetry, 1995; (with A. Toledo) Kindness of Cybernetics, 1998; Volver a imaginarlas, 1998; (ed.) Mujeres y cambio desde la letra, 2005; Sagatara mio, 2005; Culture and Customs of Honduras, 2009. Contributor to books. **Address:** Department of Spanish, University of New Hampshire, 210D Murkland Hall, Durham, NH 03824, U.S.A. **Online address:** jng@unh.edu

GOLD, Jerome. American (born United States), b. 1943. **Genres:** Novels, Novellas/Short Stories, Poetry, Autobiography/Memoirs, Essays, Writing/Journalism. **Career:** Black Heron Press, publisher and co-founder, 1984-. Writer. **Publications:** NOVELS: The Negligence of Death, 1984; The Inquisitor, 1991; The Prisoner's Son: Homage to Anthony Burgess, 1996; Sergeant Dickinson, 1999. STORIES: (with L. Galloway) Of Great Spaces, 1987; War Stories, 1990; Life at the End of Time (and essays), 1992; Prisoners (and poems), 1999. OTHERS: (ed.) Hurricanes, 1994; Publishing Lives: Interviews with Independent Book Publishers in the Pacific Northwest and British Columbia, 1996; Obscure in the Shade of the Giants: Publishing Lives, 2 vols., 2000; How I Learned That I Could Push the Button (memoirs/essays), 2003; Stillness, 2005; Paranoia & Heartbreak: Fifteen Years in a Juvenile Facility, 2009. Contributor of articles to periodicals. Works appear in anthologies. **Address:** Black Heron Press, PO Box 13396, Mill Creek, WA 98082-1396, U.S.A.

GOLD, Judy. American (born United States), b. 1962. **Genres:** Plays/Screenplays, Theology/Religion. **Career:** Home Box Office, At the Multiplex

with Judy Gold (television program), host. Writer. **Publications:** (With K.M. Ryan) 25 Questions for a Jewish Mother, 2007. **Address:** Abrams Artists Agency, 275 7th Ave., 26th Fl., New York, NY 10001-6708, U.S.A.

GOLD, Michael. American (born United States), b. 1950. **Genres:** Medicine/Health, Cultural/Ethnic Topics, Theology/Religion, Human Relations/Parenting. **Career:** Congregation Sons of Israel, rabbi, 1978-84; Beth El Congregation, rabbi, 1984-90; Temple Beth Torah, rabbi, 1990-; Heartfelt Communications, founder. Writer. **Publications:** And Hannah Wept: Infertility, Adoption and the Jewish Couple, 1988; Does God Belong in the Bedroom?, 1992; God, Love, Sex, and Family: A Rabbi's Guide for Building Relationships that Last, 1998; The Ten Journeys of Life: Walking the Path of Abraham: A Guide to Being Human, 2001; The Kabbalah of Love: The Journey of a Soul, 2008. **Address:** Heartfelt Communications, 2147 Eisenhower Dr. N, Ste. A, Goshen, IN 46526, U.S.A. **Online address:** rabbigold@aol.com

GOLD, Michael Evan. American (born United States), b. 1943. **Genres:** Law, Industrial Relations, Social Sciences. **Career:** English and Mathematics teacher; University of Liberia, School of Law, faculty of civil procedure and evidence; Cornell University, associate professor of industrial and labor relations. Writer. **Publications:** Some Terms from Liberian Speech, rev. ed., 1971; A Dialogue on Comparable Worth, 1983; An Introduction to Labor Law, 1989, 2nd ed., 1998; An Introduction to the Law of Employment Discrimination, 1993, 2nd ed., 2001; Labor and Employment Discrimination Law, 2006; A Student's Introduction to Legal Reasoning, forthcoming. Works appear in anthologies. Contributor to law journals. **Address:** Department of Labor Relations, Law & History, Cornell University, 362 Ives Faculty Bldg., Ithaca, NY 14853-3901, U.S.A. **Online address:** meg3@cornell.edu

GOLD, Nora. Canadian (born Canada), b. 1952. **Genres:** Novellas/Short Stories, Novels, Social Work. **Career:** Jewish Fiction .net, founder and editor; McMaster University, associate professor of social work, 1990-2000. Activist. **Publications:** FICTION: Marrow and Other Stories, 1998. Contributor of articles to books and journals. **Address:** Centre for Women's Studies in Education, Ontario Institute for Studies in Education, University of Toronto, 252 Bloor St. W, Toronto, ON M5S 1V6, Canada. **Online address:** nora.gold@jewishfiction.net

GOLD, Penny Schine. American (born United States), b. 1947. **Genres:** History, Social Sciences, Education, Business/Trade/Industry. **Career:** University of Cincinnati, instructor in history, 1975-76; Knox College, instructor, assistant professor, associate professor, professor of history, 1976-, chair of women's studies program, 1986-96, 2000-04, history department chair, 1994-99, 2000-02, coordinator of faculty development program, 2002-; University of Iowa, visiting assistant professor, 1982; Newberry Library, director of program in the humanities, 1983-84; University of Chicago, visiting associate professor, 1985; University of Chicago, Institute for Advanced Studies in Religion, senior fellow, 1997-98. Writer. **Publications:** The Lady and the Virgin: Image, Attitude, and Experience in Twelfth-Century France, 1985; (ed. with B.C. Sax) Cultural Visions: Essays in the History of Culture, 2000; Americanization and The Transformation of Jewish Education, 2000; (with J. Goldsmith and J. Komlos) The Chicago Guide to Your Academic Career: A Portable Mentor for Scholars from Graduate School through Tenure, 2001; Making the Bible Modern: Children's Bibles and Jewish Education in Twentieth-Century America, 2004. **Address:** Department of History, Knox College, Galesburg, IL 61401, U.S.A. **Online address:** pgold@knox.edu

GOLD, Scott. American (born United States), b. 1976. **Genres:** Food And Wine. **Career:** ShamelessCarnivore.com, founder, 2005. Writer. **Publications:** The Shameless Carnivore: A Manifesto for Meat Lovers, 2008. Contributor to periodicals. **Address:** Brooklyn, NY , U.S.A. **Online address:** scott@shamelesscarnivore.com

GOLD, Steven J(ames). American (born United States), b. 1955. **Genres:** Sociology, Politics/Government. **Career:** Off Track Betting Corp., Market Research Department, staff, 1977-78; University of California, Institute of Business and Economic Research, research assistant, 1978-79; Lawrence Berkeley Laboratory, research assistant in applied science division, 1980-85; Institute of International Studies, research assistant, 1981-82, Center for Southeast Asian Refugee Resettlement, program developer, 1982-84; Whittier College, Department of Sociology, Anthropology and Social work, assistant professor, 1985-91, associate professor of sociology, 1991-94, chair, 1993-94; Wilstein Institute on Jewish Policy Studies, senior fellow, 1991-99; Michigan State University, Department of Sociology, associate professor, 1994-99, acting associate chair and graduate program director, 1999, acting chair, 2003-04, professor, 1999-, associate chair, 1999-2008, graduate program director, 2002-. Writer. **Publications:** Refugee Communities: A Comparative Field Study, 1992; (with M. Tuan) Jews from the Former U.S.S.R. in the United States, 1993; From the Workers State to the Golden State, 1995; (ed. with N. Foner and R.G. Rumbaut) Immigration Research for a New Century, 2000; (with I. Light) Ethnic Economies, 2000; The Israeli Diaspora, 2002; The Store in the Hood: Ethnic Businesses and Conflict in the US, 1900 to 2005, 2010; (ed. with S.J. Nawyn) The International Handbook of Migration Studies, 2011. Contributor of articles to books and journals. **Address:** Department of Sociology, Michigan State University, 462 Berkey Hall, East Lansing, MI 48824-1111, U.S.A. **Online address:** gold@msu.edu

GOLDACRE, Ben. British (born England), b. 1974?. **Genres:** Sciences. **Career:** British National Health Service, Physician; The Guardian (London, England), columnist, 2003-; King's College London, Institute of Psychiatry, research fellow, 2008. Writer. **Publications:** Bad Science, 2008 in US as Bad Science: Quacks, Hacks, and Big Pharma Flacks, 2010; The Drug Pushers, 2012. **Address:** The Guardian, Kings Pl., 90 York Way, London, GL N1 9GU, England. **Online address:** ben@badscience.net

GOLDBERG, Bruce (Edward). American (born United States), b. 1948. **Genres:** Medicine/Health, Psychiatry, History, Psychology. **Career:** Dental practice, 1976-89, retired, 1989; hypnotherapy practice, 1976-; Los Angeles Academy of Clinical Hypnosis, president, 1990-. Writer. **Publications:** Past Lives, Future Lives: Accounts of Regression and Progression through Hypnosis, 1982; The Search for Grace: A Documented Case of Murder and Reincarnation, 1994; Soul Healing, 1996; Peaceful Transition, 1997; Unleash Your Psychic Powers, 1997; Sosegar el Alma, 1997; Secrets of Self-hypnosis: The Amazing New Technique to Lose Weight, Quit Smoking, Improve Memory, Change Bad Habits, 1997; Astral Voyages, 1998; Look Younger, Live Longer, 1998; New Age Hypnosis, 1998; Protected by the Light, 1998; Time Travelers from Our Future, 1998; Custom Design Your Own Destiny, 2000; Lose Weight Permanently and Naturally, 2000; Self Hypnosis, 2001, rev. ed., 2006; Dream Your Problems Away, 2003; Ascension, 2004; Spirit Guide Contact through Hypnosis, 2005; Karmic Capitalism: A Spiritual Approach to Financial Independence, 2005; Egypt: An Extraterrestrial And Time Traveler Experiment, 2007; Time Traveler Confidential: The Apocalypse, 2007. Contributor to journals. **Address:** Bruce Goldberg Inc., 4300 Natoma Ave., Woodland Hills, CA 91364, U.S.A. **Online address:** drbg@sbcglobal.net

GOLDBERG, Danny. American (born United States), b. 1950. **Genres:** Music. **Career:** Gold Mountain Entertainment, owner and president, 1983-92; Atlantic Records, senior vice president, 1992, president, 1993-94; Warner Bros Records, chair and chief executive officer, 1995; Mercury Records, president, 1996-97, chair and chief executive officer, 1994-98; Tikkun Magazine, co-publisher, 1997-2001; Artemis Records, chair and chief executive officer, 1998-; Sheridan Square Entertainment, president and chief executive officer; Swan Song Records, vice president; Modern Records, founder and co-owner; Air America Radio, chief executive officer, 2005-06; Gold Village Entertainment, president; American Symphony Orchestra, chair of the board of directors, 2008. Writer. **Publications:** (Ed. with V. Goldberg and R. Greenwald) It's a Free Country: Personal Freedom in America after September 11, 2002; Dispatches from the Culture Wars: How the Left Lost Teen Spirit, 2003; How the Left Lost Teen Spirit, 2005; Bumping into Geniuses: Inside the Rock and Roll Business, 2008. **Address:** Gold Village Entertainment, 72 Madison Ave., 8th Fl., New York, NY 10016, U.S.A. **Online address:** info@dannygoldberg.com

GOLDBERG, Harold. American (born United States) **Genres:** Novels. **Career:** Sony Online Entertainment, staff, editor-in-chief; Viacom, writer/consultant, 2006-08; American Movie Classics Website, writer, 2007. **Publications:** Advanced Commodity Spread Trading, 1985; (with H. Morrison) My Life among the Serial Killers: Inside the Minds of the World's Most Notorious Murderers, 2004; All Your Base are belong to us, 2011. Contributor to periodicals. **Address:** c/o Author Mail, William Morrow/HarperCollins, 10 E 53rd St., New York, NY 10022, U.S.A.

GOLDBERG, Jacob. (Jake Goldberg). American (born United States), b. 1943. **Genres:** Children's Non-fiction, Young Adult Non-fiction, Biography,

Humanities, Sciences, Reference, Young Adult Fiction. **Career:** Crown Publishers Inc., senior editor, 1970-90; Chelsea House Publishers, senior editor, 1990-96. **Publications:** AS JAKE GOLDBERG FOR CHILDREN: Rachel Carson: Biologist and Author, 1991; Hawaii, 1998, (with J. Hart) 2nd ed., 2007. FOR YOUNG ADULTS: Miguel de Cervantes, 1993; Economics and the Environment, 1993; The Disappearing American Farm, 1995; Albert Einstein: The Rebel behind Relativity, 1996; Food, 1997; Food: The Struggle to Sustain the Human Community, 1999. **Address:** c/o Author Mail, Watts Publishing Group, 96 Leonard St., London, GL EC2A 4XD, England.

GOLDBERG, Jake. See **GOLDBERG, Jacob.**

GOLDBERG, Jane G. American (born United States), b. 1946. **Genres:** Psychology, Medicine/Health, Human Relations/Parenting, Self Help. **Career:** Psychoanalyst, 1973-; Center for Modern Psychoanalytic Studies, faculty, 1980-; Boston Center for Modern Psychoanalytic Studies, faculty, 1980-; Institute for the Study of Violence, faculty; Boston Graduate School of Psychoanalysis, faculty; Psychoanalytic Center of Northern New Jersey, faculty; Treatment and Referral Service, faculty; Fifth Avenue Center for Counseling and Psychotherapy, faculty; City University of New York, Department of Psychology, faculty; Advanced Center for Psychotherapy, staff psychotherapist; Hillside Hospital, Art Therapy Program, staff psychotherapist; Kingsbrook Jewish Medical Center, Department of Medical Oncology, research associate; New School for Social Research, Department of Psychology, graduate faculty. Writer. **Publications:** (Ed.) Psychotherapeutic Treatment of Cancer Patients, 1981; Deceits of the Mind and Their Effects on the Body, 1991; The Dark Side of Love: The Positive Role of Our Negative Feelings, 1993. **Address:** Centre for Modern Psychoanalytic Studies, 41 E 20th St., New York, NY 10003-1324, U.S.A. **Online address:** janegoldberg@janegoldbergphd.com

GOLDBERG, Jonah Jacob. American (born United States), b. 1969. **Genres:** Politics/Government. **Career:** Lucianne Goldberg Literary Agency, vice president, 1991-; teacher, 1991-92; American Enterprise Institute, researcher, 1993-94; New River Media, producer, 1994; Think Tank with Ben Wattenberg, Public Broadcasting Service, producer, 1996-; Cable News Network, Regular political commentator, CNN's Crossfire, guest host; CNN's Late Edition with Wolf Blitzer, regular panelist. Writer. **Publications:** Liberal Fascism: The Secret History of the American Left, from Mussolini to the Politics of Meaning, 2007. Contributor to periodicals. **Address:** National Review, 221 Pennsylvania Ave. SE, Washington, DC 20003, U.S.A. **Online address:** jonahnro@aol.com

GOLDBERG, Leonard S. American (born United States), b. 1936. **Genres:** Mystery/Crime/Suspense, Science Fiction/Fantasy, Medicine/Health, Novels, Young Adult Fiction. **Career:** St. Louis City Hospital, intern and resident in medicine, 1960-61; Medical College of Virginia, resident in medicine, 1963-64; Jackson Memorial Hospital, resident in medicine, 1964-65; University of California-Los Angeles, fellow in hematology, 1965-66, research fellow in immunology, 1966-67, assistant professor, 1968-71, Veterans Administration, clinical investigator, 1968-71, associate professor, 1971-75, professor, 1975-79, clinical professor of medicine, 1979-, Medical Center, affiliate; University of California-San Francisco, research fellow in immunology, 1967-68; Veterans Administration St., clinical investigator, 1968-71; Wadsworth Veterans Hospital, consultant in rheumatology, 1971-. American Board of Internal Medicine, diplomate in internal medicine, hematology, and rheumatology. Writer. **Publications:** MEDICAL SUSPENSE NOVELS: Transplant, 1980; The Cure, 1982; Deadly Medicine, 1992; A Deadly Practice, 1994; Deadly Care, 1996; Deadly Harvest, 1997; Deadly Exposure, 1998; Lethal Measures, 2000; Fatal Care, 2001; Brainwaves, 2002; Fever Cell, 2003. OTHERS: The Setup, 1980; Patient One, 2012. Contributor to journals. **Address:** c/o Jane Jordan Browne, Multimedia Product Development Inc., 410 S Michigan Ave., Ste. 724, Chicago, IL 60605, U.S.A. **Online address:** mail@leonardgoldberg.com

GOLDBERGER, Avriel H. American (born United States), b. 1928. **Genres:** History, Women's Studies And Issues, Autobiography/Memoirs, Biography, Essays. **Career:** Hofstra University, professor of French, head of department, 1969-74, 1986-93, professor emeritus, 1993-. Writer. **Publications:** Visions of a New Hero: The Heroic Life According to Andre Malraux and Earlier Advocates of Human Grandeur, 1965; (ed.) Woman as Mediatrix: Essays on Nineteenth-Century European Woman Writers, 1987; (ed.) The Stendhal Bicentennial Papers, 1987; (ed. with M. Gutwirth and K. Szmurlo)

Germaine de Staël: Crossing the Borders, 1991. TRANSLATOR: (and intro.) Corinne, or, Italy, 1987; (intro. with E. Carles and R. Destarque) A Life of Her Own: A Countrywoman in Twentieth-Century France in UK as A Wild Herb Soup, 1991; (and intro.) G. deStaël, Delphine, 1995; (and intro.) G. de Staël, Ten Years of Exile, 2000. Contributor to journals and periodicals. **Address:** Hofstra University, 160 Hagedorn Hall, Hempstead, NY 11549-1000, U.S.A.

GOLDBLATT, Stacey. American (born United States), b. 1969?. **Genres:** Young Adult Fiction, Romance/Historical. **Career:** Encinitas Middle School, English teacher, 1992-2001. Author. **Publications:** Stray (young adult novel), 2007; Girl to the Core, 2009. **Address:** Delacorte Press Books for Young Readers, 1745 Broadway, 10th Fl., New York, NY 10019, U.S.A. **Online address:** staceygo@stacegoldblatt.com

GOLDEN, Arthur. American (born United States), b. 1956. **Genres:** Biography, Novels, Young Adult Fiction. **Career:** Writer. **Publications:** Memoirs of a Geisha, 1997. **Address:** 43 Abbottsford Rd., Brookline, MA 02446-6705, U.S.A.

GOLDEN, Mark. Canadian (born Canada), b. 1948. **Genres:** Classics, History, Sports/Fitness, Antiques/Furnishings. **Career:** University of Winnipeg, professor of classics, 1982-. Writer. **Publications:** Children and Childhood in Classical Athens, 1990; Sport and Society in Ancient Greece, 1998; Sport in Greece and Rome form A to Z, 2003. EDITOR: (with P. Toohey) Inventing Ancient Culture, 1997; (with P. Toohey) Sex and Difference in Ancient Greece and Rome, 2003; Sport in the Ancient World from A to Z, 2004; Greek Sport and Social Status, 2008. **Address:** Department of Classics, University of Winnipeg, 4G17, Graham Hall, 515 Portage Ave., Winnipeg, MB R3B 2E9, Canada. **Online address:** m.golden@uwinnipeg.ca

GOLDEN, Renny. American (born United States), b. 1937. **Genres:** Poetry, Civil Liberties/Human Rights, International Relations/Current Affairs, Politics/Government, Social Sciences, Sociology. **Career:** Malcolm X College, dean and co-founder, 1972-77; Harvard Divinity School, research/faculty associate, 1977-78; Northeastern Illinois University, associate professor, 1978, professor, 1978-2005, now professor emerita, 2005-10; Chicago Religious Task Force on Central America, co-founder, 1982; University of Arizona, Southwest Institute on Women, Rockfeller humanities fellow, 1989-90; Colombia College, Graduate Department of Educational Studies, adjunct professor, 1993-98; St. Leonard's Adult High School, co-founder, 2001-05; Dorothy Stang Adult High School, co-founder, 2005-10; University of New Mexico, adjunct professor, 2006-11, now professor emeritus. Writer. **Publications:** (With S. Collins and E. Kreutz) Half a Winter to Go: Poems, 1976; (with S. Collins) Struggle Is a Name for Hope, 1982; (with M. McConnell) Sanctuary: The New Underground Railroad, 1986; Dangerous Memories: Invasion and Resistance Since 1492, 1991; The Hour of the Poor, The Hour of Women: Salvadoran Women Speak, 1991; Disposable Children: America's Child Welfare System, 1997; The Hour of the Furnaces, 2000; (with M. Dennis and S. Wright) Oscar Romero: Reflections on His Life and Writings, 2000; Branded: Imprisoned Mothers and Children They Left Behind, 2004; War on the Family: Mothers in Prison and the Children they Leave Behind, 2005; Blood Desert, 2010. Contributor to books and periodicals. **Address:** Department of Justice Studies & Social Work, Northeastern Illinois University, 5500 N Saint Louis Ave., Chicago, IL 60625-4699, U.S.A. **Online address:** renny2213@aol.com

GOLDENTYER, Debra. American (born United States), b. 1960. **Genres:** Young Adult Non-fiction, Children's Fiction, Politics/Government. **Career:** Schaeffer and Goldentyer, partner, 1989-; Kaiser Permanente, web manager, 1994-99; University of California, Haas School of Business, web editor, 1999-2007, manager of online marketing, 2007-; CompuServe, assistant system operator. Writer. **Publications:** TEEN HOT LINE SERIES: Dropping Out of School, 1994; Gangs, 1994; Family Violence, 1995; Parental Divorce, 1995; Child Abuse, 1998; Divorce, 1998; Street Violence, 1998. OTHER: You and the Law, 1993. **Address:** Haas School of Business, University of California, 2000 Center St., 4th Fl.,, Berkeley, CA 94720-1900, U.S.A. **Online address:** goldentyer@haas.berkeley.edu

GOLDFARB, Jeffrey C. American (born United States), b. 1949. **Genres:** Politics/Government, Adult Non-fiction. **Career:** State University of New York, teaching assistant, 1971-72; University of Chicago, instructor in sociology, 1976-77; Illinois Institute of Technology, instructor in sociology, 1976-77; New School for Social Research, assistant professor, 1977-81, asso-

ciate professor, 1981-89, professor of sociology, 1989-99, Michael E. Gellert professor of sociology, 1999-, Eugene Lang College, faculty, 1986-91, chair of sociology department, 1992-95, 2003-06; sociologist and writer. **Publications:** The Persistence of Freedom: The Sociological Implications of Polish Student Theater, 1980; On Cultural Freedom: An Exploration of Public Life in Poland and America, 1982; Beyond Glasnost: The Post-Totalitarian Mind, 1989; The Cynical Society: The Culture of Politics and the Politics of Culture in American Life, 1991; After the Fall: The Pursuit of Democracy in Central Europe, 1992; (contrib.) Grappling with Democracy, 1996; Civility and Subversion: The Intellectual in Democratic Society, 1998; (contrib.) Materializing Democracy, 2001; The Politics of Small Things: The Power of the Powerless in Dark Times, 2006. Contributor to books and periodicals. **Address:** Department of Sociology, New School for Social Research, Rm. 431, 65 5th Ave., New York, NY 10011, U.S.A. **Online address:** goldfarj@newschool.edu

GOLDFARB, Michael. American (born United States), b. 1950. **Genres:** Politics/Government, History. **Career:** National Public Radio, foreign correspondent, 1991-, bureau chief, reporter, London bureau chief, 1996-98, U.S. correspondent, Boston public radio, affiliate, WBUR, senior correspondent; The Weekly Standard, contributing editor; Project for the New American Century, research associate; John McCain's deputy communications director; Joan Shorenstein Center on the Press, Politics and Public Policy, fellow; John F. Kennedy School of Government, fellow; British Broadcasting Corp., staff, News 24's program, panelist, Radio 3, essayist, Radio 4, critic; Globalpost.com, writer, London correspondent. **Publications:** Ahmad's War, Ahmad's Peace: Surviving under Saddam, Dying in the New Iraq, 2005; Emancipation: How Liberating Europe's Jews from the Ghetto Led to Revolution and Renaissance, 2009. **Address:** WBUR-FM, 890 Commonwealth Ave., Fl. 3, Boston, MA 02215, U.S.A.

GOLDFARB, Ronald (Lawrence). American (born United States), b. 1933. **Genres:** Communications/Media, Law, Politics/Government. **Career:** Twentieth Century Fund, research director, 1964-65; Goldfarb & Associates, partner, 1966-; U.S. Department of Justice, special prosecutor, 1961-64; Washington Service Bureau, vice-president, 1966-79; The Writing Co., chairman. Writer, attorney and literary agent. **Publications:** The Contempt Power, 1963; Ransom: A Critique of the American Bail System, 1965; (with A. Friendly) Crime and Publicity: The Impact of News on the Administration of Justice, 1967; (with L.R. Singer) Problems in the administration of justice in California, 1969; (with L.R. Singer) After Conviction: A Review of the American Correction System, 1973; Jails: The Ultimate Ghetto, 1975; Migrant Farm Workers, A Caste of Despair, 1981; (with J. Raymond) Clear Understandings: Guide to Legal Writing, 1982; (with G. Ross) The Writer's Lawyer, 1989; Perfect Villains, Imperfect Heroes, RFK's War against Organized Crime, 1995; TV or Not TV, Television Justice and the Courts, 1998; In Confidence: When to Protect Secrecy and When to Require Disclosure, 2009. Contributor to books. **Address:** Goldfarb & Associates, 721 Gibbon St., Alexandria, VA 22314, U.S.A. **Online address:** rglawlit@aol.com

GOLDHAGEN, Shari. American (born United States), b. 1976?. **Genres:** Novels, Psychology, Human Relations/Parenting. **Career:** Ohio State University, writing teacher; Gotham Writers Workshop, writing teacher. Writer. **Publications:** Family and Other Accidents: A Novel, 2006. Contributor to periodicals. **Address:** c/o Author Mail, Doubleday Publishers, 1745 Broadway, New York, NY 10019-4368, U.S.A. **Online address:** info@sharigoldhagen.com

GOLDIN, Barbara Diamond. American (born United States), b. 1946. **Genres:** Novellas/Short Stories, Children's Fiction, Young Adult Fiction, Theology/Religion, Humor/Satire. **Career:** Teacher, 1970-75; Children's Bookshop, co-owner and operator, 1975-76; Quaint Public Library, library assistant in children's section, 1976-78; freelance writer, 1981-; Congregation B'nai Israel Preschool, head teacher, 1986-89; Heritage Academy, language arts teacher, 1990-. **Publications:** JUVENILE: Just Enough is Plenty, 1988; The World's Birthday, 1990; Child's Book of Midrash, 1990; The Family Book of Midrash, 1990; Cakes and Miracles, 1991; Fire!: The Beginnings of the Labor Movement, 1992; The Magician's Visit: A Passover Tale, 1993; The Passover Journey, 1994; Red Means Good Fortune, 1994; Night Lights, 1995; Bat Mitzvah, 1995; Creating Angels, 1996; Coyote and the Fire Stick, 1996; While the Candles Burn, 1996; The Girl Who Lived with the Bears, 1997; Journeys with Elijah, 1999; Ten Holiday Jewish Children's Stories, 2000; A Mountain of Blintzes, 2001; One Hundred and One Read-Aloud Jewish

Stories, 2001; The Best Hanukkah Ever, 2007. Contributor to journals. **Address:** c/o Virginia Knowlton, Curtis Brown Ltd., 10 Astor Pl., New York, NY 10003, U.S.A. **Online address:** barbaradiamond@rcn.com

GOLDIN, Owen. American (born United States), b. 1957. **Genres:** Philosophy, Natural History. **Career:** University Texas, teaching assistant, 1984-87; Marquette University, Department of Philosophy, assistant professor, 1987-94, associate professor of philosophy, 1994-, professor, director graduate studies, 2004-06, Interdisciplinary Minor in Environmental Ethics, director, 2003-05. Writer. **Publications:** Explaining an Eclipse: Aristotle's Posterior Analytics 2.1-10, 1996; (ed. with P. Kilroe) Human Life and the Natural World: Readings in the History of Western Philosophy, 1997. Contributor to journals. **Address:** Department of Philosophy, Marquette University, 232 Coughlin Hall, PO Box 1881, Milwaukee, WI 53201-1881, U.S.A. **Online address:** owen.goldin@marquette.edu

GOLDIN, Paul R. (Paul Rakita Goldin). American (born United States), b. 1972. **Genres:** Philosophy. **Career:** University of Pennsylvania, Department of Asian and Middle Eastern Studies, assistant professor, 1996-2002, associate professor, 2002-04, Department of East Asian Languages and Civilizations, associate professor, 2004-07, professor, 2007-, undergraduate chair, 2003-07, department chair, 2007-. Writer and consultant. **Publications:** Rituals of the Way: The Philosophy of Xunzi, 1999; The Culture of Sex in Ancient China, 2002; (intro.) Sexual Life in Ancient China: A Preliminary Survey of Chinese Sex and Society from ca. 1500 B.C. till 1644 A.D., 2003; After Confucius: Studies in Early Chinese Philosophy, 2005; (ed. with V.H. Mair and N.S. Steinhardt) Hawai'i Reader in Traditional Chinese Culture, 2005; Confucianism, 2011. Contributor of articles to books and journals. **Address:** East Asian Languages & Civilizations, University of Pennsylvania, 847 Williams Hall, Philadelphia, PA 19104, U.S.A. **Online address:** prg@sas.upenn.edu

GOLDIN, Paul Rakita. See **GOLDIN, Paul R.**

GOLDING, Alan. American/British (born England), b. 1952. **Genres:** Literary Criticism And History. **Career:** Kishwaukee College, lecturer, 1976; Roosevelt University, lecturer, 1977-79; University of California, visiting lecturer in composition, 1980-84; University of Mississippi, assistant professor of American literature, 1984-87; University of Louisville, assistant professor, 1987-90, associate professor, 1990-96, professor of American literature, 1996-, affiliated faculty in women's and gender studies, 2004-. Writer. **Publications:** From Outlaw to Classic: Canons in American Poetry, 1995. Contributor of articles to books and periodicals. **Address:** Department of English, University of Louisville, Bingham Humanities, Belknap Campus, Rm. 312 B, Louisville, KY 40292, U.S.A. **Online address:** alan.golding@louisville.edu

GOLDING, Peter. British (born England), b. 1947. **Genres:** Communications/Media, Sociology, Social Sciences. **Career:** Leicester University, Centre for Mass Communication Research, research officer, 1970-89; Loughborough University, Department of Social Sciences, professor, 1990-, head, 1991-2006, pro-vice-chancellor, 2006-, co-chairman, Communications Research Centre, co-director; Research Assessment Exercise, chair, 2008; European Journal of Communication, co-editor; European Sociological Association, Media Research Network, chair; European Science Foundation, co-director. Writer. **Publications:** The Mass Media, 1974; (with P. Elliott) Making the News, 1979; (with S. Middleton) Images of Welfare: Press and Public Attitudes to Poverty, 1982; Excluding the Poor, 1986; Communicating Politics: Mass Communications and the Political Process, 1986; (with A. Sills, G. Taylor) The Politics of the Urban Crisis, 1988; (with D. Deacon) Taxation and Representation: Media, Political Communication and the Poll Tax, 1994; (ed. with G. Murdock) Political Economy of the Media, 1997; Beyond Cultural Imperialism, 1997; (ed. with M. Ferguson) Cultural Studies in Question, 1997; (contrib.) Europäischeb Öffentlichkeit, 1997; Researching Communications, 1999; (ed. with I. Bondebjerg)European Culture and the Media, 2004; (ed. with D. McQuail and E.D. Bens) Communication Theory and Research, 2005; (ed. with G. Murdock) Unpacking Digital Dynamics, 2010. **Address:** Department of Social Sciences, University of Loughborough, Loughborough, LE11 3TU, England. **Online address:** p.golding@lboro.ac.uk

GOLDING, Theresa Martin. American (born United States), b. 1960. **Genres:** Children's Fiction, Young Adult Fiction, Novels, Picture/Board Books, Mystery/Crime/Suspense, Social Commentary. **Career:** Writer. **Publications:** NOVELS: Kat's Surrender, 1999; The Secret Within, 2002; The Truth about Twelve, 2004; Niner, 2008. PICTURE BOOKS: Memorial Day

Surprise, 2004; Abby's Asthma and the Big Race, 2009. **Address:** c/o Author Mail, Boyds Mills Press, 815 Church St., Honesdale, PA 18431-1877, U.S.A. **Online address:** tmgolding@aol.com

GOLDMAN, Ari L. American (born United States), b. 1949?. **Genres:** Adult Non-fiction, Theology/Religion. **Career:** New York Times, copy boy, clerk, metro reporter, religion correspondent, 1973-93; Columbia University Graduate School of Journalism, professor, 1993-; Oxford University, Skirball fellow; Hebrew University, visiting Fulbright professor. Writer. **Publications:** The Search for God at Harvard, 1991; Being Jewish, 2000; Living a Year of Kaddish, 2003; In Every Generation: The JDC Haggadah: From the Archives of The Joint, the American Jewish Joint Distribution Committee, 2010. Contributor to periodicals. **Address:** Graduate School of Journalism, Columbia University, 807 Journalism, 2950 Broadway, New York, NY 10027-7004, U.S.A. **Online address:** alg18@columbia.edu

GOLDMAN, Arnold (Melvyn). British/American (born United States), b. 1936. **Genres:** Literary Criticism And History, Education, Gerontology/Senior Issues, Humanities, Institutions/Organizations, Civil Liberties/Human Rights. **Career:** University of Manchester, lecturer in English, 1961-65; Smith College, lecturer in English, 1965-66; University of Sussex, lecturer, 1966-, reader in English and American studies, through 1974; State University of New York, visiting professor, 1973; Vassar College, visiting professor and acting director of changing American culture, 1973-74, director of changing American culture, 1974-; University of Keele, professor of American studies, 1975-82; The Journal of American Studies, associate editor, 1976-82; Council for National Academic Awards, deputy chief executive, 1983-88; University of Kent, honorary professor of American studies, 1989-99, senior enterprise advisor and director quality enhancement, 1990-99; Staff and Educational Development Association, vice chairman, through 2000; Eastbourne Seniors Club, chairman of the trustees; World Education Services, trustee; Wealden Federation of Voluntary Organisations, trustee; Herstmonceux Village Information Centre, trustee; Eastbourne Symphony Orchestra, external relations manager, Eastbourne Association of Voluntary Services, trustee and director. **Publications:** The Joyce Paradox, 1966; James Joyce, 1968; Twentieth Century Interpretations of Absalom Absalom!, 1971; (co-ed.) Charles Dickens' American Notes, 1972; Tender is the Night, by F. Scott Fitzgerald, 1982; (ed.) American Literature in Context, 4 vols., 1982; Synge's the Aran Islands: A World of Grey, 1991. Contributor to periodicals. **Address:** 24 Eastport Ln., Lewes, ES BN7 1TL, England. **Online address:** a.goldman@cowbeech.f9.co.uk

GOLDMAN, E(leanor) M(aureen). Canadian/American (born United States), b. 1943. **Genres:** Young Adult Fiction, Children's Fiction, Science Fiction/Fantasy, Plays/Screenplays, Mystery/Crime/Suspense. **Career:** Litigation secretary, 1960, 1981-92. Writer. **Publications:** FOR MIDDLE GRADE READERS: Money to Burn, 1994; Shrinking Pains, 1996. FOR YOUNG ADULT READERS: The Night Room, 1995; Getting Lincoln's Goat: An Elliot Armbruster Mystery, 1995. **Address:** 295 Glassford Rd., Gibsons, BC V0N 1V8, Canada. **Online address:** emaureen2001@gmail.com

GOLDMAN, Elizabeth. American (born United States), b. 1949. **Genres:** Biography, Children's Fiction. **Career:** Oxford University Press, book publicist, 1984-88; University of New Hampshire, lecturer, 1991-93; New England College, lecturer, 1994-; McIntosh College, lecturer, 1994-; New Hampshire College, lecturer, 1994-; Temple Israel, vice president, 1995. Writer. **Publications:** Believers: Spiritual Leaders of the World, 1995. Contributor of articles to periodicals. **Address:** 41 Summer St., Dover, NH 03820, U.S.A. **Online address:** elizgo@aol.com

GOLDMAN, Francisco. American (born United States), b. 1954. **Genres:** Novels, Young Adult Non-fiction. **Career:** Harper's Magazine, contributing editor; Trinity College, faculty member, 2002, Allan K. Smith professor of English. **Publications:** The Long Night of White Chickens, 1992; The Ordinary Seaman, 1997; The Divine Husband, 2004; The Art of Political Murder: Who Killed the Bishop?, 2007. Contributor to periodicals. **Address:** Department of English, Trinity College, Rm. 302, 115 Vernon St., Hartford, CT 06106, U.S.A. **Online address:** francisco.goldman@trincoll.edu

GOLDMAN, Karla. American (born United States), b. 1960. **Genres:** Theology/Religion, Women's Studies And Issues, History, Cultural/Ethnic Topics, Social Sciences, Sociology. **Career:** Hebrew Union College, assistant professor, associate professor of American Jewish history, 1991-2000; Jewish

Women's Archive, historian-in-residence, 2000-08; University of Michigan, Sol Drachler professor of social work, University Program in Jewish Communal Leadership, director. Writer. **Publications:** Beyond the Synagogue Gallery: Finding a Place for Women in American Judaism, 2000. Contributor to periodicals. **Address:** School of Social Work, University of Michigan, Rm. 3810 SSWB, 1080 S University Ave., Ann Arbor, MI 48109-1106, U.S.A. **Online address:** kargold@umich.edu

GOLDMAN, Katherine (Wyse). American (born United States), b. 1951. **Genres:** Essays, How-to Books, Business/Trade/Industry. **Career:** Cleveland Press, intern, 1971; Taunton Daily Gazette, stringer, 1972-73; Random House Inc., copywriter, 1973-74; Wyse Advertising, senior copywriter, 1974-82; Shop, associate editor, 1979-80; Richardson, Myers and Donofrio, associate creative director, 1983-86, operator of a consulting business for advertising and promotion, 1986-. **Publications:** (Co-author) Disco Beauty, 1980; My Mother Worked and I Turned Out Okay, 1993; If You Can Raise Kids, You Can Get a Good Job, 1996; Working Mothers 101: How to Organize Your Life, Your Children, and Your Career to Stop Feeling Guilty and Start Enjoying It All, 1998; New York's 50 Best Places to Have a Kid's Party, 1999. **Address:** PO Box 560, Pound Ridge, NY 10576-0560, U.S.A.

GOLDMAN, Lawrence. British (born England), b. 1957. **Genres:** History, Politics/Government. **Career:** Trinity College, junior research fellow, 1982-; University of Oxford, Department for Continuing Education, university lecturer, 1985, Saint Peter's College, tutorial fellow and tutor in modern history; Oxford Dictionary of National Biography, editor, 2004-, historian. **Publications:** (Ed.) The Blind Victorian: Henry Fawcett and British Liberalism, 1989; Dons and Workers: Oxford and Adult Education since 1850, 1995; (contrib.) Articulating America: Fashioning a National Political Culture in Early America: Essays in Honor of J.R. Pole, 2000; Science, Reform and Politics in Victorian Britain: The Social Science Association, 1857-1886, 2002; (ed.) Oxford Dictionary of National Biography, 2004; (ed. with P. Ghosh) Politics and Culture in Victorian Britain: Essays in Memory of Colin Matthew, 2006; (ed. and intro.) Federalist Papers, 2008. Contributor to journals. **Address:** Department of History, St. Peter's College, Oxford University, New Inn Hall St., Oxford, OX OX1 2DL, England. **Online address:** lawrence.goldman@spc.ox.ac.uk

GOLDMAN, Marlene B. Canadian (born Canada), b. 1963?. **Genres:** Writing/Journalism, Women's Studies And Issues. **Career:** University of Toronto, Department of English, associate professor of English, graduate faculty and undergraduate instructor. Writer. **Publications:** Paths of Desire: Images of Exploration and Mapping in Canadian Women's Writing, 1997; Rewriting Apocalypse in Canadian Fiction, 2005; Dispossession: Haunting in Canadian Fiction, 2012; Forgotten: Age-Related Dementia and Alzheimer's in Canadian Literature, forthcoming. **Address:** Department of English, University of Toronto, H321 Jackman Humanities Bldg., 1265 Military Trail, Toronto, ON M1C 1A4, Canada. **Online address:** mgoldman@chass.utoronto.ca

GOLDMAN, Marshall I(rwin). American (born United States), b. 1930. **Genres:** Economics, Environmental Sciences/Ecology, Politics/Government, History, Social Sciences, Theology/Religion. **Career:** Harvard University, Davis Center for Russian and Eurasian Studies, associate, 1957-75, associate director, 1975-, Russian Research Center, researcher, 1957-; Wellesley College, Department of Economics, instructor, 1958-60, assistant professor, 1961-65, associate professor, 1966-68, professor, 1968-98, Kathryn Wasserman Davis professor of Russian economics, now professor emeritus, chairman of department, 1971-; International Marketing Institute, consultant, 1960-; Brandeis University, visiting professor of economics, 1961; Raytheon Corp., consultant, 1962; Arthur D. Little, consultant, 1967; Cambridge Economic Research Group, consultant, 1968-; Charles Rives Associates, consultant, 1969; Century Bank and Trust, director; Harvard University, Davis Center for Russian and Eurasian studies; Century Bank and Trust, director; Hillel Council of Greater Boston, president; Boston Baroque, president; Midland Road Corp., president. Writer. **Publications:** Soviet Marketing: Distribution in a Controlled Economy, 1963; Soviet Foreign Aid, 1967; The Soviet Economy: Myth and Reality, 1968; Critical Issues in Controlling Pollution, 1972; The Spoils of Progress: Environmental Pollution in the Soviet Union, 1972; Détente and Dollars: Doing Business with the Soviets, 1975; Changing Role of Raw Material Exports and Soviet Foreign Trade, 1979; The Enigma of Soviet Petroleum: Half Full or Half Empty, 1980; The U.S.S.R in Crisis: The Failure of an Economic System, 1983; Gorbachev's Challenge: Economic Reform in the Age of High Technology, 1987; What Went Wrong with Perestroika, 1991; The Former Soviet Republics and Eastern Europe: Struggling

for Solutions, 1993; Lost Opportunity: Why Economic Reforms in Russia Have Not Worked, 1994; The Piratization of Russia: Russian Reform goes Awry, 2003; Petrostate: Putin, Power and the New Russia, 2008. EDITOR: Comparative Economic Systems: A Reader, 1964, 2nd ed., 1971; Controlling Pollution: The Economics of a Cleaner America, 1967, rev. ed. as Ecology and Economics: Controlling Pollution in the 1970's, 1972; (with Z. Gitelman and M. Glants) Jewish Life After the U.S.S.R., 2003. Contributor of articles. **Address:** Davis Center for Russian and Eurasian Studies, Harvard University, 1730 Cambridge St., Cambridge, MA 02138, U.S.A. **Online address:** goldman3@fas.harvard.edu

GOLDMAN, Mary Elizabeth. American (born United States) **Genres:** Young Adult Fiction, Romance/Historical, Biography. **Career:** Republic of Texas Press, managing editor; Forever Texas, co-editor. **Publications:** A Trail Rider's Guide to Texas, 1993; (ed. with M. Blakely) Forever Texas: Texas History, the Way Those Who Lived It Wrote It, 2000; To Love and Die in Dallas, 2007. **Address:** Bandera County, TX , U.S.A. **Online address:** meg@maryelizabethgoldman.com

GOLDMAN, Minton F. American (born United States), b. 1933. **Genres:** Politics/Government, International Relations/Current Affairs. **Career:** Northeastern University, Department of Political Science, professor of political science, now professor emeritus. Writer. **Publications:** Global Studies: The Soviet Union and Eastern Europe, 1986, 11th ed. as Global Studies: Russia, the Eurasian Republics and Central/Eastern Europe, 2007; Revolution and Change in Central and Eastern Europe: Political, Economic, and Social Challenges, 1997; Slovakia since Independence: A Struggle for Democracy, 1999; Rivalry in Eurasia: Russia, the United States, and the War on Terror, 2009. Works appear in anthologies. Contributor of articles to periodicals. **Address:** Department of Political Science, Northeastern University, 323 Meserve Hall, 360 Huntington Ave., Boston, MA 02115-5005, U.S.A. **Online address:** m.goldman@neu.edu

GOLDMAN, Roger L. American (born United States), b. 1941. **Genres:** Law, Politics/Government, Sports/Fitness, Military/Defense/Arms Control. **Career:** St. Louis University, assistant professor, 1971-74, associate professor, 1974-77, professor of law, 1977-2004, associate dean, 1978-79, associate dean for academic affairs, 1996-98, interim dean, 1998-99, The Callis Family professor of law, 2004-; University of Pennsylvania, Gowen fellow, 1977-78; U.S. Department of Justice, researcher, 1977-78; Maryville College, lecturer, 1986. Writer. **Publications:** (With L. Riekes, S. Jenkins and P. McKissack) The Bill of Rights and You, 1989; (with J. O'Brien) Federal Criminal Trial Evidence, 1989; (with S. Jenkins, L. Riekes and S. Slane) Teacher's Resource Manual: The Bill of Rights and You, 1990; (co-author) Conflict, Courts and Trials, 3rd ed., 1991; (co-author) Teacher's Resource Guide: Conflicts, Courts and Trials, 3rd ed., 1991; (with L. Riekes and S. Slane) Teaching about the Bill of Rights in Elementary and Middle School Classrooms, 1991; Individual Rights: The Universal Challenge: 1791-1991, Bicentennial Celebration of the Bill of Rights, 1991; The Military and the Constitution, 1992; Alcohol, Drugs and the Bill of Rights, 1992; (with D. Gallen) Thurgood Marshall: Justice for All, 1992; (with D. Gallen) Justice William J. Brennan, Jr.: Freedom First, 1994; (with L. Riekes and D.B. Malcolm) Citizenship Through Sports and Law, 1995; (with S. Frankowski and E. Letowska) The Role of the United States Supreme Court in Protecting Civil Rights and Liberties, 1997. Contributor to books and periodicals. **Address:** School of Law, Saint Louis University, Rm. 202, Morrissey Hall, 3700 Lindell Blvd., Saint Louis, MO 63108, U.S.A. **Online address:** goldmanrl@slu.edu

GOLDMAN, Steven. American (born United States), b. 1964?. **Genres:** Film, Humor/Satire. **Career:** Author and educator. **Publications:** Two Parties, One Tux, and a Very Short Film about The Grapes of Wrath, 2008. Contributor to journals and magazines. **Address:** Boston, MA , U.S.A. **Online address:** steven@stevengoldmanbooks.com

GOLDMAN, William. Also writes as S. Morgenstern. American (born United States), b. 1931. **Genres:** Novels, Children's Fiction, Plays/Screenplays, Theatre, Essays, Literary Criticism And History, Young Adult Fiction, Young Adult Non-fiction, Young Adult Non-fiction. **Career:** Writer. **Publications:** NOVELS: Temple of Gold, 1957; Your Turn to Curtsy, My Turn to Bow, 1958; Soldier in the Rain, 1960; A Family Affair, 1961; No Way to Treat A Lady, 1964; Boys & Girls Together, 1964; The Thing of It Is...,

1967; Butch Cassidy and The Sundance Kid, 1969; Father's Day, 1971; The Princess Bride, 1973; Marathon Man, 1974; Wigger, 1974; The Great Waldo Pepper, 1975; Magic, 1976; Tinsel, 1979; Control, 1982; (as S. Morgenstern) The Silent Gondoliers, 1983; The Color of Light, 1984; Heat, 1985; Edged Weapons, 1985; Brothers, 1987; Misery, 1994; Chamber, 1996; Ghost and the Darkness: Only the Most Incredible Parts of the Story are True, 1996; Absolute Power, 1997; Hearts in Atlantis, 2001; Dreamcatcher: The Shooting Script, 2003. NON-FICTION: Blood Sweat and Stanley Poole, 1962; The Season: A Candid Look at Broadway, 1969; Adventures in the Screen Trade: A Personal View of Hollywood and Screenwriting, 1983; (with M. Lupica) Wait Till Next Year: The Story of a Season When What Should've Happened Didn't and What Could've Gone Wrong Did, 1988; Hype and Glory, 1990; The Big Picture: Who Killed Hollywood? And Other Essays, 1999; Which Lie Did I Tell?: More Adventures in the Screen Trade, 2000. Contributor to periodicals. **Address:** Morton L. Janklow Associates Inc., 598 Madison Ave., New York, NY 10022-1610, U.S.A.

GOLDNER, Beth. American (born United States) **Genres:** Novellas/Short Stories, Literary Criticism And History. **Career:** Rosemont College, adjunct faculty; The National Board of Medical Examiners, editor; Journal of Thoracic and Cardiovascular Surgery, assistant managing editor, managing editor; Wolters Kluwer, managing editor. **Publications:** Wake: Stories, 2003; The Number We End Up With: A Novel, 2005. Contributor of short stories to periodicals. **Address:** Counter Point, 1919 5th St., Berkeley, CA 94710, U.S.A. **Online address:** bgoldner@rosemont.edu

GOLDREIN, Iain S. British (born England) **Genres:** Law. **Career:** 7 Harrington Street Chambers, Crime Department, staff. Writer. **Publications:** (With M.R. de Haas) Property Distribution on Divorce, 2nd ed., 1985; (with M. de Haas) Personal Injury Litigation, 1985; Ship Sale and Purchase: Law and Technique, 1985, (with M. Hannaford and P. Turner) 6th ed., 2012; (with Kershaw and K.H.P. Wilkinson) Commercial Litigation: Pre-Emptive Remedies, 1987, 4th ed., 2002; Bullen and Leake and Jacob's Precedents of Pleadings, 1990; (with J. Jacob) Pleadings: Principles and Practice, 1990; (ed. with M. de Haas) Structured Settlements: A Practical Guide, 1993, 2nd ed., 1997; (with M. de Haas) Medical Negligence: Cost Effective Case Management, 1997; (co-ed.) Insurance Disputes, 1999, 3rd ed., 2012; (with M. de Haas and J. Frenkel) Personal Injury Major Claims Handling: Cost Effective Case Management, 2000; Media Access to the Family Court: A Guide to the New Rules and Their Application, 2009; Child Case Management Practice, 2009, 2nd ed., 2012; Privacy Injunctions and the Media: A Practice Manual, 2012. **Address:** 7 Harrington Street Chambers, 7 Harrington St., Liverpool, MS L2 9YH, England. **Online address:** goldhaas@tiscali.co.uk

GOLDS, Cassandra. Australian (born Australia), b. 1962?. **Genres:** Romance/Historical. **Career:** Writer. **Publications:** Michael and the Secret War, 1989; The Mostly True Story of Matthew and Trim, 2005; Clair-de-Lune, 2006; The Museum of Mary Child, 2009; The Three Loves of Perimmon, 2010. Contributor to periodicals. **Online address:** cassandragolds@yahoo.com

GOLDSBOROUGH, Robert (Gerald). American (born United States), b. 1937. **Genres:** Mystery/Crime/Suspense, Art/Art History, Business/Trade/Industry, Young Adult Fiction. **Career:** Associated Press, reporter, 1959; City News Bureau, reporter, 1959; Chicago Tribune, reporter, 1960-63, Sunday Magazine, assistant editor, 1963-66, TV Week, editor, 1966-67, assistant, 1967-71, assistant, 1971-72, Sunday editor, 1972-75, editor, 1975-82; Advertising Age, executive editor, 1982-88, special projects director, 1988. **Publications:** (Ed. and intro.) Great Railroad Paintings, 1976; Murder in E minor: A Nero Wolfe Mystery, 1986; Death on Deadline: A Nero Wolfe Mystery, 1987; The Bloodied Ivy: A Nero Wolfe Mystery, 1988; The Last Coincidence, 1989; Fade to Black, 1990; The Crain Adventure: The Making & Building of a Family Publishing Company, 1992; Silver Spire, 1992; The Missing Chapter, 1994; On Wings of Eagles: Thirty-Five Years of Spreading the Good News in Singapore and Beyond, 2003. SNAP MALEK MYSTERY SERIES: Three Strikes You're Dead, 2005; Shadow of the Bomb, 2006; A Death in Pilsen, 2007; A President in Peril, 2009; Terror at the Fair, 2011. **Address:** 360 N Michigan Ave., Chicago, IL 60601, U.S.A. **Online address:** rgoldsbo@crain.com

GOLDSCHMIDT, Arthur. American (born United States), b. 1938. **Genres:** History, Biography, Social Sciences, Translations, Education. **Career:** Pennsylvania State University, assistant professor, 1965-73, associate professor, 1973-89, professor, 1989-2000, professor emeritus of Middle East history, 2000-; Haifa University, visiting associate professor, 1973-74; University of Cairo, visiting professor, 1981-82, New Jersey Scholars Program, academic dean, 1985; Voices of Central Pennsylvania, founder, 1993, president, 1993-97. Writer. **Publications:** A Concise History of the Middle East, 1979, 9th ed., (with L. Davidson) 2009; Modern Egypt: The Formation of a Nation State, 1988, 2nd ed., 2004; (trans. and intro.) The Memoirs and Diaries of Muhammad Farid, 1992; Historical Dictionary of Egypt, 1994, 3rd ed., 2003; Biographical Dictionary of Modern Egypt, 2000; (ed. with A.J. Johnson and B.A. Salmoni) Re-Envisioning Egypt 1919-1952, 2005; Brief History of Egypt, 2008. Contributor to periodicals. **Address:** Department of History, Pennsylvania State University, 108 Weaver Bldg., 201 Old Main, University Park, PA 16802-5938, U.S.A. **Online address:** axg2@psu.edu

GOLDSCHMIDT, Tijs. Dutch (born Netherlands), b. 1953. **Genres:** Botany, Sciences. **Career:** University of Leiden, research assistant, through 1993. Writer. **Publications:** Darwins hofvijver, 1994; Oversprongen: Beschouwingen Overcultuur en Natuur, 2000; Kloten van de Engel: Beschouwingen over de Natuurlijkheid van Cultuur, 2007; (with D. Hillenius) Ademgaten, 2009. Contributor to periodicals. **Address:** The MIT Press, 55 Hayward St., Cambridge, MA 02142-1493, U.S.A.

GOLDSCHNEIDER, Gary. Dutch/American (born United States), b. 1939. **Genres:** History, Astronomy, Sciences. **Career:** Drexel University, lecturer in English and humanities, 1964-66; Philadelphia City College, assistant professor in English and Music, 1967-70; Nelson School of Music, piano faculty, 1980-81; Muziekschool Amsterdam, instructor, 1985-88; Avant Garde, astrologer, 1989-; Mirabella Magazine, astrologer, 1998-2000; Settlement Music School, piano faculty; KVMR, radio broadcaster. Writer. **Publications:** The Secret Language of Birthdays, 1994; The Secret Language of Relationships, 1997; The Secret Language of Destiny, 1999; The Astrology of Time, 2002; Charting the Times of your Life, 2004; Secret Language of Luck, 2004; Personology, 2005; Gary Goldschneider's Everyday Astrology, 2009. **Address:** Sunshower Productions, Hobbemakade 92 hs, Amsterdam, 1071 XR, Netherlands. **Online address:** gary@goldschneider.com

GOLDSMITH, Andrea. Australian (born Australia), b. 1950. **Genres:** Novels, Young Adult Fiction. **Career:** Speech pathologist, through 1987; Deakin University, creative writing teacher, 1987-, lecturer, 1995-98; La Trobe University, writer-in-residence. teacher, 1987-, lecturer, 1995-98; La Trobe University, writer-in-residence. **Publications:** NOVELS: Gracious Living, 1989; Modern Interiors, 1991; Facing the Music, 1994; Under the Knife, 1998; The Prosperous Thief, 2002; Reunion, 2009. Contributor of essays to books and periodicals. **Address:** c/o Barbara Mobbs, PO Box 126, Edgecliff, NW 2027, Australia.

GOLDSMITH, Barbara. American (born United States), b. 1931. **Genres:** Novels, History, Social Commentary, Biography, Essays. **Career:** Wellesley College, Center for Research on Women, overseer; Woman's Home Companion, entertainment editor, 1954-57; Herald Tribune, art writer for New York section, 1966-68; Kennedy Center, editorial advisor; Center for Research and Treatment of Dyslectic Children, founder; New York Magazine, founding editor, 1968-73; Harpers Bazaar, senior editor, 1970-74; Author's League, guild, 1983-; New York State Council on the Arts, director, 1992; New York Public Library, trustee; Hearst Corp., consultant. **Publications:** The Straw Man (novel), 1975; Little Gloria, Happy at Last, 1980; Johnson v. Johnson, 1987; Other Powers: The Age of Suffrage, Spiritualism, and the Scandalous Victoria Woodhull, 1998; Obsessive Genius: The Inner World of Marie Curie, 2005. Contributor of articles and essays to periodicals. **Address:** c/o Lynn Nesbit, Janklow & Nesbit Associates, 445 Park Ave., Fl. 13, New York, NY 10022, U.S.A. **Online address:** bgasst@aol.com

GOLDSMITH, Jeff Charles. American (born United States), b. 1948?. **Genres:** Medicine/Health. **Career:** State of Illinois, Office of the Governor, fiscal and policy analyst, special assistant, 1973-75; University of Chicago Medical Center, director of planning and government affairs and special assistant, 1975-82; University of Chicago Graduate School of Business, lecturer, 1979-90; Ernst and Young, national advisor for healthcare, 1982-94; Health Futures Inc., founder and president, 1982-; University of Virginia, associate professor. Writer. **Publications:** Can Hospitals Survive? The New Competitive Health Care Market, 1981; Digital Medicine: Implications for Healthcare Leaders, 2003; The Long Baby Boom: An Optimistic Vision for a Graying Generation, 2008; (with B.J. Hillman) The Sorcerer's Apprentice: How Medical Imaging Is Changing Health Care, 2011. Contributor to magazines and periodicals. **Address:** Charlottesville, VA , U.S.A. **Online address:** hfutures@healthfutures.net

GOLDSMITH, Lynn. American (born United States), b. 1948. **Genres:** Music, Photography. **Career:** Elektra Records, staff; LGI Photo Agency, founder, 1976. Photographer and writer. **Publications:** The Police, 1983; Springsteen, 1984, vol. I: Access All Areas, 2000; New Kids on the Block, 1990; Circus Dreams, 1991; Marky Mark, 1992; Photo Diary, 1995; Flower, 2000; (with M.R. Ciardi and I. Kantrov) Guiding Curriculum Decisions for Middle-Grades Language Arts, 2001; Rock and Roll, 2007; The Police: 1978-1983, 2007. Contributor to periodicals. **Address:** 40 Sunset Dr., Ste. 10A, Basalt, CO 81621-8362, U.S.A. **Online address:** lynn@lynngoldsmith.com

GOLDSTEIN, Brandt. American (born United States) **Genres:** Law, Young Adult Non-fiction. **Career:** Yale Law School, research associate, 1999-2001; Writ (online journal), co-founder; New York Law School, visiting associate professor of law. Writer and lawyer. **Publications:** (With D. Lithwick) Me v. Everybody: Absurd Contracts for an Absurd World, 2003; Storming the Court: How a Band of Yale Law Students Sued the President-and Won, 2005; (with R. Citron and M.B. Land) A Documentary Companion to Storming the Court, 2009. Contributor to periodicals. **Address:** c/o Henry Dunow, Dunow, Carlson & Lerner Literary Agency Inc., 27 W 20th St., Ste. 1107, New York, NY 10011, U.S.A. **Online address:** brandt@brandtgoldstein.com

GOLDSTEIN, Carl. American (born United States), b. 1938. **Genres:** Art/ Art History. **Career:** Wheaton College, visiting instructor in art history and acting director of art gallery, 1966; Brown University, assistant professor of art history, 1966-71; University of North Carolina, associate professor, 1971-80, professor of art history, 1980-, coordinator of art history. Writer. **Publications:** Visual Fact Over Verbal Fiction: A Study of the Carracci and the Criticism, Theory, and Practice of Art in Renaissance and Baroque Italy, 1988; (contrib.) FS-Beer, 1989; Teaching Art: Academies and Schools from Vasari to Albers (monograph), 1996; Print Culture in Early Modern France: Abraham Bosse and the Purposes of Print, 2011. Contributor to periodicals. **Address:** Department of Art, University of North Carolina, 138 Gatewood Studio Arts Bldg., PO Box 26170, Greensboro, NC 27402-6170, U.S.A. **Online address:** c_goldst@uncg.edu

GOLDSTEIN, David B. American (born United States), b. 1964. **Genres:** History. **Career:** University College London, Wolfson professor of genetics, 1999-2005, Institute of Neurology, honorary professor, 2007-; Duke University, professor of molecular genetics, microbiology and biology, Richard and Pat Johnson distinguished university professor, Center for Human Genome Variation, director. Writer. **Publications:** Jacob's Legacy: A Genetic View of Jewish History, 2008. Contributor of articles to journals. **Address:** Center for Human Genome Variation, Rm. 330, LSRC B Wing, 450 Research Dr., PO Box 91009, Durham, NC 27708, U.S.A. **Online address:** d.goldstein@duke.edu

GOLDSTEIN, Harvey. British (born England), b. 1939. **Genres:** Education, Mathematics/Statistics. **Career:** University of London, University College, Department of Statistics, research assistant, 1962-64, Institute of Child Health, lecturer in statistics, 1964-71, visiting professor, 2005-, Institute of Education, professor of statistics, 1977-2005; National Children's Bureau, head of the statistics section, 1971-77; Journal of Royal Statistical Society, joint editor, 1987-91; University of Toronto, Ontario Institute for Studies in Education, adjunct professor, 1987-90; Journal of Educational and Behavioural Statistics, associate editor, 1988-; World Health Organisation, Centre on Growth and Development, joint director, 1989-; University of East Anglia, visiting professor, 1992-, Centre for Statistics, associate director, 1998-; Assessment in Education, executive editor, 1993-; William Ellis School, founding governor, 1993-96; Journal of Multivariate Analysis, editor, 1996-98; University of Texas, School of Public Health, adjunct professor, 1998-; University of Bristol, visiting professor, 2000-05, professor of social statistics, 2005-; Royal Statistical Society, vice president, 2002-03; London School of Hygiene and Tropical Medicine, visiting professor, 2004-. **Publications:** (Coauthor) From Birth to Seven, 1972; The Design and Analysis of Longitudinal Studies, 1979; (with C. Gipps) Monitoring Children, 1983; (comp. with P. Levy) Tests in Education, 1984; Multilevel Models in Educational and Social Research, 1987; (with C. Gipps and H. Gross) Warnock's 18 Per Cent: Children with Special Needs in Primary Schools, 1987; Interpreting International Comparisons of Student Achievement, 1995; Multilevel Statistical Models, 1995, 4th ed., 2010. EDITOR: (with L. Moss) The Recall Method in Social

Surveys, 1979; (with T. Lewis) Assessment, 1996; (with A.H. Leyland) Multilevel Modelling of Health Statistics, 2001. **Address:** Graduate School of Education, University of Bristol, 2 Priory Rd., Bristol, BS8 1TX, England. **Online address:** h.goldstein@bristol.ac.uk

GOLDSTEIN, Imre. Israeli/American/Hungarian (born Hungary), b. 1938. **Genres:** Poetry, Translations, Theatre. **Career:** Hunter College, adjunct lecturer, 1972-74; Tel Aviv University, Department of Theatre Arts, professor of theatre, 1974-2003, professor emeritus, 2003-, head of acting/directing program; University of North Carolina, visiting associate professor, 1990-91; U.S. Department of State, escort and seminar interpreter (Hungarian and Hebrew), 1991-. Writer and translator. **Publications:** Kefitsah Meshuleshet: Shirim, 1984; Triple Jump (poems), 1984; Dream of the Last Moment (poems), 1998; November Spring (novel), 2000; Elmenöben: (versek), 2004. TRANSLATOR: U. Oren, Loving Strangers, 1975; F. Karinthy, Three Short Plays, 1979; A. Artzi, Godly Forces Revealed, 1981; G.B. Simhon, A Moroccan King (play), 1982; Y. Biro, Profane Mythology: The Savage Mind of the Cinema, 1982; D. Horowitz, Uncle Arthur (play), 1982; D. Horowitz, Yossele Golem (play), 1982; O. Strahl, Encounters in the Forest (play), 1984; T. Dery, The Giant Baby (play), 1986; The Dybbuk (play), 1991; G. Konrad, A Feast in the Garden, 1992; Oedipus Tyrannos (play), 1992; M. Lerner, Kastner (play), 1993; Ten Hungarian Plays, 1994; P. Salamon, The House of Sorel, 1994; (with I. Sanders) P. Nadas, A Book of Memories, 1997; P. Nadas, The End of a Family Story, 1998; P. Nadas, Burial (play), 1998; P. Nadas, A Lovely Tale of Photography, 1999; P. Nadas, Love: Novel, 2000; A. Palyi, Out of Oneself, 2003; P. Nadas, Fire and Knowledge, 2007; A. Bartis, Tranquility, 2008; P. Nadas, Parallel Stories, 2011. Contributor to periodicals. **Address:** 2 HaRav Uziel St., Tel Aviv, 62333, Israel. **Online address:** dybbuk@post.tau.ac.il

GOLDSTEIN, Joshua S. American (born United States), b. 1952. **Genres:** International Relations/Current Affairs, Politics/Government. **Career:** University of Southern California, School of International Relations, assistant professor, 1986-89, associate professor, 1989-93; Harvard University, associate, 1991-93; Yale University, fellow, 1991-93, visiting professor emeritus, 2008; American University, associate professor, 1993-95, professor of international relations, 1995-2003, professor emeritus, 2003-; Brown University, adjunct professor, 2002-07; University of Maryland, non-resident Sadat senior fellow, 2006-. Writer. **Publications:** Long Cycles: Prosperity and War in the Modern Age, 1988; (with J.R. Freeman) Three-Way Street: Strategic Reciprocity in World Politics, 1990; International Relations (textbook), 1994, (with J.C. Pevehouse) 10th ed., 2011; War and Gender: How Gender Shapes the War System and Vice Versa, 2001; Real Price of War: How You Pay for the War on Terror, 2004; (J.C. Pevehouse) Readings in International Relations, 2008; Principles of International Relations, 2008; Winning the War on War: The Decline of Armed Conflict Worldwide, 2011. Contributor to books and periodicals. **Address:** PO Box 3068, Amherst, MA 01004-3068, U.S.A. **Online address:** jg@joshuagoldstein.com

GOLDSTEIN, Larry Joel. American (born United States), b. 1944. **Genres:** Information Science/Computers, Mathematics/Statistics, Technology, Education, Reference. **Career:** Auerbach Corp., technical staff, 1960-66, consultant, 1967-69; Princeton University, teaching assistant, 1967; Yale University, Josiah Willard Gibbs instructor of mathematics, 1967-69; Analytics Inc., consultant, 1969-72; University of Maryland, associate professor of mathematics, 1969-72, professor of mathematics, 1972-84, adjunct professor of mathematics, 1984-89; Science Service Inc., Westinghouse Science Talent Search, judge, 1969-88; Robert J. Brady Co., founder and adviser for Microcomputer Series, 1980-84; Goldstein Educational Technologies, president, 1980-; Goldstein Software Inc., president, 1985-; United States Naval Academy, secretary of the navy distinguished professor, 1989-90; Montgomery College, adjunct professor of mathematics, 1992-93; Drexel University, visiting professor of mathematics, 1993-94; Villanova University, adjunct professor of mathematics and computer science, 1995-99; The Hockaday School, consultant, 1997-99; Advan Source, consultant, 1999-2000; Future Graph Inc., editorial director, 1999-2000; Diginexus Corp., principal project manager, director and consultant, 2000-01; Algorhythms L.L.C., co-founder and principal, 2004-; Web TCD, co-founder and chief technology officer, 2008-10; Advanced Patient Analytics, co-founder and chief technology officer, 2010-; CTEC Inc., consultant. Writer. **Publications:** Lectures on Analytic Number Theory (monograph), 1968; Analytic Number Theory (monograph), 1971; Abstract Algebra: A First Course, 1973; (with W. Adams) An Introduction to Number Theory, 1976; The Theory of Numbers (monograph), 1976; (with D.C. Lay and D.I. Schneider) Calculus and Its Applications, 1977, (with D.C.

Lay, N.H. Asmar and D.I. Schneider) 12th ed., 2010; (with D. Schneider) Introduction to Mathematics, 1976; (with D.I. Schneider) Finite Mathematics and Its Applications, 1980, (with D.I. Schneider and M.J. Siegel) 10th ed., 2010; (with D.C. Lay and D.I. Schneider) Modern Mathematics and Its Applications, 1980; TRS-80 Model III: Programming and Applications, 1982; IBM Personal Computer: Programming and Applications, 1982; BASIC for the Apple II, 1982; (with S. Campbell and S. Zimmerman) The Osborne Computer: Programming and Applications, 1982; (with G. Streitmatter) PET/CBM: Programming and Applications, 1983; (with S. Manetta) The Franklin ACE: Programming and Applications, 1983; (with L. Graff) Apple Soft BASIC for the Apple II and II/e, 1983; IBM PC: An Introduction to the Operating System (with software), 1983, 3rd ed. as IBM PC: An Introduction to the Operating System, BASIC Language and Applications, 1986; Advanced BASIC and Beyond (with software), 1983; IBM PCjr Buyer's Guide, 1983; The COMPAQ Computer: User's Guide, 1983; The Graphics Generator: A Business Graphics Package for the IBM PC, 1983; Mathematics for Management: Social and Biological Sciences, 2nd ed., 1984; (with D.C. Lay and D.I. Schneider) Brief Calculus & Its Applications, 3rd ed., 1984, (with D.C. Lay, N.H. Asmar and D.I. Schneider) 12th ed., 2010; IBM PCjr: An Introduction to the Operating System, BASIC Language and Applications (with software), 1984; (with F. Mosher) An Introduction to the Commodore 64, 1984; (with J. Rensin) Basically Kaypro, 1984; TRS-80 Model III/4: An Introduction to the Operating System, BASIC Language, and Applications, 1984; (with J. Rensin) Hewlett-Packard 150: User's Guide, 1984; An Introduction to ADAM Smart BASIC, 1984; (with R. Ellis and M. Ellis) The Atari 600/800/1200, 1984; (with D.I. Schneider) Macintosh: An Introduction to Microsoft BASIC, 1984, (with D.I. Schneider and G. Helzer) 2nd ed. as Microsoft BASIC for the Macintosh, 1986; (with L. Graff) Applesoft BASIC on the Apple IIc, 1984; Computers and Their Applications, 1986; TRUE BASIC: An Introduction to Structured Programming, 1986; Microcomputer Applications: A Hands-On Approach to Computer Literacy, 1987; PASCAL and Its Applications: An Introduction to Programming, 1988; Turbo Pascal and Its Applications, 1988; Hands-On Quick BASIC, 1988; Hands-On Turbo C, 1989; Hands-On Turbo BASIC, 1989; Hands-On Turbo Pascal, 1991; Algebra and Trigonometry and Their Applications, 1993, 2nd ed., 1995; College Algebra and Its Applications, 1993, 2nd ed., 1995; Trigonometry and Its Applications, 1993; The Official Student Guide to QBASIC, 1993; IBM PC and Compatibles, 5th ed., 1993; College Algebra for Students of Business and the Social Sciences, 1993; Business Statistics and Its Applications, 1993; Precalculus and Its Applications, 1994; College Algebra for the Management, Social, Biological Sciences, 1995. Contributor to periodicals. **Address:** Advanced Patient Analytics, 4 Bittersweet Dr., Doylestown, PA 18901-2767, U.S.A. **Online address:** larrygoldstein@advancedpatientanalytics.com

GOLDSTEIN, Lyle J. American (born United States), b. 1972. **Genres:** Intellectual History, International Relations/Current Affairs, Military/Defense/Arms Control. **Career:** U.S. Naval War College, Strategic Research Department, associate professor of strategic studies, China Maritime Studies Institute, director; Eurasia Studies Group, vice chair. Writer. **Publications:** Preventive Attack and Weapons of Mass Destruction: A Comparative Historical Analysis, 2006; (ed. with A.S. Erickson, A.R. Wilson and W.S. Murray) China's Future Nuclear Submarine Force, 2007; (ed. with A.S. Erickson and N. Li) China, the United States, and 21st-century Sea Power, 2008; (ed. with A.S. Erickson and C. Lord) China Goes to Sea, 2009; (with A.S. Erickson and W.S. Murray) Chinese Mine Warfare, 2009; Five Dragons Stirring Up the Sea, 2010; (ed. with A.S. Erickson) Chinese Aerospace Power: Evolving Maritime Roles, 2011. Contributor to periodicals. **Address:** U.S. Naval War College, 686 Cushing Rd., Newport, RI 02841-1207, U.S.A. **Online address:** lyle.goldstein@usnwc.edu

GOLDSTEIN, Michael S. American (born United States), b. 1944. **Genres:** Sports/Fitness, Sociology. **Career:** Brown University, lecturer, 1970-71; University of California, Department of Sociology, assistant professor, 1971-78, associate professor, 1978-88, professor of sociology, 1988-, Division of Behavioral Sciences and Health Education, head, 1978-80, School of Public Health, Department of Community Health Sciences, vice chair, 1988-89, 1989-91, professor, Center for Health Policy Research, senior research scientist and faculty associate, interim vice provost for graduate education, Graduate Division, dean, CHIS-CAM Program, co-principal investigator and director; American Civil Liberties Union of Southern California, board director, 1987-89; Society for the Study of Social Problems, Division of Health, Health Policy and Health Services, co-chair, 1991-93. Writer. **Publications:** The Health Movement: Promoting Fitness in America, 1992; Alternative Health

Care: Medicine, Miracle, or Mirage?, 1999. Contributor to periodicals. **Address:** Department of Sociology, University of California, 264 Haines Hall, 375 Portola Plz., PO Box 951551, Los Angeles, CA 90095-1551, U.S.A. **Online address:** msgoldst@ucla.edu

GOLDSTEIN, Naama. American (born United States), b. 1969?. **Genres:** Novellas/Short Stories, Literary Criticism And History. **Career:** Librarian and writer. **Publications:** The Place Will Comfort You: Stories, 2004; Busybodies: AB Yehoshua's Existential Investigators, forthcoming; Family Plots, forthcoming. **Address:** c/o Author Mail, Maria Massie Inkwell Management, 521 5th Ave., Ste. 2600, New York, NY 10175-2600, U.S.A. **Online address:** contact@naamagoldstein.com

GOLDSTEIN, Nancy. American (born United States), b. 1942. **Genres:** History, Literary Criticism And History. **Career:** Writer. **Publications:** Jackie Ormes: The First African American Woman Cartoonist, 2008. **Online address:** nancy@jackieormes.com

GOLDSTEIN, Niles Elliot. American (born United States), b. 1966. **Genres:** Psychology. **Career:** Temple Israel, assistant rabbi; The New Shul, founding rabbi and spiritual leader, 1999-2009, rabbi emeritus; New York University, faculty; Hebrew Union College, faculty; National Jewish Center for Learning and Leadership, faculty, senior fellow; The Steinhardt Foundation, program officer. Writer. **Publications:** Forests of the Night: The Fear of God in Early Hasidic Thought, 1996; (with S.S. Mason) Judaism and Spiritual Ethics, 1996; (ed.) Spiritual Manifestos: Visions for Renewed Religious Life in America from Young Spiritual Leaders of Many Faiths, 1999; (ed. and intro. with P.S. Knobel) Duties of the Soul: The Role of Commandments in Liberal Judaism, 1999; God at the Edge: Searching for the Divine in Uncomfortable and Unexpected Places, 2000; Lost Souls: Finding Hope in the Heart of Darkness, 2002; Gonzo Judaism: A Bold Path for an Ancient Faith, 2006; Craving the Divine: A Spiritual Guide for Today's Perplexed, 2007; Challenge of the Soul: A Guide for the Spiritual Warrior, 2009. **Address:** The New Shul, 505 8th Ave., Ste. 1212, New York, NY 10018, U.S.A.

GOLDSTEIN, Rebecca. American (born United States), b. 1950. **Genres:** Novels, Novellas/Short Stories, Young Adult Fiction, Young Adult Nonfiction, Essays. **Career:** Barnard College, assistant professor of philosophy, 1976-86; Rutgers University, visiting professor of philosophy, 1988-90; Columbia University, professor of creative writing, 1993-96; Trinity College, visiting professor of philosophy, 2001-06; American Academy of Arts and Sciences, fellow, 2005; Harvard University, Radcliffe Institute for Advanced Study, fellow, 2006-07, Guggenheim fellow, Department of Psychology, research associate, 2007-. Writer. **Publications:** The Mind-Body Problem, 1983; The Late-Summer Passion of a Woman of Mind, 1989; The Dark Sister, 1991; Strange Attractors, 1993; Mazel, 1995; Properties of Light: A Novel of Love, Betrayal and Quantum Physics, 2000; Incompleteness: The Proof and Paradox of Kurt Gödel, 2005; Betraying Spinoza: The Renegade Jew Who Gave us Modernity, 2006; 36 Arguments for the Existence of God: A Work of Fiction, 2010. Works appear in anthology. Contributor to books. **Address:** Department of Psychology, Harvard University, William James Hall, 33 Kirkland St., Cambridge, MA 02138, U.S.A. **Online address:** rebegolds@gmail.com

GOLDSTEIN, Robert Justin. American (born United States), b. 1947. **Genres:** Civil Liberties/Human Rights, History, Politics/Government, Law, Social Sciences. **Career:** University of Illinois-Urbana Champaign, Office of Instructional Research and Chancellor's Commission on Reform of Undergraduate Education and Living, research assistant, administrative assistant, 1972-73; San Diego State University, lecturer in political science, 1974-76; Oakland University, assistant professor, 1976-81, associate professor, 1981-87, professor of political science, 1987-, now professor emeritus. Writer. **Publications:** Political Repression in Modern America: From 1870 to the Present, 1978, as Political Repression in Modern America from 1870 to 1976, 2001; Political Repression in Nineteenth Century Europe, 1983; Political Censorship of the Arts and the Press in Nineteenth-Century Europe, 1989; Censorship of Political Caricature in Nineteenth-Century France, 1989; Saving Old Glory: The History of the American Flag Desecration Controversy, 1994, rev. ed., 1996; Burning the Flag: The Great 1989-90 American Flag Desecration Controversy, 1996; (ed.) Desecrating the American Flag: Key Documents from the Controversy from the Civil War to 1995, 1996; (ed.) The War for the Public Mind: Political Censorship in Nineteenth Century Europe, 2000; Flag Burning and Free Speech: The Case of Texas v. Johnson, 2000; (ed.) Political

Censorship: The New York Times 20th Century in Review, 2001; American Blacklist: The Attorney General's List of Subversive Organizations, 2008; (ed.) Frightful Stage: Political Censorship of the Theater in Nineteenth-century Europe, 2009. CONTRIBUTOR: Political Youth, Traditional Schools, 1972; Government and Politics in America: Perspectives from Home and Abroad, 1980; Comparative Social Research, vol. IV, 1981; Human Rights and Statistics: Getting the Record Straight, 1992; Writing and Censorship, 1992. Contributor to periodicals. **Address:** Department of Political Science, Oakland University, 418 Varner Hall, Rochester, MI 48309-4488, U.S.A. **Online address:** goldstei@oakland.edu

GOLDSTEIN, Sidney. American (born United States), b. 1927. **Genres:** Demography, Sociology, Urban Studies, Theology/Religion, History. **Career:** University of Pennsylvania, instructor in sociology, 1953-55, Wharton School of Finance and Commerce, research associate, 1955-58; Brown University, assistant professor, 1955-57, associate professor, 1957-60, professor of sociology, 1960-77, Population Studies and Training Center, founder, director, 1960-89, chair of sociology department, 1963-70, George Hazard Crooker university professor, 1977-93, professor emeritus, 1993-; National Institutes of Health, consultant, 1960-61; Institute for Neurological Diseases and Blindness, consultant, 1960-71; Ford Foundation, consultant, 1971-81; Rockefeller Foundation, consultant, 1971-81; United Nations Economic and Social Commission for Asia and the Pacific, consultant, 1971-82; Urban Institute, consultant, 1974-82; Rand Corp., consultant, 1974-82; Population Association of America, president, 1976-77. Writer. **Publications:** Patterns of Mobility, 1910-1950, 1958; (with K.B. Mayer) Migration and Economic Development in Rhode Island, 1958; (with K.B. Mayer) Population Projections, Rhode Island Cities and Towns, 1970 and 1980, 1960; (with B.G. Zimmer) Residential Displacement and Resettlement of the Aged, 1960; The Norristown Study, 1961; Metropolitanization and Population Change in Rhode Island, 1961; (with K.B. Mayer) The First Two Years: Problems of Small Business Growth and Survival, 1961; (with K.B. Mayer) People of Rhode Island, 1960, 1963; (with K.B. Mayer) Residential Mobility, Migration and Commuting in Rhode Island, 1963; (with C. Goldscheider) Jewish-Americans: Three Generations in a Jewish Community, 1968; A Population Survey of the Greater Springfield Jewish Community, 1968; Urbanization in Thailand, 1970; Interrelations between Migration and Fertility in Population Redistribution in Thailand, 1971; The Demography of Bangkok, 1972; (with A. Goldstein and P. Tirasawat) The Influence of Labor Force Participation and Education on Fertility in Thailand, 1972; (with A. Goldstein and S. Piampiti) The Effect of Broken Marriage on Fertility Levels in Thailand, 1973; (with A. Goldstein and V. Prachuabmoh) Urban-Rural Migration Differentials in Thailand, 1974; (with P. Pitaktepsombati) Migration and Urban Growth in Thailand: An Exploration of Interrelations among Origin, Recency, and Frequency of Moves, 1974; (with A. Speare, Jr. and W.H. Frey) Residential Mobility, Migration and Metropolitan Change, 1975; (with P. Tirasawat) Fertility of Migrants to Urban Places in Thailand, 1977; (with A. Goldstein and P. Pitaktepsombati) Migration to Urban Places in Thailand: Interrelations among Origin, Recency, Frequency, and Motivations, 1977; Circulation in the Context of Total Mobility in Southeast Asia, 1978; (with A. Goldstein) A Test of the Potential Use of Multiplicity in Research on Population Movement, 1979; Migration and Rural Development: Research Directions on Interrelations, 1979; (with A. Goldstein) Differentials in Repeat and Return Migration in Thailand, 1965-1970, 1980; (with A. Goldstein) Surveys of Migration in Developing Countries, 1981; (with A. Goldstein and B. Limanonda) Migration and Fertility-Related Attitudes and Behavior in Urban Thailand, 1981; (with A. Goldstein) Migration and Fertility in Peninsular Malaysia, 1983; (with A. Goldstein) Population Mobility in the People's Republic of China, 1985; (with C. Goldscheider) Jewish Americans: Three Generations in a Jewish Community, 1985; Urbanization in China, 1985; (with A. Goldstein) Migration in Thailand: A 25-Year Review, 1986; (with C. Goldscheider) The Jewish Community of Rhode Island, 1987; Demographics of American Jewry, 1987; 1990 National Jewish Population Study: Why and How, 1988; (with A. Goldstein) Permanent and Temporary Migration Differentials in China, 1990; Urbanization in China 1982-87: The Role of Migration and Reclassification, 1990; The Impact of Temporary Migration on Urban Places, 1993; (with A. Goldstein) Lithuanian Jewry, 1993: (with R. Neupert) Urbanization and Population Redistribution in Mongolia, 1994; (with A. Goldstein) Jews on the Move, 1995; A Demographic and Sociocultural Profile, 1997; (with A. Goldstein) Conservative Jewry in the United States, 1998; (with A. Goldstein and Y. Djamba) Permanent and Temporary Migration during Periods of Economic Change, 1999; (with A. Goldstein and Z. Liang) Migration, Gender, and Labor Force in Hubei Province, China, 1985-1990, 2000. EDITOR WITH D.F. SLY: Basic Data Needed for the Study of Urbanization, 1975; Measurement of Urbanization and the Projection of Urban Population, 1975; Patterns of Urbanization: Comparative Country Studies, 1977. Contributor of articles to periodicals and journals. **Address:** Department of Sociology, Brown University, Maxcy Hall, 112 George St., PO Box 1916, Providence, RI 02912-1916, U.S.A. **Online address:** sidney_goldstein@brown.edu

GOLDSTEIN-JACKSON, Kevin. British (born England), b. 1946. **Genres:** Business/Trade/Industry, Children's Non-fiction, Money/Finance, Recreation, Humor/Satire, Economics. **Career:** Southern Television, program organizer, 1970-73; freelance writer and television producer, 1973-75; Anglia Television, Drama Department, assistant, 1977-81; TSW-TV, founder, joint managing director and program controller, 1981-; Television South West Holdings P.L.C., director of programmes and chief executive, 1981-85; Television South West Music Ltd., director; Independent Television Publications Ltd., director. **Publications:** The Right Joke for the Right Occasion, 1973; (comp.) The Leslie Frewin Book of Ridiculous Facts, 1974; Encyclopaedia of Ridiculous Facts, 1975; Joke After Joke After Joke, 1977; Things to Make with Everyday Objects, 1978; (with N. Rudnick and R. Hyman) Experiments with Everyday Objects: Science Activities for Children, Parents, and Teachers, 1978; Magic with Everyday Objects, 1979; Activities with Everyday Objects, 1980; (comp.) The Dictionary of Essential Quotations, 1983; Right Joke for the Right Occasion, 1985; Jokes for Telling, 1986; Share Millions, 1989; The Public Speaker's Joke Book, 1991; The Astute Private Investor, 1994; Quick Quips and Longer Jokes, 1999. **Address:** Television South West Ltd., Derry's Cross, Branksome Pk., Plymouth, DN BH13 7DH, England.

GOLDSTONE, Patricia. American (born United States), b. 1951. **Genres:** Adult Non-fiction, Travel/Exploration, Politics/Government. **Career:** Los Angeles Times, reporter; Washington Post, writer; Maclean's, writer; Economist Intelligence Unit, writer. **Publications:** Making the World Safe for Tourism, 2001; Aaronsohn's Maps: The Untold Story of the Man Who Might Have Created Peace in the Middle East, 2007. **Address:** Yale University Press, 302 Temple St., PO Box 209040, New Haven, CT 06511-8909, U.S.A. **Online address:** patricia@patriciagoldstone.com

GOLDSWORTHY, Peter. Australian (born Australia), b. 1951. **Genres:** Novels, Novellas/Short Stories, Plays/Screenplays, Poetry. **Career:** Writer. **Publications:** POETRY: Readings from Ecclesiastes, 1982; This Goes with This, 1988; This Goes with That, 1991; If, Then, 1996. STORIES: Archipelagoes, 1982; Zooing, 1986; Bleak Rooms, 1988; Little Deaths (and novella), 1993; Navel Gazing, 1998; Collected Stories, 2004. NOVELS: Maestro, 1989; Honk If You Are Jesus, 1992; (co-author) The Stranger Inside: An Erotic Adventure, 1994; Wish, 1995; Keep It Simple Stupid, 1996; Jesus Wants me for a Sunbeam, 1999; Three Dog Night, 2003. OTHER: (with B. Matthews) Magpie, 1992; After the Ball, 1992; New Selected Poems, 2001; The List of all Answers: Collected Stories, 2004; (ed.) True Blue?: On Being Australian, 2008; Everything I knew, 2009; Gravel, 2010. **Address:** c/o Fiona Inglis, Curtis Brown Private Ltd., PO Box 19, Paddington, NW NSW 2021, Australia.

GOLDWASSER, Thomas. American (born United States), b. 1939. **Genres:** Business/Trade/Industry, Politics/Government, Ghost Writer, Young Adult Fiction, Economics. **Career:** Freelance writer and consultant, 1970-; Montgomery College, adjunct professor of political science, 1989-; Johns Hopkins University, instructor of American government; George Washington University, Graduate School of Political Management, adjunct professor, 2004-. **Publications:** Family Pride: Profiles of Five of America's Best-Run Family Businesses, 1986. Contributor of articals to periodicals. **Address:** Department of Social Science, Montgomery College, CM202, Humanities 273, 7600 Takoma Ave., Takoma Park, MD 20912, U.S.A. **Online address:** tombenton2@earthlink.net

GOLINSKI, Jan. American/British (born England), b. 1957. **Genres:** History, Sciences. **Career:** University of Lancaster, Department of History, lecturer, 1983-86; Cambridge University, Churchill College, junior research fellow, 1986-90; British Society for the History of Science, honorary secretary, 1987-88; University of California, William Andrews Clark Memorial Library, visiting fellow, 1989; University of Wisconsin, Institute for Research in the Humanities, visiting fellow, 1989; Huntington Library, V.M. Keck Foundation fellow, 1990-94; University of New Hampshire, assistant professor of history and humanities, 1990-94, associate professor, 1994-2000, professor, 2000-, chair of the department of history, 2006-; Princeton University, visiting assistant professor, 1992. Writer. **Publications:** Science as Public Culture: Chemistry and Enlightenment in Britain, 1760-1820, 1992; Making Natural Knowledge: Constructivism and the History of Science, 1998; (co-ed.) The Sciences in Enlightened Europe, 1999; (contrib.) Discussing Chemistry and Steam: The Minutes of a Coffee House Philosophical Society, 1780-1787, 2002; Making Natural Knowledge: Constructivism and the History of Science, 2005; British Weather and the Climate of Enlightenment, 2007. Contributor of articles to books and periodicals. **Address:** Department of History, Horton Social Science Center, University of New Hampshire, 20 Academic Way, Durham, NH 03824-3586, U.S.A. **Online address:** jan.golinski@unh.edu

GOLLAHER, David L. American (born United States), b. 1949. **Genres:** Biography, Medicine/Health. **Career:** Young and Rubicam (advertising agency), account executive, 1981-82; Phillips Ramsey Advertising, vice president, 1982-85; Scripps Clinic and Research Foundation, senior executive, vice president, 1985-91; San Diego State University, professor of public health, 1991-93; Harvard University, Houghton Library, fellow, 1993; California Health Care Institute, president and chief executive officer, 1993-; Vision Robotics Corp., co-founder; The Journal of Life Sciences, co-publisher and editorial director; California Biotechnology Foundation, director; San Diego BioIndustry Council, board director; The National Endowment for the Humanities, fellow. Writer and historian. **Publications:** Voice for the Mad: The Life of Dorothea Dix (biography), 1995; Circumcision: A History of the World's Most Controversial Surgery, 2000; Das verletzte Geschlecht: Die Geschichte der Beschneidung, 2002. **Address:** California Health Care Institute, 1020 Prospect St., Ste. 310, La Jolla, CA 92037, U.S.A. **Online address:** gollaher@chi.org

GOLLIN, Rita K. American (born United States), b. 1928. **Genres:** Literary Criticism And History, Bibliography, Biography. **Career:** University of Rochester, lecturer, assistant professor of English, 1955-67; State University of New York, assistant professor, 1967-68, associate professor, 1968-75, professor of English, 1975-95, distinguished professor of English, 1995-, distinguished professor of English emerita, 2002-; Yale University, Institute on Reconstructing American Literature, fellow, 1982. Writer. **Publications:** Nathaniel Hawthorne and the Truth of Dreams, 1979; Portraits of Nathaniel Hawthorne: An Iconography, 1983; (with J.L. Idol, Jr.) Prophetic Pictures: Hawthorne's Knowledge and Uses of the Visual Arts, 1991; Annie Adams Fields: Woman of Letters, 2002. EDITOR: A Little Journey in the World, 1970; Northwood, 1972; Thoreau Inter Alia: Essays in Honor of Walter Harding, 1985; The Scarlet Letter: Complete Text With Introduction, Historical Contexts, Critical Essays, 2002. Works appear in anthologies. Contributor of articles to periodicals and encyclopedias. **Address:** Department of English, State University of New York, Welles Hall 226, Geneseo, NY 14454, U.S.A. **Online address:** gollin@aol.com

GOLOGORSKY, Beverly. American (born United States) **Genres:** Young Adult Fiction, History. **Career:** Writer and activist. **Publications:** The Things We Do to Make It Home, 1999. Contributor to periodicals. **Address:** c/o Author Mail, Random House, 1745 Broadway, New York, NY 10019, U.S.A.

GOLOMB, Jacob. Israeli/Canadian (born Canada), b. 1947. **Genres:** Philosophy, Psychology, Anthropology/Ethnology, Humanities, Intellectual History. **Career:** Carleton University, visiting lecturer, 1977; Hebrew University of Jerusalem, senior lecturer of philosophy, 1985-88, associate professor, 1996-2006, Center for Austrian Studies, director, 2001-04, professor of philosophy, 2006-, Hebrew University Magnes Press, philosophical editor; Wolfson College, visiting fellow, 1987; Pennsylvania State University, visiting professor of philosophy, 1997-98. **Publications:** Masot 'al Hinukh le-Tarbut, 1988; Nietzsche's Enticing Psychology of Power, 1989; Mavo le-Filosofyot ha-Kiyum, 1990; In Search of Authenticity: From Kierkegaard to Camus, 1995; Nietzshe and Jewish Culture, 1997; (co-ed.) Nietzshe and Depth Psychology, 1999; Nitsheh ba-Tarbut ha-'Ivrit, 2002; Nietzshe, Godfather of Fascism?: On the Uses and Abuses of a Philosophy, 2002; Nietzsche and Zion, 2004; Nletzsche ha-Ivri, 2009; Beauvoir and Sartre: The Riddle of Influence, 2009; Ecce Homo: Nletzsche's Letters, forthcoming. **Address:** Department of Philosophy, Hebrew University of Jerusalem, Rm. 5604, Mount Scopus, 91905, Israel. **Online address:** jacob.golomb@huji.ac.il

GOLOMSHTOK, Igor. See **GOLOMSTOCK, Igor (Naumovitch).**

GOLOMSTOCK, Igor (Naumovitch). (Igor Golomshtok). British/Russian (born Russia), b. 1929. **Genres:** Art/Art History. **Career:** Oxford University, lecturer, 1976-80; British Broadcasting Corp., scriptwriter, 1979-87; Stanford University, visiting researcher, 1986-87; Harvard University, visiting researcher, 1988-89. **Publications:** AS IGOR GOLOMSHTOK: (with A. Sinyarskii) Picasso, 1960; Iskusstvo drevneĭ Meksiki, 1962; Cezanne, 1975; (with A. Glezer) Soviet Art in Exile, 1977; (with A. Glezer) Unofficial Art from the Soviet Union, 1977; (with M. Rueschemeyer and J. Kennedy) Soviet emigré Artists: Life and Work in the USSR and the United States, 1985; Totalitarnoe iskusstvo, 1994; The Camp Drawings of Boris Sveshnikov, 2000; (contrib.) Lagernye risunki, 2000; Iskusstvo avangarda v portretakh ego predstaviteleĭ v Evrope i Amerike, 2004. OTHER: (as Fomin) Hieronymus Bosch, 1973. Contributor of articles to periodicals. **Address:** c/o Andrew Nurnberg, Andrew Nurnberg Associates Ltd., 20-23 Greville St., London, GL EC1N 8SS, England. **Online address:** igor@golomstock.snet.co.uk

GOLUBHOFF, Risa L. (Risa Lauren Golubhoff). American (born United States), b. 1971. **Genres:** Young Adult Non-fiction, Novellas/Short Stories, Civil Liberties/Human Rights, Social Sciences. **Career:** U.S. Court of Appeals, Second Circuit, law clerk for Guido Calabresi; U.S. Supreme Court, law clerk for Stephen G. Breyer; University of Virginia Law School, professor of history, professor of law, 2002-; University Law School, visiting professor, 2008; Columbia Law School, visiting professor, 2009. Writer. **Publications:** NONFICTION: The Lost Promise of Civil Rights, 2007; (ed. with M.E. Gilles) Civil Rights Stories, 2008. **Address:** University of Virginia School of Law, 389 Withers Brown Hall, 580 Massie Rd., Charlottesville, VA 22903-1783, U.S.A. **Online address:** goluboff@virginia.edu

GOLUBHOFF, Risa Lauren. See **GOLUBHOFF, Risa L.**

GOLUBITSKY, Martin. American (born United States), b. 1945. **Genres:** Mathematics/Statistics, Education, Sciences. **Career:** University of California, instructor in mathematics, 1970-71; Massachusetts Institute of Technology, instructor in mathematics, 1971-73; Queens College of City University of New York, instructor, 1973-74, assistant professor, 1974-76, associate professor of mathematics, 1977-79; Arizona State University, professor of mathematics, 1979-83; University of Houston, professor of mathematics, Cullen professor of mathematics, 1983-2008, Cullen distinguished professor of mathematics, 1989-2008, Institute for Theoretical and Engineering Science, director, 1988-2008; Ohio State University, distinguished professor of mathematics and physical sciences, 2008-, Mathematical Biosciences Institute, director, 2008-; SIAM Journal, founding editor-in-chief, president, 2005-06. Writer. **Publications:** (With M. Rothschild) On the Convergence of the Age Structure, 1973; (with V. Guillemin) Stable Mappings and Their Singularities, 1974; (with D.G. Schaeffer) Singularities and Groups in Bifurcation Theory I, 1985; Multiparameter Bifurcation Theory, 1986; (with I. Stewart and D.G. Schaeffer) Singularities and Groups in Bifurcation Theory II, 1988; (with M. Field) Symmetry in Chaos: A Search For Pattern In Mathematics, Art And Nature, 1992, 2nd ed., 2009; (with I. Stewart) Fearful Symmetry: Is God A Geometer?, 1992; (ed. with E. Allgower and K. Böhmer) Bifurcation and Symmetry: Cross Influence between Mathematics and Applications, 1992; (ed. with D. Luss and S.H. Strogatz) Pattern Formation In Continuous And Coupled Systems: A Survey Volume, 1999; (with M. Dellnitz) Linear Algebra and Differential Equations Using MATLAB, 1999; (with I. Stewart) The Symmetry Perspective: From Equilibrium To Chaos In Phase Space And Physical Space, 2003. **Address:** Mathematical Biosciences Institute, Ohio State University, 364 Jennings Hall, 1735 Neil Ave., Columbus, TX 43210, U.S.A. **Online address:** mg@mbi.osu.edu

GOMBRICH, Richard Francis. British (born England), b. 1937. **Genres:** Theology/Religion. **Career:** Oxford University, lecturer, 1965-76, Boden professor of Sanskrit, 1976-2004, now professor emeritus; Pali Text Society, president, 1994-2004; Clay Sanskrit Library, general editor emeritus; Oxford Centre for Buddhist Studies, founder and president. **Publications:** Precept and Practice: Traditional Buddhism in the Rural Highlands of Ceylon, 1971; (with M. Cone) The Perfect Generosity of Prince Vessantara, 1977; On Being Sanskritic, 1978; Buddhist Studies, 1984; Theravada Buddhism: A Social History from Ancient Benares to Modern Colombo, 1988, 2nd ed., 2006; (with G. Obeyesekere) Buddhism Transformed: Religious Change in Sri Lanka, 1988; Buddhist Precept and Practice: Traditional Buddhism in the Rural Highlands of Ceylon, 1991; How Buddhism Began: The Conditioned Genesis of the Early Teachings, 1996; Kindness and Compassion as Means to Nirvana, 1998; What the Buddha Thought, 2009. EDITOR: (with H. Bechert) The World of

Buddhism, 1984 in UK as The World of Buddhism: Buddhist Monks and Nuns in Society and Culture, 1991; (with J. Benson) M. Coulson, Sanskrit, 2nd ed., 1992. Contributor of articles and book to magazines. **Address:** Oxford Centre for Buddhist Studies, Wolfson College, Linton Rd., Oxford, OX2 6UD, England. **Online address:** richard.gombrich@balliol.ox.ac.uk

GOMEZ, Jewelle. American (born United States), b. 1948. **Genres:** Poetry, Essays, Novels, Plays/Screenplays, Novellas/Short Stories. **Career:** WGBH-TV, production assistant, 1968-71; New York State Council on the Arts, program associate, 1983-89, director of literature program, 1989-93; Gay and Lesbian Alliance Against Defamation, founding director, 1984; Hunter College, lecturer in women's studies and English, 1989-90; San Francisco State University, Poetry Center and American Poetry Archives, executive director; Poets & Writers Inc., National Center for Lesbian Rights, advisor; San Francisco Public Library Commission, president; teacher. Writer. **Publications:** The Lipstick Papers (poetry), 1980; Flamingoes and Bears (poetry), 1986; The Gilda Stories: A Novel, 1991; Forty-three Septembers (essays), 1993; Oral Tradition (poetry), 1995; Don't Explain (short stories); Bones and Ash (play), 1996; (ed. with E. Garber) Swords of the Rainbow, 1996; Don't Explain, 1997; Televised, forthcoming. Contributor to periodicals. **Address:** San Francisco Public Library, 100 Larkin St., San Francisco, CA 94102-4733, U.S.A. **Online address:** moi@jewellegomez.com

GÓMEZ ROSA, Alexis. American (born United States), b. 1950. **Genres:** Poetry. **Career:** Colegio Onesimo Jimenez, teacher, 1972-74; Young and Rubicam Advertising Agency, copywriter, 1974; Padre Billini High School, teacher, 1975-77; RETHO Advertising Agency, copywriter, 1975; Dominican Export Promotion Center, publicist, 1978-83; Noticias del Mundo, publicist, 1983-90; poetry instructor in the public schools, 1984-85; Northern Manhattan Coalition for Immigrants Rights, community liaison, 1987-88; New York University, Spanish instructor, 1988-, doctoral candidate in Hispanic literature. Journalist. **Publications:** Oficio de post-muerte: poemas 1970-1972, 1977; Cabeza de aquiler: contra la pluma la espuma: poemas 1980-86; Opio territorio: contra la pluma la espuma: poemas 1980-86, 1990; New York City en tránsito de pie quebrado, 1993; (intro.) Las lenguas de la máscara: antología poética, 2002; High Quality, Ltd, 2004; Lápida circa y otros epitafios de la torre abolida, 2004; Tregua de los mamíferos: escrito en llamas de abril 1965, 2005; Ferryboat de una noche invertebrada, 2006. Works appear in anthologies. **Address:** Department of Spanish, New York University, 19 University Pl., 4th Fl., New York, NY 10003, U.S.A.

GOMI, Tarō. Japanese (born Japan), b. 1945. **Genres:** Children's Fiction, Essays, Illustrations, Picture/Board Books, Children's Non-fiction, Translations. **Career:** Author and illustrator of children's books. **Publications:** SELF-ILLUSTRATED FOR CHILDREN: Michi, 1973; Himitsu no Gakki, 1975; Bokuwa Zouda, 1976; Kingyo ga Nigeta, 1977, trans. as Where's the Fish?, 1986; Tabeta no Dare, 1977; Kakushita no Dare, 1977; Minna Unchi, 1977, trans. as Everyone Poops, 1993; Buta ga Bu Bu, 1977; Ojisan no Tsue, 1977; Yubikun, 1977; Chiisana Kisha, 1978, rev. ed., 1982; Kujirada!, 1978; Kakurenbo Kakurenbo, 1978, trans. as Hide and Seek, 1989; Kotoba, 1978; U(yu)shi to G(ji)shi, 1978; Umiwa Hiroine, Ojiichan, 1979; Kotoba no AI-UEO, 1979; Sora Hadakanbo!, 1979; Hito ni Tsuite, 1979; Hayaku aitai na, 1979; Obasan no Gochisou, 1979; Rappa wo Narase, 1979, trans. as Toot!, 1986; Hayaku Aitaina, 1979, trans. as Coco Can't Wait, 1983; Minna ga Oshietekuremashita, 1979, trans. as My Friends, 1990; Kimi ha Shitteiru, 1979; Futari de Hanbun, 1979, trans. as Sharing, 1981; Aka no Hon, 1979; Kuro no Hon, 1979; Shiro no Hon, 1979; Omiseyasan, 1979; Tomodachi 15 nin, 1979; Ipponbashi Wataru, 1979; Saru-Rururu, 1979; Umi no Mukouwa, 1979; Ushiro ni Irunoha Daareda, 1980; Kanji no Ehon, 1980; Kurisumasu Niwa Okurimono, 1980; Norimono, 1980; Kimono, 1980; Koushi no Haru, 1980, trans. as Spring Is Here, 1989; Denwa de Ohanashi, 1980; Sakasu Sakasu, 1980; Itadakimasu Gochisousama, 1980; Kiiro no Hon, 1980; Midori no Hon, 1980; Chairo no Hon, 1980; Natsu, 1980; Takai Takai, 1980; Nagai Nagai, 1980; Midori no Boushi, 1980; Akachan, 1980; Okasan, 1980; Doubutsu Rando, 1980; Okusan To 9 Nin No Seirusuman, 1980; Kage, 1980, trans. as Shadows, 1981; Katakana Ehon AIUEO, 1980; Tenshisama ga Oritekuru, 1980; Fuyu, 1981; Aki, 1981; Haru, 1981; Nandaka Ureshikunattekita, 1981; Noharano Terebijyon, 1981; Toriaezu Ehon ni Tsuite (essay), 1981; Helikoputatachi, 1981; Hi, 1981; Mizu, 1981; Iro, 1981; Katachi, 1981; Baku-Kukuku, 1981; Emono wa Dokoda, 1981; Gatsu no Akachan, vol. I-XII, 1981; Akachan no enon, vol. I-XII, 1981; Mominoki Sono Mi Wo Kazarinasai, 1981; Ehon Kotoba Asobi, 1982; Gaikotsusan, 1982; Gū Gū Gū, 1982; Tokidoki no Shounen (essay), 1982; Ehon ABC, 1983; Kiiroino wa Choucho, 1983, trans. as Hi,

Butterfly!, 1983; Geimu Bukku No. 1, 1983; Tamago wo Douzo, 1983; Kabusan Tonda, 1983; Geimu Bukku No. 2, 1983; Tosan Maigo, 1983; Geimu Bukku No. 3, 1983; MadoKara no Okurimono, 1983, trans. as Santa through the Window, 1995; Nakushitamono Mitsuketa, 1983; Kotoba no Ehon AI-UEO, 1983; Kazu No Ehon1-2-3, 1983, rev. ed., 1985; Gomi Taro Catalogue-ehon, 1984; Wanisan Doki Haishasan Doki, 1984, trans. as The Crocodile and the Dentist, 1994; Korewa Himo, 1984; Kore wa Hako, 1984; Tomodachi ga Kimashita, 1984; Tomodachiga Imashita, 1984; Battakun, 1984; Kore wa Te, 1984; Kore wa Atama, 1984; Ichiban Hajimeni, 1984, trans. as First Comes Harry, 1987; Chibisuke Kirakira, 1985; Omen de Asobouyo, 1985; Doubutsu Sakasudan, 1985; Basu gaKita, 1985, trans. as Bus Stops, 1988; Suji no Ehon, 1985; Sansansan, 1985; Omataseshimashita, 1985; Kyou Mo Genkisa, 1985; Kotoba Zukan 1 Ugokinokotoba (Doushi), 1985, trans. as Seeing, Saying, Doing, Playing: A Big Book of Action Words, 1985; Ba Ba Zou Diu Le, Ying Wen Han Sheng ChuBan Gong Si, 1985; Kotoba Zukan 2 Yusanokotoba (Fukushi), 1985; Nihon Kotowaza Mongatari, 1985; Sanpo no Shirushi, 1986; Kotoba Zukan 3 Kazarukotoba (A) (Keiyoushi), 1986; Kotoba Zukan 4 Kazarukotoba(B) (Keiyoushi), 1986; Ne Ohanashi Shiteyo, 1986; Kotoba Zukan 5Tsunaginokotoba (Joshi), 1986; Kotowaza Ehon 1, 1986; Gokigen Ikaga, 1986; Guruguru Doubutsuehon, 1986; Kotoba Zukan 6 Kurashinokotoba (Aisatsugo), 1986; Saru-rururu Karuta, 1986; Wo Shi Di Yi Ge, 1986; ABC Tu Hua Shu, 1986; Doubutsu Daisuki, 1987; Gomi Taro Poster Ehon, 1987; Kotoba Zukan 7 Tatoenokotoba (Hiyu), 1987; Everyone East and..., 1987; What Does This Sign Say?, 1987; Kotowaza Ehon 2, 1988; Kotoba Zukan 8, 1988; Boku ha Zouda, 1988; Aiue Obakedazo, 1988; Kumasan Home-Run, 1988; Kotoba Zukan 9 Shipponokotoba (Jodoushi), 1988; Otto Otoshimono, 1988; Gomi Taro Catalogue Ehon: Part II, 1988; Ehon wo Yondemiru, 1988; Hajimeteno Eigo 1, 1988; Hajimeteno Eigo 2, 1988; Kotoba Zukan 10 Namaenokotoba (Meishi), 1988; Jazz Song Book, 1988; Guru Guru Card (Doubutsu), 1988; Haiku PurasuAruga Zou, 1988; Node Node Node, 1989; Kakigogochi no Yoi Kutsu, 1989; Utaga Kikoetekuru, 1989; Popopopopo, 1989; Nihongo Gitaigo Jiten, 1990; Rakugaki Ehon, 1990; 12 Ko no E no Hako, 1990; Sekaijyu no Kodomotachiga, 1990; Boku no Uta, 1990; Parade, 1990; Boku Tooreruyo, 1990; Ya Minasan, 1990; Nanikashira, 1990; Jazz Song Book 2, 1991; Jyobuna Atama to KahiskoiKarad ni Narutameni, 1991; Kakakakaka, 1991; Rururururu, 1991; Hajimeteno Eigo 3, 1991; Hajimeteno Eigo 4, 1991; Shisumon Ehon, 1991; Iroirona Doubutsuni Nattemimashita, 1991; Iroirona Mononi Nattemimashita, 1991; Saru-rururu One More, 1991; Hajimenteno Piano Kyokushu, 1991; Hello!, 1991; Aisatsu Ehon, 1991; Guess Who?, 1991; Who Ate It?, 1991; Who HidIt?, 1991; Rakugaki Ehon Part 2, 1992; Ipponbashi Wataru One More, 1992; Doubutsu Sakasudan, 1992; Ashita ga Suki, 1992; Doubutsu-hen, 1992; Dougu-hen, 1992; Kotoba-hen, 1992; Kanji Jyukugo-hen, 1992; Dododododo, 1992; Rakugaki Book Rakugaki Ehon, 1992; Kesshite Soudeha Arimasen, 1992; Kotobano Ehon AIUEO, 1992; Gomi Taro Design Work, 1992; Nanika Itteruyo, 1992; Kono Yubi Naani, 1992; Tsumande Goran, 1992; Rakugaki Hagaki, 1992; Guess What?, 1992; There's a Mouse in the House, 1992; Ouchi wo Tsukurimashou, 1993; Oshare wo Shimashou, 1993; Ki wo Uemashou, 1993; Saa Itadakimashou, 1993; Hajimenteno Piano Kyokushu 2, 1993; Kaimono Ehon, 1993; Tetetetete, 1993; Tonimokakunimo Sutekin Nakama, 1993; Hahahahaha, 1993; Smile, 1993; Face Painting, 1993; Tadashii Kurashikata Dokuhon, 1993; Mouichido Sonokotowa, 1993; Sorezore no Jyoukyou, 1993; Matteimasu, 1994; Minnasorezore Kinoii Nakama, 1994; Gomi Taro Ehonsenshu Part 1, 1994; Darega Sunde Irunokana, 1994; Haiku wa Ikaga, 1994; Bibibibibi, 1994; Nununununu, 1994; Pocket ni Uta wo Tsumete, 1994; Kotoba no Ehon Aiueo Karuta, 1994; Ah Likimochi, 1995; Naniwatomoare Ganbaru Nakama, 1995; Rirririri, 1995; Kore wa Umi, 1995; Kore wa Yama, 1995; Nnnnn, 1995; Omataseshimashita 2, 1995; Sansansan Sono 2, 1995; Chikyu ha Utau, 1995; Tegami ga Kurukuru, 1995; Wakuwakusurune, 1996; Isshoni, 1996; Kochira to Sochira, 1996; Hidarinohon Miginohon, 1996; Waratteru Naiteiru, 1996; Anakara Nigeta, 1996; Dokoni Hairoukana, 1996; Tsukandegoran, 1996; Satori kun, 1996; Tanoshii Ookii Kotoba Ehon, 1996; Nuttari KaitariRakugaki Book, 1996; Otona Mondai, 1996; Rakugaki Ehon 1.2.3., 1996; Karada Shiata, 1997; Darekaga Imasu, 1997; Herikoputatachi, 1997; Todos Hacemos Caca, 1998; I Lost My Dad, 2001; Llegoó la primavera, 2006; Mis amigos, 2006. **Address:** Kai Co., 6- 34-6-406 Jingu-Mae Shibuya-Ku, Tokyo, 150, Japan.

GOMMANS, Jos J. L. Dutch (born Netherlands), b. 1963. **Genres:** History, Politics/Government, Adult Non-fiction, Essays, Local History/Rural Topics. **Career:** University of Leiden, Department of South and Central Asian Studies, faculty, 1993-; Kern Institute, Department of South and Central Asian Studies, associate professor. Writer. **Publications:** The Rise of the Indo-Afghan Empire, c. 1710-1780, 1995; (ed.) Warfare and Weaponry in South Asia, 1000-1800, 2001; Dutch Sources on South Asia, c. 1600-1825, 2001; (with L. Bes and G. Kruijtzer) Dutch Aources on South Asia, c. 1600-1825, 2001; (ed. with J. Leider) Maritime Frontier of Burma: Exploring Political, Cultural and Commercial Interaction in the Indian Ocean World, 1200-1800, 2002; Mughal Warfare: Indian Frontiers and Highroads to Empire, 1500-1700, 2002; (ed. with O. Prakash) Circumambulations in South Asian History: Essays in Honour of Dirk H.A. Kolff, 2003. Contributor of articles to periodicals. **Address:** Department of South and Central Asian Studies, Kern Institute, Nonnensteeg 1-3, PO Box 9515, Leiden, 2300 RA, Netherlands. **Online address:** j.j.l.gommans@hum.leidenuniv.nl

GONDRY, Michel. French (born France), b. 1963. **Genres:** Film, Novellas/Short Stories, Young Adult Non-fiction. **Career:** Director and writer. **Publications:** (Intro.) Eternal Sunshine of the Spotless Mind, 2004. **Address:** Partizan Ltd., 7 Westbourne Grove Mews, London, GL W11 2UR, England.

GONEN, Jay Y. American/Israeli (born Israel), b. 1934?. **Genres:** Psychology, History, Social Sciences. **Career:** University of Cincinnati, professor of psychology, now retired; University of Rochester Medical Center, professor. Writer. **Publications:** A Psychohistory of Zionism, 1975; The Roots of Nazi Psychology: Hitler's Utopian Barbarism, 2000; Yahweh Versus Yahweh: The Enigma of Jewish History, 2005. Contributor of articles to periodicals. **Address:** c/o Author Mail, University Press of Kentucky, 663 S Limestone St., Lexington, KY 40508-4008, U.S.A.

GONI, Uki. See **GOÑI, Uki.**

GOÑI, Uki. (Uki Goni). Argentine/American (born United States), b. 1953. **Genres:** History, Military/Defense/Arms Control, Social Sciences. **Career:** Writer and musician. **Publications:** Judas: La Verdadera Historia De Alfredo Astiz, El Infiltrado, 1996; Perón y los Alemanes: La Verdad Sobre el Espionaje Nazi y los Fugitivos del Reich, 1998; Auténtica Odessa: La Fuga Nazi a la Argentina de Perón, 2002, trans. as The Real Odessa: How Perón Brought the Nazi War Criminals to Argentina, 2003. Contributor to periodicals. **Address:** Granta Publications, 12 Addison Ave., London, GL W11 4QR, England. **Online address:** mail@ukinet.com

GONYEA, Mark. American (born United States) **Genres:** Design. **Career:** Heavy Metal (magazine), designer, 1995- 96; Vermont Teddy Bear Co., graphic artist, 1998-2000; assistant art director, 2002-04, art director, 2004; SendAMERICA, art director, 2000-02. Writer. **Publications:** A Book about Design: Complicated Doesn't Make It Good, 2005; Another Book about Design: Complicated Doesn't Make It Bad, 2007. **Address:** VT , U.S.A. **Online address:** mark@mroblivious.com

GONZALES, Felipe. See **GONZALES, Phillip B.**

GONZALES, Laurence. American (born United States), b. 1947?. **Genres:** Novels, Essays, Novellas/Short Stories, Young Adult Non-fiction, Information Science/Computers, Young Adult Fiction. **Career:** Freelance writer, 1970-; Medill School of Journalism, Northwestern University, adjunct lecturer; University of Missouri, artist-in-residence. **Publications:** COMPUTERS SERIES: Computers for Doctors, 1984; Computers for Lawyers, 1984; Computers for Writers, 1984; Computers for Realtors, 1984. NOVELS: Jambeaux, 1979; The Last Deal, 1981; El Vago, 1983; ESSAYS: The Still Point, 1989; One Zero Charlie: Adventures in Grass Roots Aviation, 1992; The Hero's Apprentice, 1994. SHORT STORIES: (with G. Lyons and R. Rath) 4-4-4, 1977; Artificial Horizon, 1986. NONFICTION: Deep Survival: Who Lives, Who Dies and Why: True Stories of Miraculous Endurance and Sudden Death, 2003; Everyday Survival: Why Smart People Do Stupid Things, 2008. OTHER: Lucy, 2010. Contributor to periodicals. **Address:** c/o Gail Hochman, Brandt & Hochman, 1501 Broadway, New York, NY 10036, U.S.A. **Online address:** deepsurvival@comcast.net

GONZALES, Phillip B. Also writes as Felipe Gonzales. American (born United States), b. 1946. **Genres:** Sociology. **Career:** University of California, Institute for the Study of Social Change, Graduate Field Research Training, field researcher, 1978-79; BART Research Project, field researcher, 1978-79; National Science Foundation, co-researcher, 1985-86; Insurance Institute for Highway Safety, field researcher, 1986-87; University of New Mexico, Department of Sociology, assistant professor, 1987-2003, associate professor, 1996-2003, professor, 2003-, chair, 2004-, Southwest Hispanic Research Institute, director, 1996-2003, College of Arts and Sciences, senior associate dean for faculty. Writer. **Publications:** (With L. Lamphere, P. Zavella and P.B. Evans as Felipe Gonzales) Sunbelt Working Mothers: Reconciling Family and Factory, 1993; Forced Sacrifice as Ethnic Protest: The Hispano Cause in New Mexico and the Racial Attitude Confrontation of 1933, 2001; (ed.) Expressing New Mexico: Nuevomexicano Creativity, Ritual, and Memory, 2007; Política: The Native Son Cause Struggle for Political Inclusion, Equality, and Justice in New Mexico, 1848-1935, forthcoming. Works appear in anthologies. Contributor to periodicals. **Address:** Department of Sociology, University of New Mexico, Rm. 201, Ortega Hall, 1915 Roma NE, Ste. 1103, PO Box 03 2120, Albuquerque, NM 87131-1166, U.S.A. **Online address:** gonzales@unm.edu

GONZALES-DAY, Ken. American (born United States), b. 1964?. **Genres:** Architecture. **Career:** Scripps College, professor of studio art, 1995-, chair of the art and art history departments, 2003-06, chair of the art department, 2006-08, 2009-; College Art Association, director, 2007-. Writer. **Publications:** (With T. Stallings, A. Jones and D.R. Roediger) Whiteness, a Wayward Construction, 2003; Lynching in the West: 1850-1935, 2006. Contributor of articles to journals. **Address:** Scripps College, 1030 Columbia Ave., Claremont, CA 91711, U.S.A. **Online address:** ken@kengonzalesday.com

GONZALEZ, Alexander G. American (born United States), b. 1952. **Genres:** Literary Criticism And History, Young Adult Fiction, inspirational/Motivational Literature, Humanities. **Career:** City University of New York, Queens College, team teacher of English composition, 1975-76; University of Oregon, director of writing laboratory, 1978-79; University of California, visiting lecturer in English, 1980-81; University of Oregon, instructor in writing and composition, 1982-83; Ohio State University, assistant professor of English, 1983-88; State University of New York College, assistant professor, 1988-91, associate professor, 1991-94, professor of English, 1994-2003, distinguished teaching professor, 2003-; Central New York Conference on Language and Literature, director, 1995-2001. Writer. **Publications:** Darrell Figgis: A Study of His Novels, 1992; Short Stories from the Irish Renaissance: An Anthology, 1993; (ed.) Assessing the Achievement of J.M.Synge, 1996; Peadar O'Donnell: A Reader's Guide, 1997; Modern Irish Writers: A Bio-Critical Sourcebook, 1997; (contrib.) That Other World: The Fantastic and the Supernatural in Irish Literature, 1998; Contemporary Irish Women Poets: Some Male Perspectives, 1999; (ed.) Irish Women Writers: An A-to-Z Guide, 2005. Contributor to periodicals. **Address:** Department of English, State University of New York College, 117-B Old Main, PO Box 2000, Cortland, NY 13045, U.S.A. **Online address:** gonzalez@cortland.edu

GONZÁLEZ, Aníbal. American/Puerto Rican (born Puerto Rico), b. 1956. **Genres:** Literary Criticism And History, Politics/Government, Romance/Historical, Social Sciences, Young Adult Fiction. **Career:** University of Texas, assistant professor, 1982-87, tenured associate professor of Spanish, 1987-90, Institute of Latin American Studies, chair, University of Texas Press, reader; Michigan State University, tenured associate professor, 1990-93, professor of Spanish, 1993; Pennsylvania State University, Department of Spanish, Italian and Portuguese, Edwin Erle Sparks professor of Spanish, 1994-, graduate advisor, 1998-2001; Cambridge University Press, Cambridge Studies in Latin American and Iberian Literature Series, general editor, 1995-97, reader; Bucknell University Press, Bucknell Studies in Latin American Literature and Theory, general editor, 1998, reader; Yale University, professor; Columbia University Press, reader; University of California Press, reader; Oxford University Press, reader. **Publications:** (With J.M.M. Martínez and J.M.D. Taboada) Literatura Española, 1978; (co-author) Repertorium Litterarum Graecarum: Ex Codicibus, Papyris, Epigraphis, 1982; La Crónica Modernista Hispanoamericana, 1983; La Novela Nodernista Hispanoamericana, 1987; Journalism and the Development of Spanish American Narrative, 1993; (trans.) J.L. Borges, Un Ensayo Autobiografico, 1999; Killer Books, 2001; Abusos y Admoniciones: Ética y Escritura en la Narrativa Hispanoamericana Moderna, 2001; Killer Books: Writing, Violence, and Ethics in Modern Spanish American Narrative, 2001; Companion to Spanish American Modernismo, 2007; Redentores, 2009; Love and Politics in the Contemporary Spanish American Novel, 2010. Contributor to books and journals. **Address:** Department of Spanish, Italian and Portuguese, Pennsylvania State University, 211 Burrowes Bldg., University Park, PA 16802, U.S.A. **Online address:** axg20@psu.edu

GONZALEZ, Genaro. American (born United States), b. 1949. **Genres:** Novels, Novellas/Short Stories. **Career:** Pan American University Edinburg

Texas, instructor in psychology, 1976-79, 1979-82; Universidad de las Américas Puebla Mexico, associate professor of psychology, 1983-85; University of Texas, Texas Governor's School, instructor, 1986; Wichita State University, assistant professor of minority studies, 1986-88; University of Texas at Pan American, associate professor in psychology, 1988-97, professor in psychology, 1997-. Writer. **Publications:** Rainbow's End, 1988; Only Sons (short story collection), 1991; The Quixote Cult, 1998; So-called Vacation, 2009. Contributor of articles to periodicals. Works appear in anthologies. **Address:** Department of Psychology, University of Texas, SBSC 339, 1201 W University Dr., Edinburg, TX 78539, U.S.A. **Online address:** ggonzalez@panam.edu

GONZALEZ, Jose Manuel Prieto. *See* **PRIETO, Jose Manuel.**

GONZÁLEZ, Justo L(uis). American/Cuban (born Cuba), b. 1937. **Genres:** Theology/Religion. **Career:** Evangelical Seminary of Puerto Rico, professor of historical theology, 1961-69, dean, 1967-69; Yale University, research fellow, 1968; Church of the Province of the West Indies, consultant, 1969-74; Ninth Province of the Episcopal Church, consultant, 1969-74; Emory University, assistant professor, 1969-71, associate professor, 1971-77; Interdenominational Theological Center, visiting professor of theology, 1977-88; Columbia Theological Seminary, visiting professor, 1987-91, adjunct professor of theology, 1988-90; Fund for Theological Education, consultant, 1987-88. Writer. **Publications:** The Development of Christianity in the Latin Caribbean, 1969; (with C.G. Gonzalez) Their Souls Did Magnify the Lord, 1977; Sus almas engrandecieron al Señor, 1977; Luces bajo el almud, 1977; (with C.G. Gonzalez) Vision at Patmos, 1978; Era de las tinieblas, 1978; (with C.G. Gonzalez) Rejoice in Your Savior, 1979; (with C.G. Gonzalez) Liberation Preaching, 1980; (with C.G. Gonzalez) In Accord, 1981; The Story of Christianity, 1984, 2nd ed.; The Story of Christianity, vol. I: The Early Church to the Reformation, 2010; A History of Christian Thought, 3 vols., 1970-79, 1987; The Crusades: Piety Misguided, 1988; Monasticism: Patterns of Piety, 1988; Christian Thought Revisited, 1989; Faith and Wealth, 1990; Manana: Christian Theology from a Hispanic Perspective, 1990; Out of Every Tribe and Nation: Christian Theology at the Ethnic Roundtable, 1992; Mentors as Instruments of God's Call: Biblical Reflections, 1992, rev. ed., 2009; Santa Biblia, 1996; Church History, 1996; (with C.G. Gonzalez) Revelation, 1997; For the Healing of the Nations, 1999; Mark's Message for the New Millennium, 2000; Jonas, 2000; Acts: The Gospel of the Spirit, 2001; Changing Shape of Church History, 2002; (with Z.M. Prez) Introduction to Christian Theology Three Months with Matthew, 2002; Three Months with the Spirit, 2003; Three Months with Revelation, 2004; Three Months with John, 2005; Essential Theological Terms, 2005; Concise History of Christian Doctrine, 2005; Hechos de los Apóstoles, 2006; Three Months with Paul, 2006; Apostles' Creed for Today, 2007; (with O.E. González) Christianity in Latin America: A History, 2008; Heretics for Armchair Theologians, 2008; Luke, 2010; For the Love of God, 2010. EDITOR: Proclaiming the Acceptable Years, 1982; Reformation to the Present Day, 1984; Early Church to the Dawn of the Reformation, 1984; Each in Our Own Tongue: A History of Hispanic United Methodism, 1991; Voices: Voices from the Hispanic Church, 1992; (with P.A. Jiménez) Púlpito: An Introduction to Hispanic Preaching, 2005; Hispanic Christian Thought at the Dawn of the 21st Century, 2005; (co-ed.) The Westminster Dictionary of Theologians, 2006. **Address:** 336 S Columbia Dr., Decatur, GA 30030, U.S.A.

GONZÁLEZ, Ray. American (born United States), b. 1952. **Genres:** Poetry, Literary Criticism And History. **Career:** La Voz, editor-in-chief, 1981-82; Bloomsbury Review, poetry editor, 1980-; Mesilla Press, founder, editor and publisher, 1984-; Guadalupe Cultural Arts Center, director, 1989-; University of Illinois, assistant professor of English and Latin American studies, 1996-98; University of Minnesota, assistant professor, 1998-2000, associate professor, 2000-02, professor of English, 2002-, director of creative writing program, Emerson House Detention Center, instructor; Luna Journal, editor. **Publications:** From the Restless Roots, 1986; Twilights and Chants: Poems, 1987; (with Koptcho and Mills) Falling Into, 1992; Memory Fever: A Journey Beyond El Paso del Norte, 1993; The Heat of Arrivals, 1996; Cabato Sentora, 1998; Turtle Pictures, 2000; The Ghost of John Wayne and Other Stories, 2001; Circling the Tortilla Dragon: Short-Short Fiction, 2002; The Underground Heart: A Return to a Hidden Landscape: Essays, 2002; The Hawk Temple at Tierra Grande: Poems, 2002; Human Crying Daisies: Prose Poems, 2003; The Religion of Hands: Prose Poems and Short Fictions, 2005; Consideration of the Guitar: New and Selected Poems, 2005; Renaming the Earth: Personal Essays, 2008; Cool Auditor: Prose Poems, 2009; Faith Run: Poems, 2009. EDITOR: City Kite on a Wire: 38 Denver Poets, 1986; Cross-

ing the River: Poets of the Western U.S., 1987; Tracks in the Snow, 1988; Without Discovery: A Native Response to Columbus, 1992; After Aztlan: Latino Poets of the Nineties, 1992; Mirrors Beneath the Earth: Short Fiction by Chicano Writers, 1992; Currents from the Dancing River: Contemporary Latino Fiction, Nonfiction and Poetry, 1994; Under the Pomegranate Tree: The Best New Latino Erotica, 1996; Inheritance of Light, 1996; Muy Macho: Latino Men Confront Their Manhood, 1996; (and intro.) Touching the Fire: Fifteen Poets of Today's Latino Renaissance, 1998; No Boundaries: Prose Poems by 24 American Poets, 2003; (with R. Shapard and J. Thomas) Sudden Fiction Latino: Short-short Stories from the United States and Latin America, 2010. **Address:** Department of English, University of Minnesota, 310E Lind, 207 Church St. SE, Minneapolis, MN 55455, U.S.A. **Online address:** gonza049@umn.edu

GONZALEZ-BALADO, Jose Luis. Spanish (born Spain), b. 1933. **Genres:** Biography, Theology/Religion, History, Social Sciences. **Career:** Ediciones Paulinas, editor. **Publications:** Cristo en los arrabales: Madre Teresa de Calcuta, 1974; Me llaman el obispo rojo: Dom Hélder Camara, 1974; El desafío de Taizé, 1976; Le défi de Taizè: frére Roger, 1977; Ernesto Cardenal poeta revolucionario monje, 1978; Always the Poor: Mother Teresa, Her Life and Message, 1980; (with K. Spink) Spirit of Bethlehem: Brother Andrew and the Missionary Brothers of Charity, 1987; Ruiz-Giménez, talante y figura: Trayectoria de un hombre discutido, 1989; Padre Llanos: Un jesuita en el suburbio, 1991; (comp.) In my Own Words, 1996; Mother Teresa: Her Life, Her Work, Her Message: A Memoir, 1997; El Bendito Juan XXIII, 2003; Teresa of Calcutta: A Personal Memoir, 2007. EDITOR: (with J.N. Playfoot) My Life for the Poor, 1985; Heart of Joy, 1987; One Heart Full of Love, 1988; Loving Jesus, 1991; My Life for the Poor: An Autobiography, 2005. **Address:** Parque Eugenia de Montijo 55, Madrid, 28047, Spain.

GONZÁLEZ-ECHEVARRIA, Roberto. American/Cuban (born Cuba), b. 1943. **Genres:** Literary Criticism And History. **Career:** Yale University, instructor, 1969-70, assistant professor of Latin American studies, 1970-71, assistant professor of Spanish, 1970-71, associate professor, 1977-80, professor, 1980-85, director of undergraduate studies in Latin American studies, 1979-80, Council on Latin American Studies, chairman, 1981-83, 1984-85, Department of Spanish and Portuguese, chairman, 1983-89, 1990-93, R. Selden Rose professor of Spanish, 1985-91, Bass professor of Hispanic and comparative literatures, 1991-95, Sterling professor of Hispanic and comparative literatures, 1995-, William Clyde DeVane professor, 2001; Cornell University, assistant professor, 1971-75, associate professor, 1975-77, Department of Romance Studies, director of graduate studies, 1973-74; Stanford University, lecturer, 1974; New School for Social Research, lecturer, 1975; Brown University, lecturer, 1978; Universidad Simon Bolivar, lecturer, 1980; University of Ottawa, lecturer, 1980; Johns Hopkins University, lecturer, 1980. Writer. **Publications:** (With M. Duran) Calderón Y la Crítica, Historia Y Antología, 1976; Relecturas, Estudios de Literatura Cubana, 1976; Alejo Carpentier: The Pilgrim at Home, 1977; (with K. Muller-Bergh) Alejo Carpentier: Bibliographical Guide, 1983; Isla a su Vuelo Fugitiva: Ensayos Críticos sobre Literatura Hispanoamericana, 1983; Estatuas Sepultada yOtros Relatos, 1984; (ed.) Estatuas sepultadas y otros relatos, 1984; Historia y Ficción en la Narrativa Hispanoamericana, 1985; (ed.) Los Pasos Perididos, 1985; The Voice of the Masters: Writing and Authority in Modern Latin American Literature, 1985; La ruta de Severo Sarduy, 1987; Myth and Archive: A Theory of Latin American Narrative, 1990; Celestina's Brood: Continuities of the Baroquein Spanish and Latin American Literatures, 1993; Alejo Carpentier, El Peregrino En Su Patria, 1993; (ed.) De Donde Son Los Cantantes, 1993; (ed. with E. Pupo-Walker) The Cambridge History of Latin American Literature, 3 vols., 1996; (ed.) The Oxford Book of Latin American Short Stories, 1997; Miguel de Cervantes, 1998; The Pride of Havana: A History of Cuban Baseball, 1999; (ed.) Borges: Desesperaciones Aparentes Y Consuelos Secretos, 1999; (contrib.) En un lugar de la Mancha: Estudios Cervantinos En Honor De Manuel Durán, 1999; (contrib.) Acerca de Miguel Barnet, 2000; Voz De Los Maestros: Escritura y Autoridad En La Literatura Latinoamericana Moderna, 2001; (intro.) Ingenious Hidalgo Don Quixote De La Mancha, 2001; Critica Practica/Practica Critica, 2002; (intro.) José Martí: Selected Writings, 2002; (contrib.) Ensayo Cubano del siglo XX: Antología, 2002; Gabriel García Márquez's One Hundred Years of Solitude, 2003; Cuba, un siglo de Literatura (1902-2002), 2004; (ed.) Cervantes' Don Quixote: A Casebook, 2005; Love and the Law in Cervantes, 2005; Oye mi son: ensayos y testimonios sobre literatura hispanoamericana, 2008; Cartas de Carpentier, 2008; (ed. and intro.) Celestina, 2009; Cuban Fiestas, 2010; Modern Latin American Literature, 2012. Contributor to periodicals. **Address:** Department of Spanish and Portuguese,

Yale University, 82-90 Wall St., 120 High St., New Haven, CT 06511-8944, U.S.A. **Online address:** roberto.echevarria@yale.edu

GONZALEZ (MANDRI), Flora. American/Cuban (born Cuba), b. 1948. **Genres:** Literary Criticism And History, History, Social Sciences, Poetry, Women's Studies And Issues, Politics/Government. **Career:** Dartmouth College, lecturer, 1974-76, visiting assistant professor of Spanish and Portuguese, 1982-83; University of Chicago, assistant professor of romance languages, 1983-86; Middlebury College, assistant professor, 1984-89, associate professor, 1993; Emerson College, assistant professor, 1986-91, associate professor of humanities and social sciences, 1991-98, professor, 1998-, acting dean of graduate studies, 1994-95, director of honors program, 1995-96; Harvard University, W.E.B. Du Bois Institute, resident fellow, 1997-98, David Rockefeller Center of Latin American Studies, affiliate; Calvin College, lecturer; Yale University, lecturer; Tufts University, lecturer; University of Michigan, lecturer; Florida International University, lecturer. Writer. **Publications:** Jose Donoso's House of Fiction: A Dramatic Construction of Time and Place, 1995; (ed. and trans. with R. Rosenmeier) In the Vortex of the Cyclone: Selected Poems by Excilia Saldana, 2002; Guarding Cultural Memory: Afro-Cuban Women in Literature and the Arts, 2006; On the Other Side of the Glass, forthcoming. Contributor of articles to books and periodicals. **Address:** Department of Writing, Literature and Publishing, Emerson College, 80 Tremont St., 10th Fl., Boston, MA 02116-4624, U.S.A. **Online address:** flora_gonzalez@emerson.edu

GOOCH, Brad. American (born United States), b. 1952. **Genres:** Novels, Novellas/Short Stories, Poetry, Gay And Lesbian Issues, Biography, Travel/Exploration, Young Adult Non-fiction, Young Adult Fiction, Young Adult Fiction. **Career:** William Paterson University, professor of English. Freelance writer. **Publications:** The Daily News, 1977; Jailbait and Other Stories, 1984; Hall & Oates (biography), 1985; Billy Idol (biography), 1985; Scary Kisses (novel), 1988; City Poet: The Life and Times of Frank O'Hara, 1993; The Golden Age of Promiscuity, 1996; Finding the Boyfriend Within, 1999; Zombie00, 2000; Godtalk: Travels in Spiritual America, 2002; Dating the Greek Gods: Empowering Spiritual Sex and Love, Creativity and Wisdom, 2003; Flannery: A Life of Flannery O'Connor, 2009. Contributor to magazines. **Address:** Department of English, William Paterson University, 230 Atrium, 300 Pompton Rd., Wayne, NJ 07470, U.S.A. **Online address:** goochb@wpunj.edu

GOOCH, Paul W(illiam). Canadian (born Canada), b. 1941. **Genres:** Philosophy, Theology/Religion, Social Sciences. **Career:** University of Toronto, department of philosophy, instructor, 1966, Centre for Religious Studies, director, 1986-88, professor, 1988, School of Graduate Studies, associate dean, 1988-90, acting assistant dean, 1989-90, assistant dean, 1990-92, acting dean, 1992-93, vice-dean, 1993-94, vice-provost, 1994-2001; Scarborough College, division of humanities, lecturer, 1967, assistant professor, 1970, associate professor, 1973, chairman, 1977-82; Saint John's College, Cambridge, Commonwealth fellow, 1982-83; Victoria University, president, 2001-. **Publications:** Partial Knowledge: Philosophical Studies in Paul, 1987; Reflections on Jesus and Socrates: Word and Silence, 1996. Contributor to periodicals. **Address:** Office of the President, Victoria University, Northrop Frye Hall, 73 Queen's Pk. Cres., Toronto, ON M5S 1K7, Canada. **Online address:** paul.gooch@utoronto.ca

GOOCH, Steve. British (born England), b. 1945. **Genres:** Plays/Screenplays, Translations, Writing/Journalism, Essays. **Career:** Freelance writer and theatrical director, 1969-72; Plays and Players Magazine, assistant editor, 1972-73; Half Moon Theatre, resident dramatist, 1973-74; Greenwich Theatre, resident dramatist, 1974-75; Platform magazine, co-editor, 1979-82; Solent Peoples Theatre, resident dramatist, 1981-82; Theatre Venture, resident dramatist, 1983-84; writer, 1984-; Warehouse Theatre, resident dramatist, 1986-87; Gate Theatre, resident dramatist, 1990-91; Freehand Theatre, cofounder, 1999. **Publications:** (Trans.) Big Wolf, 1972; (trans.) The Mother, 1973; Female Transport, 1974, 2nd ed., 1983; (with P. Thompson) The Motor Show, 1974; Will Wat, If Not, Wat Will?, 1975; (trans.) Wolf Biermann: Poems and Ballads, 1977; The Women Pirates, Ann Bonney and Mary Read, 1978; (trans.) Wallraff: The Undesirable Journalist, 1978; Fast One, 1982; Landmark, 1982; (trans.) Gambit 39, 1982; All Together Now: An Alternative View of Theatre and the Community, 1984; Taking Liberties, 1984; Writing a Play, 1988, 3rd ed., 2004; (trans.) Lulu and the Marquis of Keith, 1990; Massa, 1990; Stages of Translation, 1996. Contributor to books. **Address:** Steve Gooch Publications, PO Box 5, Robertsbridge, ES TN32 5ZS, England.

GOOD, Deirdre Joy. American (born United States) **Genres:** Theology/Religion. **Career:** Valparaiso University, instructor in theology, 1982-83; Agnes Scott College, assistant professor of bible and religion, 1983-86, department chair, 1985-86; General Theological Seminary of the Episcopal Church, assistant professor of New Testament, 1986-87, associate professor, 1987-92, professor, 1992-. Writer. **Publications:** Reconstructing the Tradition of Sophia in Gnostic Literature, 1987; Jesus the Meek King, 1999; (ed.) Mariam, the Magdalen and the Mother, 2005; Jesus Family Values, 2006; (with B. Chilton) Studying the New Testament, 2010. Contributor to books and periodicals. **Address:** General Theological Seminary, 440 W 21st St., New York, NY 10011, U.S.A. **Online address:** good@gts.edu

GOOD, Howard. American (born United States), b. 1951. **Genres:** Documentaries/Reportage, Young Adult Non-fiction, Social Sciences, Reference. **Career:** Ann Arbor News, editor, 1977-78; Charlotte Observer, editor, 1978-80; Grand Forks Herald, editor, 1980-83; University of North Dakota, assistant professor of journalism, 1980-83; State University of New York, Department of journalism, associate professor, 1985-, professor, 1992-. **Publications:** Acquainted with the Night, 1986; Outcasts: The Image of Journalists in Contemporary Film, 1989; The Journalist as Autobiographer, 1993; Diamonds in the Dark, 1997; Girl Reporter: Gender, Journalism, and the Movies, 1998; The Drunken Journalist: The Biography of Film Stereotype, 2000; (with M.J. Dillon) Media Ethics Goes to the Movies, 2002; Educated Guess: A School Board Member Reflects, 2003; (ed.) Desperately Seeking Ethics: A Guide to Media Conduct, 2003; Theory of Oz: Rediscovering the Aims of Education, 2005; Inside the Board Room: Reflections of a Former School Board Member, 2006; Mis-Education in Schools: Beyond the Slogans and Double-Talk, 2007; (ed.) Journalism Ethics Goes to the Movies, 2008; (ed. with S.L. Borden) Ethics and Entertainment: Essays on Media Culture and Media Morality, 2010. **Address:** Communication and Media, State University of New York, CSB 43, Service Bldg., 75 S Manheim Blvd., New Paltz, NY 12561, U.S.A. **Online address:** goodh@newpaltz.edu

GOOD, Timothy. British (born England), b. 1942?. **Genres:** Novellas/Short Stories, International Relations/Current Affairs. **Career:** London Symphony Orchestra, professional violinist; London Philharmonic Orchestra, professional violinist; Mantovani Orchestra, professional violinist; Philharmonia Orchestra, professional violinist; U.S. Congress Investigations, consultant. Journalist, public speaker, researcher and broadcaster. **Publications:** (With L. Zinsstag) George Adamski: The Untold Story, 1983; Above Top Secret: The Worldwide UFO Cover-Up, 1987; Alien Liaison: The Ultimate Secret, 1991 in US as Alien Contact: Top-Secret UFO Files Revealed, 1993; Beyond Top Secret: The Worldwide UFO Security Threat, 1996; Alien Base: Earth's Encounters with Extraterrestrials, 1998; Unearthly Disclosure: Conflicting Interests in the Control of Extraterrestrial Intelligence, 2000; Need to Know: UFOs, the Military and Intelligence, 2006. EDITOR: The UFO Report 1990, 1989; The UFO Report 1991, 1990; The UFO Report 1992, 1991; Alien Update, 1993. **Address:** William Morrow, 10 E 53rd St., New York, NY 10022, U.S.A. **Online address:** info@timothygood.co.uk

GOODALL, Jane. (Jane van Lawick-Goodall). American/South African/British (born England), b. 1934. **Genres:** Animals/Pets, Children's Non-fiction, Zoology, Autobiography/Memoirs, Biology, Young Adult Non-fiction, Sciences, Adult Non-fiction, Natural History. **Career:** National Museum of Natural History, assistant curator, 1960; Gombe Stream Research Center, scientific director, 1967-2003; Stanford University, Department of Psychiatry and Human Biology, visiting professor, 1970-75; Gombe National Park, director of research, 1972-2003; University of Dar es Salaam, honorary visiting professor in zoology, 1973-; L.S.B. Leakey Foundation, trustee, 1974-; Jane Goodall Institute, founder, 1977-; Chicago Academy of Sciences, scientific governor, 1981-; Chimpan Zoo, international director, 1984-; Tufts University, School of Veterinary Medicine, Department of Environmental Studies, adjunct professor, 1987-88; Cleveland Natural History Museum, associate, 1990-; University of Southern California, Department of Anthropology, distinguished adjunct professor, 1990-, Department of Occupational Therapy, distinguished adjunct professor, 1990-; Whole Child Initiative Intl., founder, 1995-; Cornell University, A.D. White professor-at-large, 1996-2002; Whole Child Initiative USA, advisor and founder, 2001-; EETA-CRABS, co-founder, 2001-; U.S. Laboratories, Great Chapter at Grace Cathedral, leading founder, 2007-. Writer. **Publications:** ADULT NON-FICTION: (as Jane van Lawick-Goodall) My Friends, The Wild Chimpanzees, 1967; (as Jane van Lawick-Goodall) The Behavior of Free-Living Chimpanzees in the Gombe Stream Reserve, 1968; (as Jane van Lawick-Goodall with H. VanLawick) Innocent

Killers, 1970; (as Jane van Lawick-Goodall) Grub: The Bush Baby, 1970; In the Shadow of Man, 1971; The Chimpanzees of Gombe: Patterns of Behavior, 1986; Through a Window: My Thirty Years with the Chimpanzees of Gombe, 1990 in UK as Through the Window: Thirty Years with the Chimpanzees of Gombe, 1998; The Chimpanzee: The Living Links between Man and Beast: The Third Edinburgh Medal Address, 1992; (with D. Peterson) Visions of Caliban: On Chimpanzees and People, 1993, 2nd ed., 2003; With Love: Ten Heartwarming Stories of Chimpanzees in the Wild, 1994, 3rd ed., 2002; With Love, 1998; Dr. White, 1999; (contrib.) Brutal Kinship, 1999; (with P. Berman) A Reason for Hope: A Spiritual Journey, 1999; Africa in My Blood: An Autobiography in Letters: The Early Years, 2000; Beyond Innocence: An Autobiography in Letters: The Later Years, 2001; Performance and Evolution in the Age of Darwin: Out of the Natural Order, 2002; (with M. Bekoff) The Ten Trusts: What We Must do to Care for the Animals We Love, 2002; (foreword) Heart of the Horse, 2004; Rickie & Henri, 2005; (with G. McAvoy and G. Hudson) Harvest for Hope: A Guide to Mindful Eating, 2005; (intro.) Black Market: Inside the Endangered Species Trade in Asia, 2005; (with T. Maynard and G. Hudson) Hope for Animals and Their World: How Endangered Species Are Being Rescued from the Brink, 2009; (contrib.) The Mind of the Chimpanzee: Ecological and Experimental Perspectives, 2010. JUVENILE NON-FICTION: My Life with the Chimpanzees, 1988; The Chimpanzee Family Book, 1989; Chimps, 1989; Jane Goodall's Animal World: Chimps, 1980; Lion Family, 1989; Chimpanzee Family, 1990; Giraffe Family, 1990; Baboon Family, 1990; Elephant Family, 1990; Gorillas, 1990; Zebra Family, 1990; Sea Otters, 1990; Hyena Family, 1990; Wildebeast Family, 1990; Tigers, 1990; (reteller) The Eagle and the Wren, 2000; The Chimpanzees I Love: Saving Their World and Ours, 2001. OTHERS: Jane Goodall: 50 Years at Gombe, a Tribute to Fire Decades of Wildfire Research, Education, and Conservation, 2010. Contributor to journals. **Address:** Jane Goodall Institute, 4245 N Fairfax Dr., Ste. 600, Arlington, VA 22203, U.S.A. **Online address:** jgoodall@janegoodall.org

GOODAVAGE, Maria. American (born United States), b. 1962?. **Genres:** Film, Animals/Pets, Travel/Exploration. **Career:** USA Today, staff writer. **Publications:** The California Dog Lover's Companion, 1994, rev. ed. as The Dog Lover's Companion to California: The Inside Scoop on Where to Take Your Dog in the Golden State, 2002; (intro.) A Dog's World, 1998; The Dog Lover's Companion in the Bay Area, 2002; (with J. Gordon) Good Nights: The Happy Parents' Guide to the Family Bed and a Peaceful Night's Sleep!, 2002; Dog Lover's Companion to the San Francisco Bay Area, 6th ed., 2008, 7th ed., 2011; Soldier Dogs: The Untold Story of America's Canine Heroes, 2012. Contributor to periodicals. **Address:** c/o Author Mail, St. Martin's Griffin, 175 5th Ave., New York, NY 10010, U.S.A. **Online address:** contact@caldogtravel.com

GOODE, Carolyn. See VORNHOLT, John.

GOODENOUGH, Ward Hunt. American (born United States), b. 1919. **Genres:** Anthropology/Ethnology, Language/Linguistics, Cultural/Ethnic Topics. **Career:** University of Wisconsin, instructor, 1948-49; University of Pennsylvania, assistant professor, 1949-54, associate professor, 1954-62, professor, 1962-80, university professor, 1980-89, university professor emeritus of anthropology, 1989-, University Museum, Oceania Section, consulting curator emeritus; Cornell University, visiting professor, 1961-62. Writer. **Publications:** Property, Kin and Community on Truk, 1951, 2nd ed., 1978; Native astronomy in the Central Carolines, 1953; Cooperation in Change: An Anthropological Approach to Community Development, 1963; (ed.) Explorations in Cultural Anthropology, 1964; Description and Comparison in Cultural Anthropology, 1970; Culture, Language and Society, 1971, 2nd ed., 1981; (comp. with H. Sugita) Trukese-English Dictionary=Pwpwuken tettenin fóós, Chuuk-Ingenes, 1980; (contrib. with P. Charoenwongsa) Ban Chiang: Discovery of a Lost Bronze Age, 1982; (contrib.) Culture, Kin and Cognition in Oceania: Essays in Honor of Ward H. Goodenough, 1989; (ed.) Prehistoric Settlement of the Pacific, 1996; Under Heaven's Brow: Pre-Christian Religious Tradition in Chuuk, 2002. **Address:** Department of Anthropology, University of Pennsylvania, 3451 Walnut St., Philadelphia, PA 19104, U.S.A. **Online address:** whgooden@sas.upenn.edu

GOODFIELD, (Gwyneth) June. British (born England), b. 1927. **Genres:** Novels, Sciences, Young Adult Fiction, Adult Non-fiction. **Career:** Medical Research Council, research assistant in zoology, 1949-50; Cheltenham Ladies College, senior biology mistress, 1950-54; Benenden School, physics mistress, 1954-56; University of Leeds, Leverhulme research fellow and lecturer

in history of science, 1956-60; Nuffield Foundation, Unit for the History of Ideas, assistant director, 1960-64; Wellesley College, professor of the history and philosophy of science, Rebecca Bachrach Treves professor, 1965-68; Michigan State University, College of Human Medicine, professor of philosophy and medicine, 1968-77; Rockefeller University, senior research associate, 1976-83; Cornell University Medical College, adjunct professor, 1977-89; International Health and Biomedicine Ltd., president, 1982-96; George Mason University, Clarence J. Robinson professor, 1990-; Royal Society of Medicine, fellow; Zoological Society of London, fellow. Writer. **Publications:** The Growth of Scientific Physiology, 1960; (with S.E. Toulmin) The Fabric of the Heavens, 1961; (with S.E. Toulmin) The Architect of Matter, 1962; (with S.E. Toulmin) The Discovery of Time, 1965; Courier to Peking, 1973; Behvarz: A New Iranian Answer to the Health and Medical Needs of the Millions: The Story of a Challenging Pilot Project in the Tribal Areas of Fars Province, 1974; Cancer under Siege: A Unique Account of the Lives and Ideas of the Scientists Who are Striving to Lessen the Price We Pay for Life, 1975; Growth of Scientific Physiology: Physiological Method and the Mechanist-Vitalist Controversy, Illustrated by the Problems of Respiration and Animal Heat, 1975; The Siege of Cancer, 1975; Playing God: Genetic Engineering and the Manipulation of Life, 1977; Reflections on Science and the Media, 1981; An Imagined World: A Story of Scientific Creativity, 1981; Wissenschaft und Medien, 1983; From the Face of the Earth, 1984; Quest for the Killers, 1985; The Planned Miracle, 1991; A Chance to Live, 1991; Rotten at the Core, 2001. **Address:** The Manor House, Alfriston, Polegate, ES BN26 6SF, England.

GOODHEART, Eugene. American (born United States), b. 1931. **Genres:** Literary Criticism And History, Politics/Government, Social Sciences. **Career:** City College (now City College of the City University of New York), instructor in English, 1955-56, 1957-58; Bard College, instructor, 1958-60, assistant professor, 1960-62; University of Chicago, assistant professor of English, 1962-66; Wesleyan University, visiting assistant professor, 1963; Mount Holyoke College, associate professor of English, 1966-67; Massachusetts Institute of Technology, associate professor, 1967-70, professor, 1970-74, Cambridge humanities seminar, co-director, 1973-82; Boston University, professor of English and chairman of department, 1974-83; Brandeis University, Edytha Macy Gross professor of humanities, through 1983, Brandeis Center for the Humanities, director, 1986-92, department chairman, 1989-94, now Edythe Macy professor of humanities emeritus, professor emeritus of English; National Humanities Center, fellow, 1987. Writer. **Publications:** The Utopian Vision of D.H. Lawrence, 1963, rev. ed., 2006; The Cult of the Ego: The Self in Modern Literature, 1968, rev. ed., 2005; Culture and the Radical Conscience, 1973, rev. ed., 2001; The Failure of Criticism, 1978; The Skeptic Disposition in Contemporary Criticism, 1984; Pieces of Resistance, 1987; Skeptic Disposition: Deconstruction, Ideology, and Other Matters, 1991; Desire and Its Discontents, 1992; The Reign of Ideology, 1997; Does Literary Studies Have a Future, 1999; Modernism and the Critical Spirit, 2000; Confessions of a Secular Jew: A Memoir, 2001, 2nd. ed., 2005; Novel Practices: Classic Modern Fiction, 2004; Darwinian Misadventures in the Humanities, 2007; (ed.) Great Expectations, 2009; (ed.) Ernest Hemingway, 2010; (ed.) Charles Dickens, 2011. **Address:** Department of English, Brandeis University, Rabb 266a, 415 South St., Waltham, MA 02453, U.S.A. **Online address:** goodhear@brandeis.edu

GOODHUE, Thomas W. American (born United States), b. 1949. **Genres:** Children's Non-fiction, Theology/Religion, Biography, History, Autobiography/Memoirs. **Career:** Windward Coalition of Churches, clergy coordinator, 1975-77; United Methodist churches, pastor, 1975-77, 1985-92, 1992-99; Kahaluu, 1977-78; teacher, 1978-85; Long Island Council of Churches, presenter of weekly radio commentary, 1988-91, vice president, 1991-94, president, 1994-97, executive director, 1999-; United Methodist Center of Far Rockaway, vice president, 1985-92; Long Island Interfaith Disaster Response, founder, 2001. Writer. **Publications:** Kaahumanu: Queen of Hawaii, 1985; Stories for the Children of Light, 1986; Sharing the Good News with Children, 1992; Curious Bones: Mary Anning and the Birth of Paleontology, 2002; Fossil Hunter: The Life and Times of Mary Anning, 2004. Contributor of articles to magazines. **Address:** Long Island Council of Churches, 1644 Denton Green, Hempstead, NY 11550, U.S.A. **Online address:** tgoodhue@suffolk.lib.ny.us

GOODING, Mel. British (born England), b. 1941. **Genres:** Art/Art History. **Career:** Sidney Webb College of Education, lecturer in English, 1972-80; London Polytechnic, lecturer in English, 1980-94; Edinburgh College of

Art, senior resident fellow, 1998-2005; Wimbledon School of Art, professor, 2006-. Writer, art critic, consultant and exhibition organiser. **Publications:** (With B. McLean) Ladder, 1986; Michael Upton, Paintings 1977-1987, 1987; F.E. McWilliam: Sculpture, 1932-1989, 1989; Bruce McLean, 1990; A Vertical Balcony: A Real Gazebo, 1990; William Alsop: Buildings and Projects, 1992; (ed.) Surrealist Games, 1993; Alphabets & Other Signs, 1993; The Paradox Box: Optical Illusions, Puzzling Pictures, Verbal Diversions, 1994; John Carter, Norman Dilworth, Michael Kidner, Eric Snell, Gary Woodley: Blick über den Ärmelkanal-via Guernsey, 1994; Patrick Heron, 1994; Mary Fedden, 1995; Book of Surrealist Games: Including the Little Surrealist Dictionary, 1995; National and University Library, Ljubljana: Joze Plecnik, 1997; (intro.) Public-art-space: A Decade of Public Art Commissions Agency, 1987-1997, 1998; Painter as Critic, Patrick Heron: Selected Writings, 1998; Artists, 1999; (ed. with J. Rothenstein) The Playful Eye, 2000; Matériau: couleur: Stéphane Bordarier, Antonio Scaccabarozzi, SeainShanahan, 2000; (with J. Hulme and K. Powell) Alsop: Not Architecture, 2001; Gillian Ayres, 2001; Abstract Art, 2001; Song of the Earth, 2002; (with W. Furlong) Artists, Land, Nature, 2002; Ceri Richards, 2002; (ed. with J. Rothenstein) ABZ: More Alphabets and Other Signs, 2003; (with D. Elliott) Sylvia Edwards, 2003; The Psychobox, 2004; Patrick Hayman: Visionary Artist, 2005; Wihelmina Barnes-Graham, 2005; (with J.D. Goede and C. Lotz) Jules de Goede, 2006; John Hoyland, 2006; (with H. Vries) Herman de Vries, 2006; Prunella Clough: 50 Years of Making Art, 2009; Alan Gouk: Principle, Appearance, Style: A Career Survey, 2009; (intro.) Speaking of Art: Four Decades of Art in Conversation, 2010; (contrib.) Alphabets, 2010; Merlyn Evans, 2010; Frank Bowling, 2011. **Address:** Wimbledon College of Art, Main Bldg., Merton Hall Rd., London, GL SW19 3QA, England. **Online address:** gooding@braque.demon.co.uk

GOODISON, Lorna (Gaye). Jamaican (born Jamaica), b. 1947. **Genres:** Novels, Novellas/Short Stories, Poetry, Young Adult Fiction. **Career:** University of the West Indies, writer-in-residence, 1973; CARIFESTA 76 Magazine, editor, 1976; freelance writer and painter, 1977-; University of Iowa, International Writing Program, fellow, 1983; Radcliffe College, Bunting Institute, fellow, 1986-87; University of Toronto, visiting fellow in women's studies, 1990-91; University of Michigan, visiting professor of English, 1992-93, 1995, professor of creative writing. **Publications:** SELF-ILLUSTRATOR: Tamarind Season, 1980. OTHERS: I Am Becoming My Mother, 1986; Heartease, 1988; Lorna Goodison: Chapbook of Poems, 1989; Baby Mother and the King of Swords, 1990; Selected Poems, 1992; (with E.K. Brathwaite and M. Morris) Three Caribbean Poets on Their Work, 1993; Quartet of Poems, 1994; To Us, All Flowers Are Roses, 1995; The Book of Amber, 1995; Turn Thanks, 1999; Guinea Woman, 2000; Travelling Mercies, 2001; Controlling the Silver: Poems, 2005; Goldengrove, 2006; From Harvey River, 2007; I Come Through, 2009; By Love Possessed, 2011. STORIES: (co-author) Quartet of Stories, 1993; Fool-Fool Rose is Leaving Labour-in-Vain Savannah, 2005. Contributor to periodicals. **Address:** Department of English Language and Literature, University of Michigan, 3232 Angell Hall, 435 S State St., Ann Arbor, MI 48109-1003, U.S.A. **Online address:** goodison@umich.edu

GOODKIN, Richard E. (Richard Elliot Goodkin). American (born United States), b. 1953. **Genres:** Literary Criticism And History, Classics, Language/Linguistics. **Career:** Yale University, assistant professor, 1980-86, associate professor, 1986-89; University of Wisconsin-Madison, associate professor, 1989-92, professor of French, 1992-; Guggenheim Fellow, 2005-06; Institute for Research in the Humanities, senior fellow, 2009-. Writer. **Publications:** The Symbolist Home and the Tragic Home: Mallarme and Oedipus, 1984; Around Proust, 1991; The Tragic Middle: Racine, Aristotle, Euripides, 1991; (trans.) Antoine Campagnon, Proust between Two Centuries, 1992; Birth Marks: The Tragedy of Primogeniture in Pierre Corneille, Thomas Corneille, and Jean Racine, 2000; In Memory of Elaine Marks: Life Writing, Writing Death, 2007. **Address:** Department of French and Italian, University of Wisconsin, 618 Van Hise Hall, 1220 Linden Dr., Madison, WI 53706, U.S.A. **Online address:** rgoodkin@wisc.edu

GOODKIN, Richard Elliot. See **GOODKIN, Richard E.**

GOODKIND, Terry. American (born United States), b. 1948?. **Genres:** Science Fiction/Fantasy, Novels, Young Adult Fiction. **Career:** Novelist. **Publications:** NOVELS. THE SWORD OF TRUTH SERIES: Wizard's First Rule, 1994; Stone of Tears, 1995; Blood of the Fold, 1996; Temple of the Winds, 1997; Soul of the Fire, 1999; Faith of the Fallen, 2000; Debt of Bones, 2001; The Pillars of Creation, 2001; Naked Empire, 2003; Chainfire, 2005; Phantom, 2006; Confessor, 2007; Law of Nines, 2009; The Omen Machine, 2011.

Address: c/o Russell Galen, Scovil Chichak Galen Literary Agency Inc., 276 5th Ave., Ste. 708, New York, NY 10001, U.S.A.

GOODLAD, John I. American/Canadian (born Canada), b. 1920. **Genres:** Education. **Career:** Emory University, associate professor, 1949-50, professor, Division of Teacher Education, director; New Standard Encyclopedia, chairman, 1953-; Progressive Education, contributing editor, 1955-58; University of Chicago, professor and director of center for teacher education, 1956-60; American Council on Education, chairman, 1959-62; University of California, professor of education, 1960-85, University Elementary School, director, 1960-85, Graduate School of Education, dean, 1967-83; National Society of College Teachers of Education, president, 1962-63; Institute for Development of Educational Activities, Research and Development Division, director, 1966-81; American Educational Research Association, president, 1967-68; Journal of Curriculum Studies, editorial consultant, 1967-75; National Foundation for the Improvement of Education, board director, 1970-74; National Academy of Education, secretary and treasurer, 1971-77; National Society for the Study of Education, chairman, 1972-73; Global Perspectives in Education Inc., founding member, 1974-86; Institute for Educational Inquiry, president; Encyclopaedia Britannica Educational Corp., board director, 1984-; International Institute of Arts and Letters, fellow; University of Washington, Center for Educational Renewal, co-founder, professor of education, 1984-, now emeritus; American Association of Colleges for Teacher Education, president, 1989-90. **Publications:** The Elementary School, 1956; Educational Leadership and the Elementary School Principal, 1956; The Nongraded Elementary School, 1959, (with R.H. Anderson) rev. ed., 1963; Planning and Organizing for Teaching, 1963; School Curriculum Reform in the United States, 1964; School, Curriculum, and the Individual, 1966; (with J.F. O'Toole, Jr. and L.L. Tyler) Computers and Information Systems in Education, 1966; (with R. von Stoephasius and M.F. Klein) The Changing School Curriculum, 1966; (with M.N. Richter, Jr.) The Development of a Conceptual System for Dealing with Problems of Curriculum and Instruction, 1966; (co-author) Behind the Classroom Door, 1970, rev. ed. as Looking behind the Classroom Door, 1974; (co-author) Early Schooling in England and Israel, 1973; (co-author) Early Schooling in the United States, 1973; (co-author) Toward a Mankind School, 1974; The Dynamics of Educational Change, 1975; (co-author) The Conventional and the Alternative in Education, 1975; Facing the Future, 1976; What Schools Are For, 1979; (co-author) Curriculum Inquiry, 1979; A Place Called School, 1984, rev. ed., 2004; Teachers for Our Nations Schools, 1990; Educational Renewal: Better Teachers, Better Schools, 1994; In Praise of Education, 1997; Romances with Schools, 2004; Education for Everyone, 2004. EDITOR: The Changing American School, 1966; (with H.G. Shane) The Elementary School in the United States, 1973; Alternatives in Education, 1973; (with G.D. Fenstermacher) Individual Differences and the Common Curriculum, 1983; The Ecology of School Renewal, 1987; (with K.A. Sirotnik) School-University Partnerships in Action, 1988; (with P. Keating) Access to Knowledge, 1990; (with R. Soder and K.A. Sirotnik) The Moral Dimensions of Teaching, 1990; (with R. Soder and K.A. Sirotnik) Places Where Teachers are Taught, 1990; (with T.C. Lovitt) Integrating General and Special Education, 1993; (with T.J. McMannon) The Public Purpose of Education and Schooling, 1997; (with R. Soder and T.J. McMannon) Developing Democratic Character in the Young, 2001; (with T.J. McMannon) The Teaching Career, 2004; (with R. Soder and B. McDaniel) Education and the Making of a Democratic People, 2008. Contributor to periodicals. **Address:** Institute for Educational Inquiry, 117 E Louisa St., Ste. 371, Seattle, WA 98102, U.S.A. **Online address:** paulam@ieiseattle.org

GOODLAND, Katharine. American (born United States), b. 1958. **Genres:** Literary Criticism And History, Theatre, History. **Career:** United States Military Academy, instructor, 1990-; City University of New York, College of Staten Island, associate professor of English and dramatic literature advisor. Writer. **Publications:** NONFICTION: Female Mourning and Tragedy in Medieval and Renaissance English Drama: From the Raising of Lazarus to King Lear, 2006; (with J. O'Connor) A Directory of Shakespeare in Performance, 1970-2005, 2008. Contributor to books and journals. **Address:** Department of English, College of Staten Island, City University of New York, 2800 Victory Blvd., Staten Island, NY 10314-6609, U.S.A. **Online address:** goodland@mail.csi.cuny.edu

GOODMAN, Allegra. American (born United States), b. 1967. **Genres:** Novels, Novellas/Short Stories, Young Adult Fiction. **Career:** Boston University, faculty. Writer. **Publications:** STORIES: Total Immersion: Stories, 1989; The Family Markowitz, 1996. NOVELS: Kaaterskill Falls, 1998; Paradise Park: A Novel, 2001; Intuition, 2006; The Other Side of the Island, 2008; The Cookbook Collector, 2010. Contributor to periodicals. **Address:** c/o Author Mail, Dial Press/Random House, 1745 Broadway, New York, NY 10019, U.S.A. **Online address:** allegra@allegragoodman.com

GOODMAN, Amy. American (born United States), b. 1957. **Genres:** Politics/Government, Sciences, History. **Career:** WBAI (radio station), news director, 1985-; Democracy Now!, founder and executive producer, 1996-. Journalist. **Publications:** (With D. Goodman) The Exception to the Rulers: Exposing Oily Politicians, War Profiteers, and the Media That Love Them, 2004; (with N. Chomsky and P. Farmer) Getting Haiti Right This Time: The U.S. and the Coup, 2004; (with D. Goodman) Static: Government Liars, Media Cheerleaders, and the People Who Fight Back, 2006; (with D. Goodman) Standing Up to the Madness: Ordinary Heroes in Extraordinary Times, 2008; Breaking the Sound Barrier, 2009. **Address:** Democracy Now!, 207 W 25th St., 11th Fl., New York, NY 10001, U.S.A.

GOODMAN, Carol. American (born United States) **Genres:** Novels, Mystery/Crime/Suspense. **Career:** Teachers & Writers, writer-in-residence. Educator. **Publications:** The Lake of Dead Languages, 2002; The Seduction of Water, 2003; The Drowning Tree, 2004; The Ghost Orchid, 2006; The Sonnet Lover, 2007; Night Villa, 2008; Arcadia Falls: A Novel, 2010; Black Swan Rising, 2010. Contributor to periodicals. **Address:** Loretta Barrett Books Inc., 101 Fifth Ave., 11th Fl., New York, NY 10003, U.S.A.

GOODMAN, Ellen (Holtz). American (born United States), b. 1941. **Genres:** Social Commentary, Essays, Young Adult Fiction, Politics/Government. **Career:** Newsweek Magazine, researcher and reporter, 1963-65; Detroit Free Press, feature writer, 1965-67; Boston Globe, feature writer and columnist, 1967-, associate editor, 1986-; Washington Post Writers Group, syndicated columnist, 1976-; Stanford University, Lorry I. Lokey visiting professor in professional journalism, 1996; Harvard's Kennedy School of Government, Shorenstein fellow, 2007. **Publications:** Close to Home, 1979; Turning Points, 1979; At Large, 1981; Keeping in Touch, 1985; Making Sense, 1989; Value Judgments, 1993; (with P. O'Brien) I Know Just What You Mean: The Power of Friendship in Women's Lives, 2000; Paper Trail: Common Sense in Uncommon Times, 2004. **Address:** c/o Boston Globe, PO Box 55819, Boston, MA 02205-5819, U.S.A. **Online address:** ellengoodman1@me.com

GOODMAN, Eric. (Eric K. Goodman). American (born United States), b. 1953. **Genres:** Novels, Plays/Screenplays, Young Adult Fiction. **Career:** Miami University, associate professor of English, professor, director of creative writing external programs. Writer. **Publications:** (As Eric K. Goodman) High on the Energy Bridge (novel), 1980; (as Eric K. Goodman with J.D. Snyder) Friend of the Court, 1947-1982; The Anti-Defamation League of B'nai B'rith: To Secure Justice and Fair Treatment for All (monograph), 1983; (as Eric K. Goodman) The First Time I Saw Jenny Hall (novel), 1983; In Days of Awe (novel), 1991; The Pressure To Be Perfect, 1996; The Fruits of Summer, 2001; Child of My Right Hand, 2004; Sleeper, 2004; A Drastic Step, 2004; Twelfth and Race, 2012; Identity Thief, forthcoming; Blue Ball, forthcoming. Contributor of articles to periodicals. **Address:** Department of English, Miami University, 313 Bachelor Hall, Oxford Campus, Oxford, OH 45056, U.S.A. **Online address:** ekg@erickgoodman.com

GOODMAN, Eric K. See GOODMAN, Eric.

GOODMAN, Hirsh. (Hirsh Benjamin Goodman). Israeli/South African (born South Africa), b. 1946?. **Genres:** Communications/Media, Autobiography/Memoirs. **Career:** Jerusalem Post, reporter to vice president, 1999-2001; Jerusalem Report, founding editor-in-chief, 1990-99; Washington Institution on Near East Policy, strategic fellow; Tel Aviv University, Jaffee Center for Strategic Studies, senior research associate, Andrea and Charles Bronfman Program on Information Strategy, deputy director, 2000-, Institute for National Security Studies, senior research fellow; Sunday Times, correspondent. **Publications:** (With W.S. Carus) The Future Battlefield and the Arab-Israeli Conflict, 1990; (ed. with J. Cummings) The Battle of Jenin: A Case Study in Israel's Communications Strategy, 2003; Let Me Create a Paradise, God Said to Himself: A Journey of Conscience from Johannesburg to Jerusalem (memoir), 2005 as Let Me Create a Paradise: A Journey of Conscience from Johannesburg to Jerusalem, 2005; Anatomy of Israel's Survival, 2011. Contributor to magazines. **Address:** The Institute for National Security Studies, Tel Aviv University, 40 Haim Levanon St., Tel Aviv, 61398, Israel. **Online address:** goodmanh@post.tau.ac.il

GOODMAN, Hirsh Benjamin. See GOODMAN, Hirsh.

GOODMAN, James. American (born United States), b. 1956. **Genres:** History, Novellas/Short Stories, Sociology. **Career:** New York City Commission on Human Rights, assistant director of public relations, 1980-81; Daniel J. Edelman Public Relations Inc., account executive, 1981-82; Harvard University, assistant professor of history and social studies, 1990-; Rutgers University, Department of History, professor, 1997-, department chair, 1999-2002. Writer. **Publications:** Stories of Scottsboro, 1994; Blackout, 2003; I Wrote the Story of Abraham and Isaac, forthcoming. Contributor of articles to periodicals. **Address:** Department of History, Rutgers University, 307 Conklin Hall, 175 University Ave., Newark, NJ 07102-1801, U.S.A. **Online address:** goodmanj@andromeda.rutgers.edu

GOODMAN, Jesse. (Jesse H. Goodman). American (born United States), b. 1948?. **Genres:** Education, History. **Career:** Indiana University, assistant professor, 1982-90, associate professor, 1990-97, professor, 1997-, Harmony Education Center, co-director, 1990-, Curriculum Studies Program, chair, 1991-97, Elementary Certification Graduate Program, co-director, 1993-. Writer. **Publications:** (with J. Kuzmic and X. Wu) Elementary Schooling for Critical Democracy, 1992; Reforming Schools: Working within a Progressive Tradition during Conservative Times, 2006. Contributor to books and periodicals. **Address:** Indiana University, 3208 Education Bldg., Bloomington, IN 47405, U.S.A. **Online address:** goodmanj@indiana.edu

GOODMAN, Jesse H. See GOODMAN, Jesse.

GOODMAN, Jo. American (born United States), b. 1953?. **Genres:** Romance/Historical, Novels. **Career:** Writer. **Publications:** ROMANCE NOVELS: Velvet Night, 1987; Midnight Princess, 1989; Passion's Sweet Revenge, 1990; (ed. with T. Gascoigne and M. Tyrrell) Dream Time: New Stories by Sixteen Award-winning Authors (anthology), 1991; Seaswept Abandon, 2000; (with H. Howell and L. Madl) Magically Delicious Kisses (omnibus), 2002; The Price of Desire, 2008; Never Love a Lawman, 2009. McCLELLAN FAMILY SERIES: Crystal Passion, 1985; Seaswept Abandon, 1986; Tempting Torment, 1989. DENNEHY SISTERS SERIES: Wild Sweet Ecstasy, 1992 as More than a Touch, 1996; Rogue's Mistress, 1993; Forever in My Heart, 1994; Always in My Dreams, 1995; Only in My Arms, 1999. THORNE BROTHERS SERIES: My Steadfast Heart, 2000; My Reckless Heart, 2001; With All My Heart, 2001. HAMILTON FAMILY SERIES: More than You Know, 2000; More than You Wished, 2001. COMPASS CLUB SERIES: Let Me Be the One, 2002; All I Ever Needed, 2003; Everything I Ever Wanted, 2003; Beyond a Wicked Kiss, 2004. GRANTHAM SERIES: Season to Be Sinful, 2005; One Forbidden Evening, 2006; If His Kiss Is Wicked, 2007. **Address:** U.S.A. **Online address:** jdobrzan@gmail.com

GOODMAN, Joanna. Canadian (born Canada), b. 1969?. **Genres:** Novels. **Career:** Toronto linen store, owner. writer, 1998-. **Publications:** Belle of the Bayou, 1998; You Made Me Love You, 2006; Harmony: A Novel, 2007. Contributor of stories to periodicals. **Address:** Beverley Slopen Literary Agency, 131 Bloor St. W, Ste. 711, Toronto, ON M5S 1S3, Canada. **Online address:** beverley@slopeagency.ca

GOODMAN, Jordan E. American (born United States), b. 1954. **Genres:** Business/Trade/Industry, Money/Finance, Economics, How-to Books. **Career:** Money, Wall Street correspondent, 1979-97; MoneyAnswers.com, affiliate program director. Writer and speaker. **Publications:** Barron's Dictionary of Finance and Investment Terms, 1985, 8th ed., 2010; Barron's Finance and Investment Handbook, 1987, 8th ed., 2010; Barron's Dictionary of Business Terms, 1990, 2nd ed., 1995; (co-author) Everyone's Money Book, 1993, 4th ed., 2001; (with J. White and J. Downes) Canadian Dictionary of Finance and Investment Terms, 1995, 2nd ed., 2000; Everyone's Money Book on Stock, Bonds and Mutual Funds, 2002; Everyone's Money Book on Retirement Planning, 2002; Everyone's Money Book on Financial Planning, 2002; Everyone's Money Book on Credit, 2002; Everyone's Money Book on College, 2002; Everyone's Money Book on Real Estate, 2002; Reading between the Lies: How to Detect Fraud and Avoid Becoming a Victim of Wall Street's Next Scandal, 2003; Master Your Money Type: Using Your Financial Personality to Create a Life of Wealth and Freedom, 2006; Fast Profits in Hard Times: 10 Secret Strategies to Make You Rich in an Up or Down

Economy, 2008; (with B. Westrom) Master your Debt: Slash Your Monthly Payments and Become Debt Free, 2010. **Address:** Amherst Enterprises Ltd., 84 Walworth Ave., Scarsdale, NY 10583-1139, U.S.A. **Online address:** jordgood@gmail.com

GOODMAN, Lizbeth (L.). British/American (born United States), b. 1964. **Genres:** Plays/Screenplays, Literary Criticism And History, Women's Studies And Issues, Photography, Humanities. **Career:** Better Half Women's Theatre Cooperative, producer, director and playwright, 1987-89; Footlights Women's Co., artistic director and executive producer, 1989-90; Open University, lecturer in literature, 1990-98, Gender in Writing and Performance Research Group, chairperson, 1992-, Shakespeare Multimedia Research Group, chair, 1995-; Agreeable Productions, artistic director and producer, 1992-93; University of British Columbia, Centre for Women's Studies and Gender Relations, visiting fellow, 1995; University of Surrey, Institute for New Media Performance Research, founder, director, 1998-; Banff Center for New Media and the Arts, visiting senior artist, 2000-02; University of East London, professor of digital media, director of studies, Central Saint Martins College of Art and Design, SMARTlab Centre, director, 2001-05, Creative Technology Innovation, director, 2005, SMARTlab Digital Media Institute and Magic Gamelab, founder and director; Too Creative Productions, associate producer; SPIRITLEVEL consortium, head; BBC, researcher, writer and presenter of learning and Arts/Media programmes; SMARTshell Project, principal investigator. **Publications:** Contemporary Feminist Theatres: To Each Her Own, 1993; Sexuality in Performance: Replaying Theatre and Culture, 1999; Presence: On being, Where You are, When You are Not, 2008; Emergenc(i)es: Practice-based Research in Media Arts, 2008; (co-author) Club-teching: Accessible Technologies for Developing Cultures, 2008. EDITOR: (and contrib.) Imagining Women: Cultural Representations and Gender, 1992; Literature and Gender, 1996; (and intro.) Feminist Stages: Interviews with Women in Contemporary British Theater, 1996; (and contrib.) Shakespeare, Aphra Behn and the Canon, 1996; (with J. de Gay) The Routledge Reader in Gender and Performance, 1998; (and intro.) Gender, Politics and Performance in South African Theatre Today, 3 vols., 1999; Women, Politics, and Performance in South African Theatre Today, 1999; (with J. de Gay) The Routledge Reader in Politics and Performance, 2000; (and intro.) Mythic Women, Real Women: Plays and Performance Pieces by Women, 2000; (with J. de Gay) Women's Comedy: Cross-Cultural Perspectives on Gender and Humour, 2000; (co-author) Voice of Theatre Shaped by Women, 2002; (with J. de Gay) Languages of Theatre Shaped by Women, 2003; (with K. Milton) A Guide to Good Practice in New Media Content and Tools Creation, 2005. Contributor to journals. Works appear in anthologies. **Address:** SMARTlab Digital Media Institute, University of East London, LD 3216, 4-6 University Way, Docklands Campus, London, GL E16 2RD, England. **Online address:** lizbeth@uel.ac.uk

GOODMAN, Louis W. (Louis Wolf Goodman). American (born United States), b. 1942. **Genres:** Sociology, International Relations/Current Affairs. **Career:** Latin American School of Sociology, faculty, 1967-68; Northwestern University, Department of Sociology, lecturer, 1969; Yale University, assistant professor of sociology, 1969-73, lecturer, 1978-81; Social Science Research Council, staff associate, 1974-78, Program on Latin America and the Caribbean, director; Princeton University, visiting lecturer, 1976; Woodrow Wilson Center, director, 1981-86, acting program secretary and senior program associate; American University, School of International Service, dean and professor of international relations, 1986-, affiliate professor of sociology, now dean emeritus; Association of Professional Schools of International Affairs, president, 1992. Writer. **Publications:** (With S.M. Davis) Workers and Managers in Latin America, 1972; The Structure of Human Society, 1975; (with R. Stevens and S.S. Mick) The Alien Doctors: Foreign Medical Graduates in American Hospitals, 1978; Small Nations, Giant Firms, 1987; International Relations Education at the Eve of the 21st Century, 1996. EDITOR: (with R.F. Winch) Selected Studies in Marriage and the Family, 1968; (with D.E. Apter) Multinational Corporation and Social Change, 1976; (with J.S.R. Mendelson and J. Rial) The Military and Democracy: The Future of Civil-Military Relations in Latin America, 1990; (with W.M. LeoGrande and J.M. Forman) Political Parties and Democracy in Central America, 1992; (co-ed.) Lessons from the Venezuelan Experience, 1995. **Address:** School of International Service, American University, Rm. 100, 4400 Massachusetts Ave. NW, Washington, DC 20016-8071, U.S.A. **Online address:** goodman@american.edu

GOODMAN, Louis Wolf. See **GOODMAN, Louis W.**

GOODMAN, Martin (David). British (born England), b. 1953. **Genres:** History. **Career:** Oxford Centre for Postgraduate Hebrew Studies, Kaye, Jr., research fellow, 1976-77; Birmingham University, lecturer in ancient history, 1977-86; Oxford Centre for Hebrew and Jewish Studies, fellow, 1986-91, governor, acting president, 1995-96, 1999-2000; Oxford University, St. Cross College, senior research fellow, 1986-91, lecturer in Roman history, 1988-, Wolfson College, fellow, 1991-, university reader in Jewish studies, 1991-96, professor of Jewish studies, 1996-; Journal of Roman Studies, editorial reviewer, 1993-98, editor, 1999-2003; Hebrew University of Jerusalem, Institute for Advanced Studies, fellow, 1993; British Association for Jewish Studies, president, 1995; Journal of Jewish Studies, joint editor, 1995-99; British Academy, fellow, 1996; European Association of Jewish Studies, secretary. **Publications:** State and Society in Roman Galilee, A.D. 132-212, 1983; The Ruling Class of Judaea: The Origins of the Jewish Revolt against Rome, A.D. 66-70, 1987; Who was a Jew?, 1989; (ed. with G. Vermes) The Essenes: According to the Classical Sources, 1989; Mission and Conversion: Proselytizing in the Religious History of the Roman Empire, 1994; (with J. Sherwood) The Roman World, 44 B.C.-A.D. 180, 1997; (ed.) Jews in a Graeco-Roman World, 1998; In Search of the Divine Mother: The Mystery of Mother Meera: Encountering a Contemporary Mystic, 1998; (ed. with M.J. Edwards and S.R.F. Price) Apologetics in the Roman Empire: Pagans, Jews and Christians, 1999; The Oxford Handbook of Jewish Studies, 2002; Rome and Jerusalem: The Clash of Ancient Civilizations, 2007; Judaism in the Roman World: Collected Essays, 2007; (ed. with P. Alexander) Rabbinic Texts and the History of Late-Roman Palestine, 2010. Contributor to periodicals. **Address:** Oriental Institute, Wolfson College, University of Oxford, Pusey Ln., Oxford, OX OX1 2LE, England. **Online address:** martin.goodman@orinst.ox.ac.uk

GOODMAN, Matthew Aaron. American (born United States), b. 1975. **Genres:** Novels. **Career:** Exalt, literacy program leader; Leadership Alliance, founder, 2007; New York City Public School System, teacher. Writer. **Publications:** Hold Love Strong (novel), 2009. **Address:** Simon & Schuster Inc., 1230 Ave. of the Americas, New York, NY 10020, U.S.A. **Online address:** matthewagoodman@gmail.com

GOODMAN, Melvin A. American (born United States), b. 1938. **Genres:** International Relations/Current Affairs, Third World, Politics/Government. **Career:** Central Intelligence Agency (CIA), soviet analyst, 1966-86; National War College, professor of national security, 1986-, professor of international security studies, Center for International Policy, senior fellow. Writer. **Publications:** Gorbachev and Soviet policy in the Third World, 1990; Gorbachev's Retreat: The Third World, 1991; The End of Superpower Conflict in the Third World, 1992; (with C.M. Ekedhal) Shevardnadze and the End of the Cold War, 1997; (with C.M. Ekedahl) Wars of Eduard Shevardnadze, 1997; Lessons of the Cold War, 1999; (with C. Eisendrath and G.E. Marsh) Phantom Defense: America's Pursuit of the Star Wars Illusion, 2001; (with C.R. Eisendrath) Bush League Diplomacy: How the Neoconservatives are Putting the World at Risk, 2004; Failure of Intelligence: The Decline and Fall of the CIA, 2008. Contributor to periodicals. **Address:** Department of International Security, National War College, 300 D St. SW, Fort Lesley J. McNair, Washington, DC 20319, U.S.A. **Online address:** goodmanm@ndu.edu

GOODMAN, Richard. American (born United States), b. 1945. **Genres:** Autobiography/Memoirs, Essays, Adult Non-fiction, Travel/Exploration, Horticulture, Writing/Journalism, Homes/Gardens, Reference, Reference, Humanities, Humor/Satire. **Career:** Spalding University's, MFA in writing program, faculty, 2003-. Writer. **Publications:** French Dirt: The Story of a Garden in the South of France, 1991, 2nd ed., 2002; The Soul of Creative Writing, 2008; A New York Memoir, 2010; The Bicycle Diaries: One New Yorker's Journey Through September 11th, 2011. **Address:** 183 Pinehurst Ave., Apt. 26, New York, NY 10033-1846, U.S.A. **Online address:** richgood711@earthlink.net

GOODMAN, Susan. American (born United States), b. 1951. **Genres:** History, Literary Criticism And History, Women's Studies And Issues. **Career:** Public school teacher, 1972-83; California State University, assistant professor, 1989-92, associate professor, 1992-94; University of Delaware, Department of English, assistant professor, 1994-96, associate professor, 1996-98, professor, 1998-, H. Fletcher Brown chair of humanities; University of New England, Dorothy M. Healy visiting professor, 2000. Writer. **Publications:** Gertrude Bell, 1985; Edith Wharton's Women: Friends & Rivals, 1990; Edith Wharton's Inner Circle, 1994; (ed. with D.Ryot) Femmes de Conscience: Aspects du Feminisme Americain, 1848-1875, 1994; Ellen Glasgow: A Biography, 1998; (ed. with C. Colquitt and C. Waid) Edith Wharton: A Forward

Glance: New Essays On Edith Wharton, 1999; (intro.) The Battle-Ground, 2000; Civil Wars: American Novelists and Manners, 1880-1940, 2003; (with C. Dawson) William Dean Howells: A Writer's Life, 2005; (with C. Dawson) Mary Austin and the American West, 2008; Republic of Words, 2011. Contributor to periodicals. **Address:** Department of English, University of Delaware, 133 Memorial Hall, Newark, DE 19716, U.S.A. **Online address:** sgoodman@udel.edu

GOODMAN, Susan E. American (born United States), b. 1952?. **Genres:** Novels, Animals/Pets, Archaeology/Antiquities, Young Adult Fiction. **Career:** Lesley University, professor; General Learning Corp., contributing editor. **Publications:** Amazing Biofacts: The Human Body, Animals, Plants, 1983; Amazing Spacefacts: Solar System-stars-space Travel, 1983; Bats, Bugs and Biodiversity: Adventures in the Amazonian Rain Forest, 1995; Unseen Rainbows, Silent Songs: The World beyond Human Senses, 1995; The Great Antler Auction, 1996; Stones, Bones and Petroglyphs: Digging into Southwest Archaeology: An Ultimate Field Trip, 1998; Pilgrims of Plymouth, 1999; Ultimate Field Trip 3: Wading into Marine Biology, 1999; Ultimate Field Trip 4: A Week in the 1800s, 2000; Animal Rescue: The Best Job There is, 2000; Chopsticks for My Noodle Soup: Eliza's Life in Malaysia, 2000; Ultimate Field Trip 5: Blasting off to Space Academy, 2001; Seeds, Stems and Stamens: The Ways Plants Fit into Their World, 2001; Claws, Coats and Camouflage: The Ways Animals Fit into Their World, 2001; What Do You Do-at the Zoo?, 2002; What Do You Do On A Farm?, 2002; Cora Frear: A True Story, 2002; Nature Did It First!, 2003; Brave Kids: True Stories from America's Past: Robert Henry Hendershot, 2003; Choppers!, 2004; On this Spot: An Expedition Back Through Time, 2004; The Truth About Poop, 2004; Skyscraper: From The Ground Up, 2004; Hazelle Boxberg, 2004; All in Just One Cookie, 2006; India in the Past and Present, 2006; Life on the Ice, 2006; Saber-Toothed Cats, 2006; Gee Whiz! it's ALL About Pee, 2006; Women Work for Change, 2006; Motorcycles!, 2007; See How They Run: Campaign Dreams, Election Schemes and the Race to the White House, 2008; Saving the Whooping Crane, 2008; Monster Trucks!, 2010; It's a Dog's Life, 2012; How do You Burp in Space?, 2012; Trains!, 2012. **Address:** 5 Oakview Terr., Boston, MA 02130, U.S.A. **Online address:** sugoodman@aol.com

GOODRICH, Amanda Jane. British (born England), b. 1957. **Genres:** Politics/Government, History, Philosophy. **Career:** University of London, Royal Holloway, Department of History, teaching associate; Open University, Department of History, associate lecturer, 2009-. Writer. **Publications:** Debating England's Aristocracy in the 1790s: Pamphlets, Polemics, and Political Ideas, 2005. Contributor to journals. **Address:** Royal Holloway, University of London, Egham, TW20 0EX, England. **Online address:** amanda.goodrich@rhul.ac.uk

GOODSON, Larry P. American (born United States) **Genres:** Area Studies, Politics/Government, International Relations/Current Affairs, History, Military/Defense/Arms Control. **Career:** Bentley College, associate professor of international studies, 2001; U.S. Army War College, Department of National Security and Strategy, director and associate professor of Middle East studies, 2002-, professor of Middle East studies, General Dwight D. Eisenhower chair of national security; Harvard University, Center for Middle East Studies, research affiliate. Writer. **Publications:** Afghanistan's Endless War: State Failure, Regional Politics, and the Rise of the Taliban, 2001; The Talibanization of Pakistan, 2002; Middle East Politics, 2005. Contributor of articles to periodicals. **Address:** Department of National Security & Strategy, U.S. Army War College, 122 Forbes Ave., Carlisle, PA 17013-5234, U.S.A. **Online address:** larry.goodson@us.army.mil

GOODSTEIN, Judith R. American (born United States), b. 1939. **Genres:** Novels. **Career:** California Institute of Technology, institute archivist, 1968-95, faculty associate, 1982-, lecturer, 1989, 2001, 2002, registrar, 1989-2003, university archivist, 1995-, now university archivist emeritus. Writer. **Publications:** (With A. Stone) Caltechs Throop Hall, 1981; (ed. with C. Kopp) The Theodore von Kármán Collection at the California Institute of Technology: Guide to the Original Collection and a Microfiche Edition, 1981; (ed. with C.H. Bugé) The Frank J. Malina Collection at the California Institute of Technology: Guide to a Microfiche Edition, 1986; Millikan's School: A History of the California Institute of Technology, 1991; (with D.L. Goodstein) Feynman's Lost Lecture: The Motion of Planets around the Sun, 1996; The Volterra Chronicles: The Life and Times of an Extraordinary Mathema-

tician, 1860-1940, 2007. **Address:** California Institute of Technology, 1200 E California Blvd., PO Box 015A-74, Pasadena, CA 91125, U.S.A. **Online address:** jrg@caltech.edu

GOODSTEIN, Phil. American (born United States), b. 1952. **Genres:** Area Studies, Adult Non-fiction, Novels, History. **Career:** University in Denver, professor; Colorado University, professor; Colorado Free University, tour guide; Naysayer, monthly newsletter editor; New Social Publications, staff. **Publications:** Theory of the General Strike from the French Revolution to Poland, 1984; Denver's Capitol Hill: One Hundred Years of Life in a Vibrant Urban Neighborhood, 1988; South Denver Saga, 1991; Exploring Jewish Colorado, 1992; The Seamy Side of Denver: Tall Tales of the Mile High City, 1993; Denver Streets: Names, Numbers, Locations, Logic, 1994; The Ghosts of Denver: Capitol Hill, 1996; Murders in the Bank Vault: The Father's Day Massacre and the Trial of James King, 1998; Denver in Our Time, vol. I: A People's History of the Modern Mile High City, 1999, vol. II: DIA and Other Scams: A People's History of the Modern Mile High City, 2000; Denver from the Bottom Up, vol. I: From Sand Creek to Ludlow, 2003, vol. II: Robert Speer's Denver, 1904-1920, 2004; Depression Denver: The Mile High City from the Klan to World War II, 2007; The History of South Denver, vol. I: The Spirits of South Broadway, 2008, vol. II: Haunts of Washington Park, 2009; North Side Story: Denver's Most Intriguing Neighborhood, 2011. Contributor to periodicals. **Address:** New Social Publications, PO Box 18026, Denver, CO 80218, U.S.A.

GOODWEATHER, Hartley. *See* KING, Thomas.

GOODWILL, Susan. American (born United States), b. 1957?. **Genres:** Mystery/Crime/Suspense. **Career:** Writer. **Publications:** Brigadoom: A Kate London Mystery, 2007; Little Shop of Murders: A Kate London Mystery, 2008. **Address:** U.S.A. **Online address:** susan@susangoodwill.com

GOODWIN, Doris (Helen) Kearns. (Doris Kearns). American (born United States), b. 1943. **Genres:** Novels, History, Autobiography/Memoirs, Biography, Social Sciences. **Career:** U.S. Government, Department of State, intern, 1963-, House of Representatives, intern, 1965, Department of Health, Education and Welfare, special assistant, 1966, Department of Labor, special assistant to Willard Wirtz, 1967; special assistant to President Lyndon B. Johnson, 1968; special consultant to President Johnson, 1969-73; Harvard University, assistant provost, 1969-71, associate provost, 1972, Institute of Politics, assistant director, 1971-; Northwest Airlines, board director, 1997-. Writer. **Publications:** (As Doris Kearns) Lyndon Johnson and the American Dream, 1976; (intro.) The Johnson Presidential Press Conferences, 1978; The Fitzgeralds and the Kennedys: An American Saga, 1987; Mortal Friends: A Novel, 1992; No Ordinary Time: Franklin and Eleanor Roosevelt-The Homefront in World War II, 1994; Wait till Next Year: A Memoir, 1997; Team of Rivals: The Political Genius of Abraham Lincoln, 2005. Contributor to books. **Address:** c/o Julia Prosser, Simon & Schuster Inc., 1230 Ave. of the Americas, New York, NY 10020, U.S.A.

GOODWIN, Frederick K(ing). American (born United States), b. 1936. **Genres:** Medicine/Health, Psychology. **Career:** National Heart Institute, fellow, 1967-68; State University of New York, Upstate Medical Center, intern in medicine and psychiatry, 1963-64; University of North Carolina, resident in psychiatry, 1964-65; National Institute of Mental Health, Adult Psychiatry Branch, clinical associate, 1965-67, Laboratory of Clinical Science, chief of clinical research unit, 1968-73, chief of section of psychiatry, 1973-77, Clinical Psychobiology Branch, chief, 1977-81, Intramural Research Program, director, 1982-88, National Depression Awareness, Recognition and Treatment Program, scientific director, 1985, director, 1992-94, senior scientific adviser to the director, 1994-97; Washington School of Psychiatry, fellow, 1969-71; George Washington University, adjunct professor, 1972-82, research professor of psychiatry, 1994-2008, Center on Neuroscience, Behavior and Society, director, 1994-, Psychopharmacology Research Center, director, 1997-, clinical professor of psychiatry, 2008-, professor of psychiatry; Uniformed Services University of the Health Sciences, adjunct professor, 1980-; Alcohol, Drug Abuse and Mental Health Administration, administrator, 1988-92; Best Practice L.L.C, principal. Writer. **Publications:** (Ed. with T.A. Wehr) Circadian Rhythms in Psychiatry, 1983; (ed. with D.Nerozzi, E. Costa) Hypothalamic Dysfunction in Neuropsychiatric Disorders, 1987; (ed. with T.P. Bridge, A.F. Mirsky) Psychological, neuropsychiatric, and Substance Abuse Aspects of AIDS, 1988; (with K.R. Jamison) Manic-Depressive Illness, 1990, 2nd ed., 2007; (ed. with A.Marneros) Bipolar Disorders: Mixed States, Rapid

Cycling and Atypical Forms, 2005, 2nd ed., 2007. Contributor to journals. **Address:** Department of Psychiatry, Center on Neurosciencey, George Washington University Medical Ctr., 5712 Warwick Pl., Bethesda, MD 20815, U.S.A. **Online address:** fred@drgoodwin.com

GOODWIN, Jan. American/British (born England) **Genres:** Documentaries/Reportage, Women's Studies And Issues. **Career:** Women's Realm, diary and features editor; London News Service, news editor; New York Times Magazine Development Co., Us Magazine, executive editor; Ladies' Home Journal, executive editor, 1978-88; Save the Children Federation, program manager, 1988-91; BBC Radio, reporter; On The Issues, editor-in-chief. **Publications:** Caught in the Crossfire (nonfiction), 1987; Price of Honor: Muslim Women Lift the Veil of Silence on the Islamic World, 1994, rev. ed., 2003. Contributor to periodicals. **Address:** New York, NY , U.S.A. **Online address:** jgoodwin@pipeline.com

GOODWIN, Joanne L. American (born United States), b. 1949. **Genres:** History. **Career:** University of Michigan, lecturer, 1989-90; University of Nevada, assistant professor of history, 1991-97, associate professor of history, 1997-, Women's Research Institute of Nevada, executive director, 1999-. Writer. **Publications:** Gender and the Politics of Welfare Reform: Mothers' Pensions in Chicago, 1911-1929, 1997; (co-ed.) Women in American History, 1585-present, 2002; In Her Own Words, forthcoming. Contributor of articles to journals. **Address:** Department of History, University of Nevada, 4505 Maryland Pkwy., PO Box 455020, Las Vegas, NV 89154-5020, U.S.A. **Online address:** jgoodwin@unlv.nevada.edu

GOODWIN, Ken(neth Leslie). Australian (born Australia), b. 1934. **Genres:** Literary Criticism And History, History, Poetry. **Career:** Teachers' College, lecturer in English, 1958; University of Queensland, lecturer, 1959-61, 1962-67, senior lecturer, 1967-69, reader, 1970-71, professor of English, 1971-92, head of English department, 1974-79; University of California, visiting lecturer, 1967; Assessors for Canada-Australia Literary Award, chairman, 1982; Queensland Art Gallery, trustee, 1983-94; University of Southern Queensland, deputy vice-chancellor, 1992-98, now professor emeritus; Southern Queensland Theology Library, president, 1996-98; University of Sydney, honorary professor, 1999-. Writer. **Publications:** The Influence of Ezra Pound, 1966; An Approach to Modern Poetry, 1968; Understanding African Poetry: A Study of Ten Poets, 1982; Selected Poems of Bruce Dawe, 1984; A Preliminary Hand list of Manuscripts and Documents of William Morris, 1984; A History of Australian Literature, 1986; Adjacent Worlds: A Literary Life of Bruce Dawe, 1988. EDITOR: National Identity: Papers Delivered at the Commonwealth Literature Conference, 1970; Commonwealth Literature in the Curriculum, 1980; (with M.Freer) A Common Wealth of Words, 1982; (with A. Lawson) The Macmillan Anthology of Australian Literature, 1990; Bruce Dawe: Essays and Opinions, 1990; (with W. Zach) Nationalism vs. Internationalism: (Inter) National Dimensions of Literatures in English, 1996. **Address:** 2 Stewart Cres., Armidale, NW 2350, Australia. **Online address:** ken_ness.goodwin@bigpond.com

GOODWIN, Michael. American (born United States), b. 1949. **Genres:** Biography, Economics. **Career:** New York Times, clerk, 1972-77, reporter, 1978-88, City Hall bureau chief; Columbia University, Graduate School of Journalism, faculty, adjunct professor; New York Daily News, executive editor, editorial page editor and political columnist, 2004-; New York Post, chief political columnist. **Publications:** (With A. Browne and D. Collins) I, Koch: A Decidedly Unauthorized Biography of the Mayor of New York City, Edward I. Koch, 1985; (with N. Wise) On the Edge: The Life and Times of Francis Coppola, Morrow, 1989; (ed.) New York Comes Back: The Mayoralty of Edward I. Koch, 2005. **Address:** New York Daily News, 450 W 33 St., New York, NY 10001, U.S.A. **Online address:** mgoodwin@nydailynews.com

GOODWIN, Neil. American (born United States), b. 1940. **Genres:** Adult Non-fiction. **Career:** Stephenson Gibney and Associates, architect; Yale Literary Magazine, chairman, 1962; F.A. Stahl and Associates, architect, 1964-72; Peace River Films, president and filmmaker, 1972-. Writer. **Publications:** (Ed. with J. Harned) Art and the craftsman; the best of the Yale literary magazine, 1836-1961, 1961; (with G. Goodwin) The Apache Diaries: A Father-Son Journey, 1999; Like a Brother: Grenville Goodwin's Apache Years, 1928-1939, 2004; We Go as Captives: The Royalton Raid and the Shadow War on the Revolutionary Frontier, 2010. **Address:** Peace River Films Inc., 240 Concord Ave., Cambridge, MA 02138, U.S.A. **Online address:** goodwin@prfi.com

GOODWIN, Robert Theodore Chorley. British (born England), b. 1969. **Genres:** Biography. **Career:** University College, visiting research fellow, research fellow, honorary research associate. Writer. **Publications:** Crossing the Continent, 1527-1540: The Story of the First African American Explorer of the American South, 2008. **Address:** Department of Spanish and Latin American Studies, School of European Languages, Culture and Society, University College London, Gower St., London, GL WC1E 6BT, England.

GOODY, Jack. *See* **GOODY, John R(ankine).**

GOODY, John R(ankine). (Jack Goody). British (born England), b. 1919. **Genres:** Anthropology/Ethnology, History, Social Sciences, Theology/Religion, Sociology, Humanities. **Career:** Cambridge University, St. John's College, assistant lecturer, 1954-59, lecturer, 1959-71, fellow, 1960-, director of the African studies centre, 1966-73, Smuts Reader in Commonwealth Studies, 1972, William Wyse Professor of Social Anthropology, 1973-84, now William Wyse Emeritus Professor of Social Anthropology. Writer. **Publications:** The Social Organisation of the Lo Wiili, 1956, 2nd ed., 1967; Death, Property and the Ancestors: A Study of The Mortuary Customs of The Lo Dagaa of West Africa, 1962; (with J.A. Braimah) Salaga: The Struggle for Power, 1968; Comparative Studies in Kinship, 1969; Technology, Tradition and the State in Africa, 1971; Domestic Groups, 1972; The Myth of the Bagre, 1972; (with S.J. Tambiah) Bride Wealth and Dowry, 1973; (with N.O. Addo) Siblings in Ghana, 1976; Production and Reproduction: A Comparative Study of The Domestic Domain, 1976; Production and Reproduction, 1977; The Domestication of the Savage Mind, 1977; (with J.W.D.K. Gandah) Une Recitation du Bagre, 1981; Cooking, Cuisine and Class: A Study in Comparative Sociology, 1982; The Development of the Family and Marriage in Europe, 1983; La logique deléscriture: Aux Origines DesSociétés Humaines, 1986; The Logic of Writing and the Organization of Society, 1986; The Interface between the Oral and the Written, 1987; The Oriental, the Ancient and the Primitive, 1989; The Oriental, the Ancient and the Primitive: Systems Of Marriage and the Family In The Pre-Industrial Societies of Eurasia, 1990; The Culture of Flowers, 1993; The Expansive Moment: The Rise of Social Anthropology in Britain and Africa, 1918-1970, 1995; The East in the West, 1996; Jack Goody: L'Homme, l'ecriture et la mort, 1996; Representations and Contradictions: Ambivalence Towards Images, Theater, Fiction, Relics And Sexuality, 1997; Food and Love, 1998; The European Family: An Historico-Anthropological Essay, 2000; The Power of The Written Tradition, 2000; Institutional and Cultural Variables In Africa's Population Growth, 2000; (with S.W.D.K. Gandah) The Third Bagre, 2002; Islam in Europe, 2004; Capitalism and Modernity: The Great Debate, 2004; Ideas in Europe, 2004; The Theft Of History, 2006; Ghana Observed, Africa Reconsidered, 2007; Renaissances: The One or the Many?, 2010; Eurasian Miracle, 2010; Myth, Ritual and the Oral, 2010. EDITOR: The Developmental Cycle in Domestic Groups, 1958; Succession to High Office, 1966; Literacy in Traditional Societies, 1968; Kinship: Selected Readings, 1971; The Developmental Cycle in Domestic Groups, 1971; The Character of Kinship, 1973; Changing Social Structure in Ghana: Essays In The Comparative Sociology of A New State and An Old Tradition, 1975; Family and Inheritance: Rural Society in Western Europe, 1200-1800, 1976; (intro.) Religion, Morality and the Person: Essays on Tallensi Religion, 1987; (with E. Marx) The Bedouin of Cyrenaica: Studies in Personal And Corporate Power, 1990. **Address:** St. John's College, Cambridge University, Cambridge, CB CB2 1TP, England. **Online address:** jrg1@hermes.cam.ac.uk

GOODY-JONES *See* **Janko, (Kathleen) Susan.**

GOOLEY, Dana. American (born United States), b. 1969. **Genres:** Music, History. **Career:** Harvard University, lecturer, 2000, visiting assistant professor of music, 2000; Amherst College, Valentine visiting assistant professor of music, 2000-03; Case Western Reserve University, assistant professor of music, 2003-06; Brown University, assistant professor of music, 2006-07, Manning assistant professor of music, 2007-, associate professor of music, 2010-. Jazz pianist and writer. **Publications:** The Virtuoso Liszt, 2004; (ed. with C.H. Gibbs) Franz Liszt and His World, 2006; (ed. with N. Dufetel, M. Haine and J. Kregor) Franz Liszt, Musicien Europeen: Art, Culture, Politique, 2012. Contributor to periodicals. **Address:** Department of Music, Brown University, Orwig Music Bldg., 1 Young Orchard Ave., PO Box 1924, Providence, RI 02912-9045, U.S.A. **Online address:** gooley@brown.edu

GOONAN, Kathleen Ann. American (born United States), b. 1952. **Genres:** Young Adult Fiction, Novels. **Career:** Writer, 1990-; Georgia Institute of Technology, School of Literature, Communication and Culture, faculty, visiting professor, 2010-11. **Publications:** Queen City Jazz, 1994; The Bones of Time, 1996; Mississippi Blues, 1997; Crescent City Rhapsody, 2000; Light Music, 2002; In War Times, 2007; (ed. with D.G. Hartwell) Year's Best SF 14, 2009; This Shared Dream, 2011; String, 2011. **Address:** c/o Martha Millard, Martha Millard Literary Agency, 50 W 67th St., Ste. 1G, New York, NY 10023, U.S.A. **Online address:** kathleen.goonan@sff.net

GOONETILLEKE, D. C. R. A. Sri Lankan (born Sri Lanka), b. 1938. **Genres:** Literary Criticism And History, Novellas/Short Stories, History, Language/Linguistics, Education. **Career:** University of Ceylon, assistant lecturer in English, 1961-62; Vidyodaya University, assistant lecturer in English, 1962-66; University of Kelaniya, lecturer in English, 1970-74, senior lecturer, 1974-79, head of department, 1978-87, 1989-95, 2002-04, associate professor, 1979-80, professor of English, 1980-90, senior professor of English, 1990-2004, professor emeritus, 2005-; Cambridge University, Churchill College, fellow commoner, 1977-78, Clare Hall, foundation visiting fellow, 1987-88; University of London, Institute of Commonwealth Studies, Henry Charles Chapman visiting fellow, 1988-89; Sri Lanka Ministry of Cultural Affairs, advisor, 1993. Writer. **Publications:** Introducing English Literature, vol. I: First Steps to Literary Criticism, 1975, vol. II: A Study of Fiction, 1976, vol. III: A Study of Poetry, 1977; Developing Countries in British Fiction, 1977; Between Cultures: Essays on Literature, Language and Education, 1987; Images of the Raj: South Asia in the Literature of the Empire, 1988; (with M. Gooneratne and M. Jayawardena) Learning English: vol. I, 1988, (with M. Gooneratne) vol. II, 2009; Joseph Conrad: Beyond Culture and Background, 1990; (ed.) Encyclopedia of Post-Colonial Literatures in English, 1994; (ed.) Heart of Darkness, 1995, 2nd ed., 1999; Salman Rushdie, 1998, 2nd ed., 2010; Sri Lankan English Literature and the Sri Lankan People, 1917-2003, 2005, 2ed., 2007; Joseph Conrad's Heart of Darkness, 2007; (ed.) Kaleidoscope: An Anthology of Sri Lankan English Literature, 2007, vol. II, 2010. CONTRIBUTOR: Honouring E.F.C. Ludowyk, 1984; ESP in Practice: Models and Challenges for Teachers, 1986; Crisis and Creativity in the New Literatures in English, 1989; Joseph Conrad: Third World Perspectives, 1990; From Commonwealth to Post-Colonial: Critical Essays, 1992; The Writers as Historical Witness: Studies in Commonwealth Literature, 1995; Commonwealth and American Women's Discourse: Essays in Criticism, 1996; A Talent(ed) Digger: Creations, Cameos, and Essays in Honour of Anna Rutherford, 1996; Crossing Cultures: Essays on Literature and Culture in the Asia-Pacific, 1996; Sharing a Commonwealth, 2001; The Politics of English as a World Language: New Horizons in Postcolonial Cultural Studies, 2003; From English Literature to Literatures in English: International Perspectives, 2005; Towards a Transcultural Future: Literature and Society in a 'Post'-Colonial World, 2005; One of Us: Studi inglesi e conradiani offerti a Mario Curreli, 2009; South Asian Literatures, 2010. EDITOR AND AUTHOR OF INTRODUCTION: Modern Sri Lankan Stories: An Anthology, 1986; Modern Sri Lankan Poetry: An Anthology, 1987; Modern Sri Lankan Drama: An Anthology, 1991; The Penguin New Writing in Sri Lanka, 1992; The Penguin Book of Modern Sri Lankan Stories, 1996; Sri Lankan Literature in English 1948-98: A 50th Independence Anniversary Anthology, 1998; Perspectives on Post Colonial Literature, 2001. Contributor to journals. **Address:** Department of English, University of Kelaniya, Kandawatta Rd., Ste. 1, Nugegoda, Kelaniya, 80212, Sri Lanka. **Online address:** dcragoonetilleke@sltnet.lk

GOOSSEN, Rachel Waltner. American (born United States), b. 1960. **Genres:** History, Social Sciences, Race Relations, Theology/Religion, Local History/Rural Topics. **Career:** Bethel College, instructor in history, 1984-85, 1987, visiting professor of history, 1999-2000; University of Kansas, assistant instructor, 1988-92, instructor in history, 1992-94, lecturer in American studies, 1999-2000; Goshen College, assistant professor of history, 1995-98, chair, associate professor of history, 1988-99; Washburn University, assistant professor of history, 2000-04, associate professor of history, 2004-09, professor, 2009-, Center for Kansas studies, fellow. Writer. **Publications:** Brick and Mortar: A History of Newton, Kansas, 1984; Meetingplace: A History of the Mennonite Church of Normal, 1912-1987, 1987; (with R. Kreider) Hungry, Thirsty, A Stranger: The Mennonite Central Committee Story, 1988; Prairie Vision: A History of the Pleasant Valley Mennonite Church, 1888-1988, 1988; (with R.S. Kreider) When Good People Quarrel: Studies of Conflict Resolution, 1989; (with W. Young) History of the United States Through the Civil War: A Study Guide, rev. ed., 1994; Women Against the Good War: Conscientious Objection and Gender on the American Home Front, 1941-1947, 1997; Prairie People: A Swiss Volhynian Kaleidoscope of Images,

2000. Contributor to books. **Address:** Department of History, Washburn University, 1700 SW College Ave., Topeka, KS 66621, U.S.A. **Online address:** rachel.goossen@washburn.edu

GOOTENBERG, Paul. American (born United States), b. 1954. **Genres:** History, Social Sciences, Politics/Government, Cultural/Ethnic Topics. **Career:** Brandeis University, assistant professor of history, 1987-90; State University of New York-Stony Brook, Department of History, associate professor, 1990-95, professor of Latin American and economic history, 1995-, co-director; Stony Brook University, Stony Brook Initiative for Historical Social Sciences, coordinator. Writer. **Publications:** Between Silver and Guano: Commercial Policy and the State in Postindependence Peru, 1989; Corazones y mentes: Tejidosy Harinas, 1989; Imagining Development: Economic Ideas in Peru's Fictitious Prosperity of Guano, 1840-1880, 1993; (ed.) Cocaine: Global Histories, 1999; Andean Cocaine: The Making of a Global Drug, 2008; (ed. with L. Reygadas) Indelible Inequalities in Latin America: Insights from History, Politics, and Culture, 2010; Invención de la cocaína: la historia olvidada de Alfredo Bignon y la ciencia nacional peruana, 1884-1890, 2010. Contributor to periodicals. **Address:** Department of History, State University of New York, N-319 Social and Behavioral Sciences Bldg., 100 Nicolls Rd., Stony Brook, NY 11794-4348, U.S.A. **Online address:** paul.gootenberg@sunysb.edu

GOPIAH See **Keys, Kerry Shawn.**

GORDIEVSKY, Oleg. British (born England), b. 1938. **Genres:** International Relations/Current Affairs, Politics/Government, Autobiography/Memoirs, Young Adult Non-fiction. **Career:** KGB, faculty of first chief directorate (KGB's foreign intelligence service), 1962-85; British Secret Intelligence Service (MI6), secret agent, 1974-85; deputy head of station in Copenhagen, 1975-78; deputy head of station in London, 1982-85; Sunday Times, reviewer; Spectator, reviewer; Literary Review, reviewer. Writer and educator. **Publications:** (With C. Andrew) KGB Dans le Monde, 1917-1990, 1990; (with C. Andrew) KGB: The Inside Story, 1990; Instructions from the Centre, 1991; (ed. with C. Andrew) More Instructions from the Centre, 1992; (ed. with C. Andrew) Comrade Kryuchkov's Instructions: Top Secret Files on KGB Foreign Operations, 1975-1985, 1993; Next Stop Execution, 1995; (with I. Rogatchi) Blind Mirror, 1998; (with J. Andersen) De Rode Spioner, 2002. **Address:** A.M. Heath & Company Ltd., 6 Warwick Ct., London, GL WC1R 5DJ, England. **Online address:** navole1@aol.com

GORDIMER, Nadine. South African (born South Africa), b. 1923. **Genres:** Novels, Novellas/Short Stories, Literary Criticism And History, Essays, Young Adult Fiction, Adult Non-fiction. **Career:** Ford Foundation, Institute of Contemporary Arts, visiting professor, 1961; University of Michigan, lecturer, 1970; American Academy in Rome, writer-in-residence, 1984; Harvard University, faculty; Princeton University, faculty; Northwestern University, faculty; Columbia University, faculty; Tulane University, faculty. Writer. **Publications:** NOVELS: The Lying Days, 1953; A World of Strangers, 1958; Occasion for Loving, 1963; The Late Bourgeois World, 1966; A Guest of Honour, 1970; The Conservationist, 1974; Burger's Daughter, 1979; July's People, 1981; A Sport of Nature, 1987; My Son's Story, 1990; None to Accompany Me, 1994; Harald, Claudia, and their Son Duncan, 1996; The House Gun, 1998; The Pickup, 2001; Get a Life, 2005; No Time Like the Present, 2012. SHORT STORIES: Face to Face: Short Stories, 1949; The Soft Voice of the Serpent and Other Stories, 1952; Six Feet of the Country, 1956; Friday's Footprint and Other Stories, 1960; Not for Publication and Other Stories, 1965; Livingstone's Companions: Stories, 1971; Selected Stories, 1975; Some Monday for Sure, 1976; A Soldier's Embrace, 1980; Town and Country Lovers, 1980; Something Out There, 1984; Reflections of South Africa: Short Stories, 1986; Crimes of Conscience: Selected Short Stories, 1991; Jump and Other Stories, 1991; Why Haven't You Written?: Selected Stories, 1950-1972, 1993; Loot and Other Stories, 2003; Beethoven was One-Sixteenth Black: And Other Stories, 2007. OTHERS: (ed. with L. Abrahams) South African Writing Today, 1967; African Literature: The Lectures Given on This Theme at the University of Cape Town's Public Summer School, February, 1972, 1972; The Black Interpreters: Notes on African Writing, 1973; On the Mines, 1973; (co-author) What Happened to Burger's Daughter or How South African Censorship Works, 1980; Lifetimes under Apartheid, 1986; The Essential Gesture: Writing, Politics and Places, 1988; Three in a Bed: Fiction, Morals and Politics, 1991; (with R. Weiss) Zimbabwe and the New Elite, 1993; Writing and Being: The Charles Eliot Norton Lectures, 1995; Living in Hope and History: Notes from Our Century (essays), 1999; The Ultimate Safari, 2001;

(ed.) Telling Tales, 2004; (intro.) Three Novels of Ancient Egypt: Khufu's Wisdom: Rhadopis of Nubia: Thebes at War, 2007; Telling Times: Writing and Living, 1950-2008, 2010; Telling Times: Writing and Living, 1954-2008, 2010; Life Times: Stories, 1952-2007, 2010. Contributor to periodicals. **Address:** A.P. Watt Ltd., 20 John St., London, GL WC1N 2DR, England.

GORDIN, Michael D. American (born United States) **Genres:** History. **Career:** Princeton University, Whitman College, Department of History, assistant professor of history, 2003-07, associate professor, 2007-09, professor, 2009-, Program in Russian and Eurasian Studies, acting director, 2008-09, director, 2009-; Harvard University, Society of Fellows, junior fellow, 2001-03, 2004-05. Writer. **Publications:** (Ed. and intro. with P. Galison and D. Kaiser) Science and Society: The History of Modern Physical Science in the Twentieth Century, 2001; The History of the Modern Physical Science in the Twentieth Century, 2001; A Well-ordered Thing: Dmitrii Mendeleev and the Shadow of the Periodic Table, 2004; Five Days in August: How World War II Became a Nuclear War, 2007; (ed. with K. Hall, A.B. Kojevnikov) Intelligentsia Science: The Russian Century, 1860-1960, 2008; Red Cloud at Dawn: Truman, Stalin and the End of the Atomic Monopoly, 2009; (ed. with H. Tilley and G. Prakash) Utopia/Dystopia: Conditions of Historical Possibility, 2010; The Pseudoscience Wars: Immanuel Velikovsky and the Birth of the Modern Fringe, 2012; The Second Superpower: How Russians Triggered the Nuclear Arms Race, forthcoming. **Address:** Department of History, Princeton University, 305 Dickinson Hall, Princeton, NJ 08544-1017, U.S.A. **Online address:** mgordin@princeton.edu

GORDINIER, Jeff. American (born United States) **Genres:** History, Sociology, Social Sciences, Essays. **Career:** Details Magazine, editor. **Publications:** X Saves the World: How Generation X Got the Shaft but Can Still Keep Everything from Sucking, 2008. Contributor to books. Works appear in anthologies. **Address:** Penguin Group (USA) Inc., 375 Hudson St., New York, NY 10014, U.S.A. **Online address:** jeff@jeffgordinier.com

GORDIS, Lisa M. American (born United States), b. 1966?. **Genres:** Theology/Religion, Geography, Literary Criticism And History, History. **Career:** Columbia University, Barnard College, Department of English, associate professor, 1993-, professor, Early American Literature, editorial staff, First-Year Seminar Program, director. **Publications:** Opening Scripture: Bible Reading and Interpretive Authority in Puritan New England, 2003. Contributor to books. **Address:** Barnard College, 3009 Broadway, New York, NY 10027, U.S.A. **Online address:** lgordis@barnard.edu

GORDON, Alan R. American (born United States), b. 1959?. **Genres:** Mystery/Crime/Suspense, Novels. **Career:** Legal Aid Society, attorney. Writer. **Publications:** Thirteenth Night: A Medieval Mystery, 1999; Jester Leaps In: A Medieval Mystery, 2000; A Death in the Venetian Quarter: A Medieval Mystery, 2002; The Widow of Jerusalem, 2003; An Antic Disposition, 2004; The Lark's Lament, 2007; The Moneylender of Toulouse: A Fools' Guild Mystery, 2008; The Parisian Prodigal, 2010. Contributor of short stories to periodicals. **Address:** Legal Aid Society, 199 Water St., New York, NY 10038, U.S.A.

GORDON, Andrew D. American (born United States), b. 1952?. **Genres:** History, Area Studies. **Career:** Harvard University, assistant professor of history, 1981-85, professor of history, 1995-2002, East Asian Studies, head tutor, 1998-2002; Edwin O. Reischauer Institute of Japanese Studies, director, 1998-2004, Department of History, chair, 2004-07, Lee and Juliet Folger Fund professor of history, 2002-; Duke University, assistant professor, 1985-87, associate professor, 1987-91, professor of history, 1991-95. Writer. **Publications:** The Evolution of Labor Relations in Japan: Heavy Industry, 1853-1955, 1985; Labor and Imperial Democracy in Prewar Japan, 1991; The Wages of Affluence: Labor and Management in Postwar Japan, 1998; A Modern History of Japan: From Tokugawa Times to Present, 2003, 2nd ed., 2009; Er shi shi ji Riben: cong Dechuan shi dai dao xian dai, 2006; The Unknown Story of Matsuzaka's Major League Revolution, 2007; Nihonjin ga shiranai Matsuzaka mejaa kakumei, 2007; Fabricating Consumers: The Sewing Machine in Modern Japan, 2011. EDITOR: Postwar Japan as History, 1993; (and trans. with M. Hane) Kumazawa Makoto, Portraits of the Japanese Workplace, 1996; (and trans with T. Boardman) Nimura Kazuo, The Ashio Riot of 1907, 1997; (with M. Goldman) Historical Perspectives on Contemporary East Asia, 2000; (with G.L. Bernstein and K.W. Nakai) Public Spheres, Private Lives in Modern Japan, 1600-1950: Essays in Honor of Albert M. Craig, 2005; Stitching in Modern Times: The Sewing Machine in Japan, 2009. Contributor to books. **Address:** Department of History,

Center for Government and International Studies, Harvard University, Rm. S236, 1730 Cambridge St., Cambridge, MA 02138, U.S.A. **Online address:** agordon@fas.harvard.edu

GORDON, Anne Wolrige. British (born England), b. 1936. **Genres:** Autobiography/Memoirs, Biography, History, Literary Criticism And History. **Career:** Writer. **Publications:** Peter Howard: Life and Letters, 1969; Blindsight, 1970; Dame Flora, 1974. **Address:** Ythan Lodge, Newburgh, Newburgh, AB41 6AD, Scotland.

GORDON, April A. American (born United States), b. 1947. **Genres:** Sociology, Social Sciences, Medicine/Health, Women's Studies And Issues, Young Adult Non-fiction, Humanities. **Career:** Coker College, assistant professor, associate professor of sociology, 1976-87; Winthrop University, assistant professor, professor of sociology, 1987-, coordinator of women's studies; University of Evansville, lecturer of Igleheart public affairs, 1992. Writer. **Publications:** Soviet Family Policy: 1944 to the Present, 1979; Agricultural Policy and Development in Cameroon, 1987; (ed. with D.L. Gordon) Understanding Contemporary Africa, 1992, 4th ed., 2007; Transforming Capitalism and Patriarchy: Gender and Development in Africa, 1996; (contrib.) Global Social Science for the Third Millennium, 2001; Women and Sustainable Development in Africa, 2001; Nigeria's Diverse Peoples: A Reference Sourcebook, 2003. **Address:** Department of Sociology, Winthrop University, 332 Kinard Hall, 701 Oakland Ave., Rock Hill, SC 29733, U.S.A. **Online address:** gordona@winthrop.edu

GORDON, Charles F. American (born United States), b. 1943. **Genres:** Plays/Screenplays, Art/Art History, Young Adult Fiction. **Career:** New Lafayette Theatre, assistant technical director, 1967-69; American Place Theatre, assistant stage manger, 1970; Black Magicians Theatre Co., founder, 1970; Negro Ensemble Co., master electrician, 1971; Afro-American Cultural Center, creative writing teacher, 1972; Street Theatre, Eastern Connecticut Correctional Institute, creative writing teacher, 1975-76; Afro-American Cultural Center, creative writing teacher, 1978; College of New Rochelle, creative writing teacher, 1979-82; Emory University, writer-in-residence, 1982-83; Playwrights Center, writer-in-residence, 1984; Playwrights Workshop, Princeton University, visiting lecturer, 1986-87; University of Michigan, adjunct associate professor of playwriting, 1989-90, associate professor, 1990-, associate professor of theatre and writer-in-residence; Theatre Communications Group, vice president and director. **Publications:** PUBLISHED PLAYS WRITTEN AS OYAMO: The Negroes, 1970; Outta Site, 1970; Willie Bignigga, 1970; The Star That Could Not Play, 1974; Hillybilly Liberation: A Grossly Understated Prayer of the Theatrical Spectacles, Social Positions, and Poetry, 1976; The Resurrection of Lady Lester: A Poetic Mood Song Based on the Legend of Lester Young, 1981; I am a Man: Powa ta da Peepas, 1995. **Address:** Department of Theatre & Drama, University of Michigan, 2550 Frieze Bldg., Ann Arbor, MI 48109-1285, U.S.A. **Online address:** oyamo@umich.edu

GORDON, Colin. (Lancaster Gordon). American (born United States), b. 1962. **Genres:** History, Biography, Autobiography/Memoirs, Politics/Government. **Career:** University of British Columbia, assistant professor of history, 1990-94; University of Iowa, Department of History, assistant professor, 1994-96, associate professor, 1996-2004, professor, 2004-, department chair, 2006-; Iowa Policy Project, senior research consultant. Writer. **Publications:** New Deals: Business, Labor, and Politics in America, 1920-1935, 1994; (with P. Kingston) The Business Culture in France, 1996; (ed.) Major Problems in American History, 1920-1945: Document and Essays, 1999, 2nd ed., 2011; (with P. Fisher) The State of Working Iowa, 2001; Dead on Arrival: The Politics of Health Care in Twentieth-Century America, 2003; Bending the Rules: The Promise and Practice of the Grow Iowa Values Fund, 2004; Working Blues: Labor Day in Iowa, 2004; (with E. Ditsler and P. Fisher) On the Fringe: The Substandard Benefits of Workers in Part-Time, Temporary, and Contract Jobs, 2005; (co-author) Nonstandard Jobs, Substandard Benefits, 2005; (with P. Fisher and E. Ditsler) No Picnic: A Labor Day 2006 Update on the State of Working Iowa, 2006. Contributor of articles to journals. **Address:** Department of History, University of Iowa, 280 Schaeffer Hall, Iowa City, IA 52242-1409, U.S.A. **Online address:** colin-gordon@uiowa.edu

GORDON, Deborah. American (born United States), b. 1959. **Genres:** History, Technology, History. **Career:** Chevron USA Inc., chemical and regulatory engineer, 1982-87; Lawrence Berkeley Laboratory, research assistant, 1988-89; Union of Concerned Scientists, director of transportation and energy programs and senior policy analyst, 1989-96; Yale School of Forestry and Environmental Studies, program director, 1996-2000; policy consultant, 1996-. Writer. **Publications:** Steering a New Course: Transportation, Energy and the Environment, 1991; (with D. Sperling) Two Billion Cars: Driving toward Sustainability, 2009. Contributor of articles to journals. **Address:** Island Press, 1718 Connecticut Ave. NW, Ste. 300, Washington, DC 20009-1148, U.S.A. **Online address:** dzgordon@aol.com

GORDON, Deborah Hannes. (Brooke Hastings). American (born United States), b. 1946. **Genres:** Mystery/Crime/Suspense, Romance/Historical, Education, Young Adult Fiction, Young Adult Non-fiction, Novels. **Career:** Columbia University, research assistant, 1968-70; The Huron Institute and Working Papers Magazine, secretary, 1971-73; CARD Consultants, researcher and writer, 1979; Sacramento Community Commission for Women and California Women's Coalition, board director; National Council of Jewish Women, president. **Publications:** AS BROOKE HASTINGS: Desert Fire, 1980; Playing for Keeps, 1980; Innocent Fire, 1980; Island Conquest, 1981; Winner Take All, 1981; Rough Diamond, 1982; Intimate Strangers, 1982; A Matter of Time, 1983; An Act of Love, 1983; Innocent Victim, 1983; Interested Parties, 1984; Reasonable Doubts, 1984; Tell Me No Lies, 1984; Hard to Handle, 1985; As Time Goes By, 1986; Double Jeopardy, 1986; Forward Pass, 1986; Too Close for Comfort, 1987; Forbidden Fruit, 1987; Both Sides Now, 1988; Catch a Falling Star, 1988; So Sweet a Sin, 1989; Reluctant Mistress, 1990; Seduction, 1990. AS DEBORAH GORDON: FICTION: Beating the Odds, 1992; Runaway Bride, 1994; Runaway Time, 1995; Runaway Magic, 1996. NON-FICTION: (with L. Ramer) How to Help Students with AD/HD Succeed in School and in Life (non-fiction), 2001. **Address:** 1240 Noonan Dr., Sacramento, CA 95822, U.S.A.

GORDON, Donald. *See* **PAYNE, Donald Gordon.**

GORDON, Eric A(rthur). American (born United States), b. 1945. **Genres:** Literary Criticism And History, Music, Autobiography/Memoirs, Art/Art History. **Career:** Manchester Community College, instructor in history, 1972-75; Hartford Advocate, writer, 1975-80; Sephardic Home for the Aged, editor, 1982-84; G. Schirmer (music publisher), publicity manager, 1984-86; Social and Public Art Resource Center, director of public information, 1990-93; Workmen's Circle/Arbeter Ring, director, 1995-; People's Voice Cafe, founder and treasurer. **Publications:** Mark the Music: The Life and Work of Marc Blitzstein, 1989; (with E. Robinson) Ballad of an American: The Autobiography of Earl Robinson, 1998. Contributor of articles to books and periodicals. **Address:** Scarecrow Press, 15200 NBN Way, PO Box 191, Blue Ridge Summit, PA 17214, U.S.A. **Online address:** ericarthur@aol.com

GORDON, Frances. *See* **WOOD, Bridget.**

GORDON, Graeme. British (born England), b. 1966. **Genres:** Plays/Screenplays, Novels, Criminology/True Crime, Mystery/Crime/Suspense, Young Adult Fiction. **Career:** Actor, writer and producer of video films and television pilots, 1988-; Feline Partnership (video production company), cofounder, 1990; London Film Makers Co-operative, staff, 1990. Librarian. **Publications:** Bayswater Bodycount, 1995; Barking Mad (crime novel), 1997. Contributor to periodicals. **Address:** c/o Author Mail, Serpents Trial, 4 Blackstock Mew, London, GL N4 2BT, England.

GORDON, Grant. British (born England), b. 1956. **Genres:** Business/Trade/Industry, Human Relations/Parenting, Administration/Management. **Career:** Institute for Family Business, general director, Drinks Sector, senior executive. Writer. **Publications:** (With N. Nicholson) Family Wars: Classic Conflicts in Family Business and How to Deal with Them, 2008; (with N. Nicholson) Family Wars: Stories and Insights from Famous Family Business Feuds, 2010. **Address:** Institute for Family Business, 32 Buckingham Palace Rd., London, GL SW1W 0RE, England.

GORDON, Haim. Israeli/Palestinian (born Palestine), b. 1936. **Genres:** Literary Criticism And History, Philosophy, Politics/Government, History, Education. **Career:** Ben-Gurion University of the Negev, lecturer, 1975-81; senior lecturer, 1981-92, associate professor, 1992-98, professor of education, 1998-, professor emeritus; University of South Alabama, visiting professor of philosophy, 1983-84; Free University of Berlin, Institute for Jewish Studies, visiting professor, 1984; Ohio University, visiting professor of philosophy, 1987; University of Notre Dame, Kroc Institute for International Peace Studies, visiting fellow, 1991-92. Writer. **Publications:** (With J. Bloch) Martin

Buber: A Centenary Volume, 1981; Dance, Dialogue, and Despair, 1986; The Other Martin Buber: Recollections of His Contemporaries, 1988; Make Room for Dreams, 1989; Naguib Mahfouz's Egypt, 1990; (with R. Gordon) Sartre and Evil: Guidelines for a Struggle, 1995; Quicksand: Israel, the Intifada and the Rise of Political Evil in Democracies, 1995; Fighting Evil: Unsung Heroes in the Novels of Graham Greene, 1997; Looking Back at the June, 1967 War, 1999; Dwelling Poetically, 2000; The Heidegger-Buber Controversy: The Status of theI-Thou, 2001; (with R. Gordon) Sartre's Philosophy and the Challenge of Education, 2001; (with R. Gordon) Sophistry and 20th Century Art, 2002; (with R. Gordon and T. Shriteh) Beyond Intifada: Narratives of Freedom Fighters in the Gaza Strip, 2003; Heroism and Friendship in the Novels of Erich Maria Remarque, 2003; (with S. Tamari) Maurice Merleau Ponty's Phenomenology of Perception, 2004; (with R. Gordon) Heidegger on Truth and Myth, 2006; Israel Today, 2007; (with R. Gordon) Hobbema and Heidegger: On Truth and Beauty, 2008. EDITOR: (with J. Bloch) Martin Buber, A Centenary Volume, 1984; (with L. Grob and contrib.) Education for Peace, 1987; (with Grob and R. Hassan and contrib.) Women's and Men's Liberation: Testimonies of Spirit, 1991; (with R. Gordon and contrib.) Israel/Palestine: The Quest for Dialogue, 1991; (and intro.) Jochanan Bloch: Jews and Judaism-A Political Philosophy (in Hebrew), 1998; (and intro.) Dictionary of Existentialism, 1999. Contributor of articles to books and journals. **Address:** Department of Education, Ben-Gurion University of the Negev, PO Box 653, Beer-Sheva, 94105, Israel.

GORDON, Jacob U. American/Nigerian (born Nigeria), b. 1939. **Genres:** History, Cultural/Ethnic Topics. **Career:** Albany State University, associate professor of history and political science and department head, 1967-70; University of Kansas, professor of African and African American studies, 1970-, chair, courtesy professor of American studies, Center for Black Leadership Development and Research, executive director, 1986-, Schiefelbusch Institute for Life Span Studies, research fellow, 1989-, now professor emeritus of African and African-American studies; Leavenworth Prison, lecturer, 1975-85; University of Missouri-Kansas City, visiting professor, 1984; National Council for the African American Male Inc., president and chief executive officer, 1990-; Big Brothers/Big Sisters of Lawrence, board director; Robert Wood Johnson Foundation, consultant. Writer. **Publications:** (Ed. with J. Rosser) The Black Studies Debate, 1974; African Studies at Kansas, 1965-75, 1977; (ed.) Multiculturalism in Alcohol and Other Drug Abuse Services, 1992; (ed.) The Role of Higher Education in Alcohol and Other Drug Abuse Prevention, 1993; Narratives of African Americans in Kansas, 1870-1992: Beyond the Exodus Movement, 1993; (ed.) Managing Multiculturalism in Substance Abuse Services, 1994; (ed. with R. Majors) The American Black Male: His Present Status and His Future, 1994; (with E. Freeman and J. Lee) Supplemental Readings for Training in Multicultural Substance Abuse: Continuum of Care for the 21st Century, 1994; (ed.) Systems Change Approach to Substance Abuse Prevention, 1997; (with E.C. Jackson, Jr.) Search for Equal Justice by African-American Lawyers: A History of the National Bar Association, 1999; (comp.) The African-American Male, 1999; Black Leadership for Social Change, 2000; (ed.) Black Male in White America, 2002; African Leadership in the Twentieth Century: An Enduring Experiment in Democracy, 2002; (ed. with F.E. Obiakor) African Perspectives in American Higher Education: Invisible Voices, 2003; (ed.) African Studies for the 21st Century, 2004; (ed.) African Presence in Black America, 2004; Winning the Future for Africa and the Diaspora, 2011. Contributor to books and academic journals. **Address:** Department of African and African-American Studies, The University of Kansas, Rm. 9, Bailey Hall, 1440 Jayhawk Blvd., Lawrence, KS 66045-7555, U.S.A.

GORDON, Jaimy. American (born United States), b. 1944. **Genres:** Novels, Novellas/Short Stories, Essays, Translations, Poetry. **Career:** Rhode Island State Council on the Arts, writer-in-residence, 1975-77; Stephens College, director of creative writing program, 1980-81; Western Michigan University, assistant professor, 1981-87, associate professor, 1987-92, professor of English, 1992-; Harvard University, Bunting Institute of Radcliffe College, fellow, 1984-85. **Publications:** NOVELS: Shamp of the City-Solo, 1974, 3rd ed., 1993; She Drove without Stopping, 1990; (trans. with P. Blickle) Lost Weddings (novel), 1990; Bogeywoman, 1999; Lord of Misrule: A Novel, 2010. OTHERS: The Bend, the Lip, the Kid (narrative poem), 1978; Circumspections from an Equestrian Statue (novella), 1979; (trans.) Hermine: An Animal Life, 2004. Contributor to periodicals. **Address:** Department of English, Western Michigan University, Kalamazoo, MI 49008, U.S.A. **Online address:** gordonj@wmich.edu

GORDON, James S(amuel). American (born United States), b. 1941. **Genres:** Medicine/Health, Self Help, Sports/Fitness. **Career:** Harvard College, teaching fellow, 1963-67; Cornell Medical College, department of pathology, teaching assistant, 1964-65; Metropolitan State Hospital, clinical researcher, 1967; Albert Einstein College of Medicine, chief resident and clinical instructor, 1968-71; National Institutes for Mental Health, Mental Health Study Center, staff psychiatrist, 1971-74, Center for Studies of Child and Family Mental Health, research psychiatrist and consultant on alternative forms of service, 1974-80, Division of Special Mental Health Programs, research psychiatrist, 1980-82, Office of Alternative Medicine, Program Advisory Council, chair, 1994-97; Catholic University of America, visiting professor, 1974-75; Community Therapy Training Center, visiting lecturer, 1975; The President's Commission on Mental Health, Special Study on Alternative Services, director, 1977-78; The Group for the Advancement of Psychiatry, Blanche Lttleson Consultant, 1979; Saint Elizabeth's Hospital, Division of Child and Adolescent Services, senior consultant on adolescence, 1979-80, Division of Child and Adolescent Services, Adolescent Services Branch, chief, 1980-82; Walter Reed Army Medical Center, The Wellness Program, medical consultant, 1980-82; Georgetown University, School of Medicine, departments of psychiatry and family medicine, clinical professor, 1980-; Latin American Youth Center, senior consultant, 1984-; Uniformed Services University of the Health Sciences, department of psychiatry, associate clinical professor, 1989-; The Fetzer Institute, fellow, 1990-96; Center for Mind-Body Medicine, founder and director, 1991-; Georgetown Medical School, clinical professor. Writer. **Publications:** Caring for Youth: Essays on Alternative Services, 1978; (ed. with A.C. Hastings and J. Fadiman) Health for the Whole Person: The Complete Guide to Holistic Medicine, 1980; (ed. with M. Beyer) Reaching Troubled Youth: Runaways and Community Mental Health, 1981; (ed. with D.T. Jaffe and D.E. Bresler) Mind, Body and Health: Toward an Integral Medicine, 1984; (with R. Rosenthal) New Directions in Medicine: A Directory of Learning Opportunities, 1984; The Golden Guru: The Strange Journey of Bhagwan Shree Rajneesh, 1987; Holistic Medicine, 1988; Stress Management, 1990; Manifesto for a New Medicine: Your Guide to Healing Partnerships and the Wise Use of Alternative Therapies, 1996; (with S. Curtin) Comprehensive Cancer Care: Integrating Alternative, Complementary and Conventional Therapies, 2000; Unstuck: Your Guide to the Seven-stage Journey out of Depression, 2008. **Address:** The Center for Mind-Body Medicine, 5225 Connecticut Ave. NW, Ste. 414, Washington, DC 20015, U.S.A. **Online address:** jgordon@cmbm.org

GORDON, Jennifer. (Jennifer Lynn Gordon). American (born United States), b. 1965. **Genres:** Business/Trade/Industry, Economics. **Career:** Workplace Project, founder and director, 1992-98; Yale Law School, J. Skelly Wright Fellow and visiting faculty lecturer, 1998-2000; consultant, 1998-2003; Fordham University, School of Law, associate professor of law, 2003-. Writer and labor law attorney. **Publications:** Suburban Sweatshops: The Fight for Immigrant Rights, 2005. Contributor of articles to books and journals. **Address:** School of Law, Fordham University, 140 W 62nd St., New York, NY 10023-7407, U.S.A.

GORDON, Jennifer Lynn. *See* **GORDON, Jennifer.**

GORDON, John (William). British (born England), b. 1925. **Genres:** Horror, Science Fiction/Fantasy, Children's Fiction, Young Adult Fiction, Autobiography/Memoirs, Natural History, Mystery/Crime/Suspense. **Career:** Isle of Ely and Wisbech Advertiser, reporter, 1947-49, sub-editor, 1949-51; Bury Free Press, chief reporter, sub-editor, 1951-58; Western Evening Herald, sub-editor, 1958-62; Eastern Evening News, columnist and subeditor, 1962-73; Eastern Daily Press, sub-editor, 1973-85. Writer. **Publications:** The Giant under the Snow, 1968; The House on the Brink, 1970; The Ghost on the Hill, 1976; The Waterfall Box, 1978; The Spitfire Grave: And Other Stories, 1979; The Edge of the World, 1983; Catch Your Death: And Other Ghost Stories, 1984; The Quelling Eye, 1986; The Grasshopper, 1987; Ride the Wind, 1989; Secret Corridor, 1990; Blood Brothers, 1991; Ordinary Seaman (autobiography), 1992; The Burning Baby and Other Ghosts, 1992; Gilray's Ghost, 1995; The Flesh Eater, 1998; The Midwinter Watch, 1998; Skinners, 1999; The Ghosts of Blacklode, 2002; Left in the Dark: The Supernatural Tales of John Gordon, 2006; Fen Runners, 2009. **Address:** 99 George Borrow Rd., Norwich, NF NR4 7HU, England.

GORDON, Lancaster. *See* **GORDON, Colin.**

GORDON, Lewis Ricardo. American/Jamaican (born Jamaica), b. 1962.

Genres: Philosophy, Humanities, Politics/Government, Race Relations, Education, Intellectual History, Cultural/Ethnic Topics, Anthropology/Ethnology, Essays, Theology/Religion, Third World, E-books. **Career:** Lehman High School, social studies teacher, 1985-89, Second Chance Program, founder and coordinator, 1987-89; Yale University, teaching fellow in philosophy and classics, 1990-93; University of Hartford, adjunct professor of philosophy, 1992; City University of New York, Lehman College, Lehman Scholars Program, adjunct assistant professor, 1993; Purdue University, assistant professor of philosophy and African-American studies, 1993-95, associate professor of philosophy and African-American studies, 1996-97; Brown University, assistant professor, 1996, associate professor, 1997, professor, 1998-2004; Temple University, Laura H. Carnell professor of philosophy, religion, and Jewish studies, 2004-, Institute for the Study of Race and Social Thought, director, 2004-, Center for Afro-Jewish Studies, director, 2004-. Writer. **Publications:** Bad Faith and Antiblack Racism, 1995; Fanon and the Crisis of European Man: An Essay on Philosophy and the Human Sciences, 1995; Her Majesty's Other Children: Sketches of Racism from a Neocolonial Age, 1997; What Fanon Really Said: An Introduction to His Life and Thought, 1998; Existentia Africana: Understanding Africana Existential Thought, 2000; Disciplinary Decadence: Living Thought in Trying Times, 2006; An Introduction to Africana Philosophy, 2008; (with J.A. Gordon) Of Divine Warning: Reading Disaster in the Modern Age, 2009. EDITOR: (and trans. with T.D. Sharpley-Whiting and R.T. White) Fanon: A Critical Reader, 1996; Existence in Black: An Anthology of Black Existential Philosophy, 1997; (with R.T. White) Black Texts and Textuality: Constructing and De-Constructing Blackness, 1998; Key Figures in African American Thought, 1998; The Edinburgh Encyclopedia of Continental Philosophy: Philosophy of Existence, 1998; (J.A. with Gordon) Not Only the Master's Tools: African-American Studies in Theory and Practice, 2006; (with J.A. Gordon) Companion to African-American Studies, 2006. **Address:** Center for Afro-Jewish Studies, Temple University, 648 Anderson Hall, 114 W Berks St., Philadelphia, PA 19122, U.S.A. **Online address:** gordonl@temple.edu

GORDON, Lois G. American (born United States), b. 1938?. **Genres:** History, Literary Criticism And History, Biography, Reference. **Career:** City College of New York, lecturer in English, 1964-66; University of Missouri, assistant professor of English, 1966-68; Fairleigh Dickinson University, assistant professor, 1968-71, associate professor, 1971-75, professor of English and comparative literature, 1975-, chairman of department, 1982-90, university distinguished professor of English, 2007-; Rutgers University, visiting professor, 1994. Writer. **Publications:** Stratagems to Uncover Nakedness: The Dramas of Harold Pinter, 1969; Donald Barthelme, 1981: Robert Coover: The Universal Fictionmaking Process, 1983; (with A. Gordon) American Chronicle: Six Decades in American Life, 1920-1980, 1987, rev. ed. as American Chronicle: Seven Decades in American Life, 1920-1989, 1990; (ed.) Harold Pinter: A Casebook, 1990; (with A. Gordon) Columbia Chronicles of American Life, 1910-1992, 1995; The Columbia World of Quotations, 1996; The World of Samuel Beckett, 1906-1946, 1996; (with A. Gordon) American Chronicle: Year by Year through the Twentieth Century, 1999; (ed.) Pinter at 70: A Casebook, 2001; Reading Godot, 2002; Nancy Cunard: Heiress, Muse, Political Idealist, 2007. **Address:** Department of English Language and Literature, Program, Fairleigh Dickinson University, 25 Robison Hall, 285 Madison Ave., Madison, NJ 07940, U.S.A. **Online address:** lgordon@fdu.edu

GORDON, Lyndall (Felicity). British/South African (born South Africa), b. 1941. **Genres:** Literary Criticism And History, Autobiography/Memoirs, Biography. **Career:** Columbia University, assistant professor of English, 1975-76; Jesus College, lecturer in English, 1977-84; St. Hilda's College, fellow and tutor in English, 1984-95, senior research fellow, 1995-; Royal Society of Literature, fellow, 2002-. Writer. **Publications:** BIOGRAPHIES: Eliot's Early Years, 1977; Virginia Woolf: A Writer's Life, 1984; Eliot's New Life, 1988, rev. ed. as T.S. Eliot: An Imperfect Life, 1998; Charlotte Bronte: A Passionate Life, 1994; Henry James: A Private Life: Two Women and His Art, 1998; Vindication: A Life of Mary Wollstonecraft, 2005; Lives Like Loaded Guns: Emily Dickinson and Her Family's Feuds, 2010. OTHER: Shared Lives (memoir), 1992. Contributor to periodicals. **Address:** St. Hilda, Cowley Pl., Oxford, OX OX4 1DY, England. **Online address:** lyndall.gordon@st-hildas.ox.ac.uk

GORDON, Mary (Catherine). American (born United States), b. 1949. **Genres:** Novels, Novellas/Short Stories, Autobiography/Memoirs, Essays, Mystery/Crime/Suspense, Education, Adult Non-fiction, Literary Criticism And History, Literary Criticism And History. **Career:** Dutchess Community College, teacher of English, 1974-78; Amherst College, teacher of English,

1979; Barnard College, Millicent C. McIntosh professor of English and writing, 1988-, department chair. Writer. **Publications:** NOVELS: Final Payments, 1978; The Company of Women, 1980; Men and Angels, 1985; The Other Side, 1989; Spending: A Utopian Divertimento, 1998; Pearl, 2005; The Stories of Mary Gordon, 2006; Circling My Mother, 2007. SHORT STORIES: Temporary Shelter, 1987; The Rest of Life: Three Novellas, 1993. OTHERS: (co-author) Spiritual Quests: The Art and Craft of Religious Writing, 1988; Good Boys and Dead Girls: And Other Essays, 1991; (co-author) Deadly Sins, 1994; The Shadow Man, 1996; Seeing through Places: Reflections On Geography And Identity, 2000; Joan of Arc, 2000; Reading Jesus: A Writer's Encounter with the Gospels, 2009; Roots of Empathy: Changing the World Child by Child, 2009; Love of My Youth, 2011. AUTHOR OF INTRODUCTION: Bridges: Poets of Dutchess and Ulster Counties, 1989; The House of Mirth, 1990; Room on One's Own, 1990; The Collected Writings, 1992; Ethan Frome and Other Short Fiction, 1994; Talk of Angels, 1997; Howards End, 2003. Contributor to periodicals. **Address:** Department of English, Barnard College, Columbia University, Office 401A, 417 Barnard Hall, 3009 Broadway, New York, NY 10027-6501, U.S.A. **Online address:** mgordon@barnard.edu

GORDON, Meryl. American (born United States), b. 1951?. **Genres:** Autobiography/Memoirs. **Career:** New York University, Arthur L. Carter Journalism Institute, director of magazine writing; Rochester Democrat & Chronicle, newspaper reporter; Cincinnati Post, newspaper reporter; Gannett News Service, economics reporter; USA Today, economics reporter. Writer. **Publications:** Mrs. Astor Regrets: The Hidden Betrayals of a Family Beyond Reproach, 2008. Contributor to periodicals. **Address:** Arthur L. Carter Journalism Institute, New York University, 20 Cooper Sq., 6th Fl., New York, NY 10003, U.S.A. **Online address:** meryl@mindspring.com

GORDON, Mike. American/British (born England), b. 1948. **Genres:** Children's Fiction, Children's Non-fiction, Illustrations, Picture/Board Books, Young Adult Fiction, Cartoons. **Career:** Illustrator and cartoonist, 1983-. Greeting card designer and writer. **Publications:** FOR CHILDREN: (with M. Gordon) Haunted House, 1989. LEARNING TOGETHER SERIES: Let's Write, 1997; Let's Read, 1997; Let's Count, 1997. FOR ADULTS: The Duffer's Guide to Coarse Fishing, 1985; The Duffer's Guide to Snooker, 1986; The Duffer's Guide to D.I.Y., 1986; The Duffer's Guide to Horse Racing, 1986; The Duffer's Guide to Squash, 1987; William Cooke, Howlers, 1988; The Duffer's Guide to Cycling, 1988; The Duffer's Guide to Boxing, 1989; (with D. Smith) Strange But True Facts about Sex: The Illustrated Book of Sexual Trivia, 1990. Illustrator of books by others. Contributor to magazines. **Address:** 321 W Pedregosa St., PO Box 91818, Santa Barbara, CA 93101, U.S.A. **Online address:** mike@gordonillustration.com

GORDON, Neve. Israeli (born Israel), b. 1965. **Genres:** Politics/Government. **Career:** Physicians for Human Rights, executive director, 1992-94; Ben-Gurion University, Department of Political Science and Government, co-director of graduate studies, lecturer, 1999-2004, senior lecturer, 2005-, chair, 2008-10; University of Michigan, Political Science Department, visiting associate professor, 2007-08. Writer. **Publications:** (Ed. with R. Marton) Torture: Human Rights, Medical Ethics and the Case of Israel, 1995; (ed. and contrib.) From the Margins of Globalization: Critical Perspectives on Human Rights, 2004; Israel's Occupation, 2008. Contributor to books and periodicals. **Address:** Ben-Gurion University of the Negev, PO Box 653, Beer Sheva, 84105, Israel. **Online address:** ngordon@bgu.ac.il

GORDON, Philip H. American (born United States), b. 1962. **Genres:** History, Translations. **Career:** National Security Council, director for European affairs, 1997-2000; Brookings Institution, senior fellow for U.S. foreign policy, 1999-2009; U.S. Department of State, assistant secretary of state for Europe and Eurasian affairs, 2009-; International Institute for Strategic Studies, faculty; Johns Hopkins University, School of Advanced International Studies, faculty; European Institute for Business Administration (INSEAD), faculty; German Society for Foreign Affairs, faculty. Writer. **Publications:** (Ed. with D.P. Calleo) From the Atlantic to the Urals: National Perspectives on the New Europe, 1992; French Security Policy after the Cold War: Continuity, Change, and Implications for the United States, 1992; A Certain Idea of France: French Security Policy and the Gaullist Legacy, 1993; France, Germany, and the Western Alliance, 1995; (ed.) NATO's Transformation: The Changing Shape of the Atlantic Alliance, 1997; The Transatlantic Allies and the Changing Middle East, 1998; (with S. Meunier) The French Challenge: Adapting to Globalization, 2001; (trans.) H. Védrine and D. Moïsi, France in an Age of

Globalization, 2001; (with J. Shapiro) Allies at War: America, Europe, and the Crisis over Iraq, 2004; (ed. with I. Daalder and N. Gnesotto) Crescent of Crisis: U.S.-European Strategy for the Greater Middle East, 2006; Winning the Right War: The Path to Security for America and the World, 2007; (trans.) N. Sarkozy, Testimony: France, Europe and the World in the Twenty-first Century, 2007; (with O. Taspinar) Winning Turkey: How America, Europe, and Turkey Can Revive a Fading Partnership, 2008. Contributor to periodicals. **Address:** Brookings Institution Press, 1775 Massachusetts Ave. NW, Washington, DC 20036, U.S.A.

GORDON, Rivca. Israeli (born Israel), b. 1945. **Genres:** International Relations/Current Affairs, Philosophy, Social Sciences, Politics/Government, Art/Art History. **Career:** Teacher of special education, 1973-83; Gaza Team for Human Rights, chairperson, 1988-; Foundation for Democratic Education in Israel, general manager, 1989-, director. Writer. **Publications:** (Ed. with H. Gordon) Israel/Palestine: The Quest for Dialogue, 1991; (with H. Gordon) Sartre and Evil: Guidelines for a Struggle, 1995; (with H. Gordon) Sartre's Philosophy and the Challenge of Education, 2001; (with H. Gordon and T. Shriteh) Beyond Intifada: Narratives of Freedom Fighters in the Gaza Strip, 2003; (with H. Gordon) Heidegger on Truth and Myth: A Rejection of Postmodernism, 2006; Existential Thinking: Blessings and Pitfalls, 2007; (with H. Gordon) Hobbema and Heidegger: On Truth and Beauty, 2008. Contributor to books and periodicals. **Address:** 258/7 Derech Metsada, Beer Sheva, 58812, Israel.

GORDON, Robert. American (born United States), b. 1961?. **Genres:** Novels, History. **Career:** Writer. **Publications:** It Came from Memphis, 1994; The King on the Road, 1996; Cant Be Satisfied: The Life and Times of Muddy Waters, 2002; The Elvis Treasures, 2002; (ed. with B. Nemerov) Lost Delta Found: Rediscovering the Fisk University-Library of Congress Coahoma County Study 1941-1942, 2005. **Address:** c/o Christy Fletcher, Fletcher and Parry L.L.C., The Carriage House, 121 E 17th St., New York, NY 10003, U.S.A.

GORDON, Robert Ellis. American (born United States), b. 1954. **Genres:** Novels, Adult Non-fiction, Autobiography/Memoirs. **Career:** Washington State Prison Writers Project, workshop director and writing teacher, 1989-96; Huffington Post, columnist. Novelist. **Publications:** When Bobby Kennedy was a Moving Man, 1993, 2nd ed. as Humping Credenzas with the Late Bobby Kennedy: A Convicts True Account, 2010; Yo Words, 1994; The Funhouse Mirror: Reflections on Prison, 2000. Contributor to periodicals. **Address:** 2413 E Lynn St., PO Box 20129, Seattle, WA 98112-2659, U.S.A. **Online address:** robertegordon@mac.com

GORDON, Sheila. American/South African (born South Africa), b. 1927. **Genres:** Young Adult Fiction, Autobiography/Memoirs, Novels, Literary Criticism And History, Novellas/Short Stories, Essays, Travel/Exploration. **Career:** Writer. **Publications:** World Problems, 1971; Unfinished Business: A Novel of South Africa, 1975; A Monster in the Mailbox (juvenile novel), 1978; A Modest Harmony: Seven Summers in a Scottish Glen (memoir), 1982; Waiting for the Rain: A Novel of South Africa (young adult novel), 1987; 3rd September 1939, 1988; The Middle of Somewhere: A Story of South Africa, 1990; Lady Anne's Way, 1995. Contributor to periodicals. **Address:** c/o Elaine Markson, 44 Greenwich Ave., New York, NY 10011, U.S.A.

GORDON, Stewart. American (born United States), b. 1945?. **Genres:** Theology/Religion. **Career:** University of Michigan, Center for South Asian Studies, senior research scholar. Consultant and writer. **Publications:** The Marathas, 1600-1818, 1993; Marathas, Marauders and State Formation in Eighteenth-Century India, 1994; Sunlight and Steel: The Story of the S.S. Constitution and the S.S. Independence, 1994; (ed.) Robes and Honor: The Medieval World of Investiture, 2001; Robes of Honor: Khil'at in Pre-Colonial and Colonial India, 2003; When Asia Was the World, 2007. **Address:** Ann Arbor, MI , U.S.A. **Online address:** stewart_gordon@mac.com

GORDON, Wendy M. American (born United States), b. 1967?. **Genres:** Women's Studies And Issues, Young Adult Fiction, History. **Career:** State University of New York-Plattsburgh, assistant professor of history, chair. Writer. **Publications:** Mill Girls and Strangers: Single Women's Independent Migration in England, Scotland and the United States, 1850-1881, 2002. **Address:** Department of History, State University of New York, 220 Champlain Valley Hall, 101 Broad St., Plattsburgh, NY 12901, U.S.A. **Online address:** gordonwm@plattsburgh.edu

GORDON, William. *See* **GORDON, William A.**

GORDON, William A. (William Gordon). American (born United States), b. 1950. **Genres:** History, Travel/Exploration, Documentaries/Reportage, Humor/Satire. **Career:** Writer. **Publications:** (Ed.) How Many Books Do You Sell in Ohio? A Quote Book for Writers, 1986; The Fourth of May: Killings and Coverups at Kent State, 1990; The Ultimate Hollywood Tour Book: The Incomparable Guide to Movie Stars? Homes, Movie and TV Locations, Scandals, Murders, Suicide and All the Famous Tourist Sites, 1992, 4th ed., 2007; Shot on This Site: A Travelers Guide to the Places and Locations Used to Film Famous Movies and TV Shows, 1995; Four Dead in Ohio: Was There a Conspiracy at Kent State?, 1995; The Quotable Writer, 2000. **Address:** PO Box 1463, Lake Forest, CA 92609, U.S.A. **Online address:** bgordonla@aol.com

GORDON, W. Terrence. Also writes as Alan R. Lintrey, Alan R. Lintrey. Canadian (born Canada), b. 1942. **Genres:** Literary Criticism And History, Language/Linguistics, Intellectual History, Humanities, Popular Culture, Speech/Rhetoric, Technology, Bibliography, Biography, Reference, Communications/Media. **Career:** University of Alberta, assistant professor of French and romance linguistics, professor, 1970-72; Dalhousie University, assistant professor of French, professor, 1972-, Alexander McLeod chair in modern languages, 1999-2002, now professor emeritus; St. Marys University, part-time lecturer in linguistics. Writer. **Publications:** Semantics: A Bibliography, 1965-1978, 1980; A History of Semantics, 1982; Semantics: A Bibliography, 1979-1985, 1987; C.K. Ogden: A Bio-Bibliographic Study, 1990; Semantics: A Bibliography, 1986-1991, 1992; C.K. Ogden and Linguistics, 1994; Saussure for Beginners, 1996; McLuhan for Beginners, 1997; Marshall McLuhan: Escape into Understanding. A Biography, 1997; In Two Words, 2000; Understanding Media: The Extensions of Man, 2003; (ed.) McLuhan Unbound, 2005; (ed.) The Classical Trivium: The Place of Thomas Nashe in The Learning of His Time, 2006; (ed.) Everyman's McLuhan, 2007; Linguistics for Beginners, 2008; Everyman's James Joyce, 2009; McLuhan: Guide for the Perplexed, 2010; From Cliche to Archetype, 2011. **Address:** Department of French, Dalhousie University, 6135 University Ave., Ste. 1114, Halifax, NS B3H 3J5, Canada. **Online address:** wtgordon@dal.ca

GORE, Ariel. American (born United States), b. 1970. **Genres:** Self Help, Reference, Travel/Exploration, Biography, Autobiography/Memoirs, Theology/Religion. **Career:** Hip Mama (magazine), founder and editor, 1994-. **Publications:** The Hip Mama Survival Guide, 1998; Mother Trip: Hip Mama's Guide to Staying Sane in the Chaos of Motherhood, 2000; (ed. with B. Lavender) Breeder: Real-Life Stories from the New Generation of Mothers, 2001; Atlas of the Human Heart, 2003; (ed.) Essential Hip Mama, 2004; Whatever, Mom: Hip Mama's Guide to Raising a Teenager, 2004; The Traveling Death and Resurrection Show, 2006; How to Become a Famous Writer Before You're Dead: Your Words in Print and Your Name in Lights, 2007; Bluebird: Women and the New Psychology of Happiness, 2010. Contributor to books. **Address:** 5 Bisbee Ct., Ste. 109, PO Box 21, Santa Fe, NM 87508, U.S.A. **Online address:** arielgore@earthlink.net

GORE, Kristin C. *See* **GORE, Kristin (C.).**

GORE, Kristin (C.). Also writes as Kristin C. Gore. American (born United States), b. 1977. **Genres:** Novels, Literary Criticism And History, Young Adult Fiction. **Career:** Futurama (animated television series), story editor and staff writer, 2000-03. **Publications:** Sammy's Hill: A Novel, 2004; Sammy's House, 2007; (co-author) Companion to the Major Motion Picture Arctic Tale, 2007; (co-author) Arctic Tale, 2007; Sweet Jiminy, 2011. Contributor to periodicals. **Address:** Miramax Books, 77 W 66th St., Fl. 11, New York, NY 10023-6201, U.S.A.

GORE, Patrick Wilson. (Rob Wilson). Canadian (born Canada), b. 1938. **Genres:** Novels, Mystery/Crime/Suspense, Young Adult Fiction. **Career:** Associated Press, editor, 1968-69; Humber College, assistant chairman, 1969-73; North Frontier Communications, president, 1971-87. Writer. **Publications:** (As Rob Wilson) Escape from Marrakesh, 1983; (as Rob Wilson) Frame-up in Belize, 1985; And Death in Erin, 2000; The Gold Miner of Magadan, 2001; Bolivar's Right Hand, 2001; In the Month of Muharram, 2001; Jango Says, 2001; Staggerbush: A Story of the New Millenium, 2001; The Valley of the Germans, 2003. **Address:** PO Box 573, Perth, ON K7H 3K4, Canada.

GOREHAM, Gary A. American (born United States), b. 1953. **Genres:** Local History/Rural Topics, Agriculture/Forestry, Social Commentary, History, Politics/Government. **Career:** North Dakota State University, State Data Center for Agricultural Economics, assistant director, 1985-87, assistant professor, 1987-94, associate professor of sociology and anthropology, 1994, professor of sociology, department chair, Rural Social Science Education program, director, Center for Rural Studies, co-director, Community Development Minor, co-director; Rural Church Network for the U.S. and Canada, treasurer; Great Plains Sociologist, co-editor. **Publications:** (With M.P. Riley and J.L Satterlee) South Dakota Population, Housing, and Farm Census Facts: Ranking of Counties on Population and Housing (1970-1980) and Farms (1978), 1983; (with M.P. Riley and J.L Satterlee) Population Change of Counties and Incorporated Places in South Dakota, 1950-1980, 1984; (with J.L. Satterlee) South Dakota School Districts, 1980: Population and Housing Information, 1984; (with S.G. Goss and R.T. Wagner) South Dakotans on The Move: Characteristics of People Leaving and Entering the State, 1970 to 1980, 1984; (with J. Daul and R.W. Rathge) Racial Minority Groups in North Dakota, 1970-1980: A Statistical Portrait, 1986; (with R.W. Rathge) Projected Prevalence of Alzheimer's Disease Among North Dakota's Elderly, 1986; (with R.W. Rathge and S.Thom) Comparative Viability of Senior Citizen Centers in North Dakota, 1988; (with F.L. Leistritz and R.W. Rathge) Labor Force Projections for North Dakota, 1980-2000, 1988; (with R.W. Rathge and S.D. Anonsen) The Red River Valley: A Socio-Demographic and Economic Profile, 1988; The Rural Church in America: A Century of Writings: A Bibliography, 1990; (with R.W. Rathge and G.D. Pederson) Distribution of Personal Income in Agriculture-Dependent Counties of Midwestern States: A Policy Variables Approach, 1990; (with D.L. Watt and R.M. Jacobsen) The Socioeconomics of Sustainable Agriculture: An Annotated Bibliography, 1992; (ed.) Encyclopedia of Rural America: The Land and People, 1997, 2nd ed., 2008. **Address:** Department of Sociology and Anthropology, North Dakota State University, 226 Richard H. Barry Hall, PO Box 6050, Fargo, ND 58108-6050, U.S.A. **Online address:** gary.goreham@ndsu.edu

GORHAM, Deborah. Canadian/American (born United States), b. 1937. **Genres:** Women's Studies And Issues, Autobiography/Memoirs, Humanities, Social Sciences. **Career:** Carleton University, Department of History, assistant professor, 1969-78, associate professor, 1978-88, professor of history, 1988-2002, professor emerita, 2002-, distinguished research professor, 2004-. Writer. **Publications:** The Victorian Girl and the Feminine Ideal, 1982; Vera Brittain: A Feminist Life, 1996. EDITOR: (with J. Williamson) Up and Doing: Canadian Women and Peace, 1990; (with D. Dodd) Caring and Curing: Historical Perspectives on Women and Healing in Canada, 1994. Contributor to books and periodicals. **Address:** Department of History, Carleton University, 400 Paterson Hall, 1125 Colonel By Dr., Ottawa, ON K1S 5B6, Canada. **Online address:** dgorham@ccs.carleton.ca

GORINI, Catherine A. American (born United States), b. 1949. **Genres:** Mathematics/Statistics. **Career:** Maharishi University of Management, professor of mathematics, 1978-, dean of faculty. Writer. **Publications:** (Ed.) Geometry at Work: A Collection of Papers Showing Applications of Geometry, 2000; The Facts on File Geometry Handbook, 2003, rev. ed., 2009; Master Math: Probability, 2010. **Address:** c/o Roger Williams, New England Publishing Associates, PO Box 66066, Lawrenceville, NJ 08648-6066, U.S.A. **Online address:** cgorini@mum.edu

GÖRLACH, Manfred. German (born Germany), b. 1937. **Genres:** Mythology/Folklore, Cultural/Ethnic Topics. **Career:** University of Heidelberg, lecturer in English, 1967-84; University of Cologne, professor of English language and medieval studies, 1984-2002, chair of English linguistics and medieval studies, through 1984, professor emeritus, 2002-. Writer. **Publications:** The South English Legendary, Gilte Legende and Golden Legend, 1972; The Textual Tradition of the South English Legendary, 1974; Einführung in die englische Sprachgeschichte, 1974; Einführung ins Frühneuenglische, 1978; Studies in the History of the English Language, 1990; Englishes: Studies in Varieties of English, 1984-1988, 1991; Eingemauert: Erinnerungen an Potsdam und Brandenburg, 1961-64, 1991; Introduction to Early Modern English, 1991; Mac ond Mauris in Old English Rhymed an Alliterative Verse, 1992; (with B. Glauser and E.W. Schneider) A New Bibliography of Writings on Varieties of English, 1984-1992/93, 1993; Max und Moritz in romanischen Sprachen, 1994; New Studies in the History of English, 1995; More Englishes: New Studies in Varieties of English, 1988-1994, 1995; Max und Moritz in aller Munde: Wandlungen eines Kinderbuches: eine Ausstellung in der Universitäts und Stadtbibliothek Köln, 27. Juni-30. September 1997, 1997; A Linguistic History of English, 1997; Even More Englishes: Studies,

1996-1997, 1998; An Annotated Bibliography of 19th-Century Grammars of English, 1998; Aspects of the History of English, 1998; Studies in Middle English Saints Legends, 1998; English in Nineteenth-Century England: An Introduction, 1999; Wilhelm Buschs Plisch und Plum: in 40 deutschen Mundarten, 1999; Explorations in English Historical Linguistics, 2002; Still More Englishes, 2002; Weltsprache Englisch: Katalog zur Ausstellung, 2002; English Words Abroad, 2003; Topics in English Historical Linguistics, 2003; Text Types and the History of English 2004. EDITOR: East Midland Revision of the South English Legendary: A Selection from MS C.U.L. Add. 3039, 1976; (with R.W. Bailey) English as a World Language, 1982; Focus on Scotland, 1985; Max and Moritz in English Dialects and Creoles, 1986; (with J. Holm) Focus on the Caribbean, 1986; Dictionary of European Anglicisms: A Usage Dictionary of Anglicisms in Sixteen European Languages, 2001; (with H. Diller) Towards a History of English as a History of Genres, 2001; English in Europe, 2002; Annotated Bibliography of European Anglicisms, 2002. **Address:** English Seminar, University of Cologne, Albertus-Magnus-Platz, Cologne, 50931, Germany.

GORLIN, Eitan. (Martin Eisenstadt). American (born United States), b. 1969?. **Genres:** Autobiography/Memoirs. **Career:** Writer, filmmaker and actor. **Publications:** (As Martin Eisenstadt with D. Mirvish) I Am Martin Eisenstadt: One Man's Wildly Inappropriate Adventures with the Last Republicans (fake memoir), 2009. **Address:** U.S.A. **Online address:** martin@eisenstadtgroup.com

GORMAN, Carol. American (born United States), b. 1952. **Genres:** Children's Fiction. **Career:** Teacher, through 1984; writer, 1984-; American School, writer-in-residence; Coe College, part-time instructor, adjunct instructor, instructor, 2002-. **Publications:** America's Farm Crisis, 1987; Chelsey and the Green-Haired Kid, 1987; Pornography, 1988; T. J. and the Pirate Who Wouldn't Go Home, 1990; The Biggest Bully in Brookdale, 1992; It's Not Fair, 1992; Die for Me, 1992; Graveyard Moon, 1993; The Great Director, 1993; Skin Deep, 1993; Nobody's Friend, 1993; The Richest Kid in the World, 1993; Brian's Footsteps, 1994; The Taming of Roberta Parsley, 1994; Million Dollar Winner, 1994; The Rumor, 1994; The Miraculous Makeover of Lizard Flanagan, 1994; Jennifer-the-Jerk Is Missing, 1994; Back from the Dead, 1995; Bugman Lives!, 1996; Lizard Flanagan, Supermodel?, 1998; Dork in Disguise, 1999; (ed. with E. Gorman) Felonious Felines, 2000; Dork on the Run, 2002; A Midsummer Night's Dork, 2004; (with R.J. Findley) Stumptown Kid, 2005; Games, 2007. **Address:** c/o Author Mail, HarperCollins Inc., 10 E 53rd St., New York, NY 10022, U.S.A. **Online address:** carol@carolgorman.com

GORMAN, Dave. British (born England), b. 1971. **Genres:** Recreation, Humor/Satire. **Career:** Stand-up comedian, 1990-. Writer. **Publications:** (With C. Aherne, C. Cash and H. Normal) Mrs. Merton's World of Television, 1997; (with D. Wallace) Are You Dave Gorman?, 2001; Dave Gorman's Googlewhack! Adventure, 2004; America Unchained, 2008; Dave Gorman Vs the Rest of the World, 2010. **Address:** c/o Author Mail, Avalon, 4A Exmoor St., London, GL W10 6BD, England. **Online address:** dave@davegorman.com

GORMAN, James. American (born United States), b. 1949?. **Genres:** Children's Fiction, Children's Non-fiction, Essays, Medicine/Health, Sciences, Young Adult Fiction, Biology. **Career:** Discover Magazine, columnist. **Publications:** Hazards to Your Health: The Problem of Environmental Disease, 1979; First Aid for Hypochondriacs (humor), 1982; (with J.R. Horner) Maia: A Dinosaur Grows Up (juvenile fiction), 1985; (with J.R. Horner) Digging Dinosaurs, 1988; The Man with No Endorphins and Other Reflections on Science, 1988; The Total Penguin, 1990; Ocean Enough and Time: Discovering the Waters around Antarctica, 1995; (with J.R. Horner) How to Build A Dinosaur: Extinction Doesn't Have to be Forever, 2009. **Address:** Discover Magazine, 114 5th Ave., New York, NY 10011, U.S.A.

GORMAN, Lyn. Australian (born Australia), b. 1947. **Genres:** Theology/Religion, Social Commentary, Bibliography, History, Film. **Career:** University of Sussex, administrator, assistant secretary, 1974-80, Institute of Development Studies, researcher, 1974-80; Brighton Polytechnic, faculty administrative officer in education studies, 1981-83; Australian Quarantine Inspection Service, technical editor, 1988-89; Charles Sturt University, lecturer in history and politics, 1991-96, senior lecturer in history and politics, 1996-2002, School of Humanities and Social Sciences, head, 1999-2002, dean of faculty of arts, 2002-, deputy vice chancellor of administration and vice president of administration, 2007-11; Deakin University, visiting fellow, 1996. **Publica-**

tions: (Comp.) Bibliography on Community and Rural Development: Europe, 1978-81, 1982; (with G.E. Gorman) Theological and Religious Reference Materials: General Resources and Biblical Studies, 1984; (with R. Israeli) Islam in China: A Critical Bibliography, 1994; (contrib.) Qualitative Research for the Information Professional, 1997; (co-author) Reasons Values and Institutions, 1999; (with D. McLean) Media and Society in the Twentieth Century: A Historical Introduction, 2003, 2nd ed. as Media and Society into the 21st Century: A Historical Introduction, 2009. EDITOR: (with M. Kiljunen) The Enlargement of the European Community: Case-studies of Greece, Portugal, and Spain, 1983; (with M.J. Kiljunen) The Second Enlargement of the EEC: The New Members, 1983; CDB: A Tribute from the Faculty of Arts, 2001; (with N. Blacklow and intro.) Arts and Ownership in the New Millennium, 2001. **Address:** Wiley-Blackwell, 350 Main St., Malden, MA 02148, U.S.A.

GORMAN, Martha. American (born United States), b. 1953. **Genres:** Adult Non-fiction, Environmental Sciences/Ecology, Sciences, Humor/Satire, Psychology, Social Sciences, Natural History, Education, Education. **Career:** Freelance writer and translator, 1979-92; Englewood-Colorado Chiropractic Association, director of public relations, 1992-. **Publications:** El Mercado del libro en Colombia, 1978; (with G. Campbell and M. Cader) Everybody for President: Everything You Need to Know to Run for the Highest Office in the Land, 1984; (with B.S. Busick) Ill, Not Insane, 1986; Environmental Hazards: Marine Pollution, 1993; (with C.S. Roberts) Euthanasia: A Reference Handbook, 1996, 2nd ed., (with J.F. McDougall), 2008. Contributor of articles to magazines. **Address:** 4282 Eldorado Springs Dr., Boulder, CO 80303-9611, U.S.A. **Online address:** marthagorman@att.net

GORMAN, Michael E. American (born United States), b. 1952. **Genres:** Sciences, Technology, Philosophy, Economics. **Career:** University of New Hampshire, Department of Psychology, graduate teaching assistant, 1976-78, instructor, 1978-80, dissertation fellow, 1980-81; Michigan Technological University, assistant professor, 1981-87, associate professor of psychology and humanities, 1987-88; University of Virginia, visiting associate professor, 1988-90, associate professor of humanities, 1990-99, Department of Science, Technology and Society, professor, 1999-, Division of Technology, Culture and Communication, chair, 2000-03. Writer. **Publications:** Simulating Science: Heuristics, Mental Models, and Technoscientific Thinking, 1992; Transforming Nature: Ethics, Invention and Discovery, 1998; (with M.M. Mehalik and P.H. Werhane) Ethical and Environmental Challenges to Engineering, 2000; (co-ed.) Scientific and Technological Thinking, 2005; (ed.) Trading Zones and Interactional Expertise: Creating New Kinds of Collaboration, 2010. Contributor to journals. **Address:** Department of Science, Technology and Society, University of Virginia, A217 Thorton Hall, 395 McCormick Rd., PO Box 400745, Charlottesville, VA 22904-4744, U.S.A. **Online address:** meg3c@virginia.edu

GORN, Elliott (J.). American (born United States), b. 1951. **Genres:** History, Biography. **Career:** University of Alabama, instructor, 1981-82, assistant professor of American studies, 1983-85; Miami University, assistant professor of history and American studies, 1985-88, associate professor of history and American studies, 1988-94, director of American studies, 1985-92, professor of history and American studies, 1994-98; Purdue University, associate professor of history, 1998-2001, professor of history, 2001-02; Brown University, Department of History, professor of history, 2003-, Department of American Civilization, chair of American civilization, 2006-08. Writer. **Publications:** The Manly Art: Bare-Knuckle Prize Fighting in America, 1986; (with W. Goldstein) A Brief History of American Sports, 1993; Mother Jones: The Most Dangerous Woman in America, 2001; Dillinger's Wild Ride, 2009. EDITOR: (with R. Roberts and T.D. Bilhartz) Constructing the American Past: A Source Book of a People's History, 1991, 7th ed., 2011; (with M.K. Cayton and P.W. Williams) The Encyclopedia of American Social History, 3 vols., 1993; Muhammad Ali: The People's Champ, 1995; (and intro.) The McGuffey Readers: Selections from the 1879 Edition, 1998; Sports in Chicago, 2008. Contributor to periodicals. **Address:** Department of History, Brown University, 79 Brown St., PO Box N, Providence, RI 02912, U.S.A. **Online address:** elliott_gorn@brown.edu

GORN, Michael H. (Michael Herman Gorn). American (born United States), b. 1950. **Genres:** History, Sciences, Technology, Biography, Astronomy. **Career:** New England Historic Genealogical Society, chief of archives, 1978-81; Headquarters Air Force Systems Command, staff historian, 1981-85, chief historian, 1989-91; Office of Air Force History, staff historian, 1985-89, senior historian, 1993-95; U.S. Environmental Protection Agency, chief historian, 1991-93; National Air and Space Museum, research collaborator, 1994-; NASA, Dryden Flight Research Center, Aviation and Spaceflight History, author and researcher, 1996-, chief historian. **Publications:** Harnessing the Genie: Science and Technology Forecasting for the Air Force, 1944-1986, 1988; The Universal Man: Theodore von Kármán's Life in Aeronautics, 1992; Hugh L. Dryden's Career in Aviation and Space, 1996; Expanding the Envelope: Flight Research at NACA and NASA, 2001; (with R.P. Hallion) On the Frontier: Flight Research at Dryden, 1946-1999, 2001; (with R.P. Hallion) On the Frontier: Experimental Flight at NASA Dryden, 2004. EDITOR: An Index and Guide to the Microfilm Edition of the Massachusetts and Maine Direct Tax Census of 1798, 1979; (and intro.) Prophecy Fulfilled: Toward New Horizons and Its Legacy, 1994. Works appear in anthologies. **Address:** Dryden Space Flight Research Center, PO Box 273, Edwards, CA 93523, U.S.A.

GORN, Michael Herman. See **GORN, Michael H.**

GORNICK, Vivian. American (born United States), b. 1935. **Genres:** Literary Criticism And History, Women's Studies And Issues, Autobiography/Memoirs, Essays, Young Adult Fiction. **Career:** State University of New York, instructor in English, 1966-67; Hunter College of the City University of New York, instructor in English, 1967-68; Village Voice, staff writer, 1969-77; The House of Elder Artists Inc., founder; The New School, visiting faculty, instructor of writing; Harvard University, Radcliffe Institute, fellow, 2007-08. **Publications:** (Ed. with B.K. Moran) Woman in Sexist Society: Studies in Power and Powerlessness, 1971; In Search of Ali Mahmoud: An American Woman in Egypt, 1973; The Romance of American Communism, 1977; Essays in Feminism, 1978; Women in Science: Portraits From a World in Transition, 1983, rev. ed. as Women in Science: 100 Journeys into the Territory, 1990; Fierce Attachments: A Memoir, 1987; Approaching Eye Level: Personal Essays, 1996; The End of the Novel of Love: Critical Essays, 1997; The Situation and the Story: The Art of Personal Narrative, 2001; Escribir Narrativa Personal, 2003; Solitude of Self: Thinking about Elizabeth Cady Stanton, 2005; Men in My Life, 2008; Women in Science: Then and Now, 2009; Emma Goldman, 2011. Contributor to periodicals. **Address:** The House of Elder Artists Inc., 175 W 12th St., Ste. 16 F, New York, NY 10011, U.S.A.

GOROKHOVA, Elena. American/Russian (born Russia), b. 1955?. **Genres:** Autobiography/Memoirs. **Career:** Writer and educator. **Publications:** A Mountain of Crumbs: A Memoir, 2010. **Address:** c/o Molly Friedrich, The Friedrich Agency, 19 W 21st St., Ste. 201, New York, NY 10010, U.S.A. **Online address:** elena@elenagorokhova.com

GORRA, Michael (Edward). American (born United States), b. 1957. **Genres:** Literary Criticism And History. **Career:** Smith College, professor of English, 1985-, Mary Augusta Jordan professor of English language and literature. Writer. **Publications:** The English Novel at Mid-Century: From the Leaning Tower, 1990; After Empire: Scott, Naipaul, Rushdie, 1997; The Bells in Their Silence: Travels through Germany, 2004; (intro.) Mani: Travels in the Southern Peloponnese, 2006; (ed. and intro.) Portable Conrad, 2007; (ed.) As I Lay Dying: Authoritative Text, Backgrounds and Contexts, Criticism, 2010; Portrait of a Novel, forthcoming. **Address:** Department of English, Smith College, 401 Seelye Hall, Northampton, MA 01063, U.S.A. **Online address:** mgorra@smith.edu

GORRELL, Gena K. Canadian (born Canada), b. 1946. **Genres:** Children's Non-fiction, Mystery/Crime/Suspense, Education, Reference. **Career:** Lester and Orpen Dennys, editor, 1978-91. **Publications:** Stories of the Witch Queen, 1985; (ed.) House on Ninth Street: Interviews and Photographs from Guatemala, 1994; North Star to Freedom: The Story of the Underground Railroad, 1997; Catching Fire: The Story of Firefighting, 1999; Heart and Soul: The Story of Florence Nightingale, 2000; Working Like a Dog: The Story of Working Dogs through History, 2003; In the Land of the Jaguar: South America and its People, 2007; Say What?: The Weird and Mysterious Journey of the English Language, 2009. **Address:** c/o Author Mail, Tundra Books, 75 Sherbourne St., 5th Fl., Toronto, ON M5A 2P9, Canada. **Online address:** gorrell@netrover.com

GORRELL, Lorraine. American (born United States) **Genres:** Music. **Career:** Winthrop University, professor of music, 1973-2008, now professor emeritus. Writer and singer. **Publications:** The Nineteenth-Century German Lied, 1993; Discordant Melody: Alexander Zemlinsky, His Songs and the Second Viennese School, 2002. Contributor to music journals. **Address:** Department of Music, Winthrop University, 129 Conservatory of

Music, 701 Oakland Ave., Rock Hill, SC 29733, U.S.A. **Online address:** gorrelll@comporium.net

GORRELL, Robert (Mark). American (born United States), b. 1914. **Genres:** Mystery/Crime/Suspense, Language/Linguistics, Literary Criticism And History. **Career:** Deep Springs College, instructor, 1939-42; Indiana University, instructor, 1942-45; University of Nevada, assistant professor, professor of English, 1945-80, professor emeritus, 1980-, Graduate School, dean, 1967-68, College of Arts and Sciences, dean, 1972-76, vice-president for academic affairs, 1976-80, distinguished faculty; University of California, visiting professor, 1953; University of Sydney, Fulbright professor, 1954-55; Portland School District, consultant, 1959-61; University of Helsinki, Fulbright professor, 1961-62. Writer. **Publications:** (With C. Emery and K.N. Cameron) Practice in English Communication, 2 vols., 1944; (with C. Laird) Modern English Handbook, 1953, (with C. Laird and M. Urie) 7th ed. as Modern English Rhetoric and Handbook, 1988; (with C. Laird) Modern English Workbook, 1957, 2nd ed., 1962; (with C. Laird) A Course in Modern English, 1960; (with C. Laird) English As Language: Backgrounds, Development, Usage, 1961; (with A. Kitzhaber and P. Roberts) Education for College, 1961; (with C. Laird and P. Pflug) A Basic Course in Modern English, 1963; (ed.) Rhetoric: Theories for Application: Papers Presented At The 1965 Convention of The National Council of Teachers of English, 1967; (with C. Laird and R.E. Freeman) Modern English Reader, 1970, (co-ed.) 2nd ed., 1977; (with C. Laird) Reading about Language, 1971; (with M.M. Brown) Writing and Language, vol. I-II, 1971; (with C. Laird) Writing Modern English, 1973; Watch Your Language!: Mother Tongue and Her Wayward Children, 1994; Murder at the Rose, 2000; What's in a Word?: Etymological Gossip about Some Interesting English Words, 2001. **Address:** Department Of English, University of Nevada, 1664 N Virginia St., Reno, NV 89557-0208, U.S.A. **Online address:** rmgorrell@aol.com

GORRINGE, Timothy. (Timothy Jervis Gorringe). British (born England), b. 1946?. **Genres:** Philosophy, Theology/Religion, Economics. **Career:** Tamil Nadu Theological Seminary, teacher of theology, 1979-86; University of St. Andrews, reader in contextual theology, 1995-98; University of Exeter, Department of Theology and Religion, St. Luke's professor of theological studies, 1998-; St. John's College, chaplain, fellow and tutor in theology. Writer and theologist. **Publications:** THEOLOGICAL NON-FICTION: Redeeming Time: Atonement through Education, 1986; (as T.J. Gorringe) Discerning Spirit: A Theology of Revelation, 1990; (as Timothy J. Gorringe) Capital and the Kingdom: Theological Ethics and Economic Order, 1994; God's Just Vengeance: Crime, Violence, and the Rhetoric of Salvation, 1996; Karl Barth: Against Hegemony, 1999; Fair Shares: Ethics and the Global Economy, 1999; (as T.J. Gorringe) A Theology of the Built Environment: Justice, Empowerment, Redemption, 2002; (as T.J. Gorringe) The Education of Desire: Towards a Theology of the Senses, 2002; (as T.J. Gorringe) Furthering Humanity: A Theology of Culture, 2004; (as T.J. Gorringe) Earthly Visions: Theology and the Challenges of Art, 2011; (as T.J. Gorringe) Common Good and the Global Emergency, 2011. **Address:** Department of Theology and Religion, University of Exeter, Amory Bldg., Rennes Dr., Exeter, DN EX4 4RJ, England. **Online address:** t.j.gorringe@exeter.ac.uk

GORRINGE, Timothy Jervis. See **GORRINGE, Timothy.**

GORRITI, Gustavo. (Gustavo Gorriti Ellenbogen). Panamanian (born Panama) **Genres:** History, Politics/Government. **Career:** Caretas (weekly magazine), staff journalist; La Prensa (newspaper), deputy editor, associate director, 2001; Instituto de Defensa Legal (IDL), journalist-in-residence. **Publications:** (As Gustavo Gorriti Ellenbogen) Sendero: Historia De La Guerra Milenaria En El Perú, 1990; The Shining Path: A History of the Millenarian War in Peru, 1999; La Batalla, 2003; La Calavera En Negro: El Traficante QueQuiso Gobernar Un País, 2006; Petroaudios: Políticos, Espías y Periodistas Detrás del Escándalo, 2009. **Address:** La Prensa Panama, Apartado 6-4586 El Dorado Ave., 12 de octubre, Hato Pintado Panama, 51562, Panama.

GORSKI, Philip S. American (born United States) **Genres:** Young Adult Non-fiction. **Career:** University of Wisconsin, assistant professor, 1996-2001, associate professor, 2001-03, professor of sociology, 2003-04, director of the Center for Comparative Social Analysis, 2001-; Yale University, professor of sociology, 2004-, co-director of the Center for Comparative Research, 2004-. Writer. **Publications:** NONFICTION: (with A.S. Markovits) The German Left: Red, Green and Beyond, 1993; The Disciplinary Revolution: Calvinism and the Rise of the State in Early Modern Europe, 2003;

(ed. with C. Camic and D.M. Trubek) Max Weber's Economy and Society: A Critical Companion, 2005. Contributor to books and journals. **Address:** Department of Sociology, Yale University, 140 Prospect St., New Haven, CT 06511, U.S.A. **Online address:** philip.gorski@yale.edu

GORUP, Radmila J(ovanović). American/Yugoslav (born United States), b. 1935?. **Genres:** Humanities, Language/Linguistics, Essays, Adult Non-fiction. **Career:** Columbia University, instructor in Slavic languages, 1980-86, lecturer, adjunct professor of Slavic languages, 1994-, senior lecturer; University of California, lecturer in Slavic languages, 1986-93. Writer. **Publications:** The Semantic Organization of the Serbocroatian Verb, 1987; (ed. with N. Obradović) The Prince of Fire: An Anthology of Contemporary Serbian Short Stories, 1998; (ed. with B. Rakić) In a Foreign Harbor: Essays in Honor of Vasa D. Mihailovich, 2000; (ed. with J. Davis and N. Stern) Advances in Functional Linguistics: Columbia School beyond Its Origins, 2006; (ed.) Slave Girl: And Other Stories about Women, 2009. Contributor of articles to periodicals. **Address:** Department of Slavic Languages, Columbia University, 718 Hamilton Hall, PO Box 2839, New York, NY 10027-6902, U.S.A. **Online address:** rjg26@columbia.edu

GOSDEN, R. G. See **GOSDEN, Roger.**

GOSDEN, Roger. Also writes as R. G. Gosden, Roger Gordon Gosden. American/British (born England), b. 1948. **Genres:** Medicine/Health, Sciences, Biology. **Career:** Duke University, Population Council, research fellow, 1974-75; Cambridge University, research fellow, 1975-76; University of Edinburgh, lecturer, senior lecturer, 1976-94; University of Leeds, professor of reproductive biology, 1994-99; McGill University, professor, 1999-, Royal Victoria Hospital, research director for obstetrics and gynecology, 1999-2001; Eastern Virginia Medical School, Jones Institute for Reproductive Medicine, scientific director, 2001-04; Cornell University, Weill Cornell Medical College, faculty. Writer. **Publications:** Biology of Menopause, 1985; Transplantation of Ovarian and Testicular Tissues, 1996; Cheating Time: Science, Sex, and Aging, 1996; Designer Babies: The Brave New World of Reproductive Technology, 1999; (ed. with A.O. Trounson) Biology and Pathology of the Oocyte: Its Role in Fertility and Reproductive Medicine, 2003. Contributor to journals. **Address:** Weill Cornell Medical College, Cornell University, Rm. S-509, 1300 York Ave., New York, NY 10065-4805, U.S.A. **Online address:** rgg2004@med.cornell.edu

GOSDEN, Roger Gordon. See **GOSDEN, Roger.**

GOSE, Peter. Canadian (born Canada), b. 1955. **Genres:** Anthropology/Ethnology, Adult Non-fiction, Agriculture/Forestry. **Career:** University of Lethbridge, assistant professor, 1987-91, associate professor of anthropology, 1991-94; University of Regina, associate professor of anthropology and head of department, 1994-2005; Memorial University of Newfoundland, lecturer; University of Calgary, lecturer; McGill University, lecturer; University of Western Ontario, lecturer; Universidad de Barcelona, lecturer; Pontificia Universidad Catolica delPeru, lecturer; Carleton University, Department of Sociology and Anthropology, professor, department chair. Writer. **Publications:** Deathly Waters and Hungry Mountains: Agrarian Ritual and Class Formation in an Andean Town, 1994; Invaders As Ancestors: On The Intercultural Making And Unmaking Of Spanish Colonialism In The Andes, 2008. Contributor to books and journals. **Address:** Department of Sociology and Anthropology, Carleton University, B759 Loeb Bldg., 1125 Colonel By Dr., Ottawa, ON K1S 5B6, Canada. **Online address:** peter_gose@carleton.ca

GOSHEN-GOTTSTEIN, Esther. (Esther Rachel Goshen-Gottstein). Israeli/British/German (born Germany), b. 1928. **Genres:** Psychology, Humanities. **Career:** Hadassah Hospital, senior clinical psychologist, 1961-68; Child Development Center, senior clinical psychologist, 1968-70; Office of the Prime Minister, head of research project, 1971-75; Bar Ilan University, senior lecturer, 1973-85. Clinical psychologist and freelance writer. **Publications:** Marriage and First Pregnancy, 1966; (as Esther Rachel Goshen-Gottstein) Coping Behavior of Mothers of Multiple Births, 1976; Recalled to Life: The Story of a Coma, 1990; Surviving Widowhood, 2002. Contributor to journals. **Address:** 17 Jabotinsky St., Jerusalem, 92141, Israel. **Online address:** egoshen@netvision.net.il

GOSHEN-GOTTSTEIN, Esther Rachel. See **GOSHEN-GOTTSTEIN, Esther.**

GOSLINE, Andrea Alban. (Andrea Alban). American (born United States), b. 1959?. **Genres:** Human Relations/Parenting, How-to Books, Theology/Religion. **Career:** Ambledance Pictures and Verse, creative director and co-owner. Writer. **Publications:** AS ANDREA ALBAN: (with L.B. Bossi and A.M. Beanland) Mother's Nature: Timeless Wisdom for the Journey into Motherhood, 1999; Little Moments of Peace: Daily Reflections for Mothers, 2002; January's Child: The Birthday Month Book, 2007; Ten Little Wishes: A Baby Animal Counting Book, 2007; The Happiness Tree: Celebrating the Gifts of Trees We Treasure, 2008; Anya's War, 2011. OTHERS: Welcoming Ways: Creating Your Baby's Welcome Ceremony with the Wisdom of World Traditions, 2000. **Address:** Feiwel and Friends, 175 5th Ave., New York, NY 10010, U.S.A. **Online address:** andreaalban@me.com

GOSLING, J. See **GOSLING, J. C. B.**

GOSLING, J. C. B. Also writes as J. Gosling, Justin Gosling. British (born England), b. 1930. **Genres:** Philosophy, Theology/Religion, Translations. **Career:** Oxford University, Wadham College, lecturer in philosophy, 1958-60, Pembroke College, lecturer in philosophy, 1958-60, St. Edmund Hall, fellow, 1960-, 1982-96, tutor, 1960-67, senior tutor in philosophy, 1967-72, senior proctor, 1977-78, principal, 1982-96, pro-vice-chancellor, 1989-95. Writer. **Publications:** (As J. Gosling) Marriage and The Love of God, 1965; Pleasure and Desire: The Case for Hedonism Reviewed, 1969; (contrib.) The Business of Reason, 1969; Plato, 1973; (trans. and intro.) Plato, Philebus, 1975; (contrib.) Nature and Conduct, 1975; (with C.C.W. Taylor) The Greeks on Pleasure, 1982; (as Justin Gosling) The Weakness of the Will, 1990. Contributor to periodicals. **Address:** St. Edmund Hall, Oxford University, Oxford, OX OX1 4AR, England.

GOSLING, Justin. See **GOSLING, J. C. B.**

GOSLING, Paula. Also writes as Ainslie Skinner. British/American (born United States), b. 1939. **Genres:** Mystery/Crime/Suspense, Young Adult Fiction. **Career:** Campbell-Ewald Advertising, copywriter trainee, 1962-64; C. Mitchell & Co., copywriter, 1964-67; Pritchard-Wood Advertising, copywriter, 1967-68; David Williams Advertising, copywriter, 1968-69; Mitchell's Advertising, copy consultant, 1969-70; ATA Advertising, copy consultant, 1976-79; writer, 1979-. **Publications:** A Running Duck in US as Fair Game, 1978; The Zero Trap, 1979; Loser's Blues, 1980 in US as Solo Blues, 1981; (as Ainslie Skinner) Mind's Eye, 1980 in US as The Harrowing, 1981; The Woman in Red, 1983; Monkey Puzzle, 1985; The Wychford Murders, 1986; Hoodwink, 1988; Backlash, 1989; Death Penalties: A Luke Abbott Mystery, 1991; The Body in Blackwater Bay, 1992; A Few Dying Words, 1993; The Dead of Winter, 1995; Death and Shadows, 1999; Cobra, 1999; Underneath Every Stone, 2000; Ricochet, 2002; Tears of the Dragon, 2004. **Address:** Greene & Heaton Ltd., 37 Goldhawk Rd, London, GL W12 8QQ, England. **Online address:** paula.gosling@virgin.net

GOSS, Glenda Dawn. Finnish/American (born United States), b. 1947. **Genres:** Music, Translations, Literary Criticism And History. **Career:** University of Georgia, lecturer, 1976-78, assistant professor, 1978-85, associate professor, 1985-93, professor of musicology, 1993-, Division of Musicology, head; University of Helsinki, Fulbright professor, 1995-96; Sibelius Academy, teacher, visiting professor, 1995-96, professor, 1998-. Writer. **Publications:** (Ed. and intro. as Glenda Thompson) Benedictus Appenzeller: Chansons, 1982; (with B. Martinů) Par T.S.F.: Pianoforte: Na Vlnách Rozhlasu, 1990; Music and the Moderns: The Life and Works of Carol Robinson, 1993; Jean Sibelius and Olin Downes: Music, Friendship, Criticism, 1995; (trans.) K. Kilpelaainen, Sibelius: Jaervenpaeae, ja Ainola, 1995; (ed.) The Sibelius Companion, 1996; (trans.) Werke Jean Sibelius, 1996; (ed. and intro.) Jean Sibelius: The Hämeenlinna Letters: Scenes From a Musical Life, 1874-1895; Jean Sibelius: Ungdomsbrev, 1997; Jean Sibelius: A Guide to Research, 1998; (ed.) Kullervo: op. 7, 2005; Sibelius: A Composer's Life and the Awakening of Finland, 2009. Contributor to books, journals and periodicals. **Address:** Sibelius Academy, 250 River Rd., PO Box 86, Helsinki, 00251, Finland. **Online address:** glenda.goss@gmail.com

GOSS, Kristin A. American (born United States), b. 1965. **Genres:** Young Adult Non-fiction. **Career:** Chronicle of Philanthropy, staff writer and senior editor, 1988-94; Georgetown University, political science instructor, 2002-05; Duke University, Sanford School of Public Policy, assistant professor of public policy and political science, 2005-. **Publications:** Disarmed: The Missing Movement for Gun Control in America (nonfiction), 2006. Contributor to books. **Address:** Sanford School of Public Policy, Duke University, PO Box 90245, Durham, NC 27708-0245, U.S.A. **Online address:** kgoss@duke.edu

GOSS, Pete. American/British (born England), b. 1962?. **Genres:** Westerns/Adventure, Biography. **Career:** Adventurer and writer. **Publications:** Close to the Wind, 1999. Contributor to periodicals. **Address:** c/o Author Mail, Carroll & Graf, 345 W 17th St., 11th Fl., New York, NY 10011-5300, U.S.A.

GOSS, Theodora. American/Hungarian (born Hungary) **Genres:** Young Adult Fiction, Novellas/Short Stories, Poetry. **Career:** Boston University, Atrs and Sciences Writing Program, lecturer. Corporate attorney and writer. **Publications:** (Intro.) Disturbing Muses, 2005; In the Forest of Forgetting, 2006; (ed. with D. Sherman) Interfictions: An Anthology of Interstitial Writing, 2007; (ed.) Voices from Fairyland: The Fantastical Poems of Mary Coleridge, Charlotte Mew and Sylvia Townsend Warner, 2008. Works appear in anthologies. **Address:** Departmentt of English, Boston University, 236 Bay State Rd., 4th Fl., Boston, MA 02215, U.S.A. **Online address:** theodora@theodoragoss.com

GOTANDA, Philip Kan. American (born United States), b. 1949. **Genres:** Plays/Screenplays. **Career:** Stanford University, artist-in-residence; University of California, artist-in-residence; Berkeley Repertory Theatre, artist-in-residence. Playwright and filmmaker. **Publications:** The Dream of Kitamura, 1983; Yankee Dawg You Die, 1991; Wash, 1992; Day Standing on Its Head, 1994; Fish Head Soup, and Other Plays, 1995; Ballad of Yachiyo, 1996; Wind Cries Mary: Loosely Adapted from Ibsen's Hedda Gabler, 2004; No More Cherry Blossoms: Sisters Matsumoto and Other Play, 2005. **Address:** 1205 Campus Dr., Berkeley, CA 94708, U.S.A. **Online address:** joeozu@philipkangotanda.com

GOTFRYD, Bernard. American/Polish (born Poland), b. 1924. **Genres:** Autobiography/Memoirs, Documentaries/Reportage. **Career:** Newsweek, photojournalist, 1957-88; writer, 1983-. **Publications:** Anton the Dove Fancier and Other Tales of the Holocaust, 1990; The Intimate Eye, 2006; Widuje ich w snach: nowe opowiadania, 2008. Contributor to periodicals. **Address:** IMG - Julian Bach Literary Agency Inc., 747 3rd Ave., New York, NY 10017, U.S.A. **Online address:** gotfrydb@aol.com

GOTO, Hiromi. Canadian (born Canada), b. 1966. **Genres:** Novels, Novellas/Short Stories, Poetry, Young Adult Fiction, Children's Fiction. **Career:** Emily Carr University of Art and Design, writer-in-residence, 2003-04; University of Northern British Columbia, writer-in-residence, 2003-04; Vancouver Public Library, writer-in-residence, 2007-08; Simon Fraser University, writer-in-residence, 2008-09; University of Alberta, writer-in-residence, 2009-10. **Publications:** (Co-ed.) The Skin on Our Tongues, 1993; Chorus of Mushrooms, 1994; (contrib.) Literary Pluralities, 1998; The Water of Possibility, 2001; The Kappa Child, 2001; Hopeful Monsters: Stories, 2004; Half World, 2009; (with D. Bateman) Wait Until Late Afternoon, or Distilled, Decanted & Debauched, 2009; Darkest Light, 2012. Works appear in anthologies. Contributor of articles to periodicals. **Address:** The Cooke Agency, 278 Bloor St. E, Ste. 305, Toronto, ON M4W 3M4, Canada. **Online address:** hiromi_goto@shaw.ca

GOTŌ, Junichi. Japanese (born Japan), b. 1951. **Genres:** Economics, Agriculture/Forestry, Business/Trade/Industry, History. **Career:** Japanese Ministry of Labor, Affiliate, 1975-86, Labor Economy Division, deputy director, 1990-91; World Bank, International Economics Department, economist, 1987-90; Kobe University, professor, 1991-, Research Institute for Economics and Business Administration, director, professor; Massachusetts Institute of Technology, visiting fellow, 1993-94; Yale University, visiting fellow, 1995; Keio University, Graduate School of Media and Governance, faculty of policy management, professor; Inter-American Development Bank, staff. Writer. **Publications:** Effects of the Multifibre Arrangement on Developing Countries: A Survey, 1988; International Trade and Imperfect Competition: Theory and Application to the Automobile Trade, 1988; Kokusai Rōdō Keizaigaku: Bōeki Mondai e no Atarashii Shiten, 1988; Gaikokujin Rōdō no Keizaigaku: Kokusai bōekiron kara no apurōchi, 1990; Formal Estimation of the Effect of the MFA on Clothing Exports from LDCs, 1990; Labor in International Trade Theory: A New Perspective on Japanese-American Issues, 1990; Gaikokujin Rōdōsha to Nihon Keizai: Maiguronomikusu, 1993; Economic Preconditions for Asian Regional Integration, 1994; Regional Economic Integration and Agricultural Trade, 1997; Regional Economic Conditions and Article XXIV of the GATT, 2000; (with A. Estevadeorkdal and R. Saez) The New

Regionalism in the Americas: The Case of MERCOSUR, 2000. Contributor to periodicals. **Address:** Graduate School of Media and Governance, KEIO University-Shonan Fujisawa Campus, 5322 Endo Fujisawa, Kanagawa, 252-0882, Japan. **Online address:** jgoto@sfc.keio.ac.jp

GOTT, Richard (Willoughby). British (born England), b. 1938. **Genres:** History, International Relations/Current Affairs, Third World, Biography, Autobiography/Memoirs, Social Sciences. **Career:** Royal Institute of International Affairs, research assistant, 1962-65; Guardian newspaper, leader writer, 1964-66; University of Chile, Institute of International Studies, research fellow, 1966-69, honorary research fellow; The Standard, foreign editor, 1970-72; Latin American Newsletters Ltd., director, 1976-80; The Guardian, features editor, 1978-89, literary editor, 1992-94; University of London, Institute for the Study of the Americas, honorary research fellow. Writer. **Publications:** (Co-ed.) Documents on International Affairs, 1960; (with M. Gilbert) The Appeasers, 1963, 2nd ed., 1967; (with J. Gittings) NATO's Final Decade, 1964; (with J. Gittings) The End of the Alliance, 1965; Mobutu's Congo, 1968; A Future for the United Nations?, 1968; Guerrilla Movements in Latin America, 1970; Rural Guerillas in Latin America, 1973; Close Your Frontiers: Development as the Ideology of Imperialism, 1983; Land Without Evil: Utopian Journeys Across the South American Watershed, 1993; In the Shadow of the Liberator: Hugo Chavez and the Transformation of Venezuela, 2000; (intro.) The African Dream: The Diaries of the Revolutionary War in the Congo, 2001; Cuba: A New History, 2004; Hugo Chávez and the Bolivarian Revolution, 2005; Britain's Empire, 2011. Contributor to magazines. **Address:** 88 Ledbury Rd., London, GL W11 2AH, England. **Online address:** rwgott@aol.com

GOTTFREDSON, Mark Alan. American (born United States), b. 1957. **Genres:** Administration/Management, Business/Trade/Industry. **Career:** Bain & Company Inc., consultant, 1983-85, manager, 1985-88, vice president, 1988-90, founder and managing director, 1990-, partner, global head. Writer. **Publications:** (With S. Schaubert, J. Case and K. Tsakalakis) The Breakthrough Imperative: How the Best Managers Get Outstanding Results, 2008. Contributor to periodicals. **Address:** Bain & Company Inc., 5215 N O'Connor Blvd., Ste. 500, Irving, TX 75039, U.S.A. **Online address:** mark.gottfredson@bain.com

GOTTFRIED, Paul Edward. American (born United States) **Genres:** Politics/Government. **Career:** Yale University, graduate fellow, 1965-66; Case Western Reserve University, assistant professor, 1968-71; New York University, assistant professor of history, 1971-72; Rockford College, Department of History, chair, 1974-86; Elizabethtown College, Department of Political Science, professor of humanities, Raffensperger chair, 1989-. Writer and political scientist. **Publications:** Conservative Millenarians: The Romantic Experience in Bavaria, 1979; The Search for Historical Meaning: Hegel and the Postwar American Right, 1986; (with T. Fleming) The Conservative Movement, 1988, rev. ed., 1993; Carl Schmitt: Politics and Theory, 1990; (intro.) Religion from Tolstoy to Camus, 1994; After Liberalism: Mass Democracy in the Managerial State, 1999; Multiculturalism and the Politics of Guilt: Toward a Secular Theocracy, 2002; The Strange Death of Marxism: The European Left in the New Millennium, 2005; Conservatism in America: Making Sense of the American Right, 2007; Encounters: My Life with Nixon, Marcuse, and Other Friends and Teachers, 2009; Leo Strauss and the American Conservative Movement: A Critical Appraisal, 2011. Contributor to periodicals and journals. **Address:** Department of Political Science, Elizabethtown College, 1 Alpha Dr., Elizabethtown, PA 17022-2298, U.S.A. **Online address:** gottfrpe@etown.edu

GOTTFRIED, Robert R(ichard). American/Mexican (born Mexico), b. 1948. **Genres:** Economics, Environmental Sciences/Ecology. **Career:** St. John's University, Department of Economics, assistant professor, 1975-78; Universidad Rafael Landivar, Fulbright lecturer in economics, 1979; University of North Carolina, Department of Economics, visiting professor, 1981-82; Sewanee: The University of the South, Department of Economics, MacArthur assistant professor, 1982-85, associate professor, 1986-, professor of economics, chair, 1994-97, Sewanee Landscape Analysis Laboratory, cofounder, 1982-, Social Science Foreign Language Program, chair, 1991-94, Environmental Studies Program, chair, 1999-2001, Center for Religion and Environment, director, 2009-; Temperate Ecosystems, U.S. Man and the Biosphere Directorate, staff, 1989-92; Universidad Nacional, Central American Commission on Forests and the Environment, researcher, 1995-96. Writer.

Publications: Report on the Final plan for the Caribbean National Forest, 1986; Economics, Ecology, and the Roots of Western Faith: Perspectives From the Garden, 1995. Contributor to books and journals. **Address:** Department of Economics, Sewanee: The University of the South, 313 Walsh-Ellet Hall, 735 University Ave., Sewanee, TN 37375-1000, U.S.A. **Online address:** rgottfri@sewanee.edu

GOTTLIEB, Alma. American (born United States), b. 1954. **Genres:** Anthropology/Ethnology, Autobiography/Memoirs. **Career:** Virginia Commonwealth University, adjunct instructor in sociology and anthropology, 1977-79; De Tocqueville Society, research assistant, 1978-79; Virginia Union University, adjunct instructor, 1978; Institut d'Ethno-sociologie, Universite Nationale de Cote d'Ivoire, chercheuse associee, 1979-80, 1993; University of Illinois, visiting assistant professor, 1983-85, assistant professor, 1985-91, associate professor, 1991-98, professor of anthropology, 1998-, director of undergraduate studies; National Endowment for the Humanities, fellow, 1985, 1991, 1992-93; The Northwest Writing Institute, Lewis and Clark College, visiting faculty, 2004; Universidade Tecnica de Lisboa, Instituto Superior de Ciencias Sociais e Politicas, visiting researcher, 2006-07; Society for Cultural Anthropology, fellow. Writer. **Publications:** Under the Kapok Tree: Identity and Difference in Beng Thought, 1992; (with P. Graham) Parallel Worlds: An Anthropologist and a Writer Encounter Africa (memoir), 1993; (with M.L. Murphy) Beng-English Dictionary, 1995; The Afterlife Is Where We Come From: The Culture of Infancy in West Africa, 2004. EDITOR AND CONTRIBUTOR: (with T. Buckley) Blood Magic: The Anthropology of Menstruation, 1988; (with J. De Loache) A World of Babies: Imagined Infant and Childcare Guides for Seven Societies, 2000. Contributor of articles and reviews to periodicals. **Address:** Department of Anthropology, University of Illinois, 109 Davenport Hall, 607 S Mathews Ave., PO Box 148, Urbana, IL 61801, U.S.A. **Online address:** ajgottli@illinois.edu

GOTTLIEB, Annie. American (born United States), b. 1946. **Genres:** Novels, Plays/Screenplays, Cultural/Ethnic Topics, Literary Criticism And History, Psychology, Theology/Religion, Philosophy, Self Help, Self Help. **Career:** Harcourt Brace Jovanovich, editorial assistant, 1967-70; writer, 1969-. **Publications:** (With J. Sandulescu) The Carpathian Caper (novel), 1975; (intro.) Women See Woman (photography), 1976; (with B. Sher) Wishcraft: How to Get What You Really Want, 1979; (contrib.) The Last Sitting, 1982; Do You Believe in Magic?: The Second Coming of the Sixties Generation, 1987 as Do You Believe in Magic?: Bringing the Sixties Back Home, 1988; (with B. Sher) Teamworks!: Building Support Groups That Guarantee Success, 1989; (intro.) Thomas McKnight: Windows On Paradise, 1990; (contrib.) Voyage to Paradise: A Visual Odyssey, 1993; (with S.D. Pešić) The Cube: Keep the Secret, 1995; The Low Oxalate Cookbook, 2 vols., 1997-2005; (with S.D. Pešić) Secrets of the Cube: The Ancient Visualization Game That Reveals Your True Self, 1998; (with J.M. Schwartz and P. Buckley) A Return to Innocence: Philosophical Guidance in an Age of Cynicism, 1998; (with J.M. Schwartz and P. Buckley) Dear Patrick: Life Is Tough, Here's Some Good Advice, 2003. Contributor to periodicals. **Address:** c/o Arielle Eckstut, Levine Greenberg Literary Agency, 307 7th Ave., Ste. 2407, New York, NY 10001-6035, U.S.A.

GOTTLIEB, Arthur. (Arthur Josephs). American (born United States), b. 1929. **Genres:** Medicine/Health, Sports/Fitness. **Career:** Teacher, 1951-52; North American Aviation, negotiator, 1956-63; Gyler, Gottlieb & Gottlieb, attorney, 1963-82; National Stroke Quality of Life Medical Education Institute, Columbia-Presbyterian Medical Center, co-chairman. Writer. **Publications:** (As Arthur Josephs) The Invaluable Guide to Life After Stroke: An Owner's Manual, 1992. **Address:** Amadeus Press, PO Box 13011, Long Beach, CA 90803-8011, U.S.A. **Online address:** amadeuspr@earthlink.net

GOTTLIEB, Beatrice. American (born United States), b. 1925. **Genres:** History, Translations, Social Sciences, Humanities. **Career:** Time Inc., Sports Illustrated, head of copy room, 1954-67; Smith College, assistant professor, 1976-77. Writer. **Publications:** (Trans. and intro.) L. Febvre, The Problem of Unbelief in the Sixteenth Century, 1980; (contrib.) Family and Sexuality in French History, 1980; The Family in the Western World from the Black Death to the Industrial Age, 1993. **Address:** c/o William B. Goodman, 26 Pickman Dr., Bedford, MA 01730, U.S.A.

GOTTLIEB, Daphne. American (born United States), b. 1968?. **Genres:** Poetry, Young Adult Fiction, Children's Fiction, Novels. **Career:** Lodestar Quarterly, poetry editor, through 2006; Other Magazine, poetry editor; Mills College, instructor; New College of California, faculty; California Institute

of Integral Studies (CIIS), instructor. **Publications:** Pelt, 1999; Why Things Burn: Poems, 2001; Final Girl, 2003; (ed.) Homewrecker: An Adultery Reader, 2005; (with D. DiMassa) Jokes and The Unconscious, 2006; Kissing Dead Girls, 2008; (ed.) Fucking Daphne: Mostly True Stories and Fictions, 2008; (ed. with L. Kester) Dear Dawn, 2011; 15 Ways to Stay Alive, 2011. Works appear in anthologies. Contributor to journals and periodicals. **Address:** Manic D Press, PO Box 410804, San Francisco, CA 94141, U.S.A. **Online address:** peek@daphnegottlieb.com

GOTTLIEB, Freema (Peninah). American/British (born England), b. 1946. **Genres:** Humanities, Mythology/Folklore, Biography, Essays. **Career:** New School for Social Research, assistant professor, 1990-91; Adam International Review, literary adviser; Skirball Center for Adult Jewish Learning, faculty. Writer. **Publications:** (With J.U. Mayerson) Jewish Folk Art: From Biblical Days to Modern Times, 1986; The Lamp of God: A Jewish Book of Light, 1989; Mystical Stonescapes: Symbols on Jewish Gravestones in Prague Old Jewish Cemetery and in Bohemia, 1997. **Address:** c/o Susan Cohen, Writers House L.L.C., 21 W 26th St., New York, NY 10010, U.S.A. **Online address:** freema@mindspring.com

GOTTLIEB, Lisa. American (born United States), b. 1971. **Genres:** Art/Art History, Young Adult Non-fiction, Literary Criticism And History. **Career:** University of Toronto, faculty. Writer. **Publications:** (With J. Dilevko) The Evolution of Library and Museum Partnerships, 2004; (with J. Dilevko) Reading and the Reference Librarian: The Importance to Library Service of Staff Reading Habits, 2004; Graffiti Art Styles: A Classification System and Theoretical Analysis, 2008. Contributor to periodicals. **Address:** c/o Author Mail, McFarland and Company Inc., PO Box 611, Jefferson, NC 28640-0611, U.S.A. **Online address:** lisa.gottlieb@utoronto.ca

GOTTLIEB, Sherry Gershon. American (born United States), b. 1948. **Genres:** Documentaries/Reportage, Novels, Young Adult Non-fiction, History. **Career:** Budget Films, executive secretary, 1970-72; United Artists, script reader, 1971-74; Change of Hobbit Bookstore, owner, 1972-91; University of California Los Angeles Extension, class coordinator, 1982. Book doctor, editor and writer. **Publications:** Hell No, We Won't Go!: Resisting the Draft during the Vietnam War, 1991; Love Bite, 1994; (contrib.) The Portable Writer's Conference, 1997; Worse Than Death, 1999; Pup Fiction, 2002. **Address:** c/o Author Mail, St. Martin's Press, 175 5th Ave., New York, NY 10010-7703, U.S.A.

GOTTLIEB, Stephen E. American (born United States), b. 1941. **Genres:** Law. **Career:** Golenbock and Barell (law firm), associate, 1967-69; Legal Aid Society, managing attorney and staff attorney, 1969-72; St. Louis University, adjunct instructor in research and writing, 1972; Community Action for Legal Services Inc., assistant general counsel and director of training, 1973-76; West Virginia University, associate professor of law, 1976-79; Albany Law School of Union University, associate professor, 1979-82, professor of law, 1982-, Jay and Ruth Caplan distinguished professor of law; Cleveland-Marshall College of Law, Joseph C. Hostetler-Baker and Hostetler visiting chair in law, 1995-96; Marquette University Law School, Robert F. Boden distinguished visiting chair, 1997; Suffolk University Law School, distinguished visiting professor, 2000; New York Civil Liberties Union, board director; WAMC Northeast Public Radio, commentator. Writer. **Publications:** Systematic Litigation Planning, 1978; Jurisprudence: Cases and Materials, 1993, 2nd ed., 2006; Morality Imposed: The Rehnquist Court and Liberty in America, 2000. EDITOR: (with P. Finkelman) Toward a Usable Past: Liberty under State Constitutions, 1991; Public Values in Constitutional Law, 1993. Contributor to journals and periodicals. **Address:** Albany Law School, Union University, 80 New Scotland Ave., Albany, NY 12208-3494, U.S.A. **Online address:** sgott@albanylaw.edu

GOTTSCHALL, Edward M(aurice). American (born United States), b. 1915. **Genres:** Advertising/Public Relations, Art/Art History, Communications/Media, Technology, Illustrations, Information Science/Computers. **Career:** Colton Press, managing editor of graphic arts production yearbook, 1937-51; Pratt Institute, lecturer, 1947-64; Art Direction, editor, 1952-69; New York University, lecturer, 1955-64; Popular Merchandising Co., senior editor, 1964-67; Advertising Trade Publications Inc., co-publisher and editorial director, 1967-69; American Institute of Graphic Arts, executive director, 1969-75; International Typeface Corp., executive vice president, 1975-86, vice chairman, 1986-89; Design Processing International Inc., vice president, 1977-85; U&lc Magazine, editor. **Publications:** (With F.C. Rodewald) Commercial Art as a Business, 1960, 2nd ed., 1971; Graphic Communication '80s, 1981; Typographic Communications Today, 1989. **Address:** 63 Highland Ave., Eastchester, NY 10709-3627, U.S.A.

GÖTZ, Ignacio L. American (born United States), b. 1933. **Genres:** Education, Philosophy, Theology/Religion. **Career:** Junior high school teacher of English, 1957-59; St. Stanislaus College, lecturer in exegesis, 1963-64; Hofstra University, adjunct assistant professor, 1966-68, assistant professor, 1968-72, associate professor, 1972-77, professor of philosophy of education, 1977, now Lawrence Stessin distinguished professor emeritus, director special studies program, Program for Academic Learning Skills, founder, 1979. Writer. **Publications:** (Trans.) Pavitra Gulabmala, 1961; Joseph Fletcher's Situation Ethics and Education, 1968; (ed.) No Schools, 1971; The Psychedelic Teacher: Drugs, Mysticism and Schools, 1972; Creativity: Theoretical and Socio-cosmic Reflections, 1978; Zen and the Art of Teaching, 1988; Conceptions of Happiness, 1995; The Culture of Sexism, 1999; Manners and Violence, 2000; Technology and the Spirit, 2001; Faith, Humor and Paradox, 2002; Richard Rorty: Education, Philosophy and Politics, 2003; Jesus the Jew, 2009; Conceptions of Happiness, 2010. Contributor to journals. **Address:** Hofstra University, 107 Barnard Hall, Hempstead, NY 11549-1000, U.S.A. **Online address:** ignaciolleo@cs.com

GOUDSOUZIAN, Aram. American (born United States), b. 1973?. **Genres:** History, Biography, Sports/Fitness. **Career:** Suffolk University, history instructor, 2001-03; University of Massachusetts, history instructor, 2002-03; Hamilton College, visiting assistant professor of history, 2003; University of Memphis, assistant professor of history, 2005-, associate professor, Graduate Association for African-American History, faculty advisor, Marcus W. Orr Center for the Humanities, interim director. Writer. **Publications:** Sidney Poitier: Man, Actor, Icon, 2004; The Hurricane of 1938, 2004; King of the Court: Bill Russell and the Basketball Revolution, 2010. **Address:** Department of History, University of Memphis, 119 Mitchell Hall, 101 Wilder Twr., 3705 Alumni Dr., Memphis, TN 38152-3450, U.S.A. **Online address:** agoudszn@memphis.edu

GOUGEON, Len (G.). American (born United States), b. 1947. **Genres:** Literary Criticism And History. **Career:** University of Massachusetts, graduate instructor in rhetoric, 1970-74; University of Scranton, assistant professor, 1974-78, associate professor, 1978-82, professor of English, 1982-, chairman of university senate, 1979-80, The Ralph Waldo Emerson Society, president, 1999-2001, professor of American literature and distinguished university fellow, 2003. **Publications:** Virtue's Hero: Emerson, Antislavery, and Reform, 1990, 2010; (ed. with J. Myerson) Emerson's Antislavery Writings, 1995, 2002; Emerson & Eros: The Making of a Cultural Hero, 2007, 2011; Emerson's Truth, Emerson's Wisdom: Transcendental Advice for Everyday Life, 2010. Contributor to books. **Address:** Department of English & Theatre, University of Scranton, CLP205, Scranton, PA 18510, U.S.A. **Online address:** gougeonL1@scranton.edu

GOUGH, Laurence. Canadian (born Canada) **Genres:** Mystery/Crime/Suspense, Horror, Young Adult Fiction. **Career:** Writer. **Publications:** WILLOWS AND PARKER POLICE PROCEDURAL MYSTERY SERIES: The Goldfish Bowl, 1987; Death on a No. 8 Hook, 1988 in the U.S. as Silent Knives; Hot Shots, 1989; Serious Crimes, 1990; Accidental Deaths, 1991; Fall Down Easy, 1992; Killers, 1993; Heartbreaker, 1996; Memory Lane, 1996; Karaoke Rap, 1997; Shutterbug, 1998; Funny Money, 2000; Cloud of Suspects, 2003. OTHER: Sandstorm, 1990. **Address:** McClelland and Stewart Ltd., 481 University Ave., Ste. 900, Toronto, ON M5G 2E9, Canada.

GOUGH, Laurie. Canadian/American (born United States), b. 1964. **Genres:** Travel/Exploration, Young Adult Non-fiction. **Career:** Writer and educator. **Publications:** Island of the Human Heart: A Woman's Travel Odyssey (nonfiction), 1998 in US as Kite Strings of the Southern Cross: A Woman's Travel Odyssey (nonfiction), 1999; Kiss the Sunset Pig: An American Road Trip with Exotic Detours (nonfiction), 2006. Contributor to periodicals. Works appear in anthologies. **Address:** 19 Lewis St., Wakefield, QC J0X 3G0, Canada. **Online address:** laurie@lauriegough.com

GOUGH, Maria. American (born United States), b. 1961. **Genres:** Art/Art History. **Career:** University of Michigan, assistant professor of art history; Stanford University, assistant professor of art history, associate professor of art history, 2003-. Writer. **Publications:** (With M. Hefferlin) Tradition Rediscovered: The Finley Collection of Russian Art, 1998; The Artist as Pro-

ducer: Russian Constructivism in Revolution, 2005. Contributor of articles to journals. **Address:** Department of Art & Art History, Stanford University, 435 Lasuen Mall, Stanford, CA 94305-2018, U.S.A. **Online address:** mgough@stanford.edu

GOUGH, Michael. American (born United States), b. 1939. **Genres:** Environmental Sciences/Ecology. **Career:** Baylor College of Medicine, assistant professor of microbiology, 1968-72; State University of New York, assistant professor, 1972-75, associate professor, 1975-76; National Institute of Health, health scientist administrator, 1976-78; United States Congressional Office of Technology Assessment, director of special projects, 1978-85; Risk Science Institute, director, 1985-86; Environ Corp., project manager, 1986-87; Center for Risk Management, Resources for the Future, director, 1987-90; U.S. Veterans Administration Advisory Committee on Health-Related Effects of Herbicides, chair, 1987-90; U.S. Department of Health and Human Services Advisory Committee, chair, 1990-95; U.S. Congress Office of Technology Assessment, senior associate, 1990-, Biological Application Program, program manager; Cato Institute, director of science and risk studies. Writer. **Publications:** Dioxin, Agent Orange: The Facts, 1986; (co-author) Technologies for Detecting Heritable Mutations in Human beings, 1988; (with A.M. Ujihara) Managing Ash from Municipal Waste Incinerators: A Report, 1989; (ed. with T.S. Glickman) Readings in Risk, 1990; (with S.J. Milloy) Silencing Science, 1998; (ed.) Politicizing Science: The Alchemy of Policymaking, 2003; The Alchemy of Policy Making: Political Manipulation of Science, forthcoming. Contributor to books. **Address:** 6404 E Halbert Rd., Bethesda, MD 20817-5423, U.S.A. **Online address:** mgough@bellatlantic.net

GOUGH, Sue. Australian/British (born England), b. 1940. **Genres:** Young Adult Fiction, Young Adult Non-fiction, Sciences, History, Biography. **Career:** Canberra Times, arts writer, 1963-68; Jacaranda Press, editor, 1970-74; National Theatre, critic, 1984-98. **Publications:** YOUNG ADULT NOVELS: A Long Way to Tipperary, 1992; Wyrd, 1993; Here Comes the Night, 1997. OTHERS: Queensland Colonial Years, 1984; (with D. Weedon) Tears in My Champagne (biography), 1984; The Book of Brisbane, 1985; Sugar, 1986; Hard Times and High Hopes, 1986; Issues of Today: Conservation, 1986; Issues of Today: AIDS, 1989; Unique Mammals of Australia, 1990; Creatures of the Antarctic, 1992; Big Beasts, Fact or Fiction, 1992; Keeping in Touch through Time, 1992; Thommo Makes His Mark, 1992; From Raw to Ready, 1992; Tell It in Print, 1992; The Daggs Meet the Bad Beasts, 1993; Punk Rocker from Hell, 1993; The Monster Manual, 1995; (ed.) Setting the Stage: Queensland Performing Arts Complex: The First Ten Years, 1995; The Nether Regions, 2001. Contributor to periodicals. **Address:** 344 Savages Rd., Brookfield, Brisbane, QL 4069, Australia. **Online address:** suegough@bigpond.net.au

GOULBOURNE, Harry. British/Jamaican (born Jamaica), b. 1948. **Genres:** Sociology, Race Relations, Politics/Government, Social Sciences, Education, Medicine/Health. **Career:** University of Dar es Salaam, lecturer, 1975-78, senior lecturer, 1978-80; University of the West Indies, senior lecturer, 1980-86; Cheltenham and Gloucester College of Higher Education, professor of political sociology, 1994-98; London South Bank University, professor of sociology, 1998-, visiting professor of sociology. Writer. **Publications:** Teachers, Education and Politics in Jamaica, 1892-1972, 1988; Ethnicity and Nationalism in Post-Imperial Britain, 1991; Race Relations in Britain since 1945, 1998; Caribbean Transnational Experience, 2002. EDITOR: Politics and State in the Third World, 1979; (with L. Sterling) Social Sciences and Caribbean Society, 2 vols., 1985; (and contrib.) Black Politics in Britain, 1990; (with R. Cohen) Democracy and Socialism in Africa, 1991; (with R. Cohen and contrib.) Taking Democracy Seriously: Socialists and Democracy in Africa, 1992; (with M. Chamberlain) Caribbean Families in the Atlantic World, 2000; Race and Ethnicity: Critical Concepts in Sociology, 2001; Transnational Families: Ethnicities, Identities and Social Capital, 2010. Contributor to journals. Works appear in anthologies. **Address:** Faculty of Humanities and Social Science, London South Bank University, 103 Borough Rd., London, GL SE1 0AA, England. **Online address:** goulbohd@lsbu.ac.uk

GOULD, Bryan. New Zealander (born New Zealand), b. 1939. **Genres:** Politics/Government, Novels, Economics. **Career:** Her Majesty's Diplomatic Service, affiliate, 1964-68; Oxford University, tutor in law and fellow of Worcester College, 1968-74, Nuffield College, visiting fellow, 2005; Thames Television, reporter, 1979-83; labour member of parliament-Southampton, 1974-79, labour member of parliament-Dagenham, 1983-94; Labour Shadow Cabinet, member, 1986-92; University of Waikato, vice-chancellor, 1994-

2004; Television New Zealand, director, 2004. Writer. **Publications:** WITH J. MILLS AND S. STEWART: Competitive Pound, 1977; Politics of Monetarism, 1979; Monetarism or Prosperity?, 1981. OTHERS: (with E. Topliss) A Charter for the Disabled, 1981; (co-author) Economic Recovery: What Labour Must Do, 1982; Socialism and Freedom, 1986; A Future for Socialism, 1989; Goodbye to All That, 1995; The Democracy Sham: How Globalisation Devalues Your Vote, 2006; Rescuing the New Zealand Economy: Where We Went Wrong and How We Can Fix It, 2008. **Address:** 239 Ohiwa Beach Rd., RD2, Opotiki, 3198, New Zealand. **Online address:** bgould@paradise.net.nz

GOULD, James L. American (born United States), b. 1945. **Genres:** Biology, Environmental Sciences/Ecology, Animals/Pets, Social Sciences. **Career:** Princeton University, assistant professor, 1975-80, associate professor, 1980-84, professor of biology, 1984-; Mathey College, senior fellow, 1997-2007. Writer. **Publications:** (With C.G. Gould) Ethology: The Mechanisms and Evolution of Behavior, 1982; (with W.T. Keeton) Biological Science, 4th ed., 1986, 6th ed., 1996; (with C.G. Gould) The Honey Bee, 1988, 2nd ed., 1995; (ed. with C.G. Gould) Life at the Edge: Readings from Scientific American, 1989; (with C.G. Gould) Sexual Selection, 1989, 2nd ed., 1997; (with C.G. Gould) The Animal Mind, 1994, 2nd ed., 1999; (with G.F. Gould) Biostats Basics, 2002; Animal Architects: Building and the Evolution of Intelligence, 2007; (with C.G. Gould) Nature's Compass: The Mystery of Animal Navigation, 2012. Contributor to books. **Address:** Department of Ecology and Evolutionary Biology, Princeton University, 330A Guyot Hall, 106A Guyot Hall, Princeton, NJ 08544-1003, U.S.A. **Online address:** gould@princeton.edu

GOULD, Janice. American (born United States), b. 1949. **Genres:** Poetry. **Career:** University of New Mexico, teaching assistant, 1988-96; College of Santa Fe, adjunct instructor, 1991-95; University of Northern Colorado, assistant professor in English, 1997-98; teacher, 1998-2001; Lewis and Clark College, adjunct instructor, 1998-2001, adjunct professor, 2001-05; Portland State University, Portland Community College, adjunct instructor, 1999-2001, lecturer, adjunct professor, 2000-02; Clackamas Community College, adjunct instructor, 2000-01; Willamette University, Hallie Ford chair in creative writing, 2001-04; University of Colorado, assistant professor, 2009-. Writer. **Publications:** Beneath My Heart: Poetry, 1990; Earthquake Weather: Poems, 1996; Alphabet, 1996; (ed. with D. Rader) Speak to Me Words: Essays On Contemporary American Indian Poetry, 2003; Doubters and Dreamers, 2011. Contributor of articles to journals and periodicals. **Address:** University of Colorado, 1420 Austin Bluffs Pkwy., Colorado Springs, CO 80918-3733, U.S.A. **Online address:** jgould@uccs.edu

GOULD, John. Canadian (born Canada), b. 1959?. **Genres:** Young Adult Fiction, Novellas/Short Stories. **Career:** University of Victoria, creative writing instructor, Victoria School of Writing, executive director; British Columbia Festival of the Arts, Otherwords Program, co-creator. Writer. **Publications:** The Kingdom of Heaven: 88 Palm-of-the-Hand Stories, 1996; Kilter: 55 Fictions, 2003; Seven Good Reasons Not to Be Good, 2010. **Address:** Department of Writing, University of Victoria, Rm. 233, Fine Arts Bldg., 3800 Finnerty Rd., PO Box 1700, Sta. CSC, Victoria, BC V8P 5C2, Canada. **Online address:** gouldj@uvic.ca

GOULD, Judith. See GALLAHER, (William) Rhea.

GOULD, Judith. See BIENES, Nicholas Peter.

GOULD, Kevin. British (born England), b. 1964. **Genres:** Theology/Religion. **Career:** Nottingham Trent University, lecturer; Society for the Study of French History, web editor. **Publications:** Catholic Activism in South-West France, 1540-1570, 2006. Contributor to books. **Address:** School of Arts and Humanities, Nottingham Trent University, Clifton Campus, Nottingham, NT NG11 8NS, England. **Online address:** kevin.gould@ntu.ac.uk

GOULD, K. Lance. American (born United States), b. 1938. **Genres:** Medicine/Health. **Career:** University of Hawaii School of Public Health, instructor, 1969; University of Washington School of Medicine, instructor, 1970, assistant professor, 1972, associate professor, 1976; VA Hospital, attending physician, 1970-79, education and research associate, 1971-74, clinical investigator, 1971-74; University of Texas Medical School, professor, 1979-, director of division of cardiology, 1979-85, vice chairman for clinical affairs, 1980-84, professor, Health Science Center, 1980-98, Weatherhead PET Center for Preventing and Reversing Atherosclerosis, director, 1997-; Positron Diagnostic and Research Center, director, 1979-87; Hermann Hospital, chief

of cardiology, attending physician, 1979-85; American College of Cardiology, board director; Positron Corp., board director; Optimal Care, board director; Institute of Clinical PET, board director; American College of Physicians, fellow. Writer. **Publications:** Coronary Artery Stenosis and Reversing Heart Disease, 1997, 2nd ed. as Coronary Artery Stenosis and Reversing Atherosclerosis, 1999; Heal Your Heart: How You Can Prevent or Reverse Heart Disease, 1998. Contributor of articles to academic journals and to film productions. **Address:** University of Texas Medical School, Rm. 4.256 MSB, 6431 Fannin St., Ste. 7.200, Houston, TX 77030, U.S.A. **Online address:** k.lance.gould@uth.tmc.edu

GOULD, Steven (Charles). American (born United States), b. 1955. **Genres:** Novels, Science Fiction/Fantasy, Mystery/Crime/Suspense, Young Adult Fiction. **Career:** Freelance writer, 1990-. **Publications:** Jumper (novel), 1992; Wildside (science fiction novel), 1996; (with L.J. Mixon) Greenwar (technical suspense novel), 1997; Helm, 1998; Blind Waves, 2000; Reflex, 2004; Jumper: Griffin's Story, 2007; 7th Sigma, 2010. Contributor to periodicals. **Address:** Ralph Vicinanza Ltd., 303 W 18th St., New York, NY 10011, U.S.A. **Online address:** stevengould@digitalnoir.com

GOULD, Terry. Canadian/American (born United States), b. 1949?. **Genres:** Novels, Romance/Historical. **Career:** Saturday Night Magazine, contributing editor, 1993-2002; CBC-TV, Front Page Challenge, editor, script writer; Vancouver Magazine, senior editor; V Magazine, senior editor. **Publications:** How the Blind Make Love, 1984; The Lifestyle: A Look at the Erotic Rites of Swingers, 2000; Paper Fan: The Hunt for Triad Gangster Steven Wong, 2004; Murder without Borders: Dying for the Story in the World's Most Dangerous Places, 2009; Marked for Death: Dying for the Story in the World's Most Dangerous Places, 2009. Contributor to books and periodicals. **Address:** c/o Author Mail, Thunders Mouth Press, 245 W 17th St., 11th Fl., New York, NY 10011-5300, U.S.A.

GOULD, William B(enjamin). American (born United States), b. 1936. **Genres:** Organized Labor, Race Relations. **Career:** United Auto Workers, assistant general counsel in labor law, 1961-62; National Labor Relations Board, attorney, 1963-65, chairman, 1994-98; Battle, Fowler, Stokes, Kheel (law firm), associate, 1965-68; Wayne State University, professor of law, 1968-71; Harvard University, visiting professor of law, 1971-72; Stanford University, professor of law, 1972-94, Charles A. Beardsley professor of law, now emeritus; Churchill College, visiting fellow and lecturer, 1975; University of Tokyo, faculty of law, 1975, 1978; Australian National University, visiting fellow and lecturer, 1985; European University Institute, visiting fellow and lecturer, 1988; Howard University, School of Law, visiting professor, 1989; University of Witwatersrand, visiting fellow and lecturer, 1991; University of Hawaii, visiting professor, 2005. Writer. **Publications:** Black Workers in White Unions: Job Discrimination in the United States, 1977; A Primer on American Labor Law, 1982, 4th ed., 2004; Japan's Reshaping of American Labor Law, 1984; Strikes, Dispute Procedures, and Arbitration: Essays on Labor Law, 1985; (co-author) Labor Relations in Professional Sports, 1986; Agenda for Reform, 1993; Shin Amerika Rōdōhō, nyūmonLabored Relations, 2000; (ed.) Diary of a Contraband: The Civil War Passage of a Black Sailor, 2002; (ed. with R.J. Flanagan) International Labor Standards: Globalization, Trade, and Public Policy, 2003; Bargaining with Baseball, 2011. **Address:** Stanford Law School, Stanford University, Crown Quadrangle, 559 Nathan Abbott Way, Stanford, CA 94305-8610, U.S.A. **Online address:** wbgould@stanford.edu

GOULDEN, Joseph C. (Henry S. A. Becket). American (born United States), b. 1934. **Genres:** History, Institutions/Organizations, Military/Defense/Arms Control, Law, Biography, Autobiography/Memoirs, Communications/Media. **Career:** Marshall New-Messenger, reporter, 1956; Dallas Morning News, reporter, 1958-61; The Philadelphia Inquirer, reporter to Washington bureau chief, 1961-68; Accuracy in Media Inc., media critic, 1989-, director of media analysis. **Publications:** The Curtis Caper, 1965; Monopoly, 1968; Truth is the First Casualty: The Gulf of Tonk in Affair-Illusion and Reality, 1969; The Money Givers, 1971; Meany: The Unchallenged Strong Man of American Labor, 1972; The Super-lawyers: The Small and Powerful World of the Great Washington Law Firms, 1972; The Benchwarmers: The Private Powerful World of the Great Federal Judges, 1974; The Best Years: 1945-50, 1976; (ed.) Mencken's Last Campaign, 1976; The Million Dollar Lawyers, 1978; Jerry Wurf: Labor's Last Angry Man, 1982; Korea: The Untold Story of the War, 1983; (with P. Dickson) There Are Alligators in Our Sewers, and Other American Credos, 1983; (with A.W. Raffio) The Death Merchant: The Rise and Fall of Edwin P. Wilson, 1984; (as H.S.A. Becket) Dictionary of Espionage: Spookspeak into English, 1986; Kaddafi, la CIA et les marchands de mort, 1987; Fit to Print: A.M. Rosenthal and His Times, 1988; (with P. Dickson) Myth-Informed: Legends, Credos, and Wrongheaded Facts We All Believe, 1993; Money Lawyers: The No-Holds-Barred World of Today's Richest and Most Powerful Lawyers, 2006; The Dictionary of Espionage: Spyspeak into English, 2012. Contributor to periodicals. **Address:** 1534 29th St. NW, Washington, DC 20007-3060, U.S.A. **Online address:** josephg894@aol.com

GOULDING, Edwin (John). British (born England), b. 1938. **Genres:** Sciences, Homes/Gardens. **Career:** Gouldings Fuchsias, owner. Writer. **Publications:** Fuchsias: The Complete Guide, 1995, new ed., 2002. Contributor to plant magazines. **Address:** Gouldings Fuchsias, W View, Link Ln., Bentley, SU 1P9 2DP, England.

GOULTER, Barbara. American (born United States) **Genres:** How-to Books, Human Relations/Parenting. **Career:** University of San Francisco, faculty; Foothill College, faculty; San Francisco Chronicle, film critic. Writer. **Publications:** (With V. Goulter) How to Keep Your Car Mechanic Honest, 1990; (with J. Minninger) The Perfect Presentation, 1992; (with Minninger) The Father-Daughter Dance: Insight, Inspiration, and Understanding for Every Woman and Her Father, 1993. Contributor of articles and reviews to magazines and newspapers. **Address:** c/o Linda Allen Agency, 1949 Green St., San Francisco, CA 94123, U.S.A.

GOURGOURIS, Stathis. American/Greek (born Greece), b. 1958. **Genres:** Poetry, Humanities, Intellectual History, Philosophy, Music, Theatre, Essays. **Career:** Planodion, associate editor, 1986-; Princeton University, Department of Comparative Literature, assistant professor, 1992-2000, Undergraduate Studies, director, 1993-94, 1995-97, Mathey College, faculty fellow and freshman adviser, 1999-2000; Eleftherotypia, correspondent, 1999-; National Technical University, visiting assistant professor, 1995; University of California, Group for the Study of Composite Cultures, supervising editor, 1989-90, literature editor, 1991, associate editor, 1998-2003, Department of Comparative Literature, professor, 2005-08, Graduate Studies, director, 2006-07; Rutgers University, Center for Critical Analysis of Contemporary Culture, senior fellow, 2000; Yale University, Department of Comparative Literature and Yale Center for International and Area Studies, visiting associate professor, 2001; Columbia University, Center for Comparative Literature and Society, associate professor, 2002-05, Undergraduate Studies, director, 2004-05, Institute of Comparative Literature and Society, director, professor, 2008-; Modern Greek Studies Association, president; University of Michigan, visiting professor; American School of Classical Studies, senior fellow; Emergences, editor. **Publications:** Dream Nation: Enlightenment, Colonization and the Institution of Modern Greece, 1996; (trans.) Y. Patilis, Camel of Darkness: Selected Poems 1970-1990, 1998; Does Literature Think?: Literature as Theory for an Antimythical Era, 2003; (ed.) Freud and Fundamentalism, 2010; Conversations with Edward Said, forthcoming; The Perils of the One, forthcoming; Nothing Sacred, forthcoming. POETRY COLLECTIONS PUBLISHED IN GREEK: Ptoseis, 1988; Autochthonies, 1993; Eisagogi stin Fysiki, 2005. Contributor of articles to books and journals. **Address:** Institute of Comparative Literature and Society, Columbia University, 608 Hamilton Hall, HB1-1 Heyman Ctr., 2960 Broadway, PO Box 5700, New York, NY 10027, U.S.A. **Online address:** ssg93@columbia.edu

GOURSAC, Olivier de. French (born France), b. 1959?. **Genres:** Astronomy, Sciences, Children's Fiction. **Career:** Jet Propulsion Laboratory, Mars Pathfinder Mission, outreach correspondent, 1993-98; Planète Mars Association, Mars Exploration Missions, outreach manager, 1999-. Writer. **Publications:** À la conquête de Mars, 2000; Space: Exploring the Moon, the Planets, and Beyond, 2006. Contributor to periodicals. **Address:** Planète Mars Association, 28 Rue de la Gaîté, Paris, 75014, France.

GOVIER, Trudy. Canadian (born Canada), b. 1944. **Genres:** Philosophy, Politics/Government, Social Sciences. **Career:** Trent University, professor of philosophy; Simon Fraser University, faculty; University of Amsterdam, faculty; Menno Simons College, Esau distinguished visiting professor, 2004-05; University of Lethbridge, associate professor of philosophy, 2005-, professor of philosophy. Writer. **Publications:** A Practical Study of Argument, 1985, 7th ed., 2010; Problems in Argument Analysis and Evaluation, 1987; (ed.) Selected Issues in Logic and Communication, 1988; God, the Devil and the Perfect Pizza: Ten Philosophical Questions, 1989; Social Trust and Human Communities, 1997; Socrates' Children: Thinking and Knowing in the Western Tradition, 1997; Dilemmas of Trust, 1998; Forgiveness and Revenge,

2002; A Delicate Balance: What Philosophy Can Tell Us About Terrorism, 2002; Taking Wrongs Seriously: Acknowledgement, Reconciliation and the Politics of Sustainable Peace, 2006. Contributor to periodicals. **Address:** Department of Philosophy, University of Lethbridge, B880 University Hall, 4401 University Dr., Lethbridge, AB T1K 3M4, Canada. **Online address:** trudy.govier@uleth.ca

GOW, Andrew Colin. Canadian (born Canada), b. 1962. **Genres:** History, Cultural/Ethnic Topics, Theology/Religion, Essays. **Career:** University of Alberta, assistant professor, 1993-99, associate professor, 1999-2003, professor of history, 2003-, Studies in Medieval and Reformation Traditions, editor-in-chief, Religious Studies Program, director; Humboldt Foundation, Humboldt research fellow, 2002-. **Publications:** (Trans.) H.A. Oberman, The Reformation: Roots and Ramifications, 1994; The Red Jews: Anti-Semitism in an Apocalyptic Age, 1200-1600, 1995; (ed. with R.J. Bast) Continuity and Change: The Harvest of Late Medieval and Reformation History, 2000; (with L. Apps) Male Witches in Early Modern Europe, 2003; (ed. with R. Landes and D.C. Van) The Apocalyptic Year 1000: Religious Expectation and Social Change, 950-1050, 2003; (ed. with R. Connors) Anglo-American Millennialism, From Milton to the Millerites, 2004; (ed.) Hyphenated histories: Articulations of Central European Bildung and Slavic Studies in The Contemporary Academy, 2007; (ed. and intro. with J. Rak) Mountain Masculinity: The Life and Writing of Nello Tex Vernon-Wood in the Canadian Rockies, 1906-1938, 2008. **Address:** Department of History and Classics, Arts 337D, 2-28 Tory Bldg., University of Alberta, Edmonton, AB T6G 2H4, Canada. **Online address:** agow@ualberta.ca

GOW, Michael. Australian (born Australia), b. 1955?. **Genres:** Plays/Screenplays, Art/Art History, How-to Books. **Career:** Thalia Theatre Co., founder; Sydney Theatre Co., associate director, 1991-93; Queensland Theatre Co., artistic director, 1999-2010. Writer. **Publications:** PLAYS: The Kid, 1983; Away, 1986; Europe, 1986; 1841, 1988; Furious, 1994; All Stops Out, 1991; Sweet Phoebe, 1995; Live Acts on Stage, 1996; The Fortunes of Richard Mahony, 2002. **Address:** RGM Artist Group, PO Box 128, Surry Hills, NW 2010, Australia.

GOWAN, Lee. Canadian (born Canada), b. 1961. **Genres:** Novellas/Short Stories, Novels, Plays/Screenplays, Young Adult Fiction. **Career:** Freelance writer, 1980-91; University of Regina, instructor in English and creative writing, 1991-96; University of Toronto, instructor and facilitator of writing program, faculty of landscape, architecture and design, 1998-, School of Continuing Studies, director of creative writing program. Writer. **Publications:** Going to Cuba (short stories), 1990; Make Believe Love (novel), 2001; Last Cowboy: A Novel, 2004; Confession, 2009; An Average Moment in the West, forthcoming. Contributor to magazines. **Address:** Westwood Creative Artists, 94 Harbord St., Toronto, ON M5S 1G6, Canada. **Online address:** lee.gowan@utoronto.ca

GOWEN, L. Kris. American (born United States), b. 1968. **Genres:** Sex. **Career:** Stanford University, Stanford Center on Adolescence, research fellow, 1996-98, visiting lecturer, 1998-99; University of California-San Francisco, Center for AIDS Prevention Studies, research and evaluation consultant, 1997-98; SERA Learning Inc., director of research and development, 1998-99; Portland State University, adjunct faculty, 2000-, School of Community Health, instructor, faculty, 2001-08, School of Social Work, Regional Research Institute of Human Services, research associate, 2006-; Womensforum.com, senior channel producer, 2000-01; Foundation for Accountability, senior research associate, 2001-04; The Commonwealth Fund, Cultural Applications Project, researcher, 2001-03; The Markle Foundation, Connecting for Health, researcher, 2002-04; Markle Foundation, Life on the Line Media Project, researcher, 2002-04; Merck, Medication Adherence Education, researcher, 2002-04; Northwest Health Foundation, Parent/Teen Communication Enhancement, researcher, 2002-05; Oregon Health and Sciences University, senior research associate, 2003-06; Acumentra Health, Research Analyst, 2004-06; OMPRO, project coordinator, 2004-; State of Oregon, Addiction and Mental Health Division, researcher, 2005-07; icouldbe.org, e-mentor, 2005-; Pacific University, adjunct faculty, 2006; Association of Sex Educators, Counselors and Therapists, section leader, 2006-08; Maltreatment and Mental Health in Older Foster Youth, researcher, 2007-08; The Virtual Mystery Tour, creator. Writer. **Publications:** Making Sexual Decisions: The Ultimate Teen Guide, 2003; (with M. McKenna) Image and Identity: Becoming the Person You Are, 2005. Contributor of articles to journals. **Address:**

School of Community Health, Portland State University, MCB 932, 2145 MetroCenter Blvd., Ste. 400, Orlando, FL 32835, U.S.A. **Online address:** gowen@pdx.edu

GOYER, David S. American (born United States), b. 1965. **Genres:** Cartoons, Film, Novels, Science Fiction/Fantasy. **Career:** Writer and producer. **Publications:** COMICS: (with J. Robinson) JSA: Justice Be Done, 2000; (coauthor) JSA: Darkness Falls, 2002; (with G. Johns) JLA, JSA: Virtue and Vice, 2002; (with G. Johns) JSA: The Return of Hawkman, 2002; (with J. Robinson) Starman: A Starry Knight, 2002; (co-author) The Justice Society Returns!, 2003; (with L. Kirk) JSA: Stealing Thunder, 2003; (with G. Johns) JSA: Savage Times, 2004. NOVELS: (co-author) Dark City, 1998; (with C. Nolan and P. Lerangis) Batman Begins: The Junior Novel, 2005. OTHERS: (with M. Cassutt) Heaven's Shadow, 2011; Ghost Rider, forthcoming. Contributor to periodicals. **Address:** c/o Author Mail, DC Comics Inc., 1700 Broadway, 7th Fl., New York, NY 10019-5905, U.S.A.

GRAB, Daphne. American (born United States), b. 1971?. **Genres:** Novels, Young Adult Fiction, Children's Fiction. **Career:** Writer. **Publications:** Alive and Well in Prague, NY (YA novel), 2008; Halftime (novel), 2010. **Address:** Laura Geringer Books, 1350 Ave. of the Americas, New York, NY 10019, U.S.A. **Online address:** daphnegrab@yahoo.com

GRABBE, Crockett L(ane). American (born United States), b. 1951. **Genres:** inspirational/Motivational Literature, Physics, Politics/Government, Sciences, Technology, Astronomy, Autobiography/Memoirs. **Career:** University of Tennessee, visiting assistant professor, 1978-79; Science Applications, research scientist, 1979-81; Naval Research Laboratory, researcher; University of Iowa, associate research scientist, 1981-88, research scientist, 1988-; public speaker on science-related issues; SeaLane Consulting, scientific consultant and trainer. Writer. **Publications:** (Ed.) Plasma Waves and Instabilities, 1986; Space Weapons and the Strategic Defense Initiative, 1991; Duck Soup for the Die Hard Soul, 2001; Power in Focus, 2004; Plasma Physics Applied, 2006. Contributor of articles to books, journals and magazines. **Address:** Department of Physics and Astronomy, University of Iowa, VAN 203 Allen Hall, Iowa City, IA 52242, U.S.A. **Online address:** grabbe@einstein.physics.uiowa.edu

GRABENSTEIN, Chris. American (born United States), b. 1955. **Genres:** Humor/Satire, Novels. **Career:** J. Walter Thompson (advertising agency), copywriter, creative director; Young & Rubicam (advertising agency), group creative director/executive vice president; Bart and Chris (radio creative services), co-founder; Columbia Broadcasting System, writer. **Publications:** Tilt-a-Whirl, 2005; Mad Mouse, 2006; Slay Ride, 2006; Whack a Mole, 2007; Hell for the Holidays, 2007; Whack-a-Mole, 2007; Crossroads, 2008; Hell Hole, 2008; Hanging Hill, 2009; Mind Scrambler: A John Ceepak Mystery, 2009; Rolling Thunder, 2010; Smoky Corridor, 2010; The Black Heart Crypt, 2011; Riley Mack and the Other Known Troublemakers, 2012. **Address:** The Spieler Agency, 154 W 57th St., Rm. 135, New York, NY 10019, U.S.A. **Online address:** author@chrisgrabenstein.com

GRABER, Mark A. American (born United States), b. 1956. **Genres:** Politics/Government, History. **Career:** University of Texas, instructor, 1987-88, assistant professor, 1988-93; University of Maryland- College Park, Department of Government and Politics, assistant professor, 1993-95, associate professor, 1995-2001, professor, 2001-07, associate department chair, director of graduate studies; University of Maryland-Baltimore, Francis King Carey School of Law, professor of law, 2003-, associate dean for research and faculty development, 2010-. Writer and lawyer. **Publications:** Transforming Free Speech: The Ambiguous Legacy of Civil Libertarianism, 1991; (co-author) 1991 Fish Tax Study, 1992; Rethinking Abortion: Equal Choice, the Constitution, and Reproductive Politics, 1996; (ed. with M. Perhac) Marbury versus Madison: Documents and Commentary, 2002; Dred Scott and the Problem of Constitutional Evil, 2006; (with H. Gillman and K.E. Whittington) American Constitutionalism, 2012. Contributor to periodicals and journals. **Address:** Department of Government and Politics, University of Maryland, Rm. 354, 500 W Baltimore St., College Park, MD 20742, U.S.A. **Online address:** mgraber@gvpt.umd.edu

GRABER MILLER, Keith Allen. (Keith G. Miller). American (born United States), b. 1959. **Genres:** Documentaries/Reportage. **Career:** Kokomo Tribune, bureau chief, 1981-83; Howard County News, editor and general manager, 1981-83; Howard-Miami Mennonite Church, co-pastor, 1983-87;

Goshen College, interim campus minister, 1987-88, assistant professor of communication, 1987-89, associate professor of bible, religion, and philosophy, 1993-, professor of bible, religion and philosophy, 1993-, department chair, 2005-; Emory University, teaching assistantships, 1989-93; Associated Mennonite Biblical Seminary, visiting faculty, 1997-. **Publications:** (As Keith G. Miller) Wise as Serpents, Innocent as Doves: American Mennonites Engage Washington, 1996; (ed. with M.E. Berry) Wrestling with the Text: Young Adult Perspectives on Scripture, 2007; (ed.) Prophetic Peacemaking: Selected Writings of J.R. Burkholder, 2010. Contributor of articles and reviews to periodicals. **Address:** Goshen College, 1700 S Main St., Goshen, IN 46526, U.S.A. **Online address:** keithgm@goshen.edu

GRABILL, Stephen J. (Stephen John Grabill). American (born United States), b. 1967?. **Genres:** Business/Trade/Industry, Money/Finance, Cultural/Ethnic Topics. **Career:** Writer and theologian. **Publications:** (with K.E. Schmiesing and G.L. Zúñiga) Doing Justice to Justice: Competing Frameworks of Interpretation in Christian Social Ethics, 2002; Rediscovering the Natural Law in Reformed Theological Ethics, 2006; (ed.) Sourcebook in Late-Scholastic Monetary Theory: The Contributions of Martín de Azpilcueta, Luis de Molina, S.J, and Juan de Mariana, S.J., 2007. **Address:** Acton Institute, 161 Ottawa Ave. NW, Ste. 301, Grand Rapids, MI 49503, U.S.A. **Online address:** sgrabill@acton.org

GRABILL, Stephen John. *See* **GRABILL, Stephen J.**

GRABOYS, Thomas B. American (born United States), b. 1945?. **Genres:** Autobiography/Memoirs. **Career:** Boston City Hospital, intern, 1970-72; Greater Boston Physicians for Social Responsibility, chair, 1980-87; United States Air Force School of Aerospace Medicine, Biodynamics Branch, research associate; Harvard Medical School, Brigham and Women's Hospital, clinical professor of medicine and attending cardiologist; Lown Cardiovascular Research Foundation, president emeritus and attending cardiologist. Writer. **Publications:** (With C.M. Blatt) Angina Pectoris: Management Strategies and Guide to Interventions, 1994, 2nd ed., 1997; (with P. Zheutlin) Life in the Balance: A Physician's Memoir of Life, Love, and Loss with Parkinson's Disease and Dementia, 2008. **Address:** U.S.A. **Online address:** tgraboys@partners.org

GRACE, Alexander M. (Bruce W. Farcau). American (born United States), b. 1951. **Genres:** Novels, Adult Non-fiction, History, Military/Defense/Arms Control, Politics/Government. **Career:** Washington Inventory Service, manager, 1973-77; U.S. Department of State, staff, 1977-; political officer-Bolivia, 1979-81, political officer-Ecuador, 1981-84, political officer-France, 1985-87, political officer-Dominican Republic, 1987-88, political officer-Spain, 1990-92. Writer. **Publications:** AS BRUCE W. FARCAU: The Transition to Democracy in Latin America: The Role of the Military, 1996; The Chaco War: Bolivia and Paraguay, 1932-1935, 1996; The Ten Cents War: Chile, Peru, and Bolivia in the War of the Pacific, 1879-1884, 2000. OTHERS: Crisis, 1991; Coup!, 1991; The Coup: Tactics in the Seizure of Power, 1993; Sky Blue, 1995; Holy War, 1996; Hegemon, 1996; A Little Empire of Their Own, 1999. **Address:** c/o Matt Bialer, William Morris Agency, 1330 Ave. of the Americas, New York, NY 10019, U.S.A.

GRACE, C. L. *See* **DOHERTY, P(aul) C.**

GRACE, Deborah. *See* **WINER, Deborah Grace.**

GRACE, Nancy McCampbell. American (born United States), b. 1952. **Genres:** Literary Criticism And History, Biography, Autobiography/Memoirs. **Career:** Women's Tribune, editor and publisher, 1978-80; Columbus Art, editor, 1980-84; Ohio State University, Writing Skills Laboratory, director, 1983-84, Department of Anesthesiology, editor, 1985-86, lecturer in English, 1986-87; Otterbein College, adjunct lecturer, 1986-87; Franklin University, adjunct lecturer, 1986-87; College of Wooster, associate professor of English, 1987-, department head, 1994-, Virginia Myers professor, founding director of program in writing, 1988-, chair of women's, gender, and sexuality studies; Beat Studies Association, founding member. **Publications:** (With T.L. Milligan) The Waiting (poetry chapbook), 1980; (with G. DeLaVars) The Tutor Handbook, 1986; The Feminized Male Character in Twentieth-century Literature, 1995; (ed. with R.C. Johnson) Girls who Wore Black: Women Writing the Beat Generation, 2002; (with R.C. Johnson) Breaking the Rule of Cool: Interviewing and Reading Women Beat Writers, 2004; Jack Kerouac and the Literary Imagination, 2007. Contributor of articles to books and periodicals. **Address:** Department of English, College of Wooster, 214 Kauke Hall, 400 E University St., Wooster, OH 44691, U.S.A. **Online address:** ngrace@wooster.edu

GRACE, Patricia (Frances). New Zealander (born New Zealand), b. 1937. **Genres:** Novels, Novellas/Short Stories, Children's Fiction, Picture/Board Books, Young Adult Fiction. **Career:** Victoria University, writing fellow, 1985; full-time writer, 1986-. **Publications:** CHILDREN'S BOOKS: The Kuia and the Spider, 1981; Wahine Toa: Women of Maori Myth, 1984; Watercress Tuna and the Children of Champion Street, 1984, as Te Tuna Watakirihi Me Nga Tamariki O Te Tiriti O Toa, 1985, as Tuna O LeKapisivai Ma Tamaiti O Champion Street, 1988; He aha te mea nui? Ma Wai?Ko ua tenei and Ahakoa he iti (Maori readers), 4 vols., 1985; The Trolleyas Te Toneke, 1993; Areta and the Kahawai, 1994; Kei Te Retireti Au, 1997; (with K. Waiariki and B. Gunson) Ko Au Tenei, 1998; (with Waiariki and Gunson) Ma Wai?, 1998. ADULT FICTION: Waiariki, 1975; Mutuwhenua: The Moon Sleeps, 1978; The Dream Sleepers and Other Stories, 1980; Potiki, 1986, new ed., 2009; Electric City and Other Stories, 1988; Selected Stories, 1991; Cousins, 1992; The Sky People, 1994; Collected Stories, 1994; Baby No-Eyes, 1998; Dogside Story, 2001; Tu, 2004; Small Holes In The Silence: Short Stories, 2006; (ed.) Huia Short Stories 6: Contemporary Maori Fiction, 2006; Maraea and the Albatrosses, 2008; Ned & Katina: A True Love Story, 2009. OTHERS: Earth, Sea, Sky: Images And Maori Proverbs from the Natural World of Aotearoa New Zealand, 2006. Works appear in anthologies. **Address:** Penguin Books, North Shore Mail Ctr., PO Box 102902, Auckland, 0745, New Zealand.

GRAD, Laurie Burrows. American (born United States), b. 1944. **Genres:** Food And Wine. **Career:** Los Angles Magazine, food editor, 1978-95; cookbook author, 1982-; Buzz Magazine, restaurant columnist, 1996-. **Publications:** (Comp.) Dining in-Los Angeles, 1979, rev. ed., 1982; Make It Easy in Your Kitchen, 1982; Make It Easy Entertaining, 1984; Make It Easy, Make It Light, 1987; Entertaining Light and Easy: Lower-Fat Recipes for Festive Meals, 1998. Contributor to magazines. and periodicals. **Address:** Maureen Lasher, Lasher Agency, PO Box 46370, Los Angeles, CA 90046, U.S.A. **Online address:** mkitezy@aol.com

GRAEF, Roger (Arthur). British/American (born United States), b. 1936. **Genres:** Documentaries/Reportage, Criminology/True Crime, Law. **Career:** Actors Studio, director, 1958-62; HarperCollins, media advisor, 1982-87; Oxford University, Communications and Broadcast Media, news international visiting professor; University of London, Royal Holloway College, visiting professor; London School of Economics and Political Science, Mannheim Centre for Criminology, visiting professor, visiting fellow, 1995-; Bournemouth University, visiting professor; Films of Record, staff, chief executive officer; Paul Hamlyn Foundation, advisor. Producer and writer. **Publications:** Central London Bus Map: Going Places, 1981; Talking Blues: The Police in Their Own Words, 1989; Living Dangerously: Young Offenders in Their Own Words, 1993; Why Restorative Justice?: Repairing The Harm Caused By Crime, 2001. **Address:** Mannheim Center for Criminology, London School of Economics & Political Science, School of the University of London, Houghton St., London, GL WC2A 2AE, England. **Online address:** rogerg@filmsofrecord.com

GRAEME, Roderic. See **JEFFRIES, Roderic.**

GRAEUB, Ralph. Swiss (born Switzerland), b. 1921. **Genres:** Environmental Sciences/Ecology, Medicine/Health, Sciences. **Career:** Faerberei AG, development engineer, 1950-72; Kammzugfaerberei AG, manager, 1972-87. Writer. **Publications:** Die sanften Möerder: Atomkraftwerke demaskiert, 1972; Der Petkau-Effekt und unsere strahlende Zukuft, 1985. **Address:** Hoeflistrasse 102, PO Box 210, Langnaua, CH-8135, Switzerland.

GRAF, Mike. American (born United States), b. 1960. **Genres:** Education. **Career:** Teacher; California Polytechnic State University, instructor and master's degree supervisor, 1994-97; California State University, instructor in child development and children's literature, 1998-, Child Development Program, lecturer, 1999; The Weather Channel, consultant; McClean Literary Agency, consultant. Writer. **Publications:** The Weather Report, 1989; National Parks Projects: A Complete Guide to National Park Education for Classroom Use, 1993; Lightning! and Thunderstorms, 1998; Cave Story: An Underground Adventure, 1998; Tornado!: The Strongest Winds on Earth, 1999; The Worlds Best Places: Classroom Explorations in Geography and

Environmental Science, 2000; Somalia, 2002; Switzerland, 2002; What Happened to Bodie?, 2002; Teachers Guide to Explorers of North America for Grades 4-6, 2002; Teachers Guide to Fifth-Grade Reading at Various Levels, 2002; Yellowstone National Park, 2003; Wolves, 2003; (with K. McFarren) Explorers of North America, 2003; Whirlwind, 2003; Africa, 2003; South America, 2003; Olympic National Park, 2003; Asia, 2003; Rocky Mountain National Park, 2003; Europe, 2003; Grand Canyon National Park, 2003; Yosemite National Park, 2003; Great Smoky Mountains National Park, 2003; White-Water Kayaking, 2004; Oregon, 2004; The Nile River, 2004; Washington, 2004; Everglades National Park, 2004; Glacier National Park, 2004; Mammoth Cave National Park, 2004; Rock Climbing, 2004; Montana, 2004; Zion National Park, 2004; The Amazon River, 2004; (with K. McFarene) Science Fair Projects and Activities: Creative Ideas Using Easy-to-Find Materials, 2005; Grand Canyon: The Tail of the Scorpion, 2006; Bryce and Zion: Danger in the Narrows, 2006; Whale Rescue, 2006; Water World, 2006; Eye of the Grizzly, 2007; Harrowing Ascent of Half Dome, 2007; Tornado Watch, 2007; How does a Waterfall become Electricity?, 2008; How does A Cloud become a Thunderstorm?, 2008; A Year of Change, 2008; Great Smoky Mountains National Park, 2009; Touch of the Tide Pool, Crack of the Glacier, 2009; Ridge Runner Rescue, 2009; Storm, 2010; Quake!, 2010; Peril on Longs Peak, 2010; Going to the Sun, 2010; My Yosemite: A Guide for Young Adventurers, 2012. **Address:** California State University, AJH 123C, 400 W 1st St., Chico, CA 95929, U.S.A. **Online address:** mgraf@csuchico.edu

GRAF, William L. American (born United States), b. 1947. **Genres:** Geography. **Career:** University of Wisconsin, Department of Geography, teacher, 1969, research assistant, 1969-70, 1970-71; Lowry Air Force Base, Armed Forces Air Intelligence Training Center, U.S. Air Force, intelligence officer, lecturer, 1971-74; University of Iowa, assistant professor, associate professor of geography, Institute of Urban and Regional Research, research associate, 1974-78, Department of Geography, assistant Professor and associate Professor, 1974-78; Arizona State University, associate professor, professor of geography, Regents professor, 1978-2001, Center for Southwest Studies, director, 1981-83; University of California, distinguished lecturer, 1986; University of London, distinguished visiting professor and Maconokie lecturer, 1992; Clark University, Atwood lecturer, 1993; McMaster University, Brown distinguished lecturer, 1994; U.S. Geological Survey, Thomas B. Nolan distinguished lecturer, 1994; University of Southampton, K. J. Gregory lecturer, 1997; University of South Carolina, professor, university foundation distinguished professor, 2001-, chair of department, 2006-10, School of the Environment, professor, 2001-, College of Arts and Sciences, Interim Associate Dean for Research, 2010-11; U.S. Department of the Interior, fellow; Geological Society of America, officer; Association of American Geographers, president; American Association for the Advancement of Science, fellow; National Academy of Sciences, national associate. Writer and consultant. **Publications:** The Colorado River: Instability and Basin Management, 1985; Fluvial Processes in Dryland Rivers, 1988; Wilderness Preservation and the Sagebrush Rebellions, 1990; Plutonium and the Rio Grande, 1994; Dam Consequences: An Environmental History of Dams and American Rivers, forthcoming; Dam Removal: Science and Decision Making, forthcoming. EDITOR: Geomorphic Systems of North America, 1987; The Salt and Gila Rivers in Central Arizona: A Geographic Field Trip Guide, 1988. Contributor of articles to books and periodicals. **Address:** Department of Geography, University of South Carolina, Rm. 220, Callcott Bldg., 709 Bull St., Columbia, SC 29208, U.S.A. **Online address:** graf@sc.edu

GRAFF, Dale E(dward). American (born United States), b. 1934. **Genres:** Paranormal, Theology/Religion. **Career:** Bendix Systems Division, aerospace engineer, 1959-61; Martin Marietta Corp., aerospace engineer, 1961-64; U.S. Air Force, Foreign Technology Division, civilian aerospace engineer and physicist, 1964-81; Project STARGATE, director; Defense Intelligence Agency, physicist, 1981-93. Writer. **Publications:** Tracks in the Psychic Wilderness, 1998; River Dreams: Wilderness and Psychic Themes, 1998; (co-author) Frank Joseph, Synchronicity and You, 1999; River Shadows, forthcoming; On the Trail of Intuition, forthcoming. **Address:** 230 St. Michaels Rd., Hamburg, PA 19526, U.S.A. **Online address:** baygraff@chesapeake.net

GRAFF, Garrett M. American (born United States), b. 1981?. **Genres:** Politics/Government. **Career:** Washingtonian magazine, editor-at-large; Georgetown University, faculty member; EchoDitto Inc., vice president of communications; Howard Dean's Presidential Campaign, deputy national press secretary; mediabistro.com, FishbowlDC, founding editor. **Publications:** The First Campaign: Globalization, the Web and the Race for the White

House, 2007. **Address:** Georgetown Univ Ctr. For Cont. & Professional Edu, 3101 Wilson Blvd., Ste. 200, Arlington, VA 22201, U.S.A. **Online address:** ggraff@washingtonian.com

GRAFF, Henry Franklin. American (born United States), b. 1921. **Genres:** History, Biography, Politics/Government, Essays. **Career:** Columbia University, faculty, 1946, Department of History, chairman, 1961-63, professor of history, 1961-91, professor emeritus of history, 1991-. Writer. **Publications:** (Ed. and intro.) Bluejackets with Perry in Japan: A Day-by-Day Account Kept by Master's Mate R. C. Lewis and Cabin Boy William B. Allen, 1952; (with J. Barzun) The Modern Researcher, 1957, 6th ed., 2004; (with C. Lord) American Themes, 1963; The Life History of the United States, 1963, 2nd ed., 1969; Thomas Jefferson, 1968; The Free and the Brave, 1967, 5th ed., 1992; (ed.) American Imperialism and the Philippine Insurrection, 1969; The Tuesday Cabinet: Deliberation and Decision on Peace and Warunder Lyndon B. Johnson, 1970; Free and The Brave, 1972; (with J.A. Krout) The Adventure of the American People, 1959, 3rd ed., 1973; (with R.B. Morris) America at 200: Essays, 1975; (with P.J. Bohannan) The Grand Experiment, vol. I: The Call of Freedom, vol. II: The Promise of Democracy, 1978; This Great Nation: A History of the United States, 1983; (ed.) The Presidents: A Reference History, 1984, 3rd ed., 2002; America: The Glorious Republic, 1985, 4th ed., 1990; Grover Cleveland, 2002; (ed.) Inaugural Addresses of the Presidents of the United States, 2005. Contributor to journals and periodicals. **Address:** 47 Andrea Ln., Scarsdale, NY 10583, U.S.A. **Online address:** preshist@aol.com

GRAFF, Laurie. American (born United States) **Genres:** Novellas/Short Stories. **Career:** Writer. **Publications:** You Have to Kiss a Lot of Frogs, 2004; Looking for Mr. Goodfrog, 2006; The Shiksa Syndrome, 2008; Charlie & Flo, 2008; (intro.) Marjorie Hillis, Live Alone and Like It: The Classic Guide for the Single Woman, 2008. Contributor to books. **Address:** New York, NY , U.S.A. **Online address:** laurie@lauriegraff.com

GRAFF, Lisa. American (born United States), b. 1981?. **Genres:** Novels, Children's Fiction, Young Adult Fiction. **Career:** Farrar, Straus & Giroux Books for Young Readers, assistant editor. **Publications:** The Thing About Georgie: A Novel, 2006; The Life and Crimes of Bernetta Wallflower: A Novel, 2008; Umbrella Summer, 2009; Sophie Simon Solves Them All, 2010; Double Dog Dare, 2012. **Address:** HarperCollins Children's Books, 10 E 53rd St., New York, NY 10022, U.S.A. **Online address:** graff.lisa@yahoo.com

GRAFTON, Anthony T(homas). American (born United States), b. 1950. **Genres:** History, Translations, Literary Criticism And History, Biography. **Career:** Cornell University, instructor in history, 1974-75; Princeton University, Department of History, assistant professor, 1975-80, associate professor, 1970-85, professor, 1985-, Andrew Mellon professor of history, 1988-93, Dodge professor of history, 1993-, Henry Putnam university professor of history, 2000-; New York Public Library, exhibit curator, 1992; Library of Congress, curator, 1993; Columbia University, Meyer Schapiro lecturer, 1996-97; British Academy, corresponding fellow, 1997; American Historical Association, president, 2011. Writer. **Publications:** Joseph Scaliger: A Study in the History of Classical Scholarship, vol. I: Textual Criticism and Exegesis, 1983, vol. II: Historical Chronology, 1993; (with L. Jardine) From Humanism to the Humanities: Education and the Liberal Arts in Fifteenth and Sixteenth Century Europe, 1986; Forgers and Critics: Creativity and Duplicity in Western Scholarship, 1990; Defenders of the Text: The Traditions of Scholarship in an Age of Science, 1450-1800, 1991; (with A. Shelford and N. Siraisi) New Worlds, Ancient Texts: The Power of Tradition and the Shock of Discovery, 1992; (with E.F. Rice) The Foundations of Early Modern Europe, 1460-1559, 1994; The Footnote: A Curious History, 1997; Commerce with the Classics, 1997; Cardano's Cosmos, 1999; Leon Battista Alberti, 2000; Bring Out Your Dead, 2001; (contrib.) The Revolt of the Bees, 2005; Magic and Technology in Early Modern Europe, 2005; (with M. Williams) Christianity and the Transformation of the Book, 2006; What Was History?, 2007; Codex in Crisis, 2008; Worlds Made by Words, 2009; Cartographies of Time, 2010; I Have Always Loved the Holy Tongue, 2011. EDITOR: (comp. with H.J. de Jonge) Joseph Scaliger: A Bibliography, 1852-1982, 1982; (with A. Blair) The Transmission of Culture in Early Modern Europe, 1990; Rome Reborn: The Vatican Library and Renaissance Culture (catalogue of an exhibition held at the Library of Congress, Washington, DC, January 6-April 30, 1993), 1993; (with N. Siraisi) Natural particulars, 1999; (with J.H.M. Salmon) Historians and Ideologues, 2001; (with M. Idel) Der Magus, 2001; (with W.R. Newman) Secrets of Nature, 2001; (with K. Mills) Conversion in Late Antiquity and the Early Middle Ages, 2003; (with K. Mills) Conversion: Old Worlds and

New, 2003; (with M.S. Rodriguez) Migration in History, 2007; (with G.W. Most and S Settis) Classical tradition, 2010. TRANSLATOR: (with G.W. Most and J.E.G. Zetzel) Prolegomena to Homer, 1795, by F.A. Wolf, 1985. Contributor to periodicals. **Address:** Department of History, Princeton University, 126 Dickinson Hall, Princeton, NJ 08544, U.S.A. **Online address:** grafton@princeton.edu

GRAFTON, Sue. American (born United States), b. 1940. **Genres:** Mystery/ Crime/Suspense, Plays/Screenplays, Novellas/Short Stories, Novels, Young Adult Non-fiction. **Career:** Los Angeles City College, lecturer; University of Dayton, City College, lecturer. Screenwriter. **Publications:** Keziah Dane, 1967; The Lolly-Madonna War: A Novel, 1969; A Is for Alibi, 1982; B Is for Burglar, 1985; C is for Corpse, 1986; D is for Deadbeat, 1987; E is for Evidence, 1988; F is for Fugitive, 1989; G is for Gumshoe, 1990; H is for Homicide, 1991; I is for Innocent, 1992; (ed.) Writing Mysteries: A Handbook, 1992, 2nd ed., 2002; Kinsey and Me (short stories), 1992; J is for Judgment, 1993; K is for Killer, 1994; L is for Lawless, 1995; M is for Malice, 1996; N is for Noose, 1998; O is for Outlaw, 1999; P is for Peril, 2000; Q is for Quarry, 2002; R is for Ricochet, 2004; (ed. with J. Deaver, R. Herbert and T. Hillerman) A New Omnibus of Crime, 2005; S is for Silence, 2005; T is for Trespass, 2007; U is for Undertow, 2009; V Is For Vengeance, 2011. Contributor to periodicals. **Address:** PO Box 41447, Santa Barbara, CA 93140-1447, U.S.A.

GRAGG, Rod. American (born United States), b. 1950. **Genres:** History, Military/Defense/Arms Control. **Career:** WWAY-TV, news director, 1973-74; WBTV-TV, news reporter, 1974-76; Montreat-Anderson College, administrator, 1977-78; Coastal Carolina University, administrator and instructor, 1978-83, The Center for Military and Veterans Studies, director, Department of History, adjunct professor; Southern Communications, president, 1983-; Conway Christian School, chair. Writer. **Publications:** Bobby Bagley P.O.W., 1978; Pirates, Planters, and Patriots: Historical Tales from the South Carolina Grand Strand, 1984; The Civil War Quiz and Fact Book, 1985; The Old West Quiz and Fact Book, 1986; The Illustrated Confederate Reader: A Remarkable Collection of Personal Experiences, Eyewitness Accounts, and Interesting Facts by and About Southern Soldiers and Civilians During the Civil War, 1989; Confederate Goliath: The Battle of Fort Fisher, 1991; The Illustrated History of Horry County, 1994; Covered with Glory: The 26th North Carolina Infantry at Gettysburg, 2000; (comp. and ed.) A Commitment to Valor: A Character Portrait of Robert E. Lee, 2001; From Foxholes and Flight Decks: Letters Home From World War II, 2002; Lewis and Clark on the Trail of Discovery: The Journey that Shaped America, 2003; (foreword and contrib.) Great Maps of the Civil War: Pivotal Battles and Campaigns Featuring 32 Removable Maps, 2004; Declaration of Independence: The Story behind America's Founding Document and the Men Who Created It, 2005; (with H.L. Reeder III) Leadership Dynamic: A Biblical Model for Raising Effective Leaders, 2008; Forged in Faith: How Faith Shaped the Birth of the Nation, 1607-1776, 2010; By the Hand of Providence: How Faith Shaped the American Revolution, 2011. Contributor to periodicals. **Address:** Coastal Carolina University, PO Box 261954, Conway, SC 29528-6054, U.S.A. **Online address:** rgragg@coastal.edu

GRAGNOLATI, Manuele. British/Italian (born Italy), b. 1968. **Genres:** Cultural/Ethnic Topics, Literary Criticism And History, Poetry. **Career:** Dartmouth College, assistant professor, 1999-2003; Somerville College, tutor, fellow and university reader in Italian literature; St. Catherine's College, university lecturer, 2003-, tutor; University of Oxford, Lady Margaret Hall, tutor. Writer. **Publications:** Experiencing the Afterlife: Soul and Body in Dante and Medieval Culture, 2005. EDITOR: (with S. Fortuna) Power of Disturbance, 2009; (with A. Suerbaum) Aspects of the Performative in Medieval Culture, 2010; (with S. Fortuna and J. Trabant) Dante's Plurilingualism: Authority, Knowledge, Subjectivity, 2010; (with F. Camilletti and F. Lampart) Metamorphosing Dante, 2011. Contributor to books. **Address:** Somerville College, Woodstock Rd., Oxford, OX OX2 6HD, England. **Online address:** manuele.gragnolati@some.ox.ac.uk

GRAHAM, Ada. American (born United States), b. 1931. **Genres:** Children's Non-fiction, Animals/Pets, Mystery/Crime/Suspense. **Career:** New York City Public Schools, teacher, 1957-58, 1964-65; Baldwin School-New York City, teacher, 1958-59; Baldwin School-Sullivan, teacher, 1965-67; Summer Head Start Program, teacher, 1967-70; Maine State Commission on the Arts and Humanities, vice-chairman, 1975-80; Audubon Adventures (National Audubon Society), developer and writer, 1984-. **Publications:**

WITH F. GRAHAM, JR.: The Great American Shopping Cart: How America Gets Its Food Today, 1969; Wildlife Rescue, 1970; Puffin Island, 1971; The Mystery of the Everglades, 1972; Let's Discover Winter Woods, 1974; Let's Discover the Floor of the Forest, 1974; Let's Discover Changes Everywhere, 1974; Let's Discover Birds in Our World, 1974; Dooryard Garden, 1974; The Careless Animal, 1975; The Milkweed and Its World of Animals, 1976; Bug Hunters, 1978; Whale Watch, 1978; Coyote Song, 1978; Falcon Flight, 1978; Audubon Readers, 6 vols., 1978-81; Alligators, 1979; Careers in Conservation, 1980; Birds of the Northern Seas, 1981; The Changing Desert, 1981; Jacob and Owl: A Story of Modern Medical Research, 1981; Bears in the Wild, 1981; Three Million Mice, 1981; Busy Bugs, 1983; The Big Stretch: The Complete Book of the Amazing Rubber Band, 1985; We Watch Squirrels, 1985; Kate Furbish and the Flora of Maine, 1995. OTHERS: Foxtails, Ferns, and Fish Scales: A Handbook of Art and Nature Projects, 1976; Six Little Chickadees: A Scientist and Her Work With Birds, 1982. **Address:** JCA Literary Agency Inc., 27 W 20th St., Ste. 1103, New York, NY 10011-3723, U.S.A.

GRAHAM, Anne. *See* **LEAMAN, Celia A.**

GRAHAM, Barbara. American (born United States), b. 1948?. **Genres:** Mystery/Crime/Suspense. **Career:** Novelist. **Publications:** Murder by Serpents: The Mystery Quilt, 2007. **Address:** WY , U.S.A. **Online address:** barbara@bgmysteries.com

GRAHAM, Billy. American (born United States), b. 1918. **Genres:** Theology/Religion, inspirational/Motivational Literature, Biography, Autobiography/Memoirs. **Career:** First Baptist Church, pastor, 1943-45; First Youth for Christ Intl., vice-president, 1945-50; Northwestern College, president, 1947-52; Billy Graham Evangelistic Association, founder, 1950-; Hour of Decision, leader of the weekly radio program, 1950-. Evangelist and author. **Publications:** Calling Youths to Christ, 1947; Chance of a lifetime: Helps for Servicemen, 1952; Peace with God, 1953, rev. ed., 1984; 7 Deadly Sins, 1955; The Secret of Happiness, 1955, rev. ed., 1985; My Answer, 1960; World A flame, 1965; Un monde en Flames, 1967; The Challenge, 1969; The Jesus Generation, 1971; Give this Man Place, 1973; Leva-sof Shalom, 1975; Angels: God's Secret Agents, 1975, rev. ed., 1986; Billy Graham Talks to Teenagers, 1976; How to Be Born Again, 1977; (with C.T. Boom) To God be the Glory: A Testimony of Living Faith From Two Famous Christian Personalities, 1977; The Holy Spirit, 1978; Till Armageddon, 1981; Approaching Hoofbeats: The Four Horseman of the Apocalypse, 1983; A Biblical Standard for Evangelists, 1984; Unto the Hills, 1986, 2nd ed., 2010; Facing Death and the Life After, 1987; Billy Graham's the Bible Says, 1988; Answers to Life's Problems, 1988; The Early Billy Graham: Sermon and Revival Accounts, 1988; Hope for the Troubled Heart, 1991; Storm Warnings, 1992; (foreword) The Master Plan of Evangelism, 1993; Flights of Angels, 1994; Breakfast with Billy Graham: 120 Daily Readings, 1996; Just as I Am, 1997, rev. ed., 2007; Hope for Each Day: Words of Wisdom and Faith, 2002; Key to Personal Peace, 2003; Living in God's love: The New York Crusade, 2005; The Journey: How To Live By Faith In An Uncertain World, 2006; Led to Believe, 2007; Searching for Hope, 2007; God's Love for You: Hope and Encouragement for Life, 2007; Billy Graham: God's Ambassador A Celebration of His Life and Ministry, 2007; Embracing the Good News, 2007; Confronting the Enemies Within, 2007; (with R. Graham) This Christmas Night: Reflections from Our Hearts to Your Home, 2007; Dealing With Doubt, 2007; Leaving a Legacy, 2007; Building a Christ-Centered Home, 2007; Learning to Pray, 2007; Living As A Christian, 2007; Wisdom for Each Day, 2008; Hope for Each Day: A 365-Day Journaling Devotional, 2009; Nearing Home: Life, Faith and Finishing Well, 2011. **Address:** Billy Graham Evangelistic Association, 1 Billy Graham Pkwy., Charlotte, NC 28201, U.S.A.

GRAHAM, Bob. Australian (born Australia), b. 1942. **Genres:** Children's Fiction, Children's Non-fiction, Illustrations, Westerns/Adventure, Adult Non-fiction. **Career:** New South Wales Government Printers, artist, 1973-75; Department of Technical Education, resource designer, 1975-82; Five Mile Press, freelance illustrator and writer, 1982-. **Publications:** SELF-ILLUSTRATED CHILDREN'S FICTION: Pete and Roland, 1981; Here Comes John, 1983; Here Comes Theo, 1983; Pearl's Place, 1983; Libby, Oscar and Me, 1984; Bath Time for John, 1985; First There was Frances, 1985; Where is Sarah?, 1985; The Wild, 1986; The Junk Book, 1986; The Adventures of Charlotte and Henry, 1987; Crusher is Coming!, 1987; The Red Woollen Blanket, 1987; Has Anyone Here Seen William?, 1988; Grandad's Magic, 1989; Greetings from Sandy Beach, 1990; Rose Meets Mr. Wintergarten, 1991; Brand New Baby, 1992; Spirit of Hope, 1993; Zoltan the Magnificent, 1994; The

Red Woolen Blanket, 1996; Queenie the Bantam, 1997; Queenie, One of the Family, 1997; Buffy, 1999; Benny, 1999; Max, 2000; Let's Get a Pup, 2001; Jethro Byrde, 2002; Tales from the Waterhole, 2004; Oscar's Half Birthday, 2005; The Trouble with Dogs, Said Dad, 2007; Dimity Dumpty: The Story of Humpty's Little Sister, 2007; How to Heal a Broken Wing, 2008; April and Esme, Tooth Fairies, 2010. NON-FICTION (readers): (ed.) A First Australian Poetry Book, 1983; I Can series: Actions 1, Actions 2, Babies, Bikes, Colour, Families, Helping, In the Water, My Senses, Pets, School, Shopping, 12 vols., 1984 in UK as Reading is Fun Series, 12 vols., 1986; Science Early Learners Series: Heat, Moving, Push, Senses, Sound, Water, Wheels, vol. VII, 1985-86; Busy Day Board Books: Playing, Sleeping, Waking, vol. III, 1988. Illustrator of books by others. **Address:** 34 Melville St., Hawthorn, VI 3122, Australia. **Online address:** bobgraham59@hotmail.com

GRAHAM, Caroline. British (born England), b. 1931. **Genres:** Novels, Mystery/Crime/Suspense, Plays/Screenplays, Romance/Historical, Literary Criticism And History. **Career:** Writer, 1971-. **Publications:** NOVELS: Fire Dance, 1982; The Envy of the Stranger, 1984; BMX Star Rider, 1985; BMX'ers Battle It Out, 1985; Murder at Madingley Grange, 1991. MYSTERIES: The Killings at Badger's Drift, 1988; Death of a Hollow Man: A Chief Inspector Barnaby Mystery, 1989; Death in Disguise 1993; Camilla: The King's Mistress: A Love Story, 1994; Written in Blood: A Chief Inspector Barnaby Mystery, 1995; Faithful unto Death, 1998; Place of Safety: A Chief Inspector Barnaby Mystery, 1999; Ghost in the Machine, 2004. Contributor to periodicals. **Address:** David Higham Associates Ltd., 5-8 Lower John St., Golden Sq., London, GL W1R 4HA, England.

GRAHAM, Carol (Lee). American (born United States), b. 1962. **Genres:** Politics/Government, Marketing, Economics. **Career:** Duke University, Department of Political Science, assistant professor of political economy, 1989-90; Georgetown University, Department of Government, adjunct professor of government, 1990-94; World Bank, Office of the Chief Economist and Vice Presidency for Human Resources, visiting fellow, 1994-95; Brookings Institution, Economic Studies Program, senior fellow in economic studies, 1995-, Governance Studies Program, vice president and director, 2002-04, Center on Social and Economic Dynamics, co-director, 1998-2006, Charles Robinson Chair in Foreign Policy Studies; Inter-American Development Bank, special advisor to executive vice president, 1997-98; Johns Hopkins University, Department of Economics, visiting professor; University of Maryland, School of Public Policy, park professor, 2005-08; Institute for the Study of Labor, research fellow. Writer. **Publications:** From Emergency Employment to Social Investment: Alleviating Poverty in Chile, 1991; Peru's APRA: Parties, Politics, and the Elusive Quest for Democracy, 1992; Safety Nets, Politics, and the Poor: Transitions to Market Economies, 1994; (with M. O'Hanlon) A Half Penny on the Federal Dollar: The Future of Development Aid, 1997; (ed. with R.H. Sabot and N. Birdsall) Beyond Tradeoffs: Efficient and Equitable Growth in Latin America, 1998; Private Markets for Public Goods: Raising the Stakes in Economic Reform, 1998; Improving the Odds: Political Strategies for Institutional Reform in Latin America, 1999; (ed. with N. Birdsall) New Markets, New Opportunities?: Economics and Social Mobility in a Changing World, 1999; (with S. Pettinato) Happiness and Hardship: Opportunity and Insecurity in New Market Economies, 2002; The Other War: Global Poverty and the Millennium Challenge Account, 2004; (ed. with S.M. Collins) Brookings Trade Forum, 2004; Happiness around the World, 2009; (ed. with E. Lora) Paradox and Perception: Measuring Quality of Life in Latin America, 2009; The Pursuit of Happiness, 2011. **Address:** The Brookings Institution, 1775 Massachusetts Ave. NW, Washington, DC 20036, U.S.A. **Online address:** cgraham@brookings.edu

GRAHAM, Cosmo. British (born England), b. 1956. **Genres:** Law, Business/Trade/Industry. **Career:** Liverpool Polytechnic, lecturer in law, 1981-82; University of Sheffield, lecturer in law, 1982-92; University of Hull, professor of law, 1993-99; University of Leicester, professor of law, 1999-, Centre for Utility Consumer Law, director; Utilities Law Review, co-editor. **Publications:** (Ed. with T. Prosser) Waiving the Rules: The Constitution under Thatcherism, 1988; (ed. with N. Lewis and D. Beyleveld) Reforming the Secret State, 1990; (ed. with N. Lewis and D. Beyleveld) Happy and Glorious: The Constitution in Transition, 1990; (ed. with N. Lewis and D. Beyleveld) Planning Appeals: A Critique, 1991; (with T. Prosser) Privatizing Public Enterprises: Constitutions, the State, and Regulation in Comparative Perspective, 1991; (ed. with N. Lewis) Contracting State, 1992; (ed.) Inner City Regeneration: The Demise of Regional and Local Government, 1992; Regulating Public Utilities: A Constitutional Approach, 2000; (ed. with F. Smith) Competition, Regulation, and the New Economy, 2004; EU and UK Competition Law, 2010. **Address:** School of Law, University of Leicester, University Rd., Leicester, LE1 7RH, England. **Online address:** cosmo.graham@leicester.ac.uk

GRAHAM, Daniel O. American (born United States), b. 1952. **Genres:** Writing/Journalism, Science Fiction/Fantasy, Humor/Satire, Biography, Military/Defense/Arms Control, Business/Trade/Industry, Economics. **Career:** Kentec Corp., president, 1983-86; Graham Associates, principal, 1986-; High Frontier Inc., director, 1983-85; Journal of Practical Applications in Space, founder. Writer. **Publications:** (With J.H. Graham) The Writing System Workbook, 1994; The Gatekeepers (science fiction), 1995; The Politics of Meaning (humor), 1995; (ed.) Confessions of a Cold Warrior (biography), 1995; (with J.H. Graham) The Writing System: A Step-By-Step Guide for Business and Technical Writers, 2002; (with J. Graham) Can Do Writing: The Proven Ten-step System for Fast and Effective Business Writing, 2009; The Father's Gift, forthcoming. SCIENCE FICTION WITH R. DAWSON: Entering Tenebrea, 2001; Tenebrea's Hope, 2001; Tenebrea Rising, 2002. **Address:** Graham Associates, 9117 Saranac Ct., Fairfax, VA 22032, U.S.A. **Online address:** daniel.graham@cox.net

GRAHAM, Desmond. British (born England), b. 1940. **Genres:** Poetry, Literary Criticism And History, Biography, Translations. **Career:** University of Tuebingen, lecturer in English literature, 1961-62; University of Rhodesia, assistant lecturer in English literature, 1962-63; University of Sierra Leone, lecturer in English literature, 1963-66; Munich University, lecturer in English literature, 1968-70; Mannheim University, lecturer in English literature, 1970-71; Gdansk University, visiting lecturer, 1984; Opera News, correspondent, 1969-71; University of Newcastle, reader in modern English poetry, 1997-2000, professor of poetry, 2000-, now professor emeritus. Writer. **Publications:** Introduction to Poetry, 1968; Keith Douglas 1920-1944: A Biography, 1974; (intro.) Alamein to Zem Zem, 1979; The Truth of War: Owen, Blunden and Rosenberg, 1984; (intro. and comp.) A Prose Miscellany, 1985; Seren Poets 2, 1990; A Set of Signs for Chopin's 24 Preludes, 1990; A Rumtopf for Summer 1990; The Lie of Horizons, 1993; (trans. with T.P. Krzeszowski) A. Kamienska, Two Darknesses: Selected Poems, 1994; The Marching Bands, 1996; Not Falling, 1999; After Shakespeare, 2001; Milena Poems, 2004; Heart Work, 2007; Making Poems and their Meanings, 2007; Green Parakeet, 2009. EDITOR: The Complete Poems, 1977, (and intro.) 3rd ed., 1998; (and intro.) Poetry of the Second World War: An International Anthology, 1995; The Letters, 2000. **Address:** School of English Literature, University of Newcastle, Percy Bldg., Newcastle upon Tyne, TW NE1 7RU, England.

GRAHAM, Frank. American (born United States), b. 1925. **Genres:** Environmental Sciences/Ecology, Natural History, Children's Fiction, Animals/Pets, Novellas/Short Stories, History, Mathematics/Statistics, Sciences, Sciences. **Career:** Brooklyn Dodgers Baseball Club, publicity director, 1951-55; Sport (magazine), assistant managing editor, 1956-58; Audubon Magazine, field editor, 1969-. **Publications:** Disaster by Default: Politics and Water Pollution, 1966; (with J.W. Hoyt) For the Love of Mike, 1966; (with S. Woodward) Sportswriter, 1967; Since Silent Spring, 1970; Man's Dominion: The Story of Conservation in America, 1971; Where the Place Called Morning Lies, 1973; Gulls: A Social History, 1975; Potomac: The Nation's River, 1976; The Adirondack Park: A Political History, 1978; A Farewell to Heroes, 1981; The Dragon Hunters, 1984; (with C.W. Buchheister) The Audubon Ark: A History of the National Audubon Society, 1992; Kate Furbish and the Flora of Maine, 1995; Farewell to Heroes, 2003; (with D.T. Jennings) Spiders (Arachnida: Araneae) of Milbridge, Washington County, Maine, 2007. CHILDREN'S BOOKS: Casey Stengel-His Half Century in Baseball, 1958; (with M. Allen) It Takes Heart, 1959; Margaret Chase Smith, Woman of Courage, 1964; Austria, 1964; Great Pennant Races of the Major Leagues, 1967; Great No-Hit Games of the Major Leagues, 1968; Great Hitters of the Major Leagues, 1969. WITH A. GRAHAM: The Great American Shopping Cart: How America Gets Its Food Today, 1969; Wildlife Rescue, 1970; Puffin Island, 1971; The Mystery of the Everglades, 1972; Dooryard Garden, 1974; Let's Discover: The Floor of the Forest, 1974; Let's Discover: Birds in Our World, 1974; Let's Discover: The Winter Woods, 1974; Let's Discover: Changes Everywhere, 1974; The Careless Animal, 1975; The Milkweed and Its World of Animals, 1976; Whale Watch, 1978; Bug Hunters, 1978; Falcon Flight, 1978; Coyote Song, 1978; Alligators, 1979; Careers in Conservation, 1980; Birds of the Northern Seas, 1980; Bears in the Wild, 1981; The Changing Desert, 1981; Three Million Mice: A Story of Modern Medical Research, 1981; Jacob and Owl: A Story, 1981; Busy Bugs, 1983; We Watch Squirrels, 1985. **Address:** JCA Literary Agency, 27 W 20th St., Ste. 1103, New York, NY 10011, U.S.A.

GRAHAM, Gael. (Gael N. Graham). American (born United States), b. 1958. **Genres:** Theology/Religion, Cultural/Ethnic Topics. **Career:** Western Carolina University, professor. Writer. **Publications:** Gender, Culture, and Christianity: American Protestant Mission Schools in China, 1880-1930, 1995; Young Activists: American High School Students in the Age of Protest, 2006. Contributor of articles to journals. **Address:** Western Carolina University, McKee Bldg. 203A, Cullowhee, NC 28723, U.S.A. **Online address:** graham@email.wcu.edu

GRAHAM, Gael N. See **GRAHAM, Gael.**

GRAHAM, Henry. British (born England), b. 1930. **Genres:** Poetry, Social Sciences. **Career:** The John Moores University (now Liverpool Polytechnic), lecturer in art history, 1969-, now retired; Ambit Magazine, poetry editor; Atkinson Art Gallery, writer-in-residence, 1996. Jazz musician. **Publications:** (With J. Mangnall) Soup City Zoo: Poems, 1968; Good Luck to You, Kafka/You'll Need It, Boss, 1969; Passport to Earth, 1971; Poker in Paradise Lose, 1977; Bomb, 1985; Europe After Rain, 1981; The Very Fragrant Death of Paul Gauguin, 1987; Everywhere You Look, 1993; The Eye of the Beholder, 1997; Bar Room Ballads, 1999; Kafka in Liverpool, 2002. Works appear in anthologies. **Address:** Ambit Magazine, 17 Priory Gardens, London, GL N6 5QY, England.

GRAHAM, Holly. See **WELLS, Shirley.**

GRAHAM, Jefferson. American (born United States), b. 1956. **Genres:** Communications/Media, Technology, Marketing, Humor/Satire, Literary Criticism And History, Young Adult Fiction. **Career:** Recycled Records, co-owner and co-founder, 1976-79; The Hollywood Reporter, columnist and reporter, 1981-84; USA Today, reporter, 1984-; Prodigy, columnist, 1992-. **Publications:** Come On Down: The TV Game Show Book, 1988; Vegas: Live and In Person, 1989; Fodor's Vegas '91, 1991; (with K. Kragen) Life is a Contact Sport: Ten Great Career Strategies that Work, 1994; (with R. Popeil) As Seen on TV: Ron Popeil, His Incredible Inventions and How to Participate in the Home Shopping Revolution, 1995; (with R. Popeil) Salesman of the Century: Inventing, Marketing and Selling on TV: How I did it and How You Can Too!, 1995; Frasier, 1996; (with A. Spelling) Aaron Spelling: A Prime-time Life, 1996; Ultimate Rugrats Fan Book, 1998; Norton, Norton & Nordovsky, forthcoming; Defrosted, forthcoming. Contributor to periodicals. **Address:** c/o Mel Berger, William Morris Agency, 1325 Ave. of the Americas, New York, NY 10019, U.S.A. **Online address:** jgraham@usatoday.com

GRAHAM, John D. American (born United States), b. 1956. **Genres:** Medicine/Health, Politics/Government. **Career:** National Research Council/National Academy of Sciences, staff associate, 1979-81; Carnegie-Mellon University, assistant professor, 1984-85; Harvard University, Harvard School of Public Health, post-doctoral fellow, assistant professor, 1985-88, associate professor, 1988-91, professor of policy and decision sciences, 1991-2003, Department of Health Policy and Management, deputy chairman, 1987-92; Center for Risk Analysis, founding director, 1989-2001, Center for Injury Control, director, 1990-97; White House Office of Management and Budget, Office of Information and Regulatory Affairs, administrator, 2001-06; Frederick S. Pardee RAND Graduate School, professor of policy analysis and dean, 2006-08; Indiana University, professor of public affairs, 2008-, School of Public and Environmental Affairs, dean, 2008-. Brookings Institution, predoctoral fellow. Writer. **Publications:** (With L.C. Green and M.J. Roberts) In Search of Safety: Chemicals and Cancer Risk, 1988; Auto Safety: Assessing America's Performance, 1989; (with D. Epstein) Polarized Politics and Policy Consequences, 2007; (with E.D. Brown) Leading the Executive Branch: Strategies and Options for Achieving Success, 2007; (with S. Montoya) Modernizing the Federal Government: Paying for Performance, 2007; Bush on the Home Front: Domestic Policy Triumphs and Failures, 2010. EDITOR: Preventing Automobile Injury: Recent Findings of Evaluation Research, 1988; Harnessing Science for Environmental Regulation, 1991; (with J.B. Wiener) Risk versus Risk: Tradeoffs in Protecting Health and the Environment, 1995; The Role of Epidemiology in Regulatory Risk Assessment, 1995; (with J.K. Hartwell) The Greening of Industry: A Risk Management Approach, 1997. Contributor to professional journals and magazines. **Address:** School of Public & Environmental Affairs, Indiana University, 1315 E 10th St., Rm. 300, Bloomington, IN 47405, U.S.A. **Online address:** grahamjd@indiana.edu

GRAHAM, Jorie. American (born United States), b. 1950. **Genres:** Poetry, Photography. **Career:** Murray State University, assistant professor of

English, 1978-79; Humboldt State University, assistant professor of English, 1979-81; Columbia University, associate professor, 1981-83, Writer's Community workshop, instructor, 1981-83; University of Iowa, professor of English, 1983-99, Writers' Workshop, instructor, 1983-99, director; The Academy of American Poets, chancellor, 1997-2003; Harvard University, Department of English, Boylston professor of rhetoric and oratory, 1999-. Writer. **Publications:** Hybrids of Plants and of Ghosts, 1980; Erosion, 1983; The End of Beauty, 1987; Region of Unlikeness, 1991; Poetry Reading, 1991; (ed. with D. Lehman) The Best American Poetry 1990, 1991; Materialism: Poems, 1993; The Dream of the Unified Field: Poems, 1974-1994, 1995; (ed.) Earth Took of Earth: A Golden Ecco Anthology, 1996; The Errancy: Poems, 1997; (with J.M. Barron) Photographs and Poems, 1998; Swarm: Poems, 2000; Never: Poems, 2002; All Things, 2002; Speaking Subject, 2002; Overlord: Poems, 2005; Sea Change: Poems, 2008. **Address:** c/o Leslie Cohen, ECCO/ HarperCollins Publishers, 10 E 53rd St., New York, NY 10022-5244, U.S.A. **Online address:** graham2@fas.harvard.edu

GRAHAM, Laurie. Irish/British (born England), b. 1947. **Genres:** Novels, Adult Non-fiction, How-to Books. **Career:** The Daily Telegraph, columnist, 1987-91; Sunday Telegraph, columnist, 1987-91; She (magazine), contributing editor; Cosmopolitan, contributing editor; British Broadcasting Corp., playwriter. **Publications:** Parents' Survival Guide, 1986; The Man for the Job, 1986; A Marriage Survival Guide, 1988; Getting It Right: A Survival Guide to Modern Manners, 1989; Generation Games, 1990; Rebuilding the House, 1990; The British Abroad: A Survival Guide, 1991; Teenagers: A Family Survival Guide, 1992; The Ten O'clock Horses (stories), 1996; Perfect Meringues (stories), 1997; The Dress Circle, 1998; Dog Days, Glen Miller Nights (stories), 2000; The Future Homemakers of America, 2001; The Unfortunates, 2002; The Great Husband Hunt, 2003; Mr. Starlight, 2004; Gone with the Windsors, 2005; The Importance of Being Kennedy, 2007; Life According to Lubka, 2009; At Sea, 2010. **Address:** The Mic Cheetham Agency, 50 Albemarle St., London, GL W1S 4BD, England. **Online address:** laurie@lauriegraham.com

GRAHAM, Patterson Toby. American (born United States), b. 1969. **Genres:** Librarianship, Social Sciences, History, Sociology, Civil Liberties/ Human Rights. **Career:** University of Southern Mississippi, associate professor and head of special collections, 1999-2003; University of Georgia, Digital Library of Georgia, deputy university librarian and director, 2003-, Hargrett Rare Book and Manuscript Library, acting director, 2008-. Writer. **Publications:** A Right to Read: Segregation and Civil Rights in Alabama's Public Libraries 1900-1965, 2002. Contributor to periodicals. **Address:** Digital Library of Georgia, University of Georgia, Athens, GA 30602-1641, U.S.A. **Online address:** tgraham@uga.edu

GRAHAM, Robert. See HALDEMAN, Joe (William).

GRAHAM, Vanessa. See FRASER, Anthea.

GRAHAM, W(illiam) Fred. American (born United States), b. 1930. **Genres:** History, Theology/Religion, Autobiography/Memoirs. **Career:** Bethel United Presbyterian Church, pastor, 1955-61; Michigan State University, instructor, 1963-64, Department of Religion, assistant professor, 1964-66, Justin Morrill College, assistant professor, 1965-69, associate professor of religious studies, 1969-73, professor of religious studies, through 1973, professor emeritus of religious studies, 1992-. Writer. **Publications:** The Constructive Revolutionary: John Calvin and His Socio-Economic Impact, 1971; Picking Up the Pieces: A Christian Stance in a Godless Age, 1975; (co-author) Reforming Economics: Calvinist Studies on Methods and Institutions, 1990; (ed.) Later Calvinism: International Perspectives, 1994. **Address:** Department of Religious Studies, Michigan State University, 116 Morrill Hall, East Lansing, MI 48824, U.S.A. **Online address:** grahamw@msu.edu

GRAHAM, Ysenda (May) Maxtone. British (born England), b. 1962. **Genres:** Adult Non-fiction, Theology/Religion, Biography. **Career:** Express on Sunday, columnist. **Publications:** The Church Hesitant: A Portrait of the Church of England Today, 1993; The Real Mrs. Miniver: The Life of Jan Struther, 2001. Contributor to periodicals. **Address:** 1 Avalon Rd., London, GL SW6 2EX, England.

GRAINGER, John D(ownie). British (born England), b. 1939. **Genres:** Archaeology/Antiquities, Classics, History, Biography, Military/Defense/Arms Control, Humanities. **Career:** Bridley Moor High School, teacher of history,

1963-90; writer and historian, 1990-. **Publications:** Seleukos Nikator (biography), 1990; (ed.) The Royal Navy in the River Plate, 1806-1807, 1996; A Seleukid Prosopography and Gazetter, 1997; Aitolian Prosopographical Studies, 2000; The Roman War of Antiochos the Great, 2002; Nerva and the Roman Imperial Succession Crisis AD 96-99, 2003. HISTORY: The Cities of Seleukid Syria, 1990; Hellenistic Phoenicia, 1991; Cromwell against the Scots: The Last Anglo-Scottish War, 1650-1652, 1997; The League of the Aitolians, 1999; (ed.) The Maritime Blockade of Germany in the Great War: The Northern Patrol, 1914-1918, 2003; The Amiens Truce: Britain and Bonaparte, 1801-1803, 2004; Battle of Yorktown, 1781: A Reassessment, 2005; The Battle for Palestine 1917, 2006; Alexander the Great Failure: The Collapse of the Macedonian Empire, 2007; First Pacific War: Britain and Russia, 1854-1856, 2008; Cities of Pamphylia, 2009; Syrian Wars, 2010. Contributor to periodicals and journals. **Address:** Boydell & Brewer Ltd., Whitwell House, St Audry's Park Rd., Melton, Woodbridge, SU IP12 1SY, England. **Online address:** john@grainger4737.freeserve.com

GRALLA, Cynthia. American (born United States) **Genres:** Adult Non-fiction, Novels, Sex. **Career:** Hostess. Writer. **Publications:** The Floating World, 2003; The demimonde in Japanese Literature: Sexuality and the Literary Karyukai, 2010. **Address:** c/o Author Mail, Ballantine Books, Random House, 1745 Broadway, Fl. 3, New York, NY 10019, U.S.A.

GRAMBO, Rebecca L(ynn). Canadian (born Canada), b. 1963. **Genres:** Animals/Pets, Zoology, Children's Non-fiction, Photography. **Career:** Grambo Photography and Design Inc., president, 1995-. Writer. **Publications:** The World of the Fox, 1995, as The Nature of Foxes, 1995; Eagles: Masters of the Sky, 1997; Mountain Lion, 1998; Exploring Weird Science (juvenile), 1998; Eagles, 1999; Birds of Prey (juvenile), 1999; (with J. Grassy and R. Matero) Animal Kingdom, 2000; Dinosaurs (juvenile), 2000; Technology, 2001; (with J.P. Resnick and T. Tallarico) The Big Book of Questions and Answers, 2002; Wapusk: White Bear of the North, 2003; Wolf: Legend, Enemy, Icon, 2005; Digging Canadian History, 2006; The Great Sand Hills: A Prairie Oasis, 2007. AMAZING ANIMALS SERIES FOR CHILDREN: Eyes, 1997; Colors, 1997; Hunters, 1997; Defenses, 1997; Families, 1998; Claws and Jaws, 1998. **Address:** 113 7th Ave. N, PO Box 910, Warman, SK S0K 4S0, Canada. **Online address:** r.grambo@sasktel.net

GRAMBS, David (Lawrence). American (born United States), b. 1938. **Genres:** Language/Linguistics, Translations, Children's Fiction. **Career:** Stratemeyer Syndicate (publisher), juvenile fiction editor, 1963-65; American Heritage Publishing Co., senior editor of American heritage dictionary, 1967-69; Funk & Wagnalls Inc., senior editor and writer of new encyclopedia, 1969-71; Charles Scribner's Sons, The Dictionary of Scientific Biography, associate editor, 1971-73; Penthouse International Inc., Penthouse, copyeditor, 1976-83; Random House Inc., Random House Dictionary of the English Language, staff editor, 1983-87. **Publications:** (Trans.) J. Grünenfelder, Cathedrals of Europe, 1976; Words about Words, 1984 in UK as Literary Companion Dictionary, 1990; Dimboxes, Epopts, and Other Quidams: Words to Describe Life's Indescribable People, 1986; (ed.) Bernstein's Reverse Dictionary, 2nd ed., 1988; Death by Spelling, 1989, rev. ed. as The Ultimate Spelling Quiz Book, 1992; (ed.) The Random House Dictionary for Writers and Readers, 1990; The Describer's Dictionary: A Treasury of Terms and Literary Quotations for Readers and Writers, 1993; Did I Say Something Wrong?, 1993; The Endangered English Dictionary, 1994; Just Ask Mr. Wordwizard, Sentences Repaired, Words Offered, Ignorance Thwarted, 1995; (with E.S. Levine) So You Think You Can Spell?: Killer Quizzes for the Incurably Competitive and Overly Confident, 2009. Contributor to books and periodicals. **Address:** 22 W 90th St., New York, NY 10024-1543, U.S.A.

GRAMER, Rod. American (born United States), b. 1953. **Genres:** Biography. **Career:** Idaho Statesman, reporter, city editor, political editor of editorial page, editor, 1975-88; KTVB-TV 7, director of news and public affairs, 1988-, executive news director; KGW TV 8, executive news director; Bay News 9, vice president and general manager, 2011. **Publications:** (With L. Ashby) Fighting the Odds: The Life of Senator Frank Church, 1994. **Address:** Bay News 9, 4400 Martin Luther King Jr. Blvd., Tampa, FL 33614, U.S.A. **Online address:** rgramer@kgw.com

GRAMPP, William D. American (born United States), b. 1914. **Genres:** Economics. **Career:** Akron Time-Press, editorial staff, 1937-38; Adelphi University, instructor in economics, 1942; Elmhurst College, assistant professor of economics, 1942-44; American Embassy, vice-consul in economics section, 1944-45; De Paul University, assistant professor, 1945-47; University of Illinois, professor, 1947-80, professor emeritus of economics, 1980-; University of Chicago, visiting professor of social sciences, 1980-94, Law School, lecturer, 1994-2001; Institute for Humane Studies, senior fellow, 1982; Lake Forest College, visiting professor; University of California, visiting professor; Indiana University, visiting professor; University of Wisconsin, visiting professor. Writer. **Publications:** Mercantilism and Laisser Faire in American Political Discussion, 1787-1829, 1944; (ed. with E.T. Weiler) Economic Policy: Readings in Political Economy, 1953, 3rd ed., 1961; The Manchester School of Economics, 1960, rev. ed., 1993; Economic Liberalism, 1965; Pricing the Priceless: Art, Artists, and Economics, 1989. **Address:** Depatment of Economics, University of Illinois, 2103UH, 601 S Morgan, PO Box 144, Chicago, IL 60607, U.S.A.

GRAN, Peter. American (born United States), b. 1941. **Genres:** History, Adult Non-fiction, inspirational/Motivational Literature, Business/Trade/Industry. **Career:** Friends World College, core faculty, 1974-75; University of California, visiting assistant professor of history, 1975-77; University of Texas, visiting assistant professor of history, 1977-79; Temple University, associate professor, 1979-97, professor of history, 1997-. Writer. **Publications:** Study in the Indigenous Origins and Early Development of Modern Culture in Egypt: The Life and Writings of Shaykh Hassan Al-c Attar, 1766-1835, 1974; Islamic Roots of Capitalism: Egypt, 1760-1840, 1979, rev. ed. as Al-Judhural-Islamiyah li-l-ra'smaliya: Misr 1760-1840, 1992; Beyond Eurocentrism: A New View of Modern World History, 1996; (ed. with A. Dirlik and V. Bahl) History After the Three Worlds: Post-Eurocentric Historiographies, 2000; Holy Land in Transit: Colonialism and the Quest for Canaan, 2006; Rise of the Rich: A New View of Modern World History, 2009; (ed.) The Large Landowning Class and the Peasantry in Egypt, 1837-1958, 2009. Contributor to books and periodicals. **Address:** Department of History, Temple University, 844 Gladfelter Hall, 9th Fl., 1115 W Berks St., Philadelphia, PA 19122, U.S.A. **Online address:** pgran@temple.edu

GRAN, Sara. American (born United States), b. 1971. **Genres:** Novels, Criminology/True Crime, Young Adult Fiction. **Career:** Shakespeare and Co., staff; Writer. **Publications:** NOVELS: Saturn's Return to New York, 2001; Come Closer, 2003; Dope, 2006; Claire DeWitt and the City of the Dead, 2011. **Address:** c/o Sita White, Artists Agency, 230 W 55th St., Ste. 29D, New York, NY 10019, U.S.A. **Online address:** sara@saragran.com

GRANDIN, Temple. American (born United States), b. 1947. **Genres:** Animals/Pets, Autobiography/Memoirs. **Career:** Arizona Farmer Ranchman, livestock editor, 1973-78; Corral Industries, equipment designer, 1974-75; Grandin Livestock Handling Systems Inc., independent consultant, 1975-; Colorado State University, lecturer, assistant professor of animal science, 1990-, professor of animal science. Writer. **Publications:** (With M.M. Scariano) Emergence, Labeled Autistic, 1986, rev. ed., 1996; Recommended Animal Handling Guidelines for Meat Packers, 1991; Thinking in Pictures: And Other Reports from my Life with Autism, 1995, rev. ed., 2006; Animal Welfare and Meat Science, 1998; (ed.) Genetics and the Behavior of Domestic Animals, 1998; (ed.) Livestock Handling and Transport, 2000; (with K. Duffy) Developing Talents: Careers for Individuals with Asperger Syndrome and High-Functioning Autaism, 2004; (with S. Barron) Unwritten Rules of Social Relationships, 2005; (with C. Johnson) Animals in Translation: Using the Mysteries of Autism to Decode Animal Behavior, 2005, rev. ed., 2006; Asperger's and Girls: World-Renowned Experts Join Those with Asperger's Syndrome to Resolve Issues that Girls and Women Face Every Day!, 2006; Animal Welfare and Meat Production, 2007; (ed.) Livestock Handling and Transport, 2007; (with M. Deesing) Humane Livestock Handling, 2008; The Way I See It: A Personal Look at Autism and Asperger's, 2008; (with C. Johnson) Animals Make Us Human: Creating the Best Life for Animals, 2009; (ed.) Improving Animal Welfare: A Practical Approach, 2010; Different...Not Less, forthcoming. **Address:** Department of Animal Science, Colorado State University, Animal Sciences Bldg., Fort Collins, CO 80523-1171, U.S.A. **Online address:** cmiller@ceres.agsci.colostate.edu

GRANDITS, John. American (born United States), b. 1949?. **Genres:** Illustrations, Poetry. **Career:** Writer. **Publications:** Pictures Tell Stories, 1995; SELF-ILLUSTRATED: Technically, It's Not My Fault: Concrete Poems, 2004; Blue Lipstick: Concrete Poems, 2007; The Travel Game, 2008. **Address:** c/o Andrea Cascardi, Transatlantic Literary Agency, 72 Glengowan Rd., Toronto, ON M4N 1G4, Canada.

GRANELLI, Roger. Welsh (born Wales), b. 1950. **Genres:** Novels, Novellas/Short Stories. **Career:** Professional musician, 1971-79; music teacher and performing musician 1984-; Writer 1992-. **Publications:** NOVELS: Crystal Spirit, 1992; Out of Nowhere, 1995; Dark Edge, 1997; Status Zero, 1999; Resolution, 2003; Losing it, 2008; Risk, 2008; Dead Pretty, 2009. Contributor of short stories to periodicals. **Address:** 60 Hopkinstown Rd., Pontypridd, MG CF37 2PS, Wales. **Online address:** rogergranelli@googlemail.com

GRANGE, William Marshall. American (born United States), b. 1947. **Genres:** Theatre, Popular Culture, Film, History, Plays/Screenplays. **Career:** Florida Southern College, assistant professor, 1981-87; Marquette University, associate professor, 1987-96; University of Nebraska, faculty, 1996-, Hixson-Lied professor, 2008-; University of Vienna, Fulbright distinguished chair in humanities and cultural studies, 2007. Writer. **Publications:** Partnership In The German Theatre: Zuckmayer and Hilpert, 1925-1961, 1991; Comedy in the Weimar Republic, 1996; Hitler Laughing: Comedy in the Third Reich, 2005; Historical Dictionary of German Theater, 2006; Cultural Chronicle of the Weimar Republic, 2008; Historical Dictionary of Postwar German Literature, 2009; Historical Dictionary of German Literature to 1945, 2011. Contributor to journals, books, magazines and periodicals. **Address:** Johnny Carson School of Theatre and Film, University of Nebraska, 207 Temple, Lincoln, NE 68588-0201, U.S.A. **Online address:** wgrange1@unl.edu

GRANGER, Michele. American (born United States), b. 1949. **Genres:** Children's Fiction, Business/Trade/Industry, Young Adult Fiction. **Career:** Williamsburg Public Schools, first grade teacher 1971-73; DeKalb County Schools, teacher, 1974-77, Department of Early Childhood/Special Education, chairperson, 1976-78; Fairfax County Adult Education, parent educator, 1980-83; Montclair State College, educational supervisor, 1984, adjunct faculty, 1985; Children's Hospital, teacher in early intervention and AIDS intervention program, 1985-98; University Hospital, teacher in early intervention and AIDS intervention program, 1985-98; Renaissance Middle School, The Writers' Room, co-director, 1999-; Missouri State University, professor. Consultant and writer. **Publications:** The Summer House Cat, 1989; Eliza the Hypnotizer: And Other Eliza and Francie Stories, 1993; Fifth Grade Fever, 1995; A Guide to Analyzing Your Fashion Industry Internship, 1996; Case Studies in Merchandising Apparel and Soft Goods, 1996; (with T. Sterling) Fashion Entrepreneurship: Retail Business Planning, 2003; The Fashion Intern, 2004; Fashion: The Industry and its Careers, 2007. **Address:** Deaprtment of Fashion and Interior Design, Missouri State University, Rm. 327, Park Central Office Bldg., 901 S National Ave., Springfield, MO 65897, U.S.A. **Online address:** michelegranger@missouristate.edu

GRANGER, (Patricia) Ann. (Ann Hulme). British (born England), b. 1939. **Genres:** Mystery/Crime/Suspense, Novels, Young Adult Fiction. **Career:** Educator and writer. **Publications:** AS ANN HULME: Interlaken Intrigue, 1986; No Place for a Lady, 1988; An Innocent Affair, 2003. MITCHELL AND MARKBY SERIES MYSTERY NOVELS: Say It with Poison, 1991; A Season for Murder, 1991; Cold in the Earth, 1992; Murder among Us, 1992; Where Old Bones Lie, 1993; A Fine Place for Death, 1994; Flowers for His Funeral, 1994; Candle for a Corpse, 1995; A Touch of Mortality, 1996; A Word after Dying, 1996; Call the Dead Again, 1998; Beneath These Stones, 1999; Shades of Murder, 2000; A Restless Evil, 2002; That Way Murder Lies: A Mitchell and Markby Mystery, 2004; Mud, Muck and Dead Things, 2009; Rack, Ruin and Murder, 2011. HISTORICAL ROMANCE NOVELS AS ANN HULME: A Poor Relation, 1979; Summer Heiress, 1981; The Gamester, 1982; The Emperor's Dragoon, 1983; Daughter of Spain, 1984; A Woman of the Regiment, 1985; The Hungarian Adventures, 1985; The Garden of the Azure Dragon, 1986; The Unexpected American, 1988; The Flying Man, 1988; A Scandalous Bargain, 1988; Captain Harland's Marriage, 1989; False Fortune, 1989; Whisper in the Wind, 1989. FRAN VARADY SERIES: Asking for Trouble, 1997; Keeping Bad Company, 1997; Running Scared, 1998; Risking It All, 2001; Watching Out, 2003; Mixing with Murder, 2005; Rattling the Bones, 2007. LIZZIE MARTIN: A Rare Interest in Corpses, 2006; A Mortal Curiosity, 2008; A Better Quality of Murder, 2010. Contributor of serials to magazines and periodicals. **Address:** c/o Al Zuckerman, Writers House, 21 W 26th St., New York, NY 10010, U.S.A.

GRANN, David. American (born United States), b. 1967. **Genres:** History. **Career:** New Republic, senior editor; The Hill, executive editor, 1995-96; New Yorker, staff writer, 2003-. **Publications:** The Lost City of Z: A Tale of Deadly Obsession in the Amazon, 2009. Works appear in anthologies. Contributor to periodicals. **Address:** New Yorker, 4 Times Sq., New York, NY 10036, U.S.A. **Online address:** davidgrann@gmail.com

GRANT, Andrew. British (born England), b. 1968. **Genres:** Young Adult Fiction, Mystery/Crime/Suspense. **Career:** Writer. **Publications:** Even, 2009; Die Twice, 2010. **Address:** Minotaur Books, 175 5th Ave., New York, NY 10010, U.S.A. **Online address:** andrew@andrewgrantbooks.com

GRANT, Anne Underwood. American (born United States), b. 1946. **Genres:** Mystery/Crime/Suspense, Novels, Young Adult Fiction, Literary Criticism And History. **Career:** North Carolina Arts Council, community associate, 1970; Good Will Publishers, communications director, 1980; Underwood Grant Advertising, president, 1980-90; Tarradiddle Players, president, 1990. Writer. **Publications:** MYSTERY NOVELS: Multiple Listing, 1998; Smoke Screen, 1998; Cuttings, 1999; (ed. with R.A. Ollar and N.D. Connell) Molecular Mycobacteriology: Techniques and Clinical Applications, 1999; Voices in the Sand, 2000. **Address:** 587 George Chastain Dr., Horse Shoe, NC 28742, U.S.A. **Online address:** annieug@sprynet.com

GRANT, Anthony. *See* **CAMPBELL, Judith.**

GRANT, Barry Keith. American/Canadian (born Canada), b. 1947. **Genres:** Film, Cultural/Ethnic Topics, Documentaries/Reportage. **Career:** Cheetah Discotheque, co-director of mixed media light show, 1966-67; Media Study, assistant director, 1974-75; Brock University, faculty, 1975-91, professor of film studies, 1991-, Department of Fine Arts, chair, 1982-85, Department of Film Studies, Drama and Visual Arts, chair, 1989-90, Film Studies Program, director, 1990-, Popular Music Archive, founder and director, 1986-; Medaille College, lecturer, 1975-; Purdue University, lecturer, 1980-; West Virginia Wesleyan College, lecturer, 1980; State University of New York, Center for Studies in Film, Mythology and Folklore, faculty, 1987-; University of Otago, Lincoln College, lecturer, 1989-; University of Waikato, Massey University, lecturer, 1989-; University of Auckland, lecturer, 1989; York University, external faculty, 1990. Writer. **Publications:** (Ed.) Zoetrope, 1969; (ed.) Film Genre: Theory and Criticism, 1977; Saturday Night at the Movies, 1980; (ed.) Film Study in the Undergraduate Curriculum, 1983; (ed. with C. Sharrett) Planks of Reason: Essays on the Horror Film, 1984, rev. ed., 2004; (ed.) Film Genre Reader, 1986; Voyages of Discovery: The Cinema of Frederick Wiseman, 1992; (ed.) Film Genre Reader II, 1995; (ed.) The Dread of Difference: Gender and the Horror Film, 1996; (ed. with J. Sloniowski) Documenting the Documentary: Close Readings of Documentary Film and Video, 1998; (with S. Blandford and J. Hillier) The Film Studies Dictionary, 2001; (ed.) Fritz Lang: Interviews, 2003; (ed.) John Ford's Stagecoach, 2003; (ed.) Film Genre Reader III, 2003; (foreword) Five Films by Frederick Wiseman, 2006; Schirmer Encyclopedia of Film, 2007; Film Genre: From Iconography to Ideology, 2007; (ed.) Auteurs and Authorship: A Film Reader, 2008; (ed.) American Cinema of the1960s: Themes and Variations, 2008. (ed.) Britton on Film: The Complete Film Criticism of Andrew Britton, 2009; (with J. Hillier) 100 Documentary Films, 2009; Shadows of Doubt: Negotiations of Masculinity in American Genre Films, 2010; Invasion of the Body Snatchers, 2010; American Film Musicals, 2012; The Technique of Terror: The Films of John Carpenter, forthcoming; Musical Moments: Film and the Performance of Song and Dance, forthcoming. Contributor to periodicals. Works appear in anthologies. **Address:** Department of Communications, Brock University, 341 Scotia Bank Hall, 500 Glenridge Ave., St. Catharines, ON L2S 3A1, Canada. **Online address:** bgrant@brocku.ca

GRANT, Bruce (Alexander). Australian (born Australia), b. 1925. **Genres:** Novels, International Relations/Current Affairs, Politics/Government, History, Essays. **Career:** The Age Newspaper, film, theatre critic, 1949-53, foreign correspondent in Europe and Middle East, 1954-57, Singapore, 1959-63, Washington correspondent, 1964-65, columnist on public affairs, 1968-73; University of Melbourne, fellow in political science, 1965-68, George Scott visiting fellow, 1976; Monash University, councillor, 1970-73, writer-in-residence, 1980, Graduate School of Government, professor, 1994-97, Department of Management, adjunct professor, 1997-2003; high commissioner for Australia in India and Ambassador to Nepal, 1973-76; International Institute for Strategic Studies, associate, 1976-77; Deakin University, councillor, 1979; Government of Victoria, arts adviser, 1982-86; Spoleto Melbourne Festival of Three Worlds, president, 1985-87; Australia-Indonesia Institute, chairman, 1989-92. Writer. **Publications:** Indonesia, 1964, 3rd ed., 1996; Foreign Af-

fairs and the Australian Press, 1969; (with G.R. Laking and L.V. Castle) New Zealand and Australia; Foreign Policy in the 1970's, 1970; A Crisis of Loyalty: A Study of Australian Foreign Policy, 1972, rev. ed., 1973; (ed.) Arthur and Eric: An Anglo-Australian Story from the Journal of Arthur Hickman, 1977; The Security of South-East Asia, 1978; The Boat People: An Age Investigation with Bruce Grant, 1979; Cherry Bloom, 1980; Gods & Politicians, 1982; The Australian Dilemma: A New Kind of Western Society, 1983; What Kind of Country?: Australia and the Twenty-first Century, 1988; (with G. Evans) Australia's Foreign Relations: In the World of the 1990s, 1991, 2nd ed., 1995; The Budd Family, 1995; A Furious Hunger: America in the 21st Century, 1999; The Great Pretender at the Bar of Justice in Best Australian Essays, 2002; Fatal Attraction: Reflections on the Alliance with the United States, 2004; Bali: Spirit of Here and Now in Best Australian Essays, 2004. Contributor to periodicals. **Address:** The Drummond Agency, PO Box 572, Woodend, VI 3442, Australia. **Online address:** profbrucegrant@compuserve.com

GRANT, Colin. British/Jamaican (born Jamaica), b. 1961. **Genres:** Biography. **Career:** British Broadcasting Corp., script editor and producer of arts programs, 1989-, Science Unit, radio producer. Writer and producer. **Publications:** Negro with a Hat: The Rise and Fall of Marcus Garvey (biography), 2008. **Address:** Tibor Jones & Associates, Piano House, Ste. 12 B, 9 Brighton Terr., London, GL SW9 8DJ, England.

GRANT, Cynthia D. American (born United States), b. 1950. **Genres:** Young Adult Fiction, Education, Self Help, Horror, Children's Fiction, Humor/Satire. **Career:** Writer, 1974-. **Publications:** YOUNG ADULT FICTION: Joshua Fortune, 1980; Summer Home, 1981; Big Time, 1982; Hard Love, 1983; Kumquat May, I'll Always Love You, 1986; Phoenix Rising, or, How to Survive Your Life, 1989; Keep Laughing, 1991; Shadow Man, 1992; Uncle Vampire, 1993; Mary Wolf, 1995; The White Horse, 1998; The Cannibals: Starring Tiffany Spratt, 2002. **Address:** PO Box 95, Cloverdale, CA 95425, U.S.A.

GRANT, Daniel. American (born United States), b. 1954. **Genres:** Art/Art History, Education. **Career:** Art and Artists, editor, 1976-84; Newsday, art critic, 1980-84; Commercial Appeal, art critic, 1984-85; Boston Herald, art critic, 1986-; Berkshire Eagle, art critic, 1986-; WFCR-Radio, writer, 1988-94; Amherst Cultural Council, chair, 1992-94. **Publications:** The Business of Being an Artist, 1991, 4th ed., 2000; On Becoming an Artist, 1993; The Artist's Resource Handbook, 1994, rev. ed., 1996; The Writer's Resource Handbook, 1996; How to Start and Succeed as an Artist, 1997; The Fine Artist's Career Guide, 1998, 2nd ed. Fine Artist's Career Guide: Making Money in the Arts and Beyond, 2004; The Artist's Guide to Making It in New York, 2001; How to Grow as an Artist, 2002; Selling Art Without Galleries: Toward Making a Living from Your Art, 2004. Contributor to magazines and newspapers. **Address:** 19 Summer St., Amherst, MA 01002, U.S.A. **Online address:** danhg@aol.com

GRANT, Gail Milissa. Italian/American (born United States), b. 1949?. **Genres:** Civil Liberties/Human Rights, History. **Career:** Howard University, assistant professor of art and architectural history; U.S. Information Agency, foreign service officer; Spotlight-On (consulting firm), founder. Writer, diplomat and public speaker. **Publications:** At the Elbows of My Elders: One Family's Journey toward Civil Rights, 2008. **Address:** Rome, Italy. **Online address:** gail_milissa@hotmail.com

GRANT, Graeme. Also writes as Tom McGregor, Nick Leon. Scottish (born Scotland), b. 1961. **Genres:** Humor/Satire, Science Fiction/Fantasy, Novels, Mystery/Crime/Suspense, Young Adult Fiction. **Career:** Writer, 1993-; University of Westminster, fellow, 2008-10. **Publications:** AS TOM McGREGOR: Between the Lines: The Chill Factor, 1993; Peak Practice 1, 1993; Between the Lines: Close Protection, 1994; The Knock 1, 1995; Roughnecks: The Official Guide to the BBC Drama Series, 1995; Kavanagh QC1, 1995; Peak Practice 2, 1995; Kavanagh QC 2, 1996; The Knock 2, 1996; An Invitation to Romance, 1996; White Ghost, 1996; Death in the Wilderness, 1996; This Life: The Companion Guide, 1997; All the Queen's Horses, 1997; Wokenwell, 1997; Vaulting North, 1997; The Making of Hornblower: The Official Companion to the ITV Series, 1998; Behind the Scenes at Who Wants to be a Millionaire, 1999; Oliver Twist: The Official Companion to the ITV Drama Series, 1999; Saving Grace, 2000; The People Detective: Discovering Your Family Roots, 2001; The Making of Master and Commander: The Far

Side of the World, 2003. AS NICK LEON: The Christmas Pox: An Immoral Fable (satire), 1995; Shooting Fish: A Novel, 1997; Randall & Hopkirk (Deceased): Ghosts from the Past, 2000; Swimming with Narcissus, a satirical novel, forthcoming. Contributor to magazines and newspapers. **Address:** c/o Laura Morris, Abner Stein, 10 Roland Gardens, London, GL SW7 3PH, England. **Online address:** graemeg@zipworld.com.au

GRANT, Helen. Belgian/British (born England), b. 1964?. **Genres:** Novels. **Career:** Novelist. **Publications:** The Vanishing of Katharina Linden (novel), 2009; The Glass Demon, 2010. Contributor of articles to periodicals and newsletters. **Address:** Brussels, Belgium. **Online address:** helengrantsays@gmail.com

GRANT, James. American (born United States), b. 1946?. **Genres:** Novels, Business/Trade/Industry, Economics. **Career:** Barron Current Yield Column, writer and originator, 1975-83; Grant's Interest Rate Observer, founder and editor, 1983-. **Publications:** Bernard M. Baruch: Adventures of a Wall Street Legend, 1983; Money of the Mind: Borrowing and Lending in America from the Civil War to Michael Milken, 1992; Minding Mr. Market: Ten Years on Wall Street with Grants Interest Rate Observer, 1993; Minding Mister Market, 1994; The Trouble with Prosperity: The Loss of Fear the Rise of Speculation and the Risk to American Savings, 1996; John Adams: Party of One, 2005; (intro.) Security Analysis, 2008; Mr. Market Miscalculates: The Bubble Years and Beyond, 2008; Mr. Speaker: The Life and Times of Thomas B. Reed, the Man Who Broke the Filibuster, 2011. **Address:** Grants Interest Rate Observer, 2 Wall St., New York, NY 10005, U.S.A.

GRANT, James Russell. Scottish (born Scotland), b. 1924. **Genres:** Poetry, Literary Criticism And History, Medicine/Health, Psychiatry, Social Sciences, Translations, History, Essays, Essays. **Career:** The Maudsley Hospital, Institute of Psychiatry, registrar, 1954-55; Provincial Guidance Clinic, psychiatrist, 1955-57; medical practitioner, 1958-; King's Cross Hostel for the Homeless, medical officer. Writer. **Publications:** Hyphens, 1958; Poems, 1959; (trans.) Guillaume Apollinaire, Zone, 1962; The Excitement of Being Sam: Earth-Poetry in English, 1977; The Cracked Weather Set, 1980; Myths of My Age (poems), 1985; Hattonrig Road (poems), 1986; In the 4 Cats, 1997; Essays on Anxiety, 2001; Jigsaw and the Art of Poetry, 2001. Contributor to journals. **Address:** Provincial Guidance Clinic, Gatesden, Cromer St., W. C. 1, London, GL N2 9BP, England. **Online address:** rusty@dircon.co.uk

GRANT, Jeanne. See GREENE, Jennifer.

GRANT, Jill. British/Canadian (born Canada), b. 1951. **Genres:** Urban Studies, Regional/Urban Planning, Geography. **Career:** Nova Scotia College of Art and Design, assistant professor, 1979-88, associate professor, 1988-95, professor of environmental planning, 1995, department head, 1980-81, 1985-87, 1992-95, vice president, 1995-98; Dalhousie University, School of Planning, honorary research associate, 1991-, adjunct faculty, 1991-94, professor, 2001-, director, 2002-08; St. Mary's University, International Development Studies Program, adjunct faculty, 1991-94. Writer. **Publications:** The Drama of Democracy: Contention and Dispute in Community Planning, 1994; Towards Sustainable Cities: East Asian, North American and European Perspectives on Managing Urban Regions, 2004; Planning the Good Community: New Urbanism in Theory and Practice, 2006; (ed.) A Reader in Canadian Planning: Linking Theory and Practice, 2008. Contributor to books. **Address:** School of Planning, Dalhousie University, PO Box 1000, Halifax, NS B3J 2X4, Canada. **Online address:** jill.grant@dal.ca

GRANT, John. See BARNETT, John Le Page.

GRANT, Jonathan A. American (born United States), b. 1963. **Genres:** Economics. **Career:** Florida State University, professor, Bryan Hall Learning Community, director, 2004-08, associate chair for undergraduate studies, 2007-. Writer. **Publications:** Big Business in Russia: The Putilov Company in Late Imperial Russia, 1868-1917, 1999; (ed. with D.J. Stoker, Jr.) Girding for Battle: The Arms Trade in a Global Perspective, 1815-1940, 2003; Rulers, Guns, and Money: The Global Arms Trade in the Age of Imperialism, 2007. **Address:** Florida State University, 600 W College Ave., Tallahassee, FL 32306, U.S.A. **Online address:** jgrant@fsu.edu

GRANT, Katharine Houghton. See HOUGHTON, Katharine.

GRANT, Kathryn. See PTACEK, Kathryn.

GRANT, Matthew G. See MAY, Julian.

GRANT, Michael Johnston. American (born United States), b. 1961. **Genres:** Agriculture/Forestry. **Career:** Kentucky Department of Agriculture, Office of Strategic Planning & Administration, staff, manager, 2002. Writer, public speaker and consultant. **Publications:** Down and Out on the Family Farm: Rural Rehabilitation in the Great Plains, 1929-1945, 2002. **Address:** Office of Strategic Planning & Administration, Kentucky Department of Agriculture, 111 Corporate Dr., Frankfort, KY 40601, U.S.A. **Online address:** michael.grant@ky.gov

GRANT, Neil. Also writes as Gail Mountfield, David Mountfield, Gail Trenton, D. M. Field. British (born England), b. 1938. **Genres:** Novellas/Short Stories, Art/Art History, Children's Non-fiction, History, Travel/Exploration. **Career:** American People Encyclopedia, associate editor, 1962-67. **Publications:** Disraeli, 1969; Benjamin Disraeli: Prime Minister Extraordinary, 1969; Emperor Charles V, 1970; English Explorers of North America, 1970; Victoria: Queen and Empress, 1970; The Renaissance, 1971; Munich 1938, 1971; Kings and Queens of England, 1971; Cathedrals, 1972; Guilds, 1972; Easter Rising, 1972; World Leaders of Today, 1972; Howards of Norfolk, 1972; Barbarossa, 1972; History Alive: Lives, 3 vols., 1972; The Industrial Revolution, 1973; Partition of Palestine, 1947-1973; Basic Atlas, 1973; The New World Held Promise, 1974; David Livingstone, 1974; The Campbells of Argyll, 1975; Neil Grant's Book of Spies and Spying, 1975; The German-Soviet Pact, August 23, 1939, 1975; Buccaneers, 1976; Stagecoaches, 1977; Children's History of Britain, 1977; Smugglers, 1978; (with N. Viney) An Illustrated History of Ball Games, 1978; The Discoverers, 1979; Explorers, 1979; The Savage Trade, 1980; (with P. Womersley) Collecting Stamps, 1980; Conquerers, 1981; Discovering the World, 1981; Great Palaces, 1982; Eighteenth Century, 1983; Scottish Clans and Tartans, 1987; Life in the Rainforest, 1987; (with N. Middleton) Atlas of the World Today, 1987; 500 Questions and Answers about the Bible, 1988; People and Places: The United Kingdom, 1988; Ireland, 1989; Heroes of World War II, 1989; The World of Odysseus, 1990; How They Lived: The Egyptians, The Greeks, The Romans, 1990; Village London, Past and Present, 1990; (comp.) James Dean in his Own Words, 1991; (comp.) Marilyn: In her Own Words, 1991; Roman Conquests, 1991; (co-author) Royal Geographical Society History of World Exploration, 1991; Great Atlas of Discovery, 1992; Explorers and Discoverers, 1992; Chronicle of 20th Century Conflict, 1992; The Egyptians, 1993; Children's Concise History Encyclopedia, 1993; Ancient Greece, 1994; Record Breakers: People and Places, 1994; Kings and Queens, 1996; Eric the Red, 1997; The Vikings, 1998; Hamlyn History of Literature, 1998; Oxford Children's History of the World, 2000; History of Theatre, 2002; Everyday Life of the Celts, 2003; Everyday Life in Ancient Rome, 2003; The Atlas of the Renaissance World, 2003; Everyday Life in Medieval Europe, 2005; Everyday Life of the Vikings, 2005; Ancient Egypt and Greece, 2009; Renaissance Europe, 2009. AS D.M. FIELD: Greek and Roman Mythology, 1977; Great Masterpieces of World Art, 1978; The Nude in Art, 1981; Great Palaces, 1982; (contrib.) Oriental Rugs, 1983; The World's Greatest Architecture, 2001; Leonardo da Vinci, 2002; Rembrandt, 2003; Van Gogh, 2004. AS GAILTRENTON: Whispers at Twilight, 1982; The White Bear, 1983; Reflections in the Stream, 1983. AS DAVID MOUNTFIELD: A History of Polar Exploration, 1974; Antique Collectors Dictionary, 1974; A History of African Exploration, 1976; The Coaching Age, 1976; Brief Histories of Great Nations: England, 1978; Everyday Life in Elizabethan England, 1978; The Partisans, 1979; London, 1979; Britain, 1979; The Railway Barons, 1979; (with R. Markus) A Vulnerable Game, 1988; Tchaikovsky, 1990; Castles and Castle Towns of Great Britain, 1993; Rossini, 1995; (co-author) Philip's Atlas of Exploration, 1996. **Address:** c/o Author Mail, McGraw-Hill Children, 8787 Orion Pl., 4th Fl., Columbus, OH 43240-4027, U.S.A. **Online address:** neildgrant@aol.com

GRANT, Patrick. Canadian/Irish (born Ireland), b. 1941. **Genres:** Literary Criticism And History, Theology/Religion, Social Sciences. **Career:** University of Illinois, visiting assistant professor of English, 1966-68; University of Victoria, assistant professor, 1968-77, associate professor, 1977-79, professor of English, 1979-, now professor emeritus. Writer. **Publications:** The Transformation of Sin: Studies in Donne, Herbert, Vaughan and Traherne, 1974; Images and Ideas in Literature of the English Renaissance, 1979; Six Modern Authors and Problems of Belief, 1979; The Literature of Mysticism in Western Tradition, 1983; Literature and the Discovery of Method in the English Renaissance, 1985; (ed.) A Dazzling Darkness: An Anthology of Western Mysticism, 1985; Reading the New Testament, 1989; Literature and Personal Values, 1992; Spiritual Discourse and the Meaning of Persons, 1994; Personalism and the Politics of Culture: Readings in Literature and Religion from the New Testament to the Poetry of Northern Ireland, 1996; Breaking Enmities: Religion, Literature and Culture in Northern Ireland, 1967-97, 1999; Literature, Rhetoric, and Violence in Northern Ireland, 1968-98: Hardened to Death, 2001; Buddhism and Ethnic Conflict in Sri Lanka, 2009. **Address:** Department of English, University of Victoria, Rm. C343, Clearihue Bldg., 3800 Finnerty Rd., PO Box 3070, Sta. CSC, Victoria, BC V8W 3P4, Canada.

GRANT, Pete. Also writes as Jon Dijon, Paul Kuehn. American (born United States) **Genres:** Law, Novels, Medicine/Health, Young Adult Fiction, Mystery/Crime/Suspense, Humanities. **Career:** Night Torpedo Squadron, pilot, 1941-45. Surgeon and author. **Publications:** Night Flying Avenger, 1990; The Surgical Arena, 1993; Destination 2020 White House, 1999; The Medical Supreme Court, 2001. AS PAUL KUEHN: Breast Care Options: A Cancer Specialist Discusses Breast Care Options, Risk Factors, and How to Cope with Breast Cancer, 1986; Breast Care Options for the 1990s, 1991; (co-author) Distant Thunder: Recollections of Lodi Area Veterans, 2004. AS JON DIJON: Who is Robin?: A Novel, 1993. **Address:** c/o Author Mail, Newmark Publishing, 729 Ellington Rd., PO Box 603, South Windsor, CT 06074, U.S.A.

GRANT, Richard. American (born United States), b. 1952?. **Genres:** Novels, Science Fiction/Fantasy, Young Adult Fiction. **Career:** Down East Magazine, contributing editor. **Publications:** Saraband of Lost Time, 1985; Rumors of Spring, 1987; Views from the Oldest House, 1989; Through the Heart, 1991; Tex and Molly in the Afterlife, 1996; In the Land of Winter, 1997; Kaspian Lost, 1999; Another Green World, 2006; (contrib.) Porch, 2011. Contributor to periodicals. **Address:** HarperCollins Publishers, 10 E 53rd St., 7th Fl., New York, NY 10022, U.S.A.

GRANT, Stephanie. American (born United States), b. 1962. **Genres:** Novels. **Career:** Ohio State University, faculty; Mount Holyoke College, writer-in-residence; Duke University, Franklin Humanities Institute, visiting writer; Lesbian and Gay Community Services Center, curator and director. **Publications:** The Passion of Alice (novel), 1995; Map of Ireland, 2008. Contributor to periodicals. **Address:** c/o Sloan Harris, International Creative Management, 40 W 57th St., New York, NY 10019, U.S.A. **Online address:** sjg13@duke.edu

GRANT, Susan. American (born United States) **Genres:** Air/Space Topics, Romance/Historical, Paranormal, Science Fiction/Fantasy, Novels, Novellas/Short Stories. **Career:** United Airlines, pilot; writer, 1997-. **Publications:** Once a Pirate, 2000; The Star King, 2000; The Star Prince, 2001; Contact, 2002; The Star Princess, 2003; The Legend of Banzai Maguire, 2004; The Scarlet Empress, 2004; Your Planet or Mine?, 2006; My Favorite Earthling, 2007; How to Lose an Extraterrestrial in 10 Days, 2007; Moonstruck, 2008; (with L. Mckenna) Mission, Christmas, 2008; The Warlord's Daughter, 2009; Sureblood: A Tale of the Borderlands, 2010; The Last Warrior, 2011. **Address:** c/o Ethan Ellenberg, The Ethan Ellenberg Literary Agency, 548 Broadway, Ste. 5E, New York, NY 10012, U.S.A. **Online address:** susan@susangrant.com

GRANT, Susan-Mary C. British/Scottish (born Scotland), b. 1962. **Genres:** History, Military/Defense/Arms Control. **Career:** University of Pittsburgh, research assistant, 1987-88; The British-American, editor, 1988-92; Institute of United State Studies RAE and TQA reviews, advisor, 1998-2002; Association of British American Nineteenth Century Historians, secretary, 1992-2001, editor, 2005-; University of Newcastle, lecturer, 1992-, history faculty and professor of American history, reader in American history, 2002-; Brunel University, academic advisor. Writer. **Publications:** North over South: Northern Nationalism and American Identity in the Antebellum Era, 2000; (ed. with B.H. Reid) The American Civil War: Explorations and Reconsiderations, 2000; (ed. with P.J. Parish) Legacy of Disunion: The Enduring Significance of the American Civil War, 2003; (ed. with A.I.P. Smith) North and the Nation in the Era of the Civil War, 2003; War for a Nation: The American Civil War, 2006; (ed. with B.H. Reid) Themes of the American Civil War, 2010. **Address:** School of Historical Studies, University of Newcastle, Newcastle, NE1 7RU, England. **Online address:** susan.grant@ncl.ac.uk

GRANT, Vanessa. Canadian/British (born England) **Genres:** Romance/Historical, Mystery/Crime/Suspense, Young Adult Non-fiction, Novels, Young Adult Fiction. **Career:** Family Life, counselor. Writer and educator. **Publications:** Pacific Disturbance, 1985; Shadows, 1986; Stray Lady, 1987; Jenny's Turn, 1987; The Chauvinist, 1987; Stranded Heart, 1988; Storm, 1988;

Takeover Man, 1988; Wild Passage, 1989; Taking Chances, 1989; Awakening Dreams, 1989; The Touch of Love, 1990; One Secret Too Many, 1990; So Much for Dreams, 1990; With Strings Attached, 1991; Angela's Affair, 1991; When Love Returns, 1991; Hidden Memories, 1992; Nothing Less than Love, 1992; Catalina's Lover, 1992; Dace of Seduction, 1993; Yesterday's Vows, 1994; Moon Lady's Lover, 1994; Writing Romance, 1997, 3rd ed., 2007; After All This Time, 1998; Strangers by Day, 1998; If You Loved Me, 1999; The Colors of Love, 2000; Think about Love, 2001; Seeing Stars, 2001; Wind Shift, 2003. **Address:** Writers Union of Canada, 90 Richmond St. E, Ste. 200, Toronto, ON M5C 1P1, Canada. **Online address:** vanessa@vanessagrant.ca

GRANT-ADAMSON, Lesley (Heycock). (Isobel Brown). British (born England), b. 1942. **Genres:** Mystery/Crime/Suspense, Education, Travel/Exploration, Young Adult Fiction. **Career:** Leonard Hill Publishing, editorial assistant, 1960, sub-editor, 1960-63; Thomson Publications, sub-editor, 1960-63; Palmers Green and Southgate Gazette, reporter, 1963-66; The Citizen, reporter, 1966-68; Rugby Advertiser, reporter, 1969-71; Herts Advertiser, news editor, 1971-73; The Guardian, feature writer, 1973-80; freelance writer, 1980-. **Publications:** Patterns in the Dust in US as Death on Widows Walk, 1985; The Face of Death, 1986; Guilty Knowledge, 1986; Wild Justice, 1987; Threatening Eye, 1988; Curse the Darkness, 1990; Flynnin in US as Too Many Questions, 1991; A Life of Adventure, 1992; The Dangerous Edge, 1993; Dangerous Games, 1995; (with A. Grant-Adamson) A Season in Spain, 1995; Wish You Were Here, 1996; Evil Acts, 1996; Writing Crime and Suspense Fiction, 1996, rev. ed., 2003; The Girl in the Case, 1997; Lipstick and Lies, 1998; Undertow, 1999; Music to Be Murdered By, 2000; (as Isobel Brown) Domestic Crime, 2001; Teach Yourself Writing Crime Fiction, 2003; How to Write Practically Anything 2004. **Address:** 22 High St., Debenham, SU IP14 6QJ, England. **Online address:** lesley@crimefiction.co.uk

GRASS, Günter (Wilhelm). German/Polish (born Poland), b. 1927. **Genres:** Novels, Plays/Screenplays, Art/Art History, Literary Criticism And History, Essays. **Career:** Columbia University, writer-in-residence, 1966; Harvard University, lecturer; Yale University, lecturer; Smith College, lecturer; Kenyon College, lecturer; YWCA. lecturer; Poetry Center of YM, lecturer. **Publications:** Die Vorzuege der Windhuehner, 1956, 3rd ed., 1967; O Susanna: Ein Jazzbilderbuch: Blues, Balladen, Spirituals, Jazz, 1959; Die Blechtrommel (novel), 1959; Gleisdreieck, 1960; Katz und Maus (novella), 1961; Hundejahre (novel), 1963; Rede ueber das Selbstverstaendliche (speech), 1965; Dich singe ich, Demokratie, 1965; Fuenf Wahlreden (speeches), 1965; Selected Poems (in German and English), 1966; Ausgefragt, 1967; Der Fall Axel C. Springer am Beispiel Arnold Zweig: Eine Rede, ihr Anlass, und die Folgen, 1967; Ueber das Selbstverstaendliche: Reden, Aufsaetze, offene Briefe, Kommentare, 1968, rev. ed as Ueber das Selbstverstaendliche: Politische Schriften, 1969; Briefe ueber die Grenze: Versuch eines Ost-West-Dialogs by Gunter Grass and Pavel Kohout (letters), 1968; Ueber meinen Lehrer Doeblin und andere Vortraege, 1968; Gunter Grass: Ausgewaehlte Texte, Abbildungen, Faksimiles, Bio-Bibliographie, 1968, also as Portraet und Poesie, 1968; Kunst oder Pornographie?, 1969; Oertlich betaeubt (novel), 1969; Die Schweinekopfsuelze, 1969; Originalgraphik (poem with illustrations), 1970; Gesammelte Gedichte (poems), 1971; Dokumente zur politischen Wirkung, 1971; Aus dem Tagebuch einer Schnecke, 1972; Mariazuehren Hommageamarie Inmarypraise, 1973; Liebe geprueft (poems), 1974; Der Buerger und seine Stimme; Gunter Grass Materialienbuch, 1976; Der Butt, 1977; Denkzettel, 1978; Das Treffen in Telgte, 1978; Werkverzeichnis der Radierungen (catalogue), 1979; (with V. Schlondorff) Die Blechtrommel als Film, 1979; Aufsaetze zur Literatur, 1957-1979, 1980; Danziger Trilogie, 1980; Kopfgeburten; oder Die Deutschen sterben aus, 1980; Zeichnen and Schreiben: Das bildnerische Werk des Schriftstellers Gunter Grass, 1982; Kinderlied (poems and etchings), 1982; Zeichnungen und Texte, 1954-1977, 1982; Ach, Butt!: Dein Maerchen geht boese aus, 1983; Radierungen und Texte, 1972-1982, 1984; Widerstand lernen: Politische Gegenreden, 1980-1983, 1984; Geschenkt Freiheit, 1985; Die Raettin, 1986; Werkausgabe, 10 vols., 1987; Die Gedichte 1955-1986, 1988; Zunge Zeigen, 1988; Deutscher Lastenausgleich: Wider das dumpfe Einheitsgebot; Reden und Gesprache, Texte zur Zeit, 1990; Ein Schnappchen namens DDR: Letzte Reden vorm Glockengelaut, 1990; Skizzenbuch, 1990; Schreiben nach Auschwitz, 1990; Two States-One Nation?, 1990; Ukenrufe: Eine Erzahlung, 1992; Unkenrufe, 1992; (with R. Hildebrandt) Schaden begrenzen, oder auf die Füsse treten: Ein Gespräch, 1993; Die Deutschen und Ihre Dichter, 1995; Der Schriftsteller als Zeitgenosse, 1996; Aesthetik des Engagements, 1996; Novemberland: 13 Sonette, 1996; Fundsachen für Nichtleser, 1997; Ohne die Feder zu wechseln: Zeichnungen, Druckgraphiken, Aquarelle, Skulpturen, 1997; Aus einem fotografischen und politischen Tabebuch: Berlin jenseits der Mauer, 1997; Rotgrüne Reder, 1998; Vom Abentauer der Aufklaerung, 1999; Für-und Widerworte, 1999; Auf einem anderen Blatt: Zeichnungen, 1999; Mein Jahrhundert, 1999; Wort und Bild: Tübinger Poetik Vorlesung & Materialien, 1999; Fortsetzung folgt-: Literature und Geschichte, 1999; (with M. Martens) Ich werde die Wunde offen halten: Ein GesprSch zur Person und über die Ziet, 1999; Weites Feld, 2000; (ed.) Gemischte Klasse, 2000; Ohne Stimme: Reder zugunsten des Volkes der Roma und Sinti, 2000; Günter Grass: Mit Wasserfarben: Aquarelle, 2001; Fünf Jahrzehnte: ein Werkstattbericht, 2001; (co-author) Die Zukunft der Erinnerung, 2001; (with D.Dahn and J. Strasser) In einem reichen Land: Zeugnisse alltSglichen Leidens an der Gessellschaft, 2002; Im Krebsgang, 2002; Crabwalk, 2002; (contrib. with L. Koerner and U. Kuhlemann) Albrecht Duürer and his Legacy: The Graphic Work of a Renaissance Artist, 2002; (contrib.) Günter Grass: Gebrannte Erde, 2002; Letzte Tänze, 2003; (with H. Wolff) Briefe 1959-1994, 2003; Diesseits und Jenseits Von Arkadien: Goethe und Grass Als Landschaftszeichner, 2004; (contrib.)The Günter Grass Reader, 2004; Der Schatten: Hans Christian Andersens Märchen, 2004; (with S. Dasgupta) Seeking Another World: Subhoranjan Dasgupta on Günter Grass & Bush's Iraq War, 2005; Beim Häuten Der Zwiebel, 2006; (with M. Döpfner) Die Springer-Kontroverse: Ein Streitgespraech über Deutschland, 2006; Dummer August, 2007; (with U. Johnson and A. Grass) Briefwechsel, 2007; Steine wälzen: Essays und Reden 1997-2007, 2007; (contrib.) Schlagt der äbtissin ein Schnippchen, wählt SPD, 2007; (contrib.) Günter Grass: Catalogue Raisonne, 2007; Peeling the Onion, 2007; Box: Dunkelkammergeschichten, 2008; (contrib.) Günter Grass-Repräsentant deutscher Literatur, deutscher Kultur, Deutschlands?, 2008; Tin Drum, 2009; Unterwegs von Deutschland nach Deutschland: Tagebuch 1990, 2009; Letze Tanze, 2009; Box: Tales from the Darkroom, 2010; Grimms Wörter, 2010. **Address:** Niedstrasse 13, Berlin-Grunewald, 41, Germany.

GRASSI, Maggi Lidchi. (Maggi Lidchi). French (born France), b. 1930. **Genres:** Novels, Novellas/Short Stories, Mythology/Folklore, History. **Career:** Sri Aurobindo Ashram, head. Teacher and editor. **Publications:** NOVELS: Man of Earth, 1968; The Battle of Kurukshetra, 1985; Legs of the Tortoise, 1989; Great Sir & the Heaven Lady: A True Story of the Experiences of an American Infantry Man Spiritually Guided through World War II (nonfiction), 1993; The Light That Shone into the Dark Abyss (paranormal), 1994; The Great Golden Sacrifice of the Mahabharata, 2001. STORIES: Jitendra the Protector, 1986. NOVELS AS MAGGI LIDCHI: Earthman, 1967; The First Wife, 1981. **Address:** Sri Aurobindo Ashram, 3 Rangapillai St., Pondicherry, PN 605 001, India. **Online address:** suramama@satya.net.in

GRASSIAN, Daniel. American (born United States), b. 1974. **Genres:** Social Commentary, Language/Linguistics, History, Social Sciences. **Career:** Manhattan Community College, faculty; The University of North Carolina, faculty; The University of Kansas, faculty; Temple University, faculty; Oklahoma State University, visiting assistant professor, 2002-03; Temple University, visiting assistant professor, 2003-04; Shippensburg University, visiting assistant professor, 2004-05; Nevada State College, assistant professor of English, 2005-, associate professor of English, department chair of humanities. Writer. **Publications:** Hybrid Fictions: American Literature and Generation X, 2003; Understanding Sherman Alexie, 2005; Writing the Future of Black America: Literature of the Hip-Hop Generation, 2009. Contributor of articles to periodicals. **Address:** Department of Humanities, Nevada State College, 1125 Nevada State Dr., Henderson, NV 89002, U.S.A. **Online address:** daniel.grassian@nsc.nevada.edu

GRATUS, Jack. British/South African (born South Africa), b. 1935?. **Genres:** Writing/Journalism, Plays/Screenplays, Communications/Media, Novels, Novellas/Short Stories, Theology/Religion, Business/Trade/Industry. **Career:** Pritchard Englefield & Co., legal executive, 1960-62; Oxford College, deputy principal and teacher of English and commercial law, 1963-66; freelance writer, 1967-; Glamorgan Summer School, organizing tutor of creative writing course, 1968-77; Regent Institute, senior tutor, 1973-76; City Literary Institute, tutor in charge of nonfiction writing, 1974-. **Publications:** (With E. Gratus) Cooking in Season, 1967; A Man in His Position, 1968; The Victims, 1969; Mister Landlord Appel, 1971; (with T. Preston) Night Hair Child, 1971; The Great White Lie: Slavery, Emancipation and Changing Racial Attitudes, 1973; The False Messiahs: Prophets of the Millenium, 1975, 2nd ed., 1976; The Jo'burgers, 1979; The Redneck Rebel, 1980; Successful Interviewing: How to Find and Keep the Best People, 1988; Give and Take, 1990; Sharpen Up Your Interviewing, 1991; Facing Your Next Interview With Confidence, 1992. **Address:** c/o Murray Pollinger, 4 Garrick St., London, GL WC26 9BH, England.

GRATZ, Alan. American (born United States), b. 1972. **Genres:** Novels. **Career:** Czech university, lecturer. Writer. **Publications:** YOUNG ADULTS NOVELS: Samurai Shortstop, 2006; Something Rotten: A Horatio Wilkes Mystery, 2007; Something Wicked: A Horatio Wilkes Mystery, 2008; The Brooklyn Nine: A Novel in Nine Innings, 2009. **Address:** Penland, NC 28765, U.S.A. **Online address:** bigcheese@alangratz.com

GRAU, Shirley Ann. American (born United States), b. 1929. **Genres:** Novels, Novellas/Short Stories, Young Adult Non-fiction, Children's Non-fiction, Young Adult Fiction, Humor/Satire, Mystery/Crime/Suspense. **Career:** University of New Orleans, creative writing teacher, 1966-67. Novelist. **Publications:** SHORT STORY COLLECTIONS: Fever Flower, 1954; The Black Prince and Other Stories, 1955, rev. ed. as 3 by 3: Masterworks of the Southern Gothic, 1985; The Wind Shifting West, 1973; Nine Women, 1985. NOVELS: The Hard Blue Sky, 1958; New Orleans Society, 1958; The House on Coliseum Street, 1961; The Keepers of the House, 1964; The Southern Mind: Black/White, 1964; The Condor Passes, 1971; Evidence of Love, 1977; Roadwalkers, 1994; Selected Stories, 2003. OTHERS: (foreword) Old Creole Days, 1961; (intro.) Cross Creek, 1966; Writers and Writing, 1988. Contributor of articles to journals and magazines. **Address:** JCA Literary Agency, 27 W 20 St., Ste. 1103, New York, NY 10011-3723, U.S.A. **Online address:** shirleygrau@bellsouth.net

GRAVELLE, Jane G(ibson). American (born United States), b. 1947. **Genres:** Economics, E-books, Business/Trade/Industry, Law. **Career:** Library of Congress, Congressional Research Service, research assistant, 1969-72, economist, analyst and senior specialist in economic policy, 1972-; U.S. Department of Labor, visiting economist, 1977; Boston University, visiting professor, 1988; U.S. Treasury Department, visiting economist, 1989-90. Writer. **Publications:** An Analysis of the Federal Tax Treatment of Oil and Gas and Some Policy Alternatives, 1974; The Economic Effects of Taxing Capital Income, 1994; (ed. with J.J. Cordes and R.D. Ebel) The Encyclopedia of Taxation and Tax Policy, 1999, 2nd ed., 2005; Enron Debacle: Lessons for Tax Policy, 2003; The Marriage Tax Penalty, 2003. Contributor to books and journals. **Address:** Congressional Research Service, Library of Congress, 101 Independence Ave. SE, Washington, DC 20540-7500, U.S.A. **Online address:** jgravelle@crs.loc.gov

GRAVER, Elizabeth. American (born United States), b. 1964. **Genres:** Novels, Novellas/Short Stories, Essays. **Career:** Freelance journalist, 1984-87; Washington University, instructor in creative writing, 1989; Cornell University, instructor in creative writing, 1991-92; Emerson College, adjunct graduate faculty, 1992; Boston College, Department of English, visiting assistant professor, 1993-95, assistant professor, 1995-99, associate professor, 1999-2005, professor, 2005-, Creative Nonfiction Program, coordinator, 1999-, Creative Writing Concentration, director, 1999-2000; Wesleyan University, visiting writer, 1993; Share Our Strength, organizer, 1993-95; State Library of South Australia, Somerville Gardens Oral History Project, chronicler, 1995; PEN American Center, PEN Prison Writing Project, writing mentor, 2002-. **Publications:** Have You Seen Me? (stories), 1991. NOVELS: Unravelling, 1997; The Honey Thief, 1999; Awake, 2004. Works appear in anthologies. Contributor of articles to periodicals. **Address:** c/o Richard Parks, The R. Parks Agency, 138 E 16th St., Ste. 5B, PO Box 693, Salem, NY 12865, U.S.A. **Online address:** graver@bc.edu

GRAVES, Joseph Lewis. American (born United States), b. 1955. **Genres:** Race Relations, Medicine/Health, Sciences, Social Sciences. **Career:** University of California, assistant professor of evolutionary biology and African-American studies, 1990-94; Arizona State University, associate professor, 1994-2000, professor of evolutionary biology and African-American studies, 2000-04; Midwestern Osteopathic Medical College, adjunct professor of biological sciences, 2001; Embry-Riddle Aeronautical University, visiting professor, 2002; Fairleigh Dickinson University, core director and professor of biological sciences, 2004-05; North Carolina Agricultural and Technical State University, University Studies, dean, 2005-10, professor of biological studies, Joint School of Nanoscience and Nanoengineering, associate dean for research, 2011-. Writer. **Publications:** The Emperors New Clothes: Biological Theories of Race at the Millennium, 2001; The Race Myth: Why We Pretend Race Exists in America, 2004. Contributor to books. **Address:** Joint School of Nanoscience and Nanoengineering, 2901 E Lee St., Ste. 2200, Greensboro, NJ 27401, U.S.A. **Online address:** gravesjl@ncat.edu

GRAVES, Ralph (Augustus). American (born United States), b. 1924.

Genres: Novels, Autobiography/Memoirs, Mystery/Crime/Suspense, Young Adult Fiction, Art/Art History, Travel/Exploration. **Career:** Life Magazine, researcher, reporter and writer, 1948-58, articles editor, 1958-61, assistant managing editor, 1961-67, managing editor, 1969-72; Time Inc., senior staff editor, 1968, associate publisher, 1975, corporate editor, 1976-78, editorial director, 1978-83. Citizen's Crime Commission, chairman. **Publications:** Thanks for the Ride, 1949; The Lost Eagles, 1955; August People, 1985; Share of Honor, 1989; Orion: The Story of a Rape, 1993; (with E. Graves) Tables of Content, 1993; (with R. Ellis) Martha's Vineyard: An Affectionate Memoir, 1995; Objects of Desire: A Portrait of Love and Marriage, 2003; The Triumph of An Idea, 2005. **Address:** Julian Bach Literary Agency, 22 E 71st St., New York, NY 10021, U.S.A.

GRAVES, Russell A. American (born United States), b. 1969. **Genres:** Environmental Sciences/Ecology, Natural History, Photography, Illustrations. **Career:** Childress Independent School District, teacher, 1993-; Childress County Historical Museum, board director. Writer. **Publications:** SELF-ILLUSTRATED: The Prairie Dog: Sentinel of the Plains, 2001. OTHERS: Managing Wildlife as an Enterprise, 1997; The Hunting Dogs: A Photographic Tribute, 2002; Communicating in the Agricultural Industry, 2005; Kodak Most Basic Book of Digital Nature Photography, 2008. **Address:** 706 Ave. 1 SE, Childress, TX 79201-6824, U.S.A. **Online address:** russell@russellgraves.com

GRAVES, Sarah. American (born United States), b. 1951?. **Genres:** Mystery/Crime/Suspense, Young Adult Fiction, Children's Fiction, Westerns/Adventure. **Career:** Yale-New Haven Hospital, respiratory therapist. Writer. **Publications:** HOME REPAIR IS HOMICIDE MYSTERY SERIES: The Dead Cat Bounce, 1997; Triple Witch, 1999; Wicked Fix, 2000; Repair to Her Grave, 2001; Wreck the Halls, 2001; Unhinged, 2003; Mallets Aforethought, 2004; Tool & Die, 2004; Nail Biter, 2005; Trap Door, 2006; The Book of Old Houses, 2007; A Face at the Window, 2008; Crawlspace: A Home Repair Is Homicide Mystery, 2009; Knockdown: A Home Repair is Homicide Myster, 2011. OTHER: Dead Level, 2012. Contributor to periodicals. **Address:** Bantam Books, 1745 Broadway, 10th Fl., New York, NY 10019, U.S.A. **Online address:** sarahgraves1@hotmail.com

GRAVITZ, Herbert L. American (born United States), b. 1942. **Genres:** Medicine/Health, Psychology. **Career:** Larue D. Carter Memorial Hospital, clinical intern, 1967-68; University of Windsor, assistant professor of psychology, 1969-72; University of California, assistant director of counseling center, 1972-79, Counseling, Career Planning and Placement Services, counseling program director, 1979-80, coordinator of training, 1980-81; Affiliated with Cottage Hospital, staff, 1974-96; Client-Centered Theory and Practice, Santa Barbara County Mental Health Center Psychiatric Residence Program, teaching psychologist, 1976; private practice of clinical psychology, 1979-; Psychiatric Emergency Team, consulting psychologist, 1980-81; Sanctuary House Inc., consulting psychologist, 1980-82; Suzanne Somers Institute, core faculty, 1989-92; Antioch University West, adjunct faculty, 1981-84. Writer. **Publications:** (With J.D. Bowden) Guide to Recovery: A Book for Adult Children of Alcoholics, 1985; Children of Alcoholics Handbook: Who They Are, What They Experience, and How They Recover, 1985; (contrib.) Growing in the Shadow, 1986; (with J.D. Bowden) Recovery: A Guide for Adult Children of Alcoholics, 1987; (with J.D. Bowden) Genesis: Spirituality in Recovery from Childhood Traumas, 1988; Obsessive Compulsive Disorder: New Help for the Family, 1998, 2nd ed., 2006; Trauma: A Crucible for Excellence, 1999; Words That Heal: More Help for the Family, 2004; Mental Illness and the Family: Unlocking the Doors to Triumph, 2004; Facing Adversity: Words That Heal, 2005. Contributor to books and periodicals. **Address:** 2020 Alameda Padre Serra, Ste. 217, Santa Barbara, CA 93103, U.S.A. **Online address:** gravitz@aol.com

GRAY, Alasdair (James). Scottish (born Scotland), b. 1934. **Genres:** Novels, Novellas/Short Stories, Plays/Screenplays, Intellectual History, Poetry, Politics/Government, Biography, Literary Criticism And History, Literary Criticism And History. **Career:** Part-time art teacher, 1958-62; Pavilion and Citizens' Theatre, scene painter, 1962-63; freelance playwright and painter, 1963-75; People's Palace Local History Museum, artist recorder, 1977; University of Glasgow, writer-in-residence, 1977-79, consulting professor of creative writing, 2001-03; freelance writer and book designer, 1979-2001; Oran Mor Arts and Leisure Centre, mural painter, 2003-. **Publications:** NOVELS: Lanark: A Life in 4 Books, 1981, 2nd ed., 1982; 1982, Janine, 1984, 2nd ed., 1985; The Fall of Kelvin Walker: A Fable of the Sixties, 1985; McGrotty

and Ludmilla; or, The Harbinger Report, 1989; Something Leather, 1990; Poor Things, 1992; A History Maker, 1994; (ed.) Old Men in Love, 2007. STORIES: The Comedy of the White Dog, 1979; Unlikely Stories, Mostly, 1983; (with A. Owens and J. Kelman) Lean Tales, 1985; Ten Tales Tall and True, 1993; Mavis Belfrage: A Romantic Tale: With Five Shorter Tales, 1996; The British Book of Popular Political Songs, 2002; The Ends of Our Tethers, 2003. OTHERS: Saltire Self-Portrait 4 (autobiographical sketch), 1988; Old Negatives (4 verse sequences), 1989; Why Scots Should Rule Scotland, 1992; (contrib.) Songs of Scotland: A Hundred of the Best, 1996; Working Legs: A Play for People Without Them, (play), 1997; (contrib.) Artist in His World: Prints, 1986-1997, 1998; (ed.) The Book of Prefaces, 2000; Sixteen Occasional Poems, 1990-2000, 2000; The Ends of Their Tethers: Thirteen Sorry Stories, 2003; A Short Survey of Classical Scottish Writing, 2001; (with A. Tomkins) How We Should Rule Ourselves, 2005; (ed. and intro.) Dear Green Place: & Fur Sadie, 2008; A Gray Play Book, 2009; A Life in Pictures, 2010; Collected Verses, 2010; Every Short Story by Alasdair Gray 1952-2012, 2012. Contributor to periodicals. **Address:** c/o Giles Gordon, 6 Ann St., Edinburgh, EH 4 1PJ, Scotland.

GRAY, Andrew. Canadian/Scottish (born Scotland), b. 1968?. **Genres:** Young Adult Fiction, Poetry. **Career:** University of British Columbia, instructor in creative writing, Booming Ground, founder and director, Optional-Residency M.F.A. Program, founder, coordinator. Author. **Publications:** Small Accidents, 2001. Contributor to magazines. **Address:** Creative Writing Program, University of British Columbia, Buchanan Rm. E471, 1866 Main Mall, Vancouver, BC V6T 1Z1, Canada. **Online address:** angray@exchange.ubc.ca

GRAY, Chris Hables. American (born United States), b. 1953. **Genres:** Ethics, History, Military/Defense/Arms Control, Philosophy, Politics/Government, Information Science/Computers. **Career:** South Africa Catalyst Project, research director and traveling organizer, 1979-81; Zetetic Software Inc., writer and consultant, 1983-90, project developer, 1987-90; University of California, lecturer, 1989-91, Crown College, lecturer, 2005-08; Square One Software Inc., lead writer and consultant, 1991-93; Oregon State University, adjunct graduate faculty and assistant professor of history, 1992-96; Goddard College, professor of interdisciplinary studies, 1994-2007; Hewlett-Packard, writer and consultant, 1994-95; University of Great Falls, associate professor of computer science and cultural studies of science and technology, 1996-2005; Union Institute and University, Graduate College, professor, 2000-. Writer. **Publications:** Power-Learning: Developing Effective Study Skills, 1992; Postmodern War: The New Politics of Conflict, 1997; Cyborg Citizen: Politics in the Posthuman Age, 2000; The New Cold War: Information, Power, and the Meaning of Peace, 2002; Peace, War, and Computers, 2005. EDITOR: (with S. Mentor and L. Wagner) Lawrence Litvak and Kathleen McTigue, 1977; The New Columbia Encyclopedia, 5th ed., 1993; (with H. Figueroa-Sarriera and S. Mentor) The Cyborg Handbook, 1995; Technohistory: Using the History of American Technology in Interdisciplinary Research, 1996. Contributor to books and periodicals. **Address:** Union Institute and University, Graduate College, 440 E McMillan St., Cincinnati, OH 45206, U.S.A. **Online address:** chris.gray@myunion.edu

GRAY, Christopher. American (born United States), b. 1950?. **Genres:** Adult Non-fiction, Architecture, History, Photography. **Career:** Office for Metropolitan History, founder and director, 1975-; Avenue magazine, columnist, 1980-92; House and Garden, columnist, 1982-85; New York Times, Streetscapes columnist, 1987-. Writer and architectural historian. **Publications:** (Comp.) Blueprints: Twenty-Six Extraordinary Structures, 1981; Changing New York: The Architectural Scene, 1992; (ed.) Fifth Avenue, 1911, from Start to Finish in Historic Block-by-Block Photographs, 1994; Sutton Place, Uncommon Community by the River, 1997; (with D. Stravitz) The Chrysler Building: Creating a New York Icon Day by Day, 2002; New York Streetscapes: Tales of Manhattan's Significant Buildings and Landmarks, 2003; New York, Empire City: 1920-1945, 2004. **Address:** Office for Metropolitan History, Broadway Studio Bldg., 246 W 80th St., Ste. 8, New York, NY 10024, U.S.A. **Online address:** christopher.gray@metrohistory.com

GRAY, Clayton. Canadian (born Canada), b. 1918?. **Genres:** History, Travel/Exploration, Adult Non-fiction. **Career:** Canadian Press News Bureau, editor, 1944-45; Concordia University, History of Canadian Literature, lecturer, 1954-61; Lake St. Louis Historical Society, vice-president, 1954-75; David M. Stewart Museum, historian, 1955-; Macdonald-Stewart Foundation, historian, 1955-; P.E.N. Canadian Centre, honorary secretary, 1979-80; National Liberal Club, staff, 1982-83. **Publications:** The Montreal Story, 1949; Montréal qui disparait, 1952; Conspiracy in Canada, 1959; Le Vieux Montréal, 1964; Montreal During the American Civil War, 1965; The Louisiana Affair, 1984; The Canadian Guide to Britain, vol. I: England, 1985; Le Castor Fait Tout, 1987. **Address:** 1495 Ste. Croix, Montreal, QC H4L 3Z5, Canada.

GRAY, Colin S. British/American (born United States), b. 1943?. **Genres:** Military/Defense/Arms Control, History, International Relations/Current Affairs, Politics/Government. **Career:** University of Reading, School of Politics and International Relations, professor of international politics and strategic studies, Centre for Strategic Studies, director; Lancaster University, faculty; University of York, faculty; University of Hull, faculty; University of British Columbia, faculty; Canadian Institute of International Affairs, executive secretary of the strategic studies commission; International Institute for Strategic Studies, assistant director, director; Hudson Institute, director of national security studies, 1976-; National Institute for Public Policy, founder, founding president and chair, 1981-, senior associate; Force Development and Integration Center, U.S. Army Space and Missile Defense Command, director, 2000; British Royal Navy, advisor; U.S. Army War College, Strategic Studies Institute, external researcher. Writer. **Publications:** Security through SALT?, 1971; Canada and NORAD: A Study in Strategy, 1972; Canadian Defence Priorities: A Question of Relevance, 1972; Canada's Maritime Forces, 1973; (ed. with R.B. Byers) Canadian Military Professionalism: The Search for Identity, 1973; The Soviet-American Arms Race, 1976; The Geopolitics of the Nuclear Era: Heartland, Rimlands and the Technological Revolution, 1977; The Future of Land-Based Missile Forces, 1977; (with L. Goure and W.G. Hyland) The Emerging Strategic Environment: Implications for Ballistic Missile Defense, 1979; SALT: Deep Force Level Reductions, 1981; The MX ICBM and National Security, 1981; Strategic Studies and Public Policy: The American Experience, 1982; Strategic Studies: A Critical Assessment, 1982; American Military Space Policy: Information Systems, Weapon Systems and Arms Control, 1982; Nuclear Strategy and Strategic Planning, Foreign Policy Research Institute, 1984; (ed. with K.B. Payne) The Nuclear Freeze Controversy, 1984; (ed. with B.R. Schneider and K.B. Payne) Missiles for the Nineties: ICBMs and Strategic Policy, 1984; Missiles against War: The ICBM Debate Today, 1985; Maritime Strategy, Geopolitics and the Defense of the West, 1986; Nuclear Strategy and National Style, 1986; The Geopolitics of Super Power, 1988; (ed. with R.W. Barnett) Seapower and Strategy, 1989; War, Peace and Victory: Strategy and Statecraft for the Next Century, 1990; The Leverage of Sea Power: The Strategic Advantage of Navies in War, 1992; House of Cards: Why Arms Control Must Fail, 1992; Weapons Don't Make War: Policy, Strategy and Military Technology, 1993; The Navy in the Post-Cold War World: The Uses and Value of Strategic Sea Power, 1994; (intro.) Military Operations and Maritime Preponderance: Their Relations and Interdependence, 1996; Explorations in Strategy, 1996; (ed. with G. Sloan) Geopolitics, Geography and Strategy, 1999; The Second Nuclear Age, 1999; Modern Strategy, 1999; Defining and Achieving Decisive Victory, 2002; Strategy for Chaos: Revolutions in Military Affairs and the Evidence of History, 2002; Maintaining Effective Deterrence, 2003; The Sheriff: America's Defense of the New World Order, 2004; Another Bloody Century: Future Warfare, 2005; Transformation and Strategic Surprise, 2005; Irregular Enemies and the Essence of Strategy: Can the American Way of War Adapt?, 2006; Strategy and History: Essays on Theory and Practice, 2006; Recognizing and Understanding Revolutionary Change in Warfare, 2006; The Implications of Preemptive and Preventive War Doctrines: A Reconsideration, 2007; War, Peace and International Relations: An Introduction to Strategic History, 2007, 2nd ed., 2011; Fighting Talk: Forty Maxims on War, Peace and Strategy, 2007; The Airpower Advantage in Future Warfare: The Need for Strategy, 2007; Schools for Strategy: Teaching Strategy for 21st Century Conflict, 2009; National Security Dilemmas: Challenges & Opportunities, 2009; Understanding Airpower: Bonfire of the Fallacies, 2009; After Iraq: The Search for a Sustainable National Security Strategy, 2009; (ed. with J. Baylis and J.J. Wirtz) Strategy in the Contemporary World: An Introduction to Strategic Atudies, 3rd ed., 2010; The Strategy Bridge: Theory for Practice, 2010; Airpower for Strategic Effect, 2011; Hard Power and Soft Power: The Utility of Military Force as an Instrument of Policy in the 21st Century, 2011. Contributor to periodicals. **Address:** Department of Politics and International Relations, University of Reading, Whiteknights, PO Box 218, Reading, BR RG6 6AA, England. **Online address:** c.s.gray@reading.ac.uk

GRAY, Deborah D. American (born United States), b. 1951. **Genres:** Social Work, Psychology. **Career:** North Slope Borough School District, counselor, 1975-76; State University of New York, Upstate Medical University, Regional Perinatal Center, social worker, 1979-81; Catholic Community Services, therapist, 1982-84; New Hope Child and Family Services, casework supervisor, 1988-93; Antioch University, Foster Care and Adoption Therapy Post-graduate Certificate Program, core faculty; Portland State University, Foster Care and Adoption Therapy Post-graduate Certificate Program, faculty. Writer. **Publications:** Attaching in Adoption: Practical Tools for Today's Parents, 2002; Nurturing Adoptions: Creating Resilience After Neglect and Trauma, 2007. Contributor to periodicals. **Address:** 9757 NE Juanita Dr., Ste. 129, Kirkland, WA 98034-8031, U.S.A. **Online address:** deborahdgray@yahoo.com

GRAY, Dianne E. American (born United States) **Genres:** Children's Fiction, Travel/Exploration. **Career:** GrayGoose Software, co-founder and software developer; University of Wisconsin, Department of Management, associate lecturer, lecturer. Writer. **Publications:** Holding Up the Earth, 2000; Together Apart, 2002; Tomorrow, the River, 2006. **Address:** GrayGoose Software, 2374 Granite Cir. NW, Rochester, MN 55901-3057, U.S.A. **Online address:** dgray@prairievoices.com

GRAY, Dulcie. (Dulcie Winifred Catherine Bailey). British/Malaysian (born Malaysia), b. 1915. **Genres:** Novels, Mystery/Crime/Suspense, Plays/Screenplays, Autobiography/Memoirs, Novellas/Short Stories, Adult Non-fiction, Young Adult Fiction. **Career:** Actress, 1939-; Chiltern Shakespeare Co., distinguished patron. Writer. **Publications:** Mark Calypso, 1957; Love Affair (play), 1957; Murder in Melbourne, 1958; Baby Face, 1959; Epitaph for a Dead Actor, 1960; Murder on a Saturday, 1961; Murder in Mind, 1963; The Devil Wore Scarlet, 1964; (with M. Denison) The Actor and His World, 1964; No Quarter for a Star, 1964; The Murder of Love, 1967; Died in the Red, 1968; Murder on Honeymoon, 1969; For Richer for Richer, 1970; Deadly Lampshade, 1971; Understudy to Murder, 1972; Dead Giveaway, 1974; Ride on a Tiger, 1975; Stage-Door Fright (stories), 1977; Death in Denims, 1977; J.B. Priestley, 1977; Butterflies On My Mind: Their Life and Conservation in Britain Today, 1978; Dark Calypso, 1979; The Glanville Women, 1982; Anna Starr, 1984; Mirror Image, 1987; Looking Forward, Looking Back (autobiography), 1991. **Address:** Barry Burrelt Associates, Prince of Wales Theatre, 31 Coventry St., London, GL W1V 8AS, England.

GRAY, Francine du Plessix. American/Polish (born Poland), b. 1930. **Genres:** Novels, History, Women's Studies And Issues, Theology/Religion, Social Sciences, Biography, Autobiography/Memoirs. **Career:** United Press Intl., reporter, 1952-54; Realities Magazine, editorial assistant, 1954-55; freelance writer, 1955-; Art in America, book editor, 1964-66; New Yorker, staff writer, 1968-; City University of New York, City College, distinguished visiting professor, 1975; Yale University, visiting professor, 1981; Columbia University, School of Fine Arts, adjunct professor, 1983-; Princeton University, Ferris Professor, 1986; St. Mary's College, Guggenheim fellow, 1991-92; University of Hartford, Guggenheim fellow, 1991-92; Brown University, Annenberg Fellow, 1997; Vassar College, distinguished visiting professor, 1999; Saybrook College, visiting lecturer, 1981. **Publications:** Divine Disobedience: Profiles in Catholic Radicalism, 1970; Hawaii: The Sugar-Coated Fortress, 1972; Lovers and Tyrants, 1976; World without End: A Novel, 1981; October Blood, 1985; Adam and Eve and the City, 1987; Soviet Women: Walking the Tightrope, 1990; Rage and Fire: A Life of Louise Colet, Pioneer Feminist, Literary Star, Flaubert's Muse, 1994; At Home with the Marquis de Sade: A Life, 1998; Simone Weil, 2001; Them: A Memoir of Parents, 2005. Contributor to periodicals. **Address:** Georges Borchardt Inc., 136 E 57th St., New York, NY 10022-2707, U.S.A.

GRAY, Ian. Australian (born Australia), b. 1951. **Genres:** Sociology, Politics/Government. **Career:** Australian Government, research officer, 1979-88; Charles Sturt University, School of Humanities and Social Sciences, lecturer in sociology, 1989-99, associate professor, 1999-, Rural Social Research, director. Writer. **Publications:** Politics in Place: Social Power Relations in an Australian Country Town, 1991; (with P. Dunn, B. Kelly and C. Williams) Immigrant Settlement in Country Areas, 1991; (with G. Lawrence and T. Dunn) Coping with Change: Australian Farmers in the 1990s, 1993; Australian Farm Families Experience of Drought, 1999; (with G. Lawrence) A Future for Regional Australia: Escaping Global Misfortune, 2001. Contributor to journals. **Address:** School of Humanities & Social Sciences, Charles Sturt University, Bldg. 26, PO Box 678, Wagga Wagga, NW 2678, Australia. **Online address:** igray@csu.edu.au

GRAY, John. British (born England), b. 1948. **Genres:** Politics/Government, Theology/Religion, Philosophy, Social Sciences. **Career:** University of Essex, lecturer; Jesus College, fellow, tutor; Oxford University, faculty; Harvard University, visiting professor, 1985-86; Bowling Green State University, Social Philosophy and Policy Center, Stranahan fellow, 1990-94; Tualane University, visiting professor, 1991; Yale University, visiting professor, 1994; London School of Economics and Political Science, professor of European, through 2008. Writer. **Publications:** Mill on Liberty: A Defence, 1983; (ed. with Z. Pelczynski) Conceptions of Liberty in Political Philosophy, 1984; Hayek on Liberty, 1984, 3rd ed., 1998; Liberalism, 1986, 2nd ed., 1995; Liberalisms: Essays in Political Philosophy, 1989; (ed. with G.W. Smith) On Liberty in Focus, 1991; Post-Liberalism: Studies in Political Thought, 1993; Beyond the New Right: Markets, Government and the Common Environment, 1993; Berlin, 1995; Enlightenment's Wake: Politics and Culture at the Close of the Modern Age, 1995; Isaiah Berlin, 1996; Endgames: Questions in Late Modern Political Thought (essays), 1997; False Dawn: The Delusions of Global Capitalism, 1998; Voltaire: Voltaire and Enlightenment, 1998; Two Faces of Liberalism, 2000; Straw Dogs: Thoughts on Humans and Other Animals, 2003; Al Qaeda and What It Means to be Modern, 2003; Heresies, 2004; Black Mass: Apocalyptic Religion and the Death of Utopia, 2007; (ed. and intro.) On Liberty and Other Essays, 1991; Gray's Anatomy: Selected Writings, 2009; The Immortalization Commission: Science and the Strange Quest to Cheat Death, 2011. **Address:** School of European Thought, London School of Economics & Political Science, Houghton St., London, GL WC2A 2AE, England.

GRAY, John. American (born United States), b. 1951?. **Genres:** Human Relations/Parenting, Self Help, Sex, Social Commentary, Romance/Historical. **Career:** American Psychological Association, president. Teacher and writer. **Publications:** What You Feel, You Can Heal, 1989; Men, Women, and Relationships: Making Peace with the Opposite Sex, 1990; Men Are from Mars, Women Are from Venus: A Practical Guide for Improving Communication and Getting What You Want in Your Relationships, 1992; What Your Mother Couldn't Tell You and What Your Father Didn't Know: Advanced Relationship Skills for Better Communication and Lasting Intimacy, 1994; Mars and Venus in the Bedroom: A Guide to Lasting Romance and Passion, 1995; Mars and Venus in Love, 1996; Mars and Venus Together Forever, 1996; Mars and Venus on a Date, 1997; Mars and Venus Starting Over, 1998; Men Are from Mars, Women Are from Venus: Book of Days, 1998; How to Get What You Want and Want What You Have, 1999; Children Are from Heaven, 1999; Practical Miracles for Mars and Venus, 2000; Men, Women and Relationships, 2001; Mars and Venus in the Workplace: A Practical Guide for Improving Communication and Getting Results at Work, 2002; The Mars and Venus Diet and Exercise Solution, 2003; Truly Mars and Venus: The Illustrated Essential Men Are from Mars, Women Are from Venus, 2003; Why Mars and Venus Collide: Improving Relationships by Understanding How Men and Women Cope Differently with Stress, 2008. **Address:** c/o Author Mail, HarperCollins Publishers, 10 E 53rd St., 7th Fl., New York, NY 10022, U.S.A. **Online address:** askjohngray@marsvenus.com

GRAY, Jordan. See **RABE, Jean.**

GRAY, Judith A(nne). American/New Zealander (born New Zealand), b. 1939?. **Genres:** Dance/Ballet, How-to Books, Education. **Career:** University of Wisconsin, assistant professor, 1979-86, professor of education; Abbott Middle School, assistant principal, 1990-94; H.M. Jackson High School, Department of Science, chairperson, 1994-; Antioch University, Center for Education, core faculty, adjunct professor, 1997-2007; Heritage Institute, instructor and consultant, 1995-2009; West Valley School District, reform consultant, 2003-10; Marysville School District, research advisor, 2008-11; City University of Seattle, faculty, 2009-. Writer. **Publications:** Dance Instruction: Science Applied to the Art of Movement, 1989; (ed.) Dance Technology: Current Applications and Future Trends, 1989; Research in Dance IV: 1900-1990, 1992; (with S. Ellison) 365 Foods Kids Love to Eat: Nutritious and Kid-Tested, 1995, 3rd ed. as 365 Foods Kids Love to Eat: Fun, Nutritious & Kid-tested!, 2005; (with S. Ellison) 365 Afterschool Activities: TV-Free Fun for Kids Ages 7-12, 1995; (with S. Ellison) 365 Days of Creative Play: For Children 2 Years and Up, 1995, 4th ed., 2005; (with S. Ellison) 365 Books Kids Will Love to Read, 1996; (with S. Ellison) 365 Puzzles and Tricks, 1996; (S. Ellison) 365 Smart Afterschool Activities: Tv-Free Fun for Kids Ages 7-12, 2005. **Address:** Sourcebooks, 1935 Brookdale Rd., Ste. 139, Naperville, IL 60563, U.S.A. **Online address:** jgray803@aol.com

GRAY, Richard A. American (born United States), b. 1927?. **Genres:** Bibliography, Reference. **Career:** Ohio State University, senior reference librarian

and associate professor, 1963-69; American Library Association, Publishing Division, senior editor, 1969-74, board chair; R.R. Bowker, acquisitions editor, 1974-75; Pierian Press, senior editor, 1986-. **Publications:** Guide to Book Review Citations: A Bibliography of Sources, 1968; (comp. with D. Villmow) Serial Bibliographies in the Humanities and Social Sciences, 1969; (ed. with J.Z. Cushman) Reference Books for Small and Medium-Sized Libraries, 2nd ed., 1973; (with H.R. Malinowski and D.A. Gray) Science and Engineering Literature, 2nd ed., 1976; (with T.C. Weiskel) Environmental Decline and Public Policy: Pattern, Trend and Prospect, 1992; (with C.M. Schmitz) The Gift of Life-Organ and Tissue Transplantation: An Introduction to Issues and Information Sources, 1993; (with Schmitz) Smoking-The Health Consequences of Tobacco Use: An Annotated Bibliography With an Analytical Introduction, 1995; (with C.M. Schultz) Alcoholism: The Health and Social Consequences of Alcohol Use, 1998. Contributor to periodicals. **Address:** Pierian Press, 3196 Maple Dr., Ypsilanti, MI 48197, U.S.A. **Online address:** dgray4307@aol.com

GRAY, Richard J(ohn). British (born England), b. 1944. **Genres:** Language/Linguistics, Biography, Literary Criticism And History, Young Adult Fiction. **Career:** University of Essex, lecturer, 1969-76, senior lecturer, 1976-80, reader, 1981-90, professor of literature, 1990-; University of Mississippi, Center for the Study of Southern Culture, faculty, 1979; University of South Carolina, Robert E. McNair visiting professor, 1993; University of Georgia, distinguished visiting professor in southern studies, 2008-09; British Academy, fellow, 1993; Journal of American Studies, editor; American Literary History, consulting editor. **Publications:** (Ed. and intro.) American Verse of the Nineteenth Century, 1973; (ed. and intro.) American Poetry of the Twentieth Century, 1976; The Literature of Memory: Modern Writers of the American South, 1977; (ed. and intro.) Robert Penn Warren: A Collection of Critical Essays, 1980; (ed.) American Fiction: New Readings, 1983; Writing the South: Ideas of an American Region, 1986; American Poetry of the Twentieth Century, 1990; The Life of William Faulkner: A Critical Biography, 1994; Southern Aberrations: Writers of the American South and the Problem of Regionalism, 2000; (ed. and intro.) Edgar Allen Poe, 2002; A History of American Literature, 2004, 2nd ed., 2011; (ed. with O. Robinson) A Companion to the Literature and Culture of the American South, 2004; Web of Words: The Great Dialogue of Southern Literature, 2007; (co-ed.) Transatlantic Exchanges: The American South in Europe-Europe in the American South, 2007; Brief History of American Literature, 2011; After the Fall, 2011. **Address:** Department of Literature, University of Essex, Rm. 5A 104, Wivenhoe Pk., Colchester, EX CO4 3SQ, England. **Online address:** grayr@essex.ac.uk

GRAY, Robert (Archibald Speir). British (born England), b. 1942. **Genres:** History, Biography, Poetry. **Career:** Writer. **Publications:** Rolls on the Rocks, 1971; (with J. Olivier) Edward VIII, The Man We Lost: A Pictorial Study, 1972; A History of London, 1978; Cardinal Manning: A Biography, 1985; (co-author) Vehicular Traffic and Air Pollution in El Paso Cd Juárez, 1989; The King's Wife: Five Queen Consorts, 1990; The Factory Question and Industrial England, 1830-1860, 1996; (ed. with A.M. Ramlal) Training Programme for Management of Child Abuse, 1997; New Selected Poems, 1998; (with T. Atkins) Melbourne Style 2, 2004; Melbourne Style 3, 2006; I Wish that I Were Langston Hughes, 2008; (ed. with G. Lehmann) Australian Poetry Since 1788, 2011. Contributor to periodicals. **Address:** 23 St. Luke's Rd., London, GL W11 1DB, England.

GRAY, Robert (Curtis). Australian (born Australia), b. 1945. **Genres:** Novels, Young Adult Fiction. **Career:** Sydney Morning Herald, staff; Meiji University, writer-in-residence; Geelong College, writer-in-residence, 1982. **Publications:** Introspect, Retrospect, 1970; Creekwater Journal, 1974; Grass Script, 1979; (ed. with G. Lehmann) The Younger Australian Poets, 1983; The Skylight, 1984; Selected Poems, 1963-1983, 1985, rev. ed., 1990; Piano, 1988; (ed. with G. Sturgeon and C. Gentle) Alun Leach-Jones, 1988; (ed. with G. Lehmann) Australian Poetry in the Twentieth Century, 1991; (ed. with V. Smith) Sydney's Poems: A Selection on the Occasion of the City's One Hundred and Fiftieth Anniversary 1842-1992, 1992; (ed. and intro.) Selected Poems, 1993; Certain Things, 1993; New and Selected Poems, 1995; Lineations, 1996; New Selected Poems, 1998; Afterimages, 2002; Nameless Earth, 2006; The Land I Came Through Last, 2008; (contrib.) What on Earth Possessed You, 2008. **Address:** c/o Author Mail, Giramondo Publishing Co., PO Box 752, Artarmon, NW 1570, Australia.

GRAY, Victor. See **CONQUEST, (George) Robert (Acworth).**

GRAYBILL, Andrew R. American (born United States), b. 1971. **Genres:** History. **Career:** University of Nebraska, associate professor of history, 2003-. Writer. **Publications:** Policing the Great Plains: Rangers, Mounties, and the North American Frontier, 1875-1910, 2007; (ed. with B.H. Johnson) Bridging National Borders in North America: Transnational and Comparative Histories, 2010. **Address:** Department of History, University of Nebraska-Lincoln, 612 Oldfather Hall, Lincoln, NE 68588, U.S.A. **Online address:** agraybill2@unl.edu

GRAYDON, Shari. Canadian (born Canada), b. 1958. **Genres:** Children's Non-fiction, Adult Non-fiction. **Career:** Burson-Marsteller, client services manager, 1985-88; freelance consultant, 1988-96; Simon Fraser University, communications instructor, 1996-2000; Premier of British Columbia, press secretary, 2000-01; Institute for Media Policy and Civil Society, associate, 2004-; MediaWatch, president, 1992-2000; Women's Future Fund, vice president, 2004, president, 2005-. Writer. **Publications:** Gender Issues in the Media, 1994; Round Table on the Portrayal of Young Women in the Media, 1997; (with D. Mitchell) British Columbia's Business Leaders of the Century, 1999; Made You Look: How Advertising Works and Why You Should Know, 2003; In Your Face: The Culture of Beauty and You, 2004; I Feel Great About My Hands, 2011. Contributor to periodicals and books. **Address:** 155 McLeod St., Ottawa, ON K2P 0Z6, Canada. **Online address:** sgraydon@uottawa.ca

GRAYSON, Donald K. American (born United States), b. 1945. **Genres:** Bibliography, Earth Sciences, History, Natural History. **Career:** University of Oregon, Division of Continuing Education, instructor in anthropology, 1969-71; Kirkland College, assistant professor of anthropology, 1971-74; Bureau of Land Management, Oregon State Office, state office archaeologist, 1974-75; University of Washington, Quaternary Sciences Center, adjunct assistant professor, 1975-78, adjunct associate professor, 1978-83, adjunct professor, 1983-, Department of Anthropology, assistant professor, 1975-78, associate professor, 1978-83, professor, 1983-, Thomas Burke Memorial Museum, adjunct assistant curator of environmental archaeology, 1977-78, adjunct associate curator, 1978-83, adjunct curator, 1983-, acting curator of archaeology, 1988-89; American Museum of Natural History, research associate in anthropology, 1979-; Academic Press, Studies in Archaeological Science, editor, 1982-85; Quaternary Research, associate editor, 1983-93. **Publications:** A Bibliography of the Literature on North American Climates of the Past 13,000 Years, 1975; (ed. with W.E. Engelbrecht) Essays in Northeastern Anthropology in Memory of Marian E. White, 1978; (ed. with P.D. Sheets) Volcanic Activity and Human Ecology, 1979; (ed. with R.C. Dunnell) Lulu Linear Punctated: Essays in Honor of George Irving Quimby, 1983; The Establishment of Human Antiquity, 1983; Quantitative Zooarchaeology: Topics in the Analysis of Archaeological Faunas, 1984; The Desert's Past: A Natural Prehistory of the Great Basin, 1993; Great Basin: A Natural Prehistory, 2011; Was there Increasing Dietary Specialization Across the Middle-to-Upper Paleolithic Transition in France?, forthcoming. Works appear in anthologies. Contributor to journals. **Address:** Department of Anthropology, University of Washington, 119 Denny Hall, PO Box 353100, Seattle, WA 98195-3100, U.S.A. **Online address:** grayson@u.washington.edu

GRAYSON, Emily. American (born United States) **Genres:** Novels, Young Adult Fiction, History, Literary Criticism And History, Romance/Historical. **Career:** Writer. **Publications:** The Gazebo, 1999; The Observatory: A Novel, 2000; The Fountain: A Novel, 2001; Waterloo Station: A Novel, 2003; Night Train to Lisbon, 2004. Contributor to periodicals. **Address:** c/o Author Mail, William Morrow-HarperCollins, 10 E 53rd St., New York, NY 10022, U.S.A.

GRAYSON, Paul. American (born United States), b. 1946. **Genres:** Psychology, Education. **Career:** New York University, University Counseling Service, director; Marymount Manhattan College, Counseling and Wellness Center, director. Writer. **Publications:** (Ed. with K. Canley) College Psychotherapy, 1989; (with P. Meilman) Beating the College Blues, 1992, 2nd ed. 1999; (with P.W. Meilman) College Mental Health Practice, 2006. **Address:** Marymount Manhattan College, 221 E 71st St., New York, NY 10021, U.S.A. **Online address:** pgrayson@mmm.edu

GRAYSON, Richard. See **GRINDAL, Richard.**

GRAZER, Gigi Levangie. American (born United States), b. 1963. **Genres:** Film, Novels, Plays/Screenplays, Romance/Historical. **Career:** Novelist. **Publications:** Rescue Me: A Love Story (novel), 2000; Maneater: A Novel, 2003; The Starter Wife (novel), 2005; Queen Takes King: A Novel, 2008;

Fairytale Ending, 2010; The After Wife, 2012. Contributor to periodicals. **Address:** c/o Author Mail, Simon & Schuster Inc., 1230 Ave. of the Americas, New York, NY 10020-1513, U.S.A.

GRAZIANO, Michael S. A. (M. S. A. Graziano). American (born United States), b. 1967. **Genres:** Novels. **Career:** Princeton University, postdoctoral fellow, 1996-98, research staff, 1998-2001, Department of Psychology, assistant professor, 2001-07, associate professor, 2007-. Writer, neuroscientist and researcher. **Publications:** (As M.S.A. Graziano with L.M. Graziano) Cretaceous Dawn: A Novel, 2008; The Love Song of Monkey: A Novel, 2008; The Divine Farce, 2009; The Intelligent Movement Machine: An Ethological Perspective on the Primate Motor System, 2009; God Soul Mind Brain: A Neuroscientist's Reflections on the Spirit World, 2010; Human Conscious Experience, forthcoming. Contributor to books and journals. **Address:** Department of Psychology, Princeton University, Green Hall, Princeton, NJ 08544-1010, U.S.A. **Online address:** graziano@princeton.edu

GRAZIANO, M. S. A. See **GRAZIANO, Michael S. A.**

GREACEN, Lavinia. Irish/British (born England) **Genres:** Biography, Young Adult Fiction, Autobiography/Memoirs. **Career:** Writer. **Publications:** Chink: A Biography, 1989; J.G. Farrell: The Making of a Writer, 1999; (ed.) J.G. Farrell in his Own Words: Selected Letters and Diaries, 2009. Contributor to periodicals. **Address:** c/o Author Mail, Bloomsbury Publishing Plc., 36 Soho Sq., London, GL W1D 3QY, England.

GREANEY, Mark. American (born United States), b. 1968?. **Genres:** Mystery/Crime/Suspense, Novels. **Career:** Writer. **Publications:** The Gray Man, 2009; On Target, 2010. **Address:** c/o Scott Miller, Trident Media Group, 41 Madison Ave., 36th Fl., New York, NY 10010, U.S.A.

GREARSON, Jessie Carroll. American (born United States), b. 1962?. **Genres:** Adult Non-fiction, Essays. **Career:** John Marshall Law School, professor of writing, 1997-, director of writing resource center, through 2001. **Publications:** (Ed. with L.B. Smith) Swaying: Essays on Intercultural Love, 1995; (with L.B. Smith) Love in a Global Village: A Celebration of Intercultural Families in the Midwest, 2001. **Address:** John Marshall Law School, 315 S Plymouth Ct., Chicago, IL 60604, U.S.A. **Online address:** 7grearson@jmls.edu

GREASEBEAM, Rowland W. See **BASE, Graeme (Rowland).**

GREAVES, Bettina Herbert Bien. American (born United States), b. 1917. **Genres:** Economics, Bibliography, Business/Trade/Industry, Politics/Government. **Career:** Foreign Economic Administration, Board of Economic Warfare, overseas worker, 1943-45; Foundation for Freedom, editorial assistant, 1946-47; Foundation for Economic Education Inc., senior staff, 1951-92; New York Institute of Credit, professor of economics, 1986-; The Library of the Works of Ludwig von Mises, Liberty Fund Series, consulting editor. **Publications:** Works of Ludwig Von Mises, 1969; Free Market Economics: A Syllabus, 1975; (trans.) L. von Mises, On the Manipulation of Money and Credit, 1978; (comp. with R.W. McGee) Mises: An Annotated Bibliography, 1993, rev. ed., 1997; (contrib.) Economics: A Free Market Reader, 2004. EDITOR: Economic Freedom and Interventionism, 1990; Austrian Economics: An Anthology, 1996; Interventionism: An Economic Analysis, 1998; Rules for Living: The Ethics of Social Cooperation, 1999; Liberalism: The Classical Tradition, 2005; Theory and History: An Interpretation of Social and Economic Evolution, 2005; Anti-Capitalistic Mentality, 2006; Nation, State and Economy: Contributions to the Politics and History of Our Time, 2006; The Ultimate Foundation of Economic Science: An Essay on Method, 2nd ed., 2006; (foreword) Bureaucracy, 2007; Human Action: A Treatise on Economics, 2007; (foreword) Planning for Freedom: Let the Market System Work: A Collection of Essays and Addresses, 2008; (foreword) Omnipotent Government: The Rise of the Total State and Total War, 2009; Economic Policy: Thoughts for Today and Tomorrow, 2010. Contributor to periodicals. **Address:** Foundation for Economic Education Inc., 30 S Broadway, Irvington on Hudson, NY 10533, U.S.A.

GREAVES, Nick. Zimbabwean/British (born England), b. 1955. **Genres:** Mythology/Folklore, Animals/Pets, Children's Fiction. **Career:** Anglo American Corp., field geologist, 1976-80; Retreatments Group, contracts manager, 1980-83; O. Connoly & Co., sales manager, 1983-88; L&L Mining and Industrial Suppliers, administrative manager, 1988-. Writer. **Publications:** SELF-

ILLUSTRATED: Hwange: Retreat of the Elephants, 1996. OTHERS: When Hippo Was Hairy and Other Tales from Africa, 1988; When Lion Could Fly: And Other Tales from Africa, 1993; When Elephant was King and Other Elephant Tales from Africa, 1996; When Bat was a Bird, 2004; The Magic Fish Bones, 2006. Contributor to periodicals. **Address:** Foxes African Safaris, PO Box 18065, Dar es Salaam, 1, Tanzania, United Republic of.

GREBSTEIN, Sheldon Norman. American (born United States), b. 1928. **Genres:** Literary Criticism And History, History, Essays. **Career:** University of Kentucky, instructor, assistant professor of English, 1953-62; University of South Florida, assistant professor of English, 1962-63; State University of New York, Purchase College, associate professor, 1963-68, professor of English, 1968-81, director of graduate English studies, 1965-72, executive assistant, 1975, dean of arts and sciences, 1975-81, president and professor of literature, 1981-93, university professor of literature, 1993-95, university professor emeritus of literature, 1995-; University of Rouen, Fulbright lecturer, 1968-69. Writer. **Publications:** Monkey Trial: Tennessee vs. John T. Scopes, 1960; Sinclair Lewis, 1962; John O'Hara, 1966; Perspectives in Contemporary Criticism: A Collection of Recent Essays by American, English and European Literary Critics, 1968; Merrill Studies in For Whom the Bell Tolls, 1971; Hemingway's Craft, 1973. Contributor to books and journals. **Address:** Purchase College, State University of New York, 735 Anderson Hill Rd., Purchase, NY 10577, U.S.A. **Online address:** whc@bestweb.net

GRECO, Lidia. Italian (born Italy), b. 1969. **Genres:** Industrial Relations, Business/Trade/Industry. **Career:** University of Bari, lecturer; Centro Ricerche per il Mezzogiorno, researcher; Centre for Urban and Regional Development Studies, researcher; Trinity College, Employment Research Centre, researcher; University of Durham, consultant; Sussex European Institute, consultant; European Union, consultant. Writer. **Publications:** Industrial Redundancies: A Comparative Analysis of the Chemical and Clothing Industries in the U.K. and Italy, 2002; (with M. Dunford) After the Three Italies: Wealth, Inequality and Industrial Change, 2005; (with E. Corigliano) Tra donne: Vecchi legami e nuovi spazi; Pratiche tradizionali e transnazionali nel lavoro delle immigrate, 2005; (with E. Corigliano) Trappole e Traiettorie Nel Mercato Del Lavoro Meridionale: Salvati Dal Telefono?: Una Ricerca in un Call Center, 2009. **Address:** Department of Social Sciences, University of Bari, Palazzo Ateneo, Piazza Umberto 1, Bari, 1-70121, Italy. **Online address:** l.greco@scienzepolitiche.uniba.it

GREELEY, Andrew (Moran). American (born United States), b. 1928. **Genres:** Novels, Education, Sociology, Theology/Religion, Mystery/Crime/Suspense, inspirational/Motivational Literature, Children's Fiction, Young Adult Fiction, Human Relations/Parenting, Social Sciences. **Career:** Church of Christ the King, assistant pastor, 1954-64; University of Chicago, National Opinion Research Center, senior study director, 1961-68, lecturer in sociology of religion, 1962-72, program director for higher education, 1968-70, research associate, 1985-, Center for the Study of American Pluralism, director, 1971-85, professor of social science, 1991-; University of Arizona, professor of sociology, 1978-, professor of sociology of education, distinguished lecturer; University of Illinois, professor of sociology of education. Writer. **Publications:** RELIGION AND THEOLOGY: The Church and the Suburbs, 1959; Strangers in the House: Catholic Youth in America, 1961, rev. ed., 1967; Religion and Career: A Study of College Graduates, 1963; Letters to a Young Man, 1964; Letters to Nancy, from Andrew M. Greeley, 1964; Priests for Tomorrow, 1964; And Young Men Shall See Visions: Letters from Andrew M. Greeley, 1964; (with P.H. Rossi) The Education of Catholic Americans, 1966; The Hesitant Pilgrim: American Catholicism after the Council, 1966; The Catholic Experience: An Interpretation of the History of American Catholicism, 1967; (with W.V. Cleve and G.A. Carroll) The Changing Catholic College, 1967; The Crucible of Change: The Social Dynamics of Pastoral Practice, 1968; Uncertain Trumpet: The Priest in Modern America, 1968; Youth Asks, Does God Talk?, 1968 as Youth Asks, Does God Still Speak?, 1970; (with M.E. Marty and S.E. Rosenberg) What Do We Believe? The Stance of Religion in America, 1968; From Backwater to Mainstream: A Profile of Catholic Higher Education, 1969; A Future to Hope In: Socio-Religious Speculations, 1969; Life for a Wanderer: A New Look at Christian Spirituality, 1969; Religion in the Year 2000, 1969; New Horizons for the Priesthood, 1970; The Life of the Spirit, 1970; (with W.E. Brown) Can Catholic Schools Survive?, 1970; The Jesus Myth, 1971; The Touch of the Spirit, 1971; What a Modern Catholic Believes About God, 1971; The Unsecular Man: The Persistence of Religion, 1972; Priests in the United States: Reflections on a Survey, 1972; The Sinai Myth, 1972; What a Modern Catholic believes about the

Church, 1972; The Catholic Priest in the United States: Sociological Investigations, 1972; (ed. with G. Baum) Persistence of Religion, 1973; The Devil, You Say! Man and His Personal Devils and Angels, 1974; (ed. with G. Baum) The Church as Institution, 1974; May the Wind Be at Your Back: The Prayer of St. Patrick, 1975; (with W.C. McCready and K. McCourt) Catholic Schools in a Declining Church, 1976; The Communal Catholic, 1976; Death and Beyond, 1976; The American Catholic: A Social Portrait, 1977; The Mary Myth: On the Femininity of God, 1977; An Ugly Little Secret: Anti-Catholicism in North America, 1977; Everything You Wanted to Know About the Catholic Church but Were Too Pious to Ask, 1978; (ed. with G. Baum) Communication in the Church, 1978; The Making of the Popes, 1978; Crisis in the Church: A Study of Religion in America, 1979; The Politics of Intrigue in the Vatican, 1979, rev. ed. as The Making of the Pope, 2005, 2005; Catholic High School and Minority Students, 1982; The Bottom Line Catechism for Contemporary Catholics, 1982; Religion: A Secular Theory, 1982; The Catholic Why? Book, 1983; How to Save the Catholic Church, 1984; (with M.G. Durkin) Angry Catholic Women, 1984; American Catholics Since the Council: An Unauthorized Report, 1985; Patience of a Saint, 1986; Catholic Contributions: Sociology and Policy, 1987; When Life Hurts: Healing Themes from the Gospels, 1988; 101 Irish-American Blessings, 1988; God in Popular Culture, 1988; Religious Indicators, 1940-1985, 1989; Myths of Religion, 1989; Religious Change in America, 1989; Complaints against God, 1989; Year of Grace, 1990; (with J. Neusner) The Bible and Us: A Priest and a Rabbi Read Scripture Together, 1990, rev. ed. as Common Ground: A Priest And A Rabbi Read Scripture Together, 1996; The Book of Irish American Prayers and Blessings, 1991; The Catholic Myth: The Behavior and Beliefs of American Catholics, 1991; Love Affair: A Prayer Journal, 1992; Religion as Poetry, 1994; Sociology and the Religion: A Collection of Readings, 1994; Sacraments of Love: A Prayer Journal, 1994; Windows: A Prayer Journal, 1994; (with A.J. Bergesen) God in the Movies: A Sociological Investigation, 2000; The Catholic Imagination, 2000; My Love: A Prayer Journal, 2001; The Great Mysteries: Experiencing Catholic Faith from the Inside Out, 2003; The Catholic Revolution: New Wine, Old Wineskins, and the Second Vatican Council, 2004; Priests: A Calling in Crisis, 2004; (with M. Hout) The Truth About Conservative Christians: What They Think And What They Believe, 2006; Jesus: A Meditation on His Stories and His Relationships with Women, 2007; Chicago Catholics and the Struggles within Their Church, 2010. SOCIOLOGY: Why Can't They Be Like Us?: Facts and Fallacies about Ethnic Differences and Group Conflicts in America, 1969; A Fresh Look at Vocations, 1969; (with J.L. Spaeth) Recent Alumni and Higher Education, 1970; Why Can't They Be Like Us?: America's White Ethnic Groups, 1971; The Denominational Society: A Sociological Approach to Religion in America, 1972; That Most Distressing Nation: The Taming of the American Irish, 1972; The New Agenda, 1973; Building Coalitions: American Politics in the 1970s, 1974; Ethnicity in the United States: A Preliminary Reconnaissance, 1974. MEDIA: Ethnic Media in the United States, 1974; The Sociology of the Paranormal: A Reconnaissance, 1975; Ethnicity, Denomination and Inequality, 1976; The Great Mysteries: Essential Catechism, 1976; (with W.C. McCready) The Ultimate Values of the American Population, 1976; Neighborhood, 1977; No Bigger than Necessary: An Alternative to Socialism, Capitalism, and Anarchism, 1977; (ed.) The Family in Crisis or in Transition: A Sociological and Theological Perspective, 1979; The Irish Americans: The Rise to Money and Power, 1980; (with W.C. McCready and G. Theisen) Ethnic Drinking Subcultures, 1980; The Sociology of Andrew M. Greeley, 1993; Religion in Europe at the End of the Second Millennium: A Sociological Profile, 2003; A Stupid, Unjust, And Criminal War: Iraq, 2001-2007, 2007. RELATIONSHIPS: The Friendship Game, 1970; Sexual Intimacy, 1973; Ecstasy: A Way of Knowing, 1974; Love and Play, 1975; Faithful Attraction: Discovering Intimacy, Love, and Fidelity in American Marriage, 1991; The Sense of Love (poems), 1992. NOVELS: Nora Maeve and Sebi, 1976; The Magic Cup: An Irish Legend, 1979; Death in April, 1980; The Cardinal Sins, 1981; Thy Brother's Wife, 1982; Ascent into Hell, 1983; Lord of the Dance, 1987; Love Song, 1988; All about Women, 1989; The Search for Maggie Ward, 1991; The Cardinal Virtues, 1991; An Occasion of Sin, 1992; Wages of Sin, 1992; Fall from Grace, 1993; Angel Light: An Old-fashioned Love Story, 1995; (co-author) Forging A Common Future: Catholic, Judaic, And Protestant Relations For A New Millennium, 1997; A Midwinter's Tale, 1998; Younger than Springtime, 1999; A Christmas Wedding, 2000; September Song, 2001; Second Spring: A Love Story, 2003; Golden Years: The Sixth Chronicle of The O'Malley Family In The Twentieth Century, 2004; The Priestly Sins, 2004; The Senator and the Priest, 2006; Home for Christmas, 2009. FATHER 'BLACKIE' RYAN MYSTERY NOVELS: Virgin and Martyr, 1985; Happy Are the Meek, 1985; Happy Are Those Who Thirst for Justice, 1987; Rite of Spring, 1987; Happy Are the Clean of

Heart, 1988; St. Valentine's Night, 1989; Happy Are the Merciful, 1992; Happy Are the Peacemakers, 1993; Happy Are the Poor in Spirit, 1994; Happy Are Those Who Mourn, 1995; White Smoke: A Novel about the Next Papal Conclave, 1996; The Bishop and the Missing L Train, 2000; The Bishop and the Beggar Girl of St. Germain, 2001; The Bishop in the West Wing, 2002; The Bishop Goes to the University, 2003; The Bishop in the Old Neighborhood, 2005; The Bishop at the Lake, 2007; The Archbishop in Andalusia, 2008. SCIENCE FICTION NOVELS: Angels of September, 1986; God Game, 1986; The Final Planet, 1987; Angel Fire, 1988. NUALA MCGRAIL NOVELS: Irish Gold, 1994; Irish Lace, 1996; Irish Whiskey, 1998; Irish Mist, 1999; Irish Eyes, 2000; Irish Love, 2001; Irish Stew!, 2002; Irish Cream, 2005; Irish Crystal, 2006; Irish Linen, 2007; Irish Tiger, 2008; Irish Tweed, 2009. OTHERS: Come Blow Your Mind with Me (essays), 1971; (with J.N. Kotre) The Best of Times, the Worst of Times, 1978; Women I've Met (poetry), 1979; A Piece of My Mind... on Just about Everything, 1983; Confessions of a Parish Priest: An Autobiography, 1986; An Andrew Greely Reader (essays), 1987; Andrew Greeley's Chicago, 1989; (intro.) Pat-Riots to Patriots: American Irish in Caricature and Comic Art, 1990; Andrew Greeley, 1990; Authors of Their Own Lives: Intellectual Autobiographies, by Twenty American Sociologists, 1990; (ed. with M. Cassutt) Sacred Visions, 1991; An Epidemic of Joy: Stories in the Spirit of Jesus, 1999; Furthermore: Memories of a Parish Priest, 1999; (with J. Neusner and M.G. Durkin) Virtues and Vices: Stories of the Moral Life, 1999; (comp. with M.G. Durkin) The Book of Love: A Treasury Inspired By The Greatest of Virtues, 2002; (ed.) Emerald Magic: Great Tales of Irish Fantasy, 2004; The Making of the Pope 2005, 2005. Contributor to journals and magazines. **Address:** Forge, 175 5th Ave., New York, NY 10010, U.S.A. **Online address:** agreel@email.arizona.edu

GREELEY, Robin Adèle. American (born United States), b. 1958?. **Genres:** Literary Criticism And History, History, Art/Art History. **Career:** University of Connecticut, assistant professor, 1998-2004, associate professor of Latin American art history, 2004-, fellow; Massachusetts Institute of Technology, faculty, visiting associate professor, 2009-10; University of California, fellow. Writer. **Publications:** Surrealism and the Spanish Civil War, 2006; (ed. with A. Anreus and L. Folgarait) Mexican Muralism: A Critical History, 2010; Between Campesino and State: The Mexican Avant-garde and Images of the Nation, 1920-1950, forthcoming, (ed. and intro.) Round de Sombra: The Writings of Abraham Cruzvillegas, forthcoming; (co-ed.) Empire in the Middle East: from Antiquity to the British Mandate, forthcoming. **Address:** School of Fine Arts, University of Connecticut, 830 Bolton Rd., Ste. 1099, Storrs, CT 06269-1099, U.S.A. **Online address:** robin.greeley@uconn.edu

GREEN, Adam. American (born United States), b. 1963?. **Genres:** History. **Career:** University of Chicago, associate professor of American history. Writer and historian. **Publications:** (Ed. with C.M. Payne) Time Longer Than Rope: A Century of African American Activism, 1850-1950, 2003; Selling the Race: Culture, Community, and Black Chicago, 1940-1955, 2007. **Address:** Department of History, University of Chicago, 1126 E 59th St., PO Box 102, Chicago, IL 60637, U.S.A. **Online address:** apgreen@uchicago.edu

GREEN, Angela. British/American (born United States), b. 1949?. **Genres:** Young Adult Fiction, Novels, Literary Criticism And History. **Career:** Public relations consultant and writer. **Publications:** Ashdon: A History Of An Essex Village, 1989; Cassandra's Disk, 2002; The Colour of Water, 2003. Contributor to periodicals. **Address:** c/o Author Mail, Peter Owen Publishers, 73 Kenway Rd., London, GL SW5 0RE, England.

GREEN, Arthur. American (born United States), b. 1941. **Genres:** Theology/Religion, Translations, Biography, Humanities. **Career:** University of Pennsylvania, faculty, 1973-84; Reconstructionist Rabbinical College, dean, 1984-86, president, 1986-93; Brandeis University, Philip W. Lown professor, 1994-, professor emeritus of Near Eastern and Judaic studies. Writer. **Publications:** (Ed. and trans. with B.W. Holtz) Your Word is Fire: The Hasidic Masters On Contemplative Prayer, 1977; Tormented Master, 1979; (trans. and intro.) Upright Practices: The Light of the Eyes, 1982; (ed.) Jewish Spirituality, 1984; Devotion and Commandment: The Faith of Abraham in the Hasidic Imagination, 1989; Seek My Face, Speak My Name, 1992, 2nd ed. as Seek My Face: A Jewish Mystical Theology, 2003; Tormented Master: The Life and Spiritual Quest of Rabbi Nahman of Bratslav, 1992; New Directions in Jewish Theology in America, 1994; Judaism for the Post-Modern Era, 1995; Keter: The Crown of God in Early Jewish Mysticism, 1997; (trans.) The Language of Truth: The Torah Commentary of the Sefat Emet, Rabbi Yehudah Leib Alter of Ger, 1998; These Are the Words: A Vocabulary of Jewish Spiri-

tual Life, 1999; Ehyeh: A Kabbalah for Tomorrow, 2003; Guide to the Zohar, 2004; Rosh Hashanah Readings, 2006; Eto slova-, Eleh Ha-Devarim, 2008; Radical Judaism: Rethinking God and Tradition, 2010. **Address:** Brandeis University, Lown 206, 415 South St., PO Box 054, Waltham, MA 02453-2728, U.S.A. **Online address:** green@brandeis.edu

GREEN, Bryan Clark. American (born United States), b. 1967?. **Genres:** Architecture. **Career:** Commonwealth Architects, architectural historian, director of historic preservation; Virginia Historical Society, associate curator for prints and photographs. Writer. **Publications:** (With C. Loth and W.M.S. Rasmunssen) Lost Virginia: Vanished Architecture of the Old Dominion, 2001; In Jefferson's Shadow: The Architecture of Thomas R. Blackburn, 2006; (with A.L. Miller) Building a President's House, 2007. **Address:** Commonwealth Architects, 101 Shockoe Slip, 3rd Fl., Richmond, VA 23219, U.S.A.

GREEN, Celia (Elizabeth). British (born England), b. 1935. **Genres:** Psychology, Sciences, History, Social Sciences. **Career:** Institute of Psychophysical Research, founder and director, 1961-; Oxford Forum, owner. Writer. **Publications:** Lucid Dreams, 1968; Out-of-the-Body Experiences, 1968; The Human Evasion, 1969; (with C. McCreery) Apparitions, 1975; The Decline and Fall of Science, 1976; Advice to Clever Children, 1981; (with C. McCreery) Lucid Dreaming: The Paradox of Consciousness During Sleep, 1994; The Lost Cause: Causation and the Mind-Body Problem, 2003; Letters from Exile: Observations on a Culture in Decline, 2005. **Address:** Institute of Psychophysical Research, 118 Banbury Rd., Oxford, OX OX2 6JU, England. **Online address:** cg@celiagreen.com

GREEN, Charles H. American (born United States), b. 1950?. **Genres:** Administration/Management, Marketing. **Career:** MAC Group, consultant and vice president, 1976-95; Trusted Advisor Associates L.L.C., founder, business strategy consultant and chief executive officer, 1996-; Gemini Consulting, strategy consultant and vice president. Writer. **Publications:** (With R.M. Galford and D.H. Maister) The Trusted Advisor, 2000; Trust-based Selling: Using Customer Focus and Collaboration to Build Long-term Relationships, 2006. Contributor to periodicals. **Address:** Trusted Advisor Associates L.L.C., 8 Lapis Cir., West Orange, NJ 07052-2116, U.S.A. **Online address:** cgreen@trustedadvisor.com

GREEN, (Charles Stuart) Jamison. American (born United States), b. 1948?. **Genres:** Sex, Gay And Lesbian Issues, Law, Medicine/Health, Psychology, Social Sciences, Autobiography/Memoirs, Novels, Novellas/Short Stories, Civil Liberties/Human Rights, Biography. **Career:** Pacific Northwest Bell, construction cable splicer, 1973-76; The Bank of California, affirmative action representative, 1978-79; Cooper Laser Sonics, medical writer and publications manager, 1979-82; North Star Computers, Technical Publications and Engineering Services, manager, 1983-86; Paperback Software Intl., publications and vice president, operations, director, 1986-88; Sun Microsystems, System Software Documentation, engineering group manager, 1988-91; FTM International Inc., president, 1991-99; consulting technical writer, 1992-99; Visa USA, Technical Publications, senior technical writer and director, 1999-2007; Jamison Green & Associates, president, 2007-; University of California San Francisco, Center of Excellence for Transgender Health, Department of Family and Community Medicine, primary care manager, 2009-10. Writer, speaker and advocate. **Publications:** Eyes, 1976; Becoming a Visible Man, 2004. FORTHCOMING: Forces in Motion: Law, Medicine, the Media and the Church in Kantaras v Kantaras; The FTM Guide to SEX; Visible Man: A Transsexual Memoir, A Transgender Life; Making Penises; Someone Else's Body (a novel). **Address:** c/o Author Mail, Vanderbilt University Press, 2014 Broadway, PO Box 1813, Sta. B, Nashville, TN 37203, U.S.A. **Online address:** james@jamisongreen.com

GREEN, Chloe. See **FRANK, J. Suzanne.**

GREEN, Christine. British (born England), b. 1944?. **Genres:** Mystery/Crime/Suspense, Novels. **Career:** Writer, 1998-. **Publications:** CHIEF INSPECTOR CONNOR O'NEILL AND DETECTIVE SGT. FRAN WILSON SERIES: Death in the Country, 1993; Die in My Dreams, 1995; Fatal Cut, 1999. KATE KINSELLA SERIES: Deadly Errand, 1991; Deadly Admirer, 1992; Deadly Practice, 1994; Deadly Partners, 1996; Deadly Bond, 2001; Deadly Echo, 2002; Deadly Choice, 2004; Deadly Night, 2004; Deadly Web, 2005; Deadly Retreat, 2007. DETECTIVE INSPECTOR THOMAS RYDELL AND SERGEANT DENISE CALDECOTE SERIES: Fire Angels, 2001; Vain Hope, 2002. OTHER: Five Centuries of Pioneering, 1989. NOVELS: Coronation Street: The Way to Victory, 2000; Coronation Street: The War Years, 2001. **Address:** c/o Author Mail, Severn House Publishers Ltd., 9-15 High St., Sutton, SR SM1 1DF, England. **Online address:** christine@christine-green.co.uk

GREEN, Cliff(ord). Australian (born Australia), b. 1934. **Genres:** Novels, Children's Fiction, Plays/Screenplays, Young Adult Fiction, Novellas/Short Stories. **Career:** Education Department of Victoria, head teacher in primary grades, 1960-69; Crawford Productions, staff writer, 1969-; freelance writer; Western Australian Institute of Technology, teacher of screen writing; Australian Film and Television School, teacher of screen writing; Victorian College of the Arts, teacher of screen writing; Victorian Council of Adult Education, teacher of screen writing. **Publications:** Marion, 1974; Picnic at Hanging Rock: A Film, 1975; The Incredible Steam-Driven Adventures of Riverboat Bill (juvenile), 1975; Break of Day (novel), 1976; Summerfield: A Film, 1977; The Sun Is Up: Memories of Country School-Days, 1978; Four Scripts, 1978; Burn the Butterflies, 1979; The Further Adventures of Riverboat Bill (juvenile), 1981; The Art of Dale Marsh, 1981; Plays for Kids, 1981; Cop Out!, 1983; Evergreen: The Story of a Family, 1984; Riverboat Bill Steams Again (juvenile), 1985; (contrib.) Senior Drama, 1985. **Address:** 23 Webb St., Warrandyte, VI 3113, Australia.

GREEN, Connie Jordan. American (born United States), b. 1938. **Genres:** Young Adult Fiction, Novels. **Career:** Woodland Elementary, teacher, 1960-61; Oak Ridge High School, teacher, 1961; Robertson Junior High, teacher, 1961-62; nursery school teacher, 1970-77; University of Tennessee, part-time instructor of composition and literature, 1986-. Writer. **Publications:** YOUNG ADULT NOVELS: The War at Home, 1989; Emmy, 1992; Slow Children Playing, 2007; Regret Comes to Tea, 2011. CONTRIBUTOR: An Encyclopedia of East Tennessee, 1981; These Are Our Voices: The Story of Oak Ridge, 1987. Contributor to periodicals. **Address:** Department of English, University of Tennessee, Knoxville, TN 37996, U.S.A. **Online address:** rejgreen@aol.com

GREEN, Daryl D. American (born United States), b. 1966. **Genres:** Administration/Management, Human Relations/Parenting, Public/Social Administration, Business/Trade/Industry, Social Commentary, Adult Non-fiction. **Career:** Tennessee Department of Energy, program manager, 1989-; Performance Management and Logistics Associates (PMLA), president, 1997-; Knoxville College, professor, 2005-09; Lincoln Memorial University, professor, 2009-; Johnson University, professor, 2011-. Writer. **Publications:** My Cup Runneth Over: Setting Goals for Single Parents and Working Couples, 1997; Awakening the Talents Within, 2001; (co-author) Fruit of the Spirit, 2003; More Than a Conqueror: Achieving Personal Fulfillment in Government Service, 2006; (with R. Jenkins) A Call to Destiny: How to Create Effective Ways to Assist Black Boys in America, 2009; Publishing for Professionals, 2009; Breaking Organizational Ties, 2010; (co-author) Impending Danger, 2011; (co-author) Second Chance, 2011; Don't Be An Old Fool, 2011. **Address:** PO Box 32733, Knoxville, TN 37930-2733, U.S.A. **Online address:** pmla@att.net

GREEN, December. American (born United States), b. 1961. **Genres:** Women's Studies And Issues, Politics/Government, Law. **Career:** University of South Carolina, associate instructor, 1985-88; The Citadel, assistant professor, 1988-92, Non-Western Studies Program, director, 1989-92; Governor's School of South Carolina, professor, 1989-93, 1995-98; Pacific Lutheran University, assistant professor, 1992-94; Wright State University, assistant professor, 1994-98, associate professor, 1998-2001, professor, 2001-, International Studies Program, director, 2001-. Writer. **Publications:** (Co-author) Somalia, 1988; (with D.L. Sparks) Namibia: The Nation at Independence, 1992; Gender Violence in Africa: African Women's Responses, 1999; (with L. Luehrmann) Comparative Politics of the Third World: Linking Concepts and Cases, 2003, 2nd ed., 2007. Contributor of articles to periodicals. **Address:** Department of Political Science, Wright State University, 317 Millett Hall, Dayton, OH 45435, U.S.A. **Online address:** december.green@wright.edu

GREEN, Denise. American/Australian (born Australia), b. 1946. **Genres:** Art/Art History. **Career:** Pennsylvania Academy of Fine Arts, graduate faculty, 1997. Writer. **Publications:** Resonating, 2001; Metonymy in Contemporary Art: A New Paradigm, 2006. **Address:** 13 Laight St., PO Box 5, New York, NY 10013, U.S.A. **Online address:** dgaussie@aol.com

GREEN, Duncan. British (born England), b. 1958. **Genres:** Adult Non-fiction, Young Adult Fiction, Social Sciences, Business/Trade/Industry, Politics/Government. **Career:** Greater London Council, policy researcher, 1985-86; freelance journalist on Latin America, 1986-88; Latin America Bureau, writer and editor, 1989-97; CAFOD, trade policy analyst, 1997-; Oxfam GB, head of research, 2004-. **Publications:** NONFICTION: Faces of Latin America, 1991, 2nd ed., 1997; Guatemala, Burden of Paradise: Account of the First Visit of the Association of Artists for Guatemala, 1992; Silent Revolution: The Rise of Market Economics in Latin America, 1995, 2nd ed., 2003; Children of Latin America, 1997; Hidden Lives: Voices of Children in Latin America and the Caribbean, 1998; (with D. Neu) Truth or Profit?: The Ethics and Business of Public Accounting, 2006; From Poverty to Power: How Active Citizens and Effective States can Change the World, 2008. Contributor to periodicals. **Address:** CAFOD, Romero house, 55 Westminster Bridge Rd., London, GL SE1 7JB, England. **Online address:** dgreen@cafod.org.uk

GREEN, Elna C. American (born United States), b. 1959. **Genres:** History, Women's Studies And Issues, Politics/Government. **Career:** Tulane University, visiting assistant professor of history, 1992-93; Sweet Briar College, assistant professor of history, 1993-98; Florida State University, associate professor, 1998-2004, professor, 2004-, Allen Morris associate professor of history, 2007-, department chair; San Jose State University, College of Humanities and Arts, associate dean, 2009-. Writer. **Publications:** Southern Strategies: Southern Women and the Woman Suffrage Question, 1997; (ed.) Before the New Deal: Social Welfare in the South, 1830-1930, 1999; (ed.) The New Deal and Beyond: Social Welfare in the South since 1930, 2003; This Business of Relief: Confronting Poverty in a Southern City, 1740-1940, 2003; (ed.) Looking for the New Deal: Florida Womens Letters during the Great Depression, 2007; (ed. and intro.) In Black and White: An Interpretation of the South, 2008. **Address:** Department of History, Florida State University, 453 Bellamy, Tallahassee, FL 32306-2200, U.S.A. **Online address:** egreen@mailer.fsu.edu

GREEN, G. Dorsey. American (born United States), b. 1949. **Genres:** Gay And Lesbian Issues, Social Sciences. **Career:** Psychotherapist and writer. **Publications:** (With M. Clunis) Lesbian Couples, 1988, 3rd ed. as Lesbian Couples: A Guide to Creating Healthy Relationships, 2000; (with M. Clunis) Lesbian Couples: Creating Healthy Relationships for the 90s, 1993; The Lesbian Parenting Book: A Guide to Creating Families and Raising Children, 1995, 2nd ed., 2003. Contributor to periodicals. **Address:** c/o Author Mail, Seal Press, 300 Queen Anne Ave. N, Ste. 375, Seattle, WA 98109, U.S.A.

GREEN, Hannah. See GREENBERG, Joanne.

GREEN, Harry. See JASPER, James M(acdonald).

GREEN, James. American (born United States), b. 1964. **Genres:** Adult Non-fiction, Self Help. **Career:** Business Express, pilot and first officer, 1992-96; TransWorld Airlines, pilot and flight engineer, 1996-97; Delta Airlines, pilot and first officer, 1997-. Writer. **Publications:** If There's One Thing I've Learned . . . How to Seize Your Once-in-a-Lifetime Chance to Get It Right, 2005. Contributor to periodicals. **Address:** c/o Author Mail, Sound View Publishing, PO Box 696, Shoreham, NY 11786, U.S.A. **Online address:** jimgreen@soundviewpublishing.com

GREEN, Jane. British (born England), b. 1968. **Genres:** Novels. **Career:** Daily Express, feature writer. Journalist. **Publications:** Straight Talking, 1997; Jemima J: A Novel about Ugly Ducklings and Swans, 1999; Mr. Maybe, 1999; Bookends, 2000; Babyville: A Novel, 2001; Spellbound, 2003 in US as To Have and To Hold, 2004; The Other Woman, 2004; (with J. Coburn and L. Ireland) This Christmas, 2005; Swapping Lives in UK as Life Swap, 2006; Second Chance, 2007; Beach House, 2008; Dune Road in UK as Girl Friday, 2009; Promises to Keep, 2010; Another Piece of My Heart, 2012. **Address:** c/o Author Mail, Random House Inc., 1745 Broadway, New York, NY 10019, U.S.A. **Online address:** askjane@janegreen.com

GREEN, Jeffrey M. (Yakov Green). Israeli/American (born United States), b. 1944. **Genres:** Novels, Translations, Language/Linguistics, Travel/Exploration. **Career:** Writer and translator. **Publications:** (With T. Birger) A Daughter's Gift of Love, 1992; Half a Baker: A Novel, 1994; Ḥazarah el Marsel Prusṭ, 1996; Sofshavua Ameriḳani, 1998; Thinking Through Translation, 2000; Largest Island in the Sea, 2009. TRANSLATOR: B. Leroy, The Jews of Navarre in the Late Middle Ages, 1985; A. Appelfeld, To the Land of the Cattails, 1986; A. Appelfeld, The Immortal Bartfuss, 1988; A. Appelfeld, For Every Sin, 1989; G. Shaked, Shmuel Yosef Agnon: A Revolutionary Traditionalist, 1989; A. Appelfeld, The Healer, 1990; A. Appelfeld, Katerina, 1992; R. Elior, The Paradoxical Ascent to God: The Kabbalistic Theosophy of Habad Hasidism, 1992; A. Appelfeld, Unto the Soul, 1994; A. Appelfeld, Beyond Despair, 1994; L. Lazare, Rescue as Resistance, 1996; A. Appelfeld, The Iron Tracks, 1998; A. Appelfeld, The Conversion, 1998; A. Appelfeld, Blooms of darkness, 2010; I. Etkes, The Gaon of Vilna: The Man and His Image, 2002. **Address:** 3 Avigayil St., Jerusalem, 93551, Israel. **Online address:** marjef@gmail.com

GREEN, Jesse. American (born United States), b. 1958. **Genres:** Novels, Novellas/Short Stories, Writing/Journalism. **Career:** Writer and freelance journalist. **Publications:** (With M. Wolitzer) Nutcrackers: Devilishly Addictive Mind Twisters for the Insatiably Verbivorous, 1991; O Beautiful: A Novel, 1992; The Velveteen Father: An Unexpected Journey to Parenthood, 1999. Contributor to periodicals. **Address:** c/o Cynthia Cannell, Janklow & Nesbit Associates, 598 Madison Ave., New York, NY 10022-2606, U.S.A.

GREEN, John C. American (born United States), b. 1953. **Genres:** Theology/Religion, Cultural/Ethnic Topics, Communications/Media, Politics/Government. **Career:** University of Akron, distinguished professor of political science, Ray C. Bliss Institute of Applied Politics, director. Writer. **Publications:** (With J.L. Guth, C.E. Schmidt and L.A. Kellstedt) Religion and the Culture Wars: Dispatches from the Front, 1996; (with J.L. Guth, C.E. Schmidt and L.A. Kellstedt) The Bully Pulpit: The Politics of Protestant Clergy, 1997; (co-author) The Diminishing Divide, 2000; (with A.L. Sherman) Fruitful Collaborations: A Survey of Government-Funded Faith-Based Programs in 15 States: Executive Summary, Faith in Communities, 2003; The Faith Factor: How Religion Influences American Elections, 2007; (with A. Zaidan) Portraits of Power: Ohio and National Politics, 1964-2004, 2007; (with M.M. Poloma) The Assemblies of God, 2010. EDITOR: (with J.L. Guth) The Bible and the Ballot Box: Religion and Politics in the 1988 Election, 1991; (with M. Margolis) Machine Politics, Sound Bites and Nostalgia: On Studying Political Parties, 1993; Politics, Professionalism and Power: Modern Party Organization and the Legacy of Ray C. Bliss, 1994; (with W. Crotty and M.A. Schwartz) Representing Interests and Interest Group Representation, 1994; (with D.M. Shea) The State of the Parties: The Changing Role of Contemporary American Parties, 1994, (with D.J. Coffey) 6th ed., 2011; (with J.K. White) The Politics of Ideas: Intellectual Challenges to the Party after 1992, 1995; (with P.S. Herrnson) Multiparty Politics in America, 1997, 2nd ed. as Multiparty Politics in America: Prospects and Performance, 2002; Financing the 1996 Election, 1999; (with M.J. Rozell and C. Wilcox) Prayers in the Precincts: The Christian Right in the 1998 Elections, 2000; (with C.P. Banks) Superintending Democracy: The Courts and the Political Process, 2001; (with P.S. Herrnson) Responsible Partisanship? The Evolution of American Political Parties since 1950, 2002; (with M.J. Rozell and C. Wilcox) The Christian Right in American Politics: Marching to the Millennium, 2003; (with R. Farmer and J.D. Rausch, Jr.) The Test of Time: Coping with Legislative Term Limits, 2003; (with C.P. Banks and D.B. Cohen) The Final Arbiter: The Consequences of Bush v. Gore for Law and Politics, 2005; (with M.J. Rozell and C. Wilcox) The Values Campaign? The Christian Right and the 2004 Elections, 2006; (with M.K. Kirtz, M.J. Kasoff and R. Farmer) The Elections of 2000: Politics, Culture and Economics in North America, 2006; (with D.M. Shea) Fountain of Youth: Strategies and Tactics for Mobilizing America's Young Voters, 2007; (with L.R. Olson) Beyond Red State, Blue State: Electoral Gaps in the Twenty-first Century American Electorate, 2009. **Address:** Pew Forum on Religion & Public Life, 1615 L St. NW, Ste. 700, Washington, DC 20036-5610, U.S.A. **Online address:** jgreen@pewforum.org

GREEN, Joseph (Lee). American (born United States), b. 1931. **Genres:** Science Fiction/Fantasy, Novellas/Short Stories, Novels, Young Adult Fiction, Technology, Literary Criticism And History. **Career:** International Paper Co., laboratory technician, 1949-51; welder and shop worker, 1952-54; construction millwright, 1955-58; Boeing Co., senior supervisor, 1959-63; NASA, Kennedy Space Center, public affairs science writer, 1965-97, Education Office, deputy chief, engineering writer, 1965-, now retired. **Publications:** The Loafers of Refuge, 1965; An Affair with Genius (short stories), 1969; Gold the Man, 1971 in US as The Mind Behind the Eye, 1971; Conscience Interplanetary, 1972; Star Probe, 1976; The Horde, 1976; Come from Away: A Novel, 1981. Contributor of short stories. **Address:** c/o Lurton Blassingame, 60 E 42nd St., Ste. 1131, New York, NY 10017, U.S.A.

GREEN, J. Paul. Canadian (born Canada), b. 1929. **Genres:** Music, Adult Non-fiction. **Career:** Mississauga High School, Music Department, head, 1955-65; Salvation Army, Dovercourt Citadel Band, conductor, 1963-65; Ontario Ministry of Education, Summer School of Music, teacher, 1964-66, consultant; University of Western Ontario, Don Wright Faculty of Music, professor of music education, 1965-, head of department, 1969-79, now professor emeritus. Writer. **Publications:** (With K. Bray) Solos for Schools, 12 vols., 1979-82; (with N.F. Vogan) Music Education in Canada: A Historical Account, 1991. Works appear in anthologies. Contributor to journals. **Address:** Don Wright Faculty of Music, University of Western Ontario, 1151 Richmond St., London, ON N6A 3K7, Canada. **Online address:** pgreen4@uwo.ca

GREEN, Kenneth Hart. Canadian (born Canada), b. 1953. **Genres:** Theology/Religion, Philosophy, Politics/Government. **Career:** York University, faculty, 1986-87; University of Toronto, Department for the Study of Religion, associate professor, professor of religion, 1987-, graduate faculty associate, 2006-; State University of New York Press, series editor. **Publications:** NONFICTION: Jew and Philosopher: The Return to Maimonides in the Jewish Thought of Leo Strauss, 1993; (ed. and intro.) The Jewish Writings of Leo Strauss, vol. I: Philosophy and Law: Contributions to the Understanding of Maimonides and His Predecessors, 1995, vol. II: Jewish Philosophy and the Crisis of Modernity: Essays and Lectures in Modern Jewish Thought, 1997, vol. III: The Early Writings, 2002; Leo Strauss and Maimonides, 2012; (ed. and intro.) Maimonides Rediscovered, 2012; Emil Fackenheim, Revelation, and Radical Evil, forthcoming; What Moses Saw: Maimonidean Meditations, forthcoming. Contributor to periodicals. **Address:** Centre for the Study of Religion, University of Toronto, 170 St. George St., 3rd Fl., Toronto, ON M5S 2M8, Canada. **Online address:** kenneth.green@utoronto.ca

GREEN, Michael D. American (born United States), b. 1941. **Genres:** History, Bibliography, Human Relations/Parenting, Geography. **Career:** University of North Carolina, Department of American Studies, professor of history and American studies, now professor emeritus. Writer and historian. **Publications:** The Creeks: A Critical Bibliography, 1979; The Politics of Indian Removal: Creek Government and Society in Crisis, 1982; The Creeks, 1990; (ed. and intro. with T. Perdue) The Cherokee Removal: A Brief History with Documents, 1995, 2nd ed., 2005; (with T. Perdue) The Columbia Guide to American Indians of the Southeast, 2001; (with T. Perdue) The Cherokee Nation and the Trail of Tears, 2007; (with T. Perdue) North American Indians: A Very Short Introduction, 2010. **Address:** Department of American Studies, University of North Carolina, CB 3195, Hamilton Hall, Chapel Hill, NC 27599-3195, U.S.A. **Online address:** mgreen@email.unc.edu

GREEN, Michael (Frederick). British (born England), b. 1927. **Genres:** Novels, Autobiography/Memoirs, Humor/Satire, Sports/Fitness. **Career:** Leicester Mercury, reporter, 1943; Northampton Chronicle and Echo, reporter, 1943-50; Birmingham Gazette, sub-editor, 1950-53; Star, sub-editor, 1953-56; freelance writer, 1956-. **Publications:** Art of Coarse Rugby, 1961; Art of Coarse Sailing, 1962, rev. ed., 1973; Even Coarser Rugby, or, What Did You do to Ronald?, 1963; Don't Print My Name Upside Down (novel), 1963; Art of Coarse Acting, 1965, rev. ed., 1987; Downwind of Upstage: The Art of Coarse Acting, 1966; Art of Coarse Sport, 1966; Art of Coarse Golf, 1967; Art of Coarse Moving, 1969; Rugby Alphabet, 1971; Art of Coarse Drinking, 1973; The Art of Coarse Sailing, 1973; Squire Haggard's Journal (satire), 1975; Art of Coarse Cruising, 1976; Even Coarser Sport, 1978; Four Plays for Coarse Actors, 1978, rev. ed., 1988; The Coarse Acting Show 2, 1980; Art of Coarse Sex, 1981; Tonight Josephine, and Other Undiscovered Letters, 1982; (ed. And comp.) The Peterborough Book, 1982; Don't Swing from the Balcony, Romeo: Further Undiscovered Letters, 1983; Never Make Love in a Suit of Armor: And Other Undiscovered Letters, 1983; The Art of Coarse Office Life, 1985; The Third Great Coarse Acting Show, 1986; The Boy Who Shot Down an Airship, 1988; Nobody Hurt in Small Earthquake: The Sequel to The Boy Who Shot Down an Airship, 1990; Coarse Acting Strikes Back, 1999; Coarse Acting Strikes Back: Four More Coarse Plays, 2000. **Address:** Anthony Sheil Associates Ltd., 43 Doughty St., London, WC1N 2LF, England.

GREEN, Norman. American (born United States), b. 1954?. **Genres:** Novels, Young Adult Fiction, Literary Criticism And History, Mystery/Crime/Suspense. **Career:** Writer. **Publications:** NOVELS: Shooting Dr. Jack, 2001; The Angel of Montague Street, 2003; Way Past Legal, 2004; Dead Cat Bounce, 2006; The Last Gig, 2009; Sick Like That, 2010. Contributor to periodicals. **Address:** c/o Author Mail, HarperCollins Publishers, 10 E 53rd St., 7th Fl., New York, NY 10022, U.S.A.

GREEN, Peter (Morris). (Denis Delaney). British (born England), b. 1924. **Genres:** Novels, Novellas/Short Stories, Poetry, Children's Non-fiction, Classics, History, Humanities, Biography, Essays, Translations. **Career:** Cambridge Review, editor, 1950-51; Selwyn College, director of studies in classics, 1952-53; Daily Telegraph, fiction critic, 1953-63; Bodley Head Ltd., literary adviser, 1956-57; Hodder & Stoughton Ltd., consultant editor, 1959-63; The Listener, television critic, 1961-63; John o'London's, film critic, 1961-63; College Year in Athens, lecturer in Greek history and literature, 1966-71, visiting professor of history, 1999; University of Texas, visiting professor of classics, 1971-72, professor, 1972-82, James R. Dougherty, Jr. Centennial Professor of Classics, 1982-97, James R. Dougherty, Jr. Centennial Professor Emeritus, 1997-; University of California, visiting professor of classics, 1976; Tulane University, Mellon Chair of Humanities, 1986; University of Iowa, visiting professor of history, 1997-98, adjunct professor, 1998-, Syllecta Classica, editor, 1999-2009, co-editor, 2010-; Princeton University, visiting research fellow and writer-in-residence, 2001; East Carolina University, King Charles II Distinguished Visiting Professor in Classics and Ancient History, 2004, Whichard Visiting Professor of Classics and Ancient History, 2006. **Publications:** EDITOR: Poetry from Cambridge, 1947-50, 1951; (and intro.) Appreciations: Essays by Clifton Fadiman, 1962; (and intro.) Hellenistic History and Culture, 1993. OTHERS: The Expanding Eye, 1953; (trans.) C. Aveline, Fountain at Marlieux, 1954; Achilles His Armour, 1955; (as Denis Delaney) Cat in Gloves, 1956; The Sword of Pleasure, 1957; (trans.) A. Devigny, Escape from Montluc, 1957; (trans.) Child of Our Time, 1958; (trans.) Mission Accomplished, 1958; (trans.) M.G. Landes, Antoine, 1959; Sir Thomas Browne, 1959; Kenneth Grahame, 1959; (trans.) J.Kessel, Lion, 1959; (trans.) M. de Saint-Pierre, Men of Letters, 1959; (trans.) P. Guimard, Lottery, 1959 as House of Happiness, 1960; Essays in Antiquity, 1960; (trans.) G. Poazzini, Children of Lilith, 1960; John Skelton, 1960; (trans.) G. Rab, Journey into the Blue, 1960; (trans.) Z. Oldenbourg, Destiny of Fire, 1961; (trans.) Z. Oldenbourg, Massacre at Montsegur: A History of the Albigensian Crusade, 1961; (trans.) S. de Beauvoir, The Prime of Life, 1962; Aspects of the Historical Novel, 1962; (trans.) S. de Beauvoir and G. Hamili, Djamila Boupacha, 1962; Habeas Corpus (short stories), 1963; World of William Golding, 1963; (trans.) S.Turno, Diamond River, 1963; Look at the Romans, 1963; The Laughter of Aphrodite, 1965; (trans. and intro.) Juvenal: The Sixteen Satires, 1967, 3rd ed., 1998; (trans.) R. Christophe, Danton, 1967; Alexander the Great, 1970; Xerxes at Salamis, 1970; The Year of Salamis, 480-479 BC, 1970 as The Greco-Persian Wars, 1996; Armada from Athens, 1971; The Shadow of the Parthenon, 1972; The Parthenon, 1973; A Concise History of Ancient Greece in US as Ancient Greece, 1973; Alexander of Macedon 356-323 BC, 1974, rev. ed., 1991; (trans. and intro.) Ovid, The Erotic Poems, 1982; Beyond the Wild Wood: The World of Kenneth Grahame, 1983; (ed. and intro.) Wind in the Willows, 1983; Classical Bearings, 1989; Alexander to Actium, 1990, rev. ed., 1993; (trans.) Y. Ritsos, The Fourth Dimension, 1993; (trans. and intro.) Ovid, The Poems of Exile, 1994; (trans. and intro.) A. Rhodios, The Argonautika, 1997; (trans. and intro.) The Argonautika: The Story of Jason and the Quest for the Golden Fleece, 1997; From Ikaria to the Stars, 2004; (trans. and intro.) The Poems of Catullus, 2005; (trans. and intro.) D. Siculus, Diodorus Siculus, Books 11-12.37.1: Greek History 480-431 B.C., The Alternative Version, 2006; The Hellenistic Age: A Short History, 2007; (trans.) E. Sotiropoulos, Zigzag through the Bitter-Orange Trees, 2007; (trans. and Intro.) D. Siculus, Persian Wars to the Fall of Athens: Books 11-14.34 (480-401 BCE), 2009. **Address:** Department of Classics, College of Arts and Sciences, University of Iowa, 210 Jefferson Bldg., Iowa City, TX 52242, U.S.A. **Online address:** peter-green-1@uiowa.edu

GREEN, Richard. British/American (born United States), b. 1936. **Genres:** Law, Psychiatry, Sex. **Career:** Imperial College School of Medicine, Charing Cross Hospital, research director, consultant psychiatrist, head, director of research, Gender Identity Clinic, Department of Psychiatry, visiting professor, honorary professor of psychiatry; University of California, Neuropsychiatric Institute, professor of psychiatry, professor emeritus of psychiatry, Law School, professor of law in residence; University of Cambridge, Faculty of Law, affiliated lecturer; State University of New York, professor of psychiatry and psychology; Archives of Sexual Behavior, founding editor, editor, 1971-2001; International Academy of Sex Research, founding president, 1975; Royal College of Psychiatrists, fellow, 1994-; Harry Benjamin International Gender Dysphoria Association, president, 1997-99; Imperial College, honorary professor. Writer. **Publications:** Sexual Identity Conflict in Children

and Adults, 1974; (with G. Wagner) Impotence: Physiological, Psychological, Surgical Diagnosis and Treatment, 1981; The Sissy Boy Syndrome and the Development of Homosexuality, 1987; Sexual Science and the Law, 1992; (with L.A.D. Walker) Y-O-U and the I-O-A Way, 1998. EDITOR: (with J. Money) Transsexualism and Sex Reassignment, 1969; Human Sexuality: A Health Practitioner's Text, 1974, 2nd ed., 1979; (with E.A. Rubinstein and E. Brecher) New Directions in Sex Research, 1976; (with J. Wiener) Methodology in Sex Research, 1980; (with D. West) Sociolegal Control of Homosexuality: A Multi-Nation Comparison, 1997. Contributor to books. **Address:** Gender Identity Clinic, Charing Cross Hospital, Claybrook Ctr., London, GL W6 8 LN, England. **Online address:** richard.green@imperial.ac.uk

GREEN, Ricky K(enneth). American (born United States), b. 1958. **Genres:** Politics/Government, Ethics, Philosophy, Social Sciences, Young Adult Nonfiction, Race Relations. **Career:** University of California, lecturer in political science, 1998; California State University, Department of Ethnic Studies, assistant professor of ethnic studies and government, 1998-, associate professor. Writer. **Publications:** Democratic Virtue in the Trial and Death of Socrates: Resistance to Imperialism in Classical Athens, 2000; (co-ed.) Ethnic America, 2003; Voices in Black Political Thought, 2005; Black Pluralism, forthcoming. **Address:** Department of Ethnic Studies, California State University, 562A Amador Hall, 6000 J St., Sacramento, CA 95819-6013, U.S.A. **Online address:** greenr@csus.edu

GREEN, Risa. American (born United States) **Genres:** Novels, Novellas/Short Stories, Science Fiction/Fantasy. **Career:** Milken Community High School, co-director of college counseling. Writer and attorney. **Publications:** Notes from the Underbelly, 2005; Tales from the Crib, 2006; The Carpenter Girls. **Address:** c/o Author Mail, NAL/Penguin Putnam, 375 Hudson St., New York, NY 10014, U.S.A.

GREEN, Roger. See GREEN, R. P. H.

GREEN, R. P. H. (Roger Green). British (born England), b. 1943. **Genres:** Literary Criticism And History, Theology/Religion, Humanities, Classics. **Career:** University of St. Andrews, lecturer, senior lecturer, 1967-95, reader in Latin and chair of department, 1992-95; University of Glasgow, professor of humanity, 1995-2008, emeritus professor and honorary professorial research fellow in classics, 2008-. Writer. **Publications:** The Poetry of Paulinus of Nola: A Study of his Latinity, 1971; Seven Versions of Carolingian Pastoral, 1980; (ed. and intro.) The Works of Ausonius, 1991; Augustine, De Doctrina Christiana, 1995; (trans. and intro.) Augustine, On Christian Teaching, 1999; Ausonii Opera, 1999; Latin Epics of the New Testament: Juvencus, Sedulius, Arator, 2006; (ed. with P.J. Ford) George Buchanan, Poet and Dramatist, 2009; George Buchanan, Poetic Paraphrase of the Psalms, 2011. **Address:** Classics, School of Humanities, University of Glasgow, 65 Oakfield Ave., Glasgow, G12 8QQ, Scotland. **Online address:** r.green@classics.arts.gla.ac.uk

GREEN, Scott E. American (born United States), b. 1951. **Genres:** Science Fiction/Fantasy, Business/Trade/Industry, History, Documentaries/Reportage, Literary Criticism And History. **Career:** Antique trader, correspondent; Atlantic Flyer (general aviation tabloid), correspondent; New England Entertainment Digest, Rising Star (newsletter), editor and publisher; Starline, contributor; Southern New Hampshire Services, board director; National Writers Union, vice-president. Science Fiction Poetry Association, president; Small Press Writers and Artists Organization, vice president. Journalist. **Publications:** Private Worlds (poems), 1983; Baby Sale at the 7-11 (poems), 1984; Contemporary Science Fiction, Fantasy, and Horror Poetry: A Resource Guide and Biographical Directory, 1989; A Directory of Depositories of Family History in New Hampshire, 1995; Isaac Asimov: An Annotated Bibliography, 1995. **Address:** 70 W River Dr., Apt. 4, Manchester, NH 03104-1919, U.S.A. **Online address:** sgreen@grolen.com

GREEN, Sharony Andrews. American (born United States), b. 1967?. **Genres:** Biography, Autobiography/Memoirs, Music, Literary Criticism And History. **Career:** Miami Herald, staff, 1984-, journalist; Detroit Free Press, reporter and assistant national editor, through 1997; visual artist. **Publications:** Cuttin' the Rug under the Moonlit Sky: Stories and Drawings about a Bunch of Women Named Mae, 1997; Grant Green: Rediscovering the Forgotten Genius of Jazz Guitar, 1999. Contributor to periodicals. **Address:** Doubleday, 1540 Broadway, New York, NY 10036, U.S.A. **Online address:** sharonee@aol.com

GREEN, Simon R(ichard). British (born England), b. 1955. **Genres:** Novels, Sciences. **Career:** Writer. **Publications:** FOREST KINGDOM SERIES: Blue Moon Rising, 1991; Blood and Honour, 1992; Down Among the Dead Men, 1993. TWILIGHT OF THE EMPIRE SERIES: Mistworld, 1992; Ghostworld, 1993; Hellworld, 1993; Twilight of the Empire, 1997; Deathstalker Prelude, 1998. NOVELS: Kevin Costner is Robin Hood, Prince of Thieves, 1991; Shadows Fall, 1994; Drinking Midnight Wine, 2001. DEATHSTALKER SERIES: Deathstalker: Being the First Part of the Life and Times of Owen Deathstalker, 1995; Deathstalker Rebellion: Being the Second Part of the Life and Times of Owen Deathstalker, 1996; Deathstalker War, 1997; Deathstalker Honour: Being the Fourth Part of the Life and Times of Owen Deathstalker, 1998; Deathstalker Destiny: Being the Fifth and Last Part of the Life and Times of Owen Deathstalker, 1999; The Man Who Had Everything, 2002; Friends, Enemies and Allies, 2002; Under the Ashes, the City, 2002. DEATHSTALKER LEGACY SERIES: Deathstalker Legacy, 2002; Deathstalker Return, 2004; Deathstalker Coda, 2005. NIGHTSIDE SERIES: Something from the Nightside, 2003; Agents of Light and Darkness, 2003; Nightingale's Lament, 2004; Hex and the City, 2005; Paths Not Taken, 2005; Sharper Than A Serpent's Tooth, 2006; Hell to Pay, 2006; The Unnatural Inquirer, 2008; A Walk on the Nightside, 2006; Just Another Judgement Day, 2009; The Good, the Bad, and the Uncanny, 2010; A Hard Day's Knight, 2011; The Bride Wore Black Leather, 2012. SECRET HISTORIES: The Man With The Golden Torc, 2007; Daemons Are Forever, 2008; The Spy Who Haunted Me, 2009; From Hell with Love, 2010; For Heaven's Eyes Only, 2011; Live and Let Drood, 2012. NIGHTSIDE OMNIBUS: Into the Nightside, 2008; Haunting the Nightside, 2008; The Dark Heart of the Nightside, 2008. THE GHOSTFINDERS SERIES: Ghost of a Chance, 2010. OTHERS: Guard Against Dishonor, 1991; Beyond the Blue Moon, 2000. **Address:** 40 St. Laurence Rd., Bradford-on-Avon, Bradford-on-Avon, BA15 1JQ, England. **Online address:** info@simonrgreen.co.uk

GREEN, Stephen J(ohn). American (born United States), b. 1940. **Genres:** Education, Politics/Government, Military/Defense/Arms Control, Natural History. **Career:** Gaffin and Weiss (law firm), clerk, 1964; American Friends of the Middle East, assistant director of programs, 1965-67; United Nations Children's Fund (UNICEF), Area Office for the Philippines and Pacific Territories, assistant program and supply officer, 1967-69, Area Office for Ethiopia and Somalia, planning and program officer, 1973-74, Europe Office, assistant to the deputy director, 1974-75; Vermont Office on Aging, director, 1970-71; Vermont Department of Employment, chief of manpower support services, 1971-72; United Nations Association, National Policy Panel on International Disaster Relief, project director, 1976-77; United Nations Development Program, Office of Projects Execution in Chad, regional coordinator, 1978; writer, 1978-80, 1981-; Basswood Associates, president, 1979-80; World Food Programme, senior relief officer, 1990-94, senior evaluation officer, 1997-99, Russia Federation, coordinator, 2000; United Nations Department of Humanitarian Affairs, senior policy officer 1994-96, deputy head, civil affairs. Writer. **Publications:** Hospital, an Organizational Analysis, 1974; Acts of Nature, Acts of Man, 1977; International Disaster Relief: Toward a Responsive System, 1977; (ed. with L.H. Stephens) Disaster Assistance, Appraisal, Reform, and New Approaches, 1979; Taking Sides, 1984; Living by the Sword, 1988; Sexual Dead-End, 1992; Bahrain Seashells, 1994; Conservation of Natural Resources: Perspective of the American West, 1994. Contributor to periodicals. **Address:** c/o Carl Brandt, Brandt & Brandt Literary Agents Inc., 1501 Broadway, Ste. 2310, New York, NY 10036, U.S.A. **Online address:** sgreen@leg.state.vt.us

GREEN, Terence M(ichael). Canadian (born Canada), b. 1947. **Genres:** Novels, Novellas/Short Stories, Science Fiction/Fantasy, Young Adult Fiction. **Career:** East York Collegiate Institute, English teacher, 1968-99; Mohawk College, writer-in-residence, 2003-04; The University of Western Ontario, lecturer in creative writing, 2005-. Writer. **Publications:** SHORT STORIES: The Woman Who Is the Midnight Wind, 1987. NOVELS: Barking Dogs, 1988; Children of the Rainbow, 1992; Shadow of Ashland, 1996; Blue Limbo, 1997; A Witness to Life, 1999; St. Patrick's Bed, 2001; Sailing Time's Ocean, 2006. Works appear in anthologies. Contributor of articles to periodicals. **Address:** 154 Randolph Rd., Toronto, ON M4G 3S4, Canada. **Online address:** tmgreen@sympatico.ca

GREEN, Timothy. American (born United States), b. 1953. **Genres:** Young Adult Fiction, Novels, Illustrations, Mystery/Crime/Suspense. **Career:** Bureau of Indian Affairs, junior high school English teacher, 1989-; Denver School for Gifted and Talented Students, faculty. Writer. **Publications:**

SELF-ILLUSTRATED: Mystery of Navajo Moon, 1991; Mystery of Coyote Canyon, 1993. OTHERS: Twilight Boy, 1997; The Legend of Wingz, 2001; Matrix of Existence: A Commonsense Theory of Everything, 2007; Average Joe, 2008. Contributor to periodicals. **Address:** Northland Publishing, 2900 N Fort Valley Rd., PO Box 1389, Flagstaff, AZ 86002-1389, U.S.A.

GREEN, Timothy (S.). (Timothy (Seton) Green). British (born England), b. 1936. **Genres:** Money/Finance, Natural History, Travel/Exploration. **Career:** Horizon, London correspondent, 1959-62; American Heritage, London correspondent, 1959-62; Life, London correspondent, 1962-64; Illustrated London News, editor, 1964-66; Consolidated Gold Fields, consultant on gold markets, 1969-; Gold Fields Mineral Services (now GFMS), consultant. Woodrow Wilson visiting fellow. **Publications:** The World of Gold, 1968, rev. ed., 1993; The Smugglers: An Investigation into the World of the Contemporary Smuggler, 1969; Restless Spirit: Profiles in Adventure, 1970; Adventures: Four Profiles of Contemporary Travellers, 1970; The Universal Eye: The World of Television, 1972; World of Gold Today, 1973; How to Buy Gold, 1975; The Smuggling Business, 1977; The World of Diamonds, 1981; The New World of Gold: The Inside Story of the Mines, the Markets, the Politics, the Investors, 1982, rev. ed., 1984; (with M. Green) The Good Water Guide, 1985, rev. ed., 1994; The Prospect for Gold: The View to the Year 2000, 1987; The Gold Companion, 1991, rev. ed., 1997; (with D. Duval and R. Louthean) New Frontiers in Diamonds, 1996; The Millennium in Gold 1000-1999, 2000; The Millennium in Silver 1000-1999, 2000; The Ages of Gold, 2007. Contributor to periodicals. **Address:** GFMS Ltd., Hedges House, 153 - 155 Regent St., London, GL W1B 4JE, England.

GREEN, Timothy (Seton). See **GREEN, Timothy (S.).**

GREEN, Toby. British (born England), b. 1974?. **Genres:** Novels, Adult Non-fiction, History. **Career:** King's College London, Leverhulme early career fellow. Travel writer and historian. **Publications:** Saddled with Darwin: A Journey Through South America, 1999; Meeting the Invisible Man: Secrets and Magic in West Africa, 2001; Thomas More's Magician: A Novel Account of Utopia in Mexico, 2004; Inquisition: The Reign of Fear, 2009; Rise of the Trans-Atlantic Slave Trade in Western Africa, 1300-1589, 2012. Contributor to periodicals. **Address:** King's College London, Rm. S 3.08, Strand, London, GL WC2R 2LS, England. **Online address:** tobias.green@kcl.ac.uk

GREEN, Yakov. See **GREEN, Jeffrey M.**

GREENBERG, Allan. American/South African (born South Africa), b. 1938. **Genres:** Architecture. **Career:** Architect, 1965-; Connecticuts Chief Justice, architectural consultant, 1967-79; Allan Greenberg L.L.C., sole proprietor, 1972-; Yale University, School of Architecture, faculty, School of Law, professor; University of Pennsylvania, faculty; Columbia University, Deparrtment of Historic Preservation, faculty; University of Notre Dame, faculty. Writer. **Publications:** Courthouse Design: A Handbook for Judges and Court Administrators, 1975; Standards Relating to Architecture of Facilities, 1977; George Washington, Architect, 1999; The Architecture of Democracy: American Architecture and the Legacy of the Revolution, 2006; Lutyens and the Modern Movement, 2007. **Address:** Allan Greenberg Architect L.L.C., 1050 Thomas Jefferson St. NW, Ste. 2100, Washington, CT 20007-3800, U.S.A. **Online address:** info@allangreenberg.com

GREENBERG, Alvin. American (born United States), b. 1932. **Genres:** Songs/Lyrics And Libretti, Novels, Poetry, Novellas/Short Stories, Young Adult Fiction, Essays. **Career:** University of Kentucky, assistant professor of English, 1963-65; Macalester College, professor of English, 1965-99, department head, 1988-93; University of Kerala, Fulbright lecturer, 1966-67; National Endowment for the Arts, fellow, 1972, 1992. Writer. **Publications:** NOVELS: The Small Waves, 1965; Going Nowhere, 1971; The Invention of the West, 1976; Time Lapse: A Novels, 2003. POETRY: The Metaphysical Giraffe, 1968; The House of the Would-Be Gardener, 1972; Dark Lands: A Book of Poems, 1973; Metaform, 1975; In Direction, 1978; And Yet, 1981; Heavy Wings: A Poems, 1988; Why We Live with Animals: A Poems, 1990; Hurry Back: Poems, 2005. OPERA LIBRETTI: Horspfal, 1969; The Jealous Cellist, 1979; Apollonia's Circus, 1994. STORIES: The Discovery of America and Other Tales of Terror and Self-Exploration: Stories, 1980; Delta Q: Stories, 1983; The Man in the Cardboard Mask: Short Stories, 1985; How the Dead Live: Stories, 1998. ESSAYS: The Dog of Memory: A Family Album of Secrets and Silences, 2002. Contributor of articles to periodicals. **Address:** 1304 N 26th St., Boise, ID 83702, U.S.A. **Online address:** alvindg@cs.com

GREENBERG, Cheryl. American (born United States), b. 1958. **Genres:** History. **Career:** Trinity College, assistant professor of African American and twentieth-century American history, 1986-92, associate professor, 1992-2000, professor of history, 2000-06, Paul E. Raether distinguished professor of history, 2006-, American Studies Program, director, 1998-2000, 2011; Harvard University, Department of Afro-American Studies, visiting associate professor, 1996-97; University of Helsinki, Renvall Institute, bicentennial Fulbright distinguished chair in American studies, 2002-03, visiting professor, 2008; Nankai University, Institute of American History and Culture, Fulbright distinguished lecturer, 2010-11. Writer and historian. **Publications:** Or Does It Explode?: Black Harlem in the Great Depression, 1991, 2nd ed., 1997; (ed.) Circle of Trust: Remembering SNCC, 1997; Troubling the Waters: Black-Jewish Relations in the American Century, 2006; To Ask for an Equal Chance: African Americans in the Great Depression, 2009. **Address:** Department of History, Trinity College, 300 Summit St., Hartford, CT 06106, U.S.A. **Online address:** cheryl.greenberg@trincoll.edu

GREENBERG, Elinor Miller. American (born United States), b. 1932. **Genres:** Education, Human Relations/Parenting, Institutions/Organizations, Psychology, Self Help, Women's Studies And Issues, Autobiography/Memoirs, Essays, Essays. **Career:** Loretto Heights College, director of university without walls, 1971-79, assistant academic dean for adult education and public service, 1981-84, assistant, 1984-85; Council for Adult and Experimental Learning, regional manager and executive officer for mountains and plains region, 1979-91; Pathways to the Future, founding executive director, 1986-91, project leadership, executive director, 1986-; Women's Forum of Colorado, president, 1986; EMG and Associates, president and chief executive officer, 1991-; University of Maryland, Institute for Research on Adults in Higher Education, research associate, 1991; Colorado Mathematics, Science, and Technology Commission, co-chairman, 1992-; University of Memphis, Leadership Institute For Judicial Education, consultant, 2004-08; University of Colorado Health Science Center, Mountain and Plains Partnership (MAPP), educational innovator, theorist and writer. **Publications:** (With W.H. Bergquist and R.A. Gould) Designing Undergraduate Education, 1981; (co-author) Enhancing Leadership, 1989; Weaving: The Fabric of a Woman's Life, 1991; Journey for Justice, 1993; (with W.H. Bergquist and G.A. Klaum) In Our Fifties: Voices of Men and Women Reinventing Their Lives, 1993; (with M.S. Barber and M.B. Scott) The Parent's Guide to Food Allergies: Clear and Complete Advice from the Experts on Raising Your Food-Allergic Child, 2001; (with F.W. Whitney) A Time of Our Own: In Celebration of Women Over Sixty, 2008. EDITOR AND CONTRIBUTOR: (with K.M. O'Donnell and W.H. Bergquist) Educating Learners of All Ages, 1980; (co-ed.) New Partnerships: Higher Education and the Nonprofit Sector, 1982. Contributor to periodicals. **Address:** EMG and Associates, 6725 S Adams Way, Littleton, CO 80122, U.S.A. **Online address:** ellie.greenberg@ucdenver.edu

GREENBERG, Gerald S(tuart). American (born United States), b. 1946. **Genres:** Popular Culture, Bibliography, Librarianship, History, Language/Linguistics, Writing/Journalism. **Career:** New York City Public Schools, teacher, 1969-71; Ohio City Schools, teacher, 1971-84; Ohio State University, University Libraries, reference and bibliographic instruction librarian, 1987-2004, collection manager for physical education, 1997-2004, collection manager for library science, 2005, Information Services Department, head, 2004-06, collection manager for reference and physical education, 2004-06, Thompson Library, Sullivant Library, subject specialist for education, 2006-, acting collection manager for film studies, 2007-, professor; Kent State University, adjunct faculty, 2000-. Writer. **Publications:** Tabloid Journalism: An Annotated Bibliography of English-Language Sources, 1996; (ed.) Historical Encyclopedia of U.S. Independent Counsel Investigations, 2000; Poststructuralism and Communication: An Annotated Bibliography, 2005. Contributor to books and periodicals. **Address:** Sullivant Library, Ohio State University, 222D Thompson Library, 1858 Neil Ave. Mall, Columbus, OH 43210, U.S.A. **Online address:** greenberg.3@osu.edu

GREENBERG, Joanne. (Hannah Green). American (born United States), b. 1932. **Genres:** Novels, Novellas/Short Stories, Poetry, Children's Fiction. **Career:** Colorado School of Mines, adjunct professor of anthropology, 1983-, assistant professor of anthropology and creative writing, 1985-, distinguished lecturer. Writer. **Publications:** The King's Persons, 1963; (as Hannah Green) I Never Promised You a Rose Garden, 1964; The Monday Voices, 1965; Summering, 1966; In This Sign, 1970; Rites of Passage, 1971; (as Hannah Green) Dead of the House, 1972; Founder's Praise, 1976; High Crimes and Misdemeanours, 1979; A Season of Delight, 1981; The Far Side of Victory,

1983; (as Hannah Green) In the City of Paris, 1985; Simple Gifts, 1986; Age of Consent, 1987; Of Such Small Differences, 1988; With the Snow Queen (short stories), 1991; No Reck'ning Made, 1993; Where the Road Goes, 1998; (as Hannah Green) Little Saint, 2000; Season of delight, 2003; Appearances, 2006; Miri, Who Charms, 2009. Works appear in anthologies. **Address:** Colorado School of Mines, 1500 Illinois St., Golden, CO 80401, U.S.A. **Online address:** jgreenbe@mines.edu

GREENBERG, Karen. American (born United States), b. 1955. **Genres:** Young Adult Non-fiction. **Career:** New York University School of Law, Center on Law and Security, founder and executive director, 2003-; New York University, Department of European studies, faculty; Bard College, faculty. Writer and consultant. **Publications:** NONFICTION: (ed.) Al Qaeda Now: Understanding Today's Terrorists, 2005; (ed. with J.L. Dratel) The Torture Papers: The Road to Abu Ghraib, 2005; (ed.) The Torture Debate in America, 2006; (ed, with J.L. Dratel) The Enemy Combatant Papers: American Justice, the Courts and the War on Terror, 2008; The Least Worst Place: Guantanamo's First 100 Days, 2009. Contributor to newspapers and magazines. **Address:** Center on Law and Security, New York University School of Law, 110 W 3rd St., Ste. 224/5, New York, NY 10012, U.S.A. **Online address:** karen.greenberg@nyu.edu

GREENBERG, Martin. American (born United States), b. 1918. **Genres:** Literary Criticism And History, Translations. **Career:** Schocken Books, editor, 1946-49; Gnome Press, co-founder, 1948; Commentary (magazine), editor, 1953-60; The New School, lecturer, 1961-67; C.W. Post College, assistant professor, professor of English literature, 1963-88, professor emeritus, 1988-. **Publications:** The Terror of Art: Kafka and Modern Literature, 1968; The Hamlet Vocation of Coleridge and Wordsworth, 1986. TRANSLATOR: The Diaries of Franz Kafka 1914-23, 1948; Heinrich von Kleist, The Marquise of O- and Other Stories, 1960; Heinrich von Kleist, Five Plays, 1988; J.W. von Goethe, Faust, vol. I, 1992; J.W. von Goethe, Faust, vol. II, 1998; H.V. Kleist, Michael Kohlhaas, 2004. **Address:** C. W. Post College, Long Island University, 720 Northern Blvd., Greenvale, NY 11548, U.S.A.

GREENBERG, Mike. American (born United States), b. 1967. **Genres:** Novels, Autobiography/Memoirs. **Career:** WMAQ-Radio, sports anchor and reporter, 1989-92; WSCR Radio, reporter and talk show host, 1992-96; Copley News Service, sports columnist, 1993-95; Sports Channel, sports reporter, 1994-95; CLTV cable news network, sports anchor and reporter, 1995-96; ESPN, ESPN News, anchor, 1996-99, ESPN Radio, Mike and Mike in the Morning, co-host, 1999-. **Publications:** Why My Wife Thinks I'm an Idiot: Sports, Family, and the Pursuit of Sanity, 2006; Why My Wife Thinks I'm an Idiot: The Life and Times of a Sportscaster Dad, 2006; (with M. Golic and A. Chaikivsky) Mike and Mike's Rules for Sports and Life, 2010. **Address:** c/o Author Mail, Random House, 1745 Broadway, 3rd Fl., New York, NY 10019-4368, U.S.A. **Online address:** mikeandmike@espnradio.com

GREENBERG, Peter. American (born United States) **Genres:** Travel/Exploration. **Career:** National Geographic Traveler Magazine, travel editor and correspondent; Newsweek, correspondent; ABCs Good Morning America, travel correspondent, 1988-95; MSNBC.com, columnist and travel editor, 1995-2009; United Paramount Network News, travel editor; Avenues Magazine, contributing editor; KABC Radio, host; Columbia Broadcasting System News, travel editor; Mens Health magazine, contributing editor; Consumer News and Business Channel, creator, co-executive producer and host; Paramount Television, vice-president of television development. **Publications:** The Travel Detective: How to Get the Best Service and the Best Deals from Airlines, Hotels, Cruise Ships and Car Rental Agencies, 2001; The Travel Detective Flight Crew Confidential: People Who Fly for a Living Reveal Insider Secrets and Hidden Values in Cities and Airports around the World, 2002; Hotel Secrets from the Travel Detective: Insider Tips on Getting the Best Value, Service, and Security in Accommodations from Bed-and-Breakfasts to Five-Star Resorts, 2004; Real U Guide to Traveling On Your Own, 2004; Traveler's Diet: Eating Right and Staying Fit on the Road, 2006; Complete Travel Detective Bible: The Consummate Insider Tells You What You Need To Know In An Increasingly Complex World!, 2007; Don't Go There!: The Travel Detective's Essential Guide to the Must-Miss Places of the World, 2009; Tough times, Great Travels: the Travel Detective's Guide to Hidden Deals, Unadvertised Bargains and Great Experiences, 2009. **Address:** c/o Author Mail, Random House Publishing Group/Villard, 1745 Broadway, 18th Fl., New York, NY 10019, U.S.A. **Online address:** peter@petergreenberg.com

GREENBERG, Roger P(aul). American (born United States), b. 1941. **Genres:** Psychology, Sciences, Social Sciences. **Career:** Syracuse Veterans Administration Hospital, intern in clinical psychology, 1966-67; State University New York, Health Science Center, assistant professor, 1968-72, associate professor, 1972-78, professor of psychiatry, director of psychology internship training, 1978-, Division of Clinical Psychology, professor, head, 1993-; Upstate Medical University, distinguished teaching professor of psychiatry and behavioral Sciences. Writer. **Publications:** (With S. Fisher) The Scientific Credibility of Freud's Theories and Therapy, 1977, rev. ed., 1985; (with S. Fisher) Freud Scientifically Reappraised: Testing the Theories and Therapy, 1996. EDITOR: (with S. Fisher) The Scientific Evaluation of Freud's Theories and Therapy: A Book of Readings, 1978; (with S. Fisher) The Limits of Biological Treatments for Psychological Distress: Comparisons with Psychotherapy and Placebo, 1989; (with S. Fisher) From Placebo to Panacea: Putting Psychiatric Drugs to the Test, 1997; (with M.J. Dewan and B.N. Steenbarger) The Art and Science of Brief Psychotherapies: A Practioner's Guide, 2004. Contributor to periodicals. **Address:** Department of Psychiatry & Behavioral Sciences, Upstate Medical University, 312 Psychiatry And Behavioral Sciences Bldg., 713 Harrison St., Syracuse, NY 13210, U.S.A. **Online address:** greenber@upstate.edu

GREENBERGER, Evelyn Barish. See BARISH, Evelyn.

GREENE, Amy. American (born United States), b. 1975. **Genres:** Novels. **Career:** Writer. **Publications:** Bloodroot (novel), 2010. **Address:** Russellville, TN , U.S.A. **Online address:** amygreenebloodroot@gmail.com

GREENE, A. Wilson. American (born United States), b. 1949. **Genres:** Military/Defense/Arms Control, History, Social Sciences. **Career:** Association for the Preservation of Civil War Sites, president and chief executive officer, 1990-94; Pamplin Historical Park and National Museum of the Civil War Soldier, executive director, 1995-; Mary Washington College, faculty; Germanna Community College, faculty; St. Bernard Community College, faculty; Fredericksburg National Military Park, historian; Petersburg National Battlefield, historian. Writer. **Publications:** (With G.W. Gallagher) National Geographic Guide to the Civil War National Battlefield Parks, 1992; Whatever You Resolve to Be: Essays on Stonewall Jackson, 1992; The Second Battle of Manassas, 1995; Breaking the Backbone of the Rebellion: The Final Battles of the Petersburg Campaign, 2000, 2nd ed. as The Final Battles of the Petersburg Campaign: Breaking the Backbone of the Rebellion, 2008; Civil War Petersburg: Confederate City in the Crucible of War, 2006; Pamplin Historical Park and the National Museum of the Civil War Soldier: A Visitor's Guide, 2006. **Address:** Pamplin Historical Park, 6125 Boydton Plank Rd., Petersburg, VA 23803, U.S.A.

GREENE, Bette. American (born United States), b. 1934. **Genres:** Children's Fiction, Young Adult Fiction, Romance/Historical, Novels. **Career:** Hebrew Watchman, contributor and reporter, 1950-52; Memphis Commercial Appeal, reporter, 1950-52; United Press Intl., reporter, 1953-54; American Red Cross, public information officer, 1958-59; Boston State Psychiatric Hospital, information officer, 1959-61. Writer. **Publications:** Summer of My German Soldier, 1973; Philip Hall Likes Me, I Reckon Maybe, 1974, 2nd ed., 1989; Morning is a Long Time Coming, 1978; Beat The Turtle Drum, 1979; Bette Greene's Survival Kit: 303 Tips from One Writer to Another, 1980; Get on Out of Here, Philip Hall, 1981; Them That Glitter and Them That Don't, 1983; I've Already Forgotten Your Name, Philip Hall!, 1983; Drowning of Stephan Jones, 1991; Get On Out of Here Philip Hall, 1999. Contributor of articles to periodicals. **Address:** c/o Susan Schulman, Susan Schulman Literary Agency, 454 W 44th St., New York, NY 10036-5205, U.S.A.

GREENE, Bryan A. Canadian (born Canada), b. 1938. **Genres:** Biography, Autobiography/Memoirs. **Career:** Government of Newfoundland and Labrador Wilderness, field geologist, senior mapping geologist, director of the geological survey, 1970-96. Writer and geologist. **Publications:** (Ed. and intro. with R. Buchanan) The Woman Who Mapped Labrador: The Life and Expedition Diary of Mina Hubbard, 2005. **Address:** McGill-Queen's University Press, 1010 Sherbrooke W, Ste. 1720, Montreal, QC H3A 2R7, Canada. **Online address:** bgreene@nfld.com

GREENE, Constance C(larke). American (born United States), b. 1924. **Genres:** Novels, Novellas/Short Stories, Young Adult Fiction, Ghost Writer, Children's Fiction, Adult Non-fiction. **Career:** Associated Press, reporter, 1944-46; writer, 1968-. **Publications:** A Girl Called Al, 1969; Leo the Li-

oness, 1970; The Good-luck Bogie Hat, 1971; Unmaking of Rabbit, 1972; Isabelle the Itch, 1973; The Ears of Louis, 1974; I Know You, Al, 1975; Beat the Turtle Drum, 1976; Getting Nowhere, 1977; I and Sproggy, 1978; Your Old Pal, Al, 1979; Dotty's Suitcase, 1980; Double-Dare O'Toole, 1981; Al(exandra) the Great, 1982; Ask Anybody, 1983; Isabelle Shows Her Stuff, 1984; Star Shine, 1985; Other Plans (for adults), 1985; Just Plain Al, 1986; The Love Letters of J. Timothy Owen, 1986; Monday I Love You, 1988; Isabelle and Little Orphan Frannie, 1988; Al's Blind Date, 1989; Odds on Oliver, 1992; Nora: Maybe a Ghost Story, 1993. Contributor to periodicals. **Address:** Curtis Brown Ltd., 10 Astor Pl., New York, NY 10003, U.S.A.

GREENE, Don. American (born United States) **Genres:** Music, Psychology, Self Help. **Career:** Juilliard School of Music, faculty, 1998-; U.S. Olympic Diving Team, sports psychologist; World Championship Swimming Team, sports psychologist; Golf Digest Schools, sports psychologist; Vail Ski School, sports psychologist; New School Music Theater Program, faculty; New World Symphony, performance psychology coach. Writer. **Publications:** Audition Success: An Olympic Sports Psychologist Teaches Performing Artists How to Win, 2001; Fight Your Fear and Win: Seven Skills for Performing Your Best Under Pressure-At Work, in Sports, on Stage, 2001; Performance Success: Performing Your Best Under Pressure, 2002. **Address:** New World Symphony, 541 Lincoln Rd., Miami Beach, FL 33139, U.S.A. **Online address:** drdgreene@aol.com

GREENE, Douglas G. American (born United States), b. 1944. **Genres:** Mystery/Crime/Suspense, History, Bibliography, Biography, Novels. **Career:** University of Montana, instructor in history, 1970-71; Old Dominion University, professor, 1971-83, Institute for Humanities, director, 1983-99, professor of history, 1999-, Department of History, chair, 2010-; Crippen & Landru Books, publisher, 1994-. Writer. **Publications:** The Earl of Castlehaven's Memoirs of the Irish Wars, 1974; (with P.E. Hanff) Bibliographia Oziana, A Concise Bibliography of the Oz Books by L. Frank Baum and His Successors, 1976, rev. ed., 1988; (with M.P. Hearn) W.W. Denslow, 1976; John Dickson Carr: The Man Who Explained Miracles, 1995. EDITOR: Diaries of the Popish Plot: Being the Diaries of Israel Tonge, Sir Robert Southwell, John Joyne, Edmund Warcup, and Thomas Dangerfield: And Including Titus Oates's A True Narrative of the Horrid Plot (1679), 1977; (intro.) The Meditations of Lady Elizabeth Delaval: Written between 1662 and 1671, 1978; (and intro.) The Door to Doom and Other Detections, 1980; (and intro.) The Dead Sleep Lightly, 1983; (with J.E. Haff) The Wizard of Way-Up and Other Wonders, 1985; (with R.C.S. Adey) Death Locked In: An Anthology of Locked Room Stories, 1987, 2nd ed., 1994; (and intro.)The Collected Short Fiction of Ngaio Marsh, 1989; (and intro.) Merrivale, March and Murder, 1991; (and intro.) Fell and Foul Play, 1991; (and intro.) Toughboy and Sister, 1992; (and intro.) Detectionby Gaslight: Detection by Gaslight, 1997; (and intro.) The Detections of Miss Cusack, 1998; (and intro.) The Dead Hand and Other Uncollected Stories, 1999; (and intro.) Classic Mystery Stories, 1999; (intro.) Grand Guignol (in Japanese), 1999; The Romance of the Secret Service Fund, 2003; Sissajig and Other Surprises, 2003; The Adventures of Rogan Kincaid Omnibus, 2009; The Compleat Deteckative Cases of Philo Gubb Omnibus, 2010. **Address:** Department of History, Old Dominion University, 8000 Batten Arts & Letters, 5115 Hampton Blvd., Norfolk, VA 23508, U.S.A. **Online address:** dgreene@odu.edu

GREENE, Gayle. American (born United States), b. 1943. **Genres:** Literary Criticism And History, Women's Studies And Issues, Medicine/Health, Sports/Fitness, Biography. **Career:** Harper & Row Publishers, editorial assistant, 1967-68; Queens College of the City University of New York, lecturer, 1968-72; Brooklyn College of the City University of New York, lecturer, 1972-74; Scripps College, Department of English, assistant professor, associate professor, professor, faculty, 1974-, chair, 1979-80, director of humanities colloquium, 1976; University of California, Beatrice M. Bain visiting fellow, 1992-93. **Publications:** (Ed. with C.R.S. Lenz and C.T. Neely) The Woman's Part: Feminist Criticism of Shakespeare, 1980; (ed. with C. Kahn) Making a Difference: Feminist Literary Criticism, 1985; Changing the Story: Feminist Fiction and the Tradition, 1991; (ed. with C. Kahn) Changing Subjects: The Making of Feminist Literary Criticism, 1993; Doris Lessing: The Poetics of Change: The Fiction of Doris Lessing, 1994; The Woman Who Knew Too Much: Alice Stewart and the Secrets of Radiation, 1999; Insomniac, 2008; Missing Persons: A Silicon Valley Memoir, forthcoming; Sleep Savvy, forthcoming. Works appear in anthologies. **Address:** Department of English, Scripps College, 311 Balch Hall, 1030 Columbia Ave., Claremont, CA 91711-3948, U.S.A. **Online address:** gaylegreene@earthlink.net

GREENE, Harlan. American (born United States), b. 1953. **Genres:** Local History/Rural Topics, Gay And Lesbian Issues, Young Adult Fiction. **Career:** South Carolina Historical Society, archivist and assistant director, 1976-89; North Carolina Preservation Consortium, director, 1990-. Writer. **Publications:** Why We Never Danced the Charleston, 1984; Charleston: City of Memory, 1987; What the Dead Remember, 1991; Mr. Skylark: John Bennett and The Charleston Renaissance, 2001; (ed. with J. Hutchisson) Renaissance in Charleston: Art and Life in the Carolina Low Country, 1900-1940, 2003; (with H.S. Hutchins, Jr. and B.E. Hutchins) Slave Badges and the Slave-Hire System in Charleston, South Carolina, 1783-1865, 2004; (contrib.) Southern Sisters: The Art of Charleston and Savannah, 2004; The German Officer's Boy, 2005; (comp.) Explorations in Charleston's Jewish History, 2005. **Address:** 133 1/2 Wintworth St., Charleston, SC 29401, U.S.A.

GREENE, Jacqueline Dembar. American (born United States), b. 1946. **Genres:** Children's Fiction, Children's Non-fiction, History, Picture/Board Books, Young Adult Fiction, Animals/Pets. **Career:** French teacher, 1967-69; reporter, columnist and feature writer, 1971-80; author, 1980-. **Publications:** A Classroom Hanukah, 1980; The Hanukah Tooth, 1981; Butchers and Bakers, Rabbis and Kings, 1984; The Leveller, 1984; Nathan's Hanukkah Bargain, 1984; Out of Many Waters, 1988; The Maya, 1992; What His Father Did, 1992; The Chippewa, 1993; One Foot Ashore, 1994; Manabozho's Gifts, 1994; Marie: Mystery at the Paris Ballet, 1997; Marie: Summer in the Country, 1997; The Tohono O'odham (Papago), 1998; Powwow: A Good Day to Dance, 1998; Slavery in Ancient Egypt and Mesopotamia, 2000; Slavery in Ancient Greece and Rome, 2000; The Emperor's Teacup, 2002; 2001 World Trade Center Attack, 2007; Triangle Shirtwaist Factory Fire, 2007; Grizzly Bears: Saving the Silvertip, 2008; Secret Shofar of Barcelona, 2009; Rebecca to the Rescue, 2009; Rebecca and the Movies, 2009; Rebecca and Ana, 2009; Changes for Rebecca, 2009; Meet Rebecca: An American Girl, 2009; Candlelight for Rebecca, 2009; Secrets at Camp Nokomis: A Rebecca Mystery, 2010. Contributor to periodicals. Works appear in anthologies. **Address:** 5 Astra, Wayland, MA 01778, U.S.A. **Online address:** mailbox@jdgbooks.com

GREENE, Jennifer. Also writes as Jessica Massey, Jeanne Grant. American (born United States), b. 1948?. **Genres:** Romance/Historical. **Career:** Writer, 1980-. Educator. **Publications:** AS JEANNE GRANT: Man from Tennessee, 1983; A Daring Proposition, 1983; Kisses from Heaven, 1984; Sunburst, 1984; Wintergreen, 1984; Trouble in Paradise, 1984; Silver and Spice, 1984; Conquer the Memories, 1984; Cupid's Confederates, 1984; Ain't Misbehaving, 1985; Can't Say No, 1985; Pink Satin, 1985; Sweets to the Sweet, 1986; No More Mr. Nice Guy, 1986; Tender Loving Care, 1987. OTHERS: (as Jessica Massey) Stormy Surrender, 1984; Madam's Room, 1986; Body and Soul, 1986; Foolish Pleasure, 1986; Lady Be Good, 1987; Secrets, 1987; Dear Reader, 1987; Minx, 1987; The Castle Keep, 1988; Lady of the Island, 1988; Love Potion, 1988; Night of the Hunter, 1989; Dancing in the Dark, 1989; Devil's Night, 1989; Broken Blossom, 1990; (with K. Keast and E. Richards) Birds, Bees and Babies, 1990; Heat Wave, 1990; Slow Dance, 1990; Falconer, 1991; Night Light, 1991; It Had to Be You, 1992; Pink Topaz, 1992; Just Like Old Times, 1992; Quicksand, 1993; A Groom for Red Riding Hood, 1994; Bewitched, 1994; Bothered, 1994; Bewildered, 1995; Arizona Heat, 1995; Single Dad Seeks, 1995; Riley's Baby, 1996; Bachelor Mom, 1997; The Unwilling Bride, 1996; Nobody's Princess, 1997; 200 Per Cent Wife, 1997; The Baby Chase, 1997; A Baby in His In-box, 1998; Her Holiday Secret, 1998; The Honour-Bound Groom, 1998; Kiss Your Prince Charming, 1999; You Belong to Me, 2000; Prince Charming's Child, 1999; Millionaire MD, 2001; Rock Solid, 2001; The Woman Most Likely To ..., 2002; Where is He Now?, 2003; Wild in the Field, 2003; Wild in the Moment, 2004; Wild in the Moonlight, 2004; Hot to the Touch, 2005; Lucky, 2005; Blame It on Chocolate, 2006; The Soon-to-Be-Disinherited Wife, 2006; Sparkle, 2006; Blame It on Cupid, 2007; (with S. Mittman and K. Austin) Summer Dreams, 2007; Born in My Heart, 2007; Blame It on Paris, 2008; Blame It On The Blizzard, 2009; Secretive Stranger, 2010; Mesmerizing Strange, 2010; Irresistible Stranger, 2010; The Billionaire's Handler, 2010; (with M. Lovelace and C. Myers) Baby, it's Cold Outside, 2010. **Address:** Harlequin.com, PO Box 5190, Buffalo, NY 14240-5190, U.S.A. **Online address:** jennifer@jennifergreene.com

GREENE, Jody. American (born United States) **Genres:** Social Sciences, History, Literary Criticism And History. **Career:** National Outdoor Leadership School, instructor; University of California, Department of Literature and Feminist Studies, assistant professor, associate professor. Writer. **Publications:** (Ed.) The Work of Friendship: In Memoriam: Alan Bray, 2004; The Trouble with Ownership: Literary Property and Authorial Liability in

England, 1660-1730, 2005. Contributor to books and journals. **Address:** Department of Literature and Feminist Studies, University of California, 635 Humanities 1, 1156 High St., Santa Cruz, CA 95064, U.S.A. **Online address:** jgreene@ucsc.edu

GREENE, Jonathan (Edward). American (born United States), b. 1943. **Genres:** Poetry, Essays. **Career:** Gnomon Press, publisher, 1965-; University Press of Kentucky, production manager and designer, 1967-75. Writer. **Publications:** The Reckoning, 1966; Instance, 1968; The Lapidary, 1969; A 17th Century Garner, 1969; An Unspoken Complaint, 1970; (trans.) A. Rimbaud, The Poor in Church, 1973; Scaling the Walls, 1974; Glossary of the Everyday, 1974; (ed.) Kentucky Renaissance: An Anthology of Contemporary Writing, 1976; Peripatetics, 1978; (ed.) Jonathan Williams: A 50th Birthday Celebration, 1979; Once a Kingdom Again, 1979; Quiet Goods, 1980; Idylls, 1983; Small Change for the Long Haul, 1984; Trickster Tales, 1985; Les Chambres des Poetes, 1990; The Robert C. May Photography Collection: With Essays, 1995; The Man Came to Haul Stone, 1995; Of Moment, 1998; Inventions of Necessity: Selected Poems, 1998; Incidents of Travel in Japan, 1999; A Little Ink in the Paper Sea, 2001; Book of Correspondences, 2002; Watching Dewdrops Fall, 2003; Hummingbird's Water Trough, 2003; Fault Lines, 2004; On the Banks of Monks Pond: The Thomas Merton/Jonathan Greene Correspondence, 2004; The Death of a Kentucky Coffee Tree and Other Poems, 2006; The Hut Poems, 2006; Gists, Orts, Shards, A Commonplace Book, 2006; Hut Poems, 2007; Heart Matters, 2008; Feed the Lotus, 2009; Distillations and Siphonings, 2010; Gists, Orts, Shards II, 2011. **Address:** PO Box 475, Frankfort, KY 40602-0475, U.S.A. **Online address:** jgnomon@bellsouth.net

GREENE, Julie. American (born United States), b. 1956. **Genres:** Politics/Government, History. **Career:** University of Maryland, professor; Labor: Studies in Working-class History of the Americas, founding reviews editor, 2004, editor. **Publications:** (Ed. with E. Arnesen and B. Laurie) Labor Histories: Class, Politics, and the Working Class Experience, 1998; Pure and Simple Politics: The American Federation of Labor and Political Activism, 1881-1917, 1998; The Canal Builders: Making America's Empire at the Panama Canal, 2009. Contributor to periodicals. **Address:** Department of History, University of Maryland, 2115 Francis Scott Key, College Park, MD 20742, U.S.A. **Online address:** jmg@umd.edu

GREENE, Meg. See MALVASI, Meg Greene.

GREENE, Melissa Fay. American (born United States), b. 1952. **Genres:** Adult Non-fiction, Medicine/Health, Sports/Fitness, Social Sciences, History, Autobiography/Memoirs, Military/Defense/Arms Control, Race Relations, Race Relations. **Career:** Paralegal for General Assistance Legal Services Program, 1975-79, 1980-81. Writer. **Publications:** Praying for Sheetrock, 1991; The Temple Bombing, 1996; Last Man Out, 2003; There is No Me Without You: One Woman's Odyssey to Rescue Africa's Children, 2006; No Biking In The House Without A Helmet, 2011. Contributor of articles to magazines and newspapers. **Address:** 1708 E Clifton Rd. NE, Atlanta, GA 30307-1252, U.S.A. **Online address:** mfgreene1@aol.com

GREENE, Nathanael. American (born United States), b. 1935. **Genres:** History, Politics/Government, Social Commentary. **Career:** Wesleyan University, Department of History, instructor, 1963-64, assistant professor, 1964-68, associate professor, 1968-74, professor, 1974-, chair of department, 1973-78. Writer. **Publications:** Fascism: An Anthology, 1968; Crisis and Decline: The French Socialist Party in the Popular Front Era, 1969; From Versailles to Vichy: The Third French Republic, 1919-1940, 1970; (ed. and intro.) European Socialism since World War II, 1971. **Address:** Department of History, Wesleyan University, Public Affairs Ctr. 215, Middletown, CT 06457, U.S.A. **Online address:** ngreene@wesleyan.edu

GREENE, Rhonda Gowler. American (born United States), b. 1955. **Genres:** Children's Fiction, Young Adult Fiction, Young Adult Non-fiction, Reference, Picture/Board Books. **Career:** Goodridge Elementary School, learning disabilities teacher, 1977-79; Covenant Nursery School, teacher, 1990-93. Writer, 1985-. **Publications:** Barnyard Song, 1997; When a Line Bends Shape Begins, 1997; The Stable Where Jesus Was Born, 1999; Jamboree Day, 2001; Eek! Creak! Snicker, Sneak, 2002; The Beautiful World That God Made, 2002; The Very First Thanksgiving Day, 2002; At Grandma's, 2003; This Is the Teacher, 2004; Santa's Stuck, 2004; Firebears: The Rescue Team, 2005; Sing Praise, 2006; Mail Monkeys, 2006, Noah and the Mighty Ark, 2007; One Lost Sheep, 2007; Jonah and the Great Big Fish, 2007, Zacchaeus and the Happy Day, 2007; Daddy is a Cozy Hug, 2009; Mommy is a Soft, Warm Kiss, 2010. Contributor to magazines. **Address:** Marilyn E. Marlow, Curtis Brown Ltd., 10 Astor Pl., Fl. 3, New York, NY 10003-6935, U.S.A. **Online address:** rhonda@rhondagowlergreene.com

GREENE, Ross W. American (born United States), b. 1957. **Genres:** Psychology, Human Relations/Parenting. **Career:** Cambridge Health Alliance, staff psychologist; Tufts University, Department of Education, senior lecturer of school psychology program; Lives in the Balance, founder and director; Massachusetts General Hospital, Collaborative Problem Solving Institute, Department of Psychiatry, director; Harvard Medical School, Department of Psychiatry, associate clinical professor of psychology; University of Massachusetts, Medical Center, assistant professor in psychiatry and pediatrics; Virginia Tech University, visiting assistant professor of clinical psychology, Department of Psychology, adjunct associate professor. Writer. **Publications:** The Explosive Child: A New Approach for Understanding and Parenting Easily Frustrated, Chronically Inflexible Children, 1998; (with R.R. Abidin and T.R. Konold) ITS, Index of Teaching Stress: Professional Manual, 2004; (with J.S. Ablon) Treating Explosive Kids: The Collaborative Problem-solving Approach, 2006; Lost at School: Why Our Kids with Behavioral Challenges Are Falling through the Cracks and How We Can Help Them, 2008. Contributor to journals. **Address:** Department of Psychiatry, Collaborative Problem Solving Institute, Massachusetts General Hospital, 313 Washington St., Ste. 402, Newton, MA 02458, U.S.A. **Online address:** drrossgreene@gmail.com

GREENE, Sheldon L. American (born United States), b. 1934. **Genres:** Novels, Mystery/Crime/Suspense, Young Adult Fiction. **Career:** Court of Common Pleas, law clerk; Insurance of the State of Ohio, warden; Pennsylvania Life Insurance Co., house counsel; Greene & Allison, co-partner; Oak Creek Energy Systems Inc., executive vice president and director; California Rural Legal Assistance, general counsel. Writer. **Publications:** Two Lost Tribes, 1978. NOVELS: Lost and Found, 1980; Burnt Umber: A Novel, 2001; Prodigal Sons, 2009. Contributor of law review articles. **Address:** 1195 Sterling Ave., Berkeley, CA 94708-1756, U.S.A. **Online address:** sheldon7@pacbell.net

GREENE, Thomas Christopher. American (born United States), b. 1968. **Genres:** Novels. **Career:** Vermont College of Fine Arts, staff, senior staff, founding president; Norwich University, director of public relations. Writer. **Publications:** NOVELS: Mirror Lake, 2003; After the Rain, 2004; I'll Never Be Long Gone, 2005; Envious Moon, 2007; Acrimony, forthcoming; The Reluctant Thief, forthcoming. **Address:** c/o Nick Ellison, Nicholas Ellison Inc., 55 5th Ave., New York, NY 10003, U.S.A. **Online address:** thomaschristophergreene@comcast.net

GREENE, Victor. (Victor R. Greene). American (born United States), b. 1933. **Genres:** Cultural/Ethnic Topics, Music, History. **Career:** Kansas State University, assistant professor, 1963-68, associate professor, 1968-71; University of Wisconsin, associate professor of history, 1971-77, professor of history, 1977-, now professor emeritus; Immigration and Ethnic History Society, president, 1985-88. Writer. **Publications:** Slavic Community on Strike: Immigrant Labor in Pennsylvania Anthracite, 1968; For God and Country: The Rise of Polish and Lithuanian Ethnic Consciousness in America, 1860-1910, 1975; American Immigrant Leaders, 1800-1910: Marginality and Identity, 1987; A Passion for Polka: Old-Time Ethnic Music in America, 1992; A Singing Ambivalence: American Immigrants Between Old World and New, 1830-1930, 2004; (ed. with M. Anderson) Perspectives on Milwaukee's Past, 2009. **Address:** Department of History, University of Wisconsin, 383 Holton Hall, 2200 E Kenwood Blvd., PO Box 413, Milwaukee, WI 53201-0413, U.S.A. **Online address:** vicgre@uwm.edu

GREENE, Victor R. See **GREENE, Victor.**

GREENER, Michael John. Welsh (born Wales), b. 1931. **Genres:** Business/Trade/Industry, Law, Administration/Management, Economics. **Career:** Deloitte, Plender, Griffiths & Co., senior audit clerk, 1953-56; Institute Chartered Accountants, associate, 1957; Western Mail and Echo Ltd., assistant, 1957-60; College of Commerce, assistant lecturer, lecturer in accounting, 1960-63; Greener & Sons Ltd., director and secretary, 1961-, managing director, 1972-2001; Barry Art & Book Centre, proprietor, 1973-. Writer. **Publications:** Between the Lines of the Balance Sheet: The Plain Man's Guide to Published Accounts, 1968, 2nd ed., 1980; Problems for Discussion on Mercantile Law, 1968; Penguin Dictionary of Commerce, 1971. **Address:** 33 Glan Hafren, Maes-Y-Coed, Barry, SG CF62 6TA, Wales.

GREENFELD, Liah. American (born United States), b. 1954. **Genres:** Social Sciences, Sociology, History, Humanities. **Career:** Hebrew University, Department of Sociology, teaching assistant, 1976-81, graduate teaching and research assistant and instructor, 1979-82, School for Overseas Students, lecturer, 1981-82; University of Chicago, visiting lecturer, 1982-83; Rensselaer Polytechnic Institute, Department of Science and Technology Studies, visiting assistant professor of sociology, 1984-85; Harvard University, Russian Research Center, post-doctoral fellow, 1984-85, fellow, 1985-97, assistant professor, 1985-89, associate professor of sociology and social studies, 1989-94, John L. Loeb associate professor of social sciences, 1989-92; Massachusetts Institute of Technology, visiting associate professor, 1992-93; Boston University, fellow of the university professors, 1994-, university professor and professor of sociology, political science and anthropology 2009-, Institute for the Advancement of the Social Sciences, director; Woodrow Wilson International Center for Scholars, fellow, 1998; University of Fribourg, Institute of Federalism, Law School, visiting professor, 2004-05; St. George University, visiting professor, 2009. Writer. **Publications:** (Ed. with M. Martin) Center: Ideas and Institutions, 1988; Different Worlds: A Sociological Study of Taste, Choice, and Success in Art, 1989; Nationalism: Five Roads to Modernity, 1992; Nationalisme i Modernitat, 1999; The Spirit of Capitalism: Nationalism and Economic Growth, 2001; Nationalism and the Mind: Essays on Modern Culture, 2006. Contributor to journals. **Address:** Boston University, UNI 604, 745 Commonwealth Ave., Boston, MA 02215, U.S.A. **Online address:** lvg@bu.edu

GREENFIELD, Darby. See **WARD, Philip.**

GREENFIELD, Jeanette. Australian (born Australia) **Genres:** Area Studies, Cultural/Ethnic Topics, Environmental Sciences/Ecology, Law, Natural History. **Career:** Monash University, Law School, teaching fellow, 1970-71. Writer. **Publications:** China and the Law of the Sea, Air, and Environment, 1979; The Return of Cultural Treasures, 1989, 3rd ed., 2007; China's Practice in the Law of the Sea, 1992. Contributor to periodicals. **Address:** 59 River Ct., Upper Ground, London, GL SE1 9PB, England.

GREENHALGH, Paul. British (born England), b. 1955. **Genres:** Art/Art History, Area Studies, Crafts. **Career:** Cardiff College of Art and Design, lecturer in the history and theory of art and design, 1980-87; Victoria and Albert Museum, tutor, head of research, 1988-2000; Royal College of Art, tutor, 1988-90; Camberwell College of Arts, head of art history, 1992-94; Nova Scotia College of Art and Design, president, 2001-10, Corcoran director. Writer. **Publications:** Ephemeral Vistas: The Expositions Universelles, Great Exhibitions and World's Fairs, 1851-1939, 1988; (comp. and intro.) Quotations on Design and Material Culture in US as Quotations and Sources on Design and the Decorative Arts, 1993; The Essence of Art Nouveau, 2000; Essential Art Nouveau, 2000; Looking Forward: New Views of the Craft Object, 2000; The Modern Ideal: The Rise and Collapse of Idealism in the Visual Arts from the Enlightenment to Postmodernism, 2005; (co-author) Essential Modernism, 2007; (co-author) Turner to Cezanne: Masterpieces from the Davies Collection, National Museum Wales, 2009; Fair World: A History of World's Fairs and Expositions, From London to Shanghai, 1851-2010, 2011. EDITOR: Modernism in Design, 1990; Art Nouveau: 1890-1914, 2000; The Persistence of Craft: The Applied Arts Today, 2003. Contributor to magazines. **Address:** Papadakis Publisher, Kimber Studio, Winterbourne, BR RG20 8AN, England.

GREENHALGH, Susan. American (born United States), b. 1949?. **Genres:** Adult Non-fiction, International Relations/Current Affairs, Medicine/Health. **Career:** University of California, Chinese Studies Center, postdoctoral fellow, 1982-83, associate professor, 1994-2001, professor of anthropology, 2001-, faculty-in-residence, 2005-06; Population Council, Center for Policy Studies, Berelson fellow, 1983-84, staff research associate, 1984-86, research associate, 1987-89, Research Division, senior research associate, 1990-94; Princeton University, visiting instructor, 1993, 1994; Open Society Institute, individual project fellow. Writer and anthropologist. **Publications:** (Ed. with E.A. Winckler) Contending Approaches to the Political Economy of Taiwan, 1988; (ed.) Situating Fertility: Anthropology and Demographic Inquiry, 1995; Under the Medical Gaze: Facts and Fictions of Chronic Pain, 2001; (with E.A. Winckler) Governing China's Population: From Leninist to Neoliberal Biopolitics, 2005; Just One Child: Science and Policy in Deng's China, 2008; Cultivating Global Citizens: Population in the Rise of China, 2010. Contributor to periodicals and journals. **Address:** Department of Anthropology, University of California, 3308 Social and Behavioral Sciences Gateway, Irvine, CA 92697, U.S.A. **Online address:** smgreenh@uci.edu

GREENHALL, Ken. (Jessica Hamilton). American (born United States), b. 1928. **Genres:** Novels, Young Adult Fiction, Horror. **Career:** Writer. **Publications:** Childgrave, 1982; The Companion, 1988; Death Chain, 1991; Lenoir: A Novel, 1998; Rumors of Sanctity, forthcoming. AS JESSICA HAMILTON: Elizabeth, 1976; Baxter, 1977. **Address:** c/o Susan Llewellyn, 310 W 85th St., New York, NY 10024, U.S.A. **Online address:** kgreenhall@hotmail.com

GREENHILL, Pauline. Canadian (born Canada), b. 1955. **Genres:** Anthropology/Ethnology, Cultural/Ethnic Topics, Mythology/Folklore, Women's Studies And Issues. **Career:** University of Waterloo, assistant professor, 1986-90, adjunct professor of anthropology, 1987-91, adjunct professor of English, 1989, associate professor of Canadian studies, 1990-91; St. Pauls United College, dean of residence, 1986-90; University of Winnipeg, Institute for Women's and Gender Studies, associate professor, 1991-96, coordinator, 1992-94, professor of women's and gender studies, 1996-98, 1999-, acting chair, associate professor of anthropology, 1995-97, professor of anthropology, 1996-98; University of Manitoba, adjunct faculty, 1994-99; Memorial University of Newfoundland, visiting professor of folklore, 1998; University of Guelph, associated graduate faculty in sociology and anthropology, 2001-. Writer. **Publications:** So We Can Remember: Showing Family Photographs, 1981; Lots of Stories: Maritime Narratives from the Creighton Collection, 1985; True Poetry: Traditional and Popular Verse in Ontario, 1989; Ethnicity in the Mainstream: Three Studies of English Canadian Culture in Ontario, 1994; (ed. with D. Tye) Undisciplined Women: Tradition and Culture in Canada, 1997; (ed. with L. Locke and T.A. Vaughan) Encyclopedia of Women's Folklore and Folklife, 2009; Fairy Tale Films: Visions of Ambiguity, 2010; Make the Night Hideous: Four English-Canadian Charivaris, 1881-1940, 2010. Contributor to books. **Address:** Women's Studies, University of Winnipeg, Rm. 4G19, 515 Portage Ave., Winnipeg, MB R2B 2E9, Canada. **Online address:** p.greenhill@uwinnipeg.ca

GREENHOUSE, Carol J(ane). American (born United States), b. 1950. **Genres:** Anthropology/Ethnology, Social Commentary, Education. **Career:** Georgia State University, Department of Anthropology, instructor, 1975; United States Bureau of Social Science Research, research analyst, 1976-77; George Mason University, Department of Anthropology, instructor, 1977; Cornell University, assistant professor, 1977-83, associate professor of anthropology, 1983-91; Indiana University, professor of anthropology, 1991-2001, chair, 1995-96; American Ethnologist, editor, 1998-; Princeton University, professor of anthropology, 2001-, chair; école des hautes études en sciences sociales, visiting professor. **Publications:** Praying for Justice: Faith, Order, and Community in an American Town, 1986; (with B. Yugresson and D.M. Engel) Law and Community in Three American Towns, 1994; A Moment's Notice: Time Politics across Cultures, 1996; (ed. with R. Kheshti) Democracy and Ethnography: Constructing Identities in Multicultural States, 1998; (ed. with E. Mertz and K.B. Warren) Ethnography in Unstable Places: Everyday Lives in Contexts of Dramatic Political Change, 2002; (ed.) Ethnographies of Neoliberalism, 2010; The Paradox of Relevance: Ethnography and Citizenship in the United States, 2011. **Address:** Department of Anthropology, Princeton University, 116 Aaron Burr Hall, Princeton, NJ 08544-1011, U.S.A. **Online address:** cgreenho@princeton.edu

GREENING, John. American/British (born England), b. 1954?. **Genres:** Poetry. **Career:** Writer and educator. **Publications:** COLLECTIONS OF POEMS: Westerners, 1984; The Tutankhamun Variations, 1991; Fotheringhay and Other Poems, 1995; The Bocase Stone, 1996; Nightflights: New and Selected Poems, 1998; Gascoigne's Egg, 2000; Omm Sety, 2001; Poetry of Ted Hughes, 2007; Thomas Hardy: Poems of 1912-13: The "Emma" Poems, 2007; Iceland Spar, 2008; Elizabethan Love Poets, 2010. Contributor to periodicals. Works appear in anthologies. **Address:** Cargo Press, The Annex, Penhaver House, Cliff Rd., Helston, Gorran Haven, CW PL26 6JN, England.

GREENLAW, Lavinia (Elaine). British (born England), b. 1962. **Genres:** Novels, Poetry, Travel/Exploration. **Career:** Imperial College of Science and Technology, publications editor, 1985-86; Allison and Busby, desk editor, 1986-87; Earthscan, managing editor, 1988-90; South Bank Centre, assistant literature officer, 1990-91; London Arts Board, principal literature officer, 1991-94; Freelance writer and reviewer, 1994-; London Science Museum, writer-in-residence, 1994-95; Aldeburgh Festival, poet-in-residence, 1997;

Royal Festival Hall, reader-in-residence, 2000; University of London, Goldsmiths College, visiting lecturer in creative writing, 2002-. **Publications:** POETRY: The Cost of Getting Lost in Space, 1991; Love from a Foreign City, 1992; Night Photograph, 1993; A World Where News Travelled Slowly, 1997; Minsk, 2003; (ed.) Signs and Humours: The Poetry of Medicine, 2007; The Casual Perfect, 2011. NOVEL: Mary George of All Northover, 2001. OTHER: Thoughts of a Night Sea: Photographs by Garry Fabian Miller (artist's book), 2002; Irresponsible Age, 2006; The Bridport Prize, 2006; The Importance of Music to Girls, 2007; Questions of Travel: William Morris in Iceland, 2011. Contributor to periodicals. **Address:** c/o Derek Johns, A.P. Watt Ltd., 20 John St., London, GL WC1N 2DR, England.

GREENLEAF, Stephen (Howell). American (born United States), b. 1942. **Genres:** Mystery/Crime/Suspense, Novels, Children's Fiction, Literary Criticism And History. **Career:** Bar of California, attorney, 1968; Multnomah County Legal Aid, researcher, 1969-70; Thompson & Hubbard, associate attorney, 1970-71; Sullivan, Jones & Archer, associate attorney, 1972-76; Bar of Iowa, attorney, 1977; University of Iowa, adjunct professor of trial advocacy, 1979-80; University of Washington Extension, instructor, 1993-96; Iowa Summer Writing Festival, instructor, 1995-2000. Writer. **Publications:** JOHN MARSHALL TANNER NOVEL: Grave Error, 1979; Death Bed: A Detective Story, 1980; State's Evidence, 1982; Fatal Obsession, 1983; Beyond Blame, 1986; Toll Call, 1987; Book Case, 1991; Blood Type, 1992; Southern Cross, 1993; False Conception, 1994; Flesh Wounds, 1996; Past Tense, 1997; Strawberry Sunday, 1999; Ellipsis, 2000. OTHER: Child Proof, 1981; The Ditto List, 1985; Impact, 1989. **Address:** c/o Scribner, 1230 Ave. of the Americas, New York, NY 10020, U.S.A.

GREENLEE, J(acob) Harold. American (born United States), b. 1918. **Genres:** Language/Linguistics, Theology/Religion, Essays. **Career:** Asbury Theological Seminary, professor of new testament Greek, 1944-65; Oxford University, senior Fulbright fellow, 1950-51; American Bible Society, research associate, 1955-65; Oral Roberts University, Graduate School of Theology, professor of New Testament Greek, 1965-69; Seminario Biblico, professor, 1965, 1970-74; OMS International (formerly The Oriental Missionary Society), ordained minister, 1969-; Wycliffe Bible Translators, translation consultant, 1971-; University of Texas, adjunct professor of linguistics, 1974-. Writer. **Publications:** Concise Exegetical Grammar of New Testament Greek, 1948, 5th ed., 1986; The Gospel Text of Cyril of Jerusalem, 1955; An Introduction to New Testament Textual Criticism, 1964, rev. ed., 1995; (with T.M. Anderson) How to Build Expository Sermons, 1965; Nine Uncial Palimpsests of the Greek New Testament, 1968; A New Testament Greek Morpheme Lexicon, 1983; Scribes, Scrolls and Scripture, 1985; An Exegetical Summary of Titus and Philemon, 1992, 2nd ed., 2008; An Exegetical Summary of Philippians, 1992, 2nd ed., 2008; Scribes and Scripture: New Testament Essays in Honor of J. Harold Greenlee, 1992; An Exegetical Summary of James, 1993, 2nd ed., 2008; What the New Testament Says about Holiness, 1994; (with R. Greenlee) With Two Suitcases and a Carry-On, 1994; An Exegetical Summary of Hebrews, 1998, 2nd ed., 2008; An Exegetical Summary of Jude, 1999, 2nd ed., 2008; Words from the Word, 2000; Text of the New Testament: From Manuscript to Modern Edition, 2008; Exegetical Summaries of Titus and Philemon, 2008. **Address:** c/o Author Mail, Zondervan, 5300 Patterson Ave. SE, Grand Rapids, MI 49530, U.S.A. **Online address:** haroldgreenlee@compuserve.com

GREENLEE, Sharon. American (born United States), b. 1935. **Genres:** Self Help, Education, Children's Fiction. **Career:** Freelance consultant and leader, 1983-; counselor, 1984-; University of Wyoming, instructor, 1985-. Writer. **Publications:** When Someone Dies, 1992; Self-Esteem, Communication and High-level Thinking Skills, 1992; Ways to Help Yourself and Others, forthcoming; Images of Me: A Guide for Those Who Work with Pre-School Age Children, forthcoming. **Address:** 2020 Grand Ave., PO Box 104, Laramie, WY 82070-4383, U.S.A. **Online address:** sharongr104@aol.com

GREEN MUSSELMAN, Elizabeth. American (born United States), b. 1971. **Genres:** History, Sciences. **Career:** Indiana University, associate instructor and National Science Foundation fellow, 1993; Georgetown Voice, editor-in-chief, 1990-91; Blue and Gray, associate editor, 1992-93; Southwestern University, associate professor. **Publications:** Nervous Conditions: Science and the Body Politic in Early Industrial Britain, 2006. Contributor to books and periodicals. **Address:** Department of History, Southwestern University, 1001 E University Ave., Georgetown, TX 78626-6100, U.S.A. **Online address:** greenmue@southwestern.edu

GREENO, Gayle. American (born United States), b. 1949. **Genres:** Science Fiction/Fantasy, Novels, Young Adult Fiction. **Career:** G.P. Putnam's Sons, sales and marketing manager, 1973-75; Praeger Publishers, sales and marketing manager, 1975-78; Fawcett Books, sales and marketing manager, 1979-80; New American Library, sales and marketing manager, 1980-90. Writer and publishing consultant, 1991-. **Publications:** GHATTI'S TALE: Finders-Seekers, 1993; Mind-speakers' Call, 1994; Exiles' Return, 1995. GHATTEN'S GAMBIT: Sunderlies Seeking, 1998; The Farthest Seeking, 2000. NOVEL: Mind Snare, 1997. **Address:** DAW Books Inc., 375 Hudson St., New York, NY 10014, U.S.A.

GREENSIDE, Mark. American (born United States), b. 1944. **Genres:** Novellas/Short Stories, Travel/Exploration. **Career:** Peralta Community College District, teacher of history, political science, English, creative writing and humanities, 1971-, staff development officer, 1992-94, 1996-98; Vista College, director of older adult program, 1978-84. Writer. **Publications:** I Saw a Man Hit His Wife (short stories), 1997; I'll Never be French (No Matter What I do): Living in a Small Village in Brittany, 2008. Contributor to periodicals. **Address:** Peralta Community College District, 333 E 8th St., Oakland, CA 94606, U.S.A. **Online address:** mark@markgreenside.com

GREENSTEIN, George. American (born United States), b. 1940. **Genres:** Astronomy, Sciences, Autobiography/Memoirs. **Career:** Yeshiva University, research associate, 1968-70; Princeton University, Observatory, research associate, 1970-71; Amherst College, Department of Astronomy, assistant professor, 1971-77, associate professor, 1977-83, professor, 1983-93, chairman for five-college astronomy department, 1981-84, Sidney Dillon professor of astronomy, 1993-; Air and Space/Smithsonian Magazine, contributing editor. **Publications:** Frozen Star: Of Pulsars, Black Holes, and the Fate of Stars, 1983; The Symbiotic Universe: Life and Mind in the Cosmos, 1988; (with A.G. Zajonc) The Quantum Challenge: Modern Research on the Foundations of Quantum Mechanics, 1997, 2nd ed., 2006; Portraits of Discovery: Profiles in Scientific Genius, 1998. Contributor to scientific journals and magazines. **Address:** Department of Astronomy, Amherst College, Amherst, MA 01002, U.S.A. **Online address:** gsgreenstein@amherst.edu

GREENWALD, Bruce C. American (born United States), b. 1946. **Genres:** Economics. **Career:** Harvard Business School, professor; Columbia University, Business School, Robert Heilbrunn Professor of Finance and Asset Management, 1991-, Heilbrunn Center for Graham & Dodd Investing, director. Writer. **Publications:** Adverse Selection in the Labor Market, 1979; (co-author) Value Investing: From Graham to Buffett and Beyond, 2001; (with J. Stiglitz) Towards a New Paradigm in Monetary Economics, 2003; (with J. Kahn) Competition Demystified: A Radically Simplified Approach to Business Strategy, 2005; (with J.A. Knee and A. Seave) The Curse of the Mogul: What's Wrong with the World's Leading Media Companies, 2009; (with J. Kahn) Glob-ali-za'tion: n. the Irrational Fear That Someone in China Will Take Your Job, 2009. Contributor to periodicals and journals. **Address:** Business School, Columbia University, 3022 Broadway, New York, NY 10027, U.S.A. **Online address:** bg7@columbia.edu

GREENWALD, G. Jonathan. American (born United States), b. 1943. **Genres:** International Relations/Current Affairs, Economics, Biography. **Career:** U.S. Defense Department, legal adviser, 1968-69; U.S. State Department, staff, 1969-97; Lawrence University, Stephen Edward Scarff memorial visiting professor, 1998-99; U.S. Mission to the European Community, political counselor; International Crisis Group, vice president, 2001-. Writer. **Publications:** (With L. Sullivan, Jr.) Western Stake in the Future of the Soviet Economy, 1987; Berlin Witness: An American Diplomat's Chronicle of East Germany's Revolution, 1993. Contributor to periodicals. **Address:** International Crisis Group, 1629 K St. NW, Ste. 450, Washington, DC 20006-1677, U.S.A.

GREENWALD, Glenn. American (born United States), b. 1967. **Genres:** Politics/Government. **Career:** Attorney, 1996-; Greenwald Christoph & Holland, co-founder, 1996; Wachtell, Lipton, Rosen & Katz, intern. Writer. **Publications:** How Would a Patriot Act? Defending American Values from a President Run Amok, 2006; A Tragic Legacy: How a Good vs. Evil Mentality Destroyed the Bush Presidency, 2007; Great American Hypocrites: Toppling the Big Myths of Republican Politics, 2008; Drug Decriminalization In Portugal: Lessons For Creating Fair and Successful Drug Policies, 2009; With Liberty and Justice for Some: How the Law is Used to Destroy Equality and Protect the Powerful, 2011. Contributor to periodicals. **Address:** Wachtell, Lipton, Rosen & Katz, 51 W 52nd St., New York, NY 10019, U.S.A. **Online address:** ggreenwald@gclaw.us

GREENWALD, Jeff. American (born United States), b. 1954. **Genres:** Cultural/Ethnic Topics, Sciences, Travel/Exploration, Writing/Journalism, Essays, History. **Career:** Santa Barbara News & Review, cultural and features editor, 1980; Art/Life, editor, 1981-83; Global Network, contributing travel editor, 1993-95; Wired magazine, contributing editor, 1993-98; Adventure Zone Network, columnist and digital video producer, 1999-2000; Tricycle magazine, contributing editor, 2002-; Ethical Traveler, founder and executive director, 2003. World traveler, photographer, videographer, artist and writer. **Publications:** Mister Raja's Neighborhood: Letters from Nepal, 1986; Shopping for Buddhas, 1990; (ed.) Burma: The Next Killing Fields?, 1992; The Size of the World: Once Around Without Leaving the Ground, 1995; Future Perfect: How Star Trek Conquered Planet Earth, 1998; Snake Lake, 2010. Work represented in anthologies. Contributor to magazines. **Address:** PO Box 5883, Berkeley, CA 94705-0883, U.S.A. **Online address:** jeff@jeffgreenwald.com

GREENWALD, Marilyn S. American (born United States), b. 1954. **Genres:** Writing/Journalism, Social Sciences, Biography. **Career:** The Telegraph, copy editor and entertainment editor, 1976-78; Columbus Citizen-Journal, business reporter and news reporter, 1978-85; Columbus Dispatch, business reporter, 1986-87; Ohio University, professor of journalism, 1987-. **Publications:** (With R. Izsard) Public Affairs Reporting: The Citizen's News, 2nd ed., 1991; A Woman of the Times: Journalism, Feminism and the Career of Charlotte Curtis, 1999; (ed. with J. Bernt) The Big Chill: Investigative Reporting in the Current Media Environment, 2000; The Secret of the Hardy Boys: Leslie McFarlane and the Stratemeyer Syndicate, 2004; Cleveland Amory: Media Curmudgeon and Animal Crusader, 2009. **Address:** E. W. Scripps School of Journalism, Ohio University, 230 Scripps Hall, 32 Park Pl., Athens, OH 45701, U.S.A. **Online address:** greenwal@ohio.edu

GREENWALD, Ricky. American (born United States), b. 1958. **Genres:** Psychiatry, Psychology, Social Sciences. **Career:** Wediko Children's Services, staff, 1989; Children's Day Treatment Center, therapist, 1989; Neuro-Psychology Associates, neuropsychological examiner, 1990; Institute at Newton, outreach child and family therapist, 1990-91; Forest Family Clinic-Springfield, consultant and therapist, 1991; Forest Family Clinic-Honolulu, consultant and therapist, 1991-92; Queen's Medical Center, Queen's Mental Health Clinic, consultant and therapist, 1992; Chaminade University, adjunct faculty, 1993; Affiliated Psychological Consultants, employee assistance program therapist, 1995; Community Services Institute, post-doctoral fellow in child and adolescent trauma, 1995-96; Suicide Prevention and Crisis Service, consultant, 1996-99; Crisis Management Intl., crisis management associate, 1996-2004; Tompkins-Cortland Community College, adjunct faculty, 1997; American School of Professional Psychology, adjunct faculty, 1997; Kauai Department of Education, Mokihana Project, senior psychologist, 1997-99; Mount Sinai School of Medicine, Department of Psychiatry, assistant clinical professor of psychiatry, 2000-02; Children After Trauma Care and Health (CATCH) Program, director, 2000-02; Sidran Institute, Child and Adolescent Trauma Programs, consultant, 2001-03; Intensive Aftercare Program, Office of Children and Family Services, consultant and therapist, 2002-04; Trauma Institute and Child Trauma Institute Inc., founder, executive director and faculty chair, 2002-; State University of New York, University at Buffalo, School of Social Work, affiliate professor, 2007-; Journal of Child and Adolescent Trauma, associate editor, 2008-. **Publications:** Eye Movement Desensitization and Reprocessing (EMDR) in Child and Adolescent Psychotherapy, 1999; (ed.) Trauma and Juvenile Delinquency: Theory, Research, and Interventions, 2002; Child Trauma Handbook: A Guide for Helping Trauma-exposed Children and Adolescents, 2005; EMDR: Within A Phase Model of Trauma-Informed Treatment, 2007; (with K.J. Baden) A Fairy Tale, 2007; Treating Problem Behaviors: A Trauma-informed Approach, 2009. Contributor to periodicals. **Address:** Trauma Institute & Child Trauma Institute Inc., PO Box 544, Greenfield, MA 01302, U.S.A. **Online address:** rg@childtrauma.com

GREENWALD, Sheila. American (born United States), b. 1934. **Genres:** Young Adult Fiction, Illustrations, Humor/Satire. **Career:** Writer and illustrator. **Publications:** SELF-ILLUSTRATED YOUNG ADULT FICTION: A Metropolitan Love Story, 1962; Willie Bryant and the Flying Otis, 1971; The Hot Day, 1972; Miss Amanda Snap, 1972; Mat Pit and the Tunnel Tenants, 1972; The Secret Museum, 1974; The Secret in Miranda's Closet, 1977; The Mariah Delany Lending Library Disaster, 1977; The Atrocious Two, 1978; All the Way to Wit's End, 1979; It All Began with Jane Eyre or the Secret Life of Franny Dillman, 1980; Give Us a Great Big Smile, Rosy Cole, 1981; Blissful Joy and the SATs: A Multiple-Choice Romance, 1982; Will the Real Gertrude Hollings Please Stand Up?, 1983; Valentine Rosy, 1984; Rosy Cole's Great American Guilt Club, 1985; Alvin Webster's Sure Fire Plan for Success and How It Failed, 1987; Write on Rosy!, 1988; Rosy's Romance, 1989; The Meriah Delany's Author-of-the-Month Club, 1990; Here's Hermione, A Rosy Cole Production, 1991; Rosy Cole Discovers America!, 1992; My Fabulous New Life, 1993; Rosy Cole! She Walks in Beauty, 1994; Rosy Cole: She Grows and Graduates, 1997; Stucksville, 2000; Rosy Cole's Worst Ever, Best Yet Tour of New York City, 2003; Rosy Cole's Memoir Explosion, 2006; Watch Out World- Rosy Cole is Going Green!, 2010. Illustrator of books by others. **Address:** 175 Riverside Dr., New York, NY 10024, U.S.A. **Online address:** sheilagreenwald@usa.net

GREENWOOD, Barbara. Canadian (born Canada), b. 1940. **Genres:** Children's Fiction, Young Adult Fiction, Children's Non-fiction, Biography, History. **Career:** Davisville Public School, Kindergarten, founder; Ryerson Polytechnical Institute, visiting lecturer, 1984-2004; University of New Brunswick, visiting lecturer, 1989, 1991-; Markham Library System, writer-in-residence, 1989-90; University of Toronto, visiting lecturer, 1990-92. **Publications:** A Question of Loyalty, 1984; (with A. McKim) Her Special Vision: A Biography of Jean Little, 1987; Jeanne Sauve, 1989; Spy in the Shadows, 1990; Klondike Challenge: Rachel Hanna, Frontier Nurse, 1990; (ed.) Presenting Children's Authors, Illustrators, and Performers, 1990; (with P. Hancock) The Other Side of the Story, 1990; A Pioneer Story: The Daily Life of a Canadian Family in 1840, 1994; (with B. Greenwood) Speak Up! Speak Out!, 1995; A Pioneer Sampler: The Daily Life of a Pioneer Family in 1840, 1995; The Kids Book of Canada: Exploring the Land and Its People, 1997, rev. ed. 1999; Pioneer Crafts, 1997; The Last Safe House: A Story of the Underground Railroad, 1998; A Pioneer Thanksgiving: A Story of Harvest Celebrations in 1841, 1999; Gold Rush Fever: A Story of the Klondike, 1898, 2001; A Pioneer Christmas: Celebrations in the Backwoods in 1841, 2003; Factory Girl, 2007. EDITOR: Presenting Children's Authors, Illustrators, and Performers, 1990; CANSCAIP Companion: A Biographical Record of Canadian Children's Authors, Illustrators, and Performers, 1991; Behind the Story: The Creators of Our Best Children's Books and How They Do it, 1995. Contributor to periodicals. **Address:** Kids Can Press, 25 Dockside Dr., Toronto, ON M5A 0B5, Canada. **Online address:** bgrwood@interlog.com

GREENWOOD, David Luis Valdes. American (born United States), b. 1967?. **Genres:** Plays/Screenplays, Human Relations/Parenting, Gay And Lesbian Issues, Adult Non-fiction. **Career:** Tufts University, lecturer in English. Writer. **Publications:** Brave Navigator, 2000; Homo Domesticus: Notes from a Same-Sex Marriage, 2007; A Little Fruitcake: A Boyhood in Holidays, 2007; The Rhinestone Sisterhood: A Journey Through Small Town America, One Tiara at a Time, 2010. **Address:** English Department, Tufts University, 210 East Hall, Medford, MA 02155, U.S.A. **Online address:** impersonalstuff@aol.com

GREENWOOD, Judith. *See* **GREENWOOD-WALLER, Judith.**

GREENWOOD, Leigh. American (born United States), b. 1942. **Genres:** Romance/Historical, Novels. **Career:** Writer and music teacher. **Publications:** ROMANCE NOVELS: Wyoming Wildfire, 1987; The Captain's Caress, 1988; Wicked Wyoming Nights, 1989; Colorado Bride, 1990; Seductive Wager, 1990; Sweet Temptation, 1991; Rebel Enchantress, 1992; Scarlet Sunset, Silver Nights, 1992; Arizona Embrace, 1993; (with P. Sutherland) Only You, 1997; Just What the Doctor Ordered, 1999; Married by High Noon, 1999; Winner's Circle, 1999; Love on the Run, 2000; Texas Bride, 2002; Texas Homecoming, 2002; Undercover Honeymoon, 2002; Born to Love, 2003; Family Merger, 2003; Independent Bride, 2004; Reluctant Bride, 2005; A Someone Like You, 2009; When Love Comes, 2010; Texas Pride, 2012. THE COWBOYS SERIES: Jake, 1997; Ward, 1997; Chet, 1998; Buck, 1998; Pete, 1999; Sean, 1999; Drew, 2000; Luke, 2000; Matt, 2001; The Mavericks, 2005; Texan's Honor, 2006; Texas Tender, 2007; Texas Loving, 2008. SEVEN BRIDES SERIES: Rose, 1993; A Fairy-Tale Christmas in An Old-Fashioned Southern Christmas, 1994; Fern, 1994; Iris, 1994; Daisy, 1995; Father Christmas in Their First Noel, 1995; Laurel, 1995; Lily, 1996; Violet, 1996; Bah, Humbug! in The Christmas Spirit, 1997; Here Comes Santa Claus in Winter Wonderland, 1999. **Address:** PO Box 470761, Charlotte, NC 28226, U.S.A. **Online address:** leighgwood@aol.com

GREENWOOD, Norman Neill. Australian/British (born England), b. 1925. **Genres:** Chemistry, Education, Biography, Sciences. **Career:** Trinity College, resident tutor and lecturer of chemistry, 1946-48; University of Nottingham, lecturer, senior lecturer of inorganic chemistry, 1953-61; University of Newcastle-upon-Tyne, Department of Inorganic Chemistry, professor and head, 1961-71; University of Leeds, Department of Inorganic and Structural Chemistry, professor and head, 1971-90, professor emeritus, 1990-. Writer. **Publications:** Principles of Atomic Orbitals, 1964, 4th ed., 1980; (co-author) Spectroscopic Properties of Inorganic and Organometallic Compounds, 9 vols., 1967-75; Ionic Crystals, Lattice Defects and Nonstoichiometry, 1968; (with T.C. Gibb) Mössbauer Spectroscopy, 1971; (with W.A. Campbell) Contemporary British Chemists, 1971; Periodicity and Atomic Structure, 1971; (with E.J.F. Ross and B.P. Straughan) Index of Vibrational Spectra of Inorganic and Organometallic Compounds, 3 vols., 1972-77; Boron, 1973; (with A. Earnshaw) Chemistry of the Elements, 1984, 2nd ed., 1997. **Address:** School of Chemistry, University of Leeds, Woodhouse Ln., Leeds, WY LS2 9JT, England. **Online address:** n.n.greenwood@chemistry.leeds.ac.uk

GREENWOOD, T. American (born United States), b. 1969?. **Genres:** Novels. **Career:** George Washington University, teacher of creative writing. Writer. **Publications:** NOVELS: Breathing Water, 1999; Nearer Than the Sky, 2000; Undressing the Moon, 2002; Two Rivers, 2009; This Glittering World, 2011. **Address:** Department of English, George Washington University, Rome Hall, 760801 22nd St. NW, Washington, DC 20052, U.S.A. **Online address:** stewbalms@verizon.net

GREENWOOD-WALLER, Judith. (Judith Greenwood). American (born United States), b. 1941. **Genres:** Medicine/Health, Social Sciences, Politics/Government. **Career:** West Virginia University, Medical Center, research associate, 1977-79, clinical associate professor, 1983-; West Virginia Department of Health, director of human resource development, 1979-82; West Virginia Bureau of Employment Programs, director of workers compensation research, 1982-2000; Health Management Systems, senior consultant, 1989. Writer. **Publications:** Role of the Physician Assistants in Primary Care, 1980; (ed. with A. Taricco) Workers' Compensation Health Care Cost Containment, 1992. Contributor to periodicals. **Address:** 9 Vail Dr., Ripley, WV 25271-1338, U.S.A.

GREER, Andrew Sean. American (born United States), b. 1970?. **Genres:** Novels, Young Adult Fiction. **Career:** Novelist. **Publications:** How It Was for Me, 2000; The Path of Minor Planets, 2001; The Confessions of Max Tivoli, 2004; The Story of a Marriage, 2008. Contributor to periodicals. Works appear in anthologies. **Address:** c/o Lynn Nesbit, Janklow & Nesbit Associates, 445 Park Ave., New York, NY 10022-2606, U.S.A.

GREER, Gaylon. American (born United States), b. 1936?. **Genres:** Novels. **Career:** Writer and educator. **Publications:** The Real Estate Investor and the Federal Income Tax, 1978; The Real Estate Investment Decision, 1979, 2nd ed., 1982; (with M.D. Farrell) Contemporary Real Estate: Theory and Practice, 1983; (with M.D. Farrell) Investment Analysis for Real Estate Decisions, 1984, (with P.T. Kolbe) 7th ed., 2009; (with M.D. Farrell) Tax Shelters: Illusions, Delusions, and Economic Reality, 1985; The New Dow Jones-Irwin Guide to Real Estate Investing, 1989; (with P.T. Kolbe and H.G. Rudner III) Real Estate Finance, 2003; The Price of Sanctuary (novel), 2009. **Address:** Austin, TX , U.S.A. **Online address:** gaylon@gaylongreer.com

GREER, Germaine. British/Australian (born Australia), b. 1939. **Genres:** Literary Criticism And History, Women's Studies And Issues, Poetry, Biography, Autobiography/Memoirs, Sex, Philosophy. **Career:** Sydney University, senior tutor, 1963-64; University of Warwick, assistant lecturer, lecturer in English, 1968-72, professor of English and comparative studies, 1998-2003, professor emeritus, 2003-; Sunday Times Newspaper, columnist, 1971-73; American Program Bureau, lecturer, 1973-78; University of Tulsa, visiting professor, graduate faculty of modern letters, 1979, professor of modern letters, 1980-83; Tulsa Centre for the Study of Women's Literature, founder and director, 1979-82, editor, 1981; Stump Cross Books, director, 1988-; Newnham College, special lecturer, 1989-98. **Publications:** The Female Eunuch, 1969; The Obstacle Race, 1979; Sex and Destiny: The Politics of Human Fertility, 1984; Shakespeare, 1986; The Madwoman's Underclothes: Essays and Occasional Writings, 1986; Daddy, We Hardly Knew You, 1989; The Change: Women, Aging and Menopause, 1991; Slip-shod Sybils: Recognition, Rejection and the Woman Poet, 1995; The Whole Woman, 1999; John Wilmot, Earl of Rochester, 1999; Shakespeare: A Very Short Introduction,

2002; The Beautiful Boy, 2003; Whitefella Jump Up: The Shortest Way to Nationhood, 2004; Shakespeare's Wife, 2007; (contrib.) The On-nibus, 2009. EDITOR: (and intro. with J. Medoff, M. Sansone and S. Hasting) Kissing the Rod: An Anthology of Seventeenth-Century Women's Verse, 1989; (and intro.) The Uncollected Verse of Aphra Behn, 1989; (with S. Hastings) The Surviving Works of Anne Wharton, 1997; (with E. Showalter) Cambridge Guide to Women's Writing in English, 1999; Lines of Life: 101 Poems by 101 Women, 2001; Poems for Gardeners, 2003. Contributor to periodicals. Address: Gillon Aitken Associates Ltd., 29 Fernshaw Rd., London, GL SW10 0TG, England. Online address: ensce@snow.csv.warwick.ac.uk

GREER, Jane. American (born United States), b. 1951?. Genres: Human Relations/Parenting, Medicine/Health. Career: Adelphi University School of Social Work, adjunct assistant professor; Redbook Magazine, contributing editor. Writer. Publications: (With E. Myers) Adult Sibling Rivalry: Understanding the Legacy of Childhood, 1992; (with M.D. Rosen) How Could You Do This to Me?: Learning to Trust after Betrayal, 1997; (with M.D. Rosen) Gridlock: Finding the Courage to Move on in Love, Work and Life, 2000; (intro.) What Women Really Want and How They Can Get It, 2000; The Afterlife Connection: A Therapist Reveals How to Communicate With Departed Loved Ones, 2003; What about Me?: Stop Selfishness From Ruining Your Relationship, 2010. Address: c/o Author Mail, Doubleday Publicity, 245 Park Ave., New York, NY 10017, U.S.A. Online address: drjanegreer@drjanegreer.com

GREER, John Michael. American (born United States), b. 1962. Genres: Paranormal, Mythology/Folklore, Theology/Religion, Intellectual History. Career: Academia Duellatoria, teacher; freelance writer, 1995-. Publications: Paths of Wisdom: The Magical Cabala in the Western Tradition, 1996; Circles of Power: Ritual Magic in the Western Tradition, 1997; Inside a Magical Lodge: Group Ritual in the Western Tradition, 1998; (trans.) G. Thibault, Academy of the Sword (martial arts book originally published 1630), 1999; Earth Divination, Earth Magic: A Practical Guide to Geomancy, 1999; Natural Magic: Potions and Powers from the Magical Garden, 2000; Monsters: An Investigator's Guide to Magical Beings, 2001; Techniques for Geometric Transformation, 2001; The New Encyclopedia of the Occult, 2003; (with E. King, Jr. and C. Vaughn) Learning Ritual Magic: Fundamental Theory and Practice for the Solitary Apprentice, 2004; A World Full of Gods: An Inquiry into Polytheism, 2005; The Element Encyclopedia of Secret Societies, 2006; The Druidry Handbook, 2006; (with C. Vaughn) Pagan Prayer Beads, 2007; Atlantis: Ancient Legacy, Hidden Prophecy, 2007; The Druid Magic Handbook, 2007; The Long Descent: A User's Guide to the End of the Industrial Age, 2008; Fires of Shalsa, 2009; The Art and Practice of Geomancy, 2009; Secrets of the Lost Symbol: The Unauthorized Guide to Secret Societies, Hidden Symbols & Mysticism, 2009; The UFO Phenomenon: Fact, Fantasy and Disinformation, 2009; The Ecotechnic Future: Envisioning a Post-Peak World, 2009; Apocalypse Not, 2011; Wealth of Nature, 2011. Address: PO Box 387, Ashland, OR 97520, U.S.A. Online address: threelynx@earthlink.net

GREER, Robert O. American (born United States), b. 1944. Genres: Mystery/Crime/Suspense, Novels, Horror. Career: University of Colorado Health Services Center, professor of pathology, medicine, surgery and dentistry, cancer research; The High Plains Literary Review, founder and editor-in-chief, 1986-; KUVO (National Public Radio affiliate), book reviewer. Mystery novelist. Publications: (With G.W. Mierau and B.E. Favara) Tumors of the Head and Neck in Children: Clinicopathologic Perspectives, 1983; The Devil's Hatband, 1996; The Devil's Red Nickel, 1997; The Devil's Backbone, 1998; Limited Time, 2000; Isolation and Other Stories, 2001; Heat Shock, 2003; Resurrecting Langston Blue, 2005; The Fourth Perspective, 2006; The Mongoose Deception, 2007; Blackbird, Farewell, 2008; Spoon: A Novel, 2009; First of State, 2010; Astride a Pink Horse, 2012. Contributor to periodicals. Address: c/o Allegra Harris, North Atlantic Books, 1435 4th St., Berkeley, CA 94710, U.S.A. Online address: robert@robertgreerbooks.com

GREER, Steven (Crawford). British/Irish (born Ireland), b. 1956. Genres: Law, Civil Liberties/Human Rights, Politics/Government. Career: University of Sussex, lecturer in law, 1985-86; University of Bristol, lecturer in law, 1986-96, reader in law, 1996-2005, professor, 2005-; University of Hannover, visiting lecturer, 1988. Writer. Publications: (With A. White) Abolishing the Diplock Courts: The Case for Restoring Jury Trial to Scheduled Offences in Northern Ireland, 1986; (ed. with R. Morgan and contrib.) The Right to Silence Debate, 1990; Supergrasses: A Study in Anti-Terrorist Law Enforcement in Northern Ireland, 1995; The Exceptions to Articles 8 to 11 of the European Convention on Human Rights, 1997; The Margin of Appreciation: Interpreta-

tion and Discretion Under The European Convention on Human Rights, 2000; The European Convention on Human Rights: Achievements, Problems, and Prospects, 2006. Contributor of articles to journals. Address: School of Law, University of Bristol, Rm. 3.40, Wills Memorial Bldg., Queens Rd., Bristol, AV BS8 1RJ, England. Online address: steven.greer@bristol.ac.uk

GREET, Kenneth Gerald. British (born England), b. 1918. Genres: Theology/Religion. Career: Bristol Corp., clerk, 1935-40; Kingstone Methodist Church, methodist minister, 1940-42; Ogmore Vale Methodist Church, methodist minister, 1942-45; Methodist Department of Christian Citizenship, secretary, 1954-71; Temperance Council of Christian Churches, chair, 1961-71; World Christian Temperance Foundation, chair, 1962-72; Free Church Federal Council, moderator, 1982-83; World Disarmament Campaign, co-chair, 1984-. Writer. Publications: Mutual Society: Aspects of the Relationship of Men and Women, 1962; Man and Wife Together, 1962; Large Petitions, 1964; Guide to Loving, 1964; The Debate About Drink, 1969; The Sunday Question, 1970; The Art of Moral Judgement, 1970; When the Spirit Moves, 1975; A Lion from a Thicket, 1978; The Big Sin, 1982; Under the Rainbow Arch, 1984; What Shall I Cry?, 1986; Jabez Bunting, 1995; Fully Connected, 1997. Contributor to journals. Address: 89 Broadmark Ln., Rustington, WS BN16 2JA, England.

GREETHAM, David. American (born United States), b. 1941. Genres: Writing/Journalism, History, Humanities, Intellectual History, Law, Music, Philosophy, Politics/Government, Popular Culture, Social Sciences, Technology, Theatre, Theology/Religion, Autobiography/Memoirs, Bibliography, Autobiography/Memoirs, E-books, Architecture. Career: Procter and Gamble, public relations officer, 1963-65; International Schule, English Department, head, 1965-67; City University of New York, instructor, distinguished professor, 1967-. Writer. Publications: Textual Scholarship: An Introduction, 1992, 2nd ed., 2011; Text: Transactions of the Society for Textual Scholarship, 1981-96; Textual Transgressions: Essays toward the Construction of a Bio-bibliography, 1998; Theories of the Text, 1999; The Pleasures of Contamination: Evidence, Text and Voice in Textual Studies, 2010; Incompletes: The Nature of the Unfinished Work, forthcoming. EDITOR: Scholarly Editing: A Guide to Research, 1995; The Margins of the Text, 1997. Address: Graduate Center, City University of New York, 365 5th Ave., New York, NY 10016-4309, U.S.A. Online address: dgreetham@gc.cuny.edu

GREGERSON, Linda. American (born United States), b. 1950. Genres: Poetry, Literary Criticism And History. Career: Atlantic Monthly, staff editor, 1982-87, assistant poetry editor, 1982-86; Boston University, Department of English, visiting assistant professor, 1985-86; Massachusetts Institute of Technology, faculty and instructor, 1985-87; University of Michigan, assistant professor, 1987-94, William Wilhartz assistant professor of English, 1991-94, associate professor, 1994-2001, professor of English, 2001-03, Frederick G.L. Huetwell professor of English, 2003-08, Caroline Walker Bynum distinguished university professor of English, 2008-, MFA Program in Creative Writing, director, 1997-2000, Institute for the Humanities, A. Bartlett Giamatti faculty fellow, 1996-97, John Rich professor, 2004-05; Washington University, visiting Hurst professor, 2006; Beloit College, Visiting Mackey Chair, 2010. Publications: The Reformation of the Subject: Spenser, Milton, and the English Protestant Epic, 1995. POETRY: Fire in the Conservatory, 1982; The Woman Who Died in Her Sleep, 1996; Negative Capability: Contemporary American Poetry, 2001; Waterborne, 2002; Magneic North, 2007. (ed. with S. Juster) Empires of God: Religious Encounters in the Early Modern Atlantic, 2011. Works appear in anthologies. Contributor of articles to journals and newspapers. Address: Department of English Language and Literature, University of Michigan, 3147 Angell Hall, 435 S State St., Ann Arbor, MI 48109-1003, U.S.A. Online address: gregerso@umich.edu

GREGG, Clark. American (born United States), b. 1962. Genres: Film, Plays/Screenplays, Young Adult Fiction. Career: Writer, actor and director. Publications: What Lies Beneath, 2000; Natural Selection, 2000. Contributor to periodicals. Address: c/o Dan Aloni, United Talent Agency, 9560 Wilshire Blvd., 5th Fl., Beverly Hills, CA 90212, U.S.A.

GREGOR, Arthur. French/Austrian (born Austria), b. 1923. Genres: Children's Fiction, Plays/Screenplays, Poetry, Autobiography/Memoirs, Young Adult Fiction, Literary Criticism And History. Career: Electronic Transformer Corp., engineer, 1947-54; Whitney Publications, technical editor, 1956-61; Macmillan Co. (publishers), senior editor, 1962-70; California State University, visiting professor, 1972-73; Hofstra University, professor, 1974.

Publications: Octavian Shooting Targets, 1954; 1 2 3 4 5, 1956; The Little Elephant, 1956; Declensions of a Refrain, 1957; Animal Babies, 1959; Basic Movements, 1966; Figure in the Door, 1968; A Bed by the Sea, 1970; Selected Poems, 1971; Bell Laboratories: Inside the World's Largest Communications Center, 1972; The Past Now, 1975; Embodiment, and Other Poems, 1982; A Longing in the Land: Memoir of a Quest, 1983; Secret Citizen: Poems, 1989; The River Serpent and Other Poems, 1994; That Other Side of Things, 2001; The Hand upon His Head: Selected Poems, 1947-2003, 2004. **Address:** 9 bis rue Gelee, Chatillon-sur-Loire, 45360, France. **Online address:** arthur.gregor@wanadoo.fr

GREGOR, Neil. British (born England), b. 1969. **Genres:** History, Young Adult Fiction, Humanities. **Career:** University of Southampton, reader in modern German history, professor, James Parkes Centre, lecturer in jewish history, coordinator. Writer. **Publications:** Daimler-Benz in the Third Reich, 1998; (ed.) Nazism: A Reader, 2000; (ed.) Nazism, War and Genocide: Essays in Honour of Jeremy Noakes, 2005; How to Read Hitler, 2005; (ed. with N. Roemer and M. Roseman) German History From the Margins, 2006; Haunted City: Nuremberg and the Nazi Past, 2008. Contributor to Periodicals. **Address:** Department of History, School of Humanities, University of Southampton, Rm. 2057, University Rd., Southampton, HM S017 1BJ, England. **Online address:** ng1@soton.ac.uk

GREGORIAN, Raffi. American (born United States), b. 1964. **Genres:** Politics/Government, Military/Defense/Arms Control, History. **Career:** U.S. Army Center for Military History, historian, 1986-88; Science Applications International Corp., senior analyst, 1990-98; U.S. Department of Defense, Interagency Task Force for Military Stabilization in the Balkans, senior adviser, 1999; Office of the Special Adviser to the President and Secretary of State for Kosovo and Dayton Implementation, senior adviser and chief of staff, Kosovo Implementation office, acting director, 2001; United States Department of State, Department of Defense BiH Section, director, 2001-04; Defence Reform Commission of Bosnia and Herzegovina, co-chairman, 2005; NATO Brcko Final Award Office (BFAO), Brcko Supervisor and deputy high representative, 2006-, principal deputy high representative, 2007-10. Writer. **Publications:** The British Army, the Gurkhas, and Cold War Strategy in the Far East, 1947-1954, 2002. Contributor to books and journals. **Address:** Office of the EU Special Representative for BiH, Council of the European Union, 133 Rue Froissart, Brussels, 1040, Belgium.

GREGORY, Derek John. British (born England), b. 1951. **Genres:** Geography. **Career:** University of Cambridge, Sidney Sussex College, Department of Geography, university assistant lecturer, 1973-78, university lecturer, 1978-88, fellow, 1973-88; University of British Columbia, professor of geography, 1989-; University of London, lecturer; University of Sheffield, lecturer; University of Manchester, lecturer; University of Washington, lecturer; Karlstad University, lecturer. Educator and author. **Publications:** Ideology, Science and Human Geography, 1978; Regional Transformation and Industrial Revolution: A Geography of the Yorkshire Woolen Industry, 1982; Geographical Imaginations, 1994; Explorations in Critical Human Geography: Hettner Lecture 1997, 1998; The Colonial Present: Afghanistan, Palestine and Iraq, 2004. EDITOR: (with R.J. Johnson and D.M. Smith) The Dictionary of Human Geography, 2nd ed., 1986; (with A.R.H. Baker) Explorations in Historical Geography: Interpretative Essays, 1984; (with M. Billinge and R. Martin) Recollections of a Revolution: Geography as Spatial Science, 1984; (with J. Urry) Social Relations and Spatial Structures, 1985; (with R. Walford) Horizons in Human Geography, 1989; (with R. Martin and G. Smith) Human Geography: Society, Space and Social Science, 1994; (with T. Barnes) Reading Human Geography: The Poetics and Politics of Inquiry, 1997; (with J. Duncan) Writes of Passage: Reading Travel Writing, 1999; (with A. Pred) Violent Geographies: Fear, Terror and Political Violence, 2007. **Address:** Department of Geography, University of British Columbia, 1984 West Mall, Vancouver, BC V6T 1Z2, Canada. **Online address:** gregory@geog.ubc.ca

GREGORY, Dick. American (born United States), b. 1932. **Genres:** Civil Liberties/Human Rights, Race Relations, Social Commentary, Novels, Autobiography/Memoirs. **Career:** Roberts Show Club, master of ceremonies, 1959-60; Dick Gregory Health Enterprises, chairman, 1984-. Writer. **Publications:** From the Back of the Bus, 1962; (with R. Lipsyte) Nigger: An Autobiography, 1964; What's Happening?, 1965; The Shadow That Scares Me, 1968; Write Me In!, 1971; No More Lies: The Myth and Reality of American History, 1971; Dick Gregory's Political Primer, 1972; Dick Gregory's Natural Diet for Folks Who Eat: Cookin' with Mother Nature, 1973; Dick Gregory's Bible Tales, 1974; (with McGraw) Up from Nigger, 1976; (with M. Lane) Code Name Zorro: The Murder of Martin Luther King Jr., 1971; Dick Gregory's Bible Tales, 1978; (with M. Lane) Murder in Memphis: The FBI and the Assassination of Martin Luther King, 1993; (with S.P. Moses) Callus on My Soul: A Memoir, 2000; National Visionary Leadership Project Oral History, 2002-04-29, 2002. **Address:** Dick Gregory Health Enterprises, 39 S LaSalle, Chicago, IL 60603, U.S.A.

GREGORY, Frederick. American (born United States), b. 1942. **Genres:** History, Biography. **Career:** Eisenhower College, assistant professor of mathematics and history of science, 1973-78; University of Florida, Department of History, associate professor, 1978-91, associate chair, 1984-88, chair, 1991-95, professor of history of science, 1992-, now professor emeritus of history of science and European history; History of Science Society, vice president, 1994-95, president, 1996-97; Massachusetts Institute of Technology, Dibner Institute, visiting fellow, 1995. Writer. **Publications:** Scientific Materialism in Nineteenth-Century Germany, 1977; (ed. and intro.) Knowledge, Belief, and Aesthetic Sense, 1989; Nature Lost: Natural Science and the German Theological Traditions, 1992; Extending Kant, 2006; Mystik Methodisch Maskieren, 2007; Questioning Scientific Faith in the Late Nineteenth Century, 2008; Natural Science in Western Civilization, vol. I: Ancient Times to Newton, vol. II: Newton to the Present, 2008; Natural Science in Western History, 2008; J.F. Fries: An Intellectual Biography, forthcoming. **Address:** Department of History, University of Florida, 225 Keene-Flint Hall, PO Box 117320, Gainesville, FL 32611-7329, U.S.A. **Online address:** fgregory@ufl.edu

GREGORY, Kristiana. American (born United States), b. 1951. **Genres:** Westerns/Adventure, Children's Fiction, Young Adult Fiction, History. **Career:** Gardena Valley News, freelance feature writer, 1977-79, freelance reporter, 1978; Southern California Business, associate editor, 1978; Los Angeles Times, book reviewer and columnist, 1978-91; San Luis Obispo County Telegram-Tribune, reporter, 1980-81; writer, 1982-. **Publications:** Jenny of the Tetons, 1989; The Legend of Jimmy Spoon, 1990; Earthquake at Dawn, 1992; Jimmy Spoon and the Pony Express, 1994; The Stowaway: A Tale of California Pirates, 1995; The Winter of Red Snow: The Revolutionary War Diary of Abigail Jane Stewart, 1996; Across the Wide and Lonesome Prairie: The Oregon Trail Diary of Hattie Campbell, 1997; Orphan Runaways, 1998; The Great Railroad Race: The Diary of Libby West, 1999; Cleopatra VII: Daughter of the Nile, 1999; Five Smooth Stones: The Revolutionary War Diary of Hope Penny Potter, 2001; Seeds of Hope: The Gold Rush Diary of Susanna Fairchild, California Territory, 1849, 2001; Eleanor, Crown Jewel of Aquitane, 2002; We Are Patriots: Hope's Revolutionary War Diary, 2002; When Freedom Comes: Hope's Revolutionary War Diary, 2004; Winter Tidings, 2004; Catherine: The Great Journey, 2005; Bronte's Book Club, 2008; Clue at the Bottom of the Lake, 2008; Legend Of Skull Cliff, 2008; My Darlin' Clementine, 2009; Secret of the Junkyard Shadow, 2009; The Dear America: The Winter of Red Snow, 2010; Dear America: Cannons at Dawn, 2010; Cannons At Dawn: The Second Diary of Abigail Jane Stewart, 2011. PRAIRIE RIVER: Prairie River: Journey of Faith, 2003; Prairie River: A Grateful Harvest, 2003; Prairie River: Winter Tidings, 2004; Prairie River: Hope Springs Eternal, 2005. **Address:** PO Box 46021, Boise, ID 83711, U.S.A. **Online address:** kgregorybooks@yahoo.com

GREGORY, Patrick. American (born United States) **Genres:** Novels, Translations, Literary Criticism And History. **Career:** Writer. **Publications:** (Trans. with J. Gregory) Fables of Aesop, 1975; (intro.) Diaries of Marya Zaturenska, 1938-1944, 2002; The Daguerreotype, 2004. Contributor to periodicals. **Address:** c/o Author Mail, Syracuse University Press, 621 Skytop Rd., Ste. 110, Syracuse, NY 13244-5290, U.S.A.

GREGORY, Philippa. British/Kenyan (born Kenya), b. 1954. **Genres:** Novels, Novellas/Short Stories. **Career:** Provincial journalist for newspapers, 1971-75; BBC-Radio, radio journalist, 1978-80, 1984-; Portsmouth News, senior reporter; Hartlepool People, founding member and vice-president; Kingston University, fellow, 1994; University of Durham, faculty; Open University, faculty; Teeside Polytechnic, faculty; Gardens for the Gambia, founder; Guardian, columnist. **Publications:** WIDEACRE TRILOGY: Wideacre, 1987; The Favoured Child, 1989; Meridon, 1990. EARTHLY JOYS SERIES: Earthly Joys, 1998; Virgin Earth, 1999. OTHERS: Mrs. Hartley and the Growth Centre, 1992; The Wise Woman, 1993; Fallen Skies, 1995; A Respectable Trade, 1995; The Little House: A Novel, 1996; Perfectly Correct,

1996; Midlife Mischief, 1998; Zelda's Cut, 2000; Bread and Chocolate, 2000; The Other Boleyn Girl: A Novel, 2002; Queen's Fooll, 2004; Virgin's Lover, 2004; Constant Princess, 2005; The Boleyn Inheritance, 2006; The Other Queen, 2008; The Women of the Cousins' War: The Duchess, the Queen, and the King's Mother, 2011. CHILDREN'S NOVELS: Princess Florizella, 1988; Florizella and the Wolves, 1993; Florizella and the Giant, 2000. COUSINS' WAR: The White Queen, 2009; Red Queen, 2010; The Lady of the Rivers, 2011; Wars of the Roses (2-book boxed set), 2011; The Kingmaker's Daughter, 2012 Contributor of articles to periodicals. **Address:** Simon and Schuster UK, 222 Grays Inn Rd., London, GL WC1X 8HE, England. **Online address:** info@philippagregory.com

GREGORY, Susanna. (Simon Beaufort). Welsh/British (born England), b. 1958. **Genres:** Novels, Young Adult Fiction. **Career:** Cambridge University, Scott Polar Research Institute, research associate. Writer. **Publications:** MATTHEW BARTHOLOMEW SERIES: A Plague on Both Your Houses 1996; An Unholy Alliance, 1996; A Bone of Contention, 1997; A Deadly Brew, Little, 1998; A Wicked Deed, 1999; A Masterly Murder, 2000; The First Matthew Bartholomew Omnibus, 2001; An Order for Death, 2001; A Summer of Discontent, 2002; A Killer in Winter, 2003; The Hand of Justice: The Tenth Chronicle of Matthew Bartholomew, 2004; The Mark of a Murderer: The Eleventh Chronicle of Matthew Bartholomew, 2005; The Tarnished Chalice, 2006; To Kill or Cure, 2007; A Plague on Both Your Houses and Unholy Alliance, 2007; Devil's Disciples, 2008; A Vein of Deceit, 2009; A Killer of Pilgrims, 2010. SIR GEOFFREY DE MAPPESTONE SERIES AS SIMON BEAUFORT: Murder in the Holy City, 1998; A Head for Poisoning, 1999; The Bishop's Brood, 2003; The King's Spies, 2003; The Coiners' Quarrel, 2004. THOMAS CHALONER SERIES: A Conspiracy of Violence, 2006; Blood on the Strand, 2006; Butcher of Smithfield, 2008; The Westminster Poisoner, 2008; A Murder on London Bridge, 2009; The Body in the Thames, 2011. OTHERS: The White Ship Murders, 1999; The Tainted Relic: An Historical Mystery, 2006; House of Shadows, 2007; (co-author) King Arthur's Bones: A Historical Mystery, 2009; Murder in the Minster, 2011; Mystery in the Minster, 2011; (co-author) Hill of Bones, 2011. **Address:** c/o Euan Thorneycroft, A.M. Heath & Company Ltd., 6 Warwick Ct., London, GL WC1R 5DJ, England.

GREGORY, Tobias. (Tobias Bolton Gregory). American (born United States), b. 1971?. **Genres:** Literary Criticism And History, Theology/Religion. **Career:** California State University, assistant professor of English, 1999-2003; Claremont McKenna College, assistant professor of literature, 2003-07; Catholic University of America, associate professor of English, 2007-, director of graduate studies. Writer. **Publications:** From Many Gods to One: Divine Action in Renaissance Epic, 2006. Contributor to periodicals and journals. **Address:** Department of English, Catholic University of America, 323 Marist Hall, 620 Michigan Ave., Washington, DC 20064-0001, U.S.A. **Online address:** gregoryt@cua.edu

GREGORY, Tobias Bolton. *See* **GREGORY, Tobias.**

GREGORY, Valiska. American (born United States), b. 1940. **Genres:** Children's Fiction, Poetry, inspirational/Motivational Literature. **Career:** White Oak Elementary School, music and drama teacher, 1962-64; Oak Lawn Memorial High School, teacher, 1965-68; University of Wisconsin, lecturer in English, 1968-74; University of Indianapolis, adjunct professor of English, 1974-83; Butler University, adjunct professor of English, 1983-85, Midwinter Children's Literature Conference, founding director, 1989-92, writer-in-residence, 1993-; Butler Writers' Studio, fellow, 1989-92. Writer and producer. **Publications:** FOR CHILDREN: Terribly Wonderful, 1986; Sunny Side Up, 1986; Riddle Soup, 1987; The Oatmeal Cookie Giant, 1987; Happy Burpday, Maggie McDougal!, 1992; Through the Mickle Woods, 1992; Babysitting for Benjamin, 1993; Stories from a Time Before, 1995; Kate's Giants, 1995; Looking for Angels, 1996; When Stories Fell Like Shooting Stars, 1996; A Valentine for Norman Noggs, 1999; Shirley's Wonderful Baby, 2000; The Mystery of the Grindlecat, 2003. OTHER: The Words Like Angels Come (poetry for adults), 1987. Contributor to periodicals. **Address:** Butler University, 4600 Sunset Ave., Indianapolis, IN 46208, U.S.A. **Online address:** vgregory@butler.edu

GREGORY, Vicki L. American (born United States), b. 1950. **Genres:** Librarianship, Bibliography. **Career:** Auburn University, audio-visual librarian, 1976-78, Department of Systems and Operations, head, 1976-88, coordinator

of technical services, 1978-86, Department of Systems and Operations, head, 1986-88; University of South Florida, School of Library and Information Science, head, 1988-, assistant professor, 1988-94, associate professor, 1994-2000, director, 1999-, professor, 2000-; Florida Library Association, director, 2001-03; The American Society for Information Science and Technology, SIG cabinet director, 2003-07. Writer. **Publications:** (Co-ed.) A Dynamic Tradition: The History of Alabama Academic Libraries from Their Establishment through 1988, 1991; (ed.) The State and the Academic Library, 1993; (with M. Stauffer and T. Keene) Multicultural Resources on the Internet: The United States and Canada, 1999; Selecting and Managing Electronic Resources, 2000, rev. ed., 2006. Contributor to books and periodicals. **Address:** School of Library and Information Science, University of South Florida, CIS 1040, 4202 E Fowler Ave., Tampa, FL 33620-8100, U.S.A. **Online address:** gregory@shell.cas.usf.edu

GREGSON, Julia. Welsh (born Wales), b. 1948?. **Genres:** Novels. **Career:** Sungravure (Australian magazine group), New York foreign correspondent; Rolling Stone magazine, reporter; Hardy Amies, house model. **Publications:** The Water Horse (novel), 2005 as Band of Angels: A Novel, 2010; East of the Sun, 2009. Contributor to periodicals. **Address:** Monmouthshire, Wales. **Online address:** julia@juliagregson.net

GREHAN, Ida. Irish (born Ireland), b. 1916. **Genres:** Area Studies, History, Theology/Religion, Reference. **Career:** Radio broadcaster; Irish Times, feature writer. **Publications:** Irish Family Names: Highlights of 50 Family Histories, 1973; Waterford, An Irish Art: The History of Waterford Crystal, 1981; Pocket Guide to Irish Family Names, 1985; (with P.W. Joyce and R. Coghlan) The Book of Irish Names: First, Family and Place Names, 1989; Irish Family Histories, 1993; Dictionary of Irish Family Names, 1997; A Little Book of Irish Family Names, 1997. Contributor to periodicals. **Address:** Milk Wood, Sandycove Ave. E, Dublin, 26376, Ireland.

GREIF, Geoffrey L. American (born United States), b. 1949. **Genres:** Social Work, Human Relations/Parenting. **Career:** Child Study Team, chair, 1974-76; Philadelphia College of the Performing Arts, adjunct instructor, 1974-76; Drenk Memorial Guidance Center, clinical social worker, 1976-79; Widener University, adjunct instructor, 1982-84; Cabrini College, adjunct instructor, 1983-84; University of Maryland, assistant professor, 1984-89, associate professor of social work, 1989-95, professor, 1995-, associate dean, 1996-2007; Community Counseling and Resource Center, clinical supervisor, 1985-90; Sinai Hospital, Drug Dependency Program, trainer and clinician, 1990-92, 1996; Epoch House, family therapy consultant, 1991-; Jewish Family Services, divorce support group, co-leader, 1991-; Juvenile Justice Resource Center, consultant, 1992-; Maryland Correctional Adjustment Center, Baltimore's SuperMax Prison, co-leader of fathering groups, 2011-. Writer. **Publications:** Single Fathers, 1985; (with M.S. Pabst) Mothers without Custody, 1988; The Daddy Track and the Single Father, 1990; (with R.L. Hegar) When Parents Kidnap: The Families behind the Headlines, 1993; (with R.L. Hegar) Understanding Abducted Children, 1993; (with Hegar) Parents Who Abduct (monograph), 1994; (ed. with P. Ephross) Group Work with Populations at Risk, 1997, 3rd ed., 2011; Out of Touch: When Parents and Children Lose Contact after Divorce, 1997; (with F. Hrabowksi and K. Maton) Beating the Odds: Raising Academically Successful African American Males, 1998; (co-author) Overcoming the Odds: Raising Academically Successful African American Women, 2002; Group Work With Populations at Risk, 2005, 3rd ed., 2011; Buddy System: Understanding Male Friendships, 2009; (with K.H. Deal) Two Plus Two, 2012. **Address:** School of Social Work, University of Maryland, Rm. 3W01, 525 W Redwood St., Baltimore, MD 21201, U.S.A. **Online address:** ggreif@ssw.umaryland.edu

GREIF, Karen F. (Karen Faye Greif). American (born United States), b. 1952. **Genres:** Information Science/Computers, Sciences, Adult Non-fiction. **Career:** California Institute of Technology, Division of Biology, postdoctoral fellow, 1978; University of California Medical Center, Department of Physiology, postdoctoral fellow, 1978-81, 1981-82; Bryn Mawr College, faculty, 1982-, assistant professor 1982-89, associate professor, 1989-94, professor of biology, 1994-, department chair, 1993-96, 2006-09; Medical College of Pennsylvania, Department of Anatomy, visiting assistant professor, 1983-84; University of California, Department of Biology, visiting associate professor, 1989-90; National Research Council, National Academy of Sciences, Office of Scientific and Engineering Personnel, program officer, 1996-97; Saunders Publishing Co., textbook reviewer, 1998; University of Pennsylvania, Center for Bioethics, visiting fellow, 2003-04. Writer. **Publications:** (With

J.F. Merz) Current Controversies in the Biological Sciences: Case Studies of Policy Challenges from New Technologies, 2007. Contributor to journals. **Address:** Department of Biology, Bryn Mawr College, Park Science Bldg., 101 N Merion Ave., Bryn Mawr, PA 19010, U.S.A. **Online address:** kgreif@brynmawr.edu

GREIF, Karen Faye. *See* **GREIF, Karen F.**

GREIFF, Barrie S(anford). American (born United States), b. 1935. **Genres:** Human Relations/Parenting, Psychology. **Career:** Jewish General Hospital, intern, 1960-61; Institute of Living, resident, 1961-64; University of Hartford, adjunct assistant professor, 1963-64; Georgetown University, clinical instructor in psychiatry, 1964-66; Veterans Administration Hospital, consultant, 1964-66; Harvard University, fellow in psychiatry, 1964-66; University Health Service, psychiatrist, 1966-, consultant; Massachusetts General Hospital, clinical assistant psychiatrist, 1966-68; Harvard Business School, lecturer in occupational psychiatry, 1970-. Writer. **Publications:** (With P.K. Munter) Tradeoffs: Executive, Family, and Organizational Life, 1980; (with N. Kates and D.Q. Hagen) Psychosocial Impact of Job Loss, 1990; Introduction of Occupational Psychiatry, 1993; Legacy: The Giving of Life's Greatest Treasures, 1999; A Life Worth Living, 2001. **Address:** 25 Montrose St., Newton, MA 02458-2717, U.S.A.

GREIL, Arthur L(awrence). American (born United States), b. 1949. **Genres:** Sociology, Social Sciences, Philosophy, Human Relations/Parenting, Medicine/Health. **Career:** Alfred University, instructor, assistant professor, associate professor, professor, full professor of sociology and health policy, 1977-, director of honors program, 1982-85, College of Liberal Arts and Sciences, associate dean, 1985-92, division chair of social sciences, 1997-, 2005-08; New Jersey Institute of Technology, lecturer, 1989. Writer. **Publications:** Georges Sorel and the Sociology of Virtue, 1981; Not Yet Pregnant: Infertile Couples in Contemporary America, 1991; (ed. with T. Robbins) Religion and Social Order, vol. IV: Between Sacred and Secular: Theory and Research on Quasi-Religion, 1994, (ed. with D.G. Bromley) vol. X: Defining Religion: Critical Perspectives on Drawing Boundaries between Sacred and Secular, 2003. Works appear in anthologies. Contributor to sociology journals and popular magazines. **Address:** Social Sciences Department, Alfred University, 1 Saxon Dr., Olin Bldg. 208B, Alfred, NY 14802, U.S.A. **Online address:** fgreil@alfred.edu

GREMILLION, Helen. American (born United States), b. 1965. **Genres:** Anthropology/Ethnology, Self Help. **Career:** Stanford University, fellow, 1994-95, lecturer in anthropology, 1996-98; Indiana University, assistant professor, 1998-2004, Peg Zeglin Brand chair, 1998-, adjunct professor of anthropology, 1998, adjunct professor of cultural studies, 2000, adjunct professor of American studies, 2003, associate professor of gender studies, 2004-, Graduate Studies, director, University Graduate School, fellow of research, 2001, Progressive Faculty Coalition, staff, 2001-, Freshman Learning Project, fellow of research, 2004. Writer. **Publications:** Feeding Anorexia: Gender and Power at a Treatment Center, 2003; Ethnographic Therapies: Lessons for an Engaged Anthropology, forthcoming. Contributor of articles to journals. **Address:** Department of Gender Studies, Indiana University, Memorial Hall E, Rm. 130, 1021 E 3rd St., Bloomington, IN 47405-2201, U.S.A.

GRENFELL, Michael J. (Michael James Grenfell). British (born England), b. 1953. **Genres:** Education, Language/Linguistics, How-to Books, Philosophy. **Career:** Bristol United Hospitals, scientific officer, 1970-76; Aérospatiale Industry, instructor and translator, 1978-79; Oxford School of English, tutor in English as a foreign language, 1980-81; Pace Ltd., tutor in English, 1981-83; Langley Park Boys' School, teacher of French and German, 1983-89, department head, 1985-89; University of Southampton, faculty, 1989-. Writer. **Publications:** Partners, 1993; Reflections on Reading, 1995; (with D. James) Bourdieu and Education: Acts of Practical Theory, 1998; Training Teachers in Practice, 1998; (ed. with M. Kelly) Pierre Bourdieu: Language, Culture and Education, 1999; (with V. Harris) Modern Languages and Learning Strategies: In Theory and Practice, 1999; (co-author) Aspectos didácticaos de Inglés, 2002; (ed.) Modern Languages across the Curriculum, 2002; (with M. Kelly and D. Jones) The European Language Teacher, 2003; Pierre Bourdieu-Agent Provocateur, 2004; (with C. Hardy) Art rules: Pierre Bourdieu and the Visual Arts, 2007; Pierre Bourdieu: Education and Training, 2007; Bourdieu, Language and Linguistics, 2010; (co-author) Language, Eth-

nography, and Education, 2011. Contributor to journals. **Address:** School of Education, University of Southampton, Bldg. 32, Southampton, SO17 1BJ, England. **Online address:** grenfell@soton.ac.uk

GRENFELL, Michael James. *See* **GRENFELL, Michael J.**

GRENHAM, John. Irish (born Ireland), b. 1954. **Genres:** Area Studies, History, Genealogy/Heraldry, Poetry, Reference. **Career:** National University of Ireland, University College, tutor, 1981-85; Irish Genealogical Project, project manager, 1990-. Writer. **Publications:** Daedalus: Introductions, 1990; The Cloverdale Anthology of Irish Poetry, 1991; Tracing Your Irish Ancestors: The Complete Guide, 1992, 4th ed., 2012; Clans and Families of Ireland: The Heritage and Heraldry of Irish Clans and Families, 1993; The Little Book of Irish Clans, 1994; Generations: The Story of a Family, 1996; Pocket Reference: Irish Family Names, 1996; An Illustrated History of Ireland, 1997; Grenham's Irish Surnames, 2003; Irish Ancestors, 2004. **Address:** National Library of Ireland, 2 Kildare St., Dublin, DU 2, Ireland.

GRENHOLM, Cristina. Swedish (born Sweden) **Genres:** Theology/Religion. **Career:** Karlstad University, faculty. Writer. **Publications:** Romans Interpreted: A Comparative Analysis of the Commentaries of Barth, Nygren, Cranfield, and Wilckens on Paul's Epistle to the Romans, 1990; The Old Testament, Christianity, and Pluralism, 1996; (ed. with D. Patte) Reading Israel in Romans: Legitimacy and Plausibility of Divergent Interpretations, 2000; (ed. with D. Patte) Gender, Tradition, and Romans: Shared Ground, Uncertain Borders, 2005; Motherhood and Love: Beyond the Gendered Stereotypes of Theology, 2011. **Address:** Karlstad University, Universitetsgatan 2, Karlstad, 651 88, Sweden. **Online address:** cristina.grenholm@kau.se

GRENIER, John. American (born United States), b. 1967?. **Genres:** History, Military/Defense/Arms Control. **Career:** United States Air Force Academy, associate professor of history, professor; Norwich University, Master of Arts in Military History, senior professor in American military history and capstone director. Writer. **Publications:** The First Way of War: American War Making on the Frontier, 1607-1814, 2005; The Far Reaches of Empire: War in Nova Scotia, 1710-1760, 2008. Contributor to periodicals. **Address:** Master of Arts in Military History, Norwich University, 158 Harmon Dr., Northfield, VT 05663, U.S.A. **Online address:** john.grenier@comcast.net

GRENNAN, Eamon. American/Irish (born Ireland), b. 1941. **Genres:** Poetry, Translations, Literary Criticism And History. **Career:** Vassar College, professor of English, 1974-2007, Dexter M. Ferry Jr. professor of English, through 2004, professor emeritus, 2007-; Villanova University, Heimbold professor of Irish studies, 2002; Columbia University, Graduate Writing Program, adjunct professor, 2005-; New York University, Graduate Writing Program, adjunct professor, 2005-; City University of New York, Lehman College, professor. Writer. **Publications:** Wildly for Days, 1983; What Light There Is, 1987; Twelve Poems, 1988; Cat Scat, 1988; What Light There is and Other Poems, 1989; (ed. with J.D. Brophy) New Irish Writing, 1989; ACCTEST New Irish Writing, 1989; As If It Matters, 1991; So It Goes, 1995; (trans.) Selected Poems of Giacomo Leopardi, 1995; Leopardi: Selected Poems, 1997; Relations: New and Selected Poems, 1998; Facing the Music: Irish Poetry in the Twentieth Century, 1999; Still Life with Waterfall, 2001; Poems, 2002; The Quick of It, 2004; (trans. with R. Kitzinger) Oedipus at Colonus, 2004; Out of Breath, 2007; Matter of Fact, 2008; Out of Sight, 2010. **Address:** Vassar College, 124 Raymond Ave., PO Box 352, Poughkeepsie, NY 12604-0352, U.S.A. **Online address:** grennan@vassar.edu

GRESCOE, Paul. Canadian (born Canada), b. 1939?. **Genres:** History, Travel/Exploration, Novels, Money/Finance, Romance/Historical. **Career:** Canadian Press, staff; Brandon Sun, staff; Winnipeg Tribune, staff; Toronto Telegram, staff; The Canadian Magazine, staff writer and editor; Maclean's Magazine, staff. **Publications:** (With D. Cruise) The Money Rustlers: Self-Made Millionaires of the New West, 1985; Flesh Wound (novel), 1991; Blood Vessel (novel), 1993; (with A. Grescoe) Alaska: The Cruise-Lover's Guide, 1994, 3rd. ed., 2002; (with A. Grescoe) Fragments of Paradise: British Columbia's Wild and Wondrous Islands, 1995; The Merchants of Venus: Inside Harlequin and the Empire of Romance, 1996; The Mavericks: Lessons Learned from the West's Winning Entrepreneurs, 1999; Trip of a Lifetime: The Making of the Rocky Mountaineer, 2000, rev. ed., 2005; Flight Path: How West Jet is Flying High in Canada's Most Turbulent Industry, 2004; Pass It On: The Astonishing Story of Savers and Value Village, 2005. COMPILED AND EDITED WITH A. GRESCOE: The Book of Letters: 150 Years of Private Canadian Correspondence, 2002; Book of War Letters: 100 Years of Private Canadian Correspondence, 2003; The Book of Love Letters: Canadian Kinship, Friendship and Romance, 2005. Contributor to periodicals. **Address:** Raincoast Books, 8680 Cambie St., Vancouver, BC V6P 6M9, Canada.

GRESHAKE, Gisbert. German (born Germany), b. 1933. **Genres:** Theology/Religion, History. **Career:** University of Munster and Tubingen, assistant professor, 1966-73; University of Vienna, professor, 1974-85, dean of theology faculty, 1979-83, 1989-90; University of Freiburg, professor, 1985-99, emeritus professor, 1999-. Writer. **Publications:** Historie wird Geschichte, 1963; Auferstehung der Toten, 1969; Zum Thema: Busse und Bussfeier, 1971; Gnade als konkrete Freiheit, 1972; (with G. Lohfink) Naherwartung-Auferstehung-Untersterblichkeit, 1975; Staerker als der Tod, 1976; Geschenkte Freiheit, 1977; Der Preis der Liebe, 1978; (with G. Lohfink) Bittgebet: Testfall des Glaubens, 1978; Die Wueste bestehen, 1979; Signale des Glaubens, 1980; (with W. Geerlings and J. Weismayer) Quellen geistlichen Lebens, 4 vols., 1980-89; Priestersein, 1982; Wer ist der Mensch?, 1983; Gottes Heil: Gluck des Menschen, 1983; Gottes Willen tun, 1984; Ungewisses Jenseits?, 1986; Gott in allen Dingen finden, 1986; (with J. Kremer) Resurrectio mortuorum, 1986; Erloest in einer unerloester Welt?, 1987; Tod-und dann?, 1988; The Meaning of Christian Priesthood, 1989; Zur Frage der Bischofsernennung, 1990; Ruf Gottes: Anwort des Menschen, 1991; Wenn Leid mein Leben laehmt, 1992; Des dreieine Gott, 1997; Au den dreieinen Gott glauben, 1998; Priester sein in dienes Zeit, 2000; Spiritualitat der Wuste, 2002; Guade-Geschenk der Freiheit, 2004; Kleine Hinfuhrung zum Glauben an der drei-liven Gott, 2005. Contributor to journals. **Address:** Institute of Theology, University of Freiburg, Werthmannplatz, Freiburg, D-79085, Germany. **Online address:** gisbert.greshake@theol.uni-freiburg.de

GRESHAM, Eddie. American (born United States), b. 1968. **Genres:** Horror. **Career:** IBM Corp., staff; Niborex Inc., staff. Writer and networking consultant. **Publications:** Footfalls, 2007. **Address:** Plano, TX , U.S.A. **Online address:** etg@eddiegresham.com

GRESHAM, Stephen. Also writes as J. V. Lewton, John Newland. American (born United States), b. 1947?. **Genres:** Horror, Novels, Novellas/Short Stories, Young Adult Fiction. **Career:** Auburn University, professor of English. Writer. **Publications:** HORROR NOVELS: Moon Lake, 1982; Rockabye Baby, 1984; Half Moon Down, 1985; Dew Claws, 1986; The Shadow Man, 1986; Midnight Boy, 1987; Abracadabra, 1988; Runaway, 1988; Night Touch, 1988; Demon's Eye, 1989; Blood Wings, 1990; The Living Dark, 1991; In the Blood, 2001; Dark Magic, 2002; Haunted Ground, 2003; The Fraternity, 2004. OTHERS: (as J.V. Lewton) Just Pretend (young adult novel), 1994; (as John Newland) Primal Instinct, 1994; (as J.V. Lewton) Called to Darkness, 1995; Night Shapes, 2001; Crossing the River of Good Mind, 2007; The Book of Moonlight and Other Dark Fantasy Tales (stories), 2007; Deadrise, 2011. Works appear in anthologies. **Address:** Department of English, Auburn University, 9030 Haley Ctr., Auburn, AL 36849-5203, U.S.A. **Online address:** greshsl@auburn.edu

GRESKOVIC, Robert. American (born United States) **Genres:** Dance/Ballet, Art/Art History. **Career:** Lewis Center for the Arts, lecturer in theatre and dance; Dance Magazine, reviewer and New York correspondent; Wall Street Journal, columnist; DanceView, consulting editor; Dance Intl., New York correspondent; City University of New York, faculty, Hunter College, faculty; Sarah Lawrence College, faculty; Ballet Review, associate. **Publications:** Looking at Ballet: Ashton and Balanchine, 1926-1936, 1992; Ballet 101: A Complete Guide to Learning and Loving the Ballet, 1998; (contrib.) Dorothea Tanning: Early Designs for the Stage, 2010. **Address:** Hyperion, 114 5th Ave., New York, NY 10011, U.S.A.

GRESSER, Seymour. American (born United States), b. 1926. **Genres:** Poetry, Biography, Autobiography/Memoirs, Homes/Gardens, Theology/Religion, Young Adult Fiction. **Career:** U.S. Merchant Marines, radio operator, 1944-46; Sculptor's Studio, part-time instructor in sculpture, 1958-63; Yale University, sculptor-in-residence, 1969. Sculptor and writer. **Publications:** Stone Elegies, 1955; Coming of the Atom, 1957; Letters from Mexico, 1964; Voyages, 1969; A Garland for Stephen, 1970; Departure for Sons, 1973; Fragments and Other Poems, 1982; (ed.) Bio-gardener's Bible, 1982; Hagar and Her Elders, 1989. Contributor to magazines. **Address:** 1015 Ruatan St., Silver Spring, MD 20903-3216, U.S.A. **Online address:** sygr@erols.com

GRETSCH, Mechthild. German (born Germany), b. 1945. **Genres:** Literary

Criticism And History, Theology/Religion. **Career:** Georg-August-Universität Göttingen, professor, head and chair. Writer. **Publications:** Die Regula Sancti Benedicti in England und ihre altenglische übersetzung, 1973; The Intellectual Foundations of the English Benedictine Reform, 1999; Aelfric and the Cult of Saints in Late Anglo-Saxon England, 2005. Contributor to books and journals. **Address:** Seminar für Englische Philologie, Georg-August-Universität Göttingen, Käte-Hamburger-Weg 3, Göttingen, 37073, Germany. **Online address:** mechthild.gretsch@phil.uni-goettingen.de

GREWAL, David Singh. American/Indian (born India), b. 1976. **Genres:** Social Sciences. **Career:** Harvard University, Society of Fellows, junior fellow; Yale Law School, professor, 2011-, Information Society Project, affiliated fellow. Writer and political scientist. **Publications:** Network Power: The Social Dynamics of Globalization, 2008. **Address:** Society of Fellows, Harvard University, 78 Mount Auburn St., Cambridge, MA 02138, U.S.A. **Online address:** dsgrewal@post.harvard.edu

GREY, Amelia. *See* **SKINNER, Gloria Dale.**

GREY, Anthony. British (born England), b. 1938. **Genres:** Novels, Autobiography/Memoirs, Novellas/Short Stories, Plays/Screenplays, Romance/Historical, Politics/Government, Young Adult Fiction, Sex, Sex. **Career:** Eastern Daily Press, journalist, 1960-64; Reuters News Agency, foreign correspondent, 1965-69; British Broadcasting Corporation World Service, presenter, 1974-79; independent radio and television reporter and presenter. Writer. **Publications:** Hostage in Peking (autobiography), 1970; A Man Alone (short stories), 1972; Some Put Their Trust in Chariots, 1973; Crosswords from Peking, 1975; The Bulgarian Exclusive, 1976; The Chinese Assassin, 1978; Saigon, 1982; The Prime Minister was a Spy (non-fiction), 1983; Peking: A Novel of China's Revolution, 1921-1978, 1988; The Bangkok Secret (novel), 1990; The Naked Angels (novel), 1990; A Gallery of Nudes, 1992; Quest for Justice: Towards Homosexual Emancipation, 1992; Speaking of Sex: The Limits of Language, 1993; Tokyo Bay (novel) 1996; The German Stratagem, 1998; Tokyo Imperial, 1999; What is the Universe In? (short stories), 2003; The Thoughts of Chairman Grey, 2007; Hostage in Peking Plus, 2008; The Hostage Handbook: The Secret Diary of a Two-Year Ordeal in China, 2009. Contributor of articles to books and periodicals. **Address:** c/o Michael Sissons, A. D. Peters, 5th Fl., Chelsea Harbour, Lots Rd., London, GL SW10 0XF, England. **Online address:** anthony.grey@virgin.net

GREY, Beryl (Elizabeth). British (born England), b. 1927. **Genres:** Novellas/Short Stories, Dance/Ballet, Travel/Exploration. **Career:** Royal Ballet (formerly Sadlers Wells Ballet), Prima Ballerina, staff, 1941-57; writer, 1958-; Arts Education Trust, artistic director, 1966-68; London College of Dance, governor, 1966-, vice-chairman, 1984-93, retired, 1993; London Festival Ballet (now English National Ballet), artistic director, 1968-79; Royal Academy of Dancing, vice-president, 1980; Dance Council of Wales, president, 1981; Imperial Society of Teachers of Dancing, chairwoman, 1981-91, president, 1991-2001, life president, 2001; Keep Fit Society, president, 1992; Birmingham Royal Ballet, governor, 1995-99, director; Royal Opera House, Covent Garden, director, 1999-2003. Writer. **Publications:** Red Curtain Up, 1958; Through the Bamboo Curtain, 1965; (ed.) My Favourite Ballet Stories, 1981. **Address:** David Higham Associates Ltd., 5-8 Lower John St., Golden Sq., London, GL W1F 9HA, England.

GREY, Jerry. American (born United States), b. 1926. **Genres:** Air/Space Topics, Engineering, Sciences, Technology, Industrial Relations, Information Science/Computers. **Career:** Cornell University, instructor in thermodynamics, 1947-49; Fairchild Corp., Engine Division, staff, 1949-50; California Institute of Technology, Guggenheim Aerospace Laboratory, hypersonic aerodynamicist, 1950-51; Marquardt Aircraft Co., senior engineer, 1951-52; Princeton University, School of Engineering and Applied Science, research associate, 1952-56, assistant professor, 1956-59, associate professor of aerospace science, 1960-67, Nuclear Propulsion Research Laboratory, director, 1962-67, visiting professor, 1990-; Greyrad Corp., president, 1959-71; American Institute of Aeronautics and Astronautics, administrator for technical activities and communications, 1971-82, director of science and technology policy, 1987-; Calprobe Corp. (high-temperature instrumentation), president, 1972-83; Applied Solar Energy Corp., director, 1978-92; Aerospace America, publisher, 1982-87. Writer. **Publications:** Nuclear Propulsion, 1970; The Race for Electric Power, 1972; The Facts of Flight, 1973; Noise, Noise, Noise!, 1975; Enterprise, 1979; Aeronautics in China: An AIAA Report Based on an AIAA Visit to the People's Republic of China, August

30-September 18, 1980, 1981; Space Tracking and Data Systems: Proceedings of the AIAS/NASA Symposium on Space Tracking and Data Systems, Pentagon City, Virginia, June 16-18, 1981, 1981; Beachheads in Space, 1983; A Compilation of Selected Nuclear Space Power Reactor Characteristics: Sp-100 Project, 1983; Government vs. Free Enterprise in Space, 1987; Highlights in Space Technology and Applications (annually), 1988; Issues in Strategic Planning for Commercial Space Growth, 1989; Basis for R&D Planning for Civil Aviation in the 21st Century, 1989; Assessment of Strategic Defense Initiative Technologies, 1989; The Role of Technology in Revitalizing Civil Aviation, 1990; Issues in Planning Mission to Planet Earth, 1990; Assessment of New Technologies for the Space Exploration Initiative, 1990; Atmospheric Effects of Chemical Rocket Propulsion, 1991; Assessment of Technologies for Ballistic Missile Defense, 1993; Interactive Effects of Noise and Emission Reduction Technologies on Other Aviation System Technologies, 1993. EDITOR: (with V. Grey) Space Flight Report to the Nation, 1962; Offshore Airport Center Planning, 1971; (with J.P. Layton) New Space Transportation Systems, 1973; (with A. Henderson) Exploration of the Solar System, 1974; Aircraft Fuel Conservation, 1974; Solar Energy for Earth, 1975; The Role of Technology in Civil Aviation Policy, 1976; Advanced Energy Conservation Technology, 1976; (with R. Downey and B. Davis) Space: A Resource for Earth, 1976; Space Manufacturing Facilities, 4 vols., 1977-81; (with M. Newman) Aerospace Technology Transfer to the Public Sector, 1978; (with R. Salkeld and D. Patterson) Space Transportation 1980-2000, 1978; Alternative Fuels for Transportation, 1979; (with C. Krop) Aerospace Technology and Marine Transport, 1979; International Aerospace Review, 1982; Working in Space, 1982; Global Implications of Space Activities, 1982; Aerospace Technology and Commercial Nuclear Power, 1983; Hybrid Rocket Propulsion, 1995; Space Launch Integration, 1998; Assessment of NASA Studies of Space Solar Power Concerts, 1998; Export Control Policy and the US Satellite Industry, 1999; Defense Excellence, 2002. **Address:** American Institute of Aeronautics and Astronautics, 1801 Alexander Bell Dr., Ste. 500, Reston, VA 20191-4344, U.S.A.

GREY, Patricia. See EVANS, Liz.

GREY, Rudolph. American (born United States) **Genres:** Biography. **Career:** Freelance writer, 1992-. **Publications:** Nightmare of Ecstasy: The Life and Art of Edward D. Wood Jr. (biography), 1992. **Address:** Feral House, 2532 Lincoln Blvd., Ste. 359, PO Box 39910, Venice, CA 90291-5043, U.S.A.

GREY-WILSON, C. See GREY-WILSON, Christopher.

GREY-WILSON, Christopher. (C. Grey-Wilson). British (born England), b. 1944?. **Genres:** Botany, Horticulture, Sciences. **Career:** Royal Botanic Gardens, principal scientific officer, 1968-90, research botanist, Curtis Magazine, editor; The Alpine Garden Society, editor, 1990-; Royal Horticultural Society, The Plantsman Magazine, editor. **Publications:** Dionysia, 1970; (ed. with R.C. Elliott) Saxifrages: The Genus Saxifraga in the Wild and in Cultivation, 1976; Alpine Flowers of Britain and Europe, 1979; Impatiens of Africa, 1980; (with B. Mathew) Bulbs, 1981; (with V. Matthews) Gardening on Walls, 1983; Garden Flowers, 1986; The Genus Cyclamen, 1988; (ed.) A Manual of Alpine and Rock Garden Plants, 1988; (with M. Blamey) The Illustrated Flora of Britain and Northern Europe, 1988; (with M. Blamey) The Genus Dionysia, 1989; Mediterranean Wild Flowers, 1993; Poppies: A Guide to the Poppy Family in the Wild and in Cultivation, 1993, rev. ed., 2000; (with V. Matthews) Gardening with Climbers, 1997; Cyclamen, 1997, new ed., 2003; Clematis, the Genus: A Comprehensive Guide for Gardeners, Horticulturists and Botanists, 2000; Annuals & Biennials, 2000; The Rock Garden Plant Primer: Easy, Small Plants for Containers, Patios and the Open Garden, 2009. **Address:** The Alpine Garden Society, AGS Ctr., Avon Bank, Pershore, WR10 3JP, England. **Online address:** kit@agsbull.demon.co.uk

GRICE, Gordon. American (born United States), b. 1965. **Genres:** Zoology, Sciences, Animals/Pets. **Career:** Teacher, 1994-97; Panhandle Times, reporter and columnist, 1995-97; Oklahoma Today Magazine, contributing editor, 1998-; California Institute of the Arts, faculty; University of California Los Angeles, Extension, faculty. **Publications:** The Red Hourglass: Lives of the Predators, 1998; Deadly Kingdom: The Book of Dangerous Animals, 2010. Contributor of articles to periodicals. **Address:** c/o Elyse Cheney, Sanford J. Greenburger Associates, 55 5th Ave., New York, NY 10003-4301, U.S.A.

GRIDNEFF, Ilya. Papua New Guinean/Australian (born Australia), b. 1979?. **Genres:** Essays. **Career:** Australian Associated Press, journalist and field re-

porter. **Publications:** (With H. DeWitt) Your Name Here, 2008. **Address:** Port Moresby, Papua New Guinea. **Online address:** ilyagridneff@hotmail.com

GRIEB, Kenneth J. American (born United States), b. 1939. **Genres:** History, International Relations/Current Affairs, Literary Criticism And History, Politics/Government, Third World, Bibliography, Reference, Area Studies, Area Studies. **Career:** Indiana University-South Bend, resident lecturer in history, 1965-66; University of Wisconsin, assistant professor, 1966-70, coordinator of Latin American studies, 1968-77, associate professor, 1970-74, professor of history, 1974-, coordinator of international studies, 1977-, Interdisciplinary Center, director, 1978-91, John McNaughton Rosebush university professor, 1983-; SNC Corp., professor of international relations, 1993-. Writer. **Publications:** The United States and Huerta, 1969; (with G. Flynn) Essays on Miguel Angel Asturias, 1973; The Latin American Policy of Warren G. Harding, 1976, rev. ed., 2000; Guatemalan Caudillo: The Regime of Jorge Ubico, Guatemala, 1931-1944, 1979; Central America in the Nineteenth and Twentieth Centuries: An Annotated Bibliography, 1988. EDITOR: Latin American Government Leaders, 1970; Research Guide to Central America and the Caribbean, 1985. Contributor of articles to journals. **Address:** International Studies Program, University of Wisconsin-Oshkosh, Polk 58, 800 Algoma Blvd., Oshkosh, WI 54901, U.S.A. **Online address:** grieb@uwosh.edu

GRIERSON, Bruce. Canadian (born Canada) **Genres:** Psychology, Self Help, Medicine/Health. **Career:** Adbusters, contributing editor. **Publications:** (With K. Lasn) Culture Jam, 1999; U-turn: What If You Woke Up One Morning and Realized You Were Living the Wrong Life?, 2007. Contributor to periodicals. **Address:** Adbusters, 1243 W 7th Ave., Vancouver, BC V6H 1B7, Canada. **Online address:** brucegrierson@telus.net

GRIESEMER, John. American (born United States), b. 1947. **Genres:** Novels, Novellas/Short Stories, Young Adult Fiction, Romance/Historical. **Career:** Newspaper journalist, 1973-76; actor and writer, 1973-. **Publications:** NOVELS: No One Thinks of Greenland, 2001; Signal & Noise, 2003. Contributor to periodicals. **Address:** Eastern Alliance Talent, 1501 Broadway, Ste. 404, New York, NY 10036, U.S.A.

GRIEST, Stephanie Elizondo. American (born United States), b. 1974. **Genres:** Women's Studies And Issues, Reference. **Career:** Seattle Post-Intelligencer, freelance journalist, 1996; China Daily, journalism instructor and editor, 1997-98; Associated Press, political reporter, 1998-99; The Odyssey: U.S. Trek, national correspondent, 2000-01; Youth Free Expression Network, co-founder and director, 2002-05; Gotham Writers Workshop, instructor, 2004-; Princeton University, Hodder Fellow, writer-in-residence, 2005-06; Media Bistro, instructor, 2006-; University of Iowa, MFA in the Nonfiction Writing Program, dean's graduate fellow, Department of English, instructor, 2010-. **Publications:** Around the Bloc: My Life in Moscow, Beijing and Havana, 2004; 100 Places Every Woman Should Go, 2007; 100 Destinos Imprescindibles Para Las Singles De Hoy, 2007; 100 Viagens Que Toda Mulher Precisa Fazer, 2008; Mexican Enough: My Life Between the Borderlines, 2008; Best Women's Travel Writing, 2010. CONTRIBUTOR: Bookmark Now: Writing in Unreaderly Times, 2004; Lengua Fresca: Latinos Writing on the Edge, 2006; Go Your Own Way, 2007. Contributor to periodicals. **Address:** c/o Author Mail, Random House, 1745 Broadway, New York, NY 10019, U.S.A. **Online address:** stephanie@aroundthebloc.com

GRIFFIN, Adele. American (born United States), b. 1970. **Genres:** Children's Fiction, Young Adult Fiction. **Career:** Clarion Books, assistant editor, 1996-98, freelance manuscript reader, 1996-99. **Publications:** Rainy Season, 1996; Split Just Right, 1997; Sons of Liberty, 1997; The Other Shepards, 1998; Dive, 1999; Amandine, 2001; Witch Twins, 2001; Witch Twins at Camp Bliss, 2002; Hannah, Divided, 2002; Witch Twins and Melody Malady, 2003; Overnight, 2003; Where I Want to Be, 2004; Witch Twins and the Ghost of Glenn Bly, 2004; My Almost Epic Summer, 2006; Vampire Island, 2007; Knaveheart's Curse: A Vampire Island Story, 2008; V is for Vampire: A Vampire Island Story, 2009; Picture the Dead, 2010; The Julian Game, 2010; Tighter, 2011; All You Never Wanted, 2012. Contributor to periodicals. **Address:** c/o Charlotte Sheedy, Sheedy Literary Agency Inc., 65 Bleecker St., Fl. 12, New York, NY 10012, U.S.A. **Online address:** erichmauff@aol.com

GRIFFIN, Alice. American (born United States), b. 1924?. **Genres:** Theatre, Biography, Literary Criticism And History. **Career:** City University of New York, Hunter College, temporary tutor, 1948, faculty, 1948-68, Herbert H. Lehman College, professor of English and director of graduate studies, 1968-

91, now professor emeritus. Writer. **Publications:** Pageantry on the Shakespearean Stage, 1951; Living Theatre: A Study Guide to Great Plays, 1951; Living Theatre: An Anthology of Great Plays, 1953; (ed.) The Sources of Ten Shakespearean Plays, 1966; Rebels and Lovers: Shakespeare's Young Heroes and Heroines: A New Approach to Acting and Teaching, 1976; Understanding Tennessee Williams, 1995; Understanding Arthur Miller, 1996; (with G. Thorsten) Understanding Lillian Hellman, 1999; Shakespeare's Women in Love, 2001. Contributor of articles to periodicals. **Address:** University of South Carolina Press, 718 Devine St., Columbia, SC 29208, U.S.A. **Online address:** alice@theaterpro.com

GRIFFIN, Farah Jasmine. American (born United States), b. 1963. **Genres:** Literary Criticism And History, Mystery/Crime/Suspense, Photography, Music. **Career:** University of Pennsylvania, associate professor of English, 1994-2000; Columbia University, professor of English and comparative literature and African American studies, 2000-, Institute for Research in African-American Studies, director; Bunting Institute of Radcliffe College, fellow. Writer. **Publications:** Who Set You Flowin'?: The African-American Migration Narrative, 1995; (with C.J. Fish) A Stranger in the Village: Two Centuries of African-American Travel Writings, 1998; (ed.) Beloved Sisters and Loving Friends: Letters from Rebecca Primus of Royal Oak, Maryland and Addie Brown of Hartford, Connecticut, 1854-1868, 1999; If You Can't Be Free, Bea Mystery: In Search of Billie Holiday, 2001; (ed. with R.G. O'Meally and B.H. Edwards) Uptown Conversation: The New Jazz Studies, 2004; (intro.) Incidents in the Life of a Slave Girl, 2005; (intro.) Inclusive Scholarship: Developing Black Studies in the United States, 2007; (with S. Washington) Clawing at the Limits of Cool: Miles Davis, John Coltrane and the Greatest Jazz Collaboration Ever, 2008. **Address:** Department of English and Comparative Literature, Columbia University, 508B Philosophy Hall, 763 Schermerhorn Ext., 1200 Amsterdam Ave., PO Box 4927, New York, NY 10027, U.S.A. **Online address:** fjg8@columbia.edu

GRIFFIN, H. Terrell. American (born United States), b. 1942. **Genres:** Mystery/Crime/Suspense. **Career:** Trial lawyer in Orlando, Florida. **Publications:** MATT ROYAL MYSTERY SERIES: Longboat Blues, 2005; Murder Key, 2006; Blood Island, 2008; Wyatt's Revenge, 2009. Bitter Legacy, 2010; Collateral Damage, 2011-. **Address:** PO Box 940158, Maitland, FL 32794, U.S.A. **Online address:** tgriffin@hterrellgriffin.com

GRIFFIN, Jasper. British (born England), b. 1937. **Genres:** History, Classics. **Career:** University of Oxford, Balliol College, fellow and tutor, 1963-, Department of Classics, university reader, 1989-, professor of classical literature, 1992-, public orator, 1992-2004, Sub-Faculty of Languages and Literature, public orator. Writer. **Publications:** Homer on Life and Death, 1980; Homer, 1980; A Critical Spirit, the View from Oxford, 1982; (comp.) Snobs, 1982; Latin Poets and Roman Life, 1985; The Mirror of Myth: Classical Themes & Variations, 1986; Virgil, 1986; (ed. with J. Boardman and O. Murray) The Oxford History of the Classical World, 1986, vol. I: Oxford History of Greece and the Hellenistic World, 1991, vol. II: The Oxford History of the Roman World, 1991; Homer, The Odyssey, 1987; (ed.) The Iliad: Book Nine, 1995; (ed.) Sophocles Revisited: Essays Presented to Sir Hugh Lloyd-Jones, 1999; (ed. with J. Boardman and O. Murray) Oxford Illustrated History of the Roman World, 2001; (ed. with J. Boardman and O. Murray) Oxford Illustrated History of Greece and the Hellenistic World, 2001. OTHERS: Tragedy and History, forthcoming. Contributor to journals and periodicals. **Address:** Departmentt of Classics, Balliol College, University of Oxford, Broad St., Oxford, OX OX1 3BJ, England. **Online address:** jasper.griffin@balliol.ox.ac.uk

GRIFFIN, Jill. American (born United States), b. 1955. **Genres:** Business/Trade/Industry, Adult Non-fiction. **Career:** R.J.R. Nabisco Inc., senior brand manager, 1979-85; AmeriSuite Hotels, director of marketing and sales, 1985-87; Griffin Group, president, 1987-; University of Texas, marketing faculty, 1988-90. Writer. **Publications:** NONFICTION: Power Packed Promotion, 1990; Selling the Sizzle, 1993; Customer Loyalty: How to Earn It, How to Keep It, 1995, rev. ed., 2002; Customer Winback: How to Recapture Lost Customers and Keep Them Loyal, 2001; Taming The Search-and-Switch Customer: Earning Customer Loyalty In a Compulsion-To-Compare World, 2009. **Address:** Griffin Group, 2727 Exposition Blvd., Ste. 119, Austin, TX 78703, U.S.A. **Online address:** jill@loyaltysolutions.com

GRIFFIN, Keith B(roadwell). American/British/Panamanian (born Panama), b. 1938. **Genres:** Economics, Third World, Business/Trade/Industry. **Career:** University of Chile, Institute of Economics and Planning, visiting professor, 1962-63, 1964-65; Expert on Agricultural Planning, acting chief FAO mission, 1963-64; Pakistan Institute of Development Economics, research adviser, 1965, 1970; Magdalen College, fellow and tutor in economics, 1965-76, acting warden and director, 1973, 1977-78, president, 1979-88, honorary fellow, 1988; U.S. Agency for International Development on Investment Allocation, advisor, 1966; AO/ICO/IBRD World Coffee Study, advisor, 1967; Nited Nations Research Institute for Social Development, senior consultant, 1971-72; World Bank on land, consultant, 1973; ILO, Rural development, consultant, 1974; Rural and Urban Employment Policies Branch, chief, 1975-76, Employment Advisory Mission, chief, 1982, Social Policy Review Mission, leader, 1994-96, Employment and Social Protection Mission, leader, 1997; Queen Elizabeth House, warden/director, 1978-79; Development Studies Association, president, 1978-80; OECD Development Centre, senior adviser, 1986-91; United Nations Research Institute for Social Development, chairman of the board, 1988-95; economic adviser, 1989-91; University of California, Economics Department, distinguished professor, 1988-2004, chair, 1988-2004, professor emeritus, 2004-; UNDP Mission, Human Development Report, consultant, 1989, 1991-94, Poverty Alleviation Mission, leader, 1994, advisor, 1995, Macroeconomic Policy and Poverty Reduction Mission, leader, 1997, Human Development Report, consultant, 1998, leader, 2001; Oxford Centre for Islamic Studies, visiting fellow, 1998. Writer. **Publications:** (With B. Glassburner) An Evaluation of Pakistan's Third Five Year Plan, 1965; Underdevelopment in Spanish America, 1969; (with J. Enos) Planning Development, 1970; Green Revolution: An Economic Analysis, 1972; The Political Economy of Agrarian Change, 1974, 2nd ed., 1979; Land Concentration and Rural Poverty, 1976, 2nd ed., 1981; International Inequality and National Poverty, 1978; (with A. Saith) Pattern of Income Inequality in Rural China, 1980; (with J. James) The Transition to Egalitarian Development, 1981; (with A. Saith) Growth and Equality in Rural China, 1981; World Hunger and the World Economy, 1987; Zhongguo nong cun de ti zhi gai ge he jing ji fa zhan, 1987; Alternative Strategies for Economic Development, 1989, 2nd ed., 1999; (with T. McKinley) Implementing a Human Development Strategy, 1994; Studies in Globalization and Economic Transitions, 1996; Alternative Strategies for Economic Development, 1999; Studies in Development Strategy and Systemic Transformation, 2000; Human Development in the Era of Globalization, 2006. EDITOR: Financing Development in Latin America, 1971; (with A.R. Khan) Growth and Inequality in Pakistan, 1972; (with E.A.G. Robinson) The Economic Development of Bangladesh within a Socialist Framework, 1974; Institutional Reform and Economic Development in the Chinese Countryside, 1984; (with J. Knight) Human Development and the International Development Strategy for the 1990s, 1990; The Economy of Ethiopia, 1992; (with A.R. Khan) Globalisation and the Developing World, 1992; (with Z. Renwei) The Distribution of Income in China, 1993; Poverty and the Transition to a Market Economy in Mongolia, 1995; Social Policy and Economic Transformation in Uzbekistan, 1996; Economic Reform in Vietnam, 1998; Growth, Inequality and Poverty in Armenia, 2002; Poverty Reduction in Mongolia, 2003. **Address:** Department of Economics, University of California, 4108 Sproul Hall, Riverside, CA 92502, U.S.A. **Online address:** keith.griffin@mail.ucr.edu

GRIFFIN, Laura. American (born United States), b. 1973?. **Genres:** Novels. **Career:** Journalist. **Publications:** One Last Breath, 2007; Thread of Fear, 2007; One Wrong Step, 2008; Whisper of Warning, 2009; Untraceable, 2009; Unspeakable, 2010; Deadly Promises, 2010; Unforgivable, 2010; Snapped, 2011; Twisted, 2012. Contributor to periodicals. **Address:** Pocket Books, 1230 Ave. of the Americas, New York, NY 10020-1586, U.S.A. **Online address:** laura@lauragriffin.com

GRIFFIN, Patrick. American (born United States), b. 1965?. **Genres:** History. **Career:** Ohio University, Department of History, assistant professor, 2000-04, associate professor, 2004-06; National University of Ireland, Moore Institute for Research in the Humanities and Social Sciences, senior fellow and visiting professor, 2004-06; University of Virginia, Corcoran Department of History, director of graduate studies, associate professor, 2006-08; University of Notre Dame, Madden-Hennebry professor, 2008-, Department of History, chair, 2011. Writer. **Publications:** The People with No Name: Ireland's Ulster Scots, America's Scots Irish and the Creation of a British Atlantic World, 1689-1764, 2001; American Leviathan: Empire, Nation and Revolutionary Frontier, 2007; America's Revolution, 2012; The American Revolution: A Brief History, forthcoming. **Address:** Department of History, University of Notre Dame, 479 Decio, 219 O'Shaughnessy Hall, Notre Dame, IN 46556, U.S.A. **Online address:** pgriffi4@nd.edu

GRIFFIN, P(auline) M. American (born United States), b. 1947. **Genres:** Novels, Novellas/Short Stories, Science Fiction/Fantasy, Mystery/Crime/Suspense, Science Fiction/Fantasy, Anthropology/Ethnology. **Career:** Sweet's, McGraw-Hill, manager, administrator for technical support, 1966-. Writer. **Publications:** STAR COMMANDOS SERIES: Star Commandos, 1986; Colony in Peril, 1987; Mission Underground, 1988; Death Planet, 1989; Mind Slaver, 1990; Return to War, 1990; Fire Planet, 1990; Jungle Assault, 1991; Call to Arms, 1991; Watchdogs of Space, 2001; Pariah, 2004; War Prince, 2004. WITH A. NORTON: Storms of Victory, 1991; Port of Dead Ships, 1991; Seakeep, 1991; Falcon Hope, 1992; (with M.H. Schaub) Flight of Vengeance, 1992; Redline The Stars, 1993; Firehand, 1994. **Address:** Archeobooks Publishing Inc., 6081 Silver King Blvd., Ste. 903, Cape Coral, FL 33914, U.S.A. **Online address:** pmgriffin@pmgriffin.com

GRIFFIN, Peni R(ae). American (born United States), b. 1961. **Genres:** Mystery/Crime/Suspense, Science Fiction/Fantasy, Children's Fiction, Novels, Horror, Travel/Exploration, Young Adult Fiction. **Career:** City Public Service, clerk, 1985-89; Masco/MSA Survey, production assistant, 1991-95. Writer. **Publications:** Hobkin, 1992; The Switching Well (time travel fantasy), 1993; The Truth in the Case of Eliza Mary Muller, by Herself, 1993; The Brick House Burglars (mystery), 1994; Vikki Vanishes (YA suspense), 1995. FOR CHILDREN: Otto from Otherwhere (science fiction), 1990; A Dig in Time (science fiction), 1991; Treasure Bird (mystery), 1992; The Maze (fantasy), 1994; Margo's House (fantasy), 1996; The Ghost Sitter (ghost story), 2001; The Music Thief, 2002; 11,000 Years Lost, 2004; Vision Quest, 2005. **Address:** 1123 W Magnolia Ave., San Antonio, TX 78201, U.S.A. **Online address:** griffin@idworld.net

GRIFFIN, Steven A(rthur). American (born United States), b. 1953. **Genres:** Sports/Fitness, Children's Non-fiction, Travel/Exploration, Children's Fiction, Young Adult Fiction. **Career:** Freelance writer and photographer, 1975-; Central Michigan University, part-time instructor, 1987-; The Oxford Eagle, sports writer. **Publications:** OUTDOOR KIDS SERIES WITH E.M. GRIFFIN: Fishing for Kids: A Family Fishing Guide, 1993; Camping for Kids: A Family Camping Guide, 1994; Bird Watching for Kids: A Family Bird Watching Guide, 1995; Hiking for Kids: A Family Hiking Guide, 1996. OTHERS: Ice Fishing: Methods and Magic, 1985; (with B. Tilton) First Aid for Youths, 1994; The Fishing Sourcebook: Your One-Stop Resource for Everything to Feed Your Fishing Habit, 1996; The Camping Sourcebook: Your One-Stop Resource for Everything You Need for Great Camping, 1997; Snowshoeing, 1998. Contributor to periodicals. **Address:** 1310 Jefferson Ave., Midland, MI 48640-5525, U.S.A.

GRIFFIN, Susan M. (Susan Mary Griffin). American (born United States), b. 1953. **Genres:** Literary Criticism And History, Biography. **Career:** University of Louisville, Department of English, assistant professor, 1982-87, associate professor, 1987-92, professor, 1992-, department chair, 2003-, Justus Bier professor of humanities, 2004-. Writer. **Publications:** (Ed. with W. Veeder) The Art of Criticism: Henry James on the Theory and the Practice of Fiction, 1986; The Historical Eye: The Texture of the Visual in Late James, 1991; (ed.) Henry James Goes to the Movies, 2002; Anti-Catholicism and Nineteenth-Century Fiction, 2004; (ed. with A. Nadel) Men Who Knew Too Much: Henry James and Alfred Hitchcock, 2011. **Address:** Department of English, University of Louisville, 315 Bingham Humanities, Belknap Campus, 2211 S Brook St., Louisville, KY 40292, U.S.A. **Online address:** smgrif01@louisville.edu

GRIFFIN, Susan Mary. *See* **GRIFFIN, Susan M.**

GRIFFITH, Arthur Leonard. Canadian/British (born England), b. 1920. **Genres:** Theology/Religion. **Career:** Ordained to ministry of United Church of Canada, 1945; pastor of churches, 1945-60; City Temple, minister, 1960-66; Deer Park United Church, minister, 1966-75; ordained to ministry of Anglican Church of Canada, 1975; St. Paul's Church, associate minister, 1975-; Toronto School of Theology, lecturer in homiletics, 1977-. Writer. **Publications:** The Roman Letter Today, 1959; God and His People: The Renewal of the Church, 1961; Beneath the Cross of Jesus, 1961; What is a Christian? Sermons on the Christian Life, 1962; Barriers to Christian Belief, 1962, rev. ed., 1969; A Pilgrimage to the Holy Land, 1962; The Eternal Legacy From an Upper Room, 1963; Pathways to Happiness: A Devotional Study of the Beatitudes, 1964; God's Time and Ours: Sermons for the Christian Year, 1964; The Crucial Encounter: The Personal Ministry of Jesus, 1965 in US as Encounters with Christ: The Personal Ministry of Jesus, 1966; This is Living: Paul's Letter to the Philippians, 1966; God In Man's Experience: The Activity of God in the Psalms, 1968; Illusions of Our Culture, 1969, rev. ed., 1972; The Need to Preach, 1971; Hang on to the Lord's Prayer, 1973; We Have this Ministry, 1973; Ephesians: A Positive Affirmation: The Ephesian Letter Today, 1975; Gospel Characters: The Personalities Around Jesus, 1976; Reactions to God: Man's Response to God's Activity in the Psalms, 1979; Take Hold of the Treasure: Life in the Christian Faith, 1983; From Sunday to Sunday: Fifty Years in the Pulpit, 1987. **Address:** St. Paul's Church, 227 Bloor St. E, Toronto, ON M4W 1C8, Canada.

GRIFFITH, Gail. American (born United States), b. 1950?. **Genres:** Biography, Human Relations/Parenting. **Career:** Writer, lawyer and consultant. **Publications:** Will's Choice: A Suicidal Teen, a Desperate Mother, and a Chronicle of Recovery, 2005. **Address:** c/o Gail Ross, Gail Ross Literary Agency, 1666 Connecticut Ave., 5th Fl., Washington, DC 20009, U.S.A. **Online address:** gail@gailgriffith.com

GRIFFITH, Helen V(irginia). American (born United States), b. 1934. **Genres:** Children's Fiction, Human Relations/Parenting, Humor/Satire. **Career:** S.G. Williams & Brothers Co., secretary and treasurer, 1976-. Writer. **Publications:** Mine Will, Said John, 1980; Alex and the Cat, 1982; Alex Remembers, 1983; More Alex and the Cat, 1983; Foxy, 1985; Nata, 1985; Georgia Music, 1986; Grandaddy's Place, 1987; Journal of a Teenage Genius, 1987; Emily and the Enchanted Frog, 1989; Plunk's Dreams, 1990; Caitlin's Holiday, 1990; Grandaddy and Janetta, 1993; Doll Trouble, 1993; Dream Meadow, 1994; Grandaddy's Stars, 1995; Alex and the Cat (The 3 Alex Books in One Volume), 1997; Dinosaur Habitat, 1998; Cougar, 1999; How Many Candles?, 1999; Grandaddy and Janetta Together: The Three Stories in One Book, 2001; Moonlight, 2012. **Address:** 410 Country Club Dr., Wilmington, DE 19803, U.S.A.

GRIFFITH, Ivelaw L(loyd). American/Guyanese (born Guyana), b. 1955. **Genres:** Politics/Government. **Career:** Lehman College, assistant professor, 1990-94; Florida International University, assistant professor of political science, 1994-96, associate professor of political science, 1996-2000, professor of political science, College of Arts and Sciences, associate dean for budget and facilities, The Honors college, dean; Caribbean Studies Association, president, 2001-02; Council on Undergraduate Research, councilor, 2005-07; Radford University, provost, 2006-07; City University of New York, York College, provost and senior vice president for academic affairs, 2007-, professor of political science. Writer. **Publications:** The Quest for Security in the Caribbean: Problems and Promises in Subordinate States, 1993; Caribbean Security on the Eve of the 21st Century, 1996; Drugs and Security in the Caribbean: Sovereignty under Siege, 1997. EDITOR AND CONTRIBUTOR: Strategy and Security in the Caribbean, 1991; (with B.N. Sedoc-Dahlberg) Democracy and Human Rights in the Caribbean, 1997; Political Economy of Drugs in the Caribbean, 2000; Caribbean Security in the Age of Terror: Challenge and Change, 2004. Contributor of articles to books, journals and newspapers. **Address:** York College, City University of New York, AC2H06, 94-20 Guy R. Brewer Blvd., Jamaica, NY 11451-0001, U.S.A. **Online address:** provost@york.cuny.edu

GRIFFITH, Jim. American (born United States) **Genres:** Business/Trade/Industry, Law, Theology/Religion, Information Science/Computers. **Career:** EBay, customer relations, 1996-; Customer Support Training program, manager, 1999-; eBay University, trainer, dean, 2000-. Writer. **Publications:** The Official eBay Bible: The Most Up-to-Date, Comprehensive How-to Manual for Everyone from First-Time Users to People Who Want to Run Their Own Business, 2003, 3rd ed. as The Official Ebay Bible: The Newly Revised and Updated Version of the Most Comprehensive EBay How-to Manual for Everyone from First-Time Users to eBay Experts, 2007; (with B. Easum) Ten Most Common Mistakes Made by New Church Starts, 2008. **Address:** eBay Inc., 2145 Hamilton Ave., San Jose, CA 95125, U.S.A.

GRIFFITH, Marlene. American/Austrian (born Austria), b. 1928. **Genres:** Education, Writing/Journalism, Politics/Government. **Career:** San Francisco State College, professor in English, 1962-64; University of California, professor in English, 1964-66; Laney College, professor in English, 1966-87. Writer. **Publications:** (Ed. with C. Muscatine) The Borzoi College Reader, 1966, 7th ed., 1992; (ed. with C. Muscatine) First Person Singular, 1973; Writing for the Inexperienced Writer: Fluency, Shape, Correctness, 1979; Writing to Think, 1982; (with A. Connor) Democracy's Open Door: The Community

College in America's Future, 1994. **Address:** 25 Stonewall Rd., Berkeley, CA 94705-1414, U.S.A.

GRIFFITH, Nicola. British (born England), b. 1960. **Genres:** Novels, Science Fiction/Fantasy, History. **Career:** Janes Plane (music group), singer and lyricist, 1981-82; freelance writer, 1988-. **Publications:** NOVELS: Ammonite, 1993; Slow River, 1995; Stay, 2002. OTHER: (ed. with S. Pagel) Bending the Landscape: Fantasy, (anthology), vol. I, 1997; (ed. with S. Pagel) Science Fiction, 1998; Penny in My Mouth, 1998; The Blue Place (novel), 1998; (ed. with S. Pagel) The Horror, 2001; With Her Body, 2004; (ed. with S. Pagel) Fantasy, 2004; Always, 2007; And Now We Are Going to Have a Party: Liner Notes to a Writer's Early Life, 2007. Contributor to periodicals and books. **Address:** c/o Shawna McCarthy, Scovil Chichak Galen, 381 Park Ave. S, Ste. 1020, New York, NY 10016, U.S.A. **Online address:** nicolaz@aol.com

GRIFFITH, Thomas Gwynfor. British/Welsh (born Wales), b. 1926. **Genres:** Language/Linguistics, Literary Criticism And History, Translations, Young Adult Fiction. **Career:** University of Leeds, lecturer in Italian, 1948-52; University of Dublin, lecturer, 1952-55, reader in Italian, 1955-58; Trinity College, fellow, 1955-58; Oxford University, lecturer in Italian, 1958-65; St. Cross College, fellow, 1965; University of Hull, professor of Italian, 1966-71; University of Manchester, chair, professor, 1971-88, professor emeritus of Italian language and literature, 1988-. Writer. **Publications:** (Ed. and trans.) Boccaccio: Detholion o'r Decameron, 1951; Bandello's Fiction: An Examination of the Novelle, 1955; Avventure Linguistiche del Cinquecento, 1961; The Italian Language, 1966, (with B. Migliorini) rev. ed., 1984; Italian Writers and the Italian Language: An Inaugural Lecture Delivered in the University of Hull, 9th November 1966, 1967; (ed. and intro. with P.R.J. Hainsworth) Selected Poems of Petrarch, 1971; Dau Beny Daith, 1995; O Hendrefigillt i Livorno: Penodau yn Hanes Llewelyn Lloyd a Llwydiaid Toscana, 2000. Contributor to periodicals. **Address:** Department of Italian Studies, University of Manchester, Oxford Rd., Manchester, GM M13 9PL, England.

GRIFFITHS, Bill. See **GRIFFITHS, William G.**

GRIFFITHS, Fiona J. American (born United States) **Genres:** Women's Studies And Issues. **Career:** New York University, Department of History, assistant professor, associate professor, director of graduate studies, Faculty of Arts and Science, academic director of history, Religious Studies Program, faculty, Medieval and Renaissance Center, faculty. Writer. **Publications:** The Garden of Delights: Reform and Renaissance for Women in the Twelfth Century, 2007; Nuns and Priests: Mutuality and Dependence in the Medieval Monastery, 1050-1250, forthcoming. Contributor to journals. **Address:** Department of History, New York University, Rm. 524, King Juan Carlos I of Spain Ctr., 53 Washington Sq. S, 4E Fl., New York, NY 10012, U.S.A. **Online address:** fjg3@nyu.edu

GRIFFITHS, Jane. British (born England), b. 1970?. **Genres:** Poetry. **Career:** Oxford University, instructor; Edinburgh University, instructor; Oxford English Dictionary, editor; bookbinder; University of Bristol, Department of English, lecturer, 2007-, senior lecturer. Poet and writer. **Publications:** POETRY: The House, 1990; A Grip on Thin Air, 2000; Icarus on Earth, 2005; Another Country: New and Selected Poems, 2008; Terrestrial Variations, 2012. CONTRIBUTOR: Reactions: New Poetry, 2000; Magdalen Poets: Five Centuries of Poetry from Magdalen College, 2000; Self-Presentation and Social Identification: The Rhetoric and Pragmatics of Letter-Writing in Early Modern Times, 2001; Staying Alive: Real Poems for Unreal Times, 2002; Nothing but Papers, My Lord: Studies in Early Modern English Language and Literature, 2003; The Oxford Dictionary of National Biography, 2004; John Stow: Author, Editor, and Reader, 2004; The New Dictionary of National Biography, 2004; And Not Just a Game: Sporting Poetry, 2006. OTHERS: John Skelton and Poetic Authority: Defining the Liberty to Speak, 2006; Diverting Authorities: The Marginal Gloss from Manuscript to Print, forthcoming. Contributor to periodicals. **Address:** Department of English, University of Bristol, Rm. G.12, 11 Woodland Rd., Bristol, GL BS8 1TB, England. **Online address:** jane.griffiths@bristol.ac.uk

GRIFFITHS, Linda. Canadian (born Canada), b. 1956. **Genres:** Plays/Screenplays, Film, Theatre. **Career:** Duchess Productions, owner, 1996; York University, staff, 2001; University of Toronto, adjunct faculty, 2005. Writer. **Publications:** PLAYS: (with P. Thompson) Maggie & Pierre: A Fantasy of Love, Politics and the Media, 1980; The Darling Family, 1991;

Chronic, 2004; Age of Arousal, 2007. OTHERS: (with M. Campbell) Book of Jessica: A Theatrical Transformation, 1989; (with P. Brymer) Dangerous Traditions: O.D. on Paradise (anthology), 1993; The Speed Christmas, 1994; The Dirty Theatre Stories, 2003; The Duchess: A.k.a. Wallis Simpson, 1998; Sheer Nerve: Seven Plays, 1999; Alien Creature: A Visitation from Gwendolyn MacEwen, 2000. Works appear in anthologies. **Address:** c/o Micheal Petrasek, Kensington Literary Representation, 34 St. Andrew St., Toronto, ON M5T 1K6, Canada. **Online address:** lgriff@sympatico.ca

GRIFFITHS, Niall. British (born England), b. 1966?. **Genres:** Novels, Novellas/Short Stories, Young Adult Fiction. **Career:** Writer. **Publications:** Grits, 2000; Sheepshagger, 2001; Kelly + Victor, 2002; Stump, 2003; Wreckage, 2005; Runt, 2006; Bring it Back Home, 2007; (with P. Finch) Real Liverpool, 2008; (with P. Finch) Real Aberystwyth, 2008; Ten Pound Pom, 2009; The Dreams of Max and Ronnie: New Stories from the Mabinogion, 2010. **Address:** United Agents, 12-26 Lexington St., London, GL W1F 0LE, England.

GRIFFITHS, Paul E(dmund). Welsh (born Wales), b. 1962. **Genres:** Psychology, Biology, Medicine/Health. **Career:** Otago University, assistant lecturer, senior lecturer, 1988-98; University of Maryland, visiting assistant professor of philosophy, 1992; University of Sydney, director of unit for history of philosophy of science, 1998-2000; Konrad Lorenz Institute for Evolution and Cognition Research, fellow, 1999-, School of Philosophical and Historical Inquiry, fellow, 2007-; University of Pittsburgh, adjunct professor, 2000-, Department of History and Philosophy of Science, professor, 2000-04, Centre for Philosophy of Science, associate director, 2002-; Biology and Philosophy, associate editor, 2000-; University of Exeter, ESRC Centre for Genomics in Society, visiting professor of philosophy of science, 2004-; University of Queensland, ARC federation fellow and professor of philosophy, 2004-07. Writer. **Publications:** What Emotions Really Are: The Problem of Psychological Categories, 1997; (with K. Sterelny) Sex and Death: An Introduction to Philosophy of Biology, 1999; (ed. with S. Oyama and R.D. Gray) Cycles of Contingency: Developmental Systems and Evolution, 2001. Contributor of articles to books. **Address:** Department of Philosophy, University of Sydney, Main Quadrangle A14, Sydney, NW 2006, Australia. **Online address:** paul.griffiths@usyd.edu.au

GRIFFITHS, Paul J. American/British (born England), b. 1955?. **Genres:** Psychology, Reference, Theology/Religion. **Career:** University of Wisconsin, Department of South Asian Studies, visiting assistant professor, 1983-84; University of Chicago, Department of South Asian Languages and Civilizations, assistant professor, 1984-86, associate professor, professor, 1990-2000; University of Notre Dame, assistant professor of theology, 1986-90; University of Illinois, Schmitt chair of Catholic studies, 2000-07; Duke Divinity School, Warren chair of Catholic theology, 2008-. Writer. **Publications:** On Being Mindless: Buddhist Meditation and the Mind-Body Problem, 1986; (trans. and intro.) The Realm of Awakening: A Translation and Study of the Tenth Chapter of Asanga's Mahayanasangraha, 1989; (ed.) Christianity through Non-Christian Eyes, 1990; An Apology for Apologetics: A Study in the Logic of Interreligious Dialogue, 1991; On Being Buddha: The Classical Doctrine of Buddhahood, 1994; Religious Reading: The Place of Reading in the Practice of Religion, 1999; Problems of Religious Diversity, 2001; (ed. with C. Taliaferro) Philosophy of Religion: An Anthology, 2003; Lying: An Augustinian Theology of Duplicity, 2004; (ed. with R. Hütter) Reason and the Reasons of Faith, 2005; The Vice of Curiosity: An Essay on Intellectual Appetite, 2006; Intellectual Appetite: A Theological Grammar, 2009; Song of Songs, 2011. Contributor to periodicals. **Address:** Duke Divinity School, 056 Langford, 407 Chapel Dr., PO Box 90968, Durham, NC 27708-0968, U.S.A. **Online address:** pgriffiths@div.duke.edu

GRIFFITHS, Stephen Gareth. See **GRIFFITHS, Steve.**

GRIFFITHS, Steve. (Stephen Gareth Griffiths). British/Welsh (born Wales), b. 1949. **Genres:** Poetry, Politics/Government, Public/Social Administration. **Career:** North Thames Gas, leader, 1970-72; community worker, 1973-77; Islington Council, staff, 1978-; Welsh Academy, vice chair; ODPM, consultant, 2000-03; U.K. Department of Health, consultant, 2002-03. Writer and freelance researcher. **Publications:** Poetry: (contrib.) The Green Horse, 1978; Anglesey Material: Poems, 1975-1978, 1980; Civilised Airs: Poems, 1973-1982, 1984; (contrib.) Poetry Book Society Anthology, 1990; Uncontrollable Fields, 1990; (contib.) The Bright Field, 1991; Selected Poems, 1993; (contrib.) One Hundred Poets from Wales, 2007; Elusive State: Entering al-

Chwm, 2008; Surfacing, 2011. Works appears in anthologies. Contributor to magazines. **Address:** 3 John Campbell Rd., Stoke Newington, London, GL N16, England. **Online address:** stevegriffiths@clara.co.uk

GRIFFITHS, Tom. Australian (born Australia), b. 1957?. **Genres:** History. **Career:** Australian National University, Research School of Social Sciences, professor of history, Centre for Environmental History, director, Australian Dictionary of Biography, chair; State Library of Victoria, field officer; University of Copenhagen, adjunct professor of climate research; National Museum of Australia, Centre for Historical Research, affiliate. Writer. **Publications:** Secrets of the Forest: Discovering History in Melbourne's Ash Range, 1992; Hunters and Collectors: The Antiquarian Imagination in Australia, 1996; Forests of Ash: An Environmental History, 2001; Slicing the Silence: Voyaging to Antarctica, 2007. EDITOR: (with A. Platt and intro.) The Life and Adventures of Edward Snell: The Illustrated Diary of an Artist, Engineer and Adventurer in the Australian Colonies 1849 to 1859, 1988; (with L. Robin) Ecology and Empire: The Environmental History of Settler Societies, 1997; (with T. Bonyhady) Prehistory to Politics: John Mulvaney, the Humanities and the Public Intellectual, 1997; (with T. Bonyhady) Words for Country: Landscape & Language in Australia, 2001; (co-ed.) Change in the Weather: Climate and Culture in Australia, 2005; (with B. Attwood) Frontier, Race, Nation: Henry Reynolds & Australian History, 2005. **Address:** Department of History, Australian National University, Rm. 3129, Coombs Bldg., Canberra, AC 0200, Australia. **Online address:** tom.griffiths@anu.edu.au

GRIFFITHS, Trevor. (Ben Rae). British (born England), b. 1935. **Genres:** Plays/Screenplays, Music, History. **Career:** Stockport Technical College, lecturer in liberal studies, 1962-65; British Broadcasting Corp., education officer, 1965-72. Writer. **Publications:** (Co-author) Layby, 1971; Occupations: The Big House, 1972; Sam Sam, 1972; The Party, 1974; Comedians, 1976; Through the Night and Such Impossibilities: Two Plays for Television, 1977; 1935 All Good Men and Absolute Beginners: Two Plays for Television, 1977; Cherry Orchard, 1978; Apricots & Thermidor: Two Plays, 1978; Occupations, 1980; Oi for England, 1982; Sons and Lovers: Trevor Griffith's Screenplay of the Novel by D.H. Lawrence, 1982; Last Place On Earth. Episode Two, Leading Men, 1985; Last Place On Earth. Episode Three, Gentlemen & Players, 1985; Last Place On Earth. Episode One, Poles Apart, 1985; Judgement Over the Dead: The Screenplay of The Last Place On Earth, 1986; Real Dreams, 1987; (with J. Pikser) Revolution in Cleveland, 1987; Fatherland, 1987; Collected Plays for Television, 1988; Last Place on Earth. Episode Six, Rejoice, 1988; Last Place on Earth. Episode Four, The Glories of the Race, 1988; Last Place on Earth. Episode Five, Foregone Conclusion, 1988; Piano: A New Play for Theatre Based on the Film Unfinished Piece for Mechanical Piano by A. Adabashyan and N. Mikhalkov, 1990; Gulf Between Us, or, The Truth and Other Fictions, 1992; Hope in the Year Two, and Thatcher's Children, 1994; Who Shall Be Happy?, 1997; Food for Ravens: A Film for Television, 1998; Theatre Plays One, 2007; Theatre Plays Two, 2007. AS BEN RAE: Adam Smith, 1972; Don't Make Waves, 1975. **Address:** c/o Robert Kirby, United Agents, 12-26 Lexington St., London, GL W1F 0LE, England. **Online address:** tgriffPost@aol.com

GRIFFITHS, William G. (Bill Griffiths). American (born United States) **Genres:** Autobiography/Memoirs, Novels. **Career:** Writer. **Publications:** The Witness (novel), 2000; (as Bill Griffiths with C. Griffiths) Road to Forgiveness (memoir), 2001; Malchus, 2002; Driven: A Novel (supernatural thriller), 2002; Takedown: A Gavin Pierce Novel, 2003; Stingers (novel), 2003; Methuselah's Pillar (novel), 2010; Talons, 2011; Guilty Conscience, forthcoming; Angel of Death, forthcoming; Under Eden, forthcoming. **Address:** c/o Author Mail, Warner Books Inc., 1271 Ave. of the Americas, New York, NY 10020, U.S.A. **Online address:** wggriffiths@gmail.com

GRIGELY, Joseph Constantine. American (born United States), b. 1956. **Genres:** Art/Art History. **Career:** Gallaudet University, associate professor of English, 1983-; Stanford University, Mellon postdoctoral fellow in English, 1985-87; University of Michigan, professor of history of art; National Endowment for the Humanities, fellow, 1992-93; School of the Art Institute of Chicago (SAIC), professor of visual and critical studies, faculty of art history and theory and criticism. Writer. **Publications:** Textualterity: Art, Theory and Textual Criticism, 1995; Joseph Grigely: Portraits for Dublin, 1997; Joseph Grigely: Imbrie, 2009. **Address:** School of the Art Institute of Chicago, 37 S Wabash Ave., Chicago, IL 60603-3002, U.S.A. **Online address:** jgrigely@saic.edu

GRIGG, Ray. Canadian (born Canada), b. 1938. **Genres:** Philosophy, Poetry, Human Relations/Parenting, Theology/Religion. **Career:** Omega Institute for Holistic Studies, teacher; Hollyhock Farm Experiential Learning Institute, teacher; University of Victoria, Centre for Studies in Religion and Society, director. Writer. **Publications:** The Tao of Relationships: A Balancing of Man and Woman, 1988; The Tao of Being: A Think and Do Workbook, 1989; The Tao of Sailing: A Bamboo Way of Life, 1990; Zen Brushpoems, 1991; The Tao of Zen, 1994; The New Lao Tzu: A Contemporary Tao Te Ching, 1995; The Sage's Way: Teachings and Commentaries, 2004. **Address:** 1087 Topcliff Rd., PO Box 362, Quathiaski Cove, BC V0P 1N0, Canada. **Online address:** raygrigg@island.net

GRIGGS, Barbara. See **VAN DER ZEE, Barbara (Blanche).**

GRIGGS, Terry. Canadian (born Canada), b. 1951. **Genres:** Novellas/Short Stories, Novels, Young Adult Fiction, Mystery/Crime/Suspense, Picture/Board Books. **Career:** Writer. **Publications:** Harrier, 1982; Quickening, 1990; The Lusty Man, 1995; Cat's Eye Corner, 2000; Rogues' Wedding, 2002; The Silver Door, 2004; Bigmouth, 2005; Invisible Ink, 2006; Thought You were Dead, 2009; Nieve, 2010. **Address:** The Bukowski Agency, 14 Prince Arthur Ave., Ste. 202, Toronto, ON M5R 1A9, Canada. **Online address:** griggsbu@kanservu.ca

GRIGGS, Vanessa Davis. American (born United States), b. 1959. **Genres:** inspirational/Motivational Literature, Novels, Autobiography/Memoirs, Young Adult Non-fiction. **Career:** BellSouth Telecommunications, staff, 1978-96; freelance author and motivational speaker, 1996-; Free to Soar, founder. **Publications:** Destiny Unlimited, 1999; The Rose of Jericho, 2000; Promises Beyond Jordan, 2004; Wings of Grace, 2005; Blessed Trinity, 2007; (with G.J. Owen) Tara and The Place of Irish Kings, 2008; Strongholds, 2008; If Memory Serves, 2008; Goodness and Mercy, 2009; Practicing what You Preach, 2009; The Truth Is the Light, 2010; Redeeming Waters, 2011; Ray of Hope, 2011; Forever Soul Ties, 2012. **Address:** Free to Soar, Department RV, PO Box 101328, Birmingham, AL 35210-6328, U.S.A. **Online address:** vanessa@vanessadavisgriggs.com

GRIHM, Amanda. American (born United States), b. 1952. **Genres:** E-books, Science Fiction/Fantasy, Novels, Mystery/Crime/Suspense. **Career:** JAG Enterprise, consultant, 2000-02; Project Match Inc., executive director, 2002-. Writer. **Publications:** The Wolf, 2003. **Address:** Project Match Inc., 5502 Peachtree Rd., Ste. 207-A, Chamblee, GA 30341, U.S.A. **Online address:** agrihm34@attbi.com

GRIM, Ryan. American (born United States), b. 1978. **Genres:** History. **Career:** Washington City Paper, staff writer; Politico, staff writer; Huffington Post, senior congressional correspondent; Wall Street Journal, staff. **Publications:** This Is Your Country on Drugs: The Secret History of Getting High in America, 2009. Contributor to periodicals. **Address:** Huffington Post, PO Box 447, Herndon, VA 20172-0447, U.S.A. **Online address:** ryan@huffingtonpost.com

GRIMALDI, David. American (born United States), b. 1957. **Genres:** Earth Sciences, Biology, Botany. **Career:** American Museum of Natural History, curator of entomology; City University of New York, adjunct professor; Columbia University, adjunct professor; Cornell University, adjunct professor; Earth Institute, Center for Environmental Research and Conservation, adjunct senior research scientist. Writer. **Publications:** Amber: Window to the Past, 1996; Studies on Fossils in Amber, 2000; (with M.S. Engel) Evolution of the Insects, 2005; (with M.S. Engel) Diverse Neuropterida in Cretaceous amber, with Particular Reference to the Paleofauna of Myanmar (Insecta), 2008. Contributor to journals. **Address:** Department of Entomology, American Museum of Natural History, Central Park W, 79th St., New York, NY 10024-5192, U.S.A. **Online address:** grimaldi@amnh.org

GRIMALDI, Janette Pienkny. (Janette Habel). French (born France), b. 1938. **Genres:** Social Sciences, Third World. **Career:** University of Havana, faculty, 1964-65; Societe d'Etudes de Mathematiques Appliquees (SEMA), director of studies. Writer. **Publications:** (As Janette Habel) Cuba, 1989, rev. ed., 1991. Contributor to periodicals. **Address:** 21 Blvd. Richard Lenoir, Paris, 75011, France. **Online address:** Janette.habel@wanadoo.fr

GRIMBERG, Tina. Canadian/Ukranian (born Ukraine), b. 1962?. **Genres:** Autobiography/Memoirs. **Career:** Congregation Beth Elohim, assistant rabbi; Congregation Darchei Noam, rabbi, 2002-. **Publications:** Out of Line: Growing Up Soviet (memoir), 2007. **Address:** Toronto, ON , Canada. **Online address:** darcheinoam@bellnet.ca

GRIMES, Martha. American (born United States), b. 1931. **Genres:** Mystery/Crime/Suspense, Novels, Novellas/Short Stories, Horror, Young Adult Fiction, Poetry. **Career:** Montgomery College, professor of English, 1970-, now retired; University of Iowa, English instructor; Frostburg State College, assistant professor of English. Writer. **Publications:** RICHARD JURY SERIES: The Man with a Load of Mischief, 1981; The Old Fox Deceiv'd, 1982; The Anodyne Necklace, 1983; The Dirty Duck, 1984; Jerusalem Inn, 1984; Help the Poor Struggler, 1985; The Deer Leap, 1985; I Am the Only Running Footman, 1986; The Five Bells and Bladebone, 1987; The Old Silent, 1989; The Old Contemptibles, 1991; The Horse You Came In On, 1993; Rainbow's End, 1995; The Case Has Altered, 1997; The Stargazey, 1998; The Lamorna Wink, 1999; Blue Last, 2001; The Grave Maurice, 2002; The Winds of Change, 2004; Dust, 2007; Old Wine Shades, 2006; Black Cat, 2010. EMMA GRAHAM SERIES: Hotel Paradise, 1996; Cold Flat Junction, 2001; Belle Ruin, 2005; Fadeaway Girl, 2011. ANDI OLIVER SERIES: Biting the Moon, 1999; Dakota: A Novel, 2008. NOVELS: Send Bygraves, 1989; The End of the Pier, 1992; The Train Now Departing: Two Novellas, 2000; Foul Matter, 2003. **Address:** Viking Press, 375 Hudson St., New York, NY 10014-3658, U.S.A. **Online address:** grimesinfo@plesser.com

GRIMES, Michael D. American (born United States), b. 1942. **Genres:** Sociology, Social Sciences, Children's Fiction. **Career:** University of Houston, assistant professor, 1970-73; Louisiana State University, Department of Sociology, associate professor, professor of sociology, 1973-, director of graduate studies, 1990-95, director of undergraduate studies, 1999-2000, 2002-05, State Police Degree Program, coordinator, 1999-2003, chair of undergraduate studies, 2000-02, 2005-. Writer. **Publications:** Class in Twentieth-Century American Sociology: An Analysis of Theories and Measurement Strategies, 1991; (with J.M. Morris) Caught in the Middle: Contradictions in the Lives of Sociologists from Working-Class Backgrounds, 1997; Patching Up the Cracks: A Case Study of Juvenile Court Reform, 2005. Contributor of articles to periodicals. **Address:** Department of Sociology, Louisiana State University, 105B Stubbs Hall, Baton Rouge, LA 70803-5411, U.S.A. **Online address:** mgrimes@lsu.edu

GRIMES, Thomas J. See **GRIMES, Tom.**

GRIMES, Tom. (Thomas J. Grimes). American (born United States), b. 1954. **Genres:** Novels, Plays/Screenplays, Young Adult Fiction. **Career:** Private Papers Inc., general manager, 1980-83; Wolfman-Gold and Good Co., general manager, 1983-86; Louie's Backyard, waiter, 1986-89; University of Iowa, Writers Workshop, visiting professor, 1991-92; Southwest Texas State University, assistant professor of English, 1992-95, associate professor, 1995-, professor, MFA Program in Creative Writing, director, 1996-. Writer. **Publications:** A Stone of the Heart, 1990; Four Walls Eight Windows, 1990; Spec (play), 1991; Season's End (novel), 1992; City of God (novel), 1995; (ed.) The Workshop: Seven Decades of the Iowa Writers' Workshop, 1999; WILL@epicqwest.com: A Medicated Memoir, 2003; Mentor: A Memoir, 2010. **Address:** Department of English, Southwest Texas State University, M-25 Flowers Hall, 601 University Dr., San Marcos, TX 78666, U.S.A. **Online address:** tg02@txstate.edu

GRIMSLEY, Jim. American (born United States), b. 1955. **Genres:** Novels, Plays/Screenplays. **Career:** ACME Theatre Co., founding member, 1983-87; Seven Stages Theater, playwright-in-residence, 1986-; Celeste Miller and Co., president, 1989-94; Regional Organization of Theaters-South (ROOTS), chairman, 1990-91; Emory University, Department of English and Creative Writing, senior writer-in-residence, professor, senior resident fellow in creative writing, director of creative writing program and senior lecturer in creative writing; About Face Theater, playwright-in-residence, 1999-2004. **Publications:** The Existentialists, 1983; The Earthlings, 1984; The Receptionist in Hell, 1985; Estelle and Otto, 1985; Dead of Winter, 1986, as Beam Angel, 1993; On the Appearance of a Fire in the West, 1987; Math and Aftermath, 1988; Man with a Gun, 1989; White People, 1989; The Lizard of Tarsus, 1990; The Fall of the House of Usher, 1991; Belle Ives, 1991; Aurora Be Mine, 1992; The Borderland, 1994. NOVELS: Winter Birds, 1994; Dream Boy, 1995; My Drowning, 1997; Kirith Kirin, 2000; Boulevard, 2002; Comfort & Joy, 2003; The Ordinary, 2004; The Last Green Tree, 2006; Forgiveness, 2007. OTHERS: True Fiction: An Essay, 1994; Mr. Universe and Other

Plays, 1998; Free in Asveroth, 1998; Making Our Way: A Southern Lesbian And Gay Reader, 2001. Contributor to periodicals. **Address:** Department of English, Emory University, N315 Callaway Ctr., 537 Kilgo Cir., Atlanta, GA 30322, U.S.A. **Online address:** jgrimsl@emory.edu

GRIMSTONE, David. See **STONE, David Lee.**

GRINDAL, Richard. (Richard Grayson). British/Scottish (born Scotland), b. 1922. **Genres:** Novels, Mystery/Crime/Suspense, Horror, Young Adult Fiction, Young Adult Non-fiction. **Career:** P.E. Management Consulting Group, consultant, 1961-63. Writer. **Publications:** JOHN BRYANT SERIES: The Spiral Path, 1955; Death in Melting, 1957; Madman's Whisper, 1958; Dead So Soon, 1960. NOVELS: Death Stalk, 1982; Whisky Murders, 1987; Over the Sea to Die, 1990; The Tartan Conspiracy, 1992. INSPECTOR GAUTIER SERIES AS RICHARD GRAYSON: The Murders at Impasse Louvain: A Novel, 1978; The Monterant Affair, 1980; The Death of Abbé Didier, 1981; The Montmartre Murders: A Novel, 1982; Crime Without Passion, 1983; Death en Voyage, 1986; Death on the Cards, 1988; Death Off Stage, 1991; Death Au Gratin, 1994; Death in the Skies, 1998. NONFICTION: Return to the Glen, 1989; The Spirit of Whisky, 1992. NOVELS AS RICHARD GRAYSON: Murder Red-handed, 1965; Spy in Camera, 1968; Play the Roman Fool and Die, 1970; A Taste of Death, 1973; And Death the Prize, 1996; For Blood and Wine Are Red, 2000; Let Slip the Dogs of War, 2002. **Address:** A M Heath & Company Ltd., 6 Warwick Ct., Holborn, London, GL WC1R 5DJ, England.

GRINDE, Donald A(ndrew). American (born United States), b. 1946. **Genres:** History, Race Relations, Social Sciences, Young Adult Non-fiction, Politics/Government. **Career:** Buffalo North American Indian Culture Center, board director, 1974-77; California Polytechnic State University, professor of history, 1977-; University of California-Los Angeles, visiting associate professor, 1978-79; University of Utah, director of native American studies, 1981-84; Salt Lake City Indian Center, chair, 1983-84; Gettysburg College, distinguished professor of interdisciplinary studies, 1987-88; New York State Department of Education, American Indian History Curriculum Project, consultant, 1988-91; University of California-Riverside, Rupert Costo professor of American Indian affairs, 1989-91; American College Testing, test consultant, 1994-; State University of New York, Department of American Studies, professor and chair of American studies; National Park Service, consultant; Smithsonian Institution, consultant. Writer. **Publications:** The Iroquois and the Founding of the American Nation, 1977; (with B.E. Johansen) Exemplar of Liberty: Native America and the Evolution of Democracy, 1991; (co-author) Exiles in the Land of the Free, 1992; (with B.E. Johansen) Ecocide of Native America: Environmental Destruction of Indian lands and Peoples, 1995; (with B.E. Johansen) Encyclopedia of Native American Biography: Six Hundred Life Stories of Important People from Powhatan to Wilma Mankiller, 1997; The Mission Indian Federation, 1920-1970, forthcoming. EDITOR: (with C.M. Gentry) Unheard Voices: American Indian Responses to the Columbian Quincentenary, 1492-1992, 1994; (with R. Griffin) Apocalypse of Chiokoyhikoy, 1997; Native Americans, 2002. **Address:** Department of American Studies, State University of New York, 442 Main St., 1010 Clemens Hall, Buffalo, NY 14260-4630, U.S.A. **Online address:** dgrinde@buffalo.edu

GRINER, Paul. American (born United States) **Genres:** Novellas/Short Stories. **Career:** University of Louisville, associate professor and director of creative writing program, professor of creative writing. Writer. **Publications:** Follow Me, 1996; Collectors: A Novel, 1999; The German Woman, 2009. **Address:** Department of English, University of Louisville, Belknap Campus, 319C Bingham Humanities, 2211 S Brook St., Louisville, KY 40292, U.S.A. **Online address:** pfgrin01@louisville.edu

GRINSPOON, David H. (David Harry Grinspoon). American (born United States), b. 1959?. **Genres:** Air/Space Topics, Science Fiction/Fantasy. **Career:** National Aeronautics and Space Administration, Ames Research Center, postdoctoral research associate, 1989-91; European Space Agency's, Venus Express Mission, interdisciplinary scientist; Laboratory for Atmospheric and Space Physics, senior research associate, 1991-99; University of Colorado, Astrophysical and Planetary Sciences, assistant professor, 1991-99, adjunct professor, 2000-, adjunct associate professor; Southwest Research Institute, principal scientist, 1995-2005; Denver Museum of Nature and Science, curator of astrobiology; Sky & Telescope Magazine, contributing editor. **Publications:** Venus Revealed: A New Look below the Clouds of Our Mysterious Twin Planet, 1997; (with M.Y. Marov) The planet Venus, 1998;

Lonely Planets: The Natural Philosophy of Alien Life, 2003. **Address:** Department of Astrophysical and Planetary Sciences, University of Colorado, 1416 Broadway St., PO Box 391, Boulder, CO 80309, U.S.A. **Online address:** david@boulder.edu

GRINSPOON, David Harry. *See* **GRINSPOON, David H.**

GRIPPO, Charles. American (born United States) **Genres:** Adult Nonfiction, Law, Business/Trade/Industry, Plays/Screenplays. **Career:** Showstopper Magazine, founder and editor-in-chief, 1989; Chicago Alliance for Playwrights, director emeritus. Writer, producer, composer and lyricist. **Publications:** The Stage Producer's Business and Legal Guide, 2002; Business and Legal Forms for Theater, 2004; Sex Marks the Spot, 2011. **Address:** c/o Author Mail, Allworth Press, 307 W 36th St., 11th Fl., New York, NY 10018, U.S.A. **Online address:** readermail@charlesgrippo.org

GRISHAM, John. American (born United States), b. 1955. **Genres:** Mystery/Crime/Suspense, Novels, Children's Fiction, Young Adult Non-fiction. **Career:** Lawyer, 1981-90; Mississippi House of Representatives, staff, 1984-90; writer, 1984-. **Publications:** A Time to Kill, 1989; The Firm, 1991; The Pelican Brief, 1992; The Client, 1993; The Chamber, 1994; The Rainmaker, 1995; The Runaway Jury, 1996; The Partner, 1997; The Street Lawyer, 1998; The Testament, 1999; The Brethren, 2000; A Painted House: A Novel, 2001; Skipping Christmas, 2001; The Summons, 2002; The King of Torts, 2003; Bleachers, 2003; The Last Juror, 2004; The Broker, 2005; The Innocent Man: Murder and Injustice in a Small Town, 2006; Playing for Pizza, 2007; La apelación, 2008; The Appeal, 2008; The Associate, 2009; Asociado, 2009; Ford County: Stories, 2009; The Confession: A Novel, 2010; The Litigators, 2011; Calico Joe, 2012; The Jailhouse Lawyer, 2012. THEODORE BOONE SERIES: Theodore Boone: Kid Lawyer, 2010; The Abduction, 2011; The Accused, 2012. **Address:** Pinder Lane & Garon-Brooke Associates Ltd., 159 W 53rd St., New York, NY 10019, U.S.A.

GRISSO, Thomas. American (born United States), b. 1942. **Genres:** Humanities, Civil Liberties/Human Rights, Adult Non-fiction, Social Sciences. **Career:** Ashland University, assistant professor, 1969-, associate professor, through 1974; St. Louis University, associate professor of psychology and law, 1974-87; professor of psychology, through 1987; University of Massachusetts, Center for Mental Health Services Research, Mental Health and Law Core, director; University of Massachusetts Medical School, professor of psychiatry, director of psychology, Law-Psychiatry Program Psychiatry Department, director, Law-Psychiatry Program, coordinator, 1987-. Writer. **Publications:** Juveniles Waiver of Rights: Legal and Psychological Competence, 1981; Evaluating Competencies: Forensic Assessments and Instruments, 1986, 2nd ed., 2003; Competency to Stand Trial Evaluations: A Manual for Practice, 1988; (ed. with C.F. Ferris) Understanding Aggressive Behavior in Children, 1996; (with P.S. Appelbaum) Assessing Competence to Consent to Treatment: A Guide for Physicians and Other Health Care Professionals, 1998; Forensic Evaluation of Juveniles, 1998; Instruments for Assessing Understanding & Appreciation of Miranda Rights, 1998; (ed. with R.G. Schwartz) Youth on Trial: A Developmental Perspective on Juvenile Justice, 2000; (co-author) Rethinking Risk Assessment: The MacArthur Study of Mental Disorder and Violence, 2001; (with P.S. Appelbaum) MacArthur Competence Assessment Tool for Clinical Research (MacCAT-CR), 2001; Double Jeopardy: Adolescent Offenders with Mental Disorders, 2004; (ed. with G. Vincent and D. Seagrave) Mental Health Screening and Assessment in Juvenile Justice, 2005; Evaluating Juveniles Adjudicative Competence: A Guide for Clinical Practice, 2005; Clinical Evaluations for Juveniles Competence to Stand Trial: A Guide for Legal Professionals, 2005; (with R. Barnum) Massachusetts Youth Screening Instrument, Version 2: MAYSI-2: Users Manual and Technical Report, 2006; (with I. Kruh) Evaluation of juveniles Competence to Stand Trial, 2009; (with K. Heilbrun and A.M. Goldstein) Foundations of Forensic Mental Health Assessment, 2009; (with I. Packer) Specialty Competencies in Forensic Psychology, 2011. Contributor to journals. **Address:** Center for Mental Health Services Research, S7-864, 55 Lake Ave. N, Worcester, MA 01655, U.S.A. **Online address:** thomas.grisso@umassmed.edu

GRISWOLD, Jerome. American (born United States), b. 1947. **Genres:** Literary Criticism And History, Children's Fiction. **Career:** Northeastern University, instructor in English, 1976-79; San Diego State University, assistant professor, 1980-83, associate professor, 1983-87, professor of English, 1987, now professor emeritus, National Center for the Study of Children's Literature, director; University of California, visiting assistant professor,

1983; University of California, visiting associate professor, 1984-86, visiting professor, 1988-; University of Connecticut-Storrs, visiting professor, 1989. Writer. **Publications:** The Children's Books of Randall Jarrell, 1988; Audacious Kids: Coming of Age in America's Classic Children's Books, 1992 as The Classic American Children's Story: Novels of the Golden Age, 1996; (ed. and intro.) The Prince and the Pauper, 1997; (ed. and intro.) The Voyages of Doctor Dolittle, 2000; The Meanings of Beauty & the Beast: A Handbook, 2004; Feeling Like A Kid: Childhood And Children's Literature, 2006. CONTRIBUTOR: The Contemporary Literary Scene, 1974; Studies in Medieval Culture, 1976; Maurice Sendak Bilderbuchkunstler, 1987; Zen in American Life and Letters, 1987; Culture, Texte, et Jeune lecteur, 1993; International Companion Encyclopedia of Children's Literature, 1996; The Parallel Universe of English, 1996; Reflections of Change: Children's Literature since 1945, 1997. **Address:** Department of English and Comparative Literature, San Diego State University, Rm. AL 225, 5500 Campanile Dr., San Diego, CA 92182-6020, U.S.A. **Online address:** jgriswol@mail.sdsu.edu

GRIZZLE, Ralph. American (born United States), b. 1957. **Genres:** Travel/Exploration. **Career:** ASTA Agency Management, managing editor, 1990-95; Cruise Week, co-founder, 1995; Our State: Down-Home Living in North Carolina, columnist and contributing editor; Cruiser Observer, editor and publisher; Avid Cruiser Magazine, editor and publisher; Kenilworth Media, president; Avid Travel Media Inc., president. **Publications:** Remembering Charles Kuralt, 2000; Day Trips from Raleigh-Durham: Getaways Approximately Two Hours Away, 2002; (ed. and comp.) Charles Kuralt's People, 2002; (with J.L. Hoffman) Insiders' Guide Day Trips from Raleigh-Durham: Getaway Ideas for the Local Traveler, 2007. **Address:** Avid Travel Media Inc., PO Box 17577, Asheville, NC 28816-7577, U.S.A. **Online address:** ralph@kenilworthmedia.com

GROB, Gerald N. American (born United States), b. 1931. **Genres:** History, Psychiatry, Medicine/Health. **Career:** Clark University, instructor to professor of history, 1957-69; Rutgers University, professor of history, 1969-90, Henry E. Sigerist professor of history of medicine, 1990-, Henry E. Sigerist professor of history of medicine emeritus. Writer. **Publications:** Workers and Utopia: A Study of Ideological Conflict in the American Labor Movement 1865-1900, 1961; The State and the Mentally Ill: A History of Worcester State Hospital in Massachusetts, 1830-1920, 1966; Mental Institutions in America: Social Policy to 1875, 1972; Edward Jarvis and the Medical World of Nineteenth-Century America, 1978; Mental Illness and American Society 1875-1940, 1983; The Inner World of American Psychiatry 1890-1940: Selected Correspondence, 1985; From Asylum to Community: Mental Health Policy in Modern America, 1991; The Mad among Us: A History of the Care of America's Mentally Ill, 1994; The Deadly Truth: A History of Disease in America, 2002; (with H.H Goldman) Dilemma of Federal Mental Health Policy: Radical Reform or Incremental Change?, 2006; Mental Institutions in America: Social Policy to 1875, 2009; (with A.V. Horwitz) Diagnosis, Therapy and Evidence: Conundrums in Modern American Medicine, 2010. EDITOR: (with R.N. Beck) American Ideas, 2 vols., 1963; (with G.A. Billias) Interpretations of American History: Patterns and Perspectives, 1967, 6th ed., 1992; Statesmen and Statecraft of the Modern West, 1967; (with G.A. Billias) American History: Retrospect and Prospect, 1971; Insanity and Idiocy in Massachusetts: Report of the Commission on Lunacy, 1855, 1971; Immigrants and Insanity: Dissenting Views, 1883-1914, 1980; Mentally Ill in Urban America: Four Studies, 1914-1922, 1980; Psychiatry and Medical Education: Two Studies, 1980; Public Policy and Mental Illness: Four Investigations, 1915-1939, 1980; Epidemiology of Drug Addiction: Three Studies, 1924-1926, 1980; Mental Hygiene in Twentieth Century America: Four Studies, 1921-1924, 1980; American Perceptions of Drug Addiction: Five Studies, 1872-1912, 1980; Psychiatric Research in America: Two Studies, 1936-1941, 1980; Public Policy and the Problem of Addiction: Four Studies, 1914-1924, 1981; Origins of Medical Attitudes Toward Drug Addiction in America: Eight Studies, 1791-1858, 1981; Medical Professions and Drug Addiction: Six Studies, 1882-1932, 1981; Narcotic Addiction and American Foreign Policy: Seven Studies, 1924-1938, 1981; Nineteenth-Century Medical Attitudes Toward Alcoholic Addiction: Six Studies, 1814-1867, 1981. **Address:** Institute for Health, Rutgers University, 112 Paterson St., New Brunswick, NJ 08901, U.S.A. **Online address:** ggrob@rci.rutgers.edu

GROBMAN, Laurie. American (born United States), b. 1962. **Genres:** Education, Cultural/Ethnic Topics. **Career:** Penn State Berks, professor of English and women's studies. Author and educator. **Publications:** Teaching at the Crossroads: Cultures and Critical Perspectives in Literature by Women of Color, 2001; (ed. with C. Spigelman) On Location: Theory and Practice in Classroom-based Writing Tutoring, 2005; Multicultural Hybridity: Transforming American Literary Scholarship and Pedagogy, 2007. **Address:** Penn State Berks, Tulpehocken Rd., PO Box 7009, Reading, PA 19610, U.S.A. **Online address:** leg8@psu.edu

GROBSMITH, Elizabeth S. American (born United States), b. 1946. **Genres:** Anthropology/Ethnology, History, Social Sciences. **Career:** University of Arizona, graduate teaching assistant, 1971, graduate teaching associate, 1972, instructor in anthropology, 1973; Sinte Gleska College, instructor in anthropology, 1973-74; Northeast Technical Community College, instructor, 1975-76; University of Nebraska, Department of Anthropology, instructor, 1971-72, 1975-77, assistant professor, 1977-81, associate professor, 1981-91, professor of anthropology, 1991-96, College of Arts & Sciences, assistant dean, 1989-91, assistant vice-chancellor for academic affairs, 1991-94, associate vice-chancellor for academic affairs, 1994-96; Kearney State College, visiting lecturer, 1979; University of Colorado, College of Letters, Arts and Sciences, dean, 1996-2001; Utah State University, College of Humanities, Arts and Social Sciences, dean, 2001-02; Northern Arizona University, provost, vice president for academic affairs and professor of anthropology, 2002-. Writer. **Publications:** Lakota of the Rosebud: A Contemporary Ethnography, 1981; Indians in Prison: Incarcerated Native Americans in Nebraska, 1994. Contributor to books and journals. **Address:** Office of the Provost, Northern Arizona University, PO Box 4120, Flagstaff, AZ 86011-4120, U.S.A. **Online address:** liz.grobsmith@nau.edu

GRODEN, Michael (Lewis). Canadian/American (born United States), b. 1947. **Genres:** Literary Criticism And History. **Career:** University of Western Ontario, visiting assistant professor of English, 1975-77, assistant professor of English, 1977-78, associate professor of English, 1978-83, professor of English, 1983-, distinguished university professor, 2006-. Writer. **Publications:** Ulysses in Progress, 1977; (ed.) The James Joyce Archive, 63 vols., 1977-79; (comp.) James Joyce's Manuscripts: An Index, 1980; (co-ed.) Johns Hopkins Guide to Literary Theory and Criticism, 1994, 2nd ed., 2005; (co-ed.) Genetic Criticism: Texts and Avant-textes, 2004; Ulysses in Focus: Genetic, Textual, and Personal Views, 2010. **Address:** Department of English, University of Western Ontario, Rm. 173, London, ON N6A 3K7, Canada. **Online address:** mgroden@uwo.ca

GRODIN, Charles. American (born United States), b. 1935. **Genres:** Children's Fiction, Plays/Screenplays, Autobiography/Memoirs, Humor/Satire, Biography. **Career:** CNBC, host, 1995-98. Writer. **Publications:** The Opening (play), 1972, rev. ed. as One of the All-Time Greats, 1992; (with J. Bloom) 11 Harrowhouse, 1974; It Would Be So Nice If You Weren't Here: My Journey Through Show Business (memoir), 1989; Price of Fame (play), 1990; How I Get Through Life: A Wise and Witty Guide, 1992; Freddie the Fly (children's book), 1993; We're Ready for You, Mr. Grodin: Behind the Scenes at Talk Shows, Movies, and Elsewhere (memoir), 1994; I Like it Better When You're Funny: Working in Television and Other Precarious Adventures, 2002; If I Only Knew Then: Learning From our Mistakes, 2007; The Right Kind of People, 2008; How I Got to be Whoever it is I Am, 2009. **Address:** United Talent Agency, 9560 Wilshire Blvd., Ste. 500, Beverly Hills, CA 90212-2401, U.S.A.

GROEMER, Gerald. Japanese/American (born United States), b. 1957. **Genres:** Translations, Cultural/Ethnic Topics, Autobiography/Memoirs. **Career:** Edo-Tokyo Museum, research associate, 1992-94; Tokyo University of Fine Arts and Music, lecturer, 1993-94; Earlham College, Department of Music, assistant professor, 1994-98; University of Yamanashi, Department of Music, associate professor, 1998-2006, professor, 2006-, department chair, 2002-03, 2006-07, 2010-11; Faculty of Education and Human Sciences, faculty. Ethnomusicologist, pianist, composer and writer. **Publications:** (Trans. and ed.) The Autobiography of Takahashi Chikuzan: Adventures of a Tsugaru-Jamisen Musician, 1991; Bakumatsu No hayariuta: Kudokibushi tododoit-subushi No shinkenkyū, 1995; (trans. and ed.) Edo Culture: Daily Life and Diversions in Urban Japan, 1600-1868, 1997; The Spirit Of Tsugaru: Blind Musicians, Tsugaru-Jamisen, And The Folk Music of Northern Japan, With The Autobiography of Takahashi Chikuzan, 1999; (ed. with S. Addiss and J.T. Rimer) Traditional Japanese Arts and Culture: An Illustrated Sourcebook, 2006; Goze to gozeuta no kenkyū, 2007. **Address:** Department of Music, University of Yamanashi, Takeda 4-4-37, Kofu, 400-8510, Japan.

GROENEWEGEN, Peter. Australian/Dutch (born Netherlands), b. 1939.

Genres: Economics. **Career:** University of Sydney, professor of economics, 1980-2002, Centre for the Study of the History of Economic Thought, director, 1989-2002, professor emeritus, 2002-, School of Economics and Politics, honorary associate. Writer. **Publications:** The Taxable Capacity of Local Government in New South Wales, 1976; The Economics of Turgot, 1977; Public Finance in Australia, 1978, 3rd ed., 1990; (ed.) Australian Taxation Policy, 1980, 2nd ed., 1987; Everyone's Guide to Australian Taxation, 1985; (with B. McFarlane) A History of Australian Economic Thought, 1990; (trans. with B. McGilvray) Pietro Verri, Reflections on Political Economy, 1993; A Soaring Eagle: Alfred Marshall, 1842-1924, 1995; Eighteenth Century Economics: Turgot, Beccaria and Smith and Their Contemporaries, 2002; (with G. Vaggi) Il Pensiero economico: Dal Mercantilismo al monetarismo, 2002, 2nd ed. 2010; Classics and Moderns in Economics: Essays on Nineteenth and Twentieth-Century Economic Thought, 2 vols., 2003; (with G. Vaggi) Concise History of Economic Thought: From Mercantilism to Monetarism, 2003, 2nd ed. 2010; Educating for Business, Public Service and the Social Sciences: A History of the Faculty of Economics at the University of Sydney 1920-1999, 2009. EDITOR: (with G. Brennan and B.S. Grewal) Taxation and Fiscal Federalism: Essays in Honour of Russell Mathews, 1988; (intro.) The Economists Refuted and Other Early Economic Writings, 1993; Feminism and Political Economy in Victorian England, 1994; Economics and Ethics?, 1996; Official Papers of Alfred Marshall: A Supplement, 1996; Alfred Marshall: Critical Responses, 1998; Physicians and Political Economy, Six Studies of the Work of Doctor-Economists, 2001. Contributor to periodicals. **Address:** Department of Economics, University of Sydney, Rm. M432, H04 Merewether Bldg., Sydney, NW 2006, Australia. **Online address:** peter.groenewegen7@bigpond.com

GROENING, Matt. American (born United States), b. 1954. **Genres:** Humor/Satire, Cartoons, Graphic Novels. **Career:** Writer. **Publications:** LIFE IN HELL SERIES: Love Is Hell, 1984; Work Is Hell, 1986; School Is Hell, 1987; Childhood Is Hell, 1988; Akbar and Jeff's Guide to Life, 1989; Greetings from Hell, 1989; The Big Book of Hell, 1990; With Love from Hell, 1991; How to Go to Hell, 1991; The Road to Hell, 1992; Binky's Guide to Love, 1994; Love Is Still Hell: A Cartoon Book, 1994; The Huge Book of Hell, 1997; Will and Abe's Guide to the Universe: A Cartoon Book, 2007. THE SIMPSONS SERIES: The Simpsons Xmas Book, 1990; Greetings from the Simpsons, 1990; The Simpsons Rainy Day Fun Book, 1991; (with M. Groening) Maggie Simpson's Alphabet Book, 1991; (with M. Groening) Maggie Simpson's Book of Animals, 1991; (with M. Groening) Maggie Simpson's Book of Colors and Shapes, 1991; (with M. Groening) Maggie Simpson's Counting Book, 1991; The Simpsons Uncensored Family Album, 1991; The Simpsons Fun in the Sun Book, 1992; Making Faces with the Simpsons: A Book of Ready-to-Wear Masks, 1992; The Simpsons Ultra-Jumbo Rain-or-Shine Fun Book, 1993; Cartooning with the Simpsons, 1993; Bart Simpson's Guide to Life, 1993; Simpsons Comics Extravaganza, 1994; Simpson's Comics Spectacular, 1995; Bartman: The Best of the Best!, 1995; Simpsons Comics Simps-O-Rama, 1996; Simpsons Comics Strike Back, 1996; The Simpsons: A Complete Guide to Our Favorite Family, 1997; Simpsons Comics Wingding, 1997; Simpsons Comics Big Bonanza, 1998; Simpsons Comics on Parade, 1998; The Simpsons Guide to Springfield, 1998; Big Bonanza, 1999; Bart Simpson's Treehouse of Horror: Heebie-Jeebie Hullabaloo, 1999; The Simpsons Forever!: A Complete Guide to Our Favorite Family-Continued, 1999; Homer's Guide to Being a Man, 2000; Simpsons Comics A-Go-Go, 2000; (co-author) Bart Simpson's Treehouse of Horror Spine-Tingling Spooktacular, 2001; Simpsons Comics Royale, 2001 as Simpson's Comics Royale: A Super-Sized Simpson Soiree, 2001; Simpsons Comics Unchained, 2001; Simpsons Comics: Madness, 2002; The Simpsons beyond Forever!: A Complete Guide to Our Favorite Family-Still Continued, 2002; Ultimate Simpsons in a Big Ol' Box: A Complete Guide to Our Favorite Family Seasons 1-12, 2002; Big Book of Bart Simpson, 2002; Big Bad Book of Bart Simpson, 2003; Simpsons Comics Madness, 2003; The Simpsons Treehouse of Horror Fun-Filled Frightfest, 2003; Simpsons Comics Belly Buster, 2004; The Simpsons One Step Beyond Forever!: A Complete Guide to Our Favorite Family, 2005; Simpsons Comics: Beach Blanket Bongo, 2007; Simpsons Handbook: Secret Tips from the Pros, 2007; Simpsons Comics Dollars to Donuts, 2008; Bart Simpson: Son of Home, 2009; Simpsons/Futurama Crossover Crisis, 2010; Bart Simpson Class Clown, 2010; Simpsons Comics Get Some Fancy Book Learnin', 2010; Simpsons Futurama Crossover Crisis, 2010; Simpsons World: The Ultimate Episode Guide, Seasons 1-20, 2010; (co-author) Bart Simpson: Prince of Pranks, 2011. OTHERS: (with S. Vance) Postcards That Ate My Brain, 1990; (intro.) Chuck Amuck: The Life and Times of an Animated Cartoonist, 1999; (co-author) Futurama-o-rama,

2002; Da Capo Best Music Writing 2003: The Year's Finest Writing on Rock, Pop, Jazz, Country & More, 2003; Futurama Adventures, 2004; The Homer Book, 2004; The Ralph Wiggum Book, 2005; Comic Book Guy's Guide to Pop Culture, 2005; The Lisa Book, 2006; The Krusty Book, 2006; (contrib.) Futurama Conquers the Universe, 2007; The Best Radioactive Man Event Ever, 2009; The Marge Book, 2009. **Address:** c/o Sondra Gatewood, ACME Features Syndicate, 147 NE Yamhill St., Sheridan, OR 97378-1240, U.S.A. **Online address:** binky@acmefeatures.com

GROFF, Lauren. American (born United States), b. 1978. **Genres:** Novels. **Career:** Writer. **Publications:** The Monsters of Templeton: A Novel, 2008; Delicate Edible Birds and Other Stories, 2009. Works appear in anthologies. Contributor to periodicals. **Address:** c/o Bill Clegg, William Morris Agency, 1325 Ave. of the Americas, New York, NY 10019, U.S.A. **Online address:** lauren@laurengroff.com

GROIS, Boris. *See* GROYS, Boris.

GRONDAHL, Paul. American (born United States), b. 1959?. **Genres:** Politics/Government, Biography. **Career:** Times Union, staff writer, 1984-, reporter; Albany Academy For Girls, writer-in-residence, 2005-10; New York State senate, staff. **Publications:** Mayor Erastus Corning: Albany Icon, Albany Enigma, 1997; (with M.A. LoGiudice) That Place Called Home: A Very Special Love Story, 2000; I Rose like a Rocket: The Political Education of Theodore Roosevelt, 2004; Now Is The Time: A History of Parsons Child and Family Center 1829-2004, 2005. **Address:** c/o Daniel Mandel, Sanford J. Greenburger Associates, 55 5th Ave., New York, NY 10003, U.S.A. **Online address:** pgrondahl@timesunion.com

GRONEMAN, Carol. American (born United States), b. 1943. **Genres:** Women's Studies And Issues, Social Commentary, History, Business/Trade/Industry. **Career:** City University of New York, John Jay College of Criminal Justice, assistant professor, 1973-76, associate professor, 1981-90, professor, 1990-, now professor emeritus; New York Council for the Humanities, research associate, 1976-78, executive director, 1978-81; New York University, Graduate School of Arts and Sciences, adjunct associate professor, 1982-89, visiting professor, 2005-07; Institute for Research in History, chairman, 1986-89. Writer. **Publications:** (With R.N. Lear) The Corporate Ph. D., 1985; (ed. with M.B. Norton) To Toil the Livelong Day: America's Women at Work, 1780-1980, 1987; (ed.) Encyclopedia of New York City, 1995; Nymphomania: A History, 2000. Contributor to journals. **Address:** c/o Georges Borchardt, Georges Borchardt Inc., 136 E 57th St., New York, NY 10022-2940, U.S.A. **Online address:** cgroneman@jjay.cuny.edu

GROOM, Gloria. American (born United States) **Genres:** Art/Art History. **Career:** Art Institute of Chicago, research assistant, 1984-85, David and Mary Winton Green Curator of 19th Century European Painting & Sculpture, 1985-, assistant, 1986-89, assistant curator, 1989-94, associate curator, 1994-, Mary and Winton Green Curator of Medieval through Modern European Painting and Sculpture. Writer. **Publications:** Edouard Vuillard: Painter-Decorator: Patrons and Projects, 1892-1912, 1993; Beyond the Easel: Decorative Paintings by Bonnard, Vuillard, Denis, and Roussel, 1890-1930, 2000; (contrib.) Pierre Bonnard: Observing Nature, 2003; (with D. Druick, D. Chudzicka and J. Shaw) Impressionists, 2008; (with D. Druick, D. Chudzicka and J. Shaw) Age of Impressionism at the Art Institute of Chicago, 2008; (with D. Druick, D. Chudzicka and J. Shaw) The Age of French Impressionism: Masterpieces from the Art Institute of Chicago, 2010. Contributor to journals. **Address:** Art Institute of Chicago, 111 S Michigan Ave., Chicago, IL 60603-6404, U.S.A.

GROOM, Winston (Francis). American (born United States), b. 1944. **Genres:** Novels, History, Adult Non-fiction, Sports/Fitness. **Career:** Washington Star, reporter, columnist, 1967-76; full-time novelist, 1976-. **Publications:** NOVELS: Better Times Than These, 1978; As Summers Die, 1980; (with D. Spencer) Conversations with the Enemy: The Story of P. F. C. Robert Garwood, 1983; Only, 1984; Gone the Sun, 1988; Such a Pretty, Pretty Girl, 1999. FORREST GUMP SERIES: Forrest Gump; 1986; The Bubba Gump Shrimp Co. Cookbook: Recipes and Reflections from Forrest Gump, 1994; Gumpisms: The Wit and Wisdom of Forrest Gump, 1994; Gump & Co., 1995; Forrest Gump: My Favorite Chocolate Recipes: Mama's Fudge, Cookies, Cakes and Candies, 1995. NON-FICTION: Shrouds of Glory: From Atlanta to Nashville: The Last Great Campaign of the Civil War, 1995; (foreword) James Jones: A Friendship, 1999; The Crimson Tide: An Illustrated History of Football at the University of Alabama, 2000; A Storm in Flanders: Tragedy

and Triumph on the Western Front, 2002; 1942: The Year That Tried Men's Souls, 2005; Patriotic Fire: Andrew Jackson and Jean Laffite at the Battle of New Orleans, 2006; Vicksburg, 1863, 2009; The Crimson Tide: The Official Illustrated History of Alabama Football, 2010. OTHERS: (intro.) Horses Don't Fly: A Memoir of World War I, 2002; Kearny's March, 2011; Ronald Reagan: Our Fortieth President, 2012; Shiloh 1862: The First Great and Terrible Battle of the Civil War, 2012. **Address:** c/o Theron Raines, Raines & Raines, 71 Park Ave., New York, NY 10016-2507, U.S.A. **Online address:** info@winstongroombooks.com

GROS, Jean-Germain. American/Haitian (born United States), b. 1964. **Genres:** Social Sciences, Business/Trade/Industry. **Career:** University of Missouri, Department of Political Science, associate professor of political science and public policy, 1994-, Center for International Studies, research fellow. Writer and consultant. **Publications:** (Ed.) Democratization in Late Twentieth-Century Africa: Coping with Uncertainty, 1998; (ed.) Cameroon: Politics and Society in Critical Perspectives, 2003; (with O. Prokopovych) When Reality Contradicts Rhetoric: World Bank Lending Practices in Developing Countries in Historical, Theoretical, and Empirical Perspectives, 2005; State Failure, Underdevelopment, and Foreign Intervention in Haiti, 2012. Contributor to periodicals. **Address:** Department of Political Science, University of Missouri, 905 Twr., 347 SSB, 1 University Blvd., St. Louis, MO 63121-4400, U.S.A. **Online address:** jg.gros@umsl.edu

GROSBARD, Ofer. Israeli (born Israel), b. 1954. **Genres:** Translations, Psychology, History, Politics/Government, Social Sciences. **Career:** Clinical psychologist, 1995-2001; University of Haifa, Department of Community Mental Health, Social Welfare and Health Sciences, faculty, 2004-05, 2007-, The Strategic Research and Policy Center, research fellow, 2006-. Writer. **Publications:** Heter Le-Shigàon, 1994; Yisráel al ha-sapah: Ha-Psikhologyah Shel Tahalikh Ha-Shalom, 2000; Ha-àrvi Sheba-Lev, 2000; Israel on the Couch: The Psychology of the Peace Process, 2003; Menahem Begin: Deyoḳano Shel Manhig: Biyografyah, 2006; Pitsuaḥ Ha-Tsofen Ha-Tarbuti, 2007; Díalog: 123 Sipurim ṭipuliyim Meha-ḥevrah Ha-Masortit U-Fitronam, 2007. **Address:** c/o Author Mail, State University of New York Press, 90 State St., Ste. 700, Albany, NY 12207-1707, U.S.A. **Online address:** grosbard@netvision.net.il

GROSE, Peter (Bolton). American (born United States), b. 1934. **Genres:** International Relations/Current Affairs, History. **Career:** Associated Press, London correspondent, 1959-60, Congo and West Africa correspondent, 1961-62; New York Times, correspondent-Paris, 1963, chief correspondent-Saigon, Vietnam, 1964-65, chief of Moscow bureau, 1965-67, diplomatic correspondent, 1967-70, chief of Jerusalem bureau, 1970-72, chief of United Nations bureau, 1976-77; United States Department of State, policy planning staff, deputy director, 1977-78; Columbia University, Rockefeller Foundation, research associate, 1978-80, Middle East Institute, research associate, 1978-81; Seven Springs Center, director of studies, 1981-82, director of Middle East studies, 1982-84; Foreign Affairs, editor; Harvard University, John F. Kennedy School of Government, fellow, International Security Program, research fellow, 1997-2004, associate, 2004-10; Vineyard Haven Yacht Club, governor. **Publications:** The Next Steps toward Peace between Israel and Its Neighbors: A Symposium at Seven Springs Center, Mount Kisco, New York, February 7-9, 1980: A Report of the Proceedings, 1980; The United States, NATO, and Israeli-Arab Peace: A Symposium at Seven Springs Center, Mount Kisco, New York, October 12-14, 1980: A Report of the Proceedings, 1981; Israel in the Mind of America, 1983; A Changing Israel, 1985; Gentleman Spy: The Life of Allen Dulles, 1994; Continuing the Inquiry: The Council on Foreign Relations from 1921 to 1996, 1996; Operation Rollback: America's Secret War Behind the Iron Curtain, 2000; Power To People: The Inside Story of AES And The Globalization Of Electricity, 2007. Contributor to newspapers. **Address:** Island Press, 1718 Connecticut Ave. NW, Ste. 300, Washington, DC 20009-1148, U.S.A.

GROSECLOSE, Barbara. (Barbara S. Groseclose). American (born United States), b. 1944. **Genres:** Art/Art History, Theology/Religion. **Career:** University of Wisconsin, special lecturer in art history, 1972-74; Ohio State University, Department of History of Art, assistant professor, 1974-80, associate professor, 1980-90, professor, 1991-, now professor emeritus; U.S. Agency for International Development, lecturer in India and Sri Lanka, 1985; Smithsonian Institution, Travelling Exhibition Service, curator, 1988-89; University of Utrecht, Fulbright professor and Walt Whitman professor of American studies, 1994, Fulbright distinguished chair in history and civilization in

Florence, 2002. Writer. **Publications:** (As Barbara S. Groseclose) Emanuel Leutze, 1816-1868: Freedom is the Only King, 1975; (ed. with S. Ferguson) Literature and the Visual Arts in Contemporary Society, 1985; British Sculpture and the Company Raj: Church Monuments and Public Statuary in Madras, Calcutta and Bombay to 1858, 1995; Nineteenth-Century American Art, 2000; (ed. with J. Wierich) Internationalizing The History Of American Art: Views, 2009. Contributor to periodicals. **Address:** Department of History of Art, Ohio State University, 3180 Smith Laboratory, 174 W. 18th Ave., Columbus, OH 43210, U.S.A. **Online address:** groseclose.1@osu.edu

GROSECLOSE, Barbara S. *See* **GROSECLOSE, Barbara.**

GROSS, Andrew. American (born United States), b. 1952?. **Genres:** Novels, Mystery/Crime/Suspense. **Career:** Writer. **Publications:** NOVELS: (with J. Patterson) 2nd Chance, 2002; (with J. Patterson) The Jester, 2003; (with J. Patterson) 3rd Degree, 2004; (with J. Patterson) Lifeguard, 2005; (with J. Patterson) Judge & Jury, 2006; The Blue Zone, 2007; The Dark Tide, 2008; Don't Look Twice, 2009; Reckless, 2010; Eyes Wide Open in UK as Killing Hour, 2011; 15 Seconds, 2012. **Address:** c/o Author Mail, HarperCollins Publishers, 10 E 53rd St., New York, NY 10022, U.S.A. **Online address:** andrew@andrewgrossbooks.com

GROSS, Ariela J. American (born United States), b. 1965?. **Genres:** History. **Career:** University of Southern California, John B. and Alice R. Sharp professor of law and history, 1996-. Writer. **Publications:** Double Character: Slavery and Mastery in the Antebellum Southern Courtroom, 2000; (co-author) America Past & Present, 8th ed., 2008; (with W. Brand, T. Breen and H. Williams) American Stories, 2008; What Blood Won't Tell: A History of Race on Trial in America, 2008. Contributor of articles to periodicals and journals. **Address:** Department of Law, University of Southern California, Los Angeles, CA 90089-0074, U.S.A. **Online address:** agross@law.usc.edu

GROSS, David. American (born United States), b. 1940. **Genres:** History, Politics/Government, Cultural/Ethnic Topics, Philosophy. **Career:** University of Wisconsin-Madison, instructor in history, 1968-69; University of Colorado, assistant professor, 1969-73, associate professor, 1973-81, professor of history, 1981-; University of California, visiting associate professor, 1979. Writer. **Publications:** The Writer and Society: Heinrich Mann and Literary Politics in Germany, 1890-1940, 1980; The Past in Ruins: Tradition and the Critique of Modernity, 1992; Lost Time: On Remembering and Forgetting in Late Modern Culture, 2000. Contributor of articles to journals. Works appear in anthologies. **Address:** Department of History, University of Colorado, Rm. HLMS 204, PO Box 234, Boulder, CO 80309-0234, U.S.A. **Online address:** david.l.gross@colorado.edu

GROSS, Emanuel. Israeli/Romanian (born Romania), b. 1948. **Genres:** Law, Politics/Government. **Career:** Israel Defence Force, Central Command, deputy district military attorney, 1972-80; District Military Court, deputy chief judge, 1980-87, chief judge, 1987-93; Haifa University, professor of criminal law, 1994-, Clinical Studies In Criminal Law, academic consultant; Villanova Law School, visiting professor of law, 1995; John Marshall Law School, visiting professor of law, 1997; American University, Washington College of Law, visiting professor of law, 2002; York University, Osgoode Hall Law School, visiting professor of law, 2003. Writer. **Publications:** Ed-ha-medinah, 1988; The Struggle of Democracy against Terrorism: Lessons from the United States, the United Kingdom, and Israel, 2006. Contributor to periodicals. **Address:** Faculty of Law, University of Haifa, Rm. 3001, Haifa, 31905, Israel. **Online address:** egross@law.haifa.ac.il

GROSS, Ernie. American/Hungarian (born Hungary), b. 1913. **Genres:** History, Theology/Religion, Humanities, Social Sciences. **Career:** Lincoln Star, reporter, 1937-41; Buffalo Evening News, reporter, 1941-63; New York State Labor Department, public relations director, 1963-64; U.S. Office of Economic Opportunity, public relations director of Job Corps, 1964-67; U.S. Department of Housing and Urban Development, director of new services, 1967-75. **Publications:** This Day in Religion, 1990; This Day in American History, 1990, (with R.H. Worth, Jr.) 3rd ed., 2008; From Plymouth Rock to Election 1992: Timetables of American History, 1993; The American Years: A Chronology of United States History, 1999, (co-author) 2nd ed. as The American Years: Chronologies of American History and Experience, 2002; This Day in Sports, 2000; Advances and Innovations in American Daily Life, 1600s-1930s, 2002. **Address:** c/o Publicity Director, Neal-Schuman Publishers Inc., 100 William St., Ste. 2004, New York, NY 10038-4512, U.S.A.

GROSS, Jonathan David. American (born United States), b. 1962. **Genres:** Literary Criticism And History, Novels. **Career:** Columbia University, preceptor, 1991-92; New York University, adjunct faculty, 1992; DePaul University, assistant professor of English, 1992-97, associate professor of English, 1998-2003, professor, 2005-, M.A. in English, director, 1997-2000, Humanities Center, Fulbright Program, director, 2009-. Writer. **Publications:** (Ed.) Byron's Corbeau Blanc: The Life and Letters of Lady Elizabeth Milbanke, Lady of Melbourne (1751-1818), 1997; Byron: The Erotic Liberal, 2001; (ed. and intro.) Emma, or, The Unfortunate Attachment: A Sentimental Novel, 2004; (ed. and intro.) Thomas Jefferson's Scrapbooks: Poems of Nation, Family, and Romantic Love Collected by America's Third President, 2006; (ed. and intro.) The Sylph, 2007; (ed. and intro.) Belmour: A Modern Edition, 2011. Contributor of articles to books and journals. **Address:** Department of English, DePaul University, 2347 N Racine, 246C McGaw, 802 W Belden Ave., Ste. 255, Chicago, IL 60614-3280, U.S.A. **Online address:** jgross@depaul.edu

GROSS, Kali N. American (born United States), b. 1972. **Genres:** Women's Studies And Issues. **Career:** Drexel University, assistant professor, associate professor of history & director of Africana studies. Writer. **Publications:** Colored Amazons: Crime, Violence and Black Women in the City of Brotherly Love, 1880-1910, 2006. **Address:** Drexel University, University City Main Campus, 3141 Chestnut St., Philadelphia, PA 19104, U.S.A. **Online address:** kng25@drexel.edu

GROSS, Michael L. Israeli (born Israel), b. 1954?. **Genres:** Adult Nonfiction, History, Ethics, Social Sciences. **Career:** University of Haifa, Department of International Relations, lecturer, professor of political science and chair, Graduate Program in Applied and Professional Ethics, co-director. Writer. **Publications:** Ethics and Activism: The Theory and Practice of Political Morality, 1997; Bioethics and Armed Conflict: Moral Dilemmas of Medicine and War, 2006; Moral Dilemmas of Modern War: Torture, Assassination and Blackmail in an Age of Asymmetric Conflict, 2010. **Address:** Division of International Relations, School of Political Sciences, The University of Haifa, Rm. 407, Terrace Bldg., Mount Carmel, Haifa, 31905, Israel. **Online address:** mgross@poli.haifa.ac.il

GROSS, Miss Anne Lasko. American (born United States), b. 1977. **Genres:** Novels. **Career:** Writer. **Publications:** Escape from "Special" (graphic novel), 2007; A Mess of Everything (graphic novel), 2009. Contributor to periodicals. **Address:** New York, NY , U.S.A. **Online address:** miss@houseoftwelve.com

GROSS, Neil. Canadian/American (born United States), b. 1971. **Genres:** Biography, Philosophy. **Career:** University of Southern California, faculty; Harvard University, faculty; University of British Columbia, associate professor, 2008-; Sociological Theory, editor. **Publications:** (Ed. and trans. with R.A. Jones) Durkheim's Philosophy Lectures: Notes from the Lycée de Sens Course, 1883-1884, 2004; Richard Rorty: The Making of an American Philosopher, 2008. **Address:** Canada. **Online address:** ngross@interchange.ubc.ca

GROSS, Philip (John). British (born England), b. 1952. **Genres:** Poetry, Communications/Media, Children's Fiction, Young Adult Fiction, Adult Non-fiction, Children's Non-fiction, Reference. **Career:** Collier Macmillan Ltd., editorial assistant, 1973-76; Croydon Public Libraries, librarian, 1976-84; freelance writer and tutor of creative writing, 1984-; Bath Spa University, College of Higher Education, lecturer, 1991-2004; University of Glamorgan, professor of creative writing, 2004-. **Publications:** Familiars (poems), 1983; The Ice Factory (poems), 1984; Cat's Whisker (poems), 1987; (with S. Kantaris) The Air Mines of Mistila, 1988; Manifold Manor, 1989; The Song of Gail and Fludd, 1991; The Son of the Duke of Nowhere (poems), 1991; The All-Nite Café, 1994; Plex, 1994; I.D. (poems), 1994; The Wind Gate, 1995; Coniunctio: A Spell, 1995; Nature Studies, 1995; Scratch City, 1995; A Cast of Stones, 1996; Transformer, 1996; The Wasting Game, 1998; Psylicon Beach, 1998; Facetaker, 1999; Changes of Address: Poems, 1980-1998, 2001; Going for Stone, 2002; Mappa Mundi, 2003; The Lastling, 2003; Marginaliens, 2003; Turn to Stone, 2005; The Storm Garden, 2006; The Egg of Zero, 2006; The Abstract Garden, 2006; I Spy Pinhole Eye, 2009; The Water Table, 2009; Off Road to Everywhere, 2010. **Address:** University of Glamorgan, Llantwit Rd., Treforest, Pontypridd, CF37 1DL, England. **Online address:** contact@philipgross.co.uk

GROSSCUP, Beau. American (born United States) **Genres:** International

Relations/Current Affairs, History. **Career:** Boston University, adjunct assistant professor of international relations, 1973-75; Ithaca College, assistant professor of international relations, 1975-82; University of California, Irvine, visiting faculty, 1983-86; University of California, Santa Barbara, visiting faculty, 1983-86; California State University, lecturer, 1988-90, assistant professor, 1990-93, associate professor of international relations, 1993-, Department of Political Science, faculty, vice-chairperson; University of Redlands, visiting associate professor, 1980-81. Writer. **Publications:** The Explosion of Terrorism, 1987; New Explosion of Terrorism, 1991; The Newest Explosions of Terrorism: Latest Sites of Terrorism in the 1990s and Beyond, 1998; Strategic Terror: The Politics and Ethics of Aerial Bombardment, 2006. Contributor to books and periodicals. **Address:** Department of Political Science, California State University, 716 BUTE, 400 W 1st St., Chico, CA 95929-0455, U.S.A. **Online address:** bgrosscup@csuchico.edu

GROSSE, W. Jack. American (born United States), b. 1923. **Genres:** Law, Environmental Sciences/Ecology, Photography. **Career:** Dun & Bradstreet, credit reporter, 1946-47; Fifth-Third Bank, credit manager, 1947-54; Chase College of Commerce, professor and associate dean, 1954-62; Underwriters Publishing Co., author of insurance summaries, 1962-82, editor, 1962-; Clarkson College of Technology, professor, 1964-66; Northern Kentucky University, professor of law, 1966-68, 1970-91, Salmon P. Chase College of Law, professor of law and assistant dean, 1962-64, dean, 1970-78, interim dean, 1992-93, professor emeritus of law, 1991-; Xavier University, professor and assistant dean, 1968-70; Ohio Valley Environmental and Natural Resources Law Institute, president; Ohio State Bar Foundation, fellow. **Publications:** (Co-author) Government Contract Law, 1970; School Law Handbook, 1981; The Protection and Management of Our Natural Resources: Wildlife and Habitat, 1992, 2nd ed., 1997; Natural Resource Law: Cases and Materials, 2 vols., 1993; (with C.M. Dieffenbach and S.E. Harper) A Centennial History of Chase College of Law, 1994. Contributor to journals. **Address:** Northern Kentucky University, Salmon P. Chase College of Law, Nunn Dr., Highland Heights, KY 41099, U.S.A. **Online address:** grosse@nku.edu

GROSSINGER, Harvey L. American (born United States), b. 1948?. **Genres:** Novellas/Short Stories, Young Adult Fiction. **Career:** R.R. Bowker Co., editorial associate, 1968-72; Indiana University, instructor in English, 1974-80; Globe Distributing Co., supervisor and manager, 1980-82; American University, writing instructor, 1990-95, adjunct professor in literature and creative writing, 1995-; University of Maryland, Honors College, adjunct professor, 1995-97; Johns Hopkins University, Graduate Program in Writing, adjunct professor, 1999-. **Publications:** Home Burial: Five Stories, 1990; The Quarry (stories), 1997; The Caretaker's Niece. Contributor to periodicals. **Address:** Johns Hopkins University, 1717 Massachusetts Ave., Ste. 101, Washington, DC 20036-2005, U.S.A. **Online address:** harvlg@aol.com

GROSSINGER, Tania. American (born United States), b. 1937. **Genres:** Novels, Advertising/Public Relations, Food And Wine, Human Relations/Parenting, Psychology, Travel/Exploration, Writing/Journalism, Autobiography/Memoirs, Autobiography/Memoirs. **Career:** Barcas & Shalit, account executive, 1961-62; Playboy Magazine, Broadcast Promotion, director, 1963-69; Sherut La'am, consultant, 1969-72; Stein and Day Inc., director of publicity, 1970-72; Israel Ministry of Tourism, public relations counsel, 1990-. Writer. **Publications:** The Book of Gadgets, 1974; Growing Up at Grossinger's, 1975; The Great Gadget Catalogue, 1977; (with A. Neiderman) Weekend, 1980. Contributor of articles to magazines and newspapers. **Address:** 1 Christopher St., Ste. 7E, New York, NY 10017, U.S.A. **Online address:** taniagrossinger@verizon.net

GROSSKURTH, Phyllis. Canadian (born Canada), b. 1924. **Genres:** Literary Criticism And History, Biography, Women's Studies And Issues. **Career:** Carleton University, lecturer, 1964-65; University of Toronto, New College, Department of English, professor of English, 1965-87, now professor emeritus, Humanities and Psychoanalysis Programme, faculty, 1987-; University College, honorary research fellow; Order of Canada, officer, 2000. Writer. **Publications:** John Addington Symonds: A Biography, 1964 in US as The Woeful Victorian, 1965; Notes on Browning's Works, 1967; Leslie Stephen, 1968; Gabrielle Roy, 1969; Havelock Ellis: A Biography, 1980; (ed. and intro.) The Memoirs of John Addington Symonds: The Secret Homosexual Life of a Leading 19th Century Man of Letters, 1984; Melanie Klein: Her World and Her Work, 1986; Margaret Mead: A Life of Controversy, 1988; The Secret Ring: Freud's Inner Circle and the Politics of Psychoanalysis, 1991; Byron: The Flawed Angel, 1997; Elusive Subject: A Biographer's Life, 1999. Con-

tributor to periodicals. **Address:** Department of English, New College, University of Toronto, Wetmore Hall, 170 St. George St., Toronto, ON M5R 2M8, Canada. **Online address:** phyllis.grosskurth@utoronto.ca

GROSSMAN, Austin. American (born United States), b. 1969. **Genres:** Novels, Young Adult Fiction, Humor/Satire. **Career:** Looking Glass Games, video game designer; freelance game design consultant; editor; novelist. **Publications:** (Ed.) Postmortems from Game Developer, 2003; Soon I Will Be Invincible, 2007. Contributor to periodicals. **Address:** c/o Author Mail, Pantheon Books, 1745 Broadway, New York, NY 10019, U.S.A.

GROSSMAN, David. Israeli (born Israel), b. 1954. **Genres:** Novels, Novellas/Short Stories, Adult Non-fiction, Young Adult Fiction, Translations. **Career:** Israel Radio, editor and broadcaster. **Publications:** Yehudah ye-Shomron, 1977; Ratz (title means: Jogger), 1983; ḥiyukh ha-gedi (novel), 1983; aḥ ḥadash legamre, 1986; 'Ayen ' erekh-ahavah, 1990; Ha-Zeman ha-tsahov (non fiction), 1987; Gan Riḳi, 1988; Hanochachim hanifkadim (nonfiction), 1992; Nokheḥim nifḳadim, 1992; Sefer ha-diḳduḳ ha-pnimi (novel), 1992; Ha-'Safah ha-meyuḥedet shel Uri (title means: 'Uri's Special Language'), 1996; She-tihyi li ha-sakin (title means: 'Words into Flesh'), 1998; (with H.I. Ajaegbu and L.M. van den Berg) Market Gardening, Urban Development and Income Generation on the Jos Plateau, 2000; Mishehu La-Ruts Ito, 2000; Be My Knife (novel), 2001; Ba-guf Ani Mevinah: Tsemed Novelot, 2002; Her Body Knows: Two Novellas, 2005; Momiḳ, 2005; Lion's Honey: The Myth of Samson, 2006; Ishah boraḥat mi-beśorah, 2008; Until the End of the Land, 2008; To the End of the Land, 2010; Mi rotseh sak kemah, 2011; Falling Out of Time, 2011. FOR CHILDREN: Du-krav (title means: 'Duel'), 1984; Itamar metayel 'al kirot, 1986; Ach chadash l'gamrei, 1986; Itamar pogesh arnav, 1988; Itamar mikhtav, 1988; Itamar ye'koval ha'ksamimha'shachor, 1992; Yesh Yeladim Zigzag (novel), 1994, trans. as The ZigzagKid, 1997; Pajama Sam the Magic Hat Tree, 2000. Contributor to periodicals. **Address:** c/o Deborah Harris, The Harris/Elon Agency, PO Box 8528, Jerusalem, 91083, Israel.

GROSSMAN, Dina. American/Russian (born Russia), b. 1954. **Genres:** History, Travel/Exploration, Theology/Religion. **Career:** Tzipora Publications, founder, publisher, president, illustrator and designer, 2002-. Writer. **Publications:** How We Returned to Egypt: From the Totalitarian Soviet Regime to Totalist Cult in Israel, 2003. **Address:** Tzipora Publications, 1890 E 5th St., PO Box 115, Brooklyn, NY 11223-2833, U.S.A. **Online address:** tziporapub@groups.msn.com

GROSSMAN, Karl (H.). American (born United States), b. 1942. **Genres:** Writing/Journalism, Documentaries/Reportage. **Career:** New Voice, founder and editor, 1961-62; League Against Obnoxious Television Commercials, national director, 1961-63; Babylon Town Leader, reporter, 1962-64; Sunrise Press, reporter and associate editor, 1964; Long Island Press, investigative reporter, 1964-70, columnist, 1970-77; Island Closeup News Service, founder and editor, 1977-; Suffolk Cablevision, reporter, 1977-78; WRCN-Radio, reporter and commentator, 1979; WSNL TV, anchorperson, 1979-84; State University of New York College at Old Westbury, instructor, 1979-81, assistant professor in American studies, 1981-86, associate professor of American studies, 1986-92, professor in American studies, coordinator of media and communications, 1992-, full professor of journalism; EnviroVideo, program host, program director and vice president, 1991-; WBAZ-Radio, political commentator, 1992-97; WVVH-TV, chief investigative reporter. Writer. **Publications:** Cover Up: What You Are Not Supposed to Know about Nuclear Power, 1980, rev. ed., 1982; The Poison Conspiracy, 1983; (contrib.) Nicaragua: America's New Vietnam?, 1984, rev. ed., 1988; (with A. Kitaeff and V. Howell) Making It in the Hamptons, 1985; Power Crazy: How Lilco is Turning Shoreham into America's Chernobyl?, 1986; The Wrong Stuff: The Space Program's Nuclear Threat to Our Planet, 1997; Weapons in Space, 2001. Contributor to books, magazines and newspapers. **Address:** College at Old Westbury, State University of New York, Rm. B321, 223 Store Hill Rd., PO Box 210, Old Westbury, NY 11568-1700, U.S.A. **Online address:** kgrossman@hamptons.com

GROSSMAN, Lev (Thomas). American (born United States), b. 1969. **Genres:** Novels. **Career:** Time Magazine, book reviewer, senior writer, 2002-. **Publications:** Warp, 1997; Codex, 2004; The Magicians: A Novel, 2009; The Magician King, 2011. **Address:** c/o Author Mail, Harcourt School Publishers, 6277 Sea Harbor Dr., Orlando, FL 32887, U.S.A.

GROSSMAN, Richard. American (born United States), b. 1943. **Genres:** Novels, Poetry. **Career:** Gelco, financial executive in charge of administration and acquisitions, 1967-76; poet and novelist, 1976-. **Publications:** POETRY: Tycoon Boy, 1977; The Animals, 1983, rev. ed., 2011. AMERICAN LETTERS TRILOGY: The Alphabet Man, 1993; The Book of Lazarus, 1997. **Address:** 2000 DeMille Dr., Los Angeles, CA 90027, U.S.A. **Online address:** richardgrossman@earthlink.net

GROSSMAN, Wendy. (Wendy M. Grossman). British/American (born United States), b. 1954. **Genres:** Poetry, Technology. **Career:** Folksinger, 1975-83; The Skeptic (British periodical), founder and founding editor, 1987-, editor, 1999-2001; Internet Today, columnist, 1996-97; Fleet Street Forum (online), site manager. **Publications:** (Ed.) Remembering the Future: Interviews from Personal Computer World, 1997; (as Wendy M. Grossman) Net.Wars, 1997; (as Wendy M. Grossman) From Anarchy to Power: The Net Comes of Age, 2001. Contributor of articles to periodicals. **Address:** The Skeptic, 10 Crescent View, Loughton, EX IG10 4PZ, England. **Online address:** wendyg@skeptic.demon.co.uk

GROSSMAN, Wendy M. See **GROSSMAN, Wendy.**

GROSSMANN, Atina. American (born United States), b. 1950. **Genres:** Biology, Sciences. **Career:** Mount Holyoke College, assistant professor, 1983-88; Columbia University, assistant professor, 1988-93, associate professor, 1993-96, adjunct associate professor, 1996-99; New York University, Remarque Institute for European Studies, faculty associate, 1996-; Cooper Union for the Advancement of Science and Art, associate professor, 1996-2005, professor of history, 2005-. Writer. **Publications:** (Ed. with R. Bridenthal and M. Kaplan) When Biology Became Destiny: Women in Weimar and Nazi Germany, 1984; Reforming Sex: The German Movement for Birth Control and Abortion Reform, 1920-1950, 1999; (ed. with O. Bartov and M. Nolan) Crimes of War: Guilt and Denial in the Twentieth Century, 2002; Jews, Germans, and Allies: Close Encounters in Occupied Germany, 2007. Contributor to books and periodicals. **Address:** Cooper Union, Cooper Sq., New York, NY 10003, U.S.A. **Online address:** grossm@cooper.edu

GROSSMITH, Robert (Anthony). Scottish/British (born England), b. 1954. **Genres:** Novels, Novellas/Short Stories. **Career:** Word and Action (community theater company), actor and organizer, 1976-77; British Institute, Stockholm, English teacher, 1977-80; Swedish-English translator, 1980-81; University of Keele, lecturer in American literature, 1987; Harper Collins Ltd., bilingual dictionary editor, 1991-. **Publications:** The Empire of Lights (novel), 1990. Contributor to journals. Works appear in anthologies. **Address:** Curtis Brown Group Ltd., 37 Queensferry St., Edinburgh, EH2 4QS, England. **Online address:** bgrossmith@aol.com

GROSZ, Terry. American (born United States) **Genres:** Novels, Animals/Pets, Zoology, Biography, Autobiography/Memoirs, History. **Career:** California Department of Fish and Game, state game warden, 1966-70; U.S. Fish and Wildlife Service, special agent and assistant regional director for law enforcement, 1970-98. Writer. **Publications:** Wildlife Wars: The Life and Times of a Fish and Game Warden, 1999; For Love of Wilderness: The Journal of a U.S. Game Management Agent, 2000; Defending Our Wildlife Heritage: The Life and Times of a Special Agent, 2001; A Sword for Mother Nature: The Further Adventures of a Fish and Game Warden, 2002; No Safe Refuge: Man as Predator in the World of Wildlife, 2003; The Thin Green Line: Outwitting Poachers, Smugglers and Market Hunters, 2004; Genesis of a Duck Cop: Memories & Milestones, 2006; Slaughter in the Sacramento Valley: Poaching and Commercial Market Hunting-Stories and Conversations, 2008; Crossed Arrows, 2010. **Address:** Johnson Books, 3360 Mitchell n., Ste. E, Boulder, CO 80301, U.S.A. **Online address:** mperrizo@bigearthpublishing.com

GROSZMANN, Lore. See **SEGAL, Lore.**

GROTE, David (G.). American (born United States), b. 1945. **Genres:** Theatre, Plays/Screenplays, Literary Criticism And History, Education. **Career:** Centre Theatre, director, 1964-65; Curtain Theater, director, 1965-67; Wichita Falls Summer Musical Theater, director, 1966-67; Wichita Falls Summer Musical Theater, director, 1966-67, 1971; teacher, 1968-80; Bakersfield Youth Theater Project, director, 1973; Bakersfield Community Theater, director, 1973-79; Scripps College, professor of theater, 1980-81; Pomona College, assistant professor of theater, 1981-82; writer, 1982-; Long Beach Playhouse, director, 1983; Classic Theater Project of San Francisco, artistic director,

1992-. **Publications:** The Undercover Lover, 1978; Rome is Where the Heart Is; Widget's Worries, 1980; Help: The Medicine Man, 1980; The Women of Troy, 1981; Theater: Preparation and Performance, 1981, rev. ed., 1988; The End of Comedy, 1983; Script Analysis: Reading and Understanding the Playscript for Production, 1985; Staging the Musical: Organizing, Planning, and Rehearsing the Amateur Production, 1986; Common Knowledge: A Readers Guide to Literary Allusions, 1987; Harlequin Holds the Bag, 1990; British English for American Readers: A Dictionary of the Language, Customs, and Places of British Life and Literature, 1992; Play Directing in the School: A Drama Director's Survival Guide, 1997; The Best Actors in the World: Shakespeare and his Acting Company, 2002. **Address:** Greenwood Publishing Group Inc., 88 Post Rd. W, PO Box 5007, Westport, CT 06880-4208, U.S.A.

GROTENSTEIN, Jonathan. American (born United States), b. 1970?. **Genres:** Novels, Sports/Fitness. **Career:** Professional poker player and writer. **Publications:** Phil Gordon's Little Black Book, 2004; (with P. Gordon) Poker: The Real Deal, 2004; (with S. Reback) All In: The (Almost) Entirely True Story of the World Series of Poker, 2005; (with H. Moody) God Hates Us All, 2009; (with G. Wendt) Drinking with George: A Barstool Professional's Guide to Beer, 2009; (with T. Geller) 30 Days to a Well-Mannered Dog, 2010. **Address:** c/o Author Mail, Publicity Department, Thomas Dunne Books, 175 5th Ave., New York, NY 10010, U.S.A.

GROTH, Janet. American (born United States), b. 1936. **Genres:** Literary Criticism And History, Biography. **Career:** New Yorker, editorial staff, 1957-78; City University of New York, Queensborough Community College, adjunct lecturer, 1970; Brooklyn College, City University of New York, adjunct lecturer, 1970-74, instructor, 1971; Vassar College, visiting lecturer, 1976-77; University of Cincinnati, assistant professor of English, 1978-82; State University of New York College, associate professor, 1982-95, professor of English, 1995-2000, emeritus professor of English; University of Norway, Fulbright lecturer, 1996; Yale University, Beineke Library, visiting fellow, 1997. Writer. **Publications:** Edmund Wilson: A Critic for Our Time, 1989; (ed. with D. Castronovo and intro.) From the Uncollected Edmund Wilson, 1995; (intro.) The Wound and the Bow: Seven Studies in Literature, 1997; (ed. with D. Castronova and intro.) Edmund Wilson, The Man in Letters, 2001; (with D. Castronova) Critic in Love: A Romantic Biography of Edmund Wilson, 2005. Contributor of articles to periodicals. **Address:** Department of English, State University of New York College, 101 Broad St., Plattsburgh, NY 12901, U.S.A.

GROULT, Benoite. French (born France), b. 1920. **Genres:** Novels, Autobiography/Memoirs, Biography. **Career:** Teacher of French and Latin, 1944-46; radio journalist, 1946-51. **Publications:** (With F. Groult) Il etait deux fois (novel), 1968; Le Journal a 4 mains, 1968; (with F. Groult) La Feminin pluriel, 1972; La part des choses, 1972; Journal à quatre mains, 1973; Les 3/4 du Temps, 1975; (co-author) Des nouvelles de la famille, 1980; Le Féminisme au masculin, 1980; La moitié de la terre, 1981; Les trois quarts du temps: roman, 1983; Les vais seaux du coeur (novel), 1988; Comment la liberte vint aux femmes (biography), 1991; Pauline Roland, ou, Comment la liberté vint aux femmes, 1991; Annuaire de la misogynie, 1993; Histoire d'une evasion (autobiography), 1997; Ainsi soit-elle, 1975, rev. ed., 2000; La touche étoile, 2006; Mon évasion, 2008; Une Femme Parmi Les Siennes, 2010. **Address:** 54 rue de Bourgogne, Paris, 75007, France.

GROUNDS, Roger. British (born England), b. 1938. **Genres:** Horticulture, Homes/Gardens. **Career:** Ward Lock Ltd., gardening editor, 1971-76; Braydon Hall, head gardener, 1979; Moundsmere Manor, head gardener. **Publications:** Plants, 1971; Agriculture, 1971; Gardening for Beginners, 1972; Simple Greenhouse Gardening, 1972; The Perfect Lawn, 1974; Shrubs and Decorative Evergreens, 1974; Trees for Smaller Gardens, 1974; Ferns, 1974; Chilton's Encyclopedia of Gardening, 1975; Grow Your Own Vegetables, 1976; Bottle Gardens, 1976; The Natural Garden, 1976; Growing Vegetables and Herbs, 1977; Everyday Gardening, 1977; Ornamental Grasses, 1979; The Private Life of Plants, 1980; The Multi-Coloured Garden, 1982; (with D. Grenfell) The White Garden, 1990; Small Garden, 1993; The Plantfinder's Guide to Ornamental Grasses, 1998; Grasses and Bamboos, 2002. EDITOR: Complete Handbook of Pruning, 1973; Making and Planning a Small Garden, 1973; Gardening in Colour, 1973; The Pruning Handbook, 1975; The Garden Planner, 1975; The 2 Hour Garden, 1976; Gardening for Everyone, 1978; Gardening With Ornamental Grasses, 2004. **Address:** 1 Southwood Cottages, Moundsmere, Basingstoke, RG25 2HE, England.

GROUNDWATER, Beth. American (born United States) **Genres:** Mystery/Crime/Suspense, Novels. **Career:** Mystery author. **Publications:** A Real Basket Case (novel), 2007; To Hell in a Handbasket (novel), 2009; The Epsilon Eridani Alternative (novella), 2009; Deadly Currents (novel) 2011; Basketful of Troubles, Wicked Eddies, Cataract Canyon, fothcoming. **Online address:** website07@bethgroundwater.com

GROVE, Richard H(ugh). British (born England), b. 1955. **Genres:** Business/Trade/Industry, Agriculture/Forestry, Environmental Sciences/Ecology, Natural History, Technology, Engineering. **Career:** Cambridge University, research fellow, 1986-89, Churchill College, fellow and director of studies, 1989-94, Global Environmental History Unit, coordinator; Woodrow Wilson Center for International Scholars, fellow, 1992-93; Australian National University, Institute of Advanced Studies, senior fellow, 1993-, visiting fellow; National Humanities Center, fellow, 1995-96; National Institute of Science, Technology and Development, research associate. Writer. **Publications:** The Cambridgeshire Coprolite Mining Rush, 1976; The Future for Forestry, 1983; The SSSI Handbook, 1985; (ed. with D. Anderson) Conservation in Africa: People, Policies and Practice, 1987; Green Imperialism: Science, Colonial Expansion and the Emergence of Global Environmentalism, 1660-1880, 1995; Ecology, Climate and Empire: Colonialism and Global Environmental History, 1400-1940, 1997; (co-ed.) Nature and the Orient: The Environmental History of South and Southeast Asia, 1998; (ed. with J. Chappell) En Niño, History and Crisis: Studies from the Asia-Pacific Region, 2000. **Address:** Cambridge University, Clare Hall, Herschel Rd., Cambridge, CB3 9AL, England. **Online address:** richardfgrove@hotmail.com

GROVER, Jan(ice) Zita. American (born United States), b. 1945?. **Genres:** Adult Non-fiction. **Career:** San Francisco General Hospital, AIDS worker, medical editor. **Publications:** (As Janice Zita Grover) Silver Lining, 1983; North Enough: AIDS and Other Clear-Cuts, 1997; Northern Waters, 1999; Jo Spence: Beyond the Perfect Image, 2005; A Home for Dakota, 2008. Contributor to periodicals. **Address:** Graywolf Press, 2402 University Ave., Ste. 203, Saint Paul, MN 55114, U.S.A.

GROVER, Wayne. American (born United States), b. 1934. **Genres:** Children's Fiction, Young Adult Fiction, Adult Non-fiction, Environmental Sciences/Ecology, Novels, Animals/Pets. **Career:** Journalist, 1978-; news correspondent, 1978-86; senior international correspondent, 1986-. **Publications:** NOVELS: Dolphin Adventure: A True Story, 1990; Ali and the Golden Eagle, 1993; Dolphin Treasure, 1996; Dolphin Freedom, 1999. Contributor to newspapers and magazines. **Address:** Greenwillow Books, 10 E 53rd St., New York, NY 10022, U.S.A. **Online address:** author001@authorwaynehgrover.com

GROVES, Annie. See **JORDAN, Penny.**

GROVIER, Kelly. Welsh/American (born United States), b. 1968?. **Genres:** Poetry, History. **Career:** Aberystwyth University, lecturer, 2004-; European Romantic Review, co-founder. Poet and historian. **Publications:** A Lens in the Palm (poetry collection), 2008; The Gaol: The Story of Newgate, London's Most Notorious Prison, 2008. Contributor to periodicals. **Address:** Department of English & Creative Writing, Aberystwyth University, Hugh Owen Bldg., Aberystwyth, SY23 3DY, Wales. **Online address:** nkg@aber.ac.uk

GROW, L(ynn) M(erle). American (born United States), b. 1945?. **Genres:** Literary Criticism And History, Autobiography/Memoirs, Adult Non-fiction, inspirational/Motivational Literature. **Career:** Wichita State University, assistant professor, 1972-77; University of Maryland, Far East Division, lecturer, 1977-81; College of the Bahamas, lecturer in English, 1981-82, English language coordinator, 1982-83; Broward Community College (now Broward College), senior professor of English, 1983-, adjunct faculty. Writer. **Publications:** Consistency of the Biographia Literaria, 1973; Dream Scenes of Invisible Man, 1974; The Prose Style of Samuel Taylor Coleridge, 1976; Harrowed and Hallowed Ground: An Interview with Bienvenido N. Santos, 1977; (comp.) The Epistolary Criticism of Manuel A. Viray: In Memoriam, 1998; The Novels of Bienvenido N. Santos, 1999; World Enough and Time: Epistemologies and Ontologies in Modern Philippine Poetry, 2000; Distillation & Essence: World View in Modern Philippine Literature, 2002; And Quiet Flows the Dawn, 2003. Contributor to periodicals. **Address:** Broward College, 3501 SW Davie Rd., Central Campus, Davie, FL 33314, U.S.A. **Online address:** lgrow@broward.edu

GROWE, Sarah Jane. Canadian/American (born United States), b. 1939. **Genres:** Medicine/Health, Biography. **Career:** High school teacher, 1961-64; CFRO-Radio, host of live radio show, 1977; Vancouver Sun, journalist, 1978; Richmond Review, journalist, 1978-83; Kingston Whig Standard, stringer, 1981-82; Star, reporter and feature writer, 1983-88, editor on foreign-national-city desk team, 1989-, columnist/feature writer, 1998-; Frontier College, literacy tutor. **Publications:** Who Cares? The Crisis in Canadian Nursing, 1991. Contributor to periodicals. **Address:** c/o Elaine Markson, Elaine Markson Literary Agency Inc., 44 Greenwich Ave., New York, NY 10011, U.S.A. **Online address:** growe@sympatico.ca

GROYS, Boris. (Boris Groïs). German (born Germany), b. 1947. **Genres:** History. **Career:** Moscow State University, research fellow, 1976-81; Karlsruhe Institute of Technology, professor, 1994-; New York University, Global distinguished professor of Russian and Slavic studies; Munster University, faculty. Writer. **Publications:** AS BORIS GROÏS: Dnevnik Filosofa, 1989; Utopiia i obmen, 1993; (with I. Kabakov) Dialogi (1990-1994), 1999; Kommunisticheskiĭ postkriptum, 2007. OTHERS: Zeitgenössische Kunst aus Moskau: von der Neo-Avantgarde zum Post-Stalinismus, 1991; The Total Art of Stalinism: Avant-garde, Aesthetic Dictatorship, and Beyond, 1992; über das Neue: Versuch einer Kulturökonomie, 1992; (contrib. with D.B. Kuspit) Milan Kunc, Milan Kunc: Peinlicher Realismus, Ost-Pop (1974-1979): Verfeinerte Malerei (1986-1992), 1992; (contrib. with C. Haenlein and N. Smolik) Richard Prince: Photographien 1977- 1993, 1994; (with M. Tupitsyn and V. Misiano) Kräftsmessen: eine Ausstellung ost-östlicher Positionen innerhalb der westlichen Welt, 1995; (with T. Duve and A. Pelenc) Jeff Wall, 1996; Kunst-Kommentare, 1997; (with D.A. Ross and I. Blazwick) Ilya Kabakov, 1998; Unter Verdacht: eine Phänomenologie der Medien, 2000; Politik der Unsterblichkeit: vier Gespräche mit Thomas Knoefel, 2000; (contrib.) Nackt für Stalin: Körperbilder in der russischen Fotografie der 20er und 30er Jahre, 2003; (contrib.) Postmodernism and the Postsocialist Condition: Politicized Art under Late Socialism, 2003; (contrib. with O. Bätschmann) Ilya Kabakov: Installations 1983-2000: Catalogue Raisonné, 2003; Privatisierungen: Zeitgenössische Kunst aus Osteuropa, 2004; (contrib. with S. Berg and S. Eiblmayr) Peter Kogler, 2004; (contrib. with A. Kaernbach) Politik & Kunst, Kunst & Politik: Künstler und ihre Werke im Reichstagsgebaüde: Fotografien, 2004; (contrib. with J. Burton and M. Godfrey) Open Systems: Rethinking Art c. 1970, 2005; Das kommunistische Postskriptum, 2006; (with A. Heiden and P. Weibel) Zurúck aus der Zukunft: osteuropäische Kulturen im Zeitalter des Postkommunismus, 2006; (ed. with M. Fontán del Junco and M. Hollein) La Ilustración Total: Arte Conceptual de Moscú, 1960-1990, 2008; Art Power, 2008; History Becomes Form: Moscow Conceptualism, 2010; (contrib. with M. Babias) Project Europa: Imagining the (Im)possible, 2010. **Address:** Massachusetts Institute of Technology Press, 55 Hayward St., Cambridge, MA 02142-1493, U.S.A. **Online address:** groys@aol.com

GRUBB, Jeff. American (born United States), b. 1957. **Genres:** Novels. **Career:** TSR Inc., game designer; Wizards of Coast Inc., game designer. Writer. **Publications:** City in Darkness, 1986; Manual of the Planes: Advanced Dungeons and Dragons, 1987; (with K. Novak) Azure Bonds, 1988; (with K. Novak) The Wyverns Spur, 1990; Adventures: An Updated Tour of the Heartlands AD&D 2nd Edition Game, 1990; Forgotten Realms: Song of the Saurials, 1991; (with A. Allston and T.M. Reid) Karameikos: Kingdom of Adventure, 1994; (wtih E. Greenwoood) Cormyr: A Novel, 1996; Knorrman Steel and Charonti Bone, 1997; Tymora's Luck, 1997; The Brothers War, 1998; The Gathering Dark, 1999; Wrath of the Minotaur, 1999; Eye of the Wyvern, 1999; The Shattered Alliance: Ice Age Cycle 3, 2000; Enemies and Allies: A Dungeons and Dragons Accessory, 2001; Liberty's Crusade, 2001; Tempest Feud, 2002; Power of the Jedi Sourcebook, 2002; Last Guardian, 2002; (ed. with E. Greenwood and J.M. Ward) We Three Dragons: A Trio of Dragon Tales for the Holiday Season, 2005; (contrib.) The Further Adventures of Beowulf, 2006; (co-author) Last Guardian, 2007; (with G. Mesta, T. Hickman and M. Neilson) Starcraft Archive, 2007; Artifacts Cycle. I. The Thran, 2009; Ghosts of Ascalon, 2010; Chronicles of War, 2010; (with M. Forbeck) Guild Wars, 2010; (with C. Golden and A. Rosenberg) World of Warcraft, 2010. **Address:** Wizards of the Coast Inc., PO Box 707, Renton, WA 98057, U.S.A.

GRUBB, Michael (J.). British (born England), b. 1960. **Genres:** Sciences, Business/Trade/Industry, Economics, Earth Sciences, Mathematics/Statistics. **Career:** Imperial College, Department of Electrical Engineering, postdoctoral research assistant, 1986-88, professor of climate change and energy policy, 1999-2002; Royal Institute of International Affairs, Energy and Environmental Programme, research fellow, 1998-92, senior fellow, 1992-93, head, 1993-98; Climate Policy, editor-in-chief, 2001-; U.K. Carbon Trust, associated director of policy, 2002-05, chief economist, 2002-09; Climate

Strategies, chair, 2005-; University of Cambridge, professor, senior research associate, faculty of economics. Writer. **Publications:** Energy Policies and the Greenhouse Effect, vol. I: Policy Appraisal, 1990, vol. II: Country Studies and Technical Options, 1991; (co-author) Emerging Energy Technologies: Impacts and Policy Implications, 1992; (ed. with R.L. Garwin and E. Matanle) Managing The Plutonium Surplus: Applications and Technical Options, 1994; Renewable Energy Strategies for Europe, 1995; (with C. Vrolijk and D. Brack) The Kyoto Protocol: A Guide and Assessment, 1999; (ed. with J. Gupta) Climate Change and European Leadership: A Sustainable Role for Europe?, 2000; (ed. with A. Korppoo and J. Karas) Russia and the Kyoto Protocol: Opportunities and Challenges, 2006; (with T. Jamasb and M.G. Pollitt) Delivering a Low-carbon Electricity System: Technologies, Economics and Policy, 2008. **Address:** Faculty of Economics, University of Cambridge, Austin Robinson Bldg., Sidgwick Ave., Prince Consort Rd., Cambridge, CB CB3 9DD, England. **Online address:** mjg7@econ.cam.ac.uk

GRUBER, William E. American (born United States), b. 1943. **Genres:** Theatre, Autobiography/Memoirs. **Career:** Courier-Post, reporter, 1968-69; Age, reporter, 1969-70; Emory University, professor of English and adjunct professor of theater studies, 1980-. Writer. **Publications:** Comic Theaters: Studies in Performance and Audience Response, 1986; Missing Persons: Character and Characterization in Modern Drama, 1994; On All Sides Nowhere: Building a Life in Rural Idaho, 2002; Offstage Space, Narrative and the Theatre of the Imagination, 2010. **Address:** Department of English, Emory University, N 302 Callaway Ctr., 537 Kilgo Cir., Atlanta, GA 30322, U.S.A. **Online address:** wegrube@emory.edu

GRUBERG, Martin. American (born United States), b. 1935. **Genres:** Politics/Government. **Career:** U.S. Department of State, Passport Agency, agent-adjudicator, 1960-61; City University of New York, Hunter College, instructor in political science, 1961-62; University of Wisconsin, Department of Political Science, assistant professor, 1963-66, associate professor, 1966-69, professor of political science, 1969-, chair, 1969-72, director of pre-law. Writer. **Publications:** Women in American Politics, 1968; (ed.) The Encyclopedia of American Government, 3rd ed., 1985; A Case Study in U.S. Urban Leadership: The Incumbency of Milwaukee Mayor Henry Maier, 1996; A History of Winnebago County Government, 1998; Introduction to Law, 2003; Record of Natural and Social Disasters and Their Political Implications: An New Issue for Public Policy Planners, 2009. Contributor to books. **Address:** Department of Political Science, University of Wisconsin, Clow 424, Oshkosh, WI 54901-8673, U.S.A. **Online address:** gruberg@uwosh.edu

GRUDIN, Robert. American (born United States), b. 1938. **Genres:** Novels, Novellas/Short Stories, Poetry, Literary Criticism And History, Essays. **Career:** University of Oregon, assistant professor, 1971-78, associate professor, 1978-90, professor of English, 1990-98, professor emeritus, 1998-; University of South Florida, Humanities Section, chairman, 1984, 1985; Hellas, contributing editor, 1992-88; Bennington College, instructor in fiction workshop, 1994. **Publications:** Mighty Opposites: Shakespeare and Renaissance Contrariety, 1979; Time and the Art of Living, 1982, 2nd ed., 1988; The Grace of Great Things: Creativity and Innovation, 1990; Book: A Novel, 1992; On Dialogue: An Essay in Free Thought, 1996; The Most Amazing Thing (novel), 2002; American Vulgar: The Politics of Manipulation Versus the Culture of Awareness, 2006; Design and truth, 2010; (with M.P. Grudin) Boccaccio's Decameron and the Ciceronian Renaissance, 2012. Contributor of articles to periodicals. **Address:** Palgrave Macmillan Ltd., Houndmills, Basingstoke, Hampshire, RG21 6XS, England. **Online address:** rgrudin@yahoo.com

GRUEN, Bob. American (born United States), b. 1945?. **Genres:** Photography. **Career:** Rock Scene Magazine, photographer, 1970. Writer. **Publications:** (Intro. with S. Mieses) Listen to These Pictures: Photographs of John Lennon, 1985; Chaos, the Sex Pistols, 1991; (with Y. Ono) Sometime in New York, 1995; Crossfire Hurricane, 25 Years with the Rolling Stones, 1998; (contrib.) John Lennon: The New York Years, 2005; Rockers, 2007; New York Dolls: Photographs, 2008; Rock Seen, 2011. **Address:** Bob Gruen Studio, 55 Bethune St., Ste. A202, New York, NY 10014, U.S.A. **Online address:** websitemail01@aol.com

GRUENENFELDER, Kim. American (born United States) **Genres:** Young Adult Fiction, Novels. **Career:** Writer. **Publications:** CHARLIE EDWARDS SERIES: A Total Waste of Makeup, 2006; Misery Loves Cabernet, 2009.

NOVELS: There's Cake in My Future, 2010; Wedding Fever, 2011. **Address:** c/o Rachel Ekstrom, St. Martin's Press, 175 5th Ave., New York, NY 10010-7703, U.S.A. **Online address:** kim@kimgruenenfelder.com

GRUESSER, John Cullen. American (born United States), b. 1959. **Genres:** Literary Criticism And History. **Career:** Seton Hall University, lecturer in English, 1982-84; Purdue University, visiting assistant professor of English, 1989-90; Kean University, assistant professor of English, 1990-96, associate professor of English, 1996-2000, professor of English 2000-, M.A. in Liberal Studies Program, coordinator. Writer. **Publications:** White on Black: Contemporary Literature about Africa, 1992; Black on Black: Twentieth-Century African American Writing about Africa, 2000; Confluences: Postcolonialism, African American Literary Studies, and the Black Atlantic, 2005. EDITOR: The Unruly Voice: Rediscovering Pauline Elizabeth Hopkins, 1996; (and intro.) The Black Sleuth, 2002; (with H. Wallinger) Loopholes and Retreats: African American Writers and the Nineteenth Century, 2009; A Century of Detection: Twenty Great Mystery Stories, 1841-1940, 2010. Works appear in anthologies. Contributor of articles to journals. **Address:** Department of English, Kean University, CAS 227, 1000 Morris Ave., Union, NJ 07083, U.S.A. **Online address:** jgruesse@kean.edu

GRUHN, George. American (born United States), b. 1945. **Genres:** Music, History, Photography, Reference. **Career:** Gruhn Guitars Inc., president, 1970-; Guild Guitars, executive vice president of research and development and artist relations, 1986-88, owner. Writer and consultant. **Publications:** (Ed.) The 1940 Martin Catalog, 1973; (with D.B. Green) Roy Acuff's Musical Collection at Opryland, 1982; (with W. Carter) Gruhn's Guide to Vintage Guitars, 1991 as Gruhn's Guide to Vintage Guitars: An Identification Guide for American Fretted Instruments, 1999, 3rd ed., 2010; (with W. Carter) Acoustic Guitars and Other Fretted Instruments: A Photographic History, 1993; (with W. Carter) Electric Guitars and Basses: A Photographic History, 1994. Contributor of articles to periodicals. **Address:** Gruhn Guitars Inc., 400 Broadway, Nashville, TN 37203, U.S.A. **Online address:** gruhn@gruhn.com

GRULEY, Bryan. American (born United States), b. 1957. **Genres:** Mystery/Crime/Suspense. **Career:** Kalamazoo Gazette, staff, 1981-84; Detroit News, reporter, 1984-95; Wall Street Journal, reporter and editor, 1995-2005, Chicago bureau chief, 2005-. Journalist. **Publications:** Paper Losses: A Modern Epic of Greed and Betrayal at America's Two Largest Newspaper Companies, 1993; Starvation Lake: A Mystery, 2009. **Address:** Chicago, IL , U.S.A. **Online address:** grules@bryangruley.com

GRUMBACH, Doris. American (born United States), b. 1918. **Genres:** Novels, Literary Criticism And History, Biography, Autobiography/Memoirs. **Career:** Metro-Goldwyn-Mayer, title-writer, 1940-41; Time Inc., proofreader and copy editor, 1941-42; Architectural Forum, associate editor, 1942-43; Albany Academy for Girls, teacher of English, 1952-55; College of St. Rose, instructor, professor of English, 1952-73; Critic, columnist, 1960-64; National Catholic Reporter, columnist, 1968-76; The New Republic, literary editor, 1973-75; American University, professor of American literature, 1975-85; New York Times Books Review, columnist, 1976-83; Saturday Review, columnist, 1977-78; Chronicle of Higher Education, columnist, 1979-84; Wayward Books, owner, 1990-; University of Iowa, Writers Workshop, faculty. **Publications:** NOVELS: The Spoil of the Flowers, 1962; The Short Throat, the Tender Mouth, 1964; Chamber Music, 1979; The Missing Person, 1981; The Ladies, 1984; The Magician's Girl, 1987; The Book of Knowledge, 1989. OTHERS: The Company She Kept, 1967; Coming into the End Zone, 1991; Extra Innings, 1993; Fifty Days of Solitude, 1994; Life in a Day, 1996; The Presence of Absence, 1998; The Pleasure of Their Company, 2000. Contributor of articles to periodicals. **Address:** c/o Tim Seldes, Russell and Volkening, 50 W 29th St., New York, NY 10001, U.S.A.

GRUMBINE, R. Edward. American (born United States), b. 1953. **Genres:** Environmental Sciences/Ecology, Animals/Pets. **Career:** U.S. Forest Service, Sequoia National Forest, research intern in fire ecology, 1974, Mount Baker-Snoqualmie National Forest, fire fighter, 1977; Antioch College, instructor in environmental studies, 1975, 1977; National Park Service, Sitka National Historical Park, interpretive naturalist, 1976, Olympic National Park, backcountry ranger, 1978, North Cascades National Park, backcountry ranger, 1982; Evergreen State College, instructor in environmental studies, 1979; University of Montana, Wilderness Institute, administrative assistant, 1979-80, instructor, 1981; University of California Extension, instructor in environmental studies, 1982-, Sierra Institute, director, 1982-. Writer. **Publications:**

Ghost Bears: Exploring the Biodiversity Crisis, 1992; (ed.) Environmental Policy and Biodiversity, 1994; Where the Dragon Meets the Angry River: Nature and Power in the People's Republic of China, 2010. Contributor of articles to periodicals. **Address:** University of California Extension, 740 Front St., Ste. 155, Santa Cruz, CA 95060, U.S.A.

GRUMMAN, Bob. American (born United States), b. 1941. **Genres:** Plays/Screenplays, Poetry, Psychology, Literary Criticism And History, Science Fiction/Fantasy, Novels. **Career:** Datagraphic Computer Services, computer operator, 1971-76; Charlotte County School Board, substitute teacher, 1994-2009. Writer. **Publications:** Poems (visual haiku), 1966; Preliminary Rough Draft of a Total Psychology (theoretical psychology), 1967; A Straynge Book (children's book), 1987; An April Poem (visual poetry), 1989; Spring Poem No. 3,719,242 (visual poetry), 1990; Of Manywhere-at-Once, vol. I (memoir/criticism), 1990; Mathemaku 1-5 (mathematical poetry), 1992; Mathemaku 6-12 (mathematical poetry), 1994; Of Poem (solitextual poetry), 1994; Mathemaku 13-19 (mathematical poetry), 1996; A Selection of Visual Poems (visual poetry), 1998; min. kolt., matemakuk, 2000; Cryptographiku 1-5 (cryptographic poetry), 2003; Excerpts from Poem's Search for Meaning (solitextual poetry), 2004; Greatest Hits of Bob Grumman (mixture of poetries), 2006; Shakespeare and the Rigidniks (theoretical psychology), 2006; From Haiku To Lyriku, 2007; April to the Power of the Quantity Pythagoras Times Now (collection of mathemaku), 2007; This Is Visual Poetry (visual Poetry), 2010; Poem Demerging (solitextual poetry), 2010; A Preliminary Taxonomy of Poetry, 2011. EDITOR: (with C. Hill) Vispo auf Deutsch, 1995; Writing to Be Seen, vol. I, 2001. **Address:** PO Box 495597, Port Charlotte, FL 33949, U.S.A. **Online address:** bobgrumman@nut-n-but.net

GRUNBAUM, Adolf. American (born United States), b. 1923. **Genres:** Philosophy, Psychology. **Career:** Lehigh University, instructor, 1950-51, assistant professor, 1951-53, associate professor, 1953-55, professor of philosophy, 1955-56, William Wilson Selfridge Professor of Philosophy, 1956-60; University of Minnesota, Center for Philosophy of Science, visiting research professor, 1956, 1959; University of Pittsburgh, Department of History and Philosophy of Science, Andrew Mellon Professor of Philosophy of Science, 1960-, research professor of psychiatry, 1979-, primary research professor, 2006-, Center for Philosophy of Science, director, 1960-78, chairman, 1978-; Michigan State University, Arnold Isenberg Memorial Lecturer, 1965; Wesleyan University, Matchette Lecturer, 1966; Princeton University, Louis Clark Vanuxem Lecturer, 1967; Stanford University, Summer Institute for College Teachers in Philosophy and the Sciences, visiting professor, 1967, Center for Advanced Study in the Behavioral Sciences, visiting fellow, 1967; University of Chicago, Monday Lecturer, 1968; Indiana University, Mahlon Powell Lecturer, 1968, Alberto J. Coffa Memorial Lecturer, 1986; Johns Hopkins University, Thalheimer Lecturer, 1969; University of Iowa, Everett W. Hall Lecturer, 1973, Gustav Bergmann Memorial Lecturer, Beam Visiting Professor, 1993; University of Notre Dame, visiting lecturer in philosophy, 1976; University of Duesseldorf, visiting lecturer in philosophy, 1976; Institute for Advanced Study, Einstein Centennial Lecturer, 1979-80; University of Konstanz, Konstanz Dialogues Lecturer, 1983; Bavarian Academy of Sciences, Werner Heisenberg Lecturer, 1985; University of St. Andrews, St. Andrews College, Gifford Lecturer, 1985; University of Alberta, visiting distinguished professor, 1988; California Institute of Technology, Visiting Mellon Professor, 1990; University of Hannover, Leibniz Lecturer, 2003. Writer. **Publications:** Philosophical Problems of Space and Time, 1963, 2nd ed., 1973; Modern Science and Zeno's Paradoxes, 1967, rev. ed., 1968; (contrib.) A Sophisticate's Primer of Relativity, 1967; Geometry and Chronometry in Philosophical Perspective, 1968; (ed. with E. Nagel and S. Bromberger) Observation and Theory in Science, 1971; The Foundations of Psychoanalysis: A Philosophical Critique, 1984; Psychoanalyse in Wissenschafts-theoretischer sicht-Zum werk Sigmund Freuds und seiner rezeption, 1987; Psicoanalisi: Obiezioni E Risposte, 1988; (ed. with W.C. Salmon) The Limitations of Deductivism, 1988; (ed.) Kritische Betrachtungen zur Psychoanalyse, 1991; Psicoanalisi e il Teismo, 1991; Validation in the Clinical Theory of Psychoanalysis: A Study in the Philosophy of Psychoanalysis, 1993; La Psychanalyse a l Epreuve, 1993; Philosophy of Science in Action, forthcoming. FESTSCHRIFT VOLUMES: (ed. with R.S. Cohen and L. Laudan) Physics, Philosophy, and Psychoanalysis: Essays in Honor of Adolf Grunbaum, 1983; (ed. with J. Earman) Philosophical Problems of the Internal and External Worlds: Essays in Honor of Adolf Grunbam, 1993; (ed. with A. Jokic) Philosophy of Religion, Physics and Psychology: Essays in Honor of Adolf Grunbaum, 2009. Contributor of

articles to periodicals. Works appear in anthologies. **Address:** University of Pittsburgh, 2510 Cathedral of Learning, Pittsburgh, PA 15260-2510, U.S.A. **Online address:** grunbaum@pitt.edu

GRUNDY, Joan. British (born England), b. 1920. **Genres:** Literary Criticism And History, Poetry, Philosophy, Literary Criticism And History, Young Adult Fiction. **Career:** University of Edinburgh, assistant lecturer in English, 1947-50; University of Liverpool, lecturer in English, 1950-65; University of London, Royal Holloway College, reader, 1965-79, professor of English literature, 1979-80, professor emeritus of English literature, 1980-. Writer. **Publications:** (Ed.) The Poems of Henry Constable, 1960; The Spenserian Poets: A Study in Elizabethan and Jacobean Poetry, 1969; Hardy and the Sister Arts, 1979. Contributor of articles to periodicals. **Address:** Rose Cottage, Lamb Pk., Rosside, Ulverston, CM LA12 7NR, England.

GRUNDY, Pamela C. American (born United States), b. 1962. **Genres:** Education, History, Local History/Rural Topics, Race Relations, Sports/Fitness, Women's Studies And Issues, Politics/Government. **Career:** Star, reporter, 1986-87; Davidson College, adjunct assistant professor of history, 2006-, visiting assistant professor. Writer. **Publications:** (With B. Carlin) Musical Change in the Western Piedmont: A Research Summary, 1991; You Always Think of Home: A Portrait of Clay County, Alabama, 1991; Learning to Win: Sports, Education and Social Change in Twentieth-Century North Carolina, 2001; (with S. Shackelford) Shattering the Glass: The Remarkable History of Women's Basketball, 2005. **Address:** Davidson College, PO Box 7145, Davidson, NC 28035, U.S.A.

GRUNER, Charles R. American (born United States), b. 1931. **Genres:** Communications/Media, Speech/Rhetoric, Language/Linguistics, Humor/Satire. **Career:** High school teacher of speech and drama, 1956-57; St. Lawrence University, instructor, 1957-60, assistant professor of speech, 1960-64, Hulett Hall Dormitory, head resident, 1958-59, Debate Society, advisor; University of Nebraska, assistant professor, 1964-66, associate professor of speech, 1966-69, special assistant to the chairman for graduate matters, 1965-69; University of Georgia, associate professor, 1969-74, professor of speech, 1974-97, professor emeritus, 1997-, General Sandy Beaver teaching professor, 1994-97, undergraduate advisor, 1974-75, graduate coordinator, 1974-83; Georgia Speech Communication Journal, editor, 1975-77; Southern Speech Communication Journal, associate editor, 1975-77. **Publications:** (With C.M. Logue, D.L. Freshley and R.C. Huseman) Speech Communication in Society, 1972, 2nd ed., 1977; (with C.M. Logue, D.L. Freshley and R.C. Huseman) Speaking: Back to Fundamentals, 1976, 4th ed. as Briefly Speaking, 1992; Understanding Laughter: The Workings of Wit and Humor, 1978; Plain Public Speaking, 1982; Essentials of Public Speaking, 1993; The Game of Humor: A Comprehensive Theory of Why We Laugh, 1997. Contributor of articles to journals. **Address:** Department of Speech Communication, University of Georgia, 138 Terrell Hall, Athens, GA 30602, U.S.A. **Online address:** cgruner@arches.uga.edu

GRUNER, Wolf. German (born Germany), b. 1960. **Genres:** Novels. **Career:** Historische Kommission, researcher, 1994-95; Technical University, researcher, 1997-2002; German Federal Foundation, consultant; Webster University, Desmond E. Lee distinguished visiting professor for global awareness, 2003; Institute for Contemporary History, researcher and co-editor, 2004-07. **Publications:** Judenverfolgung in Berlin 1933-1945: Eine chronologie der Behordenmassnahmen in der reichshauptstadt, 1996; Der geschlossene arbeitseinsatz deutscher Juden: Zur zwangsarbeit als element der verfolgung 1938-1943, 1997; Zwangsarbeit und verfolgung: Osterreichische Juden im NS-Staat 1938-43, 2000; Offentliche Wohlfahrt und Judenverfolgung. Wechselwirkungen lokaler und zentraler Politik im NS-Staat (1933-1942), 2002; Widerstand in der rosenstrasse: die fabrikaktion und die verfolgung der mischehen 1943, 2005; Jewish Forced Labor under the Nazis: Economic Needs and Racial Aims, 1938-1944, 2006, rev. ed., 2008; (co-ed.) Die Verfolgung und Ermordung der europaischen Juden durch das national-sozialistische Deutschland 1933-1945, vol. I: Das Deutsche Reich 1933 bis 1937, 2008. **Address:** Department of History, University of Southern California, 3520 Trousdale Pkwy., SOS Rm. 262, Los Angeles, CA 90089-0034, U.S.A. **Online address:** gruner@usc.edu

GRUNTMAN, Mike. American (born United States), b. 1954. **Genres:** Air/Space Topics, History, Engineering, Sciences, Biography. **Career:** USSR Academy of Sciences, Space Research Institute, research fellow, 1977-86, Institute for Problems in Mechanics, research fellow, 1987-90; FOM-Institute for Atomic and Molecular Physics, visiting scientist, 1988; University of Southern California, Space Sciences Center, research scientist, 1990-93, Viterbi School of Engineering, professor of astronautics, aerospace engineering, and systems architecture engineering, 1993-, Astronautics Program, founder, 1994-95, chair, 2004-07. Writer. **Publications:** Blazing the Trail: The Early History of Spacecraft and Rocketry, 2004; From Astronautics to Cosmonautics, 2007; Enemy Amongst Trojans: A Soviet Spy at USC, 2011. Contributor to books and journals. **Address:** Department of Astronautical Engineering, Viterbi School of Engineering, University of Southern California, RRB-224, MC-1192, 854 Downey Way, Los Angeles, CA 90089-1192, U.S.A. **Online address:** mikeg@usc.edu

GRUSKY, Scott T. American (born United States), b. 1961. **Genres:** Novels, Young Adult Fiction. **Career:** Web developer and writer. **Publications:** Silicon Sunset, 1998. **Address:** InfoNet Publication, 23852 Pacific Coast Hwy., Ste. 330, Malibu, CA 90265, U.S.A. **Online address:** soulsurfer@gmail.com

GRYLLS, Bear. British (born England), b. 1974. **Genres:** Travel/Exploration, Human Relations/Parenting, Environmental Sciences/Ecology, Natural History. **Career:** The Scout Association, chief scout, 2009-; United Kingdom Special Forces Reserve, part-time survival instructor, 1994-97. Writer. **Publications:** Facing Up: A Remarkable Journey to the Summit of Mount Everest (autobiography), 2000 in US as The Kid Who Climbed Everest: The Incredible Story of a Twenty-three Year Old's Summit of Mt. Everest, 2001; Facing the Frozen Ocean, 2003, new ed. 2005; Born Survivor: Bear Grylls Transworld, 2007; Man vs. Wild: Survival Techniques from the Most Dangerous Places on Earth, 2008; Mission Survival: Gold of the Gods, 2008; Sands of the Scorpion, 2009; Living Wild: The Ultimate Guide to Scouting and Fieldcraft, 2009; Great Outdoor Adventures, 2009; Mission Survival: Way of the Wolf, 2009; Mission Survival: Tracks of the Tiger, 2010; With Love, Papa, 2010. **Address:** Chief Scout's Office, The Scout Association, Gilwell Park, Chingford, London, GL E4 7QW, England. **Online address:** bear@beargrylls.com

GUARDINO, Peter. (Peter F. Guardino). American (born United States), b. 1963?. **Genres:** History, Law, Politics/Government, Humanities. **Career:** University of Chicago, Department of Economy, research assistant, 1986, teaching assistant, 1987-88, Department of Sociology, visiting professor, 1989, Department of History, research assistant, 1990; Central Washington University, research assistant, 1991; California Institute for Rural Studies, research assistant, 1991; Loyola University, lecturer, 1992; University of Illinois, Center for Latin American Studies, visiting assistant professor, 1992-93; Indiana University, Department Of History, assistant professor, 1993-99, associate professor, 1999-, professor, chair, director of graduate studies, American Historical Review, associate editor, 1994-96. Writer and historian. **Publications:** Peasants, Politics and the Formation of Mexico's National State: Guerrero, 1800-1857, 1996; (contrib.) After Spanish Rule: Postcolonial Predicaments in the Americas, 2003; The Time of Liberty: Popular Political Culture in Oaxaca, 1750-1850, 2005; (contrib.) Honor, Status and Law in Modern Latin America, 2005. Contributor to periodicals and journals. **Address:** Department of History, Indiana University, Rm. 709 Ballantine Hall, 1020 E Kirkwood Ave., Bloomington, IN 47405-7103, U.S.A. **Online address:** pguardin@indiana.edu

GUARDINO, Peter F. *See* **GUARDINO, Peter.**

GUARE, John. American (born United States), b. 1938. **Genres:** Plays/Screenplays, Homes/Gardens, Young Adult Fiction, Literary Criticism And History. **Career:** Eugene O'Neill Theatre Center, founding member, 1965; New York Shakespeare Festival, resident playwright, 1976; Yale University, School of Drama, adjunct professor of playwriting, 1978-81; Harvard University, visiting artist, 1990-91; Juilliard School, fellow, 1993-94; New York University, lecturer; City College of New York, lecturer. Writer. **Publications:** Muzeeka and Other Plays, 1969; Kissing Sweet, and A Day for Surprises, 1970; The House of Blue Leaves, 1971; Rich and Famous, 1977; (with M. Shapiro) Two Gentlemen of Verona, 1973; Marco Polo Sings a Solo, 1977; The Landscape of the Body, 1978; Bosoms and Neglect, 1979, rev. ed., 1999; In Fireworks Lie Secret Codes, 1981; Three Exposures: Plays, 1982; Lydie Breeze, 1982; Gardenia, 1982; The Talking Dog, 1986; Six Degrees of Separation: A Play, 1990; (intro.) The Locusts Have No King, 1990; Women and Water, 1990; (intro.) The Substance of Fire and Other Plays, 1991; Four Baboons Adoring the Sun and Other Plays, 1993; Moon under Miami, 1995; Chuck Close: Life and Work, 1988-1995, 1995; The War against the Kitchen

Sink, 1996; The General of Hot Desire and Other Plays, 1999; Lake Hollywood, 2000; Chaucer in Rome, 2002; A Few Stout Individuals, 2003; (foreword) Three Plays: Dividing the Estate, The Trip to Bountiful, and The Young Man from Atlanta, 2008; (intro.) Enemy of the People: An Adaptation of the Play by Henrik Ibsen, 2010. Contributor to periodicals. **Address:** International Creative Management Inc., 730 5th Ave., New York, NY 10019, U.S.A.

GUARNIERI, Carlo. Italian (born Italy), b. 1949. **Genres:** Politics/Government, Law, Public/Social Administration. **Career:** University of Bologna, Department of Political Science, professor, 1990-, dean, 1997-2000, chairman, 2001-07. Writer. **Publications:** L'indipendenza della magistratura, 1981; Pubblico ministero e sistema politico, 1984; Magistratura e politica in italia: pesi senza contrappesi, 1993; (with P. Pederzoli) La puissance de juger: pouvoir judiciaire et democratie, 1996; La giustizia in Italia, 2001; La magistratura nelle democrazie contemporanee, 2002; (with P. Pederzoli) The Power of Judges: A Comparative Study of Courts and Democracy, 2002; (with J.L. Newell) Italian Politics: Quo Vadis?, 2005; Il sistema politico italiano: radiografia politica di un paese, 2006; The Italian Political System, 2007; Judicial Independence in Authoritarian Regimes: Lessons from Continental Europe, 2009. **Address:** Department of Political Science, University of Bologna, Strada Maggiore 45, Bologna, 40125, Italy. **Online address:** carlo.guarniericalbo@unibo.it

GUARNIERI, Patrizia. Italian (born Italy), b. 1954. **Genres:** History, Criminology/True Crime, Psychology, Women's Studies And Issues, Medicine/Health, Intellectual History. **Career:** University of Florence, Centro di Cultura per Stranieri, lecturer, 1978-81; Stanford University, Program in Italy, lecturer in Italian, 1982-93, lecturer in history of science, 1986-93; University College London, Wellcome Trust Center for the History of Medicine, C.N.R.-Nato Fellow, 1983; University of Trieste, professor of history of science, 1988-91; European University Institute, Jean Monnet fellow, 1989, visiting professor, 2000; University of Firenze, Department of Psychology, professor of history, 2004-; Medicina & Storia, editor-in-chief, 2010-. Historian. **Publications:** Luigi Credaro: Lo studioso e il politico, 1979; Filosofia e scuola nell'eta giolittiana, 1980; La Rivista Filosofica, 1899-1908: Conoscenza evalori nel neokantismo italiano, 1981; Introduzione a James, 1985; (ed.) Luigi Credaro nella scuola e nella storia, 1986; Individualita difformi: La psichiatria antropologica di Enrico Morselli, 1986; L'ammazzabambini: Legge e scienza in un processo toscano dell'Ottocento, 1988, rev. ed., 2006, trans. as A Case of Child Murder: Law and Science in Nineteenth-Century Tuscany, 1993; The Psyche in Trance: Inquiries into Hypnotism, 1990; La Storia della Psichiatria: Un Secolo di Studi in Italia, 1991, trans. as The History of Psychiatry in Italy: A Century of Studies, 1994; Dangerous Girls: Family Secrets and Incest Law, 1998; Bambini e Salute in Europa 1750-2000/ Children and Health in Europe 1750-2000, 2004; (ed.) In scienza e coscienza. Maternità nascite e aborti tra esperienze e bioetica, 2009; Men Committing Female Crime: Infanticide, Family and Honor in Italy, 2009. Works appear in anthologies. Contributor to periodicals. **Address:** Department of Psychology, University of Firenze, via San Salvi 12, Firenze, 50133, Italy. **Online address:** patrizia.guarnieri@unifi.it

GUASPARI, John. American (born United States) **Genres:** Business/Trade/Industry, Young Adult Fiction, Administration/Management. **Career:** Rath & Strong, senior associate, vice president; Guaspari & Salz Inc., co-founder and president, 1986-. Writer. **Publications:** I Know It When I See It: A Modern Fable about Quality, 1985; Theory Why: In Which the Boss Solves the Riddle of Quality, 1986; The Customer Connection: Quality for the Rest of Us, 1988; It's about Time: A Fable about the Next Dimension of Quality, 1992; The Value Effect: A Murder Mystery about the Pursuit of The Next Big Thing, 2000. Contributor to periodicals. **Address:** Guaspari & Salz Inc., 53 Bradford St., Concord, MA 01742, U.S.A. **Online address:** jguaspari@qualitydigest.com

GUBAR, Susan (David). American (born United States), b. 1944. **Genres:** Literary Criticism And History, Women's Studies And Issues, Theology/Religion, History, Biography. **Career:** University of Illinois, faculty, through 1973; Indiana University, faculty, 1973-, distinguished professor of English and women's studies, Ruth N. Halls Professor Emeritus of English, now distinguished professor emeritus of English. Writer. **Publications:** WITH S.M. GILBERT: The Madwoman in the Attic: The Woman Writer and the Nineteenth-Century Literary Imagination, 1979, 2nd ed., 2000; (ed. and intro.) Shakespeare's Sisters: Feminist Essays on Poets, 1979; (comp.) The Norton Anthology of Literature by Women: The Tradition in English, 1985, 3rd ed., 2007; (ed.) The Female Imagination and the Modernist Aesthetic, 1986; No Man's Land: The Place of the Woman Writer in the Twentieth Century, 3 vols., 1988-94; Masterpiece Theatre: An Academic Melodrama, 1995; (ed. with D. O'Hehir) Mothersongs: Poems For, By and About Mothers, 1995; (ed.) Feminist Literary Theory And Criticism: A Norton Reader, 2007. OTHERS: (ed. with J. Hoff) For Adult Users Only: The Dilemma of Violent Pornography, 1989; (ed. and intro. with J. Kamholtz) English Inside and Out: The Places of Literary Criticism, 1993; Racechanges: White Skin, Black Face in American Culture, 1997; Critical Condition: Feminism at the Turn of the Century, 2000; Poetry after Auschwitz: Remembering What One Never Knew, 2003; Room of One's Own, 2005; Rooms of Our Own, 2006; Judas: A Biography, 2009; True Confessions: Feminist Professors Tell Stories out of Schools, 2011. Contributor to periodicals and journals. **Address:** Department of English, Indiana University, 442 Ballantine Hall, 1020 E Kirkwood Ave., Bloomington, IN 47405-7103, U.S.A. **Online address:** gubar@indiana.edu

GUDORF, Christine E. American (born United States), b. 1949. **Genres:** Theology/Religion, Women's Studies And Issues, Sex, Cultural/Ethnic Topics. **Career:** Xavier University, assistant professor, 1978-83, associate professor, 1983-88, professor of religious studies, 1988-93; Mount St. Mary's Seminary, adjunct professor, 1979-89; Temple University, visiting professor, 1989; Florida International University, associate professor, 1993-95, professor of religious studies, 1995-, department chair, 2004-; Seattle University, visiting professor, 1995. Writer. **Publications:** Catholic Social Teaching on Liberation Themes, 1980; (ed. with B. Andolsen and M. Pellauer) Women's Consciousness, Women's Conscience: A Reader in Feminist Ethics, 1985; (co-author) Christian Ethics: A Case Method Approach, 1989, 3rd ed., 2005; Victimization: Examining Christian Complicity, 1992; Body, Sex and Pleasure: Reconstructing Christian Sexual Ethics, 1994; (with R. Wolfe) Ethics and World Religions: Cross-Cultural Case Studies, 1999; (with J. Huchingson) Boundaries: A Casebook in Environmental Ethics, 2003, 2nd ed., 2009. Contributor to books and periodicals. **Address:** Department of Religious Studies, Florida International University, University Pk. DM 303, Miami, FL 33199, U.S.A. **Online address:** gudorf@fiu.edu

GUELKE, Adrian. Irish/South African (born South Africa), b. 1947. **Genres:** Business/Trade/Industry. **Career:** University of the Witwatersrand, Jan Smuts professor of international relations, 1993-95; Queen's University, School of Politics, International Studies and Philosophy, professor of comparative politics, Center for Study of Ethnic Conflict, director of research, MA in Comparative Ethnic Conflict, director. Writer. **Publications:** (With S. Siebert) The Control of Wages in South Africa, 1973; Northern Ireland: The International Perspective, 1989; Interdependence and Transition: The Cases of South Africa and Northern Ireland, 1993; (ed.) New Perspectives on the Northern Ireland Conflict, 1994; The Age of Terrorism and the International Political System, 1995; South Africa in Transition: The Misunderstood Miracle, 1999; (ed. with M. Cox and F. Stephen) A Farewell to Arms?: From 'Long War' to Long Peace in Northern Ireland, 2000; (ed.) Democracy and Ethnic Conflict: Advancing Peace in Deeply Divided Societies, 2004; Rethinking the Rise and Fall of Apartheid: South Africa and World Politics, 2005; Terrorism and Global Disorder: Political Violence in the Contemporary World, 2006; (ed.) The Challenges of Ethno-nationalism: Case Studies in Identity Politics, 2010. Contributor of articles to journals. **Address:** School of Politics, Intl. Studies and Philosophy, Queen's University Belfast, Rm. 19.102, 21 University Sq., Belfast, BT7 1PA, Northern Ireland. **Online address:** a.guelke@qub.ac.uk

GUÉRIF, François. French (born France), b. 1944. **Genres:** Film, Biography. **Career:** Editions Fayard, editor; Editions Fleuve Noire, editor; Editions PAC, editor; Editions Rivages, editorial director; Journal Polar, editor. **Publications:** Paul Newman, 1975; Robert Redford, 1976; Marlon Brando, 1976; (with P. Merigeau) John Wayne: le Dernier Géant, 1979; Le Film Noir Américain, 1979; Le Cinéma Policier Francais, 1981; (with R. Boyer) Brigitte Bardot: And God Created Woman, 1983; Clint Eastwood, 1983; Vincente Minnelli, 1984; François Truffaut, 1988; Steve McQueen, 1988; Sans Espoir de Retour: Samuel Fuller, 1989; Le film Policier, 1989; Passéla Loire, c'est l'aventure: 50 ans de cinéma Gilles Grangier, 1989; James M. Cain: Biographie, 1992; Conversations with Claude Chabrol, 1997; Claude Chabrol: un jardin bien à moi, 1999; Le film noir americain, 1999; (with S. Bourgoin and J. Deloux) Dahlia Noir, 2006; (with C. Chabrol) Comment faire un film, 2003; Ciné miscellanées, 2007. **Address:** 106 Blvd., Saint Germain, Paris, 75006, France.

GUERNSEY, Thomas F. American (born United States), b. 1951. **Genres:** Law. **Career:** Vermont Law School, instructor in law, 1976-78; Temple University, Honorable Abraham L. Freedman Fellow and lecturer in law, 1978-

80, Temple Legal Aid Office, assistant general counsel, 1978-80; Offender Aid and Restoration of Richmond, board director, 1984-87, vice president, 1985-87; University of Richmond, assistant professor, 1980-83, associate professor, 1983-86, professor of law, 1986-, associate dean for academic affairs, 1992-95, dean, president; Southern Illinois University School of Law, dean and professor, 1996-2002, interim provost and vice chancellor for academic affairs, 1999-2000; Albany Law School, president, 2002-, dean, 2002-11, professor of law. Writer and consultant. **Publications:** (With R.J. Bacigal) Admissibility of Evidence in Virginia: A Manual for Virginia Trial Lawyers, 1990, (with T.F. Guernsey and J.S. Tate) 2nd ed., 1998; Problems and Simulations in Evidence, with Instructor's Manual, 1991, 4th ed., 2010; (with L.A. Dubin) Trial Practice, 1991, (co-author) 2nd ed., forthcoming; Virginia Evidence, with supplements, 1992; (with K. Klare) Special Education Law, 1993, 3rd ed., 2008; (with Klare) Negotiations for Health Care Materials Managers: A Systematic Approach, 1993; (with Harbaugh and Zwier) Negotiate for Success! (interactive computer program), 1994; A Practical Guide to Negotiation, 1996; (with K. Klare) Special Education Law, 2001, 3rd ed., 2008; (with P.J. Zwier) Advanced Negotiation and Mediation Theory and Practice: A Realistic Integrated Approach, 2005; (foreword) Pioneering Women Lawyers, 2008. Contributor of articles to journals. **Address:** Albany Law School, 80 New Scotland Ave., Albany, NY 12208-3494, U.S.A. **Online address:** tguer@albanylaw.edu

GUEST, Christopher. American (born United States), b. 1948. **Genres:** Plays/Screenplays, Songs/Lyrics And Libretti, Novels, Humor/Satire. **Career:** Writer. **Publications:** (Intro.) Death by Laughter, 2008. Contributor to periodicals. **Address:** Creative Artists Agency, 9830 Wilshire Blvd., Beverly Hills, CA 90212-1825, U.S.A.

GUEST, Harry. British/Welsh (born Wales), b. 1932. **Genres:** Novels, Poetry, Literary Criticism And History, Translations, Travel/Exploration, Plays/Screenplays. **Career:** Felsted School, assistant master, 1955-61; Lancing College, Modern Languages Department, head, 1961-66; Yokohama National University, assistant lecturer, 1966-72; Exeter School, teacher and head of modern languages, 1972-91; Exeter University, honorary university fellow, 1994-. Writer. **Publications:** Private View, 1962; A Different Darkness, 1964; Arrangements, 1968; Another Island Country, 1970; The Cutting-Room, 1970; (with M. Mead and J. Beeching) Penguin Modern Poets 16, 1970; (M. Mead) Jack Beeching, 1970; The Place, 1971; (ed. and trans. with L. Guest and K. Shôzô) Post-War Japanese Poetry, 1972; The Achievements of Memory, 1974; The Enchanted Acres, 1975; Mountain Journal, 1975; A House Against the Night, 1976; English Poems, 1976; Two Poems, 1977; Days: Novel, 1978; The Hidden Change, 1978; Zeami in Exile, 1978; Elegies, 1980; (trans.) V. Hugo, The Distance, The Shadows: Selected Poems, 1981; Lost and Found: Poems 1975-1982, 1983; The Emperor of Outer Space, 1983; Dealings with the Real World, 1987; Mastering Japanese, 1989; Lost Pictures (novel), 1991; Coming to Terms, 1994; Literary Companion to Japan, 1994; Japan, 1995; So Far, 1998; Versions, 1999; The Artist on the Artist, 2000; A Puzzling Harvest, Collected Poems 1955-2000, 2002; Comparisons & Conversions, 2009; Some Times, 2010. **Address:** 1 Alexandra Terr., Exeter, DN EX4 6SY, England.

GUEST, Ivor (Forbes). British (born England), b. 1920. **Genres:** Dance/Ballet, Classics. **Career:** Tweedie & Prideaux, partner, 1951-85; Royal Academy of Dancing, chairman, 1969-93, vice president, 1993-; British Theatre Museum, vice-chairman, 1966-77; Society of Dance Research, chairman, 1982-97; Radcliffe Trust, trustee, 1997-; Ordre des Arts et des Lettres, chevalier, 1998. Writer and solicitor. **Publications:** Napoleon III in England, 1952; The Ballet of the Second Empire, 1858-70, 1953; The Romantic Ballet in England, 1954; The Ballet of the Second Empire, 1847-58, 1955; Fanny Cerrito, 1956, 2nd ed., 1974; Victorian Ballet Girl, 1957; Adeline Genee, 1958; The Alhambra Ballet, 1959; The Dancer's Heritage, 1960, 5th ed., 1977; (ed. and co-author) La Fille mal Gardee, 1960; The Empire Ballet, 1962; A Gallery of Romantic Ballet, 1965; The Romantic Ballet in Paris, 1966, 2nd ed., 1980; Dandies and Dancers, 1969; Carlotta Zambelli, 1969; Two Coppelias, 1970; Fanny Elssler, 1970; Pas de Quatre, 1970; Le Ballet de l'Opera de Paris, 1976, rev. ed., 2001; The Divine Virginia, 1977; Adeline Genee: A Pictorial Record, 1978; Lettres d'un Maitre de Ballet, 1978; (ed.) Letters from a Ballet-Master, 1981; Adventures of a Ballet Historian, 1982; Jules Perrot, 1984; Gautier on Dance, 1986; Gautier on Spanish Dancing, 1987; Dr. John Radcliffe and His Trust, 1991; Ballet in Leicester Square, 1992; The Ballet of the Enlightenment, 1996; (intro.) Les cancans de l'Opéra, 2000; Ballet under Napoleon, 2002. Contributor to magazines. **Address:** 17 Holland Pk., London, GL W11 3TD, England. **Online address:** ivorguest@lodc.org

GUEST, Jacqueline. Canadian (born Canada), b. 1952?. **Genres:** Children's Fiction, Young Adult Fiction, History, Sports/Fitness. **Career:** Writer. **Publications:** Hat Trick, 1997; Free Throw, 1999; Triple Threat, 1999; Rookie Season, 2000; Lightning Rider, 2000; Rink Rivals, 2001; A Goal in Sight, 2002; Soccer Star, 2003; Racing Fear, 2004; At Risk, 2004; Bell of Batoche, 2004; Wild Ride, 2005; Dream Racer, 2006; Secret Signs, 2006; War Games, 2009; Ghost Messages, 2011. **Address:** PO Box 522, Bragg Creek, AB T0L 0K0, Canada. **Online address:** writer@jacquelineguest.com

GUEST, Judith. American (born United States), b. 1936. **Genres:** Novels, Essays, Plays/Screenplays, Young Adult Non-fiction, Young Adult Fiction, Mystery/Crime/Suspense. **Career:** Teacher, 1964-75; Palantine press, staff; Daily Herald, staff. Writer. **Publications:** Ordinary People, 1976; Second Heaven, 1982; (contrib.) Judith Guest's Ordinary people: A Full Length Play, 1983; (with R. Hill) Killing Time in St. Cloud, 1988; The Mythic Family: Essay, 1988; Errands, 1996; Ice Walk (essay), 2001; The Tarnished Eye, 2004; White in The Moon, forthcoming; Don't be Too Sure, forthcoming. Contributor to periodicals. **Address:** Patricia Karlan Agency, 3575 Cahvenga Blvd., Ste. 210, Los Angeles, CA 90068-1341, U.S.A. **Online address:** judy@judithguest.com

GUEST, Paul. American (born United States) **Genres:** Novellas/Short Stories. **Career:** University of West Georgia, teacher of English; University of Tennessee, teacher of English. Poet and educator. **Publications:** The Resurrection of the Body and the Ruin of the World, 2003; Notes for My Body Double, 2007. Contributor to journals. **Address:** Carrollton, GA, U.S.A. **Online address:** paulmguest@hotmail.com

GUEVARA, Maurice Kilwein. American/Colombian (born Colombia), b. 1961. **Genres:** Poetry, Literary Criticism And History, Education. **Career:** Indiana University, assistant professor, 1991-97, associate professor of English, 1997-99, professor of English, through 2002; Vermont College, poetry faculty, 2002-03; University of Wisconsin, professor of English, 2003-. Writer. **Publications:** Postmortem: Poems, 1994; Poems of the River Spirit, 1996; The Best of Cream City Rev, 1997; Learning By Heart, 1999; Autobiography of So-and-So: Poems in Prose, 2001; To Box Clouds, 2002; Poema: Poems, 2009. Contributor to magazines. Works appear in anthologies. **Address:** Department of English, University of Wisconsin, 512 Curtin Hall, 3243 N Downer Ave., PO Box 413, Milwaukee, WI 53201, U.S.A. **Online address:** maurice@uwm.edu

GUGGENBÜHL, Allan. Swiss (born Switzerland), b. 1952. **Genres:** Psychology, Social Sciences, Medicine/Health, Children's Fiction. **Career:** Jung Institute of Zurich, lecturer; University of Education, professor. Writer. **Publications:** The Incredible Fascination of Violence, 1996; Men, Power and Myths: The Quest for Male Identity, 1997; Dem Dämon in die Augen schauen: Gewaltprävention in der Schule, 1998; Moderationsanleitung fürPolizeikräfte im Rahmen der Kampagne Gemeinsam gegen Gewalt, 1999. **Address:** Unter Zaunel, Zurich, 8001, Switzerland. **Online address:** algugg@swissonline.ch

GUGLER, Laurel Dee. Canadian/American (born United States) **Genres:** Children's Fiction, Young Adult Fiction, Novels, Picture/Board Books, Animals/Pets. **Career:** Whimsical Words, owner; Hamilton Children's Museum, education coordinator and teacher; SHAIR International Resource Centre, co-founder and coordinator. Writer. **Publications:** Mashed Potato Mountain, 1988; Casey's Carousel, 1989; Little Wynne's Giggly Thing, 1995; Muddle Cuddle, 1997; Monkey Tales, 1998; Facing the Day, 1999; There's a Billy Goat in the Garden, 2003; Catching Forever, 2007; A Piece of Forever, 2008; Where the River Meets the Sea, forthcoming. Contributor to magazines. **Address:** Whimsical Words, 219 College St., Apt. 342, Toronto, ON M5T 1R1, Canada. **Online address:** lgugler@primus.ca

GUHA-THAKURTA, Tapati. Indian (born India) **Genres:** Art/Art History. **Career:** Centre for Studies in Social Sciences, professor of history. Educator and writer. **Publications:** The Making of a New Indian Art: Artists, Aesthetics and Nationalism in Bengal, 1850-1920, 1992; Traversing Past and Present in the Victoria Memorial, 1995; Archaeology as Evidence: Looking Back from the Ayodhya Debate, 1997; Culture and the Disciplines: Papers from the Cultural Studies Workshops, 1999; Culture and Democracy: Papers from the Cul-

tural Studies Workshops, 1999; In Her Own Right: Remembering the Artist Karuna Shaha, 2001; Visual Worlds of Modern Bengal: Selections from the Documentation Archive of the Centre for Studies in Social Sciences, 2002; Monuments, Objects, Histories: Institutions of Art in Colonial and Postcolonial India, 2004; Calcutta, Repossessing the City, 2006; Iconography Now: Rewriting Art History?, 2006. Contributor to magazines. **Address:** Ctr. for Studies in Social Sciences, Calcutta R-1, Baishnabghata Patuli Township, Kolkata, 700 094, India. **Online address:** tapati@cssscal.org

GUHRKE, Laura Lee. American (born United States) **Genres:** Novels, Romance/Historical. **Career:** Novelist. **Publications:** GUILTY SERIES: Guilty Pleasures, 2004; His Every Kiss, 2004; The Marriage Bed, 2005; She's No Princess, 2006; Wedding of the Season, 2011; Scandal of the Year, 2011; Trouble at the Wedding, 2012. GIRL-BACHELOR SERIES: And Then He Kissed Her, 2007; The Wicked Ways of a Duke, 2008; Secret Desires of a Gentleman, 2008; With Seduction in Mind, 2009. OTHER: Prelude to Heaven, 1994; To Dream Again, 1995; Conor's Way, 1996; The Seduction, 1997; Breathless, 1999; The Charade, 2000; Not So Innocent, 2002. **Address:** Harper Collins, 10 E 53rd St., New York, NY 10022, U.S.A. **Online address:** laura@lauraleeguhrke.com

GUIDRY, Cindy. American (born United States), b. 1965?. **Genres:** Autobiography/Memoirs, Biography, International Relations/Current Affairs, Essays. **Career:** Writer. **Publications:** The Last Single Woman in America (essays, memoir), 2008. **Address:** CA, U.S.A. **Online address:** cindy@cindyguidry.com

GUIGNON, Charles B(urke). American (born United States), b. 1944. **Genres:** Literary Criticism And History, Philosophy, Psychology. **Career:** Princeton University, lecturer in philosophy, 1976-77; University of Texas, instructor and assistant professor of philosophy, 1977-84; University of California, visiting assistant professor, 1984-85; University of Vermont, associate professor, 1985-93, professor of philosophy, 1993-2001, College of Arts and Sciences, secretary, 1988-89, John Dewey Honors Program, director, 1996-99; University of Auckland, visiting professor, 1999; University of South Florida, professor, 2001-. Writer. **Publications:** Heidegger and the Problem of Knowledge, 1983; (with F. Richardson and B. Fowers) Re-envisioning Psychology: Moral Dimensions of Theory and Practice, 1999; On Being Authentic, 2004. EDITOR: The Cambridge Companion to Heidegger, 1993, 2nd ed., 2006; (intro.) The Grand Inquisitor: With Related Chapters from the Brothers Karamazov, 1993; (with D. Pereboom and intro.) Existentialism: Basic Writings, 1995; (intro.) The Good Life, 1999; (with D.R. Hiley) Richard Rorty, 2003; The Existentialists: Critical Essays on Kierkegaard, Nietzsche, Heidegger, and Sartre, 2004; (with K. Aho and intro.) Dostoevsky's Notes from the Underground, 2009. **Address:** Department of Philosophy, University of South Florida, 4202 E Fowler Ave., Tampa, FL 33620-7926, U.S.A. **Online address:** guignon@chuma1.cas.usf.edu

GUILD, Elspeth. British/Canadian (born Canada), b. 1954. **Genres:** Politics/Government, Law, Sociology. **Career:** Baileys Shaw & Gillett Solicitors, solicitor, 1989-97; Kingsley Napley Solicitors, partner, 1997-; University of Nijmegen, professor of European migration law, 2000-; London School of Economics, visiting professor, 2003-; Centre for European Policy Studies, senior research fellow, 2005-; College of Europe, visiting professor, 2007-08; King's College London, Department of War Studies, faculty. Writer. **Publications:** The Developing Immigration and Asylum Policies of the European Union: Adopted Conventions, Resolutions, Recommendations, Decisions, and Conclusions, 1996; (with G. Lesieur) The European Court of Justice on the European Convention on Human Rights: Who Said What, When?, 1998; (ed.) The Legal Framework and Social Consequences of Free Movement of Persons in the European Union, 1999; (ed. with C. Harlow) Implementing Amsterdam: Immigration and Asylum Rights in EC Law, 2001; Immigration Law in the European Community, 2001; (ed. with K. Groenendijk and P. Minderhound) In Search of Europe's Borders, 2003; The Legal Elements of European Identity: EU Citizenship and Migration Law, 2004; (ed. with D. Bigo) Controlling Frontiers: Free Movement into and within Europe, 2005; (ed. with J. van Selm) International Migration and Security: Opportunities and Challenges, 2005; (ed. with P. Minderhoud) Immigration and Criminal Law in the European Union: The Legal Measures and Social Consequences of Criminal Law in Member States on Trafficking and Smuggling in Human Beings, 2006; (ed. with A. Baldaccini and H. Toner) Whose Freedom, Security and Justice? EU Immigration and Asylum Law and Policy, 2007; (ed. with A. Baldaccini) Terrorism and the Foreigner: A Decade of Tension around the

Rule of Law in Europe, 2007; (ed. with F. Geyer) Security versus Justice? Police and Judicial Cooperation in the European Union, 2008. Contributor to journals. **Address:** King's College London, Strand, London, GL WC2R 2LS, England. **Online address:** e.guild@jur.kun.nl

GUILE, Melanie. Australian (born Australia), b. 1949?. **Genres:** Children's Fiction, Children's Non-fiction, History. **Career:** Melbourne University, tutor in English literature, 1972-75, lecturer in children's literature, 1988-94; Royal Melbourne Institute of Technology, instructional designer and educational editor, 1995-98; full-time author, 2002-. **Publications:** CHILDREN'S FICTION: Revenge of the Green Genie, 1996; Mr. Venus-Computer Wizard, 1997; Ghost Granny, 2005. CHILDREN'S NON-FICTION: AUSTRALIA'S NEIGHBOURS SERIES: Indonesia, 2000; Japan, 2000; New Zealand, 2000; China, 2000; Vietnam, 2001; Papua New Guinea, 2001. CULTURE IN SERIES: New Zealand, 2002; Papua New Guinea, 2002; Japan, 2002; Indonesia, 2002; North and South Korea, 2003; China, 2003; Thailand, 2003; Singapore, 2003; India, 2005; Vietnam, 2005; Australia, 2005; Malaysia, 2005. CHILDREN IN AUSTRALIAN HISTORY SERIES: Little Felons, 2005; Bush Boys and Girls, 2005; Another Mouth to Feed, 2005; Baby Boomers, 2005. ISLANDS OF THE SOUTH PACIFIC SERIES: Micronesia, 2005; Solomon Islands, 2005; Tonga, 2005; Fiji, 2005; Vanuatu, 2005; Samoa and Tuvalu, 2005. GOLD IN AUSTRIA SERIES: The Gold Rushes, 2006; Life on the Goldfields, 2006; Famous People of the Goldrush Era, 2006; How Gold Shaped Australia, 2006. WHAT IS AUSTRALIA? SERIES: The Land, 2009; The People, 2009; The Nation, 2009; Plants & Animals, 2009. WORLD ISSUES COME TO AUSTRALIA SERIES: Drought and El Nino, 2008; Violence, 2010; Extremism, 2010. DISASTERS IN AUSTRALIA: Flood, 2010. STORIES FROM AUSTRALIA'S HISTORY SERIES: Vida Goldstein's Fight for Women's Rights, 2010; Douglas Mawson's Antarctic Expedition, 2010; Vincent Lingiari and the Wave Hill Walkout, 2010; Peter Lalor and the Eureka Stockade, 2010; Captain Arthur Phillip and the First Fleet, 2010; The Anzacs and the Battle for Gallipoli, 2010; Ned Kelly and the Kelly Gang, 2011; Burke and Wills' Expedition to Cross Australia, 2011; Fanny Durack's Olympic Quest, 2011; C.Y.O'Connor and the Goldfields Pipeline, 2011; Weary Dunlop and the Burma-Thailand Railway, 2011; Charles Perkins and the Freedom Ride, 2011. ADULT NON-FICTION: Clyde School 1910-1975: An Uncommon History, 2006. **Address:** 47 Tongue St., Yarraville, VI 3013, Australia. **Online address:** melanieguile@iinet.net.au

GUILFOILE, Kevin. American (born United States), b. 1968. **Genres:** Novels, Literary Criticism And History, Mystery/Crime/Suspense. **Career:** Writer. **Publications:** SELF-ILLUSTRATED: (with J. Warner) Modern Humorist Presents My First Presidentiary: A Scrapbook by George W. Bush, 2001. OTHERS: Cast of Shadows, 2005 in UK as Wicker, 2005; The Thousand, 2010. Contributor to periodicals. **Address:** c/o Author Mail, Alfred A. Knopf Inc., 1745 Broadway, New York, NY 10019-4368, U.S.A. **Online address:** kevin@guilfoile.net

GUILHOT, Nicolas. American/British/French (born France), b. 1970. **Genres:** Civil Liberties/Human Rights, Business/Trade/Industry. **Career:** London School of Economics, lecturer in sociology; Centre National de la Recherche Scientifique-Centre de Sociologie Européenne, director of research, senior researcher, 2003-; Social Science Research Council, research fellow, 2007-; Institute for Public Knowledge, program officer; Columbia University, Department of Sociology, faculty. Writer. **Publications:** Financiers, Philanthropes: Vocations Ethiques et Reproduction du Capital A Wall Street depuis 1970, 2004, rev. ed. as Financiers, Philanthropes: Sociologie de Wall Street, 2006; The Democracy Makers: Human Rights and International Order, 2005; (ed.) Invention of International Relations Theory: Realism The Rockefeller Foundation and The 1954 Conference On Theory, 2011. **Address:** Institute for Public Knowledge, 20 Cooper Sq., 5th Fl., Houghton St., New York, NY 10003, U.S.A. **Online address:** guilhot@ssrc.org

GUILL, Jane. American (born United States) **Genres:** Novels, History. **Career:** Graphic designer, archaeological illustrator and writer. **Publications:** Nectar from a Stone, 2005. Contributor to magazines. Works appear in anthologies. **Address:** Simon & Schuster Inc., 1230 Ave. of the Americas, New York, NY 10020, U.S.A.

GUILLAUMIN, Colette. French (born France), b. 1934?. **Genres:** Social Commentary, Sociology, Young Adult Non-fiction, Anthropology/Ethnology. **Career:** University of Paris VII, Centre National de la Recherche Scientifique, researcher; French National Centre for Scientific Research, sociologist. Writer. **Publications:** L'idéologie raciste: Genèse et langage actuel, 1972; Sexe, race et pratique du pouvoir, L'idee de nature, 1992, trans. as Racism, Sexism, Power and Ideology, 1995. Works appear in anthologies. Contributor to journals. **Address:** Unite de Recherche Migrations et Societes, Centre National de la Recherche Scientifique, Universite de Paris VII Denis Diderot, 2 Pl. Jussieu Tour Centrale, Paris Cedex, 05, France.

GUILLEMIN, Jeanne (Harley). American (born United States), b. 1943. **Genres:** Anthropology/Ethnology, Sociology. **Career:** Radcliffe Institute, Bunting fellow, 1972-73; The Hastings Center for the Study of Society, Ethics and the Life Sciences, National Endowment for the Humanities research fellow, 1980-81; Brigham & Women's Hospital, Decision Systems Group, editorial associate, 1996-99; Massachusetts Institute of Technology, Dibner Institute for the Study of the History of Science and Technology, senior fellow, 2002-03, Security Studies Program, senior advisor; Boston College, research professor of sociology. Writer. **Publications:** Urban Renegades: The Cultural Strategy of American Indians, 1975; (ed.) Anthropological Realities: Readings in the Science of Culture, 1981; (contrib.) Anspruchsspirale, 1983; (with L.L. Holmstrom) Mixed Blessings: Intensive Care for Newborns, 1986, rev. ed., 1991; Anthrax: The Investigation of a Deadly Outbreak, 1999; Biological Weapons: From the Invention of State-sponsored Programs to Contemporary Bioterrorism, 2005; American Anthrax: Fear, Crime, and the Investigation of the Nation's Deadliest Bioterror Attack, 2011. **Address:** Department of Sociology, Boston College, 426 McGuinn Hall, 140 Commonwealth Ave., Chestnut Hill, MA 02467-3807, U.S.A. **Online address:** jeanne.guillemin.1@bc.edu

GUILLEN, Michael (Arthur). American (born United States), b. 1940?. **Genres:** Mathematics/Statistics, Sciences, Plays/Screenplays, Theology/Religion. **Career:** Harvard University, teacher of physics and mathematics in core curriculum program, 1985-; WCVB-TV, science editor, 1985-; ABC-TV, science editor, 1988-, ABC News, science correspondent for programs, 1990-; Spectacular Science Productions Inc., president; Filmanthropy Media Inc., president. Writer. **Publications:** NONFICTION: Bridges to Infinity: The Human Side of Mathematics, 1983; Five Equations that Changed the World: The Power and Poetry of Mathematics, 1995; Dr. Universe Tells U about Ur Body, 1999; Dr. Universe Tells U about the Solar System, 2000; Can a Smart Person Believe in God?, 2004. Contributor to periodicals. **Address:** c/o Good Morning America, ABC-TV, 147 Columbus Ave., New York, NY 10023, U.S.A. **Online address:** info@MichaelGuillen.com

GUILLERMOPRIETO, Alma. Mexican (born Mexico), b. 1949. **Genres:** Area Studies, Essays. **Career:** Guardian, reporter, journalist; Washington Post, reporter; New Yorker, contributing writer, 1989-, staff correspondent; University of Chicago, Center for Latin American Studies, Tinker visiting professor in history, 2008; Newsweek, South American bureau chief; New York Review of Books, writer. **Publications:** Samba, 1990; The Heart That Bleeds: Latin America Now (essays), 1994; Al pie de unvolcán te escribo, 2000; Looking for History: Dispatches from Central America (essays), 2001; La Habana en un espejo, 2005. Contributor to periodicals. **Address:** c/o Author Mail, Alfred A. Knopf Inc., 299 Park Ave., 4th Fl., New York, NY 10171, U.S.A.

GUILLORY, Dan. American (born United States), b. 1944. **Genres:** Essays, Poetry, Novels, History. **Career:** Louisiana State University, instructor in English, 1967-70, special lecturer, 1969-70; Tulane University, teaching assistant, 1970-71; Millikin University, Department of English, assistant professor, 1972-78, associate professor, 1978-82, professor of English, 1982-2004, Hardy distinguished professor of English, 1984-86, emeritus professor of English, 2004-; Omar Bongo University, Fulbright senior lecturer, 1989-90. Writer. **Publications:** Living with Lincoln: Life and Art in the Heartland (essays), 1989; The Alligator Inventions (poems), 1992; When the Waters Recede: Rescue and Recovery during the Great Flood, 1996; Introduction to the Lemon Jelly Cake (novel), 1997; Introduction to Tramping across America (essays), 1999; Decatur, 2004; Wartime Decatur, 1832-1945, 2006; Macon County, 2007; Lincoln Poems, 2008; People & Places in the Land of Lincoln, 2010. Contributor to periodicals. **Address:** Department of English, Millikin University, 1184 W Main St., Decatur, IL 62522, U.S.A. **Online address:** dguillory@mail.millikin.edu

GUILLOU, Jan. Swedish (born Sweden), b. 1944. **Genres:** Politics/Government, Novels. **Career:** FIB aktuellt, writer, 1966-67; Folket i Bild/Kulturfront Magazine, co-founder and writer, 1970-77; Aftonbladet, columnist; Piratforlaget, co-owner. **Publications:** Halvfärdig bok, 1971; Om kriget kommer. En dokumentär roman, 1971; Journalistik 1967-1976, 1976; (with M. Stagh) Irak-det nya Arabien, 1977; (with J.H. Dahlström) Artister: Intervjuer och porträytt, 1979; Reporter, 1979; Ondskan, 1981; Justitiemord: Fallet Keith Cederholm, 1983; (with G. Skytte) Nya berättelser: Från Geijer till Rainer, 1984; Demokratiske terroristen: Coq Rouge, 1987; I nationens intresse: Coq Rouge, 1988; Fiendens fiende, 1989; Vendetta: Coq Rouge VI, 1991; Ingen mans land: Coq Rouge VII, 1992; Enemy's Enemy: A Novel, 1992; Den enda segern: Coq Rouge VIII, 1993; I hennes majestäts tjänst: Coq Rouge IX, 1994; Medborgare höjd över varje misstanke: Coq Rouge X, 1995; Svenskarna, invandrarna och svartskallarna: mitt livs viktigaste reportage, 1996; Vägen till Jerusalem, 1998; Tempelriddaren, 1999; Riket vid vägens slut, 2000; Arvet efter Arn, 2001; Häxornas försvarare: ett historiskt reportage, 2002; Madame Terror, 2006; Den Hedervärde mördaren, 2006; Fienden inom oss, 2007; Men inte om det gäller din dotter, 2008; Birth of the Kingdom, 2010. **Address:** Norstedt Publishers, PO Box 2052, Stockholm, 10312, Sweden.

GUINIER, Lani. American (born United States), b. 1950. **Genres:** Law, History, Social Sciences. **Career:** U.S. Court of Appeals, Sixth Circuit, law clerk, 1974-76; Wayne County Juvenile Court, juvenile court referee, 1976-77; U.S. Department of Justice, Civil Rights Division, special assistant, 1977-81; National Association for the Advancement of Colored People (NAACP) Legal Defense and Educational Fund, assistant counsel, 1981-88; New York University School of Law, adjunct professor, 1985-89; Lawyers Committee for International Human Rights, board director, 1985-93; University of Pennsylvania Law School, associate professor, 1988-92, professor of law, 1992-98; NOW Legal Defense Fund, board director, 1990-96; Juvenile Law Center, board director, 1992-98; Commonplace Inc., founder and president, 1994-99; RACETALKS, principal investigator, 1996-2002; Harvard University, visiting professor of law, 1996, professor of law, 1998-2001, Bennett Boskey professor of law, 2001-. Writer. **Publications:** The Tyranny of the Majority: Fundamental Fairness in Representative Democracy, 1994; (with M. Fine and J. Balin) Becoming Gentleman: Women, Law School, and Institutional Change, 1998; Lift Every Voice: Turning a Civil Rights Setback into a New Vision of Social Justice, 1998; Reflecting all of Us: The Case for Proportional Representation, 1999; (with S. Strum) Who's Qualified?: A New Democracy Forum on Creating Equal Opportunity in School and Jobs, 2001; (with G. Torres) The Miner's Canary: Enlisting Race, Resisting Power, Transforming Democracy, 2002; Meritocracy Inc.: How Wealth Became Merit, Class Became Race and Higher Education Became a Gift From the Poor to the Rich, forthcoming. Contributor to journals. **Address:** Harvard Law School, 1563 Massachusetts Ave., Cambridge, MA 02138, U.S.A. **Online address:** lguinier@law.harvard.edu

GUINN, Jeff Mason. American (born United States), b. 1951. **Genres:** Autobiography/Memoirs, Young Adult Non-fiction. **Career:** Fort Worth Star-Telegram, books editor. Journalist. **Publications:** (Ed.) The Autobiography of Santa Claus: It's Better to Give, 1994; (reteller) How Mrs. Claus Saved Christmas, 2005; (ed. with J. Alter) Noah's Ride: A Collaborative Western Novel, 2006; (reteller) The Great Santa Search, 2006; (reteller) Santa's North Pole Cookbook: Classic Christmas Recipes from Saint Nicholas Himself, 2007; The Christmas Chronicles, 2008. NONFICTION: (reteller) You Can't Hit the Ball with the Bat on Your Shoulder: The Baseball Life and Times of Bobby Bragan, 1992; Sometimes a Fantasy: Midlife Misadventures with Baseball Heroes, 1994; (with A. Grieser) Something in the Blood: The Underground World of Today's Vampires, 1996; Dallas Cowboys: The Authorized Pictorial History, 1996; (with B. Bragan) When Panthers Roared: The Fort Worth Cats and Minor League Baseball, 1999; Our Land before We Die: The Proud Story of the Seminole Negro, 2002; (with D. Perry) The Sixteenth Minute: Life in the Aftermath of Fame, 2005; Go Down Together: The True, Untold Story of Bonnie and Clyde, 2009; Last Gunfight, 2011. **Address:** Fort Worth Star-Telegram, 400 W 7th St., Fort Worth, TX 76102, U.S.A. **Online address:** jguinn@star-telegram.com

GUINNESS, Desmond. Irish/British (born England), b. 1931. **Genres:** Architecture, History. **Career:** Irish Georgian Society, co-founder, 1958; Metropolitan Museum, lecturer; Boston Museum of Fine Arts, lecturer; Philadelphia Museum of Art, lecturer; Art Museum of Chicago, lecturer; Los Angeles County Museum, lecturer. Writer. **Publications:** Portrait of Dublin, 1967; (with W. Ryan) Irish Houses and Castles, 1971; (with J.T. Sadler, Jr.) Mr.

Jefferson, Architect, 1973; Irish House, 1975; (with J.T. Sadler, Jr.) Palladio: A Western Progress, 1976; Georgian Dublin, 1979; (with W. Ryan) The White House: An Architectural History, 1980; (with J.T. Sadler, Jr.) Newport Preserved: Architecture of the 18th Century, 1982; (with D. Donoghue) Ascendancy Ireland: Papers Read at a Clark Library Seminar, 28 September 1985, 1986; (with J. O'Brien) Great Irish Houses and Castles, 1992; (with J. O'Brien) Dublin: A Grand Tour, 1994. Contributor to periodicals. **Address:** Leixlip Castle, Leixlip, KL 26376, Ireland.

GUINNESS, Jonathan (Bryan). British (born England), b. 1930. **Genres:** Biography, Business/Trade/Industry, Economics, History. **Career:** Reuters, journalist, 1953-56; Erlangers Ltd., merchant banker trainee, 1956-59; Philip Hill, merchant banker trainee, 1959-62; Arthur Guinness Son and Comapny Ltd., director, 1961-88; Leopold Joseph, executive director, 1962-64, non-executive director, 1964-91. Writer. **Publications:** (With C. Guinness) The House of Mitford (biography), 1984, reissued, 2004; Shoe: The Odyssey of a Sixties Survivor (biography), 1989; Requiem for a Family Business, 1997. **Address:** c/o Gillon Aitken, 29 Fernshaw Rd., London, GL SW10-OTG, England.

GUISTA, Michael. American (born United States) **Genres:** Novellas/Short Stories, Psychology. **Career:** Allan Hancock College, faculty. Writer. **Publications:** Brain Work: Stories, 2005. Contributor to journals. **Address:** Allan Hancock College, Santa Maria Campus, 800 S College Dr., Santa Maria, CA 93454, U.S.A. **Online address:** mguista@hancockcollege.edu

GULBEKIAN, Sevak E(dward). British (born England), b. 1964. **Genres:** inspirational/Motivational Literature, Cultural/Ethnic Topics, Theology/Religion. **Career:** Temple Lodge Publishing Ltd., chief editor, 1990-, Clairview Books Ltd., chief editor; Rudolf Steiner Press, chief editor. **Publications:** At the Grave of Civilization? A Spiritual Approach to Popular Culture, 1996; The Future Is Now: Anthroposophy at the New Millennium, 2000; In the Belly of the Beast: Holding Your Own in Mass Culture, 2004. **Address:** c/o Author Mail, Clairview Books Ltd., Temple Lodge Publishing, Hillside House, The Square, Forest Row, ES RH18 5ES, England. **Online address:** sevak@clairviewbooks.com

GULLOTTA, Thomas P. American (born United States), b. 1948. **Genres:** Medicine/Health, Education. **Career:** Child and Family Services of Connecticut, child care worker, 1971-73; Glastonbury Youth and Family Resource Center, assistant director, 1974-75, director of clinical services, 1975-81; Central Connecticut State University, lecturer, 1974-81; Net (runaway shelter), director, 1975-77; Friends of Glastonbury Youth, board director, 1976-86, board chair, 1981-83; University of Connecticut, field instructor, 1976-80, 1989-92, lecturer, 1984; Manchester Community College, lecturer, 1978-79; United Social and Mental Health Services, director of consultation and education, 1981-84; Eastern Connecticut State University, lecturer, 1982-; Child & Family Agency of Southeast Connecticut Inc., chief executive officer, 1985-; National Institute of Mental Health, consultant; Town of Glastonbury, vice chair of town council, 1986-91. Writer. **Publications:** (With G.R. Adams) Adolescent Life Experiences, 1983, (with Adams and C. Markstrom-Adams) 3rd ed., 1994; (with G.R. Adams and S. Alexander) Today's Marriages and Families: A Wellness Approach, 1986; (co-author) Issues in Children's and Families' Lives, vol. I: Family Violence: Prevention and Treatment, 1993; (with G.R. Adams and C.A. Markstrom) The Adolescent Experience, 2000. EDITOR: (with G.R. Adams and R. Montemayor) The Biology of Adolescent Behavior and Development, 1989; (with G.R. Adams and R. Montemayor) From Childhood to Adolescence, 1990; (with G.R. Adams and R. Montemayor) Developing Social Competency in Adolescence, 1990; (with G.R. Adams and R. Montemayor) Adolescent Identity Formation, 1992; (with G.R. Adams and R. Montemayor) Adolescent Sexuality, 1993; Substance Misuse in Adolescence, 1994; (with R.L. Hampton and P. Jenkins) Preventing Violence in America, 1996; (with G.M. Blau) Adolescent Dysfunctional Behavior: Causes, Interventions, and Prevention, 1996; (with G.W. Albee) Primary Prevention Works, 1997; (with R.L. Hampton and V. Senatore) Substance Abuse, Family Violence, and Child Welfare: Bridging Perspectives, 1998; (with S.J. McElhaney) Violence in Homes and Communities: Prevention, Intervention, and Treatment, 1999; (co-ed.) Children's Health Care: Issues for the Year 2000 and Beyond, 1999; (with G.R. Adams) Delinquent Violent Youth: Theory and Interventions, 1999; (with G.R. Adams and R. Montemayor) Adolescent Diversity in Ethnic, Economic, and Cultural Contexts, 2000; (with S.J. Danish) Developing Competent Youth and Strong Communities through After-School Programming, 2000; (with M. Bloom) Promoting Creativity across the Life Span, 2001; (with M. Bloom) The Encyclopedia of Primary Prevention and Health Promotion, 2003; (with R.W. DuCharme) Asperger Syndrome: A Guide for Professionals and Families, 2003; (with R.L. Hampton) Promoting Racial, Ethnic, and Religious Understanding and Reconciliation, 2004; (with G.R. Adams) Handbook of Adolescent Behavioral Problems: Evidence-Based Approaches to Prevention and Treatment, 2005; (with R.L. Hampton) Interpersonal Violence in the African American Community: Evidence-based Prevention and Treatment Practices, 2006; (with G.M. Blau) Family Influences on Childhood Behavior and Development: Evidence-Based Prevention and Treatment Approaches, 2008; (with M. Bloom, C.F. Gullotta and J.F. Messina) A Blueprint for Promoting Academic and Social Competence in After-School Programs, 2008; (with G.M. Blau) Handbook of Childhood Behavioral Issues: Evidence-based Approaches to Prevention and Treatment, 2008; (co-ed.) Adolescent Substance Abuse: Evidence-Based Approaches to Prevention and Treatment, 2009; (with R.L. Hampton and R.L. Crowel) Handbook of African American Health, 2010. Works appear in anthologies. Contributor of articles to periodicals. **Address:** Child & Family Agency of Southeastern CT Inc., 255 Hempstead St., New London, CT 06320-6290, U.S.A.

GULVIN, Jeff. *See* **ARMSTRONG, Adam.**

GUMBRECHT, Hans Ulrich. American/German (born Germany), b. 1948. **Genres:** Novels. **Career:** University of Bochum, professor, 1975-82; University of Siegen, professor, 1983-89; Stanford University, professor, 1989-; University of Montreal, associate professor. Writer. **Publications:** Funktionswandel und Rezeption; Studien zur Hyperbolik in literarischen Texten des romanischen Mittelalters, 1972; Zola Im Historischen Kontext: Fur Eine Neue Lekture Des Rougon-Macquart-Zyklus, 1978; Funktionen Parlamentarischer Rhetorik in Der FranzOsischen Revolution: Vorstudien Zur Entwicklung Einer Historischen Textpragmatik, 1978; Literatur in Der Gesellschaft Des Spatmittelalters, 1980; (with K. Stierle and R. Warning) Honore De Balzac, 1980; (with R. Reichardt und T. Schleich) Sozialgeschichte Der Aufklarung in Frankreich: 12 Original-Beitrage, 1981; (with B. Cerquiglini) Der Diskurs Der Literatur Und Sprachhistorie: Wissenschaftsgeschichte Als Innovationsvorgabe, 1983; (with U. Link-Heer) Epochenschwellen Und Epochenstrukturen Im Diskurs Der Literatur Und Sprachhistorie, 1985; La Litterature Historiographique Des Origines A 1500, 1986; (with K.L. Pfeiffer) Stil: Geschichten Und Funktionen Eines Kulturwissenschaftlichen Diskurselements, 1986; Dabei Sein Ist Alles: uberwith N. Luhmann Die Geschichte Von Medien, Sport, Publikum, 1988; (with N. Luhmann, H. Heckhausen and S.J. Schmidt) Kreativitat, Ein Verbrauchter Begriff?, 1988; Eine Geschichte Der Spanischen Literatur, 1990; (with K.L. Pfeiffer) Paradoxien, Dissonanzen, Zusammenbruche: Situationen Offener Epistemologie, 1991; (with R. Weimann) Postmoderne: Globale Differenz, 1991; Making Sense in Life and Literature, 1992; (ed. with K.L. Pfeiffer) Materialities of Communication, 1994; (with C. Wulf and D. Kamper) Ethik Der asthetik, 1994; (ed. with M.S. Brownlee) Cultural Authority in Golden Age Spain, 1995; (with F. Kittler und B. Siegert) Der Dichter Als Kommandant: D Annunzio Erobert Fiume, 1996; In 1926: Living on the Edge of Time, 1997; (ed. with D. Palumbo-Liu) Streams of Cultural Capital: Transnational Cultural Studies, 1997; (ed. with J.C. De C. Rocha) MAscaras Da Mimesis: A Obra De Luiz Costa Lima, 1999; Warum Fussball? Kulturwissenschaftliche Beschreibungen Eines Sports, 2002; ParisBerlin: Europa, 2002; Vom Leben Und Sterben Der Grossen Romanisten: Karl Vossler, Ernst Robert Curtius, Leo Spitzer, Erich Auerbach, Werner Krauss, 2002; (ed. with M. Marrinan) Mapping Benjamin: The Work of Art in the Digital Age, 2003; The Powers of Philology: Dynamics of Textual Scholarship, 2003; (intro.) Intermedialidad E Hispanistica, 2003; (ed. with T. Lenoi) Experiments, Models, Paper Tools: Cultures of Organic Chemistry in the Nineteenth Century, 2003; (ed. with D.E. Wellbery and J. Ryan) A New History of German Literature, 2004; Production of Presence: What Meaning Cannot Convey, 2004; In Praise of Athletic Beauty, 2006. **Address:** Stanford University, 112 Pigott Hall, Stanford, CA 94305-2010, U.S.A. **Online address:** sepp@stanford.edu

GUMMER, Scott. American (born United States) **Genres:** Sports/Fitness. **Career:** Golf magazine, travel editor & senior writer. Journalist. **Publications:** The Seventh at St. Andrews: How Scotsman David McLay Kidd and His Ragtag Band Built the First New Course on Golf's Holy Soil in Nearly a Century, 2007. Contributor to periodicals. **Address:** c/o Scott Waxman, Waxman Literary Agency, 80 5th Ave., Ste. 1101, New York, NY 10011, U.S.A. **Online address:** scottgummer@yahoo.com

GUNDY, Jeff(rey Gene). American (born United States), b. 1952. **Genres:** Poetry, Adult Non-fiction, Essays. **Career:** Indiana University, associate instructor in English, 1977-80; Goshen College, assistant professor of English, 1980, visiting professor of English, 2004; Hesston College, instructor in English, 1980-84; Bluffton University, Department of English and Language, associate professor, 1984-89, professor of English, 1989-, coordinator of peace studies, 1985-93, C. Henry Smith Peace lecturer, 1989, 1999, Humanities Division, chair; Ohio Northern University, visiting lecturer in English, 1987; Ohio State University, visiting assistant professor of English, 1989; University of Salzburg, Fulbright lecturer, 2008. Writer. **Publications:** POETRY: Inquiries, 1992; Flatlands, 1995; Rhapsody with Dark Matter, 2000; Greatest Hits 1986-2003, 2003; Deerflies, 2004; Spoken among the Trees, 2007. OTHER: Surrendering to the Real Things: The Archetypal Experience of C. Wordsworth Crockett, 1986; A Community of Memory: My Days with George and Clara (nonfiction), 1996; Scattering Point: The World in a Mennonite Eye (nonfiction), 2003; Walker in the Fog: On Mennonite Writing, 2005. Contributor to periodicals. **Address:** Department of English and Language, Bluffton University, 318 Centennial Hall, 1 University Dr., Bluffton, OH 45817-2104, U.S.A. **Online address:** gundyj@bluffton.edu

GUNETTI, Daniele. Italian (born Italy), b. 1963. **Genres:** Information Science/Computers, Engineering, Technology. **Career:** Ministry of Communication, technician, 1983-87; University of Turin, technician, 1987-95, assistant professor of computer science, 1995-, associate professor in computer science. Writer. **Publications:** (With F. Bergadano) Inductive Logic Programming: From Machine Learning to Software Engineering, 1995. **Address:** Department of Computer Science, University of Turin, Corso Svizzera 185, Turin, 10149, Italy. **Online address:** gunetti@di.unito.it

GUNN, Ali. (Ally O'Brien). British (born England), b. 1969?. **Genres:** Mystery/Crime/Suspense. **Career:** Curtis Brown, literary agent, 1996-2006; Gunn Media, founder and literary agent, 2006-, director. Writer. **Publications:** (As Ally O'Brien) The Agency, 2009. **Address:** St. Martin's Press, 175 5th Ave., New York, NY 10010, U.S.A. **Online address:** ali@gunnmedia.co.uk

GUNN, Brooke. *See* **BROOKS-GUNN, Jeanne.**

GUNN, Eileen. American (born United States), b. 1945. **Genres:** Novellas/Short Stories, Young Adult Fiction, Science Fiction/Fantasy. **Career:** Advertising copy writer, 1969-; Microsoft Corp., director of advertising and sales promotion, 1980-; Clarion West Writers Workshop, director, 1988-; The Infinite Matrix, editor and publisher, 2001-; Global Automation, director of marketing; Gorp, managing editor. **Publications:** Stable Strategies and Others, 2004; (ed. with L.T. Duchamp) The WisCon Chronicles, 2008. **Address:** c/o Jacob Weisman, Tachyon Publications, 518 Connecticut St., San Francisco, CA 94107-2833, U.S.A.

GUNN, James E(dwin). American (born United States), b. 1923. **Genres:** Novels, Novellas/Short Stories, Science Fiction/Fantasy, Literary Criticism And History. **Career:** Western Printing and Lithographing Co., editor, 1951-52; Assistant director of civil defense, 1952; full-time writer, 1953-55; University of Kansas, administrative assistant for university elations and instrucrtor in English, 1958-70, lecturer in English and journalism, 1970-73, professor of English, 1974-93, Mellon Fellow, 1981, 1984, professor emeritus, 1993-, Center for the Study of Science Fiction, head and director; Science Fiction Writers of America, president, 1971-72. **Publications:** This Fortress World, 1955; (with J. Williamson) Star Bridge, 1955; Station in Space, 1958; The Joy Makers, 1961; The Immortals, 1962; Future Imperfect (short stories), 1964; The Immortal, 1970; The Witching Hour (short stories), 1970; The Burning, 1972; Breaking Point (short stories), 1972; The Listeners, 1972; Some Dreams Are Nightmares (short stories), 1974; Alternate Worlds: The Illustrated History of Science Fiction, 1975; The End of the Dreams: Three Short Novels About Space, Happiness, and Immortality, 1975; The Magicians, 1976; Kampus, 1977; The Dreamers, 1980 as The Mind Master, 1982; Isaac Asimov: The Foundations of Science Fiction, 1982; Tiger! Tiger! A Short Novel, 1984; Crisis!, 1986; Inside Science Fiction: Essays on Fantastic Literature, 1992, rev. ed., 1996; The Unpublished Gunn, vol. I, 1992, vol. II, 1996; The Joy Machine, 1996; The Science of Science-Fiction Writing, 2000; The Millennium Blues, 2001; Human Voices: Science Fiction Stories, 2002; Gift From the Stars, 2005; Inside Science Fiction, 2006. EDITOR: Man and the Future, 1968; Nebula Award Stories 10, 1975; The Road to Science Fiction (short stories), 6 vols., 1977-99; The New Encyclopedia of Science Fiction, 1988; The Best of Astounding: Classic Short Novels from the Golden

Age of Science Fiction, 1992; The Millennium Blues, 2001; Speculations on Speculation: Theories of Science Fiction, 2005; (with M.S. Barr and M. Candelaria) Reading Science Fiction, 2009. **Address:** English Department, University of Kansas, Wescoe Hall, 1445 Jayhawk Bldg., Rm. 3001, Lawrence, KS 66045-7590, U.S.A. **Online address:** jgunn@ku.edu

GUNN, Kirsty. British (born England), b. 1960. **Genres:** Novels. **Career:** Oxford University, professor of creative writing; University of Dundee, professor of creative writing. Writer. **Publications:** NOVELS: Rain, 1995; The Keepsake, 1997; This Place you Return to is Home, 1999; Featherstone, 2002; The Boy and the Sea, 2006; 44 Things: A Year of Life at Home, 2007. **Address:** Department of Creative Writing, University of Dundee, Perth Rd., Nethergate, Dundee, DD1 4HN, Scotland. **Online address:** k.j.gunn@dundee.ac.uk

GUNN, Moira A. American (born United States), b. 1949?. **Genres:** Sciences. **Career:** National Aeronautics and Space Administration, Institute for Advanced Computation, staff, 1974-80, scientist and engineer; University of San Francisco, College of Professional Studies, adjunct faculty, 1983-, program director of information systems, 2006-, Global Information Systems and Biotechnology, assistant professor; National Public Radio, Tech Nation, host, BioTech Nation, host, 1993-; The Tech Nation Group, president and chief executive officer; Tech Museum of Innovation, board member emeritus; Purdue University, staff. Writer. **Publications:** Welcome to Bio Tech Nation: My Unexpected Odyssey into the Land of Small Molecules, Lean Genes, and Big Ideas, 2007. **Address:** Tech Nation Media, KQED-FM, 2601 Mariposa St., San Francisco, CA 94110, U.S.A. **Online address:** technation@aol.com

GUNN, Robin Jones. American (born United States), b. 1955. **Genres:** Novels, Young Adult Fiction, Children's Fiction, Travel/Exploration, Romance/Historical. **Career:** Writer and radio host. **Publications:** BILLY 'N' BEAR SERIES: Billy 'n' Bear Go to Birthday Party, 1985; Billy 'n' Bear Go to Church, 1985; Billy 'n' Bear Go to Sunday School, 1985; Billy 'n' Bear Go to Doctor, 1985; Billy 'n' Bear Go to Grocery Store, 1985; Billy 'n' Bear Visits Grandpa and Grandma, 1985. JESUS IS WITH ME SERIES: Jesus Is with Me When I Celebrate His Birthday, 1988; Jesus Is with Me When I Go to the Park, 1988; Jesus Is with Me When I Have a Babysitter, 1988; Jesus Is with Me When I Help My Mommy, 1988; God's Mountains, Meadows, and More: A Book about Places God Has Made, 1994; (with T. Goyer) Praying for Your Future Husband: Preparing Your Heart for His, 2011. CHRISTY MILLER SERIES: Summer Promise, 1988, rev. ed., 1998; A Whisper and a Wish, 1989, rev. ed., 1998; Yours Forever, 1990, rev. ed., 1998; Surprise Endings, 1991, rev. ed., 1998; Island Dreamer, 1992, rev. ed., 1999; A Heart Full of Hope, 1992, rev. ed., 1999; True Friends, 1993, rev. ed., 1999; Starry Night, 1993, rev. ed., 1999; Seventeen Wishes, 1993, rev. ed., 1999; A Time to Cherish, 1993; rev. ed., 1999; Sweet Dreams, 1994, rev. ed., 1999; A Promise Is Forever, 1994, rev. ed., 1999; From the Secret Place in My Heart: Christy Miller's Diary, 1999; Until Tomorrow, 2000; As You Wish, 2000; I Promise, 2001; The Christy Miller Collection, 2005; Christy & Todd: The College Years, 2009; Departures: Two Rediscovered Stories, 2011. THE GLEN BROOKE SERIES: Secrets, 1995; Whispers, 1995; Echoes, 1996; Sunsets, 1997; Clouds, 1997; Waterfalls, 1998; Woodlands, 2000; Wildflowers, 2001. SISTERCHICKS SERIES: Sisterchicks on the Loose! 2003; Sisterchicks Do the Hula!, 2004; Sisterchicks in Sombreros!: A Sisterchicks Novel, 2004; Sisterchicks Down Under!: A Sisterchicks Novel, 2005; Sisterchicks Say Ooh La La!: A Sisterchicks Novel, 2005; Sisterchicks in Gondolas!, 2006; (with C. Hannan) Take Flight!: A Sisterchicks Devotional, 2006; Sisterchicks Go Brit!: A Novel, 2008; Sisterchicks in Wooden Shoes!: A Sisterchicks Novel, 2009. CHILDREN'S BOOKS: MRS. ROSEY-POSEY SERIES: Mrs. Rosey-Posey and the Chocolate Cherry Treat, 1991; Mrs. Rosey-Posey and the Treasure Hunt, 1991; Mrs. Rosey-Posey and the Empty Nest, 1993; Mrs. Rosey Posey and the Baby Bird, 2008; Mrs. Rosey Posey and the Fine China Plate, 2008; Mrs.Rosey Posey and the Hidden Treasure, 2008; Mrs. Rosey Posey and the Yum-Yummy Birthday Cake, 2008. SIERRA JENSEN SERIES: Only You, Sierra, 1995; In Your Dreams, 1996; Don't You Wish, 1996; Close Your Eyes, 1996; Without a Doubt, 1997; With This Ring, 1997; Open Your Heart, 1997; Time Will Tell, 1998; Now Picture This, 1998; Hold on Tight, 1998; Closer than Ever, 1999; Take My Hand, 1999; The Sierra Jensen Collection, vol. I, 2006. GIFT BOOKS: Mothering by Heart: Celebrating the Moments That Last Forever, 1996; Tea at Glenbrooke: A Quiet Place Where Souls are Refreshed, 2001. OTHER NOVELS: Departures, 1999; Gardenias for Breakfast, 2005; Finding Father Christmas, 2007; Peculiar Treasures, 2008; Coming Attractions, 2009; Canary Island Song, 2011. HIDEAWAY: Under a Maui Moon, 2010. Contributor to books and periodicals. **Address:**

Robin's Nest, PO Box 2902, Kahului, HI 96733, U.S.A. **Online address:** robinsnest@robingunn.com

GUNNING, Sally (Carlson). American (born United States), b. 1951. **Genres:** Novels, Literary Criticism And History. **Career:** Writer. **Publications:** PETER BARTHOLOMEW SERIES: Hot Water, 1990; Under Water, 1992; Ice Water, 1993; Troubled Water, 1993; Rough Water, 1994; Still Water, 1995; Deep Water, 1996; Muddy Water, 1997; Dirty Water, 1998; Fire Water, 1999. SATUCKET SERIES: The Widow's War: A Novel, 2006; The Rebellion of Jane Clarke, 2010. NOVEL: Bound, 2008. Contributor to periodicals. **Address:** c/o Christine Maddalena, HarperCollins Publishers, 10 E 53rd St., 11th Fl., New York, NY 10022-5244, U.S.A.

GUNSTON, Bill. British (born England), b. 1927. **Genres:** Air/Space Topics, Military/Defense/Arms Control, Technology, Transportation, Biography. **Career:** Flight Inl., technical editor, 1951-63; Science Journal, technology editor, 1964-70; Jane's All the World's Aircraft, compiler, 1968-, Jane's Aero-Engines, editor, 1995-2007, associate editor, 2007-; Aircraft (Australia), European editor, 1973-; So Few Ltd., director, 1990; Order of the British Empire, officer, 1995; Circle of Aviation Writers, chairman. **Publications:** Your Book of Light, 1968; Hydrofoils and Hovercraft, 1969; The Jet Age, 1971; Transport Technology, 1972; Transport Problems and Prospects, 1972; (with F. Howard) Conquest of the Air, 1973; Bombers of the West, 1973; Shaping Metals, 1974; Attack Aircraft of the West, 1974; Philatelist's Companion, 1975; Supersonic Fighters, 1975; Submarines in Colour, 1975; F-4 Phantom, 1976; Night Fighters: A Development and Combat History, 1976, rev. ed., 2003; Encyclopedia of Combat Aircraft, 1976; Modern Military Aircraft, 1977; Aircraft of World War II, 1978; (with B. Sweetman) Soviet Air Power, 1978; Spotting Planes, 1978; F-111, 1978; Bombers, 1978; By Jupiter, 1978; Tornado, 1979; Encyclopedia of Missiles and Rockets, 1979; Find Out about Trains and Railways, 1979; Find Out about Aircraft, 1979; Water, 1980; Aircraft of World War 2, 1980; The Plane Makers, 1980; Jane's Aerospace Dictionary, 1980, 3rd ed., 1988; Harrier, 1980; Coal, 1981; Motor Cycles, 1981; Modern Warplanes, 1981; Airliners, 1981; Fighters of the Fifties, 1981; Bombers of World War II, 1981; Military Helicopters, 1981; Fighters 1914-1945, 1982; Record Breakers (Land), 1982; (with A. Wood) Hitler's Luftwaffe, 1982; St. Michael Airliners, 1982; Aeroplanes, Balloons and Rockets, 1982; The Israeli Air Force, 1982; Family Library of Aviation, 1982; St. Michael Modern Air Combat, 1982; F-16 Fighting Falcon, 1982; Air-Launched Missiles, 1982; Warships, 1982; (contrib.) The Arms Yearbook, 1982; Fighter Aircraft in Colour, 1983; Aircraft of the Soviet Union, 1983; Spy Planes and RPVs, 1983; Fact File F-111, 1983; Missiles and Rockets of World War III, 1983; Encyclopedia of Modern Air Combat, 1983; Helicopters of the World, 1983; Naval and Maritime Aircraft, 1983; Falklands: The Aftermath, 1984; Fact File Harrier, 1984; Not Much of an Engineer (biography), 1984; Big Book of Fighter Planes, 1984; First Questions: Transport, 1984; Future Fighters and Combat Aircraft, 1984; Encyclopedia of Modern Fighting Aircraft, 1984; (with D. Taylor) The Guinness Book of Speed Facts and Feats, 1984; Aircraft of the RAF: Phantom, 1984; Air Superiority, 1985; F/A-18 Hornet, 1985; (co-author) Advanced Technology Warfare, 1985; Commercial Aircraft, 1985; Military Aircraft, 1985; A Century of Flight, 1985; Warplanes of the Future, 1985; (co-author) Encyclopedia of Modern Weapons, 1985; Modern Technology Aircraft, 1985; Grumman X-29, 1985; World Encyclopedia of Aero Engines, 1986, 5th ed., 2006; Water Travel, 1986; EAP, 1986; Encyclopedia of Modern Fighting Helicopters, 1986, 2nd ed., 1997; Encyclopedia of American Warplanes, 1986, 2nd ed., 1997; MiG-21, 1986; British, German, Japanese, U.S. Aircraft of World War 2, 4 vols., 1986; Modern European Aircraft, 1986; Modern Soviet Aircraft, 1986; Modern U.S. Aircraft, 1986; (ed.) Whittle: The True Story, 1987 as Genesis of the Jet, 1996; MiG-23 Flogger, 1987; AH-64A Apache, 1987; Aircraft of the Vietnam War, 1987; Encyclopedia of Aircraft Armament, 1987; Diamond Flight: British Midland (airways), 1987; Topics: Railways, 1987; Stealth Warplanes, 1987; One of a Kind (history of Grumman aircraft), 1987; Airbus, 1988, 2nd ed. as Airbus: The Complete History, 2009; Modern Combat Arms, 2 vols., 1988; American Military Aircraft, 1988; Guide to Modern Bombers, 1988; Anatomy of Aircraft, 1988; (with L. Peacock) Encyclopedia of Fighter Missions, 1988; Flight without Formulae, 5th ed., 1988; Rolls-Royce Aero Engines, 1989; Avionics, 1990; Stingers, F/A-18, 1990; Combat Arms: Helicopters, 1990; Classic Warplanes: P-51 Mustang, 1990; Combat Arms: Attack Aircraft, 1990; Flights of Fantasy, 1990; (co-author) So Few, 1990; Plane Speaking, 1991; Jet Bombers, 1991; Giants of the Sky, 1991; Passenger Airliners, 1991; Faster than Sound, 1992, 2nd ed. as Faster than Sound: The Story of Supersonic Flight, 2008; Aircraft Piston Engines, 1992, 2nd ed., 1999; Visual Dictionary of Flight,

1992; How It Works: Flight, 1993; Encyclopedia of Piston Aero Engines, 1993, 2nd ed., 1999; World Encyclopedia of Aircraft Manufacturers, 1993; (co-author) Spirit in the Sky: F-4 Phantom, 1993; World Encyclopaedia of Aircraft Manufacturers: From the Pioneers to the Present Day, 1993, 2nd ed., 2005; Tupolev Aircraft since 1922, 1995; Encyclopedia of Russian aircraft, 1875-1995, 1995; (with J. Golley and ed.) So Many: A Folio Dedicated to All Who Served with RAF Bomber Command, 1939-45, 1995; Back to the Drawing Board, 1996; (ed.) Genesis of the Jet: Frank Whittle and the Invention of the Jet Engine, 1996; (with Y. Gordon) Yakovlev Aircraft since 1924, 1997; Development of Jet and Turbine Aero Engines, 1997; World Encyclopaedia of Aero Engines: All Major Aircraft Power Plants, from the Wright Brothers to the Present Day, 1998; Modern Fighting Helicopters, 1998; (with Y. Gordon) MiG Aircraft since 1937, 1998; Fedden: The Life of Sir Roy Fedden, 1998; (with M. Badrocke) Boeing Aircraft Cutaways: The History of Boeing Aircraft Company, 1998; Illustrated Directory of Fighting Aircraft of World War II, 1999; Fighter Planes, 1999; Development of Piston Aero Engines: From the Wrights to Microlights: A Century of Evolution and Still a Power to be Reckoned With, 1999; Classic World War II Aircraft Cutaways, 1999; History of Military Aviation, 2000; (with Y. Gordon) Soviet X-Planes, 2000; Jane's Aero Engines, 2000; World of Flight, 2001; (ed.) Aviation Year by Year, 2001; (with P. Masefield) Flight Path: The Autobiography of Sir Peter Masefield, 2002; Aviation: The First 100 Years, 2002; (with D.A. Anderton and F.K. Mason) Warplanes and Fighters of World War II, 2002; Cambridge Aerospace Dictionary, 2004, 2nd ed., 2009; Aero-mania!, 2004; Nimrod: The Centenarian Aircraft, 2009. Contributor to books, magazines, periodicals and newspapers. **Address:** Jane's Aero-Engines, Sentinel House, 163 Brighton Rd., Coulsdon, SR CR5 2YH, England.

GUNSTONE, Frank Denby. Scottish/British (born England), b. 1923. **Genres:** Chemistry. **Career:** University of Glasgow, lecturer, 1946-54; St. Andrews University, lecturer 1954-59, senior lecturer 1959-65, reader 1965-70, professor, 1971-89, dean of the faculty of science, 1973-76, vice-principal, 1977-81, honorary research professor, 1989-96; professor emeritus of chemistry, 1989-; Scottish Crop Research Institute, honorary fellow, 1996; Lipid Technology, editor. **Publications:** An Introduction to the Chemistry of Fats and Fatty Acids, 1958; (with J. Read) A Text-Book of Organic Chemistry, 1958, 2nd ed., 1968; Programmes in Organic Chemistry, 6 vols., 1966-74; An Introduction to the Chemistry and Biochemistry of Fatty Acids and Their Glycerides, 1967; (with J.T. Sharp and D.M. Smith) An Introductory Course in Practical Organic Chemistry, 1970; Reactions of Amines, Alcohols, and Alkyl Halides, 1970; Basic Stereochemistry, 1974; Guidebook to Stereochemistry, 1975; (with F.A. Norris) Lipids in Foods, 1983; (with B.G. Herslof) A Lipid Glossary, 1992, rev. ed., 2000; Fatty Acid and Lipid Chemistry, 1995; Chemistry of Oils and Fats: Sources, Composition, Properties, and Uses, 2004; Oils and Fats in the Food Industry, 2008. EDITOR: Topics in Lipid Chemistry, 3 vols., 1970-72; (with J.T. Harwood and F.B. Padley) The Lipid Handbook, 1986, 3rd ed., 2007; Palm Oil, 1987; (with F.B. Padley) Lipid Technologies and Applications, 1997; Lipid Synthesis and Manufacture, 1999; (with D. Firestone) Scientia Gras: A Select History of Fat Science and Technology, 2000; Structured and Modified Lipids, 2001; Oleochemical Manufacture and Applications, 2001; Vegetable Oils in Food Technology, 2002, 2nd ed., 2011; Lipids for Functional Foods and Nutraceticals, 2003; Rapeseed and Canola Oil: Production, Processing, Properties and Uses, 2004; Chemistry of Oils and Fats Sources, Composition, Properties and Uses, 2004; Modifying Lipids for Use in Foods, 2006; (with J.L. Harwood and A.J. Dijkstra) The Lipid Handbook with CD-ROM, 3rd ed., 2007. **Address:** 3 Dempster Ct., St Andrews, FF KY16 9EU, Scotland. **Online address:** fdg1@st-and.ac.uk

GUNTER, Pete (Addison Yancey). American (born United States), b. 1936. **Genres:** Novels, Environmental Sciences/Ecology, Philosophy, Bibliography, Translations, Young Adult Fiction. **Career:** Auburn University, assistant professor of philosophy, 1962-65; University of Tennessee, associate professor of philosophy, 1965-69; University of North Texas, professor of philosophy and chairman, 1969-74, professor, 1970-87, Regents' university professor, 1987-2005, professor, 2005-, now professor emeritus; Foundation for Philosophy of Creativity, executive director, 1982-92. Writer. **Publications:** EDITOR: (trans. and intro.) Bergson and the Evolution of Physics, 1969; (with R. Calvert) The Memoirs of W.R. Strong, 1982; Present, Tense, Future, Perfect? A Symposium on Widening Choices for the Visual Environmental Resource, 1984; (with A. Papanicolaou) Bergson and Modern Thought: Towards a Unification of the Sciences, 1987; Creativity in George Herbert Mead, 1990. OTHERS: The Big Thicket: A Challenge for Conservation, 1972; Henri Bergson: A Bibliography, 1974, 2nd ed., 1986; (with J.R. Sibley)

Process Philosophy: Basic Writings, 1978; Creative Evolution, 1983; River in Dry Grass (novel), 1984; (M.P. Ford, P. Ochs and D.R. Griffin) Founders of Constructive Postmodern Philosophy: Peirce, James, Bergson, Whitehead and Hartshorne, 1992; The Big Thicket: An Ecological Reevaluation, 1993; (with M.F. Oelschlaeger) Texas Land Ethics, 1997; (contrib.) The Big Thicket Guidebook, 2011. Contributor of articles to journals and periodicals. **Address:** Department of Philosophy and Religion Studies, University of North Texas, EESAT 225, PO Box 310920, Denton, TX 76203-0920, U.S.A. **Online address:** pete.gunter@unt.edu

GUNTHER, Robert E. American (born United States), b. 1960?. **Genres:** Business/Trade/Industry. **Career:** Wharton School of Business, director of communications; Gunther Communications, founder; The Press of Atlantic City, reporter and editor. Journalist and writer. **Publications:** (With J.W. Gould) Reinventing Fatherhood, 1993; (with R.A. D'Aveni) Hypercompetition: Managing the Dynamics of Strategic Maneuvering, 1994; (with M.M. Klepper) I'd Rather Die than Give a Speech, 1994; (with R.A. D'Aveni) Hypercompetitive Rivalries: Competing in Highly Dynamic Environments, 1995; (ed. with G.S. Day and D.J. Reibstein) Wharton on Dynamic Competitive Strategy, 1997; (ed. with G.S. Day and P.J.H. Schoemaker) Wharton on Managing Emerging Technologies, 2000; (ed. with S.J. Hoch and H.G. Kunreuther) Wharton on Making Decisions, 2001; (with R.A. D'Aveni and J. Cole) Strategic Supremacy: How Industry Leaders Create Growth, Wealth and Power through Spheres of Influence, 2001; (with R. Rickertsen) Buyout: The Insider's Guide to Buying Your Own Company, 2001; (with P.J.H. Schoemaker) Profiting from Uncertainty: Strategies for Succeeding No Matter What the Future Brings, 2002; (with Y. Wind and V. Mahajan) Convergence Marketing: Running with the Centaurs, 2002; (ed. with H. Gatignon and J.R. Kimberly) INSEAD-Wharton Alliance on Globalizing: Strategies for Building Successful Global Businesses, 2004; (with Y. Wind and C. Crook) Power of Impossible Thinking: Transform the Business of Your Life and the Life of Your Business, 2005; (co-author) 2015: Scenarios for the Future of Human Resource Management, 2005; (with V. Mahajan and K. Banga) 86 Percent Solution: How to Succeed in the Biggest Market Opportunity of the Next 50 Years, 2006; (with R. Rickertsen) Sell Your Business Your Way: Getting Out, Getting Rich and Getting On With Your Life, 2006; Truth About Making Smart Decisions, 2008; (with G. Shea) Your Job Survival Guide: A Manual for Thriving in Change, 2009. **Address:** c/o Author Mail, Free Press, 1230 Ave. of the Americas, New York, NY 10020, U.S.A.

GUO, Xiaolin. Swedish (born Sweden), b. 1955?. **Genres:** Social Sciences. **Career:** Harvard University, John King Fairbank Center for East Asian Research, postdoctoral fellow, 1997-98; University of Aarhus, adjunct professor, 1998-2000; Lund University, lecturer in anthropology; Institute for Security and Development Policy, senior research fellow. Writer. **Publications:** Hu Sheng: Jin Ri Zhongguo She Hui Wen Ti Bao Gao, 1998; (with J. Alvin) Engaging with the Issue of Myanmar: A New Perspective, 2007; (with M. Schoenhals) Cadres and Discourse in the People's Republic of China, 2007; State and Ethnicity in China's Southwest, 2008. Contributor to books, periodicals and journals. **Address:** Silk Road Studies Program, Central Asia-Caucasus Institute, PO Box 514, Uppsala, SE-751 20, Sweden. **Online address:** xguo@isdp.eu

GUO, Xiaolu. British/Chinese (born China), b. 1973?. **Genres:** Novels, Essays. **Career:** Writer, film director and producer. **Publications:** ESSAYS: Flying in My Dreams, 2000; Movie Map, 2001; Notes on Movie Theory, 2002. NOVELS: Fenfang's 37.2 Degrees, 2000; A Concise Chinese-English Dictionary for Lovers, 2007. OTHERS: Who is My Mother's Boyfriend? (collected film scripts), 1999; 20 Fragments of a Ravenous Youth, 2008; UFO in Her Eyes, 2009; (co-author) Ox-Tales: Fire, 2009; Lovers in the Age of Indifference, 2010; (co-author) Because I am a Girl, 2010. **Address:** Chatto & Windus, 20 Vauxhall Bridge Rd., London, GL SW1V 2SA, England. **Online address:** contact@guoxiaolu.com

GUP, Ted (S.). American (born United States), b. 1950. **Genres:** Documentaries/Reportage, History, Young Adult Non-fiction. **Career:** Akron Beacon-Journal, news reporter, 1974-75; Washington Post, staff writer, 1978-86; Time Magazine, correspondent, 1987-93; Case Western Reserve University, Shirley Wormser professor of journalism, 1999-2009; Emerson College, Department of Journalism, professor and chair, 2009-. Writer. **Publications:** The Book of Honor: Covert Lives and Classified Deaths at the CIA, 2000; Book of Honor: The Secret Lives and Deaths of CIA Operatives, 2001; Nation of secrets: The Threat to Democracy and The American Way of Life, 2007; Mr. B. Virdot's

Gift, 2010; Secret Gift: How One Man's Kindness and a Trove of Letters Revealed the Hidden History of the Great Depression, 2010. Works appear in anthologies. Contributor to periodicals. **Address:** Department of Journalism, Emerson College, 120 Boylston St., 6th Fl., Boston, MA 02116-4624, U.S.A. **Online address:** ted_gup@emerson.edu

GUPPY, Stephen (Anthony). Canadian (born Canada), b. 1951. **Genres:** Poetry, Novellas/Short Stories, Novels, Young Adult Fiction. **Career:** Freelance editor and consultant, 1972-82; School District No. 69, secondary school teacher, 1982-85; Vancouver Island University (formerly Malaspina University College), Department of Creative Writing and Journalism, college professor, 1986-. **Publications:** POETRY: Ghostcatcher, 1979; Blind Date with the Angel: The Diane Arbus Poems, 1998; Understanding Heaven, 2002; OTHER: (ed. with R. Smith) Rainshadow: Stories from Vancouver Island (anthology), 1982; FICTION: Another Sad Day at the Edge of the Empire (short stories), 1985; The Fire Thief (novel), 2004; The Work of Mercy (short stories), 2006. Works appear in anthologies. **Address:** Department of Creative Writing & Journalism, Vancouver Island University, 900 5th St., Bldg. 340, Rm. 127, Nanaimo, BC V9R 5S5, Canada. **Online address:** steve.guppy@viu.ca

GUPTA, Anil K. American (born United States), b. 1949. **Genres:** Philosophy. **Career:** McGill University, assistant professor of philosophy, 1975-79, associate professor of philosophy, 1980-82; University of Pittsburgh, visiting assistant professor of philosophy, 1979-80, distinguished professor of philosophy, 2001-; University of Illinois, associate professor of philosophy, 1982-89, Institute for the Humanities, fellow, 1985-86; University of Padua, visiting professor, 1985; Indiana University, professor of philosophy, 1989-95, Rudy professor of philosophy, 1995-2000. Writer. **Publications:** The Logic of Common Nouns, 1980; (ed. with J.M. Dunn and contrib.) Truth or Consequences: Essays in Honor of Nuel Belnap, 1990; (with N. Belnap) The Revision Theory of Truth, 1993; (ed. with A. Chapuis) Circularity, Definition & Truth, 2000; Empiricism and Experience, 2006; Truth, Meaning, Experience, 2011. Works appear in anthologies. Contributor of articles to journals. **Address:** Department of Philosophy, University of Pittsburgh, 1009-H, 1001 Cathedral of Learning, Pittsburgh, PA 15260, U.S.A. **Online address:** agupta@pitt.edu

GUPTA, Sunetra. British/Indian (born India), b. 1965. **Genres:** Novels, Biology. **Career:** University of Oxford, Department of Zoology, Wellcome Training fellow in mathematical biology, 1992-95, Wellcome senior research fellow, 1995-99, professor of theoretical epidemiology, 1999-. Writer. **Publications:** Memories of Rain, 1992; The Glass Blower's Breath, 1993; Moonlight into Marzipan, 1995; A Sin of Colour, 1999; A Sin of Color: A Novel of Obsession, 2001; So Good in Black, 2009. Contributor to scientific journals. **Address:** c/o Esmond Harmsworth, Zachary Shuster Harmsworth L.L.C., 1776 Broadway, New York, NY 10019, U.S.A. **Online address:** sunetra.gupta@zoo.ox.ac.uk

GUPTA, U. S. Nigerian/Indian (born India), b. 1940. **Genres:** Agriculture/ Forestry, Sciences, Biology, Botany, Technology. **Career:** Haryana Agricultural University, assistant professor, 1965-74, associate professor, 1975-76; University of Khartoum, associate professor of crop production, 1976-78; Ahmadu Bello University, reader in crop physiology, 1978-90, professor of crop physiology, 1990-. Writer. **Publications:** (Ed.) Physiological Aspects of Dryland Farming, 1975; Physiological Aspects of Crop Nutrition and Resistance, 1977; Crop Physiology, 1978; Crop Physiology-Advancing Frontiers, 1984; Progress in Crop Physiology, 1988; Crop Improvement, vol. I: Physiological Attributes, 1992; Production and Improvement of Crops for Dryland, 1994; Physiology of Stressed Crops, 2005; What's New About Crop Plants: Novel Discoveries of the 21st Century, 2010. **Address:** Department of Plant Science, Faculty of Agriculture, Ahmadu Bello University, PO Box 1044, Zaria, 1, Nigeria.

GURALNICK, Peter. American (born United States), b. 1943. **Genres:** Music, Biography, Travel/Exploration. **Career:** Boston University, classics instructor, 1967-73; Camp Alton, director, 1971-92. Music journalist. **Publications:** Almost Grown, 1694; Mister Downchild, 1967; Feel Like Going Home: Portraits in Blues and Rock n Roll, 1971; Lost Highway: Journeys & Arrivals of American Musicians, 1979; Nighthawk Blues, 1980; The Listener's Guide to the Blues, 1982; Sweet Soul Music: Rhythm and Blues and the Southern Dream of Freedom, 1986; Searching for Robert Johnson, 1989; Last Train to Memphis: The Rise of Elvis Presley, 1994; Careless Love: The Un-

making of Elvis, 1999; (with E. Jorgensen) Elvis Day by Day: The Definitive Record of His Life and Music, 1999; (contrib. with C. Hirshberg) Elvis Then & Now, 2002; (foreword) Elvis at 21: New York to Memphis, 2003; Dream Boogie: The Triumph of Sam Cooke, 2005; (contrib.) Rockabilly, 2011. EDITOR: Da Capo Best Music Writing 2000, 2000; (co-ed.) Martin Scorsese Presents the Blues: A Musical Journey, 2003. Works appear in anthologies. Contributor to periodicals. **Address:** c/o Richard P. McDonough, 812 Centre St., PO Box 1950, Boston, MA 02205-1950, U.S.A.

GURDON, Martin. British/American (born United States) **Genres:** Zoology, Technology, Humor/Satire, Animals/Pets. **Career:** Classic Cars Magazine, columnist. Journalist. **Publications:** HUMOR: Hen and the Art of Chicken Maintenance: Reflections on Raising Chickens, 2003; Travels with My Chicken: A Man and His Companion Take to the Road, 2005; Fowl! From Clucking Useless to a Success to Crow About!, 2006; Hope is a Strategy: The Empire Builder's Guide to Selling, 2006; Write on!, 2008; Doing Bird, 2013. Contributor to periodicals. **Address:** c/o Author Mail, Lyons Press, 246 Goose Ln., PO Box 480, Guilford, CT 06437-0480, U.S.A. **Online address:** wingofwang@btinternet.com

GUREWITSCH, Edna P. (Edna Perkel Gurewitsch). American (born United States) **Genres:** Biography, Human Relations/Parenting. **Career:** E. & A. Silberman Galleries Inc., staff, 1948-, vice president, 1953-61; E. P. Gurewitsch Works of Art Inc., president, 1973-. Writer. **Publications:** Kindred Souls: The Friendship of Eleanor Roosevelt and David Gurewitsch, 2002; Kindred Souls: The Devoted Friendship of Eleanor Roosevelt and Dr. David Gurewitsch, 2003. Contributor to periodicals. **Address:** Georges Borchardt Inc., 136 E 57th St., New York, NY 10022-2940, U.S.A.

GUREWITSCH, Edna Perkel. See **GUREWITSCH, Edna P.**

GURGANUS, Allan. American (born United States), b. 1947. **Genres:** Novels, Novellas/Short Stories, Essays, Young Adult Fiction. **Career:** University of Iowa, professor of fiction writing, 1972-74; Stanford University, professor of fiction writing, 1974-76; Duke University, professor of fiction writing, 1976-78; Sarah Lawrence College, professor of fiction writing, 1978-86; University of Iowa Writers' Workshop, professor of fiction writing, 1989-90, visiting faculty, 2009-10. Writer and artist. **Publications:** Breathing Lessons, 1981; Good Help, 1988; Oldest Living Confederate Widow Tells All (novel), 1989; Blessed Assurance: A Moral Tale (novella), 1990; White People: Stories and Novellas, 1991; The Practical Heart (novellas), 1993; Plays Well with Others (novel), 1997; Plays Well with Others, 1997; (with J. Holding) Oldest Living Confederate Widow: Her Confession, 2008. **Address:** c/o Amanda Urban, International Creative Management, 40 W 57th St., 17th Fl., New York, NY 10019-4001, U.S.A.

GURIAN, Naomi. (Cady Kalian). American (born United States), b. 1933. **Genres:** Novels. **Career:** Writers Guild of America, associate attorney and assistant executive director, 1978-82, executive director, 1982-90, vice president; Women in Film, president. Lawyer and writer. **Publications:** AS CADY KALIAN: As Dead as It Gets, 2005; A Few Good Murders, 2007. **Address:** c/o Author Mail, Forge Books, 175 5th Ave., New York, NY 10010, U.S.A. **Online address:** cadykalian@gmail.com

GURNEY, Alan. British (born England) **Genres:** Travel/Exploration, History, Sciences, Sports/Fitness. **Career:** Writer. **Publications:** Below the Convergence: Voyages toward Antarctica, 1699-1839, 1997; The Race to the White Continent, 2000; Compass: A Story of Exploration and Innovation, 2004. Contributor to periodicals. **Address:** c/o Author Mail, W. W. Norton & Co Ltd., 500 5th Ave., New York, NY 10110, U.S.A.

GURNEY, A(lbert) R(amsdell). American (born United States), b. 1930. **Genres:** Novels, Plays/Screenplays, Biography, Novellas/Short Stories, Music. **Career:** Massachusetts Institute of Technology, professor of humanities, 1960-70, professor of literature, 1970-96. Writer. **Publications:** Love in Buffalo, 1958; Tom Sawyer, 1959; The Bridal Dinner, 1962; Around the World in Eighty Days, 1962; The Rape of Bunny Stuntz, 1964; The Comeback, 1965; The David Show, 1966; The Golden Fleece, 1968; The Problem, 1968; The Open Meeting, 1968; Tonight in Living Color, 1969; The Love Course, 1970; Scenes from American Life, 1970, rev. ed., 1991; The Old One-Two, 1973; Children, 1974; The Gospel According to Joe (novel), 1974; Who Killed Richard Cory?, 1976; Entertaining Strangers (novel), 1976; The Wayside Motor Inn, 1978; The Middle Ages, 1978; O Youth and Beauty, 1979; What

I Did Last Summer, 1983; The Golden Age, 1984; The Dining Room, 1984; The Snow Ball (novel), 1984, rev. ed., 1992; Four Plays, 1985; Sweet Sue, 1986; The Perfect Party: A Comedy in Two Acts, 1986; Another Antigone, 1988; The Hit List, 1988; The Cocktail Hour, 1988; Love Letters, 1989; (intro.) The Cocktail Hour and Two Other Plays: Another Antigone and The Perfect Party, 1989; (intro.) Love Letters and Two Other Plays: The Golden Age and What I Did Last Summer, 1990; The Snow Ball (play), 1991; Public Affairs, 1992; The Old Boy, 1992; The Fourth Wall, 1992, rev. ed., 2003; Later Life, 1994; (intro.) Later Life and Two Other Plays: The Snow Ball and The Old Boy, 1994; A Cheever Evening: A Play Based on the Stories of John Cheever, 1994; Nine Early Plays, 1961-1973, 1995; Collected works, 1995; Sylvia, 1996; Overtime: A Modern Sequel to The Merchant of Venice, 1996; Let's Do It, 1996; A.R. Gurney: Early Plays, 2 vols., 1997; Labor Day, 1999; Far East, 1999; Strawberry Fields (opera), 1999; Ancestral Voices: A Family Story, 2000; Human Events, 2000; Buffalo Gal, 2001; Collected Plays, 5 vols., 2002; Strictly Academic, 2003; Fouth Wall, 2003; O Jerusalem, 2003; Big Bill, 2004; Mrs. Farnsworth, 2004; Screen Play, 2005; A Light Lunch, 2006; (intro.) 4 Plays, 2007; Crazy Mary, 2007; Indian Blood, 2008; The Grand Manner, 2010. **Address:** c/o Gilbert Parker, William Morris Agency, 1325 Ave. of the Americas, New York, NY 10019, U.S.A. **Online address:** a.r.gurney@charter.net

GURR, A(ndrew) J(ohn). New Zealander/British (born England), b. 1936. **Genres:** Literary Criticism And History, Theatre. **Career:** Victoria University of Wellington, lecturer in English, 1959; University of Leeds, lecturer in English, 1962-69; University of Nairobi, Department of Literature, professor and head, 1969-73; University of Reading, Department of English Language and Literature, professor, 1976-, department chairman, 1979-86; Globe Project, chief academic advisor, 1981-, director of globe research, 1998-, now retired; Folger Shakespeare Library, visiting fellow, 1986, 1990, 1994; University of California, distinguished visiting professor, 1989. Writer. **Publications:** The Shakespearean Stage, 1574-1642, 1970, 4th ed., 2008; Hamlet and the Distracted Globe, 1978; Writers in Exile, 1981; (with C. Hanson) Katherine Mansfield, 1981; Playgoing in Shakespeare's London, 1987, 3rd ed., 2004; Studying Shakespeare: An Introduction, 1988; (with J. Orrell) Rebuilding Shakespeare's Globe, 1989; William Shakespeare: The Extraordinary Life of the Most Successful Writer of All Time, 1995; The Shakespearian Playing Companies, 1996; (with M. Ichikawa) Staging in Shakespeare's Theatres, 2000; Shakespeare Company, 1594-1642, 2004; Shakespeare's Opposites: The Admiral's Company 1594-1625, 2009. EDITOR: The Knight of the Burning Pestle, 1968; The Maid's Tragedy, 1969; Philaster, 1969; (with P. Zirimu) Black Aesthetics, 1973; (with A. Calder) Writers in East Africa, 1974; King Richard II, 1984; King Henry V, 1992; The First Quarto of King Henry V, 2000. **Address:** Department of English, University of Reading, Whiteknights Pk., Reading, RG6 2AA, England. **Online address:** ajgurr@reading.ac.uk

GURR, David. Also writes as D. G. Courtney, William Breton. Canadian/British (born England), b. 1936. **Genres:** Novels, Plays/Screenplays. **Career:** Computer Devices of Canada, systems analyst and project manager, 1970-71; writer, 1978-. **Publications:** NOVELS: Troika, 1979; A Woman Called Scylla, 1981; An American Spy Story, 1984; The Action of the Tiger, 1984; On the Endangered List, 1985; The Ring Master, 1987; The Voice of the Crane, 1989; Arcadia West, 1993; The Time of the Seventh Angel, 2007; The Charlatan Variations, 2008; In the Mill I, forthcoming; In the Mill II, forthcoming. AS WILLIAM BRETON: Ten Days to Zero Zero, 1989; Countdown, 1992. AS D.G. COURTNEY: Kings Cross, 1993. **Address:** 3914 Ansell Rd., Victoria, BC V8P 4W3, Canada. **Online address:** dgurr@shaw.ca

GURR, Michael. Australian (born Australia), b. 1961. **Genres:** Plays/Screenplays, Literary Criticism And History, Young Adult Fiction. **Career:** Melbourne Theatre Co., playwright-in-residence, 1982; Playbox Theatre, artistic counsel, 1993-95. Writer. **Publications:** A Pair of Claws, 1983; (with intro. by R. Lawler) Magnetic North and Imitation Real, 1983; Sex Diary of an Infidel, 1992; Jerusalem, 1996; Days Like These, 2006. Contributor to periodicals. **Address:** Curtis Brown Australia Pty Ltd., Level 1, 2 Boundary St., PO Box 19, Paddington, NW 2021, Australia.

GURTOV, Mel. See **GURTOV, Melvin.**

GURTOV, Melvin. (Mel Gurtov). American (born United States), b. 1941. **Genres:** Area Studies, Politics/Government. **Career:** Rand Corp., research associate in social science, 1966-71; University of California-Santa Barbara, visiting lecturer, 1969; University of California-Riverside, associate profes-

sor, 1971-76, department chair, 1973-74, professor of political science, 1976-86; California Institute of Technology, visiting lecturer, 1971-72; Haynes Foundation fellow, 1972; University of California-Davis, visiting professor, 1975; University of California-Berkeley, visiting lecturer, 1975; Portland State University, professor of political science, 1986-, director of international studies program, 1986-92, director of Asia programs, 1992-96, now professor emeritus of political science; Northwest Regional China Council, president, 1993-95; Waseda University, visiting professor; Hankuk Foreign Studies University, visiting professor; Asian Perspective, editor-in-chief. Writer. **Publications:** AS MEL GURTOV: NONFICTION: The First Vietnam Crisis: Chinese Communist Strategy and United States Involvement, 1953-1954, 1967; Recent Developments on Taiwan, 1967; Problems and Prospects of United States Policy in Southeast Asia, 1969; Southeast Asia Tomorrow: Problems and Prospects for U.S. Policy, 1970; China and Southeast Asia, the Politics of Survival: A Study of Foreign Policy Interaction, 1971; (with H. Harding) Purge of Lo Jui-ching: the Politics of Chinese Strategic Planning, 1971; The United States Against the Third World: Antinationalism and Intervention, 1974; Viet Cong Cadres and the Cadre System: A Study of the Main and Local Forces, 1975; War in the Delta: Views from Three Viet Cong Battalions, 1975; Tōnan Ajia to Kokusai Seiji, 1976; Making Changes: The Politics of Self Liberation, 1979; (with B. Hwang) China under Threat: The Politics of Strategy and Diplomacy, 1980; (with R. Maghroori) The Roots of Failure: United States Policy in the Third World, 1984; (with D. Haghighat) Global Politics in the Human Interest, 1988, 5th ed., 2007; (with J.F. Larson and R.R. Swartout, Jr.) Korea's Amazing Century: From Kings to Satellites, 1996; (with Byong-Moo Hwang) China's Security: The New Roles of the Military, 1998; Pacific Asia? Prospects for Security and Cooperation in East Asia, 2002; Superpower on Crusade: The Bush Doctrine in U.S. Foreign Policy, 2006. EDITOR: (with S. Chawla and A. Marsot) Southeast Asia under the New Balance of Power, 1974; (with J.K. Park) Southeast Asia in Transition: Regional and International Politics, 1977; (and contrib.) The Transformation of Socialism: Perestroika and Reform in the Soviet Union and China, 1990; (with D. Lieberman and contrib.) Revealing the World: An Interdisciplinary Reader for International Studies, 1992; (with Tae-Hwan Kwak) Future of China and Northeast Asia, 1997; (with P.V. Ness) Confronting the Bush Doctrine: Critical Views from the Asia-Pacific, 2005. Contributor of articles to books. **Address:** Department of Political Science, Hatfield School of Government, Portland State University, 650 C-D Urban Ctr., Portland, OR 97207-0751, U.S.A. **Online address:** mgurtov@aol.com

GURVAL, Robert Alan. American (born United States), b. 1958. **Genres:** Classics, Politics/Government. **Career:** University of Oregon, assistant professor of classics, 1989-90; University of California, assistant professor, 1990-96, associate professor of classics, 1996-; Gamble House, docent. Writer. **Publications:** Actium and Augustus: The Politics and Emotions of Civil War, 1995. **Address:** Department of Classics, University of California, 100 Dodd Hall, 6265 Bunche Hall, PO Box 951473, Los Angeles, CA 90095-1473, U.S.A. **Online address:** gurval@humnet.ucla.edu

GURVIS, Sandra J. American (born United States), b. 1951. **Genres:** Novels, Medicine/Health, Popular Culture, Ghost Writer, Humor/Satire, Popular Culture, Travel/Exploration, Writing/Journalism, Writing/Journalism, E-books, Essays, Adult Non-fiction, Communications/Media. **Career:** Defense Construction Supply Center, job classification analyst, 1973-78; freelance writer, 1978-83, 1984-; Charles Merrill Publishing, textbook editor, 1983-84. **Publications:** Cockroach Hall of Fame: And 101 Other Off-the-Wall Museums, 1994; The Off-the-Beaten Path Job Book, 1995; America's Strangest Museums: A Traveler's Guide to the Most Unusual and Eccentric Collections, 1996, rev. ed., 1998; Way Stations to Heaven: 50 Major Visionary Shrines in the United States, 1996; 30 Great Cities to Start out In, 1997; Careers for Nonconformists: A Practical Guide to Finding and Developing a Career Outside the Mainstream, 2000; The Well-Traveled Dog, 2001; The Pipe Dreamers, 2001; Day Trips from Columbus, 2002, 3rd ed., 2009; Where Have All the Flower Children Gone?, 2006; Ohio Curiosities, 2007, 2nd ed., 2011; Management Basics, 2007; (with M. Amigoni) Managing the Telecommuting Employee, 2009; Paris Hilton: A Biography, 2011; Country Club Wives, 2011. Contributor to books. Works appear in anthologies. **Address:** 6251 Albany Brooke Dr., Westerville, OH 43081, U.S.A. **Online address:** sgurvis@sgurvis.com

GUSCHOV, Stephen D. American (born United States), b. 1965?. **Genres:** Plays/Screenplays, Sports/Fitness, Mystery/Crime/Suspense. **Career:** Grenier and McCarron (law firm), attorney, 1990-; Massachusetts School of Law, adjunct professor, 1992-; WCCM-AM Radio, talk show host, 1998-. Writer. **Publications:** (Adaptation) The Diary of Adam and Eve (play), 1997; The Prodigal (play), 1998; The Red Stockings of Cincinnati: Base Ball's First All-professional Team and Its Historic 1869 and 1870 Seasons, 1998; Second Chances, 2002. **Address:** Grenier & McCarron, 491 Maple St., Ste. 100, Danvers, MA 01923-1065, U.S.A.

GÜSE, Ernst Gerhard. German (born Germany) **Genres:** Art/Art History, History, Crafts. **Career:** Saarland Museum, director. Art historian and writer. **Publications:** Das Frühwerk Max Beckmanns: Zur Thematik Seiner Bilder Aus Den Jahren 1904-1914, 1977; 96 Künstler Aus Westfalen: Westfälisches Landesmuseum für Kunst und Kulturgeschichte, Landschaftsverband Westfalen-Lippe, 1982; Die Tunisreise: Klee, Macke, Moilliet, 1982; Wilhelm Morgner, 1983; (with E. Schumacher) Djerba, 1983; Arnulf Rainer, Malerei 1980-1990, 1990; Matisse: Drawings and Sculpture, 1991; Emil Schumacher: Die Gouachen Der 80er Jahre: Mit Einem Beitrag Des Künstlers, 1992; Pablo Picasso: Der Artistische Prozess, Das Lithographische Werk, 1993; Klaus Graubner: Völklingen, 1998; Ottweiler Porzellan: Katalog Zurgleichnamingen Ausstellung Der Alten Sammlung, 2000; Kultur Des Biedermeier: Der Maler Louis Krevel, 2001. EDITOR: Paul Klee: Dialogue with Nature, 1991; Erste Blick, 2006; (with M. Siebenbrodt) Lyonel Feininger in Weimar, 2006; Rokokoschloss Dornburg, 2006; (with J. Maatsch) Schillers Wohnhaus, 2006; Emil Schumacher: Leben in der Malerei, 2008; (with F.A. Morat) Giorgio Morandi: Paintings, Watercolours, Drawings, Etchings, 2008; Victor Hugo, 2008; (with M. Oppel) Goethes Gartenhaus Klassik-Stiftung Weimar, 2008; Landschaftszeichnungen, 2009. **Address:** c/o Author Mail, Prestel Art Books, 26 Mandlstrasse, Munich, 80802, Germany.

GUSHEE, David P. (David Paul Gushee). American/German (born Germany), b. 1962. **Genres:** Politics/Government, Novels. **Career:** Walnut Hills Baptist Church, youth minister, 1983-84; Saint Matthews Baptist Church, youth minister, 1984-86; Evangelicals for Social Action, staff, 1990-93; Southern Baptist Theological Seminary, assistant professor of Christian ethics, 1993-96, School of Theology, acting associate dean and acting director of professional studies, 1995-96; Union University, associate professor of Christian studies, 1996-99, Department of Moral Philosophy, Graves associate professor, 1999-2003, Graves professor, 2003-07, university fellow, 2006-07; Carl F.H. Henry Center for Christian Leadership, senior fellow, 2000-; First Presbyterian Church, interim pastor, 2004-05; Mercer University, McAfee School of Theology, distinguished university professor of Christian ethics, 2007-, Center for Theology and Public Life, director; Evangelicals for Human Rights, president; U.S. Holocaust Memorial Museum, staff. Writer. **Publications:** The Righteous Gentiles of the Holocaust: A Christian Interpretation, 1994, 2nd ed. as Righteous Gentiles of the Holocaust: Genocide and Moral Obligation, 2003; (ed. with W.C. Jackson) Preparing for Christian Ministry: An Evangelical Approach, 1996; (with R.H. Long) A Bolder Pulpit: Reclaiming the Moral Dimension of Preaching, 1998; (ed.) Toward a Just and Caring Society: Christian Responses to Poverty in America, 1999; (ed. with D.S. Dockery) The Future of Christian Higher Education, 1999; (ed.) Christians and Politics beyond the Culture Wars: An Agenda for Engagement, 2000; (with G.H. Stassen) Kingdom Ethics: Following Jesus in Contemporary Context, 2003; Getting Marriage Right: Realistic Counsel for Saving and Strengthening Relationships, 2004; Only Human: Christian Reflections on the Journey toward Wholeness (Enduring Questions in Christian Life series), 2005; Future of Faith in American Politics: The Public Witness of the Evangelical Center, 2008; (co-author) Jewish-Christian Dialogue: Drawing Honey from the Rock, 2008; (ed. with R. Ward) Scholarly Vocation and the Baptist Academy: Essays on the Future of Baptist Higher Education, 2008; (ed. with J.H. Zimmer and J.D. Zimmer) Religious Faith, Torture and Our National Soul, 2010; The Sanctity of Life: A Christian Exploration; Moral Philosophy: Tracing the Traditions, forthcoming. **Address:** McAfee School of Theology, Mercer University, 3001 Mercer University Dr., Atlanta, GA 30341-4115, U.S.A. **Online address:** gushee_dp@mercer.edu

GUSHEE, David Paul. See GUSHEE, David P.

GUSSIN, Patricia. (Patricia Stewart). American (born United States) **Genres:** Novels. **Career:** Johnson & Johnson Co., vice president, worldwide research & development, consumer pharmaceuticals division; McNeil Consumer Healthcare, director; Sarnoff Corp., trustee; Pennsylvania Dental School, member of board of overseers & associate trustee of the univer-

sity. Writer. **Publications:** Shadow of Death, 2006; Twisted Justice, 2007; The Test, 2009. **Address:** Longboat Key, FL , U.S.A. **Online address:** patg@patriciagussin.com

GUSTAFSON, Chris. American (born United States), b. 1950. **Genres:** Education, Reference. **Career:** Elementary school teacher, 1990-2000; Whitman Middle School, librarian, 2000-, teaching and technology coach, 2002-. Writer. **Publications:** Acting Out: Readers Theatre across the Curriculum, 2002; Acting Cool! Using Readers Theatre to Teach Math and Science in Your Classroom, 2003; Acting Cool! Using Readers Theatre to Teach Language Arts and Social Studies in Your Classroom, 2003. **Address:** Whitman Middle School, 9201 15th Ave. NW, Seattle, WA 98117, U.S.A. **Online address:** cgustafson@seattleschools.org

GUSTAFSON, Sid. American (born United States), b. 1954. **Genres:** Novels, Novellas/Short Stories, Ethics, Animals/Pets, Medicine/Health, Social Commentary, Anthropology/Ethnology, Writing/Journalism, Writing/Journalism. **Career:** Writer, veterinarian and educator. **Publications:** First Aid for the Active Dog: Canine Health and Prevention, 2003; Prisoners of Flight (novel), 2003; Horses They Rode (novel), 2006; Poems Across the Big Sky: An Anthology of Montana Poets, 2007; Oregon Stories, 2010; The Language of Horsemanship, 2012; Swift Dam, 2012. Contributor of articles to magazines and journals. Works appear in anthologies. **Address:** Veterinary Behavior Services, 918 S Church, Bozeman, MT 59715, U.S.A. **Online address:** swgustafson@yahoo.com

GUSTAINIS, Justin. American (born United States), b. 1951. **Genres:** Novels. **Career:** Plattsburgh State University, professor of communication. Writer. **Publications:** American Rhetoric and the Vietnam War, 1993; The Hades Project (novel), 2003. MORRIS AND CHASTAIN SERIES: SUPERNATURAL NOVELS: Black Magic Woman, 2007; Evil Ways, 2009. Contributor to journals. **Address:** Plattsburgh, NY , U.S.A. **Online address:** justingustainis@yahoo.com

GUSTE, Roy F(rancis). American (born United States), b. 1951?. **Genres:** Food And Wine, Adult Non-fiction, History, Travel/Exploration. **Career:** Loyola university, faculty; Tulane University, faculty; Antoine's Restaurant, proprietor, 1975-84. Writer. **Publications:** Antoine's Restaurant, since 1840, Cookbook: A Collection of the Original Recipes from New Orleans Oldest and Most Famous Restaurant, 1978; The Restaurants of New Orleans, 1982, rev. ed., 1990; The 100 Greatest Dishes of Louisiana Cookery, 1988; (co-author) Louisiana Light: Low-Fat, Low-Calorie, Low-Cholesterol, Low-Salt: Cajun and Creole Cookery, 1990; The Secret Gardens of the Vieux Carre: The Historic French Quarter of New Orleans, 1993, 2nd ed., 2006; The Fish of the Gulf Coast Cookbook, 1993; The 100 Greatest New Orleans Creole Recipes, 1994; The Tomato Cookbook, 1995; Gulf Coast Fish: A Cookbook, 1996; (with T.J. Fisher) The Bean Book, 2001; (with T.J Fisher and L. Sahuc) Orléans Embrace: The Secret Gardens of the Vieux Carré, 2006. **Address:** W.W. Norton & Co., 500 5th Ave., New York, NY 10110, U.S.A. **Online address:** gust4681@bellsouth.net

GUTERSON, David. American (born United States), b. 1956. **Genres:** Novels, Novellas/Short Stories, Education, Young Adult Fiction. **Career:** Teacher, 1984-94; Field's End, co-founder. Writer. **Publications:** The Country Ahead of Us, the Country Behind: Stories, 1989; Family Matters: Why Homeschooling Makes Sense, 1992; Snow Falling on Cedars, 1994; The Drowned Son, 1996; East of the Mountains, 1999; Snow Falling on Cedars: The Shooting Script, 1999; Our Lady of the Forest, 2003; The Other, 2008; Ed King, 2011. Contributor to periodicals. **Address:** Georges Borchardt Inc., 136 E 57th St., New York, NY 10022, U.S.A.

GUTFREUND, Owen D. American (born United States), b. 1963. **Genres:** Urban Studies, History, Geography. **Career:** Lazard Freres and Co., vice president, 1985-88; Barnard College, assistant professor of history and urban studies, 1998-2007, associate professor of history and urban studies, 2008-09, director of urban studies program, 2000-09; City University of New York, Hunter College, associate professor of urban affairs and planning, 2009-, director of graduate program in urban affairs, 2011-. Writer. **Publications:** Twentieth Century Sprawl: Highways and the Reshaping of the American Landscape, 2004. FORTHCOMING: Cities Take Flight: Airports, Aviation and Modern American Urbanism; Go Team Go: Major League Sports Arenas, Stadiums and Downtown Revitalization. **Address:** Department of Urban

Affairs & Planning, Hunter College, 695 Park Ave., New York, NY 10065, U.S.A. **Online address:** odg1@columbia.edu

GUTHMAN, Julie. (Julie Harriet Guthman). American (born United States) **Genres:** Sciences, Geography. **Career:** East Bay Organizing Committee, Citizens' Party, Tax Big Oil campaign, staff, 1979-80; Financial management consultant, 1980-93; Nuclear Weapons Freeze Campaign, Northern California director, 1981-82; Voting P.O.W.E.R., organizer, financial manager, administrative and fundraising director, 1982-85; Herrick Hospital, staff, 1985-86; Contra Costa County Hospital, staff, 1985-86; University of California, reader in business administration, 1987, graduate student instructor, 1995-96, Graduate Opportunity Program student mentor, 1997, lecturer and research assistant, 1999, lecturer, 2001-03, associate professor, 2003-, assistant professor; KQED, television division financial administrator, 1988-90; Child Care Coordinating Council of San Mateo County, fiscal manager, 1990-92. Writer. **Publications:** Agrarian Dreams: The Paradox of Organic Farming in California, 2004; Weighing In: Obesity, Food Justice, and The Limits of Capitalism, 2011. CONTRIBUTOR: Engineering Trouble: Biotechnology and Its Discontents, 2003; Geographies of Commodity Chains, 2004; Agribusiness and Society, 2004; Constructing Alternative Food Geographies: Representation and Practice, 2007. Contributor of articles to books and journals. **Address:** Department of Community Studies, University of California, 1156 High St., Santa Cruz, CA 95064, U.S.A. **Online address:** jguthman@ucsc.edu

GUTHMAN, Julie Harriet. *See* GUTHMAN, Julie.

GUTHRIE, Allan. Scottish (born Scotland), b. 1965. **Genres:** Mystery/ Crime/Suspense, Novels, Novellas/Short Stories. **Career:** Point Blank Press, commissioning editor; Jenny Brown Associates, commissioning editor. **Publications:** NOVELS: Two-Way Split, 2004; Savage Night, 2008; Slammer, 2009. PEARCE SERIES: Kiss Her Goodbye, 2005; Hard Man, 2007. NOVELLAS: Kill Clock, 2007; Killing Mum, 2009; Bye Bye Baby, 2010. **Address:** Jenny Brown Associates, 33 Argyle Pl., Edinburgh, LT EH9 1JT, Scotland. **Online address:** allan@allanguthrie.co.uk

GUTHRIE, Donna W. American (born United States), b. 1946. **Genres:** Children's Fiction, Children's Non-fiction, Picture/Board Books. **Career:** Teacher, 1968-75; Colorado Springs Montessori School, vice president of education, 1976-77; Kids Corner Ltd. (audio visual company), founder and president, 1980-90; freelance writer and author, 1980-2000; Pikes Peak Library District, president. **Publications:** PICTURE BOOKS: The Witch Who Lives Down the Hall, 1985; Grandpa Doesn't Know It's Me, 1986; This Little Pig Stayed Home, 1987; While I'm Waiting, 1988; A Rose for Abby, 1988; Mrs. Gigglebelly Is Coming for Tea, 1990; The Witch Has an Itch, 1990; Not for Babies, 1993; Nobiah's Well: A Modern African Folk Tale, 1993; The Secret Admirer, 1996. OTHER: (with K.K. Arnsteen) I Can't Believe It's History! Fun Facts from around the World, 1993; Frankie Murphy's Kiss List (chapter book), 1993; (with N. Bentley and K.K. Arnsteen) The Young Author's Do It Yourself Book: How to Write, Illustrate, and Produce Your Own Book, 1993; How to Promote Your Book on a Shoe String, 1994; The Better Letter Book, 1994; One Hundred and Two Steps, 1995; (with N. Bentley) The Young Producer's Video Book: How to Write, Direct, and Shoot Your Own Video, 1995; Donna Guthrie: An Author's Story, 1995; (with J.N. Hulme) How to Write, Recite, and Delight in All Kinds of Poetry, 1996; How to Write, Recite and Delight in Poetry, 1996; (with N. Bentley) Putting on a Play: The Young Playwright's Guide to Scripting, Directing, and Performing, 1996; (with J. Stiles) Real World Math: Money and Other Numbers in Your Life, 1998; (with N. Bentley) The Young Journalist's Book: How to Write and Produce Your Own Newspaper, 1998; (with J.N. Hulme) Supermarket Math, 2000; (with N. Bentley) Writing Mysteries, Movies, Monsters Stories, and More, 2001; Mysteries, Maps & Monsters, 2001; Collect This!, A Kid's Guide to Collecting, 2001. Contributor of articles to periodicals. **Address:** 7622 Eads Ave., La Jolla, CA 92037, U.S.A. **Online address:** donnag6113@aol.com

GUTHRIE, Randolph H. American (born United States), b. 1934. **Genres:** Medicine/Health, Women's Studies And Issues, Sports/Fitness. **Career:** New York Hospital, intern, 1961-62, resident, 1962-63, 1969-71; St. Luke's Hospital, resident, 1963-66; Memorial Sloan-Kettering Cancer Center, chief of plastic surgery, 1971-77; New York State Supreme Court, Malpractice Panel, plastic surgery representative, 1971-80; New York Downtown Hospital, chief of plastic surgery, 1981-2000; New York Hospital, attending surgeon, 1988-2000; Cornell University, clinical professor of surgery, 1988-; Save Venice Inc., president, chief executive officer, chairman emeritus. Writer. **Publica-**

tions: (With G.F. Schwartz) Reconstructive and Aesthetic Mammoplasty, 1989; (with D. Podolsky) The Truth about Breast Implants, 1994; (with G.F. Schwartz) Atlas of Breast Surgery, 1996. Contributor of articles to journals. **Address:** Save Venice Inc., 1104 Lexington Ave., 4C, New York, NY 10075, U.S.A.

GUTMAN, Dan. (Herb Dunn). American (born United States), b. 1955. **Genres:** Children's Fiction, Children's Non-fiction. **Career:** Video Review Publications, Electronic Fun, co-editor, 1982-83; Carnegie Publications, Computer Games, founder and editor-in-chief, 1983-84; freelance writer, 1984-. **Publications:** The Greatest Games: The 93 Best Computer Games of All Time, 1985; I Didn't Know You Could Do That with a Computer!: Practical, Unusual and Wonderful Software You Can Buy, 1986; It Ain't Cheating If You Don't Get Caught: Scuffing, Corking, Spitting, Gunking, Razzing and Other Fundamentals of Our National Pastime, 1990; (ed.) Super Memory, 1991; Baseball Babylon: From the Black Sox to Pete Rose, The Real Stories Behind the Scandals that Rocked the Game, 1992; Baseball's Biggest Bloopers: The Games that Got Away, 1993; (with D. Herrmann and D. Raybeck) Improving Student Memory, 1993; Baseball's Greatest Games, 1994; World Series Classics, 1994; Banana Bats and Ding Dong Balls: A Century of Unique Baseball Inventions, 1995; They Came from Center Field, 1995; Taking Flight: My Story, 1995; Ice Skating: From Axels to Zambonis, 1996; Gymnastics, 1996; The Way Baseball Works, 1996; The Kid Who Ran for President, 1996; Honus & Me: A Baseball Card Adventure, 1997; The Shortstop Who Knew Too Much, 1997; The Green Monster in Left Field, 1997; The Catcher Who Shocked the World, 1997; The Pitcher Who Went Out of His Mind, 1997; The Million Dollar Shot, 1997, 2nd ed., 2006; Ice Skating: An Inside Look at the Stars, The Sport and the Spectacle, 1997; Virtually Perfect, 1998; (co-author) Katy's Gift, 1998; (comp.) Cal Ripken, Jr.: My Story, 1999; Jackie & Me: A Baseball Card Adventure, 1999; Funny Boy Meets the Airsick Alien from Andromeda, 1999; The Kid Who Became President, 1999; (as Herb Dunn) Joe DiMaggio, 1999; (as Herb Dunn) Jackie Robinson, 1999; Funny Boy versus the Bubble-Brained Barbers from the Big Bang, 2000; Funny Boy Meets the Chit-chatting Cheese from Chattanooga, 2000; Babe & Me, 2000; Landslide! A Kids' Guide to The U.S. Elections, 2000; Johnny Hang Time, 2000; The Secret Life of Dr. Demented, 2001; The Million-Dollar Kick, 2001, 2nd ed., 2006; Qwerty Stevens: The Edison Mystery, 2001; Qwerty Stevens Stuck in Time with Benjamin Franklin, 2002; Shoeless Joe & Me, 2002; Race for the Sky: The Kitty Hawk Diaries of Johnny Moore, 2003; Mickey & Me, 2003; Million Dollar Goal, 2003, 2nd ed., 2006; Babe Ruth and the Ice Cream Mess, 2004; The Get-Rich-Quick Club, 2004; Miss Daisy Is Crazy!, 2004; Mr. Klutz Is Nuts!, 2004; Miss Roopy Is Loopy!, 2004; Million Dollar Strike, 2004; Jackie Robinson and the Big Game, 2005; Abner & Me: A Baseball Card Adventure, 2005; Miss Lazar is Bizarre!, 2005; Miss Small is Off The Wall!, 2005; Mr. Hynde is Out of His Mind!, 2005; Mrs. Cooney is Loony!, 2005; Ms. Hannah is Bananas!, 2005; Ms. LaGrange is Strange!, 2005; Mrs. Kormel Is Not Normal!, 2006; Mrs. Patty is Batty!, 2006; Ms. Todd is Odd!, 2006; Satch & Me: A Baseball Card Adventure, 2006; The Homework Machine, 2006; Jackie Robinson and the Big Game, 2006; The Million Dollar Putt, 2006, rev. ed., 2007; Miss Holly is Too Jolly!, 2006; Mr. Docker is Off His Rocker!, 2006; Mrs. Yonkers is Bonkers!, 2007; Ms. Coco is Loco!, 2007; My Weird School Daze!, 2007; Casey Back at Bat, 2007; Dr. Carbles is Losing His Marbles!, 2007; Getting Air, 2007; Miss Suki is Kooky!, 2007; Mr. Louie is Screwy!, 2007; Mr. Macky is Wacky!, 2007; Mrs. Yonkers is Bonkers!, 2007; Jim & Me: A Baseball Card Adventure, 2008; Nightmare at the Bookfair, 2008; Ray & Me, 2009; The Christmas Genie, 2009; Recycle This Book, 2009. **Address:** NJ , U.S.A. **Online address:** dangut@comcast.net

GUTMAN, Judith Mara. American (born United States), b. 1928. **Genres:** Art/Art History, Intellectual History, Photography, Biography, Social Sciences. **Career:** University of Wisconsin, instructor in psychology, 1952-54; Montefiore (Hospital) Nursery School, director, 1954-58; Hunter College (now of the City University of New York), lecturer in education, 1959-60; International Herald Tribune, contributor, 1983-85; New School for Social Research, adjunct professor, 1990-95, 1999-; New York University, adjunct professor, 1996; Parsons-New School, adjunct professor, 1999. Writer. **Publications:** The Colonial Venture, 1966; Lewis W. Hine, and the American Social Conscience, 1967; (with E. Rozwenc) The Making of American Society, 1972; Is America Used Up?, 1973; Lewis W. Hine, 1874-1940: Two Perspectives, 1974; Buying, 1975; Ethnic Heritage: Immigration, Migration and the Growth of Cities, 1975; Through Indian Eyes, 1982; Alfred Stieglitz and Dorothy Norman, Passion and Power, forthcoming. Contributor to periodicals. **Address:** 97 6th Ave., Nyack, NY 10960, U.S.A. **Online address:** gutmanj@aol.com

GUTMAN, Robert W. American (born United States), b. 1925. **Genres:** Biography, Music, Autobiography/Memoirs, Romance/Historical. **Career:** New School for Social Research, faculty of art department and human relations workshop, 1955-57; City College (now City College of the City University of New York), instructor in art history, 1955-57; State University of New York, Fashion Institute of Technology, Art and Design Division, assistant professor, professor, Master Classes of Bayreuth Festival, founder and lecturer, faculty, 1957-88, dean, 1974-80, dean of graduate studies, 1980-88; Duchesne College, teacher of music history, 1966-67; Bard College, visiting professor, 1991. Writer. **Publications:** (Intro.) Volsunga Saga: The Story of the Volsungs and Niblungs, 1962; Richard Wagner: The Man, His Mind, and His Music, 1968; Mozart: A Cultural Biography, 1999. Contributor to journals. **Address:** Houghton Mifflin Harcourt, 222 Berkeley St., Boston, MA 02116, U.S.A.

GUTMANN, David L(eo). American (born United States), b. 1925. **Genres:** Gerontology/Senior Issues, Psychology, Social Commentary. **Career:** University of Illinois, Neuro-Psychiatric Institute, intern clinical psychology, 1956-57, clinical instructor psychology, 1959-60; private practice psychotherapist, 1956-60, 1963-; Michael Reese Hospital, Psychosomatic and Psychiatric Institute, fellow in clinical psychology, 1958-59; Presbyterian-Saint Luke's Hospital, staff psychologist, 1959-60; Massachusetts Mental Health Center, staff psychologist, 1960-62; Harvard University, lecturer social relations, 1961-62; University of Michigan, Psychological Clinic, senior staff psychologist, 1962-66, assistant professor, 1962-67, associate professor, 1967-70, professor of psychology, 1970-78; Center for Psychosocial Studies, visiting fellow, 1974-75; University of Chicago, visiting professor, 1975, Research and Clinical Practice in the Mental Health of Later Life Training Program, co-director, 1977-79, Center for the Study of the Behavioral Sciences, visiting professor, 1985-86; Northwestern University Medical School, professor, psychiatry, education, 1976-, Division of Psychology, chief, 1976-81, Older Adult Program, director, 1977-, Human Development and Social Policy, associate faculty, 1986-, now emeritus. Writer. **Publications:** Reclaimed Powers: Toward a New Psychology of Men and Women in Later Life, 1987, rev. ed. 1994; The Human Elder, 1997; Ha-im iḥarti et ha-rakevet?: mashmáut ha-ḥayim ba-maḥatsit ha-sheniyah shel ha-ḥayim, 2007. Works appear in anthologies. **Address:** Department of Psychology, Northwestern University, Ward Bldg., Rm. 12-150, 303 E Chicago Ave., Chicago, IL 60611-3008, U.S.A.

GUTTENPLAN, D. D. American (born United States), b. 1957. **Genres:** Documentaries/Reportage, Writing/Journalism, History, Politics/Government. **Career:** Pantheon Books, staff; Village Voice, senior editor; Vanity Fair and Newsweek, staff; New York Newsday, media columnist, 1988-91; Granta Magazine, staff; Nation, co-chief, 1997-, London correspondent; International Herald Tribune, education writer, 2010-. **Publications:** The Holocaust on Trial: History, Justice, and the David Irving Libel Case, 2001; American Radical: The Life and Times of I.F. Stone, 2009. Contributor to periodicals. **Address:** The Wylie Agency L.L.C., 250 W 57th St., Ste. 2114, New York, NY 10107, U.S.A. **Online address:** don@ddguttenplan.com

GUTTERIDGE, Don(ald George). Canadian (born Canada), b. 1937. **Genres:** Novels, Poetry, Education, Literary Criticism And History, Young Adult Fiction. **Career:** University of Western Ontario, assistant professor, 1975-77, professor of English education, 1977-93, professor emeritus, 1993-; Althouse Press, director, 1990-93. Writer. **Publications:** Riel: A Poem for Voices, 1968; The Village Within, 1970; Language and Expression, 1970; Death at Quebec, 1971; Saying Grace, An Elegy, 1972; The Quest for North Coppermine, 1973; Bus-Ride, 1974; Borderlands, 1975; Tecumseh, 1976; A True History of Lambton County, 1977; Mountain and Plain, 1978; The Country of the Young, 1978; Rites of Passage, 1979; All in Good Time, 1980; God's Geography, 1982; Brave Season, 1983; The Exiled Heart, 1986; Incredible Journeys, 1986; St. Vitus Dance, 1987; Shaman's Ground, 1988; The Dimension of Delight, 1988; Love in the Wintertime, 1990; How the World Began, 1991; Summer's Idyll, 1993; Stubborn Pilgrimage, 1994; Winter's Descent, 1996; Flute Music in the Cello's Belly, 1997; Bewilderment (novel), 2000; Teaching English, 2000; Bloodlines (poetry), 2001; Turncoat, 2003; Solemn Vows, 2003; Something More Miraculous, 2004; Still Magical, 2007.

Address: University of Western Ontario, 1151 Richmond St., London, ON N6A 3K7, Canada. **Online address:** dongutteridge@rogers.com

GUTTERIDGE, Thomas G. American (born United States), b. 1942. **Genres:** Business/Trade/Industry, Economics. **Career:** General Motors Corp., Buick Motor Division, assistant safety engineer and production supervisor, 1960-65; Industrial Nucleonics Corp., assistant to the vice president for marketing and corporate recruiter, 1966-67; Purdue University, instructor in personnel and industrial relations, 1967-69; State University of New York, assistant professor, 1970-, associate professor of human resources and industrial relations, through 1983, director of Human Resources Institute, 1981-83, 1984, Regional Economic Assistance Center, executive director, 1978-83, Development Center for Business, director, 1982-83; New York State Public Employment Relations Board, labor mediator, fact-finder and arbitrator, 1972-83; WEBR-Radio, labor commentator, 1976-77; Southern Illinois University, professor of management, College of Business and Administration, dean, 1983-92; University of Connecticut, distinguished professor of management, School of Business Administration, dean, 1992-; University of Toledo, College of Business Administration, dean. Writer. **Publications:** Career planning practices, 1979; Career Planning and Development: Perspectives of the Individual and the Organization, 1980; (with F. Otte) Organizational Career Development: State of the Practice, 1983; (with U. Sekaran) Career Planning and Development: A Multi-Dimensional Perspective, 1986; (with Z. Leibowitz and J. Shore) Organizational Career Development: On the Brink of the Twenty-First Century, 1994. Contributor of journals. **Address:** College of Business Administration, The University of Toledo, 5021 Stranahan Hall, 2801 Bancroft, PO Box 103, Toledo, OH 43606-3390, U.S.A. **Online address:** thomas.gutteridge@utoledo.edu

GUTTMANN, Allen. American (born United States), b. 1932. **Genres:** History, Literary Criticism And History, Sports/Fitness. **Career:** Amherst College, instructor, 1959-62, assistant professor, 1962-66, associate professor, 1966-71, professor of English and American studies, 1971-, Emily C. Jordan Folger professor of English and American studies. Writer. **Publications:** The Wound in the Heart: America and the Spanish Civil War, 1962; (ed. with L. Filler) Removal of the Cherokee Nation: Manifest Destiny or National Dishonor?, 1962; American Neutrality and the Spanish Civil War, 1963; (ed. and intro. with B.M. Ziegler) Communism, the Courts, and the Constitution, 1964; States' Rights and Indian Removal, 1965; Korea and the Theory of Limited War, 1967; The Conservative Tradition in America, 1967; The Jewish Writer in America, 1971; Korea: Cold War and Limited War, 1972; From Ritual to Record: The Nature of Modern Sports, 1978, rev. ed., 2004; (ed. with J.A. Sappenfield) Life of George Washington, 5 vols., 1982; The Games Must Go On: Avery Brundage and the Olympic Movement, 1984; Sports Spectators, 1986; A Whole New Ball Game: An Interpretation of American Sports, 1988; Essays on Sport History and Sport Mythology, 1990; Women's Sports: A History, 1991; The Olympics: A History of the Modern Games, 1992, 2nd ed., 2002; Games and Empires: Modern Sports and Cultural Imperialism, 1994; The Erotic in Sports, 1996; (ed. with K. Christensen and G. Pfister) International Encyclopedia of Women and Sport, 3 vols., 2000; (with L. Thompson) Japanese Sports: A History, 2001; Olympics, a History of the Modern Games, 2002; Sports: The First Five Millennia, 2004; Sports and American art from Benjamin West to Andy Warhol, 2011. Contributor to periodicals. **Address:** Department of English, Amherst College, 4 Johnson Chapel, PO Box 2234, Amherst, MA 01002, U.S.A. **Online address:** aguttmann@amherst.edu

GUTTMANN, Hadassah. American (born United States), b. 1952?. **Genres:** Music. **Career:** Nassau Community College, adjunct professor and applied associate professor of music, 1984-, now professor emeritus; Lucy Moses Music School, Abraham Goodman House, Merkin Concert Hall, teacher, director and coordinator, 1992-95; Yeshiva University High School for Girls, music director, 2000-; The Guttmann Trio, director. Writer. **Publications:** The Music of Paul Ben-Haim: A Performance Guide, 1992. **Address:** Department of Music, Nassau Community College, Bldg. Z, 1 Education Dr., Garden City, NY 11530-6793, U.S.A. **Online address:** hadassah.guttmann@ncc.edu

GUTTMANN, Robert. American (born United States), b. 1951?. **Genres:** Business/Trade/Industry, Economics, Industrial Relations, Cultural/Ethnic Topics. **Career:** Hofstra University, professor of economics, 1984-, chair; U.F.R. de Sciences Economiques et de Gestion, Université de Paris-Nord, Villetaneuse, visiting professor, 1993-. Writer. **Publications:** (Ed.) Reforming Money and Finance: Institutions and Markets in Flux, 1989, 2nd ed. as Reforming Money and Finance: Toward a New Monetary Regime, 1997; How

Credit-Money Shapes the Economy: The United States in a Global System, 1994; Cybercash: The Coming Era of Electronic Money, 2003. Contributor to periodicals. **Address:** Department of Economics, Hofstra University, 200D Barnard Hall, 104 Hofstra University, Hempstead, NY 11549, U.S.A. **Online address:** ecorpg@hofstra.edu

GUTZMAN, Kevin R.C. American (born United States), b. 1963. **Genres:** Politics/Government, History. **Career:** City University of New York, John Jay College, assistant professor of history; New College, distinguished visiting professor of history, 2008; Western Connecticut State University, professor of history, 2009-. Writer and attorney. **Publications:** The Politically Incorrect Guide to the Constitution, 2007; Virginia's American Revolution: From Dominion to Republic, 1776-1840, 2007; (with T.E. Woods, Jr.) Who Killed the Constitution? The Fate of American Liberty from World War I to George W. Bush, 2008. Contributor to books and periodicals. **Address:** Department of History, Western Connecticut State University, 181 White St., Danbury, CT 06810, U.S.A. **Online address:** gutzmank@wcsu.edu

GUY, Mary E. American (born United States), b. 1947. **Genres:** Ethics, Institutions/Organizations, Public/Social Administration, Social Sciences. **Career:** Georgia Department of Human Resources, counselor, 1970-73; South Carolina State Hospital, clinical counselor, 1973-75, psychologist, 1975-78; supervising psychologist, 1978-80, quality assurance coordinator, 1980-82, South Carolina Department of Mental Health, psychologist, 1973-82; University of Alabama in Birmingham, Department of Government and Public Service, assistant professor, 1982-86, associate professor, 1986-91, professor, 1991-97; Florida State University, Askew School of Public Administration and Policy, professor, 1997-, Jerry Collins eminent scholar chair, 1997-, Doctoral Program, director; American Society for Public Administration, president, 1997-98; Southern Political Science Association, president, 2001-02. Writer. **Publications:** Professionals in Organizations: Debunking a Myth, 1985; From Organizational Decline to Organizational Renewal: The Phoenix Syndrome, 1989; Ethical Decision Making in Everyday Work Situations, 1990; (ed.) Women and Men of the States: Public Administrators at the State Level, 1992; (with M.A. Newman and S.H. Mastracci) Emotional Labor: Putting the Service in Public Service, 2008; (with S.H. Mastracci and M.A. Newman) Emotional Labor and Crisis Response: Working on the Razor's Edge, 2011. Contributor to journals. **Address:** Askew School of Public Administration & Policy, Florida State University, 642 Bellamy Bldg., Tallahassee, FL 32306-2250, U.S.A. **Online address:** mguy@fsu.edu

GUY, Ray. Canadian (born Canada), b. 1939. **Genres:** Local History/Rural Topics, Plays/Screenplays, Humor/Satire, Young Adult Non-fiction, Travel/Exploration. **Career:** Evening Telegraph, general reporter, writer of commentary, 1963-75; Sunday Express, reporter. Writer and actor. **Publications:** You May Know Them as Sea Urchins, Ma'am: Writings, 1975, rev. ed., 1985; That Far Greater Bay, 1976, rev. ed., 1985; Beneficial Vapours, 1981; An Heroine for Our Time, 1983; Newfoundland/Labrador, 1984; This Dear and Fine Country, 1985; Young Triffie's Been Made Away With, 1985; Ray Guy's Best, 1987; Outhouses of the East, 1988; Ray Guy: The Smallwood Years, 2008. Contributor to magazines. **Address:** Breakwater Books, 277 Duckworth St., PO Box 2188, Saint John's, NL A1C 6E6, Canada.

GUY, Rosa (Cuthbert). American/Trinidadian (born Trinidad and Tobago), b. 1925. **Genres:** Children's Fiction, Plays/Screenplays, Translations, Literary Criticism And History, Novels, Young Adult Fiction. **Career:** Writer, 1950-; Harlem Writer's Guild, co-founder and president. **Publications:** Bird at My Window, 1966; (ed.) Children of Longing, 1971; The Friends, 1973; Ruby: A Novel, 1976; Edith Jackson, 1978; The Disappearance, 1979; Mirror of Her Own, 1981; (trans.) B. Diop, Mother Crocodile, 1981; New Guys around the Block, 1983; A Measure of Time, 1983; Paris, Pee Wee and Big Dog, 1984; My Love, My Love, or The Peasant Girl, 1985; And I Heard a Bird Sing, 1987; The Ups and Downs of Carl Davis III, 1989; The Music of Summer, 1992; Billy the Great, 1992; The Sun, the Sea, a Touch of the Wind, 1995. Contributor to periodicals. **Address:** c/o Ellen Levine, Trident Media Group L.L.C., 41 Madison Ave., 36th Fl., New York, NY 10010-2257, U.S.A.

GUYATT, Nicholas. British (born England), b. 1973. **Genres:** History, Young Adult Fiction. **Career:** Princeton University, lecturer, 2003-04; Simon Fraser University, assistant professor of history, 2004-07; University of York, lecturer, 2007-, Stanford Humanities Center, external faculty fellow, 2009-10.

Writer. **Publications:** The Absence of Peace: Understanding the Israeli-Palestinian Conflict, 1998; Another American Century? The United States and the World after 2000, 2000, rev. ed., 2003; Have a Nice Doomsday: Why Millions of Americans Are Looking Forward to the End of the World, 2007; Providence and the Invention of the United States, 1607-1876, 2007; (ed. with R. Bessel and J. Rendal) War, Empire, and Slavery, 1770-1830, 2010. Contributor of articles to periodicals. **Address:** Department of History, University of York, Vanbrugh College V/115, Heslington, SY Y010 5DD, England. **Online address:** nicholas.guyatt@york.ac.uk

GUZZETTI, Alfred F. American (born United States), b. 1942. **Genres:** Film, Art/Art History. **Career:** Harvard University, assistant professor, 1971-, associate professor, professor of visual environmental studies, 1975-, Osgood Hooker professor of visual arts. Writer. **Publications:** Two or Three Things I Know About Her: Analysis of a Film by Godard, 1981. **Address:** Department of Visual Environmental Studies, Harvard University, 24 Quincy St., Cambridge, MA 02138-3804, U.S.A.

GUZZO, Lou(is Richard). American (born United States), b. 1919. **Genres:** Communications/Media, Environmental Sciences/Ecology, Military/Defense/Arms Control, Writing/Journalism, Women's Studies And Issues, Politics/Government. **Career:** Plain Dealer, reporter, 1936-42; Seattle Times, reporter, editor and copyreader, 1946-50, music, film, theater, and arts critic, 1947-65; Seattle Post-Intelligencer, managing editor, executive editor, chief editorial writer, and columnist, 1965-75; freelance writer, 1976-; University of Washington, teacher, 1976; Seattle University, teacher, 1976; Warehouse Container Systems, vice-president, 1981-89; Analytics Corp., vice-president and director, 1981-89; Grizzly Publishing Co., vice-president and director, 1981-89; Louis R. Guzzo and Associates Inc., president, 1984-; Governor's Cultural-Affairs, director. Writer. **Publications:** (With D. Bodansky and F. Schmidt) The Fight over Nuclear Power, 1976; Arts Plan of Washington State, 1979; Is it True What They Say About Dixy?: A Biography of Dixy Lee Ray, 1980; (ed.) Partnership Power, 1984; Severo Antonelli, Photographer, 1988; (with T.C. Liberman) The Catalyst, 1989; (with D.L. Ray) Trashing the Planet: How Science Can Help Us Deal with Acid Rain, Depletion of the Ozone, and Nuclear Waste, 1990; (with D.L. Ray) Environmental Overkill: Whatever Happened to Common Sense?, 1993; A Soul Reclaimed, 1999; Memoirs of Virginia and Milton Katims, 2000; When Did I Die?: Biography of Artist Richard Lachman, 2001; F!D!F! (Fire! Dammit! Fire!), A Feast of New Ideas, 2005; She Should Have Been President: The Wisdom of Dixy Lee Ray, 2006; Romulus and Remus: A Modern Parable, 2007; Masseur!, 2007. Contributor to periodicals. **Address:** Outskirts Press Inc., 10940 S Parker Rd., Ste. 515, Parker, CO 80134, U.S.A. **Online address:** lou@louguzzo.com

GWARTNEY, Debra. American (born United States), b. 1957?. **Genres:** Autobiography/Memoirs, Human Relations/Parenting. **Career:** Newsweek, correspondent; Oregonian, correspondent; Nonfiction faculty, Pacific University, MFA in Writing Program, faculty. **Publications:** (Ed.) Home Ground: Language for an American Landscape, 2006; Live through This: A Mother's Memoir of Runaway Daughters and Reclaimed Love, 2009. Contributor to periodicals. **Address:** OR , U.S.A. **Online address:** debra@debragwartney.com

GWYN, Richard. British/Welsh (born Wales), b. 1956. **Genres:** Young Adult Fiction, Essays, Poetry. **Career:** Cardiff University, School of English, Communication and Philosophy, senior lecturer in creative writing, through 2006, reader, MA Program in Creative Writing, director. Writer. **Publications:** POETRY: One Night in Icarus Street, 1995; Stone Dog, Flower Red/Gos Depedra, Flor Vermella, 1995; Walking on Bones, 2000; Being in Water, 2001; (ed.) The Pterodactyl's Wing: Welsh World Poetry, 2003. OTHERS: Communicating Health and Illness, 2002; (ed. with J. Coupland) Discourse, the Body, and Identity, 2003; The Colour of a Dog Running Away, 2005; Deep Hanging Out, 2007; Sad Giraffe Café, 2010; The Vagabond's Breakfast, 2011. Contributor to periodicals. **Address:** c/o Ivan Mulcahy, Mulcahy Conway Associates Ltd., 7 Meard St., 1st Fl., London, GL W1F 0EW, England. **Online address:** gwyn@cf.ac.uk

GWYN, William Brent. American (born United States), b. 1927. **Genres:** Politics/Government, Philosophy. **Career:** University of Tennessee, assistant professor of political science, 1956-57; Bucknell University, assistant professor of political science, 1957-63; Tulane University of Louisiana, associate professor, 1963-69, professor of political science, 1969-93, professor emeritus, 1993-, chairperson of department, 1975-79. Writer. **Publications:** Democracy and the Cost of Politics in Britain, 1962; The Meaning of the Separation of Powers: An Analysis of the Doctrine from Its Origin to the Adoption of the United States Constitution, 1965; Barriers to Establishing Urban Ombudsmen: The Case of Newark, 1974; (ed. with G.C. Edwards III) Perspectives on Public Policy, 1975; (ed. with R. Rose) Britain: Progress and Decline, 1980; Ombudsman Policy Innovation in the English-Speaking World, 1980. CONTRIBUTOR: Ombudsmen for American Government?, 1968; The Ombudsman: An International Handbook, 1980; Does the Separation of Powers Still Work?, 1986; Political Culture and Constitutionalism, 1995. Contributor to periodicals and journals. **Address:** Department of Political Science, Tulane University of Louisiana, New Orleans, LA 70118, U.S.A.

GWYNELLE (DISMUKES), Gwynelle. American (born United States) **Genres:** Cultural/Ethnic Topics, Human Relations/Parenting, Philosophy, Sociology, Social Sciences. **Career:** Brite Moments, publisher/editor, 1995-97; Sankofa African Heritage Museum, assistant curator. **Publications:** Affirmations for a Year-Round Kwanzaa, 1993; Afrikan Alkhemy: Spiritual and Soul Transformation in America, 1995; The African Centered Family Unity Guide, 1998; Practicing Kwanzaa Year Round: Affirmations and Activities around the Seven Principles, 2000; Black 2 the Future; The Sustainable Seven African-based Principles of Social Sustainability for the 21st Century. Contributor to books. **Address:** 20 The Farm, Summertown, TN 38483, U.S.A. **Online address:** c2dismukes@hotmail.com

GWYNN, R(obert) S(amuel). American (born United States), b. 1948. **Genres:** Poetry, Literary Criticism And History, Young Adult Fiction. **Career:** Southwest Texas State University, instructor in English, 1973-76; Lamar University, faculty, 1976-, university professor of English, 1997-, poet-in-residence. **Publications:** POETRY: Bearing and Distance, 1977; The Narcissiad, 1981; The Drive-In, 1986; (comp.) Fiction, 1993, (ed.) 7th ed., 2012; The Area Code of God, 1994; (comp. with D. Gioia) The Longman Anthology of Short Fiction, 2001; No Word of Farewell: Selected Poems 1970-2000, 2001. EDITOR: Drama, 1993, 5th ed., 2012; (and intro.) Poetry: A Longman Pocket Anthology, 1993, 6th ed. as Poetry: A Pocket Anthology, 2009; The Advocates of Poetry: A Reader of American Poet-Critics of the Modernist Era, 1996; New Expansive Poetry: Theory, Criticism, History, 1999; Literature: A Pocket Anthology, 2002, 4th ed., 2010; (with D. Gioia) The Longman Masters of Short Fiction, 2002; (with A. Lindner) Contemporary American Poetry: A Pocket Anthology, 2005; (with D. Gioia) Art of the Short Story, 2006. EDITOR AND CONTRIBUTOR: American Poets Since World War II, vol. II, 1991, vol. III, 1992. OTHERS: (with J.E. Seale, N.S. Nye and W.V. Davis) Texas Poets in Concert, 1990; Longman Anthology of Short Fiction: Stories and Authors in Context, 2001; (with S. Zani) Inside Literature Reading, Responding, Arguing, 2007; (contrib.) Pale Fire: A Poem in Four Cantos by John Shade, 2010. Works appear in anthologies. Contributor of articles to books and periodicals. **Address:** Department of English and Modern Languages, Lamar University, MA 050, PO Box 10023, Beaumont, TX 77710-0023, U.S.A. **Online address:** rsgwynn@my.lamar.edu

GYATSO, Palden. American/Tibetan (born Tibet), b. 1933?. **Genres:** Autobiography/Memoirs. **Career:** Writer. **Publications:** (With T. Shakya) Fire Under the Snow: The Autobiography of a Tibetan Monk, 1997; Fire Under The Snow: True Story of a Tibetan Monk (Panther), 1998. **Address:** Grove/Atlantic Inc., 841 Broadway, 4th Fl., New York, NY 10003, U.S.A.

GYLFASON, Thorvaldur. Icelander (born Iceland), b. 1951. **Genres:** Economics, Politics/Government. **Career:** Princeton University, assistant in instruction, 1975-76; International Monetary Fund, economist, 1976-81, lecturer and consultant, 1993-; University of Stockholm, Institute for International Economic Studies, research fellow, 1978-79, senior research fellow, 1981-96, International Graduate School, instructor, 1982-83; University of Iceland, professor of economics, 1983-, research professor of economics, 1998-2005, Faculty of Economics and Business Administration, chairman, 1988-90; Central Bank of Iceland, consultant, 1984-93; Kaupthing Ltd., chairman, 1986-90; European Economic Review, associate editor, 1986-92, editor, 2002-10; Centre for Economic Policy Research, research fellow, 1987-; Icelandic Opera Society, chairman, 1988-94; Japan and the World Economy, associate editor, 1989-; New York University, Center for U.S.-Japan Business and Economic Studies, research associate, 1989-; Auolind Ltd., chairman, 1990-92; SNS-Center for Business and Policy Studies, research associate, 1994-2004, Economic Policy Group, head, 1996-97; Scandinavian Journal of Economics, associate editor, 1995-2005; Macroeconomic Dynamics, associate editor, 1997-; University of Munich, Center for Economic Studies, research fellow, 1999-; CESifo Economic Studies, associate editor, 2003-. **Publications:** Interest, Inflation, and the Aggregate Consumption Function, 1979; Credit Policy and Economic Activity in Developing Countries with IMF Stabilization Programs, 1987; Almannahagur (Public Interest), 1990; Hagfraeoi, stjórnmál og menning, 1991; (with A.J. Isachsen and C.B. Hamilton) Understanding the Market Economy, 1992; Hagkvaemni og réttlaeti, 1993; Sidustu forvod, 1995; The Macroeconomics of European Agriculture, 1995; (ed.) The Swedish Model under Stress: A View from the Stands, 1997; Understanding Economic Growth, 1998; Ad byggja land, 1998; Vidskiptin efla alla dad, 1999; Principles of Economic Growth, 1999; Framtíoin er annao land, 2001; Tveir heimar, 2005; (co-author) Nordics in Global Crisis, 2010. Contributor of articles to books and journals. **Address:** Department of Economics, University of Iceland, Saemundargötu 2, Reykjavík, 101, Iceland. **Online address:** gylfason@hi.is

GYOHTEN, Toyoo. Japanese (born Japan), b. 1931. **Genres:** Economics, International Relations/Current Affairs, Business/Trade/Industry. **Career:** Japan Ministry of Finance, staff, 1955-, director of public loan and investment department, finance bureau, 1975-77, deputy director general of international finance bureau, 1980-83, deputy director general of banking bureau, 1983-84, director general of international finance bureau, 1984-86, vice minister of finance for international affairs, 1986-89, special adviser, 1989-90; International Monetary Fund, trainee, 1960-61, Japan Desk, staff, 1964-66; Morioka Tax Office, director, 1962-63; Asian Development Bank, special assistant, 1966-69; Tokyo International Airport, customs commissioner, 1972-73; Harvard University, Harvard Business School, visiting professor, 1990; Princeton University, visiting professor, 1990-91; University of St. Gallen, visiting professor, 1991; Bank of Tokyo, adviser, 1991-, senior adviser, chairman, 1992-96; The Bank of Tokyo-Mitsubishi Ltd., senior advisor, 1996-; Institute for International Monetary Affairs, president, 1996-. Writer. **Publications:** Regionalism in a Converging World: A Report to the Trilateral Commission, 1992; (with P. Volcker) Changing Fortunes: The World's Money and the Threat to American Leadership, 1992; (ed. with M. Kuroda) One Hundred Key Words to Understand U.S.-Japan Economic Relations, 1992; Nihon Keizai noShiza, 1993; The Yen: Destination Unknown-Personal Perspective, 1996. **Address:** Institute for International Monetary Affairs, 1-3-2 Nihombashi Hongokucho 1-chome, Chuo-ku, Tokyo, 103-0021, Japan.